For Reference

Do Not Take From the Library

Oxford Rhyming Dictionary

Oxford
Rhyming Dictionary

Clive Upton
Eben Upton

OXFORD
UNIVERSITY PRESS

OXFORD

UNIVERSITY PRESS

Great Clarendon Street, Oxford OX2 6DP

Oxford University Press is a department of the University of Oxford.
It furthers the University's objective of excellence in research, scholarship,
and education by publishing worldwide in

Oxford New York

Auckland Cape Town Dar es Salaam Hong Kong Karachi Kuala Lumpur
Madrid Melbourne Mexico City Nairobi New Delhi Shanghai Taipei Toronto

With offices in

Argentina Austria Brazil Chile Czech Republic France Greece
Guatemala Hungary Italy Japan South Korea Poland Portugal
Singapore Switzerland Thailand Turkey Ukraine Vietnam

Oxford is a registered trade mark of Oxford University Press
in the UK and in certain other countries

Published in the United States
by Oxford University Press Inc., New York

© Oxford University Press 2004

British Library Cataloguing in Publication Data

Data available

Library of Congress Cataloging in Publication Data

Data available

ISBN 0-19-280115-5

2

Designed by Jane Stevenson
typeset in Swift and Frutiger
by Kolam Information Services
Printed in Great Britain
by Clays Ltd, Bungay, Suffolk

Contents

Preface

Introducing rhymes

It's the endings of words that rhyme.

But what do we mean by 'endings'? *Stumpy*, *jumpy*, and *grumpy* end the same, and they rhyme. So *-umpy*, what the three words have in common, must be their ending.

We could also call *-umpy* a sound. But we know that it's really several sounds together, four to be precise; there's an **uh**, an **m**, a **p**, and an **ee**. Sharing these four sounds is what makes the words rhyme.

Let's change the first of these four sounds, making the **uh** into an **o**, and think of a word with the **o** sound in it, but still ending in *-mpy*, alongside our earlier ones. Take the word *swampy*. Does this still rhyme with *stumpy*, *jumpy*, and *grumpy*? It's certainly not as close to them as they are to each other, but it's a lot closer than most other words.

And if we think of other words with *-mpy* at the end, we'd be happy to run a lot of them together, and to play with their connection by sound. We could picture a *jumpy impi*. Or complain about *skimpy scampi*. Was *Pompey wimpy*? Or *dumpy*? Or fond of *rumpy-pumpy*?

Now, do we dare to lose the *m*, and just keep the *-py* ending, and still talk about rhyming? Obviously the connection to the *-mpy* words won't be as great as the one those words have with each other—we're moving away in rhyme, just as we did going from *-umpy* to just *-mpy*. But there's still similarity of sorts. *Gillespie* might be *grumpy*. We could complain about *pulpy skimpy scampi*.

And even if we change some sounds, and replace them with ones of a similar kind, then a rhyme of sorts remains. Let's replace *-py* with *-by*. If other sounds in the words are the same, we have a rhyme that is quite close: we have, perhaps, a *wimpy nimby*, or a *happy tabby*. If the rhyme relies on only the *-py* and *-by*, we're getting further away, but a connection remains: *frumpy* and *baby*, *Debbie* and *waspie*.

And that's how the *Oxford Rhyming Dictionary* works. It groups the best or strongest rhymes closest together, by putting together words that share a lot of sounds. Words that share some sounds or have sounds that are made in similar ways (such as *b* and *p*, which are both produced at the front of the mouth) are grouped together, but not as closely. The *Oxford Rhyming Dictionary* organises the words phonetically. We simply consider the sounds, and are not dictated to by any alphabetical or spelling considerations, working always from the last syllable backwards through the words. This means that *moustachio* is as good a rhyme as *peepshow* for the word *quizshow*.

... and a bit of theory

The rhymes in the *Oxford Rhyming Dictionary* are based directly on the pronunciations given in the *Oxford Dictionary of Pronunciation for Current English*, which means that they're based on sounds rather than spellings. This is important, for a number of reasons. First, using sounds as the organizing principle is the most accurate and scientific means of proceeding, because it ensures that sounds that are closest together are grouped together. The order of letters in the alphabet does not relate to sounds, so that *f* and *v*, which are very close in sound, are far apart in terms of their position in the alphabet, while *f* and *g*, although adjacent in the alphabet, do not represent similar sounds at all.

Second, English spelling is notoriously irregular in the way in which letters represent sounds. If spellings of words, rather than sounds, were used as the organizing principle for a rhyming dictionary, that would tend to elevate a 'same-spelling' rhyme over a rhyme which had a very different spelling. Part of the beauty and the delight of rhyme is the way in which it cuts across how a word looks on the page. It can bring unlikely bedfellows together—*Chloe* is spelled very differently but it is just as good a rhyme for *showy* as *snowy* is, and *clayey*, despite its appearance, is a very strong rhyme for *Pompeii*. The *Oxford Rhyming Dictionary* goes beyond spelling and orders words according to the way in which they're produced in the mouth and the throat.

Vowels are produced by forming the mouth into a particular shape and passing through it air that has been set vibrating by the vocal cords. Crucial to the sound produced is just where the tongue is in the mouth, and vowels are typically described as 'high' when the tongue is raised towards the roof of the mouth, 'low' when it is lowered, 'front' when it is pushed forwards, 'back' when it is pulled back. Vowel positions can be plotted on a diagram called the 'vowel quadrilateral' to show the tongue position when each sound is made. In the *Oxford Rhyming Dictionary*, we first take note of the grouping of words by vowel sound, working our way round the diagram from the 'high front' vowel ([iː], the sound in *beat*), through the other lower front vowels (such as [a] in *bat*), then across to the lower back vowels (such as [ɑː] in *bark*), up to the 'high back' vowel ([uː] in *boot*) and so to the 'central', very neutral-sounding vowel [ə], the *er* in *father*. Arranging matters in this way puts *beat* and *bit* close to *bait*, which is followed by *bet* and then *bat*; these are followed in turn by *Bart* and *bite* and *but*. Everything is focused on the sound: spelling has nothing to do with the ordering.

Finally, because the rhymes given in the *Oxford Rhyming Dictionary* are based on the *Oxford Dictionary of Pronunciation for Current English*, they relate to the standard pronunciation of British English, so-called Received Pronunciation or RP. The emphasis in the *Oxford Rhyming Dictionary* is on the most up-to-date, unmarked variety of that accent, such as that often used by television newsreaders. In some cases a word can have two different possible pronunciations, both correct. For example the word *poor* can be pronounced so that it rhymes with *bore* but it can also be pronounced (the more traditional pronunciation in RP) so that it rhymes with *lure*. Therefore, the word *poor* will be found listed in two different places, reflecting the two different pronunciations.

After vowel ordering has been considered in any syllable, the types of consonant become relevant. There are several ways in which consonants are created: by 'exploding' sounds out of the mouth (the so-called 'plosives' such as *p* and *b*), rubbing air through the mouth past differently-created obstructions (the 'fricatives' such as *f* and *v*) and so on. Many of the consonants are paired too, depending on whether the air associated with their creation has been vibrated or 'voiced' by the vocal cords or not. All such considerations are brought into play in our organization of the words. So the plosive [p], created by damming up air behind the lips and letting it out suddenly but *without* the air vibrating, precedes and is paired with the sound [b], made in the same way as [p] except with voiced, vibrating air: this will place *nip* close to *nib*, *rope* close to *robe*. The other differently-made plosives [t] and [d], [k] and [g] are similarly paired, as are the fricatives [s] and [z], [ʃ] and [ʒ] and so on. Although these are only given as examples, they show that meaningful groupings of sounds have been created throughout the book.

Who needs rhymes?

There are professionals who will most obviously benefit on a day-to-day basis from this book: the composers and translators of poetry, of song lyrics and of advertisement jingles, the creators of word puzzles and games, to name a few. But almost everybody needs information about rhymes at some time in their lives; perhaps to compose a little ditty as a joke for family or friends, when constructing a quiz, or to settle an argument such as whether there's an exact rhyme for orange (there is, incidentally, though there isn't for *butcher*). So this dictionary is for everyone. Anyone, who enjoys the sounds of the language, whether or not they have a professional purpose or a pressing personal need for a rhyme, could find themselves browsing far beyond the immediate confines of any target word they look up.

Finding rhymes: how to use this dictionary

When you need a rhyme for a word, first look up the word in the index (with 85,000 words to choose from you've a good chance of finding the one you're interested in). Then go to the section or sections indicated—a section holding a large number of words will have small-print 'fine tuning' numbers to help you to find your word in it. For example, if you want a word that rhymes with *radiate*, you will be directed to **22.4.2(.4)** in the main text. The ordering of the numbers is sequential before each full stop, so that, for example, **1.9.16** comes before **1.23** and after **1.4.6**. When you've found your word, its closest neighbours, above and below it in the list, will be its closest rhymes. The further you go in either direction the more words you'll discover that might be useful to you, although the strength with which they rhyme will of course decrease as you go further afield.

Although you'll find what you need in the sections you've been directed to by the index and the plus signs (these flag further sections where you'll find other rhymes relevant to the words you're looking at), because of the way the lists are structured you'll find it worth your while to roam about in the area of your target word. You'll also, of course, be able to create more rhymes for yourself by adding endings such as *-s*, *-ed*, and *-ing*. For instance you can find very strong rhymes for *landing* by looking up land and adding *-ing* to the words you find in that section. This leaves you *expanding* your *understanding* of a good *landing*. By exploring, you'll find many rhymes of different sorts—you'll probably spot all kinds of connections you'd never thought of before!

1
.1 Sheehy **.2** sprayey, clayey, Pompeii **.3** bowie, Tawe, Towy, Douai, Douay, Cowie, Howie, Sirhowy, Pontardawe **.4** strawy **.5** skyey **.6** hokonui, tui, Tuohy, Twohy, gooey, phooey, chewy, hooey, rouille, screwy, U-ey, Dewey, dewy, Huey, Hughey, Hughie, Louie, louis, bluey, St Louis, gluey, Drambuie®, Anouilh, chop suey, Matsui®, feng shui, mildewy, sinewy, Cimabue, Wanganui **.7** toey, towy, doughy, snowy, Zoë, showy, joey, Hoey, blowy, Chloë, meadowy, shadowy, echoey, arrowy, furrowy, pillowy, billowy, willowy, yellowy, tallowy, sallowy, tomatoey, kalenchoe, pahoehoe

1.8.1
cheapie, weepie, weepy, creepie, creepy, sleepy, orthoepy

1.8.2
tippy, dippy, nippy, snippy, zippy, chippie, chippy, gippy, hippie, hippy, whippy, trippy, drippy, grippy, Lippi, lippy, clippie, slippy, Xanthippe, Mississippi

1.8.3
kepi, crapy, crêpey, scrapie, grapey

1.8.4
peppy, kepi, Sheppey, preppie, preppy, orthoepy, Tío Pepe®, Giuseppe

1.8.5
pappy, tapis, gappy, nappy, snappy, sappy, zappy, chappie, chappy, happi, happy, strappy, crappie, crappy, scrappy, yappy, flappy, slaphappy, unhappy

1.8.6
sharpie, harpy, okapi, serape

1.8.7
poppy, copy, kopje, koppie, moppy, soppy, shoppy, choppy, stroppy, loppy, floppy, sloppy, miscopy, jalopy, photocopy, microcopy, microfloppy

1.8.8
puppy, buppie, duppy, guppy, yuppie, hiccupy, chirrupy

1.8.9
pipy, stripy, stereotypy

1.8.10
Tupi, goopy, snoopy, soupy, roupy, droopy, croupy, groupie, Kewpie®, NUPE, loopy

1.8.11
.1 calliope **.2** cacoepy, orthoepy **.3** tittuppy, metope, isotopy **.4** Rhodope **.5** syncope, pericope, apocope, episcope, colposcopy, cystoscopy, endoscopy, bronchoscopy, stethoscopy, horoscopy, fluoroscopy, uroscopy, spectroscopy, necroscopy, microscopy, arthroscopy, radioscopy, stereoscopy, metoposcopy, sigmoidoscopy, laryngoscopy, ophthalmoscopy, colonoscopy, ornithoscopy, laparoscopy **.6** canopy, turnipy **.7** praecipe,

recipe, gossipy, Príncipe **.8** syrupy, therapy, satrapy, entropy, pleiotropy, isotropy, thixotropy, allotropy, aeolotropy, lycanthropy, misanthropy, philanthropy, physiotherapy, radiotherapy, heliotherapy, psychotherapy, chemotherapy, hypnotherapy, hydrotherapy, sclerotherapy, anisotropy, aromatherapy, immunotherapy, organotherapy, thalassotherapy, electrotherapy **.9** malope, trollopy, Penelope

1.8.12
chirpy, Euterpe

1.8.13
Opie, taupy, dopey, dopy, kopi, mopey, soapy, Hopi, ropey, ropy, Rhodope, cacoepy

1.8.14
impi, skimpy, gimpy, wimpy, crimpy, scrimpy, kempy, campy, scampi, vampy, Pompey, swampy, rompy, bumpy, stumpy, dumpy, jumpy, humpy, rumpy, scrumpy, grumpy, frumpy, lumpy, plumpy, clumpy, rumpy-pumpy

1.8.15
wispy, crispy, raspy, waspie, Gillespie

1.8.16
kelpie, pulpy, gulpy, enthalpy

1.9.1
Beebe, phoebe, Hebe, freebie

1.9.2
Libby

1.9.3
baby, Blaby, crybaby, bushbaby, tsessebi, Achebe

1.9.4
Debbie, webby, plebby, Entebbe, cobwebby

1.9.5
abbey, Abby, tabby, cabbie, cabby, scabby, gabby, shabby, Rabbie, crabby, grabby, yabby, flabby, Newtownabbey

1.9.6
Babi, Darby, derby, Mugabe, Punjabi, Wahabi, kohlrabi, Abu Dhabi, Hammurabi

1.9.7
Bobbie, bobby, Gobbi, gobby, knobby, snobby, hobby, squabby, swabbie, Robbie, lobby

1.9.8
bawbee, dauby, corbie, Corby, mauby, warby

1.9.9
tubby, stubby, cubby, nubby, chubby, hubby, scrubby, grubby, shrubby, clubby

1.9.10
booby, jube, ruby, Newby, balas ruby

1.9.11
Sowerby, Niobe, Suddaby, Enderby, Jacobi, Lockerbie, Barnaby, Thornaby, Burnaby, Wetherby, Sotheby, tsessebi, sassaby, Araby, oribi, Willoughby, wallaby, Anlaby

1.9.12
Kirby, Kirkby, Furby, Herbie, herby

1.9.13
obi, toby, dhobi, dobe, Kobe, Scobie, Scoby, goby, mauby, Robey, Roby, adobe, Jacobi, Nairobi

1.9.14
VitBe®, Whitby

1.9.15
Oadby

1.9.16
Kirkby, Rokeby

1.9.17
Digby, Rigby, rugby

1.9.18
nimby, Dombey, combi, zombie, Crombie, Formby, brumby, namby-pamby, Abercrombie

1.9.19
Tenby, Denbigh, Denby, Danby, Hornby, Toynbee, Ponsonby, Lazonby, renminbi, Allenby

1.9.20
Boothby

1.9.21
Crosby, Catesby, Saxby

1.9.22
Visby, Thisbe, Naseby, Crosbie, Crosby, Moresby, busby, Buzby, Ingoldsby, Rigsby, Grimsby, Ormesby, Ormsby, Hornsby, Coningsby

1.9.23
Ashby

1.9.24
Philby, Wilby, trilby, Selby, Albee, Dolby®, Colby, Bowlby, Appleby, Dimbleby, Nickleby, Duggleby, astilbe

1.10.1
peaty, Beatty, meaty, sweetie, rete, treaty, sleety, Haiti, Papeete, granite, Venite, graffiti, Tahiti, entreaty, Nefertiti, spermaceti, Test-Ban Treaty

1.10.2
Pitti, pity, spitty, bitty, titty, ditty, kitty, Mitty, city, shitty, chitty, Whitty, witty, pretty, gritty, smriti, slitty, self-pity, McVitie, tri-city, Sun City, itty-bitty, subcommittee, inter-city, Salt Lake City, Vatican City, vulgarity, pretty-pretty, nitty-gritty

1.10.3
eighty, Beatty, Katie, Katy, matey, Haiti, weighty, pratie, Leyte, platy, slaty, Kuwaiti, Papeete, Albacete

1.10.4
petit, petty, Betti, Betty, Getty, Nettie, SETI, jetty, Hettie, sweaty, yeti, spaghetti, Dalgetty, confetti, cavetti, terzetti, Rossetti, machete, Serengeti, Giacometti, Olivetti®, spermaceti, Donizetti, amaretti, amoretti

1.10.5
Ghiberti

1.10.6
paté, pattée, Patti, Pattie, patty, batty, Tati, tattie, tatty, catty, scatty, natty, fatty, Satie, chatty, Hattie, ratty, bratty, flattie, chapatti, Bugatti, basmati, Marathi, Hanratty, Scarlatti, Cincinnati, Dolcelatte®

1.10.7
outie, pouty, doughty, gouty, snouty, trouty, droughty

1.10.8
arty, parti, party, tarty, Smartie, smarty, jati, hearty, lathi, clarty, coati, chapatti, ex parte, Astarte, McCarty, Clancarty, Frascati, Amati, basmati, karate, Marathi, Moriarty, multi-party, Kiribati, obbligati, literati, glitterati, Maserati®, Gujarati

1.10.9
potty, spotty, totty, dotty, Scottie, knotty, snotty, hottie, grotty, yachtie, Lottie, zloty, Menotti, manicotti, Pavarotti, Lanzarote

1.10.10
Auty, sporty, Corti, naughty, forty, sortie, shorty, haughty, warty, rorty, panforte, UB40, pianoforte

1.10.11
hoity-toity

1.10.12
putty, butty, tutty, cutty, gutty, smutty, nutty, rutty

1.10.13
mighty, mity, nightie, Haiti, whitey, whity, Blighty, flighty, high-and-mighty, almighty, Venite, Aphrodite, over-mighty, Amphitrite

1.10.14
tutti, sooty, Così Fan Tutte

1.10.15
booty, tutti, cootie, snooty, duty, rooty, fruity, beauty, cutie, loti, fluty, Djibouti, agouti, point duty, maloti, Funafuti, tutti-frutti

1.10.16
.1 deity, aseity, haecceity, velleity, spontaneity, simultaneity, femineity, corporeity, instantaneity, homogeneity, heterogeneity, contemporaneity, incorporeity, inhomogeneity .2 gaiety, gayety, laity .3 moiety .4 piety, impiety, dubiety, ubiety, satiety, society, anxiety, variety, propriety, sobriety, overanxiety, notoriety, subvariety, contrariety, impropriety, inebriety, insobriety .5 suety, Trimurti, circuity, fortuity, fatuity, gratuity, congruity, vacuity, acuity, tenuity, annuity, Krishnamurti, ambiguity, innocuity, perpetuity, assiduity, incongruity, perspicuity, promiscuity, amibiguity, contiguity, exiguity, continuity, ingenuity, superfluity, discontinuity .6 snippety, wapiti, property, uppity, champerty, serendipity .7 liberty,

rabbity, rubbity, puberty, probity, pre-puberty, acerbity, improbity **.8** sanctity, entity, quantity, chastity, identity, nonentity, unchastity, sacrosanctity **.9** quiddity, fluidity, superfluidity, tepidity, vapidity, torpidity, stupidity, cupidity, sapidity, rapidity, limpidity, intrepidity, insipidity, morbidity, rabidity, turbidity, humidity, tumidity, timidity, avidity, lividity, viscidity, flaccidity, lucidity, acidity, placidity, rancidity, subacidity, pellucidity, rigidity, frigidity, turgidity, algidity, liquidity, illiquidity, floridity, aridity, torridity, viridity, hybridity, putridity, acridity, stolidity, squalidity, pallidity, validity, solidity, invalidity, heredity, oddity, commodity, crudity, nudity, surdity, absurdity, rotundity, fecundity, jocundity, profundity, moribundity, rubicundity **.10** rickety, Hecate, rackety, pockety, Doherty, blankety, biscuity, pernickety, finickity **.11** Peggotty, Hegarty, maggoty, faggoty, Fogarty **.12** dimity, amity, comity, Cromarty, furmety, enmity, proximity, sublimity, Yosemite, extremity, calamity, enormity, abnormity, deformity, conformity, infirmity, pseudonymity, longanimity, synonymity, anonymity, unanimity, magnanimity, equanimity, multiformity, uniformity, nonconformity, unconformity, disconformity, pusillanimity **.13** amenity, disamenity, trinity, feminity, affinity, infinity, divinity, vicinity, concinnity, virginity, sanguinity, felinity, salinity, clandestinity, femininity, asininity, Patavinity, exsanguinity, consanguinity, crystallinity, alkalinity, masculinity, unfemininity, mundanity, seniti, lenity, obscenity, serenity, vanity, sanity, urbanity, humanity, inanity, profanity, insanity, Christianity, inhumanity, unity, triunity, impunity, immunity, community, disunity, importunity, opportunity, autoimmunity, intercommunity, eternity, paternity, maternity, quaternity, fraternity, modernity, sempiternity, taciturnity, confraternity, postmodernity, dignity, indignity, benignity, malignity, indemnity, solemnity **.14** Rafferty **.15** naivety, privity, creativity, nativity, motivity, captivity, activity, festivity, reactivity, proactivity, negativity, ergativity, permittivity, sensitivity, transitivity, positivity, iterativity, relativity, emotivity, receptivity, perceptivity, absorptivity, eruptivity, objectivity, connectivity, effectivity, affectivity, subjectivity, selectivity, collectivity, reflectivity, radioactivity, retroactivity, inactivity, self-activity, overactivity, productivity, conductivity, resistivity, associativity, insensitivity, intransitivity, correlativity, hyperactivity, hypersensitivity, photosensitivity, superconductivity, photoconductivity, passivity, expressivity, impassivity, diffusivity, exclusivity, emissivity, reflexivity, expansivity, acclivity, declivity, proclivity, brevity, levity, longevity, cavity, gravity, concavity, depravity, biconcavity, antigravity, suavity, poverty, velvety **.16.1** cecity,

obesity, Tricity®, laicity, syllabicity, vorticity, rhoticity, septicity, spasticity, plasticity, causticity, rusticity, pneumaticity, chromaticity, ellipticity, authenticity, domesticity, elasticity, automaticity, aromaticity, achromaticity, inauthenticity, inelasticity, mendicity, periodicity, spheroidicity, impudicity, aperiodicity, rhythmicity, seismicity, atomicity, endemicity, chronicity, tonicity, ethnicity, iconicity, volcanicity, canonicity, synchronicity, carcinogenicity, hypertonicity, isotonicity, ecumenicity, oecumenicity, toxigenicity, isochronicity, specificity, prolificity, stereospecificity, basicity, toxicity, sphericity, historicity, lubricity, centricity, eccentricity, electricity, chronicity, egocentricity, triboelectricity, photoelectricity, thermoelectricity, pyroelectricity, piezoelectricity, ferroelectricity, hydroelectricity, ethnocentricity, phallocentricity, helicity, felicity, triplicity, duplicity, simplicity, complicity, publicity, infelicity, Catholicity, hydraulicity, multiplicity, quadruplicity, necessity, scarcity, opacity, capacity, rapacity, audacity, mordacity, edacity, predacity, mendacity, fugacity, sagacity, tenacity, minacity, pugnacity, vivacity, sequacity, loquacity, veracity, voracity, salacity, radiopacity, incapacity, perspicacity, efficacity, pertinacity, undercapacity, overcapacity **.16.2** sparsity, varsity, hideosity, grandiosity, funniosity, speciosity, graciosity, preciosity, curiosity, flexuosity, tortuosity, virtuosity, sumptuosity, sinuosity, religiosity, incuriosity, impetuosity, anfractuosity, impecuniosity, pomposity, adiposity, gibbosity, verbosity, nodosity, mucosity, jocosity, precocity, viscosity, varicosity, bellicosity, rugosity, animosity, vinosity, venosity, luminosity, voluminosity, serosity, porosity, ferocity, scirrhosity, atrocity, monstrosity, tuberosity, ponderosity, generosity, reciprocity, villosity, pilosity, callosity, velocity, scrupulosity, nebulosity, fabulosity, paucity, russety, nicety, benedicite, obtusity, caducity, diversity, perversity, adversity, multiversity, biodiversity, university **.16.3** fixity, laxity, prolixity, convexity, biconvexity, perplexity, complexity, tensity, density, propensity, intensity, immensity, falsity **.17** witchetty, crotchety **.18** fidgety, gadgety **.19** Flaherty **.20** equity, ubiquity, antiquity, iniquity, obliquity, inequity, propinquity **.21.1** jequirity, ferrety, verity, sincerity, prosperity, asperity, austerity, posterity, dexterity, temerity, severity, insincerity, celerity, ambidexterity, rarity, parity, carroty, charity, clarity, linearity, subsidiarity, collinearity, familiarity, peculiarity, rectilinearity, unfamiliarity, overfamiliarity, disparity, oviparity, viviparity, fissiparity, ovoviviparity, barbarity, unitarity, complementarity, solidarity, coplanarity, polarity, molarity, hilarity, capillarity, bipolarity, pupilarity, pupillarity, similarity, osmolarity, modularity, popularity, globularity, secularity, jocularity, circularity, vascularity, muscularity, regularity, singularity, angularity, triangularity, granularity, insularity, cellularity, unipolarity, dissimilarity, unpopularity, orbicularity, particularity, perpendicularity, molecularity, vernacularity, oracularity, irregularity, rectangularity **.21.2** priority, minority, sonority, authority, majority, sorority, seniority, juniority, superiority, anteriority, posteriority, exteriority, inferiority, entirety, surety, purity, maturity, futurity, impurity, security, obscurity, immaturity, prematurity, insecurity **.21.3** celebrity, salubrity, muliebrity, insalubrity, lithotrity, alacrity, mediocrity, integrity **.22.1** lability, nubility, ability, playability, viability, friability, liability, pliability, suability, stability, debility, mobility, nobility, memorability, amiability, permeability, variability, malleability, printability, foreseeability, enjoyability, employability, deniability, unviability, reliability, renewability, capability, palpability, culpability, probability, clubbability, ratability, rateability, portability, suitability, mutability, potability, notability, quotability, floatability, temptability, actability, tractability, collectability, rentability, testability, instability, readability, biddability, gradability, edibility, credibility, audibility, laudability, roadability, weldability, stickability, peccability, placability, shockability, likability, likeability, cookability, workability, bankability, immobility, tameability, flammability, inability, trainability, tenability, learnability, ignobility, listenability, fashionability, affability, liveability, lovability, movability, provability, solvability, disability, miscibility, traceability, passibility, possibility, flexibility, taxability, vincibility, sensibility, feasibility, visibility, risibility, plausibility, usability, useability, fusibility, washability, sociability, changeability, frangibility, fungibility, teachability, stretchability, stageability, legibility, tangibility, equability, bearability, wearability, durability, curability, separability, reparability, operability, comparability, ponderability, venerability, vulnerability, preferability, transferability, mensurability, answerability, measurability, tolerability, scalability, saleability, fallibility, gullibility, handleability, volubility, solubility **.22.2** impermeability, associability, negotiability, invariability, unemployability, quantifiability, justifiability, falsifiability, satisfiability, unreliability, incapability, unflappability, unstoppability, impalpability, improbability, absorbability, repeatability, creditability, translatability, resettability, compatibility, supportability, exportability, transportability, ignitability, ignitibility, excitability, unsuitability, inscrutability, inscrutibility, computability, immutability, commutability, transmutability, refutability, habitability,

marketability, imitability, profitability, pivotability, irritability, heritability, palatability, invertibility, convertibility, promotability, perceptibility, susceptibility, acceptability, adaptability, corruptibility, discerptibility, contemptibility, reputability, predictability, respectability, perfectibility, delectability, attractability, intractability, extractability, deductibility, conductibility, destructibility, preventability, presentability, accountability, uncountability, resistibility, digestibility, suggestibility, exhaustibility, combustibility, adjustability, metastability, unreadability, persuadability, degradability, inedibility, incredibility, inaudibility, affordability, dependability, expendability, extendability, extendibility, fecundability, despicability, applicability, unshakability, unshakeability, impeccability, implacability, unshockability, practicability, predicability, vindicability, amicability, revocability, replicability, unworkability, educability, unthinkability, unsinkability, unshrinkability, fatiguability, navigability, programmability, inflammability, performability, conformability, amenability, machinability, alienability, attainability, retainability, obtainability, maintainability, sustainability, untenability, governability, pensionability, questionability, impregnability, ungovernability, impressionability, unmentionability, ineffability, conceivability, believability, survivability, immovability, removability, improvability, unprovability, unsolvability, resolvability, immiscibility, permissibility, admissibility, transmissibility, accessibility, compressibility, impassability, impassibility, irascibility, impossibility, enforceability, reducibility, producibility, serviceability, reversibility, collapsibility, reflexibility, inflexibility, invincibility, dispensability, distensibility, extensibility, defensibility, insensibility, expansibility, responsibility, defeasibility, infeasibility, unfeasibility, divisibility, invisibility, implausibility, advisability, realizability, realisability, infusibility, confusability, disposability, insatiability, perishability, unsociability, exchangeability, intangibility, refrangibility, infrangibility, untouchability, approachability, manageability, marriageability, eligibility, knowledgability, knowledgeability, negligibility, insurability, perdurability, endurability, incurability, desirability, inerrability, inseparability, irreparability, inoperability, insuperability, incomparability, penetrability, demonstrability, inalterability, imponderability, integrability, innumerability, denumerability, invulnerability, recoverability, manoeuvrability, inexorability, commensurability, immeasurability, availability, unsaleability, indelibility, infallibility, reconcilability, inviolability, controllability, calculability, dissolubility, insolubility **.22.3** inescapability, equiprobability, indescribability, imperturbability, unrepeatability, biocompatibility, substitutability, precipitability, inhabitability, inimitability, illimitability, indomitability, inevitability, inheritability, interpretability, unpalatability, inconvertibility, unpredictability, ineluctability, representability, biodegradability, understandability, inextricability, inapplicability, inexplicability, impracticability, communicability, irrevocability, ineducability, irrefragability, irredeemability, inalienability, unquestionability, indiscernibility, inconceivability, irretrievability, ineffaceability, irrepressibility, irreducibility, reproducibility, unserviceability, indispensability, indefensibility, reprehensibility, apprehensibility, comprehensibility, irresponsibility, indefeasibility, recognisability, recognizability, inadvisability, generalisability, generalizability, imperishability, interchangeability, irreproachability, incorrigibility, intelligibility, ineligibility, interoperability, impenetrability, indecipherability, incommensurability, manufacturability, unassailability, irreconcilability, inconsolability, manipulability, incalculability, indissolubility, incontrovertibility, incommunicability, indefatigability, incomprehensibility, unintelligibility, universalizability **.23** utility, futility, fertility, motility, tactility, ductility, gentility, infantility, hostility, disutility, infertility, versatility, volatility, retractility, contractility **.24** humility **.25** anility, senility, juvenility **.26** civility, servility, incivility **.27** fissility, gracility, docility, facility, flexility, tensility, imbecility, indocility, prehensility **.28** agility, fragility **.29** nihility **.30** tranquillity **.31** puerility, scurrility, sterility, virility, febrility, fidelity, infidelity **.32.1** reality, duality, labiality, bestiality, cordiality, ideality, veniality, geniality, triviality, joviality, axiality, spatiality, speciality, partiality, cruciality, sociality, seriality, aeriality, surreality, patriality, unreality, sexuality, sensuality, mutuality, virtuality, actuality, factuality, punctuality, textuality, visuality, connubiality, proverbiality, primordiality, parochiality, congeniality, perenniality, conviviality, impartiality, commerciality, provinciality, potentiality, essentiality, sequentiality, substantiality, collegiality, materiality, ethereality, corporeality, mercuriality, asexuality, bisexuality, eventuality, spirituality, effectuality, unpunctuality, contextuality, superficiality, artificiality, confidentiality, consequentiality, referentiality, insubstantiality, consubstantiality, unsubstantiality, circumstantiality, immateriality, incorporeality, territoriality, unisexuality, intersexuality, homosexuality, heterosexuality, unspirituality,

ineffectuality, intellectuality, intertextuality, individuality, inconsequentiality, exterritoriality, extraterritoriality **.32.2** principality, municipality **.32.3** mortality, vitality, brutality, totality, natality, fatality, mentality, immortality, hospitality, sentimentality, sacrementality, inhospitality, fundamentality, sacramentality, instrumentality, monumentality, horizontality, unsentimentality **.32.4** feudality, modality, sodality, bipedality, bimodality **.32.5** vocality, locality, fiscality, rascality, quizzicality, typicality, topicality, criticality, verticality, practicality, comicality, finicality, technicality, ethicality, classicality, farcicality, physicality, musicality, whimsicality, logicality, clericality, theatricality, grammaticality, pragmaticality, impracticality, fantasticality, veridicality, equivocality, nonsensicality, unmusicality, illogicality, reciprocality, univocality, ungrammaticality **.32.6** regality, legality, frugality, prodigality, illegality, conjugality **.32.7** normality, formality, abnormality, subnormality, informality, optimality, animality **.32.8** venality, carnality, finality, banality, tonality, nationality, atonality, cardinality, criminality, liminality, feminality, commonality, personality, seasonality, rationality, optionality, fictionality, functionality, marginality, eternality, internality, externality, communality, polytonality, impersonality, additionality, conditionality, irrationality, proportionality, emotionality, exceptionality, directionality, intentionality, extensionality, dimensionality, conventionality, provisionality, occasionality, originality, supranationality, unconditionality, internationality, constitutionality, unconventionality, Aboriginality, unoriginality, unconstitutionality, unidirectionality, multidimensionality **.32.9** coevality, ovality **.32.10** lethality **.32.11** transversality, commensality, universality **.32.12** nasality, causality **.32.13** orality, plurality, spirality, chirality, rurality, morality, neutrality, centrality, dextrality, corporality, temporality, liberality, literality, gutturality, pastorality, immorality, amorality, generality, sinistrality, integrality, illiberality, collaterality, ephemerality, peripherality **.32.14** molality, osmolality **.33** polity, jollity, quality, frivolity, equality, coequality, inequality **.34** nullity **.35** sedulity, credulity, garrulity, incredulity **.36** chocolatey **.37** ringlety

1.10.17
Bertie, dirty, Gertie, thirty, Sirte, shirty, cherty, qwerty, flirty, Alberti, Krishnamurti

1.10.18
oaty, dhoti, goaty, roti, throaty, loti, floaty, peyote, coyote, chayote, Capote, cenote, Quixote, maloti

1.10.19
Mopti, empty, umpty, humpty-dumpty

1.10.20
ushabti

1.10.21
dicty, Sakti, bhakti

1.10.22
Naughtie, Auchtermuchty

1.10.23
.1 minty, shinty, squinty, linty, flinty, McGinty, pepperminty .2 painty, dainty, suzerainty .3 sente, Henty, twenty, plenty, al dente, lisente, aplenty, pentimenti, San Clemente, prominenti, cognoscenti, twenty-twenty, dolce far niente .4 ante, anti, Dante, scanty, Fante, Fanti, Zante, chanty, chantey, shanty, Chianti, andante, bacchante, diamanté, Bramante, spumante, infante, Ashanti, Durante, meranti, Ferranti, flagrante, penny-ante, concertante, dilettante, dilettanti, Alicante, figurante, figuranti, vigilante, Asti Spumante, pococurante .5 bounty, county, Mountie, Mounty, viscounty, intercounty .6 auntie, aunty .7 Conteh, Monte, Monty, Brontë, Visconti, Del Monte, Belafonte, Capo di Monte .8 jaunty, flaunty .9 pointy .10 Bunty, runty .11 ninety .12 certainty, frumenty, guaranty, warranty, seventy, sovereignty, peasanty, uncertainty

1.10.24
nifty, fifty, shifty, swiftie, rifty, thrifty, safety, hefty, leftie, lefty, drafty, draughty, crafty, softie, softy, lofty, tufty, mufti, shufti, shufty, unthrifty, toplofty, fifty-fifty, arty-crafty

1.10.25
naivety

1.10.26
.1 beastie, yeasty .2 misty, twisty, wristy, Christi, Christie, Christy, Corpus Christi, lachryma Christi .3 pastie, pasty, tasty, Hastie, hasty, overhasty .4 testy, zesty, chesty, Tibesti .5 Asti, nasty, contrasty, epinasty, hyponasty, pederasty, angioplasty, otoplasty, rhinoplasty .6 frowsty .7 frosty .8 busty, dusty, gusty, musty, fusty, rusty, trustie, trusty, crusty, lusty .9 feisty .10 Carnoustie .11 modesty, dynasty, honesty, amnesty, travesty, majesty, touristy, sacristy, immodesty, dishonesty, lèse-majesté .12 Kirstie, thirsty, bloodthirsty .13 postie, toastie, toasty .14 sixty .15 Anstey

1.10.27
deputy

1.10.28
kiltie, guilty, silty, realty, frailty, felty, shelty, Welty, balti, malty, faulty, salty, Solti, McNulty, fealty, royalty, loyalty, cruelty, viceroyalty, disloyalty, personalty, mayoralty, admiralty, severalty, jolty, subtlety, faculty, difficulty, penalty, commonalty, sheriffalty, shrievalty, novelty, specialty, casualty

1.11.1
Eadie, Edie, speedy, beady, needy, vide, cedi, seedy, weedy, tweedy, reedy, Preedy, greedy, Macready, McCready, McReady, Coober Pedy

1.11.2
Biddie, biddy, diddy, kiddie, giddy, middy, MIDI, midi, vide, Dinwiddie, Dinwiddy, chickabiddy

1.11.3
beardie, weirdie

1.11.4
Adie, Sadie, shady, Brady, Grady, lady, O'Brady, O'Grady, chairlady, charlady, forelady, milady, Toplady, landlady, dragonlady, saleslady, maravedi

1.11.5
Eddie, eddy, teddy, steady, neddy, heady, ready, reddy, Freddie, Freddy, thready, unsteady, rough-and-ready, make-ready, unready, oven-ready, already, teledu

1.11.6
Verdi, Monteverdi, Mesa Verde

1.11.7
Addie, Addy, paddy, baddy, daddy, caddie, Maddie, Maddy, faddy, haddie, laddie, gladdie, kabaddi, granddaddy, finnanhaddie

1.11.8
Audi®, dowdy, Gaudí, Goudy, Saudi, howdy, rowdy, cloudy, pandowdy

1.11.9
bardy, tardy, cadi, cardy, kadi, Maerdy, Mahdi, mardy, Saadi, Hardie, hardy, Guardi, Yardie, lardy, Lombardi, Bacardi®, Coolgardie, samadhi, Sephardi, foolhardy, irade, Lollardy, lardy-dardy, Chorlton-cum-Hardy, autostrade, Makgadikgadi

1.11.10
Oddie, poddy, body, toddy, noddy, Soddy, shoddy, hoddie, waddy, wadi, wady, squaddie, swaddie, swaddy, Roddy, cloddy, Peabody, Goodbody, embody, somebody, homebody, disembody, dogsbody, Kirkcaldy, antibody, busybody, underbody, anybody, everybody, Irrawaddy, Irrawady, Passamaquoddy

1.11.11
Audie, bawdy, gaudy, Geordie, Brawdy, Lordy, Kirkcaldy, O'Brady

1.11.12
ploidy, diploidy, triploidy, polyploidy

1.11.13
buddy, study, cuddy, muddy, nuddy, ruddy, cruddy, restudy, unbloody, understudy, overstudy, fuddy-duddy

1.11.14
tidy, didy, vide, Heidi, Friday, untidy, bona fide, mala fide

1.11.15
goody, hoodie, woody, Dunwoody

1.11.16
Moodie, moody, foodie, Judi, Judy, Rudi, Rudy, broody, Trudi, Trudy, Mudie, Punch and Judy, Yehudi

1.11.17
jeopardy, Peabody, nobody, Lombardy, somebody, Saturday, yesterday, bastardy, custody, Picardy, Arcady, raggedy, remedy, psalmody, comedy, threnody, Kennedy, monody, hymnody, perfidy, Cassidy, prosody, rhapsody, subsidy, accidie, tragedy, parody, melody, malady, holiday, Lollardy, hexapody, chiropody, anybody, everybody, Schenectady, self-parody, tragicomedy

1.11.18
Purdie, Purdy, birdie, sturdy, curdy, nerdy, wordy, hurdy-gurdy, Monteverdi, paloverde, vinho verde

1.11.19
toady, tody, Cody, Jodie, Jody, roadie, Brodie, polypody

1.11.20
.1 indie, Indy, Mindy, Cindy, Sindhi, Sindy, shindy, Hindi, windy, Lindy, Rawalpindi .2 Maendy .3 bendy, Hendy, Wendy, trendy, Allende, effendi, Gassendi, untrendy .4 Andy, bandy, Tandy, dandy, candy, Kandy, Gandhi, Mandy, Nandi, sandhi, sandy, shandy, handy, randy, brandy, yandy, jim-dandy, rock-candy, unhandy, Río Grande, Tonypandy, jaborandi .5 tondi, blondie, bassi profondi .6 Maundy .7 undy, Bundy, gundi, gundy, Monday, Fundy, sundae, Sunday, Grundy, Lundy, salmagundi, coatimundi, barramundi, jaguarundi, bassi profundi .8 Kirundi, Burundi, Mappa Mundi, anima mundi .9 organdie, burgundy, Normandy

1.11.21
Tuesday, Thursday, Wednesday

1.11.22
Rushdie

1.11.23
wieldy, tilde, Caldy, baldy, worlde, oldie, Goldie, moldy, mouldy, unwieldy, alcalde, Vivaldi, Grimaldi, Fittipaldi, Garibaldi, olde worlde, higgledy-piggledy

1.12.1
peaky, peeky, beaky, tiki, Geikie, sneaky, cheeky, squeaky, reeky, streaky, creaky, freaky, Leakey, leaky, cliquey, sleeky, Kon-Tiki, tzatziki, cock-a-leekie, Thessaloníki

1.12.2
icky, ikky, picky, sticky, Dickie, dicky, mickey, Nicki, Nicky, Nikki, Vikki, thickie, sickie, hickey, quickie, rickey, Ricky, Rikki, brickie, tricky, hei-tiki, dashiki, doohickey, Billericay

1.12.3
achy, snaky, shaky, quaky, Blackie, Blakey, flaky, headachy, wakey-wakey

1.12.4
Becky, techie, recce

1.12.5
ackee, akee, Paki, baccy, backy, tacky, Mackey, Mackie, Jackie, Jacqui, wacky, raki, cracky, lackey, Blackie, Coxsackie, Iraqi, gimcracky, ticky-tacky, Taranaki, Nagasaki, Kawasaki, sukiyaki, teriyaki

1.12.6
thearchy, diarchy, dyarchy, parky, sparky, Starkey, Starkie, darkie, khaki, narky, saké, saki, sarky, raki, larky, patriarchy, matriarchy, eparchy, autarchy, autarky, plutarchy, heptarchy, octarchy, synarchy, menarche, ethnarchy, Iraqi, hierarchy, squirarchy, squirearchy, trierarchy, tetrarchy, malarkey, malarky, souvlaki, oligarchy, Taranaki, Nagasaki, Kawasaki, sukiyaki, teriyaki

1.12.7
oche, pocky, stocky, cocky, gnocchi, choccy, jockey, hockey, rocky, flocky, schlocky, outjockey, jabberwocky

1.12.8
pawky, porky, balky, baulky, talkie, stalky, corky, gawky, Gorky, chalky, Treorchy, Milwaukee, walkie-talkie

1.12.9
Buckie, ducky, mucky, truckie, yucky, lucky, plucky, clucky, Kentucky, unlucky, happy-go-lucky

1.12.10
spiky, Tyche, Nike, psyche, crikey

1.12.11
bookie, cookie, kooky, nooky, hookey, Wookey, rookie, netsuke

1.12.12
spooky, Stiffkey, kooky, Sukey, Sukie, pukey, fluky, kabuki, adsuki, azuki, bouzouki, Suzuki®, adzuki, saluki

1.12.13
schipperke, plasticky, gimmicky, hummocky, finicky, anarchy, panicky, monarchy, picnicky, tussocky, physicky, dashiki, hillocky, Malachy, garlicky, colicky, bullocky, rheumaticky, Diadochi, synecdoche, skiamachy, sciamachy, theomachy, logomachy, tauromachy, Andromache, McConachie, Fifth Monarchy, entelechy, smart-alecky

1.12.14
perky, turkey, Turki, murky, smirky, jerky, quirky, Albuquerque, herky-jerky

1.12.15
Okie, poky, smoky, folkie, folky, chokey, jokey, hokey, hoki, roquet, croaky, croquet, yolky, Loki, karaoke, hokey-pokey, okey-dokey, hokey-cokey, Okefenokee

1.12.16
inky, pinkie, stinky, dinky, Kinki, kinky, minke, zincy, Chinky, slinky, manky, Sankey, hanky,

Wankie, wanky, Twankey, swanky, cranky,
Frankie, Yankee, lanky, blanky, donkey, shonky,
honky, wonky, punky, spunky, monkey, funky,
chunky, junkie, hunky, flunkey, stotinki,
Helsinki, Palenque, hanky-panky, catananche,
Killiecranckie

1.12.17
.1 whisky, risky, frisky **.2** Esky®, pesky,
kromesky **.3** asci, ASCII, Askey, Laski, Pulaski
.4 Tarski **.5** bosky **.6** Sikorsky **.7** tusky, dusky,
musky, husky, Russki, McCluskie **.8** netsuke,
Gretzky, Trotsky, Radetsky, Górecki, Blavatsky,
Penderecki **.9** Brodsky **.10** Mussorgsky
.11 Chomsky **.12** Bronski, Kandinsky,
Stravinsky, Nijinsky, Brzezinski,
Dzerzhinsky, kolinsky, Kerensky, Polanski
.13 Tchaikovsky, Bukowski, Stokowski,
Minkowski, Dostoevsky, Dostoyevsky,
Paderewski, Malinowski **.14** Nevsky,
Stanislavsky **.15** Volski, Topolsky, Przewalski,
Kamensk-Uralski

1.12.18
droshky

1.12.19
milky, silky, Wilkie, Elkie, talcy, Khalki, baulky,
bulky, sulky, pulque

1.13
Haughey, Mulcaghey, McGahey, Maconachie,
Maconochie

1.14.1
Respighi, Malpighi, Carnegie

1.14.2
piggy, biggie, ciggy, twiggy, spriggy

1.14.3
Craigie, plaguy

1.14.4
eggy, Peggy, dreggy, leggy

1.14.5
Aggie, baggy, Maggie, knaggy, snaggy, saggy,
shaggy, jaggy, quaggy, swaggie, draggy, craggy,
scraggy, slaggy

1.14.6
boggy, doggy, moggy, smoggy, foggy, soggy,
quaggy, groggy, Froggie, froggy, cloggy,
pedagogy, demagogy

1.14.7
porgy, corgi

1.14.8
puggy, buggy, Dougie, muggy, fuggy, vuggy,
druggy

1.14.9
Ciba-Geigy®

1.14.10
boogie, Googie, sastrugi, boogie-woogie

1.14.11
Lalage

1.14.12
Fergie, lurgy

1.14.13
pogey, bogey, bogie, stogy, dogie, fogey, hoagie,
yogi, pierogi

1.14.14
dinghy, dengue, Changi, Hwange, Bangui,
Bungay, lungi, Ubange, sarangi

1.15.1
beamy, steamy, Mimi, seamy, REME, preemie,
dreamy, creamy, gleamy, polysemy

1.15.2
Timmy, gimme, shimmy, Jimmie, jimmy

1.15.3
Aimée, Amy, gamey, gamy, Mamie, samey,
Jamie, flamy, cockamamie

1.15.4
Emmy, semé, semi, gemmy, jemmy, lemme,
Clemmie, phlegmy, maremme

1.15.5
fermi

1.15.6
Tammie, tammy, gammy, mammee, mammy,
Sammy, chammy, chamois, shammy, jammy,
hammy, whammy, ramee, ramie, rammy,
trammie, Grammy, clammy, Miami

1.15.7
army, palmy, balmy, barmy, smarmy, swami,
tatami, tsunami, ex-army, gourami, pastrami,
macrame, macramé, salami, origami,
Yanomami, Salvation Army

1.15.8
pommy, tommy, Commie, commis, mommy

1.15.9
stormy, dormy

1.15.10
tummy, dummy, scummy, gummy, mummy,
chummy, rummy, Brummie, crumby, crummy,
scrummy, thrummy, yummy, lumme, plummy,
slummy

1.15.11
thymy, stymie, rimy, grimy, limey, blimey,
slimy, cor blimey, gorblimey

1.15.12
Twomey, rheumy, roomy, Rumi, spumy, fumy,
plumy, gloomy, mushroomy, perfumy

1.15.13
.1 epitome, atomy, anatomy, neuroanatomy,
zootomy, colpotomy, lobotomy, phlebotomy,
autotomy, phytotomy, cystotomy, dichotomy,
trichotomy, leucotomy, vagotomy, splenotomy,
tenotomy, splanchnotomy, lithotomy,
neurotomy, sclerotomy, nephrotomy, colotomy,
tracheotomy, craniotomy, pharyngotomy,
laryngotomy, laparotomy, enterotomy,
sequestrotomy, urethrotomy, omphalotomy,
episiotomy, ovariotomy, ureterotomy,

lumpectomy, tubectomy, lobectomy, cystectomy, mastectomy, appendectomy, splenectomy, vasectomy, gastrectomy, nephrectomy, colectomy, tonsillectomy, prostatectomy, clitoridectomy, pneumonectomy, sympathectomy, salpingectomy, hysterectomy, oophorectomy, ovariectomy, cholecystectomy, appendicectomy, ostomy, colostomy, tracheostomy, ileostomy, enterostomy **.2** sodomy, taxidermy, academy **.3** alchemy **.4** bigamy, digamy, trigamy, syngamy, polygamy, oogamy, autogamy, cleistogamy, endogamy, homogamy, xenogamy, monogamy, misogamy, exogamy, allogamy, hypergamy, anisogamy, heterogamy **.5** enemy, anomie, antinomy, McMenemy, arch-enemy, toponymy, hyponymy, autonomy, metonymy, antonymy, economy, homonymy, synonymy, teknonymy, isonomy, taxonomy, aeronomy, meronymy, gastronomy, astronomy, agronomy, pathognomy, physiognomy, anthroponymy, diseconomy, heteronomy, Deuteronomy **.6** thingummy **.7** infamy, blasphemy **.8** trisomy, sesame, blossomy, polysemy **.9** bosomy **.10** sashimi **.11** Jeremy, Laramie, gourami **.12** elemi, Bellamy, Ptolemy

1.15.14
fermi, germy, wormy, squirmy, diathermy, taxidermy, homoeothermy, homeothermy, homoiothermy, endothermy, agamospermy, poikilothermy

1.15.15
foamy, homey, loamy, Naomi, Dahomey, Salome, polychromy

1.15.16
acme

1.15.17
pygmy, borborygmi

1.15.18
AFSCME

1.15.19
Esme

1.15.20
Lakshmi

1.15.21
filmy, elmy, salmis

1.16.1
beanie, teeny, meanie, Feeney, sheeny, Cheney, genie, Jeannie, Heaney, weenie, weeny, wienie, tweeny, queenie, Sweeney, Renée, Trini, greeny, spleeny, capellini, Mitylene, tortellini, cannellini **.1** scaloppine **.2** bambini, Cherubini **.3** martini, spaghettini **.4** Houdini, Dandini **.5** zucchini, bikini, monokini **.6** Lamborghini® **.7** Borromini **.8** Panini, Bernini, Toscanini, Paganini **.9** Athene **.10** Rossini, grissini, Mazzini **.11** Tetrazzini **.12** Puccini, Gambaccini, fettuccine **.13** wahine **.14** linguine, McSweeney, teeny-weeny **.15** Cyrene, nerine, Santoríni,

Boccherini **.16** Bellini, Fellini, Cellini, Selene, Mitilíni, Magdalene, Rossellini, Mussolini, paraselene

1.16.2
Pinney, pinny, spinney, Binnie, tinny, Kinney, skinny, guinea, mini, Minnie, ninny, Finney, finny, Vinney, cine, shinny, Ginny, jinnee, jinni, Jinny, hinny, whinny, Winnie, Linnhe, Pliny, blini, McKinney, Niu Gini, dominee, Blue Vinney, Mawhinny, Dalwhinnie, supermini, piccaninny, telecine, Papua New Guinea

1.16.3
Tierney, amphictyony

1.16.4
veiny, zany, Chaney, Cheney, Cheyne, Janey, Haney, waney, rainy, brainy, grainy, Na-Dene, Khomeini, McIlvaney, Eugénie, Bahraini, Bahreini, Delaney, Allegheny, lilangeni

1.16.5
any, penne, penni, penny, benni, Benny, tenné, Dene, Denny, Kenney, Kenny, many, fenny, jenny, Rennie, Lennie, Lenny, blenny, two-a-penny, pinchpenny, catchpenny, Na-Dene, Kilkenny, McIlvenny, over-many, Abergavenny

1.16.6
Annie, Danny, canny, nanny, Fannie, fanny, shanny, tranny, cranny, granny, Mitanni, ca'canny, uncanny, Afghani, hootenanny, Giovanni, Durante, Pakistani

1.16.7
townie, towny, Downey, Downie, downy, brownie

1.16.8
ani, barney, Carney, carny, Kearney, Kearny, Varney, sarnie, blarney, Afghani, Armani, Omani, Giovanni, Galvani, maharani, Sobranie®, Killarney, Fulani, biriani, Cipriani, Zakopane, frangipani, Mbabane, Hindustani, Pakistani, Rajasthani, Mantovani, Don Giovanni, Rafsanjani, Modigliani, Azerbaijani

1.16.9
Bonnie, bonny, Connie, Johnnie, johnny, Suwannee, Swanee, Ronnie, Lonnie, ca'canny, gyronny, quadraphony

1.16.10
tawny, tourney, corny, thorny, horny, brawny, scrawny, lawny, Trelawney, mulligatawny

1.16.11
koiné

1.16.12
bunny, Tunney, tunny, dunny, gunny, money, funny, sonny, Sunni, sunny, honey, runny, beer money, baldmoney, hush money, unfunny, Ballymoney, loadsamoney

1.16.13
piny, spiny, tiny, viny, shiny, Heine, Heiney, whiny, winy, briny, liny, sunshiny, nerine, porcupiny

1.16.14
spoony, Cooney, gooney, Nguni, Mooney, Moonie, moony, Rooney, uni, puisne, puny, loony, Clunie, Cluny, cartoony, Río Muni

1.16.15
.1 peony, Léonie .2 Mahoney .3 Briony, bryony, Hermione .4 tourney .5 threepenny, fourpenny, tuppenny, twopenny, timpani, company, tenpenny, fivepenny, sixpenny, accompany, tuppenny-ha'penny, twopenny-halfpenny .6 ebony, Albany .7 dittany, prytany, Brittany, litany, betony, tetany, atony, satiny, rhatany, botany, cottony, buttony, muttony, gluttony, scrutiny, mutiny, Anthony, Antony, mountainy, destiny, brimstony, neoteny, geobotany, monotony, palaeobotany, astrobotany .8 Alderney, chalcedony .9 Gascony, Tuscany, balcony .10 agony, garganey, Antigone, telegony, theogony, cosmogony, mahogany, heterogony .11 simony, jiminy, Rimini, Emeny, Yemeni, lemony, Tammany, scammony, salmony, harmony, dominie, hominy, Germany, Romany, postliminy, hegemony, anemone, Gethsemane, disharmony, Melpomene, phillumeny, sanctimony, antimony, testimony, ignominy, parsimony, ceremony, patrimony, matrimony, acrimony, agrimony, alimony, palimony, agapemone, miminy-piminy, niminy-piminy .12 tiffany, epiphany, antiphony, Tisiphone, polyphony, Stephanie, Persephone, telephony, aphony, Zoffany, theophany, tautophony, Christophany, cacophony, homophony, quadraphony, quadrophony, colophony, stereophony, heterophony, euphony, symphony .13 Bethany .14 larceny, saxony, Mnemosyne, monopsony, oligopsony .15 raisiny, rosiny .16 cushiony .17 progeny, polygeny, polygyny, phytogeny, ontogeny, histogeny, endogeny, homogeny, monogeny, monogyny, pathogeny, misogyny, schizogeny, orogeny, androgyny, phylogeny, aborigine, osteogeny, anthropogeny, teratogeny, epeirogeny, epirogeny, heterogeny .18 tyranny, barony, Guarani, irony, synchrony, saffrony, diachrony, isochrony .19 oniony .20 villainy, Melanie, felony, colony, miscellany

1.16.16
Ernie, Burney, tourney, Kearney, Kearny, gurney, ferny, Verney, Verny, Czerny, journey, attorney, McInerney

1.16.17
pony, bony, Toni, tony, stony, coney, phoney, crony, yoni, Sloaney, Léonie, Dione, Kuoni, tortelloni, cannelloni, Giorgione, Antonioni, Sierra Leone, conversazione .1 Volpone, mascarpone .2 Zamboni .3 Buitoni®, brimstony, rigatoni, panettone .4 bordone, Bodoni .5 Marconi .6 Annigoni .7 spumoni, sanctimony .8 Albinoni .9 canzone, calzone .10 Manzoni, Ardizzone .11 Shoshone .12 Mahoney .13 Moroni, padrone, Mulroney, pepperoni, Gaborone, macaroni, cicerone,

minestrone .14 zabaglione .15 polony, baloney, bologna, boloney, Maloney, Moloney, abalone

1.16.18
halfpenny, ha'penny, Stepney, threepenny, fourpenny, tuppenny, twopenny, Ampney, company, shove-ha'penny, accompany, tuppenny-ha'penny, twopenny-halfpenny

1.16.19
Pitney, jitney, Whitney, Witney, Watney, Courtney, Putney, chutney, Pountney, Poultney, McCartney, monotony, Novotny

1.16.20
kidney, Sidney, Sydney, Adeney, Rodney, Evadne, Ariadne

1.16.21
Blakeney, acne, hackney, Cockney, hockney, Rockne, Procne, Orkney, Cuckney, McKechnie, chloracne, Arachne, pyrotechny

1.16.22
Agni, Cagney

1.16.23
chimney, Romney, Rhymney, calumny

1.16.24
Ifni, daphne, Gaffney

1.16.25
Graveney

1.16.26
Eithne

1.16.27
Disney, Chesney, Lesney, Grozny

1.17
stingy, dinghy, thingy, zingy, swingy, springy, stringy, lingy, clingy, tangy, hangi, twangy, slangy, pongy, Lange, puddingy, Missolonghi

1.18.1
beefy, leafy

1.18.2
iffy, spiffy, stiffy, niffy, sniffy, jiffy, whiffy, squiffy, Liffey, cliffy

1.18.3
Effie

1.18.4
taffy, daffy, cafe, NAAFI, cybercafé, echocardiography, echoencephalography, Raffi, chaffy, Kaddafi, Gaddafi, Cavafy

1.18.5
toffee, coffee, Coffey, Roffey, strophe

1.18.6
Morphy, wharfie, ectomorphy, endomorphy, homomorphy, mesomorphy

1.18.7
puffy, toughie, stuffy, Duffy, snuffy, huffy, roughy, scruffy, fluffy, sloughy, unstuffy

1.18.8
oofy, poofy, Dufy, goofy, Sufi

1.18.9
.1 salsify, theosophy, gymnosophy, philosophy
.2 atrophy, eutrophy, dystrophy, mycotrophy, hypertrophy, epistrophe, antistrophe, catastrophe, anastrophe, apostrophe, amyotrophy, oligotrophy **.3.1** epigraphy, stratigraphy, scintigraphy, tachygraphy, lexigraphy, serigraphy, calligraphy, telegraphy, radiotelegraphy, sciagraphy **.3.2** geography, biography, zoography, metallography, crystallography, osteography, radiography, cardiography, hagiography, ichthyography, physiography, angiography, zoogeography, biogeography, stereography, oreography, choreography, heliography, palaeography, paleography, bibliography, cholangiography, palaeogeography, phytogeography, historiography, autobiography, cholecysto-graphy, autoradiography, echoencephalography, electrocardiography, topography, typography, lipography, prosopography, anthropography, autotypography, dittography, cartography, autography, phytography, photography, cryptography, glyptography, pictography, chromatography, cinematography, telephotography, macrophotography, cacography, zincography, discography, lexicography, mammography, tomography, demography, nomography, thermography, sphygmography, cosmography, seismography, filmography, stenography, planography, pornography, phonography, ichnography, hymnography, ethnography, iconography, röntgenography, oceanography, uranography, selenography, orthography, mythography, lithography, opisthography, photolithography, chromolithography, nosography, hypsography, flexography, chirography, xerography, orography, chorography, pyrography, cerography, reprography, petrography, spectrography, hydrography, polarography, photomicrography, holography, xylography, haplography, dactylography, oscillography, electroencephalography

1.18.10
turfy, scurfy, murphy, furphy, surfy

1.18.11
Sophie, Brophy, trophy, strophe

1.18.12
comfy

1.18.13
Delphi, Malfi, Amalfi

1.19.1
peavey, Revie, Levi, Donlevy

1.19.2
spivvy, bivvy, divi, divvy, skivvy, civvy, chivvy, privy, Livy, tantivy, divi-divi

1.19.3
Pavey, Davie, Davy, Devi, cave, cavy, navy, wavy, gravy, slavey, agave, alla breve, Rikki-Tiki-Tavi

1.19.4
bevvy, bevy, Chevy, chevy, heavy, levee, Levi, levy, top-heavy, replevy

1.19.5
navvy, savvy, lavvy

1.19.6
ave, Garvey, Harvey, peccavi, agave, Mohave, Mojave, Rikki-Tiki-Tavi

1.19.7
Tovey, Dovey, covey, lovey, luvvy, lovey-dovey, Aberdovey

1.19.8
Iveagh, ivy

1.19.9
movie, groovy

1.19.10
Muscovy, anchovy, Pahlavi

1.19.11
Turvey, curvy, scurvy, Nervi, nervy, topsy-turvy

1.19.12
Povey, Tovey, grovy

1.19.13
envy, Canvey

1.19.14
Sylvie, moolvi, moolvie, Ogilvy

1.20.1
heathy, Lethe, Abernethy

1.20.2
pithy, smithy

1.20.3
breathy, Abernethy

1.20.4
Cathy, Kathy, Abernathy

1.20.5
McCarthy

1.20.6
bothy, Cothi, mothy, wrathy, frothy

1.20.7
toothy

1.20.8
apathy, sympathy, empathy, timothy, Dorothy, antipathy, telepathy, psychopathy, leucopathy, trichopathy, adenopathy, lymphopathy, neuropathy, hydropathy, nephropathy, allopathy, opsimathy, polymathy, chrestomathy, osteopathy, idiopathy, homeopathy, homoeopathy, retinopathy, naturopathy, encephalopathy

1.20.9
earthy

1.20.10
Xanthe, nepenthe, Iolanthe

1.20.11
lengthy

1.20.12
filthy, stealthy, healthy, wealthy, unhealthy

1.21
smithy, withy, lathy, mouthy, Southey, swarthy, smoothie, worthy, Honddu, seaworthy, airworthy, noteworthy, trustworthy, roadworthy, blameworthy, unworthy, loveworthy, praiseworthy, newsworthy, Elsworthy, Galsworthy, unseaworthy, creditworthy, untrustworthy

1.22.1
Treacy, Creasy, greasy, fleecy, divisi, Assisi, Tbilisi

1.22.2
kissy, missy, Cissie, Sissie, sissy, prissy, Chrissie

1.22.3
Piercy, idiocy, immediacy, intermediacy

1.22.4
pace, pacy, spacey, Basie, Stacy, Casey, racy, Tracy, Gracie, lacy, Candace, O'Casey, theocrasy, Sulawesi, Bovey Tracy

1.22.5
Bessie, messy, Nessie, jesse, Jessie, tressy, dressy, Crécy

1.22.6
Bassey, bassi, tassie, dassie, Cassie, gassy, massé, Massey, massy, sassy, chassis, Brassey, brassie, brassy, grassy, lassie, Plassey, classy, glacis, glassie, glassy, Manasseh, Malagasy, Tallahassee, Haile Selassie

1.22.7
mousey, mousy

1.22.8
Parcae, Darcy, farcy, brassy, grassy, Iasi, classy, glassie, glassy, sannyasi, sanyasi, dalasi, Adivasi

1.22.9
Ossie, posse, bossy, mossie, mossy, phossy, Rossi, drossy, glossy, Flossie, flossy

1.22.10
fainéancy

1.22.11
Dorsey, causey, gorsy, saucy, horsey, horsy, De Courcy

1.22.12
mussy, fussy, Hussey, hussy, unfussy

1.22.13
icy, spicey, spicy, dicey, vice, pricey, pricy, Berenice, pro hac vice

1.22.14
pussy

1.22.15
goosey, juicy, Lucey, Lucie, Lucy, Debussy, Watusi, Senussi, acey-deucy

1.22.16
.1 Chambourcy®. .2 papacy, haruspicy, episcopacy, archiepiscopacy .3 abbacy, embassy, celibacy

.4 statice, courtesy, fantasy, phantasy, testacy, eustasy, ecstasy, discourtesy, intestacy, apostasy, isostasy .5 odyssey, Chalcidice, Eurydice, theodicy, geodesy, candidacy .6 efficacy, graphicacy, advocacy, intricacy, delicacy, complicacy, prolificacy, inefficacy, equivocacy, indelicacy .7 legacy, argosy, surrogacy, delegacy, profligacy .8 pharmacy, primacy, Christmassy, supremacy, intimacy, ultimacy, diplomacy, contumacy, legitimacy, illegitimacy .9 Hennessy, Shaughnessy, lunacy, obstinacy, governessy, effeminacy, determinacy, pharmacognosy, indeterminacy .10 prophecy .11 privacy, controversy .12 adequacy, inadequacy .13 conspiracy, heresy, clerisy, Morrissey, oracy, phoresy, curacy, pleurisy, piracy, retiracy, literacy, numeracy, obduracy, accuracy, illiteracy, inveteracy, confederacy, immoderacy, innumeracy, itineracy, degeneracy, inaccuracy, unregeneracy, leprosy, actress, schoolmistressy, magistracy, secrecy, theocracy, theocrasy, hypocrisy, mobocracy, autocracy, plutocracy, stratocracy, landocracy, timocracy, democracy, monocracy, gynocracy, technocracy, isocracy, adhocracy, bureaucracy, hierocracy, ochlocracy, hagiocracy, physiocracy, meritocracy, gerontocracy, aristocracy, gynaecocracy, idiosyncrasy .14 jealousy, prelacy, Palissy, fallacy, policy, Wallasey, anglice, impolicy, inviolacy, articulacy, immaculacy, inarticulacy

1.22.17
Percy, pursy, mercy, Circe, Hersey, arsy-versy, controversy

1.22.18
Josie, viva-voce

1.22.19
tipsy, kipsie, gypsy, Pepsi®, biopsy, popsy, Topsy, copsy, dropsy, Dempsey, Campsie, Poughkeepsie, autopsy, necropsy, bankruptcy, lithotripsy, epilepsy, catalepsy, narcolepsy, nympholepsy, acatalepsy

1.22.20
Wibsey, fubsy

1.22.21
Uffizi, Pizzey, ditzy, Mitzi, ritzy, glitzy, itsy-bitsy, etc, Betsy, tsetse, baronetcy, patsy, flatsie, Nazi, Pestalozzi, gutsy, tootsie, footsie, FT-SE, Watutsi, Abruzzi, Tutsi, rootsy, cornetcy, curtsy, Surtsey, Chertsey, Yangtze, artsy-craftsy

1.22.22
pixie, Dixey, dixie, tricksy, Trixie, sexy, prexy, cachexy, unsexy, apoplexy, cataplexy, electroplexy, taxi, maxi, Haxey, waxy, Laxey, ataxy, Cotopaxi, stereotaxy, epitaxy, heterotaxy, phyllotaxy, ataraxy, Oxhey, poxy, boxy, doxy, moxie, foxy, Roxy, proxy, epoxy, hydroxy, Biloxi, amphioxi, orthodoxy, heterodoxy, unorthodoxy, Orczy, booksy, galaxy, Oaksey, folksy, bonxie

1.22.23

.1 chintzy, wincey, De Quincey **.2** sentiency, radiancy, leniency, fainéancy, deviancy, transiency, pruriency, recreancy, brilliancy, saliency, recipiency, incipiency, expediency, subserviency, esuriency, resiliency, ebulliency, circumambiency, inexpediency **.3** Montmorency **.4** antsy, Nancy, nancy, fancy, chancy, Clancey, Clancy, geomancy, zoomancy, bibliomancy, cartomancy, rhabdomancy, pyromancy, chiromancy, necromancy, oneiromancy **.5** bouncy, viscountcy, paramountcy **.6** poncey, poncy, sonsie, sonsy **.7** sprauncy **.8** Muncie, Runcie **.9** ensigncy **.10.1** buoyancy, flamboyancy, pliancy, compliancy, congruency, constituency, truancy, fluency **.10.2** flippancy, rampancy, discrepancy, occupancy, unoccupancy, under-occupancy, lambency, absorbency, recumbency, incumbency, patency, latency, blatancy, potency, captaincy, chieftaincy, instancy, constancy, appetency, impotency, competency, renitency, hesitancy, irritancy, militancy, advertency, prepotency, adjutancy, expectancy, accountancy, persistency, insistency, consistency, inconstancy, consultancy, exultancy, intermittency, precipitancy, inappetency, incompetency, inhabitancy, concomitancy, impenitency, inadvertency, inconsistency, self-consistency, cadency, ardency, mordancy, stridency, pudency, verdancy, pendency, tendency, discordancy, precedency, residency, presidency, dependency, impendency, intendancy, ascendancy, transcendency, resplendency, despondency, respondency, redundancy, codependency, independency, superintendency, interdependency, piquancy, vacancy, peccancy, impeccancy, mendicancy, significancy, insignificancy, arrogancy, extravagancy **.10.3** clemency, dormancy, inclemency, adamancy, diathermancy, tenancy, sonancy, pregnancy, stagnancy, subtenancy, lieutenancy, pertinency, abstinency, immanency, prominency, permanency, opponency, benignancy, malignancy, oppugnancy, undertenancy, locum tenency, impermanency **.10.4** infancy, sycophancy, fervency, solvency, relevancy, conservancy, insolvency, irrelevancy, decency, recency, nascency, lucency, indecency, adjacency, complacency, quiescency, incessancy, translucency, innocency, conversancy, effervescency, alkalescency, recusancy, trenchancy, efficiency, deficiency, sufficiency, proficiency, inefficiency, insufficiency, self-sufficiency, immuno-deficiency, regency, agency, sergeancy, urgency, cogency, stringency, tangency, plangency, pungency, reagency, subagency, exigency, emergency, divergency, convergency, insurgency, contingency, astringency, intransigency, counterinsurgency, frequency, infrequency, eigenfrequency, delinquency, coherency, incoherency, errancy, aberrancy,

transparency, currency, iterancy, itinerancy, belligerency, nonbelligerency, vibrancy, vagrancy, fragrancy, flagrancy, poignancy, valency, bivalency, divalency, trivalency, covalency, multivalency, monovalency, electrovalency, repellency, water-repellency, equipollency, sibilancy, somnolency, excellency, flatulency, purulency, corpulency, truculency, ambivalency, equivalency, chaplaincy

1.22.24
Livesey

1.22.25
Rothesay

1.22.26
Elsie, Delsey, Selsey, Chelsea, Dulcie, schmaltzy, normalcy, colonelcy, minstrelsy

1.23.1
easy, Kesey, sneezy, Vesey, cheesy, wheezy, queasy, Sqezy, breezy, greasy, sleazy, Sleepeezee, Zambezi, speakeasy, uneasy, Assisi, Parcheesi®, pachisi, easy-peasy

1.23.2
Izzy, Pizzey, busy, tizzy, dizzy, fizzy, frizzy, Lizzie, Lizzy

1.23.3
Basie, daisy, Maisie, mazy, Vaizey, hazy, crazy, lazy, glazy, Farnese, stir-crazy, Bel Paese®, ups-a-daisy, upsy-daisy, oops-a-daisy, Piranesi, Veronese, Buthelezi

1.23.4
prezzie

1.23.5
snazzy, jazzy, Anasazi

1.23.6
drowsy, frowzy, lousy, blowsy, Dalhousie, housey-housey

1.23.7
Stasi, carzey, khazi, Ghazi, quasi, Swazi, Nastase, Abkhazi, Benghazi, kamikaze, Ashkenazi, Ashkenazy, Anasazi, Esterhazy

1.23.8
Aussie, Ozzie, cossie, mossie

1.23.9
causey, gauzy

1.23.10
Boise, noisy, malvoisie

1.23.11
SCSI, scuzzy, muzzy, fuzzy, hussy, huzzy, fuzzy-wuzzy

1.23.12
oozy, Uzi®, Boosey, boozy, doozy, snoozy, Susie, Suzy, choosy, woozy, Pewsey, Pusey, newsy, bluesy, floozie, jacuzzi, Dalhousie

1.23.13
poesy, Brindisi, euphrasy

1.23.14
durzi, kersey, Mersey, furzy, jersey, Stogursey

1.23.15
posey, posy, bosie, dozy, COHSE, cosy, cozy, mosey, nosy, Josie, Rosie, rosy, prosy, Losey

1.23.16
Wibsey, Abse

1.23.17
klutzy

1.23.18
Pudsey, sudsy, woodsy, Lindsay, Lindsey, Bermondsey

1.23.19
whimsy, flimsy, Ramsay, Ramsey, malmsey, Romsey, clumsy

1.23.20
teensy, Kinsey, quinsy, Lindsay, Lindsey, Lynsey, frenzy, pansy, Tansey, tansy, Swansea, bronzy, Guernsey, Pevensey, Mackenzie, Firenze, Bermondsey, teensy-weensy

1.23.21
Livesey

1.23.22
palsy, ballsy, Wolsey, woolsey, Molesey, palsy-walsy, linsey-woolsey

1.24.1
specie

1.24.2
dishy, fishy, Vichy, squishy, swishy, rishi, maharishi, Mitsubishi®

1.24.3
Swadeshi

1.24.4
fleshy, Bangladeshi

1.24.5
ashy, mashie, trashy, plashy, splashy, flashy, bimbashi, Lubumbashi

1.24.6
marshy, Ustashe

1.24.7
washy, squashy, sloshy, wishy-washy

1.24.8
Givenchy

1.24.9
gushy, mushy, rushy, brushy, plushy, slushy

1.24.10
pushy, Bushey, bushy, cushy

1.24.11
sushi

1.24.12
rubbishy, flourishy

1.24.13
Hershey

1.24.14
imshi, Gramsci

1.24.15
Binchy, Vinci, Frenchy, Ranchi, branchy, conchie, paunchy, raunchy, punchy, bunchy, crunchy, da Vinci, Comanche, Givenchy

1.24.16
bolshie

1.25.1
Peachey, peachy, beechy, preachy, screechy, Campeachy, Campeche, obeche, Radice, caliche, Eurydice, Berenice

1.25.2
itchy, pitchy, bitchy, titchy, kitschy, twitchy, Richie, Ritchie

1.25.3
Strachey

1.25.4
tetchy, sketchy, vetchy, stretchy

1.25.5
arrivederci

1.25.6
patchy, catchy, snatchy, scratchy, fratchy, Apache, shakuhachi

1.25.7
pouchy, grouchy, slouchy

1.25.8
Archie, starchy, hibachi, vivace, Karachi, Pagliacci, Fibonacci, shakuhachi, Liberace

1.25.9
notchy, splotchy, blotchy

1.25.10
touchy, duchy

1.25.11
Gucci, smoochy, Vespucci, Noguchi, penuche, Bertolucci

1.25.12
spinachy, semplice

1.25.13
churchy

1.25.14
viva-voce, sotto voce

1.25.15
kimchi

1.25.16
squelchy

1.26.1
widgie, squidgy, ridgy

1.26.2
Agee, stagey, stagy, cagey, sagy

1.26.3
edgy, veggie, vegie, sedgy, wedgie, ledgy

1.26.4
haji, koradji, komitadji

1.26.5
Argie, bhaji, haji, Panaji, argy-bargy

1.26.6
podgy, stodgy, dodgy, splodgy, pedagogy, demagogy, anagoge, anagogy

1.26.7
orgy, Georgie

1.26.8
pudgy, bhaji, budgie, smudgy, sludgy

1.26.9
Fuji

1.26.10
.1 cabbagy .2 liturgy, strategy, cottagey .3 prodigy .4 romaji .5 spinachy, synergy, energy .6 effigy, geophagy, hippophagy, ichthyophagy, anthropophagy .7 lethargy .8 syzygy .9 porridgy, koradji .10 villagey, trilogy, antilogy, brachylogy, elegy, allergy, Lalage, hypallage, metallurgy, mammalogy, analogy, tetralogy, genealogy, mineralogy .11.1 ology, rheology, neology, theology, geology, chaology, biology, myology, bryology, zoology, oology, symbolology, aetiology, etiology, osteology, deltiology, ideology, radiology, cardiology, audiology, archaeology, hagiology, semeiology, semiology, craniology, balneology, ophiology, ichthyology, speciology, glaciology, sociology, axiology, physiology, phraseology, museology, Mariology, choreology, embryology, speleology, teleology, cryobiology, bryozoology, satanology, amphibiology, ethnoarchaeology, kinesiology, semasiology, heresiology, ecclesiology, crustaceology, liturgiology, hydrogeology, Assyriology, soteriology, bacteriology, venereology, radiobiology, sociobiology, aerobiology, microbiology, photobiology, psychobiology, exobiology, neurobiology, astrobiology, protozoology, epidemiology, onomasiology, anaesthesiology, anesthesiology, psychophysiology, neurophysiology, electrobiology, electrophysiology
.11.2 carpology, topology, typology, apology, tropology, escapology, anthropology, palaeoanthropology, tribology, symbology, amphibology, cetology, scatology, heortology, tautology, cytology, otology, cryptology, proctology, pantology, ontology, deontology, neontology, Scientology®, neonatology, herpetology, eschatology, haematology, hematology, thremmatology, thaumatology, primatology, climatology, rheumatology, pneumatology, dermatology, stomatology, somatology, cosmetology, thanatology, planetology, erotology, teratology, Egyptology, insectology, dialectology, palaeontology, paleontology, odontology, gerontology, protistology, parasitology, symptomatology, numismatology, periodontology, palaeoclimatology, histology, Christology, pestology, kidology, pedology, Indology, orchidology, methodology, iridology,

pteridology, ethnomethodology .11.3 cacology, mycology, phycology, psychology, ecology, trichology, oncology, conchology, muscology, palaeoecology, paleoecology, codicology, pharmacology, myrmecology, synecology, gynaecology, gynecology, lexicology, toxicology, musicology, malacology, Etruscology, metapsychology, parapsychology, neuropsychology, psychopharmacology, ethnomusicology, algology, laryngology, otolaryngology, otorhinolaryngology .11.4 gemmology, pomology, homology, zymology, sphygmology, cosmology, seismology, victimology, enzymology, etymology, potamology, entomology, ophthalmology, epistemology, enology, oenology, penology, splenology, Sinology, menology, phenology, phonology, chronology, phrenology, hypnology, technology, splanchnology, hymnology, limnology, ethnology, campanology, sindonology, iconology, lichenology, volcanology, vulcanology, röntgenology, demonology, criminology, terminology, biocoenology, geochronology, selenology, palynology, Kremlinology, immunology, biotechnology, arachnology, phenomenology, endocrinology, glottochronology, dendrochronology, radioimmunology, nanotechnology, electrotechnology .11.5 psephology, nephology, graphology, carphology, morphology, ufology, geomorphology, ethology, pathology, mythology, lithology, anthology, ornithology, helminthology, sociopathology, phytopathology, histopathology, psychopathology, neuropathology, nosology, glossology, misology, posology, sexology, doxology, reflexology, serology, aerology, orology, horology, chorology, virology, hierology, neurology, coprology, ombrology, urology, metrology, patrology, petrology, astrology, hydrology, dendrology, necrology, hygrology, nephrology, meteorology, oneirology, papyrology, heterology, martyrology, acarology, numerology, futurology, characterology, gastroenterology, philology, haplology, dactylology, vexillology, eulogy

1.26.11
theurgy, clergy, chemurgy, zymurgy, micrurgy, telergy, dramaturgy, thaumaturgy, metallurgy

1.26.12
anagoge, anagogy, paragoge

1.26.13
bougie, stingy, dingy, mingy, whingey, whingy, fringy, mangey, mangy, rangy, Angie, kanji, spongy, bungee, scungy, gungy, grungy, lozengy, basenji, satranji, Ranjitsinhji

1.26.14
Algie, Algy, Golgi, bulgy

1.27
Sheehy, Leahy, Caughey, Fahy, Brahe, Haughey, bohea, Mulcahy, McGahey, Rajshahi, surahi, takahe, tarakihi

1.28
Dewi, Kabwe, Bequia, segue, Conwy, Mynwy, Vyrnwy, Malawi, Zimbabwe, colloquy, obloquy, tu quoque, Deganwy, Myfanwy, Goronwy, Lilongwe, McElwie, ventriloquy, soliloquy, Filioque, virginibus puerisque

1.29.1
Pirie, piripiri, hara-kiri

1.29.2
eerie, Erie, aerie, eyrie, Peary, peri, Pery, beery, teary, dearie, Geary, smeary, theory, cheery, weary, quaere, query, dreary, leery, bleary, Cleary, Clery, Dun Laoghaire **.1** apiary, topiary, vespiary **.2** bestiary, vestiary **.3** presidiary, subsidiary, incendiary, intermediary **.4** knopkierie **.5** Kashmiri **.6** laniary, herniary, balneary, praemunire **.7** breviary, aviary **.8** braziery, graziery, glaziery, hosiery **.9** retiary, justiciary, fiduciary, beneficiary **.10** aweary, unweary **.11** farriery, furriery, miserere **.12** biliary, miliary, ciliary, O'Leary, nobiliary, mobiliary, homiliary, auxiliary, superciliary, domiciliary

1.29.3
perry, Pery, beret, berry, bury, terry, Derry, Ceri, Kerry, skerry, merry, ferry, very, sherry, cherry, Gerry, jerry, wherry, rebury, blueberry, snowberry, soapberry, loganberry, boysenberry, spiceberry, whortleberry, knobkerrie, carferry, Horseferry, Queensferry, choke cherry, equerry, beriberi, elderberry, checkerberry, serviceberry, secretary, Londonderry, Pondicherry, unnecessary, undersecretary

1.29.4
airy, aerie, eyrie, Pery, dairy, Dari, Carew, Carey, Cary, scary, Mary, nary, faerie, faery, fairy, vary, chary, hairy, wary, prairie, lairy, clary, glairy, glary, unbury, costmary, Guarneri, canary, Azeri, unwary, Nyerere, contrary, Salieri, cassowary, Tipperary, Inveraray, miserere, condottiere, carabiniere, Abertillery

1.29.5
parry, Barrie, Barry, tarry, Carrie, carry, Cary, karri, Garry, Gary, gharry, marry, harry, Larry, Clarrie, miscarry, glengarry, remarry, intermarry

1.29.6
sparry, Bari, tarry, starry, mare, Mari, sari, Campari®, Qatari, Atari®, Scutari, shikari, askari, Zanskari, tamari, safari, Vasari, Nizari, Bihari, Ferrari®, Harare, curare, Cagliari, Zanzibari, ricercare, terramare, calamari, Rastafari, Stradivari, charivari, Mata Hari, Kalahari, certiorari, in statu pupillari

1.29.7
corrie, Snorri, sorry, zori, whare, quarry, Laurie, Lawrey, Lawrie, lorry, Florrie, Macquarie

1.29.8
Pori, Tory, storey, story, dory, Corey, Cory, gory, Maury, moory, saury, zori, hoary, Rory, Ruaridh, curie, fury, lory, glory, Florey, flory, satori, centaury, Suntory®, clearstory, clerestory, tandoori, Ruwenzori, furore, outlawry, vainglory, Maggiore, Manipuri, cacciatore, multistorey, understorey, hunky-dory, amphigori, Tobermory, Montessori, monsignore, Montefiore

1.29.9
spurrey, dhurrie, durrie, durry, Currie, curry, scurry, Murray, murrey, surrey, hurry, worry, plurry, flurry, slurry, hurry-scurry

1.29.10
matsuri

1.29.11
.1 bowery, towery, dowry, cowrie, kauri, Gowrie, Maori, showery, loury, Lowery, Lowrie, Lowry, floury, flowery, Blairgowrie **.2** aerie, eyrie, spiry, diary, miry, fiery, wiry, priory, briery, friary, transire, expiry, inquiry, enquiry **.3** moory, Jewry, jury, houri, Ruaridh, Drury, Urey, curie, Newry, fury, fleury, de jure, Manipuri, fioriture, tandoori, amphigouri, Missouri, statuary, mortuary, sumptuary, actuary, sanctuary, venturi, obituary, voluptuary, electuary, tumultuary, usufructuary, residuary, Inverurie, Allbeury, Dioscuri **.4** brewery **.5** zedoary **.6** frippery, slippery, apery, papery, napery, vapory, vapoury, japery, drapery, grapery, peppery, coppery, foppery, dupery, popery, blimpery, temporary, trumpery, polypary, contemporary, extemporary, extempore **.7.1** Ebury, Cleobury, bayberry, tayberry, blaeberry, cowberry, Barbary, barberry, snobbery, jobbery, robbery, slobbery, Horbury, strawberry, rubbery, shrubbery, blubbery, bribery, Rubery, dewberry, Newbury, blueberry, Canterbury, elderberry, Overbury, syllabary, Burberry®, turbary, snowberry, crowberry **.7.2** Tetbury, Westbury, Astbury, Ledbury, Padbury, Cadbury, Bradbury, cloudberry, Sudbury, Oldbury, hackberry, blackberry, chokeberry, dogberry, Embury, baneberry, Tenbury, fen-berry, anbury, Banbury, Stanbury, Danbury, cranberry, Bunbury, Sunbury, wineberry, Turnberry, Rattenbury, Chanctonbury, Glastonbury, Roddenberry, Brackenbury, Alconbury, loganberry, Canonbury, Avebury, Asbury, Shaftesbury, waxberry, Tewkesbury, naseberry, raspberry, Fosbury, gooseberry, Dewsbury, Shrewsbury, Rosebery, Amesbury, Samlesbury, Malmesbury, Bloomsbury, Queensberry, Finsbury, Sainsbury, Wednesbury, Lansbury, Lounsbury, Doonesbury, Kingsbury, Spilsbury, Aylesbury, Salisbury, Haight-Ashbury, bilberry, tilbury, Albury, mulberry, Soulbury, whortleberry, Pendlebury, huckleberry **.8.1** eatery, secretory, excretory, skittery, jittery, twittery, littery, glittery, nitwittery, expiatory, mediatory, deviatory, aleatory, spoliatory, calumniatory,

abbreviatory, alleviatory, appreciatory, associatory, denunciatory, renunciatory, depreciatory, propitiatory, initiatory, conciliatory, reconciliatory, retaliatory **.8.2** participatory, anticipatory, emancipatory, approbatory, incubatory, disapprobatory, hortatory, citatory, rotatory, gestatory, gustatory, sternutatory, incantatory, commendatory, depredatory, intimidatory, elucidatory, consolidatory, placatory, masticatory, dedicatory, indicatory, vindicatory, reificatory, deprecatory, imprecatory, supplicatory, confiscatory, communicatory, justificatory, modificatory, unificatory, pacificatory, classificatory, clarificatory, purificatory, qualificatory, equivocatory, nugatory, mitigatory, castigatory, confirmatory, cachinnatory, condemnatory, hallucinatory, innovatory, elevatory, compensatory, pulsatory, accusatory, gyratory, vibratory, castratory, migratory, celebratory, execratory, consecratory, transmigratory, emigratory, denigratory, reverberatory, revelatory, flagellatory, adulatory, undulatory, stipulatory, circulatory, regulatory, congratulatory, articulatory, self-congratulatory **.8.3** rettery, battery, tattery, cattery, mattery, chattery, flattery, Slattery, self-flattery **.8.4** artery, Tartary, martyry, Òttery, pottery, tottery, lottery, Godwottery, cautery, mortary, watery, buttery, spluttery, fluttery, niterie, Scutari, bijouterie, contributory, distributary, persecutory, circumlocutory **.8.5** dietary, proprietary, insinuatory, extenuatory, pituitary **.8.6** repertory, raspatory, inculpatory, exculpatory, presbytery, exhibitory, prohibitory, inhibitory, potatory, saltatory, exhortatory, invitatory, excitatory, salutatory, auscultatory, laevorotatory, dextrorotatory, predatory, auditory, laudatory, sudatory, feudatory, mandatary, mandatory, hereditary, retardatory, transudatory, amendatory, emendatory, recommendatory, precatory, piscatory, judicatory, explicatory, evocatory, advocatory, invocatory, predicatory, revocatory, vesicatory, manducatory, obfuscatory, prognosticatory, certificatory, excommunicatory, negatory, purgatory, obligatory, derogatory, compurgatory, expurgatory, objurgatory, interrogatory, investigatory, supererogatory **.8.7** limitary, cemetery, crematory, amatory, cometary, vomitory, dormitory, fumitory, termitary, defamatory, desquamatory, acclamatory, declamatory, proclamatory, exclamatory, inflammatory, performatory, reformatory, informatory, lachrymatory, affirmatory, anti-inflammatory, minatory, divinatory, primogenitary, vanitory, sanatory, sanitary, planetary, unsanitary, insanitary, explanatory, interplanetary, self-explanatory, monitory, protonotary, premonitory, admonitory, prothonotary, monetary, unitary, punitory, combinatory, criminatory,

comminatory, fulminatory, procrastinatory, recriminatory, incriminatory, discriminatory, eliminatory, exterminatory, vaticinatory, phonatory, dignitary, signatory, cosignatory, recognitory, damnatory **.8.8** prefatory, offertory, lavatory, conservatory, observatory, plebiscitary, dispensatory, transitory, depositary, depository, repository, suppository, expository, excusatory, improvisatory, budgetary **.8.9** territory, feretory, oratory, separatory, libratory, secretary, respiratory, inspiratory, preparatory, declaratory, laboratory, exploratory, adjuratory, perspiratory, transpiratory, expiratory, procuratory, corroboratory, impetratory, immigratory, remuneratory, refrigeratory, inauguratory, undersecretary **.8.10** tributary, statutory, locutory, salutary, retributory, executory, interlocutory, dilatory, military, depilatory, distillatory, unmilitary, oscillatory, paramilitary, pellitory, solitary, consolatory, gratulatory, copulatory, ambulatory, osculatory, stimulatory, ovulatory, assimilatory, dissimilatory, capitulatory, expostulatory, manipulatory, confabulatory, deambulatory, perambulatory, gesticulatory, matriculatory, ejaculatory, emasculatory, self-regulatory, coagulatory, recapitulatory, circumambulatory, condolatory, oblatory **.8.11** otary, coterie, motory, notary, votary, rotary, locomotory **.8.12** scriptory, preemptory, peremptory, interruptory, victory, nectary, sectary, rectory, factory, refectory, insectary, trajectory, directory, enactory, olfactory, refractory, phylactery, perfunctory, interdictory, benedictory, contradictory, maledictory, valedictory, interjectory, ex-directory, genuflectory, calefactory, manufactory, satisfactory, introductory, self-contradictory, dissatisfactory, unsatisfactory, wintery, printery, splintery, sedentary, commentary, promontory, momentary, inventory, dysentery, mesentery, effrontery, pigmentary, segmentary, voluntary, testamentary, sedimentary, rudimentary, ligamentary, tenementary, filamentary, elementary, alimentary, parliamentary, supplementary, complementary, compli-mentary, documentary, tegumentary, involuntary, unparliamentary, uncomplimentary, integumentary, Europarliamentary, bistoury, mystery, history, blistery, clerestory, mastery, plastery, blustery, huckstery, consistory, prehistory, self-mastery, baptistery, monastery, phalanstery, upholstery, ethnohistory, overmastery, smeltery, psaltery, desultory, adultery: (+ **1.29.15**) **.9** powdery, Chaudhury, doddery, shuddery, spidery, rudery, prudery, tindery, cindery, boundary, quandary, thundery, bindery, prebendary, secondary, legendary, bouldery, del credere, embroidery, do-goodery, lapidary, dromedary, camaraderie: (+ **1.29.16**) **.10** mickerie, mickery, Vickery, chicory, hickory, trickery, bakery, fakery, jacquerie, peccary, daiquiri, knackery, Thackeray, Zachary, hackery, quackery, mockery, rockery, crockery, puckery, succory, cookery, rookery, crookery, Tanqueray, monkery, piscary, whiskery, brusquerie, Valkyrie, Terpsichore, knick-knackery, gimcrackery, peacockery, grotesquerie, grotesquery, hypothecary, apothecary, jiggery-pokery, mountebankery: (+ **1.29.17**) **.11** piggery, whiggery, priggery, vagary, beggary, Gregory, waggery, toggery, hoggery, puggaree, buggery, snuggery, thuggery, sugary, roguery, angary, Hungary, Calgary, amphigori, humbuggery, skulduggery, category, vinegary, allegory, ironmongery, Devanagari, demagoguery, pettifoggery, subcategory: (+ **1.29.18**) **.12** creamery, shimmery, Amory, emery, Emory, memory, mammary, armoury, Montgomery, mummery, nummary, summary, summery, flummery, primary, plumery, bloomery, spermary, rosemary, flimflammery, gendarmerie, parfumerie, perfumery, customary, gossamery, calamary, infirmary, supernumerary **.13.1** beanery, centenary, deanery, denary, venery, scenery, senary, greenery, plenary, catenary, septenary, bicentenary, tercentenary, quingentenary, duodenary, subdeanery, machinery, tricentenary, septcentenary, sexcentenary, quincentenary, septuagenary, bimillenary, quatercentenary, sesquicentenary, octocentenary, disciplinary, interdisciplinary, chicanery, antennary, millenary, tannery, stannary, cannery, granary, clownery, Connery, swannery, ornery, joinery, gunnery, nunnery, pinery, binary, finery, vinery, winery, quinary, swinery, refinery, goonery, unary, lampoonery, festoonery, cocoonery, buffoonery, poltroonery, lacunary, sublunary, translunary, superlunary **.13.2** concubinary, octonary, ordinary, subordinary, unordinary, extraordinary, cotyledonary, consuetudinary, valetudinary, seminary, luminary, pulmonary, preliminary, prolegomenary, cardiopulmonary, antiphonary, mercenary, eleemosynary, concretionary, tuitionary, prohibitionary, petitionary, seditionary, traditionary, missionary, commissionary, transitionary, repetitionary, expeditionary, stationary, stationery, probationary, geostationary, deflationary, reflationary, inflationary, disinflationary, cessionary, confessionary, recessionary, processionary, concessionary, discretionary, cautionary, precautionary, ablutionary, substitutionary, executionary, elocutionary, evolutionary, devolutionary, revolutionary, dissolutionary, circumlocutionary, pre-revolutionary, unrevolutionary, counterrevolutionary, excursionary, diversionary, reversionary, dictionary, lectionary, fractionary, functionary, confectionary, confectionery, reactionary, interjectionary, insurrectionary, pensionary, expansionary, convulsionary, visionary,

enginery, divisionary, revisionary, exclusionary, questionary, legionary, paginary, imaginary, sexagenary, quinquagenary, sanguinary, coronary, urinary, veterinary, genito-urinary, millinery, culinary **.13.3** ternary, turnery, fernery, quaternary, nonary, zonary, signary, hymnary: (+ **1.29.20**) **.14** wafery, porphyry, puffery, spoofery, sulfury, sulphury, midwifery, housewifery, periphery **.15** thievery, spivvery, shivery, quivery, livery, Avery, knavery, Savery, savory, savoury, wavery, quavery, Lavery, slavery, severy, reverie, carvery, ivory, Bouverie, servery, ovary, Bovary, silvery, calvary, delivery, unsavory, unsavoury, Llandovery, recovery, discovery, salivary, olivary, rediscovery, self-discovery: (+ **1.29.22**) **.16** smithery **.17** dithery, slithery, feathery, heathery, leathery, lathery, smothery **.18** pâtisserie, rotisserie, tracery, pessary, accessory, possessory, intercessory, brasserie, tracasserie, glossary, sorcery, spicery, derisory, dimissory, emissary, lamasery, commissary, promissory, janissary, vavasory, adversary, necessary, unnecessary, bursary, cursory, mercery, nursery, precursory, anniversary, grocery, greengrocery, sensory, chancery, dispensary, suspensory, ostensory, condensery, incensory, responsory, extrasensory, caravanserai, compulsory **.19** misery, causerie, hosiery, rosary, chinoiserie, revisory, provisory, advisory, illusory, delusory, prolusory, janizary, supervisory **.20** fishery, trashery, noshery, washery, tertiary, gaucherie, luxury, justiciary, judiciary, fiduciary, beneficiary, haberdashery, penitentiary, evidentiary, residentiary, plenipotentiary **.21** braziery, treasury, lingerie, usury, injury, gingery, scavengery, orangery **.22** pituri, stitchery, witchery, treachery, lechery, hatchery, archery, butchery, bestiary, debauchery **.23** Margery, Marjorie, forgery, drudgery, perjury, surgery, soldiery, menagerie, imagery, savagery, cryosurgery, incendiary, neurosurgery, microsurgery, psychosurgery **.24** equerry, cassowary, antiquary, reliquary **.25** orrery, horary, February, library, literary, contrary, cinerary, honorary, funerary, vulnerary, Makerere, bizarrerie, unliterary, arbitrary, subcontrary, registrary, itinerary, interlibrary **.26** estuary, mercury, augury, strangury, signory, seigneury, seigniory, penury, January, ossuary, colliery, stipendiary, pecuniary **.27** sealery, Tuileries, pillory, Hilary, Hillary, frillery, papillary, capillary, artillery, fritillary, distillery, armillary, bacillary, axillary, maxillary, ancillary, fibrillary, codicillary, domiciliary, subaxillary, premaxillary, submaxillary, supramaxillary, nailery, quailery, raillery, Ellery, celery, vitellary, calorie, gallery, Malory, Valerie, Valéry, salary, low-calorie, intercalary, kilocalorie, owlery, corollary, coloury, scullery, gullery, medullary, foolery, tomfoolery, carpellary, pupillary, tutelary, pistillary, mamillary, chancellery, epistolary, drollery, cajolery, exemplary, diablerie, cartulary, scapulary, formulary, capitulary, constabulary, vocabulary, tintinnabulary, cutlery, pedlary, saddlery, chandlery, jugglery, burglary

1.29.12
spurry, myrrhy, firry, furry, blurry

1.29.13
Capri, lamprey

1.29.14
Aubrey, Kirkcudbright, ambry, hombre, aumbry

1.29.15
Petrie, phratry, Rattray, Hawtrey **.1** podiatry, psychiatry **.2** poetry **.3** puppetry **.4** Babbittry, hobbitry **.5** banditry, punditry **.6** parquetry, marquetry, coquetry, rocketry, circuitry, trinketry, basketry, musketry, microcircuitry **.7** bigotry, faggotry **.8** symmetry, altimetry, tachymetry, planimetry, gravimetry, asymmetry, dissymmetry, dosimetry, acidimetry, saccharimetry, calorimetry, colorimetry, polarimetry, alkalimetry, telemetry, photogrammetry, geometry, biometry, zoometry, radiometry, audiometry, eudiometry, stoichiometry, craniometry, goniometry, sociometry, stereometry, potentiometry, anthropometry, photometry, optometry, magnetometry, refractometry, spectrophotometry, odometry, psychometry, viscometry, thermometry, seismometry, anemometry, clinometry, chronometry, iconometry, trigonometry, uranometry, morphometry, isometry, hypsometry, pyrometry, barometry, spectrometry, hydrometry, micrometry, hygrometry, saccharometry, electrometry, interferometry, coulometry, bolometry, nephelometry, alcoholometry, summitry **.9** cabinetry, gannetry, vanitory **.10** corsetry **.11** gadgetry **.12** barratry **.13** zealotry, helotry, varletry, harlotry, zoolatry, plutolatry, Christolatry, bardolatry, idolatry, monolatry, pyrolatry, hierolatry, necrolatry, hagiolatry, ophiolatry, ichthyolatry, mariolatry, bibliolatry, iconolatry, demonolatry, toiletry **.14** McMurtry **.15** wintry, entry, sentry, gentry, re-entry, pantry, gantry, chantry, gauntry, country, upcountry, West Country, carpentry, sedentary, pedantry, tenantry, infantry, pageantry, errantry, gallantry, knight-errantry, Daventry, Coventry, peasantry, pheasantry, pleasantry, unpleasantry **.16** Langtry **.17** pastry, Destry, vestry, McNestry, ancestry, casuistry, papistry, tapestry, artistry, baptistry, dentistry, industry, chemistry, palmistry, ministry, tanistry, monastery, sophistry, registry, Oswestry, forestry, floristry, biochemistry, geochemistry, agro-industry, radiochemistry, stereochemistry, photo-chemistry, spectrochemistry, phytochemistry, histochemistry, thermochemistry, petrochemistry, astrochemistry, agroforestry, immunochemistry, electrochemistry

.18 peltry, paltry, sultry, poultry, deviltry: (+ **1.29.11**(.8))

1.29.16
Deirdre, Airdrie, Cowdray, Cowdrey, compadre, Rhodri, Audrey, bawdry, tawdry, Cawdrey, wizardry, balladry, indri, Hendry, Landry, foundry, laundry, sundry, brigandry, legendry, polyandry, monandry, husbandry, Baldry, ribaldry, cuckoldry, heraldry: (+ **1.29.11**(.9))

1.29.17
Pitlochry, kukri, gimmickry, mimicry, Conakry, ochry: (+ **1.29.11**(.10))

1.29.18
angry, hungry: (+ **1.29.11**(.11))

1.29.19
Comrie, Cymru, bottomry, coxcombry

1.29.20
henry, weaponry, charlatanry, falconry, archdeaconry, almonry, yeomanry, aldermanry, cannonry, canonry, pigeonry, heronry, felonry, slovenry, heathenry, masonry, blazonry, emblazonry, citizenry: (+ **1.29.11**(.13))

1.29.21
Geoffrey, Jeffery, Jeffrey, orphrey, Godfrey, Pumphrey, comfrey, Humphrey, belfry, palfrey, gallimaufry

1.29.22
every, McGillivray: (+ **1.29.11**(.15))

1.29.23
Guthrie

1.29.24
missilery, jewellery, chapelry, hostelry, camelry, chivalry, devilry, revelry, cavalry, rivalry

1.30
bouilli, Daubigny, Mascagni

1.31.1
eely, Ely, steely, stele, dele, Keeley, Keighley, Kiely, mealie, mealy, vealy, Sealey, Seeley, Seely, Gigli, Healey, Healy, wheelie, tweely, really, Creeley, Greeley, Greely, freely, Lely, sapele, Keneally, fusilli, Swahili, carefreely, Ismaili, Matabele, Indebele, Sindebele, Ndebele, KwaNdebele, campanile, Kiswahili

1.31.2
Billie, billy, Tilley, Tilly, stilly, Dili, dilly, skilly, ghillie, gillie, gilly, Millie, filly, Philly, Scilly, silly, Chile, chile, chili, chilli, chilly, Gilly, hilly, Willey, willie, willy, frilly, Lillee, Lilley, Lillie, Lilly, lily, Lyly, hillbilly, Chantilly, rustily, rowdily, Rhossili, gingili, Goonhilly, rockabilly, Piccadilly, willy-nilly, willy-willy, piccalilli

1.31.3
dearly, merely, nearly, sheerly, cheerly, queerly, really, Brearley, Brierley, Brierly, yearly, clearly, austerely, ideally, severely, sincerely, insincerely, surreally, unreally **.1** participially **.2** labially, bilabially, connubially, proverbially,

adverbially **.3** bestially, celestially **.4** medially, radially, cordially, remedially, primordially, exordially, sympodially **.5** parochially **.6** binomially **.7** menially, venially, genially, lineally, linearly, cranially, congenially, collinearly, biennially, triennially, octennially, decennially, quinquennially, perennially, quadrennially, colonially, uncongenially, curvilinearly, rectilinearly, matrilineally, intracranially, ceremonially, patrimonially, matrimonially **.8** trivially, jovially, convivially, antediluvially **.9** mesially, glacially, axially, fiducially, coaxially, uniaxially **.10** colloquially, ventriloquially **.11** serially, superiorly, imperially, materially, interiorly, anteriorly, posteriorly, exteriorly, ulteriorly, funereally, venereally, inferiorly, ethereally, immaterially, ministerially, magisterially, managerially, aerially, notarially, actuarially, corporeally, sartorially, tutorially, pictorially, factorially, marmoreally, censorially, sensorially, tenurially, incorporeally, reportorially, proprietorially, dictatorially, editorially, piscatorially, senatorially, equatorially, territorially, immemorially, professorially, inquisitorially, conspiratorially, mercurially, entrepreneurially, terrestrially, industrially **.12** filially, unclearly, familiarly, unfilially, peculiarly, cavalierly

1.31.4
Eilidh, paly, bailey, bailie, Baillie, Bailly, tailie, Dailey, daily, Daley, Daly, Cayley, ceilidh, kali, scaly, gaily, feyly, shaley, shaly, Hailey, haily, Haley, Hayley, Waley, Whaley, Whalley, Rayleigh, greyly, Ndebele, Adélie, Israeli, Disraeli, shillelagh, Indebele, Sindebele, KwaNdebele, capercaillie, triticale, ukulele

1.31.5
Ellie, belly, tele, telly, Delhi, deli, delly, Kelley, kelly, Melly, smelly, Nellie, nelly, felly, Shelley, shelly, gelly, jelly, wellie, welly, Grappelli, beer belly, sowbelly, potbelly, Leadbelly, underbelly, yellow-belly, tagliatelle, Kelly, Pengelly, Abergele, Minelli, Clovelly, Machiavelli, Pwllheli, Preseli, Botticelli, vermicelli, Torricelli, Kidwelly, Mahaweli, Corelli, Schiaparelli, Zeffirelli

1.31.6
sparely, barely, Fairley, Fairlie, fairly, squarely, rarely, unfairly, debonairly

1.31.7
Ali, alley, Ally, ally, palais, pally, bally, Talley, tally, dally, Calais, kali, galley, mallee, valley, sallee, sally, chalet, challis, Halle, Hallé, Halley, Ralegh, Raleigh, rally, teocalli, tomalley, O'Malley, McNally, farfalle, reveille, trevally, dilly-dally, Mexicali, Tin Pan Alley, McAnally, Napa Valley, Silicon Valley, shilly-shally

1.31.8
Pauli, Cowley, jowly

1.31.9
Ali, Pali, parley, Bali, barley, Dali, Cali, Carly, Kali, Mali, Marley, marly, gnarly, snarly, Farleigh, Farley, Varley, Charlie, charlie, Ralegh, Raleigh, bialy, Gurkhali, Kigali, Svengali, tamale, Somali, finale, bizarrely, Diwali, Mexicali, pastorale

1.31.10
Ollie, pollie, polly, poly, Tolley, dollie, dolly, Colley, collie, golly, Mollie, molly, folly, volley, Jolley, Jollie, jolly, Holley, holly, wally, Whalley, brolly, trolley, lolly, chromoly, loblolly, Barbirolli

1.31.11
poorly, Cawley, Corley, Morley, Smalley, Fawley, sorely, surely, Chorley, Hawley, Warley, Whalley, squally, Ralegh, Raleigh, rawly, crawly, scrawly, purely, Lawley, Nepali, Macaulay, Bengali, cocksurely, unsurely, maturely, impurely, securely, obscurely, demurely, immaturely, prematurely, creepy-crawly, insecurely

1.31.12
oily, doily, doyley, doyly, coyly, soily

1.31.13
Tully, Sculley, Scully, gulley, gully, Mulley, sully

1.31.14
kylie, smiley, Smily, Filey, shyly, highly, Wiley, wily, Wylie, Wylye, Reilly, Riley, wrily, wryly, spryly, drily, slyly, sedile, O'Reilly, membrum virile

1.31.15
pulley, bully, fully, Woolley, woolly, Lully

1.31.16
Pooley, puli, boule, Thule, stoolie, Dooley, Cooley, coolie, coulée, schoolie, goolie, mooli, muli, duly, Julie, Hooley, truly, cruelly, newly, Friuli, guayule, Grand Coulee, Bernouilli, patchouli, unduly, untruly, unruly, douroucouli

1.31.17
.1 hourly, dourly, sourly **.2** royally, loyally **.3** direly, squirely, Brierley, Brierly, friarly, entirely **.4** poorly, Gourlay, Gourley, surely, purely, cocksurely, unsurely, maturely, impurely, securely, obscurely, demurely, immaturely, prematurely, insecurely, Kalgoorlie **.5** gooeyly, jewelly, cruelly, dewily, glueyly **.6** snowily, showily, blowily **.7** weepily, creepily, sleepily, nippily, snippily, zippily, ripply, tripoli, drippily, Gallipoli, papally, peppily, dapperly, snappily, sappily, happily, crappily, scrappily, unhappily, Tarporley, soppily, choppily, properly, stroppily, floppily, sloppily, duopoly, monopoly, improperly, bibliopoly, oligopoly, Trichinopoly, archetypally, soupily, droopily, principally, episcopally, municipally, purply, chirpily, dopily, mopily, soapily, ropily, dimply, skimpily, crimpily, Temperley, campily, bumpily, stumpily, dumpily, jumpily, rumply, grumpily, frumpily, lumpily, wispily **.8** Cybele, dribbly, scribbly, stably, neighborly, neighbourly, pebbly, shabbily, crabbily, flabbily,

marbly, bobbly, Mobberley, knobbly, wobbly, bubbly, stubbily, stubbly, chubbily, rubbly, scrubbily, grubbily, lubberly, tribally, verbally, Moberly, soberly, globally, Kimberley, Kimberly, somberly, sombrely, Stromboli, unneighborly, unneighbourly, cantabile, hyperbole, preverbally, primum mobile, perpetuum mobile **.9.1** meatily, skeletally, centripetally, Italy, spittly, bitterly, bittily, wittily, prettily, brittly, grittily, matily, fatally, weightily, prenatally, palatally, pettily, sweatily, battily, tattily, cattily, scattily, Natalie, Nathalie, nattily, fattily, Chatterley, chattily, rattily, rattly, latterly, philately, sal volatile, doughtily, goutily **.9.2** artily, tartily, heartily, spottily, dottily, knottily, snottily, grottily, sportily, daughterly, mortally, naughtily, haughtily, quarterly, immortally, utterly, smuttily, subtly, unsubtly, Maithili, mightily, vitally, writerly, flightily, sootily, snootily, brutally, fruitily, pre-coitally, societally, varietally, capitally, ricketily, genitally, digitally, maritally, basipetally, occipitally, acropetally, congenitally, premaritally, interparietally, interdigitally, extramaritally, dirtily, shirtily, totally, throatily, teetotally, sacerdotally, anecdotally **.9.3** emptily, rectally, doctorly, syndactyly, basilectally, winterly, flintily, painterly, daintily, mentally, orientally, transcendentally, accidentally, occidentally, incidentally, coincidentally, segmentally, governmentally, judgementally, judgmentally, sentimentally, fundamentally, ornamentally, regimentally, temperamentally, detrimentally, sacramentally, incrementally, elementally, supplementally, instrumentally, monumentally, departmentally, compartmentally, unsentimentally, experimentally, developmentally, environmentally, intergovernmentally, interdepartmentally, continentally, transcontinentally, intercontinentally, parentally, scantily, consonantly, quantally, horizontally, jauntily, frontally, contrapuntally, niftily, shiftily, thriftily, heftily, draftily, draughtily, craftily, loftily, easterly, yeastily, distally, mistily, sisterly, systole, twistily, pastily, tastily, hastily, testily, festally, chestily, westerly, masterly, nastily, frowstily, frostily, dustily, gustily, mustily, fustily, trustily, crustily, lustily, thirstily, postally, southeasterly, northeasterly, southwesterly, northwesterly, diastole, headmasterly, schoolmasterly, sinisterly, bloodthirstily, overhastily, intercostally, guiltily, faultily, joltily **.10** speedily, beadily, needily, seedily, tweedily, reedily, greedily, tiddly, giddily, fiddly, Siddeley, twiddly, shadily, steadily, headily, readily, unsteadily, unreadily, faddily, dowdily, cloudily, tardily, hardily, foolhardily, bodily, shoddily, twaddly, orderly, bawdily, caudally, gaudily, disorderly, rhomboidally, adenoidally, toroidally, sinusoidally, puddly, muddily, ruddily, bloodily, tidally, tidily, bridally, untidily, suicidally,

homicidally, moodily, broodily, feudally, pyramidally, hebdomadally, sturdily, wordily, modally, windily, tenderly, trendily, slenderly, handily, randily, unhandily, elderly, unwieldily **.11** peekily, sneakily, cheekily, squeakily, treacly, streakily, creakily, freakily, tickly, stickily, fickly, prickly, trickily, trickly, classically, snakily, shakily, Quakerly, quakily, flakily, tackily, wackily, Fazackerley, sarkily, patriarchally, stockily, cockily, rockily, broccoli, pawkily, gawkily, chalkily, duckily, muckily, knuckly, luckily, pluckily, cluckily, unluckily, spikily, kookily, spookily, flukily, perkily, mirkily, murkily, smirkily, jerkily, quirkily, pokily, smokily, vocally, chokily, jokily, hokily, croakily, locally, univocally, inkily, tinkly, dinkily, kinkily, twinkly, slinkily, swankily, crankily, lankily, wonkily, spunkily, funkily, chunkily, melancholy, fiscally, riskily, friskily, peskily, rascally, duskily, huskily, milkily, silkily, bulkily, sulkily **.12** eagerly, meagerly, meagrely, regally, legally, viceregally, illegally, overeagerly, jiggly, wiggly, squiggly, wriggly, plagueily, plaguily, beggarly, splenomegaly, acromegaly, hepatomegaly, baggily, Baguley, shaggily, waggly, straggly, craggily, scraggily, scraggly, argali, nargile, nargileh, foggily, soggily, groggily, cloggily, snuggly, frugally, fugally, centrifugally, prodigally, conjugally, tingly, spangly, diphthongally, monophthongally, vulgarly **.13** steamily, dreamily, creamily, simile, facsimile, gamily, Emily, Semele, family, clammily, stepfamily, balmily, barmily, smarmily, homily, anomaly, stormily, normally, formally, formerly, abnormally, informally, conformally, paranormally, gummily, summerly, chummily, rummily, crummily, plummily, primally, grimily, slimily, roomily, gloomily, contumely, optimally, minimally, decimally, maximally, proximally, centesimally, duodecimally, vigesimally, millesimally, hexadecimally, sexagesimally, infinitesimally, thermally, geothermally, isothermally, exothermally, hydrothermally, homeyly, dismally, abysmally, phantasmally, filmily **.14.1** penally, venally, officinally, innerly, tinnily, marginally, anally, zanily, rainily, grainily, decanally, cannily, mannerly, flannelly, flannely, uncannily, unmannerly, downily, carnally, bonnily, Donnelly, Connolly, cornily, thornily, funnily, sunnily, unfunnily, spinally, tinily, finally, shinily, vaginally, doctrinally, spoonily, moonily, punily, communally **.14.2** cardinally, libidinally, latitudinally, longitudinally, trigonally, diagonally, octagonally, pentagonally, hexagonally, tetragonally, orthogonally, criminally, seminally, geminally, noumenally, nominally, terminally, germinally, subliminally, abdominally, phenomenally, pronominally, antiphonally, personally, medicinally, impersonally, interpersonally, seasonally **.14.3** additionally, traditionally, conditionally, unconditionally, definitionally, transitionally, positionally, prepositionally, propositionally, suppositionally, compositionally, nutritionally, volitionally, radiationally, ideationally, variationally, recreationally, situationally, occupationally, mutationally, rotationally, presentationally, gravitationally, computationally, confrontationally, gradationally, vocationally, educationally, informationally, transformationally, denominationally, interdenominationally, motivationally, observationally, sensationally, conversationally, unsensationally, organisationally, organizationally, operationally, inspirationally, relationally, translationally, professionally, obsessionally, unprofessionally, nationally, rationally, irrationally, multinationally, internationally, torsionally, proportionally, disproportionally, institutionally, constitutionally, evolutionally, unconstitutionally, notionally, emotionally, devotionally, unemotionally, optionally, exceptionally, conceptionally, unexceptionally, fictionally, frictionally, sectionally, affectionally, directionally, selectionally, inflectionally, inflexionally, unidirectionally, factionally, fractionally, transactionally, constructionally, functionally, conjunctionally, tensionally, intensionally, intentionally, dimensionally, conventionally, unintentionally, unconventionally, multidimensionally, divisionally, provisionally, occasionally, regionally, virginally, originally, aboriginally, unoriginally, inguinally, isochronally, vernally, diurnally, supernally, eternally, coeternally, paternally, maternally, fraternally, nocturnally, internally, externally, infernally, sempiternally, tonally, stonily, phonily, zonally, atonally, hormonally, autumnally **.15** springily, stringily, clingingly, slangily **.16.1** beefily, gleefully, spiffily, sniffily, sniffly, pitifully, tearfully, fearfully, cheerfully, playfully, brachycephaly, macrocephaly, microcephaly, anencephaly, dolichocephaly, carefully, prayerfully, daffily, Offaly, waffly, cartophily, toxophily, necrophily, bibliophily, heterophylly, awfully, lawfully, unlawfully, joyfully, puffily, stuffily, snuffly, huffily, scruffily, fluffily, goofily, ruefully, powerfully, irefully, direfully, dutifully, beautifully, plentifully, bountifully, masterfully, wonderfully, flavorfully, flavourfully, mercifully, fancifully, sorrowfully, colorfully, colourfully, undutifully, unbeautifully, characterfully, unmercifully, apocryphally, woefully **.16.2** hopefully, helpfully, worshipfully, unhelpfully, fitfully, fatefully, hatefully, gratefully, fretfully, doubtfully, artfully, thoughtfully, spitefully, rightfully, frightfully, fruitfully, hurtfully, tactfully, wistfully, tastefully, wastefully, zestfully, restfully, trustfully, lustfully, boastfully, deceitfully, ungratefully, forgetfully, regretfully,

unthoughtfully, despitefully, insightfully, delightfully, unfruitfully, effortfully, respectfully, neglectfully, eventfully, resentfully, distastefully, unrestfully, distrustfully, mistrustfully, disrespectfully, uneventfully, needfully, heedfully, dreadfully, pridefully, mindfully, regardfully, unmindfully, disregardfully, wakefully, thankfully, shamefully, blamefully, harmfully, comfily, triumphally, sinfully, painfully, banefully, gainfully, manfully, scornfully, mournfully, tunefully, disdainfully, untunefully, songfully, wrongfully, meaningfully, faithfully, wrathfully, ruthfully, truthfully, youthfully, mirthfully, slothfully, healthfully, unfaithfully, untruthfully, peacefully, blissfully, gracefully, stressfully, forcefully, usefully, ungracefully, disgracefully, successfully, distressfully, remorsefully, resourcefully, purposefully, unsuccessfully, unremorsefully, easefully, reposefully, wishfully, bashfully, pushfully, watchfully, reproachfully, vengefully, revengefully, skilfully, skillfully, wilfully, willfully, balefully, guilefully, dolefully, soulfully, unskilfully **.17** evilly, weevily, Tivoli, civilly, privily, navally, wavily, Everley, Everly, Beverley, Beverly, heavily, levelly, cleverly, gravelly, Calverley, Coverley, groovily, scurvily, nervily, ovally, overly, coevally, primevally, uncivilly, top-heavily, datavally, medievally, genitivally, adjectivally, topsy-turvily, infinitivally **.18** lethally, pithily, breathily, frothily, toothily, earthily, lengthily, filthily, stealthily, healthily, wealthily, unhealthily **.19** weatherly, Hatherley, fatherly, northerly, swarthily, motherly, southerly, brotherly, worthily, grandfatherly, unfatherly, grandmotherly, unmotherly, Osmotherley, Osmotherly, unbrotherly, trustworthily, unworthily, praiseworthily, untrustworthily **.20** greasily, fleecily, thistly, Cicely, cicely, Sicily, prissily, gristly, remissly, racily, lacily, messily, Thessaly, Cecily, dressily, sassily, brassily, classily, glassily, mousily, bossily, glossily, colossally, dorsally, saucily, horsily, muscly, fussily, unfussily, icily, spicily, dicily, juicily, transversally, universally, tipsily, ritzily, glitzily, gutsily, chintzily, tricksily, sexily, waxily, foxily, folksily, tinselly, fancily, chancily, bouncily, commensally **.21** easily, cheesily, weaselly, wheezily, queasily, breezily, sleazily, busily, dizzily, fizzily, frizzily, frizzly, mazily, nasally, hazily, crazily, lazily, snazzily, jazzily, drowsily, frowsily, frowzily, lousily, blowsily, blowzily, causally, gauzily, clausally, noisily, muzzily, fuzzily, miserly, oozily, boozily, choosily, woozily, dozily, cosily, nosily, Rosalie, rosily, prosily, flimsily, clumsily, uneasily **.22** dishily, fishily, swishily, judicially, initially, officially, surficially, interstitially, prejudicially, superficially, artificially, beneficially, unofficially, sacrificially, extrajudicially, spatially, facially, racially, glacially, palatially,

interfacially, multiracially, interracially, specially, especially, trashily, splashily, flashily, partially, martially, impartially, squashily, gushily, mushily, plushily, pushily, bushily, cushily, crucially, fiducially, commercially, controversially, uncontroversially, socially, asocially, unsocially, antisocially, psychosocially, sexually, asexually, unisexually, intersexually, homosexually, heterosexually, psychosexually, provincially, sensually, influentially, experientially, potentially, penitentially, existentially, prudentially, confidentially, evidentially, providentially, residentially, presidentially, exponentially, essentially, consensually, quintessentially, tangentially, sequentially, consequentially, inconsequentially, torrentially, differentially, deferentially, referentially, preferentially, inferentially, reverentially, circumferentially, pestilentially, substantially, financially, insubstantially, unsubstantially, circumstantially, quincuncially, bolshily
.23 visually, leisurely, casually, usually, unusually **.24** teacherly, creaturely, bitchily, Wycherley, twitchily, ritually, habitually, techily, tetchily, sketchily, perpetually, patchily, catchily, snatchily, scratchily, grouchily, starchily, blotchily, touchily, mutually, spiritually, virtually, churchily, perceptually, conceptually, actually, tactually, factually, punctually, aspectually, effectually, contractually, instinctually, unpunctually, ineffectually, intellectually, raunchily, punchily, crunchily, eventually, accentually, textually, contextually **.25** stagily, cagily, edgily, gradually, podgily, stodgily, dodgily, pudgily, smudgily, stingily, dingily, mingily, gingerly, mangily, spongily, soldierly, vestigially, residually, unsoldierly, individually **.26** equally, tranquilly, lingually, unequally, multilingually, unilingually **.27.1** squirrelly, eerily, beerily, neroli, cheerily, wearily, drearily, blearily, subsidiarily, merrily, verily, momentarily, primarily, militarily, necessarily, arbitrarily, unnecessarily, airily, scarily, charily, hairily, warily, unwarily, contrarily, Farrelly, starrily, morally, sorrily, immorally, amorally, unmorally, aurally, orally, chorally, Coralie, gorily, hoarily, rurally, neurally, plurally, florally, monaurally, intramurally, extramurally, propitiatorily, thoroughly, spirally, virally, flowerily, fierily, wirily, slipperily, corporally, temporally, temporarily, contemporarily, spatio-temporally, liberally, illiberally, literally, laterally, bilaterally, trilaterally, collaterally, multilaterally, unilaterally, gutturally, predatorily, mandatorily, sanitarily, monetarily, unitarily, statutorily, transitorily, dilatorily, solitarily, hereditarily, obligatorily, derogatorily, insanitarily, explanatorily, premonitorily, preparatorily, peremptorily, tributarily, electorally, refractorily, perfunctorily, contradictorily, satisfactorily, unsatisfactorily,

sedentarily, fragmentarily, parenterally, testamentarily, elementarily, supplementarily, complementarily, complimentarily, documentarily, rudimentarily, federally, secondarily **.27.2** summarily, ephemerally, customarily, plenarily, generally, ordinarily, sanguinarily, culinarily, extraordinarily, preliminarily, imaginarily, evolutionarily, peripherally, savorily, savourily, severally, unsavorily, unsavourily, viscerally, cursorily, sensorily, derisorily, illusorily, compulsorily, provisorily, naturally, scripturally, sculpturally, structurally, texturally, culturally, connaturally, unnaturally, unscripturally, conjecturally, supernaturally, preternaturally, horticulturally, architecturally, multiculturally, socioculturally, viticulturally, agriculturally, procedurally, literarily, extemporarily, pecuniarily, behaviourally, exemplarily **.27.3** cerebrally, vertebrally, neutrally, spectrally, wintrily, ventrally, centrally, voluntarily, involuntarily, astrally, pastorally, rostrally, dextrally, orchestrally, ancestrally, sinistrally, paltrily, sultrily, desultorily, tawdrily, scoundrelly, legendarily, sepulchrally, angrily, mongrelly, hungrily, integrally **.28** lawyerly, nebuly, raguly, annually, manually, biannually, continually, televisually **.29** sillily, sailorly, scholarly, jollily, unscholarly, oilily, wilily, similarly, dissimilarly, surlily, polarly, holily, lowlily, titularly, popularly, tabularly, globularly, secularly, ocularly, jocularly, circularly, vascularly, muscularly, tegularly, regularly, singularly, angularly, annularly, granularly, insularly, unpopularly, orbicularly, particularly, perpendicularly, vesicularly, auricularly, molecularly, spectacularly, vernacularly, oracularly, monocularly, irregularly, triangularly, rectangularly, unspectacularly, ghastlily, friendlily, kindlily, uglily, cleanlily, lovelily, livelily

1.31.18
Earley, early, pearly, Purley, Berlei, Burghley, Burleigh, Burley, burly, Curley, curly, girlie, girly, surly, Shirley, hurley, twirly, swirly, yearly, biyearly, hurly-burly

1.31.19
coaly, coley, goalie, moly, Foley, soli, shoaly, choli, holey, holy, Rowley, Crowley, lowly, slowly, aioli, anole, pinole, cannoli, unholy, narrowly, mellowly, callowly, shallowly, hollowly, ravioli, roly-poly, guacamole

1.31.20
steeply, deeply, cheaply, Shipley, Ripley, ripply, triply, shapely, haply, sharply, popply, Copley, properly, ripely, purply, pimply, dimply, simply, limply, amply, damply, crumply, plumply, crisply, unshapely, quadruply, panoply, principally, quintuply, sextuply, nondescriptly, fait accompli

1.31.21
.1 feebly, Sibley, dribbly, scribbly, glibly, pitiably, amiably, enviably, variably, malleably,

inexpiably, impermeably, unenviably, appreciably, insatiably, invariably, irremediably, inappreciably, ably, stably, sably, unstably, pebbly, Webley®, Weobley, trebly, drably, knobbly, wobbly, bubbly, doubly, nubbly **.2** foreseeably, agreeably, disagreeably, unplayably, allowably, enjoyably, viably, pliably, deniably, reliably, undeniably, certifiably, justifiably, classifiably, verifiably, unreliably, identifiably, unjustifiably, arguably, valuably, inarguably, unarguably, invaluably **.3** capably, palpably, culpably, incapably, unflappably, unstoppably, impalpably, inescapably, probably, clubbably, improbably, indescribably, imperturbably **.4.1** unbeatably, unrepeatably, hospitably, inhospitably, ratably, rateably, debatably, equatably, untranslatably, regrettably, unforgettably, compatibly, incompatibly, redoubtably, undoubtably, portably, supportably, insupportably, unsupportably, excitably, suitably, unsuitably, statutably, inscrutably, computably, disputably, immutably, unstatutably, indisputably, incommutably, irrefutably **.4.2** habitably, creditably, profitably, comfortably, equitably, irritably, veritably, heritably, charitably, palatably, indubitably, discreditably, inimitably, illimitably, indomitably, unprofitably, uncomfortably, inevitably, inequitably, unequitably, uncharitably, unpalatably, convertibly, indivertibly, inconvertibly, incontrovertibly, notably **.4.3** perceptibly, susceptibly, acceptably, adaptably, corruptibly, contemptibly, imperceptibly, unacceptably, incorruptibly, reputably, disreputably, attributably, unattributably, tractably, predictably, respectably, detectably, delectably, intractably, unpredictably, undetectably, indestructibly, ineluctably, lamentably, unprintably, presentably, accountably, uncountably, warrantably, unaccountably, insurmountably, unwarrantably, resistibly, detestably, exhaustibly, combustibly, irresistibly, incontestably, indigestibly, inexhaustibly **.4.4** readably, credibly, audibly, laudably, slidably, unreadably, formidably, inedibly, incredibly, inaudibly, affordably, avoidably, dependably, expendably, commendably, unavoidably, understandably **.5** unspeakably, despicably, applicably, explicably, inextricably, inapplicably, inexplicably, mistakably, unshakably, unshakeably, unbreakably, unmistakably, unmistakeably, impeccably, placably, implacably, remarkably, unshockably, likeably, practicably, amicably, impracticably, immedicably, communicably, irrevocably, ineradicably, incommunicably, workably, ineducably, unthinkably, immitigably, irrefragably, indefatigably **.6** blamably, blameably, inflammably, conformably, presumably, estimably, irredeemably, unredeemably, irreclaimably, unconformably,

inestimably, unfathomably, amenably, inalienably, unalienably, sustainably, unattainably, unobtainably, unsustainably, unexplainably, unascertainably, untenably, definably, indefinably, undefinably, pardonably, unpardonably, abominably, interminably, indeterminably, ungovernably, personably, seasonably, reasonably, treasonably, unseasonably, unreasonably, fashionably, actionably, impressionably, unfashionably, proportionably, exceptionably, objectionably, unmentionably, unconscionably, unexceptionably, unobjectionably, questionably, unquestionably, imaginably, unimaginably, companionably, discernibly, indiscernibly, impregnably, damnably **.7.1** affably, laughably, ineffably, lovably, loveably, movably, provably, perceivably, conceivably, retrievably, believably, forgivably, immovably, immoveably, observably, inconceivably, irretrievably, unbelievably, unforgivably, unforgiveably, irremovably **.7.2** peaceably, immiscibly, permissibly, irremissibly, inadmissibly, untraceably, ineffaceably, irreplaceably, accessibly, inaccessibly, irrepressibly, inexpressibly, unexpressibly, passably, impassably, impassibly, irascibly, unsurpassably, possibly, impossibly, forcibly, enforceably, irreducibly, reproducibly, noticeably, serviceably, unnoticeably, coercibly, reversibly, irreversibly, flexibly, inflexibly, sensibly, invincibly, convincibly, ostensibly, defensibly, insensibly, responsibly, indispensably, indefensibly, reprehensibly, comprehensibly, unpronounceably, irresponsibly, incomprehensibly, feasibly, visibly, risibly, plausibly, sizeably, defeasibly, unfeasibly, divisibly, invisibly, implausibly, cognisably, cognizably, advisably, excusably, confusably, indefeasibly, indivisibly, recognisably, recognizably, inexcusably, unrecognisably, unrecognizably **.7.3** sociably, perishably, unsociably, unquenchably, distinguishably, imperishableness, indistinguishably, inextinguishably, changeably, tangibly, unchangeably, intangibly, infrangibly, interchangeably, unchallengeably **.7.4** unreachably, unmatchably, unsearchably, unimpeachably, unapproachably, irreproachably, legibly, chargeably, illegibly, manageably, corrigibly, eligibly, knowledgably, knowledgeably, negligibly, unmanageably, incorrigibly, intelligibly, ineligibly, unintelligibly **.7.5** equably **.8** terribly, bearably, unbearably, incomparably, horribly, adorably, durably, curably, perdurably, incurably, deplorably, unendurably, desirably, undesirably, separably, reparably, operably, comparably, inseparably, irreparably, inoperably, insuperably, unutterably, inalterably, unalterably, considerably, imponderably, inconsiderably, unconquerably, memorably, numerably, admirably, unmemorably,

innumerably, denumerably, venerably,
honorably, honourably, vulnerably,
dishonorably, dishonourably, invulnerably,
preferably, insufferably, indecipherably,
favorably, favourably, unfavorably,
unfavourably, irrecoverably, undiscoverably,
answerably, inexorably, commensurably,
unanswerably, incommensurably, miserably,
measurably, pleasurably, immeasurably,
unmeasurably, conjecturably, tolerably,
colorably, colourably, intolerably, inerrably,
demonstrably, impenetrably, execrably
.9 volubly, dissolubly, insolubly, indissolubly,
fallibly, gullibly, availably, indelibly, infallibly,
reconcilably, inviolably, controllably, calculably,
unassailably, irreconcilably, inconsolably,
unconsolably, uncontrollably, incalculably
.10 superbly **.11** nobly, Hobley, ignobly
.12 nimbly, Wembley, trembly, Hambly, brambly,
jumbly, humbly, crumbly, grumbly, assembly,
reassembly, self-assembly, disassembly

1.31.22
.1 meetly, neatly, Wheatley, sweetly, Streatley,
fleetly, concretely, discreetly, discretely,
completely, indiscreetly, obsoletely,
incompletely **.2** fitly, Whitley, Witley, unfitly
.3 mediately, immediately, collegiately,
appropriately, intermediately, inappropriately
.4 Pateley, stately, straightly, straitly, lately,
radiately, inchoately, sedately, truncately,
innately, pinnately, ornately, ternately,
cognately, irately, prolately, insensately
.5 Tetley, wetly **.6** Attlee, patly, fatly, rattly, flatly
.7 stoutly, devoutly **.8** partly, tartly, smartly,
Hartley **.9** Otley, motley, hotly, squatly **.10** portly,
tautly, courtly, shortly, uncourtly **.11** adroitly,
maladroitly **.12** Utley, Uttley, subtly **.13** tightly,
knightly, nightly, sightly, Whiteley, whitely,
rightly, sprightly, spritely, brightly, tritely,
lightly, slightly, reconditely, finitely, fortnightly,
unsightly, uprightly, contritely, forthrightly,
politely, Golightly, tripartitely, eruditely,
compositely, impolitely **.14** cutely, mutely,
astutely, acutely, argutely, minutely, subacutely,
dissolutely, resolutely, absolutely, irresolutely
.15 quietly, unquietly, digitately, precipitately,
intricately, delicately, indelicately, profligately,
conjugately, consummately, intimately,
ultimately, proximately, legitimately,
penultimately, inanimately, approximately,
illegitimately, obstinately, definitely, infinitely,
passionately, fortunately, coordinately,
subordinately, inordinately, discriminately,
effeminately, predominately, determinately,
indefinitely, compassionately, dispassionately,
proportionately, extortionately, affectionately,
importunately, unfortunately, insubordinately,
indiscriminately, indeterminately,
disproportionately, alternately, covertly,
privately, licitly, tacitly, illicitly, implicitly,
explicitly, oppositely, inexplicitly, exquisitely,
appositely, requisitely, inappositely, stalwartly,

adequately, inadequately, separately,
corporately, temperately, disparately,
desperately, literately, moderately,
intemperately, deliberately, elaborately,
illiterately, inveterately, considerately,
immoderately, degenerately, commensurately,
inconsiderately, unregenerately,
incommensurately, obdurately, accurately,
inaccurately, secretly, desolately, inviolately,
undulately, disconsolately, articulately,
reticulately, immaculately, triangulately,
inarticulately **.16** pertly, curtly, Wortley,
expertly, inertly, overtly, alertly, inexpertly
.17 remotely **.18** aptly, raptly, promptly, adeptly,
ineptly, inaptly, unaptly, corruptly, abruptly,
unkemptly, nondescriptly **.19** strictly, abjectly,
directly, erectly, correctly, compactly, exactly,
abstractly, perfectly, distinctly, succinctly,
circumspectly, indirectly, incorrectly, matter-of-
factly, inexactly, imperfectly, indistinctly
.20.1 sapiently, sentiently, radiantly, leniently,
presciently, transiently, pruriently, recreantly,
brilliantly, saliently, valiantly, suppliantly,
percipiently, incipiently, expediently,
obediently, preveniently, conveniently,
subserviently, omnisciently, insouciantly,
esuriently, luxuriantly, resiliently, ebulliently,
disobediently, inconveniently, faintly, saintly,
quaintly, Bentley, gently, intently, ungently,
accidentally, occidentally, incidentally,
coincidently, scantly, Grantley, paramountly,
gauntly, jointly, conjointly, Huntley, bluntly,
buoyantly, flamboyantly, clairvoyantly, pliantly,
defiantly, compliantly, self-reliantly,
congruently, affluently, fluently, pursuantly
.20.2 flippantly, rampantly, lambently,
absorbently, latently, distantly, instantly,
constantly, impotently, competently,
penitently, hesitantly, militantly, advertently,
expectantly, reluctantly, repentantly,
persistently, insistently, consistently,
inconstantly, exultantly, concomitantly,
intermittently, self-importantly, omnipotently,
precipitantly, incompetently, exorbitantly,
impenitently, inadvertently, unrepentantly,
equidistantly, inconsistently, ardently,
mordantly, stridently, prudently, verdantly,
accordantly, concordantly, discordantly,
imprudently, decadently, diffidently,
confidently, evidently, providently, precedently,
impudently, dependently, transcendently,
resplendently, despondently, abundantly,
redundantly, antecedently, self-confidently,
self-evidently, improvidently, independently,
correspondently, superabundantly,
overabundantly, overconfidently,
interdependently, piquantly, vacantly,
significantly, insignificantly, arrogantly,
elegantly, extravagantly, inelegantly
.20.3 clamantly, clemently, vehemently,
momently, inclemently, adamantly, pregnantly,
stagnantly, pertinently, continently,
abstinently, imminently, eminently,

dominantly, prominently, permanently, dissonantly, resonantly, indignantly, benignantly, malignantly, repugnantly, impertinently, incontinently, preeminently, predominantly, impermanently, inconsonantly, supereminently **.20.4** triumphantly, fervently, relevantly, irrelevantly, unobservantly, decently, absently, adjacently, reticently, innocently, magnificently, beneficently, presently, pleasantly, complaisantly, unpleasantly, patiently, anciently, trenchantly, efficiently, deficiently, sufficiently, proficiently, impatiently, inefficiently, insufficiently, self-sufficiently, urgently, cogently, stringently, plangently, pungently, indigently, exigently, diligently, negligently, emergently, divergently, contingently, astringently, indulgently, effulgently, refulgently, intransigently, intelligently, self-indulgently, overindulgently, unintelligently **.20.5** sequently, frequently, infrequently, subsequently, consequently, eloquently, delinquently, magniloquently, inconsequently, grandiloquently, coherently, inherently, incoherently, errantly, arrantly, apparently, transparently, abhorrently, currently, recurrently, concurrently, ignorantly, differently, reverently, tolerantly, exuberantly, protuberantly, reverberantly, preponderantly, indifferently, irreverently, belligerently, intolerantly, vibrantly, remonstrantly, recalcitrantly, vagrantly, fragrantly, flagrantly, poignantly, covalently, repellently, gallantly, ungallantly, silently, violently, jubilantly, pestilently, redolently, indolently, somnolently, prevalently, ambivalently, equivalently, benevolently, malevolently, unambivalently, excellently, insolently, superexcellently, nonchalantly, vigilantly, petulantly, flatulently, fraudulently, virulently, purulently, crapulently, opulently, turbulently, flocculently, succulently, truculently, luculently, somnambulantly **.21** swiftly, deftly, daftly, softly, softly-softly **.22** beastly, Priestley, priestly, istle, chastely, Astley, ghastly, vastly, lastly, costly, moistly, justly, Christly, deucedly, firstly, ghostly, mostly, barefacedly, shamefacedly, unchastely, steadfastly, stedfastly, robustly, augustly, unjustly, modestly, honestly, earnestly, manifestly, unsteadfastly, immodestly, dishonestly, embarrassedly **.23** Saltley, saltly, occultly, adultly, difficultly

1.31.23
.1 fluidly, tiddly, fiddly, twiddly, Ridley, unweariedly **.2** weirdly **.3** staidly, Madeley, Cradley, comradely, retrogradely **.4** deadly, medley, Smedley, Hedley, redly, chance-medley **.5** badly, madly, sadly, Hadlee, Hadley, Radley, Bradley, gladly **.6** proudly, loudly **.7** hardly, Yardley, blackguardly **.8** oddly, Bodley, godly, ungodly **.9** Audley, broadly, lordly, self-assuredly, untowardly **.10** puddly, Budleigh, Studley, Dudley, cuddly **.11** idly, snidely, widely,

impliedly, dignifiedly, horrifiedly, satisfiedly, dissatisfiedly, self-satisfiedly **.12** goodly, Woodley **.13** rudely, crudely, shrewdly, Bewdley, lewdly **.14.1** cowardly, allowedly, tiredly, inspiredly, leewardly, frowardly **.14.2** tepidly, vapidly, rapidly, torpidly, stupidly, limpidly, temperedly, insipidly, intrepidly, rabidly, crabbedly, morbidly, turbidly, absorbedly, unperturbedly **.14.3** heatedly, repeatedly, conceitedly, admittedly, half-wittedly, statedly, fixatedly, concentratedly, frustratedly, elatedly, belatedly, inflatedly, unabatedly, agitatedly, irritatedly, dedicatedly, complicatedly, animatedly, exasperatedly, unrelatedly, calculatedly, premeditatedly, sophisticatedly, unmitigatedly, opinionatedly, exaggeratedly, unpremeditatedly, unsophisticatedly, fetidly, mattedly, undoubtedly, light-heartedly, hard-heartedly, kind-heartedly, warm-heartedly, downheartedly, wholeheartedly, tenderheartedly, besottedly, reportedly, purportedly, distortedly, unsupportedly, unitedly, benightedly, clear-sightedly, foresightedly, shortsightedly, excitedly, delightedly, uninvitedly, unrequitedly, surefootedly, light-footedly, reputedly, convolutedly, limitedly, spiritedly, unlimitedly, dispiritedly, uninhibitedly, unsolicitedly, pervertedly, concertedly, disconcertedly, devotedly, uninterruptedly, restrictedly, connectedly, affectedly, dejectedly, collectedly, protractedly, distractedly, abstractedly, unrestrictedly, unsuspectedly, unexpectedly, unconnectedly, disconnectedly, unaffectedly, disaffectedly, pointedly, jointedly, unstintedly, contentedly, tormentedly, dementedly, self-centeredly, self-centredly, enchantedly, unwontedly, undauntedly, disjointedly, discontentedly, disappointedly, unprecedentedly, giftedly, dastardly, tight-fistedly, interestedly, disgustedly, unresistedly, uncontestedly, uninterestedly, disinterestedly, stiltedly, exaltedly **.14.4** jadedly, guardedly, sordidly, studiedly, splendidly, candidly, hotheadedly, light-headedly, hard-headedly, wrong-headedly, unguardedly, unstudiedly, hot-bloodedly, cold-bloodedly, misguidedly, decidedly, lopsidedly, one-sidedly, outmodedly, intendedly, offendedly, surehandedly, high-handedly, right-handedly, light-handedly, backhandedly, offhandedly, unboundedly, unfoundedly, confoundedly, broad-mindedly, like-mindedly, small-mindedly, simple-mindedly, single-mindedly, unimpededly, undecidedly, heavy-handedly, underhandedly **.14.5** wickedly, nakedly, markedly, crookedly, niggardly, jaggedly, haggardly, raggedly, laggardly, doggedly, ruggedly, sluggardly **.14.6** timidly, tumidly, humidly, ashamedly, informedly, assumedly, presumedly, unashamedly, feignedly, learnedly, sustainedly, unfeignedly, restrainedly, constrainedly, ingrainedly, designedly, resignedly, concernedly, unlearnedly, unrestrainedly, unconstrainedly,

undesignedly, unconcernedly .**14.7** bifidly,
vividly, lividly, avidly, fervidly, aggrievedly,
perfervidly, deservedly, reservedly, resolvedly,
unrelievedly, undeservedly, unreservedly,
unobservedly, unresolvedly, blessedly, acidly,
placidly, flaccidly, cussedly, deucedly, lucidly,
cursedly, fixedly, vexedly, barefacedly,
shamefacedly, professedly, confessedly,
enforcedly, unforcedly, pellucidly, accursedly,
perplexedly, relaxedly, pronouncedly,
embarrassedly, wizardly, dazedly, frenziedly,
haphazardly, advisedly, surprisedly, bemusedly,
confusedly, supposedly, composedly,
undisguisedly, unadvisedly, unabashedly,
measuredly, wretchedly, good-naturedly, ill-
naturedly, detachedly, rigidly, frigidly, turgidly,
allegedly, waywardly, forwardly, upwardly,
outwardly, eastwardly, westwardly, liquidly,
backwardly, awkwardly, languidly, inwardly,
downwardly, southwardly, avowedly,
straightforwardly, variedly, aridly, torridly,
horridly, floridly, luridly, hurriedly, worriedly,
putridly, sacredly, acridly, declaredly, assuredly,
unhurriedly, unpreparedly, pallidly, validly,
stolidly, solidly, squalidly, invalidly,
uncontrolledly .**15** Eardley, thirdly, absurdly
.**16** unaccustomedy .**17** spindly, Findlay,
Hindley, Brindley, Lindley, friendly, Handley,
grandly, blandly, soundly, roundly, fondly,
kindly, blindly, secondly, jocundly, unfriendly,
profoundly, unsoundly, rotundly, secundly,
unkindly, husbandly, user-friendly, eco-friendly,
overfondly, determinedly .**18** baldly, mildly,
wildly, worldly, boldly, coldly, unworldly,
overboldly, manifoldly

1.31.24
.**1** meekly, chicly, weakly, Weekley, weekly,
treacly, bleakly, sleekly, uniquely, biweekly,
tri-weekly, obliquely .**2** tickly, thickly, sickly,
quickly, prickly, trickly, strictly, slickly,
politicly, ritualistically .**3** opaquely .**4** Checkley,
freckly .**5** hackly, crackly, blackly, slackly,
exactly .**6** sparkly, Barclay, Barkley, Barkly,
Berkeley, starkly, darkly, clerkly .**7** Buckley,
knuckly .**8** likely, unlikely .**9.1** onomatopoeically,
laically, archaically, prosaically, Hebraically,
Pharisaically, algebraically, paranoiacally,
paranoically, maniacally, demoniacally,
simoniacally, elegiacally, stoically, echoically,
heroically, unheroically .**9.2** typically, atypically,
untypically, stereotypically, prototypically,
archetypically, phenotypically, apically,
epically, topically, tropically, myopically,
entropically, misanthropically, isotopically,
stereoscopically, stroboscopically,
endoscopically, stethoscopically, periscopically,
stauroscopically, macroscopically,
microscopically, hygroscopically, telescopically,
heliotropically, isotropically, philanthropically,
radioisotopically, kaleidoscopically,
laryngoscopically, ophthalmoscopically,
anisotropically, cubically, syllabically,

cherubically, acerbically, aerobically,
trisyllabically, claustrophobically,
polysyllabically, monosyllabically .**9.3** critically,
dendritically, diacritically, uncritically,
politically, proclitically, enclitically, Jesuitically,
sporophytically, parasitically, sybaritically,
hypocritically, hypercritically, apolitically,
geopolitically, unpolitically, analytically,
paralytically, hydrolytically, psychoanalytically,
electrolytically, poetically, unpoetically,
alphabetically, quodlibetically, analphabetically,
dietetically, peripatetically, eidetically,
catechetically, mimetically, hermetically,
cosmetically, arithmetically, kinetically,
tonetically, phonetically, genetically,
frenetically, phrenetically, splenetically,
magnetically, geomagnetically, diamagnetically,
cytogenetically, ectogenetically,
phylogenetically, ontogenetically,
orthogenetically, parthenogenetically,
electromagnetically, aphetically, prophetically,
pathetically, prothetically, synthetically,
aesthetically, esthetically, prosthetically,
antithetically, epithetically, apathetically,
hypothetically, sympathetically, empathetically,
parenthetically, kinaesthetically, kinesthetically,
anaesthetically, anesthetically, antipathetically,
unsympathetically, photosynthetically,
ascetically, energetically, epexegetically,
apologetically, unapologetically, theoretically,
heretically, cataphoretically, phyletically,
athletically .**9.4** statically, sciatically, sabbatically,
adiabatically, acrobatically, ecstatically, anti-
statically, homeostatically, homoeostatically,
apostatically, hypostatically, fungistatically,
thermostatically, aerostatically, hydrostatically,
schematically, thematically, traumatically,
climatically, rheumatically, pneumatically,
somatically, dramatically, chromatically,
grammatically, stigmatically, phlegmatically,
pragmatically, dogmatically, mathematically,
asthmatically, schismatically, prismatically,
judgematically, idiomatically, axiomatically,
automatically, symptomatically, systematically,
kinematically, cinematically, aromatically,
achromatically, diagrammatically,
programmatically, ungrammatically,
diplomatically, problematically, emblematically,
enigmatically, syntagmatically, numismatically,
charismatically, microclimatically,
unsystematically, psychosomatically,
melodramatically, monochromatically,
epigrammatically, anagrammatically,
undiplomatically, unproblematically,
paradigmatically, apophthegmatically,
fanatically, morganatically, emphatically,
unemphatically, piratically, hieratically,
erratically, theocratically, Socratically,
operatically, autocratically, plutocratically,
democratically, technocratically,
bureaucratically, aristocratically,
undemocratically, idiosyncratically,
cathartically, chaotically, meiotically,

despotically, robotically, narcotically, psychotically, zygotically, zymotically, osmotically, hypnotically, quixotically, exotically, erotically, neurotically, symbiotically, idiotically, semiotically, patriotically, asymptotically, unpatriotically, antibiotically, macrobiotically, nautically, vortically, aeronautically, astronautically, scorbutically, pharmaceutically, therapeutically, hermeneutically, vertically **.9.5** cryptically, sceptically, skeptically, septically, optically, elliptical, elliptically, ecliptically, aseptically, sylleptically, synaptically, synoptically, antiseptically, apocalyptically, hectically, tactically, practically, dialectically, eclectically, syntactically, didactically, climactically, impractically, unpractically, apodictically, apoplectically, paratactically, apodeictically, anticlimactically, intergalactically, frantically, franticly, identically, authentically, pedantically, gigantically, semantically, romantically, unauthentically, unromantically, sycophantically **.9.6** pantheistically, mystically, deistically, theistically, touristically, mechanistically, fatalistically, mentalistically, feudalistically, legalistically, journalistically, socialistically, atheistically, archaistically, casuistically, altruistically, euphuistically, egoistically, modernistically, expressionistically, vandalistically, annalistically, mutualistically, moralistically, pluralistically, naturalistically, cannibalistically, capitalistically, paternalistically, monotheistically, communalistically, nationalistically, rationalistically, evangelistically, individualistically, artistically, statistically, inartistically, unartistically, egotistically, sadistically, propagandistically, masochistically, atomistically, optimistically, euphemistically, pessimistically, pianistically, hedonistically, agonistically, humanistically, chauvinistically, Calvinistically, synchronistically, communistically, opportunistically, antagonistically, deterministically, impressionistically, anachronistically, exhibitionistically, sophistically, atavistically, positivistically, relativistically, narcissistically, solipsistically, logistically, synergistically, syllogistically, eulogistically, dyslogistically, linguistically, sociolinguistically, eristically, floristically, voyeuristically, heuristically, aprioristically, manneristically, aphoristically, futuristically, terroristically, militaristically, militeristically, characteristically, behavioristically, behaviouristically, uncharacteristically, realistically, holistically, stylistically, dualistically, ballistically, idealistically, surrealistically, unrealistically, cabalistically, cabbalistically, imperialistically, materialistically, somnambulistically, simplistically, domestically, majestically, spastically, drastically, plastically, bombastically, fantastically, sarcastically,

stochastically, orgastically, pleonastically, dynastically, monastically, gymnastically, elastically, scholastically, orgiastically, periphrastically, paraphrastically, inelastically, ecclesiastically, enthusiastically, iconoclastically, unenthusiastically, overenthusiastically, caustically, prognostically, diagnostically, encaustically, rustically, acoustically, peristaltically **.9.7** medically, radically, comedically, veridically, juridically, triadically, nomadically, sporadically, spasmodically, synodically, methodically, prosodically, rhapsodically, melodically, heraldically, cyclopaedically, cyclopedically, pyramidically, periodically, unmethodically, episodically, encyclopaedically, encyclopedically, psychically, anarchically, monarchically, hierarchically, oligarchically, pedagogically, demagogically **.9.8** systemically, tonemically, graphemically, morphemically, epistemically, diaphonemically, morphophonemically, inimically, metonymically, patronymically, chemically, endemically, polemically, epidemically, academically, electrochemically, dynamically, cleistogamically, panoramically, psychodynamically, thermodynamically, aerodynamically, electrodynamically, comically, atomically, anatomically, tragicomically, serio-comically, physiognomically, economically, ergonomically, taxonomically, astronomically, gastronomically, agronomically, socio-economically, uneconomically, thermically, endermically, hypodermically, endothermically, exothermically, gnomically, rhythmically, biorhythmically, unrhythmically, logarithmically, algorithmically, osmically, cosmically, seismically, miasmically, orgasmically, cataclysmically, macrocosmically, microcosmically, scenically, hygienically, unhygienically, photogenically, finically, finickily, cynically, clinically, rabbinically, arsenically, eugenically, ecumenically, oecumenically, radiogenically, ectogenically, ontogenically, carcinogenically, oestrogenically, abiogenically, manically, tetanically, titanically, botanically, satanically, mechanically, volcanically, organically, galvanically, tyrannically, messianically, puritanically, inorganically, photomechanically, tonically, conically, phonically, sonically, chronically, ionically, bionically, psionically, embryonically, histrionically, hydroponically, diatonically, Platonically, tectonically, monotonically, isotonically, sardonically, draconically, laconically, demonically, mnemonically, harmonically, pulmonically, enharmonically, canonically, uncanonically, diaphonically, symphonically, polyphonically, stereophonically, homophonically, monophonically, quadraphonically, quadrophonically, telephonically, thrasonically, subsonically, hypersonically, supersonically,

29

1.31.25

ultrasonically, infrasonically, ironically, Byronically, moronically, acronycally, acronychally, diachronically, synchronically, electronically, cyclonically, technically, untechnically, pyrotechnically, ethnically
.9.9 beatifically, pontifically, scientifically, pacifically, specifically, terrifically, horrifically, prolifically, unscientifically, soporifically, honorifically, calorifically, hieroglyphically, stereospecifically, dermatoglyphically, graphically, seraphically, geographically, biographically, radiographically, physiographically, zoogeographically, choreographically, palaeographically, paleographically, bibliographically, epigraphically, topographically, typographically, photographically, cryptographically, demographically, nomographically, kymographically, sphygmographically, seismographically, pornographically, phonographically, ethnographically, lithographically, orthographically, xerographically, barographically, chorographically, spirographically, reprographically, spectrographically, hydrographically, telegraphically, calligraphically, holographically, autobiographically, chromatographically, lexicographically, iconographically, metallographically, cinematographically, telephotographically, photolithographically, cartographically, theosophically, philosophically, catastrophically, unphilosophically, homomorphically, isomorphically, allomorphically, anthropomorphically, civically, unequivocally
.9.10 mythically, ethically, Gothically, unethically, empathically, monolithically, osteopathically, homeopathically, homoeopathically, psychopathically, hydropathically, naturopathically, telepathically, basically, classically, farcically, lexically, toxically, nonsensically, anorexically, paradoxically, physically, quizzically, musically, whimsically, geophysically, biophysically, unmusically, intrinsically, extrinsically, forensically, hyperphysically, metaphysically, lackadaisically **.9.11** strategically, magically, tragically, lethargically, logically, anagogically, illogically, geologically, alogically, theologically, biologically, zoologically, seismologically, aetiologically, etiologically, osteologically, ideologically, archaeologically, archeologically, genealogically, sociologically, physiologically, embryologically, teleologically, topologically, tautologically, cytologically, ontologically, ecologically, mycologically, psychologically, conchologically, phrenologically, analogically, phonologically, chronologically, technologically, ethnologically, psephologically, morphologically, ethologically, mythologically, pathologically, chorologically, virologically, neurologically, astrologically, hydrologically,

philologically, unphysiologically, bacteriologically, radiobiologically, sociobiologically, microbiologically, anthropologically, herpetologically, climatologically, dermatologically, methodologically, codicologically, pharmacologically, gynaecologically, gynecologically, lexicologically, musicologically, etymologically, entomologically, terminologically, immunologically, ornithologically, meteorologically, parapsychologically, epistemologically, phenomenologically, surgically, liturgically, metallurgically, nostalgically, equivocally
.9.12 lyrically, empirically, satirically, spherically, hysterically, chimerically, numerically, mesmerically, generically, clerically, cholerically, esoterically, exoterically, hemispherically, atmospherically, alphanumerically, barbarically, rhetorically, historically, euphorically, plethorically, meteorically, oratorically, unhistorically, prehistorically, categorically, allegorically, metaphorically, semaphorically, reciprocally, metrically, obstetrically, geometrically, diametrically, symmetrically, stoichiometrically, goniometrically, pluviometrically, sociometrically, psychometrically, viscometrically, thermometrically, manometrically, chronometrically, asymmetrically, isometrically, unsymmetrically, barometrically, pyrometrically, hydrometrically, hygrometrically, volumetrically, econometrically, trigonometrically, axonometrically, interferometrically, theatrically, psychiatrically, electrically, dielectrically, thermoelectrically, piezoelectrically, hydroelectrically, geocentrically, eccentrically, concentrically, heliocentrically, endocentrically, egocentrically, ethnocentrically, anthropocentrically, cylindrically, helically, phallically, biblically, publically, publicly, cyclically, catholically, catholicly, umbilically, idyllically, angelically, metallically, diabolically, symbolically, shambolically, bucolically, hydraulically, philatelically, psychedelically, evangelically, hyperbolically, metabolically, catabolically, parabolically, apostolically, melancholically **.10** Berkley
.11 Oakley **.12** pinkly, tinkly, Hinckley, twinkly, wrinkly, crinkly, dankly, Shankly, rankly, frankly, lankly, Dunkley **.13** briskly, brusquely, grotesquely, statuesquely, picturesquely

1.31.25
giggly, niggly, jiggly, wiggly, Wigley, Quigley, squiggly, wriggly, Wrigley, vaguely, waggly, straggly, scraggly, Mowgli, ugli, ugly, smugly, snuggly, snugly, googly, Hooghly, singly, shingly, jingly, Zwingli, spangly, dangly, gangly, jungly, plug-ugly

1.31.26

.1 seemly, unseemly, supremely, extremely **.2** dimly, primly, trimly, grimly, slimly **.3** tamely, gamely, namely, lamely **.4** Emley **.5** family, Hamley, Bramley **.6** Armley, calmly **.7** Bromley **.8** Gormley, warmly, lukewarmly, uniformly **.9** dumbly, comely, numbly, Cholmeley, Cholmondeley, rumly, Lumley, Plomley, glumly **.10** timely, untimely, sublimely **.11** Bottomley, randomly, welcomely, lissomly, fearsomely, awesomely, noisomely, gruesomely, tiresomely, lightsomely, gladsomely, buxomly, irksomely, gamesomely, winsomely, handsomely, lonesomely, toothsomely, loathsomely, toilsomely, fulsomely, wholesomely, troublesomely, meddlesomely, solemnly, unwelcomely, wearisomely, worrisomely, cumbersomely, humorsomely, venturesomely, frolicsomely, quarrelsomely, unwholesomely **.12** termly, firmly **.13** homely

1.31.27

.1 keenly, meanly, queenly, greenly, leanly, cleanly, routinely, obscenely, serenely, uncleanly **.2** inly, Finlay, thinly, Brynley, Linley, McKinley **.3** medianly, ruffianly, Dickensianly **.4** mainly, vainly, sanely, plainly, urbanely, mundanely, arcanely, ungainly, humanely, germanely, inanely, profanely, insanely, inhumanely **.5** Henley **.6** Stanley, Manley, manly, Hanley, Cranleigh, Cranley, Port Stanley, Winstanley, unmanly, Osmanli **.7** Townley **.8** Darnley, Farnley **.9** Conley, wanly, Swanley **.10** Thornley, forlornly **.11** finely, supinely, condignly, benignly, divinely, bovinely, malignly, clandestinely **.12** jejunely, opportunely **.13** genuinely **.14** openly, misshapenly, stubbornly, slatternly, rottenly, certainly, wantonly, uncertainly, maidenly, leadenly, modernly, soddenly, suddenly, woodenly, goldenly, unmaidenly, brokenly, drunkenly, mistakenly, unshakenly, outspokenly, unbrokenly, seamanly, commonly, womanly, humanly, yeomanly, statesmanly, sportsmanly, gentlemanly, uncommonly, unwomanly, inhumanly, ungentlemanly, superhumanly, femininely, evenly, cravenly, heavenly, slovenly, unevenly, vixenly, brazenly, cousinly, frozenly, citizenly, musicianly, Christianly, unchristianly, curmudgeonly, sanguinely, barrenly, matronly, sovereignly, sullenly, masculinely **.15** Ernle, Burnley, sternly, taciturnly **.16** only, Stoneleigh, pronely, lonely

1.31.28

.1 Bingley, tingly, Dingley, kingly **.1.1** unseeingly, pityingly, wearyingly, varyingly, worryingly, unpityingly, self-pityingly, unwearyingly, unvaryingly, gnawingly, cloyingly, annoyingly, pryingly, tryingly, lyingly, undyingly, stupefyingly, gratifyingly, mortifyingly, mystifyingly, edifyingly, terrifyingly, horrifyingly, satisfyingly, unedifyingly,

unsatisfyingly, cooingly, knowingly, flowingly, unknowingly, harrowingly **.1.2** weepingly, sweepingly, trippingly, grippingly, gapingly, snappingly, gripingly, gropingly, limpingly, rompingly, lispingly, raspingly, graspingly, gulpingly, unsleepingly **.1.3** sobbingly, snubbingly, probingly, absorbingly, perturbingly, disturbingly **.1.4** cheatingly, bleatingly, fleetingly, entreatingly, fittingly, wittingly, befittingly, unfittingly, unwittingly, unremittingly, unbefittingly, gratingly, nauseatingly, undeviatingly, depreciatingly, ingratiatingly, excruciatingly, infuriatingly, humiliatingly, insinuatingly, extenuatingly, hesitatingly, irritatingly, devastatingly, unhesitatingly, debilitatingly, intimidatingly, accommodatingly, placatingly, suffocatingly, deprecatingly, intoxicatingly, self-deprecatingly, fascinatingly, incriminatingly, discriminatingly, illuminatingly, captivatingly, aggravatingly, frustratingly, exasperatingly, penetratingly, invigoratingly, exaggeratingly, exhilaratingly, titillatingly, scintillatingly, calculatingly, stimulatingly, upsettingly, poutingly, doubtingly, smartingly, sportingly, supportingly, unsportingly, ripsnortingly, cuttingly, struttingly, bitingly, slightingly, invitingly, excitingly, uninvitingly, off-puttingly, disquietingly, comfortingly, dispiritingly, inspiritingly, divertingly, disconcertingly, dotingly, gloatingly, floatingly, temptingly, affectingly, exactingly, unsuspectingly, unreflectingly, pantingly, rantingly, tauntingly, dauntingly, vauntingly, hauntingly, unstintingly, tormentingly, lamentingly, dissentingly, enchantingly, disenchantingly, unrelentingly, disappointingly, questingly, lastingly, trustingly, boastingly, insistingly, protestingly, arrestingly, interestingly, unrestingly, contrastingly, disgustingly, unresistingly, unprotestingly, unarrestingly, uninterestingly, everlastingly, meltingly, haltingly, insultingly, exultingly, revoltingly **.1.5** pleadingly, kiddingly, ploddingly, thuddingly, chidingly, glidingly, broodingly, grindingly, blindingly, woundingly, yieldingly, exceedingly, unheedingly, misleadingly, forbiddingly, unfadingly, degradingly, accordingly, rewardingly, abidingly, confidingly, deridingly, intrudingly, forebodingly, unbendingly, unendingly, outstandingly, demandingly, commandingly, astoundingly, resoundingly, spellbindingly, unyieldingly, unrewardingly, unpretendingly, condescendingly, understandingly, correspondingly, uncomprehendingly **.1.6** sneakingly, creakingly, achingly, takingly, mockingly, shockingly, strikingly, smirkingly, jokingly, stinkingly, shrinkingly, clankingly, breathtakingly, painstakingly, rebukingly, rollickingly, provokingly, unthinkingly,

unwinkingly, unshrinkingly, unblinkingly,
naggingly, braggingly, intriguingly, unflaggingly
.1.7 schemingly, seemingly, screamingly,
gleamingly, swimmingly, shamingly,
damningly, charmingly, numbingly, fumingly,
disarmingly, alarmingly, heartwarmingly,
becomingly, assumingly, consumingly,
presumingly, welcomingly, unbecomingly,
unassumingly, overwhelmingly, meaningly,
unmeaningly, overweeningly, Finningley,
winningly, grinningly, complainingly,
entertainingly, uncomplainingly, fawningly,
warningly, yawningly, punningly, stunningly,
cunningly, shiningly, whiningly, designingly,
underminingly, threateningly, hearteningly,
frighteningly, maddeningly, sickeningly,
deafeningly, questioningly, dishearteningly,
unreasoningly, unquestioningly, burningly,
yearningly, discerningly, concerningly,
moaningly, groaningly, stingingly, singingly,
swingingly, ringingly, longingly **.1.8** sniffingly,
laughingly, scoffingly **.1.9** ravingly, lovingly,
movingly, forgivingly, unlovingly, approvingly,
reprovingly, unnervingly, deservingly,
unswervingly, unbelievingly, disbelievingly,
unforgivingly, disapprovingly, undeservingly
.1.10 seethingly, scathingly, soothingly
.1.11 piercingly, pressingly, passingly, vexingly,
taxingly, coaxingly, mincingly, wincingly,
glancingly, unceasingly, decreasingly,
increasingly, caressingly, depressingly,
distressingly, surpassingly, harassingly,
rejoicingly, enticingly, promisingly,
menacingly, perplexingly, convincingly,
entrancingly, self-effacingly, acquiescingly,
unpromisingly, embarrassingly,
unconvincingly **.1.12** teasingly, wheezingly,
pleasingly, blazingly, rousingly, musingly,
unpleasingly, displeasingly, amazingly,
appraisingly, surprisingly, accusingly,
amusingly, confusingly, imposingly,
appetisingly, appetizingly, compromisingly,
agonisingly, agonizingly, patronisingly,
patronizingly, mesmerisingly,
mesmerizingly, enterprisingly,
unsurprisingly, tantalisingly, tantalizingly,
paralysingly, paralyzingly, moralisingly,
moralizingly, unimposingly, unappetisingly,
unappetizingly, uncompromisingly,
demoralisingly, demoralizingly **.1.13** dashingly,
smashingly, lashingly, gushingly, rushingly,
crushingly, pushingly, flinchingly, refreshingly,
unblushingly, punishingly, ravishingly,
languishingly, perishingly, nourishingly,
unflinchingly, astonishingly
.1.14 whingeingly, whingingly, swingeingly,
unchangingly, challengingly **.1.15** fetchingly,
scorchingly, touchingly, searchingly,
bewitchingly, reproachingly
.1.16 grudgingly, engagingly, begrudgingly,
ungrudgingly, obligingly, damagingly,
disobligingly, disparagingly, encouragingly,
discouragingly **.1.17** sneeringly, searingly,

jeeringly, leeringly, endearingly, domineeringly,
interferingly, sparingly, daringly, wearingly,
glaringly, despairingly, unsparingly,
forbearingly, uncaringly, overbearingly,
boringly, snoringly, soaringly, roaringly,
luringly, adoringly, reassuringly, enduringly,
riproaringly, deploringly, imploringly, louringly,
devouringly, overpoweringly, inspiringly,
retiringly, untiringly, admiringly, enquiringly,
uninspiringly, stirringly, unerringly, simperingly,
whimperingly, blubberingly, soberingly,
titteringly, glitteringly, shatteringly, flatteringly,
stutteringly, mutteringly, splutteringly,
hectoringly, swelteringly, falteringly,
earthshatteringly, unflatteringly, unfalteringly,
shudderingly, thunderingly, wonderingly,
blunderingly, smolderingly, smoulderingly,
bewilderingly, snickeringly, sniggeringly,
staggeringly, swaggeringly, lingeringly,
shimmeringly, glimmeringly, stammeringly,
murmuringly, unmurmuringly, shiveringly,
quiveringly, waveringly, quaveringly,
unwaveringly, witheringly **.1.18** feelingly,
appealingly, unfeelingly, revealingly,
unappealingly, killingly, chillingly, willingly,
thrillingly, unwillingly, wailingly, unfailingly,
prevailingly, unavailingly, tellingly,
compellingly, growlingly, snarlingly, gallingly,
sprawlingly, crawlingly, appallingly, smilingly,
beguilingly, unsmilingly, gruellingly,
cripplingly, quibblingly, tremblingly,
ramblingly, stumblingly, mumblingly,
fumblingly, grumblingly, dissemblingly,
startlingly, belittlingly, wheedlingly,
middlingly, riddlingly, muddlingly, sparklingly,
nigglingly, bafflingly, stiflingly, triflingly,
snivellingly, grovelingly, grovellingly,
dazzlingly, puzzlingly, whirlingly, consolingly
.2 tangly, Langley **.3** wrongly, strongly,
headstrongly

1.31.29

chiefly, briefly, stiffly, sniffly, safely, deafly,
carefully, waffly, awfully, toughly, Cuffley,
snuffly, roughly, gruffly, bluffly, wifely,
unsafely, housewifely, aloofly, beautifully,
disgracefully, characterfully

1.31.30

.1 naively **.2** cognitively, constitutively **.3** bravely,
gravely, concavely **.4** suavely **.5** lovely, unlovely
.6 lively **.7.1** palliatively, appreciatively,
associatively, enunciatively, natively, creatively,
rotatively, illatively, quantitatively, denotatively,
connotatively, qualitatively, implicatively,
propagatively, innovatively, illustratively,
combatively, sportively, supportively,
abortively, intuitively, prohibitively,
partitively, putatively, optatively, tentatively,
quantitively, facultatively, repetitively,
competitively, exploitatively, dubitatively,
meditatively, imitatively, vegetatively,
preventatively, authoritatively,
argumentatively, representatively,

unrepresentatively, talkatively, predicatively, indicatively, evocatively, provocatively, communicatively, incommunicatively, uncommunicatively, negatively, ergatively, interrogatively, primitively, normatively, formatively, informatively, affirmatively, approximatively, unitively, punitively, definitively, ruminatively, culminatively, alternatively, determinatively, imaginatively, unimaginatively, privatively, derivatively, conservatively, sensitively, transitively, adversatively, insensitively, unsensitively, intransitively, positively, causatively, acquisitively, inquisitively, appositively, postpositively, accusatively, fugitively, imperatively, narratively, preparatively, comparatively, declaratively, restoratively, pejoratively, operatively, iteratively, decoratively, figuratively, generatively, cooperatively, vituperatively, deliberatively, collaboratively, commemoratively, regeneratively, uncooperatively, unremuneratively, interpretively, penetratively, demonstratively, administratively, undemonstratively, secretively, lucratively, relatively, ablatively, isolatively, appellatively, irrelatively, correlatively, superlatively, contemplatively, copulatively, speculatively, cumulatively, legislatively, manipulatively, accumulatively, furtively, assertively, nonassertively, unassertively, emotively
.7.2 descriptively, prescriptively, perceptively, deceptively, receptively, adaptively, adoptively, eruptively, disruptively, preemptively, consumptively, presumptively, unperceptively, attributively, retributively, distributively, consecutively, executively, diminutively, inconsecutively, fictively, predictively, vindictively, restrictively, afflictively, perspectively, respectively, prospectively, protectively, affectively, effectively, defectively, invectively, projectively, subjectively, objectively, correctively, electively, collectively, selectively, reflectively, irrespectively, retrospectively, introspectively, ineffectively, actively, reactively, proactively, inactively, attractively, diffractively, radioactively, retroactively, interactively, unattractively, deductively, seductively, productively, inductively, conductively, destructively, obstructively, instructively, constructively, reproductively, unproductively, self-destructively, counterproductively, distinctively, instinctively, adjunctively, subjunctively, conjunctively, disjunctively, indistinctively **.7.3** plaintively, substantively, attentively, retentively, preventively, inventively, inattentively, unretentively, uninventively **.7.4** festively, restively, costively, digestively, suggestively, exhaustively, cohesively, adhesively, permissively, submissively, dismissively, evasively, pervasively, invasively, persuasively, abrasively,

unpersuasively, recessively, obsessively, excessively, successively, possessively, oppressively, repressively, impressively, expressively, regressively, digressively, aggressively, progressively, ingressively, unimpressively, inexpressively, retrogressively, passively, massively, impassively, percussively, divisively, decisively, incisively, derisively, indecisively, conducively, protrusively, obtrusively, intrusively, abusively, effusively, diffusively, illusively, allusively, elusively, delusively, collusively, inclusively, conclusively, exclusively, unobtrusively, inconclusively, purposively, cursively, coercively, abstersively, recursively, discursively, excursively, aversively, subversively, erosively, corrosively, explosively, reflexively, pensively, suspensively, expensively, intensively, ostensively, extensively, offensively, defensively, expansively, responsively, inexpensively, inoffensively, apprehensively, comprehensively, irresponsively, unresponsively, repulsively, impulsively, compulsively, convulsively

1.31.31
Keighley, deathly, fourthly, earthly, eighthly, tenthly, monthly, ninthly, seventhly, fifthly, twelfthly, sixthly, Dolgellau, Llanelli, uncouthly, unearthly, bimonthly

1.31.32
lithely, blithely, smoothly

1.31.33
.1.1 fiercely, copiously, impiously, dubiously, amphibiously, piteously, duteously, beauteously, courteously, plenteously, bounteously, discourteously, rumbustiously, tediously, hideously, studiously, odiously, fastidiously, perfidiously, invidiously, insidiously, commodiously, melodiously, compendiously, incommodiously, unmelodiously
.1.2 abstemiously, ingeniously, spontaneously, instantaneously, simultaneously, extraneously, harmoniously, euphoniously, erroneously, feloniously, homogeneously, heterogeneously, ignominiously, consanguineously, percutaneously, subcutaneously, subterraneously, miscellaneously, impecuniously, inharmoniously, disharmoniously, sanctimoniously, parsimoniously, ceremoniously, acrimoniously, contemporaneously, extemporaneously, unceremoniously **.1.3** deviously, previously, perviously, obviously, enviously, lasciviously, obliviously, imperviously, nauseously, aqueously, obsequiously **.1.4** deliriously, seriously, imperiously, mysteriously, deleteriously, variously, vicariously, precariously, gregariously, nefariously, hilariously, burglariously, multifariously, spuriously, curiously, furiously, gloriously, laboriously, notoriously, victoriously, uxoriously, censoriously, usuriously,

uproariously, incuriously, ingloriously, vaingloriously, meritoriously, luxuriously, injuriously, penuriously, lugubriously, salubriously, opprobriously, industriously, illustriously **.1.5** biliously, punctiliously, contumeliously, superciliously **.2** Wesley, expressly **.3** scarcely **.4** crassly **.5** parsley, sparsely **.6** crossly **.7** coarsely, hoarsely, retrorsely, sinistrorsely **.8** choicely **.9** nicely, precisely, concisely, imprecisely **.10** otiosely, grandiosely **.11** sprucely, loosely, obtusely, abstrusely, diffusely, profusely **.12.1** joyously, piously, flexuously, sensuously, fatuously, tortuously, virtuously, sumptuously, unctuously, impetuously, voluptuously, contemptuously, presumptuously, tempestuously, incestuously, tumultuously, congruously, incongruously, arduously, vacuously, sinuously, tenuously, strenuously, assiduously, perspicuously, innocuously, promiscuously, ambiguously, contiguously, exiguously, continuously, ingenuously, disingenuously, inconspicuously, unambiguously, discontinuously, mellifluously, superfluously **.12.2** purposely, pompously, gibbously, riotously, fortuitously, gratuitously, circuitously, covetously, portentously, momentously, precipitously, calamitously, felicitously, solicitously, necessitously, ubiquitously, iniquitously, serendipitously, infelicitously, hazardously, stupendously, tremendously, horrendously, raucously, viscously, analogously **.12.3** famously, squamously, timeously, enormously, bigamously, venomously, infamously, blasphemously, posthumously, polygamously, monogamously, unanimously, magnanimously, autonomously, pseudonymously, homonymously, anonymously, synonymously, pusillanimously, venously, heinously, intravenously, ruinously, cretinously, gluttonously, mutinously, glutinously, gelatinously, monotonously, libidinously, multitudinously, vertiginously, ominously, numinously, luminously, verminously, voluminously, coterminously, conterminously, diaphanously, cavernously, ravenously, larcenously, poisonously, indigenously, fuliginously, exogenously, tyrannously, synchronously, isochronously, asynchronously, villainously **.12.4** amorphously, grievously, nervously, mischievously, speciously, dioeciously, facetiously, viciously, propitiously, auspiciously, suspiciously, conspicuously, ambitiously, fictitiously, factitiously, adventitiously, seditiously, judiciously, perniciously, officiously, flagitiously, capriciously, nutritiously, deliciously, maliciously, unpropitiously, inauspiciously, unsuspiciously, unambitiously, overambitiously, repetitiously, surreptitiously, superstitiously, expeditiously, injudiciously, supposititiously, avariciously, meretriciously, supposititiously, spaciously, graciously, capaciously, rapaciously,

flirtatiously, ostentatiously, audaciously, bodaciously, mendaciously, fugaciously, sagaciously, tenaciously, pugnaciously, vivaciously, curvaceously, curvaciously, vexatiously, sequaciously, loquaciously, veraciously, voraciously, ungraciously, hellaciously, fallaciously, salaciously, disputatiously, unostentatiously, perspicaciously, efficaciously, contumaciously, pertinaciously, inefficaciously, preciously, tortiously, cautiously, incautiously, overcautiously, lusciously, precociously, ferociously, atrociously, captiously, bumptiously, scrumptiously, factiously, fractiously, noxiously, anxiously, infectiously, innoxiously, obnoxiously, compunctiously, rambunctiously, overanxiously, consciously, pretentiously, sententiously, contentiously, tendenciously, tendentiously, licentiously, subconsciously, unconsciously, self-consciously, conscientiously, unpretentiously, uncontentiously, superconsciously, unselfconsciously, righteously, unrighteously, self-righteously, gorgeously, frabjously, egregiously, litigiously, prestigiously, prodigiously, religiously, rampageously, contagiously, advantageously, courageously, outrageously, irreligiously, sacrilegiously, sacriligiously, disadvantageously **.12.5** porously, vaporously, prosperously, viviparously, oviparously, fissiparously, obstreperously, unprosperously, barbarously, traitorously, stertorously, boisterously, blusterously, dexterously, preposterously, adulterously, murderously, odorously, slanderously, ponderously, thunderously, malodorously, decorously, rancorously, indecorously, cantankerously, vigorously, rigorously, languorously, clangorously, clangourously, timorously, amorously, clamorously, glamorously, glamourously, numerously, humorously, generously, onerously, sonorously, ungenerously, overgenerously, pestiferously, splendiferously, vociferously, odoriferously, flavorously, flavourously, carnivorously, omnivorously, cancerously, precancerously, venturously, adventurously, dangerously, treacherously, lecherously, torturously, rapturously, unadventurously, valorously, dolorously, scabrously, fibrously, cumbrously, lustrously, dextrously, monstrously, disastrously, idolatrously, ambidextrously, wondrously, ludicrously, chivalrously, unchivalrously **.12.6** rebelliously, villously, pitilessly, peerlessly, tearlessly, fearlessly, cheerlessly, zealously, jealously, airlessly, carelessly, callously, parlously, lawlessly, flawlessly, joylessly, cluelessly, powerlessly, tirelessly, libellously, libelously, scandalously, humorlessly, humourlessly, anomalously, pennilessly, frivolously, marvellously, marvelously, mercilessly, measurelessly, sedulously, credulously, pendulously, incredulously, perilously, querulously, garrulously, scurrilously, populously, scrupulously, nebulously, fabulously, patulously, emulously, tremulously, scrofulously, unscrupulously, meticulously, ridiculously, miraculously, colorlessly, colourlessly, sleeplessly, shapelessly, haplessly, hopelessly, helplessly, witlessly, weightlessly, doubtlessly, artlessly, heartlessly, spotlessly, thoughtlessly, gutlessly, sightlessly, fruitlessly, tactlessly, dauntlessly, pointlessly, shiftlessly, thriftlessly, listlessly, tastelessly, restlessly, guiltlessly, faultlessly, limitlessly, effortlessly, spiritlessly, eventlessly, relentlessly, resistlessly, needlessly, heedlessly, cloudlessly, godlessly, bloodlessly, wordlessly, endlessly, boundlessly, soundlessly, groundlessly, mindlessly, childlessly, regardlessly, fecklessly, recklessly, lucklessly, thanklessly, seamlessly, dreamlessly, aimlessly, namelessly, shamelessly, blamelessly, charmlessly, harmlessly, gormlessly, formlessly, timelessly, sinlessly, painlessly, stainlessly, brainlessly, spinelessly, tunelessly, tonelessly, motionlessly, expressionlessly, meaninglessly, lifelessly, selflessly, lovelessly, nervelessly, motivelessly, faithlessly, deathlessly, breathlessly, ruthlessly, mirthlessly, worthlessly, ceaselessly, baselessly, facelessly, gracelessly, voicelessly, pricelessly, uselessly, sexlessly, senselessly, remorselessly, purposelessly, defencelessly, defenselessly, causelessly, noiselessly, speechlessly, matchlessly, changelessly, guilelessly, soullessly, tersely, diversely, aversely, perversely, reversely, obversely, adversely, inversely, conversely, transversely **.13** grossly, closely, verbosely, globosely, jocosely, rugosely, morosely, comatosely, bellicosely, lachrymosely **.14** Apsley **.15** Bexley, laxly, Oxley, Locksley, Loxley, Huxley, prolixly, convexly, complexly, orthodoxly, unorthodoxly **.16** princely, tensely, densely, prepensely, intensely, immensely **.17** falsely

1.31.34
Beasley, measly, Bisley, Disley, mizzly, Sisley, Wisley, drizzly, grisly, grizzly, frizzly, paisley, Wesley, Presley, Lesley, Leslie, Parsley, Mosley, Guiseley, wisely, unwisely, otiosely, grandiosely, muesli, Hattersley, Baddesley, Eckersley, Annesley, Worsley, Moseley, rugosely, comatosely, bellicosely, lachrymosely, Beardsley, Cloudesley, Maudsley, Tyldesley, Walmesley, Tinsley, Ainsley, Hensley, Barnsley, Kingsley, Wellesley, Wolseley

1.31.35
.1 Corbishley **.2** specially, freshly, fleshly **.3** Ashley, rashly, brashly **.4** harshly **.5** poshly **.6** lushly, plushly **.7.1** babyishly, boyishly, Jewishly, shrewishly, sheepishly, apishly, snappishly, foppishly, uppishly, popishly, impishly, wimpishly, grumpishly,

frumpishly, lumpishly, waspishly, snobbishly, yobbishly, skittishly, pettishly, cattishly, loutishly, sottishly, sluttishly, brutishly, doltishly, coltishly, coquettishly, caddishly, faddishly, cloddishly, prudishly, modishly, fiendishly, childishly, outlandishly, freakishly, rakishly, peckishly, blockishly, mawkishly, puckishly, bookishly, monkishly, piggishly, priggishly, waggishly, doggishly, hoggishly, thuggishly, sluggishly, roguishly **.7.2** squeamishly, mannishly, clannishly, clownishly, donnishly, swinishly, kittenishly, womanishly, heathenishly **.7.3** raffishly, offishly, huffishly, oafishly, elfishly, selfishly, wolfishly, standoffishly, unselfishly, peevishly, thievishly, knavishly, slavishly, lavishly, elvishly **.7.4** minxishly, garishly, boorishly, whorishly, currishly, liquorishly, tigerishly, ogreishly, feverishly, liverishly, nightmarishly, amateurishly, shamateurishly, hellishly, owlishly, stylishly, bullishly, ghoulishly, foolishly, mulishly, girlishly, churlishly, ticklishly, devilishly, gauchely

1.31.36
richly, Critchley, Sketchley, Bletchley, archly, muchly, Finchley, staunchly

1.31.37
Midgley, sagely, largely, Rugeley, hugely, strangely, savagely, averagely

1.31.38
stilly, shrilly, palely, stalely, frailly, foully, vowelly, dully, vilely, coolly, dually, solely, wholely, wholly, drolly, supplely, brittlely, genteelly, ideally, banally, futilely, hostilely, servilely, facilely, docilely, agilely, fragilely, sterilely, puerilely, fickly, evilly, imbecilely, versatilely, juvenilely, unsterilely

1.32
Dolgellau, Llanelli

2
e, he, p, pea, pee, b, be, Bea, bee, t, te, tea, tee, ti, d, Dee, dee, cay, key, quay, ski, ghee, ghi, gie, me, Mee, mi, knee, fee, v, vee, the, thee, c, sea, see, si, zee, she, shea, shchi, g, gee, we, wee, whee, puy, twee, Twi, re, Rea, prix, spree, Brie, tree, dree, Cree, cri, scree, free, three, ye, Lea, lea, lee, Leigh, Ley, ley, plea, Blea, glee, flea, flee, payee, drawee, i.e., cooee, cooey, tant pis, herb tea, ID, loanee, whangee, tai chi, t'ai chi, Grand Prix, Grands Prix, Wee Free, pollee, OBE, s.a.e., employee, PAYE, Anouilh, R & B, maître d', maîtres d', R & D, Wounded Knee, c'est la vie, C. of E., eau-de-vie, Caspian Sea, Zuider Zee, parti pris, upas tree, dernier cri, appellee, fleur-de-lis, evacuee, interviewee, South China Sea, Caribbean Sea

2.1
fimbriae

2.2
tracheae

2.3
tibiae, tracheae, branchiae, bronchiae, taeniae, Danae, foveae, torii, scoriae, ochreae, paleae, nauplii, cochleae, trochleae, petechiae, actiniae, gorgoniae, Pasiphaë, exuviae, rickettsiae, facetiae, minutiae, reliquiae, cercariae, denarii, filariae, injuriae, prima facie, differentiae, retiarii, maculae luteae

2.4
Danae, cicisbei, Agnus Dei, Pasiphaë

2.5
employee

2.6
striae, Hawaii, sine die

2.7
cooee, Louis

2.8
psoai

2.9
tepee, yippee, OAP, tapis, rappee, cowpea, VIP, whoopee, rupee, pupae, topi, scopae, chickpea, MP, tempi, USP, OHP, EDP, GDP, escapee, RIP, cap-à-pie, agape, calipee

2.10
maybe, rabi, Nabi, bawbee, would-be, frisbee®, bumblebee, amoebae, KGB, honeybee, wannabe, succubae, SOB

2.11
PET, TT, titi, VAT, metis, settee, puttee, suttee, hutia, bootee, tutee, q.t., petit, coatee, goatee, TNT, grantee, patentee, absentee, presentee, draftee, testee, trustee, UHT, remittee, SAT®, repartee, allottee, deportee, indictee, invitee, NUT, dilutee, picotee, legatee, permittee, manatee, muffetee, devotee, amputee, billetee, MOT, adoptee, selectee, inductee, appointee, guarantee, warrantee, consultee, cohabitee, dedicatee

2.12.1
titi, chaetae, setae, sgraffiti, Docetae

2.12.2
vittae, lyttae, banditti, committee

2.12.3
metis

2.12.4
cornetti, Marinetti, vaporetti

2.12.5
ciabatte, sfumati, castrati, obbligati, illuminati

2.12.6
démenti

2.12.7
suttee

2.12.8
aqua vitae, arbor vitae, lignum vitae

2.12.9
putti

2.12.10
bootee, bootie, ritenuti

2.12.11
manatee, transmutability

2.12.12
coatee

2.12.13
stacte, svarabhakti

2.12.14
portamenti, prominenti, cognoscenti, divertimenti

2.12.15
cristae, testae, vestee, cesti, bustee, trustee, ballistae

2.12.16
peltae

2.13
QED, TD, three-D, Midi, Gardaí, guardee, O'Dea, OD, Litt.D., Hindi, OED, OND, vendee, standee, grandee, spondee, Dundee, secondee, PhD, Chaldee, Tweedledee, LED, Zebedee, fiddle-de-dee, chickadee, kiskadee, keskidee, solidi, attendee, glissandi, sforzandi, secondi, Ynys-ddu, arachnidae, primigravidae, modi vivendi, modus vivendi, modi operandi, modus operandi

2.14
thecae, Bacchae, maquis, marquee, marquis, coquille, loci, Torquay, Newquay, McKee, McKie, raki, trochee, croci, turnkey, conchae, bronchi, Stiffkey, miskey, passkey, Volski, latchkey, sulci, Waikiki, cloacae, verrucae, Manichee, tunicae, Cherokee, tarakihi, après-ski, spermathecae, horti sicci, gonococci, diplococci, noctilucae

2.15
ragee, raggee, thuggee, Magee, McGee, whangee, Bangui, Belgae, algae

2.16
squamae, rami, gemmae, mammae, strumae, thermae, drachmae, en famille, bonhomie, Otomi, McNamee, ginglymi, excuse-me, hypothalami

2.17
trainee, ranee, rani, Pawnee, Shawnee, donee, detainee, distrainee, assignee, consignee, nominee, Guarani, returnee, internee, bouquet garni, abandonee, examinee

2.17.1
venae, catenae, sordini, trichinae, Mycenae, porcini, carinae, stellini, paraselenae

2.17.2
pinnae

2.17.3
antennae

2.17.4
Cannae

2.17.5
rani

2.17.6
Chamonix

2.17.7
koiné

2.17.8
minae, trichinae, carinae, globigerinae

2.17.9
lacunae

2.17.10
retinae, Gemini, Chamonix, laminae, Panini

2.17.11
personae, coronae, panettoni, conversazioni

2.17.12
thicknee

2.17.13
Temne, alumnae

2.17.14
ulnae

2.18
feoffee, Fifi, hyphae, McFee, McPhee, nymphae, McAfee

2.19
larvae, q.v., novae, sylvae, peccavi, vis-à-vis, gingivae, venae cavae, conjunctivae, supernovae

2.20
mythi

2.21
prithee, Ynys-ddu

2.22
cc, Jaycee, lessee, Parsee, foresee, Q.C., Coetzee, emcee, ONC, Shensi, Shansi, Shanxi, licensee, BSc, THC, plc, UPC, releasee, addressee, sub-lessee, SERC, endorsee, divorcé, divorcée, WC, undersea, fricassee, promisee, Tennessee, oversea, oversee, USMC, sub-licensee, MSc

2.22.1
thecae

2.22.2
abscissae, vibrissae

2.22.3
precis

2.22.4
Parsee, Farsi

2.22.5
fossae, concerti grossi

2.22.6
medusae, verrucae

2.22.7
Battersea, fricassee, Sadducee, Pharisee, gallice, Eurydice, sub judice, loci classici

2.22.8
bursae

2.22.9
loci, mafiosi

2.22.10
Pitsea, sightsee, paparazzi

2.22.11
coxae, look-see, gonococci, diplococci

2.22.12
Withernsea

2.22.13
Brightlingsea

2.22.14
sulci, Anglesey, Winchelsea

2.23
fusee, fuzee, appraisee, chalazae, booboisie, bourgeoisie, malvoisie, devisee, advisee, franchisee, jalousie, medusae, chimpanzee, mycorrhizae, mafiosi, petty bourgeoisie, petite bourgeoisie

2.24
specie, chichi, rushee, O'Shea, buckshee, banshee, munshi, debauchee, garnishee, prima facie

2.25
sitringee

2.26
Geechee, lychee, bocce, Medici, debauchee, chincherinchee

2.27
e.g., Fiji, gee-gee, squeegee, pledgee, bargee, burgee, ogee, pongee, Belgae, algae, anti-g, solfeggi, refugee, apogee, Chatterjee, mortgagee, perigee, obligee, sitringee, Murrumbidgee

2.28
tee-hee, spahi, towhee, sandhi

2.29
peewee, pewee, kiwi, weewee, Pertwee, aiguille, Anhui, ennui, ratatouille, siliquae

2.30
Chérie, Tiree, Marie, sirree, flânerie, retiree, rapparee, potpourri, jamboree, stingaree, sangaree, dungaree, bain-marie, bummaree, Annemarie, referee, conferee, shivaree, kedgeree, transferee, corroboree, Annamarie, chinoiserie

2.30.1
hetaerae

2.30.2
serrae

2.30.3
condottieri

2.30.4
monsignori

2.30.5
Nyree

2.30.6
potpourri

2.30.7
chickaree, stingaree, zingari, amphorae, tesserae, kedgeree, primiparae, corroboree, charcuterie, chelicerae, umbelliferae

2.30.8
Capri, esprit, primiparae, jeu d'esprit, bel esprit

2.30.9
débris, terebrae, vertebrae, tenebrae, penumbrae

2.30.10
Portree, shoetree, firtree, Plumptre, Crabtree, figtree, Plumtre, Aintree, Braintree, Rountree, Rowntree, pinetree, rooftree, crosstree, Elstree, whippletree, doubletree, singletree, swingletree, whiffletree, triquetrae, charcuterie, fenestrae

2.30.11
decree

2.30.12
gree-gree, gris-gris, agree, degree, pedigree, verdigris, disagree, filigree

2.30.13
carefree, VAT-free, scot-free, frost-free, lead-free, smoke-free, unfree

2.30.14
tesserae, chelicerae

2.30.15
Tishri

2.31
come-all-ye

2.32
bailee, Ali, alee, Tralee, Eastleigh, expellee, wagon-lit, appellee, libellee, Peterlee, fleur-de-lys, parolee, enrollee, Buckfastleigh, Trincomalee

2.32.1
stelae, chelae, sequelae

2.32.2
papillae, morbilli, mamillae, axillae, maxillae

2.32.3
alveoli

2.32.4
bailee

2.32.5
glabellae, patellae, lamellae, novelle, sequelae, casus belli, ritornelli, legionellae, saltarelli

2.32.6
phalli, thalli, prothalli

2.32.7
strobilae

2.32.8
bullae, ampullae, torulae

2.32.9
.1 foveolae, areolae **.2** Thermopylae **.3** jubilee, emboli, discoboli **.4** amygdalae **.5** ovoli
.6 cypselae **.7** shiralee, morulae, gastrulae

.8 papulae, scapulae, scopulae, serpulae, nebulae, tabulae, spatulae, blastulae, radulae, moduli, maculae, loculi, reguli, ungulae, stimuli, famuli, hamuli, formulae, cannulae, lunulae, infulae, uvulae, lazuli, torulae, vox populi, corbiculae, fasciculi, trabeculae, valleculae, ranunculi, glomeruli **.9** Galilee **.10** stolae, Holi, alveoli **.11** Chablis **.12** Eastleigh **.13** agley

3
ear, 'ere, peer, pier, Pierre, spear, Speir, beer, Bere, bier, tear, tier, Tyr, steer, stere, dear, Deare, deer, Deere, Keir, kier, kir, gear, mere, Mia, Mir, smear, shmear, near, sneer, fear, sphere, veer, Vere, cere, sear, seer, sere, Zia, shear, sheer, Shere, -shire, cheer, jeer, hear, here, Wear, weir, we're, queer, rear, rhea, Trier, drear, Greer, Grier, Freer, Frere, year, Lear, leer, lehr, blear, clear, fleer, FLIR, Meir, Zaïre, De Vere, scrutineer, Tyne and Wear, Baile Átha Cliath

3.1
appear, reappear, Sapir, disappear

3.2.1
sepia

3.2.2
Principia

3.2.3
tapir, Napier, Sapir, rapier, tilapia

3.2.4
Apia, tilapia

3.2.5
copier, photocopier

3.2.6
croupier

3.2.7
myopia, utopia, subtopia, dystopia, sinopia, presbyopia, Ethiopia, oxyopia, polyopia, amblyopia, cornucopia, hemianopia, tritanopia, protanopia, deuteronopia, hyperopia, emmetropia, nyctalopia, hypermetropia

3.2.8
Dampier, compeer, Olympia

3.2.9
Shakespeare, Breakspear

3.2.10
Robespierre

3.3
sabir, Manorbier

3.3.1
akebia

3.3.2
tibia, Libya, Namibia, Conybeare, amphibia

3.3.3
Fabia, Swabia, labia, Arabia, Bessarabia, Saudi Arabia

3.3.4
lobbyer, della Robbia

3.3.5
euphorbia

3.3.6
Nubia

3.3.7
Meyerbeer

3.3.8
Serbia, suburbia, exurbia

3.3.9
obeah, phobia, Zenobia, neophobia,
hippophobia, sitophobia, photophobia,
Francophobia, homophobia, xenophobia,
gynophobia, Sinophobia, technophobia,
aquaphobia, claustrophobia, hydrophobia,
necrophobia, acrophobia, Negrophobia,
agoraphobia, Gallophobia, Anglophobia,
Russophobia, ailurophobia, symmetrophobia

3.3.10
rootbeer

3.3.11
cambia, Gambia, gambier, Zambia, cumbia,
Colombia, Columbia

3.4
McTeer, frontier, charioteer, puppeteer,
pulpiteer, McAteer, racketeer, marketeer,
rocketeer, musketeer, summiteer, sonneteer,
profiteer, privateer, corsetière, gazetteer,
gadgeteer, Galatea, muleteer, pamphleteer,
orienteer, volunteer, peripeteia

3.4.1
meteor, wheatear, retia

3.4.2
Whittier, syncytia

3.4.3
Ossetia, poinsettia

3.4.4
Katia

3.4.5
hamartia, Dei gratia

3.4.6
cottier

3.4.7
courtier, consortia

3.4.8
Yakutia

3.4.9
macula lutea, corpora lutea

3.4.10
sestertia

3.4.11
protea

3.4.12
strontia, frontier, Parmentier, astrantia, in
absentia, tradescantia, explanantia, orthodontia,
North-West Frontier, bona vacantia

3.4.13
Bastia, austere, Ostia, Izvestia, understeer,
Monastir, oversteer, periostea, gynaecomastia,
gynecomastia

3.5
idea, Judaea, Judea, bayadère, Medea, endear,
bombardier, halberdier, brigadier, Agadir,
grenadier, belvedere, balladeer, commandeer

3.5.1
media, bi-media, via media, acedia,
hypnopaedia, hypnopedia, cyclopaedia,
cyclopedia, multimedia, intermedia, epicedia,
encyclopaedia, encyclopedia

3.5.2
Lydia, oidia, ommatidia, Numidia, chlamydia,
conidia, Ophidia, Pisidia, praesidia, basidia,
pyxidia, peridia, clostridia, nephridia,
enchiridia, hesperidia, antheridia,
cryptosporidia

3.5.3
stadia, Nadia, nadir, Arcadia, Acadia

3.5.4
steadier

3.5.5
Nadia, myocardia, La Guardia, gaillardia,
tachycardia, pericardia, bradycardia,
endocardia

3.5.6
Claudia, primordia, exordia

3.5.7
belvedere

3.5.8
odea, podia, roe-deer, sympodia, Cambodia,
plasmodia, allodia, pseudopodia

3.5.9
India, reindeer, Scandia, compendia, Finlandia,
antependia, Fennoscandia, latifundia

3.6
fakir, Bashkir

3.6.1
petechia

3.6.2
Nausicaa

3.6.3
fakir, trachea, Wallachia

3.6.4
rudbeckia

3.6.5
fakir, dieffenbachia, Slovakia, Czechoslovakia

3.6.6
clarkia, souvlakia

3.6.7
lochia

3.6.8
branchia, bronchia, funkia

3.6.9
Ischia, Saskia

3.7
logia, footgear, headgear, switchgear, collegia

3.8
emir, amir, Taimyr, Crimea, ameer, Vermeer, Shamir, chimere, Izmir, cashmere, Kashmir

3.8.1
premia, pyaemia, parasitaemia, academia, hyperlipidaemia, leukaemia, ischaemia, anaemia, Euphemia, anthemia, polycythaemia, acaemia, toxaemia, septicaemia, thalassaemia, hypoxaemia, anoxaemia, hyperglycaemia, hypoglycaemia, Bohemia, uraemia, hyperaemia, bacteraemia, tularaemia

3.8.2
Ymir, skimmia, kerseymere, bulimia

3.8.3
macadamia, prothalamia, Mesopotamia, epithalamia

3.8.4
Emyr, premier

3.8.5
dysthymia, schizothymia, cyclothymia

3.8.6
costumier, perfumier

3.8.7
metamere, Buttermere, Vladimir, Windermere, Rothermere, centromere, telomere, Delamere

3.8.8
Hermia, panspermia, hyperthermia, hypothermia, poikilothermia

3.8.9
encomia, centromere

3.8.10
Tranmere

3.8.11
Tangmere

3.8.12
arrhythmia

3.8.13
Grasmere, besmear

3.8.14
anosmia, cosmea, Ellesmere, anorgasmia

3.8.15
cashmere

3.8.16
kalmia, Fowlmere, Thirlmere, Haslemere, ophthalmia, anophthalmia, exophthalmia

3.9
paneer, anear, pioneer, Kinnear, veneer, Rainier, caponier, carbineer, scrutineer, mutineer, mountaineer, buccaneer, domineer, cannoneer, chiffonier, muffineer, souvenir, auctioneer, engineer, re-engineer, bioengineer,

carabineer, electioneer, conventioneer, gonfalonier

3.9.1
taenia, senior, xenia, leucopenia, neutropenia, actinia, gardenia, bergenia, Armenia, hymenia, Slovenia, Ruthenia, asthenia, myasthenia, neurasthenia, proscenia, Encaenia, sarracenia, Eugenia, Kyrenia, schizophrenia

3.9.2
tinea, zinnia, linear, robinia, Sardinia, Gdynia, delphinia, Lavinia, Bithynia, vaccinia, gloxinia, Virginia, fourdrinier, collinear, trilinear, pollinia, triclinia, pleurodynia, Abyssinia, curvilinear, rectilinear, interlinear

3.9.3
mania, Rainier, crania, Oceania, Lithuania
.1 Albania **.2** Titania, Lusitania, Aquitania, Mauritania, Ruritania, collectanea, Tripolitania
.3 succedanea **.4** Lucania, Hyrcania, calcanea
.5 Romania, Tasmania, bibliomania, hypomania, kleptomania, egomania, monomania, Sinomania, nymphomania, infomania, mythomania, dipsomania, pyromania, Gallomania, megalomania, Anglomania, Graecomania, Francomania, erotomania, balletomania, toxicomania, decalcomania, theomania, hydromania, Grecomania
.6 Pennsylvania, Transylvania **.7** Azania, gazania
.8 Urania, Pomerania, pericrania **.9** miscellanea

3.9.4
denier, sthenia, xenia, biennia, triennia, septennia, decennia, quinquennia, quadrennia, millenia

3.9.5
pannier, Tania, Tanya, Goiânia, Campania, Catania

3.9.6
Tania, Tanya, Narnia, Titania, Christiania, Oceania

3.9.7
cornea, California

3.9.8
moneyer

3.9.9
junior, petunia

3.9.10
vernier, journeyer, hernia, Calpurnia, Hibernia

3.9.11
bonier, Ionia, Catalonia, myotonia, Antonia, Estonia, hypertonia, catatonia, Snowdonia, Rondônia, Macedonia, syconia, Laconia, zirconia, Franconia, gorgonia, begonia, Patagonia, archegonia, spermogonia, Paphlagonia, spermatogonia, pneumonia, ammonia, philharmonia, bronchopneumonia, pleuropneumonia, aphonia, sinfonia, Livonia, Slavonia, danthonia, watsonia, Amazonia,

mahonia, boronia, Wallonia, paulownia,
valonia, Babylonia, escallonia, Cephalonia

3.9.12
apnoea

3.9.13
insignia, algolagnia

3.9.14
romneya, insomnia, Polyhymnia, epilimnia,
hypolimnia

3.9.15
daphnia

3.9.16
Bothnia

3.9.17
Bosnia

3.10
ratafia, interfere

3.10.1
greffier

3.10.2
tafia, Mafia, raffia, dysgraphia

3.10.3
morphia

3.10.4
Sofia, kniphofia

3.10.5
geosphere, biosphere, troposphere,
stratosphere, photosphere, hemisphere,
thermosphere, chromosphere, atmosphere,
planisphere, infosphere, lithosphere,
bathysphere, mesosphere, exosphere,
barysphere, hydrosphere, ecosphere,
magnetosphere, asthenosphere, ionosphere

3.10.6
Montgolfier, Philadelphia

3.11
klavier, severe, revere, revers, clavier, persevere,
Guadalquivír

3.11.1
hevea

3.11.2
trivia, Livia, quadrivia, Olivia, Olivier, Bolivia

3.11.3
Avia®, pavior, paviour, Xavier, Flavia, Batavia,
Octavia, Moldavia, Moravia, Belgravia,
Scandinavia

3.11.4
Xavier, clavier

3.11.5
Yugoslavia

3.11.6
uvea, diluvia, alluvia, colluvia, effluvia

3.11.7
Guinevere, Elzevir, Retrovir, Olivia, acyclovir

3.11.8
fovea, Segovia, synovia, Retrovir, Monrovia,
Fitzrovia

3.11.9
Latvia

3.11.10
envier

3.11.11
Sylvia, salvia

3.12
Pythia, lithia, Parthia, Boothia, Cynthia, Anthea,
Althea, forsythia, dinothere, isothere, Dorothea,
Orinthia, Carinthia, stichomythia

3.13
Scythia, clothier

3.14
sincere, Coetzee, insincere, plumassier, panacea,
cuirassier, adipocere, harquebusier

3.14.1
Moesia, gynoecia, androecia, paramecia

3.14.2
Mysia, Lycia, indicia, Cilicia, Alicia, Galicia,
Felicia

3.14.3
Dacia, fascia, glacier

3.14.4
cassia, quassia

3.14.5
tarsia, tarsier, mahseer, Marcia, intarsia

3.14.6
dossier, diglossia

3.14.7
nausea

3.14.8
Lucia, Belorussia, Andalusia

3.14.9
overseer

3.14.10
Mercia

3.14.11
Procea, agnosia, Cappadocia

3.14.12
dyspepsia, eclampsia, pre-eclampsia, polydipsia,
chromatopsia, hemianopsia

3.14.13
fatsia, bartsia, deutzia, strelitzia, rickettsia,
bilharzia, eschscholtzia

3.14.14
Landseer

3.14.15
ixia, banksia, asphyxia, elixir, cachexia, pyrexia,
alexia, dyslexia, ataxia, Vent-Axia®, apraxia,
dyspraxia, hypoxia, anoxia, anorexia, ataraxia,
bulimarexia

3.14.16
fancier, Lancia®, Landseer, hortensia, valencia, estancia, financier, intelligentsia

3.14.17
excelsior, sidalcea

3.15
vizier, Hosea

3.15.1
Moesia, freesia, Frisia, trapezia, framboesia, artemisia, magnesia®, amnesia, Indonesia, Micronesia, Melanesia, Polynesia, paramnesia, tardive dyskinesia, hypoaesthesia, hypaesthesia, kinaesthesia, synaesthesia, anaesthesia, phonaesthesia, paraesthesia, hyperaesthesia, telaesthesia, analgesia, Silesia, ecclesia, rafflesia: (+ **17.27.1**)

3.15.2
vizier, Frisia, Kirghizia, Tunisia, artemisia

3.15.3
brazier, grazier, Frazier, glazier, fantasia, Anastasia, Transcaucasia, monochasia, antonomasia, paronomasia, gymnasia, euthanasia, aphasia, dysphasia, dyscrasia, Malaysia, aplasia, dysplasia, hyperplasia, metaplasia, achondroplasia: (+ **17.27.2**)

3.15.4
razzia, brassiere

3.15.5
Abkhazia, bilharzia, Anastasia

3.15.6
nausea

3.15.7
Hoosier, indusia

3.15.8
osier, hosier, crozier, symposia, agnosia, ambrosia, afrormosia

3.16
cashier

3.16.1
retia, godetia, Helvetia, alopecia, paramoecia

3.16.2
bichir, Leticia, Letitia, indicia, Cilicia, Alicia, Galicia

3.16.3
fascia, Hypatia, Sarmatia, Horatia, Dei gratia, Galatia, solatia, Appalachia, osteomalacia

3.16.4
fascia, quassia

3.16.5
quassia

3.16.6
Lucia, St Lucia, minutia

3.16.7
dystocia, Cappadocia

3.16.8
strontia, amentia, opuntia, differentia, vasa deferentia

3.17
osier, nemesia, rafflesia

3.18
breccia, Appalachia

3.19
Tangier

3.19.1
collegia, aquilegia, florilegia, hemiplegia, paraplegia, tetraplegia, quadriplegia: (+ **17.29.1**)

3.19.2
Phrygia, steatopygia

3.19.3
dysphagia, menorrhagia, metrorrhagia

3.19.4
aqua regia

3.19.5
Borgia

3.19.6
steatopygia

3.19.7
Perugia

3.19.8
loggia, eulogia, apologia, menologia

3.19.9
Thuringia, sporangia, gametangia

3.19.10
myalgia, nostalgia, coxalgia

3.20
rehear, cohere, adhere, inhere, menhir, mishear, overhear

3.21
Kingswear, colloquia

3.22
chorea, arrear, diarrhoea, career, Korea, Maria, gonorrhoea, dysmenorrhoea

3.22.1
Styria, Syria, gaultheria, porphyria, Assyria, Illyria, deliria, collyria, subdeliria

3.22.2
superior, imperia, Iberia, Siberia, Liberia, criteria, bacteria, interior, anterior, posterior, hysteria, wistaria, wisteria, listeria, exterior, psalteria, ulterior, cafeteria, washeteria, eubacteria, Cyanobacteria, corynebacteria, Bashkiria, armeria, cryptomeria, alstroemeria, inferior, echeveria, diphtheria, prototheria, megatheria, Nigeria, Algeria

3.22.3
terrier, Ferrier

3.22.4
area, Caria, varia, miliaria, herbaria, columbaria, Carpentaria, termitaria, sanataria, sanitaria,

planetaria, militaria, insectaria,
armamentaria, sudaria, caldaria, tepidaria,
frigidaria, cercaria, araucaria, urticaria,
Berengaria, Bulgaria, Samaria, Gran Canaria,
pulmonaria, oceanaria, vivaria, Bavaria,
leprosaria, rosaria, fusaria, aquaria, terraria,
sacraria, cineraria, honoraria, talaria, malaria,
filaria, solaria, radiolaria, calceolaria,
armillaria

3.22.5
barrier, tarrier, carrier, garrya, farrier, harrier

3.22.6
Maurya

3.22.7
aria, maria, Zaria, Amu Darya, charivaria

3.22.8
warrior, Laurier

3.22.9
coria, scoria, thoria, curia, Gloria, emporia,
ciboria, praetoria, Vitoria, Pretoria, scriptoria,
victoria, Astoria, natatoria, auditoria, sudatoria,
crematoria, vomitoria, sanatoria, sanitoria,
moratoria, conservatoria, phantasmagoria,
triforia, euphoria, dysphoria, sensoria,
aspersoria, glycosuria

3.22.10
spurrier, courier, currier, furrier, worrier

3.22.11
courier, Fourier

3.22.12
Surya, curia, couturier, couturière, Manchuria,
injuria, Etruria, pyuria, Liguria, dysuria,
glycosuria, haematuria, ketonuria,
phenylketonuria, albuminuria

3.22.13
spurrier

3.22.14
fimbria, Cambria, Umbria, Cumbria, Cantabria,
Calabria, Northumbria, disequilibria

3.22.15
atria, Kshatriya, nutria, Bactria, Istria, destrier,
Austria, Aspatria, gematria, endometria,
epigastria, hypogastria

3.22.16
Andrea, scolopendria, Alexandria, perichondria,
hypochondria, mitochondria

3.22.17
ochrea

3.22.18
sangría

3.23
Goodyear, yesteryear

3.24
Melilla, pistoleer, Cordelier, bandoleer,
bandolier, chandelier, gondolier, cameleer,
chevalier, cavalier, fusilier

3.24.1
Elia, Delia, Melia, Celia, quelia, stapelia,
Montpelier, abelia, lobelia, Cordelia, sedilia,
psychedelia, Rumelia, Amelia, Camelia,
camellia, bromelia, Cornelia, Ophelia, aphelia,
epithelia, endothelia, mycelia, Cecilia, parhelia,
Aurelia, Karelia

3.24.2
ILEA, ilia, cilia, Hillier, epyllia, memorabilia,
sedilia, achillea, familiar, unfamiliar,
overfamiliar, juvenilia, Pamphylia, paedophilia,
haemophilia, coprophilia, necrophilia,
Anglophilia, bougainvillea, Sicilia, conciliar,
penicillia, Brasília

3.24.3
palea, dahlia, galea, Thalia, inter alia, dentalia,
Castalia, genitalia, Dhekelia, Lupercalia,
pontificalia, regalia, saturnalia, bacchanalia,
marginalia, paraphernalia, Westphalia, azalea,
Mahalia, Australia, penetralia, Eulalia, dyslalia,
echolalia, glossolalia, palilalia

3.24.4
St Helier, Montpellier, hotelier, sommelier,
camellia, subsellia

3.24.5
pallia, dallier, rallier, espalier, Antalya,
prothallia, Alitalia®, shilly-shallyer

3.24.6
Gwalia, Somalia, Himalaya, passacaglia

3.24.7
collier, volleyer

3.24.8
haulier, saintpaulia

3.24.9
sedilia

3.24.10
dulia, Julia, abulia, Apulia, peculiar, dyscalculia

3.24.11
olea, scholia, folia, foliar, Grolier, Mongolia,
magnolia, Anatolia, melancholia

3.24.12
cattleya

3.24.13
buddleia

3.24.14
cochlea, cochlear, trochlea, trochlear, Highclere,
nuclear, unclear, sub-nuclear, chanticleer, anti-
nuclear, internuclear, thermonuclear

3.24.15
Anglia, ganglia, gangliar, neuroglia

3.24.16
Novaya Zemlya

4
a, aye, eh, pay, Pei, spae, spay, Spey, bay, bey,
Tay, stay, day, dey, cay, k, Kay, Kaye, gay, Gaye,
Mae, may, nae, nay, né, Neagh, nee, née, neigh,

Ney, fay, Faye, fey, they, say, sei, chez, shay, Che, j, jay, Haigh, hay, heigh, hey, hey, Hué, way, Wei, weigh, wey, whey, qua, Sui, sway, Rae, ray, re, Rea, Reary, Rey, Wray, pray, prey, spray, brae, bray, trait, tray, trey, stray, dray, drey, Cray, Kray, gray, grey, fray, Frey, yea, Lae, lay, lei, Ley, ley, play, splay, clay, Cley, Klee, gley, flay, vlei, slay, sleigh, sley, PA, TA, CIA, Hawke Bay, Hawke's Bay, Mossel Bay, Twelfth Day, MA, Lough Neagh, FA, au fait, USA, per se, feng shui, IRA, cy pres, du Pré, in re, Man Ray, YMCA, LEA, ILEA, aka, USIA, Thunder Bay, Prudhoe Bay, Walvis Bay, light of day, Santa Fé, Morgan le Fay, Icknield Way, Appian Way, Skara Brae, fromage frais, UCLA, INLA, UCCA, Aboukir Bay, Montego Bay, cafe au lait, YWCA

4.1
mouillé, plié, déshabillé

4.2.1
croupier

4.2.2
métier, Cartier, Poitier, Poitiers, rentier, bustier, Sabatier, Parmentier

4.2.3
perruquier

4.2.4
Rainier, denier, fourdrinier

4.2.5
Escoffier, Montgolfier

4.2.6
Cuvier, Plouviez, Olivier

4.2.7
dossier

4.2.8
Lavoisier, Courvoisier®, Le Corbusier

4.2.9
kyrie, Perrier®, Laurier, Fourier, Chabrier, Le Verrier, Du Maurier, couturier, opere serie

4.2.10
tablier, Montpellier, Tortelier, atelier, hotelier, sommelier, espalier, Duvalier, Chevalier, esprit de l'escalier

4.3
foyer

4.4
Benue, habitué

4.5
Douai, Douay, Coué, roué, Niue, Cimabue

4.6
Soay

4.7
repay, prepay, épée, Pepe, frappé, shar-pei, Taipei, toupée, coupé, Nupe, Hupeh, Pompeii, jaspé, strathspey, sarape, Saint-Tropez, underpay, agape, canapé, overpay, Príncipe

4.8
Tebay, thebe, abbé, Torbay, sorbet, Hubei, obey, Kobe, sickbay, embay, flambé, flambée, pombe, Bombay, rosebay, mangabey, disobey, yohimbe, Dushanbe

4.9
crudités, décolleté, enfant gâté

4.9.1
jeté, fouetté, mantellette

4.9.2
pâté, pattée, maté, satay

4.9.3
écarté, Jubilate, commedia dell'arte

4.9.4
Franche-Comté

4.9.5
forte, panforte, prêt-à-porter, pianoforte, mezzo forte

4.9.6
velouté

4.9.7
fouetté, Timotei®, naiveté, décolleté, cinéma-vérité

4.9.8
sauté, cenote

4.9.9
Dante, Conteh, andante, diamanté, Deo volente, concertante, Belo Horizonte

4.9.10
forestay, bobstay, outstay, shortstay, backstay, mainstay, overstay

4.10
Bordet, coudé, O'Dea, today, present-day, midday, same-day, Muscadet, everyday

4.10.1
bidet, vide

4.10.2
payday, mayday, heyday

4.10.3
summa cum laude, magna cum laude

4.10.4
Vendée

4.10.5
Corday

4.10.6
Friday

4.10.7
nowaday, Saturday, yesterday, workaday, Muscadet, faraday, Halliday, holiday, Holliday

4.10.8
Daudet, godet, démodé

4.10.9
hobday

4.10.10
weekday, workday

4.10.11
someday

4.10.12
man-day, Monday, sundae, Sunday, noonday, Allende, duende, Whit Sunday, Yaoundé

4.10.13
Loveday

4.10.14
birthday

4.10.15
Tuesday, Thursday, Domesday, doomsday, Wednesday

4.10.16
washday

4.10.17
Doubleday

4.11
piqué, saké, pace, parquet, tokay, UK, piquet, bouquet, decay, McKay, OK, okay, roquet, croquet, cloqué, manqué, Biscay, risqué, pulque, appliqué, tourniquet, sobriquet, Malplaquet, communiqué

4.12
reggae, Sergei, margay, maguey, Hwange, nosegay, distingué, distinguée, Fotheringay, Tenzing Norgay

4.13
Niamey, Aimée, semé, semée, gamay, lamé, gourmet, Fiume, Lomé, drachmae, dismay, Ismay, FNMA, macramé, Mallarmé, consommé, résumé, animé, entremets, São Tomé

4.14
Binet, chiné, nene, Dene, René, Renée, Manet, Carné, carnet, donné, donnée, Monet, borné, Mornay, koiné, Tournai, Genet, pince-nez, Na-Dene, Dubonnet®, cloisonné, Cabernet, matinée, gratiné, gratinée, Chardonnay, Hogmanay, Massenet, violone, nota bene, roche moutonnée, estaminet, panettone, catalogue raisonné

4.15
café, parfait, buffet, Dufay, ofay, Recife, étouffée, Nescafé®, coryphée, réchauffé, cybercafé, opere buffe, auto-da-fé

4.16
névé, levee, pavé, ave, Yahveh, corvée, Iveagh, Bouvet, duvet, cuvée, survey, chevet, purvey, Beauvais, McVay, McVey, inveigh, convey, Solvay, resurvey, relevé, champlevé

4.17
Pathé, Cathay

4.18
glissé, essay, daresay, passé, chassé, Marseille, Marseilles, pensée, assay, José, gainsay, unsay, Yenisey, pas glissé, déclassé, déclassée, Quai d'Orsay, radio-assay, ballon d'essai, ballons

d'essai, arrière-pensée, arrière-pensées, immunoassay

4.18.1
nisei, lycée, plissé

4.18.2
hearsay

4.18.3
naysay

4.18.4
essay, medrese

4.18.5
daresay

4.18.6
assay, passé, chassé, glacé, déclassé, radio-assay, laissez-passer, marron glacé, immunoassay

4.18.7
Raasey

4.18.8
pensée, arrière-pensée

4.18.9
repoussé, retroussé

4.18.10
Vatersay

4.18.11
Ronaldsay

4.18.12
fiancé, fiancée, Oronsay, Colonsay, arrière-pensée

4.18.13
Rothesay, soothsay

4.19
Bizet, frisé, blasé, José, rosé, Élysée, dépaysé, San José, exposé, vin rosé, Oronsay, Colonsay, Champs Élysées

4.20
cliché, cachet, sachet, sashay, Crawshay, Boucher, touché, Suchet, O'Shea, crochet, McShea, recherché, attaché, Beaumarchais, Leclanché, écorché, ricochet, Pinochet, papier-mâché

4.21
dragée, Roget, Angers, congé, rangé, Piaget, dégagé, engagé, d'Erlanger, Fabergé, protégé, negligee

4.22
pace, Duce, Croce, Elche, seviche, vivace, semplice, Eurydice, Berenice, mezza voce

4.23
deejay, blue jay, popinjay

4.24
Roundhay, Oxhey, Delahaye

4.25
reweigh, three-way, two-way, wu-wei, away, aweigh, lwei, noway, straightway, outweigh,

part-way, midway, halfway, straightaway, faraway, everyway

4.25.1
keyway, seaway, freeway, leeway

4.25.2
taxiway, entryway, alleyway

4.25.3
clearway, areaway

4.25.4
airway, stairway, fairway

4.25.5
Yahweh

4.25.6
doorway, Norway

4.25.7
byway, skyway, highway, flyway, superhighway

4.25.8
throughway, thruway

4.25.9
flyaway, stowaway, throwaway, straightaway, getaway, Chataway, waterway, cutaway, motorway, huntaway, castaway, fadeaway, Reddaway, hideaway, foldaway, takeaway, breakaway, walkaway, soakaway, Wimoweh, Greenaway, anyway, Stornoway, runaway, giveaway, Hathaway, tearaway, caraway, carraway, Alloway, galloway, Holloway, colourway, mulloway, rollaway

4.25.10
shipway, slipway, ropeway

4.25.11
Kabwe, subway, Ojibway, Zimbabwe

4.25.12
Kitwe, gateway, Otway, footway

4.25.13
speedway, Midway, Medway, headway, Broadway, tideway, guideway, slideway, roadway

4.25.14
Bequia, trackway, parkway, walkway, folkway

4.25.15
segue, Skagway, maguey

4.25.16
tramway, someway

4.25.17
Stanway, Anhwei, Conway, runway, Steinway®, sternway, companionway

4.25.18
gangway, Hemingway, Lilongwe

4.25.19
Safeway

4.25.20
driveway

4.25.21
pathway

4.25.22
raceway, sluiceway, expressway

4.25.23
breezeway, causeway, cruiseway, Ronaldsway, Queensway, Kingsway, Garmondsway

4.25.24
hatchway, archway

4.25.25
ridgeway, Ridgway, carriageway, passageway, steerageway

4.25.26
spillway, railway, Galway, hallway, tollway, cableway, bridleway

4.26
moray, array, hooray, Dounreay, Monterrey, Whangarei, disarray, jeunesse dorée, hip-hip-hooray

4.26.1
ciré, Dies Irae, Desirée

4.26.2
beret

4.26.3
affairé, condottiere

4.26.4
barré, Le Carré

4.26.5
mare, moiré, soirée, ricercare

4.26.6
moray, foray

4.26.7
Doré, Gor-Ray, moray, Fauré, purée, curé, cacciatore, jeunesse dorée, con amore, oboe d'amore

4.26.8
bourrée, purée, curé, de jure, tabouret, cabaret, Thackeray, Tanqueray, Tavaré, fioriture, pro tempore, villeggiature

4.26.9
kouprey, sempre, respray, hairspray, osprey, pro tempore

4.26.10
ombré, Mowbray, chambray, chambré, hombre, terebrae, vertebrae, tenebrae

4.26.11
Littré, Rattray, entrée, portray, outré, betray, in-tray, distrait, astray, ashtray, Ballantrae

4.26.12
Cowdray, Cowdrey, padre, André, Sierra Madre

4.26.13
Thackeray, sucre, McCrea

4.26.14
Tigray, Maigret, émigré

4.26.15
sunray

4.26.16
stingray

4.26.17
affray, defray

4.26.18
Vouvray, McGillivray

4.26.19
X-ray

4.26.20
Castlereagh

4.27
mouillé, oyez, Spanier, soignée, sommelier, ukiyo-e, boulevardier

4.28
relay, gilet, waylay, melee, allay, belay, Bellay, delay, Malay, olé, outlay, inlay, unlay, mislay, Roslea, crème brûlée, Mandalay, underlay, Nicolet, chevalet, overlay, cassoulet, cabriolet, appellation contrôlée

4.28.1
Millais, Millay, filet, nargileh

4.28.2
Pelé, melee, Mont Pelée, pappardelle

4.28.3
palais, ballet, Calais, valet, chalet, Hallé, farfalle, pis aller, laisser-aller, corps de ballet

4.28.4
parlay, pourparler, Don Pasquale

4.28.5
volet

4.28.6
boule, Boulez, coulée, Kawthulei

4.28.7
piolet, Rabelais, Mandalay, roundelay, underlay, nargile, Mingulay, overlay, cassoulet, Beaujolais, virelay, Charolais, Chevrolet®, papabile, cantabile, piano nobile

4.28.8
pinole

4.28.9
replay, airplay, foreplay, byplay, outplay, swordplay, wordplay, endplay, strokeplay, screenplay, downplay, gunplay, misplay, horseplay, display, matchplay, role-play, teleplay, interplay, underplay, overplay

4.28.10
paso doble

4.28.11
outlay

4.28.12
Barclay, bouclé, fireclay, pipeclay, underclay, roman-à-clef

4.28.13
agley, franglais, cor anglais

4.28.14
inlay, Finlay

4.28.15
soufflé, reflet

4.28.16
Nestlé®, bobsleigh

5
yeah, Valais

6
air, Ayer, Ayr, e'er, ere, Eyre, heir, pair, pare, pear, père, spare, bare, bear, tare, tear, stair, stare, dare, care, Kerr, scare, mare, mayor, Khmer, ne'er, snare, fair, fare, fayre, vair, their, there, they're, Cher, share, Sher, chair, chare, hair, hare, Herr, ware, wear, where, square, sware, swear, rare, prayer, Frere, yeah, Pierre, lair, lehr, Blair, blare, Claire, Clare, glair, glaire, glare, flair, flare, whoe'er, au pair, pigeon pair, whate'er, midair, Finnair, plein-air, Dan-Air®, Bonaire, where'er, en clair, portière, Armentières, lumière, Meniere, rivière, derrière, Soufrière, wheresoe'er, whatsoe'er, whensoe'er, ventre à terre, nom de guerre, de la Mare, mal de mer, savoir faire, boutonnière, lavaliere, surface-to-air, concessionaire, chemin de fer, chemins de fer, Tiananmen Square, trahison des clercs

6.1
Robespierre, première, lumière, Meniere, Molière, couturière, son et lumière

6.2
repair, prepare, impair, ampere, compère, compare, despair, disrepair, self-despair, milliampere

6.3
Rambert, forbear, forebear, Flaubert, threadbare, cudbear, bugbear, Colbert, woolly-bear, overbear, Camembert

6.4
parterre, hectare, Astaire, upstair, outstare, backstair, Altair, Voltaire, Saltaire, Lapotaire, pied-à-terre, secretaire, solitaire, wear-and-tear, Finisterre, Alisdair, Alistair, cordon sanitaire

6.5
bayadère, outdare, Kildare, Aberdare, Frigidaire®, Santander

6.6
haircare, childcare, skincare, devil-may-care, aftercare, Medicare

6.7
Daguerre, Gelligaer

6.8
commère, Khmer, nightmare, bêche-de-mer, Weston-super-Mare

6.9
Finnair, whene'er, McNair, ensnare, debonair, ordinaire, luminaire, questionnaire, legionnaire, doctrinaire, billionaire, millionaire, vin

ordinaire, commissionaire, concessionaire, Apollinaire

6.10
Mayfair, Playfair, airfare, carfare, warfare, Tailleferre, affair, affaire, fieldfare, workfare, fanfare, unfair, funfair, welfare, laissez-faire, thoroughfare, chargé d'affaires

6.11
Anvers, couvert, Convair

6.12
Swissair®, corsair, Althusser

6.13
misère

6.14
ploughshare, torchère, timeshare, porte-cochère, Labouchere

6.15
Niger, Folies-Bergère

6.16
flatshare, co-chair, deckchair, armchair, pushchair, wheelchair

6.17
O'Hare, mohair, shorthair, maidenhair, longhair, horsehair, camel hair

6.18
aware, beware, outwear, wash-and-wear, elsewhere, unaware, self-aware, ready-to-wear

6.18.1
skiwear, freeware

6.18.2
playwear

6.18.3
shareware

6.18.4
Tupperware®, outerwear, lustreware, underwear, lacquerware, dinnerware, anywhere, chinaware, silverware, leatherwear, otherwhere, leisurewear, everywhere, Delaware, holloware, hollowware

6.18.5
nowhere, hollowware

6.18.6
sleepwear, slip-ware, groupware

6.18.7
knitwear, wetware, flatware, nightwear, footwear, giftware, software, delftware, graniteware, telesoftware

6.18.8
hardware

6.18.9
neckwear, cookware, workwear, tee-square, T-square, foursquare, chi-square, setsquare, headsquare, root-mean-square

6.18.10
creamware, swimwear, stemware, somewhere, firmware

6.18.11
tinware, rainwear, ironware, stoneware, ovenware, earthenware, kitchenware

6.18.12
brassware, glassware, foreswear, forswear, sportswear, dancewear, elsewhere

6.18.13
menswear, womenswear

6.18.14
beachwear

6.18.15
Edgware

6.18.16
pearlware, tableware, enamelware

6.19
confrère, au contraire

6.20
tuyère, Gruyère, cafetière, meunière, La Bruyère, boutonnière, jardinière, lavaliere

6.21
éclair, declare, Sinclair, Rosslare, Baudelaire

7
à la, voilà, embonpoint

8
vin, Chopin, Pétain, gratin, Cardin, Rodin, Gauguin, Balmain, dauphin, Louvain, Poussin, Perrin, serein, au gratin, Chambertin, coq au vin, Limousin, mise au point, Couperin, Teilhard de Chardin

9
ow, pow, bough, bow, Tao, tau, Dão, dhow, Dow, cow, scow, Gow, mow, now, vow, thou, sough, sow, chow, ciao, Hough, how, Howe, wow, row, prow, brow, trow, Frau, Lao, plough, plow, Slough, slough, meow, miaow, Liao, Mau Mau

9.1
luau

9.2
Bilbao, Concertgebouw

9.3
kotow, kowtow

9.4
endow, Spandau, landau, disendow, Moldau

9.5
Dachau, Cracow, Kraków, moocow, cacao, Macao, Macau, Fischer-Dieskau

9.6
Aargau, Thurgau, hoosegow, Oberammergau

9.7
Donau, Lucknow, Mindanao

9.8
avow, disavow

9.9
Dessau, Nassau, Bissau, Guinea-Bissau

9.10
Yangshao

9.11
Hangzhou

9.12
Foochow, Lanchow, Hangchow

9.13
Hangzhou

9.14
know-how, nohow, somehow, Greenhough, anyhow

9.15
powwow, bow-wow

9.16
gherao, Arrau, eyebrow, highbrow, lowbrow, Löwenbräu, middlebrow, Jungfrau, Hausfrau

9.17
pilau, Belau, Palau, allow, pulao, snowplough, Breslau, Tokelau, disallow

10
aah, aargh, ah, are, our, r, pa, pah, par, parr, pas, spa, spar, baa, bah, bar, Barr, barre, ta, tahr, tar, thar, star, Starr, dah, car, Carr, ka, Kerr, scar, ska, gar, ma, maar, Maher, mar, Marr, knar, fa, fah, far, Farr, schwa, shwa, Saar, Sarre, tsar, shah, cha, char, charr, jar, ha, haar, hah, Twa, Kwa, qua, guar, moire, loir, Loire, rah, bra, Kra, Fra, yah, pya, la, lah, blah, faux pas, slot car, Del Mar, Zsa Zsa, Du Bois, Du Toit, bête noire, bêtes noires, film noir, foie gras, à la, Leamington Spa, objet d'art, objets d'art, touring car, USSR, pas de chat, langue de chat, langues de chat, petits pois, famille noire, cafe noir, Pinot Noir, fille de joie, feu de joie, Mardi Gras, UNHCR, de haut en bas, comme ci, comme ça, je ne sais quoi, ménage à trois, embarras de choix, pâté de foie gras

10.1
penniä, caviar, Boléat

10.2
boyar

10.3
guar

10.4
pipa, papa, grandpa, oompah, fluorspar, feldspar, calcspar, grandpapa

10.5
debar, pooh-bah, unbar, Dunbar, disbar, Castlebar, Zanzibar, Calabar

10.5.1
rebar

10.5.2
minibar, millibar

10.5.3
baba

10.5.4
Aqaba, cinnabar, isobar, Hephzibah, Zanzibar, Calabar, Malabar, coolibah

10.5.5
durbar

10.5.6
towbar, crowbar, isobar

10.5.7
typebar

10.5.8
sidebar, sandbar

10.5.9
Akbar

10.5.10
mimbar, hors de combat

10.5.11
minbar, Finbar

10.5.12
crossbar, busbar

10.5.13
casbah, kasbah

10.5.14
heelbar, rollbar, handlebar

10.6
sitar, pietà, ta-ta, tartare, catarrh, Qatar, guitar, coup d'état, Alma-Ata, Bogotá, al-Fatah, Al Fatah, avatar, waratah

10.6.1
UNITAR

10.6.2
attar, Qatar

10.6.3
tartar

10.6.4
Utah

10.6.5
UNITAR, avatar

10.6.6
JICTAR

10.6.7
plantar

10.6.8
daystar, Tri-Star, co-star, WordStar, loadstar, lodestar, instar, sunstar, earthstar, Telstar®, Pole Star, superstar, podestà, megastar

10.6.9
Ishtar

10.7
deodar, radar, Ardagh, Dada, Kádáar, Godard, lidar, doodah, purdah, sirdar, Pindar, havildar, la-di-da, subahdar, chowkidar, Haggadah, Krasnodar, zamindar, tahsildar

10.8
Bekaa, shikar, in-car, ricercar

10.8.1
Indycar

10.8.2
Neckar

10.8.3
Dacca, Dakar, fracas

10.8.4
taka, kaka, markka, Farquhar, Halakah, Titicaca

10.8.5
tricar

10.8.6
chukar

10.8.7
hookah

10.8.8
autocar, motorcar, rent-a-car, advocaat, Issachar, ricercar, Bullokar

10.8.9
sircar

10.8.10
trocar, autocar

10.8.11
streetcar, flatcar

10.8.12
Redcar, sidecar, handcar

10.8.13
stockcar

10.8.14
tramcar

10.8.15
Shankar

10.8.16
eschar, NASCAR, boxcar, Zanskar

10.8.17
lashkar

10.8.18
railcar, cable car, Hamilcar

10.9
agar, Degas, Hagar, bagarre, gaga, taiga, cougar, nougat, cigar, Elgar, Bulgar, Trafalgar, Chandigarh, bedeguar, budgerigar, realgar

10.10
Braemar, Shema, Armagh, Dumas, mama, mamma, Omagh, ujamaa, Panama, ulema, Beach-la-mar

10.10.1
Tamar

10.10.2
Weimar

10.10.3
Dumas

10.10.4
Valdemar, Waldemar, grandmama, Panama, Kostroma, Palomar, ulema, Bislama

10.10.5
Fermat

10.10.6
grandma

10.10.7
Dagmar

10.10.8
Ingmar

10.10.9
Kretzschmar

10.10.10
palmar, Kalmar, fulmar

10.11
dinar, thenar, Sana'a, Bonnard, sonar, Fragonard, seminar, jacana, Paraná, proseminar

10.12
Afar, cafard, afar, Dhofar, Sofar, sol-fa, Potiphar, insofar, nenuphar, tonic sol-fa

10.13
Avar, Navarre, sheva, Invar®, Alvar, halva, shalwar, cultivar, samovar, Bolívar, bolivar, Lochinvar

10.14
Cathar

10.15
paisa, Ronsard, pulsar, commissar, collapsar, Amritsar, ahimsa

10.16
César, quasar, bazaar, bizarre, hussar, huzza, beaux-arts, maquisard, kala-azar, Alcazar, Balthasar, Balthazar, Salazar

10.17
Suchard, Changsha, entrechat, Khorramshahr

10.18
Sharjah

10.19
cha-cha, cha-cha-cha

10.20
Sharjah, ajar, nightjar

10.21
Lehár, aha, ha-ha, Praha, lahar, hoo-ha, Bihar, Doha, Mudéjar, brouhaha, Kandahar, pakeha, Yamaha, Omaha, Minnehaha, satyagraha

10.22
jowar, aide-memoire, de Beauvoir, Seychellois

10.22.1
wah-wah

10.22.2
Chippewa

10.22.3
mirepoix, avoirdupois

10.22.4
pourboire

10.22.5
patois, fatwa, Artois, trottoir, repertoire,
abattoir, escritoire, Directoire, conservatoire

10.22.6
Hardwar, Vaudois, boudoir

10.22.7
Farquhar, Québecois

10.22.8
memoir, chamois, armoire, tous-les-mois,
aide-memoire, aides-memoire

10.22.9
peignoir, baignoire, Renoir, Anwar,
rouge-et-noir, tamanoir

10.22.10
devoir, renvoi, reservoir, au revoir

10.22.11
pissoir, voussoir, François, Françoise, poult-de-
soie, peau-de-soie

10.22.12
bourgeois, petit bourgeois

10.22.13
octroi, chaud-froid, sang-froid, Delacroix

10.22.14
Gallois, Valois, couloir

10.23
Pará, Torah, hurrah, Stranraer, haftorah,
baccara, baccarat

10.23.1
Marat

10.23.2
rah-rah

10.23.3
baccarat, Aymara

10.23.4
Seurat

10.23.5
haphtorah

10.23.6
chapeau-bras

10.23.7
registrar

10.23.8
Accra

10.23.9
bajra

10.24
Iyyar, Villa, boyar, Magyar, Grignard, Chechnya,
assignat

10.25
Villa, challah, tra-la, voilà, foulard, galah, Shangri-
La, Hezbollah, cervelat, Aguilar, Baha Ullah

10.25.1
alar

10.25.2
Mylar

10.25.3
Baha Ullah

10.25.4
foulard

10.25.5
cervelat

10.25.6
hoopla

10.25.7
blah-blah

10.25.8
éclat

10.25.9
verglas

10.25.10
kevlar

10.25.11
ashlar

11
ton, Caen, Sand, Jean, blanc, Le Mans, au fond,
Mont Blanc, Pinot Blanc, fromage blanc,
chateaubriand, Cabernet Franc

11.1
Lyons, Coeur de Lion

11.2
Amiens, insouciant

11.3
fainéant

11.4
Rouen

11.5
piton, feuilleton, Danton, contretemps

11.6
dedans

11.7
Mâcon, aide-de-camp

11.8
virement, roulement, dénouement,
debridement, acharnement, rapprochement,
accouchement, divertissement, arrondissement,
éclaircissement

11.9
Simenon

11.10
plafond, bouffant

11.11
bon vivant, ci-devant, vol-au-vent, tableau vivant

11.12
croissant, Saint-Saëns, garçon, chanson,
soupçon, en passant, Maupassant, thé dansant,
Besançon, Cartier-Bresson

11.13
soi-disant, liaison

11.14
penchant, Duchamp

11.15
Dijon, goujons

11.16
embonpoint

11.17
perron, restaurant, au courant, Mitterrand

11.18
Villon, bouillon, chignon, Avignon, Évian®,
Messiaen, pension, Semillon, Roussillon,
sabayon, court-bouillon, papillon, Sauvignon,
Cro-Magnon, par avion, en pension, filet
mignon, boeuf bourgignon, demi-pension,
Cabernet Sauvignon

11.19
élan, salon, Toulon, Leblanc

12
awe, oar, or, ore, Orr, paw, poor, pore, pour,
spoor, spore, boar, Boer, Bohr, boor, bore, tau,
taw, tor, tore, torr, tour, store, Storr, daw, Dawe,
door, caw, cor, CORE, core, corps, scaur, score,
gore, maw, Mawer, moor, Moore, mor, more,
gnaw, Noah, nor, Nore, snore, for, fore, four,
thaw, Thor, saw, soar, sore, pshaw, shaw, shore,
sure, chaw, chore, jaw, Haugh, haw, hoar,
Hoare, whore, war, Waugh, wore, squaw, swore,
raw, roar, braw, straw, draw, drawer, craw,
crore, frore, yaw, yore, your, pure, cure, Muir,
mure, lure, law, lor, lore, claw, flaw, floor, slaw,
Dior, velour, Rough Tor, tout court, Z score, Bryn
Mawr, pi jaw, sea floor, petit four, overawe,
either/or, Mosaic Law, esprit de corps, Afrika
Korps

12.1
Eeyore, Dior

12.2
Melchior, Gwalior, excelsior

12.3
sapor, rapport, papaw, pawpaw, forepaw, Jaipur,
Jodhpur, downpour, Cawnpore, southpaw,
zoospore, diaspore, Jabalpur, Manipur, en
rapport, Singapore, madrepore, millepore,
nullipore, endospore, zygospore, megaspore,
microspore, nephridiopore

12.4
Ebor, rebore, Trebor, tabor, forbore, LIBOR,
abhor, Gábor, tambour, Tombaugh, smooth-
bore, Dukhobor, usquebaugh, hellebore

12.5
grantor, guarantor, warrantor, Ulan Bator

12.5.1
detour, praetor, pretor

12.5.2
détour

12.5.3
imperator

12.5.4
Utah

12.5.5
Minotaur, Wichita

12.5.6
caveat emptor

12.5.7
lictor, lector, Choctaw

12.5.8
stentor, mentor, centaur, cantor, contour,
warrantor, hippocentaur

12.5.9
quaestor, toystore, restore, cold store,
bookstore, drugstore, in-store, superstore,
megastore

12.5.10
realtor

12.6
moidore, adore, trapdoor, outdoor, indoor,
Indore, bandore, tandoor, Salvador, mirador,
comprador

12.6.1
Skiddaw

12.6.2
toreador

12.6.3
chador

12.6.4
Cawdor, Wardour

12.6.5
moidore

12.6.6
Theodore, Pompadour, cuspidor, troubadour,
matador, picador, commodore, humidor,
thermidor, stevedore, Salvador, Isadore,
Ecuador, mirador, parador, corridor, Labrador,
conquistador, San Salvador, lobster thermidor

12.6.7
Sodor

12.6.8
trapdoor

12.6.9
jackdaw

12.6.10
stormdoor

12.6.11
vendor, bandore, tandoor, landau, Landor,
condor

12.6.12
USDAW

12.6.13
Appledore, battledore

12.7
décor, markhor, ichor, macaw, softcore, hardcore, Angkor, encore, Goncourt, threescore, fourscore, kwashiorkor, albacore, manticore, Agincourt, underscore, Securicor®

12.8
Igor, nagor, rigor, gewgaw, Tagore, nylghau, Ruddigore, obligor

12.9
amour, Dromore, Ardmore, unmoor, Newtonmore, Strathmore, Aviemore, anymore, evermore, nevermore, furthermore, for evermore

12.9.1
Timor, Seymour

12.9.2
Aviemore, Barrymore

12.9.3
claymore

12.9.4
mattamore, Baltimore, Scudamore, sycomore, hackamore, blackamoor, sagamore, Fenimore, Fennimore, sophomore, nevermore, furthermore, paramour, Tullamore

12.9.5
Fermor

12.9.6
Growmore

12.9.7
Whitmore, Patmore, Dartmoor

12.9.8
Padmore, Broadmoor

12.9.9
Blakemore, Blackmore

12.9.10
Wigmore, Ogmore, Frogmore

12.9.11
Brynmor, Stanmore

12.9.12
Pasmore, Cottesmore, Exmoor, Hawksmoor

12.9.13
Rushmore, Winchmore

12.9.14
Winchmore

12.9.15
Sedgemoor

12.9.16
Gilmore, Gilmour, Fillmore, Michelmore

12.10
unau, Koh-i-noor, Lenor®, Lenore, ignore, Wichnor, consignor, Mackinac, mackinaw, Saginaw, Elsinore

12.11
therefor, afore, before, guffaw, Balfour, two-by-four, heretofore, theretofore, hereinbefore, thereinbefore

12.11.1
ephor

12.11.2
therefore, wherefore

12.11.3
metaphor, semaphore, spermophore, ctenophore, pinafore, anaphor, lophophore, sporophore, pneumatophore, spermatophore, ionophore, siphonophore, coccolithophore

12.11.4
lophophore, spermatophore, ionophore, siphonophore

12.11.5
unhoped-for, unlooked-for, unasked-for

12.11.6
uncared-for, uncalled-for

12.11.7
Roquefort®

12.11.8
Balfour

12.12
Ifor, Cavour, Gwynfor, herbivore, granivore, carnivore, omnivore, Aznavour, detritivore, insectivore

12.13
Hathor

12.14
lessor, foresaw, Mysore, oversaw

12.14.1
Esau, seesaw

12.14.2
ichthyosaur, plesiosaur

12.14.3
lessor

12.14.4
Nassau

12.14.5
Warsaw

12.14.6
tussore

12.14.7
eyesore

12.14.8
brontosaur, Chickasaw, stegosaur, dinosaur, vavasour, mosasaur, pterosaur, hadrosaur, megalosaur, tyrannosaur

12.14.9
bowsaw

12.14.10
whipsaw, ripsaw

12.14.11
fretsaw, heartsore, sightsaw, footsore

12.14.12
bedsore, padsaw, handsaw

12.14.13
hacksaw, bucksaw, Luxor

12.14.14
jigsaw

12.14.15
chainsaw, Ensor, Arkansas, tenon-saw, Fidei Defensor

12.15
bezoar

12.16
ashore, assure, reassure, footsure, cocksure, inshore, insure, reinsure, ensure, onshore, unsure, offshore, ship-to-shore, overinsure

12.16.1
seashore

12.16.2
Wishaw

12.16.3
Crashaw

12.16.4
foreshore, Forshaw, Crawshaw

12.16.5
trishaw

12.16.6
Kershaw

12.16.7
Trubshaw

12.16.8
Bradshaw

12.16.9
kickshaw, rickshaw, lakeshore

12.16.10
Bagshaw, dogshore

12.16.11
scrimshaw, Grimshaw

12.16.12
Henshaw, Renshaw, Fanshawe, Featherstonehaugh, Earnshaw, Openshaw, Birkenshaw, Wythenshawe, Ollerenshaw

12.16.13
longshore, alongshore

12.17
couture, mature, sepulture, haute couture, ligature, immature, premature, armature, crenature, confiture, coverture, couverture, overture, filature, prefecture, calenture, caricature

12.18
adjure, abjure, stickjaw, crack-jaw, lockjaw, endure, mortgagor

12.19
hee-haw, haw-haw, Johor, Lahore, abhor, Featherstonehaugh

12.20
prewar, outwore, postwar, forswore, interwar, tug-of-war, man-o'-war

12.21
furore, uproar, bedstraw, jackstraw, INSTRAW, windlestraw, redraw, wiredraw, withdraw, Magraw, McGraw, overdraw

12.22
impure, mature, endure, secure, procure, liqueur, obscure, immure, demure, Tweedsmuir, signor, inure, Senhor, señor, enure, manure, gravure, allure, simon-pure, immature, premature, epicure, pedicure, sinecure, manicure, insecure, Lammermuir, Monsignor

12.23
velour, Delors, galore, Bangalore

12.23.1
by-law

12.23.2
roquelaure

12.23.3
deplore, implore, explore

12.23.4
temblor

12.23.5
outlaw, Whitelaw

12.23.6
Laidlaw

12.23.7
de-claw, roquelaure, dewclaw, folklore

12.23.8
in-law, Danelaw

12.23.9
shop-floor, subfloor, underfloor

12.23.10
coleslaw, overslaugh

13
oi, poi, boy, buoy, toy, coy, koi, goy, Moy, Fowey, soy, joy, hoy, Roy, troy, ploy, cloy, Gloy, langue d'oïl, Rob Roy

13.1
naoi, pronaoi

13.2
teapoy, sepoy, charpoy, topoi

13.3
playboy, cowboy, ploughboy, carboy, poorboy, toyboy, highboy, choirboy, hautboy, doughboy, lowboy, bootboy, rentboy, liftboy, sandboy, blackboy, tomboy, homeboy, nun-buoy, lifebuoy, houseboy, busboy, newsboy, pageboy, bellboy, ballboy, tallboy, call boy, schoolboy, copyboy, bully boy, paperboy, attaboy, sonobuoy, breeches buoy

13.4
Mettoy®, Tolstoy

13.5
decoy, Khoikhoi, McCoy, didicoi, Trubetskoy

13.6
Quemoy, dromoi, Amoy, Fermoy

13.7
tannoy®, Hanoi, annoy, Portnoy, Illinois

13.8
travois, savoy, envoi, envoy, convoy, McAvoy, cunjevoi

13.9
pithoi

13.10
borzoi, Chedzoy

13.11
Bolshoi

13.12
Mountjoy, enjoy, Lovejoy, killjoy

13.13
ahoy, hobbledehoy

13.14
Iroquois

13.15
Leroy, Norroy, destroy, Conroy, viceroy, Fitzroy, Kilroy, Gilroy, Elroy, McIlroy, corduroy, Pomeroy, Fauntleroy

13.16
Yayoi

13.17
teloi, alloy, Molloy, tholoi, trompe l'oeil, deploy, employ, re-employ, Remploy®, hoi polloi, Permalloy, omphaloi, saveloy, redeploy, misemploy

14
ai, ay, aye, eye, i, pi, pie, Pye, spy, bi, buy, by, bye, Tai, Thai, tie, Tighe, Tye, sty, stye, Dai, Di, die, dye, chi, kai, sky, Skye, guy, my, nigh, Nye, fie, phi, Vi, vie, thigh, thy, Cy, psi, sigh, xi, Shuy, shy, hi, hie, high, why, Wye, y, swy, rai, rye, wry, pry, spry, braai, try, dry, cry, scry, fry, Frye, lie, lye, ply, Bligh, Bly, Cley, fly, vlei, sly, aye aye, ao dai, p.s.i., UPI, UDI, haere mai, weather eye, pie in the sky

14.1
uraei, scarabaei, coryphaei

14.2
clypei, radii, bindi-eye, Haggai, genii, splenii, Sinai, congii, galeae, mallei, pilei, nauplii, nuclei, sestertii, rhomboidei, leylandii, calcanei, exuviae, caducei, minutiae, denarii, senarii, sartorii, injuriae, retiarii, septenarii, octonarii, pons Varolii, amicus curiae, lex domicilii, pontes Varolii, petitio principii

14.3
Haggai

14.4
aye-aye

14.5
psoae

14.6
pappi, carpi, Popeye, potpie, woodpie, magpie, espy, I-spy, sweetie-pie, occupy, Philippi, polypi, counterspy, streptocarpi, reoccupy, preoccupy, hippocampi

14.7
nearby, hereby, lay-by, thereby, whereby, rabbi, forbye, bye-bye, flyby, Dubai, go-by, blowby, goodbye, standby, nimbi, limbi, rhombi, thrombi, overbuy, passer-by, hushaby, succubae, succubi, incubi, syllabi, alibi, lullaby, passers-by, choriambi, dithyrambi

14.8
Khitai, vitae, retie, strati, shut-eye, Eyetie, titi, white-eye, necktie, recti, cacti, hogtie, Yantai, untie, Xingtai, tongue-tie, xysti, cesti, crosstie, pigsty, Altai, habutai, Sukhotai, dziggetai, conducti, aqua vitae, nimbostrati, corpus delicti, curriculum vitae

14.9
redye, deadeye, red-eye, do-or-die, tie-dye, nidi, Kodály, nodi, Sendai, Bondi, fundi, Hyundai®, solidi, eisteddfodau, locus standi, modi vivendi, modi operandi

14.10
Akai, Bacchae, Sakai, cocci, sockeye, trochi, loci, buckeye, Mackay, McKie, rocaille, cerci, foci, croci, pinkeye, bronchi, Ciskei, asci, Transkei, sulci, abaci, didakai, Mordecai, Malachi, horti sicci, streptococci, gonococci, diplococci, Diadochi, diplodoci

14.11
vagi, tragi, Haggai, fungi, gilgai, nilgai, Belgae, Milngavie, mamaguy, assegai, sarcophagi, esophagi, oesophagi, Areopagi, anthropophagi

14.12
rami, thymi, demy, Momi, Chiangmai, calami, ginglymi, lapsus calami, hypothalami

14.13
Sinai, Brunei, Dunaj, anigh, deny, Iceni, carinae, scaleni, sileni, decani, antennae, lacunae, goldeneye, Gemini, laminae, termini, acini, cotherni, personae, alumni, trigemini, Anno Domini, dramatis personae

14.14
defy

14.14.1
rubify, citify, ladyfy

14.14.2
kowhai

14.14.3
sci-fi, hi-fi

14.14.4
.1 deify, reify **.2** typify, torpefy, yuppify, stupefy, obstupefy **.3** rubefy, syllabify **.4** prettify, ratify, stratify, gratify, mortify, fortify, beautify, certify,

notify, rectify, fructify, sanctify, quantify, mystify, testify, justify, stultify, acetify, beatify, decertify, self-certify, objectify, identify, demystify, misidentify **.5** nidify, edify, modify, codify, dandify, fluidify, humidify, acidify, rigidify, solidify, reedify, remodify, commodify, dehumidify **.6** ramify, mummify, tumefy, humify **.7** minify, vinify, sanify, unify, tonify, dignify, signify, lignify, magnify, damnify, saponify, personify, reunify, resinify, indeminify **.8** vivify, revivify **.9** specify, pacify, gasify, classify, ossify, Russify, crucify, versify, Nazify, calcify, falsify, dulcify, silicify, opacify, declassify, reclassify, humusify, diversify, denazify, detoxify, intensify, decalcify, emulsify **.10** prosify **.11** Frenchify **.12** speechify, preachify **.13** liquefy **.14** terrify, verify, scarify, rarefy, clarify, torrefy, horrify, scorify, purify, glorify, vitrify, petrify, nitrify, putrefy, gentrify, esterify, repurify, devitrify, denitrify, electrify, transmogrify **.15** argufy **.16** vilify, jellify, salify, mollify, jollify, qualify, nullify, simplify, amplify, uglify, alkalify, disqualify, exemplify, preamplify, oversimplify

14.14.5
tophi

14.14.6
satisfy, dissatisfy

14.14.7
Delphi

14.15
naevae, Levi

14.16
mythi, canthi, lecythi, acanthi

14.17
Cleddau

14.18
byssi, Desai, Versailles, assai, Masai, tarsi, nisi, fuci, thyrsi, foci, loci, cocci, flocci, bonsai, unci, sulci, narcissi, colossi, molossi, abaci, prophesy, lex loci, tibiotarsi, gonococci, diplococci, ex hypothesi, loci classici, Canes Venatici

14.19
quasi, grisaille, Birdseye, bird's-eye, banzai, tiger's-eye

14.20
cockshy, workshy, gunshy

14.21
magi, vagi, tragi, fungi, sarcophagi, esophagi, oesophagi

14.22
Baha'i, sky-high, Tsinghai, Qinghai, shanghai, hi-de-hi

14.23
kowhai, siliquae, Paraguay, Uruguay, Ross-on-Wye, lapsus linguae, nolle prosequi

14.24
awry, terai, serai

14.24.1
cirri, scirrhi

14.24.2
hetaerae

14.24.3
certiorari

14.24.4
tori, sori, lex fori, thesauri, pylori, a priori, brachiosauri, ichthyosauri, plesiosauri, brontosauri, mosasauri, a fortiori, memento mori, dolichosauri, tyrannosauri, a posteriori, Proxima Centauri

14.24.5
gyri, papyri, hetairai

14.24.6
Dioscuri, uteri, samurai, ephori, caravanserai

14.24.7
retry

14.24.8
spray-dry, blow-dry, wet-and-dry, spin-dry, high-and-dry, tumble-dry

14.24.9
decry, outcry, descry

14.24.10
stir-fry, panfry

14.25
ally, belie, July, rely, underlie, overlie, misally

14.25.1
Eli, Ely

14.25.2
villi, lapilli, morbilli, bacilli, lactobacilli

14.25.3
alveoli, nucleoli

14.25.4
tali, kali

14.25.5
vitelli, ocelli, casus belli

14.25.6
ally, phalli, thalli, prothalli

14.25.7
wall-eye

14.25.8
stili, styli, strobilae

14.25.9
malleoli, Dolgellau, obeli, strobili, emboli, Naphtali, alkali, moduli, Lorelei, loculi, flocculi, calculi, reguli, stimuli, limuli, famuli, hamuli, tumuli, annuli, cannulae, lazuli, discoboli, antalkali, astragali, glomeruli, funiculi, fasciculi, ranunculi, cynocephali, stratocumuli, lapis lazuli

14.25.10
tholi, Rollei, E. coli, gladioli, alveoli, nucleoli

14.25.11
three-ply, apply, reapply, supply, reply, imply,

comply, crossply, multiply, resupply, misapply, oversupply

14.25.12
Adlai

14.25.13
agley

14.25.14
deerfly, mayfly, barfly, sawfly, shoofly, firefly, blowfly, outfly, botfly, whitefly, gadfly, sandfly, blackfly, greenfly, stonefly, dragonfly, housefly, horsefly, catchfly, damselfly, butterfly, thunderfly, hoverfly, overfly

14.25.15
Dolgellau

15.1
Cleo

15.1.1
Scipio, Scorpio

15.1.2
patio, Subbuteo®

15.1.3
video, radio, audio, studio, rodeo, presidio, Palladio

15.1.4
Tokyo, radicchio, Pinocchio

15.1.5
mimeo, cameo, Romeo

15.1.6
Borneo, Tornio, Bonio, roneo, Antonio, San Antonio

15.1.7
Casio®, Lazio, nuncio, senecio, Ajaccio, internuncio

15.1.8
physio, Anzio

15.1.9
ratio, senecio, Horatio, fellatio, pistachio, mustachio, Mercutio, ab initio, ex officio, ex silentio

15.1.10
capriccio, Carpaccio, pistachio, Boccaccio, braggadocio, ex silentio

15.1.11
agio, Sergio, Fangio, Algeo, arpeggio, solfeggio, Correggio, adagio, DiMaggio, Caravaggio

15.1.12
vireo, stereo, Blériot, barrio, Mario, Florio, Oreo®, curio, vibrio, embryo, etaerio, Ontario, scenario, Lotharío, Rosario, impresario, Polisario, oratorio

15.1.13
billy-o, billy-oh, oleo, olio, polio, folio, fabliau, punctilio, Fidelio, intaglio, seraglio, portfolio, in folio, Malvolio, rosolio, imbroglio

16
ooh, poo, pooh, boo, to, too, two, do, coo, coup,

goo, moo, moue, gnu, sault, Sioux, sou, Su, sue, zoo, choux, shoe, shoo, chew, stew, Jew, who, woo, Wu, roo, roux, rue, Pru, Prue, sprue, brew, true, strew, drew, crew, Crewe, cru, Kroo, Kru, screw, grew, threw, thro', through, thru, shrew, Ewe, ewe, u, yew, you, pew, più, Pugh, Pughe, spew, spue, dew, due, cue, Kew, q, queue, skew, meu, mew, mu, smew, knew, new, nu, feu, few, phew, view, thew, Heugh, hew, hue, Hugh, Huw, whew, lieu, lieux, loo, Looe, Lou, plew, blew, blue, clew, clou, clue, glue, flew, flu, flue, slew, slue, ryu, skean dhu, scean dhu, chez nous, kung fu, au jus, Sutton Hoo, Who's Who, thank you, toodle-oo, entre nous, déjà vu, de la Rue

16.1
Diu

16.2
leu

16.3
prau

16.4
bayou

16.5
quipu, ZAPU, tapu, coypu, pooh-pooh, hoopoe, OGPU, shampoo, pakapoo, pakapu, Winnie-the-Pooh

16.6
zebu, baboo, babu, boo-boo, taboo, tabu, bamboo, peekaboo, jigaboo, bugaboo, caribou, marabou, marabout, Malibu, tickety-boo

16.7
hereto, K2, thereto, whereto, battue, tattoo, Poitou, too-too, U-2, vertu, virtu, set-to, stand-to, Bantu, mangetout, passe-partout, cockatoo, thitherto, hitherto, Timbuktu, thereunto

16.7.1
tatou, Vanuatu

16.7.2
passe-partout, Manawatu, Nosferatu

16.7.3
too-too, tutu, Sotho, Hutu, Mobutu, Basotho, Lesotho

16.7.4
manitou, hitherto

16.7.5
surtout

16.7.6
Motu

16.7.7
lean-to, into, gentoo, Bantu, unto, thereinto, hereunto, thereunto

16.7.8
pistou

16.7.9
Pushtu

16.8
redo, skidoo, nardoo, ado, to-do, outdo, Hindu, wandoo, undo, billet-doux, compte rendu, well-to-do, underdo, overdo, how-do-you-do, how-d'ye-do, Kathmandu, derring-do, didgeridoo, cock-a-doodle-doo

16.8.1
hairdo

16.8.2
nardoo, sadhu, Tamil Nadu

16.8.3
pudu, kudu, voodoo, hoodoo

16.8.4
Urdu, Pompidou, amadou, Xanadu, teledu

16.8.5
fondu, fondue

16.9
Baku, raku, hokku, buchu, haiku, cuckoo, juku, puku, roucou, Turku, nunchaku, seppuku, sabicu, Shikoku

16.10
ragout, fugu, Magoo, burgoo, fogau, congou, Enugu, Telugu, Ouagadougou

16.11
rimu, Camus, Shamu, Jammu, muu-muu, tinamou

16.12
Manu, ZANU, KANU, Ainu, canoe, Vishnu, ingénue, parvenu, Fashanu

16.13
snafu, Corfu, Typhoo®, Khufu, tofu, samfu

16.14
Kivu, shivoo, rendezvous, Viti Levu

16.15
sissoo, Jesu, lasso, shih-tzu, Lao-tzu, Meng-tzu, Ginsu, Kiangsu, Iguaçu, aperçu, Fujitsu, jujitsu, keiretsu, shiatsu, zaibatsu, Daihatsu®, jujutsu, ninjutsu, Herstmonceaux, Hurstmonceux, Clarenceux, pari passu, tiramisu

16.16
Jesu, kazoo, razoo, kudzu, Kalamazoo

16.17
fichu, issue, tissue, cachou, cashew, horseshoe, Kyushu, snowshoe, sandshoe, gumshoe, Honshu, reissue, atishoo, catechu, overshoe, Mogadishu, overissue

16.18
bijou, Anjou, Lanzhou, acajau, carcajou

16.19
fitchew, choo-choo, achoo, atchoo, Manchu, eschew, catechu, Fu Manchu, Machu Picchu: (+ **16.24.5**)

16.20
juju, sapajou, carcajou, kinkajou: (+ **16.24.6**)

16.21
wahoo, prahu, yahoo, Lahu, boohoo, yoo-hoo, erhu, ballyhoo, Oahu, you-know-who

16.22
tu-whit tu-whoo

16.23
Nauru, Peru, Carew, karoo, Karroo, Theroux, hooroo, jabiru, jamberoo, Brian Ború, potoroo, candiru, wanderoo, smackeroo, jackaroo, buckaroo, kangaroo, switcheroo, jillaroo, wallaroo

16.23.1
chiru

16.23.2
Nehru, Maseru

16.23.3
Subaru®, Kota Baharu

16.23.4
guru

16.23.5
Nauru, Nakuru

16.23.6
jabiru, Subaru®, Timaru, Devereux, haleru

16.23.7
Hebrew, imbrue, Irnbru

16.23.8
untrue, bestrew, construe, misconstrue, Mersa Matruh

16.23.9
redrew, wiredrew, Andrew, withdrew, overdrew

16.23.10
écru, aircrew, accrue, airscrew, setscrew, woodscrew, jackscrew, corkscrew, thumbscrew, twin-screw, unscrew

16.23.11
regrew, outgrew, Pettigrew, overgrew

16.23.12
froufrou, Renfrew

16.23.13
see-through, therethrough, readthrough, breakthrough, walk-through, downthrew, runthrough, pullthrough, overthrew

16.23.14
beshrew

16.24
IOU, non-U, OGPU

16.24.1
Kikuyu

16.24.2
shoyu

16.24.3
coypu

16.24.4
zebu, début, imbue

16.24.5
situ, battue, statue, virtue, in situ, impromptu:
(+ **16.19**)

16.24.6
Cardew, adieu, bedew, Purdue, subdue, indue,
endue, vendue, fondu, fondue, undue, sundew,
mildew, honeydew, overdue, residue, cire
perdue: (+ **16.20**)

16.24.7
ecu, miscue, fescue, rescue, Askew, askew,
barbecue, Autocue®, curlicue, Montesquieu,
Fortescue

16.24.8
ague, Pegu, argue, Montague

16.24.9
emu, seamew, Bartholomew

16.24.10
sinew, menu, venue, foreknew, anew, renew,
Agnew, continue, ingénue, retinue, revenue,
avenue, parvenu, Molyneux, discontinue

16.24.11
nephew, Corfu, curfew, feverfew

16.24.12
preview, prevue, rearview, nephew, review,
revue, purview, worldview, Bellevue, interview,
overview, teleview

16.24.13
Matthew

16.24.14
issue, tissue, pursue, ensue, reissue, aperçu,
Herstmonceaux, Hurstmonceaux, Clarenceux,
overissue, idée reçue

16.24.15
Jesu

16.24.16
Jehu, Mayhew, McHugh, Elihu, Donahue,
Donoghue, Donohue, clerihew

16.24.17
value, purlieu, curlew, w, verdelho, devalue,
revalue, R-value, outvalue, eigenvalue,
Mallalieu, UAW, countervalue, undervalue,
overvalue

16.25
Yalu, poilu, tolu, sulu, Zulu, lulu, Selous, halloo,
curlew, Oulu, Lamplugh, true-blue, Buccleugh,
igloo, outflew, Tuvalu, KwaZulu, Peterloo,
Waterloo, vindaloo, Bakerloo, Pagalu, ormolu,
Angelou, calalu, overblew, superglue, overflew,
Kinabalu, Amazulu, Honolulu, hullabaloo, Kota
Kinabalu

17.1
kea, keyer, skier, Thea, seer, Shi'a, Shiah, Gaea,
Rea, rhea, ria, freer, Leah, glia, mens rea

17.1.1
Apia, Tarpeia, rupiah, Cassiopeia,
mythopoeia, prosopopoeia, pharmacopoeia,
onomatopoeia

17.1.2
Euboea

17.1.3
Plataea, garreteer, Oresteia

17.1.4
Chaldea

17.1.5
IKEA®, Achaea, toquilla, trachea, Latakia

17.1.6
ipomoea

17.1.7
cornea, dyspnoea, sinfonia, Tanzania, perinea,
peritonea, Iphigenia

17.1.8
keffiyeh, Sofia, Sophia, ratafia

17.1.9
Nivea®

17.1.10
barathea, Dorothea, calathea, Arimathea

17.1.11
García, ossia, foreseer, Nicaea, Phocaea,
sightseer, Boadicea, Nicosia, panacea, gynaecea,
Andalucía, arquebusier

17.1.12
fantasia

17.1.13
Lucia, Kampuchea

17.1.14
Hygeia, Pangaea, hypogea

17.1.15
Bahía

17.1.16
sharia, Oriya, spiraea, pyorrhoea, sheria, urea,
seborrhoea, trattoria, steatorrhoea, taqueria,
leucorrhoea, logorrhoea, Tia Maria®, Almería,
menorrhoea, Cytherea, pizzeria, Caesarea,
thiourea, dysuria, galleria, amenorrhoea,
Pantelleria, destrier, Eritrea, sangría

17.1.17
aliyah, Hialeah, Ismailia, propylaea, achillea,
mausolea

17.2
payer, Bayer, stayer, kea, Maher, Maia, Maya,
Mayer, Meyer, sayer, weigher, prayer, preyer,
sprayer, strayer, Freya, Freyr, layer, player,
flayer, slayer, Mauna Kea, Malpighian layer

17.2.1
ratepayer, taxpayer

17.2.2
Marbella, abaya, obeyer, disobeyer

17.2.3
Oresteia

17.2.4
Nausicaa

17.2.5
Nouméa

17.2.6
surveyor, purveyor, conveyor

17.2.7
naysayer, assayer, gainsayer, soothsayer

17.2.8
crocheter

17.2.9
portrayer, betrayer, Eritrea

17.2.10
waylayer, delayer, Malaya, displayer, gamesplayer, ballplayer, platelayer, bricklayer, tracklayer, inlayer, minelayer, bobsleigher, Himalaya, monolayer, record-player, Penthesilea

17.3
hour, our, paua, power, Bauer, bower, tower, Stour, dour, dower, cower, scour, gaur, Gower, fawr, sour, shower, giaour, lour, lower, plougher, plower, glower, flour, flower, watt-hour, pasque flower, quarter-hour

17.3.1
firepower, empower, disempower, brainpower, manpower, gunpower, horsepower, willpower, candlepower, superpower, waterpower, overpower

17.3.2
embower, Beckenbauer

17.3.3
watchtower

17.3.4
endower, Glendower

17.3.5
Brynmawr, Penmaenmawr

17.3.6
man-hour, Adenauer

17.3.7
devour

17.3.8
sweet-and-sour

17.3.9
rush-hour, thundershower

17.3.10
Schopenhauer, Eisenhower

17.3.11
deflower, mayflower, safflower, windflower, cornflour, cornflower, sunflower, passionflower, bellflower, wallflower, gillyflower, cauliflower, elderflower, satinflower

17.4
tawer, Mawer, drawer, clawer, withdrawer, overdrawer

17.5
Boyer, toea, Toyah, coir, Goya, Moir, Moya, Moyer, foyer, sawyer, soya, hoya, lawyer, loir, Latoya, Nagoya, annoyer, enjoyer, La Jolla, sequoia, destroyer, employer, Kamenskoye, paranoia

17.6
ayah, ire, pyre, spire, buyer, byre, tier, tire, tyre, dire, dyer, skyer, Gaia, Maia, Mair, Maya, Mayer, Meier, Meyer, mire, fire, via, sire, shire, shyer, gyre, hire, hiya, wire, Wyre, twyer, Dwyer, choir, quire, squire, rayah, Praia, prior, briar, brier, trier, stria, drier, dryer, crier, scryer, friar, fryer, liar, lyre, playa, glia, flyer, town crier, Saint Elmo's fire, Irian Jaya

17.6.1
papaya, empire, vampire, umpire, aspire, perspire, suspire, respire, expire, inspire, transpire, conspire, occupier

17.6.2
homebuyer, housebuyer, Surabaya

17.6.3
satire, attire, retire, Kintyre, entire, Pentire, Blantyre, saltire, overtire, McIntyre, Oresteia, peripeteia

17.6.4
Obadiah

17.6.5
Zedekiah, Hezekiah

17.6.6
lammergeier, Gelligaer

17.6.7
Niemeyer, Nehemiah, bemire, admire, quagmare, pismire, Biedermeier, Jeremiah

17.6.8
denier, Zephaniah, Iphigenia

17.6.9
afire, defier, Sophia, backfire, ceasefire, misfire, hellfire, rapid-fire **.1** speechifier **.2** sapphire **.3** surefire **.4** typifier, stupefier, prettifier, ratifier, gratifier, fortifier, beautifier, rectifier, sanctifier, quantifier, testifier, justifier, stultifier, identifier, modifier, codifier, humidifier, solidifier, dehumidifier, granophyre, unifier, signifier, magnifier, personifier, indemnifier, specifier, pacifier, classifier, crucifier, versifier, opacifier, intensifier, decalcifier, emulsifier, liquefier, terrifier, verifier, scarifier, clarifier, scorifier, purifier, glorifier, gentrifier, electrifier, vilifier, mollifier, qualifier, nullifier, amplifier, preamplifier **.5** campfire **.6** spitfire **.7** portfire **.8** rimfire, samphire, drumfire **.9** bonfire, gunfire **.10** crossfire, foxfire **.11** brushfire, bush fire **.12** watchfire **.13** shellfire, wildfire

17.6.10
messiah, Josiah, grandsire, transire, prophesier

17.6.11
Isaiah, desire, Josiah, transire

17.6.12
patagia

17.6.13
rewire, haywire, tripwire, barbwire, O'Dwyer, acquire, reacquire, require, inquire, enquire, esquire, Maguire, McGuire, underwire, retrochoir

17.6.14
pariah, Maria, Soraya, Uriah, subprior, sweetbriar, latria, hairdryer, spin-dryer, tumble-dryer, decrier, Zechariah, Zachariah, Black Maria, washer/dryer

17.6.15
dulia, Thalia, applier, supplier, replier, outlier, inlier, jambalaya, multiplier, hyperdulia, oligodendroglia

17.7
poor, spoor, Boer, boor, tour, Tours, Stour, dour, Sgurr, moor, Moore, sure, who're, Ruhr, Ure, your, you're, pure, Tyr, cure, Muir, mure, lure, lur, Marston Moor, plat du jour, de nos jours

17.7.1
Papua, Jaipur, Jodhpur, Nagpur, Rampur, Jabalpur, Manipur, Yom Kippur, Kolhapur, Bahawalpur, Kuala Lumpur

17.7.2
tambour

17.7.3
detour, Fraktur, contour, dastur, Kultur

17.7.4
tandoor, Pompadour, troubadour, tamandua, Borobudur

17.7.5
hors concours, Prix Goncourt

17.7.6
Uighur, langur, kieselguhr

17.7.7
Amur, amour, Dartmoor, Broadmoor, unmoor, Exmoor, Hawksmoor, paramour

17.7.8
Koh-i-noor

17.7.9
Cavour, Aznavour

17.7.10
Nashua, hachure, Joshua, assure, reassure, brochure, footsure, cocksure, insure, reinsure, ensure, unsure, embouchure, commissure, cynosure, annexure, overinsure

17.7.11
menstrua, Karlsruhe

17.7.12
.1 dasyure **.2** guipure, Papua, Capua, purpure, impure, simon-pure **.3** couture, mature, mantua, sepulture, nunciature, haute couture, ligature, immature, premature, armature, crenature, confiture, coverture, couverture, curvature, overture, filature, prefecture, Gargantua, calenture, investiture, caricature **.4** Padua, adjure, abjure, ordure, bordure, endure,

grandeur, conjure, residua, tamandua **.5** vacua, secure, procure, liqueur, obscure, epicure, pedicure, sinecure, manicure, insecure **.6** jaguar, arguer, Aconcagua, Managua, Nicaragua **.7** immure, demure, Namur, Saumur, Langmuir, Tweedsmuir, Kilmuir, Kirriemuir, Walpamur, Lammermuir **.8** inure, conure, enure, manure, continua, continuer **.9** coiffure **.10** gravure, nervure, heliogravure, photogravure, rotogravure **.11** tressure, Saussure, tonsure, commissure, paradoxure **.12** Côte d'Azur, cynosure **.13** Joshua **.14** valuer, allure, colure, craquelure, cannelure, anomalure

17.7.13
velour, doublure, McClure

17.8
doer, Nuer, sewer, suer, chewer, who're, wooer, brewer, strewer, screwer, ewer, spewer, Dewar, dewar, skewer, skua, viewer, hewer, gluer, tattooer, wrongdoer, evildoer, Amur, lassoer, issuer, snowshoer, rescuer, renewer, reviewer, pursuer, Kahlua®, tamandua, Rotorua, interviewer, televiewer

17.9
o'er, boa, Boer, tower, stoa, Stour, Doha, koa, goa, goer, moa, mower, knower, Noah, sewer, sower, shower, hoer, rower, proa, grower, thrower, loa, lower, blower, Van Der Rohe, Mauna Loa, Mies van der Rohe

17.9.1
jerboa, Lebowa, Balboa, Nova Lisboa

17.9.2
vetoer, Krakatoa

17.9.3
widower, shadower, Shenandoah

17.9.4
echoer

17.9.5
playgoer, foregoer, filmgoer, racegoer, churchgoer, Algoa, moviegoer, theatregoer, picturegoer, Delagoa, concert-goer

17.9.6
Samoa, lawnmower

17.9.7
winnower, genoa, anoa

17.9.8
lassoer

17.9.9
epizoa, protozoa, spermozoa, spermatozoa

17.9.10
feijoa

17.9.11
harrower, borrower, sorrower, burrower, winegrower, Figueroa, Mururoa

17.9.12
feijoa

17.9.13
Alloa, follower, wallower, swallower, aloha, snowblower, Hornblower, Batticaloa

17.10.1
peeper, beeper, keeper, Dnieper, nipa, weeper, sweeper, reaper, creeper, leaper, bleeper, sleeper, barkeeper, storekeeper, doorkeeper, scorekeeper, zookeeper, shopkeeper, gatekeeper, bookkeeper, gamekeeper, timekeeper, greenkeeper, innkeeper, peacekeeper, housekeeper, greenskeeper, watchkeeper, goalkeeper, minesweeper, treecreeper, Arequipa, wicketkeeper, hotelkeeper

17.10.2
Pippa, tipper, dipper, kipper, skipper, nipper, snipper, sipper, zipper, shipper, chipper, hipper, whipper, ripper, tripper, stripper, gripper, clipper, flipper, slipper, mudskipper, equipper, Agrippa

17.10.3
paper, taper, tapir, caper, gaper, vapor, vapour, sapor, shaper, raper, draper, scraper, repaper, flypaper, notepaper, endpaper, sandpaper, glasspaper, newspaper, touchpaper, wallpaper, escaper, skyscraper, transfer-paper, voting paper

17.10.4
pepper, leper, salt-and-pepper, Culpeper, high-stepper, sidestepper

17.10.5
tapa, tapper, dapper, kappa, mapper, knapper, napa, nappa, napper, snapper, sapper, Zappa, schappe, rapper, wrapper, trapper, strapper, crapper, scrapper, grappa, yapper, clapper, flapper, petnapper, kidnaper, kidnapper, Harappa, entrapper, palapa, handicapper, whippersnapper, understrapper, Phi Beta Kappa

17.10.6
Cowper

17.10.7
tapa, carper, scarper, sharper, harper, Hunkpapa, macrocarpa, jipijapa

17.10.8
poppa, popper, bopper, topper, stopper, Dopper, copper, koppa, shopper, chopper, Joppa, hopper, whopper, swapper, proper, dropper, cropper, lopper, bebopper, doorstopper, showstopper, unstopper, woodchopper, clodhopper, rockhopper, froghopper, leafhopper, grasshopper, hedgehopper, improper, eyedropper, name-dropper, eavesdropper, sharecropper, teenybopper, weeny-bopper, window-shopper

17.10.9
pauper, torpor, scauper, scorper, gawper, warper, yawper

17.10.10
keuper

17.10.11
upper, cuppa, scupper, supper, crupper

17.10.12
pipa, piper, nipa, sniper, viper, wiper, swiper, griper, Pied Piper, sandpiper, bagpiper, electrotyper

17.10.13
BUPA, stupa, cooper, Couper, Cowper, Cupar, scooper, snooper, super, stupor, duper, Hooper, whooper, trooper, trouper, grouper, pupa, looper, blooper, pea-souper, mosstrooper, party-pooper, superduper, pooper-scooper, paratrooper

17.10.14
diaper, juniper, gossiper, worshiper, worshipper, Philippa, caliper, calliper, scalloper, galloper, walloper, developer, redeveloper

17.10.15
sherpa, chirper, usurper

17.10.16
opah, toper, dopa, doper, coper, scopa, moper, Soper, hoper, Roper, groper, l-dopa, horse-coper, NATSOPA, no-hoper, Europa, eloper, padloper, landloper, laevodopa, interloper

17.10.17
simper, whimper, Whymper, crimper, shrimper, temper, Semper, pamper, Tampa, tamper, stamper, damper, camper, scamper, hamper, tramper, stomper, romper, bumper, stumper, dumper, thumper, jumper, humper, lumper, attemper, distemper, top-hamper, gazumper, showjumper

17.10.18
whisper, Wispa®, crisper, lisper, Vespa®, vesper, Casper, gasper, jasper, rasper, grasper, clasper, RoSPA, prosper, chutzpah

17.10.19
helper, yelper, BALPA, kalpa, scalper, pulper, gulper, catalpa, mea culpa, Atahualpa, Tegucigalpa

17.11.1
Ciba, Sheba, Geber, Weber, Bourguiba, amoeba, ameba, Beersheba, Bathsheba, Kariba, zareba, zariba, Curitiba

17.11.2
bibber, dibber, fibber, gibber, jibba, jibber, ribber, cribber, libber, winebibber, women's libber

17.11.3
tabor, caber, neighbour, weber, sabre, labour, belabour

17.11.4
Webber, Weber, rebbe

17.11.5
aba, abba, stabber, dabber, Caaba, gabber, jabber, grabber, yabber, blabber

17.11.6
carnauba, Pickelhaube

17.11.7
arbour, baba, barber, Barbour®, Caaba, Kaaba, Saba, Sabah, Shaba, harbor, harbour, rum baba, indaba, Annaba, unharbour, Pearl Harbor, Lualaba, Ali Baba

17.11.8
cobber, mobber, sobber, jobber, robber, clobber, slobber, ski-bobber, stockjobber, beslobber

17.11.9
dauber, catawba, Micawber, carnauba, absorber

17.11.10
snubber, rubber, scrubber, grubber, lubber, blubber, clubber, landlubber

17.11.11
Tiber, fibre, giber, briber, scriber, Schreiber, liber, copaiba, imbiber, describer, prescriber, subscriber, inscriber, transcriber, circumscriber

17.11.12
Buber, scuba, goober, tuba, tuber, Juba, Cuba, cuber, Nuba, Huber, Aruba

17.11.13
mastaba, Córdoba, Aqaba, Bathsheba, Yoruba, Hecuba, succuba, djellaba, calibre, Excalibur, Addis Ababa

17.11.14
Berber, Thurber, Djerba, disturber, ipsissima verba

17.11.15
sober, prober, Kroeber, lobar, October, jojoba, Manitoba

17.11.16
agba

17.11.17
.1 timber, timbre, Kimber, limber, marimba
.2 chamber, bedchamber, gas chamber, antechamber .3 ember, Pemba, Bemba, member, September, remember, dismember, November, December, misremember .4 amber, tamber, camber, gamba, mamba, samba, clamber, caramba, Maramba, Cochabamba, liquidambar, sambar, sambhar, sambur
.5 ombre, scomber, sombre, Zomba .6 umber, cumber, number, Humber, rhumba, rumba, lumbar, lumber, slumber, cucumber, encumber, disencumber, Stogumber, renumber, outnumber, Columba .7 Toowoomba

17.11.18
Drouzhba

17.11.19
Bar-Cochba

17.11.20
Wilbur, Elba, melba, Alba, Galba, bulbar, pêche Melba, terra alba

17.12.1
eater, eta, Peta, peter, pita, beater, beta, teeter, Dieter, chaeta, skeeter, meeter, meter, metre, fetor, vita, theta, seta, Sita, zeta, cheater, cheetah, heater, tweeter, rhetor, Rita, praetor, treater, Streeter, greeter, Greta, litre, dolce vita .1 tapeta, copita, nepeta, repeater, saltpetre, Struwwelpeter .2 browbeater .3 partita, anteater .4 Akita .5 Bhagavadgita .6 ammeter, trimeter, Demeter, tripmeter, wattmeter, voltmeter, Machmeter, ohmmeter, taximeter, hectometre, femtometre, centimetre, altimeter, decametre, gigametre, nanometre, decimetre, terametre, kilometre, millimetre, telemeter, micrometre .7 granita, pineta, UNITA, Anita, Bonita, Juanita, amanita, manzanita, terra incognita .8 beefeater, counterfeiter .9 Evita, Ryvita®, Bournvita .10 masseter, two-seater .11 Peshitta, Matsushita® .12 windcheater .13 reheater, superheater .14 Arita, ureter, propraetor, maltreater, secretor, excreta, excreter, señorita, arboreta, margarita .15 Lolita, valeta, veleta, millilitre, hectolitre, centilitre, decalitre, decilitre, corallita, kilolitre

17.12.2
pitta, spitter, bitter, titter, skitter, knitter, fitter, vitta, sitter, jitter, hitter, witter, twitter, quitter, Ritter, critter, gritter, fritter, litter, lytta, splitter, glitter, flitter, slitter, embitter, Perdita, Birgitta, sagitta, emitter, permitter, committer, remitter, submitter, transmitter, photoemitter, neurotransmitter, shopfitter, outfitter, steamfitter, counterfeiter, bedsitter, housesitter, babysitter, bullshitter, pinch-hitter, atwitter

17.12.3
theatre, amphitheatre

17.12.4
pater, tater, stater, stator, data, cater, skater, gaiter, gator, geta, mater, saeter, Chater, hater, Hayter, waiter, prater, traitor, crater, krater, grater, freighter, later, plater, slater, creator, pia mater, dura mater .1 expiator, mediator, radiator, gladiator, brachiator, permeator, deviator, aviator, vitiator, procreator, palliator, spoliator, repudiator, delineator, calumniator, alleviator, appreciator, negotiator, associator, asphyxiator, annunciator, enunciator, denunciator, propitiator, initiator, officiator, appropriator, impropriator, expropriator, humiliator, conciliator, retaliator, defoliator, intermediator, differentiator .2 actuator, graduator, valuator, perpetuator, evacuator, continuator, insinuator, attenuator, evaluator .3 extirpator, syncopator, dissipator, participator, anticipator, emancipator .4 rebater, debater, albata, masturbator, incubator .5 scrutator, rotator, dictator, spectator, cunctator, commentator, testator, upstater, meditator, imitator, annotator, levitator, hesitater, agitator, cogitator, irritator, amputator, commutator, sternutator, understater, devastator, precipitator, decapitator, resuscitator, facilitator, prestidigitator .6 viewdata, biodata, updater,

mandator, liquidator, depredator, emendator, intimidator, elucidator, consolidator **.7** Decatur, Mercator, locator, rubricator, demarcator, masticator, dedicator, predicator, abdicator, indicator, vindicator, fornicator, defecator, trafficator, desiccator, educator, deprecator, fabricator, lubricator, allocator, replicator, applicator, duplicator, explicator, authenticator, prognosticator, eradicator, adjudicator, communicator, scarificator, purificator, equivocator, hypothecator, prevaricator, reciprocator, excommunicator, confiscator, inculcator, defalcator **.8** negator, legator, tailgater, promulgator, litigator, propagator, expurgator, mitigator, castigator, instigator, fumigator, abnegator, navigator, subjugator, irrigator, corrugator, abrogator, delegator, alligator, obligator, compurgator, investigator, interrogator, circumnavigator **.9** cremator, intimater, estimator, ultimata, animator, decimator, imprimatur, lachrymator, consummator, collimator, monochromator **.10** donator, pronator, ruminator, alienator, supinator, hibernator, detonator, alternator, procrastinator, coordinator, laminator, dominator, nominator, terminator, germinator, discriminator, eliminator, disseminator, inseminator, contaminator, abominator, denominator, illuminator, exterminator, Kelvinator, rejuvenator, fascinator, personator, vaccinator, buccinator, vaticinator, assassinator, hallucinator, impersonator, ratiocinator, resonator, machinator, fractionator, oxygenator, originator, chlorinator, indoctrinator, peregrinator, self-pollinator, designator **.11** levator, motivator, Rotavator®, activator, cultivator, excavator, innovator, renovator, conservator, elevator, deactivator **.12** glossator, peseta, compensator, pulsator, inspissator, tergiversator **.13** pulverizator, totalizator **.14** tidewaiter, equator, dumbwaiter, exequatur **.15** aerator, gyrator, narrator, curator, Chelicerata, ameliorator, instaurator, separator, operator, respirator, aspirator, inspirator, evaporator, cooperator, incorporator, recuperator, vituperator, liberator, deliberator, elaborator, collaborator, corroborator, reverberator, literator, obliterator, transliterator, expectorator, adulterator, moderator, decorator, invigorator, numerator, commemorator, enumerator, venerator, generator, incinerator, regenerator, perforator, vociferator, proliferator, macerator, incarcerator, commiserator, triturator, obturator, refrigerator, exaggerator, depurator, procurator, sulfurator, sulphurator, inaugurator, tolerator, decelerator, accelerator, vibrator, lucubrator, celebrator, calibrator, equilibrator, concentrator, castrator, frustrater, substrata, infiltrator, perpetrator, arbitrator, penetrator, orchestrator, sequestrator, superstrata, illustrator, demonstrator, remonstrator, administrator, coadministrator, hydrator,

desecrator, consecrator, migrator, transmigrator, integrator, denigrator, deflagrator, disintegrator **.16** fellator, collator, dilator, elater, delator, relater, relator, translator, vasodilator, terra sigillata, violator, annihilator, extrapolator, interpellator, interpolator, mutilator, ventilator, percolator, escalator, immolator, assimilator, desolator, vacillator, oscillator, isolator, postulator, capitulator, congratulator, flagellator, modulator, invigilator, demodulator, adulator, defibrillator, stipulator, tabulator, peculator, speculator, circulator, calculator, regulator, stimulator, simulator, emulator, formulator, granulator, insulator, manipulator, perambulator, articulator, gesticulator, ejaculator, inoculator, emasculator, coagulator, dissimulator, accumulator, contemplator, electroplater, Linklater, deflator, inflater, inflator, insufflator, legislator

17.12.5

ETA, petter, better, bettor, tetter, debtor, getter, feta, fetta, fetter, saeter, setter, whetter, Quetta, sweater, Greta, letter, Loretta, arietta, Henrietta, sinfonietta **.1** abetter, Leadbetter **.2** vendetta **.3** bruschetta **.4** begetter, forgetter, go-getter **.5** canzonetta **.6** enfetter, unfetter **.7** anchoveta **.8** upsetter, typesetter, trendsetter, filmsetter, insetter, pinsetter, pacesetter, photosetter, phototypesetter **.9** biretta, Lambretta®, operetta, carburettor, Alexandretta **.10** vignetter **.11** Valletta, newsletter, mantelletta

17.12.6

attar, patter, spatter, batter, tatter, scatter, matter, smatter, natter, Al Fatah, satyr, shatter, chatter, hatter, ratter, spratter, yatter, latter, platter, splatter, clatter, flatter, Mar del Plata, bespatter, pitter-patter, teeter-tatter, Mocatta, regatta, Matmata, antimatter, matamata, paramatta, Parramatta, anatta, al-Fatah, Maratha, Kenyatta

17.12.7

outer, pouter, spouter, touter, doubter, scouter, shouter, grouter, out-and-outer

17.12.8

Sparta, barter, Bata, tartar, Tatar, starter, darter, dartre, data, carter, garter, martyr, sonata, charter, rata, strata, IATA, pro rata, Traviata, Magna Carta, alma mater, persona grata, Río de la Plata, persona non grata **.1** Zapata **.2** ciabatta **.3** batata, cantata, self-starter **.4** viewdata **.5** toccata, Djakarta, Inkatha, Jogjakarta **.6** alpargata, medulla oblongata **.7** stomata, fermata, stigmata, imprimatur, protomartyr **.8** piñata, Renata, caponata, Odonata, serenata, appassionata **.9** passata, cassata **.10** errata, Maratha, substrata, superstrata, desiderata, inamorata **.11** balata, chipolata, taramasalata

17.12.9

ottar, otter, potter, spotter, totter, dotter, cotta, cottar, cotter, gotta, knotter, jotter, hotter, squatter, swatter, swotter, rotter, trotter, lotta, plotter, blotter, Flotta, pinspotter, ricotta, flyswatter, garrotter, globetrotter, pelota, teeter-totter, terracotta

17.12.10

oughta, porter, sporter, torte, daughter, mortar, snorter, sorta, sorter, Shorter, Horta, water, quarter, slaughter, aorta, tap water, Semer Water, Javelle water **.1** supporter, reporter, importer, exporter, transporter, colporteur, re-exporter **.2** distorter, extorter, Sachertorte **.3** stepdaughter, granddaughter **.4** ripsnorter **.5** kicksorter **.6** resorter, exhorter **.7** seawater, shearwater, firewater, Bowater, cutwater, Whitewater, Wastwater, meltwater, saltwater, headwater, tidewater, groundwater, Goldwater, three-quarter, breakwater, backwater, forequarter, McWhorter, headquarter, Drinkwater, rainwater, springwater, bathwater, rosewater, dishwater, freshwater, ditchwater, Bridgewater, Bridgwater, underwater, overwater, Derwentwater **.8** manslaughter, self-slaughter

17.12.11

goitre, Reuter, loiter, exploiter, reconnoitre

17.12.12

utter, putter, sputter, butter, stutter, cutter, scutter, gutter, mutter, nutter, Sutter, shutter, strutter, splutter, clutter, flutter, abutter, rebutter, woodcutter, stonecutter, leafcutter, Calcutta, Agutter, constructor, aflutter, surrebutter

17.12.13

biter, titre, mitre, smiter, nitre, fighter, vita, sighter, righter, writer, lighter, blighter **.1** backbiter **.2** indicter, expediter **.3** dynamiter **.4** first-nighter, igniter, all-nighter, amanita, overnighter **.5** dogfighter, infighter, gunfighter, prizefighter, bullfighter, Rhodophyta **.6** inviter **.7** reciter, exciter, inciter **.8** baryta, scriptwriter, typewriter, ghostwriter, screenwriter, signwriter, songwriter, sportswriter, copywriter, underwriter, teletypewriter, singer-songwriter **.9** gauleiter, highlighter, firelighter, uplighter, lamplighter, downlighter, moonlighter

17.12.14

putter, footer, inputter, six-footer, pussyfooter

17.12.15

Pooter, tooter, scooter, Ceuta, souter, Souttar, Soutter, suitor, shooter, Shuter, tutor, hooter, rooter, router, fruiter, pewter, sputa, scuta, neuter, looter **.1** freebooter **.2** accoutre, likuta, barracouta **.3** Desoutter **.4** peashooter, trapshooter, crapshooter, sharpshooter, six-shooter, lineshooter, troubleshooter **.5** prostitutor, constitutor **.6** Herrnhuter **.7** uprooter, recruiter **.8** Laputa, computer,

disputer, transputer, commuter, transmuter, refuter, diluter, polluter, valuta, saluter, contributor, distributor, prosecutor, persecutor, collocutor, minicomputer, supercomputer, microcomputer, telecommuter

17.12.16

.1 dieter, rioter, proprietor **.2** Botha **.3** Jupiter, Lampeter, trumpeter, accipiter, per capita, spanakopita **.4** arbiter, obiter, orbiter, presbyter, exhibitor, prohibiter, prohibitor, inhibitor, cohabiter **.5** competitor **.6** editor, predator, creditor, adyta, traditor, auditor, verditer, subeditor **.7** picketer, cricketer, marketer, telemarketer **.8** Agutter **.9.1** bemata, schemata, treponemata, dimeter, scimitar, trimeter, limiter, tachymeter, planimeter, gravimeter, dosimeter, tensimeter, pulsimeter, perimeter, delimiter, acidimeter, prosenchymata, viscosimeter, velocimeter, vaporimeter, saccharimeter, calorimeter, colorimeter, polarimeter, alkalimeter, telemeter, amateur, shamateur, diameter, heptameter, octameter, pentameter, voltameter, hexameter, parameter, tetrameter, milliammeter, semidiameter, traumata, Parmiter **.9.2** vomiter, geometer, swingometer, radiometer, cardiometer, audiometer, eudiometer, goniometer, pluviometer, fluviometer, areometer, variometer, heliometer, oleometer, potentiometer, pyrheliometer, radio-goniometer, tribometer, automata, photometer, optometer, Comptometer, lactometer, magnetometer, cathetometer, densitometer, sensitometer, olfactometer, refractometer, diffractometer, spectrophotometer, speedometer, pedometer, hodometer, udometer, odometer, tachometer, viscometer, thermometer, tromometer, seismometer, anemometer, dynamometer, katathermometer, planometer, clinometer, tonometer, manometer, phonometer, sonometer, chronometer, actinometer, iconometer, galvanometer, auxanometer, salinometer, declinometer, inclinometer, sphygmomanometer, bathometer, Fathometer®, gasometer, hypsometer, Pulsometer, opisometer, extensometer, piezometer, spherometer, pyrometer, spirometer, barometer, sclerometer, ombrometer, spectrometer, hydrometer, micrometer, psychrometer, hygrometer, saccharometer, electrometer, monochromator, interferometer, decelerometer, accelerometer, milometer, bolometer, kilometre, cyclometer, nephelometer, alcoholometer **.9.3** sclerenchymata, hypodermata, stomata, stromata, glomata, adenomata, angiomata, lipomata, scotomata, teratomata, sarcomata, zygomata, lymphomata, xanthomata, myxomata, neuromata, scleromata, fibromata, chondromata, atheromata, neurofibromata, myelomata, papillomata, condylomata, stigmata, kerygmata, syntagmata, melismata, plasmodesmata **.10** senator, janitor, monitor, progenitor, premonitor, terra incognita, primogenitor **.11** taffeta, forfeiter, comforter, Job's comforter **.12** riveter, servitor, conservator **.13** catheter **.14** Cirencester, masseter, Rossiter, circiter, Exeter, Wroxeter, elicitor, solicitor, capacitor, Uttoxeter **.15** visitor, inquisitor, depositor, compositor, expositor, ovipositor **.16** sagitta, Pargiter, coadjutor **.17** sequitur, loquitur, banqueter, non sequitur **.18** ferreter, heritor, barrator, orator, ureter, conspirator, inheritor, co-inheritor, apparitor, comparator, interpreter, Lysistrata, Mahabharata, misinterpreter **.19** contributor, distributor, executor, collocutor, prolocutor, interlocutor **.20** billeter, filleter, balata, Ballater, Findlater, Linklater, Hippolyta, bardolater, idolater, hagiolater, bibliolater, iconolater

17.12.17
stertor, kurta, Goethe, Murtagh, squirter, Roberta, Alberta, Ethelberta, frankfurter, perverter, reverter, subverter, inverter, converter, asserter, inserter, Bizerta, deserter, McWhirter

17.12.18
boater, Botha, toter, doter, Kota, scoter, jota, Gotha, motor, voter, chota, quota, rota, rotor, scrota, bloater, gloater, floater, Toyota®, iota, biota, Dakota, scapegoater, Saxe-Coburg-Gotha, emoter, promoter, locomotor, psychomotor, vasomotor, Minnesota, Serota, pelota

17.12.19
descriptor, lithotripter, Anaglypta, sceptre, septa, lepta, receptor, preceptor, accepter, acceptor, inceptor, interceptor, nociceptor, photoreceptor, mechanoreceptor, captor, chapter, raptor, adapter, adaptor, velociraptor, dioptre, 'copter, adopter, helicopter, corrupter, disrupter, interrupter, Gupta, tempter, prompter, sumpter, Sumter, preemptor, verkrampte, teleprompter, sculptor

17.12.20
ABTA

17.12.21
.1 dicta, victor, Richter, lictor, depicter, predictor, evictor, constrictor, verligte, inflicter, contradictor, obiter dicta, vasoconstrictor **.2** Spector, spectre, nectar, vector, sector, hector, recta, rector, prospector, respecter, inspector, detector, protector, connector, trifecta, effector, perfecta, perfecter, defector, infector, superfecta, convector, bisector, dissector, trisector, prosector, sub-sector, vivisector, ejecta, ejector, rejector, projector, objector, injector, director, erector, corrector, elector, collector, selector, prelector, deflector, reflector, analecta, genuflector **.3** acta, actor, facta, factor, tractor, reactor, compactor, redactor, enactor, transactor, exacta, exactor, varactor, attractor, detractor, retractor, protractor, subtracter, contractor, distractor, abstractor, extractor,

refractor, infractor, benefactor, malefactor, chiropractor, subcontractor, campylobacter **.4** Sakta **.5** okta, doctor, Procter, proctor, witchdoctor, concocter, concoctor, pro-proctor **.6** Bukta, adducter, abductor, inductor, conductor, destructor, obstructor, instructor, reconstructor, semiconductor, superconductor, photoconductor **.7** character **.8** sphincter, sancta, puncta, functor

17.12.22
.1 inter, into, pinta, Pinter, tinter, stinter, quinta, Minter, sinter, winter, Wintour, squinter, printer, sprinter, linter, splinter, Jacinta, calc-sinter, midwinter, reprinter, mezzotinter, Araminta, overwinter, teleprinter **.2** painter **.3** enter, tenter, stentor, centre, renter, re-enter, scienter, Rowenta®, repenter, indentor, commenter, tormentor, amenta, tomenta, momenta, fermenter, fomenter, cementer, lamenter, omenta, augmenter, indumenta, implementer, rejectamenta, impedimenta, experimenter, eventer, preventer, inventor, decentre, precentor, assenter, dissenter, placenta, jobcentre, accentor, succentor, concentre, epicentre, metacentre, presenter, magenta, frequenter, polenta **.4** banter, canter, cantor, manta, Fanta®, Santa, chanter, ranter, tranter, Granta, grantor, plantar, planter, instanter, Vedanta, decanter, recanter, trochanter, infanta, levanter, enchanter, maranta, supplanter, transplanter, Atlanta, almucantar, tam-o'-shanter, Atalanta **.5** counter, mounter, encounter, rencounter, revcounter, discounter, Geiger counter, under-the-counter **.6** granter **.7** Zonta, wanter, quanta, rencontre **.8** taunter, vaunter, saunter, haunter, flaunter **.9** pointer, jointer, three-pointer, appointer, anointer, point-to-pointer **.10** punter, Bunter, stunter, Gunter, shunter, chunter, junta, hunter, Grantha, grunter, headhunter, Todhunter, Arunta **.11** Gunther **.12** carpenter, patentor, Parmenter, covenanter, covenantor, warranter

17.12.23
snifter, Sifta, sifter, shifter, drifter, grifter, lifter, EFTA, after, BAFTA, rafter, drafter, grafter, laughter, softa, crofter, lofter, poofter, sceneshifter, shoplifter, uplifter, weightlifter, sought-after, hereafter, whereafter, thereafter, hereinafter, thereinafter

17.12.24
.1 Easter, keister, Dniester, feaster, quaestor, leister, Batista, southeaster, northeaster, autopista **.2** Bicester, bistre, mister, vista, sister, twister, tryster, crista, Krista, lister, blister, clyster, glister, demister, thermistor, Sandinista, assister, stepsister, insister, transistor, phototransistor, resistor, polyhistor, varistor, thyristor, ballista, enlister **.3** taster, Caistor, waster, poetaster, shirtwaister **.4** ester, Esther, pester, testa, tester, Nesta, Nestor, fester, vesta, cesta, zester, Chester, jester, Hester, wester, cuesta, quester, questor, Prester, Leicester,

Leister, Lester, fiesta, siesta, polyester, attestor, detester, protester, protestor, contester, trimester, semester, Silvester, Avesta, investor, ancestor, Cirencester, Dorchester, winchester, Manchester, Silchester, digester, suggester, sou'wester, nor'-wester, sequester, requester, arrester, molester, celesta **.5** aster, Astor, pasta, pastor, caster, castor, master, faster, Shasta, Rasta, raster, plaster, blaster, piaster, piastre, oleaster, Zoroaster, cotoneaster, alabaster, forecaster, Jocasta, Tadcaster, broadcaster, Lancaster, Doncaster, sportscaster, newscaster, criticaster, telecaster, narrowcaster, mesogaster, Antofagasta, remaster, paymaster, whoremaster, spymaster, choirmaster, shipmaster, submaster, Scoutmaster, pastmaster, postmaster, toastmaster, headmaster, yardmaster, bandmaster, grandmaster, Buckmaster, McMaster, taskmaster, ironmaster, ringmaster, housemaster, quizmaster, bushmaster, drillmaster, schoolmaster, harbourmaster, quartermaster, burgomaster, overmaster, concertmaster, whaling-master, pinaster, canasta, philosophaster, disaster, Alastor, pilaster, sandblaster **.6** ouster, jouster, frowster **.7** Costa, coster, foster, zoster, hosta, roster, Gloster, Gloucester, praepostor, impostor, defroster, paternoster, herpes zoster **.8** Forster, Vorster, exhauster **.9** oyster, hoister, roister, cloister **.10** buster, duster, Custer, muster, rustre, truster, frusta, thruster, lustre, bluster, cluster, fluster, chartbuster, trustbuster, ghostbuster, sodbuster, blockbuster, Dambuster, gangbuster, Augusta, adjuster, distruster, Lincrusta®, delustre, lacklustre, filibuster **.11** shyster, Hofmeister, Kapellmeister **.12** Worcester, Famagusta **.13** Shuster, Wooster, booster, rooster, brewster **.14** Lankester, minister, sinister, banister, canister, ganister, sophister, breakfaster, harvester, Sylvester, Chichester, Rochester, Porchester, Winchester, Grantchester, Lanchester, Ilchester, Colchester, register, barrister, chorister, forester, Forrester, fillister, Alisdair, Alistair, baluster, administer, deregister, preregister, McAlister, maladminister **.15** poster, boaster, toaster, Towcester, coaster, roaster, throwster, billposter **.16** tipster, hipster, whipster, quipster, tapster, dopester, Dempster, dumpster **.17** Webster, dabster, mobster, lobster, daubster **.18** maltster **.19** speedster, fraudster, roadster, oldster **.20** trickster, dexter, Baxter, oxter, huckster, Pinkster, prankster, funkster, youngster, Poindexter, ambidexter **.21** gagster, dragster **.22** teamster, deemster, gamester, Leominster, hamster, rhymester, rimester, doomster **.23** scenester, spinster, minster, Anstruther, Leinster, monster, punster, funster, Münster, Warminster, Sturminster, Westminster, Buckminster, Axminster, Ilminster, Kidderminster, Gila monster **.24** ringster, gangster, Sangster, songster **.25** Falster, holster,

Alcester, Ulster, pollster, bolster, soulster, upholster, reupholster

17.12.25
Tánaiste

17.12.26
.1 tilter, kilter, milter, filter, philtre, quilter **.2** realtor **.3** pelta, spelter, belter, delta, kelter, melter, smelter, Shelta, shelter, welter, swelter, backvelder, helter-skelter **.4** Yalta **.5** altar, alter, palter, Malta, falter, vaulter, Volta, volta, psalter, salter, halter, Walter, defaulter, asphalter, Minolta®, pole-vaulter, assaulter, exalter, Fitzwalter, Gibraltar, Upper Volta, superaltar **.6** insulter **.7** Poulter, bolter, Boulter, colter, coulter, moulter

17.13.1
speeder, kneader, feeder, Veda, cedar, seeder, Ouida, weeder, reader, Breda, breeder, Creda®, leader, Leda, Lieder, pleader, bleeder, Aïda, stampeder, sheetfeeder, self-feeder, seceder, reseda, succeeder, conceder, interceder, corrida, Derrida, stockbreeder, sight-reader, mind-reader, Etheldreda, proofreader, Elfreda, newsreader, copyreader, olla podrida, cheerleader, bearleader, Vileda, bandleader, ringleader, misleader, interpleader, follow-my-leader

17.13.2
bidder, kidder, Jiddah, whydah, outbidder, candida, consider, underbidder, overbidder, reconsider

17.13.3
Ada, aider, Nader, fader, Veda, Seder, wader, raider, braider, Breda, trader, grader, Hodeida, blockader, Grenada, evader, Rigveda, invader, Darth Vader, crusader, persuader, dissuader, parader, abrader, degrader, upgrader, serenader, Sama-Veda, masquerader, rollerblader

17.13.4
Edda, bedder, tedder, Kedah, Vedda, shedder, Cheddar, Jedah, Jeddah, header, spreader, treader, threader, shredder, homesteader, Kilfedder, Enzedder, triple-header, doubleheader

17.13.5
adder, khaddar, madder, ladder, bladder, stepladder, yadda-yadda

17.13.6
powder, Gouda, chowder, howdah, Lauda, gunpowder

17.13.7
Ardagh, ardour, Bader, cadre, carder, Garda, guarder, chadar, RADA, Lada®, larder, Dalriada, lambada, retarder, tostada, cicada, Haggadah, armada, Hamada, Torquemada, panada, Granada, promenader, intifada, Nevada, Theravada, Sierra Nevada, pousada, Masada, Scheherazade, autostrada, gelada, enchilada, piña colada

17.13.8
dodder, fodder, Hodder, prodder, plodder, hot-rodder

17.13.9
order, boarder, border, Cawdor, Korda, sordor, hoarder, warder, Wardour, reorder, keyboarder, suborder, snowboarder, skateboarder, sailboarder, short-order, recorder, camcorder, disorder, awarder, marauder, defrauder, mail order, superorder, video recorder

17.13.10
avoider, embroider, Schadenfreude

17.13.11
udder, shudder, chador, chuddar, judder, rudder

17.13.12
eider, Ida, spider, Guider, Snyder, Schneider, cider, Saida, chider, Haida, hider, rider, Ryder, strider, stridor, glider, slider, Oneida, divider, provider, decider, outsider, insider, Tynesider, ringsider, offsider, joyrider, derider, outrider, nightrider, roughrider, collider, backslider, Sydneysider, overrider, paraglider

17.13.13
Buddha, do-gooder, garuda

17.13.14
Cooder, Gouda, Tudor, Judah, brooder, Luda, Neruda, mouthbrooder, obtruder, intruder, Magruder, Barbuda, Bermuda, deluder, colluder, excluder, barracuda, Buxtehude

17.13.15
Drogheda, Rhayader, Amphipoda, Cephalopoda, asafoetida, coloquintida, Phasmida, Andromeda, Canada, Kannada, arachnida, spina bifida, Sepulveda, primigravida, reseda, Cressida, ambassador, forwarder, Mérida, forrader, Florida, Phyllida, Cadwallader

17.13.16
purdah, birder, Gerda, girder, murder, herder, Schroeder, self-murder

17.13.17
Oder, odour, coda, coder, Skoda®, soda, Rhoda, Schroeder, Yoder, loader, Clodagh, decoder, vocoder, encoder, Sargodha, pagoda, Fashoda, Baroda, freeloader, exploder, unloader, self-loader, Hexapoda, Diplopoda

17.13.18
Magda

17.13.19
lambda, LAMDA, numdah

17.13.20
.1 tinder, Kinder, cinder, hinder, Linda, Cabinda, Lucinda, Dorinda, Clarinda, Belinda, Melinda .2 attainder, remainder .3 ender, spender, bender, tender, mender, fender, Venda, vendor, sender, gender, Wenda, Gwenda, render, Brenda, Länder, lender, splendor, splendour, blender, Glenda, slender, weekender, tail-ender, hacienda, suspender, bartender, attender, pretender, contender, extender, goaltender, pudenda, addenda, corrigenda, amender, recommender, offender, defender, newsvendor, ascender, descender, descendeur, parascender, fazenda, agenda, engender, surrender, referenda, self-surrender, moneylender .4 panda, pander, Banda, stander, dander, candour, Skanda, gander, Vanda, sander, zander, brander, Landor, slander, meander, Leander, Rwanda, Luanda, coriander, oleander, compander, expander, dittander, Santander, bystander, withstander, understander, Afrikander, Uganda, Baganda, Buganda, propaganda, pomander, Amanda, demander, commander, germander, gerrymander, allamanda, calamander, salamander, Alexander, Anaximander, Menander, explananda, Lysander, goosander, right-hander, backhander, Aranda, Miranda, veranda, jacaranda, memoranda, Thailander, philander, solander, Yolanda, Laplander, uitlander, plattelander, flatlander, outlander, inlander, mainlander, Queenslander, overlander, Netherlander .5 pounder, bounder, founder, sounder, hounder, rounder, grounder, flounder, propounder, impounder, compounder, expounder, rebounder, typefounder .6 Lahnda .7 ponder, nonda, Fonda, zonda, Honda®, Wanda, wander, squander, Rhondda, yonder, responder, transponder, de-bonder, Golconda, Lagonda, Deronda, La Gioconda, anaconda, absconder .8 maunder, launder .9 joinder, rejoinder, nonjoinder, surrejoinder .10 under, bunder, thunder, Sunda, sunder, chunder, wonder, plunder, blunder, rotunda, up-and-under, osmunda, refunder, asunder, gazunder, hereunder, thereunder, floribunda, barramunda .11 binder, kinda, minder, finder, winder, grinder, blinder, highbinder, bookbinder, ringbinder, self-binder, Fassbinder, spellbinder, reminder, childminder, goalminder, viewfinder, faultfinder, wordfinder, pathfinder, rangefinder, rewinder, sidewinder .12 Munda, Kaunda, Peenemunde .13 husbander, seconder, Falkender, lavender, provender, Warrender, cylinder, calendar, calender, Callander, Hollander, colander, islander, Highlander, lowlander, Shetlander, midlander, woodlander, Newfoundlander, Greenlander, Icelander, Little Englander, semicylinder, supercalender

17.13.21
Pravda

17.13.22
Asda®, Mazda®, Bethesda

17.13.23
.1 Kielder, fielder, wielder, yielder, outfielder, midfielder, brickfielder, infielder .2 builder, Tilda, tilde, St Kilda, gilder, guilder, Hilda, wilder, rebuilder, shipbuilder, boatbuilder, housebuilder, coachbuilder, Mathilda, Brünhilde, bewilder, bodybuilder .3 elder, Zelda, Schelde, welder, backvelder, Griselda,

spotwelder, van de Velde **.4** Valda, Esmeralda
.5 alder, polder, Balder, Calder, solder,
unsolder, Isolde **.6** scalder **.7** Wilder **.8** Boldre,
boulder, scolder, Golda, molder, moulder,
smolder, smoulder, folder, shoulder, holder,
empolder, impolder, householder, keyholder,
freeholder, shareholder, beholder, upholder,
jobholder, stadtholder, cardholder,
landholder, bondholder, fundholder,
stakeholder, stockholder, loanholder,
slaveholder, withholder, leaseholder,
placeholder, gasholder, stallholder,
smallholder, titleholder, candleholder,
copyholder, unitholder, commonholder,
officeholder, policyholder

17.14.1
pika, speaker, beaker, tikka, sneaker, theca,
caeca, ceca, seeker, sika, squeaker, wreaker,
streaker, Griqua, shrieker, leaker, Costa Rica,
Topeka, loudspeaker, Guernica, Dominica,
spermatheca, self-seeker, Mochica, areca,
eureka, paprika, Frederica, Ash Shariqah,
Tanganyika, Zuleika

17.14.2
picker, bicker, ticker, tikka, sticker, dicker,
kicker, knicker, nicker, snicker, vicar, shicker,
whicker, Wicca, wicker, pricker, tricker, licker,
liquor, clicker, flicker, slicker, pigsticker,
billsticker, Konika, McVicar, bootlicker,
hepatica, Thessalonica

17.14.3
acre, baker, taker, staker, Dacre, maker, nacre,
naker, faker, saker, shaker, waker, Quaker,
raker, breaker, Laker, cloaca, bellyacher
.1 Studebaker **.2** caretaker, partaker, piss-taker,
grubstaker, undertaker, wicket-taker
.3 haymaker, playmaker, carmaker, lawmaker,
toymaker, shoemaker, Jamaica, printmaker,
bedmaker, brickmaker, clockmaker,
bookmaker, homemaker, filmmaker,
rainmaker, planemaker, gunmaker, winemaker,
kingmaker, peacemaker, pacemaker,
lacemaker, dressmaker, glassmaker,
cheesemaker, noisemaker, matchmaker,
watchmaker, sailmaker, toolmaker,
troublemaker, moneymaker, moviemaker,
merrymaker, papermaker, widow-maker,
Wanamaker, boilermaker, automaker, mischief-
maker, holidaymaker, cabinetmaker **.4** conacre
.5 forsaker, Chandrasekhar **.6** wiseacre,
stavesacre **.7** saltshaker,
boneshaker **.8** jawbreaker, tie-breaker,
heartbreaker, Windbreaker®, strikebreaker,
safebreaker, housebreaker, horsebreaker,
icebreaker, muckraker **.9** Zuleika

17.14.4
ekka, pecker, Becker, Decca, decker, Dekker,
mecca, Neckar, Necker, Secker, checker, Cheka,
chequer, weka, wrecker, trekker, Flecker,
woodpecker, Quebecker, Rebecca, three-decker,
Baedeker, exchequer, Voortrekker, Rijeka

17.14.5
aka, paca, packer, backer, tacker, stacker, Dacca,
Dakar, Dhaka, smacker, knacker, sacker,
hacker, Hakka, wacke, whacker, tracker,
cracker, yakka, lacker, lacquer, clacker,
claqueur, slacker, backpacker, unpacker, alpaca,
outbacker, linebacker, Rickenbacker,
Ansbacher, attacker, Schumacher, kanaka,
sifaka, ransacker, skyjacker, hijacker,
greywacke, bushwhacker, illywhacker, maraca,
backtracker, firecracker, nutcracker,
safecracker, wisecracker, polacca, malacca

17.14.6
Bowker

17.14.7
Acre, paca, parka, parker, barker, Tarka, kaka,
marker, markka, Zarqa, Shaka, haka, Kabaka,
waymarker, backmarker, bookmarker,
moussaka, Lusaka, Osaka, Oaxaca, polacre, nosy
parker, Tripitaka, Titicaca

17.14.8
ocker, tocher, stocker, docker, cocker, mocha,
mocker, knocker, Fokker®, soccer, shocker,
chocker, hougher, quokka, rocker, Crocker,
locker, blocker, Rioja, doorknocker, footlocker,
Knickerbocker, saltimbocca, interlocker

17.14.9
orca, porker, baulker, talker, stalker, caulker,
corker, Chalker, hawker, walker, squawker,
yorker, Lorca, deerstalker, Menorca, Minorca,
Majorca, jaywalker, firewalker, sleepwalker,
shopwalker, streetwalker, hillwalker, Mallorca

17.14.10
troika, perestroika

17.14.11
UCCA, pucker, pukka, bucker, tucker, ducker,
mucker, fucker, succour, sucker, shucker,
chukka, chukker, trucker, yucca, Loughor,
plucker, seersucker, sapsucker, lumpsucker,
goatsucker, bloodsucker, cocksucker, felucca,
motherfucker

17.14.12
pica, pika, piker, spica, biker, Byker, duiker,
mica, hiker, striker, Leica®, Schleicher,
Formica®, vesica, Zuleika, balalaika

17.14.13
booker, cooker, Sukkur, hookah, hooker, looker,
onlooker, overlooker

17.14.14
pooka, Stuka, snooker, spruiker, euchre, lucre,
Blücher, Paducah, bazooka, verruca, farruca,
rebuker, palooka, involucre, noctiluca

17.14.15
.1 perestroika **.2** Cyrenaica, Bandaranaike
.3 Gurkha, mazurka **.4** Eroica **.5** abaca
.6 Whittaker, Attica, Jataka, swastika, Tripitaka,
viatica, sciatica, Karnataka, exotica, erotica,
Antarctica, Areopagitica **.7** Baedeker, Boudicca,
melodica, materia medica **.8** mimicker,

stomacher, nux vomica **.9** spinnaker, Linacre, Lineker, Dominica, Seneca, Anneka, Hanukkah, manuka, arnica, Monica, moniker, Honecker, japonica, santonica, harmonica, veronica, Salonica, tunica, Guernica, picnicker, memoria technica **.10** trafficker **.11** Ithaca **.12** vesica, Jessica, massacre, brassica, fossicker, Corsica **.13** Fujica **.14** erica, areca, paprika, ostraca, Africa, America, Armorica **.15** silica, frolicker, Bullokar, replica, basilica, angelica, majolica, maiolica, res publica, vox angelica

17.14.16
burka, Gurkha, smirker, nerka, circa, shirker, jerker, worker, lurker, berserker, mazurka, tearjerker, shopworker, networker, outworker, craftworker, woodworker, fieldworker, farmworker, timeworker, homeworker, mineworker, stoneworker, caseworker, faceworker, steelworker, millworker, metalworker, teleworker, autoworker

17.14.17
ochre, poker, Stoker, stoker, coca, Coker, smoker, soaker, soca, choker, joker, Roker, broker, croaker, Croker, Rioja, EOKA, judoka, Avoca, evoker, revoker, provoker, invoker, Asoka, shipbroker, stockbroker, pawnbroker, tapioca, mediocre, carioca

17.14.18
Sitka, Kotka, latke, Nootka, kibitka, Kamchatka

17.14.19
Redcar, vodka

17.14.20
Simca®

17.14.21
.1 Inca, inker, tinker, stinker, minke, finca, vinca, thinker, sinker, jinker, winker, drinker, shrinker, blinker, clinker, Glinka, Soyinka, stotinka, freethinker, lip-syncer, headshrinker, Treblinka **.2** Cuenca **.3** anchor, anker, spanker, banker, tanka, tanker, canker, chancre, hanker, wanker, rancor, rancour, ranker, franker, flanker, Bianca, up-anchor, scrimshanker, Sri Lanka, Lubyanka, supertanker, Salamanca, lingua franca, Capablanca, Costa Blanca, Casablanca **.4** bonker, stonker, concha, conker, conquer, Dzongkha, plonker, reconquer **.5** punkah, bunker, hunker, younker, lunker, debunker, coal bunker, spelunker, Minya Konka **.6** Junker

17.14.22
Kafka

17.14.23
whisker, Risca, frisker, esker, Wesker, asker, Tasker, masker, masquer, lascar, Lasker, Oscar, busker, tusker, britzka, lansker, Francesca, burlesquer, unmasker, Nebraska, Alaska, McCusker, Athabasca, Madagascar

17.14.24
kishke, lashkar, Kokoschka, babushka

17.14.25
bilker, milker, Rilke, polka, baulker, skulker, sulker, sepulchre, yarmulka, yarmulke

17.15
dagga, tocher, Clogher, Loughor, Schleicher, simcha, Halacha, Halakah, Rioja, Gallagher

17.16.1
eager, eagre, meagre, Vega, Seeger, Riga, leaguer, Ortega, Antigua, bodega, Tredegar, reneger, Swarfega®, intriguer, quadriga, beleaguer, overeager

17.16.2
digger, nigger, snigger, figure, vigor, vigour, chigger, jigger, swigger, rigger, rigor, rigour, trigger, Frigga, ligger, gravedigger, prefigure, configure, disfigure, transfigure, square-rigger, outrigger, thimblerigger, reconfigure

17.16.3
agar, maigre, Vega, Sagar, Sager, saiga, Hagar, Jaeger®, yager, Ortega, reneger, Noriega, Meleager, rutabaga, Kabalega

17.16.4
eggar, egger, beggar, mega, Megger®, Gregor, legger, Heidegger, McGregor, bootlegger

17.16.5
stagger, dagga, dagger, nagger, saggar, shagger, Jagger, jagger, quagga, swagger, bragger, lagger, blagger, flagger, three-bagger, four-bagger, sandbagger, carpetbagger

17.16.6
Aga®, dagga, dargah, naga, saga, raga, Braga, laager, lager, Seaga, Onondaga, Balenciaga

17.16.7
dogger, jogger, hogger, logger, flogger, slogger, defogger, footslogger, pettifogger, Wagga Wagga, cataloguer

17.16.8
auger, augur, sauger, Mississauga, massasauga

17.16.9
bugger, tugger, mugger, hugger, rugger, lugger, plugger, slugger, debugger, Srinagar, hugger-mugger

17.16.10
Eiger, taiga, tiger, Steiger, saiga, liger, braunschweiger, Auriga, quadriga

17.16.11
sugar, Zeebrugge

17.16.12
cougar, Kruger, Luger®, Chattanooga, ajuga, beluga, Kaluga

17.16.13
Heidegger, omega, vinegar, onager, Honegger, alegar, Gallagher, Málaga

17.16.14
Urga, Berger, burger, burgher, turgor, Limburger, hamburger, Luxemburger,

Weinberger, beefburger, cheeseburger, Ethelburga, parerga, Vegeburger, Erzgebirge

17.16.15
ogre, toga, yoga, Ladoga, Cuyahoga, Saratoga, conestoga, hatha-yoga, Ticonderoga

17.16.16
Edgar

17.16.17
.1 finger, linga, linger, forefinger, Muchinga, churinga, seringa, syringa, malinger, ladyfinger, Minnesinger, alcheringa **.2** anger, panga, Bangor, tanga, kanga, sanga, sangar, sangha, hangar, languor, clangour, Katanga, inanga, Northanger, Betteshanger, Tauranga, Erlanger, Zamboanga **.3** tonga, donga, conga, conger, Rarotonga **.4** monger, hunger, Younger, scaremonger, whoremonger, warmonger, ironmonger, cheesemonger, newsmonger, fishmonger, fellmonger, scandalmonger, costermonger, gossipmonger **.5** Kanchenjunga, sitatunga

17.16.18
Pisgah

17.16.19
wilga, Elgar, Helga, alga, Olga, Volga, brolga, bulghur, mulga, vulgar, realgar, Trafalgar

17.17.1
Pima, beamer, bema, steamer, schema, schemer, femur, seamer, reamer, streamer, dreamer, creamer, screamer, lemur, Lima, seriema, empyema, Iwo Jima, terza rima, ottava rima, oedema, redeemer, myxoedema, treponima, blasphemer, erythema, enanthema, exanthema, emphysema, Tsushima, Kagoshima, Hiroshima, extrema, daydreamer, Tolima, Colima, Selima

17.17.2
dimmer, skimmer, simmer, zimmer, shimmer, chimer, swimmer, Rimmer, trimmer, strimmer®, krimmer, limber, limner, glimmer, slimmer

17.17.3
enantiomer

17.17.4
tamer, Shema, Hamer, squama, Cramer, Kramer, framer, claimer, lion-tamer, testamur, defamer, reclaimer, acclaimer, declaimer, proclaimer, disclaimer, inflamer

17.17.5
Emma, emmer, stemma, gemma, Jemma, tremor, lemma, pip emma, contemner, ack emma, maremma, trilemma, dilemma, analemma

17.17.6
stammer, dammar, gamma, gammer, mama, mamma, gnamma, namma, shammer, jammer, hammer, rammer, crammer, grammar, yammer, lamber, clamour, glamour, slammer, Alabama, Tsitsikamma, digamma, enamour, windjammer, tilt-hammer, jackhammer, sledgehammer, yellowhammer, programmer, flimflammer

17.17.7
amah, armour, Palma, palmer, Parma, dharma, Kama, karma, farmer, Samar, charmer, Harmer, Rama, Brahma, Bramah, drama, Yama, lama, llama, Gama, da, disarmer, cariama, Dalai Lama, Panchen lama, Vasco da Gama, embalmer, Atacama, Surinamer, share-farmer, snake-charmer, pajama, pyjama, Sajama, Yokohama, diorama, stripperama, Cinerama®, panorama, cyclorama, psychodrama, monodrama, docudrama, melodrama, Fujiyama, pranayama, Matsuyama

17.17.8
bomber, comma, momma, prommer

17.17.9
ormer, stormer, dormer, korma, Norma, former, warmer, trauma, barnstormer, performer, reformer, pro-forma, informer, conformer, sixth-former, transformer

17.17.10
bummer, comer, gumma, Gummer, mummer, summa, summer, hummer, rummer, strummer, drummer, thrummer, plumber, Plummer, newcomer, latecomer, incomer, downcomer, breastsummer, midsummer, kettledrummer

17.17.11
timer, dimer, mimer, cyma, sima, rhymer, primer, trimer, climber, two-timer, part-timer, old-timer, Jemima, Horkheimer, Oppenheimer, wisenheimer, Roraima, arapaima

17.17.12
summa, roomer

17.17.13
boomer, Duma, Sumer, tumour, stumer, roomer, rumour, struma, Nkrumah, puma, humour, Plomer, bloomer, satsuma, perfumer, consumer, Koluma, Montezuma

17.17.14
.1 epimer **.2** etyma, metamer, Fatima, Latimer, Gautama, tautomer, Mortimer, optima, customer, ultima, ambystoma, elastomer **.3** Tadema, Gordimer, Dodoma, Aceldama, Alma-Tadema **.4** Yakima, welcomer, prosenchyma, sclerenchyma, aerenchyma, parenchyma, collenchyma **.5** agama, oligomer **.6** minima, cinema, enema, anima, monomer, astronomer **.7** anathema, exanthema **.8** Bessemer, gossamer, isomer, eczema, maxima, ransomer, dulcimer, Septuagesima, Sexagesima, Quinquagesima, Quadragesima, stereoisomer **.9** Hiroshima **.10** lorimer, ashrama **.11** curcuma **.12** polymer, ulema, copolymer

17.17.15
Irma, Burma, termor, derma, murmur, wormer, squirmer, Valderma, affirmer, hypoderma, leucoderma, xeroderma, scleroderma, terra firma

17.17.16
Omagh, omer, Tomor, stoma, coma, comber, Gomer, vomer, soma, homa, Homer, roamer, Roma, romer, stroma, chroma, Cromer, Plomer, glioma, adenoma, carcinoma, angioma, enantiomer **.1** lipoma **.2** scotoma, haematoma, teratoma **.3** Kardomah **.4** glaucoma, sarcoma, leucoma, Tacoma, trachoma, beachcomber **.5** zygoma, oligomer **.6** misnomer, melanoma, adenocarcinoma **.7** lymphoma **.8** xanthoma **.9** myxoma, opisthosoma **.10** Oklahoma **.11** aroma, neuroma, scleroma, fibroma, chondroma, atheroma, neurofibroma **.12** myeloma, diploma, papilloma, condyloma

17.17.17
mahatma

17.17.18
Padma, Bodmer

17.17.19
chacma, drachma

17.17.20
stigma, sigma, smegma, agma, magma, dogma, zeugma, enigma, kerygma, syntagma

17.17.21
Cranmer

17.17.22
asthma

17.17.23
Mesmer, plasma, charisma, melisma, miasma, chiasma, coprosma, plasmodesma

17.17.24
Wilma, Wilmer, Aylmer, Elmer, Velma, Thelma, Selma, Chelmer, Alma, Palma, palmar, halma, Kalmar, dolma, Bulmer, fulmar

17.18.1
Ena, Ina, Deanna, kina, Nina, vena, vina, thenar, Zena, Sheena, Shena, Gina, Heanor, weaner, wiener, preener, screener, fraena, frena, Lena, plena, cleaner, gleaner, hyaena, hyena, Raina, Rowena, Adelina **.1** subpoena, Filipina, philippina **.2** Robina, Ribena®, verbena, Sabina, carabiner, Karabiner, amphisbaena **.3** Martina, Cortina®, patina, Bettina, catena, cantina, Clementina, Argentina, Christina, sestina, sonatina, cavatina, concertina, guillotiner, scarlatina **.4** Medina, duodena, Pasadena, phagedaena **.5** trichina, Burkina, coquina **.6** Taormina, demeanour, Traminer, misdemeanour, Philomena, Ballymena, Wilhelmina, Gewürztraminer, Seraphina, Petrofina **.7** novena, convener, intervener, intervenor, Bukovina, contravener, Herzegovina **.8** Athena **.9** piscina, Messina, retsina, Thomasina, Teresina **.10** rendzina **.11** deus ex machina **.12** kachina **.13** Georgina, Hygena, congener, Cartagena **.14** Edwina **.15** czarina, tsarina, arena, carina, marina, farina, Serena, signorina, casuarina, Caterina, ocarina, Riverina, ballerina, Santa Catarina,

prima ballerina, Sabrina, Catriona, Catrina, Katrina, orchestrina, Palestrina **.16** doline, galena, Melina, Selena, Selina, St Helena, pipecleaner, euglena, Catalina, cantilena, santolina, Magdalena, semolina, Messalina, Angelina

17.18.2
inner, pinna, Pinner, spinner, tinner, dinner, skinner, Minna, finner, thinner, sinner, ginner, Jinnah, winner, Brynner, grinner, beginner, breadwinner, prizewinner, Corinna, Berliner, Savonlinna, Proserpina

17.18.3
stainer, Dana, Cana, caner, Gaenor, gainer, Gaynor, seiner, scena, Raina, Rayner, trainer, strainer, drainer, grainer, Jena, Lena, planar, planer, Sinn Feiner, yerba buena, campaigner, detainer, retainer, curtana, obtainer, maintainer, maintainor, lantana, container, sustainer, entertainer, abstainer, ordainer, arcana, N'Djamena, Cunene, profaner, purse-seiner, Cartagena, cordwainer, distrainer, restrainer, Marlene, coplanar, complainer, explainer, cantilena, uniplanar

17.18.4
tenner, tenor, tenour, Venner, senna, Jenna, Jenner, henna, Vienna, Siena, sienna, duenna, antenna, Heldentenor, McKenna, Ravenna, Gehenna, Morwenna, countertenor, Avicenna

17.18.5
Verner

17.18.6
Anna, panner, spanner, banner, tanner, canna, canner, scanner, manna, manner, manor, nana, nanna, fanner, Hanna, Hannah, Branagh, lanner, planner, Deanna, Diana, Guiana, Guyana, goanna, Joanna, Indiana, Louisiana, Arianna, Pollyanna, Santa Ana, ipecacuanha, Copacabana, Montana, bandanna, Fata Morgana, Fermanagh, Cavanagh, Kavanagh, savannah, Havana, caravanner, Roxanna, Susannah, Suzanna, hosanna, Rosanna, Susquehanna, Alana, wallplanner

17.18.7
downer, sauna, frowner, uptowner, sundowner

17.18.8
ana, Dana, darner, kana, garner, Ghana, mana, Marner, nana, varna, bwana, Tswana, prana, Lana, Guiana, liana, Tatiana, Christiana, poinciana, Georgiana, Mariana, Haryana, Oriana, Gloriana, Ljubljana, iguana, nicotiana, Edwardiana, varsoviana, Shakespeareana, Victoriana, siciliana, ipecacuanha **.1** cabana, ikebana **.2** sultana, curtana, lantana, Fontana, Rajputana, tramontana **.3** arcana, Chicana, Turkana, gymkhana, Toscana, katakana, Africana, Afrikaner, Americana **.4** nagana, hiragana, caragana **.5** vox humana, Bildungsromane **.6** banana, zenana **.7** nirvana

.8 Roxana, Lipizzaner **.9** Rosh Hashana
.10 Tijuana, Gondwana, Setswana, Botswana, marijuana, Bophuthatswana **.11** Tirana, Purana, piranha, pacarana, Weimaraner, Carmina Burana **.12** mañana, Santayana, Hinayana, Mahayana **.13** pozzolana

17.18.9
honour, Bonner, Doner, donna, Connor, goner, gonna, Shona, wanna, madonna, McDonagh, O'Connor, dishonour, Mashona, prima donna, Maradona, belladonna, Tarragona

17.18.10
spawner, corner, scorner, Morna, mourner, fauna, fawner, Thorner, sauna, horner, warner, yawner, Lorna, suborner, infauna, forewarner, epifauna, avifauna

17.18.11
coiner, joiner, amboyna, purloiner

17.18.12
punner, stunner, scunner, gunner, Sunna, oner, runner, forerunner, Corunna, front-runner, roadrunner, rumrunner, gunrunner, pinch-runner

17.18.13
Ina, Steiner, Dinah, diner, mina, miner, minor, mynah, Viner, Weiner, signer, shiner, china, Heine, whiner, twiner, Shriner, liner, Ursa Minor, Canis Minor **.1** Niersteiner, Liechtensteiner, Landsteiner, mediastina **.2** Medina **.3** Shekinah, trichina **.4** coalminer, underminer **.5** forty-niner **.6** definer, refiner **.7** diviner **.8** assigner, assignor, cosigner, consignor, countersigner **.9** designer, resigner **.10** moonshiner **.11** Indo-China, Cochin-China **.12** vagina, Regina, angina **.13** carina, farina, casuarina, globigerina **.14** airliner, eyeliner, maligner, salina, freightliner, jetliner, headliner, hardliner, roadliner, decliner, recliner, incliner, mainliner, bodyliner, Carolina

17.18.14
Sunna

17.18.15
Oonagh, Poona, puna, spooner, Buna, schooner, tuna, tuner, Junor, pruner, crooner, Una, Luna, lunar, Tristan da Cunha, harpooner, lampooner, Altoona, induna, honeymooner, mizuna, yokozuna, kahuna, oppugner, vicuña, lacuna, lacunar, cislunar, circumlunar, calluna, translunar

17.18.16
gonna **.1** ironer **.2** xoana **.3** sharpener, opener, tympana, dampener **.4** sweetener, straightener, Smetana, retina, threatener, patina, flattener, tightener, whitener, frightener, easterner, westerner, Pristina, enlightener, south-easterner, Midwesterner, southwesterner: (+ **17.18.21**) **.5** deadener, gladdener, pardoner, gardener, hardener, Modena, widener,

Londoner, abandoner: (+ **17.18.22**) **.6** weakener, thickener, sickener, reckoner, jacana, darkener, falconer: (+ **17.18.23**) **.7** wagoner, bargainer, organa, tobogganer: (+ **17.18.24**) **.8** limina, gravamina, stamina, lamina, laminar, examiner, foramina, trilaminar, velamina, noumena, almoner, Brahmana, commoner, nomina, phenomena, prolegomena, paralipomena, properispomena, hapax legomena, epiphenomena, summoner, rumina, numina, alumina, determiner: (+ **17.18.25**) **.9** tenoner **.10** stiffener, softener, toughener: (+ **17.18.26**) **.11** scrivener, Taverner, Cavanagh, Kavanagh, governor, Grosvenor, enlivener, Hercegovina, Herzegovina: (+ **17.18.27**) **.12** strengthener, lengthener **.13** southerner, northerner **.14** christener, listener, chastener, fastener, larcener, Porsena, loosener, retsina; zip-fastener: (+ **17.18.28**) **.15** seasoner, reasoner, prisoner, poisoner **.16** missioner, stationer, feiseanna, fashioner, pensioner, tensioner, partitioner, petitioner, practitioner, conditioner, commissioner, munitioner, positioner, parishioner, probationer, foundationer, vacationer, extortioner, reversioner, confectioner, exhibitioner, reconditioner, subcommissioner, requisitioner, executioner: (+ **17.18.30**) **.17** provisioner **.18** Kitchener, Michener, questioner **.19** sojourner, religioner, imaginer **.20** mariner, coroner, koruna, foreigner, warrener, submariner **.21** Ramayana **.22** milliner, Eleanor, Elinor, Helena, Callenor, Challoner, Dubliner

17.18.17
earner, spurner, burner, turner, sterna, Myrna, Smyrna, Verner, Werner, yearner, learner, returner, woodturner, taverna, discerner, Annapurna, afterburner, xiphisterna

17.18.18
owner, boner, toner, stoner, Stonor, dona, donor, moaner, Mona, phono, Shona, Jonah, rhona, rona, trona, krona, krone, kroner, kronor, kronur, groaner, loaner, loner, Fiona, Leona, Iona, co-owner, disowner, Catriona **.1** shipowner, postponer **.2** Daytona, Latona, intoner **.3** landowner, condoner **.4** cinchona, Ascona **.5** Pomona, Ramona, Cremona, homeowner, Desdemona **.6** Anona, Winona **.7** persona **.8** Arizona **.9** Mashona **.10** corona, Verona, madrona, madrone **.11** Ilona, Valona, coal owner, Pamplona, Barcelona

17.18.19
Dympna

17.18.20
Abner

17.18.21
Etna, Patna, Shatner, Ratner, Ventnor, centner, Costner, Gestetner: (+ **17.18.16(.4)**)

17.18.22
Edna, Radner, Radnor, pardner, Gardner, Lardner, echidna: (+ **17.18.16(.5)**)

17.18.23
Faulkner, Buckner, Brookner, Bruckner:
(+ **17.18.16**(.6))

17.18.24
Wagner, Bognor, Bugner, interregna, Leptis
Magna: (+ **17.18.16**(.7))

17.18.25
limner, Bremner, damna, Cumnor, numnah,
Sumner, alumna, columnar: (+ **17.18.16**(.8))

17.18.26
Jaffna: (+ **17.18.16**(.10))

17.18.27
guvnor, guv'nor, czarevna, tsarevna:
(+ **17.18.16**(.11))

17.18.28
Cessna®, Flexner, pilsner: (+ **17.18.16**(.14))

17.18.29
visna, Pevsner, pilsner

17.18.30
Mishnah, Krishna, Hare Krishna, Ramakrishna:
(+ **17.18.16**(.16))

17.18.31
Wichnor

17.18.32
Kilner®, Milner, ulna, ulnar

17.19.1
Inga, pinger, stinger, singer, zinger, winger,
swinger, ringer, wringer, springer, bringer,
stringer, clinger, flinger, slinger, Schrödinger,
humdinger, Helsingor, out-swinger, inswinger,
klipspringer, bell ringer, mudslinger,
gunslinger, mastersinger, Meistersinger

17.19.2
banger, ganger, Sanger, hangar, hanger, clanger,
headbanger, doppelgänger, double-ganger,
Stavanger, straphanger, cliffhanger,
Betteshanger, haranguer, paperhanger

17.19.3
tonga, wronger, prolonger

17.19.4
ponga

17.20.1
feoffor, FIFA, reefer

17.20.2
differ, sniffer

17.20.3
Schaefer, Schaeffer, chafer, wafer, trefa, UEFA,
cockchafer, rose-chafer

17.20.4
feoffor, zephyr, heifer

17.20.5
Staffa, staffer, kaffir, kafir, gaffer, zaffre, Shaffer,
chaffer, Jaffa, Mustafa, Mustapha, Luftwaffe

17.20.6
staffer, laugher

17.20.7
Offa, offer, coffer, cougher, scoffer, goffer,
quaffer, Swaffer, proffer, Gasthöfe, Bonhoeffer,
counteroffer

17.20.8
Forfar, Altdorfer, amorpha

17.20.9
puffer, buffer, stuffer, duffer, snuffer, suffer,
luffa, bluffer

17.20.10
knifer, fifer, cipher, Haifa, hypha, lifer,
decipher, encipher

17.20.11
spoofer, chufa, tufa, hoofer, woofer, roofer,
loofa, loofah, opera buffa, waterproofer

17.20.12
.1 Pettifer, metaphor, Potiphar, rotifer,
Christopher, Mustafa, Mustapha .2 Jennifer,
conifer, foraminifer .3 crucifer, Lucifer, lucifer,
theosopher, philosopher .4 aquifer .5 porifer,
thurifer, Apocrypha, tachygrapher, serigrapher,
calligrapher, pseudepigrapha, telegrapher,
agrapha, geographer, biographer,
crystallographer, radiographer, cardiographer,
Hagiographa, hagiographer, ichthyographer,
physiographer, choreographer, palaeographer,
paleographer, bibliographer, historiographer,
autobiographer, topographer, typographer,
prosopographer, cartographer, photographer,
cryptographer, cinematographer,
cacographer, discographer, lexicographer,
logographer, demographer, cosmographer,
seismographer, stenographer, monographer,
pornographer, phonographer, hymnographer,
ethnographer, iconographer, oceanographer,
uranographer, selenographer, orthographer,
mythographer, lithographer, chromolithographer, glossographer, chorographer,
chirographer, reprographer, petrographer,
hydrographer, xylographer .6 umbellifer

17.20.13
surfer, windsurfer, Bonhoeffer

17.20.14
Ophir, gofer, gopher, sofa, chauffeur, shofar,
loafer, Fraunhofer, Nuku'alofa

17.20.15
titfer

17.20.16
Agfa®

17.20.17
nympha, camphor, chamfer

17.20.18
phosphor

17.20.19
pilfer, telfer, telpher, alfa, alpha, Balfour, golfer,
sulpha, sulphur, alfalfa, Wadi Halfa

17.21.1
Eva, beaver, Belvoir, deva, diva, Neva, fever, viva, Shiva, heaver, weaver, weever, reiver, griever, leaver, lever, cleaver, Geneva, genever, perceiver, deceiver, receiver, transceiver, self-deceiver, misconceiver, yeshiva, achiever, underachiever, overachiever, coalheaver, retriever, believer, reliever, unbeliever, disbeliever, cantilever, Unilever®

17.21.2
giver, shiver, quiver, river, liver, flivver, sliver, lawgiver, forgiver, aquiver, Guadalquivír, upriver, downriver, deliver

17.21.3
Ava, paver, deva, caver, Neva, favor, favour, saver, savor, savour, shaver, haver, waiver, waver, quaver, raver, craver, graver, laver, flavor, flavour, slaver, cadaver, disfavor, disfavour, lifesaver, engraver, beslaver, enslaver, vena cava, misbehaver, semiquaver, demisemiquaver, semidemisemiquaver, hemidemisemiquaver

17.21.4
ever, never, sever, Trevor, leva, clever, however, whoever, soever, whosoever, whatever, endeavor, endeavour, Micheldever, whomever, whenever, Dynefor, assever, dissever, whichever, wherever, forever, Rostrevor, wheresoever, howsoever, whatsoever, whomsoever, whencesoever, whensoever, whosesoever, whichsoever, never-never, whithersoever

17.21.5
slaver, cadaver, beslaver

17.21.6
carver, kava, Java, guava, larva, lava, cadaver, woodcarver, piassava, cassava, palaver, Costa Brava, balaclava, Bratislava

17.21.7
bovver, hover, windhover

17.21.8
Morfa

17.21.9
cover, lover, plover, Glover, recover, slipcover, softcover, hardcover, uncover, discover, gill cover, fun-lover, sun-lover, undercover, rediscover

17.21.10
Ifor, Iver, Ivor, stiver, diver, skiver, guiver, gyver, fiver, viva, jiver, river, striver, driver, Liver, sliver, skydiver, Godiva, McIver, conniver, survivor, reviver, gingiva, contriver, screwdriver, co-driver, cabdriver, slave-driver, piledriver, saliva, conjunctiva

17.21.11
Tuva, mover, Suva, hoover, groover, louvre, Vancouver, remover, manoeuvre, reprover, improver, outmanoeuvre, disapprover

17.21.12
Vltava, vetiver, Cordova, sandiver, Dynefor, miniver, Nineveh, Genova, Hanover, Vaishnava, gingiva, Ostrava, helluva, Oliver, Gulliver, baklava, Pavlova, Ulanova

17.21.13
Nerva, fervour, server, swerver, Minerva, timeserver, deserver, reserver, preserver, observer

17.21.14
ova, over, Dover, nova, rover, trover, drover, Grover, clover, left-over, warmed-over, up-and-over, moreover, over-and-over, bossa nova **.1** layover **.2** flyover **.3** slipover, popover, stopover **.4** leftover **.5** Wendover, handover, Moldova, holdover **.6** tickover, Rickover, takeover, Markova, walkover, strikeover **.7** Hannover, Hanover, Canova, turnover, supernova, Casanova **.8** wingover, hangover **.9** Passover, crossover, once-over, Bolsover **.10** flashover, pushover **.11** switch-over **.12** changeover **.13** Jehovah **.14** Land-Rover® **.15** spillover, pullover, Mickleover, Pavlova, Navratilova

17.21.15
Moskva

17.21.16
triumvir, duumvir

17.21.17
Gwynfor, Denver

17.21.18
mitzvah

17.21.19
Silva, silver, sylva, Wylfa, elver, delver, shelver, salver, salvor, halva, halvah, solver, Culver, vulva, vulvar, re-silver, quicksilver, Gabalfa, revolver, resolver, absolver

17.22.1
ether, Ibiza, bequeather, Aretha

17.22.2
cither

17.22.3
Cather

17.22.4
souther

17.22.5
Arthur, Martha, MacArthur

17.22.6
Hiawatha

17.22.7
author

17.22.8
Luther, anacolutha

17.22.9
Tabitha, Agatha, Golgotha

17.22.10
Eartha, Bertha, rebirther, Jugurtha

17.22.11
Gotha, quotha

17.22.12
naphtha

17.22.13
anther, panther, Gunther, Jacintha, Samantha, polyantha, pyracantha

17.22.14
Jephthah, aphtha, naphtha

17.22.15
Esther

17.22.16
maltha

17.23.1
either, neither, breather, bequeather

17.23.2
dither, thither, zither, hither, whither, wither, swither, slither

17.23.3
bather, Mather, sunbather

17.23.4
tether, nether, feather, heather, weather, wether, whether, leather, blether, untether, together, pinfeather, pen-feather, wet-weather, bellwether, shoeleather, whitleather, altogether, Pennyfeather, Merryweather, hell-for-leather

17.23.5
gather, Mather, lather, blather, slather, regather, foregather, forgather, ingather

17.23.6
mouther, Crowther

17.23.7
farther, father, rather, lather, forefather, stepfather, godfather, grandfather

17.23.8
pother, bother, Rother, Golgotha

17.23.9
norther

17.23.10
other, t'other, mother, smother, brother, stepmother, godmother, grandmother, housemother, another, Fairbrother, stepbrother, Anstruther

17.23.11
either, neither

17.23.12
smoother, soother

17.23.13
murther, further

17.23.14
loather

17.23.15
Rhondda

17.24.1
piecer, greaser, leaser, Lisa, Raisa, Teresa, Theresa, Nerissa, increaser, degreaser, releaser, releasor

17.24.2
kisser, mantissa, abscissa, Orissa, Marisa, Larissa, Clarissa, Alissa, Melissa, reminiscer

17.24.3
piercer

17.24.4
acer, Asa, pacer, spacer, macer, mesa, facer, chaser, racer, bracer, tracer, placer, debaser, grimacer, omasa, defacer, steeplechaser, Teresa, embracer, replacer, abomasa

17.24.5
TESSA, guesser, Nessa, cesser, Hesse, dresser, lesser, plessor, Slessor, contessa, Edessa, Odessa, Vanessa, professor, confessor, assessor, processor, successor, intercessor, predecessor, pre-processor, coprocessor, multiprocessor, microprocessor, possessor, repossessor, oppressor, depressor, suppressor, represser, repressor, compressor, expresser, hairdresser, addresser, redresser, vine-dresser, digresser, aggressor, transgressor, decompressor, sub-lessor

17.24.6
Assur, Asur, passer, tassa, casa, gasser, NASA, Nasser, Lhasa, Nyasa, El Paso, Mombasa, macassar, Makassar, amasser, Manasseh, kirschwasser, Kinshasa, harasser, madrasa, Panthalassa, Cabora Bassa, antimacassar

17.24.7
dowser, Scouser, mouser, Hausa, grouser, degausser

17.24.8
Asa, passer, casa, Vaasa, Lhasa, Kinshasa, Bahasa, Tarrasa

17.24.9
Ossa, tosser, dosser, fossa, josser, Rosser, Prosser, glosser, embosser, Saragossa, Zaragoza, Barbarossa

17.24.10
dorsa, courser, Xhosa, forcer, saucer, Chaucer, Horsa, endorser, reinforcer, enforcer

17.24.11
voicer, rejoicer

17.24.12
tussah, tusser, tussore, fusser, trusser, discusser

17.24.13
paisa, paise, dicer, vice, shicer, twicer, ricer, pricer, gricer, splicer, slicer, de-icer, enticer

17.24.14
Susa, juicer, rusa, sprucer, samosa, medusa, seducer, reducer, producer, traducer, inducer,

transducer, Abu Musa, reproducer, introducer, babirusa, Appaloosa, katharevousa

17.24.15
trespasser, practiser, focuser, grimacer, promiser, promisor, menacer, harnesser, thicknesser, officer, surfacer, vavasour, traverser, canvasser, purchaser, harasser, artificer, returning officer

17.24.16
Ursa, purser, bursa, bursar, curser, cursor, mercer, versa, coercer, disperser, reimburser, disburser, precursor, reverser, traverser, converser, vice versa, rehearser

17.24.17
Xhosa, grocer, pigmentosa, Formosa, mimosa, samosa, serosa, greengrocer, curiosa, ponderosa, Via Dolorosa, bulimia nervosa, anorexia nervosa

17.24.18
lapser, eclipser, relapser

17.24.19
pizza, Katowice, howitzer, spritzer, Chichén Itzá, Maritsa, Amritsar, Wurlitzer®, carezza, matza, matzo, piazza, schnauzer, tazza, lotsa, Hakenkreuze, gutser, Schweitzer, kibitzer, Vinnitsa, Pulitzer, Henze, Faenza, petuntse, seltzer, Kielce, waltzer, Alka-Seltzer®

17.24.20
mixer, fixer, sixer, shicksa, shiksa, vexer, sexer, plexor, flexor, taxa, taxer, Saxa, waxer, oxer, boxer, coxa, moxa, coaxer, hoaxer, remixer, elixir, indexer, adnexa, Alexa, relaxer, kick-boxer, multiplexer, multiplexor, chionodoxa, bobby-soxer

17.24.21
Tecumseh

17.24.22
.1 pincer, mincer, wincer, rinser, convincer
.2 ENSA, spencer, Spenser, tensor, Mensa, fencer, censer, censor, sensa, sensor, Despenser, dispenser, extensor, condenser, biosensor
.3 cancer, Hansa, merganser, romancer, chiromancer, necromancer, oneiromancer, answer, dancer, chancer, prancer, lancer, tap-dancer, ropedancer, advancer, enhancer
.4 pouncer, bouncer, trouncer, announcer, denouncer, renouncer, pronouncer **.5** sponsor, Bonser, Bonsor **.6** oncer **.7** conveyancer, influencer, Odense, licensor, sequencer, balancer, silencer, remembrancer

17.24.23
Gafsa

17.24.24
Ailsa, Elsa, Kielce, salsa, waltzer, ulcer, Tulsa, propulsor

17.25.1
easer, Pisa, teaser, Keyser, geezer, geyser, sneezer, visa, Caesar, seizer, wheezer, tweezer, squeezer, greaser, freezer, Lisa, Liza, Louisa, El

Giza, appeaser, stripteaser, mestiza, Malteser, genizah, Ebenezer, Shalmaneser, tortfeasor, Hispano-Suiza, Theresa, crowd-pleaser, Tiglath-pileser

17.25.2
fizzer, scissor, whizzer, quizzer

17.25.3
Asa, beisa, gazer, maser, mazer, Weser, razor, praiser, brazer, grazer, Fraser, Frazer, laser, blazer, Glaser, glazer, stargazer, eraser, Teresa, appraiser, hellraiser, chalaza, trailblazer, Spätlese, salmanazar, Maria Theresa

17.25.4
Nebuchadnezzar

17.25.5
jazzer, lazar, Alcazar, Balthasar, Balthazar, Belshazzar

17.25.6
bowser®, dowser, Mauser®, schnauzer, Hausa, wowser, rouser, browser, trouser, espouser, arouser, carouser, rabble-rouser, honoris causa

17.25.7
parser, Garza, Gaza, plaza, dopiaza, tabula rasa

17.25.8
rozzer

17.25.9
causer, Xhosa, hawser

17.25.10
Gasthäuser, Tannhäuser

17.25.11
buzzer

17.25.12
Tizer®, Kaiser, Keyser, geyser, miser, visor, sizar, sizer, riser, Dreiser, Lisa, Liza, Mount Isa
.1 despiser **.2** chastiser, appetizer, sanitizer, magnetizer, privatizer, advertiser, sensitizer, complementizer, systematizer, proselytizer
.3 gormandizer, merchandizer, standardizer, anodizer, methodizer, subsidizer, oxidizer, liquidizer, melodizer, aggrandizer **.4** catechizer
.5 atomizer, itemizer, victimizer, systemizer, minimizer, maximizer, compromiser, economizer **.6** Latinizer, mechanizer, ionizer, lionizer, scrutinizer, westernizer, modernizer, vulcanizer, organizer, womanizer, sermonizer, Germanizer, galvanizer, homogenizer, patronizer, synchronizer, immunizer, colonizer, recognizer **.7** philosophizer **.8** deviser, devisor, divisor, reviser, provisor, adviser, supervisor, improviser, televisor **.9** sympathizer **.10** incisor, criticizer, plasticizer, synthesizer, exerciser, hypothesizer **.11** franchiser **.12** energizer, mythologizer **.13** Budweiser® **.14** coryza, mycorrhiza, theorizer, vaporizer, temporizer, pasteurizer, rasterizer, tenderizer, memorizer, summarizer, mesmerizer, pulverizer, moisturizer, plagiarizer, terrorizer, polarizer, bowdlerizer, deodorizer, popularizer,

enterpriser **.15** Eliza, realizer, idealizer, monopolizer, stabilizer, verbalizer, mobilizer, immobilizer, catalyser, utilizer, fertilizer, totalizer, tantalizer, idolizer, vocalizer, normalizer, analyser, nationalizer, rationalizer, civilizer, breathalyser, Breathalyzer®, evangelizer, equalizer, tranquilizer, sterilizer, moralizer, liberalizer, neutralizer, generalizer, electrolyser, electrolyzer, nebulizer

17.25.13
mezuzah

17.25.14
boozer, snoozer, Sousa, Susa, chooser, bruiser, cruiser, user, loser, Marcuse, yakuza, anchusa, De Souza, mezuzah, medusa, peruser, battlecruiser, abuser, accuser, diffuser, refuser, infuser, misuser, Arethusa, lollapalooza

17.25.15
poser, Tozer, dozer, Xhosa, Moser, Rosa, proser, opposer, proposer, composer, disposer, exposer, transposer, Mendoza, bulldozer, angledozer, mucosa, rugosa, Formosa, mimosa, Somoza, Spinoza, anorexia nervosa, sub rosa, discloser, curiosa, ponderosa, retinitis pigmentosa

17.25.16
Shevardnadze

17.25.17
hamza

17.25.18
Windsor, Penza, cleanser, Panzer, stanza, kwanza, Lanza, bonzer, Monza, cadenza, credenza, Constanza, organza, Braganza, merganser, bonanza, influenza, extravaganza

17.25.19
colza, Demelza

17.26.1
Esher, retia, godetia, Rhodesia, Phoenicia, Venetia, magnesia®, Helvetia, Ossetia, maxixe, aubretia, montbretia, Lucretia, Silesia, alopecia, paramoecia

17.26.2
Fischer, fisher, fissure, wisher, Tricia, Trisha, Derbyshire, Laetitia, Leticia, Letitia, justiciar, Phoenicia, kingfisher, well-wisher, Patricia, Alicia, Galicia, militia

17.26.3
Asia, Dacia, geisha, facia, Brasher, Croatia, Hypatia, Cetacea, Crustacea, acacia, Sarmatia, Dalmatia, Ganesha, Laurasia, Horatia, ex gratia, Galatia, solatia, Appalachia, Australasia, osteomalacia

17.26.4
Cheshire, pressure, tressure, fresher, thresher, flesher, refresher, acupressure

17.26.5
Ayrshire

17.26.6
Asher, Ashur, pacha, pasha, masher, smasher, gnasher, Sacha, Sasha, hachure, quassia, rasher,

thrasher, lasher, clasher, flasher, slasher, earbasher, Natasha, gatecrasher, Falasha, haberdasher

17.26.7
pacha, Marcia, Marsha

17.26.8
cosher, josher, washer, quassia, whitewasher, dishwasher, bottlewasher

17.26.9
Porsche®, Portia, consortia

17.26.10
usher, gusher, rusher, Russia, Prussia, crusher, blusher, flusher, Belorussia

17.26.11
Elisha

17.26.12
pusher, penpusher

17.26.13
fuchsia, St Lucia, minutia

17.26.14
Udmurtia, Darbishire, furbisher, Frobisher, Britisher, Leicestershire, Worcestershire, Yiddisher, brandisher, Lancashire, skirmisher, finisher, planisher, varnisher, punisher, burnisher, furnisher, Radnorshire, Forfarshire, ravisher, vanquisher, languisher, perisher, nourisher, flourisher, polisher, publisher, replenisher, extinguisher, embellisher, abolisher, demolisher, establisher

17.26.15
Persia, Mercia, Quercia, sestertia, inertia

17.26.16
OSHA, kosher, Scotia, brochure, Boeotia, Vitosha, dystocia, Durocher, Cappadocia, Nova Scotia

17.26.17
Shropshire, Hampshire

17.26.18
Staffordshire, Hertfordshire, Bedfordshire, Oxfordshire, Herefordshire

17.26.19
flexure, Berkshire, moksha, Yorkshire, Berwickshire, jinricksha, Lanarkshire, Brecknockshire, Warwickshire

17.26.20
Nottinghamshire, Buckinghamshire

17.26.21
censure, amentia, dementia, differentia, vasa deferentia, tonsure, strontia, Wigtownshire, Lincolnshire, Northamptonshire, Huntingdonshire, Breconshire, Devonshire, Caernarvonshire

17.26.22
Monmouthshire

17.26.23
Inverness-shire

17.26.24
Cambridgeshire

17.26.25
Wilsher, welsher, Argyllshire

17.27.1
seizure, Rhodesia: (+ **3.15.1**)

17.27.2
Asia, azure, Laurasia, erasure, embrasure,
Australasia: (+ **3.15.3**)

17.27.3
measure, treasure, leisure, pleasure, remeasure,
outmeasure, admeasure, mismeasure,
displeasure, made-to-measure, countermeasure,
overmeasure

17.27.4
azure

17.27.5
Sharjah, arbitrager

17.27.6
Borgia

17.27.7
Hoosier

17.27.8
Persia

17.27.9
osier, crozier, closure, composure, exposure,
foreclosure, inclosure, enclosure, disclosure,
exclosure, discomposure, overexposure,
underexposure

17.28.1
teacher, Meacher, Nietzsche, feature,
reacher, preacher, creature,
screecher, leacher, bleacher, headteacher,
schoolteacher

17.28.2
pitcher, stitcher, ditcher, snitcher, hitcher,
twitcher, switcher, gyttja, vestiture

17.28.3
nunciature

17.28.4
nature, denature, magistrature, Appalachia

17.28.5
etcher, betcha, sketcher, fetcher,
kvetcher, breccia, stretcher, lecher, fletcher

17.28.6
patcher, stature, dacha, catcher, snatcher,
thatcher, Hatcher, kwacha, scratcher,
dispatcher, attacher, cowcatcher,
spycatcher, flycatcher, focaccia, ratcatcher,
dogcatcher, viscacha, vizcacha, backscratcher,
oystercatcher

17.28.7
Boucher, voucher

17.28.8
archer, starcher, marcher, kwacha, departure,
viscacha

17.28.9
botcher, gotcha, notcher, watcher, wotcha,
wotcher, top-notcher, firewatcher, birdwatcher,
doomwatcher

17.28.10
torture, scorcher, lorcha, debaucher,
self-torture

17.28.11
toucher, kuccha, scutcher, retoucher

17.28.12
kurdaitcha

17.28.13
butcher

17.28.14
moocher, smoocher, suture, future, Blücher,
cachucha

17.28.15
striature, aperture, divestiture, investiture,
candidature, expenditure, judicature,
explicature, implicature, ligature, premature,
amateur, shamateur, armature, crenature,
miniature, garniture, signature, furniture,
subminiature, progeniture, primogeniture,
countersignature, ultimogeniture, forfeiture,
confiture, discomfiture, coverture, couverture,
curvature, overture, decurvature, recurvature,
temperature, literature, portraiture, quadrature,
magistrature, filature, prelature, tablature,
musculature, entablature, nomenclature,
legislature

17.28.16
percher, nurture, searcher, lurcher, researcher,
guttapercha

17.28.17
poacher, cloture, reproacher, encroacher

17.28.18
scripture, capture, rapture, rupture, sculpture,
recapture, enrapture

17.28.19
Chibcha

17.28.20
picture, stricture, lecture, facture, fracture,
structure, tincture, cincture, puncture,
juncture, prefecture, conjecture, restructure,
substructure, conjuncture, disjuncture,
architecture, manufacture, superstructure,
ultrastructure, microstructure,
infrastructure, venepuncture, venipuncture,
acupuncture

17.28.21
simcha

17.28.22
Pincher, wincher, lyncher, clincher, flincher,
Flintshire, bencher, denture, venture,
wencher, quencher, trencher, rancher, slàinte,
launcher, jointure, puncher, cruncher, luncher,
affenpinscher, debenture, front-bencher,

backbencher, cross-bencher, indenture, adventure, peradventure, keypuncher, cowpuncher, calenture, Bonaventure, misadventure

17.28.23
tincture, cincture, puncture, juncture, conjuncture, disjuncture, venepuncture, venipuncture, acupuncture

17.28.24
vesture, gesture, pasture, posture, moisture, mixture, fixture, texture, divesture, depasture, imposture, immixture, commixture, admixture, prefixture, affixture, retexture, intermixture

17.28.25
Tánaiste

17.28.26
filcher, Wiltshire, belcher, squelcher, culture, multure, vulture, sepulture, subculture, apiculture, stirpiculture, viticulture, horticulture, counterculture, pomiculture, viniculture, monoculture, aviculture, silviculture, pisciculture, aquaculture, aquiculture, sericulture, floriculture, arboriculture, agriculture

17.29.1
besieger, procedure, supersedure, aquilegia, hemiplegia, paraplegia, tetraplegia, quadriplegia: (+ **3.19.1**)

17.29.2
Bridger, abridger

17.29.3
ager, pager, stager, gauger, major, wager, rampager, upstager, old-stager, engager, sergeant-major, town-major, teenager, golden-ager, dysphagia, Alsager, assuager, Ursa Major, Canis Major

17.29.4
edger, hedger, dredger, ledger, leger, pledger, pledgor, St Leger

17.29.5
badger, cadger

17.29.6
gouger

17.29.7
sparger, Sharjah, charger, raja, rajah, recharger, discharger, maharaja, enlarger, supercharger, turbocharger

17.29.8
todger, dodger, codger, Rodger, roger, lodger, loggia

17.29.9
ordure, Borgia, gorger, forger, Georgia

17.29.10
nudger, trudger, grudger, bludger, dole-bludger

17.29.11
Niger, Elijah, obliger

17.29.12
puja, thuja, Abuja, Perugia

17.29.13
dowager, voyager, potager, cottager, integer, vintager, frontager, bondager, packager, mortgagor, scrimmager, armiger, rummager, scrummager, tanager, manager, onager, ravager, salvager, presager, massager, Alsager, forager, pillager, villager, Scaliger, colleger, encourager, chronologer, mythologer, horologer, astrologer, philologer, under-manager, campanologer

17.29.14
urger, perjure, purger, Berger, scourger, merger, verdure, verger, demerger

17.29.15
Scrimgeour, Scrimger

17.29.16
.1 injure, ninja, ginger, whinger, winger, cringer, impinger, harbinger, wharfinger, infringer **.2** danger, manger, changer, ranger, stranger, Grainger, endanger, shapechanger, exchanger, arranger, hydrangea, bushranger, moneychanger, autochanger **.3** avenger, revenger **.4** ganja, grandeur, Njanja, phalanger, gametangia **.5** scrounger, lounger, sunlounger **.6** slàinte **.7** sponger, conjure, plunger, blunger, expunger **.8** scavenger, Kissinger, messenger, Schlesinger, passenger, Massinger, Slazenger, derringer, porringer, Salinger, challenger, Bolinger, Bollinger® **.9** Alger, Folger, soldier, myalgia, nostalgia, coxalgia, neuralgia, indulger

17.30
Brahe, Clogher, uh-huh, Fatiha, Fatihah, Kelleher, Gallagher, aloha

17.31.1
Chichewa, rewarewa

17.31.2
tawa, Hayakawa, Kanawa, Massawa, Ozawa, chihuahua, kawakawa, Tokugawa, Okinawa, Kurosawa

17.31.3
Iowa, Kiowa, Chippewa, Ottawa, Medawar, Te Kanawa

17.31.4
Ojibwa

17.31.5
fatwa

17.31.6
Griqua, aqua, Qwaqwa, subaqua, chautauqua, siliqua

17.31.7
Aconcagua, Managua, piragua, Interlingua

17.31.8
Quichua, Quechua

17.32.1
Pyrrha, mirror, sirrah, Indira

17.32.2
era, steerer, smearer, sneerer, Vera, Thera, Thira, sera, shearer, hearer, Hera, rearer, Lehrer, lira, lire, clearer, sclera, lempira, hetaera, monstera, rangatira, Madeira, Indira, chimera, O'Meara, Altamira, scorzonera, interferer, Elvira, Depo-Provera®, Cythera, Utsire, antisera, phylloxera, Megaera, pereira

17.32.3
eyra, capoeira

17.32.4
error, Berra, terra, terror, Ferrer, serra, sierra, aloe vera, Ystalyfera

17.32.5
airer, Éire, parer, Perak, sparer, bearer, tearer, starer, darer, carer, scarer, snarer, Sara, Sarah, sharer, wearer, squarer, swearer, Lehrer, Clara, Riviera, repairer, preparer, cupbearer, swordbearer, mace-bearer, torch-bearer, talebearer, pallbearer, ciguatera, caldera, O'Meara, habanera, seafarer, wayfarer, Rivera, primavera, Halmahera, pereira, Herrera, Demerara, cordillera, declarer, de Valera

17.32.6
para, Farrah, Farrar, jarrah

17.32.7
Tara, Cara, Nara, Varah, Sara, Zara, Lara, tiara, Honiara, capybara, Qattara, tuatara, solfatara, Bukhara, shikara, cascara, mascara, samskara, toxocara, caracara, Gemara, O'Mara, Tamara, Damara, samara, Samarra, Asmara, Connemara, McNamara, terramara, Glaramara, carbonara, marinara, Guevara, samsara, vihara, O'Hara, Sahara, Guadalajara, gurdwara, Timisoara, Carrara, Ferrara

17.32.8
orra, schnorrer, horror, Andorra, begorra, Gomorrah

17.32.9
genre

17.32.10
aura, pourer, spoorer, bora, borer, Torah, storer, Dora, Cora, corer, scorer, Maura, Nora, snorer, fora, Thora, soarer, sora, Zora, Zorah, whorer, roarer, Euro-, Laura, pleura, flora, Vlorë, Kia-Ora® **.1** abhorrer, tamboura, bombora, Bora-Bora **.2** Atora®, restorer **.3** adorer, Theodora, fedora, rhodora, Eudora, Andorra, Pandora, Contadora, Isadora, maquilladora **.4** pakora **.5** angora, Stara Zagora **.6** Camorra, remora **.7** Leonora, menorah, Sonora, Lenora, ignorer, Eleonora, labia minora **.8** Masorah **.9** ski-jorer, labia majora **.10** aurora, Tuscarora **.11** signora, señora **.12** explorer, grandiflora

17.32.11
Moira

17.32.12
borough, burgh, Burra, currach, thorough, surra, demurrer, kookaburra, Fraserburgh

17.32.13
Ira, Pyrah, Beira, tayra, Tyrer, Mira, Myra, naira, Lyra, hetaira, almirah, palmyra, Deianira, Elvira, Corcyra, CoSIRA, Ancyra, Fujairah, Hegira, spirogyra

17.32.14
.1 scourer, flowerer, devourer **.2** firer, hirer, wirer, inspirer, retirer, admirer, acquirer, requirer, inquirer, enquirer **.3** spoorer, tourer, Dürer, durra, sura, surah, surra, dura, Jura, juror, curer, führer, pleura, tempura, tamboura, Bujumbura, assurer, insurer, ensurer, caesura, nonjuror, Estremadura, datura, scordatura, tessitura, fioritura, coloratura, Angostura, villeggiatura, appoggiatura, acciaccatura, imprimatura, nomenklatura, Bonaventura, Madura, procurer, Cuticura®, camera obscura, figura, Thysanura, Arafura, bravura **.4** Tripura, paperer, caperer, vaporer, vapourer, opera, corpora, whimperer, emperor, tempera, temperer, tempora, Klemperer, pamperer, Tampere, tamperer, whisperer, primipara, nullipara, Diaspora: (+ **17.32.17**) **.5** labara, Deborah, jabberer, laborer, labourer, Barbara, Scarborough, yarborough, blubberer, Newborough, Newburgh, Peterborough, Fraserburgh, Berbera, gerbera, Crowborough, Sedburgh, Jedburgh, Aldeburgh, Shuckburgh, Flamborough, Sumburgh, lumberer, slumberer, rememberer, Digambara, Queenborough, Spenborough, Canberra, Farnborough, Attenborough, Edinburgh, Wellingborough, Loughborough, Conisbrough, Vosburgh, Mexborough, Roxburgh, Conisborough, Risborough, Happisburgh, Knaresborough, Gainsborough, Hillsborough, Middlesbrough, Marlboro, Marlborough, Pulborough, Musselburgh: (+ **17.32.18**) **.6** titterer, witterer, twitterer, caterer, letterer, batterer, scatterer, smatterer, natterer, shatterer, chatterer, flatterer, barterer, charterer, potterer, putterer, totterer, waterer, slaughterer, loiterer, utterer, sputterer, stutterer, mutterer, splutterer, flutterer, fruiterer, pewterer, Diptera, Hemiptera, Dermaptera, Trichoptera, Homoptera, Orthoptera, Neuroptera, Dictyoptera, Coleoptera, Lepidoptera, Hymenoptera, Thysanoptera, Heteroptera, Ephemeroptera, winterer, enterer, banterer, saunterer, pesterer, plasterer, fosterer, roisterer, musterer, monstera, bolsterer, upholsterer, filibusterer, shelterer, palterer, falterer, poulterer, adulterer: (+ **17.32.19**) **.7** dodderer, orderer, borderer, murderer, verderer, tenderer, renderer, flounderer, slanderer, wanderer, squanderer, launderer, thunderer, wonderer, plunderer, blunderer, Kundera, solderer, caldera, embroiderer, self-murderer, philanderer, gerrymanderer: (+ **17.32.20**) **.8** bickerer, dickerer, lacquerer, heuchera, tinkerer, Ankara, hankerer, conqueror: (+ **17.32.21**) **.9** sniggerer, staggerer, swaggerer, lingerer, mandragora, malingerer: (+ **17.32.22**)

.10 femora, remora, stammerer, camera, hammerer, armourer, Marmara, woomera, kumara, murmurer, ephemera, in camera, cinecamera, telecamera: (+ **17.32.23**) **.11** genera, gunnera, subgenera: (+ **17.32.24**) **.12** chafferer, offerer, offeror, sufferer, amphora, pilferer, Rotifera, cataphora, anaphora, exophera: (+ **17.32.25**) **.13** shiverer, favourer, waverer, Devereux, hoverer, coverer, Carnivora, deliverer, Mauleverer, recoverer, discoverer, manoeuvrer, rediscoverer: (+ **17.32.26**) **.14** cithara, plethora **.15** ditherer, gatherer, blatherer, furtherer **.16** viscera, tessera, sorcerer, lonicera, chelicera, phylloxera, phyloxera **.17** venturer, adventurer **.18** treasurer, usurer, injurer, conjuror, Lemesurier **.19** torturer, nurturer, capturer, lecturer, gesturer, posturer, manufacturer **.20** perjurer, conjurer **.21** purpura **.22** cellarer, cholera

17.32.15
öre, stirrer, demurrer, deferrer, referrer, transferor, transferrer

17.32.16
Torah, sora, haphtorah

17.32.17
Ypres, chypre, Capra, copra, supra, Oprah, amour propre: (+ **17.32.14**(.4))

17.32.18
zebra, Libra, terebra, cerebra, vers libre, Aqua Libra®, labra, Debra, cause célèbre, Aldabra, abracadabra, sabra, macabre, danse macabre, candelabra, cobra, Rubbra, lubra, vertebra, algebra, Coimbra, umbra, Alhambra, penumbra, disjecta membra, Vanbrugh: (+ **17.32.14**(.5))

17.32.19
.1 triquetra **.2** fête champêtre, petit-maître **.3** Petra, tetra, belles-lettres, raison d'être **.4** Tatra, Sartre, Chartres, Cleopatra, Montmartre, Sumatra, Sinatra **.5** Le Nôtre **.6** sutra, Brahmaputra, bumiputra, Kama Sutra **.7** elytra, et cetera **.8** Socotra **.9** spectra, plectra, Electra **.10** Sintra, centra, antra, tantra, mantra, yantra, contra, dicentra, per contra, Iran-Contra **.11** sistra, astra, Shastra, rostra, lustra, extra, palaestra, orchestra, fenestra, sequestra, palestra, aspidistra, Clytemnestra, Cosa Nostra, Zarathustra **.12** Maharashtra **.13** ultra: (+ **17.32.14**(.6))

17.32.20
cathedra, trihedra, ex cathedra, polyhedra, rhombohedra, heptahedra, octahedra, pentahedra, decahedra, hexahedra, tetrahedra, icosidodecahedra, Sidra, clepsydra, Deirdre, Phaedra, ephedra, entendre, Audra, hydra, Sudra, Indra, Sandra, Zandra, tundra, Felindre, Cassandra, pachysandra, Alexandra, double entendre: (+ **17.32.14**(.7))

17.32.21
sacra, chakra, okra, buckra, Lycra®, fulcra, fiacre, simulacra: (+ **17.32.14**(.8))

17.32.22
Agra, Ingres, bhangra, pellagra, Niagara, Viagra, podagra, chaulmoogra, Tanagra, Porto Alegre: (+ **17.32.14**(.9))

17.32.23
CAMRA: (+ **17.32.14**(.10))

17.32.24
genre, UNNRA, UNRRA, UNRWA: (+ **17.32.14**(.11))

17.32.25
tephra, Aphra, infra, Biafra: (+ **17.32.14**(.12))

17.32.26
Sèvres, Devereux, chèvre, Louvre, oeuvre, Le Havre, chef-d'œuvre, savoir vivre, joie de vivre: (+ **17.32.14**(.13))

17.32.27
urethra, Blencathra

17.32.28
Ezra, Basra

17.32.29
Hijra

17.33.1
tortilla, toquilla, ouguiya, keffiyeh, camarilla, cuadrilla, seguidilla

17.33.2
ayah, De Falla

17.33.3
thuja, hallelujah

17.33.4
bowyer

17.33.5
Libya

17.33.6
stature, Katya, courtier

17.33.7
ordure, verdure

17.33.8
Lockyer, Antakya

17.33.9
Kenya, Monsignor, Tigrinya, polynya, Peña, mania, seigneur, Mantegna, Montagna, malagueña, tenure, Sardegna, Spanier, Vanya, Britannia, lasagne, doña, Sonia, bologna, bunya, gunyah, chikungunya, vicuña, Tristan da Cunha, La Coruña, Bastogne

17.33.10
saviour, nervure, behaviour, misbehaviour

17.33.11
ossia, Vaisya, tonsure

17.33.12
azure, Micronesia, Melanesia, Polynesia

17.33.13
failure, polje, Colyer, cuadrilla, derailleur, seguidilla, manzanilla, banderilla

17.34.1
peeler, spieler, stealer, stela, stelar, dealer, chela, Keeler, Keillor, Miele, kneeler, feeler, vela, velar, Vila, sealer, Schiele, sheila, Shelagh, healer, HeLa, wheeler, squealer, reeler, Leila, appealer, candela, wheeler-dealer, tequila, Philomela, annealer, revealer, labiovelar, concealer, Monongahela, freewheeler, three-wheeler, two-wheeler, Coahuila, sequela, stern-wheeler

17.34.2
pillar, spiller, tiller, killer, Millar, miller, filler, villa, thiller, Cilla, psylla, scilla, siller, zillah, Schiller, chiller, Hiller, Willa, willer, swiller, driller, griller, thriller **.1** papilla, caterpillar **.2** scintilla, Attila, flotilla, mantilla, potentilla, distiller, instiller, pulsatilla **.3** Padilla, cedilla, sapodilla, sabadilla, granadilla, serradilla **.4** orchilla, weedkiller, painkiller, ladykiller **.5** megillah **.6** mamilla, Camilla **.7** manila, manilla, vanilla, manzanilla **.8** fulfiller, Polyfilla® **.9** bacillar, Priscilla, Drusilla, vexilla, axilla, maxilla **.10** Godzilla **.11** chinchilla **.12** aspergilla **.13** downhiller **.14** Aquila, Anguilla **.15** guerrilla, zorilla, spirilla, barilla, gorilla, fibrillar, pralltriller, sarsaparilla, cascarilla, camarilla

17.34.3
viola, bronchiolar, alveolar, nucleolar

17.34.4
alar, bailer, bailor, baler, tailor, Taylor, scalar, scaler, gala, galla, mailer, malar, nailer, Naylor, sailer, sailor, Scheele, chela, gaoler, jailer, hailer, wailer, whaler, kwela, railer, trailer, Leila, retailer, Adela, Akela, Michaela, blackmailer, greenmailer, Pharsala, wassailer, abseiler, boardsailer, wholesaler, parasailer, loudhailer, inhaler, vihuela, bewailer, Benguela, zarzuela, Venezuela, derailleur, karela, semitrailer, shillelagh

17.34.5
Ella, speller, Bella, teller, Stella, stellar, Della, Keller, Mellor, smeller, Kneller, fellah, feller, fellow, cellar, Sellar, seller, Heller, Weller, dweller, queller, paella, Viyella®, Louella, Floella, Ben Bella, Daniela, klebsiella **.1** Capella, repeller, propeller, impeller, dispeller, expeller, a cappella, alla cappella **.2** rubella, cribella, glabella, glabellar, umbellar, Annabella, Isabella, cerebella, cerebellar, Arabella, Clarabella **.3** foreteller, scutella, patella, patellar, Estella, taleteller, storyteller, panatella, tarantella, interstellar, fenestella, Santiago de Compostela **.4** Clydella, predella, Abdela, candela, Mandela, mortadella, serradella **.5** McKellar, Ratskeller, rathskeller **.6** shigella **.7** lamella, lamellar **.8** prunella, Fenella, quinella, fustanella, soldanella, salmonella, fraxinella, legionella, citronella, Petronella, villanella **.9** Rockefeller **.10** novella, favela **.11** reseller, Marcella, ocellar, best-seller, saltcellar, bookseller, Kinsella, vorticella, varicella

.12 rosella **.13** Nigella, flagella, flagellar **.14** indweller, sequela, Benguela **.15** corella, karela, chlorella, umbrella, Cinderella, mozzarella

17.34.6
Allah, pallor, Bala, calla, calor, Galla, valour, Haller, Whyalla, inshallah, Valhalla, Caracalla

17.34.7
scowler, fowler, howler, prowler, growler, wildfowler

17.34.8
parlor, parlour, Bala, tala, thaler, Carla, gala, galla, Mahler, snarler, challah, háler, nyala, Douala, koala, La Scala, impala, Kampala, kabbala, tambala, Mergenthaler, Emmentaler, akala, cicala, Tlaxcala, cigala, Lingala, Guatemala, Transvaaler, Marsala, Pharsala, Musala, masala, Uppsala, garam masala, Sinhala, Gujranwala, inyala

17.34.9
dollar, dolour, choler, collar, scholar, holla, holler, wallah, Waller, squalor, Zwolle, troller, loller, Hezbollah, ayatollah, extoller, white-collar, corolla, Eurodollar, petrodollar, punkah-wallah

17.34.10
Paula, bawler, caller, mauler, faller, hauler, sprawler, brawler, trawler, drawler, crawler, Lawler, Lawlor, spitballer, footballer, forestaller, installer, mandorla, stonewaller, nightcrawler

17.34.11
Euler, oiler, spoiler, boiler, toiler, broiler, despoiler, potboiler

17.34.12
bulla, colour, culler, sculler, Gullah, mullah, muller, nullah, Sulla, cruller, medulla, Abdullah, recolour, bicolour, tricolour, discolour, multicolour, unicolour, watercolour, technicolour, nulla-nulla

17.34.13
Isla, tiler, Tyler, styler, Schuyler, miler, smiler, filer, phyla, hila, stockpiler, compiler, strobila, freestyler, beguiler, defiler, profiler, subphyla, reviler, abseiler, reconciler, Rottweiler, Delilah

17.34.14
pula, puller, bulla, Buller, mullah, Müller, fuller, Sulla, Wooler, petiolar, wirepuller, ampulla, Abdullah, Niemöller, Weissmuller

17.34.15
Thule, tooler, Tula, cooler, moolah, Foula, sooler, Shula, jeweler, jeweller, hula, ruler, Euler, Beulah, gular, pre-schooler, Petula, torula, scheduler, Tallulah, intercooler, hula-hula

17.34.16
.1 tropaeola, rubeola, foveola, roseola, roseolar, aureola, areola, areolar **.2** dialler, viola, variola, variolar **.3** vacuolar **.4** dueller, jeweller **.5** Coppola, propyla, pupillar, cupola, gospeller

.6 labeller, Cabbala, libeller, falbala, parabola, hyperbola: (+ **17.34.20**) **.7** victualler, tutelar, hosteller, hospitaller, teetotaller, epistoler, youth hosteller, Knight Hospitaller, Perissodactyla: (+ **17.34.21**) **.8** Adela, modeller, udaller, yodeller, Magdala, amygdala, candela, mandala, condylar, gondola, oropendola: (+ **17.34.22**) **.9** Nicola, tricolor, tricolour, snorkeller, rucola, Agricola, Dallapiccola: (+ **17.34.23**) **.10** argala, rugola, pergola: (+ **17.34.24**) **.11** similar, Pamela, dissimilar, enameller, verisimilar: (+ **17.34.25**) **.12** Ranelagh, tunneller, signaller **.13** Wulfila, drosophila, gypsophila: (+ **17.34.26**) **.14** sniveller, driveller, reveller, leveller, Ávila, caviller, traveller, marveller, groveller, shoveller **.15** bacillar, basilar, wassailer, cypsela, Kinsella, penciller, canceller, chancellor, councillor, counsellor, tonsillar: (+ **17.34.27**) **.16** teaseler, chiseller, methuselah: (+ **17.34.28**) **.17** Angela **.18** titular, spatula, bachelor, fistula, fistular, Vistula, blastula, pustular, capitula, capitular, tarantula **.19** scheduler, radula, radular, flagellar, modular, nodular, glandular, calendula **.20** Kerala, caroller, quarreler, quarreller, fibrillar, gastrula **.21.1** stipular, papula, papular, scapula, scapular, popular, copula, copular, scopula, serpula, discipular, unpopular, fibula, fibular, nebula, nebular, tabula, tabular, lobular, globular, tubular, vestibular, mandibular, preambular, infundibular, acetabula, tintinnabula, tintinnabular, incunabula, incunabular, interlobular **.21.2** spicular, vehicular, orbicular, corbicula, articular, vorticular, cuticular, particular, reticula, reticular, lenticular, testicular, interarticular, diverticula, diverticular, subcuticular, pedicular, radicular, perpendicular, vermicular, canicular, funicular, adminicular, clavicular, navicular, acicula, acicular, fascicular, versicular, vesicular, auricula, auricular, curricula, curricular, utricular, ventricular, extracurricular, follicular, pellicular, specula, specular, secular, trabecula, trabecular, Benbecula, vallecula, vallecular, molecular, intermolecular, monomolecular, intramolecular, macromolecular, macula, macular, facula, facular, saccular, Dracula, piacular, spectacular, tentacular, tenacula, vernacular, oracular, spiracula, spiracular, vibracula, vibracular, unspectacular, supernacular, ocular, jocular, locular, preocular, subocular, inocula, monocular, binocular, trilocular, unilocular, circular, opercula, opercular, tubercular, semicircular, vincula, carbuncular, peduncular, avuncular, caruncular, furuncular, vascula, vascular, oscula, oscular, floscular, muscular, corpuscular, crepuscular, minuscular, majuscular, cardiovascular, intramuscular, neuromuscular, cerebrovascular, animalcular **.21.3** tegular, regular, vugular, jugular, cingula, singular, angular, ungula, Caligula, irregular, coagula, arugula, triangular, rectangular, multangular, sexangular,

quadrangular, equiangular **.21.4** primula, formula, nummular, tumular, plumular, fraenula, pinnular, frenula, annular, cannula, granular, lunula, campanula, penannular, scrofula, infula, ovular, uvula, uvular, valvular, Ursula, capsular, insular, consular, peninsula, peninsular, proconsular, ferula, spherular, sporular, torula, morula, glomerular, pillular, stellular, cellular, acellular, multicellular, intercellular, unicellular, intracellular, extracellular

17.34.17
pearler, purler, curler, whirler, twirler, Ertebolle

17.34.18
polar, bola, bowler, tola, stola, coaler, cola, kola, molar, Nola, volar, sola, solar, Zola, roller, troller, stroller, scroller, Lola, viola, criolla, payola, Crayola®, Viola, rock and roller, rock 'n roller, Abiola, rubeola, bronchiolar, alveolar, roseola, roseolar, aureola, nucleolar, Hispaniola **.1** bipolar, dipolar, multipolar, unipolar, homopolar, heteropolar, circumpolar **.2** barbola, Ebola, tombola, carambola **.3** Tortola, extoller **.4** eidola, idola, mandola, Ndola **.5** Pepsi-Cola®, Coca-Cola®, Pensacola **.6** plugola, Angola **.7** premolar **.8** pianola®, granola, canola, Finola **.9** boffola **.10** consoler, lunisolar, circumsolar **.11** Gorgonzola **.12** cajoler **.13** potholer **.14** patroller, comptroller, Victrola®, controller, roadroller, logroller, steamroller, enroller, Motorola, Savonarola **.15** Vignola, scagliola

17.34.19
tippler, stippler, crippler, stapler, pepla, Kepler, grappler, poplar, Doppler, coupler, Templar, sampler, trampler, hexapla, Knight Templar, Knights Templar, exempla, exemplar

17.34.20
enfant terrible, kiblah, nibbler, quibbler, dribbler, scribbler, fabler, enabler, Puebla, Ebla, babbler, tabla, dabbler, gabbler, garbler, amende honorable, cobbler, gobbler, nobbler, hobbler, wobbler, squabbler, warbler, bubbler, doubler, troubler, burbler, trembler, ambler, gambler, rambler, scrambler, bumbler, tumbler, stumbler, mumbler, fumbler, rumbler, grumbler, assembler, dissembler, resembler, knee-trembler, descrambler, unscrambler: (+ **17.34.16(.6)**)

17.34.21
Mitla, Hitler, littler, Fetlar, fettler, settler, settlor, battler, tatler, tattler, rattler, prattler, startler, bottler, throttler, butler, cutler, sutler, tootler, antler, Koestler, belittler, dismantler: (+ **17.34.16(.7)**)

17.34.22
Fidler, Fiedler, wheedler, piddler, tiddler, diddler, twiddler, riddler, ladler, peddler, pedlar, meddler, medlar, Adler, paddler, saddler, Sadler, straddler, Bowdler, toddler, waddler, dawdler, puddler, muddler, idler, doodler, curdler,

hurdler, yodeller, kindler, swindler, Ländler, chandler, handler, fondler, bundler: (+ **17.34.16**(.8))

17.34.23
pickler, tickler, stickler, trickler, heckler, Hekla, cackler, sparkler, buckler, suckler, chuckler, truckler, circler, winkler, twinkler, sprinkler, swashbuckler, recycler, chronicler, bicycler, fin de siècle, tackler: (+ **17.34.16**(.9))

17.34.24
beagler, Ziegler, giggler, niggler, sigla, wiggler, wriggler, kegler, haggler, straggler, smuggler, juggler, struggler, bugler, burglar, gurgler, ogler, mingler, Swingler, angler, dangler, mangler, wangler, wrangler, strangler, bungler, finagler: (+ **17.34.16**(.10))

17.34.25
Simla, Himmler, Daimler®: (+ **17.34.16**(.11))

17.34.26
piffler, sniffler, whiffler, baffler, waffler, muffler, snuffler, shuffler, stifler, trifler: (+ **17.34.16**(.13))

17.34.27
whistler, tesla, Kessler, wrestler, hostler, Osler, ostler, hustler, rustler, Geissler, Koestler, Spätzle: (+ **17.34.16**(.15))

17.34.28
sizzler, Rizla®, grizzler, dazzler, puzzler, guzzler, muzzler, Chrysler®, Kreisler, embezzler, bamboozler, foozler: (+ **17.34.16**(.16))

17.34.29
ashlar, acushla

18
er, err, Ur, per, purr, spur, birr, bur, burr, stir, cur, Kerr, skirr, murre, myrrh, knur, knurr, fir, fur, sir, Sher, shirr, jeu, chirr, churr, her, were, whir, whirr, 'twere, year, lur, blur, Fleur, slur, Shloer®, à deux, vieux jeu, tant mieux, tirailleur, sauve qui peut, pas de deux, cri de coeur, cris de coeur, faute de mieux, cordon-bleu, au sérieux, affaire de cœur, affaires de cœur, au grand sérieux

18.1
hotspur, larkspur

18.2
clotbur, cocklebur, butterbur

18.3
auteur, hauteur, deter, inter, reinter, chanteur, disinter, pisteur, Pasteur, astir, bestir, rapporteur, saboteur, amateur, shamateur, littérateur, restaurateur, raconteur, restauranteur, répétiteur, provocateur, agent provocateur

18.4
pudeur, frondeur, frondeurs

18.5
occur, co-occur, recur, incur, concur

18.6
blagueur, langur, longueur, Chandigarh, de rigueur

18.7
demur

18.8
flâneur, proneur, souteneur, infopreneur, entrepreneur, intrapreneur

18.9
Darfur, coiffeur, defer, refer, prefer, infer, confer, transfer, pot-au-feu, underfur

18.10
aver, bon viveur

18.11
masseur, chasseur, farceur, douceur, danseur, régisseur, connoisseur, Vavasseur

18.12
diseur, poseur

18.13
accoucheur

18.14
force majeure, voyageur, arbitrageur

18.15
sabreur, Montreux

18.16
voyeur, prie-dieu, prie-dieux, Goodyear, liqueur, seigneur, monsieur, milieu, milieux, Richelieu, yesteryear, Montesquieu, Monseigneur, juste milieu, droit de seigneur

18.17
jongleur, siffleur, bateleur

19
o, oh, owe, po, Poe, beau, beaux, bo, Bow, bow, toe, tow, stow, Stowe, doe, doh, dough, Co., Coe, go, mho, mo, Mohs, mot, mow, schmo, schmoe, know, no, Noh, snow, Faux, foe, Vaux, voe, tho', though, sault, sew, so, soh, sow, dzho, dzo, zho, show, jo, Joe, Zhou, ho, hoe, whoa, wo, woe, rho, roe, row, Rowe, pro, bro, trow, strow, crow, Crowe, grow, fro, froe, frow, throe, throw, yo, lo, Loew, Loewe, low, blow, glow, Flo, floe, flow, sloe, slow, PO, CO, c/o, kayo, KO, maillot, Rouault, Li Po, Li Bo, right-ho, righto, goodo, good-oh, whacko, MO, bon mot, bons mots, UFO, USO, PRO, per pro., de trop, skid row, Joe Blow, cheerio, TKO, Li T'ai Po, saddle bow, Fertö Tó, tae kwon do, comme il faut, Sullom Voe, WHO, quid pro quo, status quo, Scapa Flow, Fernando Póo, galanty show, eeny meeny miny mo

19.1
Kehoe, Keogh, Milhaud, Theo, Rio, brio, trio, Krio, Leo, Clio, Castillo, con brio

19.2
Deo, Mayo, rodeo, cacao, paseo, cicisbeo, Bulawayo, Galileo, Montevideo, Alfa Rome®, Bartolomeo

19.3
Tao, Dão, cacao

19.4
boyo, arroyo

19.5
Io, bio, ngaio, thio, Clio, Ohio, Cetshwayo

19.6
in vacuo, continuo, moto perpetuo

19.7
duo, Luo

19.8
Ipoh, peep-bo, cheapo, repo, gippo, hippo, pepo, depot, Grępo, capo, Taupo, SWAPO, oppo, topo, troppo, typo, hypo, WIPO, hoopoe, Vopo, tempo, compo, Expo, cachepot, Aleppo, Gestapo, da capo, kakapo, apropos, entrepôt, Limpopo, a tempo, up-tempo, genipapo, ma non troppo, malapropos

19.9
procès-verbaux

19.9.1
Ibo, cribo, grebo, placebo, gazebo, Essequibo

19.9.2
Strabo, lavabo

19.9.3
Abo, sabot, jabot

19.9.4
Gabo, Garbo, lavabo

19.9.5
yobbo

19.9.6
sorbo, theorbo

19.9.7
Maracaibo

19.9.8
bubo

19.9.9
Mirabeau, Malabo, angwantibo

19.9.10
turbo

19.9.11
oboe, hobo, lobo

19.9.12
peep-bo

19.9.13
Igbo, fog-bow

19.9.14
bimbo, limbo, ambo, Tambo, mambo, sambo, Rambo, Rimbaud, crambo, flambeau, combo, umbo, dumbo, gumbo, jumbo, akimbo, Ovambo, Negombo, Colombo, nelumbo, mumbo-jumbo

19.9.15
rainbow, sunbow

19.9.16
longbow

19.9.17
crossbow, oxbow

19.9.18
bilbo, elbow

19.10
bateau, plateau, tic-tac-toe

19.10.1
Ito, Peto, Tito, Quito, veto, SEATO, Lobito, bandito, coquito, mosquito, Miskito, Benito, bonito, Veneto, magneto, sgraffito, graffito, burrito, Negrito, sanbenito, incognito, Esposito, Hirohito

19.10.2
ditto, pettitoe, Sillitoe

19.10.3
Ayto, Cato, NATO, JATO, Plato, potato

19.10.4
ghetto, stretto, zucchetto, fianchetto, larghetto, palmetto, cornetto, cavetto, terzetto, falsetto, Soweto, Loreto, libretto, Orvieto, stiletto, vaporetto, Tintoretto, amaretto, amoretto, lazaretto, allegretto, Canaletto

19.10.5
concerto

19.10.6
bateau, Catto, gateau, chateau, Chatto, plateau, anatto, sforzato, mulatto, gelato

19.10.7
Sarto, esparto, rubato, Ambato, marcato, Waikato, spiccato, staccato, legato, sfumato, tomato, annatto, vibrato, castrato, agitato, pizzicato, obbligato, ostinato, moderato, inamorato

19.10.8
Otto, potto, motto, Giotto, Watteau, grotto, lotto, blotto, risotto

19.10.9
auto, Porto, quarto, Oporto

19.10.10
putto, Bhutto

19.10.11
Bhutto, Pluto, Maputo, Basuto, prosciutto, tenuto, ritenuto, sostenuto

19.10.12
undertow, cogito, Erato, aerotow, paletot

19.10.13
concerto

19.10.14
toto, koto, photo, Sotho, Soto, Kyoto, in toto, con moto, ex voto, Sesotho, Lesotho, aerotow, Yamamoto, Kumamoto, telephoto

19.10.15
tiptoe, crypto, Steptoe

19.10.16
recto, facto, Cocteau, perfecto, de facto, sensu stricto, ipso facto, ex post facto, in flagrante delicto

19.10.17
pinto, Minto®, Shinto, cento, Trento, lento, panto, canto, manteau, Tonto, pronto, pimento, memento, seicento, trecento, Sorrento, pimiento, bel canto, portmanteau, Otranto, Toronto, San Jacinto, portamento, pentimento, Sacramento, cinquecento, quattrocento, Esperanto, pronunciamento, divertimento, aggiornamento, Risorgimento

19.10.18
Shafto

19.10.19
Bisto®, Bristow, Plaistow, pesto, presto, Bairstow, gusto, Cousteau, bestow, Chepstow, Padstow, sexto, Callisto, Modesto, hey presto, impasto, Felixstowe, Walthamstow, Edwinstowe, fritto misto, manifesto, antipasto, capo tasto, Ariosto

19.10.20
Pashto

19.10.21
alto, molto, Sholto, mistletoe, rialto, contralto, Palo Alto, Trentino-Alto

19.11
Bardot, Bordeaux, do-si-do, bushido, dos-à-dos

19.11.1
Ido, speedo, Guido, Phaedo, credo, lido, torpedo, libido, albedo, Escondido, aikido, comedo, tuxedo, bushido, teredo, Toledo, desaparecido

19.11.2
kiddo, widow

19.11.3
weirdo

19.11.4
dado, Feydeau, credo, strappado, gambado, tornado, Laredo, Toledo, Oviedo, carbonado, bastinado

19.11.5
eddo, Edo, meadow

19.11.6
spado, shadow, foreshadow, eyeshadow, overshadow

19.11.7
Pardoe, Bardo, Prado, strappado, Le Bardo, gambado, pintado, tostado, Ricardo, Mikado, Delgado, Leonardo, Barnardo, stifado, bravado, cruzado, Dorado, avocado, renegado, carbonado, bastinado, muscovado, desperado, eldorado, Colorado, zapateado, aficionado, amontillado, incommunicado

19.11.8
gordo

19.11.9
dido, Fido, lido, Hokkaido

19.11.10
pseudo, judo, Trudeau, ludo, testudo, escudo

19.11.11
sourdough, comedo, tournedos, UNIDO

19.11.12
McMurdo

19.11.13
Odo, dodo, Komodo, Ferodo, Quasimodo

19.11.14
window, kendo, bandeau, Dando, Brando, tondo, condo, rondeau, rondo, fricandeau, Nintendo®, crescendo, stringendo, commando, glissando, scherzando, smorzando, sforzando, Orlando, calando, secondo, Belmondo, innuendo, decrescendo, rallentando, ritardando, San Fernando, diminuendo, accelerando, basso profondo

19.11.15
dildo, Faldo, Waldo, Essoldo

19.12
Akko, Foucault, Glencoe, Bamako

19.12.1
pekoe, Pico, picot, Biko, Ricoh, tricot, Graeco-, Tampico, matico, Gromyko, Puerto Rico

19.12.2
Vico, thicko, sicko, tricot, Stilicho

19.12.3
mako, shako, Waco, Draco, macaco, Iveco®

19.12.4
echo, Eco, Ekco, deco, dekko, gecko, secco, Graeco-, re-echo, pre-echo, art deco, pukeko, El Greco, fresco secco

19.12.5
tacho, taco, mako, shako, wacko, squacco, tobacco, Bamako

19.12.6
Arco, taco, mako, Monaco, Gran Chaco

19.12.7
socko, Rocco, Morocco, sirocco

19.12.8
bucko, stucco

19.12.9
Tycho, psycho, Graeco-

19.12.10
osso buco

19.12.11
basuco, pachuco, Pernambuco

19.12.12
portico, medico, zydeco, Amoco®, guanaco, Monaco, Mexico, Jericho, haricot, touraco, turaco, Jellicoe, calico, Pimlico, politico, simpatico, magnifico, Angelico

19.12.13
Burco, Turco

19.12.14
poco, coco, cocoa, moko, smoko, choko, loco, rococo, iroko, Orinoco

19.12.15
pinko, stinko, ginkgo, zinco, Tenko, Kenco, Franco, blanco, bronco, plonko, unco, bunco, junco, pachinko, flamenco, Lysenko, Yevtushenko, calamanco

19.12.16
Rothko

19.12.17
pisco, disco, Disko, cisco, Brisco, Briscoe, Tesco, fresco, Pascoe, Moscow, roscoe, Cuzco, finnesko, finneskoe, Nabisco®, San Francisco, Morisco, Ionesco, UNESCO, Enesco, Moresco, alfresco, fiasco, Tabasco, churrasco, Lambrusco, Kosciuszko

19.12.18
wilco, salchow, Acapulco

19.13
forgo, ago, stop-go, outgo, stop-and-go, touch-and-go, undergo, have-a-go

19.13.1
ego, Vigo, sego, amigo, Oswego, Abednego, superego

19.13.2
GIGO, chigoe

19.13.3
dago, sago, Jago, Diego, Tobago, lumbago, plumbago, imago, galago, San Diego, Winnebago, solidago, pichiciago, Tierra del Fuego, Trinidad and Tobago

19.13.4
Lego®, alter ego

19.13.5
Argo, argot, cargo, Margo, Fargo, largo, embargo, Otago, botargo, Chicago, escargot, imago, Zhivago, farrago, virago, Key Largo, Santiago, supercargo

19.13.6
doggo, logo

19.13.7
Sligo, lentigo, prurigo, impetigo, intertrigo, vitiligo

19.13.8
Yugo, Hugo, lanugo

19.13.9
vertigo, indigo, Bendigo, Inigo, Abednego, archipelago, Chagos Archipelago

19.13.10
ergo, Virgo

19.13.11
pogo, Togo, go-go, fogau, logo, agogo

19.13.12
pingo, bingo, dingo, jingo, gringo, lingo, tango, mango, Sango, quango, Lango, pongo, bongo,

Congo, congou, mongo, drongo, mungo, fungo, Mandingo, Domingo, flamingo, eryngo, olingo, Marengo, Cubango, contango, fandango, Durango, charango, camerlingo, Okavango, Niger-Congo, Santo Domingo

19.13.13
Lithgow, Linlithgow

19.13.14
Glasgow

19.13.15
Stilgoe, NALGO, Hidalgo

19.14
trumeau, barleymow

19.14.1
Nemo, primo, supremo, Frelimo

19.14.2
Nimmo, limo

19.14.3
haymow

19.14.4
demo, memo

19.14.5
Palermo

19.14.6
ammo, Gamow, Rameau

19.14.7
Rameau

19.14.8
commo, Homo

19.14.9
Pontormo, twenty-fourmo, sixty-fourmo

19.14.10
Dymo, Flymo®, Nanaimo

19.14.11
sumo, Profumo, thirty-two-mo

19.14.12
centimo, ultimo, Eskimo, Esquimau, Bergamo, dynamo, proximo, paramo, Alamo, chalumeau, Guantánamo, Geronimo, fortissimo, prestissimo, altissimo, pianissimo, duodecimo, generalissimo, octodecimo, sextodecimo

19.14.13
Palermo

19.14.14
Como, Nkomo, Homo, homo, duomo, promo, chromo, slo-mo, Sumitomo, majordomo, Ecce Homo

19.14.15
Whatmough

19.14.16
Dunmow, eighteenmo, sixteenmo

19.14.17
twelvemo

19.14.18
gizmo, Cosmo, machismo, verismo, gran turismo

19.14.19
Elmo, Malmö

19.15
foreknow, dunno, Brno

19.15.1
Eno®, beano, keno, kino, fino, vino, Zeno, chino, Gino, Reno, Greenough, leno, Filipino, bambino, albino, Latino, concertino, andantino, Valentino, Ladino, con sordino, Borodino, San Bernardino, maraschino, amino, Comino, palomino, sopranino, Parmigianino, Trevino, Sansovino, Orsino, casino, campesino, Monte Cassino, Pacino, Ticino, cappuccino, Torino, Marino, merino, Moreno, neutrino, peperino, pecorino, San Marino, Navarino, Borsalino®

19.15.2
minnow, winnow

19.15.3
volcano, Moreno, ripieno

19.15.4
tenno, steno, Renault®, Meiji Tenno

19.15.5
Pernod®

19.15.6
Mano, piano, cyano, player-piano, Altiplano, forte-piano

19.15.7
Arno, Carnot, Kano, Karno, guano, piano, llano, Sukarno, meccano, Chicano, Locarno, Lugano, Romano, Cinzano®, Bolzano, Pisano, Marrano, soprano, poblano, Marciano, oregano, Verrazano, Parmigiano, Capistrano, forte-piano, portolano, Altiplano, boliviano, siciliano, mezzo soprano

19.15.8
tonneau, mono, phono

19.15.9
porno, Livorno, Mezzogiorno

19.15.10
Sino-, wino, rhino, lino, amino

19.15.11
uno, Gounod, Juneau, Juno, Bruno, UNO

19.15.12
cyano, pompano, Gobineau, Martineau, Pocono, Huguenot, amino, domino, Romano, Molyneaux, oregano, avgolemono

19.15.13
Pernod®, Brno, Sterno®, Furneaux, journo, inferno, Salerno, Mebyon Kernow

19.15.14
Mono, no-no, phono, cui bono, kimono, kakemono, Odo-Ro-No

19.15.15
Grodno, Llandudno

19.15.16
techno

19.15.17
Fresno

19.16
FIFO, LIFO, Biffo, Sappho, Yafo, boffo, buffo, Truffaut, UFO, Defoe, nympho, info, Castel Gandolfo

19.17
vivo, Rievaulx, dévot, arvo, bravo, servo, Jervaulx, Provo, zemstvo, Wenvoe, galvo, salvo, Volvo®, in vivo, relievo, octavo, rilievo, centavo, art nouveau, de nouveau, Kosovo, ab ovo, de novo, Denovo, Sarajevo, Porto Novo, alto-relievo, basso-relievo, mezzorilievo, multum in parvo, Beaujolais Nouveau, Antananarivo

19.18
metho, litho, Otho, Clotho, Bolitho

19.19
although

19.20
Marceau, so-so, undersow, oversew

19.20.1
Tissot

19.20.2
peso, say-so

19.20.3
Esso®, gesso, espresso

19.20.4
basso, Tasso, Brasso®, lasso, Picasso, Sargasso, Burkina Faso

19.20.5
Brasso®, Picasso

19.20.6
mosso, Mato Grosso, concerto grosso

19.20.7
torso

19.20.8
Russo

19.20.9
whoso, Rousseau, trousseau, Caruso, Robinson Crusoe

19.20.10
Curaçao, curassow

19.20.11
verso, Thurso

19.20.12
so-so, maestoso, mafioso, arioso, virtuoso, amoroso, oloroso, doloroso, capriccioso

19.20.13
dipso, calypso, lhasa apso

19.20.14
schizo, mezzo, scherzo, matzo, fatso, terrazzo, intermezzo, paparazzo

19.20.15
Paxo®, Saxo, Glaxo, Oxo

19.20.16
ponceau, so-and-so, Colenso, Alfonso, Clarenceux, in extenso

19.20.17
Silsoe, Kelso, also

19.21
whizzo, ouzo, muso, Clouzot, bozo, Gozo, Bonzo, gonzo, mestizo, diazo, proviso, Caruso, rebozo, maestoso, corozo, Lorenzo, Colenso, garbanzo, Alfonso, Alonzo, Chimborazo, Valparaiso, mafioso, arioso, virtuoso, doloroso

19.22
Saisho, basho, foreshow, no-show, peepshow, chat show, sideshow, roadshow, dumbshow, Sancho, rancho, poncho, quizshow, raree-show, Horatio, moustachio

19.23
Peugeot®, Zhengzhou

19.24
macho, nacho, gaucho, Groucho, chocho, Sancho, rancho, poncho, honcho, pasticcio, gazpacho, quebracho, Ayacucho

19.25
Gorgio, Xuzhou, Tojo, dojo, banjo

19.26
heigh-ho, Heyhoe, Tahoe, Tajo, oho, boho, coho, Moho, Soho, ho-ho, yo-ho, right-ho, smoke-ho, Greenhough, Aynho, Wivenhoe, Ivanhoe, Hwang-Ho, gung-ho, heave-ho, Ferneyhough, tally-ho, Idaho, tuckahoe, Donohoe, Navajo, yo-ho-ho, yo-heave-ho, Arapaho

19.27
Miró, Perrault, Thoreau, Perot, Monroe, Munro, Heathrow, bordereau

19.27.1
Pierrot, Nero, zero, gyro, hero, Shapiro, Pinero, De Niro, sub-zero, Herero, Trocadero, anti-hero, superhero, Rio de Janeiro

19.27.2
Perrault, kero, Meroe, serow, Polperro

19.27.3
aero, faro, Faroe, pharaoh, pampero, vaquero, Romero, llanero, Pinero, dinero, cruzeiro, ranchero, Guerrero, Herero, torero, sombrero, potrero, bolero, forastero, Trocadero, caballero, Lilliburlero

19.27.4
arrow, sparrow, barrow, taro, tarot, Darrow, marrow, narrow, farrow, Varro, Jarrow, harrow, yarrow, wheelbarrow, Nancarrow, Tupamaro

19.27.5
Faro, charro, Poirot, Nabarro, Pissarro, Pizarro, saguaro, Tupamaro, Cannizzaro, Kilimanjaro

19.27.6
borrow, Corot, morrow, sorrow, tomorrow

19.27.7
Moro, Thoreau, euro, bureau, Sapporo, Mindoro, enduro, Río de Oro, Politburo

19.27.8
burro, Burrough, burrow, Murrow, furrow

19.27.9
pyro, biro®, tyro, Cairo, chi-rho, giro, gyro, Clyro, autogiro

19.27.10
burro

19.27.11
Douro, Truro, euro, bureau, bureaux, enduro, Oruro, gaspereau, Prospero, hetero, Diderot, Figaro, vigoro, zingaro, Comoro, Jivaro, Devereux, Clitheroe, Prothero, Protheroe, Cicero, guacharo, bolero, chiaroscuro, Ishiguro, Politburo, in utero

19.27.12
ro-ro

19.27.13
repro, appro, impro, sanpro, Aspro®, Prospero

19.27.14
Ebro, gabbro, fibro, Hambro

19.27.15
vitro, metro, hetero, retro, Quattro, LAUTRO, nitro, Sutro, note-row, intro, Cointreau, bistro, Castro, Austro-, maestro, in vitro, in utero, electro, cilantro

19.27.16
Pedro, hydro, Woodrow, windrow, UNDRO, Avogadro

19.27.17
scarecrow, macro, NACRO, micro, mucro, cockcrow, synchro, escrow, velcro, Yamoussoukro

19.27.18
Negro, regrow, aggro, outgrow, Babygro®, allegro, overgrow, Montenegro, Petulengro

19.27.19
windrow, Lonrho®, tone-row, McEnroe

19.27.20
Afro, to-and-fro

19.27.21
Jethro, upthrow, downthrow, overthrow

19.27.22
hedgerow

19.28
Milhaud, noyau, noyaux, yo-yo®, bagnio, Sanyo®, Castillo, caudillo, cursillo, Trujillo, El Niño, dal segno, verdelho, jalapeño, tomatillo

19.29
hello, Boileau, rouleau, alow, below, Fanagalo

19.29.1
kilo, filo, Hilo

19.29.2
pillow, billow, Gillow, willow, Brillo®, caudillo, Murillo, Utrillo, Negrillo, tomatillo, peccadillo, armadillo, cigarillo, Amarillo, tamarillo

19.29.3
halo

19.29.4
bellow, mellow, felloe, fellow, cello, jello, yellow, niello, martello, Otello, Costello, bordello, pomelo, playfellow, bedfellow, Oddfellow, Goodfellow, blackfellow, Longfellow, schoolfellow, Novello, Othello, Uccello, Bargello, morello, Portobello, Donatello, Pirandello, ritornello, Punchinello, Monticello, violoncello, saltarello, Robin Goodfellow

19.29.5
aloe, tallow, callow, Gallo, mallow, fallow, sallow, shallow, hallow, marshmallow, lign-aloe

19.29.6
São Paulo

19.29.7
Barlow, Carlo, Carlow, Marlow, Marlowe, Saint-Malo, Harlow, Lalo, Monte Carlo

19.29.8
follow, jollo, hollow, wallow, swallow, Rollo, Apollo

19.29.9
stylo, kyloe, milo, silo, Shiloh, Hilo, lilo, Llandeilo

19.29.10
Bullough

19.29.11
Hulot, rouleau

19.29.12
ex nihilo, tupelo, Tiepolo, bibelot, furbelow, cymbalo, cembalo, Rumbelow, diabolo, clavicembalo, matelot, Costello, pedalo, piccolo, Bigelow, gigolo, brigalow, bungalow, Fanagalo, tremolo, pomelo, bummalo, Manilow, beefalo, buffalo, ovolo, Angelo, tangelo, Michelangelo, modulo, regulo, coram populo

19.29.13
furlough

19.29.14
polo, bolo, solo, Rolo®, Iolo, criollo, tombolo, palolo, Marco Polo

19.29.15
Taplow

19.29.16
bibelot, pueblo, Pablo, tableau, deathblow, counterblow, overblow, Fontainebleau

19.29.17
whitlow, matelot

19.29.18
Ludlow

19.29.19
Wicklow

19.29.20
Day-Glo®, airglow, aglow, alpenglow, Anglo, Nant-y-glo, afterglow

19.29.21
airflow, upflow, outflow, mudflow, inflow, onflow, cash flow, uniflow, interflow, underflow, overflow, contraflow

19.29.22
go-slow, Cottesloe

19.29.23
Oslo, Wilmslow, Winslow, Onslow, Cottesloe

20.1
peep, beep, steep, deep, keep, neap, neep, veep, seep, sheep, cheap, cheep, Jeep®, heap, Heep, weep, sweep, reap, Streep, creep, grippe, leap, bleep, sleep, skin-deep, barkeep, upkeep, housekeep, Eastcheap, scrapheap, ant heap, muckheap, slagheap, asleep, chimney sweep, cassareep, oversleep, overleap

20.2
pip, tip, DIP, dip, kip, skip, nip, snip, sip, zip, ship, chip, gip, gyp, hip, whip, quip, rip, trip, Tripp, strip, drip, scrip, grip, grippe, yip, lip, blip, clip, flip, slip, Möbius strip

20.2.1
toodle-pip

20.2.2
wingtip, fingertip

20.2.3
sheepdip, Mendip, skinny-dip

20.2.4
turnip, catnip, parsnip, Worsnip

20.2.5
gossip

20.2.6
unzip

20.2.7
reship, transship, unship, tranship
.1 trusteeship, traineeship, lesseeship **.2** ladyship, jockeyship, prebendaryship, suretyship, deputyship, attorneyship, secretaryship, commissaryship **.3** premiership, viziership, engineership **.4** airship, heirship, mayorship **.5** starship, registrarship **.6** warship, praetorship **.7** envoyship, viceroyship **.8** Q-ship **.9** surveyorship, fireship, squireship, priorship, umpireship, Messiahship, viewership, membership, tutorship, rectorship, doctorship, proctorship, quaestorship, pastorship, mastership, dictatorship, curatorship, proprietorship, presbytership, editorship, senatorship, monitorship, servitorship, preceptorship, inspectorship, protectorship,

directorship, electorship, conductorship,
instructorship, precentorship, succentorship,
apprenticeship, ministership, moderatorship,
procuratorship, arbitratorship, subeditorship,
progenitorship, executorship, prolocutorship,
administratorship, readership, leadership,
foundership, eldership, recordership,
commandership, stadtholdership,
ambassadorship, speakership, vicarship,
ownership, partnership, governorship,
coronership, co-ownership, landownership,
probationership, ephorship, receivership,
survivorship, authorship, fathership, pursership,
bursarship, censorship, sponsorship,
professorship, self-censorship, kaisership,
sizarship, ushership, rangership, lectureship,
indentureship, majorship, rajaship, vergership,
soldiership, managership, emperorship,
treasurership, lecturership, dealership,
tellership, fellowship, scholarship, rulership,
chancellorship, councillorship,
controllership **.10** worship, connoisseurship,
entrepreneurship **.11** virtuosoship **.12** troopship
.13 sibship **.14** primateship **.15** midship,
headship, lairdship, hardship, godship,
wardship, lordship, stewardship, friendship,
comradeship, husbandship, overlordship
.16 clerkship **.17** flagship **.18** steamship,
mediumship **.19** queenship, kinship,
championship, guardianship, custodianship,
librarianship, thaneship, clanship, partisanship,
bipartisanship, township, archonship, gunship,
sonship, tribuneship, captainship, chieftainship,
wardenship, deaconship, Blankenship,
archdeaconship, suffraganship, seamanship,
chairmanship, showmanship, ropemanship,
workmanship, brinkmanship, penmanship,
horsemanship, statesmanship, batsmanship,
sportsmanship, grantsmanship, draftsmanship,
draughtsmanship, craftsmanship,
marksmanship, brinksmanship, oarsmanship,
swordsmanship, gamesmanship,
salesmanship, churchmanship,
aldermanship, one-upmanship, coxswainship,
cousinship, citizenship, musicianship,
relationship, interrelationship, companionship,
chamberlainship, internship **.20** kingship,
longship **.21** sheriffship **.22** spaceship,
princeship, prenticeship, justiceship,
acquaintanceship **.23** sageship, judgeship,
hostageship **.24** battleship, beadleship,
consulship, marshalship, aedileship,
admiralship, generalship, discipleship,
principalship, cardinalship, apostleship,
proconsulship

20.2.8
mateship, courtship, lightship, biochip,
woodchip, saintship, countship, clientship,
studentship, regentship, sergeantship,
serjeantship, guestship, prophetship,
laureateship, cadetship, abbotship, rocketship,
legateship, microchip, viscountship,
residentship, presidentship, provostship,

associateship, surrogateship, magistrateship,
advocateship

20.2.9
unhip, rosehip

20.2.10
equip, re-equip, horsewhip, bullwhip

20.2.11
cantrip, airstrip, outstrip, filmstrip, hairgrip,
handgrip, unrip, weatherstrip, kirby-grip®

20.2.12
bunyip

20.2.13
Philip, harelip, tulip, Cudlipp, circlip, unclip,
payslip, cowslip, Ruislip, sideslip, landslip, oxlip,
gymslip, wheelslip, underlip, paperclip,
pillowslip

20.3
ape, tape, cape, scape, gape, nape, Snape,
SHAPE, shape, chape, jape, rape, drape, crape,
crêpe, scrape, grape, seascape, skyscape, escape,
snowscape, cloudscape, landscape, inscape,
townscape, moonscape, roofscape, Inchcape,
agape, reshape, shipshape, misshape,
broomrape, videotape, audiotape, tickertape,
sellotape®, cityscape

20.4
pep, step, steppe, skep, cep, hep, rep, repp,
prep, strep, crêpe, yep, schlepp, shlep,
Dieppe, doorstep, outstep, footstep, sidestep,
quickstep, instep, one-step, misstep,
goosestep, UNEP, recep, sitrep, salep, julep,
Imhotep, step-by-step, overstep, demirep,
Amenhotep

20.5
pap, Papp, bap, tap, Tapp, dap, cap, gap, map,
knap, Knapp, nap, nappe, sap, zap,
schappe, shap, chap, Jap, hap, rap, wrap, trap,
strap, crap, scrap, frap, yap, yapp, lap, Lapp, clap,
flap, slap

20.5.1
kneecap, recap, skycap, toecap, snowcap,
hubcap, ratecap, nightcap, whitecap, redcap,
madcap, blackcap, uncap, ASCAP, baasskap,
dunce cap, foolscap, skullcap, handicap

20.5.2
stopgap

20.5.3
bitmap

20.5.4
Carnap, catnap, kidnap

20.5.5
mayhap, mishap

20.5.6
rewrap, riprap, satrap, flytrap, firetrap, claptrap,
entrap, mantrap, suntrap, giftwrap, deathtrap,
mousetrap, footstrap, bootstrap, backstrap,
jockstrap, chinstrap, unstrap, watchstrap,

rattletrap, wentletrap, enwrap, unwrap, Saranwrap

20.5.7
lagniappe

20.5.8
dewlap, burlap, shiplap, handclap, Dunlap, earflap, mudflap, interlap, overlap, thunderclap

20.6
Arp, tarp, carp, scarp, sharp, Sharpe, harp, syncarp, escarp, baasskap, card sharp, unsharp, epicarp, pericarp, Polycarp, pseudocarp, endocarp, mesocarp, schizocarp, xylocarp, rhizocarp, counterscarp, autoharp

20.7
op, op., pop, bop, top, stop, dop, cop, kop, mop, knop, fop, sop, shop, chop, hop, whap, whop, wop, swap, swop, prop, strop, drop, crop, lop, plop, clop, glop, flop, slop, pre-op, vox pop, post-op, Spion Kop

20.7.1
co-op

20.7.2
mom-and-pop, lollipop

20.7.3
bebop

20.7.4
treetop, foretop, screwtop, screw-top, atop, tiptop, laptop, flattop, hardtop, blacktop, worktop, tanktop, desktop, pegtop, ragtop, palmtop, maintop, clifftop, rooftop, wavetop, estop, housetop, doorstop, ripstop, shortstop, backstop, nonstop, unstop, longstop, whistle-stop, hilltop, rolltop, tabletop, overtop, mountaintop, over-the-top

20.7.5
Boskop

20.7.6
rollmop

20.7.7
coin-op

20.7.8
Aesop, Warsop, soursop, sweetsop, Worksop, milksop, Allsop, Blenkinsop

20.7.9
teashop, toyshop, hockshop, tuckshop, bookshop, cookshop, workshop, pawnshop, barbershop, window-shop

20.7.10
sweetshop, sweatshop, muttonchop

20.7.11
carhop, hiphop, longhop, hedgehop, bellhop, hippety-hop

20.7.12
Ribbentrop, eardrop, teardrop, airdrop, dewdrop, snowdrop, backdrop, namedrop, gumdrop, raindrop, eavesdrop, sharecrop, outcrop,

maincrop, stonecrop, Heythrop, Northrop, Winthrop, underprop, malaprop, turboprop, agitprop, paradrop, intercrop, overcrop

20.7.13
orlop, clip-clop, Dunlop, flipflop, Hislop, escallop, escalope, bellyflop, gigaflop, megaflop, teraflop

20.8
dorp, Corp., scaup, scorp, gawp, Thorpe, warp, whaup, yawp, Klerksdorp, Grimethorpe, Scunthorpe, Palethorpe, Calthorpe, Oglethorpe, upwarp, downwarp, Citicorp

20.9
up, pup, tup, cup, scup, sup, hup, Krupp, yup, two-up, slap-up, straight-up, het up, souped-up, trumped-up, washed up, fed up, warmed-up, up-and-up, stuck-up, World Cup, grown-up, Seven Up®, thumbs-up, shoot'em up, totting-up, summing-up, washing-up

20.9.1
wickiup, pick-me-up

20.9.2
fry-up

20.9.3
screwup

20.9.4
zip-up, slap-up, top-up

20.9.5
sit-up, split-up, setup, letup, start-up, cutup, shoot-up

20.9.6
roundup, wind-up, fold-up, holdup

20.9.7
teacup, pickup, stick-up, hiccup, take-up, makeup, shakeup, break-up, check-up, backup, crackup, markup, cock-up, lockup, walkup, hookup, lookup, Sidcup, eggcup, kingcup, linkup, wassail-cup, buttercup

20.9.8
warm-up

20.9.9
clean-up, pinup, ton-up, sunup, run-up, lineup, turnup, grownup

20.9.10
hangup

20.9.11
rave-up, carve-up

20.9.12
piss-up, press-up, toss-up, catsup

20.9.13
nosh-up, wash-up, hush-up, punchup

20.9.14
ketchup, catchup, matchup, punchup

20.9.15
chirrup, clear-up

20.9.16
fill-up, snarl-up, pileup, pull-up

20.10
pipe, type, stipe, snipe, sipe, hype, wipe, swipe, ripe, tripe, stripe, gripe, slype

20.10.1
blowpipe, windpipe, standpipe, bagpipe, drainpipe, panpipe, downpipe, hornpipe, stovepipe, nosepipe, hosepipe, pitchpipe, tailpipe, soilpipe, liripipe

20.10.2
retype, mistype, antitype, stereotype, karyotype, heliotype, autotype, prototype, archetype, zincotype, logotype, phenotype, stenotype, genotype, Monotype®, linotype, phonotype, schizotype, serotype, teletype, collotype, holotype, somatotype, platinotype, diazotype, daguerreotype, electrotype, subtype, tintype, syntype

20.10.3
jacksnipe, guttersnipe

20.10.4
sideswipe, wash/wipe

20.10.5
pinstripe, unripe, rathe-ripe, underripe, overripe

20.11
Krupp

20.12
poop, stoep, stoop, stoup, coop, Coope, scoop, goop, snoop, soup, dupe, hoop, whoop, swoop, roup, troop, troupe, droop, drupe, croup, group, stupe, loop, loupe, bloop, sloop, recoup, hencoop, pea-soup, regroup, peer-group, playgroup, subgroup, in-group, housegroup, battlegroup, nincompoop, cock-a-hoop, hula-hoop, paratroop, cantaloupe, Guadeloupe

20.13.1
tittup

20.13.2
Sidcup

20.13.3
Stanhope

20.13.4
hyssop, Jessop, Mossop, Glossop, catsup

20.13.5
bishop, archbishop

20.13.6
stirrup, syrup, Harrap, larrup, Europe, satrap, caltrop, Northrup

20.13.7
fillip, callop, scallop, gallop, Gallup, galop, salep, Salop, shallop, jalap, polyp, dollop, collop, scollop, gollop, wallop, trollop, Trollope, lollop, julep, Hislop, develop, envelop, escallop, escalope, codswallop, redevelop, overdevelop

20.14
Earp, burp, chirp, twerp, slurp, usurp, Antwerp

20.15
ope, pope, taupe, tope, stope, dope, cope, scope, mope, nope, soap, hope, rope, trope, grope, lope, slope

20.15.1
myope

20.15.2
antipope

20.15.3
metope, isotope, radioisotope

20.15.4
.1 episcope, hagioscope, stereoscope, spectrohelioscope, bioscope, diascope, epidiascope, snooperscope, colposcope, stroboscope, statoscope, otoscope, rotorscope, proctoscope, cystoscope, tachistoscope, endoscope, sigmoidoscope, kaleidoscope, phonendoscope, bronchoscope, laryngoscope, pharyngoscope, seismoscope, CinemaScope®, ophthalmoscope, kinescope, chronoscope, rhinoscope, phonoscope, stethoscope, periscope, horoscope, auriscope, stauroscope, fluoroscope, gyroscope, laparoscope, spectroscope, gastroscope, microscope, hygroscope, arthroscope, spinthariscope, polariscope, electroscope, ultramicroscope, telescope, oscilloscope, riflescope

20.15.5
tritanope, protanope, deuteronope

20.15.6
sandsoap

20.15.7
Bramhope, Stanhope

20.15.8
pyrope, towrope, tightrope, zoetrope, unrope, lycanthrope, misanthrope, bellrope, phalarope, azeotrope, heliotrope, thaumatrope, allotrope, skipping-rope, philanthrope

20.15.9
elope, aslope, interlope, antelope, escalope, envelope, triantelope

20.16.1
imp, pimp, skimp, gimp, guimpe, simp, chimp, wimp, primp, crimp, scrimp, shrimp, limp, blimp

20.16.2
temp, kemp, hemp

20.16.3
amp, preamp, tamp, stamp, damp, camp, scamp, gamp, vamp, samp, champ, ramp, tramp, cramp, lamp, clamp, firedamp, decamp, encamp, revamp, blowlamp, spotlamp, headlamp, sidelamp, wheel-clamp, sunlamp, gaslamp, flash lamp, tail lamp, table lamp, Tilley lamp®

20.16.4
pomp, stomp, comp, chomp, whomp, swamp, romp, tromp, trompe, yomp, clomp

20.16.5
ump, pump, bump, tump, stump, dump, thump, sump, chump, jump, hump, whump, rump, trump, crump, scrump, grump, frump, lump, plump, clump, flump, slump, cryopump, handpump, bilgepump, gazump, ski-jump, showjump, outjump, long jump, mugwump, no-trump, overtrump

20.17
wisp, crisp, lisp, thesp, asp, gasp, hasp, rasp, grasp, clasp, Wasp, wasp, cusp, unhasp, enclasp, unclasp, woodwasp, gall-wasp, galliwasp, will-o'-the-wisp

20.18
Quilp, kelp, help, whelp, yelp, alp, palp, scalp, pulp, sculp, gulp, megilp, self-help

21.1
Beeb, dweeb, grebe, plebe, glebe, Antibes, ephebe, Maghrib, Delibes

21.2
sahib, bib, dib, Gibb, nib, snib, fib, sib, gib, jib, squib, rib, crib, lib, glib, memsahib, sparerib, Carib, midrib, corn crib, ad-lib, women's lib, Sennacherib

21.3
Abe, babe, McCabe, astrolabe

21.4
ebb, deb, Seb, web, Webb, reb, pleb, bleb, cubeb, Deneb, cobweb, Horeb, Zagreb, Caleb, celeb, Aurangzeb, mahaleb

21.5
fines herbes, Malherbe

21.6
ab, Moab, tab, stab, dab, cab, scab, gab, nab, fab, jab, drab, crab, Crabbe, grab, lab, blab, flab, slab, baobab, kebab, Cantab, crosstab, De Kalb, vocab, McNab, dag-nab, prefab, confab, rehab, Ahab, smash-and-grab, Skylab, Lib-Lab, spacelab, shish kebab, pedicab, minicab, taxicab

21.7
arb, barb, carb, garb, Saab®, sahib, rhubarb, kabob, bicarb, memsahib, Punjab, nawab, mihrab, sodium bicarb

21.8
Ob, bob, stob, dob, cob, Cobb, gob, mob, knob, nob, snob, fob, sob, job, hob, squab, swab, swob, rob, Robb, throb, yob, lob, blob, glob, slob, skibob, nabob, corncob, demob, doorknob, hobnob, heartthrob, thingamabob

21.9
orb, daub, forb, sorb, warb, bedaub, desorb, resorb, absorb, reabsorb, adsorb, nawab

21.10
bombe

21.11
pub, bub, tub, stub, dub, cub, nub, snub, sub, chub, Chubb®, hub, rub, drub, scrub, grub, shrub, blub, club, flub, slub, hubbub, twintub, bathtub, washtub, wolfcub, subshrub, nightclub, syllabub, rub-a-dub, overdub, undershrub, Beelzebub, rub-a-dub-dub

21.12
kibe, gibe, gybe, jibe, bribe, tribe, scribe, imbibe, diatribe, escribe, ascribe, describe, prescribe, proscribe, subscribe, inscribe, transcribe, conscribe, superscribe, misdescribe, circumscribe, oversubscribe

21.13
boob, tube, jube, rube, droob, cube, lube, j'adoube, jujube, flashcube, Danube, hypercube

21.14
Jacob, kincob, cherub, Arab, carob, scarab, Mozarab, Shatt al-Arab

21.15
burb, curb, kerb, verb, Serb, herb, Loeb, blurb, superb, suburb, perturb, disturb, uncurb, proverb, reverb, pro-verb, adverb, converb, acerb, exurb, potherb, willowherb

21.16
daube, Job, robe, probe, strobe, lobe, Loeb, globe

21.16.1
Turcophobe, Francophobe, homophobe, xenophobe, Sinophobe, technophobe, Russophobe, claustrophobe, agoraphobe, Gallophobe, Anglophobe, Slavophobe, ailurophobe

21.16.2
aerobe, Latrobe, wardrobe, microbe, enrobe, unrobe, bathrobe, disrobe, anaerobe, chifforobe

21.16.3
earlobe

21.17
iamb, bombe, rhomb, corymb, choriamb, choliamb, dithyramb

21.18
stilb, Elbe, alb, bulb, De Kalb, flashbulb

22.1
eat, peat, Pete, beat, beet, teat, Skeat, skeet, meat, meet, mete, neat, feat, feet, seat, sheet, gîte, cheat, heat, wheat, tweet, suite, sweet, treat, St., street, Crete, greet, frites, leat, leet, pleat, bleat, cleat, fleet, sleet, score sheet, en suite, tout de suite, overeat, Harley Street, Watling Street, Carnaby Street

22.1.1
repeat, compete, outcompete

22.1.2
browbeat, upbeat, heartbeat, deadbeat, dead-beat, drumbeat, downbeat, offbeat, hoofbeat, sugarbeet

22.1.3
petite

22.1.4
mesquite, polychaete, parakeet, lorikeet,
spirochaete

22.1.5
gamete, sheepmeat, helpmeet, crabmeat,
sweetmeat, nutmeat, pigmeat, forcemeat,
horsemeat, mincemeat

22.1.6
splay-feet, forefeet, effete, defeat, club feet,
flatfeet, Blackfeet, counterfeit

22.1.7
aquavit

22.1.8
aesthete, esthete

22.1.9
reseat, deceit, receipt, unseat, conceit,
windowseat, self-deceit, self-conceit,
phycomycete, ascomycete, schizomycete,
myxomycete, actinomycete

22.1.10
marcasite, carte de visite

22.1.11
freesheet, flysheet, flowsheet, dopesheet,
jobsheet, spreadsheet, broadsheet, groundsheet,
worksheet, timesheet, mainsheet, dustsheet,
newssheet, undersheet

22.1.12
Brigitte

22.1.13
escheat, dustsheet

22.1.14
exegete

22.1.15
reheat, preheat, superheat, overheat

22.1.16
buckwheat, wholewheat, semisweet, bitter-
sweet, Nutrasweet®, meadowsweet

22.1.17
terete, pretreat, retreat, entreat, mistreat,
estreat, backstreet, Greenstreet, maltreat,
accrete, secrete, concrete, discreet, discrete,
excrete, calcrete, Magritte, afreet, Margeurite,
marguerite, Masorete, trick-or-treat, indiscreet,
indiscrete, Chester-le-Street, ferroconcrete

22.1.18
élite, delete, deplete, replete, kick-pleat,
compleat, complete, Longleat, Byfleet, Purfleet,
Wainfleet, Benfleet, Northfleet, athlete, corps
d'élite, obsolete, incomplete, paraclete,
biathlete, triathlete, heptathlete, pentathlete,
decathlete

22.2
it, pit, Pitt, spit, bit, bitt, tit, dit, kit, skit, git,
mitt, smit, Schmidt, Schmitt, knit, nit, snit, fit,
fytte, sit, zit, shit, chit, hit, whit, wit, Witt, twit,
quit, squit, rit., writ, Pritt, sprit, Brit, Britt, crit,
grit, frit, lit, split, flit, slit, MLitt

22.2.1
howbeit, albeit

22.2.2
Slaithwaite

22.2.3
Inuit, Jesuit, floruit, conduit

22.2.4
suet, Pruitt, cruet, Yuit, Hewett, Hewitt, Blewitt,
bluet, Bluett, sluit, intuit

22.2.5
fleapit, pipit, tippet, Tippett, skippet, snippet,
whippet, bear pit, tappet, lappet, carpet, poppet,
moppet, sawpit, puppet, Cupitt, sandpit,
cockpit, limpet, armpit, trumpet, strumpet,
crumpet, limepit, stone-pit, cesspit, respite,
turnspit, pulpit, incipit, decrepit, cuckoo-spit

22.2.6
Tibbett, exhibit, prohibit, adhibit, inhibit,
Tebbitt, debit, rarebit, Babbitt, habit, rabbet,
rabbit, rebate, cohabit, inhabit, jackrabbit,
barbet, obit, Cobbett, gobbet, hobbit, probit,
orbit, two-bit, cubit, Cubitt, gigabit, turbit,
cucurbit, Tobit, infobit, titbit, tidbit, backbit,
hawkbit, frogbit, gambit, sheep's-bit, Nesbit,
shell-bit

22.2.7
Pettitt, blue tit, tomtit, wrentit

22.2.8
edit, credit, adit, audit, plaudit, Chindit, pandit,
bandit, conduit, pundit, re-edit, subedit,
accredit, discredit

22.2.9
.1 picket, Pickett, picquet, piquet, ticket,
snicket, thicket, wicket, Rickett, pricket, cricket,
midwicket .2 Becket .3 jacket, Hackett, racket,
racquet, bracket, placket, Blackett, paypacket,
bluejacket, straitjacket, bedjacket, lifejacket,
leatherjacket .4 market, Haymarket,
Newmarket, Stowmarket, upmarket,
downmarket, hypermarket, supermarket,
aftermarket, Euromarket .5 pocket, docket,
socket, rocket, sprocket, brocket, crocket,
Crockett, air pocket, pickpocket, skyrocket,
retro-rocket, Drumnadrochit .6 Puckett, bucket,
tucket, Duckett, rustbucket .7 identikit®
.8 Birkett, circuit, short-circuit, microcircuit
.9 trinket, blanket, junket, Plunket, Blunkett,
underblanket .10 biscuit, brisket, casket, clothes
basket .11 toolkit

22.2.10
target, hogget, Tlingit, Gilgit

22.2.11
demit, remit, limit, semmit, dammit, comet,
vomit, summit, plummet, emit, omit, permit,
commit, Kermit, thermit, hermit, submit, admit,

readmit, transmit, Goldschmidt, delimit, Mahomet, pretermit, intermit, Hindemith, recommit, intromit, manumit, resubmit, retransmit, Messerschmitt, overcommit

22.2.12
spinet, minute, linnet, Bennett, sennet, Sennett, sennit, genet, jennet, planet, Barnett, bonnet, cornet, cornett, punnet, unit, burnet, Burnett, gurnet, unknit, blue bonnet, unbonnet, sunbonnet, whodunit, whodunnit, sub-unit, interknit, up-to-the-minute

22.2.13
refit, Parfitt, soffit, profit, prophet, buffet, tuffet, befit, Tophet, outfit, Kwik-Fit, comfit, unfit, misfit, Wolfit, photofit, counterfeit, benefit, retrofit, disbenefit

22.2.14
civet, rivet, privet, trivet, brevet, davit, velvet, unrivet, aquavit, affidavit

22.2.15
with-it

22.2.16
resit, licit, Blissett, tacet, cresset, asset, tacit, Ossett, posset, cosset, corset, gusset, russet, scripsit, op. cit., outsit, whatsit, wotsit, bedsit, exit, loc. cit., transit, Tilsit, babysit, illicit, elicit, solicit, implicit, complicit, explicit, accessit, opposite, plebiscite, assumpsit, inexplicit, Blennerhassett, ipse dixit, proxime accessit

22.2.17
visit, posit, closet, exit, transit, Tilsit, revisit, deposit, opposite, composite, requisite, perquisite, oviposit, prerequisite

22.2.18
horseshit, bullshit

22.2.19
Brigitte

22.2.20
Datchet, matchet, hatchet, ratchet, Cratchit, Watchet

22.2.21
eegit, eejit, digit, widget, Brigit, parget, budget, legit

22.2.22
mishit, pinch-hit

22.2.23
peewit, nitwit, outwit, godwit, conduit, acquit, banquet, dimwit, halfwit, Chuzzlewit

22.2.24
spirit, territ, merit, Merritt, worrit, bowsprit, Prakrit, Sanskrit, afrit, dispirit, inspirit, demerit, inherit, hypocrite, haematocrit

22.2.25
D.Litt., relit, millet, filet, pellet, starlit, daleth, Pollitt, Smollett, twilit, Hewlett, lamplit, floodlit, backlit, unlit, sunlit, moonlit, torchlit, candlelit, Shepton Mallet, underlit, decuplet, Duraglit®,

lickety-split, what-do-you-call-it, what-you-may-call-it

22.3
peart

22.3.1
clypeate, opiate, parsley-piert

22.3.2
labiate, chalybeate, trilabiate

22.3.3
bracteate

22.3.4
idiot, immediate, dimidiate, intermediate

22.3.5
brachiate, branchiate

22.3.6
craniate, Uniate, cuneate, laciniate

22.3.7
Teviot, cheviot, breviate, soviet, foveate, landgraviate, Sino-Soviet

22.3.8
associate

22.3.9
roseate

22.3.10
satiate, cruciate, initiate, novitiate, patriciate, insatiate, associate, licentiate

22.3.11
orgeat, collegiate, fastigiate, intercollegiate

22.3.12
seriate, heriot, Heriott, Herriot, variate, Marriott, Marryat, chariot, Harriet, lariat, laureate, aureate, Cypriot, fimbriate, patriot, vicariate, salariat, eukaryote, Iscariot, phanariot, Poet Laureate, appropriate, inebriate, expatriate, compatriot, secretariat, proletariat, multivariate, commissariat, professoriate, baccalaureate, inappropriate, Judas Iscariot, lumpenproletariat

22.3.13
pileate, galeate, Eliot, Elliot, galliot, foliot, Juliet, Boléat, foliate, affiliate, Italiot, aculeate, bifoliate, trifoliate, perfoliate, curvifoliate

22.4
ait, ate, eight, eyot, Pate, pate, spate, Speaight, Speight, bait, bate, Tait, Tate, state, date, cate, Kate, skate, gait, gate, mate, fate, fête, sate, Haight, hate, wait, Waite, weight, Thwaite, rate, prate, spruit, trait, straight, strait, crate, grate, great, freight, late, plate, slate, create, straight-eight, recreate, uncreate, welfare state, member state, sell-by date, overate, Menai Strait

22.4.1
tracheate

22.4.2
.1 expiate .2 trabeate, labiate .3 tritiate
.4 mediate, radiate, ideate, irradiate, repudiate

.5 brachiate, tracheate, branchiate **.6** permeate
.7 miniate, Uniate, cuneate, delineate, calumniate **.8** deviate, aviate, obviate, abbreviate, alleviate, lixiviate, exuviate
.9 glaciate, nauseate, croceate, appreciate, emaciate, negotiate, associate, dissociate, consociate, asphyxiate, substantiate, annunciate, enunciate, denunciate, renegotiate, disassociate, transubstantiate, consubstantiate **.10** roseate
.11 vitiate, satiate, fasciate, cruciate, depreciate, propitiate, initiate, officiate, expatiate, ingratiate, excruciate, potentiate, instantiate, differentiate, circumstantiate **.12** brecciate
.13 fastigiate **.14** seriate, variate, aureate, floriate, fimbriate, recreate, procreate, excoriate, infuriate, luxuriate, appropriate, impropriate, expropriate, inebriate, expatriate, repatriate, elutriate, misappropriate **.15** ciliate, palliate, oleate, foliate, nucleate, humiliate, affiliate, conciliate, retaliate, defoliate, bifoliate, exfoliate, enucleate, disaffiliate, uninucleate

22.4.3
striate

22.4.4
situate, actuate, fluctuate, punctuate, graduate, menstruate, arcuate, sinuate, valuate, eventuate, accentuate, habituate, perpetuate, infatuate, effectuate, evacuate, insinuate, attenuate, extenuate, devaluate, evaluate, re-evaluate, individuate, disambiguate, superannuate

22.4.5
floriate

22.4.6
inchoate

22.4.7
pupate, baldpate, crispate, cuspate, palpate, extirpate, constipate, syncopate, dissipate, nuncupate, inculpate, exculpate, participate, anticipate, emancipate

22.4.8
rebate, barbate, abate, debate, probate, lobate, whitebait, groundbait, plumbate, jailbait, stereobate, adsorbate, masturbate, intubate, reprobate, approbate, incubate, stylobate, bilobate, trilobate, exacerbate

22.4.9
mutate, notate, rotate, dictate, spectate, lactate, tête-à-tête **.1** vittate **.2** apartheid
.3 guttate **.4** scutate **.5** crepitate, palpitate, precipitate, decrepitate, decapitate, nictitate, meditate, premeditate, imitate, palmitate, delimitate, annotate, sanitate, levitate, gravitate, dissertate, acetate, felicitate, necessitate, triacetate, capacitate, resuscitate, incapacitate, hesitate, digitate, vegetate, agitate, sagittate, cogitate, tridigitate, excogitate, regurgitate, ingurgitate, interdigitate, irritate, amputate, commutate, permutate, militate, rehabilitate, debilitate, habilitate, facilitate
.6 septate **.7** tractate, punctate, pernoctate

.8 dentate, potentate, commentate, orientate, tridentate, edentate, reorientate, disorientate
.9 restate, cristate, estate, testate, gestate, hastate, costate, prostate, Grosseteste, upstate, instate, reinstate, downstate, tungstate, misstate, intestate, apostate, superstate, interstate, understate, devastate, overstate
.10 peltate, auscultate

22.4.10
pre-date, sedate, predate, gradate, update, postdate, backdate, mandate, misdate, up-to-date, pedate, airdate, retardate, caudate, cordate, acaudate, obcordate, subcordate, iodate, periodate, lapidate, cuspidate, antedate, candidate, vanadate, oxidate, liquidate, fluoridate, depredate, exudate, validate, dilapidate, bicuspidate, intimidate, accommodate, elucidate, invalidate, consolidate, reconsolidate, molybdate, fecundate, inundate

22.4.11
vacate, locate, placate, furcate, truncate, relocate, translocate **.1** thecate **.2** quintuplicate
.3 baccate, saccate **.4** demarcate, exarchate, tetrarchate **.5** spicate, plicate **.6** auspicate, corticate, urticate, masticate, rusticate, altercate, decorticate, authenticate, sophisticate, domesticate, fantasticate, prognosticate, dedicate, medicate, predicate, abdicate, indicate, vindicate, syndicate, rededicate, eradicate, adjudicate, contraindicate, fornicate, tunicate, communicate, excommunicate, intercommunicate, defecate, suffocate, bifurcate, trifurcate, certificate, pontificate, eutrophicate, nidificate, advocate, equivocate, hypothecate, desiccate, vesicate, exsiccate, detoxicate, intoxicate, loricate, suricate, deprecate, imprecate, fabricate, rubricate, lubricate, imbricate, metricate, extricate, divaricate, prevaricate, reciprocate, prefabricate, educate, manducate, re-educate, miseducate, silicate, allocate, collocate, triplicate, replicate, supplicate, duplicate, implicate, complicate, explicate, spifflicate, dislocate, umbilicate, reallocate, echolocate, reduplicate, quadruplicate, sesquiplicate, borosilicate, photoduplicate **.7** cheapskate, obfuscate, confiscate, bletherskate, coruscate **.8** falcate, sulcate, inculcate, defalcate, trisulcate

22.4.12
negate, ligate, lockgate **.1** variegate
.2 Margate **.3** Highgate, Reigate **.4** Newgate
.5 propagate, expurgate, mitigate, litigate, watergate, castigate, fustigate, instigate, Newdigate, fumigate, Unigate®, runagate, abnegate, levigate, navigate, divagate, objurgate, subjugate, conjugate, irrigate, derogate, arrogate, Harrogate, corrugate, surrogate, abrogate, subrogate, segregate, aggregate, congregate, delegate, relegate, colligate, obligate, investigate, reinvestigate, defumigate, interrogate, desegregate, disaggregate, homologate, circumnavigate

.**6** virgate, compurgate .**7** liftgate, Westgate, Postgate .**8** Lydgate, Ludgate, floodgate, Sandgate, Aldgate .**9** Wingate, Irangate, elongate .**10** sluicegate, Bishopsgate .**11** Ramsgate, Stansgate, Aldersgate, Billingsgate .**12** lychgate .**13** tailgate, Colgate®, vulgate, Polegate, tollgate, promulgate

22.4.13
cremate, checkmate, selfmate .**1** playmate .**2** sulphamate .**3** palmate .**4** formate .**5** primate .**6** carbamate, automate, glutamate, intimate, estimate, guesstimate, animate, sulfamate, decimate, desquamate, consummate, coelomate, collimate, diplomate, sublimate, cyclamate, acclimate, amalgamate, reanimate, approximate, underestimate, overestimate, monosodium glutamate .**7** bromate, chromate, bichromate, dichromate, cyclostomate .**8** shipmate, helpmate .**9** seatmate, flatmate .**10** workmate .**11** sigmate .**12** teammate, roommate .**13** inmate .**14** casemate, racemate, messmate, classmate, housemate .**15** stalemate, schoolmate, soulmate, stablemate

22.4.14
innate, connate, ornate, donate, phonate, stagnate .**1** crenate, septenate .**2** pinnate, bipinnate, tripinnate, Latinate, marginate, predestinate .**3** neonate, propionate, alienate .**4** tannate, stannate, artisanate .**5** khanate, incarnate, reincarnate .**6** binate, quinate .**7** lunate .**8** thionate, thiocyanate .**9.1** supinate, rabbinate, carbonate, cybernate, hibernate, turbinate, umbonate, polycarbonate, detonate, catenate, titanate, protonate, intonate, consternate, alternate, sultanate, concatenate, agglutinate, procrastinate, metropolitanate, iodinate, odonate, coordinate, subordinate, cachinnate, machinate, diaconate, subdiaconate, archidiaconate, shogunate, permanganate .**9.2** criminate, emanate, geminate, laminate, dominate, nominate, ruminate, terminate, verminate, germinate, culminate, fulminate, recriminate, incriminate, discriminate, eliminate, disseminate, inseminate, degeminate, ingeminate, contaminate, decontaminate, foraminate, abominate, predominate, renominate, denominate, illuminate, exterminate, regerminate, transilluminate .**9.3** raffinate, hyphenate, sulphonate, decaffeinate, pulvinate, rejuvenate, assonate, fascinate, arsenate, personate, circinate, vaccinate, succinate, lancinate, uncinate, vaticinate, assassinate, deracinate, hallucinate, impersonate, revaccinate, ratiocinate, resinate, resonate, fractionate, functionate, paginate, alginate, oxygenate, originate, repaginate, evaginate, invaginate, homogenate, hydrogenate, dehydrogenate, deoxygenate, exsanguinate .**9.4** carinate, marinate, chlorinate, urinate, fluorinate, mandarinate, mucronate,

dechlorinate, indoctrinate, peregrinate, tribunate, Italianate, selenate, pollinate, stolonate, reclinate, desalinate .**10** ternate, triternate .**11** zonate, pronate .**12** adnate .**13** agnate, magnate, cognate, impregnate, designate, redesignate

22.4.15
phosphate, sulfate, sulphate, caliphate, triphosphate, thiosulphate, bisulphate, polyphosphate, superphosphate, organophosphate

22.4.16
clavate, nervate, ovate, bovate, valvate, solvate, pyruvate, titivate, motivate, rotavate, captivate, activate, aestivate, cultivate, excavate, innervate, innovate, enervate, renovate, passivate, aggravate, margravate, elevate, salivate, recurvate, coacervate, obovate, demotivate, deactivate, reactivate, inactivate

22.4.17
xanthate

22.4.18
fixate, luxate, sensate, compensate, condensate, pulsate, inspissate, incrassate, decussate, insensate, intravasate, extravasate, tergiversate, methotrexate, overcompensate

22.4.19
solmizate

22.4.20
self-hate

22.4.21
flyweight, await, Kuwait, shortweight, lightweight, makeweight, torquate, equate, liquate, unweight, Braithwaite, Slaithwaite, birthweight, Micklethwaite, Postlethwaite, catchweight, middleweight, pennyweight, heavyweight, paperweight, counterweight, welterweight, underweight, summer-weight, overweight, featherweight, cruiserweight, hundredweight, bantamweight, Satterthwaite

22.4.22
derate, rerate, aerate, orate, irate, gyrate, berate, narrate, serrate, prorate, uprate, tenth-rate, disrate, underrate, overrate .**1** stearate, emirate, amirate, vizierate, meliorate, deteriorate, ameliorate .**2** ferrate .**3** de-aerate .**4** borate, quorate, urate, chlorate, inquorate, perchlorate .**5** lyrate .**6** separate, operate, respirate, aspirate, evaporate, cooperate, incorporate, reincorporate, disincorporate, recuperate, vituperate, exasperate, liberate, aberrate, deliberate, elaborate, collaborate, corroborate, exuberate, reverberate, iterate, deuterate, butyrate, reiterate, alliterate, obliterate, transliterate, expectorate, coelenterate, adulterate, federate, moderate, desiderate, confederate, preponderate, equiponderate, decorate, redecorate, edulcorate, invigorate, glomerate, commemorate, agglomerate, conglomerate,

enumerate, venerate, generate, itinerate, incinerate, regenerate, degenerate, exonerate, remunerate, perforate, camphorate, phosphorate, vociferate, proliferate, asseverate, perseverate, macerate, lacerate, ulcerate, eviscerate, incarcerate, commiserate, indurate, refrigerate, exaggerate, perorate, depurate, suppurate, triturate, maturate, saturate, obturate, sulphurate, tellurate, inaugurate, supersaturate, polyunsaturate, valerate, tolerate, exhilarate, decelerate, accelerate **.7** vibrate, librate, vertebrate, cerebrate, lucubrate, celebrate, calibrate, adumbrate, equilibrate, invertebrate, decerebrate, concelebrate **.8** citrate, tartrate, portrait, titrate, nitrate, concentrate, distraite, castrate, rostrate, prostrate, frustrate, lustrate, substrate, filtrate, infiltrate, self-portrait, perpetrate, impetrate, arbitrate, penetrate, orchestrate, sequestrate, superstrate, fenestrate, magistrate, illustrate, demonstrate, remonstrate, exfiltrate, sodium nitrate, impenetrate, administrate, defenestrate, acrylonitrate, interpenetrate **.9** quadrate, hydrate, dehydrate, rehydrate, carbohydrate **.10** picrate, desecrate, obsecrate, execrate, consecrate, deconsecrate, reconsecrate **.11** regrate, migrate, ingrate, transmigrate, integrate, immigrate, emigrate, denigrate, deflagrate, reintegrate, redintegrate, disintegrate **.12** airfreight **.13** clathrate, birth rate **.14** piece-rate

22.4.23
fellate, collate, dilate, elate, delate, relate, prolate, translate, regelate, retranslate, mistranslate, intercalate, interrelate **.1** chelate **.2** etiolate, urceolate, lanceolate, variolate **.3** alate **.4** stellate, interpellate **.5** phthalate, circumvallate **.6** bullate **.7.1** violate, annihilate, Merthiolate®, epilate, depilate, papillate, extrapolate, interpolate, sibilate, jubilate, umbellate, assibilate, titillate, scutellate, mutilate, scintillate, ventilate, cantillate, pistillate, distillate, constellate, apostolate, hyperventilate, decollate, percolate, escalate, alkylate, machicolate, de-escalate **.7.2** immolate, mamillate, assimilate, dissimilate, crenellate, methylate, tessellate, desolate, vacillate, oscillate, isolate, oxalate, pedicellate, salicylate, carboxylate, sigillate, stridulate, adulate, flagellate, modulate, pendulate, undulate, invigilate, acidulate, demodulate, arillate, correlate, fibrillate, phosphorylate, defibrillate, intercorrelate **.7.3** stipulate, populate, copulate, manipulate, depopulate, repopulate, overpopulate, tabulate, subulate, ambulate, mandibulate, infibulate, confabulate, perambulate, discombobulate, circumambulate, postulate, pustulate, capitulate, congratulate, absquatulate, expostulate, recapitulate, peculate, speculate, sacculate, flocculate, circulate, osculate, calculate, scrobiculate, articulate, particulate, reticulate, denticulate, gesticulate, vermiculate,

fasciculate, vesiculate, auriculate, matriculate, valleculate, ejaculate, inoculate, recirculate, pedunculate, emasculate, inosculate, recalculate, miscalculate, disarticulate, interosculate, ligulate, regulate, jugulate, strangulate, ungulate, deregulate, coagulate, triangulate, stimulate, simulate, emulate, formulate, cumulate, dissimulate, reformulate, accumulate, annulate, cannulate, granulate, degranulate, ovulate, insulate, encapsulate, serrulate, cellulate, ululate, pullulate **.8** doorplate, hotplate, footplate, breastplate, bedplate, bookplate, nameplate, template, vamplate, terne-plate, baseplate, faceplate, fishplate, soleplate, baffle-plate, copperplate, numberplate, fingerplate, silver-plate, chromium-plate, contemplate, electroplate **.9** oblate, ablate **.10** Benlate **.11** reflate, deflate, inflate, conflate, insufflate **.12** legislate

22.5
ate, PET, pet, bet, Bette, stet, debt, get, met, net, nett, vet, set, sett, jet, het, wet, whet, sweat, ret, Rett, Rhett, Brett, tret, fret, threat, yet, let, Lett, Fayette, layette, duet, diskette, luncheonette, en fête, flannelette, novelette, serviette, winceyette, paillette, Juliet, oubliette, statuette, pirouette, minuet, silhouette, overate

22.5.1
pipette, salopette

22.5.2
Tibet, barbette, abet, alphabet, quodlibet

22.5.3
quartet, motet, septet, octet, quintet, sestet, sextet

22.5.4
Claudette, Odette, Burdett, cadet, vedette, godet, Bernadette

22.5.5
briquette, maquette, hackette, plaquette, Marquette, coquette, moquette, shochet, croquette, Phuket, picquet, piquet, Bosanquet, banquette, blanquette, diskette, etiquette, scilicet, videlicet

22.5.6
shochet

22.5.7
baguette, beget, forget

22.5.8
Mehmet, palmette, roomette, cermet, unmet, kismet, calumet

22.5.9
de-net, spinet, Annette, Nanette, Barnett, nonet, dinette, Mynett, brunet, brunette, lunette, bayonet, Burnett, genette, Janette, Jeanette, Lynette, satinette, midinette, marionette, martinet, castanet, stockinet, wagonette, sermonette, basinet, bassinet, maisonette, canzonet, luncheonette, kitchenette, Antoinette, serinette, baronet, Bart., clarinet,

coronet, mignonette, caravanette, Marie
Antoinette **.1** hairnet **.2** jaconet, lansquenet,
alkanet, Ethernet, Intranet **.3** keepnet **.4** drift
net, Fastnet **.5** dragnet **.6** fishnet **.7** gill-net,
telnet, Cellnet®

22.5.10
mofette, nymphet

22.5.11
Yvette, Tevet, corvette, cuvette, Chevette®,
revet, curvet, Ovett, Olivet

22.5.12
epithet

22.5.13
reset, preset, pincette, poussette, beset, cassette,
upset, thickset, quickset, inset, Dansette, on-set,
unset, offset, anisette, heavyset, underset,
overset **.1** teaset **.2** placet, hic jacet, non placet
.3 asset, facet **.4** photoset, render-set, Somerset,
thermoset, avocet, Exocet®, Letraset®, scilicet,
salicet, video cassette, audio cassette, videlicet
.5 coset **.6** typeset **.7** subset **.8** outset **.9** headset,
handset, mindset **.10** filmset **.11** twinset, onset,
Consett, sunset, moonset **.12** photo-offset

22.5.14
noisette, Suzette, musette, gazette, rosette,
grisette, anisette, marquisette, marmoset, crêpe
suzette

22.5.15
pochette, brochette, planchette, fourchette,
couchette, trebuchet, ricochet

22.5.16
courgette

22.5.17
Georgette, trijet, propjet, ramjet, scramjet,
suffragette, turbojet

22.5.18
superhet

22.5.19
arête, barrette, fleurette, syrette®, burette,
curette, soubrette, Debrett, umbrette,
launderette, aigrette, regret, Everett, Carteret,
cigarette, swimmeret, amourette, spinneret,
minaret, banneret, leatherette, lazaret,
usherette, majorette, pillaret, collarette, solleret,
vinaigrette, musique concrète

22.5.20
rillettes, paupiette, vignette, lorgnette, paillette,
vilayet, La Fayette, aiguillette

22.5.21
relet, Arlette, toilette, Colette, Paulette,
roulette, briolette, triolet, galette, Gillette,
sublet, outlet, raclette, inlet, unlet, landaulette,
epaulette, underlet, Nicolette, flannelette,
novelette, isolette, flageolet, rivulet, eau de
toilette

22.6
terre-verte, famille verte

22.7
at, pat, spat, bat, tat, stat, cat, scat, skat, gat,
GATT, mat, matt, matte, gnat, Nat, fat, VAT, vat,
that, sat, shat, chat, hat, twat, rat, prat, Pratt,
sprat, Spratt, brat, drat, frat, lat, plait, plat, Platt,
splat, flat, slat, hereat, whereat, thereat,
Symonds Yat, stove-pipe hat, ten-gallon hat

22.7.1
fiat

22.7.2
Uniat, caveat, exeat, floreat, Boléat, secretariat

22.7.3
fiat, Rubáiyát

22.7.4
Croat, Serbo-Croat

22.7.5
repat, cowpat, expat, pit-a-pat

22.7.6
Sebat, shabbat, Rabat, fruitbat, brickbat, combat,
wombat, numbat, dingbat, tittlebat, acrobat,
Nanga Parbat

22.7.7
rat-tat, diktat, rheostat, cryostat, Randstad,
Darmstadt, Kronstadt, Eisenstadt, Hallstatt,
habitat, rat-a-tat, tit-for-tat, aegrotat, heliostat,
appestat, photostat®, haemostat, hemostat,
thermostat, aerostat, siderostat, coelostat,
Willemstadt, rat-a-tat-tat, nihil obstat

22.7.8
adat, Sadat, concordat, samizdat

22.7.9
she-cat, firecat, meerkat, bearcat, UCATT,
Sno-Cat®, snow cat, tipcat, bobcat, Kit-Kat, fat cat,
wildcat, tomcat, muscat, hellcat, polecat, copycat,
scaredy-cat, pussycat, Magnificat, requiescat

22.7.10
begat, SOGAT, Kattegat

22.7.11
doormat, format, Fermat, Zermatt, Brinks-Mat®,
reformat, automat, laundromat, achromat,
diplomat, Dürrenmatt, apochromat, anastigmat,
apostigmat

22.7.12
Donat, aplanat, assignat

22.7.13
defat, butterfat, Arafat, marrowfat,
Jehoshaphat

22.7.14
Shevat, vivat, cravat, amadavat, avadavat

22.7.15
resat, Passat®, outsat, Comsat®, babysat,
Inmarsat, Intelsat

22.7.16
howzat

22.7.17
chit-chat, backchat, whinchat, stonechat

22.7.18
high-hat, hardhat, sunhat

22.7.19
paraquat

22.7.20
Surat, jurat, firebrat, quadrat, theocrat, muskrat, apparat, nacarat, ziggurat, Montserrat, Ararat, Ballarat, physiocrat, autocrat, plutocrat, landocrat, democrat, technocrat, Eurocrat, bureaucrat, ochlocrat, aristocrat

22.7.21
Eilat, unplait, mudflat, cervelat, interplait

22.8
quinte, pointe, enceinte

22.9
out, owt, pout, spout, bout, tout, stout, doubt, scout, gout, knout, nowt, snout, shout, rout, Prout, sprout, trout, drought, Kraut, grout, lout, clout, flout, way-out, throughout, straight-out, spaced-out, washed out, out-and-out, pig-out, time-out, without, thereout, unthought-out, down-and-out, passing-out, chucker-out

22.9.1
payout, layout

22.9.2
buyout

22.9.3

22.9.4
throw-out, blowout

22.9.5
cop-out, dropout, wipeout, downspout, eelpout, waterspout

22.9.6
about, layabout, rightabout, eastabout, westabout, roustabout, gadabout, roundabout, knockabout, walkabout, runabout, turnabout, rouseabout, hereabout, thereabout

22.9.7
cutout, shut-out, white-out, shoot-out, opt-out, printout

22.9.8
readout, hideout, Rideout, redoubt, standout, handout, groundout, self-doubt, misdoubt, foldout, holdout, down-and-out

22.9.9
takeout, stakeout, breakout, checkout, blackout, stockout, knockout, lockout, walkout, strikeout, cookout, lookout, workout

22.9.10
dugout

22.9.11
spin-out, brown-out, lineout, turnout, down-and-out

22.9.12
hangout

22.9.13
devout

22.9.14
phaseout, closeout

22.9.15
washout

22.9.16
pitchout

22.9.17
mahout

22.9.18
clear-out, share-out, bean sprout, bull trout, sauerkraut

22.9.19
bailout, sellout, fallout, pullout, ablaut, umlaut, litterlout

22.10
art, part, pâte, baht, Bart, Barthes, tart, START, start, dart, cart, carte, kart, quarte, Scart, ghat, Maat, mart, smart, fart, chart, Jat, hart, Harte, heart, clart, kyat, spare part, op art, D'Oyly Carte, à la carte, state-of-the-art

22.10.1
forepart, apart, depart, impart, rampart, mouthpart, Unipart, counterpart, afterpart, underpart, Bonaparte

22.10.2
Rabat, Hobart

22.10.3
restart, stop-start, upstart, redstart, kickstart, pushstart, Hallstatt

22.10.4
Stoddart, Geldart

22.10.5
Descartes, zakat, go-cart, go-kart, tip-cart, dustcart, handcart, dogcart, Cathcart, oxcart, pushcart, applecart, undercart

22.10.6
Bogart, Stuttgart

22.10.7
foumart, outsmart

22.10.8
savate

22.10.9
Mansart, Robsart, Mozart, Dysart

22.10.10
flowchart, wallchart

22.10.11
Earhart, sweetheart, Goodhart, Eckhart, Lockhart, Leichhardt, Burckhardt, greenheart, Reinhardt, Bernhardt, Tugendhat, beefheart, oxheart, heart-to-heart

22.10.12
Gujrat, apparat, Gujarat, Bundesrat

22.10.13
Eilat, salat

22.11
Ott, pot, spot, bot, bott, tot, stot, Stott, dot, cot, Scot, Scott, got, Mott, motte, knot, Knott, not, Nott, snot, sot, shot, jot, hot, Wat, Watt, watt, what, wot, twat, squat, swat, swot, rot, trot, grot, yacht, lot, plot, Splott, blot, clot, slot, Shavuoth

22.11.1
eukaryote, prokaryote

22.11.2
teapot, repot, beerpot, stewpot, flowerpot, capot, hotpot, jackpot, crackpot, stockpot, inkpot, stinkpot, swankpot, tompot, compote, tinpot, pisspot, despot, tosspot, saucepot, fusspot, hotspot, nightspot, findspot, sexpot, black spot, sunspot, fishpot, fleshpot, dashpot, cachepot, hotchpot, smudgepot, Phillpott, chimney pot, talipot, galipot, gallipot, pepperpot, lobsterpot, on-the-spot

22.11.3
robot

22.11.4
Hottentot

22.11.5
Wyandot, peridot, polka dot, Bernadotte, microdot, Turandot

22.11.6
Draycott, cocotte, boycott, dicot, Grocott, Epcot®, Westcott, Didcot, dovecote, Prescott, ascot, mascot, Truscott, wainscot, Calcot, Calcott, Alcott, Walcot, Walcott, carrycot, Caldecote, Caldecott, monocot, massicot, apricot

22.11.7
begot, forgot, ergot

22.11.8
motmot, Willmott, bergamot, guillemot

22.11.9
cannot, slipknot, topknot, whatnot, unknot, have-not, touch-me-not, Hoddinott, Arbuthnot, forget-me-not

22.11.10
fylfot

22.11.11
dévote, gavotte

22.11.12
earshot, eyeshot, bowshot, chip shot, grapeshot, snapshot, slapshot, upshot, outshot, potshot, bloodshot, Oxshott, buckshot, Bagshot, mugshot, gunshot, moonshot, slingshot, spaceshot, mailshot, troubleshot, scattershot, undershot, Aldershot, overshot

22.11.13
hotshot

22.11.14
loquat, kumquat, somewhat, Watson-Watt, Ofwat, milliwatt, gigawatt, megawatt, terawatt,
kilowatt, you-know-what, paraquat, aliquot, diddly-squat

22.11.15
garrotte, gutrot, dogtrot, jogtrot, foxtrot, tommyrot

22.11.16
Mayotte

22.11.17
culotte, allot, reallot, calotte, shallot, marplot, subplot, Simplot, inkblot, feedlot, woodlot, sandlot, melilot, Camelot, Winalot®, ocelot, Lancelot, cachalot, sans-culotte, scatterplot, counterplot, underplot, polyglot, heptaglot, monoglot, Aeroflot®

22.12
entente, vicomte, passant, nuée ardente, trente-et-quarante

22.13
aught, Oort, ought, port, Porte, sport, boart, bort, bought, taught, taut, tort, torte, caught, Cort, court, ghat, mort, naught, nought, snort, fort, fought, thought, sort, sought, short, wart, quart, thwart, swart, rort, wrought, brought, fraught, Hampton Court, St Peter Port, Sublime Porte, Inns of Court

22.13.1
apport, deport, support, report, purport, import, reimport, comport, self-support, misreport, under-report, seaport, Freeport, Maryport, heliport, sally port, airport, Fairport, carport, Newport, viewport, Stourport, hoverport, teleport, Europort, outport, Bridport, Stockport, Kennebunkport, Devonport, davenport, Shreveport, passport, Gosport, disport, export, transport, spoilsport, watersport, re-export, Bridgeport, Alport, Coalport

22.13.2
abort, shop-bought, overbought

22.13.3
retaught, retort, untaught, contort, self-taught, bistort, mistaught, distort, extort

22.13.4
Harcourt, forecourt, backcourt, uncaught, escort, Port Harcourt, Dovercourt, Delacourt, Agincourt

22.13.5
Aigues-Mortes

22.13.6
Hainault, Connacht, Connaught, dreadnought, Argonaut, juggernaut, cosmonaut, aquanaut, aeronaut, astronaut

22.13.7
Beaufort, outfought

22.13.8
cavort

22.13.9
rethought, methought, forethought, bethought, unthought, aforethought, afterthought

22.13.10
resort, assort, besought, consort, unsought

22.13.11
resort, exhort

22.13.12
cohort

22.13.13
Kleinwort, athwart, worrywart

22.13.14
distraught, inwrought, unwrought, overwrought

22.13.15
onslaught

22.14
doit, coit, quoit, droit, dacoit, Bayreuth, Detroit, introit, adroit, exploit, maladroit

22.15
putt, but, butt, tut, cut, scut, ghat, gut, Mut, mutt, smut, nut, Knut, phut, phutt, shut, jut, hut, rut, strut, Strutt, glut, slut

22.15.1
put-put, putt-putt, sinciput, occiput, Lilliput

22.15.2
abut, rebut, sackbut, scuttlebutt, holibut

22.15.3
tut-tut

22.15.4
pre-cut, haircut, sawcut, crewcut, Whitcutt, shortcut, woodcut, uncut, offcut, crosscut, uppercut, intercut, undercut, anicut, annicut, Calicut, linocut

22.15.5
catgut, rotgut, midgut, Vonnegut

22.15.6
peanut, donut, doughnut, cobnut, chestnut, groundnut, locknut, pignut, wingnut, earthnut, beechnut, gallnut, walnut, hazelnut, butternut, coconut

22.15.7
phut-phut

22.15.8
unshut

22.16
spite, bight, bite, byte, tight, dight, kite, skite, might, mite, smite, knight, night, nite, fight, cite, sight, site, shite, Haight, height, hight, white, Whyte, wight, twite, Dwight, quite, right, rite, wright, write, sprite, bright, trite, krait, fright, light, lite, plight, blight, flight, sleight, slight, Twelfth Night, Isle of Wight, Very light

22.16.1
Shiite

22.16.2
Trotskyite, Paisleyite, McCarthyite, galleryite

22.16.3
Vishnuite

22.16.4
Vishnuite

22.16.5
Sivaite, Baha'ite, Karaite

22.16.6
sporozoite

22.16.7
respite, Warspite, despite

22.16.8
fleabite, Moabite, frostbite, soundbite, snakebite, backbite, lovebite, stilbite, albite, Rechabite, Jacobite, gigabyte, Mb, megabyte, coenobite, terabyte, kilobyte, trilobite, columbite

22.16.9
Hittite, steatite, airtight, ratite, partite, biotite, uptight, tektite, skintight, tungstite, bipartite, tripartite, apartheid, sexpartite, apatite, appetite, watertight, enstatite, haematite, hematite, migmatite, pegmatite, magnetite, weathertight, stalactite, cementite, transvestite, multipartite, unipartite, quadripartite, peridotite, carbonatite

22.16.10
lyddite, jadeite, cordite, Luddite, bedight, indict, indite, endite, recondite, expedite, erudite, extradite, troglodyte, incondite, Araldite®, hermaphrodite

22.16.11
trachyte, Melchite, malachite, blatherskite, Amalekite

22.16.12
dugite, Areopagite

22.16.13
Semite, samite, Hamite, marmite, termite, thermite, somite, chromite, catamite, Fatimite, Benthamite, Edomite, tridymite, Adamite, sodomite, dynamite, Gothamite, Hashemite, Vegemite®, eremite, hellgrammite, wolframite, Elamite, dolomite, Islamite, stalagmite, diatomite, pre-adamite, Adullamite

22.16.14
unite, tonight, lenite, goodnight, McKnight, ignite, reignite, reunite, overnight, disunite
.1 Gibeonite, Midianite .2 sennight .3 stannite
.4 Sunnite .5 kainite, finite, twi-night, echinite, transfinite .6 kyanite, syenite, dithionite, ebonite, urbanite, bentonite, yesternight, aconite, taconite, vulcanite, manganite, ammonite, Mammonite, Buchmanite, ilmenite, Canaanite, Mennonite, Leninite, Maronite, encrinite, mylonite, selenite, allanite, xylonite, kaolinite, suburbanite, exurbanite, molybdenite, sillimanite, gadolinite, porphyrogenite, montmorillonite .7 fortnight

.8 midnight .9 weeknight .10 lignite, gelignite
.11 Samnite, belemnite .12 watchnight

22.16.15
Irvingite, quislingite

22.16.16
outfight, chamaephyte, neophyte, osteophyte,
graphite, ophite, bryophyte, zoophyte, epiphyte,
protophyte, entophyte, spermophyte,
lithophyte, mesophyte, xerophyte, sporophyte,
saprophyte, hydrophyte, microphyte,
hygrophyte, thallophyte, halophyte, holophyte,
gametophyte, spermatophyte, pteridophyte,
cockfight, dogfight, gunfight, phosphite,
prizefight, sulphite, bullfight, bisulphite,
hyposulphite, metabisulphite

22.16.17
Levite, Servite, invite, sylvite, Muscovite,
stishovite, Stakhanovite

22.16.18
anorthite

22.16.19
resite, recite, excite, incite, overexcite
.1 histiocyte .2 dacite .3 Kassite .4 foresight,
Forsyte .5 zoisite .6 Hussite .7 eyesight .8 brucite,
Lucite® .9 lewisite, oocyte, composite, plebiscite,
thrombocyte, andesite, marcasite, leucocyte,
phagocyte, spermocyte, plasmacyte, monocyte,
magnesite, lymphocyte, oversight, parasite,
anthracite, gametocyte, hepatocyte,
spermatocyte, Monophysite, anorthosite,
erythrocyte, granulocyte, ectoparasite,
entoparasite, endoparasite, reticulocyte,
oligodendrocyte .10 rhodochrosite .11 campsite
.12 quartzite .13 hindsight .14 backsight,
bauxite, worksite .15 bombsight, bomb site
.16 insight, gunsight .17 calcite

22.16.20
composite, andesite, monazite, martensite

22.16.21
augite

22.16.22
gesundheit, Fahrenheit

22.16.23
Snow-white, bobwhite, requite, Hepplewhite,
Micklewhite, lillywhite

22.16.24
rewrite, aright, outright, read-write, alright,
underwrite, overwrite .1 copyright .2 sclerite,
meteorite .3 playwright .4 ferrite .5 barite
.6 Plowright .7 thorite, chlorite, fluorite,
hypochlorite .8 pyrite, chalcopyrite .9 diorite,
azurite, sybarite, Labourite, laterite, Hutterite,
siderite, anchorite, ankerite, margarite,
Amorite, Minorite, phosphorite, Nazirite,
Thatcherite, fulgurite, tellurite, sphalerite,
dolerite, Hitlerite, cassiterite, ozokerite
.10 shipwright, upright .11 eyebright, Albright,
Fulbright .12 cartwright, nitrite, contrite
.13 Goodwright, dendrite, chondrite, anhydrite,

archimandrite, alexandrite .14 Arkwright
.15 wainwright, Enright, downright
.16 nephrite, affright .17 forthright,
birthright .18 Cheesewright .19 wheelwright,
millwright

22.16.25
relight, alight, polite, delight, impolite,
self-delight .1 Peelite, pelite, scheelite
.2 phyllite .3 ophiolite, ichthyolite, variolite,
Pre-Raphaelite, Ishmaelite .4 daylight
.5 covellite .6 halite .7 starlight, marlite .8 stylite,
skylight, highlight, twilight .9 zeolite,
firelight, hyalite, rhyolite, cryolite, oolite,
cosmopolite, rubellite, kimberlite,
amphibolite, metabolite, cristobalite,
antimetabolite, satellite, quarterlight,
graptolite, troctolite, tantalite, afterlight,
crystallite, stromatolite, sodalite, lepidolite,
crocidolite, theodolite, Bakelite®, acolyte,
Armalite®, Carmelite, marmolite, phonolite,
toxophilite, Monothelite, featherlight,
chrysolite, proselyte, topazolite, socialite,
Keralite, spherulite, aerolite, corallite,
staurolite, coprolite, microlight, Israelite,
electrolyte, nummulite, cellulite, vermiculite
.10 pearlite, perlite .11 Coalite®, lowlight
.12 stoplight, hoplite, lamplight .13 streetlight,
spotlight, nightlight .14 deadlight, headlight,
floodlight, sidelight .15 jacklight, heteroclite
.16 limelight .17 penlight, fanlight, sunlight,
moonlight .18 preflight, in-flight, spaceflight,
overflight .19 gaslight, wax-light .20 flashlight,
rushlight .21 torchlight, searchlight .22 taillight,
candlelight

22.17
put, foot, Foote, soot, amniote, throughput,
kaput, output, input, Rajput, Yakut, splay-foot,
barefoot, forefoot, afoot, crowfoot, club foot,
flatfoot, hotfoot, lightfoot, Blackfoot,
wrong-foot, goosefoot, coltsfoot, cocksfoot,
Landshut, procaryote, prokaryote, per caput,
Lilliput, pussyfoot, tenderfoot, underfoot,
Saundersfoot, Inuktitut

22.18
boot, toot, coot, Coote, scoot, moot, knout,
snoot, suit, chute, shoot, Shute, jute, hoot, root,
route, bruit, brut, brute, fruit, Ute, beaut, Bute,
butte, cute, scute, mute, newt, lute, loot, flute,
sloot, Paiute, zoot suit, square root, en route, ugli
fruit, kiwi fruit

22.18.1
Aleut

22.18.2
Paiute

22.18.3
skiboot, seaboot, reboot, freeboot, snowboot,
topboot, jackboot, gumboot, unboot, overboot,
marabout

22.18.4
bandicoot, babacoote, Tonton Macoute

22.18.5
Knut, droop-snoot

22.18.6
playsuit, lawsuit, drysuit, snowsuit, jumpsuit, wetsuit, sweatsuit, catsuit, pantsuit, tracksuit, tanksuit, swimsuit, nonsuit, sunsuit, spacesuit, bodysuit, Hatshepsut

22.18.7
outshoot, beanshoot, offshoot, troubleshoot, undershoot, overshoot, parachute

22.18.8
mahout

22.18.9
re-route, Beirut, cheroot, taproot, uproot, clubroot, imbrute, beetroot, bloodroot, snakeroot, choucroute, recruit, unroot, grapefruit, breadfruit, jackfruit, passionfruit, bitterroot, arrowroot, autoroute

22.18.10
Paiute, Salyut, depute, repute, impute, compute, dispute, disrepute, tribute, attribute, deattribute, contribute, distribute, redistribute, statute, astute, destitute, prostitute, substitute, institute, constitute, reinstitute, reconstitute, acute, subacute, prosecute, persecute, execute, electrocute, argute, permute, commute, transmute, malamute, telecommute, minute, Canute, Cnut, comminute, Hardicanute, refute, confute

22.18.11
dilute, Aleut, elute, pollute, galoot, volute, salute, Hakluyt, archlute, evolute, devolute, revolute, involute, dissolute, absolute, resolute, irresolute

22.19.1
Piat

22.19.2
Ayot, eyot

22.19.3
Jowett, Jowitt

22.19.4
Byatt, diet, Hyatt, Wyatt, quiet, riot, ryot, unquiet, disquiet, isohyet

22.19.5
Oort, Verwoerd, situate, graduate, arcuate, eluate, postgraduate, attenuate, undergraduate

22.19.6
Stewart, Stuart, Ewart

22.19.7
poet, Jowett, inchoate, ethanoate

22.19.8
sippet, frippet, Capet, Rupert, purport, occiput, principate, parapet, episcopate, archiepiscopate

22.19.9
Hebert, zibet, gibbet, flibbertigibbet, abbot, Abbott, Cabot, Newton Abbott, Tarbert, Garbett, nobbut, Robert, Corbett, Norbert, sorbet, adsorbate, Schubert, Hubert, celibate, halibut, burbot, turbot, sherbet, Herbert, Egbert, Imbert, ambit, lambert, Humbert, Cuthbert, Nisbett, Osbert, Gilbert, filbert, Hilbert, Wilbert, Elbert, Delbert, Albert, talbot, Port Talbot

22.19.10
testate, Bastet, Vansittart, stipitate, intestate, precipitate

22.19.11
pedate, Stoddart, chordate, candidate, incondite

22.19.12
.1 thecate **.2** Sickert **.3** Draycott **.4** Hecate **.5** packet **.6** patriarchate **.7** locket, Lockhart **.8** ducat, Nantucket **.9** spicate, plicate **.10** etiquette, predicate, syndicate, Caldecote, advocate, intricate, affricate, silicate, delicate, Calicut, collocate, triplicate, duplicate, Connecticut, sophisticate, canonicate, certificate, pontificate, umbilicate, indelicate, quadruplicate, sesquiplicate, borosilicate, aluminosilicate **.11** Urquhart, bifurcate **.12** Didcot, Hidcote **.13** Heathcote **.14** frisket, Westcott, Prescot, Prescott, ascot, basket, gasket, mascot, musket, Truscott, wainscot, wastebasket, breadbasket, workbasket **.15** Calcott, Charlecote, Alcott, Walcott

22.19.13
Piggott, spigot, bigot, gigot, jigot, frigate, legate, Leggatt, agate, Taggart, maggot, faggot, Swaggart, braggart, garget, margate, Hoggart, yogurt, nougat, nugget, drugget, Highgate, Reigate, ergot, Kirkgate, virgate, Ludgate, Aldgate, ingot, vulgate, McTaggart, conjugate, Harrogate, surrogate, abrogate, aggregate, delegate, profligate

22.19.14
squamate, emmet, gamut, Mamet, Hammett, marmot, grommet, primate, climate, Dermot, kismet, Elmet, pelmet, helmet, imamate, consummate, intimate, estimate, guesstimate, ultimate, animate, proximate, McDermott, microclimate, ecoclimate, legitimate, penultimate, inanimate, approximate, illegitimate, underestimate, overestimate, antepenultimate

22.19.15
.1 pinnate, sinnet, Sinnott, bipinnate, tripinnate, cabinet, bobbinet **.2** tenet, Kennet, senate, rennet **.3** cannot, gannet, Thanet, Janet, granite, pomegranate **.4** garnet, Garnett, Barnet, incarnate, reincarnate, discarnate **.5** Connaught, sonnet **.6** hornet **.7** Mynett, Mynott **.8** lunate **.9** bayonet, lionet, resupinate, tabinet, rabbinate, carbonate, turbinate, umbonate, bicarbonate, polycarbonate, pectinate, obstinate, sultanate, Palatinate, agglutinate, ordinate, coordinate, subordinate, inordinate, insubordinate, superordinate, deaconate, falconet, diaconate, subdiaconate, archidiaconate, dragonet, shogunate, permanganate, geminate, staminate, laminate, pulmonate, discriminate, effeminate,

innominate, acuminate, determinate, indiscriminate, predeterminate, indeterminate, definite, infinite, indefinite, basinet, arsenate, sarsenet, circinate, uncinate, runcinate, passionate, compassionate, dispassionate, proportionate, extortionate, affectionate, disproportionate, unaffectionate, fortunate, importunate, unfortunate, alginate, Plantagenet, baronet, carinate, coronet, mucronate, tribunate, companionate **.10** ternate, triternate, alternate **.11** cygnet, signet, magnate, magnet, impregnate, designate, electromagnet **.12** Hamnett **.13** Arbuthnot

22.19.16
Seifert, effort, Moffatt, forfeit, surfeit, Beaufort, Montfort, Frankfurt, comfort, de Montfort, discomfit, discomfort

22.19.17
sievert, pivot, divot, Evert, covert, covet, lovat, private, vervet, Ovett, Calvert, culvert, Glenlivet, feme covert, Olivet, semiprivate

22.19.18
tiercet, placet, Knesset, basset, facet, Dorset, faucet, Fawcett, Dysart, tercet, verset, Quixote, lancet, concert, Consett, Quonset®, dulcet, deficit, marquessate, marquisate, Don Quixote, insensate, Narragansett

22.19.19
desert, exquisite, apposite, inapposite

22.19.20
Wishart, freshet, ashet, cushat, lynchet, planchet, associate

22.19.21
Pritchett, latchet, rochet, crotchet, lynchet, planchet, Melchett

22.19.22
midget, fidget, Bridget, pledget, Paget, Bagehot, gadget, gorget

22.19.23
loquat, stalwart, adequate, inadequate

22.19.24
.1 skirret, levirate **.2** Meerut, juniorate, vizierate **.3** terret, ferret, disinherit **.4** parrot, Parrott, barret, carat, caret, carrot, karat, Garratt, garret, Jarratt, claret, Ballymacarrett **.5** floret **.6** curate **.7** turret **.8** pirate, lyrate, Epirot **.9** floweret, priorate, separate, corporate, temperate, disparate, desperate, aspirate, incorporate, intemperate, tabaret, tabouret, carburet, deliberate, elaborate, literate, preterite, Carteret, rectorate, doctorate, pastorate, presbyterate, preliterate, illiterate, inveterate, inspectorate, protectorate, directorate, electorate, coelenterate, moderate, desiderate, considerate, confederate, immoderate, inconsiderate, emirate, amirate, glomerate, numerate, agglomerate, conglomerate, innumerate, banneret, lanneret, degenerate, regenerate, governorate, unregenerate,

ephorate, perforate, pomfret, imperforate, favourite, Everett, leveret, unfavourite, triumvirate, duumvirate, centumvirate, professorate, commensurate, incommensurate, Gennesaret, obdurate, indurate, accurate, barbiturate, monounsaturate, inaccurate, cellaret **.10** culprit, interpret, reinterpret, misinterpret **.11** labret, vertebrate, invertebrate **.12** portrait, rostrate, self-portrait, electret, magistrate **.13** quadrat, quadrate **.14** secret **.15** egret, Margaret

22.19.25
panchayat

22.19.26
.1 billet, skillet, fillet, willet, papillate, verticillate, penicillate **.2** petiolate, alveolate, urceolate, lanceolate, calceolate, oblanceolate **.3** raylet, playlet **.4** stellate, Kellet, Kellett, zealot, Helot, prelate, appellate, stipellate, patellate **.5** Allott, palate, palette, pallet, ballot, Malet, mallet, valet, sallet **.6** owlet, Howlett **.7** starlet, scarlet, Scarlett, varlet, charlotte, harlot **.8** Colet, collet, wallet **.9** toilet **.10** cullet, gullet, mullet, surmullet **.11** eyelet, islet, Pilate, pilot, stylet, co-pilot, autopilot, gyropilot **.12** pullet, bullet **.13** triolet, foveolate, violet, squirelet, inviolate, ultraviolet, umbellate, mantelet, scutellate, pistillate, distillate, apostolate, lamellate, cardinalate, coverlet, desolate, ocellate, isolate, Lancelot, disconsolate, flagellate, flageolet, arillate, correlate, lobulate, spatulate, postulate, spiculate, oculate, ungulate, amulet, annulet, rivulet, capsulate, consulate, serrulate, orbiculate, scrobiculate, articulate, particulate, reticulate, straticulate, denticulate, testiculate, pediculate, fasciculate, vesiculate, unguiculate, auriculate, folliculate, trabeculate, tentaculate, immaculate, ejaculate, operculate, tuberculate, pedunculate, triangulate, campanulate, proconsulate, inarticulate, solidungulate, Capulet **.14** sterlet, Merlot, murrelet **.15** ripplet, triplet, Caplet®, chaplet, droplet, couplet, drupelet, template, templet, septuplet, quintuplet, sextuplet, quadruplet **.16** triblet, driblet, gablet, tablet, goblet, doublet **.17** statelet, platelet, flatlet, troutlet, Bartlett, tartlet, martlet, cutlet, nutlet, rootlet, fruitlet, notelet, gantlet, mantlet, plantlet, gauntlet, frontlet, swiftlet, wristlet **.18** Radlett, cloudlet, rodlet, toadlet **.19** lakelet, necklet, sparklet, chocolate, rocklet, auklet, stalklet, pikelet, spikelet, booklet, hooklet, rooklet, brooklet, circlet, anklet **.20** eaglet, piglet, shiglet, aiglet, reglet, aglet, goglet, buglet, singlet **.21** streamlet, gimlet, stemlet, Tremlett, samlet, hamlet, armlet, omelet, omelette, boomlet **.22** greenlet, inlet, veinlet, townlet, runlet **.23** kinglet, winglet, ringlet, springlet **.24** leaflet, pamphlet **.25** wavelet **.26** bracelet, harslet, corselet, corselette, verselet, lancelet **.27** haslet, Haslett, Hazlitt, Hunslet **.28** branchlet

22.20

pert, spirt, spurt, Bert, Birt, Burt, Sturt, dirt, curt, Kurt, skirt, girt, vert, cert, shirt, chert, hurt, wert, wort, quirt, squirt, yurt, blurt, flirt

22.20.1

expert, malapert, inexpert

22.20.2

Osbert, Colbert, Engelbert, Ethelbert

22.20.3

paydirt

22.20.4

Eckert, miniskirt, underskirt, overskirt

22.20.5

begirt

22.20.6

émeute

22.20.7

inert

22.20.8

Frankfurt

22.20.9

divert, avert, evert, overt, pervert, revert, covert, obvert, subvert, advert, invert, convert, ambivert, retrovert, introvert, controvert, extravert, extrovert, reconvert, animadvert, seroconvert

22.20.10

assert, reassert, exsert, insert, reinsert, concert, preconcert, disconcert

22.20.11

desert, dessert, exert, overexert

22.20.12

teeshirt, redshirt, Blackshirt, Brownshirt, undershirt

22.20.13

sweatshirt, sportshirt, nightshirt

22.20.14

unhurt

22.20.15

spearwort, starwort, spurwort, dropwort, soapwort, limpwort, ribwort, saltwort, leadwort, sandwort, woundwort, milkwort, figwort, ragwort, mugwort, lime-wort, spleenwort, danewort, hornwort, stonewort, lungwort, toothwort, glasswort, lousewort, sneezewort, stitchwort, pillwort, felwort, pilewort, pearlwort, nipplewort, navelwort, pennywort, moneywort, slipperwort, pepperwort, setterwort, butterwort, bladderwort, spiderwort, liverwort, squinancywort

22.20.16

alert

22.21

oat, boat, Thoth, tote, stoat, dote, Caute, coat, cote, goat, moat, mote, smote, note, phot, vote, shoat, quote, rote, wrote, groat, throat, bloat, gloat, float, flote, table d'hôte, Terre Haute

22.21.1

capote, compote

22.21.2

sea-boat, U-boat, Q-boat, powerboat, towboat, showboat, rowboat, catboat, flatboat, speedboat, foldboat, stakeboat, cockboat, workboat, tugboat, steamboat, dreamboat, bumboat, gunboat, swingboat, longboat, lifeboat, surfboat, houseboat, sauceboat, iceboat, keelboat, mailboat, sailboat, whaleboat, ferryboat, jolly boat, motorboat, riverboat

22.21.3

asymptote

22.21.4

Haggadoth, antidote, anecdote

22.21.5

Succoth, blue coat, surcoat, topcoat, greatcoat, waistcoat, redcoat, Wilmcote, raincoat, turncoat, dovecote, housecoat, tailcoat, gelcoat, Charlecote, happi-coat, petticoat, undercoat, overcoat, entrecôte, Swadlincote

22.21.6

zygote, scapegoat, nanny goat, redingote, heterozygote, homozygote

22.21.7

demote, emote, remote, promote, witenagemot

22.21.8

keynote, denote, connote, footnote, headnote, woodnote, endnote, banknote

22.21.9

isophote, holophote

22.21.10

devote, outvote, mitzvoth

22.21.11

creosote, myosote, Quixote

22.21.12

mezuzoth

22.21.13

unquote, misquote, underquote

22.21.14

rewrote, shofroth, bluethroat, cutthroat, whitethroat, haphtaroth, Epirote, overwrote

22.21.15

refloat, afloat, matelote, pardalote, Fomalhaut

22.22.1

hipped, crypt, script, untipped, Egypt, unwhipped, unstripped, decrypt, encrypt, rescript, prescript, typescript, subscript, postscript, transcript, conscript, harelipped, ellipt, unequipped, underequipped, superscript, nondescript, manuscript, eucalypt

22.22.2

pearshaped, U-shaped, wedge-shaped, undraped

22.22.3
kept, sept, wept, swept, crept, leapt, slept, adept,
unkept, housekept, inept, precept, percept,
except, accept, reaccept, incept, transept,
concept, unwept, upswept, windswept,
rainswept, unswept, yclept, intercept,
nympholept, overleaped, overslept

22.22.4
apt, rapt, periapt, untapped, adapt,
readapt, snow-capped, unmapped, inapt,
unapt, enrapt

22.22.5
opt, Copt, co-opt, adopt, readopt, uncropped

22.22.6
irrupt, erupt, corrupt, abrupt, bankrupt, disrupt,
interrupt

22.22.7
unwiped

22.22.8
undeveloped, underdeveloped

22.22.9
excerpt

22.22.10
sculpt

22.23.1
hollow-cheeked

22.23.2
Pict, strict, depict, handpicked, edict, addict,
predict, verdict, evict, convict, district,
Maastricht, restrict, constrict, delict, relict,
afflict, inflict, conflict, interdict, Benedict,
contradict, pluperfect, word-perfect, Peak
District, derestrict, derelict

22.23.3
unbaked, sun-baked, unslaked

22.23.4
echt, sect, Brecht **.1** aspect, prospect, suspect,
respect, expect, inspect, reinspect, retrospect,
introspect, self-respect, disrespect,
circumspect **.2** detect, protect, architect
.3 pandect **.4** connect, bull-necked, reconnect,
disconnect, interconnect **.5** defect, prefect,
affect, effect, perfect, infect, reinfect, confect,
disinfect **.6** advect **.7** bisect, dissect, trisect,
resect, insect, transect, intersect, vivisect
.8 unchecked **.9** reject, project, eject, deject,
abject, object, subject, inject, reinject, interject,
retroject **.10** direct, erect, re-erect, porrect,
correct, Utrecht, Dordrecht, redirect, indirect,
misdirect, suberect, incorrect, resurrect,
hypercorrect **.11** collect, elect, re-elect,
pre-elect, dialect, select, prelect, neglect, deflect,
reflect, inflect, idiolect, intellect, recollect,
analect, deselect, mesolect, reselect, basilect,
unselect, acrolect, self-neglect, genuflect,
president-elect

22.23.5
act, pact, tact, fact, bract, tract, react, outact,

enact, abreact, retroact, interact, counteract,
underact, overact, overreact **.1** play-act **.2** epact,
impact, compact, subcompact **.3** barebacked,
humpbacked, unbacked, hunchbacked
.4 intact, contact **.5** redact, autodidact **.6** re-enact
.7 artefact, artifact, ventifact, matter-of-fact
.8 transact, exact, inexact **.9** entr'acte, attract,
detract, retract, protract, subtract, contract,
untracked, distract, abstract, extract, uncracked,
diffract, refract, infract, cataract, subcontract,
Pontefract

22.23.6
marked, Wehrmacht, unmarked, infarct,
unremarked

22.23.7
unstocked, decoct, concoct, dreadlocked,
landlocked

22.23.8
duct, product, adduct, viaduct, deduct, subduct,
abduct, induct, conduct, destruct, obstruct,
instruct, construct, deconstruct, unplucked,
oviduct, ventiduct, aqueduct, safe-conduct,
misconduct, reconduct, self-destruct,
reconstruct, usufruct, autodestruct

22.23.9
uncooked, Sehnsucht, unlooked

22.23.10
conduct, perfect, object, subject, imperfect

22.23.11
handworked, unworked

22.23.12
unsmoked, unsoaked, unprovoked, unrevoked,
uninvoked

22.23.13
distinct, extinct, instinct, precinct, succinct,
unthanked, defunct, adjunct, injunct, conjunct,
disjunct, indistinct, unit-linked, sacrosanct

22.23.14
unasked

22.23.15
mulct

22.24
Fichte, echt, Brecht, Maastricht, Utrecht,
Dordrecht, Gaeltacht, Kristallnacht,
Wehrmacht, Sehnsucht

22.25
Klimt, tempt, kempt, dreamed, dreamt, prompt,
preempt, attempt, reattempt, contempt,
unkempt, exempt, undreamt, unstamped,
undamped, vicomte, self-contempt, teleprompt

22.26.1
bint, tint, stint, dint, quint, skint, mint, vint,
hint, squint, suint, print, sprint, lint, splint,
clint, glint, flint, undertint, monotint, aquatint,
mezzotint, remint, spearmint, catmint,
peppermint, calamint, Septuagint, asquint,
forint, reprint, preprint, blueprint, footprint,

imprint, thumbprint, screen-print, enprint, offprint, misprint, voiceprint, newsprint, fingerprint, overprint, ELINT, skinflint

22.26.2
.1 sapient, percipient, recipient, excipient, incipient, impercipient **.2** ambient, circumambient **.3** mediant, radiant, gradient, expedient, obedient, submediant, ingredient, irradiant, clairaudient, inexpedient, disobedient **.4** permeant **.5** lenient, fainéant, prevenient, convenient, supervenient, intervenient, inconvenient **.6** deviant, subservient **.7** nescient, prescient, transient, omniscient, insouciant, insousiant, asphyxiant, renunciant **.8** officiant, negotiant: (+ **22.26.15**(.19)) **.9** variant, Orient, prurient, nutrient, recreant, procreant, miscreant, aperient, invariant, euphoriant, disorient, esurient, luxuriant, parturient **.10** brilliant, salient, valiant, suppliant, resilient, emollient, ebullient, defoliant

22.26.3
ain't, paint, taint, mayn't, faint, feint, saint, quaint, spraint, plaint, repaint, spray-paint, warpaint, greasepaint, attaint, acquaint, reacquaint, distraint, restraint, constraint, complaint, overpaint, unrestraint, self-restraint, unconstraint

22.26.4
pent, spent, bent, tent, stent, dent, kent, Ghent, meant, vent, cent, scent, sent, gent, went, Gwent, rent, brent, Trent, leant, lent, blent **.1** orient, reorient, disorient **.2** repent, outspent, unspent, misspent, underspent, overspent **.3** Broadbent, unbent **.4** portent, detent, intent, content, extent, self-content, discontent, malcontent **.5** indent, Mentadent®, Pepsodent®, Steradent **.6** Tashkent **.7** Penyghent **.8** ament, comment, torment, dement, ferment, foment, cement, lament, loment, pigment, segment, fragment, augment, unmeant, ornament, regiment, decrement, document, supplement, implement, compliment, experiment **.9** anent, thereanent **.10** event, prevent, advent, invent, reinvent, circumvent **.11** precent, ascent, assent, percent, descent, dissent, absent, accent, unsent, consent **.12** wisent, resent, present, re-present, represent, misrepresent **.13** forwent, outwent, frequent, underwent **.14** quitrent, Stoke-on-Trent **.15** relent

22.26.5
daren't

22.26.6
ant, pant, cant, Kant, scant, chant, rand, rant, Brandt, brant, grant, Land, plant, slant, Brabant, corybant, extant, confidant, confidante, commandant, decant, bacchante, recant, descant, predikant, Bodnant, sycophant, hierophant, levant, gallivant, Durrant, Morant, Rembrandt, jimmygrant, gallant, replant, supplant, eggplant, implant, houseplant,

explant, waxplant, transplant, ashplant, aslant, underplant, homotransplant, heterotransplant

22.26.7
count, mount, fount, Blount, recount, viscount, accompt, account, acct, no-account, headcount, discount, miscount, demount, remount, amount, surmount, dismount, catamount, tantamount, paramount

22.26.8
aren't, aunt, can't, Nantes, shan't, chant, rand, grant, plant, slant, détente, entente, débutant, débutante, commandant, en passant, plainchant, enchant, disenchant, courante, restaurant, jimmygrant, replant, supplant, eggplant, implant, houseplant, explant, waxplant, transplant, ashplant, aslant, fête galante, underplant, homotransplant, heterotransplant

22.26.9
pont, Comte, conte, Nantes, font, fount, want, wont, quant, rand, Du Pont, symbiont, Hellespont, Broederbond, Penybont, Talybont, détente, entente, poste restante, glyptodont, conodont, lophodont, selenodont, dicynodont, hypsilophodont, Frémont, Claremont, Clermont, Stormont, Vermont, Lamont, Beaumont, Grosmont, piedmont, Egmont, Belmont, Egremont, bouffant, Delfont, Chalfont, bon vivant, schizont, restaurant, diplont

22.26.10
taunt, daunt, Comte, gaunt, vaunt, jaunt, haunt, flaunt, avaunt

22.26.11
point, joint, repoint, three-point, waypoint, dewpoint, viewpoint, appoint, reappoint, powerpoint, outpoint, midpoint, endpoint, standpoint, breakpoint, checkpoint, tuckpoint, pinpoint, gunpoint, strongpoint, reefpoint, knifepoint, cashpoint, flashpoint, sealpoint, vowel-point, ballpoint, needlepoint, telepoint, Hurstpierpoint, point-to-point, counterpoint, disappoint, vantage point, anoint, T-joint, subjoint, conjoint, unjoint, disjoint, aroint

22.26.12
punt, bunt, stunt, cunt, shunt, hunt, runt, brunt, grunt, front, Lunt, Blount, blunt, exeunt, mahant, headhunt, manhunt, foxhunt, witch-hunt, seafront, storefront, forefront, shorefront, affront, shopfront, up-front, shirtfront, lakefront, confront, oceanfront, wavefront, beachfront, Adi Granth, waterfront, riverfront

22.26.13
pint, Geraint

22.26.14
punt, munt, bergschrund

22.26.15
.1 exeunt **.2** mayn't, naiant, abeyant **.3** buoyant, flamboyant, clairvoyant **.4** giant, Bryant, pliant,

client, affiant, defiant, reliant, compliant, supergiant, self-reliant **.5** issuant, congruent, unguent, diluent, eluent, effluent, refluent, affluent, influent, confluent, substituent, constituent, evacuant, continuant, mellifluent, interfluent, circumfluent **.6** truant, fluent, pursuant **.7** flippant, serpent, dopant, rampant, occupant, participant, anticipant **.8** lambent, desorbent, resorbent, absorbent, adsorbent, decumbent, recumbent, procumbent, incumbent, superincumbent **.9** remittent, concomitant, intermittent, latent, blatant, supernatant, patent, combatant, oughtn't, portent, important, unimportant, self-important, mightn't, excitant, mutant, nutant, disputant, pollutant, annuitant, crepitant, appetent, impotent, competent, palpitant, habitant, penitent, renitent, visitant, hesitant, adjutant, equitant, irritant, militant, volitant, totipotent, omnipotent, precipitant, inappetent, incompetent, cohabitant, inhabitant, exorbitant, impenitent, coadjutant, executant, omnicompetent, incapacitant, counterirritant, immunocompetent, advertent, inadvertent, potent, prepotent, reptant, optant, acceptant, octant, expectant, protectant, humectant, annectent, disinfectant, reactant, surfactant, attractant, reluctant, interactant, repentant, accountant, remontant, unrepentant, distant, extant, sextant, instant, constant, assistant, persistent, subsistent, insistent, consistent, resistant, existent, preexistent, coexistent, contestant, decongestant, Protestant, inconstant, equidistant, inconsistent, self-consistent, self-existent, nonexistent, water-resistant, consultant, resultant, exultant **.10** needn't, decedent, precedent, antecedent, retrocedent, didn't, pedant, hadn't, ardent, guardant, retardant, regardant, mordant, mordent, accordant, concordant, discordant, trident, strident, couldn't, shouldn't, wouldn't, student, prudent, imprudent, protrudent, jurisprudent, decadent, diffident, confident, evident, provident, dissident, Pepsodent®, accident, occident, oxidant, incident, resident, president, impudent, unconfident, self-confident, self-evident, improvident, coincident, ex-president, overconfident, antioxidant, verdant, rodent, pendant, pendent, splendent, fondant, appendant, dependant, dependent, impendent, attendant, intendant, defendant, ascendant, descendant, descendent, transcendent, resplendent, demandant, despondent, respondent, abundant, redundant, commandant, codependent, independent, self-dependent, superintendent, correspondent, co-respondent, superabundant, overabundant, interdependent **.11** piquant, secant, vacant, peccant, bacchant, cosecant, impeccant, vesicant, predicant, abdicant, mendicant, desiccant, toxicant, lubricant, applicant, supplicant, communicant, significant, intoxicant, insignificant **.12** litigant, fumigant,

termagant, arrogant, intrigant, congregant, elegant, noctivagant, extravagant, inelegant **.13.1** agreement, disagreement, worriment, embodiment, disembodiment, cerement, endearment, lineament, payment, raiment, claimant, clamant, repayment, prepayment, embayment, defrayment, underpayment, overpayment, clement, inclement, Claremont, impairment, ensnarement, Lamont, endowment, disendowment, garment, varmint, disbarment, undergarment, overgarment, torment, Stormont, dormant, formant, informant, securement, procurement, immurement, inurement, allurement, enjoyment, deployment, employment, re-employment, redeployment, misemployment, unemployment, self-employment, underemployment, Dymont, vehement, empowerment, virement, retirement, acquirement, requirement **.13.2** orpiment, dissepement, dismemberment, encumberment, betterment, sentiment, testament, embitterment, accoutrement, presentiment, hereditament, pediment, sediment, adamant, rudiment, condiment, fundament, wonderment, impediment, bewilderment, medicament, predicament, ligament, prefigurement, disfigurement, armament, firmament, rearmament, disarmament, liniment, tenement, ornament, tournament, muniment, accompaniment, decipherment, encipherment, approximant, measurement, remeasurement, admeasurement, mismeasurement, endangerment, regiment, diriment, merriment, temperament, detriment, nutriment, instrument, decrement, sacrament, increment, excrement, Egremont, experiment, arbitrament, document, tegument, argument, monument, integument, emolument, filament, element, aliment, parliament, supplement, implement, complement, compliment, habiliment, monofilament, Europarliament, determent, interment, reinterment, disinterment, deferment, preferment, conferment, averment, moment, Grosmont, loment, bestowment, spur-of-the-moment **.13.3** shipment, transshipment, transhipment, equipment, escapement, entrapment, escarpment, recoupment, regroupment, elopement, decampment, encampment, development, envelopment, redevelopment, self-development, underdevelopment, treatment, pretreatment, mistreatment, maltreatment, fitment, commitment, refitment, recommitment, statement, abatement, restatement, reinstatement, misstatement, affreightment, understatement, overstatement, abetment, revetment, besetment, apartment, department, impartment, compartment, allotment, reallotment, deportment, comportment, assortment, hutment, abutment, rebutment, indictment, excitement, incitement, overexcitement, recruitment, disconcertment, tapotement, devotement, ejectment, enactment, re-enactment, debarkment, embankment, ointment, contentment, resentment, presentment, enchantment, disenchantment, appointment, reappointment, discontentment, disappointment, vestment, encystment, agistment, enlistment, re-enlistment, divestment, investment, reinvestment, disinvestment, arrestment, adjustment, readjustment, entrustment, encrustment, self-adjustment, maladjustment, oddment, bodement, debridement, embedment, bombardment, retardment, rescindment, intendment, amendment, disbandment, commandment, impoundment, secondment, refundment, unfoldment, pigment, figment, segment, fragment **.13.4** enjambment, embalmment, entombment, disentombment, attainment, reattainment, detainment, retainment, obtainment, containment, sustainment, ordainment, enchainment, arraignment, detrainment, entrainment, distrainment, refrainment, entertainment, infotainment, ascertainment, edutainment, self-containment, adornment, enjoinment, refinement, confinement, assignment, reassignment, consignment, entwinement, enshrinement, alignment, alinement, realignment, reconsignment, intertwinement, nonalignment, misalignment, cantonment, impugnment, enlightenment, abandonment, environment, self-abandonment, internment, discernment, concernment, adjournment, postponement, atonement, dethronement, enthronement, disheartenment, government, self-government, misgovernment, enlivenment, anti-government, disseverment, blazonment, imprisonment, emblazonment, apportionment, reapportionment, proportionment, provisionment, disillusionment **.13.5** feoffment, enfeoffment, engulfment, engraftment, pavement, movement, achievement, bereavement, enslavement, improvement, evolvement, devolvement, involvement, underachievement, overachievement, countermovement, self-improvement, noninvolvement, self-involvement, enswathement, basement, casement, placement, abasement, debasement, encasement, effacement, defacement, embracement, replacement, outplacement, emplacement, displacement, misplacement, enlacement, self-abasement, self-effacement, interlacement, assessment, reassessment, impressment, redressment, amassment, harassment, embossment, indorsement, endorsement, reinforcement, enforcement, re-enforcement, divorcement, enticement, traducement, inducement, conducement, encompassment, divertissement, advertisement, arrondissement, embarrassment, disembarrassment,

self-advertisement, reimbursement, disbursement, amercement, engrossment, convincement, commencement, advancement, enhancement, entrancement, announcement, enouncement, denouncement, renouncement, pronouncement, recommencement, self-advancement, easement, appeasement, amazement, appraisement, chastisement, disguisement, amusement, bemusement, aggrandizement, enfranchisement, disfranchisement, disenfranchisement, self-aggrandizement **.13.6** enmeshment, refreshment, abashment, encashment, debouchment, blandishment, banishment, garnishment, punishment, ravishment, languishment, nourishment, retrenchment, entrenchment, embranchment, refurbishment, replenishment, astonishment, admonishment, relinquishment, extinguishment, malnourishment, impoverishment, embellishment, abolishment, accomplishment, establishment, re-establishment, anti-establishment, undernourishment, disestablishment, preachment, catchment, hatchment, parchment, impeachment, enrichment, attachment, reattachment, detachment, avouchment, encroachment, abridgement, engagement, re-engagement, preengagement, disengagement, assuagement, enragement, enlargement, lodgement, dislodgement, engorgement, disgorgement, judgement, prejudgement, adjudgement, misjudgement, management, mismanagement, envisagement, disparagement, encouragement, discouragement, acknowledgement, impingement, infringement, arrangement, rearrangement, prearrangement, derangement, estrangement, disarrangement, divulgement **.13.7** concealment, congealment, instilment, fulfilment, self-fulfilment, wish-fulfilment, overfulfilment, ailment, bailment, impalement, curtailment, entailment, regalement, derailment, disembowelment, extolment, forestalment, instalment, enthralment, disenthralment, despoilment, embroilment, annulment, disannulment, beguilement, defilement, revilement, reconcilement, cajolement, enrolment, babblement, enfeeblement, entablement, enablement, disablement, ennoblement, settlement, battlement, embrittlement, belittlement, resettlement, unsettlement, entitlement, disentitlement, dismantlement, disgruntlement, befuddlement, tracklement, encirclement, inveiglement, entanglement, disentanglement, embranglement, empanelment, bafflement, devilment, bedevilment, dishevelment, dazzlement, puzzlement, embezzlement, bedazzlement, bamboozlement **.14** misdemeanant, recombinant, complainant, pennant, tenant, Tennant, subtenant, lieutenant, undertenant, sublieutenant, pertinent, continent, abstinent, alternant, appertinent, appurtenant, impertinent, subcontinent, incontinent, supercontinent, immanent, imminent, eminent, remanent, dominant, prominent, ruminant, permanent, germinant, culminant, fulminant, discriminant, preeminent, contaminant, predominant, subdominant, illuminant, impermanent, determinant, supereminent, revenant, covenant, dissonant, assonant, consonant, unisonant, hallucinant, inconsonant, resonant, sonant, opponent, deponent, proponent, imponent, component, exponent, regnant, pregnant, stagnant, indignant, benignant, malignant, oppugnant, repugnant, remnant **.15** infant, sycophant, elephant, Oliphant, triumphant **.16** fervent, servant, advent, convent, solvent, Sturtevant, pursuivant, adjuvant, relevant, maidservant, manservant, insolvent, dissolvent, resolvent, irrelevant, unobservant **.17.1** decent, recent, obeisant, indecent, puissant, dehiscent, impuissant, reminiscent, reviviscent, indehiscent, nascent, renascent, adjacent, coadjacent, subjacent, complacent, superjacent, unadjacent, circumjacent **.17.2** Besant, Cheshunt, crescent, quiescent, acquiescent, pubescent, albescent, prepubescent, erubescent, frutescent, lactescent, candescent, recrudescent, turgidescent, iridescent, viridescent, incandescent, tumescent, detumescent, intumescent, senescent, luminescent, evanescent, juvenescent, bioluminescent, rejuvenescent, triboluminescent, chemiluminescent, thermoluminescent, electroluminescent, rufescent, confessant, flavescent, fulvescent, effervescent, ingravescent, marcescent, acescent, incessant, turgescent, liquescent, deliquescent, virescent, fluorescent, depressant, suppressant, vitrescent, putrescent, decrescent, concrescent, excrescent, nigrescent, arborescent, phosphorescent, efflorescent, antidepressant, immunosuppressant, coalescent, pearlescent, opalescent, adolescent, pre-adolescent, alkalescent, convalescent, obsolescent **.17.3** passant, mustn't, discussant, usedn't, usen't, lucent, relucent, translucent, noctilucent, corposant, reticent, innocent, Stuyvesant, Millicent, concupiscent, munificent, magnificent, beneficent, maleficent, versant, dispersant, conversant, docent, absent, accent, relaxant, Patuxent, Vincent, St Vincent, demulcent, convulsant, anticonvulsant **.18** wisent, isn't, peasant, bezant, pheasant, present, pleasant, hasn't, wasn't, doesn't, malfeasant, complaisant, unpleasant, cognizant, recusant, omnipresent, everpresent, recognizant, incognizant **.19** patient, Ushant, couchant, quotient, ancient, sentient, efficient, coefficient, deficient, sufficient, proficient, outpatient, impatient, in-patient, negotiant, assentient, dissentient, presentient, insentient, consentient, inefficient, tax-efficient,

insufficient, self-sufficient, stupefacient, sorbefacient, rubefacient, tumefacient, liquefacient, putrefacient, calefacient, abortifacient, immunodeficient: (+ **22.26.2**(.8))
.20 etchant, Marchant, merchant, trenchant
.21 sejant, regent, allegiant, indigent, agent, reagent, subagent, newsagent, pageant, argent, Sargant, sergeant, serjeant, Nugent, exigent, diligent, negligent, intransigent, intelligent, unintelligent, urgent, detergent, abstergent, emergent, re-emergent, divergent, convergent, resurgent, insurgent, cogent, ringent, stringent, tangent, plangent, pungent, contingent, astringent, refringent, cotangent, birefringent, fulgent, indulgent, effulgent, refulgent, self-indulgent, overindulgent **.22** Derwent, sequent, frequent, infrequent, subsequent, consequent, eloquent, aliquant, delinquent, inconsequent, grandiloquent, magniloquent
.23.1 sederunt, coherent, adherent, inherent, incoherent, errant, aberrant, knight-errant, deterrent, inerrant, parent, step-parent, godparent, grandparent, houseparent, transparent, declarant, arrant, apparent, unapparent **.23.2** Arendt, torrent, horrent, warrant, abhorrent, insurant, Durrant, currant, current, occurrent, recurrent, upcurrent, whitecurrant, redcurrant, blackcurrant, concurrent, crosscurrent, intercurrent, undercurrent, spirant, tyrant, aspirant
.23.3 operant, cooperant, antiperspirant, roborant, exuberant, protuberant, reverberant, restaurant, expectorant, adulterant, deodorant, preponderant, equiponderant, cormorant, sonorant, ignorant, itinerant, different, efferent, deferent, referent, afferent, indifferent, vociferant, reverent, irreverent, saturant, denaturant, refrigerant, belligerent, nonbelligerent, carburant, obscurant, figurant, tolerant, colourant, exhilarant, accelerant, intolerant **.23.4** vibrant, terebrant, celebrant, concelebrant, titrant, entrant, penetrant, re-entrant, ministrant, registrant, remonstrant, recalcitrant, administrant, quadrant, hydrant, vagrant, fragrant, flagrant, migrant, transmigrant, integrant, immigrant, emigrant
.24 poignant, brilliant **.25** sealant, bivalent, divalent, trivalent, tervalent, covalent, sexvalent, multivalent, univalent, polyvalent, septivalent, heptavalent, octavalent, pentavalent, monovalent, sexivalent, hexavalent, quinquevalent, tetravalent, quadrivalent, electrovalent, assailant, inhalant, appellant, repellent, propellant, propellent, impellent, expellent, flagellant, water-repellant, water-repellent, talent, gallant, topgallant, ungallant, equipollent, installant, silent, coolant, violent, nonviolent, sibilant, libellant, jubilant, scintillant, pestilent, redolent, indolent, somnolent, prevalent, ambivalent, equivalent, benevolent, malevolent, unambivalent, excellent, insolent, superexcellent, nonchalant, vigilant, stridulant,

fraudulent, undulant, crapulent, opulent, corpulent, turbulent, ambulant, somnambulant, petulant, flatulent, postulant, pustulant, congratulant, feculent, flocculent, succulent, truculent, luculent, esculent, osculant, matriculant, coagulant, anticoagulant, stimulant, tremulant, anovulant, virulent, purulent, pulverulent, ululant, pullulant, volant, Solent, resemblant

22.26.16
burnt, weren't, learned, learnt, mowburnt, unburnt, sunburnt

22.26.17
don't, wont, won't

22.27.1
gift, sift, shift, squiffed, swift, rift, drift, grift, thrift, shrift, lift, Whitgift, upshift, stickshift, makeshift, downshift, adrift, snowdrift, spindrift, spendthrift, Festschrift, ski lift, airlift, stairlift, chairlift, shoplift, uplift, boatlift, forklift, facelift

22.27.2
eft, deft, theft, heft, weft, reft, Dreft, left, cleft, klepht, bereft

22.27.3
Taft

22.27.4
aft, daft, shaft, haft, waft, raft, draft, draught, craft, kraft, graft **.1** abaft **.2** unstaffed, understaffed **.3** layshaft, air shaft, Shakeshaft, jackshaft, crankshaft, camshaft, downshaft, driveshaft, countershaft, turboshaft **.4** redraft, updraught, updraught, backdraught, indraft, indraught, downdraft, aircraft, Hopcraft, statecraft, priestcraft, woodcraft, handcraft, Wollstonecraft, kingcraft, spacecraft, housecraft, bushcraft, leechcraft, witchcraft, stagecraft, needlecraft, ingraft, engraft, overdraft, handicraft, watercraft, hovercraft, mothercraft, autograft, homograft, xenograft, heterograft, allograft

22.27.5
oft, toft, soft, waft, croft, loft, Lowestoft, Cockcroft, Cockroft, Moorcroft, Rycroft, Hopcroft, Wheatcroft, Bancroft, Foxcroft, Ashcroft, hayloft, aloft, semisoft, Microsoft®, Thorneycroft, undercroft

22.27.6
tuft, unstuffed, candytuft

22.27.7
Delft

22.28
wry-mouthed, widemouthed, sawtoothed, snaggle-toothed

22.29.1
east, piste, beast, feast, priest, triste, yeast, least, batiste, artiste, Mideast, modiste, beanfeast, southeast, northeast, archpriest, uncreased,

south-southeast, anapaest, hartebeest, wildebeest, arriviste, north-northeast, dirigiste, unreleased

22.29.2
kist, mist, fist, cist, cyst, schist, gist, hist, whist, wist, twist, wrist, tryst, grist, list, Liszt **.1** deist, theist, ditheist, tritheist, misoneist, antitheist, polytheist, monotheist **.2** copyist, hobbyist, lobbyist, fideist, hockeyist, Trotskyist, atheist, pantheist, entryist, voluntaryist, accompanyist **.3** archaist, essayist, prosaist, Hebraist, Mithraist, algebraist **.4** Taoist, Maoist **.5** Dadaist **.6** Baha'ist **.7** casuist, altruist, euphuist **.8** Uist, cueist, tattooist, voodooist, canoeist **.9** Lamaist **.10** oboist, Titoist, Shintoist, judoist, egoist, jingoist, banjoist, soloist, seicentoist, hylozoist **.11** papist, rapist, Trappist, harpist, typist, orthoepist, escapist, landscapist, therapist, audio typist, stenotypist, endoscopist, stethoscopist, spectroscopist, microscopist, misanthropist, psilanthropist, philanthropist, physiotherapist, radiotherapist, psychotherapist, chemotherapist, hypnotherapist, hydrotherapist, aromatherapist, electrotherapist **.12** Babist, vibist, cubist, cambist, theorbist, Arabist **.13** defeatist, graffitist, Docetist, élitist, completist, exegetist, statist, fatist, portraitist, duettist, cornetist, phonetist, librettist, vignettist, clarinettist, fattist, abattised, artist, Chartist, Scotist, flautist, rightist, finitist, chutist, flutist, parachutist, therapeutist, absolutist, pietist, quietist, varietist, fortuitist, nepotist, abatised, egotist, Semitist, dramatist, stigmatist, pragmatist, dogmatist, Donatist, hypnotist, spiritist, separatist, corporatist, syncretist, Sanskritist, automatist, systematist, diplomatist, numismatist, anaesthetist, comparatist, melodramatist, epigrammatist, protist, unnoticed, Baptist, synoptist, orthoptist, Anabaptist, unpractised, Comtist, dentist, scientist, Adventist, seicentist, trecentist, Vedantist, geoscientist, irredentist, cinquecentist, quattrocentist, Esperantist, obscurantist, periodontist, orthodontist, contrapuntist, neuroscientist, immanentist, indifferentist, leftist, transvestist, cultist, occultist, gestaltist **.14** orthopaedist, velocipedist, encyclopedist, sadist, faddist, Mahdist, avant-gardist, keyboardist, recordist, harpsichordist, Talmudist, Buddhist, nudist, feudist, orchidist, psalmodist, comedist, threnodist, monodist, hymnodist, Methodist, prosodist, rhapsodist, orchardist, parodist, melodist, chiropodist, unprejudiced, orologist, absurdist, Girondist, unjaundiced, Bollandist, contrabandist, propagandist, heraldist **.15** oecist, stockist, Yorkist, tychist, unkissed, Sunkist, autarkist, catechist, Butterkist®, anarchist, monarchist, masochist, sadomasochist **.16** druggist, fuguist, epilogist **.17** demist, extremist, chemist, biochemist, geochemist, radiochemist, phytochemist, electrochemist,

ceramist, palmist, psalmist, alarmist, reformist, conformist, nonconformist, rhymist, pantomimist, atomist, totemist, optimist, Wykehamist, alchemist, bigamist, digamist, trigamist, Targumist, animist, dynamist, euphemist, pessimist, Islamist, epitomist, legitimist, anatomist, phlebotomist, lithotomist, Soroptimist, taxidermist, polygamist, monogamist, misogamist, autonomist, economist, ergonomist, taxonomist, agronomist, palindromist, physiognomist, Deuteronomist, Thomist, rhythmist **.18.1** routinist, machinist, hygienist, tambourinist, trampolinist, Latinist, violinist, mandolinist, pianist, Fabianist, unionist, alienist, Orleanist, accordionist, trade unionist, trades unionist, traducianist, millenarianist, Jainist, Zenist, eugenist, tanist, Hispanist, sopranist, monist, mnemonist, corniced, faunist, hornist, lampoonist, cartoonist, bassoonist, Neptunist, balloonist, opportunist, Zionist, timpanist, alpinist, accompanist, rabbinist, urbanist, satanist, Platonist, botanist, lutanist, lutenist, Montanist, Neoplatonist, geobotanist, Byzantinist, ultramontanist, hedonist, modernist, postmodernist, mechanist, tokenist, Vulcanist, tobacconist, Vaticanist, Africanist, americanist, agonist, organist, tritagonist, protagonist, antagonist, theogonist, tobogganist, cosmogonist, deuteragonist, shamanist, feminist, Mammonist, harmonist, humanist, terminist, Germanist, Romanist, eudaemonist, eudemonist, illuminist, phillumenist, determinist, indeterminist, Leninist, canonist, onanist, Marxist–Leninist, symphonist, telephonist, saxophonist, xylophonist, chauvinist, Calvinist, galvanist, arsonist, larcenist, Saxonist, Jansenist **.18.2** prohibitionist, partitionist, seditionist, traditionist, nutritionist, coalitionist, intuitionist, exhibitionist, expeditionist, requisitionist, abolitionist, demolitionist, creationist, deviationist, variationist, situationist, associationist, appropriationist, emancipationist, presentationist, transmutationist, sanitationist, representationist, accommodationist, vacationist, educationist, negationist, segregationist, preformationist, salvationist, conservationist, preservationist, conversationist, inspirationist, liberationist, restorationist, federationist, integrationist, collaborationist, relationist, deflationist, inflationist, revelationist, isolationist, secessionist, processionist, impressionist, expressionist, progressionist, Passionist, abortionist, contortionist, extortionist, percussionist, constructionist, Confucianist, elocutionist, evolutionist, devolutionist, revolutionist, circumlocutionist, excursionist, diversionist, receptionist, underconsumptionist, fictionist, restrictionist, protectionist, connectionist, perfectionist, resectionist, rejectionist, projectionist, reactionist, abstractionist,

reductionist, obstructionist, deconstructionist, vivisectionist, insurrectionist, antivivisectionist, ascentionist, expansionist, interventionist **.18.3** visionist, fusionist, revisionist, precisionist, intrusionist, diffusionist, illusionist, seclusionist, exclusionist, polygenist, religionist, misogynist, philogynist, irreligionist, co-religionist, abiogenist, Darwinist, Pyrrhonist, Peronist, ironist, doctrinist, communist, anti-communist, Eurocommunist, Hellenist, Stalinist, colonist, philhellenist, internist, bonist, trombonist, sousaphonist, vibraphonist, pyrotechnist, hymnist, columnist **.19** sophist, pacifist, Lagerkvist, paragraphist, theosophist, deipnosophist, gymnosophist, catastrophist, epigraphist, calligraphist, telegraphist, monographist, chirographist, anthropomorphist **.20** Yahvist, fauvist, nativist, activist, archivist, Bolshevist, reservist, Jehovist, cognitivist, intuitivist, negativist, primitivist, positivist, corporativist, relativist, prescriptivist, subjectivist, objectivist, collectivist, constructivist, recidivist, Stakhanovist, progressivist, logical positivist **.21** Baathist, empathist, amethyst, telepathist, hydropathist, allopathist, homeopathist, homoeopathist **.22** assist, persist, desist, subsist, insist, encyst, consist, bassist, racist, anti-racist, classist, exorcist, mosaicist, Spartacist, Vorticist, fantasist, phoneticist, geneticist, pneumatocyst, nematocyst, semanticist, romanticist, Atlanticist, cyberneticist, cytogeneticist, geodesist, psychicist, pharmacist, phonemicist, supremacist, polemicist, dynamicist, ceramicist, thermodynamicist, aerodynamicist, hydrodynamicist, technicist, eugenicist, Hispanicist, mythicist, ethicist, synthesist, bioethicist, hypothesist, classicist, narcissist, neoclassicist, physicist, geophysicist, biophysicist, astrophysicist, lyricist, rubricist, empiricist, historicist, esotericist, solecist, publicist, Anglicist, metempsychosist, solipsist, sexist, saxist, Marxist, heterosexist **.23** resist, exist, preexist, coexist, speciesist, Spinozist **.24** fascist, fetishist, mica-schist, revanchist, anti-fascist **.25** collagist, Falangist, phalangist **.26.1** ageist, agist, Swarajist, theurgist, liturgist, strategist, imagist, synergist, suffragist, elegist, allergist, dialogist, metallurgist, analogist, paralogist, genealogist, mineralogist **.26.2** rheologist, neologist, theologist, geologist, biologist, bryologist, zoologist, oologist, osteologist, deltiologist, ideologist, radiologist, cardiologist, audiologist, archaeologist, archeologist, hagiologist, semiologist, craniologist, balneologist, ophiologist, ichthyologist, glaciologist, sociologist, axiologist, physiologist, choreologist, embryologist, speleologist, teleologist, cryobiologist, ethnoarchaeologist, ecclesiologist, hydrogeologist, Assyriologist, bacteriologist, venereologist, radiobiologist, sociobiologist, aerobiologist, microbiologist, psychobiologist, exobiologist, epidemiologist, anaesthesiologist, anesthesiologist, neurophysiologist **.26.3** topologist, typologist, apologist, escapologist, anthropologist, palaeoanthropologist, tribologist, cetologist, scatologist, heortologist, tautologist, cytologist, otologist, cryptologist, proctologist, ontologist, deontologist, neontologist, Scientologist, histologist, pestologist, sovietologist, herpetologist, eschatologist, haematologist, primatologist, climatologist, rheumatologist, dermatologist, stomatologist, cosmetologist, planetologist, teratologist, Egyptologist, dialectologist, palaeontologist, odontologist, gerontologist, parasitologist, pedologist, Indologist, methodologist, iridologist, pteridologist, ethnomethodologist, mycologist, phycologist, psychologist, ecologist, trichologist, oncologist, conchologist, muscologist, palaeoecologist, pharmacologist, synecologist, gynaecologist, lexicologist, toxicologist, musicologist, parapsychologist, ethnomusicologist, algologist, otolaryngologist, otorhinolaryngologist **.26.4** gemmologist, gemologist, pomologist, zymologist, cosmologist, seismologist, etymologist, entomologist, ophthalmologist, epistemologist, enologist, oenologist, penologist, Sinologist, menologist, monologist, phenologist, phonologist, chronologist, phrenologist, hypnologist, technologist, hymnologist, limnologist, ethnologist, campanologist, volcanologist, vulcanologist, demonologist, criminologist, terminologist, geochronologist, immunologist, selenologist, palynologist, Kremlinologist, biotechnologist, arachnologist, phenomenologist, endocrinologist, dendrochronologist, psephologist, graphologist, morphologist, ufologist, geomorphologist, ethologist, pathologist, mythologist, lithologist, anthologist, ornithologist, helminthologist, neuropathologist, misologist, sexologist, reflexologist, serologist, aerologist, horologist, chorologist, virologist, neurologist, urologist, patrologist, petrologist, hydrologist, dendrologist, necrologist, meteorologist, oneirologist, papyrologist, martyrologist, numerologist, futurologist, philologist, vexillologist, eulogist, thaumaturgist **.27** Elohist **.28** Yahwist, UWIST, untwist, Rehnquist, linguist, intertwist, ventriloquist, soliloquist, sociolinguist, psycholinguist **.29.1** lyrist, panegyrist, theorist, querist, apiarist, topiarist, plagiarist, careerist, meliorist, verist, aorist, Marist, plein-airist, welfarist **.29.2** czarist, tsarist, sitarist, guitarist, scenarist, Catharist, memoirist, florist, rainforest, disforest, disafforest, aurist, tourist, Maurist, purist, petaurist, folklorist, pedicurist, sinecurist, manicurist, caricaturist **.29.3** diarist, jurist, satirist, scooterist, motorist, votarist, dipterist, monetarist, militarist, Redemptorist, detectorist, voluntarist, coleopterist, lepidopterist,

documentarist, Eucharist, eucharist, allegorist **.29.4** amorist, armorist, summarist, humorist, mesmerist, ephemerist, consumerist, tenorist, mannerist, seminarist, aphorist, zitherist, glossarist, Lazarist, naturist, futurist, obituarist, miniaturist, adventurist, acupuncturist, apiculturist, viticulturist, horticulturist, viniculturist, aviculturist, silviculturist, pisciculturist, sericulturist, floriculturist, arboriculturist, agriculturist, aquarist, terrorist, eco-terrorist, narcoterrorist, Accurist®, behaviourist, colourist, solarist, artillerist, secularist, ocularist, watercolourist, particularist, auteurist **.29.5** Octobrist, Decembrist, equilibrist, metrist, entrist, centrist, tantrist, belletrist, paediatrist, podiatrist, psychiatrist, geriatrist, hexametrist, optometrist, psychometrist, econometrist, photogrammetrist, sociometrist, sacrist, phenocryst **.30** pointillist **.31.1** enlist, re-enlist, mercantilist, idyllist, realist, idealist, serialist, aerialist, surrealist, millennialist, colonialist, diluvialist, imperialist, materialist, industrialist, premillennialist, ceremonialist, neocolonialist, immaterialist, ministerialist, editorialist, playlist, cellist, violoncellist, cabbalist, foilist, disloyalist, stylist, hairstylist, profilist, nihilist, royalist, loyalist, violist, sciolist, trialist, dualist, duellist **.31.2** papalist, oligopolist, kabbalist, tribalist, libellist, verbalist, herbalist, cymbalist, symbolist, diabolist, probabilist, hyperbolist, indissolubilist, fatalist, bimetallist, catalyst, philatelist, autocatalyst, vitalist, recitalist, brutalist, capitalist, sacerdotalist, anecdotalist, mentalist, transcendentalist, orientalist, occidentalist, sentimentalist, fundamentalist, ornamentalist, instrumentalist, sacramentalist, documentalist, experimentalist, environmentalist, pastellist, Pentecostalist, medallist, feudalist, vocalist, syndicalist, classicalist, physicalist, clericalist, legalist, madrigalist **.31.3** homilist, formalist, animalist, maximalist, minimalist, analyst, annalist, panellist, cryptanalyst, psychoanalyst, finalist, semifinalist, communalist, nominalist, phenomenalist, traditionalist, conversationalist, intuitionalist, sensationalist, representationalist, educationalist, Congregationalist, denominationalist, nationalist, rationalist, internationalist, proportionalist, constitutionalist, notionalist, emotionalist, sectionalist, functionalist, conventionalist, occasionalist, regionalist, virginalist, journalist, paternalist, photojournalist **.31.4** cartophilist, oenophilist, necrophilist, triumphalist, novelist, survivalist, revivalist, medievalist, universalist, racialist, specialist, socialist, sexualist, sensualist, unsocialist, provincialist, prudentialist, essentialist, substantialist, controversialist, existentialist, consequentialist, experientialist, gradualist, pugilist, evangelist, individualist, tele-evangelist, televangelist, moralist, amoralist, oralist, muralist, pluralist, ruralist, liberalist, literalist, pastoralist, federalist, generalist, naturalist, scripturalist, structuralist, culturalist, behaviouralist, multilateralist, unilateralist, supernaturalist, multiculturalist, horticulturalist, agriculturalist, neutralist, centralist, decentralist **.31.5** populist, fabulist, mutualist, factualist, textualist, oculist, masculist, formulist, noctambulist, funambulist, somnambulist, spiritualist, conceptualist, contextualist, intellectualist, Gaullist, holist **.31.6** disablist, shortlist, handlist, sicklist, checklist, backlist, blacklist, stocklist, cyclist, booklist, bicyclist, tricyclist, unicyclist, motorcyclist, Anglist, wish-list

22.29.3
unpierced

22.29.4
paste, baste, taste, mayst, chaste, haste, waist, waste, toothpaste, shore-based, lambaste, foretaste, distaste, barefaced, po-faced, whitefaced, red-faced, boldfaced, shamefaced, self-faced, smooth-faced, pale-faced, unchaste, posthaste, shirtwaist, untraced, unplaced, straightlaced, straitlaced, aftertaste, overhaste, pantywaist

22.29.5
pest, best, test, guest, nest, vest, zest, chest, gest, jest, hest, west, quest, rest, wrest, breast, Brest, crest, lest, blessed, blest, Trieste, beau geste, Key West, Mae West, Sunday best, Rorschach test, chanson de geste **.1** anapaest, Budapest, rinderpest **.2** t-test, retest, pretest, attest, detest, protest, roadtest, contest, Grosseteste **.3** houseguest **.4** gabfest, talkfest, slugfest, infest, disinfest, songfest, Hammerfest, manifest, self-confessed **.5** divest, invest, reinvest, disinvest, transvest, undervest **.6** incest, Alceste, unprocessed, palimpsest, self-obsessed **.7** unpossessed, self-possessed **.8** toolchest **.9** digest, egest, suggest, ingest, congest, predigest, Almagest **.10** behest, alkahest **.11** NatWest®, East-West, Midwest, acquest, bequest, request, inquest, conquest, southwest, northwest, reconquest, self-conquest, Haverfordwest **.12** arrest, rearrest, imprest, unpressed, abreast, redbreast, footrest, interest, prestressed, unstressed, headrest, backrest, firecrest, hillcrest, armrest, unrest, Bucharest, unsuppressed, unimpressed, unexpressed, chimney breast, self-interest, disinterest, unaddressed, self-addressed, unredressed, immunodepressed, immunosuppressed **.13** molest, celeste, unblessed, unblest, arbalest, Mary Celeste

22.29.6
past, bast, cast, caste, mast, fast, vast, hast, last, blast **.1** cineaste, chiliast, scholiast, encomiast, ecdysiast, enthusiast, symposiast **.2** flypast, repast, unsurpassed **.3** lambast, bombast **.4** fantast **.5** recast, precast, forecast, upcast,

typecast, outcast, outcaste, broadcast, worm-cast, downcast, opencast, off-cast, roughcast, miscast, sportscast, newscast, Qualcast®, simulcast, telecast, unforecast, overcast, narrowcast, rebroadcast **.6** aghast, flabbergast, Prendergast **.7** foremast, durmast, topmast, mainmast, mizzenmast, dismast, beechmast, onomast, maintopmast **.8** dynast, gymnast **.9** sit-fast, lightfast, bedfast, steadfast, headfast, holdfast, lockfast, sunfast, Belfast, colour fast, unsteadfast **.10** avast **.11** contrast, pederast **.12** symplast, arblast, oblast, sandblast, outlast, protoplast, leucoplast, chloroplast, epiblast, hypoblast, ectoblast, counterblast, leucoblast, spermoblast, trophoblast, mesoblast, meroblast, pyroclast, Elastoplast®, spermatoblast, erythroblast, iconoclast

22.29.7
oust, Faust, joust, roust, frowst

22.29.8
past, cast, caste, karst, mast, fast, vast, last, blast **.1** flypast, repast, unsurpassed **.2** rat-arsed **.3** recast, precast, forecast, upcast, typecast, outcast, outcaste, broadcast, worm-cast, downcast, opencast, off-cast, roughcast, miscast, sportscast, newscast, Qualcast®, simulcast, telecast, unforecast, thermokarst, overcast, narrowcast, rebroadcast **.4** aghast, flabbergast, Prendergast **.5** foremast, durmast, topmast, mainmast, mizzenmast, dismast, beechmast, maintopmast **.6** avast **.7** contrast **.8** arblast, sandblast, outlast, leucoplast, epiblast, hypoblast, ectoblast, counterblast, leucoblast, spermoblast, trophoblast, mesoblast, meroblast, pyroclast, Elastoplast®, spermatoblast, erythroblast, iconoclast

22.29.9
cost, wast, Prost, frost, lost, teleost, riposte, impost, compost, storm-tossed, accost, oncost, alecost, glasnost, provost, star-crossed, defrost, hoarfrost, Jack Frost, Van der Post, Pentecost, permafrost

22.29.10
Aust, horst, unforced, exhaust, hypocaust, holocaust, unenforced, unreinforced, under-resourced

22.29.11
moist, foist, joist, hoist, unvoiced

22.29.12
bust, dost, dust, gust, must, musth, just, rust, trust, crust, thrust, lust, unit trust, robust, combust, bundobust, stardust, sawdust, brickdust, angel dust, undiscussed, august, disgust, self-disgust, adjust, readjust, unjust, intrust, entrust, distrust, mistrust, piecrust, shortcrust, incrust, encrust, upthrust, antitrust, overthrust, bloodlust, wanderlust

22.29.13
heist, Christ, Kleist, Zeitgeist, unpriced, unsliced, poltergeist, underpriced, Antichrist

22.29.14
boost, deuced, roost, Proust, used, langouste, mot juste, mots justes, unused, starch-reduced, self-induced

22.29.15
.1 freest .2 boniest, veriest .3 mayest .4 unbiased .5 wurst, bierwurst, bratwurst, knackwurst, knockwurst, liverwurst .6 doest .7 goest .8 tempest .9 mightest .10 modest, damnedest, darnedest, durndest, eldest, immodest .11 locust, varicosed, focused .12 August, Hengist .13 dynast, honest, earnest, Ernest, dishonest, unwitnessed, miscellanist, antivivisectionist .14 steadfast, breakfast .15 harvest, provost .16 farthest, furthest .17 forest, Forrest, interest, Everest, deforest, reforest, afforest, reafforest, self-interest, disinterest, unembarrassed .18 ballast, Sallust, arbalest, memorialist, monopolist

22.29.16
erst, burst, durst, cursed, curst, first, verst, thirst, hurst, worst, wurst, airburst, starburst, outburst, cloudburst, rockburst, sunburst, toneburst, microburst, accursed, headfirst, twenty-first, safety-first, bierwurst, bratwurst, knackwurst, knockwurst, liverwurst, unversed, reversed, Fairhurst, Dewhurst, Ewhurst, Midhurst, Broadhurst, Sandhurst, Pankhurst, Amherst, Brockenhurst, Smethurst, Bathurst, Penshurst, Tilehurst, Staplehurst, Chislehurst, unrehearsed, Billingshurst, under-rehearsed

22.29.17
oast, post, boast, toast, coast, ghost, most, host, roast .1 Freepost, doorpost, lamp-post, gatepost, outpost, bedpost, guidepost, impost, signpost, sternpost, milepost, newelpost, goalpost, Datapost®, fingerpost, Intelpost .2 milquetoast .3 seacoast, varicosed .4 rearmost, foremost, lowermost, topmost, upmost, outmost, utmost, rightmost, leftmost, midmost, headmost, endmost, hindmost, backmost, inmost, downmost, sternmost, easternmost, westernmost, northernmost, southernmost, almost, uppermost, outermost, bottommost, uttermost, centermost, centremost, aftermost, undermost, innermost, nethermost, weathermost, furthermost

22.29.18
wouldst

22.29.19
didst, midst, hadst, couldst, wouldst, amidst

22.29.20
sixte, 'twixt, text, next, sext, Bakst, angst, unmixed, suffix, betwixt, pretext, subtext, context, unflexed, untaxed, unwaxed, videotext, hypertext, teletext, unindexed, undersexed, oversexed, unrelaxed

22.29.21
inst., 'gainst, Ernst, canst, Unst, Nernst, fragranced, against, unfenced, valanced,

unlicensed, unconvinced, unannounced, unrenounced, uninfluenced, unsilenced, unbeknownst, unrecompensed, underfinanced

22.29.22
angst, 'mongst, amongst

22.29.23
whilst, Holst, discalced

22.30
whisht, borscht, unthreshed, unfleshed, uncashed, caboshed, unwashed, stonewashed, unbrushed, uncrushed, unquenched, sundrenched, unblemished, unfinished, untarnished, unvarnished, unpunished, unfurnished, unvanquished, malnourished, unpolished, unpublished, unrefreshed, unabashed, undiminished, undistinguished, undernourished, unembellished, unaccomplished, unestablished

22.31
unreached, unbleached, far-fetched, upstretched, outstretched, unstretched, unmatched, unthatched, unhatched, unscratched, unstarched, unwatched, untouched, unsearched, unquenched, sundrenched, unattached, unresearched, semidetached

22.32.1
spilt, built, tilt, stilt, kilt, gilt, guilt, milt, silt, jilt, hilt, wilt, quilt, lilt, unspilt, rebuilt, square-built, upbuilt, inbuilt, unbuilt, atilt, uptilt, regilt, Vanderbilt, overbuilt

22.32.2
pelt, spelt, belt, dealt, Celt, kelt, Scheldt, gelt, melt, smelt, knelt, felt, veld, veldt, svelte, welt, dwelt, snowbelt, seatbelt, rust-belt, swordbelt, fanbelt, unbelt, Sunbelt, lifebelt, undealt, misdealt, forefelt, heartfelt, unfelt, Weidenfeld, backveld, bushveld, Copperbelt, underfelt, Magherafelt, Bielefeld, Roosevelt

22.32.3
alt, shalt, gestalt, asphalt

22.32.4
gestalt

22.32.5
Balt, Galt, gault, malt, smalt, fault, vault, volt, volte, salt, halt, cobalt, Hainault, polevault, desalt, assault, exalt, stringhalt, millivolt, megavolt, oxysalt, somersault, summersault, Eversholt

22.32.6
Balt, Galt, gault, malt, smalt, fault, vault, salt, halt, cobalt, Hainault, default, asphalt, polevault, desalt, basalt, assault, exalt, stringhalt, strike-slip fault, oxysalt, somersault, summersault

22.32.7
spoilt, unspoilt

22.32.8
ult, cult, adult, indult, occult, incult, tumult, penult, insult, consult, result, exult, catapult, antepenult, jurisconsult

22.32.9
poult, catapult

22.32.10
poult, Iseult

22.32.11
cobalt, asphalt

22.32.12
poult, bolt, boult, dolt, colt, molt, moult, smolt, volt, volte, jolt, holt, U-bolt, Newbolt, deadbolt, Shadbolt, Humboldt, unbolt, kingbolt, ringbolt, revolt, Northolt, thunderbolt, millivolt, archivolt, megavolt, kilovolt, Eversholt, electronvolt

22.32.13
cobalt

22.32.14
difficult

22.32.15
basalt, Hasselt

23.1
Eid, speed, bead, Bede, steed, deed, mead, Mede, meed, knead, need, feed, cede, seed, she'd, Gide, he'd, heed, we'd, weed, tweed, Swede, Read, read, Reade, rede, reed, Reid, breed, creed, screed, greed, lead, Lied, plead, bleed, sous vide

23.1.1
impede, stampede, airspeed, god-speed, centipede, palmipede, millipede, velocipede

23.1.2
Flamsteed

23.1.3
Candide, indeed, misdeed

23.1.4
Diomede, Runnymede, Ganymede

23.1.5
weak-kneed

23.1.6
dripfeed, breastfeed, greenfeed, linefeed, spoonfeed, chicken feed, Sylphides, tractorfeed, overfeed

23.1.7
deseed, re-cede, reseed, precede, hayseed, secede, recede, proceed, rapeseed, grapeseed, birdseed, exceed, accede, flaxseed, succeed, wormseed, linseed, concede, cottonseed, self-seed, allseed, oilseed, coleseed, supersede, intercede, aniseed, retrocede, pumpkinseed

23.1.8
Rashid, Jamshid

23.1.9
Lockheed

23.1.10
seaweed, mayweed, oarweed, oreweed, shoreweed, fireweed, knapweed, goutweed, smartweed, knotweed, cudweed, pondweed, bindweed, stickweed, chickweed, hawkweed, duckweed, brookweed, pokeweed, stinkweed, slinkweed, pigweed, ragweed, hogweed, greenweed, daneweed, stoneweed, gulfweed, flixweed, sneezeweed, tumbleweed, waterweed, silverweed, locoweed, blanket weed

23.1.11
re-read, sub-breed, outbreed, inbreed, crossbreed, sight-read, mind-read, proofread, Siegfried, misread, copyread, interbreed, overbreed, filigreed

23.1.12
fairlead, implead, nosebleed, mislead, invalid, interplead, Nibelungenlied

23.2
id, bid, did, kid, Kidd, Kyd, skid, gid, mid, fid, vid, Sid, chid, hid, quid, squid, rid, grid, yid, lid, Lydd, slid, El Cid, tertium quid

23.2.1
Aeneid, Eneid, scarabaeid

23.2.2
clupeid, Aeneid, Eneid, cepheid, nereid, saturniid

23.2.3
noctuid

23.2.4
zooid, Druid, Clwyd, fluid, superfluid

23.2.5
spermatozoid

23.2.6
lipid, tepid, vapid, sapid, rapid, poppied, torpid, stupid, cupid, limpid, hispid, cuspid, insipid, intrepid, canopied, elapid, bicuspid, tricuspid, phospholipid, unicuspid

23.2.7
rebid, ibid, rabid, morbid, forbid, turbid, outbid, underbid, overbid, carabid

23.2.8
foetid, nitid, fetid, mantid, plastid, Hampstead, Wheathampstead, Grinstead, Wanstead, unpitied, hydatid, parotid, carotid, proglottid, Llanwrtyd, propertied, spermatid, chromatid, unemptied, Armistead, caryatid, unpropertied

23.2.9
redid, gadid, sordid, sturdied, outdid, splendid, candid, candied, undid, katydid, disembodied, underdid, overdid

23.2.10
wicked, orchid, whizz-kid, alkyd, schoolkid

23.2.11
sphingid

23.2.12
timid, tumid, humid, amid, desmid, phasmid, plasmid, Mahommed, Fatimid, pyramid, MacDiarmid, cyanamid

23.2.13
Enid, crannied, honeyed, Leonid, Oceanid, braconid, salmonid, hominid, Sassanid, serranid, arachnid, Achaemenid, unaccompanied, vespertilionid

23.2.14
triffid, aphid, bifid, trifid, syrphid, trophied, multifid, quadrifid, hypertrophied

23.2.15
vivid, livid, David, avid, gravid, Ovid, ivied, scurvied, fervid, bovid, Mogen David, perfervid, unenvied

23.2.16
viscid, inviscid, acid, Chasid, Hasid, placid, flaccid, triacid, subacid, Abbasid, antacid, oxyacid, lucid, Seleucid, capsid, therapsid, rancid, unfancied, alcid

23.2.17
quinsied, frenzied, palsied

23.2.18
Jamshid

23.2.19
sphingid

23.2.20
rigid, Brigid, frigid, turgid, sphingid, algid, fulgid, carangid

23.2.21
liquid, equid, pinguid, languid, illiquid

23.2.22
mirid, unwearied, serried, unburied, viverrid, varied, unvaried, arid, sparid, married, unmarried, torrid, horrid, florid, storeyed, storied, lurid, hurried, unhurried, unworried, unflurried, satyrid, acarid, ascarid, liveried, ivoried, traceried, unsalaried, hybrid, scombrid, monohybrid, putrid, Astrid, Madrid, acrid, Tancred, diagrid, Winfred, Wilfrid, Winifred

23.2.23
psyllid, gelid, pallid, valid, stolid, solid, squalid, eyelid, bolide, skidlid, cichlid, Euclid, backslid, pyralid, invalid, unsullied, Attalid, annelid, chrysalid, Ozalid®, panoplied, yellow-bellied

23.3
eared, beard, fyrd, Sheard, weird, greybeard, Bluebeard, goatsbeard, afeard, myriad, period, Iliad, chiliad, Hilliard, Olympiad, unidea'd, photoperiod

23.4
aid, aide, paid, spade, bade, staid, cade, made, maid, fade, they'd, shade, jade, hade, wade, Quaid, suede, raid, braid, trade, grade, lade, laid, blade, clade, glade, Slade, limeade, down grade, belle laide, orangeade

23.4.1
repaid, postpaid, unpaid, reply-paid, underpaid, escapade, overpaid

23.4.2
Ubaid, forbade, forbad, gambade

23.4.3
rodomontade

23.4.4
McDade, alidade

23.4.5
decade, arcade, stockade, cockade, blockade, brocade, Kincaid, cascade, cavalcade, autocade, motorcade, Medicaid, barricade, ambuscade

23.4.6
brigade, renegade

23.4.7
remade, barmaid, mermaid, handmade, handmaid, milkmaid, homemade, man-made, unmade, self-made, housemaid, nursemaid, Teasmade®, bridesmaid, dairymaid, scullerymaid, chambermaid, metermaid, tailor-made, parlourmaid, undismayed

23.4.8
Sinéad, grenade, Whipsnade, gabionade, tamponade, carbonade, gasconade, dragonnade, lemonade, cannonade, pasquinade, serenade, carronade, marinade, colonnade, esplanade, harlequinade, fanfaronade

23.4.9
evade, pervade, invade, unsurveyed

23.4.10
glissade, passade, crusade, palisade

23.4.11
Lucozade®

23.4.12
eyeshade, lampshade, sunshade

23.4.13
nightshade

23.4.14
unweighed, persuade, dissuade, unswayed, Biggleswade, Ultrasuede®

23.4.15
Noraid, tirade, parade, Mairead, unsprayed, abrade, upbraid, regrade, degrade, upgrade, downgrade, Belgrade, ram-raid, comrade, afraid, masquerade, antitrade, stock-in-trade, balustrade, plantigrade, multigrade, intergrade, centigrade, saltigrade, tardigrade, pinnigrade, retrograde, unafraid, digitigrade

23.4.16
new-laid, grillade, unplayed, twayblade, switchblade, inlaid, unlade, unlaid, Greenslade, Lechlade, Adelaide, accolade, escalade, marmalade, defilade, enfilade, overlaid, fusillade, razorblade, rollerblade

23.5
Ed, sped, bed, ted, stead, dead, ked, sked, Med, Ned, fed, said, z, zed, shed, head, wed, read, red, redd, spread, bread, bred, tread, dread, cred, Fred, thread, shred, lead, led, pled, bled, fled, sled, coed, Dip Ed, Op-Ed, Cert Ed, Samoyed, Beachy Head

23.5.1
biped, moped, pinniped, uniped, cirriped, palmiped, quadruped, soliped, parallelepiped

23.5.2
seabed, daybed, air bed, abed, flowerbed, flatbed, hotbed, footbed, seedbed, reed-bed, roadbed, childbed, sickbed, trackbed, rock-bed, streambed, embed, imbed, sunbed, deathbed, waterbed, interbed, slugabed, sofabed, riverbed, featherbed

23.5.3
Newstead, oersted, Hampstead, bedstead, roadstead, Buxted, farmstead, Olmsted, Plumstead, homestead, Wheathampstead, Rothamsted, instead, Grinstead, Stansted, Wanstead, Felstead, Halstead, Sanderstead, Armistead, Hemel Hempstead, Moretonhampstead, Finchampstead, Berkhampstead

23.5.4
undead

23.5.5
Szeged

23.5.6
pre-med, Ahmed

23.5.7
Eluned

23.5.8
dripfed, sheetfed, breastfed, unfed, spoonfed, underfed, overfed

23.5.9
Elfed

23.5.10
gainsaid, unsaid, soothsaid, aforesaid

23.5.11
Enzed

23.5.12
cowshed, Shepshed, bloodshed, woodshed, unshed, woolshed, toolshed, watershed, Evershed, Holinshed

23.5.13
ahead, behead, Spithead, short-head, Birkenhead, Gateshead, Hillhead, Peterhead, overhead **.1** sleepyhead, Holyhead
.2 spearhead **.3** airhead, stairhead
.4 Moorhead, forehead, sorehead, warhead, Muirhead **.5** go-ahead, copperhead, letterhead, dunderhead, thunderhead, figurehead, loggerhead, hammerhead, featherhead, Weatherhead, Leatherhead, arrowhead

.6 bowhead, towhead **.7** mophead, hophead, drophead, Lochgilphead **.8** subhead
.9 meathead, pithead, cathead, fathead, Flathead, pothead, hothead, whitehead, printhead, masthead, bonnethead **.10** bedhead, deadhead, redhead, godhead, Broadhead, Woodhead, Roundhead, Hindhead, baldhead **.11** dickhead, thickhead, blackhead, blockhead, lunkhead, bulkhead **.12** big-head, egghead **.13** dumbhead, drumhead
.14 greenhead, pinhead, skinhead, Minehead, bonehead, muttonhead, fountainhead, maidenhead, woodenhead **.15** basehead, Portishead **.16** Brideshead, hogshead, Holinshed **.17** beachhead **.18** bridgehead **.19** steelhead, billhead, railhead, wellhead, bullhead, knucklehead, chucklehead, bufflehead, shovelhead, barrelhead

23.5.14
unwed, newlywed

23.5.15
re-read, outspread, bedspread, widespread, wingspread, teabread, waybread, sowbread, purebred, shewbread, crispbread, sweetbread, Whitbread, flatbread, outbred, shortbread, inbred, cornbread, spoon-bread, crossbred, retread, sight-read, mind-read, street-cred, Tancred, unread, proofread, packthread, unthread, misread, Ethelred, infrared, overspread, interbred, underbred, overbred, gingerbread, thoroughbred, Standardbred

23.5.16
blacklead, misled, bobsled

23.6
Baird, Sheard, laird, unpaired, scared, unshared, short-haired, tousle-haired, unprepared, unrepaired, unimpaired, undeclared, under-prepared

23.7
ad, add, pad, bad, bade, tad, dad, cad, scad, gad, mad, fad, sad, shad, Chad, had, rad, prad, brad, trad, Strad, grad, lad, plaid, clad, glad, Vlad, Novi Sad, superadd

23.7.1
Riyadh

23.7.2
ennead, Lusiad, Dunciad, oread, Iliad, chiliad, Gilead, tele-ad, Asclepiad, Olympiad, gesnieriad, bromeliad, pedophiliad

23.7.3
dyad, naiad, triad, dryad, jeremiad, hamadryad

23.7.4
ogdoad

23.7.5
keypad, footpad, notepad, inkpad, tonepad, launchpad, sketchpad, scratchpad, touchpad, helipad, scribbling-pad

23.7.6
forbad, forbade, forebad, forebade, Sinbad,
Carlsbad, Karlsbad, Ashkhabad, Hyderabad,
Faisalabad, Marienbad, Faridabad, Ahmadabad,
Islamabad, Allahabad, Secunderabad, Jalalabad

23.7.7
heptad, octad, UNCTAD, pentad

23.7.8
aoudad, crawdad, Ciudad, doodad, bedad,
stepdad, Baghdad, grandad, Trinidad, alidad,
Soledad

23.7.9
ecad, Akkad, nicad, cycad

23.7.10
egad, begad

23.7.11
nomad

23.7.12
maenad, gonad, monad, trichomonad

23.7.13
Assad, Mossad, hexad

23.7.14
Upanishad

23.7.15
jihad, Galahad

23.7.16
farad, NORAD, tetrad, Amstrad®, postgrad,
Conrad, Konrad, Titograd, undergrad,
Volgograd, Petrograd, Leningrad, Stalingrad,
Kaliningrad

23.7.17
snowclad, unclad, ironclad

23.8
Saud, proud, Stroud, crowd, shroud, loud, cloud,
unbowed, O'Dowd, lowbrowed, in-crowd,
enshroud, aloud, unploughed, becloud, McLeod,
unendowed, unavowed, overcrowd,
thundercloud, overcloud

23.9
pard, bard, card, guard, nard, Fahd, Sade, sard,
shard, chard, hard, yard, lard, Briard, wild card,
en garde, Savoyard

23.9.1
grillade

23.9.2
milliard, Hilliard, galliard

23.9.3
Bayard

23.9.4
Savoyard

23.9.5
Peppard, Stoppard, camelopard

23.9.6
tabard, aubade, gambade, bombard, bombarde,
Lombard, Isambard, Svalbard, Ashkhabad,
Hyderabad, Faisalabad, statute-barred,
Faridabad, Ahmadabad, Islamabad, Allahabad,
Secunderabad, Jalalabad

23.9.7
retard, leotard, petard, Ostade, croustade,
ill-starred, Coulthard, rodomontade

23.9.8
Stoddard, Goddard, Woodard, Ciudad

23.9.9
Picard, Rickard, Packard, saccade, Jacquard,
placard, scorecard, becard, showcard, postcard,
phonecard, discard, Liskeard, racecard,
unscarred, flashcard, punchcard, railcard,
Microcard®

23.9.10
blackguard, Lugard, fireguard, regard, Bogarde,
coastguard, Midgard, mudguard, vanguard,
unguard, safeguard, lifeguard, Asgard,
Horseguard, Fishguard, bodyguard, avant-garde,
Kierkegaard, self-regard, disregard

23.9.11
pomade, unmarred

23.9.12
Maynard, reynard, canard, Barnard, Cunard,
Bernard, spikenard, Oxnard, carbonade,
Oudenarde, promenade, communard

23.9.13
couvade, boulevard

23.9.14
Gothard, Coulthard

23.9.15
glissade, Assad, brassard, façade, mansard,
Hansard

23.9.16
Izzard, Tizard

23.9.17
Suchard, Trenchard, Blanchard

23.9.18
Pritchard, Trenchard, Blanchard

23.9.19
diehard, jihad, blowhard

23.9.20
Gerard, Garrard, charade, estrade, Everard,
piperade

23.9.21
Riyadh, dooryard, foreyard, grillade, oeillade,
shipyard, scrapyard, courtyard, boatyard,
tiltyard, Rudyard, woodyard, brickyard,
backyard, stockyard, dockyard, junkyard,
farmyard, Bromyard, greenyard, vineyard,
lanyard, barnyard, poniard, graveyard,
switchyard, churchyard, steelyard, kaleyard,
schoolyard, lumberyard, Montagnard

23.9.22
Dillard, Gillard, Millard, Willard, ballade,
Ballard, mallard, pollard, bollard, Lollard,

Woollard, roulade, poulard, foulard, salade,
Abelard, interlard, fusillade

23.10
od, odd, pod, bod, tod, Todd, Dodd, cod, god,
mod, nod, sod, shod, hod, wad, quad, quod,
squad, rod, prod, trod, scrod, yod, plod, clod

23.10.1
tripod, unipod, polypod, brachiopod, myriapod,
copepod, chaetopod, octopod, pseudopod,
decapod, lycopod, megapod, monopod,
amphipod, isopod, hexapod, rhizopod,
theropod, pteropod, sauropod, tetrapod,
gasteropod, gastropod, macropod, arthropod,
phyllopod, tylopod, cephalopod

23.10.2
Ichabod

23.10.3
fantod

23.10.4
Ashdod

23.10.5
peascod

23.10.6
sun-god, demigod

23.10.7
synod

23.10.8
ephod

23.10.9
Hafod, eisteddfod

23.10.10
slipshod, unshod, roughshod

23.10.11
tightwad, Aswad

23.10.12
retrod, hotrod, Nimrod, ramrod, Ormerod, con
rod, goldenrod, pushrod, Novgorod, Iditarod,
Nizhni Novgorod

23.10.13
Bacolod

23.11
Landes, seconde

23.12
baud, bawd, board, chord, cord, gaud, Gawd,
gourd, maud, Maude, Foord, ford, Forde, sword,
hoard, horde, ward, sward, broad, fraud, fiord,
fjord, laud, lord, Claud, Claude, unawed, ouija
board

23.12.1
fjord

23.12.2
aboard, above board **.1** keyboard, seaboard,
freeboard **.2** Contiboard, storyboard **.3** starboard,
garboard, larboard **.4** scoreboard, strawboard,
floorboard **.5** scraperboard, clapperboard,

fibreboard, teeterboard, mortarboard,
centerboard, centreboard, plasterboard,
checkerboard, chequerboard, daggerboard,
fingerboard, Beaverboard, overboard,
weatherboard, motherboard **.6** snowboard
.7 shipboard, chipboard, clipboard, clapboard
.8 skateboard, fretboard, outboard, dartboard,
whiteboard, footboard, draughtboard,
pasteboard **.9** headboard, breadboard,
cardboard, hardboard, sideboard, soundboard,
mouldboard **.10** backboard, tackboard,
blackboard, blockboard, chalkboard, buckboard,
duckboard **.11** pegboard **.12** inboard, drainboard,
funboard, signboard **.13** springboard,
stringboard, gangboard, longboard,
runningboard, divingboard **.14** surfboard
.15 baseboard, chessboard, pressboard,
saxboard, noticeboard, smorgasbord
.16 cheeseboard **.17** dashboard, splashboard,
washboard **.18** switchboard, patchboard,
matchboard, scratchboard, sandwich-board
.19 bargeboard **.20** billboard, millboard,
tailboard, sailboard, wobble-board, flannelboard,
baffleboard, shuffleboard, shovelboard

23.12.3
unrestored

23.12.4
record, drawcord, trichord, accord, whipcord,
ripcord, concord, uncord, Concorde, discord,
needlecord, notochord, heptachord, octachord,
pentachord, monochord, clavichord, disaccord,
harpsichord, hexachord, re-record, prerecord,
urochord, tape-record, tetrachord, telerecord,
misericord

23.12.5
afford, Oxenford

23.12.6
broadsword

23.12.7
assured, insured

23.12.8
award, toward, reward, greensward, Aylward,
untoward

23.12.9
maraud, abroad, defraud

23.12.10
cured, matured, secured, obscured

23.12.11
warlord, milord, applaud, landlord, slumlord,
overlord, unexplored

23.13
Boyd, Coed, void, Freud, Lloyd, Floyd, sloid, Pink
Floyd, Betws-y-Coed

23.13.1
geoid

23.13.2
scorpioid, clupeoid, opioid, taenioid, ichthyoid,
embryoid, botryoid

23.13.3
pyoid, hyoid

23.13.4
zooid

23.13.5
lipoid, hypoid, lupoid, polypoid, anthropoid

23.13.6
cuboid, globoid, rhomboid, amoeboid

23.13.7
mattoid, factoid, lentoid, cestoid, mastoid, deltoid, rheumatoid, dermatoid, granitoid, planetoid, demantoid, allantoid, odontoid, parasitoid, elephantoid

23.13.8
gadoid, turdoid

23.13.9
placoid, coccoid, cricoid, fucoid, percoid, vocoid, trochoid, Cyncoed, conchoid, discoid, eunuchoid, pithecoid, coracoid, helicoid, meniscoid, molluscoid, cercopithecoid

23.13.10
fungoid, algoid, pemphigoid

23.13.11
sigmoid, ethmoid, prismoid, sesamoid, epidermoid

23.13.12
ctenoid, sphenoid, splenoid, crinoid, ganoid, conoid, echinoid, tetanoid, retinoid, platinoid, adenoid, salmonoid, hominoid, humanoid, delphinoid, resinoid, benzenoid, paranoid, cyprinoid, fibrinoid, solenoid, drumlinoid, arachnoid, arytenoid, carotenoid, albuminoid, bioflavonoid, cartilaginoid

23.13.13
xiphoid, scaphoid, typhoid, lymphoid, paratyphoid

23.13.14
naevoid, avoid, devoid, ovoid

23.13.15
feldspathoid, helminthoid

23.13.16
cissoid, gneissoid, schizoid, coccoid, Caucasoid, sinusoid, ellipsoid

23.13.17
sleazoid, rhizoid, trapezoid, spermozoid

23.13.18
overjoyed

23.13.19
viroid, scirrhoid, steroid, spheroid, scleroid, tapiroid, meteoroid, aroid, scaroid, sparoid, choroid, toroid, thyroid, hyperthyroid, hypothyroid, parathyroid, asteroid, acaroid, accaroid, haemorrhoid, Osmiroid, aneroid, diphtheroid, leatheroid, sciuroid, lemuroid, Polaroid®, gabbroid, fibroid, scombroid, centroid, sistroid, Murgatroyd, hydroid,

dendroid, android, salamandroid, Ackroyd, cancroid, chancroid, negroid, Mytholmroyd, pyrethroid, erythroid, Boothroyd, Holroyd

23.13.20
unalloyed, keloid, varioloid, squaloid, thalloid, colloid, styloid, myeloid, hyaloid, petaloid, metalloid, crystalloid, condyloid, alkaloid, mongoloid, bungaloid, amyloid, syphiloid, coralloid, Australoid, celluloid, paraboloid, hyperboloid, amygdaloid, diploid, triploid, haploid, euploid, polyploid, tetraploid, heteroploid, unemployed, self-employed, underemployed, allopolyploid, autopolyploid, tabloid, cycloid, epicycloid, hypocycloid

23.14
spud, bud, stud, dud, cud, scud, mud, thud, sudd, Judd, rudd, crud, blood, m'lud, flood, taste bud, redbud, disbud, rosebud, Talmud, pureblood, Wildblood, lifeblood, stick-in-the-mud

23.15
I'd, ide, pied, bide, tide, guide, nide, snide, Said, side, shied, chide, hide, Hyde, wide, ride, Ryde, pride, Pryde, bride, tried, stride, dried, cried, lied, Clyde, glide, slide, pie-eyed, sloe-eyed, popeyed, wild-eyed, cockeyed, stalk-eyed, Port Said, square-eyed, park and ride, wall-eyed, starry-eyed, hollow-eyed, tender-eyed

23.15.1
oroide

23.15.2
unoccupied

23.15.3
carbide, Ubaid, abide

23.15.4
betide, riptide, peptide, ebb-tide, Hocktide, noontide, eventide, Whitsuntide, Passiontide, springtide, Shrovetide, Yuletide, nucleotide, apartheid, Eastertide, dipeptide, Rogationtide, Ascensiontide, Christmastide, polypeptide, oligopeptide, oligonucleotide

23.15.5
iodide, undyed

23.15.6
waveguide, misguide, honeyguide

23.15.7
imide, amide, bromide, frusemide, polyamide, tolbutamide, thalidomide, cyanamide, sulphonamide, nicotinamide, sulphanilamide

23.15.8
cyanide, actinide, undenied, lanthanide, selenide

23.15.9
confide, cityfied, Gypsyfied, countrified, raphide, dignified, signified, sissified, unstratified, unratified, unfortified, uncertified, unrectified, unsanctified, unquantified, unjustified, unmodified, undignified, unspecified, unclassified, unverified, unpurified,

unqualified, unsimplified, preamplified, unamplified, unidentified, overqualified, phosphide, unsatisfied, self-satisfied, sulphide, disulphide

23.15.10
divide, provide, redivide, subdivide

23.15.11
aside, beside, decide, subside, outside, backside, Brookside, inside, onside, coincide, Kelvinside, offside, five-a-side, alongside **.1** Teesside, Deeside, quayside, seaside **.2** Heaviside, Merseyside, countryside **.3** nearside, Wearside, nucleoside **.4** Tayside, dayside, wayside **.5** airside **.6** deicide, fireside, suicide, lapicide, herbicide, Humberside, foeticide, set-aside, waterside, pesticide, insecticide, rodenticide, infanticide, parasiticide, underside, glycoside, glucoside, fungicide, Barmecide, homicide, spermicide, vermicide, germicide, genocide, tyrannicide, riverside, larvicide, ovicide, overside, silverside, regicide, algicide, parricide, patricide, matricide, fratricide, bactericide, acaricide, sororicide, uxoricide, cerebroside, stillicide, filicide, silicide **.7** Cheapside, topside, diopside **.8** curbside, kerbside **.9** stateside **.10** bedside, broadside, roadside **.11** lakeside, Exide, trackside, oxide, dockside, lochside, dioxide, trioxide, epoxide, suboxide, monoxide, peroxide, tetroxide, hydroxide, carbon monoxide, sodium hydroxide **.12** downside, Tyneside, lineside, Ironside, Burnside, turnside, Whernside, mountainside **.13** ringside **.14** cliffside **.15** graveside **.16** beachside **.17** hillside, poolside, Ambleside, canalside

23.15.12
azide, thiazide, reside, preside

23.15.13
cowhide, rawhide, greenhide, horsehide, oxhide, aldehyde, naugahyde, formaldehyde, paraldehyde, acetaldehyde, urea-formaldehyde

23.15.14
statewide, worldwide, nationwide

23.15.15
hayride, chloride, fluoride, joyride, deride, McBride, Kirkbride, Kilbride, outride, nitride, untried, astride, bestride, hydride, sun-dried, refried, pan-fried, bichloride, trichloride, saccharide, override, glyceride, telluride, anhydride, tetrachloride, hydrochloride, sodium chloride, borofluoride, trisaccharide, triglyceride, polysaccharide, monosaccharide, oligosaccharide, mucopolysaccharide

23.15.16
halide, allied, elide, collide, bolide, applied, implied, nuclide, Strathclyde, landslide, backslide, unallied, unapplied, unsupplied, ophicleide, paraglide, acetylide, radionuclide, acetanilide

23.16
pud, stood, could, Godd, good, Goode, should, hood, wood, would, 'twould, Robin Hood, balsa wood

23.16.1
withstood, understood, misunderstood

23.16.2
Likud

23.16.3
Toogood, Habgood, Osgood, Gielgud, Thorogood

23.16.4
Malamud

23.16.5
.1 puppyhood, babyhood, ladyhood, hardihood, Gypsyhood, likelihood, livelihood, unlikelihood **.2** boyhood **.3** squirehood, neighbourhood, daughterhood, doctorhood, sisterhood, masterhood, spinsterhood, fatherhood, motherhood, brotherhood, toddlerhood **.4** widowhood **.5** cubhood **.6** statehood, knighthood, sainthood, priesthood, Christhood, colthood, prophethood, parenthood, adulthood **.7** godhood, childhood, husbandhood **.8** monkhood **.9** lambhood, victimhood **.10** queenhood, manhood, nunhood, lionhood, maidenhood, orphanhood, personhood, cousinhood, nationhood, matronhood, virginhood, womanhood, citizenhood **.11** kinghood **.12** calfhood, wifehood, serfhood, selfhood, sheriffhood **.13** monkshood, falsehood **.14** girlhood, cripplehood

23.16.6
Burtonwood **.1** cherrywood, Hollywood **.2** Cawood, Haywood, Heywood **.3** Sharwood, Harewood, Harwood, Yarwood, Larwood **.4** Norwood **.5** plywood **.6** firewood, briarwood, brierwood, cedarwood, underwood, Boldrewood, Isherwood **.7** Sherwood **.8** sapwood, Hopwood, pulpwood, tulipwood **.9** Fleetwood, Chetwode, Atwood, heartwood, whitewood, lightwood, fruitwood, bentwood, Brentwood, driftwood, softwood, Eastwood, Westwood, giltwood **.10** redwood, hardwood, cordwood, Broadwood, Goodwood, wildwood **.11** Blackwood, Stockwood, Lockwood, corkwood, Brookwood, Kirkwood, stinkwood, muskwood **.12** Dagwood, dogwood, logwood **.13** camwood, wormwood, Holmwood, Elmwood **.14** greenwood, Linwood, Kenwood®, pinewood, ironwood, cottonwood, buttonwood, southernwood, satinwood, sapanwood, sappanwood **.15** Ringwood, Collingwood **.16** beefwood **.17** lacewood, basswood, copsewood, Spottiswoode, boxwood, lancewood **.18** cheesewood, Grisewood, rosewood, Kingswood **.19** ashwood, brushwood **.20** beechwood, Wychwood, matchwood, Scratchwood, larchwood, touchwood, birchwood, coachwood **.21** Wedgwood **.22** Hailwood, Halewood, Smallwood, Fulwood,

Littlewood, sandalwood, Inglewood, Englewood, Tanglewood, Hinshelwood

23.17
oud, Oudh, mood, snood, food, pseud, Jude, who'd, rood, rude, prude, brood, Strood, crude, shrewd, you'd, Bude, dude, nude, feud, lewd, lude

23.17.1
étude

23.17.2
seafood, catfood, wholefood

23.17.3
protrude, Gertrude, obtrude, intrude, extrude, pultrude, Holyrood, Ermintrude

23.17.4
.1 étude, quietude, inquietude, disquietude, turpitude, decrepitude, hebetude, habitude, attitude, gratitude, latitude, platitude, fortitude, certitude, aptitude, promptitude, rectitude, sanctitude, vastitude, altitude, Bultitude, multitude, beatitude, ingratitude, incertitude, ineptitude, inaptitude, correctitude, exactitude, inexactitude, longitude, finitude, plenitude, magnitude, infinitude, servitude, crassitude, lassitude, vicissitude, solicitude, oversolicitude, desuetude, mansuetude, consuetude, pulchritude, nigritude, negritude, solitude, amplitude, similitude, dissimilitude, verisimilitude **.2** subdued **.3** unargued **.4** denude, unrenewed **.5** transude, unissued **.6** exude **.7** prelude

23.17.5
illude, Quaalude®, allude, elude, delude, collude, postlude, occlude, seclude, preclude, include, conclude, exclude, unglued, interlude

23.18.1
multi-layered

23.18.2
coward, Howard, Howerd, unpowered, unsoured, underpowered

23.18.3
dryad, pleiad, untired, unwired, time-expired, unexpired, uninspired, jeremiad, undesired, underwired, hamadryad, semiretired

23.18.4
gourd, Lourdes, cured, assured, insured, matured, secured, obscured

23.18.5
steward, Seward, leeward

23.18.6
froward

23.18.7
Shepard, shepherd, Sheppard, leopard

23.18.8
tribade, tabard, scabbard, larboard, starboard, cupboard, Hubbard, halberd, unlaboured, unnumbered

23.18.9
.1 conceited, unheated, treated **.2** nitwitted, thick-witted, quick-witted, half-witted **.3** striated, self-created, herniated, glaciated, storiated, fimbriated, pileated, ciliated, galeated, laciniated, ammoniated, historiated, outdated, short-dated, spicated, plicated, corticated, dedicated, unlocated, alembicated, elasticated, uneducated, educated, unmated, mismated, consummated, semipalmated, pinnated, ganglionated, patinated, pectinated, columnated, foraminated, opinionated, self-pollinated, polychlorinated, trade-weighted, long-awaited, antiquated, rostrated, unrated, X-rated, unconsecrated, uncorroborated, unadulterated, stellated, elated, belated, violated, castellated, mentholated, ocellated, pixilated, nodulated, unrelated, over-inflated, folliculated **.4** indebted, minareted, sulphuretted **.5** matted, fatted, dratted, cravatted, top-hatted, superfatted **.6** undoubted **.7** uncharted, light-hearted, hard-hearted, good-hearted, kind-hearted, warm-hearted, downhearted, lion-hearted, wholehearted, simple-hearted, overparted, unimparted, stony-hearted, heavy-hearted, tenderhearted, hollow-hearted **.8** St Gotthard, besotted, unallotted **.9** unexploited, underexploited **.10** benighted, clear-sighted, shortsighted, unsighted, detrited, uninvited, unrequited **.11** splay-footed, barefooted, surefooted, web-footed, club-footed, light-footed, wrong-footed, heavy-footed **.12** unsuited, untutored, reputed, voluted, undisputed, convoluted, self-constituted, maldistributed **.13** habited, limited, velveted, faceted, facetted, ringletted, carpeted, unedited, unaudited, unlimited, uncomforted, unvisited, unmerited, uninhibited, uninhabited, unsolicited, multifaceted, uninterpreted **.14** concerted, introverted, extroverted, unconverted, uncontroverted **.15** dotard, sugarcoated **.16** Apted, unscripted, unprompted, unaccepted, unadapted, unadopted, uncorrupted, uninterrupted **.17** nectared, aspected, invected, complected, protracted, distracted, unpredicted, unrestricted, unconstricted, self-inflicted, unsuspected, unexpected, undetected, unprotected, unconnected, disconnected, unperfected, unaffected, disaffected, uninfected, undirected, uncorrected, uncollected, unelected, uninflected, unobstructed, unreconstructed **.18** tempted, unattempted **.19** hand-painted, unstinted, unprinted, sainted, unpainted, untainted, unacquainted, undented, unvented, unscented, self-centred, unrepented, self-contented, discontented, malcontented, precedented, unfermented, filamented, unlamented, unaccented, unfrequented, unprecedented, unornamented, unregimented, undocumented, unrepresented, under-represented, uncounted, unmounted, unaccounted, unwanted, unwonted, undaunted,

unpointed, self-appointed, untenanted, unwarranted, untalented, uncovenanted **.20** tight-fisted, limp-wristed, unlisted, unassisted, unresisted, waisted, untasted, Quested, untested, unrested, unattested, uncontested, uninvested, predigested, undigested, uncongested, unrequested, uninterested, self-interested, unmolested, tuberculin-tested, dastard, bastard, unplastered, costard, unexhausted, bustard, custard, mustard, unflustered, unadjusted, maladjusted, worsted, Newstead, Sanderstead, unharvested, unregistered, oersted, posted, toasted, roasted, Buxted, Plumstead, Moretonhampstead, Finchampstead, Stansted, Halstead **.21** stilted, sheltered, unaltered, unsalted

23.18.10
.1 reeded, unneeded, unseeded, unheeded, unimpeded, pleaded **.2** unaided, unfaded, unshaded, persuaded, voluntary-aided **.3** bareheaded, tow-headed, fatheaded, hotheaded, light-headed, hardheaded, baldheaded, thickheaded, blockheaded, pigheaded, pinheaded, boneheaded, woodenheaded, wrong-headed, chuckleheaded, unwedded, unleaded, woolly-headed, dunderheaded **.4** plaided, unpadded **.5** uncrowded, unclouded **.6** farded, retarded, unregarded **.7** Stoddard, Goddard **.8** unrewarded **.9** embroidered **.10** unstudied, pureblooded, hot-blooded, red-blooded, cold-blooded, warm-blooded **.11** unguided, misguided, lopsided, slab-sided, one-sided, undivided, undecided **.12** wooded, hooded **.13** uncoded, outmoded, spring-loaded, unexploded **.14** unhindered, intended, untended, unmended, unfriended, blended, unattended, unintended, amended, undefended, undescended, befriended, apprehended, uncomprehended, standard, glandered, substandard, nonstandard, uncandid, three-handed, surehanded, high-handed, shorthanded, right-handed, light-handed, redhanded, backhanded, offhanded, unbranded, heavy-handed, underhanded, unbounded, unfounded, unsounded, ungrounded, unrounded, uncompounded, unfunded, underfunded, broad-minded, like-minded, tough-minded, small-minded, simple-minded, single-minded, literal-minded, wounded, seconded **.15** unshielded, gilded, round-shouldered, unheralded

23.18.11
nacred, naked, becard, marked, cycad, crooked, stinkard, tankard, drunkard, unconquered, bewhiskered

23.18.12
niggard, legged, jagged, haggard, ragged, laggard, blackguard, dogged, rugged, sluggard, three-legged, barelegged, cross-legged, unsugared, Ladefoged

23.18.13
Talmud, enamored, enamoured, Muhammad, ill-humoured

23.18.14
synod, reynard, Leonard, Stannard, Seanad, Sioned, Bernard, gurnard, learned, Oxnard, patinaed, mannered, honoured, three-cornered, unlearned, cater-cornered

23.18.15
winged

23.18.16
.1 Seaford, Sleaford **.2** Lifford, Clifford, Mudeford, Hunniford **.3** Heyford, Crayford **.4** Fairford **.5** Stafford, Trafford, Strafford **.6** Orford, Stortford, Crawford, Lawford **.7** Rufford **.8** Twyford, undeciphered **.9** Waterford, Stuttaford, Bideford, Hungerford, Rutherford, Hereford **.10** Burford, Herford, Hurford **.11** Mitford, Deptford, Retford, Stretford, Catford, Dartford, Hartford, Hertford, Watford **.12** Bedford, Redford, Radford, Bradford, Woodford, Sandford, Blandford, Guildford, eisteddfod **.13** Pickford, Beckford, Crockford **.14** Mogford **.15** Cromford, Mumford **.16** Winford, Wynford, Linford, Rainford, Stanford, Sanford, Kingswinford **.17** Chingford, Strangford, Langford, Longford, Wallingford **.18** Cosford, Knutsford, Wexford, Oxford, Beresford **.19** Chelmsford, Eynsford, Alresford, Woodlesford **.20** Ashford **.21** Stechford, Blatchford, Rochford **.22** Wilford, Telford, Welford, Alford, Salford, Holford, Walford, Fulford, Coleford, Stapleford, Stableford, Camelford, Castleford

23.18.17
Harvard, Dyfed, unflavoured, unsevered, beloved, lily-livered, undelivered, unrecovered, undiscovered, unbeloved

23.18.18
method

23.18.19
withered, unfathered, unbothered

23.18.20
blessed, cussed, deuced, cursed, monoacid, pellucid, accursed, censored, unanswered

23.18.21
izard, Izzard, Tizard, gizzard, vizard, wizard, lizard, blizzard, mazzard, hazard, Hazzard, buzzard, haphazard

23.18.22
Trenchard, Blanchard, uncensured

23.18.23
pongid, unmeasured, uninjured

23.18.24
Richard, Pritchard, natured, wretched, pochard, orchard, strictured, Trenchard, Blanchard, pilchard, good-natured, ill-natured, unstructured, uncultured

23.18.25
aged, Rudyard, pongid, alleged, uninjured

23.18.26
.1 seaward, Seward, leeward .2 cityward
.3 rearward .4 Hayward, Haywood, wayward
.5 forward, shoreward, straightforward, wing
forward, thenceforward, henceforward
.6 skyward .7 afterward, thitherward,
hitherward, whitherward, Hereward .8 upward
.9 streetward, outward, rightward, frontward,
leftward, eastward, westward .10 Edward,
headward, godward, sideward, Woodward,
windward, landward .11 backward, awkward
.12 homeward .13 inward, townward,
downward, onward, sunward, sternward,
heavenward, oceanward .14 graveward
.15 southward, northward, earthward
.16 spaceward .17 Aylward, hellward, poleward

23.18.27
Herod, Garrard, farad, Harrod, forehead, hatred,
Ystrad, Mordred, kindred, hundred, Mildred,
sacred, Ingrid, comrade, Manfred, Alfred,
Angharad, self-hatred

23.18.28
Rudyard, vineyard, Spaniard, lanyard, poniard,
Hesiod, billiard, steelyard, halyard, tenured

23.18.29
ballad, mallard, salad, pollard, bollard, collard,
Lollard, dullard, Coloured, bicoloured,
tricoloured, uncoloured, self-coloured,
particoloured, multicoloured, versicoloured,
varicoloured

23.19
bird, Byrd, turd, curd, Kurd, gird, nerd, nurd,
fyrd, verd, third, surd, Sheard, sherd, Heard,
herd, word, Cape Verde, word for word

23.19.1
seabird, jaybird, cowbird, shorebird, bluebird,
bowerbird, firebird, lyrebird, snowbird, catbird,
nightbird, yardbird, tick-bird, blackbird,
rainbird, sunbird, ovenbird, kingbird, songbird,
surfbird, lovebird, cage bird, gaolbird, jailbird,
bellbird, wattlebird, ladybird, dicky bird,
whirlybird, waterbird, thunderbird, weaverbird,
widow-bird, mockingbird, hummingbird

23.19.2
unstirred, undeterred

23.19.3
Sigurd, begird, engird, ungird, undergird

23.19.4
absurd

23.19.5
absurd

23.19.6
potsherd

23.19.7
reheard, cowherd, goatherd, unheard, swineherd,
misheard, gooseherd, oxherd, overheard

23.19.8
keyword, reword, swearword, foreword,
byword, headword, codeword, loanword,
password, crossword, buzzword, catchword,
watchword, afterword

23.20
ode, Spode®, baud, bode, toad, code, goad, mode,
node, woad, road, rode, Troad, strode, load, lode,
Morse code, offload, à la mode

23.20.1
geode

23.20.2
diode, triode, Zener diode, photodiode

23.20.3
epode, antipode, megapode

23.20.4
forebode, abode

23.20.5
web-toed, pentode, cestode, trematode,
nematode

23.20.6
cladode

23.20.7
decode, recode, bar code, zip-code, postcode,
encode, transcode, autocode, microcode

23.20.8
commode, Kermode, incommode,
discommode

23.20.9
threnode, anode, antinode, internode, palinode

23.20.10
cathode, hydathode, anticathode

23.20.11
rhapsode, hexode, episode

23.20.12
byroad, highroad, erode, corrode, sarod, tetrode,
outrode, bestrode, Bulstrode, inroad, crossroad,
railroad, tollroad, overrode, electrode, middle-
of-the-road

23.20.13
reload, freeload, phyllode, payload, carload,
shipload, upload, implode, explode, cartload,
boatload, peakload, truckload, workload,
armload, trainload, planeload, vanload,
download, unload, wagonload, Evenlode,
baseload, caseload, coachload, lorryload,
unhallowed, unswallowed, overload,
barrowload, waggonload

23.21
bilobed, unabsorbed, self-absorbed,
undescribed, prescribed, perturbed, disturbed,
undersubscribed, circumscribed

23.22
legged, jagged, bewigged, square-rigged,
ship-rigged, outrigged, barelegged, gatelegged,
cross-legged, waterlogged

23.23.1
dreamed, meseemed, unstreamed, undreamed, unredeemed

23.23.2
undimmed, unskimmed, broadbrimmed, untrimmed

23.23.3
untamed, unnamed, ashamed, inflamed, unframed, unclaimed, unashamed, unacclaimed, unproclaimed, self-proclaimed, unreclaimed

23.23.4
self-condemned

23.23.5
unarmed, unharmed, alarmed

23.23.6
unformed, malformed, unwarmed, performed, deformed, reformed, uninformed, transformed

23.23.7
unplumbed

23.23.8
unperfumed, unconsumed

23.23.9
unfathomed, ransomed, unaccustomed

23.23.10
unconfirmed

23.24.1
fiend, unweaned, unscreened

23.24.2
poind, Mynd, Sind, Sindh, wind, Lind, Rifkind, thick-skinned, thin-skinned, prescind, rescind, exscind, upwind, Chetwynd, tradewind, headwind, woodwind, downwind, crosswind, tailwind, whirlwind, tamarind, Wedekind, wunderkind, ensanguined, Amerind, Rosalind

23.24.3
Trobriand

23.24.4
maned, tearstained, unstained, unfeigned, harebrained, crackbrained, untrained, ingrained, unattained, self-contained, unsustained, self-sustained, ordained, featherbrained, undertrained, restrained, self-restrained, constrained, unexplained, ascertained

23.24.5
end, pend, spend, bend, tend, mend, fend, vend, scend, send, Zend, wend, rend, trend, friend, lend, blend, blende, upend, weekend, tag end, scrag-end, Southend, Gravesend, Bridgend, tail-end **.1** minuend **.2** stipend, append, perpend, depend, impend, suspend, outspend, expend, misspend, underspend, overspend, interdepend **.3** U-bend, Z-bend, unbend, S-bend **.4** portend, attend, pretend, subtend,

intend, contend, Ostend, distend, extend, coextend, repetend, superintend, overextend **.5** dividend **.6** bookend **.7** emend, amend, commend, recommend, ill-omened **.8** bin-end **.9** forfend, offend, reoffend, defend **.10** Demavend **.11** ascend, reascend, descend, godsend, transcend, redescend, condescend, parascend **.12** Townsend **.13** reprehend, apprehend, comprehend, subtrahend, misapprehend **.14** boyfriend, befriend, penfriend, girlfriend **.15** hornblende, pitchblende, interblend

23.24.6
and, band, stand, manned, NAND, sand, hand, rand, brand, strand, grand, Land, land, bland, gland, whip hand, second hand, own brand, Río Grande, Franz Joseph Land, Van Diemen's Land **.1** Trobriand **.2** graduand **.3** repand, expand **.4** showband, proband, sweatband, hatband, wristband, waistband, headband, broadband, sideband, neckband, armband, trainband, waveband, disband, passband, jazzband, noseband, watchband, bellyband, saraband, contraband **.5** untanned, hatstand, bandstand, handstand, grandstand, kickstand, bookstand, inkstand, withstand, newsstand, washstand, hallstand, understand, misunderstand **.6** deodand **.7** Samarkand, multiplicand **.8** demand, command, remand, unmanned, countermand, undermanned, confirmand, reprimand, allemande **.9** ordinand, Ferdinand **.10** Streisand, quicksand, greensand, ampersand, analysand **.11** freehand, cowhand, forehand, shorthand, righthand, firsthand, shedhand, thirdhand, deckhand, backhand, farmhand, unhand, longhand, offhand, stagehand, chargehand, millhand, beforehand, underhand, overhand, behindhand **.12** firebrand, Talleyrand, operand, Krugerrand, honorand, magistrand, integrand, Witwatersrand **.13** inland, overland, Ngamiland, Disneyland®, Dixieland, Swaziland, fairyland, Maoriland, Somaliland, Matabeleland, ploughland, Saarland, Thailand, Zululand, Basotholand, Oberland, timberland, platteland, hinterland, borderland, wonderland, Gelderland, Griqualand, Nagaland, Helgoland, fatherland, motherland, pastureland, Manicaland, Heligoland, Gondwanaland, Mashonaland, Nyasaland, Namaqualand, Damaraland, Bechuanaland, Öland, meadowland, Ovamboland, Basutoland, Lapland, swampland, unplanned, scrubland, clubland, peatland, wetland, flatland, heartland, Gotland, wasteland, coastland, cloudland, tideland, lackland, parkland, dockland, dreamland, farmland, homeland, Vinland, mainland, fenland, downland, Rhineland, Sudetenland, gangland, elfland, heathland, southland, grassland, Queensland, no-man's-land, marshland, washland, rangeland, tableland

23.24.7
pound, bound, mound, found, sound, hound, wound, round, ground, Puget Sound
.1 propound, impound, compound, expound, decompound **.2** rebound, abound, snowbound, outbound, potbound, softbound, eastbound, westbound, frostbound, hardbound, hidebound, windbound, rockbound, strikebound, fogbound, stormbound, homebound, inbound, unbound, southbound, clothbound, northbound, earthbound, disbound, case-bound, brassbound, housebound, icebound, spellbound, weatherbound, superabound **.3** astound
.4 redound **.5** profound, dumbfound, confound
.6 unsound, ultrasound, infrasound **.7** resound
.8 deerhound, greyhound, horehound, bloodhound, elkhound, staghound, wolfhound, sleuthhound, foxhound, newshound, hellhound
.9 rewound, unwound, interwound, overwound
.10 around, surround, go-round, whip-round, wrapround, playground, fairground, foreground, aground, showground, campground, background, stoneground, battleground, turnround, changeround, wraparound, runaround, turnaround, underground, overground, aboveground, merry-go-round, theatre-in-the-round

23.24.8
demand, command, remand, countermand, self-command, reprimand

23.24.9
pond, bond, fond, sonde, wand, ronde, frond, Fronde, Frondes, yond, blonde, dewpond, despond, respond, millpond, de-bond, second, abscond, haut monde, beau monde, plafond, keeshond, mete-wand, Gironde, beyond, correspond, Broederbond, vagabond, Eurobond, demi-monde, overfond, radiosonde, Trebizond, chateaubriand

23.24.10
unmourned, unwarned, adorned

23.24.11
poind

23.24.12
bund, fund, Lund, rotund, obtund, fecund, jocund, secund, refund, re-fund, gerund, cummerbund, moribund, orotund, rubicund, Rosamund

23.24.13
bind, kind, mind, find, hind, Hinde, wind, wynd, rind, grind, blind, rebind, woodbind, unbind, spellbind, mankind, unkind, womenkind, womankind, humankind, remind, mastermind, affined, undefined, hydrofined, unrefined, unconfined, undersigned, unassigned, resigned, designed, behind, rewind, enwind, unwind, interwind, overwind, dripgrind, Gradgrind, purblind, snowblind, sunblind, unlined, nonaligned, unaligned, colour-blind, streamlined

23.24.14
Lund, Dortmund, bergschrund

23.24.15
wound, untuned, unpruned, unimpugned

23.24.16
.1 viand, unironed **.2** riband, prebend, proband, husband, beribboned, Younghusband, househusband **.3** sweetened, threatened, patterned, whitened, enlightened **.4** dividend
.5 fecund, second, jocund, weakened, rubicund, unthickened, wakened, split-second, unreckoned, unawakened, millisecond, nanosecond, microsecond, picosecond
.6 brigand, ligand **.7** Crimond, Grimond, Raymond, Hammond, almond, Armand, dromond, Ormond, gourmand, Drummond, Dymond, diamond, Dortmund, Edmund, Redmond, Sigmund, Esmond, Desmond, Osmond, osmund, Richmond, summoned, ill-omened, Sigismund, unexamined, undetermined, self-determined **.8** ordinand, Ferdinand **.9** ungoverned, self-governed, unleavened **.10** Streisand, dachshund, unchastened **.11** wizened, thousand, unseasoned **.12** old-fashioned, unsanctioned, unmentioned, unconditioned, commissioned, impassioned, proportioned, intentioned, aforementioned, undermentioned **.13** escutcheoned, unquestioned **.14** legend, imagined **.15** errand, gerund, operand, Bertrand, reverend **.16.1** eland, Zealand, Zeeland, Wieland, Leland, Cleland, Ponteland, Nayland, Wayland, Leyland, Elland, Welland, Yelland, McClelland, Dowland
.16.2 garland, Harland, engarland, McFarland, Tollund, Dollond, Holland, Mulholland, moorland, Morland, norland, foreland, Westmorland, island, Thailand, highland, Hyland, Ryland, dry land, Burntisland, Rhode Island, Robben Island, Staten Island, Coalisland, Ireland, Courland, Cumberland, Sunderland, Haviland, Sutherland, Switzerland, Maryland, Northumberland, de Havilland, Poland, Roland, Rowland, lowland **.16.3** upland, Coupland, Copeland, Maitland, Zetland, Shetland, wetland, Cartland, Hartland, heartland, Scotland, Portland, Jutland, Rutland, Pentland, Priestland, Westland, midland, headland, Studland, woodland, Newfoundland, Port Hedland, Strickland, Lakeland, Checkland, Breckland, lackland, parkland, dockland, Auckland, Buckland, Kirkland, Oakland, Frankland, England
.16.4 Greenland, inland, Finland, Vinland, mainland, fenland, downland, Langland, Cleveland, heathland, Northland, Goathland, Crosland, Iceland, Friesland, Queensland, marshland

23.24.17
learned, burned, upturned, unturned

23.24.18
pre-owned, unowned, atoned, chaperoned

23.25
winged, smooth-tongued, unstockinged

23.26
broadleaved, paved, saved, unshaved,
sexstarved, beloved, gloved, unloved, unmoved,
unproved, unsolved, perceived, believed,
unrelieved, Wellbeloved, contrived, dived,
approved, deserved, involved

23.27
unscathed, wry-mouthed, loudmouthed,
widemouthed, unsmoothed, mealy-mouthed

23.28.1
unfazed, amazed

23.28.2
tub-sized, unsized, undersized, unplasticized,
unpublicized, uncircumcised, pearlized

23.28.3
used, bruised, co-accused, unused, underused,
unamused

23.28.4
ptosed, unposed, snub-nosed, sclerosed,
unopposed, self-imposed, undisposed,
unexposed, varicosed, snotty-nosed,
toffee-nosed, undiagnosed, unenclosed,
undisclosed

23.28.5
uncleansed

23.29
tinged, unchanged, unavenged, challenged

23.30
aged, privileged, unwaged, gilt-edged,
unfledged, alleged, unabridged, unassuaged,
undischarged, unavenged, unacknowledged,
underprivileged

23.31.1
field, shield, heald, weald, wield, yield, Flodden
Field **.1** unaneled **.2** afield, midfield,
track-and-field, misfield, crossfield, Driffield,
Mayfield, hayfield, Sheffield, airfield, Garfield,
Caulfield, Duffield, Nuffield, Byfield, Fifield,
Scourfield, Copperfield, Satterfield, Butterfield,
chesterfield, Delderfield, Somerfield,
Summerfield, Dangerfield, Delafield, Sellafield,
Fallowfield, Mirfield, Schofield, snowfield,
upfield, Whitefield, Whitfield, Streatfield,
Hatfield, outfield, Westfield, Padfield, Hadfield,
Oldfield, goldfield, Sutton Coldfield, brickfield,
Wakefield, backfield, Uckfield, Cuckfield,
Brookfield, Armfield, Blomfield, Bloomfield,
Greenfield, infield, Winfield, grainfield, Enfield,
Shenfield, Anfield, Cranfield, brownfield,
Dronfield, cornfield, minefield, urnfield,
Leconfield, Lee–Enfield, Wingfield, Springfield,
Lingfield, Heathfield, Smithfield, Masefield,
gasfield, Stansfield, Mansfield, Wednesfield,
Wivelsfield, Petersfield, Huddersfield, Lichfield,
Burchfield, Sedgefield, oilfield, coalfield,
Scholfield, battlefield, Englefield **.3** unrevealed

.4 unsealed, concealed **.5** windshield, gumshield
.6 unhealed

23.31.2
build, gild, guild, sild, unspilled, rebuild,
upbuild, unbuild, tooth-billed, untilled,
deskilled, Roskilde, unskilled, regild, wergild,
unfilled, Brunhild, weak-willed, unwilled,
self-willed, overbuild, unfulfilled,
Townswomen's Guild

23.31.3
draggle-tailed, unscaled, uncurtailed

23.31.4
eld, Schelde, geld, meld, held, weld, Dunkeld,
Threlkeld, Salkeld, wergeld, Danegeld, Krefeld,
Blofeld, Ziegfeld, beheld, upheld, withheld,
spotweld, self-propelled, Bielefeld, unparalleled

23.31.5
skald, Buchenwald, Schwarzwald

23.31.6
bald, scald, skald, ribald, Theobald, piebald,
skewbald, so-called, walled, Rosenwald,
Archibald, Cumbernauld

23.31.7
soiled, spoiled, unoiled, shopsoiled

23.31.8
culled, thick-skulled

23.31.9
mild, Fylde, child, Childe, wild, Wilde, Wyld,
Wylde, self-styled, Fairchild, stepchild, godchild,
Goodchild, grandchild, brainchild, love child,
Rothschild, schoolchild, defiled, reconciled

23.31.10
Ould, Gould, unschooled, unscheduled

23.31.11
Roald, kobold, cuckold, Tynwald, Griswold,
Oswald, Gerald, herald, Jarrold, Harold, emerald,
Archibald, Fitzgerald

23.31.12
world, worlde, dreamworld, Transworld,
afterworld, underworld, netherworld

23.31.13
old, Ould, bold, told, cold, scold, gold, mold,
mould, fold, sold, hold, wold **.1** Leopold,
unpolled **.2** Cobbold, Newbold, Newbould,
Rumbold, overbold **.3** retold, Courtauld,
foretold, untold **.4** cuckold, Prestcold **.5** Gingold,
mangold, marigold **.6** remould, Wormold,
Detmold **.7** refold, threefold, enfold, unfold,
eightyfold, fortyfold, thirtyfold, twentyfold,
ninetyfold, seventyfold, fiftyfold, sixtyfold,
manyfold, scaffold, fourfold, twofold,
centrefold, manifold, overfold, sheepfold,
upfold, eightfold, gatefold, blindfold,
thousandfold, hundredfold, pinfold, Penfold,
tenfold, fanfold, downfold, onefold, ninefold,
sevenfold, linenfold, millionfold, elevenfold,
fivefold, twelvefold, sixfold, billfold, Nettlefold
.8 resold, Clissold, outsold, unsold, undersold,

oversold **.9** freehold, forehold, ahold, behold, toehold, uphold, shorthold, foothold, handhold, stokehold, stronghold, withhold, leasehold, household, threshold, throttlehold, stranglehold, copyhold, anchorhold, commonhold, lo and behold **.10** Southwold, Cotswold, Griswold, Stow-on-the-Wold **.11** uncontrolled, self-controlled

23.31.14
trampled, crumpled, unprincipled, unexampled

23.31.15
ribald, kobold, labelled, troubled, Archibald

23.31.16
metalled, embattled, untitled, disgruntled

23.31.17
bemedaled, bemedalled, unfuddled

23.31.18
cuckold, wrinkled, bespectacled

23.31.19
unmingled, newfangled

23.31.20
Wormald, Wormold, untrammelled

23.31.21
Arnold, Donald, Ronald, McDonald, Dundonald, Reginald

23.31.22
scaffold, ruffled, stifled

23.31.23
untravelled, unrivalled

23.31.24
sozzled

24.1
eke, peak, Peake, peek, peke, pique, speak, Speke, beak, teak, keek, geek, meek, sneak, Sneek, seek, Sikh, chic, sheikh, cheek, Cheke, weak, week, tweak, squeak, reek, wreak, streak, creak, creek, Greek, freak, shriek, leak, leek, bleak, cleek, clique, sleek, caique, shit creek

24.1.1
forepeak, apeak, repique, newspeak, bespeak, doublespeak, Chesapeake, technospeak

24.1.2
debeak, Mozambique, spoonbeak, grosbeak, stickybeak

24.1.3
batik, pratique, boutique, critique, triptyque, antique, Mustique, mystique, verd-antique, Ostpolitik, corps diplomatique, Realpolitik

24.1.4
opéra comique

24.1.5
Monique, unique, technique, Martinique, ortanique, Dominique, veronique, microtechnique

24.1.6
cacique, hide-and-seek

24.1.7
bezique, physique

24.1.8
Aguecheek, tongue-in-cheek

24.1.9
Tajik

24.1.10
midweek, workweek, pipsqueak

24.1.11
perique, hairstreak, tugrik, fenugreek, téléphérique

24.1.12
Lalique®, silique, oblique, houseleek

24.2
pic, pick, spic, spick, spik, Bic®, tic, tick, stick, shtick, dick, kick, mick, nick, snick, Vic, Vick, thick, sic, sick, Schick, chick, hic, hick, wick, KWIC, quick, rick, wrick, prick, brick, trick, strick, crick, lick, click, flick, slick, pea stick, Old Vic, Moby Dick, Ding an sich, three-card trick

24.2.1
dyspnoeic, maleic, nucleic, mythopoeic, seborrhoeic, logorrhoeic, onomatopoeic, deoxyribonucleic

24.2.2
diarrhoeic

24.2.3
laic, deltaic, Altaic, voltaic, Judaic, spondaic, archaic, trochaic, Incaic, alcaic, Romaic, Mishnaic, mosaic, prosaic, stanzaic, Hebraic, Mithraic, nucleic, faradaic, Aramaic, Ptolemaic, Cyrenaic, Pharisaic, choleraic, algebraic, formulaic, apotropaic, Ural-Altaic, photovoltaic, ribonucleic, deoxyribonucleic

24.2.4
haik

24.2.5
paranoic

24.2.6
Bewick, Buick®, Luick, toluic

24.2.7
Stoic, zoic, echoic, azoic, Neozoic, benzoic, heroic, caproic, valproic, gabbroic, pleochroic, dichroic, trichroic, allantoic, anechoic, butanoic, ethanoic, Palaeozoic, Paleozoic, protozoic, cryptozoic, Caenozoic, Cenozoic, Cainozoic, Mesozoic, Proterozoic, Phanerozoic, unheroic, spermatozoic

24.2.8
hand-pick, unpick **.1** philippic, stereotypic, prototypic, phenotypic, genotypic, monotypic **.2** epic, orthoepic **.3** priapic **.4** Harpic®, endocarpic, monocarpic, schizocarpic **.5** topic, tropic, myopic, presbyopic, Ethiopic, amblyopic,

photopic, ectopic, isotopic, radioisotopic, radioscopic, hagioscopic, stereoscopic, stroboscopic, otoscopic, pantoscopic, cystoscopic, endoscopic, megascopic, seismoscopic, stethoscopic, periscopic, horoscopic, stauroscopic, gyroscopic, spectroscopic, necroscopic, macroscopic, microscopic, hygroscopic, arthroscopic, telescopic, tachistoscopic, sigmoidoscopic, kaleidoscopic, laryngoscopic, ophthalmoscopic, polariscopic, electroscopic, submicroscopic, oscilloscopic, ultramicroscopic, Canopic, hyperopic, geotropic, rheotropic, pleiotropic, entropic, isentropic, azeotropic, heliotropic, phototropic, nyctitropic, psychotropic, emmetropic, thermotropic, xenotropic, isotropic, thixotropic, allotropic, gonadotropic, corticotropic, hypermetropic, anisotropic, adrenocorticotropic, hydropic, theanthropic, misanthropic, therianthropic, psilanthropic, philanthropic **.6** Yupik, Inupik **.7** biopic **.8** nitpick, nutpick **.9** Olympic **.10** toothpick **.11** aspic

24.2.9

.1 amoebic, ephebic **.2** syllabic, dissyllabic, disyllabic, trisyllabic, parisyllabic, polysyllabic, heptasyllabic, decasyllabic, monosyllabic, sexisyllabic, hexasyllabic, tetrasyllabic, quadrisyllabic, octosyllabic, hendecasyllabic, imparisyllabic **.3** sorbic, ascorbic **.4** Rubik, pubic, cubic, cherubic **.5** Arabic, Mozarabic **.6** acerbic **.7** phobic, niobic, lyophobic, aerobic, microbic, photophobic, homophobic, xenophobic, technophobic, claustrophobic, hydrophobic, acrophobic, Negrophobic, agoraphobic, anaerobic **.8** limbic, rhombic, plumbic, alembic, iambic, choriambic, galliambic, choliambic, dithyrambic, orthorhombic

24.2.10

artic **.1** Rhaetic, cretic, luetic, acetic, Docetic, copacetic, spermacetic **.2.1** critic, lytic, clitic, satellitic, Sinaitic, jesuitic, theodolitic, phlebitic, coenobitic, steatitic, stalactitic, troglodytic, endocarditic, hermaphroditic, rachitic, trachytic, bronchitic **.2.2** Hamitic, palmitic, Semitic, somitic, hermitic, eremitic, dolomitic, Islamitic, stalagmitic, Hamito-Semitic, Sinitic, granitic, kyanitic, syenitic, lignitic, tympanitic, aconitic, selenitic **.2.3** graphitic, ophitic, zoophytic, bryophytic, mephitic, epiphytic, sporophytic, saprophytic, hygrophytic, holophytic, gametophytic, bauxitic, calcitic, leucocytic, phagocytic, lymphocytic, parasitic, fibrositic, anthracitic, anorthositic, granulocytic, Cushitic, meningitic, laryngitic **.2.4** chloritic, pyritic, dioritic, pruritic, neuritic, pleuritic, barytic, ferritic, dendritic, diacritic, Sanskritic, nephritic, arthritic, meteoritic, sybaritic, lateritic, anchoritic, Ugaritic, porphyritic, diphtheritic, osteoarthritic, antipruritic, polyneuritic, oneirocritic **.2.5** zeolitic, dialytic, oolitic,

proclitic, enclitic, typhlitic, proteolytic, variolitic, catalytic, autolytic, photolytic, histolytic, Glagolitic, haemolytic, hemolytic, thermolytic, analytic, syphilitic, spherulitic, paralytic, pyrolytic, hydrolytic, bacteriolytic, psychoanalytic, cryptanalytic, encephalitic, electrolytic **.3.1** metic, thetic, Lettic, poetic, noetic, unpoetic, anoetic, aloetic, erythropoietic, onomatopoetic, herpetic, diabetic, tabetic, alphabetic, analphabetic, dietetic, zetetic, peripatetic, geodetic, eidetic, syndetic, asyndetic, catechetic, gametic, mimetic, emetic, hermetic, cosmetic, arithmetic, homogametic, kinetic, tonetic, phonetic, genetic, frenetic, phrenetic, splenetic, magnetic, cybernetic, biogenetic, oogenetic, geomagnetic, diamagnetic, hyperkinetic, telekinetic, psychokinetic, photokinetic, epigenetic, polygenetic, osteogenetic, metagenetic, cytogenetic, ectogenetic, frontogenetic, homogenetic, monogenetic, morphogenetic, pathogenetic, heterogenetic, phylogenetic, ontogenetic, histogenetic, orthogenetic, orogenetic, palingenetic, ferrimagnetic, ferromagnetic, aeromagnetic, paramagnetic, gyromagnetic, hydromagnetic, agamogenetic, parthenogenetic, spermatogenetic, electromagnetic **.3.2** aphetic, Japhetic, prophetic, unprophetic, Helvetic, pathetic, bathetic, prothetic, synthetic, aesthetic, esthetic, prosthetic, antithetic, epithetic, apathetic, sympathetic, empathetic, metathetic, nomothetic, biosynthetic, epenthetic, parenthetic, unaesthetic, hypaesthetic, kinaesthetic, synaesthetic, anaesthetic, paraesthetic, hyperaesthetic, telaesthetic, antipathetic, unsympathetic, polysynthetic, photosynthetic, parasynthetic, parasympathetic, Ossetic, ascetic, Gangetic, synergetic, energetic, bioenergetic, exegetic, epexegetic, apologetic, unapologetic **.3.3** theoretic, pyretic, paretic, phoretic, syncretic, anchoretic, diaphoretic, Masoretic, diuretic, enuretic, antipyretic, natriuretic, cataphoretic, electrophoretic, antidiuretic, balletic, phyletic, athletic, homiletic, polyphyletic **.4.1** attic, batik, static, phatic, vatic, phreatic, sciatic, ischiatic, Asiatic, Hanseatic, psoriatic, muriatic, Adriatic, pancreatic, Eleatic, hepatic, sabbatic, adiabatic, katabatic, anabatic, aerobatic, acrobatic, protatic, astatic, prostatic, eustatic, rheostatic, diastatic, ecstatic, anti-static, homeostatic, homoeostatic, heliostatic, apostatic, hypostatic, metastatic, photostatic, fungistatic, haemostatic, hemostatic, thermostatic, orthostatic, isostatic, aerostatic, gyrostatic, hydrostatic, bacteriostatic, electrostatic, mithridatic **.4.2** schematic, thematic, haematic, hematic, traumatic, climatic, rheumatic, pneumatic, sematic, somatic, stromatic, dramatic, chromatic, spermatic, stigmatic, sigmatic, smegmatic, phlegmatic, magmatic, pragmatic, dogmatic, zeugmatic, asthmatic, schismatic, prismatic, miasmatic, plasmatic, judgematic, dalmatic, athematic, idiomatic, axiomatic, enzymatic, automatic, symptomatic, systematic, zygomatic, kinematic, cinematic, graphematic, theorematic, aromatic, undramatic, achromatic, dichromatic, trichromatic, panchromatic, diagrammatic, programmatic, engrammatic, diaphragmatic, diplomatic, problematic, emblematic, astigmatic, tristigmatic, enigmatic, kerygmatic, syntagmatic, undogmatic, fantasmatic, numismatic, charismatic, porismatic, melismatic, unidiomatic, analemmatic, microclimatic, hydropneumatic, semiautomatic, asymptomatic, unsystematic, meristematic, erythematic, episematic, aposematic, psychosomatic, melodramatic, apochromatic, monochromatic, isochromatic, polychromatic, orthochromatic, heterochromatic, epigrammatic, anagrammatic, monogrammatic, chronogrammatic, undiplomatic, unproblematic, anastigmatic, paradigmatic, apophthegmatic, synallagmatic, protoplasmatic, uncharismatic **.4.3** Carnatic, fanatic, agnatic, cognatic, morganatic, aplanatic **.4.4** emphatic, lymphatic, phosphatic, apophatic, aliphatic, unemphatic, sylvatic, aquatic, semiaquatic, subaquatic **.4.5** piratic, hieratic, erratic, quadratic, theocratic, Socratic, operatic, leviratic, biquadratic, physiocratic, Hippocratic, autocratic, plutocratic, timocratic, democratic, monocratic, technocratic, pre-Socratic, isocratic, bureaucratic, ochlocratic, meritocratic, aristocratic, undemocratic, idiosyncratic, prelatic **.5** Partick, aspartic, cathartic **.6** otic, chaotic, biotic, diotic, meiotic, miotic, symbiotic, idiotic, semiotic, amniotic, ichthyotic, patriotic, scoliotic, abiotic, enzootic, eucaryotic, eukaryotic, procaryotic, prokaryotic, unpatriotic, compatriotic, antibiotic, gnotobiotic, anabiotic, parabiotic, necrobiotic, macrobiotic, epizootic, despotic, robotic, thrombotic, ketotic, mitotic, asymptotic, lordotic, acidotic, anecdotic, narcotic, dichotic, mycotic, psychotic, silicotic, zygotic, indigotic, heterozygotic, phimotic, zymotic, demotic, osmotic, stenotic, cyanotic, kenotic, hypnotic, albinotic, biocoenotic, melanotic, kyphotic, bathotic, quixotic, exotic, chlorotic, erotic, neurotic, cirrhotic, sclerotic, fibrotic, hidrotic, necrotic, dicrotic, tricrotic, amaurotic, auto-erotic, homoerotic, monocrotic, psychoneurotic, rhinocerotic, atherosclerotic, arteriosclerotic, Nilotic, ankylotic, polyglottic, epiglottic **.7** quartic, aortic, aeronautic **.8** erythrocytic **.9** toreutic, maieutic, scorbutic, pharmaceutic, propaedeutic, halieutic, therapeutic, trigoneutic, hermeneutic, antiscorbutic, radiotherapeutic, psychotherapeutic, aromatherapeutic, electrotherapeutic **.10** lunatic, heretic, politic, impolitic, unpolitic **.11** ptotic, photic, rhotic, lotic **.12** styptic, diptych, triptych, tryptic,

cryptic, glyptic, polyptych, elliptic, ecliptic, lithotriptic, apocalyptic, peptic, sceptic, skeptic, septic, eupeptic, dyspeptic, aseptic, sylleptic, proleptic, cataleptic, antiseptic, epileptic, narcoleptic, analeptic, nympholeptic, acataleptic, organoleptic, haptic, synaptic, optic, Coptic, sarcoptic, panoptic, synoptic, orthoptic, stereoptic, eclamptic, pre-eclamptic **.13** anaptyctic, apodictic, apomictic, amphimictic, pectic, smectic, hectic, eutectic, cachectic, cathectic, orectic, dialectic, catalectic, eclectic, dyslectic, demodectic, anorectic, apoplectic, cataplectic, acatalectic, hypercatalectic, tactic, lactic, syntactic, didactic, climactic, stalactic, galactic, stereotactic, hypotactic, thermotactic, paratactic, phyllotactic, ataractic, chiropractic, prophylactic, parallactic, autodidactic, anticlimactic, intergalactic, extragalactic, anaphylactic, arctic, Nearctic, subarctic, Antarctic, Holarctic, Palaearctic, subantarctic, deictic, epideictic, apodeictic, elenctic **.14** antic, mantic, frantic, quantic, identic, authentic, crescentic, Vedantic, pedantic, bacchantic, gigantic, geomantic, semantic, romantic, Atlantic, deontic, anthelmintic, inauthentic, unauthentic, corybantic, necromantic, unromantic, sycophantic, hierophantic, cisatlantic, transatlantic, mastodontic, orthodontic, anacreontic **.15.1** nonstick, unstick, anapaestic, distich, mystic, fistic, cystic, deistic, theistic, Taoistic, truistic, fideistic, atheistic, pantheistic, archaistic, Hebraistic, Dadaistic, casuistic, altruistic, euphuistic, egoistic, jingoistic, polytheistic, monotheistic **.15.2** papistic, artistic, autistic, pietistic, quietistic, statistic, scientistic, inartistic, unartistic, nepotistic, egotistic, chrematistic, pragmatistic, syncretistic, Buddhistic, sadistic, Methodistic, syllogistic, propagandistic, anarchistic, masochistic, sadomasochistic, Thomistic, mediumistic, atomistic, totemistic, optimistic, animistic, euphemistic, pessimistic, pianistic, monistic, faunistic, unionistic, hedonistic, modernistic, mechanistic, tokenistic, agonistic, jargonistic, shamanistic, harmonistic, humanistic, onanistic, chauvinistic, Calvinistic, diachronistic, synchronistic, communistic, Hellenistic, opportunistic, antagonistic, eudaemonistic, deterministic, impressionistic, expressionistic, reductionistic, expansionistic, illusionistic, misogynistic, anachronistic, indeterministic, exhibitionistic, evolutionistic, sophistic, atavistic, negativistic, positivistic, relativistic, objectivistic, collectivistic, recidivistic, narcissistic, solecistic, publicistic, solipsistic, Spinozistic, fascistic, fetishistic, logistic, phlogistic, imagistic, synergistic, eulogistic, dyslogistic, antiphlogistic, linguistic, ventriloquistic, sociolinguistic, metalinguistic, paralinguistic, extralinguistic, psycholinguistic, neurolinguistic, eristic, veristic, aoristic, floristic, touristic, puristic, voyeuristic, diaristic, heuristic, juristic, hubristic, patristic, plagiaristic, aprioristic, eucharistic, humoristic, manneristic, aphoristic, futuristic, terroristic, folkloristic, belletristic, militaristic, characteristic, hypocoristic, behaviouristic, uncharacteristic **.15.3** realistic, holistic, stylistic, nihilistic, royalistic, sciolistic, dualistic, ballistic, idealistic, surrealistic, unrealistic, ritualistic, mutualistic, gradualistic, ritualistically, cabbalistic, tribalistic, verbalistic, symbolistic, fatalistic, vitalistic, mentalistic, pointillistic, feudalistic, vandalistic, legalistic, formalistic, annalistic, finalistic, journalistic, sensationalistic, nationalistic, rationalistic, novelistic, specialistic, socialistic, pugilistic, moralistic, pluralistic, liberalistic, literalistic, naturalistic, populistic, oculistic, formulistic, imperialistic, materialistic, monopolistic, probabilistic, cannibalistic, capitalistic, physicalistic, anomalistic, animalistic, communalistic, criminalistic, nominalistic, paternalistic, maternalistic, traditionalistic, revivalistic, evangelistic, spiritualistic, somnambulistic, individualistic, oligopolistic, phenomenalistic, universalistic, simplistic **.15.4** gearstick, orchestic, domestic, Avestic, majestic, catachrestic, spastic, mastic, nastic, drastic, plastic, clastic, chiastic, orgiastic, chiliastic, scholiastic, encomiastic, ecclesiastic, enthusiastic, unenthusiastic, overenthusiastic, bombastic, fantastic, sarcastic, stochastic, orgastic, onomastic, pleonastic, dynastic, monastic, gymnastic, hyponastic, prednastic, doxastic, paederastic, Hudibrastic, metaphrastic, periphrastic, paraphrastic, elastic, scholastic, aplastic, neoplastic, dysplastic, inelastic, metaplastic, protoplastic, homoplastic, rhinoplastic, poroplastic, heteroplastic, thermoplastic, ceroplastic, ectoblastic, plagioclastic, cataclastic, pyroclastic, achondroplastic, iconoclastic, Bostik®, caustic, gnostic, agnostic, prognostic, diagnostic, acrostic, Austick, encaustic, apolaustic, joystick, fustic, rustic, acoustic, hemistich, tetrastich, Evo-stik®, dipstick, lipstick, slapstick, chopstick, knobstick, nightstick, paintstick, yardstick, swordstick, flagstick, drumstick, broomstick, greenstick, panstick, tungstic, fishstick, matchstick, mahlstick, fiddlestick, candlestick, singlestick **.16** Celtic, Baltic, cultic, systaltic, asphaltic, cobaltic, basaltic, peristaltic

24.2.11
.1 medick, Vedic, comedic, logopaedic, orthopaedic, cyclopedic, encyclopedic **.2** Druidic, fluidic, Glenfiddich, hasidic, acidic, nuclidic, pyramidic, glycosidic, glucosidic, aldehydic **.3** vanadic **.4** Eddic, medic, Samoyedic, paramedic **.5** Chadic, dyadic, triadic, decadic, saccadic, Haggadic, nomadic, maenadic, monadic, tornadic, sporadic, faradic, Helladic, Cycladic, ischiadic **.6** bardic, Lombardic, Sephardic, Langobardic **.7** Roddick, geodic, iodic,

spasmodic, psalmodic, anodic, monodic, synodic, threnodic, cathodic, methodic, prosodic, rhapsodic, parodic, melodic, periodic, eisteddfodic, episodic, aperiodic, antispasmodic, photoperiodic **.8** Nordic **.9** hyperthyroidic, hypothyroidic **.10** Talmudic **.11** pudic, ludic **.12** Benedick **.13** sodic **.14** molybdic **.15** dik-dik **.16** Indic, syndic, Wendic, Icelandic, Amerindic **.17** asdic, Fosdick **.18** skaldic, heraldic

24.2.12
Bacchic, psychic, Turkic, dropkick, sidekick, miskick, stomachic, tribrachic, diarchic, autarchic, autarkic, heptarchic, anarchic, monarchic, hierarchic, Halachic, amphibrachic, oligarchic, synecdochic

24.2.13
yogic, Pelasgic, pedagogic, demagogic

24.2.14
.1 pyaemic, systemic, leukaemic, ischaemic, anaemic, tonemic, phonemic, chronemic, graphemic, morphemic, racemic, lexemic, toxaemic, proxemic, uraemic, epistemic, diaphonemic, polysemic, septicaemic, hyperaemic, tularaemic, morphophonemic, hyperglycaemic, hypoglycaemic, hyperlipidaemic **.2** gimmick, mimic, bulimic, pantomimic, toponymic, metonymic, homonymic, synonymic, metronymic, patronymic **.3** totemic, endemic, pandemic, alchemic, polemic, epidemic, academic, unacademic **.4** potamic, glutamic, agamic, dynamic, balsamic, dioramic, ceramic, thalamic, Islamic, polygamic, cryptogamic, cleistogamic, phanerogamic, undynamic, panoramic, bioceramic, cycloramic, photodynamic, psychodynamic, haemodynamic, thermodynamic, isodynamic, aerodynamic, hydrodynamic, epithalamic, electrodynamic, magnetohydrodynamic **.5** karmic, psalmic, alexipharmic **.6** comic, atomic, preatomic, diatomic, triatomic, entomic, polyatomic, subatomic, trichotomic, dichotomic, anatomic, monatomic, tetratomic, interatomic, heroi-comic, tragicomic, serio-comic, anomic, bionomic, physiognomic, autonomic, economic, ergonomic, taxonomic, metronomic, Deuteronomic, astronomic, gastronomic, agronomic, socio-economic, macroeconomic, microeconomic, uneconomic, prodromic, syndromic, loxodromic, palindromic **.7** formic, McCormick **.8** enzymic, schizothymic, cyclothymic **.9** humic **.10** hypothalamic **.11** dermic, thermic, endermic, diathermic, epidermic, hypodermic, endodermic, taxidermic, homeothermic, homoiothermic, hyperthermic, endothermic, exothermic, poikilothermic **.12** ohmic, gnomic, bromic, chromic, polychromic, photochromic, monochromic **.13** cadmic **.14** syntagmic, nystagmic, borborygmic **.15** rhythmic, biorhythmic, eurhythmic, logarithmic, algorithmic **.16** anosmic **.17** chasmic, plasmic,

osmic, cosmic, seismic, strabismic, miasmic, phantasmic, orgasmic, marasmic, embolismic, cataclysmic, cytoplasmic, protoplasmic, ectoplasmic, macrocosmic, microcosmic, isoseismic **.18** filmic, Kalmyk, ophthalmic, exophthalmic

24.2.15
.1 scenic, splenic, proteinic, naphthenic, hygienic, irenic, selenic, phagedaenic, unhygienic, photogenic, philhellenic **.2** Finnic, cynic, clinic, rabbinic, platinic, actinic, phosphinic, succinic, alginic, kaolinic, pollinic, triclinic, aclinic, Jacobinic, nicotinic, histaminic, polyclinic, monoclinic, isoclinic **.3** morainic **.4** fennec, Fenwick, sthenic, genic, Renwick, phrenic, neotenic, asthenic, myasthenic, pantothenic, neurasthenic, callisthenic, arsenic, Saracenic, eugenic, biogenic, myogenic, cryogenic, dysgenic, transgenic, antigenic, polygenic, mediagenic, cariogenic, radiogenic, autogenic, cytogenic, mutagenic, ectogenic, ontogenic, histogenic, gestagenic, psychogenic, glycogenic, oncogenic, cyanogenic, carcinogenic, morphogenic, pathogenic, toxigenic, orogenic, pyrogenic, neurogenic, saprogenic, iatrogenic, oestrogenic, androgenic, necrogenic, saccharogenic, telegenic, allergenic, halogenic, phylogenic, abiogenic, anthropogenic, somatogenic, teratogenic, erotogenic, adaptogenic, leukaemogenic, hallucinogenic, epeirogenic, hypo-allergenic, immunogenic, schizophrenic, Hellenic, galenic, panhellenic, ethylenic **.5** Alnwick, panic, tannic, stannic, Stanwick, manic, cyanic, messianic, Ossianic, oceanic, transoceanic, interoceanic, tympanic, Hispanic, tetanic, titanic, botanic, satanic, Britannic, puritanic, mechanic, volcanic, vulcanic, organic, manganic, inorganic, shamanic, Brahmanic, Germanic, Romanic, hypomanic, aldermanic, talismanic, Indo-Germanic, Rhaeto-Romanic, epiphanic, galvanic, Quranic, Puranic, Koranic, uranic, transuranic **.6.1** tonic, conic, phonic, chthonic, sonic, chronic, clonic, paeonic, ionic, pionic, bionic, psionic, muonic, thermionic, avionic, baryonic, chorionic, embryonic, pre-embryonic, histrionic, nucleonic, ganglionic, Pharaonic, cationic, anionic, amphictyonic, chameleonic, Napoleonic, hydroponic, carbonic, bubonic, ketonic, pretonic, atonic, Metonic, Teutonic, Plutonic, diatonic, myotonic, Platonic, protonic, leptonic, subtonic, tectonic, planktonic, Miltonic, hypertonic, supertonic, catatonic, pentatonic, monotonic, isotonic, viscerotonic, Neoplatonic, somatotonic, architectonic, hedonic, sardonic, chalcedonic, iconic, Tychonic, laconic, obconic, cinchonic, aniconic, agonic, cosmogonic, isogonic, telegonic **.6.2** demonic, mnemonic, harmonic, daimonic, pneumonic, daemonic, gnomonic, pulmonic, eudaemonic, antimonic, inharmonic, enharmonic, anharmonic, philharmonic, hegemonic, Solomonic,

pathognomonic, canonic **.6.3** aphonic, typhonic, siphonic, euphonic, diaphonic, symphonic, sulphonic, polyphonic, radiophonic, stereophonic, gramophonic, homophonic, monophonic, saxophonic, quadraphonic, quadrophonic, microphonic, telephonic, allophonic, xylophonic, dodecaphonic, electrophonic, radio-telephonic, Slavonic, pythonic, Brythonic, autochthonic, Masonic, opsonic, subsonic, transonic, trans-sonic, hypersonic, supersonic, Panasonic, ultrasonic, infrasonic, mesonic, ozonic **.6.4** ironic, Byronic, neuronic, Pyrrhonic, moronic, Saronic, hadronic, diachronic, synchronic, hyperonic, macaronic, positronic, electronic, anachronic, animatronic, microelectronic, colonic, cyclonic, anticyclonic **.7** tunic, runic, Punic, Munich **.8** Metternich, Dominic **.9** saturnic **.10** beatnik, Chetnik, sputnik **.11** nudnik **.12** picnic, pycnic, pyknic, strychnic, technic, splanchnic, pyrotechnic, polytechnic, electrotechnic **.13** algolagnic **.14** hymnic **.15** Dubrovnik **.16** ethnic, multi-ethnic **.17** peacenik, kibbutznik **.18** Iznik, Selznick, refusenik

24.2.16
.1 glyphic, morbific, beatific, pontific, scientific, omnific, ossific, pacific, specific, calcific, terrific, horrific, prolific, triglyphic, unscientific, subspecific, transpacific, conspecific, unspecific, felicific, vaporific, soporific, torporific, sudorific, honorific, calorific, colorific, anaglyphic, hieroglyphic, pseudo-scientific, Indo-Pacific, stereospecific, interspecific, dermatoglyphic **.2** Efik, benefic, malefic **.3** maffick, Sapphic, traffic, graphic, edaphic, seraphic, geographic, digraphic, biographic, sciagraphic, dysgraphic, ideographic, radiographic, hagiographic, physiographic, zoogeographic, biogeographic, choreographic, palaeographic, bibliographic, epigraphic, topographic, typographic, dittographic, stratigraphic, autographic, photographic, cryptographic, pictographic, pantographic, tachygraphic, cacographic, demographic, tomographic, nomographic, homographic, kymographic, thermographic, sphygmographic, cosmographic, seismographic, stenographic, planographic, monographic, chronographic, pornographic, phonographic, ethnographic, oceanographic, lithographic, orthographic, hypsographic, flexographic, xerographic, paragraphic, barographic, orographic, chorographic, spirographic, chirographic, reprographic, petrographic, spectrographic, hydrographic, telegraphic, allographic, calligraphic, holographic, stylographic, historiographic, autobiographic, pseudepigraphic, prosopographic, chromatographic, lexicographic, anemographic, iconographic, uranographic, selenographic, polarographic, oscillographic, metallographic, crystallographic, autoradiographic, cinematographic, telephotographic,

chromolithographic, photolithographic, electrocardiographic, cartographic **.4** trophic, strophic, theosophic, atrophic, eutrophic, dystrophic, geostrophic, philosophic, hypertrophic, autotrophic, heterotrophic, antistrophic, apostrophic, catastrophic, monostrophic, unphilosophic, gonadotrophic, corticotrophic, oligotrophic, adreno-corticotrophic **.5** Orphic, pleomorphic, dimorphic, trimorphic, zoomorphic, biomorphic, skeuomorphic, polymorphic, theriomorphic, metamorphic, ectomorphic, pantomorphic, pseudomorphic, endomorphic, zygomorphic, homomorphic, anamorphic, monomorphic, mesomorphic, isomorphic, heteromorphic, allomorphic, enantiomorphic, anthropomorphic, actinomorphic, anisomorphic, gynandromorphic, allelomorphic **.6** Kufic, Sufic, Cufic **.7** Elphick, Delphic, Guelphic

24.2.17
civic, Narvik, Slavic, Norvic, Jorvik, Britvic®, pelvic, Ludovic, Menshevik, Bolshevik, Reykjavik, Keflavik

24.2.18
.1 mythic, lithic, ornithic, Trevithick, trilithic, Eolithic, neolithic, heliolithic, Palaeolithic, otolithic, Chalcolithic, megalithic, granolithic, monolithic, Mesolithic, microlithic **.2** ethic, Trevethick **.3** pathic, spathic, gnathic, empathic, feldspathic, prognathic, osteopathic, idiopathic, homeopathic, sociopathic, antipathic, trichopathic, psychopathic, amphipathic, neuropathic, heteropathic, hydropathic, naturopathic, telepathic, allopathic, polymathic **.4** Gothic, Sothic, hypothec, Visigothic, Ostrogothic **.5** anacoluthic **.6** benthic, xanthic, helminthic, anthelminthic, epicanthic

24.2.19
Smethwick

24.2.20
.1 seasick, geodesic, amnesic, electrophoresic **.2** silicic **.3** basic, dibasic, tribasic, diastasic, polybasic, monobasic **.4** airsick **.5** classic, Triassic, liassic, potassic, thoracic, boracic, Jurassic, anthracic, thalassic, neoclassic, osteomalacic **.6** carsick **.7** fossick, diglossic, virtuosic, cellulosic **.8** banausic **.9** prusik, prussic **.10** phthisic, gneissic **.11** Tungusic **.12** heartsick **.13** toxic, pyrexic, dyslexic, ataxic, hypoxic, anoxic, anorexic, stereotaxic, thermotaxic, ataraxic, antitoxic, phytotoxic, cytotoxic, autotoxic, bulimarexic, hepatotoxic **.14** homesick **.15** greensick, brainsick, trainsick, Phensic, turnsick, intrinsic, extrinsic, forensic **.16** lovesick **.17** alsike

24.2.21
mesic, physic, Chiswick, phasic, Beswick, Keswick, music, Phensic, geodesic, amnesic, analgesic, biophysic, aphasic, dysphasic, dyscrasic, banausic, Tungusic, Zaqaziq, intrinsic,

extrinsic, forensic, metaphysic, polyphasic, Ashkenazic, achondroplasic

24.2.22
moujik, muzhik

24.2.23
peachick, dabchick, squab-chick, apparatchik

24.2.24
.1 strategic, hemiplegic, paraplegic, tetraplegic, quadriplegic **.2** magic, tragic, pelagic, haemorrhagic, bathypelagic **.3** Tajik, lethargic **.4** logic, geologic, dialogic, mystagogic, pedagogic, demagogic, anagogic, isagogic, paragogic, aetiologic, radiologic, archaeologic, embryologic, teleologic, tautologic, pantologic, analogic, monologic, chronologic, ethnologic, mythologic, pathologic, horologic, urologic, petrologic, metrologic, astrologic, hydrologic, philologic, haematologic, climatologic, gynaecologic, etymologic, immunologic **.5** georgic **.6** theurgic, liturgic, chemurgic, synergic, lysergic, allergic, demiurgic, dramaturgic, thaumaturgic, cholinergic, metallurgic **.7** laryngic **.8** Pelasgic **.9** Belgic, myalgic, nostalgic, neuralgic

24.2.25
Warwick, Lerwick, Gatwick, Prestwick, Chadwick, Hardwick, Herdwick, Pickwick, Fenwick, Renwick, Stanwick, Borthwick, Brunswick, Giggleswick, Fishwick, Sidgewick, Sedgewick, candlewick, Shufflewick, bailiwick, Dinorwic, Pennycuick

24.2.26
.1 Pyrrhic, lyric, empiric, vampiric, butyric, satiric, satyric, panegyric **.2** steric, spheric, xeric, Balearic, valeric **.3** hayrick **.4** Eric, Berwick, Derek, derrick, Deryck, skerrick, Merrick, Meyrick, ferric, Seric, Herrick, cleric, suberic, neoteric, icteric, sphincteric, enteric, dysenteric, mesenteric, hysteric, amphoteric, esoteric, exoteric, ureteric, climacteric, gastroenteric, dimeric, chimeric, trimeric, numeric, Homeric, mesmeric, epimeric, polymeric, metameric, tautomeric, monomeric, isomeric, enantiomeric, alphanumeric, elastomeric, generic, subgeneric, congeneric, tropospheric, stratospheric, photospheric, hemispheric, chromospheric, atmospheric, planispheric, ionospheric, lithospheric, etheric, diphtheric, choleric **.5** baric, Tariq, daric, carrick, Garrick, stearic, barbaric, tartaric, Pindaric, fumaric, Dinaric, samsaric, Amharic, hyperbaric, isobaric, laevotartaric **.6** Doric, Warwick, Yorick, historic, euphoric, theophoric, camphoric, dysphoric, phosphoric, plethoric, caloric, pyloric, meteoric, madreporic, aleatoric, unhistoric, prehistoric, ahistoric, categoric, paregoric, allegoric, sophomoric, metaphoric, semaphoric, anaphoric, exophoric, pyrophoric, phantasmagoric, spermatophoric **.7** boric, toric, chloric, auric, zoosporic, folkloric **.8** Zürich, Rurik, uric, purpuric, mercuric, sulfuric,

sulphuric, telluric **.9** oneiric **.10** rhetoric, Catterick, deuteric, Frederick, Roderick, Broderick, agaric, limerick, turmeric, maverick, Laverick, Petherick, Masaryk, Alaric, glycosuric, barbituric, Theodoric, cadaveric **.11** myrrhic **.12** capric, cupric, pinprick, bishopric, archbishopric **.13** airbrick, fabric, Swarbrick, Kubrick, rubric, firebrick, redbrick, mudbrick, cambric, Scarisbrick **.14.1** matric, Dietrich, citric, McKittrick, allopatric, Ettrick **.14.2** metric, obstetric, geometric, trimetric, biometric, diametric, cliometric, symmetric, dosimetric, radiometric, eudiometric, stoichiometric, craniometric, goniometric, pluviometric, sociometric, hypermetric, photometric, optometric, psychometric, viscometric, tromometric, thermometric, seismometric, planimetric, manometric, chronometric, clinometric, gravimetric, asymmetric, isometric, hypsometric, hexametric, perimetric, parametric, barometric, pyrometric, spectrometric, hydrometric, hygrometric, calorimetric, volumetric, kilometric, telemetric, bolometric, coulometric, potentiometric, anthropometric, refractometric, anemometric, econometric, trigonometric, galvanometric, axonometric, colorimetric, polarimetric, electrometric, nephelometric, granulometric, spectrophotometric, sphygmomanometric, interferometric **.14.3** Patrick, theatric, Kirkpatrick, sympatric, Downpatrick, Fitzpatrick, Kilpatrick, paediatric, psychiatric, geriatric, nitric, undertrick, overtrick, dioptric, catoptric, catadioptric, electric, dielectric, photoelectric, thermoelectric, piezoelectric, ferroelectric, pyroelectric, hydroelectric, centric, tantric, con trick **.14.4** geocentric, dicentric, theocentric, eccentric, excentric, concentric, heliocentric, metacentric, endocentric, egocentric, homocentric, ethnocentric, exocentric, androcentric, phallocentric, Anglocentric, Eurocentric, Afrocentric, anthropocentric, selenocentric **.14.5** Raistrick, gastric, Rastrick, digastric, Scalextric, epigastric, hypogastric, pneumogastric **.15** Cedric, Friedrich, quadric, hydric, Kendrick, baldric, dihydric, trihydric, McKendrick, calendric, theandric, McGoldrick, polyhedric, monohydric **.16** Ugric, podagric, Finno-Ugric **.17** Cymric **.18** Kenrick **.19** Leofric, afric, Aelfric **.20** chivalric

24.2.27
.1 velic, parhelic, allelic **.2** Tillich, killick, dactylic, idyllic, lyophilic, methylic, exilic, Cyrillic, acrylic, cacodylic, bibliophilic, haemophilic, thermophilic, basophilic, hydrophilic, necrophilic, imbecilic, salicylic, carboxylic, acidophilic, electrophilic, acetylsalicylic **.3** Gaelic, malic, Salic **.4** melic, melick, Sellick, relic, Gadhelic, Goidelic, angelic, autotelic, philatelic, psychedelic, archangelic, evangelic **.5** Ehrlich **.6** Alec, Alick, Gallic, phallic, thallic, italic, metallic, tantalic, bimetallic,

organometallic, medallic, Vandalic, vocalic, prevocalic, postvocalic, acromegalic, cephalic, encephalic, ithyphallic, brachycephalic, plagiocephalic, megacephalic, macrocephalic, microcephalic, leptocephalic, orthocephalic, mesocephalic, hydrocephalic, anencephalic, dolichocephalic, intervallic, naphthalic, oxalic, Uralic **.7** cowlick **.8** garlic, pashalic **.9** cholic, colic, folic, Follick, rollick, frolic, Aeolic, carbolic, diabolic, symbolic, embolic, shambolic, diastolic, systolic, glycolic, glycollic, bucolic, phenolic, petrolic, hydraulic, vitriolic, hyperbolic, metabolic, catabolic, anabolic, parabolic, apostolic, melancholic, hypergolic, shopaholic, chocaholic, chocoholic, workaholic, alcoholic, fumarolic, unapostolic, nonalcoholic **.10** aulic **.11** hylic **.12** abulic **.13** nickelic, catholic, anticatholic, Roman Catholic **.14** niblick, public, republic **.15** catlick, saltlick, gemütlich **.16** cyclic, tricyclic, encyclic, acyclic, clickety-click, polycyclic, epicyclic, isocyclic, tetracyclic, heterocyclic, alicyclic **.17** tiglic **.18** skinflick **.19** souslik **.20** shashlik

24.3
ache, spake, bake, take, stake, steak, cake, make, snake, fake, sake, shake, sheikh, jake, haick, haik, hake, wake, quaich, quake, rake, brake, break, strake, drake, crake, vraic, lake, splake, Blake, flake, slake, hot cake, Lyke Wake

24.3.1
bellyache

24.3.2
opaque, radiopaque, radio-opaque

24.3.3
hardbake, clambake

24.3.4
retake, caretake, partake, heartache, betake, uptake, out-take, stocktake, intake, wapentake, mistake, sweepstake, Copestake, grubstake, beefsteak, undertake, overtake

24.3.5
headache

24.3.6
teacake, backache, cupcake, shortcake, fruitcake, oatcake, seedcake, rock-cake, pancake, beefcake, cheesecake, fishcake, oilcake, griddlecake, johnnycake, coffee cake, tipsy-cake, pat-a-cake, stomachache

24.3.7
remake, unmake

24.3.8
rattlesnake

24.3.9
toothache

24.3.10
forsake, keepsake, namesake

24.3.11
handshake

24.3.12
awake, seaquake, moonquake, earthquake, kittiwake, wideawake

24.3.13
earache, daybreak, air brake, tiebreak, firebreak, outbreak, heartbreak, footbrake, windbreak, handbrake, canebrake, canebreak, jailbreak, mandrake, sheldrake, muckrake, corncrake, bugrake, make-or-break

24.3.14
Hoylake, Mortlake, Widlake, snowflake, cornflake, Timberlake

24.4
pec, peck, spec, speck, beck, tec, tech, Teck, DEC, deck, keck, neck, sneck, sec, Zech., zek, check, cheque, Czech, heck, rec, reck, wreck, trek, dreck, yecch, yech, Lec®, lek, fleck, well deck, Hon. Sec.

24.4.1
Hayek

24.4.2
OAPEC, OPEC, kopek, henpeck

24.4.3
xebec, rebec, rebeck, Warbeck, Brubeck, Lübeck, Québec, Purbeck, Birkbeck, crombec, Steinbeck, Uzbek, pinchbeck, Baalbek, Beiderbecke

24.4.4
hitech, MTech, Mixtec, Aztec, Toltec, Zapotec, discotheque, infotech, cinematheque

24.4.5
foredeck, bedeck, sundeck, helideck, quarterdeck, afterdeck, Melchizedek

24.4.6
Olmec, Chichimec

24.4.7
V-neck, rooinek, wryneck, redneck, neck-and-neck, breakneck, roughneck, swan-neck, bottleneck, turtleneck, rubberneck, halterneck, leatherneck

24.4.8
parsec, cusec, cosec

24.4.9
exec

24.4.10
Hasek, Chiang Kai-shek

24.4.11
recheck, paycheque, háček, Dubček, spot-check, soundcheck, crosscheck, vapour-check, countercheck, Janáček, overcheck, Eurocheque

24.4.12
varec, shipwreck, tenrec, tanrec, Toulouse-Lautrec

24.4.13
Hayek

24.4.14
Palekh, Dalek, fartlek, Auchinleck

24.5
de Klerk

24.6
ack, pack, back, tach, tack, stack, mac, mach, mack, smack, knack, snack, vac, sac, sack, Zack, shack, Jacques, jack, hack, WAC, wack, whack, KWAC, quack, thwack, rack, WRAC, wrack, brack, Braque, track, drack, crack, yack, yak, lac, lack, lakh, plaque, black, clack, claque, flack, flak, slack, Kai Tak, sits vac, Union Jack

24.6.1
Pontiac, cardiac, Kodiak, zodiac, pericardiac, oomiak, umiak, maniac, Cluniac, ammoniac, demoniac, simoniac, insomniac, bibliomaniac, hypomaniac, kleptomaniac, egomaniac, monomaniac, nymphomaniac, mythomaniac, dipsomaniac, pyromaniac, Gallomaniac, megalomaniac, Graecomaniac, Anglomaniac, sal ammoniac, erotomaniac, Dionysiac, amnesiac, symposiac, aphrodisiac, anaphrodisiac, Syriac, theriac, Mauriac, celeriac, hypochondriac, coeliac, ileac, iliac, sacroiliac, paedophiliac, haemophiliac, hemophiliac, coprophiliac, necrophiliac

24.6.2
paranoiac

24.6.3
Dayak, kayak, guaiac, chiack, chyack

24.6.4
bivouac, Kerouac

24.6.5
repack, prepack, powerpack, Lurpak®, mudpack, backpack, shrinkpack, Compaq, unpack, woolpack

24.6.6
aback, Nagorno-Karabakh **.1** zwieback
.2 piggyback **.3** payback, wayback, playback
.4 bareback **.5** sowback **.6** Orbach, drawback, clawback **.7** tieback, dieback, flyback
.8 skewback **.9** fireback, paperback, quarterback, pickaback, huckaback, cornerback, leatherback, razorback, yellowback **.10** throwback, blowback **.11** sweepback, humpback **.12** setback, wetback, fatback, outback, slotback, cutback, fightback, right-back, softback, fastback
.13 feedback, redback, hardback, foldback, holdback, biofeedback, diamondback
.14 kickback, talkback, crookback **.15** hogback
.16 tombac, tombak, comeback
.17 greenback, thornback, runback, turnback, Blumenbach **.18** wingback, slingback
.19 halfback **.20** leaseback, mossback, horseback **.21** splashback, flashback, hunchback **.22** switchback, hatchback, touchback **.23** tailback, whaleback, shellback, callback, fallback, pullback, fullback, rollback, saddleback, stickleback, huckle-back, camelback

24.6.7
Atack, Blu-tack®, attack, hardtack, tic-tac, thumbtack, tintack, Contac, untack, haystack, smokestack, hackmatack, nunatak, counterattack, chimney stack, Enewetak

24.6.8
Ladakh, Kodak®, NASDAQ, Adirondack

24.6.9
ack-ack, macaque, ipecac

24.6.10
Tarmac®, Cormac, sumac, gobsmack, yashmak, Dannimac, Merrimac, Merrimack, McCormack, tokamak, Potomac

24.6.11
Carnac, Karnak, Nanak, knick-knack, nicknack, Pasternak, almanac, Savernake, Sassenach, Pontianak

24.6.12
Novak, Slovak, Univac, Medevac, Czechoslovak

24.6.13
Mawddach

24.6.14
daysack, Barsac, Cossack, corsac, Husák, Cusack, knapsack, hopsack, rucksack, ransack, woolsack, coalsack, gunnysack, Gay-Lussac, cul-de-sac, haversack

24.6.15
Tyzack, Kazakh, Cusack, Muzak®, Prozac®, Anzac, Balzac

24.6.16
Meshach, Toshack

24.6.17
Dvořák

24.6.18
skyjack, hijack, Kojak, cheapjack, skipjack, flapjack, slapjack, bootjack, muntjac, blackjack, steeplejack, applejack, supplejack, amberjack, lumberjack, natterjack, crackerjack

24.6.19
tacamahac

24.6.20
bushwhack, paddywack, Sarawak, Arawak

24.6.21
Iraq, hayrack, Perak, serac, borak, Dirac, tribrach, shabrack, barmbrack, sidetrack, soundtrack, backtrack, amtrac, Amtrak®, halftrack, racetrack, toast rack, Shadrach, rickrack, ricrac, gimcrack, wisecrack, Mubarak, bladderwrack, sandarac, Bacharach, Skagerrak, tamarack, anorak, Coverack, Bergerac, bric-a-brac, amphibrach, Cyrano de Bergerac

24.6.22
cognac, timberjack, Armagnac, yackety-yack

24.6.23
shellac, kulak, alack, Polack, Brolac, eyeblack,

shoeblack, lampblack, bootblack, pitchblack, click-clack, Senlac, Cadillac®

24.7
gowk, padouk

24.8
arc, ark, park, Parke, spark, Sparke, Bach, bark, barque, stark, dark, mach, marc, mark, marque, narc, nark, snark, sark, shark, hark, quark, Braque, lark, plaque, Clarke, clerk, Vlach, Newark, red bark, Jeanne d'Arc, Joan of Arc, Cutty Sark

24.8.1
patriarch, matriarch, heresiarch, symposiarch

24.8.2
eparch, car park, skatepark, impark, ballpark

24.8.3
debark, zwieback, soapbark, shagbark, embark, re-embark, disembark, tanbark, ironbark, Offenbach, ringbark, stringy-bark

24.8.4
Plutarch

24.8.5
Ladakh

24.8.6
macaque

24.8.7
oligarch

24.8.8
seamark, remark, earmark, waymark, Lamarck, Newmark, tyremark, Steiermark, Kitemark®, footmark, Ostmark, postmark, skidmark, Widmark, trademark, tidemark, landmark, Goldmark, check mark, pockmark, bookmark, Denmark, scuffmark, hoofmark, proofmark, birthmark, pressmark, sitzmark, Bismarck, benchmark, Deutschmark, hallmark, watermark, monomark, telemark

24.8.9
anarch, ethnarch

24.8.10
aardvark

24.8.11
futharc

24.8.12
Pesach, exarch

24.8.13
Ozark

24.8.14
loanshark

24.8.15
Iraq, hierarch, squirearch, Petrarch, tetrarch, Oistrakh

24.8.16
skylark, titlark, mudlark, woodlark, sales clerk, meadowlark

24.9
pock, Spock, bock, stock, doc, dock, Coch, cock, Koch, mock, smock, knock, nock, Nok, sock, shock, choc, chock, jock, hock, hough, wok, KWOC, roc, rock, broch, brock, croc, crock, frock, loch, lock, Locke, lough, bloc, Bloch, block, Blok, clock, floc, flock, schlock, langue d'oc, post hoc, ad hoc, en bloc, postman's knock, speaking clock

24.9.1
Antioch, manioc

24.9.2
epoch, kapok, yapok, belle époque

24.9.3
reebok, rhebok, bontbok, sjambok, Lombok, steenbok, steinbock, springbok, grysbok, blesbok, gemsbok, bontebok

24.9.4
Bartók, tick-tock, Quantock, destock, restock, Bostock, nostoc, Vostok, Rostock, whipstock, fatstock, rootstock, feedstock, deadstock, headstock, bloodstock, Woodstock, sandstock, Comstock, linstock, penstock, gunstock, vinestock, Weinstock, alpenstock, livestock, drillstock, tailstock, McClintock, Tavistock, overstock, laughing stock, Eniwetok, Vladivostok

24.9.5
Médoc, Zadok, burdock, Murdoch, postdoc, undock, boondock, Baldock, Caradoc, Languedoc, dramadoc, opodeldoc

24.9.6
peacock, seacock, Leacock, Hickok, haycock, Lacock, Laycock, gorcock, moorcock, Pocock, stopcock, Babcock, petcock, Adcock, woodcock, blackcock, gamecock, draincock, Hancock, turncock, Bangkok, spitchcock, Hitchcock, spatchcock, Wilcock, Alcock, ballcock, shuttlecock, poppycock, turkeycock, billycock, monocoque, weathercock

24.9.7
torgoch

24.9.8
amok

24.9.9
Enoch, Charnock, Dornoch, Warnock, Brecknock, anti-knock, Kilmarnock, monadnock

24.9.10
bedsock, windsock, Abersoch

24.9.11
shellshock, aftershock

24.9.12
bubbly-jock

24.9.13
forehock, Mohock, hollyhock

24.9.14
jabberwock

24.9.15
baroque, pibroch, Sheetrock®, bedrock, rimrock, shamrock, defrock, Prufrock, unfrock, disfrock, Ragnarök

24.9.16
Kinloch, unlock, interlock **.1** Belloc **.2** airlock, Gairloch, Gareloch **.3** charlock **.4** oarlock, Porlock, forelock, warlock **.5** Shylock **.6** firelock, fetterlock, hammerlock **.7** sherlock **.8** moloch, rowlock **.9** Diplock, zip-lock **.10** wrest-block, woodblock, roadblock, unblock, sunblock, breeze block, chock-a-block **.11** Whitlock, fetlock, Matlock, putlock, flintlock **.12** gridlock, deadlock, headlock, wedlock, padlock **.13** picklock, o'clock **.14** daglock **.15** hemlock, armlock **.16** genlock, gunlock **.17** elflock **.18** havelock, lovelock **.19** Fishlock **.20** matchlock

24.10
auk, orc, ork, pork, baulk, Bork, talk, torc, torque, stalk, stork, dork, calk, Calke, caulk, cork, gawk, nork, Falk, fork, chalk, hawk, Hawke, walk, squawk, Rorke, Rourke, york, Yorke

24.10.1
morepork

24.10.2
pep talk, shoptalk, sweet-talk, outtalk, back talk, smooth-talk, crosstalk, footstalk, beanstalk, cornstalk, smalltalk

24.10.3
Dundalk

24.10.4
uncork

24.10.5
mollymawk

24.10.6
hayfork, pitchfork

24.10.7
futhorc

24.10.8
mohawk, nighthawk, goshawk, ballhawk, winklehawk, tomahawk, sparrowhawk

24.10.9
jaywalk, skywalk, sheepwalk, sleepwalk, ropewalk, catwalk, outwalk, boardwalk, sidewalk, cakewalk, spacewalk, crosswalk

24.11
oick, oik, Hawick, hoick

24.12
puck, buck, tuck, stuck, duck, DUKW, muck, schmuck, snuck, fuck, suck, shuck, chuck, Huck, ruck, truck, Truk, struck, cruck, yuck, luck, pluck, cluck, Fluck

24.12.1
Tarbuck, sawbuck, roebuck, reedbuck, blackbuck, jumbuck, blesbuck, bushbuck, Clutterbuck, megabuck

24.12.2
untuck, unstuck

24.12.3
shelduck

24.12.4
Habakkuk

24.12.5
amok, Kalmuck, mallemuck,
high-muck-a-muck

24.12.6
Canuck

24.12.7
upchuck, woodchuck

24.12.8
awestruck, dumbstruck, sunstruck,
moonstruck, stagestruck, thunderstruck

24.12.9
mukluk

24.13
pike, spike, bike, tyke, dyke, kike, mike,
Smike, psych, haick, haik, hike, Wyke, Reich,
trike, strike, grike, shrike, like, Van Dyck, van
Eyck

24.13.1
garpike, turnpike, handspike, turnspike,
marlinspike

24.13.2
pushbike, minibike, motorbike

24.13.3
Updike, vandyke, Klondike, Thorndike,
Fosdyke

24.13.4
hitchhike

24.13.5
Heckmondwike

24.13.6
Österreich, Oberösterreich

24.13.7
alike, belike, unlike, dislike, mislike, unalike
.1 ladylike **.2** tearlike **.3** clay-like **.4** hairlike
.5 starlike **.6** sawlike, warlike, unwarlike
.7 toylike **.8** flowerlike, viper-like, lubberlike,
soundalike, lookalike, loverlike, fatherlike,
motherlike, umbrella-like **.9** snowlike
.10 sheeplike, liplike, ape-like, tapelike, steplike,
traplike, soaplike, wasplike **.11** scablike,
crablike, knoblike, tubelike, herblike, globelike
.12 catlike, snoutlike, nutlike, hutlike,
knightlike, rootlike, flutelike, saintlike, antlike,
plantlike, priestlike, yeastlike, mistlike,
nestlike, Christlike, ghostlike **.13** threadlike,
godlike, rodlike, cordlike, swordlike, lordlike,
hoodlike, toadlike, fiendlike, sandlike, childlike,
husbandlike **.14** sticklike, snakelike, sacklike,
rocklike, stalklike, corklike, hawklike, pucklike,
hooklike, trunklike, silklike **.15** piglike, doglike,
hoglike **.16** dreamlike, flamelike, stemlike,

gemlike, lamblike, womb-like, plumelike,
wormlike, domelike, homelike **.17** queenlike,
skinlike, veinlike, panlike, manlike, fanlike,
swanlike, hornlike, nunlike, sunlike, lion-like,
maidenlike, machinelike, seamanlike,
womanlike, workmanlike, statesmanlike,
sportsmanlike **.18** stinglike, kinglike, winglike,
springlike, stringlike **.19** leaflike, cliff-like,
waif-like, calf-like, rufflike, knifelike, wifelike,
lifelike, nymphlike, sylphlike, wolf-like
.20 sievelike, cave-like, wavelike, dovelike
.21 heathlike, wraithlike, deathlike,
toothlike **.22** grasslike, glasslike, mouselike,
mosslike, horselike, vicelike, wax-like, foxlike,
lynxlike, princelike, tortoise-like, businesslike
.23 roselike **.24** dishlike, fishlike, rushlike,
brush-like, branch-like **.25** witchlike, suchlike
.26 wedgelike, judgelike, spongelike
.27 scalelike, hell-like, wool-like, petal-like

24.14
book, took, stook, shtuck, doek, Coke®, cook,
Cooke, nook, schnook, shook, chook, hook,
Hooke, rook, Rooke, brook, Brooke, Bruch,
crook, Crooke, look, Gluck, Flook

24.14.1
Holyoake

24.14.2
Volapük

24.14.3
pre-book, overbook, copybook, storybook,
yearbook, daybook, playbook, prayerbook,
scorebook, boobook, picturebook, transfer-book,
chapbook, scrapbook, notebook, textbook,
pocketbook, studbook, guidebook, wordbook,
handbook, chequebook, cookbook, workbook,
bank book, logbook, hymnbook, gamebook,
psalmbook, formbook, hornbook, songbook,
casebook, passbook, sourcebook, phrasebook,
cash book, sketchbook, matchbook, stylebook,
schoolbook, rulebook

24.14.4
retook, partook, betook, mistook, undertook,
overtook

24.14.5
precook, Pennycuick, pastrycook, undercook,
overcook

24.14.6
Inuk, Sihanouk, Chinook, inglenook, gerenuk

24.14.7
forsook, nainsook

24.14.8
caoutchouc

24.14.9
skyhook, pothook, Windhoek, unhook,
buttonhook, fishhook, billhook, tenterhook

24.14.10
Uruk, Tobruk, Sherbrooke, Stradbroke,
Ladbroke, Cranbrook, Colnbrook, Innsbruck,

Washbrook, Rael-Brook, Walbrook, Colebrook, Holbrook, donnybrook, Osnabrück, Beaverbrook, Hinchingbrooke, Bolingbroke, Carisbrooke

24.14.11
Shilluk, wetlook, outlook, Amlwch, overlook

24.15
Pook, spook, stook, kook, gook, snoek, snook, souk, zouk, tuque, duke, spruik, puke, cuce, nuke, Luke, Flook, fluke

24.15.1
Volapük

24.15.2
dybbuk, chibouk

24.15.3
gobbledegook

24.15.4
Chinook

24.15.5
bashi-bazouk

24.15.6
Seljuk

24.15.7
peruke, Farouk

24.15.8
Dubuque, rebuke, archduke, Heptateuch, Octateuch, Pentateuch, Hexateuch, Marmaduke, Pennycuick, Mameluke

24.15.9
sail-fluke

24.16

24.16.1
guaiac, elegiac

24.16.2
Newark

24.16.3
dybbuk, Lubbock

24.16.4
mattock, buttock, futtock, Quantock

24.16.5
piddock, Clydach, paddock, Maddock, shaddock, haddock, Craddock, Marduk, puddock, ruddock, Portmadoc, Caradoc

24.16.6
Dimmock, Dymock, hammock, Cormac, stomach, hummock, slummock

24.16.7
Greenock, Kinnock, bannock, Cannock, Zanuck, Rannoch, Lanark, Charnock, monarch, Dornoch, dunnock, eunuch, Cumnock, Kilmarnock, draconic, coronach, Rappahannock

24.16.8
Norfolk, Suffolk

24.16.9
havoc

24.16.10
Southwark, Rhydderch

24.16.11
cassock, hassock, tussock

24.16.12
wazzock, Isaac

24.16.13
Taoiseach

24.16.14
bulwark, timberwork

24.16.15
arrack, barrack, Baruch, carrack, Thurrock, Pembroke, laverock

24.16.16
pillock, hillock, charlock, Harlech, pollack, pollock, ballock, Walach, rowlock, Tulloch, mullock, lilac, bullock, cromlech, havelock, Bonallack, McCullough

24.17
erk, irk, perk, berk, Bourke, Buerk, burk, Burke, Turk, stirk, dirk, kirk, Merck, murk, smirk, cirque, shirk, Chirk, jerk, work, quirk, Quirke, lurk

24.17.1
hauberk

24.17.2
Atatürk

24.17.3
Diekirch, steenkirk, Dunkirk, Ormskirk, Selkirk, Falkirk

24.17.4
McGurk

24.17.5
berserk

24.17.6
rework, outwork, interwork, overwork
.1 bodywork, handiwork, donkey work, fancy-work, busywork, telework **.2** daywork
.3 pairwork **.4** firework, paperwork, masterwork, plasterwork, underwork, wickerwork, pokerwork, camerawork
.5 stuccowork **.6** pipework **.7** cribwork, jobwork
.8 network, fretwork, artwork, part-work, knotwork, brightwork, footwork, paintwork, craftwork, breastwork, frost-work, basketwork
.9 beadwork, spadework, headwork, woodwork, roadwork, handwork, groundwork, fieldwork
.10 brickwork, hackwork, clockwork, bookwork, deskwork **.11** legwork **.12** teamwork, framework, farmwork, formwork, timework, homework
.13 chainwork, brainwork, ironwork, stonework, openwork **.14** earthwork **.15** piecework, casework, lacework, guesswork, glasswork, housework, coursework, waxwork, falsework, trellis-work **.16** brushwork **.17** stitchwork,

patchwork, coachwork **.18** bridgework
.19 steelwork, grillwork, bulwark, schoolwork, crewelwork, scrollwork, rubblework, metalwork, needlework, enamelwork

24.17.7
Ragnarök

24.18
oak, poke, Polk, spoke, toke, toque, stoke, Coke®, coke, Koch, moke, smoke, folk, soak, soke, choke, joke, woke, roque, broke, stroke, croak, yoke, yolk, bloke, cloak

24.18.1
cowpoke, mopoke, slowpoke, bespoke

24.18.2
Greystoke

24.18.3
okey-doke

24.18.4
decoke, Ocrecoke

24.18.5
holm oak, woodsmoke

24.18.6
Roanoke

24.18.7
kinfolk, menfolk, kinsfolk, townsfolk, dalesfolk, gentlefolk, countryfolk, fisherfolk, womenfolk

24.18.8
evoke, revoke, provoke, invoke, convoke, equivoque

24.18.9
presoak, Abersoch

24.18.10
artichoke

24.18.11
in-joke

24.18.12
awoke

24.18.13
Pembroke, keystroke, upstroke, heatstroke, breaststroke, sidestroke, backstroke, downstroke, sunstroke, stony-broke, counterstroke, masterstroke

24.18.14
unyoke

24.18.15
uncloak

24.19.1
Inc., ink, PINC, pink, Spink, stink, dink, kink, skink, gink, mink, fink, think, cinque, sink, sync, zinc, chink, jink, wink, twink, Quink®, rink, prink, brink, drink, Frink, shrink, link, plink, blink, clink, slink, pen-and-ink **.1** rinky-dink, Humperdinck **.2** unkink **.3** ratfink **.4** rethink, bethink, unthink, doublethink **.5** lip-sync, countersink

.6 hoodwink, kiddiewink, tiddledywink, tiddlywink **.7** soft-drink, overdrink, skating-rink **.8** Sealink, iceblink, unlink, cufflink, bobolink, Maeterlinck, interlink

24.19.2
Eysenck

24.19.3
ankh, spank, banc, bank, tank, stank, dank, thank, sank, shank, hank, wank, swank, rank, prank, drank, crank, franc, frank, shrank, yank, lank, Planck, plank, blank, clank, flank, Jodrell Bank **.1** Ewbank, Burbank, snowbank, stopbank, cloudbank, mudbank, Clydebank, sandbank, Brockbank, fogbank, embank, Millbank, Brocklebank, Citibank®, piggybank, databank, interbank, mountebank, riverbank, Bundesbank **.2** think-tank **.3** Unthank **.4** countersank **.5** sheepshank, redshank, Cruikshank, scrimshank, greenshank **.6** outrank, flag-rank, lophobranch, overdrank, lamellibranch, elasmobranch **.7** Poulenc, gangplank, point-blank, outflank

24.19.4
Franck, blanc, Leblanc

24.19.5
bonk, conch, conk, gonk, zonk, honk, bronc, tronc, cronk, plonk, clonk, pétanque, Leblanc, honky-tonk

24.19.6
oink, boink

24.19.7
punk, spunk, bunk, stunk, dunk, skunk, gunk, Monck, monk, funk, thunk, sunk, chunk, junk, hunk, trunk, drunk, shrunk, plunk, clunk, flunk, slunk, debunk, podunk, chipmunk, quidnunc, bohunk, punchdrunk, preshrunk, kerplunk, cyberpunk, countersunk, overdrunk

24.19.8
Munch

24.20.1
bisk, bisque, disc, disk, fisc, Fiske, whisk, RISC, risk, brisk, frisk, lentisc, flywhisk, eggwhisk, asterisk, tamarisk, videodisc, laserdisc, obelisk, odalisque, basilisk

24.20.2
Novosibirsk

24.20.3
Esk, desk, grotesque, Dantesque, gardenesque, Moresque, burlesque, novelesque, Disneyesque, statuesque, Kafkaesque, Junoesque, arabesque, gigantesque, copydesk, rubenesque, Normanesque, Romanesque, Pythonesque, Bunyanesque, plateresque, Tudoresque, picaresque, humoresque, sculpturesque, picturesque, Alhambresque, Guignolesque, madrigalesque, Churrigueresque, unpicturesque

24.20.4
ask, bask, Basque, task, cask, casque, mask,
masque, lasque, flask, abask, unmask, facemask,
overtask, Monégasque, antimasque,
bergamasque, Krasnoyarsk

24.20.5
kiosk, Bosc, Tosk, mosque

24.20.6
torsk

24.20.7
Usk, busk, tusk, dusk, musk, husk, rusk,
brusque, subfusc, cornhusk, unhusk

24.20.8
damask, mollusc

24.20.9
Thirsk

24.20.10
Vitebsk

24.20.11
Donetsk, Okhotsk, Irkutsk, Yakutsk,
Novokuznetsk

24.20.12
Omsk, Tomsk

24.20.13
Minsk, Smolensk, Gdansk, Murmansk, Saransk,
Chelyabinsk

24.20.14
Sverdlovsk, Brest-Litovsk, Khabarovsk,
Aleksandrovsk

24.20.15
Komsomolsk

24.21
ilk, bilk, Dilke, milk, silk, elk, whelk, talc,
calque, Volk, baulk, Falk, bulk, skulk, sulk, hulk,
Bwlch, wolf's-milk, Liebfraumilch, buttermilk,
Ostermilk, VisiCalc, catafalque

25.1
Munich, Dietrich, Ehrlich, Glenfiddich,
Metternich, gemütlich

25.2
quaich

25.3
yech

25.4
Mawddach, Sassenach

25.5
Bach, Pesach, Oistrakh

25.6
och, Coch, Koch, broch, loch, lough, Bloch,
Clough, torgoch, Dornoch, pibroch, Gairloch,
Gareloch, Kinloch

25.7
Reich, Österreich, Oberösterreich

25.8
Amlwch

25.9
Tough

25.10
Clydach, Murdoch, Rannoch, Dornoch,
Rhydderch, Taoiseach, currach, curragh,
Harlech, Tulloch, cromlech, coronach,
McCullough

25.11
Bwlch, Liebfraumilch

26.1
gigue, Grieg, league, klieg, fatigue, renege,
intrigue, Sitzkrieg, Blitzkrieg, colleague,
overfatigue

26.2
pig, big, tig, dig, gig, MiG, snig, fig, Figg, cig, jig,
Whig, wig, twig, swig, rig, Rigg, prig, sprig, brig,
Brigg, trig, grig, frig, Frigg, lig, infra dig

26.2.1
Liebig

26.2.2
shindig, Grundig, Nantgaredig

26.2.3
fizgig, whirligig, sheela-na-gig

26.2.4
Pfennig, Arenig

26.2.5
Ludwig, Schleswig

26.2.6
Leipzig

26.2.7
Danzig, Zagazig

26.2.8
rejig, thingamajig

26.2.9
earwig, Ludwig, bigwig, Schleswig, piggywig,
WYSIWYG, periwig

26.2.10
Gehrig, Meurig, Askrigg, unrig, oilrig,
thimblerig

26.3
taig, vague, Hague, Haigh, Sprague, Craig,
plague, Maesteg, renege, Mallaig

26.4
egg, Eigg, peg, Pegg, beg, teg, keg, skeg, Gheg,
Meg, neg., dreg, Gregg, Greig, yegg, leg, Legge,
cleg, Clegg, JPEG, hatpeg, unpeg, clothes peg,
duckegg, muskeg, nutmeg, thalweg, areg,
Tuareg, foreleg, Oleg, proleg, gateleg, bootleg,
redleg, jackleg, blackleg, peg-leg, dogleg,
Winnipeg, Scanderbeg, filibeg

26.5
bag, tag, stag, Stagg, dag, gag, mag, knag, nag,
snag, Snagge, fag, vag, sag, zag, shag, jag, hag,
wag, quag, swag, rag, sprag, Spragge, brag,
Bragg, drag, crag, scrag, YAG, lag, blag, blague,
flag, Flagg, slag

26.5.1
teabag, debag, seabag, fleabag, air bag, bluebag, Gro-bag®, growbag, kitbag, shitbag, ratbag, postbag, feedbag, windbag, sandbag, handbag, ragbag, bumbag, scumbag, beanbag, gasbag, nosebag, washbag, punchbag, mailbag, sailbag, saddlebag, dillybag, polybag, litterbag, tuckerbag, carpet bag

26.5.2
ragtag, dogtag, Sontag, dibatag

26.5.3
Agag, lallygag

26.5.4
tutenag, Brobdingnag

26.5.5
brainfag

26.5.6
zigzag

26.5.7
wigwag, chinwag, scallywag

26.5.8
Morag, dishrag, bullyrag

26.5.9
greylag, Stalag, gulag, jetlag, reflag

26.6
darg, Kharg, Prague, Reichstag, Camargue, Den Haag, Bundestag

26.7
bog, tog, dog, cog, Gog, mog, Mogg, smog, nog, snog, fog, Fogg, Zog, jog, hog, Hogg, wog, quag, prog, sprog, trog, grog, frog, yogh, log, clog, flog, slog, yule log

26.7.1
Ffestiniog, Blaenau Ffestiniog

26.7.2
peatbog

26.7.3
tautog

26.7.4
seadog, pye-dog, firedog, sheepdog, lapdog, hotdog, red-dog, gundog, hangdog, housedog, watchdog, bulldog, shaggy-dog, Porthmadog, Caradog, underdog

26.7.5
incog

26.7.6
Magog, agog, goosegog, mystagogue, pedagogue, demagogue, Gogmagog, synagogue, galactagogue, sialagogue

26.7.7
eggnog

26.7.8
befog, pettifog

26.7.9
Herzog

26.7.10
phizog, fizog

26.7.11
quahog, warthog, roadhog, sandhog, groundhog, hedgehog

26.7.12
polliwog, golliwog

26.7.13
leapfrog, bullfrog, Taganrog

26.7.14
Kellogg, dialogue, duologue, PROLOG, prologue, putlog, eclogue, backlog, unclog, footslog, antilog, ideologue, Tagalog, epilogue, apologue, catalogue, Decalogue, magalogue, grammalogue, homologue, Sinologue, analogue, monolog, monologue, travelogue

26.8
langue

26.9
Borg, morgue, Cherbourg, cyborg, Swedenborg, Aalborg, quahog, Helsingborg

26.10
pug, bug, tug, Doug, dug, mug, smug, snug, fug, vug, thug, chug, jug, hug, rug, trug, drug, shrug, lug, plug, glug, slug, debug, firebug, bedbug, shieldbug, humbug, doodlebug, hearthrug, earplug, fireplug, unplug, Rawlplug®, ladybug, mealybug, jitterbug, litterbug, shutterbug, thunderbug, sulfa drug, chugalug

26.11
Graig, Braunschweig

26.12
goog, Moog, fugue

26.13
Cherbourg, faubourg

26.14
erg, berg, burg

26.14.1
.1 Warburg .2 Freiburg .3 Newburg .4 Magdeburg, osnaburg .5 coburg, Joburg .6 Wartburg .7 Sedburgh, Strindberg, Lindbergh, Sandburg, Goldberg .8 Limburg, Hamburg, homburg, Romberg, Bromberg, Luxembourg, Luxemburg, Württemberg, Nuremberg .9 Steinberg, Schönberg, Wittenberg, Battenberg, Gutenberg, Brandenburg, Oldenburg, Gothenburg, Heisenberg, Rosenberg, Hindenburg, Vandenderg, Cronenberg, Orenburg, Wallenberg, Mecklenburg, Charlottenburg, Ekaterinburg, Yekaterinburg .10 Louisburg, Pressburg, Strasberg, iceberg, Duisburg, Habsburg, Hapsburg, Pittsburgh, Würzburg, Salzburg, Vicksburg, Harrisburg, Johannesburg, Pietermaritzburg .11 Strasbourg, Augsburg, Ginsberg, Finsberg, Drakensberg, Carlsberg®, Gettysburg, Petersburg, St Petersburg,

Königsberg, Williamsburg .12 Spielberg, Tilburg, Heidelberg, Inselberg, Vorarlberg

26.14.2
simurg

26.14.3
exergue

26.14.4
Esbjerg

26.15
Pogue, vogue, rogue, brogue, drogue, Logue, disembogue, Minogue, pirogue, prorogue, collogue

27.1
Eyam, beam, team, teem, steam, deem, deme, scheme, Nîmes, feme, theme, seam, seem, Cheam, haem, ream, rheme, bream, stream, dream, cream, scream, gleam, ice cream

27.1.1
I-beam, abeam, whitebeam, sealed-beam, hornbeam, sunbeam, moonbeam, crossbeam, hammerbeam

27.1.2
septime, centime, esteem, semanteme, disesteem, self-esteem

27.1.3
redeem, academe

27.1.4
hakim

27.1.5
sememe, tagmeme, enthymeme

27.1.6
moneme, toneme, phoneme, chroneme, treponeme, diaphoneme

27.1.7
grapheme, morpheme, blaspheme

27.1.8
raceme, glosseme, beseem, lexeme, inseam

27.1.9
régime, ancien régime

27.1.10
Ibrahim, Elohim

27.1.11
Pittenweem

27.1.12
harem, bireme, trireme, Purim, supreme, airstream, slipstream, upstream, jetstream, midstream, bloodstream, Coldstream, extreme, mainstream, downstream, onstream, millstream, daydream, Brylcreem®, quinquereme, quadrireme, monotreme, buttercream

27.1.13
kilim, agleam

27.2
him, Pimm, Pym, Tim, dim, Kim, skim, nim, vim, Sim, shim, gym, Jim, hymn, whim,

quim, swim, rim, prim, brim, trim, crim, scrim, grim, Grimm, limb, limn, Lymm, Lympne, glim, slim

27.2.1
goyim

27.2.2
cherubim

27.2.3
shittim, victim, verbatim, seriatim, literatim

27.2.4
bedim, Chasidim, Hasidim, Sephardim

27.2.5
Sikkim, Joachim

27.2.6
minim, paynim, eponym, toponym, typonym, hypernym, hyponym, metonym, antonym, pseudonym, homonym, synonym, anonym, paronym, acronym

27.2.7
teraphim, seraphim

27.2.8
moshavim

27.2.9
passim, maxim, kibbutzim

27.2.10
Ashkenazim

27.2.11
Midrashim

27.2.12
slim-jim

27.2.13
Ibrahim, Elohim

27.2.14
corymb, urim, Purim, retrim, Leitrim, interim, Antrim, overbrim, ad interim, Sanhedrim

27.2.15
goyim

27.2.16
Elim, prelim, Baalim, forelimb

27.3.1
opium, europium

27.3.2
labium, erbium, terbium, cambium, ytterbium, niobium, columbium

27.3.3
tritium, Latium, protium, strontium, syncytium, consortium, sestertium, sclerotium, cementium, Byzantium, cerastium, corpus luteum, periosteum

27.3.4
.1 tedium, medium, cypripedium, intermedium, epicedium .2 idiom, oidium, rubidium, cymbidium, conidium, Praesidium, basidium, Presidium, pyxidium, iridium, peridium,

clostridium, nephridium, ommatidium, hesperidium, post meridiem, antheridium, cryptosporidium **.3** stadium, radium, vanadium, palladium **.4** Padiham **.5** myocardium, pericardium, endocardium **.6** Bodiam **.7** Gordium, primordium, exordium, rutherfordium **.8** odeum, Odiham, odium, podium, sodium, rhodium, sympodium, plasmodium, allodium, collodium, pseudopodium, lycopodium **.9** indium, scandium, compendium, antependium, latifundium

27.3.5
ischium

27.3.6
collegium

27.3.7
premium, phormium, fermium, chromium, cadmium, osmium, holmium, gelsemium, neodymium, didymium, encomium, praseodymium, prothalamium, Verulamium, epithalamium

27.3.8
.1 rhenium, hymenium, ruthenium, proscenium, selenium, helenium, asplenium **.2** minium, actinium, delphinium, pollinium, triclinium, protactinium, condominium, dockominium, aluminium, gadolinium **.3** cranium, titanium, calcaneum, germanium, geranium, uranium, succedaneum, pericranium, chondrocranium, Herculaneum **.4** biennium, triennium, septennium, decennium, quinquennium, quadrennium, millennium **.5** hahnium **.6** californium **.7** einsteinium **.8** neptunium **.9** Capernaum **.10** conium, ionium, plutonium, iconium, syconium, meconium, zirconium, harmonium, ammonium, stramonium, euphonium, oxonium, polonium, archegonium, spermogonium, pelargonium, pandemonium, cuprammonium, positronium, spermatogonium **.11** hafnium

27.3.9
trivium, quadrivium, diluvium, alluvium, colluvium, effluvium, mendelevium, kurchatovium

27.3.10
lithium, promethium

27.3.11
axiom, francium, calcium, lutecium, lutetium, gynoecium, androecium, indicium, potassium, lawrencium, paramecium, perimysium, americium

27.3.12
caesium, trapezium, magnesium, Elysium, gymnasium, indusium, symposium, dysprosium, monochasium

27.3.13
Latium, strontium, lutetium, technetium, indicium, solatium, lutecium, consortium,

sestertium, cementium, ad initium, americium

27.3.14
sporangium, gametangium

27.3.15
collegium, eulogium, sporangium, florilegium, uropygium, menologium, gametangium

27.3.16
requiem, colloquium

27.3.17
.1 Miriam, delirium, collyrium, subdelirium **.2** cerium, imperium, deuterium, bacterium, psalterium, eubacterium, magisterium, megatherium, cyanobacterium, corynebacterium **.3** barium, herbarium, sudarium, caldarium, samarium, vivarium, rosarium, fusarium, aquarium, terrarium, sacrarium, solarium, columbarium, termitarium, sanitarium, planetarium, insectarium, armamentarium, tepidarium, frigidarium, dolphinarium, oceanarium, leprosarium, cinerarium, honorarium **.4** corium, thorium, emporium, ciborium, nielsbohrium, praetorium, scriptorium, triforium, sensorium, auditorium, sudatorium, crematorium, vomitorium, sanatorium, sanitorium, moratorium, aspersorium, conservatorium, curium, tellurium **.5** Librium®, opprobrium, equilibrium, disequilibrium **.6** yttrium, atrium, endometrium, epigastrium, hypogastrium **.7** scolopendrium, perichondrium

27.3.18
Sealyham, helium, ileum, ilium, cilium, psyllium, trillium, bdellium, allium, pallium, gallium, valium, thallium, thulium, oleum, scholium, folium, Bethlehem, nobelium, berkelium, mycelium, Fitzwilliam, beryllium, dentalium, subsellium, prothallium, linoleum, petroleum, epithelium, endothelium, mesothelium, penicillium, hyracotherium

27.4
aim, tame, Thame, dame, came, kame, game, maim, name, fame, same, shame, frame, lame, blame, claim, flame, Bohème

27.4.1
aspartame

27.4.2
grandame

27.4.3
became, misbecame, overcame

27.4.4
endgame

27.4.5
rename, forename, byname, surname, nickname, misname, filename, what's-her-name, what's-its-name, what's-his-name

27.4.6
defame

27.4.7
selfsame

27.4.8
Ephraim, airframe, doorframe, sub-frame, bedframe, mainframe, underframe

27.4.9
reclaim, acclaim, declaim, proclaim, quitclaim, disclaim, exclaim, aflame, inflame, counterclaim

27.5
em, m, stem, feme, femme, them, SEM, Shem, gem, Jem, hem, Wem, rem, LEM, Clem, phlegm, a.m., Bohème, pro tem, ad rem, in rem, IBM®, REM, ICBM, crème de la crème

27.5.1
per diem, carpe diem

27.5.2
requiem

27.5.3
proem, phloem

27.5.4
contemn, brainstem, meristem

27.5.5
idem, diadem, modem, Lib Dem, condemn, ibidem

27.5.6
ad hominem

27.5.7
apophthegm, apothem

27.5.8
Snowcem®

27.5.9
chernozem

27.5.10
Horsham

27.5.11
stratagem

27.5.12
mayhem, ahem, Bethlehem

27.5.13
suprême, ad valorem

27.5.14
Belém, Angoulême

27.6
am, Pam, Spam®, TAM, tam, dam, damn, cam, cham, scam, gam, ma'am, mam, Nam, femme, Sam, sham, jam, jamb, ham, wham, swam, ram, praam, pram, Bram, tram, drachm, dram, cram, scram, gram, gramme, yam, lam, lamb, clam, glam, flam, slam, Khayyam, Siam, pro-am, Pan-Am, Uncle Sam, Kompong Cham, Omar Khayyám

27.6.1
choliamb, ad nauseam, in memoriam

27.6.2
iamb, Priam

27.6.3
diazepam, nitrazepam

27.6.4
Etam®, tam-tam, syntagm, Mandelstam, Seringapatam

27.6.5
Edam, Schiedam, mesdames, goddam, grandam, quondam, Potsdam, milldam, Rotterdam, Amsterdam, cofferdam

27.6.6
Nicam, CADCAM, minicam

27.6.7
cryptogam, phanerogam

27.6.8
imam, hammam

27.6.9
Vietnam, Suriname, ad personam

27.6.10
Oxfam

27.6.11
Assam, cheongsam

27.6.12
exam

27.6.13
Babycham®

27.6.14
doorjamb, logjam

27.6.15
Abraham, Birmingham

27.6.16
wigwam, whim-wham

27.6.17
.1 DRAM .2 dirham .3 dithyramb .4 Abram, Vibram® .5 milligram, ideogram, radiogram, cardiogram, phraseogram, angiogram, heliogram, myocardiogram, arteriogram, echocardiogram, electrocardiogram, trigram, diagram, skiagram, sciagram, epigram, scattergram, cartogram, photogram, cryptogram, pictogram, hectogram, scintigram, pentagram, centigram, histogram, chromatogram, logogram, mammogram, tomogram, nomogram, kymogram, thermogram, sphygmogram, seismogram, anagram, nanogram, monogram, sonagram, sonogram, chronogram, phonogram, ethogram, kissogram, decigram, hexagram, aerogramme, hierogram, tetragram, spectrogram, dendrogram, microgram, kilogram, telegram, hologram, pyelogram, oscillogram, parallelogram, encephalogram, echoencephalogram, electroencephalogram, program, programme, echogram, deprogramme, reprogram, subprogram, microprogram,

engram, tangram, cablegram **.6** diaphragm
.7 ashram

27.6.18
Eelam, Elam, flimflam, Islam, oriflamme,
alprazolam

27.7
Baum, Greenbaum, Mandelbaum, Lebensraum

27.8
arm, palm, balm, barm, calm, ma'am, malm,
smarm, Nam, farm, psalm, charm, harm, qualm,
Guam, praam, Yarm, rearm, Khayyam,
short-arm, unarm, disarm, forearm,
Notre-Dame, Fleet Air Arm

27.8.1
napalm

27.8.2
embalm

27.8.3
short-arm, Sidebotham, Sidebottom,
Seringapatam

27.8.4
yardarm, gendarme, sidearm, Madame,
round-arm

27.8.5
becalm, Montcalm

27.8.6
imam, hammam, schoolmarm

27.8.7
tonearm

27.8.8
windfarm

27.8.9
forearm, Bairam, firearm, underarm, overarm

27.8.10
alarm, salaam, Islam, Dar es Salaam

27.9
om, pom, bomb, bombe, Thom, tom, dom,
mom, Somme, rhomb, ROM, Rom, prom, from,
glom, pompom, firebomb, stinkbomb, diatom,
tomtom, Uncle Tom, condom, COCOM,
sitcom, satcom, non-com, EAROM, EPROM,
angstrom, maelstrom, pogrom, therefrom,
wherefrom, shalom, coulomb, aplomb,
honnête homme, Minicom, intercom,
CARICOM, Telecom®, Kompong Som,
Panmunjom, CD-ROM

27.10
Orm, Orme, Baum, storm, dorm, corm,
Maugham, norm, form, forme, shawm, halm,
haulm, warm, swarm

27.10.1
Hobsbawm

27.10.2
firestorm, snowstorm, windstorm, sandstorm,
rainstorm, brainstorm, barnstorm, hailstorm,
thunderstorm

27.10.3
Benidorm

27.10.4
cairngorm

27.10.5
reform, preform, perform, deform, inform,
conform, transform, outperform, misinform,
underperform **.1** triform **.2** proteiform, deiform,
stipiform, lupiform, tubiform, cubiform,
cymbiform, retiform, scutiform, multiform,
stipitiform, stalactiform, serpentiform,
pediform, iodoform, hydatidiform,
proboscidiform, fungiform, mammiform,
vermiform, bromoform, reniform, graniform,
coniform, uniform, cuneiform, ligniform,
resiniform, scyphiform, claviform, curviform,
oviform, pisiform, cruciform, plexiform,
sacciform, ensiform, unciform, falciform,
vasiform, fusiform, spongiform, linguiform,
aeriform, variform, chloroform, vaporiform,
viperiform, scalpriform, fibriform, cribriform,
vitriform, rostriform, microform, scalariform,
villiform, aliform, stelliform, coliform, piliform,
filiform, gangliform, moniliform, bacilliform,
lamelliform, flagelliform **.3** subform **.4** platform
.5 landform, Cominform **.6** springform
.7 waveform

27.10.6
meerschaum

27.10.7
lukewarm

27.11
um, bum, tum, stum, dumb, come, cum,
scum, gum, mum, numb, thumb, some, sum,
chum, hum, swum, Rhum, rhumb, rum, Brum,
strum, drum, crumb, scrum, thrum, yum, lum,
Lumb, plum, plumb, glum, slum, dim sum,
Kara Kum

27.11.1
natatorium

27.11.2
stumblebum

27.11.3
tumtum

27.11.4
dumdum, Tweedledum

27.11.5
become, succumb, outcome, income,
misbecome, overcome

27.11.6
degum, bluegum, ungum, bubblegum

27.11.7
hammam

27.11.8
benumb, lanthanum

27.11.9
hop-o'-my-thumb

27.11.10
adsum, Aksum, Axum

27.11.11
ho-hum

27.11.12
angstrom, eardrum, humdrum, kettledrum, McCrum, breadcrumb

27.11.13
yum-yum

27.11.14
sugarplum

27.12
I'm, thyme, time, dime, chyme, Chaim, mime, cyme, chime, rhyme, rime, prime, crime, grime, lime, climb, clime, slime

27.12.1
teatime, daytime, playtime, airtime, spare-time, wartime, showtime, uptime, part-time, nighttime, bedtime, ragtime, dreamtime, sometime, meantime, downtime, one-time, noontime, springtime, halftime, lifetime, peacetime, mistime, pastime, flextime, lunchtime, mealtime, schooltime, whole-time, flexitime, beforetime, suppertime, wintertime, summertime, dinnertime, anytime, overtime, maritime, Christmastime

27.12.2
paradigm

27.12.3
isocheim

27.12.4
pantomime

27.12.5
abzyme, enzyme, lysozyme, isoenzyme, holoenzyme

27.12.6
Sondheim, Trondheim, Waldheim, Durkheim, Mannheim, Oppenheim, Guggenheim, Niflheim, Anaheim, Hildesheim

27.12.7
begrime, monorhyme, pararhyme

27.12.8
sublime, birdlime, quicklime, brooklime

27.13
shtum, cwm, Qum, room, cogito ergo sum

27.13.1
adsum, Aksum, Axum

27.14
boom, tomb, doom, doum, combe, khoum, zoom, whom, womb, rheum, room, Roome, broom, Broome, brougham, brume, Croom, Croome, groom, Frome, vroom, spume, neum, neume, fume, Hulme, Hume, loom, plume, bloom, Blum, gloom, glume, flume, post room, nom de plume

27.14.1
Khartoum, entomb, disentomb, hecatomb

27.14.2
predoom, foredoom

27.14.3
catacomb

27.14.4
Targum

27.14.5
simoom

27.14.6
.1 tearoom .2 anteroom .3 dayroom, playroom .4 storeroom .5 showroom, elbowroom .6 taproom .7 clubroom, whiskbroom, pushbroom .8 stateroom, courtroom, guestroom, restroom .9 bedroom, headroom, guardroom, boardroom, wardroom, mudroom .10 sickroom, checkroom, back room, darkroom, stockroom, workroom, cloakroom .11 legroom, bridegroom .12 homeroom .13 greenroom, gunroom, sunroom, common room .14 strongroom .15 staffroom .16 bathroom .17 pressroom, classroom, houseroom, box room .18 newsroom, salesroom .19 washroom, mushroom, lunchroom .20 stillroom, grillroom, saleroom, ballroom, poolroom, toolroom, schoolroom

27.14.7
costume, vacuum, legume, perfume, assume, reassume, subsume, consume, resume, presume, exhume, inhume, volume, Leverhulme, illume

27.14.8
heirloom, deplume, abloom, broadloom, handloom, filoplume

27.15.1
geum, Liam, Te Deum, lyceum, museum, Athenaeum, perineum, Erechtheum, gynaeceum, coliseum, Rijksmuseum, hypogeum, propylaeum, mausoleum, peritoneum

27.15.2
Graeme, graham, Grahame, Te Deum

27.15.3
Higham, Priam, patagium

27.15.4
menstruum, triduum, residuum, continuum

27.15.5
brougham, Newham

27.15.6
poem, Boehm, Noam, Rehoboam, Siloam, jeroboam

27.15.7
Shippam, Meopham, Clapham, Popham, Topham, wampum

27.15.8
sebum, Brabham, Cobham, Chobham, plumbum, album, ad verbum

27.15.9
.1 Chetham, Cheetham, tapetum, Antietam, pinetum, excretum, arboretum **.2** Tatum, datum, satem, stratum, pomatum, substratum, ultimatum, ageratum, superstratum, petrolatum **.3** Streatham **.4** atom, Tatham, Chatham, Euratom **.5** post-partum, erratum, antepartum, desideratum **.6** bottom, Gotham, Rowbotham, Rowbottom, Sidebotham, Sidebottom, rock-bottom, Higginbotham, Higginbottom, Longbottom, Ramsbotham, Ramsbottom, Shufflebottom, Winterbotham, Winterbottom **.7** autumn, postmortem, ante-mortem **.8** Ightham, item, ad litem, ad infinitum **.9** sputum, scutum, Aquascutum® **.10** diatom, libitum, adytum, ad libitum **.11** totem, scrotum, teetotum, factotum **.12** septum, symptom **.13** dictum, rectum, factum, sanctum, punctum, obiter dictum **.14** Bentham, centum, Trentham, bantam, phantom, quantum, amentum, tomentum, momentum, cementum, omentum, indumentum, adiantum **.15** system, custom, frustum, subsystem, accustom, reaccustom, Chrysostom, solar system, ecosystem, disaccustom **.16** Eltham, Feltham

27.15.10
.1 Edom, Needham, sedum, freedom, unfreedom **.2** yuppiedom, jockeydom, fogeydom, Gypsydom, Nazidom **.3** heirdom **.4** Adam, madam, Madame, macadam, tarmacadam **.5** stardom, tsardom, shahdom, superstardom **.6** Odham, Sodom, Wadham, rodham **.7** boredom, Fordham, whoredom **.8** squiredom, poppadom, pauperdom, martyrdom, masterdom, junkerdom **.9** reductio ad absurdum **.10** Odom **.11** popedom **.12** saintdom **.13** sheikhdom, clerkdom, dukedom, archdukedom **.14** queendom, Wymondham, Wyndham, thanedom, tandem, fandom, random, condom, quondam, heathendom, Christendom, Saxondom, pudendum, addendum, agendum, Saxmundham, corundum, corrigendum, referendum, explanandum, avizandum, memorandum, ad eundem, Carborundum®, nil desperandum **.15** kingdom **.16** fiefdom, chiefdom, serfdom, sheriffdom **.17** princedom **.18** wisdom, unwisdom **.19** savagedom **.20** Gaeldom, beldam, seldom, thraldom, earldom, Oldham, crippledom, bumbledom, rascaldom, devildom, scoundreldom, officialdom

27.15.11
.1 caecum, Secombe **.2** stickum, Wickham, Wycombe, Illyricum **.3** vade mecum **.4** Peckham, Beckham **.5** Rackham **.6** Occam **.7** Duckham **.8** skookum, Newcombe, Newcome **.9** guaiacum, practicum, Widdecombe, modicum, colchicum, capsicum, Woolacombe, viaticum, arsenicum,

doronicum, taraxacum, hypericum, Eboricum **.10** Kirkham **.11** Oakham, oakum, Skokholm, hokum, Holcombe, locum, Slocombe, Slocum **.12** income **.13** dinkum, bunkum **.14** Ascham, Askham, Anscombe, Wiveliscombe **.15** Swanscombe **.16** Edgecombe **.17** welcome, Wellcome, talcum, Malcolm, Salcombe, unwelcome

27.15.12
begum, Brigham, Egham, Targum, Margam, ogham, sorghum, lingam, Pengam, Fotheringham, amalgam

27.15.13
extremum, optimum, cardamom, Pergamum, minimum, sesamum, maximum, chrysanthemum, xeranthemum, helianthemum, mesembryanthemum

27.15.14
.1 Greenham, frenum, plenum, duodenum **.2** Houyhnhnm **.3** Fanum, arcanum **.4** Denham, denim, venom, Wenham, Blenheim, envenom **.5** per annum **.6** Downham **.7** Arnhem, Barnum, Farnham **.8** Bonham **.9** Lynam, mediastinum, antirrhinum **.10** Newnham, jejunum **.11** Chippenham, tympanum, galbanum, platinum, Tottenham, Puttenham, Cheltenham, Tidenham, ladanum, laudanum, Twickenham, Pakenham, Fakenham, Dagenham, organum, Shrivenham, olibanum, molybdenum, origanum, polygonum, aluminum **.12** Burnham, sternum, viburnum, laburnum, alburnum, xiphisternum **.13** summum bonum **.14** Puttnam **.15** lignum, sphagnum, magnum, interregnum **.16** damnum **.17** Woosnam

27.15.15
Ingham, Bingham, gingham, thingum, Uppingham, Nottingham, Buckingham, Wokingham, Birmingham, Cunningham, Effingham, Walsingham, Wolsingham, Sheringham, Altrincham, Sandringham, Billingham, Gillingham, Collingham, Hurlingham, Framlingham

27.15.16
Swaffham

27.15.17
ovum, sempervivum

27.15.18
Tatham, Statham, Latham, Gotham, Botham, Bentham, anthem, Grantham, Feltham, Waltham, Ramsbotham, Sidebotham

27.15.19
Witham, rhythm, Lytham, Tatham, Statham, Latham, fathom, Southam, Bootham, polyrhythm, logarithm, algorithm, antilogarithm

27.15.20
.1 threesome, gleesome **.2** lissom, wearisome, worrisome **.3** fearsome **.4** omasum, abomasum **.5** Masham **.6** possum, blossom, opossum,

odontoglossum **.7** awesome, dorsum, foursome **.8** noisome **.9** helichrysum **.10** twosome, gruesome, Newsome **.11** tiresome, tempersome, cumbersome, lumbersome, humoursome, flavoursome, Hilversum, bothersome, venturesome, alyssum, adventuresome **.12** gypsum, Epsom **.13** eightsome, jetsam, flotsam, lightsome **.14** gladsome **.15** Brixham, Wrexham, darksome, Wroxham, buxom, irksome, pranksome, frolicsome **.16** plaguesome **.17** gamesome **.18** winsome, sensum, Wensum, Sansom, handsome, hansom, ransom, Ransome, transom, lonesome, burdensome, unhandsome, overburdensome **.19** lovesome **.20** toothsome, loathsome **.21** lithesome, blithesome **.22** chillsome, balsam, Folsom, toilsome, fulsome, wholesome, troublesome, mettlesome, nettlesome, meddlesome, cuddlesome, quarrelsome, unwholesome

27.15.21
.1 dirigisme, besom **.2.1** ism, schism, Chisholm, prism, chrism, chrisom, constitutionalism, deism, theism, Shiism, absenteeism, ditheism, tritheism, Parseeism, Manichaeism, misoneism, antitheism, polytheism, monotheism, hylotheism, henotheism, Sadduceeism, lobbyism, prettyism, rowdyism, fideism, toadyism, dandyism, Grundyism, flunkeyism, Trotskyism, cronyism, cockneyism, atheism, pantheism, Naziism, Toryism, entryism, McCarthyism, voluntaryism, pococuranteism, Couéism, Judaism, archaism, prosaism, Hebraism, Mithraism, Pharisaism, Taoism, Maoism, Baha'ism, Vishnuism, altruism, euphuism, truism, voodooism, Hinduism, Sabaism, Dadaism, Mazdaism, Lamaism, Krishnaism, Sivaism, ultraism, Pollyannaism, echoism, Titoism, Shintoism, egoism, jingoism, heroism, Castroism, pleochroism, dichroism, trichroism, Jim Crowism, Negroism, hylozoism **.2.2** papism, priapism, tropism, escapism, sinapism, rheotropism, pleiotropism, geotropism, malapropism, psilanthropism, philanthropism, heliotropism, phototropism, thermotropism, hydrotropism **.2.3** Babism, cubism, abysm, plumbism, Arabism **.2.4** defeatism, Docetism, élitism, obsoletism, prophetism, eremitism, hermaphroditism, patriotism, statism, fatism, mithridatism, fattism, Chartism, Scotism, sans-culottism, polyglottism, autism, rightism, Ludditism, finitism, Hussitism, troglodytism, sybaritism, satellitism, Pre-Raphaelitism, mutism, hirsutism, absolutism, Pietism, quietism, fortuitism, nepotism, despotism, Jacobitism, narcotism, egotism, ergotism, schematism, Semitism, traumatism, rheumatism, hermetism, chromatism, pragmatism, dogmatism, suprematism, automatism, systematism, achromatism, dichromatism, trichromatism, astigmatism, polychromatism, monochromatism, Donatism, hypnotism,

magnetism, diamagnetism, geomagnetism, ferrimagnetism, palaeomagnetism, paleomagnetism, paramagnetism, ferromagnetism, electromagnetism, conservatism, quixotism, parasitism, spiritism, erotism, separatism, corporatism, moderatism, syncretism, favoritism, favouritism, democratism, helotism, proselytism, photism, peyotism, baptism, Anabaptism, Saktism, Comtism, scientism, giantism, Adventism, gigantism, tarantism, Protestantism, decadentism, irredentism, dilettantism, obscurantism, vigilantism, immanentism, indifferentism, pococurantism, leftism, casteism, transvestism, cultism, occultism, gestaltism **.2.5** sadism, cladism, faddism, Mahdism, Luddism, Buddhism, foodism, nudism, iodism, Druidism, brigandism, gourmandism, Chasidism, Hasidism, Lollardism, do-goodism, tribadism, nomadism, monadism, Methodism, hybridism, paludism, absurdism, invalidism, avant-gardism, propagandism, encyclopedism, photoperiodism, hyperthyroidism, hypothyroidism **.2.6** Sikhism, cliquism, tychism, caciquism, patriarchism, Lamarckism, hierarchism, panpsychism, catechism, anarchism, monachism, monarchism, masochism, monopsychism, sadomasochism **.2.7** whiggism, priggism, thuggism, yogism, pedagogism **.2.8** Thomism, bromism, extremism, mediumism, alarmism, reformism, conformism, atomism, totemism, optimism, Benthamism, endemism, animism, dynamism, euphemism, dysphemism, pessimism, Islamism, pancosmism, nonconformism, legitimism, academism **.2.9** routinism, Latinism, libertinism, Ghibellinism, pianism, utopianism, Fabianism, lesbianism, Erastianism, Freudianism, Arcadianism, Palladianism, Bohemianism, antinomianism, Fenianism, unionism, Arminianism, trade unionism, ruffianism, traducianism, Keynesianism, Cartesianism, magianism, Pelagianism, Arianism, histrionism, sectarianism, Tractarianism, Victorianism, Nestorianism, pedestrianism, equestrianism, Presbyterianism, libertarianism, sabbatarianism, Trinitarianism, Unitarianism, vegetarianism, proletarianism, millenarianism, Rastafarianism, necessarianism, antiquarianism, Zoroastrianism, humanitarianism, necessitarianism, ubiquitarianism, authoritarianism, utilitarianism, totalitarianism, egalitarianism, equalitarianism, establishmentarianism, uniformitarianism, latitudinarianism, valetudinarianism, alienism, Wesleyanism, Hegelianism, Australianism, Machiavellianism, episcopalianism, Jainism, cocainism, monism, moronism, opportunism, plebeianism, Europeanism, Epicureanism, Zionism, Messianism, alpinism, rabbinism, urbanism, albinism, Jacobinism, satanism, Platonism, cretinism, saturnism, Plutonism, actinism, Montanism, daltonism, Neoplatonism,

nicotinism, puritanism, charlatanism, Byzantinism, Philistinism, Samaritanism, ultramontanism, cosmopolitanism, metropolitanism, hedonism, modernism, Cobdenism, postmodernism, Muhammadanism, mechanism, laconism, tokenism, volcanism, Vaticanism, Africanism, Gallicanism, Anglicanism, Americanism, republicanism, un-Americanism, veganism, paganism, organism, antagonism, hooliganism, micro-organism, demonism, shamanism, feminism, Mammonism, Brahmanism, Mormonism, Normanism, humanism, terminism, Germanism, Romanism, Rachmanism, Buchmanism, Weismannism, Pelmanism, eudaemonism, ecumenism, illuminism, determinism, polydaemonism, indeterminism, Leninism, onanism, strychninism, Marxism–Leninism, morphinism, chauvinism, Calvinism, galvanism, heathenism, Saxonism, Jansenism, Parkinsonism, prohibitionism, intuitionism, exhibitionism, abolitionism, creationism, presentationism, salvationism, relationism, inflationism, deviationism, situationism, representationism, inspirationism, restorationism, annihilationism, isolationism, secessionism, impressionism, expressionism, constructionism, Confucianism, Rosicrucianism, evolutionism, revolutionism, protectionism, connectionism, perfectionism, abstractionism, reductionism, obstructionism, deconstructionism, insurrectionism, antivivisectionism, abstentionism, expansionism, interventionism, divisionism, revisionism, precisianism, precisionism, illusionism, polygenism, religionism, Darwinism, Pyrrhonism, Peronism, uranism, doctrinism, prochronism, synchronism, Lutheranism, diachronism, anachronism, parachronism, communism, Eurocommunism, melanism, Hellenism, Stalinism, panhellenism, philhellenism, bonism, strychnism
.2.10 Sapphism, sophism, Orphism, dwarfism, Sufism, Guelphism, pleomorphism, dimorphism, trimorphism, amorphism, zoomorphism, pacifism, polymorphism, homeomorphism, metamorphism, pseudomorphism, homomorphism, monomorphism, isomorphism, heteromorphism, hylomorphism, theosophism, catastrophism, enantiomorphism, anthropomorphism, gynandromorphism
.2.11 Slavism, fauvism, arrivisme, incivism, panslavism, nativism, atavism, activism, Bolshevism, cognitivism, intuitivism, negativism, primitivism, positivism, corporativism, relativism, descriptivism, prescriptivism, subjectivism, objectivism, collectivism, constructivism, recidivism, Stakhanovism, progressivism, logical positivism
.2.12 prognathism, erethism, Graecism, racism, anti-racism, classism, exorcism, Stoicism, Arabicism, witticism, Briticism, criticism,

Atticism, Scotticism, Vorticism, scepticism, mysticism, gnosticism, Celticism, self-criticism, phoneticism, propheticism, aestheticism, estheticism, asceticism, athleticism, chromaticism, fanaticism, erraticism, exoticism, eroticism, neuroticism, eclecticism, didacticism, semanticism, romanticism, Atlanticism, fantasticism, monasticism, scholasticism, neo-plasticism, agnosticism, hypercriticism, auto-eroticism, peripateticism, ecclesiasticism, lambdacism, psychicism, supremacism, academicism, cynicism, Germanicism, Teutonicism, sardonicism, laconicism, Hibernicism, ecumenicism, histrionicism, mythicism, Gothicism, classicism, narcissism, neoclassicism, lyricism, rubricism, ostracism, empiricism, historicism, esotericism, exotericism, Gallicism, phallicism, solecism, publicism, Anglicism, Catholicism, Roman Catholicism, solipsism, Nazism, sexism, Marxism, bruxism, paroxysm, heterosexism, speciesism, Spinozism **.2.13** tachism, fascism, Britishism, fetishism, Yiddishism, revanchism, ageism, imagism, synergism, suffragism, syllogism, Falangism, Orangeism, paralogism, neologism, teleologism, ventriloquism
.2.14 hetaerism, plagiarism, Fourierism, careerism, meliorism, volunteerism, incendiarism, verism, welfarism, doctrinairism, tsarism, porism, tourism, purism, sinecurism, hetairism, vampirism, apriorism, pauperism, labourism, barbarism, Micawberism, asterism, hipsterism, huckterism, gangsterism, amateurism, shamateurism, monetarism, militarism, voluntarism, Shakerism, Quakerism, rigorism, vulgarism, mesmerism, euhemerism, epimerism, metamerism, tautomerism, isomerism, consumerism, polymerism, Skinnerism, mannerism, spoonerism, aphorism, Catharism, adventurism, naturism, Thatcherism, futurism, Majorism, terrorism, eco-terrorism, narcoterrorism, voyeurism, aneurysm, epicurism, behaviourism, solarism, Hitlerism, bowdlerism, popularism, secularism, insularism, particularism, vernacularism, auteurism, pentaprism, entrism, centrism, tantrism, belletrism, theocentrism, egocentrism, ethnocentrism, androcentrism, phallocentrism, Eurocentrism, anthropocentrism **.2.15** genteelism, realism, labialism, bestialism, idealism, serialism, surrealism, unrealism, parochialism, trinomialism, colonialism, Pre-Raphaelism, colloquialism, imperialism, materialism, mercurialism, photorealism, industrialism, premillennialism, ceremonialism, neocolonialism, immaterialism, territorialism, entrepreneurialism, Baalism, malism, parallelism, phallism, cabbalism, alcoholism, troilism, gargoylism, mercantilism, nihilism, royalism, loyalism, myalism, sciolism, sensualism, ritualism, mutualism, factualism, textualism, gradualism, transsexualism,

perpetualism, conceptualism, intellectualism, individualism, dualism, papalism, episcopalism, ableism, Cabalism, tribalism, verbalism, herbalism, Froebelism, symbolism, embolism, diabolism, metabolism, catabolism, katabolism, anabolism, probabilism, cannibalism, hyperbolism, immobilism, fatalism, bimetallism, monometallism, vitalism, brutalism, hospitalism, teetotalism, sacerdotalism, syndactylism, bidialectalism, mentalism, pointillism, transcendentalism, infantilism, orientalism, occidentalism, sentimentalism, fundamentalism, ornamentalism, sacramentalism, monumentalism, elementalism, departmentalism, experimentalism, environmentalism, Pentecostalism, feudalism, Mendelism, vandalism, bipedalism, vocalism, localism, rascalism, physicalism, radicalism, syndicalism, classicalism, clericalism, mechanicalism, theatricalism, ecumenicalism, anticlericalism, evangelicalism, regalism, legalism, mongolism, formalism, minimalism, animalism, finalism, communalism, nominalism, phenomenalism, traditionalism, intuitionalism, sensationalism, vocationalism, representationalism, Congregationalism, denominationalism, professionalism, obsessionalism, unprofessionalism, nationalism, rationalism, internationalism, supranationalism, institutionalism, emotionalism, sectionalism, factionalism, functionalism, conventionalism, unconventionalism, occasionalism, regionalism, journalism, paternalism, maternalism, fraternalism, photojournalism, necrophilism, triumphalism, devilism, survivalism, revivalism, medievalism, commensalism, universalism, racialism, specialism, socialism, initialism, officialism, commercialism, provincialism, prudentialism, essentialism, substantialism, controversialism, existentialism, consequentialism, experientialism, evangelism, tele-evangelism, televangelism, botulism, spiritualism, pugilism, populism, formulism, noctambulism, somnambulism, bilingualism, trilingualism, multilingualism, virilism, moralism, amoralism, oralism, pluralism, ruralism, liberalism, literalism, gutturalism, pastoralism, federalism, naturalism, scripturalism, structuralism, culturalism, bilateralism, bicameralism, multilateralism, unilateralism, supernaturalism, preternaturalism, multiculturalism, neutralism, centralism, scoundrelism, mongrelism, Gaullism, holism, simplism, cataclysm **.3** spasm, chasm, plasm, chiliasm, phantasm, sarcasm, orgasm, pleonasm, neoplasm, symplasm, enthusiasm, metaplasm, cataplasm, cytoplasm, protoplasm, ectoplasm, endoplasm, sarcoplasm, exoplasm, cataclasm, overenthusiasm, iconoclasm **.4** macrocosm, microcosm **.5** bradyseism, microseism **.6** bosom, embosom

27.15.22
Measham, Heysham, meerschaum, Latium, Chesham, Gresham, pashm, Masham, Lewisham, Frodsham, Melksham, Eynsham, Keynsham, strontium, Evesham, Aylesham, Hailsham, Walsham, Windlesham, technetium, solatium, lutecium, petersham, Amersham, Caversham, Faversham, sestertium, nasturtium

27.15.23
Beecham, Meacham, Mitcham, Mitchum, sachem

27.15.24
dodgem, Belgium, stratagem, Brummagem

27.15.25
Nahum, Odiham, Wilbraham

27.15.26
.1 Dereham, dirham, theorem, serum, antiserum **.2** arum, Fareham, Sarum, harem, Wareham, Old Sarum, harum-scarum **.3** carom, marram **.4** alarum **.5** Boreham, Coram, forum, Shoreham, jorum, quorum, decorum, Mizoram, valorem, variorum, indecorum, Karakoram, Karakorum, cockalorum, sanctum sanctorum, pons asinorum **.6** Durham, durum **.7** Hiram **.8** labarum, Caterham, Westerham, Rotherham, marjoram, pittosporum **.9** Abram, labrum, Vibram®, Wilbraham, cerebrum, candelabrum **.10** Outram, Mottram, Bertram, spectrum, plectrum, centrum, antrum, tantrum, oestrum, sistrum, Tristram, åstrom, nostrum, rostrum, lustrum, angstrom, maelstrom, broad-spectrum, electrum, sequestrum, colostrum, ligustrum, hippeastrum, ocular spectrum **.11** Meldrum, panjandrum, conundrum **.12** sacrum, buckram, fulcrum, simulacrum **.13** megrim, Wigram, pogrom, grogram, Ingram, pilgrim, pre-programme, subprogram **.14** wolfram **.15** pyrethrum **.16** ashram

27.15.27
William

27.15.28
.1 velum, coelom **.2** chillum, vexillum, spirillum, aspergillum **.3** Balaam, Salem **.4** pelham, vellum, cribellum, scutellum, flagellum, antebellum, cerebellum **.5** alum, Balham, Calum, Malham, mallam, vallum, Hallam, McCallum **.6** Haarlem, Harlem, slalom, Malayalam **.7** Colum, column, solemn **.8** golem **.9** phylum, xylem, hilum, whilom, subphylum, asylum **.10** Fulham **.11** tropaeolum, paspalum, cimbalom, tantalum, Absalom, pendulum, pabulum, speculum, vinculum, vasculum, osculum, cingulum, frenulum, Jerusalem, capitulum, reticulum, curriculum, tenaculum, spiraculum, vibraculum, inoculum, operculum, coagulum, acetabulum, tintinnabulum, incunabulum, diverticulum, supernaculum **.12** Irlam **.13** Bolam, mowlem, idolum **.14** peplum, exemplum **.15** Pablum®, problem, emblem **.16** Whitlam **.17** bedlam, Audlem, Ludlum, hoodlum

.18 siglum .19 Muslim .20 Haslam, Moslem, Burslem

27.16
perm, sperm, berm, berme, Boehm, term, derm, firm, therm, germ, herm, worm, squirm, tube worm

27.16.1
oosperm, perisperm, angiosperm, endosperm, gymnosperm

27.16.2
pre-term, midterm

27.16.3
pachyderm, ectoderm, endoderm, mesoderm, exoderm, ostracoderm, malacoderm, echinoderm

27.16.4
affirm, reaffirm, infirm, confirm, disaffirm, reconfirm, disconfirm

27.16.5
homeotherm, isotherm, isogeotherm, poikilotherm

27.16.6
wheatgerm

27.16.7
mawworm, screwworm, wireworm, slowworm, shipworm, whipworm, tapeworm, gapeworm, lobworm, flatworm, cutworm, threadworm, bloodworm, woodworm, roundworm, blindworm, muckworm, bookworm, hookworm, silkworm, ragworm, lugworm, pinworm, ringworm, lungworm, earthworm, inchworm, eelworm, mealworm, angleworm, bristle worm, cankerworm

27.17
ohm, om, pome, Boehm, tome, dome, comb, gnome, Noam, Nome, foam, holm, Holme, hom, home, roam, Rom, Rome, brome, drome, chrome, Crome, Frome, loam

27.17.1
Guillaume

27.17.2
biome

27.17.3
Beerbohm

27.17.4
leucotome, microtome, plagiostome, peristome, phyllostome, cyclostome

27.17.5
radome, astrodome

27.17.6
trichome, backcomb, Lancôme®, toothcomb, cockscomb, coxcomb, honeycomb

27.17.7
megohm

27.17.8
genome, metronome, gastronome

27.17.9
Styrofoam®

27.17.10
liposome, ribosome, schistosome, chromosome, lysosome, centrosome, microsome, trypanosome

27.17.11
rhizome

27.17.12
rehome, stay-at-home, take-home, Stockholm, Skokholm, Bornholm, Wolstenholme, Oxenholme, Axholme, Rusholme, motorhome

27.17.13
Jerome, prodrome, syndrome, Nichrome®, hippodrome, loxodrome, aerodrome, velodrome, palindrome, polychrome, Cibachrome, phytochrome, cytochrome, Ektachrome®, Kodachrome, monochrome, Mercurochrome®, lymphadenopathy syndrome

27.17.14
shalom

27.18
film, elm, helm, realm, olm, culm, Hulme, Ulm, cling film, Kenelm, Anselm, witchelm, wychelm, Denholme, cinefilm, telefilm, microfilm, underwhelm, overwhelm

28.1
e'en, peen, bean, been, teen, Teign, Steen, dean, Dene, dene, Kean, Keane, keen, Keene, skean, gean, mean, mesne, mien, Nene, sphene, scene, seen, sheen, Sheene, gene, Jean, jean, wean, ween, Wheen, 'tween, quean, queen, preen, Breen, treen, screen, green, Greene, yean, lean, lien, Lleyn, spleen, clean, glean, Bethnal Green, vaseline®, fedayeen, Halloween, crêpe de Chine, Gretna Green

28.1.1
theine

28.1.2
cysteine, coniine, phenolphthalein

28.1.3
diene, triene, butadiene, leukotriene

28.1.4
toluene, trinitrotoluene

28.1.5
ibogaine

28.1.6
ligroine

28.1.7
terpene, propene, spalpeen, lycopene, reserpine, clozapine, atropine, Philippine, polypropene, benzodiazepine

28.1.8
Rabin, soybean, Sabine, shebeen, buckbean, gombeen, horsebean, stilbene, yohimbine, might-have-been

28.1.9
preteen, eighteen, sateen, lateen, Martine,
poteen, potheen, fourteen, routine, thirteen,
umpteen, Bakhtin, canteen, tontine, nineteen,
seventeen, fifteen, Christine, sixteen, saltine,
nougatine, velveteen, guillotine, galantine
.1 pachytene **.2** butene, subroutine **.3** creatine,
libertine, cabotine, leptotene, astatine, nicotine,
zygotene, nemertean, nemertine, travertine,
spessartine, carotene, gelatine, diplotene,
aconitine **.4** protein, nucleoprotein,
lactoprotein, flavoprotein, scleroprotein,
lipoprotein, glycoprotein **.5** Benedictine
.6 dentine, barquentine, brigantine, Byzantine,
Argentine, brilliantine, diamantine, quarantine,
Florentine, eglantine **.7** cystine, Sistine, pristine,
Presteigne, Justine, Goldstein, Sixtine,
Bronstein, Bernstein, Springsteen,
langoustine, Trappistine, Modestine, Augustine,
mangosteen, Ernestine, celestine **.8** Ovaltine®

28.1.10
Nadine, Ladin, sardine, Claudine, subdean,
Aberdeen, gaberdine, grenadine, Rottingdean,
mujahedin, gradine, Jardine, iodine, cytidine,
histidine, Engadine, spermidine, sanidine,
pethidine, pyridine, acridine, cimetadine,
pyrimidine, pentamidine, piperidine,
sulphadimidine, codeine, Roedean, indene,
undine, brigandine, almandine, Aldine,
Geraldine, emeraldine

28.1.11
achene, nankeen, piscine, alkene, Tolkien,
palanquin

28.1.12
beguine, carrageen

28.1.13
imine, Amin, amine, gamine, ramin, thymine,
thiamine, demean, spermine, bromine,
hyoscyamine, dopamine, protamine, histamine,
rhodamine, Pergamene, Dramamine®,
tyramine, chloramine, spodumene, melamine,
theobromine, neostigmine, amphetamine,
arsphenamine, nitrosamine, scopolamine,
physostigmine, methamphetamine,
antihistamine, catecholamine

28.1.14
quinine, threonine, Benin, guanine, Dineen,
Janine, Jeannine, strychnine, methionine,
adenine, cinchonine, oscinine, mezzanine,
arginine, safranine, alanine, antivenene,
phenylalanine

28.1.15
caffeine, dauphine, morphine, trephine,
phosphene, phosphine, Delphine, clomiphene,
toxaphene, Josephine, olefine

28.1.16
flavine, Devine, ravine, Levine, nervine, Slovene,
convene, sylvine, supervene, intervene,
contravene, margravine, landgravine, olivine,
reconvene, riboflavine, acriflavine

28.1.17
ethene, naphthene, xanthine, polyethene,
polythene, hypersthene

28.1.18
Essene, Massine, fascine, Racine, foreseen,
Nicene, piscine, obscene, hoatzin, Maxine,
Francine, unseen, unforeseen, overseen
.1 Neocene, Palaeocene **.2** casein **.3** arsine,
glassine **.4** lysine, glycine **.5** leucine, isoleucine
.6 Eocene, Miocene, hyoscine, Pliocene, epicene,
cytosine, Plasticine®, Pleistocene, colchicine,
damascene, kerosene, tyrosine, anthracene,
salicine, Holocene, thylacine, Oligocene,
adenosine, dryopithecine, cercopithecine,
australopithecine **.7** Rexine®, vaccine, Loxene,
fuchsine, alexine, pyroxene, thyroxine,
pyridoxine

28.1.19
azine, cuisine, Vosene, benzene, benzine,
fanzine, organzine, bombazine, magazine,
limousine, simazine, haute cuisine, Thorazine®,
tartrazine, hydrazine, chlorpromazine,
promethazine, azobenzine, nitrobenzene,
paradichlorobenzene

28.1.20
machine, Balanchine

28.1.21
aubergine

28.1.22
poteen, Balanchine

28.1.23
hygiene, Eugene, Stergene, phosgene, indigene,
polygene, epigene, hypogene, oncogene,
plasmagene

28.1.24
between, McQueen, go-between, in-between,
totaquine

28.1.25
terrine, sarin, moreen, Irene, squireen, tureen,
Tyrrhene, Doreen, careen, marine, serene,
tambourine, leaderene, Gadarene, figurine,
margarine, submarine, transmarine,
mazarine, Nazarene, tangerine, aquamarine,
ultramarine, oleomargarine **.1** taurine,
chorine, scoreine, Maureen, Noreen, purine,
chlorine, fluorine, organochlorine **.2** styrene,
polystyrene **.3** berberine, nectarine,
Listerine®, saccharine, muscarine, wolverine,
glycerine, curarine, pelerine, helleborine,
papaverine, alizarine, nitroglycerine
.4 neoprene **.5** Atebrin® **.6** citrine, Catrine,
latrine, veratrine **.7** ephedrine, Methedrine®,
Dexedrine, Benzedrine® **.8** viewscreen,
sightscreen, roodscreen, windscreen,
smokescreen, silkscreen, sunscreen,
Hippocrene, quinacrine **.9** regreen,
shagreen, ungreen, gangrene, wintergreen,
evergreen, putting-green **.10** epinephrine

28.1.26
fedayeen, Medellín

28.1.27
Alleyne, Tallinn, Malines, colleen, baleen,
Moline, Jolene, trampoline, Sakhalin, gasoline,
vaseline® **.1** theophylline **.2** Aileen, scalene,
valine, Rayleen, praline, thermohaline
.3 Hellene, philhellene, isabelline **.4** Arlene,
Darlene, Marlene, Charlene **.5** Pauline **.6** Eileen,
xylene **.7** hyaline, propylene, polypropylene,
Ghibelline, Abilene, lobeline, Cymbeline,
Mytilene, pistilline, acetylene, oxyacetylene,
amitriptyline, Windolene®, Hölderlin,
Jacqueline, mescaline, Emeline, tourmaline,
Germolene, quinoline, aniline, lanoline,
rosaniline, nepheline, ethylene, methylene,
naphthalene, polyethylene,
perchloroethylene, tetrachloroethylene,
polytetrafluoroethylene, Rosaleen, rosaline,
Evangeline, terylene® **.8** choline, proline,
acetylcholine **.9** crimplene® **.10** Maclean,
unclean, spring-clean, tetracycline **.11** Kathleen
.12 mousseline

28.2
in, inn, PIN, pin, spin, bin, Teign, tin, DIN, din,
kin, skin, Ginn, Min, fin, Finn, thin, sin, shin,
chin, djinn, gin, Jin, jinn, whin, win, Wyn,
Wynn, Wynne, twin, quin, Quinn, Gwyn,
Gwynn, Prynne, Bryn, grin, yin, linn, llyn, Lyn,
Lynn, Lynne, Glyn, Glynn, Flinn, Flynn, lie-in,
ad fin., thick and thin, within, Ne Win, herein,
wherein, therein, Gunga Din, Ho Chi Minh,
Mickey Finn, Aksai Chin, whipper-in, sitter-in

28.2.1
theine, zein

28.2.2
lutein, casein, ossein, phenolphthalein

28.2.3
weigh-in, papain

28.2.4
Towyn

28.2.5
lie-in, papain

28.2.6
Menuhin, genuine, Islwyn

28.2.7
shoo-in, ruin, bruin, Skewen, sewin

28.2.8
Bowen, Cohen, throw-in, benzoin, heroin,
heroine, fibroin, ligroin, hydantoin, allantoin

28.2.9
unpin, underpin, pippin, shearpin, Pepin,
hairpin, rapine, Chaliapin, orpine, tiepin, lupin,
reserpine, terrapin, atropine, somatotropin,
Turpin, thyrotropin, corticotropin, hatpin,
wrest-pin, headpin, stickpin, crankpin,
rifampin, tenpin, ninepin, kingpin, Crispin,
topspin, backspin, wheelspin, tailspin, isospin,
clothes pin, pushpin, linchpin, Gilpin, Halpin,
sculpin, tholepin

28.2.10
Sabin, Sabine, Brabin, cabin, rabbin, bobbin,
dobbin, robin, Corbin, dubbin, Rubin, turbine,
Tobin, Probyn, dustbin, thrombin, sin-bin,
swingbin, ashbin, Philbin, Scriabin, Skryabin,
round robin, wake-robin, litterbin, Jacobin,
Horabin, myoglobin, Drumalbyn, Portakabin®,
psilocybin, bilirubin, haemoglobin, hemoglobin,
oxyhaemoglobin

28.2.11
.1 Chloromycetin® **.2** sit-in **.3** pancreatin **.4** cretin
.5 satin, Latin, Prestatyn **.6** martin, freemartin,
pine marten **.7** shut-in **.8** chitin **.9** Tutin, rutin,
gluten, Rasputin, highfalutin **.10** biotin, cabotin,
astatine, bouquetin, legatine, haematin,
chromatin, kinetin, isatin, sclerotin, keratin,
gelatin, bulletin, precipitin, phenacetin
.11 Curtin **.12** pecten, pectin, actin, prolactin,
protopectin, avermectin **.13** Quintin, Quentin,
Pontin, San Quentin **.14** Iestyn, Austen, Austin,
Mostyn, Dustin, Justin, clandestine

28.2.12
read-in, lead-in, gradin, Hardin, iodin, Odin,
stand-in, Blondin, Dunedin, Aladdin, muscadine,
Anadin®, Borodin, paladin, Saladin, Girondin,
unlived-in, piperidine, prostaglandin

28.2.13
Pekin, akin, Tonkin **.1** Deakin, Meakin,
Wrekin, Brechin **.2** Aitken, take-in, Dakin
.3 parkin, Larkin **.4** walk-in, Dworkin
.5 interleukin **.6** lambrequin, Peterkin,
sooterkin, kilderkin, baldachin, ramekin,
minikin, pannikin, cannikin, manakin,
manikin, mannequin, mannikin, larrikin,
Zworykin, spillikin **.7** Perkin, gherkin,
merkin, firkin, Serkin, jerkin **.8** pipkin,
Hopkin, Simpkin, limpkin, pumpkin,
bumpkin **.9** Atkin, catkin, Watkin, Kropotkin
.10 bodkin, Nordkinn, Yudkin **.11** lambkin,
Potemkin **.12** Donkin **.13** Jenkin, Rankin,
Junkin, Algonquin **.14** Miskin, siskin, griskin,
deerskin, bearskin, Baskin, gaskin, foreskin,
buskin, Ruskin, doeskin, sheepskin, capeskin,
goatskin, kidskin, redskin,
snakeskin, sharkskin, buckskin, pigskin,
dogskin, lambskin, cleanskin, wineskin,
coonskin, calfskin, wolfskin, sealskin, oilskin,
moleskin, tigerskin, Rumpelstiltskin,
onionskin **.15** Pushkin **.16** Hodgkin **.17** Silkin,
welkin, calkin, grimalkin

28.2.14
Brechin

28.2.15
piggin, Wiggin, Begin, Fagin, noggin, hoggin,
agin, begin, McGinn, tanghin, Elgin, Kosygin,
Eugene Onegin

28.2.16
Vietminh, maximin

28.2.17
.1 women, maximin, jurywomen, countrywomen, committeewomen, laywomen, airwomen, chairwomen, charwomen, forewomen, firewomen, superwomen, Ulsterwomen, alderwomen, anchorwomen, fisherwomen, washerwomen, Yorkshirewomen, scrubwomen, clubwomen, batwomen, draughtswomen, postwomen, aircraftwomen, freedwomen, madwomen, bondwomen, workwomen, policewomen, spacewomen, horsewomen, stateswomen, Scotswomen, yachtswomen, sportswomen, draftswomen, craftswomen, spokeswomen, Manxwomen, cragswomen, servicewomen, businesswomen, congresswomen, aircraftswomen, oarswomen, tribeswomen, bondswomen, guildswomen, kinswomen, plainswomen, clanswomen, townswomen, daleswomen, saleswomen, frontierswomen, freshwomen, Frenchwomen, Welshwomen, Cornishwomen, Irishwomen, Englishwomen, Scotchwomen, Dutchwomen, churchwomen, noblewomen, gentlewomen, needlewomen, councilwomen **.2** amine, gamin, examine, re-examine **.3** Brahmin **.4** cumin, illumine **.5** thiamine, hyoscyamine, vitamin, histamine, sycamine, jessamin, theremin, amphetamine, arsphenamine, Duralumin®, scopolamine, methamphetamine, antihistamine, cyanocobalamin **.6** ermine, vermin, Jermyn **.7** theobromine **.8** admin, Bodmin **.9** jasmine, Yasmin

28.2.18
linen, rennin, Lenin, tannin, run-in, kinin, phone-in, ronin, Cronin, lignin, Kalinin, bedlinen, Killanin, Bakunin, methionine, saponin, santonin, opsonin, safranin, melanin, underlinen, antivenin, bradykinin, haemocyanin, hemocyanin, agglutinin, unfeminine, serotonin

28.2.19
biffin, tiffin, griffin, Baffin, boffin, coffin, dauphin, puffin, muffin, perfin, bowfin, threadfin, elfin, dolphin, Corstorphine, endorphin, paraffin, yellowfin, Godolphin, ragamuffin, gonadotrophin, cycloparaffin, somatotrophin, corticotrophin, adrenocorticotrophin

28.2.20
flavin, Bevin, Kevin, Previn, levin, spavin, Gavin, savin, savine, ravin, ravine, Marvin, covin, Irvine, Merfyn, Mervyn, Mordvin, kelvin, Melvin, Alvin, Calvin, Colvin, replevin, Angevin, riboflavin, acriflavine, griseofulvin

28.2.21
Gethin, strophanthin

28.2.22
Swithin, Bleddyn

28.2.23
Tientsin **.1** ricin, Tok Pisin **.2** sasine, bacitracin **.3** vasopressin **.4** sasin **.5** oscine **.6** orcin, resorcin

.7 lysin, glycin, aureomycin, streptomycin, Terramycin®, tyrothricin, erythromycin **.8** mucin **.9** eosin, moccasin, Anacin®, ceresin, characin, allicin, salicin, salicine, thylacine, folacin, rifampicin, amphotericin **.10** versin, hircine **.11** oxytocin **.12** trypsin, pepsin, rhodopsin, chymotrypsin, amylopsin **.13** Yeltsin, hoatzin, rebbetzin, Solzhenitsyn **.14** tocsin, toxin, auxin, alexin, dioxin, phytoalexin, antitoxin, autotoxin, phytotoxin, cytotoxin, mycotoxin, aflatoxin, pyridoxine, tetrodotoxin **.15** khamsin, hamsin **.16** Wisconsin **.17** calcine

28.2.24
seisin, resin, rosin, hoisin, benzin, disseisin, muezzin, oleo-resin

28.2.25
Balchin, Capuchin, Ilyushin

28.2.26
teach-in, Hitchin, Machin, Cochin, urchin, chin-chin, Balchin, Capuchin

28.2.27
margin, gaijin, Pugin, virgin

28.2.28
Berwyn, Samhain, Arwyn, Darwen, Darwin, Irwin, Urwin, no-win, Chetwyn, Chatwin, Edwin, Medwin, Cledwyn, Gladwin, Godwin, Blodwen, Goodwin, Chindwin, Baldwin, Goldwyn, sequin, Tecwyn, Tarquin, Alcuin, Chegwin, pinguin, penguin, anguine, sanguine, Brangwyn, Unwin, Gershwin, Dilwyn, Delwyn, Selwyn, Alwyn, Olwen, Colwyn, chloroquine, harlequin, Algonquin, palanquin

28.2.29
wherein, Turin, Corinne, Penrhyn **.1** stearin, Kirin, serine **.2** Erin, Perrin, serin, Sherrin, transferrin **.3** Darin, sarin **.4** Corin **.5** cyclosporin, urine, burin, murine, aneurin, heparin, tambourin, nectarine, mandarin, saccharin, saccharine, muscarine, tamarin, Comorin, coumarin, sapphirine, porphyrin, warfarin, perforin, epinephrine, savarin, culverin, glycerine, Mazarin, sciurine, purpurin, pelerine, luciferin, papaverine, alizarin, nitroglycerine **.6** Disprin® **.7** fibrin, Atebrin® **.8** citrine, Catrin, Katrine, dextrin, veratrine, lacustrine, alabastrine, cyclodextrin **.9** Aldrin, Sanhedrin, ephedrine, Methedrine®, Dexedrine, Benzedrine®, Paludrine®, meandrine, salamandrine, alexandrine **.10** eccrine, mepacrine, apocrine, endocrine, quinacrine, Silvikrin®, exocrine **.11** Lohengrin, peregrine, Montenegrin **.12** pyrethrin

28.2.30
Pinyin

28.2.31
Kweilin, violin, Boleyn, Berlin, mandolin, Sakhalin, Tal-y-llyn **.1** kylin **.2** fill-in, vanillin, theophylline, Enniskillen, podophyllin, ampicillin, penicillin **.3** Palin, digitalin **.4** Welwyn, Llewelyn, vitellin,

vitelline, Helvellyn, isabelline, gibberellin
.5 Tallinn, Malin **.6** Stalin, Carlin, carline, marlin, marline **.7** Bollin, Dolin, Colin **.8** tarpaulin
.9 moulin, Newlyn **.10** kaolin, ptyalin, myelin, hyalin, hyaline, sphingomyelin, cipolin, capelin, zeppelin, Ritalin®, Ottoline, Ventolin®, pistilline, oxyacetylene, madeleine, Madeline, Gwendolen, Gwendoline, Jacqueline, francolin, mescaline, pangolin, Hamelin, formalin, quinoline, crinoline, aniline, lanolin, adrenalin, rosaniline, enkephalin, Evelyn, Rivelin, javelin, ravelin, Jocelyn, pyroxylin, Rosalyn, Michelin®, Caroline, globulin, masculine, insulin, calmodulin, tuberculin, immunoglobulin
.11 purlin, merlin, Merlyn **.12** bowline, acetylcholine **.13** Taplin, poplin, Joplin
.14 goblin, Dublin, Lublin, hobgoblin **.15** Caitlin, ratline **.16** codlin, maudlin, Candlin **.17** Wakelin, Mechlin, Jacklin, Shanklin, tetracycline
.18 metheglin **.19** Emlyn, Kremlin, gremlin, Tomlin, drumlin, Crumlin **.20** O'Flynn **.21** Devlin
.22 Rathlin **.23** Glaslyn, Rosslyn

28.2.32
Tal-y-llyn

28.3.1
apian, trappean, Scorpian, scorpion, tampion, Campion, champion, rampion, Grampian, tompion, Crispian, thespian, Ulpian, Philippian, Utopian, subtopian, dystopian, fallopian, Salopian, Cyclopean, Olympian, Mississippian, Aesculapian, Guadeloupian, Ethiopian, cornucopian

28.3.2
Gibeon, Libyan, gabion, Fabian, Sabian, Swabian, Sorbian, Nubian, Serbian, Grobian, Gambian, Zambian, lesbian, Albion, amoebean, Namibian, amphibian, Caribbean, Arabian, Danubian, Colombian, Columbian, Bessarabian, pre-Columbian, Saudi Arabian

28.3.3
Haitian, Fortean, Goethean, protean, Brechtian, Fichtean, Dantean, Kantian, Zontian, bastion, Faustian, fustian, Tacitean, Gravettian, himation, Mozartian, Djiboutian, Schubertian, Gilbertian, nemertean, lacertian, amphictyon, Atlantean, Thyestean, Sebastian, Erastian, Procrustean, Montserratian, anti-christian

28.3.4
Judaean, Antipodean **.1** median, comedian, tragedian, Archimedean, epicedian **.2** Gideon, Midian, Lydian, Clwydian, quotidian, Numidian, ophidian, Dravidian, Pisidian, ascidian, obsidian, Floridian, Derridean, meridian, viridian, Euclidean, euclidean, solifidian, nullifidian, proboscidean, enchiridion, post meridian
.3 Badian, Hadean, radian, Barbadian, Akkadian, Arcadian, Orcadian, Acadian, circadian, gammadion, Canadian, Grenadian, steradian, ultradian, infradian, Palladian **.4** Verdian
.5 Chadian, McFadyean, McFadzean, Trinidadian
.6 guardian **.7** Gordian, Claudian, accordion,

Edwardian, piano-accordion **.8** Freudian
.9 Bermudian **.10** Odeon, Rhodian, Cambodian, custodian, collodion, melodeon, nickelodeon
.11 Indian, Andean, pandean, Kandyan, Shandean, Burgundian, Burundian, Amerindian

28.3.5
piscean, Chomskyan, Volscian, Pickwickian, batrachian, Wallachian, selachian, Lamarckian, Kentuckian, Seljukian, Gulbenkian, Algonquian, saurischian, ornithischian, Czechoslovakian

28.3.6
logion, Jungian, Trisagion, Swedenborgian, Muskogean, Pelasgian, Brobdingnagian, Carolingian

28.3.7
Simeon, simian, Bamian, Damian, Samian, camion, Marmion, Charmian, Crimean, Permian, fermion, vermian, thermion, isthmian, anthemion, Bohemian, Endymion, prosimian, Bahamian, Durkheimian, prothalamion, Alabamian, antinomian, Mesopotamian

28.3.8
.1 Fenian, Armenian, Slovenian, Athenian, Mycenaean, Cyrenian, sirenian, Tyrrhenian, Magdalenian **.2** Guinean, minion, Ninian, Argentinian, Justinian, Sardinian, Arminian, dominion, Socinian, Hercynian, Virginian, Darwinian, Valentinian, Augustinian, Palestinian, Eleusinian, Carthaginian, Papua New Guinean **.3** Albanian, Jordanian, Vulcanian, Romanian, Tasmanian, Pennsylvanian, Transylvanian, Sassanian, Azanian, Iranian, Turanian, Ukrainian, Oceanian, Lithuanian, Occitanian, Mauritanian, Ruritanian, Transjordanian, Araucanian, Panamanian, Indo-Iranian, subterranean, Pomeranian, Tripolitanian, Mediterranean **.4** monogenean
.5 Mannion, Mitannian **.6** Brownian **.7** Bornean, Capricornian, Californian **.8** Moynihan **.9** union, Neptunian, Réunion, reunion, trade union, Mancunian, communion, disunion, trades union, Cameroonian, Soviet Union, self-communion, intercommunion
.10 Hibernian, Saturnian, quaternion, Falernian
.11 chthonian, aeonian, Ionian, Catalonian, Sierra Leonian, Serbonian, Etonian, Newtonian, Plutonian, Estonian, Bostonian, Miltonian, Meltonian®, Washingtonian, Sheldonian, Aberdonian, Macedonian, Chalcedonian, Caledonian, Baconian, Tychonian, draconian, Laconian, gorgonian, Tobagonian, Patagonian, Oregonian, Paphlagonian, Devonian, Slavonian, Oxonian, Johnsonian, Smithsonian, Wilsonian, Grandisonian, Tennysonian, Amazonian, Shoshonean, Pyrrhonian, Neronian, Ciceronian, chelonian, Scillonian, Apollonian, Babylonian, Thessalonian **.12** amnion, epilimnion, hypolimnion **.13** Bosnian

28.3.9
Graafian, Orphean, ruffian, nymphean,

Delphian, Falstaffian, Halafian, Natufian, Christadelphian, Philadelphian

28.3.10
Vivian, Vivien, Vyvyan, avian, Évian®, Shavian, Flavian, Servian, Jovian, Latvian, Maldivian, Bolivian, oblivion, Batavian, Octavian, Moldavian, Moravian, Belgravian, subclavian, Labovian, Peruvian, Vitruvian, Vesuvian, diluvian, alluvion, Chekhovian, Varsovian, Harrovian, Monrovian, Pavlovian, Scandinavian, Yugoslavian, antediluvian

28.3.11
Lethean, Pythian, Parthian, pantheon, Promethean, Carpathian, Hogarthian, Corinthian, labyrinthian

28.3.12
Scythian, Lothian, Wordsworthian, Midlothian

28.3.13
panacean, piscean, Mysian, Lycian, Odyssean, Dionysian, Cilician, Galician, Ordovician, Dacian, Athanasian, Hessian, Circassian, Parnassian, Gaussian, homoiousian, homoousian, Ossian, Roscian, Joycean, Piscean, Lucian, homousian, traducian, Venusian, Belorussian, Andalusian, Mercian, Phocian, Procyon, Cappadocian, Maglemosian, Capsian, Keatsian, Yeatsian, Leibnizian, Marxian, Waldensian, Valencian, Albigensian, Premonstratensian, halcyon

28.3.14
Miesian, Frisian, artesian, Cartesian, Etesian, magnesian, Belizean, Milesian, Silesian, Salesian, Indonesian, Tunisian, Dionysian, Parisian, Elysian, nasion, Vespasian, Caucasian, Malaysian, Transcaucasian, Athanasian, Rabelaisian, Abkhazian, Levalloisean, Tardenoisian, Venusian, Carthusian, Malthusian, homoiousian, homoousian, ambrosian, Maglemosian, Holmesian, Keynesian, Dickensian

28.3.15
Decian, Rhaetian, Priscian, Haitian, Roscian, Lucian, Mercian, Phocian, gentian, Domitian, Cilician, Galician, Ordovician, ornithischian, Appalachian, Cappadocian

28.3.16
Etesian, Thuringian, Varangian, Merovingian, Carlovingian, Carolingian

28.3.17
Nietzschean, Appalachian

28.3.18
Stygian, Phrygian, magian, Fujian, collegian, Ogygian, Pelagian, Swedenborgian, neologian, theologian, Thuringian, Varangian, Pelasgian, callipygian, Cantabrigian, philologian, Merovingian, Carlovingian, Carolingian

28.3.19
Malawian, Zimbabwean, Algonquian

28.3.20
Korean **.1** Irian, Tyrian, Syrian, empyrean, Assyrian, Illyrian **.2** Zairian, Pierian, Napierian, Hyperion, Hesperian, Shakespearean, Iberian, Siberian, Liberian, criterion, Mousterian, Cimmerian, Sumerian, Skinnerian, Wagnerian, eutherian, Chaucerian, Spenserian, Cancerian, mezereon, Nigerian, Nigerien, Algerian, valerian, Keplerian, Hitlerian, Adlerian, Whistlerian, trans-Siberian, Presbyterian, phalansterian, Hanoverian, metatherian, prototherian **.3** Merrion, Portmeirion **.4** Arian, Aryan, Parian, Darien, Marian, apiarian, topiarian, Ripuarian, Indo-Aryan, riparian, barbarian, fruitarian, Rotarian, nectarean, sectarian, Tractarian, tractarian, libertarian, sabbatarian, Trinitarian, sanitarian, Unitarian, Sauveterrian, vegetarian, Sagittarian, proletarian, unsectarian, parliamentarian, Gibraltarian, quodlibetarian, humanitarian, communitarian, necessitarian, ubiquitarian, authoritarian, majoritarian, utilitarian, futilitarian, totalitarian, egalitarian, equalitarian, sacramentarian, establishmentarian, antisabbatarian, uniformitarian, antitrinitarian, inegalitarian, Europarliamentarian, abecedarian, Tocharian, Hungarian, Bulgarian, vulgarian, grammarian, planarian, octonarian, centenarian, seminarian, veterinarian, doctrinarian, millenarian, predestinarian, septuagenarian, octogenarian, nonagenarian, sexagenarian, quinquagenarian, quadragenarian, disciplinarian, latitudinarian, platitudinarian, valetudinarian, Rastafarian, ovarian, Bavarian, Althusserian, necessarian, prelapsarian, sublapsarian, supralapsarian, infralapsarian, caesarean, rosarian, Aquarian, antiquarian, librarian, contrarian, agrarian, sub-librarian, malarian, radiolarian, turbellarian **.5** Carian, carrion, Marion, clarion **.6** morion, quarrian **.7** Taurean, Dorian, chorion, saurian, praetorian, pretorian, Victorian, suctorian, stentorian, historian, Nestorian, Gregorian, censorian, centurion, Arthurian, tellurian, Silurian, Delorean, Singaporean, Hyperborean, oratorian, prehistorian, Salvadorean, Ecuadorean, Terpsichorean, dinosaurian, holothurian, salutatorian, valedictorian **.8** Missourian, Manchurian, Marlburian, Ligurian, Khachaturian, turion, durian, Ben-Gurion **.9** Cyprian **.10** Cambrian, Umbrian, Cumbrian, Cantabrian, Calabrian, Precambrian, neo-Cambrian, Northumbrian **.11** Sartrean, Bactrian, Istrian, Austrian, Amphitryon, Solutrean, pedestrian, equestrian, Lancastrian, Maharashtrian, Zoroastrian, Zarathustrian **.12** Adrian, Adrienne, Hadrian, Mondriaan, salamandrian, Alexandrian, mitochondrion **.13** Anacreon **.14** Ugrian, Finno-Ugrian

28.3.21
.1 Pelion, Delian, abelian, Froebelian, Mendelian, Handelian, chameleon, carnelian, cornelian, aphelion, anthelion, parhelion, Sahelian,

Aurelian, Karelian, perihelion, Aristotelian, Mephisthophelean, Mephisthophelian **.2** pillion, billion, gillion, million, zillion, Chilean, Gillian, jillion, Jillian, squillion, trillion, hellion, stallion, Lilian, Lillian, epyllion, cotillion, septillion, reptilian, quintillion, Quintilian, Antillean, Castilian, postilion, postillion, sextillion, modillion, Tamilian, vermilion, Pamphylian, pavilion, civilian, Abbevillian, vaudevillian, Bougainvillian, caecilian, coecilian, Sicilian, Tresillian, Azilian, Brazilian, Churchillian, Vergilian, Virgilian, carillon, quatrillion, quadrillion, lacertilian, crocodilian, Maximilian, rebellion, Italian, medallion, slumgullion, multimillion **.3** alien, Salian, Walian, Castalian, Daedalian, Deucalion, Hegelian, mammalian, Pygmalion, Westphalian, Thessalian, Australian, madrigalian, saturnalian, bacchanalian, episcopalian, Sardanapalian, sesquipedalian, tatterdemalion **.4** Chellean, Sabellian, triskelion, Trevelyan, Orwellian, Cromwellian, Machiavellian **.5** talion, scallion, galleon, battalion, rapscallion **.6** Dalian, Malian, Somalian, Himalayan **.7** Jolyon, Apollyon **.8** scullion, mullion, Tertullian **.9** bullion **.10** Boolean, Julian, Julien, Friulian, Acheulian, cerulean **.11** aeolian, eolian, napoleon, Mongolian, simoleon, Ashmolean, Tyrolean, capitolian, Anatolian **.12** Bodleian, Liverpudlian **.13** Heraklion **.14** Zwinglian, Anglian, ganglion **.15** penillion **.16** Wesleyan

28.3.22
Gwenllian, penillion

28.4
ain, pain, Paine, pane, Payn, Payne, Spain, Bain, bane, ta'en, stain, Dane, deign, Cain, Caine, cane, Kane, skein, gain, main, Maine, mane, Mayne, fain, fane, feign, vain, vane, vein, thane, thegn, sane, Seine, seine, Zane, Shane, chain, Jain, Jane, jane, Jayne, Hain, wain, Waine, wane, Wayne, twain, Duane, Dwane, swain, rain, Raine, reign, rein, sprain, brain, Braine, train, strain, drain, crane, grain, Frayn, Frayne, lain, lane, plain, plane, blain, slain, chow mein, Sinn Fein, coup de main, mise en scène

28.4.1
propane, campaign, champagne, champaign, marchpane, counterpane, windowpane, frangipane, Port-of-Spain, cyclopropane, elecampane

28.4.2
fleabane, cowbane, urbane, McBain, henbane, ratsbane, wolfsbane

28.4.3
cetane, butane, attain, reattain, pertain, detain, retain, heptane, obtain, octane, maintain, pentane, plantain, Montaigne, montane, Fonteyn, contain, Bloemfontein, cysteine, Costain, sustain, abstain, bloodstain, sextain, Holstein, Beltane, appertain, entertain, ascertain, Aquitaine, chevrotain, neopentane,

tramontane, transmontane, La Fontaine, elastane, isooctane, ultramontane

28.4.4
ordain, preordain, chlordane, lindane, mondaine, mundane, disdain, Haldane, foreordain, transpadane, demi-mondaine, antemundane, supermundane, supramundane, extramundane, ultramundane

28.4.5
decane, arcane, Duquesne, cocaine, McCain, chicane, procain, procaine, Biscayne, alkane, lidocaine, sugarcane, lignocaine, Novocaine®, benzocaine, marocain, cycloalkane

28.4.6
regain, again, salangane

28.4.7
pearmain, Charmaine, humane, amain, Pomagne®, ptomaine, demesne, domain, domaine, germane, Jermaine, remain, romaine, Tremain, Germaine, mortmain, Moulmein, Castlemaine, inhumane, Quartermaine, codomain, Alamein, Charlemagne, balletomane, legerdemain

28.4.8
inane, Dunsinane

28.4.9
profane, hydrophane, Cellophane®

28.4.10
vervain, Alfvén, weathervane, paravane

28.4.11
ethane, methane, urethane, ethoxyethane, trichloroethane, polyurethane

28.4.12
Hussein, sixain, hexane, insane, purse-seine, dioxane, cyclohexane

28.4.13
quatorzain

28.4.14
Duchesne, McShane

28.4.15
enchain, unchain, push-chain, pull-chain, watchchain

28.4.16
Ujjain

28.4.17
haywain, Gawain, cordwain, McIlwain

28.4.18
terrain, terrane, Bahrain, arraign, moraine, Lorraine, unrein, vicereine, Coleraine, borane, murrain, souterrain, riverain, suzerain, forebrain, midbrain, birdbrain, hindbrain, McBrain, lamebrain, membrane, scatterbrain, detrain, seatrein, retrain, quatrain, entrain, restrain, eye strain, distrain, constrain, Coltrane, linertrain, hovertrain, overtrain, aerotrain, overstrain, check rein, Ukraine, migraine,

grosgrain, ingrain, engrain, wholegrain,
Cassegrain, refrain

28.4.19
Spillane, Verlaine, Alleyne, Elaine, delaine,
Faslane, Coeur d'Alene, underlain, overlain,
villein, air lane, mullein, silane, chatelaine,
Madelaine, madeleine, Tamerlane, porcelain,
purslane, Tamburlaine, deplane, ski-plane,
seaplane, airplane, terreplein, warplane,
biplane, triplane, towplane, floatplane,
emplane, Champlain, complain, mainplane,
enplane, proof-plane, explain, tailplane,
sailplane, volplane, peneplain, monoplane,
aquaplane, aeroplane, gyroplane, hydroplane,
Dunblane, chilblain, McLean

28.5
en, n, pen, Penn, Spen, Behn, Ben, Benn, ten,
den, ken, men, Nene, fen, then, Zen, gen, hen,
wen, when, Gwen, Rennes, wren, Bren, yen, Len,
glen, Glenn, cayenne, doyenne, Nguyen, UN,
Phnom Penh, but and ben, La Tène, white men,
Etienne, Vivienne, persiennes, Adrienne,
julienne, mise en scène, comedienne,
tragedienne, varsovienne, Valenciennes,
equestrienne, ticket-of-leave men

28.5.1
doyen

28.5.2
playpen, Inkpen, pigpen, fountainpen,
cattlepen

28.5.3
pecten

28.5.4
Ardennes, Ogaden

28.5.5
henequen

28.5.6
again

28.5.7
amen **.1** he-men **.2** shantymen, safetymen,
handymen, bogeymen, bogymen, dairymen,
tallymen, committeemen, deliverymen
.3 Indiamen **.4** stamen, flamen, gravamen,
examen, foramen **.5** repairmen **.6** Carmen,
ramen **.7** strawmen, lawmen **.8** hymen, limen
.9 Shumen, rumen, lumen, cerumen,
catechumen **.10** firemen, wiremen,
supermen, lumbermen, motormen,
spidermen, anchormen, hammermen,
overmen, weathermen, regimen,
cameramen, newspapermen **.11** mermen
.12 nomen, snowmen, foemen, praenomen,
agnomen, cognomen, absit omen **.13** apemen,
topmen **.14** submen **.15** hitmen, gatemen,
nightmen, stuntmen, frontmen, liftmen,
Minutemen, selectmen **.16** freedmen,
headmen, admen, yardmen, sidemen,
roadmen **.17** packmen, trackmen, linkmen,
milkmen **.18** legmen, bagmen, gagmen,

swagmen, ragmen, dogmen **.19** binmen,
trainmen, fenmen, con men, gunmen
.20 wingmen, hangmen, strongmen
.21 wolf-men **.22** cavemen **.23** Northmen,
earthmen **.24** pacemen, spacemen, chessmen,
pressmen, gasmen, Norsemen, icemen, axemen,
taxmen, businessmen, ambulancemen
.25 jazzmen, newsmen **.26** trashmen
.27 sandwich-men **.28** wheelmen, mailmen,
oilmen, schoolmen, stablemen, middlemen,
patrolmen

28.5.8
Nurofen®, acetaminophen

28.5.9
Cévennes, Leuven

28.5.10
Tlemcen, samisen, Sun Yat-sen

28.5.11
zazen

28.5.12
Duchenne

28.5.13
Shenzhen

28.5.14
Chechen

28.5.15
cryogen, cultigen, pathogen, Origen, androgen,
allergen, Sanatogen®

28.5.16
peahen, greyhen, moorhen

28.5.17
Corwen, Blodwen, Ogwen, somewhen, Anwen,
Ceinwen

28.5.18
Karen, Dairen, paren, Loren, Opren®

28.5.19
Guyenne, Saint-Étienne

28.5.20
Crossmaglen

28.6
bairn, Bern, Berne, cairn, Nairn, Fairbairn,
Pitcairn, Auvergne

28.7
an, Ann, Anne, Pan, pan, panne, span, ban, tan,
dan, can, Cannes, scan, man, Mann, nan, fan,
van, vin, Schwann, tanh, than, san, Shan, Xian,
Chan, Jan, Han, WAN, ran, bran, cran, scran,
gran, Fran, Llan, plan, clan, Klan, flan, Leanne,
liane, Lianne, Dayan, Diane, Cheyenne, yuan,
Joanne, CAT scan, white man, Ariane, Marianne,
Adrianne, Peter Pan, Isle of Man, Kunlun Shan,
Ku Klux Klan, ticket-of-leave man

28.7.1
ASEAN

28.7.2
cyan

28.7.3
koan

28.7.4
claypan, sapan, tarpan, taipan, Saipan, frypan, stewpan, Japan, trepan, Chopin, pitpan, dustpan, saltpan, skidpan, bedpan, deadpan, hardpan, tampan, sampan, brainpan, outspan, spick-and-span, inspan, wingspan, lifespan, dishpan, ash pan, pattypan, Matapan, tragopan, Belmopan, marzipan, Algipan

28.7.5
Laban, Strabane, kanban, unban, Martaban, Caliban, Seremban

28.7.6
rattan, Powhatan, fan-tan, suntan, constantan, kaftan, mercaptan, Athelstan, orangutan: (+ **28.9.2**)

28.7.7
Friedan, Cardin, sedan, Sudan, redan, Rodin, randan, Abadan, Ramadan, shandrydan

28.7.8
pecan, Lacan, toucan, McCann, Spokane, cancan, ashcan, trashcan, Alcan®, oilcan, jerrycan, billycan, Arakan, astrakhan, ryokan, scintiscan, Leninakan

28.7.9
Sagan, began, Gauguin, Afghan

28.7.10
deman, reman, Amman, unman, Gell-Mann, man-to-man, Omdurman, overman **.1** he-man **.2** shantyman, safetyman, handyman, bogeyman, bogyman, dairyman, tallyman, committeeman, deliveryman **.3** Indiaman **.4** repairman **.5** strawman, lawman **.6** wireman, Superman, lumberman, motorman, spiderman, Turkoman, anchorman, hammerman, weatherman, cameraman, everyman, Telemann, newspaperman **.7** merman **.8** snowman **.9** apeman, topman **.10** subman **.11** gateman, Batman, nightman, stuntman, frontman, liftman, Minuteman, selectman **.12** freedman, headman, adman, yardman, sideman, roadman, sandman **.13** packman, Pac-man®, trackman, linkman **.14** legman, bagman, gagman, swagman, ragman, dogman **.15** binman, trainman, fenman, con man, gunman **.16** wingman, hangman, strongman **.17** wolf-man **.18** caveman **.19** earthman **.20** paceman, spaceman, chessman, pressman, gasman, iceman, axeman, taxman, businessman, ambulanceman **.21** jazzman, newsman **.22** trashman **.23** sandwich-man **.24** wheelman, mailman, oilman, schoolman, stableman, middleman, Winckelmann, patrolman

28.7.11
Tsinan, Jinan, Tainan, Hunan, Yunnan, Onan, Honan, Poznan

28.7.12
tryptophan, Kordofan, turbofan

28.7.13
Ivan, Louvain, pavane, divan, brake van, Ativan®, minivan, Aberfan, Yerevan, caravan

28.7.14
Nissan®, Nisan, Poussin, Pusan, Roxanne, Elsan®, Salvarsan, Phyllosan

28.7.15
tisane, ptisan, Cézanne, Suzanne, Kazan, Hazan, Rosanne, Roseanne, Lausanne, artisan, partisan, bartizan, courtesan, parmesan, bipartisan

28.7.16
Anshan, Zhongshan

28.7.17
Abidjan, Harijan, Birobidzhan

28.7.18
Wuhan, Cohan, Moynihan, Hanrahan, Callaghan

28.7.19
Aswan

28.7.20
reran, Iran, Tehran, Dhahran, shoran, foreran, Oran, Moran, saran, serein, outran, Fortran, Couperin, Alcoran, trimaran, overran, Mazarin, catamaran

28.7.21
banyan

28.7.22
élan, Elan, courlan, Milan, replan, pre-plan, Catalan, gamelan, Acrilan®, rataplan, Ameslan

28.8
town, Towne, down, gown, noun, Braun, brown, Browne, drown, crown, frown, clown, triple crown, Camden Town

28.8.1
Freetown, cowtown, toytown, Newtown, Motown®, uptown, midtown, Yorktown, boomtown, hometown, downtown, Longtown, crosstown, Princetown, Kingstown, Jamestown, Grahamstown, Queenstown, Youngstown, Bridgetown, Georgetown, shantytown, Chinatown, Levittown, Charlottetown, Allentown, Cooperstown, Tinseltown, Tamla Motown®

28.8.2
adown, low-down, sitdown, cutdown, run-down, thumbs-down, upside-down **.1** eiderdown **.2** godown, showdown, hoedown, slowdown **.3** step-down, clampdown **.4** rubdown **.5** letdown, shutdown, putdown, countdown, pastedown, Piltdown, meltdown **.6** kickdown, takedown, shakedown, breakdown, crackdown, markdown **.7** comedown, climbdown **.8** pin-down, Sandown, sundown, rundown, wind-down, turndown, Southerndown **.9** Southdown **.10** phasedown, close-down, Lansdowne, swansdown **.11** Ashdown, splashdown, pushdown **.12** touchdown, Churchdown

.13 pulldown, hold-down, tumbledown, thistledown

28.8.3
nightgown

28.8.4
renown, pronoun

28.8.5
embrown, uncrown

28.9
Arne, Avon, pan, barn, tarn, darn, Caen, Calne, Kahn, khan, skarn, Mahon, Marne, Shan, Siân, Hahn, guan, Juan, yarn, larn, Laugharne, liane, Tai'an, Dayan, douane, yuan, San Juan, Vientiane, Aga Khan, Kublai Khan, Ayub Khan, Genghis Khan, t'ai chi ch'uan

28.9.1
Iban, Autobahn

28.9.2
Bhutan, soutane, Pathan, Yucatán, Hindustan, Bantustan, Tatarstan, Baltistan, Kurdistan, Pakistan, Turkestan, Kyrgyzstan, Dagestan, Rajasthan, Nuristan, Kazakhstan, Tajikistan, Uzbekistan, Turkmenistan, Afghanistan, Baluchistan: (+ **28.7.6**)

28.9.3
maidan, Sudan, Abadan, Ramadan, Ramadhan, Port Sudan

28.9.4
lucarne, Michoacán, Taklimakan

28.9.5
tzigane, Kurgan, Dingaan, Trefgarne

28.9.6
Amman, Oman, McMahon, Othman, hanuman, Omdurman, Turkoman, nouveau roman, Bildungsroman

28.9.7
Kordofan, Lindisfarne

28.9.8
Ivan, pavane

28.9.9
Nisan, Hassan, Khoisan

28.9.10
Abidjan, Azerbaijan, Birobidzhan

28.9.11
Isfahan

28.9.12
Taiwan, dewan, Antoine, Bhagwan, Aswan, Sichuan, Yinchuan, macédoine

28.9.13
Iran, Tehran, Dhahran, Wahran, Koran, Oran, Qumran, Huascarán, Alcoran

28.9.14
Vientiane, Karajan

28.9.15
uhlan, Tenochtitlán

28.10
Hon., on, 'pon, Bonn, don, con, conn, scone, gone, Mon, non, phon, von, shone, john, Jon, St John, wan, won, swan, Swann, Schwann, Ron, Fron, yon, León, Bayonne, spot-on, side-on, off and on, nem con, logon, dies non, odds-on, whereon, thereon, Nuevo León, Asunción, chateaubriand, sine qua non

28.10.1
aeon, peon, neon, jeon, prion, Creon, Freon®, Leon

28.10.2
dupion, tachyon, logion, fermion, thermion, baryon, chorion, Pelion, nucleon, himation, Apollyon, Ceredigion, Mabinogion, epilimnion

28.10.3
kaon, rayon, crayon, Leon

28.10.4
ion, pion, Psion®, parathion

28.10.5
muon, gluon, Fluon®

28.10.6
Laocoon, epizoon, protozoon, ectozoon, spermozoon, spermatozoon

28.10.7
Nippon, zip-on, capon, yaupon, coupon, upon, tampon, kampong, crampon, pompon, sit-upon, hereupon, thereupon, whereupon

28.10.8
Narbonne, Bourbon, Sorbonne, Gabon, bonbon, Audubon

28.10.9
piton, Teton, Breton, cretonne, baton, chiton, futon, croûton, muton, pluton, photon, proton, krypton, lepton, nekton, Anton, Danton, Canton, canton, wonton, neuston, Ikhnaton, eschaton, Benetton®, magneton, graviton, exciton, Balaton, phlogiston, hyperbaton, antiproton, Tetragrammaton

28.10.10
radon, Proudhon, codon, glyptodon, mastodon, Mogadon®, Chalcedon, mylodon, pteranodon, iguanodon, anticodon

28.10.11
Nikon®, racon, chaconne, archon, walk-on, icon, ikon, Yukon, zircon, ancon, mascon, Rubicon, Comecon, ostracon, Helicon, Oerlikon®, emoticon, eirenicon, catholicon, stereopticon

28.10.12
Dagon, argon, Sargon, doggone, logon, foregone, bygone, tigon, Saigon, trigon, begone, trogon, outgone, Elgon, Wobegon, woebegone, heptagon, undergone, decagon, nonagon, tetragon, estragon, polygon, parergon, dodecagon, hendecagon, undecagon

28.10.13
Ramón, Timon, gnomon, Jomon, etymon, telamon

28.10.14
ninon, xenon, Trianon, guenon, anon, xoanon, phonon, Memnon, Rhiannon, Maintenon, organon, Simenon, noumenon, Parthenon, Algernon, olecranon, Agamemnon, properispomenon

28.10.15
chiffon, antiphon, Xenophon, Ctesiphon, agraphon, balafon, colophon, Bellerophon

28.10.16
Evonne, Yvonne, Avon, afon, Arfon, bon vivant, elevon

28.10.17
talkathon, walkathon, trilithon, telethon, autochthon, anacoluthon

28.10.18
frisson, caisson, garçon, Tucson, Epson, boson, soupçon, exon, Exxon®, axon, taxon, Oxon, chanson, Besançon, Carcassonne, Aubusson

28.10.19
meson, Quezon, raisons d'être, blouson, Luzon, K-meson, pi-meson, mu-meson, liaison, Barbizon, borazon

28.10.20
torchon, outshone, cabochon

28.10.21
Inchon

28.10.22
Upjohn, Brownjohn, Fitzjohn, Littlejohn, Meiklejohn, demijohn

28.10.23
Taiwan, Erewhon

28.10.24
Perón, whereon, Caron, Garonne .1 interferon .2 Charon .3 boron, moron, oxymoron .4 Styron .5 neuron, Huron, pleuron, fleuron, operon, hyperon, Auberon, Oberon, deuteron, Calderón, Acheron, megaron, Percheron, longeron, vigneron, aileron, ephemeron, diatessaron, erigeron, hysteron proteron .6 Hebron, Heilbronn .7 natron, neutron, cistron, klystron, ignitron, betatron, kenotron, dynatron, magnetron, bevatron, mesotron, positron, thyratron, synchrotron, elytron, mellotron, cyclotron, electron, animatron, anti-electron, photoelectron, synchrocyclotron .8 hadron .9 macron, Akron, Dacron®, micron, omicron, millimicron .10 neophron, nephron

28.10.25
bouillon, piñon, mignon, chignon, court-bouillon, Sauvignon, Cro-Magnon, Concepción, carillon

28.10.26
Colón, colon, Ceylon, halon, Dralon®, salon, Marlon, Orlon®, pylon, nylon, bri-nylon, papillon, propylon, Babylon, etalon, petalon, Miquelon, Ashqelon, Semillon, Avalon, epsilon, echelon, carillon, abutilon, encephalon, mesencephalon, prosencephalon, stolon, Solon, roll-on, eidolon, semicolon, Simplon, Fablon®, Teflon®, mouflon, Revlon®, Savlon®, biathlon, triathlon, heptathlon, pentathlon, decathlon, tetrathlon, Caslon

28.11
Alne, awn, pawn, porn, spawn, born, borne, bourn, torn, dawn, corn, scorn, Maughan, morn, mourn, Mourne, Norn, faun, fawn, Vaughan, Vaughn, thorn, Thorne, sawn, Sean, Shaun, shorn, horn, Horne, warn, worn, Quorn®, sworn, prawn, Braun, brawn, Strachan, drawn, thrawn, yawn, lawn, lorn, Bjorn, famille jaune

28.11.1
frogspawn

28.11.2
reborn, freeborn, forborne, highborn, newborn, suborn, inborn, unborn, self-born, baseborn, stillborn, overborne, seaborne, Caborn, Brabourne, Claiborne, airborne, Fairbourne, waterborne, Winterbourne, Sherbourne, Ayckbourn, Wimborne, Camborne, Cranborne, Glyndebourne, Pangbourne, Sittingbourne, Eastbourne, firstborn, Broxbourne, Osborn, Usborne, Wellesbourne, Washbourne, Tichborne, Melbourne, Selborne, Golborne

28.11.3
wartorn, althorn

28.11.4
adorn, Apeldoorn

28.11.5
acorn, tricorne, popcorn, sweetcorn, seedcorn, Runcorn, einkorn, barleycorn, peppercorn, tubicorn, unicorn, longicorn, leprechaun, Capricorn, lamellicorn

28.11.6
yestermorn

28.11.7
Siobhan

28.11.8
Crathorne, hawthorn, Crowthorne, whitethorn, Pickthorne, quickthorn, blackthorn, buckthorn, Worsthorne

28.11.9
unshorn

28.11.10
dehorn, shoehorn, alphorn, shorthorn, Whitehorn, posthorn, althorn, Findhorn, inkhorn, stinkhorn, bighorn, leghorn, foghorn, krummhorn, greenhorn, tinhorn, alpenhorn, pronghorn, longhorn, hartshorn, Hartshorne, saxhorn, bullhorn, Flügelhorn, Matterhorn, Little Bighorn

28.11.11
way-worn, careworn, forewarn, warworn,
shopworn, outworn, timeworn, unworn,
foresworn, unsworn, toilworn, weatherworn

28.11.12
redrawn, wiredrawn, indrawn, withdrawn,
overdrawn

28.11.13
Allaun, forlorn, lovelorn

28.12
Boyne, coign, coin, quoin, Moyne, join, groin,
groyne, loin, Ardoyne, Dordogne, recoin,
Gascoigne, Burgoyne, Des Moines, sainfoin,
rejoin, adjoin, subjoin, enjoin, conjoin, unjoin,
disjoin, Boulogne, purloin, sirloin, talapoin,
tenderloin

28.13
pun, spun, bun, ton, tonne, tun, stun, done,
Donne, dun, Dunn, Dunne, gun, Gunn, none,
nun, Nunn, fun, son, sun, sunn, shun, hon, Hun,
one, won, run, Lunn, Clun, sten gun, Bren gun,
no one, trial run, dummy run, Sally Lunn,
submachine gun

28.13.1
homespun, fine-spun

28.13.2
honeybun

28.13.3
megaton, kiloton

28.13.4
redone, Verdun, outdone, undone, underdone,
overdone

28.13.5
speargun, air gun, begun, shogun, blowgun,
popgun, outgun, shotgun, handgun, sixgun,
flashgun, supergun, scattergun, son-of-a-gun

28.13.6
Altarnun

28.13.7
stepson, godson, grandson, Intasun

28.13.8
someone, one-to-one, anyone, everyone

28.13.9
rerun, forerun, sheeprun, outrun, endrun,
tip-and-run, hit-and-run, pressrun, pinch-run,
overrun

28.13.10
balun

28.14
pine, spine, bine, tine, Tyne, stein, dine, dyne,
kine, Main, mine, nine, fine, Fyne, vine, thine,
sign, sine, syne, shine, sinh, chine, whine, wine,
twine, swine, Rhine, brine, trine, Strine, shrine,
line, spline, cline, Clyne, Klein, Kline, auld lang
syne, party line, leger line, Mason–Dixon Line,
Maginot Line, Newcastle upon Tyne

28.14.1
Hirwaun

28.14.2
Owain

28.14.3
rapine, orpine, supine, lupine, opine, repine,
vespine, pitchpine, alpine, vulpine, Proserpine,
porcupine, subalpine, McAlpine, cisalpine,
transalpine

28.14.4
Sabine, carbine, turbine, hop-bine, woodbine,
combine, Holbein, concubine, recombine,
columbine

28.14.5
vespertine, serotine, Palatine, nemertine,
lacertine, tontine, turpentine, serpentine,
Constantine, clementine, infantine, Levantine,
Byzantine, Argentine, Tridentine, diamantine,
Diophantine, cispontine, transpontine,
Florentine, Ballantine, valentine, eglantine,
adamantine, elephantine, chryselephantine,
Epstein, Goldstein, Sixtine, Bechstein, Einstein,
Bernstein, Rubinstein, Lichtenstein,
Liechtenstein, Wildenstein, Frankenstein,
Wittgenstein, Eisenstein, Finkelstein, asbestine,
clandestine, Augustine, Hammerstein,
Philistine, celestine, Palestine, amethystine,
Heseltine

28.14.6
Gardyne, sardine, Jardine, Pendine, condign,
Aldine, Haseldine, muscadine, anodyne,
Sensodyne®, Considine, aerodyne, chlorodyne,
heterodyne, acridine, hirundine, almandine,
celandine, incarnadine, superheterodyne

28.14.7
piscine, alkyne

28.14.8
carmine, landmine, goldmine, coalmine,
coppermine, countermine, undermine,
sycamine, melamine, calamine

28.14.9
canine, Pennine, leonine, benign, trans-Pennine,
saturnine, Antonine, adenine, pavonine,
Fescennine, asinine, oscinine, arginine, alanine,
phenylalanine

28.14.10
define, refine, trephine, confine, superfine,
redefine, overfine

28.14.11
Torfaen, corvine, Glühwein, Devine, divine,
Irvine, nervine, cervine, ovine, bovine,
grapevine, ovibovine

28.14.12
Jugurthine, hyacinthine, acanthine,
terebinthine, labyrinthine, Rhadamanthine,
amaranthine

28.14.13
V-sign, resign, piscine, oscine, porcine, assign,
reassign, ursine, versine, hircine, cosine, Euxine,

ensign, consign, calcine, psittacine, countersign, undersign, sphingosine, haversine, thylacine, brank-ursine, reconsign, internecine, asbestosine, australopithecine

28.14.14
design, resign

28.14.15
shoeshine, outshine, sunshine, moonshine, earthshine, monkeyshine

28.14.16
androgyne

28.14.17
entwine, untwine, equine, Boscawen, intertwine

28.14.18
taurine, murine, murrhine, caprine, zebrine, eccrine, enshrine, viverrine, estuarine, leporine, viperine, catarrhine, platyrrhine, uterine, sapphirine, zollverein, riverine, passerine, anserine, vulturine, sciurine, lemurine, colubrine, lacustrine, adulterine, meandrine, apocrine, endocrine, exocrine, helleborine, aventurine, alabastrine, salamandrine, alexandrine, intrauterine

28.14.19
reline, align, realign, malign, moline, frontline, hardline, on-line, interline, underline, misalign, Ashton-under-Lyne **.1** beeline, feline, treeline **.2** bodyline, storyline **.3** saline, thermohaline **.4** vitelline, isabelline **.5** airline, Baerlein, hairline **.6** ralline **.7** carline **.8** Pauline, shoreline, jawline **.9** Fräulein **.10** byline, skyline **.11** hyaline, opaline, Ghibelline, sibylline, timberline, petaline, metalline, Catiline, waterline, quarter-line, centreline, crystalline, Capitoline, polycrystalline, microcrystalline, cryptocrystalline, Adeline, borderline, alkaline, saxicoline, rosaniline, penduline, aquiline, inquiline, Caroline, coralline, reguline, Ursuline **.12** towline, snowline **.13** hipline, strapline, pipeline, helpline **.14** dateline, chatline, outline, hotline, nightline, sightline, buntline, waistline, coastline **.15** midline, deadline, headline, redline, breadline, yardline, bloodline, tideline, guideline, sideline, handline, landline **.16** neckline, decline, recline, incline, disincline, syncline, anticline, thermocline, monocline, microcline **.17** dragline **.18** streamline, slimline, hemline, tramline, rhumb-line, plumbline **.19** mainline, Heinlein **.20** lifeline, roofline **.21** baseline **.22** clothes line **.23** catchline, touchline, punchline

28.15
tabun

28.16
poon, spoon, boon, Boone, Doone, coon, Kuhn, Scone, goon, moon, noon, soon, tune, dune, June, hoon, swoon, rune, prune, Troon, croon, loon, lune

28.16.1
harpoon, lampoon, teaspoon, soupspoon, tablespoon, dessertspoon

28.16.2
baboon

28.16.3
spittoon, Béthune, ratoon, cartoon, platoon, pontoon, spontoon, festoon, Saskatoon, musketoon

28.16.4
cardoon, lardoon, bridoon, vodun, Muldoon, rigadoon, Brigadoon

28.16.5
raccoon, puccoon, tycoon, cocoon, racoon, Cancún, veldskoen, barracoon

28.16.6
jargoon, dragoon, lagoon, Irgun, Rangoon

28.16.7
simoon, honeymoon, Tutankhamun

28.16.8
forenoon, Dunoon, kanoon, afternoon

28.16.9
typhoon, buffoon

28.16.10
gossoon, bassoon, caisson, Sassoon, monsoon

28.16.11
jejune

28.16.12
Calhoun, cohune, Colquhoun

28.16.13
maroon, patroon, bestrewn, poltroon, quadroon, Gudrun, gadroon, octaroon, octoroon, picaroon, macaroon, Cameroon

28.16.14
triune, oppugn, impugn, tribune, detune, retune, Béthune, fortune, attune, Neptune, commune, immune, Bethune, picayune, importune, misfortune, opportune, autoimmune, perilune, inopportune, Changchun

28.16.15
Kowloon, Walloon, balloon, galloon, saloon, shalloon, doubloon, perilune, apolune, pantaloon

28.17.1
aeon, eon, Ian, paean, paeon, peon, Behan, skean, Meehan, Meon, Creon, Leon, lien **.1** Tarpeian, European, Cyclopean, pan-European, Indo-European **.2** Sabaean, plebeian, Rugbeian, Maccabean, Jacobean, Caribbean **.3** protean, Actaeon, Dantean, Nabataean, nemertean, Tacitean **.4** Andean, Mandaean, Chaldean, Hebridean **.5** Archaean, Achaean, Manichaean, Nicomachean **.6** Cadmean, pygmean **.7** Minaean, Linnaean, Geminian, Hasmonean, Tanzanian, Pyrenean, monogenean **.8** Orphean, Sisyphean **.9** piscean,

Circean, lyncean, theodicean, Laodicean, Pegasean, Tennesseean, panacean, Sadducean, Andalusian **.10** Kampuchean, Medicean **.11** Aegean, Fijian, Augean, hygeian, apogean, hypogean, perigean **.12** Taurean, empyrean, Eritrean, Hyperborean, Terpsichorean, Pythagorean, epicurean **.13** Berkeleian, Aeschylean, Tyrolean, Carolean, Herculean, Galilean, Sophoclean, Periclean

28.17.2
rayon, crayon, Leon, Ghanaian, Linnaean, Tigrayan, Malayan, Zimbabwean, Eritrean, Himalayan

28.17.3
Cowan, Cowen, gowan, Samhain, rowan, rowen, McCowan, McGowan, Palawan

28.17.4
doyen, Saroyan, Illinoisan, Iroquoian

28.17.5
ion, iron, Gaian, Mayan, cion, cyan, scion, Sion, Syon, Zion, Ryan, prion, Brian, Bryan, Ieuan, lion, Lyon, cation, flatiron, wrought-iron, midiron, gridiron, sad-iron, andiron, anion, Bruneian, Ixion, Hawaiian, Orion, Narayan, O'Brien, ant lion, Geminian, malathion, Marazion, Paraguayan, Uruguayan, zwitterion, dandelion

28.17.6
Papuan, Paduan, Bedouin, Don Juan, Methuen, Saskatchewan, gargantuan, Tuvaluan, Nicaraguan

28.17.7
Siouan, Euan, Labuan, McGoohan, Nauruan, McEwan, Methuen, McLuhan

28.17.8
Owen, powan, Cowen, Goan, Rohan, rowan, Ohioan, Boscawen, Virgoan, Samoan, Minoan, Trethowan, bryozoan, Halesowen, Citroën®, Laocoon, Chicagoan, polyzoan, metazoan, protozoan, protozoon, spermozoon, scyphozoan, anthozoan, hydrozoan, Idahoan, spermatozoan, spermatozoon

28.17.9
steepen, deepen, cheapen, Ripon, Rippon, Crippen, capon, weapon, cap'n, happen, parpen, tarpon, sharpen, ripen, open, tympan, hempen, tampon, dampen, crampon, lampern, lumpen, aspen, saucepan, Halpern, misshapen, reopen, overripen

28.17.10
Theban, gibbon, ribbon, Clibborn, Fitzgibbon, Brabourne, Laban, Eben, ebon, Hepburn, Ruabon, carbon, Harben, graben, radiocarbon, fluorocarbon, hydrocarbon, chlorofluorocarbon, auburn, Bourbon, stubborn, Tyburn, Steuben, Woburn, Reuben, Ruben, Cuban, Marylebone, urban, bourbon, turban, Durban, Sherbourne, suburban, exurban, Cockburn, Manitoban, Hogben, Brisbane, Lisbon, Kilburn, Melbourne, Shelburne, Alban, Breadalbane

28.17.11
.1 Eaton, Eton, beaten, Beaton, Beeton, Bethune, Keaton, neaten, Seaton, seton, Heaton, wheaten, sweeten, Cretan, browbeaten, unbeaten, uneaten, Nuneaton, Cleckheaton, weather-beaten, polychaetan, overeaten **.2** bitten, bittern, Ditton, kitten, mitten, smitten, witan, Witton, written, Britain, Briton, Brittain, Brittan, Britten, Britton, Litton, Lytton, Flitton, Surbiton, frostbitten, hardbitten, backbitten, Crediton, rewritten, typewritten, handwritten, unwritten, underwritten, overwritten, Bulwer-Lytton **.3** Paton, Payton, Peyton, Deighton, phaeton, Satan, straighten, straiten, Drayton, Creighton, laten, Layton, Leighton, Leyton, Clayton **.4** jeton, jetton, Breton, Bretton, Stretton, cretin, threaten, Tibetan, Sowetan, Sino-Tibetan **.5** Ayrton **.6** paten, patten, pattern, Patton, baton, batten, Tatton, Catton, fatten, Saturn, Hatton, Grattan, Gratton, latten, platan, platen, flatten, slattern, Mountbatten, harmattan, Powhatan, Manhattan **.7** Stoughton, Coughton, Houghton, Rowton, Broughton **.8** Aten, partan, Parton, spartan, Barton, tartan, carton, marten, smarten, hearten, Dumbarton, pine marten, Ikhnaton, Akhenaten, dishearten, sauerbraten, Akhetaten, kindergarten **.9** cotton, gotten, rotten, shotten, Wotton, begotten, forgotten, ill-gotten, polycotton, unbegotten, self-begotten, misbegotten, unforgotten, only-begotten **.10** Orton, Porton, boughten, Bourton, tauten, torten, Corton, Gorton, Morton, Naughton, Norton, shorten, chorten, Haughton, Horton, Warton, Wharton, quartan, quartern, Sproughton, Laughton, Lawton, verboten, Throgmorton, McNaghten, McNaughton, Brize Norton, foreshorten, Sachertorten **.11** button, Dutton, mutton, Sutton, Hutton, Clutton, glutton, unbutton, pushbutton **.12** tighten, titan, chitin, chiton, Knighton, heighten, Huyton, whiten, righten, Ryton, Wrighton, brighten, Brighton, triton, Crichton, frighten, lighten, Blyton, enlighten **.13** Wootton **.14** Teuton, Scruton, newton, Luton, gluten, rambutan, Laputan **.15** Ireton, quieten, Temperton, Warburton, Pemberton, hyperbaton, Betterton, Chatterton, Winterton, Chesterton, Salterton, Alderton, asyndeton, Bickerton, Pinkerton, Homerton, automaton, Mahometan, Tetragrammaton, Swinnerton, Benetton®, Honiton, Woofferton, Tiverton, Everton, Claverton, Overton, Yelverton, Dulverton, Wolverton, Atherton, Brotherton, Occitan, Egerton, Sheraton, Coryton, puritan, Alfreton, Samaritan, skeleton, Allerton, tarlatan, charlatan, Ollerton, Colyton, Northallerton, Neapolitan, exoskeleton, endoskeleton, cosmopolitan, metropolitan, megalopolitan **.16** burton, Turton, Stourton, curtain, Curtin, Girton, Merton, certain, Albertan, uncertain **.17** oaten, Coton, croton, Dakotan, Lofoten, Minnesotan **.18** Skipton, Shipton, Lipton, Shepton, Repton, captain, Clapton, Upton,

Shrimpton, Hampton, Rampton, Brampton, Frampton, Compton, Brompton, Crompton, Plumpton, mercaptan, Southampton, Northampton, Roehampton, Rockhampton, Okehampton, Littlehampton, Cullompton, Wolverhampton, Lambton **.19** Geraldton **.20** nekton, lectern, acton, Clacton, Stockton, Buckton, plankton, Monckton, Moncton, Monkton, Fredericton, zooplankton, phytoplankton **.21** Wigton **.22** Tintern, Minton, Hinton, Winton, quintain, quintan, Quinton, Swinton, Frinton, Linton, Lynton, Clinton, Paignton, Stainton, Benton, Denton, Kenton, Fenton, Renton, Trenton, Lenten, Stanton, Staunton, Canton, canton, Scranton, lantern, plantain, Plantin, mountain, fountain, wanton, Swanton, Taunton, Thornton, Pointon, Brunton, fronton, Hunstanton, Wincanton, Table Mountain, Normanton, Edmonton, badminton, jack-o'-lantern, catamountain **.23** Newington, Orpington, Babington, Whittington, Partington, Huntington, Eddington, Teddington, Addington, Paddington, Haddington, Boddington, Waddington, Workington, Pilkington, Symington, Lymington, Remington®, lamington, Wilmington, Pennington, Kennington, Bonington, Donington, Mornington, Skeffington, Chevington, Bravington, Bovington, Withington, Worthington, Blessington, Grassington, Lexington, Easington, Kensington, Ashington, Washington, Sherrington, Carrington, Charrington, Harrington, Warrington, Accrington, Hetherington, Ellington, wellington, Arlington, Darlington, Burlington, Bridlington, Bedlington, Pocklington, Drighlington, Framlington, Islington, Langton, Longton **.24** chieftain, Clifton, Grafton, often, Crofton, Festschriften **.25** eastern, Easton, piston, cistern, Wiston, Wystan, Tristan, Liston, Eddystone, Germiston, Penistone, phlogiston, destine, Keston, Heston, western, Weston, Preston, sebesten, intestine, predestine, Avestan, Midwestern, Aston, pastern, Paston, Edgbaston, Aldermaston, postern, Boston, Royston, Augustan, Syston, Fryston, Houston, Euston, Huston, Palmerston, Coniston, Burnaston, Silverstone, Galveston, Ulverston, Atherstone, Featherstone, Lauriston, sacristan, Wollaston, Kirsten, Thurston, Hurston, Shipston, capstan, Maidstone, Gladstone, Flixton, Exton, sexton, Paxton, Caxton, Saxton, Blackstone, Parkstone, Oxton, Foxton, Hoxton, Buxton, Kirkstone, Folkestone, brimstone, Urmston, Winston, Princeton, Menston, Branston, Cranston, Launceston, Johnston, Dunstan, Gordonstoun, Kingston, tungsten, Livingston, Livingstone, Charleston, Alston, Dalston, Wulstan, Coulston, Huddleston, Ecclestone, Athelstan **.26** Ashton, Rushton **.27** Pilton, Stilton®, Milton, Filton, Shilton, Chiltern, Chilton, Hilton, Hylton, Wilton, Elton, Skelton, melton, Felton, Shelton, Tarleton, Carlton, Charlton, Alton, Dalton, Galton, saltern, Halton, Walton, Chorlton, Carshalton, sultan,

Fulton, Hamilton, Oulton, Poulton, Bolton, Boulton, Doulton®, molten, Molton, Moulton, Kimbolton, Stapleton, Appleton, Poppleton, simpleton, Templeton, doubleton, subaltern, Littleton, Lyttleton, Middleton, Pendleton, Shackleton, Ingleton, singleton, Castleton

28.17.12
.1 Eden, Weedon, Sweden, Bredon, cedarn, Yeadon, Dunedin, boustrophedon, cotyledon, acotyledon, dicotyledon, monocotyledon **.2** bidden, midden, hidden, ridden, stridden, forbidden, unbidden, unhidden, outridden, bestridden, bedridden, hagridden, unridden, overridden **.3** Reardon, Riordan **.4** Aden, Aidan, Baden, Badon, Gaydon, maiden, Hayden, Haydn, Braden, laden, Leiden, Bladon, Blaydon, handmaiden, menhaden, unladen, overladen **.5** deaden, Sneddon, Seddon, redden, leaden, Armageddon **.6** madden, sadden, Haddon, gladden, gladdon, Ibadan, Abaddon, McFadden **.7** Bowden, Howden, louden, Plowden **.8** Arden, pardon, garden, Vardon, harden, lardon, Baden-Baden, Wiesbaden, Kincardine, teagarden, bear garden, Covent Garden, Nevadan, Dolly Varden, Coloradan **.9** modern, sodden, hodden, trodden, postmodern, retrodden, downtrodden, untrodden, Culloden **.10** Auden, bourdon, cordon, Gordon, Norden, Jordan, Hordern, warden, Rawdon, broaden, Transjordan, churchwarden, Invergordon **.11** hoyden, Croydon **.12** sudden **.13** guidon, Phaidon, Sidon, widen, Bryden, Dryden, Leyden, Poseidon **.14** wooden **.15** Barbudan, Bermudan **.16** oppidan, bombardon, Tenterden, mastodon, Myrmidon, Todmorden, Macedon, Chalcedon, Meriden, harridan, Corydon, celadon, mylodon, decapodan, Muhammadan, solenodon, pteranodon, arachnidan, annelidan **.17** Purdon, burden, Burdon, guerdon, unburden, disburden, overburden **.18** Snowden, Snowdon, Foden, Woden, loden **.19** Hebden, Cobden **.20** Walkden, Buckden, Mukden **.21** Ogden **.22** Campden, Cramden **.23** Findon, Swindon, linden, Lindon, tendon, Hendon, Brendan, Grendon, Brandon, Landon, bounden, Spondon, Quarndon, London, Blunden, Hughenden, Harpenden, Cruttenden, Wolfenden, Ovenden, Northenden, Missenden, Essendon, Oxenden, Rwandan, Luandan, abandon, Ugandan, Bagandan, Bugandan, Burundan, Benenden, Clarendon, self-abandon **.24** Longden, Abingdon, Huntingdon, Bovingdon, Farringdon, Hillingdon **.25** Clevedon, Cliveden **.26** Neasden, Wisden, Dresden, Marsden, Hoddesdon, Ramsden, Lumsden, Willesden, Harlesden, Droylsden, Coulsdon **.27** Fielden, wealden, Tilden, Baildon, Eldon, Sheldon, Weldon, Shaldon, Alden, Malden, Maldon, Walden, milden, gulden, olden, golden, Holden, Wimbledon, embolden, beholden

28.17.13
.1 pecan, beacon, deacon, weaken, Mozambican, subdeacon, archdeacon, Mohican, Dominican,

Puerto Rican, Costa Rican, Tanganyikan
.2 dicken, Dickon, thicken, sicken, chicken,
Wiccan, quicken, stricken, Rubicon, requicken,
awestricken, dumbstricken **.3** Aiken, bacon,
taken, Macon, shaken, waken, retaken,
partaken, betaken, untaken, mistaken,
Jamaican, forsaken, unshaken, awaken,
reawaken, overtaken, unmistaken, godforsaken
.4 pekan, beckon, Deccan, reckon, Brecon,
Aztecan, Toltecan **.5** Mackin, bracken, Strachan,
blacken, clachan, slacken, Kilbracken,
McCracken **.6** Aachen, archon, darken, Marcan,
hearken, kraken, Monacan, Petrarchan,
Interlaken **.7** Brocken, lochan, Moroccan
.8 falcon, Lorcan, Menorcan, Minorcan,
Majorcan **.9** Buchan, Abersychan **.10** Steichen,
lichen, liken **.11** Saarbrücken **.12** toucan, Lucan,
Finucane **.13** barbican, Vatican, Optacon,
pemmican, Heineken®, Corsican, Mexican,
lexicon, hurricane, African, Millikan, silicon,
pelican, spellican, Helicon, Gallican, Oerlikon®,
publican, Anglican, Copernican, pantechnicon,
American, ulotrichan, Pan-African, South
African, basilican, republican, Pan-Anglican,
Meso-American, Pan-American, un-American,
South American, interAmerican, malacostracan,
Ibero-American, Spanish-American
.14 Ardnamurchan **.15** oaken, spoken, token,
woken, broken, ryokan, bespoken, outspoken,
plainspoken, unspoken, Hoboken, foretoken,
betoken, awoken, heartbroken, unbroken
.16 napkin **.17** Incan, Lincoln, Mencken, ancon,
Duncan, sunken, drunken, shrunken, Sri
Lankan **.18** brisken, Gascon, Tuscan, Franciscan,
Nebraskan, Alaskan, Etruscan, molluscan,
Athabascan, Madagascan, Della Cruscan
.19 silken, Balcon, Balkan, tulchan, Vulcan,
gerfalcon, gyrfalcon

28.17.14
Strachan, clachan, lochan, tulchan

28.17.15
.1 Egan, Keegan, vegan, Regan, Antiguan
.2 Wigan, Lygon, Newbiggin, Kentigern,
McGuigan, Balbriggan, McGilligan **.3** pagan,
Kagan, Fagan, Hagan, Reagan, Tobagan,
Nijmegen, O'Hagan, Copenhagen **.4** Megan
.5 Bergen **.6** wagon, dragon, lagan, flagon,
bandwagon, Volkswagen®, snapdragon,
pendragon **.7** argon, bargain, jargon **.8** logan,
toboggan **.9** organ, gorgon, Mawgan, Morgan,
morgen, Horgan, Glamorgan, sense-organ
.10 Duggan, Cadogan **.11** tigon, trigon
.12 Dougan **.13** Rattigan, yataghan, martagon,
Vortigern, heptagon, octagon, pentagon,
cardigan, decagon, ptarmigan, Finnegan,
Branigan, brannigan, Flanagan, Donnegan,
nonagon, hexagon, Michigan, Kerrigan, Aragon,
paragon, tarragon, Oregon, origan, Corrigan,
tetragon, estragon, suffragan, Milligan, polygon,
mulligan, hooligan, hendecagon, undecagon,
shenanigan, Magilligan, Penhaligon **.14** Cogan,
shogun, hogan, Wogan, Brogan, Grogan, Logan,

slogan **.15** röntgen **.16** Mangan, Tongan,
Rarotongan

28.17.16
.1 Piman, Beamon, daemon, demon, Niemann,
seaman, semen, Riemann, freeman, Lehmann,
leman, Schliemann, penstemon, Philemon,
cacodemon **.2** Rimmon, Simon, journeyman,
persimmon, Runciman, clergyman, ferryman,
wherryman, dairyman, quarryman, juryman,
liveryman, nurseryman, salaryman,
deliveryman, artilleryman, pantryman,
countryman, infantryman, vestryman,
poultryman, West Countryman, Palfreyman,
cavalryman, tallyman, Plinlimmon, Plynlimon,
assemblyman **.3** spearman, Shearman **.4** Eamon,
Damon, caiman, shaman, Hayman, Bremen,
drayman, layman, gravamen, highwayman,
checkweighman, railwayman, duramen,
Suleiman, velamen **.5** Yemen, Lemmon, lemon
.6 airman, chairman **.7** Amman, Ammon,
gammon, Mammon, famine, salmon, Drammen,
backgammon, Alabaman **.8** bowman, cowman,
ploughman **.9** barman, carman, Carmen,
Scarman, Garman, Sharman, Jarman, Harman,
Harmon, Rahman, Brahman, Tutankhamun
.10 common, uncommon, Roscommon
.11 Bormann, storeman, doorman, Gorman,
Moorman, Mormon, Norman, foreman, lawman,
O'Gorman, longshoreman **.12** summon,
Newcomen **.13** pieman, Timon, Symon, Hyman,
hymen, Wyman, Ryman, limen **.14** woman,
jurywoman, countrywoman, committeewoman,
laywoman, airwoman, chairwoman,
charwoman, forewoman, firewoman,
superwoman, Ulsterwoman, alderwoman,
anchorwoman, fisherwoman, washerwoman,
Yorkshirewoman, everywoman, scrubwoman,
clubwoman, batwoman, postwoman,
aircraftwoman, freedwoman, madwoman,
bondwoman, workwoman, policewoman,
spacewoman, horsewoman, stateswoman,
Scotswoman, yachtswoman, sportswoman,
draftswoman, draughtswoman, craftswoman,
spokeswoman, Manxwoman, cragswoman,
servicewoman, businesswoman,
congresswoman, aircraftswoman, oarswoman,
tribeswoman, bondswoman, guildswoman,
kinswoman, plainswoman, clanswoman,
townswoman, daleswoman, saleswoman,
frontierswoman, freshwoman, Frenchwoman,
Welshwoman, Cornishwoman, Irishwoman,
Englishwoman, Scotchwoman, Dutchwoman,
churchwoman, noblewoman, gentlewoman,
needlewoman, councilwoman **.15** Schumann,
rumen, Trueman, crewman, Neumann,
Newman, numen, human, lumen, cerumen,
ichneumon, subhuman, inhuman, unhuman,
catechumen, energumen, superhuman,
preterhuman **.16** Layamon, fireman,
Doberman, lumberman, peterman, etymon,
Letterman, ottoman, waterman, Quarterman,
lighterman, lobsterman, Ulsterman, abdomen,
Omdurman, Lindemann, Andaman, alderman,

Akerman, checkerman, Ackerman, Zuckerman, Turkoman, dragoman, Pergamon, Zimmerman, cinnamon, Chinaman, Chinamen, Heinemann, Campbell-Bannerman, overman, Silverman, specimen, fisherman, washerman, Yorkshireman, militiaman, Benjamin, bitumen, Betjeman, trencherman, regimen, Harriman, cameraman, albumen, albumin, acumen, telamon, cellarman, Solomon, trawlerman, cyclamen **.17** Burman, firman, sermon, Sherman, German, germen, germon, Herman, Hermon, determine, redetermine, predetermine, Franco-German, overdetermine **.18** Oman, omen, nomen, foeman, showman, Roman, yeoman, Lowman, Sloman, crossbowman, praenomen, cognomen, Oklahoman, Graeco-Roman, Gallo-Roman **.19** Shipman, Lippmann, chapman, shopman, Helpmann, midshipman **.20** cabman, Tubman, clubman **.21** pitman, Pittman, Whitman, hetman, batman, atman, Hartman, Cotman, footman, boatman, Hauptmann, merchantman, Eastman, dustman, postman, beltman, lifeboatman, selectman, aircraftman, harvestman **.22** freedman, Friedman, Steadman, headman, Readman, Caedmon, madman, Bradman, Godman, hodman, goodman, woodman, roadman, bondman, Feldman, Goldman, orchardman, husbandman, Highlandman **.23** Hickman, brakeman, Beckmann, packman, trackman, stockman, Walkman®, Eichmann, pikeman, bookman, kirkman, workman, milkman **.24** ragman, flagman, dogman, frogman, Bergman, Seligman **.25** penman, fenman, gunman, Feynman, lineman **.26** hangman, Longman **.27** Kauffmann, Hoffman, Huffman, turfman **.28** Othman, Rothman, Northman, Guzmán, lengthman **.29** policeman, serviceman, paceman, spaceman, baseman, chessman, pressman, upperclassman, houseman, Housman, warehouseman, Osman, Crossman, Norseman, horseman, busman, musmon, Weismann, businessman, congressman, talisman, agribusinessman, statesman, batsman, Scotsman, yachtsman, sportsman, Weizmann, pointsman, huntsman, raftsman, draftsman, draughtsman, craftsman, Boltzmann, aircraftsman, brakesman, axeman, cracksman, Flaxman, marksman, locksman, spokesman, Manxman **.30** Cheeseman, sundriesman, steersman, frontiersman, privateersman, desman, Tasman, oarsman, outdoorsman, Wiseman, prizeman, exciseman, tribesman, beadsman, seedsman, tradesman, headsman, guardsman, swordsman, sidesman, bridesman, woodsman, herdsman, bandsman, landsman, roundsman, groundsman, bondsman, fieldsman, guildsman, coastguardsman, ombudsman, backwoodsman, cragsman, magsman, gamesman, almsman, groomsman, helmsman, kinsman, plainsman, lensman, clansman, Klansman, townsman, gownsman,

linesman, Ku Klux Klansman, wheelsman, bailsman, talesman, dalesman, salesman, spoilsman **.31** Leishman, freshman, Cashman, Flashman, Bushman, Welshman, Cornishman, Englishman, Irishman **.32** Orangeman **.33** pitchman, switchman, Scotchman, watchman, Dutchman, churchman, coachman, henchman, Frenchman **.34** liegeman, Bridgeman, bargeman **.35** Gilman, railman, Spellman, bellman, Hellman, dolman, Colman, Ullmann, Pullman, schoolman, Perelman, coalman, Coleman, Holman, nobleman, cattleman, gentleman, udalman, fugleman, signalman, rifleman, Mussulman, councilman, patrolman

28.17.17
.1 Keenan, Henan, Burkinan **.2** finnan, McKinnon, Dunsinane **.3** Canaan **.4** pennon, tenon, Brennan, Lennon, McLennan **.5** cannon, canon, Gannon, Shannon, Channon, Hannon, Rhiannon, Montanan, Buchanan, Concannon, colcannon, Dungannon, Clackmannan, Louisianan **.6** Botswanan **.7** Cynan **.8** Eynon, Beynon, Tynan, Gorseinon **.9** Noonan **.10** Lebanon, feminine, Heffernan, Parthenon, Algernon, Saarinen, Cullinan, phenomenon, prolegomenon, hapax legomenon, epiphenomenon **.11** Vernon **.12** Onan, Conan, Ronan, Arizonan **.13** Cro-Magnon **.14** Memnon, Agamemnon

28.17.18
Bingen, Tongan, wrong'un, Groningen, Vlissingen, Weltanschauungen, Völkerwanderungen

28.17.19
Biffen, stiffen, griffin, griffon, gryphon, deafen, Wilhelmshafen, often, soften, orphan, toughen, roughen, siphon, hyphen, antiphon, colophon, olefin, Wilhelmshaven, Bellerophon, ibuprofen

28.17.20
.1 even, Stephen, Steven, Sivan, Kesteven, uneven, Genevan, Strathleven **.2** given, Niven, riven, Ruthven, Tryfan, driven, thriven, shriven, forgiven, Godgiven, misgiven, unshriven, unforgiven **.3** Avon, maven, shaven, haven, raven, craven, graven, unshaven, Fairhaven, Newhaven, Whitehaven, Stonehaven, Milford Haven, Stratford-upon-Avon **.4** Evan, Bevan, Devon, Nefyn, Nevin, leaven, seven, Severn, heaven, Pleven, eleven **.5** afon, pavane, spavin, tavern, Cavan, cavern, Aberavon, Glanyrafon **.6** Arfon, carven, Javan, Dungarvan, Caernarfon, Cuxhaven, Tórshavn, Wilhelmshaven **.7** oven, coven, Govan, govern, sloven, McGovern, misgovern **.8** Ivan, wyvern, liven, enliven **.9** proven, unproven **.10** cordovan, Canavan, Donovan, Sullivan, O'Donovan, O'Sullivan **.11** woven, cloven, Beethoven, Eindhoven, enwoven, unwoven, interwoven **.12** Alfven **.13** Hesvan **.14** silvan, silvern, sylvan, Malvern, Resolven

28.17.21
Ethan, Tudorbethan, Elizabethan, Nathan,
Bethan, Cauthen, python, anacoluthon,
Phaethon, earthen, strengthen, lengthen,
leviathan, Jonathan, lecithin, marathon,
autochthon, Melanchthon

28.17.22
heathen, Swithin, Swithun, leathern, Hathern,
northern, southern, earthen, burthen,
Carmarthen

28.17.23
.1 Thyssen, Gleason **.2** Nissan®, Nisan, Nissen,
Wiston, christen, listen, glisten, rechristen
.3 Pearson, Pierson, Grierson **.4** basin, caisson,
mason, chasten, Jason, hasten, Grayson,
diapason, handbasin, washbasin, Freemason,
stonemason, wash-hand basin, Donets Basin,
Kuznetz Basin, Fortnum and Mason **.5** Essen,
Hessen, Wesson, Bresson, lessen, lesson,
delicatessen **.6** Casson, Masson, Hassan, assassin
.7 fasten, unfasten, arson, parson, Carson,
sarsen, Sarson, Larsen, Larson **.8** Ardrossan
.9 Orson, Porson, Dawson, coarsen, Mawson,
hoarsen, whoreson, Rawson, Lawson **.10** Boyson,
moisten **.11** Cusson **.12** bison, Tyson, Dyson,
Meissen, Fison, hyson, Bryson, grison, neomycin
.13 Jewson, Hooson, loosen, medusan, unloosen
.14 niacin, Jespersen, Roberson, Peterson,
jettison, Paterson, Pattison, Waterson,
Widdowson, Edison, medicine, Addison,
Madison, Goodison, Henderson, Anderson,
Sanderson, Grandison, Alderson, biomedicine,
Dickerson, Mackeson, Farquharson, Huskisson,
Wilkerson, Ferguson, Jamieson, Emerson,
Rasmussen, benison, Tennyson, Dennison,
venison, unison, Jefferson, Davison, cavesson,
Salvesen, Matheson, Mathieson, diocesan,
archdiocesan, Aitchison, Acheson, Hutchison,
Murchison, parison, garrison, Saracen, Harrison,
Morrison, Margerison, caparison, comparison,
Ellison, Alison, Allison, malison, Finlayson
.15 person, worsen, layperson, chairperson,
unperson, statesperson, sportsperson,
craftsperson, spokesperson, salesperson,
McPherson, person-to-person, anchorperson
.16 boatswain, bosun, Formosan **.17** Epson,
Timpson, Simpson, jimpson, Empson, Sampson,
Hampson, Thompson **.18** Ibsen, Gibson, Dobson,
Hobson, Robson, Robeson, Hobson-Jobson,
Jacobson **.19** Kitson, Whitsun, Ritson, Bateson,
Stetson®, Datsun®, Dotson, Watson, Ibbotson,
Robertson, Cuthbertson **.20** Dodson, Hodson,
Hudson, Donaldson, Davidson, Richardson,
Amundsen, Edmondson, Edmundson,
Rowlandson **.21** Dixon, Nixon, vixen, Hickson,
Blixen, Texan, Sachsen, Saxon, Jackson, waxen,
klaxon, flaxen, Clarkson, oxen, Oxon, coxswain,
Cookson, Ericsson, Hendrickson, dioxan,
Wilcoxon **.22** Grigson, Gregson, Bergson
.23 Stimson, Gimson, Simson, jimson, Jameson,
Samson, ramson, Thomson, Mommsen,
Adamson, Williamson **.24** Robinson, Dickinson,

Parkinson, Hopkinson, Simpkinson,
Tompkinson, Atkinson, Watkinson, Jenkinson,
Hodgkinson, Wilkinson, Hutchinson, Allinson,
Rawlinson, Tomlinson, Swainson, ensign,
Benson, tenson, Jensen, Henson, Anson,
Manson, Nansen, Sanson, Jansen, Hansen,
Hanson, Branson, Downson, sponson, Johnson,
Johnston, Jonson, Swanson, Ronson®, Bunsen,
Christensen, Sorensen, Collinson, Stephenson,
Stevenson **.25** Wolfson, Gustafson **.26** Smithson
.27 Dodgson, Hodgson **.28** keelson, Neilson,
Nielsen, Ilson, Pilsen, Stillson, Nilsson, Wilson,
Belsen, telson, kelson, Nelson, Carlson, Olsen,
Coulson, Poulson, Jolson, Mendelssohn,
Nicholson, Michelson

28.17.24
.1 Pisan, season, reason, treason, pre-season,
disseisin, Hoseason, low season, unreason
.2 mizzen, risen, prison, grison, arisen, uprisen,
unrisen, imprison **.3** scazon, raisin, Raison,
brazen, blazon, liaison, diapason, emblazon,
Spätlesen **.4** basan **.5** blouson, advowson,
Munchausen, Stockhausen **.6** Tarzan **.7** gossan
.8 poison **.9** dozen, cousin, cozen **.10** kaizen,
greisen, bedizen, horizon, spiegeleisen **.11** Susan,
medusan **.12** Brabazon, citizen, jettison,
partisan, bartizan, Amazon, benison, denizen,
venison, unison, orison, malison, bipartisan,
diocesan **.13** Curzon **.14** chosen, Rosen, frozen,
Formosan, unchosen, refrozen, unfrozen,
Lederhosen **.15** crimson, damson, ramson
.16 tenzon, Kansan **.17** Pilsen

28.17.25
.1 Rhaetian, Grecian, Haitian, Capetian,
Rhodesian, Phoenician, venetian, magnesian,
Helvetian, Tahitian, accretion, secretion,
concretion, excretion, Silesian, deletion,
depletion, suppletion, repletion, completion,
Diocletian, Syro-Phoenician **.2.1** Titian, mission,
fission, scission, Priscian, tuition, fruition,
coition, intuition, circuition, suspicion,
prohibition, ambition, imbibition, adhibition,
inhibition, exhibition, overambition
.2.2 partition, mortician, sortition, beautician,
dietician, petition, optician, tactician, dentition,
semiotician, repartition, tripartition, repetition,
competition, mathematician, cosmetician,
phonetician, aesthetician, esthetician,
theoretician, politician, dialectician, semantician,
diagnostician, acoustician, superstition,
statistician, linguistician, equipartition,
arithmetician, cybernetician, geopolitician
.2.3 audition, addition, edition, perdition,
sedition, tradition, rendition, condition,
subaudition, expedition, erudition, extradition,
recondition, precondition, superaddition
.2.4 dormition, emission, omission, permission,
demission, Domitian, commission, Hermitian,
remission, submission, admission, readmission,
dismission, transmission, photoemission,
pretermission, intermission, decommission,
recommission, intromission, manumission,

retransmission, academician, monition, munition, lenition, clinician, technician, ignition, cognition, mechanician, premonition, admonition, inanition, definition, tribunician, ammunition, precognition, recognition, redefinition, derecognition **.2.5** abscission, transition, musician, position, physician, deposition, reposition, pre-position, preposition, apposition, opposition, proposition, supposition, postposition, imposition, reimposition, composition, disposition, exposition, transposition, requisition, acquisition, reacquisition, inquisition, disquisition, oviposition, presupposition, superposition, interposition, juxtaposition, contraposition, decomposition, predisposition, indisposition, metaphysician, derequisition, superimposition, photocomposition **.2.6** logician, magician, Mauritian, rubrician, metrician, nutrition, attrition, patrician, detrition, contrition, apparition, preterition, rhetorician, parturition, micturition, paediatrician, geriatrician, obstetrician, innutrition, geometrician, biometrician, malnutrition, electrician, econometrician, coalition, Galician, volition, ebullition, abolition, demolition **.3.1** Asian, station, Dacian, nation, Thracian, creation, striation, Croatian, personation, cantillation, castellation, crenellation, expiation, trabeation, tritiation, mediation, radiation, ideation, brachiation, permeation, lineation, deviation, aviation, obviation, caseation, glaciation, speciation, vitiation, satiation, fasciation, brecciation, seriation, variation, storiation, recreation, procreation, self-creation, filiation, ciliation, palliation, spoliation, foliation, nucleation, situation, actuation, fluctuation, punctuation, graduation, menstruation, valuation, inchoation, detonation, impersonation, mutilation, irradiation, repudiation, laciniation, alineation, allineation, delineation, calumniation, abbreviation, alleviation, exuviation, appreciation, emaciation, negotiation, association, dissociation, consociation, asphyxiation, substantiation, annunciation, enunciation, denunciation, renunciation, pronunciation, depreciation, propitiation, initiation, officiation, expatiation, ingratiation, excruciation, instantiation, excoriation, infuriation, appropriation, impropriation, expropriation, inebriation, expatriation, repatriation, elutriation, humiliation, affiliation, conciliation, reconciliation, retaliation, despoliation, defoliation, exfoliation, enucleation, eventuation, accentuation, perpetuation, infatuation, effectuation, habituation, evacuation, continuation, insinuation, attenuation, extenuation, devaluation, revaluation, evaluation, re-evaluation, lixiviation, Serbo-Croatian, deracination, intermediation, interlineation, inappreciation, self-appreciation, renegotiation, disassociation,

transubstantiation, consubstantiation, mispronunciation, self-renunciation, beneficiation, differentiation, misappropriation, disaffiliation, dishabituation, self-perpetuation, individuation, disambiguation, discontinuation, superannuation, undervaluation, overvaluation, supercolumniation **.3.2** pupation, palpation, extirpation, constipation, syncopation, dissipation, occupation, reoccupation, preoccupation, nuncupation, usurpation, inculpation, exculpation, participation, anticipation, emancipation, libation, probation, lobation, prelibation, perturbation, masturbation, conurbation, titubation, intubation, reprobation, approbation, incubation, exacerbation, self-approbation, disapprobation **.3.3** hortation, quartation, citation, mutation, nutation, potation, natation, notation, cetacean, quotation, rotation, flotation, flirtation, septation, coaptation, co-optation, temptation, dictation, jactation, lactation, coarctation, punctation, cunctation, mentation, plantation, ostentation, sustentation, lamentation, fermentation, fomentation, pigmentation, fragmentation, augmentation, presentation, frequentation, siltation, saltation, occultation, auscultation, exultation, consultation, dilatation, impartation, deportation, importation, reimportation, exportation, re-exportation, transportation, exhortation, exploitation, sexploitation, excitation, incitation, transmutation, crepitation, capitation, palpitation, habitation, dubitation, nictitation, jactitation, constatation, meditation, imitation, limitation, denotation, annotation, sanitation, connotation, levitation, cavitation, gravitation, invitation, dissertation, recitation, oscitation, visitation, hesitation, digitation, vegetation, agitation, cogitation, gurgitation, equitation, misquotation, irritation, deputation, reputation, imputation, amputation, computation, disputation, commutation, permutation, sternutation, refutation, confutation, salutation, velitation, acceptation, adaptation, readaptation, expectation, affectation, delectation, retractation, pernoctation, eructation, orientation, reorientation, indentation, cementation, segmentation, recantation, incantation, implantation, explantation, transplantation, confrontation, sedimentation, ornamentation, regimentation, instrumentation, documentation, argumentation, alimentation, supplementation, implementation, complementation, re-presentation, representation, exaltation, superfetation, teleportation, precipitation, decrepitation, decapitation, cohabitation, inhabitation, premeditation, accreditation, delimitation, acclimatation, elicitation, felicitation, solicitation, resuscitation, pollicitation, excogitation, regurgitation, ingurgitation, autorotation, dextrorotation, interpretation, reinterpretation, rehabilitation, debilitation, habilitation, facilitation, maladaptation, disorientation, compartmentation, experimentation, incapacitation, prestidigitation, counterirritation, misinterpretation, misrepresentation, testation, gestation, vastation, gustation, crustacean, eustachian, substation, outstation, workstation, detestation, attestation, contestation, infestation, disinfestation, arrestation, molestation, encrustation, protestation, devastation, encystation, forestation, manifestation, deforestation, reforestation, afforestation, reafforestation, disforestation, disafforestation **.3.4** laudation, sedation, predation, gradation, foundation, fecundation, commendation, retardation, denudation, trepidation, lapidation, oxidation, liquidation, backwardation, fluoridation, depredation, degradation, infeudation, exudation, transudation, validation, emendation, inundation, recommendation, dilapidation, intimidation, accommodation, elucidation, autoxidation, biodegradation, intergradation, retrogradation, invalidation, consolidation, superfecundation, reconsolidation **.3.5** vacation, plication, vocation, location, placation, furcation, truncation, inculcation, debarkation, embarkation, disembarkation, demarcation, manducation, urtication, mastication, rustication, altercation, dedication, medication, predication, claudication, abdication, indication, vindication, syndication, formication, fornication, defecation, suffocation, deification, reification, evocation, revocation, avocation, provocation, advocation, invocation, convocation, desiccation, vesication, education, re-education, co-education, deprecation, imprecation, fabrication, rubrication, lubrication, imbrication, embrocation, metrication, extrication, affrication, relocation, allocation, reallocation, collocation, triplication, replication, application, reapplication, supplication, duplication, implication, complication, explication, publication, spifflication, dislocation, translocation, bifurcation, defalcation, syllabication, alembication, decortication, authentication, sophistication, domestication, fantastication, prognostication, rededication, premedication, eradication, adjudication, contraindication, revendication, communication, pontification, typification, yuppification, prettification, beatification, ratification, stratification, gratification, mortification, fortification, beautification, certification, notification, rectification, fructification, sanctification, quantification, mystification, testification, justification, stultification, nidification, edification, reedification, modification, codification, ramification, mummification, humification, vinification, unification,

signification, lignification, magnification, damnification, vivification, specification, pacification, gasification, classification, ossification, Russification, versification, Nazification, calcification, falsification, dulcification, Frenchification, speechification, sanguification, verification, scarification, rarefication, clarification, horrification, scorification, purification, thurification, glorification, vitrification, petrification, nitrification, eutrophication, gentrification, vilification, jellification, mollification, jollification, qualification, nullification, simplification, amplification, uglification, equivocation, hypothecation, detoxication, intoxication, self-education, miseducation, divarication, prevarication, reciprocation, self-deprecation, prefabrication, radiolocation, echolocation, misapplication, quintuplication, reduplication, quadruplication, multiplication, republication, pre-publication, self-justification, unsophistication, miscommunication, excommunication, syllabification, acetification, self-gratification, self-certification, desertification, objectification, identification, demystification, humidification, acidification, solidification, remodification, commodification, saponification, personification, reunification, resinification, indemnification, revivification, silicification, declassification, reclassification, subclassification, diversification, denazification, detoxification, intensification, decalcification, emulsification, calorification, repurification, self-glorification, devitrification, denitrification, electrification, transmogrification, disqualification, exemplification, autointoxication, photoduplication, intercommunication, telecommunication, misidentification, dehumidification, oversimplification, obfuscation, confiscation, coruscation **.3.6** ligation, negation, rogation, legation, purgation, promulgation, variegation, propagation, expurgation, mitigation, litigation, castigation, fustigation, instigation, fumigation, abnegation, levigation, navigation, divagation, objurgation, subjugation, conjugation, irrigation, derogation, arrogation, corrugation, prorogation, abrogation, subrogation, segregation, aggregation, congregation, delegation, relegation, allegation, colligation, obligation, compurgation, elongation, prolongation, divulgation, investigation, reinvestigation, self-abnegation, interrogation, desegregation, disaggregation, centrifugation, homologation, circumnavigation, supererogation **.3.7** gemmation, Sarmatian, formation, summation, cremation, Dalmatian, deformation, re-formation, preformation, conformation, malformation, inhumation, automation, intimation, estimation, animation, reanimation, defamation, reformation, affirmation, reaffirmation, information, confirmation, transformation, decimation, desquamation, lachrymation, exhumation, consummation, collimation, sublimation, declamation, reclamation, acclamation, acclimation, proclamation, exclamation, inflammation, legitimation, amalgamation, inanimation, self-affirmation, disaffirmation, misinformation, reconfirmation, approximation, disinformation, disconfirmation, illegitimation, underestimation, overestimation **.3.8** tarnation, carnation, lunation, ruination, pinnation, donation, conation, phonation, venation, crenation, vernation, zonation, pronation, agnation, stagnation, cognation, damnation, alienation, incarnation, reincarnation, subornation, trepanation, supination, carbonation, cybernation, hibernation, turbination, combination, patination, catenation, pectination, intonation, destination, festination, consternation, alternation, iodination, ordination, coordination, condonation, cachinnation, machination, crimination, emanation, gemination, deamination, lamination, domination, commination, nomination, rumination, termination, vermination, germination, culmination, fulmination, trephination, profanation, hyphenation, sulphonation, divination, Athanasian, fascination, vaccination, calcination, fractionation, pagination, margination, marination, coronation, chlorination, urination, fluorination, pollination, myelination, explanation, declination, inclination, indignation, Aurignacian, impregnation, oppugnation, assignation, designation, resignation, condemnation, recombination, concatenation, agglutination, predestination, procrastination, incoordination, subordination, foreordination, recrimination, incrimination, discrimination, elimination, dissemination, insemination, degemination, contamination, decontamination, examination, re-examination, abomination, predomination, renomination, denomination, illumination, determination, extermination, regermination, rejuvenation, vaticination, assassination, ratiocination, hallucination, revaccination, origination, miscegenation, repagination, imagination, evagination, invagination, hydrogenation, oxygenation, deoxygenation, halogenation, exsanguination, dechlorination, indoctrination, peregrination, desalination, self-pollination, disinclination, redesignation, self-condemnation, insubordination, indiscrimination, self-examination, transillumination, redetermination, predetermination, indetermination, self-determination, dehydrogenation, overdetermination **.3.9** starvation, nivation, privation, ovation, nervation, lavation, salvation, solvation, titivation, motivation, captivation, activation, deactivation, reactivation,

aestivation, estivation, cultivation, excavation, innervation, innovation, enervation, renovation, coacervation, passivation, conservation, reservation, preservation, observation, derivation, depravation, deprivation, aggravation, elevation, salivation, incurvation, demotivation, self-motivation, inactivation, self-preservation, superelevation **.3.10** sensation, cessation, cassation, fixation, vexation, taxation, luxation, compensation, dispensation, condensation, Alsatian, pulsation, inspissation, decussation, conversation, malversation, prefixation, suffixation, infixation, indexation, annexation, complexation, relaxation, subluxation, incensation, precompensation, intravasation, extravasation, tergiversation, overcompensation, causation **.3.11** Judaization, quantization, potentization, iodization, fluidization, ionization, deionization, lionization, laicization, theorization, vaporization, pauperization, temporization, arborization, barbarization, martyrization, cauterization, motorization, vectorization, factorization, winterization, rasterization, deodorization, vulgarization, glamourization, pulverization, etherization, authorization, pressurization, velarization, valorization, realization, stylization, creolization, solmization, accusation, concretization, mediatization, Sovietization, narcotization, amortization, sabbatization, robotization, schematization, Semitization, lemmatization, dramatization, traumatization, stigmatization, sanitization, monetization, magnetization, privatization, sensitization, digitization, prioritization, palletization, periodization, bastardization, standardization, subsidization, oxidization, fluoridization, hybridization, diphthongization, Islamization, atomization, itemization, optimization, victimization, systemization, randomization, minimization, dynamization, maximization, routinization, Latinization, unionization, carbonization, urbanization, fraternization, platinization, scrutinization, westernization, modernization, preconization, mechanization, Balkanization, vulcanization, organization, reorganization, demonization, feminization, harmonization, humanization, Germanization, romanization, canonization, galvanization, ozonization, Russianization, Christianization, pidginization, patronization, synchronization, immunization, communization, Hellenization, salinization, colonization, enthronization, solemnization, improvisation, exorcization, cliticization, plasticization, Anglicization, villagization, satirization, notarization, pasteurization, memorization, summarization, mesmerization, terrorization, sulphurization, polarization, solarization, bowdlerization, cicatrization, militarization **.3.12** characterization, categorization, allegorization, desulphurization, depressurization, repressurization, miniaturization, labialization, idealization, trivialization, serialization, self-realization, decreolization, actualization, ritualization, stabilization, verbalization, mobilization, globalization, symbolization, metallization, cartelization, glottalization, subtilization, vitalization, brutalization, utilization, fertilization, totalization, tantalization, crystallization, idolization, feudalization, focalization, vocalization, localization, legalization, normalization, formalization, thermalization, penalization, canalization, finalization, vernalization, personalization, nationalization, rationalization, fictionalization, regionalization, civilization, novelization, fossilization, nasalization, podzolization, specialization, socialization, equalization, tranquilization, tranquillization, sterilization, paralyzation, moralization, pluralization, ruralization, liberalization, neutralization, centralization, federalization, mongrelization, mineralization, generalization, naturalization, visualization, self-accusation, alphabetization, automatization, acclimatization, systematization, problematization, aromatization, demonetization, remonetization, demagnetization, anaesthetization, parasitization, desensitization, securitization, democratization, bureaucratization, epitomization, legitimization, macadamization, economization, keratinization, pedestrianization, Europeanization, decarbonization, suburbanization, gelatinization, Africanization, antagonization, disorganization, bituminization, dehumanization, aluminization, Egyptianization, dechristianization, indigenization, homogenization, decommunization, desalinization, de-stalinization, decolonization, recolonization, masculinization, relativization, objectivization, collectivization, politicization, phoneticization, romanticization, phonemicization, italicization, chronologization, familiarization, denuclearization, extemporization, computerization, catheterization, transistorization, polymerization, containerization, alveolarization, revalorization, decolorization, modularization, popularization, secularization, circularization, regularization, singularization, depolarization, demilitarization, depolymerization, arterialization, materialization, industrialization, desexualization, conceptualization, contextualization, monopolization, destabilization, cannibalization, solubilization, demobilization, immobilization, volatilization, immortalization, devitalization, revitalization, reutilization, capitalization, hospitalization, palatalization, segmentalization, topicalization, radicalization, theatricalization, animalization, decimalization, caramelization, marginalization,

communalization, criminalization, nominalization, internalization, externalization, depersonalization, professionalization, denationalization, renationalization, initialization, commercialization, evangelization, spiritualization, demoralization, decentralization, demineralization, denaturalization, legitimatization, anathematization, proletarianization, Americanization, comprehensivization, depoliticization, demythologization, subcategorization, copolymerization, particularization, microminiaturization, dematerialization, territorialization, individualization, municipalization, under-utilization, recapitalization, sentimentalization, departmentalization, compartmentalization, decriminalization, internationalization, institutionalization, deinstitutionalization, universalization, overspecialization, overgeneralization
.3.13 liquation, aeration, de-aeration, oration, gyration, duration, neuration, narration, serration, Horatian, proration, Eurasian, curation, melioration, instauration, defloration, susurration, separation, reparation, preparation, operation, cooperation, corporation, desperation, respiration, aspiration, suspiration, perspiration, expiration, inspiration, transpiration, liberation, aberration, carburation, iteration, reiteration, literation, deuteration, restoration, alteration, federation, adoration, moderation, ponderation, decoration, Amerasian, numeration, admiration, veneration, generation, perforation, botheration, maceration, laceration, mensuration, ulceration, trituration, maturation, saturation, obturation, pejoration, adjuration, abjuration, induration, conjuration, peroration, depuration, suppuration, procuration, obscuration, figuration, fulguration, sulfuration, sulphuration, toleration, coloration, colouration, exploration, declaration, immoderation, deterioration, amelioration, evaporation, incorporation, reincorporation, recuperation, vituperation, exasperation, deliberation, elaboration, collaboration, corroboration, reverberation, alliteration, obliteration, transliteration, expectoration, adulteration, consideration, confederation, redecoration, edulcoration, prefiguration, configuration, transfiguration, invigoration, reinvigoration, commemoration, agglomeration, conglomeration, enumeration, self-admiration, itineration, incineration, regeneration, degeneration, exoneration, remuneration, vociferation, proliferation, asseveration, perseveration, evisceration, incarceration, commiseration, denaturation, unsaturation, acculturation, inculturation, refrigeration, exaggeration, inauguration, exhilaration, deceleration, acceleration, discoloration, discolouration, misdeclaration,

reconsideration, inconsideration, reconfiguration, supersaturation, vibration, libration, vertebration, cerebration, lucubration, celebration, calibration, adumbration, equilibration, concelebration, titration, nitration, concentration, castration, prostration, frustration, lustration, filtration, infiltration, perpetration, impetration, arbitration, penetration, orchestration, sequestration, ministration, fenestration, registration, illustration, demonstration, remonstration, exfiltration, administration, defenestration, deregistration, preregistration, interpenetration, maladministration, hydration, dehydration, rehydration, desecration, obsecration, execration, consecration, deconsecration, reconsecration, migration, transmigration, integration, reintegration, immigration, emigration, denigration, deflagration, conflagration, redintegration, disintegration **.3.14** chelation, illation, fellation, gelation, lallation, collation, spallation, dilation, elation, violation, delation, Galatian, halation, relation, translation, etiolation, annihilation, vacuolation, epilation, depilation, appellation, cupellation, compilation, sibilation, jubilation, titillation, scutellation, scintillation, ventilation, distillation, installation, instillation, constellation, decollation, percolation, escalation, de-escalation, immolation, revelation, methylation, tessellation, desolation, vacillation, oscillation, isolation, exhalation, insolation, cancellation, consolation, postulation, pustulation, regelation, stridulation, adulation, flagellation, modulation, nodulation, congelation, undulation, inhalation, correlation, fibrillation, Australasian, ululation, stipulation, population, copulation, tribulation, tabulation, ambulation, deambulation, peculation, speculation, maculation, sacculation, flocculation, circulation, osculation, calculation, regulation, coagulation, triangulation, strangulation, stimulation, simulation, emulation, formulation, cumulation, annulation, granulation, ovulation, insulation, serrulation, cellulation, pullulation, retranslation, mistranslation, circumvallation, vasodilation, horripilation, extrapolation, interpellation, interpolation, assibilation, self-mutilation, machicolation, intercalation, self-immolation, assimilation, dissimilation, self-revelation, disconsolation, capitulation, congratulation, expostulation, invigilation, acidulation, demodulation, phosphorylation, interrelation, defibrillation, manipulation, depopulation, repopulation, infibulation, confabulation, perambulation, articulation, reticulation, gesticulation, vermiculation, fasciculation, vesiculation, matriculation, ejaculation, inoculation, tuberculation, recirculation, emasculation, inosculation, recalculation, miscalculation, deregulation, self-regulation, dissimulation, reformulation,

accumulation, degranulation, encapsulation, hyperventilation, hypoventilation, recapitulation, self-congratulation, intercorrelation, overpopulation, tintinnabulation, circumambulation, disarticulation, contemplation, oblation, ablation, deflation, reflation, stagflation, inflation, conflation, disinflation, insufflation, anti-inflation, legislation **.4** cession, session, freshen, profession, confession, secession, recession, precession, procession, obsession, accession, deaccession, succession, concession, supersession, intercession, retrocession, possession, repossession, prepossession, self-possession, dispossession, oppression, depression, suppression, repression, impression, compression, expression, discretion, egression, regression, digression, aggression, progression, ingression, transgression, decompression, self-expression, indiscretion, nonagression, retrogression, introgression, immunodepression, immunosuppression **.5** ashen, passion, fashion, ration, impassion, compassion, refashion, deration, K-ration **.6** Martian, harshen **.7** Roscian, groschen **.8** portion, torchon, torsion, caution, apportion, reapportion, proportion, abortion, retortion, contortion, distortion, extortion, precaution, incaution, disproportion, overcaution **.9** Russian, Prussian, percussion, succussion, concussion, discussion, repercussion, Belorussian **.10** cushion, pincushion **.11** crucian, Lucian, traducian, Rosicrucian, Ilyushin, Lilliputian, retribution, attribution, deattribution, contribution, distribution, redistribution, maldistribution, Poisson distribution, destitution, restitution, prostitution, substitution, institution, reinstitution, constitution, reconstitution, locution, prosecution, persecution, execution, consecution, elocution, allocution, perlocution, electrocution, interlocution, circumlocution, diminution, comminution, Confucian, transfusion, dilution, Aleutian, elution, pollution, volution, solution, ablution, evolution, devolution, revolution, involution, convolution, dissolution, absolution, resolution, circumvolution, redissolution, irresolution, counterrevolution **.12** Persian, tertian, Mercian, version, coercion, Revised Standard Version, aspersion, dispersion, interspersion, Cistercian, abstersion, recursion, incursion, excursion, emersion, immersion, submersion, diversion, aversion, eversion, perversion, reversion, obversion, subversion, inversion, conversion, ambiversion, retroversion, introversion, extraversion, extroversion, reconversion, animadversion, interconversion, assertion, reassertion, lacertian, insertion, reinsertion, self-assertion, disconcertion, desertion, exertion, overexertion **.13** ocean, potion, Goshen, motion, notion, lotion, Boeotian, Laotian, demotion, premotion, emotion, commotion, promotion, self-motion, devotion, Cappadocian, Nova Scotian, locomotion **.14** conniption, Egyptian, decryption, encryption, ascription, description, prescription, proscription, subscription, inscription, transcription, conscription, superscription, misdescription, circumscription, perception, deception, reception, exception, inception, conception, subreption, proprioception, apperception, interception, self-deception, contraception, preconception, misconception, intussusception, introsusception, photoreception, caption, contraption, usucaption, option, co-option, adoption, readoption, sorption, desorption, resorption, absorption, reabsorption, adsorption, chemisorption, malabsorption, self-absorption, irruption, eruption, corruption, abruption, disruption, interruption, incorruption, discerption, excerption, gumption, preemption, coemption, redemption, exemption, assumption, reassumption, subsumption, consumption, presumption, resumption, underconsumption **.15.1** diction, fiction, friction, depiction, addiction, prediction, indiction, prefixion, nonfiction, transfixion, eviction, conviction, restriction, constriction, affliction, infliction, confliction, interdiction, benediction, contradiction, malediction, valediction, jurisdiction, crucifixion, derestriction, dereliction, self-contradiction, magnetostriction, vasoconstriction **.15.2** section, lection, flexion, inspection, retrospection, introspection, circumspection, detection, protection, self-protection, connection, reconnection, disconnection, interconnection, affection, perfection, defection, refection, infection, reinfection, confection, disinfection, imperfection, disaffection, evection, advection, convection, bisection, dissection, trisection, resection, subsection, midsection, transection, venesection, intersection, vivisection, antivivisection, ejection, dejection, rejection, projection, abjection, objection, subjection, injection, interjection, introjection, direction, erection, re-erection, correction, redirection, indirection, misdirection, insurrection, resurrection, hypercorrection, election, re-election, pre-election, bolection, collection, selection, prelection, complexion, deflection, reflection, inflection, Euro-election, intellection, predilection, recollection, deselection, reselection, self-selection, retroflexion, introflexion, genuflection **.15.3** action, faction, traction, fraction, reaction, coaction, proaction, inaction, enaction, self-action, abreaction, retroaction, interaction, counteraction, overreaction, impaction, compaction, redaction, olfaction, stupefaction, labefaction, rubefaction, tumefaction, benefaction, liquefaction, rarefaction, torrefaction, vitrifaction, petrifaction, putrefaction, calefaction, malefaction, satisfaction, obstupefaction, dissatisfaction, self-satisfaction, exaction,

transaction, attraction, detraction, retraction, protraction, subtraction, contraction, distraction, abstraction, extraction, diffraction, refraction, infraction, counterattraction **.15.4** infarction, auction, decoction, concoction **.15.5** suction, ruction, fluxion, adduction, eduction, deduction, seduction, reduction, production, subduction, abduction, induction, conduction, transduction, destruction, obstruction, instruction, construction, deconstruction, effluxion, reproduction, pre-production, introduction, reintroduction, self-induction, liposuction, self-destruction, microinstruction, macroinstruction, reconstruction, misconstruction, solifluction, underproduction, overproduction **.15.6** sanction, unction, function, junction, intinction, distinction, extinction, compunction, expunction, inunction, eigenfunction, dysfunction, malfunction, T-junction, injunction, conjunction, disjunction, multifunction, contradistinction **.16** pension, tension, mention, gentian, salientian, suspension, attention, detention, retention, pretension, obtention, intension, intention, contention, distension, abstention, extension, coextension, hypertension, hypotension, inattention, dimension, Übermenschen, Untermenschen, prevention, subvention, invention, reinvention, convention, supervention, intervention, contravention, circumvention, ascension, reascension, dissension, recension, condescension, prehension, reprehension, apprehension, comprehension, misapprehension, incomprehension, uncomprehension, Laurentian, declension, stanchion, scansion, mansion, expansion, sponsion, München **.17** falchion, repulsion, propulsion, impulsion, compulsion, expulsion, emulsion, avulsion, evulsion, revulsion, convulsion

28.17.26
.1 Friesian, Frisian, lesion, artesian, Cartesian, Etesian, Rhodesian, magnesian, Ephesian, cohesion, adhesion, inhesion, Milesian, Silesian, Salesian, Indonesian, Austronesian, Micronesian, Melanesian, Polynesian, Peloponnesian, Malayo-Polynesian **.2** vision, scission, division, revision, prevision, provision, envision, tunnel vision, decision, recision, rescission, precisian, precision, excision, incision, concision, derision, misprision, elision, collision, supervision, redivision, subdivision, LaserVision®, Eurovision, television, indecision, imprecision, circumcision, under-provision, uncircumcision **.3** Asian, suasion, Vespasian, Caucasian, occasion, evasion, pervasion, invasion, equation, persuasion, dissuasion, corrasion, Eurasian, abrasion, Malaysian, Transcaucasian, Athanasian, Amerasian, Rabelaisian, Australasian **.4** fusion, contusion, protrusion, obtrusion, intrusion, extrusion, affusion, effusion, perfusion, diffusion,

suffusion, profusion, infusion, confusion,
transfusion, illusion, allusion, delusion,
collusion, prolusion, occlusion, seclusion,
reclusion, preclusion, inclusion, conclusion,
exclusion, interfusion, rediffusion, self-delusion,
disillusion **.5** Persian, aspersion, recursion,
incursion, immersion, submersion, perversion,
animadversion **.6** plosion, erosion, corrosion,
implosion, explosion, eclosion

28.17.27
Itchen, kitchen, richen, lichen, fortune,
scutcheon, birchen, puncheon, scuncheon,
truncheon, luncheon, München, Christian,
question, falchion, misfortune, escutcheon,
unchristian, digestion, suggestion, ingestion,
congestion, exhaustion, combustion,
Appalachian, inescutcheon, anti-christian,
Judaeo-Christian, predigestion, indigestion,
self-suggestion, moxibustion

28.17.28
.1 region, legion, Norwegian, Glaswegian,
subregion **.2** pidgin, pigeon, smidgen, wigeon,
woodpigeon, Harijan, religion, irreligion
.3 Bajan, Cajun, Trajan, Barbadian, contagion,
Pelagian **.4** imagine **.5** Farjeon, largen **.6** Georgian
.7 dudgeon, gudgeon, sojourn, trudgen,
bludgeon, curmudgeon **.8** Rügen **.9** cryogen,
habergeon, Vortigern, mutagen, antigen,
gestagen, cultigen, Sanatogen®, teratogen,
adaptogen, progestogen, endogen, glycogen,
Imogen, leukaemogen, Energen, caseinogen,
carcinogen, trypsinogen, fibrinogen, cyanogen,
hallucinogen, pathogen, exogen, oxygen, origin,
nitrogen, estrogen, oestrogen, hydrogen,
androgen, acrogen, oxy-hydrogen,
parahydrogen, ortho-hydrogen, allergen,
halogen, collagen **.10** Spurgeon, burgeon,
sturgeon, gurjun, surgeon **.11** Trojan, neologian,
theologian **.12** Injun, engine, donjon, dungeon,
aero engine, Carlovingian **.13** Belgian

28.17.29
Sheehan, Linehan, Lenihan, Monaghan,
Moynihan, Brosnahan, Hanrahan, Callaghan,
Houlihan

28.17.30
Corwen, Iowan, Kirwan, Boscawen, Ogwen,
Anwen, Bronwen, Ceinwen, Quechuan,
Antiguan, Bandar Seri Begawan

28.17.31
.1 Mirren **.2** Kieran, Theran, schlieren, Madeiran
.3 perron, serran, heron **.4** Aaron, Charon,
Sharon, Dáil Eireann **.5** Aran, baron, barren,
Barron, Darren, Caron, Karen, yarran, Tregaron,
Maclaren, Aberdaron **.6** Gagarin, Saharan,
sub-Saharan **.7** sporran, foreign, warren, Lauren,
florin, Andorran **.8** Doran, Coren, Moran, Horan,
loran, Loren, Salvadoran, Ecuadoran **.9** Burren,
Curran, murrain, murrhine **.10** Byron, Chiron,
Myron, siren, Aneurin, environ, Aberaeron
.11 Honduran, Van Buren, anuran, thysanuran,
Auberon, Aldebaran, veteran, cateran, Lateran,

dipteran, hemipteran, dermapteran,
trichopteran, homopteran, orthopteran,
chiropteran, neuropteran, dictyopteran,
coleopteran, lepidopteran, hymenopteran,
thysanopteran, heteropteran, ephemeropteran,
Acheron, Corcoran, mascaron, camaron,
Cameron, Decameron, hexameron, poriferan,
foraminiferan, Catherine, Katherine, Lutheran,
Ramsaran, suzerain, aleuron, O'Halloran
.12 apron, Opren®, aspirin **.13** Libran
.14 Citroën®, citron, patron, matron, natron,
Sumatran, elytron, plectron, doctrine, cistron,
plastron, dextran **.15** hadron, squadron,
chaudron, Gudrun, dieldrin, children, caldron,
cauldron, Waldron, chaldron, trihedron,
stepchildren, godchildren, grandchildren, love
children, schoolchildren, polyhedron,
rhombohedron, heptahedron, octahedron,
pentahedron, decahedron, hexahedron,
tetrahedron, rhododendron, philodendron,
dodecahedron, icosahedron, icosidodecahedron
.16 macron, Akron, Cochrane, omicron
.17 chagrin **.18** Conran **.19** saffron, Dyffryn,
Wulfrun, Biafran **.20** chevron, navarin,
sovereign **.21** Cathryn, Kathryn **.22** brethren

28.17.32
Libyan, röntgen, McFadyean, McFadzean,
pinion, piñon, Binyon, minion, Kenyan, Kenyon,
banian, banyan, cañon, canyon, Mannion,
lorgnon, onion, bunion, Bunyan, munnion,
Runyon, trunnion, grunion, opinion,
rack-and-pinion, companion, d'Artagnan,
self-opinion, Old Dominion, Austronesian,
Micronesian, Melanesian, Polynesian,
Peloponnesian, Malayo-Polynesian

28.17.33
.1 Elan, Phelan, Whelan **.2** billon, Dillon, Dylan,
villain, villein, Macmillan, Anguillan **.3** Galen,
O'Faolain, Venezuelan **.4** Ellen, Mellon, melon,
felon, Helen, McKellen, Magellan, muskmelon,
Castlewellan, McClellan, McLellan, pademelon,
watermelon **.5** Alan, Allen, Alleyne, Alun, talon,
gallon, Fallon, Lallan, Rowallan, Van Allen
.6 Marlon, McFarlane, Guatemalan **.7** pollan,
pollen, Stollen, Hohenzollern **.8** fallen, befallen,
chap-fallen, chop-fallen, crestfallen **.9** Cullen,
Mullan, mullein, Mullen, sullen, Cúchulainn,
Lucullan **.10** pylon, epsilon, upsilon **.11** Pullen,
Boleyn, Bullen, woolen, woollen **.12** Doolan,
Cuillin, koulan, kulan, Zebulon **.13** Babylon,
chamberlain, petalon, ortolan, portolan,
castelan, castellan, magdelen, Askelon,
Kerguelen, mamelon, gonfalon, Josceline,
porcelain, Marilyn, myrobalan, abutilon, Mary
Magdalene, noradrenaline **.14** merlon **.15** stolen,
stolon, Dolan, colon, Nolan, solan, Solon,
swollen, Angolan, semicolon **.16** Caplan, Kaplan,
chaplain, Chaplin, compline, discipline,
indiscipline, undiscipline, self-discipline
.17 Veblen **.18** Nahuatlan **.19** Magdalen,
Magdalene **.20** Declan, Lachlan, Coughlan,
Loughlin, Brooklyn, franklin, Franklyn,

McLachlan, McLaughlin **.21** raglan
.22 Dunfermline **.23** Quinlan, Scanlon, Conlon, dunlin, O'Hanlon **.24** biathlon, triathlon, heptathlon, pentathlon, decathlon, tetrathlon, Llangollen **.25** Rhuddlan **.26** purslane **.27** muslin

28.18
earn, ern, erne, urn, spurn, Bern, Berne, burn, Burne, Byrne, tern, terne, turn, Stearn, Stearne, stern, Sterne, Dearne, durn, kern, fern, foehn, fohn, föhn, Verne, CERN, churn, Hearne, Hern, quern, yearn, learn, lierne, star turn, vingt-et-un, pay-as-you-earn, three-point turn

28.18.1
Bayern

28.18.2
epergne

28.18.3
Raeburn, Rayburn, Leyburn, Hebburn, Hepburn, Thorburn, Tyburn, Cliburn, Woburn, Cockburn, heartburn, Saltburn, sideburn, windburn, slash-and-burn, Blackburn, lean-burn, Swinburne, sunburn, Gisborne, Lisburn, Washburn, Kilburn, Milburn, Shelburne, Otterburn, Bannockburn

28.18.4
bittern, gittern, cittern, Vättern, slattern, U-turn, return, Sauternes, upturn, lectern, nocturn, nocturne, intern, downturn, pastern, astern, extern, overturn, taciturn, Comintern

28.18.5
Crewkerne

28.18.6
Kentigern, Vortigern

28.18.7
Redfern, lady-fern

28.18.8
wyvern, Auvergne

28.18.9
Lucerne, discern, concern, unconcern

28.18.10
casern

28.18.11
sojourn, adjourn, Vortigern

28.18.12
Aherne, Traherne, Mulhearn

28.18.13
relearn, unlearn

28.19
own, pone, Beaune, bone, tone, stone, Coen, Cohn, Colne, cone, scone, moan, Mon, mown, known, phone, sewn, Soane, sone, sown, zone, shown, Joan, hone, Rhône, roan, rone, prone, strown, drone, crone, groan, grown, throne, thrown, loan, lone, blown, clone, flown, Sloane, leone, Bayonne, co-own, disown, pick-your-own, Sierra Leone, Rosetta Stone

28.19.1
Dione, androstenedione

28.19.2
Capone, postpone, lithopone

28.19.3
debone, jawbone, thighbone, hipbone, splint-bone, breastbone, blade bone, rag-and-bone, cheekbone, backbone, spoke-bone, hambone, trombone, shinbone, Rathbone, wishbone, aitchbone, tailbone, whalebone, cuttlebone, knucklebone, marrowbone, collarbone, herringbone, Marylebone

28.19.4
pretone, atone, intone, halftone, Boca Raton **.1** ketone **.2** semitone, Movietone®, oxytone **.3** tritone **.4** two-tone **.5** duotone, barbitone, undertone, monotone, overtone, orthotone, acetone, dulcitone, baritone, barytone, microtone, paroxytone, pentobarbitone, phenobarbitone, proparoxytone **.6** peptone **.7** lactone **.8** thiopentone **.9** Bastogne, keystone, freestone, histone, cherrystone, holystone, hoarstone, drystone, bluestone, cornerstone, Silverstone, Yellowstone, flowstone, Clipstone, capstone, lapstone, copestone, soapstone, curbstone, kerbstone, Wheatstone, gritstone, whetstone, potstone, siltstone, Ingatestone, headstone, mudstone, bloodstone, toadstone, lodestone, sandstone, bondstone, grindstone, fieldstone, Wealdstone, jackstone, Blackstone, chockstone, cookstone, clinkstone, ragstone, flagstone, brimstone, gemstone, limestone, tombstone, greenstone, tinstone, whinstone, veinstone, brownstone, Johnstone, cornstone, hornstone, sunstone, rhinestone, moonstone, ironstone, turnstone, Leytonstone, clingstone, stepping-stone, coping stone, gravestone, hearthstone, birthstone, pitchstone, touchstone, sealstone, millstone, hailstone, gallstone, oilstone, milestone, cobblestone

28.19.5
condone, amidone, methadone

28.19.6
snowcone, windcone, pinecone, nosecone, silicone

28.19.7
ochone

28.19.8
orgone, epigone

28.19.9
hormone, daimon, new-mown, bemoan, Simone, unmown, pheromone, neurohormone

28.19.10
Oenone, quinone, foreknown, unknown, propanone, unbeknown, butanone, rotenone, menaquinone, hydroquinone, phylloquinone

28.19.11
Freefone®, freephone, earphone, payphone, diphone, geophone, diaphone, headphone,

cardphone, cellphone, sulfone, sulphone, heckelphone, entryphone®, polyphone, videophone, optophone, Dictaphone, Vodaphone®, speakerphone, francophone, megaphone, lagerphone, gramophone, homophone, saxophone, Ansafone®, answerphone, sousaphone, Linguaphone®, vibraphone, hydrophone, microphone, telephone, allophone, Parlophone, xylophone, Anglophone, sarrusophone, metallophone, radiotelephone

28.19.12
flavone

28.19.13
dapsone, Saxone, unsewn, unsown, self-sown

28.19.14
ozone, endzone, evzone, cortisone, prednisone, parozone, hydrocortisone

28.19.15
foreshown

28.19.16
ochone

28.19.17
Tyrone, neurone, regrown, outgrown, homegrown, ingrown, mossgrown, dethrone, enthrone, downthrown, unthrone, chaperone, camaron, coumarone, Navarone, aleurone, Toblerone®, tautochrone, overgrown, overthrown, androsterone, progesterone, testosterone, aldosterone, brachistochrone

28.19.18
McKeown

28.19.19
alone, violone, Cologne, Malone, flyblown, windblown, unblown, cyclone, outflown, Athlone, stand-alone, overblown, overflown, eau de Cologne, anticyclone

28.20
kiln, Milne, Alne, shuln, Köln, Colne, limekiln, Hardcastle

29.1
ping, bing, Byng, ting, sting, ding, king, ging, Ming, thing, sing, Singh, Synge, zing, wing, swing, ring, wring, spring, bring, Tring, string, ling, pling, cling, fling, sling, I Ching, teething ring, vortex ring

29.1.1
being, far-seeing, sightseeing, unseeing

29.1.2
wellbeing, dairying, unpitying, self-pitying, heli-skiing, unwearying, blackberrying, unvarying, unhurrying

29.1.3
maying, saying, slaying, taxpaying, bricklaying, tracklaying, minelaying

29.1.4
Gowing

29.1.5
drawing, underdrawing

29.1.6
annoying, self-destroying

29.1.7
tying, dying, vying, hying, lying, housebuying, retying, untying, undying, belying, uplying, outlying, inlying, self-denying, overlying, self-gratifying, self-justifying, unedifying, unsatisfying

29.1.8
doing, Ewing, bluing, wrongdoing, misdoing, evildoing

29.1.9
Boeing®, going, mowing, knowing, sowing, showing, froing, flowing, seagoing, foregoing, outgoing, ingoing, ongoing, ocean-going, racegoing, churchgoing, unknowing, borrowing, ingrowing, toing and froing, following, inflowing, easygoing, theatregoing, thoroughgoing

29.1.10
Taiping, Teng Hsiao-p'ing **.1** deeping, sweeping, shopkeeping, bookkeeping, gamekeeping, timekeeping, greenkeeping, station-keeping, safekeeping, peacekeeping, housekeeping, goalkeeping, minesweeping, unsleeping, wicketkeeping **.2** snipping, chipping, whipping, dripping, clipping **.3** shaping, scraping **.4** Epping **.5** tapping, wrapping, phonetapping, self-tapping, kneecapping, petnapping, kidnapping, handclapping, backslapping **.6** topping, stopping, sopping, Wapping, dropping, showstopping, clodhopping, wife-swapping, teleshopping **.7** swan-upping **.8** audio typing **.9** grouping **.10** Norrköping **.11** coping, roping **.12** camping, showjumping **.13** helping

29.1.11
ribbing, stabbing, zorbing, rubbing, tubing, probing, winebibbing, stockjobbing

29.1.12
.1 beating, Keating, meeting, sweeting, greeting, fleeting, self-defeating **.2** fitting, sitting, witting, shopfitting, pipefitting, unfitting, unwitting, sidesplitting, unremitting, unbefitting **.3** weighting, rating, grating, plating, slating, uprating, stimulating, accommodating, discriminating, illuminating, undeviating, suffocating, self-perpetuating, unhesitating, self-deprecating, self-propagating, self-pollinating, self-generating, concelebrating, vasodilating, self-immolating, uncalculating, self-regulating **.4** setting, wetting, letting, typesetting, trendsetting, pace-setting, bloodletting, photosetting, thermosetting, phototypesetting **.5** Gatting, matting **.6** outing, undoubting **.7** parting **.8** knotting **.9** unsporting, ripsnorting, self-supporting **.10** cutting, Nutting,

woodcutting, linocutting **.11** sighting, whiting, writing, lighting, flyting, dogfighting, infighting, prizefighting, bullfighting, playwriting, skywriting, scriptwriting, typewriting, handwriting, screenwriting, signwriting, songwriting, self-righting, backlighting, uninviting, unexciting, copywriting **.12** footing, off-putting **.13** Tooting, suiting, shooting, luting, trapshooting, sharpshooting, biocomputing, highfaluting, supercomputing, self-executing **.14** disquieting, carpeting, trumpeting, marketing, spirketing, visiting, pickpocketing, telemarketing **.15** skirting, shirting, self-asserting, disconcerting **.16** coating **.17** tempting, prompting, excepting **.18** self-acting, exacting, unsuspecting, self-respecting, self-correcting, self-selecting, unreflecting, unexacting, semiconducting, superconducting **.19** printing, painting, Banting, ranting, planting, monting, Ponting, bunting, unstinting, reprinting, enchanting, accounting, underpainting, unconsenting, unrelenting, disappointing **.20** weightlifting **.21** easting, twisting, listing, pasting, tasting, westing, fasting, lasting, costing, frosting, trusting, posting, roasting, arresting, unresting, trustbusting, ghostbusting, blockbusting, disgusting, untrusting, billposting, unresisting, unprotesting, unarresting, uninteresting, narrowcasting, everlasting, self-adjusting **.22** malting, salting, Boulting, revolting

29.1.13

.1 sheading, reading, reeding, leading, pleading, self-feeding, exceeding, unheeding, stockbreeding, inbreeding, misleading **.2** Rhydding, Ridding, forbidding **.3** shading, grading, lading, arcading, unfading, upbraiding, Armatrading **.4** steading, heading, wedding, Reading, subheading **.5** Dowding **.6** Harding, self-regarding **.7** wadding, hot-rodding **.8** hoarding, snowboarding, sailboarding, according, recording, self-recording, unrewarding, video recording, telerecording **.9** siding, hiding, riding, confiding, paragliding **.10** pudding, peasepudding **.11** orcharding **.12** wording **.13** loading, foreboding, self-loading **.14** ending, standing, stranding, landing, sounding, grounding, binding, finding, wounding, impending, goaltending, unending, heartrending, freestanding, upstanding, outstanding, hardstanding, surrounding, bookbinding, fact-finding, faultfinding, self-winding, unpretending, unoffending, moneylending, understanding, notwithstanding, undemanding, three-point landing, corresponding, underfunding, uncomprehending, self-understanding, misunderstanding **.15** wingding **.16** Fielding, yielding, building, gelding, Spalding, wilding, scolding, Golding, moulding, holding, scaffolding, unyielding, rebuilding, shipbuilding, outbuilding, stakebuilding, housebuilding, shareholding, roadholding,

hand-holding, landholding, fundholding, stockholding, smallholding, bodybuilding

29.1.14

Peking, Nanking, unking, Chungking **.1** unspeaking, self-seeking **.2** ticking, licking, pigsticking, arse-kicking, arse-licking, politicking **.3** taking, making, stocktaking, breathtaking, piss-taking, painstaking, haymaking, shoemaking, snowmaking, printmaking, brickmaking, clockmaking, bookmaking, home-making, filmmaking, rainmaking, planemaking, winemaking, lovemaking, peacemaking, pacemaking, lacemaking, dressmaking, cheesemaking, matchmaking, watchmaking, toolmaking, trouble-making, earthshaking, tie-breaking, heartbreaking, back-breaking, strikebreaking, housebreaking, undertaking, wicket-taking, moneymaking, merrymaking, papermaking, cabinetmaking **.4** packing, backing, sacking, whacking, tracking, blacking, hopsacking, whipcracking, nerve-racking, nerve-wracking **.5** parking, carking, marking, sarking **.6** stocking, shocking, bluestocking, self-cocking, self-mocking, self-locking **.7** Dorking, Hawking, firewalking, sleepwalking, streetwalking, hillwalking **.8** bloodsucking, motherfucking **.9** Viking, liking **.10** booking, Brooking, onlooking **.11** finicking, Mafeking, bollocking **.12** working, tear-jerking, reworking, outworking, hardworking, woodworking, metalworking **.13** soaking, Woking, stockbroking, pawnbroking, thought-provoking **.14** sinking, shrinking, spanking, ranking, stonking, trunking, freethinking, unthinking, unwinking, unshrinking, unblinking, spelunking, telebanking **.15** erl-king

29.1.15

digging, wigging, rigging, legging, lagging, nogging, frogging, mugging, de-rigging, unflagging, Vereeniging

29.1.16

steaming, Deeming, scheming, trimming, lemming, Fleming, charming, coming, Cumming, mumming, timing, coaming, homing, gloaming, Kunming, Godalming, disarming, uncharming, heartwarming, housewarming, becoming, upcoming, shortcoming, up-and-coming, homecoming, incoming, oncoming, forthcoming, mind-numbing, assuming, Wyoming, unbecoming, unforthcoming, unassuming, unpresuming, multiprogramming

29.1.17

Xining **.1** meaning, screening, greening, leaning, unmeaning, spring-cleaning, self-cleaning, overweening **.2** inning, thinning, winning, twinning, Glendinning, beginning, prizewinning, underpinning **.3** caning, entertaining, self-sustaining, uncomplaining **.4** Steyning, Denning, kenning,

Glendenning **.5** Canning, Manning, Channing, undermanning **.6** Downing, Browning, drowning **.7** Sonning **.8** awning, spawning, dawning, Corning, morning, mourning, warning, aborning **.9** cunning, up and running, gunrunning **.10** vining, signing, Twining, lining, designing, hydrofining, bodylining, interlining **.11** tuning, de Kooning **.12** happening, sharpening, opening, sweetening, lightening, widening, thickening, awakening, reckoning, stiffening, christening, fastening, seasoning, reasoning, poisoning, questioningly, reopening, unthreatening, unfrightening, self-governing, unreasoning, unquestioning, unenlightening, self-determining **.13** turning, Herning, yearning, woodturning, discerning, undiscerning **.14** landowning **.15** lightning **.16** evening, Chevening

29.1.18
hanging, longing, tonguing, part-singing, sight-singing, upbringing, bell ringing, mudslinging, gunslinging, headbanging, straphanging, cliffhanging, suffix, overhanging

29.1.19
spiffing, strafing, offing, morphing, stuffing, roofing, debriefing, understaffing

29.1.20
weaving, sleeving, living, paving, saving, shaving, raving, craving, carving, roofing, Erving, Irving, serving, coving, delving, misgiving, thanksgiving, timesaving, engraving, woodcarving, unloving, fun-loving, skydiving, piledriving, unmoving, self-moving, approving, reproving, timeserving, self-serving, deserving, unswerving, self-deceiving, unbelieving, unforgiving, photoengraving, undeserving

29.1.21
plaything, nothing, something, anything, everything, rebirthing, silversmithing, pennyfarthing, twentysomething

29.1.22
sheathing, scathing, southing, farthing, northing, tithing, writhing, Worthing, clothing, underclothing

29.1.23
unceasing, Gissing, spacing, casing, facing, bracing, tracing, lacing, placing, steeplechasing, interfacing, self-effacing, pressing, dressing, Lessing, blessing, depressing, distressing, hairdressing, vine-dressing, well-dressing, multiprocessing, unprepossessing, passing, surpassing, crossing, voicing, rejoicing, icing, enticing, top-slicing, self-sufficing, self-sacrificing, latticing, defocussing, unpromising, embarrassing, waxing, suffix, kick-boxing, Lansing, conveyancing, unconvincing, underfinancing, teleconferencing, videoconferencing

29.1.24
phrasing, Dowsing, housing, rising, musing, unpleasing, stargazing, self-raising, hellraising,

trailblazing, uprising, surprising, self-rising, amusing, confusing, self-closing, appetizing, enterprising, unsurprising, unamusing, unimposing, unappetizing, self-aggrandizing, uncompromising, unpatronizing, unenterprising, self-fertilizing, self-analysing

29.1.25
dashing, thrashing, lashing, flashing, gushing, Flushing, Cushing, Pershing, lynching, square-bashing, tongue-lashing, inrushing, onrushing, unblushing, garnishing, furnishing, ravishing, unflinching, union-bashing

29.1.26
Beijing, shapechanging, unchanging, unchallenging

29.1.27
teaching, preaching, etching, hatching, churching, lynching, felching, team-teaching, misteaching, schoolteaching, backscratching, potlatching, firewatching, birdwatching, whale-watching, heartsearching, unflinching

29.1.28
ageing, Beijing, staging, edging, lodging, urging, Hsing-king, Nanjing, engaging, ungrudging, obliging, cottaging, managing, shapechanging, unchanging, radiopaging, turbocharging, unobliging, discouraging, unchallenging

29.1.29
forewing, viewing, lapwing, batwing, redwing, hindwing, lacewing, upswing, outswing, waxwing, inswing, downswing, beeswing, underwing

29.1.30
.1 keyring **.2** earring, gearing, shearing, clearing, godfearing, unhearing, child-rearing, puppeteering, privateering, orienteering, unendearing, auctioneering, engineering, electioneering **.3** herring **.4** airing, pairing, paring, sparing, bearing, Behring, Bering, daring, caring, fairing, Waring, wearing, raring, unsparing, cheese-paring, childbearing, talebearing, ball bearing, uncaring, seafaring, wayfaring, worksharing, time-sharing, hardwearing, Mainwaring, overbearing **.5** Bowring **.6** ashlaring **.7** boring, scoring, Goring, mooring, shoring, roaring, flooring, outpouring, goalscoring, ski-joring, riproaring, underflooring **.8** firing, wiring, retiring, untiring, uninspiring, Turing, during, reassuring, nonjuring, whimpering, tampering, whispering, wittering, Kettering, smattering, watering, quartering, muttering, roistering, faltering, self-catering, earthshattering, unflattering, self-flattering, schoolmastering, unaltering, unfaltering, self-registering, ordering, rendering, pondering, wandering, maundering, thundering, wondering, plundering, meandering, Pickering, flickering, tinkering, hankering, unflickering, fingering, scaremongering, glimmering, hammering,

Angmering, unmurmuring, offering, suffering, thank-offering, quivering, Havering, Clavering, flavouring, covering, unwavering, wallcovering, manoeuvring, blithering, gathering, ingathering, woolgathering, posturing, restructuring, sailoring **.9** stirring, Goering, furring, unerring **.10** O-ring **.11** hairspring, headspring, handspring, mainspring, offspring, watchspring, wellspring **.12** Sebring **.13** gee-string, G-string, restring, drawstring, shoestring, bowstring, lutestring, hamstring, unstring **.14** sacring **.15** nosering **.16** bullring

29.1.31
dingaling **.1** Ealing, peeling, dealing, Keeling, feeling, ceiling, shieling, wheeling, appealing, unfeeling, revealing, self-sealing, Darjeeling, unappealing, wheeler-dealing, unrevealing, self-revealing **.2** Pilling, killing, filling, Schilling, shilling, willing, quilling, Trilling, grilling, frilling, painkilling, deskilling, unwilling, unfulfilling, self-fulfilling, wish-fulfilling **.3** shearling, yearling **.4** paling, tailing, mailing, failing, veiling, sailing, Hayling, wailing, railing, grayling, unfailing, boardsailing, unavailing, oversailing, parasailing **.5** spelling, telling, Schelling, dwelling, swelling, misspelling, upwelling, self-propelling, storytelling **.6** lalling **.7** Dowling, cowling, fowling, towelling, wildfowling **.8** sparling, starling, darling, rosemaling **.9** Pauling, calling **.10** piling, tiling, filing, hireling, squireling, hairstyling, unsmiling, reviling **.11** schooling, ruling, gruelling, intercooling **.12** bitterling, chitterling, fosterling, sanderling, underling, fingerling, atheling, enamelling, eco-labelling **.13** Spurling, sterling, Stirling **.14** tenpin bowling **.15** Kipling, stripling, sapling, Jopling, coupling, sampling, dumpling **.16** sibling, scribbling, babbling, dabbling, marbling, Jobling, trembling, rambling, brambling, mumbling, rumbling, grumbling **.17** witling, Catling, Gatling, fatling, rattling, troutling, goatling, saintling, scantling, mantling, priestling, firstling **.18** seedling, reedling, middling, Stradling, codling, Maudling, lordling, doodling, kindling, brandling, foundling, groundling, worldling **.19** weakling, chickling, Hickling, crackling, darkling, rockling, porkling, buckling, duckling, Suckling, suckling, rookling, inkling, tinkling, sprinkling, swashbuckling, motorcycling **.20** pigling, gangling, wrangling, strangling **.21** weanling, yeanling **.22** kingling, youngling **.23** piffling, shuffling, rifling **.24** shaveling, starveling **.25** earthling **.26** Riesling, brisling, nestling, wrestling, rustling, nursling, princeling, unsling **.27** quisling, gosling, puzzling **.28** vetchling, hatchling **.29** fledgling, changeling

29.2
spraing

29.3
Boateng, ronggeng, Kaifeng, ginseng, Hang Seng, Yen-cheng, Yancheng

29.4
pang, spang, bang, bhang, tang, dang, gang, gangue, fang, vang, sang, Shang, Chang, Zhang, hang, wang, whang, twang, rang, prang, sprang, Strang, thrang, yang, Laing, Lang, Lange, clang, slang, kiang, Da Nang, Sturm und Drang

29.4.1
trepang

29.4.2
shebang, gobang, probang, slap-bang, slambang, Battambang, whiz-bang, charabanc, Luang Prabang, Palembang

29.4.3
Sittang, satang, gratin, mustang, Kuomintang, orang-utan

29.4.4
Madang, seladang, Guomindang

29.4.5
tongkang

29.4.6
sirgang, chain gang, Wolfgang, pressgang

29.4.7
siamang

29.4.8
Penang

29.4.9
sight-sang, linsang, parasang

29.4.10
Xizang

29.4.11
Nanchang

29.4.12
Xinjiang, Zhenjiang, Zhanjiang

29.4.13
rehang, Pahang, strap-hang, unhang, overhang

29.4.14
zugzwang, Zaozhuang, burrawang

29.4.15
parang, meringue, serang, harangue, Semarang, boomerang

29.4.16
Kweiyang, bowyang, Sinkiang, Shenyang, Pyongyang

29.4.17
Salang, Erlang, boomslang, ylang-ylang

29.5
langue, zugzwang

29.6
pong, Spong, bong, tong, Tonge, dong, gong, nong, thong, song, Wong, wrong, prong, strong, throng, Jong, langue, long, flong, King Kong, Hong Kong, chaise longue

29.6.1
kampong, pingpong

29.6.2
billabong

29.6.3
biltong

29.6.4
dingdong, Guangdong, Mao Zedong

29.6.5
Mekong, Vietcong

29.6.6
dugong, bogong, wobbegong, Chittagong,
Wollongong

29.6.7
Haiphong

29.6.8
diphthong, triphthong, monophthong

29.6.9
part-song, birdsong, folksong, plainsong,
swansong, evensong, singsong

29.6.10
souchong, Lapsang Souchong

29.6.11
souchong

29.6.12
mah-jong, kurrajong

29.6.13
morwong, currawong

29.6.14
sarong, headstrong, Armstrong, overstrong

29.6.15
Geelong, Shillong, yearlong, kalong, Heilong,
oolong, along, belong, prolong, furlong, oblong,
nightlong, headlong, sidelong, endlong,
week-long, lifelong, livelong, tagalong,
singalong, overlong, cacholong

29.7
boing

29.8
bung, Tonge, tongue, tung, stung, dung, mung,
sung, hung, swung, rung, wrung, sprung,
strung, Yonge, young, lung, clung, flung, slung,
shantung, ox tongue, among, Hoffnung,
Samsung, unsung, rehung, Pahang, strap-hung,
unhung, wall-hung, unsprung, restrung,
hamstrung, unstrung, unwrung, outflung,
unslung, underhung, overhung, overstrung,
aqualung, underslung, Götterdämmerung

29.9
Kung, Jung, Weltanschauung, Bandung,
Hornung, Hoffnung, Samsung, Taichung, Mao
Tse-tung, Gleichschaltung, bremsstrahlung,
Nibelung, Sturmabteilung, Völkerwanderung,
Götterdämmerung

29.10
mung

29.11
vingt-et-un

30.1
beef, Keefe, feoff, fief, thief, seif, sheaf, chief,
reef, brief, Crieff, grief, leaf, Leif, lief, naif

30.1.1
metif, sportif, motif, leitmotif, aperitif

30.1.2
O'Keefe

30.1.3
Hanif

30.1.4
enfeoff

30.1.5
sneak-thief

30.1.6
massif

30.1.7
wheatsheaf, kerchief, neckerchief,
handkerchief

30.1.8
sharif, debrief, newsbrief, Tenerife,
Mazar-e-Sharif

30.1.9
tealeaf, caliph, flyleaf, belief, relief, dropleaf,
broadleaf, figleaf, unbelief, disbelief,
misbelief, interleaf, overleaf, cloverleaf,
bas-relief

30.2
if, iff, biff, tiff, stiff, kif, skiff, miff, niff, sniff, ziff,
Jif®, jiff, whiff, quiff, Rif, riff, griff, griffe, spliff,
cliff, Cliffe, glyph

30.2.1
caitiff, plaintiff, pontiff, mastiff

30.2.2
Cardiff

30.2.3
Braniff, Pecksniff

30.2.4
skew-whiff

30.2.5
tariff, midriff, hippogriff

30.2.6
bailiff, khalif, aleph, Wyclif, Wycliffe, Aycliffe,
Highcliffe, Ratcliffe, Sutcliffe, Radcliffe,
Heathcliff, Northcliffe, Hinchcliffe, triglyph,
McAuliffe, undercliff, anaglyph, hieroglyph,
petroglyph

30.3
safe, seif, SHAEF, chafe, waif, Rafe, Ralph, strafe,
unsafe, vouchsafe

30.4
eff, f, Kiev, teff, deaf, def, kef, Neff®, feoff, chef,
Geoff, Jeff, ref, clef, Nureyev, tone-deaf,
Brezhnev, enfeoff, UHF, aleph, treble clef, Kislev,
ASLEF, Ipatieff, Prokofiev, RAF, TGIF, UNICEF,
Turgenev, Diaghilev

30.5
Taff, DAF®, daff, caff, gaff, gaffe, MAFF, naff, faff, WAAF, WAF, RAF, WRAF, draff, Graf, piaffe: (+ **30.7**)

30.5.1
Piaf

30.5.2
Llandaff

30.5.3
decaf, bathyscaphe

30.5.4
shandygaff

30.5.5
Asaph

30.5.6
chiffchaff

30.5.7
Najaf

30.5.8
paraph, riffraff

30.5.9
pilaf, Olaf

30.6
langlauf

30.7
barf, staff, calf, scarf, Scarfe, chaff, half, coif, strafe, Graf, graph, laugh, Van de Graaff: (+ **30.5**)

30.7.1
Langbaurgh

30.7.2
distaff, tipstaff, jackstaff, pikestaff, flagstaff, Falstaff, epitaph, cenotaph, quarterstaff, overstaff

30.7.3
Metcalf, Metcalfe, mooncalf, headscarf, boxcalf

30.7.4
behalf, scrum-half, wing-half

30.7.5
carafe, giraffe .1 polygraph, ideograph, radiograph, cardiograph, mimeograph, stereograph, choreograph, heliograph, oleograph, autoradiograph, echocardiograph, spectroheliograph, electrocardiograph, bar graph, bigraph, digraph, trigraph, viewgraph, biograph, sciagraph, epigraph, autograph, photograph, pictograph, hectograph, pantograph, magnetograph, chromatograph, phonautograph, cinematograph, telephotograph, microphotograph, hodograph, pseudograph, tachograph, psychograph, zincograph, tomograph, nomograph, homograph, kymograph, thermograph, sphygmograph, seismograph, anemograph, stenograph, monograph, sonograph, chronograph, Chinagraph, phonograph, coronagraph, lithograph, opisthograph, chromolithograph, Addressograph®, xerograph, Ferrograph®, serigraph, paragraph, barograph, spirograph, chirograph, gyrograph, hierograph, spectrograph, micrograph, meteorograph, sub-paragraph, photomicrograph, telegraph, allograph, holograph, stylograph, xylograph, cyclograph, oscillograph, encephalograph, electroencephalograph, shadowgraph, echograph, stevengraph, flannelgraph

30.8
off, boff, toff, doff, cough, scoff, Gough, Hough, coif, quaff, Prof., trough, van Gogh, in-off, on-off, far-off, whooping cough, sending-off, telling-off, roll-on roll-off

30.8.1
payoff, lay-off, playoff

30.8.2
show-off, throw-off

30.8.3
rip-off, stop-off

30.8.4
cutoff, shut-off, Molotov

30.8.5
Tordoff, stand-off, Geldof

30.8.6
pickoff, kickoff, takeoff, Chekhov, Cracow, Zhukov, Kirchhoff, Schwarzkopf, Tretchikoff, Korsakoff, Sholokhov, Cerenkov, Cherenkov, Baryshnikov, Kalashnikov, Rimsky-Korsakov

30.8.7
spin-off, Ustinov, Godunov, Stroganoff, Romanov, Rachmaninov

30.8.8
theosoph

30.8.9
Khrushchev, Gorbachev

30.8.10
Meyerhof, Gasthof, Greenhough, Baader-Meinhof

30.8.11
Kirov, tear-off, eavestrough, Sakharov

30.8.12
Karloff, Wolof

30.9
orfe, Orff, corf, Corfe, morph, Haugh, wharf, Wharfe, Whorf, dwarf, swarf

30.9.1
Ludendorff, Nixdorf®, Waldorf, Düsseldorf, Dahrendorf

30.9.2
biomorph, skeuomorph, polymorph, ectomorph, pseudomorph, endomorph, lagomorph, homomorph, mesomorph, isomorph, tetramorph, allomorph, enantiomorph, gynandromorph, allelomorph

30.10
coif, Cruyff

30.11
puff, buff, Tough, tough, tuff, stuff, duff, cuff, scuff, guff, muff, snuff, sough, chough, chuff, Hough, huff, rough, ruff, Brough, scruff, gruff, luff, bluff, clough, fluff, slough, sluff

30.11.1
puff-puff, powderpuff

30.11.2
rebuff

30.11.3
calc-tuff, dyestuff, feedstuff, foodstuff, greenstuff, overstuff

30.11.4
McDuff

30.11.5
handcuff

30.11.6
earmuff, Whatmough

30.11.7
enough, Goodenough, sure-enough

30.11.8
dischuff

30.11.9
Greenhough, Fernihough

30.11.10
woodruff, dandruff, overruff

30.11.11
Fairclough, Coleclough

30.12
knife, fife, Fyfe, wife, rife, strife, life, bowie knife, jack-knife, penknife, spaewife, midwife, goodwife, housewife, fishwife, alewife, loosestrife, true-life, pro-life, lowlife, nightlife, wildlife, shelf-life, still-life, paperknife, butter knife, Yellowknife, afterlife

30.13
oof, poof, pouf, pouffe, spoof, goof, hoof, woof, roof, proof, yoof, Heugh, loof, kloof

30.13.1
Tartuffe

30.13.2
shadoof

30.13.3
behoof

30.13.4
re-roof, reproof, showerproof, fireproof, heatproof, shotproof, rot-proof, lightproof, rustproof, burstproof, skidproof, windproof, soundproof, childproof, leakproof, shockproof, shrinkproof, flameproof, bombproof, stormproof, rainproof, thornproof, sunproof, ovenproof, mothproof, greaseproof, disproof, gasproof, Chilpruf, shellproof, foolproof,

pent-roof, unroof, sunroof, tamper-proof, shatterproof, waterproof, underproof, overproof, weatherproof, bulletproof

30.13.5
aloof, witloof

30.14
Asaph, Joseph, kerchief, mischief, teraph, seraph, serif, sheriff, paraph, caliph, Olaf, neckerchief, handkerchief, sans serif

30.15
turf, kerf, scurf, smurf, serf, surf, returf, windsurf, sang-de-boeuf, AstroTurf®

30.16
oaf, loaf, Lagerlöf, sugarloaf

30.17
Dummkopf, Schwarzkopf, Kulturkampf

30.18
nymph, lymph, umph, triumph, bumf, humph, oomph, harrumph, galumph, perilymph, endolymph, Kulturkampf, Arc de Triomphe

30.19
Banff

30.20.1
sylph, Wilf

30.20.2
elf, pelf, self, themself, shelf, Guelph, ourself, yourself, myself, thyself, herself, itself, himself, oneself, bookshelf, mantelshelf

30.20.3
Ralph

30.20.4
golf, Wolf, Rolf, Botolph, Rudolph, Randolph

30.20.5
gulf, Biddulph, ingulf, engulf, Ranulf

30.20.6
wolf, Wolfe, Woolf, she-wolf, werewolf, Beowulf, aardwolf, Cynewulf

31.1
eve, Yves, peeve, steeve, Steve, Neave, thieve, sheave, heave, weave, we've, reave, reeve, reive, breve, greave, grieve, leave, cleave, Gleave, sleeve, naive, qui vive

31.1.1
recitative

31.1.2
khedive, Maldive, Laccadive

31.1.3
Genevieve, Tel Aviv

31.1.4
perceive, deceive, receive, conceive, apperceive, undeceive, preconceive, misconceive

31.1.5
achieve, underachieve, overachieve

31.1.6
upheave

31.1.7
folkweave, inweave, enweave, interweave

31.1.8
bereave, reprieve, portreeve, retrieve, Orgreave, aggrieve, Congreve, yestereve, semibreve, Tananarive

31.1.9
way leave, believe, relieve, shirtsleeve, make-believe, disbelieve, interleave, oversleeve

31.2
spiv, give, Viv, sieve, chiv, shiv, we've, live

31.2.1
.1 accretive, excretive, suppletive, completive, expletive **.2** radiative, recreative, procreative, palliative, irradiative, alleviative, appreciative, associative, dissociative, enunciative, denunciative, renunciative, appropriative, conciliative, retaliative, exfoliative, inappreciative, unappreciative **.3** stative, dative, native, creative, uncreative, inchoative, dissipative, approbative, incubative, disapprobative, rotative, gustative, quantitative, denotative, annotative, connotative, hesitative, commutative, qualitative, oxidative, exudative, elucidative, vindicative, implicative, propagative, segregative, consummative, emanative, innovative, renovative, compensative, concentrative, castrative, adumbrative, illustrative, execrative, commiserative, redintegrative, illative, prolative, ventilative, nomenclative **.4** Etive **.5** sportive, supportive, abortive, extortive, unsupportive **.6** exploitive **.7** constructive **.8** restitutive, substitutive, constitutive, evolutive, resolutive, redistributive **.9.1** evacuative, continuative, insinuative, evaluative, stick-to-it-ive, intuitive, nuncupative, inculpative, participative, anticipative, probative, combative, prohibitive, inhibitive, rebarbative, perturbative, appetitive, repetitive, competitive, uncompetitive, partitive, portative, hortative, assortative, exhortative, exploitative, excitative, putative, imputative, transmutative, dubitative, entitative, meditative, imitative, limitative, vegetative, cogitative, irritative, delimitative, capacitative, resuscitative, excogitative, authoritative, interpretative, rehabilitative, debilitative, facilitative, quotative, optative, factitive, tentative, quantitive, fermentative, augmentative, preventative, presentative, frequentative, argumentative, representative, unrepresentative, misrepresentative, manifestative, facultative, consultative, sedative, additive, auditive, laudative, degradative, retardative, denudative, siccative, fricative, precative, vocative, locative, talkative, predicative, indicative, affricative, explicative, evocative, provocative, dedicative, medicative,

judicative, desiccative, educative, deprecative, lubricative, replicative, unprovocative, prognosticative, adjudicative, communicative, significative, reduplicative, multiplicative, incommunicative, uncommunicative, excommunicative, intercommunicative, negative, ergative, purgative, colligative, derogative, prerogative, instigative, irrigative, aggregative, seronegative, rhesus-negative, interrogative, investigative, electronegative **.9.2** primitive, amative, calmative, normative, formative, desquamative, preformative, performative, reformative, informative, transformative, estimative, affirmative, confirmative, uninformative, approximative, definitive, infinitive, genitive, lenitive, progenitive, philoprogenitive, sanative, unitive, punitive, combinative, detonative, criminative, carminative, nominative, ruminative, germinative, culminative, concatenative, agglutinative, procrastinative, coordinative, subordinative, recriminative, discriminative, denominative, illuminative, determinative, originative, imaginative, opinionative, indiscriminative, ratiocinative, unimaginative, alternative, donative, conative, cognitive, precognitive **.9.3** privative, derivative, conservative, preservative, fixative, laxative, sensitive, transitive, pulsative, capacitive, adversative, insensitive, unsensitive, intransitive, hypersensitive, photosensitive, positive, causative, acquisitive, inquisitive, prepositive, appositive, oppositive, diapositive, postpositive, expositive, transpositive, accusative, contrapositive, seropositive, rhesus-positive, electropositive, initiative, fugitive **.9.4** meliorative, deteriorative, ameliorative, imperative, narrative, reparative, preparative, comparative, declarative, pejorative, explorative, restorative, durative, curative, maturative, depurative, separative, operative, corporative, temperative, evaporative, preoperative, cooperative, postoperative, inoperative, recuperative, vituperative, interpretive, uncooperative, vibrative, deliberative, elaborative, collaborative, corroborative, reverberative, iterative, nutritive, alterative, reiterative, alliterative, obliterative, federative, desiderative, penetrative, ministrative, demonstrative, remonstrative, administrative, undemonstrative, interpenetrative, secretive, decorative, lucrative, figurative, prefigurative, invigorative, integrative, disintegrative, numerative, commemorative, agglomerative, enumerative, generative, degenerative, regenerative, exonerative, remunerative, unremunerative, perforative, proliferative, ulcerative, acculturative, indurative, refrigerative, exaggerative, suppurative, exhilarative, accelerative, attributive, retributive, contributive, distributive, consecutive, executive, diminutive, inconsecutive, relative, volitive, ablative, isolative, appellative, irrelative, correlative, mutilative, copulative, speculative, circulative, calculative, regulative, stimulative, simulative, emulative, cumulative, superlative, contemplative, legislative, extrapolative, interpolative, assimilative, congratulative, manipulative, gesticulative, inoculative, coagulative, accumulative, recapitulative **.10** furtive, assertive, introvertive, nonassertive, unassertive, self-assertive **.11** motive, votive, emotive, promotive, leitmotive, automotive, locomotive, magnetomotive, electromotive **.12** descriptive, prescriptive, proscriptive, inscriptive, transcriptive, perceptive, deceptive, susceptive, receptive, preceptive, inceptive, conceptive, proprioceptive, apperceptive, unperceptive, interceptive, self-deceptive, interoceptive, contraceptive, unreceptive, exteroceptive, captive, adaptive, maladaptive, co-optive, adoptive, resorptive, absorptive, adsorptive, irruptive, eruptive, corruptive, disruptive, interruptive, preemptive, redemptive, assumptive, consumptive, presumptive, resumptive **.13.1** fictive, depictive, addictive, predictive, vindictive, convictive, restrictive, constrictive, afflictive, maledictive, nonrestrictive, vasoconstrictive **.13.2** perspective, respective, prospective, detective, protective, connective, affective, effective, perfective, defective, infective, advective, invective, convective, ejective, rejective, projective, subjective, objective, directive, corrective, elective, collective, selective, reflective, inflective, irrespective, retrospective, introspective, self-protective, imperfective, ineffective, intellective, recollective, self-elective, unselective, unreflective, overprotective **.13.3** active, tractive, reactive, coactive, proactive, inactive, enactive, olfactive, attractive, detractive, retractive, subtractive, contractive, abstractive, extractive, diffractive, refractive, abreactive, unreactive, radioactive, psychoactive, vasoactive, retroactive, stupefactive, liquefactive, rarefactive, putrefactive, hyperactive, interactive, counteractive, overactive, unattractive **.13.4** octave, adductive, eductive, deductive, seductive, reductive, productive, inductive, conductive, destructive, obstructive, instructive, deconstructive, reproductive, unproductive, self-inductive, self-destructive, reconstructive, unconstructive, counterproductive, superconductive, photoconductive, adjective **.13.5** distinctive, extinctive, instinctive, adjunctive, subjunctive, injunctive, conjunctive, disjunctive, indistinctive **.14** plaintive, substantive, attentive, retentive, pendentive, preventive, inventive, incentive, disincentive, appointive, inattentive, irretentive, unretentive, overattentive, uninventive **.15** festive, restive, costive, resistive,

digestive, suggestive, ingestive, congestive, contrastive, exhaustive, combustive, indigestive, unsuggestive **.16** assaultive

31.2.2
endive, Laccadive, gerundive

31.2.3
forgive, misgive

31.2.4
.1 cohesive, adhesive, self-adhesive **.2** missive, emissive, omissive, permissive, remissive, submissive, admissive, dismissive, transmissive, derisive **.3** suasive, evasive, pervasive, invasive, assuasive, persuasive, dissuasive, abrasive, appraisive, unpersuasive **.4** essive, recessive, obsessive, excessive, successive, concessive, possessive, oppressive, depressive, suppressive, repressive, impressive, compressive, expressive, egressive, regressive, digressive, aggressive, degressive, progressive, ingressive, transgressive, retrocessive, unimpressive, inexpressive, unexpressive, self-expressive, nonaggressive, unaggressive, unprogressive, retrogressive, immunosuppressive **.5** passive, massive, impassive **.6** tussive, jussive, percussive, concussive, repercussive **.7** divisive, decisive, incisive, indecisive **.8** conducive, protrusive, obtrusive, intrusive, extrusive, abusive, amusive, effusive, diffusive, perfusive, infusive, illusive, allusive, elusive, delusive, collusive, occlusive, seclusive, reclusive, preclusive, inclusive, conclusive, exclusive, unobtrusive, inconclusive, unexclusive **.9** purposive **.10** cursive, coercive, dispersive, abstersive, precursive, recursive, incursive, discursive, excursive, aversive, perversive, subversive, inversive, introversive **.11** plosive, erosive, corrosive, implosive, explosive **.12** reflexive **.13** pensive, evincive, suspensive, expensive, intensive, ostensive, extensive, coextensive, offensive, defensive, expansive, responsive, inexpensive, hypertensive, hypotensive, self-defensive, inoffensive, counteroffensive, apprehensive, comprehensive, irresponsive, unresponsive, · misapprehensive **.14** repulsive, propulsive, impulsive, compulsive, expulsive, emulsive, revulsive, convulsive, electroconvulsive

31.2.5
relive, olive, outlive, Palmolive®

31.3
pave, stave, Dave, Cave, cave, gave, Maeve, knave, nave, fave, they've, save, shave, waive, wave, rave, brave, crave, grave, lave, clave, glaive, slave

31.3.1
octave, palstave

31.3.2
concave, biconcave, planoconcave

31.3.3
agave, forgave, misgave

31.3.4
spokeshave, aftershave

31.3.5
behave, misbehave

31.3.6
airwave, heatwave, shortwave, tidewave, brainwave, microwave

31.3.7
deprave, outbrave, Segrave, margrave, Wargrave, burgrave, Redgrave, landgrave, Waldegrave, engrave, Cosgrave, Musgrave, palsgrave, Palgrave, Sulgrave, architrave

31.3.8
Olave, enclave, conclave, exclave, enslave, autoclave

31.4
Kiev, Rev., rev, lev, Nureyev, Laptev, Negev, Brezhnev, maglev, Mendeleev

31.5
have, lav, satnav, Olav, Wroclaw

31.6
Zouave, starve, calve, carve, varve, halve, suave, grave, Graves, Slav, Gustave, Algarve, moshav, Wroclaw, Yugoslav

31.7
of, Lvov, Karpov, Labov, Lermontov, Chekhov, Cracow, Kharkov, Zhukov, Zhdanov, Azov, Kirov, hereof, whereof, c/o, thereof, improv, Pavlov, unthought-of, Maksutov, Molotov, undreamt-of, unheard-of, undreamed-of, Nabokov, Tretyakov, Cherenkov, Asimov, Ustinov, Romanov, Kasparov, Sakharov, Baryshnikov

31.8
dove, guv, shove, love, luv, glove, above, ring-dove, turtledove, true love, foxglove, self-love, light-o'-love, tug-of-love

31.9
I've, dive, skive, five, chive, gyve, jive, hive, wive, swive, rive, strive, drive, thrive, shrive, live, Clive, skydive, skin-dive, endive, swandive, nosedive, archive, Argive, connive, survive, revive, ogive, beehive, arrive, derive, deprive, contrive, self-drive, alive, scuba-dive, swallow-dive, MI5, overdrive, rear-wheel drive

31.10
poove, move, who've, prove, groove, you've, Louvre, remove, behoove, approve, reprove, improve, disprove, tongue-and-groove, countermove, disapprove, microgroove, interfluve

31.11
perv, derv, curve, MIRV, nerve, verve, serve, swerve, chef-d'oeuvre, hors-d'oeuvre, decurve, recurve, incurve, Deneuve, unnerve, re-serve, disserve, šubserve, conserve, deserve, reserve, preserve, observe, unreserve, roman-fleuve, ready-to-serve

31.12
stove, dove, cove, mauve, fauve, Jove, hove, wove, rove, trove, strove, drove, grove, throve, shrove, clove, Labov, crash-dove, alcove, behove, inwove, enwove, mangrove, Musgrove, Bromsgrove, Snelgrove, unrove, Cazenove, interwove, Aldergrove

31.13
delve, shelve, helve, twelve, valve, salve, solve, bivalve, check valve, lipsalve, evolve, devolve, revolve, involve, convolve, exsolve, dissolve, resolve, absolve, multivalve, univalve, redissolve

32.1
teeth, Keith, Meath, neath, sheath, heath, Reith, wreath, Leith, Cowdenbeath, eyeteeth, buck teeth, dogteeth, Monteith, Hadith, Dalkeith, Westmeath, beneath, Polzeath, unsheathe, Blackheath, Lakenheath, bequeath, Portreath, underneath, Bexleyheath, B'nai B'rith

32.2
pith, kith, myth, smith, Smyth, withe, frith

32.2.1
Lapith

32.2.2
Edith, Meredith

32.2.3
Naismith, Grossmith, whitesmith, wordsmith, goldsmith, blacksmith, locksmith, jokesmith, tinsmith, gunsmith, songsmith, Hindemith, Ladysmith, coppersmith, Hammersmith, silversmith, Arrowsmith

32.2.4
zenith

32.2.5
Griffith, Japheth

32.2.6
Osyth

32.2.7
Blawith, Sopwith, outwith, Ystwyth, Asquith, forthwith, Aberystwyth

32.2.8
Winfrith, Hollerith, Chapel-en-le-Frith

32.2.9
Delyth, tallith, trilith, eolith, oolith, lopolith, phytolith, otolith, laccolith, coccolith, megalith, regolith, xenolith, monolith, batholith, microlith, peristalith

32.3
Criccieth

32.4
Snaith, faith, saithe, wraith, Galbraith, inter-faith

32.5
Beth, death, 'sdeath, saith, Seth, breath, Criccieth, Macbeth, Lisbeth, Toxteth, Japheth, Polzeath, Jerez, Brandreth, megadeath, shibboleth, isopleth

32.6
Cath, Kath, math, hath, strath, lath, Plath,
De'ath: (+ **32.8**)

32.6.1
Díaz

32.6.2
telepath, osteopath, homeopath, homoeopath,
sociopath, psychopath, neuropath, naturopath,
allopath

32.6.3
polymath, aftermath, opsimath

32.6.4
chaetognath

32.7
mouth, south, Routh, drouth, Louth,
Wearmouth, wry-mouth, bad-mouth,
loudmouth, widemouth, big mouth, frogmouth,
Tynemouth, Avonmouth, Alnmouth, Exmouth,
Grangemouth, goalmouth, Lossiemouth,
blabbermouth, motormouth, mouth-to-mouth,
Oystermouth, Cockermouth

32.8
path, Baath, Barth, bath, garth, hearth, lath,
warpath, bypath, towpath, footpath, eyebath,
hipbath, footbath, mudbath, bloodbath, bird
bath, sand-bath, sitz-bath, Hogarth, Aysgarth,
Talgarth, Penarth, McGrath, condylarth,
Rabindranath: (+ **32.6**)

32.9
coth, Goth, moth, Thoth, Wath, swath, Roth,
wrath, wroth, broth, troth, froth, cloth, Sabaoth,
Naboth, hawkmoth, snow-broth, cerecloth,
J-cloth®, haircloth, floorcloth, waist-cloth,
broadcloth, backcloth, sackcloth, loincloth,
facecloth, grasscloth, waxcloth, cheesecloth,
dishcloth, washcloth, sailcloth, oilcloth,
tablecloth, saddlecloth, Visigoth, Ostrogoth,
behemoth, tiger moth, leathercloth

32.10
Porth, Borth, north, forth, fourth, swath,
Bridgnorth, Seaforth, Garforth, Cutforth,
Stainforth, Carnforth, Gosforth, thenceforth,
henceforth, Dishforth, Ampleforth, Aberporth,
Perranporth, Palmerston North

32.11
doth

32.12
Rosyth, Forsyth, Gwendraeth

32.13
booth, Boothe, tooth, couth, sooth, ruth, truth,
strewth, struth, youth, sleuth, tolbooth,
tollbooth, sawtooth, eyetooth, buck tooth,
dogtooth, houndstooth, snaggletooth, uncouth,
vermouth, Maynooth, forsooth, untruth,
Redruth, Duluth, sabretooth

32.14.1
eightieth, fortieth, thirtieth, twentieth,
ninetieth, seventieth, fiftieth, sixtieth

32.14.2
Haworth, Howarth

32.14.3
Goliath

32.14.4
doeth

32.14.5
goeth

32.14.6
ha'p'orth, Morpeth, turpeth, Elspeth

32.14.7
zibeth, sabbath, Narberth, Digbeth, Lambeth,
Elsbeth, Lisbeth, Elisabeth, Elizabeth

32.14.8
Toxteth

32.14.9
Judith

32.14.10
Succoth, Hesketh

32.14.11
Plymouth, Weymouth, mammoth, Yarmouth,
vermouth, Dartmouth, Sidmouth,
Teignmouth, Lynmouth, Monmouth,
Bournemouth, Portsmouth, Exmouth,
bismuth, Falmouth, behemoth, azimuth,
altazimuth

32.14.12
Gwyneth, pennyworth, Kenneth,
Gwenyth, twopennyworth, halfpennyworth,
Merioneth

32.14.13
Garforth, Spofforth, Cutforth, Holmfirth,
Stainforth, Gosforth, Horseforth, Dishforth

32.14.14
Culceth

32.14.15
Hayworth, Haworth, Iorwerth, Hepworth,
Papworth, Knebworth, Whitworth, Petworth,
Wentworth, Warkworth, Duckworth,
Dankworth, Tamworth, Farnworth,
Wirksworth, Bosworth, jobsworth, Wadsworth,
Wordsworth, Wandsworth, Holdsworth,
Emsworth, Hainsworth, Harmsworth,
Unsworth, Halesworth, Molesworth,
Wigglesworth, Ashworth, Rushworth,
Letchworth, Edgeworth, Walworth, Lulworth,
Woolworth, Shuttleworth, Kenilworth,
Isleworth, twopennyworth, Butterworth,
Lutterworth, pennyworth, Illingworth,
Hollingsworth, Sawbridgeworth

32.14.16
Gareth, Brandreth, Nazareth

32.14.17
Silloth, Lilith, shibboleth, Watendlath

32.14.18
Machynlleth

32.15
earth, Perth, berth, birth, dearth, girth, mirth, firth, worth, unearth, Moray Firth, Solway Firth

32.15.1
rebirth, childbirth, stillbirth, afterbirth

32.15.2
self-worth, halfpennyworth, twopennyworth

32.16
oath, both, Thoth, quoth, Roath, Roth, wroth, troth, growth, loath, sloth, zeroth, betroth, regrowth, upgrowth, outgrowth, ingrowth, intergrowth, undergrowth, overgrowth

32.17
depth, in-depth

32.18
width, eighth, breadth, thousandth, bandwidth, hairbreadth, handbreadth, hairsbreadth, handsbreadth, hundredth

32.19
strength, length, calf-length, wavelength, under-strength

32.20
warmth

32.21
plinth, nth, tenth, month, ninth, seventh, thousandth, dozenth, Corinth, eighteenth, fourteenth, thirteenth, umpteenth, nineteenth, seventeenth, fifteenth, sixteenth, helminth, jacinth, hyacinth, absinth, absinthe, labyrinth, perianth, chrysanth, twelvemonth, billionth, millionth, zillionth, trillionth, eleventh, terebinth, aschelminth, colocynth, tragacanth, coelacanth, amaranth, crème de menthe, quintillionth, sextillionth, platyhelminth

32.22
fifth, twelfth

32.23
sixth

32.24
spilth, tilth, filth, stealth, health, wealth, coolth, commonwealth

33.1
teethe, Meath, seethe, sheathe, wreathe, breathe, unsheathe, bequeath, inbreathe, inwreathe, enwreathe, Pontypridd

33.2
with, withe, Gruffydd, Dafydd, herewith, therewith, wherewith, outwith, forthwith, Meredydd, Senghenydd, Trawsfynydd

33.3
spathe, bathe, staithe, scathe, saithe, swathe, rathe, lathe, sunbathe, enswathe, unswathe

33.4
eth, Gorsedd

33.5
mouth, bad-mouth

33.6
Blawith

33.7
tithe, Smythe, scythe, Hythe, withe, writhe, lithe, blithe, Blyth, Rotherhithe

33.8
booth, Boothe, smooth, smoothe, soothe, tollbooth

33.9
Gwynedd, cynghanedd

33.10
loathe, clothe, betroth, reclothe, unclothe

34.1
peace, piece, geese, Nice, niece, fils, cease, Rees, Rhys, Preece, crease, creese, Cris, kris, grease, Greece, lease, police, fleece, de Vries

34.1.1
T-piece, earpiece, hairpiece, eyepiece, two-piece, apiece, showpiece, set-piece, headpiece, codpiece, sidepiece, Makepeace, workpiece, timepiece, Greenpeace, crownpiece, mouthpiece, crosspiece, tailpiece, Smallpiece, mantelpiece, chimney piece, centrepiece, masterpiece, altarpiece, frontispiece

34.1.2
obese

34.1.3
metis, Matisse, pastis

34.1.4
anis, Bernice, Denise, MacNeice, chersonese, Berenice

34.1.5
cassis, decease, surcease, predecease, crème de cassis

34.1.6
Cochise

34.1.7
Terese, cerise, Charisse, caprice, Patrice, Dotrice, lectrice, Castries, decrease, Lucrece, increase, degrease, Dumfries, calabrese, cantatrice, ambergris, verdigris

34.1.8
release, coulisse, pelisse, police, sublease, underlease, McAleese, re-release

34.2
piss, bis, Diss, kiss, miss, vis, this, sis, hiss, cuisse, Swiss, Chris, bliss

34.2.1
dais

34.2.2
Powys

34.2.3
tenuis

34.2.4
Brewis, Lewes, lewis, Louis, St Louis

34.2.5
Lois, allantois

34.2.6
apis, Pepys, coppice, Kempis, Thespis, hospice, auspice, Serapis, precipice

34.2.7
Forbes, ibis, pubis, abyss, mons pubis, Anubis, cannabis, arabis

34.2.8
Thetis, treatise, diabetes, aetatis, clematis, Lettice, Attis, brattice, abattis, cottise, glottis, proglottis, epiglottis, mortise, fortis, rigor mortis, aqua fortis, neuritis, nephritis, cutis, abatis, Curtis, Otis, myosotis, haliotis, stephanotis, factice, practice, practise, malpractice, prentice, Prentiss, mantis, Atlantis, Propontis, compos mentis, in loco parentis, testis, pastis, justice, Alcestis, injustice, armistice, pneumocystis, ovotestis

34.2.9
Geddes, caddis, Gladys, Tardis, Sardis, cowardice, stewardess, Landis, jaundice, Aldis, hendiadys, prejudice, Charybdis, de profundis, Scylla and Charybdis, mutatis mutandis

34.2.10
rachis, orchis, Hotchkiss, Colchis, Dukakis, Theodorákis

34.2.11
Figgis, haggis, Boggis, Menzies, Walpurgis

34.2.12
Amis, premise, premiss, airmiss, amice, pomace, commis, promise, pumice, koumiss, amiss, remiss, dermis, kermis, hit-and-miss, dismiss, extremis, Artemis, Salamis, in extremis, Semiramis, epidermis, hypodermis, epididymis

34.2.13
penis, finis, lenis, Glynis, Ennis, tennis, Denis, Denys, Venice, Glenys, anise, cornice, Tunis, lychnis, Daphnis, Maginnis, McGuinness, Pendennis, Wincarnis, Kiwanis, reminisce, Erinys, Adonis, aepyornis, Barrow-in-Furness, Issigonis, lex talionis

34.2.14
aphis, office, Memphis, artifice, edifice, benefice, orifice

34.2.15
Bevis, Nevis, Divis, Avis®, Davies, Davis, mavis, crevice, clevis, Travis, parvis, parvise, Jarvis, Purves, Purvis, service, Servis, Jervis, Bovis, Hovis®, Clovis, Elvis, pelvis, St Kitts-Nevis, Ben Nevis, disservice, self-service, social service, rara avis

34.2.16
Tethys, Glenrothes

34.2.17
.1 tmesis, thesis, noesis, mimesis, prosthesis, ascesis, paresis, anoesis, catechesis, diakinesis, anamnesis, synizesis, exegesis, hysteresis, diaphoresis, diuresis, enuresis, anuresis, catachresis, epiclesis, aposiopesis, amniocentesis, telekinesis, psychokinesis, karyokinesis, epexegesis, natriuresis, cataphoresis, iontophoresis, plasmapheresis, electrophoresis **.2** basis, stasis, crasis, oasis, trichiasis, mydriasis, parabasis, homoeostasis, haemostasis, cataclasis, filariasis, bacteriostasis **.3** askesis **.4** glacis, Onassis **.5** arsis, catharsis **.6** proboscis, salpiglossis **.7** pertussis **.8** Isis, phthisis, crisis, lysis **.9** Trefusis, Eleusis, Valle Crucis, anacrusis **.10.1** diocese, giardiasis, archdiocese, psoriasis, elephantiasis, candidiasis, leishmaniasis, helminthiasis, bilharziasis, babesiasis, pityriasis, satyriasis, schistosomiasis, trichomoniasis, urolithiasis, toxocariasis, trypanosomiasis **.10.2** anabasis, protasis, entasis, metastasis, hypostasis, aelectasis, iconostasis, ecdysis, syndesis, apodosis, arthrodesis, Lachesis **.10.3** emesis, nemesis, synesis, enosis, genesis, regenesis, biogenesis, diagenesis, oogenesis, syngenesis, epigenesis, polygenesis, osteogenesis, embryogenesis, abiogenesis, metagenesis, mutagenesis, ectogenesis, ontogenesis, frontogenesis, histogenesis, endogenesis, glycogenesis, spermogenesis, thermogenesis, monogenesis, hypnogenesis, carcinogenesis, morphogenesis, mythogenesis, pathogenesis, orthogenesis, orogenesis, sporogenesis, neurogenesis, petrogenesis, heterogenesis, phylogenesis, phytogenesis, psychogenesis, palingenesis, anthropogenesis, gametogenesis, spermatogenesis, agamogenesis, parthenogenesis, epeirogenesis **.10.4** aphesis, symphysis, emphasis, epiphysis, hypophysis, apophysis, re-emphasis, metamorphosis, anamorphosis, underemphasis, overemphasis, prothesis, synthesis, antithesis, diathesis, metathesis, hypothesis, biosynthesis, epenthesis, parenthesis, photosynthesis, chemosynthesis, parasynthesis, diaeresis, syneresis, apheresis, antiphrasis, periphrasis, anagnorisis **.10.5** dialysis, catalysis, analysis, reanalysis, paralysis, thrombolysis, autolysis, photolysis, histolysis, glycolysis, haemolysis, thermolysis, plasmolysis, pyrolysis, hydrolysis, psychoanalysis, microanalysis, cryptanalysis, self-analysis, urinalysis, proteolysis, electrolysis, haemodialysis, bacteriolysis, electrodialysis **.11.1** ptosis, gnosis, Phocis, pyosis, meiosis, miosis, symbiosis, ichthyosis, scoliosis, babesiosis, coccidiosis, apotheosis, listeriosis, berylliosis, antibiosis, anabiosis, parabiosis, necrobiosis, pneumoconiosis, endometriosis, mononucleosis, polyposis, thrombosis, ketosis, steatosis, mitosis, kurtosis, proptosis, amitosis, athetosis, keratosis, halitosis, asbestosis, synostosis, phagocytosis, myxomatosis, sarcomatosis, neurofibromatosis, lordosis, lipidosis, acidosis, ketoacidosis, narcosis, mycosis, psychosis, sycosis, syssarcosis, psittacosis, silicosis, metempsychosis,

thyrotoxicosis, zygosis **.11.2** phimosis, zymosis, osmosis, syndesmosis, anastomosis, toxoplasmosis, stenosis, zoonosis, cyanosis, kenosis, hypnosis, prognosis, diagnosis, trichinosis, byssinosis, biocoenosis, melanosis, misdiagnosis, acrocyanosis, avitaminosis, kyphosis, chlorosis, fluorosis, pyrosis, neurosis, cirrhosis, sorosis, sclerosis, fibrosis, hidrosis, necrosis, nephrosis, amaurosis, heterosis, synchondrosis, synarthrosis, enarthrosis, atherosclerosis, leptospirosis, psychoneurosis, trophoneurosis, osteoporosis, arteriosclerosis, psilosis, ankylosis, alkalosis, brucellosis, salmonellosis, pediculosis, tuberculosis, furunculosis, diverticulosis **.12** sepsis, apsis, ellipsis, asepsis, syllepsis, prolepsis, synapsis, synopsis, paralipsis, antisepsis, periapsis, stereopsis, caryopsis, coreopsis, ampelopsis **.13** abscess **.14** pyxis, deixis, lexis, axis, taxis, praxis, Zeuxis, cathexis, Alexis, sparaxis, anaptyxis, apomixis, amphimixis, stereotaxis, hypotaxis, chemotaxis, thermotaxis, parataxis, phyllotaxis, epistaxis, prophylaxis, anaphylaxis **.15** Jancis, Francis, amanuensis, Giraldus Cambrensis **.16** Chalcis, Dolcis®, diastalsis, peristalsis

34.2.18
aegis, Lyme Regis

34.2.19
dehisce

34.2.20
unguis

34.2.21
Eris, derris, Ferris, Llanberis, Apollinaris, arris, Paris, Farris, Harries, Harris, Clarice, Beaumaris, Polaris, lupus vulgaris, orris, Boris, Torres, Torrez, Corris, Maurice, morris, Norris, doch-an-dorris, loris, Flores, cantoris, iris, Osiris, sui juris, clitoris, Charteris, liquorice, eucharis, ascaris, Seféris, dentifrice, avarice, ephemeris, Emrys, mons veneris, sui generis, hubris, ex libris, Cader Idris, mistigris

34.2.22
.1 hamamelis **.2** Dilys, fillis, Phyllis, cilice, Willis, amaryllis **.3** Baylis, Fidelis, physalis, borealis, digitalis, cum grano salis **.4** Ellice, Ellis, trellis **.5** Alice, Tallis, malice, Sallis, challis, oxalis, hemerocallis, tallith **.6** polis, Collis, Hollis, Wallis, Cornwallis, torticollis **.7** schizostylis, arcus senilis **.8** Eirlys, Tripolis, propolis, syphilis, chrysalis, Persepolis, Annapolis, cosmopolis, metropolis, necropolis, acropolis, Minneapolis, Indianapolis, Heliopolis, megalopolis, annus horribilis, annus mirabilis **.9** Perlis **.10** Margolis, Coriolis **.11** Inglis **.12** Tiflis **.13** Majlis

34.3
Pearce, Peirce, pierce, Bierce, tierce, fierce

34.3.1
clypeus, capias, Scorpius, copious, Gropius, impious, transpierce, Asclepius, Procopius

34.3.2
scabious, Fabius, dubious, plumbeous, Eusebius, triphibious, amphibious, Polybius

34.3.3
piteous, Statius, Porteous, duteous, beauteous, luteous, gluteus, courteous, Photius, Proteus, Grotius, plenteous, bounteous, Pontius, Deo gratias, sestertius, discourteous, robustious, rumbustious, galimatias, ignotum per ignotius

34.3.4
tedious, hideous, radius, Thaddeus, sardius, Claudius, studious, studiously, odious, fastidious, perfidious, invidious, insidious, rhomboideus, commodious, Methodius, Herodias, melodious, compendious, incommodious, discommodious, unmelodious, Ozymandias

34.3.5
abstemious, eximious

34.3.6
.1 genius, splenius, Comenius, arsenious, ingenious, Irenaeus, selenious, homogeneous, heterogeneous **.2** Phineas, vimineous, Arminius, gramineous, sanguineous, ignominious, consanguineous **.3** sanious, cutaneous, spontaneous, instantaneous, consentaneous, simultaneous, calcaneus, Pausanias, membraneous, extraneous, percutaneous, subcutaneous, transcutaneous, succedaneous, miscellaneous, porcellaneous, contemporaneous, extemporaneous **.4** Ennius, Nennius **.5** corneous **.6** impecunious **.7** Suetonius, Antonius, harmonious, euphonious, symphonious, erroneous, Petronius, Polonius, felonious, antimonious, inharmonious, unharmonious, disharmonious, sanctimonious, parsimonious, ceremonious, acrimonious, Apollonius, unceremonious **.8** igneous, ligneous, pyroligneous **.9** calumnious **.10** Vilnius

34.3.7
Cepheus, Xiphias, Orpheus, Morpheus

34.3.8
devious, previous, niveous, Flavius, pluvious, pervious, obvious, envious, lascivious, oblivious, Octavius, Vitruvius, Vesuvius, impervious

34.3.9
Pythias, struthious, Boethius, Prometheus, Erechtheus

34.3.10
Theseus, caseous, gaseous, Cassius, osseous, Roscius, nauseous, Lucius, Perseus, gypseous, Celsius, Alcaeus, Tiresias, Odysseus, Dionysius, caduceus, Theodosius, Athanasius, interosseous

34.3.11
caesious, nauseous, Dionysius, Athanasius

34.3.12
Statius, Roscius, Tertius, caduceus, Propertius, sestertius

34.3.13
Regius, Sergius, congius, Pelagius, Hippo Regius, callipygous

34.3.14
aqueous, obsequious, subaqueous, superaqueous

34.3.15
.1 Sirius, delirious **.2** Nereus, serious, imperious, Tiberias, Tiberius, subereous, mysterious, Guarnerius, cinereous, unserious, deleterious, subdelirious **.3** Arius, carious, scarious, various, nectareous, vicarious, precarious, calcareous, vagarious, gregarious, denarius, senarius, nefarious, Aquarius, malarious, hilarious, burglarious, retiarius, Sagittarius, septenarius, octonarius, multifarious, omnifarious, Stradivarius, Belisarius, temerarious, Darius **.4** Marius **.5** spurious, curious, furious, glorious, arboreous, laborious, sartorius, notorious, victorious, Nestorius, uxorious, censorious, usurious, uproarious, incurious, strangurious, penurious, sulphureous, inglorious, vainglorious, meritorious **.6** cupreous **.7** lugubrious, salubrious, opprobrious, insalubrious **.8** vitreous, Atreus, Demetrius, industrious, illustrious **.9** nacreous, ochreous, pancreas

34.3.16
Peleus, Delius, ileus, bilious, alias, malleus, pileus, Julius, coleus, nauplius, Publius, nucleus, Cornelius, Berzelius, Aurelius, punctilious, Sibelius, Vesalius, Vitellius, Equuleus, contumelious, atrabilious, supercilious, Marcus Aurelius

34.4
ace, pace, space, base, bass, dace, dais, case, Scase, mace, face, Sayce, chase, Wace, Weiss, race, brace, trace, grace, Thrace, lace, place, plaice, ambs-ace, wild-goose chase, trotting race

34.4.1
protease

34.4.2
lipase, apace, outpace, airspace, headspace, backspace, workspace, carapace, hyperspace, interspace, aerospace

34.4.3
dBase, rebase, freebase, airbase, abase, debase, wheelbase, database, gynobase, contrabass, bouillabaisse

34.4.4
phosphatase, Fuentes

34.4.5
vendace

34.4.6
staircase, doorcase, ukase, showcase, slipcase, nutcase, suitcase, notecase, bookcase, crankcase, encase, incase, uncase, briefcase, watchcase, uppercase, pillowcase, packing case

34.4.7
zymase, grimace

34.4.8
tenace, hydrogenase

34.4.9
reface, efface, deface, typeface, outface, whiteface, postface, boldface, dogface, paleface, coalface, interface, Boniface, in-your-face

34.4.10
Gervaise, Gervase

34.4.11
rosace, ambs-ace

34.4.12
enchase, steeplechase, paperchase

34.4.13
embrace, vambrace, unbrace, retrace, ratrace, scapegrace, disgrace, millrace, Samothrace

34.4.14
shoelace, replace, fireplace, noplace, showplace, workplace, someplace, birthplace, displace, misplace, bootlace, enlace, unlace, Lovelace, interlace, anyplace, everyplace, marketplace, commonplace, resting-place, plagioclase, orthoclase, periclase

34.5
s, Bes, Bess, Tess, Kes, guess, mess, ness, fess, fesse, cess, sess, chess, jess, Hess, Hesse, press, tress, stress, dress, cress, yes, less, bless, prowess, Jewess, US, clerkess, USS, heiress, stop press, USPS, acquiesce, SAS, SOS, Titaness, Waffen SS, Shakeress, WRVS

34.5.1
abbess, bouillabaisse

34.5.2
Cortes, poetess, countess, giantess, priestess, tristesse, hostess, vicomtesse, prophetess, politesse, viscountess

34.5.3
goddess, stewardess, Druidess, recrudesce, shepherdess, leopardess, incandesce, demigoddess

34.5.4
Borges, outguess

34.5.5
kermess, intumesce

34.5.6
lioness, Lyonnesse, finesse, Furness, senesce, Bowness, Skegness, Stromness, Caithness, Dungeness, Shoeburyness, deaconess, luminesce, canoness, evanesce, governess, Inverness, marchioness, baroness, patroness, rejuvenesce

34.5.7
profess, confess

34.5.8
effervesce

34.5.9
recess, assess, reassess, process, abscess, obsess, excess, access, success, princess, reprocess,

preprocess, subprocess, unsuccess, pterygoid process

34.5.10
possess, repossess, prepossess, dispossess

34.5.11
duchesse, embarras de richesse

34.5.12
largesse

34.5.13
deliquesce

34.5.14
peeress, mayoress, fluoresce, duress, prioress, flouresce, caress, murderess, phosphoresce, authoress, tailoress, effloresce, manageress **.1** heiress, billionairess, millionairess **.2** Mudéjares **.3** procuress, votaress, Shakeress, anchoress, sorceress **.4** oppress, depress, suppress, repress, impress, compress, winepress, express, letterpress, decompress **.5** distress, protectress, overstress, progenitress **.6** redress, tendresse, address, readdress, top-dress, nightdress, shirtdress, headdress, laundress, undress, sundress, housedress, battledress, minidress, underdress, overdress, misaddress, ambassadress **.7** watercress **.8** egress, Negress, regress, tigress, digress, aggress, progress, ogress, ingress, congress, transgress, retrogress

34.5.15
oyez

34.5.16
unless, coalesce, noblesse, opalesce, recalesce, convalesce, nonetheless, nontheless, frijoles, nevertheless

34.6
scarce

34.7
bass, tass, gas, mass, vas, SAS, sass, chasse, Haas, wrasse, trass, strass, crass, frass, lass, en masse, paillasse, Vanden Plas: (+ **34.9**)

34.7.1
Díaz

34.7.2
Phidias, Lysias, Pelias, palliasse, Herodias, Tiresias, Tiberias, Asturias, Ozymandias, Aphrodisias, scire facias, fieri facias, paterfamilias, materfamilias

34.7.3
Trias, hamadryas

34.7.4
psoas, SOAS, Troas

34.7.5
Malpas, Antipas

34.7.6
Donbas, anabas, Kiribati

34.7.7
Gabbitas, demitasse, Kensitas, tarantass

34.7.8
Adidas®, Badedas®, Lycidas, Epaminondas

34.7.9
ACAS, jackass

34.7.10
degas, teargas, bagasse, Vargas, biogas, outgas, Ofgas

34.7.11
Hamas, Mimas, amass, biomass, Lomas, admass, landmass, Candlemas, Quatermass, Childermas, Martinmas

34.7.12
Dinas

34.7.13
Cephas, Caiaphas, volte-face

34.7.14
Chivas, Chavasse, crevasse

34.7.15
Alsace

34.7.16
wiseass

34.7.17
Rojas

34.7.18
IRAS, morass, harass, cuirass, Fortinbras, Madras, Esdras, Mithras, Stallybrass, Hudibras, hippocras, sassafras, Protagoras, Anaxagoras

34.7.19
Hellas, Pallas, alas, Laplace, Ulfilas, Stanislas, Wenceslas

34.8
spouse, Taos, douse, dowse, Gauss, mouse, nous, souse, house, Rowse, Prowse, Strauss, Kraus, grouse, Laos, louse, Klaus, White House, movie house

34.8.1
Windaus

34.8.2
lobscouse

34.8.3
degauss

34.8.4
dormouse, titmouse, fieldmouse, coalmouse, colemouse, Die Fledermaus

34.8.5
Manaus

34.8.6
in-house **.1** teahouse, treehouse **.2** beerhouse **.3** playhouse **.4** warehouse **.5** Bauhaus **.6** storehouse, Moorhouse, whorehouse **.7** poorhouse, powerhouse, firehouse, Charterhouse, porterhouse,

Waterhouse, slaughterhouse, Oosterhuis, sugarhouse, summerhouse, Claverhouse, treasurehouse **.8** rowhouse **.9** chophouse, flophouse **.10** clubhouse **.11** shithouse, statehouse, gatehouse, cathouse, outhouse, pothouse, hothouse, courthouse, nuthouse, Whitehouse, lighthouse, boathouse, penthouse, Lofthouse, guesthouse, resthouse, Gasthaus, oasthouse, malthouse, Salthouse, pilothouse **.12** madhouse, guardhouse, Wodehouse, Woodhouse, roadhouse, roundhouse **.13** bakehouse, steakhouse, deckhouse, Backhouse, Stackhouse, Parkhouse, blockhouse, cookhouse, workhouse, smokehouse, bunkhouse, Monkhouse **.14** Brighouse, doghouse, bughouse **.15** farmhouse, Limehouse **.16** greenhouse, henhouse, townhouse, funhouse, Stonehouse **.17** springhouse, longhouse, meeting house, counting house, Westinghouse, clearing house **.18** roughhouse **.19** bathhouse **.20** gashouse, glasshouse, dosshouse, doll's house, icehouse **.21** almshouse **.22** washhouse **.23** coach house **.24** wheelhouse, alehouse, jailhouse, dollhouse, schoolhouse, tollhouse, coalhouse, barrelhouse

34.8.7
woodgrouse, sandgrouse

34.8.8
delouse, woodlouse, Stanislaus

34.9
arse, pass, sparse, baas, carse, Kars, Maas, farce, kvas, kvass, chasse, Haas, brass, grass, Grasse, class, glass, kick-ass, Khyber Pass, Brenner Pass, coup de grâce, cheval glass

34.9.1
repass, bypass, surpass, impasse, underpass, overpass

34.9.2
smart-arse, smart-ass, demitasse, gravitas

34.9.3
badass, lardass

34.9.4
bagasse

34.9.5
volte-face

34.9.6
Madras, sawgrass, ryegrass, bluegrass, crabgrass, wheatgrass, knotgrass, Snodgrass, lyme-grass, goosegrass, eelgrass, Stallybrass, supergrass, aftergrass

34.9.7
alas, Laplace, declass, subclass, outclass, eyeglass, spyglass, hourglass, stained-glass, sandglass, handglass, wineglass, Ravenglass, tooth-glass, watch-glass, upper-class, inter-class, masterclass, underclass, infraclass, superclass, Plexiglass®, fibreglass, weatherglass, gallowglass, isinglass, Stanislas

34.10
poss., boss, toss, DOS, doss, Cos, cos, Kos, Goss, Gosse, moss, foss, fosse, Voss, joss, Ross, Bros, dross, cross, crosse, loss, gloss, floss, en brosse, weight loss, adios

34.10.1
Eos, Chios

34.10.2
Helios, Makarios

34.10.3
chaos, naos, pronaos, Áyios Nikólaos

34.10.4
Laos

34.10.5
Chios

34.10.6
EPOS, topos, tripos, Atropos

34.10.7
strawboss, rooibos, Phobos, emboss, Lesbos, Cerebos®, Villa-Lobos

34.10.8
Santos, Fray Bentos, asbestos, Domestos®

34.10.9
reredos, kudos, Chandos, Barbados, extrados, Granados, Abydos, Tenedos, Calvados, parados, intrados, MS-DOS®

34.10.10
Pecos, Caicos, Marcos

34.10.11
Lagos, Argos, logos

34.10.12
Demos, Amos, Deimos, Sámos, Ramos, dromos, clubmoss, peatmoss, Pátmos, cosmos, scale-moss, Los Alamos, exophthalmos

34.10.13
Kronos, Minos, Hypnos, Lemnos, Mykonos, Torremolinos

34.10.14
ethos, pithos, Athos, pathos, bathos, benthos, Kórinthos

34.10.15
Knossos, Hyksos, Náxos, Dos Passos

34.10.16
Eros, pharos, Saros, Imbros, recross, Shawcross, across, lacrosse, Cairncross, uncross, crisscross, Greengross, Kinross, albatross, rallycross, motocross, intercross, cyclo-cross, autocross, polocrosse, Ballesteros, monopteros

34.10.17
Delos, Melos, telos, tholos, Pylos, Vólos, Byblos, bugloss, Kinloss, omphalos, semigloss, isogloss, candyfloss

34.11
séance, ambience, faience, Provence, puissance, Saint-Saëns, insouciance, par excellence,

Aix-en-Provence, pièce de résistance, mariage de convenance

34.12
bourse, torse, coarse, corse, course, gorse, morse, Norse, force, sauce, source, hoarse, horse, Trojan Horse, tour de force, tartar sauce, charley horse

34.12.1
indorse, endorse

34.12.2
recourse, midcourse, concourse, discourse, racecourse, minicourse, telecourse, watercourse, intercourse

34.12.3
premorse, remorse

34.12.4
afforce, perforce, workforce, reinforce, enforce, re-enforce, Wilberforce

34.12.5
divorce

34.12.6
resource, outsource'

34.12.7
seahorse, sawhorse, warhorse, shire-horse, carthorse, Whitehorse, draughthorse, packhorse, cockhorse, workhorse, unhorse, racehorse, trace-horse, clothes horse, hobby horse

34.12.8
retrorse, introrse, dextrorse, sinistrorse

34.12.9
Stanislaus

34.13
Boyce, voice, choice, Joyce, Royce, tortoise, devoice, invoice, pro-choice, rejoice, bourgeois, Rolls-Royce®

34.14
us, pus, bus, buss, cuss, Gus, muss, fuss, thus, sus, suss, huss, Russ, truss, plus, debus, airbus, postbus, embus, schoolbus, battlebus, percuss, concuss, cuscus, discuss, untruss, walrus, nonplus, midibus, minibus, trolleybus, blunderbuss, omnibus, overplus

34.15
ice, pice, speiss, spice, bice, tice, dice, mice, gneiss, nice, vice, Weiss, sice, syce, Zeiss, twice, rice, price, Pryce, Bryce, trice, thrice, lice, splice, slice, de-ice

34.15.1
allspice

34.15.2
entice

34.15.3
Fordyce, Brandeis, Jarndyce, merchandise, paradise

34.15.4
pack ice, choc ice

34.15.5
Cemaes, dormice, titmice, fieldmice, coalmice, colemice

34.15.6
suffice, sacrifice, self-sacrifice

34.15.7
device, advice, edelweiss

34.15.8
precise, concise, imprecise

34.15.9
reprice, underprice, overprice, Haltemprice, cockatrice

34.15.10
Dulais, Dowlais, woodlice, topslice, Ystradgynlais

34.16
puss, schuss, sourpuss, Cottbus, Tungus, Anschluss, platypus, Belarus

34.17
douce, goose, moose, mousse, noose, Sousse, Zeus, schuss, deuce, juice, Rhoose, Rousse, russe, spruce, Bruce, truce, use, puce, loose, luce, sluice, au jus, Ballets Russes, charlotte russe

34.17.1
cayuse

34.17.2
papoose

34.17.3
caboose, calaboose

34.17.4
ventouse

34.17.5
Peaudouce®

34.17.6
soukous, couscous

34.17.7
mongoose, wayzgoose

34.17.8
vamoose

34.17.9
burnous

34.17.10
verjuice, bugjuice, limejuice, Betelgeuse: (+ **34.17.13**)

34.17.11
Aarhus

34.17.12
ceruse, Larousse, abstruse, Belarus

34.17.13
re-use, disuse, misuse, overuse, cayuse, prepuce, abuse, self-abuse, retuse, obtuse, produce, adduce, educe, deduce, seduce, reduce, traduce, Peaudouce®, induce, conduce, transduce, reproduce, introduce, reintroduce, superinduce,

overproduce: (+ **34.17.10**), excuse, Syracuse,
hypotenuse, Idomeneus, refuse, diffuse,
profuse

34.17.14
Palouse, footloose, recluse, unloose

34.18
us, this

34.18.1
Zacchaeus, Aeneas, Eneas, Alcaeus, Piraeus,
uraeus, scarabaeus, coryphaeus, Apuleius, Judas
Maccabaeus

34.18.2
Linnaeus, Piraeus, Apuleius, Laius, Antaeus,
Emmaus, Andreas, San Andreas, Archelaus,
Menelaus

34.18.3
prowess

34.18.4
joyous

34.18.5
eyas, pious, Pius, bias, Caius, Gaius, dryas, Lias,
impious, Tobias, Matthias, Arius, Darius, Elias,
Ananias, hamadryas

34.18.6
bourse, menstruous, congruous, incongruous,
fatuous, tortuous, virtuous, sumptuous,
fructuous, unctuous, impetuous, spirituous,
voluptuous, contemptuous, presumptuous,
anfractuous, tempestuous, incestuous,
tumultuous, ignis fatuus, self-contemptuous,
unpresumptuous, arduous, assiduous,
deciduous, vacuous, nocuous, perspicuous,
innocuous, promiscuous, inconspicuous,
ambiguous, contiguous, exiguous,
unambiguous, sinuous, tenuous, strenuous,
continuous, ingenuous, disingenuous,
discontinuous, flexuous, sensuous, sensuously,
mellifluous, superfluous

34.18.7
Jewess, Ewyas, Shavuoth

34.18.8
psoas, loess

34.18.9
.1 Lepus **.2** Lysippus, eohippus, polypous,
Aristippus **.3** Priapus **.4** pappus, Chiapas
.5 carpus, acarpous, syncarpous, oxycarpous,
apocarpous, metacarpus, streptocarpus,
monocarpous, schizocarpous, xylocarpous,
oligocarpous **.6** porpoise, corpus, Malpas, habeas
corpus **.7** upas, lupous, lupus **.8** platypus,
octopus, Oedipus, Atropos, polypus,
Sinanthropus, Zinjanthropus, Paranthropus,
Pithecanthropus **.9** purpose, multipurpose
.10 opus, Scopus, Canopus, magnum opus
.11 pampas, campus, grampus, pompous,
compass, rumpus, Olympus, unpompous, bow
compass, encompass, hippocampus,
gyrocompass **.12** trespass **.13** palpus, pulpous

34.18.10
Phoebus, rebus, gibbous, Abbas, abbess,
shabbos, Arbus, Forbes, niobous, nimbus,
limbus, rhombus, thrombus, plumbous,
bulbous, Cerne Abbas, Barabbas, Barnabas,
omnibus, arquebus, harquebus, Erebus,
Antrobus, succubus, incubus, syllabus, colobus,
iambus, Columbus, virginibus puerisque,
choriambus, dithyrambus, ceteris paribus,
cumulonimbus

34.18.11
.1 foetus, Cetus, quietus, acetous, Miletus,
boletus, Epictetus, polychaetous **.2** Nunc
Dimittis **.3** status, stratus, gratis, flatus, meatus,
hiatus, Donatus, De Freitas, afflatus, apparatus,
saleratus, cirrostratus, nimbostratus, altostratus,
cumulostratus **.4** Bettws, lettuce **.5** lattice
.6 Pilatus, posse comitatus **.7** tortoise, Plautus
.8 Titus, Vitus, St Vitus, duodenitis, osteitis,
fasciitis, ileitis, colpitis, phlebitis, otitis, scrotitis,
cystitis, mastitis, pancreatitis, hepatitis,
dermatitis, stomatitis, sclerotitis, parotitis,
periostitis, myocarditis, mastoiditis, pericarditis,
endocarditis, rachitis, orchitis, bronchitis,
ophthalmitis, splenitis, rhinitis, tinnitus,
tympanitis, retinitis, tendinitis, pneumonitis,
vaginitis, peritonitis, lymphadenitis, mephitis,
vulvitis, synovitis, gingivitis, conjunctivitis,
tenosynovitis, glossitis, myositis, caecitis,
bursitis, sinusitis, fibrositis, appendicitis,
lymphangitis, salpingitis, meningitis,
pharyngitis, laryngitis, scleritis, iritis, pyritous,
pruritis, detritus, metritis, gastritis, arthritis,
arteritis, uteritis, enteritis, mesenteritis,
blepharitis, ovaritis, osteoarthritis, urethritis,
polyneuritis, ureteritis, gastroenteritis,
endometritis, pyelonephritis, colitis, pyelitis,
myelitis, typhlitis, spondylitis, tonsillitis,
valvulitis, cellulitis, Polyclitus, Heraclitus,
osteomyelitis, poliomyelitis, encephalitis,
epicondilitis, diverticulitis, encephalomyelitis
.9 Brutus, arbutus **.10** riotous, fortuitous,
gratuitous, circuitous, poetess, coitus, crepitus,
impetus, champertous, precipitous, Iapetus,
serendipitous, decubitus, Herodotus, fremitus,
vomitus, gummatous, oedematous, eczematous,
calamitous, glaucomatous, sarcomatous,
trachomatous, carcinomatous,
prosenchymatous, parenchymatous,
pachydermatous, prophetess, covetous,
acclivitous, declivitous, Tacitus, felicitous,
solicitous, duplicitous, necessitous, infelicitous,
oversolicitous, ubiquitous, iniquitous, spiritous,
emeritus, Philostratus, Theocritus, Democritus,
Hippolytus **.11** notice, lotus, Duns Scotus
.12 conceptus, eucalyptus, coitus interruptus
.13 ictus, rictus, rectus, cactus, linctus, Sanctus,
prospectus, conspectus, conductus, Oireachtas,
Benedictus, cunnilinctus **.14** Quintus, countess,
Pontus, Qantas®, giantess, tomentous,
portentous, sarmentous, momentous,
apprentice, Diophantus, viscountess,
ligamentous, filamentous, Pocahontas

.15 Lofthouse, Loftus **.16** priestess, cistus, xystus, Festus, cestus, Rastus, Fastus, Eustace, hostess, Sixtus, solstice, Hephaestus, asbestos, Theophrastus, Augustus, interstice **.17** saltus, cultus, poultice, cobaltous

34.18.12
Cardus, bodice, goddess, Midas, nidus, Judas, nodus, Indus, Pindus, Findus, vendace, Candace, Candice, Dundas, fundus, Aldous, Barbados, Badedas®, shepherdess, Lepidus, vanadous, exodus, hazardous, liquidus, solidus, stupendous, tremendous, horrendous, demigoddess, tetrapodous, gastropodous, tylopodous, Enceladus

34.18.13
.1 distichous, hortus siccus **.2** Pecos, Caicos, Zacatecas **.3** Bacchus, Gracchus, Caracas **.4** carcass, Marcus, sarcous, clerkess, Hipparchus, Aristarchus **.5** coccus, trochus, locus, floccus, streptococcus, pneumococcus, gonococcus, diplococcus, staphylococcus, meningococcus **.6** Orcus, Dorcas, caucus, raucous, glaucous **.7** succuss, ruckus **.8** monostichous **.9** soukous, mucous, mucus, fucous, fucus, Lucas, caducous, verrucous, Ophiuchus **.10** Antiochus, abacus, Spartacus, tristichous, classicus, varicose, Leviticus, Caratacus, diplodocus, Callimachus, Telemachus, Nicomachus, Germanicus, deinonychus, Copernicus, Dryopithecus, ulotrichous, umbilicus, Autolycus, locus classicus, Ecclesiasticus, Gigantopithecus, Australopithecus **.11** cercus, circus **.12** focus, hocus, crocus, defocus, refocus, hocus-pocus, autofocus, Archilochus **.13** incus, Pincus, bronchus, uncus, elenchus, Oxyrhynchus, odontorhynchous, ornithorhynchus **.14** discus, viscous, viscus, ascus, fuscous, hibiscus, meniscus, Damascus, molluscous **.15** talcous, sulcus

34.18.14
.1 negus **.2** Tagus, magus, vagus, tragus, Las Vegas **.3** Argus, Vargas **.4** steatopygous, heterozygous, homozygous **.5** pemphigous, pemphigus, azygous, Galapagos, polyphagous, scatophagous, phytophagous, sarcophagus, monophagous, esophagus, oesophagus, coprophagous, saprophagous, necrophagous, xylophagous, phyllophagous, noctivagous, asparagus, nidifugous, analogous, autologous, tautologous, homologous, Areopagus, ichthyophagous, anthropophagous, anthropophagus, entomophagous, heterologous **.6** Burgas, Fergus, Lycurgus, Carrickfergus **.7** bogus **.8** dingus, Mingus, Angus, fungous, fungus, Aer Lingus®, humongous, anilingus, cunnilingus **.9** valgus, ad captandum vulgus

34.18.15
.1 Remus, Nicodemus, Polyphemus, polysemous **.2** grimace, Hieronymus **.3** famous, Seamus, shamus, squamous, ramus, mandamus,

ignoramus **.4** Lammas **.5** gaudeamus, Nostradamus **.6** Thomas **.7** ginormous, enormous **.8** timeous, chymous, Mimas, thymus, rimous, primus **.9** hummus, brumous, strumose, strumous, grumous, spumous, humus **.10** mittimus, Artemus, Septimus, dichotomous, trichotomous, hippopotamus, vidimus, bigamous, digamous, trigamous, agamous, syngamous, amphigamous, polygamous, oogamous, autogamous, cryptogamous, endogamous, homogamous, xenogamous, monogamous, exogamous, heterogamous, phanerogamous, venomous, animus, onymous, bonhomous, unanimous, magnanimous, equanimous, euonymus, hyponymous, eponymous, autonomous, antonymous, pseudonymous, homonymous, anonymous, synonymous, teknonymous, paronymous, pusillanimous, heteronomous, infamous, blasphemous, Decimus, maximus, Onesimus, Pyramus, catadromous, anadromous, posthumous, non possumus, calamus, thalamus, ginglymus, hypothalamus **.11** Thermos®, diathermous, angiospermous, monospermous, gymnospermous **.12** Momus, Lomas, polychromous **.13** Titmus, litmus **.14** Cadmus **.15** nystagmus, borborygmus **.16** isthmus **.17** Christmas **.18** trismus, strabismus, tenesmus, chiasmus, Erasmus, marasmus, vaginismus **.19** Las Palmas, exophthalmus

34.18.16
.1 venous, Venus, genus, heinous, tweeness, freeness, threeness, proteinous, Longinus, saphenous, Malvinas, Maecenas, subgenus, carefreeness, scalenus, silenus, Salinas, intravenous, Cunobelinus **.2.1** Innes, pinnace, Guinness, McInnes, clayiness, gooeyness, chewiness, screwiness, dewiness, glueyness, doughiness, snowiness, showiness, blowiness, shadowiness **.2.2** weepiness, creepiness, sleepiness, nippiness, snippiness, zippiness, chippiness, whippiness, drippiness, slippiness, peppiness, snappiness, sappiness, happiness, crappiness, scrappiness, soppiness, choppiness, stroppiness, floppiness, sloppiness, goopiness, soupiness, droopiness, loopiness, chirpiness, dopiness, mopiness, soapiness, ropiness, skimpiness, crimpiness, campiness, swampiness, bumpiness, stumpiness, dumpiness, jumpiness, humpiness, grumpiness, frumpiness, lumpiness, wispiness, crispiness, pulpiness, unhappiness, scabbiness, shabbiness, crabbiness, flabbiness, knobbiness, tubbiness, stubbiness, chubbiness, srubbiness, grubbiness, shrubbiness **.2.3** peatiness, meatiness, sleetiness, bittiness, wittiness, prettiness, grittiness, mateyness, weightiness, pettiness, sweatiness, battiness, tattiness, cattiness, scattiness, nattiness, fattiness, chattiness, rattiness, doughtiness, goutiness, artiness, tartiness, heartiness, pottiness, spottiness, dottiness, knottiness, snottiness, grottiness, sportiness, naughtiness, haughtiness, smuttiness, nuttiness,

mightiness, flightiness, almightiness, sootiness, snootiness, fruitiness, ricketiness, crotchetiness, fidgetiness, pernicketiness, dirtiness, shirtiness, throatiness, emptiness, mintiness, flintiness, daintiness, scantiness, jauntiness, niftiness, shiftiness, thriftiness, heftiness, draughtiness, craftiness, loftiness, tuftiness, unthriftiness, yeastiness, mistiness, twistiness, pastiness, tastiness, hastiness, testiness, zestiness, chestiness, nastiness, frowstiness, frostiness, bustiness, dustiness, gustiness, mustiness, fustiness, rustiness, trustiness, crustiness, lustiness, feistiness, thirstiness, bloodthirstiness, guiltiness, maltiness, faultiness, saltiness, joltiness, speediness, beadiness, neediness, seediness, weediness, tweediness, reediness, greediness, giddiness, shadiness, steadiness, headiness, readiness, faddiness, dowdiness, rowdiness, cloudiness, tardiness, hardiness, shoddiness, bawdiness, gaudiness, muddiness, ruddiness, bloodiness, tidiness, woodiness, moodiness, broodiness, sturdiness, wordiness, windiness, bendiness, trendiness, sandiness, handiness, randiness, moldiness, mouldiness, unsteadiness, unreadiness, foolhardiness, untidiness, unhandiness, unwieldiness **.2.4** peakiness, sneakiness, cheekiness, squeakiness, streakiness, creakiness, freakiness, leakiness, cliqueyness, pickiness, stickiness, trickiness, snakiness, shakiness, quakiness, flakiness, tackiness, wackiness, crackiness, sarkiness, larkiness, stockiness, cockiness, rockiness, pawkiness, baulkiness, corkiness, gawkiness, chalkiness, duckiness, muckiness, yuckiness, luckiness, pluckiness, cluckiness, unluckiness, spikiness, kookiness, spookiness, flukiness, finickiness, perkiness, murkiness, jerkiness, quirkiness, pokiness, smokiness, folkiness, chokiness, jokiness, hokeyness, croakiness, inkiness, dinkiness, kinkiness, slinkiness, swankiness, crankiness, lankiness, wonkiness, spunkiness, funkiness, chunkiness, riskiness, friskiness, peskiness, boskiness, duskiness, muskiness, huskiness, milkiness, silkiness, bulkiness, sulkiness, plagueiness, egginess, legginess, bagginess, shagginess, jagginess, cragginess, scragginess, bogginess, dogginess, fogginess, sogginess, grogginess, clogginess, mugginess, fugginess, McGinnis **.2.5** steaminess, seaminess, dreaminess, creaminess, gaminess, sameyness, gamminess, jamminess, clamminess, balminess, barminess, smarminess, storminess, gumminess, chumminess, rumminess, crumminess, plumminess, slumminess, griminess, sliminess, roominess, gloominess, worminess, foaminess, homeyness, loaminess, filminess, tinniness, skinniness, zaniness, raininess, braininess, graininess, canniness, downiness, bonniness, tawniness, corniness, thorniness, horniness, brawniness, scrawniness, funniness, sunniness, runniness, spininess, tininess, shininess, brininess, spooniness, puniness, looniness,

boniness, stoniness, phoniness, uncanniness, unfunniness, springiness, stringiness, clinginess, tanginess, slanginess **.2.6** beefiness, leafiness, spiffiness, sniffiness, whiffiness, cliffiness, daffiness, chaffiness, puffiness, stuffiness, huffiness, scruffiness, fluffiness, oofiness, goofiness, scurfiness, comfiness, waviness, heaviness, grooviness, curviness, scurviness, nerviness, top-heaviness, topsy-turviness, pithiness, breathiness, frothiness, toothiness, earthiness, lengthiness, filthiness, stealthiness, healthiness, wealthiness, unhealthiness, swarthiness, worthiness, seaworthiness, airworthiness, noteworthiness, trustworthiness, roadworthiness, blameworthiness, unworthiness, praiseworthiness, newsworthiness, unseaworthiness, creditworthiness, untrustworthiness **.2.7** greasiness, fleeciness, sissiness, priciness, prissiness, raciness, laciness, messiness, dressiness, gassiness, massiness, sassiness, brassiness, grassiness, classiness, glassiness, mousiness, bossiness, mossiness, glossiness, sauciness, horsiness, fussiness, iciness, spiciness, diciness, juiciness, pursiness, tipsiness, ritziness, glitziness, gutsiness, chintziness, tricksiness, sexiness, waxiness, foxiness, folksiness, fanciness, chanciness, bounciness, concinnous, easiness, cheesiness, wheeziness, queasiness, breeziness, sleaziness, busyness, dizziness, fizziness, frizziness, maziness, haziness, craziness, laziness, snazziness, jazziness, drowsiness, frowziness, lousiness, blowsiness, gauziness, noisiness, muzziness, fuzziness, ooziness, booziness, choosiness, wooziness, newsiness, doziness, cosiness, nosiness, rosiness, prosiness, flimsiness, clumsiness, uneasiness **.2.8** dishiness, fishiness, squishiness, swishiness, fleshiness, ashiness, trashiness, splashiness, flashiness, marshiness, squashiness, gushiness, mushiness, plushiness, slushiness, pushiness, bushiness, cushiness, bolshiness, peachiness, preachiness, itchiness, bitchiness, titchiness, kitschiness, twitchiness, techiness, tetchiness, sketchiness, stretchiness, patchiness, catchiness, scratchiness, fratchiness, grouchiness, starchiness, splotchiness, blotchiness, touchiness, churchiness, paunchiness, raunchiness, punchiness, crunchiness, squelchiness, squidginess, staginess, caginess, edginess, podginess, stodginess, dodginess, splodginess, pudginess, smudginess, stinginess, dinginess, manginess, ranginess, sponginess, bulginess **.2.9** eeriness, beeriness, smeariness, cheeriness, weariness, dreariness, leeriness, bleariness, subsidiariness, merriness, airiness, scariness, chariness, hairiness, wariness, glairiness, unwariness, contrariness, tarriness, starriness, sorriness, goriness, hoariness, flouriness, floweriness, miriness, fieriness, wiriness, slipperiness, pepperiness, temporariness, contemporariness, slobberiness, rubberiness, jitteriness, wateriness, butteriness, momentariness, sedentariness, predatoriness, transitoriness, tributariness, dilatoriness, militariness, solitariness, peremptoriness, refractoriness, perfunctoriness, desultoriness, consiliatoriness, hereditariness, sanitariness, contradictoriness, satisfactoriness, rudimentariness, elementariness, complementariness, voluntariness, unsatisfactoriness, powderiness, dodderiness, thunderiness, secondariness, sugariness, summariness, customariness, orneriness, mercenariness, ordinariness, stationariness, visionariness, sanguinariness, extraordinariness, savouriness, quaveriness, silveriness, unsavouriness, featheriness, leatheriness, cursoriness, illusoriness, necessariness, compulsoriness, unnecessariness, literariness, extemporariness, arbitrariness, exemplariness, furriness, wintriness, paltriness, sultriness, tawdriness, hungriness **.2.10** steeliness, mealiness, silliness, chilliness, hilliness, frilliness, scaliness, shaliness, smelliness, jolliness, oiliness, wiliness, woolliness, unruliness, neighbourliness, wobbliness, painterliness, sisterliness, masterliness, orderliness, elderliness, treacliness, giggliness, beggarliness, mannerliness, weatherliness, fatherliness, motherliness, southerliness, brotherliness, miserliness, leisureliness, gingerliness, scholarliness, unneighbourliness, disorderliness, unmannerliness, unfatherliness, unscholarliness, earliness, pearliness, burliness, curliness, surliness, holiness, lowliness, unholiness, shapeliness, pimpliness, unshapeliness, knobbliness, crumbliness, stateliness, portliness, courtliness, knightliness, sightliness, sprightliness, saintliness, beastliness, priestliness, ghastliness, costliness, ghostliness, unsightliness, deadliness, godliness, lordliness, cuddliness, goodliness, cowardliness, friendliness, kindliness, worldliness, ungodliness, dastardliness, niggardliness, sluggardliness, unfriendliness, unworldliness, user-friendliness, weakliness, sickliness, prickliness, likeliness, wrinkliness, crinkliness, unlikeliness, niggliness, ugliness, seemliness, comeliness, timeliness, homeliness, unseemliness, untimeliness, queenliness, cleanliness, manliness, loneliness, slatternliness, heavenliness, slovenliness, ungainliness, uncleanliness, unmanliness, womanliness, gentlemanliness, unwomanliness, ungentlemanliness, kingliness, wifeliness, housewifeliness, loveliness, liveliness, unloveliness, deathliness, earthliness, unearthliness, bristliness, princeliness, measliness, grisliness, fleshliness **.3** dearness, nearness, sincereness, sheerness, queerness, clearness, austereness, unclearness, anteriorness **.4** anus, gayness, feyness, Janus, greyness, Silvanus, Sejanus, Uranus, migrainous, Coriolanus, Punta Arenas **.5** tenace, menace

.6 spareness, bareness, fairness, squareness, rareness, unfairness, awareness, unawareness, self-awareness **.7** annus, pannus, stannous, Janice, Janis, pandanus, McManus, ananas **.8** Taunus, Kaunas **.9** farness, harness, bizarreness, unharness **.10** Faunus, soreness, rawness, Capricornus, Cassivelaunus: (+ **34.18.16(.15.1)**) **.11** coyness **.12** Ynys **.13** spinous, minus, vinous, sinus, shyness, highness, wryness, spryness, dryness, Linus, flyness, slyness, Plotinus, echinus, Delphinus, Socinus, Aquinas, Quirinus, laurustinus, Antoninus, botulinus **.14** twoness, Souness, trueness, Eunice, skewness, newness, fewness, blueness **.15.1** Oceanus, sourness, direness, lioness, poorness, dourness, sureness, pureness, cocksureness, unsureness, matureness, impureness, demureness, prematureness, ruinous: (+ **34.18.16(.10)**) **.15.2** dapperness, properness, limberness, sombreness, bitterness, tetanus, cretinous, patinous, utterness, gluttonous, Titaness, chitinous, mutinous, glutinous, mountainous, gelatinous, neotenous, monotonous, velutinous, sinisterness, anti-tetanus, tenderness, tendinous, slenderness, wilderness, Holderness, libidinous, Eridanus, cotyledonous, tricotyledonous, platitudinous, multitudinous, pulchritudinous, acotyledonous, dicotyledonous, vicissitudinous, monocotyledonous, trichinous, lichenous, eagerness, meagreness, manganous, overeagerness, heterogonous **.15.3** bimanous, ominous, numinous, luminous, terminus, verminous, germanous, trigeminous, abdominous, bituminous, ceruminous, quadrumanous, albuminous, leguminous, aluminous, voluminous, coterminous, conterminous, diathermanous, prolegomenous, innerness, polyphonous, diaphanous, cacophonous, homophonous, cleverness, cavernous, ravenous, governess, autochthonous, allochthonous, otherness, togetherness, acinus, larcenous, unisonous, treasonous, resinous, poisonous, trigynous, serpiginous, rubiginous, vertiginous, indigenous, omnigenous, oxygenous, terrigenous, pruriginous, perigynous, polygynous, uliginous, fuliginous, impetiginous, cageyness, plumbaginous, pentagynous, decagynous, farraginous, tetragynous, cartilaginous, oleaginous, mucilaginous, autogenous, protogynous, ectogenous, endogenous, trichogenous, oncogenous, homogenous, monogynous, pathogenous, misogynous, schizogenous, exogenous, erogenous, pyrogenous, sporogenous, nitrogenous, hydrogenous, androgynous, acrogenous, erotogenous, aeruginous, ferruginous, tyrannous, baroness, uranous, urinous, thoroughness, membranous, patroness, synchronous, gangrenous, diachronous, isochronous, asynchronous, geosynchronous, villainess, villainous, yellowness, mercilessness, porcellanous

.16 Bernice, furnace, Furness, Avernus, cothernus, cupola-furnace **.17** onus, bonus, tonus, Jonas, Cronus, lowness, Clones, clonus, slowness, Tithonus, narrowness, mellowness, callowness, fallowness, sallowness, shallowness, hollowness, chlamydomonas **.18** steepness, deepness, cheapness, hipness, sharpness, ripeness, limpness, dampness, plumpness, crispness, unsharpness, unripeness, overripeness **.19** glibness, drabness, superbness **.20.1** meetness, neatness, sweetness, fleetness, effeteness, concreteness, discreetness, discreteness, repleteness, completeness, indiscreetness, obsoleteness, incompleteness, fitness, witness, unfitness, eyewitness, decrepitness, immediateness, appropriateness, intermediateness, inappropriateness, straightness, straitness, greatness, lateness, inchoateness, sedateness, innateness, ornateness, cognateness, irateness, wetness, patness, fatness, flatness **.20.2** stoutness, devoutness, tartness, smartness, apartness, Totnes, hotness, squatness, tautness, shortness, adroitness, maladroitness, tightness, whiteness, rightness, brightness, triteness, lightness, slightness, reconditeness, finiteness, uprightness, outrightness, downrightness, forthrightness, politeness, compositeness, impoliteness, cuteness, muteness, astuteness, acuteness, minuteness, hirsuteness, dissoluteness, resoluteness, absoluteness, irresoluteness **.20.3** quietness, unquietness, precipitateness, delicateness, indelicateness, profligateness, ultimateness, definiteness, infiniteness, passionateness, indefiniteness, inordinateness, determinateness, dispassionateness, indiscriminateness, indeterminateness, disproportionateness, covertness, tacitness, illicitness, implicitness, explicitness, oppositeness, inexplicitness, exquisiteness, appositeness, requisiteness, inappositeness, stalwartness, adequateness, separateness, corporateness, temperateness, disparateness, desperateness, literateness, moderateness, obdurateness, accurateness, intemperateness, deliberateness, elaborateness, illiterateness, inveterateness, immoderateness, commensurateness, inconsiderateness, incommensurateness, desolateness, inviolateness, disconsolateness, articulateness, immaculateness, inarticulateness, pertness, curtness, expertness, inertness, overtness, alertness, inexpertness, remoteness **.20.4** aptness, raptness, promptness, adeptness, ineptness, corruptness, abruptness, unkemptness, nondescriptness, strictness, abjectness, directness, erectness, correctness, selectness, compactness, intactness, exactness, abstractness, perfectness, distinctness, succinctness, defunctness, circumspectness, indirectness, incorrectness, matter-of-factness, inexactness, imperfectness, indistinctness, faintness, quaintness, scantness, gauntness,

bluntness, pliantness, flippantness, distantness, ferventness, recentness, absentness, presentness, pleasantness, ancientness, fragrantness, brilliantness, transientness, intentness, currentness, differentness, incessantness, unpleasantness, transparentness, apparentness, swiftness, deftness, daftness, softness, chasteness, fastness, vastness, moistness, justness, barefacedness, shamefacedness, unchasteness, steadfastness, robustness, augustness, unjustness, earnestness, colour fastness, unsteadfastness, farfetchedness, saltness, occultness, adultness, difficultness **.21.1** fluidness, Widnes, unweariedness, weirdness, staidness, deadness, redness, badness, madness, sadness, gladness, proudness, loudness, hardness, oddness, broadness, untowardness, voidness, snideness, wideness, unsatisfiedness, goodness, rudeness, crudeness, shrewdness, lewdness, tiredness, retiredness, frowardness, tepidness, vapidness, rapidness, torpidness, limpidness, insipidness, rabidness, crabbedness, morbidness, turbidness, conceitedness, nitwittedness, quick-wittedness, half-wittedness, outdatedness, elatedness, belatedness, relatedness, inflatedness, complicatedness, unrelatedness, opinionatedness, unsophisticatedness, fetidness, indebtedness, mattedness, light-heartedness, hard-heartedness, good-heartedness, kind-heartedness, warm-heartedness, downheartedness, wholeheartedness, tenderheartedness, spottedness, besottedness, distortedness, benightedness, clear-sightedness, foresightedness, shortsightedness, excitedness, unrequitedness, surefootedness, light-footedness, rootedness, limitedness, spiritedness, unlimitedness, dispiritedness, uninhibitedness, devotedness, uninterruptedness, addictedness, restrictedness, connectedness, collectedness, protractedness, distractedness, abstractedness, unrestrictedness, unexpectedness, unprotectedness, unconnectedness, disconnectedness, unaffectedness, pointedness, jointedness, stuntedness, contentedness, dementedness, self-centeredness, self-centredness, unwontedness, undauntedness, disjointedness, discontentedness, giftedness, tight-fistedness, interestedness, uninterestedness, disinterestedness, stiltedness, exaltedness, jadedness, hotheadedness, light-headedness, hard-headedness, thickheadedness, big-headedness, pinheadedness, wooden-headedness, wrong-headedness, unweddedness, crowdedness, guardedness, unguardedness, sordidness, studiedness, red-bloodedness, cold-bloodedness, warm-bloodedness, sidedness, misguidedness, decidedness, lopsidedness, one-sidedness, undecidedness, outmodedness, splendidness, candidness, handedness, woundedness, surehandedness, high-handedness, right-handedness, light-handedness, offhandedness, unboundedness, unfoundedness, broad-mindedness, like-mindedness, tough-mindedness, small-mindedness, simple-mindedness, single-mindedness, heavy-handedness, underhandedness, wickedness, nakedness, markedness, crookedness, unmarkedness, jaggedness, haggardness, raggedness, laggardness, doggedness, ruggedness, timidness, tumidness, humidness, ashamedness, informedness, unashamedness, learnedness, resignedness, concernedness, unlearnedness, unrestrainedness, vividness, lividness, fervidness, perfervidness, deservedness, reservedness, resolvedness, undeservedness, unreservedness, unresolvedness, blessedness, acidness, placidness, flaccidness, cussedness, lucidness, cursedness, mixedness, fixedness, rancidness, pellucidness, relaxedness, haphazardness, unadvisedness, wretchedness, rigidness, frigidness, turgidness, waywardness, forwardness, outwardness, liquidness, backwardness, awkwardness, languidness, inwardness, straightforwardness, aridness, torridness, horridness, floridness, luridness, hurriedness, putridness, sacredness, acridness, preparedness, assuredness, unpreparedness, pallidness, validness, stolidness, solidness, squalidness, absurdness, grandness, blandness, soundness, roundness, fondness, blondness, kindness, blindness, jocundness, profoundness, unsoundness, rotundness, unkindness, purblindness, overfondness, determinedness, baldness, mildness, wildness, oldness, boldness, coldness, unsettledness, manifoldness, unprincipledness **.22** meekness, chicness, weakness, Greekness, bleakness, sleekness, uniqueness, obliqueness, thickness, sickness, quickness, slickness, seasickness, airsickness, carsickness, heartsickness, homesickness, greensickness, trainsickness, lovesickness, specificness, prolificness, opaqueness, blackness, slackness, starkness, darkness, Harkness, likeness, unlikeness, lifelikeness, prosaicness, franticness, graphicness, pinkness, dankness, rankness, frankness, lankness, blankness, briskness, brusqueness, grotesqueness, statuesqueness, picturesqueness **.23** bigness, Cygnus, vagueness, Agnes, Magnus, smugness, snugness **.24** supremeness, extremeness, dimness, primness, trimness, grimness, slimness, tameness, gameness, sameness, lameness, calmness, warmness, lukewarmness, dumbness, numbness, rumness, glumness, alumnus, primeness, randomness, welcomeness, lissomness, fearsomeness, awesomeness, noisomeness, gruesomeness, tiresomeness, lightsomeness, gladsomeness, buxomness, irksomeness, gamesomeness, winsomeness, handsomeness, lonesomeness, burdensomeness, toothsomeness,

loathsomeness, toilsomeness, fulsomeness, wholesomeness, troublesomeness, meddlesomeness, solemnness, unwelcomeness, wearisomeness, cumbersomeness, humorsomeness, venturesomeness, frolicsomeness, quarrelsomeness, unwholesomeness, firmness **.25** keenness, meanness, greenness, leanness, obsceneness, sereneness, uncleanness, vainness, saneness, plainness, urbaneness, mundaneness, humaneness, germaneness, inaneness, profaneness, insaneness, fineness, supineness, divineness, jejuneness, opportuneness, genuineness, openness, stubbornness, wantonness, modernness, goldenness, brokenness, drunkenness, commonness, humanness, cravenness, Russianness, sanguineness, barrenness, foreignness, fallenness, sullenness, misshapenness, mistakenness, outspokenness, unbrokenness, uncommonness, inhumanness, feminineness, masculineness, sternness, proneness, unknownness, aloneness, rottenness, hiddenness, leadenness, soddenness, suddenness, woodenness, forsakenness, evenness, unevenness, brazenness **.26** knowingness, ongoingness, sweepingness, graspingness, fittingness, lastingness, trustingness, unwittingness, unsportingness, invitingness, excitingness, exactingness, interestingness, disgustingness, unremittingness, unbefittingness, unsuspectingness, unreflectingness, unrelentingness, unresistingness, uninterestingness, everlastingness, unhesitatingness, yieldingness, misleadingness, unbendingness, unendingness, unyieldingness, unpretendingness, undemandingness, takingness, shockingness, strikingness, painstakingness, unthinkingness, becomingness, forthcomingness, presumingness, unbecomingness, unassumingness, overwhelmingness, winningness, cunningness, unmeaningness, overweeningness, belongingness, lovingness, unlovingness, deservingness, unbelievingness, unforgivingness, nothingness, bracingness, amazingness, surprisingness, imposingness, uncompromisingness, dashingness, touchingness, grudgingness, engagingness, obligingness, unchangingness, sparingness, glaringness, boringness, unsparingness, unerringness, overbearingness, willingness, sterlingness, triflingness, unfeelingness, unwillingness, unfailingness, unsmilingness, wrongness, headstrongness **.27** briefness, stiffness, safeness, deafness, toughness, roughness, gruffness, bluffness, rifeness, helpfulness, selfness, unsafeness, aloofness, waterproofness **.28.1** forgiveness, braveness, graveness, suaveness, aliveness, nativeness, creativeness, innovativeness, sportiveness, supportiveness, abortiveness, constructiveness,

stick-to-it-iveness, intuitiveness, combativeness, prohibitiveness, tentativeness, repetitiveness, competitiveness, meditativeness, imitativeness, vegetativeness, uncompetitiveness, authoritativeness, argumentativeness, representativeness, unrepresentativeness, talkativeness, evocativeness, provocativeness, communicativeness, incommunicativeness, uncommunicativeness, negativeness, primitiveness, amativeness, normativeness, informativeness, punitiveness, definitiveness, determinativeness, imaginativeness, unimaginativeness, conservativeness, sensitiveness, transitiveness, insensitiveness, hypersensitiveness, positiveness, acquisitiveness, inquisitiveness, appreciativeness, operativeness, iterativeness, secretiveness, decorativeness, lucrativeness, figurativeness, generativeness, imperativeness, declarativeness, cooperativeness, inoperativeness, deliberativeness, demonstrativeness, uncooperativeness, undemonstrativeness, unremunerativeness, consecutiveness, diminutiveness, inconsecutiveness, relativeness, speculativeness, cumulativeness, superlativeness, manipulativeness, furtiveness, assertiveness, unassertiveness, self-assertiveness, emotiveness, descriptiveness, prescriptiveness, perceptiveness, deceptiveness, receptiveness, adaptiveness, absorptiveness, disruptiveness, unperceptiveness, fictiveness, activeness, addictiveness, vindictiveness, restrictiveness, prospectiveness, protectiveness, affectiveness, effectiveness, defectiveness, infectiveness, invectiveness, subjectiveness, objectiveness, collectiveness, selectiveness, reflectiveness, attractiveness, seductiveness, productiveness, inductiveness, destructiveness, obstructiveness, instructiveness, distinctiveness, introspectiveness, ineffectiveness, unattractiveness, reproductiveness, unproductiveness, indistinctiveness, counterproductiveness, plaintiveness, substantiveness, attentiveness, retentiveness, inventiveness, inattentiveness, unretentiveness, uninventiveness, festiveness, restiveness, costiveness, suggestiveness, exhaustiveness
.28.2 cohesiveness, adhesiveness, permissiveness, submissiveness, dismissiveness, evasiveness, pervasiveness, invasiveness, persuasiveness, abrasiveness, recessiveness, obsessiveness, excessiveness, successiveness, possessiveness, oppressiveness, repressiveness, impressiveness, expressiveness, regressiveness, digressiveness, aggressiveness, progressiveness, ingressiveness, unimpressiveness, inexpressiveness, passiveness, massiveness, impassiveness, divisiveness, decisiveness, incisiveness, derisiveness, indecisiveness, conduciveness, protrusiveness, obtrusiveness, intrusiveness, abusiveness, effusiveness, diffusiveness, illusiveness, allusiveness,

elusiveness, delusiveness, collusiveness, reclusiveness, inclusiveness, conclusiveness, exclusiveness, unobtrusiveness, inconclusiveness, cursiveness, coerciveness, discursiveness, excursiveness, subversiveness, corrosiveness, explosiveness, pensiveness, suspensiveness, expensiveness, intensiveness, ostensiveness, extensiveness, offensiveness, defensiveness, expansiveness, responsiveness, inexpensiveness, inoffensiveness, apprehensiveness, comprehensiveness, irresponsiveness, unresponsiveness, repulsiveness, impulsiveness, compulsiveness
.29 Caithness, uncouthness **.30** litheness, blitheness, smoothness **.31.1** fierceness, copiousness, impiousness, dubiousness, piteousness, duteousness, beauteousness, courteousness, plenteousness, bounteousness, discourteousness, rumbustiousness, tediousness, hideousness, studiousness, odiousness, fastidiousness, perfidiousness, invidiousness, insidiousness, commodiousness, melodiousness, compendiousness, incommodiousness, abstemiousness, ingeniousness, spontaneousness, instantaneousness, simultaneousness, extraneousness, harmoniousness, erroneousness, feloniousness, homogeneousness, heterogeneousness, ignominiousness, miscellaneousness, impecuniousness, inharmoniousness, sanctimoniousness, parsimoniousness, ceremoniousness, acrimoniousness, contemporaneousness, extemporaneousness, unceremoniousness, deviousness, previousness, perviousness, obviousness, lasciviousness, obliviousness, imperviousness, gaseousness, nauseousness, obsequiousness, seriousness, imperiousness, mysteriousness, deleteriousness, nefariousness, variousness, vicariousness, precariousness, calcareousness, gregariousness, hilariousness, multifariousness, spuriousness, curiousness, furiousness, luxuriousness, gloriousness, laboriousness, notoriousness, victoriousness, uxoriousness, censoriousness, uproariousness, incuriousness, penuriousness, usuriousness, ingloriousness, vaingloriousness, meritoriousness, lugubriousness, salubriousness, opprobriousness, vitreousness, industriousness, illustriousness, biliousness, punctiliousness, atrabiliousness, superciliousness, unrebelliousness
.31.2 baseness, commonplaceness, scarceness, crassness, sparseness, crossness, coarseness, hoarseness, choiceness, niceness, preciseness, conciseness, impreciseness, otioseness, spruceness, looseness, obtuseness, abstruseness, diffuseness, profuseness, joyousness, piousness, congruousness, incongruousness, fatuousness, tortuousness, virtuousness, sumptuousness, unctuousness, arduousness, vacuousness, sinuousness, tenuousness, strenuousness, sensuousness, impetuousness, spirituousness,

voluptuousness, contemptuousness, presumptuousness, tempestuousness, incestuousness, tumultuousness, assiduousness, deciduousness, perspicuousness, conspicuousness, innocuousness, promiscuousness, ambiguousness, contiguousness, exiguousness, continuousness, ingenuousness, disingenuousness, inconspicuousness, mellifluousness, superfluousness **.31.3** pompousness, gibbousness, bulbousness, riotousness, fortuitousness, gratuitousness, circuitousness, covetousness, portentousness, momentousness, precipitousness, calamitousness, felicitousness, solicitousness, necessitousness, ubiquitousness, iniquitousness, hazardousness, stupendousness, tremendousness, horrendousness, raucousness, viscousness, bogusness, analogousness, famousness, squamousness, enormousness, venomousness, unanimousness, synonymousness, pusillanimousness, heinousness, ruinousness, poisonousness, glutinousness, ominousness, numinousness, luminousness, verminousness, ravenousness, synchronousness, villainousness, monotonousness, libidinousness, voluminousness, indigenousness, multitudinousness, amorphousness, grievousness, nervousness, mischievousness **.31.4** speciousness, facetiousness, viciousness, propitiousness, auspiciousness, suspiciousness, ambitiousness, fictitiousness, factitiousness, seditiousness, judiciousness, perniciousness, officiousness, flagitiousness, capriciousness, nutritiousness, deliciousness, maliciousness, unpropitiousness, inauspiciousness, unsuspiciousness, unambitiousness, repetitiousness, surreptitiousness, superstitiousness, expeditiousness, injudiciousness, supposititiousness, avariciousness, meretriciousness, supposititiousness, spaciousness, graciousness, capaciousness, rapaciousness, flirtatiousness, audaciousness, bodaciousness, predaciousness, mendaciousness, fugaciousness, sagaciousness, tenaciousness, pugnaciousness, vivaciousness, vexatiousness, loquaciousness, veraciousness, voraciousness, ungraciousness, fallaciousness, salaciousness, disputatiousness, unostentatiousness, perspicaciousness, efficaciousness, pertinaciousness, inefficaciousness, preciousness, cautiousness, incautiousness, overcautiousness, lusciousness, precociousness, ferociousness, atrociousness, captiousness, bumptiousness, scrumptiousness, factiousness, fractiousness, noxiousness, anxiousness, infectiousness, innoxiousness, obnoxiousness, rambunctiousness, consciousness, pretentiousness, sententiousness, contentiousness, tendenciousness, tendentiousness, licentiousness, preconsciousness, subconsciousness, unconsciousness,

self-consciousness, conscientiousness, unpretentiousness, superconsciousness, unselfconsciousness **.31.5** righteousness, unrighteousness, self-righteousness, gorgeousness, egregiousness, litigiousness, prestigiousness, prodigiousness, religiousness, rampageousness, contagiousness, advantageousness, courageousness, outrageousness, irreligiousness, disadvantageousness, porousness, vaporousness, prosperousness, viviparousness, fissiparousness, obstreperousness, barbarousness, traitorousness, stertorousness, boisterousness, dexterousness, preposterousness, adulterousness, murderousness, odorousness, slanderousness, ponderousness, thunderousness, malodorousness, decorousness, indecorousness, cantankerousness, vigorousness, rigorousness, timorousness, amorousness, clamorousness, numerousness, humorousness, generousness, onerousness, sonorousness, congenerousness, ungenerousness, splendiferousness, vociferousness, odoriferousness, carnivorousness, omnivorousness, cadaverousness, venturousness, adventurousness, dangerousness, treacherousness, lecherousness, rapturousness, dolorousness, ludicrousness, chivalrousness, rebelliousness **.31.6** treelessness, pitilessness, peerlessness, tearlessness, fearlessness, cheerlessness, zealousness, jealousness, airlessness, carelessness, hairlessness, callousness, parlousness, awelessness, lawlessness, flawlessness, joylessness, cluelessness, valuelessness, powerlessness, tirelessness, scandalousness, humorlessness, humourlessness, pennilessness, frivolousness, marvellousness, marvelousness, fatherlessness, motherlessness, patulousness, sedulousness, credulousness, perilousness, querulousness, garrulousness, scurrilousness, populousness, scrupulousness, bibulousness, nebulousness, fabulousness, emulousness, tremulousness, scrofulousness, anomalousness, incredulousness, unscrupulousness, meticulousness, ridiculousness, miraculousness, sleeplessness, shapelessness, haplessness, toplessness, hopelessness, helplessness, joblessness, witlessness, statelessness, weightlessness, artlessness, heartlessness, spotlessness, plotlessness, thoughtlessness, gutlessness, sightlessness, rightlessness, rootlessness, fruitlessness, tactlessness, dauntlessness, pointlessness, shiftlessness, thriftlessness, listlessness, tastelessness, restlessness, guiltlessness, faultlessness, limitlessness, effortlessness, spiritlessness, relentlessness, needlessness, heedlessness, beardlessness, cloudlessness, godlessness, cordlessness, bloodlessness, wordlessness, endlessness, friendlessness, boundlessness, soundlessness, groundlessness, mindlessness, childlessness, regardlessness, fecklessness, recklessness, tracklessness, lucklessness, thanklessness, seamlessness, dreamlessness, aimlessness, namelessness, shamelessness, blamelessness, charmlessness, harmlessness, gormlessness, formlessness, timelessness, homelessness, bottomlessness, sinlessness, chinlessness, painlessness, stainlessness, brainlessness, sunlessness, spinelessness, tunelessness, tonelessness, motionlessness, expressionlessness, meaninglessness, leaflessness, lifelessness, selflessness, lovelessness, nervelessness, motivelessness, faithlessness, deathlessness, breathlessness, ruthlessness, mirthlessness, worthlessness, ceaselessness, baselessness, facelessness, gracelessness, classlessness, voicelessness, pricelessness, uselessness, sexlessness, senselessness, remorselessness, resourcelessness, purposelessness, defencelessness, defenselessness, noiselessness, changelessness, speechlessness, agelessness, stylelessness, guilelessness, soullessness **.31.7** terseness, averseness, perverseness, adverseness, grossness, closeness, verboseness, globoseness, jocoseness, moroseness, laxness, tenseness, denseness, intenseness, immenseness, falseness **.32** business, outsizeness, agribusiness **.33.1** freshness, rashness, brashness, harshness, poshness, lushness, plushness, flushness, babyishness, boyishness, tomboyishness, Jewishness, shrewishness **.33.2** sheepishness, apishness, snappishness, foppishness, uppishness, popishness, impishness, wimpishness, lumpishness, waspishness, snobbishness, yobbishness **.33.3** skittishness, Britishness, pettishness, cattishness, loutishness, Scottishness, sottishness, sluttishness, whitishness, brutishness, doltishness, coltishness, coquettishness, reddishness, caddishness, faddishness, laddishness, cloddishness, prudishness, modishness, fiendishness, childishness, outlandishness **.33.4** freakishness, cliquishness, rakishness, peckishness, brackishness, blockishness, mawkishness, hawkishness, puckishness, bookishness, monkishness, piggishness, whiggishness, priggishness, waggishness, doggishness, hoggishness, thuggishness, sluggishness, voguishness, roguishness **.33.5** squeamishness, greenishness, Spanishness, mannishness, clannishness, clownishness, donnishness, swinishness, kittenishness, womanishness, heathenishness **.33.6** raffishness, offishness, huffishness, oafishness, elfishness, selfishness, wolfishness, standoffishness, unselfishness, peevishness, thievishness, knavishness, slavishness, lavishness, elvishness, bearishness, garishness, boorishness, whorishness, Irishness, currishness, spinsterishness, liquorishness, feverishness, liverishness, nightmarishness, amateurishness,

shamateurishness, hellishness, owlishness, stylishness, bullishness, ghoulishness, foolishness, mulishness, girlishness, churlishness, ticklishness, Englishness, devilishness, gaucheness, Welshness **.34** strangeness **.35** richness, archness, muchness, Frenchness, staunchness **.36** sageness, largeness, hugeness, savageness **.37.1** genteelness, illness, stillness, chillness, shrillness, realness, venialness, trivialness, filialness, paleness, staleness, maleness, haleness, frailness, femaleness, wellness, foulness, tallness, smallness, dullness, vileness, futileness, facileness, worthwhileness, volatileness, fullness, undutifulness, coolness, cruelness, sensualness, casualness, usualness, factualness, gradualness, unusualness, habitualness, spiritualness, effectualness, unspiritualness, ineffectualness, dismalness, eternalness, provisionalness **.37.2** gleefulness, pitifulness, tearfulness, fearfulness, cheerfulness, playfulness, carefulness, prayerfulness, awfulness, lawfulness, joyfulness, ruefulness, powerfulness, irefulness, dutifulness, plentifulness, bountifulness, masterfulness, wonderfulness, mercifulness, fancifulness, sorrowfulness, colourfulness, unmercifulness, woefulness, hopefulness, worshipfulness, unhelpfulness, fitfulness, fatefulness, hatefulness, gratefulness, fretfulness, doubtfulness, artfulness, thoughtfulness, spitefulness, rightfulness, frightfulness, fruitfulness, hurtfulness, tactfulness, wistfulness, tastefulness, wastefulness, zestfulness, restfulness, trustfulness, lustfulness, boastfulness, deceitfulness, ungratefulness, forgetfulness, regretfulness, unthoughtfulness, despitefulness, delightfulness, unfruitfulness, respectfulness, neglectfulness, eventfulness, resentfulness, distastefulness, unrestfulness, mistrustfulness, distrustfulness, self-forgetfulness, uneventfulness, needfulness, heedfulness, dreadfulness, mindfulness, regardfulness, unmindfulness, wakefulness, thankfulness, unthankfulness, shamefulness, harmfulness, sinfulness, painfulness, banefulness, gainfulness, manfulness, scornfulness, mournfulness, tunefulness, disdainfulness, untunefulness, wrongfulness, meaningfulness, faithfulness, wrathfulness, slothfulness, ruthfulness, truthfulness, youthfulness, mirthfulness, healthfulness, unfaithfulness, untruthfulness, unhealthfulness, peacefulness, blissfulness, gracefulness, stressfulness, forcefulness, usefulness, ungracefulness, successfulness, remorsefulness, resourcefulness, purposefulness, easefulness, reposefulness, wishfulness, bashfulness, pushfulnes, changefulness, vengefulness, revengefulness, watchfulness, reproachfulness, skilfulness, wilfulness, balefulness, guilefulness, dolefulness, soulfulness **.37.3** unequalness, liberalness, literalness, generalness, naturalness, trilateralness, ephemeralness, unnaturalness, supernaturalness, preternaturalness, wholeness, drollness **.37.**4 suppleness, purpleness, simpleness, ampleness, feebleness, pitiableness, amiableness, variableness, malleableness, impermeableness, invariableness, stableness, unstableness, agreeableness, allowableness, enjoyableness, friableness, pliableness, reliableness, appliableness, undeniableness, justifiableness, invaluableness, capablness, clubbableness, imperturbableness, uneatableness, inhospitableness, incompatibleness, portableness, insupportableness, excitableness, suitableness, inscrutableness, indisputableness, habitableness, profitableness, comfortableness, equitableness, charitableness, palatableness, inimitableness, illimitableness, indomitableness, unprofitableness, uncomfortableness, inevitableness, uncharitableness, disreputableness, attributableness, unpalatableness, uninhabitableness, potableness, notableness, acceptableness, adaptableness, corruptibleness, unacceptableness, tractableness, respectableness, intractableness, unpredictableness, presentableness, accountableness, warrantableness, irresistibleness, incombustibleness, readableness, edibleness, audibleness, formidableness, incredibleness, dependableness, unavoidableness, placableness, likableness, likeableness, workableness, unspeakableness, applicableness, implacableness, remarkableness, practicableness, amicableness, unworkableness, unthinkableness, unmistakableness, impracticableness, incommunicableness, navigableness, irrefragableness, indefatigableness, tameableness, inflammableness, estimableness, unconformableness, unfathomableness, amenableness, inalienableness, attainableness, unattainableness, tenableness, untenableness, unpardonableness, terminableness, abominableness, interminableness, governableness, personableness, seasonableness, reasonableness, treasonableness, unseasonableness, unreasonableness, fashionableness, unfashionableness, exceptionableness, objectionableness, unmentionableness, unconscionableness, unexceptionableness, unobjectionableness, questionableness, unquestionableness, companionableness, liveableness, lovableness, movableness, provableness, retrievableness, immovableness, immoveableness, unprovableness, unsolvableness, inconceivableness, unbelievableness, peaceableness, traceableness, passableness, forcibleness, flexibleness, sensibleness, permissibleness, impassableness,

impassibleness, irascibleness, serviceableness, reversibleness, invincibleness, insensibleness, responsibleness, inaccessibleness, irrepressibleness, indispensableness, comprehensibleness, incomprehensibleness, visibleness, usableness, useableness, invisibleness, advisableness, unrecognisableness, unrecognizableness, sociableness, perishableness, unsociableness, imperishably, indistinguishableness, changeableness, frangibleness, unchangeableness, infrangibleness, interchangeableness, teachableness, unreachableness, untouchableness, unsearchableness, unapproachableness, irreproachableness, chargeableness, tangibleness, manageableness, knowledgableness, knowledgeableness, unmanageableness, incorrigibleness, unintelligibleness, equableness, terribleness, unbearableness, incomparableness, horribleness, durableness, incurableness, desirableness, undesirableness, separableness, superableness, comparableness, irreparableness, unutterableness, unalterableness, inconsiderableness, unconquerableness, memorableness, admirableness, venerableness, honourableness, vulnerableness, dishonourableness, insufferableness, favorableness, favourableness, unfavorableness, unfavourableness, commensurableness, unanswerableness, miserableness, measurableness, pleasurableness, immeasurableness, tolerableness, intolerableness, volubleness, insolubleness, fallibleness, availableness, unsalableness, unsaleableness, inviolableness, unavailableness, unassailableness, irreconcilableness, inconsolableness, uncontrollableness, nobleness, nimbleness, humbleness **.37.**5 brittleness, littleness, fatalness, subtleness, gentleness, ungentleness, incidentalness, horizontalness, idleness, fickleness, localness, criticalness, practicalness, radicalness, finicalness, technicalness, classicalness, physicalness, quizzicalness, musicalness, whimsicalness, Pharisaicalness, grammaticalness, identicalness, mechanicalness, equivocalness, unmusicalness, reciprocalness, symmetricalness, unpoeticalness, ungrammaticalness, unequivocalness, lackadaisicalness, frugalness, singleness, prodigalness, formalness, evilness, levelness, ovalness, specialness, partialness, impartialness, essentialness, substantialness, superficialness, inconsequentialness

34.18.17
Dreyfus, preface, typhous, typhus, scyphus, rufous, Rufus, surface, tophus, lymphous, dimorphous, trimorphous, amorphous, Sisyphus, resurface, subsurface, diadelphous, triadelphous, polymorphous, pseudomorphous, zygomorphous, homomorphous,

monomorphous, isomorphous, undersurface, polyadelphous, monadelphous, philadelphus, enantiomorphous, anthropomorphous, surface-to-surface

34.18.18
Stevas, naevus, Chivas, grievous, Leavis, traverse, novice, nervous, Jervaulx, canvas, canvass, Selvas, fulvous, Gustavus, mischievous, redivivus, luteofulvous

34.18.19
mythus, Mathis, canthus, aphthous, Malthus, prognathous, syngnathous, lecythus, ceanothus, Hyacinthus, clianthus, dianthus, acanthus, synanthous, schizanthus, ailanthus, Aegisthus, orthognathous, amianthus, helianthus, polyanthus, agapanthus, Rhadamanthus

34.18.20
rhesus, Croesus, byssus, Crassus, Lassus, tarsus, lusus, versus, thyrsus, Texas, nexus, plexus, Oxus, princess, census, Frances, narcissus, Marquesas, Parnassus, colossus, molossus, Dionysus, Hattusas, petasus, Caucasus, Pegasus, Ephesus, excursus, prolapsus, abraxus, consensus, tibiotarsus, metatarsus, solar plexus, amphioxus, Paracelsus, Halicarnassus, numerus clausus

34.18.21
Jesus, Anzus, Kansas

34.18.22
.1 specious, dioecious, trioecious, monoecious, synoecious, facetious, paroecious, Lucretius
.2 vicious, propitious, auspicious, suspicious, conspicuous, ambitious, fictitious, factitious, adventitious, spadiceous, seditious, judicious, pumiceous, pernicious, officious, flagitious, Mauritius, sericeous, capricious, lubricious, nutritious, delicious, malicious, siliceous, Aloysius, unpropitious, inauspicious, unsuspicious, unambitious, overambitious, repetitious, adscititious, surreptitious, cementitious, superstitious, expeditious, injudicious, inofficious, supposititious, avaricious, innutritious, meretricious, supposititious
.3 spacious, Statius, gracious, coriaceous, scoriaceous, liliaceous, alliaceous, oleaceous, foliaceous, drupaceous, capacious, rapacious, sebaceous, herbaceous, bulbaceous, cetaceous, setaceous, Cretaceous, myrtaceous, flirtatious, cactaceous, ostentatious, lomentaceous, testaceous, crustaceous, disputatious, unostentatious, cucurbitaceous, audacious, mordacious, edacious, bodacious, rudaceous, predacious, mendacious, orchidaceous, iridaceous, micaceous, perspicacious, efficacious, ericaceous, inefficacious, fugacious, sagacious, palmaceous, glumaceous, diatomaceous, contumacious, galimatias, vinaceous, spinaceous, tenacious, minacious, Ignatius, pugnacious, saponaceous, carbonaceous, pertinacious, proteinaceous, graminaceous, Athanasius, arenaceous,

farinaceous, membranaceous, gallinaceous, solanaceous, papilionaceous, tuffaceous, tufaceous, vivacious, curvaceous, malvaceous, olivaceous, spathaceous, vexatious, musaceous, rosaceous, sequacious, loquacious, veracious, voracious, ungracious, papyraceous, arboraceous, stercoraceous, furfuraceous, papaveraceous, hellacious, violaceous, fallacious, salacious, argilaceous, argillaceous, plumulaceous, ranunculaceous **.4** precious, semiprecious **.5** tortious, cautious, incautious, overcautious **.6** luscious **.7** Lucius, Confucius **.8** Tertius, Propertius, sestertius **.9** stotious, precocious, ferocious, atrocious **.10** captious, bumptious, scrumptious **.11** factious, fractious, noxious, anxious, infectious, innoxious, obnoxious, compunctious, rambunctious, contradictious, overanxious **.12** Pontius, conscious, pretentious, sententious, contentious, tendencious, tendentious, licentious, preconscious, foreconscious, subconscious, unconscious, self-conscious, conscientious, unpretentious, uncontentious, semi-conscious, hyperconscious, superconscious, unselfconscious

34.18.23
duchess, righteous, purchase, Pontius, archduchess, unrighteous, self-righteous, repurchase, robustious, rumbustious

34.18.24
Regius, gorgeous, burgess, frabjous, egregious, litigious, prestigious, prodigious, religious, rampageous, contagious, advantageous, courageous, outrageous, umbrageous, irreligious, sacrilegious, sacriligious, unreligious, disadvantageous

34.18.25
Carajás

34.18.26
equus, marquess, marquis, siliquous, ventriloquous

34.18.27
.1 Pyrrhus, cirrous, cirrus, scirrhous, scirrhus, stratocirrus **.2** peeress, serous, sclerous, Severus, Algeciras, superioress, Ahasuerus **.3** terrace, Nerys, ferrous **.4** heiress, scarus, mayoress, varus, glaireous, Carreras, billionairess, millionairess **.5** arras, harass, embarrass, disembarrass **.6** charas **.7** Doris, Forres, Horace **.8** porous, Taurus, torus, chorus, sorus, Horus, Centaurus, canorous, thesaurus, procuress, pylorus, pelorus, Dolores, Epidaurus, brachiosaurus, ichthyosaurus, plesiosaurus, brontosaurus, stegosaurus, mosasaurus, megalosaurus, Epicurus, atlantosaurus, dolichosaurus, elasmosaurus, tyrannosaurus **.9** susurrus **.10** MIRAS, virus, Cyrus, gyrus, Epirus, papyrus, antivirus, rotavirus, echovirus, parvovirus, myxovirus, retrovirus, enterovirus, filovirus, morbillivirus **.11** prioress, desirous, undesirous, Honduras, Arcturus, thysanurous,

verdurous, mercurous, sulphurous, tellurous
.12 biparous, vaporous, leprous, copperas,
viperous, cypress, Cyprus, stuporous, cuprous,
empress, Hesperus, Bosporus, prosperous,
pupiparous, multiparous, gemmiparous,
primiparous, uniparous, viviparous, oviparous,
fissiparous, nulliparous, obstreperous,
unprosperous, ovoviviparous **.13** scabrous,
glabrous, barbarous, fibrous, tuberous, berberis,
Cerberus, sombrous, cumbrous, slumberous,
slumbrous, tenebrous **.14** triquetrous, citrous,
citrus, Beatrice, waitress, traitorous, traitress,
craterous, petrous, Tatras, matrass, mattress,
Hatteras, Tartarus, fortress, slaughterous,
goitrous, buttress, nitrous, tutoress, uterus,
proprietress, arbitress, cockatrice, barratrous,
progenitress, inheritress, idolatress, idolatrous,
stertorous, votaress, dipterous, apterous,
temptress, sculptress, hemipterous, preceptress,
dermapterous, tetrapterous, trichopterous,
homopterous, orthopterous, chiropterous,
neuropterous, dictyopterous, coleopterous,
lepidopterous, hymenopterous, thysanopterous,
heteropterous, ephemeropterous, icterus,
nectarous, actress, protectress, directress,
Electress, seductress, conductress, instructress,
benefactress, jointress, huntress, inventress,
enchantress, oestrous, oestrus, mistress,
boisterous, roisterous, lustrous, blusterous,
sempstress, dexterous, dextrous, seamstress,
monstrous, songstress, postmistress,
toastmistress, headmistress, taskmistress,
housemistress, schoolmistress, ancestress,
disastrous, preposterous, impostorous,
impostrous, ambidextrous, adulteress,
adulterous **.15** Phaedrus, wardress, hydrous,
murderess, murderous, odorous, Pandarus,
glanderous, slanderous, foundress, ponderous,
laundress, thunderous, wondrous, plunderous,
Esdras, anhydrous, inodorous, malodorous,
diandrous, triandrous, protandrous,
pentandrous, decandrous, monandrous,
anandrous, gynandrous, tetrandrous,
ambassadress, polyandrous **.16** Icarus, nacrous,
Shakeress, decorous, ichorous, ochreous,
ochrous, anchoress, Pancras, cankerous,
rancorous, indecorous, ludicrous, cantankerous
.17 Negress, vigorous, rigorous, tigress, Tigris,
ogress, languorous, clangourous, congress,
pellagrous, Protagoras, podagrous, Pythagoras,
Anaxagoras **.18** timorous, dimerous, trimerous,
amorous, clamorous, glamorous, glamourous,
tumorous, numerous, humerus, humorous,
murmurous, polymerous, octamerous,
pentamerous, tetramerous, unglamorous,
isomerous, oligomerous, heteromerous
.19 generous, onerous, sonorous, congenerous,
ungenerous, overgenerous **.20** resiniferous,
metalliferous, oleiferous, herbiferous,
plumbiferous, setiferous, lactiferous,
fructiferous, argentiferous, pestiferous,
pyritiferous, diamantiferous, splendiferous,
diamondiferous, proboscidiferous,

gemmiferous, pomiferous, culmiferous,
balsamiferous, graniferous, laniferous,
coniferous, ligniferous, somniferous,
Carboniferous, seminiferous, staminiferous,
luminiferous, polliniferous, stoloniferous,
foraminiferous, cruciferous, nuciferous,
vociferous, gypsiferous, bacciferous, calciferous,
siliciferous, floriferous, auriferous, thuriferous,
cupriferous, umbriferous, rostriferous,
soporiferous, nectariferous, sudoriferous,
odoriferous, piliferous, melliferous, saliferous,
proliferous, umbelliferous, pistilliferous,
mammaliferous, fossiliferous, Zephyrus,
electrophorus, Bosphorus, phosphorous,
phosphorus, organophosphorus **.21** feverous,
flavourous, herbivorous, vermivorous,
granivorous, carnivorous, omnivorous,
piscivorous, nucivorous, fungivorous,
frugivorous, cadaverous, insectivorous,
graminivorous **.22** authoress, synantherous
.23 sorceress, sorcerous, cancerous, ulcerous,
rhinoceros, Monoceros, precancerous **.24** Lazarus
.25 venturous, adventuress, adventurous
.26 treacherous, lecherous, torturous, rapturous,
vulturous, unadventurous **.27** dangerous,
setigerous, armigerous, lanigerous **.28** valorous,
dolorous, walrus, chivalrous, unchivalrous

34.18.28
Peleus, rebellious

34.18.29
.1 keyless, treeless, degreeless **.2** Dulais, villous,
villus, pitiless, bodiless, moneyless, aphyllous,
triphyllous, symphyllous, bacillus, merciless,
weariless, Pontardulais, remediless,
chlorophyllous, lactobacillus **.3** earless, peerless,
tearless, fearless, cheerless, frontierless, idealess,
alveolus, variolous, nucleolus **.4** talus, dayless,
rayless **.5** zealous, jealous, vitellus, entellus,
Marcellus, ocellus, Bucelas, overzealous **.6** airless,
heirless, careless, hairless, prayerless **.7** palace,
Pallas, Dallas, Callas, callous, callus, phallus,
thallous, thallus, chalice, Challes, prothallus
.8 Dowlais **.9** parlous, starless, scarless, braless
.10 solace, Wallace **.11** aweless, oarless,
scoreless, thawless, shoreless, lawless, clawless,
flawless, floorless **.12** joyless, Troilus, recoilless
.13 Dulles, Catullus, portcullis, Agulhas
.14 eyeless, pilous, tieless, stylus, chylous,
skyless, Silas, tristylous **.15** bullace, Tibullus
.16 shoeless, ruleless, pewless, viewless, hueless,
clueless, issueless, virtueless, sinewless,
valueless **.17.1** Aeolus, roseolous, malleolus,
powerless, dowerless, flowerless, tireless,
fireless, wireless **.17.2** paperless, supperless,
erysipelas, Sardanapalus, harborless,
harbourless, obelus, fibreless, libellous,
strobilus, embolus, memberless, numberless,
discobolus, Heliogabalus, holometabolous,
letterless, mortarless, nautilus, fortalice,
waterless, shutterless, winterless, tantalous,
tantalus, sisterless, masterless, lustreless,
shelterless, apetalous, tripetalous, sympetalous,

tridactylous, syndactylous, characterless, monopetalous, zygodactylous, monodactylous, tetradactylous, Daedalus, leaderless, rudderless, riderless, odorless, odourless, windowless, scandalous, thunderless, Nicholas, nickelous, succourless, Aeschylus, tubicolous, stagnicolous, saxicolous, terricolous, figureless, vigourless, sugarless, fingerless, astragalus **.17.3** hammerless, grammarless, summerless, humourless, anomalous, penniless, mannerless, ownerless, partnerless **.17.4** acephalous, bicephalous, Bucephalus, brachycephalous, autocephalous, cynocephalus, monocephalous, hydrocephalus, macrocephalous, microcephalous, leptocephalous, dolichocephalous, Theophilus, xerophilous, sclerophyllous, saprophilous, hygrophilous, acidophilus, entomophilous, anemophilous, heterophyllous, riverless, frivolous, liverless, savourless, flavourless, marvellous, loverless, driverless **.17.5** featherless, fatherless, motherless, saucerless, cancellous, trouserless, visorless, measureless, leisureless, angelus, featureless, futureless, structureless, fistulous, moistureless, pustulous, textureless, sedulous, credulous, modulus, pendulous, acidulous, incredulous, errorless, perilous, querulous, carolus, garrulous, scurrilous, glomerulus **.17.6** papulous, crapulous, populace, populous, scrupulous, unscrupulous, overscrupulous, bibulous, nebulous, fabulous, globulous, tubulous, tintinnabulous, patulous, faculous, loculus, flocculus, flosculous, calculous, calculus, meticulous, pediculous, ridiculous, funiculus, fasciculus, miraculous, tuberculous, homunculus, ranunculus, furunculous, regulus, orgulous, stimulus, mimulus, limulus, emulous, tremulous, famulus, hamulus, Romulus, tumulus, cumulous, cumulus, stratocumulus, cirrocumulus, altocumulus, annulus, spinulous, scrofulous, convolvulus, pilulous, cellulous, sailorless, collarless, colourless **.18** spurless, stirless, furless **.19** bolas, bolus, toeless, snowless, pholas, tholus, SOLAS, solus, shadowless, echoless, furrowless, gladiolus, holus-bolus **.20** sleepless, pipless, tipless, shipless, hipless, whipless, lipless, tapeless, shapeless, tapless, mapless, sapless, hapless, strapless, topless, stopless, shopless, pipeless, surplice, surplus, popeless, soapless, hopeless, lampless, humpless, rumpless, helpless, scalpless, pulpless, accomplice **.21** ribless, Nablus, barbless, jobless, troublous, tubeless, herbless, lobeless **.22** meatless, seatless, shitless, witless, pocketless, riotless, stateless, dateless, mateless, sateless, weightless, plateless, fretless, atlas, fatless, hatless, spoutless, doubtless, artless, heartless, spotless, knotless, plotless, thoughtless, supportless, cutlass, gutless, sightless, rightless, riteless, lightless, flightless, footless, bootless, rootless, fruitless, trumpetless, ticketless, limitless, summitless, effortless, profitless, comfortless, spiritless, pilotless,

skirtless, shirtless, hurtless, coatless, noteless, voteless, tactless, ductless, prospectless, objectless, subjectless, stintless, printless, taintless, ventless, scentless, countless, dauntless, pointless, jointless, frontless, eventless, relentless, tenantless, parentless, talentless, shiftless, riftless, thriftless, priestless, yeastless, listless, tasteless, waistless, wasteless, restless, breastless, crestless, frostless, dustless, rustless, thirstless, textless, resistless, stiltless, guiltless, faultless, saltless, resultless **.23** needless, seedless, heedless, weedless, leadless, lidless, beardless, fadeless, shadeless, headless, shroudless, cloudless, guardless, godless, rodless, cordless, fordless, lordless, bloodless, tideless, sideless, prideless, hoodless, woodless, wordless, roadless, windlass, windless, endless, friendless, handless, landless, boundless, soundless, groundless, mindless, rindless, woundless, shieldless, childless, regardless, rewardless, husbandless, irregardless **.24** tickless, stickless, Nicklaus, trickless, brakeless, lakeless, speckless, necklace, feckless, reckless, backless, sackless, trackless, sparkless, stockless, sockless, rockless, lockless, stalkless, luckless, pluckless, hookless, workless, Toklas, smokeless, yolkless, tankless, thankless, trunkless, diskless, Patroclus, stomachless, trafficless **.25** eggless, legless, Douglas, fatigueless **.26** seamless, streamless, dreamless, rimless, brimless, limbless, aimless, nameless, shameless, frameless, blameless, flameless, stemless, armless, charmless, harmless, stormless, gormless, formless, thumbless, plumbless, timeless, rhymeless, limeless, fumeless, plumeless, termless, foamless, homeless, rhythmless, fathomless, bottomless, symptomless, victimless, systemless **.27** kinless, skinless, finless, sinless, chinless, winless, painless, stainless, maneless, vaneless, veinless, chainless, rainless, reinless, brainless, trainless, grainless, anlace, manless, townless, thornless, hornless, gunless, sonless, sunless, spineless, wineless, moonless, tuneless, ironless, weaponless, womanless, portionless, tensionless, engineless, questionless, pollenless, dimensionless, religionless, fernless, returnless, boneless, toneless, stoneless, throneless, buttonless, seasonless, reasonless, passionless, torsionless, motionless, frictionless, flexionless, functionless, pensionless, traditionless, professionless, possessionless, expressionless, proportionless, distortionless, emotionless, directionless, complexionless, inflectionless, visionless, provisionless **.28** stingless, kingless, wingless, ringless, springless, stringless, fangless, songless, tongueless, rungless, lungless, stockingless, meaningless, feelingless **.29** briefless, leafless, wifeless, lifeless, roofless, proofless, selfless **.30** sleeveless, waveless, graveless, marvelous, loveless, nerveless, swerveless, valveless, motiveless **.31** sheathless, heathless, pithless, faithless, deathless, breathless, pathless, mouthless, toothless, ruthless, truthless, mirthless, worthless, depthless, strengthless .**32** scatheless .**33** ceaseless, greaseless, baseless, faceless, traceless, graceless, placeless, stressless, massless, grassless, classless, glassless, houseless, sauceless, horseless, remorseless, resourceless, voiceless, viceless, priceless, juiceless, truceless, useless, purposeless, Stanislas, Wenceslas, sexless, taxless, coxless, indexless, tenseless, fenceless, senseless, conscienceless, offenceless, offenseless, defenceless, defenseless, pulseless .**34** breezeless, causeless, noiseless, newsless, fuseless, noseless, roseless, lensless .**35** fleshless, cashless, lashless, brushless, quenchless, perishless .**36** speechless, stitchless, matchless, porchless, searchless .**37** ageless, edgeless, smudgeless, hingeless, fringeless, changeless, flangeless, imageless .**38** keelless, heelless, wheelless, skill-less, will-less, tailless, scaleless, nailless, veilless, sailless, railless, smell-less, shell-less, vowelless, wall-less, oilless, soil-less, styleless, guileless, smileless, goalless, soulless, saddleless, victualless, muscleless

34.19
Erse, perse, purse, burse, terce, terse, curse, nurse, verse, hearse, worse, loess, coerce, Nez Percé

34.19.1
cutpurse, asperse, disperse, intersperse, monodisperse

34.19.2
reimburse, disburse

34.19.3
sesterce

34.19.4
commerce, amerce, emerse, immerse, submerse

34.19.5
wet-nurse

34.19.6
reverse, diverse, averse, perverse, traverse, obverse, adverse, inverse, converse, transverse, universe

34.19.7
rehearse

34.20
Bose, dose, Voce, chausses, Rhos, gross, Grosz, close, adios, otiose, grandiose, religiose

34.20.1
Ríos

34.20.2
pappose, adipose

34.20.3
sorbose, ribose, verbose, globose, thrombose, corymbose

34.20.4
setose, pectose, lactose, fructose, pentose, sarmentose, tomentose, schistose, crustose,

maltose, comatose, acetose, keratose, galactose, edematose, oedematose

34.20.5
nodose, frondose, overdose

34.20.6
arkose, glucose, jocose, viscose, talcose, verrucose, vorticose, fruticose, spadicose, varicose, ventricose, bellicose

34.20.7
strigose, rugose

34.20.8
squamose, ramose, glumose, cymose, rimose, strumose, plumose, comose, racemose, lachrymose

34.20.9
venose, spinose, pruinose, lacunose, laminose, raffinose, anthracnose, arabinose, uliginose

34.20.10
scyphose

34.20.11
Davos, inter vivos

34.20.12
spathose

34.20.13
gneissose, hexose

34.20.14
chaparejos

34.20.15
siliquose

34.20.16
cirrose, squarrose, torose, morose, suberose, dextrose, necrose, sucrose, engross, Penrhos, saccharose

34.20.17
villose, pilose, xylose, lamellose, trehalose, papillose, ankylose, nodulose, nodulous, papulose, surculose, spinulose, laevulose, cellulose, reticulose, hemicellulose, nitrocellulose

34.21.1
Pepys

34.21.2
Phipps, Chips, Cripps, thrips, tinsnips, midships, Phillips®, ellipse, eclipse, amidships, apocalypse

34.21.3
traipse, sour grapes, jackanapes

34.21.4
Pepys, Schweppes®, Lesseps, forceps, biceps, triceps, quadriceps, editio princeps

34.21.5
apse, caps, schnapps, perhaps, craps, lapse, synapse, relapse, elapse, collapse, prolapse

34.21.6
copse, Cheops, Pelops, Cyclops, Keystone Kops, triceratops

34.21.7
corpse, Cleethorpes

34.21.8
cripes, Stars and Stripes

34.21.9
oops

34.21.10
whoops, paratroops

34.21.11
turps, stirps, SERPS

34.21.12
Stopes

34.21.13
glimpse, mumps, goosebumps

34.21.14
Phelps

34.22.1
eats, Keats, foresheets, ascomycetes

34.22.2
its, it's, blewits, Pitts, spitz, St Kitts, Fitz, sitz, Ritz, spritz, Fritz, blitz, glitz, Tirpitz, Tibbitts, kibits, Colditz, rickets, Ricketts, Doenitz, Leibniz, Chemnitz, Auschwitz, Biarritz, Saint-Moritz, Berlitz, with-profits, slivovitz, Clausewitz, Horowitz, Austerlitz, Rabinowitz

34.22.3
Bates, Gates, Fates, Waites, Wates, Yates, Yeats, Trucial States, annates, United States

34.22.4
Betts, Metz, Odets, godets, Lil-lets®, pantalettes

34.22.5
stats, Katz, ersatz, congrats

34.22.6
therabouts, whereabouts

34.22.7
Harz, Herts, Graz

34.22.8
Potts, Scots, Notts, Watts

34.22.9
orts, quartz, Schwartz, Cinque Ports, allsorts, undershorts

34.22.10
Hakenkreuz

34.22.11
putz, Smuts, futz, klutz

34.22.12
Knights, footlights, houselights, Golan Heights

34.22.13
putz, Lutz, kibbutz, Perutz

34.22.14
Schütz, Rootes, Lutz, slyboots, cahoots, first fruits, smarty-boots, Der Freischütz

34.22.15
Roberts, Nimitz, Hodgetts, Willetts, giblets, quill-coverts, Massachusetts, polyunsaturates

34.22.16
hertz, outskirts, Weltschmerz, deserts, megahertz, kilohertz

34.22.17
Oates, Coates, John o'Groats

34.22.18
chintz, Linz, blintz, pants, Hants, Mainz, Clements, shinsplints, sweatpants, Northants, Rosencrantz, Y-fronts®, Barents, Lorentz, emblements, smarty-pants, underpants, Liederkrantz, bons vivants, arrondissements

34.22.19
draughts, Crufts

34.22.20
Wilts, waltz, schmaltz, Schultz, krummholz, Helmholtz

34.23.1
Weekes, breeks, maxixe, idée fixe, Macgillicuddy's Reeks

34.23.2
pix, pyx, Styx, mix, nix, Nyx, Pnyx, fix, six, Hicks, Wicks, Ricks, Rix, prix fixe **.1** tropics, Paralympics **.2** Weetabix®, Aquarobics® **.3** Celtics, Dianetics, mathematics, cladistics, ekistics, sphragistics, Anglistics, informatics, biomathematics, semeiotics, semiotics, astronautics, geopolitics, periodontics, metapolitics, lexicostatistics **.4** spadix, radix, Bendix®, appendix **.5** remix, commix, admix, tagmemics, intermix **.6** phoenix, Xenix, onyx, fornix, UNIX®, vernix, cami-nicks, cryonics, Ebonics, photonics, sardonyx, biomechanics, radionics, ambisonics, mechatronics, hydromechanics, microelectronics **.7** prefix, affix, suffix, postfix, infix, unfix, transfix, crucifix **.8** cervix, Chenevix **.9** bioethics **.10** Essex, Wessex, Sussex, coccyx, kinesics, MI**6 .11** geophysics, psychophysics, astrophysics **.12** varix, oryx, Beatrix, matrix, tortrix, apteryx, tectrix, rectrix, Hendrix, Asterix, mediatrix, aviatrix, creatrix, testatrix, cicatrix, directrix, precentrix, dominatrix, Vercingetorix, morphometrics, prosecutrix, progenitrix, inheritrix, executrix, archaeopteryx, administratrix, interlocutrix **.13** Felix, helix, calyx, Alex, Alix, Horlicks®, kylix, prolix, spondulicks

34.23.3
Jacques, Jaques, Raikes

34.23.4
ex, Exe, x, specs, Tex, kex, vex, sex, hex, Rex, prex, lex, flex, Tyrannosaurus Rex **.1** Tipp-Ex®,

apex, Ampex®, perspex, haruspex .2 ibex
.3 Sweetex®, latex, Playtex®, Aertex®, cortex,
Gore-tex®, vortex, frutex, Cutex, vertex,
Semtex®, videotex, Teletex® .4 Hedex®, codex,
'tween decks, index, Copydex®, Nikkei index
.5 remex, Amex®, Timex®, Tex-Mex, Shell-Mex
.6 Kleenex®, annex, Gannex, Moulinex®
.7 tubifex, pontifex, spinifex .8 convex,
biconvex, planoconvex .9 narthex .10 desex,
same-sex, unsex, Middlesex, intersex, unisex
.11 Durex®, murex, Lurex®, Pyrex®, NIREX,
Optrex® .12 Halex®, Telex, pollex, ilex, silex,
scolex, Rolex®, triplex, duplex, perplex,
Dimplex®, simplex, Amplex®, complex, reflex,
multiplex, dorsiflex, retroflex, circumflex,
radiotelex, herpes simplex, single-lens reflex

34.23.5
axe, pax, Backs, Bax, tax, DAKS, max, fax, Sfax,
Sachs, sax, saxe, zax, Jacques, wax, Drax, lax, flax
.1 co-ax .2 Kippax, hapax .3 pretax, surtax, syntax,
Pentax®, supertax, overtax .4 addax, hand-axe
.5 pickaxe .6 IMAX®, climax, Lomax, minimax,
Betamax®, anticlimax .7 Astyanax, opopanax
.8 Ceefax®, Fairfax, carfax, Telefax®, Halifax,
Filofax® .9 vivax .10 Tay-Sachs .11 nunchaks
.12 Ajax, banjax .13 earwax, AWACS, beeswax,
thorow-wax .14 borax, storax, thorax, styrax,
hyrax, anthrax, pneumothorax, hydrothorax,
cephalothorax .15 smilax, relax, pole-axe,
toadflax, gravlax, Ex-lax, battleaxe, parallax,
gravadlax

34.23.6
Foulkes, Fowkes

34.23.7
Parkes, Sparks, Berks, Marks, Marx, Lourenço
Marques

34.23.8
ox, pox, box, Stocks, cox, Coxe, Knox, fox, Foxe,
Vaux, sox, prox., lox, phlox, Fort Knox .1 cowpox,
chickenpox, smallpox .2 gearbox, haybox,
shoebox, firebox, soapbox, sweatbox, hatbox,
paintbox, postbox, saltbox, breadbox, bandbox,
sandbox, soundbox, lockbox, tuckbox, jukebox,
workbox, brainbox, strongbox, snuffbox,
saucebox, horsebox, icebox, loosebox,
squeezebox, cash box, matchbox, pillbox,
mailbox, toolbox, rattlebox, moneybox,
pepperbox, letterbox, chatterbox, shadowbox,
tinderbox, thunderbox, pillar box, pouncet-box
.3 detox .4 redox, Radox®, orthodox, paradox,
heterodox, unorthodox .5 praecox, Simcox,
Hancox, Silcox, Wilcocks, Wilcox, dementia
praecox .6 Magnox, equinox .7 outfox .8 volvox
.9 bobby sox .10 xerox, aurochs, Ibrox
.11 backblocks, dreadlocks, Westclox, Goldilocks

34.23.9
Faux, Vaux, Hawkes, Guy Fawkes

34.23.10
yoicks

34.23.11
Bucks, tux, dux, crux, lux, luxe, flux,

redux, Dulux®, deluxe, de luxe, reflux, efflux,
afflux, influx, conflux, Benelux, Electrolux®

34.23.12
Sykes, yikes

34.23.13
Brookes, Crookes, luxe

34.23.14
Ffoulkes, Fookes, Fuchs, Jukes, gadzooks,
Devereux

34.23.15
Maddox, lummox, flummox, Lennox, Trossachs,
Isaacs, barracks, hallux, Pollux, bollocks,
Appomattox

34.23.16
Perks, Merckx, circs, dyeworks, printworks,
gasworks, steelworks, waterworks

34.23.17
Oakes, Boakes, stokes, coax, Noakes, Ffoulkes,
Fowkes, hoax, Cheyne-Stokes, Sevenoaks

34.23.18
Spinks, minx, sphinx, jinks, jinx, Lincs, lynx,
Manx, Shanks, Hanks, Franks, Lancs, Tonks,
conches, Bronx, yonks, Monks, meninx,
methinks, hijinks, syrinx, pharynx, larynx,
Fairbanks, Marjoribanks, spindleshanks,
phalanx, Gollancz, quincunx, pilliwinks,
oropharynx

34.23.19
Wilkes, calx

34.24.1
mince, Vince, since, wince, quince, rinse, prince,
province, evince, convince, Port-au-Prince

34.24.2
sapience, percipience, incipience,
impercipience, ambience, circumambience,
radiance, gradience, audience, expedience,
obedience, irradiance, clairaudience,
inexpedience, disobedience, permeance,
lenience, provenience, convenience,
inconvenience, deviance, subservience,
nescience, prescience, transience, omniscience,
insouciance, variance, prurience, experience,
covariance, invariance, esurience, luxuriance,
inexperience, brilliance, salience, dalliance,
consilience, resilience, mésalliance, emollience,
ebullience

34.24.3
pence, spence, tense, dense, fence, thence,
cense, sense, hence, whence, flense, prepense,
dispense, suspense, expense, Hortense,
pretence, pretense, intense, condense,
immense, commence, offence, offense, defence,
defense, ring-fence, rail fence, incense,
frankincense, recompense, recommence,
self-defence, self-defense, common sense

34.24.4
manse, nance, Vance, Hans, rance, Penzance,
Rosencrantz, expanse, underpants, Romance,

romance, Rhaeto-Romance, finance, refinance, self-finance

34.24.5
ounce, pounce, bounce, jounce, trounce, flounce, fluid ounce, announce, enounce, denounce, renounce, pronounce, mispronounce

34.24.6
séance, nuance, stance, dance, Vance, chance, prance, trance, krantz, France, lance, glance, faience, happenstance, askance, Provence, advance, perchance, mumchance, off-chance, mischance, enhance, entrance, freelance, circumstance, Afrikaans, convenance, Renaissance, à outrance, fer de lance, par excellence

34.24.7
ponce, bonce, sconce, nonce, ambience, response, ensconce

34.24.8
Caunce, launce

34.24.9
dunce, once

34.24.10
.1 creance **.2** abeyance, purveyance, conveyance **.3** allowance, disallowance **.4** flamboyance, annoyance, clairvoyance **.5** science, affiance, defiance, geoscience, social science, alliance, reliance, appliance, compliance, neuroscience, pseudo-science, misalliance, self-reliance **.6** issuance, congruence, effluence, refluence, affluence, influence, confluence, perpetuance, continuance, mellifluence, circumfluence, discontinuance **.7** fluence, pursuance **.8** halfpence, threepence, fourpence, tuppence, twopence, fivepence, comeuppance **.9** resorbence, absorbance, disturbance, recumbence **.10** pittance, quittance, immittance, remittance, admittance, readmittance, acquittance, intermittence, importance, unimportance, self-importance, appetence, impotence, competence, penitence, renitence, hesitance, omnipotence, precipitance, inappetence, incompetence, inhabitance, exorbitance, concomitance, impenitence, capacitance, inheritance, disinheritance, omnicompetence, immunocompetence, advertence, inadvertence, potence, prepotence, acceptance, reacceptance, nonacceptance, expectance, reflectance, reactance, inductance, conductance, reluctance, self-inductance, sentence, acquaintance, reacquaintance, repentance, distance, substance, instance, Constance, outdistance, assistance, persistence, subsistence, insistence, consistence, resistance, existence, preexistence, coexistence, circumstance, water-resistance **.11** credence, impedance, supersedence, antecedence, retrocedence, riddance, forbiddance, improvidence, cadence, accordance, concordance, discordance, voidance, avoidance, guidance, stridence, abidance, misguidance,

subsidence, prudence, imprudence, jurisprudence, decadence, diffidence, confidence, evidence, providence, dissidence, precedence, accidence, incidence, residence, impudence, self-confidence, self-evidence, coincidence, overconfidence, tendance, dependence, impendence, attendance, ascendance, transcendence, resplendence, despondence, respondence, abundance, redundance, independence, self-dependence, nonattendance, superintendence, correspondence, superabundance, overabundance, interdependence **.12** significance, insignificance **.13** arrogance, elegance, extravagance, inelegance **.14** Clemence, Clements, vehemence, performance, conformance, transhumance, adamance, outperformance, underperformance **.15** chrominance, penance, pertinence, maintenance, countenance, continence, sustenance, abstinence, alternance, appurtenance, impertinence, discountenance, incontinence, ordinance, ordonnance, ordnance, immanence, imminence, eminence, remanence, dominance, prominence, luminance, permanence, preeminence, predominance, illuminance, impermanence, supereminence, provenance, governance, dissonance, desinence, assonance, consonance, inconsonance, resonance, oppugnance, repugnance **.16** clearance, appearance, reappearance, coherence, adherence, inherence, nonappearance, disappearance, interference, perseverance, incoherence, Terence, aberrance, deterrence, Behrens, transparence, forbearance, clarence, Torrance, Laurence, Lorentz, St Lawrence, Florence, abhorrence, self-abhorrence, durance, assurance, reassurance, insurance, reinsurance, endurance, procurance, self-assurance, self-insurance, overinsurance, occurrence, reoccurrence, co-occurrence, recurrence, concurrence, intercurrence, temperance, intemperance, exuberance, protuberance, remembrance, encumbrance, iterance, utterance, entrance, monstrance, penetrance, re-entrance, remonstrance, recalcitrance, hindrance, preponderance, fragrance, ignorance, difference, efference, deference, reference, preference, sufferance, inference, conference, transference, indifference, vociferance, pre-preference, circumference, teleconference, counter-transference, severance, reverence, deliverance, disseverance, irreverence, furtherance, belligerence, tolerance, intolerance **.17** grievance, contrivance, relevance, observance, irrelevance, inobservance **.18** puissance, dehiscence, impuissance, reminiscence, reviviscence, indehiscence, obeisance, Renaissance, renascence, complacence, essence, quiescence, in essence, acquiescence, pubescence, albescence, prepubescence, erubescence, lactescence,

quintessence, infructescence, candescence,
recrudescence, turgidescence, iridescence,
viridescence, incandescence, tumescence,
detumescence, intumescence, senescence,
luminescence, evanescence, juvenescence,
bioluminescence, rejuvenescence,
triboluminescence, chemiluminescence,
thermoluminescence, electroluminescence,
rufescence, effervescence, ingravescence,
marcescence, acescence, turgescence,
deliquescence, virescence, florescence,
fluorescence, vitrescence, putrescence,
concrescence, excrescence, nigrescence,
arborescence, phosphorescence, efflorescence,
inflorescence, coalescence, opalescence,
adolescence, pre-adolescence, recalescence,
alkalescence, convalescence, obsolescence,
licence, license, nuisance, translucence,
reticence, innocence, concupiscence,
reconnaissance, munificence, magnificence,
beneficence, maleficence, conversance, absence,
nonsense **.19** presence, pleasance, pleasaunce,
usance, defeasance, nonfeasance, misfeasance,
malfeasance, complaisance, cognisance,
cognizance, recusance, pluripresence,
omnipresence, recognizance, incognizance
.20 patience, sentience, conscience, impatience,
insentience **.21** mergence, vergence, vengeance,
allegiance, indigence, exigence, diligence,
negligence, emergence, re-emergence,
submergence, divergence, convergence,
resurgence, insurgence, indulgence, effulgence,
refulgence, divulgence, intransigence,
intelligence, birefringence, self-indulgence,
overindulgence, counterintelligence
.22 sequence, sub-sequence, subsequence,
consequence, eloquence, inconsequence,
grandiloquence, magniloquence **.23** poignance,
brilliance **.24** valence, bivalence, surveillance,
covalence, polyvalence, monovalence,
electrovalence, repellence, balance, valance,
Vallance, rebalance, outbalance, imbalance,
unbalance, counterbalance, overbalance,
parlance, equipollence, silence, violence,
nonviolence, sibilance, jubilance, pestilence,
redolence, indolence, somnolence, prevalence,
ambivalence, equivalence, benevolence,
malevolence, excellence, insolence,
superexcellence, nonchalance, petulance,
flatulence, vigilance, fraudulence, virulence,
purulence, crapulence, opulence, corpulence,
turbulence, ambulance, feculence, flocculence,
succulence, truculence, condolence, semblance,
dissemblance, resemblance

34.25
Staffs, Buffs, handkerchiefs, fisticuffs

34.26
meths, maths, cloths, Griffiths

34.27
grilse, else, valse, Hals, false, waltz, pulse, dulse,
Hulse, rinkhals, ringhals, repulse, impulse,
convulse

35.1
ease, pease, tease, Tees, Caius, Keays, Keyes,
Keys, sneeze, these, seise, seize, she's, cheese,
jeez, he's, wheeze, squeeze, res, prix, breeze,
grease, freeze, Fries, frieze, lees, please, Cleese,
sleaze, Louise, unease, Grands Prix, vocalese,
legalese, journalese, novelese, Genoese,
Faeroese, Faroese, Eloise, Héloïse, Timorese,
officialese, computerese, éminence grise

35.1.1
sanies, facies, superficies

35.1.2
Euphues

35.1.3
lues

35.1.4
Eloise, Héloïse, Averroës

35.1.5
stapes, stipes, appease, trapeze, stirpes, herpes,
talipes, editiones principes

35.1.6
tabes, scabies, rabies, pubes, Celebes, Maccabees

35.1.7
bêtise, Ortiz, striptease, Maltese, expertise,
Piedmontese, Stockton-on-Tees **.1** diabetes,
tagetes, Philoctetes, ascomycetes **.2** nates,
Achates, penates, Euphrates, Mithridates, fidus
Achates **.3** abattis **.4** démentis **.5** CITES,
ascites, pyrites, barytes, sorites, Stylites,
troglodytes, tympanites **.6** abatis, litotes,
fomites, Socrates, Polycrates, Hippocrates,
Harpocrates, Isocrates **.7** certes, Surtees,
Laertes **.8** Boötes, Zelotes **.9** gentes, pontes,
Cervantes, atlantes, Orontes **.10** testes,
Thyestes, Orestes, cerastes, Procrustes,
Agonistes, ovotestes, Ecclesiastes

35.1.8
Hades, Hyades, Pleiades, Andes, Rwandese,
glandes, Valdez, Culdees, aedes, stapedes,
Diomedes, apsides, Mercedes, Sporades, incudes,
Danaides, aphides, pyxides, Hebrides, Cyclades,
Archimedes, Aristides, bona fides, Alcibiades,
allantoides, antipodes, Pheidippides, Euripides,
Thucydides, Parmenides, Eumenides,
Maimonides, Simonides, Hesperides,
cantharides, chrysalides, epididymides

35.1.9
marquise

35.1.10
Portuguese

35.1.11
Siamese, chemise, Burmese, kermes, Hermes,
Sikkimese, Annamese, Vietnamese, Assamese,
Surinamese

35.1.12
Chinese, Viennese, Sienese, Guianese,
Guyanese, Goanese, Denise, Bernese, Beninese,
Amboinese, Nipponese, Japanese, Lebanese,

Gabonese, Ambonese, Bhutanese, Cantonese,
Sudanese, Sundanese, Pekinese, pekingese,
Macanese, manganese, Javanese, chersonese,
Achinese, Taiwanese, Pyrenees, Milanese,
Celanese®, Ceylonese, Balinese, Malayo-
Chinese, Indo-Chinese, Peloponnese,
Dodecanese, Andamanese, Sino-Japanese
.1 Menes **.2** manes **.3** pectines, Aeschines,
Ximenes, Cleisthenes, testudines, Xenophanes,
Holofernes, Antisthenes, Demosthenes,
imagines, Diogenes, Anaximenes,
Aristophanes, Eratosthenes **.4** ambones,
umbones, ancones

35.1.13
telegraphese

35.1.14
Dives

35.1.15
nepenthes, Cleanthes, cacoethes

35.1.16
disseise, disseize **.1** species, faeces, theses,
subspecies, asceses, anoeses, synizeses,
exegeses, diaphoreses, epicleses, aposiopeses,
epexegeses, electrophoreses **.2** bases, stases,
crases, oases, thoraces, parabases, bacteriostases
.3 askeses **.4** fasces **.5** arses **.6** probosces **.7** fauces
.8 Pisces, crises, Cambyses, Anchises, Polynices,
cicatrices **.9** cruces, anacruses **.10** diocese,
schistosomiases, apices, haruspices, anabases,
latices, protases, cortices, vortices, frutices,
vertices, entases, metastases, iconostases,
radices, codices, indices, syndeses, apodoses,
appendices, nemeses, Rameses, fornices,
regeneses, diageneses, metageneses,
heterogeneses, epeirogeneses, symphyses,
emphases, epiphyses, pontifices, apophyses,
re-emphases, metamorphoses, anamorphoses,
underemphases, overemphases, cervices,
protheses, syntheses, antitheses, diatheses,
hypotheses, biosyntheses, epentheses,
parentheses, chemosyntheses, parasyntheses,
varices, matrices, tortrices, tectrices, rectrices,
diaereses, synaereses, creatrices, testatrices,
directrices, precentrices, periphrases,
anagnorises, mediatrices, aviatrices,
dominatrices, prosecutrices, progenitrices,
inheritrices, executrices, administratrices,
halluces, calyces, helices, Ulysses, scolices,
dialyses, analyses, reanalyses, paralyses,
autolyses, glycolyses, microanalyses, urinalyses,
proteolyses, bacteriolyses **.11** gnoses, meioses,
mioses, symbioses, apotheoses, antibioses,
anabioses, parabioses, thromboses, proptoses,
synostoses, lipidoses, psychoses, sycoses,
syssarcoses, syndesmoses, anastomoses,
stenoses, zoonoses, cyanoses, hypnoses,
prognoses, diagnoses, biocoenoses, melanoses,
misdiagnoses, avitaminoses, neuroses, soroses,
scleroses, amauroses, synchondroses,
synarthroses, enarthroses, atheroscleroses,
psychoneuroses, trophoneuroses,

arterioscleroses, ankyloses, alkaloses **.12** sepses,
ellipses, syllepses, prolepses, synapses, synopses,
paralipses, periapses **.13** heartsease **.14** axes,
y-axes, taxes, praxes, Xerxes, z-axes, x-axes,
sparaxes, anaptyxes, amphimixes, hypotaxes,
epistaxes, Artaxerxes **.15** menses, Waldenses,
Albigenses, amanuenses **.16** calces

35.1.17
Aziz, disease

35.1.18
species, subspecies, superficies

35.1.19
meninges, larynges, pharanges, phalanges,
oropharynges

35.1.20
headcheese

35.1.21
Ganges, compages, Boanerges, meninges,
larynges, pharanges, phalanges, oropharynges

35.1.22
Ceres, Ares, Aries, caries, nares, lares, Flores,
vires, Terese, cerise, reprise, Tabriz, Castries,
refreeze, unfreeze, Antares, Benares, Silures,
Timorese, Canarese, Kanarese, Madurese,
calabrese, antifreeze, traditores, ultra vires,
Buenos Aires, prima inter pares, primus inter
pares, literae humaniores

35.1.23
Belize, valise, Kirklees, Nepalese, vocalese,
legalese, Togolese, Cingalese, Sinhalese,
Congolese, journalese, novelese, Senegalese,
officialese, Antilles, Achilles, tales, Thales,
Actinomycetales, Apelles, Ramillies, Hercules,
Praxiteles, anopheles, isosceles, Los Angeles,
Mephistopheles, displease, Damocles,
Sophocles, Pericles, Heracles, Androcles,
Themistocles, Empedocles

35.2
he's, his, is, biz, 'tis, tiz, tizz, fizz, phiz, viz, zizz,
chiz, jizz, whizz, quiz, squiz, swizz, frizz, Liz

35.2.1
Suez, Ruiz, louis

35.2.2
scabies, Jabez, rabies, showbiz, Celebes,
heebie-jeebies

35.2.3
treatise, Cortes, panties, scanties, Estes,
Cervantes

35.2.4
Cadíz, Indies, undies, social studies

35.2.5
Rockies, walkies, Yerkes, Henriques

35.2.6
Kyrgyz, Menzies

35.2.7
Amies, jammies, kermes

35.2.8
pennies, monies, boonies, Clunies,
Champneys

35.2.9
hafiz

35.2.10
Skivvies, civvies

35.2.11
species, missis, chassis, glacis, falsies, subspecies

35.2.12
Aziz, cosies, Menzies

35.2.13
species, munchies, subspecies

35.2.14
munchies

35.2.15

35.2.16
gee-whiz, Jaques, obsequies, exequies

35.2.17
series, Harries, Torres, Furies, Flores, Potteries,
Minories, Jefferies, Jeffreys, Humphries,
congeries, Canaries, furores, transires, Tuileries,
miniseries

35.2.18
Benzies

35.2.19
Gillies, Scillies, Morales

35.3
Piers, Spears, Sears, cheers, Squeers, De Beers,
Armentières, halteres, Pamirs, Teniers, revers,
Tangiers, Algiers

35.4
baize, daze, gaze, maize, Mays, maze, naze, faze,
phase, chaise, Jeyes, Hayes, Hays, haze, Heyes,
raise, raze, res, Reyes, praise, prase, braise,
braze, craze, graze, fraise, phrase, laze, Blaise,
blaze, glaze, liaise, Marseillaise, in medias res

35.4.1
protease, nuclease

35.4.2
lipase

35.4.3
Cathays, lactase, Estes, diastase, penates,
phosphatase, invertase, equites, elastase,
Trás-os-Montes

35.4.4
nowadays, godets, schooldays, hollandaise,
peroxidase

35.4.5
ukase

35.4.6
stargaze, agaze

35.4.7
zymase, amaze, Lamaze

35.4.8
Béarnaise, manes, Lyonnais, lyonnaise,
mayonnaise, pince-nez, polonaise, Bolognese,
cojones, hydrogenase, catalogues raisonnés

35.4.9
prophase, multiphase, polyphase, metaphase,
anaphase

35.4.10
Gervaise

35.4.11
écossaise, arrière-pensées

35.4.12
post-chaise

35.4.13
PJ's

35.4.14
Summerhayes

35.4.15
crabways, slantways, leastways, sideways,
endways, eques, longways, widthways,
breadthways, lengthways, crossways,
Strangeways, edgeways, always, cornerways

35.4.16
Terese, lares, mores, erase, upraise, appraise,
reappraise, self-praise, dispraise, rephrase,
catchphrase, Senhores, señores, overpraise,
chrysoprase, overgraze, metaphrase,
paraphrase, polymerase, isomerase,
conquistadores

35.4.17
Marseillaise, Bolognese

35.4.18
malaise, ablaze, outblaze, deglaze, reglaze,
onglaze, catalase, amylase, Marseillaise,
hydrolase, cellulase, plagioclase, orthoclase,
periclase, underglaze, overglaze, alguaciles,
alguaziles, carboxylase, oligoclase, broderie
anglaise

35.5
Kes, Fès, fez, says, sez, fraise, fraises, Les, des
res

35.5.1
Ge'ez

35.5.2
Baez

35.5.3
López

35.5.4
Jabez

35.5.5
Cortés, Montez

35.5.6
Méndez, Fernández, Hernández

35.5.7
Rodrigues

35.5.8
Gómez

35.5.9
Inez, Martínez, Jiménez

35.5.10
Chavez

35.5.11
Sánchez

35.5.12
Vásquez, Velázquez

35.5.13
Peres, Pérez, Juárez, Varèse, Ramírez, Alvarez, Gutiérrez

35.5.14
oyez

35.5.15
Boulez, González

35.6
Ayers, Pears®, theirs, Carstairs, upstairs, Broadstairs, backstairs, downstairs, housewares, smallwares, understairs, unawares, chargés d'affaires

35.7
as, Boas, Boaz, SOAS, Baz, Daz®, Chaz, jazz, has, razz, La Paz, topaz, Abkhaz, pizzazz, Shiraz, whereas, razzmatazz, Alcatraz

35.8
spouse, dowse, Cowes, house, Howes, rouse, Prowse, browse, browze, drowse, drowze, blouse, Clowes, espouse, rehouse, unhouse, arouse, carouse, overblouse

35.9
ours, parse, Paz, Mars, vase, Lars, three R's, Stars and Bars, fracas, Abkhaz, Lamaze, patois, turquoise, chauds-froids, Gauloise, aides-memoires, champenoise, vichyssoise, Seychelloise

35.10
Oz, Boz, cos, mozz, schnozz, was, 'twas, Ros, Bros, EPOS, Sandoz, because, kolkhoz

35.11
Saint-Saëns, bons vivants, arrondissements, tableaux vivants

35.12
pause, taws, tawse, Storrs, Dawes, Dors, cause, Coors®, gauze, Hawes, hawse, drawers, yaws, yours, Lawes, Laws, clause, diapause, quatorze, indoors, kolkhoz, plus-fours, Azores, furores, applause, sub-clause, tropopause, stratopause, menopause, mesopause, Helsingfors, underdrawers, Santa Claus

35.13
poise, noise, Noyes, Anglepoise®, Warboys, tortoise, travois, turquoise, counterpoise, equipoise, Dotheboys, avoirdupois

35.14
buzz, does, coz, muzz, fuzz, abuzz, redoes, outdoes, because, D.Mus., Ormuz, M.Mus., Buzfuz, underdoes, overdoes

35.15
guise, size, wise, Reyes, rise, prise, prize, lyse, flies

35.15.1
archaize, Hebraize

35.15.2
Hinduize

35.15.3
Judaize

35.15.4
jumboize, ghettoize, heroize

35.15.5
despise, misanthropize, philanthropize

35.15.6
bye-byes, syllabize

35.15.7
baptize **.1** concretize **.2** mediatize, Sovietize **.3** mithridatize **.4** alphabetize **.5** amortize **.6** pyritize, phagocytize **.7** poetize, appetize, expertize, sabbatize, robotize, hypostatize, apostatize, narcotize, egotize, schematize, Semitize, lemmatize, emblematize, dramatize, diagrammatize, overdramatize, melodramatize, epigrammatize, anagrammatize, traumatize, acclimatize, automatize, systematize, problematize, legitimatize, anathematize, aromatize, achromatize, diplomatize, stigmatize, pragmatize, dogmatize, enigmatize, schismatize, sanitize, monetize, unitize, hypnotize, magnetize, demonetize, remonetize, demagnetize, graphitize, privatize, advertise, synthetize, anaesthetize, anesthetize, quixotize, sensitize, parasitize, desensitize, photosensitize, digitize, prioritize, necrotize, syncretize, securitize, democratize, bureaucratize, deputize, pelletize, palletize, proselytize **.8** quantize, potentize, fragmentize, Protestantize, permanentize **.9** chastise

35.15.8
periodize, iodize, fluidize, jeopardize, bastardize, standardize, psalmodize, nomadize, anodize, methodize, rhapsodize, subsidize, oxidize, liquidize, sherardize, hybridize, melodize, gourmandize, merchandize, aggrandize, propagandize

35.15.9
hierarchize, catechize

35.15.10
disguise, prologize, diphthongize

35.15.11
demise, surmise, remise, premise, opiumize, atomize, itemize, optimize, victimize, systemize, customize, epitomize, legitimize,

anatomize, lobotomize, phlebotomize, dichotomize, trichotomize, leucotomize, lithotomize, vasectomize, illegitimize, hysterectomize, sodomize, randomize, macadamize, alchemize, minimize, dynamize, economize, euphemize, racemize, maximize, compromise, pilgrimize, Islamize

35.15.12
cognize **.1** routinize **.2** Latinize, keratinize **.3** unionize, sectarianize, pedestrianize, Australianize, proletarianize **.4** Normanize **.5** Europeanize, luteinize, ionize, kyanize, lionize, deionize, caponize, ebonize, carbonize, urbanize, decarbonize, suburbanize, satanize, tetanize, cretinize, fraternize, platinize, gelatinize, botanize, monotonize, gluttonize, scrutinize, nicotinize, skeletonize, peptonize, westernize, Daltonize, modernize, iodinize, attitudinize, platitudinize, preconize, mechanize, Balkanize, vulcanize, Africanize, Americanize, paganize, agonize, jargonize, organize, gorgonize, antagonize, reorganize, disorganize, demonize, feminize, harmonize, simonize, womanize, humanize, sermonize, Germanize, romanize, Pelmanize, disharmonize, bituminize, dehumanize, aluminize, vitaminize, canonize, euphonize, divinize, Calvinize, galvanize, Saxonize, ozonize, Russianize, fractionize, Egyptianize, emulsionize, revolutionize, disillusionize, Christianize, dechristianize, pidginize, indigenize, homogenize, oxygenize, tyrannize, ironize, heparinize, patronize, synchronize, Lutheranize, isochronize, immunize, communize, decommunize, civilianize, Hellenize, colonize, kaolinize, desalinize, decolonize, recolonize, masculinize **.6** eternize **.7** recognize **.8** solemnize

35.15.13
theosophize, philosophize, apostrophize, anthropomorphize, bibliographize

35.15.14
Levi's®, devise, revise, previse, advise, supervise, improvise, televise, misadvise, relativize, objectivize, collectivize, comprehensivize

35.15.15
sympathize, empathize, telepathize

35.15.16
resize, assize, capsize, outsize, excise, incise, downsize, undersize, oversize **.1** Graecize **.2** apotheosize **.3** exorcize **.4** laicize, criticize, cliticize, Scotticize, fantasize, plasticize, causticize, gnosticize, ecstasize, politicize, poeticize, phoneticize, grammaticize, fanaticize, eroticize, semanticize, romanticize, metastasize, monasticize, elasticize, hypostasize, depoliticize, phonemicize, polemicize, Hispanicize, emphasize, de-emphasize, re-emphasize, underemphasize, overemphasize, mythicize, ethicize, Gothicize, synthesize, hypothesize, parenthesize,

photosynthesize, classicize, exercise, metaphysicize, metricize, ostracize, dehistoricize, Gallicize, publicize, Anglicize, italicize, Catholicize **.5** synopsize **.6** circumcise **.7** queen-size, twin-size

35.15.17
franchise, fetishize, affranchise, enfranchise, disenfranchise, disfranchise

35.15.18
energize, syllogize, elegize, eulogize, analogize, paralogize, neologize, theologize, geologize, apologize, tautologize, psychologize, homologize, monologize, chronologize, mythologize, anthologize, philologize, genealogize, archaeologize, etymologize, demythologize

35.15.19
nowise, stepwise, slopewise, crabwise, streetwise, slantwise, leastwise, coastwise, broadwise, sidewise, endwise, clockwise, likewise, spokewise, unwise, longwise, widthwise, breadthwise, lengthwise, crosswise, hingewise, edgewise, wedgewise, saltirewise, anywise, cornerwise, otherwise, scissorwise, contrariwise, anticlockwise, counterclockwise, ventriloquize, soliloquize

35.15.20
highrise, arise, low-rise, uprise **.1** theorize, linearize, plagiarize, interiorize, exteriorize, familiarize, denuclearize **.2** diarize, vaporize, pauperize, temporize, contemporize, extemporize, barbarize, rubberize, satirize, tartarize, martyrize, cauterize, motorize, notarize, vectorize, factorize, winterize, pasteurize, rasterize, computerize, catheterize, militarize, characterize, transistorize, demilitarize, tenderize, slenderize, deodorize, vulgarize, categorize, allegorize, subcategorize, memorize, glamorize, summarize, mesmerize, epimerize, isomerize, polymerize, oligomerize, depolymerize, copolymerize, containerize, aphorize, sanforize, pulverize, etherize, authorize, weatherize, mercerize, accessorize, pressurize, depressurize, moisturize, texturize, miniaturize, panegyrize, terrorize, curarize, sulphurize, velarize, valorize, colorize, polarize, solarize, bowdlerize, burglarize, alveolarize, revalorize, modularize, popularize, secularize, circularize, vascularize, regularize, singularize, formularize, depolarize, particularize, vernacularize **.3** apprise, apprize, surprise, comprise, misprize, enterprise **.4** cicatrize, symmetrize, geometrize, parametrize **.5** sunrise, moonrise

35.15.21
.1 idyllize **.2** realize, labialize, bestialize, idealize, trivialize, serialize, imperialize, arterialize, materialize, etherealize, memorialize, industrialize, dematerialize, immaterialize, editorialize, territorialize **.3** stylize **.4.1** creolize, vowelize, dialyse, dualize **.4.2** monopolize,

municipalize, stabilize, destabilize, diabolize, metabolize, catabolize, obelize, detribalize, cannibalize, solubilize, verbalize, mobilize, globalize, demobilize, immobilize, symbolize **.4.3** metallize, catalyse, catalyze, volatilize, cartelize, glottalize, immortalize, subtilize, vitalize, devitalize, revitalize, brutalize, utilize, reutilize, under-utilize, capitalize, hospitalize, digitalize, palatalize, recapitalize, overcapitalize, fertilize, totalize, photolyze, dentalize, tantalize, transcendentalize, segmentalize, orientalize, occidentalize, sentimentalize, monumentalize, departmentalize, compartmentalize, experimentalize, crystallize, recrystallize, idolize, feudalize, scandalize, vandalize **.4.4** focalize, vocalize, localize, topicalize, verticalize, radicalize, musicalize, delocalize, theatricalize, legalize, prodigalize **.4.5** normalize, formalize, thermalize, plasmolyze, animalize, decimalize, caramelize, penalize, marginalize, analyse, canalize, channelize, reanalyse, psychoanalyse, carnalize, finalize, communalize, criminalize, nominalize, decriminalize, phenomenalize, pronominalize, personalize, depersonalize, sensationalize, vocationalize, operationalize, professionalize, nationalize, rationalize, denationalize, renationalize, internationalize, irrationalize, institutionalize, deinstitutionalize, constitutionalize, emotionalize, fictionalize, sectionalize, factionalize, fractionalize, conventionalize, regionalize, vernalize, journalize, internalize, externalize, eternalize, signalize **.4.6** syphilize, lyophilize, civilize, novelize, medievalize, breathalyse, breathalyze, fossilize, universalize, dieselize, nasalize, podzolize, initialize, artificialize, spatialize, specialize, overspecialize, martialize, commercialize, socialize, sensualize, provincialize, substantialize, evangelize, individualize, equalize, tranquillize, lingualize **.4.7** sterilize, paralyse, paralyze, moralize, demoralize, pluralize, pyrolyze, ruralize, liberalize, literalize, gutturalize, collateralize, federalize, mineralize, generalize, demineralize, overgeneralize, naturalize, denaturalize, supernaturalize, neutralize, centralize, electrolyse, electrolyze, decentralize, hydrolyze, mongrelize **.4.8** ritualize, actualize, formulize, annualize, capsulize, sexualize, visualize, spiritualize, conceptualize, contextualize, decontextualize, decasualize, intellectualize **.5** manyplies

35.16
otiose, grandiose, Berlioz, Thammuz, Hormuz, Soyuz

35.17
ooze, Ouse, booze, do's, schmooze, snooze, choose, who's, whose, roux, ruse, bruise, trews, Druze, cruise, cruse, Cruz, use, youse, Bewes, 'scuse, Skues, mews, muse, news, fuse, fuze, Hughes, lose, blues, Clewes, Clowes, BMus, Santa Cruz

35.17.1
Vaduz, billets-doux, comptes rendus

35.17.2
Tungus

35.17.3
Hormuz

35.17.4
Mahfouz

35.17.5
bijoux

35.17.6
peruse, Andrews, St Andrews, Veracruz

35.17.7
re-use, abuse, contuse, adieux, accuse, incuse, excuse, amuse, bemuse, defuse, effuse, perfuse, diffuse, suffuse, refuse, infuse, confuse, transfuse, Mathews, Matthews, enthuse, disuse, misuse, ill-use, purlieux, under-use, overuse, disabuse, Syracuse, interfuse, rediffuse, circumfuse, hypotenuse

35.17.8
Toulouse, rhythm-and-blues

35.18

35.18.1
Meyers, Sayers

35.18.2
ours, Powers, Bowers, Towers, Flowers

35.18.3
Moyers

35.18.4
Byers, Myers, Briers, pliers, transires, Greyfriars, Whitefriars, Blackfriars

35.18.5
Tours, yours

35.18.6
jeepers, jodhpurs, Pampers®, champers, Gompers

35.18.7
Sobers, Chambers, nos, Olbers, bejabers, bejabbers, Fochabers

35.18.8
Peters, squitters, Charteris, Waters, Butters, certes, Winters, Masters, Klosters, Walters, headquarters, hindquarters, Cockfosters

35.18.9
flinders, Enders, sanders, Randers, Landers, glanders, Flanders, Saunders, Childers, Bermudas, malanders, mallenders, sallenders, alexanders

35.18.10
Snickers®, Vickers, Chequers, starkers, Leuchars, bluchers, jankers, Yonkers, Whiskas®, Moluccas, camiknickers

35.18.11
Tigers, Rutgers, butterfingers

35.18.12
Chalmers, Somers, Summers, Bahamas, Alzheimer's

35.18.13
Innes, Connors, Berners, Taverners, Marianas

35.18.14
Bofors

35.18.15
cleavers, Chivers, Rievaulx, Rivers, clivers, Havers, Evers, Travers, divers, vivers, Redvers, Danvers, Pitt-Rivers, estovers

35.18.16
Smithers, withers, Carruthers, druthers

35.18.17
missus, Messrs, molasses, sunglasses, fracases, premises, marquises, galluses, abatises, cephalothoraxes

35.18.18
Moses, Joneses, Marquesas, Devizes, elevenses

35.18.19
conches, Pontine Marshes

35.18.20
breeches, britches, laches, Marches, bluchers, Scriptures, conches, Weightwatchers®, sons-of-bitches, rags-to-riches

35.18.21
Bridges, Hedges, Clarges, Hodges, Rogers, Judges, ambages, Claridge's

35.18.22
Elwes, always, Velázquez

35.18.23
Benares, Dolores, danses macabres, fêtes champêtres

35.18.24
de Villiers

35.18.25
Sillars, Mellors, Sellars, González, binoculars

35.19
Meuse, furze, hers, chanteurs, chanteuse, chanteuses, vendeuse, frondeurs, charmeuse, coiffeurs, coiffeuse, coiffeuses, chauffeuse, divers, berceuse, masseuse, danseuse, diseuse, poseuse, poseuses, Betelgeuse, chartreuse, prie-dieux, messieurs, milieux, siffleuse, mitrailleuse, secateurs, raconteuse, accoucheuse, au sérieux, agents provocateurs

35.20
pose, beaux, Bose, Bowes, doze, Mohs, noes, nose, those, chose, hose, squoze, rose, pros, prose, brose, froze, close, Clowes, cloze, bons mots

35.20.1
prepose, appose, oppose, depose, suppose, repose, propose, impose, reimpose, compose, dispose, expose, transpose, superpose, interpose, juxtapose, adipose, presuppose,

decompose, recompose, discompose, superimpose, predispose, indispose, overexpose, underexpose

35.20.2
sorbose, ribose, flambeaux, thrombose

35.20.3
setose, bateaux, gateaux, chateaux, plateaux, pectose, lactose, fructose, pentose, manteaux, sarmentose, maltose, comatose, keratose, galactose, portmanteaux, phagocytose

35.20.4
Beddoes, bandeaux, rondeaux, fricandeaux, bulldoze

35.20.5
arkose, glucose, viscose, talcose, fruticose, bellicose

35.20.6
rugose

35.20.7
trumeaux, Esquimaux, lachrymose, chalumeaux, anastomose

35.20.8
tonneaux, diagnose, Brasenose, bottlenose, Quaglino's®, raffinose, anthracnose, misdiagnose, arabinose

35.20.9
metamorphose

35.20.10
trousseaux, hexose, ponceaux

35.20.11
MacLehose, pantyhose

35.20.12
Faeroes, bureaux, Burroughs, arose, uprose, Ambrose, Waitrose, Montrose, dextrose, sucrose, primrose, Camrose, cornrows, refroze, unfroze, Melrose, gaspereaux, tuberose, bordereaux, guelder-rose, saccharose, Jaques-Dalcroze

35.20.13
noyaux, Muñoz

35.20.14
Fellowes, gallows, Hallowes, pilose, xylose, rouleaux, tableaux, parclose, foreclose, nightclothes, bedclothes, inclose, plainclothes, enclose, unclose, disclose, papillose, ankylose, papulose, laevulose, cellulose, underclothes, hemicellulose, nitrocellulose

35.21
Thebes, PIBS, Tibbs, Gibbs, Hibs, Krebs, Babs, Hobbes, Hobbs, Forbes, Stubbs, vibes, Zubes, dribs and drabs, Jacobs, Proverbs, mulligrubs

35.22
Stieglitz

35.23.1
Leeds, proceeds

35.23.2
SIDS, Perseids, Geminids

35.23.3
Aids, Palisades, Everglades

35.23.4
adze

35.23.5
Ards, Rickards

35.23.6
Dodds, Mods, NACODS

35.23.7
Lourdes, Tussaud's

35.23.8
Lloyd's, adenoids

35.23.9
suds, soapsuds

35.23.10
ides, upsides, classifieds

35.23.11
goods, Woods, piece-goods, smallgoods, backwoods

35.23.12
Lourdes, innards, Richards, forwards, Edwards, backwards, downwards

35.23.13
Byrds

35.23.14
Rhodes, Tussaud's, Hampton Roads

35.23.15
Sandes, Sandys, badlands, zounds, grounds, Lowndes, Simmonds, Symonds, Edmonds, calends, kalends, Hollands, Rylands, Newlands, Rowlands, Falklands, Brooklands, Bury St Edmunds, Netherlands, Fields, Shields, Faulds, Childs, Foulds, Reynolds, Bluefields, Spitalfields

35.24
Biggs, Higgs, Riggs, Briggs, Griggs, Largs, jougs, sheerlegs, Joe Bloggs, yellowlegs, moneybags, daddy-long-legs

35.25.1
Eames, Wemyss, Reims, meseems

35.25.2
Timms, Sims

35.25.3
Ames, James, hames

35.25.4
jimjams, Abrahams

35.25.5
alms, Brahms, Glamis, man-at-arms

35.25.6
Toms, comms, coms, telecoms

35.25.7
Worms, Cairngorms

35.25.8
Times, Simes, Grimes, betimes, oftentimes, Maritimes, betweentimes

35.25.9
Toombs, Coombes

35.25.10
diddums, Adams, Abrams, doldrums, Ingrams, Williams, Debenhams, McWilliams

35.25.11
Soames, Holmes

35.26.1
Keynes, means, Jeans, Queens, Macleans®, Phillipines, smithereens

35.26.2
Binns, Robbins, Robins, gubbins, Gittins, matins, mattins, Dickens, Akins, Eakins, Dawkins, Hawkins, Perkins, Hopkins, Simpkins, Tompkins, Atkins, Watkins, Adkins, Jenkins, Wilkins, Elkins, Higgins, Wiggins, muggins, juggins, Huggins, Cummins, Blevins, Hutchins, Hollins, Rollins, Rawlins, Mullins, chitlins, Butlin's, O'Higgins, widdershins, Gobelins, galligaskins

35.26.3
Trinian's, Orléans, Colossians

35.26.4
Baines, Staines, Keynes, Gaines, Haynes, Raynes, afterpains

35.26.5
Spens, Benz, mens, Fens, gens, WRNS, lens, cleanse, sapiens, Serpens, Ardennes, impatiens, persiennes, deferens, Homo sapiens, locum tenens, vas deferens, nolens volens, delirium tremens

35.26.6
Cairns, Mearns

35.26.7
banns, sans, Hans, glans, Prestonpans, Octans, explanans, Langerhans, Liederkrantz

35.26.8
Townes, Downes, hash-browns

35.26.9
Parnes, Barnes, Afrikaans

35.26.10
pons, bonze, Mons, Johns, St John's, bronze, mod cons, goujons

35.26.11
sons-of-guns

35.26.12
Fiennes, Heinz, Hines, confines, Apennines, Nazca Lines, Newnes, Clunes

35.26.13
.1 Orléans, New Orleans .2 Lyons, Onions
.3 Youens .4 Owens .5 Serpens .6 Gibbons, Rubens, Robens, St Albans .7 Martens, Buttons, Sextans, Rocky Mountains .8 Siddons .9 Huygens

.10 Siemens, Simmons, Symons, Clemens, commons, summons, Simons, Tromans, Yeomans, Fitzsimmons **.11** Stephens, Stevens, avens, Evans, Jevons, Strevens, Ovens, Ivens **.12** Athens **.13** Sissons, Parsons, Goossens **.14** Cousins, Cozens **.15** Lamentations, Colossians, United Nations **.16** Hitchens **.17** goujons, imagines **.18** Behrens, Lorenz, environs **.19** Lutyens **.20** St Helens, Collins

35.26.14
Burns, Kearns

35.26.15
nones, Jones, barebones, sawbones, crossbones, Flintstones, fivestones, lazybones

35.27
Springs, toings and froings, trappings, beestings, Hastings, hustings, tidings, pickings, Cummings, combings, gleanings, gainings, Jennings, earnings, leavings, Livings, fixings, fleshings, scratchings, Hutchings, scourings, Palm Springs, heartstrings, purse-strings, feelings, Rawlings, filings, proceedings, belongings, underthings, arisings, furnishings, waterwings, imaginings

35.28.1
eaves, beeves, thieves, Jeeves, Reeves, Greaves, leaves, sneak-thieves, wheatsheaves, Hargreaves, tealeaves, flyleaves, figleaves, Greensleeves, handkerchiefs, cloverleaves

35.28.2
Graves, tipstaves, jackstaves, Hargraves, Bygraves

35.28.3
haves

35.28.4
calves, scarves

35.28.5
corves, wharves, dwarves

35.28.6
Ives, knives, wives, lives, jackknives, penknives, spaewives, midwives, goodwives, housewives, fishwives, alewives, under-fives, afterlives

35.28.7
hooves, rooves

35.28.8
turves

35.28.9
Groves, loaves, sugarloaves

35.28.10
elves, selves, themselves, shelves, wolves, theirselves, ourselves, yourselves, bookshelves, mantelshelves, she-wolves, werewolves, aardwolves

35.29
cloths, clothes, nightclothes, bedclothes, plainclothes, underclothes

35.30.1
Galashiels

35.30.2
Mills, Sills, Hills, Wills, Brownhills

35.30.3
tales, Smails, Hales, Wales, Swales, entrails, Bloomingdale's, Fylingdales, telesales, New South Wales, cat-o'-nine-tails

35.30.4
Kells, Wells, Kwells, Dardanelles, Seychelles, Builth Wells, Tunbridge Wells, crimes passionnels, Llandrindod Wells

35.30.5
Hals, Casals

35.30.6
Fowles, Vowles

35.30.7
Arles, Charles

35.30.8
hols, Consols

35.30.9
balls, Walls, Rawls

35.30.10
Iles, Styles, Miles, Myles, Smiles, Giles, Ryles, Wade-Giles

35.30.11
Jools, Jules, gules, McNaghten rules

35.30.12
Howells, Samuels, Daniels

35.30.13
Bowles, Coles, Scholes, Knollys, Knowles, Vowles, Rolls

35.30.14
Naples, Sharples

35.30.15
Peebles, Gorbals, Goebbels, Mumbles, Venables, collywobbles

35.30.16
Beatles, battels, bristols

35.30.17
Needles, Tiddles, oodles

35.30.18
Pickles, Nichols, Eccles

35.30.19
Biggles, Engels, Gleneagles

35.30.20
Ennals

35.30.21
Raffles

35.30.22
Brussels

35.30.23
measles

36.1
quiche, niche, fiche, Laois, leash, Leix, babiche, potiche, schottische, pastiche, postiche,

corniche, Rajneesh, affiche, hasheesh, hashish, backsheesh, baksheesh, McLeish, Dalgleish, Dalglish, unleash, ouananiche, microfiche, nouveau riche, nouveaux riches

36.2
pish, bish, Bysshe, dish, Gish, knish, fish, wish, cuish, squish, swish, Trish, Frisch, goyisch, goyish, Petri dish, gefilte fish

36.2.1
puppyish, babyish, shabbyish, tubbyish, boobyish, prettyish, toadyish, dandyish, sandyish, monkeyish, fogeyish, fogyish, nannyish, toffeeish, heavyish, sissyish, Gypsyish

36.2.2
greyish, clayish

36.2.3
boyish, tomboyish

36.2.4
dryish

36.2.5
aguish, Melhuish

36.2.6
Jewish, trueish, shrewish, newish, bluish, Melhuish

36.2.7
Pollyannaish, prima donna-ish

36.2.8
lowish, slowish, narrowish, yellowish, tallowish, sallowish

36.2.9
steepish, sheepish, cheapish, apish, snappish, Lappish, sharpish, foppish, uppish, popish, mopish, impish, wimpish, blimpish, dampish, scampish, vampish, trampish, mumpish, grumpish, frumpish, lumpish, plumpish, waspish, trollopish

36.2.10
nebbish, mobbish, snobbish, yobbish, slobbish, tubbish, rubbish, furbish, refurbish

36.2.11
sweetish, skittish, twittish, British, straightish, lateish, latish, pettish, fetish, wettish, Lettish, cattish, fattish, flattish, stoutish, loutish, smartish, Scottish, sottish, hottish, shortish, ruttish, sluttish, whitish, rightish, brightish, lightish, slightish, Jutish, brutish, goatish, Pictish, Kentish, leftish, softish, saltish, doltish, coltish, un-British, coquettish, novelettish

36.2.12
Swedish, Yiddish, maidish, old-maidish, reddish, baddish, caddish, kaddish, faddish, saddish, radish, laddish, horseradish, loudish, hardish, oddish, cloddish, widish, goodish, rudish, prudish, dudish, butterdish, Kurdish, toadish, modish, sidedish, fiendish, Wendish, Standish, brandish, blandish, houndish, roundish,

tundish, brigandish, Cavendish, outlandish, inlandish, Netherlandish, baldish, mildish, childish, wildish, oldish, coldish

36.2.13
peakish, weakish, freakish, cliquish, thickish, sickish, trickish, rakish, peckish, quackish, brackish, blackish, sparkish, darkish, clerkish, blockish, gawkish, mawkish, hawkish, puckish, bookish, Turkish, quirkish, folkish, pinkish, prankish, Frankish, punkish, monkish, völkisch, knick-knackish, textbookish, unbookish

36.2.14
piggish, biggish, whiggish, priggish, vaguish, haggish, waggish, doggish, hoggish, puggish, thuggish, sluggish, voguish, roguish, Luxemburgish

36.2.15
squeamish, Rhemish, dimmish, slimmish, Hamish, lamish, blemish, Flemish, Amish, famish, qualmish, Squamish, warmish, skirmish, gnomish, Romish, Carchemish, schoolmarmish

36.2.16
.1 greenish, cleanish **.2** finish, Finnish, thinnish, diminish, refinish, photo finish **.3** Danish **.4** Rhenish, replenish **.5** Spanish, banish, tannish, mannish, vanish, planish, clannish **.6** townish, brownish, clownish **.7** tarnish, garnish, varnish, revarnish **.8** donnish, astonish, admonish **.9** Cornish **.10** punish, nunnish, Hunnish **.11** swinish, porcupinish **.12** soonish, cartoonish, buffoonish **.13** kittenish, maidenish, hoydenish, paganish, dragonish, Mammonish, womanish, Romanish, heathenish, vixenish **.14** burnish, furnish, refurnish **.15** tonish

36.2.17
strongish, longish, youngish

36.2.18
overfish **.1** stiffish, killifish, jellyfish **.2** spearfish **.3** waifish, crayfish **.4** raffish **.5** starfish, calfish, garfish **.6** offish, standoffish **.7** oarfish, sawfish, dwarfish, crawfish **.8** toughish, muffish, huffish, roughish **.9** wifish **.10** jewfish, bluefish **.11** butterfish, triggerfish, silverfish **.12** oafish, blowfish **.13** pipefish, lumpfish **.14** globefish **.15** sheatfish, catfish, flatfish, whitefish, parrotfish **.16** redfish, threadfish, codfish, swordfish, mudfish, toadfish, goldfish, scabbard-fish **.17** weakfish, jackfish, blackfish, stockfish, rockfish, monkfish **.18** hagfish, dogfish, frogfish **.19** panfish, sunfish, moonfish, bonefish, stonefish, ribbonfish, dragonfish **.20** kingfish, lungfish **.21** sailfish, elfish, selfish, shellfish, filefish, wolfish, coalfish, cuttlefish, devilfish, damselfish, angelfish, unselfish

36.2.19
peevish, thievish, spivish, spivvish, knavish, slavish, ravish, lavish, dervish, mauvish, elvish, McTavish

36.2.20
smoothish

36.2.21
missish, coarsish, niceish, nicish, loosish, closish, minxish

36.2.22
hashish, Tarshish

36.2.23
largish

36.2.24
vanquish, anguish, languish, unwish, relinquish, distinguish, extinguish, contradistinguish

36.2.25
nearish, queerish, buccaneerish, perish, cherish, bearish, garish, fairish, squarish, nightmarish, parish, Parrish, tovarish, boorish, Moorish, moreish, whorish, nourish, flourish, Irish, sourish, vaporish, vapourish, viperish, gibberish, Pooterish, spinsterish, spiderish, lickerish, liquorice, liquorish, Quakerish, muckerish, ochreish, vigorish, tigerish, ogreish, feverish, liverish, vulturish, Micawberish, amateurish, shamateurish, vinegarish, impoverish, currish

36.2.26
goyish

36.2.27
palish, Salish, Melhuish, Mellish, hellish, swellish, relish, embellish, owlish, polish, repolish, spit-and-polish, abolish, demolish, tallish, Dawlish, Gaulish, smallish, dullish, stylish, bullish, coolish, ghoulish, foolish, mulish, Ballachulish, purplish, ticklish, devilish, girlish, churlish, Polish, accomplish, feeblish, stablish, publish, establish, disestablish, gemütlich, English, Spanglish, Janglish

36.3
kirsch

36.4
Paish, kesh, feis, seiche, crèche, Leix, flèche

36.5
Kesh, mesh, nesh, feis, crèche, fresh, thresh, flèche, flesh, tête-bêche, Ardèche, enmesh, afresh, refresh, crème fraîche, parfleche, horseflesh, gooseflesh, Bangladesh, Marrakesh, intermesh, Gilgamesh, micromesh, synchromesh, Madhya Pradesh, Uttar Pradesh, Andhra Pradesh

36.6
ash, Ashe, pash, bash, stash, dash, cache, cash, gash, MASH, mash, smash, gnash, Nash, Nashe, sash, hash, rash, brash, trash, crash, thrash, lash, plash, splash, clash, flash, slash

36.6.1
calipash

36.6.2
earbash, Wabash, abash, kurbash, calabash

36.6.3
potash, soutache, Saltash, sabretache, succotash

36.6.4
csárdás, slapdash, pebbledash, spatterdash, balderdash

36.6.5
encash, Balkhash

36.6.6
quamash, camas, mishmash

36.6.7
Monash, panache

36.6.8
rehash

36.6.9
cornbrash, Midrash, gatecrash, waterbrash

36.6.10
eyelash, goulash, calash, whiplash, backlash, unlash, newsflash, backslash, thunderflash, synchroflash

36.7
stoush

36.8
marsh, harsh, gouache, moustache, démarche, Titmarsh, Saltmarsh, Tidmarsh, Hindmarsh, Killamarsh

36.9
posh, Boche, Bosch, bosh, tosh, dosh, cosh, gosh, nosh, Foch, josh, wash, quash, Quosh, squash, swash, Roche, frosh, splosh, cloche, slosh, brioche

36.9.1
brioche

36.9.2
kibosh, Haber-Bosch

36.9.3
McIntosh, mackintosh

36.9.4
cohosh

36.9.5
rewash, pre-wash, car wash, eyewash, Siwash, awash, outwash, whitewash, backwash, musquash, pigwash, bagwash, hogwash, Pugwash, limewash, brainwash, mouthwash, wish-wash, colour wash

36.9.6
Milosz, guilloche, galosh

36.10
carte blanche, arme blanche

36.11
Porsche®, borsch

36.12
tush, gush, mush, shush, hush, rush, brush, crush, thrush, lush, plush, blush, flush, slush, hush-hush, uprush, airbrush, hairbrush, tarbrush, paintbrush, toothbrush, clothes brush,

sagebrush, nailbrush, outrush, Midrash, woodrush, Windrush, inrush, onrush, songthrush, mistle thrush, bulrush, ablush, underbrush

36.13
push, bush, cush, Kush, mush, shush, whoosh, swoosh, bell push, saltbush, shadbush, Wimbush, ambush, spicebush, rosebush, kiddush, cush-cush, kurus, sugarbush, Hindu Kush

36.14
douche, whoosh, swoosh, ruche, louche, sploosh, sloosh, capuche, debouch, tarboosh, bonne bouche, cartouche, gobemouche, barouche, kurus, farouche, scaramouch, Ashby-de-la-Zouch

36.15
kirsch, Smersh

36.16
brioche, gauche, Roche, troche, guilloche

36.17
welsh, Walsh, Greenhalgh, Liebfraumilch: (+ **38.19**)

37.1
prestige, noblesse oblige

37.2
beige, Liège, cortège, manège, Courrèges, saxifrage

37.3
concierge, auberge, barège

37.4
taj, raj, plage, maquillage, bon voyage

37.4.1
triage

37.4.2
découpage

37.4.3
potage, frottage, montage, agiotage, marcottage, reportage, cabotage, sabotage, curettage, décolletage, photomontage

37.4.4
bocage

37.4.5
ménage, espionage, badinage, counterespionage

37.4.6
dressage, corsage, Lesage, vernissage

37.4.7
paysage

37.4.8
repêchage

37.4.9
mirage, barrage, garage, entourage, effleurage, arbitrage

37.4.10
maquillage

37.4.11
collage, fuselage, camouflage, persiflage

37.5
mélange, plus ça change

37.6
Nuits-Saint-George

37.7
rouge, Bruges, luge, Cluj, gamboge, Khmer Rouge, Baton Rouge, deluge, Moulin Rouge, vermifuge, calcifuge

37.8
demi-vierge

37.9
doge, Vosges, loge, gamboge, Limoges

38.1
each, peach, speech, beach, beech, teach, reach, preach, breach, breech, screech, leach, leech, Leitch, pleach, bleach, impeach, Long Beach, Wisbech, Holbeach, Holbech, Holbeche, reteach, unteach, misteach, beseech, outreach, horseleech, overreach

38.2
itch, pitch, bitch, titch, stitch, ditch, kitsch, Mitch, niche, snitch, fitch, hitch, which, witch, twitch, quitch, squitch, switch, rich, glitch, flitch

38.2.1
overpitch

38.2.2
son-of-a-bitch

38.2.3
slipstitch, topstitch, backstitch, lockstitch, hemstitch, unstitch

38.2.4
Redditch, Shoreditch, Houndsditch

38.2.5
West Bromwich

38.2.6
spinach, Greenwich

38.2.7
Mickiewicz, tsarevich, Rostropovich, Shostakovich

38.2.8
unhitch

38.2.9
bewitch, Droitwich, Nantwich, Prestwich, Sandwich, Aldwych, Magwitch, sandwich, Northwich, Ipswich, dip switch, Middlewich, microswitch, Cesarewitch

38.2.10
Harwich, Norwich, ostrich, Edrich, Goodrich, eldrich, eldritch, enrich

38.2.11
Dulwich, Woolwich

38.3
aitch, h, pH, coth, Toc H, tanh, sinh, cosh, Rh, mph

38.4
etch, ketch, sketch, fetch, vetch, kvetch, retch, wretch, stretch, lech, Dolmetsch, outstretch, backstretch, overstretch

38.5
patch, batch, catch, match, natch, snatch, thatch, hatch, ratch, brach, cratch, scratch, latch, eyepatch, crosspatch, dispatch, Sandbach, ambatch, attach, reattach, detach, Lukács, rematch, outmatch, mismatch, crossmatch, Wasatch, nuthatch, stonehatch, crosshatch, Brands Hatch, sasquatch, potlatch, unlatch, overmatch, astrohatch, coffee klatch

38.6
ouch, pouch, couch, vouch, crouch, grouch, slouch, debouch, avouch

38.7
arch, parch, starch, march, Marche, larch, cornstarch, frogmarch, inarch, countermarch, overarch

38.8
potch, botch, Koch, scotch, notch, watch, swatch, crotch, splotch, blotch, hotchpotch, hopscotch, topnotch, skywatch, stopwatch, fobwatch, outwatch, wristwatch, sasquatch, dogwatch, doomwatch, deathwatch, butterscotch

38.9
porch, bortsch, torch, scorch, nautch, lorch, debauch, blowtorch

38.10
Plattdeutsch

38.11
touch, Dutch, cutch, scutch, much, mutch, such, Sutch, hutch, crutch, thrutch, clutch, retouch, forasmuch, such-and-such, nonsuch, nonesuch, declutch, overmuch, insomuch, inasmuch

38.12
Crich

38.13
putsch, butch, Lódz

38.14
pooch, Couch, couch, Gooch, mooch, smooch, hooch, hootch, capuche, Quiller-Couch

38.15
orache

38.16
perch, birch, Burch, smirch, search, church, lurch, pikeperch, besmirch, research, wordsearch, Whitchurch, Christchurch, Dymchurch, Fenchurch, Hornchurch, unchurch, silver birch

38.17
poach, coach, roach, Roche, broach, brooch, loach, slowcoach, stagecoach, approach, reproach, abroach, cockroach, encroach, motorcoach, self-reproach

38.18.1
inch, pinch, Minch, finch, cinch, sinh, chinch, winch, squinch, Linch, lynch, clinch, flinch, chaffinch, hawfinch, goldfinch, greenfinch, bullfinch, unclinch

38.18.2
bench, tench, stench, Dench, wench, quench, wrench, trench, drench, French, blench, clench, sawbench, frontbench, front bench, backbench, workbench, crossbench, retrench, intrench, entrench, unclench, Übermensch, Untermensch

38.18.3
tanh

38.18.4
stanch, ranch, branch, tranche, blanch, Blanche, flanch, Rumansh, Romansh, sub-branch, anabranch, avalanche

38.18.5
conch

38.18.6
paunch, staunch, haunch, raunch, graunch, launch, flaunch, relaunch

38.18.7
punch, bunch, munch, hunch, brunch, crunch, scrunch, lunch, keypunch, cardpunch, counterpunch, honeybunch

38.19
pilch, milch, filch, zilch, belch, welch, squelch, gulch, mulch: (+ **36.17**)

39.1
siege, liege, prestige, besiege

39.2
midge, ridge, bridge, fridge

39.2.1
quayage, triage

39.2.2
verbiage, lineage, ferriage, foliage

39.2.3
cowage, cowhage

39.2.4
buoyage

39.2.5
triage

39.2.6
sewage, pewage

39.2.7
towage, stowage, flowage

39.2.8
seepage, slippage, wrappage, stoppage, warpage, groupage, estoppage, equipage

39.2.9
cribbage, Babbage, cabbage, garbage, Burbage, herbage

39.2.10
metage, agiotage, freightage, baronetage, curettage, outage, cartage, pottage, cottage,

wattage, frottage, marcottage, telecottage,
portage, shortage, reportage, knightage,
footage, rootage, fruitage, scutage, adjutage,
cabotage, Armitage, hermitage, heritage,
pilotage, dotage, floatage, sacerdotage,
anecdotage, mintage, vintage, tentage, ventage,
vantage, Wantage, frontage, percentage,
advantage, parentage, disadvantage, driftage,
wastage, vestige, hostage, postage, meltage,
voltage

39.2.11
headage, adage, yardage, cordage, wordage,
windage, bandage, poundage, groundage,
pondage, bondage, frondage, brigandage,
appendage, vagabondage

39.2.12
leakage, breakage, wreckage, package, trackage,
dockage, socage, soccage, lockage, blockage,
corkage, truckage, soakage, sinkage, shrinkage,
linkage, tankage, boscage, repackage,
prepackage

39.2.13
baggage, mortgage, luggage, burgage,
remortgage

39.2.14
image, scrimmage, damage, Gamage, homage,
Bromwich, Gummidge, rummage, scrummage,
plumage, ohmage, self-image, West Bromwich,
pilgrimage

39.2.15
spinach, Prinknash, Greenwich, libertinage,
gabionage, alienage, thanage, drainage,
cranage, underdrainage, empennage, pannage,
tannage, manage, mismanage, stage-manage,
carnage, nonage, Swanage, coinage, tonnage,
dunnage, linage, peonage, apanage,
appanage, tamponage, commonage,
orphanage, siphonage, Stevenage, vicinage,
parsonage, personage, cozenage, baronage,
patronage, villeinage, gallonage, concubinage,
chaperonage

39.2.16
leafage, staffage, wharfage, roughage, roofage,
serfage, Alphege

39.2.17
cleavage, pavage, savage, ravage, lavage, lovage,
selvedge, salvage

39.2.18
Carthage

39.2.19
message, presage, passage, brassage, sausage,
usage, dosage, misusage, Hathersage,
surplusage, telemessage, overdosage

39.2.20
visage, usage, envisage

39.2.21
Sandwich, language, sandwich, messuage,
metalanguage, interlanguage, paralanguage

39.2.22
.1 peerage, steerage, arrearage **.2** Berridge
.3 lairage **.4** carriage, garage, marriage, Harwich,
disparage, miscarriage, remarriage,
mismarriage, undercarriage, intermarriage
.5 porridge, borage, Norwich, forage **.6** storage,
moorage, murage **.7** courage, Surridge,
encourage, discourage, demurrage **.8** umpirage
.9 sewerage, cooperage, amperage, harbourage,
metreage, litreage, porterage, quarterage,
lighterage, tutorage, hectarage, factorage,
fosterage, vicarage, acreage, brokerage,
anchorage, stockbrokerage, Muggeridge,
hangarage, haemorrhage, pilferage, telpherage,
leverage, beverage, Beveridge, average,
Doveridge, coverage, Loveridge, overage,
Etheridge, pasturage, depasturage, seigniorage,
cellarage, Coleridge **.10** weighbridge,
Weybridge, Cowbridge, harborage, Corbridge,
drawbridge, Newbridge, abridge, Stourbridge,
Trowbridge, footbridge, Coatbridge,
Wadebridge, Redbridge, Woodbridge,
Stockbridge, Cambridge, Bembridge, umbrage,
Bainbridge, Tonbridge, Stonebridge, Longbridge,
Lethbridge, Knightsbridge, Oxbridge,
Stocksbridge, Uxbridge, Kingsbridge, Delbridge,
tollbridge, Ferrybridge, Stalybridge,
Casterbridge, Fordingbridge **.11** partridge,
cartridge, ostrich **.12** Edridge, Eldridge, Aldridge,
Wooldridge **.13** Breckenridge **.14** suffrage,
Selfridge, ossifrage

39.2.23
pillage, spillage, tillage, stillage, millage, village,
grillage, haylage, railage, pelage, tallage, college,
knowledge, foreknowledge, acknowledge,
self-knowledge, stallage, smallage, haulage,
spoilage, ullage, Dulwich, sullage, mileage,
silage, ensilage, Woolwich, Coolidge, pupillage,
Cumberledge, cartilage, sortilege, tutelage,
curtilage, privilege, vassalage, mucilage,
fuselage, sacrilege, assemblage, Routledge,
Sutlej, Rutledge, kentledge

39.3
demiurge

39.4
age, page, Paige, stage, cage, gage, gauge, mage,
phage, sage, wage, swage, rage, off stage, tire
gauge, tyre guage, Iron Age, school-age,
under-age, overage

39.4.1
frontpage, rampage, interpage

39.4.2
restage, upstage, soundstage, backstage,
downstage, offstage, multistage

39.4.3
ribcage, birdcage, encage, uncage

39.4.4
greengage, raingauge, engage, disengage

39.4.5
teenage

39.4.6
macrophage, bacteriophage

39.4.7
space-age, Osage, Hathersage

39.4.8
assuage

39.4.9
outrage, enrage, saxifrage

39.4.10
school-age

39.5
edge, kedge, veg, sedge, hedge, wedge, reg, dredge,
ledge, pledge, fledge, sledge, straight edge,
foredge, fore-edge, allege, Wenlock Edge,
Cumberledge

39.6
badge, cadge, Madge, fadge, hajj, rebadge

39.7
gouge

39.8
sparge, barge, taj, marg, marge, sarge, charge,
hajj, raj, large, litharge, dressage, massage,
paysage, recharge, surcharge, discharge, barrage,
garage, Swaraj, enlarge, reportage, sabotage,
espionage, supercharge, turbocharge,
countercharge, undercharge, covercharge,
overcharge, priest-in-charge, overlarge,
camouflage

39.9
bodge, stodge, dodge, Hodge, wadge, wodge,
lodge, splodge, hodgepodge, dislodge,
Travelodge®, horologe

39.10
gorge, forge, George, St George, regorge,
engorge, disgorge, reforge

39.11
pudge, budge, Mudge, smudge, nudge, fudge,
judge, Rudge, trudge, drudge, grudge, bludge,
cludge, sludge, prejudge, forejudge, adjudge,
misjudge, begrudge

39.12
oblige, disoblige

39.13
stooge, Goodge, smoodge, scrooge, huge, luge,
cludge, kludge, refuge, deluge, subterfuge,
vermifuge, calcifuge, febrifuge, centrifuge,
ultracentrifuge

39.14
voyage, careenage, semiology

39.15
urge, purge, spurge, Burge, dirge, scourge,
merge, verge, serge, surge, splurge, reurge,
asperge, demerge, emerge, re-emerge,
submerge, diverge, converge, upsurge,
dramaturge, thaumaturge

39.16
doge, gamboge

39.17.1
binge, tinge, dinge, singe, hinge, whinge, winge,
twinge, swinge, springe, cringe, fringe, impinge,
unhinge, syringe, infringe, Collinge

39.17.2
mange, change, range, strange, grange,
short-change, exchange, arrange, rearrange,
prearrange, derange, outrange, estrange,
Lagrange, autochange, interchange,
counterchange, part-exchange, stock exchange,
Whalley Range, disarrange

39.17.3
Penge, henge, avenge, revenge, Stonehenge

39.17.4
flange, Falange, Phalange

39.17.5
scrounge, lounge

39.17.6
mélange

39.17.7
Tonge, longe, blancmange, maskinonge

39.17.8
sponge, scunge, gunge, grunge, longe, lunge,
plunge, blunge, expunge, muskellunge

39.17.9
scavenge, lozenge, orange, challenge

39.17.10
scavenge

39.18
bilge, bulge, Greenhalgh, indulge, promulge,
divulge, overindulge

40.1
eel, peal, peel, pele, spiel, Beale, teal, steal, steel,
Steele, stele, deal, keel, Keele, Kiel, meal, kneel,
Neal, Neale, Neil, feel, veal, Veale, seal, Seale,
seel, zeal, she'll, heal, heel, hele, he'll, weal,
Weighell, Weill, we'll, wheal, wheel, squeal,
hwyl, reel, creel, leal, Lille, square deal,
eau-de-Nil

40.1.1
appeal, repeal, kriegspiel, bonspiel,
Glockenspiel

40.1.2
abele, Mobile, airmobile, Dormobile®,
snowmobile, Popemobile, bookmobile,
Oldsmobile, déshabillé, automobile

40.1.3
genteel, Bastille, Castile, cockatiel, Jugendstil

40.1.4
ordeal, ideal, misdeal, urodele

40.1.5
Guayaquil

40.1.6
Emile, Camille, schlemiel, wheatmeal,
sweetmeal, oatmeal, cornmeal, bonemeal,
piecemeal, fishmeal, inchmeal, wholemeal

40.1.7
anele, anneal, O'Neil, chenille, McNeil, manchineel, cochineal

40.1.8
forefeel

40.1.9
reveal

40.1.10
reseal, Cecile, tahsil, Lucille, unseal, conceal, imbecile, scrotocele, underseal, bronchocele, alguacil, hydrocele, haematocele, varicocele, meningocele, bubonocele

40.1.11
Dalziel, overzeal, alguazil

40.1.12
congeal

40.1.13
reheel, cowheel, Tarheel, self-heal

40.1.14
freewheel, gearwheel, flywheel, awheel, cartwheel, printwheel, treadwheel, aiguille, cogwheel, pinwheel, millwheel, tailwheel, waterwheel

40.1.15
Kurile, unreel, Jezreel, newsreel

40.1.16
allele

40.2
ill, pill, spill, bill, til, 'til, till, still, dill, kill, skill, ghyll, Gill, gill, mil, mill, nil, fill, Phil, vill, thill, cill, sill, shill, chill, jill, hill, we'll, will, twill, 'twill, quill, squill, swill, Rhyl, rill, rille, brill, trill, drill, krill, grill, grille, frill, thrill, shrill, de Mille, per mil, BPhil

40.2.1
hwyl

40.2.2
benzoyl

40.2.3
minipill, overspill, cyclopropyl, isopropyl

40.2.4
sibyl, shearbill, waybill, playbill, habile, sawbill, twibill, wrybill, shoebill, gerbil, swordbill, handbill, duckbill, bank bill, thornbill, hornbill, spoonbill, crossbill, waxbill, storksbill, hawksbill, cranesbill, bulbil, Chernobyl, razorbill, yellow-bill

40.2.5
until, butyl, trotyl, Ampthill, octyl, dentil, ventil, lentil, tormentil, pistil, pastille, postil, distil, standstill, stock-still, instil, acetyl, saxatile, syndactyl, Largactil®, apostil, apostille, zygodactyl, tetradactyl

40.2.6
idyll, spadille, condyle, cacodyl, daffodil, minoxidil

40.2.7
Jekyll, archil, orchil, Shankill, deskill, Catskill, alkyl, Rentokil®, Danakil, overkill

40.2.8
Cowgill, Cargill, Scargill, Coghill, bluegill, McGill, Trudgill, Fothergill

40.2.9
Tamil, Hamill, sawmill, flourmill, Camille, vermeil, gristmill, treadmill, windmill, watermill

40.2.10
phenyl, pennill, vinyl, thionyl, manille, biphenyl, carbonyl, polyvinyl

40.2.11
D.Phil., refill, landfill, backfill, M.Phil., infill, fulfil, bibliophil, fibrefill, monofil, overfill, xanthophyll, mesophyll, sclerophyll, chlorophyll, neutrophil, hydrophil, necrophil, eosinophil, overfulfil

40.2.12
Seville, Bournville, Louisville, Stanleyville, Orville, Torvill, Abbeville, vaudeville, Mandeville, Baskerville, Somerville, Bonneville, Hooverville, Brazzaville, Libreville, Deauville, Yeovil, Sharpeville, Fayetteville, Léopoldville, Sackville, Tocqueville, Oakville, Sihanoukville, Granville, Glanville, Gonville, Cliftonville, bidonville, Bougainville, Jacksonville, Pentonville, Elisabethville, Huntsville, Knoxville, Townsville, Nashville, Melville, Colville

40.2.13
methyl, diethyl

40.2.14
Cecil, cresyl, scissile, decile, acyl, gracile, whinsill, verticil, codicil, windowsill, alguacil, Clearasil®, uracil, Yggdrasil, carboxyl, hydroxyl, utensil, chlorambucil

40.2.15
frazil, fusil, Brazil, alguazil

40.2.16
orchil, Churchill, windchill, cook-chill

40.2.17
argil, aspergill

40.2.18
Cahill, uphill, foothill, Ampthill, anthill, Redhill, sidehill, Coghill, Rainhill, downhill, Cornhill, Thornhill, Dunhill, Jordanhill, dunghill, Bexhill, Edgehill, molehill, Underhill, Summerhill, Haverhill

40.2.19
freewill, goodwill, self-will, pigswill, whippoorwill

40.2.20
zoril, quadrille, Estoril, myofibril, espadrille, escadrille

40.2.21
allyl, Callil

40.3
real

40.3.1
clypeal, marsupial, participial

40.3.2
tibial, labial, cambial, bilabial, connubial, proverbial, adverbial, microbial

40.3.3
luteal, gluteal, bracteal, lacteal, bestial, celestial, periosteal, supercelestial

40.3.4
medial, praedial, radial, cordial, ideal, prandial, mondial, remedial, rachidial, chlamydial, conidial, basidial, myocardial, precordial, uncordial, primordial, exordial, beau idéal, unideal, preludial, sympodial, custodial, plasmodial, threnodial, allodial, preprandial, postprandial, gerundial, pericardial, anteprandial

40.3.5
brachial, tracheal, lochial, branchial, bronchial, ischial, petechial, Ezekiel, monarchial, parochial

40.3.6
gremial, shlemiel, Ishmael, proemial, monomial, binomial, trinomial, nosocomial, multinomial, polynomial, quadrinomial, epithalamial

40.3.7
.1 menial, venial, genial, splenial, ungenial, congenial, uncongenial **.2** pineal, finial, lineal, rectilineal, patrilineal, matrilineal **.3** cranial, calcaneal, domanial, subcranial, intracranial, extracranial **.4** Tenniel, centennial, biennial, triennial, septennial, octennial, bicentennial, tercentennial, vicennial, decennial, sexennial, quinquennial, perennial, quadrennial, millennial, quincentennial, premillennial, sesquicentennial **.5** Nathaniel **.6** corneal **.7** cuneal **.8** hernial **.9** monial, baronial, colonial, antimonial, testimonial, ceremonial, patrimonial, matrimonial, neocolonial, intercolonial **.10** balniel

40.3.8
trivial, gavial, pluvial, fluvial, foveal, jovial, Khedivial, convivial, exuvial, diluvial, alluvial, synovial, antediluvial

40.3.9
bathyal, Lostwithiel

40.3.10
mesial, glacial, loessial, axial, uncial, preglacial, postglacial, carnassial, fiducial, rickettsial, asphyxial, pyrexial, biaxial, triaxial, coaxial, abaxial, adaxial, periglacial, interglacial, multiaxial, uniaxial, epitaxial, internuncial

40.3.11
mesial, ecclesial, symphyseal, gymnasial, indusial, symposial, ambrosial, hypophyseal

40.3.12
collegial, vestigial, coccygeal, meningeal, pharyngeal, syringeal, laryngeal, sporangial, phalangeal, rhinopharyngeal, glosso-laryngeal

40.3.13
obsequial, colloquial, ventriloquial

40.3.14
diarrhoeal, surreal, unreal, gonorrhoeal **.1** empyreal **.2** ferial, cereal, serial, imperial, arterial, criterial, material, bacterial, sphincterial, mesenterial, sidereal, funereal, venereal, ethereal, diphtherial, vizierial, presbyterial, immaterial, biomaterial, non-material, ministerial, magisterial, uniserial, managerial, antibacterial **.3** burial, Meriel, reburial **.4** aerial, areal, ariel, gharial, nareal, narial, Squarial, notarial, vicarial, glossarial, bursarial, malarial, filarial, actuarial, secretarial, commissarial, adversarial, obituarial, antimalarial **.5** oriel, boreal, corporeal, incorporeal, arboreal, sartorial, tutorial, motorial, raptorial, scriptorial, pictorial, tectorial, vectorial, sectorial, rectorial, factorial, doctorial, proctorial, auctorial, suctorial, tinctorial, cantorial, mediatorial, gladiatorial, reportorial, proprietorial, natatorial, dictatorial, spectatorial, gestatorial, saltatorial, editorial, auditorial, piscatorial, purgatorial, senatorial, janitorial, monitorial, prefatorial, lavatorial, advertorial, visitorial, equatorial, territorial, oratorial, curatorial, grallatorial, preceptorial, inspectorial, prefectorial, directorial, visitatorial, sub-editorial, expurgatorial, progenitorial, gubernatorial, combinatorial, inquisitorial, accusatorial, conspiratorial, imperatorial, exterritorial, procuratorial, executorial, prosecutorial, improvisatorial, extraterritorial, quaestorial, consistorial, ambassadorial, Escorial, categorial, armorial, marmoreal, memorial, immemorial, manorial, authorial, gressorial, fossorial, cursorial, uxorial, tensorial, censorial, sensorial, scansorial, sponsorial, tonsorial, assessorial, accessorial, professorial, intercessorial **.6** Uriel, Curial, Muriel, mercurial, seigneurial, tenurial, manurial **.7** entrepreneurial **.8** Gabriel, Umbriel, funebrial **.9** vitriol, atrial, patrial, terrestrial, industrial, endometrial, superterrestrial, extraterrestrial, circumterrestrial **.10** Jezreel

40.3.15
Belial, ileal, filial, Balliol, pallial, mycelial, familial, unfilial, Gamaliel, epithelial, endothelial

40.4
ail, ale, pail, pale, Baal, bail, bale, tail, tale, stale, dale, kail, kale, scale, Gael, Gail, gale, Gayle, mail, male, Smail, Smale, nail, snail, fail, faille, vail, vale, veil, they'll, sail, sale, shale, gaol, jail, hail, hale, Hayle, wail, wale, Weighell, whale, dwale, quail, Quayle, squail, swale, rail, brail, Braille, trail, drail, Grail, grail, frail, Yale, flail, junk mail, fire sale,

sperm whale, Fine Gael, Ebbw Vale, Maida Vale, ginger ale

40.4.1
impale

40.4.2
detail, retail, sheartail, hightail, curtail, bobtail, cattail, white-tail, shirttail, swordtail, broadtail, cocktail, ducktail, folktale, pigtail, sprigtail, wagtail, pintail, entail, fantail, thorntail, cottontail, disentail, ringtail, springtail, bangtail, shavetail, dovetail, horsetail, rat's-tail, oxtail, foxtail, fishtail, telltale, tattletale, draggletail, bristletail, ponytail, swallowtail

40.4.3
Edale, Airedale, Tweeddale, Stockdale, Eskdale, Tindale, Glendale, Arndale, Mondale, rundale, Chippendale, Rossendale, Passchendaele, Langdale, Wharfedale, Dovedale, Teasdale, Teesdale, Bleasdale, Drysdale, Grizedale, Redesdale, Clydesdale, Lonsdale, Rochdale, Swaledale, Wensleydale, Patterdale, Lauderdale, Calderdale, Armadale, Armidale, Coverdale, Borrowdale, Coalbrookdale, Sunningdale, Skelmersdale, McCorquodale

40.4.4
seakale, percale, descale, Seascale, upscale, Windscale, timescale, downscale

40.4.5
regale, Abigail, farthingale, galingale, martingale, nightingale

40.4.6
email, female, airmail, vermeil, blackmail, bulk mail, greenmail, chain mail, Ishmael

40.4.7
treenail, doornail, toenail, hobnail, agnail, thumbnail, unnail, hangnail, fingernail

40.4.8
Raphael, McPhail, Innisfail

40.4.9
travail, avail, prevail, unveil, countervail, Perivale

40.4.10
resale, staysail, wassail, foresail, skysail, trysail, assail, abseil, topsail, spritsail, outsail, headsail, windsail, lugsail, Kinsale, mainsail, mizzen-sail, wholesale, studding-sail

40.4.11
jezail, grisaille

40.4.12
inhale, exhale

40.4.13
bewail

40.4.14
derail, cantrail, contrail, guardrail, handrail, landrail, checkrail, engrail, sangrail, taffrail, crossrail, Israel, nonpareil, monorail

40.5
el, ell, l, spell, bel, bell, belle, tell, dell, Gell, mel, smell, knell, Nell, Snell, fell, cell, sell, shell, gel, jell, hell, well, dwell, quell, swell, yell, Dalyell, Dalziel, vielle, Noel, Nowell, personnel, Danielle, Arielle, Gabrielle, Lutine Bell, show-and-tell, matériel, spirituel, spirituelle, Pantagruel

40.5.1
rappel, repel, propel, lapel, impel, compel, respell, dispel, expel, misspell, Aix-la-Chapelle

40.5.2
harebell, gabelle, cowbell, barbell, doorbell, bluebell, rebel, Dobell, Nobel, Sobell, handbell, Pachelbel, Christabel, Boscobel, Annabel, decibel, Isabel, Jezebel, mirabelle, Clarabelle

40.5.3
retell, artel, cartel, Courtelle®, foretell, Patel, hotel, boatel, motel, Pentel®, clientele, Quantel, Oftel, Estelle, Prestel®, Extel, immortelle, brocatel, brocatelle, moschatel, muscatel, bagatelle, Novotel, maître d'hôtel

40.5.4
Biddell, sardelle, Waddell, bordel, Cordell, Wardell, Adele, Odell, Badel, bedel, Cadell, Fidel, Riddell, Tindell, chandelle, Blondel, Zinfandel, citadel, muscadel, infidel, asphodel, aludel

40.5.5
Raquel

40.5.6
Miguel

40.5.7
Carmel, Cartmel, Clonmel, pell-mell, Cozumel, béchamel, caramel, hydromel, philomel, calomel, crème caramel

40.5.8
spinel, Fresnel, Parnell, Cornell, Brunel, Connell, quenelle, Chanel, crenelle, Purnell, pimpernel, fontanelle, jargonelle, organelle, mangonel, personnel, villanelle, crime passionnel, anti-personnel

40.5.9
Snaefell, Scafell, befell, Grenfell

40.5.10
carvel, Cavell, Ravel, Kap Farvel, caravel

40.5.11
resell, marcel, sarcelle, micelle, Tricel®, nacelle, Purcell, outsell, excel, lenticel, Polycell®, photocell, pedicel, undersell, oversell, carousel, Duracell®, filoselle

40.5.12
gazelle, Moselle, Giselle, mademoiselle, Mlle, Dalzell, demoiselle, damozel

40.5.13
seashell, Rochelle, Michel, Michelle, rachel, hardshell, eggshell, clamshell, bombshell, unshell, turtleshell, cockleshell, La Rochelle,

oystershell, razorshell, tortoiseshell, Mont-Saint-Michel

40.5.14
nutshell

40.5.15
plasmagel

40.5.16
Sahel, isohel

40.5.17
farewell, upwell, Manuel, unwell, Buñuel
.1 Holywell **.2** stairwell **.3** Arwel, Cherwell
.4 Orwell **.5** Camberwell, ne'er-do-well,
Motherwell, Halliwell **.6** Irwell **.7** Sitwell,
Atwell, Chartwell, Fontwell **.8** speedwell,
Shadwell, Bradwell, Cardwell, bridewell, indwell,
Caldwell **.9** Bakewell, Blackwell, Stockwell,
Rockwell, inkwell **.10** Chigwell **.11** Bramwell,
Cromwell, gromwell, Wombwell **.12** Greenwell,
Shinwell, Stanwell, Cranwell, Clerkenwell
.13 wishing-well **.14** Southwell, Bothwell,
Rothwell **.15** groundswell, Maxwell **.16** Creswell,
Boswell, Roswell, Sizewell, Tideswell
.17 Thelwell, Falwell, Fulwell, Popplewell

40.5.18
morel, Cantrell, chanterelle, Canderel®,
aquarelle, pipistrelle, au naturel

40.5.19
Hillel, allel, parallel

40.6
Al, pal, gal, mall, Val, sal, shall, Hal, rale, riyal, et
al., grand mal, Pall Mall, La Salle, petit mal

40.6.1
riyal

40.6.2
L'Oréal®, Escorial

40.6.3
Ashurbanipal

40.6.4
cabal, Iqbal, Hasdrubal

40.6.5
Natal, Chantal, Amytal®, acetal, Nembutal®

40.6.6
decal, Baikal, low-cal, mescal, pascal, musicale,
caracal

40.6.7
Chagall

40.6.8
pall-mall

40.6.9
banal, canal, bacchanal, Guadalcanál, ethanal,
methanal, rationale, Internationale

40.6.10
Parsifal

40.6.11
Laval, Sandoval, Roncesvalles, Alfa-Laval

40.6.12
Pentothal®

40.6.13
quetzal, thimerosal

40.6.14
corral, citral, chaparral, falderal

40.6.15
gayal

40.6.16
halal

40.7
owl, cowl, scowl, foul, fowl, vowel, jowl, howl,
prowl, growl, yowl, Rabaul, peafowl, moorfowl,
afoul, befoul, wildfowl, gamefowl, waterfowl

40.8
Arles, Paarl, Baal, Basle, Taal, dahl, dhal, Carl,
Karl, marl, gnarl, snarl, farl, Vaal, Waal, harl,
harle, toile, voile, rale, kraal, rial, real, gharial,
Escorial, Entente Cordiale

40.8.1
gharial

40.8.2
Bhopal

40.8.3
Iqbal, timbale, procès-verbal

40.8.4
hartal, Natal, cantal, Chantal, Wiesenthal,
Rosenthal, Wuppertal, femme fatale, Lilienthal,
Emmental, Hofmannsthal, neanderthal

40.8.5
Myrdal, Heyerdahl, Vidal, Amdahl, Stendhal,
succès de scandale

40.8.6
Baikal, coucal, percale, locale, pascal, Pascale,
housecarl, musicale

40.8.7
Chagall

40.8.8
Amal, Jamal, Albemarle

40.8.9
banal, ensnarl, unsnarl, rationale, Internationale

40.8.10
Transvaal, Roncesvalles

40.8.11
Kursaal, Provençal, Barisal

40.8.12
Kursaal

40.8.13
Funchal

40.8.14
Taj Mahal

40.8.15
chorale, corral, morale, mistral, pastorale, Massif
Central

40.8.16
gayal

40.8.17
halal

40.9
pol, poll, boll, STOL, doll, col, Coll, skol, moll,
knoll, vol, sol, Scholl, troll, loll, rag doll, Costa
del Sol

40.9.1
Sheol

40.9.2
vitriol

40.9.3
diol, thiol

40.9.4
toluol, trinitrotoluol

40.9.5
redpoll, clodpoll, Interpol, Sebastopol

40.9.6
obol, COBOL, SNOBOL

40.9.7
VTOL, Dettol®, metol, atoll, V/STOL, STOL, extol,
capitol, sorbitol, amatol, Nembutal®, inositol,
pentobarbitol

40.9.8
Ragdoll, aldol, Amidol®, Panadol®, Oxydol

40.9.9
glycol, Bluecol, McColl, Ibcol, haute école,
catechol, protocol, chloramphenicol

40.9.10
argol, googol, Gogol, Algol

40.9.11
thymol, Komsomol, salbutamol, paracetamol

40.9.12
phenol, quinol, pinol, nitinol, retinol, butanol,
ethanol, methanol, orcinol, Cuprinol®,
resorcinol, isoproterenol

40.9.13
Athol, Atholl, naphthol, menthol

40.9.14
ESOL, cresol, TESOL, Lysol®, podsol, taxol®,
spodosol, Ingersoll®, Limassol, plasmasol, alfisol,
girasol, aerosol, parasol, entresol, aridisol

40.9.15
podzol, benzol

40.9.16
catechol

40.9.17
Warhol, alcohol, gasohol

40.9.18
AWOL

40.9.19
Berol®, Virol, Chabrol, Castrol®, folderol,
glycerol, stilboestrol, cholesterol, clenbuterol,

ergosterol, calciferol, tocopherol,
cholecalciferol, ergocalciferol

40.9.20
Grand Guignol

40.9.21
pyrogallol

40.10
all, awl, orle, pall, Paul, pawl, spall, ball, bawl,
tall, stall, call, caul, gall, Galle, Gaul, mall, maul,
small, knawel, fall, Saul, schorl, shawl, hall,
haul, wall, waul, wawl, squall, Rawle, sprawl,
brawl, trawl, drawl, crawl, scrawl, thrall, yawl,
you-all, miaul, de Gaulle, withal, town hall,
curtain wall, Montreal, therewithal, overall

40.10.1
carryall

40.10.2
Mayall

40.10.3
Naipaul, appal, Nepal

40.10.4
teaball, volleyball, eyeball, highball, screwball,
cueball, fireball, butterball, thunderball,
rollerball, no-ball, snowball, lowball, trap-ball,
meatball, spitball, netball, patball, football,
paintball, softball, fastball, racketball,
basketball, speedball, hardball, oddball,
handball, stickball, blackball, pinball, cornball,
cannonball, korfball, puffball, goofball,
mothball, baseball, punchball, heelball,
stoolball, goalball, paddleball, knuckleball

40.10.5
Crittall, Nuttall, laystall, forestall, Burstall,
headstall, bookstall, Kirkstall, thumbstall,
install, reinstall, Rawtenstall, fingerstall

40.10.6
Siddall, bradawl, Goodall, Woodall, Udall,
Tindall, holdall

40.10.7
recall, Rockall, Bacall, McCall, catcall, Porthcawl,
miscall, rollcall, photocall, overcall, amplexicaul

40.10.8
nutgall, Bengal, Senegal, Donegal

40.10.9
Bokmål, Landsmål

40.10.10
Aspinall

40.10.11
dewfall, befall, snowfall, pitfall, pratfall, outfall,
shortfall, nightfall, footfall, deadfall, windfall,
landfall, rockfall, rainfall, downfall, icefall,
Threlfall, waterfall, overfall

40.10.12
Southall, Rosenthal

40.10.13
therewithal, wherewithal

40.10.14
Vauxhall, Walsall, tattersall

40.10.15
catch-all, Stivichall

40.10.16
uphaul, shorthaul, Whitehall, Woodhall, guildhall, downhaul, Leadenhall, Mildenhall, Vauxhall, keelhaul, Sauchiehall, overhaul, Willenhall

40.10.17
seawall, drywall, whitewall, gadwall, Lindwall, Childwall, Blackwall, Kirkwall, Cornwall, stonewall, Tingwall, Dingwall, Rosewall, Millwall, Thelwall, caterwaul

40.10.18
pubcrawl, inthrall, enthral, enthrall, disenthral, Wetherall, coverall, overall

40.11
oil, spoil, boil, Boyle, toil, Dáil, Doyle, coil, Koil, moil, noil, foil, Foyle, voile, soil, Hoyle, roil, Royle, broil, langue d'oïl, Fianna Fáil, cod liver oil

40.11.1
despoil

40.11.2
parboil, O'Boyle, gumboil

40.11.3
Britoil, estoile

40.11.4
recoil, uncoil

40.11.5
gargoyle

40.11.6
palm-oil, turmoil

40.11.7
trefoil, airfoil, septfoil, jetfoil, cinquefoil, tinfoil, clingfoil, sexfoil, milfoil, multifoil, counterfoil, Bacofoil, aerofoil, quatrefoil, hydrofoil

40.11.8
assoil, topsoil, subsoil

40.11.9
charbroil, embroil, disembroil, viceroyal

40.11.10
whale-oil, coaloil, disloyal

40.12
Tull, dull, cull, scull, skull, gull, mull, null, hull, trull, lull, numbskull, numskull, seagull, annul, ahull, Elul, caracul, disannul, multihull, Solihull, monohull

40.13
aisle, I'll, isle, pile, Pyle, spile, bile, tile, stile, style, chyle, kyle, guile, mile, smile, Nile, file, vile, Weil, while, wile, rile, Ryle, lisle, Lyell, Lyle, De Stijl, Sieg Heil, De Lisle

40.13.1
woodpile, stockpile, compile, thermopile, micropyle, isopropyl

40.13.2
stabile, labile, nubile, Kabyle, mobile, strobile, immobile, thermolabile

40.13.3
.1 fluviatile .2 quartile .3 rutile, utile, butyl, futile .4 acetyl, versatile, saxatile, pulsatile, vibratile, volatile .5 fertile, infertile, self-fertile .6 motile, trotyl .7 reptile, coleoptile .8 fictile, tactile, octyl, ductile, insectile, projectile, erectile, retractile, protractile, contractile .9 quintile, pentyl, gentile, pantile, mercantile, infantile, percentile .10 restyle, freestyle, hairstyle, hostile, prostyle, textile, sextile, homestyle, turnstile, lifestyle, epistyle, hypostyle, octastyle, decastyle, hexastyle, peristyle, tetrastyle, cyclostyle, bissextile, amphiprostyle

40.13.4
aedile, redial, audile, condyle, cacodyl, crocodile

40.13.5
Mikhail, alkyl

40.13.6
Argyle, Argyll, beguile

40.13.7
amyl, train-mile, ton-mile, chamomile

40.13.8
penile, phenyl, senile, anile, biphenyl, carbonyl, juvenile

40.13.9
defile, rank-and-file, interfile, cinephile, videophile, audiophile, bibliophile, hippophile, datafile, paedophile, pedophile, Graecophile, Turcophile, Francophile, homophile, thermophile, oenophile, xenophile, Sinophile, technophile, Slavophile, Russophile, xerophile, Europhile, saprophile, hydrophile, necrophile, Gallophile, Anglophile, myrmecophile, eosinophile, ailurophile, electrophile, profile

40.13.10
revile, servile, Kurzweil, Tonyrefail

40.13.11
ethyl, methyl, tetraethyl

40.13.12
cresyl, missile, fissile, scissile, acyl, decile, sessile, facile, gracile, docile, abseil, flexile, ensile, pensile, tensile, reconcile, protrusile, extrusile, domicile, indocile, carboxyl, hydroxyl, extensile, prehensile, expansile

40.13.13
jezail, resile, grisaille, exile

40.13.14
agile, fragile

40.13.15
awhile, erstwhile, meanwhile, worthwhile, Kurzweil

40.13.16
virile, sterile, puerile, febrile, laetrile, nitrile, unsterile, self-sterile, antifebrile

40.13.17
allyl, Carlisle, Carlyle

40.14
pull, bull, full, shul, wool, Sitting Bull

40.14.1
petiole, bronchiole, alveole, variole, dariole, carriole, aureole, oriole, gloriole, capriole, cabriole, centriole, foliole, arteriole

40.14.2
ringpull, push-pull

40.14.3
Kabul, cock-and-bull, Turnbull, Knatchbull, bulbul, Istanbul, Ynysybwl

40.14.4
Abdul

40.14.5
karakul

40.14.6
brimful, overfull **.1** bellyful **.2** earful **.3** trayful **.4** carful, jarful **.5** drawerful **.6** eyeful **.7** quiverful, saucerful, pitcherful, tumblerful **.8** capful, lapful, cupful, pipeful, scoopful, teacupful **.9** tubful **.10** crateful, plateful, netful, vatful, hatful, cartful, potful, boatful, fistful, nestful, jestful, pocketful, bucketful, basketful **.11** spadeful, gourdful, handful **.12** sackful, forkful, tankful, trunkful, stomachful **.13** bagful, mugful, jugful **.14** armful, palmful, roomful **.15** skinful, panful, spoonful, urnful, wagonful, basinful, apronful, teaspoonful, tablespoonful, saucepanful, dessertspoonful **.16** lungful **.17** shelfful **.18** mouthful **.19** glassful, houseful, purseful, boxful, suitcaseful, wineglassful, teacupsful **.20** vaseful, spoonsful, teaspoonsful, tablespoonsful **.21** dishful **.22** pailful, vialful, bowlful, tableful, stableful, thimbleful, kettleful, bottleful, needleful, ladleful, shovelful, bushelful, barrelful

40.14.7
rock-wool, lambswool

40.14.8
sexual, visual, casual, Emanuel, asexual, bisexual, transexual, transsexual, unisexual, intersexual, homosexual, heterosexual, psychosexual, audio-visual, televisual

40.15
pool, Poole, pul, spool, Boole, boule, boulle, buhl, tool, stool, cool, school, ghoul, Goole, fool, sool, shul, tulle, joule, rule, Sproule, drool, you'll, yule, pule, mewl, mule, Thule, Raoul, damn fool, Sunday school

40.15.1
Blackpool, ampoule, cesspool, Welshpool, whirlpool, Pontypool, Liverpool, Ullapool, Hartlepool

40.15.2
Stamboul

40.15.3
retool, O'Toole, Rintoul, stepstool, footstool, toadstool, faldstool, Tomintoul, cucking-stool

40.15.4
pre-cool, uncool, preschool, playschool, supercool, intercool

40.15.5
cagoule

40.15.6
befool, tomfool, Sprachgefühl

40.15.7
bejewel, Banjul, kilojoule

40.15.8
ferrule, ferule, spherule, sporule, curule, self-rule, misrule, work-to-rule, glomerule, overrule

40.15.9
.1 stipule, papule, cupule, ampoule **.2** barbule, lobule, globule, tubule, vestibule, microtubule **.3** mutule, noctule, pustule, frustule, intitule **.4** schedule, module, nodule, glandule, reschedule **.5** spicule, saccule, floccule, bascule, reticule, graticule, monticule, ridicule, lodicule, fascicule, molecule, homuncule, opuscule, minuscule, majuscule, animalcule, macromolecule **.6** ligule, virgule **.7** squamule, gemmule, plumule **.8** pinnule, spinule, venule, granule, antennule, gallinule **.9** ovule, valvule **.10** capsule, Spansule® **.11** pillule, pilule, cellule, umbellule

40.16.1
glial, ideal, tracheal, corneal, pineal, genial, ureal, popliteal, unideal, hymeneal, perineal, peroneal, epigeal, hypogeal, pharyngeal, laryngeal, empyreal, pharmacopoeial, peritoneal, oesophageal, glosso-laryngeal

40.16.2
Baal, Mayall, Weighell, Raphael, portrayal, betrayal, defrayal, self-betrayal

40.16.3
Powell, bowel, towel, dowel, Dowell, Cowell, vowel, Howell, Hywel, rowel, trowel, Trowell, Baden-Powell, embowel, disembowel, McDowell, avowal, Crickhowell, semivowel, disavowal

40.16.4
knawel, withdrawal

40.16.5
royal, loyal, unroyal, viceroyal, disloyal, pennyroyal, Uniroyal®

40.16.6
dial, myall, Niall, phial, vial, viol, sial, trial, Lyall, Lyell, glial, espial, redial, predial, sundial, misdial, denial, genial, retrial, pretrial, mistrial, decrial, self-denial

40.16.7
eschewal, menstrual, premenstrual, Pantagruel, ungual

40.16.8
Sewell, dual, duel, jewel, Jewell, crewel, cruel, gruel, Youell, newel, Newell, fuel, Whewell, bejewel, subdual, construal, accrual, renewal, refuel, fossil fuel, reviewal

40.16.9
Powell, koel, Noel, Nowell, Trowell, Lowell, bestowal, protozoal, spermatozoal: (+ **40.18**)

40.16.10
sexual, indicial, fiducial, asexual, bisexual, transexual, transsexual, prenuptial, antenuptial, unisexual, intersexual, homosexual, heterosexual, psychosexual, equinoctial

40.16.11
visual, casual, usual, brinjal, angel, unusual, archangel, evangel, audio-visual, televisual, rhinopharyngeal

40.16.12
Mitchell, ritual, Rachael, Rachel, Tatchell, satchel, Stivichall, mutual, mutuel, virtual, Churchill, nuptial, actual, tactual, factual, punctual, bestial, textual, habitual, perpetual, spiritual, perceptual, conceptual, conflictual, aspectual, effectual, contractual, instinctual, unpunctual, eventual, conventual, accentual, tangential, contextual, pari-mutuel, unspiritual, antenuptial, ineffectual, intellectual, artefactual, artifactual, anti-intellectual, unintellectual

40.16.13
.1 Tyrol, Tyrrell, Cyril, Wirral, squirrel **.2** spheral, scleral **.3** Errol, peril, beryl, Terrell, Merrill, Meryl, feral, ferrel, Ferrell, ferrule, ferule, Cheryl, Sheryl, imperil, chrysoberyl **.4** mayoral **.5** Aral, aril, aryl, parol, barrel, Darrell, Daryl, carol, Carole, carrel, Carroll, Caryl, Farrell, Harrell, apparel, cracker-barrel **.6** catarrhal **.7** Orrell, coral, moral, sorel, sorrel, Sorrell, Worrall, quarrel, laurel, immoral, amoral, unmoral, Balmoral **.8** aural, oral, choral, goral, loral, chloral, floral, aboral, adoral, monaural, stercoral, binaural, auroral **.9** Spurrell, bharal, burhel, Burrell, Durrell, demurral **.10** spiral, chiral, viral, achiral, antiviral, retiral **.11** sural, jural, rural, crural, Ural, mural, neural, pleural, plural, caesural, subdural, procural, commissural, epidural, intercrural, intramural, extramural, caricatural **.12.1** corporal, temporal, nonpareil, puerperal, atemporal, spatio-temporal, supertemporal, liberal, illiberal, literal, littoral, clitoral, presbyteral, triliteral, sublittoral, uniliteral, circumlittoral, lateral, bilateral, trilateral, collateral, multilateral, ipsilateral, septilateral, unilateral, equilateral, quinquelateral, quadrilateral, dotterel, Cotterel, Cottrell, guttural, dipteral, peripteral, pectoral, sectoral, rectoral, doctoral, sphincteral, protectoral, prefectoral, electoral, postdoctoral, parenteral, pastoral, federal, ruderal, pickerel, mackerel, cockerel, doggerel **.12.2** femoral, numeral, humeral, humoral,

admiral, ephemeral, bicameral, tricameral, interfemoral, unicameral, superhumeral, mineral, general, Goneril, funeral, outgeneral, major general, secretary-general, Registrar General, Solicitor-General, Quartermaster General, peripheral, Haverhill, Peveril, several, Canaveral, triumviral, Weatherall, visceral, tesseral, mensural, flexural **.12.3** natural, connatural, unnatural, supernatural, preternatural, nomenclatural, sutural, scriptural, sculptural, unscriptural, antiscriptural, structural, prefectural, conjectural, substructural, architectural, superstructural, infrastructural, gestural, postural, textural, cultural, bicultural, subcultural, multicultural, piscicultural, socio-cultural, apicultural, viticultural, horticultural, vinicultural, silvicultural, sericultural, floricultural, arboricultural, agricultural, procedural **.12.4** figural, augural, inaugural, behavioural **.13** deferral, referral, conferral, transferral **.14** April **.15** fibril, timbrel, whimbrel, gambrel, nombril, umbral, tumbril, cerebral, palpebral, vertebral, penumbral, intervertebral **.16** retral, triquetral, ureteral, citral, laetrile, petrel, petrol, mitral, neutral, arbitral, diametral, spectral, ventral, central, antral, epicentral, oestral, mistral, wastrel, kestrel, vestral, astral, Castrol®, plastral, austral, nostril, rostral, claustral, cloistral, lustral, dextral, minstrel, menstrual, stilbestrol, stilboestrol, orchestral, trimestral, ancestral, sequestral, cholesterol, subastral, cadastral, sinistral, magistral, premenstrual, curvirostral **.17** tendril, spandrel, mandrel, mandril, mandrill, scoundrel, cathedral, dihedral, trihedral, anhedral, hemihedral, polyhedral, rhombohedral, heptahedral, octahedral, pentahedral, decahedral, hexahedral, merohedral, tetrahedral, holohedral, dodecahedral, icosahedral **.18** sacral, sepulchral, involucral **.19** mongrel, integral, podagral **.20** taffrail **.21** Avril, Bovril® **.22** antheral, hypaethral, hypethral, urethral

40.16.14
Lemuel, Samuel, annual, spaniel, Daniel, manual, continual, biannual, Emmanuel, Immanuel, capsule, sensual, consensual

40.16.15
Hillel, molal, sewellel

40.17
earl, Earle, pearl, purl, birl, burl, curl, skirl, girl, merle, knurl, furl, Searle, ceorl, churl, herl, hurl, whirl, whorl, twirl, squirl, swirl, uncurl, playgirl, cowgirl, bar girl, choirgirl, showgirl, shopgirl, newsgirl, salesgirl, ballgirl, call girl, schoolgirl, unfurl, pas seul, Husserl, weathergirl

40.18
pole, poll, bole, boll, bowl, toll, stole, dhole, dole, coal, Cole, kohl, skol, goal, mol, mole, knoll, Knowle, foal, vole, thole, Seoul, sole, soul, Scholl,

shoal, Joel, hole, whole, rôle, roll, prole, Sproule, troll, stroll, droll, scroll, North Pole, feme sole, femes sole, rock 'n roll, cabriole, Super Bowl

40.18.1
Sheol, creole

40.18.2
vacuole

40.18.3
maypole, dipole, redpoll, tadpole, flagpole, Wimpole, Rumpole, beanpole, catchpole, ridgepole, bargepole, Walpole, rantipole, bibliopole, antipole, Monopole, Metropole, quadrupole

40.18.4
dustbowl, rocambole, rosebowl, fishbowl, washbowl, punchbowl, wassail-bowl, amphibole

40.18.5
citole, pistole, extol

40.18.6
indole, condole, girandole, farandole

40.18.7
clearcole, charcoal, Nicole, splint-coal, caracole, pratincole

40.18.8
touch-in-goal

40.18.9
pinole, Seminole

40.18.10
resole, rissole, plimsole, insole, console, turnsole, camisole, oversoul, girasole

40.18.11
benzole, thiazole, carbazole, imidozole, metronidazole

40.18.12
cajole

40.18.13
keyhole, kneehole, earhole, airhole, borehole, Warhol, eyehole, spyhole, Mohole, blowhole, peephole, loophole, rathole, pothole, knothole, porthole, vent-hole, priesthole, pesthole, posthole, bolt-hole, soundhole, chuckhole, stokehole, sinkhole, lughole, plughole, armhole, wormhole, pinhole, manhole, buttonhole, pigeonhole, bunghole, mousehole, arsehole, asshole, foxhole, hellhole, coal-hole, cubbyhole, hidey-hole, waterhole, Hetton-le-Hole, swallow-hole, toad-in-the-hole

40.18.14
payroll, parol, parole, Tyrol, patrol, control, decontrol, bedroll, bankroll, logroll, enrol, enroll, unroll, banderole, barcarole, fumarole, rigmarole, casserole, Coloroll®, biocontrol, self-control, profiterole: (+ **40.16.9**)

40.19.1
peepul, people, pipal, steeple, sepal, repeople, workpeople, unpeople, sportspeople,

craftspeople, tribespeople, tradespeople, townspeople

40.19.2
tipple, stipple, nipple, fipple, swipple, ripple, triple, cripple

40.19.3
papal, staple, maple

40.19.4
Keppel, sepal

40.19.5
apple, dapple, chapel, chappal, Chappell, scrapple, grapple, pineapple, Whitechapel, antechapel

40.19.6
carpal, carpel, Marple, metacarpal

40.19.7
popple, topple, stopple, hopple, estoppel, cyclopropyl

40.19.8
couple, supple, decouple, uncouple, thermocouple

40.19.9
typal, stipel, disciple, prototypal, archetypal

40.19.10
duple, drupel, scruple, pupal, pupil, cupel, septuple, quintuple, centuple, sextuple, quadruple, octuple, decuple

40.19.11
multiple, Oedipal, syncopal, maniple, principal, principle, manciple, Sebastopol, submultiple, episcopal, participle, municipal, archiepiscopal

40.19.12
purple, Serpell, empurple

40.19.13
opal, Opel®, copal, nopal, propyl, cyclopropyl, Constantinople

40.19.14
pimple, dimple, simple, wimple, temple, stemple, Semple, ample, sample, trample, rumple, crumple, scrumple, Dalrymple, example

40.19.15
Aspel, gospel

40.19.16
palpal, scalpel

40.20.1
Keble, feeble, enfeeble

40.20.2
dibble, kibble, nibble, sibyl, quibble, Ribble, dribble, scribble, Gribble

40.20.3
copiable, expiable, pitiable, dutiable, amiable, permeable, leviable, enviable, fanciable, variable, malleable, uncopiable, inexpiable, remediable, repudiable, unamiable,

impermeable, unenviable, amerciable, associable, appreciable, justiciable, insatiable, negotiable, invariable, unmalleable, photocopiable, irremediable, semipermeable, inappreciable, unappreciable, renegotiable

40.20.4
Abel, abele, able, Babel, table, stable, cable, gable, Mabel, fable, sable, label, retable, timetable, astable, bistable, unstable, enable, unable, disable, relabel, metastable, thermostable, eco-label

40.20.5
pebble, rebel, treble

40.20.6
babble, dabble, gabble, rabble, drabble, scrabble, grabble, bedabble, technobabble, psychobabble

40.20.7
barbel, Kabul, garble, marble, amende honorable

40.20.8
ensemble

40.20.9
obol, cobble, gobble, knobble, nobble, hobble, wobble, squabble, Chernobyl

40.20.10
bauble, corbel, warble

40.20.11
foible

40.20.12
bubble, stubble, double, nubble, Hubble, rubble, trouble, redouble

40.20.13
Bible, tribal, scribal, libel, intertribal

40.20.14
Hasdrubal

40.20.15
tubal, rouble, bubal, Hasdrubal

40.20.16
.1 skiable, seeable, foreseeable, unseeable, agreeable, unforeseeable, disagreeable
.2 payable, sayable, weighable, sprayable, playable, repayable, pre-payable, decayable, conveyable, assayable, unsayable, portrayable, defrayable, unplayable **.3** ploughable, avowable, allowable, unallowable **.4** enjoyable, destroyable, employable, unenjoyable, unemployable **.5** buyable, dyeable, viable, triable, friable, liable, pliable, flyable, deniable, undeniable, ratifiable, fortifiable, certifiable, notifiable, rectifiable, quantifiable, justifiable, modifiable, unifiable, magnifiable, specifiable, classifiable, falsifiable, liquefiable, verifiable, vitrifiable, nitrifiable, qualifiable, satisfiable, identifiable, unquantifiable, unjustifiable, solidifiable, saponifiable, unclassifiable, diversifiable, emulsifiable, unverifiable, unidentifiable, unviable, reliable, appliable,

unreliable, multipliable **.6** issuable, rescuable, arguable, valuable, inarguable, unarguable, continuable, invaluable, superannuable
.7 doable, suable, chewable, wooable, screwable, viewable, subduable, construable, renewable, reviewable, pursuable, unrenewable **.8** towable, mowable, knowable, growable, throwable, unknowable, swallowable **.9** keepable, shippable, clippable, tapeable, capable, shapable, shapeable, tappable, mappable, snappable, stoppable, wipeable, dupable, ropeable, jumpable, graspable, palpable, culpable, incapable, escapable, unflappable, unstoppable, recoupable, worshipable, ungraspable, impalpable, inescapable, unescapable, developable **.10** probable, tubbable, clubbable, bribable, probeable, improbable, absorbable, adsorbable, unbribable, ascribable, describable, inscribable, perturbable, equiprobable, indescribable, circumscribable, imperturbable **.11.1** eatable, beatable, treatable, repeatable, unbeatable, uneatable, untreatable, unrepeatable, hospitable, creditable, committable, remittable, admittable, transmittable, inhospitable, statable, datable, hatable, ratable, rateable, creatable, rebatable, abatable, debatable, rotatable, unstatable, vacatable, locatable, equatable, narratable, titratable, hydratable, dilatable, relatable, inflatable, translatable, annotatable, educatable, unlocatable, impregnatable, cultivatable, rehydratable, isolatable, untranslatable, manipulatable, gettable, wettable, forgettable, resettable, regrettable, unforgettable, compatible, get-at-able, come-at-able, biocompatible, incompatible, un-get-at-able, uncome-at-able, doubtable, redoubtable, undoubtable, partible **.11.2** impartable, impartible, portable, sortable, deportable, supportable, reportable, importable, exportable, transportable, insupportable, unsupportable, unexportable, untransportable, exploitable, rebuttable, citable, rightable, writable, indictable, ignitable, excitable, unwritable, extraditable, unexcitable, suitable, shootable, scrutable, mutable, unsuitable, statutable, recruitable, inscrutable, imputable, computable, disputable, immutable, permutable, commutable, transmutable, refutable, confutable, unstatutable, substitutable, indisputable, distributable, prosecutable, executable, incommutable, irrefutable
.11.3 intuitable, precipitable, habitable, inhabitable, indubitable, uninhabitable, hereditable, discreditable, marketable, pocketable, unmarketable, targetable, imitable, limitable, inimitable, illimitable, indomitable, profitable, forfeitable, comfortable, unprofitable, uncomfortable, pivotable, covetable, inevitable, visitable, vegetable, cogitable, excogitable, equitable, inequitable, unequitable, irritable, veritable, heritable, charitable, inheritable, uncharitable,

interpretable, uninterpretable, reputable, disreputable, attributable, unattributable, palatable, unpalatable, avertable, revertible, invertible, convertible, insertable, indivertible, controvertible, inconvertible, unconvertible, incontrovertible, uncontrovertible, interconvertible, potable, notable, votable, quotable, floatable, promotable, unquotable **.11.4** temptable, perceptible, susceptible, acceptable, adaptable, corruptible, discerptible, excerptible, attemptable, contemptible, imperscriptible, imprescriptible, imperceptible, insusceptible, unsusceptible, unacceptable, unadaptable, interruptible, incorruptible, oversusceptible, uninterruptible **.11.5** actable, tractable, predictable, inflictable, respectable, expectable, detectable, connectable, perfectible, rejectable, injectable, erectable, electable, delectable, collectable, selectable, contactable, enactable, exactable, attractable, retractable, intractable, contractable, extractable, deductible, conductible, destructible, unpredictable, contradictable, undetectable, indefectible, unelectable, uncontactable, tax-deductible, indestructible, reconstructable, ineluctable **.11.6** printable, paintable, rentable, grantable, plantable, countable, mountable, patentable, lamentable, merchantable, unprintable, fermentable, preventable, inventable, presentable, transplantable, accountable, uncountable, discountable, demountable, surmountable, tenantable, warrantable, unmerchantable, unpreventable, representable, unpresentable, unaccountable, insurmountable, unsurmountable, unwarrantable **.11.7** shiftable, liftable, unshiftable, twistable, listable, tasteable, wastable, testable, trustable, Whitstable, Huxtable, constable, Dunstable, resistible, attestable, detestable, contestable, untestable, comestible, investable, digestible, suggestible, arrestable, exhaustible, combustible, adjustable, harvestable, irresistible, incontestable, indigestible, inexhaustible, incombustible, meltable **.12** kneadable, feedable, readable, leadable, pleadable, re-readable, unreadable, biddable, unbiddable, formidable, wadable, tradable, gradable, evadable, persuadable, degradable, upgradeable, unpersuadable, biodegradable, nonbiodegradable, photodegradable, edible, beddable, spreadable, credible, inedible, incredible, discardable, audible, fordable, laudable, recordable, inaudible, affordable, unfordable, unrecordable, unaffordable, voidable, avoidable, unavoidable, guidable, rideable, slidable, decidable, unrideable, undecidable, includable, excludable, decodable, corrodible, undecodable, spendable, bendable, mendable, vendible, sendable, lendable, mandible, findable, rescindable, dependable, expendable, extendable, amendable, commendable, defendable, descendible, expandable, demandable,

impoundable, compoundable, refundable, undependable, recommendable, understandable, weldable, mouldable, foldable, holdable **.13** speakable, unspeakable, pickable, kickable, despicable, extricable, applicable, explicable, inextricable, inapplicable, inexplicable, takable, makable, shakeable, breakable, partakable, mistakable, unshakeable, unbreakable, unslakeable, unmistakable, peccable, checkable, impeccable, packable, stackable, sackable, placable, unbackable, unsackable, uncrackable, implacable, unattackable, remarkable, mockable, shockable, lockable, unshockable, walkable, strikable, likeable, unlikeable, dislikeable, bookable, cookable, pre-bookable, practicable, medicable, predicable, abdicable, vindicable, amicable, revocable, invocable, educable, allocable, replicable, duplicable, impracticable, domesticable, prognosticable, immedicable, eradicable, communicable, irrevocable, ineducable, uneducable, multiplicable, ineradicable, incommunicable, uncommunicable, workable, smokable, vocable, provokable, thinkable, sinkable, drinkable, shrinkable, bankable, frankable, unthinkable, unsinkable, undrinkable, unshrinkable, cascabel, confiscable **.14** huggable, luggable, fatiguable, mitigable, litigable, navigable, subjugable, irrigable, segregable, delegable, relegable, immitigable, unnavigable, irrefragable, indefatigable **.15** redeemable, irredeemable, unredeemable, swimmable, tameable, nameable, framable, blameable, claimable, untameable, unnameable, reclaimable, irreclaimable, flammable, programmable, inflammable, reprogrammable, uninflammable, farmable, performable, deformable, reformable, conformable, transformable, unconformable, hummable, unplumbable, climbable, unclimbable, assumable, subsumable, consumable, resumable, presumable, estimable, customable, fathomable, inestimable, unfathomable, affirmable, filmable **.16.1** screenable, cleanable, amenable, convenable, machinable, unamenable, winnable, alienable, inalienable, unalienable, companionable, stainable, gainable, trainable, strainable, attainable, retainable, obtainable, maintainable, containable, sustainable, untrainable, restrainable, explainable, unattainable, ascertainable, unobtainable, uncontainable, unsustainable, unrestrainable, unexplainable, unascertainable, tenable, untenable, tannable, cannibal, scannable, Hannibal, unputdownable **.16.2** joinable, runnable, fineable, signable, combinable, definable, refinable, assignable, declinable, reclinable, inclinable, indefinable, undefinable, unassignable, indeclinable, tunable, untunable, impugnable, incunable **.16.3** openable, pardonable, commonable, summonable, terminable, eliminable,

examinable, abominable, determinable,
interminable, predeterminable, indeterminable,
ungovernable, listenable, personable,
unlistenable, seasonable, reasonable,
treasonable, unseasonable, unreasonable,
fissionable, fashionable, actionable,
sanctionable, pensionable, mentionable,
conscionable, petitionable, impressionable,
unfashionable, apportionable, proportionable,
exceptionable, objectionable, unmentionable,
unconscionable, unimpressionable,
unexceptionable, unobjectionable,
questionable, imaginable, unimaginable,
disciplinable, learnable, returnable, discernible,
nonreturnable, indiscernible, loanable,
postponable, pregnable, impregnable,
inexpugnable, damnable, condemnable
.17 singable **.18** sniffable, effable, affable,
laughable, quaffable, ineffable, photographable
.19 cleavable, perceivable, deceivable,
receivable, conceivable, achievable, retrievable,
believable, relievable, inconceivable,
unachievable, irretrievable, unbelievable,
giveable, liveable, forgivable, unliveable,
unforgivable, savable, lovable, drivable,
survivable, revivable, derivable, deprivable,
contrivable, undrivable, unsurvivable, movable,
provable, immovable, removable, unmovable,
reprovable, improvable, unprovable,
disprovable, irremovable, unremovable,
cultivable, reservable, preservable, observable,
unobservable, salvable, solvable, evolvable,
revolvable, insolvable, unsolvable, dissolvable,
resolvable, irresolvable, unresolvable
.20 breathable, tithable, smoothable,
unbreathable **.21.1** peaceable, leasable,
fleeceable, increasable, releasable, kissable,
miscible, missable, immiscible, omissible,
permissible, remissible, admissible, unmissable,
dismissible, transmissible, impermissible,
irremissible, inadmissible, traceable, effaceable,
defaceable, unfaceable, embraceable,
untraceable, replaceable, unplaceable,
ineffaceable, irreplaceable, decibel, guessable,
unguessable, assessable, processable, accessible,
depressible, suppressible, repressible,
impressible, compressible, expressible,
putrescible, addressable, redressable,
inaccessible, irrepressible, incompressible,
inexpressible, unexpressible, passable, passible,
classable, surpassable, impassable, impassible,
irascible **.21.2** possible, impossible, compossible,
uncrossable, forceable, forcible, endorsable,
enforceable, unenforceable, discussable,
discussible, sliceable, derisible, crucible,
adducible, educible, deducible, seducible,
reducible, producible, inducible, protrusible,
diffusible, irreducible, reproducible,
introducible, compassable, noticeable,
traversable, serviceable, purchasable,
purchaseable, unnoticeable, unserviceable,
coercible, dispersible, reimbursable,
submersible, reversible, irreversible,

introversible **.21.3** collapsible, mixable, fixable,
flexible, taxable, indexible, reflexible, inflexible,
intermixable, vincible, fencible, sensible,
danceable, runcible, licensable, evincible,
invincible, convincible, dispensable,
suspensible, ostensible, distensible, extensible,
condensable, defensible, insensible, expansible,
renounceable, pronounceable, responsible,
influenceable, balanceable, experienceable,
indispensable, incondensable, indefensible,
reprehensible, apprehensible, comprehensible,
unpronounceable, irresponsible,
inapprehensible, incomprehensible **.22** feasible,
seizable, squeezable, freezable, defeasible,
infeasible, unfeasible, inappeasable,
unappeasable, indefeasible, visible, risible,
divisible, invisible, indivisible, raisable,
persuasible, erasable, appraisable, rousable,
arousable, causable, plausible, implausible,
unplausible, sizeable, amortizable,
hypnotizable, magnetizable, merchandizable,
standardizable, oxidizable, hybridizable,
ionizable, cognizable, vulcanizable, organizable,
recognizable, unrecognizable, devisable,
revisable, advisable, televisable, inadvisable,
unadvisable, excisable, criticizable, exercisable,
vaporizable, comprisable, memorizable,
summarizable, pulverizable, polarizable,
uncategorizable, realizable, verbalizable,
mobilizable, metabolizable, utilizable,
fertilizable, crystallizable, volatilizable,
localizable, analysable, civilizable, sterilizable,
generalizable, visualizable, usable, fusible,
losable, reusable, excusable, unusable, refusable,
infusable, infusible, confusable, confusible,
irrecusable, inexcusable, closable, opposable,
supposable, disposable, transposable,
diagnosable, reclosable, decomposable
.23 appreciable, inappreciable, unappreciable,
fishable, justiciable, satiable, insatiable,
cashable, encashable, washable, uncrushable,
tarnishable, punishable, vanquishable,
perishable, cherishable, relishable, polishable,
publishable, diminishable, unpunishable,
distinguishable, extinguishable, imperishable,
abolishable, unpublishable, indistinguishable,
undistinguishable, inextinguishable, sociable,
negotiable, associable, unsociable, renegotiable,
quenchable, unquenchable **.24** teachable,
reachable, preachable, switchable, stretchable,
catchable, matchable, watchable, touchable,
searchable, impeachable, unteachable,
unbreachable, unreachable, attachable,
detachable, uncatchable, unmatchable,
unwatchable, untouchable, researchable,
unsearchable, approachable, reproachable,
unimpeachable, unapproachable,
irreproachable **.25** bridgeable, abridgeable,
unbridgeable, stageable, gaugeable,
unassuageable, legible, pledgeable, illegible,
chargeable, rechargeable, dischargeable,
enlargeable, forgeable, fudgeable, voyageable,
mortgageable, imageable, damageable,

manageable, salvageable, exigible, dirigible,
marriageable, corrigible, eligible,
knowledgeable, negligible, unmanageable,
unsalvageable, unmarriageable, incorrigible,
re-eligible, intelligible, ineligible,
acknowledgeable, unintelligible, submergible,
changeable, tangible, frangible, spongeable,
fungible, unchangeable, exchangeable,
arrangeable, intangible, refrangible, infrangible,
challengeable, interchangeable, irrefrangible,
inexpungible, unchallengeable **.26** equable,
inequable, unequable **.27.1** steerable, hearable,
clearable, terrible, bearable, tearable, shareable,
wearable, repairable, unbearable, untearable,
unwearable, declarable, unrepairable, arable,
parable, sparable, incomparable **.27.2** horrible,
pourable, storable, restorable, adorable,
deplorable, durable, curable, thurible, assurable,
insurable, perdurable, endurable, securable,
procurable, incurable, uninsurable,
unendurable, hireable, transpirable, desirable,
rewirable, acquirable, undesirable
.27.3 separable, reparable, operable, superable,
temperable, comparable, respirable,
inseparable, irreparable, evaporable, inoperable,
recuperable, insuperable, interoperable,
rememberable, utterable, motorable, factorable,
enterable, filterable, alterable, unutterable,
inalterable, unalterable, ponderable, solderable,
considerable, imponderable, inconsiderable,
conquerable, unconquerable **.27.4** memorable,
numerable, admirable, unmemorable,
innumerable, enumerable, denumerable,
venerable, generable, honourable, vulnerable,
dishonourable, invulnerable **.27.5** referable,
preferable, sufferable, transferable, insufferable,
decipherable, untransferable, indecipherable,
undecipherable, favourable, severable,
coverable, deliverable, unfavourable,
recoverable, discoverable, manoeuvrable,
irrecoverable, undiscoverable, unmanoeuvrable,
lacerable, mensurable, answerable, ulcerable,
inexorable, commensurable, unanswerable,
incommensurable, miserable, censurable,
measurable, pleasurable, immeasurable,
unmeasurable, unpleasurable, triturable,
saturable, torturable, rupturable, conjecturable,
unconjecturable, manufacturable, tolerable,
colourable, intolerable, incurrable, demurrable,
inerrable, deferrable, inferable, conferrable
.27.6 filtrable, perpetrable, penetrable,
sequestrable, ministrable, registrable,
demonstrable, impenetrable, administrable,
indemonstrable, undemonstrable, execrable,
integrable **.28** chasuble, voluble, soluble,
resoluble, dissoluble, insoluble, water-soluble,
indissoluble **.29** sealable, healable, appealable,
repealable, revealable, resealable, congealable,
unappealable, billable, tillable, millable,
syllable, unkillable, refillable, fulfillable,
dissyllable, disyllable, trisyllable, unfulfillable,
polysyllable, decasyllable, monosyllable,
sexisyllable, tetrasyllable, quadrisyllable,

octosyllable, hendecasyllable, bailable, scalable,
mailable, sailable, saleable, unscalable, available,
resaleable, assailable, unsaleable, exhalable,
unavailable, unassailable, spellable, tellable,
smellable, sellable, compellable, expellable,
indelible, unsellable, inappellable, fallible,
infallible, recallable, gullible, reconcilable,
irreconcilable, unreconcilable, schoolable,
violable, inviolable, settleable, handleable,
isolable, calculable, regulable, assimilable,
manipulable, inoculable, incalculable,
coagulable, accumulable, unassimilable,
furlable, smoleable, rollable, consolable,
controllable, inconsolable, unconsolable,
uncontrollable, semblable, recyclable

40.20.17
burble, verbal, gerbil, herbal, preverbal, Froebel

40.20.18
coble, Mobil®, noble, global, ennoble,
Chernobyl, Grenoble, ignoble

40.20.19
timbal, timbale, gimbal, thimble, cymbal,
symbol, wimble, Brimble, Trimble, Abu Simbel,
Kemble, tremble, assemble, reassemble,
dissemble, resemble, disassemble, amble,
preamble, Campbell, gamble, gambol, shamble,
ramble, bramble, scramble, descramble,
unscramble, ensemble, tout ensemble, umbel,
umble, bumble, tumble, stumble, mumble,
fumble, jumble, humble, rumble, Trumbull,
Strumble, crumble, grumble, rough-and-tumble

40.21.1
beetle, betel, foetal, chital, maybeetle, black
beetle, decretal, skeletal, centripetal

40.21.2
it'll, spittle, tittle, kittle, victual, skittle, brittle,
whittle, little, hospital, lickspittle, committal,
remittal, submittal, transmittal, revictual,
acquittal, embrittle, Doolittle, belittle,
recommittal

40.21.3
statal, natal, fatal, ratel, stratal, hiatal, prenatal,
neonatal, palatal, antenatal, perinatal

40.21.4
petal, kettle, metal, mettle, nettle, fettle, settle,
Gretel, teakettle, gunmetal, Muntz metal, misch
metal, hemp-nettle, resettle, unsettle,
Popocatépetl

40.21.5
battle, tattle, cattle, chattel, rattle, prattle,
Seattle, embattle, tittle-tattle, Quetzalcóatl

40.21.6
startle, ratel, stratal, Nahuatl

40.21.7
pottle, bottle, dottle, Cottle, mottle, wattle,
throttle, glottal, bluebottle, inkbottle,
greenbottle, Aristotle, epicotyl, hypocotyl,
axolotl, polyglottal, epiglottal

40.21.8
portal, mortal, sortal, chortle, aortal, immortal

40.21.9
buttle, Tuttle, cuttle, scuttle, guttle, subtle, shuttle, abuttal, rebuttal, coal scuttle, unsubtle, surrebuttal, supersubtle, oversubtle

40.21.10
title, vital, retitle, surtitle, subtitle, entitle, disentitle, mistitle, recital, requital, detrital, supertitle, epiphytal

40.21.11
pootle, Bootle, Tootal, tootle, footle, rootle, brutal, scutal, recruital, refutal

40.21.12
societal, parietal, varietal, interparietal, coital, pre-coital, sincipital, centripetal, capital, capitol, basipetal, occipital, ancipital, acropetal, barbital, orbital, pubertal, cubital, suborbital, pre-pubertal, pentobarbital, phenobarbital, supraorbital, stomatal, genital, congenital, primogenital, urogenital, pivotal, digital, vegetal, sagittal, interdigital, marital, premarital, extramarital, skeletal, palatal, exoskeletal, musculoskeletal

40.21.13
turtle, kirtle, myrtle, hurtle

40.21.14
total, scrotal, teetotal, subtotal, antidotal, sacerdotal, anecdotal

40.21.15
glyptal, septal, transeptal, interseptal

40.21.16
ictal, fictile, rictal, rectal, dactyl, cactal, fractal, octal, edictal, dialectal, tridactyl, syndactyl, colorectal, bidialectal, mesolectal, basilectal, polydactyl, pentadactyl, zygodactyl, pterodactyl, tetradactyl, leptodactyl, oviductal, perissodactyl

40.21.17
.1 pintle, quintal, quintile, lintel .2 dental, dentil, mental, cental, gentle, rental, trental, lentil, Oriental, transcendental, labiodental, accidental, occidental, incidental, coincidental, linguodental, omental, submental, pigmental, segmental, fragmental, governmental, judgemental, judgmental, sentimental, testamental, pedimental, nidamental, rudimental, fundamental, ligamental, firmamental, tenemental, ornamental, regimental, temperamental, detrimental, nutrimental, instrumental, sacramental, incremental, excremental, documental, tegumental, argumental, monumental, elemental, alimental, supplemental, complemental, departmental, compartmental, unsentimental, impedimental, unornamental, experimental, integumental, developmental, suprasegmental, environmental, intergovernmental, interdepartmental,

unenvironmental, continental, subcontinental, transcontinental, epicontinental, intercontinental, placental, ungentle, parental .3 cantle, mantel, mantle, Prandtl, Fremantle, Bluemantle, dismantle, quadrantal, overmantel, covenantal, consonantal .4 fontal, quantal, periodontal, horizontal .5 buntal, frontal, prefrontal, contrapuntal, naso-frontal

40.21.18
pistil, pistol, distal, Bristol, Chrystal, crystal, listel, pestle, festal, vestal, pastel, pastille, Austell, costal, hostel, Borstal, crustal, Burstall, postal, coastal, Kirkstall, precostal, subcostal, youth hostel, pedestal, polycrystal, intercostal, Pentecostal

40.22.1
pedal, beadle, bedel, needle, Cheadle, wheedle, credal, bipedal, Threadneedle, quadrupedal

40.22.2
idyll, zooidal, piddle, Biddell, Biddle, diddle, kiddle, middle, fiddle, twiddle, Riddell, riddle, griddle, Liddell, unriddle, paradiddle, taradiddle, pig in the middle, piggy in the middle

40.22.3
cradle, ladle, gonadal

40.22.4
pedal, peddle, medal, meddle, heddle, Weddell, reddle, treadle, bipedal, back-pedal, quadrupedal

40.22.5
addle, paddle, staddle, Cadell, saddle, raddle, straddle, skedaddle, sidesaddle, packsaddle, unsaddle, astraddle

40.22.6
McArdle

40.22.7
toddle, doddle, coddle, model, noddle, Hoddle, waddle, twaddle, swaddle, remodel, mollycoddle, supermodel

40.22.8
dawdle, caudal, chordal, Wardle, acaudal, subcaudal

40.22.9
Goidel, zooidal, cuboidal, rhomboidal, trochoidal, conchoidal, ethmoidal, prismoidal, crinoidal, conoidal, sphenoidal, adenoidal, typhoidal, steroidal, toroidal, spheroidal, colloidal, cycloidal, botryoidal, anthropoidal, solenoidal, sinusoidal, ellipsoidal, trapezoidal, meteoroidal, asteroidal, haemorrhoidal, alkaloidal, paraboloidal, hyperboloidal, epicycloidal, hypocycloidal

40.22.10
puddle, cuddle, muddle, fuddle, ruddle, huddle, Tolpuddle, befuddle

40.22.11
idle, idol, tidal, sidle, Rydal, bridal, bridle, suicidal, unbridle, intertidal, spermatidal, herbicidal, pesticidal, fungicidal, barmecidal,

homicidal, spermicidal, germicidal, genocidal, regicidal, parricidal, patricidal, matricidal, fratricidal, Moorish idol, tyrannicidal, insecticidal, infanticidal, bactericidal, sororicidal, uxoricidal

40.22.12
poodle, boodle, doodle, noodle, strudel, udal, Udall, feudal, caboodle, flapdoodle, canoodle, Apfelstrudel, Yankee Doodle

40.22.13
tripodal, apodal, cuspidal, citadel, decadal, synodal, infidel, apsidal, antipodal, quadrupedal, pyramidal, hebdomadal

40.22.14
curdle, girdle, hurdle, engirdle, Bracegirdle, pantie-girdle

40.22.15
odal, Odell, Gödel, modal, nodal, jodel, yodel, bimodal, anodal, cathodal

40.22.16
spindle, tindal, Tindall, Tyndale, kindle, Hindle, dwindle, swindle, brindle, rekindle, enkindle, McCrindle, Pendle, Kendall, Mendel, sendal, Wendell, Rendell, Brendel, Grendel, Lendl, pudendal, dandle, candle, scandal, vandal, sandal, Handel, handle, Randall, footcandle, rehandle, panhandle, manhandle, mishandle, Coromandel, Oundle, poundal, roundel, fondle, rondel, bundle, Rundle, trundle, Blundell, unbundle, prebendal, Arundel, dirndl

40.23.1
Meikle, faecal, caecal, Jekyll, treacle

40.23.2
pickle, tickle, mickle, Nichol, nickel, nicol, Nicoll, fickle, sickle, chicle, prickle, trickle, strickle, mispickel, pumpernickel, cupronickel, numerical, apodictical, hieroglyphical, chronological

40.23.3
cloacal

40.23.4
speckle, deckle, shekel, Jekyll, heckle, freckle

40.23.5
tackle, cackle, mackle, macle, shackle, jackal, hackle, crackle, grackle, ramshackle, unshackle, tabernacle

40.23.6
sparkle, diarchal, débâcle, monarchal, hierarchal, patriarchal, matriarchal

40.23.7
coccal, cockle, socle, grockle, epochal, corncockle, pinochle, streptococcal, gonococcal, staphylococcal, meningococcal

40.23.8
snorkel

40.23.9
buccal, buckle, muckle, knuckle, ruckle, suckle, chuckle, huckle, truckle,

parbuckle, unbuckle, turnbuckle, honeysuckle

40.23.10
Michael, cycle, Carmichael, cervical, recycle, vesical, hemicycle, unicycle, epicycle, autocycle, motorcycle, megacycle, monocycle, kilocycle, menstrual cycle, umbilical

40.23.11
coucal, ducal, nuchal, archducal, pentateuchal, oviducal

40.23.12
.1 vehicle .2 laical, Pharisaical, algebraical .3 cardiacal, zodiacal, maniacal, heliacal, demoniacal, simoniacal, ammoniacal, elegiacal, parheliacal, egomaniacal, monomaniacal, megalomaniacal, paradisiacal .4 stoical .5 typical, apical, epical, epochal, topical, tropical, atypical, untypical, neotropical, subtropical, misanthropical, antitypical, stereotypical, prototypical, archetypical, phenotypical, stroboscopical, stethoscopical, horoscopical, spectroscopical, microscopical, semitropical, allotropical, kaleidoscopical .6 tubercle, cubical, cubicle .7.1 critical, Levitical, soritical, diacritical, subcritical, uncritical, self-critical, political, Jesuitical, Jacobitical, coenobitical, troglodytical, eremitical, parasitical, sybaritical, hypocritical, hypercritical, supercritical, overcritical, apolitical, geopolitical, unpolitical, analytical, hermaphroditical, socio-political, psychoanalytical, cryptanalytical, electrolytical, metical, reticle, poetical, prophetical, synthetical, aesthetical, theoretical, heretical, unpoetical, alphabetical, quodlibetical, catechetical, arithmetical, antithetical, epithetical, apathetical, hypothetical, metathetical, parenthetical, anaesthetical, exegetical, atheoretical, untheoretical, analphabetical, cytogenetical, antipathetical, epexegetical, apologetical, statical, sabbatical, climatical, grammatical, pragmatical, mathematical, asthmatical, schismatical, judgematical, fanatical, piratical, prelatical, apostatical, hypostatical, hydrostatical, kinematical, ungrammatical, problematical, emblematical, enigmatical, leviratical, autocratical, anagrammatical, paradigmatical .7.2 article, particle, antiparticle, semiotical, cortical, nautical, vortical, subcortical, aeronautical, astronautical, cuticle, pharmaceutical, propaedeutical, therapeutical, hermeneutical, vertical .7.3 sceptical, skeptical, optical, receptacle, synoptical, apocalyptical, spectacle, tactical, practical, dialectical, syntactical, climactical, impractical, unpractical, apoplectical, apodeictical, pentacle, tentacle, denticle, canticle, identical, conventicle, romantical, mystical, fistical, testicle, obstacle, deistical, theistical, papistical, artistical, pietistical, statistical, Buddhistical, Thomistical, faunistical, sophistical, logistical, juristical, fantastical, acoustical, atheistical, pantheistical,

casuistical, egoistical, egotistical, Methodistical, Calvinistical, Eucharistical, manneristical, cabbalistical, catachrestical, ecclesiastical **.8** pedicle, medical, radical, radicle, nodical, syndical, Druidical, fatidical, veridical, juridical, premedical, biomedical, synodical, methodical, rhapsodical, Talmudical, paramedical, periodical, unmethodical, phonological **.9** psychical, autarchical, autarkical, heptarchical, anarchical, monarchical, hierarchical, squirearchical, tetrarchical, oligarchical, antimonarchical **.10** chemical, comical, rhythmical, cosmical, seismical, inimical, biochemical, geochemical, alchemical, polemical, dynamical, unrhythmical, metonymical, epidemical, academical, agrichemical, radiochemical, photochemical, agrochemical, phytochemical, histochemical, thermochemical, petrochemical, anatomical, heroi-comical, tragicomical, physiognomical, economical, taxonomical, Deuteronomical, astronomical, gastronomical, agronomical, physico-chemical, electrochemical, thermodynamical, hydrodynamical, neuroanatomical, uneconomical **.11** irenical, pinnacle, binnacle, finical, cynical, clinical, rabbinical, dominical, adminicle, preclinical, subclinical, Jacobinical, cenacle, arsenical, galenical, ecumenical, oecumenical, panicle, manacle, sanicle, botanical, mechanical, Brahmanical, tyrannical, puritanical, photomechanical, electromechanical, barnacle, conical, monacal, monachal, monocle, chronicle, platonical, obconical, subconical, demonical, canonical, parsonical, thrasonical, ironical, achronical, acronycal, acronychal, cosmogonical, uncanonical, tunicle, funicle, vernicle, technical, geotechnical, untechnical, pyrotechnical, electrotechnical, ethnical **.12** pontifical, triglyphical, graphical, seraphical, geographical, biographical, ideographical, hagiographical, physiographical, biogeographical, choreographical, palaeographical, bibliographical, zoogeographical, epigraphical, topographical, typographical, stratigraphical, photographical, tachygraphical, cacographical, demographical, cosmographical, seismographical, phonographical, ethnographical, oceanographical, orthographical, hypsographical, barographical, orographical, petrographical, hydrographical, calligraphical, historiographical, autobiographical, pseudepigraphical, prosopographical, lexicographical, iconographical, metallographical, cartographical, theosophical, philosophical, unphilosophical **.13** clavicle, cervical, equivocal, unequivocal **.14** mythical, ethical, unethical **.15** vesical, vesicle, fascicle, classical, farcical, ossicle, icicle, bicycle, phthisical, tricycle, versicle, Popsicle®, dropsical, lexical, preclassical, neoclassical, indexical,

pyrexical, nonsensical, paradisical, paradoxical, commonsensical **.16** physical, quizzical, musical, whimsical, geophysical, biophysical, unmusical, hyperphysical, superphysical, metaphysical, extraphysical, psychophysical, astrophysical, lackadaisical **.17.1** strategical, magical, tragical **.17.2** logical, mystagogical, pedagogical, demagogical, synagogical, anagogical, illogical, geological, rheological, alogical, theological, biological, bryological, zoological, oological, aetiological, etiological, osteological, ideological, radiological, audiological, archaeological, hagiological, semiological, genealogical, craniological, balneological, ichthyological, untheological, speciological, glaciological, sociological, axiological, physiological, phraseological, embryological, speleological, teleological, cryobiological, non-biological, topological, tropological, typological, cetological, scatological, tautological, cytological, otological, proctological, ontological, deontological, histological, Christological, pestological, pedological, ecological, trichological, mycological, phycological, psychological, conchological, algological, pomological, homological, zymological, sphygmological, cosmological, seismological, oenological, penological, phenological, sinological, phrenological, analogical, monological, technological, limnological, ethnological, psephological, graphological, morphological, ethological, mythological, lithological, pathological, anthological, posological, nosological, sexological, doxological, serological, aerological, orological, chorological, horological, virological, neurological, petrological, metrological, patrological, martyrological, astrological, hydrological, dendrological, necrological, numerological, mineralogical, philological, ethnoarchaeological, semasiological, ecclesiological, unphysiological, hydrogeological, soteriological, bacteriological, venereological, radiobiological, sociobiological, microbiological, psychobiological, neurobiological, anthropological, eschatological, herpetological, haematological, hematological, climatological, rheumatological, pneumatological, dermatological, stomatological, teratological, palaeontological, odontological, gerontological, methodological, pteridological, palaeoecological, synecological, codicological, pharmacological, gynaecological, lexicological, toxicological, musicological, etymological, entomological, ophthalmological, geochronological, campanological, volcanological, vulcanological, daemonological, demonological, criminological, terminological, immunological, palynological, geomorphological, ornithological, papyrological, meteorological, vexillological, epidemiological, psychophysiological, neurophysiological, palaeoanthropological, metapsychological, parapsychological, neuropsychological, epistemological, endocrinological, dendrochronological, phenomenological, psychopathological, electrophysiological, ethnomethodological, otolaryngological **.17.3** fudgicle, surgical, theurgical, liturgical, dramaturgical, thaumaturgical, neurosurgical, microsurgical, psychosurgical, metallurgical **.18** miracle, lyrical, empirical, satirical, panegyrical, spherical, clerical, hysterical, chimerical, esoterical, exoterical, climacterical, hemispherical, atmospherical, anticlerical, alphanumerical, karakul, oracle, coracle, rhetorical, historical, oratorical, unhistorical, ahistorical, categorical, allegorical, metaphorical, phantasmagorical, auricle, thoracal, spiracle, curricle, reciprocal, rubrical, lumbrical, metrical, utricle, ventricle, centrical, obstetrical, geometrical, trimetrical, biometrical, diametrical, symmetrical, unmetrical, theatrical, electrical, eudiometrical, stoichiometrical, goniometrical, pluviometrical, hypermetrical, thermometrical, seismometrical, planimetrical, manometrical, chronometrical, dissymmetrical, asymmetrical, unsymmetrical, barometrical, hydrometrical, volumetrical, psychiatrical, econometrical, trigonometrical, cylindrical, calendrical, semicylindrical **.19** pellicle, helical, calicle, follicle, biblical, cyclical, parhelical, umbilical, angelical, diabolical, symbolical, unbiblical, encyclical, evangelical, hyperbolical, parabolical, apostolical

40.23.13
Köchel, circle, encircle, semicircle, diphycercal, circumcircle

40.23.14
Ochil, focal, vocal, socle, trochal, yokel, local, bifocal, trifocal, varifocal, hyperfocal, multivocal, univocal, matrilocal

40.23.15
tinkle, Finchale, winkle, twinkle, wrinkle, sprinkle, crinkle, ankle, Wankel, rankle, uncle, truncal, Heinkel, besprinkle, carbuncle, peduncle, granduncle, Garfunkel, siphuncle, furuncle, caruncle, periwinkle, Rip van Winkle

40.23.16
fiscal, Driscoll, paschal, Gaskell, mascle, Maskell, rascal, Gaitskell, O'Driscoll, McCaskill, procurator fiscal, procurators fiscal

40.24.1
eagle, Spiegl, beagle, Segal, Siegel, Sigal, regal, legal, porbeagle, spread-eagle, inveigle, viceregal, illegal, paralegal

40.24.2
giggle, niggle, sniggle, jiggle, higgle, wiggle, squiggle, wriggle

40.24.3
bagel, beigel, Nagle, vagal, Hegel, plagal, Schlegel, finagle, inveigle

40.24.4
gaggle, haggle, waggle, raggle, straggle, draggle, raggle-taggle, bedraggle

40.24.5
gargle, argle-bargle, Invercargill

40.24.6
boggle, toggle, goggle, joggle, woggle, boondoggle, hornswoggle, synagogal

40.24.7
Bruegel

40.24.8
guggle, smuggle, snuggle, juggle, struggle

40.24.9
Rigel

40.24.10
Dougall, Mughal, frugal, bugle, fugal, fugle, McDougall, febrifugal, centrifugal

40.24.11
prodigal, Portugal, conjugal, warrigal, astragal, madrigal, McGonagall, febrifugal, centrifugal

40.24.12
burghal, burgle, tergal, gurgle, Fergal, exergual

40.24.13
ogle, bogle, mogul, Vogel, aasvogel

40.24.14
.1 tingle, dingle, mingle, Fingal, single, shingle, jingle, swingle, Pringle, cringle, atingle, Christingle, commingle, surcingle, pharyngal, intermingle **.2** angle, triangle, spangle, bangle, tangle, dangle, gangle, mangel, mangle, jangle, wangle, twangle, Wrangel, wrangle, strangle, bespangle, rightangle, rectangle, entangle, pentangle, untangle, disentangle, wide-angle, fandangle, embrangle, quadrangle **.3** pongal, dongle, Mongol, diphthongal, triphthongal, monophthongal **.4** bungle, fungal, jungle

40.24.15
algal

40.25.1
haemal, extremal, erythemal

40.25.2
ramal

40.25.3
Gemmell

40.25.4
amyl, Tamil, camel, Scammell, mammal, samel, Hamill, trammel, enamel, entrammel

40.25.5
pommel, Rommel, trommel

40.25.6
normal, formal, abnormal, subnormal, informal, conformal, supernormal, paranormal

40.25.7
pommel, pummel, Brummell

40.25.8
primal

40.25.9
Kümmel

40.25.10
septimal, optimal, minimal, animal, decimal, maximal, proximal, caramel, lachrymal, prosenchymal, parenchymal, centesimal, duodecimal, vicesimal, vigesimal, millesimal, planetesimal, hexadecimal, sexagesimal, quadragesimal, infinitesimal

40.25.11
dermal, thermal, geothermal, pachydermal, epidermal, hypodermal, ectodermal, endodermal, taxidermal, homoeothermal, isothermal, exothermal, hydrothermal, isogeothermal, poikilothermal, electrothermal

40.25.12
stomal, prodromal, ribosomal, chromosomal

40.25.13
Cartmel

40.25.14
dismal, prismal, seismal, abysmal, strabismal, baptismal, coseismal, miasmal, phantasmal, catechismal, paroxysmal, aneurysmal, cataclysmal, protoplasmal, isoseismal

40.25.15
Richmal

40.26.1
penal, phenyl, venal, renal, duodenal, carinal, adrenal, officinal, suprarenal, infrarenal

40.26.2
meridional

40.26.3
anal, Meynell, decanal, bimanal, morainal, ruridecanal

40.26.4
kennel, Meynell, fennel, phenyl, treenail, crenel, antennal

40.26.5
anil, annal, panel, Pannal, Pannell, cannel, flannel, channel, impanel, empanel, multichannel

40.26.6
nounal

40.26.7
darnel, carnal, charnel

40.26.8
cantonal, O'Donnell, McDonnell, O'Connell, McConnell

40.26.9
cornel, faunal

40.26.10
tunnel, gunwale, funnel, Chunnel, runnel, trunnel, Eurotunnel

40.26.11
spinal, final, vinyl, rhinal, trinal, clinal, vaginal, carinal, urinal, doctrinal, synclinal, interspinal, matutinal, mediastinal, intestinal, semifinal, quarterfinal, polyvinyl, anticlinal, periclinal, monoclinal, isoclinal, cerebrospinal, gastrointestinal

40.26.12
lagoonal, monsoonal, tribunal, lacunal, communal

40.26.13
.1 Lionel, embryonal **.2** Aspinall **.3** turbinal **.4** retinal, dentinal, sentinel, cantonal, matutinal, intestinal, gastrointestinal **.5** cardinal, ordinal, libidinal, subordinal, testudinal, superordinal, attitudinal, latitudinal, altitudinal, longitudinal **.6** decanal, bacchanal, subdecanal, diaconal, ruridecanal, archidiaconal **.7** trigonal, mangonel, polygonal, diagonal, heptagonal, octagonal, pentagonal, decagonal, hexagonal, tetragonal, orthogonal **.8** bimanal, criminal, liminal, feminal, seminal, geminal, staminal, noumenal, nominal, hymenal, luminal, terminal, germinal, subliminal, trigeminal, abdominal, binominal, phenomenal, pronominal, adnominal, cognominal, cacuminal, subterminal, subabdominal, superluminal, epiphenomenal **.9** siphonal, antiphonal **.10** Juvenal **.11** autochthonal **.12** vicinal, arsenal, personal, vaccinal, vaticinal, medicinal, officinal, impersonal, transpersonal, unipersonal, interpersonal **.13** seasonal **.14.1** tuitional, intuitional, repetitional, additional, traditional, conditional, untraditional, unconditional, commissional, cognitional, definitional, transitional, positional, depositional, prepositional, appositional, oppositional, propositional, suppositional, postpositional, compositional, expositional, transpositional, inquisitional, disquisitional, juxtapositional, nutritional, attritional, volitional, salicional **.14.2** radiational, ideational, deviational, variational, recreational, situational, associational, occupational, probational, incubational, mutational, notational, rotational, presentational, transmutational, gravitational, dissertational, vegetational, computational, permutational, salutational, orientational, incantational, confrontational, representational, interpretational, gradational, foundational, oxidational, vocational, locational, pre-vocational, convocational, educational, co-educational, communicational, stratificational, rogational, navigational, conjugational, segregational, congregational, obligational, investigational, interrogational, formational, summational, deformational, reformational, informational, transformational, venational, combinational, intonational, terminational, declinational, examinational, denominational, undenominational, interdenominational, ovational, motivational,

innovational, conservational, observational,
derivational, elevational, sensational,
compensational, dispensational, conversational,
unsensational, organizational, improvisational,
durational, narrational, vibrational, migrational,
operational, aspirational, inspirational,
generational, maturational, explorational,
illustrational, demonstrational, configurational,
relational, oblational, translational, revelational,
correlational **.14.**3 sessional, professional,
confessional, secessional, recessional,
precessional, processional, obsessional,
successional, consessional, impressional,
expressional, progressional, congressional,
transgressional, preprofessional, unprofessional,
intercessional, semi-professional,
paraprofessional **.14.4** passional, national,
rational, unnational, transnational, irrational,
arational, multinational, international,
supranational, intranational **.14.5** torsional,
proportional, distortional, disproportional,
prostitutional, substitutional, institutional,
constitutional, distributional, evolutional,
involutional, convolutional, unconstitutional,
circumlocutional, anti-constitutional, versional,
excursional, diversional, reversional, notional,
emotional, commotional, promotional,
devotional, unemotional **.14.6** optional,
inscriptional, transcriptional, perceptional,
exceptional, conceptional, unexceptional,
fictional, frictional, jurisdictional, sectional,
flexional, connectional, convectional,
resectional, intersectional, vivisectional,
interjectional, directional, correctional,
insurrectional, resurrectional, multidirectional,
unidirectional, omnidirectional, selectional,
reflectional, inflectional, factional, tractional,
fractional, redactional, transactional,
interactional, fluxional, productional,
instructional, constructional, functional,
dysfunctional, conjunctional,
multifunctional **.14.7** tensional, attentional,
intensional, intentional, extensional,
dimensional, conventional, ascensional,
declensional, unintentional,
three-dimensional, tridimensional,
two-dimensional, unconventional,
multidimensional, unidimensional
.14.8 visional, fusional, divisional,
previsional, provisional, collisional,
occasional, equational, illusional, delusional,
erosional, regional, paginal, marginal,
virginal, subregional, original, imaginal,
submarginal, aboriginal, unoriginal,
inguinal, veronal, coronal, urinal, neuronal,
matronal, petronel, isochronal, communal,
disciplinal

40.26.14
sternal, colonel, kernel, vernal, journal,
diurnal, supernal, hibernal, eternal,
coeternal, paternal, maternal, fraternal,
nocturnal, internal, external, infernal,
hodiernal, sempiternal, retrosternal

40.26.15
tonal, Donal, Monel®, zonal, clonal, umbonal,
atonal, hormonal, neuronal, patronal, polytonal,
pheromonal, monoclonal

40.26.16
grapnel, shrapnel

40.26.17
Hartnell

40.26.18
spicknel, Bracknell, cracknel, Bucknell

40.26.19
spignel, signal, regnal, Pagnell, Bagnall,
Wagnall, resignal

40.26.20
simnel, hymnal, autumnal

40.26.21
Tuffnell

40.26.22
Bushnell

40.27.1
gleeful

40.27.2
piffle, skiffle, sniffle, whiffle, riffle, pitiful

40.27.3
tearful, fearful, cheerful

40.27.4
playful

40.27.5
TEFL

40.27.6
careful, prayerful, overcareful

40.27.7
baffle, snaffle, raffle, yaffle, falafel

40.27.8
offal, coffle, waffle

40.27.9
awful, lawful, unlawful

40.27.10
joyful

40.27.11
duffel, scuffle, muffle, snuffle, shuffle, ruffle,
truffle, unmuffle, kerfuffle, reshuffle

40.27.12
Eiffel, stifle, hyphal, rifle, trifle

40.27.13
souffle, rueful

40.27.14
powerful, ireful, direful, dutiful, beautiful,
plentiful, bountiful, masterful, wonderful,
flavourful, Parsifal, merciful, fanciful, sorrowful,
colourful, undutiful, unbeautiful, characterful,
unmerciful, apocryphal, pseudepigraphal

40.27.15
purfle

40.27.16
woeful, sorrowful

40.27.17
sapful, hopeful, helpful, worshipful, unhopeful, unhelpful

40.27.18
deceitful, fitful, fateful, hateful, grateful, ungrateful, fretful, forgetful, regretful, self-forgetful, doubtful, artful, thoughtful, unthoughtful, spiteful, rightful, frightful, despiteful, insightful, delightful, fruitful, unfruitful, effortful, hurtful, tactful, respectful, neglectful, disrespectful, eventful, resentful, uneventful, mistful, wistful, tasteful, wasteful, zestful, restful, trustful, lustful, boastful, distasteful, unrestful, disgustful, distrustful, mistrustful, resultful

40.27.19
needful, heedful, dreadful, prideful, bodeful, mindful, unheedful, regardful, remindful, unmindful, disregardful

40.27.20
wakeful, thankful, prankful, respectful, neglectful, unthankful, disrespectful

40.27.21
dreamful, nymphal, shameful, blameful, harmful, unharmful, triumphal

40.27.22
spleenful, sinful, painful, baneful, gainful, Grenfell, manful, scornful, mournful, mindful, tuneful, moanful, disdainful, remindful, unmindful, untuneful

40.27.23
songful, wrongful, meaningful

40.27.24
faithful, Faithfull, wrathful, ruthful, truthful, youthful, mirthful, slothful, healthful, unfaithful, untruthful, unhealthful

40.27.25
peaceful, blissful, graceful, stressful, forceful, voiceful, useful, unpeaceful, ungraceful, disgraceful, successful, distressful, remorseful, resourceful, purposeful, suspenseful, unsuccessful, unremorseful

40.27.26
easeful, praiseful, reposeful

40.27.27
wishful, bashful, blushful, pushful

40.27.28
changeful, vengeful, prestigeful, revengeful

40.27.29
speechful, watchful, unwatchful, reproachful, self-reproachful

40.27.30
dirgeful, changeful, vengeful, prestigeful, revengeful

40.27.31
skilful, wilful, baleful, wailful, guileful, doleful, soulful

40.28.1
evil, weevil, shrieval, coeval, Khedival, primeval, upheaval, retrieval, medieval

40.28.2
snivel, civil, swivel, drivel, frivol, shrivel, uncivil

40.28.3
naval, navel, Favell

40.28.4
bevel, devil, kevel, Neville, Seville, revel, Greville, level, she-devil, daredevil, bedevil, dishevel, eyelevel, split-level, multilevel

40.28.5
cavil, Cavell, gavel, snavel, Savile, ravel, travel, gravel, unravel

40.28.6
carvel, marvel, Marvell, Havel, larval, rondavel

40.28.7
novel, hovel, grovel, antinovel, photonovel

40.28.8
shovel, Lovell, steamshovel

40.28.9
nival, rival, datival, substantival, aestival, estival, archival, survival, revival, ogival, gingival, arrival, deprival, outrival, arch-rival, genitival, nominatival, relatival, ablatival, objectival, adjectival, conjunctival, gerundival, infinitival, accusatival, imperatival, diminutival

40.28.10
removal, approval, reproval, disproval, self-approval, disapproval

40.28.11
interval, aestival, festival, carnival, Furnivall, Percival, gingival, perspectival

40.28.12
serval, chervil

40.28.13
oval, Yeovil

40.28.14
Merthyr Tydfil

40.28.15
Grenville, anvil, Granville

40.28.16
vulval

40.29
lethal, Ethel, ethyl, Bethel, methyl, Atholl, brothel, diethyl, zenithal, tetraethyl, azimuthal

40.30
Southall, Southwell, betrothal

40.31.1
Wiesel, Cecil

40.31.2
Bissell, scissel, missal, thistle, Cecil, scissile, whistle, bristle, gristle, epistle, abyssal, dismissal, sowthistle, dickcissel, Birtwistle, Oswaldtwistle, cacomistle

40.31.3
Pearsall, tiercel

40.31.4
basal, staysail, vasal

40.31.5
pestle, Bessel, TESL, deasil, Nestlé®, nestle, vessel, Cecil, chessel, Jessel, wrestle, trestle, redressal

40.31.6
passel, tassel, Cassell, castle, Kassel, vassal, Hassall, hassle, Newcastle, sandcastle, Oldcastle, Horncastle, Boscastle

40.31.7
parcel, tarsal, castle, Newcastle, Hardcastle, sandcastle, Oldcastle, Horncastle, Boscastle, metatarsal

40.31.8
dossal, fossil, jostle, throstle, glossal, wassail, apostle, colossal

40.31.9
torsel, dorsal, morsel, foresail, Walsall, predorsal

40.31.10
bustle, tussle, muscle, mussel, hustle, Russell, rustle, corpuscle, Jack Russell

40.31.11
Geisel, Faisal, Feisal, sisal, trysail, paradisal

40.31.12
tattersall, pedicel

40.31.13
Persil®, Purcell, bursal, tercel, tiercel, Kursaal, dispersal, disbursal, succursal, demersal, reversal, traversal, transversal, rehearsal, universal, quaquaversal

40.31.14
Mosul

40.31.15
Tapsell, capsule, topsail

40.31.16
schnitzel, spritsail, Spätzle, quetzal, pretzel, Brezel, Herzl, Wiener schnitzel

40.31.17
Edsel, windsail, groundsel

40.31.18
pixel, Texel, Drexel, axel, axil, axle, Coggeshall, coxal, fo'c'sle, forecastle, adnexal, biaxal, transaxle, pyridoxal

40.31.19
lugsail

40.31.20
plimsole, plimsoll

40.31.21
tinsel, mainsail, pencil, stencil, Kensal, Ansell, cancel, Mansell, chancel, Hänsel, hansel, council, counsel, tonsil, consul, studding-sail/stunsail, gunsel, mizzen-sail, utensil, commensal, proconsul, intercensal

40.31.22
Walsall

40.32.1
easel, teasel, diesel, weasel, turbo-diesel

40.32.2
pizzle, mizzle, fizzle, sizzle, chisel, twizzle, swizzle, drizzle, grizzle, frizzle

40.32.3
nasal, vasal, hazel, frazil, phrasal, witch hazel, appraisal, reappraisal, orinasal, oculonasal

40.32.4
bezel, Hessle, embezzle

40.32.5
basil, dazzle, razzle, frazzle, bedazzle, razzle-dazzle, antidazzle

40.32.6
spousal, tousle, Mousehoule, espousal, arousal, carousal

40.32.7
Basel

40.32.8
mozzle, nozzle, schnozzle, shemozzle

40.32.9
causal, clausal, acausal, menopausal, monocausal

40.32.10
streusel

40.32.11
puzzle, guzzle, muzzle, nuzzle, unmuzzle

40.32.12
sisal, revisal, capsizal, reprisal, paradisal, mycorrhizal

40.32.13
ouzel, foozle, streusel, fusel, fusil, bamboozle, perusal, accusal, refusal

40.32.14
Kursaal, mangel-wurzel

40.32.15
deposal, reposal, proposal, disposal, transposal, interposal, counter-proposal

40.32.16
damsel

40.32.17
benzyl, Denzil, Rapunzel, influenzal

40.33.1
solstitial, judicial, indicial, initial, official, surficial, syncytial, altricial, interstitial, prejudicial, tribunicial, tribunitial, superficial,

artificial, beneficial, unofficial, sacrificial, cicatricial, extrajudicial

40.33.2
spatial, facial, fascial, racial, glacial, abbatial, primatial, trifacial, palatial, preglacial, subglacial, postglacial, interfacial, multiracial, interracial, periglacial, fluvioglacial, interglacial

40.33.3
special, deasil, especial, unspecial

40.33.4
raschel

40.33.5
partial, Marischal, marshal, martial, impartial, court-martial, provost-marshall

40.33.6
faucial

40.33.7
bushel

40.33.8
trucial, crucial, fiducial, preputial

40.33.9
Coggeshall, seneschal

40.33.10
Herschel, commercial, inertial, uncommercial, infomercial, controversial, uncontroversial

40.33.11
social, precocial, asocial, unsocial, antisocial, psychosocial

40.33.12
.1 provincial **.2** sciential, sapiential, congruential, affluential, influential, experiential, uninfluential, potential, sentential, penitential, existential, pluripotential, equipotential **.3** cadential, prudential, rodential,

credential, confidential, evidential, providential, residential, presidential, jurisprudential, componential, exponential, eventual, conventual, essential, coessential, accentual, quintessential, inessential, nonessential, unessential, excrescential, reminiscential, agential, tangential, intelligential, sequential, consequential, inconsequential, torrential, differential, deferential, referential, preferential, inferential, conferential, reverential, coreferential, interferential, circumferential, irreverential, pestilential **.4** substantial, financial, insubstantial, consubstantial, unsubstantial, circumstantial, unfinancial **.5** uncial, quincuncial

40.34
vigil, sigil, ridgel, strigil, schedule, gradual, nodule, cudgel, Nigel, Rigel, Vergil, Virgil, brinjal, angel, strongyle, vestigial, residual, Tintagel, archangel, evangel, individual, rhinopharyngeal

40.35.1
narwhal, Cherwell

40.35.2
Sitwell, setwall

40.35.3
equal, sequel, prequel, Bakewell, rorqual, tranquil, jonquil, coequal, unequal

40.35.4
Chigwell, lingual, ungual, bilingual, trilingual, sublingual, multilingual, audiolingual, tubilingual, monolingual, unilingual, quadrilingual

40.35.5
Anwyl, Stanwell

Index

a 4
Aachen 28.17.13(.6)
aah 10
Aalborg 26.9
aardvark 24.8.10
aardwolf 30.20.6
aardwolves 35.28.10
Aargau 9.6
aargh 10
Aarhus 34.17.11
Aaron 28.17.31(.4)
aasvogel 40.24.13
ab 21.6
aba 17.11.5
abaca 17.14.15(.5)
abaci 14.10, 14.18
aback 24.6.6
abacus 34.18.13(.10)
Abadan 28.7.7, 28.9.3
Abaddon 28.17.12(.6)
abaft 22.27.4(.1)
abalone 1.16.17(.15)
abandon 28.17.12(.23)
abandonee 2.17
abandoner 17.18.16(.5)
abandonment
    22.26.15(.13.4)
abase 34.4.3
abasement 22.26.15(.13.5)
abash 36.6.2
abashment
    22.26.15(.13.6)
abask 24.20.4
abatable 40.20.16(.11.1)
abate 22.4.8
abatement 22.26.15(.13.3)
abatis 34.2.8, 35.1.7(.6)
abatised 22.29.2(.13)
abatises 35.18.17
abattis 34.2.8, 35.1.7(.3)
abattised 22.29.2(.13)
abattoir 10.22.5
abaxial 40.3.10
abaya 17.2.2
abba 17.11.5
abbacy 1.22.16(.3)
Abbas 34.18.10
Abbasid 23.2.16
abbatial 40.33.2
abbé 4.8
abbess 34.5.1, 34.18.10
Abbeville 40.2.12
Abbevillian 28.3.21(.2)
abbey 1.9.5
abbot 22.19.9
abbotship 20.2.8
Abbott 22.19.9
abbreviate 22.4.2(.8)
abbreviation
    28.17.25(.3.1)

abbreviatory 1.29.11(.8.1)
Abby 1.9.5
Abdela 17.34.5(.4)
abdicable 40.20.16(.13)
abdicant 22.26.15(.11)
abdicate 22.4.11(.6)
abdication 28.17.25(.3.5)
abdicator 17.12.4(.7)
abdomen 28.17.16(.16)
abdominal 40.26.13(.8)
abdominally
    1.31.17(.14.2)
abdominous
    34.18.16(.15.3)
abduct 22.23.8
abduction 28.17.25(.15.5)
abductor 17.12.21(.6)
Abdul 40.14.4
Abdullah 17.34.12,
    17.34.14
Abe 21.3
abeam 27.1.1
abecedarian 28.3.20(.4)
abed 23.5.2
Abednego 19.13.1, 19.13.9
Abel 40.20.4
Abelard 23.9.22
abele 40.1.2, 40.20.4
abelia 3.24.1
abelian 28.3.21(.1)
Aberaeron 28.17.31(.10)
Aberavon 28.17.20(.5)
Abercrombie 1.9.18
Aberdare 6.5
Aberdaron 28.17.31(.5)
Aberdeen 28.1.10
Aberdonian 28.3.8(.11)
Aberdovey 1.19.7
Aberfan 28.7.13
Abergavenny 1.16.5
Abergele 1.31.5
Abernathy 1.20.4
Abernethy 1.20.1, 1.20.3
Aberporth 32.10
aberrance 34.24.10(.16)
aberrancy 1.22.23(.10.4)
aberrant 22.26.15(.23.1)
aberrate 22.4.22(.6)
aberration 28.17.25(.3.13)
Abersoch 24.9.10, 24.18.9
Abersychan 28.17.13(.9)
Abertillery 1.29.4
Aberystwyth 32.2.7
abet 22.5.2
abetment 22.26.15(.13.3)
abetter 17.12.5(.1)
abeyance 34.24.10(.2)
abeyant 22.26.15(.2)
abhor 12.4, 12.19
abhorrence 34.24.10(.16)

abhorrent 22.26.15(.23.2)
abhorrently 1.31.22(.20.5)
abhorrer 17.32.10(.1)
abidance 34.24.10(.11)
abide 23.15.3
abidingly 1.31.28(.1.5)
Abidjan 28.7.17, 28.9.10
Abigail 40.4.5
Abilene 28.1.27(.7)
ability 1.10.16(.22.1)
Abingdon 28.17.12(.24)
ab initio 15.1.9
abiogenesis 34.2.17(.10.3)
abiogenic 24.2.15(.4)
abiogenically
    1.31.24(.9.8)
abiogenist 22.29.2(.18.3)
Abiola 17.34.18
abiotic 24.2.10(.6)
abject 22.23.4(.9)
abjection 28.17.25(.15.2)
abjectly 1.31.22(.19)
abjectness 34.18.16(.20.4)
abjuration 28.17.25(.3.13)
abjure 12.18, 17.7.12(.4)
Abkhaz 35.7, 35.9
Abkhazi 1.23.7
Abkhazia 3.15.5
Abkhazian 28.3.14
ablate 22.4.23(.9)
ablation 28.17.25(.3.14)
ablatival 40.28.9
ablative 31.2.1(.9.4)
ablatively 1.31.30(.7.1)
ablaut 22.9.19
ablaze 35.4.18
able 40.20.4
ableism 27.15.21(.2.15)
abloom 27.14.8
ablush 36.12
ablution 28.17.25(.11)
ablutionary 1.29.11(.13.2)
ably 1.31.21(.1)
abnegate 22.4.12(.5)
abnegation 28.17.25(.3.6)
abnegator 17.12.4(.8)
Abner 17.18.20
abnormal 40.25.6
abnormality
    1.10.16(.32.7)
abnormally 1.31.17(.13)
abnormity 1.10.16(.12)
Abo 19.9.3
aboard 23.12.2
abode 23.20.4
abolish 36.2.27
abolishable 40.20.16(.23)
abolisher 17.26.14
abolishment
    22.26.15(.13.6)

abolition 28.17.25(.2.6)
abolitionism
    27.15.21(.2.9)
abolitionist 22.29.2(.18.2)
abomasa 17.24.4
abomasum 27.15.20(.4)
abominable
    40.20.16(.16.3)
abominableness
    34.18.16(.37.4)
abominably 1.31.21(.6)
abominate 22.4.14(.9.2)
abomination
    28.17.25(.3.8)
abominator 17.12.4(.10)
aboral 40.16.13(.8)
aboriginal 40.26.13(.14.8)
Aboriginality
    1.10.16(.32.8)
aboriginally
    1.31.17(.14.3)
aborigine 1.16.15(.17)
aborning 29.1.17(.8)
abort 22.13.2
abortifacient
    22.26.15(.19)
abortion 28.17.25(.8)
abortionist 22.29.2(.18.2)
abortive 31.2.1(.5)
abortively 1.31.30(.7.1)
abortiveness
    34.18.16(.28.1)
Aboukir Bay 4
abound 23.24.7(.2)
about 22.9.6
above 31.8
above board 23.12.2
aboveground 23.24.7(.10)
ab ovo 19.17
abracadabra 17.32.18
abrade 23.4.15
abrader 17.13.3
Abraham 27.6.15
Abrahams 35.25.4
Abram 27.6.17(.4),
    27.15.26(.9)
Abrams 35.25.10
abrasion 28.17.26(.3)
abrasive 31.2.4(.3)
abrasively 1.31.30(.7.4)
abrasiveness
    34.18.16(.28.2)
abraxus 34.18.20
abreact 22.23.5
abreaction
    28.17.25(.15.3)
abreactive 31.2.1(.13.3)
abreast 22.29.5(.12)
abridge 39.2.22(.10)
abridgeable 40.20.16(.25)

abridgement
22.26.15(.13.6)
abridger 17.29.2
abroach 38.17
abroad 23.12.9
abrogate 22.4.12(.5),
22.19.13
abrogation 28.17.25(.3.6)
abrogator 17.12.4(.8)
abrupt 22.22.6
abruption 28.17.25(.14)
abruptly 1.31.22(.18)
abruptness 34.18.16(.20.4)
Abruzzi 1.22.21
Absalom 27.15.28(.11)
abscess 34.2.17(.13), 34.5.9
abscissa 17.24.2
abscissae 2.22.2
abscission 28.17.25(.2.5)
abscond 23.24.9
absconder 17.13.20(.7)
Abse 1.23.16
abseil 40.4.10, 40.13.12
abseiler 17.34.4, 17.34.13
absence 34.24.10(.18)
absent 22.26.4(.11),
22.26.15(.17.3)
absentee 2.11
absenteeism
27.15.21(.2.1)
absently 1.31.22(.20.4)
absentness 34.18.16(.20.4)
absinth 32.21
absinthe 32.21
absit omen 28.5.7(.12)
absolute 22.18.11
absolutely 1.31.22(.14)
absoluteness
34.18.16(.20.2)
absolution 28.17.25(.11)
absolutism 27.15.21(.2.4)
absolutist 22.29.2(.13)
absolve 31.13
absolver 17.21.19
absorb 21.9
absorbability
1.10.16(.22.2)
absorbable 40.20.16(.10)
absorbance 34.24.10(.9)
absorbedly 1.31.23(.14.2)
absorbency 1.22.23(.10.2)
absorbent 22.26.15(.8)
absorbently 1.31.22(.20.2)
absorber 17.11.9
absorbingly 1.31.28(.1.3)
absorption 28.17.25(.14)
absorptive 31.2.1(.12)
absorptiveness
34.18.16(.28.1)
absorptivity 1.10.16(.15)
absquatulate 22.4.23(.7.3)

abstain 28.4.3
abstainer 17.18.3
abstemious 34.3.5
abstemiously
1.31.33(.1.2)
abstemiousness
34.18.16(.31.1)
abstention 28.17.25(.16)
abstentionism
27.15.21(.2.9)
abstergent 22.26.15(.21)
abstersion 28.17.25(.12)
abstersive 31.2.4(.10)
abstersively 1.31.30(.7.4)
abstinence 34.24.10(.15)
abstinency 1.22.23(.10.3)
abstinent 22.26.15(.14)
abstinently 1.31.22(.20.3)
abstract 22.23.5(.9)
abstractedly
1.31.23(.14.3)
abstractedness
34.18.16(.21.1)
abstraction
28.17.25(.15.3)
abstractionism
27.15.21(.2.9)
abstractionist
22.29.2(.18.2)
abstractive 31.2.1(.13.3)
abstractly 1.31.22(.19)
abstractness
34.18.16(.20.4)
abstractor 17.12.21(.3)
abstruse 34.17.12
abstrusely 1.31.33(.11)
abstruseness
34.18.16(.31.2)
absurd 23.19.4, 23.19.5
absurdism 27.15.21(.2.5)
absurdist 22.29.2(.14)
absurdity 1.10.16(.9)
absurdly 1.31.23(.15)
absurdness
34.18.16(.21.1)
ABTA 17.12.20
Abu Dhabi 1.9.6
Abuja 17.29.12
abulia 3.24.10
abulic 24.2.27(.12)
Abu Musa 17.24.14
abundance 34.24.10(.11)
abundant 22.26.15(.10)
abundantly
1.31.22(.20.2)
abuse 34.17.13, 35.17.7
abuser 17.25.14
Abu Simbel 40.20.19
abusive 31.2.4(.8)
abusively 1.31.30(.7.4)
abusiveness
34.18.16(.28.2)

abut 22.15.2
abutilon 28.10.26,
28.17.33(.13)
abutment 22.26.15(.13.3)
abuttal 40.21.9
abutter 17.12.12
abuzz 35.14
Abydos 34.10.9
abysm 27.15.21(.2.3)
abysmal 40.25.14
abysmally 1.31.17(.13)
abyss 34.2.7
abyssal 40.31.2
Abyssinia 3.9.2
abzyme 27.12.5
acacia 17.26.3
academe 27.1.3
academia 3.8.1
academic 24.2.14(.3)
academical 40.23.12(.10)
academically
1.31.24(.9.8)
academician
28.17.25(.2.4)
academicism
27.15.21(.2.12)
academism 27.15.21(.2.8)
academy 1.15.13(.2)
Acadia 3.5.3
Acadian 28.3.4(.3)
acaemia 3.8.1
acajau 16.18
acanthi 14.16
acanthine 28.14.12
acanthus 34.18.19
a cappella 17.34.5(.1)
Acapulco 19.12.18
acaricide 23.15.11(.6)
acarid 23.2.22
acaroid 23.13.19
acarology 1.26.10(.11.5)
acarpous 34.18.9(.5)
ACAS 34.7.9
acatalectic 24.2.10(.13)
acatalepsy 1.22.19
acataleptic 24.2.10(.12)
acaudal 40.22.8
acaudate 22.4.10
acausal 40.32.9
accaroid 23.13.19
accede 23.1.7
accelerando 19.11.14
accelerant
22.26.15(.23.3)
accelerate 22.4.22(.6)
acceleration
28.17.25(.3.13)
accelerative 31.2.1(.9.4)
accelerator 17.12.4(.15)
accelerometer
17.12.16(.9.2)

accent 22.26.4(.11),
22.26.15(.17.3)
accentor 17.12.22(.3)
accentual 40.16.12,
40.33.12(.3)
accentually 1.31.17(.24)
accentuate 22.4.4
accentuation
28.17.25(.3.1)
accept 22.22.3
acceptability
1.10.16(.22.2)
acceptable
40.20.16(.11.4)
acceptableness
34.18.16(.37.4)
acceptably 1.31.21(.4.3)
acceptance 34.24.10(.10)
acceptant 22.26.15(.9)
acceptation
28.17.25(.3.3)
accepter 17.12.19
acceptor 17.12.19
access 34.5.9
accessibility
1.10.16(.22.2)
accessible 40.20.16(.21.1)
accessibly 1.31.21(.7.2)
accession 28.17.25(.4)
accessit 22.2.16
accessorial 40.3.14(.5)
accessorize 35.15.20(.2)
accessory 1.29.11(.18)
acciaccatura 17.32.14(.3)
accidence 34.24.10(.11)
accident 22.26.15(.10)
accidental 40.21.17(.2)
accidentally 1.31.17(.9.3),
1.31.22(.20.1)
accidie 1.11.17
accipiter 17.12.16(.3)
acclaim 27.4.9
acclaimer 17.17.4
acclamation
28.17.25(.3.7)
acclamatory 1.29.11(.8.7)
acclimatation
28.17.25(.3.3)
acclimate 22.4.13(.6)
acclimation
28.17.25(.3.7)
acclimatization
28.17.25(.3.12)
acclimatize 35.15.7(.7)
acclivitous 34.18.11(.10)
acclivity 1.10.16(.15)
accolade 23.4.16
accommodate 22.4.10
accommodating
29.1.12(.3)
accommodatingly
1.31.28(.1.4)

accommodation **28.17.25(.3.4)**
accommodationist **22.29.2(.18.2)**
accompaniment **22.26.15(.13.2)**
accompanist **22.29.2(.18.1)**
accompany **1.16.15(.5), 1.16.18**
accompanyist **22.29.2(.2)**
accomplice **34.18.29(.20)**
accomplish **36.2.27**
accomplishment **22.26.15(.13.6)**
accompt **22.26.7**
accord **23.12.4**
accordance **34.24.10(.11)**
accordant **22.26.15(.10)**
accordantly **1.31.22(.20.2)**
according **29.1.13(.8)**
accordingly **1.31.28(.1.5)**
accordion **28.3.4(.7)**
accordionist **22.29.2(.18.1)**
accost **22.29.9**
accouchement **11.8**
accoucheur **18.13**
accoucheuse **35.19**
account **22.26.7**
accountability **1.10.16(.22.2)**
accountable **40.20.16(.11.6)**
accountableness **34.18.16(.37.4)**
accountably **1.31.21(.4.3)**
accountancy **1.22.23(.10.2)**
accountant **22.26.15(.9)**
accounting **29.1.12(.19)**
accoutre **17.12.15(.2)**
accoutrement **22.26.15(.13.2)**
Accra **10.23.8**
accredit **22.2.8**
accreditation **28.17.25(.3.3)**
accrete **22.1.17**
accretion **28.17.25(.1)**
accretive **31.2.1(.1)**
Accrington **28.17.11(.23)**
accrual **40.16.8**
accrue **16.23.10**
acct **22.26.7**
acculturation **28.17.25(.3.13)**
acculturative **31.2.1(.9.4)**
accumulable **40.20.16(.29)**
accumulate **22.4.23(.7.3)**

accumulation **28.17.25(.3.14)**
accumulative **31.2.1(.9.4)**
accumulatively **1.31.30(.7.1)**
accumulator **17.12.4(.16)**
accuracy **1.22.16(.13)**
accurate **22.19.24(.9)**
accurately **1.31.22(.15)**
accurateness **34.18.16(.20.3)**
Accurist® **22.29.2(.29.4)**
accursed **22.29.16, 23.18.20**
accursedly **1.31.23(.14.7)**
accusal **40.32.13**
accusation **28.17.25(.3.11)**
accusatival **40.28.9**
accusative **31.2.1(.9.3)**
accusatively **1.31.30(.7.1)**
accusatorial **40.3.14(.5)**
accusatory **1.29.11(.8.2)**
accuse **35.17.7**
accuser **17.25.14**
accusingly **1.31.28(.1.12)**
accustom **27.15.9(.15)**
ace **34.4**
acedia **3.5.1**
Aceldama **17.17.14(.3)**
acellular **17.34.16(.21.4)**
acephalous **34.18.29(.17.4)**
acer **17.24.4**
acerb **21.15**
acerbic **24.2.9(.6)**
acerbically **1.31.24(.9.2)**
acerbity **1.10.16(.7)**
acescence **34.24.10(.18)**
acescent **22.26.15(.17.2)**
acetabula **17.34.16(.21.1)**
acetabulum **27.15.28(.11)**
acetal **40.6.5**
acetaldehyde **23.15.13**
acetaminophen **28.5.8**
acetanilide **23.15.16**
acetate **22.4.9(.5)**
acetic **24.2.10(.1)**
acetification **28.17.25(.3.5)**
acetify **14.14.4(.4)**
acetone **28.19.4(.5)**
acetose **34.20.4**
acetous **34.18.11(.1)**
acetyl **40.2.5, 40.13.3(.4)**
acetylcholine **28.1.27(.8), 28.2.31(.12)**
acetylene **28.1.27(.7)**
acetylide **23.15.16**
acetylsalicylic **24.2.27(.2)**
acey-deucy **1.22.15**
Achaea **17.1.5**

Achaean **28.17.1(.5)**
Achaemenid **23.2.13**
acharnement **11.8**
Achates **35.1.7(.2)**
ache **24.3**
Achebe **1.9.3**
achene **28.1.11**
Acheron **28.10.24(.5), 28.17.31(.11)**
Acheson **28.17.23(.14)**
Acheulian **28.3.21(.10)**
achievable **40.20.16(.19)**
achieve **31.1.5**
achievement **22.26.15(.13.5)**
achiever **17.21.1**
achillea **3.24.2, 17.1.17**
Achilles **35.1.23**
Achinese **35.1.12**
achingly **1.31.28(.1.6)**
achiral **40.16.13(.10)**
achondroplasia **3.15.3**
achondroplasic **24.2.21**
achondroplastic **24.2.10(.15.4)**
achoo **16.19**
achromat **22.7.11**
achromatic **24.2.10(.4.2)**
achromatically **1.31.24(.9.4)**
achromaticity **1.10.16(.16.1)**
achromatism **27.15.21(.2.4)**
achromatize **35.15.7(.7)**
achronical **40.23.12(.11)**
achy **1.12.3**
acicula **17.34.16(.21.2)**
acicular **17.34.16(.21.2)**
acid **23.2.16**
acidic **24.2.11(.2)**
acidification **28.17.25(.3.5)**
acidify **14.14.4(.5)**
acidimeter **17.12.16(.9.1)**
acidimetry **1.29.15(.8)**
acidity **1.10.16(.9)**
acidly **1.31.23(.14.7)**
acidness **34.18.16(.21.1)**
acidophilic **24.2.27(.2)**
acidophilus **34.18.29(.17.4)**
acidosis **34.2.17(.11.1)**
acidotic **24.2.10(.6)**
acidulate **22.4.23(.7.2)**
acidulation **28.17.25(.3.14)**
acidulous **34.18.29(.17.5)**
acini **14.13**
acinus **34.18.16(.15.3)**
ack **24.6**

ack-ack **24.6.9**
ackee **1.12.5**
ack emma **17.17.5**
Ackerman **28.17.16(.16)**
acknowledge **39.2.23**
acknowledgeable **40.20.16(.25)**
acknowledgement **22.26.15(.13.6)**
Ackroyd **23.13.19**
aclinic **24.2.15(.2)**
acme **1.15.16**
acne **1.16.21**
acolyte **22.16.25(.9)**
Aconcagua **17.7.12(.6), 17.31.7**
aconite **22.16.14(.6)**
aconitic **24.2.10(.2.2)**
aconitine **28.1.9(.3)**
acorn **28.11.5**
acotyledon **28.17.12(.1)**
acotyledonous **34.18.16(.15.2)**
acoustic **24.2.10(.15.4)**
acoustical **40.23.12(.7.3)**
acoustically **1.31.24(.9.6)**
acoustician **28.17.25(.2.2)**
acquaint **22.26.3**
acquaintance **34.24.10(.10)**
acquaintanceship **20.2.7(.22)**
acquest **22.29.5(.11)**
acquiesce **34.5**
acquiescence **34.24.10(.18)**
acquiescent **22.26.15(.17.2)**
acquiescingly **1.31.28(.1.11)**
acquirable **40.20.16(.27.2)**
acquire **17.6.13**
acquirement **22.26.15(.13.1)**
acquirer **17.32.14(.2)**
acquisition **28.17.25(.2.5)**
acquisitive **31.2.1(.9.3)**
acquisitively **1.31.30(.7.1)**
acquisitiveness **34.18.16(.28.1)**
acquit **22.2.23**
acquittal **40.21.2**
acquittance **34.24.10(.10)**
Acre **17.14.7**
acre **17.14.3**
acreage **39.2.22(.9)**
acrid **23.2.22**
acridine **28.1.10, 28.14.6**
acridity **1.10.16(.9)**
acridly **1.31.23(.14.7)**
acridness **34.18.16(.21.1)**

acriflavine 28.1.16,
28.2.20
Acrilan® 28.7.22
acrimonious 34.3.6(.7)
acrimoniously
1.31.33(.1.2)
acrimoniousness
34.18.16(.31.1)
acrimony 1.16.15(.11)
acrobat 22.7.6
acrobatic 24.2.10(.4.1)
acrobatically 1.31.24(.9.4)
acrocyanosis
34.2.17(.11.2)
acrogen 28.17.28(.9)
acrogenous
34.18.16(.15.3)
acrolect 22.23.4(.11)
acromegalic 24.2.27(.6)
acromegaly 1.31.17(.12)
acronycal 40.23.12(.11)
acronycally 1.31.24(.9.8)
acronychal 40.23.12(.11)
acronychally 1.31.24(.9.8)
acronym 27.2.6
acropetal 40.21.12
acropetally 1.31.17(.9.2)
acrophobia 3.3.9
acrophobic 24.2.9(.7)
acropolis 34.2.22(.8)
across 34.10.16
acrostic 24.2.10(.15.4)
acrylic 24.2.27(.2)
acrylonitrate 22.4.22(.8)
act 22.23.5
acta 17.12.21(.3)
actability 1.10.16(.22.1)
actable 40.20.16(.11.5)
Actaeon 28.17.1(.3)
actin 28.2.11(.12)
actinia 3.9.1
actiniae 2.3
actinic 24.2.15(.2)
actinide 23.15.8
actinism 27.15.21(.2.9)
actinium 27.3.8(.2)
actinometer17.12.16(.9.2)
actinomorphic
24.2.16(.5)
Actinomycetales 35.1.23
actinomycete 22.1.9
action 28.17.25(.15.3)
actionable 40.20.16(.16.3)
actionably 1.31.21(.6)
activate 22.4.16
activation 28.17.25(.3.9)
activator 17.12.4(.11)
active 31.2.1(.13.3)
actively 1.31.30(.7.2)
activeness 34.18.16(.28.1)
activism 27.15.21(.2.11)

activist 22.29.2(.20)
activity 1.10.16(.15)
acton 28.17.11(.20)
actor 17.12.21(.3)
actress 34.18.27(.14)
actressy 1.22.16(.13)
actual 40.16.12
actuality 1.10.16(.32.1)
actualization
28.17.25(.3.12)
actualize 35.15.21(.4.8)
actually 1.31.17(.24)
actuarial 40.3.14(.4)
actuarially 1.31.3(.11)
actuary 1.29.11(.3)
actuate 22.4.4
actuation 28.17.25(.3.1)
actuator 17.12.4(.2)
acuity 1.10.16(.5)
aculeate 22.3.13
acumen 28.17.16(.16)
acuminate 22.19.15(.9)
acupressure 17.26.4
acupuncture 17.28.20,
17.28.23
acupuncturist
22.29.2(.29.4)
acushla 17.34.29
acute 22.18.10
acutely 1.31.22(.14)
acuteness 34.18.16(.20.2)
acyclic 24.2.27(.16)
acyclovir 3.11.7
acyl 40.2.14, 40.13.12
ad 23.7
Ada 17.13.3
adage 39.2.11
adagio 15.1.11
Adam 27.15.10(.4)
adamance 34.24.10(.14)
adamancy 1.22.23(.10.3)
adamant 22.26.15(.13.2)
adamantine 28.14.5
adamantly 1.31.22(.20.3)
Adamite 22.16.13
Adams 35.25.10
Adamson 28.17.23(.23)
adapt 22.22.4
adaptability
1.10.16(.22.2)
adaptable 40.20.16(.11.4)
adaptableness
34.18.16(.37.4)
adaptably 1.31.21(.4.3)
adaptation 28.17.25(.3.3)
adapter 17.12.19
adaptive 31.2.1(.12)
adaptively 1.31.30(.7.2)
adaptiveness
34.18.16(.28.1)
adaptogen 28.17.28(.9)

adaptogenic 24.2.15(.4)
adaptor 17.12.19
adat 22.7.8
adaxial 40.3.10
ad captandum vulgus
34.18.14(.9)
Adcock 24.9.6
add 23.7
addax 34.23.5(.4)
addenda 17.13.20(.3)
addendum 27.15.10(.14)
adder 17.13.5
addict 22.23.2
addictedness
34.18.16(.21.1)
addiction 28.17.25(.15.1)
addictive 31.2.1(.13.1)
addictiveness
34.18.16(.28.1)
Addie 1.11.7
Addington 28.17.11(.23)
Addis Ababa 17.11.13
Addison 28.17.23(.14)
addition 28.17.25(.2.3)
additional 40.26.13(.14.1)
additionality
1.10.16(.32.8)
additionally
1.31.17(.14.3)
additive 31.2.1(.9.1)
addle 40.22.5
address 34.5.14(.6)
addressable
40.20.16(.21.1)
addressee 2.22
addresser 17.24.5
Addressograph®
30.7.5(.1)
adduce 34.17.13
adducible 40.20.16(.21.2)
adduct 22.23.8
adduction 28.17.25(.15.5)
adductive 31.2.1(.13.4)
adductor 17.12.21(.6)
Addy 1.11.7
Adela 17.34.4, 17.34.16(.8)
Adelaide 23.4.16
Adele 40.5.4
Adélie 1.31.4
Adelina 17.18.1
Adeline 28.14.19(.11)
Aden 28.17.12(.4)
Adenauer 17.3.6
Adeney 1.16.20
adenine 28.1.14, 28.14.9
adenocarcinoma
17.17.16(.6)
adenoid 23.13.12
adenoidal 40.22.9
adenoidally 1.31.17(.10)
adenoids 35.23.8

adenoma 17.17.16
adenomata 17.12.16(.9.3)
adenopathy 1.20.8
adenosine 28.1.18(.6)
adept 22.22.3
adeptly 1.31.22(.18)
adeptness 34.18.16(.20.4)
adequacy 1.22.16(.12)
adequate 22.19.23
adequately 1.31.22(.15)
adequateness
34.18.16(.20.3)
ad eundem 27.15.10(.14)
à deux 18
ad fin. 28.2
adhere 3.20
adherence 34.24.10(.16)
adherent 22.26.15(.23.1)
adhesion 28.17.26(.1)
adhesive 31.2.4(.1)
adhesively 1.31.30(.7.4)
adhesiveness
34.18.16(.28.2)
adhibit 22.2.6
adhibition 28.17.25(.2.1)
ad hoc 24.9
adhocracy 1.22.16(.13)
ad hominem 27.5.6
adiabatic 24.2.10(.4.1)
adiabatically
1.31.24(.9.4)
adiantum 27.15.9(.14)
Adidas® 34.7.8
Adie 1.11.4
adieu 16.24.6
adieux 35.17.7
Adi Granth 22.26.12
ad infinitum 27.15.9(.8)
ad initium 27.3.13
ad interim 27.2.14
adiós 34.10, 34.20
adipocere 3.14
adipose 34.20.2, 35.20.1
adiposity 1.10.16(.16.2)
Adirondack 24.6.8
adit 22.2.8
Adivasi 1.22.8
adjacency 1.22.23(.10.4)
adjacent 22.26.15(.17.1)
adjacently 1.31.22(.20.4)
adjectival 40.28.9
adjectivally 1.31.17(.17)
adjective 31.2.1(.13.4)
adjoin 28.12
adjourn 28.18.11
adjournment
22.26.15(.13.4)
adjudge 39.11
adjudgement
22.26.15(.13.6)

adjudicate 22.4.11(.6)
adjudication 28.17.25(.3.5)
adjudicative 31.2.1(.9.1)
adjudicator 17.12.4(.7)
adjunct 22.23.13
adjunctive 31.2.1(.13.5)
adjunctively 1.31.30(.7.2)
adjuration 28.17.25(.3.13)
adjuratory 1.29.11(.8.9)
adjure 12.18, 17.7.12(.4)
adjust 22.29.12
adjustability 1.10.16(.22.2)
adjustable 40.20.16(.11.7)
adjuster 17.12.24(.10)
adjustment 22.26.15(.13.3)
adjutage 39.2.10
adjutancy 1.22.23(.10.2)
adjutant 22.26.15(.9)
adjuvant 22.26.15(.16)
Adkins 35.26.2
Adlai 14.25.12
Adler 17.34.22
Adlerian 28.3.20(.2)
ad-lib 21.2
ad libitum 27.15.9(.10)
ad litem 27.15.9(.8)
adman 28.7.10(.12)
admass 34.7.11
admeasure 17.27.3
admeasurement 22.26.15(.13.2)
admen 28.5.7(.16)
admin 28.2.17(.8)
adminicle 40.23.12(.11)
adminicular 17.34.16(.21.2)
administer 17.12.24(.14)
administrable 40.20.16(.27.6)
administrant 22.26.15(.23.4)
administrate 22.4.22(.8)
administration 28.17.25(.3.13)
administrative 31.2.1(.9.4)
administratively 1.31.30(.7.1)
administrator 17.12.4(.15)
administratorship 20.2.7(.9)
administratrices 35.1.16(.10)
administratrix 34.23.2(.12)
admirable 40.20.16(.27.4)
admirableness 34.18.16(.37.4)

admirably 1.31.21(.8)
admiral 40.16.13(.12.2)
admiralship 20.2.7(.24)
admiralty 1.10.28
admiration 28.17.25(.3.13)
admire 17.6.7
admirer 17.32.14(.2)
admiringly 1.31.28(.1.17)
admissibility 1.10.16(.22.2)
admissible 40.20.16(.21.1)
admission 28.17.25(.2.4)
admissive 31.2.4(.2)
admit 22.2.11
admittable 40.20.16(.11.1)
admittance 34.24.10(.10)
admittedly 1.31.23(.14.3)
admix 34.23.2(.5)
admixture 17.28.24
admonish 36.2.16(.8)
admonishment 22.26.15(.13.6)
admonition 28.17.25(.2.4)
admonitory 1.29.11(.8.7)
adnate 22.4.14(.12)
ad nauseam 27.6.1
adnexa 17.24.20
adnexal 40.31.18
adnominal 40.26.13(.8)
ado 16.8
adobe 1.9.13
adolescence 34.24.10(.18)
adolescent 22.26.15(.17.2)
Adonis 34.2.13
adopt 22.22.5
adoptee 2.11
adopter 17.12.19
adoption 28.17.25(.14)
adoptive 31.2.1(.12)
adoptively 1.31.30(.7.2)
adorable 40.20.16(.27.2)
adorably 1.31.21(.8)
adoral 40.16.13(.8)
adoration 28.17.25(.3.13)
adore 12.6
adorer 17.32.10(.3)
adoringly 1.31.28(.1.17)
adorn 28.11.4
adorned 23.24.10
adornment 22.26.15(.13.4)
adown 28.8.2
ad personam 27.6.9
ad rem 27.5
adrenal 40.26.1
adrenalin 28.2.31(.10)
adrenocorticotrophic 24.2.16(.4)
adrenocorticotrophin 28.2.19

adrenocorticotropic 24.2.8(.5)
Adrian 28.3.20(.12)
Adrianne 28.7
Adriatic 24.2.10(.4.1)
Adrienne 28.3.20(.12), 28.5
adrift 22.27.1
adroit 22.14
adroitly 1.31.22(.11)
adroitness 34.18.16(.20.2)
adscititious 34.18.22(.2)
adsorb 21.9
adsorbable 40.20.16(.10)
adsorbate 22.4.8, 22.19.9
adsorbent 22.26.15(.8)
adsorption 28.17.25(.14)
adsorptive 31.2.1(.12)
adsuki 1.12.12
adsum 27.11.10, 27.13.1
adulate 22.4.23(.7.2)
adulation 28.17.25(.3.14)
adulator 17.12.4(.16)
adulatory 1.29.11(.8.2)
Adullamite 22.16.13
adult 22.32.8
adulterant 22.26.15(.23.3)
adulterate 22.4.22(.6)
adulteration 28.17.25(.3.13)
adulterator 17.12.4(.15)
adulterer 17.32.14(.6)
adulteress 34.18.27(.14)
adulterine 28.14.18
adulterous 34.18.27(.14)
adulterously 1.31.33(.12.5)
adulterousness 34.18.16(.31.5)
adultery 1.29.11(.8.12)
adulthood 23.16.5(.6)
adultly 1.31.22(.23)
adultness 34.18.16(.20.4)
adumbrate 22.4.22(.7)
adumbration 28.17.25(.3.13)
adumbrative 31.2.1(.3)
ad valorem 27.5.13
advance 34.24.6
advancement 22.26.15(.13.5)
advancer 17.24.22(.3)
advantage 39.2.10
advantageous 34.18.24
advantageously 1.31.33(.12.4)
advantageousness 34.18.16(.31.5)
advect 22.23.4(.6)
advection 28.17.25(.15.2)
advective 31.2.1(.13.2)

advent 22.26.4(.10), 22.26.15(.16)
Adventism 27.15.21(.2.4)
Adventist 22.29.2(.13)
adventitious 34.18.22(.2)
adventitiously 1.31.33(.12.4)
adventure 17.28.22
adventurer 17.32.14(.17)
adventuresome 27.15.20(.11)
adventuress 34.18.27(.25)
adventurism 27.15.21(.2.14)
adventurist 22.29.2(.29.4)
adventurous 34.18.27(.25)
adventurously 1.31.33(.12.5)
adventurousness 34.18.16(.31.5)
adverb 21.15
adverbial 40.3.2
adverbially 1.31.3(.2)
ad verbum 27.15.8
adversarial 40.3.14(.4)
adversary 1.29.11(.18)
adversative 31.2.1(.9.3)
adversatively 1.31.30(.7.1)
adverse 34.19.6
adversely 1.31.33(.12.6)
adverseness 34.18.16(.31.7)
adversity 1.10.16(.16.2)
advert 22.20.9
advertence 34.24.10(.10)
advertency 1.22.23(.10.2)
advertent 22.26.15(.9)
advertently 1.31.22(.20.2)
advertise 35.15.7(.7)
advertisement 22.26.15(.13.5)
advertiser 17.25.12(.2)
advertorial 40.3.14(.5)
advice 34.15.7
advisability 1.10.16(.22.2)
advisable 40.20.16(.22)
advisableness 34.18.16(.37.4)
advisably 1.31.21(.7.2)
advise 35.15.14
advisedly 1.31.23(.14.7)
advisee 2.23
adviser 17.25.12(.8)
advisory 1.29.11(.19)
advocaat 10.8.8
advocacy 1.22.16(.6)
advocate 22.4.11(.6), 22.19.12(.10)
advocateship 20.2.8

advocation 28.17.25(.3.5)
advocatory 1.29.11(.8.6)
advowson 28.17.24(.5)
adyta 17.12.16(.6)
adytum 27.15.9(.10)
adze 35.23.4
adzuki 1.12.12
aedes 35.1.8
aedile 40.13.4
aedileship 20.2.7(.24)
Aegean 28.17.1(.11)
aegis 34.2.18
Aegisthus 34.18.19
aegrotat 22.7.7
aelectasis 34.2.17(.10.2)
Aelfric 24.2.26(.19)
Aeneas 34.18.1
Aeneid 23.2.1, 23.2.2
aeolian 28.3.21(.11)
Aeolic 24.2.27(.9)
aeolotropy 1.8.11(.8)
Aeolus 34.18.29(.17.1)
aeon 28.10.1, 28.17.1
aeonian 28.3.8(.11)
aepyornis 34.2.13
aerate 22.4.22
aeration 28.17.25(.3.13)
aerator 17.12.4(.15)
aerenchyma 17.17.14(.4)
aerial 40.3.14(.4)
aerialist 22.29.2(.31.1)
aeriality 1.10.16(.32.1)
aerially 1.31.3(.11)
aerie 1.29.2, 1.29.4,
  1.29.11(.2)
aeriform 27.10.5(.2)
Aer Lingus® 34.18.14(.8)
aero 19.27.3
aerobatic 24.2.10(.4.1)
aerobe 21.16.2
aerobic 24.2.9(.7)
aerobically 1.31.24(.9.2)
aerobiologist
  22.29.2(.26.2)
aerobiology 1.26.10(.11.1)
aerodrome 27.17.13
aerodynamic 24.2.14(.4)
aerodynamically
  1.31.24(.9.8)
aerodynamicist
  22.29.2(.22)
aerodyne 28.14.6
aero engine 28.17.28(.12)
Aeroflot® 22.11.17
aerofoil 40.11.7
aerogramme 27.6.17(.5)
aerolite 22.16.25(.9)
aerological 40.23.12(.17.2)
aerologist 22.29.2(.26.4)
aerology 1.26.10(.11.5)

aeromagnetic
  24.2.10(.3.1)
aeronaut 22.13.6
aeronautic 24.2.10(.7)
aeronautical
  40.23.12(.7.2)
aeronautically
  1.31.24(.9.4)
aeronomy 1.15.13(.5)
aeroplane 28.4.19
aerosol 40.9.14
aerospace 34.4.2
aerostat 22.7.7
aerostatic 24.2.10(.4.1)
aerostatically
  1.31.24(.9.4)
aerotow 19.10.12, 19.10.14
aerotrain 28.4.18
Aertex® 34.23.4(.3)
aeruginous 34.18.16(.15.3)
Aeschines 35.1.12(.3)
Aeschylean 28.17.1(.13)
Aeschylus 34.18.29(.17.2)
Aesculapian 28.3.1
Aesop 20.7.8
aesthete 22.1.8
aesthetic 24.2.10(.3.2)
aesthetical 40.23.12(.7.1)
aesthetically 1.31.24(.9.3)
aesthetician 28.17.25(.2.2)
aestheticism
  27.15.21(.2.12)
aestival 40.28.9, 40.28.11
aestivate 22.4.16
aestivation 28.17.25(.3.9)
aetatis 34.2.8
aetiologic 24.2.24(.4)
aetiological
  40.23.12(.17.2)
aetiologically
  1.31.24(.9.11)
aetiology 1.26.10(.11.1)
Afar 10.12
afar 10.12
afeard 23.3
affability 1.10.16(.22.1)
affable 40.20.16(.18)
affably 1.31.21(.7.1)
affair 6.10
affaire 6.10
affairé 4.26.3
affaire de cœur 18
affaires de cœur 18
affect 22.23.4(.5)
affectation 28.17.25(.3.3)
affectedly 1.31.23(.14.3)
affectingly 1.31.28(.1.4)
affection 28.17.25(.15.2)
affectionally
  1.31.17(.14.3)
affectionate 22.19.15(.9)

affectionately
  1.31.22(.15)
affective 31.2.1(.13.2)
affectively 1.31.30(.7.2)
affectiveness
  34.18.16(.28.1)
affectivity 1.10.16(.15)
affenpinscher 17.28.22
afferent 22.26.15(.23.3)
affiance 34.24.10(.5)
affiant 22.26.15(.4)
affiche 36.1
affidavit 22.2.14
affiliate 22.3.13, 22.4.2(.15)
affiliation 28.17.25(.3.1)
affined 23.24.13
affinity 1.10.16(.13)
affirm 27.16.4
affirmable 40.20.16(.15)
affirmation 28.17.25(.3.7)
affirmative 31.2.1(.9.2)
affirmatively
  1.31.30(.7.1)
affirmatory 1.29.11(.8.7)
affirmer 17.17.15
affix 34.23.2(.7)
affixture 17.28.24
afflatus 34.18.11(.3)
afflict 22.23.2
affliction 28.17.25(.15.1)
afflictive 31.2.1(.13.1)
afflictively 1.31.30(.7.2)
affluence 34.24.10(.6)
affluent 22.26.15(.5)
affluential 40.33.12(.2)
affluently 1.31.22(.20.1)
afflux 34.23.11
afforce 34.12.4
afford 23.12.5
affordability
  1.10.16(.22.2)
affordable 40.20.16(.12)
affordably 1.31.21(.4.4)
afforest 22.29.15(.17)
afforestation
  28.17.25(.3.3)
affranchise 35.15.17
affray 4.26.17
affreightment
  22.26.15(.13.3)
affricate 22.19.12(.10)
affrication 28.17.25(.3.5)
affricative 31.2.1(.9.1)
affright 22.16.24(.16)
affront 22.26.12
affusion 28.17.26(.4)
Afghan 28.7.9
Afghani 1.16.6, 1.16.8
Afghanistan 28.9.2
aficionado 19.11.7
afield 23.31.1(.2)

afire 17.6.9
aflame 27.4.9
aflatoxin 28.2.23(.14)
afloat 22.21.15
aflutter 17.12.12
afon 28.10.16, 28.17.20(.5)
afoot 22.17
afore 12.11
aforementioned
  23.24.16(.12)
aforesaid 23.5.10
aforethought 22.13.9
a fortiori 14.24.4
afoul 40.7
afraid 23.4.15
afreet 22.1.17
afresh 36.5
afric 24.2.26(.19)
Africa 17.14.15(.14)
African 28.17.13(.13)
Africana 17.18.8(.3)
Africanism 27.15.21(.2.9)
Africanist 22.29.2(.18.1)
Africanization
  28.17.25(.3.12)
Africanize 35.15.12(.5)
Afrikaans 34.24.6, 35.26.9
Afrika Korps 12
Afrikander 17.13.20(.4)
Afrikaner 17.18.8(.3)
afrit 22.2.24
Afro 19.27.20
Afrocentric 24.2.26(.14.4)
afrormosia 3.15.8
AFSCME 1.15.18
aft 22.27.4
after 17.12.23
afterbirth 32.15.1
afterburner 17.18.17
aftercare 6.6
afterdeck 24.4.5
afterglow 19.29.20
aftergrass 34.9.6
afterlife 30.12
afterlight 22.16.25(.9)
afterlives 35.28.6
aftermarket 22.2.9(.4)
aftermath 32.6.3
aftermost 22.29.17(.4)
afternoon 28.16.8
afterpains 35.26.4
afterpart 22.10.1
aftershave 31.3.4
aftershock 24.9.11
aftertaste 22.29.4
afterthought 22.13.9
afterward 23.18.26(.7)
afterword 23.19.8
afterworld 23.31.12
Aga® 17.16.6

Agadir **3.5**
Agag **26.5.3**
again **28.4.6, 28.5.6**
against **22.29.21**
Aga Khan **28.9**
agama **17.17.14(.5)**
Agamemnon **28.10.14, 28.17.17(.14)**
agamic **24.2.14(.4)**
agamogenesis **34.2.17(.10.3)**
agamogenetic **24.2.10(.3.1)**
agamospermy **1.15.14**
agamous **34.18.15(.10)**
agapanthus **34.18.19**
agape **2.9, 4.7, 20.3**
agapemone **1.16.15(.11)**
agar **10.9, 17.16.3**
agaric **24.2.26(.10)**
agate **22.19.13**
Agatha **17.22.9**
agave **1.19.3, 1.19.6, 31.3.3**
agaze **35.4.6**
agba **17.11.16**
age **39.4**
aged **23.18.25, 23.30**
Agee **1.26.2**
ageing **29.1.28**
ageism **27.15.21(.2.13)**
ageist **22.29.2(.26.1)**
ageless **34.18.29(.37)**
agelessness **34.18.16(.31.6)**
agency **1.22.23(.10.4)**
agenda **17.13.20(.3)**
agendum **27.15.10(.14)**
agent **22.26.15(.21)**
agential **40.33.12(.3)**
agent provocateur **18.3**
agents provocateurs **35.19**
ager **17.29.3**
ageratum **27.15.9(.2)**
Agfa® **17.20.16**
Aggie **1.14.5**
aggiornamento **19.10.17**
agglomerate **22.4.22(.6), 22.19.24(.9)**
agglomeration **28.17.25(.3.13)**
agglomerative **31.2.1(.9.4)**
agglutinate **22.4.14(.9.1), 22.19.15(.9)**
agglutination **28.17.25(.3.8)**
agglutinative **31.2.1(.9.2)**
agglutinin **28.2.18**
aggrandize **35.15.8**

aggrandizement **22.26.15(.13.5)**
aggrandizer **17.25.12(.3)**
aggravate **22.4.16**
aggravatingly **1.31.28(.1.4)**
aggravation **28.17.25(.3.9)**
aggregate **22.4.12(.5), 22.19.13**
aggregation **28.17.25(.3.6)**
aggregative **31.2.1(.9.1)**
aggress **34.5.14(.8)**
aggression **28.17.25(.4)**
aggressive **31.2.4(.4)**
aggressively **1.31.30(.7.4)**
aggressiveness **34.18.16(.28.2)**
aggressor **17.24.5**
aggrieve **31.1.8**
aggrievedly **1.31.23(.14.7)**
aggro **19.27.18**
aghast **22.29.6(.6), 22.29.8(.4)**
agile **40.13.14**
agilely **1.31.38**
agility **1.10.16(.28)**
agin **28.2.15**
Agincourt **12.7, 22.13.4**
agio **15.1.11**
agiotage **37.4.3, 39.2.10**
agist **22.29.2(.26.1)**
agistment **22.26.15(.13.3)**
agitate **22.4.9(.5)**
agitatedly **1.31.23(.14.3)**
agitation **28.17.25(.3.3)**
agitato **19.10.7**
agitator **17.12.4(.5)**
agitprop **20.7.12**
agleam **27.1.13**
aglet **22.19.26(.20)**
agley **2.32.9(.13), 4.28.13, 14.25.13**
aglow **19.29.20**
agma **17.17.20**
agnail **40.4.7**
agnate **22.4.14(.13)**
agnatic **24.2.10(.4.3)**
agnation **28.17.25(.3.8)**
Agnes **34.18.16(.23)**
Agnew **16.24.10**
Agni **1.16.22**
agnomen **28.5.7(.12)**
agnosia **3.14.11, 3.15.8**
agnostic **24.2.10(.15.4)**
agnosticism **27.15.21(.2.12)**
Agnus Dei **2.4**
ago **19.13**
agog **26.7.6**
agogo **19.13.11**
agonic **24.2.15(.6.1)**

agonisingly **1.31.28(.1.12)**
agonist **22.29.2(.18.1)**
Agonistes **35.1.7(.10)**
agonistic **24.2.10(.15.2)**
agonistically **1.31.24(.9.6)**
agonize **35.15.12(.5)**
agonizingly **1.31.28(.1.12)**
agony **1.16.15(.10)**
agoraphobe **21.16.1**
agoraphobia **3.3.9**
agoraphobic **24.2.9(.7)**
agouti **1.10.15**
Agra **17.32.22**
agrapha **17.20.12(.5)**
agraphon **28.10.15**
agrarian **28.3.20(.4)**
agree **2.30.12**
agreeable **40.20.16(.1)**
agreeableness **34.18.16(.37.4)**
agreeably **1.31.21(.2)**
agreement **22.26.15(.13.1)**
agribusiness **34.18.16(.32)**
agribusinessman **28.17.16(.29)**
agrichemical **40.23.12(.10)**
Agricola **17.34.16(.9)**
agricultural **40.16.13(.12.3)**
agriculturalist **22.29.2(.31.4)**
agriculturally **1.31.17(.27.2)**
agriculture **17.28.26**
agriculturist **22.29.2(.29.4)**
agrimony **1.16.15(.11)**
Agrippa **17.10.2**
agrochemical **40.23.12(.10)**
agroforestry **1.29.15(.17)**
agro-industry **1.29.15(.17)**
agronomic **24.2.14(.6)**
agronomical **40.23.12(.10)**
agronomically **1.31.24(.9.8)**
agronomist **22.29.2(.17)**
agronomy **1.15.13(.5)**
aground **23.24.7(.10)**
ague **16.24.8**
Aguecheek **24.1.8**
Aguilar **10.25**
aguish **36.2.5**
Agulhas **34.18.29(.13)**
Agutter **17.12.12, 17.12.16(.8)**
ah **10**
aha **10.21**

Ahab **21.6**
Ahasuerus **34.18.27(.2)**
ahead **23.5.13**
ahem **27.5.12**
Aherne **28.18.12**
ahimsa **10.15**
ahistoric **24.2.26(.6)**
ahistorical **40.23.12(.18)**
Ahmadabad **23.7.6, 23.9.6**
Ahmed **23.5.6**
ahold **23.31.13(.9)**
ahoy **13.13**
ahull **40.12**
ai **14**
aid **23.4**
Aïda **17.13.1**
Aidan **28.17.12(.4)**
aide **23.4**
aide-de-camp **11.7**
aide-memoire **10.22, 10.22.8**
aider **17.13.3**
aides-memoire **10.22.8**
aides-memoires **35.9**
Aids **35.23.3**
aiglet **22.19.26(.20)**
aigrette **22.5.19**
Aigues-Mortes **22.13.5**
aiguille **2.29, 40.1.14**
aiguillette **22.5.20**
Aiken **28.17.13(.3)**
aikido **19.11.1**
ail **40.4**
ailanthus **34.18.19**
Aileen **28.1.27(.2)**
aileron **28.10.24(.5)**
ailment **22.26.15(.13.7)**
Ailsa **17.24.24**
ailurophile **40.13.9**
ailurophobe **21.16.1**
ailurophobia **3.3.9**
aim **27.4**
Aimée **1.15.3, 4.13**
aimless **34.18.29(.26)**
aimlessly **1.31.33(.12.6)**
aimlessness **34.18.16(.31.6)**
ain **28.4**
Ainsley **1.31.34**
ain't **22.26.3**
Aintree **2.30.10**
Ainu **16.12**
aioli **1.31.19**
air **6**
air bag **26.5.1**
airbase **34.4.3**
air bed **23.5.2**
airborne **28.11.2**
air brake **24.3.13**
airbrick **24.2.26(.13)**

airbrush 36.12
airburst 22.29.16
airbus 34.14
aircraft 22.27.4(.4)
aircraftman 28.17.16(.21)
aircraftsman 28.17.16(.29)
aircraftswoman 28.17.16(.14)
aircraftswomen 28.2.17(.1)
aircraftwoman 28.17.16(.14)
aircraftwomen 28.2.17(.1)
aircrew 16.23.10
airdate 22.4.10
Airdrie 1.29.16
airdrop 20.7.12
Airedale 40.4.3
airer 17.32.5
airfare 6.10
airfield 23.31.1(.2)
airflow 19.29.21
airfoil 40.11.7
airframe 27.4.8
airfreight 22.4.22(.12)
airglow 19.29.20
air gun 28.13.5
airhead 23.5.13(.3)
airhole 40.18.13
airily 1.31.17(.27.1)
airiness 34.18.16(.2.9)
airing 29.1.30(.4)
air lane 28.4.19
airless 34.18.29(.6)
airlessly 1.31.33(.12.6)
airlessness 34.18.16(.31.6)
airlift 22.27.1
airline 28.14.19(.5)
airliner 17.18.13(.14)
airlock 24.9.16(.2)
airmail 40.4.6
airman 28.17.16(.6)
airmiss 34.2.12
airmobile 40.1.2
airplane 28.4.19
airplay 4.28.9
air pocket 22.2.9(.5)
airport 22.13.1
airscrew 16.23.10
air shaft 22.27.4(.3)
airship 20.2.7(.4)
airsick 24.2.20(.4)
airsickness 34.18.16(.22)
airside 23.15.11(.5)
airspace 34.4.2
airspeed 23.1.1
airstream 27.1.12
airstrip 20.2.11
airtight 22.16.9

airtime 27.12.1
airwave 31.3.6
airway 4.25.4
airwoman 28.17.16(.14)
airwomen 28.2.17(.1)
airworthiness 34.18.16(.2.6)
airworthy 1.21
airy 1.29.4
aisle 40.13
ait 22.4
aitch 38.3
aitchbone 28.19.3
Aitchison 28.17.23(.14)
Aitken 28.2.13(.2)
Aix-en-Provence 34.11
Aix-la-Chapelle 40.5.1
Ajaccio 15.1.7
ajar 10.20
Ajax 34.23.5(.12)
ajuga 17.16.12
aka 4, 17.14.5
Akai 14.10
akala 17.34.8
Akbar 10.5.9
akebia 3.3.1
akee 1.12.5
Akela 17.34.4
Akerman 28.17.16(.16)
Akhenaten 28.17.11(.8)
Akhetaten 28.17.11(.8)
akimbo 19.9.14
akin 28.2.13
Akins 35.26.2
Akita 17.12.1(.4)
Akkad 23.7.9
Akkadian 28.3.4(.3)
Akko 19.12
Akron 28.10.24(.9), 28.17.31(.16)
Aksai Chin 28.2
Aksum 27.11.10, 27.13.1
Al 40.6
à la 7, 10
Alabama 17.17.6
Alabaman 28.17.16(.7)
Alabamian 28.3.7
alabaster 17.12.24(.5)
alabastrine 28.2.29(.8), 28.14.18
à la carte 22.10
alack 24.6.23
alacrity 1.10.16(.21.3)
Aladdin 28.2.12
Alamein 28.4.7
Alamo 19.14.12
à la mode 23.20
Alan 28.17.33(.5)
Alana 17.18.6
alanine 28.1.14, 28.14.9

alar 10.25.1, 17.34.4
Alaric 24.2.26(.10)
alarm 27.8.10
alarmed 23.23.5
alarmingly 1.31.28(.1.7)
alarmism 27.15.21(.2.8)
alarmist 22.29.2(.17)
alarum 27.15.26(.4)
alas 34.7.19, 34.9.7
Alaska 17.14.23
Alaskan 28.17.13(.18)
Alastor 17.12.24(.5)
alate 22.4.23(.3)
alb 21.18
Alba 17.11.20
Albacete 1.10.3
albacore 12.7
Alban 28.17.10
Albania 3.9.3(.1)
Albanian 28.3.8(.3)
Albany 1.16.15(.6)
albata 17.12.4(.4)
albatross 34.10.16
albedo 19.11.1
Albee 1.9.24
albeit 22.2.1
Albemarle 40.8.8
Albert 22.19.9
Alberta 17.12.17
Albertan 28.17.11(.16)
Alberti 1.10.17
albescence 34.24.10(.18)
albescent 22.26.15(.17.2)
Albigenses 35.1.16(.15)
Albigensian 28.3.13
albinism 27.15.21(.2.9)
albino 19.15.1
Albinoni 1.16.17(.8)
albinotic 24.2.10(.6)
Albion 28.3.2
albite 22.16.8
Albright 22.16.24(.11)
album 27.15.8
albumen 28.17.16(.16)
albumin 28.17.16(.16)
albuminoid 23.13.12
albuminous 34.18.16(.15.3)
albuminuria 3.22.12
Albuquerque 1.12.14
alburnum 27.15.14(.12)
Albury 1.29.11(.7.2)
Alcaeus 34.3.10, 34.18.1
alcaic 24.2.3
alcalde 1.11.23
Alcan® 28.7.8
Alcatraz 35.7
Alcazar 10.16, 17.25.5
Alceste 22.29.5(.6)
Alcester 17.12.24(.25)

Alcestis 34.2.8
alchemic 24.2.14(.3)
alchemical 40.23.12(.10)
alchemist 22.29.2(.17)
alchemize 35.15.11
alchemy 1.15.13(.3)
alcheringa 17.16.17(.1)
Alcibiades 35.1.8
alcid 23.2.16
Alcock 24.9.6
alcohol 40.9.17
alcoholic 24.2.27(.9)
alcoholism 27.15.21(.2.15)
alcoholometer 17.12.16(.9.2)
alcoholometry 1.29.15(.8)
Alconbury 1.29.11(.7.2)
Alcoran 28.7.20, 28.9.13
Alcott 22.11.6, 22.19.12(.15)
alcove 31.12
Alcuin 28.2.28
Aldabra 17.32.18
Aldebaran 28.17.31(.11)
Aldeburgh 17.32.14(.5)
aldehyde 23.15.13
aldehydic 24.2.11(.2)
Alden 28.17.12(.27)
al dente 1.10.23(.3)
alder 17.13.23(.5)
Aldergrove 31.12
alderman 28.17.16(.16)
aldermanic 24.2.15(.5)
aldermanry 1.29.20
aldermanship 20.2.7(.19)
Aldermaston 28.17.11(.25)
Alderney 1.16.15(.8)
Aldersgate 22.4.12(.11)
Aldershot 22.11.12
Alderson 28.17.23(.14)
Alderton 28.17.11(.15)
alderwoman 28.17.16(.14)
alderwomen 28.2.17(.1)
Aldgate 22.4.12(.8), 22.19.13
Aldine 28.1.10, 28.14.6
Aldis 34.2.9
aldol 40.9.8
aldosterone 28.19.17
Aldous 34.18.12
Aldridge 39.2.22(.12)
Aldrin 28.2.29(.9)
Aldwych 38.2.9
ale 40.4
aleatoric 24.2.26(.6)
aleatory 1.29.11(.8.1)
Alec 24.2.27(.6)
alecost 22.29.9

alee **2.32**
alegar **17.16.13**
alehouse **34.8.6(.24)**
Aleksandrovsk **24.20.14**
alembic **24.2.9(.8)**
alembicated **23.18.9(.3)**
alembication **28.17.25(.3.5)**
aleph **30.2.6, 30.4**
Aleppo **19.8**
alert **22.20.16**
alertly **1.31.22(.16)**
alertness **34.18.16(.20.3)**
aleuron **28.17.31(.11)**
aleurone **28.19.17**
Aleut **22.18.1, 22.18.11**
Aleutian **28.17.25(.11)**
alewife **30.12**
alewives **35.28.6**
Alex **34.23.2(.13)**
Alexa **17.24.20**
Alexander **17.13.20(.4)**
alexanders **35.18.9**
Alexandra **17.32.20**
Alexandretta **17.12.5(.9)**
Alexandria **3.22.16**
Alexandrian **28.3.20(.12)**
alexandrine **28.2.29(.9), 28.14.18**
alexandrite **22.16.24(.13)**
alexia **3.14.15**
alexin **28.2.23(.14)**
alexine **28.1.18(.7)**
alexipharmic **24.2.14(.5)**
Alexis **34.2.17(.14)**
alfa **17.20.19**
Alfa-Laval **40.6.11**
alfalfa **17.20.19**
AlfaRomeo® **19.2**
al-Fatah **10.6, 17.12.6**
alfisol **40.9.14**
Alfonso **19.20.16, 19.21**
Alford **23.18.16(.22)**
Alfred **23.18.27**
alfresco **19.12.17**
Alfreton **28.17.11(.15)**
Alfven **28.17.20(.12)**
Alfvén **28.4.10**
alga **17.16.19**
algae **2.15, 2.27**
algal **40.24.15**
Algarve **31.6**
algebra **17.32.18**
algebraic **24.2.3**
algebraical **40.23.12(.2)**
algebraically **1.31.24(.9.1)**
algebraist **22.29.2(.3)**
Algeciras **34.18.27(.2)**
Algeo **15.1.11**
Alger **17.29.16(.9)**

Algeria **3.22.2**
Algerian **28.3.20(.2)**
Algernon **28.10.14, 28.17.17(.10)**
algicide **23.15.11(.6)**
algid **23.2.20**
algidity **1.10.16(.9)**
Algie **1.26.14**
Algiers **35.3**
alginate **22.4.14(.9.3), 22.19.15(.9)**
alginic **24.2.15(.2)**
Algipan **28.7.4**
Algoa **17.9.5**
algoid **23.13.10**
Algol **40.9.10**
algolagnia **3.9.13**
algolagnic **24.2.15(.13)**
algological **40.23.12(.17.2)**
algologist **22.29.2(.26.3)**
algology **1.26.10(.11.3)**
Algonquian **28.3.5, 28.3.19**
Algonquin **28.2.13(.13), 28.2.28**
algorithm **27.15.19**
algorithmic **24.2.14(.15)**
algorithmically **1.31.24(.9.8)**
alguacil **40.1.10, 40.2.14**
alguaciles **35.4.18**
alguazil **40.1.11, 40.2.15**
alguaziles **35.4.18**
Algy **1.26.14**
Alhambra **17.32.18**
Alhambresque **24.20.3**
Ali **1.31.7, 1.31.9, 2.32**
alias **34.3.16**
Ali Baba **17.11.7**
alibi **14.7**
Alicante **1.10.23(.4)**
Alice **34.2.22(.5)**
Alicia **3.14.2, 3.16.2, 17.26.2**
Alick **24.2.27(.6)**
alicyclic **24.2.27(.16)**
alidad **23.7.8**
alidade **23.4.4**
alien **28.3.21(.3)**
alienability **1.10.16(.22.2)**
alienable **40.20.16(.16.1)**
alienage **39.2.15**
alienate **22.4.14(.3)**
alienation **28.17.25(.3.8)**
alienator **17.12.4(.10)**
alienism **27.15.21(.2.9)**
alienist **22.29.2(.18.1)**
aliform **27.10.5(.2)**
alight **22.16.25**
align **28.14.19**
alignment **22.26.15(.13.4)**

alike **24.13.7**
aliment **22.26.15(.13.2)**
alimental **40.21.17(.2)**
alimentary **1.29.11(.8.12)**
alimentation **28.17.25(.3.3)**
alimony **1.16.15(.11)**
alineation **28.17.25(.3.1)**
alinement **22.26.15(.13.4)**
aliphatic **24.2.10(.4.4)**
aliquant **22.26.15(.22)**
aliquot **22.11.14**
Alisdair **6.4, 17.12.24(.14)**
Alison **28.17.23(.14)**
Alissa **17.24.2**
Alistair **6.4, 17.12.24(.14)**
Alitalia® **3.24.5**
alive **31.9**
aliveness **34.18.16(.28.1)**
Alix **34.23.2(.13)**
aliyah **17.1.17**
alizarin **28.2.29(.5)**
alizarine **28.1.25(.3)**
alkahest **22.29.5(.10)**
alkalescence **34.24.10(.18)**
alkalescency **1.22.23(.10.4)**
alkalescent **22.26.15(.17.2)**
alkali **14.25.9**
alkalify **14.14.4(.16)**
alkalimeter **17.12.16(.9.1)**
alkalimetry **1.29.15(.8)**
alkaline **28.14.19(.11)**
alkalinity **1.10.16(.13)**
alkaloid **23.13.20**
alkaloidal **40.22.9**
alkaloses **35.1.16(.11)**
alkalosis **34.2.17(.11.2)**
alkane **28.4.5**
alkanet **22.5.9(.2)**
Alka-Seltzer® **17.24.19**
alkene **28.1.11**
alkyd **23.2.10**
alkyl **40.2.7, 40.13.5**
alkylate **22.4.23(.7.1)**
alkyne **28.14.7**
all **40.10**
alla breve **1.19.3**
alla cappella **17.34.5(.1)**
Allah **17.34.6**
Allahabad **23.7.6, 23.9.6**
allamanda **17.13.20(.4)**
allanite **22.16.14(.6)**
allantoic **24.2.7**
allantoid **23.13.7**
allantoides **35.1.8**
allantoin **28.2.8**
allantois **34.2.5**

Allaun **28.11.13**
allay **4.28**
Allbeury **1.29.11(.3)**
allegation **28.17.25(.3.6)**
allege **39.5**
alleged **23.18.25, 23.30**
allegedly **1.31.23(.14.7)**
Allegheny **1.16.4**
allegiance **34.24.10(.21)**
allegiant **22.26.15(.21)**
allegoric **24.2.26(.6)**
allegorical **40.23.12(.18)**
allegorically **1.31.24(.9.12)**
allegorist **22.29.2(.29.3)**
allegorization **28.17.25(.3.12)**
allegorize **35.15.20(.2)**
allegory **1.29.11(.11)**
allegretto **19.10.4**
allegro **19.27.18**
allel **40.5.19**
allele **40.1.16**
allelic **24.2.27(.1)**
allelomorph **30.9.2**
allelomorphic **24.2.16(.5)**
allemande **23.24.6(.8)**
Allen **28.17.33(.5)**
Allenby **1.9.19**
Allende **1.11.20(.3), 4.10.12**
Allentown **28.8.1**
allergen **28.5.15, 28.17.28(.9)**
allergenic **24.2.15(.4)**
allergic **24.2.24(.6)**
allergist **22.29.2(.26.1)**
allergy **1.26.10(.10)**
Allerton **28.17.11(.15)**
alleviate **22.4.2(.8)**
alleviation **28.17.25(.3.1)**
alleviative **31.2.1(.2)**
alleviator **17.12.4(.1)**
alleviatory **1.29.11(.8.1)**
alley **1.31.7**
Alleyne **28.1.27, 28.4.19, 28.17.33(.5)**
alleyway **4.25.2**
alliaceous **34.18.22(.3)**
alliance **34.24.10(.5)**
allicin **28.2.23(.9)**
allied **23.15.16**
alligator **17.12.4(.8)**
allineation **28.17.25(.3.1)**
Allinson **28.17.23(.24)**
Allison **28.17.23(.14)**
alliterate **22.4.22(.6)**
alliteration **28.17.25(.3.13)**
alliterative **31.2.1(.9.4)**
allium **27.3.18**

all-nighter 17.12.13(.4)
Alloa 17.9.13
allocable 40.20.16(.13)
allocate 22.4.11(.6)
allocation 28.17.25(.3.5)
allocator 17.12.4(.7)
allochthonous
    34.18.16(.15.3)
allocution 28.17.25(.11)
allodia 3.5.8
allodial 40.3.4
allodium 27.3.4(.8)
allogamy 1.15.13(.4)
allograft 22.27.4(.4)
allograph 30.7.5(.1)
allographic 24.2.16(.3)
allomorph 30.9.2
allomorphic 24.2.16(.5)
allomorphically
    1.31.24(.9.9)
allopath 32.6.2
allopathic 24.2.18(.3)
allopathist 22.29.2(.21)
allopathy 1.20.8
allopatric 24.2.26(.14.1)
allophone 28.19.11
allophonic 24.2.15(.6.3)
allopolyploid 23.13.20
allot 22.11.17
allotment
    22.26.15(.13.3)
allotrope 20.15.8
allotropic 24.2.8(.5)
allotropical 40.23.12(.5)
allotropy 1.8.11(.8)
Allott 22.19.26(.5)
allottee 2.11
allow 9.17
allowable 40.20.16(.3)
allowableness
    34.18.16(.37.4)
allowably 1.31.21(.2)
allowance 34.24.10(.3)
Alloway 4.25.9
allowedly 1.31.23(.14.1)
alloy 13.17
allseed 23.1.7
Allsop 20.7.8
allsorts 34.22.9
allspice 34.15.1
allude 23.17.5
allure 12.22, 17.7.12(.14)
allurement
    22.26.15(.13.1)
allusion 28.17.26(.4)
allusive 31.2.4(.8)
allusively 1.31.30(.7.4)
allusiveness
    34.18.16(.28.2)
alluvia 3.11.6
alluvial 40.3.8

alluvion 28.3.10
alluvium 27.3.9
Ally 1.31.7
ally 1.31.7, 14.25, 14.25.6
allyl 40.2.21, 40.13.17
Alma 17.17.24
Alma-Ata 10.6
Almagest 22.29.5(.9)
alma mater 17.12.8
almanac 24.6.11
almandine 28.1.10,
    28.14.6
Alma-Tadema
    17.17.14(.3)
Almería 17.1.16
almightiness
    34.18.16(.2.3)
almighty 1.10.13
almirah 17.32.13
almond 23.24.16(.7)
almoner 17.18.16(.8)
almonry 1.29.20
almost 22.29.17(.4)
alms 35.25.5
almshouse 34.8.6(.21)
almsman 28.17.16(.30)
almucantar 17.12.22(.4)
Alne 28.11, 28.20
Alnmouth 32.7
Alnwick 24.2.15(.5)
aloe 19.29.5
aloetic 24.2.10(.3.1)
aloe vera 17.32.4
aloft 22.27.5
alogical 40.23.12(.17.2)
alogically 1.31.24(.9.11)
aloha 17.9.13, 17.30
alone 28.19.19
aloneness 34.18.16(.25)
along 29.6.15
alongshore 12.16.13
alongside 23.15.11
Alonzo 19.21
aloof 30.13.5
aloofly 1.31.29
aloofness 34.18.16(.27)
alopecia 3.16.1, 17.26.1
aloud 23.8
alow 19.29
Aloysius 34.18.22(.2)
alp 20.18
alpaca 17.14.5
alpargata 17.12.8(.6)
alpenglow 19.29.20
alpenhorn 28.11.10
alpenstock 24.9.4
alpha 17.20.19
alphabet 22.5.2
alphabetic 24.2.10(.3.1)
alphabetical
    40.23.12(.7.1)

alphabetically
    1.31.24(.9.3)
alphabetization
    28.17.25(.3.12)
alphabetize 35.15.7(.4)
alphanumeric 24.2.26(.4)
alphanumerical
    40.23.12(.18)
alphanumerically
    1.31.24(.9.12)
Alphege 39.2.16
alphorn 28.11.10
alpine 28.14.3
alpinism 27.15.21(.2.9)
alpinist 22.29.2(.18.1)
Alport 22.13.1
alprazolam 27.6.18
already 1.11.5
Alresford 23.18.16(.19)
alright 22.16.24
Alsace 34.7.15
Alsager 17.29.3, 17.29.13
Alsatian 28.17.25(.3.10)
alsike 24.2.20(.17)
also 19.20.17
Alston 28.17.11(.25)
alstroemeria 3.22.2
alt 22.32.3
Altai 14.8
Altaic 24.2.3
Altair 6.4
Altamira 17.32.2
altar 17.12.26(.5)
Altarnun 28.13.6
altarpiece 34.1.1
altazimuth 32.14.11
Altdorfer 17.20.8
alter 17.12.26(.5)
alterable 40.20.16(.27.3)
alteration 28.17.25(.3.13)
alterative 31.2.1(.9.4)
altercate 22.4.11(.6)
altercation 28.17.25(.3.5)
alter ego 19.13.4
alternance 34.24.10(.15)
alternant 22.26.15(.14)
alternate 24.4.14(.9.1),
    22.19.15(.10)
alternately 1.31.22(.15)
alternation 28.17.25(.3.8)
alternative 31.2.1(.9.2)
alternatively
    1.31.30(.7.1)
alternator 17.12.4(.10)
Althea 3.12
althorn 28.11.3, 28.11.10
although 19.19
Althusser 6.12
Althusserian 28.3.20(.4)
altimeter 17.12.1(.6)
altimetry 1.29.15(.8)

Altiplano 19.15.6, 19.15.7
altissimo 19.14.12
altitude 23.17.4(.1)
altitudinal 40.26.13(.5)
alto 19.10.21
altocumulus
    34.18.29(.17.6)
altogether 17.23.4
Alton 28.17.11(.27)
Altoona 17.18.15
alto-relievo 19.17
altostratus 34.18.11(.3)
altricial 40.33.1
Altrincham 27.15.15
altruism 27.15.21(.2.1)
altruist 22.29.2(.7)
altruistic 24.2.10(.15.1)
altruistically 1.31.24(.9.6)
aludel 40.5.4
alum 27.15.28(.5)
alumina 17.18.16(.8)
aluminium 27.3.8(.2)
aluminization
    28.17.25(.3.12)
aluminize 35.15.12(.5)
aluminosilicate
    22.19.12(.10)
aluminous 34.18.16(.15.3)
aluminum 27.15.14(.11)
alumna 17.18.25
alumnae 2.17.13
alumni 14.13
alumnus 34.18.16(.24)
Alun 28.17.33(.5)
Alvar 10.13
Alvarez 35.5.13
alveolar 17.34.3, 17.34.18
alveolarization
    28.17.25(.3.12)
alveolarize 35.15.20(.2)
alveolate 22.19.26(.2)
alveole 40.14.1
alveoli 2.32.3,
    2.32.9(.10),
    14.25.3, 14.25.10
alveolus 34.18.29(.3)
Alvin 28.2.20
always 35.4.15, 35.18.22
Alwyn 28.2.28
alyssum 27.15.20(.11)
Alzheimer's 35.18.12
a.m. 27.5
am 27.6
amadavat 22.7.14
amadou 16.8.4
amah 17.17.7
amain 28.4.7
Amal 40.8.8
Amalekite 22.16.11
Amalfi 1.18.13
amalgam 27.15.12

amalgamate **22.4.13(.6)**
amalgamation **28.17.25(.3.7)**
Amanda **17.13.20(.4)**
amanita **17.12.1(.7), 17.12.13(.4)**
amanuenses **35.1.16(.15)**
amanuensis **34.2.17(.15)**
amaranth **32.21**
amaranthine **28.14.12**
amaretti **1.10.4**
amaretto **19.10.4**
Amarillo **19.29.2**
amaryllis **34.2.22(.2)**
amass **34.7.11**
amasser **17.24.6**
amassment **22.26.15(.13.5)**
amateur **17.12.16(.9.1), 17.28.15, 18.3**
amateurish **36.2.25**
amateurishly **1.31.35(.7.4)**
amateurishness **34.18.16(.33.6)**
amateurism **27.15.21(.2.14)**
Amati **1.10.8**
amative **31.2.1(.9.2)**
amativeness **34.18.16(.28.1)**
amatol **40.9.7**
amatory **1.29.11(.8.7)**
amauroses **35.1.16(.11)**
amaurosis **34.2.17(.11.2)**
amaurotic **24.2.10(.6)**
amaze **35.4.7**
amazed **23.28.1**
amazement **22.26.15(.13.5)**
amazingly **1.31.28(.1.12)**
amazingness **34.18.16(.26)**
Amazon **28.17.24(.12)**
Amazonia **3.9.11**
Amazonian **28.3.8(.11)**
Amazulu **16.25**
ambages **35.18.21**
ambassador **17.13.15**
ambassadorial **40.3.14(.5)**
ambassadorship **20.2.7(.9)**
ambassadress **34.5.14(.6), 34.18.27(.15)**
ambatch **38.5**
Ambato **19.10.7**
amber **17.11.17(.4)**
ambergris **34.1.7**
amberjack **24.6.18**
ambidexter **17.12.24(.20)**

ambidexterity **1.10.16(.21.1)**
ambidextrous **34.18.27(.14)**
ambidextrously **1.31.33(.12.5)**
ambience **34.11, 34.24.2, 34.24.7**
ambient **22.26.2(.2)**
ambiguity **1.10.16(.5)**
ambiguous **34.18.6**
ambiguously **1.31.33(.12.1)**
ambiguousness **34.18.16(.31.2)**
ambisonics **34.23.2(.6)**
ambit **22.19.9**
ambition **28.17.25(.2.1)**
ambitious **34.18.22(.2)**
ambitiously **1.31.33(.12.4)**
ambitiousness **34.18.16(.31.4)**
ambivalence **34.24.10(.24)**
ambivalency **1.22.23(.10.4)**
ambivalent **22.26.15(.25)**
ambivalently **1.31.22(.20.5)**
ambiversion **28.17.25(.12)**
ambivert **22.20.9**
amble **40.20.19**
ambler **17.34.20**
Ambleside **23.15.11(.17)**
amblyopia **3.2.7**
amblyopic **24.2.8(.5)**
ambo **19.9.14**
Amboinese **35.1.12**
ambones **35.1.12(.4)**
Ambonese **35.1.12**
amboyna **17.18.11**
Ambrose **35.20.12**
ambrosia **3.15.8**
ambrosial **40.3.11**
ambrosian **28.3.14**
ambry **1.29.14**
ambs-ace **34.4, 34.4.11**
ambulance **34.24.10(.24)**
ambulanceman **28.7.10(.20)**
ambulancemen **28.5.7(.24)**
ambulant **22.26.15(.25)**
ambulate **22.4.23(.7.3)**
ambulation **28.17.25(.3.14)**
ambulatory **1.29.11(.8.10)**
ambuscade **23.4.5**
ambush **36.13**
ambystoma **17.17.14(.2)**

Amdahl **40.8.5**
ameba **17.11.1**
ameer **3.8**
Amelia **3.24.1**
ameliorate **22.4.22(.1)**
amelioration **28.17.25(.3.13)**
ameliorative **31.2.1(.9.4)**
ameliorator **17.12.4(.15)**
amen **28.5.7**
amenability **1.10.16(.22.2)**
amenable **40.20.16(.16.1)**
amenableness **34.18.16(.37.4)**
amenably **1.31.21(.6)**
amend **23.24.5(.7)**
amendable **40.20.16(.12)**
amendatory **1.29.11(.8.6)**
amended **23.18.10(.14)**
amende honorable **17.34.20, 40.20.7**
amender **17.13.20(.3)**
amendment **22.26.15(.13.3)**
Amenhotep **20.4**
amenity **1.10.16(.13)**
amenorrhoea **17.1.16**
ament **22.26.4(.8)**
amenta **17.12.22(.3)**
amentia **3.16.8, 17.26.21**
amentum **27.15.9(.14)**
Amerasian **28.17.25(.3.13), 28.17.26(.3)**
amerce **34.19.4**
amercement **22.26.15(.13.5)**
amerciable **40.20.3**
America **17.14.15(.14)**
American **28.17.13(.13)**
Americana **17.18.8(.3)**
Americanism **27.15.21(.2.9)**
americanist **22.29.2(.18.1)**
Americanization **28.17.25(.3.12)**
Americanize **35.15.12(.5)**
americium **27.3.11, 27.3.13**
Amerind **23.24.2**
Amerindian **28.3.4(.11)**
Amerindic **24.2.11(.16)**
Amersham **27.15.22**
Ames **35.25.3**
Amesbury **1.29.11(.7.2)**
Ameslan **28.7.22**
amethyst **22.29.2(.21)**
amethystine **28.14.5**
Amex® **34.23.4(.5)**
Amharic **24.2.26(.5)**
Amherst **22.29.16**

amiability **1.10.16(.22.1)**
amiable **40.20.3**
amiableness **34.18.16(.37.4)**
amiably **1.31.21(.1)**
amianthus **34.18.19**
amibiguity **1.10.16(.5)**
amicability **1.10.16(.22.2)**
amicable **40.20.16(.13)**
amicableness **34.18.16(.37.4)**
amicably **1.31.21(.5)**
amice **34.2.12**
amicus curiae **14.2**
amid **23.2.12**
amide **23.15.7**
Amidol® **40.9.8**
amidone **28.19.5**
amidships **34.21.2**
amidst **22.29.19**
Amiens **11.2**
Amies **35.2.7**
amigo **19.13.1**
Amin **28.1.13**
amine **28.1.13, 28.2.17(.2)**
amino **19.15.1, 19.15.10, 19.15.12**
amir **3.8**
amirate **22.4.22(.1), 22.19.24(.9)**
Amis **34.2.12**
Amish **36.2.15**
amiss **34.2.12**
amitosis **34.2.17(.11.1)**
amitriptyline **28.1.27(.7)**
amity **1.10.16(.12)**
Amlwch **24.14.11, 25.8**
Amman **28.7.10, 28.9.6, 28.17.16(.7)**
ammo **19.14.6**
Ammon **28.17.16(.7)**
ammonia **3.9.11**
ammoniac **24.6.1**
ammoniacal **40.23.12(.3)**
ammoniated **23.18.9(.3)**
ammonite **22.16.14(.6)**
ammonium **27.3.8(.10)**
ammunition **28.17.25(.2.4)**
amnesia **3.15.1**
amnesiac **24.6.1**
amnesic **24.2.20(.1), 24.2.21**
amnesty **1.10.26(.11)**
amniocentesis **34.2.17(.1)**
amnion **28.3.8(.12)**
amniote **22.17**
amniotic **24.2.10(.6)**
Amoco® **19.12.12**

analyst 22.29.2(.31.3)
analytic 24.2.10(.2.5)
analytical 40.23.12(.7.1)
analytically 1.31.24(.9.3)
anamnesis 34.2.17(.1)
anamorphic 24.2.16(.5)
anamorphoses 35.1.16(.10)
anamorphosis 34.2.17(.10.4)
ananas 34.18.16(.7)
anandrous 34.18.27(.15)
Ananias 34.18.5
anapaest 22.29.1, 22.29.5(.1)
anapaestic 24.2.10(.15.1)
anaphase 35.4.9
anaphor 12.11.3
anaphora 17.32.14(.12)
anaphoric 24.2.26(.6)
anaphrodisiac 24.6.1
anaphylactic 24.2.10(.13)
anaphylaxis 34.2.17(.14)
anaptyctic 24.2.10(.13)
anaptyxes 35.1.16(.14)
anaptyxis 34.2.17(.14)
anarch 24.8.9
anarchic 24.2.12
anarchical 40.23.12(.9)
anarchically 1.31.24(.9.7)
anarchism 27.15.21(.2.6)
anarchist 22.29.2(.15)
anarchistic 24.2.10(.15.2)
anarchy 1.12.13
Anasazi 1.23.5, 1.23.7
Anastasia 3.15.3, 3.15.5
anastigmat 22.7.11
anastigmatic 24.2.10(.4.2)
anastomose 35.20.7
anastomoses 35.1.16(.11)
anastomosis 34.2.17(.11.2)
anastrophe 1.18.9(.2)
anathema 17.17.14(.7)
anathematization 28.17.25(.3.12)
anathematize 35.15.7(.7)
Anatolia 3.24.11
Anatolian 28.3.21(.11)
anatomic 24.2.14(.6)
anatomical 40.23.12(.10)
anatomically 1.31.24(.9.8)
anatomist 22.29.2(.17)
anatomize 35.15.11
anatomy 1.15.13(.1)
anatta 17.12.6
anatto 19.10.6
Anaxagoras 34.7.18, 34.18.27(.17)

Anaximander 17.13.20(.4)
Anaximenes 35.1.12(.3)
anbury 1.29.11(.7.2)
ancestor 17.12.24(.4)
ancestral 40.16.13(.16)
ancestrally 1.31.17(.27.3)
ancestress 34.18.27(.14)
ancestry 1.29.15(.17)
Anchises 35.1.16(.8)
anchor 17.14.21(.3)
anchorage 39.2.22(.9)
anchoress 34.5.14(.3), 34.18.27(.16)
anchoretic 24.2.10(.3.3)
anchorhold 23.31.13(.9)
anchorite 22.16.24(.9)
anchoritic 24.2.10(.2.4)
anchorman 28.7.10(.6)
anchormen 28.5.7(.10)
anchorperson 28.17.23(.15)
anchorwoman 28.17.16(.14)
anchorwomen 28.2.17(.1)
anchoveta 17.12.5(.7)
anchovy 1.19.10
anchusa 17.25.14
ancien régime 27.1.9
ancient 22.26.15(.19)
anciently 1.31.22(.20.4)
ancientness 34.18.16(.20.4)
ancillary 1.29.11(.27)
ancipital 40.21.12
ancon 28.10.11, 28.17.13(.17)
ancones 35.1.12(.4)
Ancyra 17.32.13
and 23.24.6
Andalucía 17.1.11
Andalusia 3.14.8
Andalusian 28.3.13, 28.17.1(.9)
Andaman 28.17.16(.16)
Andamanese 35.1.12
andante 1.10.23(.4), 4.9.9
andantino 19.15.1
Andean 28.3.4(.11), 28.17.1(.4)
Anderson 28.17.23(.14)
Andes 35.1.8
andesite 22.16.19(.9), 22.16.20
Andhra Pradesh 36.5
andiron 28.17.5
Andorra 17.32.8, 17.32.10(.3)
Andorran 28.17.31(.7)
André 4.26.12

Andrea 3.22.16
Andreas 34.18.2
Andrew 16.23.9
Andrews 35.17.6
androcentric 24.2.26(.14.4)
androcentrism 27.15.21(.2.14)
Androcles 35.1.23
androecia 3.14.1
androecium 27.3.11
androgen 28.5.15, 28.17.28(.9)
androgenic 24.2.15(.4)
androgyne 28.14.16
androgynous 34.18.16(.15.3)
androgyny 1.16.15(.17)
android 23.13.19
Andromache 1.12.13
Andromeda 17.13.15
androstenedione 28.19.1
androsterone 28.19.17
Andy 1.11.20(.4)
anear 3.9
anecdotage 39.2.10
anecdotal 40.21.14
anecdotalist 22.29.2(.31.2)
anecdotally 1.31.17(.9.2)
anecdote 22.21.4
anecdotic 24.2.10(.6)
anechoic 24.2.7
anele 40.1.7
anemograph 30.7.5(.1)
anemographic 24.2.16(.3)
anemometer 17.12.16(.9.2)
anemometric 24.2.26(.14.2)
anemometry 1.29.15(.8)
anemone 1.16.15(.11)
anemophilous 34.18.29(.17.4)
anencephalic 24.2.27(.6)
anencephaly 1.31.17(.16.1)
anent 22.26.4(.9)
aneroid 23.13.19
anesthesiologist 22.29.2(.26.2)
anesthesiology 1.26.10(.11.1)
anesthetically 1.31.24(.9.3)
anesthetize 35.15.7(.7)
Aneurin 28.17.31(.10)
aneurin 28.2.29(.5)
aneurysm 27.15.21(.2.14)
aneurysmal 40.25.14

anew 16.24.10
Anfield 23.31.1(.2)
anfractuosity 1.10.16(.16.2)
anfractuous 34.18.6
angary 1.29.11(.11)
angel 40.16.11, 40.34
Angela 17.34.16(.17)
angel dust 22.29.12
angelfish 36.2.18(.21)
angelic 24.2.27(.4)
angelica 17.14.15(.15)
angelical 40.23.12(.19)
angelically 1.31.24(.9.12)
Angelico 19.12.12
Angelina 17.18.1(.16)
Angelo 19.29.12
Angelou 16.25
angelus 34.18.29(.17.5)
anger 17.16.17(.2)
Angers 4.21
Angevin 28.2.20
Angharad 23.18.27
Angie 1.26.13
angina 17.18.13(.12)
angiogram 27.6.17(.5)
angiography 1.18.9(.3.2)
angioma 17.17.16
angiomata 17.12.16(.9.3)
angioplasty 1.10.26(.5)
angiosperm 27.16.1
angiospermous 34.18.15(.11)
Angkor 12.7
angle 40.24.14(.2)
angledozer 17.25.15
Anglepoise® 35.13
angler 17.34.24
Anglesey 2.22.14
angleworm 27.16.7
Anglia 3.24.15
Anglian 28.3.21(.14)
Anglican 28.17.13(.13)
Anglicanism 27.15.21(.2.9)
anglice 1.22.16(.14)
Anglicism 27.15.21(.2.12)
Anglicist 22.29.2(.22)
Anglicization 28.17.25(.3.11)
Anglicize 35.15.16(.4)
Anglist 22.29.2(.31.6)
Anglistics 34.23.2(.3)
Anglo 19.29.20
Anglocentric 24.2.26(.14.4)
Anglomania 3.9.3(.5)
Anglomaniac 24.6.1

Anstruther 17.12.24(.23), 17.23.10
answer 17.24.22(.3)
answerability 1.10.16(.22.1)
answerable 40.20.16(.27.5)
answerably 1.31.21(.8)
answerphone 28.19.11
ant 22.26.6
antacid 23.2.16
Antaeus 34.18.2
antagonism 27.15.21(.2.9)
antagonist 22.29.2(.18.1)
antagonistic 24.2.10(.15.2)
antagonistically 1.31.24(.9.6)
antagonization 28.17.25(.3.12)
antagonize 35.15.12(.5)
Antakya 17.33.8
antalkali 14.25.9
Antalya 3.24.5
Antananarivo 19.17
Antarctic 24.2.10(.13)
Antarctica 17.14.15(.6)
Antares 35.1.22
ante 1.10.23(.4)
anteater 17.12.1(.3)
antebellum 27.15.28(.4)
antecedence 34.24.10(.11)
antecedent 22.26.15(.10)
antecedently 1.31.22(.20.2)
antechamber 17.11.17(.2)
antechapel 40.19.5
antedate 22.4.10
antediluvial 40.3.8
antediluvially 1.31.3(.8)
antediluvian 28.3.10
antelope 20.15.9
ante-mortem 27.15.9(.7)
antemundane 28.4.4
antenatal 40.21.3
antenna 17.18.4
antennae 2.17.3, 14.13
antennal 40.26.4
antennary 1.29.11(.13.1)
antennule 40.15.9(.8)
antenuptial 40.16.10, 40.16.12
antepartum 27.15.9(.5)
antependia 3.5.9
antependium 27.3.4(.9)
antepenult 22.32.8
antepenultimate 22.19.14
anteprandial 40.3.4
anterior 3.22.2

anteriority 1.10.16(.21.2)
anteriorly 1.31.3(.11)
anteriorness 34.18.16(.3)
anteroom 27.14.6(.2)
Anthea 3.12
ant heap 20.1
anthelion 28.3.21(.1)
anthelminthic 24.2.18(.6)
anthelmintic 24.2.10(.14)
anthem 27.15.18
anthemia 3.8.1
anthemion 28.3.7
anther 17.22.13
antheral 40.16.13(.22)
antheridia 3.5.2
antheridium 27.3.4(.2)
anthill 40.2.18
anthological 40.23.12(.17.2)
anthologist 22.29.2(.26.4)
anthologize 35.15.18
anthology 1.26.10(.11.5)
Anthony 1.16.15(.7)
anthozoan 28.17.8
anthracene 28.1.18(.6)
anthracic 24.2.20(.5)
anthracite 22.16.19(.9)
anthracitic 24.2.10(.2.3)
anthracnose 34.20.9, 35.20.8
anthrax 34.23.5(.14)
anthropocentric 24.2.26(.14.4)
anthropocentrically 1.31.24(.9.12)
anthropocentrism 27.15.21(.2.14)
anthropogenesis 34.2.17(.10.3)
anthropogenic 24.2.15(.4)
anthropogeny 1.16.15(.17)
anthropography 1.18.9(.3.2)
anthropoid 23.13.5
anthropoidal 40.22.9
anthropological 40.23.12(.17.2)
anthropologically 1.31.24(.9.11)
anthropologist 22.29.2(.26.3)
anthropology 1.26.10(.11.2)
anthropometric 24.2.26(.14.2)
anthropometry 1.29.15(.8)
anthropomorphic 24.2.16(.5)

anthropomorphically 1.31.24(.9.9)
anthropomorphism 27.15.21(.2.10)
anthropomorphist 22.29.2(.19)
anthropomorphize 35.15.13
anthropomorphous 34.18.17
anthroponymy 1.15.13(.5)
anthropophagi 14.11
anthropophagous 34.18.14(.5)
anthropophagus 34.18.14(.5)
anthropophagy 1.26.10(.6)
anti 1.10.23(.4)
antibacterial 40.3.14(.2)
Antibes 21.1
antibioses 35.1.16(.11)
antibiosis 34.2.17(.11.1)
antibiotic 24.2.10(.6)
antibiotically 1.31.24(.9.4)
antibody 1.11.10
antic 24.2.10(.14)
anticathode 23.20.10
anticatholic 24.2.27(.13)
Antichrist 22.29.13
anti-christian 28.3.3, 28.17.27
anticipant 22.26.15(.7)
anticipate 22.4.7
anticipation 28.17.25(.3.2)
anticipative 31.2.1(.9.1)
anticipator 17.12.4(.3)
anticipatory 1.29.11(.8.2)
anticlerical 40.23.12(.18)
anticlericalism 27.15.21(.2.15)
anticlimactic 24.2.10(.13)
anticlimactically 1.31.24(.9.5)
anticlimax 34.23.5(.6)
anticlinal 40.26.11
anticline 28.14.19(.16)
anticlockwise 35.15.19
anticoagulant 22.26.15(.25)
anticodon 28.10.10
anti-communist 22.29.2(.18.3)
anti-constitutional 40.26.13(.14.5)
anticonvulsant 22.26.15(.17.3)
anticyclone 28.19.19
anticyclonic 24.2.15(.6.4)

antidazzle 40.32.5
antidepressant 22.26.15(.17.2)
antidiuretic 24.2.10(.3.3)
antidotal 40.21.14
antidote 22.21.4
antielectron 28.10.24(.7)
anti-establishment 22.26.15(.13.6)
Antietam 27.15.9(.1)
anti-fascist 22.29.2(.24)
antifebrile 40.13.16
antifreeze 35.1.22
anti-g 2.27
antigen 28.17.28(.9)
antigenic 24.2.15(.4)
Antigone 1.16.15(.10)
anti-government 22.26.15(.13.4)
antigravity 1.10.16(.15)
Antigua 17.16.1
Antiguan 28.17.15(.1), 28.17.30
anti-hero 19.27.1
antihistamine 28.1.13, 28.2.17(.5)
anti-inflammatory 1.29.11(.8.7)
anti-inflation 28.17.25(.3.14)
anti-intellectual 40.16.12
anti-knock 24.9.9
Antillean 28.3.21(.2)
Antilles 35.1.23
antilog 26.7.14
antilogarithm 27.15.19
antilogy 1.26.10(.10)
antimacassar 17.24.6
antimalarial 40.3.14(.4)
antimasque 24.20.4
antimatter 17.12.6
antimetabolite 22.16.25(.9)
antimonarchical 40.23.12(.9)
antimonial 40.3.7(.9)
antimonic 24.2.15(.6.2)
antimonious 34.3.6(.7)
antimony 1.16.15(.11)
antinode 23.20.9
antinomian 28.3.7
antinomianism 27.15.21(.2.9)
antinomy 1.15.13(.5)
antinovel 40.28.7
anti-nuclear 3.24.14
Antioch 24.9.1
Antiochus 34.18.13(.10)
antioxidant 22.26.15(.10)
antiparticle 40.23.12(.7.2)
Antipas 34.7.5

antipasto 19.10.19
antipathetic 24.2.10(.3.2)
antipathetical 40.23.12(.7.1)
antipathetically 1.31.24(.9.3)
antipathic 24.2.18(.3)
antipathy 1.20.8
anti-personnel 40.5, 40.5.8
antiperspirant 22.26.15(.23.3)
antiphlogistic 24.2.10(.15.2)
antiphon 28.10.15, 28.17.19
antiphonal 40.26.13(.9)
antiphonally 1.31.17(.14.2)
antiphonary 1.29.11(.13.2)
antiphony 1.16.15(.12)
antiphrasis 34.2.17(.10.4)
antipodal 40.22.13
antipode 23.20.3
Antipodean 28.3.4
antipodes 35.1.8
antipole 40.18.3
antipope 20.15.2
antiproton 28.10.9
antipruritic 24.2.10(.2.4)
antipyretic 24.2.10(.3.3)
antiquarian 28.3.20(.4)
antiquarianism 27.15.21(.2.9)
antiquary 1.29.11(.24)
antiquated 23.18.9(.3)
antique 24.1.3
antiquity 1.10.16(.20)
anti-racism 27.15.21(.2.12)
anti-racist 22.29.2(.22)
antirrhinum 27.15.14(.9)
antisabbatarian 28.3.20(.4)
antiscorbutic 24.2.10(.9)
antiscriptural 40.16.13(.12.3)
antisepsis 34.2.17(.12)
antiseptic 24.2.10(.12)
antiseptically 1.31.24(.9.5)
antisera 17.32.2
antiserum 27.15.26(.1)
antisocial 40.33.11
antisocially 1.31.17(.22)
antispasmodic 24.2.11(.7)
anti-static 24.2.10(.4.1)
anti-statically 1.31.24(.9.4)
Antisthenes 35.1.12(.3)

antistrophe 1.18.9(.2)
antistrophic 24.2.16(.4)
anti-tetanus 34.18.16(.15.2)
antitheism 27.15.21(.2.1)
antitheist 22.29.2(.1)
antitheses 35.1.16(.10)
antithesis 34.2.17(.10.4)
antithetic 24.2.10(.3.2)
antithetical 40.23.12(.7.1)
antithetically 1.31.24(.9.3)
antitoxic 24.2.20(.13)
antitoxin 28.2.23(.14)
antitrade 23.4.15
antitrinitarian 28.3.20(.4)
antitrust 22.29.12
antitype 20.10.2
antitypical 40.23.12(.5)
antivenene 28.1.14
antivenin 28.2.18
antiviral 40.16.13(.10)
antivirus 34.18.27(.10)
antivivisection 28.17.25(.15.2)
antivivisectionism 27.15.21(.2.9)
antivivisectionist 22.29.2(.18.2), 22.29.15(.13)
antler 17.34.21
antlike 24.13.7(.12)
ant lion 28.17.5
Antofagasta 17.12.24(.5)
Antoine 28.9.12
Antoinette 22.5.9
Anton 28.10.9
Antonia 3.9.11
Antonine 28.14.9
Antoninus 34.18.16(.13)
Antonio 15.1.6
Antonioni 1.16.17
Antonius 34.3.6(.7)
antonomasia 3.15.3
Antony 1.16.15(.7)
antonym 27.2.6
antonymous 34.18.15(.10)
antonymy 1.15.13(.5)
antra 17.32.19(.10)
antral 40.16.13(.16)
Antrim 27.2.14
Antrobus 34.18.10
antrum 27.15.26(.10)
antsy 1.22.23(.4)
Antwerp 20.14
Anubis 34.2.7
anuran 28.17.31(.11)
anuresis 34.2.17(.1)
anus 34.18.16(.4)

Anvers 6.11
anvil 40.28.15
Anwar 10.22.9
Anwen 28.5.17, 28.17.30
Anwyl 40.35.5
anxiety 1.10.16(.4)
anxious 34.18.22(.11)
anxiously 1.31.33(.12.4)
anxiousness 34.18.16(.31.4)
any 1.16.5
anybody 1.11.10, 1.11.17
anyhow 9.14
anymore 12.9
anyone 28.13.8
anyplace 34.4.14
anything 29.1.21
anytime 27.12.1
anyway 4.25.9
anywhere 6.18.4
anywise 35.15.19
Anzac 24.6.15
Anzio 15.1.8
Anzus 34.18.21
ao dai 14
aorist 22.29.2(.29.1)
aoristic 24.2.10(.15.2)
aorta 17.12.10
aortal 40.21.8
aortic 24.2.10(.7)
aouadad 23.7.8
à outrance 34.24.6
apace 34.4.2
Apache 1.25.6
apanage 39.2.15
apart 22.10.1
apartheid 22.4.9(.2), 22.16.9, 23.15.4
apartment 22.26.15(.13.3)
apartness 34.18.16(.20.2)
apathetic 24.2.10(.3.2)
apathetical 40.23.12(.7.1)
apathetically 1.31.24(.9.3)
apathy 1.20.8
apatite 22.16.9
ape 20.3
apeak 24.1.1
Apeldoorn 28.11.4
ape-like 24.13.7(.10)
Apelles 35.1.23
apeman 28.7.10(.9)
apemen 28.5.7(.13)
Apennines 35.26.12
aperçu 16.15, 16.24.14
aperient 22.26.2(.9)
aperiodic 24.2.11(.7)
aperiodicity 1.10.16(.16.1)
aperitif 30.1.1

aperture 17.28.15
apery 1.29.11(.6)
apetalous 34.18.29(.17.2)
apex 34.23.4(.1)
Apfelstrudel 40.22.12
aphasia 3.15.3
aphasic 24.2.21
aphelia 3.24.1
aphelion 28.3.21(.1)
apheresis 34.2.17(.10.4)
aphesis 34.2.17(.10.4)
aphetic 24.2.10(.3.2)
aphetically 1.31.24(.9.3)
aphid 23.2.14
aphides 35.1.8
aphis 34.2.14
aphonia 3.9.11
aphonic 24.2.15(.6.3)
aphony 1.16.15(.12)
aphorism 27.15.21(.2.14)
aphorist 22.29.2(.29.4)
aphoristic 24.2.10(.15.2)
aphoristically 1.31.24(.9.6)
aphorize 35.15.20(.2)
Aphra 17.32.25
aphrodisiac 24.6.1
Aphrodisias 34.7.2
Aphrodite 1.10.13
aphtha 17.22.14
aphthous 34.18.19
aphyllous 34.18.29(.2)
Apia 3.2.4, 17.1.1
apian 28.3.1
apiarian 28.3.20(.4)
apiarist 22.29.2(.29.1)
apiary 1.29.2(.1)
apical 40.23.12(.5)
apically 1.31.24(.9.2)
apices 35.1.16(.10)
apicultural 40.16.13(.12.3)
apiculture 17.28.26
apiculturist 22.29.2(.29.4)
apiece 34.1.1
apis 34.2.6
apish 36.2.9
apishly 1.31.35(.7.1)
apishness 34.18.16(.33.2)
aplanat 22.7.12
aplanatic 24.2.10(.4.3)
aplasia 3.15.3
aplastic 24.2.10(.15.4)
aplenty 1.10.23(.3)
aplomb 27.9
apnoea 3.9.12
apocalypse 34.21.2
apocalyptic 24.2.10(.12)
apocalyptical 40.23.12(.7.3)

apocalyptically 1.31.24(.9.5)
apocarpous 34.18.9(.5)
apochromat 22.7.11
apochromatic 24.2.10(.4.2)
apocope 1.8.11(.5)
apocrine 28.2.29(.10), 28.14.18
Apocrypha 17.20.12(.5)
apocryphal 40.27.14
apocryphally 1.31.17(.16.1)
apodal 40.22.13
apodeictic 24.2.10(.13)
apodeictical 40.23.12(.7.3)
apodeictically 1.31.24(.9.5)
apodictic 24.2.10(.13)
apodictical 40.23.2
apodictically 1.31.24(.9.5)
apodoses 35.1.16(.10)
apodosis 34.2.17(.10.2)
apogean 28.17.1(.11)
apogee 2.27
apolaustic 24.2.10(.15.4)
apolitical 40.23.12(.7.1)
apolitically 1.31.24(.9.3)
Apollinaire 6.9
Apollinaris 34.2.21
Apollo 19.29.8
Apollonian 28.3.8(.11)
Apollonius 34.3.6(.7)
Apollyon 28.3.21(.7), 28.10.2
apologetic 24.2.10(.3.2)
apologetical 40.23.12(.7.1)
apologetically 1.31.24(.9.3)
apologia 3.19.8
apologist 22.29.2(.26.3)
apologize 35.15.18
apologue 26.7.14
apology 1.26.10(.11.2)
apolune 28.16.15
apomictic 24.2.10(.13)
apomixis 34.2.17(.14)
apophatic 24.2.10(.4.4)
apophthegm 27.5.7
apophthegmatic 24.2.10(.4.2)
apophthegmatically 1.31.24(.9.4)
apophyses 35.1.16(.10)
apophysis 34.2.17(.10.4)
apoplectic 24.2.10(.13)
apoplectical 40.23.12(.7.3)

apoplectically 1.31.24(.9.5)
apoplexy 1.22.22
aposematic 24.2.10(.4.2)
aposiopeses 35.1.16(.1)
aposiopesis 34.2.17(.1)
apostasy 1.22.16(.4)
apostate 22.4.9(.9)
apostatic 24.2.10(.4.1)
apostatical 40.23.12(.7.1)
apostatically 1.31.24(.9.4)
apostatize 35.15.7(.7)
a posteriori 14.24.4
apostigmat 22.7.11
apostil 40.2.5
apostille 40.2.5
apostle 40.31.8
apostleship 20.2.7(.24)
apostolate 22.4.23(.7.1), 22.19.26(.13)
apostolic 24.2.27(.9)
apostolical 40.23.12(.19)
apostolically 1.31.24(.9.12)
apostrophe 1.18.9(.2)
apostrophic 24.2.16(.4)
apostrophize 35.15.13
apothecary 1.29.11(.10)
apothem 27.5.7
apotheoses 35.1.16(.11)
apotheosis 34.2.17(.11.1)
apotheosize 35.15.16(.2)
apotropaic 24.2.3
appal 40.10.3
Appalachia 3.16.3, 3.18, 17.26.3, 17.28.4
Appalachian 28.3.15, 28.3.17, 28.17.27
appallingly 1.31.28(.1.18)
Appaloosa 17.24.14
appanage 39.2.15
apparat 22.7.20, 22.10.12
apparatchik 24.2.23
apparatus 34.18.11(.3)
apparel 40.16.13(.5)
apparent 22.26.15(.23.1)
apparently 1.31.22(.20.5)
apparentness 34.18.16(.20.4)
apparition 28.17.25(.2.6)
apparitor 17.12.16(.18)
appassionata 17.12.8(.8)
appeal 40.1.1
appealable 40.20.16(.29)
appealer 17.34.1
appealing 29.1.31(.1)
appealingly 1.31.28(.1.18)
appear 3.1
appearance 34.24.10(.16)
appease 35.1.5

appeasement 22.26.15(.13.5)
appeaser 17.25.1
appellant 22.26.15(.25)
appellate 22.19.26(.4)
appellation 28.17.25(.3.14)
appellation contrôlée 4.28
appellative 31.2.1(.9.4)
appellatively 1.31.30(.7.1)
appellee 2, 2.32
append 23.24.5(.2)
appendage 39.2.11
appendant 22.26.15(.10)
appendectomy 1.15.13(.1)
appendicectomy 1.15.13(.1)
appendices 35.1.16(.10)
appendicitis 34.18.11(.8)
appendix 34.23.2(.4)
apperceive 31.1.4
apperception 28.17.25(.14)
apperceptive 31.2.1(.12)
appertain 28.4.3
appertinent 22.26.15(.14)
appestat 22.7.7
appetence 34.24.10(.10)
appetency 1.22.23(.10.2)
appetent 22.26.15(.9)
appetisingly 1.31.28(.1.12)
appetite 22.16.9
appetitive 31.2.1(.9.1)
appetize 35.15.7(.7)
appetizer 17.25.12(.2)
appetizing 29.1.24
appetizingly 1.31.28(.1.12)
Appian Way 4
applaud 23.12.11
applause 35.12
apple 40.19.5
Appleby 1.9.24
applecart 22.10.5
Appledore 12.6.13
applejack 24.6.18
Appleton 28.17.11(.27)
appliable 40.20.16(.5)
appliableness 34.18.16(.37.4)
appliance 34.24.10(.5)
applicability 1.10.16(.22.2)
applicable 40.20.16(.13)
applicableness 34.18.16(.37.4)
applicably 1.31.21(.5)
applicant 22.26.15(.11)

application 28.17.25(.3.5)
applicator 17.12.4(.7)
applied 23.15.16
applier 17.6.15
appliqué 4.11
apply 14.25.11
appoggiatura 17.32.14(.3)
appoint 22.26.11
appointee 2.11
appointer 17.12.22(.9)
appointive 31.2.1(.14)
appointment 22.26.15(.13.3)
Appomattox 34.23.15
apport 22.13.1
apportion 28.17.25(.8)
apportionable 40.20.16(.16.3)
apportionment 22.26.15(.13.4)
appose 35.20.1
apposite 22.19.19
appositely 1.31.22(.15)
appositeness 34.18.16(.20.3)
apposition 28.17.25(.2.5)
appositional 40.26.13(.14.1)
appositive 31.2.1(.9.3)
appositively 1.31.30(.7.1)
appraisable 40.20.16(.22)
appraisal 40.32.3
appraise 35.4.16
appraisee 2.23
appraisement 22.26.15(.13.5)
appraiser 17.25.3
appraisingly 1.31.28(.1.12)
appraisive 31.2.4(.3)
appreciable 40.20.3, 40.20.16(.23)
appreciably 1.31.21(.1)
appreciate 22.4.2(.9)
appreciation 28.17.25(.3.1)
appreciative 31.2.1(.2)
appreciatively 1.31.30(.7.1)
appreciativeness 34.18.16(.28.1)
appreciator 17.12.4(.1)
appreciatory 1.29.11(.8.1)
apprehend 23.24.5(.13)
apprehended 23.18.10(.14)
apprehensibility 1.10.16(.22.3)
apprehensible 40.20.16(.21.3)
apprehension 28.17.25(.16)

apprehensive 31.2.4(.13)
apprehensively
1.31.30(.7.4)
apprehensiveness
34.18.16(.28.2)
apprentice 34.18.11(.14)
apprenticeship 20.2.7(.9)
apprise 35.15.20(.3)
apprize 35.15.20(.3)
appro 19.27.13
approach 38.17
approachability
1.10.16(.22.2)
approachable
40.20.16(.24)
approbate 22.4.8
approbation
28.17.25(.3.2)
approbative 31.2.1(.3)
approbatory 1.29.11(.8.2)
appropriate 22.3.12,
22.4.2(.14)
appropriately 1.31.22(.3)
appropriateness
34.18.16(.20.1)
appropriation
28.17.25(.3.1)
appropriationist
22.29.2(.18.2)
appropriative 31.2.1(.2)
appropriator 17.12.4(.1)
approval 40.28.10
approve 31.10
approved 23.26
approving 29.1.20
approvingly 1.31.28(.1.9)
approximant
22.26.15(.13.2)
approximate 22.4.13(.6),
22.19.14
approximately
1.31.22(.15)
approximation
28.17.25(.3.7)
approximative
31.2.1(.9.2)
approximatively
1.31.30(.7.1)
appurtenance
34.24.10(.15)
appurtenant
22.26.15(.14)
apraxia 3.14.15
après-ski 2.14
apricot 22.11.6
April 40.16.13(.14)
a priori 14.24.4
apriorism 27.15.21(.2.14)
aprioristic 24.2.10(.15.2)
aprioristically
1.31.24(.9.6)
apron 28.17.31(.12)

apronful 40.14.6(.15)
apropos 19.8
apse 34.21.5
apsidal 40.22.13
apsides 35.1.8
apsis 34.2.17(.12)
Apsley 1.31.33(.14)
apt 22.22.4
Apted 23.18.9(.16)
apterous 34.18.27(.14)
apteryx 34.23.2(.12)
aptitude 23.17.4(.1)
aptly 1.31.22(.18)
aptness 34.18.16(.20.4)
Apuleius 34.18.1, 34.18.2
Apulia 3.24.10
Aqaba 10.5.4, 17.11.13
aqua 17.31.6
aquaculture 17.28.26
aqua fortis 34.2.8
Aqua Libra® 17.32.18
aqualung 29.8
aquamarine 28.1.25
aquanaut 22.13.6
aquaphobia 3.3.9
aquaplane 28.4.19
aqua regia 3.19.4
aquarelle 40.5.18
aquaria 3.22.4
Aquarian 28.3.20(.4)
aquarist 22.29.2(.29.4)
aquarium 27.3.17(.3)
Aquarius 34.3.15(.3)
Aquarobics® 34.23.2(.2)
Aquascutum® 27.15.9(.9)
aquatic 24.2.10(.4.4)
aquatint 22.26.1
aquavit 22.1.7, 22.2.14
aqua vitae 2.12.8, 14.8
aqueduct 22.23.8
aqueous 34.3.14
aqueously 1.31.33(.1.3)
aquiculture 17.28.26
aquifer 17.20.12(.4)
Aquila 17.34.2(.14)
aquilegia 3.19.1, 17.29.1
aquiline 28.14.19(.11)
Aquinas 34.18.16(.13)
Aquitaine 28.4.3
Aquitania 3.9.3(.2)
aquiver 17.21.2
Arab 21.14
Arabella 17.34.5(.2)
arabesque 24.20.3
Arabia 3.3.3
Arabian 28.3.2
Arabic 24.2.9(.5)
Arabicism 27.15.21(.2.12)
arabinose 34.20.9, 35.20.8
arabis 34.2.7

Arabism 27.15.21(.2.3)
Arabist 22.29.2(.12)
arable 40.20.16(.27.1)
Araby 1.9.11
Arachne 1.16.21
arachnid 23.2.13
Arachnida 17.13.15
arachnidae 2.13
arachnidan 28.17.12(.16)
arachnoid 23.13.12
arachnologist
22.29.2(.26.4)
arachnology
1.26.10(.11.4)
Arafat 22.7.13
Arafura 17.32.14(.3)
Aragon 28.17.15(.13)
Arakan 28.7.8
Aral 40.16.13(.5)
Araldite® 22.16.10
Aramaic 24.2.3
Araminta 17.12.22(.1)
Aran 28.17.31(.5)
Aranda 17.13.20(.4)
Arapaho 19.26
arapaima 17.17.11
Ararat 22.7.20
arational 40.26.13(.14.4)
Araucanian 28.3.8(.3)
araucaria 3.22.4
Arawak 24.6.20
arb 21.7
arbalest 22.29.5(.13),
22.29.15(.18)
arbiter 17.12.16(.4)
arbitrage 37.4.9
arbitrager 17.27.5
arbitrageur 18.14
arbitral 40.16.13(.16)
arbitrament
22.26.15(.13.2)
arbitrarily 1.31.17(.27.1)
arbitrariness
34.18.16(.2.9)
arbitrary 1.29.11(.25)
arbitrate 22.4.22(.8)
arbitration 28.17.25(.3.13)
arbitrator 17.12.4(.15)
arbitratorship 20.2.7(.9)
arbitress 34.18.27(.14)
arblast 22.29.6(.12),
22.29.8(.8)
arboraceous 34.18.22(.3)
arboreal 40.3.14(.5)
arboreous 34.3.15(.5)
arborescence
34.24.10(.18)
arborescent
22.26.15(.17.2)
arboreta 17.12.1(.14)
arboretum 27.15.9(.1)

arboricultural
40.16.13(.12.3)
arboriculture 17.28.26
arboriculturist
22.29.2(.29.4)
arborization
28.17.25(.3.11)
arbor vitae 2.12.8
arbour 17.11.7
Arbus 34.18.10
Arbuthnot 22.11.9,
22.19.15(.13)
arbutus 34.18.11(.9)
arc 24.8
arcade 23.4.5
Arcadia 3.5.3
Arcadian 28.3.4(.3)
Arcadianism
27.15.21(.2.9)
arcading 29.1.13(.3)
Arcady 1.11.17
arcana 17.18.3, 17.18.8(.3)
arcane 28.4.5
arcanely 1.31.27(.4)
arcanum 27.15.14(.3)
Arc de Triomphe 30.18
arch 38.7
Archaean 28.17.1(.5)
archaeologic 24.2.24(.4)
archaeological
40.23.12(.17.2)
archaeologically
1.31.24(.9.11)
archaeologist
22.29.2(.26.2)
archaeologize 35.15.18
archaeology
1.26.10(.11.1)
archaeopteryx
34.23.2(.12)
archaic 24.2.3
archaically 1.31.24(.9.1)
archaism 27.15.21(.2.1)
archaist 22.29.2(.3)
archaistic 24.2.10(.15.1)
archaistically
1.31.24(.9.6)
archaize 35.15.1
archangel 40.16.11, 40.34
archangelic 24.2.27(.4)
archbishop 20.13.5
archbishopric
24.2.26(.12)
archdeacon 28.17.13(.1)
archdeaconry 1.29.20
archdeaconship
20.2.7(.19)
archdiocesan
28.17.23(.14)
archdiocese
34.2.17(.10.1)
archducal 40.23.11

archduchess 34.18.23
archduke 24.15.8
archdukedom 27.15.10(.13)
archegonia 3.9.11
archegonium 27.3.8(.10)
Archelaus 34.18.2
arch-enemy 1.15.13(.5)
archeologically 1.31.24(.9.11)
archeologist 22.29.2(.26.2)
archer 17.28.8
archery 1.29.11(.22)
archetypal 40.19.9
archetypally 1.31.17(.7)
archetype 20.10.2
archetypical 40.23.12(.5)
archetypically 1.31.24(.9.2)
Archibald 23.31.6, 23.31.11, 23.31.15
archidiaconal 40.26.13(.6)
archidiaconate 22.4.14(.9.1), 22.19.15(.9)
Archie 1.25.8
archiepiscopacy 1.22.16(.2)
archiepiscopal 40.19.11
archiepiscopate 22.19.8
archil 40.2.7
Archilochus 34.18.13(.12)
archimandrite 22.16.24(.13)
Archimedean 28.3.4(.1)
Archimedes 35.1.8
archipelago 19.13.9
architect 22.23.4(.2)
architectonic 24.2.15(.6.1)
architectural 40.16.13(.12.3)
architecturally 1.31.17(.27.2)
architecture 17.28.20
architrave 31.3.7
archival 40.28.9
archive 31.9
archivist 22.29.2(.20)
archivolt 22.32.12
archlute 22.18.11
archly 1.31.36
archness 34.18.16(.35)
archon 28.10.11, 28.17.13(.6)
archonship 20.2.7(.19)
archpriest 22.29.1
arch-rival 40.28.9
archway 4.25.24
Arco 19.12.6

arctic 24.2.10(.13)
Arcturus 34.18.27(.11)
arcuate 22.4.4, 22.19.5
arcus senilis 34.2.22(.7)
Ardagh 10.7, 17.13.7
Ardèche 36.5
Arden 28.17.12(.8)
ardency 1.22.23(.10.2)
Ardennes 28.5.4, 35.26.5
ardent 22.26.15(.10)
ardently 1.31.22(.20.2)
Ardizzone 1.16.17(.10)
Ardmore 12.9
Ardnamurchan 28.17.13(.14)
ardour 17.13.7
Ardoyne 28.12
Ardrossan 28.17.23(.8)
Ards 35.23.5
arduous 34.18.6
arduously 1.31.33(.12.1)
arduousness 34.18.16(.31.2)
are 10
area 3.22.4
areal 40.3.14(.4)
areaway 4.25.3
areca 17.14.1, 17.14.15(.14)
areg 26.4
arena 17.18.1(.15)
arenaceous 34.18.22(.3)
Arendt 22.26.15(.23.2)
Arenig 26.2.4
aren't 22.26.8
areola 17.34.16(.1)
areolae 2.32.9(.1)
areolar 17.34.16(.1)
areometer 17.12.16(.9.2)
Areopagi 14.11
Areopagite 22.16.12
Areopagitica 17.14.15(.6)
Areopagus 34.18.14(.5)
Arequipa 17.10.1
Ares 35.1.22
arête 22.5.19
Aretha 17.22.1
Arethusa 17.25.14
Arfon 28.10.16, 28.17.20(.6)
argala 17.34.16(.10)
argali 1.31.17(.12)
argent 22.26.15(.21)
argentiferous 34.18.27(.20)
Argentina 17.18.1(.3)
Argentine 28.1.9(.6), 28.14.5
Argentinian 28.3.8(.2)
Argie 1.26.5
argil 40.2.17
argilaceous 34.18.22(.3)

argillaceous 34.18.22(.3)
arginine 28.1.14, 28.14.9
Argive 31.9
argle-bargle 40.24.5
Argo 19.13.5
argol 40.9.10
argon 28.10.12, 28.17.15(.7)
Argonaut 22.13.6
Argos 34.10.11
argosy 1.22.16(.7)
argot 19.13.5
arguable 40.20.16(.6)
arguably 1.31.21(.2)
argue 16.24.8
arguer 17.7.12(.6)
argufy 14.14.4(.15)
argument 22.26.15(.13.2)
argumental 40.21.17(.2)
argumentation 28.17.25(.3.3)
argumentative 31.2.1(.9.1)
argumentatively 1.31.30(.7.1)
argumentativeness 34.18.16(.28.1)
Argus 34.18.14(.3)
argute 22.18.10
argutely 1.31.22(.14)
argy-bargy 1.26.5
Argyle 40.13.6
Argyll 40.13.6
Argyllshire 17.26.25
aria 3.22.7
Ariadne 1.16.20
Arian 28.3.20(.4)
Ariane 28.7
Arianism 27.15.21(.2.9)
Arianna 17.18.6
arid 23.2.22
aridisol 40.9.14
aridity 1.10.16(.9)
aridly 1.31.23(.14.7)
aridness 34.18.16(.21.1)
ariel 40.3.14(.4)
Arielle 40.5
Aries 35.1.22
arietta 17.12.5
aright 22.16.24
aril 40.16.13(.5)
arillate 22.4.23(.7.2), 22.19.26(.13)
Arimathea 17.1.10
arioso 19.20.12, 19.21
Ariosto 19.10.19
arise 35.15.20
arisen 28.17.24(.2)
arisings 35.27
Aristarchus 34.18.13(.4)
Aristides 35.1.8

Aristippus 34.18.9(.2)
aristocracy 1.22.16(.13)
aristocrat 22.7.20
aristocratic 24.2.10(.4.5)
aristocratically 1.31.24(.9.4)
Aristophanes 35.1.12(.3)
Aristotelian 28.3.21(.1)
Aristotle 40.21.7
Arita 17.12.1(.14)
arithmetic 24.2.10(.3.1)
arithmetical 40.23.12(.7.1)
arithmetically 1.31.24(.9.3)
arithmetician 28.17.25(.2.2)
Arius 34.3.15(.3), 34.18.5
Arizona 17.18.18(.8)
Arizonan 28.17.17(.12)
ark 24.8
Arkansas 12.14.15
arkose 34.20.6, 35.20.5
Arkwright 22.16.24(.14)
Arlene 28.1.27(.4)
Arles 35.30.7, 40.8
Arlette 22.5.21
Arlington 28.17.11(.23)
arm 27.8
armada 17.13.7
Armadale 40.4.3
armadillo 19.29.2
Armageddon 28.17.12(.5)
Armagh 10.10
Armagnac 24.6.22
Armalite® 22.16.25(.9)
armament 22.26.15(.13.2)
armamentaria 3.22.4
armamentarium 27.3.17(.3)
Armand 23.24.16(.7)
Armani 1.16.8
Armatrading 29.1.13(.3)
armature 12.17, 17.7.12(.3), 17.28.15
armband 23.24.6(.4)
armchair 6.16
arme blanche 36.10
Armenia 3.9.1
Armenian 28.3.8(.1)
Armentières 6, 35.3
armeria 3.22.2
Armfield 23.31.1(.2)
armful 40.14.6(.14)
armhole 40.18.13
Armidale 40.4.3
armiger 17.29.13
armigerous 34.18.27(.27)
armillaria 3.22.4
armillary 1.29.11(.27)
Arminian 28.3.8(.2)

Arminianism 27.15.21(.2.9)
Arminius 34.3.6(.2)
Armistead 23.2.8, 23.5.3
armistice 34.2.8
Armitage 39.2.10
armless 34.18.29(.26)
armlet 22.19.26(.21)
Armley 1.31.26(.6)
armload 23.20.13
armlock 24.9.16(.15)
armoire 10.22.8
armorial 40.3.14(.5)
Armorica 17.14.15(.14)
armorist 22.29.2(.29.4)
armour 17.17.7
armourer 17.32.14(.10)
armoury 1.29.11(.12)
armpit 22.2.5
armrest 22.29.5(.12)
Armstrong 29.6.14
army 1.15.7
Arndale 40.4.3
Arne 28.9
Arnhem 27.15.14(.7)
arnica 17.14.15(.9)
Arno 19.15.7
Arnold 23.31.21
aroid 23.13.19
aroint 22.26.11
aroma 17.17.16(.11)
aromatherapeutic 24.2.10(.9)
aromatherapist 22.29.2(.11)
aromatherapy 1.8.11(.8)
aromatic 24.2.10(.4.2)
aromatically 1.31.24(.9.4)
aromaticity 1.10.16(.16.1)
aromatization 28.17.25(.3.12)
aromatize 35.15.7(.7)
arose 35.20.12
around 23.24.7(.10)
arousable 40.20.16(.22)
arousal 40.32.6
arouse 35.8
arouser 17.25.6
Arp 20.6
arpeggio 15.1.11
arquebus 34.18.10
arquebusier 17.1.11
arrack 24.16.15
arraign 28.4.18
arraignment 22.26.15(.13.4)
arrange 39.17.2
arrangeable 40.20.16(.25)
arrangement 22.26.15(.13.6)
arranger 17.29.16(.2)

arrant 22.26.15(.23.1)
arrantly 1.31.22(.20.5)
arras 34.18.27(.5)
Arrau 9.16
array 4.26
arrear 3.22
arrearage 39.2.22(.1)
arrest 22.29.5(.12)
arrestable 40.20.16(.11.7)
arrestation 28.17.25(.3.3)
arrester 17.12.24(.4)
arresting 29.1.12(.21)
arrestingly 1.31.28(.1.4)
arrestment 22.26.15(.13.3)
arrhythmia 3.8.12
arrière-pensée 4.18, 4.18.8, 4.18.12
arrière-pensées 4.18, 35.4.11
arris 34.2.21
arrival 40.28.9
arrive 31.9
arrivederci 1.25.5
arrivisme 27.15.21(.2.11)
arriviste 22.29.1
arrogance 34.24.10(.13)
arrogancy 1.22.23(.10.2)
arrogant 22.26.15(.12)
arrogantly 1.31.22(.20.2)
arrogate 22.4.12(.5)
arrogation 28.17.25(.3.6)
arrondissement 11.8, 22.26.15(.13.5)
arrondissements 34.22.18, 35.11
arrow 19.27.4
arrowhead 23.5.13(.5)
arrowroot 22.18.9
Arrowsmith 32.2.3
arrowy 1(.7)
arroyo 19.4
arse 34.9
arsehole 40.18.13
arse-kicking 29.1.14(.2)
arse-licking 29.1.14(.2)
arsenal 40.26.13(.12)
arsenate 22.4.14(.9.3), 22.19.15(.9)
arsenic 24.2.15(.4)
arsenical 40.23.12(.11)
arsenically 1.31.24(.9.8)
arsenicum 27.15.11(.9)
arsenious 34.3.6(.1)
arses 35.1.16(.5)
arsine 28.1.18(.3)
arsis 34.2.17(.5)
arson 28.17.23(.7)
arsonist 22.29.2(.18.1)
arsphenamine 28.1.13, 28.2.17(.5)

arsy-versy 1.22.17
art 22.10
Artaxerxes 35.1.16(.14)
art deco 19.12.4
artefact 22.23.5(.7)
artefactual 40.16.12
artel 40.5.3
Artemis 34.2.12
artemisia 3.15.1, 3.15.2
Artemus 34.18.15(.10)
arterial 40.3.14(.2)
arterialization 28.17.25(.3.12)
arterialize 35.15.21(.2)
arteriogram 27.6.17(.5)
arteriole 40.14.1
arterioscleroses 35.1.16(.11)
arteriosclerosis 34.2.17(.11.2)
arteriosclerotic 24.2.10(.6)
arteritis 34.18.11(.8)
artery 1.29.11(.8.4)
artesian 28.3.14, 28.17.26(.1)
artful 40.27.18
artfully 1.31.17(.16.2)
artfulness 34.18.16(.37.2)
arthritic 24.2.10(.2.4)
arthritis 34.18.11(.8)
arthrodesis 34.2.17(.10.2)
arthropod 23.10.1
arthroscope 20.15.4(.1)
arthroscopic 24.2.8(.5)
arthroscopy 1.8.11(.5)
Arthur 17.22.5
Arthurian 28.3.20(.7)
artic 24.2.10
artichoke 24.18.10
article 40.23.12(.7.2)
articulacy 1.22.16(.14)
articular 17.34.16(.21.2)
articulate 22.4.23(.7.3), 22.19.26(.13)
articulately 1.31.22(.15)
articulateness 34.18.16(.20.3)
articulation 28.17.25(.3.14)
articulator 17.12.4(.16)
articulatory 1.29.11(.8.2)
artifact 22.23.5(.7)
artifactual 40.16.12
artifice 34.2.14
artificer 17.24.15
artificial 40.33.1
artificiality 1.10.16(.32.1)
artificialize 35.15.21(.4.6)
artificially 1.31.17(.22)
artillerist 22.29.2(.29.4)

artillery 1.29.11(.27)
artilleryman 28.17.16(.2)
artily 1.31.17(.9.2)
artiness 34.18.16(.2.3)
artisan 28.7.15
artisanate 22.4.14(.4)
artist 22.29.2(.13)
artiste 22.29.1
artistic 24.2.10(.15.2)
artistical 40.23.12(.7.3)
artistically 1.31.24(.9.6)
artistry 1.29.15(.17)
artless 34.18.29(.22)
artlessly 1.31.33(.12.6)
artlessness 34.18.16(.31.6)
art nouveau 19.17
Artois 10.22.5
artsy-craftsy 1.22.21
artwork 24.17.6(.8)
arty 1.10.8
arty-crafty 1.10.24
Aruba 17.11.12
arugula 17.34.16(.21.3)
arum 27.15.26(.2)
Arundel 40.22.16
Arunta 17.12.22(.10)
arvo 19.17
Arwel 40.5.17(.3)
Arwyn 28.2.28
Aryan 28.3.20(.4)
aryl 40.16.13(.5)
arytenoid 23.13.12
as 35.7
Asa 17.24.4, 17.24.8, 17.25.3
asafoetida 17.13.15
Asaph 30.5.5, 30.14
asbestine 28.14.5
asbestos 34.10.8, 34.18.11(.16)
asbestosine 28.14.13
asbestosis 34.2.17(.11.1)
Asbury 1.29.11(.7.2)
ASCAP 20.5.1
ascarid 23.2.22
ascaris 34.2.21
ascend 23.24.5(.11)
ascendance 34.24.10(.11)
ascendancy 1.22.23(.10.2)
ascendant 22.26.15(.10)
ascender 17.13.20(.3)
ascension 28.17.25(.16)
ascensional 40.26.13(.14.7)
Ascensiontide 23.15.4
ascent 22.26.4(.11)
ascentionist 22.29.2(.18.2)
ascertain 28.4.3
ascertainable 40.20.16(.16.1)
ascertained 23.24.4

ascertainment 22.26.15(.13.4)
asceses 35.1.16(.1)
ascesis 34.2.17(.1)
ascetic 24.2.10(.3.2)
ascetically 1.31.24(.9.3)
asceticism 27.15.21(.2.12)
Ascham 27.15.11(.14)
aschelminth 32.21
asci 1.12.17(.3), 14.10
ascidian 28.3.4(.2)
ASCII 1.12.17(.3)
ascites 35.1.7(.5)
Asclepiad 23.7.2
Asclepius 34.3.1
ascomycete 22.1.9
ascomycetes 34.22.1, 35.1.7(.1)
Ascona 17.18.18(.4)
ascorbic 24.2.9(.3)
ascot 22.11.6, 22.19.12(.14)
ascribable 40.20.16(.10)
ascribe 21.12
ascription 28.17.25(.14)
ascus 34.18.13(.14)
Asda® 17.13.22
asdic 24.2.11(.17)
ASEAN 28.7.1
aseity 1.10.16(.1)
asepsis 34.2.17(.12)
aseptic 24.2.10(.12)
aseptically 1.31.24(.9.5)
asexual 40.14.8, 40.16.10
asexuality 1.10.16(.32.1)
asexually 1.31.17(.22)
Asgard 23.9.10
ash 36.6
ashamed 23.23.3
ashamedly 1.31.23(.14.6)
ashamedness 34.18.16(.21.1)
Ashanti 1.10.23(.4)
ashbin 28.2.10
Ashby 1.9.23
Ashby-de-la-Zouch 36.14
ashcan 28.7.8
Ashcroft 22.27.5
Ashdod 23.10.4
Ashdown 28.8.2(.11)
Ashe 36.6
ashen 28.17.25(.5)
Asher 17.26.6
ashet 22.19.20
Ashford 23.18.16(.20)
ashiness 34.18.16(.2.8)
Ashington 28.17.11(.23)
Ashkenazi 1.23.7
Ashkenazic 24.2.21
Ashkenazim 27.2.10
Ashkenazy 1.23.7

Ashkhabad 23.7.6, 23.9.6
ashlar 10.25.11, 17.34.29
ashlaring 29.1.30(.6)
Ashley 1.31.35(.3)
Ashmolean 28.3.21(.11)
ashore 12.16
ash pan 28.7.4
ashplant 22.26.6, 22.26.8
Ashqelon 28.10.26
ashram 27.6.17(.7), 27.15.26(.16)
ashrama 17.17.14(.10)
Ash Shariqah 17.14.1
Ashton 28.17.11(.26)
Ashton-under-Lyne 28.14.19
ashtray 4.26.11
Ashur 17.26.6
Ashurbanipal 40.6.3
ashwood 23.16.6(.19)
Ashworth 32.14.15
ashy 1.24.5
Asia 17.26.3, 17.27.2
Asian 28.17.25(.3.1), 28.17.26(.3)
Asiatic 24.2.10(.4.1)
aside 23.15.11
Asimov 31.7
asinine 28.14.9
asininity 1.10.16(.13)
ask 24.20.4
askance 34.24.6
askari 1.29.6
Askelon 28.17.33(.13)
asker 17.14.23
askeses 35.1.16(.3)
askesis 34.2.17(.3)
Askew 16.24.7
askew 16.24.7
Askey 1.12.17(.3)
Askham 27.15.11(.14)
Askrigg 26.2.10
aslant 22.26.6, 22.26.8
asleep 20.1
ASLEF 30.4
aslope 20.15.9
Asmara 17.32.7
asocial 40.33.11
asocially 1.31.17(.22)
Asoka 17.14.17
asp 20.17
asparagus 34.18.14(.5)
aspartame 27.4.1
aspartic 24.2.10(.5)
Aspatria 3.22.15
aspect 22.23.4(.1)
aspected 23.18.9(.17)
aspectual 40.16.12
aspectually 1.31.17(.24)
Aspel 40.19.15

aspen 28.17.9
asperge 39.15
aspergill 40.2.17
aspergilla 17.34.2(.12)
aspergillum 27.15.28(.2)
asperity 1.10.16(.21.1)
asperse 34.19.1
aspersion 28.17.25(.12), 28.17.26(.5)
aspersoria 3.22.9
aspersorium 27.3.17(.4)
asphalt 22.32.3, 22.32.6, 22.32.11
asphalter 17.12.26(.5)
asphaltic 24.2.10(.16)
asphodel 40.5.4
asphyxia 3.14.15
asphyxial 40.3.10
asphyxiant 22.26.2(.7)
asphyxiate 22.4.2(.9)
asphyxiation 28.17.25(.3.1)
asphyxiator 17.12.4(.1)
aspic 24.2.8(.11)
aspidistra 17.32.19(.11)
Aspinall 40.10.10, 40.26.13(.2)
aspirant 22.26.15(.23.2)
aspirate 22.4.22(.6), 22.19.24(.9)
aspiration 28.17.25(.3.13)
aspirational 40.26.13(.14.2)
aspirator 17.12.4(.15)
aspire 17.6.1
aspirin 28.17.31(.12)
asplenium 27.3.8(.1)
Aspro® 19.27.13
asquint 22.26.1
Asquith 32.2.7
Assad 23.7.13, 23.9.15
assai 14.18
assail 40.4.10
assailable 40.20.16(.29)
assailant 22.26.15(.25)
Assam 27.6.11
Assamese 35.1.11
assassin 28.17.23(.6)
assassinate 22.4.14(.9.3)
assassination 28.17.25(.3.8)
assassinator 17.12.4(.10)
assault 22.32.5, 22.32.6
assaulter 17.12.26(.5)
assaultive 31.2.1(.16)
assay 4.18, 4.18.6
assayable 40.20.16(.2)
assayer 17.2.7
assegai 14.11
assemblage 39.2.23
assemble 40.20.19

assembler 17.34.20
assembly 1.31.21(.12)
assemblyman 28.17.16(.2)
assent 22.26.4(.11)
assenter 17.12.22(.3)
assentient 22.26.15(.19)
assert 22.20.10
asserter 17.12.17
assertion 28.17.25(.12)
assertive 31.2.1(.10)
assertively 1.31.30(.7.1)
assertiveness 34.18.16(.28.1)
assess 34.5.9
assessable 40.20.16(.21.1)
assessment 22.26.15(.13.5)
assessor 17.24.5
assessorial 40.3.14(.5)
asset 22.2.16, 22.5.13(.3)
assever 17.21.4
asseverate 22.4.22(.6)
asseveration 28.17.25(.3.13)
asshole 40.18.13
assibilate 22.4.23(.7.1)
assibilation 28.17.25(.3.14)
assiduity 1.10.16(.5)
assiduous 34.18.6
assiduously 1.31.33(.12.1)
assiduousness 34.18.16(.31.2)
assign 28.14.13
assignable 40.20.16(.16.2)
assignat 10.24, 22.7.12
assignation 28.17.25(.3.8)
assignee 2.17
assigner 17.18.13(.8)
assignment 22.26.15(.13.4)
assignor 17.18.13(.8)
assimilable 40.20.16(.29)
assimilate 22.4.23(.7.2)
assimilation 28.17.25(.3.14)
assimilative 31.2.1(.9.4)
assimilator 17.12.4(.16)
assimilatory 1.29.11(.8.10)
Assisi 1.22.1, 1.23.1
assist 22.29.2(.22)
assistance 34.24.10(.10)
assistant 22.26.15(.9)
assister 17.12.24(.2)
assize 35.15.16
associability 1.10.16(.22.2)
associable 40.20.3, 40.20.16(.23)

associate 22.3.8,
22.3.10, 22.4.2(.9),
22.19.20
associateship 20.2.8
association 28.17.25(.3.1)
associational
40.26.13(.14.2)
associationist
22.29.2(.18.2)
associative 31.2.1(.2)
associatively 1.31.30(.7.1)
associativity 1.10.16(.15)
associator 17.12.4(.1)
associatory 1.29.11(.8.1)
assoil 40.11.8
assonance 34.24.10(.15)
assonant 22.26.15(.14)
assonate 22.4.14(.9.3)
assort 22.13.10
assortative 31.2.1(.9.1)
assortment
22.26.15(.13.3)
assuage 39.4.8
assuagement
22.26.15(.13.6)
assuager 17.29.3
assuasive 31.2.4(.3)
assumable 40.20.16(.15)
assume 27.14.7
assumedly 1.31.23(.14.6)
assuming 29.1.16
assumingly 1.31.28(.1.7)
assumpsit 22.2.16
assumption 28.17.25(.14)
assumptive 31.2.1(.12)
Assur 17.24.6
assurable 40.20.16(.27.2)
assurance 34.24.10(.16)
assure 12.16, 17.7.10
assured 23.12.7, 23.18.4
assuredly 1.31.23(.14.7)
assuredness
34.18.16(.21.1)
assurer 17.32.14(.3)
Assyria 3.22.1
Assyrian 28.3.20(.1)
Assyriologist
22.29.2(.26.2)
Assyriology 1.26.10(.11.1)
astable 40.20.4
Astaire 6.4
Astarte 1.10.8
astatic 24.2.10(.4.1)
astatine 28.1.9(.3),
28.2.11(.10)
Astbury 1.29.11(.7.2)
aster 17.12.24(.5)
asterisk 24.20.1
asterism 27.15.21(.2.14)
Asterix 34.23.2(.12)
astern 28.18.4

asteroid 23.13.19
asteroidal 40.22.9
asthenia 3.9.1
asthenic 24.2.15(.4)
asthenosphere 3.10.5
asthma 17.17.22
asthmatic 24.2.10(.4.2)
asthmatical 40.23.12(.7.1)
asthmatically
1.31.24(.9.4)
Asti 1.10.26(.5)
astigmatic 24.2.10(.4.2)
astigmatism
27.15.21(.2.4)
astilbe 1.9.24
astir 18.3
Asti Spumante
1.10.23(.4)
Astley 1.31.22(.22)
Aston 28.17.11(.25)
astonish 36.2.16(.8)
astonishingly
1.31.28(.1.13)
astonishment
22.26.15(.13.6)
Astor 17.12.24(.5)
Astoria 3.22.9
astound 23.24.7(.3)
astoundingly
1.31.28(.1.5)
astra 17.32.19(.11)
astraddle 40.22.5
astragal 40.24.11
astragali 14.25.9
astragalus 34.18.29(.17.2)
astrakhan 28.7.8
astral 40.16.13(.16)
astrally 1.31.17(.27.3)
astrantia 3.4.12
astray 4.26.11
Astrid 23.2.22
astride 23.15.15
astringency 1.22.23(.10.4)
astringent 22.26.15(.21)
astringently
1.31.22(.20.4)
astrobiology
1.26.10(.11.1)
astrobotany 1.16.15(.7)
astrochemistry
1.29.15(.17)
astrodome 27.17.5
astrohatch 38.5
astrolabe 21.3
astrologer 17.29.13
astrologic 24.2.24(.4)
astrological
40.23.12(.17.2)
astrologically
1.31.24(.9.11)
astrology 1.26.10(.11.5)

åstrom 27.15.26(.10)
astronaut 22.13.6
astronautical
40.23.12(.7.2)
astronautically
1.31.24(.9.4)
astronautics 34.23.2(.3)
astronomer 17.17.14(.6)
astronomic 24.2.14(.6)
astronomical
40.23.12(.10)
astronomically
1.31.24(.9.8)
astronomy 1.15.13(.5)
astrophysical
40.23.12(.16)
astrophysicist
22.29.2(.22)
astrophysics 34.23.2(.11)
AstroTurf® 30.15
Asturias 34.7.2
astute 22.18.10
astutely 1.31.22(.14)
astuteness 34.18.16(.20.2)
Astyanax 34.23.5(.7)
Asunción 28.10
asunder 17.13.20(.10)
Asur 17.24.6
Aswad 23.10.11
Aswan 28.7.19, 28.9.12
asylum 27.15.28(.9)
asymmetric 24.2.26(.14.2)
asymmetrical
40.23.12(.18)
asymmetrically
1.31.24(.9.12)
asymmetry 1.29.15(.8)
asymptomatic
24.2.10(.4.2)
asymptote 22.21.3
asymptotic 24.2.10(.6)
asymptotically
1.31.24(.9.4)
asynchronous
34.18.16(.15.3)
asynchronously
1.31.33(.12.3)
asyndetic 24.2.10(.3.1)
asyndeton 28.17.11(.15)
at 22.7
Atacama 17.17.7
Atack 24.6.7
Atahualpa 17.10.19
Atalanta 17.12.22(.4)
ataractic 24.2.10(.13)
ataraxia 3.14.15
ataraxic 24.2.20(.13)
ataraxy 1.22.22
Atari® 1.29.6
Atatürk 24.17.2
atavism 27.15.21(.2.11)

atavistic 24.2.10(.15.2)
atavistically 1.31.24(.9.6)
ataxia 3.14.15
ataxic 24.2.20(.13)
ataxy 1.22.22
atchoo 16.19
ate 22.4, 22.5
Atebrin® 28.1.25(.5),
28.2.29(.7)
atelier 4.2.10
a tempo 19.8
atemporal 40.16.13(.12.1)
Aten 28.17.11(.8)
Athabasca 17.14.23
Athabascan 28.17.13(.18)
Athanasian 28.3.13,
28.3.14, 28.17.25(.3.8),
28.17.26(.3)
Athanasius 34.3.10,
34.3.11, 34.18.22(.3)
atheism 27.15.21(.2.1)
atheist 22.29.2(.2)
atheistic 24.2.10(.15.1)
atheistical 40.23.12(.7.3)
atheistically 1.31.24(.9.6)
atheling 29.1.31(.12)
Athelstan 28.7.6,
28.17.11(.25)
athematic 24.2.10(.4.2)
Athena 17.18.1(.8)
Athenaeum 27.15.1
Athene 1.16.1(.9)
Athenian 28.3.8(.1)
Athens 35.26.13(.12)
atheoretical
40.23.12(.7.1)
atheroma 17.17.16(.11)
atheromata 17.12.16(.9.3)
atheroscleroses
35.1.16(.11)
atherosclerosis
34.2.17(.11.2)
atherosclerotic
24.2.10(.6)
Atherstone 28.17.11(.25)
Atherton 28.17.11(.15)
athetosis 34.2.17(.11.1)
athlete 22.1.18
athletic 24.2.10(.3.3)
athletically 1.31.24(.9.3)
athleticism
27.15.21(.2.12)
Athlone 28.19.19
Athol 40.9.13
Atholl 40.9.13, 40.29
Athos 34.10.14
athwart 22.13.13
atilt 22.32.1
atingle 40.24.14(.1)
atishoo 16.17
Ativan® 28.7.13

Atkin 28.2.13(.9)

Atkins 35.26.2

Atkinson 28.17.23(.24)

Atlanta 17.12.22(.4)

Atlantean 28.3.3

atlantes 35.1.7(.9)

Atlantic 24.2.10(.14)

Atlanticism 27.15.21(.2.12)

Atlanticist 22.29.2(.22)

Atlantis 34.2.8

atlantosaurus 34.18.27(.8)

atlas 34.18.29(.22)

atman 28.17.16(.21)

atmosphere 3.10.5

atmospheric 24.2.26(.4)

atmospherical 40.23.12(.18)

atmospherically 1.31.24(.9.12)

atoll 40.9.7

atom 27.15.9(.4)

atomic 24.2.14(.6)

atomically 1.31.24(.9.8)

atomicity 1.10.16(.16.1)

atomism 27.15.21(.2.8)

atomist 22.29.2(.17)

atomistic 24.2.10(.15.2)

atomistically 1.31.24(.9.6)

atomization 28.17.25(.3.11)

atomize 35.15.11

atomizer 17.25.12(.5)

atomy 1.15.13(.1)

atonal 40.26.15

atonality 1.10.16(.32.8)

atonally 1.31.17(.14.3)

atone 28.19.4

atoned 23.24.18

atonement 22.26.15(.13.4)

atonic 24.2.15(.6.1)

atony 1.16.15(.7)

atop 20.7.4

Atora® 17.32.10(.2)

atrabilious 34.3.16

atrabiliousness 34.18.16(.31.1)

Atreus 34.3.15(.8)

atria 3.22.15

atrial 40.3.14(.9)

atrium 27.3.17(.6)

atrocious 34.18.22(.9)

atrociously 1.31.33(.12.4)

atrociousness 34.18.16(.31.4)

atrocity 1.10.16(.16.2)

atrophic 24.2.16(.4)

atrophy 1.18.9(.2)

atropine 28.1.7, 28.2.9

Atropos 34.10.6, 34.18.9(.8)

attaboy 13.3

attach 38.5

attachable 40.20.16(.24)

attaché 4.20

attacher 17.28.6

attachment 22.26.15(.13.6)

attack 24.6.7

attacker 17.14.5

attain 28.4.3

attainability 1.10.16(.22.2)

attainable 40.20.16(.16.1)

attainableness 34.18.16(.37.4)

attainder 17.13.20(.2)

attainment 22.26.15(.13.4)

attaint 22.26.3

Attalid 23.2.23

attar 10.6.2, 17.12.6

attemper 17.10.17

attempt 22.25

attemptable 40.20.16(.11.4)

Attenborough 17.32.14(.5)

attend 23.24.5(.4)

attendance 34.24.10(.11)

attendant 22.26.15(.10)

attendee 2.13

attender 17.13.20(.3)

attention 28.17.25(.16)

attentional 40.26.13(.14.7)

attentive 31.2.1(.14)

attentively 1.31.30(.7.3)

attentiveness 34.18.16(.28.1)

attenuate 22.4.4, 22.19.5

attenuation 28.17.25(.3.1)

attenuator 17.12.4(.2)

attest 22.29.5(.2)

attestable 40.20.16(.11.7)

attestation 28.17.25(.3.3)

attestor 17.12.24(.4)

attic 24.2.10(.4.1)

Attica 17.14.15(.6)

Atticism 27.15.21(.2.12)

Attila 17.34.2(.2)

attire 17.6.3

Attis 34.2.8

attitude 23.17.4(.1)

attitudinal 40.26.13(.5)

attitudinize 35.15.12(.5)

Attlee 1.31.22(.6)

attorney 1.16.16

attorneyship 20.2.7(.2)

attract 22.23.5(.9)

attractability 1.10.16(.22.2)

attractable 40.20.16(.11.5)

attractant 22.26.15(.9)

attraction 28.17.25(.15.3)

attractive 31.2.1(.13.3)

attractively 1.31.30(.7.2)

attractiveness 34.18.16(.28.1)

attractor 17.12.21(.3)

attributable 40.20.16(.11.3)

attributableness 34.18.16(.37.4)

attributably 1.31.21(.4.3)

attribute 22.18.10

attribution 28.17.25(.11)

attributive 31.2.1(.9.4)

attributively 1.31.30(.7.2)

attrition 28.17.25(.2.6)

attritional 40.26.13(.14.1)

attune 28.16.14

Atwell 40.5.17(.7)

atwitter 17.12.2

Atwood 23.16.6(.9)

atypical 40.23.12(.5)

atypically 1.31.24(.9.2)

aubade 23.9.6

auberge 37.3

aubergine 28.1.21

Auberon 28.10.24(.5), 28.17.31(.11)

Aubrey 1.29.14

aubretia 17.26.1

auburn 28.17.10

Aubusson 28.10.18

Auchinleck 24.4.14

Auchtermuchty 1.10.22

Auckland 23.24.16(.16.3)

au contraire 6.19

au courant 11.17

auction 28.17.25(.15.4)

auctioneer 3.9

auctioneering 29.1.30(.2)

auctorial 40.3.14(.5)

audacious 34.18.22(.3)

audaciously 1.31.33(.12.4)

audaciousness 34.18.16(.31.4)

audacity 1.10.16(.16.1)

Auden 28.17.12(.10)

Audi® 1.11.8

audibility 1.10.16(.22.1)

audible 40.20.16(.12)

audibleness 34.18.16(.37.4)

audibly 1.31.21(.4.4)

Audie 1.11.11

audience 34.24.2

audile 40.13.4

audio 15.1.3

audio cassette 22.5.13(.4)

audiolingual 40.35.4

audiological 40.23.12(.17.2)

audiologist 22.29.2(.26.2)

audiology 1.26.10(.11.1)

audiometer 17.12.16(.9.2)

audiometry 1.29.15(.8)

audiophile 40.13.9

audiotape 20.3

audio typing 29.1.10(.8)

audio typist 22.29.2(.11)

audio-visual 40.14.8, 40.16.11

audit 22.2.8

audition 28.17.25(.2.3)

auditive 31.2.1(.9.1)

auditor 17.12.16(.6)

auditoria 3.22.9

auditorial 40.3.14(.5)

auditorium 27.3.17(.4)

auditory 1.29.11(.8.6)

Audlem 27.15.28(.17)

Audley 1.31.23(.9)

Audra 17.32.20

Audrey 1.29.16

Audubon 28.10.8

au fait 4

au fond 11

Augean 28.17.1(.11)

auger 17.16.8

aught 22.13

augite 22.16.21

augment 22.26.4(.8)

augmentation 28.17.25(.3.3)

augmentative 31.2.1(.9.1)

augmenter 17.12.22(.3)

au grand sérieux 18

au gratin 8

Augsburg 26.14.1(.11)

augur 17.16.8

augural 40.16.13(.12.4)

augury 1.29.11(.26)

August 22.29.15(.12)

august 22.29.12

Augusta 17.12.24(.10)

Augustan 28.17.11(.25)

Augustine 28.1.9(.7), 28.14.5

Augustinian 28.3.8(.2)

augustly 1.31.22(.22)

augustness 34.18.16(.20.4)

Augustus 34.18.11(.16)

au jus 16, 34.17

auk 24.10

auklet 22.19.26(.19)

auld lang syne 28.14

autumnal **40.26.20**
autumnally **1.31.17(.14.3)**
Auty **1.10.10**
Auvergne **28.6, 28.18.8**
auxanometer **17.12.16(.9.2)**
auxiliary **1.29.2(.12)**
auxin **28.2.23(.14)**
Ava **17.21.3**
avadavat **22.7.14**
avail **40.4.9**
availability **1.10.16(.22.2)**
available **40.20.16(.29)**
availableness **34.18.16(.37.4)**
availably **1.31.21(.9)**
avalanche **38.18.4**
Avalon **28.10.26**
avant-garde **23.9.10**
avant-gardism **27.15.21(.2.5)**
avant-gardist **22.29.2(.14)**
Avar **10.13**
avarice **34.2.21**
avaricious **34.18.22(.2)**
avariciously **1.31.33(.12.4)**
avariciousness **34.18.16(.31.4)**
avast **22.29.6(.10), 22.29.8(.6)**
avatar **10.6, 10.6.5**
avaunt **22.26.10**
ave **1.19.6, 4.16**
Avebury **1.29.11(.7.2)**
avenge **39.17.3**
avenger **17.29.16(.3)**
avens **35.26.13(.11)**
aventurine **28.14.18**
avenue **16.24.10**
aver **18.10**
average **39.2.22(.9)**
averagely **1.31.37**
avermectin **28.2.11(.12)**
averment **22.26.15(.13.2)**
Avernus **34.18.16(.16)**
Averroës **35.1.4**
averse **34.19.6**
aversely **1.31.33(.12.6)**
averseness **34.18.16(.31.7)**
aversion **28.17.25(.12)**
aversive **31.2.4(.10)**
aversively **1.31.30(.7.4)**
avert **22.20.9**
avertable **40.20.16(.11.3)**
Avery **1.29.11(.15)**
Avesta **17.12.24(.4)**
Avestan **28.17.11(.25)**

Avestic **24.2.10(.15.4)**
avgolemono **19.15.12**
Avia® **3.11.3**
avian **28.3.10**
aviary **1.29.2(.7)**
aviate **22.4.2(.8)**
aviation **28.17.25(.3.1)**
aviator **17.12.4(.1)**
aviatrices **35.1.16(.10)**
aviatrix **34.23.2(.12)**
Avicenna **17.18.4**
aviculture **17.28.26**
aviculturist **22.29.2(.29.4)**
avid **23.2.15**
avidity **1.10.16(.9)**
avidly **1.31.23(.14.7)**
Aviemore **12.9, 12.9.2**
avifauna **17.18.10**
Avignon **11.18**
Ávila **17.34.16(.14)**
avionic **24.2.15(.6.1)**
Avis® **34.2.15**
avitaminoses **35.1.16(.11)**
avitaminosis **34.2.17(.11.2)**
avizandum **27.15.10(.14)**
Avoca **17.14.17**
avocado **19.11.7**
avocation **28.17.25(.3.5)**
avocet **22.5.13(.4)**
Avogadro **19.27.16**
avoid **23.13.14**
avoidable **40.20.16(.12)**
avoidably **1.31.21(.4.4)**
avoidance **34.24.10(.11)**
avoider **17.13.10**
avoirdupois **10.22.3, 35.13**
Avon **28.9, 28.10.16, 28.17.20(.3)**
Avonmouth **32.7**
avouch **38.6**
avouchment **22.26.15(.13.6)**
avow **9.8**
avowable **40.20.16(.3)**
avowal **40.16.3**
avowedly **1.31.23(.14.7)**
Avril **40.16.13(.21)**
avulsion **28.17.25(.17)**
avuncular **17.34.16(.21.2)**
AWACS **34.23.5(.13)**
await **22.4.21**
awake **24.3.12**
awaken **28.17.13(.3)**
awakening **29.1.17(.12)**
award **23.12.8**

awarder **17.13.9**
aware **6.18**
awareness **34.18.16(.6)**
awash **36.9.5**
away **4.25**
awe **12**
aweary **1.29.2(.10)**
aweigh **4.25**
aweless **34.18.29(.11)**
awelessness **34.18.16(.31.6)**
awesome **27.15.20(.7)**
awesomely **1.31.26(.11)**
awesomeness **34.18.16(.24)**
awestricken **28.17.13(.2)**
awestruck **24.12.8**
awful **40.27.9**
awfully **1.31.17(.16.1), 1.31.29**
awfulness **34.18.16(.37.2)**
awheel **40.1.14**
awhile **40.13.15**
awkward **23.18.26(.11)**
awkwardly **1.31.23(.14.7)**
awkwardness **34.18.16(.21.1)**
awl **40.10**
awn **28.11**
awning **29.1.17(.8)**
awoke **24.18.12**
awoken **28.17.13(.15)**
AWOL **40.9.18**
awry **14.24**
axe **34.23.5**
axel **40.31.18**
axeman **28.7.10(.20), 28.17.16(.29)**
axemen **28.5.7(.24)**
axes **35.1.16(.14)**
Axholme **17.17.12**
axial **40.3.10**
axiality **1.10.16(.32.1)**
axially **1.31.3(.9)**
axil **40.31.18**
axilla **17.34.2(.9)**
axillae **2.32.2**
axillary **1.29.11(.27)**
axiological **40.23.12(.17.2)**
axiologist **22.29.2(.26.2)**
axiology **1.26.10(.11.1)**
axiom **27.3.11**
axiomatic **24.2.10(.4.2)**
axiomatically **1.31.24(.9.4)**
axis **34.2.17(.14)**
axle **40.31.18**
Axminster **17.12.24(.23)**

axolotl **40.21.7**
axon **28.10.18**
axonometric **24.2.26(.14.2)**
axonometrically **1.31.24(.9.12)**
Axum **27.11.10, 27.13.1**
ay **14**
Ayacucho **19.24**
ayah **17.6, 17.33.2**
ayatollah **17.34.9**
Ayckbourn **28.11.2**
Aycliffe **30.2.6**
aye **4, 14**
aye aye **14**
aye-aye **14.4**
Ayer **6**
Ayers **35.6**
Áyios Nikólaos **34.10.3**
Aylesbury **1.29.11(.7.2)**
Aylesham **27.15.22**
Aylmer **17.17.24**
Aylward **23.12.8, 23.18.26(.17)**
Aymara **10.23.3**
Aynho **19.26**
Ayot **22.19.2**
Ayr **6**
Ayrshire **17.26.5**
Ayrton **28.17.11(.5)**
Aysgarth **32.8**
Ayto **19.10.3**
Ayub Khan **28.9**
azalea **3.24.3**
Azania **3.9.3(.7)**
Azanian **28.3.8(.3)**
azeotrope **20.15.8**
azeotropic **24.2.8(.5)**
Azerbaijan **28.9.10**
Azerbaijani **1.16.8**
Azeri **1.29.4**
azide **23.15.12**
Azilian **28.3.21(.2)**
azimuth **32.14.11**
azimuthal **40.29**
azine **28.1.19**
Aziz **35.1.17, 35.2.12**
Aznavour **12.12, 17.7.9**
azobenzine **28.1.19**
azoic **24.2.7**
Azores **35.12**
Azov **31.7**
Aztec **24.4.4**
Aztecan **28.17.13(.4)**
azuki **1.12.12**
azure **17.27.2, 17.27.4, 17.33.12**
azurite **22.16.24(.9)**
azygous **34.18.14(.5)**

b 2
baa **10**
Baader-Meinhof **30.8.10**
Baal **40.4, 40.8, 40.16.2**
Baalbek **24.4.3**
Baalim **27.2.16**
Baalism **27.15.21(.2.15)**
baas **34.9**
baasskap **20.5.1, 20.6**
Baath **32.8**
Baathist **22.29.2(.21)**
baba **10.5.3, 17.11.7**
babacoote **22.18.4**
Babbage **39.2.9**
Babbitt **22.2.6**
Babbittry **1.29.15(.4)**
babble **40.20.6**
babblement **22.26.15(.13.7)**
babbler **17.34.20**
babbling **29.1.31(.16)**
Babcock **24.9.6**
babe **21.3**
Babel **40.20.4**
babesiasis **34.2.17(.10.1)**
babesiosis **34.2.17(.11.1)**
Babi **1.9.6**
babiche **36.1**
Babington **28.17.11(.23)**
babirusa **17.24.14**
Babism **27.15.21(.2.3)**
Babist **22.29.2(.12)**
baboo **16.6**
baboon **28.16.2**
Babs **35.21**
babu **16.6**
babushka **17.14.24**
baby **1.9.3**
Babycham® **27.6.13**
Babygro® **19.27.18**
babyhood **23.16.5(.1)**
babyish **36.2.1**
babyishly **1.31.35(.7.1)**
babyishness **34.18.16(.33.1)**
Babylon **28.10.26, 28.17.33(.13)**
Babylonia **3.9.11**
Babylonian **28.3.8(.11)**
babysat **22.7.15**
babysit **22.2.16**
babysitter **17.12.2**
Bacall **40.10.7**
Bacardi® **1.11.9**
baccalaureate **22.3.12**
baccara **10.23**
baccarat **10.23, 10.23.3**
baccate **22.4.11(.3)**
Bacchae **2.14, 14.10**
bacchanal **40.6.9, 40.26.13(.6)**

bacchanalia **3.24.3**
bacchanalian **28.3.21(.3)**
bacchant **22.26.15(.11)**
bacchante **1.10.23(.4), 22.26.6**
bacchantic **24.2.10(.14)**
Bacchic **24.2.12**
Bacchus **34.18.13(.3)**
bacciferous **34.18.27(.20)**
baccy **1.12.5**
Bach **24.8, 25.5**
Bacharach **24.6.21**
bachelor **17.34.16(.18)**
bacillar **17.34.2(.9), 17.34.16(.15)**
bacillary **1.29.11(.27)**
bacilli **14.25.2**
bacilliform **27.10.5(.2)**
bacillus **34.18.29(.2)**
bacitracin **28.2.23(.2)**
back **24.6**
backache **24.3.6**
backbench **38.18.2**
backbencher **17.28.22**
backbit **22.2.6**
backbite **22.16.8**
backbiter **17.12.13(.1)**
backbitten **28.17.11(.2)**
backblocks **34.23.8(.11)**
backboard **23.12.2(.10)**
backbone **28.19.3**
back-breaking **29.1.14(.3)**
backchat **22.7.17**
backcloth **32.9**
backcomb **27.17.6**
backcourt **22.13.4**
backdate **22.4.10**
backdraught **22.27.4(.4)**
backdrop **20.7.12**
backer **17.14.5**
backfield **23.31.1(.2)**
backfill **40.2.11**
backfire **17.6.9**
backgammon **28.17.16(.7)**
background **23.24.7(.10)**
backhand **23.24.6(.11)**
backhanded **23.18.10(.14)**
backhandedly **1.31.23(.14.4)**
backhander **17.13.20(.4)**
Backhouse **34.8.6(.13)**
backing **29.1.14(.4)**
backlash **36.6.10**
backless **34.18.29(.24)**
backlighting **29.1.12(.11)**
backlist **22.29.2(.31.6)**
backlit **22.2.25**
backlog **26.7.14**

backmarker **17.14.7**
backmost **22.29.17(.4)**
backpack **24.6.5**
backpacker **17.14.5**
back-pedal **40.22.4**
backrest **22.29.5(.12)**
back room **27.14.6(.10)**
Backs **34.23.5**
backscratcher **17.28.6**
backscratching **29.1.27**
backsheesh **36.1**
backside **23.15.11**
backsight **22.16.19(.14)**
backslapping **29.1.10(.5)**
backslash **36.6.10**
backslid **23.2.23**
backslide **23.15.16**
backslider **17.13.12**
backspace **34.4.2**
backspin **28.2.9**
backstage **39.4.2**
backstair **6.4**
backstairs **35.6**
backstay **4.9.10**
backstitch **38.2.3**
backstop **20.7.4**
backstrap **20.5.6**
backstreet **22.1.17**
backstretch **38.4**
backstroke **24.18.13**
back talk **24.10.2**
backtrack **24.6.21**
backtracker **17.14.5**
backup **20.9.7**
backveld **22.32.2**
backvelder **17.12.26(.3), 17.13.23(.3)**
backward **23.18.26(.11)**
backwardation **28.17.25(.3.4)**
backwardly **1.31.23(.14.7)**
backwardness **34.18.16(.21.1)**
backwards **35.23.12**
backwash **36.9.5**
backwater **17.12.10(.7)**
backwoods **35.23.11**
backwoodsman **28.17.16(.30)**
backy **1.12.5**
backyard **23.9.21**
Bacofoil **40.11.7**
Bacolod **23.10.13**
bacon **28.17.13(.3)**
Baconian **28.3.8(.11)**
bacteraemia **3.8.1**
bacteria **3.22.2**
bacterial **40.3.14(.2)**
bactericidal **40.22.11**
bactericide **23.15.11(.6)**

bacteriological **40.23.12(.17.2)**
bacteriologically **1.31.24(.9.11)**
bacteriologist **22.29.2(.26.2)**
bacteriology **1.26.10(.11.1)**
bacteriolyses **35.1.16(.10)**
bacteriolysis **34.2.17(.10.5)**
bacteriolytic **24.2.10(.2.5)**
bacteriophage **39.4.6**
bacteriostases **35.1.16(.2)**
bacteriostasis **34.2.17(.2)**
bacteriostatic **24.2.10(.4.1)**
bacterium **27.3.17(.2)**
Bactria **3.22.15**
Bactrian **28.3.20(.11)**
bad **23.7**
badass **34.9.3**
Baddesley **1.31.34**
baddish **36.2.12**
baddy **1.11.7**
bade **23.4, 23.7**
Badedas® **34.7.8, 34.18.12**
Badel **40.5.4**
Baden **28.17.12(.4)**
Baden-Baden **28.17.12(.8)**
Baden-Powell **40.16.3**
Bader **17.13.7**
badge **39.6**
badger **17.29.5**
Badian **28.3.4(.3)**
badinage **37.4.5**
badlands **35.23.15**
badly **1.31.23(.5)**
badminton **28.17.11(.22)**
bad-mouth **32.7, 33.5**
badness **34.18.16(.21.1)**
Badon **28.17.12(.4)**
Baedeker **17.14.4, 17.14.15(.7)**
Baerlein **28.14.19(.5)**
Baez **35.5.2**
Baffin **28.2.19**
baffle **40.27.7**
baffleboard **23.12.2(.20)**
bafflement **22.26.15(.13.7)**
baffle-plate **22.4.23(.8)**
baffler **17.34.26**
bafflingly **1.31.28(.1.18)**
BAFTA **17.12.23**
bag **26.5**
Baganda **17.13.20(.4)**
Bagandan **28.17.12(.23)**
bagarre **10.9**
bagasse **34.7.10, 34.9.4**

bagatelle 40.5.3
Bagehot 22.19.22
bagel 40.24.3
bagful 40.14.6(.13)
baggage 39.2.13
baggily 1.31.17(.12)
bagginess 34.18.16(.2.4)
baggy 1.14.5
Baghdad 23.7.8
bagman 28.7.10(.14)
bagmen 28.5.7(.18)
Bagnall 40.26.19
bagnio 19.28
bagpipe 20.10.1
bagpiper 17.10.12
Bagshaw 12.16.10
Bagshot 22.11.12
baguette 22.5.7
Baguley 1.31.17(.12)
bagwash 36.9.5
bah 10
Baha'i 14.22
Baha'ism 27.15.21(.2.1)
Baha'ist 22.29.2(.6)
Baha'ite 22.16.5
Bahamas 35.18.12
Bahamian 28.3.7
Bahasa 17.24.8
Baha Ullah 10.25, 10.25.3
Bahawalpur 17.7.1
Bahía 17.1.15
Bahrain 28.4.18
Bahraini 1.16.4
Bahreini 1.16.4
baht 22.10
baignoire 10.22.9
Baikal 40.6.6, 40.8.6
bail 40.4
bailable 40.20.16(.29)
Baildon 28.17.12(.27)
Baile Átha Cliath 3
bailee 2.32, 2.32.4
bailer 17.34.4
bailey 1.31.4
bailie 1.31.4
bailiff 30.2.6
bailiwick 24.2.25
Baillie 1.31.4
Bailly 1.31.4
bailment 22.26.15(.13.7)
bailor 17.34.4
bailout 22.9.19
bailsman 28.17.16(.30)
Bain 28.4
Bainbridge 39.2.22(.10)
Baines 35.26.4
bain-marie 2.30
Bairam 27.8.9
Baird 23.6
bairn 28.6

Bairstow 19.10.19
bait 22.4
baize 35.4
Bajan 28.17.28(.3)
bajra 10.23.9
bake 24.3
bakehouse 34.8.6(.13)
Bakelite® 22.16.25(.9)
baker 17.14.3
Bakerloo 16.25
bakery 1.29.11(.10)
Bakewell 40.5.17(.9), 40.35.3
Bakhtin 28.1.9
baklava 17.21.12
baksheesh 36.1
Bakst 22.29.20
Baku 16.9
Bakunin 28.2.18
Bala 17.34.6, 17.34.8
Balaam 27.15.28(.3)
balaclava 17.21.6
balafon 28.10.15
balalaika 17.14.12
balance 34.24.10(.24)
balanceable 40.20.16(.21.3)
balancer 17.24.22(.7)
Balanchine 28.1.20, 28.1.22
balas ruby 1.9.10
balata 17.12.8(.11), 17.12.16(.20)
Balaton 28.10.9
Balboa 17.9.1
Balbriggan 28.17.15(.2)
Balchin 28.2.25, 28.2.26
Balcon 28.17.13(.19)
balcony 1.16.15(.9)
bald 23.31.6
baldachin 28.2.13(.6)
Balder 17.13.23(.5)
balderdash 36.6.4
baldhead 23.5.13(.10)
baldheaded 23.18.10(.3)
baldish 36.2.12
baldly 1.31.23(.18)
baldmoney 1.16.12
baldness 34.18.16(.21.1)
Baldock 24.9.5
baldpate 22.4.7
baldric 24.2.26(.15)
Baldry 1.29.16
Baldwin 28.2.28
baldy 1.11.23
bale 40.4
Balearic 24.2.26(.2)
baleen 28.1.27
baleful 40.27.31
balefully 1.31.17(.16.2)

balefulness 34.18.16(.37.2)
Balenciaga 17.16.6
baler 17.34.4
Balfour 12.11, 12.11.8, 17.20.19
Balham 27.15.28(.5)
Bali 1.31.9
Balinese 35.1.12
Balkan 28.17.13(.19)
Balkanization 28.17.25(.3.11)
Balkanize 35.15.12(.5)
Balkhash 36.6.5
balky 1.12.8
ball 40.10
Ballachulish 36.2.27
ballad 23.18.29
ballade 23.9.22
balladeer 3.5
balladry 1.29.16
Ballantine 28.14.5
Ballantrae 4.26.11
Ballarat 22.7.20
Ballard 23.9.22
ballast 22.29.15(.18)
Ballater 17.12.16(.20)
ball bearing 29.1.30(.4)
ballboy 13.3
ballcock 24.9.6
ballerina 17.18.1(.15)
Ballesteros 34.10.16
ballet 4.28.3
balletic 24.2.10(.3.3)
balletomane 28.4.7
balletomania 3.9.3(.5)
Ballets Russes 34.17
ballgirl 40.17
ballhawk 24.10.8
Balliol 40.3.15
ballista 17.12.24(.2)
ballistae 2.12.15
ballistic 24.2.10(.15.3)
ballistically 1.31.24(.9.6)
ballock 24.16.16
ballon d'essai 4.18
ballons d'essai 4.18
balloon 28.16.15
balloonist 22.29.2(.18.1)
ballot 22.19.26(.5)
ballpark 24.8.2
ballplayer 17.2.10
ballpoint 22.26.11
ballroom 27.14.6(.20)
balls 35.30.9
ballsy 1.23.22
bally 1.31.7
ballyhoo 16.21
Ballymacarrett 22.19.24(.4)

Ballymena 17.18.1(.6)
Ballymoney 1.16.12
balm 27.8
Balmain 8
balmily 1.31.17(.13)
balminess 34.18.16(.2.5)
Balmoral 40.16.13(.7)
balmy 1.15.7
balneary 1.29.2(.6)
balneological 40.23.12(.17.2)
balneologist 22.29.2(.26.2)
balneology 1.26.10(.11.1)
balniel 40.3.7(.10)
baloney 1.16.17(.15)
BALPA 17.10.19
balsam 27.15.20(.22)
balsamic 24.2.14(.4)
balsamiferous 34.18.27(.20)
balsa wood 23.16
Balt 22.32.5, 22.32.6
Balthasar 10.16, 17.25.5
Balthazar 10.16, 17.25.5
balti 1.10.28
Baltic 24.2.10(.16)
Baltimore 12.9.4
Baltistan 28.9.2
Baluchistan 28.9.2
balun 28.13.10
baluster 17.12.24(.14)
balustrade 23.4.15
Balzac 24.6.15
Bamako 19.12, 19.12.5
bambini 1.16.1(.2)
bambino 19.15.1
bamboo 16.6
bamboozle 40.32.13
bamboozlement 22.26.15(.13.7)
bamboozler 17.34.28
Bamian 28.3.7
ban 28.7
banal 40.6.9, 40.8.9
banality 1.10.16(.32.8)
banally 1.31.38
banana 17.18.8(.6)
banausic 24.2.20(.8), 24.2.21
Banbury 1.29.11(.7.2)
banc 24.19.3
Bancroft 22.27.5
band 23.24.6
Banda 17.13.20(.4)
bandage 39.2.11
bandanna 17.18.6
Bandaranaike 17.14.15(.2)
Bandar Seri Begawan 28.17.30

barquentine **28.1.9(.6)**
Barr **10**
barrack **24.16.15**
barracks **34.23.15**
barracoon **28.16.5**
barracouta **17.12.15(.2)**
barracuda **17.13.14**
barrage **37.4.9, 39.8**
barramunda **17.13.20(.10)**
barramundi **1.11.20(.7)**
barrator **17.12.16(.18)**
barratrous **34.18.27(.14)**
barratry **1.29.15(.12)**
barre **10**
barré **4.26.4**
barrel **40.16.13(.5)**
barrelful **40.14.6(.22)**
barrelhead **23.5.13(.19)**
barrelhouse **34.8.6(.24)**
barren **28.17.31(.5)**
barrenly **1.31.27(.14)**
barrenness **34.18.16(.25)**
barret **22.19.24(.4)**
barrette **22.5.19**
barricade **23.4.5**
Barrie **1.29.5**
barrier **3.22.5**
barrio **15.1.12**
barrister **17.12.24(.14)**
Barron **28.17.31(.5)**
barrow **19.27.4**
Barrow-in-Furness **34.2.13**
barrowload **23.20.13**
Barry **1.29.5**
Barrymore **12.9.2**
Barsac **24.6.14**
Bart **22.10**
Bart. **22.5.9**
bartender **17.13.20(.3)**
barter **17.12.8**
barterer **17.32.14(.6)**
Barth **32.8**
Barthes **22.10**
Bartholomew **16.24.9**
bartizan **28.7.15, 28.17.24(.12)**
Bartlett **22.19.26(.17)**
Bartók **24.9.4**
Bartolomeo **19.2**
Barton **28.17.11(.8)**
bartsia **3.14.13**
Baruch **24.16.15**
baryon **28.10.2**
baryonic **24.2.15(.6.1)**
Baryshnikov **30.8.6, 31.7**
barysphere **3.10.5**
baryta **17.12.13(.8)**
barytes **35.1.7(.5)**

barytic **24.2.10(.2.4)**
barytone **28.19.4(.5)**
basal **40.31.4**
basalt **22.32.6, 22.32.15**
basaltic **24.2.10(.16)**
basan **28.17.24(.4)**
bascule **40.15.9(.5)**
base **34.4**
baseball **40.10.4**
baseboard **23.12.2(.15)**
baseborn **28.11.2**
basehead **23.5.13(.15)**
Basel **40.32.7**
baseless **34.18.29(.33)**
baselessly **1.31.33(.12.6)**
baselessness **34.18.16(.31.6)**
baseline **28.14.19(.21)**
baseload **23.20.13**
baseman **28.17.16(.29)**
basement **22.26.15(.13.5)**
baseness **34.18.16(.31.2)**
basenji **1.26.13**
baseplate **22.4.23(.8)**
bases **35.1.16(.2)**
bash **36.6**
bashful **40.27.27**
bashfully **1.31.17(.16.2)**
bashfulness **34.18.16(.37.2)**
bashi-bazouk **24.15.5**
Bashkir **3.6**
Bashkiria **3.22.2**
basho **19.22**
basic **24.2.20(.3)**
basically **1.31.24(.9.10)**
basicity **1.10.16(.16.1)**
basidia **3.5.2**
basidial **40.3.4**
basidium **27.3.4(.2)**
Basie **1.22.4, 1.23.3**
basil **40.32.5**
basilar **17.34.16(.15)**
basilect **22.23.4(.11)**
basilectal **40.21.16**
basilectally **1.31.17(.9.3)**
basilica **17.14.15(.15)**
basilican **28.17.13(.13)**
basilisk **24.20.1**
basin **28.17.23(.4)**
basinet **22.5.9, 22.19.15(.9)**
basinful **40.14.6(.15)**
basipetal **40.21.12**
basipetally **1.31.17(.9.2)**
basis **34.2.17(.2)**
bask **24.20.4**
Baskerville **40.2.12**
basket **22.19.12(.14)**
basketball **40.10.4**
basketful **40.14.6(.10)**

basketry **1.29.15(.6)**
basketwork **24.17.6(.8)**
Baskin **28.2.13(.14)**
Basle **40.8**
basmati **1.10.6, 1.10.8**
basophilic **24.2.27(.2)**
Basotho **16.7.3**
Basotholand **23.24.6(.13)**
Basque **24.20.4**
Basra **17.32.28**
bas-relief **30.1.9**
bass **34.4, 34.7**
basset **22.19.18**
Bassey **1.22.6**
bassi **1.22.6**
bassinet **22.5.9**
bassi profondi **1.11.20(.5)**
bassi profundi **1.11.20(.7)**
bassist **22.29.2(.22)**
basso **19.20.4**
bassoon **28.16.10**
bassoonist **22.29.2(.18.1)**
basso profondo **19.11.14**
basso-relievo **19.17**
basswood **23.16.6(.17)**
bast **22.29.6**
bastard **23.18.9(.20)**
bastardization **28.17.25(.3.11)**
bastardize **35.15.8**
bastardy **1.11.17**
baste **22.29.4**
Bastet **22.19.10**
Bastia **3.4.13**
Bastille **40.1.3**
bastinado **19.11.4, 19.11.7**
bastion **28.3.3**
Bastogne **17.33.9, 28.19.4(.9)**
basuco **19.12.11**
Basuto **19.10.11**
Basutoland **23.24.6(.13)**
bat **22.7**
Bata **17.12.8**
batata **17.12.8(.3)**
Batavia **3.11.3**
Batavian **28.3.10**
batch **38.5**
bate **22.4**
bateau **19.10, 19.10.6**
bateaux **35.20.3**
bateleur **18.17**
Bates **34.22.3**
Bateson **28.17.23(.19)**
bath **32.8**
bathe **33.3**
bather **17.23.3**
bathetic **24.2.10(.3.2)**
bathhouse **34.8.6(.19)**
batholith **32.2.9**

bathometer **17.12.16(.9.2)**
bathos **34.10.14**
bathotic **24.2.10(.6)**
bathrobe **21.16.2**
bathroom **27.14.6(.16)**
Bathsheba **17.11.1, 17.11.13**
bathtub **21.11**
Bathurst **22.29.16**
bathwater **17.12.10(.7)**
bathyal **40.3.9**
bathypelagic **24.2.24(.2)**
bathyscaphe **30.5.3**
bathysphere **3.10.5**
batik **24.1.3, 24.2.10(.4.1)**
Batista **17.12.24(.1)**
batiste **22.29.1**
Batman **28.7.10(.11)**
batman **28.17.16(.21)**
baton **28.10.9, 28.17.11(.6)**
Baton Rouge **37.7**
batrachian **28.3.5**
batsman **28.17.16(.29)**
batsmanship **20.2.7(.19)**
battalion **28.3.21(.5)**
Battambang **29.4.2**
battels **35.30.16**
batten **28.17.11(.6)**
Battenberg **26.14.1(.9)**
batter **17.12.6**
batterer **17.32.14(.6)**
Battersea **2.22.7**
battery **1.29.11(.8.3)**
Batticaloa **17.9.13**
battily **1.31.17(.9.1)**
battiness **34.18.16(.2.3)**
battle **40.21.5**
battleaxe **34.23.5(.15)**
battlebus **34.14**
battlecruiser **17.25.14**
battledore **12.6.13**
battledress **34.5.14(.6)**
battlefield **23.31.1(.2)**
battleground **23.24.7(.10)**
battlegroup **20.12**
battlement **22.26.15(.13.7)**
battler **17.34.21**
battleship **20.2.7(.24)**
battue **16.7, 16.24.5**
batty **1.10.6**
batwing **29.1.29**
batwoman **28.17.16(.14)**
batwomen **28.2.17(.1)**
bauble **40.20.10**
baud **23.12, 23.20**
Baudelaire **6.21**
Bauer **17.3**
Bauhaus **34.8.6(.5)**
baulk **24.10, 24.21**

baulker 17.14.9, 17.14.25
baulkiness 34.18.16(.2.4)
baulky 1.12.8, 1.12.19
Baum 27.7, 27.10
bauxite 22.16.19(.14)
bauxitic 24.2.10(.2.3)
Bavaria 3.22.4
Bavarian 28.3.20(.4)
bawbee 1.9.8, 2.10
bawd 23.12
bawdily 1.31.17(.10)
bawdiness 34.18.16(.2.3)
bawdry 1.29.16
bawdy 1.11.11
bawl 40.10
bawler 17.34.10
Bax 34.23.5
Baxter 17.12.24(.20)
bay 4
bayadère 3.5, 6.5
Bayard 23.9.3
bayberry 1.29.11(.7.1)
Bayer 17.2
Bayern 28.18.1
Baylis 34.2.22(.3)
bayonet 22.5.9, 22.19.15(.9)
Bayonne 28.10, 28.19
bayou 16.4
Bayreuth 22.14
Baz 35.7
bazaar 10.16
bazooka 17.14.14
bdellium 27.3.18
be 2
Bea 2
beach 38.1
beachcomber 17.17.16(.4)
beachfront 22.26.12
beachhead 23.5.13(.17)
Beach-la-mar 10.10
beachside 23.15.11(.16)
beachwear 6.18.14
Beachy Head 23.5
beacon 28.17.13(.1)
bead 23.1
beadily 1.31.17(.10)
beadiness 34.18.16(.2.3)
beadle 40.22.1
beadleship 20.2.7(.24)
beadsman 28.17.16(.30)
beadwork 24.17.6(.9)
beady 1.11.1
beagle 40.24.1
beagler 17.34.24
beak 24.1
beaker 17.14.1
beaky 1.12.1
Beale 40.1
beam 27.1

beamer 17.17.1
Beamon 28.17.16(.1)
beamy 1.15.1
bean 28.1
beanbag 26.5.1
beanery 1.29.11(.13.1)
beanfeast 22.29.1
beanie 1.16.1
beano 19.15.1
beanpole 40.18.3
beanshoot 22.18.7
bean sprout 22.9.18
beanstalk 24.10.2
bear 6
bearability 1.10.16(.22.1)
bearable 40.20.16(.27.1)
bearably 1.31.21(.8)
bearcat 22.7.9
beard 23.3
beardie 1.11.3
beardless 34.18.29(.23)
beardlessness 34.18.16(.31.6)
Beardsley 1.31.34
bearer 17.32.5
bear garden 28.17.12(.8)
bearing 29.1.30(.4)
bearish 36.2.25
bearishness 34.18.16(.33.6)
bearleader 17.13.1
Béarnaise 35.4.8
bear pit 22.2.5
bearskin 28.2.13(.14)
Beasley 1.31.34
beast 22.29.1
beastie 1.10.26(.1)
beastliness 34.18.16(.2.10)
beastly 1.31.22(.22)
beat 22.1
beatable 40.20.16(.11.1)
beaten 28.17.11(.1)
beater 17.12.1
beatific 24.2.16(.1)
beatifically 1.31.24(.9.9)
beatification 28.17.25(.3.5)
beatify 14.14.4(.4)
beating 29.1.12(.1)
beatitude 23.17.4(.1)
Beatles 35.30.16
beatnik 24.2.15(.10)
Beaton 28.17.11(.1)
Beatrice 34.18.27(.14)
Beatrix 34.23.2(.12)
Beatty 1.10.1, 1.10.3
beau 19
Beaufort 22.13.7, 22.19.16
beau geste 22.29.5
beau idéal 40.3.4
Beaujolais 4.28.7

Beaujolais Nouveau 19.17
Beaumarchais 4.20
Beaumaris 34.2.21
beau monde 23.24.9
Beaumont 22.26.9
Beaune 28.19
beaut 22.18
beauteous 34.3.3
beauteously 1.31.33(.1.1)
beauteousness 34.18.16(.31.1)
beautician 28.17.25(.2.2)
beautification 28.17.25(.3.5)
beautifier 17.6.9(.4)
beautiful 40.27.14
beautifully 1.31.17(.16.1), 1.31.29
beautify 14.14.4(.4)
beauty 1.10.15
Beauvais 4.16
beaux 19, 35.20
beaux-arts 10.16
beaver 17.21.1
Beaverboard 23.12.2(.5)
Beaverbrook 24.14.10
bebop 20.7.3
bebopper 17.10.8
becalm 27.8.5
became 27.4.3
becard 23.9.9, 23.18.11
because 35.10, 35.14
béchamel 40.5.7
bêche-de-mer 6.8
Bechstein 28.14.5
Bechuanaland 23.24.6(.13)
beck 24.4
Beckenbauer 17.3.2
Becker 17.14.4
Becket 22.2.9(.2)
Beckford 23.18.16(.13)
Beckham 27.15.11(.4)
Beckmann 28.17.16(.23)
beckon 28.17.13(.4)
Becky 1.12.4
becloud 23.8
become 27.11.5
becoming 29.1.16
becomingly 1.31.28(.1.7)
becomingness 34.18.16(.26)
bed 23.5
bedabble 40.20.6
bedad 23.7.8
bedaub 21.9
bedazzle 40.32.5
bedazzlement 22.26.15(.13.7)

bedbug 26.10
bedchamber 17.11.17(.2)
bedclothes 35.20.14, 35.29
beddable 40.20.16(.12)
bedder 17.13.4
Beddoes 35.20.4
Bede 23.1
bedeck 24.4.5
bedeguar 10.9
bedel 40.5.4, 40.22.1
bedevil 40.28.4
bedevilment 22.26.15(.13.7)
bedew 16.24.6
bedfast 22.29.6(.9)
bedfellow 19.29.4
Bedford 23.18.16(.12)
Bedfordshire 17.26.18
bedframe 27.4.8
bedhead 23.5.13(.10)
bedight 22.16.10
bedim 27.2.4
bedizen 28.17.24(.10)
bedjacket 22.2.9(.3)
bedlam 27.15.28(.17)
bedlinen 28.2.18
Bedlington 28.17.11(.23)
bedmaker 17.14.3(.3)
Bedouin 28.17.6
bedpan 28.7.4
bedplate 22.4.23(.8)
bedpost 22.29.17(.1)
bedraggle 40.24.4
bedridden 28.17.12(.2)
bedrock 24.9.15
bedroll 40.18.14
bedroom 27.14.6(.9)
bedside 23.15.11(.10)
bedsit 22.2.16
bedsitter 17.12.2
bedsock 24.9.10
bedsore 12.14.12
bedspread 23.5.15
bedstead 23.5.3
bedstraw 12.21
bedtime 27.12.1
bee 2
Beeb 21.1
Beebe 1.9.1
beech 38.1
Beecham 27.15.23
beechmast 22.29.6(.7), 22.29.8(.5)
beechnut 22.15.6
beechwood 23.16.6(.20)
beechy 1.25.1
beef 30.1
beefalo 19.29.12
beefburger 17.16.14

beefcake 24.3.6
beefeater 17.12.1(.8)
beefheart 22.10.11
beefily 1.31.17(.16.1)
beefiness 34.18.16(.2.6)
beefsteak 24.3.4
beefwood 23.16.6(.16)
beefy 1.18.1
beehive 31.9
beeline 28.14.19(.1)
Beelzebub 21.11
been 28.1
beep 20.1
beeper 17.10.1
beer 3
beer belly 1.31.5
Beerbohm 27.17.3
beerhouse 34.8.6(.2)
beerily 1.31.17(.27.1)
beeriness 34.18.16(.2.9)
beer money 1.16.12
beerpot 22.11.2
Beersheba 17.11.1
beery 1.29.2
beestings 35.27
beeswax 34.23.5(.13)
beeswing 29.1.29
beet 22.1
Beethoven 28.17.20(.11)
beetle 40.21.1
Beeton 28.17.11(.1)
beetroot 22.18.9
beeves 35.28.1
befall 40.10.11
befallen 28.17.33(.8)
befell 40.5.9
befit 22.2.13
befittingly 1.31.28(.1.4)
befog 26.7.8
befool 40.15.6
before 12.11
beforehand 23.24.6(.11)
beforetime 27.12.1
befoul 40.7
befriend 23.24.5(.14)
befriended 23.18.10(.14)
befuddle 40.22.10
befuddlement
    22.26.15(.13.7)
beg 26.4
begad 23.7.10
began 28.7.9
begat 22.7.10
beget 22.5.7
begetter 17.12.5(.4)
beggar 17.16.4
beggarliness
    34.18.16(.2.10)
beggarly 1.31.17(.12)
beggary 1.29.11(.11)

Begin 28.2.15
begin 28.2.15
beginner 17.18.2
beginning 29.1.17(.2)
begird 23.19.3
begirt 22.20.5
begone 28.10.12
begonia 3.9.11
begorra 17.32.8
begot 22.11.7
begotten 28.17.11(.9)
begrime 27.12.7
begrudge 39.11
begrudgingly
    1.31.28(.1.16)
beguile 40.13.6
beguilement
    22.26.15(.13.7)
beguiler 17.34.13
beguilingly 1.31.28(.1.18)
beguine 28.1.12
begum 27.15.12
begun 28.13.5
behalf 30.7.4
Behan 28.17.1
behave 31.3.5
behavioristically
    1.31.24(.9.6)
behaviour 17.33.10
behavioural
    40.16.13(.12.4)
behaviouralist
    22.29.2(.31.4)
behaviourally
    1.31.17(.27.2)
behaviourism
    27.15.21(.2.14)
behaviourist
    22.29.2(.29.4)
behaviouristic
    24.2.10(.15.2)
behaviouristically
    1.31.24(.9.6)
behead 23.5.13
beheld 23.31.4
behemoth 32.9, 32.14.11
behest 22.29.5(.10)
behind 23.24.13
behindhand 23.24.6(.11)
Behn 28.5
behold 23.31.13(.9)
beholden 28.17.12(.27)
beholder 17.13.23(.8)
behoof 30.13.3
behoove 31.10
behove 31.12
Behrens 34.24.10(.16),
    35.26.13(.18)
Behring 29.1.30(.4)
Beiderbecke 24.4.3
beige 37.2

beigel 40.24.3
Beijing 29.1.26, 29.1.28
being 29.1.1
Beira 17.32.13
Beirut 22.18.9
beisa 17.25.3
bejabbers 35.18.7
bejabers 35.18.7
bejewel 40.15.7, 40.16.8
Bekaa 10.8
bel 40.5
belabour 17.11.3
Belafonte 1.10.23(.7)
Belarus 34.16, 34.17.12
belated 23.18.9(.3)
belatedly 1.31.23(.14.3)
belatedness
    34.18.16(.21.1)
Belau 9.17
belay 4.28
bel canto 19.10.17
belch 38.19
belcher 17.28.26
beldam 27.15.10(.20)
beleaguer 17.16.1
Belém 27.5.14
belemnite 22.16.14(.11)
bel esprit 2.30.8
Belfast 22.29.6(.9)
belfry 1.29.21
Belgae 2.15, 2.27, 14.11
Belgian 28.17.28(.13)
Belgic 24.2.24(.9)
Belgium 27.15.24
Belgrade 23.4.15
Belgravia 3.11.3
Belgravian 28.3.10
Belial 40.3.15
belie 14.25
belief 30.1.9
believability
    1.10.16(.22.2)
believable 40.20.16(.19)
believably 1.31.21(.7.1)
believe 31.1.9
believed 23.26
believer 17.21.1
belike 24.13.7
Belinda 17.13.20(.1)
Belisarius 34.3.15(.3)
belittle 40.21.2
belittlement
    22.26.15(.13.7)
belittler 17.34.21
belittlingly 1.31.28(.1.18)
Belize 35.1.23
Belizean 28.3.14
bell 40.5
Bella 17.34.5
belladonna 17.18.9

Bellamy 1.15.13(.12)
Bellay 4.28
bellbird 23.19.1
bellboy 13.3
belle 40.5
belle époque 24.9.2
belle laide 23.4
Bellerophon 28.10.15,
    28.17.19
belles-lettres 17.32.19(.3)
belletrism 27.15.21(.2.14)
belletrist 22.29.2(.29.5)
belletristic 24.2.10(.15.2)
Bellevue 16.24.12
bellflower 17.3.11
bellhop 20.7.11
bellicose 34.20.6, 35.20.5
bellicosely 1.31.33(.13),
    1.31.34
bellicosity 1.10.16(.16.2)
belligerence 34.24.10(.16)
belligerency
    1.22.23(.10.4)
belligerent 22.26.15(.23.3)
belligerently
    1.31.22(.20.5)
Bellini 1.16.1(.16)
bellman 28.17.16(.35)
Belloc 24.9.16(.1)
bellow 19.29.4
bell push 36.13
bell ringer 17.19.1
bell ringing 29.1.18
bellrope 20.15.8
bellwether 17.23.4
belly 1.31.5
bellyache 24.3.1
bellyacher 17.14.3
bellyband 23.24.6(.4)
bellyflop 20.7.13
bellyful 40.14.6(.1)
Belmondo 19.11.14
Belmont 22.26.9
Belmopan 28.7.4
Belo Horizonte 4.9.9
belong 29.6.15
belongingness
    34.18.16(.26)
belongings 35.27
Belorussia 3.14.8, 17.26.10
Belorussian 28.3.13,
    28.17.25(.9)
beloved 23.18.17, 23.26
below 19.29
Bel Paese 1.23.3
Belsen 28.17.23(.28)
Belshazzar 17.25.5
belt 22.32.2
Beltane 28.4.3
belter 17.12.26(.3)
beltman 28.17.16(.21)

beluga 17.16.12
belvedere 3.5, 3.5.7
Belvoir 17.21.1
belying 29.1.7
bema 17.17.1
bemata 17.12.16(.9.1)
Bemba 17.11.17(.3)
Bembridge 39.2.22(.10)
bemedaled 23.31.17
bemedalled 23.31.17
bemire 17.6.7
bemoan 28.19.9
bemuse 35.17.7
bemusedly 1.31.23(.14.7)
bemusement
22.26.15(.13.5)
Ben 28.5
Benares 35.1.22, 35.18.23
Benbecula
17.34.16(.21.2)
Ben Bella 17.34.5
bench 38.18.2
bencher 17.28.22
benchmark 24.8.8
bend 23.24.5
bendable 40.20.16(.12)
bender 17.13.20(.3)
Bendigo 19.13.9
bendiness 34.18.16(.2.3)
Bendix® 34.23.2(.4)
bendy 1.11.20(.3)
beneath 32.1
benedicite 1.10.16(.16.2)
Benedick 24.2.11(.12)
Benedict 22.23.2
Benedictine 28.1.9(.5)
benediction
28.17.25(.15.1)
benedictory
1.29.11(.8.12)
Benedictus 34.18.11(.13)
benefaction
28.17.25(.15.3)
benefactor 17.12.21(.3)
benefactress
34.18.27(.14)
benefic 24.2.16(.2)
benefice 34.2.14
beneficence 34.24.10(.18)
beneficent 22.26.15(.17.3)
beneficently
1.31.22(.20.4)
beneficial 40.33.1
beneficially 1.31.17(.22)
beneficiary 1.29.2(.9),
1.29.11(.20)
beneficiation
28.17.25(.3.1)
benefit 22.2.13
Benelux 34.23.11
Benenden 28.17.12(.23)

Benetton® 28.10.9,
28.17.11(.15)
benevolence
34.24.10(.24)
benevolent 22.26.15(.25)
benevolently
1.31.22(.20.5)
Benfleet 22.1.18
Bengal 40.10.8
Bengali 1.31.11
Benghazi 1.23.7
Benguela 17.34.4,
17.34.5(.14)
Ben-Gurion 28.3.20(.8)
Benidorm 27.10.3
benighted 23.18.9(.10)
benightedly
1.31.23(.14.3)
benightedness
34.18.16(.21.1)
benign 28.14.9
benignancy 1.22.23(.10.3)
benignant 22.26.15(.14)
benignantly
1.31.22(.20.3)
benignity 1.10.16(.13)
benignly 1.31.27(.11)
Benin 28.1.14
Beninese 35.1.12
benison 28.17.23(.14),
28.17.24(.12)
Benito 19.10.1
Benjamin 28.17.16(.16)
Benlate 22.4.23(.10)
Benn 28.5
Bennett 22.2.12
Ben Nevis 34.2.15
benni 1.16.5
Benny 1.16.5
Benson 28.17.23(.24)
bent 22.26.4
Bentham 27.15.9(.14),
27.15.18
Benthamism
27.15.21(.2.8)
Benthamite 22.16.13
benthic 24.2.18(.6)
benthos 34.10.14
Bentley 1.31.22(.20.1)
Benton 28.17.11(.22)
bentonite 22.16.14(.6)
bentwood 23.16.6(.9)
Benue 4.4
benumb 27.11.8
Benz 35.26.5
Benzedrine® 28.1.25(.7),
28.2.29(.9)
benzene 28.1.19
benzenoid 23.13.12
Benzies 35.2.18
benzin 28.2.24

benzine 28.1.19
benzocaine 28.4.5
benzodiazepine 28.1.7
benzoic 24.2.7
benzoin 28.2.8
benzol 40.9.15
benzole 40.18.11
benzoyl 40.2.2
benzyl 40.32.17
Beowulf 30.20.6
bequeath 32.1, 33.1
bequeather 17.22.1,
17.23.1
bequest 22.29.5(.11)
Bequia 1.28, 4.25.14
berate 22.4.22
Berber 17.11.14
Berbera 17.32.14(.5)
berberine 28.1.25(.3)
berberis 34.18.27(.13)
berceuse 35.19
Bere 3
bereave 31.1.8
bereavement
22.26.15(.13.5)
bereft 22.27.2
Berengaria 3.22.4
Berenice 1.22.13, 1.25.1,
4.22, 34.1.4
Beresford 23.18.16(.18)
beret 1.29.3, 4.26.2
berg 26.14
bergamasque 24.20.4
Bergamo 19.14.12
bergamot 22.11.8
Bergen 28.17.15(.5)
bergenia 3.9.1
Berger 17.16.14, 17.29.14
Bergerac 24.6.21
Bergman 28.17.16(.24)
bergschrund 22.26.14,
23.24.14
Bergson 28.17.23(.22)
beribboned 23.24.16(.2)
beriberi 1.29.3
Bering 29.1.30(.4)
berk 24.17
Berkeleian 28.17.1(.13)
Berkeley 1.31.24(.6)
berkelium 27.3.18
Berkhampstead 23.5.3
Berkley 1.31.24(.10)
Berks 34.23.7
Berkshire 17.26.19
Berlei 1.31.18
Berlin 28.2.31
Berliner 17.18.2
Berlioz 35.16
Berlitz 34.22.2
berm 27.16
berme 27.16

Bermondsey 1.23.18,
1.23.20
Bermuda 17.13.14
Bermudan 28.17.12(.15)
Bermudas 35.18.9
Bermudian 28.3.4(.9)
Bern 28.6, 28.18
Bernadette 22.5.4
Bernadotte 22.11.5
Bernard 23.9.12, 23.18.14
Berne 28.6, 28.18
Berners 35.18.13
Bernese 35.1.12
Bernhardt 22.10.11
Bernice 34.1.4,
34.18.16(.16)
Bernini 1.16.1(.8)
Bernouilli 1.31.16
Bernstein 28.1.9(.7),
28.14.5
Berol® 40.9.19
Berra 17.32.4
Berridge 39.2.22(.2)
berry 1.29.3
berserk 24.17.5
berserker 17.14.16
Bert 22.20
berth 32.15
Bertha 17.22.10
Bertie 1.10.17
Bertolucci 1.25.11
Bertram 27.15.26(.10)
Bertrand 23.24.16(.15)
Berwick 24.2.26(.4)
Berwickshire 17.26.19
Berwyn 28.2.28
beryl 40.16.13(.3)
berylliosis 34.2.17(.11.1)
beryllium 27.3.18
Berzelius 34.3.16
Bes 34.5
Besançon 11.12, 28.10.18
Besant 22.26.15(.17.2)
beseech 38.1
beseem 27.1.8
beset 22.5.13
besetment
22.26.15(.13.3)
beshrew 16.23.14
beside 23.15.11
besiege 39.1
besieger 17.29.1
beslaver 17.21.3, 17.21.5
beslobber 17.11.8
besmear 3.8.13
besmirch 38.16
besom 27.15.21(.1)
besotted 23.18.9(.8)
besottedly 1.31.23(.14.3)
besottedness
34.18.16(.21.1)

b

biffin 28.2.19
Biffo 19.16
bifid 23.2.14
bifidly 1.31.23(.14.7)
bifocal 40.23.14
bifoliate 22.3.13,
  22.4.2(.15)
bifurcate 22.4.11(.6),
  22.19.12(.11)
bifurcation 28.17.25(.3.5)
big 26.2
bigamist 22.29.2(.17)
bigamous 34.18.15(.10)
bigamously 1.31.33(.12.3)
bigamy 1.15.13(.4)
Bigelow 19.29.12
biggie 1.14.2
biggish 36.2.14
Biggles 35.30.19
Biggleswade 23.4.14
Biggs 35.24
big head 23.5.13(.12)
big headedness
  34.18.16(.21.1)
bighorn 28.11.10
bight 22.16
big mouth 32.7
bigness 34.18.16(.23)
bigot 22.19.13
bigotry 1.29.15(.7)
bigraph 30.7.5(.1)
bigwig 26.2.9
Bihar 10.21
Bihari 1.29.6
bijou 16.18
bijouterie 1.29.11(.8.4)
bijoux 35.17.5
bike 24.13
biker 17.14.12
bikini 1.16.1(.5)
Biko 19.12.1
bilabial 40.3.2
bilabially 1.31.3(.2)
bilateral 40.16.13(.12.1)
bilateralism
  27.15.21(.2.15)
bilaterally 1.31.17(.27.1)
Bilbao 9.2
bilberry 1.29.11(.7.2)
bilbo 19.9.18
Bildungsroman 28.9.6
Bildungsromane
  17.18.8(.5)
bile 40.13
bilge 39.18
bilgepump 20.16.5
bilharzia 3.14.13, 3.15.5
bilharziasis
  34.2.17(.10.1)
biliary 1.29.2(.12)
bilingual 40.35.4

bilingualism
  27.15.21(.2.15)
bilious 34.3.16
biliously 1.31.33(.1.5)
biliousness
  34.18.16(.31.1)
bilirubin 28.2.10
bilk 24.21
bilker 17.14.25
bill 40.2
billable 40.20.16(.29)
billabong 29.6.2
billboard 23.12.2(.20)
Billericay 1.12.2
billet 22.19.26(.1)
billet-doux 16.8
billetee 2.11
billeter 17.12.16(.20)
billets-doux 35.17.1
billfold 23.31.13(.7)
billhead 23.5.13(.19)
billhook 24.14.9
billiard 23.18.28
Billie 1.31.2
Billingham 27.15.15
Billingsgate 22.4.12(.11)
Billingshurst 22.29.16
billion 28.3.21(.2)
billionaire 6.9
billionairess 34.5.14(.1),
  34.18.27(.4)
billionth 32.21
billon 28.17.33(.2)
billow 19.29.2
billowy 1(.7)
billposter 17.12.24(.15)
billposting 29.1.12(.21)
billsticker 17.14.2
billy 1.31.2
billycan 28.7.8
billycock 24.9.6
billy-o 15.1.13
billy-oh 15.1.13
bilobate 22.4.8
bilobed 23.21
Biloxi 1.22.22
biltong 29.6.3
bimanal 40.26.3,
  40.26.13(.8)
bimanous 34.18.16(.15.3)
bimbashi 1.24.5
bimbo 19.9.14
bi-media 3.5.1
bimetallic 24.2.27(.6)
bimetallism
  27.15.21(.2.15)
bimetallist 22.29.2(.31.2)
bimillenary
  1.29.11(.13.1)
bimodal 40.22.15
bimodality 1.10.16(.32.4)

bimonthly 1.31.31
bin 28.2
binary 1.29.11(.13.1)
binate 22.4.14(.6)
binaural 40.16.13(.8)
Binchy 1.24.15
bind 23.24.13
binder 17.13.20(.11)
bindery 1.29.11(.9)
bindi-eye 14.2
binding 29.1.13(.14)
bindweed 23.1.10
bine 28.14
bin-end 23.24.5(.8)
Binet 4.14
bing 29.1
binge 39.17.1
Bingen 28.17.18
Bingham 27.15.15
Bingley 1.31.28(.1)
bingo 19.13.12
binman 28.7.10(.15)
binmen 28.5.7(.19)
binnacle 40.23.12(.11)
Binnie 1.16.2
Binns 35.26.2
binocular 17.34.16(.21.2)
binoculars 35.18.25
binomial 40.3.6
binomially 1.31.3(.6)
binominal 40.26.13(.8)
bint 22.26.1
Binyon 28.17.32
bio 19.5
bioceramic 24.2.14(.4)
biochemical 40.23.12(.10)
biochemist 22.29.2(.17)
biochemistry 1.29.15(.17)
biochip 20.2.8
biocoenology
  1.26.10(.11.4)
biocoenoses 35.1.16(.11)
biocoenosis 34.2.17(.11.2)
biocoenotic 24.2.10(.6)
biocompatibility
  1.10.16(.22.3)
biocompatible
  40.20.16(.11.1)
biocomputing
  29.1.12(.13)
biocontrol 40.18.14
biodata 17.12.4(.6)
biodegradability
  1.10.16(.22.3)
biodegradable
  40.20.16(.12)
biodegradation
  28.17.25(.3.4)
biodiversity 1.10.16(.16.2)
bioenergetic 24.2.10(.3.2)
bioengineer 3.9

bioethicist 22.29.2(.22)
bioethics 34.23.2(.9)
biofeedback 24.6.6(.13)
bioflavonoid 23.13.12
biogas 34.7.10
biogenesis 34.2.17(.10.3)
biogenetic 24.2.10(.3.1)
biogenic 24.2.15(.4)
biogeographic 24.2.16(.3)
biogeographical
  40.23.12(.12)
biogeography 1.18.9(.3.2)
biograph 30.7.5(.1)
biographer 17.20.12(.5)
biographic 24.2.16(.3)
biographical
  40.23.12(.12)
biographically
  1.31.24(.9.9)
biography 1.18.9(.3.2)
biological 40.23.12(.17.2)
biologically 1.31.24(.9.11)
biologist 22.29.2(.26.2)
biology 1.26.10(.11.1)
bioluminescence
  34.24.10(.18)
bioluminescent
  22.26.15(.17.2)
biomass 34.7.11
biomaterial 40.3.14(.2)
biomathematics
  34.23.2(.3)
biome 27.17.2
biomechanics 34.23.2(.6)
biomedical 40.23.12(.8)
biomedicine
  28.17.23(.14)
biometric 24.2.26(.14.2)
biometrical 40.23.12(.18)
biometrician
  28.17.25(.2.6)
biometry 1.29.15(.8)
biomorph 30.9.2
biomorphic 24.2.16(.5)
bionic 24.2.15(.6.1)
bionically 1.31.24(.9.8)
bionomic 24.2.14(.6)
biophysic 24.2.21
biophysical 40.23.12(.16)
biophysically
  1.31.24(.9.10)
biophysicist 22.29.2(.22)
biopic 24.2.8(.7)
biopsy 1.22.19
biorhythmic 24.2.14(.15)
biorhythmically
  1.31.24(.9.8)
bioscope 20.15.4(.1)
biosensor 17.24.22(.2)
biosphere 3.10.5
biosyntheses 35.1.16(.10)

biosynthesis 34.2.17(.10.4)
biosynthetic 24.2.10(.3.2)
biota 17.12.18
biotechnologist 22.29.2(.26.4)
biotechnology 1.26.10(.11.4)
biotic 24.2.10(.6)
biotin 28.2.11(.10)
biotite 22.16.9
biparous 34.18.27(.12)
bipartisan 28.7.15, 28.17.24(.12)
bipartisanship 20.2.7(.19)
bipartite 22.16.9
biped 23.5.1
bipedal 40.22.1, 40.22.4
bipedalism 27.15.21(.2.15)
bipedality 1.10.16(.32.4)
biphenyl 40.2.10, 40.13.8
bipinnate 22.4.14(.2), 22.19.15(.1)
biplane 28.4.19
bipolar 17.34.18(.1)
bipolarity 1.10.16(.21.1)
biquadratic 24.2.10(.4.5)
birch 38.16
birchen 28.17.27
birchwood 23.16.6(.20)
bird 23.19
bird bath 32.8
birdbrain 28.4.18
birdcage 39.4.3
birder 17.13.16
birdie 1.11.18
birdlime 27.12.8
birdseed 23.1.7
bird's-eye 14.19
Birdseye 14.19
birdsong 29.6.9
birdwatcher 17.28.9
birdwatching 29.1.27
birefringence 34.24.10(.21)
birefringent 22.26.15(.21)
bireme 27.1.12
biretta 17.12.5(.9)
Birgitta 17.12.2
biriani 1.16.8
Birkbeck 24.4.3
Birkenhead 23.5.13
Birkenshaw 12.16.12
Birkett 22.2.9(.8)
birl 40.17
Birmingham 27.6.15, 27.15.15
biro® 19.27.9

Birobidzhan 28.7.17, 28.9.10
birr 18
Birt 22.20
birth 32.15
birthday 4.10.14
birthmark 24.8.8
birthplace 34.4.14
birth rate 22.4.22(.13)
birthright 22.16.24(.17)
birthstone 28.19.4(.9)
birthweight 22.4.21
Birtwistle 40.31.2
bis 34.2
Biscay 4.11
Biscayne 28.4.5
biscuit 22.2.9(.10)
biscuity 1.10.16(.10)
bisect 22.23.4(.7)
bisection 28.17.25(.15.2)
bisector 17.12.21(.2)
bisexual 40.14.8, 40.16.10
bisexuality 1.10.16(.32.1)
bish 36.2
bishop 20.13.5
bishopric 24.2.26(.12)
Bishopsgate 22.4.12(.10)
bisk 24.20.1
Bislama 10.10.4
Bisley 1.31.34
Bismarck 24.8.8
bismuth 32.14.11
bison 28.17.23(.12)
bisque 24.20.1
Bissau 9.9
Bissell 40.31.2
bissextile 40.13.3(.10)
bistable 40.20.4
Bisto® 19.10.19
bistort 22.13.3
bistoury 1.29.11(.8.12)
bistre 17.12.24(.2)
bistro 19.27.15
bisulphate 22.4.15
bisulphite 22.16.16
bit 22.2
bitch 38.2
bitchily 1.31.17(.24)
bitchiness 34.18.16(.2.8)
bitchy 1.25.2
bite 22.16
biter 17.12.13
Bithynia 3.9.2
bitingly 1.31.28(.1.4)
bitmap 20.5.3
bitt 22.2
bitten 28.17.11(.2)
bitter 17.12.2
bitterling 29.1.31(.12)
bitterly 1.31.17(.9.1)

bittern 28.17.11(.2), 28.18.4
bitterness 34.18.16(.15.2)
bitterroot 22.18.9
bitter-sweet 22.1.16
bittily 1.31.17(.9.1)
bittiness 34.18.16(.2.3)
bitty 1.10.2
bitumen 28.17.16(.16)
bituminization 28.17.25(.3.12)
bituminize 35.15.12(.5)
bituminous 34.18.16(.15.3)
bivalence 34.24.10(.24)
bivalency 1.22.23(.10.4)
bivalent 22.26.15(.25)
bivalve 31.13
bivouac 24.6.4
bivvy 1.19.2
biweekly 1.31.24(.1)
biyearly 1.31.18
biz 35.2
bizarre 10.16
bizarrely 1.31.9
bizarreness 34.18.16(.9)
bizarrerie 1.29.11(.25)
Bizerta 17.12.17
Bizet 4.19
Bjorn 28.11
blab 21.6
blabber 17.11.5
blabbermouth 32.7
Blaby 1.9.3
black 24.6
blackamoor 12.9.4
blackball 40.10.4
black beetle 40.21.1
blackberry 1.29.11(.7.2)
blackberrying 29.1.2
blackbird 23.19.1
blackboard 23.12.2(.10)
blackboy 13.3
blackbuck 24.12.1
Blackburn 28.18.3
blackcap 20.5.1
blackcock 24.9.6
blackcurrant 22.26.15(.23.2)
blacken 28.17.13(.5)
Blackett 22.2.9(.3)
Blackfeet 22.1.6
blackfellow 19.29.4
blackfish 36.2.18(.17)
blackfly 14.25.14
Blackfoot 22.17
Blackfriars 35.18.4
blackguard 23.9.10, 23.18.12
blackguardly 1.31.23(.7)
blackhead 23.5.13(.11)

Blackheath 32.1
Blackie 1.12.3, 1.12.5
blacking 29.1.14(.4)
blackish 36.2.13
blackjack 24.6.18
blacklead 23.5.16
blackleg 26.4
blacklist 22.29.2(.31.6)
blackly 1.31.24(.5)
blackmail 40.4.6
blackmailer 17.34.4
Black Maria 17.6.14
Blackmore 12.9.9
blackness 34.18.16(.22)
blackout 22.9.9
Blackpool 40.15.1
Blackshirt 22.20.12
blacksmith 32.2.3
black spot 22.11.2
Blackstone 28.17.11(.25), 28.19.4(.9)
blackthorn 28.11.8
blacktop 20.7.4
Blackwall 40.10.17
Blackwell 40.5.17(.9)
Blackwood 23.16.6(.11)
bladder 17.13.5
bladderwort 22.20.15
bladderwrack 24.6.21
blade 23.4
blade bone 28.19.3
Bladon 28.17.12(.4)
blaeberry 1.29.11(.7.1)
Blaenau Ffestiniog 26.7.1
blag 26.5
blagger 17.16.5
blague 26.5
blagueur 18.6
blah 10
blah-blah 10.25.7
blain 28.4
Blair 6
Blairgowrie 1.29.11(.1)
Blaise 35.4
Blake 24.3
Blakemore 12.9.9
Blakeney 1.16.21
Blakey 1.12.3
blamably 1.31.21(.6)
blame 27.4
blameable 40.20.16(.15)
blameably 1.31.21(.6)
blameful 40.27.21
blamefully 1.31.17(.16.2)
blameless 34.18.29(.26)
blamelessly 1.31.33(.12.6)
blamelessness 34.18.16(.31.6)

blameworthiness 34.18.16(.2.6)

blameworthy 1.21

blanc 11, 24.19.4

blanch 38.18.4

Blanchard 23.9.17, 23.9.18, 23.18.22, 23.18.24

Blanche 38.18.4

blancmange 39.17.7

blanco 19.12.15

bland 23.24.6

Blandford 23.18.16(.12)

blandish 36.2.12

blandishment 22.26.15(.13.6)

blandly 1.31.23(.17)

blandness 34.18.16(.21.1)

blank 24.19.3

Blankenship 20.2.7(.19)

blanket 22.2.9(.9)

blanket weed 23.1.10

blankety 1.10.16(.10)

blankness 34.18.16(.22)

blanky 1.12.16

blanquette 22.5.5

Blantyre 17.6.3

blare 6

blarney 1.16.8

blasé 4.19

blaspheme 27.1.7

blasphemer 17.17.1

blasphemous 34.18.15(.10)

blasphemously 1.31.33(.12.3)

blasphemy 1.15.13(.7)

blast 22.29.6, 22.29.8

blaster 17.12.24(.5)

blastula 17.34.16(.18)

blastulae 2.32.9(.8)

blatancy 1.22.23(.10.2)

blatant 22.26.15(.9)

Blatchford 23.18.16(.21)

blather 17.23.5

blatherer 17.32.14(.15)

blatherskite 22.16.11

Blavatsky 1.12.17(.8)

Blawith 32.2.7, 33.6

Blaydon 28.17.12(.4)

blaze 35.4

blazer 17.25.3

blazingly 1.31.28(.1.12)

blazon 28.17.24(.3)

blazonment 22.26.15(.13.4)

blazonry 1.29.20

Blea 2

bleach 38.1

bleacher 17.28.1

bleak 24.1

bleakly 1.31.24(.1)

bleakness 34.18.16(.22)

blear 3

blearily 1.31.17(.27.1)

bleariness 34.18.16(.2.9)

bleary 1.29.2

Bleasdale 40.4.3

bleat 22.1

bleatingly 1.31.28(.1.4)

bleb 21.4

bled 23.5

Bleddyn 28.2.22

bleed 23.1

bleeder 17.13.1

bleep 20.1

bleeper 17.10.1

blemish 36.2.15

Blencathra 17.32.27

blench 38.18.2

blend 23.24.5

blende 23.24.5

blended 23.18.10(.14)

blender 17.13.20(.3)

Blenheim 27.15.14(.4)

Blenkinsop 20.7.8

Blennerhassett 22.2.16

blenny 1.16.5

blent 22.26.4

blepharitis 34.18.11(.8)

Blériot 15.1.12

blesbok 24.9.3

blesbuck 24.12.1

bless 34.5

blessed 22.29.5, 23.18.20

blessedly 1.31.23(.14.7)

blessedness 34.18.16(.21.1)

blessing 29.1.23

Blessington 28.17.11(.23)

blest 22.29.5

Bletchley 1.31.36

blether 17.23.4

bletherskate 22.4.11(.7)

Blevins 35.26.2

blew 16

blewits 34.22.2

Blewitt 22.2.4

Bligh 14

blight 22.16

blighter 17.12.13

Blighty 1.10.13

blimey 1.15.11

blimp 20.16.1

blimpery 1.29.11(.6)

blimpish 36.2.9

blind 23.24.13

blinder 17.13.20(.11)

blindfold 23.31.13(.7)

blindingly 1.31.28(.1.5)

blindly 1.31.23(.17)

blindness 34.18.16(.21.1)

blindworm 27.16.7

blini 1.16.2

blink 24.19.1

blinker 17.14.21(.1)

blintz 34.22.18

blip 20.2

bliss 34.2

Blissett 22.2.16

blissful 40.27.25

blissfully 1.31.17(.16.2)

blissfulness 34.18.16(.37.2)

blister 17.12.24(.2)

blistery 1.29.11(.8.12)

blithe 33.7

blithely 1.31.32

blitheness 34.18.16(.30)

blithering 29.1.30(.8)

blithesome 27.15.20(.21)

blitz 34.22.2

Blitzkrieg 26.1

Blixen 28.17.23(.21)

blizzard 23.18.21

bloat 22.21

bloater 17.12.18

blob 21.8

bloc 24.9

Bloch 24.9, 25.6

block 24.9

blockade 23.4.5

blockader 17.13.3

blockage 39.2.12

blockboard 23.12.2(.10)

blockbuster 17.12.24(.10)

blockbusting 29.1.12(.21)

blocker 17.14.8

blockhead 23.5.13(.11)

blockheaded 23.18.10(.3)

blockhouse 34.8.6(.13)

blockish 36.2.13

blockishly 1.31.35(.7.1)

blockishness 34.18.16(.33.4)

Blodwen 28.2.28, 28.5.17

Bloemfontein 28.4.3

Blofeld 23.31.4

Blok 24.9

bloke 24.18

Blomfield 23.31.1(.2)

blonde 23.24.9

Blondel 40.5.4

blondie 1.11.20(.5)

Blondin 28.2.12

blondness 34.18.16(.21.1)

blood 23.14

bloodbath 32.8

bloodhound 23.24.7(.8)

bloodily 1.31.17(.10)

bloodiness 34.18.16(.2.3)

bloodless 34.18.29(.23)

bloodlessly 1.31.33(.12.6)

bloodlessness 34.18.16(.31.6)

bloodletting 29.1.12(.4)

bloodline 28.14.19(.15)

bloodlust 22.29.12

bloodroot 22.18.9

bloodshed 23.5.12

bloodshot 22.11.12

bloodstain 28.4.3

bloodstock 24.9.4

bloodstone 28.19.4(.9)

bloodstream 27.1.12

bloodsucker 17.14.11

bloodsucking 29.1.14(.8)

bloodthirstily 1.31.17(.9.3)

bloodthirstiness 34.18.16(.2.3)

bloodthirsty 1.10.26(.12)

bloodworm 27.16.7

bloom 27.14

bloomer 17.17.13

bloomery 1.29.11(.12)

Bloomfield 23.31.1(.2)

Bloomingdale's 35.30.3

Bloomsbury 1.29.11(.7.2)

bloop 20.12

blooper 17.10.13

blossom 27.15.20(.6)

blossomy 1.15.13(.8)

blot 22.11

blotch 38.8

blotchily 1.31.17(.24)

blotchiness 34.18.16(.2.8)

blotchy 1.25.9

blotter 17.12.9

blotto 19.10.8

Blount 22.26.7, 22.26.12

blouse 35.8

blouson 28.10.19, 28.17.24(.5)

blow 19

blowback 24.6.6(.10)

blowby 14.7

blow-dry 14.24.8

blower 17.9

blowfish 36.2.18(.12)

blowfly 14.25.14

blowgun 28.13.5

blowhard 23.9.19

blowhole 40.18.13

blowily 1.31.17(.6)

blowiness 34.18.16(.2.1)

blowlamp 20.16.3

blown 28.19

blowout 22.9.4

blowpipe 20.10.1

blowsily 1.31.17(.21)

blowsiness 34.18.16(.2.7)

blowsy **1.23.6**
blowtorch **38.9**
blowy **1(.7)**
blowzily **1.31.17(.21)**
blub **21.11**
blubber **17.11.10**
blubberer **17.32.14(.5)**
blubberingly
 1.31.28(.1.17)
blubbery **1.29.11(.7.1)**
Blücher **17.14.14, 17.28.14**
bluchers **35.18.10,**
 35.18.20
bludge **39.11**
bludgeon **28.17.28(.7)**
bludger **17.29.10**
blue **16**
bluebag **26.5.1**
Bluebeard **23.3**
bluebell **40.5.2**
blueberry **1.29.3,**
 1.29.11(.7.1)
bluebird **23.19.1**
blue bonnet **22.2.12**
bluebottle **40.21.7**
blue coat **22.21.5**
Bluecol **40.9.9**
Bluefields **35.23.15**
bluefish **36.2.18(.10)**
bluegill **40.2.8**
bluegrass **34.9.6**
bluegum **27.11.6**
bluejacket **22.2.9(.3)**
blue jay **4.23**
Bluemantle **40.21.17(.3)**
blueness **34.18.16(.14)**
blueprint **22.26.1**
blues **35.17**
bluestocking **29.1.14(.6)**
bluestone **28.19.4(.9)**
bluesy **1.23.12**
bluet **22.2.4**
bluethroat **22.21.14**
blue tit **22.2.7**
Bluett **22.2.4**
Blue Vinney **1.16.2**
bluey **1(.6)**
bluff **30.11**
bluffer **17.20.9**
bluffly **1.31.29**
bluffness **34.18.16(.27)**
bluing **29.1.8**
bluish **36.2.6**
Blum **27.14**
Blumenbach **24.6.6(.17)**
Blundell **40.22.16**
Blunden **28.17.12(.23)**
blunder **17.13.20(.10)**
blunderbuss **34.14**
blunderer **17.32.14(.7)**

blunderingly
 1.31.28(.1.17)
blunge **39.17.8**
blunger **17.29.16(.7)**
Blunkett **22.2.9(.9)**
blunt **22.26.12**
bluntly **1.31.22(.20.1)**
bluntness **34.18.16(.20.4)**
blur **18**
blurb **21.15**
blurry **1.29.12**
blurt **22.20**
blush **36.12**
blusher **17.26.10**
blushful **40.27.27**
bluster **17.12.24(.10)**
blusterous **34.18.27(.14)**
blusterously
 1.31.33(.12.5)
blustery **1.29.11(.8.12)**
Blu-tack **24.6.7**
Bly **14**
Blyth **33.7**
Blyton **28.17.11(.12)**
BMus **35.17**
B'nai B'rith **32.1**
bo **19**
boa **17.9**
Boadicea **17.1.11**
Boakes **34.23.17**
Boanerges **35.1.21**
boar **12**
board **23.12**
boarder **17.13.9**
boardroom **27.14.6(.9)**
boardsailer **17.34.4**
boardsailing **29.1.31(.4)**
boardwalk **24.10.9**
boart **22.13**
Boas **35.7**
boast **22.29.17**
boaster **17.12.24(.15)**
boastful **40.27.18**
boastfully **1.31.17(.16.2)**
boastfulness
 34.18.16(.37.2)
boastingly **1.31.28(.1.4)**
boat **22.21**
boatbuilder **17.13.23(.2)**
boatel **40.5.3**
Boateng **29.3**
boater **17.12.18**
boatful **40.14.6(.10)**
boathouse **34.8.6(.11)**
boatlift **22.27.1**
boatload **23.20.13**
boatman **28.17.16(.21)**
boatswain **28.17.23(.16)**
boatyard **23.9.21**
Boaz **35.7**

bob **21.8**
Bobbie **1.9.7**
bobbin **28.2.10**
bobbinet **22.19.15(.1)**
bobbly **1.31.17(.8)**
bobby **1.9.7**
bobby sox **34.23.8(.9)**
bobby-soxer **17.24.20**
bobcat **22.7.9**
bobolink **24.19.1(.8)**
bobsled **23.5.16**
bobsleigh **4.28.16**
bobsleigher **17.2.10**
bobstay **4.9.10**
bobtail **40.4.2**
bobwhite **22.16.23**
bocage **37.4.4**
Boca Raton **28.19.4**
Boccaccio **15.1.10**
bocce **2.26**
Boccherini **1.16.1(.15)**
Boche **36.9**
bock **24.9**
bod **23.10**
bodacious **34.18.22(.3)**
bodaciously **1.31.33(.12.4)**
bodaciousness
 34.18.16(.31.4)
Boddington **28.17.11(.23)**
bode **23.20**
bodeful **40.27.19**
bodega **17.16.1**
bodement **22.26.15(.13.3)**
bodge **39.9**
Bodiam **27.3.4(.6)**
bodice **34.18.12**
bodiless **34.18.29(.2)**
bodily **1.31.17(.10)**
bodkin **28.2.13(.10)**
Bodleian **28.3.21(.12)**
Bodley **1.31.23(.8)**
Bodmer **17.17.18**
Bodmin **28.2.17(.8)**
Bodnant **22.26.6**
Bodoni **1.16.17(.4)**
body **1.11.10**
bodybuilder **17.13.23(.2)**
bodybuilding **29.1.13(.16)**
bodyguard **23.9.10**
bodyline **28.14.19(.2)**
bodyliner **17.18.13(.14)**
bodylining **29.1.17(.10)**
bodysuit **22.18.6**
bodywork **24.17.6(.1)**
Boehm **27.15.6, 27.16,**
 27.17
Boeing® **29.1.9**
Boeotia **17.26.16**
Boeotian **28.17.25(.13)**
Boer **12, 17.7, 17.9**

Boethius **34.3.9**
boeuf bourguignon **11.18**
boff **30.8**
boffin **28.2.19**
boffo **19.16**
boffola **17.34.18(.9)**
Bofors **35.18.14**
bog **26.7**
Bogarde **23.9.10**
Bogart **22.10.6**
bogey **1.14.13**
bogeyman **28.7.10(.2)**
bogeymen **28.5.7(.2)**
bogginess **34.18.16(.2.4)**
Boggis **34.2.11**
boggle **40.24.6**
boggy **1.14.6**
bogie **1.14.13**
bogle **40.24.13**
Bognor **17.18.24**
bogong **29.6.6**
Bogotá **10.6**
bogus **34.18.14(.7)**
bogusness **34.18.16(.31.3)**
bogyman **28.7.10(.2)**
bogymen **28.5.7(.2)**
bohea **1.27**
Bohème **27.4, 27.5**
Bohemia **3.8.1**
Bohemian **28.3.7**
Bohemianism
 27.15.21(.2.9)
boho **19.26**
Bohr **12**
bohunk **24.19.7**
boil **40.11**
Boileau **19.29**
boiler **17.34.11**
boilermaker **17.14.3(.3)**
boing **29.7**
boink **24.19.6**
Boise **1.23.10**
boisterous **34.18.27(.14)**
boisterously
 1.31.33(.12.5)
boisterousness
 34.18.16(.31.5)
Bokmål **40.10.9**
bola **17.34.18**
Bolam **27.15.28(.13)**
bolas **34.18.29(.19)**
bold **23.31.13**
boldface **34.4.9**
boldfaced **22.29.4**
boldly **1.31.23(.18)**
boldness **34.18.16(.21.1)**
Boldre **17.13.23(.8)**
Boldrewood **23.16.6(.6)**
bole **40.18**
Boléat **10.1, 22.3.13, 22.7.2**

bolection 28.17.25(.15.2)
bolero 19.27.3, 19.27.11
boletus 34.18.11(.1)
Boleyn 28.2.31, 28.17.33(.11)
bolide 23.2.23, 23.15.16
Bolingbroke 24.14.10
Bolinger 17.29.16(.8)
Bolitho 19.18
Bolívar 10.13
bolivar 10.13
Bolivia 3.11.2
Bolivian 28.3.10
boliviano 19.15.7
boll 40.9, 40.18
Bollandist 22.29.2(.14)
bollard 23.9.22, 23.18.29
Bollin 28.2.31(.7)
Bollinger® 17.29.16(.8)
bollocking 29.1.14(.11)
bollocks 34.23.15
bolo 19.29.14
bologna 1.16.17(.15), 17.33.9
Bolognese 35.4.8, 35.4.17
bolometer 17.12.16(.9.2)
bolometric 24.2.26(.14.2)
bolometry 1.29.15(.8)
boloney 1.16.17(.15)
Bolshevik 24.2.17
Bolshevism 27.15.21(.2.11)
Bolshevist 22.29.2(.20)
bolshie 1.24.16
bolshily 1.31.17(.22)
bolshiness 34.18.16(.2.8)
Bolshoi 13.11
Bolsover 17.21.14(.9)
bolster 17.12.24(.25)
bolsterer 17.32.14(.6)
bolt 22.32.12
bolter 17.12.26(.7)
bolt-hole 40.18.13
Bolton 28.17.11(.27)
Boltzmann 28.17.16(.29)
bolus 34.18.29(.19)
Bolzano 19.15.7
bomb 27.9
bombard 23.9.6
bombarde 23.9.6
bombardier 3.5
bombardment 22.26.15(.13.3)
bombardon 28.17.12(.16)
bombast 22.29.6(.3)
bombastic 24.2.10(.15.4)
bombastically 1.31.24(.9.6)
Bombay 4.8
bombazine 28.1.19

bombe 21.10, 21.17, 27.9
bomber 17.17.8
bombora 17.32.10(.1)
bombproof 30.13.4
bombshell 40.5.13
bombsight 22.16.19(.15)
bomb site 22.16.19(.15)
bona fide 1.11.14
bona fides 35.1.8
Bonaire 6
Bonallack 24.16.16
bonanza 17.25.18
Bonaparte 22.10.1
bona vacantia 3.4.12
Bonaventura 17.32.14(.3)
Bonaventure 17.28.22
bonbon 28.10.8
bonce 34.24.7
bond 23.24.9
bondage 39.2.11
bondager 17.29.13
bondholder 17.13.23(.8)
Bondi 14.9
bondman 28.17.16(.22)
bondsman 28.17.16(.30)
bondstone 28.19.4(.9)
bondswoman 28.17.16(.14)
bondswomen 28.2.17(.1)
bondwoman 28.17.16(.14)
bondwomen 28.2.17(.1)
bone 28.19
bonefish 36.2.18(.19)
bonehead 23.5.13(.14)
boneheaded 23.18.10(.3)
boneless 34.18.29(.27)
bonemeal 40.1.6
boner 17.18.18
boneshaker 17.14.3(.7)
bonfire 17.6.9(.9)
bong 29.6
bongo 19.13.12
Bonham 27.15.14(.8)
Bonhoeffer 17.20.7, 17.20.13
bonhomie 2.16
bonhomous 34.18.15(.10)
bonier 3.9.11
boniest 22.29.15(.2)
Boniface 34.4.9
boniness 34.18.16(.2.5)
Bonington 28.17.11(.23)
Bonio 15.1.6
bonism 27.15.21(.2.9)
bonist 22.29.2(.18.3)
Bonita 17.12.1(.7)
bonito 19.10.1
bonk 24.19.5
bonker 17.14.21(.4)

bon mot 19
Bonn 28.10
Bonnard 10.11
bonne bouche 36.14
Bonner 17.18.9
bonnet 22.2.12
bonnethead 23.5.13(.9)
Bonneville 40.2.12
Bonnie 1.16.9
bonnily 1.31.17(.14.1)
bonniness 34.18.16(.2.5)
bonny 1.16.9
bonsai 14.18
Bonser 17.24.22(.5)
bons mots 19, 35.20
Bonsor 17.24.22(.5)
bonspiel 40.1.1
bonus 34.18.16(.17)
bon vivant 11.11, 22.26.9, 28.10.16
bon viveur 18.10
bon voyage 37.4
bonxie 1.22.22
bony 1.16.17
bonze 35.26.10
bonzer 17.25.18
Bonzo 19.21
boo 16
boob 21.13
booboisie 2.23
boo-boo 16.6
boobook 24.14.3
booby 1.9.10
boobyish 36.2.1
boodle 40.22.12
boogie 1.14.10
boogie-woogie 1.14.10
boohoo 16.21
book 24.14
bookable 40.20.16(.13)
bookbinder 17.13.20(.11)
bookbinding 29.1.13(.14)
bookcase 34.4.6
bookend 23.24.5(.6)
booker 17.14.13
bookie 1.12.11
booking 29.1.14(.10)
bookish 36.2.13
bookishly 1.31.35(.7.1)
bookishness 34.18.16(.33.4)
bookkeeper 17.10.1
bookkeeping 29.1.10(.1)
booklet 22.19.26(.19)
booklist 22.29.2(.31.6)
bookmaker 17.14.3(.3)

bookmaking 29.1.14(.3)
bookman 28.17.16(.23)
bookmark 24.8.8
bookmarker 17.14.7
bookmobile 40.1.2
bookplate 22.4.23(.8)
bookseller 17.34.5(.11)
bookshelf 30.20.2
bookshelves 35.28.10
bookshop 20.7.9
bookstall 40.10.5
bookstand 23.24.6(.5)
bookstore 12.5.9
booksy 1.22.22
bookwork 24.17.6(.10)
bookworm 27.16.7
Boole 40.15
Boolean 28.3.21(.10)
boom 27.14
boomer 17.17.13
boomerang 29.4.15
boomlet 22.19.26(.21)
boomslang 29.4.17
boomtown 28.8.1
boon 28.16
boondock 24.9.5
boondoggle 40.24.6
Boone 28.16
boonies 35.2.8
boor 12, 17.7
boorish 36.2.25
boorishly 1.31.35(.7.4)
boorishness 34.18.16(.33.6)
Boosey 1.23.12
boost 22.29.14
booster 17.12.24(.13)
boot 22.18
bootblack 24.6.23
bootboy 13.3
bootee 2.11, 2.12.10
Boötes 35.1.7(.8)
booth 32.13, 33.8
Bootham 27.15.19
Boothby 1.9.20
Boothe 32.13, 33.8
Boothia 3.12
Boothroyd 23.13.19
bootie 2.12.10
bootjack 24.6.18
bootlace 34.4.14
Bootle 40.21.11
bootleg 26.4
bootlegger 17.16.4
bootless 34.18.29(.22)
bootlicker 17.14.2
bootstrap 20.5.6
booty 1.10.15
booze 35.17
boozer 17.25.14

boozily **1.31.17(.21)**
booziness **34.18.16(.2.7)**
boozy **1.23.12**
bop **20.7**
Bophuthatswana **17.18.8(.10)**
bopper **17.10.8**
bora **17.32.10**
Bora-Bora **17.32.10(.1)**
boracic **24.2.20(.5)**
borage **39.2.22(.5)**
borak **24.6.21**
borane **28.4.18**
borate **22.4.22(.4)**
borax **34.23.5(.14)**
borazon **28.10.19**
borborygmi **1.15.17**
borborygmic **24.2.14(.14)**
borborygmus **34.18.15(.15)**
Bordeaux **19.11**
bordel **40.5.4**
bordello **19.29.4**
border **17.13.9**
bordereau **19.27**
bordereaux **35.20.12**
borderer **17.32.14(.7)**
borderland **23.24.6(.13)**
borderline **28.14.19(.11)**
Bordet **4.10**
bordone **1.16.17(.4)**
bordure **17.7.12(.4)**
bore **12**
boreal **40.3.14(.5)**
borealis **34.2.22(.3)**
boredom **27.15.10(.7)**
Boreham **27.15.26(.5)**
borehole **40.18.13**
borer **17.32.10**
Borg **26.9**
Borges **34.5.4**
Borgia **3.19.5, 17.27.6, 17.29.9**
boric **24.2.26(.7)**
boring **29.1.30(.7)**
boringly **1.31.28(.1.17)**
boringness **34.18.16(.26)**
Boris **34.2.21**
Bork **24.10**
Bormann **28.17.16(.11)**
born **28.11**
borne **28.11**
borné **4.14**
Bornean **28.3.8(.7)**
Borneo **15.1.6**
Bornholm **27.17.12**
Borobudur **17.7.4**
Borodin **28.2.12**
Borodino **19.15.1**
borofluoride **23.15.15**

boron **28.10.24(.3)**
boronia **3.9.11**
borosilicate **22.4.11(.6), 22.19.12(.10)**
borough **17.32.12**
Borromini **1.16.1(.7)**
borrow **19.27.6**
Borrowdale **40.4.3**
borrower **17.9.11**
borrowing **29.1.9**
Borsalino® **19.15.1**
borsch **36.11**
borscht **22.30**
Borstal **40.21.18**
bort **22.13**
Borth **32.10**
Borthwick **24.2.25**
bortsch **38.9**
borzoi **13.10**
Bosanquet **22.5.5**
Bosc **24.20.5**
boscage **39.2.12**
Boscastle **40.31.6, 40.31.7**
Boscawen **28.14.17, 28.17.8, 28.17.30**
Bosch **36.9**
Boscobel **40.5.2**
Bose **34.20, 35.20**
bosh **36.9**
bosie **1.23.15**
boskiness **34.18.16(.2.4)**
Boskop **20.7.5**
bosky **1.12.17(.5)**
Bosnia **3.9.17**
Bosnian **28.3.8(.13)**
bosom **27.15.21(.6)**
bosomy **1.15.13(.9)**
boson **28.10.18**
Bosphorus **34.18.27(.20)**
Bosporus **34.18.27(.12)**
boss **34.10**
bossa nova **17.21.14**
bossily **1.31.17(.20)**
bossiness **34.18.16(.2.7)**
bossy **1.22.9**
Bostik® **24.2.10(.15.4)**
Bostock **24.9.4**
Boston **28.17.11(.25)**
Bostonian **28.3.8(.11)**
bosun **28.17.23(.16)**
Boswell **40.5.17(.16)**
Bosworth **32.14.15**
bot **22.11**
botanic **24.2.15(.5)**
botanical **40.23.12(.11)**
botanically **1.31.24(.9.8)**
botanist **22.29.2(.18.1)**
botanize **35.15.12(.5)**
botany **1.16.15(.7)**
botargo **19.13.5**

botch **38.8**
botcher **17.28.9**
botfly **14.25.14**
both **32.16**
Botha **17.12.16(.2), 17.12.18**
Botham **27.15.18**
bother **17.23.8**
botheration **28.17.25(.3.13)**
bothersome **27.15.20(.11)**
Bothnia **3.9.16**
Bothwell **40.5.17(.14)**
bothy **1.20.6**
Botolph **30.20.4**
botryoid **23.13.2**
botryoidal **40.22.9**
Botswana **17.18.8(.10)**
Botswanan **28.17.17(.6)**
bott **22.11**
Botticelli **1.31.5**
bottle **40.21.7**
bottleful **40.14.6(.22)**
bottleneck **24.4.7**
bottlenose **35.20.8**
bottler **17.34.21**
bottlewasher **17.26.8**
bottom **27.15.9(.6)**
bottomless **34.18.29(.26)**
bottomlessness **34.18.16(.31.6)**
Bottomley **1.31.26(.11)**
bottommost **22.29.17(.4)**
bottomry **1.29.19**
botulinus **34.18.16(.13)**
botulism **27.15.21(.2.15)**
Boucher **4.20, 17.28.7**
bouclé **4.28.12**
Boudicca **17.14.15(.7)**
boudoir **10.22.6**
bouffant **11.10, 22.26.9**
Bougainville **40.2.12**
bougainvillea **3.24.2**
Bougainvillian **28.3.21(.2)**
bough **9**
bought **22.13**
boughten **28.17.11(.10)**
bougie **1.26.13**
bouillabaisse **34.4.3, 34.5.1**
bouilli **1.30**
bouillon **11.18, 28.10.25**
boulder **17.13.23(.8)**
bouldery **1.29.11(.9)**
boule **1.31.16, 4.28.6, 40.15**
boulevard **23.9.13**
boulevardier **4.27**
Boulez **4.28.6, 35.5.15**
boulle **40.15**

Boulogne **28.12**
boult **22.32.12**
Boulter **17.12.26(.7)**
Boulting **29.1.12(.22)**
Boulton **28.17.11(.27)**
bounce **34.24.5**
bouncer **17.24.22(.4)**
bouncily **1.31.17(.20)**
bounciness **34.18.16(.2.7)**
bouncy **1.22.23(.5)**
bound **23.24.7**
boundary **1.29.11(.9)**
bounden **28.17.12(.23)**
bounder **17.13.20(.5)**
boundless **34.18.29(.23)**
boundlessly **1.31.33(.12.6)**
boundlessness **34.18.16(.31.6)**
bounteous **34.3.3**
bounteously **1.31.33(.1.1)**
bounteousness **34.18.16(.31.1)**
bountiful **40.27.14**
bountifully **1.31.17(.16.1)**
bountifulness **34.18.16(.37.2)**
bounty **1.10.23(.5)**
bouquet **4.11**
bouquet garni **2.17**
bouquetin **28.2.11(.10)**
Bourbon **28.10.8, 28.17.10**
bourbon **28.17.10**
bourdon **28.17.12(.10)**
bourgeois **10.22.12, 34.13**
bourgeoisie **2.23**
Bourguiba **17.11.1**
Bourke **24.17**
bourn **28.11**
Bournemouth **32.14.11**
Bournville **40.2.12**
Bournvita **17.12.1(.9)**
bourrée **4.26.8**
bourse **34.12, 34.18.6**
Bourton **28.17.11(.10)**
boustrophedon **28.17.12(.1)**
bout **22.9**
boutique **24.1.3**
boutonnière **6, 6.20**
Bouverie **1.29.11(.15)**
Bouvet **4.16**
bouzouki **1.12.12**
Bovary **1.29.11(.15)**
bovate **22.4.16**
Bovey Tracy **1.22.4**
bovid **23.2.15**
bovine **28.14.11**
bovinely **1.31.27(.11)**
Bovingdon **28.17.12(.24)**
Bovington **28.17.11(.23)**

Bovis 34.2.15
Bovril® 40.16.13(.21)
bovver 17.21.7
Bow 19
bow 9, 19
Bowater 17.12.10(.7)
bow compass 34.18.9(.11)
Bowden 28.17.12(.7)
Bowdler 17.34.22
bowdlerism 27.15.21(.2.14)
bowdlerization 28.17.25(.3.11)
bowdlerize 35.15.20(.2)
bowdlerizer 17.25.12(.14)
bowel 40.16.3
Bowen 28.2.8
bower 17.3
bowerbird 23.19.1
Bowers 35.18.2
bowery 1.29.11(.1)
Bowes 35.20
bowfin 28.2.19
bowhead 23.5.13(.6)
bowie 1(.3)
bowie knife 30.12
Bowker 17.14.6
bowl 40.18
Bowlby 1.9.24
bowler 17.34.18
Bowles 35.30.13
bowlful 40.14.6(.22)
bowline 28.2.31(.12)
bowman 28.17.16(.8)
Bowness 34.5.6
Bowring 29.1.30(.5)
bowsaw 12.14.9
bowser® 17.25.6
bowshot 22.11.12
bowsprit 22.2.24
bowstring 29.1.30(.13)
bow-wow 9.15
bowyang 29.4.16
bowyer 17.33.4
box 34.23.8
boxcalf 30.7.3
boxcar 10.8.16
boxer 17.24.20
boxful 40.14.6(.19)
box room 27.14.6(.17)
boxwood 23.16.6(.17)
boxy 1.22.22
boy 13
boyar 10.2, 10.24
Boyce 34.13
boycott 22.11.6
Boyd 23.13
Boyer 17.5
boyfriend 23.24.5(.14)

boyhood 23.16.5(.2)
boyish 36.2.3
boyishly 1.31.35(.7.1)
boyishness 34.18.16(.33.1)
Boyle 40.11
Boyne 28.12
boyo 19.4
boysenberry 1.29.3
Boyson 28.17.23(.10)
Boz 35.10
bozo 19.21
BPhil 40.2
bra 10
braai 14
Brabant 22.26.6
Brabazon 28.17.24(.12)
Brabham 27.15.8
Brabin 28.2.10
Brabourne 28.11.2, 28.17.10
brace 34.4
Bracegirdle 40.22.14
bracelet 22.19.26(.26)
bracer 17.24.4
brach 38.5
brachial 40.3.5
brachiate 22.3.5, 22.4.2(.5)
brachiation 28.17.25(.3.1)
brachiator 17.12.4(.1)
brachiopod 23.10.1
brachiosauri 14.24.4
brachiosaurus 34.18.27(.8)
brachistochrone 28.19.17
brachycephalic 24.2.27(.6)
brachycephalous 34.18.29(.17.4)
brachycephaly 1.31.17(.16.1)
brachylogy 1.26.10(.10)
bracing 29.1.23
bracingness 34.18.16(.26)
brack 24.6
bracken 28.17.13(.5)
Brackenbury 1.29.11(.7.2)
bracket 22.2.9(.3)
brackish 36.2.13
brackishness 34.18.16(.33.4)
Bracknell 40.26.18
braconid 23.2.13
bract 22.23.5
bracteal 40.3.3
bracteate 22.3.3
brad 23.7
bradawl 40.10.6
Bradbury 1.29.11(.7.2)
Braden 28.17.12(.4)
Bradford 23.18.16(.12)

Bradley 1.31.23(.5)
Bradman 28.17.16(.22)
Bradshaw 12.16.8
Bradwell 40.5.17(.8)
Brady 1.11.4
bradycardia 3.5.5
bradykinin 28.2.18
bradyseism 27.15.21(.5)
brae 4
Braemar 10.10
brag 26.5
Braga 17.16.6
Braganza 17.25.18
Bragg 26.5
braggadocio 15.1.10
braggart 22.19.13
bragger 17.16.5
braggingly 1.31.28(.1.6)
Brahe 1.27, 17.30
Brahma 17.17.7
Brahman 28.17.16(.9)
Brahmana 17.18.16(.8)
Brahmanic 24.2.15(.5)
Brahmanical 40.23.12(.11)
Brahmanism 27.15.21(.2.9)
Brahmaputra 17.32.19(.6)
Brahmin 28.2.17(.3)
Brahms 35.25.5
braid 23.4
braider 17.13.3
brail 40.4
Braille 40.4
brain 28.4
brainbox 34.23.8(.2)
brainchild 23.31.9
Braine 28.4
brainfag 26.5.5
braininess 34.18.16(.2.5)
brainless 34.18.29(.27)
brainlessly 1.31.33(.12.6)
brainlessness 34.18.16(.31.6)
brainpan 28.7.4
brainpower 17.3.1
brainsick 24.2.20(.15)
brainstem 27.5.4
brainstorm 27.10.2
Braintree 2.30.10
brainwash 36.9.5
brainwave 31.3.6
brainwork 24.17.6(.13)
brainy 1.16.4
braise 35.4
Braithwaite 22.4.21
brake 24.3
brakeless 34.18.29(.24)
brakeman 28.17.16(.23)
brakesman 28.17.16(.29)

brake van 28.7.13
braless 34.18.29(.9)
Bram 27.6
Bramah 17.17.7
Bramante 1.10.23(.4)
bramble 40.20.19
brambling 29.1.31(.16)
brambly 1.31.21(.12)
Bramhope 20.15.7
Bramley 1.31.26(.5)
Brampton 28.17.11(.18)
Bramwell 40.5.17(.11)
bran 28.7
Branagh 17.18.6
branch 38.18.4
branchia 3.6.8
branchiae 2.3
branchial 40.3.5
branchiate 22.3.5, 22.4.2(.5)
branchlet 22.19.26(.28)
branch like 24.13.7(.24)
branchy 1.24.15
brand 23.24.6
Brandeis 34.15.3
Brandenburg 26.14.1(.9)
brander 17.13.20(.4)
brandish 36.2.12
brandisher 17.26.14
brandling 29.1.31(.18)
Brando 19.11.14
Brandon 28.17.12(.23)
Brandreth 32.5, 32.14.16
Brands Hatch 38.5
Brandt 22.26.6
brandy 1.11.20(.4)
Brangwyn 28.2.28
Braniff 30.2.3
Branigan 28.17.15(.13)
brank-ursine 28.14.13
brannigan 28.17.15(.13)
Branson 28.17.23(.24)
Branston 28.17.11(.25)
brant 22.26.6
Braque 24.6, 24.8
Brasenose 35.20.8
brash 36.6
Brasher 17.26.3
brashly 1.31.35(.3)
brashness 34.18.16(.33.1)
Brasília 3.24.2
brass 34.9
brassage 39.2.19
brassard 23.9.15
brassbound 23.24.7(.2)
brasserie 1.29.11(.18)
Brassey 1.22.6
brassica 17.14.15(.12)
brassie 1.22.6
brassiere 3.15.4

brassily **1.31.17(.20)**
brassiness **34.18.16(.2.7)**
Brasso® **19.20.4, 19.20.5**
brassware **6.18.12**
brassy **1.22.6, 1.22.8**
brat **22.7**
Bratislava **17.21.6**
brattice **34.2.8**
bratty **1.10.6**
bratwurst **22.29.15(.5), 22.29.16**
Braun **28.8, 28.11**
Braunschweig **26.11**
braunschweiger **17.16.10**
bravado **19.11.7**
brave **31.3**
bravely **1.31.30(.3)**
braveness **34.18.16(.28.1)**
Bravington **28.17.11(.23)**
bravo **19.17**
bravura **17.32.14(.3)**
braw **12**
Brawdy **1.11.11**
brawl **40.10**
brawler **17.34.10**
brawn **28.11**
brawniness **34.18.16(.2.5)**
brawny **1.16.10**
bray **4**
braze **35.4**
brazen **28.17.24(.3)**
brazenly **1.31.27(.14)**
brazenness **34.18.16(.25)**
brazer **17.25.3**
brazier **3.15.3**
braziery **1.29.2(.8), 1.29.11(.21)**
Brazil **40.2.15**
Brazilian **28.3.21(.2)**
Brazzaville **40.2.12**
breach **38.1**
bread **23.5**
Breadalbane **28.17.10**
breadbasket **22.19.12(.14)**
breadboard **23.12.2(.9)**
breadbox **34.23.8(.2)**
breadcrumb **27.11.12**
breadfruit **22.18.9**
breadline **28.14.19(.15)**
breadth **32.18**
breadthways **35.4.15**
breadthwise **35.15.19**
breadwinner **17.18.2**
break **24.3**
breakable **40.20.16(.13)**
breakage **39.2.12**
breakaway **4.25.9**
breakdown **28.8.2(.6)**
breaker **17.14.3**
breakfast **22.29.15(.14)**

breakfaster **17.12.24(.14)**
breakneck **24.4.7**
breakout **22.9.9**
breakpoint **22.26.11**
Breakspear **3.2.9**
breakthrough **16.23.13**
break-up **20.9.7**
breakwater **17.12.10(.7)**
bream **27.1**
Brearley **1.31.3**
breast **22.29.5**
breastbone **28.19.3**
breastfed **23.5.8**
breastfeed **23.1.6**
breastless **34.18.29(.22)**
breastplate **22.4.23(.8)**
breaststroke **24.18.13**
breastsummer **17.17.10**
breastwork **24.17.6(.8)**
breath **32.5**
breathable **40.20.16(.20)**
breathalyse **35.15.21**
breathalyser **17.25.12**
breathalyze **35.15.21(.4.6)**
Breathalyzer® **17.25.12(.15)**
breathe **33.1**
breather **17.23.1**
breathily **1.31.17(.18)**
breathiness **34.18.16(.2.6)**
breathless **34.18.29(.31)**
breathlessly **1.31.33(.12.6)**
breathlessness **34.18.16(.31.6)**
breathtaking **29.1.14(.3)**
breathtakingly **1.31.28(.1.6)**
breathy **1.20.3**
breccia **3.18, 17.28.5**
brecciate **22.4.2(.12)**
brecciation **28.17.25(.3.1)**
Brechin **28.2.13(.1), 28.2.14**
Brecht **22.23.4, 22.24**
Brechtian **28.3.3**
Breckenridge **39.2.22(.13)**
Breckland **23.24.16(.16.3)**
Brecknock **24.9.9**
Brecknockshire **17.26.19**
Brecon **28.17.13(.4)**
Breconshire **17.26.21**
bred **23.5**
Breda **17.13.1, 17.13.3**
Bredon **28.17.12(.1)**
breech **38.1**
breeches **35.18.20**
breeches buoy **13.3**
breed **23.1**
breeder **17.13.1**
breeks **34.23.1**

Breen **28.1**
breeze **35.1**
breeze block **24.9.16(.10)**
breezeless **34.18.29(.34)**
breezeway **4.25.23**
breezily **1.31.17(.21)**
breeziness **34.18.16(.2.7)**
breezy **1.23.1**
Bremen **28.17.16(.4)**
Bremner **17.18.25**
bremsstrahlung **29.9**
Bren **28.5**
Brenda **17.13.20(.3)**
Brendan **28.17.12(.23)**
Brendel **40.22.16**
Bren gun **28.13**
Brennan **28.17.17(.4)**
Brenner Pass **34.9**
brent **22.26.4**
Brentwood **23.16.6(.9)**
Breslau **9.17**
Bresson **28.17.23(.5)**
Brest **22.29.5**
Brest-Litovsk **24.20.14**
brethren **28.17.31(.22)**
Breton **28.10.9, 28.17.11(.4)**
Brett **22.5**
Bretton **28.17.11(.4)**
breve **31.1**
brevet **22.2.14**
breviary **1.29.2(.7)**
breviate **22.3.7**
brevity **1.10.16(.15)**
brew **16**
brewer **17.8**
brewery **1.29.11(.4)**
Brewis **34.2.4**
brewster **17.12.24(.13)**
Brezel **40.31.16**
Brezhnev **30.4, 31.4**
Brian **28.17.5**
Brian Ború **16.23**
briar **17.6**
Briard **23.9**
briarwood **23.16.6(.6)**
bribable **40.20.16(.10)**
bribe **21.12**
briber **17.11.11**
bribery **1.29.11(.7.1)**
bric-a-brac **24.6.21**
brick **24.2**
brickbat **22.7.6**
brickdust **22.29.12**
brickfield **23.31.1(.2)**
brickfielder **17.13.23(.1)**
brickie **1.12.2**
bricklayer **17.2.10**
bricklaying **29.1.3**
brickmaker **17.14.3(.3)**
brickmaking **29.1.14(.3)**

brickwork **24.17.6(.10)**
brickyard **23.9.21**
bridal **40.22.11**
bridally **1.31.17(.10)**
bride **23.15**
bridegroom **27.14.6(.11)**
Brideshead **23.5.13(.16)**
bridesmaid **23.4.7**
bridesman **28.17.16(.30)**
bridewell **40.5.17(.8)**
bridge **39.2**
bridgeable **40.20.16(.25)**
bridgehead **23.5.13(.18)**
Bridgeman **28.17.16(.34)**
Bridgend **23.24.5**
Bridgeport **22.13.1**
Bridger **17.29.2**
Bridges **35.18.21**
Bridget **22.19.22**
Bridgetown **28.8.1**
Bridgewater **17.12.10(.7)**
bridgework **24.17.6(.18)**
Bridgnorth **32.10**
Bridgwater **17.12.10(.7)**
bridle **40.22.11**
bridleway **4.25.26**
Bridlington **28.17.11(.23)**
bridoon **28.16.4**
Bridport **22.13.1**
Brie **2**
brief **30.1**
briefcase **34.4.6**
briefless **34.18.29(.29)**
briefly **1.31.29**
briefness **34.18.16(.27)**
brier **17.6**
Brierley **1.31.3, 1.31.17(.3)**
Brierly **1.31.3, 1.31.17(.3)**
Briers **35.18.4**
brierwood **23.16.6(.6)**
briery **1.29.11(.2)**
brig **26.2**
brigade **23.4.6**
brigadier **3.5**
Brigadoon **28.16.4**
brigalow **19.29.12**
brigand **23.24.16(.6)**
brigandage **39.2.11**
brigandine **28.1.10**
brigandish **36.2.12**
brigandism **27.15.21(.2.5)**
brigandry **1.29.16**
brigantine **28.1.9(.6)**
Brigg **26.2**
Briggs **35.24**
Brigham **27.15.12**
Brighouse **34.8.6(.14)**
bright **22.16**
brighten **28.17.11(.12)**
brightish **36.2.11**

Brightlingsea 2.22.13
brightly 1.31.22(.13)
brightness 34.18.16(.20.2)
Brighton 28.17.11(.12)
brightwork 24.17.6(.8)
Brigid 23.2.20
Brigit 22.2.21
Brigitte 22.1.12, 22.2.19
brill 40.2
brilliance 34.24.2,
34.24.10(.23)
brilliancy 1.22.23(.2)
brilliant 22.26.2(.10),
22.26.15(.24)
brilliantine 28.1.9(.6)
brilliantly 1.31.22(.20.1)
brilliantness
34.18.16(.20.4)
Brillo® 19.29.2
brim 27.2
Brimble 40.20.19
brimful 40.14.6
brimless 34.18.29(.26)
brimstone 28.17.11(.25),
28.19.4(.9)
brimstony 1.16.15(.7),
1.16.17(.3)
Brindisi 1.23.13
brindle 40.22.16
Brindley 1.31.23(.17)
brine 28.14
bring 29.1
bringer 17.19.1
brininess 34.18.16(.2.5)
brinjal 40.16.11, 40.34
brink 24.19.1
brinkmanship
20.2.7(.19)
brinksmanship
20.2.7(.19)
Brinks-Mat® 22.7.11
briny 1.16.13
bri-nylon 28.10.26
brio 19.1
brioche 36.9, 36.9.1, 36.16
briolette 22.5.21
Briony 1.16.15(.3)
briquette 22.5.5
Brisbane 28.17.10
Brisco 19.12.17
Briscoe 19.12.17
brisk 24.20.1
brisken 28.17.13(.18)
brisket 22.2.9(.10)
briskly 1.31.24(.13)
briskness 34.18.16(.22)
brisling 29.1.31(.26)
bristle 40.31.2
bristletail 40.4.2
bristle worm 27.16.7
bristliness 34.18.16(.2.10)

Bristol 40.21.18
bristols 35.30.16
Bristow 19.10.19
Brit 22.2
Britain 28.17.11(.2)
Britannia 17.33.9
Britannic 24.2.15(.5)
britches 35.18.20
Briticism 27.15.21(.2.12)
British 36.2.11
Britisher 17.26.14
Britishism 27.15.21(.2.13)
Britishness
34.18.16(.33.3)
Britoil 40.11.3
Briton 28.17.11(.2)
Britt 22.2
Brittain 28.17.11(.2)
Brittan 28.17.11(.2)
Brittany 1.16.15(.7)
Britten 28.17.11(.2)
brittle 40.21.2
brittlely 1.31.38
brittleness 34.18.16(.37.5)
brittly 1.31.17(.9.1)
Britton 28.17.11(.2)
Britvic® 24.2.17
britzka 17.14.23
Brixham 27.15.20(.15)
Brize Norton
28.17.11(.10)
Brno 19.15, 19.15.13
bro 19
broach 38.17
broad 23.12
broadband 23.24.6(.4)
Broadbent 22.26.4(.3)
broadbrimmed 23.23.2
broadcast 22.29.6(.5),
22.29.8(.3)
broadcaster 17.12.24(.5)
broadcloth 32.9
broaden 28.17.12(.10)
Broadhead 23.5.13(.10)
Broadhurst 22.29.16
broadleaf 30.1.9
broadleaved 23.26
broadloom 27.14.8
broadly 1.31.23(.9)
broad-minded
23.18.10(.14)
broad-mindedly
1.31.23(.14.4)
broad-mindedness
34.18.16(.21.1)
Broadmoor 12.9.8, 17.7.7
broadness 34.18.16(.21.1)
broadsheet 22.1.11
broadside 23.15.11(.10)
broad-spectrum
27.15.26(.10)

Broadstairs 35.6
broadsword 23.12.6
broadtail 40.4.2
Broadway 4.25.13
broadwise 35.15.19
Broadwood 23.16.6(.10)
Brobdingnag 26.5.4
Brobdingnagian 28.3.6
brocade 23.4.5
brocatel 40.5.3
brocatelle 40.5.3
broccoli 1.31.17(.11)
broch 24.9, 25.6
brochette 22.5.15
brochure 17.7.10, 17.26.16
brock 24.9
Brockbank 24.19.3(.1)
Brocken 28.17.13(.7)
Brockenhurst 22.29.16
brocket 22.2.9(.5)
Brocklebank 24.19.3(.1)
Broderick 24.2.26(.10)
broderie anglaise
35.4.18
Brodie 1.11.19
Brodsky 1.12.17(.9)
Broederbond 22.26.9,
23.24.9
Brogan 28.17.15(.14)
brogue 26.15
broil 40.11
broiler 17.34.11
broke 24.18
broken 28.17.13(.15)
brokenly 1.31.27(.14)
brokenness 34.18.16(.25)
broker 17.14.17
brokerage 39.2.22(.9)
Brolac 24.6.23
brolga 17.16.19
brolly 1.31.10
bromate 22.4.13(.7)
Bromberg 26.14.1(.8)
brome 27.17
bromelia 3.24.1
bromeliad 23.7.2
bromic 24.2.14(.12)
bromide 23.15.7
bromine 28.1.13
bromism 27.15.21(.2.8)
Bromley 1.31.26(.7)
bromoform 27.10.5(.2)
Brompton 28.17.11(.18)
Bromsgrove 31.12
Bromwich 39.2.14
Bromyard 23.9.21
bronc 24.19.5
bronchi 2.14, 14.10
bronchia 3.6.8
bronchiae 2.3

bronchial 40.3.5
bronchiolar 17.34.3,
17.34.18
bronchiole 40.14.1
bronchitic 24.2.10(.2.1)
bronchitis 34.18.11(.8)
bronchocele 40.1.10
bronchopneumonia
3.9.11
bronchoscope 20.15.4(.1)
bronchoscopy 1.8.11(.5)
bronchus 34.18.13(.13)
bronco 19.12.15
Bronski 1.12.17(.12)
Bronstein 28.1.9(.7)
Brontë 1.10.23(.7)
brontosaur 12.14.8
brontosauri 14.24.4
brontosaurus 34.18.27(.8)
Bronwen 28.17.30
Bronx 34.23.18
bronze 35.26.10
bronzy 1.23.20
brooch 38.17
brood 23.17
brooder 17.13.14
broodily 1.31.17(.10)
broodiness 34.18.16(.2.3)
broodingly 1.31.28(.1.5)
broody 1.11.16
brook 24.14
Brooke 24.14
Brookes 34.23.13
Brookfield 23.31.1(.2)
Brooking 29.1.14(.10)
Brooklands 35.23.15
brooklet 22.19.26(.19)
brooklime 27.12.8
Brooklyn 28.17.33(.20)
Brookner 17.18.23
Brookside 23.15.11
brookweed 23.1.10
Brookwood 23.16.6(.11)
broom 27.14
Broome 27.14
broomrape 20.3
broomstick 24.2.10(.15.4)
Brophy 1.18.11
Bros 34.10, 35.10
brose 35.20
Brosnahan 28.17.29
broth 32.9
brothel 40.29
brother 17.23.10
brotherhood 23.16.5(.3)
brotherliness
34.18.16(.2.10)
brotherly 1.31.17(.19)
Brotherton 28.17.11(.15)
Brough 30.11

brougham **27.14, 27.15.5**
brought **22.13**
Broughton **28.17.11(.7)**
brouhaha **10.21**
brow **9**
browbeat **22.1.2**
browbeaten **28.17.11(.1)**
browbeater **17.12.1(.2)**
brown **28.8**
Browne **28.8**
brownfield **23.31.1(.2)**
Brownhills **35.30.2**
Brownian **28.3.8(.6)**
brownie **1.16.7**
Browning **29.1.17(.6)**
brownish **36.2.16(.6)**
Brownjohn **28.10.22**
brown-out **22.9.11**
Brownshirt **22.20.12**
brownstone **28.19.4(.9)**
browse **35.8**
browser **17.25.6**
browze **35.8**
Broxbourne **28.11.2**
Brubeck **24.4.3**
Bruce **34.17**
brucellosis **34.2.17(.11.2)**
Bruch **24.14**
brucite **22.16.19(.8)**
Bruckner **17.18.23**
Bruegel **40.24.7**
Bruges **37.7**
bruin **28.2.7**
bruise **35.17**
bruised **23.28.3**
bruiser **17.25.14**
bruit **22.18**
Brum **27.11**
brumby **1.9.18**
brume **27.14**
Brummagem **27.15.24**
Brummell **40.25.7**
Brummie **1.15.10**
brumous **34.18.15(.9)**
brunch **38.18.7**
Brunei **14.13**
Bruneian **28.17.5**
Brunel **40.5.8**
brunet **22.5.9**
brunette **22.5.9**
Brunhild **23.31.2**
Brünhilde **17.13.23(.2)**
Bruno **19.15.11**
Brunswick **24.2.25**
brunt **22.26.12**
Brunton **28.17.11(.22)**
bruschetta **17.12.5(.3)**
brush **36.12**
brushfire **17.6.9(.11)**
brushless **34.18.29(.35)**

brush-like **24.13.7(.24)**
brushwood **23.16.6(.19)**
brushwork **24.17.6(.16)**
brushy **1.24.9**
brusque **24.20.7**
brusquely **1.31.24(.13)**
brusqueness **34.18.16(.22)**
brusquerie **1.29.11(.10)**
Brussels **35.30.22**
brut **22.18**
brutal **40.21.11**
brutalism **27.15.21(.2.15)**
brutalist **22.29.2(.31.2)**
brutality **1.10.16(.32.3)**
brutalization **28.17.25(.3.12)**
brutalize **35.15.21(.4.3)**
brutally **1.31.17(.9.2)**
brute **22.18**
brutish **36.2.11**
brutishly **1.31.35(.7.1)**
brutishness **34.18.16(.33.3)**
Brutus **34.18.11(.9)**
bruxism **27.15.21(.2.12)**
Bryan **28.17.5**
Bryant **22.26.15(.4)**
Bryce **34.15**
Bryden **28.17.12(.13)**
Brylcreem® **27.1.12**
Bryn **28.2**
Brynley **1.31.27(.2)**
Bryn Mawr **12**
Brynmawr **17.3.5**
Brynmor **12.9.11**
Brynner **17.18.2**
bryological **40.23.12(.17.2)**
bryologist **22.29.2(.26.2)**
bryology **1.26.10(.11.1)**
bryony **1.16.15(.3)**
bryophyte **22.16.16**
bryophytic **24.2.10(.2.3)**
bryozoan **28.17.8**
bryozoology **1.26.10(.11.1)**
Bryson **28.17.23(.12)**
Brythonic **24.2.15(.6.3)**
Brzezinski **1.12.17(.12)**
BSc **2.22**
bub **21.11**
bubal **40.20.15**
bubble **40.20.12**
bubblegum **27.11.6**
bubbler **17.34.20**
bubbly **1.31.17(.8), 1.31.21(.1)**
bubbly-jock **24.9.12**
Buber **17.11.12**
bubo **19.9.8**

bubonic **24.2.15(.6.1)**
bubonocele **40.1.10**
buccal **40.23.9**
buccaneer **3.9**
buccaneerish **36.2.25**
buccinator **17.12.4(.10)**
Buccleugh **16.25**
Bucelas **34.18.29(.5)**
Bucephalus **34.18.29(.17.4)**
Buchan **28.17.13(.9)**
Buchanan **28.17.17(.5)**
Bucharest **22.29.5(.12)**
Buchenwald **23.31.5**
Buchmanism **27.15.21(.2.9)**
Buchmanite **22.16.14(.6)**
buchu **16.9**
buck **24.12**
buckaroo **16.23**
buckbean **28.1.8**
buckboard **23.12.2(.10)**
Buckden **28.17.12(.20)**
bucker **17.14.11**
bucket **22.2.9(.6)**
bucketful **40.14.6(.10)**
buckeye **14.10**
Buckfastleigh **2.32**
Buckie **1.12.9**
Buckingham **27.15.15**
Buckinghamshire **17.26.20**
Buckland **23.24.16(.16.3)**
buckle **40.23.9**
buckler **17.34.23**
Buckley **1.31.24(.7)**
buckling **29.1.31(.19)**
Buckmaster **17.12.24(.5)**
Buckminster **17.12.24(.23)**
Bucknell **40.26.18**
Buckner **17.18.23**
bucko **19.12.8**
buckra **17.32.21**
buckram **27.15.26(.12)**
Bucks **34.23.11**
bucksaw **12.14.13**
buckshee **2.24**
buckshot **22.11.12**
buckskin **28.2.13(.14)**
buck teeth **32.1**
buckthorn **28.11.8**
Buckton **28.17.11(.20)**
buck tooth **32.13**
buckwheat **22.1.16**
bucolic **24.2.27(.9)**
bucolically **1.31.24(.9.12)**
bud **23.14**
Budapest **22.29.5(.1)**
Buddha **17.13.13**

Buddhism **27.15.21(.2.5)**
Buddhist **22.29.2(.14)**
Buddhistic **24.2.10(.15.2)**
Buddhistical **40.23.12(.7.3)**
buddleia **3.24.13**
buddy **1.11.13**
Bude **23.17**
budge **39.11**
budgerigar **10.9**
budget **22.2.21**
budgetary **1.29.11(.8.8)**
budgie **1.26.8**
Budleigh **1.31.23(.10)**
Budweiser® **17.25.12(.13)**
Buenos Aires **35.1.22**
Buerk **24.17**
buff **30.11**
buffalo **19.29.12**
buffer **17.20.9**
buffet **4.15, 22.2.13**
bufflehead **23.5.13(.19)**
buffo **19.16**
buffoon **28.16.9**
buffoonery **1.29.11(.13.1)**
buffoonish **36.2.16(.12)**
Buffs **34.25**
bug **26.10**
bugaboo **16.6**
Buganda **17.13.20(.4)**
Bugandan **28.17.12(.23)**
Bugatti **1.10.6**
bugbear **6.3**
bugger **17.16.9**
buggery **1.29.11(.11)**
buggy **1.14.8**
bughouse **34.8.6(.14)**
bugjuice **34.17.10**
bugle **24.34.10**
bugler **17.34.24**
buglet **22.19.26(.20)**
bugloss **34.10.17**
Bugner **17.18.24**
bugrake **24.3.13**
buhl **40.15**
Buick® **24.2.6**
build **23.31.2**
builder **17.13.23(.2)**
building **29.1.13(.16)**
built **22.32.1**
Builth Wells **35.30.4**
Buitoni® **1.16.17(.3)**
Bujumbura **17.32.14(.3)**
Bukhara **17.32.7**
Bukovina **17.18.1(.7)**
Bukowski **1.12.17(.13)**
Bukta **17.12.21(.6)**
Bulawayo **19.2**
bulb **21.18**
bulbaceous **34.18.22(.3)**

bulbar **17.11.20**
bulbil **40.2.4**
bulbous **34.18.10**
bulbousness
 34.18.16(.31.3)
bulbul **40.14.3**
Bulgar **10.9**
Bulgaria **3.22.4**
Bulgarian **28.3.20(.4)**
bulge **39.18**
bulghur **17.16.19**
bulginess **34.18.16(.2.8)**
bulgy **1.26.14**
bulimarexia **3.14.15**
bulimarexic
 24.2.20(.13)
bulimia **3.8.2**
bulimia nervosa
 17.24.17
bulimic **24.2.14(.2)**
bulk **24.21**
bulkhead **23.5.13(.11)**
bulkily **1.31.17(.11)**
bulkiness **34.18.16(.2.4)**
bulk mail **40.4.6**
bulky **1.12.19**
bull **40.14**
bulla **17.34.12, 17.34.14**
bullace **34.18.29(.15)**
bullae **2.32.8**
bullate **22.4.23(.6)**
bulldog **26.7.4**
bulldoze **35.20.4**
bulldozer **17.25.15**
Bullen **28.17.33(.11)**
Buller **17.34.14**
bullet **22.19.26(.12)**
bulletin **28.2.11(.10)**
bulletproof **30.13.4**
bullfight **22.16.16**
bullfighter **17.12.13(.5)**
bullfighting **29.1.12(.11)**
bullfinch **38.18.1**
bullfrog **26.7.13**
bullhead **23.5.13(.19)**
bullhorn **28.11.10**
bullion **28.3.21(.9)**
bullish **36.2.27**
bullishly **1.31.35(.7.4)**
bullishness
 34.18.16(.33.6)
bull-necked **22.23.4(.4)**
bullock **24.16.16**
bullocky **1.12.13**
Bullokar **10.8.8,**
 17.14.15(.15)
Bullough **19.29.10**
bullring **29.1.30(.16)**
bullshit **22.2.18**
bullshitter **17.12.2**
bull trout **22.9.18**

bullwhip **20.2.10**
bully **1.31.15**
bully boy **13.3**
bullyrag **26.5.8**
Bulmer **17.17.24**
bulrush **36.12**
Bulstrode **23.20.12**
Bultitude **23.17.4(.1)**
bulwark **24.16.14,**
 24.17.6(.19)
Bulwer-Lytton
 28.17.11(.2)
bum **27.11**
bumbag **26.5.1**
bumble **40.20.19**
bumblebee **2.10**
bumbledom **27.15.10(.20)**
bumbler **17.34.20**
bumboat **22.21.2**
bumf **30.18**
bumiputra **17.32.19(.6)**
bummalo **19.29.12**
bummaree **2.30**
bummer **17.17.10**
bump **20.16.5**
bumper **17.10.17**
bumpily **1.31.17(.7)**
bumpiness **34.18.16(.2.2)**
bumpkin **28.2.13(.8)**
bumptious **34.18.22(.10)**
bumptiously
 1.31.33(.12.4)
bumptiousness
 34.18.16(.31.4)
bumpy **1.8.14**
bun **28.13**
Buna **17.18.15**
Bunbury **1.29.11(.7.2)**
bunch **38.18.7**
bunchy **1.24.15**
bunco **19.12.15**
bund **23.24.12**
bunder **17.13.20(.10)**
Bundesbank **24.19.3(.1)**
Bundesrat **22.10.12**
Bundestag **26.6**
bundle **40.22.16**
bundler **17.34.22**
bundobust **22.29.12**
Bundy **1.11.20(.7)**
bung **29.8**
bungaloid **23.13.20**
bungalow **19.29.12**
Bungay **1.14.14**
bungee **1.26.13**
bunghole **40.18.13**
bungle **40.24.14(.4)**
bungler **17.34.24**
bunion **28.17.32**
bunk **24.19.7**
bunker **17.14.21(.5)**

bunkhouse **34.8.6(.13)**
bunkum **27.15.11(.13)**
bunny **1.16.12**
Bunsen **28.17.23(.24)**
bunt **22.26.12**
buntal **40.21.17(.5)**
Bunter **17.12.22(.10)**
bunting **29.1.12(.19)**
buntline **28.14.19(.14)**
Bunty **1.10.23(.10)**
Buñuel **40.5.17**
bunya **17.33.9**
Bunyan **28.17.32**
Bunyanesque **24.20.3**
bunyip **20.2.12**
buoy **13**
buoyage **39.2.4**
buoyancy **1.22.23(.10.1)**
buoyant **22.26.15(.3)**
buoyantly **1.31.22(.20.1)**
BUPA **17.10.13**
buppie **1.8.8**
bur **18**
burb **21.15**
Burbage **39.2.9**
Burbank **24.19.3(.1)**
Burberry® **1.29.11(.7.1)**
burble **40.20.17**
burbler **17.34.20**
burbot **22.19.9**
Burch **38.16**
Burchfield **23.31.1(.2)**
Burckhardt **22.10.11**
Burco **19.12.13**
burden **28.17.12(.17)**
burdensome
 27.15.20(.18)
burdensomeness
 34.18.16(.24)
Burdett **22.5.4**
burdock **24.9.5**
Burdon **28.17.12(.17)**
bureau **19.27.7, 19.27.11**
bureaucracy **1.22.16(.13)**
bureaucrat **22.7.20**
bureaucratic **24.2.10(.4.5)**
bureaucratically
 1.31.24(.9.4)
bureaucratization
 28.17.25(.3.12)
bureaucratize **35.15.7(.7)**
bureaux **19.27.11,**
 35.20.12
burette **22.5.19**
Burford **23.18.16(.10)**
burg **26.14**
burgage **39.2.13**
Burgas **34.18.14(.6)**
Burge **39.15**
burgee **2.27**
burgeon **28.17.28(.10)**

burger **17.16.14**
burgess **34.18.24**
burgh **17.32.12**
burghal **40.24.12**
burgher **17.16.14**
Burghley **1.31.18**
burglar **17.34.24**
burglarious **34.3.15(.3)**
burglariously
 1.31.33(.1.4)
burglarize **35.15.20(.2)**
burglary **1.29.11(.27)**
burgle **40.24.12**
burgomaster **17.12.24(.5)**
burgoo **16.10**
Burgoyne **28.12**
burgrave **31.3.7**
Burgundian **28.3.4(.11)**
burgundy **1.11.20(.9)**
burhel **40.16.13(.9)**
burial **40.3.14(.3)**
burin **28.2.29(.5)**
burk **24.17**
burka **17.14.16**
Burke **24.17**
Burkina **17.18.1(.5)**
Burkina Faso **19.20.4**
Burkinan **28.17.17(.1)**
burl **40.17**
burlap **20.5.8**
Burleigh **1.31.18**
burlesque **24.20.3**
burlesquer **17.14.23**
Burley **1.31.18**
burliness **34.18.16(.2.10)**
Burlington **28.17.11(.23)**
burly **1.31.18**
Burma **17.17.15**
Burman **28.17.16(.17)**
Burmese **35.1.11**
burn **28.18**
Burnaby **1.9.11**
Burnaston **28.17.11(.25)**
Burne **28.18**
burned **23.24.17**
burner **17.18.17**
burnet **22.2.12**
Burnett **22.2.12, 22.5.9**
Burney **1.16.16**
Burnham **27.15.14(.12)**
burningly **1.31.28(.1.7)**
burnish **36.2.16(.14)**
burnisher **17.26.14**
Burnley **1.31.27(.15)**
burnous **34.17.9**
Burns **35.26.14**
Burnside **23.15.11(.12)**
burnt **22.26.16**
Burntisland
 23.24.16(.16.2)

burp 20.14
burr 18
Burra 17.32.12
burrawang 29.4.14
Burrell 40.16.13(.9)
Burren 28.17.31(.9)
burrito 19.10.1
burro 19.27.8, 19.27.10
Burrough 19.27.8
Burroughs 35.20.12
burrow 19.27.8
burrower 17.9.11
bursa 17.24.16
bursae 2.22.8
bursal 40.31.13
bursar 17.24.16
bursarial 40.3.14(.4)
bursarship 20.2.7(.9)
bursary 1.29.11(.18)
burse 34.19
bursitis 34.18.11(.8)
Burslem 27.15.28(.20)
burst 22.29.16
Burstall 40.10.5, 40.21.18
burstproof 30.13.4
Burt 22.20
burthen 28.17.22
burton 28.17.11(.16)
Burtonwood 23.16.6
Burundan 28.17.12(.23)
Burundi 1.11.20(.8)
Burundian 28.3.4(.11)
bury 1.29.3
Bury St Edmunds 35.23.15
bus 34.14
busbar 10.5.12
busboy 13.3
busby 1.9.22
bush 36.13
bushbaby 1.9.3
bushbuck 24.12.1
bushcraft 22.27.4(.4)
bushel 40.33.7
bushelful 40.14.6(.22)
Bushey 1.24.10
bush fire 17.6.9(.11)
bushido 19.11, 19.11.1
bushily 1.31.17(.22)
bushiness 34.18.16(.2.8)
Bushman 28.17.16(.31)
bushmaster 17.12.24(.5)
Bushnell 40.26.22
bushranger 17.29.16(.2)
bushveld 22.32.2
bushwhack 24.6.20
bushwhacker 17.14.5
bushy 1.24.10
busily 1.31.17(.21)
business 34.18.16(.32)

businesslike 24.13.7(.22)
businessman 28.7.10(.20), 28.17.16(.29)
businessmen 28.5.7(.24)
businesswoman 28.17.16(.14)
businesswomen 28.2.17(.1)
busk 24.20.7
busker 17.14.23
buskin 28.2.13(.14)
busman 28.17.16(.29)
buss 34.14
bust 22.29.12
bustard 23.18.9(.20)
bustee 2.12.15
buster 17.12.24(.10)
bustier 4.2.2
bustiness 34.18.16(.2.3)
bustle 40.31.10
busty 1.10.26(.8)
busy 1.23.2
busybody 1.11.10
busyness 34.18.16(.2.7)
busywork 24.17.6(.1)
but 22.15
butadiene 28.1.3
but and ben 28.5
butane 28.4.3
butanoic 24.2.7
butanol 40.9.12
butanone 28.19.10
butch 38.13
butcher 17.28.13
butchery 1.29.11(.22)
Bute 22.18
butene 28.1.9(.2)
Buthelezi 1.23.3
butler 17.34.21
Butlin's 35.26.2
butt 22.15
butte 22.18
butter 17.12.12
butterball 40.10.4
butterbur 18.2
buttercream 27.1.12
buttercup 20.9.7
butterdish 36.2.12
butterfat 22.7.13
Butterfield 23.31.1(.2)
butterfingers 35.18.11
butterfish 36.2.18(.11)
butterfly 14.25.14
butteriness 34.18.16(.2.9)
Butterkist® 22.29.2(.15)
butter knife 30.12
Buttermere 3.8.7
buttermilk 24.21
butternut 22.15.6
Butters 35.18.8

butterscotch 38.8
butterwort 22.20.15
Butterworth 32.14.15
buttery 1.29.11(.8.4)
buttle 40.21.9
buttock 24.16.4
button 28.17.11(.11)
buttonhole 40.18.13
buttonhook 24.14.9
buttonless 34.18.29(.27)
Buttons 35.26.13(.7)
buttonwood 23.16.6(.14)
buttony 1.16.15(.7)
buttress 34.18.27(.14)
butty 1.10.12
butyl 40.2.5, 40.13.3(.3)
butyrate 22.4.22(.6)
butyric 24.2.26(.1)
buxom 27.15.20(.15)
buxomly 1.31.26(.11)
buxomness 34.18.16(.24)
Buxted 23.5.3, 23.18.9(.20)
Buxtehude 17.13.14
Buxton 28.17.11(.25)
buy 14
buyable 40.20.16(.5)
buyer 17.6
buyout 22.9.2
Buzby 1.9.22
Buzfuz 35.14
buzz 35.14
buzzard 23.18.21
buzzer 17.25.11
buzzword 23.19.8
bwana 17.18.8
Bwlch 24.21, 25.11
by 14
Byatt 22.19.4
Byblos 34.10.17
bye 14
bye-bye 14.7
bye-byes 35.15.6
Byers 35.18.4
Byfield 23.31.1(.2)
Byfleet 22.1.18
bygone 28.10.12
Bygraves 35.28.2
Byker 17.14.12
by-law 12.23.1
byline 28.14.19(.10)
byname 27.4.5
Byng 29.1
bypass 34.9.1
bypath 32.8
byplay 4.28.9
Byrd 23.19
Byrds 35.23.13
byre 17.6
Byrne 28.18
byroad 23.20.12

Byron 28.17.31(.10)
Byronic 24.2.15(.6.4)
Byronically 1.31.24(.9.8)
Bysshe 36.2
byssi 14.18
byssinosis 34.2.17(.11.2)
byssus 34.18.20
bystander 17.13.20(.4)
byte 22.16
byway 4.25.7
byword 23.19.8
Byzantine 28.1.9(.6), 28.14.5
Byzantinism 27.15.21(.2.9)
Byzantinist 22.29.2(.18.1)
Byzantium 27.3.3
c 2
c/o 19, 31.7
Caaba 17.11.5, 17.11.7
cab 21.6
cabal 40.6.4
Cabalism 27.15.21(.2.15)
cabalistically 1.31.24(.9.6)
caballero 19.27.3
cabana 17.18.8(.1)
cabaret 4.26.8
cabbage 39.2.9
cabbagy 1.26.10(.1)
Cabbala 17.34.16(.6)
cabbalism 27.15.21(.2.15)
cabbalist 22.29.2(.31.1)
cabbalistic 24.2.10(.15.3)
cabbalistical 40.23.12(.7.3)
cabbalistically 1.31.24(.9.6)
cabbie 1.9.5
cabby 1.9.5
cabdriver 17.21.10
caber 17.11.3
Cabernet 4.14
Cabernet Franc 11
Cabernet Sauvignon 11.18
cabin 28.2.10
Cabinda 17.13.20(.1)
cabinet 22.19.15(.1)
cabinetmaker 17.14.3(.3)
cabinetmaking 29.1.14(.3)
cabinetry 1.29.15(.9)
cable 40.20.4
cable car 10.8.18
cablegram 27.6.17(.5)
cableway 4.25.26
cabman 28.17.16(.20)
cabochon 28.10.20
caboodle 40.22.12
caboose 34.17.3

Canaanite 22.16.14(.6)
Canada 17.13.15
Canadian 28.3.4(.3)
canal 40.6.9
Canaletto 19.10.4
canalization 28.17.25(.3.12)
canalize 35.15.21(.4.5)
canalside 23.15.11(.17)
canapé 4.7
canard 23.9.12
Canarese 35.1.22
Canaries 35.2.17
canary 1.29.4
canasta 17.12.24(.5)
Canavan 28.17.20(.10)
Canaveral 40.16.13(.12.2)
Canberra 17.32.14(.5)
cancan 28.7.8
cancel 40.31.21
cancellation 28.17.25(.3.14)
canceller 17.34.16(.15)
cancellous 34.18.29(.17.5)
cancer 17.24.22(.3)
Cancerian 28.3.20(.2)
cancerous 34.18.27(.23)
cancerously 1.31.33(.12.5)
cancroid 23.13.19
Cancún 28.16.5
Candace 1.22.4, 34.18.12
candela 17.34.1, 17.34.5(.4), 17.34.16(.8)
candelabra 17.32.18
candelabrum 27.15.26(.9)
Canderel® 40.5.18
candescence 34.24.10(.18)
candescent 22.26.15(.17.2)
Candice 34.18.12
candid 23.2.9
candida 17.13.2
candidacy 1.22.16(.5)
candidate 22.4.10, 22.19.11
candidature 17.28.15
Candide 23.1.3
candidiasis 34.2.17(.10.1)
candidly 1.31.23(.14.4)
candidness 34.18.16(.21.1)
candied 23.2.9
candiru 16.23
candle 40.22.16
candleholder 17.13.23(.8)
candlelight 22.16.25(.22)
candlelit 22.2.25
Candlemas 34.7.11
candlepower 17.3.1
candlestick 24.2.10(.15.4)

candlewick 24.2.25
Candlin 28.2.31(.16)
candour 17.13.20(.4)
candy 1.11.20(.4)
candyfloss 34.10.17
candytuft 22.27.6
cane 28.4
canebrake 24.3.13
canebreak 24.3.13
caner 17.18.3
Canes Venatici 14.18
canicular 17.34.16(.21.2)
canine 28.14.9
caning 29.1.17(.3)
Canis Major 17.29.3
Canis Minor 17.18.13
canister 17.12.24(.14)
canker 17.14.21(.3)
cankerous 34.18.27(.16)
cankerworm 27.16.7
canna 17.18.6
cannabis 34.2.7
Cannae 2.17.4
cannel 40.26.5
cannellini 1.16.1
cannelloni 1.16.17
cannelure 17.7.12(.14)
canner 17.18.6
cannery 1.29.11(.13.1)
Cannes 28.7
cannibal 40.20.16(.16.1)
cannibalism 27.15.21(.2.15)
cannibalistic 24.2.10(.15.3)
cannibalistically 1.31.24(.9.6)
cannibalization 28.17.25(.3.12)
cannibalize 35.15.21(.4.2)
cannikin 28.2.13(.6)
cannily 1.31.17(.14.1)
canniness 34.18.16(.2.5)
Canning 29.1.17(.5)
Cannizzaro 19.27.5
Cannock 24.16.7
cannoli 1.31.19
cannon 28.17.17(.5)
cannonade 23.4.8
cannonball 40.10.4
cannoneer 3.9
cannonry 1.29.20
cannot 22.11.9, 22.19.15(.3)
cannula 17.34.16(.21.4)
cannulae 2.32.9(.8), 14.25.9
cannulate 22.4.23(.7.3)
canny 1.16.6
canoe 16.12
canoeist 22.29.2(.8)

canola 17.34.18(.8)
canon 28.17.17(.5)
cañon 28.17.32
Canonbury 1.29.11(.7.2)
canoness 34.5.6
canonic 24.2.15(.6.2)
canonical 40.23.12(.11)
canonically 1.31.24(.9.8)
canonicate 22.19.12(.10)
canonicity 1.10.16(.16.1)
canonist 22.29.2(.18.1)
canonization 28.17.25(.3.11)
canonize 35.15.12(.5)
canonry 1.29.20
canoodle 40.22.12
Canopic 24.2.8(.5)
canopied 23.2.6
Canopus 34.18.9(.10)
canopy 1.8.11(.6)
canorous 34.18.27(.8)
Canova 17.21.14(.7)
canst 22.29.21
can't 22.26.8
cant 22.26.6
Cantab 21.6
cantabile 1.31.17(.8), 4.28.7
Cantabria 3.22.14
Cantabrian 28.3.20(.10)
Cantabrigian 28.3.18
cantal 40.8.4
cantaloupe 20.12
cantankerous 34.18.27(.16)
cantankerously 1.31.33(.12.5)
cantankerousness 34.18.16(.31.5)
cantata 17.12.8(.3)
cantatrice 34.1.7
canteen 28.1.9
canter 17.12.22(.4)
Canterbury 1.29.11(.7.1)
cantharides 35.1.8
canthi 14.16
canthus 34.18.19
canticle 40.23.12(.7.3)
cantilena 17.18.1(.16), 17.18.3
cantilever 17.21.1
cantillate 22.4.23(.7.1)
cantillation 28.17.25(.3.1)
cantina 17.18.1(.3)
cantle 40.21.17(.3)
canto 19.10.17
Canton 28.10.9, 28.17.11(.22)
canton 28.10.9, 28.17.11(.22)

cantonal 40.26.8, 40.26.13(.4)
Cantonese 35.1.12
cantonment 22.26.15(.13.4)
cantor 12.5.8, 17.12.22(.4)
cantorial 40.3.14(.5)
cantoris 34.2.21
cantrail 40.4.14
Cantrell 40.5.18
cantrip 20.2.11
Canuck 24.12.6
Canute 22.18.10
canvas 34.18.18
canvass 34.18.18
canvasser 17.24.15
Canvey 1.19.13
canyon 28.17.32
canzone 1.16.17(.9)
canzonet 22.5.9
canzonetta 17.12.5(.5)
caoutchouc 24.14.8
cap 20.5
capability 1.10.16(.22.1)
Capablanca 17.14.21(.3)
capable 40.20.16(.9)
capablness 34.18.16(.37.4)
capably 1.31.21(.3)
capacious 34.18.22(.3)
capaciously 1.31.33(.12.4)
capaciousness 34.18.16(.31.4)
capacitance 34.24.10(.10)
capacitate 22.4.9(.5)
capacitative 31.2.1(.9.1)
capacitive 31.2.1(.9.3)
capacitor 17.12.16(.14)
capacity 1.10.16(.16.1)
cap-à-pie 2.9
caparison 28.17.23(.14)
cape 20.3
capelin 28.2.31(.10)
Capella 17.34.5(.1)
capellini 1.16.1
caper 17.10.3
capercaillie 1.31.4
caperer 17.32.14(.4)
Capernaum 27.3.8(.9)
capeskin 28.2.13(.14)
Capet 22.19.8
Capetian 28.17.25(.1)
Cape Verde 23.19
capful 40.14.6(.8)
capias 34.3.1
capillarity 1.10.16(.21.1)
capillary 1.29.11(.27)
Capistrano 19.15.7
capital 40.21.12
capitalist 22.29.2(.31.2)
capitalistic 24.2.10(.15.3)

capitalistically
1.31.24(.9.6)
capitalization
28.17.25(.3.12)
capitalize 35.15.21(.4.3)
capitally 1.31.17(.9.2)
capitation 28.17.25(.3.3)
capitol 40.9.7, 40.21.12
capitolian 28.3.21(.11)
Capitoline 28.14.19(.11)
capitula 17.34.16(.18)
capitular 17.34.16(.18)
capitulary 1.29.11(.27)
capitulate 22.4.23(.7.3)
capitulation
28.17.25(.3.14)
capitulator 17.12.4(.16)
capitulatory
1.29.11(.8.10)
capitulum 27.15.28(.11)
Caplan 28.17.33(.16)
Caplet® 22.19.26(.15)
cap'n 28.17.9
capo 19.8
Capo di Monte
1.10.23(.7)
capoeira 17.32.3
capon 28.10.7, 28.17.9
caponata 17.12.8(.8)
Capone 28.19.2
caponier 3.9
caponize 35.15.12(.5)
capot 22.11.2
capo tasto 19.10.19
Capote 1.10.18
capote 22.21.1
Cappadocia 3.14.11,
3.16.7, 17.26.16
Cappadocian 28.3.13,
28.3.15, 28.17.25(.13)
cappuccino 19.15.1
Capra 17.32.17
Capri 1.29.13, 2.30.8
capric 24.2.26(.12)
capriccio 15.1.10
capriccioso 19.20.12
caprice 34.1.7
capricious 34.18.22(.2)
capriciously
1.31.33(.12.4)
capriciousness
34.18.16(.31.4)
Capricorn 28.11.5
Capricornian 28.3.8(.7)
Capricornus 34.18.16(.10)
caprine 28.14.18
capriole 40.14.1
caproic 24.2.7
caps 34.21.5
Capsian 28.3.13
capsicum 27.15.11(.9)

capsid 23.2.16
capsizal 40.32.12
capsize 35.15.16
capstan 28.17.11(.25)
capstone 28.19.4(.9)
capsular 17.34.16(.21.4)
capsulate 22.19.26(.13)
capsule 40.15.9(.10),
40.16.14, 40.31.15
capsulize 35.15.21(.4.8)
captain 28.17.11(.18)
captaincy 1.22.23(.10.2)
captainship 20.2.7(.19)
caption 28.17.25(.14)
captious 34.18.22(.10)
captiously 1.31.33(.12.4)
captiousness
34.18.16(.31.4)
captivate 22.4.16
captivatingly
1.31.28(.1.4)
captivation 28.17.25(.3.9)
captive 31.2.1(.12)
captivity 1.10.16(.15)
captor 17.12.19
capture 17.28.18
capturer 17.32.14(.19)
Capua 17.7.12(.2)
capuche 36.14, 38.14
Capuchin 28.2.25, 28.2.26
Capulet 22.19.26(.13)
capybara 17.32.7
car 10
Cara 17.32.7
carabid 23.2.7
carabineer 3.9
carabiner 17.18.1(.2)
carabiniere 1.29.4
caracal 40.6.6
Caracalla 17.34.6
caracara 17.32.7
Caracas 34.18.13(.3)
caracole 40.18.7
caracul 40.12
Caradoc 24.9.5, 24.16.5
Caradog 26.7.4
carafe 30.7.5
caragana 17.18.8(.4)
Carajás 34.18.25
caramba 17.11.17(.4)
carambola 17.34.18(.2)
caramel 40.5.7, 40.25.10
caramelization
28.17.25(.3.12)
caramelize 35.15.21(.4.5)
carangid 23.2.20
carapace 34.4.2
carat 22.19.24(.4)
Caratacus 34.18.13(.10)
Caravaggio 15.1.11

caravan 28.7.13
caravanette 22.5.9
caravanner 17.18.6
caravanserai 1.29.11(.18),
14.24.6
caravel 40.5.10
caraway 4.25.9
carb 21.7
carbamate 22.4.13(.6)
carbazole 40.18.11
carbide 23.15.3
carbine 28.14.4
carbineer 3.9
carbohydrate 22.4.22(.9)
carbolic 24.2.27(.9)
carbon 28.17.10
carbonaceous
34.18.22(.3)
carbonade 23.4.8,
23.9.12
carbonado 19.11.4,
19.11.7
carbonara 17.32.7
carbonate 22.4.14(.9.1),
22.19.15(.9)
carbonation
28.17.25(.3.8)
carbonatite 22.16.9
carbonic 24.2.15(.6.1)
Carboniferous
34.18.27(.20)
carbonization
28.17.25(.3.11)
carbonize 35.15.12(.5)
carbon monoxide
23.15.11(.11)
carbonyl 40.2.10, 40.13.8
Carborundum®
27.15.10(.14)
carboxyl 40.2.14, 40.13.12
carboxylase 35.4.18
carboxylate 22.4.23(.7.2)
carboxylic 24.2.27(.2)
carboy 13.3
carbuncle 40.23.15
carbuncular
17.34.16(.21.2)
carburant 22.26.15(.23.3)
carburation
28.17.25(.3.13)
carburet 22.19.24(.9)
carburettor 17.12.5(.9)
carcajou 16.18, 16.20
carcass 34.18.13(.4)
Carcassonne 28.10.18
Carchemish 36.2.15
carcinogen 28.17.28(.9)
carcinogenesis
34.2.17(.10.3)
carcinogenic 24.2.15(.4)
carcinogenically
1.31.24(.9.8)

carcinogenicity
1.10.16(.16.1)
carcinoma 17.17.16
carcinomatous
34.18.11(.10)
card 23.9
cardamom 27.15.13
cardboard 23.12.2(.9)
carder 17.13.7
Cardew 16.24.6
cardholder 17.13.23(.8)
cardiac 24.6.1
cardiacal 40.23.12(.3)
Cardiff 30.2.2
cardigan 28.17.15(.13)
Cardin 8, 28.7.7
cardinal 40.26.13(.5)
cardinalate 22.19.26(.13)
cardinality 1.10.16(.32.8)
cardinally 1.31.17(.14.2)
cardinalship 20.2.7(.24)
cardiogram 27.6.17(.5)
cardiograph 30.7.5(.1)
cardiographer
17.20.12(.5)
cardiography 1.18.9(.3.2)
cardiologist 22.29.2(.26.2)
cardiology 1.26.10(.11.1)
cardiometer
17.12.16(.9.2)
cardiopulmonary
1.29.11(.13.2)
cardiovascular
17.34.16(.21.2)
cardoon 28.16.4
cardphone 28.19.11
cardpunch 38.18.7
card sharp 20.6
Cardus 34.18.12
Cardwell 40.5.17(.8)
cardy 1.11.9
care 6
careen 28.1.25
careenage 39.14
career 3.22
careerism 27.15.21(.2.14)
careerist 22.29.2(.29.1)
carefree 2.30.13
carefreely 1.31.1
carefreeness 34.18.16(.1)
careful 40.27.6
carefully 1.31.17(.16.1),
1.31.29
carefulness
34.18.16(.37.2)
careless 34.18.29(.6)
carelessly 1.31.33(.12.6)
carelessness
34.18.16(.31.6)
carer 17.32.5
caress 34.5.14

caressingly 1.31.28(.1.11)
caret 22.19.24(.4)
caretake 24.3.4
caretaker 17.14.3(.2)
Carew 1.29.4, 16.23
careworn 28.11.11
Carey 1.29.4
carezza 17.24.19
carfare 6.10
carfax 34.23.5(.8)
carferry 1.29.3
carful 40.14.6(.4)
Cargill 40.2.8
cargo 19.13.5
carhop 20.7.11
Caria 3.22.4
cariama 17.17.7
Carian 28.3.20(.5)
Carib 21.2
Caribbean 28.3.2, 28.17.1(.2)
Caribbean Sea 2
caribou 16.6
caricatural 40.16.13(.11)
caricature 12.17, 17.7.12(.3)
caricaturist 22.29.2(.29.2)
CARICOM 27.9
caries 35.1.22
carillon 28.3.21(.2), 28.10.25, 28.10.26
carina 17.18.1(.15), 17.18.13(.13)
carinae 2.17.1, 2.17.8, 14.13
carinal 40.26.1, 40.26.11
carinate 22.4.14(.9.4), 22.19.15(.9)
caring 29.1.30(.4)
Carinthia 3.12
carioca 17.14.17
cariogenic 24.2.15(.4)
carious 34.3.15(.3)
Carisbrooke 24.14.10
carking 29.1.14(.5)
Carl 40.8
Carla 17.34.8
Carlin 28.2.31(.6)
carline 28.2.31(.6), 28.14.19(.7)
Carlisle 40.13.17
Carlo 19.29.7
carload 23.20.13
Carlovingian 28.3.16, 28.3.18, 28.17.28(.12)
Carlow 19.29.7
Carlsbad 23.7.6
Carlsberg® 26.14.1(.11)
Carlson 28.17.23(.28)
Carlton 28.17.11(.27)
Carly 1.31.9

Carlyle 40.13.17
carmaker 17.14.3(.3)
carman 28.17.16(.9)
Carmarthen 28.17.22
Carmel 40.5.7
Carmelite 22.16.25(.9)
Carmen 28.5.7(.6), 28.17.16(.9)
Carmichael 40.23.10
Carmina Burana 17.18.8(.11)
carminative 31.2.1(.9.2)
carmine 28.14.8
Carnaby Street 22.1
Carnac 24.6.11
carnage 39.2.15
carnal 40.26.7
carnality 1.10.16(.32.8)
carnalize 35.15.21(.4.5)
carnally 1.31.17(.14.1)
Carnap 20.5.4
carnassial 40.3.10
Carnatic 24.2.10(.4.3)
carnation 28.17.25(.3.8)
carnauba 17.11.6, 17.11.9
Carné 4.14
Carnegie 1.14.1
carnelian 28.3.21(.1)
carnet 4.14
Carney 1.16.8
Carnforth 32.10
carnival 40.28.11
Carnivora 17.32.14(.13)
carnivore 12.12
carnivorous 34.18.27(.21)
carnivorously 1.31.33(.12.5)
carnivorousness 34.18.16(.31.5)
Carnot 19.15.7
Carnoustie 1.10.26(.10)
carny 1.16.8
carob 21.14
carol 40.16.13(.5)
Carole 40.16.13(.5)
Carolean 28.17.1(.13)
Carolina 17.18.13(.14)
Caroline 28.2.31(.10), 28.14.19(.11)
Carolingian 28.3.6, 28.3.16, 28.3.18
caroller 17.34.16(.20)
carolus 34.18.29(.17.5)
carom 27.15.26(.3)
Caron 28.10.24, 28.17.31(.5)
carotene 28.1.9(.3)
carotenoid 23.13.12
carotid 23.2.8
carousal 40.32.6
carouse 35.8

carousel 40.5.11
carouser 17.25.6
carp 20.6
Carpaccio 15.1.10
carpal 40.19.6
car park 24.8.2
Carpathian 28.3.11
carpe diem 27.5.1
carpel 40.19.6
carpellary 1.29.11(.27)
Carpentaria 3.22.4
carpenter 17.12.22(.12)
carpentry 1.29.15(.15)
carper 17.10.7
carpet 22.2.5
carpet bag 26.5.1
carpetbagger 17.16.5
carpeted 23.18.9(.13)
carpeting 29.1.12(.14)
carphology 1.26.10(.11.5)
carpi 14.6
carpology 1.26.10(.11.2)
carport 22.13.1
carpus 34.18.9(.5)
Carr 10
carrack 24.16.15
carrageen 28.1.12
Carrara 17.32.7
carraway 4.25.9
carrel 40.16.13(.5)
Carreras 34.18.27(.4)
carriage 39.2.22(.4)
carriageway 4.25.25
carrick 24.2.26(.5)
Carrickfergus 34.18.14(.6)
Carrie 1.29.5
carrier 3.22.5
Carrington 28.17.11(.23)
carriole 40.14.1
carrion 28.3.20(.5)
Carroll 40.16.13(.5)
carronade 23.4.8
carrot 22.19.24(.4)
carroty 1.10.16(.21.1)
Carruthers 35.18.16
carry 1.29.5
carryall 40.10.1
carrycot 22.11.6
carse 34.9
Carshalton 28.17.11(.27)
carsick 24.2.20(.6)
carsickness 34.18.16(.22)
Carson 28.17.23(.7)
Carstairs 35.6
cart 22.10
cartage 39.2.10
Cartagena 17.18.1(.13), 17.18.3
carte 22.10

carte blanche 36.10
carte de visite 22.1.10
cartel 40.5.3
cartelization 28.17.25(.3.12)
cartelize 35.15.21(.4.3)
carter 17.12.8
Carteret 22.5.19, 22.19.24(.9)
Cartesian 28.3.14, 28.17.26(.1)
Cartesianism 27.15.21(.2.9)
cartful 40.14.6(.10)
Carthage 39.2.18
Carthaginian 28.3.8(.2)
carthorse 34.12.7
Carthusian 28.3.14
Cartier 4.2.2
Cartier-Bresson 11.12
cartilage 39.2.23
cartilaginoid 23.13.12
cartilaginous 34.18.16(.15.3)
Cartland 23.24.16(.16.3)
cartload 23.20.13
Cartmel 40.5.7, 40.25.13
cartogram 27.6.17(.5)
cartographer 17.20.12(.5)
cartographic 24.2.16(.3)
cartographical 40.23.12(.12)
cartographically 1.31.24(.9.9)
cartography 1.18.9(.3.2)
cartomancy 1.22.23(.4)
carton 28.17.11(.8)
cartoon 28.16.3
cartoonish 36.2.16(.12)
cartoonist 22.29.2(.18.1)
cartoony 1.16.14
cartophilist 22.29.2(.31.4)
cartophily 1.31.17(.16.1)
cartouche 36.14
cartridge 39.2.22(.11)
cartulary 1.29.11(.27)
cartwheel 40.1.14
cartwright 22.16.24(.12)
caruncle 40.23.15
caruncular 17.34.16(.21.2)
Caruso 19.20.9, 19.21
carve 31.6
carvel 40.5.10, 40.28.6
carven 28.17.20(.6)
carver 17.21.6
carvery 1.29.11(.15)
carve-up 20.9.11
carving 29.1.20
car wash 36.9.5
Cary 1.29.4, 1.29.5
caryatid 23.2.8

Caryl **40.16.13(.5)**
caryopsis **34.2.17(.12)**
carzey **1.23.7**
casa **17.24.6, 17.24.8**
Casablanca **17.14.21(.3)**
Casals **35.30.5**
Casanova **17.21.14(.7)**
casbah **10.5.13**
cascabel **40.20.16(.13)**
cascade **23.4.5**
cascara **17.32.7**
cascarilla **17.34.2(.15)**
case **34.4**
caseation **28.17.25(.3.1)**
casebook **24.14.3**
case-bound **23.24.7(.2)**
casein **28.1.18(.2), 28.2.2**
caseinogen **28.17.28(.9)**
caseload **23.20.13**
casemate **22.4.13(.14)**
casement **22.26.15(.13.5)**
caseous **34.3.10**
casern **28.18.10**
casework **24.17.6(.15)**
caseworker **17.14.16**
Casey **1.22.4**
cash **36.6**
cashable **40.20.16(.23)**
cash book **24.14.3**
cash box **34.23.8(.2)**
cashew **16.17**
cash flow **19.29.21**
cashier **3.16**
cashless **34.18.29(.35)**
Cashman **28.17.16(.31)**
cashmere **3.8, 3.8.15**
cashpoint **22.26.11**
casing **29.1.23**
casino **19.15.1**
Casio® **15.1.7**
cask **24.20.4**
casket **22.2.9(.10)**
Caslon **28.10.26**
Casper **17.10.18**
Caspian Sea **2**
casque **24.20.4**
Cassandra **17.32.20**
cassareep **20.1**
cassata **17.12.8(.9)**
cassation **28.17.25(.3.10)**
cassava **17.21.6**
Cassegrain **28.4.18**
Cassell **40.31.6**
casserole **40.18.14**
cassette **22.5.13**
cassia **3.14.4**
Cassidy **1.11.17**
Cassie **1.22.6**
Cassiopeia **17.1.1**
cassis **34.1.5**

cassiterite **22.16.24(.9)**
Cassius **34.3.10**
Cassivelaunus **34.18.16(.10)**
cassock **24.16.11**
Casson **28.17.23(.6)**
cassoulet **4.28, 4.28.7**
cassowary **1.29.4, 1.29.11(.24)**
cast **22.29.6, 22.29.8**
Castalia **3.24.3**
Castalian **28.3.21(.3)**
castanet **22.5.9**
castaway **4.25.9**
caste **22.29.6, 22.29.8**
casteism **27.15.21(.2.4)**
castelan **28.17.33(.13)**
Castel Gandolfo **19.16**
castellan **28.17.33(.13)**
castellated **23.18.9(.3)**
castellation **28.17.25(.3.1)**
caster **17.12.24(.5)**
Casterbridge **39.2.22(.10)**
·castigate **22.4.12(.5)**
castigation **28.17.25(.3.6)**
castigator **17.12.4(.8)**
castigatory **1.29.11(.8.2)**
Castile **40.1.3**
Castilian **28.3.21(.2)**
Castillo **19.1, 19.28**
castle **40.31.6, 40.31.7**
Castlebar **10.5**
Castleford **23.18.16(.22)**
Castlemaine **28.4.7**
Castlereagh **4.26.20**
Castleton **28.17.11(.27)**
Castlewellan **28.17.33(.4)**
castor **17.12.24(.5)**
castrate **22.4.22(.8)**
castrati **2.12.5**
castration **28.17.25(.3.13)**
castrative **31.2.1(.3)**
castrato **19.10.7**
castrator **17.12.4(.15)**
castratory **1.29.11(.8.2)**
Castries **34.1.7, 35.1.22**
Castro **19.27.15**
Castroism **27.15.21(.2.1)**
Castrol® **40.9.19, 40.16.13(.16)**
casual **40.14.8, 40.16.11**
casually **1.31.17(.23)**
casualness **34.18.16(.37.1)**
casualty **1.10.28**
casuarina **17.18.1(.15), 17.18.13(.13)**
casuist **22.29.2(.7)**
casuistic **24.2.10(.15.1)**
casuistical **40.23.12(.7.3)**
casuistically **1.31.24(.9.6)**
casuistry **1.29.15(.17)**

casus belli **2.32.5, 14.25.5**
cat **22.7**
catabolic **24.2.27(.9)**
catabolically **1.31.24(.9.12)**
catabolism **27.15.21(.2.15)**
catabolize **35.15.21(.4.2)**
catachresis **34.2.17(.1)**
catachrestic **24.2.10(.15.4)**
catachrestical **40.23.12(.7.3)**
cataclasis **34.2.17(.2)**
cataclasm **27.15.21(.3)**
cataclastic **24.2.10(.15.4)**
cataclysm **27.15.21(.2.15)**
cataclysmal **40.25.14**
cataclysmic **24.2.14(.17)**
cataclysmically **1.31.24(.9.8)**
catacomb **27.14.3**
catadioptric **24.2.26(.14.3)**
catadromous **34.18.15(.10)**
catafalque **24.21**
Catalan **28.7.22**
catalase **35.4.18**
catalectic **24.2.10(.13)**
catalepsy **1.22.19**
cataleptic **24.2.10(.12)**
Catalina **17.18.1(.16)**
catalogue **26.7.14**
cataloguer **17.16.7**
catalogue raisonné **4.14**
catalogues raisonnés **35.4.8**
Catalonia **3.9.11**
Catalonian **28.3.8(.11)**
catalpa **17.10.19**
catalyse **35.15.12**
catalyser **17.25.12(.15)**
catalysis **34.2.17(.10.5)**
catalyst **22.29.2(.31.2)**
catalytic **24.2.10(.2.5)**
catalyze **35.15.21(.4.3)**
catamaran **28.7.20**
catamite **22.16.13**
catamount **22.26.7**
catamountain **28.17.11(.22)**
catananche **1.12.16**
Catania **3.9.5**
cataphora **17.32.14(.12)**
cataphoresis **34.2.17(.1)**
cataphoretic **24.2.10(.3.3)**
cataphoretically **1.31.24(.9.3)**
cataplasm **27.15.21(.3)**
cataplectic **24.2.10(.13)**
cataplexy **1.22.22**

catapult **22.32.8, 22.32.9**
cataract **22.23.5(.9)**
catarrh **10.6**
catarrhal **40.16.13(.6)**
catarrhine **28.14.18**
catastrophe **1.18.9(.2)**
catastrophic **24.2.16(.4)**
catastrophically **1.31.24(.9.9)**
catastrophism **27.15.21(.2.10)**
catastrophist **22.29.2(.19)**
catatonia **3.9.11**
catatonic **24.2.15(.6.1)**
catawba **17.11.9**
catbird **23.19.1**
catboat **22.21.2**
catcall **40.10.7**
catch **38.5**
catchable **40.20.16(.24)**
catch-all **40.10.15**
catcher **17.28.6**
catchfly **14.25.14**
catchily **1.31.17(.24)**
catchiness **34.18.16(.2.8)**
catchline **28.14.19(.23)**
catchment **22.26.15(.13.6)**
catchpenny **1.16.5**
catchphrase **35.4.16**
catchpole **40.18.3**
catchup **20.9.14**
catchweight **22.4.21**
catchword **23.19.8**
catchy **1.25.6**
cate **22.4**
catechesis **34.2.17(.1)**
catechetic **24.2.10(.3.1)**
catechetical **40.23.12(.7.1)**
catechetically **1.31.24(.9.3)**
catechism **27.15.21(.2.6)**
catechismal **40.25.14**
catechist **22.29.2(.15)**
catechize **35.15.9**
catechizer **17.25.12(.4)**
catechol **40.9.9, 40.9.16**
catecholamine **28.1.13**
catechu **16.17, 16.19**
catechumen **28.5.7(.9), 28.17.16(.15)**
categorial **40.3.14(.5)**
categoric **24.2.26(.6)**
categorical **40.23.12(.18)**
categorically **1.31.24(.9.12)**
categorization **28.17.25(.3.12)**
categorize **35.15.20(.2)**
category **1.29.11(.11)**
catena **17.18.1(.3)**

catenae 2.17.1
catenary 1.29.11(.13.1)
catenate 22.4.14(.9.1)
catenation 28.17.25(.3.8)
cater 17.12.4
cateran 28.17.31(.11)
cater-cornered 23.18.14
caterer 17.32.14(.6)
Caterham 27.15.26(.8)
Caterina 17.18.1(.15)
caterpillar 17.34.2(.1)
caterwaul 40.10.17
Catesby 1.9.21
catfish 36.2.18(.15)
catfood 23.17.2
Catford 23.18.16(.11)
catgut 22.15.5
Cath 32.6
Cathar 10.14
Catharism 27.15.21(.2.14)
Catharist 22.29.2(.29.2)
catharsis 34.2.17(.5)
cathartic 24.2.10(.5)
cathartically 1.31.24(.9.4)
Cathay 4.17
Cathays 35.4.3
Cathcart 22.10.5
cathead 23.5.13(.9)
cathectic 24.2.10(.13)
cathedra 17.32.20
cathedral 40.16.13(.17)
Cather 17.22.3
Catherine 28.17.31(.11)
catheter 17.12.16(.13)
catheterization
    28.17.25(.3.12)
catheterize 35.15.20(.2)
cathetometer
    17.12.16(.9.2)
cathexis 34.2.17(.14)
cathodal 40.22.15
cathode 23.20.10
cathodic 24.2.11(.7)
catholic 24.2.27(.13)
catholically 1.31.24(.9.12)
Catholicism
    27.15.21(.2.12)
Catholicity 1.10.16(.16.1)
Catholicize 35.15.16(.4)
catholicly 1.31.24(.9.12)
catholicon 28.10.11
cathouse 34.8.6(.11)
Cathryn 28.17.31(.21)
Cathy 1.20.4
Catiline 28.14.19(.11)
cation 28.17.5
cationic 24.2.15(.6.1)
catkin 28.2.13(.9)
catlick 24.2.27(.15)
catlike 24.13.7(.12)

Catling 29.1.31(.17)
catmint 22.26.1
catnap 20.5.4
catnip 20.2.4
Cato 19.10.3
cat-o'-nine-tails 35.30.3
catoptric 24.2.26(.14.3)
Catrin 28.2.29(.8)
Catrina 17.18.1(.15)
Catrine 28.1.25(.6)
Catriona 17.18.1(.15),
    17.18.18
CAT scan 28.7
Catskill 40.2.7
catsuit 22.18.6
catsup 20.9.12, 20.13.4
cattail 40.4.2
Catterick 24.2.26(.10)
cattery 1.29.11(.8.3)
cattily 1.31.17(.9.1)
cattiness 34.18.16(.2.3)
cattish 36.2.11
cattishly 1.31.35(.7.1)
cattishness
    34.18.16(.33.3)
cattle 40.21.5
cattleman 28.17.16(.35)
cattlepen 28.5.2
cattleya 3.24.12
Catto 19.10.6
Catton 28.17.11(.6)
catty 1.10.6
Catullus 34.18.29(.13)
catwalk 24.10.9
Caucasian 28.3.14,
    28.17.26(.3)
Caucasoid 23.13.16
Caucasus 34.18.20
caucus 34.18.13(.6)
caudal 40.22.8
caudally 1.31.17(.10)
caudate 22.4.10
caudillo 19.28, 19.29.2
Caughey 1.27
caught 22.13
caul 40.10
cauldron 28.17.31(.15)
Caulfield 23.31.1(.2)
cauliflower 17.3.11
caulk 24.10
caulker 17.14.9
Caunce 34.24.8
causable 40.20.16(.22)
causal 40.32.9
causality 1.10.16(.32.12)
causally 1.31.17(.21)
causation 28.17.25(.3.10)
causative 31.2.1(.9.3)
causatively 1.31.30(.7.1)
cause 35.12

cause célèbre 17.32.18
causeless 34.18.29(.34)
causelessly 1.31.33(.12.6)
causer 17.25.9
causerie 1.29.11(.19)
causeway 4.25.23
causey 1.22.11, 1.23.9
caustic 24.2.10(.15.4)
caustically 1.31.24(.9.6)
causticity 1.10.16(.16.1)
causticize 35.15.16(.4)
Caute 22.21
cauterization
    28.17.25(.3.11)
cauterize 35.15.20(.2)
cautery 1.29.11(.8.4)
Cauthen 28.17.21
caution 28.17.25(.8)
cautionary 1.29.11(.13.2)
cautious 34.18.22(.5)
cautiously 1.31.33(.12.4)
cautiousness
    34.18.16(.31.4)
Cavafy 1.18.4
cavalcade 23.4.5
cavalier 3.24
cavalierly 1.31.3(.12)
cavalry 1.29.24
cavalryman 28.17.16(.2)
Cavan 28.17.20(.5)
Cavanagh 17.18.6,
    17.18.16(.11)
cavatina 17.18.1(.3)
Cave 31.3
cave 1.19.3, 31.3
caveat 22.7.2
caveat emptor 12.5.6
cave-like 24.13.7(.20)
Cavell 40.5.10, 40.28.5
caveman 28.7.10(.18)
cavemen 28.5.7(.22)
Cavendish 36.2.12
caver 17.21.3
cavern 28.17.20(.5)
cavernous 34.18.16(.15.3)
cavernously
    1.31.33(.12.3)
Caversham 27.15.22
cavesson 28.17.23(.14)
cavetti 1.10.4
cavetto 19.10.4
caviar 10.1
cavil 40.28.5
caviller 17.34.16(.14)
cavitation 28.17.25(.3.3)
cavity 1.10.16(.15)
cavort 22.13.8
Cavour 12.12, 17.7.9
cavy 1.19.3
caw 12

Cawdor 12.6.4, 17.13.9
Cawdrey 1.29.16
Cawley 1.31.11
Cawnpore 12.3
Cawood 23.16.6(.2)
Caxton 28.17.11(.25)
cay 2, 4
cayenne 28.5
Cayley 1.31.4
cayuse 34.17.1, 34.17.13
Cazenove 31.12
cc 2.22
CD-ROM 27.9
ceanothus 34.18.19
cease 34.1
ceasefire 17.6.9
ceaseless 34.18.29(.33)
ceaselessly 1.31.33(.12.6)
ceaselessness
    34.18.16(.31.6)
ceca 17.14.1
Cecil 40.2.14, 40.31.1,
    40.31.2, 40.31.5
Cecile 40.1.10
Cecilia 3.24.1
Cecily 1.31.17(.20)
cecity 1.10.16(.16.1)
cedar 17.13.1
cedarn 28.17.12(.1)
cedarwood 23.16.6(.6)
cede 23.1
cedi 1.11.1
cedilla 17.34.2(.3)
Cedric 24.2.26(.15)
Ceefax® 34.23.5(.8)
ceilidh 1.31.4
ceiling 29.1.31(.1)
Ceinwen 28.5.17, 28.17.30
celadon 28.17.12(.16)
celandine 28.14.6
Celanese® 35.1.12
celeb 21.4
Celebes 35.1.6, 35.2.2
celebrant 22.26.15(.23.4)
celebrate 22.4.22(.7)
celebration
    28.17.25(.3.13)
celebrator 17.12.4(.15)
celebratory 1.29.11(.8.2)
celebrity 1.10.16(.21.3)
celeriac 24.6.1
celerity 1.10.16(.21.1)
celery 1.29.11(.27)
celesta 17.12.24(.4)
celeste 22.29.5(.13)
celestial 40.3.3
celestially 1.31.3(.3)
celestine 28.1.9(.7),
    28.14.5
Celia 3.24.1

celibacy 1.22.16(.3)
celibate 22.19.9
cell 40.5
cellar 17.34.5
cellarage 39.2.22(.9)
cellarer 17.32.14(.22)
cellaret 22.19.24(.9)
cellarman 28.17.16(.16)
Cellini 1.16.1(.16)
cellist 22.29.2(.31.1)
Cellnet® 22.5.9(.7)
cello 19.29.4
Cellophane® 28.4.9
cellphone 28.19.11
cellular 17.34.16(.21.4)
cellularity 1.10.16(.21.1)
cellulase 35.4.18
cellulate 22.4.23(.7.3)
cellulation 28.17.25(.3.14)
cellule 40.15.9(.11)
cellulite 22.16.25(.9)
cellulitis 34.18.11(.8)
celluloid 23.13.20
cellulose 34.20.17,
   35.20.14
cellulosic 24.2.20(.7)
cellulous 34.18.29(.17.6)
Celsius 34.3.10
Celt 22.32.2
Celtic 24.2.10(.16)
Celticism 27.15.21(.2.12)
Celtics 34.23.2(.3)
Cemaes 34.15.5
cembalo 19.29.12
cement 22.26.4(.8)
cementation
   28.17.25(.3.3)
cementer 17.12.22(.3)
cementite 22.16.9
cementitious 34.18.22(.2)
cementum 27.3.3,
   27.3.13
cementum 27.15.9(.14)
cemetery 1.29.11(.8.7)
cenacle 40.23.12(.11)
cenotaph 30.7.2
cenote 1.10.18, 4.9.8
Cenozoic 24.2.7
cense 34.24.3
censer 17.24.22(.2)
censor 17.24.22(.2)
censored 23.18.20
censorial 40.3.14(.5)
censorially 1.31.3(.11)
censorian 28.3.20(.7)
censorious 34.3.15(.5)
censoriously 1.31.33(.1.4)
censoriousness
   34.18.16(.31.1)
censorship 20.2.7(.9)

censurable 40.20.16(.27.5)
censure 17.26.21
census 34.18.20
cent 22.26.4
cental 40.21.17(.2)
centaur 12.5.8
Centaurus 34.18.27(.8)
centaury 1.29.8
centavo 19.17
centenarian 28.3.20(.4)
centenary 1.29.11(.13.1)
centennial 40.3.7(.4)
centerboard 23.12.2(.5)
centermost 22.29.17(.4)
centesimal 40.25.10
centesimally 1.31.17(.13)
centigrade 23.4.15
centigram 27.6.17(.5)
centilitre 17.12.1(.15)
centime 27.1.2
centimetre 17.12.1(.6)
centimo 19.14.12
centipede 23.1.1
centner 17.18.21
cento 19.10.17
centra 17.32.19(.10)
central 40.16.13(.16)
centralism 27.15.21(.2.15)
centralist 22.29.2(.31.4)
centrality 1.10.16(.32.13)
centralization
   28.17.25(.3.12)
centralize 35.15.21(.4.7)
centrally 1.31.17(.27.3)
centre 17.12.22(.3)
centreboard 23.12.2(.5)
centrefold 23.31.13(.7)
centreline 28.14.19(.11)
centremost 22.29.17(.4)
centrepiece 34.1.1
centric 24.2.26(.14.3)
centrical 40.23.12(.18)
centricity 1.10.16(.16.1)
centrifugal 40.24.10,
   40.24.11
centrifugally 1.31.17(.12)
centrifugation
   28.17.25(.3.6)
centrifuge 39.13
centriole 40.14.1
centripetal 40.21.1,
   40.21.12
centripetally 1.31.17(.9.1)
centrism 27.15.21(.2.14)
centrist 22.29.2(.29.5)
centroid 23.13.19
centromere 3.8.7, 3.8.9
centrosome 27.17.10
centrum 27.15.26(.10)
centum 27.15.9(.14)

centumvirate
   22.19.24(.9)
centuple 40.19.10
centurion 28.3.20(.7)
ceorl 40.17
cep 20.4
cephalic 24.2.27(.6)
Cephalonia 3.9.11
cephalopod 23.10.1
Cephalopoda 17.13.15
cephalothorax
   34.23.5(.14)
cephalothoraxes
   35.18.17
Cephas 34.7.13
cepheid 23.2.2
Cepheus 34.3.7
ceramic 24.2.14(.4)
ceramicist 22.29.2(.22)
ceramist 22.29.2(.17)
cerastes 35.1.7(.10)
cerastium 27.3.3
Cerberus 34.18.27(.13)
cercaria 3.22.4
cercariae 2.3
cerci 14.10
cercopithecine
   28.1.18(.6)
cercopithecoid 23.13.9
cercus 34.18.13(.11)
cere 3
cereal 40.3.14(.2)
cerebella 17.34.5(.2)
cerebellar 17.34.5(.2)
cerebellum 27.15.28(.4)
Cerebos® 34.10.7
cerebra 17.32.18
cerebral 40.16.13(.15)
cerebrally 1.31.17(.27.3)
cerebrate 22.4.22(.7)
cerebration
   28.17.25(.3.13)
cerebroside 23.15.11(.6)
cerebrospinal 40.26.11
cerebrovascular
   17.34.16(.21.2)
cerebrum 27.15.26(.9)
cerecloth 32.9
Ceredigion 28.10.2
cerement 22.26.15(.13.1)
ceremonial 40.3.7(.9)
ceremonialism
   27.15.21(.2.15)
ceremonialist
   22.29.2(.31.1)
ceremonially 1.31.3(.7)
ceremonious 34.3.6(.7)
ceremoniously
   1.31.33(.1.2)
ceremoniousness
   34.18.16(.31.1)

ceremony 1.16.15(.11)
Cerenkov 30.8.6
Ceres 35.1.22
ceresin 28.2.23(.9)
Ceri 1.29.3
cerise 34.1.7, 35.1.22
cerium 27.3.17(.2)
cermet 22.5.8
CERN 28.18
Cerne Abbas 34.18.10
cerography 1.18.9(.3.2)
ceroplastic 24.2.10(.15.4)
cert 22.20
certain 28.17.11(.16)
certainly 1.31.27(.14)
certainty 1.10.23(.12)
CertEd 23.5
certes 35.1.7(.7), 35.18.8
certifiable 40.20.16(.5)
certifiably 1.31.21(.2)
certificate 22.4.11(.6),
   22.19.12(.10)
certification
   28.17.25(.3.5)
certificatory 1.29.11(.8.6)
certify 14.14.4(.4)
certiorari 1.29.6, 14.24.3
certitude 23.17.4(.1)
cerulean 28.3.21(.10)
cerumen 28.5.7(.9),
   28.17.16(.15)
ceruminous
   34.18.16(.15.3)
ceruse 34.17.12
Cervantes 35.1.7(.9),
   35.2.3
cervelat 10.25, 10.25.5,
   22.7.21
cervical 40.23.10,
   40.23.12(.13)
cervices 35.1.16(.10)
cervine 28.14.11
cervix 34.23.2(.8)
César 10.16
Cesarewitch 38.2.9
cess 34.5
cessation 28.17.25(.3.10)
cesser 17.24.5
cession 28.17.25(.4)
cessionary 1.29.11(.13.2)
Cessna® 17.18.28
cesspit 22.2.5
cesspool 40.15.1
cesta 17.12.24(.4)
cesti 2.12.15, 14.8
cestode 23.20.5
cestoid 23.13.7
cestus 34.18.11(.16)
Cetacea 17.26.3
cetacean 28.17.25(.3.3)

cetaceous 34.18.22(.3)
cetane 28.4.3
ceteris paribus 34.18.10
cetological 40.23.12(.17.2)
cetologist 22.29.2(.26.3)
cetology 1.26.10(.11.2)
Cetshwayo 19.5
Cetus 34.18.11(.1)
Ceuta 17.12.15
Cévennes 28.5.9
Ceylon 28.10.26
Ceylonese 35.1.12
Cézanne 28.7.15
cha 10
Chablis 2.32.9(.11)
Chabrier 4.2.9
Chabrol 40.9.19
cha-cha 10.19
cha-cha-cha 10.19
chacma 17.17.19
chaconne 28.10.11
Chad 23.7
chadar 17.13.7
Chadian 28.3.4(.5)
Chadic 24.2.11(.5)
chador 12.6.3, 17.13.11
Chadwick 24.2.25
chaeta 17.12.1
chaetae 2.12.1
chaetognath 32.6.4
chaetopod 23.10.1
chafe 30.3
chafer 17.20.3
chaff 30.7
chaffer 17.20.5
chafferer 17.32.14(.12)
chaffinch 38.18.1
chaffiness 34.18.16(.2.6)
chaffy 1.18.4
Chagall 40.6.7, 40.8.7
Chagos Archipelago 19.13.9
chagrin 28.17.31(.17)
Chaim 27.12
chain 28.4
chain gang 29.4.6
chainless 34.18.29(.27)
chain mail 40.4.6
chainsaw 12.14.15
chainwork 24.17.6(.13)
chair 6
chairlady 1.11.4
chairlift 22.27.1
chairman 28.17.16(.6)
chairmanship 20.2.7(.19)
chairperson 28.17.23(.15)
chairwoman 28.17.16(.14)
chairwomen 28.2.17(.1)
chaise 35.4

chaise longue 29.6
chakra 17.32.21
chalaza 17.25.3
chalazae 2.23
Chalcedon 28.10.10, 28.17.12(.16)
Chalcedonian 28.3.8(.11)
chalcedonic 24.2.15(.6.1)
chalcedony 1.16.15(.8)
Chalcidice 1.22.16(.5)
Chalcis 34.2.17(.16)
Chalcolithic 24.2.18(.1)
chalcopyrite 22.16.24(.8)
Chaldea 17.1.4
Chaldean 28.17.1(.4)
Chaldee 2.13
chaldron 28.17.31(.15)
chalet 1.31.7, 4.28.3
Chalfont 22.26.9
Chaliapin 28.2.9
chalice 34.18.29(.7)
chalk 24.10
chalkboard 23.12.2(.10)
Chalker 17.14.9
chalkily 1.31.17(.11)
chalkiness 34.18.16(.2.4)
chalky 1.12.8
challah 10.25, 17.34.8
challenge 39.17.9
challengeable 40.20.16(.25)
challenged 23.29
challenger 17.29.16(.8)
challengingly 1.31.28(.1.14)
Challes 34.18.29(.7)
challis 1.31.7, 34.2.22(.5)
Challoner 17.18.16(.22)
Chalmers 35.18.12
chalumeau 19.14.12
chalumeaux 35.20.7
chalybeate 22.3.2
cham 27.6
chamaephyte 22.16.16
chamber 17.11.17(.2)
chamberlain 28.17.33(.13)
chamberlainship 20.2.7(.19)
chambermaid 23.4.7
Chambers 35.18.7
Chambertin 8
Chambourcy® 1.22.16(.1)
chambray 4.26.10
chambré 4.26.10
chameleon 28.3.21(.1)
chameleonic 24.2.15(.6.1)
chamfer 17.20.17
chammy 1.15.6
chamois 1.15.6, 10.22.8

chamomile 40.13.7
Chamonix 2.17.6, 2.17.10
champ 20.16.3
champagne 28.4.1
champaign 28.4.1
champenoise 35.9
champers 35.18.6
champertous 34.18.11(.10)
champerty 1.10.16(.6)
champion 28.3.1
championship 20.2.7(.19)
Champlain 28.4.19
champlevé 4.16
Champneys 35.2.8
Champs Élysées 4.19
Chan 28.7
chance 34.24.6
chancel 40.31.21
chancellery 1.29.11(.27)
chancellor 17.34.16(.15)
chancellorship 20.2.7(.9)
chance-medley 1.31.23(.4)
chancer 17.24.22(.3)
chancery 1.29.11(.18)
chancily 1.31.17(.20)
chanciness 34.18.16(.2.7)
chancre 17.14.21(.3)
chancroid 23.13.19
Chanctonbury 1.29.11(.7.2)
chancy 1.22.23(.4)
chandelier 3.24
chandelle 40.5.4
Chandigarh 10.9, 18.6
chandler 17.34.22
chandlery 1.29.11(.27)
Chandos 34.10.9
Chandrasekhar 17.14.3(.5)
Chanel 40.5.8
Chaney 1.16.4
Chang 29.4
Changchun 28.16.14
change 39.17.2
changeability 1.10.16(.22.1)
changeable 40.20.16(.25)
changeableness 34.18.16(.37.4)
changeably 1.31.21(.7.3)
changeful 40.27.28, 40.27.30
changefulness 34.18.16(.37.2)
changeless 34.18.29(.37)
changelessly 1.31.33(.12.6)

changelessness 34.18.16(.31.6)
changeling 29.1.31(.29)
changeover 17.21.14(.12)
changer 17.29.16(.2)
changeround 23.24.7(.10)
Changi 1.14.14
Changsha 10.17
channel 40.26.5
channelize 35.15.21(.4.5)
Channing 29.1.17(.5)
Channon 28.17.17(.5)
chanson 11.12, 28.10.18
chanson de geste 22.29.5
chant 22.26.6, 22.26.8
Chantal 40.6.5, 40.8.4
chanter 17.12.22(.4)
chanterelle 40.5.18
chanteur 18.3
chanteurs 35.19
chanteuse 35.19
chanteuses 35.19
chantey 1.10.23(.4)
chanticleer 3.24.14
Chantilly 1.31.2
chantry 1.29.15(.15)
chanty 1.10.23(.4)
chaology 1.26.10(.11.1)
chaos 34.10.3
chaotic 24.2.10(.6)
chaotically 1.31.24(.9.4)
chap 20.5
chaparejos 34.20.14
chaparral 40.6.14
chapatti 1.10.6, 1.10.8
chapbook 24.14.3
chape 20.3
chapeau-bras 10.23.6
chapel 40.19.5
Chapel-en-le-Frith 32.2.8
chapelry 1.29.24
chaperonage 39.2.15
chaperone 28.19.17
chaperoned 23.24.18
chap-fallen 28.17.33(.8)
chaplain 28.17.33(.16)
chaplaincy 1.22.23(.10.4)
chaplet 22.19.26(.15)
Chaplin 28.17.33(.16)
chapman 28.17.16(.19)
chappal 40.19.5
Chappell 40.19.5
chappie 1.8.5
chappy 1.8.5
chapter 17.12.19
char 10
charabanc 29.4.2
characin 28.2.23(.9)

character 17.12.21(.7)
characterful 40.27.14
characterfully
1.31.17(.16.1), 1.31.29
characteristic
24.2.10(.15.2)
characteristically
1.31.24(.9.6)
characterization
28.17.25(.3.12)
characterize 35.15.20(.2)
characterless
34.18.29(.17.2)
characterology
1.26.10(.11.5)
charade 23.9.20
charango 19.13.12
charas 34.18.27(.6)
charbroil 40.11.9
charcoal 40.18.7
charcuterie 2.30.7,
2.30.10
chard 23.9
Chardonnay 4.14
chare 6
charge 39.8
chargeable 40.20.16(.25)
chargeableness
34.18.16(.37.4)
chargeably 1.31.21(.7.4)
chargé d'affaires 6.10
chargehand 23.24.6(.11)
charger 17.29.7
chargés d'affaires 35.6
charily 1.31.17(.27.1)
chariness 34.18.16(.2.9)
chariot 22.3.12
charioteer 3.4
charisma 17.17.23
charismatic 24.2.10(.4.2)
charismatically
1.31.24(.9.4)
Charisse 34.1.7
charitable 40.20.16(.11.3)
charitableness
34.18.16(.37.4)
charitably 1.31.21(.4.2)
charity 1.10.16(.21.1)
charivari 1.29.6
charivaria 3.22.7
charlady 1.11.4
charlatan 28.17.11(.15)
charlatanism
27.15.21(.2.9)
charlatanry 1.29.20
Charlecote 22.19.12(.15),
22.21.5
Charlemagne 28.4.7
Charlene 28.1.27(.4)
Charles 35.30.7
Charleston 28.17.11(.25)

charley horse 34.12
Charlie 1.31.9
charlie 1.31.9
charlock 24.9.16(.3),
24.16.16
charlotte 22.19.26(.7)
Charlottenburg
26.14.1(.9)
charlotte russe 34.17
Charlottetown 28.8.1
Charlton 28.17.11(.27)
charm 27.8
Charmaine 28.4.7
charmer 17.17.7
charmeuse 35.19
Charmian 28.3.7
charming 29.1.16
charmingly 1.31.28(.1.7)
charmless 34.18.29(.26)
charmlessly
1.31.33(.12.6)
charmlessness
34.18.16(.31.6)
charnel 40.26.7
Charnock 24.9.9, 24.16.7
Charolais 4.28.7
Charon 28.10.24(.2),
28.17.31(.4)
charpoy 13.2
charr 10
Charrington 28.17.11(.23)
charro 19.27.5
chart 22.10
chartbuster 17.12.24(.10)
charter 17.12.8
charterer 17.32.14(.6)
Charterhouse 34.8.6(.7)
Charteris 34.2.21, 35.18.8
Chartism 27.15.21(.2.4)
Chartist 22.29.2(.13)
Chartres 17.32.19(.4)
chartreuse 35.19
Chartwell 40.5.17(.7)
charwoman 28.17.16(.14)
charwomen 28.2.17(.1)
chary 1.29.4
Charybdis 34.2.9
chase 34.4
chaser 17.24.4
Chasid 23.2.16
Chasidim 27.2.4
Chasidism 27.15.21(.2.5)
chasm 27.15.21(.3)
chasmic 24.2.14(.17)
chasse 34.7, 34.9
chassé 4.18, 4.18.6
chasseur 18.11
chassis 1.22.6, 35.2.11
chaste 22.29.4
chastely 1.31.22(.22)
chasten 28.17.23(.4)

chastener 17.18.16(.14)
chasteness 34.18.16(.20.4)
chastise 35.15.7(.9)
chastisement
22.26.15(.13.5)
chastiser 17.25.12(.2)
chastity 1.10.16(.8)
chasuble 40.20.16(.28)
chat 22.7
Chataway 4.25.9
chateau 19.10.6
chateaubriand 11,
23.24.9, 28.10
chateaux 35.20.3
chatelaine 28.4.19
Chater 17.12.4
Chatham 27.15.9(.4)
chatline 28.14.19(.14)
chat show 19.22
Chattanooga 17.16.12
chattel 40.21.5
chatter 17.12.6
chatterbox 34.23.8(.2)
chatterer 17.32.14(.6)
Chatterjee 2.27
Chatterley 1.31.17(.9.1)
Chatterton 28.17.11(.15)
chattery 1.29.11(.8.3)
chattily 1.31.17(.9.1)
chattiness 34.18.16(.2.3)
Chatto 19.10.6
chatty 1.10.6
Chatwin 28.2.28
Chaucer 17.24.10
Chaucerian 28.3.20(.2)
chaud-froid 10.22.13
Chaudhury 1.29.11(.9)
chaudron 28.17.31(.15)
chauds-froids 35.9
chauffeur 17.20.14
chauffeuse 35.19
chaulmoogra 17.32.22
chausses 34.20
chautauqua 17.31.6
chauvinism 27.15.21(.2.9)
chauvinist 22.29.2(.18.1)
chauvinistic
24.2.10(.15.2)
chauvinistically
1.31.24(.9.6)
Chavasse 34.7.14
Chavez 35.5.10
chaw 12
chayote 1.10.18
Chaz 35.7
Che 4
Cheadle 40.22.1
Cheam 27.1
cheap 20.1
cheapen 28.17.9
cheapie 1.8.1

cheapish 36.2.9
cheapjack 24.6.18
cheaply 1.31.20
cheapness 34.18.16(.18)
cheapo 19.8
Cheapside 23.15.11(.7)
cheapskate 22.4.11(.7)
cheat 22.1
cheater 17.12.1
cheatingly 1.31.28(.1.4)
Chechen 28.5.14
Chechnya 10.24
check 24.4
checkable 40.20.16(.13)
checker 17.14.4
checkerberry 1.29.3
checkerboard 23.12.2(.5)
checkerman
28.17.16(.16)
Checkland 23.24.16(.16.3)
Checkley 1.31.24(.4)
checklist 22.29.2(.31.6)
check mark 24.8.8
checkmate 22.4.13
checkout 22.9.9
checkpoint 22.26.11
checkrail 40.4.14
check rein 28.4.18
checkroom 27.14.6(.10)
check-up 20.9.7
check valve 31.13
checkweighman
28.17.16(.4)
Cheddar 17.13.4
Chedzoy 13.10
cheek 24.1
cheekbone 28.19.3
cheekily 1.31.17(.11)
cheekiness 34.18.16(.2.4)
cheeky 1.12.1
cheep 20.1
cheer 3
cheerful 40.27.3
cheerfully 1.31.17(.16.1)
cheerfulness
34.18.16(.37.2)
cheerily 1.31.17(.27.1)
cheeriness 34.18.16(.2.9)
cheerio 19
cheerleader 17.13.1
cheerless 34.18.29(.3)
cheerlessly 1.31.33(.12.6)
cheerlessness
34.18.16(.31.6)
cheerly 1.31.3
cheers 35.3
cheery 1.29.2
cheese 35.1
cheeseboard 23.12.2(.16)
cheeseburger 17.16.14

chili 1.31.2
chiliad 23.3, 23.7.2
chiliasm 27.15.21(.3)
chiliast 22.29.6(.1)
chiliastic 24.2.10(.15.4)
chill 40.2
chiller 17.34.2
chilli 1.31.2
chilliness 34.18.16(.2.10)
chillingly 1.31.28(.1.18)
chillness 34.18.16(.37.1)
chillsome 27.15.20(.22)
chillum 27.15.28(.2)
chilly 1.31.2
Chilpruf 30.13.4
Chiltern 28.17.11(.27)
Chilton 28.17.11(.27)
Chimborazo 19.21
chime 27.12
chimer 17.17.2
chimera 17.32.2
chimere 3.8
chimeric 24.2.26(.4)
chimerical 40.23.12(.18)
chimerically
  1.31.24(.9.12)
chimney 1.16.23
chimney breast
  22.29.5(.12)
chimney piece 34.1.1
chimney pot 22.11.2
chimney stack 24.6.7
chimney sweep 20.1
chimp 20.16.1
chimpanzee 2.23
chin 28.2
china 17.18.13
Chinagraph 30.7.5(.1)
Chinaman 28.17.16(.16)
Chinamen 28.17.16(.16)
Chinatown 28.8.1
chinaware 6.18.4
chinch 38.18.1
chincherinchee 2.26
chinchilla 17.34.2(.11)
chin-chin 28.2.26
Chindit 22.2.8
Chindwin 28.2.28
chine 28.14
chiné 4.14
Chinese 35.1.12
Chingford 23.18.16(.17)
chink 24.19.1
Chinky 1.12.16
chinless 34.18.29(.27)
chinlessness
  34.18.16(.31.6)
chino 19.15.1
chinoiserie 1.29.11(.19),
  2.30
Chinook 24.14.6, 24.15.4

chinstrap 20.5.6
chintz 34.22.18
chintzily 1.31.17(.20)
chintziness 34.18.16(.2.7)
chintzy 1.22.23(.1)
chinwag 26.5.7
chionodoxa 17.24.20
Chios 34.10.1, 34.10.5
chip 20.2
chipboard 23.12.2(.7)
chipmunk 24.19.7
chipolata 17.12.8(.11)
Chippendale 40.4.3
Chippenham
  27.15.14(.11)
chipper 17.10.2
Chippewa 10.22.2, 17.31.3
chippie 1.8.2
chippiness 34.18.16(.2.2)
chipping 29.1.10(.2)
chippy 1.8.2
Chips 34.21.2
chip shot 22.11.12
chiral 40.16.13(.10)
chirality 1.10.16(.32.13)
chi-rho 19.27.9
Chirk 24.17
chirograph 30.7.5(.1)
chirographer 17.20.12(.5)
chirographic 24.2.16(.3)
chirographist
  22.29.2(.19)
chirography 1.18.9(.3.2)
chiromancer 17.24.22(.3)
chiromancy 1.22.23(.4)
Chiron 28.17.31(.10)
chiropodist 22.29.2(.14)
chiropody 1.11.17
chiropractic 24.2.10(.13)
chiropractor 17.12.21(.3)
chiropteran
  28.17.31(.11)
chiropterous
  34.18.27(.14)
chirp 20.14
chirper 17.10.15
chirpily 1.31.17(.7)
chirpiness 34.18.16(.2.2)
chirpy 1.8.12
chirr 18
chirrup 20.9.15
chirrupy 1.8.8
chiru 16.23.1
chisel 40.32.2
chiseller 17.34.16(.16)
Chisholm 27.15.21(.2.1)
Chislehurst 22.29.16
chi-square 6.18.9
Chiswick 24.2.21
chit 22.2
chital 40.21.1

chit-chat 22.7.17
chitin 28.2.11(.8),
  28.17.11(.12)
chitinous 34.18.16(.15.2)
chitlins 35.26.2
chiton 28.10.9,
  28.17.11(.12)
Chittagong 29.6.6
chitterling 29.1.31(.12)
chitty 1.10.2
chiv 31.2
chivalric 24.2.26(.20)
chivalrous 34.18.27(.28)
chivalrously
  1.31.33(.12.5)
chivalrousness
  34.18.16(.31.5)
chivalry 1.29.24
Chivas 34.7.14, 34.18.18
chive 31.9
Chivers 35.18.15
chivvy 1.19.2
chiz 35.2
chlamydia 3.5.2
chlamydial 40.3.4
chlamydomonas
  34.18.16(.17)
Chloë 1(.7)
chloracne 1.16.21
chloral 40.16.13(.8)
chlorambucil 40.2.14
chloramine 28.1.13
chloramphenicol 40.9.9
chlorate 22.4.22(.4)
chlordane 28.4.4
chlorella 17.34.5(.15)
chloric 24.2.26(.7)
chloride 23.15.15
chlorinate 22.4.14(.9.4)
chlorination
  28.17.25(.3.8)
chlorinator 17.12.4(.10)
chlorine 28.1.25(.1)
chlorite 22.16.24(.7)
chloritic 24.2.10(.2.4)
chlorodyne 28.14.6
chlorofluorocarbon
  28.17.10
chloroform 27.10.5(.2)
Chloromycetin®
  28.2.11(.1)
chlorophyll 40.2.11
chlorophyllous
  34.18.29(.2)
chloroplast 22.29.6(.12)
chloroquine 28.2.28
chlorosis 34.2.17(.11.2)
chlorotic 24.2.10(.6)
chlorpromazine 28.1.19
Chobham 27.15.8
choc 24.9

chocaholic 24.2.27(.9)
choccy 1.12.7
chocho 19.24
choc ice 34.15.4
chock 24.9
chock-a-block
  24.9.16(.10)
chocker 17.14.8
chockstone 28.19.4(.9)
chocoholic 24.2.27(.9)
chocolate 22.19.26(.19)
chocolatey 1.10.16(.36)
Choctaw 12.5.7
choice 34.13
choicely 1.31.33(.8)
choiceness 34.18.16(.31.2)
choir 17.6
choirboy 13.3
choirgirl 40.17
choirmaster 17.12.24(.5)
choke 24.18
chokeberry 1.29.11(.7.2)
choke cherry 1.29.3
choker 17.14.17
chokey 1.12.15
chokily 1.31.17(.11)
chokiness 34.18.16(.2.4)
choko 19.12.14
cholangiography
  1.18.9(.3.2)
cholecalciferol 40.9.19
cholecystectomy
  1.15.13(.1)
cholecystography
  1.18.9(.3.2)
choler 17.34.9
cholera 17.32.14(.22)
choleraic 24.2.3
choleric 24.2.26(.4)
cholerically 1.31.24(.9.12)
cholesterol 40.9.19,
  40.16.13(.16)
choli 1.31.19
choliamb 21.17, 27.6.1
choliambic 24.2.9(.8)
cholic 24.2.27(.9)
choline 28.1.27(.8)
cholinergic 24.2.24(.6)
Cholmeley 1.31.26(.9)
Cholmondeley
  1.31.26(.9)
chomp 20.16.4
Chomsky 1.12.17(.11)
Chomskyan 28.3.5
chondrite 22.16.24(.13)
chondrocranium
  27.3.8(.3)
chondroma 17.17.16(.11)
chondromata
  17.12.16(.9.3)
choo-choo 16.19

chook 24.14
choose 35.17
chooser 17.25.14
choosily 1.31.17(.21)
choosiness 34.18.16(.2.7)
choosy 1.23.12
chop 20.7
chop-fallen 28.17.33(.8)
chophouse 34.8.6(.9)
Chopin 8, 28.7.4
chopper 17.10.8
choppily 1.31.17(.7)
choppiness 34.18.16(.2.2)
choppy 1.8.7
chopstick 24.2.10(.15.4)
chop suey 1(.6)
choral 40.16.13(.8)
chorale 40.8.15
chorally 1.31.17(.27.1)
chord 23.12
chordal 40.22.8
chordate 22.19.11
chore 12
chorea 3.22
choreograph 30.7.5(.1)
choreographer 17.20.12(.5)
choreographic 24.2.16(.3)
choreographical 40.23.12(.12)
choreographically 1.31.24(.9.9)
choreography 1.18.9(.3.2)
choreologist 22.29.2(.26.2)
choreology 1.26.10(.11.1)
choriamb 21.17
choriambi 14.7
choriambic 24.2.9(.8)
choriambus 34.18.10
chorine 28.1.25(.1)
chorion 28.3.20(.7), 28.10.2
chorionic 24.2.15(.6.1)
chorister 17.12.24(.14)
Chorley 1.31.11
Chorlton 28.17.11(.27)
Chorlton-cum-Hardy 1.11.9
chorographer 17.20.12(.5)
chorographic 24.2.16(.3)
chorographically 1.31.24(.9.9)
chorography 1.18.9(.3.2)
choroid 23.13.19
chorological 40.23.12(.17.2)

chorologically 1.31.24(.9.11)
chorologist 22.29.2(.26.4)
chorology 1.26.10(.11.5)
chorten 28.17.11(.10)
chortle 40.21.8
chorus 34.18.27(.8)
chose 35.20
chosen 28.17.24(.14)
chota 17.12.18
choucroute 22.18.9
chough 30.11
choux 16
chow 9
chowder 17.13.6
chowkidar 10.7
chow mein 28.4
chrematistic 24.2.10(.15.2)
chrestomathy 1.20.8
Chris 34.2
chrism 27.15.21(.2.1)
chrisom 27.15.21(.2.1)
Chrissie 1.22.2
Christ 22.29.13
Christabel 40.5.2
Christadelphian 28.3.9
Christchurch 38.16
christen 28.17.23(.2)
Christendom 27.15.10(.14)
christener 17.18.16(.14)
christening 29.1.17(.12)
Christensen 28.17.23(.24)
Christhood 23.16.5(.6)
Christi 1.10.26(.2)
Christian 28.17.27
Christiana 17.18.8
Christiania 3.9.6
Christianity 1.10.16(.13)
Christianization 28.17.25(.3.11)
Christianize 35.15.12(.5)
Christianly 1.31.27(.14)
Christie 1.10.26(.2)
Christina 17.18.1(.3)
Christine 28.1.9
Christingle 40.24.14(.1)
Christlike 24.13.7(.12)
Christly 1.31.22(.22)
Christmas 34.18.15(.17)
Christmassy 1.22.16(.8)
Christmastide 23.15.4
Christmastime 27.12.1
Christolatry 1.29.15(.13)
Christological 40.23.12(.17.2)
Christology 1.26.10(.11.2)
Christophany 1.16.15(.12)
Christopher 17.20.12(.1)

Christy 1.10.26(.2)
chroma 17.17.16
chromate 22.4.13(.7)
chromatic 24.2.10(.4.2)
chromatically 1.31.24(.9.4)
chromaticism 27.15.21(.2.12)
chromaticity 1.10.16(.16.1)
chromatid 23.2.8
chromatin 28.2.11(.10)
chromatism 27.15.21(.2.4)
chromatogram 27.6.17(.5)
chromatograph 30.7.5(.1)
chromatographic 24.2.16(.3)
chromatographically 1.31.24(.9.9)
chromatography 1.18.9(.3.2)
chromatopsia 3.14.12
chrome 27.17
chromic 24.2.14(.12)
chrominance 34.24.10(.15)
chromite 22.16.13
chromium 27.3.7
chromium-plate 22.4.23(.8)
chromo 19.14.14
chromolithograph 30.7.5(.1)
chromolithographer 17.20.12(.5)
chromolithographic 24.2.16(.3)
chromolithography 1.18.9(.3.2)
chromoly 1.31.10
chromosomal 40.25.12
chromosome 27.17.10
chromosphere 3.10.5
chromospheric 24.2.26(.4)
chroneme 27.1.6
chronemic 24.2.14(.1)
chronic 24.2.15(.6.1)
chronically 1.31.24(.9.8)
chronicity 1.10.16(.16.1)
chronicle 40.23.12(.11)
chronicler 17.34.23
chronogram 27.6.17(.5)
chronogrammatic 24.2.10(.4.2)
chronograph 30.7.5(.1)
chronographic 24.2.16(.3)
chronologer 17.29.13

chronologic 24.2.24(.4)
chronological 40.23.2
chronologically 1.31.24(.9.11)
chronologist 22.29.2(.26.4)
chronologization 28.17.25(.3.12)
chronologize 35.15.18
chronology 1.26.10(.11.4)
chronometer 17.12.16(.9.2)
chronometric 24.2.26(.14.2)
chronometrical 40.23.12(.18)
chronometrically 1.31.24(.9.12)
chronometry 1.29.15(.8)
chronoscope 20.15.4(.1)
chrysalid 23.2.23
chrysalides 35.1.8
chrysalis 34.2.22(.8)
chrysanth 32.21
chrysanthemum 27.15.13
chryselephantine 28.14.5
Chrysler® 17.34.28
chrysoberyl 40.16.13(.3)
chrysolite 22.16.25(.9)
chrysoprase 35.4.16
Chrysostom 27.15.9(.15)
Chrystal 40.21.18
chthonian 28.3.8(.11)
chthonic 24.2.15(.6.1)
chub 21.11
Chubb® 21.11
chubbily 1.31.17(.8)
chubbiness 34.18.16(.2.2)
chubby 1.9.9
chuck 24.12
chucker-out 22.9
chuckhole 40.18.13
chuckle 40.23.9
chucklehead 23.5.13(.19)
chuckleheaded 23.18.10(.3)
chuckler 17.34.23
chuddar 17.13.11
chufa 17.20.11
chuff 30.11
chug 26.10
chugalug 26.10
chukar 10.8.6
chukka 17.14.11
chukker 17.14.11
chum 27.11
chummily 1.31.17(.13)
chumminess 34.18.16(.2.5)

chummy **1.15.10**
chump **20.16.5**
chunder **17.13.20(.10)**
Chungking **29.1.14**
chunk **24.19.7**
chunkily **1.31.17(.11)**
chunkiness **34.18.16(.2.4)**
chunky **1.12.16**
Chunnel **40.26.10**
chunter **17.12.22(.10)**
church **38.16**
Churchdown **28.8.2(.12)**
churchgoer **17.9.5**
churchgoing **29.1.9**
Churchill **40.2.16, 40.16.12**
Churchillian **28.3.21(.2)**
churchily **1.31.17(.24)**
churchiness **34.18.16(.2.8)**
churching **29.1.27**
churchman **28.17.16(.33)**
churchmanship **20.2.7(.19)**
churchwarden **28.17.12(.10)**
churchwoman **28.17.16(.14)**
churchwomen **28.2.17(.1)**
churchy **1.25.13**
churchyard **23.9.21**
churinga **17.16.17(.1)**
churl **40.17**
churlish **36.2.27**
churlishly **1.31.35(.7.4)**
churlishness **34.18.16(.33.6)**
churn **28.18**
churr **18**
churrasco **19.12.17**
Churrigueresque **24.20.3**
chute **22.18**
chutist **22.29.2(.13)**
chutney **1.16.19**
chutzpah **17.10.18**
Chuzzlewit **22.2.23**
chyack **24.6.3**
chyle **40.13**
chylous **34.18.29(.14)**
chyme **27.12**
chymotrypsin **28.2.23(.12)**
chymous **34.18.15(.8)**
chypre **17.32.17**
CIA **4**
ciabatta **17.12.8(.2)**
ciabatte **2.12.5**
ciao **9**
Ciba **17.11.1**

Cibachrome **27.17.13**
Ciba-Geigy® **1.14.9**
ciboria **3.22.9**
ciborium **27.3.17(.4)**
cicada **17.13.7**
cicala **17.34.8**
cicatrices **35.1.16(.8)**
cicatricial **40.33.1**
cicatrix **34.23.2(.12)**
cicatrization **28.17.25(.3.11)**
cicatrize **35.15.20(.4)**
Cicely **1.31.17(.20)**
cicely **1.31.17(.20)**
Cicero **19.27.11**
cicerone **1.16.17(.13)**
Ciceronian **28.3.8(.11)**
cichlid **23.2.23**
cicisbei **2.4**
cicisbeo **9.6**
cider **17.13.12**
ci-devant **11.11**
cig **26.2**
cigala **17.34.8**
cigar **10.9**
cigarette **22.5.19**
cigarillo **19.29.2**
ciggy **1.14.2**
ciguatera **17.32.5**
cilantro **19.27.15**
cilia **3.24.2**
ciliary **1.29.2(.12)**
ciliate **22.4.2(.15)**
ciliated **23.18.9(.3)**
ciliation **28.17.25(.3.1)**
cilice **34.2.22(.2)**
Cilicia **3.14.2, 3.16.2**
Cilician **28.3.13, 28.3.15**
cilium **27.3.18**
cill **40.2**
Cilla **17.34.2**
Cimabue **1(.6), 4.5**
cimbalom **27.15.28(.11)**
cimetadine **28.1.10**
Cimmerian **28.3.20(.2)**
cinch **38.18.1**
cinchona **17.18.18(.4)**
cinchonic **24.2.15(.6.1)**
cinchonine **28.1.14**
Cincinnati **1.10.6**
cincture **17.28.20, 17.28.23**
cinder **17.13.20(.1)**
Cinderella **17.34.5(.15)**
cindery **1.29.11(.9)**
Cindy **1.11.20(.1)**
cine **1.16.2**
cineaste **22.29.6(.1)**
cinecamera **17.32.14(.10)**
cinefilm **27.18**
cinema **17.17.14(.6)**

CinemaScope® **20.15.4(.1)**
cinematheque **24.4.4**
cinematic **24.2.10(.4.2)**
cinematically **1.31.24(.9.4)**
cinematograph **30.7.5(.1)**
cinematographer **17.20.12(.5)**
cinematographic **24.2.16(.3)**
cinematographically **1.31.24(.9.9)**
cinematography **1.18.9(.3.2)**
cinéma-vérité **4.9.7**
cinephile **40.13.9**
Cinerama® **17.17.7**
cineraria **3.22.4**
cinerarium **27.3.17(.3)**
cinerary **1.29.11(.25)**
cinereous **34.3.15(.2)**
Cingalese **35.1.23**
cingula **17.34.16(.21.3)**
cingulum **27.15.28(.11)**
cinnabar **10.5.4**
cinnamon **28.17.16(.16)**
cinque **24.19.1**
cinquecentist **22.29.2(.13)**
cinquecento **19.10.17**
cinquefoil **40.11.7**
Cinque Ports **34.22.9**
Cinzano® **19.15.7**
cion **28.17.5**
cipher **17.20.10**
cipolin **28.2.31(.10)**
Cipriani **1.16.8**
circa **17.14.16**
circadian **28.3.4(.3)**
Circassian **28.3.13**
Circe **1.22.17**
Circean **28.17.1(.9)**
circinate **24.4.14(.9.3), 22.19.15(.9)**
circiter **17.12.16(.14)**
circle **40.23.13**
circler **17.34.23**
circlet **22.19.26(.19)**
circlip **20.2.13**
circs **34.23.16**
circuit **22.2.9(.8)**
circuition **28.17.25(.2.1)**
circuitous **34.18.11(.10)**
circuitously **1.31.33(.12.2)**
circuitousness **34.18.16(.31.3)**
circuitry **1.29.15(.6)**
circuity **1.10.16(.5)**
circular **17.34.16(.21.2)**
circularity **1.10.16(.21.1)**

circularization **28.17.25(.3.12)**
circularize **35.15.20(.2)**
circularly **1.31.17(.29)**
circulate **22.4.23(.7.3)**
circulation **28.17.25(.3.14)**
circulative **31.2.1(.9.4)**
circulator **17.12.4(.16)**
circulatory **1.29.11(.8.2)**
circumambience **34.24.2**
circumambiency **1.22.23(.2)**
circumambient **22.26.2(.2)**
circumambulate **22.4.23(.7.3)**
circumambulation **28.17.25(.3.14)**
circumambulatory **1.29.11(.8.10)**
circumcircle **40.23.13**
circumcise **35.15.16(.6)**
circumcision **28.17.26(.2)**
circumference **34.24.10(.16)**
circumferential **40.33.12(.3)**
circumferentially **1.31.17(.22)**
circumflex **34.23.4(.12)**
circumfluence **34.24.10(.6)**
circumfluent **22.26.15(.5)**
circumfuse **35.17.7**
circumjacent **22.26.15(.17.1)**
circumlittoral **40.16.13(.12.1)**
circumlocution **28.17.25(.11)**
circumlocutional **40.26.13(.14.5)**
circumlocutionary **1.29.11(.13.2)**
circumlocutionist **22.29.2(.18.2)**
circumlocutory **1.29.11(.8.4)**
circumlunar **17.18.15**
circumnavigate **22.4.12(.5)**
circumnavigation **28.17.25(.3.6)**
circumnavigator **17.12.4(.8)**
circumpolar **17.34.18(.1)**
circumscribable **40.20.16(.10)**
circumscribe **21.12**
circumscribed **23.21**
circumscriber **17.11.11**

circumscription 28.17.25(.14)

circumsolar 17.34.18(.10)

circumspect 22.23.4(.1)

circumspection 28.17.25(.15.2)

circumspectly 1.31.22(.19)

circumspectness 34.18.16(.20.4)

circumstance 34.24.6, 34.24.10(.10)

circumstantial 40.33.12(.4)

circumstantiality 1.10.16(.32.1)

circumstantially 1.31.17(.22)

circumstantiate 22.4.2(.11)

circumterrestrial 40.3.14(.9)

circumvallate 22.4.23(.5)

circumvallation 28.17.25(.3.14)

circumvent 22.26.4(.10)

circumvention 28.17.25(.16)

circumvolution 28.17.25(.11)

circus 34.18.13(.11)

ciré 4.26.1

Cirencester 17.12.16(.14), 17.12.24(.4)

cire perdue 16.24.6

cirque 24.17

cirrhosis 34.2.17(.11.2)

cirrhotic 24.2.10(.6)

cirri 14.24.1

cirriped 23.5.1

cirrocumulus 34.18.29(.17.6)

cirrose 34.20.16

cirrostratus 34.18.11(.3)

cirrous 34.18.27(.1)

cirrus 34.18.27(.1)

cisalpine 28.14.3

cisatlantic 24.2.10(.14)

cisco 19.12.17

Ciskei 14.10

cislunar 17.18.15

cispontine 28.14.5

Cissie 1.22.2

cissoid 23.13.16

cist 22.29.2

Cistercian 28.17.25(.12)

cistern 28.17.11(.25)

cistron 28.10.24(.7), 28.17.31(.14)

cistus 34.18.11(.16)

citable 40.20.16(.11.2)

citadel 40.5.4, 40.22.13

citation 28.17.25(.3.3)

citatory 1.29.11(.8.2)

cite 22.16

CITES 35.1.7(.5)

cithara 17.32.14(.14)

cither 17.22.2

Citibank® 24.19.3(.1)

Citicorp 20.8

citify 14.14.1

citizen 28.17.24(.12)

citizenhood 23.16.5(.10)

citizenly 1.31.27(.14)

citizenry 1.29.20

citizenship 20.2.7(.19)

citole 40.18.5

citral 40.6.14, 40.16.13(.16)

citrate 22.4.22(.8)

citric 24.2.26(.14.1)

citrine 28.1.25(.6), 28.2.29(.8)

Citroën® 28.17.8, 28.17.31(.14)

citron 28.17.31(.14)

citronella 17.34.5(.8)

citrous 34.18.27(.14)

citrus 34.18.27(.14)

cittern 28.18.4

city 1.10.2

cityfied 23.15.9

cityscape 20.3

cityward 23.18.26(.2)

Ciudad 23.7.8, 23.9.8

civet 22.2.14

civic 24.2.17

civically 1.31.24(.9.9)

civil 40.28.2

civilian 28.3.21(.2)

civilianize 35.15.12(.5)

civility 1.10.16(.26)

civilizable 40.20.16(.22)

civilization 28.17.25(.3.12)

civilize 35.15.21(.4.6)

civilizer 17.25.12(.15)

civilly 1.31.17(.17)

civvies 35.2.10

civvy 1.19.2

clachan 28.17.13(.5), 28.17.14

clack 24.6

clacker 17.14.5

Clackmannan 28.17.17(.5)

Clacton 28.17.11(.20)

clad 23.7

clade 23.4

cladism 27.15.21(.2.5)

cladistics 34.23.2(.3)

cladode 23.20.6

Claiborne 28.11.2

claim 27.4

claimable 40.20.16(.15)

claimant 22.26.15(.13.1)

claimer 17.17.4

clairaudience 34.24.2

clairaudient 22.26.2(.3)

Claire 6

clairvoyance 34.24.10(.4)

clairvoyant 22.26.15(.3)

clairvoyantly 1.31.22(.20.1)

clam 27.6

clamant 22.26.15(.13.1)

clamantly 1.31.22(.20.3)

clambake 24.3.3

clamber 17.11.17(.4)

clammily 1.31.17(.13)

clamminess 34.18.16(.2.5)

clammy 1.15.6

clamorous 34.18.27(.18)

clamorously 1.31.33(.12.5)

clamorousness 34.18.16(.31.5)

clamour 17.17.6

clamp 20.16.3

clampdown 28.8.2(.3)

clamshell 40.5.13

clan 28.7

Clancarty 1.10.8

Clancey 1.22.23(.4)

Clancy 1.22.23(.4)

clandestine 28.2.11(.14), 28.14.5

clandestinely 1.31.27(.11)

clandestinity 1.10.16(.13)

clang 29.4

clanger 17.19.2

clangorously 1.31.33(.12.5)

clangour 17.16.17(.2)

clangourous 34.18.27(.17)

clangourously 1.31.33(.12.5)

clank 24.19.3

clankingly 1.31.28(.1.6)

clannish 36.2.16(.5)

clannishly 1.31.35(.7.2)

clannishness 34.18.16(.33.5)

clanship 20.2.7(.19)

clansman 28.17.16(.30)

clanswoman 28.17.16(.14)

clanswomen 28.2.17(.1)

clap 20.5

clapboard 23.12.2(.7)

Clapham 27.15.7

clapper 17.10.5

clapperboard 23.12.2(.5)

Clapton 28.17.11(.18)

claptrap 20.5.6

claque 24.6

claqueur 17.14.5

Clara 17.32.5

Clarabella 17.34.5(.2)

Clarabelle 40.5.2

Clare 6

Claremont 22.26.9, 22.26.15(.13.1)

clarence 34.24.10(.16)

Clarenceux 16.15, 16.24.14, 19.20.16

Clarendon 28.17.12(.23)

claret 22.19.24(.4)

Clarges 35.18.21

Claridge's 35.18.21

clarification 28.17.25(.3.5)

clarificatory 1.29.11(.8.2)

clarifier 17.6.9(.4)

clarify 14.14.4(.14)

Clarinda 17.13.20(.1)

clarinet 22.5.9

clarinettist 22.29.2(.13)

clarion 28.3.20(.5)

Clarissa 17.24.2

clarity 1.10.16(.21.1)

Clarke 24.8

clarkia 3.6.6

Clarkson 28.17.23(.21)

Clarrie 1.29.5

clart 22.10

clarty 1.10.8

clary 1.29.4

clash 36.6

clasher 17.26.6

clasp 20.17

clasper 17.10.18

class 34.9

classable 40.20.16(.21.1)

classic 24.2.20(.5)

classical 40.23.12(.15)

classicism 27.15.21(.2.15)

classicalist 22.29.2(.31.2)

classicality 1.10.16(.32.5)

classically 1.31.17(.11), 1.31.24(.9.10)

classicalness 34.18.16(.37.5)

classicism 27.15.21(.2.12)

classicist 22.29.2(.22)

classicize 35.15.16(.4)

classicus 34.18.13(.10)

classifiable 40.20.16(.5)

classifiably 1.31.21(.2)

classification 28.17.25(.3.5)

classificatory 1.29.11(.8.2)
classifieds 35.23.10
classifier 17.6.9(.4)
classify 14.14.4(.9)
classily 1.31.17(.20)
classiness 34.18.16(.2.7)
classism 27.15.21(.2.12)
classist 22.29.2(.22)
classless 34.18.29(.33)
classlessness 34.18.16(.31.6)
classmate 22.4.13(.14)
classroom 27.14.6(.17)
classy 1.22.6, 1.22.8
clastic 24.2.10(.15.4)
clathrate 22.4.22(.13)
clatter 17.12.6
Claud 23.12
Claude 23.12
Claudette 22.5.4
Claudia 3.5.6
Claudian 28.3.4(.7)
claudication 28.17.25(.3.5)
Claudine 28.1.10
Claudius 34.3.4
clausal 40.32.9
clausally 1.31.17(.21)
clause 35.12
Clausewitz 34.22.2
claustral 40.16.13(.16)
claustrophobe 21.16.1
claustrophobia 3.3.9
claustrophobic 24.2.9(.7)
claustrophobically 1.31.24(.9.2)
clavate 22.4.16
clave 31.3
Claverhouse 34.8.6(.7)
Clavering 29.1.30(.8)
Claverton 28.17.11(.15)
clavicembalo 19.29.12
clavichord 23.12.4
clavicle 40.23.12(.13)
clavicular 17.34.16(.21.2)
clavier 3.11, 3.11.4
claviform 27.10.5(.2)
claw 12
clawback 24.6.6(.6)
clawer 17.4
clawless 34.18.29(.11)
clay 4
clayey 1(.2)
clayiness 34.18.16(.2.1)
clayish 36.2.2
clay-like 24.13.7(.3)
claymore 12.9.3
claypan 28.7.4
Clayton 28.17.11(.3)

clean 28.1
cleanable 40.20.16(.16.1)
cleaner 17.18.1
cleanish 36.2.16(.1)
cleanlily 1.31.17(.29)
cleanliness 34.18.16(.2.10)
cleanly 1.31.27(.1)
cleanse 35.26.5
cleanser 17.25.18
cleanskin 28.2.13(.14)
Cleanthes 35.1.15
clean-up 20.9.9
clear 3
clearable 40.20.16(.27.1)
clearance 34.24.10(.16)
Clearasil® 40.2.14
clearcole 40.18.7
clearer 17.32.2
clearing 29.1.30(.2)
clearing house 34.8.6(.17)
clearly 1.31.3
clearness 34.18.16(.3)
clear-out 22.9.18
clear-sighted 23.18.9(.10)
clear-sightedly 1.31.23(.14.3)
clear-sightedness 34.18.16(.21.1)
clearstory 1.29.8
clear-up 20.9.15
clearway 4.25.3
Cleary 1.29.2
cleat 22.1
cleavable 40.20.16(.19)
cleavage 39.2.17
cleave 31.1
cleaver 17.21.1
cleavers 35.18.15
Cleckheaton 28.17.11(.1)
Cleddau 14.17
Cledwyn 28.2.28
cleek 24.1
Cleese 35.1
Cleethorpes 34.21.7
clef 30.4
cleft 22.27.2
cleg 26.4
Clegg 26.4
Cleisthenes 35.1.12(.3)
cleistogamic 24.2.14(.4)
cleistogamically 1.31.24(.9.8)
cleistogamy 1.15.13(.4)
Cleland 23.24.16(.16.1)
Clem 27.5
clematis 34.2.8
Clemence 34.24.10(.14)
clemency 1.22.23(.10.3)
Clemens 35.26.13(.10)

clement 22.26.15(.13.1)
Clementina 17.18.1(.3)
clementine 28.14.5
clemently 1.31.22(.20.3)
Clements 34.22.18, 34.24.10(.14)
Clemmie 1.15.4
clenbuterol 40.9.19
clench 38.18.2
Cleo 15.1
Cleobury 1.29.11(.7.1)
Cleopatra 17.32.19(.4)
clepsydra 17.32.20
clerestory 1.29.8, 1.29.11(.8.12)
clergy 1.26.11
clergyman 28.17.16(.2)
cleric 24.2.26(.4)
clerical 40.23.12(.18)
clericalism 27.15.21(.2.15)
clericalist 22.29.2(.31.2)
clericality 1.10.16(.32.5)
clerically 1.31.24(.9.12)
clerihew 16.24.16
clerisy 1.22.16(.13)
clerk 24.8
clerkdom 27.15.10(.13)
Clerkenwell 40.5.17(.12)
clerkess 34.5, 34.18.13(.4)
clerkish 36.2.13
clerkly 1.31.24(.6)
clerkship 20.2.7(.16)
Clermont 22.26.9
Clery 1.29.2
Clevedon 28.17.12(.25)
Cleveland 23.24.16(.16.4)
clever 17.21.4
cleverly 1.31.17(.17)
cleverness 34.18.16(.15.3)
clevis 34.2.15
clew 16
Clewes 35.17
Cley 4, 14
clianthus 34.18.19
Clibborn 28.17.10
Cliburn 28.18.3
cliché 4.20
click 24.2
click-clack 24.6.23
clicker 17.14.2
clickety-click 24.2.27(.16)
client 22.26.15(.4)
clientele 40.5.3
clientship 20.2.8
cliff 30.2
Cliffe 30.2
cliffhanger 17.19.2
cliffhanging 29.1.18
cliffiness 34.18.16(.2.6)
cliff-like 24.13.7(.19)

Clifford 23.18.16(.2)
cliffside 23.15.11(.14)
clifftop 20.7.4
cliffy 1.18.2
Clifton 28.17.11(.24)
Cliftonville 40.2.12
climacteric 24.2.26(.4)
climacterical 40.23.12(.18)
climactic 24.2.10(.13)
climactical 40.23.12(.7.3)
climactically 1.31.24(.9.5)
climate 22.19.14
climatic 24.2.10(.4.2)
climatical 40.23.12(.7.1)
climatically 1.31.24(.9.4)
climatologic 24.2.24(.4)
climatological 40.23.12(.17.2)
climatologically 1.31.24(.9.11)
climatologist 22.29.2(.26.3)
climatology 1.26.10(.11.2)
climax 34.23.5(.6)
climb 27.12
climbable 40.20.16(.15)
climbdown 28.8.2(.7)
climber 17.17.11
clime 27.12
clinal 40.26.11
clinch 38.18.1
clincher 17.28.22
cline 28.14
cling 29.1
clinger 17.19.1
cling film 27.18
clingfoil 40.11.7
clinginess 34.18.16(.2.5)
clingingly 1.31.17(.15)
clingstone 28.19.4(.9)
clingy 1.17
clinic 24.2.15(.2)
clinical 40.23.12(.11)
clinically 1.31.24(.9.8)
clinician 28.17.25(.2.4)
clink 24.19.1
clinker 17.14.21(.1)
clinkstone 28.19.4(.9)
clinometer 17.12.16(.9.2)
clinometric 24.2.26(.14.2)
clinometry 1.29.15(.8)
clint 22.26.1
Clinton 28.17.11(.22)
Clio 19.1, 19.5
cliometric 24.2.26(.14.2)
clip 20.2
clipboard 23.12.2(.7)
clip-clop 20.7.13
clippable 40.20.16(.9)

clipper **17.10.2**
clippie **1.8.2**
clipping **29.1.10(.2)**
Clipstone **28.19.4(.9)**
clique **24.1**
cliquey **1.12.1**
cliqueyness **34.18.16(.2.4)**
cliquish **36.2.13**
cliquishness
  34.18.16(.33.4)
cliquism **27.15.21(.2.6)**
Clissold **23.31.13(.8)**
Clitheroe **19.27.11**
clitic **24.2.10(.2.1)**
cliticization
  28.17.25(.3.11)
cliticize **35.15.16(.4)**
clitoral **40.16.13(.12.1)**
clitoridectomy
  1.15.13(.1)
clitoris **34.2.21**
Clive **31.9**
Cliveden **28.17.12(.25)**
clivers **35.18.15**
cloaca **17.14.3**
cloacae **2.14**
cloacal **40.23.3**
cloak **24.18**
cloakroom **27.14.6(.10)**
clobber **17.11.8**
cloche **36.9**
clock **24.9**
clockmaker **17.14.3(.3)**
clockmaking **29.1.14(.3)**
clockwise **35.15.19**
clockwork **24.17.6(.10)**
clod **23.10**
Clodagh **17.13.17**
cloddish **36.2.12**
cloddishly **1.31.35(.7.1)**
cloddishness
  34.18.16(.33.3)
cloddy **1.11.10**
clodhopper **17.10.8**
clodhopping **29.1.10(.6)**
clodpoll **40.9.5**
clog **26.7**
cloggily **1.31.17(.12)**
clogginess **34.18.16(.2.4)**
cloggy **1.14.6**
Clogher **17.15, 17.30**
cloisonné **4.14**
cloister **17.12.24(.9)**
cloistral **40.16.13(.16)**
clomiphene **28.1.15**
clomp **20.16.4**
clonal **40.26.15**
clone **28.19**
Clones **34.18.16(.17)**
clonic **24.2.15(.6.1)**

clonk **24.19.5**
Clonmel **40.5.7**
clonus **34.18.16(.17)**
clop **20.7**
cloqué **4.11**
closable **40.20.16(.22)**
close **34.20, 35.20**
close-down **28.8.2(.10)**
closely **1.31.33(.13)**
closeness **34.18.16(.31.7)**
closeout **22.9.14**
closet **22.2.17**
closish **36.2.21**
clostridia **3.5.2**
clostridium **27.3.4(.2)**
closure **17.27.9**
clot **22.11**
clotbur **18.2**
cloth **32.9**
clothbound **23.24.7(.2)**
clothe **33.10**
clothes **35.29**
clothes basket **22.2.9(.10)**
clothes brush **36.12**
clothes horse **34.12.7**
clothes line **28.14.19(.22)**
clothes peg **26.4**
clothes pin **28.2.9**
clothier **3.13**
clothing **29.1.22**
Clotho **19.18**
cloths **34.26, 35.29**
cloture **17.28.17**
clou **16**
cloud **23.8**
cloudbank **24.19.3(.1)**
cloudberry **1.29.11(.7.2)**
cloudburst **22.29.16**
Cloudesley **1.31.34**
cloudily **1.31.17(.10)**
cloudiness **34.18.16(.2.3)**
cloudland **23.24.6(.13)**
cloudless **34.18.29(.23)**
cloudlessly **1.31.33(.12.6)**
cloudlessness
  34.18.16(.31.6)
cloudlet **22.19.26(.18)**
cloudscape **20.3**
cloudy **1.11.8**
Clough **25.6**
clough **30.11**
clout **22.9**
Clouzot **19.21**
clove **31.12**
Clovelly **1.31.5**
cloven **28.17.20(.11)**
clover **17.21.14**
cloverleaf **30.1.9**
cloverleaves **35.28.1**
Clovis **34.2.15**

Clowes **35.8, 35.17, 35.20**
clown **28.8**
clownery **1.29.11(.13.1)**
clownish **36.2.16(.6)**
clownishly **1.31.35(.7.2)**
clownishness
  34.18.16(.33.5)
cloy **13**
cloyingly **1.31.28(.1.1)**
clozapine **28.1.7**
cloze **35.20**
club **21.11**
clubbability **1.10.16(.22.1)**
clubbable **40.20.16(.10)**
clubbableness
  34.18.16(.37.4)
clubbably **1.31.21(.3)**
clubber **17.11.10**
clubby **1.9.9**
club feet **22.1.6**
club foot **22.17**
club-footed **23.18.9(.11)**
clubhouse **34.8.6(.10)**
clubland **23.24.6(.13)**
clubman **28.17.16(.20)**
clubmoss **34.10.12**
clubroom **27.14.6(.7)**
clubroot **22.18.9**
clubwoman **28.17.16(.14)**
clubwomen **28.2.17(.1)**
cluck **24.12**
cluckily **1.31.17(.11)**
cluckiness **34.18.16(.2.4)**
clucky **1.12.9**
cludge **39.11, 39.13**
clue **16**
clueless **34.18.29(.16)**
cluelessly **1.31.33(.12.6)**
cluelessness
  34.18.16(.31.6)
Cluj **37.7**
clump **20.16.5**
clumpy **1.8.14**
clumsily **1.31.17(.21)**
clumsiness **34.18.16(.2.7)**
clumsy **1.23.19**
Clun **28.13**
Clunes **35.26.12**
clung **29.8**
Cluniac **24.6.1**
Clunie **1.16.14**
Clunies **35.2.8**
clunk **24.19.7**
Cluny **1.16.14**
clupeid **23.2.2**
clupeoid **23.13.2**
cluster **17.12.24(.10)**
clutch **38.11**
clutter **17.12.12**
Clutterbuck **24.12.1**

Clutton **28.17.11(.11)**
Clwyd **23.2.4**
Clwydian **28.3.4(.2)**
Clydach **24.16.5, 25.10**
Clyde **23.15**
Clydebank **24.19.3(.1)**
Clydella **17.34.5(.4)**
Clydesdale **40.4.3**
Clyne **28.14**
clypeal **40.3.1**
clypeate **22.3.1**
clypei **14.2**
clypeus **34.3.1**
Clyro **19.27.9**
clyster **17.12.24(.2)**
Clytemnestra
  17.32.19(.11)
Cnut **22.18.10**
CO **19**
Co. **19**
co-accused **23.28.3**
coacervate **22.4.16**
coacervation
  28.17.25(.3.9)
coach **38.17**
coachbuilder
  17.13.23(.2)
coach house **34.8.6(.23)**
coachload **23.20.13**
coachman **28.17.16(.33)**
coachwood **23.16.6(.20)**
coachwork **24.17.6(.17)**
coaction **28.17.25(.15.3)**
coactive **31.2.1(.13.3)**
coadjacent **22.26.15(.17.1)**
coadjutant **22.26.15(.9)**
coadjutor **17.12.16(.16)**
coadministrator
  17.12.4(.15)
coagula **17.34.16(.21.3)**
coagulable **40.20.16(.29)**
coagulant **22.26.15(.25)**
coagulate **22.4.23(.7.3)**
coagulation
  28.17.25(.3.14)
coagulative **31.2.1(.9.4)**
coagulator **17.12.4(.16)**
coagulatory **1.29.11(.8.10)**
coagulum **27.15.28(.11)**
Coahuila **17.34.1**
coal **40.18**
Coalbrookdale **40.4.3**
coal bunker **17.14.21(.5)**
coaler **17.34.18**
coalesce **34.5.16**
coalescence **34.24.10(.18)**
coalescent **22.26.15(.17.2)**
coalface **34.4.9**
coalfield **23.31.1(.2)**
coalfish **36.2.18(.21)**

coffin 28.2.19
coffle 40.27.8
cog 26.7
Cogan 28.17.15(.14)
cogency 1.22.23(.10.4)
cogent 22.26.15(.21)
cogently 1.31.22(.20.4)
Coggeshall 40.31.18, 40.33.9
Coghill 40.2.8, 40.2.18
cogitable 40.20.16(.11.3)
cogitate 22.4.9(.5)
cogitation 28.17.25(.3.3)
cogitative 31.2.1(.9.1)
cogitator 17.12.4(.5)
cogito 19.10.12
cogito ergo sum 27.13
cognac 24.6.22
cognate 22.4.14(.13)
cognately 1.31.22(.4)
cognateness 34.18.16(.20.1)
cognatic 24.2.10(.4.3)
cognation 28.17.25(.3.8)
cognisably 1.31.21(.7.2)
cognisance 34.24.10(.19)
cognition 28.17.25(.2.4)
cognitional 40.26.13(.14.1)
cognitive 31.2.1(.9.2)
cognitively 1.31.30(.2)
cognitivism 27.15.21(.2.11)
cognitivist 22.29.2(.20)
cognizable 40.20.16(.22)
cognizably 1.31.21(.7.2)
cognizance 34.24.10(.19)
cognizant 22.26.15(.18)
cognize 35.15.12
cognomen 28.5.7(.12), 28.17.16(.18)
cognominal 40.26.13(.8)
cognoscenti 1.10.23(.3), 2.12.14
cogwheel 40.1.14
cohabit 22.2.6
cohabitant 22.26.15(.9)
cohabitation 28.17.25(.3.3)
cohabitee 2.11
cohabiter 17.12.16(.4)
Cohan 28.7.18
Cohen 28.2.8
cohere 3.20
coherence 34.24.10(.16)
coherency 1.22.23(.10.4)
coherent 22.26.15(.23.1)
coherently 1.31.22(.20.5)
cohesion 28.17.26(.1)
cohesive 31.2.4(.1)
cohesively 1.31.30(.7.4)

cohesiveness 34.18.16(.28.2)
Cohn 28.19
coho 19.26
cohort 22.13.12
cohosh 36.9.4
COHSE 1.23.15
cohune 28.16.12
coif 30.7, 30.8, 30.10
coiffeur 18.9
coiffeurs 35.19
coiffeuse 35.19
coiffeuses 35.19
coiffure 17.7.12(.9)
coign 28.12
coil 40.11
Coimbra 17.32.18
coin 28.12
coinage 39.2.15
coincide 23.15.11
coincidence 34.24.10(.11)
coincident 22.26.15(.10)
coincidental 40.21.17(.2)
coincidentally 1.31.17(.9.3)
coincidently 1.31.22(.20.1)
coiner 17.18.11
co-inheritor 17.12.16(.18)
coin-op 20.7.7
Cointreau 19.27.15
coir 17.5
coit 22.14
coital 40.21.12
coition 28.17.25(.2.1)
coitus 34.18.11(.10)
coitus interruptus 34.18.11(.12)
cojones 35.4.8
Coke® 24.14, 24.18
coke 24.18
Coker 17.14.17
col 40.9
cola 17.34.18
colander 17.13.20(.13)
Colbert 6.3, 22.20.2
Colby 1.9.24
colcannon 28.17.17(.5)
Colchester 17.12.24(.14)
colchicine 28.1.18(.6)
colchicum 27.15.11(.9)
Colchis 34.2.10
cold 23.31.13
cold-blooded 23.18.10(.10)
cold-bloodedly 1.31.23(.14.4)
cold-bloodedness 34.18.16(.21.1)
coldish 36.2.12
Colditz 34.22.2

coldly 1.31.23(.18)
coldness 34.18.16(.21.1)
cold store 12.5.9
Coldstream 27.1.12
Cole 40.18
Colebrook 24.14.10
Coleclough 30.11.11
colectomy 1.15.13(.1)
Coleford 23.18.16(.22)
Coleman 28.17.16(.35)
colemice 34.15.5
colemouse 34.8.4
Colenso 19.20.16, 19.21
Coleoptera 17.32.14(.6)
coleopteran 28.17.31(.11)
coleopterist 22.29.2(.29.3)
coleopterous 34.18.27(.14)
coleoptile 40.13.3(.7)
Coleraine 28.4.18
Coleridge 39.2.22(.9)
Coles 35.30.13
coleseed 23.1.7
coleslaw 12.23.10
Colet 22.19.26(.8)
Colette 22.5.21
coleus 34.3.16
coley 1.31.19
Colgate® 22.4.12(.13)
colic 24.2.27(.9)
colicky 1.12.13
coliform 27.10.5(.2)
Colima 17.17.1
Colin 28.2.31(.7)
coliseum 27.15.1
colitis 34.18.11(.8)
Coll 40.9
collaborate 22.4.22(.6)
collaboration 28.17.25(.3.13)
collaborationist 22.29.2(.18.2)
collaborative 31.2.1(.9.4)
collaboratively 1.31.30(.7.1)
collaborator 17.12.4(.15)
collage 37.4.11
collagen 28.17.28(.9)
collagist 22.29.2(.25)
collapsar 10.15
collapse 34.21.5
collapsibility 1.10.16(.22.2)
collapsible 40.20.16(.21.3)
collar 17.34.9
collarbone 28.19.3
collard 23.18.29
collarette 22.5.19
collarless 34.18.29(.17.6)
collate 22.4.23

collateral 40.16.13(.12.1)
collaterality 1.10.16(.32.13)
collateralize 35.15.21(.4.7)
collaterally 1.31.17(.27.1)
collation 28.17.25(.3.14)
collator 17.12.4(.16)
colleague 26.1
collect 22.23.4(.11)
collectability 1.10.16(.22.1)
collectable 40.20.16(.11.5)
collectanea 3.9.3(.2)
collectedly 1.31.23(.14.3)
collecteness 34.18.16(.21.1)
collection 28.17.25(.15.2)
collective 31.2.1(.13.2)
collectively 1.31.30(.7.2)
collectiveness 34.18.16(.28.1)
collectivism 27.15.21(.2.11)
collectivist 22.29.2(.20)
collectivistic 24.2.10(.15.2)
collectivity 1.10.16(.15)
collectivization 28.17.25(.3.12)
collectivize 35.15.14
collector 17.12.21(.2)
colleen 28.1.27
college 39.2.23
colleger 17.29.13
collegia 3.7, 3.19.1
collegial 40.3.12
collegiality 1.10.16(.32.1)
collegian 28.3.18
collegiate 22.3.11
collegiately 1.31.22(.3)
collegium 27.3.6, 27.3.15
collenchyma 17.17.14(.4)
collet 22.19.26(.8)
Colley 1.31.10
collide 23.15.16
collider 17.13.12
collie 1.31.10
collier 3.24.7
colliery 1.29.11(.26)
colligate 22.4.12(.5)
colligation 28.17.25(.3.6)
colligative 31.2.1(.9.1)
collimate 22.4.13(.6)
collimation 28.17.25(.3.7)
collimator 17.12.4(.9)
collinear 3.9.2
collinearity 1.10.16(.21.1)
collinearly 1.31.3(.7)
Collinge 39.17.1
Collingham 27.15.15

Collingwood 23.16.6(.15)
Collins 35.26.13(.20)
Collinson 28.17.23(.24)
Collis 34.2.22(.6)
collision 28.17.26(.2)
collisional 40.26.13(.14.8)
collocate 22.4.11(.6),
   22.19.12(.10)
collocation 28.17.25(.3.5)
collocutor 17.12.15(.8),
   17.12.16(.19)
collodion 28.3.4(.10)
collodium 27.3.4(.8)
collogue 26.15
colloid 23.13.20
colloidal 40.22.9
collop 20.13.7
colloquia 3.21
colloquial 40.3.13
colloquialism
   27.15.21(.2.15)
colloquially 1.31.3(.10)
colloquium 27.3.16
colloquy 1.28
collotype 20.10.2
collude 23.17.5
colluder 17.13.14
collusion 28.17.26(.4)
collusive 31.2.4(.8)
collusively 1.31.30(.7.4)
collusiveness
   34.18.16(.28.2)
colluvia 3.11.6
colluvium 27.3.9
collyria 3.22.1
collyrium 27.3.17(.1)
collywobbles 35.30.15
Colman 28.17.16(.35)
Colnbrook 24.14.10
Colne 28.19, 28.20
colobus 34.18.10
colocynth 32.21
Cologne 28.19.19
Colombia 3.3.11
Colombian 28.3.2
Colombo 19.9.14
colon 28.10.26,
   28.17.33(.15)
Colón 28.10.26
colonel 40.26.14
colonelcy 1.22.26
colonial 40.3.7(.9)
colonialism
   27.15.21(.2.15)
colonialist 22.29.2(.31.1)
colonially 1.31.3(.7)
colonic 24.2.15(.6.4)
colonist 22.29.2(.18.3)
colonization
   28.17.25(.3.11)
colonize 35.15.12(.5)

colonizer 17.25.12(.6)
colonnade 23.4.8
colonoscopy 1.8.11(.5)
Colonsay 4.18.12, 4.19
colony 1.16.15(.20)
colophon 28.10.15,
   28.17.19
colophony 1.16.15(.12)
coloquintida 17.13.15
colorably 1.31.21(.8)
Coloradan 28.17.12(.8)
Colorado 19.11.7
coloration 28.17.25(.3.13)
coloratura 17.32.14(.3)
colorectal 40.21.16
colorfully 1.31.17(.16.1)
colorific 24.2.16(.1)
colorimeter 17.12.16(.9.1)
colorimetric
   24.2.26(.14.2)
colorimetry 1.29.15(.8)
colorize 35.15.20(.2)
colorlessly 1.31.33(.12.6)
Coloroll® 40.18.14
colossal 40.31.8
colossally 1.31.17(.20)
colossi 14.18
Colossians 35.26.3,
   35.26.13(.15)
colossus 34.18.20
colostomy 1.15.13(.1)
colostrum 27.15.26(.10)
colotomy 1.15.13(.1)
colour 17.34.12
colourable 40.20.16(.27.5)
colourably 1.31.21(.8)
colourant 22.26.15(.23.3)
colouration
   28.17.25(.3.13)
colour-blind 23.24.13
Coloured 23.18.29
colour fast 22.29.6(.9)
colour fastness
   34.18.16(.20.4)
colourful 40.27.14
colourfully 1.31.17(.16.1)
colourfulness
   34.18.16(.37.2)
colourist 22.29.2(.29.4)
colourless 34.18.29(.17.6)
colourlessly 1.31.33(.12.6)
colour wash 36.9.5
colourway 4.25.9
coloury 1.29.11(.27)
colpitis 34.18.11(.8)
colporteur 17.12.10(.1)
colposcope 20.15.4(.1)
colposcopy 1.8.11(.5)
colpotomy 1.15.13(.1)
Colquhoun 28.16.12
colt 22.32.12

colter 17.12.26(.7)
colthood 23.16.5(.6)
coltish 36.2.11
coltishly 1.31.35(.7.1)
coltishness
   34.18.16(.33.3)
Coltrane 28.4.18
coltsfoot 22.17
colubrine 28.14.18
Colum 27.15.28(.7)
Columba 17.11.17(.6)
columbaria 3.22.4
columbarium 27.3.17(.3)
Columbia 3.3.11
Columbian 28.3.2
columbine 28.14.4
columbite 22.16.8
columbium 27.3.2
Columbus 34.18.10
column 27.15.28(.7)
columnar 17.18.25
columnated 23.18.9(.3)
columnist 22.29.2(.18.3)
colure 17.7.12(.14)
Colville 40.2.12
Colvin 28.2.20
Colwyn 28.2.28
Colyer 17.33.13
Colyton 28.17.11(.15)
colza 17.25.19
coma 17.17.16
Comanche 1.24.15
comatose 34.20.4, 35.20.3
comatosely 1.31.33(.13),
   1.31.34
comb 27.17
combat 22.7.6
combatant 22.26.15(.9)
combative 31.2.1(.9.1)
combatively 1.31.30(.7.1)
combativeness
   34.18.16(.28.1)
combe 27.14
comber 17.17.16
combi 1.9.18
combinable
   40.20.16(.16.2)
combination
   28.17.25(.3.8)
combinational
   40.26.13(.14.2)
combinative 31.2.1(.9.2)
combinatorial 40.3.14(.5)
combinatory
   1.29.11(.8.7)
combine 28.14.4
combings 35.27
combo 19.9.14
combust 22.29.12
combustibility
   1.10.16(.22.2)

combustible
   40.20.16(.11.7)
combustibly 1.31.21(.4.3)
combustion 28.17.27
combustive 31.2.1(.15)
come 27.11
come-all-ye 2.31
come-at-able
   40.20.16(.11.1)
comeback 24.6.6(.16)
Comecon 28.10.11
comedian 28.3.4(.1)
comedic 24.2.11(.1)
comedically 1.31.24(.9.7)
comedienne 28.5
comedist 22.29.2(.14)
comedo 19.11.1, 19.11.11
comedown 28.8.2(.7)
comedy 1.11.17
comeliness
   34.18.16(.2.10)
comely 1.31.26(.9)
Comenius 34.3.6(.1)
comer 17.17.10
comestible 40.20.16(.11.7)
comet 22.2.11
cometary 1.29.11(.8.7)
comeuppance
   34.24.10(.8)
comfily 1.31.17(.16.2)
comfiness 34.18.16(.2.6)
comfit 22.2.13
comfort 22.19.16
comfortable
   40.20.16(.11.3)
comfortableness
   34.18.16(.37.4)
comfortably 1.31.21(.4.2)
comforter 17.12.16(.11)
comfortingly
   1.31.28(.1.4)
comfortless
   34.18.29(.22)
comfrey 1.29.21
comfy 1.18.12
comic 24.2.14(.6)
comical 40.23.12(.10)
comicality 1.10.16(.32.5)
comically 1.31.24(.9.8)
Cominform 27.10.5(.5)
coming 29.1.16
Comino 19.15.1
Comintern 28.18.4
comity 1.10.16(.12)
comma 17.17.8
command 23.24.6(.8),
   23.24.8
commandant 22.26.6,
   22.26.8, 22.26.15(.10)
commandeer 3.5
commander 17.13.20(.4)

commandership
20.2.7(.9)
commandingly
1.31.28(.1.5)
commandment
22.26.15(.13.3)
commando **19.11.14**
comme ci, comme ça **10**
commedia dell'arte
4.9.3
comme il faut **19**
commemorate
22.4.22(.6)
commemoration
28.17.25(.3.13)
commemorative
31.2.1(.9.4)
commemoratively
1.31.30(.7.1)
commemorator
17.12.4(.15)
commence **34.24.3**
commencement
22.26.15(.13.5)
commend **23.24.5(.7)**
commendable
40.20.16(.12)
commendably
1.31.21(.4.4)
commendation
28.17.25(.3.4)
commendatory
1.29.11(.8.2)
commensal **40.31.21**
commensalism
27.15.21(.2.15)
commensality
1.10.16(.32.11)
commensally
1.31.17(.20)
commensurability
1.10.16(.22.2)
commensurable
40.20.16(.27.5)
commensurableness
34.18.16(.37.4)
commensurably
1.31.21(.8)
commensurate
22.19.24(.9)
commensurately
1.31.22(.15)
commensurateness
34.18.16(.20.3)
comment **22.26.4(.8)**
commentary
1.29.11(.8.12)
commentate **22.4.9(.8)**
commentator **17.12.4(.5)**
commenter **17.12.22(.3)**
commerce **34.19.4**
commercial **40.33.10**

commercialism
27.15.21(.2.15)
commerciality
1.10.16(.32.1)
commercialization
28.17.25(.3.12)
commercialize
35.15.21(.4.6)
commercially
1.31.17(.22)
commère **6.8**
Commie **1.15.8**
commination
28.17.25(.3.8)
comminatory
1.29.11(.8.7)
commingle **40.24.14(.1)**
comminute **22.18.10**
comminution
28.17.25(.11)
commis **1.15.8, 34.2.12**
commiserate **22.4.22(.6)**
commiseration
28.17.25(.3.13)
commiserative
31.2.1(.3)
commiserator
17.12.4(.15)
commissar **10.15**
commissarial **40.3.14(.4)**
commissariat **22.3.12**
commissary **1.29.11(.18)**
commissaryship
20.2.7(.2)
commission
28.17.25(.2.4)
commissionaire **6.9**
commissional
40.26.13(.14.1)
commissionary
1.29.11(.13.2)
commissioned
23.24.16(.12)
commissioner
17.18.16(.16)
commissural
40.16.13(.11)
commissure **17.7.10,
17.7.12(.11)**
commit **22.2.11**
commitment
22.26.15(.13.3)
committable
40.20.16(.11.1)
committal **40.21.2**
committee **2.12.2**
committeeman
28.7.10(.2)
committeemen
28.5.7(.2)
committeewoman
28.17.16(.14)

committeewomen
28.2.17(.1)
committer **17.12.2**
commix **34.23.2(.5)**
commixture **17.28.24**
commo **19.14.8**
commode **23.20.8**
commodification
28.17.25(.3.5)
commodify **14.14.4(.5)**
commodious **34.3.4**
commodiously
1.31.33(.1.1)
commodiousness
34.18.16(.31.1)
commodity **1.10.16(.9)**
commodore **12.6.6**
common **28.17.16(.10)**
commonable
40.20.16(.16.3)
commonage **39.2.15**
commonality
1.10.16(.32.8)
commonalty **1.10.28**
commoner **17.18.16(.8)**
commonhold
23.31.13(.9)
commonholder
17.13.23(.8)
commonly **1.31.27(.14)**
commonness
34.18.16(.25)
commonplace **34.4.14**
commonplaceness
34.18.16(.31.2)
common room
27.14.6(.13)
commons **35.26.13(.10)**
common sense **34.24.3**
commonsensical
40.23.12(.15)
commonwealth **32.24**
commotion **28.17.25(.13)**
commotional
40.26.13(.14.5)
comms **35.25.6**
communal **40.26.12,
40.26.13(.14.8)**
communalism
27.15.21(.2.15)
communalist
22.29.2(.31.3)
communalistic
24.2.10(.15.3)
communalistically
1.31.24(.9.6)
communality
1.10.16(.32.8)
communalization
28.17.25(.3.12)
communalize
35.15.21(.4.5)

communally
1.31.17(.14.1)
communard **23.9.12**
commune **28.16.14**
communicability
1.10.16(.22.3)
communicable
40.20.16(.13)
communicably
1.31.21(.5)
communicant
22.26.15(.11)
communicate **22.4.11(.6)**
communication
28.17.25(.3.5)
communicational
40.26.13(.14.2)
communicative
31.2.1(.9.1)
communicatively
1.31.30(.7.1)
communicativeness
34.18.16(.28.1)
communicator
17.12.4(.7)
communicatory
1.29.11(.8.2)
communion **28.3.8(.9)**
communiqué **4.11**
communism
27.15.21(.2.9)
communist **22.29.2(.18.3)**
communistic
24.2.10(.15.2)
communistically
1.31.24(.9.6)
communitarian
28.3.20(.4)
community **1.10.16(.13)**
communization
28.17.25(.3.11)
communize **35.15.12(.5)**
commutability
1.10.16(.22.2)
commutable
40.20.16(.11.2)
commutate **22.4.9(.5)**
commutation
28.17.25(.3.3)
commutative **31.2.1(.3)**
commutator **17.12.4(.5)**
commute **22.18.10**
commuter **17.12.15(.8)**
Como **19.14.14**
Comorin **28.2.29(.5)**
Comoro **19.27.11**
comose **34.20.8**
comp **20.16.4**
compact **22.23.5(.2)**
compaction
28.17.25(.15.3)
compactly **1.31.22(.19)**

compactness 34.18.16(.20.4)
compactor 17.12.21(.3)
compadre 1.29.16
compages 35.1.21
compander 17.13.20(.4)
companion 28.17.32
companionable 40.20.16(.16.1)
companionableness 34.18.16(.37.4)
companionably 1.31.21(.6)
companionate 22.19.15(.9)
companionship 20.2.7(.19)
companionway 4.25.17
company 1.16.15(.5), 1.16.18
Compaq 24.6.5
comparability 1.10.16(.22.1)
comparable 40.20.16(.27.3)
comparableness 34.18.16(.37.4)
comparably 1.31.21(.8)
comparatist 22.29.2(.13)
comparative 31.2.1(.9.4)
comparatively 1.31.30(.7.1)
comparator 17.12.16(.18)
compare 6.2
comparison 28.17.23(.14)
compartment 22.26.15(.13.3)
compartmental 40.21.17(.2)
compartmentalization 28.17.25(.3.12)
compartmentalize 35.15.21(.4.3)
compartmentally 1.31.17(.9.3)
compartmentation 28.17.25(.3.3)
compass 34.18.9(.11)
compassable 40.20.16(.21.2)
compassion 28.17.25(.5)
compassionate 22.19.15(.9)
compassionately 1.31.22(.15)
compatibility 1.10.16(.22.2)
compatible 40.20.16(.11.1)
compatibly 1.31.21(.4.1)
compatriot 22.3.12
compatriotic 24.2.10(.6)

compeer 3.2.8
compel 40.5.1
compellable 40.20.16(.29)
compellingly 1.31.28(.1.18)
compendia 3.5.9
compendious 34.3.4
compendiously 1.31.33(.1.1)
compendiousness 34.18.16(.31.1)
compendium 27.3.4(.9)
compensate 22.4.18
compensation 28.17.25(.3.10)
compensational 40.26.13(.14.2)
compensative 31.2.1(.3)
compensator 17.12.4(.12)
compensatory 1.29.11(.8.2)
compère 6.2
compete 22.1.1
competence 34.24.10(.10)
competency 1.22.23(.10.2)
competent 22.26.15(.9)
competently 1.31.22(.20.2)
competition 28.17.25(.2.2)
competitive 31.2.1(.9.1)
competitively 1.31.30(.7.1)
competitiveness 34.18.16(.28.1)
competitor 17.12.16(.5)
compilation 28.17.25(.3.14)
compile 40.13.1
compiler 17.34.13
complacence 34.24.10(.18)
complacency 1.22.23(.10.4)
complacent 22.26.15(.17.1)
complain 28.4.19
complainant 22.26.15(.14)
complainer 17.18.3
complainingly 1.31.28(.1.7)
complaint 22.26.3
complaisance 34.24.10(.19)
complaisant 22.26.15(.18)
complaisantly 1.31.22(.20.4)
compleat 22.1.18
complected 23.18.9(.17)

complement 22.26.15(.13.2)
complemental 40.21.17(.2)
complementarily 1.31.17(.27.1)
complementariness 34.18.16(.2.9)
complementarity 1.10.16(.21.1)
complementary 1.29.11(.8.12)
complementation 28.17.25(.3.3)
complementizer 17.25.12(.2)
complete 22.1.18
completely 1.31.22(.1)
completeness 34.18.16(.20.1)
completion 28.17.25(.1)
completist 22.29.2(.13)
completive 31.2.1(.1)
complex 34.23.4(.12)
complexation 28.17.25(.3.10)
complexion 28.17.25(.15.2)
complexionless 34.18.29(.27)
complexity 1.10.16(.16.3)
complexly 1.31.33(.15)
compliance 34.24.10(.5)
compliancy 1.22.23(.10.1)
compliant 22.26.15(.4)
compliantly 1.31.22(.20.1)
complicacy 1.22.16(.6)
complicate 22.4.11(.6)
complicatedly 1.31.23(.14.3)
complicatedness 34.18.16(.21.1)
complication 28.17.25(.3.5)
complicit 22.2.16
complicity 1.10.16(.16.1)
compliment 22.26.4(.8), 22.26.15(.13.2)
complimentarily 1.31.17(.27.1)
complimentary 1.29.11(.8.12)
compline 28.17.33(.16)
comply 14.25.11
compo 19.8
component 22.26.15(.14)
componential 40.33.12(.3)
comport 22.13.1
comportment 22.26.15(.13.3)

compose 35.20.1
composedly 1.31.23(.14.7)
composer 17.25.15
composite 22.2.17, 22.16.19(.9), 22.16.20
compositely 1.31.22(.13)
compositeness 34.18.16(.20.2)
composition 28.17.25(.2.5)
compositional 40.26.13(.14.1)
compositionally 1.31.17(.14.3)
compositor 17.12.16(.15)
compos mentis 34.2.8
compossible 40.20.16(.21.2)
compost 22.29.9
composure 17.27.9
compote 22.11.2, 22.21.1
compound 23.24.7(.1)
compoundable 40.20.16(.12)
compounder 17.13.20(.5)
comprador 12.6
comprehend 23.24.5(.13)
comprehensibility 1.10.16(.22.3)
comprehensible 40.20.16(.21.3)
comprehensibleness 34.18.16(.37.4)
comprehensibly 1.31.21(.7.2)
comprehension 28.17.25(.16)
comprehensive 31.2.4(.13)
comprehensively 1.31.30(.7.4)
comprehensiveness 34.18.16(.28.2)
comprehensivization 28.17.25(.3.12)
comprehensivize 35.15.14
compress 34.5.14(.4)
compressibility 1.10.16(.22.2)
compressible 40.20.16(.21.1)
compression 28.17.25(.4)
compressive 31.2.4(.4)
compressor 17.24.5
comprisable 40.20.16(.22)
comprise 35.15.20(.3)
compromise 35.15.11
compromiser 17.25.12(.5)

compromisingly
1.31.28(.1.12)
compte rendu 16.8
comptes rendus 35.17.1
Comptometer
17.12.16(.9.2)
Compton 28.17.11(.18)
comptroller 17.34.18(.14)
compulsion 28.17.25(.17)
compulsive 31.2.4(.14)
compulsively
1.31.30(.7.4)
compulsiveness
34.18.16(.28.2)
compulsorily
1.31.17(.27.2)
compulsoriness
34.18.16(.2.9)
compulsory 1.29.11(.18)
compunction
28.17.25(.15.6)
compunctious
34.18.22(11)
compunctiously
1.31.33(.12.4)
compurgate 22.4.12(.6)
compurgation
28.17.25(.3.6)
compurgator 17.12.4(.8)
compurgatory
1.29.11(.8.6)
computability
1.10.16(.22.2)
computable
40.20.16(.11.2)
computably 1.31.21(.4.1)
computation
28.17.25(.3.3)
computational
40.26.13(.14.2)
computationally
1.31.17(.14.3)
compute 22.18.10
computer 17.12.15(.8)
computerese 35.1
computerization
28.17.25(.3.12)
computerize 35.15.20(.2)
comrade 23.4.15, 23.18.27
comradely 1.31.23(.3)
comradeship 20.2.7(.15)
Comrie 1.29.19
coms 35.25.6
Comsat® 22.7.15
Comstock 24.9.4
Comte 22.26.9, 22.26.10
Comtism 27.15.21(.2.4)
Comtist 22.29.2(.13)
con 28.10
conacre 17.14.3(.4)
Conakry 1.29.17
con amore 4.26.7

Conan 28.17.17(.12)
conation 28.17.25(.3.8)
conative 31.2.1(.9.2)
con brio 19.1
Concannon 28.17.17(.5)
concatenate 22.4.14(.9.1)
concatenation
28.17.25(.3.8)
concatenative
31.2.1(.9.2)
concave 31.3.2
concavely 1.31.30(.3)
concavity 1.10.16(.15)
conceal 40.1.10
concealed 23.31.1(.4)
concealer 17.34.1
concealment
22.26.15(.13.7)
concede 23.1.7
conceder 17.13.1
conceit 22.1.9
conceited 23.18.9(.1)
conceitedly 1.31.23(.14.3)
conceitedness
34.18.16(.21.1)
conceivability
1.10.16(.22.2)
conceivable 40.20.16(.19)
conceivably 1.31.21(.7.1)
conceive 31.1.4
concelebrant
22.26.15(.23.4)
concelebrate 22.4.22(.7)
concelebrating
29.1.12(.3)
concelebration
28.17.25(.3.13)
concentrate 22.4.22(.8)
concentratedly
1.31.23(.14.3)
concentration
28.17.25(.3.13)
concentrative 31.2.1(.3)
concentrator
17.12.4(.15)
concentre 17.12.22(.3)
concentric 24.2.26(.14.4)
concentrically
1.31.24(.9.12)
concentricity
1.10.16(.16.1)
Concepción 28.10.25
concept 22.22.3
conception 28.17.25(.14)
conceptional
40.26.13(.14.6)
conceptionally
1.31.17(.14.3)
conceptive 31.2.1(.12)
conceptual 40.16.12
conceptualism
27.15.21(.2.15)

conceptualist
22.29.2(.31.5)
conceptualization
28.17.25(.3.12)
conceptualize
35.15.21(.4.8)
conceptually 1.31.17(.24)
conceptus 34.18.11(.12)
concern 28.18.9
concernedly
1.31.23(.14.6)
concernedness
34.18.16(.21.1)
concerningly
1.31.28(.1.7)
concernment
22.26.15(.13.4)
concert 22.19.18, 22.20.10
concertante 1.10.23(.4),
4.9.9
concerted 23.18.9(.14)
concertedly 1.31.23(.14.3)
Concertgebouw 9.2
concert-goer 17.9.5
concerti grossi 2.22.5
concertina 17.18.1(.3)
concertino 19.15.1
concertmaster
17.12.24(.5)
concerto 19.10.5, 19.10.13
concerto grosso 19.20.6
concession 28.17.25(.4)
concessionaire 6, 6.9
concessionary
1.29.11(.13.2)
concessive 31.2.4(.4)
conch 24.19.5, 38.18.5
concha 17.14.21(.4)
conchae 2.14
conches 34.23.18,
35.18.19, 35.18.20
conchie 1.24.15
conchoid 23.13.9
conchoidal 40.22.9
conchological
40.23.12(.17.2)
conchologically
1.31.24(.9.11)
conchologist
22.29.2(.26.3)
conchology 1.26.10(.11.3)
concierge 37.3
conciliar 3.24.2
conciliate 22.4.2(.15)
conciliation
28.17.25(.3.1)
conciliative 31.2.1(.2)
conciliator 17.12.4(.1)
conciliatory 1.29.11(.8.1)
concinnity 1.10.16(.13)
concinnous 34.18.16(.2.7)
concise 34.15.8

concisely 1.31.33(.9)
conciseness
34.18.16(.31.2)
concision 28.17.26(.2)
conclave 31.3.8
conclude 23.17.5
conclusion 28.17.26(.4)
conclusive 31.2.4(.8)
conclusively 1.31.30(.7.4)
conclusiveness
34.18.16(.28.2)
concoct 22.23.7
concocter 17.12.21(.5)
concoction
28.17.25(.15.4)
concoctor 17.12.21(.5)
concomitance
34.24.10(.10)
concomitancy
1.22.23(.10.2)
concomitant 22.26.15(.9)
concomitantly
1.31.22(.20.2)
concord 23.12.4
concordance
34.24.10(.11)
concordant 22.26.15(.10)
concordantly
1.31.22(.20.2)
concordat 22.7.8
Concorde 23.12.4
concourse 34.12.2
concrescence
34.24.10(.18)
concrescent
22.26.15(.17.2)
concrete 22.1.17
concretely 1.31.22(.1)
concreteness
34.18.16(.20.1)
concretion 28.17.25(.1)
concretionary
1.29.11(.13.2)
concretization
28.17.25(.3.11)
concretize 35.15.7(.1)
concubinage 39.2.15
concubinary
1.29.11(.13.2)
concubine 28.14.4
concupiscence
34.24.10(.18)
concupiscent
22.26.15(.17.3)
concur 18.5
concurrence
34.24.10(.16)
concurrent
22.26.15(.23.2)
concurrently
1.31.22(.20.5)
concuss 34.14

concussion 28.17.25(.9)
concussive 31.2.4(.6)
condemn 27.5.5
condemnable 40.20.16(.16.3)
condemnation 28.17.25(.3.8)
condemnatory 1.29.11(.8.2)
condensable 40.20.16(.21.3)
condensate 22.4.18
condensation 28.17.25(.3.10)
condense 34.24.3
condenser 17.24.22(.2)
condensery 1.29.11(.18)
condescend 23.24.5(.11)
condescendingly 1.31.28(.1.5)
condescension 28.17.25(.16)
condign 28.14.6
condignly 1.31.27(.11)
condiment 22.26.15(.13.2)
condition 28.17.25(.2.3)
conditional 40.26.13(.14.1)
conditionality 1.10.16(.32.8)
conditionally 1.31.17(.14.3)
conditioner 17.18.16(.16)
condo 19.11.14
condolatory 1.29.11(.8.10)
condole 40.18.6
condolence 34.24.10(.24)
condom 27.9, 27.15.10(.14)
condominium 27.3.8(.2)
condonation 28.17.25(.3.8)
condone 28.19.5
condoner 17.18.18(.3)
condor 12.6.11
condottiere 1.29.4, 4.26.3
condottieri 2.30.3
conduce 34.17.13
conducement 22.26.15(.13.5)
conducive 31.2.4(.8)
conducively 1.31.30(.7.4)
conduciveness 34.18.16(.28.2)
conduct 22.23.8, 22.23.10
conductance 34.24.10(.10)
conducti 14.8
conductibility 1.10.16(.22.2)

conductible 40.20.16(.11.5)
conduction 28.17.25(.15.5)
conductive 31.2.1(.13.4)
conductively 1.31.30(.7.2)
conductivity 1.10.16(.15)
conductor 17.12.21(.6)
conductorship 20.2.7(.9)
conductress 34.18.27(.14)
conductus 34.18.11(.13)
conduit 22.2.3, 22.2.8, 22.2.23
condylar 17.34.16(.8)
condylarth 32.8
condyle 40.2.6, 40.13.4
condyloid 23.13.20
condyloma 17.17.16(.12)
condylomata 17.12.16(.9.3)
cone 28.19
conestoga 17.16.15
coney 1.16.17
confab 21.6
confabulate 22.4.23(.7.3)
confabulation 28.17.25(.3.14)
confabulatory 1.29.11(.8.10)
confect 22.23.4(.5)
confection 28.17.25(.15.2)
confectionary 1.29.11(.13.2)
confectioner 17.18.16(.16)
confectionery 1.29.11(.13.2)
confederacy 1.22.16(.13)
confederate 22.4.22(.6), 22.19.24(.9)
confederation 28.17.25(.3.13)
confer 18.9
conferee 2.30
conference 34.24.10(.16)
conferential 40.33.12(.3)
conferment 22.26.15(.13.2)
conferrable 40.20.16(.27.5)
conferral 40.16.13(.13)
confess 34.5.7
confessant 22.26.15(.17.2)
confessedly 1.31.23(.14.7)
confession 28.17.25(.4)
confessional 40.26.13(.14.3)
confessionary 1.29.11(.13.2)
confessor 17.24.5
confetti 1.10.4
confidant 22.26.6

confidante 22.26.6
confide 23.15.9
confidence 34.24.10(.11)
confident 22.26.15(.10)
confidential 40.33.12(.3)
confidentiality 1.10.16(.32.1)
confidentially 1.31.17(.22)
confidently 1.31.22(.20.2)
confiding 29.1.13(.9)
confidingly 1.31.28(.1.5)
configuration 28.17.25(.3.13)
configurational 40.26.13(.14.2)
configure 17.16.2
confine 28.14.10
confinement 22.26.15(.13.4)
confines 35.26.12
confirm 27.16.4
confirmand 23.24.6(.8)
confirmation 28.17.25(.3.7)
confirmative 31.2.1(.9.2)
confirmatory 1.29.11(.8.2)
confiscable 40.20.16(.13)
confiscate 22.4.11(.7)
confiscation 28.17.25(.3.5)
confiscator 17.12.4(.7)
confiscatory 1.29.11(.8.2)
confiture 12.17, 17.7.12(.3), 17.28.15
conflagration 28.17.25(.3.13)
conflate 22.4.23(.11)
conflation 28.17.25(.3.14)
conflict 22.23.2
confliction 28.17.25(.15.1)
conflictual 40.16.12
confluence 34.24.10(.6)
confluent 22.26.15(.5)
conflux 34.23.11
conform 27.10.5
conformability 1.10.16(.22.2)
conformable 40.20.16(.15)
conformably 1.31.21(.6)
conformal 40.25.6
conformally 1.31.17(.13)
conformance 34.24.10(.14)
conformation 28.17.25(.3.7)
conformer 17.17.9
conformism 27.15.21(.2.8)
conformist 22.29.2(.17)

conformity 1.10.16(.12)
confound 23.24.7(.5)
confoundedly 1.31.23(.14.4)
confraternity 1.10.16(.13)
confrère 6.19
confront 22.26.12
confrontation 28.17.25(.3.3)
confrontational 40.26.13(.14.2)
confrontationally 1.31.17(.14.3)
Confucian 28.17.25(.11)
Confucianism 27.15.21(.2.9)
Confucianist 22.29.2(.18.2)
Confucius 34.18.22(.7)
confusability 1.10.16(.22.2)
confusable 40.20.16(.22)
confusably 1.31.21(.7.2)
confuse 35.17.7
confusedly 1.31.23(.14.7)
confusible 40.20.16(.22)
confusing 29.1.24
confusingly 1.31.28(.1.12)
confusion 28.17.26(.4)
confutable 40.20.16(.11.2)
confutation 28.17.25(.3.3)
confute 22.18.10
conga 17.16.17(.3)
congé 4.21
congeal 40.1.12
congealable 40.20.16(.29)
congealment 22.26.15(.13.7)
congelation 28.17.25(.3.14)
congener 17.18.1(.13)
congeneric 24.2.26(.4)
congenerous 34.18.27(.19)
congenerousness 34.18.16(.31.5)
congenial 40.3.7(.1)
congeniality 1.10.16(.32.1)
congenially 1.31.3(.7)
congenital 40.21.12
congenitally 1.31.17(.9.2)
conger 17.16.17(.3)
congeries 35.2.17
congest 22.29.5(.9)
congestion 28.17.27
congestive 31.2.1(.15)
congii 14.2
congius 34.3.13
conglomerate 22.4.22(.6), 22.19.24(.9)

conglomeration 28.17.25(.3.13)
Congo 19.13.12
Congolese 35.1.23
congou 16.10, 19.13.12
congrats 34.22.5
congratulant 22.26.15(.25)
congratulate 22.4.23(.7.3)
congratulation 28.17.25(.3.14)
congratulative 31.2.1(.9.4)
congratulator 17.12.4(.16)
congratulatory 1.29.11(.8.2)
congregant 22.26.15(.12)
congregate 22.4.12(.5)
congregation 28.17.25(.3.6)
congregational 40.26.13(.14.2)
Congregationalism 27.15.21(.2.15)
Congregationalist 22.29.2(.31.3)
congress 34.5.14(.8), 34.18.27(.17)
congressional 40.26.13(.14.3)
congressman 28.17.16(.29)
congresswoman 28.17.16(.14)
congresswomen 28.2.17(.1)
Congreve 31.1.8
congruence 34.24.10(.6)
congruency 1.22.23(.10.1)
congruent 22.26.15(.5)
congruential 40.33.12(.2)
congruently 1.31.22(.20.1)
congruity 1.10.16(.5)
congruous 34.18.6
congruously 1.31.33(.12.1)
congruousness 34.18.16(.31.2)
conic 24.2.15(.6.1)
conical 40.23.12(.11)
conically 1.31.24(.9.8)
conidia 3.5.2
conidial 40.3.4
conidium 27.3.4(.2)
conifer 17.20.12(.2)
coniferous 34.18.27(.20)
coniform 27.10.5(.2)
coniine 28.1.2
Coningsby 1.9.22

Conisborough 17.32.14(.5)
Conisbrough 17.32.14(.5)
Coniston 28.17.11(.25)
conium 27.3.8(.10)
conjecturable 40.20.16(.27.5)
conjecturably 1.31.21(.8)
conjectural 40.16.13(.12.3)
conjecturally 1.31.17(.27.2)
conjecture 17.28.20
conjoin 28.12
conjoint 22.26.11
conjointly 1.31.22(.20.1)
conjugal 40.24.11
conjugality 1.10.16(.32.6)
conjugally 1.31.17(.12)
conjugate 22.4.12(.5), 22.19.13
conjugately 1.31.22(.15)
conjugation 28.17.25(.3.6)
conjugational 40.26.13(.14.2)
conjunct 22.23.13
conjunction 28.17.25(.15.6)
conjunctional 40.26.13(.14.6)
conjunctionally 1.31.17(.14.3)
conjunctiva 17.21.10
conjunctivae 2.19
conjunctival 40.28.9
conjunctive 31.2.1(.13.5)
conjunctively 1.31.30(.7.2)
conjunctivitis 34.18.11(.8)
conjuncture 17.28.20, 17.28.23
conjuration 28.17.25(.3.13)
conjure 17.7.12(.4), 17.29.16(.7)
conjurer 17.32.14(.20)
conjuror 17.32.14(.18)
conk 24.19.5
conker 17.14.21(.4)
Conley 1.31.27(.9)
Conlon 28.17.33(.23)
con man 28.7.10(.15)
con men 28.5.7(.19)
con moto 19.10.14
conn 28.10
Connacht 22.13.6
connate 22.4.14
connatural 40.16.13(.12.3)
connaturally 1.31.17(.27.2)

Connaught 22.13.6, 22.19.15(.5)
connect 22.23.4(.4)
connectable 40.20.16(.11.5)
connectedly 1.31.23(.14.3)
connectedness 34.18.16(.21.1)
Connecticut 22.19.12(.10)
connection 28.17.25(.15.2)
connectional 40.26.13(.14.6)
connectionism 27.15.21(.2.9)
connectionist 22.29.2(.18.2)
connective 31.2.1(.13.2)
connectivity 1.10.16(.15)
connector 17.12.21(.2)
Connell 40.5.8
Connemara 17.32.7
Connery 1.29.11(.13.1)
Connie 1.16.9
conniption 28.17.25(.14)
connive 31.9
conniver 17.21.10
connoisseur 18.11
connoisseurship 20.2.7(.10)
Connolly 1.31.17(.14.1)
Connor 17.18.9
Connors 35.18.13
connotation 28.17.25(.3.3)
connotative 31.2.1(.3)
connotatively 1.31.30(.7.1)
connote 22.21.8
connubial 40.3.2
connubiality 1.10.16(.32.1)
connubially 1.31.3(.2)
conodont 22.26.9
conoid 23.13.12
conoidal 40.22.9
conquer 17.14.21(.4)
conquerable 40.20.16(.27.3)
conqueror 17.32.14(.8)
conquest 22.29.5(.11)
conquistador 12.6.6
conquistadores 35.4.16
Conrad 23.7.16
Conran 28.17.31(.18)
con rod 23.10.12
Conroy 13.15
consanguineous 34.3.6(.2)
consanguineously 1.31.33(.1.2)

consanguinity 1.10.16(.13)
conscience 34.24.10(.20)
conscienceless 34.18.29(.33)
conscientious 34.18.22(.12)
conscientiously 1.31.33(.12.4)
conscientiousness 34.18.16(.31.4)
conscionable 40.20.16(.16.3)
conscious 34.18.22(.12)
consciously 1.31.33(.12.4)
consciousness 34.18.16(.31.4)
conscribe 21.12
conscript 22.22.1
conscription 28.17.25(.14)
consecrate 22.4.22(.10)
consecration 28.17.25(.3.13)
consecrator 17.12.4(.15)
consecratory 1.29.11(.8.2)
consecution 28.17.25(.11)
consecutive 31.2.1(.9.4)
consecutively 1.31.30(.7.2)
consecutiveness 34.18.16(.28.1)
consensual 40.16.14
consensually 1.31.17(.22)
consensus 34.18.20
consent 22.26.4(.11)
consentaneous 34.3.6(.3)
consentient 22.26.15(.19)
consequence 34.24.10(.22)
consequent 22.26.15(.22)
consequential 40.33.12(.3)
consequentialism 27.15.21(.2.15)
consequentialist 22.29.2(.31.4)
consequentiality 1.10.16(.32.1)
consequentially 1.31.17(.22)
consequently 1.31.22(.20.5)
conservancy 1.22.23(.10.4)
conservation 28.17.25(.3.9)
conservational 40.26.13(.14.2)
conservationist 22.29.2(.18.2)

conservatism
27.15.21(.2.4)
conservative 31.2.1(.9.3)
conservatively
1.31.30(.7.1)
conservativeness
34.18.16(.28.1)
conservatoire 10.22.5
conservator 17.12.4(.11),
17.12.16(.12)
conservatoria 3.22.9
conservatorium
27.3.17(.4)
conservatory
1.29.11(.8.8)
conserve 31.11
consessional
40.26.13(.14.3)
Consett 22.5.13(.11),
22.19.18
consider 17.13.2
considerable
40.20.16(.27.3)
considerably 1.31.21(.8)
considerate 22.19.24(.9)
considerately
1.31.22(.15)
consideration
28.17.25(.3.13)
Considine 28.14.6
consign 28.14.13
consignee 2.17
consignment
22.26.15(.13.4)
consignor 12.10,
17.18.13(.8)
consiliatoriness
34.18.16(.2.9)
consilience 34.24.2
consist 22.29.2(.22)
consistence 34.24.10(.10)
consistency 1.22.23(.10.2)
consistent 22.26.15(.9)
consistently
1.31.22(.20.2)
consistorial 40.3.14(.5)
consistory 1.29.11(.8.12)
consociate 22.4.2(.9)
consociation
28.17.25(.3.1)
consolable 40.20.16(.29)
consolation
28.17.25(.3.14)
consolatory 1.29.11(.8.10)
console 40.18.10
consoler 17.34.18(.10)
consolidate 22.4.10
consolidation
28.17.25(.3.4)
consolidator 17.12.4(.6)
consolidatory
1.29.11(.8.2)

consolingly 1.31.28(.1.18)
Consols 35.30.8
consommé 4.13
consonance 34.24.10(.15)
consonant 22.26.15(.14)
consonantal 40.21.17(.3)
consonantly 1.31.17(.9.3)
con sordino 19.15.1
consort 22.13.10
consortia 3.4.7, 17.26.9
consortium 27.3.3,
27.3.13
conspecific 24.2.16(.1)
conspectus 34.18.11(.13)
conspicuous 34.18.22(.2)
conspicuously
1.31.33(.12.4)
conspicuousness
34.18.16(.31.2)
conspiracy 1.22.16(.13)
conspirator 17.12.16(.18)
conspiratorial 40.3.14(.5)
conspiratorially
1.31.3(.11)
conspire 17.6.1
constable 40.20.16(.11.7)
constabulary 1.29.11(.27)
Constance 34.24.10(.10)
constancy 1.22.23(.10.2)
constant 22.26.15(.9)
constantan 28.7.6
Constantine 28.14.5
Constantinople 40.19.13
constantly 1.31.22(.20.2)
Constanza 17.25.18
constatation
28.17.25(.3.3)
constellate 22.4.23(.7.1)
constellation
28.17.25(.3.14)
consternate 22.4.14(.9.1)
consternation
28.17.25(.3.8)
constipate 22.4.7
constipation
28.17.25(.3.2)
constituency
1.22.23(.10.1)
constituent 22.26.15(.5)
constitute 22.18.10
constitution 28.17.25(.11)
constitutional
40.26.13(.14.5)
constitutionalism
27.15.21(.2.1)
constitutionalist
22.29.2(.31.3)
constitutionality
1.10.16(.32.8)
constitutionalize
35.15.21(.4.5)

constitutionally
1.31.17(.14.3)
constitutive 31.2.1(.8)
constitutively 1.31.30(.2)
constitutor 17.12.15(.5)
constrain 28.4.18
constrained 23.24.4
constrainedly
1.31.23(.14.6)
constraint 22.26.3
constrict 22.23.2
constriction
28.17.25(.15.1)
constrictive 31.2.1(.13.1)
constrictor 17.12.21(.1)
construable 40.20.16(.7)
construal 40.16.8
construct 22.23.8
construction
28.17.25(.15.5)
constructional
40.26.13(.14.6)
constructionally
1.31.17(.14.3)
constructionism
27.15.21(.2.9)
constructionist
22.29.2(.18.2)
constructive 31.2.1(.7)
constructively
1.31.30(.7.2)
constructiveness
34.18.16(.28.1)
constructivism
27.15.21(.2.11)
constructivist
22.29.2(.20)
constructor 17.12.12
construe 16.23.8
consubstantial
40.33.12(.4)
consubstantiality
1.10.16(.32.1)
consubstantiate
22.4.2(.9)
consubstantiation
28.17.25(.3.1)
consuetude 23.17.4(.1)
consuetudinary
1.29.11(.13.2)
consul 40.31.21
consular 17.34.16(.21.4)
consulate 22.19.26(.13)
consulship 20.2.7(.24)
consult 22.32.8
consultancy
1.22.23(.10.2)
consultant 22.26.15(.9)
consultation
28.17.25(.3.3)
consultative 31.2.1(.9.1)
consultee 2.11

consumable 40.20.16(.15)
consume 27.14.7
consumer 17.17.13
consumerism
27.15.21(.2.14)
consumerist
22.29.2(.29.4)
consumingly
1.31.28(.1.7)
consummate 22.4.13(.6),
22.19.14
consummated
23.18.9(.3)
consummately
1.31.22(.15)
consummation
28.17.25(.3.7)
consummative 31.2.1(.3)
consummator 17.12.4(.9)
consumption
28.17.25(.14)
consumptive 31.2.1(.12)
consumptively
1.31.30(.7.2)
Contac 24.6.7
contact 22.23.5(.4)
contactable
40.20.16(.11.5)
Contadora 17.32.10(.3)
contagion 28.17.28(.3)
contagious 34.18.24
contagiously
1.31.33(.12.4)
contagiousness
34.18.16(.31.5)
contain 28.4.3
containable
40.20.16(.16.1)
container 17.18.3
containerization
28.17.25(.3.12)
containerize 35.15.20(.2)
containment
22.26.15(.13.4)
contaminant
22.26.15(.14)
contaminate 22.4.14(.9.2)
contamination
28.17.25(.3.8)
contaminator
17.12.4(.10)
contango 19.13.12
conte 22.26.9
Conteh 1.10.23(.7), 4.9.9
contemn 27.5.4
contemner 17.17.5
contemplate 22.4.23(.8)
contemplation
28.17.25(.3.14)
contemplative
31.2.1(.9.4)
contemplatively
1.31.30(.7.1)

contemplator **17.12.4(.16)**

contemporaneity **1.10.16(.1)**

contemporaneous **34.3.6(.3)**

contemporaneously **1.31.33(.1.2)**

contemporaneousness **34.18.16(.31.1)**

contemporarily **1.31.17(.27.1)**

contemporariness **34.18.16(.2.9)**

contemporary **1.29.11(.6)**

contemporize **35.15.20(.2)**

contempt **22.25**

contemptibility **1.10.16(.22.2)**

contemptible **40.20.16(.11.4)**

contemptibly **1.31.21(.4.3)**

contemptuous **34.18.6**

contemptuously **1.31.33(.12.1)**

contemptuousness **34.18.16(.31.2)**

contend **23.24.5(.4)**

contender **17.13.20(.3)**

content **22.26.4(.4)**

contentedly **1.31.23(.14.3)**

contentedness **34.18.16(.21.1)**

contention **28.17.25(.16)**

contentious **34.18.22(.12)**

contentiously **1.31.33(.12.4)**

contentiousness **34.18.16(.31.4)**

contentment **22.26.15(.13.3)**

conterminous **34.18.16(.15.3)**

conterminously **1.31.33(.12.3)**

contessa **17.24.5**

contest **22.29.5(.2)**

contestable **40.20.16(.11.7)**

contestant **22.26.15(.9)**

contestation **28.17.25(.3.3)**

contester **17.12.24(.4)**

context **22.29.20**

contextual **40.16.12**

contextualist **22.29.2(.31.5)**

contextuality **1.10.16(.32.1)**

contextualization **28.17.25(.3.12)**

contextualize **35.15.21(.4.8)**

contextually **1.31.17(.24)**

Contiboard **23.12.2(.2)**

contiguity **1.10.16(.5)**

contiguous **34.18.6**

contiguously **1.31.33(.12.1)**

contiguousness **34.18.16(.31.2)**

continence **34.24.10(.15)**

continent **22.26.15(.14)**

continental **40.21.17(.2)**

continentally **1.31.17(.9.3)**

continently **1.31.22(.20.3)**

contingency **1.22.23(.10.4)**

contingent **22.26.15(.21)**

contingently **1.31.22(.20.4)**

continua **17.7.12(.8)**

continuable **40.20.16(.6)**

continual **40.16.14**

continually **1.31.17(.28)**

continuance **34.24.10(.6)**

continuant **22.26.15(.5)**

continuation **28.17.25(.3.1)**

continuative **31.2.1(.9.1)**

continuator **17.12.4(.2)**

continue **16.24.10**

continuer **17.7.12(.8)**

continuity **1.10.16(.5)**

continuo **19.6**

continuous **34.18.6**

continuously **1.31.33(.12.1)**

continuousness **34.18.16(.31.2)**

continuum **27.15.4**

contort **22.13.3**

contortion **28.17.25(.8)**

contortionist **22.29.2(.18.2)**

contour **12.5.8, 17.7.3**

contra **17.32.19(.10)**

contraband **23.24.6(.4)**

contrabandist **22.29.2(.14)**

contrabass **34.4.3**

contraception **28.17.25(.14)**

contraceptive **31.2.1(.12)**

contract **22.23.5(.9)**

contractable **40.20.16(.11.5)**

contractile **40.13.3(.8)**

contractility **1.10.16(.23)**

contraction **28.17.25(.15.3)**

contractive **31.2.1(.13.3)**

contractor **17.12.21(.3)**

contractual **40.16.12**

contractually **1.31.17(.24)**

contradict **22.23.2**

contradictable **40.20.16(.11.5)**

contradiction **28.17.25(.15.1)**

contradictious **34.18.22(.11)**

contradictor **17.12.21(.1)**

contradictorily **1.31.17(.27.1)**

contradictoriness **34.18.16(.2.9)**

contradictory **1.29.11(.8.12)**

contradistinction **28.17.25(.15.6)**

contradistinguish **36.2.24**

contraflow **19.29.21**

contrail **40.4.14**

contraindicate **22.4.11(.6)**

contraindication **28.17.25(.3.5)**

contralto **19.10.21**

contraposition **28.17.25(.2.5)**

contrapositive **31.2.1(.9.3)**

contraption **28.17.25(.14)**

contrapuntal **40.21.17(.5)**

contrapuntally **1.31.17(.9.3)**

contrapuntist **22.29.2(.13)**

contrarian **28.3.20(.4)**

contrariety **1.10.16(.4)**

contrarily **1.31.17(.27.1)**

contrariness **34.18.16(.2.9)**

contrariwise **35.15.19**

contrary **1.29.4, 1.29.11(.25)**

contrast **22.29.6(.11), 22.29.8(.7)**

contrastingly **1.31.28(.1.4)**

contrastive **31.2.1(.15)**

contrasty **1.10.26(.5)**

contravene **28.1.16**

contravener **17.18.1(.7)**

contravention **28.17.25(.16)**

contretemps **11.5**

contribute **22.18.10**

contribution **28.17.25(.11)**

contributive **31.2.1(.9.4)**

contributor **17.12.15(.8), 17.12.16(.19)**

contributory **1.29.11(.8.4)**

con trick **24.2.26(.14.3)**

contrite **22.16.24(.12)**

contritely **1.31.22(.13)**

contrition **28.17.25(.2.6)**

contrivable **40.20.16(.19)**

contrivance **34.24.10(.17)**

contrive **31.9**

contrived **23.26**

contriver **17.21.10**

control **40.18.14**

controllability **1.10.16(.22.2)**

controllable **40.20.16(.29)**

controllably **1.31.21(.9)**

controller **17.34.18(.14)**

controllership **20.2.7(.9)**

controversial **40.33.10**

controversialism **27.15.21(.2.15)**

controversialist **22.29.2(.31.4)**

controversially **1.31.17(.22)**

controversy **1.22.16(.11), 1.22.17**

controvert **22.20.9**

controvertible **40.20.16(.11.3)**

contumacious **34.18.22(.3)**

contumaciously **1.31.33(.12.4)**

contumacy **1.22.16(.8)**

contumelious **34.3.16**

contumeliously **1.31.33(.1.5)**

contumely **1.31.17(.13)**

contuse **35.17.7**

contusion **28.17.26(.4)**

conundrum **27.15.26(.11)**

conurbation **28.17.25(.3.2)**

conure **17.7.12(.8)**

Convair **6.11**

convalesce **34.5.16**

convalescence **34.24.10(.18)**

convalescent **22.26.15(.17.2)**

convection **28.17.25(.15.2)**

convectional **40.26.13(.14.6)**

convective **31.2.1(.13.2)**

convector **17.12.21(.2)**

convenable
40.20.16(.16.1)
convenance **34.24.6**
convene **28.1.16**
convener **17.18.1(.7)**
convenience **34.24.2**
convenient **22.26.2(.5)**
conveniently
1.31.22(.20.1)
convent **22.26.15(.16)**
conventicle **40.23.12(.7.3)**
convention **28.17.25(.16)**
conventional
40.26.13(.14.7)
conventionalism
27.15.21(.2.15)
conventionalist
22.29.2(.31.3)
conventionality
1.10.16(.32.8)
conventionalize
35.15.21(.4.5)
conventionally
1.31.17(.14.3)
conventioneer **3.9**
conventual **40.16.12,
40.33.12(.3)**
converb **21.15**
converge **39.15**
convergence
34.24.10(.21)
convergency
1.22.23(.10.4)
convergent **22.26.15(.21)**
conversance
34.24.10(.18)
conversancy
1.22.23(.10.4)
conversant
22.26.15(.17.3)
conversation
28.17.25(.3.10)
conversational
40.26.13(.14.2)
conversationalist
22.29.2(.31.3)
conversationally
1.31.17(.14.3)
conversationist
22.29.2(.18.2)
conversazione **1.16.17**
conversazioni **2.17.11**
converse **34.19.6**
conversely **1.31.33(.12.6)**
converser **17.24.16**
conversion **28.17.25(.12)**
convert **22.20.9**
converter **17.12.17**
convertibility
1.10.16(.22.2)
convertible
40.20.16(.11.3)

convertibly **1.31.21(.4.2)**
convex **34.23.4(.8)**
convexity **1.10.16(.16.3)**
convexly **1.31.33(.15)**
convey **4.16**
conveyable **40.20.16(.2)**
conveyance **34.24.10(.2)**
conveyancer **17.24.22(.7)**
conveyancing **29.1.23**
conveyor **17.2.6**
convict **22.23.2**
conviction **28.17.25(.15.1)**
convictive **31.2.1(.13.1)**
convince **34.24.1**
convincement
22.26.15(.13.5)
convincer **17.24.22(.1)**
convincible
40.20.16(.21.3)
convincibly **1.31.21(.7.2)**
convincingly
1.31.28(.1.11)
convivial **40.3.8**
conviviality **1.10.16(.32.1)**
convivially **1.31.3(.8)**
convocation
28.17.25(.3.5)
convocational
40.26.13(.14.2)
convoke **24.18.8**
convoluted **23.18.9(.12)**
convolutedly
1.31.23(.14.3)
convolution **28.17.25(.11)**
convolutional
40.26.13(.14.5)
convolve **31.13**
convolvulus
34.18.29(.17.6)
convoy **13.8**
convulsant
22.26.15(.17.3)
convulse **34.27**
convulsion **28.17.25(.17)**
convulsionary
1.29.11(.13.2)
convulsive **31.2.4(.14)**
convulsively **1.31.30(.7.4)**
Conway **4.25.17**
Conwy **1.28**
Conybeare **3.3.2**
coo **16**
Coober Pedy **1.11.1**
co-occur **18.5**
co-occurrence
34.24.10(.16)
Cooder **17.13.14**
cooee **2, 2.7**
cooey **2**
cooingly **1.31.28(.1.1)**
cook **24.14**

cookability **1.10.16(.22.1)**
cookable **40.20.16(.13)**
cookbook **24.14.3**
cook-chill **40.2.16**
Cooke **24.14**
cooker **17.14.13**
cookery **1.29.11(.10)**
cookhouse **34.8.6(.13)**
cookie **1.12.11**
cookout **22.9.9**
cookshop **20.7.9**
Cookson **28.17.23(.21)**
cookstone **28.19.4(.9)**
cookware **6.18.9**
cool **40.15**
coolant **22.26.15(.25)**
cooler **17.34.15**
Cooley **1.31.16**
Coolgardie **1.11.9**
coolibah **10.5.4**
Coolidge **39.2.23**
coolie **1.31.16**
coolish **36.2.27**
coolly **1.31.38**
coolness **34.18.16(.37.1)**
coolth **32.24**
Coombes **35.25.9**
coon **28.16**
Cooney **1.16.14**
coonskin **28.2.13(.14)**
co-op **20.7.1**
coop **20.12**
Coope **20.12**
cooper **17.10.13**
cooperage **39.2.22(.9)**
cooperant **22.26.15(.23.3)**
cooperate **22.4.22(.6)**
cooperation
28.17.25(.3.13)
cooperative **31.2.1(.9.4)**
cooperatively
1.31.30(.7.1)
cooperativeness
34.18.16(.28.1)
cooperator **17.12.4(.15)**
Cooperstown **28.8.1**
co-opt **22.22.5**
co-optation **28.17.25(.3.3)**
co-option **28.17.25(.14)**
co-optive **31.2.1(.12)**
coordinate **22.4.14(.9.1),
22.19.15(.9)**
coordinately
1.31.22(.15)
coordination
28.17.25(.3.8)
coordinative **31.2.1(.9.2)**
coordinator **17.12.4(.10)**
Coors® **35.12**
coot **22.18**
Coote **22.18**

cootie **1.10.15**
co-own **28.19**
co-owner **17.18.18**
co-ownership **20.2.7(.9)**
cop **20.7**
Copacabana **17.18.6**
copacetic **24.2.10(.1)**
copaiba **17.11.11**
copal **40.19.13**
cope **20.15**
Copeland **23.24.16(.16.3)**
Copenhagen **28.17.15(.3)**
copepod **23.10.1**
coper **17.10.16**
Copernican **28.17.13(.13)**
Copernicus **34.18.13(.10)**
Copestake **24.3.4**
copestone **28.19.4(.9)**
copiable **40.20.3**
copier **3.2.5**
co-pilot **22.19.26(.11)**
coping **29.1.10(.11)**
coping stone **28.19.4(.9)**
copious **34.3.1**
copiously **1.31.33(.1.1)**
copiousness
34.18.16(.31.1)
copita **17.12.1(.1)**
coplanar **17.18.3**
coplanarity **1.10.16(.21.1)**
Copley **1.31.20**
copolymer **17.17.14(.12)**
copolymerization
28.17.25(.3.12)
copolymerize
35.15.20(.2)
cop-out **22.9.5**
copper **17.10.8**
copperas **34.18.27(.12)**
Copperbelt **22.32.2**
Copperfield **23.31.1(.2)**
copperhead **23.5.13(.5)**
coppermine **28.14.8**
copperplate **22.4.23(.8)**
coppersmith **32.2.3**
coppery **1.29.11(.6)**
coppice **34.2.6**
Coppola **17.34.16(.5)**
copra **17.32.17**
coprocessor **17.24.5**
coprolite **22.16.25(.9)**
coprology **1.26.10(.11.5)**
coprophagous
34.18.14(.5)
coprophilia **3.24.2**
coprophiliac **24.6.1**
coprosma **17.17.23**
copse **34.21.6**
copsewood **23.16.6(.17)**
copsy **1.22.19**

Copt 22.22.5
'copter 17.12.19
Coptic 24.2.10(.12)
copula 17.34.16(.21.1)
copular 17.34.16(.21.1)
copulate 22.4.23(.7.3)
copulation 28.17.25(.3.14)
copulative 31.2.1(.9.4)
copulatively 1.31.30(.7.1)
copulatory 1.29.11(.8.10)
copy 1.8.7
copybook 24.14.3
copyboy 13.3
copycat 22.7.9
copydesk 24.20.3
Copydex® 34.23.4(.4)
copyhold 23.31.13(.9)
copyholder 17.13.23(.8)
copyist 22.29.2(.2)
copyread 23.1.11
copyreader 17.13.1
copyright 22.16.24(.1)
copywriter 17.12.13(.8)
copywriting 29.1.12(.11)
coq au vin 8
coquetry 1.29.15(.6)
coquette 22.5.5
coquettish 36.2.11
coquettishly 1.31.35(.7.1)
coquettishness 34.18.16(.33.3)
coquille 2.14
coquina 17.18.1(.5)
coquito 19.10.1
cor 12
Cora 17.32.10
coracle 40.23.12(.18)
coracoid 23.13.9
coral 40.16.13(.7)
Coralie 1.31.17(.27.1)
coralline 28.14.19(.11)
corallita 17.12.1(.15)
corallite 22.16.25(.9)
coralloid 23.13.20
Coram 27.15.26(.5)
coram populo 19.29.12
cor anglais 4.28.13
corbel 40.20.10
Corbett 22.19.9
corbicula 17.34.16(.21.2)
corbiculae 2.32.9(.8)
corbie 1.9.8
Corbin 28.2.10
Corbishley 1.31.35(.1)
cor blimey 1.15.11
Corbridge 39.2.22(.10)
Corby 1.9.8
Corcoran 28.17.31(.11)
Corcyra 17.32.13
cord 23.12

cordage 39.2.11
cordate 22.4.10
Corday 4.10.5
Cordelia 3.24.1
Cordelier 3.24
Cordell 40.5.4
cordial 40.3.4
cordiality 1.10.16(.32.1)
cordially 1.31.3(.4)
cordillera 17.32.5
cordite 22.16.10
cordless 34.18.29(.23)
cordlessness 34.18.16(.31.6)
cordlike 24.13.7(.13)
Córdoba 17.11.13
cordon 28.17.12(.10)
cordon-bleu 18
cordon sanitaire 6.4
Cordova 17.21.12
cordovan 28.17.20(.10)
corduroy 13.15
cordwain 28.4.17
cordwainer 17.18.3
cordwood 23.16.6(.10)
CORE 12
core 12
coreferential 40.33.12(.3)
co-religionist 22.29.2(.18.3)
corella 17.34.5(.15)
Corelli 1.31.5
Coren 28.17.31(.8)
coreopsis 34.2.17(.12)
corer 17.32.10
co-respondent 22.26.15(.10)
Corey 1.29.8
corf 30.9
Corfe 30.9
Corfu 16.13, 16.24.11
corgi 1.14.7
coria 3.22.9
coriaceous 34.18.22(.3)
coriander 17.13.20(.4)
Corin 28.2.29(.4)
Corinna 17.18.2
Corinne 28.2.29
Corinth 32.21
Corinthian 28.3.11
Coriolanus 34.18.16(.4)
Coriolis 34.2.22(.10)
corium 27.3.17(.4)
cork 24.10
corkage 39.2.12
corker 17.14.9
corkiness 34.18.16(.2.4)
corklike 24.13.7(.14)
corkscrew 16.23.10
corkwood 23.16.6(.11)

corky 1.12.8
Corley 1.31.11
corm 27.10
Cormac 24.6.10, 24.16.6
cormorant 22.26.15(.23.3)
corn 28.11
cornball 40.10.4
cornbrash 36.6.9
cornbread 23.5.15
corncob 21.8
corncockle 40.23.7
corncrake 24.3.13
corn crib 21.2
cornea 3.9.7, 17.1.7
corneal 40.3.7(.6), 40.16.1
cornel 40.26.9
Cornelia 3.24.1
cornelian 28.3.21(.1)
Cornelius 34.3.16
Cornell 40.5.8
corneous 34.3.6(.5)
corner 17.18.10
cornerback 24.6.6(.9)
cornerstone 28.19.4(.9)
cornerways 35.4.15
cornerwise 35.15.19
cornet 22.2.12
cornetcy 1.22.21
cornetist 22.29.2(.13)
cornett 22.2.12
cornetti 2.12.4
cornetto 19.10.4
cornfield 23.31.1(.2)
cornflake 24.3.14
cornflour 17.3.11
cornflower 17.3.11
Cornhill 40.2.18
cornhusk 24.20.7
cornice 34.2.13
corniced 22.29.2(.18.1)
corniche 36.1
cornily 1.31.17(.14.1)
corniness 34.18.16(.2.5)
Corning 29.1.17(.8)
Cornish 36.2.16(.9)
Cornishman 28.17.16(.31)
Cornishwoman 28.17.16(.14)
Cornishwomen 28.2.17(.1)
cornmeal 40.1.6
cornrows 35.20.12
cornstalk 24.10.2
cornstarch 38.7
cornstone 28.19.4(.9)
cornucopia 3.2.7
cornucopian 28.3.1
Cornwall 40.10.17
Cornwallis 34.2.22(.6)

corny 1.16.10
corolla 17.34.9
corollary 1.29.11(.27)
Coromandel 40.22.16
corona 17.18.18(.10)
coronach 24.16.7, 25.10
coronae 2.17.11
coronagraph 30.7.5(.1)
coronal 40.26.13(.14.8)
coronary 1.29.11(.13.2)
coronation 28.17.25(.3.8)
coroner 17.18.16(.20)
coronership 20.2.7(.9)
coronet 22.5.9, 22.19.15(.9)
Corot 19.27.6
corozo 19.21
Corp. 20.8
corpora 17.32.14(.4)
corporal 40.16.13(.12.1)
corporality 1.10.16(.32.13)
corporally 1.31.17(.27.1)
corpora lutea 3.4.9
corporate 22.19.24(.9)
corporately 1.31.22(.15)
corporateness 34.18.16(.20.3)
corporation 28.17.25(.3.13)
corporatism 27.15.21(.2.4)
corporatist 22.29.2(.13)
corporative 31.2.1(.9.4)
corporativism 27.15.21(.2.11)
corporativist 22.29.2(.20)
corporeal 40.3.14(.5)
corporeality 1.10.16(.32.1)
corporeally 1.31.3(.11)
corporeity 1.10.16(.1)
corposant 22.26.15(.17.3)
corps 12
corps de ballet 4.28.3
corps d'élite 22.1.18
corps diplomatique 24.1.3
corpse 34.21.7
corpulence 34.24.10(.24)
corpulency 1.22.23(.10.4)
corpulent 22.26.15(.25)
corpus 34.18.9(.6)
Corpus Christi 1.10.26(.2)
corpuscle 40.31.10
corpuscular 17.34.16(.21.2)
corpus delicti 14.8
corpus luteum 27.3.3
corral 40.6.14, 40.8.15

corrasion 28.17.26(.3)
correct 22.23.4(.10)
correction 28.17.25(.15.2)
correctional
  40.26.13(.14.6)
correctitude 23.17.4(.1)
corrective 31.2.1(.13.2)
correctively 1.31.30(.7.2)
correctly 1.31.22(.19)
correctness
  34.18.16(.20.4)
corrector 17.12.21(.2)
Correggio 15.1.11
correlate 22.4.23(.7.2),
  22.19.26(.13)
correlation
  28.17.25(.3.14)
correlational
  40.26.13(.14.2)
correlative 31.2.1(.9.4)
correlatively 1.31.30(.7.1)
correlativity 1.10.16(.15)
correspond 23.24.9
correspondence
  34.24.10(.11)
correspondent
  22.26.15(.10)
correspondently
  1.31.22(.20.2)
corresponding
  29.1.13(.14)
correspondingly
  1.31.28(.1.5)
corrida 17.13.1
corridor 12.6.6
corrie 1.29.7
Corrigan 28.17.15(.13)
corrigenda 17.13.20(.3)
corrigendum
  27.15.10(.14)
corrigible 40.20.16(.25)
corrigibly 1.31.21(.7.4)
Corris 34.2.21
corroborate 22.4.22(.6)
corroboration
  28.17.25(.3.14)
corroborative 31.2.1(.9.4)
corroborator 17.12.4(.15)
corroboratory
  1.29.11(.8.9)
corroboree 2.30, 2.30.7
corrode 23.20.12
corrodible 40.20.16(.12)
corrosion 28.17.26(.6)
corrosive 31.2.4(.11)
corrosively 1.31.30(.7.4)
corrosiveness
  34.18.16(.28.2)
corrugate 22.4.12(.5)
corrugation
  28.17.25(.3.6)
corrugator 17.12.4(.8)

corrupt 22.22.6
corrupter 17.12.19
corruptibility
  1.10.16(.22.2)
corruptible
  40.20.16(.11.4)
corruptibleness
  34.18.16(.37.4)
corruptibly 1.31.21(.4.3)
corruption 28.17.25(.14)
corruptive 31.2.1(.12)
corruptly 1.31.22(.18)
corruptness
  34.18.16(.20.4)
corsac 24.6.14
corsage 37.4.6
corsair 6.12
corse 34.12
corselet 22.19.26(.26)
corselette 22.19.26(.26)
corset 22.2.16
corsetière 3.4
corsetry 1.29.15(.10)
Corsica 17.14.15(.12)
Corsican 28.17.13(.13)
Corstorphine 28.2.19
Cort 22.13
cortège 37.2
Cortes 34.5.2, 35.2.3
Cortés 35.5.5
cortex 34.23.4(.3)
Corti 1.10.10
cortical 40.23.12(.7.2)
corticate 22.4.11(.6)
corticated 23.18.9(.3)
cortices 35.1.16(.10)
corticotrophic
  24.2.16(.4)
corticotrophin 28.2.19
corticotropic 24.2.8(.5)
corticotropin 28.2.9
Cortina® 17.18.1(.3)
cortisone 28.19.14
Corton 28.17.11(.10)
corundum 27.15.10(.14)
Corunna 17.18.12
coruscate 22.4.11(.7)
coruscation
  28.17.25(.3.5)
corvée 4.16
corves 35.28.5
corvette 22.5.11
corvine 28.14.11
Corwen 28.5.17, 28.17.30
Cory 1.29.8
corybant 22.26.6
corybantic 24.2.10(.14)
Corydon 28.17.12(.16)
corymb 21.17, 27.2.14
corymbose 34.20.3
corynebacteria 3.22.2

corynebacterium
  27.3.17(.2)
coryphaei 14.1
coryphaeus 34.18.1
coryphée 4.15
Coryton 28.17.11(.15)
coryza 17.25.12(.14)
Cos 34.10
cos 34.10, 35.10
Cosa Nostra 17.32.19(.11)
cosec 24.4.8
cosecant 22.26.15(.11)
coseismal 40.25.14
coset 22.5.13(.5)
Cosford 23.18.16(.18)
Cosgrave 31.3.7
cosh 36.9, 38.3
cosher 17.26.8
cosies 35.2.12
Così Fan Tutte 1.10.14
cosignatory 1.29.11(.8.7)
cosigner 17.18.13(.8)
cosily 1.31.17(.21)
cosine 28.14.13
cosiness 34.18.16(.2.7)
CoSIRA 17.32.13
cosmea 3.8.14
cosmetic 24.2.10(.3.1)
cosmetically 1.31.24(.9.3)
cosmetician
  28.17.25(.2.2)
cosmetologist
  22.29.2(.26.3)
cosmetology
  1.26.10(.11.2)
cosmic 24.2.14(.17)
cosmical 40.23.12(.10)
cosmically 1.31.24(.9.8)
Cosmo 19.14.18
cosmogonic 24.2.15(.6.1)
cosmogonical
  40.23.12(.11)
cosmogonist
  22.29.2(.18.1)
cosmogony 1.16.15(.10)
cosmographer
  17.20.12(.5)
cosmographic 24.2.16(.3)
cosmographical
  40.23.12(.12)
cosmography 1.18.9(.3.2)
cosmological
  40.23.12(.17.2)
cosmologist 22.29.2(.26.4)
cosmology 1.26.10(.11.4)
cosmonaut 22.13.6
cosmopolis 34.2.22(.8)
cosmopolitan
  28.17.11(.15)
cosmopolitanism
  27.15.21(.2.9)

cosmopolite 22.16.25(.9)
cosmos 34.10.12
Cossack 24.6.14
cosset 22.2.16
cossie 1.23.8
cost 22.29.9
Costa 17.12.24(.7)
Costa Blanca 17.14.21(.3)
Costa Brava 17.21.6
Costa del Sol 40.9
Costain 28.4.3
costal 40.21.18
co-star 10.6.8
costard 23.18.9(.20)
Costa Rica 17.14.1
Costa Rican 28.17.13(.1)
costate 22.4.9(.9)
Costello 19.29.4, 19.29.12
coster 17.12.24(.7)
costermonger
  17.16.17(.4)
costing 29.1.12(.21)
costive 31.2.1(.15)
costively 1.31.30(.7.4)
costiveness
  34.18.16(.28.1)
costliness 34.18.16(.2.10)
costly 1.31.22(.22)
costmary 1.29.4
Costner 17.18.21
costume 27.14.7
costumier 3.8.6
cosy 1.23.15
cot 22.11
cotangent 22.26.15(.21)
cote 22.21
Côte d'Azur 17.7.12(.12)
coterie 1.29.11(.8.11)
coterminous
  34.18.16(.15.3)
coterminously
  1.31.33(.12.3)
coth 32.9, 38.3
cotherni 14.13
cothernus 34.18.16(.16)
Cothi 1.20.6
cotillion 28.3.21(.2)
Cotman 28.17.16(.21)
Coton 28.17.11(.17)
cotoneaster 17.12.24(.5)
Cotopaxi 1.22.22
Cotswold 23.31.13(.10)
cotta 17.12.9
cottage 39.2.10
cottager 17.29.13
cottagey 1.26.10(.2)
cottaging 29.1.28
cottar 17.12.9
Cottbus 34.16
cotter 17.12.9

coverage 39.2.22(.9)
coverall 40.10.18
covercharge 39.8
Coverdale 40.4.3
coverer 17.32.14(.13)
covering 29.1.30(.8)
coverlet 22.19.26(.13)
Coverley 1.31.17(.17)
covert 22.19.17, 22.20.9
covertly 1.31.22(.15)
covertness 34.18.16(.20.3)
coverture 12.17,
  17.7.12(.3), 17.28.15
covet 22.19.17
covetable 40.20.16(.11.3)
covetous 34.18.11(.10)
covetously 1.31.33(.12.2)
covetousness
  34.18.16(.31.3)
covey 1.19.7
covin 28.2.20
coving 29.1.20
cow 9
cowage 39.2.3
Cowan 28.17.3
coward 23.18.2
cowardice 34.2.9
cowardliness
  34.18.16(.2.10)
cowardly 1.31.23(.14.1)
cowbane 28.4.2
cowbell 40.5.2
cowberry 1.29.11(.7.1)
cowbird 23.19.1
cowboy 13.3
Cowbridge 39.2.22(.10)
cowcatcher 17.28.6
Cowdenbeath 32.1
Cowdray 1.29.16, 4.26.12
Cowdrey 1.29.16, 4.26.12
Cowell 40.16.3
Cowen 28.17.3, 28.17.8
cower 17.3
Cowes 35.8
Cowgill 40.2.8
cowgirl 40.17
cowhage 39.2.3
cowhand 23.24.6(.11)
cowheel 40.1.13
cowherd 23.19.7
cowhide 23.15.13
Cowie 1(.3)
cowl 40.7
Cowley 1.31.8
cowlick 24.2.27(.7)
cowling 29.1.31(.7)
cowman 28.17.16(.8)
cowpat 22.7.5
cowpea 2.9
Cowper 17.10.6, 17.10.13

cowpoke 24.18.1
cowpox 34.23.8(.1)
cowpuncher 17.28.22
cowrie 1.29.11(.1)
cowshed 23.5.12
cowslip 20.2.13
cowtown 28.8.1
cox 34.23.8
coxa 17.24.20
coxae 2.22.11
coxal 40.31.18
coxalgia 3.19.10,
  17.29.16(.9)
coxcomb 27.17.6
coxcombry 1.29.19
Coxe 34.23.8
coxless 34.18.29(.33)
Coxsackie 1.12.5
coxswain 28.17.23(.21)
coxswainship 20.2.7(.19)
coy 13
coyly 1.31.12
coyness 34.18.16(.11)
coyote 1.10.18
coypu 16.5, 16.24.3
coz 35.14
cozen 28.17.24(.9)
cozenage 39.2.15
Cozens 35.26.13(.14)
Cozumel 40.5.7
cozy 1.23.15
crab 21.6
Crabbe 21.6
crabbedly 1.31.23(.14.2)
crabbedness
  34.18.16(.21.1)
crabbily 1.31.17(.8)
crabbiness 34.18.16(.2.2)
crabby 1.9.5
crabgrass 34.9.6
crablike 24.13.7(.11)
crabmeat 22.1.5
Crabtree 2.30.10
crabways 35.4.15
crabwise 35.15.19
crack 24.6
crackbrained 23.24.4
crackdown 28.8.2(.6)
cracker 17.14.5
cracker-barrel
  40.16.13(.5)
crackerjack 24.6.18
crackiness 34.18.16(.2.4)
crack-jaw 12.18
crackle 40.23.5
crackling 29.1.31(.19)
crackly 1.31.24(.5)
cracknel 40.26.18
crackpot 22.11.2
cracksman 28.17.16(.29)
crackup 20.9.7

cracky 1.12.5
Cracow 9.5, 30.8.6, 31.7
Craddock 24.16.5
cradle 40.22.3
Cradley 1.31.23(.3)
craft 22.27.4
craftily 1.31.17(.9.3)
craftiness 34.18.16(.2.3)
craftsman 28.17.16(.29)
craftsmanship
  20.2.7(.19)
craftspeople 40.19.1
craftsperson
  28.17.23(.15)
craftswoman
  28.17.16(.14)
craftswomen 28.2.17(.1)
craftwork 24.17.6(.8)
craftworker 17.14.16
crafty 1.10.24
crag 26.5
craggily 1.31.17(.12)
cragginess 34.18.16(.2.4)
craggy 1.14.5
cragsman 28.17.16(.30)
cragswoman
  28.17.16(.14)
cragswomen 28.2.17(.1)
Craig 26.3
Craigie 1.14.3
crake 24.3
cram 27.6
crambo 19.9.14
Cramden 28.17.12(.22)
Cramer 17.17.4
crammer 17.17.6
cramp 20.16.3
crampon 28.10.7, 28.17.9
cran 28.7
cranage 39.2.15
cranberry 1.29.11(.7.2)
Cranborne 28.11.2
Cranbrook 24.14.10
crane 28.4
cranesbill 40.2.4
Cranfield 23.31.1(.2)
crania 3.9.3
cranial 40.3.7(.3)
cranially 1.31.3(.7)
craniate 22.3.6
craniological
  40.23.12(.17.2)
craniologist 22.29.2(.26.2)
craniology 1.26.10(.11.1)
craniometric
  24.2.26(.14.2)
craniometry 1.29.15(.8)
craniotomy 1.15.13(.1)
cranium 27.3.8(.3)
crank 24.19.3
crankcase 34.4.6

crankily 1.31.17(.11)
crankiness 34.18.16(.2.4)
crankpin 28.2.9
crankshaft 22.27.4(.3)
cranky 1.12.16
Cranleigh 1.31.27(.6)
Cranley 1.31.27(.6)
Cranmer 17.17.21
crannied 23.2.13
cranny 1.16.6
Cranston 28.17.11(.25)
Cranwell 40.5.17(.12)
crap 20.5
crape 20.3
crapper 17.10.5
crappie 1.8.5
crappily 1.31.17(.7)
crappiness 34.18.16(.2.2)
crappy 1.8.5
craps 34.21.5
crapshooter 17.12.15(.4)
crapulence 34.24.10(.24)
crapulent 22.26.15(.25)
crapulently 1.31.22(.20.5)
crapulous 34.18.29(.17.6)
crapy 1.8.3
craquelure 17.7.12(.14)
crases 35.1.16(.2)
crash 36.6
Crashaw 12.16.3
crash-dove 31.12
crasis 34.2.17(.2)
crass 34.7
crassitude 23.17.4(.1)
crassly 1.31.33(.4)
crassness 34.18.16(.31.2)
Crassus 34.18.20
cratch 38.5
Cratchit 22.2.20
crate 22.4
crateful 40.14.6(.10)
crater 17.12.4
craterous 34.18.27(.14)
Crathorne 28.11.8
cravat 22.7.14
cravatted 23.18.9(.5)
crave 31.3
craven 28.17.20(.3)
cravenly 1.31.27(.14)
cravenness 34.18.16(.25)
craver 17.21.3
craving 29.1.20
craw 12
crawdad 23.7.8
crawfish 36.2.18(.7)
Crawford 23.18.16(.6)
crawl 40.10
crawler 17.34.10
crawlingly 1.31.28(.1.18)
crawly 1.31.11

Crawshaw 12.16.4
Crawshay 4.20
Cray 4
crayfish 36.2.18(.3)
Crayford 23.18.16(.3)
Crayola® 17.34.18
crayon 28.10.3, 28.17.2
craze 35.4
crazily 1.31.17(.21)
craziness 34.18.16(.2.7)
crazy 1.23.3
creak 24.1
creakily 1.31.17(.11)
creakiness 34.18.16(.2.4)
creakingly 1.31.28(.1.6)
creaky 1.12.1
cream 27.1
creamer 17.17.1
creamery 1.29.11(.12)
creamily 1.31.17(.13)
creaminess 34.18.16(.2.5)
creamware 6.18.10
creamy 1.15.1
creance 34.24.10(.1)
crease 34.1
Creasy 1.22.1
creatable 40.20.16(.11.1)
create 22.4
creatine 28.1.9(.3)
creation 28.17.25(.3.1)
creationism 27.15.21(.2.9)
creationist 22.29.2(.18.2)
creative 31.2.1(.3)
creatively 1.31.30(.7.1)
creativeness
34.18.16(.28.1)
creativity 1.10.16(.15)
creator 17.12.4
creatrices 35.1.16(.10)
creatrix 34.23.2(.12)
creature 17.28.1
creaturely 1.31.17(.24)
crèche 36.4, 36.5
Crécy 1.22.5
cred 23.5
Creda® 17.13.1
credal 40.22.1
credence 34.24.10(.11)
credential 40.33.12(.3)
credenza 17.25.18
credibility 1.10.16(.22.1)
credible 40.20.16(.12)
credibly 1.31.21(.4.4)
credit 22.2.8
creditability
1.10.16(.22.2)
creditable 40.20.16(.11.1)
creditably 1.31.21(.4.2)
Crediton 28.17.11(.2)
creditor 17.12.16(.6)

creditworthiness
34.18.16(.2.6)
creditworthy 1.21
credo 19.11.1, 19.11.4
credulity 1.10.16(.35)
credulous 34.18.29(.17.5)
credulously 1.31.33(.12.6)
credulousness
34.18.16(.31.6)
Cree 2
creed 23.1
creek 24.1
creel 40.1
Creeley 1.31.1
creep 20.1
creeper 17.10.1
creepie 1.8.1
creepily 1.31.17(.7)
creepiness 34.18.16(.2.2)
creepy 1.8.1
creepy-crawly 1.31.11
creese 34.1
Creighton 28.17.11(.3)
cremate 22.4.13
cremation 28.17.25(.3.7)
cremator 17.12.4(.9)
crematoria 3.22.9
crematorium 27.3.17(.4)
crematory 1.29.11(.8.7)
crème brûlée 4.28
crème caramel 40.5.7
crème de cassis 34.1.5
crème de la crème 27.5
crème de menthe 32.21
crème fraîche 36.5
Cremona 17.18.18(.5)
crenate 22.4.14(.1)
crenation 28.17.25(.3.8)
crenature 12.17,
17.7.12(.3), 17.28.15
crenel 40.26.4
crenellate 22.4.23(.7.2)
crenellation
28.17.25(.3.1)
crenelle 40.5.8
creole 40.18.1
creolization
28.17.25(.3.11)
creolize 35.15.21(.4.1)
Creon 28.10.1, 28.17.1
creosote 22.21.11
crêpe 20.3, 20.4
crêpe de Chine 28.1
crêpe suzette 22.5.14
crêpey 1.8.3
crepitant 22.26.15(.9)
crepitate 22.4.9(.5)
crepitation 28.17.25(.3.3)
crepitus 34.18.11(.10)
crept 22.22.3

crepuscular
17.34.16(.21.2)
crescendo 19.11.14
crescent 22.26.15(.17.2)
crescentic 24.2.10(.14)
cresol 40.9.14
cress 34.5
cresset 22.2.16
Cressida 17.13.15
crest 22.29.5
crestfallen 28.17.33(.8)
crestless 34.18.29(.22)
Creswell 40.5.17(.16)
cresyl 40.2.14, 40.13.12
Cretaceous 34.18.22(.3)
Cretan 28.17.11(.1)
Crete 22.1
cretic 24.2.10(.1)
cretin 28.2.11(.4),
28.17.11(.4)
cretinism 27.15.21(.2.9)
cretinize 35.15.12(.5)
cretinous 34.18.16(.15.2)
cretinously 1.31.33(.12.3)
cretonne 28.10.9
crevasse 34.7.14
crevice 34.2.15
crew 16
crewcut 22.15.4
Crewe 16
crewel 40.16.8
crewelwork 24.17.6(.19)
Crewkerne 28.18.5
crewman 28.17.16(.15)
cri 2
crib 21.2
cribbage 39.2.9
cribber 17.11.2
cribella 17.34.5(.2)
cribellum 27.15.28(.4)
cribo 19.9.1
cribriform 27.10.5(.2)
cribwork 24.17.6(.7)
Criccieth 32.3, 32.5
Crich 38.12
Crichton 28.17.11(.12)
crick 24.2
cricket 22.2.9(.1)
cricketer 17.12.16(.7)
Crickhowell 40.16.3
cricoid 23.13.9
cri de coeur 18
cried 23.15
Crieff 30.1
crier 17.6
crikey 1.12.10
crim 27.2
crime 27.12
Crimea 3.8
Crimean 28.3.7

crime passionnel 40.5.8
crimes passionnels
35.30.4
criminal 40.26.13(.8)
criminalistic
24.2.10(.15.3)
criminality 1.10.16(.32.8)
criminalization
28.17.25(.3.12)
criminalize 35.15.21(.4.5)
criminally 1.31.17(.14.2)
criminate 22.4.14(.9.2)
crimination 28.17.25(.3.8)
criminative 31.2.1(.9.2)
criminatory 1.29.11(.8.7)
criminological
40.23.12(.17.2)
criminologist
22.29.2(.26.4)
criminology
1.26.10(.11.4)
Crimond 23.24.16(.7)
crimp 20.16.1
crimper 17.10.17
crimpily 1.31.17(.7)
crimpiness 34.18.16(.2.2)
crimplene® 28.1.27(.9)
crimpy 1.8.14
crimson 28.17.24(.15)
cringe 39.17.1
cringer 17.29.16(.1)
cringle 40.24.14(.1)
crinkle 40.23.15
crinkliness
34.18.16(.2.10)
crinkly 1.31.24(.12)
crinoid 23.13.12
crinoidal 40.22.9
crinoline 28.2.31(.10)
criolla 17.34.18
criollo 19.29.14
cripes 34.21.8
Crippen 28.17.9
cripple 40.19.2
crippledom 27.15.10(.20)
cripplehood 23.16.5(.14)
crippler 17.34.19
cripplingly 1.31.28(.1.18)
Cripps 34.21.2
Cris 34.1
cris de coeur 18
crises 35.1.16(.8)
crisis 34.2.17(.8)
crisp 20.17
crispate 22.4.7
crispbread 23.5.15
crisper 17.10.18
Crispian 28.3.1
Crispin 28.2.9
crispiness 34.18.16(.2.2)
crisply 1.31.20

crispness 34.18.16(.18)
crispy 1.8.15
crisscross 34.10.16
crista 17.12.24(.2)
cristae 2.12.15
cristate 22.4.9(.9)
cristobalite 22.16.25(.9)
crit 22.2
Critchley 1.31.36
criteria 3.22.2
criterial 40.3.14(.2)
criterion 28.3.20(.2)
critic 24.2.10(.2.1)
critical 40.23.12(.7.1)
criticality 1.10.16(.32.5)
critically 1.31.24(.9.3)
criticalness
    34.18.16(.37.5)
criticaster 17.12.24(.5)
criticism 27.15.21(.2.12)
criticizable 40.20.16(.22)
criticize 35.15.16(.4)
criticizer 17.25.12(.10)
critique 24.1.3
Crittall 40.10.5
critter 17.12.2
croak 24.18
croaker 17.14.17
croakily 1.31.17(.11)
croakiness 34.18.16(.2.4)
croaky 1.12.15
Croat 22.7.4
Croatia 17.26.3
Croatian 28.17.25(.3.1)
croc 24.9
Croce 4.22
croceate 22.4.2(.9)
crochet 4.20
crocheter 17.2.8
croci 2.14, 14.10
crocidolite 22.16.25(.9)
crock 24.9
Crocker 17.14.8
crockery 1.29.11(.10)
crocket 22.2.9(.5)
Crockett 22.2.9(.5)
Crockford 23.18.16(.13)
crocodile 40.13.4
crocodilian 28.3.21(.2)
crocus 34.18.13(.12)
Croesus 34.18.20
croft 22.27.5
crofter 17.12.23
Crofton 28.17.11(.24)
croissant 11.12
Croker 17.14.17
Cro-Magnon 11.18,
    28.10.25, 28.17.17(.13)
Cromarty 1.10.16(.12)
crombec 24.4.3

Crombie 1.9.18
Crome 27.17
Cromer 17.17.16
Cromford 23.18.16(.15)
cromlech 24.16.16, 25.10
Crompton 28.17.11(.18)
Cromwell 40.5.17(.11)
Cromwellian 28.3.21(.4)
crone 28.19
Cronenberg 26.14.1(.9)
Cronin 28.2.18
cronk 24.19.5
Cronus 34.18.16(.17)
crony 1.16.17
cronyism 27.15.21(.2.1)
crook 24.14
crookback 24.6.6(.14)
Crooke 24.14
crooked 23.18.11
crookedly 1.31.23(.14.5)
crookedness
    34.18.16(.21.1)
crookery 1.29.11(.10)
Crookes 34.23.13
Croom 27.14
Croome 27.14
croon 28.16
crooner 17.18.15
crop 20.7
cropper 17.10.8
croquet 12.15, 4.11
croquette 22.5.5
crore 12
Crosbie 1.9.22
Crosby 1.9.21, 1.9.22
Crosland 23.24.16(.16.4)
cross 34.10
crossbar 10.5.12
crossbeam 27.1.1
crossbench 38.18.2
cross-bencher 17.28.22
crossbill 40.2.4
crossbones 35.26.15
crossbow 19.9.17
crossbowman
    28.17.16(.18)
crossbred 23.5.15
crossbreed 23.1.11
crosscheck 24.4.11
crosscurrent
    22.26.15(.23.2)
crosscut 22.15.4
crosse 34.10
crossfield 23.31.1(.2)
crossfire 17.6.9(.10)
crosshatch 38.5
crossing 29.1.23
cross-legged 23.18.12,
    23.22
crossly 1.31.33(.6)

Crossmaglen 28.5.20
Crossman 28.17.16(.29)
crossmatch 38.5
crossness 34.18.16(.31.2)
crossover 17.21.14(.9)
crosspatch 38.5
crosspiece 34.1.1
crossply 14.25.11
crossrail 40.4.14
crossroad 23.20.12
crosstab 21.6
crosstalk 24.10.2
crosstie 14.8
crosstown 28.8.1
crosstree 2.30.10
crosswalk 24.10.9
crossways 35.4.15
crosswind 23.24.2
crosswise 35.15.19
crossword 23.19.8
crotch 38.8
crotchet 22.19.21
crotchetiness
    34.18.16(.2.3)
crotchety 1.10.16(.17)
croton 28.17.11(.17)
crouch 38.6
croup 20.12
croupier 3.2.6, 4.2.1
croupy 1.8.10
croustade 23.9.7
croûton 28.10.9
crow 19
crowbar 10.5.6
crowberry 1.29.11(.7.1)
Crowborough
    17.32.14(.5)
crowd 23.8
crowdedness
    34.18.16(.21.1)
crowd-pleaser 17.25.1
Crowe 19
crowfoot 22.17
Crowley 1.31.19
crown 28.8
crownpiece 34.1.1
Crowther 17.23.6
Crowthorne 28.11.8
Croydon 28.17.12(.11)
crozier 3.15.8, 17.27.9
cru 16
cruces 35.1.16(.9)
crucial 40.33.8
cruciality 1.10.16(.32.1)
crucially 1.31.17(.22)
crucian 28.17.25(.11)
cruciate 22.3.10,
    22.4.2(.11)
crucible 40.20.16(.21.2)
crucifer 17.20.12(.3)

cruciferous 34.18.27(.20)
crucifier 17.6.9(.4)
crucifix 34.23.2(.7)
crucifixion 28.17.25(.15.1)
cruciform 27.10.5(.2)
crucify 14.14.4(.9)
cruck 24.12
crud 23.14
cruddy 1.11.13
crude 23.17
crudely 1.31.23(.13)
crudeness 34.18.16(.21.1)
crudités 4.9
crudity 1.10.16(.9)
cruel 40.16.8
cruelly 1.31.16,
    1.31.17(.5)
cruelness 34.18.16(.37.1)
cruelty 1.10.28
cruet 22.2.4
Crufts 34.22.19
Cruikshank 24.19.3(.5)
cruise 35.17
cruiser 17.25.14
cruiserweight 22.4.21
cruiseway 4.25.23
cruller 17.34.12
crumb 27.11
crumble 40.20.19
crumbliness
    34.18.16(.2.10)
crumbly 1.31.21(.12)
crumby 1.15.10
Crumlin 28.2.31(.19)
crummily 1.31.17(.13)
crumminess
    34.18.16(.2.5)
crummy 1.15.10
crump 20.16.5
crumpet 22.2.5
crumple 40.19.14
crumpled 23.31.14
crumply 1.31.20
crunch 38.18.7
cruncher 17.28.22
crunchily 1.31.17(.24)
crunchiness
    34.18.16(.2.8)
crunchy 1.24.15
crupper 17.10.11
crural 40.16.13(.11)
crusade 23.4.10
crusader 17.13.3
cruse 35.17
crush 36.12
crusher 17.26.10
crushingly 1.31.28(.1.13)
crust 22.29.12
Crustacea 17.26.3
crustacean 28.17.25(.3.3)

Cunene 17.18.3
cunjevoi 13.8
cunnilinctus 34.18.11(.13)
cunnilingus 34.18.14(.8)
cunning 29.1.17(.9)
Cunningham 27.15.15
cunningly 1.31.28(.1.7)
cunningness 34.18.16(.26)
Cunobelinus 34.18.16(.1)
cunt 22.26.12
cup 20.9
Cupar 17.10.13
cupbearer 17.32.5
cupboard 23.18.8
cupcake 24.3.6
cupel 40.19.10
cupellation 28.17.25(.3.14)
cupful 40.14.6(.8)
cupid 23.2.6
cupidity 1.10.16(.9)
Cupitt 22.2.5
cupola 17.34.16(.5)
cupola-furnace 34.18.16(.16)
cuppa 17.10.11
cuprammonium 27.3.8(.10)
cupreous 34.3.15(.6)
cupric 24.2.26(.12)
cupriferous 34.18.27(.20)
Cuprinol® 40.9.12
cupronickel 40.23.2
cuprous 34.18.27(.12)
cupule 40.15.9(.1)
cur 18
curability 1.10.16(.22.1)
curable 40.20.16(.27.2)
curably 1.31.21(.8)
Curaçao 19.20.10
curacy 1.22.16(.13)
curare 1.29.6
curarine 28.1.25(.3)
curarize 35.15.20(.2)
curassow 19.20.10
curate 22.19.24(.6)
curation 28.17.25(.3.13)
curative 31.2.1(.9.4)
curator 17.12.4(.15)
curatorial 40.3.14(.5)
curatorship 20.2.7(.9)
curb 21.15
curbside 23.15.11(.8)
curbstone 28.19.4(.9)
curcuma 17.17.14(.11)
curd 23.19
curdle 40.22.14
curdler 17.34.22
curdy 1.11.18

cure 12, 17.7
curé 4.26.7, 4.26.8
cured 23.12.10, 23.18.4
curer 17.32.14(.3)
curettage 37.4.3, 39.2.10
curette 22.5.19
curfew 16.24.11
curia 3.22.9, 3.22.12
Curial 40.3.14(.6)
curie 1.29.8, 1.29.11(.3)
curio 15.1.12
curiosa 17.24.17, 17.25.15
curiosity 1.10.16(.16.2)
curious 34.3.15(.5)
curiously 1.31.33(.1.4)
curiousness 34.18.16(.31.1)
Curitiba 17.11.1
curium 27.3.17(.4)
curl 40.17
curler 17.34.17
curlew 16.24.17, 16.25
Curley 1.31.18
curlicue 16.24.7
curliness 34.18.16(.2.10)
curly 1.31.18
curmudgeon 28.17.28(.7)
curmudgeonly 1.31.27(.14)
currach 17.32.12, 25.10
curragh 25.10
Curran 28.17.31(.9)
currant 22.26.15(.23.2)
currawong 29.6.13
currency 1.22.23(.10.4)
current 22.26.15(.23.2)
currently 1.31.22(.20.5)
currentness 34.18.16(.20.4)
curricle 40.23.12(.18)
curricula 17.34.16(.21.2)
curricular 17.34.16(.21.2)
curriculum 27.15.28(.11)
curriculum vitae 14.8
Currie 1.29.9
currier 3.22.10
currish 36.2.25
currishly 1.31.35(.7.4)
currishness 34.18.16(.33.6)
curry 1.29.9
curse 34.19
cursed 22.29.16, 23.18.20
cursedly 1.31.23(.14.7)
cursedness 34.18.16(.21.1)
curser 17.24.16
cursillo 19.28
cursive 31.2.4(.10)
cursively 1.31.30(.7.4)
cursiveness 34.18.16(.28.2)

cursor 17.24.16
cursorial 40.3.14(.5)
cursorily 1.31.17(.27.2)
cursoriness 34.18.16(.2.9)
cursory 1.29.11(.18)
curst 22.29.16
curt 22.20
curtail 40.4.2
curtailment 22.26.15(.13.7)
curtain 28.17.11(.16)
curtain wall 40.10
curtana 17.18.3, 17.18.8(.2)
curtilage 39.2.23
Curtin 28.2.11(.11), 28.17.11(.16)
Curtis 34.2.8
curtly 1.31.22(.16)
curtness 34.18.16(.20.3)
curtsy 1.22.21
curule 40.15.8
curvaceous 34.18.22(.3)
curvaceously 1.31.33(.12.4)
curvaciously 1.31.33(.12.4)
curvature 17.7.12(.3), 17.28.15
curve 31.11
curvet 22.5.11
curvifoliate 22.3.13
curviform 27.10.5(.2)
curvilinear 3.9.2
curvilinearly 1.31.3(.7)
curviness 34.18.16(.2.6)
curvirostral 40.16.13(.16)
curvy 1.19.11
Curzon 28.17.24(.13)
Cusack 24.6.14, 24.6.15
cuscus 34.14
cusec 24.4.8
cush 36.13
cushat 22.19.20
cush-cush 36.13
cushily 1.31.17(.22)
cushiness 34.18.16(.2.8)
Cushing 29.1.25
cushion 28.17.25(.10)
cushiony 1.16.15(.16)
Cushitic 24.2.10(.2.3)
cushy 1.24.10
cusp 20.17
cuspate 22.4.7
cuspid 23.2.6
cuspidal 40.22.13
cuspidate 22.4.10
cuspidor 12.6.6
cuss 34.14
cussed 23.18.20
cussedly 1.31.23(.14.7)

cussedness 34.18.16(.21.1)
Cusson 28.17.23(.11)
custard 23.18.9(.20)
Custer 17.12.24(.10)
custodial 40.3.4
custodian 28.3.4(.10)
custodianship 20.2.7(.19)
custody 1.11.17
custom 27.15.9(.15)
customable 40.20.16(.15)
customarily 1.31.17(.27.2)
customariness 34.18.16(.2.9)
customary 1.29.11(.12)
customer 17.17.14(.2)
customize 35.15.11
cut 22.15
cutaneous 34.3.6(.3)
cutaway 4.25.9
cutback 24.6.6(.12)
cutch 38.11
cutdown 28.8.2
cute 22.18
cutely 1.31.22(.14)
cuteness 34.18.16(.20.2)
Cutex 34.23.4(.3)
Cutforth 32.10, 32.14.13
Cuthbert 22.19.9
Cuthbertson 28.17.23(.19)
cuticle 40.23.12(.7.2)
cuticular 17.34.16(.21.2)
Cuticura® 17.32.14(.3)
cutie 1.10.15
cutis 34.2.8
cutlass 34.18.29(.22)
cutler 17.34.21
cutlery 1.29.11(.27)
cutlet 22.19.26(.17)
cutoff 30.8.4
cutout 22.9.7
cutpurse 34.19.1
cutter 17.12.12
cutthroat 22.21.14
cutting 29.1.12(.10)
cuttingly 1.31.28(.1.4)
cuttle 40.21.9
cuttlebone 28.19.3
cuttlefish 36.2.18(.21)
cutty 1.10.12
Cutty Sark 24.8
cutup 20.9.5
cutwater 17.12.10(.7)
cutworm 27.16.7
cuvée 4.16
cuvette 22.5.11
Cuvier 4.2.6
Cuxhaven 28.17.20(.6)
Cuyahoga 17.16.15

Cuzco **19.12.17**
cwm **27.13**
Cy **14**
cyan **28.7.2, 28.17.5**
cyanamid **23.2.12**
cyanamide **23.15.7**
cyanic **24.2.15(.5)**
cyanide **23.15.8**
cyano **19.15.6, 19.15.12**
Cyanobacteria **3.22.2**
cyanobacterium
 27.3.17(.2)
cyanocobalamin
 28.2.17(.5)
cyanogen **28.17.28(.9)**
cyanogenic **24.2.15(.4)**
cyanoses **35.1.16(.11)**
cyanosis **34.2.17(.11.2)**
cyanotic **24.2.10(.6)**
Cybele **1.31.17(.8)**
cybercafé **1.18.4, 4.15**
cybernate **22.4.14(.9.1)**
cybernation
 28.17.25(.3.8)
cybernetic **24.2.10(.3.1)**
cybernetician
 28.17.25(.2.2)
cyberneticist **22.29.2(.22)**
cyberpunk **24.19.7**
cyborg **26.9**
cycad **23.7.9, 23.18.11**
Cyclades **35.1.8**
Cycladic **24.2.11(.5)**
cyclamate **22.4.13(.6)**
cyclamen **28.17.16(.16)**
cycle **40.23.10**
cyclic **24.2.27(.16)**
cyclical **40.23.12(.19)**
cyclically **1.31.24(.9.12)**
cyclist **22.29.2(.31.6)**
cycloalkane **28.4.5**
cyclo-cross **34.10.16**
cyclodextrin **28.2.29(.8)**
cyclograph **30.7.5(.1)**
cyclohexane **28.4.12**
cycloid **23.13.20**
cycloidal **40.22.9**
cyclometer **17.12.16(.9.2)**
cyclone **28.19.19**
cyclonic **24.2.15(.6.4)**
cyclonically **1.31.24(.9.8)**
cyclopaedia **3.5.1**
cyclopaedically
 1.31.24(.9.7)
cycloparaffin **28.2.19**
Cyclopean **28.3.1,
 28.17.1(.1)**
cyclopedia **3.5.1**
cyclopedic **24.2.11(.1)**
cyclopedically
 1.31.24(.9.7)

cyclopropane **28.4.1**
cyclopropyl **40.2.3,
 40.19.7, 40.19.13**
Cyclops **34.21.6**
cyclorama **17.17.7**
cycloramic **24.2.14(.4)**
cyclosporin **28.2.29(.5)**
cyclostomate **22.4.13(.7)**
cyclostome **27.17.4**
cyclostyle **40.13.3(.10)**
cyclothymia **3.8.5**
cyclothymic **24.2.14(.8)**
cyclotron **28.10.24(.7)**
cygnet **22.19.15(.11)**
Cygnus **34.18.16(.23)**
cylinder **17.13.20(.13)**
cylindrical **40.23.12(.18)**
cylindrically
 1.31.24(.9.12)
cyma **17.17.11**
cymbal **40.20.19**
cymbalist **22.29.2(.31.2)**
cymbalo **19.29.12**
Cymbeline **28.1.27(.7)**
cymbidium **27.3.4(.2)**
cymbiform **27.10.5(.2)**
cyme **27.12**
cymose **34.20.8**
Cymric **24.2.26(.17)**
Cymru **1.29.19**
Cynan **28.17.17(.7)**
Cyncoed **23.13.9**
Cynewulf **30.20.6**
cynghanedd **33.9**
cynic **24.2.15(.2)**
cynical **40.23.12(.11)**
cynically **1.31.24(.9.8)**
cynicism **27.15.21(.2.12)**
cynocephali **14.25.9**
cynocephalus
 34.18.29(.17.4)
cynosure **17.7.10,
 17.7.12(.12)**
Cynthia **3.12**
cy pres **4**
cypress **34.18.27(.12)**
Cyprian **28.3.20(.9)**
cyprinoid **23.13.12**
Cypriot **22.3.12**
cypripedium **27.3.4(.1)**
Cyprus **34.18.27(.12)**
cypsela **17.34.16(.15)**
cypselae **2.32.9(.6)**
Cyrano de Bergerac
 24.6.21
Cyrenaic **24.2.3**
Cyrenaica **17.14.15(.2)**
Cyrene **1.16.1(.15)**
Cyrenian **28.3.8(.1)**
Cyril **40.16.13(.1)**

Cyrillic **24.2.27(.2)**
Cyrus **34.18.27(.10)**
cyst **22.29.2**
cystectomy **1.15.13(.1)**
cysteine **28.1.2, 28.4.3**
cystic **24.2.10(.15.1)**
cystine **28.1.9(.7)**
cystitis **34.18.11(.8)**
cystoscope **20.15.4(.1)**
cystoscopic **24.2.8(.5)**
cystotomy **1.8.11(.5)**
cystotomy **1.15.13(.1)**
Cythera **17.32.2**
Cytherea **17.1.16**
cytidine **28.1.10**
cytochrome **27.17.13**
cytogenetic **24.2.10(.3.1)**
cytogenetical
 40.23.12(.7.1)
cytogenetically
 1.31.24(.9.3)
cytogeneticist
 22.29.2(.22)
cytogenic **24.2.15(.4)**
cytological **40.23.12(.17.2)**
cytologically
 1.31.24(.9.11)
cytologist **22.29.2(.26.3)**
cytology **1.26.10(.11.2)**
cytoplasm **27.15.21(.3)**
cytoplasmic **24.2.14(.17)**
cytosine **28.1.18(.6)**
cytotoxic **24.2.20(.13)**
cytotoxin **28.2.23(.14)**
czarevna **17.18.27**
czarina **17.18.1(.15)**
czarist **22.29.2(.29.2)**
Czech **24.4**
Czechoslovak **24.6.12**
Czechoslovakia **3.6.5**
Czechoslovakian **28.3.5**
Czerny **1.16.16**
d **2**
DA **4**
dab **21.6**
dabber **17.11.5**
dabble **40.20.6**
dabbler **17.34.20**
dabbling **29.1.31(.16)**
dabchick **24.2.23**
dabster **17.12.24(.17)**
da capo **19.8**
Dacca **10.8.3, 17.14.5**
dace **34.4**
dacha **17.28.6**
Dachau **9.5**
dachshund **23.24.16(.10)**
Dacia **3.14.3, 17.26.3**
Dacian **28.3.13,
 28.17.25(.3.1)**

dacite **22.16.19(.2)**
dacoit **22.14**
Dacre **17.14.3**
Dacron® **28.10.24(.9)**
dactyl **40.21.16**
dactylic **24.2.27(.2)**
dactylography
 1.18.9(.3.2)
dactylology **1.26.10(.11.5)**
dad **23.7**
Dada **10.7**
Dadaism **27.15.21(.2.1)**
Dadaist **22.29.2(.5)**
Dadaistic **24.2.10(.15.1)**
daddy **1.11.7**
daddy-long-legs **35.24**
dado **19.11.4**
Daedalian **28.3.21(.3)**
Daedalus **34.18.29(.17.2)**
daemon **28.17.16(.1)**
daemonic **24.2.15(.6.2)**
daemonological
 40.23.12(.17.2)
DAF® **30.5**
daff **30.5**
daffily **1.31.17(.16.1)**
daffiness **34.18.16(.2.6)**
daffodil **40.2.6**
daffy **1.18.4**
daft **22.27.4**
daftly **1.31.22(.21)**
daftness **34.18.16(.20.4)**
Dafydd **33.2**
dag **26.5**
Dagenham **27.15.14(.11)**
Dagestan **28.9.2**
dagga **17.15, 17.16.5,
 17.16.6**
dagger **17.16.5**
daggerboard **23.12.2(.5)**
daglock **24.9.16(.14)**
Dagmar **10.10.7**
dag-nab **21.6**
dago **19.13.3**
Dagon **28.10.12**
Daguerre **6.7**
daguerreotype **20.10.2**
Dagwood **23.16.6(.12)**
dah **10**
dahl **40.8**
dahlia **3.24.3**
Dahomey **1.15.15**
Dahrendorf **30.9.1**
Dai **14**
Daihatsu® **16.15**
Dáil **40.11**
Dáil Eireann **28.17.31(.4)**
Dailey **1.31.4**
daily **1.31.4**
Daimler® **17.34.25**

daimon 28.19.9
daimonic 24.2.15(.6.2)
daintily 1.31.17(.9.3)
daintiness 34.18.16(.2.3)
dainty 1.10.23(.2)
daiquiri 1.29.11(.10)
Dairen 28.5.18
dairy 1.29.4
dairying 29.1.2
dairymaid 23.4.7
dairyman 28.7.10(.2), 28.17.16(.2)
dairymen 28.5.7(.2)
dais 34.2.1, 34.4
daisy 1.23.3
Dakar 10.8.3, 17.14.5
Dakin 28.2.13(.2)
Dakota 17.12.18
Dakotan 28.17.11(.17)
DAKS 34.23.5
Dalai Lama 17.17.7
dalasi 1.22.8
dale 40.4
Dalek 24.4.14
dalesfolk 24.18.7
dalesman 28.17.16(.30)
daleswoman 28.17.16(.14)
daleswomen 28.2.17(.1)
daleth 22.2.25
Daley 1.31.4
Dalgetty 1.10.4
Dalgleish 36.1
Dalglish 36.1
Dalhousie 1.23.6, 1.23.12
Dali 1.31.9
Dalian 28.3.21(.6)
Dalkeith 32.1
Dallapiccola 17.34.16(.9)
Dallas 34.18.29(.7)
dalliance 34.24.2
dallier 3.24.5
dally 1.31.7
Dalmatia 17.26.3
Dalmatian 28.17.25(.3.7)
dalmatic 24.2.10(.4.2)
Dalriada 17.13.7
Dalrymple 40.19.14
dal segno 19.28
Dalston 28.17.11(.25)
Dalton 28.17.11(.27)
daltonism 27.15.21(.2.9)
Daltonize 35.15.12(.5)
Dalwhinnie 1.16.2
Daly 1.31.4
Dalyell 40.5
Dalzell 40.5.12
Dalziel 40.1.11, 40.5
dam 27.6
damage 39.2.14

damageable 40.20.16(.25)
damagingly 1.31.28(.1.16)
Damara 17.32.7
Damaraland 23.24.6(.13)
damascene 28.1.18(.6)
Damascus 34.18.13(.14)
damask 24.20.8
Dambuster 17.12.24(.10)
dame 27.4
Damian 28.3.7
dammar 17.17.6
dammit 22.2.11
damn 27.6
damna 17.18.25
damnable 40.20.16(.16.3)
damnably 1.31.21(.6)
damnation 28.17.25(.3.8)
damnatory 1.29.11(.8.7)
damnedest 22.29.15(.10)
damn fool 40.15
damnification 28.17.25(.3.5)
damnify 14.14.4(.7)
damningly 1.31.28(.1.7)
damnum 27.15.14(.16)
Damocles 35.1.23
Damon 28.17.16(.4)
damozel 40.5.12
damp 20.16.3
dampen 28.17.9
dampener 17.18.16(.3)
damper 17.10.17
Dampier 3.2.8
dampish 36.2.9
damply 1.31.20
dampness 34.18.16(.18)
damsel 40.32.16
damselfish 36.2.18(.21)
damselfly 14.25.14
damson 28.17.24(.15)
dan 28.7
Dana 17.18.3, 17.18.8
Danae 2.3, 2.4
Danaides 35.1.8
Dan-Air® 6
Danakil 40.2.7
Da Nang 29.4
Danbury 1.29.11(.7.2)
Danby 1.9.19
dance 34.24.6
danceable 40.20.16(.21.3)
dancer 17.24.22(.3)
dancewear 6.18.12
dandelion 28.17.5
dander 17.13.20(.4)
dandify 14.14.4(.5)
Dandini 1.16.1(.4)
dandle 40.22.16
Dando 19.11.14
dandruff 30.11.10

dandy 1.11.20(.4)
dandyish 36.2.1
dandyism 27.15.21(.2.1)
Dane 28.4
Danegeld 23.31.4
Danelaw 12.23.8
daneweed 23.1.10
danewort 22.20.15
dang 29.4
danger 17.29.16(.2)
Dangerfield 23.31.1(.2)
dangerous 34.18.27(.27)
dangerously 1.31.33(.12.5)
dangerousness 34.18.16(.31.5)
dangle 40.24.14(.2)
dangler 17.34.24
dangly 1.31.25
Daniel 40.16.14
Daniela 17.34.5
Danielle 40.5
Daniels 35.30.12
Danish 36.2.16(.3)
dank 24.19.3
dankly 1.31.24(.12)
dankness 34.18.16(.22)
Dankworth 32.14.15
Dannimac 24.6.10
Danny 1.16.6
danse macabre 17.32.18
danses macabres 35.18.23
Dansette 22.5.13
danseur 18.11
danseuse 35.19
Dante 1.10.23(.4), 4.9.9
Dantean 28.3.3, 28.17.1(.3)
Dantesque 24.20.3
danthonia 3.9.11
Danton 11.5, 28.10.9
Danube 21.13
Danubian 28.3.2
Danvers 35.18.15
Danzig 26.2.7
Dão 9, 19.3
dap 20.5
daphne 1.16.24
daphnia 3.9.15
Daphnis 34.2.13
dapper 17.10.5
dapperly 1.31.17(.7)
dapperness 34.18.16(.15.2)
dapple 40.19.5
dapsone 28.19.13
Darbishire 17.26.14
Darby 1.9.6
Darcy 1.22.8
Dardanelles 35.30.4

dare 6
daredevil 40.28.4
daren't 22.26.5
darer 17.32.5
daresay 4.18, 4.18.5
Dar es Salaam 27.8.10
Darfur 18.9
darg 26.6
dargah 17.16.6
Dari 1.29.4
daric 24.2.26(.5)
Darien 28.3.20(.4)
Darin 28.2.29(.3)
daring 29.1.30(.4)
daringly 1.31.28(.1.17)
dariole 40.14.1
Darius 34.3.15(.3), 34.18.5
Darjeeling 29.1.31(.1)
dark 24.8
darken 28.17.13(.6)
darkener 17.18.16(.6)
darkie 1.12.6
darkish 36.2.13
darkling 29.1.31(.19)
darkly 1.31.24(.6)
darkness 34.18.16(.22)
darkroom 27.14.6(.10)
darksome 27.15.20(.15)
Darlene 28.1.27(.4)
darling 29.1.31(.8)
Darlington 28.17.11(.23)
Darmstadt 22.7.7
darn 28.9
darnedest 22.29.15(.10)
darnel 40.26.7
darner 17.18.8
Darnley 1.31.27(.8)
Darrell 40.16.13(.5)
Darren 28.17.31(.5)
Darrow 19.27.4
dart 22.10
d'Artagnan 28.17.32
dartboard 23.12.2(.8)
darter 17.12.8
Dartford 23.18.16(.11)
Darth Vader 17.13.3
Dartmoor 12.9.7, 17.7.7
Dartmouth 32.14.11
dartre 17.12.8
Darwen 28.2.28
Darwin 28.2.28
Darwinian 28.3.8(.2)
Darwinism 27.15.21(.2.9)
Darwinist 22.29.2(.18.3)
Daryl 40.16.13(.5)
dash 36.6
dashboard 23.12.2(.17)
dashiki 1.12.2, 1.12.13
dashing 29.1.25
dashingly 1.31.28(.1.13)

dashingness 34.18.16(.26)
dashpot 22.11.2
dassie 1.22.6
dastard 23.18.9(.20)
dastardliness
 34.18.16(.2.10)
dastardly 1.31.23(.14.3)
dastur 17.7.3
dasyure 17.7.12(.1)
data 17.12.4, 17.12.8
databank 24.19.3(.1)
database 34.4.3
datable 40.20.16(.11.1)
datafile 40.13.9
Datapost® 22.29.17(.1)
Datchet 22.2.20
date 22.4
dateless 34.18.29(.22)
dateline 28.14.19(.14)
datival 40.28.9
dativally 1.31.17(.17)
dative 31.2.1(.3)
Datsun® 28.17.23(.19)
datum 27.15.9(.2)
datura 17.32.14(.3)
daub 21.9
daube 21.16
dauber 17.11.9
Daubigny 1.30
daubster 17.12.24(.17)
dauby 1.9.8
Daudet 4.10.8
daughter 17.12.10
daughterhood 23.16.5(.3)
daughterly 1.31.17(.9.2)
daunt 22.26.10
dauntingly 1.31.28(.1.4)
dauntless 34.18.29(.22)
dauntlessly 1.31.33(.12.6)
dauntlessness
 34.18.16(.31.6)
dauphin 8, 28.2.19
dauphine 28.1.15
Dave 31.3
davenport 22.13.1
Daventry 1.29.15(.15)
David 23.2.15
Davidson 28.17.23(.20)
Davie 1.19.3
Davies 34.2.15
da Vinci 1.24.15
Davis 34.2.15
Davison 28.17.23(.14)
davit 22.2.14
Davos 34.20.11
Davy 1.19.3
daw 12
dawdle 40.22.8
dawdler 17.34.22
Dawe 12

Dawes 35.12
Dawkins 35.26.2
Dawlish 36.2.27
dawn 28.11
dawning 29.1.17(.8)
Dawson 28.17.23(.9)
day 4
Dayak 24.6.3
Dayan 28.7, 28.9
daybed 23.5.2
daybook 24.14.3
daybreak 24.3.13
daydream 27.1.12
daydreamer 17.17.1
Day-Glo® 19.29.20
dayless 34.18.29(.4)
daylight 22.16.25(.4)
dayroom 27.14.6(.3)
daysack 24.6.14
dayside 23.15.11(.4)
daystar 10.6.8
daytime 27.12.1
Daytona 17.18.18(.2)
daywork 24.17.6(.2)
Daz® 35.7
daze 35.4
dazedly 1.31.23(.14.7)
dazzle 40.32.5
dazzlement
 22.26.15(.13.7)
dazzler 17.34.28
dazzlingly 1.31.28(.1.18)
dBase 34.4.3
deaccession 28.17.25(.4)
deacon 28.17.13(.1)
deaconate 22.19.15(.9)
deaconess 34.5.6
deaconship 20.2.7(.19)
deactivate 22.4.16
deactivation
 28.17.25(.3.9)
deactivator 17.12.4(.11)
dead 23.5
dead-beat 22.1.2
deadbeat 22.1.2
deadbolt 22.32.12
deaden 28.17.12(.5)
deadener 17.18.16(.5)
deadeye 14.9
deadfall 40.10.11
deadhead 23.5.13(.10)
deadlight 22.16.25(.14)
deadline 28.14.19(.15)
deadliness 34.18.16(.2.10)
deadlock 24.9.16(.12)
deadly 1.31.23(.4)
deadness 34.18.16(.21.1)
deadpan 28.7.4
deadstock 24.9.4
de-aerate 22.4.22(.3)

de-aeration
 28.17.25(.3.13)
deaf 30.4
deafen 28.17.19
deafeningly 1.31.28(.1.7)
deafly 1.31.29
deafness 34.18.16(.27)
Deakin 28.2.13(.1)
deal 40.1
dealer 17.34.1
dealership 20.2.7(.9)
dealing 29.1.31(.1)
dealt 22.32.2
deambulation
 28.17.25(.3.14)
deambulatory
 1.29.11(.8.10)
deamination
 28.17.25(.3.8)
dean 28.1
deanery 1.29.11(.13.1)
Deanna 17.18.1, 17.18.6
dear 3
Deare 3
dearie 1.29.2
dearly 1.31.3
Dearne 28.18
dearness 34.18.16(.3)
dearth 32.15
deasil 40.31.5, 40.33.3
De'ath 32.6
death 32.5
deathbed 23.5.2
deathblow 19.29.16
deathless 34.18.29(.31)
deathlessly 1.31.33(.12.6)
deathlessness
 34.18.16(.31.6)
deathlike 24.13.7(.21)
deathliness
 34.18.16(.2.10)
deathly 1.31.31
deathtrap 20.5.6
deathwatch 38.8
deattribute 22.18.10
deattribution
 28.17.25(.11)
Deauville 40.2.12
deb 21.4
débâcle 40.23.6
debag 26.5.1
debar 10.5
debark 24.8.3
debarkation
 28.17.25(.3.5)
debarkment
 22.26.15(.13.3)
debase 34.4.3
debasement
 22.26.15(.13.5)
debaser 17.24.4

debatable 40.20.16(.11.1)
debatably 1.31.21(.4.1)
debate 22.4.8
debater 17.12.4(.4)
debauch 38.9
debauchee 2.24, 2.26
debaucher 17.28.10
debauchery 1.29.11(.22)
Debbie 1.9.4
debeak 24.1.2
de Beauvoir 10.22
De Beers 35.3
Debenhams 35.25.10
debenture 17.28.22
debilitate 22.4.9(.5)
debilitatingly
 1.31.28(.1.4)
debilitation 28.17.25(.3.3)
debilitative 31.2.1(.9.1)
debility 1.10.16(.22.1)
debit 22.2.6
debonair 6.9
debonairly 1.31.6
de-bond 23.24.9
de-bonder 17.13.20(.7)
debone 28.19.3
Deborah 17.32.14(.5)
debouch 36.14, 38.6
debouchment
 22.26.15(.13.6)
Debra 17.32.18
Debrett 22.5.19
debridement 11.8,
 22.26.15(.13.3)
debrief 30.1.8
debriefing 29.1.19
débris 2.30.9
debt 22.5
debtor 17.12.5
debug 26.10
debugger 17.16.9
debunk 24.19.7
debunker 17.14.21(.5)
debus 34.14
Debussy 1.22.15
début 16.24.4
débutant 22.26.8
débutante 22.26.8
DEC 24.4
decadal 40.22.13
decade 23.4.5
decadence 34.24.10(.11)
decadent 22.26.15(.10)
decadentism
 27.15.21(.2.4)
decadently
 1.31.22(.20.2)
decadic 24.2.11(.5)
decaf 30.5.3
decaffeinate
 22.4.14(.9.3)

decagon 28.10.12, 28.17.15(.13)
decagonal 40.26.13(.7)
decagynous 34.18.16(.15.3)
decahedra 17.32.20
decahedral 40.16.13(.17)
decahedron 28.17.31(.15)
decal 40.6.6
decalcification 28.17.25(.3.5)
decalcifier 17.6.9(.4)
decalcify 14.14.4(.9)
decalcomania 3.9.3(.5)
decalitre 17.12.1(.15)
Decalogue 26.7.14
Decameron 28.17.31(.11)
decametre 17.12.1(.6)
decamp 20.16.3
decampment 22.26.15(.13.3)
decanal 40.26.3, 40.26.13(.6)
decanally 1.31.17(.14.1)
decandrous 34.18.27(.15)
decane 28.4.5
decani 14.13
decant 22.26.6
decanter 17.12.22(.4)
decapitate 22.4.9(.5)
decapitation 28.17.25(.3.3)
decapitator 17.12.4(.5)
decapod 23.10.1
decapodan 28.17.12(.16)
decarbonization 28.17.25(.3.12)
decarbonize 35.15.12(.5)
decastyle 40.13.3(.10)
decasualize 35.15.21(.4.8)
decasyllabic 24.2.9(.2)
decasyllable 40.20.16(.29)
decathlete 22.1.18
decathlon 28.10.26, 28.17.33(.24)
Decatur 17.12.4(.7)
decay 4.11
decayable 40.20.16(.2)
Decca 17.14.4
Deccan 28.17.13(.4)
decease 34.1.5
decedent 22.26.15(.10)
deceit 22.1.9
deceitful 40.27.18
deceitfully 1.31.17(.16.2)
deceitfulness 34.18.16(.37.2)
deceivable 40.20.16(.19)
deceive 31.1.4
deceiver 17.21.1
decelerate 22.4.22(.6)

deceleration 28.17.25(.3.13)
decelerator 17.12.4(.15)
decelerometer 17.12.16(.9.2)
December 17.11.17(.3)
Decembrist 22.29.2(.29.5)
decency 1.22.23(.10.4)
decennia 3.9.4
decennial 40.3.7(.4)
decennially 1.31.3(.7)
decennium 27.3.8(.4)
decent 22.26.15(.17.1)
decently 1.31.22(.20.4)
decentralist 22.29.2(.31.4)
decentralization 28.17.25(.3.12)
decentralize 35.15.21(.4.7)
decentre 17.12.22(.3)
deception 28.17.25(.14)
deceptive 31.2.1(.12)
deceptively 1.31.30(.7.2)
deceptiveness 34.18.16(.28.1)
decerebrate 22.4.22(.7)
decertify 14.14.4(.4)
dechlorinate 22.4.14(.9.4)
dechlorination 28.17.25(.3.8)
dechristianization 28.17.25(.3.12)
dechristianize 35.15.12(.5)
Decian 28.3.15
decibel 40.5.2, 40.20.16(.21.1)
decidable 40.20.16(.12)
decide 23.15.11
decidedly 1.31.23(.14.4)
decidedness 34.18.16(.21.1)
decider 17.13.12
deciduous 34.18.6
deciduousness 34.18.16(.31.2)
decigram 27.6.17(.5)
decile 40.2.14, 40.13.12
decilitre 17.12.1(.15)
decimal 40.25.10
decimalization 28.17.25(.3.12)
decimalize 35.15.21(.4.5)
decimally 1.31.17(.13)
decimate 22.4.13(.6)
decimation 28.17.25(.3.7)
decimator 17.12.4(.9)
decimetre 17.12.1(.6)
Decimus 34.18.15(.10)
decipher 17.20.10

decipherable 40.20.16(.27.5)
decipherment 22.26.15(.13.2)
decision 28.17.26(.2)
decisive 31.2.4(.7)
decisively 1.31.30(.7.4)
decisiveness 34.18.16(.28.2)
deck 24.4
deckchair 6.16
decker 17.14.4
deckhand 23.24.6(.11)
deckhouse 34.8.6(.13)
deckle 40.23.4
declaim 27.4.9
declaimer 17.17.4
declamation 28.17.25(.3.7)
declamatory 1.29.11(.8.7)
Declan 28.17.33(.20)
declarable 40.20.16(.27.1)
declarant 22.26.15(.23.1)
declaration 28.17.25(.3.13)
declarative 31.2.1(.9.4)
declaratively 1.31.30(.7.1)
declarativeness 34.18.16(.28.1)
declaratory 1.29.11(.8.9)
declare 6.21
declaredly 1.31.23(.14.7)
declarer 17.32.5
declass 34.9.7
déclassé 4.18, 4.18.6
déclassée 4.18
declassification 28.17.25(.3.5)
declassify 14.14.4(.9)
de-claw 12.23.7
declension 28.17.25(.16)
declensional 40.26.13(.14.7)
declinable 40.20.16(.16.2)
declination 28.17.25(.3.8)
declinational 40.26.13(.14.2)
decline 28.14.19(.16)
decliner 17.18.13(.14)
declinometer 17.12.16(.9.2)
declivitous 34.18.11(.10)
declivity 1.10.16(.15)
declutch 38.11
deco 19.12.4
decoct 22.23.7
decoction 28.17.25(.15.4)
decodable 40.20.16(.12)
decode 23.20.7
decoder 17.13.17
decoke 24.18.4

decollate 22.4.23(.7.1)
decollation 28.17.25(.3.14)
décolletage 37.4.3
décolleté 4.9, 4.9.7
decolonization 28.17.25(.3.12)
decolonize 35.15.12(.5)
decolorization 28.17.25(.3.12)
decommission 28.17.25(.2.4)
decommunization 28.17.25(.3.12)
decommunize 35.15.12(.5)
decomposable 40.20.16(.22)
decompose 35.20.1
decomposition 28.17.25(.2.5)
decompound 23.24.7(.1)
decompress 34.5.14(.4)
decompression 28.17.25(.4)
decompressor 17.24.5
decongestant 22.26.15(.9)
deconsecrate 22.4.22(.10)
deconsecration 28.17.25(.3.13)
deconstruct 22.23.8
deconstruction 28.17.25(.15.5)
deconstructionism 27.15.21(.2.9)
deconstructionist 22.29.2(.18.2)
deconstructive 31.2.1(.13.4)
decontaminate 22.4.14(.9.2)
decontamination 28.17.25(.3.8)
decontextualize 35.15.21(.4.8)
decontrol 40.18.14
décor 12.7
decorate 22.4.22(.6)
decoration 28.17.25(.3.13)
decorative 31.2.1(.9.4)
decoratively 1.31.30(.7.1)
decorativeness 34.18.16(.28.1)
decorator 17.12.4(.15)
decorous 34.18.27(.16)
decorously 1.31.33(.12.5)
decorousness 34.18.16(.31.5)
decorticate 22.4.11(.6)
decortication 28.17.25(.3.5)
decorum 27.15.26(.5)

d

dégagé **4.21**
Deganwy **1.28**
Degas **10.9**
degas **34.7.10**
de Gaulle **40.10**
degauss **34.8.3**
degausser **17.24.7**
degeminate **22.4.14(.9.2)**
degemination **28.17.25(.3.8)**
degeneracy **1.22.16(.13)**
degenerate **22.4.22(.6), 22.19.24(.9)**
degenerately **1.31.22(.15)**
degeneration **28.17.25(.3.13)**
degenerative **31.2.1(.9.4)**
deglaze **35.4.18**
degradability **1.10.16(.22.2)**
degradable **40.20.16(.12)**
degradation **28.17.25(.3.4)**
degradative **31.2.1(.9.1)**
degrade **23.4.15**
degrader **17.13.3**
degradingly **1.31.28(.1.5)**
degranulate **22.4.23(.7.3)**
degranulation **28.17.25(.3.14)**
degrease **34.1.7**
degreaser **17.24.1**
degree **2.30.12**
degreeless **34.18.29(.1)**
degressive **31.2.4(.4)**
degum **27.11.6**
de haut en bas **10**
de Havilland **23.24.16(.16.2)**
dehisce **34.2.19**
dehiscence **34.24.10(.18)**
dehiscent **22.26.15(.17.1)**
dehistoricize **35.15.16(.4)**
dehorn **28.11.10**
dehumanization **28.17.25(.3.12)**
dehumanize **35.15.12(.5)**
dehumidification **28.17.25(.3.5)**
dehumidifier **17.6.9(.4)**
dehumidify **14.14.4(.5)**
dehydrate **22.4.22(.9)**
dehydration **28.17.25(.3.13)**
dehydrogenate **22.4.14(.9.3)**
dehydrogenation **28.17.25(.3.8)**
Deianira **17.32.13**
de-ice **34.15**
de-icer **17.24.13**

deicide **23.15.11(.6)**
deictic **24.2.10(.13)**
deification **28.17.25(.3.5)**
deiform **27.10.5(.2)**
deify **14.14.4(.1)**
Deighton **28.17.11(.3)**
deign **28.4**
Dei gratia **3.4.5, 3.16.3**
Deimos **34.10.12**
deinonychus **34.18.13(.10)**
deinstitutionalization **28.17.25(.3.12)**
deinstitutionalize **35.15.21(.4.5)**
deionization **28.17.25(.3.11)**
deionize **35.15.12(.5)**
deipnosophist **22.29.2(.19)**
Deirdre **1.29.16, 17.32.20**
deism **27.15.21(.2.1)**
deist **22.29.2(.1)**
deistic **24.2.10(.15.1)**
deistical **40.23.12(.7.3)**
deistically **1.31.24(.9.6)**
deity **1.10.16(.1)**
deixis **34.2.17(.14)**
déjà vu **16**
deject **22.23.4(.9)**
dejectedly **1.31.23(.14.3)**
dejection **28.17.25(.15.2)**
de jure **1.29.11(.3), 4.26.8**
De Kalb **21.6, 21.18**
Dekker **17.14.4**
dekko **19.12.4**
de Klerk **24.5**
de Kooning **29.1.17(.11)**
Delacourt **22.13.4**
Delacroix **10.22.13**
Delafield **23.31.1(.2)**
Delagoa **17.9.5**
Delahaye **4.24**
delaine **28.4.19**
de la Mare **6**
Delamere **3.8.7**
Delaney **1.16.4**
de la Rue **16**
delate **22.4.23**
delation **28.17.25(.3.14)**
delator **17.12.4(.16)**
Delaware **6.18.4**
delay **4.28**
delayer **17.2.10**
Delbert **22.19.9**
Delbridge **39.2.22(.10)**
del credere **1.29.11(.9)**
Delderfield **23.31.1(.2)**
dele **1.31.1**
delectability **1.10.16(.22.2)**

delectable **40.20.16(.11.5)**
delectably **1.31.21(.4.3)**
delectation **28.17.25(.3.3)**
delegable **40.20.16(.14)**
delegacy **1.22.16(.7)**
delegate **22.4.12(.5), 22.19.13**
delegation **28.17.25(.3.6)**
delegator **17.12.4(.8)**
delete **22.1.18**
deleterious **34.3.15(.2)**
deleteriously **1.31.33(.1.4)**
deleteriousness **34.18.16(.31.1)**
deletion **28.17.25(.1)**
Delfont **22.26.9**
Delft **22.27.7**
delftware **6.18.7**
Delgado **19.11.7**
Delhi **1.31.5**
deli **1.31.5**
Delia **3.24.1**
Delian **28.3.21(.1)**
deliberate **22.4.22(.6), 22.19.24(.9)**
deliberately **1.31.22(.15)**
deliberateness **34.18.16(.20.3)**
deliberation **28.17.25(.3.13)**
deliberative **31.2.1(.9.4)**
deliberatively **1.31.30(.7.1)**
deliberativeness **34.18.16(.28.1)**
deliberator **17.12.4(.15)**
Delibes **21.1**
delicacy **1.22.16(.6)**
delicate **22.19.12(.10)**
delicately **1.31.22(.15)**
delicateness **34.18.16(.20.3)**
delicatessen **28.17.23(.5)**
delicious **34.18.22(.2)**
deliciously **1.31.33(.12.4)**
deliciousness **34.18.16(.31.4)**
delict **22.23.2**
delight **22.16.25**
delightedly **1.31.23(.14.3)**
delightful **40.27.18**
delightfully **1.31.17(.16.2)**
delightfulness **34.18.16(.37.2)**
Delilah **17.34.13**
delimit **22.2.11**
delimitate **22.4.9(.5)**
delimitation **28.17.25(.3.3)**
delimitative **31.2.1(.9.1)**

delimiter **17.12.16(.9.1)**
delineate **22.4.2(.7)**
delineation **28.17.25(.3.1)**
delineator **17.12.4(.1)**
delinquency **1.22.23(.10.4)**
delinquent **22.26.15(.22)**
delinquently **1.31.22(.20.5)**
deliquesce **34.5.13**
deliquescence **34.24.10(.18)**
deliquescent **22.26.15(.17.2)**
deliria **3.22.1**
delirious **34.3.15(.1)**
deliriously **1.31.33(.1.4)**
delirium **23.17.3(.1)**
delirium tremens **35.26.5**
De Lisle **40.13**
Delius **34.3.16**
deliver **17.21.2**
deliverable **40.20.16(.27.5)**
deliverance **34.24.10(.16)**
deliverer **17.32.14(.13)**
delivery **1.29.11(.15)**
deliveryman **28.7.10(.2), 28.17.16(.2)**
deliverymen **28.5.7(.2)**
dell **40.5**
Della **17.34.5**
Della Cruscan **28.17.13(.18)**
della Robbia **3.3.4**
delly **1.31.5**
Del Mar **10**
Del Monte **1.10.23(.7)**
delocalize **35.15.21(.4.4)**
Delorean **28.3.20(.7)**
Delors **12.23**
Delos **34.10.17**
delouse **34.8.8**
Delphi **1.18.13, 14.14.7**
Delphian **28.3.9**
Delphic **24.2.16(.7)**
Delphine **28.1.15**
delphinia **3.9.2**
delphinium **27.3.8(.2)**
delphinoid **23.13.12**
Delphinus **34.18.16(.13)**
Delsey **1.22.26**
delta **17.12.26(.3)**
deltaic **24.2.3**
deltiologist **22.29.2(.26.2)**
deltiology **1.26.10(.11.1)**
deltoid **23.13.7**
delude **23.17.5**
deluder **17.13.14**
deluge **37.7, 39.13**

delusion 28.17.26(.4)
delusional 40.26.13(.14.8)
delusive 31.2.4(.8)
delusively 1.31.30(.7.4)
delusiveness 34.18.16(.28.2)
delusory 1.29.11(.19)
delustre 17.12.24(.10)
de luxe 34.23.11
deluxe 34.23.11
delve 31.13
delver 17.21.19
delving 29.1.20
Delwyn 28.2.28
Delyth 32.2.9
demagnetization 28.17.25(.3.12)
demagnetize 35.15.7(.7)
demagogic 24.2.13, 24.2.24(.4)
demagogical 40.23.12(.17.2)
demagogically 1.31.24(.9.7)
demagogue 26.7.6
demagoguery 1.29.11(.11)
demagogy 1.14.6, 1.26.6
deman 28.7.10
demand 23.24.6(.8), 23.24.8
demandable 40.20.16(.12)
demandant 22.26.15(.10)
demander 17.13.20(.4)
demandingly 1.31.28(.1.5)
demantoid 23.13.7
demarcate 22.4.11(.4)
demarcation 28.17.25(.3.5)
demarcator 17.12.4(.7)
démarche 36.8
dematerialization 28.17.25(.3.12)
dematerialize 35.15.21(.2)
Demavend 23.24.5(.10)
deme 27.1
demean 28.1.13
demeanour 17.18.1(.6)
Demelza 17.25.19
dement 22.26.4(.8)
dementedly 1.31.23(.14.3)
dementedness 34.18.16(.21.1)
démenti 2.12.6
dementia 17.26.21
dementia praecox 34.23.8(.5)
démentis 35.1.7(.4)

Demerara 17.32.5
demerge 39.15
demerger 17.29.14
demerit 22.2.24
demersal 40.31.13
demesne 28.4.7
Demeter 17.12.1(.6)
Demetrius 34.3.15(.8)
demigod 23.10.6
demigoddess 34.5.3, 34.18.12
demijohn 28.10.22
demilitarization 28.17.25(.3.12)
demilitarize 35.15.20(.2)
de Mille 40.2
demi-mondaine 28.4.4
demi-monde 23.24.9
demineralization 28.17.25(.3.12)
demineralize 35.15.21(.4.7)
demi-pension 11.18
demirep 20.4
demise 35.15.11
demisemiquaver 17.21.3
demission 28.17.25(.2.4)
demist 22.29.2(.17)
demister 17.12.24(.2)
demit 22.2.11
demitasse 34.7.7, 34.9.2
demiurge 39.3
demiurgic 24.2.24(.6)
demi-vierge 37.8
demo 19.14.4
demob 21.8
demobilization 28.17.25(.3.12)
demobilize 35.15.21(.4.2)
democracy 1.22.16(.13)
democrat 22.7.20
democratic 24.2.10(.4.5)
democratically 1.31.24(.9.4)
democratism 27.15.21(.2.4)
democratization 28.17.25(.3.12)
democratize 35.15.7(.7)
Democritus 34.18.11(.10)
démodé 4.10.8
demodectic 24.2.10(.13)
demodulate 22.4.23(.7.2)
demodulation 28.17.25(.3.14)
demodulator 17.12.4(.16)
demographer 17.20.12(.5)
demographic 24.2.16(.3)
demographical 40.23.12(.12)

demographically 1.31.24(.9.9)
demography 1.18.9(.3.2)
demoiselle 40.5.12
demolish 36.2.27
demolisher 17.26.14
demolition 28.17.25(.2.6)
demolitionist 22.29.2(.18.2)
demon 28.17.16(.1)
demonetization 28.17.25(.3.12)
demonetize 35.15.7(.7)
demoniac 24.6.1
demoniacal 40.23.12(.3)
demoniacally 1.31.24(.9.1)
demonic 24.2.15(.6.2)
demonical 40.23.12(.11)
demonically 1.31.24(.9.8)
demonism 27.15.21(.2.9)
demonization 28.17.25(.3.11)
demonize 35.15.12(.5)
demonolatry 1.29.15(.13)
demonological 40.23.12(.17.2)
demonologist 22.29.2(.26.4)
demonology 1.26.10(.11.4)
demonstrability 1.10.16(.22.2)
demonstrable 40.20.16(.27.6)
demonstrably 1.31.21(.8)
demonstrate 22.4.22(.8)
demonstration 28.17.25(.3.13)
demonstrational 40.26.13(.14.2)
demonstrative 31.2.1(.9.4)
demonstratively 1.31.30(.7.1)
demonstrativeness 34.18.16(.28.1)
demonstrator 17.12.4(.15)
de Montfort 22.19.16
demoralisingly 1.31.28(.1.12)
demoralization 28.17.25(.3.12)
demoralize 35.15.21(.4.7)
demoralizingly 1.31.28(.1.12)
Demos 34.10.12
Demosthenes 35.1.12(.3)
demote 22.21.7
demotic 24.2.10(.6)
demotion 28.17.25(.13)

demotivate 22.4.16
demotivation 28.17.25(.3.9)
demount 22.26.7
demountable 40.20.16(.11.6)
Dempsey 1.22.19
Dempster 17.12.24(.16)
demulcent 22.26.15(.17.3)
demur 18.7
demure 12.22, 17.7.12(.7)
demurely 1.31.11, 1.31.17(.4)
demureness 34.18.16(.15.1)
demurrable 40.20.16(.27.5)
demurrage 39.2.22(.7)
demurral 40.16.13(.9)
demurrer 17.32.12, 17.32.15
demy 14.12
demystification 28.17.25(.3.5)
demystify 14.14.4(.4)
demythologization 28.17.25(.3.12)
demythologize 35.15.18
den 28.5
denarii 2.3, 14.2
denarius 34.3.15(.3)
denary 1.29.11(.13.1)
denationalization 28.17.25(.3.12)
denationalize 35.15.21(.4.5)
denaturalization 28.17.25(.3.12)
denaturalize 35.15.21(.4.7)
denaturant 22.26.15(.23.3)
denaturation 28.17.25(.3.13)
denature 17.28.4
denazification 28.17.25(.3.5)
denazify 14.14.4(.9)
Denbigh 1.9.19
Denby 1.9.19
Dench 38.18.2
dendrite 22.16.24(.13)
dendritic 24.2.10(.2.4)
dendritically 1.31.24(.9.3)
dendrochronological 40.23.12(.17.2)
dendrochronologist 22.29.2(.26.4)
dendrochronology 1.26.10(.11.4)
dendrogram 27.6.17(.5)
dendroid 23.13.19

dendrological
40.23.12(.17.2)
dendrologist
22.29.2(.26.4)
dendrology 1.26.10(.11.5)
Dene 1.16.5, 4.14, 28.1
dene 28.1
Deneb 21.4
de-net 22.5.9
Deneuve 31.11
dengue 1.14.14
Den Haag 26.6
Denham 27.15.14(.4)
Denholme 27.18
deniability 1.10.16(.22.1)
deniable 40.20.16(.5)
deniably 1.31.21(.2)
denial 40.16.6
denier 3.9.4, 4.2.4, 17.6.8
denigrate 22.4.22(.11)
denigration
28.17.25(.3.13)
denigrator 17.12.4(.15)
denigratory 1.29.11(.8.2)
denim 27.15.14(.4)
De Niro 19.27.1
Denis 34.2.13
Denise 34.1.4, 35.1.12
denitrification
28.17.25(.3.5)
denitrify 14.14.4(.14)
denizen 28.17.24(.12)
Denmark 24.8.8
Denning 29.1.17(.4)
Dennison 28.17.23(.14)
Denny 1.16.5
denominate 22.4.14(.9.2)
denomination
28.17.25(.3.8)
denominational
40.26.13(.14.2)
denominationalism
27.15.21(.2.15)
denominationalist
22.29.2(.31.3)
denominationally
1.31.17(.14.3)
denominative
31.2.1(.9.2)
denominator 17.12.4(.10)
de nos jours 17.7
denotation 28.17.25(.3.3)
denotative 31.2.1(.3)
denotatively 1.31.30(.7.1)
denote 22.21.8
dénouement 11.8
denounce 34.24.5
denouncement
22.26.15(.13.5)
denouncer 17.24.22(.4)
de nouveau 19.17

de novo 19.17
Denovo 19.17
dense 34.24.3
densely 1.31.33(.16)
denseness 34.18.16(.31.7)
densitometer
17.12.16(.9.2)
density 1.10.16(.16.3)
dent 22.26.4
dental 40.21.17(.2)
dentalia 3.24.3
dentalium 27.3.18
dentalize 35.15.21(.4.3)
dentate 22.4.9(.8)
denticle 40.23.12(.7.3)
denticulate 22.4.23(.7.3),
22.19.26(.13)
dentifrice 34.2.21
dentil 40.2.5, 40.21.17(.2)
dentinal 40.26.13(.4)
dentine 28.1.9(.6)
dentist 22.29.2(.13)
dentistry 1.29.15(.17)
dentition 28.17.25(.2.2)
Denton 28.17.11(.22)
denture 17.28.22
denuclearization
28.17.25(.3.12)
denuclearize 35.15.20(.1)
denudation 28.17.25(.3.4)
denudative 31.2.1(.9.1)
denude 23.17.4(.4)
denumerability
1.10.16(.22.2)
denumerable
40.20.16(.27.4)
denumerably 1.31.21(.8)
denunciate 22.4.2(.9)
denunciation
28.17.25(.3.1)
denunciative 31.2.1(.2)
denunciator 17.12.4(.1)
denunciatory
1.29.11(.8.1)
Denver 17.21.17
deny 14.13
Denys 34.2.13
Denzil 40.32.17
Deo 19.2
deodand 23.24.6(.6)
deodar 10.7
deodorant
22.26.15(.23.3)
deodorization
28.17.25(.3.11)
deodorize 35.15.20(.2)
deodorizer 17.25.12(.14)
Deo gratias 34.3.3
deontic 24.2.10(.14)
deontological
40.23.12(.17.2)

deontologist
22.29.2(.26.3)
deontology 1.26.10(.11.2)
Deo volente 4.9.9
deoxygenate 22.4.14(.9.3)
deoxygenation
28.17.25(.3.8)
deoxyribonucleic 24.2.1,
24.2.3
depart 22.10.1
department
22.26.15(.13.3)
departmental
40.21.17(.2)
departmentalism
27.15.21(.2.15)
departmentalization
28.17.25(.3.12)
departmentalize
35.15.21(.4.3)
departmentally
1.31.17(.9.3)
departure 17.28.8
depasturage 39.2.22(.9)
depasture 17.28.24
dépaysé 4.19
depend 23.24.5(.2)
dependability
1.10.16(.22.2)
dependable 40.20.16(.12)
dependableness
34.18.16(.37.4)
dependably 1.31.21(.4.4)
dependant 22.26.15(.10)
dependence 34.24.10(.11)
dependency
1.22.23(.10.2)
dependent 22.26.15(.10)
dependently
1.31.22(.20.2)
depersonalization
28.17.25(.3.12)
depersonalize
35.15.21(.4.5)
depict 22.23.2
depicter 17.12.21(.1)
depiction 28.17.25(.15.1)
depictive 31.2.1(.13.1)
depilate 22.4.23(.7.1)
depilation 28.17.25(.3.14)
depilatory 1.29.11(.8.10)
deplane 28.4.19
deplete 22.1.18
depletion 28.17.25(.1)
deplorable 40.20.16(.27.2)
deplorably 1.31.21(.8)
deplore 12.23.3
deploringly 1.31.28(.1.17)
deploy 13.17
deployment
22.26.15(.13.1)
deplume 27.14.8

depolarization
28.17.25(.3.12)
depolarize 35.15.20(.2)
depoliticization
28.17.25(.3.12)
depoliticize 35.15.16(.4)
depolymerization
28.17.25(.3.12)
depolymerize
35.15.20(.2)
deponent 22.26.15(.14)
Depo-Provera® 17.32.2
depopulate 22.4.23(.7.3)
depopulation
28.17.25(.3.14)
deport 22.13.1
deportable 40.20.16(.11.2)
deportation 28.17.25(.3.3)
deportee 2.11
deportment
22.26.15(.13.3)
deposal 40.32.15
depose 35.20.1
deposit 22.2.17
depositary 1.29.11(.8.8)
deposition 28.17.25(.2.5)
depositional
40.26.13(.14.1)
depositor 17.12.16(.15)
depository 1.29.11(.8.8)
depot 19.8
depravation
28.17.25(.3.9)
deprave 31.3.7
depravity 1.10.16(.15)
deprecate 22.4.11(.6)
deprecatingly
1.31.28(.1.4)
deprecation
28.17.25(.3.5)
deprecative 31.2.1(.9.1)
deprecator 17.12.4(.7)
deprecatory 1.29.11(.8.2)
depreciate 22.4.2(.11)
depreciatingly
1.31.28(.1.4)
depreciation
28.17.25(.3.1)
depreciatory 1.29.11(.8.1)
depredate 22.4.10
depredation
28.17.25(.3.4)
depredator 17.12.4(.6)
depredatory 1.29.11(.8.2)
depress 34.5.14(.4)
depressant 22.26.15(.17.2)
depressible
40.20.16(.21.1)
depressing 29.1.23
depressingly
1.31.28(.1.11)
depression 28.17.25(.4)

depressive 31.2.4(.4)
depressor 17.24.5
depressurization 28.17.25(.3.12)
depressurize 35.15.20(.2)
deprivable 40.20.16(.19)
deprival 40.28.9
deprivation 28.17.25(.3.9)
deprive 31.9
de profundis 34.2.9
deprogramme 27.6.17(.5)
Deptford 23.18.16(.11)
depth 32.17
depthless 34.18.29(.31)
depurate 22.4.22(.6)
depuration 28.17.25(.3.13)
depurative 31.2.1(.9.4)
depurator 17.12.4(.15)
deputation 28.17.25(.3.3)
depute 22.18.10
deputize 35.15.7(.7)
deputy 1.10.27
deputyship 20.2.7(.2)
De Quincey 1.22.23(.1)
deracinate 22.4.14(.9.3)
deracination 28.17.25(.3.1)
derail 40.4.14
derailleur 17.33.13, 17.34.4
derailment 22.26.15(.13.7)
derange 39.17.2
derangement 22.26.15(.13.6)
derate 22.4.22
deration 28.17.25(.5)
derby 1.9.6
Derbyshire 17.26.2
derecognition 28.17.25(.2.4)
deregister 17.12.24(.14)
deregistration 28.17.25(.3.13)
deregulate 22.4.23(.7.3)
deregulation 28.17.25(.3.14)
Dereham 27.15.26(.1)
Derek 24.2.26(.4)
derelict 22.23.2
dereliction 28.17.25(.15.1)
derequisition 28.17.25(.2.5)
derestrict 22.23.2
derestriction 28.17.25(.15.1)
Der Freischütz 34.22.14
deride 23.15.15
derider 17.13.12
deridingly 1.31.28(.1.5)

de-rigging 29.1.15
de rigueur 18.6
derisible 40.20.16(.21.2)
derision 28.17.26(.2)
derisive 31.2.4(.2)
derisively 1.31.30(.7.4)
derisiveness 34.18.16(.28.2)
derisorily 1.31.17(.27.2)
derisory 1.29.11(.18)
derivable 40.20.16(.19)
derivation 28.17.25(.3.9)
derivational 40.26.13(.14.2)
derivative 31.2.1(.9.3)
derivatively 1.31.30(.7.1)
derive 31.9
d'Erlanger 4.21
derm 27.16
derma 17.17.15
dermal 40.25.11
Dermaptera 17.32.14(.6)
dermapteran 28.17.31(.11)
dermapterous 34.18.27(.14)
dermatitis 34.18.11(.8)
dermatoglyphic 24.2.16(.1)
dermatoglyphically 1.31.24(.9.9)
dermatoid 23.13.7
dermatological 40.23.12(.17.2)
dermatologically 1.31.24(.9.11)
dermatologist 22.29.2(.26.3)
dermatology 1.26.10(.11.2)
dermic 24.2.14(.11)
dermis 34.2.12
Dermot 22.19.14
dernier cri 2
derogate 22.4.12(.5)
derogation 28.17.25(.3.6)
derogative 31.2.1(.9.1)
derogatorily 1.31.17(.27.1)
derogatory 1.29.11(.8.6)
Deronda 17.13.20(.7)
derrick 24.2.26(.4)
Derrida 17.13.1
Derridean 28.3.4(.2)
derrière 6
derring-do 16.8
derringer 17.29.16(.8)
derris 34.2.21
Derry 1.29.3
derv 31.11
dervish 36.2.19

Derwent 22.26.15(.22)
Derwentwater 17.12.10(.7)
Deryck 24.2.26(.4)
Desai 14.18
desalinate 22.4.14(.9.4)
desalination 28.17.25(.3.8)
desalinization 28.17.25(.3.12)
desalinize 35.15.12(.5)
desalt 22.32.5, 22.32.6
desaparecido 19.11.1
descale 40.4.4
descant 22.26.6
Descartes 22.10.5
descend 23.24.5(.11)
descendant 22.26.15(.10)
descendent 22.26.15(.10)
descender 17.13.20(.3)
descendeur 17.13.20(.3)
descendible 40.20.16(.12)
descent 22.26.4(.11)
descramble 40.20.19
descrambler 17.34.20
describable 40.20.16(.10)
describe 21.12
describer 17.11.11
description 28.17.25(.14)
descriptive 31.2.1(.12)
descriptively 1.31.30(.7.2)
descriptiveness 34.18.16(.28.1)
descriptivism 27.15.21(.2.11)
descriptor 17.12.19
descry 14.24.9
Desdemona 17.18.18(.5)
desecrate 22.4.22(.10)
desecration 28.17.25(.3.13)
desecrator 17.12.4(.15)
deseed 23.1.7
desegregate 22.4.12(.5)
desegregation 28.17.25(.3.6)
deselect 22.23.4(.11)
deselection 28.17.25(.15.2)
desensitization 28.17.25(.3.12)
desensitize 35.15.7(.7)
desert 22.19.19, 22.20.11
deserter 17.12.17
desertification 28.17.25(.3.5)
desertion 28.17.25(.12)
deserts 34.22.16
deserve 31.11
deserved 23.26
deservedly 1.31.23(.14.7)

deservedness 34.18.16(.21.1)
deserver 17.21.13
deserving 29.1.20
deservingly 1.31.28(.1.9)
deservingness 34.18.16(.26)
desex 34.23.4(.10)
desexualization 28.17.25(.3.12)
déshabillé 4.1, 40.1.2
desiccant 22.26.15(.11)
desiccate 22.4.11(.6)
desiccation 28.17.25(.3.5)
desiccative 31.2.1(.9.1)
desiccator 17.12.4(.7)
desiderata 17.12.8(.10)
desiderate 22.4.22(.6), 22.19.24(.9)
desiderative 31.2.1(.9.4)
desideratum 27.15.9(.5)
design 28.14.14
designate 22.4.14(.13), 22.19.15(.11)
designation 28.17.25(.3.8)
designator 17.12.4(.10)
designed 23.24.13
designedly 1.31.23(.14.6)
designer 17.18.13(.9)
designing 29.1.17(.10)
designingly 1.31.28(.1.7)
desinence 34.24.10(.15)
desirability 1.10.16(.22.2)
desirable 40.20.16(.27.2)
desirableness 34.18.16(.37.4)
desirably 1.31.21(.8)
desire 17.6.11
Desirée 4.26.1
desirous 34.18.27(.11)
desist 22.29.2(.22)
desk 24.20.3
deskill 40.2.7
deskilled 23.31.2
deskilling 29.1.31(.2)
desktop 20.7.4
deskwork 24.17.6(.10)
desman 28.17.16(.30)
desmid 23.2.12
Des Moines 28.12
Desmond 23.24.16(.7)
desolate 22.4.23(.7.2), 22.19.26(.13)
desolately 1.31.22(.15)
desolateness 34.18.16(.20.3)
desolation 28.17.25(.3.14)
desolator 17.12.4(.16)
desorb 21.9
desorbent 22.26.15(.8)
desorption 28.17.25(.14)

d

De Vere 3
Devereux 16.23.6,
  17.32.14(.13), 17.32.26,
  19.27.11, 34.23.14
Devi 1.19.3
deviance 34.24.2
deviancy 1.22.23(.2)
deviant 22.26.2(.6)
deviate 22.4.2(.8)
deviation 28.17.25(.3.1)
deviational
  40.26.13(.14.2)
deviationism
  27.15.21(.2.9)
deviationist 22.29.2(.18.2)
deviator 17.12.4(.1)
deviatory 1.29.11(.8.1)
device 34.15.7
devil 40.28.4
devildom 27.15.10(.20)
devilfish 36.2.18(.21)
devilish 36.2.27
devilishly 1.31.35(.7.4)
devilishness
  34.18.16(.33.6)
devilism 27.15.21(.2.15)
de Villiers 35.18.24
devil-may-care 6.6
devilment 22.26.15(.13.7)
devilry 1.29.24
deviltry 1.29.15(.18)
Devine 28.1.16, 28.14.11
devious 34.3.8
deviously 1.31.33(.1.3)
deviousness
  34.18.16(.31.1)
devisable 40.20.16(.22)
devise 35.15.14
devisee 2.23
deviser 17.25.12(.8)
devisor 17.25.12(.8)
devitalization
  28.17.25(.3.12)
devitalize 35.15.21(.4.3)
devitrification
  28.17.25(.3.5)
devitrify 14.14.4(.14)
Devizes 35.18.18
Devlin 28.2.31(.21)
devoice 34.13
devoid 23.13.14
devoir 10.22.10
devolute 22.18.11
devolution 28.17.25(.11)
devolutionary
  1.29.11(.13.2)
devolutionist
  22.29.2(.18.2)
devolve 31.13
devolvement
  22.26.15(.13.5)

Devon 28.17.20(.4)
Devonian 28.3.8(.11)
Devonport 22.13.1
Devonshire 17.26.21
dévot 19.17
devote 22.21.10
dévote 22.11.11
devotedly 1.31.23(.14.3)
devotedness
  34.18.16(.21.1)
devotee 2.11
devotement
  22.26.15(.13.3)
devotion 28.17.25(.13)
devotional 40.26.13(.14.5)
devotionally
  1.31.17(.14.3)
devour 17.3.7
devourer 17.32.14(.1)
devouringly
  1.31.28(.1.17)
devout 22.9.13
devoutly 1.31.22(.7)
devoutness
  34.18.16(.20.2)
de Vries 34.1
dew 16
dewan 28.9.12
Dewar 17.8
dewar 17.8
dewberry 1.29.11(.7.1)
dewclaw 12.23.7
dewdrop 20.7.12
Dewey 1(.6)
dewfall 40.10.11
Dewhurst 22.29.16
Dewi 1.28
dewily 1.31.17(.5)
dewiness 34.18.16(.2.1)
dewlap 20.5.8
dewpoint 22.26.11
dewpond 23.24.9
Dewsbury 1.29.11(.7.2)
dewy 1(.6)
Dexedrine 28.1.25(.7),
  28.2.29(.9)
dexter 17.12.24(.20)
dexterity 1.10.16(.21.1)
dexterous 34.18.27(.14)
dexterously 1.31.33(.12.5)
dexterousness
  34.18.16(.31.5)
dextral 40.16.13(.16)
dextrality 1.10.16(.32.13)
dextrally 1.31.17(.27.3)
dextran 28.17.31(.14)
dextrin 28.2.29(.8)
dextrorotation
  28.17.25(.3.3)
dextrorotatory
  1.29.11(.8.6)

dextrorse 34.12.8
dextrose 34.20.16,
  35.20.12
dextrous 34.18.27(.14)
dextrously 1.31.33(.12.5)
dey 4
Dhahran 28.7.20, 28.9.13
Dhaka 17.14.5
dhal 40.8
dharma 17.17.7
Dhekelia 3.24.3
dhobi 1.9.13
Dhofar 10.12
dhole 40.18
dhoti 1.10.18
dhow 9
dhurrie 1.29.9
Di 14
diabetes 34.2.8, 35.1.7(.1)
diabetic 24.2.10(.3.1)
diablerie 1.29.11(.27)
diabolic 24.2.27(.9)
diabolical 40.23.12(.19)
diabolically 1.31.24(.9.12)
diabolism 27.15.21(.2.15)
diabolist 22.29.2(.31.2)
diabolize 35.15.21(.4.2)
diabolo 19.29.12
diachronic 24.2.15(.6.4)
diachronically
  1.31.24(.9.8)
diachronism
  27.15.21(.2.9)
diachronistic
  24.2.10(.15.2)
diachronous
  34.18.16(.15.3)
diachrony 1.16.15(.18)
diaconal 40.26.13(.6)
diaconate 22.4.14(.9.1),
  22.19.15(.9)
diacritic 24.2.10(.2.4)
diacritical 40.23.12(.7.1)
diacritically 1.31.24(.9.3)
diadelphous 34.18.17
diadem 27.5.5
Diadochi 1.12.13, 14.10
diaereses 35.1.16(.10)
diaeresis 34.2.17(.10.4)
diageneses 35.1.16(.10)
diagenesis 34.2.17(.10.3)
Diaghilev 30.4
diagnosable 40.20.16(.22)
diagnose 35.20.8
diagnoses 35.1.16(.11)
diagnosis 34.2.17(.11.2)
diagnostic 24.2.10(.15.4)
diagnostically
  1.31.24(.9.6)
diagnostician
  28.17.25(.2.2)

diagonal 40.26.13(.7)
diagonally 1.31.17(.14.2)
diagram 27.6.17(.5)
diagrammatic
  24.2.10(.4.2)
diagrammatically
  1.31.24(.9.4)
diagrammatize
  35.15.7(.7)
diagrid 23.2.22
diakinesis 34.2.17(.1)
dial 40.16.6
dialect 22.23.4(.11)
dialectal 40.21.16
dialectic 24.2.10(.13)
dialectical 40.23.12(.7.3)
dialectically 1.31.24(.9.5)
dialectician 28.17.25(.2.2)
dialectologist
  22.29.2(.26.3)
dialectology
  1.26.10(.11.2)
dialler 17.34.16(.2)
dialogic 24.2.24(.4)
dialogist 22.29.2(.26.1)
dialogue 26.7.14
dialyse 35.15.21(.4.1)
dialyses 35.1.16(.10)
dialysis 34.2.17(.10.5)
dialytic 24.2.10(.2.5)
diamagnetic 24.2.10(.3.1)
diamagnetically
  1.31.24(.9.3)
diamagnetism
  27.15.21(.2.4)
diamanté 1.10.23(.4), 4.9.9
diamantiferous
  34.18.27(.20)
diamantine 28.1.9(.6),
  28.14.5
diameter 17.12.16(.9.1)
diametral 40.16.13(.16)
diametric 24.2.26(.14.2)
diametrical 40.23.12(.18)
diametrically
  1.31.24(.9.12)
diamond 23.24.16(.7)
diamondback 24.6.6(.13)
diamondiferous
  34.18.27(.20)
Diana 17.18.6
diandrous 34.18.27(.15)
Diane 28.7
Dianetics 34.23.2(.3)
dianthus 34.18.19
diapason 28.17.23(.4),
  28.17.24(.3)
diapause 35.12
diaper 17.10.14
diaphanous
  34.18.16(.15.3)

diaphanously 1.31.33(.12.3)
diaphone 28.19.11
diaphoneme 27.1.6
diaphonemic 24.2.14(.1)
diaphonemically 1.31.24(.9.8)
diaphonic 24.2.15(.6.3)
diaphonically 1.31.24(.9.8)
diaphoreses 35.1.16(.1)
diaphoresis 34.2.17(.1)
diaphoretic 24.2.10(.3.3)
diaphragm 27.6.17(.6)
diaphragmatic 24.2.10(.4.2)
diapositive 31.2.1(.9.3)
diarchal 40.23.6
diarchic 24.2.12
diarchy 1.12.6
diarist 22.29.2(.29.3)
diaristic 24.2.10(.15.2)
diarize 35.15.20(.2)
diarrhoea 3.22
diarrhoeal 40.3.14
diarrhoeic 24.2.2
diary 1.29.11(.2)
diascope 20.15.4(.1)
Diaspora 17.32.14(.4)
diaspore 12.3
diastalsis 34.2.17(.16)
diastase 35.4.3
diastasic 24.2.20(.3)
diastatic 24.2.10(.4.1)
diastole 1.31.17(.9.3)
diastolic 24.2.27(.9)
diatessaron 28.10.24(.5)
diathermancy 1.22.23(.10.3)
diathermanous 34.18.16(.15.3)
diathermic 24.2.14(.11)
diathermous 34.18.15(.11)
diathermy 1.15.14
diatheses 35.1.16(.10)
diathesis 34.2.17(.10.4)
diatom 27.9, 27.15.9(.10)
diatomaceous 34.18.22(.3)
diatomic 24.2.14(.6)
diatomite 22.16.13
diatonic 24.2.15(.6.1)
diatonically 1.31.24(.9.8)
diatribe 21.12
Díaz 32.6.1, 34.7.1
diazepam 27.6.3
diazo 19.21
diazotype 20.10.2
dib 21.2
dibasic 24.2.20(.3)

dibatag 26.5.2
dibber 17.11.2
dibble 40.20.2
dice 34.15
dicentra 17.32.19(.10)
dicentric 24.2.26(.14.4)
dicer 17.24.13
dicey 1.22.13
dichotic 24.2.10(.6)
dichotomic 24.2.14(.6)
dichotomize 35.15.11
dichotomous 34.18.15(.10)
dichotomy 1.15.13(.1)
dichroic 24.2.7
dichroism 27.15.21(.2.1)
dichromate 22.4.13(.7)
dichromatic 24.2.10(.4.2)
dichromatism 27.15.21(.2.4)
dicily 1.31.17(.20)
diciness 34.18.16(.2.7)
dick 24.2
dickcissel 40.31.2
dicken 28.17.13(.2)
Dickens 35.26.2
Dickensian 28.3.14
Dickensianly 1.31.27(.3)
dicker 17.14.2
dickerer 17.32.14(.8)
Dickerson 28.17.23(.14)
dickhead 23.5.13(.11)
Dickie 1.12.2
Dickinson 28.17.23(.24)
Dickon 28.17.13(.2)
dicky 1.12.2
dicky bird 23.19.1
dicot 22.11.6
dicotyledon 28.17.12(.1)
dicotyledonous 34.18.16(.15.2)
dicrotic 24.2.10(.6)
dicta 17.12.21(.1)
Dictaphone 28.19.11
dictate 22.4.9
dictation 28.17.25(.3.3)
dictator 17.12.4(.5)
dictatorial 40.3.14(.5)
dictatorially 1.31.3(.11)
dictatorship 20.2.7(.9)
diction 28.17.25(.15.1)
dictionary 1.29.11(.13.2)
dictum 27.15.9(.13)
dicty 1.10.21
Dictyoptera 17.32.14(.6)
dictyopteran 28.17.31(.11)
dictyopterous 34.18.27(.14)
dicynodont 22.26.9

did 23.2
didactic 24.2.10(.13)
didactically 1.31.24(.9.5)
didacticism 27.15.21(.2.12)
didakai 14.10
Didcot 22.11.6, 22.19.12(.12)
diddle 40.22.2
diddler 17.34.22
diddly-squat 22.11.14
diddums 35.25.10
diddy 1.11.2
Diderot 19.27.11
didgeridoo 16.8
didicoi 13.5
didn't 22.26.15(.10)
dido 19.11.9
didst 22.29.19
didy 1.11.14
didymium 27.3.7
die 14
dieback 24.6.6(.7)
dieffenbachia 3.6.5
Die Fledermaus 34.8.4
Diego 19.13.3
diehard 23.9.19
Diekirch 24.17.3
dieldrin 28.17.31(.15)
dielectric 24.2.26(.14.3)
dielectrically 1.31.24(.9.12)
diene 28.1.3
Dieppe 20.4
diesel 40.32.1
dieselize 35.15.21(.4.6)
Dies Irae 4.26.1
dies non 28.10
diet 22.19.4
dietary 1.29.11(.8.5)
Dieter 17.12.1
dieter 17.12.16(.1)
dietetic 24.2.10(.3.1)
dietetically 1.31.24(.9.3)
diethyl 40.2.13, 40.29
dietician 28.17.25(.2.2)
Dietrich 24.2.26(.14.1), 25.1
differ 17.20.2
difference 34.24.10(.16)
different 22.26.15(.23.3)
differentia 3.16.8, 17.26.21
differentiae 2.3
differential 40.33.12(.3)
differentially 1.31.17(.22)
differentiate 22.4.2(.11)
differentiation 28.17.25(.3.1)
differentiator 17.12.4(.1)
differently 1.31.22(.20.5)

differentness 34.18.16(.20.4)
difficult 22.32.14
difficultly 1.31.22(.23)
difficultness 34.18.16(.20.4)
difficulty 1.10.28
diffidence 34.24.10(.11)
diffident 22.26.15(.10)
diffidently 1.31.22(.20.2)
diffract 22.23.5(.9)
diffraction 28.17.25(.15.3)
diffractive 31.2.1(.13.3)
diffractively 1.31.30(.7.2)
diffractometer 17.12.16(.9.2)
diffuse 34.17.13, 35.17.7
diffusely 1.31.33(.11)
diffuseness 34.18.16(.31.2)
diffuser 17.25.14
diffusible 40.20.16(.21.2)
diffusion 28.17.26(.4)
diffusionist 22.29.2(.18.3)
diffusive 31.2.4(.8)
diffusively 1.31.30(.7.4)
diffusiveness 34.18.16(.28.2)
diffusivity 1.10.16(.15)
dig 26.2
Digambara 17.32.14(.5)
digamist 22.29.2(.17)
digamma 17.17.6
digamous 34.18.15(.10)
digamy 1.15.13(.4)
digastric 24.2.26(.14.5)
Digbeth 32.14.7
Digby 1.9.17
digest 22.29.5(.9)
digester 17.12.24(.4)
digestibility 1.10.16(.22.2)
digestible 40.20.16(.11.7)
digestion 28.17.27
digestive 31.2.1(.15)
digestively 1.31.30(.7.4)
digger 17.16.2
digging 29.1.15
dight 22.16
digit 22.2.21
digital 40.21.12
digitalin 28.2.31(.3)
digitalis 34.2.22(.3)
digitalize 35.15.21(.4.3)
digitally 1.31.17(.9.2)
digitate 22.4.9(.5)
digitately 1.31.22(.15)
digitation 28.17.25(.3.3)
digitigrade 23.4.15
digitization 28.17.25(.3.11)
digitize 35.15.7(.7)

directionality
1.10.16(.32.8)
directionally
1.31.17(.14.3)
directionless
34.18.29(.27)
directive **31.2.1(.13.2)**
directly **1.31.22(.19)**
directness
34.18.16(.20.4)
Directoire **10.22.5**
director **17.12.21(.2)**
directorate **22.19.24(.9)**
directorial **40.3.14(.5)**
directorship **20.2.7(.9)**
directory **1.29.11(.8.12)**
directress **34.18.27(.14)**
directrices **35.1.16(.10)**
directrix **34.23.2(.12)**
direful **40.27.14**
direfully **1.31.17(.16.1)**
direly **1.31.17(.3)**
direness **34.18.16(.15.1)**
dirge **39.15**
dirgeful **40.27.30**
dirham **27.6.17(.2),
27.15.26(.1)**
dirigible **40.20.16(.25)**
dirigisme **27.15.21(.1)**
dirigiste **22.29.1**
diriment **22.26.15(.13.2)**
dirk **24.17**
dirndl **40.22.16**
dirt **22.20**
dirtily **1.31.17(.9.2)**
dirtiness **34.18.16(.2.3)**
dirty **1.10.17**
disability **1.10.16(.22.1)**
disable **40.20.4**
disablement
22.26.15(.13.7)
disablist **22.29.2(.31.6)**
disabuse **35.17.7**
disaccord **23.12.4**
disaccustom **27.15.9(.15)**
disadvantage **39.2.10**
disadvantageous
34.18.24
disadvantageously
1.31.33(.12.4)
disadvantageousness
34.18.16(.31.5)
disaffected **23.18.9(.17)**
disaffectedly
1.31.23(.14.3)
disaffection
28.17.25(.15.2)
disaffiliate **22.4.2(.15)**
disaffiliation
28.17.25(.3.1)
disaffirm **27.16.4**

disaffirmation
28.17.25(.3.7)
disafforest **22.29.2(.29.2)**
disafforestation
28.17.25(.3.3)
disaggregate **22.4.12(.5)**
disaggregation
28.17.25(.3.6)
disagree **2.30.12**
disagreeable **40.20.16(.1)**
disagreeably **1.31.21(.2)**
disagreement
22.26.15(.13.1)
disallow **9.17**
disallowance **34.24.10(.3)**
disambiguate **22.4.4**
disambiguation
28.17.25(.3.1)
disamenity **1.10.16(.13)**
disannul **40.12**
disannulment
22.26.15(.13.7)
disappear **3.1**
disappearance
34.24.10(.16)
disappoint **22.26.11**
disappointedly
1.31.23(.14.3)
disappointing
29.1.12(.19)
disappointingly
1.31.28(.1.4)
disappointment
22.26.15(.13.3)
disapprobation
28.17.25(.3.2)
disapprobative **31.2.1(.3)**
disapprobatory
1.29.11(.8.2)
disapproval **40.28.10**
disapprove **31.10**
disapprover **17.21.11**
disapprovingly
1.31.28(.1.9)
disarm **27.8**
disarmament
22.26.15(.13.2)
disarmer **17.17.7**
disarming **29.1.16**
disarmingly **1.31.28(.1.7)**
disarrange **39.17.2**
disarrangement
22.26.15(.13.6)
disarray **4.26**
disarticulate **22.4.23(.7.3)**
disarticulation
28.17.25(.3.14)
disassemble **40.20.19**
disassembly **1.31.21(.12)**
disassociate **22.4.2(.9)**
disassociation
28.17.25(.3.1)

disaster **17.12.24(.5)**
disastrous **34.18.27(.14)**
disastrously **1.31.33(.12.5)**
disavow **9.8**
disavowal **40.16.3**
disband **23.24.6(.4)**
disbandment
22.26.15(.13.3)
disbar **10.5**
disbarment
22.26.15(.13.1)
disbelief **30.1.9**
disbelieve **31.1.9**
disbeliever **17.21.1**
disbelievingly
1.31.28(.1.9)
disbenefit **22.2.13**
disbound **23.24.7(.2)**
disbud **23.14**
disburden **28.17.12(.17)**
disbursal **40.31.13**
disburse **34.19.2**
disbursement
22.26.15(.13.5)
disburser **17.24.16**
disc **24.20.1**
discalced **22.29.23**
discard **23.9.9**
discardable **40.20.16(.12)**
discarnate **22.19.15(.4)**
discern **28.18.9**
discerner **17.18.17**
discernible
40.20.16(.16.3)
discernibly **1.31.21(.6)**
discerning **29.1.17(.13)**
discerningly **1.31.28(.1.7)**
discernment
22.26.15(.13.4)
discerptibility
1.10.16(.22.2)
discerptible
40.20.16(.11.4)
discerption **28.17.25(.14)**
discharge **39.8**
dischargeable
40.20.16(.25)
discharger **17.29.7**
dischuff **30.11.8**
disciple **40.19.9**
discipleship **20.2.7(.24)**
disciplinable
40.20.16(.3)
disciplinal **40.26.13(.14.8)**
disciplinarian **28.3.20(.4)**
disciplinary **1.29.11(.13.1)**
discipline **28.17.33(.16)**
discipular **17.34.16(.21.1)**
disclaim **27.4.9**
disclaimer **17.17.4**
disclose **35.20.14**

discloser **17.25.15**
disclosure **17.27.9**
disco **19.12.17**
discoboli **2.32.9(.3),
14.25.9**
discobolus **34.18.29(.17.2)**
discographer **17.20.12(.5)**
discography **1.18.9(.3.2)**
discoid **23.13.9**
discoloration
28.17.25(.3.13)
discolour **17.34.12**
discolouration
28.17.25(.3.13)
discombobulate
22.4.23(.7.3)
discomfit **22.19.16**
discomfiture **17.28.15**
discomfort **22.19.16**
discommode **23.20.8**
discommodious **34.3.4**
discompose **35.20.1**
discomposure **17.27.9**
disconcert **22.20.10**
disconcertedly
1.31.23(.14.3)
disconcerting
29.1.12(.15)
disconcertingly
1.31.28(.1.4)
disconcertion
28.17.25(.12)
disconcertment
22.26.15(.13.3)
disconfirm **27.16.4**
disconfirmation
28.17.25(.3.7)
disconformity
1.10.16(.12)
disconnect **22.23.4(.4)**
disconnected **23.18.9(.17)**
disconnectedly
1.31.23(.14.3)
disconnectedness
34.18.16(.21.1)
disconnection
28.17.25(.15.2)
disconsolate **22.19.26(.13)**
disconsolately
1.31.22(.15)
disconsolateness
34.18.16(.20.3)
disconsolation
28.17.25(.3.14)
discontent **22.26.4(.4)**
discontented **23.18.9(.19)**
discontentedly
1.31.23(.14.3)
discontentedness
34.18.16(.21.1)
discontentment
22.26.15(.13.3)

discontinuance **34.24.10(.6)**
discontinuation **28.17.25(.3.1)**
discontinue **16.24.10**
discontinuity **1.10.16(.5)**
discontinuous **34.18.6**
discontinuously **1.31.33(.12.1)**
discord **23.12.4**
discordance **34.24.10(.11)**
discordancy **1.22.23(.10.2)**
discordant **22.26.15(.10)**
discordantly **1.31.22(.20.2)**
discotheque **24.4.4**
discount **22.26.7**
discountable **40.20.16(.11.6)**
discountenance **34.24.10(.15)**
discounter **17.12.22(.5)**
discourage **39.2.22(.7)**
discouragement **22.26.15(.13.6)**
discouraging **29.1.28**
discouragingly **1.31.28(.1.16)**
discourse **34.12.2**
discourteous **34.3.3**
discourteously **1.31.33(.1.1)**
discourteousness **34.18.16(.31.1)**
discourtesy **1.22.16(.4)**
discover **17.21.9**
discoverable **40.20.16(.27.5)**
discoverer **17.32.14(.13)**
discovery **1.29.11(.15)**
discredit **22.2.8**
discreditable **40.20.16(.11.3)**
discreditably **1.31.21(.4.2)**
discreet **22.1.17**
discreetly **1.31.22(.1)**
discreetness **34.18.16(.20.1)**
discrepancy **1.22.23(.10.2)**
discrete **22.1.17**
discretely **1.31.22(.1)**
discreteness **34.18.16(.20.1)**
discretion **28.17.25(.4)**
discretionary **1.29.11(.13.2)**
discriminant **22.26.15(.14)**
discriminate **22.4.14(.9.2), 22.19.15(.9)**

discriminately **1.31.22(.15)**
discriminating **29.1.12(.3)**
discriminatingly **1.31.28(.1.4)**
discrimination **28.17.25(.3.8)**
discriminative **31.2.1(.9.2)**
discriminator **17.12.4(.10)**
discriminatory **1.29.11(.8.7)**
discursive **31.2.4(.10)**
discursively **1.31.30(.7.4)**
discursiveness **34.18.16(.28.2)**
discus **34.18.13(.14)**
discuss **34.14**
discussable **40.20.16(.21.2)**
discussant **22.26.15(.17.3)**
discusser **17.24.12**
discussible **40.20.16(.21.2)**
discussion **28.17.25(.9)**
disdain **28.4.4**
disdainful **40.27.22**
disdainfully **1.31.17(.16.2)**
disdainfulness **34.18.16(.37.2)**
disease **35.1.17**
diseconomy **1.15.13(.5)**
disembark **24.8.3**
disembarkation **28.17.25(.3.5)**
disembarrass **34.18.27(.5)**
disembarrassment **22.26.15(.13.5)**
disembodied **23.2.9**
disembodiment **22.26.15(.13.1)**
disembody **1.11.10**
disembogue **26.15**
disembowel **40.16.3**
disembowelment **22.26.15(.13.7)**
disembroil **40.11.9**
disempower **17.3.1**
disenchant **22.26.8**
disenchantingly **1.31.28(.1.4)**
disenchantment **22.26.15(.13.3)**
disencumber **17.11.17(.6)**
disendow **9.4**
disendowment **22.26.15(.13.1)**
disenfranchise **35.15.17**
disenfranchisement **22.26.15(.13.5)**

disengage **39.4.4**
disengagement **22.26.15(.13.6)**
disentail **40.4.2**
disentangle **40.24.14(.2)**
disentanglement **22.26.15(.13.7)**
disenthral **40.10.18**
disenthralment **22.26.15(.13.7)**
disentitle **40.21.10**
disentitlement **22.26.15(.13.7)**
disentomb **27.14.1**
disentombment **22.26.15(.13.4)**
disequilibria **3.22.14**
disequilibrium **27.3.17(.5)**
disestablish **36.2.27**
disestablishment **22.26.15(.13.6)**
disesteem **27.1.2**
diseur **18.12**
diseuse **35.19**
disfavor **17.21.3**
disfavour **17.21.3**
disfigure **17.16.2**
disfigurement **22.26.15(.13.2)**
disforest **22.29.2(.29.2)**
disforestation **28.17.25(.3.3)**
disfranchise **35.15.17**
disfranchisement **22.26.15(.13.5)**
disfrock **24.9.15**
disgorge **39.10**
disgorgement **22.26.15(.13.6)**
disgrace **34.4.13**
disgraceful **40.27.25**
disgracefully **1.31.17(.16.2), 1.31.29**
disgruntled **23.31.16**
disgruntlement **22.26.15(.13.7)**
disguise **35.15.10**
disguisement **22.26.15(.13.5)**
disgust **22.29.12**
disgustedly **1.31.23(.14.3)**
disgustful **40.27.18**
disgusting **29.1.12(.21)**
disgustingly **1.31.28(.1.4)**
disgustingness **34.18.16(.26)**
dish **36.2**
dishabituation **28.17.25(.3.1)**
disharmonious **34.3.6(.7)**

disharmoniously **1.31.33(.1.2)**
disharmonize **35.15.12(.5)**
disharmony **1.16.15(.11)**
dishcloth **32.9**
dishearten **28.17.11(.8)**
dishearteningly **1.31.28(.1.7)**
disheartenment **22.26.15(.13.4)**
dishevel **40.28.4**
dishevelment **22.26.15(.13.7)**
Dishforth **32.10, 32.14.13**
dishful **40.14.6(.21)**
dishily **1.31.17(.22)**
dishiness **34.18.16(.2.8)**
dishlike **24.13.7(.24)**
dishonest **22.29.15(.13)**
dishonestly **1.31.22(.22)**
dishonesty **1.10.26(.11)**
dishonorably **1.31.21(.8)**
dishonour **17.18.9**
dishonourable **40.20.16(.27.4)**
dishonourableness **34.18.16(.37.4)**
dishonourably **1.31.21(.8)**
dishpan **28.7.4**
dishrag **26.5.8**
dishwasher **17.26.8**
dishwater **17.12.10(.7)**
dishy **1.24.2**
disillusion **28.17.26(.4)**
disillusionize **35.15.12(.5)**
disillusionment **22.26.15(.13.4)**
disincentive **31.2.1(.14)**
disinclination **28.17.25(.3.8)**
disincline **28.14.19(.16)**
disincorporate **22.4.22(.6)**
disinfect **22.23.4(.5)**
disinfectant **22.26.15(.9)**
disinfection **28.17.25(.15.2)**
disinfest **22.29.5(.4)**
disinfestation **28.17.25(.3.3)**
disinflation **28.17.25(.3.14)**
disinflationary **1.29.11(.13.2)**
disinformation **28.17.25(.3.7)**
disingenuous **34.18.6**
disingenuously **1.31.33(.12.1)**

disingenuousness **34.18.16(.31.2)**
disinherit **22.19.24(.3)**
disinheritance **34.24.10(.10)**
disintegrate **22.4.22(.11)**
disintegration **28.17.25(.3.13)**
disintegrative **31.2.1(.9.4)**
disintegrator **17.12.4(.15)**
disinter **18.3**
disinterest **22.29.5(.12), 22.29.15(.17)**
disinterestedly **1.31.23(.14.3)**
disinterestedness **34.18.16(.21.1)**
disinterment **22.26.15(.13.2)**
disinvest **22.29.5(.5)**
disinvestment **22.26.15(.13.3)**
disjecta membra **17.32.18**
disjoin **28.12**
disjoint **22.26.11**
disjointedly **1.31.23(.14.3)**
disjointedness **34.18.16(.21.1)**
disjunct **22.23.13**
disjunction **28.17.25(.15.6)**
disjunctive **31.2.1(.13.5)**
disjunctively **1.31.30(.7.2)**
disjuncture **17.28.20, 17.28.23**
disk **24.20.1**
diskette **22.5, 22.5.5**
diskless **34.18.29(.24)**
Disko **19.12.17**
Disley **1.31.34**
dislike **24.13.7**
dislikeable **40.20.16(.13)**
dislocate **22.4.11(.6)**
dislocation **28.17.25(.3.5)**
dislodge **39.9**
dislodgement **22.26.15(.13.6)**
disloyal **40.11.10, 40.16.5**
disloyalist **22.29.2(.31.1)**
disloyalty **1.10.28**
dismal **40.25.14**
dismally **1.31.17(.13)**
dismalness **34.18.16(.37.1)**
dismantle **40.21.17(.3)**
dismantlement **22.26.15(.13.7)**
dismantler **17.34.21**
dismast **22.29.6(.7), 22.29.8(.5)**
dismay **4.13**

dismember **17.11.17(.3)**
dismemberment **22.26.15(.13.2)**
dismiss **34.2.12**
dismissal **40.31.2**
dismissible **40.20.16(.21.1)**
dismission **28.17.25(.2.4)**
dismissive **31.2.4(.2)**
dismissively **1.31.30(.7.4)**
dismissiveness **34.18.16(.28.2)**
dismount **22.26.7**
Disney **1.16.27**
Disneyesque **24.20.3**
Disneyland® **23.24.6(.13)**
disobedience **34.24.2**
disobedient **22.26.2(.3)**
disobediently **1.31.22(.20.1)**
disobey **4.8**
disobeyer **17.2.2**
disoblige **39.12**
disobligingly **1.31.28(.1.16)**
disorder **17.13.9**
disorderliness **34.18.16(.2.10)**
disorderly **1.31.17(.10)**
disorganization **28.17.25(.3.12)**
disorganize **35.15.12(.5)**
disorient **22.26.2(.9), 22.26.4(.1)**
disorientate **22.4.9(.8)**
disorientation **28.17.25(.3.3)**
disown **28.19**
disowner **17.18.18**
disparage **39.2.22(.4)**
disparagement **22.26.15(.13.6)**
disparagingly **1.31.28(.1.16)**
disparate **22.19.24(.9)**
disparately **1.31.22(.15)**
disparateness **34.18.16(.20.3)**
disparity **1.10.16(.21.1)**
dispassionate **22.19.15(.9)**
dispassionately **1.31.22(.15)**
dispassionateness **34.18.16(.20.3)**
dispatch **38.5**
dispatcher **17.28.6**
dispel **40.5.1**
dispeller **17.34.5(.1)**
dispensability **1.10.16(.22.2)**

dispensable **40.20.16(.21.3)**
dispensary **1.29.11(.18)**
dispensation **28.17.25(.3.10)**
dispensational **40.26.13(.14.2)**
dispensatory **1.29.11(.8.8)**
dispense **34.24.3**
dispenser **17.24.22(.2)**
dispersal **40.31.13**
dispersant **22.26.15(.17.3)**
disperse **34.19.1**
disperser **17.24.16**
dispersible **40.20.16(.21.2)**
dispersion **28.17.25(.12)**
dispersive **31.2.4(.10)**
dispirit **22.2.24**
dispiritedly **1.31.23(.14.3)**
dispiritedness **34.18.16(.21.1)**
dispiritingly **1.31.28(.1.4)**
displace **34.4.14**
displacement **22.26.15(.13.5)**
display **4.28.9**
displayer **17.2.10**
displease **35.1.23**
displeasingly **1.31.28(.1.12)**
displeasure **17.27.3**
disport **22.13.1**
disposability **1.10.16(.22.2)**
disposable **40.20.16(.22)**
disposal **40.32.15**
dispose **35.20.1**
disposer **17.25.15**
disposition **28.17.25(.2.5)**
dispossess **34.5.10**
dispossession **28.17.25(.4)**
dispraise **35.4.16**
Disprin® **28.2.29(.6)**
disproof **30.13.4**
disproportion **28.17.25(.8)**
disproportional **40.26.13(.14.5)**
disproportionally **1.31.17(.14.3)**
disproportionate **22.19.15(.9)**
disproportionately **1.31.22(.15)**
disproportionateness **34.18.16(.20.3)**
disprovable **40.20.16(.19)**
disproval **40.28.10**
disprove **31.10**
disputable **40.20.16(.11.2)**

disputably **1.31.21(.4.1)**
disputant **22.26.15(.9)**
disputation **28.17.25(.3.3)**
disputatious **34.18.22(.3)**
disputatiously **1.31.33(.12.4)**
disputatiousness **34.18.16(.31.4)**
dispute **22.18.10**
disputer **17.12.15(.8)**
disqualification **28.17.25(.3.5)**
disqualify **14.14.4(.16)**
disquiet **22.19.4**
disquieting **29.1.12(.14)**
disquietingly **1.31.28(.1.4)**
disquietude **23.17.4(.1)**
disquisition **28.17.25(.2.5)**
disquisitional **40.26.13(.14.1)**
Disraeli **1.31.4**
disrate **22.4.22**
disregard **23.9.10**
disregardful **40.27.19**
disregardfully **1.31.17(.16.2)**
disrepair **6.2**
disreputable **40.20.16(.11.3)**
disreputableness **34.18.16(.37.4)**
disreputably **1.31.21(.4.3)**
disrepute **22.18.10**
disrespect **22.23.4(.1)**
disrespectful **40.27.18, 40.27.20**
disrespectfully **1.31.17(.16.2)**
disrobe **21.16.2**
disrupt **22.22.6**
disrupter **17.12.19**
disruption **28.17.25(.14)**
disruptive **31.2.1(.12)**
disruptively **1.31.30(.7.2)**
disruptiveness **34.18.16(.28.1)**
Diss **34.2**
dissatisfaction **28.17.25(.15.3)**
dissatisfactory **1.29.11(.8.12)**
dissatisfiedly **1.31.23(.11)**
dissatisfy **14.14.6**
dissect **22.23.4(.7)**
dissection **28.17.25(.15.2)**
dissector **17.12.21(.2)**
disseise **35.1.16**
disseisin **28.2.24, 28.17.24(.1)**
disseize **35.1.16**

dissemblance 34.24.10(.24)
dissemble 40.20.19
dissembler 17.34.20
dissemblingly 1.31.28(.1.18)
disseminate 22.4.14(.9.2)
dissemination 28.17.25(.3.8)
disseminator 17.12.4(.10)
dissension 28.17.25(.16)
dissent 22.26.4(.11)
dissenter 17.12.22(.3)
dissentient 22.26.15(.19)
dissentingly 1.31.28(.1.4)
dissepement 22.26.15(.13.2)
dissertate 22.4.9(.5)
dissertation 28.17.25(.3.3)
dissertational 40.26.13(.14.2)
disserve 31.11
disservice 34.2.15
dissever 17.21.4
disseverance 34.24.10(.16)
disseverment 22.26.15(.13.4)
dissidence 34.24.10(.11)
dissident 22.26.15(.10)
dissimilar 17.34.16(.11)
dissimilarity 1.10.16(.21.1)
dissimilarly 1.31.17(.29)
dissimilate 22.4.23(.7.2)
dissimilation 28.17.25(.3.14)
dissimilatory 1.29.11(.8.10)
dissimilitude 23.17.4(.1)
dissimulate 22.4.23(.7.3)
dissimulation 28.17.25(.3.14)
dissimulator 17.12.4(.16)
dissipate 22.4.7
dissipation 28.17.25(.3.2)
dissipative 31.2.1(.3)
dissipator 17.12.4(.3)
dissociate 22.4.2(.9)
dissociation 28.17.25(.3.1)
dissociative 31.2.1(.2)
dissolubility 1.10.16(.22.2)
dissoluble 40.20.16(.28)
dissolubly 1.31.21(.9)
dissolute 22.18.11
dissolutely 1.31.22(.14)
dissoluteness 34.18.16(.20.2)
dissolution 28.17.25(.11)

dissolutionary 1.29.11(.13.2)
dissolvable 40.20.16(.19)
dissolve 31.13
dissolvent 22.26.15(.16)
dissonance 34.24.10(.15)
dissonant 22.26.15(.14)
dissonantly 1.31.22(.20.3)
dissuade 23.4.14
dissuader 17.13.3
dissuasion 28.17.26(.3)
dissuasive 31.2.4(.3)
dissyllabic 24.2.9(.2)
dissyllable 40.20.16(.29)
dissymmetrical 40.23.12(.18)
dissymmetry 1.29.15(.8)
distaff 30.7.2
distal 40.21.18
distally 1.31.17(.9.3)
distance 34.24.10(.10)
distant 22.26.15(.9)
distantly 1.31.22(.20.2)
distantness 34.18.16(.20.4)
distaste 22.29.4
distasteful 40.27.18
distastefully 1.31.17(.16.2)
distastefulness 34.18.16(.37.2)
distemper 17.10.17
distend 23.24.5(.4)
distensibility 1.10.16(.22.2)
distensible 40.20.16(.21.3)
distension 28.17.25(.16)
distich 24.2.10(.15.1)
distichous 34.18.13(.1)
distil 40.2.5
distillate 22.4.23(.7.1), 22.19.26(.13)
distillation 28.17.25(.3.14)
distillatory 1.29.11(.8.10)
distiller 17.34.2(.2)
distillery 1.29.11(.27)
distinct 22.23.13
distinction 28.17.25(.15.6)
distinctive 31.2.1(.13.5)
distinctively 1.31.30(.7.2)
distinctiveness 34.18.16(.28.1)
distinctly 1.31.22(.19)
distinctness 34.18.16(.20.4)
distingué 4.12
distinguée 4.12
distinguish 36.2.24
distinguishable 40.20.16(.23)

distinguishably 1.31.21(.7.3)
distort 22.13.3
distortedly 1.31.23(.14.3)
distortedness 34.18.16(.21.1)
distorter 17.12.10(.2)
distortion 28.17.25(.8)
distortional 40.26.13(.14.5)
distortionless 34.18.29(.27)
distract 22.23.5(.9)
distracted 23.18.9(.17)
distractedly 1.31.23(.14.3)
distractedness 34.18.16(.21.1)
distraction 28.17.25(.15.3)
distractor 17.12.21(.3)
distrain 28.4.18
distrainee 2.17
distrainer 17.18.3
distrainment 22.26.15(.13.4)
distraint 22.26.3
distrait 4.26.11
distraite 22.4.22(.8)
distraught 22.13.14
distress 34.5.14(.5)
distressful 40.27.25
distressfully 1.31.17(.16.2)
distressing 29.1.23
distressingly 1.31.28(.1.11)
distributable 40.20.16(.11.2)
distributary 1.29.11(.8.4)
distribute 22.18.10
distribution 28.17.25(.11)
distributional 40.26.13(.14.5)
distributive 31.2.1(.9.4)
distributively 1.31.30(.7.2)
distributor 17.12.15(.8), 17.12.16(.19)
district 22.23.2
distrust 22.29.12
distruster 17.12.24(.10)
distrustful 40.27.18
distrustfully 1.31.17(.16.2)
distrustfulness 34.18.16(.37.2)
disturb 21.15
disturbance 34.24.10(.9)
disturbed 23.21
disturber 17.11.14
disturbingly 1.31.28(.1.3)
disulphide 23.15.9

disunion 28.3.8(.9)
disunite 22.16.14
disunity 1.10.16(.13)
disuse 34.17.13, 35.17.7
disutility 1.10.16(.23)
disyllabic 24.2.9(.2)
disyllable 40.20.16(.29)
dit 22.2
ditch 38.2
ditcher 17.28.2
ditchwater 17.12.10(.7)
ditheism 27.15.21(.2.1)
ditheist 22.29.2(.1)
dither 17.23.2
ditherer 17.32.14(.15)
dithery 1.29.11(.17)
dithionite 22.16.14(.6)
dithyramb 21.17, 27.6.17(.3)
dithyrambi 14.7
dithyrambic 24.2.9(.8)
dithyrambus 34.18.10
dittander 17.13.20(.4)
dittany 1.16.15(.7)
ditto 19.10.2
dittographic 24.2.16(.3)
dittography 1.18.9(.3.2)
Ditton 28.17.11(.2)
ditty 1.10.2
ditzy 1.22.21
Diu 16.1
diuresis 34.2.17(.1)
diuretic 24.2.10(.3.3)
diurnal 40.26.14
diurnally 1.31.17(.14.3)
diva 17.21.1
divagate 22.4.12(.5)
divagation 28.17.25(.3.6)
divalency 1.22.23(.10.4)
divalent 22.26.15(.25)
divan 28.7.13
divaricate 22.4.11(.6)
divarication 28.17.25(.3.5)
dive 31.9
dived 23.26
diver 17.21.10
diverge 39.15
divergence 34.24.10(.21)
divergency 1.22.23(.10.4)
divergent 22.26.15(.21)
divergently 1.31.22(.20.4)
divers 35.18.15, 35.19
diverse 34.19.6
diversely 1.31.33(.12.6)
diversifiable 40.20.16(.5)
diversification 28.17.25(.3.5)
diversify 14.14.4(.9)
diversion 28.17.25(.12)

diversional
40.26.13(.14.5)
diversionary
1.29.11(.13.2)
diversionist **22.29.2(.18.2)**
diversity **1.10.16(.16.2)**
divert **22.20.9**
diverticula **17.34.16(.21.2)**
diverticular
17.34.16(.21.2)
diverticulitis **34.18.11(.8)**
diverticulosis
34.2.17(.11.2)
diverticulum
27.15.28(.11)
divertimenti **2.12.14**
divertimento **19.10.17**
divertingly **1.31.28(.1.4)**
divertissement **11.8,
22.26.15(.13.5)**
Dives **35.1.14**
divest **22.29.5(.5)**
divestiture **17.28.15**
divestment
22.26.15(.13.3)
divesture **17.28.24**
divi **1.19.2**
divide **23.15.10**
dividend **23.24.5(.5),
23.24.16(.4)**
divider **17.13.12**
divi-divi **1.19.2**
divination **28.17.25(.3.8)**
divinatory **1.29.11(.8.7)**
divine **28.14.11**
divinely **1.31.27(.11)**
divineness **34.18.16(.25)**
diviner **17.18.13(.7)**
divingboard **23.12.2(.13)**
divinity **1.10.16(.13)**
divinize **35.15.12(.5)**
Divis **34.2.15**
divisi **1.22.1**
divisibility **1.10.16(.22.2)**
divisible **40.20.16(.22)**
divisibly **1.31.21(.7.2)**
division **28.17.26(.2)**
divisional **40.26.13(.14.8)**
divisionally **1.31.17(.14.3)**
divisionary **1.29.11(.13.2)**
divisionism **27.15.21(.2.9)**
divisive **31.2.4(.7)**
divisively **1.31.30(.7.4)**
divisiveness
34.18.16(.28.2)
divisor **17.25.12(.8)**
divorce **34.12.5**
divorcé **2.22**
divorcée **2.22**
divorcement
22.26.15(.13.5)

divot **22.19.17**
divulgation **28.17.25(.3.6)**
divulge **39.18**
divulgement
22.26.15(.13.6)
divulgence **34.24.10(.21)**
divvy **1.19.2**
Diwali **1.31.9**
Dixey **1.22.22**
dixie **1.22.22**
Dixieland **23.24.6(.13)**
Dixon **28.17.23(.21)**
dizzily **1.31.17(.21)**
dizziness **34.18.16(.2.7)**
dizzy **1.23.2**
Djakarta **17.12.8(.5)**
djellaba **17.11.13**
Djerba **17.11.14**
Djibouti **1.10.15**
Djiboutian **28.3.3**
djinn **28.2**
D.Litt. **22.2.25**
D.Mus. **35.14**
Dnieper **17.10.1**
Dniester **17.12.24(.1)**
do **16**
doable **40.20.16(.7)**
dob **21.8**
dobbin **28.2.10**
dobe **1.9.13**
Dobell **40.5.2**
Dobermann **28.17.16(.16)**
Dobson **28.17.23(.18)**
doc **24.9**
docent **22.26.15(.17.3)**
Docetae **2.12.1**
Docetic **24.2.10(.1)**
Docetism **27.15.21(.2.4)**
Docetist **22.29.2(.13)**
doch-an-dorris **34.2.21**
docile **40.13.12**
docilely **1.31.38**
docility **1.10.16(.27)**
dock **24.9**
dockage **39.2.12**
docker **17.14.8**
docket **22.2.9(.5)**
dockland **23.24.6(.13),
23.24.16(.16.3)**
dockominium **27.3.8(.2)**
dockside **23.15.11(.11)**
dockyard **23.9.21**
doctor **17.12.21(.5)**
doctoral **40.16.13(.12.1)**
doctorate **22.19.24(.9)**
doctorhood **23.16.5(.3)**
doctorial **40.3.14(.5)**
doctorly **1.31.17(.9.3)**
doctorship **20.2.7(.9)**
doctrinaire **6.9**

doctrinairism
27.15.21(.2.14)
doctrinal **40.26.11**
doctrinally **1.31.17(.14.1)**
doctrinarian **28.3.20(.4)**
doctrine **28.17.31(.14)**
doctrinism **27.15.21(.2.9)**
doctrinist **22.29.2(.18.3)**
docudrama **17.17.7**
document **22.26.4(.8),
22.26.15(.13.2)**
documental **40.21.17(.2)**
documentalist
22.29.2(.31.2)
documentarily
1.31.17(.27.1)
documentarist
22.29.2(.29.3)
documentary
1.29.11(.8.12)
documentation
28.17.25(.3.3)
Dodd **23.10**
dodder **17.13.8**
dodderer **17.32.14(.7)**
dodderiness
34.18.16(.2.9)
doddery **1.29.11(.9)**
doddle **40.22.7**
Dodds **35.23.6**
dodecagon **28.10.12**
dodecahedral
40.16.13(.17)
dodecahedron
28.17.31(.15)
Dodecanese **35.1.12**
dodecaphonic
24.2.15(.6.3)
dodge **39.9**
dodgem **27.15.24**
dodger **17.29.8**
dodgily **1.31.17(.25)**
dodginess **34.18.16(.2.8)**
Dodgson **28.17.23(.27)**
dodgy **1.26.6**
dodo **19.11.13**
Dodoma **17.17.14(.3)**
Dodson **28.17.23(.20)**
doe **19**
doek **24.14**
Doenitz **34.22.2**
doer **17.8**
does **35.14**
doeskin **28.2.13(.14)**
doesn't **22.26.15(.18)**
doest **22.29.15(.6)**
doeth **32.14.4**
doff **30.8**
dog **26.7**
dogberry **1.29.11(.7.2)**
dogcart **22.10.5**

dogcatcher **17.28.6**
doge **37.9, 39.16**
dogface **34.4.9**
dogfight **22.16.16**
dogfighter **17.12.13(.5)**
dogfighting **29.1.12(.11)**
dogfish **36.2.18(.18)**
dogged **23.18.12**
doggedly **1.31.23(.14.5)**
doggedness
34.18.16(.21.1)
dogger **17.16.7**
doggerel **40.16.13(.12.1)**
dogginess **34.18.16(.2.4)**
doggish **36.2.14**
doggishly **1.31.35(.7.1)**
doggishness
34.18.16(.33.4)
doggo **19.13.6**
doggone **28.10.12**
doggy **1.14.6**
doghouse **34.8.6(.14)**
dogie **1.14.13**
dogleg **26.4**
doglike **24.13.7(.15)**
dogma **17.17.20**
dogman **28.7.10(.14),
28.17.16(.24)**
dogmatic **24.2.10(.4.2)**
dogmatically
1.31.24(.9.4)
dogmatism
27.15.21(.2.4)
dogmatist **22.29.2(.13)**
dogmatize **35.15.7(.7)**
dogmen **28.5.7(.18)**
do-gooder **17.13.13**
do-goodery **1.29.11(.9)**
do-goodism **27.15.21(.2.5)**
dogsbody **1.11.10**
dogshore **12.16.10**
dogskin **28.2.13(.14)**
dogtag **26.5.2**
dogteeth **32.1**
dogtooth **32.13**
dogtrot **22.11.15**
dogwatch **38.8**
dogwood **23.16.6(.12)**
doh **19**
Doha **10.21, 17.9**
Doherty **1.10.16(.10)**
doily **1.31.12**
doing **29.1.8**
doit **22.14**
dojo **19.25**
Dolan **28.17.33(.15)**
Dolby® **1.9.24**
dolce far niente
1.10.23(.3)
Dolcelatte® **1.10.6**
dolce vita **17.12.1**

Dolcis® 34.2.17(.16)
doldrums 35.25.10
dole 40.18
dole-bludger 17.29.10
doleful 40.27.31
dolefully 1.31.17(.16.2)
dolefulness 34.18.16(.37.2)
dolerite 22.16.24(.9)
Dolgellau 1.31.31, 1.32, 14.25.9, 14.25.15
dolichocephalic 24.2.27(.6)
dolichocephalous 34.18.29(.17.4)
dolichocephaly 1.31.17(.16.1)
dolichosauri 14.24.4
dolichosaurus 34.18.27(.8)
Dolin 28.2.31(.7)
doline 17.18.1(.16)
doll 40.9
dollar 17.34.9
dollhouse 34.8.6(.24)
dollie 1.31.10
Dollond 23.24.16(.16.2)
dollop 20.13.7
doll's house 34.8.6(.20)
dolly 1.31.10
Dolly Varden 28.17.12(.8)
dolma 17.17.24
dolman 28.17.16(.35)
Dolmetsch 38.4
dolomite 22.16.13
dolomitic 24.2.10(.2.2)
Dolores 34.18.27(.8), 35.18.23
doloroso 19.20.12, 19.21
dolorous 34.18.27(.28)
dolorously 1.31.33(.12.5)
dolorousness 34.18.16(.31.5)
dolour 17.34.9
dolphin 28.2.19
dolphinarium 27.3.17(.3)
dolt 22.32.12
doltish 36.2.11
doltishly 1.31.35(.7.1)
doltishness 34.18.16(.33.3)
dom 27.9
domain 28.4.7
domaine 28.4.7
domanial 40.3.7(.3)
Dombey 1.9.18
dome 27.17
domelike 24.13.7(.16)
Domesday 4.10.15
domestic 24.2.10(.15.4)
domesticable 40.20.16(.13)

domestically 1.31.24(.9.6)
domesticate 22.4.11(.6)
domestication 28.17.25(.3.5)
domesticity 1.10.16(.16.1)
Domestos® 34.10.8
domicile 40.13.12
domiciliary 1.29.2(.12), 1.29.11(.27)
dominance 34.24.10(.15)
dominant 22.26.15(.14)
dominantly 1.31.22(.20.3)
dominate 22.4.14(.9.2)
domination 28.17.25(.3.8)
dominator 17.12.4(.10)
dominatrices 35.1.16(.10)
dominatrix 34.23.2(.12)
dominee 1.16.2
domineer 3.9
domineeringly 1.31.28(.1.17)
Domingo 19.13.12
Dominic 24.2.15(.8)
Dominica 17.14.1, 17.14.15(.9)
dominical 40.23.12(.11)
Dominican 28.17.13(.1)
dominie 1.16.15(.11)
dominion 28.3.8(.2)
Dominique 24.1.5
domino 19.15.12
Domitian 28.3.15, 28.17.25(.2.4)
don 28.10
dona 17.18.18
doña 17.33.9
Donahue 16.24.16
Donal 40.26.15
Donald 23.31.21
Donaldson 28.17.23(.20)
Donat 22.7.12
donate 22.4.14
Donatello 19.29.4
donation 28.17.25(.3.8)
Donatism 27.15.21(.2.4)
Donatist 22.29.2(.13)
donative 31.2.1(.9.2)
donator 17.12.4(.10)
Donatus 34.18.11(.3)
Donau 9.7
Donbas 34.7.6
Doncaster 17.12.24(.5)
done 28.13
donee 2.17
Donegal 40.10.8
Doner 17.18.9
Donets Basin 28.17.23(.4)
Donetsk 24.20.11
dong 29.6
donga 17.16.17(.3)

Don Giovanni 1.16.8
dongle 40.24.14(.3)
Donington 28.17.11(.23)
Donizetti 1.10.4
donjon 28.17.28(.12)
Don Juan 28.17.6
donkey 1.12.16
donkey work 24.17.6(.1)
Donkin 28.2.13(.12)
Donlevy 1.19.1
donna 17.18.9
Donne 28.13
donné 4.14
donnée 4.14
Donnegan 28.17.15(.13)
Donnelly 1.31.17(.14.1)
donnish 36.2.16(.8)
donnishly 1.31.35(.7.2)
donnishness 34.18.16(.33.5)
donnybrook 24.14.10
Donoghue 16.24.16
Donohoe 19.26
Donohue 16.24.16
donor 17.18.18
Donovan 28.17.20(.10)
Don Pasquale 4.28.4
Don Quixote 22.19.18
don't 22.26.17
donut 22.15.6
doodad 23.7.8
doodah 10.7
doodle 40.22.12
doodlebug 26.10
doodler 17.34.22
doodling 29.1.31(.18)
doohickey 1.12.2
Doolan 28.17.33(.12)
Dooley 1.31.16
Doolittle 40.21.2
doom 27.14
doomsday 4.10.15
doomster 17.12.24(.22)
doomwatch 38.8
doomwatcher 17.28.9
Doone 28.16
Doonesbury 1.29.11(.7.2)
door 12
doorbell 40.5.2
doorcase 34.4.6
do-or-die 14.9
doorframe 27.4.8
doorjamb 27.6.14
doorkeeper 17.10.1
doorknob 21.8
doorknocker 17.14.8
doorman 28.17.16(.11)
doormat 22.7.11
doornail 40.4.7
doorplate 22.4.23(.8)

doorpost 22.29.17(.1)
doorstep 20.4
doorstop 20.7.4
doorstopper 17.10.8
doorway 4.25.6
dooryard 23.9.21
doozy 1.23.12
dop 20.7
dopa 17.10.16
dopamine 28.1.13
dopant 22.26.15(.7)
dope 20.15
doper 17.10.16
dopesheet 22.1.11
dopester 17.12.24(.16)
dopey 1.8.13
dopiaza 17.25.7
dopily 1.31.17(.7)
dopiness 34.18.16(.2.2)
doppelgänger 17.19.2
Dopper 17.10.8
Doppler 17.34.19
dopy 1.8.13
Dora 17.32.10
Dorado 19.11.7
Doran 28.17.31(.8)
Dorcas 34.18.13(.6)
Dorchester 17.12.24(.4)
Dordogne 28.12
Dordrecht 22.23.4(.10), 22.24
Doré 4.26.7
Doreen 28.1.25
Dorian 28.3.20(.7)
Doric 24.2.26(.6)
Dorinda 17.13.20(.1)
Doris 34.18.27(.7)
dork 24.10
Dorking 29.1.14(.7)
dorm 27.10
dormancy 1.22.23(.10.3)
dormant 22.26.15(.13.1)
dormer 17.17.9
dormice 34.15.5
dormition 28.17.25(.2.4)
dormitory 1.29.11(.8.7)
Dormobile® 40.1.2
dormouse 34.8.4
dormy 1.15.9
Dornoch 24.9.9, 24.16.7, 25.6, 25.10
doronicum 27.15.11(.9)
Dorothea 3.12, 17.1.10
Dorothy 1.20.8
dorp 20.8
Dors 35.12
dorsa 17.24.10
dorsal 40.31.9
dorsally 1.31.17(.20)
Dorset 22.19.18

Dorsey 1.22.11
dorsiflex 34.23.4(.12)
dorsum 27.15.20(.7)
Dortmund 23.24.14, 23.24.16(.7)
dory 1.29.8
do's 35.17
DOS 34.10
dos-à-dos 19.11
dosage 39.2.19
dose 34.20
dosh 36.9
do-si-do 19.11
dosimeter 17.12.16(.9.1)
dosimetric 24.2.26(.14.2)
dosimetry 1.29.15(.8)
Dos Passos 34.10.15
doss 34.10
dossal 40.31.8
dosser 17.24.9
dosshouse 34.8.6(.20)
dossier 3.14.6, 4.2.7
dost 22.29.12
Dostoevsky 1.12.17(.13)
Dostoyevsky 1.12.17(.13)
dot 22.11
dotage 39.2.10
dotard 23.18.9(.15)
dote 22.21
doter 17.12.18
doth 32.11
Dotheboys 35.13
dotingly 1.31.28(.1.4)
Dotrice 34.1.7
Dotson 28.17.23(.19)
dotter 17.12.9
dotterel 40.16.13(.12.1)
dottily 1.31.17(.9.2)
dottiness 34.18.16(.2.3)
dottle 40.21.7
dotty 1.10.9
Douai 1(.3), 4.5
Douala 17.34.8
douane 28.9
Douay 1(.3), 4.5
double 40.20.12
Doubleday 4.10.17
double entendre 17.32.20
double-ganger 17.19.2
doubleheader 17.13.4
doubler 17.34.20
doublespeak 24.1.1
doublet 22.19.26(.16)
doublethink 24.19.1(.4)
doubleton 28.17.11(.27)
doubletree 2.30.10
doubloon 28.16.15
doublure 17.7.13
doubly 1.31.21(.1)

doubt 22.9
doubtable 40.20.16(.11.1)
doubter 17.12.7
doubtful 40.27.18
doubtfully 1.31.17(.16.2)
doubtfulness 34.18.16(.37.2)
doubtingly 1.31.28(.1.4)
doubtless 34.18.29(.22)
doubtlessly 1.31.33(.12.6)
douce 34.17
douceur 18.11
douche 36.14
Doug 26.10
Dougall 40.24.10
Dougan 28.17.15(.12)
dough 19
doughboy 13.3
doughiness 34.18.16(.2.1)
doughnut 22.15.6
doughtily 1.31.17(.9.1)
doughtiness 34.18.16(.2.3)
doughty 1.10.7
doughy 1(.7)
Dougie 1.14.8
Douglas 34.18.29(.25)
Doulton® 28.17.11(.27)
doum 27.14
Dounreay 4.26
dour 17.3, 17.7
dourly 1.31.17(.1)
dourness 34.18.16(.15.1)
Douro 19.27.11
douroucouli 1.31.16
douse 34.8
dove 31.8, 31.12
dovecote 22.11.6, 22.21.5
Dovedale 40.4.3
dovelike 24.13.7(.20)
Dover 17.21.14
Dovercourt 22.13.4
Doveridge 39.2.22(.9)
dovetail 40.4.2
Dovey 1.19.7
Dow 9
dowager 17.29.13
dowdily 1.31.17(.10)
dowdiness 34.18.16(.2.3)
Dowding 29.1.13(.5)
dowdy 1.11.8
dowel 40.16.3
Dowell 40.16.3
dower 17.3
dowerless 34.18.29(.17.1)
Dowlais 34.15.10, 34.18.29(.8)
Dowland 23.24.16(.16.1)
Dowling 29.1.31(.7)
down 28.8

down-and-out 22.9, 22.9.8, 22.9.11
downbeat 22.1.2
downcast 22.29.6(.5), 22.29.8(.3)
downcomer 17.17.10
downdraft 22.27.4(.4)
downdraught 22.27.4(.4)
downer 17.18.7
Downes 35.26.8
Downey 1.16.7
downfall 40.10.11
downfold 23.31.13(.7)
down grade 23.4
downgrade 23.4.15
Downham 27.15.14(.6)
downhaul 40.10.16
downhearted 23.18.9(.7)
downheartedly 1.31.23(.14.3)
downheartedness 34.18.16(.21.1)
downhill 40.2.18
downhiller 17.34.2(.13)
Downie 1.16.7
downily 1.31.17(.14.1)
downiness 34.18.16(.2.5)
Downing 29.1.17(.6)
downland 23.24.6(.13), 23.24.16(.16.4)
downlighter 17.12.13(.9)
download 23.20.13
downmarket 22.2.9(.4)
downmost 22.29.17(.4)
Downpatrick 24.2.26(.14.3)
downpipe 20.10.1
downplay 4.28.9
downpour 12.3
downright 22.16.24(.15)
downrightness 34.18.16(.20.2)
downriver 17.21.2
downscale 40.4.4
downshaft 22.27.4(.3)
downshift 22.27.1
downside 23.15.11(.12)
downsize 35.15.16
Downson 28.17.23(.24)
downspout 22.9.5
downstage 39.4.2
downstairs 35.6
downstate 22.4.9(.9)
downstream 27.1.12
downstroke 24.18.13
downswing 29.1.29
downthrew 16.23.13
downthrow 19.27.21
downthrown 28.19.17
downtime 27.12.1
downtown 28.8.1

downtrodden 28.17.12(.9)
downturn 28.18.4
downward 23.18.26(.13)
downwardly 1.31.23(.14.7)
downwards 35.23.12
downwarp 20.8
downwind 23.24.2
downy 1.16.7
dowry 1.29.11(.1)
dowse 34.8, 35.8
dowser 17.24.7, 17.25.6
Dowsing 29.1.24
doxastic 24.2.10(.15.4)
doxological 40.23.12(.17.2)
doxology 1.26.10(.11.5)
doxy 1.22.22
doyen 28.5.1, 28.17.4
doyenne 28.5
Doyle 40.11
doyley 1.31.12
doyly 1.31.12
D'Oyly Carte 22.10
doze 35.20
dozen 28.17.24(.9)
dozenth 32.21
dozer 17.25.15
dozily 1.31.17(.21)
doziness 34.18.16(.2.7)
dozy 1.23.15
D.Phil. 40.2.11
drab 21.6
drabble 40.20.6
drably 1.31.21(.1)
drabness 34.18.16(.19)
drachm 27.6
drachma 17.17.19
drachmae 2.16, 4.13
drack 24.6
Draco 19.12.3
draconian 28.3.8(.11)
draconic 24.16.7
draconically 1.31.24(.9.8)
Dracula 17.34.16(.21.2)
draff 30.5
draft 22.27.4
draftee 2.11
drafter 17.12.23
draftily 1.31.17(.9.3)
draftsman 28.17.16(.29)
draftsmanship 20.2.7(.19)
draftswoman 28.17.16(.14)
draftswomen 28.2.17(.1)
drafty 1.10.24
drag 26.5
dragée 4.21

draggle **40.24.4**
draggletail **40.4.2**
draggle-tailed **23.31.3**
draggy **1.14.5**
dragline **28.14.19(.17)**
dragnet **22.5.9(.5)**
dragoman **28.17.16(.16)**
dragon **28.17.15(.6)**
dragonet **22.19.15(.9)**
dragonfish **36.2.18(.19)**
dragonfly **14.25.14**
dragonish **36.2.16(.13)**
dragonlady **1.11.4**
dragonnade **23.4.8**
dragoon **28.16.6**
dragster **17.12.24(.21)**
drail **40.4**
drain **28.4**
drainage **39.2.15**
drainboard **23.12.2(.12)**
draincock **24.9.6**
drainer **17.18.3**
drainpipe **20.10.1**
drake **24.3**
Drakensberg **26.14.1(.11)**
Dralon® **28.10.26**
DRAM **27.6.17(.1)**
dram **27.6**
drama **17.17.7**
dramadoc **24.9.5**
Dramamine® **28.1.13**
dramatic **24.2.10(.4.2)**
dramatically **1.31.24(.9.4)**
dramatis personae
  14.13
dramatist **22.29.2(.13)**
dramatization
  28.17.25(.3.11)
dramatize **35.15.7(.7)**
dramaturge **39.15**
dramaturgic **24.2.24(.6)**
dramaturgical
  40.23.12(.17.3)
dramaturgy **1.26.11**
Drambuie® **1(.6)**
Drammen **28.17.16(.7)**
drank **24.19.3**
drape **20.3**
draper **17.10.3**
drapery **1.29.11(.6)**
drastic **24.2.10(.15.4)**
drastically **1.31.24(.9.6)**
drat **22.7**
dratted **23.18.9(.5)**
draught **22.27.4**
draughtboard
  23.12.2(.8)
draughthorse **34.12.7**
draughtily **1.31.17(.9.3)**
draughtiness
  34.18.16(.2.3)

draughts **34.22.19**
draughtsman
  28.17.16(.29)
draughtsmanship
  20.2.7(.19)
draughtswoman
  28.17.16(.14)
draughtswomen
  28.2.17(.1)
draughty **1.10.24**
Dravidian **28.3.4(.2)**
draw **12**
drawback **24.6.6(.6)**
drawbridge **39.2.22(.10)**
drawcord **23.12.4**
drawee **2**
drawer **12, 17.4**
drawerful **40.14.6(.5)**
drawers **35.12**
drawing **29.1.5**
drawl **40.10**
drawler **17.34.10**
drawn **28.11**
drawstring **29.1.30(.13)**
Drax **34.23.5**
dray **4**
Draycott **22.11.6,
  22.19.12(.3)**
drayman **28.17.16(.4)**
Drayton **28.17.11(.3)**
dread **23.5**
dreadful **40.27.19**
dreadfully **1.31.17(.16.2)**
dreadfulness
  34.18.16(.37.2)
dreadlocked **22.23.7**
dreadlocks **34.23.8(.11)**
dreadnought **22.13.6**
dream **27.1**
dreamboat **22.21.2**
dreamed **22.25, 23.23.1**
dreamer **17.17.1**
dreamful **40.27.21**
dreamily **1.31.17(.13)**
dreaminess **34.18.16(.2.5)**
dreamland **23.24.6(.13)**
dreamless **34.18.29(.26)**
dreamlessly **1.31.33(.12.6)**
dreamlessness
  34.18.16(.31.6)
dreamlike **24.13.7(.16)**
dreamt **22.25**
dreamtime **27.12.1**
dreamworld **23.31.12**
dreamy **1.15.1**
drear **3**
drearily **1.31.17(.27.1)**
dreariness **34.18.16(.2.9)**
dreary **1.29.2**
dreck **24.4**
dredge **39.5**

dredger **17.29.4**
dree **2**
Dreft **22.27.2**
dreg **26.4**
dreggy **1.14.4**
Dreiser **17.25.12**
drench **38.18.2**
Dresden **28.17.12(.26)**
dress **34.5**
dressage **37.4.6, 39.8**
dresser **17.24.5**
dressily **1.31.17(.20)**
dressiness **34.18.16(.2.7)**
dressing **29.1.23**
dressmaker **17.14.3(.3)**
dressmaking **29.1.14(.3)**
dressy **1.22.5**
drew **16**
Drexel **40.31.18**
drey **4**
Dreyfus **34.18.17**
dribble **40.20.2**
dribbler **17.34.20**
dribbly **1.31.17(.8),
  1.31.21(.1)**
driblet **22.19.26(.16)**
dribs and drabs **35.21**
dried **23.15**
drier **17.6**
Driffield **23.31.1(.2)**
drift **22.27.1**
driftage **39.2.10**
drifter **17.12.23**
drift net **22.5.9(.4)**
driftwood **23.16.6(.9)**
Drighlington
  28.17.11(.23)
drill **40.2**
driller **17.34.2**
drillmaster **17.12.24(.5)**
drillstock **24.9.4**
drily **1.31.14**
drink **24.19.1**
drinkable **40.20.16(.13)**
drinker **17.14.21(.1)**
Drinkwater **17.12.10(.7)**
drip **20.2**
dripfed **23.5.8**
dripfeed **23.1.6**
dripgrind **23.24.13**
drippily **1.31.17(.7)**
drippiness **34.18.16(.2.2)**
dripping **29.1.10(.2)**
drippy **1.8.2**
Driscoll **40.23.16**
drivable **40.20.16(.19)**
drive **31.9**
drivel **40.28.2**
driveller **17.34.16(.14)**
driven **28.17.20(.2)**

driver **17.21.10**
driverless **34.18.29(.17.4)**
driveshaft **22.27.4(.3)**
driveway **4.25.20**
drizzle **40.32.2**
drizzly **1.31.34**
Drogheda **17.13.15**
drogue **26.15**
droit **22.14**
droit de seigneur **18.16**
Droitwich **38.2.9**
droll **40.18**
drollery **1.29.11(.27)**
drollness **34.18.16(.37.3)**
drolly **1.31.38**
drome **27.17**
dromedary **1.29.11(.9)**
dromoi **13.6**
dromond **23.24.16(.7)**
Dromore **12.9**
dromos **34.10.12**
drone **28.19**
Dronfield **23.31.1(.2)**
drongo **19.13.12**
droob **21.13**
drool **40.15**
droop **20.12**
droopily **1.31.17(.7)**
droopiness **34.18.16(.2.2)**
droop-snoot **22.18.5**
droopy **1.8.10**
drop **20.7**
drophead **23.5.13(.7)**
dropkick **24.2.12**
dropleaf **30.1.9**
droplet **22.19.26(.15)**
dropout **22.9.5**
dropper **17.10.8**
dropping **29.1.10(.6)**
dropsical **40.23.12(.15)**
dropsy **1.22.19**
dropwort **22.20.15**
droshky **1.12.18**
drosophila **17.34.16(.13)**
dross **34.10**
drossy **1.22.9**
drought **22.9**
droughty **1.10.7**
drouth **32.7**
Drouzhba **17.11.18**
drove **31.12**
drover **17.21.14**
drown **28.8**
drowning **29.1.17(.6)**
drowse **35.8**
drowsily **1.31.17(.21)**
drowsiness **34.18.16(.2.7)**
drowsy **1.23.6**
drowze **35.8**
Droylsden **28.17.12(.26)**

drub 21.11
drudge 39.11
drudgery 1.29.11(.23)
drug 26.10
drugget 22.19.13
druggist 22.29.2(.16)
druggy 1.14.8
drugstore 12.5.9
Druid 23.2.4
Druidess 34.5.3
Druidic 24.2.11(.2)
Druidical 40.23.12(.8)
Druidism 27.15.21(.2.5)
drum 27.11
Drumalbyn 28.2.10
drumbeat 22.1.2
drumfire 17.6.9(.8)
drumhead 23.5.13(.13)
drumlin 28.2.31(.19)
drumlinoid 23.13.12
drummer 17.17.10
Drummond 23.24.16(.7)
Drumnadrochit 22.2.9(.5)
drumstick 24.2.10(.15.4)
drunk 24.19.7
drunkard 23.18.11
drunken 28.17.13(.17)
drunkenly 1.31.27(.14)
drunkenness 34.18.16(.25)
drupaceous 34.18.22(.3)
drupe 20.12
drupel 40.19.10
drupelet 22.19.26(.15)
Drury 1.29.11(.3)
Drusilla 17.34.2(.9)
druthers 35.18.16
Druze 35.17
dry 14
dryad 23.7.3, 23.18.3
dryas 34.18.5
Dryden 28.17.12(.13)
dryer 17.6
dryish 36.2.4
dry land 23.24.16(.16.2)
dryness 34.18.16(.13)
dryopithecine 28.1.18(.6)
Dryopithecus 34.18.13(.10)
Drysdale 40.4.3
drystone 28.19.4(.9)
drysuit 22.18.6
drywall 40.10.17
dual 40.16.8
dualism 27.15.21(.2.15)
dualist 22.29.2(.31.1)
dualistic 24.2.10(.15.3)
dualistically 1.31.24(.9.6)
duality 1.10.16(.32.1)

dualize 35.15.21(.4.1)
dually 1.31.38
Duane 28.4
dub 21.11
Dubai 14.7
dubbin 28.2.10
Dubček 24.4.11
dubiety 1.10.16(.4)
dubious 34.3.2
dubiously 1.31.33(.1.1)
dubiousness 34.18.16(.31.1)
dubitation 28.17.25(.3.3)
dubitative 31.2.1(.9.1)
dubitatively 1.31.30(.7.1)
Dublin 28.2.31(.14)
Dubliner 17.18.16(.22)
Du Bois 10
Dubonnet® 4.14
Dubrovnik 24.2.15(.15)
Dubuque 24.15.8
ducal 40.23.11
ducat 22.19.12(.8)
Duce 4.22
Duchamp 11.14
Duchenne 28.5.12
Duchesne 28.4.14
duchess 34.18.23
duchesse 34.5.11
duchy 1.25.10
duck 24.12
duckbill 40.2.4
duckboard 23.12.2(.10)
duckegg 26.4
ducker 17.14.11
Duckett 22.2.9(.6)
Duckham 27.15.11(.7)
duckily 1.31.17(.11)
duckiness 34.18.16(.2.4)
duckling 29.1.31(.19)
ducktail 40.4.2
duckweed 23.1.10
Duckworth 32.14.15
ducky 1.12.9
duct 22.23.8
ductile 40.13.3(.8)
ductility 1.10.16(.23)
ductless 34.18.29(.22)
dud 23.14
dude 23.17
dudgeon 28.17.28(.7)
dudish 36.2.12
Dudley 1.31.23(.10)
due 16
duel 40.16.8
dueller 17.34.16(.4)
duellist 22.29.2(.31.1)
duende 4.10.12
duenna 17.18.4
duet 22.5

duettist 22.29.2(.13)
Dufay 4.15
duff 30.11
duffel 40.27.11
duffer 17.20.9
Duffield 23.31.1(.2)
Duffy 1.18.7
Dufy 1.18.8
dug 26.10
Duggan 28.17.15(.10)
Duggleby 1.9.24
dugite 22.16.12
dugong 29.6.6
dugout 22.9.10
duiker 17.14.12
Duisburg 26.14.1(.10)
Dukakis 34.2.10
duke 24.15
dukedom 27.15.10(.13)
Dukhobor 12.4
DUKW 24.12
Dulais 34.15.10, 34.18.29(.2)
dulcet 22.19.18
Dulcie 1.22.26
dulcification 28.17.25(.3.5)
dulcify 14.14.4(.9)
dulcimer 17.17.14(.8)
dulcitone 28.19.4(.5)
dulia 3.24.10, 17.6.15
dull 40.12
dullard 23.18.29
Dulles 34.18.29(.13)
dullish 36.2.27
dullness 34.18.16(.37.1)
dully 1.31.38
dulse 34.27
Duluth 32.13
Dulux® 34.23.11
Dulverton 28.17.11(.15)
Dulwich 38.2.11, 39.2.23
duly 1.31.16
Duma 17.17.13
Dumas 10.10, 10.10.3
Du Maurier 4.2.9
dumb 27.11
Dumbarton 28.17.11(.8)
dumbfound 23.24.7(.5)
dumbhead 23.5.13(.13)
dumbly 1.31.26(.9)
dumbness 34.18.16(.24)
dumbo 19.9.14
dumbshow 19.22
dumbstricken 28.17.13(.2)
dumbstruck 24.12.8
dumbwaiter 17.12.4(.14)
dumdum 27.11.4
Dumfries 34.1.7

Dummkopf 30.17
dummy 1.15.10
dummy run 28.13
dump 20.16.5
dumper 17.10.17
dumpily 1.31.17(.7)
dumpiness 34.18.16(.2.2)
dumpling 29.1.31(.15)
dumpster 17.12.24(.16)
dumpy 1.8.14
dun 28.13
Dunaj 14.13
Dunbar 10.5
Dunblane 28.4.19
Duncan 28.17.13(.17)
dunce 34.24.9
dunce cap 20.5.1
Dunciad 23.7.2
Dundalk 24.10.3
Dundas 34.18.12
Dundee 2.13
dunderhead 23.5.13(.5)
dunderheaded 23.18.10(.3)
Dundonald 23.31.21
dune 28.16
Dunedin 28.2.12, 28.17.12(.1)
Dunfermline 28.17.33(.22)
dung 29.8
Dungannon 28.17.17(.5)
dungaree 2.30
Dungarvan 28.17.20(.6)
Dungeness 34.5.6
dungeon 28.17.28(.12)
dunghill 40.2.18
Dunhill 40.2.18
dunk 24.19.7
Dunkeld 23.31.4
Dunkirk 24.17.3
Dunkley 1.31.24(.12)
Dun Laoghaire 1.29.2
Dunlap 20.5.8
dunlin 28.17.33(.23)
Dunlop 20.7.13
Dunmow 19.14.16
Dunn 28.13
dunnage 39.2.15
Dunne 28.13
dunno 19.15
dunnock 24.16.7
dunny 1.16.12
Dunoon 28.16.8
Dunsinane 28.4.8, 28.17.17(.2)
Duns Scotus 34.18.11(.11)
Dunstable 40.20.16(.11.7)
Dunstan 28.17.11(.25)
Dunwoody 1.11.15

duo **19.7**
duodecimal **40.25.10**
duodecimally
 1.31.17(.13)
duodecimo **19.14.12**
duodena **17.18.1(.4)**
duodenal **40.26.1**
duodenary **1.29.11(.13.1)**
duodenitis **34.18.11(.8)**
duodenum **27.15.14(.1)**
duologue **26.7.14**
duomo **19.14.14**
duopoly **1.31.17(.7)**
duotone **28.19.4(.5)**
dupable **40.20.16(.9)**
dupe **20.12**
duper **17.10.13**
dupery **1.29.11(.6)**
dupion **28.10.2**
duple **40.19.10**
duplex **34.23.4(.12)**
duplicable **40.20.16(.13)**
duplicate **22.4.11(.6),
 22.19.12(.10)**
duplication **28.17.25(.3.5)**
duplicator **17.12.4(.7)**
duplicitous **34.18.11(.10)**
duplicity **1.10.16(.16.1)**
Du Pont **22.26.9**
duppy **1.8.8**
du Pré **4**
Duquesne **28.4.5**
dura **17.32.14(.3)**
durability **1.10.16(.22.1)**
durable **40.20.16(.27.2)**
durableness
 34.18.16(.37.4)
durably **1.31.21(.8)**
Duracell® **40.5.11**
Duraglit® **22.2.25**
Duralumin® **28.2.17(.5)**
dura mater **17.12.4**
duramen **28.17.16(.4)**
durance **34.24.10(.16)**
Durango **19.13.12**
Durante **1.10.23(.4), 1.16.6**
duration **28.17.25(.3.13)**
durational
 40.26.13(.14.2)
durative **31.2.1(.9.4)**
Durban **28.17.10**
durbar **10.5.5**
Dürer **17.32.14(.3)**
duress **34.5.14**
Durex® **34.23.4(.11)**
Durham **27.15.26(.6)**
durian **28.3.20(.8)**
during **29.1.30(.8)**
Durkheim **27.12.6**
Durkheimian **28.3.7**

durmast **22.29.6(.7),
 22.29.8(.5)**
durn **28.18**
durndest **22.29.15(.10)**
Durocher **17.26.16**
durra **17.32.14(.3)**
Durrant **22.26.6,
 22.26.15(.23.2)**
Durrell **40.16.13(.9)**
Dürrenmatt **22.7.11**
durrie **1.29.9**
durry **1.29.9**
durst **22.29.16**
durum **27.15.26(.6)**
durzi **1.23.14**
Dushanbe **4.8**
dusk **24.20.7**
duskily **1.31.17(.11)**
duskiness **34.18.16(.2.4)**
dusky **1.12.17(.7)**
Düsseldorf **30.9.1**
dust **22.29.12**
dustbin **28.2.10**
dustbowl **40.18.4**
dustcart **22.10.5**
duster **17.12.24(.10)**
dustily **1.31.17(.9.3)**
Dustin **28.2.11(.14)**
dustiness **34.18.16(.2.3)**
dustless **34.18.29(.22)**
dustman **28.17.16(.21)**
dustpan **28.7.4**
dustsheet **22.1.11, 22.1.13**
dusty **1.10.26(.8)**
Dutch **38.11**
Dutchman **28.17.16(.33)**
Dutchwoman
 28.17.16(.14)
Dutchwomen **28.2.17(.1)**
duteous **34.3.3**
duteously **1.31.33(.1.1)**
duteousness
 34.18.16(.31.1)
dutiable **40.20.3**
dutiful **40.27.14**
dutifully **1.31.17(.16.1)**
dutifulness **34.18.16(.37.2)**
Du Toit **10**
Dutton **28.17.11(.11)**
duty **1.10.15**
duumvir **17.21.16**
duumvirate **22.19.24(.9)**
Duvalier **4.2.10**
duvet **4.16**
dux **34.23.11**
Dvořák **24.6.17**
dwale **40.4**
Dwane **28.4**
dwarf **30.9**
dwarfish **36.2.18(.7)**

dwarfism **27.15.21(.2.10)**
dwarves **35.28.5**
dweeb **21.1**
dwell **40.5**
dweller **17.34.5**
dwelling **29.1.31(.5)**
dwelt **22.32.2**
Dwight **22.16**
dwindle **40.22.16**
Dworkin **28.2.13(.4)**
Dwyer **17.6**
dyad **23.7.3**
dyadic **24.2.11(.5)**
dyarchy **1.12.6**
dybbuk **24.15.2, 24.16.3**
dye **14**
dyeable **40.20.16(.5)**
dyer **17.6**
dyestuff **30.11.3**
dyeworks **34.23.16**
Dyfed **23.18.17**
Dyffryn **28.17.31(.19)**
dying **29.1.7**
dyke **24.13**
Dylan **28.17.33(.2)**
Dymchurch **38.16**
Dymo **19.14.10**
Dymock **24.16.6**
Dymond **23.24.16(.7)**
Dymont **22.26.15(.13.1)**
Dympna **17.18.19**
dynamic **24.2.14(.4)**
dynamical **40.23.12(.10)**
dynamically **1.31.24(.9.8)**
dynamicist **22.29.2(.22)**
dynamism **27.15.21(.2.8)**
dynamist **22.29.2(.17)**
dynamite **22.16.13**
dynamiter **17.12.13(.3)**
dynamization
 28.17.25(.3.11)
dynamize **35.15.11**
dynamo **19.14.12**
dynamometer
 17.12.16(.9.2)
dynast **22.29.6(.8),
 22.29.15(.13)**
dynastic **24.2.10(.15.4)**
dynastically
 1.31.24(.9.6)
dynasty **1.10.26(.11)**
dynatron **28.10.24(.7)**
dyne **28.14**
Dynefor **17.21.4, 17.21.12**
Dysart **22.10.9, 22.19.18**
dyscalculia **3.24.10**
dyscrasia **3.15.3**
dyscrasic **24.2.21**
dysenteric **24.2.26(.4)**
dysentery **1.29.11(.8.12)**

dysfunction
 28.17.25(.15.6)
dysfunctional
 40.26.13(.14.6)
dysgenic **24.2.15(.4)**
dysgraphia **3.10.2**
dysgraphic **24.2.16(.3)**
dyslalia **3.24.3**
dyslectic **24.2.10(.13)**
dyslexia **3.14.15**
dyslexic **24.2.20(.13)**
dyslogistic **24.2.10(.15.2)**
dyslogistically
 1.31.24(.9.6)
dysmenorrhoea **3.22**
Dyson **28.17.23(.12)**
dyspepsia **3.14.12**
dyspeptic **24.2.10(.12)**
dysphagia **3.19.3, 17.29.3**
dysphasia **3.15.3**
dysphasic **24.2.21**
dysphemism
 27.15.21(.2.8)
dysphoria **3.22.9**
dysphoric **24.2.26(.6)**
dysplasia **3.15.3**
dysplastic **24.2.10(.15.4)**
dyspnoea **17.1.7**
dyspnoeic **24.2.1**
dyspraxia **3.14.15**
dysprosium **27.3.12**
dysthymia **3.8.5**
dystocia **3.16.7, 17.26.16**
dystopia **3.2.7**
dystopian **28.3.1**
dystrophic **24.2.16(.4)**
dystrophy **1.18.9(.2)**
dysuria **3.22.12, 17.1.16**
Dzerzhinsky **1.12.17(.12)**
dzho **19**
dziggetai **14.8**
dzo **19**
Dzongkha **17.14.21(.4)**
e **2**
each **38.1**
Eadie **1.11.1**
eager **17.16.1**
eagerly **1.31.17(.12)**
eagerness **34.18.16(.15.2)**
eagle **40.24.1**
eaglet **22.19.26(.20)**
eagre **17.16.1**
Eakins **35.26.2**
Ealing **29.1.31(.1)**
Eames **35.25.1**
Eamon **28.17.16(.4)**
ear **3**
earache **24.3.13**
earbash **36.6.2**
earbasher **17.26.6**

ecosystem 27.15.9(.15)
eco-terrorism 27.15.21(.2.14)
eco-terrorist 22.29.2(.29.4)
écru 16.23.10
ecstasize 35.15.16(.4)
ecstasy 1.22.16(.4)
ecstatic 24.2.10(.4.1)
ecstatically 1.31.24(.9.4)
ectoblast 22.29.6(.12), 22.29.8(.8)
ectoblastic 24.2.10(.15.4)
ectoderm 27.16.3
ectodermal 40.25.11
ectogenesis 34.2.17(.10.3)
ectogenetic 24.2.10(.3.1)
ectogenetically 1.31.24(.9.3)
ectogenic 24.2.15(.4)
ectogenically 1.31.24(.9.8)
ectogenous 34.18.16(.15.3)
ectomorph 30.9.2
ectomorphic 24.2.16(.5)
ectomorphy 1.18.6
ectoparasite 22.16.19(.9)
ectopic 24.2.8(.5)
ectoplasm 27.15.21(.3)
ectoplasmic 24.2.14(.17)
ectozoon 28.10.6
ecu 16.24.7
Ecuador 12.6.6
Ecuadoran 28.17.31(.8)
Ecuadorean 28.3.20(.7)
ecumenical 40.23.12(.11)
ecumenicalism 27.15.21(.2.15)
ecumenically 1.31.24(.9.8)
ecumenicism 27.15.21(.2.12)
ecumenicity 1.10.16(.16.1)
ecumenism 27.15.21(.2.9)
eczema 17.17.14(.8)
eczematous 34.18.11(.10)
Ed 23.5
edacious 34.18.22(.3)
edacity 1.10.16(.16.1)
Edale 40.4.3
Edam 27.6.5
edaphic 24.2.16(.3)
Edda 17.13.4
Eddic 24.2.11(.4)
Eddie 1.11.5
Eddington 28.17.11(.23)
eddo 19.11.5
eddy 1.11.5
Eddystone 28.17.11(.25)

edelweiss 34.15.7
edematose 34.20.4
Eden 28.17.12(.1)
edentate 22.4.9(.8)
Edessa 17.24.5
Edgar 17.16.16
Edgbaston 28.17.11(.25)
edge 39.5
Edgecombe 27.15.11(.16)
Edgehill 40.2.18
edgeless 34.18.29(.37)
edger 17.29.4
edgeways 35.4.15
edgewise 35.15.19
Edgeworth 32.14.15
edgily 1.31.17(.25)
edginess 34.18.16(.2.8)
edging 29.1.28
Edgware 6.18.15
edgy 1.26.3
edibility 1.10.16(.22.1)
edible 40.20.16(.12)
edibleness 34.18.16(.37.4)
edict 22.23.2
edictal 40.21.16
Edie 1.11.1
edification 28.17.25(.3.5)
edifice 34.2.14
edify 14.14.4(.5)
edifyingly 1.31.28(.1.1)
Edinburgh 17.32.14(.5)
Edison 28.17.23(.14)
edit 22.2.8
Edith 32.2.2
edition 28.17.25(.2.3)
editiones principes 35.1.5
editio princeps 34.21.4
editor 17.12.16(.6)
editorial 40.3.14(.5)
editorialist 22.29.2(.31.1)
editorialize 35.15.21(.2)
editorially 1.31.3(.11)
editorship 20.2.7(.9)
Edmonds 35.23.15
Edmondson 28.17.23(.20)
Edmonton 28.17.11(.22)
Edmund 23.24.16(.7)
Edmundson 28.17.23(.20)
Edna 17.18.22
Edo 19.11.5
Edom 27.15.10(.1)
Edomite 22.16.13
EDP 2.9
Edrich 38.2.10
Edridge 39.2.22(.12)
Edsel 40.31.17
educability 1.10.16(.22.2)
educable 40.20.16(.13)
educatable 40.20.16(.11.1)

educate 22.4.11(.6)
educated 23.18.9(.3)
education 28.17.25(.3.5)
educational 40.26.13(.14.2)
educationalist 22.29.2(.31.3)
educationally 1.31.17(.14.3)
educationist 22.29.2(.18.2)
educative 31.2.1(.9.1)
educator 17.12.4(.7)
educe 34.17.13
educible 40.20.16(.21.2)
eduction 28.17.25(.15.5)
eductive 31.2.1(.13.4)
edulcorate 22.4.22(.6)
edulcoration 28.17.25(.3.13)
edutainment 22.26.15(.13.4)
Edward 23.18.26(.10)
Edwardian 28.3.4(.7)
Edwardiana 17.18.8
Edwards 35.23.12
Edwin 28.2.28
Edwina 17.18.1(.14)
Edwinstowe 19.10.19
eegit 22.2.21
eejit 22.2.21
eel 40.1
Eelam 27.6.18
eelgrass 34.9.6
eelpout 22.9.5
eelworm 27.16.7
eely 1.31.1
e'en 28.1
eeny meeny miny mo 19
e'er 6
eerie 1.29.2
eerily 1.31.17(.27.1)
eeriness 34.18.16(.2.9)
Eeyore 12.1
eff 30.4
effable 40.20.16(.18)
efface 34.4.9
effaceable 40.20.16(.21.1)
effacement 22.26.15(.13.5)
effect 22.23.4(.5)
effective 31.2.1(.13.2)
effectively 1.31.30(.7.2)
effectiveness 34.18.16(.28.1)
effectivity 1.10.16(.15)
effector 17.12.21(.2)
effectual 40.16.12
effectuality 1.10.16(.32.1)
effectually 1.31.17(.24)

effectualness 34.18.16(.37.1)
effectuate 22.4.4
effectuation 28.17.25(.3.1)
effeminacy 1.22.16(.9)
effeminate 22.19.15(.9)
effeminately 1.31.22(.15)
effendi 1.11.20(.3)
efference 34.24.10(.16)
efferent 22.26.15(.23.3)
effervesce 34.5.8
effervescence 34.24.10(.18)
effervescency 1.22.23(.10.4)
effervescent 22.26.15(.17.2)
effete 22.1.6
effeteness 34.18.16(.20.1)
efficacious 34.18.22(.3)
efficaciously 1.31.33(.12.4)
efficaciousness 34.18.16(.31.4)
efficacity 1.10.16(.16.1)
efficacy 1.22.16(.6)
efficiency 1.22.23(.10.4)
efficient 22.26.15(.19)
efficiently 1.31.22(.20.4)
Effie 1.18.3
effigy 1.26.10(.6)
Effingham 27.15.15
effleurage 37.4.9
effloresce 34.5.14
efflorescence 34.24.10(.18)
efflorescent 22.26.15(.17.2)
effluence 34.24.10(.6)
effluent 22.26.15(.5)
effluvia 3.11.6
effluvium 27.3.9
efflux 34.23.11
effluxion 28.17.25(.15.5)
effort 22.19.16
effortful 40.27.18
effortfully 1.31.17(.16.2)
effortless 34.18.29(.22)
effortlessly 1.31.33(.12.6)
effortlessness 34.18.16(.31.6)
effrontery 1.29.11(.8.12)
effulgence 34.24.10(.21)
effulgent 22.26.15(.21)
effulgently 1.31.22(.20.4)
effuse 35.17.7
effusion 28.17.26(.4)
effusive 31.2.4(.8)
effusively 1.31.30(.7.4)

effusiveness 34.18.16(.28.2)

Efik 24.2.16(.2)

eft 22.27.2

EFTA 17.12.23

e.g. 2.27

egad 23.7.10

egalitarian 28.3.20(.4)

egalitarianism 27.15.21(.2.9)

Egan 28.17.15(.1)

Egbert 22.19.9

Egerton 28.17.11(.15)

egest 22.29.5(.9)

egg 26.4

eggar 17.16.4

eggcup 20.9.7

egger 17.16.4

egghead 23.5.13(.12)

egginess 34.18.16(.2.4)

eggless 34.18.29(.25)

eggnog 26.7.7

eggplant 22.26.6, 22.26.8

eggshell 40.5.13

eggwhisk 24.20.1

eggy 1.14.4

Egham 27.15.12

eglantine 28.1.9(.6), 28.14.5

Egmont 22.26.9

ego 19.13.1

egocentric 24.2.26(.14.4)

egocentrically 1.31.24(.9.12)

egocentricity 1.10.16(.16.1)

egocentrism 27.15.21(.2.14)

egoism 27.15.21(.2.1)

egoist 22.29.2(.10)

egoistic 24.2.10(.15.1)

egoistical 40.23.12(.7.3)

egoistically 1.31.24(.9.6)

egomania 3.9.3(.5)

egomaniac 24.6.1

egomaniacal 40.23.12(.3)

egotism 27.15.21(.2.4)

egotist 22.29.2(.13)

egotistic 24.2.10(.15.2)

egotistical 40.23.12(.7.3)

egotistically 1.31.24(.9.6)

egotize 35.15.7(.7)

egregious 34.18.24

egregiously 1.31.33(.12.4)

egregiousness 34.18.16(.31.5)

Egremont 22.26.9, 22.26.15(.13.2)

egress 34.5.14(.8)

egression 28.17.25(.4)

egressive 31.2.4(.4)

egret 22.19.24(.15)

Egypt 22.22.1

Egyptian 28.17.25(.14)

Egyptianization 28.17.25(.3.12)

Egyptianize 35.15.12(.5)

Egyptologist 22.29.2(.26.3)

Egyptology 1.26.10(.11.2)

eh 4

Ehrlich 24.2.27(.5), 25.1

Eichmann 28.17.16(.23)

Eid 23.1

eider 17.13.12

eiderdown 28.8.2(.1)

eidetic 24.2.10(.3.1)

eidetically 1.31.24(.9.3)

eidola 17.34.18(.4)

eidolon 18.10.26

Eiffel 40.27.12

eigenfrequency 1.22.23(.10.4)

eigenfunction 28.17.25(.15.6)

eigenvalue 16.24.17

Eiger 17.16.10

Eigg 26.4

eight 22.4

eighteen 28.1.9

eighteenmo 19.14.16

eighteenth 32.21

eightfold 23.31.13(.7)

eighth 32.18

eighthly 1.31.31

eightieth 32.14.1

eightsome 27.15.20(.13)

eighty 1.10.3

eightyfold 23.31.13(.7)

Eilat 22.7.21, 22.10.13

Eileen 28.1.27(.6)

Eilidh 1.31.4

Eindhoven 28.17.20(.11)

einkorn 28.11.5

Einstein 28.14.5

einsteinium 27.3.8(.7)

Éire 17.32.5

eirenicon 28.10.11

Eirlys 34.2.22(.8)

Eisenhower 17.3.10

Eisenstadt 22.7.7

Eisenstein 28.14.5

eisteddfod 23.10.9, 23.18.16(.12)

eisteddfodau 14.9

eisteddfodic 24.2.11(.7)

either 17.23.1, 17.23.11

either/or 12

Eithne 1.16.26

ejaculate 22.4.23(.7.3), 22.19.26(.13)

ejaculation 28.17.25(.3.14)

ejaculator 17.12.4(.16)

ejaculatory 1.29.11(.8.10)

eject 22.23.4(.9)

ejecta 17.12.21(.2)

ejection 28.17.25(.15.2)

ejective 31.2.1(.13.2)

ejectment 22.26.15(.13.3)

ejector 17.12.21(.2)

Ekaterinburg 26.14.1(.9)

Ekco 19.12.4

eke 24.1

ekistics 34.23.2(.3)

ekka 17.14.4

Ektachrome® 27.17.13

el 40.5

elaborate 22.4.22(.6), 22.19.24(.9)

elaborately 1.31.22(.15)

elaborateness 34.18.16(.20.3)

elaboration 28.17.25(.3.13)

elaborative 31.2.1(.9.4)

elaborator 17.12.4(.15)

Elaine 28.4.19

Elam 27.6.18

Elamite 22.16.13

Elan 28.7.22, 28.17.33(.1)

élan 11.19, 28.7.22

eland 23.24.16(.16.1)

elapid 23.2.6

elapse 34.21.5

elasmobranch 24.19.3(.6)

elasmosaurus 34.18.27(.8)

elastane 28.4.3

elastase 35.4.3

elastic 24.2.10(.15.4)

elastically 1.31.24(.9.6)

elasticated 23.18.9(.3)

elasticity 1.10.16(.16.1)

elasticize 35.15.16(.4)

elastomer 17.17.14(.2)

elastomeric 24.2.26(.4)

Elastoplast® 22.29.6(.12), 22.29.8(.8)

elate 22.4.23

elated 23.18.9(.3)

elatedly 1.31.23(.14.3)

elatedness 34.18.16(.21.1)

elater 17.12.4(.16)

elation 28.17.25(.3.14)

Elba 17.11.20

Elbe 21.18

Elbert 22.19.9

elbow 19.9.18

elbowroom 27.14.6(.5)

Elche 4.22

El Cid 23.2

eld 23.31.4

elder 17.13.23(.3)

elderberry 1.29.3, 1.29.11(.7.1)

elderflower 17.3.11

elderliness 34.18.16(.2.10)

elderly 1.31.17(.10)

eldership 20.2.7(.9)

eldest 22.29.15(.10)

Eldon 28.17.12(.27)

eldorado 19.11.7

eldrich 38.2.10

Eldridge 39.2.22(.12)

eldritch 38.2.10

Eleanor 17.18.16(.22)

Eleatic 24.2.10(.4.1)

elecampane 28.4.1

elect 22.23.4(.11)

electable 40.20.16(.11.5)

election 28.17.25(.15.2)

electioneer 3.9

electioneering 29.1.30(.2)

elective 31.2.1(.13.2)

electively 1.31.30(.7.2)

elector 17.12.21(.2)

electoral 40.16.13(.12.1)

electorally 1.31.17(.27.1)

electorate 22.19.24(.9)

electorship 20.2.7(.9)

Electra 17.32.19(.9)

Electress 34.18.27(.14)

electret 22.19.24(.12)

electric 24.2.26(.14.3)

electrical 40.23.12(.18)

electrically 1.31.24(.9.12)

electrician 28.17.25(.2.6)

electricity 1.10.16(.16.1)

electrification 28.17.25(.3.5)

electrifier 17.6.9(.4)

electrify 14.14.4(.14)

electro 19.27.15

electrobiology 1.26.10(.11.1)

electrocardiogram 27.6.17(.5)

electrocardiograph 30.7.5(.1)

electrocardiographic 24.2.16(.3)

electrocardiography 1.18.9(.3.2)

electrochemical 40.23.12(.10)

electrochemically 1.31.24(.9.8)

electrochemist 22.29.2(.17)

electrochemistry 1.29.15(.17)

electroconvulsive 31.2.4(.14)

Elsa **17.24.24**
Elsan® **28.7.14**
Elsbeth **32.14.7**
else **34.27**
elsewhere **6.18, 6.18.12**
Elsie **1.22.26**
Elsinore **12.10**
Elspeth **32.14.6**
Elstree **2.30.10**
Elsworthy **1.21**
Eltham **27.15.9(.16)**
Elton **28.17.11(.27)**
eluate **22.19.5**
elucidate **22.4.10**
elucidation
   28.17.25(.3.4)
elucidative **31.2.1(.3)**
elucidator **17.12.4(.6)**
elucidatory **1.29.11(.8.2)**
elude **23.17.5**
eluent **22.26.15(.5)**
Elul **40.12**
Eluned **23.5.7**
elusive **31.2.4(.8)**
elusively **1.31.30(.7.4)**
elusiveness
   34.18.16(.28.2)
elute **22.18.11**
elution **28.17.25(.11)**
elutriate **22.4.2(.14)**
elutriation **28.17.25(.3.1)**
elver **17.21.19**
elves **35.28.10**
Elvira **17.32.2, 17.32.13**
Elvis **34.2.15**
elvish **36.2.19**
elvishly **1.31.35(.7.3)**
elvishness **34.18.16(.33.6)**
Elwes **35.18.22**
Ely **1.31.1, 14.25.1**
Élysée **4.19**
Elysian **28.3.14**
Elysium **27.3.12**
elytra **17.32.19(.7)**
elytron **28.10.24(.7),
   28.17.31(.14)**
Elzevir **3.11.7**
em **27.5**
emaciate **22.4.2(.9)**
emaciation **28.17.25(.3.1)**
email **40.4.6**
emanate **22.4.14(.9.2)**
emanation **28.17.25(.3.8)**
emanative **31.2.1(.3)**
emancipate **22.4.7**
emancipation
   28.17.25(.3.2)
emancipationist
   22.29.2(.18.2)
emancipator **17.12.4(.3)**

emancipatory
   1.29.11(.8.2)
Emanuel **40.14.8**
emasculate **22.4.23(.7.3)**
emasculation
   28.17.25(.3.14)
emasculator **17.12.4(.16)**
emasculatory
   1.29.11(.8.10)
embalm **27.8.2**
embalmer **17.17.7**
embalmment
   22.26.15(.13.4)
embank **24.19.3(.1)**
embankment
   22.26.15(.13.3)
embargo **19.13.5**
embark **24.8.3**
embarkation
   28.17.25(.3.5)
embarras de choix **10**
embarras de richesse
   34.5.11
embarrass **34.18.27(.5)**
embarrassedly
   1.31.22(.22), 1.31.23(.14.7)
embarrassing **29.1.23**
embarrassingly
   1.31.28(.1.11)
embarrassment
   22.26.15(.13.5)
embassy **1.22.16(.3)**
embattle **40.21.5**
embattled **23.31.16**
embay **4.8**
embayment
   22.26.15(.13.1)
embed **23.5.2**
embedment
   22.26.15(.13.3)
embellish **36.2.27**
embellisher **17.26.14**
embellishment
   22.26.15(.13.6)
ember **17.11.17(.3)**
embezzle **40.32.4**
embezzlement
   22.26.15(.13.7)
embezzler **17.34.28**
embitter **17.12.2**
embitterment
   22.26.15(.13.2)
emblazon **28.17.24(.3)**
emblazonment
   22.26.15(.13.4)
emblazonry **1.29.20**
emblem **27.15.28(.15)**
emblematic **24.2.10(.4.2)**
emblematical
   40.23.12(.7.1)
emblematically
   1.31.24(.9.4)

emblematize **35.15.7(.7)**
emblements **34.22.18**
embodiment
   22.26.15(.13.1)
embody **1.11.10**
embolden **28.17.12(.27)**
emboli **2.32.9(.3), 14.25.9**
embolic **24.2.27(.9)**
embolism **27.15.21(.2.15)**
embolismic **24.2.14(.17)**
embolus **34.18.29(.17.2)**
embonpoint **7, 11.16**
embosom **27.15.21(.6)**
emboss **34.10.7**
embosser **17.24.9**
embossment
   22.26.15(.13.5)
embouchure **17.7.10**
embowel **40.16.3**
embower **17.3.2**
embrace **34.4.13**
embraceable
   40.20.16(.21.1)
embracement
   22.26.15(.13.5)
embracer **17.24.4**
embranchment
   22.26.15(.13.6)
embrangle **40.24.14(.2)**
embranglement
   22.26.15(.13.7)
embrasure **17.27.2**
embrittle **40.21.2**
embrittlement
   22.26.15(.13.7)
embrocation
   28.17.25(.3.5)
embroider **17.13.10**
embroidered **23.18.10(.9)**
embroiderer **17.32.14(.7)**
embroidery **1.29.11(.9)**
embroil **40.11.9**
embroilment
   22.26.15(.13.7)
embrown **28.8.5**
embryo **15.1.12**
embryogenesis
   34.2.17(.10.3)
embryoid **23.13.2**
embryologic **24.2.24(.4)**
embryological
   40.23.12(.17.2)
embryologically
   1.31.24(.9.11)
embryologist
   22.29.2(.26.2)
embryology **1.26.10(.11.1)**
embryonal **40.26.13(.1)**
embryonic **24.2.15(.6.1)**
embryonically
   1.31.24(.9.8)

Embury **1.29.11(.7.2)**
embus **34.14**
emcee **2.22**
Emeline **28.1.27(.7)**
emend **23.24.5(.7)**
emendation **28.17.25(.3.4)**
emendator **17.12.4(.6)**
emendatory **1.29.11(.8.6)**
Emeny **1.16.15(.11)**
emerald **23.31.11**
emeraldine **28.1.10**
emerge **39.15**
emergence **34.24.10(.21)**
emergency **1.22.23(.10.4)**
emergent **22.26.15(.21)**
emergently **1.31.22(.20.4)**
emeritus **34.18.11(.10)**
emerse **34.19.4**
emersion **28.17.25(.12)**
Emerson **28.17.23(.14)**
emery **1.29.11(.12)**
emesis **34.2.17(.10.3)**
emetic **24.2.10(.3.1)**
émeute **22.20.6**
emigrant **22.26.15(.23.4)**
emigrate **22.4.22(.11)**
emigration
   28.17.25(.3.13)
emigratory **1.29.11(.8.2)**
émigré **4.26.14**
Emile **40.1.6**
Emily **1.31.17(.13)**
eminence **34.24.10(.15)**
éminence grise **35.1**
eminent **22.26.15(.14)**
eminently **1.31.22(.20.3)**
emir **3.8**
emirate **22.4.22(.1),
   22.19.24(.9)**
emissary **1.29.11(.18)**
emission **28.17.25(.2.4)**
emissive **31.2.4(.2)**
emissivity **1.10.16(.15)**
emit **22.2.11**
emitter **17.12.2**
Emley **1.31.26(.4)**
Emlyn **28.2.31(.19)**
Emma **17.17.5**
Emmanuel **40.16.14**
Emmaus **34.18.2**
Emmental **40.8.4**
Emmentaler **17.34.8**
emmer **17.17.5**
emmet **22.19.14**
emmetropia **3.2.7**
emmetropic **24.2.8(.5)**
Emmy **1.15.4**
emollience **34.24.2**
emollient **22.26.2(.10)**

emolument 22.26.15(.13.2)
Emory 1.29.11(.12)
emote 22.21.7
emoter 17.12.18
emoticon 28.10.11
emotion 28.17.25(.13)
emotional 40.26.13(.14.5)
emotionalism 27.15.21(.2.15)
emotionalist 22.29.2(.31.3)
emotionality 1.10.16(.32.8)
emotionalize 35.15.21(.4.5)
emotionally 1.31.17(.14.3)
emotionless 34.18.29(.27)
emotive 31.2.1(.11)
emotively 1.31.30(.7.1)
emotiveness 34.18.16(.28.1)
emotivity 1.10.16(.15)
empanel 40.26.5
empanelment 22.26.15(.13.7)
empathetic 24.2.10(.3.2)
empathetically 1.31.24(.9.3)
empathic 24.2.18(.3)
empathically 1.31.24(.9.10)
empathist 22.29.2(.21)
empathize 35.15.15
empathy 1.20.8
Empedocles 35.1.23
empennage 39.2.15
emperor 17.32.14(.4)
emperorship 20.2.7(.9)
emphases 35.1.16(.10)
emphasis 34.2.17(.10.4)
emphasize 35.15.16(.4)
emphatic 24.2.10(.4.4)
emphatically 1.31.24(.9.4)
emphysema 17.17.1
empire 17.6.1
empiric 24.2.26(.1)
empirical 40.23.12(.18)
empirically 1.31.24(.9.12)
empiricism 27.15.21(.2.12)
empiricist 22.29.2(.22)
emplacement 22.26.15(.13.5)
emplane 28.4.19
employ 13.17
employability 1.10.16(.22.1)
employable 40.20.16(.4)

employee 2, 2.5
employer 17.5
employment 22.26.15(.13.1)
empolder 17.13.23(.8)
emporia 3.22.9
emporium 27.3.17(.4)
empower 17.3.1
empowerment 22.26.15(.13.1)
empress 34.18.27(.12)
Empson 28.17.23(.17)
emptily 1.31.17(.9.3)
emptiness 34.18.16(.2.3)
empty 1.10.19
empurple 40.19.12
empyema 17.17.1
empyreal 40.3.14(.1), 40.16.1
empyrean 28.3.20(.1), 28.17.1(.12)
Emrys 34.2.21
Emsworth 32.14.15
emu 16.24.9
emulate 22.4.23(.7.3)
emulation 28.17.25(.3.14)
emulative 31.2.1(.9.4)
emulator 17.12.4(.16)
emulous 34.18.29(.17.6)
emulously 1.31.33(.12.6)
emulousness 34.18.16(.31.6)
emulsifiable 40.20.16(.5)
emulsification 28.17.25(.3.5)
emulsifier 17.6.9(.4)
emulsify 14.14.4(.9)
emulsion 28.17.25(.17)
emulsionize 35.15.12(.5)
emulsive 31.2.4(.14)
Emyr 3.8.4
en 28.5
Ena 17.18.1
enable 40.20.4
enablement 22.26.15(.13.7)
enabler 17.34.20
enact 22.23.5
enactable 40.20.16(.11.5)
enaction 28.17.25(.15.3)
enactive 31.2.1(.13.3)
enactment 22.26.15(.13.3)
enactor 17.12.21(.3)
enactory 1.29.11(.8.12)
enamel 40.25.4
enameller 17.34.16(.11)
enamelling 29.1.31(.12)
enamelware 6.18.16
enamelwork 24.17.6(.19)
enamored 23.18.13
enamour 17.17.6

enamoured 23.18.13
enanthema 17.17.1
enantiomer 17.17.3, 17.17.16
enantiomeric 24.2.26(.4)
enantiomorph 30.9.2
enantiomorphic 24.2.16(.5)
enantiomorphism 27.15.21(.2.10)
enantiomorphous 34.18.17
enarthroses 35.1.16(.11)
enarthrosis 34.2.17(.11.2)
en bloc 24.9
en brosse 34.10
Encaenia 3.9.1
encage 39.4.3
encamp 20.16.3
encampment 22.26.15(.13.3)
encapsulate 22.4.23(.7.3)
encapsulation 28.17.25(.3.14)
encase 34.4.6
encasement 22.26.15(.13.5)
encash 36.6.5
encashable 40.20.16(.23)
encashment 22.26.15(.13.6)
encaustic 24.2.10(.15.4)
encaustically 1.31.24(.9.6)
enceinte 22.8
Enceladus 34.18.12
encephalic 24.2.27(.6)
encephalitic 24.2.10(.2.5)
encephalitis 34.18.11(.8)
encephalogram 27.6.17(.5)
encephalograph 30.7.5(.1)
encephalomyelitis 34.18.11(.8)
encephalon 28.10.26
encephalopathy 1.20.8
enchain 28.4.15
enchainment 22.26.15(.13.4)
enchant 22.26.8
enchantedly 1.31.23(.14.3)
enchanter 17.12.22(.4)
enchanting 29.1.12(.19)
enchantingly 1.31.28(.1.4)
enchantment 22.26.15(.13.3)
enchantress 34.18.27(.14)
enchase 34.4.12
enchilada 17.13.7
enchiridia 3.5.2

enchiridion 28.3.4(.2)
encipher 17.20.10
encipherment 22.26.15(.13.2)
encircle 40.23.13
encirclement 22.26.15(.13.7)
en clair 6
enclasp 20.17
enclave 31.3.8
enclitic 24.2.10(.2.5)
enclitically 1.31.24(.9.3)
enclose 35.20.14
enclosure 17.27.9
encode 23.20.7
encoder 17.13.17
encomia 3.8.9
encomiast 22.29.6(.1)
encomiastic 24.2.10(.15.4)
encomium 27.3.7
encompass 34.18.9(.11)
encompassment 22.26.15(.13.5)
encore 12.7
encounter 17.12.22(.5)
encourage 39.2.22(.7)
encouragement 22.26.15(.13.6)
encourager 17.29.13
encouragingly 1.31.28(.1.16)
encrinite 22.16.14(.6)
encroach 38.17
encroacher 17.28.17
encroachment 22.26.15(.13.6)
encrust 22.29.12
encrustation 28.17.25(.3.3)
encrustment 22.26.15(.13.3)
encrypt 22.22.1
encryption 28.17.25(.14)
encumber 17.11.17(.6)
encumberment 22.26.15(.13.2)
encumbrance 34.24.10(.16)
encyclic 24.2.27(.16)
encyclical 40.23.12(.19)
encyclopaedia 3.5.1
encyclopaedically 1.31.24(.9.7)
encyclopedia 3.5.1
encyclopedic 24.2.11(.1)
encyclopedically 1.31.24(.9.7)
encyclopedism 27.15.21(.2.5)
encyclopedist 22.29.2(.14)

enjoyableness 34.18.16(.37.4)

enjoyably 1.31.21(.2)

enjoyer 17.5

enjoyment 22.26.15(.13.1)

enkephalin 28.2.31(.10)

enkindle 40.22.16

enlace 34.4.14

enlacement 22.26.15(.13.5)

enlarge 39.8

enlargeable 40.20.16(.25)

enlargement 22.26.15(.13.6)

enlarger 17.29.7

enlighten 28.17.11(.12)

enlightened 23.24.16(.3)

enlightener 17.18.16(.4)

enlightenment 22.26.15(.13.4)

enlist 22.29.2(.31.1)

enlister 17.12.24(.2)

enlistment 22.26.15(.13.3)

enliven 28.17.20(.8)

enlivener 17.18.16(.11)

enlivenment 22.26.15(.13.4)

en masse 34.7

enmesh 36.5

enmeshment 22.26.15(.13.6)

enmity 1.10.16(.12)

Ennals 35.30.20

ennead 23.7.2

Ennis 34.2.13

Enniskillen 28.2.31(.2)

Ennius 34.3.6(.4)

ennoble 40.20.18

ennoblement 22.26.15(.13.7)

ennui 2.29

Eno® 19.15.1

Enoch 24.9.9

enologist 22.29.2(.26.4)

enology 1.26.10(.11.4)

enormity 1.10.16(.12)

enormous 34.18.15(.7)

enormously 1.31.33(.12.3)

enormousness 34.18.16(.31.3)

enosis 34.2.17(.10.3)

enough 30.11.7

enounce 34.24.5

enouncement 22.26.15(.13.5)

en passant 11.12, 22.26.8

en pension 11.18

enplane 28.4.19

enprint 22.26.1

enquire 17.6.13

enquirer 17.32.14(.2)

enquiringly 1.31.28(.1.17)

enquiry 1.29.11(.2)

enrage 39.4.9

enragement 22.26.15(.13.6)

en rapport 12.3

enrapt 22.22.4

enrapture 17.28.18

enrich 38.2.10

enrichment 22.26.15(.13.6)

Enright 22.16.24(.15)

enrobe 21.16.2

enrol 40.18.14

enroll 40.18.14

enrollee 2.32

enroller 17.34.18(.14)

enrolment 22.26.15(.13.7)

en route 22.18

ENSA 17.24.22(.2)

ensanguined 23.24.2

ensconce 34.24.7

ensemble 40.20.8, 40.20.19

enshrine 28.14.18

enshrinement 22.26.15(.13.4)

enshroud 23.8

ensiform 27.10.5(.2)

ensign 28.14.13, 28.17.23(.24)

ensigncy 1.22.23(.9)

ensilage 39.2.23

ensile 40.13.12

enslave 31.3.8

enslavement 22.26.15(.13.5)

enslaver 17.21.3

ensnare 6.9

ensnarement 22.26.15(.13.1)

ensnarl 40.8.9

Ensor 12.14.15

enstatite 22.16.9

ensue 16.24.14

en suite 22.1

ensure 12.16, 17.7.10

ensurer 17.32.14(.3)

enswathe 33.3

enswathement 22.26.15(.13.5)

entablature 17.28.15

entablement 22.26.15(.13.7)

entail 40.4.2

entailment 22.26.15(.13.7)

entangle 40.24.14(.2)

entanglement 22.26.15(.13.7)

entases 35.1.16(.10)

entasis 34.2.17(.10.2)

Entebbe 1.9.4

entelechy 1.12.13

entellus 34.18.29(.5)

entendre 17.32.20

entente 22.12, 22.26.8, 22.26.9

Entente Cordiale 40.8

enter 17.12.22(.3)

enterable 40.20.16(.27.3)

enterer 17.32.14(.6)

enteric 24.2.26(.4)

enteritis 34.18.11(.8)

enterostomy 1.15.13(.1)

enterotomy 1.15.13(.1)

enterovirus 34.18.27(.10)

enterprise 35.15.20(.3)

enterpriser 17.25.12(.14)

enterprising 29.1.24

enterprisingly 1.31.28(.1.12)

entertain 28.4.3

entertainer 17.18.3

entertaining 29.1.17(.3)

entertainingly 1.31.28(.1.7)

entertainment 22.26.15(.13.4)

enthalpy 1.8.16

enthral 40.10.18

enthrall 40.10.18

enthralment 22.26.15(.13.7)

enthrone 28.19.17

enthronement 22.26.15(.13.4)

enthronization 28.17.25(.3.11)

enthuse 35.17.7

enthusiasm 27.15.21(.3)

enthusiast 22.29.6(.1)

enthusiastic 24.2.10(.15.4)

enthusiastically 1.31.24(.9.6)

enthymeme 27.1.5

entice 34.15.2

enticement 22.26.15(.13.5)

enticer 17.24.13

enticing 29.1.23

enticingly 1.31.28(.1.11)

entire 17.6.3

entirely 1.31.17(.3)

entirety 1.10.16(.21.2)

entitative 31.2.1(.9.1)

entitle 40.21.10

entitlement 22.26.15(.13.7)

entity 1.10.16(.8)

entomb 27.14.1

entombment 22.26.15(.13.4)

entomic 24.2.14(.6)

entomological 40.23.12(.17.2)

entomologically 1.31.24(.9.11)

entomologist 22.29.2(.26.4)

entomology 1.26.10(.11.4)

entomophagous 34.18.14(.5)

entomophilous 34.18.29(.17.4)

entoparasite 22.16.19(.9)

entophyte 22.16.16

entourage 37.4.9

entr'acte 22.23.5(.9)

entrails 35.30.3

entrain 28.4.18

entrainment 22.26.15(.13.4)

entrammel 40.25.4

entrance 34.24.6, 34.24.10(.16)

entrancement 22.26.15(.13.5)

entrancingly 1.31.28(.1.11)

entrant 22.26.15(.23.4)

entrap 20.5.6

entrapment 22.26.15(.13.3)

entrapper 17.10.5

entreat 22.1.17

entreatingly 1.31.28(.1.4)

entreaty 1.10.1

entrechat 10.17

entrecôte 22.21.5

entrée 4.26.11

entremets 4.13

entrench 38.18.2

entrenchment 22.26.15(.13.6)

entre nous 16

entrepôt 19.8

entrepreneur 18.8

entrepreneurial 40.3.14(.7)

entrepreneurialism 27.15.21(.2.15)

entrepreneurially 1.31.3(.11)

entrepreneurship 20.2.7(.10)

entresol 40.9.14

entrism 27.15.21(.2.14)

entrist 22.29.2(.29.5)

entropic 24.2.8(.5)

entropically 1.31.24(.9.2)

entropy **1.8.11(.8)**
entrust **22.29.12**
entrustment
  22.26.15(.13.3)
entry **1.29.15(.15)**
entryism **27.15.21(.2.1)**
entryist **22.29.2(.2)**
entryphone® **28.19.11**
entryway **4.25.2**
entwine **28.14.17**
entwinement
  22.26.15(.13.4)
enucleate **22.4.2(.15)**
enucleation **28.17.25(.3.1)**
Enugu **16.10**
enumerable
  40.20.16(.27.4)
enumerate **22.4.22(.6)**
enumeration
  28.17.25(.3.13)
enumerative **31.2.1(.9.4)**
enumerator **17.12.4(.15)**
enunciate **22.4.2(.9)**
enunciation
  28.17.25(.3.1)
enunciative **31.2.1(.2)**
enunciatively
  1.31.30(.7.1)
enunciator **17.12.4(.1)**
enure **12.22, 17.7.12(.8)**
enuresis **34.2.17(.1)**
enuretic **24.2.10(.3.3)**
envelop **20.13.7**
envelope **20.15.9**
envelopment
  22.26.15(.13.3)
envenom **27.15.14(.4)**
enviable **40.20.3**
enviably **1.31.21(.1)**
envier **3.11.10**
envious **34.3.8**
enviously **1.31.33(.1.3)**
environ **28.17.31(.10)**
environment
  22.26.15(.13.4)
environmental
  40.21.17(.2)
environmentalism
  27.15.21(.2.15)
environmentalist
  22.29.2(.31.2)
environmentally
  1.31.17(.9.3)
environs **35.26.13(.18)**
envisage **39.2.20**
envisagement
  22.26.15(.13.6)
envision **28.17.26(.2)**
envoi **13.8**
envoy **13.8**
envoyship **20.2.7(.7)**

envy **1.19.13**
enweave **31.1.7**
enwind **23.24.13**
enwove **31.12**
enwoven **28.17.20(.11)**
enwrap **20.5.6**
enwreathe **33.1**
Enzed **23.5.11**
Enzedder **17.13.4**
enzootic **24.2.10(.6)**
enzymatic **24.2.10(.4.2)**
enzyme **27.12.5**
enzymic **24.2.14(.8)**
enzymology
  1.26.10(.11.4)
Eocene **28.1.18(.6)**
eohippus **34.18.9(.2)**
EOKA **17.14.17**
eolian **28.3.21(.11)**
eolith **32.2.9**
Eolithic **24.2.18(.1)**
eon **28.17.1**
Eos **34.10.1**
eosin **28.2.23(.9)**
eosinophil **40.2.11**
eosinophile **40.13.9**
epact **22.23.5(.2)**
Epaminondas **34.7.8**
eparch **24.8.2**
eparchy **1.12.6**
epaulette **22.5.21**
Epcot® **22.11.6**
épée **4.7**
epeirogeneses
  35.1.16(.10)
epeirogenesis
  34.2.17(.10.3)
epeirogenic **24.2.15(.4)**
epeirogeny **1.16.15(.17)**
epentheses **35.1.16(.10)**
epenthesis **34.2.17(.10.4)**
epenthetic **24.2.10(.3.2)**
epergne **28.18.2**
epexegeses **35.1.16(.1)**
epexegesis **34.2.17(.1)**
epexegetic **24.2.10(.3.2)**
epexegetical
  40.23.12(.7.1)
epexegetically
  1.31.24(.9.3)
ephebe **21.1**
ephebic **24.2.9(.1)**
ephedra **17.32.20**
ephedrine **28.1.25(.7),
  28.2.29(.9)**
ephemera **17.32.14(.10)**
ephemerality
  1.10.16(.32.13)
ephemerally
  1.31.17(.27.2)

ephemeralness
  34.18.16(.37.3)
ephemeris **34.2.21**
ephemerist **22.29.2(.29.4)**
ephemeron **28.10.24(.5)**
Ephemeroptera
  17.32.14(.6)
ephemeropteran
  28.17.31(.11)
ephemeropterous
  34.18.27(.14)
Ephesian **28.17.26(.1)**
Ephesus **34.18.20**
ephod **23.10.8**
ephor **12.11.1**
ephorate **22.19.24(.9)**
ephori **14.24.6**
ephorship **20.2.7(.9)**
Ephraim **27.4.8**
epiblast **22.29.6(.12),
  22.29.8(.8)**
epic **24.2.8(.2)**
epical **40.23.12(.5)**
epically **1.31.24(.9.2)**
epicanthic **24.2.18(.6)**
epicarp **20.6**
epicedia **3.5.1**
epicedian **28.3.4(.1)**
epicedium **27.3.4(.1)**
epicene **28.1.18(.6)**
epicentral **40.16.13(.16)**
epicentre **17.12.22(.3)**
epicleses **35.1.16(.1)**
epiclesis **34.2.17(.1)**
epicondilitis **34.18.11(.8)**
epicontinental
  40.21.17(.2)
epicotyl **40.21.7**
Epictetus **34.18.11(.1)**
epicure **12.22, 17.7.12(.5)**
epicurean **28.17.1(.12)**
Epicureanism
  27.15.21(.2.9)
epicurism **27.15.21(.2.14)**
Epicurus **34.18.27(.8)**
epicycle **40.23.10**
epicyclic **24.2.27(.16)**
epicycloid **23.13.20**
epicycloidal **40.22.9**
Epidaurus **34.18.27(.8)**
epideictic **24.2.10(.13)**
epidemic **24.2.14(.3)**
epidemical **40.23.12(.10)**
epidemically **1.31.24(.9.8)**
epidemiological
  40.23.12(.17.2)
epidemiologist
  22.29.2(.26.2)
epidemiology
  1.26.10(.11.1)
epidermal **40.25.11**

epidermic **24.2.14(.11)**
epidermis **34.2.12**
epidermoid **23.13.11**
epidiascope **20.15.4(.1)**
epididymides **35.1.8**
epididymis **34.2.12**
epidural **40.16.13(.11)**
epifauna **17.18.10**
epigastria **3.22.15**
epigastric **24.2.26(.14.5)**
epigastrium **27.3.17(.6)**
epigeal **40.16.1**
epigene **28.1.23**
epigenesis **34.2.17(.10.3)**
epigenetic **24.2.10(.3.1)**
epiglottal **40.21.7**
epiglottic **24.2.10(.6)**
epiglottis **34.2.8**
epigone **28.19.8**
epigram **27.6.17(.5)**
epigrammatic
  24.2.10(.4.2)
epigrammatically
  1.31.24(.9.4)
epigrammatist
  22.29.2(.13)
epigrammatize
  35.15.7(.7)
epigraph **30.7.5(.1)**
epigraphic **24.2.16(.3)**
epigraphical
  40.23.12(.12)
epigraphically
  1.31.24(.9.9)
epigraphist **22.29.2(.19)**
epigraphy **1.18.9(.3.1)**
epilate **22.4.23(.7.1)**
epilation **28.17.25(.3.14)**
epilepsy **1.22.19**
epileptic **24.2.10(.12)**
epilimnia **3.9.14**
epilimnion **28.3.8(.12),
  28.10.2**
epilogist **22.29.2(.16)**
epilogue **26.7.14**
epimer **17.17.14(.1)**
epimeric **24.2.26(.4)**
epimerism **27.15.21(.2.14)**
epimerize **35.15.20(.2)**
epinasty **1.10.26(.5)**
epinephrine **28.1.25(.10),
  28.2.29(.5)**
epiphanic **24.2.15(.5)**
epiphany **1.16.15(.12)**
epiphenomena
  17.18.16(.8)
epiphenomenal
  40.26.13(.8)
epiphenomenon
  28.17.17(.10)
epiphyses **35.1.16(.10)**

epiphysis 34.2.17(.10.4)
epiphytal 40.21.10
epiphyte 22.16.16
epiphytic 24.2.10(.2.3)
epirogeny 1.16.15(.17)
Epirot 22.19.24(.8)
Epirote 22.21.14
Epirus 34.18.27(.10)
episcopacy 1.22.16(.2)
episcopal 40.19.11
episcopalian 28.3.21(.3)
episcopalianism
  27.15.21(.2.9)
episcopalism
  27.15.21(.2.15)
episcopally 1.31.17(.7)
episcopate 22.19.8
episcope 1.8.11(.5),
  20.15.4(.1)
episematic 24.2.10(.4.2)
episiotomy 1.15.13(.1)
episode 23.20.11
episodic 24.2.11(.7)
episodically 1.31.24(.9.7)
epistaxes 35.1.16(.14)
epistaxis 34.2.17(.14)
epistemic 24.2.14(.1)
epistemically
  1.31.24(.9.8)
epistemological
  40.23.12(.17.2)
epistemologically
  1.31.24(.9.11)
epistemologist
  22.29.2(.26.4)
epistemology
  1.26.10(.11.4)
epistle 40.31.2
epistolary 1.29.11(.27)
epistoler 17.34.16(.7)
epistrophe 1.18.9(.2)
epistyle 40.13.3(.10)
epitaph 30.7.2
epitaxial 40.3.10
epitaxy 1.22.22
epithalamia 3.8.3
epithalamial 40.3.6
epithalamic 24.2.14(.4)
epithalamium 27.3.7
epithelia 3.24.1
epithelial 40.3.15
epithelium 27.3.18
epithet 22.5.12
epithetic 24.2.10(.3.2)
epithetical 40.23.12(.7.1)
epithetically 1.31.24(.9.3)
epitome 1.15.13(.1)
epitomist 22.29.2(.17)
epitomization
  28.17.25(.3.12)
epitomize 35.15.11

epizoa 17.9.9
epizoon 28.10.6
epizootic 24.2.10(.6)
epoch 24.9.2
epochal 40.23.7,
  40.23.12(.5)
epode 23.20.3
eponym 27.2.6
eponymous 34.18.15(.10)
EPOS 34.10.6, 35.10
epoxide 23.15.11(.11)
epoxy 1.22.22
Epping 29.1.10(.4)
EPROM 27.9
epsilon 28.10.26,
  28.17.33(.10)
Epsom 27.15.20(.12)
Epson 28.10.18,
  28.17.23(.17)
Epstein 28.14.5
epyllia 3.24.2
epyllion 28.3.21(.2)
equability 1.10.16(.22.1)
equable 40.20.16(.26)
equableness
  34.18.16(.37.4)
equably 1.31.21(.7.5)
equal 40.35.3
equalitarian 28.3.20(.4)
equalitarianism
  27.15.21(.2.9)
equality 1.10.16(.33)
equalization
  28.17.25(.3.12)
equalize 35.15.21(.4.6)
equalizer 17.25.12(.15)
equally 1.31.17(.26)
equanimity 1.10.16(.12)
equanimous 34.18.15(.10)
equatable 40.20.16(.11.1)
equatably 1.31.21(.4.1)
equate 22.4.21
equation 28.17.26(.3)
equational 40.26.13(.14.8)
equator 17.12.4(.14)
equatorial 40.3.14(.5)
equatorially 1.31.3(.11)
equerry 1.29.3,
  1.29.11(.24)
eques 35.4.15
equestrian 28.3.20(.11)
equestrianism
  27.15.21(.2.9)
equestrienne 28.5
equiangular
  17.34.16(.21.3)
equid 23.2.21
equidistant 22.26.15(.9)
equidistantly
  1.31.22(.20.2)
equilateral 40.16.13(.12.1)

equilibrate 22.4.22(.7)
equilibration
  28.17.25(.3.13)
equilibrator 17.12.4(.15)
equilibrist 22.29.2(.29.5)
equilibrium 27.3.17(.5)
equine 28.14.17
equinoctial 40.16.10
equinox 34.23.8(.6)
equip 20.2.10
equipage 39.2.8
equipartition
  28.17.25(.2.2)
equipment
  22.26.15(.13.3)
equipoise 35.13
equipollence
  34.24.10(.24)
equipollency
  1.22.23(.10.4)
equipollent 22.26.15(.25)
equiponderant
  22.26.15(.23.3)
equiponderate
  22.4.22(.6)
equipotential
  40.33.12(.2)
equipper 17.10.2
equiprobability
  1.10.16(.22.3)
equiprobable
  40.20.16(.10)
equitable 40.20.16(.11.3)
equitableness
  34.18.16(.37.4)
equitably 1.31.21(.4.2)
equitant 22.26.15(.9)
equitation 28.17.25(.3.3)
equites 35.4.3
equity 1.10.16(.20)
equivalence 34.24.10(.24)
equivalency
  1.22.23(.10.4)
equivalent 22.26.15(.25)
equivalently
  1.31.22(.20.5)
equivocacy 1.22.16(.6)
equivocal 40.23.12(.13)
equivocality
  1.10.16(.32.5)
equivocally 1.31.24(.9.11)
equivocalness
  34.18.16(.37.5)
equivocate 22.4.11(.6)
equivocation
  28.17.25(.3.5)
equivocator 17.12.4(.7)
equivocatory
  1.29.11(.8.2)
equivoque 24.18.8
Equuleus 34.3.16
equus 34.18.26

er 18
era 17.32.2
eradicable 40.20.16(.13)
eradicate 22.4.11(.6)
eradication 28.17.25(.3.5)
eradicator 17.12.4(.7)
erasable 40.20.16(.22)
erase 35.4.16
eraser 17.25.3
Erasmus 34.18.15(.18)
Erastian 28.3.3
Erastianism 27.15.21(.2.9)
erasure 17.27.2
Erato 19.10.12
Eratosthenes 35.1.12(.3)
erbium 27.3.2
'ere 3
ere 6
Erebus 34.18.10
Erechtheum 27.15.1
Erechtheus 34.3.9
erect 22.23.4(.10)
erectable 40.20.16(.11.5)
erectile 40.13.3(.8)
erection 28.17.25(.15.2)
erectly 1.31.22(.19)
erectness 34.18.16(.20.4)
erector 17.12.21(.2)
eremite 22.16.13
eremitic 24.2.10(.2.2)
eremitical 40.23.12(.7.1)
eremitism 27.15.21(.2.4)
erethism 27.15.21(.2.12)
Erewhon 28.10.23
erg 26.14
ergative 31.2.1(.9.1)
ergatively 1.31.30(.7.1)
ergativity 1.10.16(.15)
ergo 19.13.10
ergocalciferol 40.9.19
ergonomic 24.2.14(.6)
ergonomically
  1.31.24(.9.8)
ergonomist 22.29.2(.17)
ergosterol 40.9.19
ergot 22.11.7, 22.19.13
ergotism 27.15.21(.2.4)
erhu 16.21
Eric 24.2.26(.4)
erica 17.14.15(.14)
ericaceous 34.18.22(.3)
Ericsson 28.17.23(.21)
Eridanus 34.18.16(.15.2)
Erie 1.29.2
erigeron 28.10.24(.5)
Erin 28.2.29(.2)
Erinys 34.2.13
Eris 34.2.21
eristic 24.2.10(.15.2)
eristically 1.31.24(.9.6)

Eritrea **17.1.16, 17.2.9**
Eritrean **28.17.1(.12),
28.17.2**
erk **24.17**
Erlang **29.4.17**
Erlanger **17.16.17(.2)**
erl-king **29.1.14(.15)**
ermine **28.2.17(.6)**
Ermintrude **23.17.3**
ern **28.18**
erne **28.18**
Ernest **22.29.15(.13)**
Ernestine **28.1.9(.7)**
Ernie **1.16.16**
Ernle **1.31.27(.15)**
Ernst **22.29.21**
erode **23.20.12**
erogenous **34.18.16(.15.3)**
Eroica **17.14.15(.4)**
Eros **34.10.16**
erosion **28.17.26(.6)**
erosional **40.26.13(.14.8)**
erosive **31.2.4(.11)**
erosively **1.31.30(.7.4)**
erotic **24.2.10(.6)**
erotica **17.14.15(.6)**
erotically **1.31.24(.9.4)**
eroticism **27.15.21(.2.12)**
eroticize **35.15.16(.4)**
erotism **27.15.21(.2.4)**
erotogenic **24.2.15(.4)**
erotogenous
34.18.16(.15.3)
erotology **1.26.10(.11.2)**
erotomania **3.9.3(.5)**
erotomaniac **24.6.1**
err **18**
errancy **1.22.23(.10.4)**
errand **23.24.16(.15)**
errant **22.26.15(.23.1)**
errantly **1.31.22(.20.5)**
errantry **1.29.15(.15)**
errata **17.12.8(.10)**
erratic **24.2.10(.4.5)**
erratically **1.31.24(.9.4)**
erraticism **27.15.21(.2.12)**
erratum **27.15.9(.5)**
Errol **40.16.13(.3)**
erroneous **34.3.6(.7)**
erroneously **1.31.33(.1.2)**
erroneousness
34.18.16(.31.1)
error **17.32.4**
errorless **34.18.29(.17.5)**
ersatz **34.22.5**
Erse **34.19**
erst **22.29.16**
erstwhile **40.13.15**
Ertebolle **17.34.17**
erubescence **34.24.10(.18)**

erubescent
22.26.15(.17.2)
eructation **28.17.25(.3.3)**
erudite **22.16.10**
eruditely **1.31.22(.13)**
erudition **28.17.25(.2.3)**
erupt **22.22.6**
eruption **28.17.25(.14)**
eruptive **31.2.1(.12)**
eruptively **1.31.30(.7.2)**
eruptivity **1.10.16(.15)**
Erving **29.1.20**
eryngo **19.13.12**
erysipelas **34.18.29(.17.2)**
erythema **17.17.1**
erythemal **40.25.1**
erythematic **24.2.10(.4.2)**
erythroblast **22.29.6(.12),
22.29.8(.8)**
erythrocyte **22.16.19(.9)**
erythrocytic **24.2.10(.8)**
erythroid **23.13.19**
erythromycin **28.2.23(.7)**
erythropoietic
24.2.10(.3.1)
Erzgebirge **17.16.14**
Esau **12.14.1**
Esbjerg **26.14.4**
escadrille **40.2.20**
escalade **23.4.16**
escalate **22.4.23(.7.1)**
escalation **28.17.25(.3.14)**
escalator **17.12.4(.16)**
escallonia **3.9.11**
escallop **20.7.13, 20.13.7**
escalope **20.7.13, 20.13.7,
20.15.9**
escapable **40.20.16(.9)**
escapade **23.4.1**
escape **20.3**
escapee **2.9**
escapement
22.26.15(.13.3)
escaper **17.10.3**
escapism **27.15.21(.2.2)**
escapist **22.29.2(.11)**
escapologist
22.29.2(.26.3)
escapology **1.26.10(.11.2)**
escargot **19.13.5**
escarp **20.6**
escarpment
22.26.15(.13.3)
eschar **10.8.16**
eschatological
40.23.12(.17.2)
eschatologist
22.29.2(.26.3)
eschatology **1.26.10(.11.2)**
eschaton **28.10.9**
escheat **22.1.13**

eschew **16.19**
eschewal **40.16.7**
eschscholtzia **3.14.13**
Escoffier **4.2.5**
Escondido **19.11.1**
Escorial **40.3.14(.5), 40.6.2,
40.8**
escort **22.13.4**
escribe **21.12**
escritoire **10.22.5**
escrow **19.27.17**
escudo **19.11.10**
esculent **22.26.15(.25)**
escutcheon **28.17.27**
escutcheoned
23.24.16(.13)
Esdras **34.7.18,
34.18.27(.15)**
Esk **24.20.3**
Eskdale **40.4.3**
esker **17.14.23**
Eskimo **19.14.12**
Esky® **1.12.17(.2)**
Esme **1.15.19**
Esmeralda **17.13.23(.4)**
Esmond **23.24.16(.7)**
ESOL **40.9.14**
esophagi **14.11, 14.21**
esophagus **34.18.14(.5)**
esoteric **24.2.26(.4)**
esoterical **40.23.12(.18)**
esoterically **1.31.24(.9.12)**
esotericism
27.15.21(.2.12)
esotericist **22.29.2(.22)**
espadrille **40.2.20**
espalier **3.24.5, 4.2.10**
esparto **19.10.7**
especial **40.33.3**
especially **1.31.17(.22)**
Esperantist **22.29.2(.13)**
Esperanto **19.10.17**
espial **40.16.6**
espionage **37.4.5, 39.8**
esplanade **23.4.8**
Esposito **19.10.1**
espousal **40.32.6**
espouse **35.8**
espouser **17.25.6**
espresso **19.20.3**
esprit **2.30.8**
esprit de corps **12**
esprit de l'escalier **4.2.10**
espy **14.6**
Esquimau **19.14.12**
Esquimaux **35.20.7**
esquire **17.6.13**
essay **4.18, 4.18.4**
essayist **22.29.2(.3)**

Essen **28.17.23(.5)**
essence **34.24.10(.18)**
Essendon **28.17.12(.23)**
Essene **28.1.18**
essential **40.33.12(.3)**
essentialism
27.15.21(.2.15)
essentialist **22.29.2(.31.4)**
essentiality **1.10.16(.32.1)**
essentially **1.31.17(.22)**
essentialness
34.18.16(.37.5)
Essequibo **19.9.1**
Essex **34.23.2(.10)**
essive **31.2.4(.4)**
Esso® **19.20.3**
Essoldo **19.11.15**
establish **36.2.27**
establisher **17.26.14**
establishment
22.26.15(.13.6)
establishmentarian
28.3.20(.4)
establishmentarianism
27.15.21(.2.9)
estaminet **4.14**
estancia **3.14.16**
estate **22.4.9(.9)**
esteem **27.1.2**
Estella **17.34.5(.3)**
Estelle **40.5.3**
ester **17.12.24(.4)**
Esterhazy **1.23.7**
esterify **14.14.4(.14)**
Estes **35.2.3, 35.4.3**
Esther **17.12.24(.4),
17.22.15**
esthete **22.1.8**
esthetic **24.2.10(.3.2)**
esthetically **1.31.24(.9.3)**
esthetician **28.17.25(.2.2)**
estheticism
27.15.21(.2.12)
estimable **40.20.16(.15)**
estimableness
34.18.16(.37.4)
estimably **1.31.21(.6)**
estimate **22.4.13(.6),
22.19.14**
estimation **28.17.25(.3.7)**
estimative **31.2.1(.9.2)**
estimator **17.12.4(.9)**
estival **40.28.9**
estivation **28.17.25(.3.9)**
estoile **40.11.3**
Estonia **3.9.11**
Estonian **28.3.8(.11)**
estop **20.7.4**
estoppage **39.2.8**
estoppel **40.19.7**
Estoril **40.2.20**

estovers 35.18.15
estrade 23.9.20
estragon 28.10.12,
  28.17.15(.13)
estrange 39.17.2
estrangement
  22.26.15(.13.6)
estreat 22.1.17
Estremadura 17.32.14(.3)
estrogen 28.17.28(.9)
estuarine 28.14.18
estuary 1.29.11(.26)
esurience 34.24.2
esuriency 1.22.23(.2)
esurient 22.26.2(.9)
esuriently 1.31.22(.20.1)
ETA 17.12.5
eta 17.12.1
etaerio 15.1.12
et al. 40.6
etalon 28.10.26
Etam® 27.6.4
etc 1.22.21
et cetera 17.32.19(.7)
etch 38.4
etchant 22.26.15(.20)
etcher 17.28.5
etching 29.1.27
eternal 40.26.14
eternality 1.10.16(.32.8)
eternalize 35.15.21(.4.5)
eternally 1.31.17(.14.3)
eternalness
  34.18.16(.37.1)
eternity 1.10.16(.13)
eternize 35.15.12(.6)
Etesian 28.3.14, 28.3.16,
  28.17.26(.1)
eth 33.4
Ethan 28.17.21
ethanal 40.6.9
ethane 28.4.11
ethanoate 22.19.7
ethanoic 24.2.7
ethanol 40.9.12
Ethel 40.29
Ethelbert 22.20.2
Ethelberta 17.12.17
Ethelburga 17.16.14
Etheldreda 17.13.1
Ethelred 23.5.15
ethene 28.1.17
ether 17.22.1
ethereal 40.3.14(.2)
ethereality 1.10.16(.32.1)
etherealize 35.15.21(.2)
ethereally 1.31.3(.11)
etheric 24.2.26(.4)
Etheridge 39.2.22(.9)

etherization
  28.17.25(.3.11)
etherize 35.15.20(.2)
Ethernet 22.5.9(.2)
ethic 24.2.18(.2)
ethical 40.23.12(.14)
ethicality 1.10.16(.32.5)
ethically 1.31.24(.9.10)
ethicist 22.29.2(.22)
ethicize 35.15.16(.4)
Ethiopia 3.2.7
Ethiopian 28.3.1
Ethiopic 24.2.8(.5)
ethmoid 23.13.11
ethmoidal 40.22.9
ethnarch 24.8.9
ethnarchy 1.12.6
ethnic 24.2.15(.16)
ethnical 40.23.12(.11)
ethnically 1.31.24(.9.8)
ethnicity 1.10.16(.16.1)
ethnoarchaeological
  40.23.12(.17.2)
ethnoarchaeologist
  22.29.2(.26.2)
ethnoarchaeology
  1.26.10(.11.1)
ethnocentric
  24.2.26(.14.4)
ethnocentrically
  1.31.24(.9.12)
ethnocentricity
  1.10.16(.16.1)
ethnocentrism
  27.15.21(.2.14)
ethnographer
  17.20.12(.5)
ethnographic
  24.2.16(.3)
ethnographical
  40.23.12(.12)
ethnographically
  1.31.24(.9.9)
ethnography 1.18.9(.3.2)
ethnohistory
  1.29.11(.8.12)
ethnologic 24.2.24(.4)
ethnological
  40.23.12(.17.2)
ethnologically
  1.31.24(.9.11)
ethnologist 22.29.2(.26.4)
ethnology 1.26.10(.11.4)
ethnomethodological
  40.23.12(.17.2)
ethnomethodologist
  22.29.2(.26.3)
ethnomethodology
  1.26.10(.11.2)
ethnomusicologist
  22.29.2(.26.3)

ethnomusicology
  1.26.10(.11.3)
ethogram 27.6.17(.5)
ethological
  40.23.12(.17.2)
ethologically
  1.31.24(.9.11)
ethologist 22.29.2(.26.4)
ethology 1.26.10(.11.5)
ethos 34.10.14
ethoxyethane 28.4.11
ethyl 40.13.11, 40.29
ethylene 28.1.27(.7)
ethylenic 24.2.15(.4)
Etienne 28.5
etiolate 22.4.23(.2)
etiolation 28.17.25(.3.14)
etiological 40.23.12(.17.2)
etiologically
  1.31.24(.9.11)
etiology 1.26.10(.11.1)
etiquette 22.5.5,
  22.19.12(.10)
Etive 31.2.1(.4)
Etna 17.18.21
Eton 28.17.11(.1)
Etonian 28.3.8(.11)
étouffée 4.15
Etruria 3.22.12
Etruscan 28.17.13(.18)
Etruscology 1.26.10(.11.3)
Ettrick 24.2.26(.14.1)
étude 23.17.1, 23.17.4(.1)
etyma 17.17.14(.2)
etymologic 24.2.24(.4)
etymological
  40.23.12(.17.2)
etymologically
  1.31.24(.9.11)
etymologist 22.29.2(.26.4)
etymologize 35.15.18
etymology 1.26.10(.11.4)
etymon 28.10.13,
  28.17.16(.16)
Euan 28.17.7
eubacteria 3.22.2
eubacterium 27.3.17(.2)
Euboea 17.1.2
eucalypt 22.22.1
eucalyptus 34.18.11(.12)
eucaryotic 24.2.10(.6)
eucharis 34.2.21
Eucharist 22.29.2(.29.3)
eucharist 22.29.2(.29.3)
eucharistic 24.2.10(.15.2)
Eucharistical
  40.23.12(.7.3)
euchre 17.14.14
Euclid 23.2.23
Euclidean 28.3.4(.2)
euclidean 28.3.4(.2)

eudaemonic 24.2.15(.6.2)
eudaemonism
  27.15.21(.2.9)
eudaemonist
  22.29.2(.18.1)
eudaemonistic
  24.2.10(.15.2)
eudemonist 22.29.2(.18.1)
eudiometer 17.12.16(.9.2)
eudiometric
  24.2.26(.14.2)
eudiometrical
  40.23.12(.18)
eudiometry 1.29.15(.8)
Eudora 17.32.10(.3)
Eugene 28.1.23
Eugene Onegin 28.2.15
Eugenia 3.9.1
eugenic 24.2.15(.4)
eugenically 1.31.24(.9.8)
eugenicist 22.29.2(.22)
Eugénie 1.16.4
eugenist 22.29.2(.18.1)
euglena 17.18.1(.16)
euhemerism
  27.15.21(.2.14)
eukaryote 22.3.12, 22.11.1
eukaryotic 24.2.10(.6)
Eulalia 3.24.3
Euler 17.34.11, 17.34.15
eulogia 3.19.8
eulogist 22.29.2(.26.4)
eulogistic 24.2.10(.15.2)
eulogistically
  1.31.24(.9.6)
eulogium 27.3.15
eulogize 35.15.18
eulogy 1.26.10(.11.5)
Eumenides 35.1.8
Eunice 34.18.16(.14)
eunuch 24.16.7
eunuchoid 23.13.9
euonymus 34.18.15(.10)
eupeptic 24.2.10(.12)
Euphemia 3.8.1
euphemism
  27.15.21(.2.8)
euphemist 22.29.2(.17)
euphemistic
  24.2.10(.15.2)
euphemistically
  1.31.24(.9.6)
euphemize 35.15.11
euphonic 24.2.15(.6.3)
euphonious 34.3.6(.7)
euphoniously
  1.31.33(.1.2)
euphonium 27.3.8(.10)
euphonize 35.15.12(.5)
euphony 1.16.15(.12)
euphorbia 3.3.5

ewe **16**
ewer **17.8**
Ewhurst **22.29.16**
Ewing **29.1.8**
Ewyas **34.18.7**
ex **34.23.4**
exacerbate **22.4.8**
exacerbation
28.17.25(.3.2)
exact **22.23.5(.8)**
exacta **17.12.21(.3)**
exactable **40.20.16(.11.5)**
exacting **29.1.12(.18)**
exactingly **1.31.28(.1.4)**
exactingness
34.18.16(.26)
exaction **28.17.25(.15.3)**
exactitude **23.17.4(.1)**
exactly **1.31.22(.19),
1.31.24(.5)**
exactness **34.18.16(.20.4)**
exactor **17.12.21(.3)**
exaggerate **22.4.22(.6)**
exaggeratedly
1.31.23(.14.3)
exaggeratingly
1.31.28(.1.4)
exaggeration
28.17.25(.3.13)
exaggerative
31.2.1(.9.4)
exaggerator **17.12.4(.15)**
exalt **22.32.5, 22.32.6**
exaltation **28.17.25(.3.3)**
exaltedly **1.31.23(.14.3)**
exaltedness
34.18.16(.21.1)
exalter **17.12.26(.5)**
exam **27.6.12**
examen **28.5.7(.4)**
examinable
40.20.16(.16.3)
examination
28.17.25(.3.8)
examinational
40.26.13(.14.2)
examine **28.2.17(.2)**
examinee **2.17**
examiner **17.18.16(.8)**
example **40.19.14**
exanthema **17.17.1,
17.17.14(.7)**
exarch **24.8.12**
exarchate **22.4.11(.4)**
ex-army **1.15.7**
exasperate **22.4.22(.6)**
exasperatedly
1.31.23(.14.3)
exasperatingly
1.31.28(.1.4)
exasperation
28.17.25(.3.13)

Excalibur **17.11.13**
ex cathedra **17.32.20**
excavate **22.4.16**
excavation **28.17.25(.3.9)**
excavator **17.12.4(.11)**
exceed **23.1.7**
exceeding **29.1.13(.1)**
exceedingly **1.31.28(.1.5)**
excel **40.5.11**
excellence **34.24.10(.24)**
excellency **1.22.23(.10.4)**
excellent **22.26.15(.25)**
excellently **1.31.22(.20.5)**
excelsior **3.14.17, 12.2**
excentric **24.2.26(.14.4)**
except **22.22.3**
excepting **29.1.12(.17)**
exception **28.17.25(.14)**
exceptionable
40.20.16(.16.3)
exceptionableness
34.18.16(.37.4)
exceptionably **1.31.21(.6)**
exceptional
40.26.13(.14.6)
exceptionality
1.10.16(.32.8)
exceptionally
1.31.17(.14.3)
excerpt **22.22.9**
excerptible
40.20.16(.11.4)
excerption **28.17.25(.14)**
excess **34.5.9**
excessive **31.2.4(.4)**
excessively **1.31.30(.7.4)**
excessiveness
34.18.16(.28.2)
exchange **39.17.2**
exchangeability
1.10.16(.22.2)
exchangeable
40.20.16(.25)
exchanger **17.29.16(.2)**
exchequer **17.14.4**
excipient **22.26.2(.1)**
excisable **40.20.16(.22)**
excise **35.15.16**
exciseman **28.17.16(.30)**
excision **28.17.26(.2)**
excitability **1.10.16(.22.2)**
excitable **40.20.16(.11.2)**
excitableness
34.18.16(.37.4)
excitably **1.31.21(.4.1)**
excitant **22.26.15(.9)**
excitation **28.17.25(.3.3)**
excitative **31.2.1(.9.1)**
excitatory **1.29.11(.8.6)**
excite **22.16.19**
excitedly **1.31.23(.14.3)**

excitedness
34.18.16(.21.1)
excitement
22.26.15(.13.3)
exciter **17.12.13(.7)**
excitingly **1.31.28(.1.4)**
excitingness
34.18.16(.26)
exciton **28.10.9**
exclaim **27.4.9**
exclamation
28.17.25(.3.7)
exclamatory **1.29.11(.8.7)**
exclave **31.3.8**
exclosure **17.27.9**
excludable **40.20.16(.12)**
exclude **23.17.5**
excluder **17.13.14**
exclusion **28.17.26(.4)**
exclusionary
1.29.11(.13.2)
exclusionist
22.29.2(.18.3)
exclusive **31.2.4(.8)**
exclusively **1.31.30(.7.4)**
exclusiveness
34.18.16(.28.2)
exclusivity **1.10.16(.15)**
excogitable
40.20.16(.11.3)
excogitate **22.4.9(.5)**
excogitation
28.17.25(.3.3)
excogitative **31.2.1(.9.1)**
excommunicate
22.4.11(.6)
excommunication
28.17.25(.3.5)
excommunicative
31.2.1(.9.1)
excommunicator
17.12.4(.7)
excommunicatory
1.29.11(.8.6)
excoriate **22.4.2(.14)**
excoriation **28.17.25(.3.1)**
excrement **22.26.15(.13.2)**
excremental **40.21.17(.2)**
excrescence **34.24.10(.18)**
excrescent
22.26.15(.17.2)
excrescential **40.33.12(.3)**
excreta **17.12.1(.14)**
excrete **22.1.17**
excreter **17.12.1(.14)**
excretion **28.17.25(.1)**
excretive **31.2.1(.1)**
excretory **1.29.11(.8.1)**
excretum **27.15.9(.1)**
excruciate **22.4.2(.11)**
excruciatingly
1.31.28(.1.4)

excruciation
28.17.25(.3.1)
exculpate **22.4.7**
exculpation **28.17.25(.3.2)**
exculpatory **1.29.11(.8.6)**
excursion **28.17.25(.12)**
excursional
40.26.13(.14.5)
excursionary
1.29.11(.13.2)
excursionist
22.29.2(.18.2)
excursive **31.2.4(.10)**
excursively **1.31.30(.7.4)**
excursiveness
34.18.16(.28.2)
excursus **34.18.20**
excusable **40.20.16(.22)**
excusably **1.31.21(.7.2)**
excusatory **1.29.11(.8.8)**
excuse **34.17.13, 35.17.7**
excuse-me **2.16**
ex-directory
1.29.11(.8.12)
Exe **34.23.4**
exeat **22.7.2**
exec **24.4.9**
execrable **40.20.16(.27.6)**
execrably **1.31.21(.8)**
execrate **22.4.22(.10)**
execration **28.17.25(.3.13)**
execrative **31.2.1(.3)**
execratory **1.29.11(.8.2)**
executable **40.20.16(.11.2)**
executant **22.26.15(.9)**
execute **22.18.10**
execution **28.17.25(.11)**
executionary
1.29.11(.13.2)
executioner **17.18.16(.16)**
executive **31.2.1(.9.4)**
executively **1.31.30(.7.2)**
executor **17.12.16(.19)**
executorial **40.3.14(.5)**
executorship **20.2.7(.9)**
executory **1.29.11(.8.10)**
executrices **35.1.16(.10)**
executrix **34.23.2(.12)**
exegeses **35.1.16(.1)**
exegesis **34.2.17(.1)**
exegete **22.1.14**
exegetic **24.2.10(.3.2)**
exegetical **40.23.12(.7.1)**
exegetist **22.29.2(.13)**
exempla **17.34.19**
exemplar **17.34.19**
exemplarily
1.31.17(.27.2)
exemplariness
34.18.16(.2.9)
exemplary **1.29.11(.27)**

e

experientially
1.31.17(.22)
experiment 22.26.4(.8),
22.26.15(.13.2)
experimental
40.21.17(.2)
experimentalism
27.15.21(.2.15)
experimentalist
22.29.2(.31.2)
experimentalize
35.15.21(.4.3)
experimentally
1.31.17(.9.3)
experimentation
28.17.25(.3.3)
experimenter
17.12.22(.3)
expert 22.20.1
expertise 35.1.7
expertize 35.15.7(.7)
expertly 1.31.22(.16)
expertness 34.18.16(.20.3)
expiable 40.20.3
expiate 22.4.2(.1)
expiation 28.17.25(.3.1)
expiator 17.12.4(.1)
expiatory 1.29.11(.8.1)
expiration 28.17.25(.3.13)
expiratory 1.29.11(.8.9)
expire 17.6.1
expiry 1.29.11(.2)
explain 28.4.19
explainable
40.20.16(.16.1)
explainer 17.18.3
explananda 17.13.20(.4)
explanandum
27.15.10(.14)
explanans 35.26.7
explanantia 3.4.12
explanation
28.17.25(.3.8)
explanatorily
1.31.17(.27.1)
explanatory 1.29.11(.8.7)
explant 22.26.6, 22.26.8
explantation
28.17.25(.3.3)
expletive 31.2.1(.1)
explicable 40.20.16(.13)
explicably 1.31.21(.5)
explicate 22.4.11(.6)
explication 28.17.25(.3.5)
explicative 31.2.1(.9.1)
explicator 17.12.4(.7)
explicatory 1.29.11(.8.6)
explicature 17.28.15
explicit 22.2.16
explicitly 1.31.22(.15)
explicitness
34.18.16(.20.3)

explode 23.20.13
exploder 17.13.17
exploit 22.14
exploitable
40.20.16(.11.2)
exploitation
28.17.25(.3.3)
exploitative 31.2.1(.9.1)
exploitatively
1.31.30(.7.1)
exploiter 17.12.11
exploitive 31.2.1(.6)
exploration
28.17.25(.3.13)
explorational
40.26.13(.14.2)
explorative 31.2.1(.9.4)
exploratory 1.29.11(.8.9)
explore 12.23.3
explorer 17.32.10(.12)
explosion 28.17.26(.6)
explosive 31.2.4(.11)
explosively 1.31.30(.7.4)
explosiveness
34.18.16(.28.2)
Expo 19.8
exponent 22.26.15(.14)
exponential 40.33.12(.3)
exponentially
1.31.17(.22)
export 22.13.1
exportability
1.10.16(.22.2)
exportable 40.20.16(.11.2)
exportation 28.17.25(.3.3)
exporter 17.12.10(.1)
expose 35.20.1
exposé 4.19
exposer 17.25.15
exposition 28.17.25(.2.5)
expositional
40.26.13(.14.1)
expositive 31.2.1(.9.3)
expositor 17.12.16(.15)
expository 1.29.11(.8.8)
ex post facto 19.10.16
expostulate 22.4.23(.7.3)
expostulation
28.17.25(.3.14)
expostulatory
1.29.11(.8.10)
exposure 17.27.9
expound 23.24.7(.1)
expounder 17.13.20(.5)
ex-president
22.26.15(.10)
express 34.5.14(.4)
expresser 17.24.5
expressible
40.20.16(.21.1)
expression 28.17.25(.4)

expressional
40.26.13(.14.3)
expressionism
27.15.21(.2.9)
expressionist
22.29.2(.18.2)
expressionistic
24.2.10(.15.2)
expressionistically
1.31.24(.9.6)
expressionless
34.18.29(.27)
expressionlessly
1.31.33(.12.6)
expressionlessness
34.18.16(.31.6)
expressive 31.2.4(.4)
expressively 1.31.30(.7.4)
expressiveness
34.18.16(.28.2)
expressivity 1.10.16(.15)
expressly 1.31.33(.2)
expressway 4.25.22
expropriate 22.4.2(.14)
expropriation
28.17.25(.3.1)
expropriator 17.12.4(.1)
expulsion 28.17.25(.17)
expulsive 31.2.4(.14)
expunction
28.17.25(.15.6)
expunge 39.17.8
expunger 17.29.16(.7)
expurgate 22.4.12(.5)
expurgation
28.17.25(.3.6)
expurgator 17.12.4(.8)
expurgatorial 40.3.14(.5)
expurgatory 1.29.11(.8.6)
exquisite 22.19.19
exquisitely 1.31.22(.15)
exquisiteness
34.18.16(.20.3)
exsanguinate
22.4.14(.9.3)
exsanguination
28.17.25(.3.8)
exsanguinity 1.10.16(.13)
exscind 23.24.2
exsert 22.20.10
exsiccate 22.4.11(.6)
ex silentio 15.1.9, 15.1.10
exsolve 31.13
extant 22.26.6,
22.26.15(.9)
Extel 40.5.3
extemporaneous
34.3.6(.3)
extemporaneously
1.31.33(.1.2)
extemporaneousness
34.18.16(.31.1)

extemporarily
1.31.17(.27.2)
extemporariness
34.18.16(.2.9)
extemporary 1.29.11(.6)
extempore 1.29.11(.6)
extemporization
28.17.25(.3.12)
extemporize 35.15.20(.2)
extend 23.24.5(.4)
extendability
1.10.16(.22.2)
extendable 40.20.16(.12)
extender 17.13.20(.3)
extendibility
1.10.16(.22.2)
extensibility
1.10.16(.22.2)
extensible 40.20.16(.21.3)
extensile 40.13.12
extension 28.17.25(.16)
extensional
40.26.13(.14.7)
extensionality
1.10.16(.32.8)
extensive 31.2.4(.13)
extensively 1.31.30(.7.4)
extensiveness
34.18.16(.28.2)
extensometer
17.12.16(.9.2)
extensor 17.24.22(.2)
extent 22.26.4(.4)
extenuate 22.4.4
extenuatingly
1.31.28(.1.4)
extenuation
28.17.25(.3.1)
extenuatory 1.29.11(.8.5)
exterior 3.22.2
exteriority 1.10.16(.21.2)
exteriorize 35.15.20(.1)
exteriorly 1.31.3(.11)
exterminate 22.4.14(.9.2)
extermination
28.17.25(.3.8)
exterminator
17.12.4(.10)
exterminatory
1.29.11(.8.7)
extern 28.18.4
external 40.26.14
externality 1.10.16(.32.8)
externalization
28.17.25(.3.12)
externalize 35.15.21(.4.5)
externally 1.31.17(.14.3)
exteroceptive 31.2.1(.12)
exterritorial 40.3.14(.5)
exterritoriality
1.10.16(.32.1)
extinct 22.23.13

extinction 28.17.25(.15.6)
extinctive 31.2.1(.13.5)
extinguish 36.2.24
extinguishable 40.20.16(.23)
extinguisher 17.26.14
extinguishment 22.26.15(.13.6)
extirpate 22.4.7
extirpation 28.17.25(.3.2)
extirpator 17.12.4(.3)
extol 40.9.7, 40.18.5
extoller 17.34.9, 17.34.18(.3)
extolment 22.26.15(.13.7)
Exton 28.17.11(.25)
extort 22.13.3
extorter 17.12.10(.2)
extortion 28.17.25(.8)
extortionate 22.19.15(.9)
extortionately 1.31.22(.15)
extortioner 17.18.16(.16)
extortionist 22.29.2(.18.2)
extortive 31.2.1(.5)
extra 17.32.19(.11)
extracellular 17.34.16(.21.4)
extracranial 40.3.7(.3)
extract 22.23.5(.9)
extractability 1.10.16(.22.2)
extractable 40.20.16(.11.5)
extraction 28.17.25(.15.3)
extractive 31.2.1(.13.3)
extractor 17.12.21(.3)
extracurricular 17.34.16(.21.2)
extraditable 40.20.16(.11.2)
extradite 22.16.10
extradition 28.17.25(.2.3)
extrados 34.10.9
extragalactic 24.2.10(.13)
extrajudicial 40.33.1
extrajudicially 1.31.17(.22)
extralinguistic 24.2.10(.15.2)
extramarital 40.21.12
extramaritally 1.31.17(.9.2)
extramundane 28.4.4
extramural 40.16.13(.11)
extramurally 1.31.17(.27.1)
extraneous 34.3.6(.3)
extraneously 1.31.33(.1.2)
extraneousness 34.18.16(.31.1)

extraordinarily 1.31.17(.27.2)
extraordinariness 34.18.16(.2.9)
extraordinary 1.29.11(.13.2)
extraphysical 40.23.12(.16)
extrapolate 22.4.23(.7.1)
extrapolation 28.17.25(.3.14)
extrapolative 31.2.1(.9.4)
extrapolator 17.12.4(.16)
extrasensory 1.29.11(.18)
extraterrestrial 40.3.14(.9)
extraterritorial 40.3.14(.5)
extraterritoriality 1.10.16(.32.1)
extravagance 34.24.10(.13)
extravagancy 1.22.23(.10.2)
extravagant 22.26.15(.12)
extravagantly 1.31.22(.20.2)
extravaganza 17.25.18
extravasate 22.4.18
extravasation 28.17.25(.3.10)
extraversion 28.17.25(.12)
extravert 22.20.9
extrema 17.17.1
extremal 40.25.1
extreme 27.1.12
extremely 1.31.26(.1)
extremeness 34.18.16(.24)
extremis 34.2.12
extremism 27.15.21(.2.8)
extremist 22.29.2(.17)
extremity 1.10.16(.12)
extremum 27.15.13
extricable 40.20.16(.13)
extricate 22.4.11(.6)
extrication 28.17.25(.3.5)
extrinsic 24.2.20(.15), 24.2.21
extrinsically 1.31.24(.9.10)
extroversion 28.17.25(.12)
extrovert 22.20.9
extroverted 23.18.9(.14)
extrude 23.17.3
extrusile 40.13.12
extrusion 28.17.26(.4)
extrusive 31.2.4(.8)
exuberance 34.24.10(.16)
exuberant 22.26.15(.23.3)

exuberantly 1.31.22(.20.5)
exuberate 22.4.22(.6)
exudate 22.4.10
exudation 28.17.25(.3.4)
exudative 31.2.1(.3)
exude 23.17.4(.6)
exult 22.32.8
exultancy 1.22.23(.10.2)
exultant 22.26.15(.9)
exultantly 1.31.22(.20.2)
exultation 28.17.25(.3.3)
exultingly 1.31.28(.1.4)
exurb 21.15
exurban 28.17.10
exurbanite 22.16.14(.6)
exurbia 3.3.8
exuviae 2.3, 14.2
exuvial 40.3.8
exuviate 22.4.2(.8)
exuviation 28.17.25(.3.1)
ex voto 19.10.14
Exxon® 28.10.18
Eyam 27.1
eyas 34.18.5
eye 14
eyeball 40.10.4
eyebath 32.8
eyeblack 24.6.23
eyebright 22.16.24(.11)
eyebrow 9.16
eyedropper 17.10.8
eyeful 40.14.6(.6)
eyeglass 34.9.7
eyehole 40.18.13
eyelash 36.6.10
eyeless 34.18.29(.14)
eyelet 22.19.26(11)
eyelevel 40.28.4
eyelid 23.2.23
eyeliner 17.18.13(.14)
eyepatch 38.5
eyepiece 34.1.1
eyeshade 23.4.12
eyeshadow 19.11.6
eyeshot 22.11.12
eyesight 22.16.19(.7)
eyesore 12.14.7
eye strain 28.4.18
eyeteeth 32.1
Eyetie 14.8
eyetooth 32.13
eyewash 36.9.5
eyewitness 34.18.16(.20.1)
Eynon 28.17.17(.8)
Eynsford 23.18.16(.19)
Eynsham 27.15.22
eyot 22.4, 22.19.2
eyra 17.32.3

Eyre 6
eyrie 1.29.2, 1.29.4, 1.29.11(.2)
Eysenck 24.19.2
Ezekiel 40.3.5
Ezra 17.32.28
f 30.4
FA 4
fa 10
fab 21.6
Fabergé 4.21
Fabia 3.3.3
Fabian 28.3.2
Fabianism 27.15.21(.2.9)
Fabianist 22.29.2(.18.1)
Fabius 34.3.2
fable 40.20.4
fabler 17.34.20
fabliau 15.1.13
Fablon 28.10.26
fabric 24.2.26(.13)
fabricate 22.4.11(.6)
fabrication 28.17.25(.3.5)
fabricator 17.12.4(.7)
fabulist 22.29.2(.31.5)
fabulosity 1.10.16(.16.2)
fabulous 34.18.29(.17.6)
fabulously 1.31.33(.12.6)
fabulousness 34.18.16(.31.6)
façade 23.9.15
face 34.4
facecloth 32.9
faceless 34.18.29(.33)
facelessly 1.31.33(.12.6)
facelessness 34.18.16(.31.6)
facelift 22.27.1
facemask 24.20.4
faceplate 22.4.23(.8)
facer 17.24.4
facet 22.5.13(.3), 22.19.18
faceted 23.18.9(.13)
facetiae 2.3
facetious 34.18.22(.1)
facetiously 1.31.33(.12.4)
facetiousness 34.18.16(.31.4)
facetted 23.18.9(.13)
faceworker 17.14.16
facia 17.26.3
facial 40.33.2
facially 1.31.17(.22)
facies 35.1.1
facile 40.13.12
facilely 1.31.38
facileness 34.18.16(.37.1)
facilitate 22.4.9(.5)
facilitation 28.17.25(.3.3)
facilitative 31.2.1(.9.1)

facilitator 17.12.4(.5)
facility 1.10.16(.27)
facing 29.1.23
facsimile 1.31.17(.13)
fact 22.23.5
facta 17.12.21(.3)
fact-finding 29.1.13(.14)
factice 34.2.8
faction 28.17.25(.15.3)
factional 40.26.13(.14.6)
factionalism 27.15.21(.2.15)
factionalize 35.15.21(.4.5)
factionally 1.31.17(.14.3)
factious 34.18.22(.11)
factiously 1.31.33(.12.4)
factiousness 34.18.16(.31.4)
factitious 34.18.22(.2)
factitiously 1.31.33(.12.4)
factitiousness 34.18.16(.31.4)
factitive 31.2.1(.9.1)
facto 19.10.16
factoid 23.13.7
factor 17.12.21(.3)
factorable 40.20.16(.27.3)
factorage 39.2.22(.9)
factorial 40.3.14(.5)
factorially 1.31.3(.11)
factorization 28.17.25(.3.11)
factorize 35.15.20(.2)
factory 1.29.11(.8.12)
factotum 27.15.9(.11)
factual 40.16.12
factualism 27.15.21(.2.15)
factualist 22.29.2(.31.5)
factuality 1.10.16(.32.1)
factually 1.31.17(.24)
factualness 34.18.16(.37.1)
factum 27.15.9(.13)
facture 17.28.20
facula 17.34.16(.21.2)
facular 17.34.16(.21.2)
faculous 34.18.29(.17.6)
facultative 31.2.1(.9.1)
facultatively 1.31.30(.7.1)
faculty 1.10.28
fad 23.7
faddily 1.31.17(.10)
faddiness 34.18.16(.2.3)
faddish 36.2.12
faddishly 1.31.35(.7.1)
faddishness 34.18.16(.33.3)
faddism 27.15.21(.2.5)
faddist 22.29.2(.14)
faddy 1.11.7
fade 23.4

fadeaway 4.25.9
fadeless 34.18.29(.23)
fader 17.13.3
fadge 39.6
faecal 40.23.1
faeces 35.1.16(.1)
Faenza 17.24.19
faerie 1.29.4
Faeroes 35.20.12
Faeroese 35.1
faery 1.29.4
faff 30.5
fag 26.5
Fagan 28.17.15(.3)
faggot 22.19.13
faggotry 1.29.15(.7)
faggoty 1.10.16(.11)
Fagin 28.2.15
fah 10
Fahd 23.9
Fahrenheit 22.16.22
Fahy 1.27
faience 34.11, 34.24.6
fail 40.4
failing 29.1.31(.4)
faille 40.4
failure 17.33.13
fain 28.4
fainéancy 1.22.10, 1.22.23(.2)
fainéant 11.3, 22.26.2(.5)
faint 22.26.3
faintly 1.31.22(.20.1)
faintness 34.18.16(.20.4)
fair 6
Fairbairn 28.6
Fairbanks 34.23.18
Fairbourne 28.11.2
Fairbrother 17.23.10
Fairchild 23.31.9
Fairclough 30.11.11
Fairfax 34.23.5(.8)
Fairford 23.18.16(.4)
fairground 23.24.7(.10)
Fairhaven 28.17.20(.3)
Fairhurst 22.29.16
fairing 29.1.30(.4)
fairish 36.2.25
fairlead 23.1.12
Fairley 1.31.6
Fairlie 1.31.6
fairly 1.31.6
fairness 34.18.16(.6)
Fairport 22.13.1
fairway 4.25.4
fairy 1.29.4
fairyland 23.24.6(.13)
Faisal 40.31.11
Faisalabad 23.7.6, 23.9.6
fait accompli 1.31.20

faith 32.4
faithful 40.27.24
Faithfull 40.27.24
faithfully 1.31.17(.16.2)
faithfulness 34.18.16(.37.2)
faithless 34.18.29(.31)
faithlessly 1.31.33(.12.6)
faithlessness 34.18.16(.31.6)
fake 24.3
Fakenham 27.15.14(.11)
faker 17.14.3
fakery 1.29.11(.10)
fakir 3.6, 3.6.3, 3.6.5
falafel 40.27.7
Falange 39.17.4
Falangism 27.15.21(.2.13)
Falangist 22.29.2(.25)
Falasha 17.26.6
falbala 17.34.16(.6)
falcate 22.4.11(.8)
falchion 28.17.25(.17), 28.17.27
falciform 27.10.5(.2)
falcon 28.17.13(.8)
falconer 17.18.16(.6)
falconet 22.19.15(.9)
falconry 1.29.20
falderal 40.6.14
Faldo 19.11.15
faldstool 40.15.3
Falernian 28.3.8(.10)
Falk 24.10, 24.21
Falkender 17.13.20(.13)
Falkirk 24.17.3
Falklands 35.23.15
fall 40.10
fallacious 34.18.22(.3)
fallaciously 1.31.33(.12.4)
fallaciousness 34.18.16(.31.4)
fallacy 1.22.16(.14)
fallback 24.6.6(.23)
fallen 28.17.33(.8)
fallenness 34.18.16(.25)
faller 17.34.10
fallibility 1.10.16(.22.1)
fallible 40.20.16(.29)
fallibleness 34.18.16(.37.4)
fallibly 1.31.21(.9)
Fallon 28.17.33(.5)
fallopian 28.3.1
fallout 22.9.19
fallow 19.29.5
Fallowfield 23.31.1(.2)
fallowness 34.18.16(.17)
Falmouth 32.14.11
false 34.27

falsehood 23.16.5(.13)
falsely 1.31.33(.17)
falseness 34.18.16(.31.7)
falsetto 19.10.4
falsework 24.17.6(.15)
falsies 35.2.11
falsifiability 1.10.16(.22.2)
falsifiable 40.20.16(.5)
falsification 28.17.25(.3.5)
falsify 14.14.4(.9)
falsity 1.10.16(.16.3)
Falstaff 30.7.2
Falstaffian 28.3.9
Falster 17.12.24(.25)
falter 17.12.26(.5)
falterer 17.32.14(.6)
faltering 29.1.30(.8)
falteringly 1.31.28(.1.17)
Falwell 40.5.17(.17)
Famagusta 17.12.24(.12)
fame 27.4
familial 40.3.15
familiar 3.24.2
familiarity 1.10.16(.21.1)
familiarization 28.17.25(.3.12)
familiarize 35.15.20(.1)
familiarly 1.31.3(.12)
famille jaune 28.11
famille noire 10
famille verte 22.6
family 1.31.17(.13), 1.31.26(.5)
famine 28.17.16(.7)
famish 36.2.15
famous 34.18.15(.3)
famously 1.31.33(.12.3)
famousness 34.18.16(.31.3)
famuli 2.32.9(.8), 14.25.9
famulus 34.18.29(.17.6)
fan 28.7
Fanagalo 19.29, 19.29.12
fanatic 24.2.10(.4.3)
fanatical 40.23.12(.7.1)
fanatically 1.31.24(.9.4)
fanaticism 27.15.21(.2.12)
fanaticize 35.15.16(.4)
fanbelt 22.32.2
fanciable 40.20.3
fancier 3.14.16
fanciful 40.27.14
fancifully 1.31.17(.16.1)
fancifulness 34.18.16(.37.2)
fancily 1.31.17(.20)
fanciness 34.18.16(.2.7)
fancy 1.22.23(.4)
fancy-work 24.17.6(.1)
fandangle 40.24.14(.2)

fandango **19.13.12**
fandom **27.15.10(.14)**
fane **28.4**
fanfare **6.10**
fanfaronade **23.4.8**
fanfold **23.31.13(.7)**
fang **29.4**
Fangio **15.1.11**
fangless **34.18.29(.28)**
fanlight **22.16.25(.17)**
fanlike **24.13.7(.17)**
fanner **17.18.6**
Fannie **1.16.6**
fanny **1.16.6**
Fanshawe **12.16.12**
Fanta® **17.12.22(.4)**
fantail **40.4.2**
fan-tan **28.7.6**
fantasia **3.15.3, 17.1.12**
fantasist **22.29.2(.22)**
fantasize **35.15.16(.4)**
fantasmatic **24.2.10(.4.2)**
fantast **22.29.6(.4)**
fantastic **24.2.10(.15.4)**
fantastical **40.23.12(.7.3)**
fantasticality **1.10.16(.32.5)**
fantastically **1.31.24(.9.6)**
fantasticate **22.4.11(.6)**
fantastication **28.17.25(.3.5)**
fantasticism **27.15.21(.2.12)**
fantasy **1.22.16(.4)**
Fante **1.10.23(.4)**
Fanti **1.10.23(.4)**
fantod **23.10.3**
Fanum **27.15.14(.3)**
fanzine **28.1.19**
far **10**
farad **23.7.16, 23.18.27**
faradaic **24.2.3**
faraday **4.10.7**
faradic **24.2.11(.5)**
farandole **40.18.6**
faraway **4.25**
farce **34.9**
farceur **18.11**
farcical **40.23.12(.15)**
farcicality **1.10.16(.32.5)**
farcically **1.31.24(.9.10)**
farcy **1.22.8**
farded **23.18.10(.6)**
fare **6**
Fareham **27.15.26(.2)**
farewell **40.5.17**
farfalle **1.31.7, 4.28.3**
far-fetched **22.31**
farfetchedness **34.18.16(.20.4)**

Fargo **19.13.5**
Faridabad **23.7.6, 23.9.6**
farina **17.18.1(.15), 17.18.13(.13)**
farinaceous **34.18.22(.3)**
Farjeon **28.17.28(.5)**
farl **40.8**
Farleigh **1.31.9**
Farley **1.31.9**
farm **27.8**
farmable **40.20.16(.15)**
farmer **17.17.7**
farmhand **23.24.6(.11)**
farmhouse **34.8.6(.15)**
farmland **23.24.6(.13)**
farmstead **23.5.3**
farmwork **24.17.6(.12)**
farmworker **17.14.16**
farmyard **23.9.21**
Farnborough **17.32.14(.5)**
Farnese **1.23.3**
farness **34.18.16(.9)**
Farnham **27.15.14(.7)**
Farnley **1.31.27(.8)**
Farnworth **32.14.15**
Faro **19.27.5**
faro **19.27.3**
Faroe **19.27.3**
Faroese **35.1**
far-off **30.8**
farouche **36.14**
Farouk **24.15.7**
Farquhar **10.8.4, 10.22.7**
Farquharson **28.17.23(.14)**
Farr **10**
farraginous **34.18.16(.15.3)**
farrago **19.13.5**
Farrah **17.32.6**
Farrar **17.32.6**
Farrell **40.16.13(.5)**
Farrelly **1.31.17(.27.1)**
farrier **3.22.5**
farriery **1.29.2(.11)**
Farringdon **28.17.12(.24)**
Farris **34.2.21**
farrow **19.27.4**
farruca **17.14.14**
far-seeing **29.1.1**
Farsi **2.22.4**
fart **22.10**
farther **17.23.7**
farthest **22.29.15(.16)**
farthing **29.1.22**
farthingale **40.4.5**
fartlek **24.4.14**
fasces **35.1.16(.4)**
fascia **3.14.3, 3.16.3, 3.16.4**
fascial **40.33.2**
fasciate **22.4.2(.11)**

fasciation **28.17.25(.3.1)**
fascicle **40.23.12(.15)**
fascicular **17.34.16(.21.2)**
fasciculate **22.4.23(.7.3), 22.19.26(.13)**
fasciculation **28.17.25(.3.14)**
fascicule **40.15.9(.5)**
fasciculi **2.32.9(.8), 14.25.9**
fasciculus **34.18.29(.17.6)**
fasciitis **34.18.11(.8)**
fascinate **22.4.14(.9.3)**
fascinatingly **1.31.28(.1.4)**
fascination **28.17.25(.3.8)**
fascinator **17.12.4(.10)**
fascine **28.1.18**
fascism **27.15.21(.2.13)**
fascist **22.29.2(.24)**
fascistic **24.2.10(.15.2)**
Fashanu **16.12**
fashion **28.17.25(.5)**
fashionability **1.10.16(.22.1)**
fashionable **40.20.16(.16.3)**
fashionableness **34.18.16(.37.4)**
fashionably **1.31.21(.6)**
fashioner **17.18.16(.16)**
Fashoda **17.13.17**
Faslane **28.4.19**
Fassbinder **17.13.20(.11)**
fast **22.29.6, 22.29.8**
fastback **24.6.6(.12)**
fastball **40.10.4**
fasten **28.17.23(.7)**
fastener **17.18.16(.14)**
fastening **29.1.17(.12)**
faster **17.12.24(.5)**
fastidious **34.3.4**
fastidiously **1.31.33(.1.1)**
fastidiousness **34.18.16(.31.1)**
fastigiate **22.3.11, 22.4.2(.13)**
fasting **29.1.12(.21)**
fastness **34.18.16(.20.4)**
Fastnet **22.5.9(.4)**
Fastus **34.18.11(.16)**
fat **22.7**
Fatah, Al **10.6, 17.12.6**
fatal **40.21.3**
fatalism **27.15.21(.2.15)**
fatalist **22.29.2(.31.2)**
fatalistic **24.2.10(.15.3)**
fatalistically **1.31.24(.9.6)**
fatality **1.10.16(.32.3)**
fatally **1.31.17(.9.1)**
fatalness **34.18.16(.37.5)**
Fata Morgana **17.18.6**
fatback **24.6.6(.12)**

fat cat **22.7.9**
fate **22.4**
fateful **40.27.18**
fatefully **1.31.17(.16.2)**
fatefulness **34.18.16(.37.2)**
Fates **34.22.3**
fathead **23.5.13(.9)**
fatheaded **23.18.10(.3)**
father **17.23.7**
fatherhood **23.16.5(.3)**
fatherland **23.24.6(.13)**
fatherless **34.18.29(.17.5)**
fatherlessness **34.18.16(.31.6)**
fatherlike **24.13.7(.8)**
fatherliness **34.18.16(.2.10)**
fatherly **1.31.17(.19)**
fathership **20.2.7(.9)**
fathom **27.15.19**
fathomable **40.20.16(.15)**
Fathometer® **17.12.16(.9.2)**
fathomless **34.18.29(.26)**
fatidical **40.23.12(.8)**
fatiguability **1.10.16(.22.1)**
fatiguable **40.20.16(.14)**
fatigue **26.1**
fatigueless **34.18.29(.25)**
Fatiha **17.30**
Fatihah **17.30**
Fatima **17.17.14(.2)**
Fatimid **23.2.12**
Fatimite **22.16.13**
fatism **27.15.21(.2.4)**
fatist **22.29.2(.13)**
fatless **34.18.29(.22)**
fatling **29.1.31(.17)**
fatly **1.31.22(.6)**
fatness **34.18.16(.20.1)**
fatsia **3.14.13**
fatso **19.20.14**
fatstock **24.9.4**
fatted **23.18.9(.5)**
fatten **28.17.11(.6)**
fattily **1.31.17(.9.1)**
fattiness **34.18.16(.2.3)**
fattish **36.2.11**
fattism **27.15.21(.2.4)**
fattist **22.29.2(.13)**
fatty **1.10.6**
fatuity **1.10.16(.5)**
fatuous **34.18.6**
fatuously **1.31.33(.12.1)**
fatuousness **34.18.16(.31.2)**
fatwa **10.22.5, 17.31.5**
faubourg **26.13**
fauces **35.1.16(.7)**
faucet **22.19.18**
faucial **40.33.6**

Faulds **35.23.15**
Faulkner **17.18.23**
fault **22.32.5, 22.32.6**
faultfinder **17.13.20(.11)**
faultfinding **29.1.13(.14)**
faultily **1.31.17(.9.3)**
faultiness **34.18.16(.2.3)**
faultless **34.18.29(.22)**
faultlessly **1.31.33(.12.6)**
faultlessness **34.18.16(.31.6)**
faulty **1.10.28**
faun **28.11**
fauna **17.18.10**
faunal **40.26.9**
faunist **22.29.2(.18.1)**
faunistic **24.2.10(.15.2)**
faunistical **40.23.12(.7.3)**
Fauntleroy **13.15**
Faunus **34.18.16(.10)**
Fauré **4.26.7**
Faust **22.29.7**
Faustian **28.3.3**
faute de mieux **18**
fauve **31.12**
fauvism **27.15.21(.2.11)**
fauvist **22.29.2(.20)**
Faux **19, 34.23.9**
faux pas **10**
fave **31.3**
favela **17.34.5(.10)**
Favell **40.28.3**
Faversham **27.15.22**
favor **17.21.3**
favorableness **34.18.16(.37.4)**
favorably **1.31.21(.8)**
favoritism **27.15.21(.2.4)**
favour **17.21.3**
favourable **40.20.16(.27.5)**
favourableness **34.18.16(.37.4)**
favourably **1.31.21(.8)**
favourer **17.32.14(.13)**
favourite **22.19.24(.9)**
favouritism **27.15.21(.2.4)**
Fawcett **22.19.18**
Fawley **1.31.11**
fawn **28.11**
fawner **17.18.10**
fawningly **1.31.28(.1.7)**
fawr **17.3**
fax **34.23.5**
fay **4**
Faye **4**
Fayette **22.5**
Fayetteville **40.2.12**
fayre **6**
Fazackerley **1.31.17(.11)**
faze **35.4**
fazenda **17.13.20(.3)**

fealty **1.10.28**
fear **3**
fearful **40.27.3**
fearfully **1.31.17(.16.1)**
fearfulness **34.18.16(.37.2)**
fearless **34.18.29(.3)**
fearlessly **1.31.33(.12.6)**
fearlessness **34.18.16(.31.6)**
fearsome **27.15.20(.3)**
fearsomely **1.31.26(.11)**
fearsomeness **34.18.16(.24)**
feasibility **1.10.16(.22.1)**
feasible **40.20.16(.22)**
feasibly **1.31.21(.7.2)**
feast **22.29.1**
feaster **17.12.24(.1)**
feat **22.1**
feather **17.23.4**
featherbed **23.5.2**
featherbrained **23.24.4**
featherhead **23.5.13(.5)**
featheriness **34.18.16(.2.9)**
featherless **34.18.29(.17.5)**
featherlight **22.16.25(.9)**
Featherstone **28.17.11(.25)**
Featherstonehaugh **12.16.12, 12.19**
featherweight **22.4.21**
feathery **1.29.11(.17)**
feature **17.28.1**
featureless **34.18.29(.17.5)**
febrifugal **40.24.10, 40.24.11**
febrifuge **39.13**
febrile **40.13.16**
febrility **1.10.16(.31)**
February **1.29.11(.25)**
feces **35.1.16(.1)**
feckless **34.18.29(.24)**
fecklessly **1.31.33(.12.6)**
fecklessness **34.18.16(.31.6)**
feculence **34.24.10(.24)**
feculent **22.26.15(.25)**
fecund **23.24.12, 23.24.16(.5)**
fecundability **1.10.16(.22.2)**
fecundate **22.4.10**
fecundation **28.17.25(.3.4)**
fecundity **1.10.16(.9)**
fed **23.5**
fedayeen **28.1, 28.1.26**
federal **40.16.13(.12.1)**
federalism **27.15.21(.2.15)**
federalist **22.29.2(.31.4)**

federalization **28.17.25(.3.12)**
federalize **35.15.21(.4.7)**
federally **1.31.17(.27.1)**
federate **22.4.22(.6)**
federation **28.17.25(.3.13)**
federationist **22.29.2(.18.2)**
federative **31.2.1(.9.4)**
fedora **17.32.10(.3)**
fed up **20.9**
fee **2**
feeble **40.20.1**
feebleness **34.18.16(.37.4)**
feeblish **36.2.27**
feebly **1.31.21(.1)**
feed **23.1**
feedable **40.20.16(.12)**
feedback **24.6.6(.13)**
feedbag **26.5.1**
feeder **17.13.1**
feedlot **22.11.17**
feedstock **24.9.4**
feedstuff **30.11.3**
feel **40.1**
feeler **17.34.1**
feeling **29.1.31(.1)**
feelingless **34.18.29(.28)**
feelingly **1.31.28(.1.18)**
feelings **35.27**
Feeney **1.16.1**
feet **22.1**
feign **28.4**
feignedly **1.31.23(.14.6)**
feijoa **17.9.10, 17.9.12**
feint **22.26.3**
feis **36.4, 36.5**
Feisal **40.31.11**
feiseanna **17.18.16(.16)**
feistiness **34.18.16(.2.3)**
feisty **1.10.26(.9)**
felching **29.1.27**
Feldman **28.17.16(.22)**
feldspar **10.4**
feldspathic **24.2.18(.3)**
feldspathoid **23.13.15**
Felicia **3.14.2**
felicific **24.2.16(.1)**
felicitate **22.4.9(.5)**
felicitation **28.17.25(.3.3)**
felicitous **34.18.11(.10)**
felicitously **1.31.33(.12.2)**
felicitousness **34.18.16(.31.3)**
felicity **1.10.16(.16.1)**
Felindre **17.32.20**
feline **28.14.19(.1)**
felinity **1.10.16(.13)**
Felix **34.23.2(.13)**
Felixstowe **19.10.19**

fell **40.5**
fellah **17.34.5**
fellate **22.4.23**
fellatio **15.1.9**
fellation **28.17.25(.3.14)**
fellator **17.12.4(.16)**
feller **17.34.5**
Fellini **1.16.1(.16)**
fellmonger **17.16.17(.4)**
felloe **19.29.4**
fellow **17.34.5, 19.29.4**
Fellowes **35.20.14**
fellowship **20.2.7(.9)**
felly **1.31.5**
felon **28.17.33(.4)**
felonious **34.3.6(.7)**
feloniously **1.31.33(.1.2)**
feloniousness **34.18.16(.31.1)**
felonry **1.29.20**
felony **1.16.15(.20)**
Felstead **23.5.3**
felt **22.32.2**
Feltham **27.15.9(.16), 27.15.18**
Felton **28.17.11(.27)**
felty **1.10.28**
felucca **17.14.11**
felwort **22.20.15**
female **40.4.6**
femaleness **34.18.16(.37.1)**
feme **27.1, 27.5**
feme covert **22.19.17**
feme sole **40.18**
femes sole **40.18**
feminal **40.26.13(.8)**
feminality **1.10.16(.32.8)**
femineity **1.10.16(.1)**
feminine **28.17.17(.10)**
femininely **1.31.27(.14)**
feminineness **34.18.16(.25)**
femininity **1.10.16(.13)**
feminism **27.15.21(.2.9)**
feminist **22.29.2(.18.1)**
feminity **1.10.16(.13)**
feminization **28.17.25(.3.11)**
feminize **35.15.12(.5)**
femme **27.5, 27.6**
femme fatale **40.8.4**
femora **17.32.14(.10)**
femoral **40.16.13(.12.2)**
femtometre **17.12.1(.6)**
femur **17.17.1**
fen **28.5**
fen-berry **1.29.11(.7.2)**
fence **34.24.3**
fenceless **34.18.29(.33)**
fencer **17.24.22(.2)**

Fenchurch **38.16**
fencible **40.20.16(.21.3)**
fend **23.24.5**
fender **17.13.20(.3)**
Fenella **17.34.5(.8)**
fenestella **17.34.5(.3)**
fenestra **17.32.19(.11)**
fenestrae **2.30.10**
fenestrate **22.4.22(.8)**
fenestration
 28.17.25(.3.13)
feng shui **1(.6), 4**
Fenian **28.3.8(.1)**
Fenianism **27.15.21(.2.9)**
Fenimore **12.9.4**
fenland **23.24.6(.13),**
 23.24.16(.16.4)
fenman **28.7.10(.15),**
 28.17.16(.25)
fenmen **28.5.7(.19)**
fennec **24.2.15(.4)**
fennel **40.26.4**
Fennimore **12.9.4**
Fennoscandia **3.5.9**
fenny **1.16.5**
Fens **35.26.5**
Fenton **28.17.11(.22)**
fenugreek **24.1.11**
Fenwick **24.2.15(.4),**
 24.2.25
feoff **30.1, 30.4**
feoffee **2.18**
feoffment **22.26.15(.13.5)**
feoffor **17.20.1, 17.20.4**
feral **40.16.13(.3)**
fer de lance **34.24.6**
Ferdinand **23.24.6(.9),**
 23.24.16(.8)
feretory **1.29.11(.8.9)**
Fergal **40.24.12**
Fergie **1.14.12**
Fergus **34.18.14(.6)**
Ferguson **28.17.23(.14)**
ferial **40.3.14(.2)**
Fermanagh **17.18.6**
Fermat **10.10.5, 22.7.11**
fermata **17.12.8(.7)**
ferment **22.26.4(.8)**
fermentable
 40.20.16(.11.6)
fermentation
 28.17.25(.3.3)
fermentative **31.2.1(.9.1)**
fermenter **17.12.22(.3)**
fermi **1.15.5, 1.15.14**
fermion **28.3.7, 28.10.2**
fermium **27.3.7**
Fermor **12.9.5**
Fermoy **13.6**
fern **28.18**
Fernández **35.5.6**

Fernando Póo **19**
fernery **1.29.11(.13.3)**
Ferneyhough **19.26**
Fernihough **30.11.9**
fernless **34.18.29(.27)**
ferny **1.16.16**
ferocious **34.18.22(.9)**
ferociously **1.31.33(.12.4)**
ferociousness
 34.18.16(.31.4)
ferocity **1.10.16(.16.2)**
Ferodo **19.11.13**
Ferranti **1.10.23(.4)**
Ferrara **17.32.7**
Ferrari® **1.29.6**
ferrate **22.4.22(.2)**
ferrel **40.16.13(.3)**
Ferrell **40.16.13(.3)**
Ferrer **17.32.4**
ferret **22.19.24(.3)**
ferreter **17.12.16(.18)**
ferrety **1.10.16(.21.1)**
ferriage **39.2.2**
ferric **24.2.26(.4)**
Ferrier **3.22.3**
ferrimagnetic
 24.2.10(.3.1)
ferrimagnetism
 27.15.21(.2.4)
Ferris **34.2.21**
ferrite **22.16.24(.4)**
ferritic **24.2.10(.2.4)**
ferroconcrete **22.1.17**
ferroelectric
 24.2.26(.14.3)
ferroelectricity
 1.10.16(.16.1)
Ferrograph® **30.7.5(.1)**
ferromagnetic
 24.2.10(.3.1)
ferromagnetism
 27.15.21(.2.4)
ferrous **34.18.27(.3)**
ferruginous
 34.18.16(.15.3)
ferrule **40.15.8,**
 40.16.13(.3)
ferry **1.29.3**
ferryboat **22.21.2**
Ferrybridge **39.2.2(.10)**
ferryman **28.17.16(.2)**
fertile **40.13.3(.5)**
fertility **1.10.16(.23)**
fertilizable **40.20.16(.22)**
fertilization
 28.17.25(.3.12)
fertilize **35.15.21(.4.3)**
fertilizer **17.25.12(.15)**
Fertö Tó **19**
ferula **17.34.16(.21.4)**
ferule **40.15.8, 40.16.13(.3)**

fervency **1.22.23(.10.4)**
fervent **22.26.15(.16)**
fervently **1.31.22(.20.4)**
ferventness
 34.18.16(.20.4)
fervid **23.2.15**
fervidly **1.31.23(.14.7)**
fervidness **34.18.16(.21.1)**
fervour **17.21.13**
Fès **35.5**
Fescennine **28.14.9**
fescue **16.24.7**
fess **34.5**
fesse **34.5**
festal **40.21.18**
festally **1.31.17(.9.3)**
fester **17.12.24(.4)**
festination **28.17.25(.3.8)**
festival **40.28.11**
festive **31.2.1(.15)**
festively **1.31.30(.7.4)**
festiveness **34.18.16(.28.1)**
festivity **1.10.16(.15)**
festoon **28.16.3**
festoonery **1.29.11(.13.1)**
Festschrift **22.27.1**
Festschriften
 28.17.11(.24)
Festus **34.18.11(.16)**
feta **17.12.5**
fetch **38.4**
fetcher **17.28.5**
fetchingly **1.31.28(.1.15)**
fête **22.4**
fête champêtre
 17.32.19(.2)
fête galante **22.26.8**
fêtes champêtres
 35.18.23
fetid **23.2.8**
fetidly **1.31.23(.14.3)**
fetidness **34.18.16(.21.1)**
fetish **36.2.11**
fetishism **27.15.21(.2.13)**
fetishist **22.29.2(.24)**
fetishistic **24.2.10(.15.2)**
fetishize **35.15.17**
Fetlar **17.34.21**
fetlock **24.9.16(.11)**
fetor **17.12.1**
fetta **17.12.5**
fetter **17.12.5**
fetterlock **24.9.16(.6)**
fettle **40.21.4**
fettler **17.34.21**
fettuccine **1.16.1(.12)**
feu **16**
feud **23.17**
feudal **40.22.12**
feudalism **27.15.21(.2.15)**
feudalist **22.29.2(.31.2)**

feudalistic **24.2.10(.15.3)**
feudalistically
 1.31.24(.9.6)
feudality **1.10.16(.32.4)**
feudalization
 28.17.25(.3.12)
feudalize **35.15.21(.4.3)**
feudally **1.31.17(.10)**
feudatory **1.29.11(.8.6)**
feu de joie **10**
feudist **22.29.2(.14)**
feuilleton **11.5**
fever **17.21.1**
feverfew **16.24.11**
feverish **36.2.25**
feverishly **1.31.35(.7.4)**
feverishness
 34.18.16(.33.6)
feverous **34.18.27(.21)**
few **16**
fewness **34.18.16(.14)**
fey **4**
Feydeau **19.11.4**
feyly **1.31.4**
feyness **34.18.16(.4)**
Feynman **28.17.16(.25)**
fez **35.5**
Ffestiniog **26.7.1**
Ffoulkes **34.23.14,**
 34.23.17
fiacre **17.32.21**
fiancé **4.18.12**
fiancée **4.18.12**
fianchetto **19.10.4**
Fianna Fáil **40.11**
fiasco **19.12.17**
fiat **22.7.1, 22.7.3**
fib **21.2**
fibber **17.11.2**
Fibonacci **1.25.8**
fibre **17.11.11**
fibreboard **23.12.2(.5)**
fibrefill **40.2.11**
fibreglass **34.9.7**
fibreless **34.18.29(.17.2)**
fibriform **27.10.5(.2)**
fibril **40.16.13(.15)**
fibrillar **17.34.2(.15),**
 17.34.16(.20)
fibrillary **1.29.11(.27)**
fibrillate **22.4.23(.7.2)**
fibrillation **28.17.25(.3.14)**
fibrin **28.2.2(.7)**
fibrinogen **28.17.28(.9)**
fibrinoid **23.13.12**
fibro **19.27.14**
fibroid **23.13.19**
fibroin **28.2.8**
fibroma **17.17.16(.11)**
fibromata **17.12.16(.9.3)**
fibrosis **34.2.17(.11.2)**

fibrositic 24.2.10(.2.3)
fibrositis 34.18.11(.8)
fibrotic 24.2.10(.6)
fibrous 34.18.27(.13)
fibrously 1.31.33(.12.5)
fibula 17.34.16(.21.1)
fibular 17.34.16(.21.1)
fiche 36.1
Fichte 22.24
Fichtean 28.3.3
fichu 16.17
fickle 40.23.2
fickleness 34.18.16(.37.5)
fickly 1.31.17(.11), 1.31.38
fictile 40.13.3(.8), 40.21.16
fiction 28.17.25(.15.1)
fictional 40.26.13(.14.6)
fictionality 1.10.16(.32.8)
fictionalization
   28.17.25(.3.12)
fictionalize 35.15.21(.4.5)
fictionally 1.31.17(.14.3)
fictionist 22.29.2(.18.2)
fictitious 34.18.22(.2)
fictitiously 1.31.33(.12.4)
fictitiousness
   34.18.16(.31.4)
fictive 31.2.1(.13.1)
fictively 1.31.30(.7.2)
fictiveness 34.18.16(.28.1)
fid 23.2
fiddle 40.22.2
fiddle-de-dee 2.13
fiddlestick 24.2.10(.15.4)
fiddly 1.31.17(.10),
   1.31.23(.1)
Fidei Defensor 12.14.15
fideism 27.15.21(.2.1)
fideist 22.29.2(.2)
fideistic 24.2.10(.15.1)
Fidel 40.5.4
Fidelio 15.1.13
Fidelis 34.2.22(.3)
fidelity 1.10.16(.31)
fidget 22.19.22
fidgetiness 34.18.16(.2.3)
fidgety 1.10.16(.18)
Fidler 17.34.22
Fido 19.11.9
fiducial 40.3.10, 40.16.10,
   40.33.8
fiducially 1.31.3(.9),
   1.31.17(.22)
fiduciary 1.29.2(.9),
   1.29.11(.20)
fidus Achates 35.1.7(.2)
fie 14
Fiedler 17.34.22
fief 30.1
fiefdom 27.15.10(.16)
field 23.31.1

Fielden 28.17.12(.27)
fielder 17.13.23(.1)
fieldfare 6.10
Fielding 29.1.13(.16)
fieldmice 34.15.5
fieldmouse 34.8.4
Fields 35.23.15
fieldsman 28.17.16(.30)
fieldstone 28.19.4(.9)
fieldwork 24.17.6(.9)
fieldworker 17.14.16
fiend 23.24.1
fiendish 36.2.12
fiendishly 1.31.35(.7.1)
fiendishness
   34.18.16(.33.3)
fiendlike 24.13.7(.13)
Fiennes 35.26.12
fierce 34.3
fiercely 1.31.33(.1.1)
fierceness 34.18.16(.31.1)
fieri facias 34.7.2
fierily 1.31.17(.27.1)
fieriness 34.18.16(.2.9)
fiery 1.29.11(.2)
fiesta 17.12.24(.4)
FIFA 17.20.1
fife 30.12
fifer 17.20.10
Fifi 2.18
Fifield 23.31.1(.2)
FIFO 19.16
fifteen 28.1.9
fifteenth 32.21
fifth 32.22
fifthly 1.31.31
Fifth Monarchy 1.12.13
fiftieth 32.14.1
fifty 1.10.24
fifty-fifty 1.10.24
fiftyfold 23.31.13(.7)
fig 26.2
Figaro 19.27.11
Figg 26.2
Figgis 34.2.11
fight 22.16
fightback 24.6.6(.12)
fighter 17.12.13
figleaf 30.1.9
figleaves 35.28.1
figment 22.26.15(.13.3)
figtree 2.30.10
Figueroa 17.9.11
figura 17.32.14(.3)
figural 40.16.13(.12.4)
figurant 22.26.15(.23.3)
figurante 1.10.23(.4)
figuranti 1.10.23(.4)
figuration 28.17.25(.3.13)
figurative 31.2.1(.9.4)

figuratively 1.31.30(.7.1)
figurativeness
   34.18.16(.28.1)
figure 17.16.2
figurehead 23.5.13(.5)
figureless 34.18.29(.17.2)
figurine 28.1.25
figwort 22.20.15
Fiji 2.27
Fijian 28.17.1(.11)
filament 22.26.15(.13.2)
filamentary 1.29.11(.8.12)
filamented 23.18.9(.19)
filamentous 34.18.11(.14)
filaria 3.22.4
filariae 2.3
filarial 40.3.14(.4)
filariasis 34.2.17(.2)
filature 12.17, 17.7.12(.3),
   17.28.15
filbert 22.19.9
filch 38.19
filcher 17.28.26
file 40.13
filefish 36.2.18(.21)
filename 27.4.5
filer 17.34.13
filet 4.28.1, 22.2.25
filet mignon 11.18
Filey 1.31.14
filial 40.3.15
filially 1.31.3(.12)
filialness 34.18.16(.37.1)
filiation 28.17.25(.3.1)
filibeg 26.4
filibuster 17.12.24(.10)
filibusterer 17.32.14(.6)
filicide 23.15.11(.6)
filiform 27.10.5(.2)
filigree 2.30.12
filigreed 23.1.11
filing 29.1.31(.10)
filings 35.27
Filioque 1.28
Filipina 17.18.1(.1)
Filipino 19.15.1
fill 40.2
fille de joie 10
filler 17.34.2
fillet 22.19.26(.1)
filleter 17.12.16(.20)
fill-in 28.2.31(.2)
filling 29.1.31(.2)
fillip 20.13.7
fillis 34.2.22(.2)
fillister 17.12.24(.14)
Fillmore 12.9.16
fill-up 20.9.16
filly 1.31.2
film 27.18

filmable 40.20.16(.15)
filmgoer 17.9.5
filmic 24.2.14(.18)
filmily 1.31.17(.13)
filminess 34.18.16(.2.5)
filmmaker 17.14.3(.3)
filmmaking 29.1.14(.3)
film noir 10
filmography 1.18.9(.3.2)
filmset 22.5.13(.10)
filmsetter 17.12.5(.8)
filmstrip 20.2.11
filmy 1.15.21
filo 19.29.1
Filofax® 34.23.5(.8)
filoplume 27.14.8
filoselle 40.5.11
filovirus 34.18.27(.10)
fils 34.1
filter 17.12.26(.1)
filterable 40.20.16(.27.3)
filth 32.24
filthily 1.31.17(.18)
filthiness 34.18.16(.2.6)
filthy 1.20.12
Filton 28.17.11(.27)
filtrable 40.20.16(.27.6)
filtrate 22.4.22(.8)
filtration 28.17.25(.3.13)
fimbria 3.22.14
fimbriae 2.1
fimbriate 22.3.12,
   22.4.2(.14)
fimbriated 23.18.9(.3)
fin 28.2
finagle 40.24.3
finagler 17.34.24
final 40.26.11
finale 1.31.9
finalism 27.15.21(.2.15)
finalist 22.29.2(.31.3)
finalistic 24.2.10(.15.3)
finality 1.10.16(.32.8)
finalization
   28.17.25(.3.12)
finalize 35.15.21(.4.5)
finally 1.31.17(.14.1)
finance 34.24.4
financial 40.33.12(.4)
financially 1.31.17(.22)
financier 3.14.16
Finbar 10.5.11
finca 17.14.21(.1)
finch 38.18.1
Finchale 40.23.15
Finchampstead 23.5.3,
   23.18.9(.20)
Finchley 1.31.36
find 23.24.13
findable 40.20.16(.12)

fixate **22.4.18**
fixatedly **1.31.23(.14.3)**
fixation **28.17.25(.3.10)**
fixative **31.2.1(.9.3)**
fixedly **1.31.23(.14.7)**
fixedness **34.18.16(.21.1)**
fixer **17.24.20**
fixings **35.27**
fixity **1.10.16(.16.3)**
fixture **17.28.24**
fizgig **26.2.3**
fizog **26.7.10**
fizz **35.2**
fizzer **17.25.2**
fizzily **1.31.17(.21)**
fizziness **34.18.16(.2.7)**
fizzle **40.32.2**
fizzy **1.23.2**
fjord **23.12, 23.12.1**
flab **21.6**
flabbergast **22.29.6(.6), 22.29.8(.4)**
flabbily **1.31.17(.8)**
flabbiness **34.18.16(.2.2)**
flabby **1.9.5**
flaccid **23.2.16**
flaccidity **1.10.16(.9)**
flaccidly **1.31.23(.14.7)**
flaccidness **34.18.16(.21.1)**
flack **24.6**
flag **26.5**
flagella **17.34.5(.13)**
flagellant **22.26.15(.25)**
flagellar **17.34.5(.13), 17.34.16(.19)**
flagellate **22.4.23(.7.2), 22.19.26(.13)**
flagellation **28.17.25(.3.14)**
flagellator **17.12.4(.16)**
flagellatory **1.29.11(.8.2)**
flagelliform **27.10.5(.2)**
flagellum **27.15.28(.4)**
flageolet **22.5.21, 22.19.26(.13)**
Flagg **26.5**
flagger **17.16.5**
flagitious **34.18.22(.2)**
flagitiously **1.31.33(.12.4)**
flagitiousness **34.18.16(.31.4)**
flagman **28.17.16(.24)**
flagon **28.17.15(.6)**
flagpole **40.18.3**
flagrancy **1.22.23(.10.4)**
flagrant **22.26.15(.23.4)**
flagrante **1.10.23(.4)**
flagrantly **1.31.22(.20.5)**
flagship **20.2.7(.17)**
flagstaff **30.7.2**

flagstick **24.2.10(.15.4)**
flagstone **28.19.4(.9)**
Flaherty **1.10.16(.19)**
flail **40.4**
flair **6**
flak **24.6**
flake **24.3**
flakily **1.31.17(.11)**
flakiness **34.18.16(.2.4)**
flaky **1.12.3**
flam **27.6**
flambé **4.8**
flambeau **19.9.14**
flambeaux **35.20.2**
flambée **4.8**
Flamborough **17.32.14(.5)**
flamboyance **34.24.10(.4)**
flamboyancy **1.22.23(.10.1)**
flamboyant **22.26.15(.3)**
flamboyantly **1.31.22(.20.1)**
flame **27.4**
flameless **34.18.29(.26)**
flamelike **24.13.7(.16)**
flamen **28.5.7(.4)**
flamenco **19.12.15**
flameproof **30.13.4**
flamingo **19.13.12**
flammability **1.10.16(.22.1)**
flammable **40.20.16(.15)**
Flamsteed **23.1.2**
flamy **1.15.3**
flan **28.7**
Flanagan **28.17.15(.13)**
flanch **38.18.4**
Flanders **35.18.9**
flânerie **2.30**
flâneur **18.8**
flange **39.17.4**
flangeless **34.18.29(.37)**
flank **24.19.3**
flanker **17.14.21(.3)**
flannel **40.26.5**
flannelboard **23.12.2(.20)**
flannelette **22.5, 22.5.21**
flannelgraph **30.7.5(.1)**
flannelly **1.31.17(.14.1)**
flannely **1.31.17(.14.1)**
flap **20.5**
flapdoodle **40.22.12**
flapjack **24.6.18**
flapper **17.10.5**
flappy **1.8.5**
flare **6**
flash **36.6**
flashback **24.6.6(.21)**
flashbulb **21.18**

flashcard **23.9.9**
flashcube **21.13**
flasher **17.26.6**
flashgun **28.13.5**
flashily **1.31.17(.22)**
flashiness **34.18.16(.2.8)**
flashing **29.1.25**
flash lamp **20.16.3**
flashlight **22.16.25(.20)**
Flashman **28.17.16(.31)**
flashover **17.21.14(.10)**
flashpoint **22.26.11**
flashy **1.24.5**
flask **24.20.4**
flat **22.7**
flatbed **23.5.2**
flatboat **22.21.2**
flatbread **23.5.15**
flatcar **10.8.11**
flatfeet **22.1.6**
flatfish **36.2.18(.15)**
flatfoot **22.17**
Flathead **23.5.13(.9)**
flatiron **28.17.5**
flatland **23.24.6(.13)**
flatlander **17.13.20(.4)**
flatlet **22.19.26(.17)**
flatly **1.31.22(.6)**
flatmate **22.4.13(.9)**
flatness **34.18.16(.20.1)**
flatshare **6.16**
flatsie **1.22.21**
flatten **28.17.11(.6)**
flattener **17.18.16(.4)**
flatter **17.12.6**
flatterer **17.32.14(.6)**
flatteringly **1.31.28(.1.17)**
flattery **1.29.11(.8.3)**
flattie **1.10.6**
flattish **36.2.11**
flattop **20.7.4**
flatulence **34.24.10(.24)**
flatulency **1.22.23(.10.4)**
flatulent **22.26.15(.25)**
flatulently **1.31.22(.20.5)**
flatus **34.18.11(.3)**
flatware **6.18.7**
flatworm **27.16.7**
Flaubert **6.3**
flaunch **38.18.6**
flaunt **22.26.10**
flaunter **17.12.22(.8)**
flaunty **1.10.23(.8)**
flautist **22.29.2(.13)**
flavescent **22.26.15(.17.2)**
Flavia **3.11.3**
Flavian **28.3.10**
flavin **28.2.20**
flavine **28.1.16**
Flavius **34.3.8**

flavone **28.19.12**
flavoprotein **28.1.9(.4)**
flavor **17.21.3**
flavorfully **1.31.17(.16.1)**
flavorously **1.31.33(.12.5)**
flavour **17.21.3**
flavourful **40.27.14**
flavourfully **1.31.17(.16.1)**
flavouring **29.1.30(.8)**
flavourless **34.18.29(.17.4)**
flavourous **34.18.27(.21)**
flavourously **1.31.33(.12.5)**
flavoursome **27.15.20(.11)**
flaw **12**
flawless **34.18.29(.11)**
flawlessly **1.31.33(.12.6)**
flawlessness **34.18.16(.31.6)**
flax **34.23.5**
flaxen **28.17.23(.21)**
Flaxman **28.17.16(.29)**
flaxseed **23.1.7**
flay **4**
flayer **17.2**
flea **2**
fleabag **26.5.1**
fleabane **28.4.2**
fleabite **22.16.8**
fleapit **22.2.5**
flèche **36.4, 36.5**
fleck **24.4**
Flecker **17.14.4**
fled **23.5**
fledge **39.5**
fledgling **29.1.31(.29)**
flee **2**
fleece **34.1**
fleeceable **40.20.16(.21.1)**
fleecily **1.31.17(.20)**
fleeciness **34.18.16(.2.7)**
fleecy **1.22.1**
fleer **3**
fleet **22.1**
Fleet Air Arm **27.8**
fleeting **29.1.12(.1)**
fleetingly **1.31.28(.1.4)**
fleetly **1.31.22(.1)**
fleetness **34.18.16(.20.1)**
Fleetwood **23.16.6(.9)**
Fleming **29.1.16**
Flemish **36.2.15**
flense **34.24.3**
flesh **36.5**
flesher **17.26.4**
fleshiness **34.18.16(.2.8)**
fleshings **35.27**
fleshless **34.18.29(.35)**
fleshliness **34.18.16(.2.10)**
fleshly **1.31.35(.2)**

fleshpot **22.11.2**
fleshy **1.24.4**
fletcher **17.28.5**
Fleur **18**
fleur-de-lis **2**
fleur-de-lys **2.32**
fleurette **22.5.19**
fleuron **28.10.24(.5)**
fleury **1.29.11(.3)**
flew **16**
flex **34.23.4**
flexibility **1.10.16(.22.1)**
flexible **40.20.16(.21.3)**
flexibleness **34.18.16(.37.4)**
flexibly **1.31.21(.7.2)**
flexile **40.13.12**
flexility **1.10.16(.27)**
flexion **28.17.25(.15.2)**
flexional **40.26.13(.14.6)**
flexionless **34.18.29(.27)**
flexitime **27.12.1**
Flexner **17.18.28**
flexographic **24.2.16(.3)**
flexography **1.18.9(.3.2)**
flexor **17.24.20**
flextime **27.12.1**
flexuosity **1.10.16(.16.2)**
flexuous **34.18.6**
flexuously **1.31.33(.12.1)**
flexural **40.16.13(.12.2)**
flexure **17.26.19**
flibbertigibbet **22.19.9**
flick **24.2**
flicker **17.14.2**
flickering **29.1.30(.8)**
flies **35.15**
flight **22.16**
flightily **1.31.17(.9.2)**
flightiness **34.18.16(.2.3)**
flightless **34.18.29(.22)**
flighty **1.10.13**
flimflam **27.6.18**
flimflammer **17.17.6**
flimflammery **1.29.11(.12)**
flimsily **1.31.17(.21)**
flimsiness **34.18.16(.2.7)**
flimsy **1.23.19**
flinch **38.18.1**
flincher **17.28.22**
flinchingly **1.31.28(.1.13)**
flinders **35.18.9**
fling **29.1**
flinger **17.19.1**
Flinn **28.2**
flint **22.26.1**
flintily **1.31.17(.9.3)**
flintiness **34.18.16(.2.3)**
flintlock **24.9.16(.11)**

Flintshire **17.28.22**
Flintstones **35.26.15**
flinty **1.10.23(.1)**
flip **20.2**
flipflop **20.7.13**
flippancy **1.22.23(.10.2)**
flippant **22.26.15(.7)**
flippantly **1.31.22(.20.2)**
flippantness **34.18.16(.20.4)**
flipper **17.10.2**
FLIR **3**
flirt **22.20**
flirtation **28.17.25(.3.3)**
flirtatious **34.18.22(.3)**
flirtatiously **1.31.33(.12.4)**
flirtatiousness **34.18.16(.31.4)**
flirty **1.10.17**
flit **22.2**
flitch **38.2**
flitter **17.12.2**
Flitton **28.17.11(.2)**
flivver **17.21.2**
Flixton **28.17.11(.25)**
flixweed **23.1.10**
Flo **19**
float **22.21**
floatability **1.10.16(.22.1)**
floatable **40.20.16(.11.3)**
floatage **39.2.10**
floater **17.12.18**
floatingly **1.31.28(.1.4)**
floatplane **28.4.19**
floaty **1.10.18**
floc **24.9**
flocci **14.18**
flocculate **22.4.23(.7.3)**
flocculation **28.17.25(.3.14)**
floccule **40.15.9(.5)**
flocculence **34.24.10(.24)**
flocculent **22.26.15(.25)**
flocculently **1.31.22(.20.5)**
flocculi **14.25.9**
flocculus **34.18.29(.17.6)**
floccus **34.18.13(.5)**
flock **24.9**
flocky **1.12.7**
Flodden Field **23.31.1**
floe **19**
Floella **17.34.5**
flog **26.7**
flogger **17.16.7**
flong **29.6**
flood **23.14**
floodgate **22.4.12(.8)**
floodlight **22.16.25(.14)**
floodlit **22.2.25**
Flook **24.14, 24.15**

floor **12**
floorboard **23.12.2(.4)**
floorcloth **32.9**
flooring **29.1.30(.7)**
floorless **34.18.29(.11)**
floozie **1.23.12**
flop **20.7**
flophouse **34.8.6(.9)**
floppily **1.31.17(.7)**
floppiness **34.18.16(.2.2)**
floppy **1.8.7**
flora **17.32.10**
floral **40.16.13(.8)**
florally **1.31.17(.27.1)**
floreat **22.7.2**
Florence **34.24.10(.16)**
Florentine **28.1.9(.6), 28.14.5**
Flores **34.2.21, 35.1.22, 35.2.17**
florescence **34.24.10(.18)**
floret **22.19.24(.5)**
Florey **1.29.8**
floriate **22.4.2(.14), 22.4.5**
floribunda **17.13.20(.10)**
floricultural **40.16.13(.12.3)**
floriculture **17.28.26**
floriculturist **22.29.2(.29.4)**
florid **23.2.22**
Florida **17.13.15**
Floridian **28.3.4(.2)**
floridity **1.10.16(.9)**
floridly **1.31.23(.14.7)**
floridness **34.18.16(.21.1)**
floriferous **34.18.27(.20)**
florilegia **3.19.1**
florilegium **27.3.15**
florin **28.17.31(.7)**
Florio **15.1.12**
florist **22.29.2(.29.2)**
floristic **24.2.10(.15.2)**
floristically **1.31.24(.9.6)**
floristry **1.29.15(.17)**
Florrie **1.29.7**
floruit **22.2.3**
flory **1.29.8**
floscular **17.34.16(.21.2)**
flosculous **34.18.29(.17.6)**
floss **34.10**
Flossie **1.22.9**
flossy **1.22.9**
flotation **28.17.25(.3.3)**
flote **22.21**
flotilla **17.34.2(.2)**
flotsam **27.15.20(.13)**
Flotta **17.12.9**
flounce **34.24.5**
flounder **17.13.20(.5)**

flounderer **17.32.14(.7)**
flour **17.3**
flouresce **34.5.14**
flouriness **34.18.16(.2.9)**
flourish **36.2.25**
flourisher **17.26.14**
flourishy **1.24.12**
flourmill **40.2.9**
floury **1.29.11(.1)**
flout **22.9**
flow **19**
flowage **39.2.7**
flowchart **22.10.10**
flower **17.3**
flowerbed **23.5.2**
flowerer **17.32.14(.1)**
floweret **22.19.24(.9)**
flowerily **1.31.17(.27.1)**
floweriness **34.18.16(.2.9)**
flowerless **34.18.29(.17.1)**
flowerlike **24.13.7(.8)**
flowerpot **22.11.2**
Flowers **35.18.2**
flowery **1.29.11(.1)**
flowing **29.1.9**
flowingly **1.31.28(.1.1)**
flown **28.19**
flowsheet **22.1.11**
flowstone **28.19.4(.9)**
Floyd **23.13**
flu **16**
flub **21.11**
Fluck **24.12**
fluctuate **22.4.4**
fluctuation **28.17.25(.3.1)**
flue **16**
fluence **34.24.10(.7)**
fluency **1.22.23(.10.1)**
fluent **22.26.15(.6)**
fluently **1.31.22(.20.1)**
fluff **30.11**
fluffily **1.31.17(.16.1)**
fluffiness **34.18.16(.2.6)**
fluffy **1.18.7**
Flügelhorn **28.11.10**
fluid **23.2.4**
fluidic **24.2.11(.2)**
fluidify **14.14.4(.5)**
fluidity **1.10.16(.9)**
fluidization **28.17.25(.3.11)**
fluidize **35.15.8**
fluidly **1.31.23(.1)**
fluidness **34.18.16(.21.1)**
fluid ounce **34.24.5**
fluke **24.15**
flukily **1.31.17(.11)**
flukiness **34.18.16(.2.4)**
fluky **1.12.12**
flume **27.14**

flummery 1.29.11(.12)
flummox 34.23.15
flump 20.16.5
flung 29.8
flunk 24.19.7
flunkey 1.12.16
flunkeyism 27.15.21(.2.1)
Fluon® 28.10.5
fluoresce 34.5.14
fluorescence 34.24.10(.18)
fluorescent 22.26.15(.17.2)
fluoridate 22.4.10
fluoridation 28.17.25(.3.4)
fluoride 23.15.15
fluoridization 28.17.25(.3.11)
fluorinate 22.4.14(.9.4)
fluorination 28.17.25(.3.8)
fluorine 28.1.25(.1)
fluorite 22.16.24(.7)
fluorocarbon 28.17.10
fluoroscope 20.15.4(.1)
fluoroscopy 1.8.11(.5)
fluorosis 34.2.17(.11.2)
fluorspar 10.4
flurry 1.29.9
flush 36.12
flusher 17.26.10
Flushing 29.1.25
flushness 34.18.16(.33.1)
fluster 17.12.24(.10)
flute 22.18
flutelike 24.13.7(.12)
flutist 22.29.2(.13)
flutter 17.12.12
flutterer 17.32.14(.6)
fluttery 1.29.11(.8.4)
fluty 1.10.15
fluvial 40.3.8
fluviatile 40.13.3(.1)
fluvioglacial 40.33.2
fluviometer 17.12.16(.9.2)
flux 34.23.11
fluxion 28.17.25(.15.5)
fluxional 40.26.13(.14.6)
fly 14
flyable 40.20.16(.5)
flyaway 4.25.9
flyback 24.6.6(.7)
flyblown 28.19.19
flyby 14.7
flycatcher 17.28.6
flyer 17.6
flyleaf 30.1.9
flyleaves 35.28.1
Flymo® 19.14.10

flyness 34.18.16(.13)
Flynn 28.2
flyover 17.21.14(.2)
flypaper 17.10.3
flypast 22.29.6(.2), 22.29.8(.1)
flysheet 22.1.11
flyswatter 17.12.9
flyting 29.1.12(.11)
flytrap 20.5.6
flyway 4.25.7
flyweight 22.4.21
flywheel 40.1.14
flywhisk 24.20.1
FNMA 4.13
foal 40.18
foam 27.17
foaminess 34.18.16(.2.5)
foamless 34.18.29(.26)
foamy 1.15.15
fob 21.8
fobwatch 38.8
focaccia 17.28.6
focal 40.23.14
focalization 28.17.25(.3.12)
focalize 35.15.21(.4.4)
Foch 36.9
Fochabers 35.18.7
foci 14.10, 14.18
fo'c'sle 40.31.18
focus 34.18.13(.12)
focused 22.29.15(.11)
focuser 17.24.15
fodder 17.13.8
Foden 28.17.12(.18)
foe 19
foehn 28.18
foeman 28.17.16(.18)
foemen 28.5.7(.12)
foetal 40.21.1
foeticide 23.15.11(.6)
foetid 23.2.8
foetus 34.18.11(.1)
fog 26.7
Fogarty 1.10.16(.11)
fogau 16.10, 19.13.11
fogbank 24.19.3(.1)
fogbound 23.24.7(.2)
fog-bow 19.9.13
fogey 1.14.13
fogeydom 27.15.10(.2)
fogeyish 36.2.1
Fogg 26.7
foggily 1.31.17(.12)
fogginess 34.18.16(.2.4)
foggy 1.14.6
foghorn 28.11.10
fogyish 36.2.1
fohn 28.18
föhn 28.18

foible 40.20.11
foie gras 10
foil 40.11
foilist 22.29.2(.31.1)
foist 22.29.11
Fokker® 17.14.8
folacin 28.2.23(.9)
fold 23.31.13
foldable 40.20.16(.12)
foldaway 4.25.9
foldback 24.6.6(.13)
foldboat 22.21.2
folder 17.13.23(.8)
folderol 40.9.19
foldout 22.9.8
fold-up 20.9.6
Foley 1.31.19
Folger 17.29.16(.9)
folia 3.24.11
foliaceous 34.18.22(.3)
foliage 39.2.2
foliar 3.24.11
foliate 22.3.13, 22.4.2(.15)
foliation 28.17.25(.3.1)
folic 24.2.27(.9)
Folies-Bergère 6.15
folio 15.1.13
foliole 40.14.1
foliot 22.3.13
folium 27.3.18
folk 24.18
Folkestone 28.17.11(.25)
folkie 1.12.15
folkiness 34.18.16(.2.4)
folkish 36.2.13
folklore 12.23.7
folkloric 24.2.26(.7)
folklorist 22.29.2(.29.2)
folkloristic 24.2.10(.15.2)
folksily 1.31.17(.20)
folksiness 34.18.16(.2.7)
folksong 29.6.9
folksy 1.22.22
folktale 40.4.2
folkway 4.25.14
folkweave 31.1.7
folky 1.12.15
Follick 24.2.27(.9)
follicle 40.23.12(.19)
follicular 17.34.16(.21.2)
folliculate 22.19.26(.13)
folliculated 23.18.9(.3)
follow 19.29.8
follower 17.9.13
following 29.1.9
follow-my-leader 17.13.1
folly 1.31.10
Folsom 27.15.20(.22)
Fomalhaut 22.21.15

foment 22.26.4(.8)
fomentation 28.17.25(.3.3)
fomenter 17.12.22(.3)
fomites 35.1.7(.6)
fond 23.24.9
Fonda 17.13.20(.7)
fondant 22.26.15(.10)
fondle 40.22.16
fondler 17.34.22
fondly 1.31.23(.17)
fondness 34.18.16(.21.1)
fondu 16.8.5, 16.24.6
fondue 16.8.5, 16.24.6
font 22.26.9
Fontainebleau 19.29.16
fontal 40.21.17(.4)
Fontana 17.18.8(.2)
fontanelle 40.5.8
Fonteyn 28.4.3
Fontwell 40.5.17(.7)
Foochow 9.12
food 23.17
foodie 1.11.16
foodism 27.15.21(.2.5)
foodstuff 30.11.3
Fookes 34.23.14
fool 40.15
foolery 1.29.11(.27)
foolhardily 1.31.17(.10)
foolhardiness 34.18.16(.2.3)
foolhardy 1.11.9
foolish 36.2.27
foolishly 1.31.35(.7.4)
foolishness 34.18.16(.33.6)
foolproof 30.13.4
foolscap 20.5.1
Foord 23.12
foot 22.17
footage 39.2.10
football 40.10.4
footballer 17.34.10
footbath 32.8
footbed 23.5.2
footboard 23.12.2(.8)
footbrake 24.3.13
footbridge 39.2.22(.10)
footcandle 40.22.16
Foote 22.17
footer 17.12.14
footfall 40.10.11
footgear 3.7
foothill 40.2.18
foothold 23.31.13(.9)
footing 29.1.12(.12)
footle 40.21.11
footless 34.18.29(.22)
footlights 34.22.12

footlocker 17.14.8
footloose 34.17.14
footman 28.17.16(.21)
footmark 24.8.8
footnote 22.21.8
footpad 23.7.5
footpath 32.8
footplate 22.4.23(.8)
footprint 22.26.1
footrest 22.29.5(.12)
footsie 1.22.21
footslog 26.7.14
footslogger 17.16.7
footsore 12.14.11
footstalk 24.10.2
footstep 20.4
footstool 40.15.3
footstrap 20.5.6
footsure 12.16, 17.7.10
footway 4.25.12
footwear 6.18.7
footwork 24.17.6(.8)
foozle 40.32.13
foozler 17.34.28
fop 20.7
foppery 1.29.11(.6)
foppish 36.2.9
foppishly 1.31.35(.7.1)
foppishness 34.18.16(.33.2)
for 12
fora 17.32.10
forage 39.2.22(.5)
forager 17.29.13
foramen 28.5.7(.4)
foramina 17.18.16(.8)
foraminate 22.4.14(.9.2)
foraminated 23.18.9(.3)
foraminifer 17.20.12(.2)
foraminiferan 28.17.31(.11)
foraminiferous 34.18.27(.20)
forasmuch 38.11
forastero 19.27.3
foray 4.26.6
forb 21.9
forbad 23.4.2, 23.7.6
forbade 23.4.2, 23.7.6
forbear 6.3
forbearance 34.24.10(.16)
forbearingly 1.31.28(.1.17)
Forbes 34.2.7, 34.18.10, 35.21
forbid 23.2.7
forbiddance 34.24.10(.11)
forbidden 28.17.12(.2)
forbidding 29.1.13(.2)

forbiddingly 1.31.28(.1.5)
forbore 12.4
forborne 28.11.2
forbye 14.7
force 34.12
forceable 40.20.16(.21.2)
forceful 40.27.25
forcefully 1.31.17(.16.2)
forcefulness 34.18.16(.37.2)
force majeure 18.14
forcemeat 22.1.5
forceps 34.21.4
forcer 17.24.10
forcible 40.20.16(.21.2)
forcibleness 34.18.16(.37.4)
forcibly 1.31.21(.7.2)
ford 23.12
fordable 40.20.16(.12)
Forde 23.12
Fordham 27.15.10(.7)
Fordingbridge 39.2.22(.10)
fordless 34.18.29(.23)
Fordyce 34.15.3
fore 12
forearm 27.8, 27.8.9
forebad 23.7.6
forebade 23.7.6
forebear 6.3
forebode 23.20.4
foreboding 29.1.13(.13)
forebodingly 1.31.28(.1.5)
forebrain 28.4.18
forecast 22.29.6(.5), 22.29.8(.3)
forecaster 17.12.24(.5)
forecastle 40.31.18
foreclose 35.20.14
foreclosure 17.27.9
foreconscious 34.18.22(.12)
forecourt 22.13.4
foredeck 24.4.5
foredge 39.5
foredoom 27.14.2
fore-edge 39.5
forefather 17.23.7
forefeel 40.1.8
forefeet 22.1.6
forefelt 22.32.2
forefinger 17.16.17(.1)
forefoot 22.17
forefront 22.26.12
foregather 17.23.5
foregoer 17.9.5
foregoing 29.1.9
foregone 28.10.12
foreground 23.24.7(.10)
forehand 23.24.6(.11)

forehead 23.5.13(.4), 23.18.27
forehock 24.9.13
forehold 23.31.13(.9)
foreign 28.17.31(.7)
foreigner 17.18.16(.20)
foreignness 34.18.16(.25)
forejudge 39.11
foreknew 16.24.10
foreknow 19.15
foreknowledge 39.2.23
foreknown 28.19.10
forelady 1.11.4
foreland 23.24.16(.16.2)
foreleg 26.4
forelimb 27.2.16
forelock 24.9.16(.4)
foreman 28.17.16(.11)
foremast 22.29.6(.7), 22.29.8(.5)
foremost 22.29.17(.4)
forename 27.4.5
forenoon 28.16.8
forensic 24.2.20(.15), 24.2.21
forensically 1.31.24(.9.10)
foreordain 28.4.4
foreordination 28.17.25(.3.8)
forepart 22.10.1
forepaw 12.3
forepeak 24.1.1
foreplay 4.28.9
forequarter 17.12.10(.7)
foreran 28.7.20
forerun 28.13.9
forerunner 17.18.12
foresail 40.4.10, 40.31.9
foresaw 12.14
foresee 2.22
foreseeability 1.10.16(.22.1)
foreseeable 40.20.16(.1)
foreseeably 1.31.21(.2)
foreseen 28.1.18
foreseer 17.1.11
foreshadow 19.11.6
foresheets 34.22.1
foreshore 12.16.4
foreshorten 28.17.11(.10)
foreshow 19.22
foreshown 28.19.15
foresight 22.16.19(.4)
foresightedly 1.31.23(.14.3)
foresightedness 34.18.16(.21.1)
foreskin 28.2.13(.14)
forest 22.29.15(.17)
forestall 40.10.5

forestaller 17.34.10
forestalment 22.26.15(.13.7)
forestation 28.17.25(.3.3)
forestay 4.9.10
forester 17.12.24(.14)
forestry 1.29.15(.17)
foreswear 6.18.12
foresworn 28.11.11
foretaste 22.29.4
foretell 40.5.3
foreteller 17.34.5(.3)
forethought 22.13.9
foretoken 28.17.13(.15)
foretold 23.31.13(.3)
foretop 20.7.4
forever 17.21.4
for evermore 12.9
forewarn 28.11.11
forewarner 17.18.10
forewing 29.1.29
forewoman 28.17.16(.14)
forewomen 28.2.17(.1)
foreword 23.19.8
foreyard 23.9.21
Forfar 17.20.8
Forfarshire 17.26.14
forfeit 22.19.16
forfeitable 40.20.16(.11.3)
forfeiter 17.12.16(.11)
forfeiture 17.28.15
forfend 23.24.5(.9)
forgather 17.23.5
forgave 31.3.3
forge 39.10
forgeable 40.20.16(.25)
forger 17.29.9
forgery 1.29.11(.23)
forget 22.5.7
forgetful 40.27.18
forgetfully 1.31.17(.16.2)
forgetfulness 34.18.16(.37.2)
forget-me-not 22.11.9
forgettable 40.20.16(.11.1)
forgetter 17.12.5(.4)
forgivable 40.20.16(.19)
forgivably 1.31.21(.7.1)
forgive 31.2.3
forgiven 28.17.20(.2)
forgiveness 34.18.16(.28.1)
forgiver 17.21.2
forgivingly 1.31.28(.1.9)
forgo 19.13
forgot 22.11.7
forgotten 28.17.11(.9)
forint 22.26.1

fork **24.10**
forkful **40.14.6(.12)**
forklift **22.27.1**
forlorn **28.11.13**
forlornly **1.31.27(.10)**
form **27.10**
formal **40.25.6**
formaldehyde **23.15.13**
formalin **28.2.31(.10)**
formalism **27.15.21(.2.15)**
formalist **22.29.2(.31.3)**
formalistic **24.2.10(.15.3)**
formality **1.10.16(.32.7)**
formalization **28.17.25(.3.12)**
formalize **35.15.21(.4.5)**
formally **1.31.17(.13)**
formalness **34.18.16(.37.5)**
formant **22.26.15(.13.1)**
format **22.7.11**
formate **22.4.13(.4)**
formation **28.17.25(.3.7)**
formational **40.26.13(.14.2)**
formative **31.2.1(.9.2)**
formatively **1.31.30(.7.1)**
formbook **24.14.3**
Formby **1.9.18**
forme **27.10**
former **17.17.9**
formerly **1.31.17(.13)**
formic **24.2.14(.7)**
Formica® **17.14.12**
formication **28.17.25(.3.5)**
formidable **40.20.16(.12)**
formidableness **34.18.16(.37.4)**
formidably **1.31.21(.4.4)**
formless **34.18.29(.26)**
formlessly **1.31.33(.12.6)**
formlessness **34.18.16(.31.6)**
Formosa **17.24.17, 17.25.15**
Formosan **28.17.23(.16), 28.17.24(.14)**
formula **17.34.16(.21.4)**
formulae **2.32.9(.8)**
formulaic **24.2.3**
formularize **35.15.20(.2)**
formulary **1.29.11(.27)**
formulate **22.4.23(.7.3)**
formulation **28.17.25(.3.14)**
formulator **17.12.4(.16)**
formulism **27.15.21(.2.15)**
formulist **22.29.2(.31.5)**
formulistic **24.2.10(.15.3)**
formulize **35.15.21(.4.8)**
formwork **24.17.6(.12)**

fornicate **22.4.11(.6)**
fornication **28.17.25(.3.5)**
fornicator **17.12.4(.7)**
fornices **35.1.16(.10)**
fornix **34.23.2(.6)**
forrader **17.13.15**
Forres **34.18.27(.7)**
Forrest **22.29.15(.17)**
Forrester **17.12.24(.14)**
forsake **24.3.10**
forsaken **28.17.13(.3)**
forsakenness **34.18.16(.25)**
forsaker **17.14.3(.5)**
Forshaw **12.16.4**
forsook **24.14.7**
forsooth **32.13**
Forster **17.12.24(.8)**
forswear **6.18.12**
forswore **12.20**
Forsyte **22.16.19(.4)**
Forsyth **32.12**
forsythia **3.12**
fort **22.13**
fortalice **34.18.29(.17.2)**
forte **4.9.5**
Fortean **28.3.3**
forte-piano **19.15.6, 19.15.7**
Fortescue **16.24.7**
forth **32.10**
forthcoming **29.1.16**
forthcomingness **34.18.16(.26)**
forthright **22.16.24(.17)**
forthrightly **1.31.22(.13)**
forthrightness **34.18.16(.20.2)**
forthwith **32.2.7, 33.2**
fortieth **32.14.1**
fortifiable **40.20.16(.5)**
fortification **28.17.25(.3.5)**
fortifier **17.6.9(.4)**
fortify **14.14.4(.4)**
Fortinbras **34.7.18**
fortis **34.2.8**
fortissimo **19.14.12**
fortitude **23.17.4(.1)**
Fort Knox **34.23.8**
fortnight **22.16.14(.7)**
fortnightly **1.31.22(.13)**
Fortnum and Mason **28.17.23(.4)**
Fortran **28.7.20**
fortress **34.18.27(.14)**
fortuitism **27.15.21(.2.4)**
fortuitist **22.29.2(.13)**
fortuitous **34.18.11(.10)**
fortuitously **1.31.33(.12.2)**

fortuitousness **34.18.16(.31.3)**
fortuity **1.10.16(.5)**
fortunate **22.19.15(.9)**
fortunately **1.31.22(.15)**
fortune **28.16.14, 28.17.27**
forty **1.10.10**
fortyfold **23.31.13(.7)**
forty-niner **17.18.13(.5)**
forum **27.15.26(.5)**
forward **23.18.26(.5)**
forwarder **17.13.15**
forwardly **1.31.23(.14.7)**
forwardness **34.18.16(.21.1)**
forwards **35.23.12**
forwent **22.26.4(.13)**
Fosbury **1.29.11(.7.2)**
Fosdick **24.2.11(.17)**
Fosdyke **24.13.3**
foss **34.10**
fossa **17.24.9**
fossae **2.22.5**
fosse **34.10**
fossick **24.2.20(.7)**
fossicker **17.14.15(.12)**
fossil **40.31.8**
fossil fuel **40.16.8**
fossiliferous **34.18.27(.20)**
fossilization **28.17.25(.3.12)**
fossilize **35.15.21(.4.6)**
fossorial **40.3.14(.5)**
foster **17.12.24(.7)**
fosterage **39.2.22(.9)**
fosterer **17.32.14(.6)**
fosterling **29.1.31(.12)**
Fothergill **40.2.8**
Fotheringay **4.12**
Fotheringham **27.15.12**
Foucault **19.12**
fouetté **4.9.1, 4.9.7**
fought **22.13**
foul **40.7**
Foula **17.34.15**
foulard **10.25, 10.25.4, 23.9.22**
Foulds **35.23.15**
Foulkes **34.23.6**
foully **1.31.38**
foulness **34.18.16(.37.1)**
foumart **22.10.7**
found **23.24.7**
foundation **28.17.25(.3.4)**
foundational **40.26.13(.14.2)**
foundationer **17.18.16(.16)**
founder **17.13.20(.5)**
foundership **20.2.7(.9)**
foundling **29.1.31(.18)**

foundress **34.18.27(.15)**
foundry **1.29.16**
fount **22.26.7, 22.26.9**
fountain **28.17.11(.22)**
fountainhead **23.5.13(.14)**
fountainpen **28.5.2**
four **12**
four-bagger **17.16.5**
fourchette **22.5.15**
fourdrinier **3.9.2, 4.2.4**
fourfold **23.31.13(.7)**
Fourier **3.22.11, 4.2.9**
Fourierism **27.15.21(.2.14)**
fourpence **34.24.10(.8)**
fourpenny **1.16.15(.5), 1.16.18**
fourscore **12.7**
foursome **27.15.20(.7)**
foursquare **6.18.9**
fourteen **28.1.9**
fourteenth **32.21**
fourth **32.10**
fourthly **1.31.31**
fovea **3.11.8**
foveae **2.3**
foveal **40.3.8**
foveate **22.3.7**
foveola **17.34.16(.1)**
foveolae **2.32.9(.1)**
foveolate **22.19.26(.13)**
Fowey **13**
Fowkes **34.23.6, 34.23.17**
fowl **40.7**
fowler **17.34.7**
Fowles **35.30.6**
fowling **29.1.31(.7)**
Fowlmere **3.8.16**
fox **34.23.8**
Foxcroft **22.27.5**
Foxe **34.23.8**
foxfire **17.6.9(.10)**
foxglove **31.8**
foxhole **40.18.13**
foxhound **23.24.7(.8)**
foxhunt **22.26.12**
foxily **1.31.17(.20)**
foxiness **34.18.16(.2.7)**
foxlike **24.13.7(.22)**
foxtail **40.4.2**
Foxton **28.17.11(.25)**
foxtrot **22.11.15**
foxy **1.22.22**
foyer **4.3, 17.5**
Foyle **40.11**
Fra **10**
frabjous **34.18.24**
frabjously **1.31.33(.12.4)**
fracas **10.8.3, 35.9**
fracases **35.18.17**

fractal **40.21.16**
fraction **28.17.25(.15.3)**
fractional **40.26.13(.14.6)**
fractionalize **35.15.21(.4.5)**
fractionally **1.31.17(.14.3)**
fractionary **1.29.11(.13.2)**
fractionate **22.4.14(.9.3)**
fractionation **28.17.25(.3.8)**
fractionator **17.12.4(.10)**
fractionize **35.15.12(.5)**
fractious **34.18.22(.11)**
fractiously **1.31.33(.12.4)**
fractiousness **34.18.16(.31.4)**
fracture **17.28.20**
fraena **17.18.1**
fraenula **17.34.16(.21.4)**
fragile **40.13.14**
fragilely **1.31.38**
fragility **1.10.16(.28)**
fragment **22.26.4(.8), 22.26.15(.13.3)**
fragmental **40.21.17(.2)**
fragmentarily **1.31.17(.27.1)**
fragmentation **28.17.25(.3.3)**
fragmentize **35.15.7(.8)**
Fragonard **10.11**
fragrance **34.24.10(.16)**
fragranced **22.29.21**
fragrancy **1.22.23(.10.4)**
fragrant **22.26.15(.23.4)**
fragrantly **1.31.22(.20.5)**
fragrantness **34.18.16(.20.4)**
frail **40.4**
frailly **1.31.38**
frailness **34.18.16(.37.1)**
frailty **1.10.28**
fraise **35.4, 35.5**
fraises **35.5**
Fraktur **17.7.3**
framable **40.20.16(.15)**
framboesia **3.15.1**
frame **27.4**
frameless **34.18.29(.26)**
framer **17.17.4**
framework **24.17.6(.12)**
Framlingham **27.15.15**
Framlington **28.17.11(.23)**
Frampton **28.17.11(.18)**
Fran **28.7**
franc **24.19.3**
France **34.24.6**
Frances **34.18.20**
Francesca **17.14.23**
Franche-Comté **4.9.4**

franchise **35.15.17**
franchisee **2.23**
franchiser **17.25.12(.11)**
Francine **28.1.18**
Francis **34.2.17(.15)**
Franciscan **28.17.13(.18)**
francium **27.3.11**
Franck **24.19.4**
Franco **19.12.15**
Franco-German **28.17.16(.17)**
François **10.22.11**
Françoise **10.22.11**
francolin **28.2.31(.10)**
Francomania **3.9.3(.5)**
Franconia **3.9.11**
Francophile **40.13.9**
Francophobe **21.16.1**
Francophobia **3.3.9**
francophone **28.19.11**
frangibility **1.10.16(.22.1)**
frangible **40.20.16(.25)**
frangibleness **34.18.16(.37.4)**
frangipane **28.4.1**
frangipani **1.16.8**
franglais **4.28.13**
frank **24.19.3**
frankable **40.20.16(.13)**
Frankenstein **28.14.5**
franker **17.14.21(.3)**
Frankfurt **22.19.16, 22.20.8**
frankfurter **17.12.17**
Frankie **1.12.16**
frankincense **34.24.3**
Frankish **36.2.13**
Frankland **23.24.16(.16.3)**
franklin **28.17.33(.20)**
frankly **1.31.24(.12)**
Franklyn **28.17.33(.20)**
frankness **34.18.16(.22)**
Franks **34.23.18**
frantic **24.2.10(.14)**
frantically **1.31.24(.9.5)**
franticly **1.31.24(.9.5)**
franticness **34.18.16(.22)**
Franz Joseph Land **23.24.6**
frap **20.5**
frappé **4.7**
Frascati **1.10.8**
Fraser **17.25.3**
Fraserburgh **17.32.12, 17.32.14(.5)**
frass **34.7**
frat **22.7**
fratchiness **34.18.16(.2.8)**
fratchy **1.25.6**
fraternal **40.26.14**

fraternalism **27.15.21(.2.15)**
fraternally **1.31.17(.14.3)**
fraternity **1.10.16(.13)**
fraternization **28.17.25(.3.11)**
fraternize **35.15.12(.5)**
fratricidal **40.22.11**
fratricide **23.15.11(.6)**
Frau **9**
fraud **23.12**
fraudster **17.12.24(.19)**
fraudulence **34.24.10(.24)**
fraudulent **22.26.15(.25)**
fraudulently **1.31.22(.20.5)**
fraught **22.13**
Fräulein **28.14.19(.9)**
Fraunhofer **17.20.14**
fraxinella **17.34.5(.8)**
fray **4**
Fray Bentos **34.10.8**
Frayn **28.4**
Frayne **28.4**
Frazer **17.25.3**
Frazier **3.15.3**
frazil **40.2.15, 40.32.3**
frazzle **40.32.5**
freak **24.1**
freakily **1.31.17(.11)**
freakiness **34.18.16(.2.4)**
freakish **36.2.13**
freakishly **1.31.35(.7.1)**
freakishness **34.18.16(.33.4)**
freaky **1.12.1**
freckle **40.23.4**
freckly **1.31.24(.4)**
Fred **23.5**
Freddie **1.11.5**
Freddy **1.11.5**
Frederica **17.14.1**
Frederick **24.2.26(.10)**
Fredericton **28.17.11(.20)**
free **2**
freebase **34.4.3**
freebie **1.9.1**
freeboard **23.12.2(.1)**
freeboot **22.18.3**
freebooter **17.12.15(.1)**
freeborn **28.11.2**
freedman **28.7.10(.12), 28.17.16(.22)**
freedmen **28.5.7(.16)**
freedom **27.15.10(.1)**
freedwoman **28.17.16(.14)**
freedwomen **28.2.17(.1)**
Freefone® **28.19.11**
freehand **23.24.6(.11)**
freehold **23.31.13(.9)**

freeholder **17.13.23(.8)**
freelance **34.24.6**
freeload **23.20.13**
freeloader **17.13.17**
freely **1.31.1**
freeman **28.17.16(.1)**
freemartin **28.2.11(.6)**
Freemason **28.17.23(.4)**
freeness **34.18.16(.1)**
freephone **28.19.11**
Freeport **22.13.1**
Freepost **22.29.17(.1)**
Freer **3**
freer **17.1**
freesheet **22.1.11**
freesia **3.15.1**
freest **22.29.15(.1)**
freestanding **29.1.13(.14)**
freestone **28.19.4(.9)**
freestyle **40.13.3(.10)**
freestyler **17.34.13**
freethinker **17.14.21(.1)**
freethinking **29.1.14(.14)**
Freetown **28.8.1**
freeware **6.18.1**
freeway **4.25.1**
freewheel **40.1.14**
freewheeler **17.34.1**
freewill **40.2.19**
freezable **40.20.16(.22)**
freeze **35.1**
freezer **17.25.1**
Freiburg **26.14.1(.2)**
freight **22.4**
freightage **39.2.10**
freighter **17.12.4**
freightliner **17.18.13(.14)**
Frelimo **19.14.1**
Fremantle **40.21.17(.3)**
fremitus **34.18.11(.10)**
Frémont **22.26.9**
frena **17.18.1**
French **38.18.2**
Frenchification **28.17.25(.3.5)**
Frenchify **14.14.4(.11)**
Frenchman **28.17.16(.33)**
Frenchness **34.18.16(.35)**
Frenchwoman **28.17.16(.14)**
Frenchwomen **28.2.17(.1)**
Frenchy **1.24.15**
frenetic **24.2.10(.3.1)**
frenetically **1.31.24(.9.3)**
frenula **17.34.16(.21.4)**
frenulum **27.15.28(.11)**
frenum **27.15.14(.1)**
frenzied **23.2.17**
frenziedly **1.31.23(.14.7)**

frenzy **1.23.20**
Freon® **28.10.1**
frequency **1.22.23(.10.4)**
frequent **22.26.4(.13),
22.26.15(.22)**
frequentation
28.17.25(.3.3)
frequentative **31.2.1(.9.1)**
frequenter **17.12.22(.3)**
frequently **1.31.22(.20.5)**
Frere **3, 6**
fresco **19.12.17**
fresco secco **19.12.4**
fresh **36.5**
freshen **28.17.25(.4)**
fresher **17.26.4**
freshet **22.19.20**
freshly **1.31.35(.2)**
freshman **28.17.16(.31)**
freshness **34.18.16(.33.1)**
freshwater **17.12.10(.7)**
freshwoman
28.17.16(.14)
freshwomen **28.2.17(.1)**
Fresnel **40.5.8**
Fresno **19.15.17**
fret **22.5**
fretboard **23.12.2(.8)**
fretful **40.27.18**
fretfully **1.31.17(.16.2)**
fretfulness **34.18.16(.37.2)**
fretless **34.18.29(.22)**
fretsaw **12.14.11**
fretwork **24.17.6(.8)**
Freud **23.13**
Freudian **28.3.4(.8)**
Freudianism
27.15.21(.2.9)
Frey **4**
Freya **17.2**
Freyr **17.2**
friability **1.10.16(.22.1)**
friable **40.20.16(.5)**
friableness
34.18.16(.37.4)
friar **17.6**
friarly **1.31.17(.3)**
friary **1.29.11(.2)**
fricandeau **19.11.14**
fricandeaux **35.20.4**
fricassee **2.22, 2.22.7**
fricative **31.2.1(.9.1)**
friction **28.17.25(.15.1)**
frictional **40.26.13(.14.6)**
frictionally **1.31.17(.14.3)**
frictionless **34.18.29(.27)**
Friday **1.11.14, 4.10.6**
fridge **39.2**
Friedan **28.7.7**
Friedman **28.17.16(.22)**
Friedrich **24.2.26(.15)**

friend **23.24.5**
friendless **34.18.29(.23)**
friendlessness
34.18.16(.31.6)
friendlily **1.31.17(.29)**
friendliness
34.18.16(.2.10)
friendly **1.31.23(.17)**
friendship **20.2.7(.15)**
Fries **35.1**
Friesian **28.17.26(.1)**
Friesland **23.24.16(.16.4)**
frieze **35.1**
frig **26.2**
frigate **22.19.13**
Frigg **26.2**
Frigga **17.16.2**
fright **22.16**
frighten **28.17.11(.12)**
frightener **17.18.16(.4)**
frighteningly
1.31.28(.1.7)
frightful **40.27.18**
frightfully **1.31.17(.16.2)**
frightfulness
34.18.16(.37.2)
frigid **23.2.20**
Frigidaire® **6.5**
frigidaria **3.22.4**
frigidarium **27.3.17(.3)**
frigidity **1.10.16(.9)**
frigidly **1.31.23(.14.7)**
frigidness **34.18.16(.21.1)**
frijoles **34.5.16**
frill **40.2**
frillery **1.29.11(.27)**
frilliness **34.18.16(.2.10)**
frilling **29.1.31(.2)**
frilly **1.31.2**
fringe **39.17.1**
fringeless **34.18.29(.37)**
fringy **1.26.13**
Frink **24.19.1**
Frinton **28.17.11(.22)**
frippery **1.29.11(.6)**
frippet **22.19.8**
frisbee® **2.10**
Frisch **36.2**
frisé **4.19**
Frisia **3.15.1, 3.15.2**
Frisian **28.3.14,
28.17.26(.1)**
frisk **24.20.1**
frisker **17.14.23**
frisket **22.19.12(.14)**
friskily **1.31.17(.11)**
friskiness **34.18.16(.2.4)**
frisky **1.12.17(.1)**
frisson **28.10.18**
frit **22.2**
frites **22.1**

frith **32.2**
fritillary **1.29.11(.27)**
fritter **17.12.2**
fritto misto **19.10.19**
Fritz **34.22.2**
Friuli **1.31.16**
Friulian **28.3.21(.10)**
frivol **40.28.2**
frivolity **1.10.16(.33)**
frivolous **34.18.29(.17.4)**
frivolously **1.31.33(.12.6)**
frivolousness
34.18.16(.31.6)
frizz **35.2**
frizzily **1.31.17(.21)**
frizziness **34.18.16(.2.7)**
frizzle **40.32.2**
frizzly **1.31.17(.21),
1.31.34**
frizzy **1.23.2**
fro **19**
Frobisher **17.26.14**
frock **24.9**
Frodsham **27.15.22**
froe **19**
Froebel **40.20.17**
Froebelian **28.3.21(.1)**
Froebelism
27.15.21(.2.15)
frog **26.7**
frogbit **22.2.6**
frogfish **36.2.18(.18)**
Froggie **1.14.6**
frogging **29.1.15**
froggy **1.14.6**
froghopper **17.10.8**
frogman **28.17.16(.24)**
frogmarch **38.7**
Frogmore **12.9.10**
frogmouth **32.7**
frogspawn **28.11.1**
froing **29.1.9**
frolic **24.2.27(.9)**
frolicker **17.14.15(.15)**
frolicsome **27.15.20(.15)**
frolicsomely
1.31.26(.11)
frolicsomeness
34.18.16(.24)
from **27.9**
fromage blanc **11**
fromage frais **4**
Frome **27.14, 27.17**
Fron **28.10**
frond **23.24.9**
frondage **39.2.11**
Fronde **23.24.9**
Frondes **23.24.9**
frondeur **18.4**
frondeurs **18.4, 35.19**
frondose **34.20.5**

front **22.26.12**
frontage **39.2.10**
frontager **17.29.13**
frontal **40.21.17(.5)**
frontally **1.31.17(.9.3)**
front bench **38.18.2**
frontbench **38.18.2**
front-bencher **17.28.22**
frontier **3.4, 3.4.12**
frontierless **34.18.29(.3)**
frontiersman
28.17.16(.30)
frontierswoman
28.17.16(.14)
frontierswomen
28.2.17(.1)
frontispiece **34.1.1**
frontless **34.18.29(.22)**
frontlet **22.19.26(.17)**
frontline **28.14.19**
frontman **28.7.10(.11)**
frontmen **28.5.7(.15)**
frontogenesis
34.2.17(.10.3)
frontogenetic
24.2.10(.3.1)
fronton **28.17.11(.22)**
frontpage **39.4.1**
front-runner **17.18.12**
frontward **23.18.26(.9)**
frore **12**
frosh **36.9**
frost **22.29.9**
frostbite **22.16.8**
frostbitten **28.17.11(.2)**
frostbound **23.24.7(.2)**
frost-free **2.30.13**
frostily **1.31.17(.9.3)**
frostiness **34.18.16(.2.3)**
frosting **29.1.12(.21)**
frostless **34.18.29(.22)**
frost-work **24.17.6(.8)**
frosty **1.10.26(.7)**
froth **32.9**
frothily **1.31.17(.18)**
frothiness **34.18.16(.2.6)**
frothy **1.20.6**
frottage **37.4.3, 39.2.10**
froufrou **16.23.12**
frow **19**
froward **23.18.6**
frowardly **1.31.23(.14.1)**
frowardness
34.18.16(.21.1)
frown **28.8**
frowner **17.18.7**
frowsily **1.31.17(.21)**
frowst **22.29.7**
frowster **17.12.24(.6)**
frowstily **1.31.17(.9.3)**
frowstiness **34.18.16(.2.3)**

frowsty **1.10.26(.6)**
frowzily **1.31.17(.21)**
frowziness **34.18.16(.2.7)**
frowzy **1.23.6**
froze **35.20**
frozen **28.17.24(.14)**
frozenly **1.31.27(.14)**
fructiferous **34.18.27(.20)**
fructification **28.17.25(.3.5)**
fructify **14.14.4(.4)**
fructose **34.20.4, 35.20.3**
fructuous **34.18.6**
frugal **40.24.10**
frugality **1.10.16(.32.6)**
frugally **1.31.17(.12)**
frugalness **34.18.16(.37.5)**
frugivorous **34.18.27(.21)**
fruit **22.18**
fruitage **39.2.10**
fruitarian **28.3.20(.4)**
fruitbat **22.7.6**
fruitcake **24.3.6**
fruiter **17.12.15**
fruiterer **17.32.14(.6)**
fruitful **40.27.18**
fruitfully **1.31.17(.16.2)**
fruitfulness **34.18.16(.37.2)**
fruitily **1.31.17(.9.2)**
fruitiness **34.18.16(.2.3)**
fruition **28.17.25(.2.1)**
fruitless **34.18.29(.22)**
fruitlessly **1.31.33(.12.6)**
fruitlessness **34.18.16(.31.6)**
fruitlet **22.19.26(.17)**
fruitwood **23.16.6(.9)**
fruity **1.10.15**
frumenty **1.10.23(.12)**
frump **20.16.5**
frumpily **1.31.17(.7)**
frumpiness **34.18.16(.2.2)**
frumpish **36.2.9**
frumpishly **1.31.35(.7.1)**
frumpy **1.8.14**
frusemide **23.15.7**
frusta **17.12.24(.10)**
frustrate **22.4.22(.8)**
frustratedly **1.31.23(.14.3)**
frustrater **17.12.4(.15)**
frustratingly **1.31.28(.1.4)**
frustration **28.17.25(.3.13)**
frustule **40.15.9(.3)**
frustum **27.15.9(.15)**
frutescent **22.26.15(.17.2)**
frutex **34.23.4(.3)**
frutices **35.1.16(.10)**
fruticose **34.20.6, 35.20.5**
fry **14**

Frye **14**
fryer **17.6**
frypan **28.7.4**
Fryston **28.17.11(.25)**
fry-up **20.9.2**
FT-SE **1.22.21**
fubsy **1.22.20**
Fuchs **34.23.14**
fuchsia **17.26.13**
fuchsine **28.1.18(.7)**
fuci **14.18**
fuck **24.12**
fucker **17.14.11**
fucoid **23.13.9**
fucous **34.18.13(.9)**
fucus **34.18.13(.9)**
fuddle **40.22.10**
fuddy-duddy **1.11.13**
fudge **39.11**
fudgeable **40.20.16(.25)**
fudgicle **40.23.12(.17.3)**
fuel **40.16.8**
Fuentes **34.4.4**
fug **26.10**
fugacious **34.18.22(.3)**
fugaciously **1.31.33(.12.4)**
fugaciousness **34.18.16(.31.4)**
fugacity **1.10.16(.16.1)**
fugal **40.24.10**
fugally **1.31.17(.12)**
fugginess **34.18.16(.2.4)**
fuggy **1.14.8**
fugitive **31.2.1(.9.3)**
fugitively **1.31.30(.7.1)**
fugle **40.24.10**
fugleman **28.17.16(.35)**
fugu **16.10**
fugue **26.12**
fuguist **22.29.2(.16)**
führer **17.32.14(.3)**
Fujairah **17.32.13**
Fuji **1.26.9**
Fujian **28.3.18**
Fujica **17.14.15(.13)**
Fujitsu **16.15**
Fujiyama **17.17.7**
Fulani **1.16.8**
Fulbright **22.16.24(.11)**
fulcra **17.32.21**
fulcrum **27.15.26(.12)**
fulfil **40.2.11**
fulfillable **40.20.16(.29)**
fulfiller **17.34.2(.8)**
fulfilment **22.26.15(.13.7)**
Fulford **23.18.16(.22)**
fulgent **22.26.15(.21)**
fulgid **23.2.20**
fulguration **28.17.25(.3.13)**

fulgurite **22.16.24(.9)**
Fulham **27.15.28(.10)**
fuliginous **34.18.16(.15.3)**
fuliginously **1.31.33(.12.3)**
full **40.14**
fullback **24.6.6(.23)**
fuller **17.34.14**
fullness **34.18.16(.37.1)**
fully **1.31.15**
fulmar **10.10.10, 17.17.24**
fulminant **22.26.15(.14)**
fulminate **22.4.14(.9.2)**
fulmination **28.17.25(.3.8)**
fulminatory **1.29.11(.8.7)**
fulsome **27.15.20(.22)**
fulsomely **1.31.26(.11)**
fulsomeness **34.18.16(.24)**
Fulton **28.17.11(.27)**
fulvescent **22.26.15(.17.2)**
fulvous **34.18.18**
Fulwell **40.5.17(.17)**
Fulwood **23.16.6(.22)**
Fu Manchu **16.19**
fumaric **24.2.26(.5)**
fumarole **40.18.14**
fumarolic **24.2.27(.9)**
fumble **40.20.19**
fumbler **17.34.20**
fumblingly **1.31.28(.1.18)**
fume **27.14**
fumeless **34.18.29(.26)**
fumigant **22.26.15(.12)**
fumigate **22.4.12(.5)**
fumigation **28.17.25(.3.6)**
fumigator **17.12.4(.8)**
fumingly **1.31.28(.1.7)**
fumitory **1.29.11(.8.7)**
fumy **1.15.12**
fun **28.13**
Funafuti **1.10.15**
funambulist **22.29.2(.31.5)**
funboard **23.12.2(.12)**
Funchal **40.8.13**
function **28.17.25(.15.6)**
functional **40.26.13(.14.6)**
functionalism **27.15.21(.2.15)**
functionalist **22.29.2(.31.3)**
functionality **1.10.16(.32.8)**
functionally **1.31.17(.14.3)**
functionary **1.29.11(.13.2)**
functionate **22.4.14(.9.3)**
functionless **34.18.29(.27)**
functor **17.12.21(.8)**

fund **23.24.12**
fundament **22.26.15(.13.2)**
fundamental **40.21.17(.2)**
fundamentalism **27.15.21(.2.15)**
fundamentalist **22.29.2(.31.2)**
fundamentality **1.10.16(.32.3)**
fundamentally **1.31.17(.9.3)**
fundholder **17.13.23(.8)**
fundholding **29.1.13(.16)**
fundi **14.9**
fundus **34.18.12**
Fundy **1.11.20(.7)**
funebrial **40.3.14(.8)**
funeral **40.16.13(.12.2)**
funerary **1.29.11(.25)**
funereal **40.3.14(.2)**
funereally **1.31.3(.11)**
funfair **6.10**
fungal **40.24.14(.4)**
fungi **14.11, 14.21**
fungibility **1.10.16(.22.1)**
fungible **40.20.16(.25)**
fungicidal **40.22.11**
fungicide **23.15.11(.6)**
fungiform **27.10.5(.2)**
fungistatic **24.2.10(.4.1)**
fungistatically **1.31.24(.9.4)**
fungivorous **34.18.27(.21)**
fungo **19.13.12**
fungoid **23.13.10**
fungous **34.18.14(.8)**
fungus **34.18.14(.8)**
funhouse **34.8.6(.16)**
funicle **40.23.12(.11)**
funicular **17.34.16(.21.2)**
funiculi **14.25.9**
funiculus **34.18.29(.17.6)**
funk **24.19.7**
funkia **3.6.8**
funkily **1.31.17(.11)**
funkiness **34.18.16(.2.4)**
funkster **17.12.24(.20)**
funky **1.12.16**
fun-lover **17.21.9**
fun-loving **29.1.20**
funnel **40.26.10**
funnily **1.31.17(.14.1)**
funniness **34.18.16(.2.5)**
funniosity **1.10.16(.16.2)**
funny **1.16.12**
funster **17.12.24(.23)**
fur **18**
furbelow **19.29.12**
furbish **36.2.10**
furbisher **17.26.14**

Furby **1.9.12**
furcate **22.4.11**
furcation **28.17.25(.3.5)**
furfuraceous **34.18.22(.3)**
Furies **35.2.17**
furious **34.3.15(.5)**
furiously **1.31.33(.1.4)**
furiousness
 34.18.16(.31.1)
furl **40.17**
furlable **40.20.16(.29)**
furless **34.18.29(.18)**
furlong **29.6.15**
furlough **19.29.13**
furmety **1.10.16(.12)**
furnace **34.18.16(.16)**
Furneaux **19.15.13**
Furness **34.5.6,**
 34.18.16(.16)
furnish **36.2.16(.14)**
furnisher **17.26.14**
furnishing **29.1.25**
furnishings **35.27**
furniture **17.28.15**
Furnivall **40.28.11**
furore **1.29.8, 12.21**
furores **35.2.17, 35.12**
furphy **1.18.10**
furrier **3.22.10**
furriery **1.29.2(.11)**
furriness **34.18.16(.2.9)**
furring **29.1.30(.9)**
furrow **19.27.8**
furrowless **34.18.29(.19)**
furrowy **1(.7)**
furry **1.29.12**
further **17.23.13**
furtherance **34.24.10(.16)**
furtherer **17.32.14(.15)**
furthermore **12.9, 12.9.4**
furthermost **22.29.17(.4)**
furthest **22.29.15(.16)**
furtive **31.2.1(.10)**
furtively **1.31.30(.7.1)**
furtiveness
 34.18.16(.28.1)
furuncle **40.23.15**
furuncular
 17.34.16(.21.2)
furunculosis
 34.2.17(.11.2)
furunculous
 34.18.29(.17.6)
fury **1.29.8, 1.29.11(.3)**
furze **35.19**
furzy **1.23.14**
fusaria **3.22.4**
fusarium **27.3.17(.3)**
fuscous **34.18.13(.14)**
fuse **35.17**
fusee **2.23**

fusel **40.32.13**
fuselage **37.4.11, 39.2.23**
fuseless **34.18.29(.34)**
fusibility **1.10.16(.22.1)**
fusible **40.20.16(.22)**
fusiform **27.10.5(.2)**
fusil **40.2.15, 40.32.13**
fusilier **3.24**
fusillade **23.4.16, 23.9.22**
fusilli **1.31.1**
fusion **28.17.26(.4)**
fusional **40.26.13(.14.8)**
fusionist **22.29.2(.18.3)**
fuss **34.14**
fusser **17.24.12**
fussily **1.31.17(.20)**
fussiness **34.18.16(.2.7)**
fusspot **22.11.2**
fussy **1.22.12**
fustanella **17.34.5(.8)**
fustian **28.3.3**
fustic **24.2.10(.15.4)**
fustigate **22.4.12(.5)**
fustigation **28.17.25(.3.6)**
fustily **1.31.17(.9.3)**
fustiness **34.18.16(.2.3)**
fusty **1.10.26(.8)**
futharc **24.8.11**
futhorc **24.10.7**
futile **40.13.3(.3)**
futilely **1.31.38**
futileness **34.18.16(.37.1)**
futilitarian **28.3.20(.4)**
futility **1.10.16(.23)**
futon **28.10.9**
futtock **24.16.4**
future **17.28.14**
futureless **34.18.29(.17.5)**
futurism **27.15.21(.2.14)**
futurist **22.29.2(.29.4)**
futuristic **24.2.10(.15.2)**
futuristically **1.31.24(.9.6)**
futurity **1.10.16(.21.2)**
futurologist **22.29.2(.26.4)**
futurology **1.26.10(.11.5)**
futz **34.22.11**
fuze **35.17**
fuzee **2.23**
fuzz **35.14**
fuzzily **1.31.17(.21)**
fuzziness **34.18.16(.2.7)**
fuzzy **1.23.11**
fuzzy-wuzzy **1.23.11**
Fyfe **30.12**
Fylde **23.31.9**
fylfot **22.11.10**
Fylingdales **35.30.3**
Fyne **28.14**
fyrd **23.3, 23.19**
fytte **22.2**

g **2**
gab **21.6**
Gabalfa **17.21.19**
gabber **17.11.5**
Gabbitas **34.7.7**
gabble **40.20.6**
gabbler **17.34.20**
gabbro **19.27.14**
gabbroic **24.2.7**
gabbroid **23.13.19**
gabby **1.9.5**
gabelle **40.5.2**
gaberdine **28.1.10**
gabfest **22.29.5(.4)**
gabion **28.3.2**
gabionade **23.4.8**
gabionage **39.2.15**
gable **40.20.4**
gablet **22.19.26(.16)**
Gabo **19.9.4**
Gabon **28.10.8**
Gabonese **35.1.12**
Gábor **12.4**
Gaborone **1.16.17(.13)**
Gabriel **40.3.14(.8)**
Gabrielle **40.5**
gad **23.7**
gadabout **22.9.6**
Gadarene **28.1.25**
Gaddafi **1.18.4**
gadfly **14.25.14**
gadget **22.19.22**
gadgeteer **3.4**
gadgetry **1.29.15(.11)**
gadgety **1.10.16(.18)**
Gadhelic **24.2.27(.4)**
gadid **23.2.9**
gadoid **23.13.8**
gadolinite **22.16.14(.6)**
gadolinium **27.3.8(.2)**
gadroon **28.16.13**
gadwall **40.10.17**
gadzooks **34.23.14**
Gaea **17.1**
Gael **40.4**
Gaeldom **27.15.10(.20)**
Gaelic **24.2.27(.3)**
Gaeltacht **22.24**
Gaenor **17.18.3**
gaff **30.5**
gaffe **30.5**
gaffer **17.20.5**
Gaffney **1.16.24**
Gafsa **17.24.23**
gag **26.5**
gaga **10.9**
Gagarin **28.17.31(.6)**
gage **39.4**
gaggle **40.24.4**
gagman **28.7.10(.14)**

gagmen **28.5.7(.18)**
gagster **17.12.24(.21)**
Gaia **17.6**
Gaian **28.17.5**
gaiety **1.10.16(.2)**
gaijin **28.2.27**
Gail **40.4**
gaillardia **3.5.5**
gaily **1.31.4**
gain **28.4**
gainable **40.20.16(.16.1)**
gainer **17.18.3**
Gaines **35.26.4**
gainful **40.27.22**
gainfully **1.31.17(.16.2)**
gainfulness
 34.18.16(.37.2)
gainings **35.27**
gainsaid **23.5.10**
gainsay **4.18**
gainsayer **17.2.7**
Gainsborough
 17.32.14(.5)
'gainst **22.29.21**
Gairloch **24.9.16(.2), 25.6**
gait **22.4**
gaiter **17.12.4**
Gaitskell **40.23.16**
Gaius **34.18.5**
gal **40.6**
gala **17.34.4, 17.34.8**
galactagogue **26.7.6**
galactic **24.2.10(.13)**
galactose **34.20.4, 35.20.3**
galago **19.13.3**
galah **10.25**
Galahad **23.7.15**
galantine **28.1.9**
galanty show **19**
Galapagos **34.18.14(.5)**
Galashiels **35.30.1**
Galatea **3.4**
Galatia **3.16.3, 17.26.3**
Galatian **28.17.25(.3.14)**
galaxy **1.22.22**
Galba **17.11.20**
galbanum **27.15.14(.11)**
Galbraith **32.4**
gale **40.4**
galea **3.24.3**
galeae **14.2**
galeate **22.3.13**
galeated **23.18.9(.3)**
Galen **28.17.33(.3)**
galena **17.18.1(.16)**
galenic **24.2.15(.4)**
galenical **40.23.12(.11)**
galette **22.5.21**
Galicia **3.14.2, 3.16.2,**
 17.26.2

Galician 28.3.13, 28.3.15, 28.17.25(.2.6)
Galilean 28.17.1(.13)
Galilee 2.32.9(.9)
Galileo 19.2
galimatias 34.3.3, 34.18.22(.3)
galingale 40.4.5
galipot 22.11.2
gall 40.10
galla 17.34.4, 17.34.8
Galla 17.34.6
Gallagher 17.15, 17.16.13, 17.30
gallant 22.26.6, 22.26.15(.25)
gallantly 1.31.22(.20.5)
gallantry 1.29.15(.15)
Galle 40.10
galleon 28.3.21(.5)
galleria 17.1.16
gallery 1.29.11(.27)
galleryite 22.16.2
galley 1.31.7
galliambic 24.2.9(.8)
galliard 23.9.2
Gallic 24.2.27(.6)
Gallican 28.17.13(.13)
Gallicanism 27.15.21(.2.9)
gallice 2.22.7
Gallicism 27.15.21(.2.12)
Gallicize 35.15.16(.4)
galligaskins 35.26.2
gallimaufry 1.29.21
gallinaceous 34.18.22(.3)
gallingly 1.31.28(.1.18)
gallinule 40.15.9(.8)
galliot 22.3.13
Gallipoli 1.31.17(.7)
gallipot 22.11.2
gallium 27.3.18
gallivant 22.26.6
galliwasp 20.17
gallnut 22.15.6
Gallo 19.29.5
Gallois 10.22.14
Gallomania 3.9.3(.5)
Gallomaniac 24.6.1
gallon 28.17.33(.5)
gallonage 39.2.15
galloon 28.16.15
gallop 20.13.7
galloper 17.10.14
Gallophile 40.13.9
Gallophobe 21.16.1
Gallophobia 3.3.9
Gallo-Roman 28.17.16(.18)
galloway 4.25.9
gallowglass 34.9.7
gallows 35.20.14

gallstone 28.19.4(.9)
Gallup 20.13.7
galluses 35.18.17
gall-wasp 20.17
galoot 22.18.11
galop 20.13.7
galore 12.23
galosh 36.9.6
Galsworthy 1.21
Galt 22.32.5, 22.32.6
Galton 28.17.11(.27)
galumph 30.18
Galvani 1.16.8
galvanic 24.2.15(.5)
galvanically 1.31.24(.9.8)
galvanism 27.15.21(.2.9)
galvanist 22.29.2(.18.1)
galvanization 28.17.25(.3.11)
galvanize 35.15.12(.5)
galvanizer 17.25.12(.6)
galvanometer 17.12.16(.9.2)
galvanometric 24.2.26(.14.2)
Galveston 28.17.11(.25)
galvo 19.17
Galway 4.25.26
gam 27.6
Gama,da 17.17.7
Gamage 39.2.14
Gamaliel 40.3.15
gamay 4.13
gamba 17.11.17(.4)
Gambaccini 1.16.1(.12)
gambade 23.4.2, 23.9.6
gambado 19.11.4, 19.11.7
Gambia 3.3.11
Gambian 28.3.2
gambier 3.3.11
gambit 22.2.6
gamble 40.20.19
gambler 17.34.20
gamboge 37.7, 37.9, 39.16
gambol 40.20.19
gambrel 40.16.13(.15)
game 27.4
gamebook 24.14.3
gamecock 24.9.6
gamefowl 40.7
gamekeeper 17.10.1
gamekeeping 29.1.10(.1)
gamelan 28.7.22
gamely 1.31.26(.3)
gameness 34.18.16(.24)
gamesman 28.17.16(.30)
gamesmanship 20.2.7(.19)
gamesome 27.15.20(.17)
gamesomely 1.31.26(.11)

gamesomeness 34.18.16(.24)
gamesplayer 17.2.10
gamester 17.12.24(.22)
gametangia 3.19.9, 17.29.16(.4)
gametangium 27.3.14, 27.3.15
gamete 22.1.5
gametic 24.2.10(.3.1)
gametocyte 22.16.19(.9)
gametogenesis 34.2.17(.10.3)
gametophyte 22.16.16
gametophytic 24.2.10(.2.3)
gamey 1.15.3
gamily 1.31.17(.13)
gamin 28.2.17(.2)
gamine 28.1.13
gaminess 34.18.16(.2.5)
gamma 17.17.6
gammadion 28.3.4(.3)
gammer 17.17.6
gamminess 34.18.16(.2.5)
gammon 28.17.16(.7)
gammy 1.15.6
Gamow 19.14.6
gamp 20.16.3
gamut 22.19.14
gamy 1.15.3
gander 17.13.20(.4)
Gandhi 1.11.20(.4)
Ganesha 17.26.3
gang 29.4
gangboard 23.12.2(.13)
gangbuster 17.12.24(.10)
ganger 17.19.2
Ganges 35.1.21
Gangetic 24.2.10(.3.2)
gangland 23.24.6(.13)
gangle 40.24.14(.2)
ganglia 3.24.15
gangliar 3.24.15
gangliform 17.10.5(.2)
gangling 29.1.31(.20)
ganglion 28.3.21(.14)
ganglionated 23.18.9(.3)
ganglionic 24.2.15(.6.1)
gangly 1.31.25
gangplank 24.19.3(.7)
gangrene 28.1.25(.9)
gangrenous 34.18.16(.15.3)
gangster 17.12.24(.24)
gangsterism 27.15.21(.2.14)
gangue 29.4
gangway 4.25.18
ganister 17.12.24(.14)
ganja 17.29.16(.4)

gannet 22.19.15(.3)
gannetry 1.29.15(.9)
Gannex 34.23.4(.6)
Gannon 28.17.17(.5)
ganoid 23.13.12
gantlet 22.19.26(.17)
gantry 1.29.15(.15)
Ganymede 23.1.4
gaol 40.4
gaolbird 23.19.1
gaoler 17.34.4
gap 20.5
gape 20.3
gaper 17.10.3
gapeworm 27.16.7
gapingly 1.31.28(.1.2)
gappy 1.8.5
gar 10
garage 37.4.9, 39.2.22(.4), 39.8
garam masala 17.34.8
garb 21.7
garbage 39.2.9
garbanzo 19.21
Garbett 22.19.9
garble 40.20.7
garbler 17.34.20
Garbo 19.9.4
garboard 23.12.2(.3)
García 1.11.11
garçon 11.12, 28.10.18
Garda 17.13.7
Gardaí 2.13
garden 28.17.12(.8)
gardener 17.18.16(.5)
gardenesque 24.20.3
gardenia 3.9.1
Gardner 17.18.22
Gardyne 28.14.6
Gareloch 24.9.16(.2), 25.6
Gareth 32.14.16
Garfield 23.31.1(.2)
garfish 36.2.18(.5)
Garforth 32.10, 32.14.13
Garfunkel 40.23.15
garganey 1.16.15(.10)
Gargantua 17.7.12(.3)
gargantuan 28.17.6
garget 22.19.13
gargle 40.24.5
gargoyle 40.11.5
gargoylism 27.15.21(.2.15)
Garibaldi 1.11.23
garish 36.2.25
garishly 1.31.35(.7.4)
garishness 34.18.16(.33.6)
garland 23.24.16(.16.2)
garlic 24.2.27(.8)
garlicky 1.12.13

Garman 28.17.16(.9)
garment 22.26.15(.13.1)
Garmondsway 4.25.23
garner 17.18.8
garnet 22.19.15(.4)
Garnett 22.19.15(.4)
garnish 36.2.16(.7)
garnishee 2.24
garnishing 29.1.25
garnishment 22.26.15(.13.6)
garniture 17.28.15
Garonne 28.10.24
garpike 24.13.1
Garrard 23.9.20, 23.18.27
Garratt 22.19.24(.4)
garret 22.19.24(.4)
garreteer 17.1.3
Garrick 24.2.26(.5)
garrison 28.17.23(.14)
garrotte 22.11.15
garrotter 17.12.9
garrulity 1.10.16(.35)
garrulous 34.18.29(.17.5)
garrulously 1.31.33(.12.6)
garrulousness 34.18.16(.31.6)
Garry 1.29.5
garrya 3.22.5
garter 17.12.8
garth 32.8
garuda 17.13.13
Garvey 1.19.6
Gary 1.29.5
Garza 17.25.7
gas 34.7
gasbag 26.5.1
gas chamber 17.11.17(.2)
Gascoigne 28.12
Gascon 28.17.13(.18)
gasconade 23.4.8
Gascony 1.16.15(.9)
gaseous 34.3.10
gaseousness 34.18.16(.31.1)
gasfield 23.31.1(.2)
gash 36.6
gasholder 17.13.23(.8)
gashouse 34.8.6(.20)
gasification 28.17.25(.3.5)
gasify 14.14.4(.9)
Gaskell 40.23.16
gasket 22.19.12(.14)
gaskin 28.2.13(.14)
gaslamp 20.16.3
gaslight 22.16.25(.19)
gasman 28.7.10(.20)
gasmen 28.5.7(.24)
gasohol 40.9.17
gasoline 28.1.27

gasometer 17.12.16(.9.2)
gasp 20.17
gasper 17.10.18
gaspereau 19.27.11
gaspereaux 35.20.12
gasproof 30.13.4
Gassendi 1.11.20(.3)
gasser 17.24.6
gassiness 34.18.16(.2.7)
gassy 1.22.6
gasteropod 23.10.1
Gasthaus 34.8.6(.11)
Gasthäuser 17.25.10
Gasthof 30.8.10
Gasthöfe 17.20.7
gastrectomy 1.15.13(.1)
gastric 24.2.26(.14.5)
gastritis 34.18.11(.8)
gastroenteric 24.2.26(.4)
gastroenteritis 34.18.11(.8)
gastroenterology 1.26.10(.11.5)
gastrointestinal 40.26.11, 40.26.13(.4)
gastronome 27.17.8
gastronomic 24.2.14(.6)
gastronomical 40.23.12(.10)
gastronomically 1.31.24(.9.8)
gastronomy 1.15.13(.5)
gastropod 23.10.1
gastropodous 34.18.12
gastroscope 20.15.4(.1)
gastrula 17.34.16(.20)
gastrulae 2.32.9(.7)
gasworks 34.23.16
gat 22.7
gate 22.4
gateau 19.10.6
gateaux 35.20.3
gatecrash 36.6.9
gatecrasher 17.26.6
gatefold 23.31.13(.7)
gatehouse 34.8.6(.11)
gatekeeper 17.10.1
gateleg 26.4
gatelegged 23.22
gateman 28.7.10(.11)
gatemen 28.5.7(.15)
gatepost 22.29.17(.1)
Gates 34.22.3
Gateshead 23.5.13
gateway 4.25.12
gather 17.23.5
gatherer 17.32.14(.15)
gathering 29.1.30(.8)
Gatling 29.1.31(.17)
gator 17.12.4
GATT 22.7

Gatting 29.1.12(.5)
Gatwick 24.2.25
gauche 36.16
gauchely 1.31.35(.7.4)
gaucheness 34.18.16(.33.6)
gaucherie 1.29.11(.20)
gaucho 19.24
gaud 23.12
gaudeamus 34.18.15(.5)
Gaudí 1.11.8
gaudily 1.31.17(.10)
gaudiness 34.18.16(.2.3)
gaudy 1.11.11
gauge 39.4
gaugeable 40.20.16(.25)
gauger 17.29.3
Gauguin 8, 28.7.9
Gaul 40.10
gauleiter 17.12.13(.9)
Gaulish 36.2.27
Gaullism 27.15.21(.2.15)
Gaullist 22.29.2(.31.5)
Gauloise 35.9
gault 22.32.5, 22.32.6
gaultheria 3.22.1
gaunt 22.26.10
gauntlet 22.19.26(.17)
gauntly 1.31.22(.20.1)
gauntness 34.18.16(.20.4)
gauntry 1.29.15(.15)
gaur 17.3
Gauss 34.8
Gaussian 28.3.13
Gautama 17.17.14(.2)
gauze 35.12
gauzily 1.31.17(.21)
gauziness 34.18.16(.2.7)
gauzy 1.23.9
gave 31.3
gavel 40.28.5
gavial 40.3.8
Gavin 28.2.20
gavotte 22.11.11
Gawain 28.4.17
Gawd 23.12
gawk 24.10
gawkily 1.31.17(.11)
gawkiness 34.18.16(.2.4)
gawkish 36.2.13
gawky 1.12.8
gawp 20.8
gawper 17.10.9
gay 4
gayal 40.6.15, 40.8.16
Gaydon 28.17.12(.4)
Gaye 4
gayety 1.10.16(.2)
Gayle 40.4

Gay-Lussac 24.6.14
gayness 34.18.16(.4)
Gaynor 17.18.3
Gaza 17.25.7
gazania 3.9.3(.7)
gaze 35.4
gazebo 19.9.1
gazelle 40.5.12
gazer 17.25.3
gazette 22.5.14
gazetteer 3.4
gazpacho 19.24
gazump 20.16.5
gazumper 17.10.17
gazunder 17.13.20(.10)
Gdansk 24.20.13
GDP 2.9
Gdynia 3.9.2
gean 28.1
gear 3
gearbox 34.23.8(.2)
gearing 29.1.30(.2)
gearstick 24.2.10(.15.4)
gearwheel 40.1.14
Geary 1.29.2
Geber 17.11.1
gecko 19.12.4
Geddes 34.2.9
gee 2
Geechee 2.26
gee-gee 2.27
geek 24.1
Geelong 29.6.15
geese 34.1
gee-string 29.1.30(.13)
gee-whiz 35.2.16
Ge'ez 35.5.1
geezer 17.25.1
gefilte fish 36.2
Gehenna 17.18.4
Gehrig 26.2.10
Geiger counter 17.12.22(.5)
Geikie 1.12.1
Geisel 40.31.11
geisha 17.26.3
Geissler 17.34.27
gel 40.5
gelada 17.13.7
gelatin 28.2.11(.10)
gelatine 28.1.9(.3)
gelatinization 28.17.25(.3.12)
gelatinize 35.15.12(.5)
gelatinous 34.18.16(.15.2)
gelatinously 1.31.33(.12.3)
gelation 28.17.25(.3.14)
gelato 19.10.6
gelcoat 22.21.5

geld **23.31.4**
Geldart **22.10.4**
Gelderland **23.24.6(.13)**
gelding **29.1.13(.16)**
Geldof **30.8.5**
gelid **23.2.23**
gelignite **22.16.14(.10)**
Gell **40.5**
Gelligaer **6.7, 17.6.6**
Gell-Mann **28.7.10**
gelly **1.31.5**
gelsemium **27.3.7**
gelt **22.32.2**
gem **27.5**
Gemara **17.32.7**
gematria **3.22.15**
geminal **40.26.13(.8)**
geminally **1.31.17(.14.2)**
geminate **22.4.14(.9.2), 22.19.15(.9)**
gemination **28.17.25(.3.8)**
Gemini **2.17.10, 14.13**
Geminian **28.17.1(.7), 28.17.5**
Geminids **35.23.2**
gemlike **24.13.7(.16)**
gemma **17.17.5**
gemmae **2.16**
gemmation **28.17.25(.3.7)**
Gemmell **40.25.3**
gemmiferous **34.18.27(.20)**
gemmiparous **34.18.27(.12)**
gemmologist **22.29.2(.26.4)**
gemmology **1.26.10(.11.4)**
gemmule **40.15.9(.7)**
gemmy **1.15.4**
gemologist **22.29.2(.26.4)**
gemsbok **24.9.3**
gemstone **28.19.4(.9)**
gemütlich **24.2.27(.15), 25.1, 36.2.27**
gen **28.5**
gendarme **27.8.4**
gendarmerie **1.29.11(.12)**
gender **17.13.20(.3)**
gene **28.1**
genealogical **40.23.12(.17.2)**
genealogically **1.31.24(.9.11)**
genealogist **22.29.2(.26.1)**
genealogize **35.15.18**
genealogy **1.26.10(.10)**
genera **17.32.14(.11)**
generable **40.20.16(.27.4)**
general **40.16.13(.12.2)**

generalisability **1.10.16(.22.3)**
generalissimo **19.14.12**
generalist **22.29.2(.31.4)**
generality **1.10.16(.32.13)**
generalizability **1.10.16(.22.3)**
generalizable **40.20.16(.22)**
generalization **28.17.25(.3.12)**
generalize **35.15.21(.4.7)**
generalizer **17.25.12(.15)**
generally **1.31.17(.27.2)**
generalness **34.18.16(.37.3)**
generalship **20.2.7(.24)**
generate **22.4.22(.6)**
generation **28.17.25(.3.13)**
generational **40.26.13(.14.2)**
generative **31.2.1(.9.4)**
generatively **1.31.30(.7.1)**
generativeness **34.18.16(.28.1)**
generator **17.12.4(.15)**
generic **24.2.26(.4)**
generically **1.31.24(.9.12)**
generosity **1.10.16(.16.2)**
generous **34.18.27(.19)**
generously **1.31.33(.12.5)**
generousness **34.18.16(.31.5)**
genesis **34.2.17(.10.3)**
Genet **4.14**
genet **22.2.12**
genetic **24.2.10(.3.1)**
genetically **1.31.24(.9.3)**
geneticist **22.29.2(.22)**
genette **22.5.9**
Geneva **17.21.1**
Genevan **28.17.20(.1)**
genever **17.21.1**
Genevieve **31.1.3**
Genghis Khan **28.9**
genial **40.3.7(.1), 40.16.1, 40.16.6**
geniality **1.10.16(.32.1)**
genially **1.31.3(.7)**
genic **24.2.15(.4)**
genie **1.16.1**
genii **14.2**
genipapo **19.8**
genital **40.21.12**
genitalia **3.24.3**
genitally **1.31.17(.9.2)**
genitival **40.28.9**
genitivally **1.31.17(.17)**
genitive **31.2.1(.9.2)**
genito-urinary **1.29.11(.13.2)**

genius **34.3.6(.1)**
genizah **17.25.1**
genlock **24.9.16(.16)**
Gennesaret **22.19.24(.9)**
genoa **17.9.7**
genocidal **40.22.11**
genocide **23.15.11(.6)**
Genoese **35.1**
genome **27.17.8**
genotype **20.10.2**
genotypic **24.2.8(.1)**
Genova **17.21.12**
genre **17.32.9, 17.32.24**
gens **35.26.5**
gent **22.26.4**
genteel **40.1.3**
genteelism **27.15.21(.2.15)**
genteelly **1.31.38**
genteelness **34.18.16(.37.1)**
gentes **35.1.7(.9)**
gentian **28.3.15, 28.17.25(.16)**
gentile **40.13.3(.9)**
gentility **1.10.16(.23)**
gentle **40.21.17(.2)**
gentlefolk **24.18.7**
gentleman **28.17.16(.35)**
gentlemanliness **34.18.16(.2.10)**
gentlemanly **1.31.27(.14)**
gentleness **34.18.16(.37.5)**
gentlewoman **28.17.16(.14)**
gentlewomen **28.2.17(.1)**
gently **1.31.22(.20.1)**
gentoo **16.7.7**
gentrification **28.17.25(.3.5)**
gentrifier **17.6.9(.4)**
gentrify **14.14.4(.14)**
gentry **1.29.15(.15)**
genuflect **22.23.4(.11)**
genuflection **28.17.25(.15.2)**
genuflector **17.12.21(.2)**
genuflectory **1.29.11(.8.12)**
genuine **28.2.6**
genuinely **1.31.27(.13)**
genuineness **34.18.16(.25)**
genus **34.18.16(.1)**
geobotanist **22.29.2(.18.1)**
geobotany **1.16.15(.7)**
geocentric **24.2.26(.14.4)**
geocentrically **1.31.24(.9.12)**
geochemical **40.23.12(.10)**

geochemist **22.29.2(.17)**
geochemistry **1.29.15(.17)**
geochronological **40.23.12(.17.2)**
geochronologist **22.29.2(.26.4)**
geochronology **1.26.10(.11.4)**
geode **23.20.1**
geodesic **24.2.20(.1), 24.2.21**
geodesist **22.29.2(.22)**
geodesy **1.22.16(.5)**
geodetic **24.2.10(.3.1)**
geodic **24.2.11(.7)**
Geoff **30.4**
Geoffrey **1.29.21**
geographer **17.20.12(.5)**
geographic **24.2.16(.3)**
geographical **40.23.12(.12)**
geographically **1.31.24(.9.9)**
geography **1.18.9(.3.2)**
geoid **23.13.1**
geologic **24.2.24(.4)**
geological **40.23.12(.17.2)**
geologically **1.31.24(.9.11)**
geologist **22.29.2(.26.2)**
geologize **35.15.18**
geology **1.26.10(.11.1)**
geomagnetic **24.2.10(.3.1)**
geomagnetically **1.31.24(.9.3)**
geomagnetism **27.15.21(.2.4)**
geomancy **1.22.23(.4)**
geomantic **24.2.10(.14)**
geometer **17.12.16(.9.2)**
geometric **24.2.26(.14.2)**
geometrical **40.23.12(.18)**
geometrically **1.31.24(.9.12)**
geometrician **28.17.25(.2.6)**
geometrize **35.15.20(.4)**
geometry **1.29.15(.8)**
geomorphological **40.23.12(.17.2)**
geomorphologist **22.29.2(.26.4)**
geomorphology **1.26.10(.11.5)**
geophagy **1.26.10(.6)**
geophone **28.19.11**
geophysical **40.23.12(.16)**
geophysically **1.31.24(.9.10)**
geophysicist **22.29.2(.22)**
geophysics **34.23.2(.11)**

g

geopolitical **40.23.12(.7.1)**
geopolitically
1.31.24(.9.3)
geopolitician
28.17.25(.2.2)
geopolitics **34.23.2(.3)**
Geordie **1.11.11**
George **39.10**
Georgetown **28.8.1**
Georgette **22.5.17**
Georgia **17.29.9**
Georgian **28.17.28(.6)**
Georgiana **17.18.8**
georgic **24.2.24(.5)**
Georgie **1.26.7**
Georgina **17.18.1(.13)**
geoscience **34.24.10(.5)**
geoscientist **22.29.2(.13)**
geosphere **3.10.5**
geostationary
1.29.11(.13.2)
geostrophic **24.2.16(.4)**
geosynchronous
34.18.16(.15.3)
geotechnical
40.23.12(.11)
geothermal **40.25.11**
geothermally
1.31.17(.13)
geotropic **24.2.8(.5)**
geotropism **27.15.21(.2.2)**
Geraint **22.26.13**
Gerald **23.31.11**
Geraldine **28.1.10**
Geraldton **28.17.11(.19)**
geranium **27.3.8(.3)**
Gerard **23.9.20**
gerbera **17.32.14(.5)**
gerbil **40.2.4, 40.20.17**
Gerda **17.13.16**
gerenuk **24.14.6**
gerfalcon **28.17.13(.19)**
geriatric **24.2.26(.14.3)**
geriatrician **28.17.25(.2.6)**
geriatrist **22.29.2(.29.5)**
germ **27.16**
Germaine **28.4.7**
German **28.17.16(.17)**
germander **17.13.20(.4)**
germane **28.4.7**
germanely **1.31.27(.4)**
germaneness
34.18.16(.25)
Germanic **24.2.15(.5)**
Germanicism
27.15.21(.2.12)
Germanicus **34.18.13(.10)**
Germanism
27.15.21(.2.9)
Germanist **22.29.2(.18.1)**
germanium **27.3.8(.3)**

Germanization
28.17.25(.3.11)
Germanize **35.15.12(.5)**
Germanizer **17.25.12(.6)**
germanous
34.18.16(.15.3)
Germany **1.16.15(.11)**
germen **28.17.16(.17)**
germicidal **40.22.11**
germicide **23.15.11(.6)**
germinal **40.26.13(.8)**
germinally **1.31.17(.14.2)**
germinant **22.26.15(.14)**
germinate **22.4.14(.9.2)**
germination
28.17.25(.3.8)
germinative **31.2.1(.9.2)**
germinator **17.12.4(.10)**
Germiston **28.17.11(.25)**
Germolene **28.1.27(.7)**
germon **28.17.16(.17)**
germy **1.15.14**
Geronimo **19.14.12**
gerontocracy **1.22.16(.13)**
gerontological
40.23.12(.17.2)
gerontologist
22.29.2(.26.3)
gerontology
1.26.10(.11.2)
Gerry **1.29.3**
gerrymander **17.13.20(.4)**
gerrymanderer
17.32.14(.7)
Gershwin **28.2.28**
Gertie **1.10.17**
Gertrude **23.17.3**
gerund **23.24.12,
23.24.16(.15)**
gerundial **40.3.4**
gerundival **40.28.9**
gerundive **31.2.2**
Gervaise **34.4.10, 35.4.10**
Gervase **34.4.10**
gesnieriad **23.7.2**
gesso **19.20.3**
gest **22.29.5**
gestagen **28.17.28(.9)**
gestagenic **24.2.15(.4)**
gestalt **22.32.3, 22.32.4**
gestaltism **27.15.21(.2.4)**
gestaltist **22.29.2(.13)**
Gestapo **19.8**
gestate **22.4.9(.9)**
gestation **28.17.25(.3.3)**
gestatorial **40.3.14(.5)**
gestatory **1.29.11(.8.2)**
Gestetner **17.18.21**
gesticulate **22.4.23(.7.3)**
gesticulation
28.17.25(.3.14)

gesticulative **31.2.1(.9.4)**
gesticulator **17.12.4(.16)**
gesticulatory
1.29.11(.8.10)
gestural **40.16.13(.12.3)**
gesture **17.28.24**
gesturer **17.32.14(.19)**
gesundheit **22.16.22**
get **22.5**
geta **17.12.4**
get-at-able **40.20.16(.11.1)**
getaway **4.25.9**
Gethin **28.2.21**
Gethsemane **1.16.15(.11)**
gettable **40.20.16(.11.1)**
getter **17.12.5**
Getty **1.10.4**
Gettysburg **26.14.1(.11)**
geum **27.15.1**
gewgaw **12.8**
Gewürztraminer
17.18.1(.6)
geyser **17.25.1, 17.25.12**
Ghana **17.18.8**
Ghanaian **28.17.2**
gharial **40.3.14(.4), 40.8,
40.8.1**
gharry **1.29.5**
ghastlily **1.31.17(.29)**
ghastliness
34.18.16(.2.10)
ghastly **1.31.22(.22)**
ghat **22.10, 22.13, 22.15**
Ghazi **1.23.7**
ghee **2**
Gheg **26.4**
Ghent **22.26.4**
gherao **9.16**
gherkin **28.2.13(.7)**
ghetto **19.10.4**
ghettoize **35.15.4**
ghi **2**
Ghibelline **28.1.27(.7),
28.14.19(.11)**
Ghibellinism
27.15.21(.2.9)
Ghiberti **1.10.5**
ghillie **1.31.2**
ghost **22.29.17**
ghostbuster **17.12.24(.10)**
ghostbusting **29.1.12(.21)**
ghostlike **24.13.7(.12)**
ghostliness
34.18.16(.2.10)
ghostly **1.31.22(.22)**
ghostwriter **17.12.13(.8)**
ghoul **40.15**
ghoulish **36.2.27**
ghoulishly **1.31.35(.7.4)**
ghoulishness
34.18.16(.33.6)

ghyll **40.2**
Giacometti **1.10.4**
giant **22.26.15(.4)**
giantess **34.5.2,
34.18.11(.14)**
giantism **27.15.21(.2.4)**
giaour **17.3**
giardiasis **34.2.17(.10.1)**
gib **21.2**
Gibb **21.2**
gibber **17.11.2**
gibberellin **28.2.31(.4)**
gibberish **36.2.25**
gibbet **22.19.9**
gibbon **28.17.10**
Gibbons **35.26.13(.6)**
gibbosity **1.10.16(.16.2)**
gibbous **34.18.10**
gibbously **1.31.33(.12.2)**
gibbousness
34.18.16(.31.3)
Gibbs **35.21**
gibe **21.12**
Gibeon **28.3.2**
Gibeonite **22.16.14(.1)**
giber **17.11.11**
giblets **34.22.15**
Gibraltar **17.12.26(.5)**
Gibraltarian **28.3.20(.4)**
Gibson **28.17.23(.18)**
gid **23.2**
giddily **1.31.17(.10)**
giddiness **34.18.16(.2.3)**
giddy **1.11.2**
Gide **23.1**
Gideon **28.3.4(.2)**
gie **2**
Gielgud **23.16.3**
gift **22.27.1**
giftedly **1.31.23(.14.3)**
giftedness **34.18.16(.21.1)**
giftware **6.18.7**
giftwrap **20.5.6**
gig **26.2**
gigabit **22.2.6**
gigabyte **22.16.8**
gigaflop **20.7.13**
gigametre **17.12.1(.6)**
gigantesque **24.20.3**
gigantic **24.2.10(.14)**
gigantically **1.31.24(.9.5)**
gigantism **27.15.21(.2.4)**
Gigantopithecus
34.18.13(.10)
gigawatt **22.11.14**
giggle **40.24.2**
giggler **17.34.24**
Giggleswick **24.2.25**
giggliness **34.18.16(.2.10)**
giggly **1.31.25**

Gigli **1.31.1**
GIGO **19.13.2**
gigolo **19.29.12**
gigot **22.19.13**
gigue **26.1**
Gila monster
　17.12.24(.23)
Gilbert **22.19.9**
Gilbertian **28.3.3**
gild **23.31.2**
gilded **23.18.10(.15)**
gilder **17.13.23(.2)**
Gilead **23.7.2**
Giles **35.30.10**
gilet **4.28**
gilgai **14.11**
Gilgamesh **36.5**
Gilgit **22.2.10**
Gill **40.2**
gill **40.2**
Gillard **23.9.22**
gill cover **17.21.9**
Gillespie **1.8.15**
Gillette **22.5.21**
Gillian **28.3.21(.2)**
gillie **1.31.2**
Gillies **35.2.19**
Gillingham **27.15.15**
gillion **28.3.21(.2)**
gill-net **22.5.9(.7)**
Gillow **19.29.2**
Gilly **1.31.2**
gilly **1.31.2**
gillyflower **17.3.11**
Gilman **28.17.16(.35)**
Gilmore **12.9.16**
Gilmour **12.9.16**
Gilpin **28.2.9**
Gilroy **13.15**
gilt **22.32.1**
gilt-edged **23.30**
giltwood **23.16.6(.9)**
gimbal **40.20.19**
gimcrack **24.6.21**
gimcrackery **1.29.11(.10)**
gimcracky **1.12.5**
gimlet **22.19.26(.21)**
gimme **1.15.2**
gimmick **24.2.14(.2)**
gimmickry **1.29.17**
gimmicky **1.12.13**
gimp **20.16.1**
gimpy **1.8.14**
Gimson **28.17.23(.23)**
gin **28.2**
Gina **17.18.1**
ging **29.1**
ginger **17.29.16(.1)**
ginger ale **40.4**
gingerbread **23.5.15**

gingerliness
　34.18.16(.2.10)
gingerly **1.31.17(.25)**
gingery **1.29.11(.21)**
gingham **27.15.15**
gingili **1.31.2**
gingiva **17.21.10, 17.21.12**
gingivae **2.19**
gingival **40.28.9, 40.28.11**
gingivitis **34.18.11(.8)**
ginglymi **2.16, 14.12**
ginglymus **34.18.15(.10)**
Gingold **23.31.13(.5)**
gink **24.19.1**
ginkgo **19.12.15**
Ginn **28.2**
ginner **17.18.2**
Ginny **1.16.2**
Gino **19.15.1**
ginormous **34.18.15(.7)**
Ginsberg **26.14.1(.11)**
ginseng **29.3**
Ginsu **16.15**
Gioconda, La **17.13.20(.7)**
Giorgione **1.16.17**
Giotto **19.10.8**
Giovanni **1.16.6, 1.16.8**
gip **20.2**
gippo **19.8**
gippy **1.8.2**
giraffe **30.7.5**
Giraldus Cambrensis
　34.2.17(.15)
girandole **40.18.6**
girasol **40.9.14**
girasole **40.18.10**
gird **23.19**
girder **17.13.16**
girdle **40.22.14**
girl **40.17**
girlfriend **23.24.5(.14)**
girlhood **23.16.5(.14)**
girlie **1.31.18**
girlish **36.2.27**
girlishly **1.31.35(.7.4)**
girlishness **34.18.16(.33.6)**
girly **1.31.18**
giro **19.27.9**
Gironde **23.24.9**
Girondin **28.2.12**
Girondist **22.29.2(.14)**
girt **22.20**
girth **32.15**
Girton **28.17.11(.16)**
Gisborne **28.18.3**
Giselle **40.5.12**
Gish **36.2**
Gissing **29.1.23**
gist **22.29.2**
git **22.2**

gîte **22.1**
gittern **28.18.4**
Gittins **35.26.2**
Giuseppe **1.8.4**
give **31.2**
giveable **40.20.16(.19)**
giveaway **4.25.9**
given **28.17.20(.2)**
Givenchy **1.24.8, 1.24.15**
giver **17.21.2**
gizmo **19.14.18**
gizzard **23.18.21**
glabella **17.34.5(.2)**
glabellae **2.32.5**
glabellar **17.34.5(.2)**
glabrous **34.18.27(.13)**
glacé **4.18.6**
glacial **40.3.10, 40.33.2**
glacially **1.31.3(.9),
　1.31.17(.22)**
glaciate **22.4.2(.9)**
glaciated **23.18.9(.3)**
glaciation **28.17.25(.3.1)**
glacier **3.14.3**
glaciological
　40.23.12(.17.2)
glaciologist **22.29.2(.26.2)**
glaciology **1.26.10(.11.1)**
glacis **1.22.6, 34.2.17(.4),
　35.2.11**
glad **23.7**
gladden **28.17.12(.6)**
gladdener **17.18.16(.5)**
gladdie **1.11.7**
gladdon **28.17.12(.6)**
glade **23.4**
gladiator **17.12.4(.1)**
gladiatorial **40.3.14(.5)**
gladioli **14.25.10**
gladiolus **34.18.29(.19)**
gladly **1.31.23(.5)**
gladness **34.18.16(.21.1)**
gladsome **27.15.20(.14)**
gladsomely **1.31.26(.11)**
gladsomeness
　34.18.16(.24)
Gladstone **28.17.11(.25)**
Gladwin **28.2.28**
Gladys **34.2.9**
Glagolitic **24.2.10(.2.5)**
glair **6**
glaire **6**
glaireous **34.18.27(.4)**
glairiness **34.18.16(.2.9)**
glairy **1.29.4**
glaive **31.3**
glam **27.6**
Glamis **35.25.5**
Glamorgan **28.17.15(.9)**
glamorize **35.15.20(.2)**

glamorous **34.18.27(.18)**
glamorously
　1.31.33(.12.5)
glamour **17.17.6**
glamourization
　28.17.25(.3.11)
glamourous **34.18.27(.18)**
glamourously
　1.31.33(.12.5)
glance **34.24.6**
glancingly **1.31.28(.1.11)**
gland **23.24.6**
glandered **23.18.10(.14)**
glanderous **34.18.27(.15)**
glanders **35.18.9**
glandes **35.1.8**
glandular **17.34.16(.19)**
glandule **40.15.9(.4)**
glans **35.26.7**
Glanville **40.2.12**
Glanyrafon **28.17.20(.5)**
Glaramara **17.32.7**
glare **6**
glaringly **1.31.28(.1.17)**
glaringness **34.18.16(.26)**
glary **1.29.4**
Glaser **17.25.3**
Glasgow **19.13.14**
Glaslyn **28.2.31(.23)**
glasnost **22.29.9**
glass **34.9**
glassful **40.14.6(.19)**
glasshouse **34.8.6(.20)**
glassie **1.22.6, 1.22.8**
glassily **1.31.17(.20)**
glassine **28.1.18(.3)**
glassiness **34.18.16(.2.7)**
glassless **34.18.29(.33)**
glasslike **24.13.7(.22)**
glassmaker **17.14.3(.3)**
glasspaper **17.10.3**
glassware **6.18.12**
glasswork **24.17.6(.15)**
glasswort **22.20.15**
glassy **1.22.6, 1.22.8**
Glastonbury
　1.29.11(.7.2)
Glaswegian **28.17.28(.1)**
glaucoma **17.17.16(.4)**
glaucomatous
　34.18.11(.10)
glaucous **34.18.13(.6)**
Glaxo **19.20.15**
glaze **35.4**
glazer **17.25.3**
glazier **3.15.3**
glaziery **1.29.2(.8)**
glazy **1.23.3**
gleam **27.1**
gleamingly **1.31.28(.1.7)**
gleamy **1.15.1**

glean **28.1**
gleaner **17.18.1**
gleanings **35.27**
Gleason **28.17.23(.1)**
Gleave **31.1**
glebe **21.1**
glee **2**
gleeful **40.27.1**
gleefully **1.31.17(.16.1)**
gleefulness **34.18.16(.37.2)**
gleesome **27.15.20(.1)**
Gleichschaltung **29.9**
glen **28.5**
Glencoe **19.12**
Glenda **17.13.20(.3)**
Glendale **40.4.3**
Glendenning **29.1.17(.4)**
Glendinning **29.1.17(.2)**
Glendower **17.3.4**
Gleneagles **35.30.19**
Glenfiddich **24.2.11(.2), 25.1**
glengarry **1.29.5**
Glenlivet **22.19.17**
Glenn **28.5**
Glenrothes **34.2.16**
Glenys **34.2.13**
gley **4**
glia **17.1, 17.6**
glial **40.16.1, 40.16.6**
glib **21.2**
glibly **1.31.21(.1)**
glibness **34.18.16(.19)**
glide **23.15**
glider **17.13.12**
glidingly **1.31.28(.1.5)**
glim **27.2**
glimmer **17.17.2**
glimmering **29.1.30(.8)**
glimmeringly **1.31.28(.1.17)**
glimpse **34.21.13**
Glinka **17.14.21(.1)**
glint **22.26.1**
glioma **17.17.16**
glissade **23.4.10, 23.9.15**
glissandi **2.13**
glissando **19.11.14**
glissé **4.18**
glisten **28.17.23(.2)**
glister **17.12.24(.2)**
glitch **38.2**
glitter **17.12.2**
glitterati **1.10.8**
glitteringly **1.31.28(.1.17)**
glittery **1.29.11(.8.1)**
glitz **34.22.2**
glitzily **1.31.17(.20)**
glitziness **34.18.16(.2.7)**

glitzy **1.22.21**
gloaming **29.1.16**
gloat **22.21**
gloater **17.12.18**
gloatingly **1.31.28(.1.4)**
glob **21.8**
global **40.20.18**
globalization **28.17.25(.3.12)**
globalize **35.15.21(.4.2)**
globally **1.31.17(.8)**
globe **21.16**
globefish **36.2.18(.14)**
globelike **24.13.7(.11)**
globetrotter **17.12.9**
globigerina **17.18.13(.13)**
globigerinae **2.17.8**
globoid **23.13.6**
globose **34.20.3**
globosely **1.31.33(.13)**
globoseness **34.18.16(.31.7)**
globular **17.34.16(.21.1)**
globularity **1.10.16(.21.1)**
globularly **1.31.17(.29)**
globule **40.15.9(.2)**
globulin **28.2.31(.10)**
globulous **34.18.29(.17.6)**
Glockenspiel **40.1.1**
glom **27.9**
glomata **17.12.16(.9.3)**
glomerate **22.4.22(.6), 22.19.24(.9)**
glomerular **17.34.16(.21.4)**
glomerule **40.15.8**
glomeruli **2.32.9(.8), 14.25.9**
glomerulus **34.18.29(.17.5)**
gloom **27.14**
gloomily **1.31.17(.13)**
gloominess **34.18.16(.2.5)**
gloomy **1.15.12**
glop **20.7**
Gloria **3.22.9**
Gloriana **17.18.8**
glorification **28.17.25(.3.5)**
glorifier **17.6.9(.4)**
glorify **14.14.4(.14)**
gloriole **40.14.1**
glorious **34.3.15(.5)**
gloriously **1.31.33(.1.4)**
gloriousness **34.18.16(.31.1)**
glory **1.29.8**
gloss **34.10**
glossal **40.31.8**
glossarial **40.3.14(.4)**
glossarist **22.29.2(.29.4)**

glossary **1.29.11(.18)**
glossator **17.12.4(.12)**
glosseme **27.1.8**
glosser **17.24.9**
glossily **1.31.17(.20)**
glossiness **34.18.16(.2.7)**
glossitis **34.18.11(.8)**
glossographer **17.20.12(.5)**
glossolalia **3.24.3**
glosso-laryngeal **40.3.12, 40.16.1**
glossology **1.26.10(.11.5)**
Glossop **20.13.4**
glossy **1.22.9**
Gloster **17.12.24(.7)**
glottal **40.21.7**
glottalization **28.17.25(.3.12)**
glottalize **35.15.21(.4.3)**
glottis **34.2.8**
glottochronology **1.26.10(.11.4)**
Gloucester **17.12.24(.7)**
glove **31.8**
gloved **23.26**
Glover **17.21.9**
glow **19**
glower **17.3**
gloxinia **3.9.2**
Gloy **13**
Gluck **24.14**
glucose **34.20.6, 35.20.5**
glucoside **23.15.11(.6)**
glucosidic **24.2.11(.2)**
glue **16**
gluer **17.8**
gluey **1(.6)**
glueyly **1.31.17(.5)**
glueyness **34.18.16(.2.1)**
glug **26.10**
Glühwein **28.14.11**
glum **27.11**
glumaceous **34.18.22(.3)**
glume **27.14**
glumly **1.31.26(.9)**
glumness **34.18.16(.24)**
glumose **34.20.8**
gluon **28.10.5**
glut **22.15**
glutamate **22.4.13(.6)**
glutamic **24.2.14(.4)**
gluteal **40.3.3**
gluten **28.2.11(.9), 28.17.11(.14)**
gluteus **34.3.3**
glutinous **34.18.16(.15.2)**
glutinously **1.31.33(.12.3)**
glutinousness **34.18.16(.31.3)**
glutton **28.17.11(.11)**

gluttonize **35.15.12(.5)**
gluttonous **34.18.16(.15.2)**
gluttonously **1.31.33(.12.3)**
gluttony **1.16.15(.7)**
glyceride **23.15.15**
glycerine **28.1.25(.3), 28.2.29(.5)**
glycerol **40.9.19**
glycin **28.2.23(.7)**
glycine **28.1.18(.4)**
glycogen **28.17.28(.9)**
glycogenesis **34.2.17(.10.3)**
glycogenic **24.2.15(.4)**
glycol **40.9.9**
glycolic **24.2.27(.9)**
glycollic **24.2.27(.9)**
glycolyses **35.1.16(.10)**
glycolysis **34.2.17(.10.5)**
glycoprotein **28.1.9(.4)**
glycoside **23.15.11(.6)**
glycosidic **24.2.11(.2)**
glycosuria **3.22.9, 3.22.12**
glycosuric **24.2.26(.10)**
Glyn **28.2**
Glyndebourne **28.11.2**
Glynis **34.2.13**
Glynn **28.2**
glyph **30.2**
glyphic **24.2.16(.1)**
glyptal **40.21.15**
glyptic **24.2.10(.12)**
glyptodon **28.10.10**
glyptodont **22.26.9**
glyptography **1.18.9(.3.2)**
gnamma **17.17.6**
gnarl **40.8**
gnarly **1.31.9**
gnash **36.6**
gnasher **17.26.6**
gnat **22.7**
gnathic **24.2.18(.3)**
gnaw **12**
gnawingly **1.31.28(.1.1)**
gneiss **34.15**
gneissic **24.2.20(.10)**
gneissoid **23.13.16**
gneissose **34.20.13**
gnocchi **1.12.7**
gnome **27.17**
gnomic **24.2.14(.12)**
gnomically **1.31.24(.9.8)**
gnomish **36.2.15**
gnomon **28.10.13**
gnomonic **24.2.15(.6.2)**
gnoses **35.1.16(.11)**
gnosis **34.2.17(.11.1)**
gnostic **24.2.10(.15.4)**
gnosticism **27.15.21(.2.12)**

gnosticize 35.15.16(.4)
gnotobiotic 24.2.10(.6)
gnu 16
go 19
goa 17.9
goad 23.20
go-ahead 23.5.13(.5)
goal 40.18
goalball 40.10.4
goalie 1.31.19
goalkeeper 17.10.1
goalkeeping 29.1.10(.1)
goalless 34.18.29(.38)
goalminder 17.13.20(.11)
goalmouth 32.7
goalpost 22.29.17(.1)
goalscoring 29.1.30(.7)
goaltender 17.13.20(.3)
goaltending 29.1.13(.14)
Goan 28.17.8
Goanese 35.1.12
goanna 17.18.6
goat 22.21
goatee 2.11
goatherd 23.19.7
Goathland 23.24.16(.16.4)
goatish 36.2.11
goatling 29.1.31(.17)
goatsbeard 23.3
goatskin 28.2.13(.14)
goatsucker 17.14.11
goaty 1.10.18
gob 21.8
gobang 29.4.2
gobbet 22.2.6
Gobbi 1.9.7
gobble 40.20.9
gobbledegook 24.15.3
gobbler 17.34.20
gobby 1.9.7
Gobelins 35.26.2
gobemouche 36.14
go-between 28.1.24
Gobineau 19.15.12
goblet 22.19.26(.16)
goblin 28.2.31(.14)
gobsmack 24.6.10
go-by 14.7
goby 1.9.13
go-cart 22.10.5
god 23.10
Godalming 29.1.16
Godard 10.7
godchild 23.31.9
godchildren 28.17.31(.15)
Godd 23.16
goddam 27.6.5
Goddard 23.9.8,
 23.18.10(.7)
goddess 34.5.3, 34.18.12

Gödel 40.22.15
godet 4.10.8, 22.5.4
godetia 3.16.1, 17.26.1
godets 34.22.4, 35.4.4
godfather 17.23.7
godfearing 29.1.30(.2)
godforsaken 28.17.13(.3)
Godfrey 1.29.21
Godgiven 28.17.20(.2)
godhead 23.5.13(.10)
godhood 23.16.5(.7)
Godiva 17.21.10
godless 34.18.29(.23)
godlessly 1.31.33(.12.6)
godlessness
 34.18.16(.31.6)
godlike 24.13.7(.13)
godliness 34.18.16(.2.10)
godly 1.31.23(.8)
Godman 28.17.16(.22)
godmother 17.23.10
Godolphin 28.2.19
godown 28.8.2(.2)
godparent 22.26.15(.23.1)
godsend 23.24.5(.11)
godship 20.2.7(.15)
godson 28.13.7
god-speed 23.1.1
Godunov 30.8.7
godward 23.18.26(.10)
Godwin 28.2.28
godwit 22.2.23
Godwottery 1.29.11(.8.4)
Godzilla 17.34.2(.10)
Goebbels 35.30.15
goer 17.9
Goering 29.1.30(.9)
goest 22.29.15(.7)
goeth 32.14.5
Goethe 17.12.17
Goethean 28.3.3
gofer 17.20.14
goffer 17.20.7
Gog 26.7
go-getter 17.12.5(.4)
goggle 40.24.6
goglet 22.19.26(.20)
Gogmagog 26.7.6
go-go 19.13.11
Gogol 40.9.10
Goiânia 3.9.5
Goidel 40.22.9
Goidelic 24.2.27(.4)
going 29.1.9
goitre 17.12.11
goitrous 34.18.27(.14)
go-kart 22.10.5
Golan Heights 34.22.12
Golborne 28.11.2
Golconda 17.13.20(.7)

gold 23.31.13
Golda 17.13.23(.8)
Goldberg 26.14.1(.7)
golden 28.17.12(.27)
golden-ager 17.29.3
goldeneye 14.13
goldenly 1.31.27(.14)
goldenness 34.18.16(.25)
goldenrod 23.10.12
goldfield 23.31.1(.2)
goldfinch 38.18.1
goldfish 36.2.18(.16)
Goldie 1.11.23
Goldilocks 34.23.8(.11)
Golding 29.1.13(.16)
Goldman 28.17.16(.22)
Goldmark 24.8.8
goldmine 28.14.8
Goldschmidt 22.2.11
goldsmith 32.2.3
Goldstein 28.1.9(.7),
 28.14.5
Goldwater 17.12.10(.7)
Goldwyn 28.2.28
golem 27.15.28(.8)
golf 30.20.4
golfer 17.20.19
Golgi 1.26.14
Golgotha 17.22.9,
 17.23.8
Goliath 32.14.3
Golightly 1.31.22(.13)
Gollancz 34.23.18
golliwog 26.7.12
gollop 20.13.7
golly 1.31.10
gombeen 28.1.8
Gomer 17.17.16
Gómez 35.5.8
Gomorrah 17.32.8
Gompers 35.18.6
gonad 23.7.12
gonadal 40.22.3
gonadotrophic
 24.2.16(.4)
gonadotrophin 28.2.19
gonadotropic 24.2.8(.5)
Goncourt 12.7
gondola 17.34.16(.8)
gondolier 3.24
Gondwana 17.18.8(.10)
Gondwanaland
 23.24.6(.13)
gone 28.10
goner 17.18.9
Goneril 40.16.13(.12.2)
gonfalon 28.17.33(.13)
gonfalonier 3.9
gong 29.6
goniometer
 17.12.16(.9.2)

goniometric
 24.2.26(.14.2)
goniometrical
 40.23.12(.18)
goniometrically
 1.31.24(.9.12)
goniometry 1.29.15(.8)
gonk 24.19.5
gonna 17.18.9, 17.18.16
gonococcal 40.23.7
gonococci 2.14, 2.22.11,
 14.10, 14.18
gonococcus 34.18.13(.5)
gonorrhoea 3.22
gonorrhoeal 40.3.14
Gonville 40.2.12
González 35.5.15, 35.18.25
gonzo 19.21
goo 16
goober 17.11.12
Gooch 38.14
good 23.16
Goodall 40.10.6
Goodbody 1.11.10
goodbye 14.7
Goodchild 23.31.9
Goode 23.16
Goodenough 30.11.7
Goodfellow 19.29.4
Goodge 39.13
Goodhart 22.10.11
good-hearted 23.18.9(.7)
good-heartedness
 34.18.16(.21.1)
goodish 36.2.12
Goodison 28.17.23(.14)
goodliness 34.18.16(.2.10)
goodly 1.31.23(.12)
goodman 28.17.16(.22)
good-natured 23.18.24
good-naturedly
 1.31.23(.14.7)
goodness 34.18.16(.21.1)
goodnight 22.16.14
goodo 19
good-oh 19
Goodrich 38.2.10
goods 35.23.11
goodwife 30.12
goodwill 40.2.19
Goodwin 28.2.28
goodwives 35.28.6
Goodwood 23.16.6(.10)
Goodwright 22.16.24(.13)
goody 1.11.15
Goodyear 3.23, 18.16
gooey 1(.6)
gooeyly 1.31.17(.5)
gooeyness 34.18.16(.2.1)
goof 30.13
goofball 40.10.4

goofily 1.31.17(.16.1)
goofiness 34.18.16(.2.6)
goofy 1.18.8
goog 26.12
Googie 1.14.10
googly 1.31.25
googol 40.9.10
gook 24.15
Goole 40.15
goolie 1.31.16
goon 28.16
goonery 1.29.11(.13.1)
gooney 1.16.14
Goonhilly 1.31.2
goop 20.12
goopiness 34.18.16(.2.2)
goopy 1.8.10
goosander 17.13.20(.4)
goose 34.17
gooseberry 1.29.11(.7.2)
goosebumps 34.21.13
gooseflesh 36.5
goosefoot 22.17
goosegog 26.7.6
goosegrass 34.9.6
gooseherd 23.19.7
goosestep 20.4
goosey 1.22.15
Goossens 35.26.13(.13)
gopher 17.20.14
goral 40.16.13(.8)
Gorbachev 30.8.9
Gorbals 35.30.15
gorblimey 1.15.11
gorcock 24.9.6
Gordian 28.3.4(.7)
Gordimer 17.17.14(.3)
Gordium 27.3.4(.7)
gordo 19.11.8
Gordon 28.17.12(.10)
Gordonstoun
    28.17.11(.25)
gore 12
Górecki 1.12.17(.8)
Gore-tex® 34.23.4(.3)
gorge 39.10
gorgeous 34.18.24
gorgeously 1.31.33(.12.4)
gorgeousness
    34.18.16(.31.5)
gorger 17.29.9
gorget 22.19.22
Gorgio 19.25
gorgon 28.17.15(.9)
gorgonia 3.9.11
gorgoniae 2.3
gorgonian 28.3.8(.11)
gorgonize 35.15.12(.5)
Gorgonzola 17.34.18(.11)
gorilla 17.34.2(.15)

gorily 1.31.17(.27.1)
goriness 34.18.16(.2.9)
Goring 29.1.30(.7)
Gorky 1.12.8
Gorman 28.17.16(.11)
gormandizer 17.25.12(.3)
gormless 34.18.29(.26)
gormlessly 1.31.33(.12.6)
gormlessness
    34.18.16(.31.6)
Gormley 1.31.26(.8)
Goronwy 1.28
go-round 23.24.7(.10)
Gor-Ray 4.26.7
gorse 34.12
Gorsedd 33.4
Gorseinon 28.17.17(.8)
gorsy 1.22.11
Gorton 28.17.11(.10)
gory 1.29.8
Gosforth 32.10, 32.14.13
gosh 36.9
goshawk 24.10.8
Goshen 28.17.25(.13)
gosling 29.1.31(.27)
go-slow 19.29.22
gospel 40.19.15
gospeller 17.34.16(.5)
Gosport 22.13.1
Goss 34.10
gossamer 17.17.14(.8)
gossamery 1.29.11(.12)
gossan 28.17.24(.7)
Gosse 34.10
gossip 20.2.5
gossiper 17.10.14
gossipmonger
    17.16.17(.4)
gossipy 1.8.11(.7)
gossoon 28.16.10
got 22.11
gotcha 17.28.9
Goth 32.9
Gotha 17.12.18, 17.22.11
Gotham 27.15.9(.6),
    27.15.18
Gothamite 22.16.13
Gothard 23.9.14
Gothenburg 26.14.1(.9)
Gothic 24.2.18(.4)
Gothically 1.31.24(.9.10)
Gothicism 27.15.21(.2.12)
Gothicize 35.15.16(.4)
Gotland 23.24.6(.13)
gotta 17.12.9
gotten 28.17.11(.9)
Götterdämmerung
    29.8, 29.9
gouache 36.8
Gouda 17.13.6, 17.13.14

Goudy 1.11.8
gouge 39.7
gouger 17.29.6
Gough 30.8
goujons 11.15, 35.26.10,
    35.26.13(.17)
goulash 36.6.10
Gould 23.31.10
Gounod 19.15.11
gourami 1.15.7,
    1.15.13(.11)
gourd 23.12, 23.18.4
gourdful 40.14.6(.11)
Gourlay 1.31.17(.4)
Gourley 1.31.17(.4)
gourmand 23.24.16(.7)
gourmandism
    27.15.21(.2.5)
gourmandize 35.15.8
gourmet 4.13
gout 22.9
goutily 1.31.17(.9.1)
goutiness 34.18.16(.2.3)
goutweed 23.1.10
gouty 1.10.7
Govan 28.17.20(.7)
govern 28.17.20(.7)
governability
    1.10.16(.22.2)
governableness
    34.18.16(.37.4)
governance 34.24.10(.15)
governess 34.5.6,
    34.18.16(.15.3)
governessy 1.22.16(.9)
government
    22.26.15(.13.4)
governmental
    40.21.17(.2)
governmentally
    1.31.17(.9.3)
governor 17.18.16(.11)
governorate 22.19.24(.9)
governorship 20.2.7(.9)
Gow 9
gowan 28.17.3
Gower 17.3
Gowing 29.1.4
gowk 24.7
gown 28.8
gownsman 28.17.16(.30)
Gowrie 1.29.11(.1)
goy 13
Goya 17.5
goyim 27.2.1, 27.2.15
goyisch 36.2
goyish 36.2, 36.2.26
Gozo 19.21
Graafian 28.3.9
grab 21.6
grabber 17.11.5

grabble 40.20.6
grabby 1.9.5
graben 28.17.10
Gracchus 34.18.13(.3)
grace 34.4
graceful 40.27.25
gracefully 1.31.17(.16.2)
gracefulness
    34.18.16(.37.2)
graceless 34.18.29(.33)
gracelessly 1.31.33(.12.6)
gracelessness
    34.18.16(.31.6)
Gracie 1.22.4
gracile 40.2.14, 40.13.12
gracility 1.10.16(.27)
graciosity 1.10.16(.16.2)
gracious 34.18.22(.3)
graciously 1.31.33(.12.4)
graciousness
    34.18.16(.31.4)
grackle 40.23.5
grad 23.7
gradability 1.10.16(.22.1)
gradable 40.20.16(.12)
gradate 22.4.10
gradation 28.17.25(.3.4)
gradational
    40.26.13(.14.2)
gradationally
    1.31.17(.14.3)
grade 23.4
grader 17.13.3
Gradgrind 23.24.13
gradience 34.24.2
gradient 22.26.2(.3)
gradin 28.2.12
gradine 28.1.10
grading 29.1.13(.3)
gradual 40.34
gradualism
    27.15.21(.2.15)
gradualist 22.29.2(.31.4)
gradualistic 24.2.10(.15.3)
gradually 1.31.17(.25)
gradualness
    34.18.16(.37.1)
graduand 23.24.6(.2)
graduate 22.4.4, 22.19.5
graduation 28.17.25(.3.1)
graduator 17.12.4(.2)
Grady 1.11.4
Graecism 27.15.21(.2.12)
Graecize 35.15.16(.1)
Graeco- 19.12.1, 19.12.4,
    19.12.9
Graecomania 3.9.3(.5)
Graecomaniac 24.6.1
Graecophile 40.13.9
Graeco-Roman
    28.17.16(.18)

g

Gravesend 23.24.5
graveside 23.15.11(.15)
gravestone 28.19.4(.9)
Gravettian 28.3.3
graveward 23.18.26(.14)
graveyard 23.9.21
gravid 23.2.15
gravimeter 17.12.16(.9.1)
gravimetric 24.2.26(.14.2)
gravimetry 1.29.15(.8)
gravitas 34.9.2
gravitate 22.4.9(.5)
gravitation 28.17.25(.3.3)
gravitational
   40.26.13(.14.2)
gravitationally
   1.31.17(.14.3)
graviton 28.10.9
gravity 1.10.16(.15)
gravlax 34.23.5(.15)
gravure 12.22, 17.7.12(.10)
gravy 1.19.3
gray 4
grayling 29.1.31(.4)
Grayson 28.17.23(.4)
Graz 34.22.7
graze 35.4
grazer 17.25.3
grazier 3.15.3
graziery 1.29.2(.8)
grease 34.1, 35.1
greaseless 34.18.29(.33)
greasepaint 22.26.3
greaseproof 30.13.4
greaser 17.24.1, 17.25.1
greasily 1.31.17(.20)
greasiness 34.18.16(.2.7)
greasy 1.22.1, 1.23.1
great 22.4
greatcoat 22.21.5
greatness 34.18.16(.20.1)
greave 31.1
Greaves 35.28.1
grebe 21.1
grebo 19.9.1
Grecian 28.17.25(.1)
Grecomania 3.9.3(.5)
Greece 34.1
greed 23.4
greedily 1.31.17(.10)
greediness 34.18.16(.2.3)
greedy 1.11.1
gree-gree 2.30.12
Greek 24.1
Greekness 34.18.16(.22)
Greeley 1.31.1
Greely 1.31.1
green 28.1
Greenaway 4.25.9
greenback 24.6.6(.17)

Greenbaum 27.7
greenbottle 40.21.7
Greene 28.1
greenery 1.29.11(.13.1)
greenfeed 23.1.6
Greenfield 23.31.1(.2)
greenfinch 38.18.1
greenfly 14.25.14
greengage 39.4.4
greengrocer 17.24.17
greengrocery 1.29.11(.18)
Greengross 34.10.16
Greenhalgh 36.17, 39.18
Greenham 27.15.14(.1)
greenhead 23.5.13(.14)
greenheart 22.10.11
greenhide 23.15.13
greenhorn 28.11.10
Greenhough 9.14, 19.26,
   30.8.10, 30.11.9
greenhouse 34.8.6(.16)
greening 29.1.17(.1)
greenish 36.2.16(.1)
greenishness
   34.18.16(.33.5)
greenkeeper 17.10.1
greenkeeping 29.1.10(.1)
Greenland 23.24.16(.16.4)
Greenlander
   17.13.20(.13)
greenlet 22.19.26(.22)
greenly 1.31.27(.1)
greenmail 40.4.6
greenmailer 17.34.4
greenness 34.18.16(.25)
Greenock 24.16.7
Greenough 19.15.1
Greenpeace 34.1.1
greenroom 27.14.6(.13)
greensand 23.24.6(.10)
greenshank 24.19.3(.5)
greensick 24.2.20(.15)
greensickness
   34.18.16(.22)
greenskeeper 17.10.1
Greenslade 23.4.16
Greensleeves 35.28.1
greenstick 24.2.10(.15.4)
greenstone 28.19.4(.9)
Greenstreet 22.1.17
greenstuff 30.11.3
greensward 23.12.8
greenweed 23.1.10
Greenwell 40.5.17(.12)
Greenwich 38.2.6, 39.2.15
greenwood 23.16.6(.14)
greeny 1.16.1
greenyard 23.9.21
Greer 3
greet 22.1

greeter 17.12.1
greeting 29.1.12(.1)
greffier 3.10.1
gregarious 34.3.15(.3)
gregariously 1.31.33(.1.4)
gregariousness
   34.18.16(.31.1)
Gregg 26.4
Gregor 17.16.4
Gregorian 28.3.20(.7)
Gregory 1.29.11(.11)
Gregson 28.17.23(.22)
Greig 26.4
greisen 28.17.24(.10)
gremial 40.3.6
gremlin 28.2.31(.19)
Grenada 17.13.3
grenade 23.4.8
Grenadian 28.3.4(.3)
grenadier 3.5
grenadine 28.1.10
Grendel 40.22.16
Grendon 28.17.12(.23)
Grenfell 40.5.9, 40.27.22
Grenoble 40.20.18
Grenville 40.28.15
Grepo 19.8
Gresham 27.15.22
gressorial 40.3.14(.5)
Greta 17.12.1, 17.12.5
Gretel 40.21.4
Gretna Green 28.1
Gretzky 1.12.17(.8)
Greville 40.28.4
grew 16
grey 4
greybeard 23.3
Greyfriars 35.18.4
greyhen 28.5.16
greyhound 23.24.7(.8)
greyish 36.2.2
greylag 26.5.9
greyly 1.31.4
greyness 34.18.16(.4)
Greystoke 24.18.2
greywacke 17.14.5
Gribble 40.20.2
gricer 17.24.13
grid 23.2
griddle 40.22.2
griddlecake 24.3.6
gridiron 28.17.5
gridlock 24.9.16(.12)
grief 30.1
Grieg 26.1
Grier 3
Grierson 28.17.23(.3)
grievance 34.24.10(.17)
grieve 31.1
griever 17.21.1

grievous 34.18.18
grievously 1.31.33(.12.4)
grievousness
   34.18.16(.31.3)
griff 30.2
griffe 30.2
griffin 28.2.19, 28.17.19
Griffith 32.2.5
Griffiths 34.26
griffon 28.17.19
grift 22.27.1
grifter 17.12.23
grig 26.2
Griggs 35.24
Grignard 10.24
Grigson 28.17.23(.22)
grike 24.13
grill 40.2
grillade 23.4.16, 23.9.1,
   23.9.21
grillage 39.2.23
grille 40.2
griller 17.34.2
grilling 29.1.31(.2)
grillroom 27.14.6(.20)
grillwork 24.17.6(.19)
grilse 34.27
grim 27.2
grimace 34.4.7,
   34.18.15(.2)
grimacer 17.24.4, 17.24.15
Grimaldi 1.11.23
grimalkin 28.2.13(.17)
grime 27.12
Grimes 35.25.8
Grimethorpe 20.8
grimily 1.31.17(.13)
griminess 34.18.16(.2.5)
grimly 1.31.26(.2)
Grimm 27.2
grimness 34.18.16(.24)
Grimond 23.24.16(.7)
Grimsby 1.9.22
Grimshaw 12.16.11
grimy 1.15.11
grin 28.2
grind 23.24.13
grinder 17.13.20(.11)
grindingly 1.31.28(.1.5)
grindstone 28.19.4(.9)
gringo 19.13.12
grinner 17.18.2
grinningly 1.31.28(.1.7)
Grinstead 23.2.8, 23.5.3
grip 20.2
gripe 20.10
griper 17.10.12
gripingly 1.31.28(.1.2)
gripper 17.10.2

grippingly **1.31.28(.1.2)**
grippy **1.8.2**
Griqua **17.14.1, 17.31.6**
Griqualand **23.24.6(.13)**
grisaille **14.19, 40.4.11, 40.13.13**
Griselda **17.13.23(.3)**
griseofulvin **28.2.20**
grisette **22.5.14**
Grisewood **23.16.6(.18)**
gris-gris **2.30.12**
griskin **28.2.13(.14)**
grisliness **34.18.16(.2.10)**
grisly **1.31.34**
grison **28.17.23(.12), 28.17.24(.2)**
grissini **1.16.1(.10)**
grist **22.29.2**
gristle **40.31.2**
gristly **1.31.17(.20)**
gristmill **40.2.9**
Griswold **23.31.11, 23.31.13(.10)**
grit **22.2**
gritstone **28.19.4(.9)**
gritter **17.12.2**
grittily **1.31.17(.9.1)**
grittiness **34.18.16(.2.3)**
gritty **1.10.2**
Grizedale **40.4.3**
grizzle **40.32.2**
grizzler **17.34.28**
grizzly **1.31.34**
groan **28.19**
groaner **17.18.18**
groaningly **1.31.28(.1.7)**
groat **22.21**
Gro-bag® **26.5.1**
Grobian **28.3.2**
grocer **17.24.17**
grocery **1.29.11(.18)**
grockle **40.23.7**
Grocott **22.11.6**
Grodno **19.15.15**
grog **26.7**
Grogan **28.17.15(.14)**
groggily **1.31.17(.12)**
grogginess **34.18.16(.2.4)**
groggy **1.14.6**
grogram **27.15.26(.13)**
groin **28.12**
Grolier **3.24.11**
grommet **22.19.14**
gromwell **40.5.17(.11)**
Gromyko **19.12.1**
Groningen **28.17.18**
groom **27.14**
groomsman **28.17.16(.30)**
groove **31.10**
groover **17.21.11**

groovily **1.31.17(.17)**
grooviness **34.18.16(.2.6)**
groovy **1.19.9**
grope **20.15**
groper **17.10.16**
gropingly **1.31.28(.1.2)**
Gropius **34.3.1**
grosbeak **24.1.2**
groschen **28.17.25(.7)**
grosgrain **28.4.18**
Grosmont **22.26.9, 22.26.15(.13.2)**
gross **34.20**
Grosseteste **22.4.9(.9), 22.29.5(.2)**
grossly **1.31.33(.13)**
Grossmith **32.2.3**
grossness **34.18.16(.31.7)**
Grosvenor **17.18.16(.11)**
Grosz **34.20**
grot **22.11**
grotesque **24.20.3**
grotesquely **1.31.24(.13)**
grotesqueness **34.18.16(.22)**
grotesquerie **1.29.11(.10)**
grotesquery **1.29.11(.10)**
Grotius **34.3.3**
grottily **1.31.17(.9.2)**
grottiness **34.18.16(.2.3)**
grotto **19.10.8**
grotty **1.10.9**
grouch **38.6**
grouchily **1.31.17(.24)**
grouchiness **34.18.16(.2.8)**
Groucho **19.24**
grouchy **1.25.7**
ground **23.24.7**
groundage **39.2.11**
groundbait **22.4.8**
grounder **17.13.20(.5)**
groundhog **26.7.11**
grounding **29.1.13(.14)**
groundless **34.18.29(.23)**
groundlessly **1.31.33(.12.6)**
groundlessness **34.18.16(.31.6)**
groundling **29.1.31(.18)**
groundnut **22.15.6**
groundout **22.9.8**
grounds **35.23.15**
groundsel **40.31.17**
groundsheet **22.1.11**
groundsman **28.17.16(.30)**
groundswell **40.5.17(.15)**
groundwater **17.12.10(.7)**
groundwork **24.17.6(.9)**
group **20.12**

groupage **39.2.8**
grouper **17.10.13**
groupie **1.8.10**
grouping **29.1.10(.9)**
groupware **6.18.6**
grouse **34.8**
grouser **17.24.7**
grout **22.9**
grouter **17.12.7**
grove **31.12**
grovel **40.28.7**
grovelingly **1.31.28(.1.18)**
groveller **17.34.16(.14)**
grovellingly **1.31.28(.1.18)**
Grover **17.21.14**
Groves **35.28.9**
grovy **1.19.12**
grow **19**
growable **40.20.16(.8)**
growbag **26.5.1**
grower **17.9**
growl **40.7**
growler **17.34.7**
growlingly **1.31.28(.1.18)**
Growmore **12.9.6**
grown **28.19**
grown-up **20.9**
grownup **20.9.9**
growth **32.16**
groyne **28.12**
Grozny **1.16.27**
grub **21.11**
grubber **17.11.10**
grubbily **1.31.17(.8)**
grubbiness **34.18.16(.2.2)**
grubby **1.9.9**
grubstake **24.3.4**
grubstaker **17.14.3(.2)**
grudge **39.11**
grudger **17.29.10**
grudgingly **1.31.28(.1.16)**
grudgingness **34.18.16(.26)**
gruel **40.16.8**
gruelling **29.1.31(.11)**
gruellingly **1.31.28(.1.18)**
gruesome **27.15.20(.10)**
gruesomely **1.31.26(.11)**
gruesomeness **34.18.16(.24)**
gruff **30.11**
gruffly **1.31.29**
gruffness **34.18.16(.27)**
Gruffydd **33.2**
grumble **40.20.19**
grumbler **17.34.20**
grumbling **29.1.31(.16)**
grumblingly **1.31.28(.1.18)**
grumbly **1.31.21(.12)**
grumous **34.18.15(.9)**

grump **20.16.5**
grumpily **1.31.17(.7)**
grumpiness **34.18.16(.2.2)**
grumpish **36.2.9**
grumpishly **1.31.35(.7.1)**
grumpy **1.8.14**
Grundig **26.2.2**
Grundy **1.11.20(.7)**
Grundyism **27.15.21(.2.1)**
grunge **39.17.8**
grungy **1.26.13**
grunion **28.17.32**
grunt **22.26.12**
grunter **17.12.22(.10)**
Gruyère **6.20**
gryphon **28.17.19**
grysbok **24.9.3**
G-string **29.1.30(.13)**
guacamole **1.31.19**
guacharo **19.27.11**
Guadalajara **17.32.7**
Guadalcanál **40.6.9**
Guadalquivír **3.11, 17.21.2**
Guadeloupe **20.12**
Guadeloupian **28.3.1**
guaiac **24.6.3, 24.16.1**
guaiacum **27.15.11(.9)**
Guam **27.8**
guan **28.9**
guanaco **19.12.12**
Guangdong **29.6.4**
guanine **28.1.14**
guano **19.15.7**
Guantánamo **19.14.12**
guar **10, 10.3**
Guarani **1.16.15(.18), 2.17**
guarantee **2.11**
guarantor **12.5**
guaranty **1.10.23(.12)**
guard **23.9**
guardant **22.26.15(.10)**
guardedly **1.31.23(.14.4)**
guardedness **34.18.16(.21.1)**
guardee **2.13**
guarder **17.13.7**
guardhouse **34.8.6(.12)**
Guardi **1.11.9**
guardian **28.3.4(.6)**
guardianship **20.2.7(.19)**
guardless **34.18.29(.23)**
guardrail **40.4.14**
guardroom **27.14.6(.9)**
guardsman **28.17.16(.30)**
Guarneri **1.29.4**
Guarnerius **34.3.15(.2)**
Guatemala **17.34.8**
Guatemalan **28.17.33(.6)**
guava **17.21.6**

Guayaquil **40.1.5**
guayule **1.31.16**
gubbins **35.26.2**
gubernatorial **40.3.14(.5)**
Gucci **1.25.11**
gudgeon **28.17.28(.7)**
Gudrun **28.16.13,
28.17.31(.15)**
guelder-rose **35.20.12**
Guelph **30.20.2**
Guelphic **24.2.16(.7)**
Guelphism
27.15.21(.2.10)
guenon **28.10.14**
guerdon **28.17.12(.17)**
Guernica **17.14.1,
17.14.15(.9)**
Guernsey **1.23.20**
Guerrero **19.27.3**
guerrilla **17.34.2(.15)**
guess **34.5**
guessable **40.20.16(.21.1)**
guesser **17.24.5**
guesstimate **22.4.13(.6),
22.19.14**
guesswork **24.17.6(.15)**
guest **22.29.5**
guesthouse **34.8.6(.11)**
guestroom **27.14.6(.8)**
guestship **20.2.8**
Guevara **17.32.7**
guff **30.11**
guffaw **12.11**
Guggenheim **27.12.6**
guggle **40.24.8**
Guiana **17.18.6, 17.18.8**
Guianese **35.1.12**
guidable **40.20.16(.12)**
guidance **34.24.10(.11)**
guide **23.15**
guidebook **24.14.3**
guideline **28.14.19(.15)**
guidepost **22.29.17(.1)**
Guider **17.13.12**
guideway **4.25.13**
Guido **19.11.1**
guidon **28.17.12(.13)**
Guignolesque **24.20.3**
guild **23.31.2**
guilder **17.13.23(.2)**
Guildford **23.18.16(.12)**
guildhall **40.10.16**
guildsman **28.17.16(.30)**
guildswoman
28.17.16(.14)
guildswomen **28.2.17(.1)**
guile **40.13**
guileful **40.27.31**
guilefully **1.31.17(.16.2)**
guilefulness
34.18.16(.37.2)

guileless **34.18.29(.38)**
guilelessly **1.31.33(.12.6)**
guilelessness
34.18.16(.31.6)
Guillaume **27.17.1**
guillemot **22.11.8**
guilloche **36.9.6, 36.16**
guillotine **28.1.9**
guillotiner **17.18.1(.3)**
guilt **22.32.1**
guiltily **1.31.17(.9.3)**
guiltiness **34.18.16(.2.3)**
guiltless **34.18.29(.22)**
guiltlessly **1.31.33(.12.6)**
guiltlessness
34.18.16(.31.6)
guilty **1.10.28**
guimpe **20.16.1**
guinea **1.16.2**
Guinea-Bissau **9.9**
Guinean **28.3.8(.2)**
Guinevere **3.11.7**
Guinness **34.18.16(.2.1)**
guipure **17.7.12(.2)**
guise **35.15**
Guiseley **1.31.34**
guitar **10.6**
guitarist **22.29.2(.29.2)**
guiver **17.21.10**
Gujarat **22.10.12**
Gujarati **1.10.8**
Gujranwala **17.34.8**
Gujrat **22.10.12**
gulag **26.5.9**
gular **17.34.15**
Gulbenkian **28.3.5**
gulch **38.19**
gulden **28.17.12(.27)**
gules **35.30.11**
gulf **30.20.5**
gulfweed **23.1.10**
gull **40.12**
Gullah **17.34.12**
gullery **1.29.11(.27)**
gullet **22.19.26(.10)**
gulley **1.31.13**
gullibility **1.10.16(.22.1)**
gullible **40.20.16(.29)**
gullibly **1.31.21(.9)**
Gulliver **17.21.12**
gully **1.31.13**
gulp **20.18**
gulper **17.10.19**
gulpingly **1.31.28(.1.2)**
gulpy **1.8.16**
gum **27.11**
gumbo **19.9.14**
gumboil **40.11.2**
gumboot **22.18.3**
gumdrop **20.7.12**

gumma **17.17.10**
gummatous **34.18.11(.10)**
Gummer **17.17.10**
Gummidge **39.2.14**
gummily **1.31.17(.13)**
gumminess **34.18.16(.2.5)**
gummy **1.15.10**
gumption **28.17.25(.14)**
gumshield **23.31.1(.5)**
gumshoe **16.17**
gun **28.13**
gunboat **22.21.2**
gundi **1.11.20(.7)**
gundog **26.7.4**
gundy **1.11.20(.7)**
gunfight **22.16.16**
gunfighter **17.12.13(.5)**
gunfire **17.6.9(.9)**
Gunga Din **28.2**
gunge **39.17.8**
gung-ho **19.26**
gungy **1.26.13**
gunk **24.19.7**
gunless **34.18.29(.27)**
gunlock **24.9.16(.16)**
gunmaker **17.14.3(.3)**
gunman **28.7.10(.15),
28.17.16(.25)**
gunmen **28.5.7(.19)**
gunmetal **40.21.4**
Gunn **28.13**
gunner **17.18.12**
gunnera **17.32.14(.11)**
gunnery **1.29.11(.13.1)**
gunny **1.16.12**
gunnysack **24.6.14**
gunplay **4.28.9**
gunpoint **22.26.11**
gunpowder **17.13.6**
gunpower **17.3.1**
gunroom **27.14.6(.13)**
gunrunner **17.18.12**
gunrunning **29.1.17(.9)**
gunsel **40.31.21**
gunship **20.2.7(.19)**
gunshot **22.11.12**
gunshy **14.20**
gunsight **22.16.19(.16)**
gunslinger **17.19.1**
gunslinging **29.1.18**
gunsmith **32.2.3**
gunstock **24.9.4**
Gunter **17.12.22(.10)**
Gunther **17.12.22(.11),
17.22.13**
gunwale **40.26.10**
gunyah **17.33.9**
Guomindang **29.4.4**
guppy **1.8.8**
Gupta **17.12.19**

gurdwara **17.32.7**
gurgitation **28.17.25(.3.3)**
gurgle **40.24.12**
gurgler **17.34.24**
gurjun **28.17.28(.10)**
Gurkha **17.14.15(.3),
17.14.16**
Gurkhali **1.31.9**
gurnard **23.18.14**
gurnet **22.2.12**
gurney **1.16.16**
guru **16.23.4**
Gus **34.14**
gush **36.12**
gusher **17.26.10**
gushily **1.31.17(.22)**
gushiness **34.18.16(.2.8)**
gushing **29.1.25**
gushingly **1.31.28(.1.13)**
gushy **1.24.9**
gusset **22.2.16**
gust **22.29.12**
Gustafson **28.17.23(.25)**
gustation **28.17.25(.3.3)**
gustative **31.2.1(.3)**
gustatory **1.29.11(.8.2)**
Gustave **31.6**
Gustavus **34.18.18**
gustily **1.31.17(.9.3)**
gustiness **34.18.16(.2.3)**
gusto **19.10.19**
gusty **1.10.26(.8)**
gut **22.15**
Gutenberg **26.14.1(.9)**
Guthrie **1.29.23**
Gutiérrez **35.5.13**
gutless **34.18.29(.22)**
gutlessly **1.31.33(.12.6)**
gutlessness
34.18.16(.31.6)
gutrot **22.11.15**
gutser **17.24.19**
gutsily **1.31.17(.20)**
gutsiness **34.18.16(.2.7)**
gutsy **1.22.21**
guttapercha **17.28.16**
guttate **22.4.9(.3)**
gutter **17.12.12**
guttersnipe **20.10.3**
guttle **40.21.9**
guttural **40.16.13(.12.1)**
gutturalism
27.15.21(.2.15)
gutturality **1.10.16(.32.13)**
gutturalize **35.15.21(.4.7)**
gutturally **1.31.17(.27.1)**
gutty **1.10.12**
guv **31.8**
guv'nor **17.18.27**
guvnor **17.18.27**

guy **14**
Guyana **17.18.6**
Guyanese **35.1.12**
Guyenne **28.5.19**
Guy Fawkes **34.23.9**
Guzmán **28.17.16(.28)**
guzzle **40.32.11**
guzzler **17.34.28**
Gwalia **3.24.6**
Gwalior **12.2**
Gwen **28.5**
Gwenda **17.13.20(.3)**
Gwendolen **28.2.31(.10)**
Gwendoline **28.2.31(.10)**
Gwendraeth **32.12**
Gwenllian **28.3.22**
Gwent **22.26.4**
Gwenyth **32.14.12**
Gwyn **28.2**
Gwynedd **33.9**
Gwyneth **32.14.12**
Gwynfor **12.12, 17.21.17**
Gwynn **28.2**
gybe **21.12**
gym **27.2**
gymkhana **17.18.8(.3)**
gymnasia **3.15.3**
gymnasial **40.3.11**
gymnasium **27.3.12**
gymnast **22.29.6(.8)**
gymnastic **24.2.10(.15.4)**
gymnastically
 1.31.24(.9.6)
gymnosophist
 22.29.2(.19)
gymnosophy **1.18.9(.1)**
gymnosperm **27.16.1**
gymnospermous
 34.18.15(.11)
gymslip **20.2.13**
gynaecea **17.1.11**
gynaeceum **27.15.1**
gynaecocracy
 1.22.16(.13)
gynaecologic **24.2.24(.4)**
gynaecological
 40.23.12(.17.2)
gynaecologically
 1.31.24(.9.11)
gynaecologist
 22.29.2(.26.3)
gynaecology
 1.26.10(.11.3)
gynaecomastia **3.4.13**
gynandromorph **30.9.2**
gynandromorphic
 24.2.16(.5)
gynandromorphism
 27.15.21(.2.10)
gynandrous
 34.18.27(.15)

gynecologically
 1.31.24(.9.11)
gynecology **1.26.10(.11.3)**
gynecomastia **3.4.13**
gynobase **34.4.3**
gynocracy **1.22.16(.13)**
gynoecia **3.14.1**
gynoecium **27.3.11**
gynophobia **3.3.9**
gyp **20.2**
gypseous **34.3.10**
gypsiferous **34.18.27(.20)**
gypsophila **17.34.16(.13)**
gypsum **27.15.20(.12)**
gypsy **1.22.19**
Gypsydom **27.15.10(.2)**
Gypsyfied **23.15.9**
Gypsyhood **23.16.5(.1)**
Gypsyish **36.2.1**
gyrate **22.4.22**
gyration **28.17.25(.3.13)**
gyrator **17.12.4(.15)**
gyratory **1.29.11(.8.2)**
gyre **17.6**
gyrfalcon **28.17.13(.19)**
gyri **14.24.5**
gyro **19.27.1, 19.27.9**
gyrocompass **34.18.9(.11)**
gyrograph **30.7.5(.1)**
gyromagnetic
 24.2.10(.3.1)
gyronny **1.16.9**
gyropilot **22.19.26(.11)**
gyroplane **28.4.19**
gyroscope **20.15.4(.1)**
gyroscopic **24.2.8(.5)**
gyrostatic **24.2.10(.4.1)**
gyrus **34.18.27(.10)**
gyttja **17.28.2**
gyve **31.9**
gyver **17.21.10**
h **38.3**
ha **10**
haar **10**
Haarlem **27.15.28(.6)**
Haas **34.7, 34.9**
Habakkuk **24.12.4**
habanera **17.32.5**
habeas corpus **34.18.9(.6)**
Haber-Bosch **36.9.2**
haberdasher **17.26.6**
haberdashery **1.29.11(.20)**
habergeon **28.17.28(.9)**
Habgood **23.16.3**
habile **40.2.4**
habiliment
 22.26.15(.13.2)
habilitate **22.4.9(.5)**
habilitation **28.17.25(.3.3)**
habit **22.2.6**

habitability **1.10.16(.22.2)**
habitable **40.20.16(.11.3)**
habitableness
 34.18.16(.37.4)
habitably **1.31.21(.4.2)**
habitant **22.26.15(.9)**
habitat **22.7.7**
habitation **28.17.25(.3.3)**
habited **23.18.9(.13)**
habitual **40.16.12**
habitually **1.31.17(.24)**
habitualness
 34.18.16(.37.1)
habituate **22.4.4**
habituation **28.17.25(.3.1)**
habitude **23.17.4(.1)**
habitué **4.4**
Habsburg **26.14.1(.10)**
habutai **14.8**
háček **24.4.11**
hachure **17.7.10, 17.26.6**
hacienda **17.13.20(.3)**
hack **24.6**
hackamore **12.9.4**
hackberry **1.29.11(.7.2)**
hacker **17.14.5**
hackery **1.29.11(.10)**
Hackett **22.2.9(.3)**
hackette **22.5.5**
hackle **40.23.5**
hackly **1.31.24(.5)**
hackmatack **24.6.7**
hackney **1.16.21**
hacksaw **12.14.13**
hackwork **24.17.6(.10)**
had **23.7**
haddie **1.11.7**
Haddington **28.17.11(.23)**
haddock **24.16.5**
Haddon **28.17.12(.6)**
hade **23.4**
Hadean **28.3.4(.3)**
Hades **35.1.8**
Hadfield **23.31.1(.2)**
Hadith **32.1**
Hadlee **1.31.23(.5)**
Hadley **1.31.23(.5)**
hadn't **22.26.15(.10)**
Hadrian **28.3.20(.12)**
hadron **28.10.24(.8), 28.17.31(.15)**
hadronic **24.2.15(.6.4)**
hadrosaur **12.14.8**
hadst **22.29.19**
haecceity **1.10.16(.1)**
haem **27.1**
haemal **40.25.1**
haematic **24.2.10(.4.2)**
haematin **28.2.11(.10)**
haematite **22.16.9**

haematocele **40.1.10**
haematocrit **22.2.24**
haematologic **24.2.24(.4)**
haematological
 40.23.12(.17.2)
haematologist
 22.29.2(.26.3)
haematology
 1.26.10(.11.2)
haematoma **17.17.16(.2)**
haematuria **3.22.12**
haemocyanin **28.2.18**
haemodialysis
 34.2.17(.10.5)
haemodynamic
 24.2.14(.4)
haemoglobin **28.2.10**
haemolysis **34.2.17(.10.5)**
haemolytic **24.2.10(.2.5)**
haemophilia **3.24.2**
haemophiliac **24.6.1**
haemophilic **24.2.27(.2)**
haemorrhage **39.2.22(.9)**
haemorrhagic **24.2.24(.2)**
haemorrhoid **23.13.19**
haemorrhoidal **40.22.9**
haemostasis **34.2.17(.2)**
haemostat **22.7.7**
haemostatic **24.2.10(.4.1)**
haere mai **14**
hafiz **35.2.9**
hafnium **27.3.8(.11)**
Hafod **23.10.9**
haft **22.27.4**
haftorah **10.23**
hag **26.5**
Hagan **28.17.15(.3)**
Hagar **10.9, 17.16.3**
hagfish **36.2.18(.18)**
Haggadah **10.7, 17.13.7**
Haggadic **24.2.11(.5)**
Haggadoth **22.21.4**
Haggai **14.2, 14.3, 14.11**
haggard **23.18.12**
haggardly **1.31.23(.14.5)**
haggardness
 34.18.16(.21.1)
haggis **34.2.11**
haggish **36.2.14**
haggle **40.24.4**
haggler **17.34.24**
hagiocracy **1.22.16(.13)**
Hagiographa **17.20.12(.5)**
hagiographer
 17.20.12(.5)
hagiographic **24.2.16(.3)**
hagiographical
 40.23.12(.12)
hagiography **1.18.9(.3.2)**
hagiolater **17.12.16(.20)**
hagiolatry **1.29.15(.13)**

hagiological **40.23.12(.17.2)**
hagiologist **22.29.2(.26.2)**
hagiology **1.26.10(.11.1)**
hagioscope **20.15.4(.1)**
hagioscopic **24.2.8(.5)**
hagridden **28.17.12(.2)**
Hague **26.3**
hah **10**
ha-ha **10.21**
Hahn **28.9**
hahnium **27.3.8(.5)**
haick **24.3, 24.13**
Haida **17.13.12**
Haifa **17.20.10**
Haigh **4, 26.3**
Haight **22.4, 22.16**
Haight-Ashbury **1.29.11(.7.2)**
haik **24.2.4, 24.3, 24.13**
haiku **16.9**
hail **40.4**
hailer **17.34.4**
Haile Selassie **1.22.6**
Hailey **1.31.4**
Hailsham **27.15.22**
hailstone **28.19.4(.9)**
hailstorm **27.10.2**
Hailwood **23.16.6(.22)**
haily **1.31.4**
Hain **28.4**
Hainault **22.13.6, 22.32.5, 22.32.6**
Hainsworth **32.14.15**
Haiphong **29.6.7**
hair **6**
hairbreadth **32.18**
hairbrush **36.12**
haircare **6.6**
haircloth **32.9**
haircut **22.15.4**
hairdo **16.8.1**
hairdresser **17.24.5**
hairdressing **29.1.23**
hairdryer **17.6.14**
hairgrip **20.2.11**
hairily **1.31.17(.27.1)**
hairiness **34.18.16(.2.9)**
hairless **34.18.29(.6)**
hairlessness **34.18.16(.31.6)**
hairlike **24.13.7(.4)**
hairline **28.14.19(.5)**
hairnet **22.5.9(.1)**
hairpiece **34.1.1**
hairpin **28.2.9**
hairsbreadth **32.18**
hairspray **4.26.9**
hairspring **29.1.30(.11)**
hairstreak **24.1.11**
hairstyle **40.13.3(.10)**

hairstyling **29.1.31(.10)**
hairstylist **22.29.2(.31.1)**
hairy **1.29.4**
Haiti **1.10.1, 1.10.3, 1.10.13**
Haitian **28.3.3, 28.3.15, 28.17.25(.1)**
haji **1.26.4, 1.26.5**
hajj **39.6, 39.8**
haka **17.14.7**
hake **24.3**
Hakenkreuz **34.22.10**
Hakenkreuze **17.24.19**
hakim **27.1.4**
Hakka **17.14.5**
Hakluyt **22.18.11**
Hal **40.6**
Halacha **17.15**
Halachic **24.2.12**
Halafian **28.3.9**
Halakah **10.8.4, 17.15**
halal **40.6.16, 40.8.17**
halation **28.17.25(.3.14)**
halberd **23.18.8**
halberdier **3.5**
halcyon **28.3.13**
Haldane **28.4.4**
hale **40.4**
haleness **34.18.16(.37.1)**
háler **17.34.8**
haleru **16.23.6**
Hales **35.30.3**
Halesowen **28.17.8**
Halesworth **32.14.15**
Halewood **23.16.6(.22)**
Halex® **34.23.4(.12)**
Haley **1.31.4**
half **30.7**
halfback **24.6.6(.19)**
halfpence **34.24.10(.8)**
halfpenny **1.16.18**
halfpennyworth **32.14.12, 32.15.2**
halftime **27.12.1**
halftone **28.19.4**
halftrack **24.6.21**
halfway **4.25**
halfwit **22.2.23**
half-witted **23.18.9(.2)**
half-wittedly **1.31.23(.14.3)**
half-wittedness **34.18.16(.21.1)**
halibut **22.19.9**
Halicarnassus **34.18.20**
halide **23.15.16**
halieutic **24.2.10(.9)**
Halifax **34.23.5(.8)**
haliotis **34.2.8**
halite **22.16.25(.6)**
halitosis **34.2.17(.11.1)**

hall **40.10**
Hallam **27.15.28(.5)**
Halle **1.31.7**
Hallé **1.31.7, 4.28.3**
hallelujah **17.33.3**
Haller **17.34.6**
Halley **1.31.7**
Halliday **4.10.7**
Halliwell **40.5.17(.5)**
hallmark **24.8.8**
halloo **16.25**
hallow **19.29.5**
Halloween **28.1**
Hallowes **35.20.14**
hallstand **23.24.6(.5)**
Hallstatt **22.7.7, 22.10.3**
halluces **35.1.16(.10)**
hallucinant **22.26.15(.14)**
hallucinate **22.4.14(.9.3)**
hallucination **28.17.25(.3.8)**
hallucinator **17.12.4(.10)**
hallucinatory **1.29.11(.8.2)**
hallucinogen **28.17.28(.9)**
hallucinogenic **24.2.15(.4)**
hallux **34.23.15**
hallway **4.25.26**
halm **27.10**
halma **17.17.24**
Halmahera **17.32.5**
halo **19.29.3**
halogen **28.17.28(.9)**
halogenation **28.17.25(.3.8)**
halogenic **24.2.15(.4)**
halon **28.10.26**
halophyte **22.16.16**
Halpern **28.17.9**
Halpin **28.2.9**
Hals **34.27, 35.30.5**
Halstead **23.5.3, 23.18.9(.20)**
halt **22.32.5, 22.32.6**
Haltemprice **34.15.9**
halter **17.12.26(.5)**
halteres **35.3**
halterneck **24.4.7**
haltingly **1.31.28(.1.4)**
Halton **28.17.11(.27)**
halva **10.13, 17.21.19**
halvah **17.21.19**
halve **31.6**
halyard **23.18.28**
ham **27.6**
Hamada **17.13.7**
hamadryad **23.7.3, 23.18.3**
hamadryas **34.7.3, 34.18.5**
hamamelis **34.2.22(.1)**

hamartia **3.4.5**
Hamas **34.7.11**
Hambly **1.31.21(.12)**
hambone **28.19.3**
Hambro **19.27.14**
Hamburg **26.14.1(.8)**
hamburger **17.16.14**
Hamelin **28.2.31(.10)**
Hamer **17.17.4**
hames **35.25.3**
Hamilcar **10.8.18**
Hamill **40.2.9, 40.25.4**
Hamilton **28.17.11(.27)**
Hamish **36.2.15**
Hamite **22.16.13**
Hamitic **24.2.10(.2.2)**
Hamito-Semitic **24.2.10(.2.2)**
hamlet **22.19.26(.21)**
Hamley **1.31.26(.5)**
hammam **27.6.8, 27.8.6, 27.11.7**
hammer **17.17.6**
hammerbeam **27.1.1**
hammerer **17.32.14(.10)**
Hammerfest **22.29.5(.4)**
hammerhead **23.5.13(.5)**
hammering **29.1.30(.8)**
hammerless **34.18.29(.17.3)**
hammerlock **24.9.16(.6)**
hammerman **28.7.10(.6)**
hammermen **28.5.7(.10)**
Hammersmith **32.2.3**
Hammerstein **28.14.5**
Hammett **22.19.14**
hammock **24.16.6**
Hammond **23.24.16(.7)**
Hammurabi **1.9.6**
hammy **1.15.6**
Hamnett **22.19.15(.12)**
hamper **17.10.17**
Hampshire **17.26.17**
Hampson **28.17.23(.17)**
Hampstead **23.2.8, 23.5.3**
Hampton **28.17.11(.18)**
Hampton Court **22.13**
Hampton Roads **35.23.14**
hamsin **28.2.23(.15)**
hamster **17.12.24(.22)**
hamstring **29.1.30(.13)**
hamstrung **29.8**
hamuli **2.32.9(.8), 14.25.9**
hamulus **34.18.29(.17.6)**
hamza **17.25.17**
Han **28.7**
Hancock **24.9.6**
Hancox **34.23.8(.5)**
hand **23.24.6**
hand-axe **34.23.5(.4)**

h

Harijan **28.7.17,
28.17.28(.2)**
hark **24.8**
Harkness **34.18.16(.22)**
harl **40.8**
Harland **23.24.16(.16.2)**
harle **40.8**
Harlech **24.16.16, 25.10**
Harlem **27.15.28(.6)**
harlequin **28.2.28**
harlequinade **23.4.8**
Harlesden **28.17.12(.26)**
Harley Street **22.1**
harlot **22.19.26(.7)**
harlotry **1.29.15(.13)**
Harlow **19.29.7**
harm **27.8**
Harman **28.17.16(.9)**
harmattan **28.17.11(.6)**
Harmer **17.17.7**
harmful **40.27.21**
harmfully **1.31.17(.16.2)**
harmfulness
34.18.16(.37.2)
harmless **34.18.29(.26)**
harmlessly **1.31.33(.12.6)**
harmlessness
34.18.16(.31.6)
Harmon **28.17.16(.9)**
harmonic **24.2.15(.6.2)**
harmonica **17.14.15(.9)**
harmonically
1.31.24(.9.8)
harmonious **34.3.6(.7)**
harmoniously
1.31.33(.1.2)
harmoniousness
34.18.16(.31.1)
harmonist **22.29.2(.18.1)**
harmonistic
24.2.10(.15.2)
harmonium **27.3.8(.10)**
harmonization
28.17.25(.3.11)
harmonize **35.15.12(.5)**
harmony **1.16.15(.11)**
Harmsworth **32.14.15**
harness **34.18.16(.9)**
harnesser **17.24.15**
Harold **23.31.11**
harp **20.6**
Harpenden **28.17.12(.23)**
harper **17.10.7**
Harpic® **24.2.8(.4)**
harpist **22.29.2(.11)**
Harpocrates **35.1.7(.6)**
harpoon **28.16.1**
harpooner **17.18.15**
harpsichord **23.12.4**
harpsichordist
22.29.2(.14)

harpy **1.8.6**
harquebus **34.18.10**
harquebusier **3.14**
Harrap **20.13.6**
Harrell **40.16.13(.5)**
harridan **28.17.12(.16)**
harrier **3.22.5**
Harries **34.2.21, 35.2.17**
Harriet **22.3.12**
Harriman **28.17.16(.16)**
Harrington **28.17.11(.23)**
Harris **34.2.21**
Harrisburg **26.14.1(.10)**
Harrison **28.17.23(.14)**
Harrod **23.18.27**
Harrogate **22.4.12(.5),
22.19.13**
Harrovian **28.3.10**
harrow **19.27.4**
harrower **17.9.11**
harrowingly **1.31.28(.1.1)**
harrumph **30.18**
harry **1.29.5**
harsh **36.8**
harshen **28.17.25(.6)**
harshly **1.31.35(.4)**
harshness **34.18.16(.33.1)**
harslet **22.19.26(.26)**
hart **22.10**
hartal **40.8.4**
Harte **22.10**
hartebeest **22.29.1**
Hartford **23.18.16(.11)**
Hartland **23.24.16(.16.3)**
Hartlepool **40.15.1**
Hartley **1.31.22(.8)**
Hartman **28.17.16(.21)**
Hartnell **40.26.17**
hartshorn **28.11.10**
Hartshorne **28.11.10**
harum-scarum
27.15.26(.2)
haruspex **34.23.4(.1)**
haruspices **35.1.16(.10)**
haruspicy **1.22.16(.2)**
Harvard **23.18.17**
harvest **22.29.15(.15)**
harvestable
40.20.16(.11.7)
harvester **17.12.24(.14)**
harvestman **28.17.16(.21)**
Harvey **1.19.6**
Harwich **38.2.10,
39.2.22(.4)**
Harwood **23.16.6(.3)**
Haryana **17.18.8**
Harz **34.22.7**
has **35.7**
Hasdrubal **40.6.4,
40.20.14, 40.20.15**
Hášek **24.4.10**

Haseldine **28.14.6**
hash **36.6**
hash-browns **35.26.8**
hasheesh **36.1**
Hashemite **22.16.13**
hashish **36.1, 36.2.22**
Hasid **23.2.16**
hasidic **24.2.11(.2)**
Hasidim **27.2.4**
Hasidism **27.15.21(.2.5)**
Haslam **27.15.28(.20)**
Haslemere **3.8.16**
haslet **22.19.26(.27)**
Haslett **22.19.26(.27)**
Hasmonean **28.17.1(.7)**
hasn't **22.26.15(.18)**
hasp **20.17**
Hassall **40.31.6**
Hassan **28.9.9, 28.17.23(.6)**
Hasselt **22.32.15**
hassle **40.31.6**
hassock **24.16.11**
hast **22.29.6**
hastate **22.4.9(.9)**
haste **22.29.4**
hasten **28.17.23(.4)**
Hastie **1.10.26(.3)**
hastily **1.31.17(.9.3)**
hastiness **34.18.16(.2.3)**
Hastings **35.27**
hasty **1.10.26(.3)**
hat **22.7**
hatable **40.20.16(.11.1)**
hatband **23.24.6(.4)**
hatbox **34.23.8(.2)**
hatch **38.5**
hatchback **24.6.6(.22)**
Hatcher **17.28.6**
hatchery **1.29.11(.22)**
hatchet **22.2.20**
hatching **29.1.27**
hatchling **29.1.31(.28)**
hatchment
22.26.15(.13.6)
hatchway **4.25.24**
hate **22.4**
hateful **40.27.18**
hatefully **1.31.17(.16.2)**
hatefulness
34.18.16(.37.2)
hater **17.12.4**
Hatfield **23.31.1(.2)**
hatful **40.14.6(.10)**
hath **32.6**
Hathaway **4.25.9**
hatha-yoga **17.16.15**
Hatherley **1.31.17(.19)**
Hathern **28.17.22**
Hathersage **39.2.19,
39.4.7**

Hathor **12.13**
hatless **34.18.29(.22)**
hatpeg **26.4**
hatpin **28.2.9**
hatred **23.18.27**
Hatshepsut **22.18.6**
hatstand **23.24.6(.5)**
hatter **17.12.6**
Hatteras **34.18.27(.14)**
Hattersley **1.31.34**
Hattie **1.10.6**
Hatton **28.17.11(.6)**
Hattusas **34.18.20**
hauberk **24.17.1**
Haugh **12, 30.9**
Haughey **1.13, 1.27**
haughtily **1.31.17(.9.2)**
haughtiness
34.18.16(.2.3)
Haughton **28.17.11(.10)**
haughty **1.10.10**
haul **40.10**
haulage **39.2.23**
hauler **17.34.10**
haulier **3.24.8**
haulm **27.10**
haunch **38.18.6**
haunt **22.26.10**
haunter **17.12.22(.8)**
hauntingly **1.31.28(.1.4)**
Hauptmann **28.17.16(.21)**
Hausa **17.24.7, 17.25.6**
Hausfrau **9.16**
hautboy **13.3**
haute couture **12.17,
17.7.12(.3)**
haute cuisine **28.1.19**
haute école **40.9.9**
hauteur **18.3**
haut monde **23.24.9**
Havana **17.18.6**
have **31.5**
have-a-go **19.13**
Havel **40.28.6**
havelock **24.9.16(.18),
24.16.16**
haven **28.17.20(.3)**
have-not **22.11.9**
haver **17.21.3**
Haverfordwest
22.29.5(.11)
Haverhill **40.2.18,
40.16.13(.12.2)**
Havering **29.1.30(.8)**
Havers **35.18.15**
haversack **24.6.14**
haversine **28.14.13**
haves **35.28.3**
Haviland **23.24.16(.16.2)**
havildar **10.7**

h

havoc **24.16.9**
haw **12**
Hawaii **2.6**
Hawaiian **28.17.5**
Hawes **35.12**
hawfinch **38.18.1**
haw-haw **12.19**
Hawick **24.11**
hawk **24.10**
hawkbit **22.2.6**
Hawke **24.10**
Hawke Bay **4**
hawker **17.14.9**
Hawkes **34.23.9**
Hawke's Bay **4**
Hawking **29.1.14(.7)**
Hawkins **35.26.2**
hawkish **36.2.13**
hawkishness
  34.18.16(.33.4)
hawklike **24.13.7(.14)**
hawkmoth **32.9**
hawksbill **40.2.4**
Hawksmoor **12.9.12,
  17.7.7**
hawkweed **23.1.10**
Hawley **1.31.11**
Haworth **32.14.2, 32.14.15**
hawse **35.12**
hawser **17.25.9**
hawthorn **28.11.8**
Hawtrey **1.29.15**
Haxey **1.22.22**
hay **4**
Hayakawa **17.31.2**
haybox **34.23.8(.2)**
haycock **24.9.6**
Hayden **28.17.12(.4)**
Haydn **28.17.12(.4)**
Hayek **24.4.1, 24.4.13**
Hayes **35.4**
hayfield **23.31.1(.2)**
hayfork **24.10.6**
haylage **39.2.23**
Hayle **40.4**
Hayley **1.31.4**
Hayling **29.1.31(.4)**
hayloft **22.27.5**
haymaker **17.14.3(.3)**
haymaking **29.1.14(.3)**
Hayman **28.17.16(.4)**
Haymarket **22.2.9(.4)**
haymow **19.14.3**
Haynes **35.26.4**
hayrack **24.6.21**
hayrick **24.2.26(.3)**
hayride **23.15.15**
Hays **35.4**
hayseed **23.1.7**
haystack **24.6.7**

Hayter **17.12.4**
haywain **28.4.17**
Hayward **23.18.26(.4)**
haywire **17.6.13**
Haywood **23.16.6(.2),
  23.18.26(.4)**
Hayworth **32.14.15**
Hazan **28.7.15**
hazard **23.18.21**
hazardous **34.18.12**
hazardously
  1.31.33(.12.2)
hazardousness
  34.18.16(.31.3)
haze **35.4**
hazel **40.32.3**
hazelnut **22.15.6**
hazily **1.31.17(.21)**
haziness **34.18.16(.2.7)**
Hazlitt **22.19.26(.27)**
hazy **1.23.3**
Hazzard **23.18.21**
he **2**
head **23.5**
headache **24.3.5**
headachy **1.12.3**
headage **39.2.11**
headband **23.24.6(.4)**
headbanger **17.19.2**
headbanging **29.1.18**
headboard **23.12.2(.9)**
headcheese **35.1.20**
headcount **22.26.7**
headdress **34.5.14(.6)**
header **17.13.4**
headfast **22.29.6(.9)**
headfirst **22.29.16**
headgear **3.7**
headhunt **22.26.12**
headhunter **17.12.22(.10)**
headily **1.31.17(.10)**
headiness **34.18.16(.2.3)**
heading **29.1.13(.4)**
headlamp **20.16.3**
headland **23.24.16(.16.3)**
headless **34.18.29(.23)**
headlight **22.16.25(.14)**
headline **28.14.19(.15)**
headliner **17.18.13(.14)**
headlock **24.9.16(.12)**
headlong **29.6.15**
headman **28.7.10(.12),
  28.17.16(.22)**
headmaster **17.12.24(.5)**
headmasterly
  1.31.17(.9.3)
headmen **28.5.7(.16)**
headmistress
  34.18.27(.14)
headmost **22.29.17(.4)**
headnote **22.21.8**

headphone **28.19.11**
headpiece **34.1.1**
headpin **28.2.9**
headquarter **17.12.10(.7)**
headquarters **35.18.8**
headrest **22.29.5(.12)**
headroom **27.14.6(.9)**
headsail **40.4.10**
headscarf **30.7.3**
headset **22.5.13(.9)**
headship **20.2.7(.15)**
headshrinker
  17.14.21(.1)
headsman **28.17.16(.30)**
headspace **34.4.2**
headspring **29.1.30(.11)**
headsquare **6.18.9**
headstall **40.10.5**
headstock **24.9.4**
headstone **28.19.4(.9)**
headstrong **29.6.14**
headstrongly **1.31.28(.3)**
headstrongness
  34.18.16(.26)
headteacher **17.28.1**
headward **23.18.26(.10)**
headwater **17.12.10(.7)**
headway **4.25.13**
headwind **23.24.2**
headword **23.19.8**
headwork **24.17.6(.9)**
heady **1.11.5**
heal **40.1**
healable **40.20.16(.29)**
heald **23.31.1**
healer **17.34.1**
Healey **1.31.1**
health **32.24**
healthful **40.27.24**
healthfully **1.31.17(.16.2)**
healthfulness
  34.18.16(.37.2)
healthily **1.31.17(.18)**
healthiness **34.18.16(.2.6)**
healthy **1.20.12**
Healy **1.31.1**
Heaney **1.16.1**
Heanor **17.18.1**
heap **20.1**
hear **3**
hearable **40.20.16(.27.1)**
Heard **23.19**
hearer **17.32.2**
hearken **28.17.13(.6)**
Hearne **28.18**
hearsay **4.18.2**
hearse **34.19**
heart **22.10**
heartache **24.3.4**
heartbeat **22.1.2**

heartbreak **24.3.13**
heartbreaker **17.14.3(.8)**
heartbreaking **29.1.14(.3)**
heartbroken
  28.17.13(.15)
heartburn **28.18.3**
hearten **28.17.11(.8)**
hearteningly **1.31.28(.1.7)**
heartfelt **22.32.2**
hearth **32.8**
hearthrug **26.10**
hearthstone **28.19.4(.9)**
heartily **1.31.17(.9.2)**
heartiness **34.18.16(.2.3)**
heartland **23.24.6(.13),
  23.24.16(.16.3)**
heartless **34.18.29(.22)**
heartlessly **1.31.33(.12.6)**
heartlessness
  34.18.16(.31.6)
heartrending **29.1.13(.14)**
heartsearching **29.1.27**
heartsease **35.1.16(.13)**
heartsick **24.2.20(.12)**
heartsickness
  34.18.16(.22)
heartsore **12.14.11**
heartstrings **35.27**
heartthrob **21.8**
heart-to-heart **22.10.11**
heartwarming **29.1.16**
heartwarmingly
  1.31.28(.1.7)
heartwood **23.16.6(.9)**
hearty **1.10.8**
heat **22.1**
heatedly **1.31.23(.14.3)**
heater **17.12.1**
heath **32.1**
Heathcliff **30.2.6**
Heathcote **22.19.12(.13)**
heathen **28.17.22**
heathendom
  27.15.10(.14)
heathenish **36.2.16(.13)**
heathenishly
  1.31.35(.7.2)
heathenishness
  34.18.16(.33.5)
heathenism
  27.15.21(.2.9)
heathenry **1.29.20**
heather **17.23.4**
heathery **1.31.11(.17)**
Heathfield **23.31.1(.2)**
heathland **23.24.6(.13),
  23.24.16(.16.4)**
heathless **34.18.29(.31)**
heathlike **24.13.7(.21)**
Heathrow **19.27**
heathy **1.20.1**

Heaton 28.17.11(.1)
heatproof 30.13.4
heatstroke 24.18.13
heatwave 31.3.6
heave 31.1
heave-ho 19.26
heaven 28.17.20(.4)
heavenliness
34.18.16(.2.10)
heavenly 1.31.27(.14)
heavenward 23.18.26(.13)
heaver 17.21.1
heavily 1.31.17(.17)
heaviness 34.18.16(.2.6)
Heaviside 23.15.11(.2)
heavy 1.19.4
heavy-footed 23.18.9(.11)
heavy-handed
23.18.10(.14)
heavy-handedly
1.31.23(.14.4)
heavy-handedness
34.18.16(.21.1)
heavy-hearted 23.18.9(.7)
heavyish 36.2.1
heavyset 22.5.13
heavyweight 22.4.21
Hebburn 28.18.3
Hebden 28.17.12(.19)
hebdomadal 40.22.13
hebdomadally
1.31.17(.10)
Hebe 1.9.1
Hebert 22.19.9
hebetude 23.17.4(.1)
Hebraic 24.2.3
Hebraically 1.31.24(.9.1)
Hebraism 27.15.21(.2.1)
Hebraist 22.29.2(.3)
Hebraistic 24.2.10(.15.1)
Hebraize 35.15.1
Hebrew 16.23.7
Hebridean 28.17.1(.4)
Hebrides 35.1.8
Hebron 28.10.24(.6)
Hecate 1.10.16(.10),
22.19.12(.4)
hecatomb 27.14.1
heck 24.4
heckelphone 28.19.11
heckle 40.23.4
heckler 17.34.23
Heckmondwike 24.13.5
hectarage 39.2.22(.9)
hectare 6.4
hectic 24.2.10(.13)
hectically 1.31.24(.9.5)
hectogram 27.6.17(.5)
hectograph 30.7.5(.1)
hectolitre 17.12.1(.15)
hectometre 17.12.1(.6)

hector 17.12.21(.2)
hectoringly 1.31.28(.1.17)
Hecuba 17.11.13
he'd 23.1
heddle 40.22.4
Hedex® 34.23.4(.4)
hedge 39.5
hedgehog 26.7.11
hedgehop 20.7.11
hedgehopper 17.10.8
hedger 17.29.4
hedgerow 19.27.22
Hedges 35.18.21
Hedley 1.31.23(.4)
hedonic 24.2.15(.6.1)
hedonism 27.15.21(.2.9)
hedonist 22.29.2(.18.1)
hedonistic 24.2.10(.15.2)
hedonistically
1.31.24(.9.6)
heebie-jeebies 35.2.2
heed 23.1
heedful 40.27.19
heedfully 1.31.17(.16.2)
heedfulness
34.18.16(.37.2)
heedless 34.18.29(.23)
heedlessly 1.31.33(.12.6)
heedlessness
34.18.16(.31.6)
hee-haw 12.19
heel 40.1
heelball 40.10.4
heelbar 10.5.14
heelless 34.18.29(.38)
Heep 20.1
Heffernan 28.17.17(.10)
heft 22.27.2
heftily 1.31.17(.9.3)
heftiness 34.18.16(.2.3)
hefty 1.10.24
Hegarty 1.10.16(.11)
Hegel 40.24.3
Hegelian 28.3.21(.3)
Hegelianism
27.15.21(.2.9)
hegemonic 24.2.15(.6.2)
hegemony 1.16.15(.11)
Hegira 17.32.13
Heidegger 17.16.4,
17.16.13
Heidelberg 26.14.1(.12)
Heidi 1.11.14
heifer 17.20.4
heigh 4
heigh-ho 19.26
height 22.16
heighten 28.17.11(.12)
Heilbronn 28.10.24(.6)
Heilong 29.6.15

Heine 1.16.13, 17.18.13
Heineken® 28.17.13(.13)
Heinemann 28.17.16(.16)
Heiney 1.16.13
Heinkel 40.23.15
Heinlein 28.14.19(.19)
heinous 34.18.16(.1)
heinously 1.31.33(.12.3)
heinousness
34.18.16(.31.3)
Heinz 35.26.12
heir 6
heirdom 27.15.10(.3)
heiress 34.5, 34.5.14(.1),
34.18.27(.4)
heirless 34.18.29(.6)
heirloom 27.14.8
heirship 20.2.7(.4)
Heisenberg 26.14.1(.9)
heist 22.29.13
hei-tiki 1.12.2
Hekla 17.34.23
HeLa 17.34.1
held 23.31.4
Heldentenor 17.18.4
hele 40.1
Helen 28.17.33(.4)
Helena 17.18.16(.22)
helenium 27.3.8(.1)
Helga 17.16.19
Helgoland 23.24.6(.13)
heliacal 40.23.12(.3)
helianthemum 27.15.13
helianthus 34.18.19
helical 40.23.12(.19)
helically 1.31.24(.9.12)
helices 35.1.16(.10)
helichrysum 27.15.20(.9)
helicity 1.10.16(.16.1)
helicoid 23.13.9
Helicon 28.10.11,
28.17.13(.13)
helicopter 17.12.19
helideck 24.4.5
Heligoland 23.24.6(.13)
heliocentric
24.2.26(.14.4)
heliocentrically
1.31.24(.9.12)
Heliogabalus
34.18.29(.17.2)
heliogram 27.6.17(.5)
heliograph 30.7.5(.1)
heliography 1.18.9(.3.2)
heliogravure 17.7.12(.10)
heliolithic 24.2.18(.1)
heliometer 17.12.16(.9.2)
Heliopolis 34.2.22(.8)
Helios 34.10.2
heliostat 22.7.7
heliostatic 24.2.10(.4.1)

heliotherapy 1.8.11(.8)
heliotrope 20.15.8
heliotropic 24.2.8(.5)
heliotropically
1.31.24(.9.2)
heliotropism
27.15.21(.2.2)
heliotype 20.10.2
helipad 23.7.5
heliport 22.13.1
heli-skiing 29.1.2
helium 27.3.18
helix 34.23.2(.13)
he'll 40.1
hell 40.5
hellacious 34.18.22(.3)
hellaciously
1.31.33(.12.4)
Helladic 24.2.11(.5)
Hellas 34.7.19
hellcat 22.7.9
hellebore 12.4
helleborine 28.1.25(.3),
28.14.18
Hellene 28.1.27(.3)
Hellenic 24.2.15(.4)
Hellenism 27.15.21(.2.9)
Hellenist 22.29.2(.18.3)
Hellenistic 24.2.10(.15.2)
Hellenization
28.17.25(.3.11)
Hellenize 35.15.12(.5)
Heller 17.34.5
Hellespont 22.26.9
hellfire 17.6.9
hell-for-leather 17.23.4
hellgrammite 22.16.13
hellhole 40.18.13
hellhound 23.24.7(.8)
hellion 28.3.21(.2)
hellish 36.2.27
hellishly 1.31.35(.7.4)
hellishness
34.18.16(.33.6)
hell-like 24.13.7(.27)
Hellman 28.17.16(.35)
hello 19.29
hellraiser 17.25.3
hellraising 29.1.24
helluva 17.21.12
hellward 23.18.26(.17)
helm 27.18
helmet 22.19.14
Helmholtz 34.22.20
helminth 32.21
helminthiasis
34.2.17(.10.1)
helminthic 24.2.18(.6)
helminthoid 23.13.15
helminthologist
22.29.2(.26.4)

helminthology
1.26.10(.11.5)
helmsman 28.17.16(.30)
Héloïse 35.1, 35.1.4
Helot 22.19.26(.4)
helotism 27.15.21(.2.4)
helotry 1.29.15(.13)
help 20.18
helper 17.10.19
helpful 40.27.17
helpfully 1.31.17(.16.2)
helpfulness 34.18.16(.27)
helping 29.1.10(.13)
helpless 34.18.29(.20)
helplessly 1.31.33(.12.6)
helplessness
34.18.16(.31.6)
helpline 28.14.19(.13)
Helpmann 28.17.16(.19)
helpmate 22.4.13(.8)
helpmeet 22.1.5
Helsingborg 26.9
Helsingfors 35.12
Helsingor 17.19.1
Helsinki 1.12.16
helter-skelter
17.12.26(.3)
helve 31.13
Helvellyn 28.2.31(.4)
Helvetia 3.16.1, 17.26.1
Helvetian 28.17.25(.1)
Helvetic 24.2.10(.3.2)
hem 27.5
he-man 28.7.10(.1)
hematic 24.2.10(.4.2)
hematite 22.16.9
hematological
40.23.12(.17.2)
hematology 1.26.10(.11.2)
Hemel Hempstead
23.5.3
he-men 28.5.7(.1)
hemerocallis 34.2.22(.5)
hemianopia 3.2.7
hemianopsia 3.14.12
hemicellulose 34.20.17,
35.20.14
hemicycle 40.23.10
hemidemisemiquaver
17.21.3
hemihedral 40.16.13(.17)
Hemingway 4.25.18
hemiplegia 3.19.1,
17.29.1
hemiplegic 24.2.24(.1)
Hemiptera 17.32.14(.6)
hemipteran 28.17.31(.11)
hemipterous
34.18.27(.14)
hemisphere 3.10.5
hemispheric 24.2.26(.4)

hemispherical
40.23.12(.18)
hemispherically
1.31.24(.9.12)
hemistich 24.2.10(.15.4)
hemline 28.14.19(.18)
hemlock 24.9.16(.15)
hemocyanin 28.2.18
hemoglobin 28.2.10
hemolytic 24.2.10(.2.5)
hemophiliac 24.6.1
hemostat 22.7.7
hemostatic 24.2.10(.4.1)
hemp 20.16.2
hempen 28.17.9
hemp-nettle 40.21.4
hemstitch 38.2.3
hen 28.5
Henan 28.17.17(.1)
henbane 28.4.2
hence 34.24.3
henceforth 32.10
henceforward
23.18.26(.5)
henchman 28.17.16(.33)
hencoop 20.12
hendecagon 28.10.12,
28.17.15(.13)
hendecasyllabic
24.2.9(.2)
hendecasyllable
40.20.16(.29)
Henderson 28.17.23(.14)
hendiadys 34.2.9
Hendon 28.17.12(.23)
Hendrickson
28.17.23(.21)
Hendrix 34.23.2(.12)
Hendry 1.29.16
Hendy 1.11.20(.3)
henequen 28.5.5
henge 39.17.3
Hengist 22.29.15(.12)
henhouse 34.8.6(.16)
Henley 1.31.27(.5)
henna 17.18.4
Hennessy 1.22.16(.9)
henotheism
27.15.21(.2.1)
henpeck 24.4.2
Henrietta 17.12.5
Henriques 35.2.5
henry 1.29.20
Henshaw 12.16.12
Hensley 1.31.34
Henson 28.17.23(.24)
Henty 1.10.23(.3)
Henze 17.24.19
heortologist
22.29.2(.26.3)
heortology 1.26.10(.11.2)

hep 20.4
heparin 28.2.29(.5)
heparinize 35.15.12(.5)
hepatic 24.2.10(.4.1)
hepatica 17.14.2
hepatitis 34.18.11(.8)
hepatocyte 22.16.19(.9)
hepatomegaly
1.31.17(.12)
hepatotoxic 24.2.20(.13)
Hepburn 28.17.10, 28.18.3
Hephaestus 34.18.11(.16)
Hephzibah 10.5.4
Hepplewhite 22.16.23
heptachord 23.12.4
heptad 23.7.7
heptaglot 22.11.17
heptagon 28.10.12,
28.17.15(.13)
heptagonal 40.26.13(.7)
heptahedra 17.32.20
heptahedral 40.16.13(.17)
heptahedron
28.17.31(.15)
heptameter 17.12.16(.9.1)
heptane 28.4.3
heptarchic 24.2.12
heptarchical 40.23.12(.9)
heptarchy 1.12.6
heptasyllabic 24.2.9(.2)
Heptateuch 24.15.8
heptathlete 22.1.18
heptathlon 28.10.26,
28.17.33(.24)
heptavalent 22.26.15(.25)
Hepworth 32.14.15
her 18
Hera 17.32.2
Heracles 35.1.23
Heraclitus 34.18.11(.8)
Heraklion 28.3.21(.13)
herald 23.31.11
heraldic 24.2.11(.18)
heraldically 1.31.24(.9.7)
heraldist 22.29.2(.14)
heraldry 1.29.16
herb 21.15
herbaceous 34.18.22(.3)
herbage 39.2.9
herbal 40.20.17
herbalism 27.15.21(.2.15)
herbalist 22.29.2(.31.2)
herbaria 3.22.4
herbarium 27.3.17(.3)
Herbert 22.19.9
herbicidal 40.22.11
herbicide 23.15.11(.6)
Herbie 1.9.12
herbiferous 34.18.27(.20)
herbivore 12.12

herbivorous 34.18.27(.21)
herbless 34.18.29(.21)
herblike 24.13.7(.11)
herb tea 2
herby 1.9.12
Hercegovina
17.18.16(.11)
Herculaneum 27.3.8(.3)
Herculean 28.17.1(.13)
Hercules 35.1.23
Hercynian 28.3.8(.2)
herd 23.19
herder 17.13.16
herdsman 28.17.16(.30)
Herdwick 24.2.25
here 3
hereabout 22.9.6
hereafter 17.12.23
hereat 22.7
hereby 14.7
hereditable
40.20.16(.11.3)
hereditament
22.26.15(.13.2)
hereditarily 1.31.17(.27.1)
hereditariness
34.18.16(.2.9)
hereditary 1.29.11(.8.6)
heredity 1.10.16(.9)
Hereford 23.18.16(.9)
Herefordshire 17.26.18
herein 28.2
hereinafter 17.12.23
hereinbefore 12.11
hereof 31.7
Herero 19.27.1, 19.27.3
heresiarch 24.8.1
heresiology 1.26.10(.11.1)
heresy 1.22.16(.13)
heretic 24.2.10(.10)
heretical 40.23.12(.7.1)
heretically 1.31.24(.9.3)
hereto 16.7
heretofore 12.11
hereunder 17.13.20(.10)
hereunto 16.7.7
hereupon 28.10.7
Hereward 23.18.26(.7)
herewith 33.2
Herford 23.18.16(.10)
heriot 22.3.12
Heriott 22.3.12
heritability 1.10.16(.22.2)
heritable 40.20.16(.11.3)
heritably 1.31.21(.4.2)
heritage 39.2.10
heritor 17.12.16(.18)
herky-jerky 1.12.14
herl 40.17
herm 27.16

Herman 28.17.16(.17)
hermaphrodite 22.16.10
hermaphroditic
24.2.10(.2.1)
hermaphroditical
40.23.12(.7.1)
hermaphroditism
27.15.21(.2.4)
hermeneutic 24.2.10(.9)
hermeneutical
40.23.12(.7.2)
hermeneutically
1.31.24(.9.4)
Hermes 35.1.11
hermetic 24.2.10(.3.1)
hermetically 1.31.24(.9.3)
hermetism 27.15.21(.2.4)
Hermia 3.8.8
Hermione 1.16.15(.3)
hermit 22.2.11
hermitage 39.2.10
Hermitian 28.17.25(.2.4)
hermitic 24.2.10(.2.2)
Hermon 28.17.16(.17)
Hern 28.18
Hernández 35.5.6
hernia 3.9.10
hernial 40.3.7(.8)
herniary 1.29.2(.6)
herniated 23.18.9(.3)
Herning 29.1.17(.13)
hero 19.27.1
Herod 23.18.27
Herodias 34.3.4, 34.7.2
Herodotus 34.18.11(.10)
heroic 24.2.7
heroically 1.31.24(.9.1)
heroi-comic 24.2.14(.6)
heroi-comical
40.23.12(.10)
heroin 28.2.8
heroine 28.2.8
heroism 27.15.21(.2.1)
heroize 35.15.4
heron 28.17.31(.3)
heronry 1.29.20
herpes 35.1.5
herpes simplex
34.23.4(.12)
herpes zoster 17.12.24(.7)
herpetic 24.2.10(.3.1)
herpetological
40.23.12(.17.2)
herpetologically
1.31.24(.9.11)
herpetologist
22.29.2(.26.3)
herpetology
1.26.10(.11.2)
Herr 6
Herrera 17.32.5

Herrick 24.2.26(.4)
herring 29.1.30(.3)
herringbone 28.19.3
Herriot 22.3.12
Herrnhuter 17.12.15(.6)
hers 35.19
Herschel 40.33.10
herself 30.20.2
Hersey 1.22.17
Hershey 1.24.13
Herstmonceaux 16.15,
16.24.14
Hertford 23.18.16(.11)
Hertfordshire 17.26.18
Herts 34.22.7
hertz 34.22.16
Herzegovina 17.18.1(.7),
17.18.16(.11)
Herzl 40.31.16
Herzog 26.7.9
he's 35.1, 35.2
Heseltine 28.14.5
Hesiod 23.18.28
hesitance 34.24.10(.10)
hesitancy 1.22.23(.10.2)
hesitant 22.26.15(.9)
hesitantly 1.31.22(.20.2)
hesitate 22.4.9(.5)
hesitater 17.12.4(.5)
hesitatingly 1.31.28(.1.4)
hesitation 28.17.25(.3.3)
hesitative 31.2.1(.3)
Hesketh 32.14.10
Hesperian 28.3.20(.2)
Hesperides 35.1.8
hesperidia 3.5.2
hesperidium 27.3.4(.2)
Hesperus 34.18.27(.12)
Hess 34.5
Hesse 17.24.5, 34.5
Hessen 28.17.23(.5)
Hessian 28.3.13
Hessle 40.32.4
hest 22.29.5
Hester 17.12.24(.4)
Heston 28.17.11(.25)
Hesvan 28.17.20(.13)
het 22.5
hetaera 17.32.2
hetaerae 2.30.1, 14.24.2
hetaerism 27.15.21(.2.14)
hetaira 17.32.13
hetairai 14.24.5
hetairism 27.15.21(.2.14)
hetero 19.27.11, 19.27.15
heterochromatic
24.2.10(.4.2)
heteroclite 22.16.25(.15)
heterocyclic 24.2.27(.16)
heterodox 34.23.8(.4)

heterodoxy 1.22.22
heterodyne 28.14.6
heterogamous
34.18.15(.10)
heterogamy 1.15.13(.4)
heterogeneity 1.10.16(.1)
heterogeneous 34.3.6(.1)
heterogeneously
1.31.33(.1.2)
heterogeneousness
34.18.16(.31.1)
heterogeneses
35.1.16(.10)
heterogenesis
34.2.17(.10.3)
heterogenetic
24.2.10(.3.1)
heterogeny 1.16.15(.17)
heterogonous
34.18.16(.15.2)
heterogony 1.16.15(.10)
heterograft 22.27.4(.4)
heterologous 34.18.14(.5)
heterology 1.26.10(.11.5)
heteromerous
34.18.27(.18)
heteromorphic
24.2.16(.5)
heteromorphism
27.15.21(.2.10)
heteronomous
34.18.15(.10)
heteronomy 1.15.13(.5)
heteropathic 24.2.18(.3)
heterophony 1.16.15(.12)
heterophyllous
34.18.29(.17.4)
heterophylly
1.31.17(.16.1)
heteroplastic
24.2.10(.15.4)
heteroploid 23.13.20
heteropolar 17.34.18(.1)
Heteroptera 17.32.14(.6)
heteropteran
28.17.31(.11)
heteropterous
34.18.27(.14)
heterosexism
27.15.21(.2.12)
heterosexist 22.29.2(.22)
heterosexual 40.14.8,
40.16.10
heterosexuality
1.10.16(.32.1)
heterosexually
1.31.17(.22)
heterosis 34.2.17(.11.2)
heterotaxy 1.22.22
heterotransplant
22.26.6, 22.26.8
heterotrophic 24.2.16(.4)

heterozygote 22.21.6
heterozygotic 24.2.10(.6)
heterozygous
34.18.14(.4)
Hetherington
28.17.11(.23)
hetman 28.17.16(.21)
Hettie 1.10.4
Hetton-le-Hole 40.18.13
het up 20.9
heuchera 17.32.14(.8)
Heugh 16, 30.13
heuristic 24.2.10(.15.2)
heuristically 1.31.24(.9.6)
hevea 3.11.1
hew 16
hewer 17.8
Hewett 22.2.4
Hewitt 22.2.4
Hewlett 22.2.25
hex 34.23.4
hexachord 23.12.4
hexad 23.7.13
hexadecimal 40.25.10
hexadecimally
1.31.17(.13)
hexagon 28.17.15(.13)
hexagonal 40.26.13(.7)
hexagonally
1.31.17(.14.2)
hexagram 27.6.17(.5)
hexahedra 17.32.20
hexahedral 40.16.13(.17)
hexahedron 28.17.31(.15)
hexameron 28.17.31(.11)
hexameter 17.12.16(.9.1)
hexametric 24.2.26(.14.2)
hexametrist
22.29.2(.29.5)
hexane 28.4.12
hexapla 17.34.19
hexapod 23.10.1
Hexapoda 17.13.17
hexapody 1.11.17
hexastyle 40.13.3(.10)
hexasyllabic 24.2.9(.2)
Hexateuch 24.15.8
hexavalent 22.26.15(.25)
hexode 23.20.11
hexose 34.20.13, 35.20.10
hey 4
heyday 4.10.2
Heyerdahl 40.8.5
Heyes 35.4
Heyford 23.18.16(.3)
Heyhoe 19.26
hey presto 19.10.19
Heysham 27.15.22
Heythrop 20.7.12
Heywood 23.16.6(.2)

Hezbollah **10.25, 17.34.9**
Hezekiah **17.6.5**
hi **14**
Hialeah **17.1.17**
hiatal **40.21.3**
hiatus **34.18.11(.3)**
Hiawatha **17.22.6**
hibachi **1.25.8**
hibernal **40.26.14**
hibernate **22.4.14(.9.1)**
hibernation **28.17.25(.3.8)**
hibernator **17.12.4(.10)**
Hibernia **3.9.10**
Hibernian **28.3.8(.10)**
Hibernicism **27.15.21(.2.12)**
hibiscus **34.18.13(.14)**
Hibs **35.21**
hic **24.2**
hiccup **20.9.7**
hiccupy **1.8.8**
hic jacet **22.5.13(.2)**
hick **24.2**
hickey **1.12.2**
Hickling **29.1.31(.19)**
Hickman **28.17.16(.23)**
Hickok **24.9.6**
hickory **1.29.11(.10)**
Hicks **34.23.2**
Hickson **28.17.23(.21)**
hid **23.2**
Hidalgo **19.13.15**
Hidcote **22.19.12(.12)**
hidden **28.17.12(.2)**
hiddenness **34.18.16(.25)**
hide **23.15**
hide-and-seek **24.1.6**
hideaway **4.25.9**
hidebound **23.24.7(.2)**
hi-de-hi **14.22**
hideosity **1.10.16(.16.2)**
hideous **34.3.4**
hideously **1.31.33(.1.1)**
hideousness **34.18.16(.31.1)**
hideout **22.9.8**
hider **17.13.12**
hidey-hole **40.18.13**
hiding **29.1.13(.9)**
hidrosis **34.2.17(.11.2)**
hidrotic **24.2.10(.6)**
hie **14**
hierarch **24.8.15**
hierarchal **40.23.6**
hierarchic **24.2.12**
hierarchical **40.23.12(.9)**
hierarchically **1.31.24(.9.7)**
hierarchism **27.15.21(.2.6)**

hierarchize **35.15.9**
hierarchy **1.12.6**
hieratic **24.2.10(.4.5)**
hieratically **1.31.24(.9.4)**
hierocracy **1.22.16(.13)**
hieroglyph **30.2.6**
hieroglyphic **24.2.16(.1)**
hieroglyphical **40.23.2**
hieroglyphically **1.31.24(.9.9)**
hierogram **27.6.17(.5)**
hierograph **30.7.5(.1)**
hierolatry **1.29.15(.13)**
hierology **1.26.10(.11.5)**
Hieronymus **34.18.15(.2)**
hierophant **22.26.6**
hierophantic **24.2.10(.14)**
hi-fi **14.14.3**
Higginbotham **27.15.9(.6)**
Higginbottom **27.15.9(.6)**
Higgins **35.26.2**
higgle **40.24.2**
higgledy-piggledy **1.11.23**
Higgs **35.24**
high **14**
Higham **27.15.3**
high-and-dry **14.24.8**
high-and-mighty **1.10.13**
highball **40.10.4**
highbinder **17.13.20(.11)**
highborn **28.11.2**
highboy **13.3**
highbrow **9.16**
Highclere **3.24.14**
Highcliffe **30.2.6**
highfalutin **28.2.11(.9)**
highfaluting **29.1.12(.13)**
Highgate **22.4.12(.3), 22.19.13**
high-handed **23.18.10(.14)**
high-handedly **1.31.23(.14.4)**
high-handedness **34.18.16(.21.1)**
high-hat **22.7.18**
highland **23.24.16(.16.2)**
Highlander **17.13.20(.13)**
Highlandman **28.17.16(.22)**
highlight **22.16.25(.8)**
highlighter **17.12.13(.9)**
highly **1.31.14**
high-muck-a-muck **24.12.5**
highness **34.18.16(.13)**
highrise **35.15.20**
highroad **23.20.12**
high-stepper **17.10.4**

hight **22.16**
hightail **40.4.2**
highway **4.25.7**
highwayman **28.17.16(.4)**
hijack **24.6.18**
hijacker **17.14.5**
hijinks **34.23.18**
Hijra **17.32.29**
hike **24.13**
hiker **17.14.12**
hila **17.34.13**
hilarious **34.3.15(.3)**
hilariously **1.31.33(.1.4)**
hilariousness **34.18.16(.31.1)**
hilarity **1.10.16(.21.1)**
Hilary **1.29.11(.27)**
Hilbert **22.19.9**
Hilda **17.13.23(.2)**
Hildesheim **27.12.6**
hill **40.2**
Hillary **1.29.11(.27)**
hillbilly **1.31.2**
hillcrest **22.29.5(.12)**
Hillel **40.5.19, 40.16.15**
Hiller **17.34.2**
Hillhead **23.5.13**
Hilliard **23.3, 23.9.2**
Hillier **3.24.2**
hilliness **34.18.16(.2.10)**
Hillingdon **28.17.12(.24)**
hillock **24.16.16**
hillocky **1.12.13**
Hills **35.30.2**
Hillsborough **17.32.14(.5)**
hillside **23.15.11(.17)**
hilltop **20.7.4**
hillwalker **17.14.9**
hillwalking **29.1.14(.7)**
hilly **1.31.2**
Hilo **19.29.1, 19.29.9**
hilt **22.32.1**
Hilton **28.17.11(.27)**
hilum **27.15.28(.9)**
Hilversum **27.15.20(.11)**
him **27.2**
Himalaya **3.24.6, 17.2.10**
Himalayan **28.3.21(.6), 28.17.2**
himation **28.3.3, 28.10.2**
Himmler **17.34.25**
himself **30.20.2**
Hinayana **17.18.8(.12)**
Hinchcliffe **30.2.6**
Hinchingbrooke **24.14.10**
Hinckley **1.31.24(.12)**
hind **23.24.13**
hindbrain **28.4.18**
Hinde **23.24.13**

Hindemith **22.2.11, 32.2.3**
Hindenburg **26.14.1(.9)**
hinder **17.13.20(.1)**
Hindhead **23.5.13(.10)**
Hindi **1.11.20(.1), 2.13**
Hindle **40.22.16**
Hindley **1.31.23(.17)**
Hindmarsh **36.8**
hindmost **22.29.17(.4)**
hindquarters **35.18.8**
hindrance **34.24.10(.16)**
hindsight **22.16.19(.13)**
Hindu **16.8**
Hinduism **27.15.21(.2.1)**
Hinduize **35.15.2**
Hindu Kush **36.13**
Hindustan **28.9.2**
Hindustani **1.16.8**
hindwing **29.1.29**
Hines **35.26.12**
hinge **39.17.1**
hingeless **34.18.29(.37)**
hingewise **35.15.19**
hinny **1.16.2**
Hinshelwood **23.16.6(.22)**
hint **22.26.1**
hinterland **23.24.6(.13)**
Hinton **28.17.11(.22)**
hip **20.2**
hipbath **32.8**
hipbone **28.19.3**
hip-hip-hooray **4.26**
hiphop **20.7.11**
hipless **34.18.29(.20)**
hipline **28.14.19(.13)**
hipness **34.18.16(.18)**
Hipparchus **34.18.13(.4)**
hippeastrum **27.15.26(.10)**
hipped **22.22.1**
hipper **17.10.2**
hippety-hop **20.7.11**
hippie **1.8.2**
hippo **19.8**
hippocampi **14.6**
hippocampus **34.18.9(.11)**
hippocentaur **12.5.8**
hippocras **34.7.18**
Hippocrates **35.1.7(.6)**
Hippocratic **24.2.10(.4.5)**
Hippocrene **28.1.25(.8)**
hippodrome **27.17.13**
hippogriff **30.2.5**
Hippolyta **17.12.16(.20)**
Hippolytus **34.18.11(.10)**
hippophagy **1.26.10(.6)**
hippophile **40.13.9**
hippophobia **3.3.9**

hippopotamus **34.18.15(.10)**

Hippo Regius **34.3.13**

hippy **1.8.2**

hipster **17.12.24(.16)**

hipsterism **27.15.21(.2.14)**

hiragana **17.18.8(.4)**

Hiram **27.15.26(.7)**

hircine **28.2.23(.10), 28.14.13**

hire **17.6**

hireable **40.20.16(.27.2)**

hireling **29.1.31(.10)**

hirer **17.32.14(.2)**

Hirohito **19.10.1**

Hiroshima **17.17.1, 17.17.14(.9)**

hirsuteness **34.18.16(.20.2)**

hirsutism **27.15.21(.2.4)**

hirundine **28.14.6**

Hirwaun **28.14.1**

his **35.2**

Hislop **20.7.13, 20.13.7**

Hispanic **24.2.15(.5)**

Hispanicist **22.29.2(.22)**

Hispanicize **35.15.16(.4)**

Hispaniola **17.34.18**

Hispanist **22.29.2(.18.1)**

Hispano-Suiza **17.25.1**

hispid **23.2.6**

hiss **34.2**

hist **22.29.2**

histamine **28.1.13, 28.2.17(.5)**

histaminic **24.2.15(.2)**

histidine **28.1.10**

histiocyte **22.16.19(.1)**

histochemical **40.23.12(.10)**

histochemistry **1.29.15(.17)**

histogenesis **34.2.17(.10.3)**

histogenetic **24.2.10(.3.1)**

histogenic **24.2.15(.4)**

histogeny **1.16.15(.17)**

histogram **27.6.17(.5)**

histological **40.23.12(.17.2)**

histologist **22.29.2(.26.3)**

histology **1.26.10(.11.2)**

histolysis **34.2.17(.10.5)**

histolytic **24.2.10(.2.5)**

histone **28.19.4(.9)**

histopathology **1.26.10(.11.5)**

historian **28.3.20(.7)**

historiated **23.18.9(.3)**

historic **24.2.26(.6)**

historical **40.23.12(.18)**

historically **1.31.24(.9.12)**

historicism **27.15.21(.2.12)**

historicist **22.29.2(.22)**

historicity **1.10.16(.16.1)**

historiographer **17.20.12(.5)**

historiographic **24.2.16(.3)**

historiographical **40.23.12(.12)**

historiography **1.18.9(.3.2)**

history **1.29.11(.8.12)**

histrionic **24.2.15(.6.1)**

histrionically **1.31.24(.9.8)**

histrionicism **27.15.21(.2.12)**

histrionism **27.15.21(.2.9)**

hit **22.2**

hit-and-miss **34.2.12**

hit-and-run **28.13.9**

hitch **38.2**

Hitchcock **24.9.6**

Hitchens **35.26.13(.16)**

hitcher **17.28.2**

hitchhike **24.13.4**

Hitchin **28.2.26**

hitech **24.4.4**

hither **17.23.2**

hitherto **16.7, 16.7.4**

hitherward **23.18.26(.7)**

Hitler **17.34.21**

Hitlerian **28.3.20(.2)**

Hitlerism **27.15.21(.2.14)**

Hitlerite **22.16.24(.9)**

hitmen **28.5.7(.15)**

hitter **17.12.2**

Hittite **22.16.9**

hive **31.9**

hiya **17.6**

ho **19**

hoagie **1.14.13**

hoar **12**

hoard **23.12**

hoarder **17.13.9**

hoarding **29.1.13(.8)**

Hoare **12**

hoarfrost **22.29.9**

hoarily **1.31.17(.27.1)**

hoariness **34.18.16(.2.9)**

hoarse **34.12**

hoarsely **1.31.33(.7)**

hoarsen **28.17.23(.9)**

hoarseness **34.18.16(.31.2)**

hoarstone **28.19.4(.9)**

hoary **1.29.8**

hoatzin **28.1.18, 28.2.23(.13)**

hoax **34.23.17**

hoaxer **17.24.20**

hob **21.8**

Hobart **22.10.2**

Hobbes **35.21**

hobbit **22.2.6**

hobbitry **1.29.15(.4)**

hobble **40.20.9**

hobbledehoy **13.13**

hobbler **17.34.20**

Hobbs **35.21**

hobby **1.9.7**

hobby horse **34.12.7**

hobbyist **22.29.2(.2)**

hobday **4.10.9**

hobgoblin **28.2.31(.14)**

Hobley **1.31.21(.11)**

hobnail **40.4.7**

hobnob **21.8**

hobo **19.9.11**

Hoboken **28.17.13(.15)**

Hobsbawm **27.10.1**

Hobson **28.17.23(.18)**

Hobson-Jobson **28.17.23(.18)**

Ho Chi Minh **28.2**

hock **24.9**

hockey **1.12.7**

hockeyist **22.29.2(.2)**

hockney **1.16.21**

hockshop **20.7.9**

Hocktide **23.15.4**

hocus **34.18.13(.12)**

hocus-pocus **34.18.13(.12)**

hod **23.10**

hodden **28.17.12(.9)**

Hodder **17.13.8**

Hoddesdon **28.17.12(.26)**

hoddie **1.11.10**

Hoddinott **22.11.9**

Hoddle **40.22.7**

Hodeida **17.13.3**

Hodge **39.9**

hodgepodge **39.9**

Hodges **35.18.21**

Hodgetts **34.22.15**

Hodgkin **28.2.13(.16)**

Hodgkinson **28.17.23(.24)**

Hodgson **28.17.23(.27)**

hodiernal **40.26.14**

hodman **28.17.16(.22)**

hodograph **30.7.5(.1)**

hodometer **17.12.16(.9.2)**

Hodson **28.17.23(.20)**

hoe **19**

hoedown **28.8.2(.2)**

hoer **17.9**

Hoey **1(.7)**

Hoffman **28.17.16(.27)**

Hoffnung **29.8, 29.9**

Hofmannsthal **40.8.4**

Hofmeister **17.12.24(.11)**

hog **26.7**

hogan **28.17.15(.14)**

Hogarth **32.8**

Hogarthian **28.3.11**

hogback **24.6.6(.15)**

Hogben **28.17.10**

Hogg **26.7**

Hoggart **22.19.13**

hogger **17.16.7**

hoggery **1.29.11(.11)**

hogget **22.2.10**

hoggin **28.2.15**

hoggish **36.2.14**

hoggishly **1.31.35(.7.1)**

hoggishness **34.18.16(.33.4)**

hoglike **24.13.7(.15)**

Hogmanay **4.14**

hogshead **23.5.13(.16)**

hogtie **14.8**

hogwash **36.9.5**

hogweed **23.1.10**

Hohenzollern **28.17.33(.7)**

ho-ho **19.26**

ho-hum **27.11.11**

hoick **24.11**

hoi polloi **13.17**

hoisin **28.2.24**

hoist **22.29.11**

hoister **17.12.24(.9)**

hoity-toity **1.10.11**

hokey **1.12.15**

hokey-cokey **1.12.15**

hokeyness **34.18.16(.2.4)**

hokey-pokey **1.12.15**

hoki **1.12.15**

hokily **1.31.17(.11)**

Hokkaido **19.11.9**

hokku **16.9**

hokonui **1(.6)**

hokum **27.15.11(.11)**

Holarctic **24.2.10(.13)**

Holbeach **38.1**

Holbech **38.1**

Holbeche **38.1**

Holbein **28.14.4**

Holbrook **24.14.10**

Holcombe **27.15.11(.11)**

hold **23.31.13**

holdable **40.20.16(.12)**

holdall **40.10.6**

holdback **24.6.6(.13)**

hold-down **28.8.2(.13)**

Holden **28.17.12(.27)**

holder **17.13.23(.8)**

Hölderlin **28.1.27(.7)**

Holderness **34.18.16(.15.2)**

holdfast 22.29.6(.9)
holding 29.1.13(.16)
holdout 22.9.8
holdover 17.21.14(.5)
Holdsworth 32.14.15
holdup 20.9.6
hole 40.18
holey 1.31.19
Holford 23.18.16(.22)
Holi 2.32.9(.10)
holibut 22.15.2
holiday 1.11.17, 4.10.7
holidaymaker 17.14.3(.3)
holily 1.31.17(.29)
holiness 34.18.16(.2.10)
Holinshed 23.5.12,
23.5.13(.16)
holism 27.15.21(.2.15)
holist 22.29.2(.31.5)
holistic 24.2.10(.15.3)
holistically 1.31.24(.9.6)
holla 17.34.9
Holland 23.24.16(.16.2)
hollandaise 35.4.4
Hollander 17.13.20(.13)
Hollands 35.23.15
holler 17.34.9
Hollerith 32.2.8
Holley 1.31.10
Holliday 4.10.7
Hollingsworth 32.14.15
Hollins 35.26.2
Hollis 34.2.22(.6)
hollow 19.29.8
holloware 6.18.4
Holloway 4.25.9
hollow-cheeked 22.23.1
hollow-eyed 23.15
hollow-hearted
23.18.9(.7)
hollowly 1.31.19
hollowness 34.18.16(.17)
hollowware 6.18.4, 6.18.5
holly 1.31.10
hollyhock 24.9.13
Hollywood 23.16.6(.1)
holm 27.17
Holman 28.17.16(.35)
Holme 27.17
Holmes 35.25.11
Holmesian 28.3.14
Holmfirth 32.14.13
holmium 27.3.7
holm oak 24.18.5
Holmwood 23.16.6(.13)
holocaust 22.29.10
Holocene 28.1.18(.6)
holoenzyme 27.12.5
Holofernes 35.1.12(.3)
hologram 27.6.17(.5)

holograph 30.7.5(.1)
holographic 24.2.16(.3)
holographically
1.31.24(.9.9)
holography 1.18.9(.3.2)
holohedral 40.16.13(.17)
holometabolous
34.18.29(.17.2)
holophote 22.21.9
holophyte 22.16.16
holophytic 24.2.10(.2.3)
holothurian 28.3.20(.7)
holotype 20.10.2
Holroyd 23.13.19
hols 35.30.8
Holst 22.29.23
Holstein 28.4.3
holster 17.12.24(.25)
holt 22.32.12
holus-bolus 34.18.29(.19)
holy 1.31.19
Holyhead 23.5.13(.1)
Holyoake 24.14.1
Holyrood 23.17.3
holystone 28.19.4(.9)
Holywell 40.5.17(.1)
hom 27.17
homa 17.17.16
homage 39.2.14
hombre 1.29.14, 4.26.10
homburg 26.14.1(.8)
home 27.17
homebody 1.11.10
homebound 23.24.7(.2)
homeboy 13.3
homebuyer 17.6.2
homecoming 29.1.16
homegrown 28.19.17
homeland 23.24.6(.13)
homeless 34.18.29(.26)
homelessness
34.18.16(.31.6)
homelike 24.13.7(.16)
homeliness
34.18.16(.2.10)
homely 1.31.26(.13)
homemade 23.4.7
homemaker 17.14.3(.3)
home-making 29.1.14(.3)
homeomorphism
27.15.21(.2.10)
homeopath 32.6.2
homeopathic 24.2.18(.3)
homeopathically
1.31.24(.9.10)
homeopathist
22.29.2(.21)
homeopathy 1.20.8
homeostatic 24.2.10(.4.1)
homeostatically
1.31.24(.9.4)

homeotherm 27.16.5
homeothermic
24.2.14(.11)
homeothermy 1.15.14
homeowner 17.18.18(.5)
Homer 17.17.16
Homeric 24.2.26(.4)
homeroom 27.14.6(.12)
Homerton 28.17.11(.15)
homesick 24.2.20(.14)
homesickness
34.18.16(.22)
homespun 28.13.1
homestead 23.5.3
homesteader 17.13.4
homestyle 40.13.3(.10)
hometown 28.8.1
homeward 23.18.26(.12)
homework 24.17.6(.12)
homeworker 17.14.16
homey 1.15.15
homeyly 1.31.17(.13)
homeyness 34.18.16(.2.5)
homicidal 40.22.11
homicidally 1.31.17(.10)
homicide 23.15.11(.6)
homiletic 24.2.10(.3.3)
homiliary 1.29.2(.12)
homilist 22.29.2(.31.3)
homily 1.31.17(.13)
homing 29.1.16
hominid 23.2.13
hominoid 23.13.12
hominy 1.16.15(.11)
Homo 19.14.8, 19.14.14
homo 19.14.14
homocentric
24.2.26(.14.4)
homoeopath 32.6.2
homoeopathically
1.31.24(.9.10)
homoeopathist
22.29.2(.21)
homoeopathy 1.20.8
homoeostasis 34.2.17(.2)
homoeostatic
24.2.10(.4.1)
homoeostatically
1.31.24(.9.4)
homoeothermal
40.25.11
homoeothermy 1.15.14
homoerotic 24.2.10(.6)
homogametic
24.2.10(.3.1)
homogamous
34.18.15(.10)
homogamy 1.15.13(.4)
homogenate 22.4.14(.9.3)
homogeneity 1.10.16(.1)
homogeneous 34.3.6(.1)

homogeneously
1.31.33(.1.2)
homogeneousness
34.18.16(.31.1)
homogenetic
24.2.10(.3.1)
homogenization
28.17.25(.3.12)
homogenize 35.15.12(.5)
homogenizer
17.25.12(.6)
homogenous
34.18.16(.15.3)
homogeny 1.16.15(.17)
homograft 22.27.4(.4)
homograph 30.7.5(.1)
homographic 24.2.16(.3)
homoiothermic
24.2.14(.11)
homoiothermy 1.15.14
homoiousian 28.3.13,
28.3.14
homologate 22.4.12(.5)
homologation
28.17.25(.3.6)
homological
40.23.12(.17.2)
homologize 35.15.18
homologous 34.18.14(.5)
homologue 26.7.14
homology 1.26.10(.11.4)
homomorph 30.9.2
homomorphic
24.2.16(.5)
homomorphically
1.31.24(.9.9)
homomorphism
27.15.21(.2.10)
homomorphous
34.18.17
homomorphy 1.18.6
homonym 27.2.6
homonymic 24.2.14(.2)
homonymous
34.18.15(.10)
homonymously
1.31.33(.12.3)
homonymy 1.15.13(.5)
homoousian 28.3.13,
28.3.14
homophile 40.13.9
homophobe 21.16.1
homophobia 3.3.9
homophobic 24.2.9(.7)
homophone 28.19.11
homophonic
24.2.15(.6.3)
homophonically
1.31.24(.9.8)
homophonous
34.18.16(.15.3)
homophony 1.16.15(.12)

h

homoplastic 24.2.10(.15.4)
homopolar 17.34.18(.1)
Homoptera 17.32.14(.6)
homopteran 28.17.31(.11)
homopterous 34.18.27(.14)
Homo sapiens 35.26.5
homosexual 40.14.8, 40.16.10
homosexuality 1.10.16(.32.1)
homosexually 1.31.17(.22)
homotransplant 22.26.6, 22.26.8
homousian 28.3.13
homozygote 22.21.6
homozygous 34.18.14(.4)
homuncule 40.15.9(.5)
homunculus 34.18.29(.17.6)
hon 28.13
Hon. 28.10
Honan 28.7.11
honcho 19.24
Honda® 17.13.20(.7)
Honddu 1.21
Honduran 28.17.31(.11)
Honduras 34.18.27(.11)
hone 28.19
Honecker 17.14.15(.9)
Honegger 17.16.13
honest 22.29.15(.13)
honestly 1.31.22(.22)
honesty 1.10.26(.11)
honey 1.16.12
honeybee 2.10
honeybun 28.13.2
honeybunch 38.18.7
honeycomb 27.17.6
honeydew 16.24.6
honeyed 23.2.13
honeyguide 23.15.6
honeymoon 28.16.7
honeymooner 17.18.15
honeysuckle 40.23.9
Hong Kong 29.6
Honiara 17.32.7
Honiton 28.17.11(.15)
honk 24.19.5
honky 1.12.16
honky-tonk 24.19.5
honnête homme 27.9
Honolulu 16.25
honorably 1.31.21(.8)
honorand 23.24.6(.12)
honoraria 3.22.4
honorarium 27.3.17(.3)
honorary 1.29.11(.25)

honorific 24.2.16(.1)
honorifically 1.31.24(.9.9)
honoris causa 17.25.6
honour 17.18.9
honourable 40.20.16(.27.4)
honourableness 34.18.16(.37.4)
honourably 1.31.21(.8)
honoured 23.18.14
Hon. Sec. 24.4
Honshu 16.17
hooch 38.14
hood 23.16
hooded 23.18.10(.12)
hoodie 1.11.15
hoodless 34.18.29(.23)
hoodlike 24.13.7(.13)
hoodlum 27.15.28(.17)
hoodoo 16.8.3
hoodwink 24.19.1(.6)
hooey 1(.6)
hoof 30.13
hoofbeat 22.1.2
hoofer 17.20.11
hoofmark 24.8.8
Hooghly 1.31.25
hoo-ha 10.21
hook 24.14
hookah 10.8.7, 17.14.13
Hooke 24.14
hooker 17.14.13
hookey 1.12.11
hookless 34.18.29(.24)
hooklet 22.19.26(.19)
hooklike 24.13.7(.14)
hookup 20.9.7
hookworm 27.16.7
Hooley 1.31.16
hooligan 28.17.15(.13)
hooliganism 27.15.21(.2.9)
hoon 28.16
hoop 20.12
Hooper 17.10.13
hoopla 10.25.6
hoopoe 16.5, 19.8
hooray 4.26
hooroo 16.23
hoosegow 9.6
Hoosier 3.15.7, 17.27.7
Hooson 28.17.23(.13)
hoot 22.18
hootch 38.14
hootenanny 1.16.6
hooter 17.12.15
hoover 17.21.11
Hooverville 40.2.12
hooves 35.28.7
hop 20.7

hop-bine 28.14.4
Hopcraft 22.27.4(.4)
Hopcroft 22.27.5
hope 20.15
hopeful 40.27.17
hopefully 1.31.17(.16.2)
hopefulness 34.18.16(.37.2)
hopeless 34.18.29(.20)
hopelessly 1.31.33(.12.6)
hopelessness 34.18.16(.31.6)
hoper 17.10.16
hophead 23.5.13(.7)
Hopi 1.8.13
Hopkin 28.2.13(.8)
Hopkins 35.26.2
Hopkinson 28.17.23(.24)
hoplite 22.16.25(.12)
hop-o'-my-thumb 27.11.9
hopper 17.10.8
hopple 40.19.7
hopsack 24.6.14
hopsacking 29.1.14(.4)
hopscotch 38.8
Hopwood 23.16.6(.8)
Horabin 28.2.10
Horace 34.18.27(.7)
Horan 28.17.31(.8)
horary 1.29.11(.25)
Horatia 3.16.3, 17.26.3
Horatian 28.17.25(.3.13)
Horatio 15.1.9, 19.22
Horbury 1.29.11(.7.1)
horde 23.12
Hordern 28.17.12(.10)
Horeb 21.4
horehound 23.24.7(.8)
Horgan 28.17.15(.9)
horizon 28.17.24(.10)
horizontal 40.21.17(.4)
horizontality 1.10.16(.32.3)
horizontally 1.31.17(.9.3)
horizontalness 34.18.16(.37.5)
Horkheimer 17.17.11
Horlicks® 34.23.2(.13)
hormonal 40.26.15
hormonally 1.31.17(.14.3)
hormone 28.19.9
Hormuz 35.16, 35.17.3
horn 28.11
hornbeam 27.1.1
hornbill 40.2.4
hornblende 23.24.5(.15)
Hornblower 17.9.13
hornbook 24.14.3
Hornby 1.9.19

Horncastle 40.31.6, 40.31.7
Hornchurch 38.16
Horne 28.11
horner 17.18.10
hornet 22.19.15(.6)
horniness 34.18.16(.2.5)
hornist 22.29.2(.18.1)
hornless 34.18.29(.27)
hornlike 24.13.7(.17)
hornpipe 20.10.1
Hornsby 1.9.22
hornstone 28.19.4(.9)
hornswoggle 40.24.6
Hornung 29.9
hornwort 22.20.15
horny 1.16.10
horologe 39.9
horologer 17.29.13
horologic 24.2.24(.4)
horological 40.23.12(.17.2)
horologist 22.29.2(.26.4)
horology 1.26.10(.11.5)
horoscope 20.15.4(.1)
horoscopic 24.2.8(.5)
horoscopical 40.23.12(.5)
horoscopy 1.8.11(.5)
Horowitz 34.22.2
horrendous 34.18.12
horrendously 1.31.33(.12.2)
horrendousness 34.18.16(.31.3)
horrent 22.26.15(.23.2)
horrible 40.20.16(.27.2)
horribleness 34.18.16(.37.4)
horribly 1.31.21(.8)
horrid 23.2.22
horridly 1.31.23(.14.7)
horridness 34.18.16(.21.1)
horrific 24.2.16(.1)
horrifically 1.31.24(.9.9)
horrification 28.17.25(.3.5)
horrifiedly 1.31.23(.11)
horrify 14.14.4(.14)
horrifyingly 1.31.28(.1.1)
horripilation 28.17.25(.3.14)
horror 17.32.8
Horsa 17.24.10
hors concours 17.7.5
hors de combat 10.5.10
hors-d'oeuvre 31.11
horse 34.12
horseback 24.6.6(.20)
horsebean 28.1.8
horsebox 34.23.8(.2)
horsebreaker 17.14.3(.8)

horse-coper **17.10.16**
Horseferry **1.29.3**
horseflesh **36.5**
horsefly **14.25.14**
Horseforth **32.14.13**
Horseguard **23.9.10**
horsehair **6.17**
horsehide **23.15.13**
horseleech **38.1**
horseless **34.18.29(.33)**
horselike **24.13.7(.22)**
horseman **28.17.16(.29)**
horsemanship **20.2.7(.19)**
horsemeat **22.1.5**
horseplay **4.28.9**
horsepower **17.3.1**
horseradish **36.2.12**
horseshit **22.2.18**
horseshoe **16.17**
horsetail **40.4.2**
horsewhip **20.2.10**
horsewoman **28.17.16(.14)**
horsewomen **28.2.17(.1)**
horsey **1.22.11**
Horsham **27.5.10**
horsily **1.31.17(.20)**
horsiness **34.18.16(.2.7)**
horst **22.29.10**
horsy **1.22.11**
Horta **17.12.10**
hortation **28.17.25(.3.3)**
hortative **31.2.1(.9.1)**
hortatory **1.29.11(.8.2)**
Hortense **34.24.3**
hortensia **3.14.16**
horticultural **40.16.13(.12.3)**
horticulturalist **22.29.2(.31.4)**
horticulturally **1.31.17(.27.2)**
horticulture **17.28.26**
horticulturist **22.29.2(.29.4)**
horti sicci **2.14, 14.10**
Horton **28.17.11(.10)**
hortus siccus **34.18.13(.1)**
Horus **34.18.27(.8)**
hosanna **17.18.6**
hose **35.20**
Hosea **3.15**
Hoseason **28.17.24(.1)**
hosepipe **20.10.1**
hosier **3.15.8**
hosiery **1.29.2(.8), 1.29.11(.19)**
hospice **34.2.6**
hospitable **40.20.16(.11.1)**
hospitably **1.31.21(.4.1)**

hospital **40.21.2**
hospitalism **27.15.21(.2.15)**
hospitality **1.10.16(.32.3)**
hospitalization **28.17.25(.3.12)**
hospitalize **35.15.21(.4.3)**
hospitaller **17.34.16(.7)**
host **22.29.17**
hosta **17.12.24(.7)**
hostage **39.2.10**
hostageship **20.2.7(.23)**
hostel **40.21.18**
hosteller **17.34.16(.7)**
hostelry **1.29.24**
hostess **34.5.2, 34.18.11(.16)**
hostile **40.13.3(.10)**
hostilely **1.31.38**
hostility **1.10.16(.23)**
hostler **17.34.27**
hot **22.11**
hotbed **23.5.2**
hot-blooded **23.18.10(.10)**
hot-bloodedly **1.31.23(.14.4)**
hot cake **24.3**
Hotchkiss **34.2.10**
hotchpot **22.11.2**
hotchpotch **38.8**
hotdog **26.7.4**
hotel **40.5.3**
hotelier **3.24.4, 4.2.10**
hotelkeeper **17.10.1**
hotfoot **22.17**
hothead **23.5.13(.9)**
hotheaded **23.18.10(.3)**
hotheadedly **1.31.23(.14.4)**
hotheadedness **34.18.16(.21.1)**
hothouse **34.8.6(.11)**
hotline **28.14.19(.14)**
hotly **1.31.22(.9)**
hotness **34.18.16(.20.2)**
hotplate **22.4.23(.8)**
hotpot **22.11.2**
hotrod **23.10.12**
hot-rodder **17.13.8**
hot-rodding **29.1.13(.7)**
hotshot **22.11.13**
hotspot **22.11.2**
hotspur **18.1**
Hottentot **22.11.4**
hotter **17.12.9**
hottie **1.10.9**
hottish **36.2.11**
Houdini **1.16.1(.4)**
Hough **9, 30.8, 30.11**
hough **24.9**
hougher **17.14.8**

Houghton **28.17.11(.7)**
Houlihan **28.17.29**
hound **23.24.7**
hounder **17.13.20(.5)**
houndish **36.2.12**
Houndsditch **38.2.4**
houndstooth **32.13**
hour **17.3**
hourglass **34.9.7**
houri **1.29.11(.3)**
hourly **1.31.17(.1)**
house **34.8, 35.8**
houseboat **22.21.2**
housebound **23.24.7(.2)**
houseboy **13.3**
housebreaker **17.14.3(.8)**
housebreaking **29.1.14(.3)**
housebuilder **17.13.23(.2)**
housebuilding **29.1.13(.16)**
housebuyer **17.6.2**
housebuying **29.1.7**
housecarl **40.8.6**
housecoat **22.21.5**
housecraft **22.27.4(.4)**
housedog **26.7.4**
housedress **34.5.14(.6)**
housefly **14.25.14**
houseful **40.14.6(.19)**
housegroup **20.12**
houseguest **22.29.5(.3)**
household **23.31.13(.9)**
householder **17.13.23(.8)**
househusband **23.24.16(.2)**
housekeep **20.1**
housekeeper **17.10.1**
housekeeping **29.1.10(.1)**
housekept **22.22.3**
houseleek **24.1.12**
houseless **34.18.29(.33)**
houselights **34.22.12**
housemaid **23.4.7**
houseman **28.17.16(.29)**
housemaster **17.12.24(.5)**
housemate **22.4.13(.14)**
housemistress **34.18.27(.14)**
housemother **17.23.10**
houseparent **22.26.15(.23.1)**
houseplant **22.26.6, 22.26.8**
houseroom **27.14.6(.17)**
housesitter **17.12.2**
housetop **20.7.4**
housewares **35.6**
housewarming **29.1.16**
housewife **30.12**

housewifeliness **34.18.16(.2.10)**
housewifely **1.31.29**
housewifery **1.29.11(.14)**
housewives **35.28.6**
housework **24.17.6(.15)**
housey-housey **1.23.6**
housing **29.1.24**
Housman **28.17.16(.29)**
Houston **28.17.11(.25)**
Houyhnhnm **27.15.14(.2)**
hove **31.12**
hovel **40.28.7**
hover **17.21.7**
hovercraft **22.27.4(.4)**
hoverer **17.32.14(.13)**
hoverfly **14.25.14**
hoverport **22.13.1**
hovertrain **28.4.18**
Hovis® **34.2.15**
how **9**
Howard **23.18.2**
Howarth **32.14.2**
howbeit **22.2.1**
howdah **17.13.6**
Howden **28.17.12(.7)**
how-do-you-do **16.8**
howdy **1.11.8**
how-d'ye-do **16.8**
Howe **9**
Howell **40.16.3**
Howells **35.30.12**
Howerd **23.18.2**
Howes **35.8**
however **17.21.4**
Howie **1(.3)**
howitzer **17.24.19**
howl **40.7**
howler **17.34.7**
Howlett **22.19.26(.6)**
howsoever **17.21.4**
howzat **22.7.16**
Hoxton **28.17.11(.25)**
hoy **13**
hoya **17.5**
hoyden **28.17.12(.11)**
hoydenish **36.2.16(.13)**
Hoylake **24.3.14**
Hoyle **40.11**
Hsing-king **29.1.28**
Huascarán **28.9.13**
hub **21.11**
Hubbard **23.18.8**
Hubble **40.20.12**
hubbub **21.11**
hubby **1.9.9**
hubcap **20.5.1**
Hubei **4.8**
Huber **17.11.12**
Hubert **22.19.9**

h

hubris 34.2.21
hubristic 24.2.10(.15.2)
Huck 24.12
huckaback 24.6.6(.9)
huckle 40.23.9
huckle-back 24.6.6(.23)
huckleberry 1.29.11(.7.2)
huckster 17.12.24(.20)
huckstery 1.29.11(.8.12)
huckterism
    27.15.21(.2.14)
Huddersfield 23.31.1(.2)
huddle 40.22.10
Huddleston 28.17.11(.25)
Hudibras 34.7.18
Hudibrastic 24.2.10(.15.4)
Hudson 28.17.23(.20)
Hué 4
hue 16
hueless 34.18.29(.16)
Huey 1(.6)
huff 30.11
huffily 1.31.17(.16.1)
huffiness 34.18.16(.2.6)
huffish 36.2.18(.8)
huffishly 1.31.35(.7.3)
huffishness
    34.18.16(.33.6)
Huffman 28.17.16(.27)
huffy 1.18.7
hug 26.10
huge 39.13
hugely 1.31.37
hugeness 34.18.16(.36)
huggable 40.20.16(.14)
hugger 17.16.9
hugger-mugger 17.16.9
Huggins 35.26.2
Hugh 16
Hughenden 28.17.12(.23)
Hughes 35.17
Hughey 1(.6)
Hughie 1(.6)
Hugo 19.13.8
Huguenot 19.15.12
hula 17.34.15
hula-hoop 20.12
hula-hula 17.34.15
hulk 24.21
hull 40.12
hullabaloo 16.25
Hulme 27.14, 27.18
Hulot 19.29.11
Hulse 34.27
hum 27.11
human 28.17.16(.15)
humane 28.4.7
humanely 1.31.27(.4)
humaneness
    34.18.16(.25)

humanism 27.15.21(.2.9)
humanist 22.29.2(.18.1)
humanistic 24.2.10(.15.2)
humanistically
    1.31.24(.9.6)
humanitarian 28.3.20(.4)
humanitarianism
    27.15.21(.2.9)
humanity 1.10.16(.13)
humanization
    28.17.25(.3.11)
humanize 35.15.12(.5)
humankind 23.24.13
humanly 1.31.27(.14)
humanness 34.18.16(.25)
humanoid 23.13.12
Humber 17.11.17(.6)
Humberside 23.15.11(.6)
Humbert 22.19.9
humble 40.20.19
humbleness
    34.18.16(.37.4)
humbly 1.31.21(.12)
Humboldt 22.32.12
humbug 26.10
humbuggery 1.29.11(.11)
humdinger 17.19.1
humdrum 27.11.12
Hume 27.14
humectant 22.26.15(.9)
humeral 40.16.13(.12.2)
humerus 34.18.27(.18)
humic 24.2.14(.9)
humid 23.2.12
humidification
    28.17.25(.3.5)
humidifier 17.6.9(.4)
humidify 14.14.4(.5)
humidity 1.10.16(.9)
humidly 1.31.23(.14.6)
humidness
    34.18.16(.21.1)
humidor 12.6.6
humification
    28.17.25(.3.5)
humify 14.14.4(.6)
humiliate 22.4.2(.15)
humiliatingly
    1.31.28(.1.4)
humiliation
    28.17.25(.3.1)
humiliator 17.12.4(.1)
humility 1.10.16(.24)
hummable 40.20.16(.15)
hummer 17.17.10
hummingbird 23.19.1
hummock 24.16.6
hummocky 1.12.13
hummus 34.18.15(.9)
humongous 34.18.14(.8)
humoral 40.16.13(.12.2)

humoresque 24.20.3
humorist 22.29.2(.29.4)
humoristic 24.2.10(.15.2)
humorlessly
    1.31.33(.12.6)
humorlessness
    34.18.16(.31.6)
humorous 34.18.27(.18)
humorously
    1.31.33(.12.5)
humorousness
    34.18.16(.31.5)
humorsomely
    1.31.26(.11)
humorsomeness
    34.18.16(.24)
humour 17.17.13
humourless
    34.18.29(.17.3)
humourlessly
    1.31.33(.12.6)
humourlessness
    34.18.16(.31.6)
humoursome
    27.15.20(.11)
hump 20.16.5
humpback 24.6.6(.11)
humpbacked 22.23.5(.3)
humper 17.10.17
Humperdinck 24.19.1(.1)
humph 30.18
Humphrey 1.29.21
Humphries 35.2.17
humpiness 34.18.16(.2.2)
humpless 34.18.29(.20)
humpty-dumpty 1.10.19
humpy 1.8.14
humus 34.18.15(.9)
humusify 14.14.4(.9)
Hun 28.13
Hunan 28.7.11
hunch 38.18.7
hunchback 24.6.6(.21)
hunchbacked 22.23.5(.3)
hundred 23.18.27
hundredfold 23.31.13(.7)
hundredth 32.18
hundredweight 22.4.21
hung 29.8
Hungarian 28.3.20(.4)
Hungary 1.29.11(.11)
hunger 17.16.17(.4)
Hungerford 23.18.16(.9)
hungrily 1.31.17(.27.3)
hungriness 34.18.16(.2.9)
hungry 1.29.18
hunk 24.19.7
hunker 17.14.21(.5)
Hunkpapa 17.10.7
hunky 1.12.16
hunky-dory 1.29.8

Hunniford 23.18.16(.2)
Hunnish 36.2.16(.10)
Hunslet 22.19.26(.27)
Hunstanton 28.17.11(.22)
hunt 22.26.12
huntaway 4.25.9
hunter 17.12.22(.10)
Huntingdon 28.17.12(.24)
Huntingdonshire
    17.26.21
Huntington 28.17.11(.23)
Huntley 1.31.22(.20.1)
huntress 34.18.27(.14)
huntsman 28.17.16(.29)
Huntsville 40.2.12
hup 20.9
Hupeh 4.7
hurdle 40.22.14
hurdler 17.34.22
hurdy-gurdy 1.11.18
Hurford 23.18.16(.10)
hurl 40.17
hurley 1.31.18
Hurlingham 27.15.15
hurly-burly 1.31.18
Huron 28.10.24(.5)
hurrah 10.23
hurricane 28.17.13(.13)
hurried 23.2.22
hurriedly 1.31.23(.14.7)
hurriedness
    34.18.16(.21.1)
hurry 1.29.9
hurry-scurry 1.29.9
hurst 22.29.16
Hurstmonceux 16.15,
    16.24.14
Hurston 28.17.11(.25)
Hurstpierpoint 22.26.11
hurt 22.20
hurtful 40.27.18
hurtfully 1.31.17(.16.2)
hurtfulness
    34.18.16(.37.2)
hurtle 40.21.13
hurtless 34.18.29(.22)
Husák 24.6.14
husband 23.24.16(.2)
husbander 17.13.20(.13)
husbandhood 23.16.5(.7)
husbandless
    34.18.29(.23)
husbandlike 24.13.7(.13)
husbandly 1.31.23(.17)
husbandman
    28.17.16(.22)
husbandry 1.29.16
husbandship 20.2.7(.15)
hush 36.12
hushaby 14.7
hush-hush 36.12

hush money **1.16.12**
hush-up **20.9.13**
husk **24.20.7**
huskily **1.31.17(.11)**
huskiness **34.18.16(.2.4)**
Huskisson **28.17.23(.14)**
husky **1.12.17(.7)**
huss **34.14**
hussar **10.16**
Hussein **28.4.12**
Husserl **40.17**
Hussey **1.22.12**
Hussite **22.16.19(.6)**
Hussitism **27.15.21(.2.4)**
hussy **1.22.12, 1.23.11**
hustings **35.27**
hustle **40.31.10**
hustler **17.34.27**
Huston **28.17.11(.25)**
hut **22.15**
hutch **38.11**
Hutchings **35.27**
Hutchins **35.26.2**
Hutchinson **28.17.23(.24)**
Hutchison **28.17.23(.14)**
hutia **2.11**
hutlike **24.13.7(.12)**
hutment **22.26.15(.13.3)**
Hutterite **22.16.24(.9)**
Hutton **28.17.11(.11)**
Hutu **16.7.3**
Huw **16**
Huxley **1.31.33(.15)**
Huxtable **40.20.16(.11.7)**
Huygens **35.26.13(.9)**
Huyton **28.17.11(.12)**
huzza **10.16**
huzzy **1.23.11**
Hwange **1.14.14, 4.12**
Hwang-Ho **19.26**
hwyl **40.1, 40.2.1**
hyacinth **32.21**
hyacinthine **28.14.12**
Hyacinthus **34.18.19**
Hyades **35.1.8**
hyaena **17.18.1**
hyalin **28.2.31(.10)**
hyaline **28.1.27(.7), 28.2.31(.10), 28.14.19(.11)**
hyalite **22.16.25(.9)**
hyaloid **23.13.20**
Hyatt **22.19.4**
hybrid **23.2.22**
hybridism **27.15.21(.2.5)**
hybridity **1.10.16(.9)**
hybridizable **40.20.16(.22)**
hybridization **28.17.25(.3.11)**
hybridize **35.15.8**

hydantoin **28.2.8**
hydathode **23.20.10**
hydatid **23.2.8**
hydatidiform **27.10.5(.2)**
Hyde **23.15**
Hyderabad **23.7.6, 23.9.6**
hydra **17.32.20**
hydrangea **17.29.16(.2)**
hydrant **22.26.15(.23.4)**
hydratable **40.20.16(.11.1)**
hydrate **22.4.22(.9)**
hydration **28.17.25(.3.13)**
hydrator **17.12.4(.15)**
hydraulic **24.2.27(.9)**
hydraulically **1.31.24(.9.12)**
hydraulicity **1.10.16(.16.1)**
hydrazine **28.1.19**
hydric **24.2.26(.15)**
hydride **23.15.15**
hydro **19.27.16**
hydrocarbon **28.17.10**
hydrocele **40.1.10**
hydrocephalic **24.2.27(.6)**
hydrocephalus **34.18.29(.17.4)**
hydrochloride **23.15.15**
hydrocortisone **28.19.14**
hydrodynamic **24.2.14(.4)**
hydrodynamical **40.23.12(.10)**
hydrodynamicist **22.29.2(.22)**
hydroelectric **24.2.26(.14.3)**
hydroelectrically **1.31.24(.9.12)**
hydroelectricity **1.10.16(.16.1)**
hydrofined **23.24.13**
hydrofining **29.1.17(.10)**
hydrofoil **40.11.7**
hydrogen **28.17.28(.9)**
hydrogenase **34.4.8, 35.4.8**
hydrogenate **22.4.14(.9.3)**
hydrogenation **28.17.25(.3.8)**
hydrogenous **34.18.16(.15.3)**
hydrogeological **40.23.12(.17.2)**
hydrogeologist **22.29.2(.26.2)**
hydrogeology **1.26.10(.11.1)**
hydrographer **17.20.12(.5)**
hydrographic **24.2.16(.3)**

hydrographical **40.23.12(.12)**
hydrographically **1.31.24(.9.9)**
hydrography **1.18.9(.3.2)**
hydroid **23.13.19**
hydrolase **35.4.18**
hydrologic **24.2.24(.4)**
hydrological **40.23.12(.17.2)**
hydrologically **1.31.24(.9.11)**
hydrologist **22.29.2(.26.4)**
hydrology **1.26.10(.11.5)**
hydrolysis **34.2.17(.10.5)**
hydrolytic **24.2.10(.2.5)**
hydrolytically **1.31.24(.9.3)**
hydrolyze **35.15.21(.4.7)**
hydromagnetic **24.2.10(.3.1)**
hydromania **3.9.3(.5)**
hydromechanics **34.23.2(.6)**
hydromel **40.5.7**
hydrometer **17.12.16(.9.2)**
hydrometric **24.2.26(.14.2)**
hydrometrical **40.23.12(.18)**
hydrometrically **1.31.24(.9.12)**
hydrometry **1.29.15(.8)**
hydropathic **24.2.18(.3)**
hydropathically **1.31.24(.9.10)**
hydropathist **22.29.2(.21)**
hydropathy **1.20.8**
hydrophane **28.4.9**
hydrophil **40.2.11**
hydrophile **40.13.9**
hydrophilic **24.2.27(.2)**
hydrophobia **3.3.9**
hydrophobic **24.2.9(.7)**
hydrophone **28.19.11**
hydrophyte **22.16.16**
hydropic **24.2.8(.5)**
hydroplane **28.4.19**
hydropneumatic **24.2.10(.4.2)**
hydroponic **24.2.15(.6.1)**
hydroponically **1.31.24(.9.8)**
hydroquinone **28.19.10**
hydrosphere **3.10.5**
hydrostatic **24.2.10(.4.1)**
hydrostatical **40.23.12(.7.1)**
hydrostatically **1.31.24(.9.4)**

hydrotherapist **22.29.2(.11)**
hydrotherapy **1.8.11(.8)**
hydrothermal **40.25.11**
hydrothermally **1.31.17(.13)**
hydrothorax **34.23.5(.14)**
hydrotropism **27.15.21(.2.2)**
hydrous **34.18.27(.15)**
hydroxide **23.15.11(.11)**
hydroxy **1.22.22**
hydroxyl **40.2.14, 40.13.12**
hydrozoan **28.17.8**
hyena **17.18.1**
Hygeia **17.1.14**
hygeian **28.17.1(.11)**
Hygena **17.18.1(.13)**
hygiene **28.1.23**
hygienic **24.2.15(.1)**
hygienically **1.31.24(.9.8)**
hygienist **22.29.2(.18.1)**
hygrology **1.26.10(.11.5)**
hygrometer **17.12.16(.9.2)**
hygrometric **24.2.26(.14.2)**
hygrometrically **1.31.24(.9.12)**
hygrometry **1.29.15(.8)**
hygrophilous **34.18.29(.17.4)**
hygrophyte **22.16.16**
hygrophytic **24.2.10(.2.3)**
hygroscope **20.15.4(.1)**
hygroscopic **24.2.8(.5)**
hygroscopically **1.31.24(.9.2)**
hying **29.1.7**
Hyksos **34.10.15**
Hyland **23.24.16(.16.2)**
hylic **24.2.27(.11)**
hylomorphism **27.15.21(.2.10)**
hylotheism **27.15.21(.2.1)**
hylozoism **27.15.21(.2.1)**
hylozoist **22.29.2(.10)**
Hylton **28.17.11(.27)**
Hyman **28.17.16(.13)**
hymen **28.5.7(.8), 28.17.16(.13)**
hymenal **40.26.13(.8)**
hymeneal **40.16.1**
hymenia **3.9.1**
hymenium **27.3.8(.1)**
Hymenoptera **17.32.14(.6)**
hymenopteran **28.17.31(.11)**
hymenopterous **34.18.27(.14)**
hymn **27.2**

hymnal **40.26.20**
hymnary **1.29.11(.13.3)**
hymnbook **24.14.3**
hymnic **24.2.15(.14)**
hymnist **22.29.2(.18.3)**
hymnodist **22.29.2(.14)**
hymnody **1.11.17**
hymnographer **17.20.12(.5)**
hymnography **1.18.9(.3.2)**
hymnologist **22.29.2(.26.4)**
hymnology **1.26.10(.11.4)**
hyoid **23.13.3**
hyoscine **28.1.18(.6)**
hyoscyamine **28.1.13, 28.2.17(.5)**
hypaesthesia **3.15.1**
hypaesthetic **24.2.10(.3.2)**
hypaethral **40.16.13(.22)**
hypallage **1.26.10(.10)**
Hypatia **3.16.3, 17.26.3**
hype **20.10**
hyperactive **31.2.1(.13.3)**
hyperactivity **1.10.16(.15)**
hyperaemia **3.8.1**
hyperaemic **24.2.14(.1)**
hyperaesthesia **3.15.1**
hyperaesthetic **24.2.10(.3.2)**
hyperbaric **24.2.26(.5)**
hyperbaton **28.10.9, 28.17.11(.15)**
hyperbola **17.34.16(.6)**
hyperbole **1.31.17(.8)**
hyperbolic **24.2.27(.9)**
hyperbolical **40.23.12(.19)**
hyperbolically **1.31.24(.9.12)**
hyperbolism **27.15.21(.2.15)**
hyperbolist **22.29.2(.31.2)**
hyperboloid **23.13.20**
hyperboloidal **40.22.9**
Hyperborean **28.3.20(.7), 28.17.1(.12)**
hypercatalectic **24.2.10(.13)**
hyperconscious **34.18.22(.12)**
hypercorrect **22.23.4(.10)**
hypercorrection **28.17.25(.15.2)**
hypercritical **40.23.12(.7.1)**
hypercritically **1.31.24(.9.3)**
hypercriticism **27.15.21(.2.12)**
hypercube **21.13**

hyperdulia **17.6.15**
hyperfocal **40.23.14**
hypergamy **1.15.13(.4)**
hyperglycaemia **3.8.1**
hyperglycaemic **24.2.14(.1)**
hypergolic **24.2.27(.9)**
hypericum **27.15.11(.9)**
Hyperion **28.3.20(.2)**
hyperkinetic **24.2.10(.3.1)**
hyperlipidaemia **3.8.1**
hyperlipidaemic **24.2.14(.1)**
hypermarket **22.2.9(.4)**
hypermetric **24.2.26(.14.2)**
hypermetrical **40.23.12(.18)**
hypermetropia **3.2.7**
hypermetropic **24.2.8(.5)**
hypernym **27.2.6**
hyperon **28.10.24(.5)**
hyperonic **24.2.15(.6.4)**
hyperopia **3.2.7**
hyperopic **24.2.8(.5)**
hyperphysical **40.23.12(.16)**
hyperphysically **1.31.24(.9.10)**
hyperplasia **3.15.3**
hypersensitive **31.2.1(.9.3)**
hypersensitiveness **34.18.16(.28.1)**
hypersensitivity **1.10.16(.15)**
hypersonic **24.2.15(.6.3)**
hypersonically **1.31.24(.9.8)**
hyperspace **34.4.2**
hypersthene **28.1.17**
hypertension **28.17.25(.16)**
hypertensive **31.2.4(.13)**
hypertext **22.29.20**
hyperthermia **3.8.8**
hyperthermic **24.2.14(.11)**
hyperthyroid **23.13.19**
hyperthyroidic **24.2.11(.9)**
hyperthyroidism **27.15.21(.2.5)**
hypertonia **3.9.11**
hypertonic **24.2.15(.6.1)**
hypertonicity **1.10.16(.16.1)**
hypertrophic **24.2.16(.4)**
hypertrophied **23.2.14**
hypertrophy **1.18.9(.2)**

hyperventilate **22.4.23(.7.1)**
hyperventilation **28.17.25(.3.14)**
hypethral **40.16.13(.22)**
hypha **17.20.10**
hyphae **2.18**
hyphal **40.27.12**
hyphen **28.17.19**
hyphenate **22.4.14(.9.3)**
hyphenation **28.17.25(.3.8)**
hypnogenesis **34.2.17(.10.3)**
hypnologist **22.29.2(.26.4)**
hypnology **1.26.10(.11.4)**
hypnopaedia **3.5.1**
hypnopedia **3.5.1**
Hypnos **34.10.13**
hypnoses **35.1.16(.11)**
hypnosis **34.2.17(.11.2)**
hypnotherapist **22.29.2(.11)**
hypnotherapy **1.8.11(.8)**
hypnotic **24.2.10(.6)**
hypnotically **1.31.24(.9.4)**
hypnotism **27.15.21(.2.4)**
hypnotist **22.29.2(.13)**
hypnotizable **40.20.16(.22)**
hypnotize **35.15.7(.7)**
hypo **19.8**
hypoaesthesia **3.15.1**
hypo-allergenic **24.2.15(.4)**
hypoblast **22.29.6(.12), 22.29.8(.8)**
hypocaust **22.29.10**
hypochlorite **22.16.24(.7)**
hypochondria **3.22.16**
hypochondriac **24.6.1**
hypocoristic **24.2.10(.15.2)**
hypocotyl **40.21.7**
hypocrisy **1.22.16(.13)**
hypocrite **22.2.24**
hypocritical **40.23.12(.7.1)**
hypocritically **1.31.24(.9.3)**
hypocycloid **23.13.20**
hypocycloidal **40.22.9**
hypoderma **17.17.15**
hypodermal **40.25.11**
hypodermata **17.12.16(.9.3)**
hypodermic **24.2.14(.11)**
hypodermically **1.31.24(.9.8)**
hypodermis **34.2.12**
hypogastria **3.22.15**

hypogastric **24.2.26(.14.5)**
hypogastrium **27.3.17(.6)**
hypogea **17.1.14**
hypogeal **40.16.1**
hypogean **28.17.1(.11)**
hypogene **28.1.23**
hypogeum **27.15.1**
hypoglycaemia **3.8.1**
hypoglycaemic **24.2.14(.1)**
hypoid **23.13.5**
hypolimnia **3.9.14**
hypolimnion **28.3.8(.12)**
hypomania **3.9.3(.5)**
hypomaniac **24.6.1**
hypomanic **24.2.15(.5)**
hyponastic **24.2.10(.15.4)**
hyponasty **1.10.26(.5)**
hyponym **27.2.6**
hyponymous **34.18.15(.10)**
hyponymy **1.15.13(.5)**
hypophyseal **40.3.11**
hypophysis **34.2.17(.10.4)**
hypostasis **34.2.17(.10.2)**
hypostasize **35.15.16(.4)**
hypostatic **24.2.10(.4.1)**
hypostatical **40.23.12(.7.1)**
hypostatically **1.31.24(.9.4)**
hypostatize **35.15.7(.7)**
hypostyle **40.13.3(.10)**
hyposulphite **22.16.16**
hypotactic **24.2.10(.13)**
hypotaxes **35.1.16(.14)**
hypotaxis **34.2.17(.14)**
hypotension **28.17.25(.16)**
hypotensive **31.2.4(.13)**
hypotenuse **34.17.13, 35.17.7**
hypothalami **2.16, 14.12**
hypothalamic **24.2.14(.10)**
hypothalamus **34.18.15(.10)**
hypothec **24.2.18(.4)**
hypothecary **1.29.11(.10)**
hypothecate **22.4.11(.6)**
hypothecation **28.17.25(.3.5)**
hypothecator **17.12.4(.7)**
hypothermia **3.8.8**
hypotheses **35.1.16(.10)**
hypothesis **34.2.17(.10.4)**
hypothesist **22.29.2(.22)**
hypothesize **35.15.16(.4)**
hypothesizer **17.25.12(.10)**

hypothetical
40.23.12(.7.1)
hypothetically
1.31.24(.9.3)
hypothyroid **23.13.19**
hypothyroidic **24.2.11(.9)**
hypothyroidism
27.15.21(.2.5)
hypoventilation
28.17.25(.3.14)
hypoxaemia **3.8.1**
hypoxia **3.14.15**
hypoxic **24.2.20(.13)**
hypsilophodont **22.26.9**
hypsographic **24.2.16(.3)**
hypsographical
40.23.12(.12)
hypsography **1.18.9(.3.2)**
hypsometer
17.12.16(.9.2)
hypsometric
24.2.26(.14.2)
hypsometry **1.29.15(.8)**
hyracotherium **27.3.18**
hyrax **34.23.5(.14)**
Hyrcania **3.9.3(.4)**
hyson **28.17.23(.12)**
hyssop **20.13.4**
hysterectomize **35.15.11**
hysterectomy **1.15.13(.1)**
hysteresis **34.2.17(.1)**
hysteria **3.22.2**
hysteric **24.2.26(.4)**
hysterical **40.23.12(.18)**
hysterically **1.31.24(.9.12)**
hysteron proteron
28.10.24(.5)
Hythe **33.7**
Hyundai® **14.9**
Hywel **40.16.3**
i **14**
iamb **21.17, 27.6.2**
iambic **24.2.9(.8)**
iambus **34.18.10**
Ian **28.17.1**
Iapetus **34.18.11(.10)**
Iasi **1.22.8**
IATA **17.12.8**
iatrogenic **24.2.15(.4)**
Ibadan **28.17.12(.6)**
Iban **28.9.1**
Ibbotson **28.17.23(.19)**
Ibcol **40.9.9**
I-beam **27.1.1**
Iberia **3.22.2**
Iberian **28.3.20(.2)**
Ibero-American
28.17.13(.13)
ibex **34.23.4(.2)**
ibid **23.2.7**
ibidem **27.5.5**

ibis **34.2.7**
Ibiza **17.22.1**
IBM® **27.5**
Ibo **19.9.1**
ibogaine **28.1.5**
Ibrahim **27.1.10, 27.2.13**
Ibrox **34.23.8(.10)**
Ibsen **28.17.23(.18)**
ibuprofen **28.17.19**
Icarus **34.18.27(.16)**
ICBM **27.5**
ice **34.15**
iceberg **26.14.1(.10)**
iceblink **24.19.1(.8)**
iceboat **22.21.2**
icebound **23.24.7(.2)**
icebox **34.23.8(.2)**
icebreaker **17.14.3(.8)**
ice cream **27.1**
icefall **40.10.11**
icehouse **34.8.6(.20)**
Iceland **23.24.16(.16.4)**
Icelander **17.13.20(.13)**
Icelandic **24.2.11(.16)**
iceman **28.7.10(.20)**
icemen **28.5.7(.24)**
Iceni **14.13**
Ichabod **23.10.2**
I Ching **29.1**
ichneumon **28.17.16(.15)**
ichnography **1.18.9(.3.2)**
ichor **12.7**
ichorous **34.18.27(.16)**
ichthyographer
17.20.12(.5)
ichthyography
1.18.9(.3.2)
ichthyoid **23.13.2**
ichthyolatry **1.29.15(.13)**
ichthyolite **22.16.25(.3)**
ichthyological
40.23.12(.17.2)
ichthyologist
22.29.2(.26.2)
ichthyology **1.26.10(.11.1)**
ichthyophagous
34.18.14(.5)
ichthyophagy **1.26.10(.6)**
ichthyosaur **12.14.2**
ichthyosauri **14.24.4**
ichthyosaurus
34.18.27(.8)
ichthyosis **34.2.17(.11.1)**
ichthyotic **24.2.10(.6)**
icicle **40.23.12(.15)**
icily **1.31.17(.20)**
iciness **34.18.16(.2.7)**
icing **29.1.23**
Icknield Way **4**
icky **1.12.2**
icon **28.10.11**

iconic **24.2.15(.6.1)**
iconicity **1.10.16(.16.1)**
iconium **27.3.8(.10)**
iconoclasm **27.15.21(.3)**
iconoclast **22.29.6(.12),
22.29.8(.8)**
iconoclastic **24.2.10(.15.4)**
iconoclastically
1.31.24(.9.6)
iconographer
17.20.12(.5)
iconographic **24.2.16(.3)**
iconographical
40.23.12(.12)
iconographically
1.31.24(.9.9)
iconography **1.18.9(.3.2)**
iconolater **17.12.16(.20)**
iconolatry **1.29.15(.13)**
iconology **1.26.10(.11.4)**
iconometer **17.12.16(.9.2)**
iconometry **1.29.15(.8)**
iconostases **35.1.16(.10)**
iconostasis **34.2.17(.10.2)**
icosahedral **40.16.13(.17)**
icosahedron **28.17.31(.15)**
icosidodecahedra
17.32.20
icosidodecahedron
28.17.31(.15)
ictal **40.21.16**
icteric **24.2.26(.4)**
icterus **34.18.27(.14)**
ictus **34.18.11(.13)**
icy **1.22.13**
I'd **23.15**
ID **2**
id **23.2**
Ida **17.13.12**
Idaho **19.26**
Idahoan **28.17.8**
ide **23.15**
idea **3.5**
ideal **40.1.4, 40.3.4, 40.16.1**
idealess **34.18.29(.3)**
idealism **27.15.21(.2.15)**
idealist **22.29.2(.31.1)**
idealistic **24.2.10(.15.3)**
idealistically **1.31.24(.9.6)**
ideality **1.10.16(.32.1)**
idealization
28.17.25(.3.12)
idealize **35.15.21(.2)**
idealizer **17.25.12(.15)**
ideally **1.31.3, 1.31.38**
ideate **22.4.2(.4)**
ideation **28.17.25(.3.1)**
ideational **40.26.13(.14.2)**
ideationally **1.31.17(.14.3)**
idée fixe **34.23.1**
idée reçue **16.24.14**

idem **27.5.5**
identic **24.2.10(.14)**
identical **40.23.12(.7.3)**
identically **1.31.24(.9.5)**
identicalness
34.18.16(.37.5)
identifiable **40.20.16(.5)**
identifiably **1.31.21(.2)**
identification
28.17.25(.3.5)
identifier **17.6.9(.4)**
identify **14.14.4(.4)**
identikit® **22.2.9(.7)**
identity **1.10.16(.8)**
ideogram **27.6.17(.5)**
ideograph **30.7.5(.1)**
ideographic **24.2.16(.3)**
ideographical
40.23.12(.12)
ideological **40.23.12(.17.2)**
ideologically
1.31.24(.9.11)
ideologist **22.29.2(.26.2)**
ideologue **26.7.14**
ideology **1.26.10(.11.1)**
ides **35.23.10**
idiocy **1.22.3**
idiolect **22.23.4(.11)**
idiom **27.3.4(.2)**
idiomatic **24.2.10(.4.2)**
idiomatically
1.31.24(.9.4)
idiopathic **24.2.18(.3)**
idiopathy **1.20.8**
idiosyncrasy **1.22.16(.13)**
idiosyncratic **24.2.10(.4.5)**
idiosyncratically
1.31.24(.9.4)
idiot **22.3.4**
idiotic **24.2.10(.6)**
idiotically **1.31.24(.9.4)**
Iditarod **23.10.12**
idle **40.22.11**
idleness **34.18.16(.37.5)**
idler **17.34.22**
idly **1.31.23(.11)**
Ido **19.11.1**
idol **40.22.11**
idola **17.34.18(.4)**
idolater **17.12.16(.20)**
idolatress **34.18.27(.14)**
idolatrous **34.18.27(.14)**
idolatrously **1.31.33(.12.5)**
idolatry **1.29.15(.13)**
idolization **28.17.25(.3.12)**
idolize **35.15.21(.4.3)**
idolizer **17.25.12(.15)**
idolum **27.15.28(.13)**
Idomeneus **34.17.13**
idyll **40.2.6, 40.22.2**
idyllic **24.2.27(.2)**

idyllically 1.31.24(.9.12)
idyllist 22.29.2(.31.1)
idyllize 35.15.21(.1)
i.e. 2
Iestyn 28.2.11(.14)
Ieuan 28.17.5
if 30.2
iff 30.2
iffy 1.18.2
Ifni 1.16.24
Ifor 12.12, 17.21.10
Igbo 19.9.13
Ightham 27.15.9(.8)
igloo 16.25
Ignatius 34.18.22(.3)
igneous 34.3.6(.8)
ignis fatuus 34.18.6
ignitability 1.10.16(.22.2)
ignitable 40.20.16(.11.2)
ignite 22.16.14
igniter 17.12.13(.4)
ignitibility 1.10.16(.22.2)
ignition 28.17.25(.2.4)
ignitron 28.10.24(.7)
ignobility 1.10.16(.22.1)
ignoble 40.20.18
ignobly 1.31.21(.11)
ignominious 34.3.6(.2)
ignominiously
  1.31.33(.1.2)
ignominiousness
  34.18.16(.31.1)
ignominy 1.16.15(.11)
ignoramus 34.18.15(.3)
ignorance 34.24.10(.16)
ignorant 22.26.15(.23.3)
ignorantly 1.31.22(.20.5)
ignore 12.10
ignorer 17.32.10(.7)
ignotum per ignotius
  34.3.3
Igor 12.8
Iguaçu 16.15
iguana 17.18.8
iguanodon 28.10.10
IKEA® 17.1.5
ikebana 17.18.8(.1)
Ikhnaton 28.10.9,
  28.17.11(.8)
ikky 1.12.2
ikon 28.10.11
Ilchester 17.12.24(.14)
ILEA 3.24.2, 4
ileac 24.6.1
ileal 40.3.15
ileitis 34.18.11(.8)
ileostomy 1.15.13(.1)
Iles 35.30.10
ileum 27.3.18
ileus 34.3.16

ilex 34.23.4(.12)
ilia 3.24.2
iliac 24.6.1
Iliad 23.3, 23.7.2
ilium 27.3.18
ilk 24.21
I'll 40.13
ill 40.2
illation 28.17.25(.3.14)
illative 31.2.1(.3)
illatively 1.31.30(.7.1)
illegal 40.24.1
illegality 1.10.16(.32.6)
illegally 1.31.17(.12)
illegible 40.20.16(.25)
illegibly 1.31.21(.7.4)
illegitimacy 1.22.16(.8)
illegitimate 22.19.14
illegitimately 1.31.22(.15)
illegitimation
  28.17.25(.3.7)
illegitimize 35.15.11
ill-gotten 28.17.11(.9)
ill-humoured 23.18.13
illiberal 40.16.13(.12.1)
illiberality 1.10.16(.32.13)
illiberally 1.31.17(.27.1)
illicit 22.2.16
illicitly 1.31.22(.15)
illicitness 34.18.16(.20.3)
illimitability
  1.10.16(.22.3)
illimitable 40.20.16(.11.3)
illimitableness
  34.18.16(.37.4)
illimitably 1.31.21(.4.2)
Illingworth 32.14.15
Illinois 13.7
Illinoisan 28.17.4
illiquid 23.2.21
illiquidity 1.10.16(.9)
illiteracy 1.22.16(.13)
illiterate 22.19.24(.9)
illiterately 1.31.22(.15)
illiterateness
  34.18.16(.20.3)
ill-natured 23.18.24
ill-naturedly
  1.31.23(.14.7)
illness 34.18.16(.37.1)
illogical 40.23.12(.17.2)
illogicality 1.10.16(.32.5)
illogically 1.31.24(.9.11)
ill-omened 23.24.5(.7),
  23.24.16(.7)
ill-starred 23.9.7
illude 23.17.5
illume 27.14.7
illuminance 34.24.10(.15)
illuminant 22.26.15(.14)
illuminate 22.4.14(.9.2)

illuminati 2.12.5
illuminating 29.1.12(.3)
illuminatingly
  1.31.28(.1.4)
illumination
  28.17.25(.3.8)
illuminative 31.2.1(.9.2)
illuminator 17.12.4(.10)
illumine 28.2.17(.4)
illuminism 27.15.21(.2.9)
illuminist 22.29.2(.18.1)
ill-use 35.17.7
illusion 28.17.26(.4)
illusional 40.26.13(.14.8)
illusionism 27.15.21(.2.9)
illusionist 22.29.2(.18.3)
illusionistic 24.2.10(.15.2)
illusive 31.2.4(.8)
illusively 1.31.30(.7.4)
illusiveness
  34.18.16(.28.2)
illusorily 1.31.17(.27.2)
illusoriness 34.18.16(.2.9)
illusory 1.29.11(.19)
illustrate 22.4.22(.8)
illustration
  28.17.25(.3.13)
illustrational
  40.26.13(.14.2)
illustrative 31.2.1(.3)
illustratively 1.31.30(.7.1)
illustrator 17.12.4(.15)
illustrious 34.3.15(.8)
illustriously 1.31.33(.1.4)
illustriousness
  34.18.16(.31.1)
Illyria 3.22.1
Illyrian 28.3.20(.1)
Illyricum 27.15.11(.2)
illywhacker 17.14.5
ilmenite 22.16.14(.6)
Ilminster 17.12.24(.23)
Ilona 17.18.18(.11)
Ilson 28.17.23(.28)
Ilyushin 28.2.25,
  28.17.25(.11)
I'm 27.12
image 39.2.14
imageable 40.20.16(.25)
imageless 34.18.29(.37)
imagery 1.29.11(.23)
imaginable
  40.20.16(.16.3)
imaginably 1.31.21(.6)
imaginal 40.26.13(.14.8)
imaginarily 1.31.17(.27.2)
imaginary 1.29.11(.13.2)
imagination
  28.17.25(.3.8)
imaginative 31.2.1(.9.2)

imaginatively
  1.31.30(.7.1)
imaginativeness
  34.18.16(.28.1)
imagine 28.17.28(.4)
imagined 23.24.16(.14)
imaginer 17.18.16(.19)
imagines 35.1.12(.3),
  35.26.13(.17)
imaginings 35.27
imagism 27.15.21(.2.13)
imagist 22.29.2(.26.1)
imagistic 24.2.10(.15.2)
imago 19.13.3, 19.13.5
imam 27.6.8, 27.8.6
imamate 22.19.14
IMAX® 34.23.5(.6)
imbalance 34.24.10(.24)
imbecile 40.1.10
imbecilely 1.31.38
imbecilic 24.2.27(.2)
imbecility 1.10.16(.27)
imbed 23.5.2
Imbert 22.19.9
imbibe 21.12
imbiber 17.11.11
imbibition 28.17.25(.2.1)
imbricate 22.4.11(.6)
imbrication 28.17.25(.3.5)
imbroglio 15.1.13
Imbros 34.10.16
imbrue 16.23.7
imbrute 22.18.9
imbue 16.24.4
Imhotep 20.4
imide 23.15.7
imidozole 40.18.11
imine 28.1.13
imitability 1.10.16(.22.2)
imitable 40.20.16(.11.3)
imitate 22.4.9(.5)
imitation 28.17.25(.3.3)
imitative 31.2.1(.9.1)
imitatively 1.31.30(.7.1)
imitativeness
  34.18.16(.28.1)
imitator 17.12.4(.5)
immaculacy 1.22.16(.14)
immaculate 22.19.26(.13)
immaculately
  1.31.22(.15)
immaculateness
  34.18.16(.20.3)
immanence 34.24.10(.15)
immanency
  1.22.23(.10.3)
immanent 22.26.15(.14)
immanentism
  27.15.21(.2.4)
immanentist 22.29.2(.13)
Immanuel 40.16.14

immaterial **40.3.14(.2)**
immaterialism
27.15.21(.2.15)
immaterialist
22.29.2(.31.1)
immateriality
1.10.16(.32.1)
immaterialize
35.15.21(.2)
immaterially **1.31.3(.11)**
immature **12.17, 12.22, 17.7.12(.3)**
immaturely **1.31.11, 1.31.17(.4)**
immaturity **1.10.16(.21.2)**
immeasurability
1.10.16(.22.2)
immeasurable
40.20.16(.27.5)
immeasurableness
34.18.16(.37.4)
immeasurably
1.31.21(.8)
immediacy **1.22.3**
immediate **22.3.4**
immediately **1.31.22(.3)**
immediateness
34.18.16(.20.1)
immedicable
40.20.16(.13)
immedicably **1.31.21(.5)**
immemorial **40.3.14(.5)**
immemorially
1.31.3(.11)
immense **34.24.3**
immensely **1.31.33(.16)**
immenseness
34.18.16(.31.7)
immensity **1.10.16(.16.3)**
immerse **34.19.4**
immersion **28.17.25(.12), 28.17.26(.5)**
immigrant **22.26.15(.23.4)**
immigrate **22.4.22(.11)**
immigration
28.17.25(.3.13)
immigratory **1.29.11(.8.9)**
imminence **34.24.10(.15)**
imminent **22.26.15(.14)**
imminently
1.31.22(.20.3)
immiscibility
1.10.16(.22.2)
immiscible
40.20.16(.21.1)
immiscibly **1.31.21(.7.2)**
immitigable **40.20.16(.14)**
immitigably **1.31.21(.5)**
immittance **34.24.10(.10)**
immixture **17.28.24**
immobile **40.13.2**

immobilism
27.15.21(.2.15)
immobility **1.10.16(.22.1)**
immobilization
28.17.25(.3.12)
immobilize **35.15.21(.4.2)**
immobilizer
17.25.12(.15)
immoderacy **1.22.16(.13)**
immoderate **22.19.24(.9)**
immoderately
1.31.22(.15)
immoderateness
34.18.16(.20.3)
immoderation
28.17.25(.3.13)
immodest **22.29.15(.10)**
immodestly **1.31.22(.22)**
immodesty **1.10.26(.11)**
immolate **22.4.23(.7.2)**
immolation
28.17.25(.3.14)
immolator **17.12.4(.16)**
immoral **40.16.13(.7)**
immorality
1.10.16(.32.13)
immorally **1.31.17(.27.1)**
immortal **40.21.8**
immortality
1.10.16(.32.3)
immortalization
28.17.25(.3.12)
immortalize
35.15.21(.4.3)
immortally **1.31.17(.9.2)**
immortelle **40.5.3**
immovability
1.10.16(.22.2)
immovable **40.20.16(.19)**
immovableness
34.18.16(.37.4)
immovably **1.31.21(.7.1)**
immoveableness
34.18.16(.37.4)
immoveably **1.31.21(.7.1)**
immune **28.16.14**
immunity **1.10.16(.13)**
immunization
28.17.25(.3.11)
immunize **35.15.12(.5)**
immunizer **17.25.12(.6)**
immunoassay **4.18, 4.18.6**
immunochemistry
1.29.15(.17)
immunocompetence
34.24.10(.10)
immunocompetent
22.26.15(.9)
immunodeficiency
1.22.23(.10.4)

immunodeficient
22.26.15(.19)
immunodepressed
22.29.5(.12)
immunodepression
28.17.25(.4)
immunogenic **24.2.15(.4)**
immunoglobulin
28.2.31(.10)
immunologic **24.2.24(.4)**
immunological
40.23.12(.17.2)
immunologically
1.31.24(.9.11)
immunologist
22.29.2(.26.4)
immunology
1.26.10(.11.4)
immunosuppressant
22.26.15(.17.2)
immunosuppressed
22.29.5(.12)
immunosuppression
28.17.25(.4)
immunosuppressive
31.2.4(.4)
immunotherapy
1.8.11(.8)
immure **12.22, 17.7.12(.7)**
immurement
22.26.15(.13.1)
immutability
1.10.16(.22.2)
immutable
40.20.16(.11.2)
immutably **1.31.21(.4.1)**
Imogen **28.17.28(.9)**
imp **20.16.1**
impact **22.23.5(.2)**
impaction **28.17.25(.15.3)**
impair **6.2**
impairment
22.26.15(.13.1)
impala **17.34.8**
impale **40.4.1**
impalement
22.26.15(.13.7)
impalpability
1.10.16(.22.2)
impalpable **40.20.16(.9)**
impalpably **1.31.21(.3)**
impanel **40.26.5**
imparisyllabic **24.2.9(.2)**
impark **24.8.2**
impart **22.10.1**
impartable
40.20.16(.11.2)
impartation
28.17.25(.3.3)
impartial **40.33.5**
impartiality **1.10.16(.32.1)**
impartially **1.31.17(.22)**

impartialness
34.18.16(.37.5)
impartible **40.20.16(.11.2)**
impartment
22.26.15(.13.3)
impassability
1.10.16(.22.2)
impassable
40.20.16(.21.1)
impassableness
34.18.16(.37.4)
impassably **1.31.21(.7.2)**
impasse **34.9.1**
impassibility
1.10.16(.22.2)
impassible **40.20.16(.21.1)**
impassibleness
34.18.16(.37.4)
impassibly **1.31.21(.7.2)**
impassion **28.17.25(.5)**
impassioned
23.24.16(.12)
impassive **31.2.4(.5)**
impassively **1.31.30(.7.4)**
impassiveness
34.18.16(.28.2)
impassivity **1.10.16(.15)**
impasto **19.10.19**
impatience **34.24.10(.20)**
impatiens **35.26.5**
impatient **22.26.15(.19)**
impatiently **1.31.22(.20.4)**
impeach **38.1**
impeachable
40.20.16(.24)
impeachment
22.26.15(.13.6)
impeccability
1.10.16(.22.2)
impeccable **40.20.16(.13)**
impeccably **1.31.21(.5)**
impeccancy
1.22.23(.10.2)
impeccant **22.26.15(.11)**
impecuniosity
1.10.16(.16.2)
impecunious **34.3.6(.6)**
impecuniously
1.31.33(.1.2)
impecuniousness
34.18.16(.31.1)
impedance **34.24.10(.11)**
impede **23.1.1**
impediment
22.26.15(.13.2)
impedimenta
17.12.22(.3)
impedimental
40.21.17(.2)
impel **40.5.1**
impellent **22.26.15(.25)**
impeller **17.34.5(.1)**

i

impend 23.24.5(.2)
impendence 34.24.10(.11)
impendency 1.22.23(.10.2)
impendent 22.26.15(.10)
impending 29.1.13(.14)
impenetrability 1.10.16(.22.3)
impenetrable 40.20.16(.27.6)
impenetrably 1.31.21(.8)
impenetrate 22.4.22(.8)
impenitence 34.24.10(.10)
impenitency 1.22.23(.10.2)
impenitent 22.26.15(.9)
impenitently 1.31.22(.20.2)
imperatival 40.28.9
imperative 31.2.1(.9.4)
imperatively 1.31.30(.7.1)
imperativeness 34.18.16(.28.1)
imperator 12.5.3
imperatorial 40.3.14(.5)
imperceptible 40.20.16(.11.4)
imperceptibly 1.31.21(.4.3)
impercipience 34.24.2
impercipient 22.26.2(.1)
imperfect 22.23.10
imperfection 28.17.25(.15.2)
imperfective 31.2.1(.13.2)
imperfectly 1.31.22(.19)
imperfectness 34.18.16(.20.4)
imperforate 22.19.24(.9)
imperia 3.22.2
imperial 40.3.14(.2)
imperialism 27.15.21(.2.15)
imperialist 22.29.2(.31.1)
imperialistic 24.2.10(.15.3)
imperialistically 1.31.24(.9.6)
imperialize 35.15.21(.2)
imperially 1.31.3(.11)
imperil 40.16.13(.3)
imperious 34.3.15(.2)
imperiously 1.31.33(.1.4)
imperiousness 34.18.16(.31.1)
imperishability 1.10.16(.22.3)
imperishable 40.20.16(.23)

imperishableness 1.31.21(.7.3)
imperishably 34.18.16(.37.4)
imperium 27.3.17(.2)
impermanence 34.24.10(.15)
impermanency 1.22.23(.10.3)
impermanent 22.26.15(.14)
impermanently 1.31.22(.20.3)
impermeability 1.10.16(.22.2)
impermeable 40.20.3
impermeableness 34.18.16(.37.4)
impermeably 1.31.21(.1)
impermissible 40.20.16(.21.1)
imperscriptible 40.20.16(.11.4)
impersonal 40.26.13(.12)
impersonality 1.10.16(.32.8)
impersonally 1.31.17(.14.2)
impersonate 22.4.14(.9.3)
impersonation 28.17.25(.3.1)
impersonator 17.12.4(.10)
impertinence 34.24.10(.15)
impertinent 22.26.15(.14)
impertinently 1.31.22(.20.3)
imperturbability 1.10.16(.22.3)
imperturbable 40.20.16(.10)
imperturbableness 34.18.16(.37.4)
imperturbably 1.31.21(.3)
impervious 34.3.8
imperviously 1.31.33(.1.3)
imperviousness 34.18.16(.31.1)
impetiginous 34.18.16(.15.3)
impetigo 19.13.7
impetrate 22.4.22(.8)
impetration 28.17.25(.3.13)
impetratory 1.29.11(.8.9)
impetuosity 1.10.16(.16.2)
impetuous 34.18.6
impetuously 1.31.33(.12.1)

impetuousness 34.18.16(.31.2)
impetus 34.18.11(.10)
impi 1.8.14
impiety 1.10.16(.4)
impinge 39.17.1
impingement 22.26.15(.13.6)
impinger 17.29.16(.1)
impious 34.3.1, 34.18.5
impiously 1.31.33(.1.1)
impiousness 34.18.16(.31.1)
impish 36.2.9
impishly 1.31.35(.7.1)
impishness 34.18.16(.33.2)
implacability 1.10.16(.22.2)
implacable 40.20.16(.13)
implacableness 34.18.16(.37.4)
implacably 1.31.21(.5)
implant 22.26.6, 22.26.8
implantation 28.17.25(.3.3)
implausibility 1.10.16(.22.2)
implausible 40.20.16(.22)
implausibly 1.31.21(.7.2)
implead 23.1.12
implement 22.26.4(.8), 22.26.15(.13.2)
implementation 28.17.25(.3.3)
implementer 17.12.22(.3)
implicate 22.4.11(.6)
implication 28.17.25(.3.5)
implicative 31.2.1(.3)
implicatively 1.31.30(.7.1)
implicature 17.28.15
implicit 22.2.16
implicitly 1.31.22(.15)
implicitness 34.18.16(.20.3)
implied 23.15.16
impliedly 1.31.23(.11)
implode 23.20.13
implore 12.23.3
imploringly 1.31.28(.1.17)
implosion 28.17.26(.6)
implosive 31.2.4(.11)
imply 14.25.11
impolder 17.13.23(.8)
impolicy 1.22.16(.14)
impolite 22.16.25
impolitely 1.31.22(.13)
impoliteness 34.18.16(.20.2)
impolitic 24.2.10(.10)

imponderability 1.10.16(.22.2)
imponderable 40.20.16(.27.3)
imponderably 1.31.21(.8)
imponent 22.26.15(.14)
import 22.13.1
importable 40.20.16(.11.2)
importance 34.24.10(.10)
important 22.26.15(.9)
importation 28.17.25(.3.3)
importer 17.12.10(.1)
importunate 22.19.15(.9)
importunately 1.31.22(.15)
importune 28.16.14
importunity 1.10.16(.13)
impose 35.20.1
imposingly 1.31.28(.1.12)
imposingness 34.18.16(.26)
imposition 28.17.25(.2.5)
impossibility 1.10.16(.22.2)
impossible 40.20.16(.21.2)
impossibly 1.31.21(.7.2)
impost 22.29.9, 22.29.17(.1)
impostor 17.12.24(.7)
impostorous 34.18.27(.14)
impostrous 34.18.27(.14)
imposture 17.28.24
impotence 34.24.10(.10)
impotency 1.22.23(.10.2)
impotent 22.26.15(.9)
impotently 1.31.22(.20.2)
impound 23.24.7(.1)
impoundable 40.20.16(.12)
impounder 17.13.20(.5)
impoundment 22.26.15(.13.3)
impoverish 36.2.25
impoverishment 22.26.15(.13.6)
impracticability 1.10.16(.22.3)
impracticable 40.20.16(.13)
impracticableness 34.18.16(.37.4)
impracticably 1.31.21(.5)
impractical 40.23.12(.7.3)
impracticality 1.10.16(.32.5)
impractically 1.31.24(.9.5)
imprecate 22.4.11(.6)

imprecation 28.17.25(.3.5)
imprecatory 1.29.11(.8.2)
imprecise 34.15.8
imprecisely 1.31.33(.9)
impreciseness 34.18.16(.31.2)
imprecision 28.17.26(.2)
impregnability 1.10.16(.22.2)
impregnable 40.20.16(.16.3)
impregnably 1.31.21(.6)
impregnatable 40.20.16(.11.1)
impregnate 22.4.14(.13), 22.19.15(.11)
impregnation 28.17.25(.3.8)
impresario 15.1.12
imprescriptible 40.20.16(.11.4)
impress 34.5.14(.4)
impressible 40.20.16(.21.1)
impression 28.17.25(.4)
impressionability 1.10.16(.22.2)
impressionable 40.20.16(.16.3)
impressionably 1.31.21(.6)
impressional 40.26.13(.14.3)
impressionism 27.15.21(.2.9)
impressionist 22.29.2(.18.2)
impressionistic 24.2.10(.15.2)
impressionistically 1.31.24(.9.6)
impressive 31.2.4(.4)
impressively 1.31.30(.7.4)
impressiveness 34.18.16(.28.2)
impressment 22.26.15(.13.5)
imprest 22.29.5(.12)
imprimatur 17.12.4(.9), 17.12.8(.7)
imprimatura 17.32.14(.3)
imprint 22.26.1
imprison 28.17.24(.2)
imprisonment 22.26.15(.13.4)
impro 19.27.13
improbability 1.10.16(.22.2)
improbable 40.20.16(.10)
improbably 1.31.21(.3)
improbity 1.10.16(.7)

impromptu 16.24.5
improper 17.10.8
improperly 1.31.17(.7)
impropriate 22.4.2(.14)
impropriation 28.17.25(.3.1)
impropriator 17.12.4(.1)
impropriety 1.10.16(.4)
improv 31.7
improvability 1.10.16(.22.2)
improvable 40.20.16(.19)
improve 31.10
improvement 22.26.15(.13.5)
improver 17.21.11
improvidence 34.24.10(.11)
improvident 22.26.15(.10)
improvidently 1.31.22(.20.2)
improvisation 28.17.25(.3.11)
improvisational 40.26.13(.14.2)
improvisatorial 40.3.14(.5)
improvisatory 1.29.11(.8.8)
improvise 35.15.14
improviser 17.25.12(.8)
imprudence 34.24.10(.11)
imprudent 22.26.15(.10)
imprudently 1.31.22(.20.2)
impudence 34.24.10(.11)
impudent 22.26.15(.10)
impudently 1.31.22(.20.2)
impudicity 1.10.16(.16.1)
impugn 28.16.14
impugnable 40.20.16(.16.2)
impugnment 22.26.15(.13.4)
impuissance 34.24.10(.18)
impuissant 22.26.15(.17.1)
impulse 34.27
impulsion 28.17.25(.17)
impulsive 31.2.4(.14)
impulsively 1.31.30(.7.4)
impulsiveness 34.18.16(.28.2)
impunity 1.10.16(.13)
impure 12.22, 17.7.12(.2)
impurely 1.31.11, 1.31.17(.4)
impureness 34.18.16(.15.1)
impurity 1.10.16(.21.2)

imputable 40.20.16(.11.2)
imputation 28.17.25(.3.3)
imputative 31.2.1(.9.1)
impute 22.18.10
imshi 1.24.14
in 28.2
Ina 17.18.1, 17.18.13
inability 1.10.16(.22.1)
in absentia 3.4.12
inaccessible 40.20.16(.21.1)
inaccessibleness 34.18.16(.37.4)
inaccessibly 1.31.21(.7.2)
inaccuracy 1.22.16(.13)
inaccurate 22.19.24(.9)
inaccurately 1.31.22(.15)
inaction 28.17.25(.15.3)
inactivate 22.4.16
inactivation 28.17.25(.3.9)
inactive 31.2.1(.13.3)
inactively 1.31.30(.7.2)
inactivity 1.10.16(.15)
inadequacy 1.22.16(.12)
inadequate 22.19.23
inadequately 1.31.22(.15)
inadmissible 40.20.16(.21.1)
inadmissibly 1.31.21(.7.2)
inadvertence 34.24.10(.10)
inadvertency 1.22.23(.10.2)
inadvertent 22.26.15(.9)
inadvertently 1.31.22(.20.2)
inadvisability 1.10.16(.22.3)
inadvisable 40.20.16(.22)
inalienability 1.10.16(.22.3)
inalienable 40.20.16(.16.1)
inalienableness 34.18.16(.37.4)
inalienably 1.31.21(.6)
inalterability 1.10.16(.22.2)
inalterable 40.20.16(.27.3)
inalterably 1.31.21(.8)
inamorata 17.12.8(.10)
inamorato 19.10.7
inane 28.4.8
inanely 1.31.27(.4)
inaneness 34.18.16(.25)
inanga 17.16.17(.2)
inanimate 22.19.14
inanimately 1.31.22(.15)
inanimation 28.17.25(.3.7)

inanition 28.17.25(.2.4)
inanity 1.10.16(.13)
inappeasable 40.20.16(.22)
inappellable 40.20.16(.29)
inappetence 34.24.10(.10)
inappetency 1.22.23(.10.2)
inappetent 22.26.15(.9)
inapplicability 1.10.16(.22.3)
inapplicable 40.20.16(.13)
inapplicably 1.31.21(.5)
inapposite 22.19.19
inappositely 1.31.22(.15)
inappositeness 34.18.16(.20.3)
inappreciable 40.20.3, 40.20.16(.23)
inappreciably 1.31.21(.1)
inappreciation 28.17.25(.3.1)
inappreciative 31.2.1(.2)
inapprehensible 40.20.16(.21.3)
inappropriate 22.3.12
inappropriately 1.31.22(.3)
inappropriateness 34.18.16(.20.1)
inapt 22.22.4
inaptitude 23.17.4(.1)
inaptly 1.31.22(.18)
inarch 38.7
inarguable 40.20.16(.6)
inarguably 1.31.21(.2)
inarticulacy 1.22.16(.14)
inarticulate 22.19.26(.13)
inarticulately 1.31.22(.15)
inarticulateness 34.18.16(.20.3)
inartistic 24.2.10(.15.2)
inartistically 1.31.24(.9.6)
inasmuch 38.11
inattention 28.17.25(.16)
inattentive 31.2.1(.14)
inattentively 1.31.30(.7.3)
inattentiveness 34.18.16(.28.1)
inaudibility 1.10.16(.22.2)
inaudible 40.20.16(.12)
inaudibly 1.31.21(.4.4)
inaugural 40.16.13(.12.4)
inaugurate 22.4.22(.6)
inauguration 28.17.25(.3.13)
inaugurator 17.12.4(.15)
inauguratory 1.29.11(.8.9)
inauspicious 34.18.22(.2)

inauspiciously **1.31.33(.12.4)**

inauspiciousness **34.18.16(.31.4)**

inauthentic **24.2.10(.14)**

inauthenticity **1.10.16(.16.1)**

in-between **28.1.24**

inboard **23.12.2(.12)**

inborn **28.11.2**

inbound **23.24.7(.2)**

inbreathe **33.1**

inbred **23.5.15**

inbreed **23.1.11**

inbreeding **29.1.13(.1)**

inbuilt **22.32.1**

Inc. **24.19.1**

Inca **17.14.21(.1)**

Incaic **24.2.3**

incalculability **1.10.16(.22.3)**

incalculable **40.20.16(.29)**

incalculably **1.31.21(.9)**

in camera **17.32.14(.10)**

Incan **28.17.13(.17)**

incandesce **34.5.3**

incandescence **34.24.10(.18)**

incandescent **22.26.15(.17.2)**

incantation **28.17.25(.3.3)**

incantational **40.26.13(.14.2)**

incantatory **1.29.11(.8.2)**

incapability **1.10.16(.22.2)**

incapable **40.20.16(.9)**

incapably **1.31.21(.3)**

incapacitant **22.26.15(.9)**

incapacitate **22.4.9(.5)**

incapacitation **28.17.25(.3.3)**

incapacity **1.10.16(.16.1)**

in-car **10.8**

incarcerate **22.4.22(.6)**

incarceration **28.17.25(.3.13)**

incarcerator **17.12.4(.15)**

incarnadine **28.14.6**

incarnate **22.4.14(.5), 22.19.15(.4)**

incarnation **28.17.25(.3.8)**

incase **34.4.6**

incaution **28.17.25(.8)**

incautious **34.18.22(.5)**

incautiously **1.31.33(.12.4)**

incautiousness **34.18.16(.31.4)**

incendiarism **27.15.21(.2.14)**

incendiary **1.29.2(.3), 1.29.11(.23)**

incensation **28.17.25(.3.10)**

incense **34.24.3**

incensory **1.29.11(.18)**

incentive **31.2.1(.14)**

incept **22.22.3**

inception **28.17.25(.14)**

inceptive **31.2.1(.12)**

inceptor **17.12.19**

incertitude **23.17.4(.1)**

incessancy **1.22.23(.10.4)**

incessant **22.26.15(.17.2)**

incessantness **34.18.16(.20.4)**

incest **22.29.5(.6)**

incestuous **34.18.6**

incestuously **1.31.33(.12.1)**

incestuousness **34.18.16(.31.2)**

inch **38.18.1**

Inchcape **20.3**

inchmeal **40.1.6**

inchoate **22.4.6, 22.19.7**

inchoately **1.31.22(.4)**

inchoateness **34.18.16(.20.1)**

inchoation **28.17.25(.3.1)**

inchoative **31.2.1(.3)**

Inchon **28.10.21**

inchworm **27.16.7**

incidence **34.24.10(.11)**

incident **22.26.15(.10)**

incidental **40.21.17(.2)**

incidentally **1.31.17(.9.3), 1.31.22(.20.1)**

incidentalness **34.18.16(.37.5)**

incinerate **22.4.22(.6)**

incineration **28.17.25(.3.13)**

incinerator **17.12.4(.15)**

incipience **34.24.2**

incipiency **1.22.23(.2)**

incipient **22.26.2(.1)**

incipiently **1.31.22(.20.1)**

incipit **22.2.5**

incise **35.15.16**

incision **28.17.26(.2)**

incisive **31.2.4(.7)**

incisively **1.31.30(.7.4)**

incisiveness **34.18.16(.28.2)**

incisor **17.25.12(.10)**

incitation **28.17.25(.3.3)**

incite **22.16.19**

incitement **22.26.15(.13.3)**

inciter **17.12.13(.7)**

incivility **1.10.16(.26)**

incivism **27.15.21(.2.11)**

inclemency **1.22.23(.10.3)**

inclement **22.26.15(.13.1)**

inclemently **1.31.22(.20.3)**

inclinable **40.20.16(.16.2)**

inclination **28.17.25(.3.8)**

incline **28.14.19(.16)**

incliner **17.18.13(.14)**

inclinometer **17.12.16(.9.2)**

inclose **35.20.14**

inclosure **17.27.9**

includable **40.20.16(.12)**

include **23.17.5**

inclusion **28.17.26(.4)**

inclusive **31.2.4(.8)**

inclusively **1.31.30(.7.4)**

inclusiveness **34.18.16(.28.2)**

incog **26.7.5**

incognito **19.10.1**

incognizance **34.24.10(.19)**

incognizant **22.26.15(.18)**

incoherence **34.24.10(.16)**

incoherency **1.22.23(.10.4)**

incoherent **22.26.15(.23.1)**

incoherently **1.31.22(.20.5)**

incombustible **40.20.16(.11.7)**

incombustibleness **34.18.16(.37.4)**

income **27.11.5, 27.15.11(.12)**

incomer **17.17.10**

incoming **29.1.16**

incommensurability **1.10.16(.22.3)**

incommensurable **40.20.16(.27.5)**

incommensurably **1.31.21(.8)**

incommensurate **22.19.24(.9)**

incommensurately **1.31.22(.15)**

incommensurateness **34.18.16(.20.3)**

incommode **23.20.8**

incommodious **34.3.4**

incommodiously **1.31.33(.1.1)**

incommodiousness **34.18.16(.31.1)**

incommunicability **1.10.16(.22.3)**

incommunicable **40.20.16(.13)**

incommunicableness **34.18.16(.37.4)**

incommunicably **1.31.21(.5)**

incommunicado **19.11.7**

incommunicative **31.2.1(.9.1)**

incommunicatively **1.31.30(.7.1)**

incommunicativeness **34.18.16(.28.1)**

incommutable **40.20.16(.11.2)**

incommutably **1.31.21(.4.1)**

incomparability **1.10.16(.22.2)**

incomparable **40.20.16(.27.1)**

incomparableness **34.18.16(.37.4)**

incomparably **1.31.21(.8)**

incompatible **40.20.16(.11.1)**

incompatibleness **34.18.16(.37.4)**

incompatibly **1.31.21(.4.1)**

incompetence **34.24.10(.10)**

incompetency **1.22.23(.10.2)**

incompetent **22.26.15(.9)**

incompetently **1.31.22(.20.2)**

incomplete **22.1.18**

incompletely **1.31.22(.1)**

incompleteness **34.18.16(.20.1)**

incomprehensibility **1.10.16(.22.3)**

incomprehensible **40.20.16(.21.3)**

incomprehensibleness **34.18.16(.37.4)**

incomprehensibly **1.31.21(.7.2)**

incomprehension **28.17.25(.16)**

incompressible **40.20.16(.21.1)**

inconceivability **1.10.16(.22.3)**

inconceivable **40.20.16(.19)**

inconceivableness **34.18.16(.37.4)**

inconceivably **1.31.21(.7.1)**

inconclusive **31.2.4(.8)**

inconclusively 1.31.30(.7.4)

inconclusiveness 34.18.16(.28.2)

incondensable 40.20.16(.21.3)

incondite 22.16.10, 22.19.11

incongruity 1.10.16(.5)

incongruous 34.18.6

incongruously 1.31.33(.12.1)

incongruousness 34.18.16(.31.2)

inconsecutive 31.2.1(.9.4)

inconsecutively 1.31.30(.7.2)

inconsecutiveness 34.18.16(.28.1)

inconsequence 34.24.10(.22)

inconsequent 22.26.15(.22)

inconsequential 40.33.12(.3)

inconsequentiality 1.10.16(.32.1)

inconsequentially 1.31.17(.22)

inconsequentialness 34.18.16(.37.5)

inconsequently 1.31.22(.20.5)

inconsiderable 40.20.16(.27.3)

inconsiderableness 34.18.16(.37.4)

inconsiderably 1.31.21(.8)

inconsiderate 22.19.24(.9)

inconsiderately 1.31.22(.15)

inconsiderateness 34.18.16(.20.3)

inconsideration 28.17.25(.3.13)

inconsistency 1.22.23(.10.2)

inconsistent 22.26.15(.9)

inconsistently 1.31.22(.20.2)

inconsolability 1.10.16(.22.3)

inconsolable 40.20.16(.29)

inconsolableness 34.18.16(.37.4)

inconsolably 1.31.21(.9)

inconsonance 34.24.10(.15)

inconsonant 22.26.15(.14)

inconsonantly 1.31.22(.20.3)

inconspicuous 34.18.6

inconspicuously 1.31.33(.12.1)

inconspicuousness 34.18.16(.31.2)

inconstancy 1.22.23(.10.2)

inconstant 22.26.15(.9)

inconstantly 1.31.22(.20.2)

incontestable 40.20.16(.11.7)

incontestably 1.31.21(.4.3)

incontinence 34.24.10(.15)

incontinent 22.26.15(.14)

incontinently 1.31.22(.20.3)

incontrovertibility 1.10.16(.22.3)

incontrovertible 40.20.16(.11.3)

incontrovertibly 1.31.21(.4.2)

inconvenience 34.24.2

inconvenient 22.26.2(.5)

inconveniently 1.31.22(.20.1)

inconvertibility 1.10.16(.22.3)

inconvertible 40.20.16(.11.3)

inconvertibly 1.31.21(.4.2)

incoordination 28.17.25(.3.8)

incorporate 22.4.22(.6), 22.19.24(.9)

incorporation 28.17.25(.3.13)

incorporator 17.12.4(.15)

incorporeal 40.3.14(.5)

incorporeality 1.10.16(.32.1)

incorporeally 1.31.3(.11)

incorporeity 1.10.16(.1)

incorrect 22.23.4(.10)

incorrectly 1.31.22(.19)

incorrectness 34.18.16(.20.4)

incorrigibility 1.10.16(.22.3)

incorrigible 40.20.16(.25)

incorrigibleness 34.18.16(.37.4)

incorrigibly 1.31.21(.7.4)

incorruptible 40.20.16(.11.4)

incorruptibly 1.31.21(.4.3)

incorruption 28.17.25(.14)

incrassate 22.4.18

increasable 40.20.16(.21.1)

increase 34.1.7

increaser 17.24.1

increasingly 1.31.28(.1.11)

incredibility 1.10.16(.22.2)

incredible 40.20.16(.12)

incredibleness 34.18.16(.37.4)

incredibly 1.31.21(.4.4)

incredulity 1.10.16(.35)

incredulous 34.18.29(.17.5)

incredulously 1.31.33(.12.6)

incredulousness 34.18.16(.31.6)

increment 22.26.15(.13.2)

incremental 40.21.17(.2)

incrementally 1.31.17(.9.3)

incriminate 22.4.14(.9.2)

incriminatingly 1.31.28(.1.4)

incrimination 28.17.25(.3.8)

incriminatory 1.29.11(.8.7)

in-crowd 23.8

incrust 22.29.12

incubate 22.4.8

incubation 28.17.25(.3.2)

incubational 40.26.13(.14.2)

incubative 31.2.1(.3)

incubator 17.12.4(.4)

incubatory 1.29.11(.8.2)

incubi 14.7

incubus 34.18.10

incudes 35.1.8

inculcate 22.4.11(.8)

inculcation 28.17.25(.3.5)

inculcator 17.12.4(.7)

inculpate 22.4.7

inculpation 28.17.25(.3.2)

inculpative 31.2.1(.9.1)

inculpatory 1.29.11(.8.6)

incult 22.32.8

inculturation 28.17.25(.3.13)

incumbency 1.22.23(.10.2)

incumbent 22.26.15(.8)

incunable 40.20.16(.16.2)

incunabula 17.34.16(.21.1)

incunabular 17.34.16(.21.1)

incunabulum 27.15.28(.11)

incur 18.5

incurability 1.10.16(.22.2)

incurable 40.20.16(.27.2)

incurableness 34.18.16(.37.4)

incurably 1.31.21(.8)

incuriosity 1.10.16(.16.2)

incurious 34.3.15(.5)

incuriously 1.31.33(.1.4)

incuriousness 34.18.16(.31.1)

incurrable 40.20.16(.27.5)

incursion 28.17.25(.12), 28.17.26(.5)

incursive 31.2.4(.10)

incurvation 28.17.25(.3.9)

incurve 31.11

incus 34.18.13(.13)

incuse 35.17.7

indaba 17.11.7

Indebele 1.31.1, 1.31.4

indebted 23.18.9(.4)

indebtedness 34.18.16(.21.1)

indecency 1.22.23(.10.4)

indecent 22.26.15(.17.1)

indecipherability 1.10.16(.22.3)

indecipherable 40.20.16(.27.5)

indecipherably 1.31.21(.8)

indecision 28.17.26(.2)

indecisive 31.2.4(.7)

indecisively 1.31.30(.7.4)

indecisiveness 34.18.16(.28.2)

indeclinable 40.20.16(.16.2)

indecorous 34.18.27(.16)

indecorously 1.31.33(.12.5)

indecorousness 34.18.16(.31.5)

indecorum 27.15.26(.5)

indeed 23.1.3

indefatigability 1.10.16(.22.3)

indefatigable 40.20.16(.14)

indefatigableness 34.18.16(.37.4)

indefatigably 1.31.21(.5)

indefeasibility 1.10.16(.22.3)

indefeasible 40.20.16(.22)

infant 22.26.15(.15)
infanta 17.12.22(.4)
infante 1.10.23(.4)
infanticidal 40.22.11
infanticide 23.15.11(.6)
infantile 40.13.3(.9)
infantilism
　27.15.21(.2.15)
infantility 1.10.16(.23)
infantine 28.14.5
infantry 1.29.15(.15)
infantryman 28.17.16(.2)
infarct 22.23.6
infarction 28.17.25(.15.4)
infatuate 22.4.4
infatuation 28.17.25(.3.1)
infauna 17.18.10
infeasibility 1.10.16(.22.2)
infeasible 40.20.16(.22)
infect 22.23.4(.5)
infection 28.17.25(.15.2)
infectious 34.18.22(.11)
infectiously 1.31.33(.12.4)
infectiousness
　34.18.16(.31.4)
infective 31.2.1(.13.2)
infectiveness
　34.18.16(.28.1)
infector 17.12.21(.2)
infelicitous 34.18.11(.10)
infelicitously
　1.31.33(.12.2)
infelicity 1.10.16(.16.1)
infer 18.9
inferable 40.20.16(.27.5)
inference 34.24.10(.16)
inferential 40.33.12(.3)
inferentially 1.31.17(.22)
inferior 3.22.2
inferiority 1.10.16(.21.2)
inferiorly 1.31.3(.11)
infernal 40.26.14
infernally 1.31.17(.14.3)
inferno 19.15.13
infertile 40.13.3(.5)
infertility 1.10.16(.23)
infest 22.29.5(.4)
infestation 28.17.25(.3.3)
infeudation 28.17.25(.3.4)
infibulate 22.4.23(.7.3)
infibulation
　28.17.25(.3.14)
infidel 40.5.4, 40.22.13
infidelity 1.10.16(.31)
infield 23.31.1(.2)
infielder 17.13.23(.1)
infighter 17.12.13(.5)
infighting 29.1.12(.11)
infill 40.2.11
infiltrate 22.4.22(.8)

infiltration
　28.17.25(.3.13)
infiltrator 17.12.4(.15)
infinite 22.19.15(.9)
infinitely 1.31.22(.15)
infiniteness
　34.18.16(.20.3)
infinitesimal 40.25.10
infinitesimally
　1.31.17(.13)
infinitival 40.28.9
infinitivally 1.31.17(.17)
infinitive 31.2.1(.9.2)
infinitude 23.17.4(.1)
infinity 1.10.16(.13)
infirm 27.16.4
infirmary 1.29.11(.12)
infirmity 1.10.16(.12)
infix 34.23.2(.7)
infixation 28.17.25(.3.10)
in flagrante delicto
　19.10.16
inflame 27.4.9
inflamed 23.23.3
inflamer 17.17.4
inflammability
　1.10.16(.22.2)
inflammable
　40.20.16(.15)
inflammableness
　34.18.16(.37.4)
inflammably 1.31.21(.6)
inflammation
　28.17.25(.3.7)
inflammatory
　1.29.11(.8.7)
inflatable 40.20.16(.11.1)
inflate 22.4.23(.11)
inflatedly 1.31.23(.14.3)
inflatedness
　34.18.16(.21.1)
inflater 17.12.4(.16)
inflation 28.17.25(.3.14)
inflationary 1.29.11(.13.2)
inflationism
　27.15.21(.2.9)
inflationist 22.29.2(.18.2)
inflator 17.12.4(.16)
inflect 22.23.4(.11)
inflection 28.17.25(.15.2)
inflectional
　40.26.13(.14.6)
inflectionally
　1.31.17(.14.3)
inflectionless
　34.18.29(.27)
inflective 31.2.1(.13.2)
inflexibility 1.10.16(.22.2)
inflexible 40.20.16(.21.3)
inflexibly 1.31.21(.7.2)
inflexionally
　1.31.17(.14.3)

inflict 22.23.2
inflictable 40.20.16(.11.5)
inflicter 17.12.21(.1)
infliction 28.17.25(.15.1)
in-flight 22.16.25(.18)
inflorescence
　34.24.10(.18)
inflow 19.29.21
inflowing 29.1.9
influence 34.24.10(.6)
influenceable
　40.20.16(.21.3)
influencer 17.24.22(.7)
influent 22.26.15(.5)
influential 40.33.12(.2)
influentially 1.31.17(.22)
influenza 17.25.18
influenzal 40.32.17
influx 34.23.11
info 19.16
infobit 22.2.6
in folio 15.1.13
infomania 3.9.3(.5)
infomercial 40.33.10
infopreneur 18.8
inform 27.10.5
informal 40.25.6
informality 1.10.16(.32.7)
informally 1.31.17(.13)
informant 22.26.15(.13.1)
informatics 34.23.2(.3)
information
　28.17.25(.3.7)
informational
　40.26.13(.14.2)
informationally
　1.31.17(.14.3)
informative 31.2.1(.9.2)
informatively
　1.31.30(.7.1)
informativeness
　34.18.16(.28.1)
informatory 1.29.11(.8.7)
informedly 1.31.23(.14.6)
informedness
　34.18.16(.21.1)
informer 17.17.9
infosphere 3.10.5
infotainment
　22.26.15(.13.4)
infotech 24.4.4
infra 17.32.25
infraclass 34.9.7
infract 22.23.5(.9)
infraction 28.17.25(.15.3)
infractor 17.12.21(.3)
infradian 28.3.4(.3)
infra dig 26.2
infralapsarian 28.3.20(.4)
infrangibility
　1.10.16(.22.2)

infrangible 40.20.16(.25)
infrangibleness
　34.18.16(.37.4)
infrangibly 1.31.21(.7.3)
infrared 23.5.15
infrarenal 40.26.1
infrasonic 24.2.15(.6.3)
infrasonically
　1.31.24(.9.8)
infrasound 23.24.7(.6)
infrastructural
　40.16.13(.12.3)
infrastructure 17.28.20
infrequency
　1.22.23(.10.4)
infrequent 22.26.15(.22)
infrequently
　1.31.22(.20.5)
infringe 39.17.1
infringement
　22.26.15(.13.6)
infringer 17.29.16(.1)
infructescence
　34.24.10(.18)
infula 17.34.16(.21.4)
infulae 2.32.9(.8)
infundibular
　17.34.16(.21.1)
infuriate 22.4.2(.14)
infuriatingly 1.31.28(.1.4)
infuriation 28.17.25(.3.1)
infusable 40.20.16(.22)
infuse 35.17.7
infuser 17.25.14
infusibility 1.10.16(.22.2)
infusible 40.20.16(.22)
infusion 28.17.26(.4)
infusive 31.2.4(.8)
Inga 17.19.1
Ingatestone 28.19.4(.9)
ingather 17.23.5
ingathering 29.1.30(.8)
ingeminate 22.4.14(.9.2)
ingenious 34.3.6(.1)
ingeniously 1.31.33(.1.2)
ingeniousness
　34.18.16(.31.1)
ingénue 16.12, 16.24.10
ingenuity 1.10.16(.5)
ingenuous 34.18.6
ingenuously
　1.31.33(.12.1)
ingenuousness
　34.18.16(.31.2)
Ingersoll® 40.9.14
ingest 22.29.5(.9)
ingestion 28.17.27
ingestive 31.2.1(.15)
Ingham 27.15.15
inglenook 24.14.6
Ingleton 28.17.11(.27)

Inglewood 23.16.6(.22)
Inglis 34.2.22(.11)
inglorious 34.3.15(.5)
ingloriously 1.31.33(.1.4)
ingloriousness
34.18.16(.31.1)
Ingmar 10.10.8
ingoing 29.1.9
Ingoldsby 1.9.22
ingot 22.19.13
ingraft 22.27.4(.4)
ingrain 28.4.18
ingrained 23.24.4
ingrainedly 1.31.23(.14.6)
Ingram 27.15.26(.13)
Ingrams 35.25.10
ingrate 22.4.22(.11)
ingratiate 22.4.2(.11)
ingratiatingly
1.31.28(.1.4)
ingratiation 28.17.25(.3.1)
ingratitude 23.17.4(.1)
ingravescence
34.24.10(.18)
ingravescent
22.26.15(.17.2)
ingredient 22.26.2(.3)
Ingres 17.32.22
ingress 34.5.14(.8)
ingression 28.17.25(.4)
ingressive 31.2.4(.4)
ingressively 1.31.30(.7.4)
ingressiveness
34.18.16(.28.2)
Ingrid 23.18.27
in-group 20.12
ingrowing 29.1.9
ingrown 28.19.17
ingrowth 32.16
inguinal 40.26.13(.14.8)
inguinally 1.31.17(.14.3)
ingulf 30.20.5
ingurgitate 22.4.9(.5)
ingurgitation
28.17.25(.3.3)
inhabit 22.2.6
inhabitability
1.10.16(.22.3)
inhabitable
40.20.16(.11.3)
inhabitance 34.24.10(.10)
inhabitancy
1.22.23(.10.2)
inhabitant 22.26.15(.9)
inhabitation
28.17.25(.3.3)
inhalant 22.26.15(.25)
inhalation 28.17.25(.3.14)
inhale 40.4.12
inhaler 17.34.4
inharmonic 24.2.15(.6.2)

inharmonious 34.3.6(.7)
inharmoniously
1.31.33(.1.2)
inharmoniousness
34.18.16(.31.1)
inhere 3.20
inherence 34.24.10(.16)
inherent 22.26.15(.23.1)
inherently 1.31.22(.20.5)
inherit 22.2.24
inheritability
1.10.16(.22.3)
inheritable
40.20.16(.11.3)
inheritance 34.24.10(.10)
inheritor 17.12.16(.18)
inheritress 34.18.27(.14)
inheritrices 35.1.16(.10)
inheritrix 34.23.2(.12)
inhesion 28.17.26(.1)
inhibit 22.2.6
inhibition 28.17.25(.2.1)
inhibitive 31.2.1(.9.1)
inhibitor 17.12.16(.4)
inhibitory 1.29.11(.8.6)
inhomogeneity
1.10.16(.1)
inhospitable
40.20.16(.11.1)
inhospitableness
34.18.16(.37.4)
inhospitably 1.31.21(.4.1)
inhospitality
1.10.16(.32.3)
in-house 34.8.6
inhuman 28.17.16(.15)
inhumane 28.4.7
inhumanely 1.31.27(.4)
inhumanity 1.10.16(.13)
inhumanly 1.31.27(.14)
inhumanness
34.18.16(.25)
inhumation
28.17.25(.3.7)
inhume 27.14.7
Inigo 19.13.9
inimical 40.23.12(.10)
inimically 1.31.24(.9.8)
inimitability
1.10.16(.22.3)
inimitable 40.20.16(.11.3)
inimitableness
34.18.16(.37.4)
inimitably 1.31.21(.4.2)
iniquitous 34.18.11(.10)
iniquitously
1.31.33(.12.2)
iniquitousness
34.18.16(.31.3)
iniquity 1.10.16(.20)
initial 40.33.1

initialism 27.15.21(.2.15)
initialization
28.17.25(.3.12)
initialize 35.15.21(.4.6)
initially 1.31.17(.22)
initiate 22.3.10, 22.4.2(.11)
initiation 28.17.25(.3.1)
initiative 31.2.1(.9.3)
initiator 17.12.4(.1)
initiatory 1.29.11(.8.1)
inject 22.23.4(.9)
injectable 40.20.16(.11.5)
injection 28.17.25(.15.2)
injector 17.12.21(.2)
in-joke 24.18.11
injudicious 34.18.22(.2)
injudiciously
1.31.33(.12.4)
injudiciousness
34.18.16(.31.4)
Injun 28.17.28(.12)
injunct 22.23.13
injunction 28.17.25(.15.6)
injunctive 31.2.1(.13.5)
injure 17.29.16(.1)
injurer 17.32.14(.18)
injuria 3.22.12
injuriae 2.3, 14.2
injuriously 1.31.33(.1.4)
injury 1.29.11(.21)
injustice 34.2.8
ink 24.19.1
Inkatha 17.12.8(.5)
inkblot 22.11.17
inkbottle 40.21.7
inker 17.14.21(.1)
inkhorn 28.11.10
inkily 1.31.17(.11)
inkiness 34.18.16(.2.4)
inkling 29.1.31(.19)
inkpad 23.7.5
Inkpen 28.5.2
inkpot 22.11.2
inkstand 23.24.6(.5)
inkwell 40.5.17(.9)
inky 1.12.16
INLA 4
inlaid 23.4.16
inland 23.24.6(.13),
23.24.16(.16.4)
inlander 17.13.20(.4)
inlandish 36.2.12
in-law 12.23.8
inlay 4.28, 4.28.14
inlayer 17.2.10
inlet 22.5.21, 22.19.26(.22)
inlier 17.6.15
in loco parentis 34.2.8
inly 1.31.27(.2)
inlying 29.1.7

Inmarsat 22.7.15
inmate 22.4.13(.13)
in medias res 35.4
in memoriam 27.6.1
inmost 22.29.17(.4)
inn 28.2
innards 35.23.12
innate 22.4.14
innately 1.31.22(.4)
innateness 34.18.16(.20.1)
inner 17.18.2
innerly 1.31.17(.14.1)
innermost 22.29.17(.4)
innerness 34.18.16(.15.3)
innervate 22.4.16
innervation 28.17.25(.3.9)
Innes 34.18.16(.2.1),
35.18.13
inning 29.1.17(.2)
Innisfail 40.4.8
innkeeper 17.10.1
innocence 34.24.10(.18)
innocency 1.22.23(.10.4)
innocent 22.26.15(.17.3)
innocently 1.31.22(.20.4)
innocuity 1.10.16(.5)
innocuous 34.18.6
innocuously
1.31.33(.12.1)
innocuousness
34.18.16(.31.2)
innominate 22.19.15(.9)
innovate 22.4.16
innovation 28.17.25(.3.9)
innovational
40.26.13(.14.2)
innovative 31.2.1(.3)
innovatively 1.31.30(.7.1)
innovativeness
34.18.16(.28.1)
innovator 17.12.4(.11)
innovatory 1.29.11(.8.2)
innoxious 34.18.22(.11)
innoxiously 1.31.33(.12.4)
innoxiousness
34.18.16(.31.4)
Innsbruck 24.14.10
Inns of Court 22.13
innuendo 19.11.14
innumerability
1.10.16(.22.2)
innumerable
40.20.16(.27.4)
innumerably 1.31.21(.8)
innumeracy 1.22.16(.13)
innumerate 22.19.24(.9)
innutrition 28.17.25(.2.6)
innutritious 34.18.22(.2)
inobservance
34.24.10(.17)
inocula 17.34.16(.21.2)

inoculable 40.20.16(.29)
inoculate 22.4.23(.7.3)
inoculation 28.17.25(.3.14)
inoculative 31.2.1(.9.4)
inoculator 17.12.4(.16)
inoculum 27.15.28(.11)
inodorous 34.18.27(.15)
in-off 30.8
inoffensive 31.2.4(.13)
inoffensively 1.31.30(.7.4)
inoffensiveness 34.18.16(.28.2)
inofficious 34.18.22(.2)
inoperability 1.10.16(.22.2)
inoperable 40.20.16(.27.3)
inoperably 1.31.21(.8)
inoperative 31.2.1(.9.4)
inoperativeness 34.18.16(.28.1)
inopportune 28.16.14
inordinate 22.19.15(.9)
inordinately 1.31.22(.15)
inordinateness 34.18.16(.20.3)
inorganic 24.2.15(.5)
inorganically 1.31.24(.9.8)
inosculate 22.4.23(.7.3)
inosculation 28.17.25(.3.14)
inositol 40.9.7
in-patient 22.26.15(.19)
input 22.17
inputter 17.12.14
inquest 22.29.5(.11)
inquietude 23.17.4(.1)
inquiline 28.14.19(.11)
inquire 17.6.13
inquirer 17.32.14(.2)
inquiry 1.29.11(.2)
inquisition 28.17.25(.2.5)
inquisitional 40.26.13(.14.1)
inquisitive 31.2.1(.9.3)
inquisitively 1.31.30(.7.1)
inquisitiveness 34.18.16(.28.1)
inquisitor 17.12.16(.15)
inquisitorial 40.3.14(.5)
inquisitorially 1.31.3(.11)
inquorate 22.4.22(.4)
in re 4
in rem 27.5
inroad 23.20.12
inrush 36.12
inrushing 29.1.25
insalubrious 34.3.15(.7)
insalubrity 1.10.16(.21.3)

insane 28.4.12
insanely 1.31.27(.4)
insaneness 34.18.16(.25)
insanitarily 1.31.17(.27.1)
insanitary 1.29.11(.8.7)
insanity 1.10.16(.13)
insatiability 1.10.16(.22.2)
insatiable 40.20.3, 40.20.16(.23)
insatiably 1.31.21(.1)
insatiate 22.3.10
inscape 20.3
inscribable 40.20.16(.10)
inscribe 21.12
inscriber 17.11.11
inscription 28.17.25(.14)
inscriptional 40.26.13(.14.6)
inscriptive 31.2.1(.12)
inscrutability 1.10.16(.22.2)
inscrutable 40.20.16(.11.2)
inscrutableness 34.18.16(.37.4)
inscrutably 1.31.21(.4.1)
inscrutibility 1.10.16(.22.2)
inseam 27.1.8
insect 22.23.4(.7)
insectaria 3.22.4
insectarium 27.3.17(.3)
insectary 1.29.11(.8.12)
insecticidal 40.22.11
insecticide 23.15.11(.6)
insectile 40.13.3(.8)
insectivore 12.12
insectivorous 34.18.27(.21)
insectology 1.26.10(.11.2)
insecure 12.22, 17.7.12(.5)
insecurely 1.31.11, 1.31.17(.4)
insecurity 1.10.16(.21.2)
Inselberg 26.14.1(.12)
inseminate 22.4.14(.9.2)
insemination 28.17.25(.3.8)
inseminator 17.12.4(.10)
insensate 22.4.18, 22.19.18
insensately 1.31.22(.4)
insensibility 1.10.16(.22.2)
insensible 40.20.16(.21.3)
insensibleness 34.18.16(.37.4)
insensibly 1.31.21(.7.2)
insensitive 31.2.1(.9.3)
insensitively 1.31.30(.7.1)

insensitiveness 34.18.16(.28.1)
insensitivity 1.10.16(.15)
insentience 34.24.10(.20)
insentient 22.26.15(.19)
inseparability 1.10.16(.22.2)
inseparable 40.20.16(.27.3)
inseparably 1.31.21(.8)
insert 22.20.10
insertable 40.20.16(.11.3)
inserter 17.12.17
insertion 28.17.25(.12)
inset 22.5.13
insetter 17.12.5(.8)
inshallah 17.34.6
inshore 12.16
inside 23.15.11
insider 17.13.12
insidious 34.3.4
insidiously 1.31.33(.1.1)
insidiousness 34.18.16(.31.1)
insight 22.16.19(.16)
insightful 40.27.18
insightfully 1.31.17(.16.2)
insignia 3.9.13
insignificance 34.24.10(.12)
insignificancy 1.22.23(.10.2)
insignificant 22.26.15(.11)
insignificantly 1.31.22(.20.2)
insincere 3.14
insincerely 1.31.3
insincerity 1.10.16(.21.1)
insinuate 22.4.4
insinuatingly 1.31.28(.1.4)
insinuation 28.17.25(.3.1)
insinuative 31.2.1(.9.1)
insinuator 17.12.4(.2)
insinuatory 1.29.11(.8.5)
insipid 23.2.6
insipidity 1.10.16(.9)
insipidly 1.31.23(.14.2)
insipidness 34.18.16(.21.1)
insist 22.29.2(.22)
insistence 34.24.10(.10)
insistency 1.22.23(.10.2)
insistent 22.26.15(.9)
insistently 1.31.22(.20.2)
insister 17.12.24(.2)
insistingly 1.31.28(.1.4)
in situ 16.24.5
insobriety 1.10.16(.4)
insofar 10.12

insolation 28.17.25(.3.14)
insole 40.18.10
insolence 34.24.10(.24)
insolent 22.26.15(.25)
insolently 1.31.22(.20.5)
insolubility 1.10.16(.22.2)
insoluble 40.20.16(.28)
insolubleness 34.18.16(.37.4)
insolubly 1.31.21(.9)
insolvable 40.20.16(.19)
insolvency 1.22.23(.10.4)
insolvent 22.26.15(.16)
insomnia 3.9.14
insomniac 24.6.1
insomuch 38.11
insouciance 34.11, 34.24.2
insouciant 11.2, 22.26.2(.7)
insouciantly 1.31.22(.20.1)
insousian 22.26.2(.7)
inspan 28.7.4
inspect 22.23.4(.1)
inspection 28.17.25(.15.2)
inspector 17.12.21(.2)
inspectorate 22.19.24(.9)
inspectorial 40.3.14(.5)
inspectorship 20.2.7(.9)
inspiration 28.17.25(.3.13)
inspirational 40.26.13(.14.2)
inspirationally 1.31.17(.14.3)
inspirationism 27.15.21(.2.9)
inspirationist 22.29.2(.18.2)
inspirator 17.12.4(.15)
inspiratory 1.29.11(.8.9)
inspire 17.6.1
inspiredly 1.31.23(.14.1)
inspirer 17.32.14(.2)
inspiringly 1.31.28(.1.17)
inspirit 22.2.24
inspiritingly 1.31.28(.1.4)
inspissate 22.4.18
inspissation 28.17.25(.3.10)
inspissator 17.12.4(.12)
inst. 22.29.21
instability 1.10.16(.22.1)
install 40.10.5
installant 22.26.15(.25)
installation 28.17.25(.3.14)
installer 17.34.10
instalment 22.26.15(.13.7)
instance 34.24.10(.10)

instancy **1.22.23(.10.2)**
instant **22.26.15(.9)**
instantaneity **1.10.16(.1)**
instantaneous **34.3.6(.3)**
instantaneously
1.31.33(.1.2)
instantaneousness
34.18.16(.31.1)
instanter **17.12.22(.4)**
instantiate **22.4.2(.11)**
instantiation
28.17.25(.3.1)
instantly **1.31.22(.20.2)**
instar **10.6.8**
instate **22.4.9(.9)**
in statu pupillari **1.29.6**
instauration
28.17.25(.3.13)
instaurator **17.12.4(.15)**
instead **23.5.3**
instep **20.4**
instigate **22.4.12(.5)**
instigation **28.17.25(.3.6)**
instigative **31.2.1(.9.1)**
instigator **17.12.4(.8)**
instil **40.2.5**
instillation **28.17.25(.3.14)**
instiller **17.34.2(.2)**
instilment **22.26.15(.13.7)**
instinct **22.23.13**
instinctive **31.2.1(.13.5)**
instinctively **1.31.30(.7.2)**
instinctual **40.16.12**
instinctually **1.31.17(.24)**
institute **22.18.10**
institution **28.17.25(.11)**
institutional
40.26.13(.14.5)
institutionalism
27.15.21(.2.15)
institutionalization
28.17.25(.3.12)
institutionalize
35.15.21(.4.5)
institutionally
1.31.17(.14.3)
in-store **12.5.9**
INSTRAW **12.21**
instruct **22.23.8**
instruction
28.17.25(.15.5)
instructional
40.26.13(.14.6)
instructive **31.2.1(.13.4)**
instructively **1.31.30(.7.2)**
instructiveness
34.18.16(.28.1)
instructor **17.12.21(.6)**
instructorship **20.2.7(.9)**
instructress **34.18.27(.14)**

instrument
22.26.15(.13.2)
instrumental **40.21.17(.2)**
instrumentalist
22.29.2(.31.2)
instrumentality
1.10.16(.32.3)
instrumentally
1.31.17(.9.3)
instrumentation
28.17.25(.3.3)
insubordinate
22.19.15(.9)
insubordinately
1.31.22(.15)
insubordination
28.17.25(.3.8)
insubstantial **40.33.12(.4)**
insubstantiality
1.10.16(.32.1)
insubstantially
1.31.17(.22)
insufferable
40.20.16(.27.5)
insufferableness
34.18.16(.37.4)
insufferably **1.31.21(.8)**
insufficiency
1.22.23(.10.4)
insufficient **22.26.15(.19)**
insufficiently
1.31.22(.20.4)
insufflate **22.4.23(.11)**
insufflation
28.17.25(.3.14)
insufflator **17.12.4(.16)**
insular **17.34.16(.21.4)**
insularism **27.15.21(.2.14)**
insularity **1.10.16(.21.1)**
insularly **1.31.17(.29)**
insulate **22.4.23(.7.3)**
insulation **28.17.25(.3.14)**
insulator **17.12.4(.16)**
insulin **28.2.31(.10)**
insult **22.32.8**
insulter **17.12.26(.6)**
insultingly **1.31.28(.1.4)**
insuperability
1.10.16(.22.2)
insuperable
40.20.16(.27.3)
insuperably **1.31.21(.8)**
insupportable
40.20.16(.11.2)
insupportableness
34.18.16(.37.4)
insupportably
1.31.21(.4.1)
insurability **1.10.16(.22.2)**
insurable **40.20.16(.27.2)**
insurance **34.24.10(.16)**
insurant **22.26.15(.23.2)**

insure **12.16, 17.7.10**
insured **23.12.7, 23.18.4**
insurer **17.32.14(.3)**
insurgence **34.24.10(.21)**
insurgency **1.22.23(.10.4)**
insurgent **22.26.15(.21)**
insurmountable
40.20.16(.11.6)
insurmountably
1.31.21(.4.3)
insurrection
28.17.25(.15.2)
insurrectional
40.26.13(.14.6)
insurrectionary
1.29.11(.13.2)
insurrectionism
27.15.21(.2.9)
insurrectionist
22.29.2(.18.2)
insusceptible
40.20.16(.11.4)
inswing **29.1.29**
inswinger **17.19.1**
intact **22.23.5(.4)**
intactness **34.18.16(.20.4)**
intaglio **15.1.13**
intake **24.3.4**
intangibility
1.10.16(.22.2)
intangible **40.20.16(.25)**
intangibly **1.31.21(.7.3)**
intarsia **3.14.5**
Intasun **28.13.7**
integer **17.29.13**
integrability
1.10.16(.22.2)
integrable **40.20.16(.27.6)**
integral **40.16.13(.19)**
integrality **1.10.16(.32.13)**
integrally **1.31.17(.27.3)**
integrand **23.24.6(.12)**
integrant **22.26.15(.23.4)**
integrate **22.4.22(.11)**
integration
28.17.25(.3.13)
integrationist
22.29.2(.18.2)
integrative **31.2.1(.9.4)**
integrator **17.12.4(.15)**
integrity **1.10.16(.21.3)**
integument
22.26.15(.13.2)
integumental
40.21.17(.2)
integumentary
1.29.11(.8.12)
intellect **22.23.4(.11)**
intellection
28.17.25(.15.2)
intellective **31.2.1(.13.2)**
intellectual **40.16.12**

intellectualism
27.15.21(.2.15)
intellectualist
22.29.2(.31.5)
intellectuality
1.10.16(.32.1)
intellectualize
35.15.21(.4.8)
intellectually **1.31.17(.24)**
intelligence **34.24.10(.21)**
intelligent **22.26.15(.21)**
intelligential **40.33.12(.3)**
intelligently
1.31.22(.20.4)
intelligentsia **3.14.16**
intelligibility
1.10.16(.22.3)
intelligible **40.20.16(.25)**
intelligibly **1.31.21(.7.4)**
Intelpost **22.29.17(.1)**
Intelsat **22.7.15**
intemperance
34.24.10(.16)
intemperate **22.19.24(.9)**
intemperately
1.31.22(.15)
intemperateness
34.18.16(.20.3)
intend **23.24.5(.4)**
intendancy **1.22.23(.10.2)**
intendant **22.26.15(.10)**
intended **23.18.10(.14)**
intendedly **1.31.23(.14.4)**
intendment
22.26.15(.13.3)
intense **34.24.3**
intensely **1.31.33(.16)**
intenseness
34.18.16(.31.7)
intensification
28.17.25(.3.5)
intensifier **17.6.9(.4)**
intensify **14.14.4(.9)**
intension **28.17.25(.16)**
intensional
40.26.13(.14.7)
intensionally
1.31.17(.14.3)
intensity **1.10.16(.16.3)**
intensive **31.2.4(.13)**
intensively **1.31.30(.7.4)**
intensiveness
34.18.16(.28.2)
intent **22.26.4(.4)**
intention **28.17.25(.16)**
intentional
40.26.13(.14.7)
intentionality
1.10.16(.32.8)
intentionally
1.31.17(.14.3)
intentioned **23.24.16(.12)**

intently 1.31.22(.20.1)
intentness 34.18.16(.20.4)
inter 17.12.22(.1), 18.3
interact 22.23.5
interactant 22.26.15(.9)
interaction 28.17.25(.15.3)
interactional 40.26.13(.14.6)
interactive 31.2.1(.13.3)
interactively 1.31.30(.7.2)
inter alia 3.24.3
interAmerican 28.17.13(.13)
interarticular 17.34.16(.21.2)
interatomic 24.2.14(.6)
interbank 24.19.3(.1)
interbed 23.5.2
interblend 23.24.5(.15)
interbred 23.5.15
interbreed 23.1.11
intercalary 1.29.11(.27)
intercalate 22.4.23
intercalation 28.17.25(.3.14)
intercede 23.1.7
interceder 17.13.1
intercellular 17.34.16(.21.4)
intercensal 40.31.21
intercept 22.22.3
interception 28.17.25(.14)
interceptive 31.2.1(.12)
interceptor 17.12.19
intercession 28.17.25(.4)
intercessional 40.26.13(.14.3)
intercessor 17.24.5
intercessorial 40.3.14(.5)
intercessory 1.29.11(.18)
interchange 39.17.2
interchangeability 1.10.16(.22.3)
interchangeable 40.20.16(.25)
interchangeableness 34.18.16(.37.4)
interchangeably 1.31.21(.7.3)
inter-city 1.10.2
inter-class 34.9.7
intercollegiate 22.3.11
intercolonial 40.3.7(.9)
intercom 27.9
intercommunicate 22.4.11(.6)
intercommunication 28.17.25(.3.5)
intercommunicative 31.2.1(.9.1)

intercommunion 28.3.8(.9)
intercommunity 1.10.16(.13)
interconnect 22.23.4(.4)
interconnection 28.17.25(.15.2)
intercontinental 40.21.17(.2)
intercontinentally 1.31.17(.9.3)
interconversion 28.17.25(.12)
interconvertible 40.20.16(.11.3)
intercool 40.15.4
intercooler 17.34.15
intercooling 29.1.31(.11)
intercorrelate 22.4.23(.7.2)
intercorrelation 28.17.25(.3.14)
intercostal 40.21.18
intercostally 1.31.17(.9.3)
intercounty 1.10.23(.5)
intercourse 34.12.2
intercrop 20.7.12
intercross 34.10.16
intercrural 40.16.13(.11)
intercurrence 34.24.10(.16)
intercurrent 22.26.15(.23.2)
intercut 22.15.4
interdenominational 40.26.13(.14.2)
interdenominationally 1.31.17(.14.3)
interdepartmental 40.21.17(.2)
interdepartmentally 1.31.17(.9.3)
interdepend 23.24.5(.2)
interdependence 34.24.10(.11)
interdependency 1.22.23(.10.2)
interdependent 22.26.15(.10)
interdependently 1.31.22(.20.2)
interdict 22.23.2
interdiction 28.17.25(.15.1)
interdictory 1.29.11(.8.12)
interdigital 40.21.12
interdigitally 1.31.17(.9.2)
interdigitate 22.4.9(.5)
interdisciplinary 1.29.11(.13.1)

interest 22.29.5(.12), 22.29.15(.17)
interestedly 1.31.23(.14.3)
interestedness 34.18.16(.21.1)
interestingly 1.31.28(.1.4)
interestingness 34.18.16(.26)
interface 34.4.9
interfacial 40.33.2
interfacially 1.31.17(.22)
interfacing 29.1.23
inter-faith 32.4
interfemoral 40.16.13(.12.2)
interfere 3.10
interference 34.24.10(.16)
interferential 40.33.12(.3)
interferer 17.32.2
interferingly 1.31.28(.1.17)
interferometer 17.12.16(.9.2)
interferometric 24.2.26(.14.2)
interferometrically 1.31.24(.9.12)
interferometry 1.29.15(.8)
interferon 28.10.24(.1)
interfile 40.13.9
interflow 19.29.21
interfluent 22.26.15(.5)
interfluve 31.10
interfuse 35.17.7
interfusion 28.17.26(.4)
intergalactic 24.2.10(.13)
intergalactically 1.31.24(.9.5)
interglacial 40.3.10, 40.33.2
intergovernmental 40.21.17(.2)
intergovernmentally 1.31.17(.9.3)
intergradation 28.17.25(.3.4)
intergrade 23.4.15
intergrowth 32.16
interim 27.2.14
interior 3.22.2
interiorize 35.15.20(.1)
interiorly 1.31.3(.11)
interject 22.23.4(.9)
interjection 28.17.25(.15.2)
interjectional 40.26.13(.14.6)
interjectionary 1.29.11(.13.2)

interjectory 1.29.11(.8.12)
interknit 22.2.12
interlace 34.4.14
interlacement 22.26.15(.13.5)
Interlaken 28.17.13(.6)
interlanguage 39.2.21
interlap 20.5.8
interlard 23.9.22
interleaf 30.1.9
interleave 31.1.9
interleukin 28.2.13(.5)
interlibrary 1.29.11(.25)
interline 28.14.19
interlinear 3.9.2
interlineation 28.17.25(.3.1)
Interlingua 17.31.7
interlining 29.1.17(.10)
interlink 24.19.1(.8)
interlobular 17.34.16(.21.1)
interlock 24.9.16
interlocker 17.14.8
interlocution 28.17.25(.11)
interlocutor 17.12.16(.19)
interlocutory 1.29.11(.8.10)
interlocutrix 34.23.2(.12)
interlope 20.15.9
interloper 17.10.16
interlude 23.17.5
intermarriage 39.2.22(.4)
intermarry 1.29.5
intermedia 3.5.1
intermediacy 1.22.3
intermediary 1.29.2(.3)
intermediate 22.3.4
intermediately 1.31.22(.3)
intermediateness 34.18.16(.20.1)
intermediation 28.17.25(.3.1)
intermediator 17.12.4(.1)
intermedium 27.3.4(.1)
interment 22.26.15(.13.2)
intermesh 36.5
intermezzo 19.20.14
interminable 40.20.16(.16.3)
interminableness 34.18.16(.37.4)
interminably 1.31.21(.6)
intermingle 40.24.14(.1)
intermission 28.17.25(.2.4)
intermit 22.2.11
intermittence 34.24.10(.16)

i

intramolecular 17.34.16(.21.2)
intramural 40.16.13(.11)
intramurally 1.31.17(.27.1)
intramuscular 17.34.16(.21.2)
intranational 40.26.13(.14.4)
Intranet 22.5.9(.2)
intransigence 34.24.10(.21)
intransigency 1.22.23(.10.4)
intransigent 22.26.15(.21)
intransigently 1.31.22(.20.4)
intransitive 31.2.1(.9.3)
intransitively 1.31.30(.7.1)
intransitivity 1.10.16(.15)
intrapreneur 18.8
intrauterine 28.14.18
intravasate 22.4.18
intravasation 28.17.25(.3.10)
intravenous 34.18.16(.1)
intravenously 1.31.33(.12.3)
in-tray 4.26.11
intrench 38.18.2
intrepid 23.2.6
intrepidity 1.10.16(.9)
intrepidly 1.31.23(.14.2)
intricacy 1.22.16(.6)
intricate 22.19.12(.10)
intricately 1.31.22(.15)
intrigant 22.26.15(.12)
intrigue 26.1
intriguer 17.16.1
intriguingly 1.31.28(.1.6)
intrinsic 24.2.20(.15), 24.2.21
intrinsically 1.31.24(.9.10)
intro 19.27.15
introduce 34.17.13
introducer 17.24.14
introducible 40.20.16(.21.2)
introduction 28.17.25(.15.5)
introductory 1.29.11(.8.12)
introflexion 28.17.25(.15.2)
introgression 28.17.25(.4)
introit 22.14
introjection 28.17.25(.15.2)
intromission 28.17.25(.2.4)

intromit 22.2.11
introrse 34.12.8
introspect 22.23.4(.1)
introspection 28.17.25(.15.2)
introspective 31.2.1(.13.2)
introspectively 1.31.30(.7.2)
introspectiveness 34.18.16(.28.1)
introsusception 28.17.25(.14)
introversible 40.20.16(.21.2)
introversion 28.17.25(.12)
introversive 31.2.4(.10)
introvert 22.20.9
introverted 23.18.9(.14)
introvertive 31.2.1(.10)
intrude 23.17.3
intruder 17.13.14
intrudingly 1.31.28(.1.5)
intrusion 28.17.26(.4)
intrusionist 22.29.2(.18.3)
intrusive 31.2.4(.8)
intrusively 1.31.30(.7.4)
intrusiveness 34.18.16(.28.2)
intrust 22.29.12
intubate 22.4.8
intubation 28.17.25(.3.2)
intuit 22.2.4
intuitable 40.20.16(.11.3)
intuition 28.17.25(.2.1)
intuitional 40.26.13(.14.1)
intuitionalism 27.15.21(.2.15)
intuitionalist 22.29.2(.31.3)
intuitionism 27.15.21(.2.9)
intuitionist 22.29.2(.18.2)
intuitive 31.2.1(.9.1)
intuitively 1.31.30(.7.1)
intuitiveness 34.18.16(.28.1)
intuitivism 27.15.21(.2.11)
intuitivist 22.29.2(.20)
intumesce 34.5.5
intumescence 34.24.10(.18)
intumescent 22.26.15(.17.2)
intussusception 28.17.25(.14)
Inuit 22.2.3
Inuk 24.14.6
Inuktitut 22.17
inunction 28.17.25(.15.6)
inundate 22.4.10

inundation 28.17.25(.3.4)
Inupik 24.2.8(.6)
inure 12.22, 17.7.12(.8)
inurement 22.26.15(.13.1)
in utero 19.27.11, 19.27.15
in vacuo 19.6
invade 23.4.9
invader 17.13.3
invaginate 22.4.14(.9.3)
invagination 28.17.25(.3.8)
invalid 23.1.12, 23.2.23
invalidate 22.4.10
invalidation 28.17.25(.3.4)
invalidism 27.15.21(.2.5)
invalidity 1.10.16(.9)
invalidly 1.31.23(.14.7)
invaluable 40.20.16(.6)
invaluableness 34.18.16(.37.4)
invaluably 1.31.21(.2)
Invar® 10.13
invariability 1.10.16(.22.2)
invariable 40.20.3
invariableness 34.18.16(.37.4)
invariably 1.31.21(.1)
invariance 34.24.2
invariant 22.26.2(.9)
invasion 28.17.26(.3)
invasive 31.2.4(.3)
invasively 1.31.30(.7.4)
invasiveness 34.18.16(.28.2)
invected 23.18.9(.17)
invective 31.2.1(.13.2)
invectively 1.31.30(.7.2)
invectiveness 34.18.16(.28.1)
inveigh 4.16
inveigle 40.24.1, 40.24.3
inveiglement 22.26.15(.13.7)
invent 22.26.4(.10)
inventable 40.20.16(.11.6)
invention 28.17.25(.16)
inventive 31.2.1(.14)
inventively 1.31.30(.7.3)
inventiveness 34.18.16(.28.1)
inventor 17.12.22(.3)
inventory 1.29.11(.8.12)
inventress 34.18.27(.14)
Inveraray 1.29.4
Invercargill 40.24.5
Invergordon 28.17.12(.10)
Inverness 34.5.6
Inverness-shire 17.26.23

inverse 34.19.6
inversely 1.31.33(.12.6)
inversion 28.17.25(.12)
inversive 31.2.4(.10)
invert 22.20.9
invertase 35.4.3
invertebrate 22.4.22(.7), 22.19.24(.11)
inverter 17.12.17
invertibility 1.10.16(.22.2)
invertible 40.20.16(.11.3)
Inverurie 1.29.11(.3)
invest 22.29.5(.5)
investable 40.20.16(.11.7)
investigate 22.4.12(.5)
investigation 28.17.25(.3.6)
investigational 40.26.13(.14.2)
investigative 31.2.1(.9.1)
investigator 17.12.4(.8)
investigatory 1.29.11(.8.6)
investiture 17.7.12(.3), 17.28.15
investment 22.26.15(.13.3)
investor 17.12.24(.4)
inveteracy 1.22.16(.13)
inveterate 22.19.24(.9)
inveterately 1.31.22(.15)
inveterateness 34.18.16(.20.3)
invidious 34.3.4
invidiously 1.31.33(.1.1)
invidiousness 34.18.16(.31.1)
invigilate 22.4.23(.7.2)
invigilation 28.17.25(.3.14)
invigilator 17.12.4(.16)
invigorate 22.4.22(.6)
invigoratingly 1.31.28(.1.4)
invigoration 28.17.25(.3.13)
invigorative 31.2.1(.9.4)
invigorator 17.12.4(.15)
invincibility 1.10.16(.22.2)
invincible 40.20.16(.21.3)
invincibleness 34.18.16(.37.4)
invincibly 1.31.21(.7.2)
inviolability 1.10.16(.22.2)
inviolable 40.20.16(.29)
inviolableness 34.18.16(.37.4)
inviolably 1.31.21(.9)
inviolacy 1.22.16(.14)
inviolate 22.19.26(.13)

inviolately **1.31.22(.15)**
inviolateness
   34.18.16(.20.3)
inviscid **23.2.16**
invisibility **1.10.16(.22.2)**
invisible **40.20.16(.22)**
invisibleness
   34.18.16(.37.4)
invisibly **1.31.21(.7.2)**
invitation **28.17.25(.3.3)**
invitatory **1.29.11(.8.6)**
invite **22.16.17**
invitee **2.11**
inviter **17.12.13(.6)**
invitingly **1.31.28(.1.4)**
invitingness **34.18.16(.26)**
in vitro **19.27.15**
in vivo **19.17**
invocable **40.20.16(.13)**
invocation **28.17.25(.3.5)**
invocatory **1.29.11(.8.6)**
invoice **34.13**
invoke **24.18.8**
invoker **17.14.17**
involucral **40.16.13(.18)**
involucre **17.14.14**
involuntarily
   1.31.17(.27.3)
involuntary **1.29.11(.8.12)**
involute **22.18.11**
involution **28.17.25(.11)**
involutional
   40.26.13(.14.5)
involve **31.13**
involved **23.26**
involvement
   22.26.15(.13.5)
invulnerability
   1.10.16(.22.2)
invulnerable
   40.20.16(.27.4)
invulnerably **1.31.21(.8)**
inward **23.18.26(.13)**
inwardly **1.31.23(.14.7)**
inwardness
   34.18.16(.21.1)
inweave **31.1.7**
inwove **31.12**
inwreathe **33.1**
inwrought **22.13.14**
inyala **17.34.8**
in-your-face **34.4.9**
Io **19.5**
iodate **22.4.10**
iodic **24.2.11(.7)**
iodide **23.15.5**
iodin **28.2.12**
iodinate **22.4.14(.9.1)**
iodination **28.17.25(.3.8)**
iodine **28.1.10**
iodinize **35.15.12(.5)**

iodism **27.15.21(.2.5)**
iodization **28.17.25(.3.11)**
iodize **35.15.8**
iodoform **27.10.5(.2)**
Iolanthe **1.20.10**
Iolo **19.29.14**
ion **28.10.4, 28.17.5**
Iona **17.18.18**
Ionesco **19.12.17**
Ionia **3.9.11**
Ionian **28.3.8(.11)**
ionic **24.2.15(.6.1)**
ionically **1.31.24(.9.8)**
ionium **27.3.8(.10)**
ionizable **40.20.16(.22)**
ionization **28.17.25(.3.11)**
ionize **35.15.12(.5)**
ionizer **17.25.12(.6)**
ionophore **12.11.3,
   12.11.4**
ionosphere **3.10.5**
ionospheric **24.2.26(.4)**
iontophoresis **34.2.17(.1)**
Iorwerth **32.14.15**
iota **17.12.18**
IOU **16.24**
Iowa **17.31.3**
Iowan **28.17.30**
Ipatieff **30.4**
ipecac **24.6.9**
ipecacuanha **17.18.6,
   17.18.8**
Iphigenia **17.1.7, 17.6.8**
Ipoh **19.8**
ipomoea **17.1.6**
ipse dixit **22.2.16**
ipsilateral **40.16.13(.12.1)**
ipsissima verba **17.11.14**
ipso facto **19.10.16**
Ipswich **38.2.9**
Iqbal **40.6.4, 40.8.3**
IRA **4**
Ira **17.32.13**
irade **1.11.9**
Iran **28.7.20, 28.9.13**
Iran-Contra **17.32.19(.10)**
Irangate **22.4.12(.9)**
Iranian **28.3.8(.3)**
Iraq **24.6.21, 24.8.15**
Iraqi **1.12.5, 1.12.6**
IRAS **34.7.18**
irascibility **1.10.16(.22.2)**
irascible **40.20.16(.21.1)**
irascibleness
   34.18.16(.37.4)
irascibly **1.31.21(.7.2)**
irate **22.4.22**
irately **1.31.22(.4)**
irateness **34.18.16(.20.1)**
ire **17.6**

ireful **40.27.14**
irefully **1.31.17(.16.1)**
irefulness **34.18.16(.37.2)**
Ireland **23.24.16(.16.2)**
Irenaeus **34.3.6(.1)**
Irene **28.1.25**
irenic **24.2.15(.1)**
irenical **40.23.12(.11)**
Ireton **28.17.11(.15)**
Irgun **28.16.6**
Irian **28.3.20(.1)**
Irian Jaya **17.6**
iridaceous **34.18.22(.3)**
iridescence **34.24.10(.18)**
iridescent **22.26.15(.17.2)**
iridium **27.3.4(.2)**
iridologist **22.29.2(.26.3)**
iridology **1.26.10(.11.2)**
iris **34.2.21**
Irish **36.2.25**
Irishman **28.17.16(.31)**
Irishness **34.18.16(.33.6)**
Irishwoman **28.17.16(.14)**
Irishwomen **28.2.17(.1)**
iritis **34.18.11(.8)**
irk **24.17**
irksome **27.15.20(.15)**
irksomely **1.31.26(.11)**
irksomeness
   34.18.16(.24)
Irkutsk **24.20.11**
Irlam **27.15.28(.12)**
Irma **17.17.15**
Irnbru **16.23.7**
iroko **19.12.14**
iron **28.17.5**
Iron Age **39.4**
ironbark **24.8.3**
ironclad **23.7.17**
ironer **17.18.16(.1)**
ironic **24.2.15(.6.4)**
ironical **40.23.12(.11)**
ironically **1.31.24(.9.8)**
ironist **22.29.2(.18.3)**
ironize **35.15.12(.5)**
ironless **34.18.29(.27)**
ironmaster **17.12.24(.5)**
ironmonger **17.16.17(.4)**
ironmongery **1.29.11(.11)**
Ironside **23.15.11(.12)**
ironstone **28.19.4(.9)**
ironware **6.18.11**
ironwood **23.16.6(.14)**
ironwork **24.17.6(.13)**
irony **1.16.15(.18)**
Iroquoian **28.17.4**
Iroquois **13.14**
irradiance **34.24.2**
irradiant **22.26.2(.3)**
irradiate **22.4.2(.4)**

irradiation **28.17.25(.3.1)**
irradiative **31.2.1(.2)**
irrational **40.26.13(.14.4)**
irrationality
   1.10.16(.32.8)
irrationalize
   35.15.21(.4.5)
irrationally **1.31.17(.14.3)**
Irrawaddy **1.11.10**
Irrawady **1.11.10**
irreclaimable
   40.20.16(.15)
irreclaimably **1.31.21(.6)**
irreconcilability
   1.10.16(.22.3)
irreconcilable
   40.20.16(.29)
irreconcilableness
   34.18.16(.37.4)
irreconcilably **1.31.21(.9)**
irrecoverable
   40.20.16(.27.5)
irrecoverably **1.31.21(.8)**
irrecusable **40.20.16(.22)**
irredeemability
   1.10.16(.22.3)
irredeemable
   40.20.16(.15)
irredeemably **1.31.21(.6)**
irredentism **27.15.21(.2.4)**
irredentist **22.29.2(.13)**
irreducibility
   1.10.16(.22.3)
irreducible
   40.20.16(.21.2)
irreducibly **1.31.21(.7.2)**
irrefragability
   1.10.16(.22.3)
irrefragable **40.20.16(.14)**
irrefragableness
   34.18.16(.37.4)
irrefragably **1.31.21(.5)**
irrefrangible
   40.20.16(.25)
irrefutable **40.20.16(.11.2)**
irrefutably **1.31.21(.4.1)**
irregardless **34.18.29(.23)**
irregular **17.34.16(.21.3)**
irregularity **1.10.16(.21.1)**
irregularly **1.31.17(.29)**
irrelative **31.2.1(.9.4)**
irrelatively **1.31.30(.7.1)**
irrelevance **34.24.10(.17)**
irrelevancy **1.29.12(.10.4)**
irrelevant **22.26.15(.16)**
irrelevantly **1.31.22(.20.4)**
irreligion **28.17.28(.2)**
irreligionist **22.29.2(.18.3)**
irreligious **34.18.24**
irreligiously
   1.31.33(.12.4)

irreligiousness 34.18.16(.31.5)
irremediable 40.20.3
irremediably 1.31.21(.1)
irremissible 40.20.16(.21.1)
irremissibly 1.31.21(.7.2)
irremovable 40.20.16(.19)
irremovably 1.31.21(.7.1)
irreparability 1.10.16(.22.2)
irreparable 40.20.16(.27.3)
irreparableness 34.18.16(.37.4)
irreparably 1.31.21(.8)
irreplaceable 40.20.16(.21.1)
irreplaceably 1.31.21(.7.2)
irrepressibility 1.10.16(.22.3)
irrepressible 40.20.16(.21.1)
irrepressibleness 34.18.16(.37.4)
irrepressibly 1.31.21(.7.2)
irreproachability 1.10.16(.22.3)
irreproachable 40.20.16(.24)
irreproachableness 34.18.16(.37.4)
irreproachably 1.31.21(.7.4)
irresistible 40.20.16(.11.7)
irresistibleness 34.18.16(.37.4)
irresistibly 1.31.21(.4.3)
irresolute 22.18.11
irresolutely 1.31.22(.14)
irresoluteness 34.18.16(.20.2)
irresolution 28.17.25(.11)
irresolvable 40.20.16(.19)
irrespective 31.2.1(.13.2)
irrespectively 1.31.30(.7.2)
irresponsibility 1.10.16(.22.3)
irresponsible 40.20.16(.21.3)
irresponsibly 1.31.21(.7.2)
irresponsive 31.2.4(.13)
irresponsively 1.31.30(.7.4)
irresponsiveness 34.18.16(.28.2)
irretentive 31.2.1(.14)
irretrievability 1.10.16(.22.3)

irretrievable 40.20.16(.19)
irretrievably 1.31.21(.7.1)
irreverence 34.24.10(.16)
irreverent 22.26.15(.23.3)
irreverential 40.33.12(.3)
irreverently 1.31.22(.20.5)
irreversible 40.20.16(.21.2)
irreversibly 1.31.21(.7.2)
irrevocability 1.10.16(.22.3)
irrevocable 40.20.16(.13)
irrevocably 1.31.21(.5)
irrigable 40.20.16(.14)
irrigate 22.4.12(.5)
irrigation 28.17.25(.3.6)
irrigative 31.2.1(.9.1)
irrigator 17.12.4(.8)
irritability 1.10.16(.22.2)
irritable 40.20.16(.11.3)
irritably 1.31.21(.4.2)
irritancy 1.22.23(.10.2)
irritant 22.26.15(.9)
irritate 22.4.9(.5)
irritatedly 1.31.23(.14.3)
irritatingly 1.31.28(.1.4)
irritation 28.17.25(.3.3)
irritative 31.2.1(.9.1)
irritator 17.12.4(.5)
irrupt 22.22.6
irruption 28.17.25(.14)
irruptive 31.2.1(.12)
Irvine 28.2.20, 28.14.11
Irving 29.1.20
Irvingite 22.16.15
Irwell 40.5.17(.6)
Irwin 28.2.28
is 35.2
Isaac 24.16.12
Isaacs 34.23.15
Isabel 40.5.2
Isabella 17.34.5(.2)
isabelline 28.1.27(.3), 28.2.31(.4), 28.14.19(.4)
Isadora 17.32.10(.3)
Isadore 12.6.6
isagogic 24.2.24(.4)
Isaiah 17.6.11
Isambard 23.9.6
isatin 28.2.11(.10)
Iscariot 22.3.12
ischaemia 3.8.1
ischaemic 24.2.14(.1)
Ischia 3.6.9
ischiadic 24.2.11(.5)
ischial 40.3.5
ischiatic 24.2.10(.4.1)
ischium 27.3.5

isentropic 24.2.8(.5)
Iseult 22.32.10
Isfahan 28.9.11
Isherwood 23.16.6(.6)
Ishiguro 19.27.11
Ishmael 40.3.6, 40.4.6
Ishmaelite 22.16.25(.3)
Ishtar 10.6.9
isinglass 34.9.7
Isis 34.2.17(.8)
Isla 17.34.13
Islam 27.6.18, 27.8.10
Islamabad 23.7.6, 23.9.6
Islamic 24.2.14(.4)
Islamism 27.15.21(.2.8)
Islamist 22.29.2(.17)
Islamite 22.16.13
Islamitic 24.2.10(.2.2)
Islamization 28.17.25(.3.11)
Islamize 35.15.11
island 23.24.16(.16.2)
islander 17.13.20(.13)
isle 40.13
Isle of Man 28.7
Isle of Wight 22.16
islet 22.19.26(.11)
Isleworth 32.14.15
Islington 28.17.11(.23)
Islwyn 28.2.6
ism 27.15.21(.2.1)
Ismaili 1.31.1
Ismailia 17.1.17
Ismay 4.13
isn't 22.26.15(.18)
isobar 10.5.4, 10.5.6
isobaric 24.2.26(.5)
isocheim 27.12.3
isochromatic 24.2.10(.4.2)
isochronal 40.26.13(.14.8)
isochronally 1.31.17(.14.3)
isochronicity 1.10.16(.16.1)
isochronize 35.15.12(.5)
isochronous 34.18.16(.15.3)
isochronously 1.31.33(.12.3)
isochrony 1.16.15(.18)
isoclinal 40.26.11
isoclinic 24.2.15(.2)
isocracy 1.22.16(.13)
Isocrates 35.1.7(.6)
isocratic 24.2.10(.4.5)
isocyclic 24.2.27(.16)
isodynamic 24.2.14(.4)
isoenzyme 27.12.5
isogeotherm 27.16.5
isogeothermal 40.25.11

isogloss 34.10.17
isogonic 24.2.15(.6.1)
isohel 40.5.16
isohyet 22.19.4
isolable 40.20.16(.29)
isolatable 40.20.16(.11.1)
isolate 22.4.23(.7.2), 22.19.26(.13)
isolation 28.17.25(.3.14)
isolationism 27.15.21(.2.9)
isolationist 22.29.2(.18.2)
isolative 31.2.1(.9.4)
isolatively 1.31.30(.7.1)
isolator 17.12.4(.16)
Isolde 17.13.23(.5)
isolette 22.5.21
isoleucine 28.1.18(.5)
isomer 17.17.14(.8)
isomerase 35.4.16
isomeric 24.2.26(.4)
isomerism 27.15.21(.2.14)
isomerize 35.15.20(.2)
isomerous 34.18.27(.18)
isometric 24.2.26(.14.2)
isometrically 1.31.24(.9.12)
isometry 1.29.15(.8)
isomorph 30.9.2
isomorphic 24.2.16(.5)
isomorphically 1.31.24(.9.9)
isomorphism 27.15.21(.2.10)
isomorphous 34.18.17
isonomy 1.15.13(.5)
isooctane 28.4.3
isophote 22.21.9
isopleth 32.5
isopod 23.10.1
isopropyl 40.2.3, 40.13.1
isoproterenol 40.9.12
isosceles 35.1.23
isoseismal 40.25.14
isoseismic 24.2.14(.17)
isospin 28.2.9
isostasy 1.22.16(.4)
isostatic 24.2.10(.4.1)
isothere 3.12
isotherm 27.16.5
isothermal 40.25.11
isothermally 1.31.17(.13)
isotonic 24.2.15(.6.1)
isotonically 1.31.24(.9.8)
isotonicity 1.10.16(.16.1)
isotope 20.15.3
isotopic 24.2.8(.5)
isotopically 1.31.24(.9.2)
isotopy 1.8.11(.3)
isotropic 24.2.8(.5)

isotropically **1.31.24(.9.2)**
isotropy **1.8.11(.8)**
I-spy **14.6**
Israel **40.4.14**
Israeli **1.31.4**
Israelite **22.16.25(.9)**
Issachar **10.8.8**
Issigonis **34.2.13**
issuable **40.20.16(.6)**
issuance **34.24.10(.6)**
issuant **22.26.15(.5)**
issue **16.17, 16.24.14**
issueless **34.18.29(.16)**
issuer **17.8**
Istanbul **40.14.3**
isthmian **28.3.7**
isthmus **34.18.15(.16)**
istle **1.31.22(.22)**
Istria **3.22.15**
Istrian **28.3.20(.11)**
it **22.2**
Italian **28.3.21(.2)**
Italianate **22.4.14(.9.4)**
italic **24.2.27(.6)**
italicization **28.17.25(.3.12)**
italicize **35.15.16(.4)**
Italiot **22.3.13**
Italy **1.31.17(.9.1)**
itch **38.2**
Itchen **28.17.27**
itchiness **34.18.16(.2.8)**
itchy **1.25.2**
item **27.15.9(.8)**
itemization **28.17.25(.3.11)**
itemize **35.15.11**
itemizer **17.25.12(.5)**
iterance **34.24.10(.16)**
iterancy **1.22.23(.10.4)**
iterate **22.4.22(.6)**
iteration **28.17.25(.3.13)**
iterative **31.2.1(.9.4)**
iteratively **1.31.30(.7.1)**
iterativeness **34.18.16(.28.1)**
iterativity **1.10.16(.15)**
Ithaca **17.14.15(.11)**
ithyphallic **24.2.27(.6)**
itineracy **1.22.16(.13)**
itinerancy **1.22.23(.10.4)**
itinerant **22.26.15(.23.3)**
itinerary **1.29.11(.25)**
itinerate **22.4.22(.6)**
itineration **28.17.25(.3.13)**
it'll **40.21.2**
Ito **19.10.1**
it's **34.22.2**
its **34.22.2**
itself **30.20.2**

itsy-bitsy **1.22.21**
itty-bitty **1.10.2**
Ivan **28.7.13, 28.9.8, 28.17.20(.8)**
Ivanhoe **19.26**
I've **31.9**
Iveagh **1.19.8, 4.16**
Iveco® **19.12.3**
Ivens **35.26.13(.11)**
Iver **17.21.10**
Ives **35.28.6**
ivied **23.2.15**
Ivor **17.21.10**
ivoried **23.2.22**
ivory **1.29.11(.15)**
ivy **1.19.8**
Iwo Jima **17.17.1**
ixia **3.14.15**
Ixion **28.17.5**
Iyyar **10.24**
izard **23.18.21**
Izmir **3.8**
Iznik **24.2.15(.18)**
Izvestia **3.4.13**
Izzard **23.9.16, 23.18.21**
Izzy **1.23.2**
j **4**
jab **21.6**
Jabalpur **12.3, 17.7.1**
jabber **17.11.5**
jabberer **17.32.14(.5)**
jabberwock **24.9.14**
jabberwocky **1.12.7**
Jabez **35.2.2, 35.5.4**
jabiru **16.23, 16.23.6**
jaborandi **1.11.20(.4)**
jabot **19.9.3**
jacana **10.11, 17.18.16(.6)**
jacaranda **17.13.20(.4)**
Jacinta **17.12.22(.1)**
jacinth **32.21**
Jacintha **17.22.13**
jack **24.6**
jackal **40.23.5**
jackanapes **34.21.3**
jackaroo **16.23**
jackass **34.7.9**
jackboot **22.18.3**
jackdaw **12.6.9**
jacket **22.2.9(.3)**
jackfish **36.2.18(.17)**
Jack Frost **22.29.9**
jackfruit **22.18.9**
jackhammer **17.17.6**
Jackie **1.12.5**
jack-knife **30.12**
jackknives **35.28.6**
jackleg **26.4**
jacklight **22.16.25(.15)**
Jacklin **28.2.31(.17)**

jack-o'-lantern **28.17.11(.22)**
jackpot **22.11.2**
jackrabbit **22.2.6**
Jack Russell **40.31.10**
jackscrew **16.23.10**
jackshaft **22.27.4(.3)**
jacksnipe **20.10.3**
Jackson **28.17.23(.21)**
Jacksonville **40.2.12**
jackstaff **30.7.2**
jackstaves **35.28.2**
jackstone **28.19.4(.9)**
jackstraw **12.21**
Jacob **21.14**
Jacobean **28.17.1(.2)**
Jacobi **1.9.11, 1.9.13**
Jacobin **28.2.10**
Jacobinic **24.2.15(.2)**
Jacobinical **40.23.12(.11)**
Jacobinism **27.15.21(.2.9)**
Jacobite **22.16.8**
Jacobitical **40.23.12(.7.1)**
Jacobitism **27.15.21(.2.4)**
Jacobs **35.21**
Jacobson **28.17.23(.18)**
jaconet **22.5.9(.2)**
Jacquard **23.9.9**
Jacqueline **28.1.27(.7), 28.2.31(.10)**
jacquerie **1.29.11(.10)**
Jacques **24.6, 34.23.3, 34.23.5**
Jacqui **1.12.5**
jactation **28.17.25(.3.3)**
jactitation **28.17.25(.3.3)**
jacuzzi **1.23.12**
jade **23.4**
jadedly **1.31.23(.14.4)**
jadedness **34.18.16(.21.1)**
jadeite **22.16.10**
j'adoube **21.13**
Jaeger® **17.16.3**
Jaffa **17.20.5**
Jaffna **17.18.26**
jag **26.5**
jagged **23.18.12, 23.22**
jaggedly **1.31.23(.14.5)**
jaggedness **34.18.16(.21.1)**
Jagger **17.16.5**
jagger **17.16.5**
jagginess **34.18.16(.2.4)**
jaggy **1.14.5**
Jago **19.13.3**
jaguar **17.7.12(.6)**
jaguarundi **1.11.20(.7)**
jail **40.4**
jailbait **22.4.8**
jailbird **23.19.1**
jailbreak **24.3.13**

jailer **17.34.4**
jailhouse **34.8.6(.24)**
Jain **28.4**
Jainism **27.15.21(.2.9)**
Jainist **22.29.2(.18.1)**
Jaipur **12.3, 17.7.1**
jake **24.3**
Jalalabad **23.7.6, 23.9.6**
jalap **20.13.7**
jalapeño **19.28**
jalopy **1.8.7**
jalousie **2.23**
jam **27.6**
Jamaica **17.14.3(.3)**
Jamaican **28.17.13(.3)**
Jamal **40.8.8**
jamb **27.6**
jambalaya **17.6.15**
jamberoo **16.23**
jamboree **2.30**
James **35.25.3**
Jameson **28.17.23(.23)**
Jamestown **28.8.1**
Jamie **1.15.3**
Jamieson **28.17.23(.14)**
jammer **17.17.6**
jammies **35.2.7**
jamminess **34.18.16(.2.5)**
Jammu **16.11**
jammy **1.15.6**
Jamshid **23.1.8, 23.2.18**
Jan **28.7**
Janáček **24.4.11**
Jancis **34.2.17(.15)**
Jane **28.4**
jane **28.4**
Janet **22.19.15(.3)**
Janette **22.5.9**
Janey **1.16.4**
jangle **40.24.14(.2)**
Janglish **36.2.27**
Janice **34.18.16(.7)**
Janine **28.1.14**
Janis **34.18.16(.7)**
janissary **1.29.11(.18)**
janitor **17.12.16(.10)**
janitorial **40.3.14(.5)**
janizary **1.29.11(.19)**
jankers **35.18.10**
Jansen **28.17.23(.24)**
Jansenism **27.15.21(.2.9)**
Jansenist **22.29.2(.18.1)**
January **1.29.11(.26)**
Janus **34.18.16(.4)**
Jap **20.5**
Japan **28.7.4**
Japanese **35.1.12**
jape **20.3**
japery **1.29.11(.6)**
Japheth **32.2.5, 32.5**

Japhetic **24.2.10(.3.2)**
japonica **17.14.15(.9)**
Jaques **34.23.3, 35.2.16**
Jaques-Dalcroze **35.20.12**
jar **10**
Jardine **28.1.10, 28.14.6**
jardinière **6.20**
jarful **40.14.6(.4)**
jargon **28.17.15(.7)**
jargonelle **40.5.8**
jargonistic **24.2.10(.15.2)**
jargonize **35.15.12(.5)**
jargoon **28.16.6**
Jarman **28.17.16(.9)**
Jarndyce **34.15.3**
jarrah **17.32.6**
Jarratt **22.19.24(.4)**
Jarrold **23.31.11**
Jarrow **19.27.4**
Jarvis **34.2.15**
jasmine **28.2.17(.9)**
Jason **28.17.23(.4)**
jaspé **4.7**
jasper **17.10.18**
Jat **22.10**
Jataka **17.14.15(.6)**
jati **1.10.8**
JATO **19.10.3**
jaundice **34.2.9**
jaunt **22.26.10**
jauntily **1.31.17(.9.3)**
jauntiness **34.18.16(.2.3)**
jaunty **1.10.23(.8)**
Java **17.21.6**
Javan **28.17.20(.6)**
Javanese **35.1.12**
javelin **28.2.31(.10)**
Javelle water **17.12.10**
jaw **12**
jawbone **28.19.3**
jawbreaker **17.14.3(.8)**
jawline **28.14.19(.8)**
jay **4**
jaybird **23.19.1**
Jaycee **2.22**
Jayne **28.4**
jaywalk **24.10.9**
jaywalker **17.14.9**
jazz **35.7**
jazzband **23.24.6(.4)**
jazzer **17.25.5**
jazzily **1.31.17(.21)**
jazziness **34.18.16(.2.7)**
jazzman **28.7.10(.21)**
jazzmen **28.5.7(.25)**
jazzy **1.23.5**
J-cloth® **32.9**
jealous **34.18.29(.5)**
jealously **1.31.33(.12.6)**

jealousness **34.18.16(.31.6)**
jealousy **1.22.16(.14)**
Jean **11, 28.1**
jean **28.1**
Jeanette **22.5.9**
Jeanne d'Arc **24.8**
Jeannie **1.16.1**
Jeannine **28.1.14**
Jeans **35.26.1**
Jedah **17.13.4**
Jedburgh **17.32.14(.5)**
Jeddah **17.13.4**
Jeep® **20.1**
jeepers **35.18.6**
jeer **3**
jeeringly **1.31.28(.1.17)**
Jeeves **35.28.1**
jeez **35.1**
Jeff **30.4**
Jefferies **35.2.17**
Jefferson **28.17.23(.14)**
Jeffery **1.29.21**
Jeffrey **1.29.21**
Jeffreys **35.2.17**
Jehoshaphat **22.7.13**
Jehovah **17.21.14(.13)**
Jehovist **22.29.2(.20)**
Jehu **16.24.16**
jejune **28.16.11**
jejunely **1.31.27(.12)**
jejuneness **34.18.16(.25)**
jejunum **27.15.14(.10)**
Jekyll **40.2.7, 40.23.1, 40.23.4**
jell **40.5**
Jellicoe **19.12.12**
jellification **28.17.25(.3.5)**
jellify **14.14.4(.16)**
jello **19.29.4**
jelly **1.31.5**
jellyfish **36.2.18(.1)**
Jem **27.5**
Jemima **17.17.11**
Jemma **17.17.5**
jemmy **1.15.4**
Jena **17.18.3**
je ne sais quoi **10**
Jenkin **28.2.13(.13)**
Jenkins **35.26.2**
Jenkinson **28.17.23(.24)**
Jenna **17.18.4**
Jenner **17.18.4**
jennet **22.2.12**
Jennifer **17.20.12(.2)**
Jennings **35.27**
jenny **1.16.5**
Jensen **28.17.23(.24)**
jeon **28.10.1**
jeopardize **35.15.8**

jeopardy **1.11.17**
Jephthah **17.22.14**
jequirity **1.10.16(.21.1)**
jerboa **17.9.1**
jeremiad **23.7.3, 23.18.3**
Jeremiah **17.6.7**
Jeremy **1.15.13(.11)**
Jerez **32.5**
Jericho **19.12.12**
jerk **24.17**
jerker **17.14.16**
jerkily **1.31.17(.11)**
jerkin **28.2.13(.7)**
jerkiness **34.18.16(.2.4)**
jerky **1.12.14**
Jermaine **28.4.7**
Jermyn **28.2.17(.6)**
jeroboam **27.15.6**
Jerome **27.17.13**
jerry **1.29.3**
jerrycan **28.7.8**
jersey **1.23.14**
Jerusalem **27.15.28(.11)**
Jervaulx **19.17, 34.18.18**
Jervis **34.2.15**
Jespersen **28.17.23(.14)**
jess **34.5**
jessamin **28.2.17(.5)**
jesse **1.22.5**
Jessel **40.31.5**
Jessica **17.14.15(.12)**
Jessie **1.22.5**
Jessop **20.13.4**
jest **22.29.5**
jester **17.12.24(.4)**
jestful **40.14.6(.10)**
Jesu **16.15, 16.16, 16.24.15**
Jesuit **22.2.3**
jesuitic **24.2.10(.2.1)**
Jesuitical **40.23.12(.7.1)**
Jesuitically **1.31.24(.9.3)**
Jesus **34.18.21**
jet **22.5**
jeté **4.9.1**
jetfoil **40.11.7**
Jethro **19.27.21**
jetlag **26.5.9**
jetliner **17.18.13(.14)**
jeton **28.17.11(.4)**
jetsam **27.15.20(.13)**
jetstream **27.1.12**
jettison **28.17.23(.14), 28.17.24(.12)**
jetton **28.17.11(.4)**
jetty **1.10.4**
jeu **18**
jeu d'esprit **2.30.8**
jeunesse dorée **4.26, 4.26.7**
Jevons **35.26.13(.11)**

Jew **16**
jewel **40.16.8**
jeweler **17.34.15**
Jewell **40.16.8**
jeweller **17.34.15, 17.34.16(.4)**
jewellery **1.29.24**
jewelly **1.31.17(.5)**
Jewess **34.5, 34.18.7**
jewfish **36.2.18(.10)**
Jewish **36.2.6**
Jewishly **1.31.35(.7.1)**
Jewishness **34.18.16(.33.1)**
Jewry **1.29.11(.3)**
Jewson **28.17.23(.13)**
Jeyes **35.4**
jezail **40.4.11, 40.13.13**
Jezebel **40.5.2**
Jezreel **40.1.15, 40.3.14(.10)**
jib **21.2**
jibba **17.11.2**
jibber **17.11.2**
jibe **21.12**
JICTAR **10.6.6**
Jiddah **17.13.2**
Jif® **30.2**
jiff **30.2**
jiffy **1.18.2**
jig **26.2**
jigaboo **16.6**
jigger **17.16.2**
jiggery-pokery **1.29.11(.10)**
jiggle **40.24.2**
jiggly **1.31.17(.12), 1.31.25**
jigot **22.19.13**
jigsaw **12.14.14**
jihad **23.7.15, 23.9.19**
jill **40.2**
jillaroo **16.23**
Jillian **28.3.21(.2)**
jillion **28.3.21(.2)**
jilt **22.32.1**
Jim **27.2**
Jim Crowism **27.15.21(.2.1)**
jim-dandy **1.11.20(.4)**
Jiménez **35.5.9**
jiminy **1.16.15(.11)**
jimjams **35.25.4**
Jimmie **1.15.2**
jimmy **1.15.2**
jimmygrant **22.26.6, 22.26.8**
jimpson **28.17.23(.17)**
jimson **28.17.23(.23)**
Jin **28.2**
Jinan **28.7.11**
jingle **40.24.14(.1)**
jingly **1.31.25**

j

Judas Maccabaeus **34.18.1**

Judd **23.14**

judder **17.13.11**

Jude **23.17**

Judea **3.5**

judge **39.11**

judgelike **24.13.7(.26)**

judgematic **24.2.10(.4.2)**

judgematical **40.23.12(.7.1)**

judgematically **1.31.24(.9.4)**

judgement **22.26.15(.13.6)**

judgemental **40.21.17(.2)**

judgementally **1.31.17(.9.3)**

Judges **35.18.21**

judgeship **20.2.7(.23)**

judgmental **40.21.17(.2)**

judgmentally **1.31.17(.9.3)**

Judi **1.11.16**

judicative **31.2.1(.9.1)**

judicatory **1.29.11(.8.6)**

judicature **17.28.15**

judicial **40.33.1**

judicially **1.31.17(.22)**

judiciary **1.29.11(.20)**

judicious **34.18.22(.2)**

judiciously **1.31.33(.12.4)**

judiciousness **34.18.16(.31.4)**

Judith **32.14.9**

judo **19.11.10**

judoist **22.29.2(.10)**

judoka **17.14.17**

Judy **1.11.16**

jug **26.10**

Jugendstil **40.1.3**

jugful **40.14.6(.13)**

juggernaut **22.13.6**

juggins **35.26.2**

juggle **40.24.8**

juggler **17.34.24**

jugglery **1.29.11(.27)**

jugular **17.34.16(.21.3)**

jugulate **22.4.23(.7.3)**

Jugurtha **17.22.10**

Jugurthine **28.14.12**

juice **34.17**

juiceless **34.18.29(.33)**

juicer **17.24.14**

juicily **1.31.17(.20)**

juiciness **34.18.16(.2.7)**

juicy **1.22.15**

jujitsu **16.15**

juju **16.20**

jujube **21.13**

jujutsu **16.15**

jukebox **34.23.8(.2)**

Jukes **34.23.14**

juku **16.9**

julep **20.4, 20.13.7**

Jules **35.30.11**

Julia **3.24.10**

Julian **28.3.21(.10)**

Julie **1.31.16**

Julien **28.3.21(.10)**

julienne **28.5**

Juliet **22.3.13, 22.5**

Julius **34.3.16**

July **14.25**

jumble **40.20.19**

jumbly **1.31.21(.12)**

jumbo **19.9.14**

jumboize **35.15.4**

jumbuck **24.12.1**

jump **20.16.5**

jumpable **40.20.16(.9)**

jumper **17.10.17**

jumpily **1.31.17(.7)**

jumpiness **34.18.16(.2.2)**

jumpsuit **22.18.6**

jumpy **1.8.14**

junco **19.12.15**

junction **28.17.25(.15.6)**

juncture **17.28.20, 17.28.23**

June **28.16**

Juneau **19.15.11**

Jung **29.9**

Jungfrau **9.16**

Jungian **28.3.6**

jungle **40.24.14(.4)**

jungly **1.31.25**

junior **3.9.9**

juniorate **22.19.24(.2)**

juniority **1.10.16(.21.2)**

juniper **17.10.14**

junk **24.19.7**

Junker **17.14.21(.6)**

junkerdom **27.15.10(.8)**

junket **22.2.9(.9)**

junkie **1.12.16**

Junkin **28.2.13(.13)**

junk mail **40.4**

junkyard **23.9.21**

Juno **19.15.11**

Junoesque **24.20.3**

Junor **17.18.15**

junta **17.12.22(.10)**

Jupiter **17.12.16(.3)**

Jura **17.32.14(.3)**

jural **40.16.13(.11)**

Jurassic **24.2.20(.5)**

jurat **22.7.20**

juridical **40.23.12(.8)**

juridically **1.31.24(.9.7)**

jurisconsult **22.32.8**

jurisdiction **28.17.25(.15.1)**

jurisdictional **40.26.13(.14.6)**

jurisprudence **34.24.10(.11)**

jurisprudent **22.26.15(.10)**

jurisprudential **40.33.12(.3)**

jurist **22.29.2(.29.3)**

juristic **24.2.10(.15.2)**

juristical **40.23.12(.7.3)**

juror **17.32.14(.3)**

jury **1.29.11(.3)**

juryman **28.17.16(.2)**

jurywoman **28.17.16(.14)**

jurywomen **28.2.17(.1)**

jussive **31.2.4(.6)**

just **22.29.12**

juste milieu **18.16**

justice **34.2.8**

justiceship **20.2.7(.22)**

justiciable **40.20.3, 40.20.16(.23)**

justiciar **17.26.2**

justiciary **1.29.2(.9), 1.29.11(.20)**

justifiability **1.10.16(.22.2)**

justifiable **40.20.16(.5)**

justifiableness **34.18.16(.37.4)**

justifiably **1.31.21(.2)**

justification **28.17.25(.3.5)**

justificatory **1.29.11(.8.2)**

justifier **17.6.9(.4)**

justify **14.14.4(.4)**

Justin **28.2.11(.14)**

Justine **28.1.9(.7)**

Justinian **28.3.8(.2)**

justly **1.31.22(.22)**

justness **34.18.16(.20.4)**

jut **22.15**

jute **22.18**

Jutish **36.2.11**

Jutland **23.24.16(.16.3)**

Juvenal **40.26.13(.10)**

juvenescence **34.24.10(.18)**

juvenescent **22.26.15(.17.2)**

juvenile **40.13.8**

juvenilely **1.31.38**

juvenilia **3.24.2**

juvenility **1.10.16(.25)**

juxtapose **35.20.1**

juxtaposition **28.17.25(.2.5)**

juxtapositional **40.26.13(.14.1)**

k **4**

K2 **16.7**

ka **10**

Kaaba **17.11.7**

kabaddi **1.11.7**

Kabaka **17.14.7**

Kabalega **17.16.3**

kabbala **17.34.8**

kabbalist **22.29.2(.31.2)**

kabob **21.7**

kabuki **1.12.12**

Kabul **40.14.3, 40.20.7**

Kabwe **1.28, 4.25.11**

Kabyle **40.13.2**

kachina **17.18.1(.12)**

Kádáar **10.7**

Kaddafi **1.18.4**

kaddish **36.2.12**

kadi **1.11.9**

kaffir **17.20.5**

kafir **17.20.5**

Kafka **17.14.22**

Kafkaesque **24.20.3**

kaftan **28.7.6**

Kagan **28.17.15(.3)**

Kagoshima **17.17.1**

Kahlua® **17.8**

Kahn **28.9**

kahuna **17.18.15**

kai **14**

Kaifeng **29.3**

kail **40.4**

kainite **22.16.14(.5)**

Kaiser **17.25.12**

kaisership **20.2.7(.9)**

Kai Tak **24.6**

kaizen **28.17.24(.10)**

kaka **10.8.4, 17.14.7**

kakapo **19.8**

kakemono **19.15.14**

kala-azar **10.16**

Kalahari **1.29.6**

Kalamazoo **16.16**

Kalashnikov **30.8.6**

kale **40.4**

kaleidoscope **20.15.4(.1)**

kaleidoscopic **24.2.8(.5)**

kaleidoscopical **40.23.12(.5)**

kaleidoscopically **1.31.24(.9.2)**

kalenchoe **1(.7)**

kalends **35.23.15**

kaleyard **23.9.21**

Kalgoorlie **1.31.17(.4)**

Kali **1.31.9**

kali **1.31.4, 1.31.7, 14.25.4**

k

Kensal 40.31.21
Kensington 28.17.11(.23)
Kensitas 34.7.7
kent 22.26.4
Kentigern 28.17.15(.2), 28.18.6
Kentish 36.2.11
kentledge 39.2.23
Kenton 28.17.11(.22)
Kentuckian 28.3.5
Kentucky 1.12.9
Kenwood® 23.16.6(.14)
Kenya 17.33.9
Kenyan 28.17.32
Kenyatta 17.12.6
Kenyon 28.17.32
Keogh 19.1
kepi 1.8.3, 1.8.4
Kepler 17.34.19
Keplerian 28.3.20(.2)
Keppel 40.19.4
kept 22.22.3
Kerala 17.34.16(.20)
Keralite 22.16.25(.9)
keratin 28.2.11(.10)
keratinization 28.17.25(.3.12)
keratinize 35.15.12(.2)
keratose 34.20.4, 35.20.3
keratosis 34.2.17(.11.1)
kerb 21.15
kerbside 23.15.11(.8)
kerbstone 28.19.4(.9)
kerchief 30.1.7, 30.14
Kerensky 1.12.17(.12)
kerf 30.15
kerfuffle 40.27.11
Kerguelen 28.17.33(.13)
kermes 35.1.11, 35.2.7
kermess 34.5.5
kermis 34.2.12
Kermit 22.2.11
Kermode 23.20.8
kern 28.18
kernel 40.26.14
kero 19.27.2
kerosene 28.1.18(.6)
Kerouac 24.6.4
kerplunk 24.19.7
Kerr 6, 10, 18
Kerrigan 28.17.15(.13)
Kerry 1.29.3
kersey 1.23.14
kerseymere 3.8.2
Kershaw 12.16.6
kerygma 17.17.20
kerygmata 17.12.16(.9.3)
kerygmatic 24.2.10(.4.2)
Kes 34.5, 35.5
Kesey 1.23.1

Kesh 36.5
kesh 36.4
keskidee 2.13
Kessler 17.34.27
Kesteven 28.17.20(.1)
Keston 28.17.11(.25)
kestrel 40.16.13(.16)
Keswick 24.2.21
ketch 38.4
ketchup 20.9.14
ketoacidosis 34.2.17(.11.1)
ketone 28.19.4(.1)
ketonic 24.2.15(.6.1)
ketonuria 3.22.12
ketosis 34.2.17(.11.1)
ketotic 24.2.10(.6)
Kettering 29.1.30(.8)
kettle 40.21.4
kettledrum 27.11.12
kettledrummer 17.17.10
kettleful 40.14.6(.22)
keuper 17.10.10
kevel 40.28.4
Kevin 28.2.20
kevlar 10.25.10
Kew 16
Kewpie® 1.8.10
kex 34.23.4
key 2
keyboard 23.12.2(.1)
keyboarder 17.13.9
keyboardist 22.29.2(.14)
keyer 17.1
Keyes 35.1
keyholder 17.13.23(.8)
keyhole 40.18.13
Key Largo 19.13.5
keyless 34.18.29(.1)
Keynes 35.26.1, 35.26.4
Keynesianism 27.15.21(.2.9)
keynote 22.21.8
Keynsham 27.15.22
keypad 23.7.5
keypunch 38.18.7
keypuncher 17.28.22
keyring 29.1.30(.1)
Keys 35.1
Keyser 17.25.1, 17.25.12
keystone 28.19.4(.9)
Keystone Kops 34.21.6
keystroke 24.18.13
keyway 4.25.1
Key West 22.29.5
keyword 23.19.8
KGB 2.10
Khabarovsk 24.20.14
Khachaturian 28.3.20(.8)

khaddar 17.13.5
khaki 1.12.6
khalif 30.2.6
Khalki 1.12.19
khamsin 28.2.23(.15)
khan 28.9
khanate 22.4.14(.5)
Kharg 26.6
Kharkov 31.7
Khartoum 27.14.1
Khayyam 27.6, 27.8
khazi 1.23.7
Khedival 40.28.1
khedive 31.1.2
Khedivial 40.3.8
Khitai 14.8
Khmer 6, 6.8
Khmer Rouge 37.7
Khoikhoi 13.5
Khoisan 28.9.9
Khomeini 1.16.4
Khorramshahr 10.17
khoum 27.14
Khrushchev 30.8.9
Khufu 16.13
Khyber Pass 34.9
kiang 29.4
Kiangsu 16.15
Kia-Ora® 17.32.10
kibble 40.20.2
kibbutz 34.22.13
kibbutzim 27.2.9
kibbutznik 24.2.15(.17)
kibe 21.12
kibitka 17.14.18
kibits 34.22.2
kibitzer 17.24.19
kiblah 17.34.20
kibosh 36.9.2
kick 24.2
kickable 40.20.16(.13)
kick-ass 34.9
kickback 24.6.6(.14)
kick-boxer 17.24.20
kick-boxing 29.1.23
kickdown 28.8.2(.6)
kicker 17.14.2
kickoff 30.8.6
kick-pleat 22.1.18
kickshaw 12.16.9
kicksorter 17.12.10(.5)
kickstand 23.24.6(.5)
kickstart 22.10.3
kid 23.2
Kidd 23.2
kidder 17.13.2
Kidderminster 17.12.24(.23)
kiddie 1.11.2
kiddiewink 24.19.1(.6)

kiddingly 1.31.28(.1.5)
kiddle 40.22.2
kiddo 19.11.2
kiddush 36.13
kidnap 20.5.4
kidnaper 17.10.5
kidnapper 17.10.5
kidnapping 29.1.10(.5)
kidney 1.16.20
kidology 1.26.10(.11.2)
kidskin 28.2.13(.14)
Kidwelly 1.31.5
Kiel 40.1
Kielce 17.24.19, 17.24.24
Kielder 17.13.23(.1)
Kiely 1.31.1
kier 3
Kieran 28.17.31(.2)
Kierkegaard 23.9.10
kieselguhr 17.7.6
Kiev 30.4, 31.4
kif 30.2
Kigali 1.31.9
kike 24.13
Kikuyu 16.24.1
Kilbracken 28.17.13(.5)
Kilbride 23.15.15
Kilburn 28.17.10, 28.18.3
Kildare 6.5
kilderkin 28.2.13(.6)
Kilfedder 17.13.4
kilim 27.1.13
Kilimanjaro 19.27.5
Kilkenny 1.16.5
kill 40.2
Killamarsh 36.8
Killanin 28.2.18
Killarney 1.16.8
killer 17.34.2
killick 24.2.27(.2)
Killiecranckie 1.12.16
killifish 36.2.18(.1)
killing 29.1.31(.2)
killingly 1.31.28(.1.18)
killjoy 13.12
Kilmarnock 24.9.9, 24.16.7
Kilmuir 17.7.12(.7)
kiln 28.20
Kilner® 17.18.32
kilo 19.29.1
kilobyte 22.16.8
kilocalorie 1.29.11(.27)
kilocycle 40.23.10
kilogram 27.6.17(.5)
kilohertz 34.22.16
kilojoule 40.15.7
kilolitre 17.12.1(.15)
kilometre 17.12.1(.6), 17.12.16(.9.2)

kilometric **24.2.26(.14.2)**
kiloton **28.13.3**
kilovolt **22.32.12**
kilowatt **22.11.14**
Kilpatrick **24.2.26(.14.3)**
Kilroy **13.15**
kilt **22.32.1**
kilter **17.12.26(.1)**
kiltie **1.10.28**
Kim **27.2**
Kimber **17.11.17(.1)**
Kimberley **1.31.17(.8)**
kimberlite **22.16.25(.9)**
Kimberly **1.31.17(.8)**
Kimbolton **28.17.11(.27)**
kimchi **1.25.15**
kimono **19.15.14**
kin **28.2**
kina **17.18.1**
Kinabalu **16.25**
kinaesthesia **3.15.1**
kinaesthetic **24.2.10(.3.2)**
kinaesthetically
1.31.24(.9.3)
Kincaid **23.4.5**
Kincardine **28.17.12(.8)**
kincob **21.14**
kind **23.24.13**
kinda **17.13.20(.11)**
Kinder **17.13.20(.1)**
kindergarten **28.17.11(.8)**
kind-hearted **23.18.9(.7)**
kind-heartedly
1.31.23(.14.3)
kind-heartedness
34.18.16(.21.1)
kindle **40.22.16**
kindler **17.34.22**
kindlily **1.31.17(.29)**
kindliness **34.18.16(.2.10)**
kindling **29.1.31(.18)**
kindly **1.31.23(.17)**
kindness **34.18.16(.21.1)**
kindred **23.18.27**
kine **28.14**
kinematic **24.2.10(.4.2)**
kinematical
40.23.12(.7.1)
kinematically
1.31.24(.9.4)
kinescope **20.15.4(.1)**
kinesics **34.23.2(.10)**
kinesiology **1.26.10(.11.1)**
kinesthetically
1.31.24(.9.3)
kinetic **24.2.10(.3.1)**
kinetically **1.31.24(.9.3)**
kinetin **28.2.11(.10)**
kinfolk **24.18.7**
king **29.1**
kingbird **23.19.1**

kingbolt **22.32.12**
kingcraft **22.27.4(.4)**
kingcup **20.9.7**
kingdom **27.15.10(.15)**
kingfish **36.2.18(.20)**
kingfisher **17.26.2**
kinghood **23.16.5(.11)**
King Kong **29.6**
kingless **34.18.29(.28)**
kinglet **22.19.26(.23)**
kinglike **24.13.7(.18)**
kingliness **34.18.16(.2.10)**
kingling **29.1.31(.22)**
kingly **1.31.28(.1)**
kingmaker **17.14.3(.3)**
kingpin **28.2.9**
Kingsbridge **39.2.22(.10)**
Kingsbury **1.29.11(.7.2)**
kingship **20.2.7(.20)**
Kingsley **1.31.34**
Kingston **28.17.11(.25)**
Kingstown **28.8.1**
Kingsway **4.25.23**
Kingswear **3.21**
Kingswinford
23.18.16(.16)
Kingswood **23.16.6(.18)**
kinin **28.2.18**
kink **24.19.1**
kinkajou **16.20**
Kinki **1.12.16**
kinkily **1.31.17(.11)**
kinkiness **34.18.16(.2.4)**
kinky **1.12.16**
kinless **34.18.29(.27)**
Kinloch **24.9.16, 25.6**
Kinloss **34.10.17**
Kinnear **3.9**
Kinney **1.16.2**
Kinnock **24.16.7**
kino **19.15.1**
Kinross **34.10.16**
Kinsale **40.4.10**
Kinsella **17.34.5(.11),
17.34.16(.15)**
Kinsey **1.23.20**
kinsfolk **24.18.7**
Kinshasa **17.24.6, 17.24.8**
kinship **20.2.7(.19)**
kinsman **28.17.16(.30)**
kinswoman **28.17.16(.14)**
kinswomen **28.2.17(.1)**
Kintyre **17.6.3**
kiosk **24.20.5**
Kiowa **17.31.3**
kip **20.2**
Kipling **29.1.31(.15)**
Kippax **34.23.5(.2)**
kipper **17.10.2**
kipsie **1.22.19**

kir **3**
Kirby **1.9.12**
kirby-grip® **20.2.11**
Kirchhoff **30.8.6**
Kirghizia **3.15.2**
Kiribati **1.10.8, 34.7.6**
Kirin **28.2.29(.1)**
kirk **24.17**
Kirkbride **23.15.15**
Kirkby **1.9.12, 1.9.16**
Kirkcaldy **1.11.10, 1.11.11**
Kirkcudbright **1.29.14**
Kirkgate **22.19.13**
Kirkham **27.15.11(.10)**
Kirkland **23.24.16(.16.3)**
Kirklees **35.1.23**
kirkman **28.17.16(.23)**
Kirkpatrick **24.2.26(.14.3)**
Kirkstall **40.10.5, 40.21.18**
Kirkstone **28.17.11(.25)**
Kirkwall **40.10.17**
Kirkwood **23.16.6(.11)**
Kirov **30.8.11, 31.7**
Kirriemuir **17.7.12(.7)**
kirsch **36.3, 36.15**
kirschwasser **17.24.6**
Kirsten **28.17.11(.25)**
Kirstie **1.10.26(.12)**
kirtle **40.21.13**
Kirundi **1.11.20(.8)**
Kirwan **28.17.30**
kishke **17.14.24**
kiskadee **2.13**
Kislev **30.4**
kismet **22.5.8, 22.19.14**
kiss **34.2**
kissable **40.20.16(.21.1)**
kisser **17.24.2**
Kissinger **17.29.16(.8)**
kissogram **27.6.17(.5)**
kissy **1.22.2**
kist **22.29.2**
Kiswahili **1.31.1**
kit **22.2**
kitbag **26.5.1**
kitchen **28.17.27**
Kitchener **17.18.16(.18)**
kitchenette **22.5.9**
kitchenware **6.18.11**
kite **22.16**
Kitemark® **24.8.8**
kith **32.2**
Kit-Kat **22.7.9**
kitsch **38.2**
kitschiness
34.18.16(.2.8)
kitschy **1.25.2**
Kitson **28.17.23(.19)**
kitten **28.17.11(.2)**
kittenish **36.2.16(.13)**

kittenishly **1.31.35(.7.2)**
kittenishness
34.18.16(.33.5)
kittiwake **24.3.12**
kittle **40.21.2**
kitty **1.10.2**
Kitwe **4.25.12**
Kivu **16.14**
Kiwanis **34.2.13**
kiwi **2.29**
kiwi fruit **22.18**
Klan **28.7**
Klansman **28.17.16(.30)**
Klaus **34.8**
klavier **3.11**
klaxon **28.17.23(.21)**
klebsiella **17.34.5**
Klee **4**
Kleenex® **34.23.4(.6)**
Klein **28.14**
Kleinwort **22.13.13**
Kleist **22.29.13**
Klemperer **17.32.14(.4)**
klephth **22.27.2**
kleptomania **3.9.3(.5)**
kleptomaniac **24.6.1**
Klerksdorp **20.8**
klieg **26.1**
Klimt **22.25**
Kline **28.14**
klipspringer **17.19.1**
Klondike **24.13.3**
kloof **30.13**
Klosters **35.18.8**
kludge **39.13**
klutz **34.22.11**
klutzy **1.23.17**
klystron **28.10.24(.7)**
K-meson **28.10.19**
knack **24.6**
knacker **17.14.5**
knackery **1.29.11(.10)**
knackwurst
22.29.15(.5), 22.29.16
knag **26.5**
knaggy **1.14.5**
knap **20.5**
Knapp **20.5**
knapper **17.10.5**
knapsack **24.6.14**
knapweed **23.1.10**
knar **10**
Knaresborough
17.32.14(.5)
Knatchbull **40.14.3**
knave **31.3**
knavery **1.29.11(.15)**
knavish **36.2.19**
knavishly **1.31.35(.7.3)**
knavishness
34.18.16(.33.6)

k

knawel **40.10, 40.16.4**
knead **23.1**
kneadable **40.20.16(.12)**
kneader **17.13.1**
Knebworth **32.14.15**
knee **2**
kneecap **20.5.1**
kneecapping **29.1.10(.5)**
kneehole **40.18.13**
kneel **40.1**
kneeler **17.34.1**
knee-trembler **17.34.20**
knell **40.5**
Kneller **17.34.5**
knelt **22.32.2**
Knesset **22.19.18**
knew **16**
knicker **17.14.2**
Knickerbocker **17.14.8**
knick-knack **24.6.11**
knick-knackery **1.29.11(.10)**
knick-knackish **36.2.13**
knife **30.12**
knifelike **24.13.7(.19)**
knifepoint **22.26.11**
knifer **17.20.10**
knight **22.16**
knightage **39.2.10**
knight-errant **22.26.15(.23.1)**
knight-errantry **1.29.15(.15)**
knighthood **23.16.5(.6)**
Knight Hospitaller **17.34.16(.7)**
knightlike **24.13.7(.12)**
knightliness **34.18.16(.2.10)**
knightly **1.31.22(.13)**
Knighton **28.17.11(.12)**
Knights **34.22.12**
Knightsbridge **39.2.22(.10)**
Knights Templar **17.34.19**
Knight Templar **17.34.19**
kniphofia **3.10.4**
knish **36.2**
knit **22.2**
knitter **17.12.2**
knitwear **6.18.7**
knives **35.28.6**
knob **21.8**
knobbiness **34.18.16(.2.2)**
knobble **40.20.9**
knobbliness **34.18.16(.2.10)**
knobbly **1.31.17(.8), 1.31.21(.1)**
knobby **1.9.7**

knobkerrie **1.29.3**
knoblike **24.13.7(.11)**
knobstick **24.2.10(.15.4)**
knock **24.9**
knockabout **22.9.6**
knocker **17.14.8**
knockout **22.9.9**
knockwurst **22.29.15(.5), 22.29.16**
knoll **40.9, 40.18**
Knollys **35.30.13**
knop **20.7**
knopkierie **1.29.2(.4)**
Knossos **34.10.15**
knot **22.11**
knotgrass **34.9.6**
knothole **40.18.13**
knotless **34.18.29(.22)**
Knott **22.11**
knotter **17.12.9**
knottily **1.31.17(.9.2)**
knottiness **34.18.16(.2.3)**
knotting **29.1.12(.8)**
knotty **1.10.9**
knotweed **23.1.10**
knotwork **24.17.6(.8)**
knout **22.9, 22.18**
know **19**
knowable **40.20.16(.8)**
knower **17.9**
know-how **9.14**
knowing **29.1.9**
knowingly **1.31.28(.1.1)**
knowingness **34.18.16(.26)**
Knowle **40.18**
knowledgability **1.10.16(.22.2)**
knowledgableness **34.18.16(.37.4)**
knowledgably **1.31.21(.7.4)**
knowledge **39.2.23**
knowledgeability **1.10.16(.22.2)**
knowledgeable **40.20.16(.25)**
knowledgeableness **34.18.16(.37.4)**
knowledgeably **1.31.21(.7.4)**
Knowles **35.30.13**
known **28.19**
Knox **34.23.8**
Knoxville **40.2.12**
knuckle **40.23.9**
knuckleball **40.10.4**
knucklebone **28.19.3**
knucklehead **23.5.13(.19)**
knuckly **1.31.17(.11), 1.31.24(.7)**

knur **18**
knurl **40.17**
knurr **18**
Knut **22.15, 22.18.5**
Knutsford **23.18.16(.18)**
KO **19**
koa **17.9**
koala **17.34.8**
koan **28.7.3**
Kobe **1.9.13, 4.8**
kobold **23.31.11, 23.31.15**
Koch **24.9, 24.18, 25.6, 38.8**
Köchel **40.23.13**
Kodachrome **27.17.13**
Kodak® **24.6.8**
Kodály **14.9**
Kodiak **24.6.1**
koel **40.16.9**
Koestler **17.34.21, 17.34.27**
Koh-i-noor **12.10, 17.7.8**
kohl **40.18**
kohlrabi **1.9.6**
koi **13**
Koil **40.11**
koiné **1.16.11, 2.17.7, 4.14**
Kojak **24.6.18**
Kokoschka **17.14.24**
kola **17.34.18**
Kolhapur **17.7.1**
kolinsky **1.12.17(.12)**
kolkhoz **35.10, 35.12**
Köln **28.20**
Koluma **17.17.13**
komitadji **1.26.4**
Komodo **19.11.13**
Kompong Cham **27.6**
Kompong Som **27.9**
Komsomol **40.9.11**
Komsomolsk **24.20.15**
Königsberg **26.14.1(.11)**
Konika **17.14.2**
Konrad **23.7.16**
Kon-Tiki **1.12.1**
kook **24.15**
kookaburra **17.32.12**
kookily **1.31.17(.11)**
kookiness **34.18.16(.2.4)**
kooky **1.12.11, 1.12.12**
kop **20.7**
kopek **24.4.2**
kopi **1.8.13**
kopje **1.8.7**
koppa **17.10.8**
koppie **1.8.7**
koradji **1.26.4, 1.26.10(.9)**
Koran **28.9.13**
Koranic **24.2.15(.5)**
Korda **17.13.9**
Kordofan **28.7.12, 28.9.7**
Korea **3.22**

Korean **28.3.20**
korfball **40.10.4**
Kórinthos **34.10.14**
korma **17.17.9**
Korsakoff **30.8.6**
koruna **17.18.16(.20)**
Kos **34.10**
Kosciuszko **19.12.17**
kosher **17.26.16**
Kosovo **19.17**
Kostroma **10.10.4**
Kosygin **28.2.15**
Kota **17.12.18**
Kota Baharu **16.23.3**
Kota Kinabalu **16.25**
Kotka **17.14.18**
koto **19.10.14**
kotow **9.3**
koulan **28.17.33(.12)**
koumiss **34.2.12**
kouprey **4.26.9**
kowhai **14.14.2, 14.23**
Kowloon **28.16.15**
kowtow **9.3**
Kra **10**
kraal **40.8**
kraft **22.27.4**
krait **22.16**
Krakatoa **17.9.2**
kraken **28.17.13(.6)**
Kraków **9.5**
Kramer **17.17.4**
krantz **34.24.6**
Krasnodar **10.7**
Krasnoyarsk **24.20.4**
krater **17.12.4**
K-ration **28.17.25(.5)**
Kraus **34.8**
Kraut **22.9**
Kray **4**
Krebs **35.21**
Krefeld **23.31.4**
Kreisler **17.34.28**
Kremlin **28.2.31(.19)**
Kremlinologist **22.29.2(.26.4)**
Kremlinology **1.26.10(.11.4)**
Kretzschmar **10.10.9**
kriegspiel **40.1.1**
krill **40.2**
krimmer **17.17.2**
Krio **19.1**
kris **34.1**
Krishna **17.18.30**
Krishnaism **27.15.21(.2.1)**
Krishnamurti **1.10.16(.5), 1.10.17**
Krista **17.12.24(.2)**
Kristallnacht **22.24**

Kroeber **17.11.15**
kromesky **1.12.17(.2)**
krona **17.18.18**
krone **17.18.18**
kroner **17.18.18**
kronor **17.18.18**
Kronos **34.10.13**
Kronstadt **22.7.7**
kronur **17.18.18**
Kroo **16**
Kropotkin **28.2.13(.9)**
Kru **16**
Kruger **17.16.12**
Krugerrand **23.24.6(.12)**
krummholz **34.22.20**
krummhorn **28.11.10**
Krupp **20.9, 20.11**
krypton **28.10.9**
Kshatriya **3.22.15**
Kuala Lumpur **17.7.1**
Kublai Khan **28.9**
Kubrick **24.2.26(.13)**
kuccha **17.28.11**
kudos **34.10.9**
kudu **16.8.3**
kudzu **16.16**
Kufic **24.2.16(.6)**
Kuhn **28.16**
Ku Klux Klan **28.7**
Ku Klux Klansman **28.17.16(.30)**
kukri **1.29.17**
kulak **24.6.23**
kulan **28.17.33(.12)**
Kultur **17.7.3**
Kulturkampf **30.17, 30.18**
Kumamoto **19.10.14**
kumara **17.32.14(.10)**
Kümmel **40.25.9**
kumquat **22.11.14**
Kundera **17.32.14(.7)**
Kung **29.9**
kung fu **16**
Kunlun Shan **28.7**
Kunming **29.1.16**
Kuomintang **29.4.3**
Kuoni **1.16.17**
kurbash **36.6.2**
kurchatovium **27.3.9**
Kurd **23.19**
kurdaitcha **17.28.12**
Kurdish **36.2.12**
Kurdistan **28.9.2**
Kurgan **28.9.5**
Kurile **40.1.15**
kurrajong **29.6.12**
Kursaal **40.8.11, 40.8.12, 40.31.13, 40.32.14**
Kurt **22.20**

kurta **17.12.17**
kurtosis **34.2.17(.11.1)**
kurus **36.13, 36.14**
Kurzweil **40.13.10, 40.13.15**
Kush **36.13**
Kuwait **22.4.21**
Kuwaiti **1.10.3**
Kuznetz Basin **28.17.23(.4)**
kvas **34.9**
kvass **34.9**
kvetch **38.4**
kvetcher **17.28.5**
Kwa **10**
KWAC **24.6**
kwacha **17.28.6, 17.28.8**
KwaNdebele **1.31.1, 1.31.4**
kwanza **17.25.18**
kwashiorkor **12.7**
KwaZulu **16.25**
Kweilin **28.2.31**
Kweiyang **29.4.16**
kwela **17.34.4**
Kwells **35.30.4**
KWIC **24.2**
Kwik-Fit **22.2.13**
KWOC **24.9**
kyanite **22.16.14(.6)**
kyanitic **24.2.10(.2.2)**
kyanize **35.15.12(.5)**
kyat **22.10**
Kyd **23.2**
kyle **40.13**
kylie **1.31.14**
kylin **28.2.31(.1)**
kylix **34.23.2(.13)**
kyloe **19.29.9**
kymogram **27.6.17(.5)**
kymograph **30.7.5(.1)**
kymographic **24.2.16(.3)**
kymographically **1.31.24(.9.9)**
Kyoto **19.10.14**
kyphosis **34.2.17(.11.2)**
kyphotic **24.2.10(.6)**
Kyrenia **3.9.1**
Kyrgyz **35.2.6**
Kyrgyzstan **28.9.2**
kyrie **4.2.9**
Kyushu **16.17**
l **40.5**
la **10**
laager **17.16.6**
lab **21.6**
Laban **28.7.5, 28.17.10**
labara **17.32.14(.5)**
labarum **27.15.26(.8)**

labefaction **28.17.25(.15.3)**
label **40.20.4**
labelled **23.31.15**
labeller **17.34.16(.6)**
labia **3.3.3**
labial **40.3.2**
labialism **27.15.21(.2.15)**
labiality **1.10.16(.32.1)**
labialization **28.17.25(.3.12)**
labialize **35.15.21(.2)**
labially **1.31.3(.2)**
labia majora **17.32.10(.9)**
labia minora **17.32.10(.7)**
labiate **22.3.2, 22.4.2(.2)**
labile **40.13.2**
lability **1.10.16(.22.1)**
labiodental **40.21.17(.2)**
labiovelar **17.34.1**
labium **27.3.2**
laboratory **1.29.11(.8.9)**
laborer **17.32.14(.5)**
laborious **34.3.15(.5)**
laboriously **1.31.33(.1.4)**
laboriousness **34.18.16(.31.1)**
Labouchere **6.14**
labour **17.11.3**
labourer **17.32.14(.5)**
labourism **27.15.21(.2.14)**
Labourite **22.16.24(.9)**
Labov **31.7, 31.12**
Labovian **28.3.10**
labra **17.32.18**
Labrador **12.6.6**
labret **22.19.24(.11)**
labrum **27.15.26(.9)**
La Bruyère **6.20**
Labuan **28.17.7**
laburnum **27.15.14(.12)**
labyrinth **32.21**
labyrinthian **28.3.11**
labyrinthine **28.14.12**
lac **24.6**
Lacan **28.7.8**
Laccadive **31.1.2, 31.2.2**
laccolith **32.2.9**
lace **34.4**
lacemaker **17.14.3(.3)**
lacemaking **29.1.14(.3)**
lacerable **40.20.16(.27.5)**
lacerate **22.4.22(.6)**
laceration **28.17.25(.3.13)**
lacertian **28.3.3, 28.17.25(.12)**
lacertilian **28.3.21(.2)**
lacertine **28.14.5**
lacewing **29.1.29**
lacewood **23.16.6(.17)**

lacework **24.17.6(.15)**
laches **35.18.20**
Lachesis **34.2.17(.10.2)**
Lachlan **28.17.33(.20)**
lachryma Christi **1.10.26(.2)**
lachrymal **40.25.10**
lachrymation **28.17.25(.3.7)**
lachrymator **17.12.4(.9)**
lachrymatory **1.29.11(.8.7)**
lachrymose **34.20.8, 35.20.7**
lachrymosely **1.31.33(.13), 1.31.34**
lacily **1.31.17(.20)**
laciness **34.18.16(.2.7)**
lacing **29.1.23**
laciniate **22.3.6**
laciniated **23.18.9(.3)**
laciniation **28.17.25(.3.1)**
lack **24.6**
lackadaisical **40.23.12(.16)**
lackadaisically **1.31.24(.9.10)**
lackadaisicalness **34.18.16(.37.5)**
lacker **17.14.5**
lackey **1.12.5**
lackland **23.24.6(.13), 23.24.16(.16.3)**
lacklustre **17.12.24(.10)**
Lacock **24.9.6**
Laconia **3.9.11**
Laconian **28.3.8(.11)**
laconic **24.2.15(.6.1)**
laconically **1.31.24(.9.8)**
laconicism **27.15.21(.2.12)**
laconism **27.15.21(.2.9)**
La Coruña **17.33.9**
lacquer **17.14.5**
lacquerer **17.32.14(.8)**
lacquerware **6.18.4**
lacrosse **34.10.16**
lactase **35.4.3**
lactate **22.4.9**
lactation **28.17.25(.3.3)**
lacteal **40.3.3**
lactescence **34.24.10(.18)**
lactescent **22.26.15(.17.2)**
lactic **24.2.10(.13)**
lactiferous **34.18.27(.20)**
lactobacilli **14.25.2**
lactobacillus **34.18.29(.2)**
lactometer **17.12.16(.9.2)**
lactone **28.19.4(.7)**
lactoprotein **28.1.9(.4)**
lactose **34.20.4, 35.20.3**
lacuna **17.18.15**

k
l

lacunae 2.17.9, 14.13
lacunal 40.26.12
lacunar 17.18.15
lacunary 1.29.11(.13.1)
lacunose 34.20.9
lacustrine 28.2.29(.8), 28.14.18
lacy 1.22.4
lad 23.7
Lada® 17.13.7
Ladakh 24.6.8, 24.8.5
ladanum 27.15.14(.11)
Ladbroke 24.14.10
ladder 17.13.5
laddie 1.11.7
laddish 36.2.12
laddishness 34.18.16(.33.3)
lade 23.4
Ladefoged 23.18.12
laden 28.17.12(.4)
la-di-da 10.7
Ladin 28.1.10
lading 29.1.13(.3)
Ladino 19.15.1
ladle 40.22.3
ladleful 40.14.6(.22)
ladler 17.34.22
Ladoga 17.16.15
lady 1.11.4
ladybird 23.19.1
ladybug 26.10
lady-fern 28.18.7
ladyfinger 17.16.17(.1)
ladyfy 14.14.1
ladyhood 23.16.5(.1)
ladykiller 17.34.2(.4)
ladylike 24.13.7(.1)
ladyship 20.2.7(.2)
Ladysmith 32.2.3
Lae 4
Laertes 35.1.7(.7)
Laetitia 17.26.2
laetrile 40.13.16, 40.16.13(.16)
laevodopa 17.10.16
laevorotatory 1.29.11(.8.6)
laevotartaric 24.2.26(.5)
laevulose 34.20.17, 35.20.14
La Fayette 22.5.20
La Fontaine 28.4.3
lag 26.5
lagan 28.17.15(.6)
lager 17.16.6
Lagerkvist 22.29.2(.19)
Lagerlöf 30.16
lagerphone 28.19.11
laggard 23.18.12

laggardly 1.31.23(.14.5)
laggardness 34.18.16(.21.1)
lagger 17.16.5
lagging 29.1.15
lagniappe 20.5.7
lagomorph 30.9.2
Lagonda 17.13.20(.7)
lagoon 28.16.6
lagoonal 40.26.12
Lagos 34.10.11
Lagrange 39.17.2
La Guardia 3.5.5
lah 10
lahar 10.21
Lahnda 17.13.20(.6)
Lahore 12.19
Lahu 16.21
laic 24.2.3
laical 40.23.12(.2)
laically 1.31.24(.9.1)
laicity 1.10.16(.16.1)
laicization 28.17.25(.3.11)
laicize 35.15.16(.4)
laid 23.4
Laidlaw 12.23.6
lain 28.4
Laing 29.4
lair 6
lairage 39.2.22(.3)
laird 23.6
lairdship 20.2.7(.15)
lairy 1.29.4
laisser-aller 4.28.3
laissez-faire 6.10
laissez-passer 4.18.6
laity 1.10.16(.2)
Laius 34.18.2
La Jolla 17.5
lake 24.3
lakefront 22.26.12
Lakeland 23.24.16(.16.3)
lakeless 34.18.29(.24)
lakelet 22.19.26(.19)
Lakenheath 32.1
Laker 17.14.3
lakeshore 12.16.9
lakeside 23.15.11(.11)
lakh 24.6
Lakshmi 1.15.20
Lalage 1.14.11, 1.26.10(.10)
Lalique® 24.1.12
Lallan 28.17.33(.5)
lallation 28.17.25(.3.14)
lalling 29.1.31(.6)
lallygag 26.5.3
Lalo 19.29.7
lam 27.6
lama 17.17.7
Lamaism 27.15.21(.2.1)

Lamaist 22.29.2(.9)
Lamarck 24.8.8
Lamarckian 28.3.5
Lamarckism 27.15.21(.2.6)
lamasery 1.29.11(.18)
Lamaze 35.4.7, 35.9
lamb 27.6
lambada 17.13.7
lambast 22.29.6(.3)
lambaste 22.29.4
lambda 17.13.19
lambdacism 27.15.21(.2.12)
lambency 1.22.23(.10.2)
lambent 22.26.15(.8)
lambently 1.31.22(.20.2)
lamber 17.17.6
lambert 22.19.9
Lambeth 32.14.7
lambhood 23.16.5(.9)
lambkin 28.2.13(.11)
lamblike 24.13.7(.16)
Lamborghini® 1.16.1(.6)
lambrequin 28.2.13(.6)
Lambretta® 17.12.5(.9)
Lambrusco 19.12.17
lambskin 28.2.13(.14)
lambswool 40.14.7
Lambton 28.17.11(.18)
LAMDA 17.13.19
lame 27.4
lamé 4.13
lamebrain 28.4.18
lamella 17.34.5(.7)
lamellae 2.32.5
lamellar 17.34.5(.7)
lamellate 22.19.26(.13)
lamellibranch 24.19.3(.6)
lamellicorn 28.11.5
lamelliform 27.10.5(.2)
lamellose 34.20.17
lamely 1.31.26(.3)
lameness 34.18.16(.24)
lament 22.26.4(.8)
lamentable 40.20.16(.11.6)
lamentably 1.31.21(.4.3)
lamentation 28.17.25(.3.3)
Lamentations 35.26.13(.15)
lamenter 17.12.22(.3)
lamentingly 1.31.28(.1.4)
lamina 17.18.16(.8)
laminae 2.17.10, 14.13
laminar 17.18.16(.8)
laminate 22.4.14(.9.2), 22.19.15(.9)
lamination 28.17.25(.3.8)
laminator 17.12.4(.10)

Lamaist 22.29.2(.9)
lamington 28.17.11(.23)
laminose 34.20.9
lamish 36.2.15
Lammas 34.18.15(.4)
lammergeier 17.6.6
Lammermuir 12.22, 17.7.12(.7)
Lamont 22.26.9, 22.26.15(.13.1)
lamp 20.16.3
lampblack 24.6.23
lampern 28.17.9
Lampeter 17.12.16(.3)
lampless 34.18.29(.20)
lamplight 22.16.25(.12)
lamplighter 17.12.13(.9)
lamplit 22.2.25
Lamplugh 16.25
lampoon 28.16.1
lampooner 17.18.15
lampoonery 1.29.11(.13.1)
lampoonist 22.29.2(.18.1)
lamp-post 22.29.17(.1)
lamprey 1.29.13
lampshade 23.4.12
Lana 17.18.8
Lanark 24.16.7
Lanarkshire 17.26.19
Lancashire 17.26.14
Lancaster 17.12.24(.5)
Lancastrian 28.3.20(.11)
lance 34.24.6
lancelet 22.19.26(.26)
Lancelot 22.11.17, 22.19.26(.13)
lanceolate 22.4.23(.2), 22.19.26(.2)
lancer 17.24.22(.3)
lancet 22.19.18
lancewood 23.16.6(.17)
Lanchester 17.12.24(.14)
Lanchow 9.12
Lancia® 3.14.16
lancinate 22.4.14(.9.3)
Lancôme® 17.17.6
Lancs 34.23.18
Land 22.26.6, 23.24.6
land 23.24.6
landau 9.4, 12.6.11
landaulette 22.5.21
Länder 17.13.20(.3)
Landers 35.18.9
Landes 23.11
landfall 40.10.11
landfill 40.2.11
landform 27.10.5(.5)
landgrave 31.3.7
landgraviate 22.3.7
landgravine 28.1.16

landholder 17.13.23(.8)
landholding 29.1.13(.16)
landing 29.1.13(.14)
Landis 34.2.9
landlady 1.11.4
Ländler 17.34.22
landless 34.18.29(.23)
landline 28.14.19(.15)
landlocked 22.23.7
landloper 17.10.16
landlord 23.12.11
landlubber 17.11.10
landmark 24.8.8
landmass 34.7.11
landmine 28.14.8
landocracy 1.22.16(.13)
landocrat 22.7.20
Landon 28.17.12(.23)
Landor 12.6.11, 17.13.20(.4)
landowner 17.18.18(.3)
landownership 20.2.7(.9)
landowning 29.1.17(.14)
landrail 40.4.14
Land-Rover® 17.21.14(.14)
Landry 1.29.16
landscape 20.3
landscapist 22.29.2(.11)
Landseer 3.14.14, 3.14.16
Landshut 22.17
landslide 23.15.16
landslip 20.2.13
Landsmål 40.10.9
landsman 28.17.16(.30)
Landsteiner 17.18.13(.1)
landward 23.18.26(.10)
lane 28.4
Lang 29.4
Langbaurgh 30.7.1
Langdale 40.4.3
Lange 1.17, 29.4
Langerhans 35.26.7
Langford 23.18.16(.17)
Langland 23.24.16(.16.4)
langlauf 30.6
Langley 1.31.28(.2)
Langmuir 17.7.12(.7)
Lango 19.13.12
Langobardic 24.2.11(.6)
langouste 22.29.14
langoustine 28.1.9(.7)
Langton 28.17.11(.23)
Langtry 1.29.15(.16)
language 39.2.21
langue 26.8, 29.5, 29.6
langue de chat 10
langue d'oc 24.9
Languedoc 24.9.5
langue d'oïl 13, 40.11
langues de chat 10

languid 23.2.21
languidly 1.31.23(.14.7)
languidness 34.18.16(.21.1)
languish 36.2.24
languisher 17.26.14
languishingly 1.31.28(.1.13)
languishment 22.26.15(.13.6)
languor 17.16.17(.2)
languorous 34.18.27(.17)
languorously 1.31.33(.12.5)
langur 17.7.6, 18.6
laniary 1.29.2(.6)
laniferous 34.18.27(.20)
lanigerous 34.18.27(.27)
lank 24.19.3
Lankester 17.12.24(.14)
lankily 1.31.17(.11)
lankiness 34.18.16(.2.4)
lankly 1.31.24(.12)
lankness 34.18.16(.22)
lanky 1.12.16
lanner 17.18.6
lanneret 22.19.24(.9)
lanolin 28.2.31(.10)
lanoline 28.1.27(.7)
Lansbury 1.29.11(.7.2)
Lansdowne 28.8.2(.10)
Lansing 29.1.23
lansker 17.14.23
lansquenet 22.5.9(.2)
lantana 17.18.3, 17.18.8(.2)
lantern 28.17.11(.22)
lanthanide 23.15.8
lanthanum 27.11.8
lanugo 19.13.8
lanyard 23.9.21, 23.18.28
Lanza 17.25.18
Lanzarote 1.10.9
Lanzhou 16.18
Lao 9
Laocoon 28.10.6, 28.17.8
Laodicean 28.17.1(.9)
Laois 36.1
Laos 34.8, 34.10.4
Laotian 28.17.25(.13)
Lao-tzu 16.15
lap 20.5
laparoscope 20.15.4(.1)
laparoscopy 1.8.11(.5)
laparotomy 1.15.13(.1)
La Paz 35.7
lapdog 26.7.4
lapel 40.5.1
lapful 40.14.6(.8)
lapicide 23.15.11(.6)
lapidary 1.29.11(.9)

lapidate 22.4.10
lapidation 28.17.25(.3.4)
lapilli 14.25.2
lapis lazuli 14.25.9
Lapith 32.2.1
Laplace 34.7.19, 34.9.7
Lapland 23.24.6(.13)
Laplander 17.13.20(.4)
Lapotaire 6.4
Lapp 20.5
lappet 22.2.5
Lappish 36.2.9
Lapsang Souchong 29.6.10
lapse 34.21.5
lapser 17.24.18
lapstone 28.19.4(.9)
lapsus calami 14.12
lapsus linguae 14.23
Laptev 31.4
laptop 20.7.4
Laputa 17.12.15(.8)
Laputan 28.17.11(.14)
lapwing 29.1.29
Lara 17.32.7
Laramie 1.15.13(.11)
larboard 23.12.2(.3), 23.18.8
larcener 17.18.16(.14)
larcenist 22.29.2(.18.1)
larcenous 34.18.16(.15.3)
larcenously 1.31.33(.12.3)
larceny 1.16.15(.14)
larch 38.7
larchwood 23.16.6(.20)
lard 23.9
lardass 34.9.3
larder 17.13.7
Lardner 17.18.22
lardon 28.17.12(.8)
lardoon 28.16.4
lardy 1.11.9
lardy-dardy 1.11.9
Laredo 19.11.4
lares 35.1.22, 35.4.16
Largactil® 40.2.5
large 39.8
largely 1.31.37
largen 28.17.28(.5)
largeness 34.18.16(.36)
largesse 34.5.12
larghetto 19.10.4
largish 36.2.23
largo 19.13.5
Largs 35.24
lariat 22.3.12
Larissa 17.24.2
lark 24.8
Larkin 28.2.13(.3)
larkiness 34.18.16(.2.4)

larkspur 18.1
larky 1.12.6
larn 28.9
La Rochelle 40.5.13
Larousse 34.17.12
larrikin 28.2.13(.6)
larrup 20.13.6
Larry 1.29.5
Lars 35.9
Larsen 28.17.23(.7)
Larson 28.17.23(.7)
larva 17.21.6
larvae 2.19
larval 40.28.6
larvicide 23.15.11(.6)
Larwood 23.16.6(.3)
laryngeal 40.3.12, 40.16.1
larynges 35.1.19, 35.1.21
laryngic 24.2.24(.7)
laryngitic 24.2.10(.2.3)
laryngitis 34.18.11(.8)
laryngology 1.26.10(.11.3)
laryngoscope 20.15.4(.1)
laryngoscopic 24.2.8(.5)
laryngoscopically 1.31.24(.9.2)
laryngoscopy 1.8.11(.5)
laryngotomy 1.15.13(.1)
larynx 34.23.18
lasagne 17.33.9
La Salle 40.6
La Scala 17.34.8
lascar 17.14.23
lascivious 34.3.8
lasciviously 1.31.33(.1.3)
lasciviousness 34.18.16(.31.1)
laser 17.25.3
laserdisc 24.20.1
LaserVision® 28.17.26(.2)
lash 36.6
lasher 17.26.6
lashing 29.1.25
lashingly 1.31.28(.1.13)
lashkar 10.8.17, 17.14.24
lashless 34.18.29(.35)
Lasker 17.14.23
Laski 1.12.17(.3)
Las Palmas 34.18.15(.19)
lasque 24.20.4
lass 34.7
lassie 1.22.6
lassitude 23.17.4(.1)
lasso 16.15, 19.20.4
lassoer 17.8, 17.9.8
Lassus 34.18.20
last 22.29.6, 22.29.8
lasting 29.1.12(.21)
lastingly 1.31.28(.1.4)
lastingness 34.18.16(.26)

leakage **39.2.12**
leaker **17.14.1**
Leakey **1.12.1**
leakiness **34.18.16(.2.4)**
leakproof **30.13.4**
leaky **1.12.1**
leal **40.1**
Leamington Spa **10**
lean **28.1**
lean-burn **28.18.3**
Leander **17.13.20(.4)**
leaning **29.1.17(.1)**
leanly **1.31.27(.1)**
Leanne **28.7**
leanness **34.18.16(.25)**
leant **22.26.4**
lean-to **16.7.7**
leap **20.1**
leaper **17.10.1**
leapfrog **26.7.13**
leapt **22.22.3**
Lear **3**
learn **28.18**
learnability **1.10.16(.22.1)**
learnable **40.20.16(.16.3)**
learned **22.26.16, 23.18.14, 23.24.17**
learnedly **1.31.23(.14.6)**
learnedness **34.18.16(.21.1)**
learner **17.18.17**
learnt **22.26.16**
leasable **40.20.16(.21.1)**
lease **34.1**
leaseback **24.6.6(.20)**
leasehold **23.31.13(.9)**
leaseholder **17.13.23(.8)**
leaser **17.24.1**
leash **36.1**
least **22.29.1**
leastways **35.4.15**
leastwise **35.15.19**
leat **22.1**
leather **17.23.4**
leatherback **24.6.6(.9)**
leathercloth **32.9**
leatherette **22.5.19**
Leatherhead **23.5.13(.5)**
leatheriness **34.18.16(.2.9)**
leatherjacket **22.2.9(.3)**
leathern **28.17.22**
leatherneck **24.4.7**
leatheroid **23.13.19**
leatherwear **6.18.4**
leathery **1.29.11(.17)**
leave **31.1**
leaven **28.17.20(.4)**
leaver **17.21.1**
leaves **35.28.1**

leavings **35.27**
Leavis **34.18.18**
Lebanese **35.1.12**
Lebanon **28.17.17(.10)**
Le Bardo **19.11.7**
Lebensraum **27.7**
Leblanc **11.19, 24.19.4, 24.19.5**
Lebowa **17.9.1**
Lec® **24.4**
Le Carré **4.26.4**
lech **38.4**
lecher **17.28.5**
lecherous **34.18.27(.26)**
lecherously **1.31.33(.12.5)**
lecherousness **34.18.16(.31.5)**
lechery **1.29.11(.22)**
Lechlade **23.4.16**
lecithin **28.17.21**
Leclanché **4.20**
Leconfield **23.31.1(.2)**
Le Corbusier **4.2.8**
lectern **28.17.11(.20), 28.18.4**
lection **28.17.25(.15.2)**
lectionary **1.29.11(.13.2)**
lector **12.5.7**
lectrice **34.1.7**
lecture **17.28.20**
lecturer **17.32.14(.19)**
lecturership **20.2.7(.9)**
lectureship **20.2.7(.9)**
lecythi **14.16**
lecythus **34.18.19**
LED **2.13**
led **23.5**
Leda **17.13.1**
Ledbury **1.29.11(.7.2)**
Lederhosen **28.17.24(.14)**
ledge **39.5**
ledger **17.29.4**
ledgy **1.26.3**
lee **2**
leech **38.1**
leechcraft **22.27.4(.4)**
Leeds **35.23.1**
Lee-Enfield **23.31.1(.2)**
leek **24.1**
leer **3**
leeriness **34.18.16(.2.9)**
leeringly **1.31.28(.1.17)**
leery **1.29.2**
lees **35.1**
leet **22.1**
leeward **23.18.5, 23.18.26(.1)**
leewardly **1.31.23(.14.1)**
leeway **4.25.1**
left **22.27.2**

leftie **1.10.24**
leftish **36.2.11**
leftism **27.15.21(.2.4)**
leftist **22.29.2(.13)**
leftmost **22.29.17(.4)**
left-over **17.21.14**
leftover **17.21.14(.4)**
leftward **23.18.26(.9)**
lefty **1.10.24**
leg **26.4**
legacy **1.22.16(.7)**
legal **40.24.1**
legalese **35.1, 35.1.23**
legalism **27.15.21(.2.15)**
legalist **22.29.2(.31.2)**
legalistic **24.2.10(.15.3)**
legalistically **1.31.24(.9.6)**
legality **1.10.16(.32.6)**
legalization **28.17.25(.3.12)**
legalize **35.15.21(.4.4)**
legally **1.31.17(.12)**
legate **22.19.13**
legatee **2.11**
legateship **20.2.8**
legatine **28.2.11(.10)**
legation **28.17.25(.3.6)**
legato **19.10.7**
legator **17.12.4(.8)**
legend **23.24.16(.14)**
legendarily **1.31.17(.27.3)**
legendary **1.29.11(.9)**
legendry **1.29.16**
leger **17.29.4**
leger line **28.14**
Leggatt **22.19.13**
Legge **26.4**
legged **23.18.12, 23.22**
legger **17.16.4**
legginess **34.18.16(.2.4)**
legging **29.1.15**
leggy **1.14.4**
leghorn **28.11.10**
legibility **1.10.16(.22.1)**
legible **40.20.16(.25)**
legibly **1.31.21(.7.4)**
legion **28.17.28(.1)**
legionary **1.29.11(.13.2)**
legionella **17.34.5(.8)**
legionellae **2.32.5**
legionnaire **6.9**
legislate **22.4.23(.12)**
legislation **28.17.25(.3.14)**
legislative **31.2.1(.9.4)**
legislatively **1.31.30(.7.1)**
legislator **17.12.4(.16)**
legislature **17.28.15**
legit **22.2.21**
legitimacy **1.22.16(.8)**

legitimate **22.19.14**
legitimately **1.31.22(.15)**
legitimation **28.17.25(.3.7)**
legitimatization **28.17.25(.3.12)**
legitimatize **35.15.7(.7)**
legitimism **27.15.21(.2.8)**
legitimist **22.29.2(.17)**
legitimization **28.17.25(.3.12)**
legitimize **35.15.11**
legless **34.18.29(.25)**
legman **28.7.10(.14)**
legmen **28.5.7(.18)**
Lego® **19.13.4**
legroom **27.14.6(.11)**
legume **27.14.7**
leguminous **34.18.16(.15.3)**
legwork **24.17.6(.11)**
Lehár **10.21**
Le Havre **17.32.26**
Lehmann **28.17.16(.1)**
lehr **3, 6**
Lehrer **17.32.2, 17.32.5**
lei **4**
Leibniz **34.22.2**
Leibnizian **28.3.13**
Leica® **17.14.12**
Leicester **17.12.24(.4)**
Leicestershire **17.26.14**
Leichhardt **22.10.11**
Leiden **28.17.12(.4)**
Leif **30.1**
Leigh **2**
Leighton **28.17.11(.3)**
Leila **17.34.1, 17.34.4**
Leinster **17.12.24(.23)**
Leipzig **26.2.6**
Leishman **28.17.16(.31)**
leishmaniasis **34.2.17(.10.1)**
Leister **17.12.24(.4)**
leister **17.12.24(.1)**
leisure **17.27.3**
leisureless **34.18.29(.17.5)**
leisureliness **34.18.16(.2.10)**
leisurely **1.31.17(.23)**
leisurewear **6.18.4**
Leitch **38.1**
Leith **32.1**
leitmotif **30.1.1**
leitmotive **31.2.1(.11)**
Leitrim **27.2.14**
Leix **36.1, 36.4**
lek **24.4**
Leland **23.24.16(.16.1)**
Lely **1.31.1**
LEM **27.5**

leman **28.17.16(.1)**
Le Mans **11**
Lemesurier **17.32.14(.18)**
lemma **17.17.5**
lemmatization **28.17.25(.3.11)**
lemmatize **35.15.7(.7)**
lemme **1.15.4**
lemming **29.1.16**
Lemmon **28.17.16(.5)**
Lemnos **34.10.13**
lemon **28.17.16(.5)**
lemonade **23.4.8**
lemony **1.16.15(.11)**
lempira **17.32.2**
Lemuel **40.16.14**
lemur **17.17.1**
lemurine **28.14.18**
lemuroid **23.13.19**
Len **28.5**
Lena **17.18.1, 17.18.3**
lend **23.24.5**
lendable **40.20.16(.12)**
lender **17.13.20(.3)**
Lendl **40.22.16**
length **32.19**
lengthen **28.17.21**
lengthener **17.18.16(.12)**
lengthily **1.31.17(.18)**
lengthiness **34.18.16(.2.6)**
lengthman **28.17.16(.28)**
lengthways **35.4.15**
lengthwise **35.15.19**
lengthy **1.20.11**
lenience **34.24.2**
leniency **1.22.23(.2)**
lenient **22.26.2(.5)**
leniently **1.31.22(.20.1)**
Lenihan **28.17.29**
Lenin **28.2.18**
Leninakan **28.7.8**
Leningrad **23.7.16**
Leninism **27.15.21(.2.9)**
Leninist **22.29.2(.18.1)**
Leninite **22.16.14(.6)**
lenis **34.2.13**
lenite **22.16.14**
lenition **28.17.25(.2.4)**
lenitive **31.2.1(.9.2)**
lenity **1.10.16(.13)**
Lennie **1.16.5**
Lennon **28.17.17(.4)**
Lennox **34.23.15**
Lenny **1.16.5**
leno **19.15.1**
Lenor® **12.10**
Lenora **17.32.10(.7)**
Lenore **12.10**
Le Nôtre **17.32.19(.5)**
lens **35.26.5**

lensless **34.18.29(.34)**
lensman **28.17.16(.30)**
lent **22.26.4**
Lenten **28.17.11(.22)**
lenticel **40.5.11**
lenticular **17.34.16(.21.2)**
lentigo **19.13.7**
lentil **40.2.5, 40.21.17(.2)**
lentisc **24.20.1**
lento **19.10.17**
lentoid **23.13.7**
Leo **19.1**
Leofric **24.2.26(.19)**
Leominster **17.12.24(.22)**
Leon **28.10.1, 28.10.3, 28.17.1, 28.17.2**
León **28.10**
Leona **17.18.18**
Leonard **23.18.14**
Leonardo **19.11.7**
leone **28.19**
Leonid **23.2.13**
Léonie **1.16.15(.1), 1.16.17**
leonine **28.14.9**
Leonora **17.32.10(.7)**
leopard **23.18.7**
leopardess **34.5.3**
Leopold **23.31.13(.1)**
Léopoldville **40.2.12**
leotard **23.9.7**
leper **17.10.4**
lepidolite **22.16.25(.9)**
Lepidoptera **17.32.14(.6)**
lepidopteran **28.17.31(.11)**
lepidopterist **22.29.2(.29.3)**
lepidopterous **34.18.27(.14)**
Lepidus **34.18.12**
leporine **28.14.18**
leprechaun **28.11.5**
leprosaria **3.22.4**
leprosarium **27.3.17(.3)**
leprosy **1.22.16(.13)**
leprous **34.18.27(.12)**
lepta **17.12.19**
Leptis Magna **17.18.24**
leptocephalic **24.2.27(.6)**
leptocephalous **34.18.29(.17.4)**
leptodactyl **40.21.16**
lepton **28.10.9**
leptonic **24.2.15(.6.1)**
leptospirosis **34.2.17(.11.2)**
leptotene **28.1.9(.3)**
Lepus **34.18.9(.1)**
Lermontov **31.7**
Leroy **13.15**
Lerwick **24.2.25**

Les **35.5**
Lesage **37.4.6**
lesbian **28.3.2**
lesbianism **27.15.21(.2.9)**
Lesbos **34.10.7**
lèse-majesté **1.10.26(.11)**
lesion **28.17.26(.1)**
Lesley **1.31.34**
Leslie **1.31.34**
Lesney **1.16.27**
Lesotho **16.7.3, 19.10.14**
less **34.5**
lessee **2.22**
lesseeship **20.2.7(.1)**
lessen **28.17.23(.5)**
Lesseps **34.21.4**
lesser **17.24.5**
Lessing **29.1.23**
lesson **28.17.23(.5)**
lessor **12.14, 12.14.3**
lest **22.29.5**
Lester **17.12.24(.4)**
let **22.5**
Letchworth **32.14.15**
letdown **28.8.2(.5)**
lethal **40.29**
lethality **1.10.16(.32.10)**
lethally **1.31.17(.18)**
lethargic **24.2.24(.3)**
lethargically **1.31.24(.9.11)**
lethargy **1.26.10(.7)**
Lethbridge **39.2.22(.10)**
Lethe **1.20.1**
Lethean **28.3.11**
Leticia **3.16.2, 17.26.2**
Letitia **3.16.2, 17.26.2**
Letraset® **22.5.13(.4)**
Lett **22.5**
letter **17.12.5**
letterbox **34.23.8(.2)**
letterer **17.32.14(.6)**
letterhead **23.5.13(.5)**
letterless **34.18.29(.17.2)**
Letterman **28.17.16(.16)**
letterpress **34.5.14(.4)**
Lettic **24.2.10(.3.1)**
Lettice **34.2.8**
letting **29.1.12(.4)**
Lettish **36.2.11**
lettuce **34.18.11(.4)**
letup **20.9.5**
leu **16.2**
Leuchars **35.18.10**
leucine **28.1.18(.5)**
leucoblast **22.29.6(.12), 22.29.8(.8)**
leucocyte **22.16.19(.9)**
leucocytic **24.2.10(.2.3)**
leucoderma **17.17.15**

leucoma **17.17.16(.4)**
leucopathy **1.20.8**
leucopenia **3.9.1**
leucoplast **22.29.6(.12), 22.29.8(.8)**
leucorrhoea **17.1.16**
leucotome **27.17.4**
leucotomize **35.15.11**
leucotomy **1.15.13(.1)**
leukaemia **3.8.1**
leukaemic **24.2.14(.1)**
leukaemogen **28.17.28(.9)**
leukaemogenic **24.2.15(.4)**
leukotriene **28.1.3**
Leuven **28.5.9**
lev **31.4**
leva **17.21.4**
Levalloisean **28.3.14**
levant **22.26.6**
levanter **17.12.22(.4)**
Levantine **28.14.5**
levator **17.12.4(.11)**
levee **1.19.4, 4.16**
level **40.28.4**
leveller **17.34.16(.14)**
levelly **1.31.17(.17)**
levelness **34.18.16(.37.5)**
lever **17.21.1**
leverage **39.2.22(.9)**
leveret **22.19.24(.9)**
Leverhulme **27.14.7**
Le Verrier **4.2.9**
Levi **1.19.1, 1.19.4, 14.15**
leviable **40.20.3**
leviathan **28.17.21**
levigate **22.4.12(.5)**
levigation **28.17.25(.3.6)**
levin **28.2.20**
Levine **28.1.16**
levirate **22.19.24(.1)**
leviratic **24.2.10(.4.5)**
leviratical **40.23.12(.7.1)**
Levi's® **35.15.14**
levitate **22.4.9(.5)**
levitation **28.17.25(.3.3)**
levitator **17.12.4(.5)**
Levite **22.16.17**
Levitical **40.23.12(.7.1)**
Leviticus **34.18.13(.10)**
Levittown **28.8.1**
levity **1.10.16(.15)**
levy **1.19.4**
lewd **23.17**
lewdly **1.31.23(.13)**
lewdness **34.18.16(.21.1)**
Lewes **34.2.4**
lewis **34.2.4**
Lewisham **27.15.22**

light-headedness
34.18.16(.21.1)
light-hearted 23.18.9(.7)
light-heartedly
1.31.23(.14.3)
light-heartedness
34.18.16(.21.1)
lighthouse 34.8.6(.11)
lighting 29.1.12(.11)
lightish 36.2.11
lightless 34.18.29(.22)
lightly 1.31.22(.13)
lightness 34.18.16(.20.2)
lightning 29.1.17(.15)
light of day 4
light-o'-love 31.8
lightproof 30.13.4
lightship 20.2.8
lightsome 27.15.20(.13)
lightsomely 1.31.26(.11)
lightsomeness
34.18.16(.24)
lightweight 22.4.21
lightwood 23.16.6(.9)
lign-aloe 19.29.5
ligneous 34.3.6(.8)
ligniferous 34.18.27(.20)
lignification
28.17.25(.3.5)
ligniform 27.10.5(.2)
lignify 14.14.4(.7)
lignin 28.2.18
lignite 22.16.14(.10)
lignitic 24.2.10(.2.2)
lignocaine 28.4.5
lignum 27.15.14(.15)
lignum vitae 2.12.8
ligroin 28.2.8
ligroine 28.1.6
ligulate 22.4.23(.7.3)
ligule 40.15.9(.6)
Liguria 3.22.12
Ligurian 28.3.20(.8)
ligustrum 27.15.26(.10)
likability 1.10.16(.22.1)
likableness
34.18.16(.37.4)
like 24.13
likeability 1.10.16(.22.1)
likeable 40.20.16(.13)
likeableness
34.18.16(.37.4)
likeably 1.31.21(.5)
likelihood 23.16.5(.1)
likeliness 34.18.16(.2.10)
likely 1.31.24(.8)
like-minded 23.18.10(.14)
like-mindedly
1.31.23(.14.4)
like-mindedness
34.18.16(.21.1)

liken 28.17.13(.10)
likeness 34.18.16(.22)
likewise 35.15.19
liking 29.1.14(.9)
Likud 23.16.2
likuta 17.12.15(.2)
lilac 24.16.16
lilangeni 1.16.4
liliaceous 34.18.22(.3)
Lilian 28.3.21(.2)
Lilienthal 40.8.4
Lilith 32.14.17
Lille 40.1
Lillee 1.31.2
Lil-lets® 34.22.4
Lilley 1.31.2
Lillian 28.3.21(.2)
Lilliburlero 19.27.3
Lillie 1.31.2
Lilliput 22.15.1, 22.17
Lilliputian 28.17.25(.11)
Lilly 1.31.2
lillywhite 22.16.23
lilo 19.29.9
Lilongwe 1.28, 4.25.18
lilt 22.32.1
lily 1.31.2
lily-livered 23.18.17
Lima 17.17.1
Limassol 40.9.14
limb 27.2
limber 17.11.17(.1), 17.17.2
limberness
34.18.16(.15.2)
limbi 14.7
limbic 24.2.9(.8)
limbless 34.18.29(.26)
limbo 19.9.14
Limburg 26.14.1(.8)
Limburger 17.16.14
limbus 34.18.10
lime 27.12
limeade 23.4
Limehouse 34.8.6(.15)
limejuice 34.17.10
limekiln 28.20
limeless 34.18.29(.26)
limelight 22.16.25(.16)
limen 28.5.7(.8),
28.17.16(.13)
limepit 22.2.5
limerick 24.2.26(.10)
limestone 28.19.4(.9)
limewash 36.9.5
lime-wort 22.20.15
limey 1.15.11
limina 17.18.16(.8)
liminal 40.26.13(.8)
liminality 1.10.16(.32.8)
limit 22.2.11

limitable 40.20.16(.11.3)
limitary 1.29.11(.8.7)
limitation 28.17.25(.3.3)
limitative 31.2.1(.9.1)
limited 23.18.9(.13)
limitedly 1.31.23(.14.3)
limitedness
34.18.16(.21.1)
limiter 17.12.16(.9.1)
limitless 34.18.29(.22)
limitlessly 1.31.33(.12.6)
limitlessness
34.18.16(.31.6)
limn 27.2
limner 17.17.2, 17.18.25
limnological
40.23.12(.17.2)
limnologist 22.29.2(.26.4)
limnology 1.26.10(.11.4)
limo 19.14.2
Limoges 37.9
Limousin 8
limousine 28.1.19
limp 20.16.1
limpet 22.2.5
limpid 23.2.6
limpidity 1.10.16(.9)
limpidly 1.31.23(.14.2)
limpidness
34.18.16(.21.1)
limpingly 1.31.28(.1.2)
limpkin 28.2.13(.8)
limply 1.31.20
limpness 34.18.16(.18)
Limpopo 19.8
limpwort 22.20.15
limp-wristed 23.18.9(.20)
limuli 14.25.9
limulus 34.18.29(.17.6)
Linacre 17.14.15(.9)
linage 39.2.15
Linch 38.18.1
linchpin 28.2.9
Lincoln 28.17.13(.17)
Lincolnshire 17.26.21
Lincrusta® 17.12.24(.10)
Lincs 34.23.18
linctus 34.18.11(.13)
Lind 23.24.2
Linda 17.13.20(.1)
lindane 28.4.4
Lindbergh 26.14.1(.7)
Lindemann
28.17.16(.10)
linden 28.17.12(.23)
Lindisfarne 28.9.7
Lindley 1.31.23(.17)
Lindon 28.17.12(.23)
Lindsay 1.23.18, 1.23.20
Lindsey 1.23.18, 1.23.20
Lindwall 40.10.17

Lindy 1.11.20(.1)
line 28.14
lineage 39.2.2
lineal 40.3.7(.2)
lineally 1.31.3(.7)
lineament 22.26.15(.13.1)
linear 3.9.2
linearity 1.10.16(.21.1)
linearize 35.15.20(.1)
linearly 1.31.3(.7)
lineation 28.17.25(.3.1)
linebacker 17.14.5
linefeed 23.1.6
Linehan 28.17.29
Lineker 17.14.15(.9)
lineman 28.17.16(.25)
linen 28.2.18
linenfold 23.31.13(.7)
lineout 22.9.11
liner 17.18.13
linertrain 28.4.18
lineshooter 17.12.15(.4)
lineside 23.15.11(.12)
linesman 28.17.16(.30)
lineup 20.9.9
Linford 23.18.16(.16)
ling 29.1
linga 17.16.17(.1)
Lingala 17.34.8
lingam 27.15.12
linger 17.16.17(.1)
lingerer 17.32.14(.9)
lingerie 1.29.11(.21)
lingeringly 1.31.28(.1.17)
Lingfield 23.31.1(.2)
lingo 19.13.12
lingua franca 17.14.21(.3)
lingual 40.35.4
lingualize 35.15.21(.4.6)
lingually 1.31.17(.26)
Linguaphone® 28.19.11
linguiform 27.10.5(.2)
linguine 1.16.1(.14)
linguist 22.29.2(.28)
linguistic 24.2.10(.15.2)
linguistically
1.31.24(.9.6)
linguistician
28.17.25(.2.2)
linguodental 40.21.17(.2)
lingy 1.17
liniment 22.26.15(.13.2)
lining 29.1.17(.10)
link 24.19.1
linkage 39.2.12
Linklater 17.12.4(.16),
17.12.16(.20)
linkman 28.7.10(.13)
linkmen 28.5.7(.17)
linkup 20.9.7

I

logo **19.13.6, 19.13.11**
logogram **27.6.17(.5)**
logographer **17.20.12(.5)**
logomachy **1.12.13**
logon **28.10, 28.10.12**
logopaedic **24.2.11(.1)**
logorrhoea **17.1.16**
logorrhoeic **24.2.1**
logos **34.10.11**
logotype **20.10.2**
logroll **40.18.14**
logroller **17.34.18(.14)**
Logue **26.15**
logwood **23.16.6(.12)**
Lohengrin **28.2.29(.11)**
loin **28.12**
loincloth **32.9**
loir **10, 17.5**
Loire **10**
Lois **34.2.5**
loiter **17.12.11**
loiterer **17.32.14(.6)**
Loki **1.12.15**
Lola **17.34.18**
Lolita **17.12.1(.15)**
loll **40.9**
lollapalooza **17.25.14**
Lollard **23.9.22, 23.18.29**
Lollardism **27.15.21(.2.5)**
Lollardy **1.11.9, 1.11.17**
loller **17.34.9**
lollipop **20.7.2**
lollop **20.13.7**
lolly **1.31.10**
Lomas **34.7.11, 34.18.15(.12)**
Lomax **34.23.5(.6)**
Lombard **23.9.6**
Lombardi **1.11.9**
Lombardic **24.2.11(.6)**
Lombardy **1.11.17**
Lombok **24.9.3**
Lomé **4.13**
loment **22.26.4(.8), 22.26.15(.13.2)**
lomentaceous **34.18.22(.3)**
London **28.17.12(.23)**
Londonderry **1.29.3**
Londoner **17.18.16(.5)**
lone **28.19**
loneliness **34.18.16(.2.10)**
lonely **1.31.27(.16)**
loner **17.18.18**
lonesome **27.15.20(.18)**
lonesomely **1.31.26(.11)**
lonesomeness **34.18.16(.24)**
long **29.6**
longanimity **1.10.16(.12)**

long-awaited **23.18.9(.3)**
Long Beach **38.1**
longboard **23.12.2(.13)**
longboat **22.21.2**
Longbottom **27.15.9(.6)**
longbow **19.9.16**
Longbridge **39.2.22(.10)**
Longden **28.17.12(.24)**
longe **39.17.7, 39.17.8**
longeron **28.10.24(.5)**
longevity **1.10.16(.15)**
Longfellow **19.29.4**
Longford **23.18.16(.17)**
longhair **6.17**
longhand **23.24.6(.11)**
longhop **20.7.11**
longhorn **28.11.10**
longhouse **34.8.6(.17)**
longicorn **28.11.5**
longing **29.1.18**
longingly **1.31.28(.1.7)**
Longinus **34.18.16(.1)**
longish **36.2.17**
longitude **23.17.4(.1)**
longitudinal **40.26.13(.5)**
longitudinally **1.31.17(.14.2)**
long jump **20.16.5**
Longleat **22.1.18**
Longman **28.17.16(.26)**
longship **20.2.7(.20)**
longshore **12.16.13**
longshoreman **28.17.16(.11)**
longstop **20.7.4**
Longton **28.17.11(.23)**
Longtown **28.8.1**
longueur **18.6**
longways **35.4.15**
longwise **35.15.19**
lonicera **17.32.14(.16)**
Lonnie **1.16.9**
Lonrho® **19.27.19**
Lonsdale **40.4.3**
loo **16**
Looe **16**
loof **30.13**
loofa **17.20.11**
loofah **17.20.11**
look **24.14**
lookalike **24.13.7(.8)**
looker **17.14.13**
lookout **22.9.9**
look-see **2.22.11**
lookup **20.9.7**
loom **27.14**
loon **28.16**
looniness **34.18.16(.2.5)**
loony **1.16.14**
loop **20.12**

looper **17.10.13**
loophole **40.18.13**
loopiness **34.18.16(.2.2)**
loopy **1.8.10**
loose **34.17**
loosebox **34.23.8(.2)**
loosely **1.31.33(.11)**
loosen **28.17.23(.13)**
loosener **17.18.16(.14)**
looseness **34.18.16(.31.2)**
loosestrife **30.12**
loosish **36.2.21**
loot **22.18**
looter **17.12.15**
lop **20.7**
lope **20.15**
López **35.5.3**
lophobranch **24.19.3(.6)**
lophodont **22.26.9**
lophophore **12.11.3, 12.11.4**
lopolith **32.2.9**
lopper **17.10.8**
loppy **1.8.7**
lopsided **23.18.10(.11)**
lopsidedly **1.31.23(.14.4)**
lopsidedness **34.18.16(.21.1)**
loquacious **34.18.22(.3)**
loquaciously **1.31.33(.12.4)**
loquaciousness **34.18.16(.31.4)**
loquacity **1.10.16(.16.1)**
loquat **22.11.14, 22.19.23**
loquitur **17.12.16(.17)**
lor **12**
loral **40.16.13(.8)**
loran **28.17.31(.8)**
Lorca **17.14.9**
Lorcan **28.17.13(.8)**
lorch **38.9**
lorcha **17.28.10**
lord **23.12**
lordless **34.18.29(.23)**
lordlike **24.13.7(.13)**
lordliness **34.18.16(.2.10)**
lordling **29.1.31(.18)**
lordly **1.31.23(.9)**
lordosis **34.2.17(.11.1)**
lordotic **24.2.10(.6)**
lordship **20.2.7(.15)**
Lordy **1.11.11**
lore **12**
L'Oréal® **40.6.2**
Lorelei **14.25.9**
Loren **28.5.18, 28.17.31(.8)**
Lorentz **34.22.18, 34.24.10(.16)**
Lorenz **35.26.13(.18)**

Lorenzo **19.21**
Loreto **19.10.4**
Loretta **17.12.5**
lorgnette **22.5.20**
lorgnon **28.17.32**
loricate **22.4.11(.6)**
lorikeet **22.1.4**
lorimer **17.17.14(.10)**
loris **34.2.21**
lorn **28.11**
Lorna **17.18.10**
Lorraine **28.4.18**
lorry **1.29.7**
lorryload **23.20.13**
lory **1.29.8**
losable **40.20.16(.22)**
Los Alamos **34.10.12**
Los Angeles **35.1.23**
lose **35.17**
loser **17.25.14**
Losey **1.23.15**
loss **34.10**
Lossiemouth **32.7**
lost **22.29.9**
Lostwithiel **40.3.9**
lot **22.11**
Lothario **15.1.12**
Lothian **28.3.12**
loti **1.10.15, 1.10.18**
lotic **24.2.10(.11)**
lotion **28.17.25(.13)**
lotsa **17.24.19**
lotta **17.12.9**
lottery **1.29.11(.8.4)**
Lottie **1.10.9**
lotto **19.10.8**
lotus **34.18.11(.11)**
Lou **16**
louche **36.14**
loud **23.8**
louden **28.17.12(.7)**
loudhailer **17.34.4**
loudish **36.2.12**
loudly **1.31.23(.6)**
loudmouth **32.7**
loudmouthed **23.27**
loudness **34.18.16(.21.1)**
loudspeaker **17.14.1**
Louella **17.34.5**
lough **24.9, 25.6**
Loughborough **17.32.14(.5)**
Loughlin **28.17.33(.20)**
Lough Neagh **4**
Loughor **17.14.11, 17.15**
Louie **1(.6)**
Louis **2.7, 34.2.4**
louis **1(.6), 35.2.1**
Louisa **17.25.1**
Louisburg **26.14.1(.10)**

Louise **35.1**
Louisiana **17.18.6**
Louisianan **28.17.17(.5)**
Louisville **40.2.12**
lounge **39.17.5**
lounger **17.29.16(.5)**
Lounsbury **1.29.11(.7.2)**
loupe **20.12**
lour **17.3**
Lourdes **23.18.4, 35.23.7,**
35.23.12
Lourenço Marques
34.23.7
louringly **1.31.28(.1.17)**
loury **1.29.11(.1)**
louse **34.8**
lousewort **22.20.15**
lousily **1.31.17(.21)**
lousiness **34.18.16(.2.7)**
lousy **1.23.6**
lout **22.9**
Louth **32.7**
loutish **36.2.11**
loutishly **1.31.35(.7.1)**
loutishness
34.18.16(.33.3)
Louvain **8, 28.7.13**
Louvre **17.32.26, 31.10**
louvre **17.21.11**
lovability **1.10.16(.22.1)**
lovable **40.20.16(.19)**
lovableness
34.18.16(.37.4)
lovably **1.31.21(.7.1)**
lovage **39.2.17**
lovat **22.19.17**
love **31.8**
loveably **1.31.21(.7.1)**
lovebird **23.19.1**
lovebite **22.16.8**
love child **23.31.9**
love children
28.17.31(.15)
Loveday **4.10.13**
Lovejoy **13.12**
Lovelace **34.4.14**
loveless **34.18.29(.30)**
lovelessly **1.31.33(.12.6)**
lovelessness
34.18.16(.31.6)
lovelily **1.31.17(.29)**
loveliness **34.18.16(.2.10)**
Lovell **40.28.8**
lovelock **24.9.16(.18)**
lovelorn **28.11.13**
lovely **1.31.30(.5)**
lovemaking **29.1.14(.3)**
lover **17.21.9**
Loveridge **39.2.22(.9)**
loverless **34.18.29(.17.4)**
loverlike **24.13.7(.8)**

lovesick **24.2.20(.16)**
lovesickness
34.18.16(.22)
lovesome **27.15.20(.19)**
loveworthy **1.21**
lovey **1.19.7**
lovey-dovey **1.19.7**
lovingly **1.31.28(.1.9)**
lovingness **34.18.16(.26)**
low **19**
lowball **40.10.4**
lowboy **13.3**
lowbrow **9.16**
lowbrowed **23.8**
low-cal **40.6.6**
low-calorie **1.29.11(.27)**
low-down **28.8.2**
Lowell **40.16.9**
Löwenbräu **9.16**
lower **17.3, 17.9**
lowermost **22.29.17(.4)**
Lowery **1.29.11(.1)**
Lowestoft **22.27.5**
lowish **36.2.8**
lowland **23.24.16(.16.2)**
lowlander **17.13.20(.13)**
lowlife **30.12**
lowlight **22.16.25(.11)**
lowlily **1.31.17(.29)**
lowliness **34.18.16(.2.10)**
lowly **1.31.19**
Lowman **28.17.16(.18)**
Lowndes **35.23.15**
lowness **34.18.16(.17)**
Lowrie **1.29.11(.1)**
low-rise **35.15.20**
Lowry **1.29.11(.1)**
low season **28.17.24(.1)**
lox **34.23.8**
Loxene **28.1.18(.7)**
Loxley **1.31.33(.15)**
loxodrome **27.17.13**
loxodromic **24.2.14(.6)**
loyal **40.16.5**
loyalism **27.15.21(.2.15)**
loyalist **22.29.2(.31.1)**
loyally **1.31.17(.2)**
loyalty **1.10.28**
lozenge **39.17.9**
lozengy **1.26.13**
Lualaba **17.11.7**
Luanda **17.13.20(.4)**
Luandan **28.17.12(.23)**
Luang Prabang **29.4.2**
luau **9.1**
lubber **17.11.10**
lubberlike **24.13.7(.8)**
lubberly **1.31.17(.8)**
Lubbock **24.16.3**
lube **21.13**

Lübeck **24.4.3**
Lublin **28.2.31(.14)**
lubra **17.32.18**
lubricant **22.26.15(.11)**
lubricate **22.4.11(.6)**
lubrication **28.17.25(.3.5)**
lubricative **31.2.1(.9.1)**
lubricator **17.12.4(.7)**
lubricious **34.18.22(.2)**
lubricity **1.10.16(.16.1)**
Lubumbashi **1.24.5**
Lubyanka **17.14.21(.3)**
Lucan **28.17.13(.12)**
Lucania **3.9.3(.4)**
lucarne **28.9.4**
Lucas **34.18.13(.9)**
luce **34.17**
lucency **1.22.23(.10.4)**
lucent **22.26.15(.17.3)**
Lucerne **28.18.9**
Lucey **1.22.15**
Lucia **3.14.8, 3.16.6, 17.1.13**
Lucian **28.3.13, 28.3.15,**
28.17.25(.11)
lucid **23.2.16**
lucidity **1.10.16(.9)**
lucidly **1.31.23(.14.7)**
lucidness **34.18.16(.21.1)**
Lucie **1.22.15**
Lucifer **17.20.12(.3)**
lucifer **17.20.12(.3)**
luciferin **28.2.29(.5)**
Lucille **40.1.10**
Lucinda **17.13.20(.1)**
Lucite® **22.16.19(.8)**
Lucius **34.3.10,**
34.18.22(.7)
luck **24.12**
luckily **1.31.17(.11)**
luckiness **34.18.16(.2.4)**
luckless **34.18.29(.24)**
lucklessly **1.31.33(.12.6)**
lucklessness
34.18.16(.31.6)
Lucknow **9.7**
lucky **1.12.9**
Lucozade® **23.4.11**
lucrative **31.2.1(.9.4)**
lucratively **1.31.30(.7.1)**
lucrativeness
34.18.16(.28.1)
lucre **17.14.14**
Lucrece **34.1.7**
Lucretia **17.26.1**
Lucretius **34.18.22(.1)**
lucubrate **22.4.22(.7)**
lucubration
28.17.25(.3.13)
lucubrator **17.12.4(.15)**
luculent **22.26.15(.25)**
luculently **1.31.22(.20.5)**

Lucullan **28.17.33(.9)**
Lucy **1.22.15**
Luda **17.13.14**
Luddism **27.15.21(.2.5)**
Luddite **22.16.10**
Ludditism **27.15.21(.2.4)**
lude **23.17**
Ludendorff **30.9.1**
Ludgate **22.4.12(.8),**
22.19.13
ludic **24.2.11(.11)**
ludicrous **34.18.27(.16)**
ludicrously **1.31.33(.12.5)**
ludicrousness
34.18.16(.31.5)
Ludlow **19.29.18**
Ludlum **27.15.28(.17)**
ludo **19.11.10**
Ludovic **24.2.17**
Ludwig **26.2.5, 26.2.9**
lues **35.1.3**
luetic **24.2.10(.1)**
luff **30.11**
luffa **17.20.9**
Luftwaffe **17.20.5**
lug **26.10**
Lugano **19.15.7**
Lugard **23.9.10**
luge **37.7, 39.13**
Luger® **17.16.12**
luggable **40.20.16(.14)**
luggage **39.2.13**
lugger **17.16.9**
lughole **40.18.13**
lugsail **40.4.10, 40.31.19**
lugubrious **34.3.15(.7)**
lugubriously **1.31.33(.1.4)**
lugubriousness
34.18.16(.31.1)
lugworm **27.16.7**
Luick **24.2.6**
Lukács **38.5**
Luke **24.15**
lukewarm **27.10.7**
lukewarmly **1.31.26(.8)**
lukewarmness
34.18.16(.24)
lull **40.12**
lullaby **14.7**
Lully **1.31.15**
lulu **16.25**
Lulworth **32.14.15**
lum **27.11**
Lumb **27.11**
lumbago **19.13.3**
lumbar **17.11.17(.6)**
lumber **17.11.17(.6)**
lumberer **17.32.14(.5)**
lumberjack **24.6.18**
lumberman **28.7.10(.6),**
28.17.16(.16)

lumbermen 28.5.7(.10)
lumbersome 27.15.20(.11)
lumberyard 23.9.21
lumbrical 40.23.12(.18)
lumen 28.5.7(.9), 28.17.16(.15)
lumière 6, 6.1
luminaire 6.9
luminal 40.26.13(.8)
luminance 34.24.10(.15)
luminary 1.29.11(.13.2)
luminesce 34.5.6
luminescence 34.24.10(.18)
luminescent 22.26.15(.17.2)
luminiferous 34.18.27(.20)
luminosity 1.10.16(.16.2)
luminous 34.18.16(.15.3)
luminously 1.31.33(.12.3)
luminousness 34.18.16(.31.3)
Lumley 1.31.26(.9)
lumme 1.15.10
lummox 34.23.15
lump 20.16.5
lumpectomy 1.15.13(.1)
lumpen 28.17.9
lumpenproletariat 22.3.12
lumper 17.10.17
lumpfish 36.2.18(.13)
lumpily 1.31.17(.7)
lumpiness 34.18.16(.2.2)
lumpish 36.2.9
lumpishly 1.31.35(.7.1)
lumpishness 34.18.16(.33.2)
lumpsucker 17.14.11
lumpy 1.8.14
Lumsden 28.17.12(.26)
Luna 17.18.15
lunacy 1.22.16(.9)
lunar 17.18.15
lunate 22.4.14(.7), 22.19.15(.8)
lunatic 24.2.10(.10)
lunation 28.17.25(.3.8)
lunch 38.18.7
luncheon 28.17.27
luncheonette 22.5, 22.5.9
luncher 17.28.22
lunchroom 27.14.6(.19)
lunchtime 27.12.1
Lund 23.24.12, 23.24.14
Lundy 1.11.20(.7)
lune 28.16
lunette 22.5.9
lung 29.8

lunge 39.17.8
lungfish 36.2.18(.20)
lungful 40.14.6(.16)
lungi 1.14.14
lungless 34.18.29(.28)
lungworm 27.16.7
lungwort 22.20.15
lunisolar 17.34.18(.10)
lunker 17.14.21(.5)
lunkhead 23.5.13(.11)
Lunn 28.13
Lunt 22.26.12
lunula 17.34.16(.21.4)
lunulae 2.32.9(.8)
Luo 19.7
Lupercalia 3.24.3
lupiform 27.10.5(.2)
lupin 28.2.9
lupine 28.14.3
lupoid 23.13.5
lupous 34.18.9(.7)
lupus 34.18.9(.7)
lupus vulgaris 34.2.21
lur 17.7, 18
lurch 38.16
lurcher 17.28.16
lure 12, 17.7
Lurex® 34.23.4(.11)
lurgy 1.14.12
lurid 23.2.22
luridly 1.31.23(.14.7)
luridness 34.18.16(.21.1)
luringly 1.31.28(.1.17)
lurk 24.17
lurker 17.14.16
Lurpak® 24.6.5
Lusaka 17.14.7
luscious 34.18.22(.6)
lusciously 1.31.33(.12.4)
lusciousness 34.18.16(.31.4)
lush 36.12
lushly 1.31.35(.6)
lushness 34.18.16(.33.1)
Lusiad 23.7.2
Lusitania 3.9.3(.2)
lust 22.29.12
lustful 40.27.18
lustfully 1.31.17(.16.2)
lustfulness 34.18.16(.37.2)
lustily 1.31.17(.9.3)
lustiness 34.18.16(.2.3)
lustra 17.32.19(.11)
lustral 40.16.13(.16)
lustrate 22.4.22(.8)
lustration 28.17.25(.3.13)
lustre 17.12.24(.10)
lustreless 34.18.29(.17.2)
lustreware 6.18.4
lustrous 34.18.27(.14)

lustrously 1.31.33(.12.5)
lustrum 27.15.26(.10)
lusty 1.10.26(.8)
lusus 34.18.20
lutanist 22.29.2(.18.1)
lute 22.18
luteal 40.3.3
lutecium 27.3.11, 27.3.13, 27.15.22
lutein 28.2.2
luteinize 35.15.12(.5)
lutenist 22.29.2(.18.1)
luteofulvous 34.18.18
luteous 34.3.3
lutestring 29.1.30(.13)
lutetium 27.3.11, 27.3.13
Luther 17.22.8
Lutheran 28.17.31(.11)
Lutheranism 27.15.21(.2.9)
Lutheranize 35.15.12(.5)
Lutine Bell 40.5
luting 29.1.12(.13)
Luton 28.17.11(.14)
Lutterworth 32.14.15
Lutyens 35.26.13(.19)
Lutz 34.22.13, 34.22.14
luv 31.8
luvvy 1.19.7
lux 34.23.11
luxate 22.4.18
luxation 28.17.25(.3.10)
luxe 34.23.11, 34.23.13
Luxembourg 26.14.1(.8)
Luxemburg 26.14.1(.8)
Luxemburger 17.16.14
Luxemburgish 36.2.14
Luxor 12.14.13
luxuriance 34.24.2
luxuriant 22.26.2(.9)
luxuriantly 1.31.22(.20.1)
luxuriate 22.4.2(.14)
luxuriously 1.31.33(.1.4)
luxuriousness 34.18.16(.31.1)
luxury 1.29.11(.20)
Luzon 28.10.19
Lvov 31.7
lwei 4.25
Lyall 40.16.6
lycanthrope 20.15.8
lycanthropy 1.8.11(.8)
lycée 4.18.1
lyceum 27.15.1
lychee 2.26
lychgate 22.4.12(.12)
lychnis 34.2.13
Lycia 3.14.2
Lycian 28.3.13
Lycidas 34.7.8

lycopene 28.1.7
lycopod 23.10.1
lycopodium 27.3.4(.8)
Lycra® 17.32.21
Lycurgus 34.18.14(.6)
Lydd 23.2
lyddite 22.16.10
Lydgate 22.4.12(.8)
Lydia 3.5.2
Lydian 28.3.4(.2)
lye 14
Lyell 40.13, 40.16.6
Lygon 28.17.15(.2)
lying 29.1.7
lyingly 1.31.28(.1.1)
Lyke Wake 24.3
Lyle 40.13,
Lyly 1.31.2
lyme-grass 34.9.6
Lyme Regis 34.2.18
Lymington 28.17.11(.23)
Lymm 27.2
lymph 30.18
lymphadenitis 34.18.11(.8)
lymphadenopathy syndrome 27.17.13
lymphangitis 34.18.11(.8)
lymphatic 24.2.10(.4.4)
lymphocyte 22.16.19(.9)
lymphocytic 24.2.10(.2.3)
lymphoid 23.13.13
lymphoma 17.17.16(.7)
lymphomata 17.12.16(.9.3)
lymphopathy 1.20.8
lymphous 34.18.17
Lympne 27.2
Lyn 28.2
Lynam 27.15.14(.9)
lyncean 28.17.1(.9)
lynch 38.18.1
lyncher 17.28.22
lynchet 22.19.20, 22.19.21
lynching 29.1.25, 29.1.27
Lynette 22.5.9
Lynmouth 32.14.11
Lynn 28.2
Lynne 28.2
Lynsey 1.23.20
Lynton 28.17.11(.22)
lynx 34.23.18
lynxlike 24.13.7(.22)
Lyon 28.17.5
Lyonnais 35.4.8
lyonnaise 35.4.8
Lyonnesse 34.5.6
Lyons 11.1, 35.26.13(.2)
lyophilic 24.2.27(.2)
lyophilize 35.15.21(.4.6)

lyophobic 24.2.9(.7)
Lyra 17.32.13
lyrate 22.4.22(.5), 22.19.24(.8)
lyre 17.6
lyrebird 23.19.1
lyric 24.2.26(.1)
lyrical 40.23.12(.18)
lyrically 1.31.24(.9.12)
lyricism 27.15.21(.2.12)
lyricist 22.29.2(.22)
lyrist 22.29.2(.29.1)
Lysander 17.13.20(.4)
lyse 35.15
Lysenko 19.12.15
lysergic 24.2.24(.6)
Lysias 34.7.2
lysin 28.2.23(.7)
lysine 28.1.18(.4)
Lysippus 34.18.9(.2)
lysis 34.2.17(.8)
Lysistrata 17.12.16(.18)
Lysol® 40.9.14
lysosome 27.17.10
lysozyme 27.12.5
Lytham 27.15.19
lytic 24.2.10(.2.1)
lytta 17.12.2
lyttae 2.12.2
Lyttleton 28.17.11(.27)
Lytton 28.17.11(.2)
m 27.5
MA 4
ma 10
ma'am 27.6, 27.8
maar 10
Maas 34.9
Maastricht 22.23.2, 22.24
Maat 22.10
Mabel 40.20.4
Mabinogion 28.10.2
mac 24.6
macabre 17.32.18
macaco 19.12.3
macadam 27.15.10(.4)
macadamia 3.8.3
macadamization 28.17.25(.3.12)
macadamize 35.15.11
Macanese 35.1.12
Macao 9.5
macaque 24.6.9, 24.8.6
macaroni 1.16.17(.13)
macaronic 24.2.15(.6.4)
macaroon 28.16.13
MacArthur 17.22.5
macassar 17.24.6
Macau 9.5
Macaulay 1.31.11
macaw 12.7

Macbeth 32.5
Maccabean 28.17.1(.2)
Maccabees 35.1.6
MacDiarmid 23.2.12
mace 34.4
mace-bearer 17.32.5
macédoine 28.9.12
Macedon 28.17.12(.16)
Macedonia 3.9.11
Macedonian 28.3.8(.11)
macer 17.24.4
macerate 22.4.22(.6)
maceration 28.17.25(.3.13)
macerator 17.12.4(.15)
Macgillicuddy's Reeks 34.23.1
mach 24.6, 24.8
machete 1.10.4
Machiavelli 1.31.5
Machiavellian 28.3.21(.4)
Machiavellianism 27.15.21(.2.9)
machicolate 22.4.23(.7.1)
machicolation 28.17.25(.3.14)
Machin 28.2.26
machinability 1.10.16(.22.2)
machinable 40.20.16(.16.1)
machinate 22.4.14(.9.1)
machination 28.17.25(.3.8)
machinator 17.12.4(.10)
machine 28.1.20
machinelike 24.13.7(.17)
machinery 1.29.11(.13.1)
machinist 22.29.2(.18.1)
machismo 19.14.18
Machmeter 17.12.1(.6)
macho 19.24
Machu Picchu 16.19
Machynlleth 32.14.18
mack 24.6
Mackay 14.10
Mackenzie 1.23.20
mackerel 40.16.13(.12.1)
Mackeson 28.17.23(.14)
Mackey 1.12.5
Mackie 1.12.5
Mackin 28.17.13(.5)
Mackinac 12.10
mackinaw 12.10
mackintosh 36.9.3
mackle 40.23.5
Maclaren 28.17.31(.5)
macle 40.23.5
Maclean 28.1.27(.10)
Macleans® 35.26.1
MacLehose 35.20.11

Macmillan 28.17.33(.2)
MacNeice 34.1.4
Macon 28.17.13(.3)
Mâcon 11.7
Maconachie 1.13
Maconochie 1.13
Macquarie 1.29.7
macrame 1.15.7
macramé 1.15.7, 4.13
Macready 1.11.1
macro 19.27.17
macrobiotic 24.2.10(.6)
macrobiotically 1.31.24(.9.4)
macrocarpa 17.10.7
macrocephalic 24.2.27(.6)
macrocephalous 34.18.29(.17.4)
macrocephaly 1.31.17(.16.1)
macrocosm 27.15.21(.4)
macrocosmic 24.2.14(.17)
macrocosmically 1.31.24(.9.8)
macroeconomic 24.2.14(.6)
macroinstruction 28.17.25(.15.5)
macromolecular 17.34.16(.21.2)
macromolecule 40.15.9(.5)
macron 28.10.24(.9), 28.17.31(16)
macrophage 39.4.6
macrophotography 1.18.9(.3.2)
macropod 23.10.1
macroscopic 24.2.8(.5)
macroscopically 1.31.24(.9.2)
macula 17.34.16(.21.2)
maculae 2.32.9(.8)
maculae luteae 2.3
macula lutea 3.4.9
macular 17.34.16(.21.2)
maculation 28.17.25(.3.14)
mad 23.7
Madagascan 28.17.13(.18)
Madagascar 17.14.23
madam 27.15.10(.4)
Madame 27.8.4, 27.15.10(.4)
Madang 29.4.4
madcap 20.5.1
madden 28.17.12(.6)
maddeningly 1.31.28(.1.7)
madder 17.13.5
Maddie 1.11.7

Maddock 24.16.5
Maddox 34.23.15
Maddy 1.11.7
made 23.4
Madeira 17.32.2
Madeiran 28.17.31(.2)
Madelaine 28.4.19
madeleine 28.2.31(.10), 28.4.19
Madeley 1.31.23(.3)
Madeline 28.2.31(.10)
mademoiselle 40.5.12
made-to-measure 17.27.3
Madge 39.6
madhouse 34.8.6(.12)
Madhya Pradesh 36.5
Madison 28.17.23(.14)
madly 1.31.23(.5)
madman 28.17.16(.22)
madness 34.18.16(.21.1)
madonna 17.18.9
Madras 34.7.18, 34.9.6
madrasa 17.24.6
madrepore 12.3
madreporic 24.2.26(.6)
Madrid 23.2.22
madrigal 40.24.11
madrigalesque 24.20.3
madrigalian 28.3.21(.3)
madrigalist 22.29.2(.31.2)
madrona 17.18.18(.10)
madrone 17.18.18(.10)
Madura 17.32.14(.3)
Madurese 35.1.22
madwoman 28.17.16(.14)
madwomen 28.2.17(.1)
Mae 4
Maecenas 34.18.16(.1)
maelstrom 27.9, 27.15.26(.10)
maenad 23.7.12
maenadic 24.2.11(.5)
Maendy 1.11.20(.2)
Maerdy 1.11.9
Maesteg 26.3
maestoso 19.20.12, 19.21
maestro 19.27.15
Maeterlinck 24.19.1(.8)
Maeve 31.3
Mae West 22.29.5
Mafeking 29.1.14(.11)
MAFF 30.5
maffick 24.2.16(.3)
Mafia 3.10.2
mafiosi 2.22.9, 2.23
mafioso 19.20.12, 19.21
mag 26.5
magalogue 26.7.14
magazine 28.1.19

Magda **17.13.18**
Magdala **17.34.16(.8)**
Magdalen **28.17.33(.19)**
Magdalena **17.18.1(.16)**
Magdalene **1.16.1(.16),**
28.17.33(.19)
Magdalenian **28.3.8(.1)**
Magdeburg **26.14.1(.4)**
magdelen **28.17.33(.13)**
mage **39.4**
Magee **2.15**
Magellan **28.17.33(.4)**
magenta **17.12.22(.3)**
Maggie **1.14.5**
Maggiore **1.29.8**
maggot **22.19.13**
maggoty **1.10.16(.11)**
Magherafelt **22.32.2**
Maghrib **21.1**
magi **14.21**
magian **28.3.18**
magianism **27.15.21(.2.9)**
magic **24.2.24(.2)**
magical **40.23.12(.17.1)**
magically **1.31.24(.9.11)**
magician **28.17.25(.2.6)**
Magilligan **28.17.15(.13)**
Maginnis **34.2.13**
Maginot Line **28.14**
magisterial **40.3.14(.2)**
magisterially **1.31.3(.11)**
magisterium **27.3.17(.2)**
magistracy **1.22.16(.13)**
magistral **40.16.13(.16)**
magistrand **23.24.6(.12)**
magistrate **22.4.22(.8),**
22.19.24(.12)
magistrateship **20.2.8**
magistrature **17.28.4,**
17.28.15
Maglemosian **28.3.13,**
28.3.14
maglev **31.4**
magma **17.17.20**
magmatic **24.2.10(.4.2)**
Magna Carta **17.12.8**
magna cum laude **4.10.3**
magnanimity
1.10.16(.12)
magnanimous
34.18.15(.10)
magnanimously
1.31.33(.12.3)
magnate **22.4.14(.13),**
22.19.15(.11)
magnesia® **3.15.1, 17.26.1**
magnesian **28.3.14,**
28.17.25(.1), 28.17.26(.1)
magnesite **22.16.19(.9)**
magnesium **27.3.12**
magnet **22.19.15(.11)**

magnetic **24.2.10(.3.1)**
magnetically
1.31.24(.9.3)
magnetism **27.15.21(.2.4)**
magnetite **22.16.9**
magnetizable
40.20.16(.22)
magnetization
28.17.25(.3.11)
magnetize **35.15.7(.7)**
magnetizer **17.25.12(.2)**
magneto **19.10.1**
magnetograph **30.7.5(.1)**
magnetohydro-
dynamic **24.2.14(.4)**
magnetometer
17.12.16(.9.2)
magnetometry
1.29.15(.8)
magnetomotive
31.2.1(.11)
magneton **28.10.9**
magnetosphere **3.10.5**
magnetostriction
28.17.25(.15.1)
magnetron **28.10.24(.7)**
magnifiable **40.20.16(.5)**
Magnificat **22.7.9**
magnification
28.17.25(.3.5)
magnificence
34.24.10(.18)
magnificent
22.26.15(.17.3)
magnificently
1.31.22(.20.4)
magnifico **19.12.12**
magnifier **17.6.9(.4)**
magnify **14.14.4(.7)**
magniloquence
34.24.10(.22)
magniloquent
22.26.15(.22)
magniloquently
1.31.22(.20.5)
magnitude **23.17.4(.1)**
magnolia **3.24.11**
Magnox **23.24.8(.6)**
magnum **27.15.14(.15)**
magnum opus
34.18.9(.10)
Magnus **34.18.16(.23)**
Magog **26.7.6**
Magoo **16.10**
magpie **14.6**
Magraw **12.21**
Magritte **22.1.17**
Magruder **17.13.14**
magsman **28.17.16(.30)**
maguey **4.12, 4.25.15**
Maguire **17.6.13**
magus **34.18.14(.2)**

Magwitch **38.2.9**
Magyar **10.24**
Mahabharata
17.12.16(.18)
mahaleb **21.4**
Mahalia **3.24.3**
mahant **22.26.12**
maharaja **17.29.7**
maharani **1.16.8**
Maharashtra
17.32.19(.12)
Maharashtrian
28.3.20(.11)
maharishi **1.24.2**
mahatma **17.17.17**
Mahaweli **1.31.5**
Mahayana **17.18.8(.12)**
Mahdi **1.11.9**
Mahdism **27.15.21(.2.5)**
Mahdist **22.29.2(.14)**
Maher **10, 17.2**
Mahfouz **35.17.4**
mah-jong **29.6.12**
Mahler **17.34.8**
mahlstick **24.2.10(.15.4)**
mahogany **1.16.15(.10)**
Mahomet **22.2.11**
Mahometan **28.17.11(.15)**
Mahommed **23.2.12**
Mahon **28.9**
Mahoney **1.16.15(.2),**
1.16.17(.12)
mahonia **3.9.11**
mahout **22.9.17, 22.18.8**
mahseer **3.14.5**
Maia **17.2, 17.6**
maid **23.4**
maidan **28.9.3**
Maida Vale **40.4**
maiden **28.17.12(.4)**
maidenhair **6.17**
maidenhead **23.5.13(.14)**
maidenhood **23.16.5(.10)**
maidenish **36.2.16(.13)**
maidenlike **24.13.7(.17)**
maidenly **1.31.27(.14)**
maidish **36.2.12**
maidservant
22.26.15(.16)
Maidstone **28.17.11(.25)**
maieutic **24.2.10(.9)**
maigre **17.16.3**
Maigret **4.26.14**
mail **40.4**
mailable **40.20.16(.29)**
mailbag **26.5.1**
mailboat **22.21.2**
mailbox **34.23.8(.2)**
mailer **17.34.4**
mailing **29.1.31(.4)**
maillot **19**

mailman **28.7.10(.24)**
mailmen **28.5.7(.28)**
mail order **17.13.9**
mailshot **22.11.12**
maim **27.4**
Maimonides **35.1.8**
Main **28.14**
main **28.4**
maincrop **20.7.12**
Maine **28.4**
mainframe **27.4.8**
mainland **23.24.6(.13),**
23.24.16(.16.4)
mainlander **17.13.20(.4)**
mainline **28.14.19(.19)**
mainliner **17.18.13(.14)**
mainly **1.31.27(.4)**
mainmast **22.29.6(.7),**
22.29.8(.5)
mainplane **28.4.19**
mainsail **40.4.10, 40.31.21**
mainsheet **22.1.11**
mainspring **29.1.30(.11)**
mainstay **4.9.10**
mainstream **27.1.12**
maintain **28.4.3**
maintainability
1.10.16(.22.2)
maintainable
40.20.16(.16.1)
maintainer **17.18.3**
maintainor **17.18.3**
maintenance
34.24.10(.15)
Maintenon **28.10.14**
maintop **20.7.4**
maintopmast **22.29.6(.7),**
22.29.8(.5)
Mainwaring **29.1.30(.4)**
Mainz **34.22.18**
maiolica **17.14.15(.15)**
Mair **17.6**
Mairead **23.4.15**
Maisie **1.23.3**
maisonette **22.5.9**
Maithili **1.31.17(.9.2)**
Maitland **23.24.16(.16.3)**
maître d' **2**
maître d'hôtel **40.5.3**
maîtres d' **2**
maize **35.4**
majestic **24.2.10(.15.4)**
majestically **1.31.24(.9.6)**
majesty **1.10.26(.11)**
Majlis **34.2.22(.13)**
majolica **17.14.15(.15)**
major **17.29.3**
Majorca **17.14.9**
Majorcan **28.17.13(.8)**
majordomo **19.14.14**
majorette **22.5.19**

major general
40.16.13(.12.2)
Majorism **27.15.21(.2.14)**
majoritarian **28.3.20(.4)**
majority **1.10.16(.21.2)**
majorship **20.2.7(.9)**
majuscular
17.34.16(.21.2)
majuscule **40.15.9(.5)**
makable **40.20.16(.13)**
Makarios **34.10.2**
Makassar **17.24.6**
make **24.3**
make-believe **31.1.9**
make-or-break **24.3.13**
Makepeace **34.1.1**
maker **17.14.3**
make-ready **1.11.5**
Makerere **1.29.11(.25)**
makeshift **22.27.1**
makeup **20.9.7**
makeweight **22.4.21**
Makgadikgadi **1.11.9**
making **29.1.14(.3)**
mako **19.12.3, 19.12.5,
19.12.6**
Maksutov **31.7**
Malabar **10.5.4**
Malabo **19.9.9**
malabsorption
28.17.25(.14)
malacca **17.14.5**
Malachi **14.10**
malachite **22.16.11**
Malachy **1.12.13**
malacoderm **27.16.3**
malacology **1.26.10(.11.3)**
malacostracan
28.17.13(.13)
maladaptation
28.17.25(.3.3)
maladaptive **31.2.1(.12)**
maladjusted **23.18.9(.20)**
maladjustment
22.26.15(.13.3)
maladminister
17.12.24(.14)
maladministration
28.17.25(.3.13)
maladroit **22.14**
maladroitly **1.31.22(.11)**
maladroitness
34.18.16(.20.2)
malady **1.11.17**
mala fide **1.11.14**
Málaga **17.16.13**
Malagasy **1.22.6**
malagueña **17.33.9**
malaise **35.4.18**
Malamud **23.16.4**
malamute **22.18.10**

malanders **35.18.9**
malapert **22.20.1**
malaprop **20.7.12**
malapropism
27.15.21(.2.2)
malapropos **19.8**
malar **17.34.4**
malaria **3.22.4**
malarial **40.3.14(.4)**
malarian **28.3.20(.4)**
malarious **34.3.15(.3)**
malarkey **1.12.6**
malarky **1.12.6**
malathion **28.17.5**
Malawi **1.28**
Malawian **28.3.19**
Malay **4.28**
Malaya **17.2.10**
Malayalam **27.15.28(.6)**
Malayan **28.17.2**
Malayo-Chinese **35.1.12**
Malayo-Polynesian
28.17.26(.1), 28.17.32
Malaysia **3.15.3**
Malaysian **28.3.14,
28.17.26(.3)**
Malcolm **27.15.11(.17)**
malcontent **22.26.4(.4)**
malcontented
23.18.9(.19)
mal de mer **6**
Malden **28.17.12(.27)**
maldistributed
23.18.9(.12)
maldistribution
28.17.25(.11)
Maldive **31.1.2**
Maldivian **28.3.10**
Maldon **28.17.12(.27)**
male **40.4**
malediction
28.17.25(.15.1)
maledictive **31.2.1(.13.1)**
maledictory
1.29.11(.8.12)
malefaction
28.17.25(.15.3)
malefactor **17.12.21(.3)**
malefic **24.2.16(.2)**
maleficence **34.24.10(.18)**
maleficent **22.26.15(.17.3)**
maleic **24.2.1**
maleness **34.18.16(.37.1)**
Malet **22.19.26(.5)**
malevolence
34.24.10(.24)
malevolent **22.26.15(.25)**
malevolently
1.31.22(.20.5)
malfeasance
34.24.10(.19)

malfeasant **22.26.15(.18)**
Malfi **1.18.13**
malformation
28.17.25(.3.7)
malformed **23.23.6**
malfunction
28.17.25(.15.6)
Malham **27.15.28(.5)**
Malherbe **21.5**
Mali **1.31.9**
Malian **28.3.21(.6)**
Malibu **16.6**
malic **24.2.27(.3)**
malice **34.2.22(.5)**
malicious **34.18.22(.2)**
maliciously **1.31.33(.12.4)**
maliciousness
34.18.16(.31.4)
malign **28.14.19**
malignancy **1.22.23(.10.3)**
malignant **22.26.15(.14)**
malignantly
1.31.22(.20.3)
maligner **17.18.13(.14)**
malignity **1.10.16(.13)**
malignly **1.31.27(.11)**
Malin **28.2.31(.5)**
Malines **28.1.27**
malinger **17.16.17(.1)**
malingerer **17.32.14(.9)**
Malinowski **1.12.17(.13)**
malism **27.15.21(.2.15)**
malison **28.17.23(.14),
28.17.24(.12)**
mall **40.6, 40.10**
Mallaig **26.3**
Mallalieu **16.24.17**
mallam **27.15.28(.5)**
mallard **23.9.22, 23.18.29**
Mallarmé **4.13**
malleability
1.10.16(.22.1)
malleable **40.20.3**
malleableness
34.18.16(.37.4)
malleably **1.31.21(.1)**
mallee **1.31.7**
mallei **14.2**
mallemuck **24.12.5**
mallenders **35.18.9**
malleoli **14.25.9**
malleolus **34.18.29(.17.1)**
mallet **22.19.26(.5)**
malleus **34.3.16**
Mallorca **17.14.9**
mallow **19.29.5**
malm **27.8**
Malmesbury **1.29.11(.7.2)**
Malmö **19.14.19**
malmsey **1.23.19**
malnourished **22.30**

malnourishment
22.26.15(.13.6)
malnutrition
28.17.25(.2.6)
malodorous **34.18.27(.15)**
malodorously
1.31.33(.12.5)
malodorousness
34.18.16(.31.5)
Malone **28.19.19**
Maloney **1.16.17(.15)**
malope **1.8.11(.9)**
Malory **1.29.11(.27)**
maloti **1.10.15, 1.10.18**
Malpas **34.7.5,
34.18.9(.6)**
Malpighi **1.14.1**
Malpighian layer **17.2**
Malplaquet **4.11**
malpractice **34.2.8**
malt **22.32.5, 22.32.6**
Malta **17.12.26(.5)**
Maltese **35.1.7**
Malteser **17.25.1**
maltha **17.22.16**
malthouse **34.8.6(.11)**
Malthus **34.18.19**
Malthusian **28.3.14**
maltiness **34.18.16(.2.3)**
malting **29.1.12(.22)**
maltose **34.20.4, 35.20.3**
maltreat **22.1.17**
maltreater **17.12.1(.14)**
maltreatment
22.26.15(.13.3)
maltster **17.12.24(.18)**
malty **1.10.28**
malvaceous **34.18.22(.3)**
Malvern **28.17.20(.14)**
malversation
28.17.25(.3.10)
Malvinas **34.18.16(.1)**
malvoisie **1.23.10, 2.23**
Malvolio **15.1.13**
mam **27.6**
mama **10.10, 17.17.6**
mamaguy **14.11**
mamba **17.11.17(.4)**
mambo **19.9.14**
mamelon **28.17.33(.13)**
Mameluke **24.15.8**
Mamet **22.19.14**
Mamie **1.15.3**
mamilla **17.34.2(.6)**
mamillae **2.32.2**
mamillary **1.29.11(.27)**
mamillate **22.4.23(.7.2)**
mamma **10.10, 17.17.6**
mammae **2.16**
mammal **40.25.4**
mammalian **28.3.21(.3)**

mammaliferous
34.18.27(.20)
mammalogy 1.26.10(.10)
mammary 1.29.11(.12)
mammee 1.15.6
mammiform 27.10.5(.2)
mammogram 27.6.17(.5)
mammography
1.18.9(.3.2)
Mammon 28.17.16(.7)
Mammonish 36.2.16(.13)
Mammonism
27.15.21(.2.9)
Mammonist
22.29.2(.18.1)
Mammonite 22.16.14(.6)
mammoth 32.14.11
mammy 1.15.6
man 28.7
mana 17.18.8
manacle 40.23.12(.11)
manage 39.2.15
manageability
1.10.16(.22.2)
manageable 40.20.16(.25)
manageableness
34.18.16(.37.4)
manageably 1.31.21(.7.4)
management
22.26.15(.13.6)
manager 17.29.13
manageress 34.5.14
managerial 40.3.14(.2)
managerially 1.31.3(.11)
managership 20.2.7(.9)
managing 29.1.28
Managua 17.7.12(.6),
17.31.7
manakin 28.2.13(.6)
mañana 17.18.8(.12)
Manasseh 1.22.6, 17.24.6
man-at-arms 35.25.5
manatee 2.11, 2.12.11
Manaus 34.8.5
Manawatu 16.7.2
Manchester 17.12.24(.4)
manchineel 40.1.7
Manchu 16.19
Manchuria 3.22.12
Manchurian 28.3.20(.8)
manciple 40.19.11
Mancunian 28.3.8(.9)
Mandaean 28.17.1(.4)
mandala 17.34.16(.8)
Mandalay 4.28, 4.28.7
mandamus 34.18.15(.3)
mandarin 28.2.29(.5)
mandarinate
22.4.14(.9.4)
mandatary 1.29.11(.8.6)
mandate 22.4.10

mandator 17.12.4(.6)
mandatorily
1.31.17(.27.1)
mandatory 1.29.11(.8.6)
man-day 4.10.12
Mandela 17.34.5(.4)
Mandelbaum 27.7
Mandelstam 27.6.4
Mandeville 40.2.12
mandible 40.20.16(.12)
mandibular
17.34.16(.21.1)
mandibulate 22.4.23(.7.3)
Mandingo 19.13.12
mandola 17.34.18(.4)
mandolin 28.2.31
mandolinist
22.29.2(.18.1)
mandorla 17.34.10
mandragora 17.32.14(.9)
mandrake 24.3.13
mandrel 40.16.13(.17)
mandril 40.16.13(.17)
mandrill 40.16.13(.17)
manducate 22.4.11(.6)
manduction
28.17.25(.3.5)
manducatory
1.29.11(.8.6)
Mandy 1.11.20(.4)
mane 28.4
maned 23.24.4
manège 37.2
maneless 34.18.29(.27)
manes 35.1.12(.2), 35.4.8
Manet 4.14
Manfred 23.18.27
manful 40.27.22
manfully 1.31.17(.16.2)
manfulness
34.18.16(.37.2)
mangabey 4.8
Mangan 28.17.15(.16)
manganese 35.1.12
manganic 24.2.15(.5)
manganite 22.16.14(.6)
manganous
34.18.16(.15.2)
mange 39.17.2
mangel 40.24.14(.2)
mangel-wurzel
40.32.14
manger 17.29.16(.2)
mangetout 16.7
mangey 1.26.13
mangily 1.31.17(.25)
manginess 34.18.16(.2.8)
mangle 40.24.14(.2)
mangler 17.34.24
mango 19.13.12
mangold 23.31.13(.5)

mangonel 40.5.8,
40.26.13(.7)
mangosteen 28.1.9(.7)
mangrove 31.12
mangy 1.26.13
manhandle 40.22.16
Manhattan 28.17.11(.6)
manhole 40.18.13
manhood 23.16.5(.10)
man-hour 17.3.6
manhunt 22.26.12
mania 3.9.3, 17.33.9
maniac 24.6.1
maniacal 40.23.12(.3)
maniacally 1.31.24(.9.1)
manic 24.2.15(.5)
Manicaland 23.24.6(.13)
manically 1.31.24(.9.8)
Manichaean 28.17.1(.5)
Manichaeism
27.15.21(.2.1)
Manichee 2.14
manicotti 1.10.9
manicure 12.22,
17.7.12(.5)
manicurist 22.29.2(.29.2)
manifest 22.29.5(.4)
manifestation
28.17.25(.3.3)
manifestative 31.2.1(.9.1)
manifestly 1.31.22(.22)
manifesto 19.10.19
manifold 23.31.13(.7)
manifoldly 1.31.23(.18)
manifoldness
34.18.16(.21.1)
manikin 28.2.13(.6)
manila 17.34.2(.7)
manilla 17.34.2(.7)
manille 40.2.10
Manilow 19.29.12
manioc 24.9.1
maniple 40.19.11
manipulability
1.10.16(.22.3)
manipulable
40.20.16(.29)
manipulatable
40.20.16(.11.1)
manipulate 22.4.23(.7.3)
manipulation
28.17.25(.3.14)
manipulative 31.2.1(.9.4)
manipulatively
1.31.30(.7.1)
manipulativeness
34.18.16(.28.1)
manipulator 17.12.4(.16)
manipulatory
1.29.11(.8.10)
Manipur 12.3, 17.7.1

Manipuri 1.29.8,
1.29.11(.3)
Manitoba 17.11.15
Manitoban 28.17.10
manitou 16.7.4
mankind 23.24.13
manky 1.12.16
manless 34.18.29(.27)
Manley 1.31.27(.6)
manlike 24.13.7(.17)
manliness 34.18.16(.2.10)
manly 1.31.27(.6)
man-made 23.4.7
Mann 28.7
manna 17.18.6
manned 23.24.6
mannequin 28.2.13(.6)
manner 17.18.6
mannered 23.18.14
mannerism
27.15.21(.2.14)
mannerist 22.29.2(.29.4)
manneristic
24.2.10(.15.2)
manneristical
40.23.12(.7.3)
manneristically
1.31.24(.9.6)
mannerless
34.18.29(.17.3)
mannerliness
34.18.16(.2.10)
mannerly 1.31.17(.14.1)
Mannheim 27.12.6
mannikin 28.2.13(.6)
Manning 29.1.17(.5)
Mannion 28.3.8(.5),
28.17.32
mannish 36.2.16(.5)
mannishly 1.31.35(.7.2)
mannishness
34.18.16(.33.5)
Mano 19.15.6
manoeuvrability
1.10.16(.22.2)
manoeuvrable
40.20.16(.27.5)
manoeuvre 17.21.11
manoeuvrer 17.32.14(.13)
manoeuvring 29.1.30(.8)
manometer
17.12.16(.9.2)
manometric
24.2.26(.14.2)
manometrical
40.23.12(.18)
manometrically
1.31.24(.9.12)
ma non troppo 19.8
manor 17.18.6
Manorbier 3.3
manorial 40.3.14(.5)

m

marketplace 34.4.14
markhor 12.7
marking 29.1.14(.5)
markka 10.8.4, 17.14.7
Markova 17.21.14(.6)
Marks 34.23.7
marksman 28.17.16(.29)
marksmanship
20.2.7(.19)
markup 20.9.7
marl 40.8
Marlboro 17.32.14(.5)
Marlborough 17.32.14(.5)
Marlburian 28.3.20(.8)
Marlene 17.18.3,
28.1.27(.4)
Marley 1.31.9
marlin 28.2.31(.6)
marline 28.2.31(.6)
marlinspike 24.13.1
marlite 22.16.25(.7)
Marlon 28.10.26,
28.17.33(.6)
Marlow 19.29.7
Marlowe 19.29.7
marly 1.31.9
Marmaduke 24.15.8
marmalade 23.4.16
Marmara 17.32.14(.10)
Marmion 28.3.7
marmite 22.16.13
marmolite 22.16.25(.9)
marmoreal 40.3.14(.5)
marmoreally 1.31.3(.11)
marmoset 22.5.14
marmot 22.19.14
Marne 28.9
Marner 17.18.8
marocain 28.4.5
Maronite 22.16.14(.6)
maroon 28.16.13
Marple 40.19.6
marplot 22.11.17
marque 24.8
marquee 2.14
Marquesas 34.18.20,
35.18.18
marquess 34.18.26
marquessate 22.19.18
marquetry 1.29.15(.6)
Marquette 22.5.5
marquis 2.14, 34.18.26
marquisate 22.19.18
marquise 35.1.9
marquises 35.18.17
marquisette 22.5.14
Marr 10
Marrakesh 36.5
marram 27.15.26(.3)
Marrano 19.15.7

marriage 39.2.22(.4)
marriageability
1.10.16(.22.2)
marriageable
40.20.16(.25)
married 23.2.22
Marriott 22.3.12
marron glacé 4.18.6
marrow 19.27.4
marrowbone 28.19.3
marrowfat 22.7.13
marry 1.29.5
Marryat 22.3.12
Mars 35.9
Marsala 17.34.8
Marsden 28.17.12(.26)
Marseillaise 35.4, 35.4.17,
35.4.18
Marseille 4.18
Marseilles 4.18
marsh 36.8
Marsha 17.26.7
marshal 40.33.5
marshalship 20.2.7(.24)
marshiness 34.18.16(.2.8)
marshland 23.24.6(.13),
23.24.16(.16.4)
marshmallow 19.29.5
marshy 1.24.6
Marston Moor 17.7
marsupial 40.3.1
mart 22.10
Martaban 28.7.5
martagon 28.17.15(.13)
martello 19.29.4
marten 28.17.11(.8)
Martens 35.26.13(.7)
martensite 22.16.20
Martha 17.22.5
martial 40.33.5
martialize 35.15.21(.4.6)
martially 1.31.17(.22)
Martian 28.17.25(.6)
martin 28.2.11(.6)
Martina 17.18.1(.3)
Martine 28.1.9
Martineau 19.15.12
martinet 22.5.9
Martínez 35.5.9
martingale 40.4.5
martini 1.16.1(.3)
Martinique 24.1.5
Martinmas 34.7.11
martlet 22.19.26(.17)
martyr 17.12.8
martyrdom 27.15.10(.8)
martyrization
28.17.25(.3.11)
martyrize 35.15.20(.2)
martyrological
40.23.12(.17.2)

martyrologist
22.29.2(.26.4)
martyrology
1.26.10(.11.5)
martyry 1.29.11(.8.4)
marvel 40.28.6
Marvell 40.28.6
marveller 17.34.16(.14)
marvellous
34.18.29(.17.4)
marvellously
1.31.33(.12.6)
marvellousness
34.18.16(.31.6)
marvelous 34.18.29(.30)
marvelously
1.31.33(.12.6)
marvelousness
34.18.16(.31.6)
Marvin 28.2.20
Marx 34.23.7
Marxian 28.3.13
Marxism 27.15.21(.2.12)
Marxism–Leninism
27.15.21(.2.9)
Marxist 22.29.2(.22)
Marxist–Leninist
22.29.2(.18.1)
Mary 1.29.4
Mary Celeste 22.29.5(.13)
Maryland 23.24.16(.16.2)
Marylebone 28.17.10,
28.19.3
Mary Magdalene
28.17.33(.13)
Maryport 22.13.1
marzipan 28.7.4
Masada 17.13.7 .
Masai 14.18
masala 17.34.8
Masaryk 24.2.26(.10)
Mascagni 1.30
mascara 17.32.7
mascaron 28.17.31(.11)
mascarpone 1.16.17(.1)
mascle 40.23.16
mascon 28.10.11
mascot 22.11.6,
22.19.12(.14)
masculine 28.2.31(.10)
masculinely 1.31.27(.14)
masculineness
34.18.16(.25)
masculinity 1.10.16(.13)
masculinization
28.17.25(.3.12)
masculinize
35.15.12(.5)
masculist 22.29.2(.31.5)
Masefield 23.31.1(.2)
maser 17.25.3
Maserati® 1.10.8

Maseru 16.23.2
MASH 36.6
mash 36.6
Masham 27.15.20(.5),
27.15.22
masher 17.26.6
mashie 1.24.5
Mashona 17.18.9,
17.18.18(.9)
Mashonaland
23.24.6(.13)
mask 24.20.4
Maskell 40.23.16
masker 17.14.23
maskinonge 39.17.7
masochism 27.15.21(.2.6)
masochist 22.29.2(.15)
masochistic 24.2.10(.15.2)
masochistically
1.31.24(.9.6)
mason 28.17.23(.4)
Mason–Dixon Line 28.14
Masonic 24.2.15(.6.3)
masonry 1.29.20
Masorah 17.32.10(.8)
Masorete 22.1.17
Masoretic 24.2.10(.3.3)
masque 24.20.4
masquer 17.14.23
masquerade 23.4.15
masquerader 17.13.3
mass 34.7
Massachusetts 34.22.15
massacre 17.14.15(.12)
massage 39.8
massager 17.29.13
massasauga 17.16.8
Massawa 17.31.2
massé 1.22.6
Massenet 4.14
masseter 17.12.1(.10),
17.12.16(.14)
masseur 18.11
masseuse 35.19
Massey 1.22.6
massicot 22.11.6
massif 30.1.6
Massif Central 40.8.15
Massine 28.1.18
massiness 34.18.16(.2.7)
Massinger 17.29.16(.8)
massive 31.2.4(.5)
massively 1.31.30(.7.4)
massiveness
34.18.16(.28.2)
massless 34.18.29(.33)
Masson 28.17.23(.6)
massy 1.22.6
mast 22.29.6, 22.29.8
mastaba 17.11.13
mastectomy 1.15.13(.1)

m

master **17.12.24(.5)**
masterclass **34.9.7**
masterdom **27.15.10(.8)**
masterful **40.27.14**
masterfully **1.31.17(.16.1)**
masterfulness **34.18.16(.37.2)**
masterhood **23.16.5(.3)**
masterless **34.18.29(.17.2)**
masterliness **34.18.16(.2.10)**
masterly **1.31.17(.9.3)**
mastermind **23.24.13**
masterpiece **34.1.1**
Masters **35.18.8**
mastership **20.2.7(.9)**
mastersinger **17.19.1**
masterstroke **24.18.13**
masterwork **24.17.6(.4)**
mastery **1.29.11(.8.12)**
masthead **23.5.13(.9)**
mastic **24.2.10(.15.4)**
masticate **22.4.11(.6)**
mastication **28.17.25(.3.5)**
masticator **17.12.4(.7)**
masticatory **1.29.11(.8.2)**
mastiff **30.2.1**
mastitis **34.18.11(.8)**
mastodon **28.10.10, 28.17.12(.16)**
mastodontic **24.2.10(.14)**
mastoid **23.13.7**
mastoiditis **34.18.11(.8)**
masturbate **22.4.8**
masturbation **28.17.25(.3.2)**
masturbator **17.12.4(.4)**
mat **22.7**
Matabele **1.31.1**
Matabeleland **23.24.6(.13)**
matador **12.6.6**
Mata Hari **1.29.6**
matamata **17.12.6**
Matapan **28.7.4**
match **38.5**
matchable **40.20.16(.24)**
matchboard **23.12.2(.18)**
matchbook **24.14.3**
matchbox **34.23.8(.2)**
matchet **22.2.20**
matchless **34.18.29(.36)**
matchlessly **1.31.33(.12.6)**
matchlock **24.9.16(.20)**
matchmaker **17.14.3(.3)**
matchmaking **29.1.14(.3)**
matchplay **4.28.9**
matchstick **24.2.10(.15.4)**
matchup **20.9.14**
matchwood **23.16.6(.20)**

mate **22.4**
maté **4.9.2**
mateless **34.18.29(.22)**
matelot **19.29.12, 19.29.17**
matelote **22.21.15**
mater **17.12.4**
materfamilias **34.7.2**
material **40.3.14(.2)**
materialism **27.15.21(.2.15)**
materialist **22.29.2(.31.1)**
materialistic **24.2.10(.15.3)**
materialistically **1.31.24(.9.6)**
materiality **1.10.16(.32.1)**
materialization **28.17.25(.3.12)**
materialize **35.15.21(.2)**
materially **1.31.3(.11)**
materia medica **17.14.15(.7)**
matériel **40.5**
maternal **40.26.14**
maternalism **27.15.21(.2.15)**
maternalistic **24.2.10(.15.3)**
maternally **1.31.17(.14.3)**
maternity **1.10.16(.13)**
mateship **20.2.8**
matey **1.10.3**
mateyness **34.18.16(.2.3)**
math **32.6**
mathematical **40.23.12(.7.1)**
mathematically **1.31.24(.9.4)**
mathematician **28.17.25(.2.2)**
mathematics **34.23.2(.3)**
Mather **17.23.3, 17.23.5**
Matheson **28.17.23(.14)**
Mathews **35.17.7**
Mathieson **28.17.23(.14)**
Mathilda **17.13.23(.2)**
Mathis **34.18.19**
maths **34.26**
matico **19.12.1**
matily **1.31.17(.9.1)**
matinée **4.14**
matins **35.26.2**
Matisse **34.1.3**
Matlock **24.9.16(.11)**
Matmata **17.12.6**
Mato Grosso **19.20.6**
matrass **34.18.27(.14)**
matriarch **24.8.1**
matriarchal **40.23.6**
matriarchy **1.12.6**
matric **24.2.26(.14.1)**

matrices **35.1.16(.10)**
matricidal **40.22.11**
matricide **23.15.11(.6)**
matriculant **22.26.15(.25)**
matriculate **22.4.23(.7.3)**
matriculation **28.17.25(.3.14)**
matriculatory **1.29.11(.8.10)**
matrilineal **40.3.7(.2)**
matrilineally **1.31.3(.7)**
matrilocal **40.23.14**
matrimonial **40.3.7(.9)**
matrimonially **1.31.3(.7)**
matrimony **1.16.15(.11)**
matrix **34.23.2(.12)**
matron **28.17.31(.14)**
matronal **40.26.13(.14.8)**
matronhood **23.16.5(.10)**
matronly **1.31.27(.14)**
Matsui® **1(.6)**
matsuri **1.29.10**
Matsushita® **17.12.1(.11)**
Matsuyama **17.17.7**
matt **22.7**
mattamore **12.9.4**
matte **22.7**
matted **23.18.9(.5)**
mattedly **1.31.23(.14.3)**
mattedness **34.18.16(.21.1)**
matter **17.12.6**
Matterhorn **28.11.10**
matter-of-fact **22.23.5(.7)**
matter-of-factly **1.31.22(.19)**
matter-of-factness **34.18.16(.20.4)**
mattery **1.29.11(.8.3)**
Matthew **16.24.13**
Matthews **35.17.7**
Matthias **34.18.5**
matting **29.1.12(.5)**
mattins **35.26.2**
mattock **24.16.4**
mattoid **23.13.7**
mattress **34.18.27(.14)**
maturate **22.4.22(.6)**
maturation **28.17.25(.3.13)**
maturational **40.26.13(.14.2)**
maturative **31.2.1(.9.4)**
mature **12.17, 12.22, 17.7.12(.3)**
matured **23.12.10, 23.18.4**
maturely **1.31.11, 1.31.17(.4)**
matureness **34.18.16(.15.1)**
maturity **1.10.16(.21.2)**

matutinal **40.26.11, 40.26.13(.4)**
matza **17.24.19**
matzo **17.24.19, 19.20.14**
mauby **1.9.8, 1.9.13**
maud **23.12**
Maude **23.12**
maudlin **28.2.31(.16)**
Maudling **29.1.31(.18)**
Maudsley **1.31.34**
Maugham **27.10**
Maughan **28.11**
maul **40.10**
mauler **17.34.10**
Mauleverer **17.32.14(.13)**
Mau Mau **9**
Mauna Kea **17.2**
Mauna Loa **17.9**
maunder **17.13.20(.8)**
maundering **29.1.30(.8)**
Maundy **1.11.20(.6)**
Maupassant **11.12**
Maura **17.32.10**
Maureen **28.1.25(.1)**
Mauriac **24.6.1**
Maurice **34.2.21**
Maurist **22.29.2(.29.2)**
Mauritania **3.9.3(.2)**
Mauritanian **28.3.8(.3)**
Mauritian **28.17.25(.2.6)**
Mauritius **34.18.22(.2)**
Maury **1.29.8**
Maurya **3.22.6**
Mauser® **17.25.6**
mausolea **17.1.17**
mausoleum **27.15.1**
mauve **31.12**
mauvish **36.2.19**
maven **28.17.20(.3)**
maverick **24.2.26(.10)**
mavis **34.2.15**
maw **12**
Mawddach **24.6.13, 25.4**
Mawer **12, 17.4**
Mawgan **28.17.15(.9)**
Mawhinny **1.16.2**
mawkish **36.2.13**
mawkishly **1.31.35(.7.1)**
mawkishness **34.18.16(.33.4)**
Mawson **28.17.23(.9)**
mawworm **27.16.7**
max **34.23.5**
maxi **1.22.22**
maxilla **17.34.2(.9)**
maxillae **2.32.2**
maxillary **1.29.11(.27)**
maxim **27.2.9**

mealie **1.31.1**
mealiness **34.18.16(.2.10)**
mealtime **27.12.1**
mealworm **27.16.7**
mealy **1.31.1**
mealybug **26.10**
mealy-mouthed **23.27**
mean **28.1**
meander **17.13.20(.4)**
meandering **29.1.30(.8)**
meandrine **28.2.29(.9), 28.14.18**
meanie **1.16.1**
meaning **29.1.17(.1)**
meaningful **40.27.23**
meaningfully **1.31.17(.16.2)**
meaningfulness **34.18.16(.37.2)**
meaningless **34.18.29(.28)**
meaninglessly **1.31.33(.12.6)**
meaninglessness **34.18.16(.31.6)**
meaningly **1.31.28(.1.7)**
meanly **1.31.27(.1)**
meanness **34.18.16(.25)**
means **35.26.1**
meant **22.26.4**
meantime **27.12.1**
meanwhile **40.13.15**
Mearns **35.26.6**
Measham **27.15.22**
measles **35.30.23**
measliness **34.18.16(.2.10)**
measly **1.31.34**
measurability **1.10.16(.22.1)**
measurable **40.20.16(.27.5)**
measurableness **34.18.16(.37.4)**
measurably **1.31.21(.8)**
measure **17.27.3**
measuredly **1.31.23(.14.7)**
measureless **34.18.29(.17.5)**
measurelessly **1.31.33(.12.6)**
measurement **22.26.15(.13.2)**
meat **22.1**
meatball **40.10.4**
Meath **32.1, 33.1**
meathead **23.5.13(.9)**
meatily **1.31.17(.9.1)**
meatiness **34.18.16(.2.3)**
meatless **34.18.29(.22)**
meatus **34.18.11(.3)**
meaty **1.10.1**

Mebyon Kernow **19.15.13**
mecca **17.14.4**
meccano **19.15.7**
mechanic **24.2.15(.5)**
mechanical **40.23.12(.11)**
mechanicalism **27.15.21(.2.15)**
mechanically **1.31.24(.9.8)**
mechanicalness **34.18.16(.37.5)**
mechanician **28.17.25(.2.4)**
mechanism **27.15.21(.2.9)**
mechanist **22.29.2(.18.1)**
mechanistic **24.2.10(.15.2)**
mechanistically **1.31.24(.9.6)**
mechanization **28.17.25(.3.11)**
mechanize **35.15.12(.5)**
mechanizer **17.25.12(.6)**
mechanoreceptor **17.12.19**
mechatronics **34.23.2(.6)**
Mechlin **28.2.31(.17)**
Mecklenburg **26.14.1(.9)**
meconium **27.3.8(.10)**
Med **23.5**
medal **40.22.4**
medallic **24.2.27(.6)**
medallion **28.3.21(.2)**
medallist **22.29.2(.31.2)**
Medawar **17.31.3**
meddle **40.22.4**
meddler **17.34.22**
meddlesome **27.15.20(.22)**
meddlesomely **1.31.26(.11)**
meddlesomeness **34.18.16(.24)**
Mede **23.1**
Medea **3.5**
Medellín **28.1.26**
Medevac **24.6.12**
media **3.5.1**
mediagenic **24.2.15(.4)**
medial **40.3.4**
medially **1.31.3(.4)**
median **28.3.4(.1)**
medianly **1.31.27(.3)**
mediant **22.26.2(.3)**
mediastina **17.18.13(.1)**
mediastinal **40.26.11**
mediastinum **27.15.14(.9)**
mediate **22.4.2(.4)**
mediately **1.31.22(.3)**

mediation **28.17.25(.3.1)**
mediatization **28.17.25(.3.11)**
mediatize **35.15.7(.2)**
mediator **17.12.4(.1)**
mediatorial **40.3.14(.5)**
mediatory **1.29.11(.8.1)**
mediatrices **35.1.16(.10)**
mediatrix **34.23.2(.12)**
medic **24.2.11(.4)**
medicable **40.20.16(.13)**
Medicaid **23.4.5**
medical **40.23.12(.8)**
medically **1.31.24(.9.7)**
medicament **22.26.15(.13.2)**
Medicare **6.6**
medicate **22.4.11(.6)**
medication **28.17.25(.3.5)**
medicative **31.2.1(.9.1)**
Medicean **28.17.1(.10)**
Medici **2.26**
medicinal **40.26.13(.12)**
medicinally **1.31.17(.14.2)**
medicine **28.17.23(.14)**
medick **24.2.11(.1)**
medico **19.12.12**
medieval **40.28.1**
medievalism **27.15.21(.2.15)**
medievalist **22.29.2(.31.4)**
medievalize **35.15.21(.4.6)**
medievally **1.31.17(.17)**
Medina **17.18.1(.4), 17.18.13(.2)**
mediocre **17.14.17**
mediocrity **1.10.16(.21.3)**
meditate **22.4.9(.5)**
meditation **28.17.25(.3.3)**
meditative **31.2.1(.9.1)**
meditatively **1.31.30(.7.1)**
meditativeness **34.18.16(.28.1)**
meditator **17.12.4(.5)**
Mediterranean **28.3.8(.3)**
medium **27.3.4(.1)**
mediumism **27.15.21(.2.8)**
mediumistic **24.2.10(.15.2)**
mediumship **20.2.7(.18)**
medlar **17.34.22**
medley **1.31.23(.4)**
Médoc **24.9.5**
medrese **4.18.4**
medulla **17.34.12**
medulla oblongata **17.12.8(.6)**
medullary **1.29.11(.27)**
medusa **17.24.14, 17.25.14**

medusae **2.22.6, 2.23**
medusan **28.17.23(.13), 28.17.24(.11)**
Medway **4.25.13**
Medwin **28.2.28**
Mee **2**
meed **23.1**
Meehan **28.17.1**
meek **24.1**
meekly **1.31.24(.1)**
meekness **34.18.16(.22)**
meerkat **22.7.9**
meerschaum **27.10.6, 27.15.22**
Meerut **22.19.24(.2)**
meet **22.1**
meeter **17.12.1**
meeting **29.1.12(.1)**
meeting house **34.8.6(.17)**
meetly **1.31.22(.1)**
meetness **34.18.16(.20.1)**
Meg **26.4**
mega **17.16.4**
megabuck **24.12.1**
megabyte **22.16.8**
megacephalic **24.2.27(.6)**
megacycle **40.23.10**
megadeath **32.5**
Megaera **17.32.2**
megaflop **20.7.13**
megahertz **34.22.16**
megalith **32.2.9**
megalithic **24.2.18(.1)**
megalomania **3.9.3(.5)**
megalomaniac **24.6.1**
megalomaniacal **40.23.12(.3)**
megalopolis **34.2.22(.8)**
megalopolitan **28.17.11(.15)**
megalosaur **12.14.8**
megalosaurus **34.18.27(.8)**
Megan **28.17.15(.4)**
megaphone **28.19.11**
megapod **23.10.1**
megapode **23.20.3**
megaron **28.10.24(.5)**
megascopic **24.2.8(.5)**
megaspore **12.3**
megastar **10.6.8**
megastore **12.5.9**
megatheria **3.22.2**
megatherium **27.3.17(.2)**
megaton **28.13.3**
megavolt **22.32.5, 22.32.12**
megawatt **22.11.14**
Megger® **17.16.4**
megillah **17.34.2(.5)**
megilp **20.18**

megohm **27.17.7**
megrim **27.15.26(.13)**
Mehmet **22.5.8**
Meier **17.6**
Meiji Tenno **19.15.4**
Meikle **40.23.1**
Meiklejohn **28.10.22**
meioses **35.1.16(.11)**
meiosis **34.2.17(.11.1)**
meiotic **24.2.10(.6)**
meiotically **1.31.24(.9.4)**
Meir **3**
Meissen **28.17.23(.12)**
Meistersinger **17.19.1**
Mekong **29.6.5**
mel **40.5**
melamine **28.1.13,
28.14.8**
melancholia **3.24.11**
melancholic **24.2.27(.9)**
melancholically
1.31.24(.9.12)
melancholy **1.31.17(.11)**
Melanchthon **28.17.21**
Melanesia **3.15.1, 17.33.12**
Melanesian **28.17.26(.1),
28.17.32**
mélange **37.5, 39.17.6**
Melanie **1.16.15(.20)**
melanin **28.2.18**
melanism **27.15.21(.2.9)**
melanoma **17.17.16(.6)**
melanoses **35.1.16(.11)**
melanosis **34.2.17(.11.2)**
melanotic **24.2.10(.6)**
melba **17.11.20**
Melbourne **28.11.2,
28.17.10**
Melchett **22.19.21**
Melchior **12.2**
Melchite **22.16.11**
Melchizedek **24.4.5**
meld **23.31.4**
Meldrum **27.15.26(.11)**
Meleager **17.16.3**
melee **4.28, 4.28.2**
Melhuish **36.2.5, 36.2.6,
36.2.27**
Melia **3.24.1**
melic **24.2.27(.4)**
melick **24.2.27(.4)**
Melilla **3.24**
melilot **22.11.17**
Melina **17.18.1(.16)**
Melinda **17.13.20(.1)**
meliorate **22.4.22(.1)**
melioration
28.17.25(.3.13)
meliorative **31.2.1(.9.4)**
meliorism **27.15.21(.2.14)**
meliorist **22.29.2(.29.1)**

melisma **17.17.23**
melismata **17.12.16(.9.3)**
melismatic **24.2.10(.4.2)**
Melissa **17.24.2**
Melksham **27.15.22**
melliferous **34.18.27(.20)**
mellifluence **34.24.10(.6)**
mellifluent **22.26.15(.5)**
mellifluous **34.18.6**
mellifluously
1.31.33(.12.1)
mellifluousness
34.18.16(.31.2)
Mellish **36.2.27**
Mellon **28.17.33(.4)**
Mellor **17.34.5**
Mellors **35.18.25**
mellotron **28.10.24(.7)**
mellow **19.29.4**
mellowly **1.31.19**
mellowness **34.18.16(.17)**
Melly **1.31.5**
melodeon **28.3.4(.10)**
melodic **24.2.11(.7)**
melodica **17.14.15(.7)**
melodically **1.31.24(.9.7)**
melodious **34.3.4**
melodiously **1.31.33(.1.1)**
melodiousness
34.18.16(.31.1)
melodist **22.29.2(.14)**
melodize **35.15.8**
melodizer **17.25.12(.3)**
melodrama **17.17.7**
melodramatic
24.2.10(.4.2)
melodramatically
1.31.24(.9.4)
melodramatist
22.29.2(.13)
melodramatize
35.15.7(.7)
melody **1.11.17**
melon **28.17.33(.4)**
Melos **34.10.17**
Melpomene **1.16.15(.11)**
Melrose **35.20.12**
melt **22.32.2**
meltable **40.20.16(.11.7)**
meltage **39.2.10**
meltdown **28.8.2(.5)**
melter **17.12.26(.3)**
meltingly **1.31.28(.1.4)**
melton **28.17.11(.27)**
Meltonian® **28.3.8(.11)**
meltwater **17.12.10(.7)**
Melville **40.2.12**
Melvin **28.2.20**
member **17.11.17(.3)**
memberless
34.18.29(.17.2)

membership **20.2.7(.9)**
member state **22.4**
membranaceous
34.18.22(.3)
membrane **28.4.18**
membraneous **34.3.6(.3)**
membranous
34.18.16(.15.3)
membrum virile **1.31.14**
memento **19.10.17**
memento mori **14.24.4**
Memnon **28.10.14,
28.17.17(.14)**
memo **19.14.4**
memoir **10.22.8**
memoirist **22.29.2(.29.2)**
memorabilia **3.24.2**
memorability
1.10.16(.22.1)
memorable
40.20.16(.27.4)
memorableness
34.18.16(.37.4)
memorably **1.31.21(.8)**
memoranda **17.13.20(.4)**
memorandum
27.15.10(.14)
memorial **40.3.14(.5)**
memorialist **22.29.15(.18)**
memorialize **35.15.21(.2)**
memoria technica
17.14.15(.9)
memorizable
40.20.16(.22)
memorization
28.17.25(.3.11)
memorize **35.15.20(.2)**
memorizer **17.25.12(.14)**
memory **1.29.11(.12)**
Memphis **34.2.14**
memsahib **21.2, 21.7**
men **28.5**
menace **34.18.16(.5)**
menacer **17.24.15**
menacingly **1.31.28(.1.11)**
ménage **37.4.5**
ménage à trois **10**
menagerie **1.29.11(.23)**
Menai Strait **22.4**
Menander **17.13.20(.4)**
menaquinone **28.19.10**
menarche **1.12.6**
Mencken **28.17.13(.17)**
mend **23.24.5**
mendable **40.20.16(.12)**
mendacious **34.18.22(.3)**
mendaciously
1.31.33(.12.4)
mendaciousness
34.18.16(.31.4)
mendacity **1.10.16(.16.1)**

Mendel **40.22.16**
Mendeleev **31.4**
mendelevium **27.3.9**
Mendelian **28.3.21(.1)**
Mendelism
27.15.21(.2.15)
Mendelssohn
28.17.23(.28)
mender **17.13.20(.3)**
Méndez **35.5.6**
mendicancy
1.22.23(.10.2)
mendicant **22.26.15(.11)**
mendicity **1.10.16(.16.1)**
Mendip **20.2.3**
Mendoza **17.25.15**
Menelaus **34.18.2**
Menes **35.1.12(.1)**
menfolk **24.18.7**
Meng-tzu **16.15**
menhaden **28.17.12(.4)**
menhir **3.20**
menial **40.3.7(.1)**
menially **1.31.3(.7)**
Meniere **6, 6.1**
meningeal **40.3.12**
meninges **35.1.19, 35.1.21**
meningitic **24.2.10(.2.3)**
meningitis **34.18.11(.8)**
meningocele **40.1.10**
meningococcal **40.23.7**
meningococcus
34.18.13(.5)
meninx **34.23.18**
meniscoid **23.13.9**
meniscus **34.18.13(.14)**
Mennonite **22.16.14(.6)**
menologia **3.19.8**
menologist **22.29.2(.26.4)**
menologium **27.3.15**
menology **1.26.10(.11.4)**
menopausal **40.32.9**
menopause **35.12**
menorah **17.32.10(.7)**
Menorca **17.14.9**
Menorcan **28.17.13(.8)**
menorrhagia **3.19.3**
menorrhoea **17.1.16**
Menotti **1.10.9**
mens **35.26.5**
Mensa **17.24.22(.2)**
menses **35.1.16(.15)**
Menshevik **24.2.17**
mens rea **17.1**
Menston **28.17.11(.25)**
menstrua **17.7.11**
menstrual **40.16.7,
40.16.13(.16)**
menstrual cycle
40.23.10
menstruate **22.4.4**

menstruation 28.17.25(.3.1)

menstruous 34.18.6

menstruum 27.15.4

mensurability 1.10.16(.22.1)

mensurable 40.20.16(.27.5)

mensural 40.16.13(.12.2)

mensuration 28.17.25(.3.13)

menswear 6.18.13

Mentadent® 22.26.4(.5)

mental 40.21.17(.2)

mentalism 27.15.21(.2.15)

mentalist 22.29.2(.31.2)

mentalistic 24.2.10(.15.3)

mentalistically 1.31.24(.9.6)

mentality 1.10.16(.32.3)

mentally 1.31.17(.9.3)

mentation 28.17.25(.3.3)

menthol 40.9.13

mentholated 23.18.9(.3)

mention 28.17.25(.16)

mentionable 40.20.16(.16.3)

mentor 12.5.8

menu 16.24.10

Menuhin 28.2.6

Menzies 34.2.11, 35.2.6, 35.2.12

Meon 28.17.1

Meopham 27.15.7

meow 9

mepacrine 28.2.29(.10)

Mephistophelean 28.3.21(.1)

Mephistopheles 35.1.23

Mephistophelian 28.3.21(.1)

mephitic 24.2.10(.2.3)

mephitis 34.18.11(.8)

meranti 1.10.23(.4)

mercantile 40.13.3(.9)

mercantilism 27.15.21(.2.15)

mercantilist 22.29.2(.31.1)

mercaptan 28.7.6, 28.17.11(.18)

Mercator 17.12.4(.7)

Mercedes 35.1.8

mercenariness 34.18.16(.2.9)

mercenary 1.29.11(.13.2)

mercer 17.24.16

mercerize 35.15.20(.2)

mercery 1.29.11(.18)

merchandise 34.15.3

merchandizable 40.20.16(.22)

merchandize 35.15.8

merchandizer 17.25.12(.3)

merchant 22.26.15(.20)

merchantable 40.20.16(.11.6)

merchantman 28.17.16(.21)

Mercia 3.14.10, 17.26.15

Mercian 28.3.13, 28.3.15, 28.17.25(.12)

merciful 40.27.14

mercifully 1.31.17(.16.1)

mercifulness 34.18.16(.37.2)

merciless 34.18.29(.2)

mercilessly 1.31.33(.12.6)

mercilessness 34.18.16(.15.3)

Merck 24.17

Merckx 34.23.16

mercurial 40.3.14(.6)

mercurialism 27.15.21(.2.15)

mercuriality 1.10.16(.32.1)

mercurially 1.31.3(.11)

mercuric 24.2.26(.8)

Mercurochrome® 27.17.13

mercurous 34.18.27(.11)

mercury 1.29.11(.26)

Mercutio 15.1.9

mercy 1.22.17

mere 3

Meredith 32.2.2

Meredydd 33.2

merely 1.31.3

meretricious 34.18.22(.2)

meretriciously 1.31.33(.12.4)

meretriciousness 34.18.16(.31.4)

Merfyn 28.2.20

merganser 17.24.22(.3), 17.25.18

merge 39.15

mergence 34.24.10(.21)

Mergenthaler 17.34.8

merger 17.29.14

Mérida 17.13.15

Meriden 28.17.12(.16)

meridian 28.3.4(.2)

meridional 40.26.2

Meriel 40.3.14(.3)

meringue 29.4.15

merino 19.15.1

Merioneth 32.14.12

meristem 27.5.4

meristematic 24.2.10(.4.2)

merit 22.2.24

meritocracy 1.22.16(.13)

meritocratic 24.2.10(.4.5)

meritorious 34.3.15(.5)

meritoriously 1.31.33(.1.4)

meritoriousness 34.18.16(.31.1)

merkin 28.2.13(.7)

merle 40.17

merlin 28.2.31(.11)

merlon 28.17.33(.14)

Merlot 22.19.26(.14)

Merlyn 28.2.31(.11)

mermaid 23.4.7

merman 28.7.10(.7)

mermen 28.5.7(.11)

meroblast 22.29.6(.12), 22.29.8(.8)

Meroe 19.27.2

merohedral 40.16.13(.17)

meronymy 1.15.13(.5)

Merovingian 28.3.16, 28.3.18

Merrick 24.2.26(.4)

Merrill 40.16.13(.3)

merrily 1.31.17(.27.1)

Merrimac 24.6.10

Merrimack 24.6.10

merriment 22.26.15(.13.2)

merriness 34.18.16(.2.9)

Merrion 28.3.20(.3)

Merritt 22.2.24

merry 1.29.3

merry-go-round 23.24.7(.10)

merrymaker 17.14.3(.3)

merrymaking 29.1.14(.3)

Merryweather 17.23.4

Mersa Matruh 16.23.8

Mersey 1.23.14

Merseyside 23.15.11(.2)

Merthiolate® 22.4.23(.7.1)

Merthyr Tydfil 40.28.14

Merton 28.17.11(.16)

Mervyn 28.2.20

Meryl 40.16.13(.3)

mesa 17.24.4

mésalliance 34.24.2

Mesa Verde 1.11.6

mescal 40.6.6

mescaline 28.1.27(.7), 28.2.31(.10)

mesdames 27.6.5

meseemed 23.23.1

meseems 35.25.1

mesembryanthemum 27.15.13

mesencephalon 28.10.26

mesenterial 40.3.14(.2)

mesenteric 24.2.26(.4)

mesenteritis 34.18.11(.8)

mesentery 1.29.11(.8.12)

mesh 36.5

Meshach 24.6.16

mesial 40.3.10, 40.3.11

mesially 1.31.3(.9)

mesic 24.2.21

Mesmer 17.17.23

mesmeric 24.2.26(.4)

mesmerically 1.31.24(.9.12)

mesmerisingly 1.31.28(.1.12)

mesmerism 27.15.21(.2.14)

mesmerist 22.29.2(.29.4)

mesmerization 28.17.25(.3.11)

mesmerize 35.15.20(.2)

mesmerizer 17.25.12(.14)

mesmerizingly 1.31.28(.1.12)

mesne 28.1

Meso-American 28.17.13(.13)

mesoblast 22.29.6(.12), 22.29.8(.8)

mesocarp 20.6

mesocephalic 24.2.27(.6)

mesoderm 27.16.3

mesogaster 17.12.24(.5)

mesolect 22.23.4(.11)

mesolectal 40.21.16

Mesolithic 24.2.18(.1)

mesomorph 30.9.2

mesomorphic 24.2.16(.5)

mesomorphy 1.18.6

meson 28.10.19

mesonic 24.2.15(.6.3)

mesopause 35.12

mesophyll 40.2.11

mesophyte 22.16.16

Mesopotamia 3.8.3

Mesopotamian 28.3.7

mesosphere 3.10.5

mesothelium 27.3.18

mesotron 28.10.24(.7)

Mesozoic 24.2.7

mesquite 22.1.4

mess 34.5

message 39.2.19

Messalina 17.18.1(.16)

messenger 17.29.16(.8)

Messerschmitt 22.2.11

Messiaen 11.18

messiah 17.6.10

Messiahship 20.2.7(.9)

messianic 24.2.15(.5)

m

metropolitanate 22.4.14(.9.1)
metropolitanism 27.15.21(.2.9)
metrorrhagia 3.19.3
Metternich 24.2.15(.8), 25.1
mettle 40.21.4
mettlesome 27.15.20(.22)
Mettoy® 13.4
Metz 34.22.4
meu 16
meunière 6.20
Meurig 26.2.10
Meuse 35.19
mew 16
mewl 40.15
mews 35.17
Mexborough 17.32.14(.5)
Mexicali 1.31.7, 1.31.9
Mexican 28.17.13(.13)
Mexico 19.12.12
Meyer 17.2, 17.6
Meyerbeer 3.3.7
Meyerhof 30.8.10
Meyers 35.18.1
Meynell 40.26.3, 40.26.4
Meyrick 24.2.26(.4)
mezereon 28.3.20(.2)
mezuzah 17.25.13, 17.25.14
mezuzoth 22.21.12
mezzanine 28.1.14
mezza voce 4.22
mezzo 19.20.14
mezzo forte 4.9.5
Mezzogiorno 19.15.9
mezzorilievo 19.17
mezzo soprano 19.15.7
mezzotint 22.26.1
mezzotinter 17.12.22(.1)
mho 19
mi 2
MI5 31.9
MI6 34.23.2(.10)
Mia 3
Miami 1.15.6
miaow 9
miasma 17.17.23
miasmal 40.25.14
miasmatic 24.2.10(.4.2)
miasmic 24.2.14(.17)
miasmically 1.31.24(.9.8)
miaul 40.10
mica 17.14.12
micaceous 34.18.22(.3)
mica-schist 22.29.2(.24)
Micawber 17.11.9
Micawberish 36.2.25
Micawberism 27.15.21(.2.14)

mice 34.15
micelle 40.5.11
Michael 40.23.10
Michaela 17.34.4
Michel 40.5.13
Michelangelo 19.29.12
Micheldever 17.21.4
Michelin® 28.2.31(.10)
Michelle 40.5.13
Michelmore 12.9.16
Michelson 28.17.23(.28)
Michener 17.18.16(.18)
Michigan 28.17.15(.13)
Michoacán 28.9.4
mick 24.2
mickerie 1.29.11(.10)
mickery 1.29.11(.10)
mickey 1.12.2
Mickey Finn 28.2
Mickiewicz 38.2.7
mickle 40.23.2
Mickleover 17.21.14(.15)
Micklethwaite 22.4.21
Micklewhite 22.16.23
micro 19.27.17
microanalyses 35.1.16(.10)
microanalysis 34.2.17(.10.5)
microbe 21.16.2
microbial 40.3.2
microbic 24.2.9(.7)
microbiological 40.23.12(.17.2)
microbiologically 1.31.24(.9.11)
microbiologist 22.29.2(.26.2)
microbiology 1.26.10(.11.1)
microburst 22.29.16
Microcard® 23.9.9
microcephalic 24.2.27(.6)
microcephalous 34.18.29(.17.4)
microcephaly 1.31.17(.16.1)
microchip 20.2.8
microcircuit 22.2.9(.8)
microcircuitry 1.29.15(.6)
microclimate 22.19.14
microclimatic 24.2.10(.4.2)
microclimatically 1.31.24(.9.4)
microcline 28.14.19(.16)
microcode 23.20.7
microcomputer 17.12.15(.8)
microcopy 1.8.7

microcosm 27.15.21(.4)
microcosmic 24.2.14(.17)
microcosmically 1.31.24(.9.8)
microcrystalline 28.14.19(.11)
microdot 22.11.5
microeconomic 24.2.14(.6)
microelectronic 24.2.15(.6.4)
microelectronics 34.23.2(.6)
microfiche 36.1
microfilm 27.18
microfloppy 1.8.7
microform 27.10.5(.2)
microgram 27.6.17(.5)
micrograph 30.7.5(.1)
microgroove 31.10
microinstruction 28.17.25(.15.5)
microlight 22.16.25(.9)
microlith 32.2.9
microlithic 24.2.18(.1)
micromesh 36.5
micrometer 17.12.16(.9.2)
micrometre 17.12.1(.6)
micrometry 1.29.15(.8)
microminiaturization 28.17.25(.3.12)
micron 28.10.24(.9)
Micronesia 3.15.1, 17.33.12
Micronesian 28.17.26(.1), 28.17.32
micro-organism 27.15.21(.2.9)
microphone 28.19.11
microphonic 24.2.15(.6.3)
microphotograph 30.7.5(.1)
microphyte 22.16.16
microprocessor 17.24.5
microprogram 27.6.17(.5)
micropyle 40.13.1
microscope 20.15.4(.1)
microscopic 24.2.8(.5)
microscopical 40.23.12(.5)
microscopically 1.31.24(.9.2)
microscopist 22.29.2(.11)
microscopy 1.8.11(.5)
microsecond 23.24.16(.5)
microseism 27.15.21(.5)
Microsoft® 22.27.5
microsome 27.17.10
microspore 12.3

microstructure 17.28.20
microsurgery 1.29.11(.23)
microsurgical 40.23.12(.17.3)
microswitch 38.2.9
microtechnique 24.1.5
microtome 27.17.4
microtone 28.19.4(.5)
microtubule 40.15.9(.2)
microwave 31.3.6
micrurgy 1.26.11
micturition 28.17.25(.2.6)
mid 23.2
midair 6
Midas 34.18.12
midbrain 28.4.18
midcourse 34.12.2
midday 4.10
midden 28.17.12(.2)
middle 40.22.2
middlebrow 9.16
middleman 28.7.10(.24)
middlemen 28.5.7(.28)
middle-of-the-road 23.20.12
Middlesbrough 17.32.14(.5)
Middlesex 34.23.4(.10)
Middleton 28.17.11(.27)
middleweight 22.4.21
Middlewich 38.2.9
middling 29.1.31(.18)
middlingly 1.31.28(.1.18)
middy 1.11.2
Mideast 22.29.1
midfield 23.31.1(.2)
midfielder 17.13.23(.1)
Midgard 23.9.10
midge 39.2
midget 22.19.22
Midgley 1.31.37
midgut 22.15.5
Midhurst 22.29.16
MIDI 1.11.2
Midi 2.13
midi 1.11.2
Midian 28.3.4(.2)
Midianite 22.16.14(.1)
midibus 34.14
midinette 22.5.9
midiron 28.17.5
midland 23.24.16(.16.3)
midlander 17.13.20(.13)
midline 28.14.19(.15)
Midlothian 28.3.12
midmost 22.29.17(.4)
midnight 22.16.14(.8)
midpoint 22.26.11
Midrash 36.6.9, 36.12

Midrashim 27.2.11
midrib 21.2
midriff 30.2.5
midsection 28.17.25(.15.2)
midship 20.2.7(.15)
midshipman 28.17.16(.19)
midships 34.21.2
midst 22.29.19
midstream 27.1.12
midsummer 17.17.10
midterm 27.16.2
midtown 28.8.1
Midway 4.25.13
midway 4.25
midweek 24.1.10
Midwest 22.29.5(.11)
Midwestern 28.17.11(.25)
Midwesterner 17.18.16(.4)
midwicket 22.2.9(.1)
midwife 30.12
midwifery 1.29.11(.14)
midwinter 17.12.22(.1)
midwives 35.28.6
Miele 17.34.1
mien 28.1
Miesian 28.3.14
Mies van der Rohe 17.9
miff 30.2
MiG 26.2
might 22.16
mightest 22.29.15(.9)
might-have-been 28.1.8
mightily 1.31.17(.9.2)
mightiness 34.18.16(.2.3)
mightn't 22.26.15(.9)
mighty 1.10.13
migmatite 22.16.9
mignon 28.10.25
mignonette 22.5.9
migraine 28.4.18
migrainous 34.18.16(.4)
migrant 22.26.15(.23.4)
migrate 22.4.22(.11)
migration 28.17.25(.3.13)
migrational 40.26.13(.14.2)
migrator 17.12.4(.15)
migratory 1.29.11(.8.2)
Miguel 40.5.6
mihrab 21.7
Mikado 19.11.7
mike 24.13
Mikhail 40.13.5
mil 40.2
milady 1.11.4
Milan 28.7.22

Milanese 35.1.12
Milburn 28.18.3
milch 38.19
mild 23.31.9
milden 28.17.12(.27)
Mildenhall 40.10.16
mildew 16.24.6
mildewy 1(.6)
mildish 36.2.12
mildly 1.31.23(.18)
mildness 34.18.16(.21.1)
Mildred 23.18.27
mile 40.13
mileage 39.2.23
milepost 22.29.17(.1)
miler 17.34.13
Miles 35.30.10
Milesian 28.3.14, 28.17.26(.1)
milestone 28.19.4(.9)
Miletus 34.18.11(.1)
milfoil 40.11.7
Milford Haven 28.17.20(.3)
Milhaud 19.1, 19.28
miliaria 3.22.4
miliary 1.29.2(.12)
milieu 18.16
milieux 18.16, 35.19
militancy 1.22.23(.10.2)
militant 22.26.15(.9)
militantly 1.31.22(.20.2)
militaria 3.22.4
militarily 1.31.17(.27.1)
militariness 34.18.16(.2.9)
militarism 27.15.21(.2.14)
militarist 22.29.2(.29.3)
militaristic 24.2.10(.15.2)
militaristically 1.31.24(.9.6)
militarization 28.17.25(.3.11)
militarize 35.15.20(.2)
military 1.29.11(.8.10)
militate 22.4.9(.5)
militeristically 1.31.24(.9.6)
militia 17.26.2
militiaman 28.17.16(.16)
milk 24.21
milker 17.14.25
milkily 1.31.17(.11)
milkiness 34.18.16(.2.4)
milkmaid 23.4.7
milkman 28.17.16(.23)
milkmen 28.5.7(.17)
milksop 20.7.8
milkwort 22.20.15
milky 1.12.19
mill 40.2

millable 40.20.16(.29)
millage 39.2.23
Millais 4.28.1
Millar 17.34.2
Millard 23.9.22
Millay 4.28.1
Millbank 24.19.3(.1)
millboard 23.12.2(.20)
milldam 27.6.5
millenarian 28.3.20(.4)
millenarianism 27.15.21(.2.9)
millenarianist 22.29.2(.18.1)
millenary 1.29.11(.13.1)
millenia 3.9.4
millennial 40.3.7(.4)
millennialist 22.29.2(.31.1)
millennium 27.3.8(.4)
millepore 12.3
miller 17.34.2
millesimal 40.25.10
millesimally 1.31.17(.13)
millet 22.2.25
millhand 23.24.6(.11)
milliammeter 17.12.16(.9.1)
milliampere 6.2
milliard 23.9.2
millibar 10.5.2
Millicent 22.26.15(.17.3)
Millie 1.31.2
Milligan 28.17.15(.13)
milligram 27.6.17(.5)
Millikan 28.17.13(.13)
millilitre 17.12.1(.15)
millimetre 17.12.1(.6)
millimicron 28.10.24(.9)
milliner 17.18.16(.22)
millinery 1.29.11(.13.2)
million 28.3.21(.2)
millionaire 6.9
millionairess 34.5.14(.1), 34.18.27(.4)
millionfold 23.31.13(.7)
millionth 32.21
millipede 23.1.1
millisecond 23.24.16(.5)
millivolt 22.32.5, 22.32.12
milliwatt 22.11.14
millpond 23.24.9
millrace 34.4.13
Mills 35.30.2
millstone 28.19.4(.9)
millstream 27.1.12
Millwall 40.10.17
millwheel 40.1.14
millworker 17.14.16
millwright 22.16.24(.19)

Milne 28.20
Milner 17.18.32
Milngavie 14.11
milo 19.29.9
milometer 17.12.16(.9.2)
milord 23.12.11
Milosz 36.9.6
milquetoast 22.29.17(.2)
milt 22.32.1
milter 17.12.26(.1)
Milton 28.17.11(.27)
Miltonian 28.3.8(.11)
Miltonic 24.2.15(.6.1)
Milwaukee 1.12.8
Mimas 34.7.11, 34.18.15(.8)
mimbar 10.5.10
mime 27.12
mimeo 15.1.5
mimeograph 30.7.5(.1)
mimer 17.17.11
mimesis 34.2.17(.1)
mimetic 24.2.10(.3.1)
mimetically 1.31.24(.9.3)
Mimi 1.15.1
mimic 24.2.14(.2)
mimicker 17.14.15(.8)
mimicry 1.29.17
miminy-piminy 1.16.15(.11)
mimosa 17.24.17, 17.25.15
mimulus 34.18.29(.17.6)
Min 28.2
mina 17.18.13
minacious 34.18.22(.3)
minacity 1.10.16(.16.1)
minae 2.17.8
Minaean 28.17.1(.7)
minaret 22.5.19
minareted 23.18.9(.4)
minatory 1.29.11(.8.7)
minbar 10.5.11
mince 34.24.1
mincemeat 22.1.5
mincer 17.24.22(.1)
Minch 38.18.1
mincingly 1.31.28(.1.11)
mind 23.24.13
Mindanao 9.7
minder 17.13.20(.11)
mindful 40.27.19, 40.27.22
mindfully 1.31.17(.16.2)
mindfulness 34.18.16(.37.2)
mindless 34.18.29(.23)
mindlessly 1.31.33(.12.6)
mindlessness 34.18.16(.31.6)
mind-numbing 29.1.16
Mindoro 19.27.7

mind-read 23.1.11, 23.5.15
mind-reader 17.13.1
mindset 22.5.13(.9)
Mindy 1.11.20(.1)
mine 28.14
minefield 23.31.1(.2)
Minehead 23.5.13(.14)
minelayer 17.2.10
minelaying 29.1.3
Minelli 1.31.5
miner 17.18.13
mineral 40.16.13(.12.2)
mineralization 28.17.25(.3.12)
mineralize 35.15.21(.4.7)
mineralogical 40.23.12(.17.2)
mineralogist 22.29.2(.26.1)
mineralogy 1.26.10(.10)
Minerva 17.21.13
minestrone 1.16.17(.13)
minesweeper 17.10.1
minesweeping 29.1.10(.1)
mineworker 17.14.16
Ming 29.1
mingily 1.31.17(.25)
mingle 40.24.14(.1)
mingler 17.34.24
Mingulay 4.28.7
Mingus 34.18.14(.8)
mingy 1.26.13
mini 1.16.2
miniate 22.4.2(.7)
miniature 17.28.15
miniaturist 22.29.2(.29.4)
miniaturization 28.17.25(.3.12)
miniaturize 35.15.20(.2)
minibar 10.5.2
minibike 24.13.2
minibus 34.14
minicab 21.6
minicam 27.6.6
Minicom 27.9
minicomputer 17.12.15(.8)
minicourse 34.12.2
minidress 34.5.14(.6)
minify 14.14.4(.7)
minikin 28.2.13(.6)
minim 27.2.6
minima 17.17.14(.6)
minimal 40.25.10
minimalism 27.15.21(.2.15)
minimalist 22.29.2(.31.3)
minimally 1.31.17(.13)
minimax 34.23.5(.6)

minimization 28.17.25(.3.11)
minimize 35.15.11
minimizer 17.25.12(.5)
minimum 27.15.13
minion 28.3.8(.2), 28.17.32
minipill 40.2.3
miniseries 35.2.17
miniskirt 22.20.4
minister 17.12.24(.14)
ministerial 40.3.14(.2)
ministerialist 22.29.2(.31.1)
ministerially 1.31.3(.11)
ministership 20.2.7(.9)
ministrable 40.20.16(.27.6)
ministrant 22.26.15(.23.4)
ministration 28.17.25(.3.13)
ministrative 31.2.1(.9.4)
ministry 1.29.15(.17)
minium 27.3.8(.2)
minivan 28.7.13
miniver 17.21.12
mink 24.19.1
minke 1.12.16, 17.14.21(.1)
Minkowski 1.12.17(.13)
Minna 17.18.2
Minneapolis 34.2.22(.8)
Minnehaha 10.21
Minnesinger 17.16.17(.1)
Minnesota 17.12.18
Minnesotan 28.17.11(.17)
Minnie 1.16.2
minnow 19.15.2
Minoan 28.17.8
Minogue 26.15
Minolta® 17.12.26(.5)
minor 17.18.13
Minorca 17.14.9
Minorcan 28.17.13(.8)
Minories 35.2.17
Minorite 22.16.24(.9)
minority 1.10.16(.21.2)
Minos 34.10.13
Minotaur 12.5.5
minoxidil 40.2.6
Minsk 24.20.13
minster 17.12.24(.23)
minstrel 40.16.13(.16)
minstrelsy 1.22.26
mint 22.26.1
mintage 39.2.10
Minter 17.12.22(.1)
mintiness 34.18.16(.2.3)
Minto® 19.10.17
Minton 28.17.11(.22)
minty 1.10.23(.1)
minuend 23.24.5(.1)

minuet 22.5
minus 34.18.16(.13)
minuscular 17.34.16(.21.2)
minuscule 40.15.9(.5)
minute 22.2.12, 22.18.10
minutely 1.31.22(.14)
Minuteman 28.7.10(.11)
Minutemen 28.5.7(.15)
minuteness 34.18.16(.20.2)
minutia 3.16.6, 17.26.13
minutiae 2.3, 14.2
minx 34.23.18
minxish 36.2.21
minxishly 1.31.35(.7.4)
Minya Konka 17.14.21(.5)
Miocene 28.1.18(.6)
mioses 35.1.16(.11)
miosis 34.2.17(.11.1)
miotic 24.2.10(.6)
Miquelon 28.10.26
Mir 3
Mira 17.32.13
Mirabeau 19.9.9
mirabelle 40.5.2
miracle 40.23.12(.18)
miraculous 34.18.29(.17.6)
miraculously 1.31.33(.12.6)
miraculousness 34.18.16(.31.6)
mirador 12.6, 12.6.6
mirage 37.4.9
Miranda 17.13.20(.4)
MIRAS 34.18.27(.10)
mire 17.6
mirepoix 10.22.3
Mirfield 23.31.1(.2)
Miriam 27.3.17(.1)
mirid 23.2.22
miriness 34.18.16(.2.9)
mirkily 1.31.17(.11)
Miró 19.27
Mirren 28.17.31(.1)
mirror 17.32.1
mirth 32.15
mirthful 40.27.24
mirthfully 1.31.17(.16.2)
mirthfulness 34.18.16(.37.2)
mirthless 34.18.29(.31)
mirthlessly 1.31.33(.12.6)
mirthlessness 34.18.16(.31.6)
MIRV 31.11
miry 1.29.11(.2)
misaddress 34.5.14(.6)
misadventure 17.28.22
misadvise 35.15.14

misalign 28.14.19
misalignment 22.26.15(.13.4)
misalliance 34.24.10(.5)
misally 14.25
misanthrope 20.15.8
misanthropic 24.2.8(.5)
misanthropical 40.23.12(.5)
misanthropically 1.31.24(.9.2)
misanthropist 22.29.2(.11)
misanthropize 35.15.5
misanthropy 1.8.11(.8)
misapplication 28.17.25(.3.5)
misapply 14.25.11
misapprehend 23.24.5(.13)
misapprehension 28.17.25(.16)
misapprehensive 31.2.4(.13)
misappropriate 22.4.2(.14)
misappropriation 28.17.25(.3.1)
misbecame 27.4.3
misbecome 27.11.5
misbegotten 28.17.11(.9)
misbehave 31.3.5
misbehaver 17.21.3
misbehaviour 17.33.10
misbelief 30.1.9
miscalculate 22.4.23(.7.3)
miscalculation 28.17.25(.3.14)
miscall 40.10.7
miscarriage 39.2.22(.4)
miscarry 1.29.5
miscast 22.29.6(.5), 22.29.8(.3)
miscegenation 28.17.25(.3.8)
miscellanea 3.9.3(.9)
miscellaneous 34.3.6(.3)
miscellaneously 1.31.33(.1.2)
miscellaneousness 34.18.16(.31.1)
miscellanist 22.29.15(.13)
miscellany 1.16.15(.20)
mischance 34.24.6
mischief 30.14
mischief-maker 17.14.3(.3)
mischievous 34.18.18
mischievously 1.31.33(.12.4)
mischievousness 34.18.16(.31.3)

m

misuse **34.17.13, 35.17.7**
misuser **17.25.14**
Mitanni **1.16.6**
Mitannian **28.3.8(.5)**
Mitch **38.2**
Mitcham **27.15.23**
Mitchell **40.16.12**
Mitchum **27.15.23**
mite **22.16**
Mitford **23.18.16(.11)**
Mithraic **24.2.3**
Mithraism **27.15.21(.2.1)**
Mithraist **22.29.2(.3)**
Mithras **34.7.18**
Mithridates **35.1.7(.2)**
mithridatic **24.2.10(.4.1)**
mithridatism **27.15.21(.2.4)**
mithridatize **35.15.7(.3)**
mitigable **40.20.16(.14)**
mitigate **22.4.12(.5)**
mitigation **28.17.25(.3.6)**
mitigator **17.12.4(.8)**
mitigatory **1.29.11(.8.2)**
Mitilíni **1.16.1(.16)**
Mitla **17.34.21**
mitochondria **3.22.16**
mitochondrion **28.3.20(.12)**
mitosis **34.2.17(.11.1)**
mitotic **24.2.10(.6)**
mitrailleuse **35.19**
mitral **40.16.13(.16)**
mitre **17.12.13**
Mitsubishi® **1.24.2**
mitt **22.2**
mitten **28.17.11(.2)**
Mitterrand **11.17**
mittimus **34.18.15(.10)**
Mitty **1.10.2**
mity **1.10.13**
Mitylene **1.16.1**
Mitzi **1.22.21**
mitzvah **17.21.18**
mitzvoth **22.21.10**
mix **34.23.2**
mixable **40.20.16(.21.3)**
mixedness **34.18.16(.21.1)**
mixer **17.24.20**
Mixtec **24.4.4**
mixture **17.28.24**
Mizoram **27.15.26(.5)**
mizuna **17.18.15**
mizzen **28.17.24(.2)**
mizzenmast **22.29.6(.7), 22.29.8(.5)**
mizzen-sail **40.4.10, 40.31.21**
mizzle **40.32.2**
mizzly **1.31.34**

M.Litt. **22.2**
Mlle **40.5.12**
m'lud **23.14**
M.Mus. **35.14**
mnemonic **24.2.15(.6.2)**
mnemonically **1.31.24(.9.8)**
mnemonist **22.29.2(.18.1)**
Mnemosyne **1.16.15(.14)**
MO **19**
mo **19**
moa **17.9**
Moab **21.6**
Moabite **22.16.8**
moan **28.19**
moaner **17.18.18**
moanful **40.27.22**
moaningly **1.31.28(.1.7)**
moat **22.21**
mob **21.8**
mobber **17.11.8**
Mobberley **1.31.17(.8)**
mobbish **36.2.10**
Moberly **1.31.17(.8)**
Mobil® **40.20.18**
Mobile **40.1.2**
mobile **40.13.2**
mobiliary **1.29.2(.12)**
mobility **1.10.16(.22.1)**
mobilizable **40.20.16(.22)**
mobilization **28.17.25(.3.12)**
mobilize **35.15.21(.4.2)**
mobilizer **17.25.12(.15)**
Möbius strip **20.2**
mobocracy **1.22.16(.13)**
mobster **17.12.24(.17)**
Mobutu **16.7.3**
Moby Dick **24.2**
Mocatta **17.12.6**
moccasin **28.2.23(.9)**
mocha **17.14.8**
Mochica **17.14.1**
mock **24.9**
mockable **40.20.16(.13)**
mocker **17.14.8**
mockery **1.29.11(.10)**
mockingbird **23.19.1**
mockingly **1.31.28(.1.6)**
mod **23.10**
modal **40.22.15**
modality **1.10.16(.32.4)**
modally **1.31.17(.10)**
mod cons **35.26.10**
mode **23.20**
model **40.22.7**
modeller **17.34.16(.8)**
modem **27.5.5**
Modena **17.18.16(.5)**

moderate **22.4.22(.6), 22.19.24(.9)**
moderately **1.31.22(.15)**
moderateness **34.18.16(.20.3)**
moderation **28.17.25(.3.13)**
moderatism **27.15.21(.2.4)**
moderato **19.10.7**
moderator **17.12.4(.15)**
moderatorship **20.2.7(.9)**
modern **28.17.12(.9)**
modernism **27.15.21(.2.9)**
modernist **22.29.2(.18.1)**
modernistic **24.2.10(.15.2)**
modernistically **1.31.24(.9.6)**
modernity **1.10.16(.13)**
modernization **28.17.25(.3.11)**
modernize **35.15.12(.5)**
modernizer **17.25.12(.6)**
modernly **1.31.27(.14)**
modernness **34.18.16(.25)**
modest **22.29.15(.10)**
Modestine **28.1.9(.7)**
modestly **1.31.22(.22)**
Modesto **19.10.19**
modesty **1.10.26(.11)**
modicum **27.15.11(.9)**
modifiable **40.20.16(.5)**
modification **28.17.25(.3.5)**
modificatory **1.29.11(.8.2)**
modifier **17.6.9(.4)**
modify **14.14.4(.5)**
Modigliani **1.16.8**
modillion **28.3.21(.2)**
modi operandi **2.13, 14.9**
modish **36.2.12**
modishly **1.31.35(.7.1)**
modishness **34.18.16(.33.3)**
modiste **22.29.1**
modi vivendi **2.13, 14.9**
Mods **35.23.6**
modular **17.34.16(.19)**
modularity **1.10.16(.21.1)**
modularization **28.17.25(.3.12)**
modularize **35.15.20(.2)**
modulate **22.4.23(.7.2)**
modulation **28.17.25(.3.14)**
modulator **17.12.4(.16)**
module **40.15.9(.4)**
moduli **2.32.9(.8), 14.25.9**
modulo **19.29.12**
modulus **34.18.29(.17.5)**

modus operandi **2.13**
modus vivendi **2.13**
Moesia **3.14.1, 3.15.1**
mofette **22.5.10**
Moffatt **22.19.16**
mog **26.7**
Mogadishu **16.17**
Mogadon® **28.10.10**
Mogen David **23.2.15**
Mogford **23.18.16(.14)**
Mogg **26.7**
moggy **1.14.6**
mogul **40.24.13**
mohair **6.17**
Mohave **1.19.6**
mohawk **24.10.8**
Mohican **28.17.13(.1)**
Moho **19.26**
Mohock **24.9.13**
Mohole **40.18.13**
Mohs **19, 35.20**
moidore **12.6, 12.6.5**
moiety **1.10.16(.3)**
moil **40.11**
Moir **17.5**
Moira **17.32.11**
moire **10**
moiré **4.26.5**
moist **22.29.11**
moisten **28.17.23(.10)**
moistly **1.31.22(.22)**
moistness **34.18.16(.20.4)**
moisture **17.28.24**
moistureless **34.18.29(.17.5)**
moisturize **35.15.20(.2)**
moisturizer **17.25.12(.14)**
Mojave **1.19.6**
moke **24.18**
moko **19.12.14**
moksha **17.26.19**
mol **40.18**
molal **40.16.15**
molality **1.10.16(.32.14)**
molar **17.34.18**
molarity **1.10.16(.21.1)**
molasses **35.18.17**
mold **23.31.13**
Moldau **9.4**
Moldavia **3.11.3**
Moldavian **28.3.10**
molder **17.13.23(.8)**
moldiness **34.18.16(.2.3)**
Moldova **17.21.14(.5)**
moldy **1.11.23**
mole **40.18**
molecular **17.34.16(.21.2)**
molecularity **1.10.16(.21.1)**
molecularly **1.31.17(.29)**

molecule 40.15.9(.5)
molehill 40.2.18
Molesey 1.23.22
moleskin 28.2.13(.14)
molest 22.29.5(.13)
molestation 28.17.25(.3.3)
molester 17.12.24(.4)
Molesworth 32.14.15
Molière 6.1
Moline 28.1.27
moline 28.14.19
moll 40.9
Mollie 1.31.10
mollification 28.17.25(.3.5)
mollifier 17.6.9(.4)
mollify 14.14.4(.16)
Molloy 13.17
mollusc 24.20.8
molluscan 28.17.13(.18)
molluscoid 23.13.9
molluscous 34.18.13(.14)
molly 1.31.10
mollycoddle 40.22.7
mollymawk 24.10.5
moloch 24.9.16(.8)
Moloney 1.16.17(.15)
molossi 14.18
molossus 34.18.20
Molotov 30.8.4, 31.7
molt 22.32.12
molten 28.17.11(.27)
molto 19.10.21
Molton 28.17.11(.27)
Moluccas 35.18.10
moly 1.31.19
molybdate 22.4.10
molybdenite 22.16.14(.6)
molybdenum 27.15.14(.11)
molybdic 24.2.11(.14)
Molyneaux 19.15.12
Molyneux 16.24.10
mom 27.9
mom-and-pop 20.7.2
Mombasa 17.24.6
moment 22.26.15(.13.2)
momenta 17.12.22(.3)
momentarily 1.31.17(.27.1)
momentariness 34.18.16(.2.9)
momentary 1.29.11(.8.12)
momently 1.31.22(.20.3)
momentous 34.18.11(.14)
momentously 1.31.33(.12.2)
momentousness 34.18.16(.31.3)
momentum 27.15.9(.14)

Momi 14.12
momma 17.17.8
Mommsen 28.17.23(.23)
mommy 1.15.8
Momus 34.18.15(.12)
Mon 28.10, 28.19
Mona 17.18.18
monacal 40.23.12(.11)
Monacan 28.17.13(.6)
monachal 40.23.12(.11)
monachism 27.15.21(.2.6)
Monaco 19.12.6, 19.12.12
monad 23.7.12
monadelphous 34.18.17
monadic 24.2.11(.5)
monadism 27.15.21(.2.5)
monadnock 24.9.9
Monaghan 28.17.29
monandrous 34.18.27(.15)
monandry 1.29.16
monarch 24.16.7
monarchal 40.23.6
monarchial 40.3.5
monarchic 24.2.12
monarchical 40.23.12(.9)
monarchically 1.31.24(.9.7)
monarchism 27.15.21(.2.6)
monarchist 22.29.2(.15)
monarchy 1.12.13
Monash 36.6.7
monastery 1.29.11(.8.12), 1.29.15(.17)
monastic 24.2.10(.15.4)
monastically 1.31.24(.9.6)
monasticism 27.15.21(.2.12)
monasticize 35.15.16(.4)
Monastir 3.4.13
monatomic 24.2.14(.6)
monaural 40.16.13(.8)
monaurally 1.31.17(.27.1)
monazite 22.16.20
Monck 24.19.7
Monckton 28.17.11(.20)
Moncton 28.17.11(.20)
mondaine 28.4.4
Mondale 40.4.3
Monday 1.11.20(.7), 4.10.12
mondial 40.3.4
Mondriaan 28.3.20(.12)
Monégasque 24.20.4
Monel® 40.26.15
moneme 27.1.6
Monet 4.14
monetarily 1.31.17(.27.1)
monetarism 27.15.21(.2.14)

monetarist 22.29.2(.29.3)
monetary 1.29.11(.8.7)
monetization 28.17.25(.3.11)
monetize 35.15.7(.7)
money 1.16.12
moneybags 35.24
moneybox 34.23.8(.2)
moneychanger 17.29.16(.2)
moneyer 3.9.8
moneylender 17.13.20(.3)
moneylending 29.1.13(.14)
moneyless 34.18.29(.2)
moneymaker 17.14.3(.3)
moneymaking 29.1.14(.3)
moneywort 22.20.15
monger 17.16.17(.4)
mongo 19.13.12
Mongol 40.24.14(.3)
Mongolia 3.24.11
Mongolian 28.3.21(.11)
mongolism 27.15.21(.2.15)
mongoloid 23.13.20
mongoose 34.17.7
mongrel 40.16.13(.19)
mongrelism 27.15.21(.2.15)
mongrelization 28.17.25(.3.12)
mongrelize 35.15.21(.4.7)
mongrelly 1.31.17(.27.3)
'mongst 22.29.22
monial 40.3.7(.9)
Monica 17.14.15(.9)
monies 35.2.8
moniker 17.14.15(.9)
moniliform 27.10.5(.2)
Monique 24.1.5
monism 27.15.21(.2.9)
monist 22.29.2(.18.1)
monistic 24.2.10(.15.2)
monition 28.17.25(.2.4)
monitor 17.12.16(.10)
monitorial 40.3.14(.5)
monitorship 20.2.7(.9)
monitory 1.29.11(.8.7)
monk 24.19.7
monkery 1.29.11(.10)
monkey 1.12.16
monkeyish 36.2.1
monkeyshine 28.14.15
monkfish 36.2.18(.17)
monkhood 23.16.5(.8)
Monkhouse 34.8.6(.13)
monkish 36.2.13
monkishly 1.31.35(.7.1)

monkishness 34.18.16(.33.4)
Monks 34.23.18
monkshood 23.16.5(.13)
Monkton 28.17.11(.20)
Monmouth 32.14.11
Monmouthshire 17.26.22
Mono 19.15.14
mono 19.15.8
monoacid 23.18.20
monobasic 24.2.20(.3)
monocarpic 24.2.8(.4)
monocarpous 34.18.9(.5)
monocausal 40.32.9
monocephalous 34.18.29(.17.4)
Monoceros 34.18.27(.23)
monochasia 3.15.3
monochasium 27.3.12
monochord 23.12.4
monochromatic 24.2.10(.4.2)
monochromatically 1.31.24(.9.4)
monochromatism 27.15.21(.2.4)
monochromator 17.12.4(.9), 17.12.16(.9.2)
monochrome 27.17.13
monochromic 24.2.14(.12)
monocle 40.23.12(.11)
monoclinal 40.26.11
monocline 28.14.19(.16)
monoclinic 24.2.15(.2)
monoclonal 40.26.15
monocoque 24.9.6
monocot 22.11.6
monocotyledon 28.17.12(.1)
monocotyledonous 34.18.16(.15.2)
monocracy 1.22.16(.13)
monocratic 24.2.10(.4.5)
monocrotic 24.2.10(.6)
monocular 17.34.16(.21.2)
monocularly 1.31.17(.29)
monoculture 17.28.26
monocycle 40.23.10
monocyte 22.16.19(.9)
monodactylous 34.18.29(.17.2)
monodic 24.2.11(.7)
monodisperse 34.19.1
monodist 22.29.2(.14)
monodrama 17.17.7
monody 1.11.17
monoecious 34.18.22(.1)
monofil 40.2.11

monofilament 22.26.15(.13.2)
monogamist 22.29.2(.17)
monogamous 34.18.15(.10)
monogamously 1.31.33(.12.3)
monogamy 1.15.13(.4)
monogenean 28.3.8(.4), 28.17.1(.7)
monogenesis 34.2.17(.10.3)
monogenetic 24.2.10(.3.1)
monogeny 1.16.15(.17)
monoglot 22.11.17
monogram 27.6.17(.5)
monogrammatic 24.2.10(.4.2)
monograph 30.7.5(.1)
monographer 17.20.12(.5)
monographic 24.2.16(.3)
monographist 22.29.2(.19)
monogynous 34.18.16(.15.3)
monogyny 1.16.15(.17)
monohull 40.12
monohybrid 23.2.22
monohydric 24.2.26(.15)
monokini 1.16.1(.5)
monolatry 1.29.15(.13)
monolayer 17.2.10
monolingual 40.35.4
monolith 32.2.9
monolithic 24.2.18(.1)
monolithically 1.31.24(.9.10)
monolog 26.7.14
monologic 24.2.24(.4)
monological 40.23.12(.17.2)
monologist 22.29.2(.26.4)
monologize 35.15.18
monologue 26.7.14
monomania 3.9.3(.5)
monomaniac 24.6.1
monomaniacal 40.23.12(.3)
monomark 24.8.8
monomer 17.17.14(.6)
monomeric 24.2.26(.4)
monometallism 27.15.21(.2.15)
monomial 40.3.6
monomolecular 17.34.16(.21.2)
monomorphic 24.2.16(.5)
monomorphism 27.15.21(.2.10)

monomorphous 34.18.17
Monongahela 17.34.1
mononucleosis 34.2.17(.11.1)
monopetalous 34.18.29(.17.2)
monophagous 34.18.14(.5)
monophonic 24.2.15(.6.3)
monophonically 1.31.24(.9.8)
monophthong 29.6.8
monophthongal 40.24.14(.3)
monophthongally 1.31.17(.12)
Monophysite 22.16.19(.9)
monoplane 28.4.19
monopod 23.10.1
Monopole 40.18.3
monopolist 22.29.15(.18)
monopolistic 24.2.10(.15.3)
monopolization 28.17.25(.3.12)
monopolize 35.15.21(.4.2)
monopolizer 17.25.12(.15)
monopoly 1.31.17(.7)
monopsony 1.16.15(.14)
monopsychism 27.15.21(.2.6)
monopteros 34.10.16
monorail 40.4.14
monorhyme 27.12.7
monosaccharide 23.15.15
monosodium glutamate 22.4.13(.6)
monospermous 34.18.15(.11)
monostichous 34.18.13(.8)
monostrophic 24.2.16(.4)
monosyllabic 24.2.9(.2)
monosyllabically 1.31.24(.9.2)
monosyllable 40.20.16(.29)
monotheism 27.15.21(.2.1)
monotheist 22.29.2(.1)
monotheistic 24.2.10(.15.1)
monotheistically 1.31.24(.9.6)
Monothelite 22.16.25(.9)
monotint 22.26.1
monotone 28.19.4(.5)

monotonic 24.2.15(.6.1)
monotonically 1.31.24(.9.8)
monotonize 35.15.12(.5)
monotonous 34.18.16(.15.2)
monotonously 1.31.33(.12.3)
monotonousness 34.18.16(.31.3)
monotony 1.16.15(.7), 1.16.19
monotreme 27.1.12
Monotype® 20.10.2
monotypic 24.2.8(.1)
monounsaturate 22.19.24(.9)
monovalence 34.24.10(.24)
monovalency 1.22.23(.10.4)
monovalent 22.26.15(.25)
monoxide 23.15.11(.11)
Monroe 19.27
Monrovia 3.11.8
Monrovian 28.3.10
Mons 35.26.10
Monseigneur 18.16
monsieur 18.16
Monsignor 12.22, 17.33.9
monsignore 1.29.8
monsignori 2.30.4
monsoon 28.16.10
monsoonal 40.26.12
mons pubis 34.2.7
monster 17.12.24(.23)
monstera 17.32.2, 17.32.14(.6)
monstrance 34.24.10(.16)
monstrosity 1.10.16(.16.2)
monstrous 34.18.27(.14)
monstrously 1.31.33(.12.5)
mons veneris 34.2.21
montage 37.4.3
Montagna 17.33.9
Montagnard 23.9.21
Montague 16.24.8
Montaigne 28.4.3
Montana 17.18.6
Montanan 28.17.17(.5)
montane 28.4.3
Montanism 27.15.21(.2.9)
Montanist 22.29.2(.18.1)
Mont Blanc 11
montbretia 17.26.1
Montcalm 27.8.5
Monte 1.10.23(.7)
Monte Carlo 19.29.7
Monte Cassino 19.15.1

Montefiore 1.29.8
Montego Bay 4
Monteith 32.1
Montenegrin 28.2.29(.11)
Montenegro 19.27.18
Monterrey 4.26
Montesquieu 16.24.7, 18.16
Montessori 1.29.8
Monteverdi 1.11.6, 1.11.18
Montevideo 19.2
Montez 35.5.5
Montezuma 17.17.13
Montfort 22.19.16
Montgolfier 3.10.6, 4.2.5
Montgomery 1.29.11(.12)
month 32.21
monthly 1.31.31
Monticello 19.29.4
monticule 40.15.9(.5)
monting 29.1.12(.19)
Montmartre 17.32.19(.4)
Montmorency 1.22.23(.3)
montmorillonite 22.16.14(.6)
Mont Pelée 4.28.2
Montpelier 3.24.1
Montpellier 3.24.4, 4.2.10
Montreal 40.10
Montreux 18.15
Montrose 35.20.12
Mont-Saint-Michel 40.5.13
Montserrat 22.7.20
Montserratian 28.3.3
Monty 1.10.23(.7)
monument 22.26.15(.13.2)
monumental 40.21.17(.2)
monumentalism 27.15.21(.2.15)
monumentality 1.10.16(.32.3)
monumentalize 35.15.21(.4.3)
monumentally 1.31.17(.9.3)
Monza 17.25.18
moo 16
mooch 38.14
moocher 17.28.14
moocow 9.5
mood 23.17
Moodie 1.11.16
moodily 1.31.17(.10)
moodiness 34.18.16(.2.3)
moody 1.11.16
Moog 26.12
moolah 17.34.15
mooli 1.31.16

moolvi 1.19.14
moolvie 1.19.14
moon 28.16
moonbeam 27.1.1
mooncalf 30.7.3
Mooney 1.16.14
moonfish 36.2.18(.19)
Moonie 1.16.14
moonily 1.31.17(.14.1)
moonless 34.18.29(.27)
moonlight 22.16.25(.17)
moonlighter 17.12.13(.9)
moonlit 22.2.25
moonquake 24.3.12
moonrise 35.15.20(.5)
moonscape 20.3
moonset 22.5.13(.11)
moonshine 28.14.15
moonshiner 17.18.13(.10)
moonshot 22.11.12
moonstone 28.19.4(.9)
moonstruck 24.12.8
moony 1.16.14
moor 12, 17.7
moorage 39.2.22(.6)
moorcock 24.9.6
Moorcroft 22.27.5
Moore 12, 17.7
moorfowl 40.7
Moorhead 23.5.13(.4)
moorhen 28.5.16
Moorhouse 34.8.6(.6)
mooring 29.1.30(.7)
Moorish 36.2.25
Moorish idol 40.22.11
moorland 23.24.16(.16.2)
Moorman 28.17.16(.11)
moory 1.29.8, 1.29.11(.3)
moose 34.17
moot 22.18
mop 20.7
mope 20.15
moped 23.5.1
moper 17.10.16
mopey 1.8.13
mophead 23.5.13(.7)
mopily 1.31.17(.7)
mopiness 34.18.16(.2.2)
mopish 36.2.9
mopoke 24.18.1
moppet 22.2.5
moppy 1.8.7
Mopti 1.10.19
moquette 22.5.5
mor 12
Morag 26.5.8
morainal 40.26.3
moraine 28.4.18
morainic 24.2.15(.3)
moral 40.16.13(.7)

morale 40.8.15
Morales 35.2.19
moralisingly 1.31.28(.1.12)
moralism 27.15.21(.2.15)
moralist 22.29.2(.31.4)
moralistic 24.2.10(.15.3)
moralistically 1.31.24(.9.6)
morality 1.10.16(.32.13)
moralization 28.17.25(.3.12)
moralize 35.15.21(.4.7)
moralizer 17.25.12(.15)
moralizingly 1.31.28(.1.12)
morally 1.31.17(.27.1)
Moran 28.7.20, 28.17.31(.8)
Morant 22.26.6
morass 34.7.18
moratoria 3.22.9
moratorium 27.3.17(.4)
Moravia 3.11.3
Moravian 28.3.10
moray 4.26, 4.26.6, 4.26.7
Moray Firth 32.15
morbid 23.2.7
morbidity 1.10.16(.9)
morbidly 1.31.23(.14.2)
morbidness 34.18.16(.21.1)
morbific 24.2.16(.1)
morbilli 2.32.2, 14.25.2
morbillivirus 34.18.27(.10)
mordacious 34.18.22(.3)
mordacity 1.10.16(.16.1)
mordancy 1.22.23(.10.2)
mordant 22.26.15(.10)
mordantly 1.31.22(.20.2)
Mordecai 14.10
mordent 22.26.15(.10)
Mordred 23.18.27
Mordvin 28.2.20
more 12
moreen 28.1.25
moreish 36.2.25
morel 40.5.18
morello 19.29.4
Moreno 19.15.1, 19.15.3
moreover 17.21.14
morepork 24.10.1
mores 35.4.16
Moresby 1.9.22
Moresco 19.12.17
Moresque 24.20.3
Moretonhampstead 23.5.3, 23.18.9(.20)
Morfa 17.21.8
Morgan 28.17.15(.9)
morganatic 24.2.10(.4.3)

morganatically 1.31.24(.9.4)
Morgan le Fay 4
morgen 28.17.15(.9)
morgue 26.9
Moriarty 1.10.8
moribund 23.24.12
moribundity 1.10.16(.9)
morion 28.3.20(.6)
Morisco 19.12.17
Morland 23.24.16(.16.2)
Morley 1.31.11
Mormon 28.17.16(.11)
Mormonism 27.15.21(.2.9)
morn 28.11
Morna 17.18.10
Mornay 4.14
morning 29.1.17(.8)
Mornington 28.17.11(.23)
Moro 19.27.7
Moroccan 28.17.13(.7)
Morocco 19.12.7
moron 28.10.24(.3)
Moroni 1.16.17(.13)
moronic 24.2.15(.6.4)
moronically 1.31.24(.9.8)
moronism 27.15.21(.2.9)
morose 34.20.16
morosely 1.31.33(.13)
moroseness 34.18.16(.31.7)
Morpeth 32.14.6
morph 30.9
morpheme 27.1.7
morphemic 24.2.14(.1)
morphemically 1.31.24(.9.8)
Morpheus 34.3.7
morphia 3.10.3
morphine 28.1.15
morphing 29.1.19
morphinism 27.15.21(.2.9)
morphogenesis 34.2.17(.10.3)
morphogenetic 24.2.10(.3.1)
morphogenic 24.2.15(.4)
morphological 40.23.12(.17.2)
morphologically 1.31.24(.9.11)
morphologist 22.29.2(.26.4)
morphology 1.26.10(.11.5)
morphometrics 34.23.2(.12)
morphometry 1.29.15(.8)

morphophonemic 24.2.14(.1)
morphophonemically 1.31.24(.9.8)
Morphy 1.18.6
morris 34.2.21
Morrison 28.17.23(.14)
Morrissey 1.22.16(.13)
morrow 19.27.6
morse 34.12
Morse code 23.20
morsel 40.31.9
mort 22.13
mortadella 17.34.5(.4)
mortal 40.21.8
mortality 1.10.16(.32.3)
mortally 1.31.17(.9.2)
mortar 17.12.10
mortarboard 23.12.2(.5)
mortarless 34.18.29(.17.2)
mortary 1.29.11(.8.4)
mortgage 39.2.13
mortgageable 40.20.16(.25)
mortgagee 2.27
mortgager 17.29.13
mortgagor 12.18, 17.29.13
mortician 28.17.25(.2.2)
mortification 28.17.25(.3.5)
mortify 14.14.4(.4)
mortifyingly 1.31.28(.1.1)
Mortimer 17.17.14(.2)
mortise 34.2.8
Mortlake 24.3.14
mortmain 28.4.7
Morton 28.17.11(.10)
mortuary 1.29.11(.3)
morula 17.34.16(.21.4)
morulae 2.32.9(.7)
Morwenna 17.18.4
morwong 29.6.13
mosaic 24.2.3
mosaicist 22.29.2(.22)
Mosaic Law 12
mosasaur 12.14.8
mosasauri 14.24.4
mosasaurus 34.18.27(.8)
moschatel 40.5.3
Moscow 19.12.17
Moseley 1.31.34
Moselle 40.5.12
Moser 17.25.15
Moses 35.18.18
mosey 1.23.15
moshav 31.6
moshavim 27.2.8
Moskva 17.21.15
Moslem 27.15.28(.20)
Mosley 1.31.34

mosque **24.20.5**
mosquito **19.10.1**
moss **34.10**
Mossad **23.7.13**
mossback **24.6.6(.20)**
Mossel Bay **4**
mossgrown **28.19.17**
mossie **1.22.9, 1.23.8**
mossiness **34.18.16(.2.7)**
mosslike **24.13.7(.22)**
mosso **19.20.6**
Mossop **20.13.4**
mosstrooper **17.10.13**
mossy **1.22.9**
most **22.29.17**
mostly **1.31.22(.22)**
Mostyn **28.2.11(.14)**
Mosul **40.31.14**
MOT **2.11**
mot **19**
mote **22.21**
motel **40.5.3**
motet **22.5.3**
moth **32.9**
mothball **40.10.4**
mother **17.23.10**
motherboard **23.12.2(.5)**
mothercraft **22.27.4(.4)**
motherfucker **17.14.11**
motherfucking
   29.1.14(.8)
motherhood **23.16.5(.3)**
motherland **23.24.6(.13)**
motherless
   34.18.29(.17.5)
motherlessness
   34.18.16(.31.6)
motherlike **24.13.7(.8)**
motherliness
   34.18.16(.2.10)
motherly **1.31.17(.19)**
Motherwell **40.5.17(.5)**
mothproof **30.13.4**
mothy **1.20.6**
motif **30.1.1**
motile **40.13.3(.6)**
motility **1.10.16(.23)**
motion **28.17.25(.13)**
motionless **34.18.29(.27)**
motionlessly
   1.31.33(.12.6)
motionlessness
   34.18.16(.31.6)
motivate **22.4.16**
motivation **28.17.25(.3.9)**
motivational
   40.26.13(.14.2)
motivationally
   1.31.17(.14.3)
motivator **17.12.4(.11)**
motive **31.2.1(.11)**

motiveless **34.18.29(.30)**
motivelessly
   1.31.33(.12.6)
motivelessness
   34.18.16(.31.6)
motivity **1.10.16(.15)**
mot juste **22.29.14**
motley **1.31.22(.9)**
motmot **22.11.8**
motocross **34.10.16**
moto perpetuo **19.6**
motor **17.12.18**
motorable **40.20.16(.27.3)**
motorbike **24.13.2**
motorboat **22.21.2**
motorcade **23.4.5**
motorcar **10.8.8**
motorcoach **38.17**
motorcycle **40.23.10**
motorcycling
   29.1.31(.19)
motorcyclist
   22.29.2(.31.6)
motorhome **27.17.12**
motorial **40.3.14(.5)**
motorist **22.29.2(.29.3)**
motorization
   28.17.25(.3.11)
motorize **35.15.20(.2)**
motorman **28.7.10(.6)**
motormen **28.5.7(.10)**
motormouth **32.7**
Motorola **17.34.18(.14)**
motorway **4.25.9**
motory **1.29.11(.8.11)**
Motown® **28.8.1**
mots justes **22.29.14**
Mott **22.11**
motte **22.11**
mottle **40.21.7**
motto **19.10.8**
Mottram **27.15.26(.10)**
Motu **16.7.6**
moue **16**
mouflon **28.10.26**
mouillé **4.1, 4.27**
moujik **24.2.22**
mould **23.31.13**
mouldable **40.20.16(.12)**
mouldboard **23.12.2(.9)**
moulder **17.13.23(.8)**
mouldiness **34.18.16(.2.3)**
moulding **29.1.13(.16)**
mouldy **1.11.23**
moulin **28.2.31(.9)**
Moulinex® **34.23.4(.6)**
Moulin Rouge **37.7**
Moulmein **28.4.7**
moult **22.32.12**
moulter **17.12.26(.7)**

Moulton **28.17.11(.27)**
mound **23.24.7**
mount **22.26.7**
mountable **40.20.16(.11.6)**
mountain **28.17.11(.22)**
mountaineer **3.9**
mountainous
   34.18.16(.15.2)
mountainside
   23.15.11(.12)
mountaintop **20.7.4**
mountainy **1.16.15(.7)**
Mountbatten **28.17.11(.6)**
mountebank **24.19.3(.1)**
mountebankery
   1.29.11(.10)
mounter **17.12.22(.5)**
Mountie **1.10.23(.5)**
Mount Isa **17.25.12**
Mountjoy **13.12**
Mounty **1.10.23(.5)**
mourn **28.11**
Mourne **28.11**
mourner **17.18.10**
mournful **40.27.22**
mournfully **1.31.17(.16.2)**
mournfulness
   34.18.16(.37.2)
mourning **29.1.17(.8)**
mouse **34.8**
mousehole **40.18.13**
Mousehoule **40.32.6**
mouselike **24.13.7(.22)**
mouser **17.24.7**
mousetrap **20.5.6**
mousey **1.22.7**
mousily **1.31.17(.20)**
mousiness **34.18.16(.2.7)**
moussaka **17.14.7**
mousse **34.17**
mousseline **28.1.27(.12)**
moustache **36.8**
moustachio **19.22**
Mousterian **28.3.20(.2)**
mousy **1.22.7**
mouth **32.7, 33.5**
mouthbrooder **17.13.14**
mouther **17.23.6**
mouthful **40.14.6(.18)**
mouthless **34.18.29(.31)**
mouthpart **22.10.1**
mouthpiece **34.1.1**
mouth-to-mouth **32.7**
mouthwash **36.9.5**
mouthy **1.21**
movability **1.10.16(.22.1)**
movable **40.20.16(.19)**
movableness
   34.18.16(.37.4)
movably **1.31.21(.7.1)**

move **31.10**
movement **22.26.15(.13.5)**
mover **17.21.11**
movie **1.19.9**
moviegoer **17.9.5**
movie house **34.8**
moviemaker **17.14.3(.3)**
Movietone® **28.19.4(.2)**
movingly **1.31.28(.1.9)**
mow **9, 19**
mowable **40.20.16(.8)**
Mowbray **4.26.10**
mowburnt **22.26.16**
mower **17.9**
Mowgli **1.31.25**
mowing **29.1.9**
mowlem **27.15.28(.13)**
mown **28.19**
moxa **17.24.20**
moxibustion **28.17.27**
moxie **1.22.22**
Moy **13**
Moya **17.5**
Moyer **17.5**
Moyers **35.18.3**
Moyne **28.12**
Moynihan **28.3.8(.8),
   28.7.18, 28.17.29**
Mozambican **28.17.13(.1)**
Mozambique **24.1.2**
Mozarab **21.14**
Mozarabic **24.2.9(.5)**
Mozart **22.10.9**
Mozartian **28.3.3**
mozz **35.10**
mozzarella **17.34.5(.15)**
mozzle **40.32.8**
MP **2.9**
mph **38.3**
MPhil **40.2.11**
MSc **2.22**
MS-DOS® **34.10.9**
MTech **24.4.4**
mu **16**
Mubarak **24.6.21**
much **38.11**
Muchinga **17.16.17(.1)**
muchly **1.31.36**
muchness **34.18.16(.35)**
mucilage **39.2.23**
mucilaginous
   34.18.16(.15.3)
mucin **28.2.23(.8)**
muck **24.12**
mucker **17.14.11**
muckerish **36.2.25**
muckheap **20.1**
muckily **1.31.17(.11)**
muckiness **34.18.16(.2.4)**
muckle **40.23.9**

muckrake **24.3.13**
muckraker **17.14.3(.8)**
muckworm **27.16.7**
mucky **1.12.9**
mucopolysaccharide **23.15.15**
mucosa **17.25.15**
mucosity **1.10.16(.16.2)**
mucous **34.18.13(.9)**
mucro **19.27.17**
mucronate **22.4.14(.9.4), 22.19.15(.9)**
mucus **34.18.13(.9)**
mud **23.14**
mudbank **24.19.3(.1)**
mudbath **32.8**
mudbrick **24.2.26(.13)**
muddily **1.31.17(.10)**
muddiness **34.18.16(.2.3)**
muddle **40.22.10**
muddler **17.34.22**
muddlingly **1.31.28(.1.18)**
muddy **1.11.13**
Mudeford **23.18.16(.2)**
Mudéjar **10.21**
Mudéjares **34.5.14(.2)**
mudfish **36.2.18(.16)**
mudflap **20.5.8**
mudflat **22.7.21**
mudflow **19.29.21**
Mudge **39.11**
mudguard **23.9.10**
Mudie **1.11.16**
mudlark **24.8.16**
mudpack **24.6.5**
mudroom **27.14.6(.9)**
mudskipper **17.10.2**
mudslinger **17.19.1**
mudslinging **29.1.18**
mudstone **28.19.4(.9)**
muesli **1.31.34**
muezzin **28.2.24**
muff **30.11**
muffetee **2.11**
muffin **28.2.19**
muffineer **3.9**
muffish **36.2.18(.8)**
muffle **40.27.11**
muffler **17.34.26**
mufti **1.10.24**
mug **26.10**
Mugabe **1.9.6**
mugful **40.14.6(.13)**
mugger **17.16.9**
Muggeridge **39.2.22(.9)**
mugginess **34.18.16(.2.4)**
mugging **29.1.15**
muggins **35.26.2**
muggy **1.14.8**
Mughal **40.24.10**

mugshot **22.11.12**
mugwort **22.20.15**
mugwump **20.16.5**
Muhammad **23.18.13**
Muhammadan **28.17.12(.16)**
Muhammadanism **27.15.21(.2.9)**
Muir **12, 17.7**
Muirhead **23.5.13(.4)**
mujahedin **28.1.10**
Mukden **28.17.12(.20)**
mukluk **24.12.9**
mulatto **19.10.6**
mulberry **1.29.11(.7.2)**
Mulcaghey **1.13**
Mulcahy **1.27**
mulch **38.19**
mulct **22.23.15**
Muldoon **28.16.4**
mule **40.15**
muleteer **3.4**
mulga **17.16.19**
Mulhearn **28.18.12**
Mulholland **23.24.16(.16.2)**
muli **1.31.16**
muliebrity **1.10.16(.21.3)**
mulish **36.2.27**
mulishly **1.31.35(.7.4)**
mulishness **34.18.16(.33.6)**
mull **40.12**
mullah **17.34.12, 17.34.14**
Mullan **28.17.33(.9)**
mullein **28.4.19, 28.17.33(.9)**
Mullen **28.17.33(.9)**
muller **17.34.12**
Müller **17.34.14**
mullet **22.19.26(.10)**
Mulley **1.31.13**
mulligan **28.17.15(.13)**
mulligatawny **1.16.10**
mulligrubs **35.21**
Mullins **35.26.2**
mullion **28.3.21(.8)**
mullock **24.16.16**
mulloway **4.25.9**
Mulroney **1.16.17(.13)**
multangular **17.34.16(.21.3)**
multiaxial **40.3.10**
multicellular **17.34.16(.21.4)**
multichannel **40.26.5**
multicolour **17.34.12**
multicoloured **23.18.29**
multicultural **40.16.13(.12.3)**

multiculturalism **27.15.21(.2.15)**
multiculturalist **22.29.2(.31.4)**
multiculturally **1.31.17(.27.2)**
multidimensional **40.26.13(.14.7)**
multidimensionality **1.10.16(.32.8)**
multidimensionally **1.31.17(.14.3)**
multidirectional **40.26.13(.14.6)**
multi-ethnic **24.2.15(.16)**
multifaceted **23.18.9(.13)**
multifarious **34.3.15(.3)**
multifariously **1.31.33(.1.4)**
multifariousness **34.18.16(.31.1)**
multifid **23.2.14**
multifoil **40.11.7**
multiform **27.10.5(.2)**
multiformity **1.10.16(.12)**
multifunction **28.17.25(.15.6)**
multifunctional **40.26.13(.14.6)**
multigrade **23.4.15**
multihull **40.12**
multilateral **40.16.13(.12.1)**
multilateralism **27.15.21(.2.15)**
multilateralist **22.29.2(.31.4)**
multilaterally **1.31.17(.27.1)**
multi-layered **23.18.1**
multilevel **40.28.4**
multilingual **40.35.4**
multilingualism **27.15.21(.2.15)**
multilingually **1.31.17(.26)**
multimedia **3.5.1**
multimillion **28.3.21(.2)**
multinational **40.26.13(.14.4)**
multinationally **1.31.17(.14.3)**
multinomial **40.3.6**
multiparous **34.18.27(.12)**
multipartite **22.16.9**
multi-party **1.10.8**
multiphase **35.4.9**
multiple **40.19.11**
multiplex **34.23.4(.12)**
multiplexer **17.24.20**
multiplexor **17.24.20**
multipliable **40.20.16(.5)**

multiplicable **40.20.16(.13)**
multiplicand **23.24.6(.7)**
multiplication **28.17.25(.3.5)**
multiplicative **31.2.1(.9.1)**
multiplicity **1.10.16(.16.1)**
multiplier **17.6.15**
multiply **14.25.11**
multipolar **17.34.18(.1)**
multiprocessing **29.1.23**
multiprocessor **17.24.5**
multiprogramming **29.1.16**
multipurpose **34.18.9(.9)**
multiracial **40.33.2**
multiracially **1.31.17(.22)**
multistage **39.4.2**
multistorey **1.29.8**
multitude **23.17.4(.1)**
multitudinous **34.18.16(.15.2)**
multitudinously **1.31.33(.12.3)**
multitudinousness **34.18.16(.31.3)**
multivalency **1.22.23(.10.4)**
multivalent **22.26.15(.25)**
multivalve **31.13**
multivariate **22.3.12**
multiversity **1.10.16(.16.2)**
multivocal **40.23.14**
multum in parvo **19.17**
multure **17.28.26**
mum **27.11**
mumble **40.20.19**
mumbler **17.34.20**
Mumbles **35.30.15**
mumbling **29.1.31(.16)**
mumblingly **1.31.28(.1.18)**
mumbo-jumbo **19.9.14**
mumchance **34.24.6**
mu-meson **28.10.19**
Mumford **23.18.16(.15)**
mummer **17.17.10**
mummery **1.29.11(.12)**
mummification **28.17.25(.3.5)**
mummify **14.14.4(.6)**
mumming **29.1.16**
mummy **1.15.10**
mumpish **36.2.9**
mumps **34.21.13**
Munch **24.19.8**
munch **38.18.7**
Munchausen **28.17.24(.5)**

m

München 28.17.25(.16), 28.17.27
munchies 35.2.13, 35.2.14
Muncie 1.22.23(.8)
Munda 17.13.20(.12)
mundane 28.4.4
mundanely 1.31.27(.4)
mundaneness 34.18.16(.25)
mundanity 1.10.16(.13)
mung 29.8, 29.10
mungo 19.13.12
Munich 24.2.15(.7), 25.1
municipal 40.19.11
municipality 1.10.16(.32.2)
municipalization 28.17.25(.3.12)
municipalize 35.15.21(.4.2)
municipally 1.31.17(.7)
munificence 34.24.10(.18)
munificent 22.26.15(.17.3)
muniment 22.26.15(.13.2)
munition 28.17.25(.2.4)
munitioner 17.18.16(.16)
munnion 28.17.32
Muñoz 35.20.13
Munro 19.27
munshi 2.24
Münster 17.12.24(.23)
munt 22.26.14
muntjac 24.6.18
Muntz metal 40.21.4
muon 28.10.5
muonic 24.2.15(.6.1)
murage 39.2.22(.6)
mural 40.16.13(.11)
muralist 22.29.2(.31.4)
Murchison 28.17.23(.14)
murder 17.13.16
murderer 17.32.14(.7)
murderess 34.5.14, 34.18.27(.15)
murderous 34.18.27(.15)
murderously 1.31.33(.12.5)
murderousness 34.18.16(.31.5)
Murdoch 24.9.5, 25.10
mure 12, 17.7
murex 34.23.4(.11)
Murgatroyd 23.13.19
muriatic 24.2.10(.4.1)
Muriel 40.3.14(.6)
Murillo 19.29.2
murine 28.2.29(.5), 28.14.18
murk 24.17

murkily 1.31.17(.11)
murkiness 34.18.16(.2.4)
murky 1.12.14
Murmansk 24.20.13
murmur 17.17.15
murmurer 17.32.14(.10)
murmuringly 1.31.28(.1.17)
murmurous 34.18.27(.18)
murphy 1.18.10
murrain 28.4.18, 28.17.31(.9)
Murray 1.29.9
murre 18
murrelet 22.19.26(.14)
murrey 1.29.9
murrhine 28.14.18, 28.17.31(.9)
Murrow 19.27.8
Murrumbidgee 2.27
Murtagh 17.12.17
murther 17.23.13
Mururoa 17.9.11
musaceous 34.18.22(.3)
Musala 17.34.8
muscadel 40.5.4
Muscadet 4.10, 4.10.7
muscadine 28.2.12, 28.14.6
muscarine 28.1.25(.3), 28.2.29(.5)
muscat 22.7.9
muscatel 40.5.3
muscle 40.31.10
muscleless 34.18.29(.38)
muscly 1.31.17(.20)
muscologist 22.29.2(.26.3)
muscology 1.26.10(.11.3)
muscovado 19.11.7
Muscovite 22.16.17
Muscovy 1.19.10
muscular 17.34.16(.21.2)
muscularity 1.10.16(.21.1)
muscularly 1.31.17(.29)
musculature 17.28.15
musculoskeletal 40.21.12
muse 35.17
museology 1.26.10(.11.1)
musette 22.5.14
museum 27.15.1
Musgrave 31.3.7
Musgrove 31.12
mush 36.12, 36.13
mushily 1.31.17(.22)
mushiness 34.18.16(.2.8)
mushroom 27.14.6(.19)
mushroomy 1.15.12
mushy 1.24.9

music 24.2.21
musical 40.23.12(.16)
musicale 40.6.6, 40.8.6
musicality 1.10.16(.32.5)
musicalize 35.15.21(.4.4)
musically 1.31.24(.9.10)
musicalness 34.18.16(.37.5)
musician 28.17.25(.2.5)
musicianly 1.31.27(.14)
musicianship 20.2.7(.19)
musicological 40.23.12(.17.2)
musicologically 1.31.24(.9.11)
musicologist 22.29.2(.26.3)
musicology 1.26.10(.11.3)
musing 29.1.24
musingly 1.31.28(.1.12)
musique concrète 22.5.19
musk 24.20.7
muskeg 26.4
muskellunge 39.17.8
musket 22.19.12(.14)
musketeer 3.4
musketoon 28.16.3
musketry 1.29.15(.6)
muskiness 34.18.16(.2.4)
muskmelon 28.17.33(.4)
Muskogean 28.3.6
muskrat 22.7.20
muskwood 23.16.6(.11)
musky 1.12.17(.7)
Muslim 27.15.28(.19)
muslin 28.17.33(.27)
musmon 28.17.16(.29)
muso 19.21
musquash 36.9.5
muss 34.14
mussel 40.31.10
Musselburgh 17.32.14(.5)
Mussolini 1.16.1(.16)
Mussorgsky 1.12.17(.10)
Mussulman 28.17.16(.35)
mussy 1.22.12
must 22.29.12
mustachio 15.1.9
Mustafa 17.20.5, 17.20.12(.1)
mustang 29.4.3
Mustapha 17.20.5, 17.20.12(.1)
mustard 23.18.9(.20)
muster 17.12.24(.10)
musterer 17.32.14(.6)
musth 22.29.12
mustily 1.31.17(.9.3)
mustiness 34.18.16(.2.3)
Mustique 24.1.3

mustn't 22.26.15(.17.3)
musty 1.10.26(.8)
Mut 22.15
mutability 1.10.16(.22.1)
mutable 40.20.16(.11.2)
mutagen 28.17.28(.9)
mutagenesis 34.2.17(.10.3)
mutagenic 24.2.15(.4)
mutant 22.26.15(.9)
mutate 22.4.9
mutation 28.17.25(.3.3)
mutational 40.26.13(.14.2)
mutationally 1.31.17(.14.3)
mutatis mutandis 34.2.9
mutch 38.11
mute 22.18
mutely 1.31.22(.14)
muteness 34.18.16(.20.2)
mutilate 22.4.23(.7.1)
mutilation 28.17.25(.3.1)
mutilative 31.2.1(.9.4)
mutilator 17.12.4(.16)
mutineer 3.9
mutinous 34.18.16(.15.2)
mutinously 1.31.33(.12.3)
mutiny 1.16.15(.7)
mutism 27.15.21(.2.4)
muton 28.10.9
mutt 22.15
mutter 17.12.12
mutterer 17.32.14(.6)
muttering 29.1.30(.8)
mutteringly 1.31.28(.1.17)
mutton 28.17.11(.11)
muttonchop 20.7.10
muttonhead 23.5.13(.14)
muttony 1.16.15(.7)
mutual 40.16.12
mutualism 27.15.21(.2.15)
mutualist 22.29.2(.31.5)
mutualistic 24.2.10(.15.3)
mutualistically 1.31.24(.9.6)
mutuality 1.10.16(.32.1)
mutually 1.31.17(.24)
mutuel 40.16.12
mutule 40.15.9(.3)
muu-muu 16.11
Muzak® 24.6.15
muzhik 24.2.22
muzz 35.14
muzzily 1.31.17(.21)
muzziness 34.18.16(.2.7)
muzzle 40.32.11
muzzler 17.34.28
muzzy 1.23.11

m

my 14
myalgia 3.19.10, 17.29.16(.9)
myalgic 24.2.24(.9)
myalism 27.15.21(.2.15)
myall 40.16.6
myasthenia 3.9.1
myasthenic 24.2.15(.4)
mycelia 3.24.1
mycelial 40.3.15
mycelium 27.3.18
Mycenae 2.17.1
Mycenaean 28.3.8(.1)
mycological 40.23.12(.17.2)
mycologically 1.31.24(.9.11)
mycologist 22.29.2(.26.3)
mycology 1.26.10(.11.3)
mycorrhiza 17.25.12(.14)
mycorrhizae 2.23
mycorrhizal 40.32.12
mycosis 34.2.17(.11.1)
mycotic 24.2.10(.6)
mycotoxin 28.2.23(.14)
mycotrophy 1.18.9(.2)
mydriasis 34.2.17(.2)
myelin 28.2.31(.10)
myelination 28.17.25(.3.8)
myelitis 34.18.11(.8)
myeloid 23.13.20
myeloma 17.17.16(.12)
myelomata 17.12.16(.9.3)
Myers 35.18.4
Myfanwy 1.28
Mykonos 34.10.13
Mylar 10.25.2
Myles 35.30.10
mylodon 28.10.10, 28.17.12(.16)
mylonite 22.16.14(.6)
mynah 17.18.13
Mynd 23.24.2
Mynett 22.5.9, 22.19.15(.7)
Mynott 22.19.15(.7)
Mynwy 1.28
myocardia 3.5.5
myocardial 40.3.4
myocardiogram 27.6.17(.5)
myocarditis 34.18.11(.8)
myocardium 27.3.4(.5)
myofibril 40.2.20
myogenic 24.2.15(.4)
myoglobin 28.2.10
myology 1.26.10(.11.1)
myope 20.15.1
myopia 3.2.7
myopic 24.2.8(.5)
myopically 1.31.24(.9.2)

myositis 34.18.11(.8)
myosote 22.21.11
myosotis 34.2.8
myotonia 3.9.11
myotonic 24.2.15(.6.1)
Myra 17.32.13
Myrdal 40.8.5
myriad 23.3
myriapod 23.10.1
myrmecology 1.26.10(.11.3)
myrmecophile 40.13.9
Myrmidon 28.17.12(.16)
Myrna 17.18.17
myrobalan 28.17.33(.13)
Myron 28.17.31(.10)
myrrh 18
myrrhic 24.2.26(.11)
myrrhy 1.29.12
myrtaceous 34.18.22(.3)
myrtle 40.21.13
myself 30.20.2
Mysia 3.14.2
Mysian 28.3.13
Mysore 12.14
mystagogic 24.2.24(.4)
mystagogical 40.23.12(.17.2)
mystagogue 26.7.6
mysterious 34.3.15(.2)
mysteriously 1.31.33(.1.4)
mysteriousness 34.18.16(.31.1)
mystery 1.29.11(.8.12)
mystic 24.2.10(.15.1)
mystical 40.23.12(.7.3)
mystically 1.31.24(.9.6)
mysticism 27.15.21(.2.12)
mystification 28.17.25(.3.5)
mystify 14.14.4(.4)
mystifyingly 1.31.28(.1.1)
mystique 24.1.3
myth 32.2
mythi 2.20, 14.16
mythic 24.2.18(.1)
mythical 40.23.12(.14)
mythically 1.31.24(.9.10)
mythicism 27.15.21(.2.12)
mythicist 22.29.2(.22)
mythicize 35.15.16(.4)
mythogenesis 34.2.17(.10.3)
mythographer 17.20.12(.5)
mythography 1.18.9(.3.2)
Mytholmroyd 23.13.19
mythologer 17.29.13
mythologic 24.2.24(.4)

mythological 40.23.12(.17.2)
mythologically 1.31.24(.9.11)
mythologist 22.29.2(.26.4)
mythologize 35.15.18
mythologizer 17.25.12(.12)
mythology 1.26.10(.11.5)
mythomania 3.9.3(.5)
mythomaniac 24.6.1
mythopoeia 17.1.1
mythopoeic 24.2.1
mythus 34.18.19
Mytilene 28.1.27(.7)
myxoedema 17.17.1
myxoma 17.17.16(.9)
myxomata 17.12.16(.9.3)
myxomatosis 34.2.17(.11.1)
myxomycete 22.1.9
myxovirus 34.18.27(.10)
n 28.5
NAAFI 1.18.4
nab 21.6
Nabarro 19.27.5
Nabataean 28.17.1(.3)
Nabi 2.10
Nabisco 19.12.17
Nablus 34.18.29(.21)
nabob 21.8
Nabokov 31.7
Naboth 32.9
nacarat 22.7.20
nacelle 40.5.11
nacho 19.24
NACODS 35.23.6
nacre 17.14.3
nacred 23.18.11
nacreous 34.3.15(.9)
NACRO 19.27.17
nacrous 34.18.27(.16)
Na-Dene 1.16.4, 1.16.5, 4.14
Nader 17.13.3
Nadia 3.5.3, 3.5.5
Nadine 28.1.10
nadir 3.5.3
nae 4
naevae 14.15
naevoid 23.13.14
naevus 34.18.18
naff 30.5
nag 26.5
naga 17.16.6
Nagaland 23.24.6(.13)
nagana 17.18.8(.4)
Nagasaki 1.12.5, 1.12.6
nagger 17.16.5
naggingly 1.31.28(.1.6)

Nagle 40.24.3
nagor 12.8
Nagorno-Karabakh 24.6.6
Nagoya 17.5
Nagpur 17.7.1
Nahuatl 40.21.6
Nahuatlan 28.17.33(.18)
Nahum 27.15.25
naiad 23.7.3
naiant 22.26.15(.2)
naif 30.1
nail 40.4
nailbrush 36.12
nailer 17.34.4
nailery 1.29.11(.27)
nailless 34.18.29(.38)
nainsook 24.14.7
Naipaul 40.10.3
naira 17.32.13
Nairn 28.6
Nairobi 1.9.13
Naismith 32.2.3
naive 31.1
naively 1.31.30(.1)
naiveté 4.9.7
naivety 1.10.16(.15), 1.10.25
Najaf 30.5.7
naked 23.18.11
nakedly 1.31.23(.14.5)
nakedness 34.18.16(.21.1)
naker 17.14.3
Nakuru 16.23.5
NALGO 19.13.15
Nam 27.6, 27.8
Namaqualand 23.24.6(.13)
namby-pamby 1.9.18
name 27.4
nameable 40.20.16(.15)
namedrop 20.7.12
name-dropper 17.10.8
nameless 34.18.29(.26)
namelessly 1.31.33(.12.6)
namelessness 34.18.16(.31.6)
namely 1.31.26(.3)
nameplate 22.4.23(.8)
namesake 24.3.10
Namibia 3.3.2
Namibian 28.3.2
namma 17.17.6
Namur 17.7.12(.7)
nan 28.7
nana 17.18.6, 17.18.8
Nanaimo 19.14.10
Nanak 24.6.11
Nancarrow 19.27.4
nance 34.24.4

navel **40.28.3**
navelwort **22.20.15**
navicular **17.34.16(.21.2)**
navigability **1.10.16(.22.2)**
navigable **40.20.16(.14)**
navigableness **34.18.16(.37.4)**
navigate **22.4.12(.5)**
navigation **28.17.25(.3.6)**
navigational **40.26.13(.14.2)**
navigator **17.12.4(.8)**
Navrátilová **17.21.14(.15)**
navvy **1.19.5**
navy **1.19.3**
nawab **21.7, 21.9**
Náxos **34.10.15**
nay **4**
Nayland **23.24.16(.16.1)**
Naylor **17.34.4**
naysay **4.18.3**
naysayer **17.2.7**
Nazarene **28.1.25**
Nazareth **32.14.16**
Nazca Lines **35.26.12**
naze **35.4**
Nazi **1.22.21**
Nazidom **27.15.10(.2)**
Nazification **28.17.25(.3.5)**
Nazify **14.14.4(.9)**
Naziism **27.15.21(.2.1)**
Nazirite **22.16.24(.9)**
Nazism **27.15.21(.2.12)**
Ndebele **1.31.1, 1.31.4**
N'Djamena **17.18.3**
Ndola **17.34.18(.4)**
né **4**
Neagh **4**
Neal **40.1**
Neale **40.1**
neanderthal **40.8.4**
neap **20.1**
Neapolitan **28.17.11(.15)**
near **3**
nearby **14.7**
Nearctic **24.2.10(.13)**
nearish **36.2.25**
nearly **1.31.3**
nearness **34.18.16(.3)**
nearside **23.15.11(.3)**
Neasden **28.17.12(.26)**
neat **22.1**
neaten **28.17.11(.1)**
neath **32.1**
neatly **1.31.22(.1)**
neatness **34.18.16(.20.1)**
Neave **31.1**
nebbish **36.2.10**
Nebraska **17.14.23**

Nebraskan **28.17.13(.18)**
Nebuchadnezzar **17.25.4**
nebula **17.34.16(.21.1)**
nebulae **2.32.9(.8)**
nebular **17.34.16(.21.1)**
nebulizer **17.25.12(.15)**
nebulosity **1.10.16(.16.2)**
nebulous **34.18.29(.17.6)**
nebulously **1.31.33(.12.6)**
nebulousness **34.18.16(.31.6)**
nebuly **1.31.17(.28)**
necessarian **28.3.20(.4)**
necessarianism **27.15.21(.2.9)**
necessarily **1.31.17(.27.1)**
necessariness **34.18.16(.2.9)**
necessary **1.29.11(.18)**
necessitarian **28.3.20(.4)**
necessitarianism **27.15.21(.2.9)**
necessitate **22.4.9(.5)**
necessitous **34.18.11(.10)**
necessitously **1.31.33(.12.2)**
necessitousness **34.18.16(.31.3)**
necessity **1.10.16(.16.1)**
neck **24.4**
neck-and-neck **24.4.7**
Neckar **10.8.2, 17.14.4**
neckband **23.24.6(.4)**
Necker **17.14.4**
neckerchief **30.1.7, 30.14**
necklace **34.18.29(.24)**
necklet **22.19.26(.19)**
neckline **28.14.19(.16)**
necktie **14.8**
neckwear **6.18.9**
necrobiosis **34.2.17(.11.1)**
necrobiotic **24.2.10(.6)**
necrogenic **24.2.15(.4)**
necrolatry **1.29.15(.13)**
necrological **40.23.12(.17.2)**
necrologist **22.29.2(.26.4)**
necrology **1.26.10(.11.5)**
necromancer **17.24.22(.3)**
necromancy **1.22.23(.4)**
necromantic **24.2.10(.14)**
necrophagous **34.18.14(.5)**
necrophil **40.2.11**
necrophile **40.13.9**
necrophilia **3.24.2**
necrophiliac **24.6.1**
necrophilic **24.2.27(.2)**
necrophilism **27.15.21(.2.15)**

necrophilist **22.29.2(.31.4)**
necrophily **1.31.17(.16.1)**
necrophobia **3.3.9**
necropolis **34.2.22(.8)**
necropsy **1.22.19**
necroscopic **24.2.8(.5)**
necroscopy **1.8.11(.5)**
necrose **34.20.16**
necrosis **34.2.17(.11.2)**
necrotic **24.2.10(.6)**
necrotize **35.15.7(.7)**
nectar **17.12.21(.2)**
nectarean **28.3.20(.4)**
nectared **23.18.9(.17)**
nectareous **34.3.15(.3)**
nectariferous **34.18.27(.20)**
nectarine **28.1.25(.3), 28.2.29(.5)**
nectarous **34.18.27(.14)**
nectary **1.29.11(.8.12)**
Ned **23.5**
neddy **1.11.5**
nee **4**
née **4**
need **23.1**
needful **40.27.19**
needfully **1.31.17(.16.2)**
needfulness **34.18.16(.37.2)**
Needham **27.15.10(.1)**
needily **1.31.17(.10)**
neediness **34.18.16(.2.3)**
needle **40.22.1**
needlecord **23.12.4**
needlecraft **22.27.4(.4)**
needleful **40.14.6(.22)**
needlepoint **22.26.11**
Needles **35.30.17**
needless **34.18.29(.23)**
needlessly **1.31.33(.12.6)**
needlessness **34.18.16(.31.6)**
needlewoman **28.17.16(.14)**
needlewomen **28.2.17(.1)**
needlework **24.17.6(.19)**
needn't **22.26.15(.10)**
needy **1.11.1**
neep **20.1**
ne'er **6**
ne'er-do-well **40.5.17(.5)**
nefarious **34.3.15(.3)**
nefariously **1.31.33(.1.4)**
nefariousness **34.18.16(.31.1)**
Nefertiti **1.10.1**
Neff® **30.4**
Nefyn **28.17.20(.4)**
neg. **26.4**

negate **22.4.12**
negation **28.17.25(.3.6)**
negationist **22.29.2(.18.2)**
negative **31.2.1(.9.1)**
negatively **1.31.30(.7.1)**
negativeness **34.18.16(.28.1)**
negativism **27.15.21(.2.11)**
negativist **22.29.2(.20)**
negativistic **24.2.10(.15.2)**
negativity **1.10.16(.15)**
negator **17.12.4(.8)**
negatory **1.29.11(.8.6)**
Negev **31.4**
neglect **22.23.4(.11)**
neglectful **40.27.18, 40.27.20**
neglectfully **1.31.17(.16.2)**
neglectfulness **34.18.16(.37.2)**
negligee **4.21**
negligence **34.24.10(.21)**
negligent **22.26.15(.21)**
negligently **1.31.22(.20.4)**
negligibility **1.10.16(.22.2)**
negligible **40.20.16(.25)**
negligibly **1.31.21(.7.4)**
Negombo **19.9.14**
negotiability **1.10.16(.22.2)**
negotiable **40.20.3, 40.20.16(.23)**
negotiant **22.26.2(.8), 22.26.15(.19)**
negotiate **22.4.2(.9)**
negotiation **28.17.25(.3.1)**
negotiator **17.12.4(.1)**
Negress **34.5.14(.8), 34.18.27(.17)**
Negrillo **19.29.2**
Negrito **19.10.1**
negritude **23.17.4(.1)**
Negro **19.27.18**
negroid **23.13.19**
Negroism **27.15.21(.2.1)**
Negrophobia **3.3.9**
Negrophobic **24.2.9(.7)**
negus **34.18.14(.1)**
Nehemiah **17.6.7**
Nehru **16.23.2**
neigh **4**
neighborly **1.31.17(.8)**
neighbour **17.11.3**
neighbourhood **23.16.5(.3)**
neighbourliness **34.18.16(.2.10)**
neighbourly **1.31.17(.8)**
Neil **40.1**

Neilson 28.17.23(.28)
neither 17.23.1, 17.23.11
nekton 28.10.9,
  28.17.11(.20)
Nell 40.5
Nellie 1.31.5
nelly 1.31.5
Nelson 28.17.23(.28)
nelumbo 19.9.14
nematocyst 22.29.2(.22)
nematode 23.20.5
Nembutal® 40.6.5, 40.9.7
nem con 28.10
nemertean 28.1.9(.3),
  28.3.3, 28.17.1(.3)
nemertine 28.1.9(.3),
  28.14.5
nemeses 35.1.16(.10)
nemesia 3.17
nemesis 34.2.17(.10.3)
Nemo 19.14.1
Nene 28.1, 28.5
nene 4.14
Nennius 34.3.6(.4)
nenuphar 10.12
neo-Cambrian
  28.3.20(.10)
Neocene 28.1.18(.1)
neoclassic 24.2.20(.5)
neoclassical 40.23.12(.15)
neoclassicism
  27.15.21(.2.12)
neoclassicist 22.29.2(.22)
neocolonial 40.3.7(.9)
neocolonialism
  27.15.21(.2.15)
neocolonialist
  22.29.2(.31.1)
neodymium 27.3.7
neolithic 24.2.18(.1)
neologian 28.3.18,
  28.17.28(.11)
neologism 27.15.21(.2.13)
neologist 22.29.2(.26.2)
neologize 35.15.18
neology 1.26.10(.11.1)
neomycin 28.17.23(.12)
neon 28.10.1
neonatal 40.21.3
neonate 22.4.14(.3)
neonatology
  1.26.10(.11.2)
neontologist
  22.29.2(.26.3)
neontology 1.26.10(.11.2)
neopentane 28.4.3
neophobia 3.3.9
neophron 28.10.24(.10)
neophyte 22.16.16
neoplasm 27.15.21(.3)
neoplastic 24.2.10(.15.4)

neo-plasticism
  27.15.21(.2.12)
Neoplatonic 24.2.15(.6.1)
Neoplatonism
  27.15.21(.2.9)
Neoplatonist
  22.29.2(.18.1)
neoprene 28.1.25(.4)
neostigmine 28.1.13
neotenic 24.2.15(.4)
neotenous 34.18.16(.15.2)
neoteny 1.16.15(.7)
neoteric 24.2.26(.4)
neotropical 40.23.12(.5)
Neozoic 24.2.7
Nepal 40.10.3
Nepalese 35.1.23
Nepali 1.31.11
nepenthe 1.20.10
nepenthes 35.1.15
nepeta 17.12.1(.1)
nepheline 28.1.27(.7)
nephelometer
  17.12.16(.9.2)
nephelometric
  24.2.26(.14.2)
nephelometry 1.29.15(.8)
nephew 16.24.11, 16.24.12
nephology 1.26.10(.11.5)
nephrectomy 1.15.13(.1)
nephridia 3.5.2
nephridiopore 12.3
nephridium 27.3.4(.2)
nephrite 22.16.24(.16)
nephritic 24.2.10(.2.4)
nephritis 34.2.8
nephrology 1.26.10(.11.5)
nephron 28.10.24(.10)
nephropathy 1.20.8
nephrosis 34.2.17(.11.2)
nephrotomy 1.15.13(.1)
nepotism 27.15.21(.2.4)
nepotist 22.29.2(.13)
nepotistic 24.2.10(.15.2)
Neptune 28.16.14
Neptunian 28.3.8(.9)
Neptunist 22.29.2(.18.1)
neptunium 27.3.8(.8)
nerd 23.19
nerdy 1.11.18
nereid 23.2.2
Nereus 34.3.15(.2)
nerine 1.16.1(.15),
  1.16.13
Nerissa 17.24.1
nerka 17.14.16
Nernst 22.29.21
Nero 19.27.1
neroli 1.31.17(.27.1)
Neronian 28.3.8(.11)
Neruda 17.13.14

Nerva 17.21.13
nervate 22.4.16
nervation 28.17.25(.3.9)
nerve 31.11
nerveless 34.18.29(.30)
nervelessly 1.31.33(.12.6)
nervelessness
  34.18.16(.31.6)
nerve-racking 29.1.14(.4)
nerve-wracking
  29.1.14(.4)
Nervi 1.19.11
nervily 1.31.17(.17)
nervine 28.1.16, 28.14.11
nerviness 34.18.16(.2.6)
nervous 34.18.18
nervously 1.31.33(.12.4)
nervousness
  34.18.16(.31.3)
nervure 17.7.12(.10),
  17.33.10
nervy 1.19.11
Nerys 34.18.27(.3)
Nesbit 22.2.6
Nescafé® 4.15
nescience 34.24.2
nescient 22.26.2(.7)
nesh 36.5
ness 34.5
Nessa 17.24.5
Nessie 1.22.5
nest 22.29.5
Nesta 17.12.24(.4)
nestful 40.14.6(.10)
Nestlé® 4.28.16, 40.31.5
nestle 40.31.5
nestlike 24.13.7(.12)
nestling 29.1.31(.26)
Nestor 17.12.24(.4)
Nestorian 28.3.20(.7)
Nestorianism
  27.15.21(.2.9)
Nestorius 34.3.15(.5)
net 22.5
netball 40.10.4
netful 40.14.6(.10)
nether 17.23.4
Netherlander
  17.13.20(.4)
Netherlandish 36.2.12
Netherlands 35.23.15
nethermost 22.29.17(.4)
netherworld 23.31.12
netsuke 1.12.11,
  1.12.17(.8)
nett 22.5
Nettie 1.10.4
nettle 40.21.4
Nettlefold 23.31.13(.7)
nettlesome 27.15.20(.22)
network 24.17.6(.8)

networker 17.14.16
neum 27.14
Neumann 28.17.16(.15)
neume 27.14
neural 40.16.13(.11)
neuralgia 17.29.16(.9)
neuralgic 24.2.24(.9)
neurally 1.31.17(.27.1)
neurasthenia 3.9.1
neurasthenic 24.2.15(.4)
neuration 28.17.25(.3.13)
neuritic 24.2.10(.2.4)
neuritis 34.2.8
neuroanatomical
  40.23.12(.10)
neuroanatomy
  1.15.13(.1)
neurobiological
  40.23.12(.17.2)
neurobiology
  1.26.10(.11.1)
neurofibroma
  17.17.16(.11)
neurofibromata
  17.12.16(.9.3)
neurofibromatosis
  34.2.17(.11.1)
neurogenesis
  34.2.17(.10.3)
neurogenic 24.2.15(.4)
neuroglia 3.24.15
neurohormone 28.19.9
neurolinguistic
  24.2.10(.15.2)
neurological
  40.23.12(.17.2)
neurologically
  1.31.24(.9.11)
neurologist 22.29.2(.26.4)
neurology 1.26.10(.11.5)
neuroma 17.17.16(.11)
neuromata 17.12.16(.9.3)
neuromuscular
  17.34.16(.21.2)
neuron 28.10.24(.5)
neuronal 40.26.13(.14.8),
  40.26.15
neurone 28.19.17
neuronic 24.2.15(.6.4)
neuropath 32.6.2
neuropathic 24.2.18(.3)
neuropathologist
  22.29.2(.26.4)
neuropathology
  1.26.10(.11.5)
neuropathy 1.20.8
neurophysiological
  40.23.12(.17.2)
neurophysiologist
  22.29.2(.26.2)
neurophysiology
  1.26.10(.11.1)

neuropsychological 40.23.12(.17.2)
neuropsychology 1.26.10(.11.3)
Neuroptera 17.32.14(.6)
neuropteran 28.17.31(.11)
neuropterous 34.18.27(.14)
neuroscience 34.24.10(.5)
neuroscientist 22.29.2(.13)
neuroses 35.1.16(.11)
neurosis 34.2.17(.11.2)
neurosurgery 1.29.11(.23)
neurosurgical 40.23.12(.17.3)
neurotic 24.2.10(.6)
neurotically 1.31.24(.9.4)
neuroticism 27.15.21(.2.12)
neurotomy 1.15.13(.1)
neurotransmitter 17.12.2
neuston 28.10.9
neuter 17.12.15
neutral 40.16.13(.16)
neutralism 27.15.21(.2.15)
neutralist 22.29.2(.31.4)
neutrality 1.10.16(.32.13)
neutralization 28.17.25(.3.12)
neutralize 35.15.21(.4.7)
neutralizer 17.25.12(.15)
neutrally 1.31.17(.27.3)
neutrino 19.15.1
neutron 28.10.24(.7)
neutropenia 3.9.1
neutrophil 40.2.11
Neva 17.21.1, 17.21.3
Nevada 17.13.7
Nevadan 28.17.12(.8)
névé 4.16
never 17.21.4
nevermore 12.9, 12.9.4
never-never 17.21.4
nevertheless 34.5.16
Neville 40.28.4
Nevin 28.17.20(.4)
Nevis 34.2.15
Nevsky 1.12.17(.14)
new 16
Newark 24.8, 24.16.2
Newbiggin 28.17.15(.2)
Newbold 23.31.13(.2)
Newbolt 22.32.12
newborn 28.11.2
Newborough 17.32.14(.5)
Newbould 23.31.13(.2)

Newbridge 39.2.22(.10)
Newburg 26.14.1(.3)
Newburgh 17.32.14(.5)
Newbury 1.29.11(.7.1)
Newby 1.9.10
Newcastle 40.31.6, 40.31.7
Newcastle upon Tyne 28.14
Newcombe 27.15.11(.8)
Newcome 27.15.11(.8)
Newcomen 28.17.16(.12)
newcomer 17.17.10
Newdigate 22.4.12(.5)
newel 40.16.8
Newell 40.16.8
newelpost 22.29.17(.1)
newfangled 23.31.19
Newfoundland 23.24.16(.16.3)
Newfoundlander 17.13.20(.13)
Newgate 22.4.12(.4)
Newham 27.15.5
Newhaven 28.17.20(.3)
Ne Win 28.2
Newington 28.17.11(.23)
newish 36.2.6
new-laid 23.4.16
Newlands 35.23.15
newly 1.31.16
Newlyn 28.2.31(.9)
newlywed 23.5.14
Newman 28.17.16(.15)
Newmark 24.8.8
Newmarket 22.2.9(.4)
new-mown 28.19.9
Newnes 35.26.12
newness 34.18.16(.14)
Newnham 27.15.14(.10)
New Orleans 35.26.13(.1)
Newport 22.13.1
Newquay 2.14
Newry 1.29.11(.3)
news 35.17
newsagent 22.26.15(.21)
newsboy 13.3
newsbrief 30.1.8
newscast 22.29.6(.5), 22.29.8(.3)
newscaster 17.12.24(.5)
newsflash 36.6.10
newsgirl 40.17
newshound 23.24.7(.8)
newsiness 34.18.16(.2.7)
newsless 34.18.29(.34)
newsletter 17.12.5(.11)
newsman 28.7.10(.21)
newsmen 28.5.7(.25)
newsmonger 17.16.17(.4)
Newsome 27.15.20(.10)

New South Wales 35.30.3
newspaper 17.10.3
newspaperman 28.7.10(.6)
newspapermen 28.5.7(.10)
newspeak 24.1.1
newsprint 22.26.1
newsreader 17.13.1
newsreel 40.1.15
newsroom 27.14.6(.18)
newssheet 22.1.11
newsstand 23.24.6(.5)
Newstead 23.5.3, 23.18.9(.20)
newsvendor 17.13.20(.3)
newsworthiness 34.18.16(.2.6)
newsworthy 1.21
newsy 1.23.12
newt 22.18
newton 28.17.11(.14)
Newton Abbott 22.19.9
Newtonian 28.3.8(.11)
Newtonmore 12.9
Newtown 28.8.1
Newtownabbey 1.9.5
next 22.29.20
nexus 34.18.20
Ney 4
Nez Percé 34.19
ngaio 19.5
Ngamiland 23.24.6(.13)
Nguni 1.16.14
Nguyen 28.5
niacin 28.17.23(.14)
Niagara 17.32.22
Niall 40.16.6
Niamey 4.13
nib 21.2
nibble 40.20.2
nibbler 17.34.20
Nibelung 29.9
Nibelungenlied 23.1.12
niblick 24.2.27(.14)
nicad 23.7.9
Nicaea 17.1.11
Nicam 27.6.6
Nicaragua 17.7.12(.6)
Nicaraguan 28.17.6
Nice 34.1
nice 34.15
niceish 36.2.21
nicely 1.31.33(.9)
Nicene 28.1.18
niceness 34.18.16(.31.2)
nicety 1.10.16(.16.2)
niche 36.1, 38.2
Nichol 40.23.2
Nicholas 34.18.29(.17.2)

Nichols 35.30.18
Nicholson 28.17.23(.28)
Nichrome® 27.17.13
nicish 36.2.21
nick 24.2
nickel 40.23.2
nickelic 24.2.27(.13)
nickelodeon 28.3.4(.10)
nickelous 34.18.29(.17.2)
nicker 17.14.2
Nicki 1.12.2
Nicklaus 34.18.29(.24)
Nickleby 1.9.24
nicknack 24.6.11
nickname 27.4.5
Nicky 1.12.2
Nicodemus 34.18.15(.1)
nicol 40.23.2
Nicola 17.34.16(.9)
Nicole 40.18.7
Nicolet 4.28
Nicolette 22.5.21
Nicoll 40.23.2
Nicomachean 28.17.1(.5)
Nicomachus 34.18.13(.10)
Nicosia 17.1.11
nicotiana 17.18.8
nicotinamide 23.15.7
nicotine 28.1.9(.3)
nicotinic 24.2.15(.2)
nicotinism 27.15.21(.2.9)
nicotinize 35.15.12(.5)
nictitate 22.4.9(.5)
nictitation 28.17.25(.3.3)
nidamental 40.21.17(.2)
nide 23.15
nidi 14.9
nidificate 22.4.11(.6)
nidification 28.17.25(.3.5)
nidifugous 34.18.14(.5)
nidify 14.14.4(.5)
nidus 34.18.12
niece 34.1
niello 19.29.4
nielsbohrium 27.3.17(.4)
Nielsen 28.17.23(.28)
Niemann 28.17.16(.1)
Niemeyer 17.6.7
Niemöller 17.34.14
Niersteiner 17.18.13(.1)
Nietzsche 17.28.1
Nietzschean 28.3.17
niff 30.2
niffy 1.18.2
Niflheim 27.12.6
niftily 1.31.17(.9.3)
niftiness 34.18.16(.2.3)
nifty 1.10.24
Nigel 40.34

noes **35.20**
noesis **34.2.17(.1)**
noetic **24.2.10(.3.1)**
nog **26.7**
noggin **28.2.15**
nogging **29.1.15**
Noguchi **1.25.11**
Noh **19**
no-hoper **17.10.16**
nohow **9.14**
noil **40.11**
noise **35.13**
noiseless **34.18.29(.34)**
noiselessly **1.31.33(.12.6)**
noiselessness
   34.18.16(.31.6)
noisemaker **17.14.3(.3)**
noisette **22.5.14**
noisily **1.31.17(.21)**
noisiness **34.18.16(.2.7)**
noisome **27.15.20(.8)**
noisomely **1.31.26(.11)**
noisomeness
   34.18.16(.24)
noisy **1.23.10**
Nok **24.9**
Nola **17.34.18**
Nolan **28.17.33(.15)**
nolens volens **35.26.5**
nolle prosequi **14.23**
nomad **23.7.11**
nomadic **24.2.11(.5)**
nomadically **1.31.24(.9.7)**
nomadism **27.15.21(.2.5)**
nomadize **35.15.8**
no-man's-land
   23.24.6(.13)
nombril **40.16.13(.15)**
nom de guerre **6**
nom de plume **27.14**
Nome **27.17**
nomen **28.5.7(.12),**
   28.17.16(.18)
nomenclative **31.2.1(.3)**
nomenclatural
   40.16.13(.12.3)
nomenclature **17.28.15**
nomenklatura
   17.32.14(.3)
nomina **17.18.16(.8)**
nominal **40.26.13(.8)**
nominalism
   27.15.21(.2.15)
nominalist **22.29.2(.31.3)**
nominalistic
   24.2.10(.15.3)
nominalization
   28.17.25(.3.12)
nominalize **35.15.21(.4.5)**
nominally **1.31.17(.14.2)**
nominate **22.4.14(.9.2)**

nomination **28.17.25(.3.8)**
nominatival **40.28.9**
nominative **31.2.1(.9.2)**
nominator **17.12.4(.10)**
nominee **2.17**
nomogram **27.6.17(.5)**
nomograph **30.7.5(.1)**
nomographic **24.2.16(.3)**
nomographically
   1.31.24(.9.9)
nomography **1.18.9(.3.2)**
nomothetic **24.2.10(.3.2)**
non **28.10**
nonacceptance
   34.24.10(.10)
nonage **39.2.15**
nonagenarian **28.3.20(.4)**
nonaggressive **31.2.4(.4)**
nonagon **28.10.12,**
   28.17.15(.13)
nonagression
   28.17.25(.4)
nonalcoholic **24.2.27(.9)**
nonaligned **23.24.13**
nonalignment
   22.26.15(.13.4)
nonappearance
   34.24.10(.16)
nonary **1.29.11(.13.3)**
nonassertive **31.2.1(.10)**
nonassertively
   1.31.30(.7.1)
nonattendance
   34.24.10(.11)
nonbelligerency
   1.22.23(.10.4)
nonbelligerent
   22.26.15(.23.3)
nonbiodegradable
   40.20.16(.12)
non-biological
   40.23.12(.17.2)
nonce **34.24.7**
nonchalance
   34.24.10(.24)
nonchalant **22.26.15(.25)**
nonchalantly
   1.31.22(.20.5)
non-com **27.9**
nonconformism
   27.15.21(.2.8)
nonconformist
   22.29.2(.17)
nonconformity
   1.10.16(.12)
nonda **17.13.20(.7)**
nondescript **22.22.1**
nondescriptly **1.31.20,**
   1.31.22(.18)
nondescriptness
   34.18.16(.20.4)
none **28.13**

nonentity **1.10.16(.8)**
nones **35.26.15**
nonessential **40.33.12(.3)**
nonesuch **38.11**
nonet **22.5.9**
nonetheless **34.5.16**
nonexistent **22.26.15(.9)**
nonfeasance
   34.24.10(.19)
nonfiction **28.17.25(.15.1)**
nong **29.6**
noninvolvement
   22.26.15(.13.5)
nonjoinder **17.13.20(.9)**
nonjuring **29.1.30(.8)**
nonjuror **17.32.14(.3)**
non-material **40.3.14(.2)**
no-no **19.15.14**
nonpareil **40.4.14,**
   40.16.13(.12.1)
non placet **22.5.13(.2)**
nonplus **34.14**
non possumus
   34.18.15(.10)
nonrestrictive
   31.2.1(.13.1)
nonreturnable
   40.20.16(.16.3)
nonsense **34.24.10(.18)**
nonsensical **40.23.12(.15)**
nonsensicality
   1.10.16(.32.5)
nonsensically
   1.31.24(.9.10)
non sequitur
   17.12.16(.17)
nonstandard
   23.18.10(.14)
nonstick **24.2.10(.15.1)**
nonstop **20.7.4**
nonsuch **38.11**
nonsuit **22.18.6**
nontheless **34.5.16**
non-U **16.24**
nonviolence **34.24.10(.24)**
nonviolent **22.26.15(.25)**
noodle **40.22.12**
nook **24.14**
nooky **1.12.11**
noon **28.16**
Noonan **28.17.17(.9)**
noonday **4.10.12**
no one **28.13**
noontide **23.15.4**
noontime **27.12.1**
noose **34.17**
Nootka **17.14.18**
nopal **40.19.13**
nope **20.15**
noplace **34.4.14**
nor **12**

Nora **17.32.10**
NORAD **23.7.16**
noradrenaline
   28.17.33(.13)
Noraid **23.4.15**
Norbert **22.19.9**
Norden **28.17.12(.10)**
Nordic **24.2.11(.8)**
Nordkinn **28.2.13(.10)**
Nore **12**
Noreen **28.1.25(.1)**
Norfolk **24.16.8**
Noriega **17.16.3**
nork **24.10**
norland **23.24.16(.16.2)**
norm **27.10**
Norma **17.17.9**
normal **40.25.6**
normalcy **1.22.26**
normality **1.10.16(.32.7)**
normalization
   28.17.25(.3.12)
normalize **35.15.21(.4.5)**
normalizer **17.25.12(.15)**
normally **1.31.17(.13)**
Norman **28.17.16(.11)**
Normandy **1.11.20(.9)**
Normanesque **24.20.3**
Normanism
   27.15.21(.2.9)
Normanize **35.15.12(.4)**
Normanton **28.17.11(.22)**
normative **31.2.1(.9.2)**
normatively **1.31.30(.7.1)**
normativeness
   34.18.16(.28.1)
Norn **28.11**
Norris **34.2.21**
Norrköping **29.1.10(.10)**
Norroy **13.15**
Norse **34.12**
Norseman **28.17.16(.29)**
Norsemen **28.5.7(.24)**
north **32.10**
Northallerton
   28.17.11(.15)
Northampton
   28.17.11(.18)
Northamptonshire
   17.26.21
Northanger **17.16.17(.2)**
Northants **34.22.18**
northbound **23.24.7(.2)**
Northcliffe **30.2.6**
northeast **22.29.1**
northeaster **17.12.24(.1)**
northeasterly
   1.31.17(.9.3)
Northenden **28.17.12(.23)**
norther **17.23.9**
northerly **1.31.17(.19)**

northern **28.17.22**
northerner **17.18.16(.13)**
northernmost
 22.29.17(.4)
Northfleet **22.1.18**
northing **29.1.22**
Northland
 23.24.16(.16.4)
Northman **28.17.16(.28)**
Northmen **28.5.7(.23)**
north-northeast **22.29.1**
Northolt **22.32.12**
North Pole **40.18**
Northrop **20.7.12**
Northrup **20.13.6**
Northumberland
 23.24.16(.16.2)
Northumbria **3.22.14**
Northumbrian
 28.3.20(.10)
northward **23.18.26(.15)**
northwest **22.29.5(.11)**
northwesterly
 1.31.17(.9.3)
North-West Frontier
 3.4.12
Northwich **38.2.9**
Norton **28.17.11(.10)**
Norvic **24.2.17**
Norway **4.25.6**
Norwegian **28.17.28(.1)**
nor'-wester **17.12.24(.4)**
Norwich **38.2.10,
 39.2.22(.5)**
Norwood **23.16.6(.4)**
nos **35.18.7**
nose **35.20**
nosebag **26.5.1**
noseband **23.24.6(.4)**
nosebleed **23.1.12**
nosecone **28.19.6**
nosedive **31.9**
nosegay **4.12**
noseless **34.18.29(.34)**
nosepipe **20.10.1**
nosering **29.1.30(.15)**
Nosferatu **16.7.2**
nosh **36.9**
noshery **1.29.11(.20)**
no-show **19.22**
nosh-up **20.9.13**
nosily **1.31.17(.21)**
nosiness **34.18.16(.2.7)**
nosocomial **40.3.6**
nosography **1.18.9(.3.2)**
nosological
 40.23.12(.17.2)
nosology **1.26.10(.11.5)**
nostalgia **3.19.10,
 17.29.16(.9)**
nostalgic **24.2.24(.9)**

nostalgically
 1.31.24(.9.11)
nostoc **24.9.4**
Nostradamus **34.18.15(.5)**
nostril **40.16.13(.16)**
nostrum **27.15.26(.10)**
nosy **1.23.15**
nosy parker **17.14.7**
not **22.11**
nota bene **4.14**
notability **1.10.16(.22.1)**
notable **40.20.16(.11.3)**
notableness
 34.18.16(.37.4)
notably **1.31.21(.4.2)**
notarial **40.3.14(.4)**
notarially **1.31.3(.11)**
notarization
 28.17.25(.3.11)
notarize **35.15.20(.2)**
notary **1.29.11(.8.11)**
notate **22.4.9**
notation **28.17.25(.3.3)**
notational **40.26.13(.14.2)**
notch **38.8**
notcher **17.28.9**
notchy **1.25.9**
note **22.21**
notebook **24.14.3**
notecase **34.4.6**
noteless **34.18.29(.22)**
notelet **22.19.26(.17)**
notepad **23.7.5**
notepaper **17.10.3**
note-row **19.27.15**
noteworthiness
 34.18.16(.2.6)
noteworthy **1.21**
nothing **29.1.21**
nothingness **34.18.16(.26)**
notice **34.18.11(.11)**
noticeable **40.20.16(.21.2)**
noticeably **1.31.21(.7.2)**
noticeboard **23.12.2(.15)**
notifiable **40.20.16(.5)**
notification **28.17.25(.3.5)**
notify **14.14.4(.4)**
notion **28.17.25(.13)**
notional **40.26.13(.14.5)**
notionalist **22.29.2(.31.3)**
notionally **1.31.17(.14.3)**
notochord **23.12.4**
notoriety **1.10.16(.4)**
notorious **34.3.15(.5)**
notoriously **1.31.33(.1.4)**
notoriousness
 34.18.16(.31.1)
Notre-Dame **27.8**
no-trump **20.16.5**
Nott **22.11**
Nottingham **27.15.15**

Nottinghamshire
 17.26.20
Notts **34.22.8**
notwithstanding
 29.1.13(.14)
nougat **10.9, 22.19.13**
nougatine **28.1.9**
nought **22.13**
Nouméa **17.2.5**
noumena **17.18.16(.8)**
noumenal **40.26.13(.8)**
noumenally
 1.31.17(.14.2)
noumenon **28.10.14**
noun **28.8**
nounal **40.26.6**
nourish **36.2.25**
nourisher **17.26.14**
nourishingly
 1.31.28(.1.13)
nourishment
 22.26.15(.13.6)
nous **34.8**
nouveau riche **36.1**
nouveau roman **28.9.6**
nouveaux riches **36.1**
nova **17.21.14**
novae **2.19**
Novak **24.6.12**
Nova Lisboa **17.9.1**
Nova Scotia **17.26.16**
Nova Scotian
 28.17.25(.13)
Novaya Zemlya **3.24.16**
novel **40.28.7**
novelese **35.1, 35.1.23**
novelesque **24.20.3**
novelette **22.5, 22.5.21**
novelettish **36.2.11**
novelist **22.29.2(.31.4)**
novelistic **24.2.10(.15.3)**
novelization
 28.17.25(.3.12)
novelize **35.15.21(.4.6)**
novella **17.34.5(.10)**
novelle **2.32.5**
Novello **19.29.4**
novelty **1.10.28**
November **17.11.17(.3)**
novena **17.18.1(.7)**
Novgorod **23.10.12**
novice **34.18.18**
Novi Sad **23.7**
novitiate **22.3.10**
Novocaine® **28.4.5**
Novokuznetsk **24.20.11**
Novosibirsk **24.20.2**
Novotel **40.5.3**
Novotny **1.16.19**
now **9**
nowaday **4.10.7**

nowadays **35.4.4**
noway **4.25**
Nowell **40.5, 40.16.9**
nowhere **6.18.5**
no-win **28.2.28**
nowise **35.15.19**
nowt **22.9**
noxious **34.18.22(.11)**
noxiously **1.31.33(.12.4)**
noxiousness
 34.18.16(.31.4)
noyau **19.28**
noyaux **19.28, 35.20.13**
Noyes **35.13**
nozzle **40.32.8**
nth **32.21**
nu **16**
nuance **34.24.6**
nub **21.11**
Nuba **17.11.12**
nubble **40.20.12**
nubbly **1.31.21(.1)**
nubby **1.9.9**
Nubia **3.3.6**
Nubian **28.3.2**
nubile **40.13.2**
nubility **1.10.16(.22.1)**
nuchal **40.23.11**
nuciferous **34.18.27(.20)**
nucivorous **34.18.27(.21)**
nuclear **3.24.14**
nuclease **35.4.1**
nucleate **22.4.2(.15)**
nucleation **28.17.25(.3.1)**
nuclei **14.2**
nucleic **24.2.1, 24.2.3**
nucleolar **17.34.3,
 17.34.18**
nucleoli **14.25.3, 14.25.10**
nucleolus **34.18.29(.3)**
nucleon **28.10.2**
nucleonic **24.2.15(.6.1)**
nucleoprotein **28.1.9(.4)**
nucleoside **23.15.11(.3)**
nucleotide **23.15.4**
nucleus **34.3.16**
nuclide **23.15.16**
nuclidic **24.2.11(.2)**
nuddy **1.11.13**
nude **23.17**
nudge **39.11**
nudger **17.29.10**
nudism **27.15.21(.2.5)**
nudist **22.29.2(.14)**
nudity **1.10.16(.9)**
nudnik **24.2.15(.11)**
nuée ardente **22.12**
Nuer **17.8**
Nuevo León **28.10**
Nuffield **23.31.1(.2)**

nugatory 1.29.11(.8.2)
Nugent 22.26.15(.21)
nugget 22.19.13
nuisance 34.24.10(.18)
Nuits-Saint-George 37.6
nuke 24.15
Nuku'alofa 17.20.14
null 40.12
nullah 17.34.12
nulla-nulla 17.34.12
nullification
     28.17.25(.3.5)
nullifidian 28.3.4(.2)
nullifier 17.6.9(.4)
nullify 14.14.4(.16)
nullipara 17.32.14(.4)
nulliparous 34.18.27(.12)
nullipore 12.3
nullity 1.10.16(.34)
numb 27.11
numbat 22.7.6
number 17.11.17(.6)
numberless
     34.18.29(.17.2)
numberplate 22.4.23(.8)
numbingly 1.31.28(.1.7)
numbly 1.31.26(.9)
numbness 34.18.16(.24)
numbskull 40.12
numdah 17.13.19
numen 28.17.16(.15)
numerable
     40.20.16(.27.4)
numerably 1.31.21(.8)
numeracy 1.22.16(.13)
numeral 40.16.13(.12.2)
numerate 22.19.24(.9)
numeration
     28.17.25(.3.13)
numerative 31.2.1(.9.4)
numerator 17.12.4(.15)
numeric 24.2.26(.4)
numerical 40.23.2
numerically
     1.31.24(.9.12)
numerological
     40.23.12(.17.2)
numerologist
     22.29.2(.26.4)
numerology
     1.26.10(.11.5)
numerous 34.18.27(.18)
numerously
     1.31.33(.12.5)
numerousness
     34.18.16(.31.5)
numerus clausus
     34.18.20
Numidia 3.5.2
Numidian 28.3.4(.2)
numina 17.18.16(.8)

numinous 34.18.16(.15.3)
numinously
     1.31.33(.12.3)
numinousness
     34.18.16(.31.3)
numismatic 24.2.10(.4.2)
numismatically
     1.31.24(.9.4)
numismatist 22.29.2(.13)
numismatology
     1.26.10(.11.2)
nummary 1.29.11(.12)
nummular 17.34.16(.21.4)
nummulite 22.16.25(.9)
numnah 17.18.25
numskull 40.12
nun 28.13
nunatak 24.6.7
nun-buoy 13.3
Nunc Dimittis
     34.18.11(.2)
nunchaks 34.23.5(.11)
nunchaku 16.9
nunciature 17.7.12(.3),
     17.28.3
nuncio 15.1.7
nuncupate 22.4.7
nuncupation
     28.17.25(.3.2)
nuncupative 31.2.1(.9.1)
Nuneaton 28.17.11(.1)
nunhood 23.16.5(.10)
nunlike 24.13.7(.17)
Nunn 28.13
nunnery 1.29.11(.13.1)
nunnish 36.2.16(.10)
NUPE 1.8.10
Nupe 4.7
nuptial 40.16.12
nurd 23.19
Nuremberg 26.14.1(.8)
Nureyev 30.4, 31.4
Nuristan 28.9.2
Nurofen® 28.5.8
nurse 34.19
nursemaid 23.4.7
nursery 1.29.11(.18)
nurseryman 28.17.16(.2)
nursling 29.1.31(.26)
nurture 17.28.16
nurturer 17.32.14(.19)
NUT 2.11
nut 22.15
nutant 22.26.15(.9)
nutation 28.17.25(.3.3)
nutcase 34.4.6
nutcracker 17.14.5
nutgall 40.10.8
nuthatch 38.5
nuthouse 34.8.6(.11)
nutlet 22.19.26(.17)

nutlike 24.13.7(.12)
nutmeat 22.1.5
nutmeg 26.4
nutpick 24.2.8(.8)
Nutrasweet® 22.1.16
nutria 3.22.15
nutrient 22.26.2(.9)
nutriment 22.26.15(.13.2)
nutrimental 40.21.17(.2)
nutrition 28.17.25(.2.6)
nutritional 40.26.13(.14.1)
nutritionally
     1.31.17(.14.3)
nutritionist 22.29.2(.18.2)
nutritious 34.18.22(.2)
nutritiously 1.31.33(.12.4)
nutritiousness
     34.18.16(.31.4)
nutritive 31.2.1(.9.4)
nutshell 40.5.14
Nuttall 40.10.5
nutter 17.12.12
nuttiness 34.18.16(.2.3)
Nutting 29.1.12(.10)
nutty 1.10.12
nux vomica 17.14.15(.8)
nuzzle 40.32.11
nyala 17.34.8
Nyasa 17.24.6
Nyasaland 23.24.6(.13)
nyctalopia 3.2.7
nyctitropic 24.2.8(.5)
Nye 14
Nyerere 1.29.4
nylghau 12.8
nylon 28.10.26
nymph 30.18
nympha 17.20.17
nymphae 2.18
nymphal 40.27.21
nymphean 28.3.9
nymphet 22.5.10
nymphlike 24.13.7(.19)
nympho 19.16
nympholepsy 1.22.19
nympholept 22.22.3
nympholeptic
     24.2.10(.12)
nymphomania 3.9.3(.5)
nymphomaniac 24.6.1
Nyree 2.30.5
nystagmic 24.2.14(.14)
nystagmus 34.18.15(.15)
Nyx 34.23.2
o 19
Oadby 1.9.15
oaf 30.16
oafish 36.2.18(.12)
oafishly 1.31.35(.7.3)
oafishness 34.18.16(.33.6)

Oahu 16.21
oak 24.18
oaken 28.17.13(.15)
Oakes 34.23.17
Oakham 27.15.11(.11)
Oakland 23.24.16(.16.3)
Oakley 1.31.24(.11)
Oaksey 1.22.22
oakum 27.15.11(.11)
Oakville 40.2.12
OAP 2.9
OAPEC 24.4.2
oar 12
oarfish 36.2.18(.7)
oarless 34.18.29(.11)
oarlock 24.9.16(.4)
oarsman 28.17.16(.30)
oarsmanship 20.2.7(.19)
oarswoman 28.17.16(.14)
oarswomen 28.2.17(.1)
oarweed 23.1.10
oases 35.1.16(.2)
oasis 34.2.17(.2)
oast 22.29.17
oasthouse 34.8.6(.11)
oat 22.21
oatcake 24.3.6
oaten 28.17.11(.17)
Oates 34.22.17
oath 32.16
oatmeal 40.1.6
oaty 1.10.18
Oaxaca 17.14.7
Ob 21.8
Obadiah 17.6.4
obbligati 1.10.8, 2.12.5
obbligato 19.10.7
obconic 24.2.15(.6.1)
obconical 40.23.12(.11)
obcordate 22.4.10
obduracy 1.22.16(.13)
obdurate 22.19.24(.9)
obdurately 1.31.22(.15)
obdurateness
     34.18.16(.20.3)
OBE 2
obeah 3.3.9
obeche 1.25.1
obedience 34.24.2
obedient 22.26.2(.3)
obediently 1.31.22(.20.1)
obeisance 34.24.10(.18)
obeisant 22.26.15(.17.1)
obeli 14.25.9
obelisk 24.20.1
obelize 35.15.21(.4.2)
obelus 34.18.29(.17.2)
Oberammergau 9.6
Oberland 23.24.6(.13)
Oberon 28.10.24(.5)

n
o

offbeat 22.1.2
off-cast 22.29.6(.5),
    22.29.8(.3)
off-chance 34.24.6
offcut 22.15.4
Offenbach 24.8.3
offence 34.24.3
offenceless 34.18.29(.33)
offend 23.24.5(.9)
offendedly 1.31.23(.14.4)
offender 17.13.20(.3)
offense 34.24.3
offenseless 34.18.29(.33)
offensive 31.2.4(.13)
offensively 1.31.30(.7.4)
offensiveness
    34.18.16(.28.2)
offer 17.20.7
offerer 17.32.14(.12)
offering 29.1.30(.8)
offeror 17.32.14(.12)
offertory 1.29.11(.8.8)
offhand 23.24.6(.11)
offhanded 23.18.10(.14)
offhandedly
    1.31.23(.14.4)
offhandedness
    34.18.16(.21.1)
office 34.2.14
officeholder 17.13.23(.8)
officer 17.24.15
official 40.33.1
officialdom 27.15.10(.20)
officialese 35.1, 35.1.23
officialism 27.15.21(.2.15)
officially 1.31.17(.22)
officiant 22.26.2(.8)
officiate 22.4.2(.11)
officiation 28.17.25(.3.1)
officiator 17.12.4(.1)
officinal 40.26.1,
    40.26.13(.12)
officinally 1.31.17(.14.1)
officious 34.18.22(.2)
officiously 1.31.33(.12.4)
officiousness
    34.18.16(.31.4)
offing 29.1.19
offish 36.2.18(.6)
offishly 1.31.35(.7.3)
offishness 34.18.16(.33.6)
offload 23.20
offprint 22.26.1
off-putting 29.1.12(.12)
off-puttingly 1.31.28(.1.4)
offset 22.5.13
offshoot 22.18.7
offshore 12.16
offside 23.15.11
offsider 17.13.12
offspring 29.1.30(.11)

off stage 39.4
offstage 39.4.2
Ofgas 34.7.10
O'Flynn 28.2.31(.20)
oft 22.27.5
Oftel 40.5.3
often 28.17.11(.24),
    28.17.19
oftentimes 35.25.8
Ofwat 22.11.14
Ogaden 28.5.4
Ogden 28.17.12(.21)
ogdoad 23.7.4
ogee 2.27
ogham 27.15.12
Ogilvy 1.19.14
ogival 40.28.9
ogive 31.9
ogle 40.24.13
ogler 17.34.24
Oglethorpe 20.8
Ogmore 12.9.10
O'Gorman 28.17.16(.11)
OGPU 16.5, 16.24
O'Grady 1.11.4
ogre 17.16.15
ogreish 36.2.25
ogreishly 1.31.35(.7.4)
ogress 34.5.14(.8),
    34.18.27(.17)
Ogwen 28.5.17, 28.17.30
Ogygian 28.3.18
oh 19
O'Hagan 28.17.15(.3)
O'Halloran 28.17.31(.11)
O'Hanlon 28.17.33(.23)
O'Hara 17.32.7
O'Hare 6.17
O'Higgins 35.26.2
Ohio 19.5
Ohioan 28.17.8
ohm 27.17
ohmage 39.2.14
ohmic 24.2.14(.12)
ohmmeter 17.12.1(.6)
oho 19.26
OHP 2.9
oi 13
oick 24.11
oidia 3.5.2
oidium 27.3.4(.2)
oik 24.11
oil 40.11
oilcake 24.3.6
oilcan 28.7.8
oilcloth 32.9
oiler 17.34.11
oilfield 23.31.1(.2)
oilily 1.31.17(.29)
oiliness 34.18.16(.2.10)

oilless 34.18.29(.38)
oilman 28.7.10(.24)
oilmen 28.5.7(.28)
oilrig 26.2.10
oilseed 23.1.7
oilskin 28.2.13(.14)
oilstone 28.19.4(.9)
oily 1.31.12
oink 24.19.6
ointment 22.26.15(.13.3)
Oireachtas 34.18.11(.13)
Oistrakh 24.8.15, 25.5
Ojibwa 17.31.4
Ojibway 4.25.11
OK 4.11
okapi 1.8.6
Okavango 19.13.12
okay 4.11
O'Keefe 30.1.2
Okefenokee 1.12.15
Okehampton
    28.17.11(.18)
okey-doke 24.18.3
okey-dokey 1.12.15
Okhotsk 24.20.11
Okie 1.12.15
Okinawa 17.31.2
Oklahoma 17.17.16(.10)
Oklahoman 28.17.16(.18)
okra 17.32.21
okta 17.12.21(.5)
Olaf 30.5.9, 30.14
Öland 23.24.6(.13)
Olav 31.5
Olave 31.3.8
Olbers 35.18.7
old 23.31.13
Oldbury 1.29.11(.7.2)
Oldcastle 40.31.6, 40.31.7
Old Dominion 28.17.32
olden 28.17.12(.27)
Oldenburg 26.14.1(.9)
olde worlde 1.11.23
old-fashioned
    23.24.16(.12)
Oldfield 23.31.1(.2)
Oldham 27.15.10(.20)
oldie 1.11.23
oldish 36.2.12
old-maidish 36.2.12
oldness 34.18.16(.21.1)
Old Sarum 27.15.26(.2)
Oldsmobile 40.1.2
old-stager 17.29.3
oldster 17.12.24(.19)
old-timer 17.17.11
Old Vic 24.2
olé 4.28
olea 3.24.11
oleaceous 34.18.22(.3)

oleaginous 34.18.16(.15.3)
oleander 17.13.20(.4)
O'Leary 1.29.2(.12)
oleaster 17.12.24(.5)
oleate 22.4.2(.15)
olecranon 28.10.14
olefin 28.17.19
olefine 28.1.15
Oleg 26.4
oleiferous 34.18.27(.20)
oleo 15.1.13
oleograph 30.7.5(.1)
oleomargarine 28.1.25
oleometer 17.12.16(.9.2)
oleo-resin 28.2.24
oleum 27.3.18
olfaction 28.17.25(.15.3)
olfactive 31.2.1(.13.3)
olfactometer
    17.12.16(.9.2)
olfactory 1.29.11(.8.12)
Olga 17.16.19
olibanum 27.15.14(.11)
oligarch 24.8.7
oligarchic 24.2.12
oligarchical 40.23.12(.9)
oligarchically
    1.31.24(.9.7)
oligarchy 1.12.6
oligocarpous 34.18.9(.5)
Oligocene 28.1.18(.6)
oligoclase 35.4.18
oligodendrocyte
    22.16.19(.9)
oligodendroglia 17.6.15
oligomer 17.17.14(.5),
    17.17.16(.5)
oligomerize 35.15.20(.2)
oligomerous
    34.18.27(.18)
oligonucleotide 23.15.4
oligopeptide 23.15.4
oligopolist 22.29.2(.31.2)
oligopolistic
    24.2.10(.15.3)
oligopoly 1.31.17(.7)
oligopsony 1.16.15(.14)
oligosaccharide 23.15.15
oligotrophic 24.2.16(.4)
oligotrophy 1.18.9(.2)
olingo 19.13.12
olio 15.1.13
Oliphant 22.26.15(.15)
olivaceous 34.18.22(.3)
olivary 1.29.11(.15)
olive 31.2.5
Oliver 17.21.12
Olivet 22.5.11, 22.19.17
Olivetti® 1.10.4
Olivia 3.11.2, 3.11.7
Olivier 3.11.2, 4.2.6

olivine **28.1.16**
olla podrida **17.13.1**
Ollerenshaw **12.16.12**
Ollerton **28.17.11(.15)**
Ollie **1.31.10**
olm **27.18**
Olmec **24.4.6**
Olmsted **23.5.3**
ology **1.26.10(.11.1)**
oloroso **19.20.12**
Olsen **28.17.23(.28)**
Olwen **28.2.28**
Olympia **3.2.8**
Olympiad **23.3, 23.7.2**
Olympian **28.3.1**
Olympic **24.2.8(.9)**
Olympus **34.18.9(.11)**
om **27.9, 27.17**
Omagh **10.10, 17.17.16**
Omaha **10.21**
O'Malley **1.31.7**
Oman **28.9.6, 28.17.16(.18)**
Omani **1.16.8**
O'Mara **17.32.7**
Omar Khayyám **27.6**
omasa **17.24.4**
omasum **27.15.20(.4)**
ombre **17.11.17(.5)**
ombré **4.26.10**
ombrology **1.26.10(.11.5)**
ombrometer
    17.12.16(.9.2)
ombudsman
    28.17.16(.30)
Omdurman **28.7.10,
    28.9.6, 28.17.16(.16)**
O'Meara **17.32.2, 17.32.5**
omega **17.16.13**
omelet **22.19.26(.21)**
omelette **22.19.26(.21)**
omen **28.17.16(.18)**
omenta **17.12.22(.3)**
omental **40.21.17(.2)**
omentum **27.15.9(.14)**
omer **17.17.16**
omicron **28.10.24(.9),
    28.17.31(.16)**
ominous **34.18.16(.15.3)**
ominously
    1.31.33(.12.3)
ominousness
    34.18.16(.31.3)
omissible **40.20.16(.21.1)**
omission **28.17.25(.2.4)**
omissive **31.2.4(.2)**
omit **22.2.11**
ommatidia **3.5.2**
ommatidium **27.3.4(.2)**
omnibus **34.14, 34.18.10**
omnicompetence
    34.24.10(.10)

omnicompetent
    22.26.15(.9)
omnidirectional
    40.26.13(.14.6)
omnifarious **34.3.15(.3)**
omnific **24.2.16(.1)**
omnigenous
    34.18.16(.15.3)
omnipotence
    34.24.10(.10)
omnipotent **22.26.15(.9)**
omnipotently
    1.31.22(.20.2)
omnipresence
    34.24.10(.19)
omnipresent
    22.26.15(.18)
omniscience **34.24.2**
omniscient **22.26.2(.7)**
omnisciently
    1.31.22(.20.1)
omnivore **12.12**
omnivorous **34.18.27(.21)**
omnivorously
    1.31.33(.12.5)
omnivorousness
    34.18.16(.31.5)
omphaloi **13.17**
omphalos **34.10.17**
omphalotomy **1.15.13(.1)**
Omsk **24.20.12**
on **28.10**
onager **17.16.13, 17.29.13**
Onan **28.7.11, 28.17.17(.12)**
onanism **27.15.21(.2.9)**
onanist **22.29.2(.18.1)**
onanistic **24.2.10(.15.2)**
Onassis **34.2.17(.4)**
ONC **2.22**
once **34.24.9**
once-over **17.21.14(.9)**
oncer **17.24.22(.6)**
oncogene **28.1.23**
oncogenic **24.2.15(.4)**
oncogenous
    34.18.16(.15.3)
oncologist **22.29.2(.26.3)**
oncology **1.26.10(.11.3)**
oncoming **29.1.16**
oncost **22.29.9**
OND **2.13**
one **28.13**
onefold **23.31.13(.7)**
Oneida **17.13.12**
O'Neil **40.1.7**
oneiric **24.2.26(.9)**
oneirocritic **24.2.10(.2.4)**
oneirologist
    22.29.2(.26.4)
oneirology **1.26.10(.11.5)**
oneiromancer
    17.24.22(.3)

oneiromancy **1.22.23(.4)**
oner **17.18.12**
onerous **34.18.27(.19)**
onerously **1.31.33(.12.5)**
onerousness
    34.18.16(.31.5)
oneself **30.20.2**
one-sided **23.18.10(.11)**
one-sidedly **1.31.23(.14.4)**
one-sidedness
    34.18.16(.21.1)
Onesimus **34.18.15(.10)**
one-step **20.4**
one-time **27.12.1**
one-to-one **28.13.8**
one-upmanship
    20.2.7(.19)
onflow **19.29.21**
onglaze **35.4.18**
ongoing **29.1.9**
ongoingness
    34.18.16(.26)
onion **28.17.32**
Onions **35.26.13(.2)**
onionskin **28.2.13(.14)**
oniony **1.16.15(.19)**
on-line **28.14.19**
onlooker **17.14.13**
onlooking **29.1.14(.10)**
only **1.31.27(.16)**
only-begotten
    28.17.11(.9)
on-off **30.8**
onomasiology
    1.26.10(.11.1)
onomast **22.29.6(.7)**
onomastic **24.2.10(.15.4)**
onomatopoeia **17.1.1**
onomatopoeic **24.2.1**
onomatopoeically
    1.31.24(.9.1)
onomatopoetic
    24.2.10(.3.1)
Onondaga **17.16.6**
onrush **36.12**
onrushing **29.1.25**
on-set **22.5.13**
onset **22.5.13(.11)**
onshore **12.16**
onside **23.15.11**
onslaught **22.13.15**
Onslow **19.29.23**
onstream **27.1.12**
Ontario **15.1.12**
on-the-spot **22.11.2**
ontogenesis
    34.2.17(.10.3)
ontogenetic **24.2.10(.3.1)**
ontogenetically
    1.31.24(.9.3)
ontogenic **24.2.15(.4)**

ontogenically
    1.31.24(.9.8)
ontogeny **1.16.15(.17)**
ontological
    40.23.12(.17.2)
ontologically
    1.31.24(.9.11)
ontologist **22.29.2(.26.3)**
ontology **1.26.10(.11.2)**
onus **34.18.16(.17)**
onward **23.18.26(.13)**
onymous **34.18.15(.10)**
onyx **34.23.2(.6)**
oocyte **22.16.19(.9)**
oodles **35.30.17**
oof **30.13**
oofiness **34.18.16(.2.6)**
oofy **1.18.8**
oogamous **34.18.15(.10)**
oogamy **1.15.13(.4)**
oogenesis **34.2.17(.10.3)**
oogenetic **24.2.10(.3.1)**
ooh **16**
oolite **22.16.25(.9)**
oolith **32.2.9**
oolitic **24.2.10(.2.5)**
oological **40.23.12(.17.2)**
oologist **22.29.2(.26.2)**
oology **1.26.10(.11.1)**
oolong **29.6.15**
oomiak **24.6.1**
oompah **10.4**
oomph **30.18**
Oonagh **17.18.15**
oophorectomy
    1.15.13(.1)
oops **34.21.9**
oops-a-daisy **1.23.3**
Oort **22.13, 22.19.5**
oosperm **27.16.1**
Oosterhuis **34.8.6(.7)**
ooze **35.17**
oozily **1.31.17(.21)**
ooziness **34.18.16(.2.7)**
oozy **1.23.12**
op **20.7**
op. **20.7**
opacifier **17.6.9(.4)**
opacify **14.14.4(.9)**
opacity **1.10.16(.16.1)**
opah **17.10.16**
opal **40.19.13**
opalesce **34.5.16**
opalescence
    34.24.10(.18)
opalescent **22.26.15(.17.2)**
opaline **28.14.19(.11)**
opaque **24.3.2**
opaquely **1.31.24(.3)**
opaqueness **34.18.16(.22)**

o

op art 22.10
op. cit. 22.2.16
ope 20.15
OPEC 24.4.2
Op-Ed 23.5
Opel® 40.19.13
open 28.17.9
openable 40.20.16(.16.3)
opencast 22.29.6(.5),
    22.29.8(.3)
opener 17.18.16(.3)
opening 29.1.17(.12)
openly 1.31.27(.14)
openness 34.18.16(.25)
Openshaw 12.16.12
openwork 24.17.6(.13)
opera 17.32.14(.4)
operability 1.10.16(.22.1)
operable 40.20.16(.27.3)
operably 1.31.21(.8)
opera buffa 17.20.11
opéra comique 24.1.4
operand 23.24.6(.12),
    23.24.16(.15)
operant 22.26.15(.23.3)
operate 22.4.22(.6)
operatic 24.2.10(.4.5)
operatically 1.31.24(.9.4)
operation 28.17.25(.3.13)
operational
    40.26.13(.14.2)
operationalize
    35.15.21(.4.5)
operationally
    1.31.17(.14.3)
operative 31.2.1(.9.4)
operatively 1.31.30(.7.1)
operativeness
    34.18.16(.28.1)
operator 17.12.4(.15)
opercula 17.34.16(.21.2)
opercular 17.34.16(.21.2)
operculate 22.19.26(.13)
operculum 27.15.28(.11)
opere buffe 4.15
opere serie 4.2.9
operetta 17.12.5(.9)
operon 28.10.24(.5)
Ophelia 3.24.1
ophicleide 23.15.16
Ophidia 3.5.2
ophidian 28.3.4(.2)
ophiolatry 1.29.15(.13)
ophiolite 22.16.25(.3)
ophiologist 22.29.2(.26.2)
ophiology 1.26.10(.11.1)
Ophir 17.20.14
ophite 22.16.16
ophitic 24.2.10(.2.3)
Ophiuchus 34.18.13(.9)
ophthalmia 3.8.16

ophthalmic 24.2.14(.18)
ophthalmitis 34.18.11(.8)
ophthalmological
    40.23.12(.17.2)
ophthalmologist
    22.29.2(.26.4)
ophthalmology
    1.26.10(.11.4)
ophthalmoscope
    20.15.4(.1)
ophthalmoscopic
    24.2.8(.5)
ophthalmoscopically
    1.31.24(.9.2)
ophthalmoscopy
    1.8.11(.5)
opiate 22.3.1
Opie 1.8.13
opine 28.14.3
opinion 28.17.32
opinionated 23.18.9(.3)
opinionatedly
    1.31.23(.14.3)
opinionatedness
    34.18.16(.21.1)
opinionative 31.2.1(.9.2)
opioid 23.13.2
opisometer 17.12.16(.9.2)
opisthograph 30.7.5(.1)
opisthography
    1.18.9(.3.2)
opisthosoma 17.17.16(.9)
opium 27.3.1
opiumize 35.15.11
opodeldoc 24.9.5
opopanax 34.23.5(.7)
Oporto 19.10.9
opossum 27.15.20(.6)
Oppenheim 27.12.6
Oppenheimer 17.17.11
oppidan 28.17.12(.16)
oppo 19.8
opponency 1.22.23(.10.3)
opponent 22.26.15(.14)
opportune 28.16.14
opportunely 1.31.27(.12)
opportuneness
    34.18.16(.25)
opportunism
    27.15.21(.2.9)
opportunist
    22.29.2(.18.1)
opportunistic
    24.2.10(.15.2)
opportunistically
    1.31.24(.9.6)
opportunity 1.10.16(.13)
opposable 40.20.16(.22)
oppose 35.20.1
opposer 17.25.15
opposite 22.2.16, 22.2.17
oppositely 1.31.22(.15)

oppositeness
    34.18.16(.20.3)
opposition 28.17.25(.2.5)
oppositional
    40.26.13(.14.1)
oppositive 31.2.1(.9.3)
oppress 34.5.14(.4)
oppression 28.17.25(.4)
oppressive 31.2.4(.4)
oppressively 1.31.30(.7.4)
oppressiveness
    34.18.16(.28.2)
oppressor 17.24.5
opprobrious 34.3.15(.7)
opprobriously
    1.31.33(.1.4)
opprobriousness
    34.18.16(.31.1)
opprobrium 27.3.17(.5)
oppugn 28.16.14
oppugnance 34.24.10(.15)
oppugnancy
    1.22.23(.10.3)
oppugnant 22.26.15(.14)
oppugnation
    28.17.25(.3.8)
oppugner 17.18.15
Oprah 17.32.17
Opren® 28.5.18,
    28.17.31(.12)
opsimath 32.6.3
opsimathy 1.20.8
opsonic 24.2.15(.6.3)
opsonin 28.2.18
opt 22.22.5
Optacon 28.17.13(.13)
optant 22.26.15(.9)
optative 31.2.1(.9.1)
optatively 1.31.30(.7.1)
optic 24.2.10(.12)
optical 40.23.12(.7.3)
optically 1.31.24(.9.5)
optician 28.17.25(.2.2)
optima 17.17.14(.2)
optimal 40.25.10
optimality 1.10.16(.32.7)
optimally 1.31.17(.13)
optimism 27.15.21(.2.8)
optimist 22.29.2(.17)
optimistic 24.2.10(.15.2)
optimistically
    1.31.24(.9.6)
optimization
    28.17.25(.3.11)
optimize 35.15.11
optimum 27.15.13
option 28.17.25(.14)
optional 40.26.13(.14.6)
optionality 1.10.16(.32.8)
optionally 1.31.17(.14.3)
optometer 17.12.16(.9.2)

optometric 24.2.26(.14.2)
optometrist 22.29.2(.29.5)
optometry 1.29.15(.8)
optophone 28.19.11
opt-out 22.9.7
Optrex® 34.23.4(.11)
opulence 34.24.10(.24)
opulent 22.26.15(.25)
opulently 1.31.22(.20.5)
opuntia 3.16.8
opus 34.18.9(.10)
opuscule 40.15.9(.5)
or 12
orache 38.15
oracle 40.23.12(.18)
oracular 17.34.16(.21.2)
oracularity 1.10.16(.21.1)
oracularly 1.31.17(.29)
oracy 1.22.16(.13)
oral 40.16.13(.8)
oralism 27.15.21(.2.15)
oralist 22.29.2(.31.4)
orality 1.10.16(.32.13)
orally 1.31.17(.27.1)
Oran 28.7.20, 28.9.13
orange 39.17.9
orangeade 23.4
Orangeism 27.15.21(.2.13)
Orangeman 28.17.16(.32)
orangery 1.29.11(.21)
orang-utan 29.4.3
orangutan 28.7.6
orate 22.4.22
oration 28.17.25(.3.13)
orator 17.12.16(.18)
oratorial 40.3.14(.5)
oratorian 28.3.20(.7)
oratorical 40.23.12(.18)
oratorically 1.31.24(.9.12)
oratorio 15.1.12
oratory 1.29.11(.8.9)
orb 21.9
Orbach 24.6.6(.6)
orbicular 17.34.16(.21.2)
orbicularity 1.10.16(.21.1)
orbicularly 1.31.17(.29)
orbiculate 22.19.26(.13)
orbit 22.2.6
orbital 40.21.12
orbiter 17.12.16(.4)
orc 24.10
orca 17.14.9
Orcadian 28.3.4(.3)
orchard 23.18.24
orcharding 29.1.13(.11)
orchardist 22.29.2(.14)
orchardman 28.17.16(.22)
orchestic 24.2.10(.15.4)
orchestra 17.32.19(.11)
orchestral 40.16.13(.16)

orchestrally **1.31.17(.27.3)**
orchestrate **22.4.22(.8)**
orchestration **28.17.25(.3.13)**
orchestrator **17.12.4(.15)**
orchestrina **17.18.1(.15)**
orchid **23.2.10**
orchidaceous **34.18.22(.3)**
orchidist **22.29.2(.14)**
orchidology **1.26.10(.11.2)**
orchil **40.2.7, 40.2.16**
orchilla **17.34.2(.4)**
orchis **34.2.10**
orchitis **34.18.11(.8)**
orcin **28.2.23(.6)**
orcinol **40.9.12**
Orcus **34.18.13(.6)**
Orczy **1.22.22**
ordain **28.4.4**
ordained **23.24.4**
ordainer **17.18.3**
ordainment **22.26.15(.13.4)**
ordeal **40.1.4**
order **17.13.9**
orderer **17.32.14(.7)**
ordering **29.1.30(.8)**
orderliness **34.18.16(.2.10)**
orderly **1.31.17(.10)**
ordinaire **6.9**
ordinal **40.26.13(.5)**
ordinance **34.24.10(.15)**
ordinand **23.24.6(.9), 23.24.16(.8)**
ordinarily **1.31.17(.27.2)**
ordinariness **34.18.16(.2.9)**
ordinary **1.29.11(.13.2)**
ordinate **22.19.15(.9)**
ordination **28.17.25(.3.8)**
ordnance **34.24.10(.15)**
ordonnance **34.24.10(.15)**
Ordovician **28.3.13, 28.3.15**
ordure **17.7.12(.4), 17.29.9, 17.33.7**
ore **12**
öre **17.32.15**
oread **23.7.2**
orectic **24.2.10(.13)**
oregano **19.15.7, 19.15.12**
Oregon **28.17.15(.13)**
Oregonian **28.3.8(.11)**
O'Reilly **1.31.14**
Orenburg **26.14.1(.9)**
Oreo® **15.1.12**
oreography **1.18.9(.3.2)**
Oresteia **17.1.3, 17.2.3, 17.6.3**

Orestes **35.1.7(.10)**
oreweed **23.1.10**
orfe **30.9**
Orff **30.9**
Orford **23.18.16(.6)**
organ **28.17.15(.9)**
organa **17.18.16(.7)**
organdie **1.11.20(.9)**
organelle **40.5.8**
organic **24.2.15(.5)**
organically **1.31.24(.9.8)**
organisationally **1.31.17(.14.3)**
organism **27.15.21(.2.9)**
organist **22.29.2(.18.1)**
organizable **40.20.16(.22)**
organization **28.17.25(.3.11)**
organizational **40.26.13(.14.2)**
organizationally **1.31.17(.14.3)**
organize **35.15.12(.5)**
organizer **17.25.12(.6)**
organochlorine **28.1.25(.1)**
organoleptic **24.2.10(.12)**
organometallic **24.2.27(.6)**
organon **28.10.14**
organophosphate **22.4.15**
organophosphorus **34.18.27(.20)**
organotherapy **1.8.11(.8)**
organum **27.15.14(.11)**
organza **17.25.18**
organzine **28.1.19**
orgasm **27.15.21(.3)**
orgasmic **24.2.14(.17)**
orgasmically **1.31.24(.9.8)**
orgastic **24.2.10(.15.4)**
orgastically **1.31.24(.9.6)**
orgeat **22.3.11**
orgiastic **24.2.10(.15.4)**
orgiastically **1.31.24(.9.6)**
orgone **28.19.8**
Orgreave **31.1.8**
orgulous **34.18.29(.17.6)**
orgy **1.26.7**
Oriana **17.18.8**
oribi **1.9.11**
oriel **40.3.14(.5)**
Orient **22.26.2(.9)**
orient **22.26.4(.1)**
Oriental **40.21.17(.2)**
orientalism **27.15.21(.2.15)**
orientalist **22.29.2(.31.2)**
orientalize **35.15.21(.4.3)**
orientally **1.31.17(.9.3)**

orientate **22.4.9(.8)**
orientation **28.17.25(.3.3)**
orientational **40.26.13(.14.2)**
orienteer **3.4**
orienteering **29.1.30(.2)**
orifice **34.2.14**
oriflamme **27.6.18**
origami **1.15.7**
origan **28.17.15(.13)**
origanum **27.15.14(.11)**
Origen **28.5.15**
origin **28.17.28(.9)**
original **40.26.13(.14.8)**
originality **1.10.16(.32.8)**
originally **1.31.17(.14.3)**
originate **22.4.14(.9.3)**
origination **28.17.25(.3.8)**
originative **31.2.1(.9.2)**
originator **17.12.4(.10)**
orinasal **40.32.3**
O-ring **29.1.30(.10)**
Orinoco **19.12.14**
Orinthia **3.12**
oriole **40.14.1**
Orion **28.17.5**
orison **28.17.24(.12)**
Orissa **17.24.2**
Oriya **17.1.16**
ork **24.10**
Orkney **1.16.21**
Orlando **19.11.14**
orle **40.10**
Orleanist **22.29.2(.18.1)**
Orléans **35.26.3, 35.26.13(.1)**
Orlon® **28.10.26**
orlop **20.7.13**
Orm **27.10**
Orme **27.10**
ormer **17.17.9**
Ormerod **23.10.12**
Ormesby **1.9.22**
ormolu **16.25**
Ormond **23.24.16(.7)**
Ormsby **1.9.22**
Ormskirk **24.17.3**
Ormuz **35.14**
ornament **22.26.4(.8), 22.26.15(.13.2)**
ornamental **40.21.17(.2)**
ornamentalism **27.15.21(.2.15)**
ornamentalist **22.29.2(.31.2)**
ornamentally **1.31.17(.9.3)**
ornamentation **28.17.25(.3.3)**
ornate **22.4.14**
ornately **1.31.22(.4)**

ornateness **34.18.16(.20.1)**
orneriness **34.18.16(.2.9)**
ornery **1.29.11(.13.1)**
ornithic **24.2.18(.1)**
ornithischian **28.3.5, 28.3.15**
ornithological **40.23.12(.17.2)**
ornithologically **1.31.24(.9.11)**
ornithologist **22.29.2(.26.4)**
ornithology **1.26.10(.11.5)**
ornithorhynchus **34.18.13(.13)**
ornithoscopy **1.8.11(.5)**
orogenesis **34.2.17(.10.3)**
orogenetic **24.2.10(.3.1)**
orogenic **24.2.15(.4)**
orogeny **1.16.15(.17)**
orographic **24.2.16(.3)**
orographical **40.23.12(.12)**
orography **1.18.9(.3.2)**
oroide **23.15.1**
orological **40.23.12(.17.2)**
orologist **22.29.2(.14)**
orology **1.26.10(.11.5)**
Oronsay **4.18.12, 4.19**
Orontes **35.1.7(.9)**
oropendola **17.34.16(.8)**
oropharynges **35.1.19, 35.1.21**
oropharynx **34.23.18**
orotund **23.24.12**
orphan **28.17.19**
orphanage **39.2.15**
orphanhood **23.16.5(.10)**
Orphean **28.3.9, 28.17.1(.8)**
Orpheus **34.3.7**
Orphic **24.2.16(.5)**
Orphism **27.15.21(.2.10)**
orphrey **1.29.21**
orpiment **22.26.15(.13.2)**
orpine **28.2.9, 28.14.3**
Orpington **28.17.11(.23)**
Orr **12**
orra **17.32.8**
Orrell **40.16.13(.7)**
orrery **1.29.11(.25)**
orris **34.2.21**
Orsino **19.15.1**
Orson **28.17.23(.9)**
ortanique **24.1.5**
Ortega **17.16.1, 17.16.3**
orthocephalic **24.2.27(.6)**
orthochromatic **24.2.10(.4.2)**
orthoclase **34.4.14, 35.4.18**

orthodontia 3.4.12
orthodontic 24.2.10(.14)
orthodontist 22.29.2(.13)
orthodox 34.23.8(.4)
orthodoxly 1.31.33(.15)
orthodoxy 1.22.22
orthoepic 24.2.8(.2)
orthoepist 22.29.2(.11)
orthoepy 1.8.1, 1.8.4, 1.8.11(.2)
orthogenesis 34.2.17(.10.3)
orthogenetic 24.2.10(.3.1)
orthogenetically 1.31.24(.9.3)
orthognathous 34.18.19
orthogonal 40.26.13(.7)
orthogonally 1.31.17(.14.2)
orthographer 17.20.12(.5)
orthographic 24.2.16(.3)
orthographical 40.23.12(.12)
orthographically 1.31.24(.9.9)
orthography 1.18.9(.3.2)
ortho-hydrogen 28.17.28(.9)
orthopaedic 24.2.11(.1)
orthopaedist 22.29.2(.14)
Orthoptera 17.32.14(.6)
orthopteran 28.17.31(.11)
orthopterous 34.18.27(.14)
orthoptic 24.2.10(.12)
orthoptist 22.29.2(.13)
orthorhombic 24.2.9(.8)
orthostatic 24.2.10(.4.1)
orthotone 28.19.4(.5)
Ortiz 35.1.7
ortolan 28.17.33(.13)
Orton 28.17.11(.10)
orts 34.22.9
Oruro 19.27.11
Orvieto 19.10.4
Orville 40.2.12
Orwell 40.5.17(.4)
Orwellian 28.3.21(.4)
oryx 34.23.2(.12)
Osage 39.4.7
Osaka 17.14.7
Osbert 22.19.9, 22.20.2
Osborn 28.11.2
Oscar 17.14.23
oscillate 22.4.23(.7.2)
oscillation 28.17.25(.3.14)
oscillator 17.12.4(.16)
oscillatory 1.29.11(.8.10)
oscillogram 27.6.17(.5)
oscillograph 30.7.5(.1)

oscillographic 24.2.16(.3)
oscillography 1.18.9(.3.2)
oscilloscope 20.15.4(.1)
oscilloscopic 24.2.8(.5)
oscine 28.2.23(.5), 28.14.13
oscinine 28.1.14, 28.14.9
oscitation 28.17.25(.3.3)
oscula 17.34.16(.21.2)
osculant 22.26.15(.25)
oscular 17.34.16(.21.2)
osculate 22.4.23(.7.3)
osculation 28.17.25(.3.14)
osculatory 1.29.11(.8.10)
osculum 27.15.28(.11)
Osgood 23.16.3
OSHA 17.26.16
O'Shea 2.24, 4.20
osier 3.15.8, 3.17, 17.27.9
Osiris 34.2.21
Osler 17.34.27
Oslo 19.29.23
Osman 28.17.16(.29)
Osmanli 1.31.27(.6)
osmic 24.2.14(.17)
osmically 1.31.24(.9.8)
Osmiroid 23.13.19
osmium 27.3.7
osmolality 1.10.16(.32.14)
osmolarity 1.10.16(.21.1)
Osmond 23.24.16(.7)
osmosis 34.2.17(.11.2)
Osmotherley 1.31.17(.19)
Osmotherly 1.31.17(.19)
osmotic 24.2.10(.6)
osmotically 1.31.24(.9.4)
osmund 23.24.16(.7)
osmunda 17.13.20(.10)
Osnabrück 24.14.10
osnaburg 26.14.1(.4)
osprey 4.26.9
Ossa 17.24.9
ossein 28.2.2
osseous 34.3.10
Ossetia 3.4.3, 17.26.1
Ossetic 24.2.10(.3.2)
Ossett 22.2.16
ossia 17.1.11, 17.33.11
Ossian 28.3.13
Ossianic 24.2.15(.5)
ossicle 40.23.12(.15)
Ossie 1.22.9
ossific 24.2.16(.1)
ossification 28.17.25(.3.5)
ossifrage 39.2.22(.14)
ossify 14.14.4(.9)
osso buco 19.12.10
ossuary 1.29.11(.26)
Ostade 23.9.7
osteitis 34.18.11(.8)
Ostend 23.24.5(.4)

ostensible 40.20.16(.21.3)
ostensibly 1.31.21(.7.2)
ostensive 31.2.4(.13)
ostensively 1.31.30(.7.4)
ostensiveness 34.18.16(.28.2)
ostensory 1.29.11(.18)
ostentation 28.17.25(.3.3)
ostentatious 34.18.22(.3)
ostentatiously 1.31.33(.12.4)
osteoarthritic 24.2.10(.2.4)
osteoarthritis 34.18.11(.8)
osteogenesis 34.2.17(.10.3)
osteogenetic 24.2.10(.3.1)
osteogeny 1.16.15(.17)
osteography 1.18.9(.3.2)
osteological 40.23.12(.17.2)
osteologically 1.31.24(.9.11)
osteologist 22.29.2(.26.2)
osteology 1.26.10(.11.1)
osteomalacia 3.16.3, 17.26.3
osteomalacic 24.2.20(.5)
osteomyelitis 34.18.11(.8)
osteopath 32.6.2
osteopathic 24.2.18(.3)
osteopathically 1.31.24(.9.10)
osteopathy 1.20.8
osteophyte 22.16.16
osteoporosis 34.2.17(.11.2)
Ostermilk 24.21
Österreich 24.13.6, 25.7
Ostia 3.4.13
ostinato 19.10.7
ostler 17.34.27
Ostmark 24.8.8
ostomy 1.15.13(.1)
Ostpolitik 24.1.3
ostraca 17.14.15(.14)
ostracism 27.15.21(.2.12)
ostracize 35.15.16(.4)
ostracoderm 27.16.3
ostracon 28.10.11
Ostrava 17.21.12
ostrich 38.2.10, 39.2.22(.11)
Ostrogoth 32.9
Ostrogothic 24.2.18(.4)
O'Sullivan 28.17.20(.10)
Oswald 23.31.11
Oswaldtwistle 40.31.2
Oswego 19.13.1
Oswestry 1.29.15(.17)

Osyth 32.2.6
Otago 19.13.5
otary 1.29.11(.8.11)
Otello 19.29.4
Othello 19.29.4
other 17.23.10
otherness 34.18.16(.15.3)
otherwhere 6.18.4
otherwise 35.15.19
Othman 28.9.6, 28.17.16(.28)
Otho 19.18
otic 24.2.10(.6)
otiose 34.20, 35.16
otiosely 1.31.33(.10), 1.31.34
otioseness 34.18.16(.31.2)
Otis 34.2.8
otitis 34.18.11(.8)
Otley 1.31.22(.9)
otolaryngological 40.23.12(.17.2)
otolaryngologist 22.29.2(.26.3)
otolaryngology 1.26.10(.11.3)
otolith 32.2.9
otolithic 24.2.18(.1)
otological 40.23.12(.17.2)
otologist 22.29.2(.26.3)
otology 1.26.10(.11.2)
Otomi 2.16
O'Toole 40.15.3
otoplasty 1.10.26(.5)
otorhinolaryngologist 22.29.2(.26.3)
otorhinolaryngology 1.26.10(.11.3)
otoscope 20.15.4(.1)
otoscopic 24.2.8(.5)
Otranto 19.10.17
Ott 22.11
ottar 17.12.9
ottava rima 17.17.1
Ottawa 17.31.3
otter 17.12.9
Otterburn 28.18.3
Ottery 1.29.11(.8.4)
Otto 19.10.8
Ottoline 28.2.31(.10)
ottoman 28.17.16(.16)
Otway 4.25.12
Ouagadougou 16.10
ouananiche 36.1
oubliette 22.5
ouch 38.6
oud 23.17
Oudenarde 23.9.12
Oudh 23.17
ought 22.13
oughta 17.12.10

oughtn't 22.26.15(.9)
ouguiya 17.33.1
Ouida 17.13.1
ouija board 23.12
Ould 23.31.10, 23.31.13
Oulton 28.17.11(.27)
Oulu 16.25
ounce 34.24.5
Oundle 40.22.16
our 10, 17.3
ours 35.9, 35.18.2
ourself 30.20.2
ourselves 35.28.10
Ouse 35.17
oust 22.29.7
ouster 17.12.24(.6)
out 22.9
outact 22.23.5
outage 39.2.10
out-and-out 22.9
out-and-outer 17.12.7
outback 24.6.6(.12)
outbacker 17.14.5
outbalance 34.24.10(.24)
outbid 23.2.7
outbidder 17.13.2
outblaze 35.4.18
outboard 23.12.2(.8)
outbound 23.24.7(.2)
outbrave 31.3.7
outbreak 24.3.13
outbred 23.5.15
outbreed 23.1.11
outbuilding 29.1.13(.16)
outburst 22.29.16
outcast 22.29.6(.5),
  22.29.8(.3)
outcaste 22.29.6(.5),
  22.29.8(.3)
outclass 34.9.7
outcome 27.11.5
outcompete 22.1.1
outcrop 20.7.12
outcry 14.24.9
outdare 6.5
outdated 23.18.9(.3)
outdatedness
  34.18.16(.21.1)
outdid 23.2.9
outdistance 34.24.10(.10)
outdo 16.8
outdoes 35.14
outdone 28.13.4
outdoor 12.6
outdoorsman
  28.17.16(.30)
outer 17.12.7
outermost 22.29.17(.4)
outerwear 6.18.4
outface 34.4.9

outfall 40.10.11
outfield 23.31.1(.2)
outfielder 17.13.23(.1)
outfight 22.16.16
outfit 22.2.13
outfitter 17.12.2
outflank 24.19.3(.7)
outflew 16.25
outflow 19.29.21
outflown 28.19.19
outflung 29.8
outfly 14.25.14
outfought 22.13.7
outfox 34.23.8(.7)
outgas 34.7.10
outgeneral 40.16.13(.12.2)
outgo 19.13
outgoing 29.1.9
outgone 28.10.12
outgrew 16.23.11
outgrow 19.27.18
outgrown 28.19.17
outgrowth 32.16
outguess 34.5.4
outgun 28.13.5
outhouse 34.8.6(.11)
outie 1.10.7
outing 29.1.12(.6)
outjockey 1.12.7
outjump 20.16.5
outlander 17.13.20(.4)
outlandish 36.2.12
outlandishly 1.31.35(.7.1)
outlandishness
  34.18.16(.33.3)
outlast 22.29.6(.12),
  22.29.8(.8)
outlaw 12.23.5
outlawry 1.29.8
outlay 4.28, 4.28.11
outlet 22.5.21
outlier 17.6.15
outline 28.14.19(.14)
outlive 31.2.5
outlook 24.14.11
outlying 29.1.7
outmanoeuvre 17.21.11
outmatch 38.5
outmeasure 17.27.3
outmoded 23.18.10(.13)
outmodedly
  1.31.23(.14.4)
outmodedness
  34.18.16(.21.1)
outmost 22.29.17(.4)
outnumber 17.11.17(.6)
outpace 34.4.2
outpatient 22.26.15(.19)
outperform 27.10.5
outperformance
  34.24.10(.14)

outplacement
  22.26.15(.13.5)
outplay 4.28.9
outpoint 22.26.11
outport 22.13.1
outpost 22.29.17(.1)
outpouring 29.1.30(.7)
output 22.17
outrage 39.4.9
outrageous 34.18.24
outrageously
  1.31.33(.12.4)
outrageousness
  34.18.16(.31.5)
Outram 27.15.26(.10)
outran 28.7.20
outrange 39.17.2
outrank 24.19.3(.6)
outré 4.26.11
outreach 38.1
outridden 28.17.12(.2)
outride 23.15.15
outrider 17.13.12
outrigged 23.22
outrigger 17.16.2
outright 22.16.24
outrightness
  34.18.16(.20.2)
outrival 40.28.9
outrode 23.20.12
outrun 28.13.9
outrush 36.12
outsail 40.4.10
outsat 22.7.15
outsell 40.5.11
outset 22.5.13(.8)
outshine 28.14.15
outshone 28.10.20
outshoot 22.18.7
outshot 22.11.12
outside 23.15.11
outsider 17.13.12
outsit 22.2.16
outsize 35.15.16
outsizeness 34.18.16(.32)
outskirts 34.22.16
outsmart 22.10.7
outsold 23.31.13(.8)
outsource 34.12.6
outspan 28.7.4
outspend 23.24.5(.2)
outspent 22.26.4(.2)
outspoken 28.17.13(.15)
outspokenly 1.31.27(.14)
outspokenness
  34.18.16(.25)
outspread 23.5.15
outstanding 29.1.13(.14)
outstandingly
  1.31.28(.1.5)
outstare 6.4

outstation 28.17.25(.3.3)
outstay 4.9.10
outstep 20.4
outstretch 38.4
outstretched 22.31
outstrip 20.2.11
outswing 29.1.29
out-swinger 17.19.1
out-take 24.3.4
outtalk 24.10.2
outvalue 16.24.17
outvote 22.21.10
outwalk 24.10.9
outward 23.18.26(.9)
outwardly 1.31.23(.14.7)
outwardness
  34.18.16(.21.1)
outwash 36.9.5
outwatch 38.8
outwear 6.18
outweigh 4.25
outwent 22.26.4(.13)
outwit 22.2.23
outwith 32.2.7, 33.2
outwore 12.20
outwork 24.17.6
outworker 17.14.16
outworking 29.1.14(.12)
outworn 28.11.11
ouzel 40.32.13
ouzo 19.21
ova 17.21.14
oval 40.28.13
ovality 1.10.16(.32.9)
ovally 1.31.17(.17)
ovalness 34.18.16(.37.5)
Ovaltine® 28.1.9(.8)
Ovambo 19.9.14
Ovamboland 23.24.6(.13)
ovarian 28.3.20(.4)
ovariectomy 1.15.13(.1)
ovariotomy 1.15.13(.1)
ovaritis 34.18.11(.8)
ovary 1.29.11(.15)
ovate 22.4.16
ovation 28.17.25(.3.9)
ovational 40.26.13(.14.2)
oven 28.17.20(.7)
ovenbird 23.19.1
Ovenden 28.17.12(.23)
ovenproof 30.13.4
oven-ready 1.11.5
Ovens 35.26.13(.11)
ovenware 6.18.11
over 17.21.14
overabundance
  34.24.10(.11)
overabundant
  22.26.15(.10)
overabundantly
  1.31.22(.20.2)

overnighter 17.12.13(.4)
overpaid 23.4.1
overpaint 22.26.3
overparted 23.18.9(.7)
overpass 34.9.1
overpay 4.7
overpayment 22.26.15(.13.1)
overpitch 38.2.1
overplay 4.28.9
overplus 34.14
overpopulate 22.4.23(.7.3)
overpopulation 28.17.25(.3.14)
overpower 17.3.1
overpoweringly 1.31.28(.1.17)
overpraise 35.4.16
overprice 34.15.9
overprint 22.26.1
overproduce 34.17.13
overproduction 28.17.25(.15.5)
overproof 30.13.4
overprotective 31.2.1(.13.2)
overqualified 23.15.9
overran 28.7.20
overrate 22.4.22
overreach 38.1
overreact 22.23.5
overreaction 28.17.25(.15.3)
overridden 28.17.12(.2)
override 23.15.15
overrider 17.13.12
overripe 20.10.5
overripen 28.17.9
overripeness 34.18.16(.18)
overrode 23.20.12
overruff 30.11.10
overrule 40.15.8
overrun 28.13.9
oversailing 29.1.31(.4)
oversaw 12.14
overscrupulous 34.18.29(.17.6)
oversea 2.22
oversee 2.22
overseen 28.1.18
overseer 3.14.9
oversell 40.5.11
overset 22.5.13
oversew 19.20
oversexed 22.29.20
overshadow 19.11.6
overshoe 16.17
overshoot 22.18.7
overshot 22.11.12

overside 23.15.11(.6)
oversight 22.16.19(.9)
oversimplification 28.17.25(.3.5)
oversimplify 14.14.4(.16)
oversize 35.15.16
overskirt 22.20.4
overslaugh 12.23.10
oversleep 20.1
oversleeve 31.1.9
overslept 22.22.3
oversold 23.31.13(.8)
oversolicitous 34.18.11(.10)
oversolicitude 23.17.4(.1)
oversoul 40.18.10
overspecialization 28.17.25(.3.12)
overspecialize 35.15.21(.4.6)
overspend 23.24.5(.2)
overspent 22.26.4(.2)
overspill 40.2.3
overspread 23.5.15
overstaff 30.7.2
overstate 22.4.9(.9)
overstatement 22.26.15(.13.3)
overstay 4.9.10
oversteer 3.4.13
overstep 20.4
overstock 24.9.4
overstrain 28.4.18
overstress 34.5.14(.5)
overstretch 38.4
overstrong 29.6.14
overstrung 29.8
overstudy 1.11.13
overstuff 30.11.3
oversubscribe 21.12
oversubtle 40.21.9
oversupply 14.25.11
oversusceptible 40.20.16(.11.4)
overt 22.20.9
overtake 24.3.4
overtaken 28.17.13(.3)
overtask 24.20.4
overtax 34.23.5(.3)
over-the-top 20.7.4
overthrew 16.23.13
overthrow 19.27.21
overthrown 28.19.17
overthrust 22.29.12
overtime 27.12.1
overtire 17.6.3
overtly 1.31.22(.16)
overtness 34.18.16(.20.3)
Overton 28.17.11(.15)
overtone 28.19.4(.5)
overtook 24.14.4

overtop 20.7.4
overtrain 28.4.18
overtrick 24.2.26(.14.3)
overtrump 20.16.5
overture 12.17, 17.7.12(.3), 17.28.15
overturn 28.18.4
overuse 34.17.13, 35.17.7
overvaluation 28.17.25(.3.1)
overvalue 16.24.17
overview 16.24.12
overwater 17.12.10(.7)
overweening 29.1.17(.1)
overweeningly 1.31.28(.1.7)
overweeningness 34.18.16(.26)
overweight 22.4.21
overwhelm 27.18
overwhelmingly 1.31.28(.1.7)
overwhelmingness 34.18.16(.26)
overwind 23.24.13
overwinter 17.12.22(.1)
overwork 24.17.6
overwound 23.24.7(.9)
overwrite 22.16.24
overwritten 28.17.11(.2)
overwrote 22.21.14
overwrought 22.13.14
overzeal 40.1.11
overzealous 34.18.29(.5)
Ovett 22.5.11, 22.19.17
ovibovine 28.14.11
ovicide 23.15.11(.6)
Ovid 23.2.15
oviducal 40.23.11
oviduct 22.23.8
oviductal 40.21.16
Oviedo 19.11.4
oviform 17.10.5(.2)
ovine 28.14.11
oviparity 1.10.16(.21.1)
oviparous 34.18.27(.12)
oviparously 1.31.33(.12.5)
oviposit 22.2.17
oviposition 28.17.25(.2.5)
ovipositor 17.12.16(.15)
ovoid 23.13.14
ovoli 2.32.9(.5)
ovolo 19.29.12
ovotestes 35.1.7(.10)
ovotestis 34.2.8
ovoviviparity 1.10.16(.21.1)
ovoviviparous 34.18.27(.12)
ovular 17.34.16(.21.4)
ovulate 22.4.23(.7.3)

ovulation 28.17.25(.3.14)
ovulatory 1.29.11(.8.10)
ovule 40.15.9(.9)
ovum 27.15.17
ow 9
Owain 28.14.2
owe 19
Owen 28.17.8
Owens 35.26.13(.4)
owl 40.7
owlery 1.29.11(.27)
owlet 22.19.26(.6)
owlish 36.2.27
owlishly 1.31.35(.7.4)
owlishness 34.18.16(.33.6)
own 28.19
own brand 23.24.6
owner 17.18.18
ownerless 34.18.29(.17.3)
ownership 20.2.7(.9)
owt 22.9
ox 34.23.8
oxalate 22.4.23(.7.2)
oxalic 24.2.27(.6)
oxalis 34.2.22(.5)
oxbow 19.9.17
Oxbridge 39.2.22(.10)
oxcart 22.10.5
oxen 28.17.23(.21)
Oxenden 28.17.12(.23)
Oxenford 23.12.5
Oxenholme 27.17.12
oxer 17.24.20
Oxfam 27.6.10
Oxford 23.18.16(.18)
Oxfordshire 17.26.18
oxheart 22.10.11
oxherd 23.19.7
Oxhey 1.22.22, 4.24
oxhide 23.15.13
oxidant 22.26.15(.10)
oxidate 22.4.10
oxidation 28.17.25(.3.4)
oxidational 40.26.13(.14.2)
oxidative 31.2.1(.3)
oxide 23.15.11(.11)
oxidizable 40.20.16(.22)
oxidization 28.17.25(.3.11)
oxidize 35.15.8
oxidizer 17.25.12(.3)
Oxley 1.31.33(.15)
oxlip 20.2.13
Oxnard 23.9.12, 23.18.14
Oxo 19.20.15
Oxon 28.10.18, 28.17.23(.21)
Oxonian 28.3.8(.11)

oxonium 27.3.8(.10)
Oxshott 22.11.12
oxtail 40.4.2
oxter 17.12.24(.20)
Oxton 28.17.11(.25)
ox tongue 29.8
Oxus 34.18.20
oxyacetylene 28.1.27(.7), 28.2.31(.10)
oxyacid 23.2.16
oxycarpous 34.18.9(.5)
Oxydol 40.9.8
oxygen 28.17.28(.9)
oxygenate 22.4.14(.9.3)
oxygenation 28.17.25(.3.8)
oxygenator 17.12.4(.10)
oxygenize 35.15.12(.5)
oxygenous 34.18.16(.15.3)
oxyhaemoglobin 28.2.10
oxy-hydrogen 28.17.28(.9)
oxymoron 28.10.24(.3)
oxyopia 3.2.7
Oxyrhynchus 34.18.13(.13)
oxysalt 22.32.5, 22.32.6
oxytocin 28.2.23(.11)
oxytone 28.19.4(.2)
oyez 4.27, 34.5.15, 35.5.14
oyster 17.12.24(.9)
oystercatcher 17.28.6
Oystermouth 32.7
oystershell 40.5.13
Oz 35.10
Ozalid® 23.2.23
Ozark 24.8.13
Ozawa 17.31.2
ozokerite 22.16.24(.9)
ozone 28.19.14
ozonic 24.2.15(.6.3)
ozonization 28.17.25(.3.11)
ozonize 35.15.12(.5)
Ozymandias 34.3.4, 34.7.2
Ozzie 1.23.8
p 2
PA 4
pa 10
Paarl 40.8
Pablo 19.29.16
Pablum® 27.15.28(.15)
pabulum 27.15.28(.11)
paca 17.14.5, 17.14.7
pacarana 17.18.8(.11)
pace 1.22.4, 4.11, 4.22, 34.4
pacemaker 17.14.3(.3)
pacemaking 29.1.14(.3)

paceman 28.7.10(.20), 28.17.16(.29)
pacemen 28.5.7(.24)
pacer 17.24.4
pacesetter 17.12.5(.8)
pace-setting 29.1.12(.4)
pacha 17.26.6, 17.26.7
Pachelbel 40.5.2
pachinko 19.12.15
pachisi 1.23.1
pachuco 19.12.11
pachyderm 27.16.3
pachydermal 40.25.11
pachydermatous 34.18.11(.10)
pachysandra 17.32.20
pachytene 28.1.9(.1)
pacific 24.2.16(.1)
pacifically 1.31.24(.9.9)
pacification 28.17.25(.3.5)
pacificatory 1.29.11(.8.2)
pacifier 17.6.9(.4)
pacifism 27.15.21(.2.10)
pacifist 22.29.2(.19)
pacify 14.14.4(.9)
Pacino 19.15.1
pack 24.6
packable 40.20.16(.13)
package 39.2.12
packager 17.29.13
Packard 23.9.9
packer 17.14.5
packet 22.19.12(.5)
packhorse 34.12.7
pack ice 34.15.4
packing 29.1.14(.4)
packing case 34.4.6
packman 28.7.10(.13), 28.17.16(.23)
packmen 28.5.7(.17)
packsaddle 40.22.5
packthread 23.5.15
Pac-man® 28.7.10(.13)
pact 22.23.5
pacy 1.22.4
pad 23.7
Padbury 1.29.11(.7.2)
Paddington 28.17.11(.23)
paddle 40.22.5
paddleball 40.10.4
paddler 17.34.22
paddock 24.16.5
paddy 1.11.7
paddywack 24.6.20
pademelon 28.17.33(.4)
Paderewski 1.12.17(.13)
Padfield 23.31.1(.2)
Padiham 27.3.4(.4)
Padilla 17.34.2(.3)

padlock 24.9.16(.12)
padloper 17.10.16
Padma 17.17.18
Padmore 12.9.8
padouk 24.7
padre 4.26.12
padrone 1.16.17(.13)
padsaw 12.14.12
Padstow 19.10.19
Padua 17.7.12(.4)
Paduan 28.17.6
Paducah 17.14.14
paean 28.17.1
paederastic 24.2.10(.15.4)
paediatric 24.2.26(.14.3)
paediatrician 28.17.25(.2.6)
paediatrist 22.29.2(.29.5)
paedophile 40.13.9
paedophilia 3.24.2
paedophiliac 24.6.1
paella 17.34.5
paeon 28.17.1
paeonic 24.2.15(.6.1)
Pagalu 16.25
pagan 28.17.15(.3)
Paganini 1.16.1(.8)
paganish 36.2.16(.13)
paganism 27.15.21(.2.9)
paganize 35.15.12(.5)
page 39.4
pageant 22.26.15(.21)
pageantry 1.29.15(.15)
pageboy 13.3
pager 17.29.3
Paget 22.19.22
paginal 40.26.13(.14.8)
paginary 1.29.11(.13.2)
paginate 22.4.14(.9.3)
pagination 28.17.25(.3.8)
Pagliacci 1.25.8
Pagnell 40.26.19
pagoda 17.13.17
pah 10
Pahang 29.4.13, 29.8
Pahlavi 1.19.10
pahoehoe 1(.7)
paid 23.4
Paige 39.4
Paignton 28.17.11(.22)
pail 40.4
pailful 40.14.6(.22)
paillasse 34.7
paillette 22.5, 22.5.20
pain 28.4
Paine 28.4
painful 40.27.22
painfully 1.31.17(.16.2)
painfulness 34.18.16(.37.2)

painkiller 17.34.2(.4)
painkilling 29.1.31(.2)
painless 34.18.29(.27)
painlessly 1.31.33(.12.6)
painlessness 34.18.16(.31.6)
painstaking 29.1.14(.3)
painstakingly 1.31.28(.1.6)
painstakingness 34.18.16(.26)
paint 22.26.3
paintable 40.20.16(.11.6)
paintball 40.10.4
paintbox 34.23.8(.2)
paintbrush 36.12
painter 17.12.22(.2)
painterliness 34.18.16(.2.10)
painterly 1.31.17(.9.3)
painting 29.1.12(.19)
paintstick 24.2.10(.15.4)
paintwork 24.17.6(.8)
painty 1.10.23(.2)
pair 6
pairing 29.1.30(.4)
pairwork 24.17.6(.3)
paisa 10.15, 17.24.13
paise 17.24.13
Paish 36.4
paisley 1.31.34
Paisleyite 22.16.2
Paiute 22.18, 22.18.2, 22.18.10
pajama 17.32.14(.6)
pakapoo 16.5
pakapu 16.5
pakeha 10.21
Pakenham 27.15.14(.11)
Paki 1.12.5
Pakistan 28.9.2
Pakistani 1.16.6, 1.16.8
pakora 17.32.10(.4)
pal 40.6
palace 34.18.29(.7)
paladin 28.2.12
Palaearctic 24.2.10(.13)
palaeoanthropological 40.23.12(.17.2)
palaeoanthropologist 22.29.2(.26.3)
palaeoanthropology 1.26.10(.11.2)
palaeobotany 1.16.15(.7)
Palaeocene 28.1.18(.1)
palaeoclimatology 1.26.10(.11.2)
palaeoecological 40.23.12(.17.2)

palaeoecologist 22.29.2(.26.3)
palaeoecology 1.26.10(.11.3)
palaeogeography 1.18.9(.3.2)
palaeographer 17.20.12(.5)
palaeographic 24.2.16(.3)
palaeographical 40.23.12(.12)
palaeographically 1.31.24(.9.9)
palaeography 1.18.9(.3.2)
Palaeolithic 24.2.18(.1)
palaeomagnetism 27.15.21(.2.4)
palaeontological 40.23.12(.17.2)
palaeontologist 22.29.2(.26.3)
palaeontology 1.26.10(.11.2)
Palaeozoic 24.2.7
palaestra 17.32.19(.11)
palais 1.31.7, 4.28.3
palanquin 28.1.11, 28.2.28
palapa 17.10.5
palatability 1.10.16(.22.2)
palatable 40.20.16(.11.3)
palatableness 34.18.16(.37.4)
palatably 1.31.21(.4.2)
palatal 40.21.3, 40.21.12
palatalization 28.17.25(.3.12)
palatalize 35.15.21(.4.3)
palatally 1.31.17(.9.1)
palate 22.19.26(.5)
palatial 40.33.2
palatially 1.31.17(.22)
Palatinate 22.19.15(.9)
Palatine 28.14.5
Palau 9.17
palaver 17.21.6
Palawan 28.17.3
pale 40.4
palea 3.24.3
paleae 2.3
paleface 34.4.9
pale-faced 22.29.4
Palekh 24.4.14
palely 1.31.38
Palembang 29.4.2
paleness 34.18.16(.37.1)
Palenque 1.12.16
paleoecology 1.26.10(.11.3)
paleographer 17.20.12(.5)
paleographically 1.31.24(.9.9)

paleography 1.18.9(.3.2)
paleomagnetism 27.15.21(.2.4)
paleontology 1.26.10(.11.2)
Paleozoic 24.2.7
Palermo 19.14.5, 19.14.13
Palestine 28.14.5
Palestinian 28.3.8(.2)
palestra 17.32.19(.11)
Palestrina 17.18.1(.15)
Palethorpe 20.8
paletot 19.10.12
palette 22.19.26(.5)
palfrey 1.29.21
Palfreyman 28.17.16(.2)
Palgrave 31.3.7
Pali 1.31.9
palilalia 3.24.3
palimony 1.16.15(.11)
palimpsest 22.29.5(.6)
Palin 28.2.31(.3)
palindrome 27.17.13
palindromic 24.2.14(.6)
palindromist 22.29.2(.17)
paling 29.1.31(.4)
palingenesis 34.2.17(.10.3)
palingenetic 24.2.10(.3.1)
palinode 23.20.9
palisade 23.4.10
Palisades 35.23.3
palish 36.2.27
Palissy 1.22.16(.14)
pall 40.10
Palladian 28.3.4(.3)
Palladianism 27.15.21(.2.9)
Palladio 15.1.3
palladium 27.3.4(.3)
Pallas 34.7.19, 34.18.29(.7)
pallbearer 17.32.5
pallet 22.19.26(.5)
palletization 28.17.25(.3.11)
palletize 35.15.7(.7)
pallia 3.24.5
pallial 40.3.15
palliasse 34.7.2
palliate 22.4.2(.15)
palliation 28.17.25(.3.1)
palliative 31.2.1(.2)
palliatively 1.31.30(.7.1)
palliator 17.12.4(.1)
pallid 23.2.23
pallidity 1.10.16(.9)
pallidly 1.31.23(.14.7)
pallidness 34.18.16(.21.1)
pallium 27.3.18
Pall Mall 40.6

pall-mall 40.6.8
pallor 17.34.6
pally 1.31.7
palm 27.8
Palma 17.17.7, 17.17.24
palmaceous 34.18.22(.3)
palmar 10.10.10, 17.17.24
palmate 22.4.13(.3)
palmer 17.17.7
Palmerston 28.17.11(.25)
Palmerston North 32.10
palmette 22.5.8
palmetto 19.10.4
palmful 40.14.6(.14)
palmiped 23.5.1
palmipede 23.1.1
palmist 22.29.2(.17)
palmistry 1.29.15(.17)
palmitate 22.4.9(.5)
palmitic 24.2.10(.2.2)
palm-oil 40.11.6
Palmolive® 31.2.5
Palm Springs 35.27
palmtop 20.7.4
palmy 1.15.7
palmyra 17.32.13
Palo Alto 19.10.21
palolo 19.29.14
Palomar 10.10.4
palomino 19.15.1
palooka 17.14.14
Palouse 34.17.14
paloverde 1.11.18
palp 20.18
palpability 1.10.16(.22.1)
palpable 40.20.16(.9)
palpably 1.31.21(.3)
palpal 40.19.16
palpate 22.4.7
palpation 28.17.25(.3.2)
palpebral 40.16.13(.15)
palpitant 22.26.15(.9)
palpitate 22.4.9(.5)
palpitation 28.17.25(.3.3)
palpus 34.18.9(.13)
palsgrave 31.3.7
palsied 23.2.17
palstave 31.3.1
palsy 1.23.22
palsy-walsy 1.23.22
palter 17.12.26(.5)
palterer 17.32.14(.6)
paltrily 1.31.17(.27.3)
paltriness 34.18.16(.2.9)
paltry 1.29.15(.18)
paludism 27.15.21(.2.5)
Paludrine® 28.2.29(.9)
paly 1.31.4
palynological 40.23.12(.17.2)

palynologist 22.29.2(.26.4)
palynology 1.26.10(.11.4)
Pam 27.6
Pamela 17.34.16(.11)
Pamirs 35.3
pampas 34.18.9(.11)
pamper 17.10.17
pamperer 17.32.14(.4)
pampero 19.27.3
Pampers® 35.18.6
pamphlet 22.19.26(.24)
pamphleteer 3.4
Pamphylia 3.24.2
Pamphylian 28.3.21(.2)
Pamplona 17.18.18(.11)
Pan 28.7
pan 28.7, 28.9
panacea 3.14, 17.1.11
panacean 28.3.13, 28.17.1(.9)
panache 36.6.7
panada 17.13.7
Panadol® 40.9.8
Pan-African 28.17.13(.13)
Panaji 1.26.5
Pan-Am 27.6
Panama 10.10, 10.10.4
Panamanian 28.3.8(.3)
Pan-American 28.17.13(.13)
Pan-Anglican 28.17.13(.13)
Panasonic 24.2.15(.6.3)
panatella 17.34.5(.3)
pancake 24.3.6
panchayat 22.19.25
Panchen lama 17.17.7
panchromatic 24.2.10(.4.2)
pancosmism 27.15.21(.2.8)
Pancras 34.18.27(.16)
pancreas 34.3.15(.9)
pancreatic 24.2.10(.4.1)
pancreatin 28.2.11(.3)
pancreatitis 34.18.11(.8)
panda 17.13.20(.4)
pandanus 34.18.16(.7)
Pandarus 34.18.27(.15)
pandean 28.3.4(.11)
pandect 22.23.4(.3)
pandemic 24.2.14(.3)
pandemonium 27.3.8(.10)
pander 17.13.20(.4)
pandit 22.2.8
Pandora 17.32.10(.3)
pandowdy 1.11.8
pane 28.4
paneer 3.9

panegyric 24.2.26(.1)
panegyrical 40.23.12(.18)
panegyrist 22.29.2(.29.1)
panegyrize 35.15.20(.2)
panel 40.26.5
panellist 22.29.2(.31.3)
panettone 1.16.17(.3), 4.14
panettoni 2.17.11
pan-European 28.17.1(.1)
panfish 36.2.18(.19)
panforte 1.10.10, 4.9.5
pan-fried 23.15.15
panfry 14.24.10
panful 40.14.6(.15)
pang 29.4
panga 17.16.17(.2)
Pangaea 17.1.14
Pangbourne 28.11.2
pangolin 28.2.31(.10)
panhandle 40.22.16
panhellenic 24.2.15(.4)
panhellenism 27.15.21(.2.9)
panic 24.2.15(.5)
panicky 1.12.13
panicle 40.23.12(.11)
Panini 1.16.1(.8), 2.17.10
panjandrum 27.15.26(.11)
Pankhurst 22.29.16
panlike 24.13.7(.17)
Panmunjom 27.9
pannage 39.2.15
Pannal 40.26.5
panne 28.7
Pannell 40.26.5
panner 17.18.6
pannier 3.9.5
pannikin 28.2.13(.6)
pannus 34.18.16(.7)
panoplied 23.2.23
panoply 1.31.20
panoptic 24.2.10(.12)
panorama 17.17.7
panoramic 24.2.14(.4)
panoramically 1.31.24(.9.8)
panpipe 20.10.1
panpsychism 27.15.21(.2.6)
panslavism 27.15.21(.2.11)
panspermia 3.8.8
panstick 24.2.10(.15.4)
pansy 1.23.20
pant 22.26.6
Pantagruel 40.5, 40.16.7
pantalettes 34.22.4
pantaloon 28.16.15

pantechnicon 28.17.13(.13)
Pantelleria 17.1.16
Panthalassa 17.24.6
pantheism 27.15.21(.2.1)
pantheist 22.29.2(.2)
pantheistic 24.2.10(.15.1)
pantheistical 40.23.12(.7.3)
pantheistically 1.31.24(.9.6)
pantheon 28.3.11
panther 17.22.13
pantie-girdle 40.22.14
panties 35.2.3
pantile 40.13.3(.9)
pantingly 1.31.28(.1.4)
panto 19.10.17
pantograph 30.7.5(.1)
pantographic 24.2.16(.3)
pantologic 24.2.24(.4)
pantology 1.26.10(.11.2)
pantomime 27.12.4
pantomimic 24.2.14(.2)
pantomimist 22.29.2(.17)
pantomorphic 24.2.16(.5)
pantoscopic 24.2.8(.5)
pantothenic 24.2.15(.4)
pantry 1.29.15(.15)
pantryman 28.17.16(.2)
pants 34.22.18
pantsuit 22.18.6
pantyhose 35.20.11
pantywaist 22.29.4
Panzer 17.25.18
pap 20.5
papa 10.4
papabile 4.28.7
papacy 1.22.16(.2)
papain 28.2.3, 28.2.5
papal 40.19.3
papalism 27.15.21(.2.15)
papalist 22.29.2(.31.2)
papally 1.31.17(.7)
paparazzi 2.22.10
paparazzo 19.20.14
papaveraceous 34.18.22(.3)
papaverine 28.1.25(.3), 28.2.29(.5)
papaw 12.3
papaya 17.6.1
Papeete 1.10.1, 1.10.3
paper 17.10.3
paperback 24.6.6(.9)
paperboy 13.3
paperchase 34.4.12
paperclip 20.2.13
paperer 17.32.14(.4)
paperhanger 17.19.2

paperknife 30.12
paperless 34.18.29(.17.2)
papermaker 17.14.3(.3)
papermaking 29.1.14(.3)
paperweight 22.4.21
paperwork 24.17.6(.4)
papery 1.29.11(.6)
Paphlagonia 3.9.11
Paphlagonian 28.3.8(.11)
papier-mâché 4.20
papilionaceous 34.18.22(.3)
papilla 17.34.2(.1)
papillae 2.32.2
papillary 1.29.11(.27)
papillate 22.4.23(.7.1), 22.19.26(.1)
papilloma 17.17.16(.12)
papillomata 17.12.16(.9.3)
papillon 11.18, 28.10.26
papillose 34.20.17, 35.20.14
papism 27.15.21(.2.2)
papist 22.29.2(.11)
papistic 24.2.10(.15.2)
papistical 40.23.12(.7.3)
papistry 1.29.15(.17)
papoose 34.17.2
Papp 20.5
pappardelle 4.28.2
pappi 14.6
pappose 34.20.2
pappus 34.18.9(.4)
pappy 1.8.5
paprika 17.14.1, 17.14.15(.14)
Papua 17.7.1, 17.7.12(.2)
Papuan 28.17.6
Papua New Guinea 1.16.2
Papua New Guinean 28.3.8(.2)
papula 17.34.16(.21.1)
papulae 2.32.9(.8)
papular 17.34.16(.21.1)
papule 40.15.9(.1)
papulose 34.20.17, 35.20.14
papulous 34.18.29(.17.6)
Papworth 32.14.15
papyraceous 34.18.22(.3)
papyri 14.24.5
papyrological 40.23.12(.17.2)
papyrologist 22.29.2(.26.4)
papyrology 1.26.10(.11.5)
papyrus 34.18.27(.10)
par 10
Pará 10.23

para 17.32.6
parabases 35.1.16(.2)
parabasis 34.2.17(.2)
parabioses 35.1.16(.11)
parabiosis 34.2.17(.11.1)
parabiotic 24.2.10(.6)
parable 40.20.16(.27.1)
parabola 17.34.16(.6)
parabolic 24.2.27(.9)
parabolical 40.23.12(.19)
parabolically 1.31.24(.9.12)
paraboloid 23.13.20
paraboloidal 40.22.9
Paracelsus 34.18.20
paracetamol 40.9.11
parachronism 27.15.21(.2.9)
parachute 22.18.7
parachutist 22.29.2(.13)
paraclete 22.1.18
parade 23.4.15
parader 17.13.3
paradichlorobenzene 28.1.19
paradiddle 40.22.2
paradigm 27.12.2
paradigmatic 24.2.10(.4.2)
paradigmatical 40.23.12(.7.1)
paradigmatically 1.31.24(.9.4)
paradisal 40.31.11, 40.32.12
paradise 34.15.3
paradisiacal 40.23.12(.3)
paradisical 40.23.12(.15)
parador 12.6.6
parados 34.10.9
paradox 34.23.8(.4)
paradoxical 40.23.12(.15)
paradoxically 1.31.24(.9.10)
paradoxure 17.7.12(.11)
paradrop 20.7.12
paraesthesia 3.15.1
paraesthetic 24.2.10(.3.2)
paraffin 28.2.19
paraglide 23.15.16
paraglider 17.13.12
paragliding 29.1.13(.9)
paragoge 1.26.12
paragogic 24.2.24(.4)
paragon 28.17.15(.13)
paragraph 30.7.5(.1)
paragraphic 24.2.16(.3)
paragraphist 22.29.2(.19)
Paraguay 14.23
Paraguayan 28.17.5

parahydrogen **28.17.28(.9)**
parakeet **22.1.4**
paralanguage **39.2.21**
paraldehyde **23.15.13**
paralegal **40.24.1**
paralinguistic **24.2.10(.15.2)**
paralipomena **17.18.16(.8)**
paralipses **35.1.16(.12)**
paralipsis **34.2.17(.12)**
parallactic **24.2.10(.13)**
parallax **34.23.5(.15)**
parallel **40.5.19**
parallelepiped **23.5.1**
parallelism **27.15.21(.2.15)**
parallelogram **27.6.17(.5)**
paralogism **27.15.21(.2.13)**
paralogist **22.29.2(.26.1)**
paralogize **35.15.18**
Paralympics **34.23.2(.1)**
paralyse **35.15.21(.4.7)**
paralyses **35.1.16(.10)**
paralysingly **1.31.28(.1.12)**
paralysis **34.2.17(.10.5)**
paralytic **24.2.10(.2.5)**
paralytically **1.31.24(.9.3)**
paralyzation **28.17.25(.3.12)**
paralyze **35.15.21(.4.7)**
paralyzingly **1.31.28(.1.12)**
paramagnetic **24.2.10(.3.1)**
paramagnetism **27.15.21(.2.4)**
paramatta **17.12.6**
paramecia **3.14.1**
paramecium **27.3.11**
paramedic **24.2.11(.4)**
paramedical **40.23.12(.8)**
parameter **17.12.16(.9.1)**
parametric **24.2.26(.14.2)**
parametrize **35.15.20(.4)**
paramilitary **1.29.11(.8.10)**
paramnesia **3.15.1**
paramo **19.14.12**
paramoecia **3.16.1, 17.26.1**
paramount **22.26.7**
paramountcy **1.22.23(.5)**
paramountly **1.31.22(.20.1)**
paramour **12.9.4, 17.7.7**
Paraná **10.11**

parang **29.4.15**
paranoia **17.5**
paranoiac **24.6.2**
paranoiacally **1.31.24(.9.1)**
paranoic **24.2.5**
paranoically **1.31.24(.9.1)**
paranoid **23.13.12**
paranormal **40.25.6**
paranormally **1.31.17(.13)**
Paranthropus **34.18.9(.8)**
parapet **22.19.8**
paraph **30.5.8, 30.14**
paraphernalia **3.24.3**
paraphrase **35.4.16**
paraphrastic **24.2.10(.15.4)**
paraphrastically **1.31.24(.9.6)**
paraplegia **3.19.1, 17.29.1**
paraplegic **24.2.24(.1)**
paraprofessional **40.26.13(.14.3)**
parapsychological **40.23.12(.17.2)**
parapsychologically **1.31.24(.9.11)**
parapsychologist **22.29.2(.26.3)**
parapsychology **1.26.10(.11.3)**
paraquat **22.7.19, 22.11.14**
pararhyme **27.12.7**
parasailer **17.34.4**
parasailing **29.1.31(.4)**
parasang **29.4.9**
parascend **23.24.5(.11)**
parascender **17.13.20(.3)**
paraselenae **2.17.1**
paraselene **1.16.1(.16)**
parasitaemia **3.8.1**
parasite **22.16.19(.9)**
parasitic **24.2.10(.2.3)**
parasitical **40.23.12(.7.1)**
parasitically **1.31.24(.9.3)**
parasiticide **23.15.11(.6)**
parasitism **27.15.21(.2.4)**
parasitization **28.17.25(.3.12)**
parasitize **35.15.7(.7)**
parasitoid **23.13.7**
parasitologist **22.29.2(.26.3)**
parasitology **1.26.10(.11.2)**
parasol **40.9.14**
parasympathetic **24.2.10(.3.2)**
parasyntheses **35.1.16(.10)**

parasynthesis **34.2.17(.10.4)**
parasynthetic **24.2.10(.3.2)**
paratactic **24.2.10(.13)**
paratactically **1.31.24(.9.5)**
parataxis **34.2.17(.14)**
parathion **28.10.4**
parathyroid **23.13.19**
paratroop **20.12**
paratrooper **17.10.13**
paratroops **34.21.10**
paratyphoid **23.13.13**
paravane **28.4.10**
par avion **11.18**
parboil **40.11.2**
parbuckle **40.23.9**
Parcae **1.22.8**
parcel **40.31.7**
parch **38.7**
parcheesi® **1.23.1**
parchment **22.26.15(.13.6)**
parclose **35.20.14**
pard **23.9**
pardalote **22.21.15**
pardner **17.18.22**
Pardoe **19.11.7**
pardon **28.17.12(.8)**
pardonable **40.20.16(.16.3)**
pardonably **1.31.21(.6)**
pardoner **17.18.16(.5)**
pare **6**
paregoric **24.2.26(.6)**
paren **28.5.18**
parenchyma **17.17.14(.4)**
parenchymal **40.25.10**
parenchymatous **34.18.11(.10)**
parent **22.26.15(.23.1)**
parentage **39.2.10**
parental **40.21.17(.2)**
parentally **1.31.17(.9.3)**
parenteral **40.16.13(.12.1)**
parenterally **1.31.17(.27.1)**
parentheses **35.1.16(.10)**
parenthesis **34.2.17(.10.4)**
parenthesize **35.15.16(.4)**
parenthetic **24.2.10(.3.2)**
parenthetical **40.23.12(.7.1)**
parenthetically **1.31.24(.9.3)**
parenthood **23.16.5(.6)**
parentless **34.18.29(.22)**
parer **17.32.5**
parerga **17.16.14**
parergon **28.10.12**

paresis **34.2.17(.1)**
paretic **24.2.10(.3.3)**
par excellence **34.11, 34.24.6**
parfait **4.15**
Parfitt **22.2.13**
parfleche **36.5**
parfumerie **1.29.11(.12)**
parget **22.2.21**
Pargiter **17.12.16(.16)**
parhelia **3.24.1**
parheliacal **40.23.12(.3)**
parhelic **24.2.27(.1)**
parhelical **40.23.12(.19)**
parhelion **28.3.21(.1)**
pariah **17.6.14**
Parian **28.3.20(.4)**
parietal **40.21.12**
pari-mutuel **40.16.12**
paring **29.1.30(.4)**
pari passu **16.15**
Paris **34.2.21**
parish **36.2.25**
parishioner **17.18.16(.16)**
Parisian **28.3.14**
parison **28.17.23(.14)**
parisyllabic **24.2.9(.2)**
parity **1.10.16(.21.1)**
park **24.8**
parka **17.14.7**
park and ride **23.15**
Parke **24.8**
parker **17.14.7**
Parkes **34.23.7**
Parkhouse **34.8.6(.13)**
parkin **28.2.13(.3)**
parking **29.1.14(.5)**
Parkinson **28.17.23(.24)**
Parkinsonism **27.15.21(.2.9)**
parkland **23.24.6(.13), 23.24.16(.16.3)**
Parkstone **28.17.11(.25)**
parkway **4.25.14**
parky **1.12.6**
parlance **34.24.10(.24)**
parlay **4.28.4**
parley **1.31.9**
parliament **22.26.15(.13.2)**
parliamentarian **28.3.20(.4)**
parliamentary **1.29.11(.8.12)**
Parlophone **28.19.11**
parlor **17.34.8**
parlour **17.34.8**
parlourmaid **23.4.7**
parlous **34.18.29(.9)**
parlously **1.31.33(.12.6)**

parlousness 34.18.16(.31.6)
Parma 17.17.7
Parmenides 35.1.8
Parmenter 17.12.22(.12)
Parmentier 3.4.12, 4.2.2
parmesan 28.7.15
Parmigianino 19.15.1
Parmigiano 19.15.7
Parmiter 17.12.16(.9.1)
Parnassian 28.3.13
Parnassus 34.18.20
Parnell 40.5.8
Parnes 35.26.9
parochial 40.3.5
parochialism 27.15.21(.2.15)
parochiality 1.10.16(.32.1)
parochially 1.31.3(.5)
parodic 24.2.11(.7)
parodist 22.29.2(.14)
parody 1.11.17
paroecious 34.18.22(.1)
parol 40.16.13(.5), 40.18.14
parole 40.18.14
parolee 2.32
paronomasia 3.15.3
paronym 27.2.6
paronymous 34.18.15(.10)
parotid 23.2.8
parotitis 34.18.11(.8)
paroxysm 27.15.21(.2.12)
paroxysmal 40.25.14
paroxytone 28.19.4(.5)
parozone 28.19.14
parpen 28.17.9
parquet 4.11
parquetry 1.29.15(.6)
parr 10
Parramatta 17.12.6
parricidal 40.22.11
parricide 23.15.11(.6)
Parrish 36.2.25
parrot 22.19.24(.4)
parrotfish 36.2.18(.15)
Parrott 22.19.24(.4)
parry 1.29.5
parse 35.9
parsec 24.4.8
Parsee 2.22, 2.22.4
Parseeism 27.15.21(.2.1)
parser 17.25.7
Parsifal 40.6.10, 40.27.14
parsimonious 34.3.6(.7)
parsimoniously 1.31.33(.1.2)
parsimoniousness 34.18.16(.31.1)
parsimony 1.16.15(.11)

Parsley 1.31.34
parsley 1.31.33(.5)
parsley-piert 22.3.1
parsnip 20.2.4
parson 28.17.23(.7)
parsonage 39.2.15
parsonical 40.23.12(.11)
Parsons 35.26.13(.13)
part 22.10
partakable 40.20.16(.13)
partake 24.3.4
partaken 28.17.13(.3)
partaker 17.14.3(.2)
partan 28.17.11(.8)
parterre 6.4
part-exchange 39.17.2
parthenogenesis 34.2.17(.10.3)
parthenogenetic 24.2.10(.3.1)
parthenogenetically 1.31.24(.9.3)
Parthenon 28.10.14, 28.17.17(.10)
Parthia 3.12
Parthian 28.3.11
parti 1.10.8
partial 40.33.5
partiality 1.10.16(.32.1)
partially 1.31.17(.22)
partialness 34.18.16(.37.5)
partible 40.20.16(.11.1)
participant 22.26.15(.7)
participate 22.4.7
participation 28.17.25(.3.2)
participative 31.2.1(.9.1)
participator 17.12.4(.3)
participatory 1.29.11(.8.2)
participial 40.3.1
participially 1.31.3(.1)
participle 40.19.11
Partick 24.2.10(.5)
particle 40.23.12(.7.2)
particoloured 23.18.29
particular 17.34.16(.21.2)
particularism 27.15.21(.2.14)
particularist 22.29.2(.29.4)
particularity 1.10.16(.21.1)
particularization 28.17.25(.3.12)
particularize 35.15.20(.2)
particularly 1.31.17(.29)
particulate 22.4.23(.7.3), 22.19.26(.13)
parting 29.1.12(.7)
Partington 28.17.11(.23)

parti pris 2
partisan 28.7.15, 28.17.24(.12)
partisanship 20.2.7(.19)
partita 17.12.1(.3)
partite 22.16.9
partition 28.17.25(.2.2)
partitioner 17.18.16(.16)
partitionist 22.29.2(.18.2)
partitive 31.2.1(.9.1)
partitively 1.31.30(.7.1)
partly 1.31.22(.8)
partnerless 34.18.29(.17.3)
partnership 20.2.7(.9)
Parton 28.17.11(.8)
partook 24.14.4
partridge 39.2.22(.11)
part-singing 29.1.18
part-song 29.6.9
part-time 27.12.1
part-timer 17.17.11
parturient 22.26.2(.9)
parturition 28.17.25(.2.6)
part-way 4.25
part-work 24.17.6(.8)
party 1.10.8
party line 28.14
party-pooper 17.10.13
parvenu 16.12, 16.24.10
parvis 34.2.15
parvise 34.2.15
parvovirus 34.18.27(.10)
pas 10
Pasadena 17.18.1(.4)
pascal 40.6.6, 40.8.6
Pascale 40.8.6
paschal 40.23.16
Pascoe 19.12.17
pas de chat 10
pas de deux 18
paseo 19.2
pas glissé 4.18
pash 36.6
pasha 17.26.6
pashalic 24.2.27(.8)
pashm 27.15.22
Pashto 19.10.20
Pasiphaë 2.3, 2.4
Pasmore 12.9.12
paso doble 4.28.10
paspalum 27.15.28(.11)
pasque flower 17.3
pasquinade 23.4.8
pass 34.9
passable 40.20.16(.21.1)
passableness 34.18.16(.37.4)
passably 1.31.21(.7.2)
passacaglia 3.24.6

passade 23.4.10
passage 39.2.19
passageway 4.25.25
Passamaquoddy 1.11.10
passant 22.12, 22.26.15(.17.3)
Passat® 22.7.15
passata 17.12.8(.9)
passband 23.24.6(.4)
passbook 24.14.3
Passchendaele 40.4.3
passé 4.18, 4.18.6
passel 40.31.6
passenger 17.29.16(.8)
passe-partout 16.7, 16.7.2
passer 17.24.6, 17.24.8
passer-by 14.7
passerine 28.14.18
passers-by 14.7
pas seul 40.17
passibility 1.10.16(.22.1)
passible 40.20.16(.21.1)
passim 27.2.9
passing 29.1.23
passingly 1.31.28(.1.11)
passing-out 22.9
passion 28.17.25(.5)
passional 40.26.13(.14.4)
passionate 22.19.15(.9)
passionately 1.31.22(.15)
passionateness 34.18.16(.20.3)
passionflower 17.3.11
passionfruit 22.18.9
Passionist 22.29.2(.18.2)
passionless 34.18.29(.27)
Passiontide 23.15.4
passivate 22.4.16
passivation 28.17.25(.3.9)
passive 31.2.4(.5)
passively 1.31.30(.7.4)
passiveness 34.18.16(.28.2)
passivity 1.10.16(.15)
passkey 2.14
Passover 17.21.14(.9)
passport 22.13.1
password 23.19.8
past 22.29.6, 22.29.8
pasta 17.12.24(.5)
paste 29.29.4
pasteboard 23.12.2(.8)
pastedown 28.8.2(.5)
pastel 40.21.18
pastellist 22.29.2(.31.2)
pastern 28.17.11(.25), 28.18.4
Pasternak 24.6.11
Pasteur 18.3

pasteurization 28.17.25(.3.11)
pasteurize 35.15.20(.2)
pasteurizer 17.25.12(.14)
pasticcio 19.24
pastiche 36.1
pastie 1.10.26(.3)
pastille 40.2.5, 40.21.18
pastily 1.31.17(.9.3)
pastime 27.12.1
pastiness 34.18.16(.2.3)
pasting 29.1.12(.21)
pastis 34.1.3, 34.2.8
pastmaster 17.12.24(.5)
Paston 28.17.11(.25)
pastor 17.12.24(.5)
pastoral 40.16.13(.12.1)
pastorale 1.31.9, 40.8.15
pastoralism 27.15.21(.2.15)
pastoralist 22.29.2(.31.4)
pastorality 1.10.16(.32.13)
pastorally 1.31.17(.27.3)
pastorate 22.19.24(.9)
pastorship 20.2.7(.9)
pastrami 1.15.7
pastry 1.29.15(.17)
pastrycook 24.14.5
pasturage 39.2.22(.9)
pasture 17.28.24
pastureland 23.24.6(.13)
pasty 1.10.26(.3)
pat 22.7
pat-a-cake 24.3.6
patagia 17.6.12
patagium 27.15.3
Patagonia 3.9.11
Patagonian 28.3.8(.11)
Patavinity 1.10.16(.13)
patball 40.10.4
patch 38.5
patchboard 23.12.2(.18)
patcher 17.28.6
patchily 1.31.17(.24)
patchiness 34.18.16(.2.8)
patchouli 1.31.16
patchwork 24.17.6(.17)
patchy 1.25.6
Pate 22.4
pate 22.4
paté 1.10.6
pâte 22.10
pâté 4.9.2
pâté de foie gras 10
Patel 40.5.3
Pateley 1.31.22(.4)
patella 17.34.5(.3)
patellae 2.32.5
patellar 17.34.5(.3)
patellate 22.19.26(.4)

paten 28.17.11(.6)
patency 1.22.23(.10.2)
patent 22.26.15(.9)
patentable 40.20.16(.11.6)
patentee 2.11
patentor 17.12.22(.12)
pater 17.12.4
paterfamilias 34.7.2
paternal 40.26.14
paternalism 27.15.21(.2.15)
paternalist 22.29.2(.31.3)
paternalistic 24.2.10(.15.3)
paternalistically 1.31.24(.9.6)
paternally 1.31.17(.14.3)
paternity 1.10.16(.13)
paternoster 17.12.24(.7)
Paterson 28.17.23(.14)
path 32.8
Pathan 28.9.2
Pathé 4.17
pathetic 24.2.10(.3.2)
pathetically 1.31.24(.9.3)
pathfinder 17.13.20(.11)
pathic 24.2.18(.3)
pathless 34.18.29(.31)
pathogen 28.5.15, 28.17.28(.9)
pathogenesis 34.2.17(.10.3)
pathogenetic 24.2.10(.3.1)
pathogenic 24.2.15(.4)
pathogenous 34.18.16(.15.3)
pathogeny 1.16.15(.17)
pathognomonic 24.2.15(.6.2)
pathognomy 1.15.13(.5)
pathologic 24.2.24(.4)
pathological 40.23.12(.17.2)
pathologically 1.31.24(.9.11)
pathologist 22.29.2(.26.4)
pathology 1.26.10(.11.5)
pathos 34.10.14
pathway 4.25.21
patience 34.24.10(.20)
patient 22.26.15(.19)
patiently 1.31.22(.20.4)
patina 17.18.1(.3), 17.18.16(.4)
patinaed 23.18.14
patinated 23.18.9(.3)
patination 28.17.25(.3.8)
patinous 34.18.16(.15.2)
patio 15.1.2
pâtisserie 1.29.11(.18)

patly 1.31.22(.6)
Patmore 12.9.7
Pátmos 34.10.12
Patna 17.18.21
patness 34.18.16(.20.1)
patois 10.22.5, 35.9
Paton 28.17.11(.3)
patrial 40.3.14(.9)
patriality 1.10.16(.32.1)
patriarch 24.8.1
patriarchal 40.23.6
patriarchally 1.31.17(.11)
patriarchate 22.19.12(.6)
patriarchism 27.15.21(.2.6)
patriarchy 1.12.6
Patrice 34.1.7
Patricia 17.26.2
patrician 28.17.25(.2.6)
patriciate 22.3.10
patricidal 40.22.11
patricide 23.15.11(.6)
Patrick 24.2.26(.14.3)
patrilineal 40.3.7(.2)
patrimonial 40.3.7(.9)
patrimonially 1.31.3(.7)
patrimony 1.16.15(.11)
patriot 22.3.12
patriotic 24.2.10(.6)
patriotically 1.31.24(.9.4)
patriotism 27.15.21(.2.4)
patristic 24.2.10(.15.2)
Patroclus 34.18.29(.24)
patrol 40.18.14
patroller 17.34.18(.14)
patrolman 28.7.10(.24), 28.17.16(.35)
patrolmen 28.5.7(.28)
patrological 40.23.12(.17.2)
patrologist 22.29.2(.26.4)
patrology 1.26.10(.11.5)
patron 28.17.31(.14)
patronage 39.2.15
patronal 40.26.15
patroness 34.5.6, 34.18.16(.15.3)
patronisingly 1.31.28(.1.12)
patronization 28.17.25(.3.11)
patronize 35.15.12(.5)
patronizer 17.25.12(.6)
patronizingly 1.31.28(.1.12)
patronymic 24.2.14(.2)
patronymically 1.31.24(.9.8)
patroon 28.16.13
patsy 1.22.21
pattée 1.10.6, 4.9.2

patten 28.17.11(.6)
patter 17.12.6
Patterdale 40.4.3
pattern 28.17.11(.6)
patterned 23.24.16(.3)
Patti 1.10.6
Pattie 1.10.6
Pattison 28.17.23(.14)
Patton 28.17.11(.6)
patty 1.10.6
pattypan 28.7.4
patulous 34.18.29(.17.6)
patulously 1.31.33(.12.6)
patulousness 34.18.16(.31.6)
Patuxent 22.26.15(.17.3)
paua 17.3
paucity 1.10.16(.16.2)
Paul 40.10
Paula 17.34.10
Paulette 22.5.21
Pauli 1.31.8
Pauline 28.1.27(.5), 28.14.19(.8)
Pauling 29.1.31(.9)
paulownia 3.9.11
paunch 38.18.6
paunchiness 34.18.16(.2.8)
paunchy 1.24.15
pauper 17.10.9
pauperdom 27.15.10(.8)
pauperism 27.15.21(.2.14)
pauperization 28.17.25(.3.11)
pauperize 35.15.20(.2)
paupiette 22.5.20
Pausanias 34.3.6(.3)
pause 35.12
pavage 39.2.17
pavane 28.7.13, 28.9.8, 28.17.20(.5)
Pavarotti 1.10.9
pave 31.3
pavé 4.16
paved 23.26
pavement 22.26.15(.13.5)
paver 17.21.3
Pavey 1.19.3
pavilion 28.3.21(.2)
paving 29.1.20
pavior 3.11.3
paviour 3.11.3
Pavlov 31.7
Pavlova 17.21.12, 17.21.14(.15)
Pavlovian 28.3.10
pavonine 28.14.9
paw 12
pawkily 1.31.17(.11)
pawkiness 34.18.16(.2.4)

p

pawky **1.12.8**
pawl **40.10**
pawn **28.11**
pawnbroker **17.14.17**
pawnbroking **29.1.14(.13)**
Pawnee **2.17**
pawnshop **20.7.9**
pawpaw **12.3**
pax **34.23.5**
Paxo® **19.20.15**
Paxton **28.17.11(.25)**
pay **4**
payable **40.20.16(.2)**
pay-as-you-earn **28.18**
payback **24.6.6(.3)**
paycheque **24.4.11**
payday **4.10.2**
paydirt **22.20.3**
PAYE **2**
payee **2**
payer **17.2**
payload **23.20.13**
paymaster **17.12.24(.5)**
payment **22.26.15(.13.1)**
Payn **28.4**
Payne **28.4**
paynim **27.2.6**
payoff **30.8.1**
payola **17.34.18**
payout **22.9.1**
paypacket **22.2.9(.3)**
payphone **28.19.11**
payroll **40.18.14**
paysage **37.4.7, 39.8**
payslip **20.2.13**
Payton **28.17.11(.3)**
Paz **35.9**
pea **2**
Peabody **1.11.10, 1.11.17**
peace **34.1**
peaceable **40.20.16(.21.1)**
peaceableness **34.18.16(.37.4)**
peaceably **1.31.21(.7.2)**
peaceful **40.27.25**
peacefully **1.31.17(.16.2)**
peacefulness **34.18.16(.37.2)**
peacekeeper **17.10.1**
peacekeeping **29.1.10(.1)**
peacemaker **17.14.3(.3)**
peacemaking **29.1.14(.3)**
peacenik **24.2.15(.17)**
peacetime **27.12.1**
peach **38.1**
Peachey **1.25.1**
peachick **24.2.23**
peachiness **34.18.16(.2.8)**
peachy **1.25.1**

peacock **24.9.6**
peacockery **1.29.11(.10)**
peafowl **40.7**
peahen **28.5.16**
peak **24.1**
Peak District **22.23.2**
Peake **24.1**
peakiness **34.18.16(.2.4)**
peakish **36.2.13**
peakload **23.20.13**
peaky **1.12.1**
peal **40.1**
peanut **22.15.6**
pear **6**
Pearce **34.3**
pearl **40.17**
pearler **17.34.17**
pearlescent **22.26.15(.17.2)**
Pearl Harbor **17.11.7**
pearliness **34.18.16(.2.10)**
pearlite **22.16.25(.10)**
pearlized **23.28.2**
pearlware **6.18.16**
pearlwort **22.20.15**
pearly **1.31.18**
pearmain **28.4.7**
Pears® **35.6**
Pearsall **40.31.3**
pearshaped **22.22.2**
Pearson **28.17.23(.3)**
peart **22.3**
Peary **1.29.2**
peasant **22.26.15(.18)**
peasantry **1.29.15(.15)**
peasanty **1.10.23(.12)**
peascod **23.10.5**
pease **35.1**
peasepudding **29.1.13(.10)**
peashooter **17.12.15(.4)**
pea-soup **20.12**
pea-souper **17.10.13**
pea stick **24.2**
peat **22.1**
peatbog **26.7.2**
peatiness **34.18.16(.2.3)**
peatland **23.24.6(.13)**
peatmoss **34.10.12**
peaty **1.10.1**
peau-de-soie **10.22.11**
Peaudouce® **34.17.5, 34.17.13**
peavey **1.19.1**
pebble **40.20.5**
pebbledash **36.6.4**
pebbly **1.31.17(.8), 1.31.21(.1)**
pec **24.4**
pecan **28.7.8, 28.17.13(.1)**

peccability **1.10.16(.22.1)**
peccable **40.20.16(.13)**
peccadillo **19.29.2**
peccancy **1.22.23(.10.2)**
peccant **22.26.15(.11)**
peccary **1.29.11(.10)**
peccavi **1.19.6, 2.19**
pêche Melba **17.11.20**
peck **24.4**
pecker **17.14.4**
Peckham **27.15.11(.4)**
peckish **36.2.13**
peckishly **1.31.35(.7.1)**
peckishness **34.18.16(.33.4)**
Pecksniff **30.2.3**
pecorino **19.15.1**
Pecos **34.10.10, 34.18.13(.2)**
pecten **28.2.11(.12), 28.5.3**
pectic **24.2.10(.13)**
pectin **28.2.11(.12)**
pectinate **22.19.15(.9)**
pectinated **23.18.9(.3)**
pectination **28.17.25(.3.8)**
pectines **35.1.12(.3)**
pectoral **40.16.13(.12.1)**
pectose **34.20.4, 35.20.3**
peculate **22.4.23(.7.3)**
peculation **28.17.25(.3.14)**
peculator **17.12.4(.16)**
peculiar **3.24.10**
peculiarity **1.10.16(.21.1)**
peculiarly **1.31.3(.12)**
pecuniarily **1.31.17(.27.2)**
pecuniary **1.29.11(.26)**
pedagogic **24.2.13, 24.2.24(.4)**
pedagogical **40.23.12(.17.2)**
pedagogically **1.31.24(.9.7)**
pedagogism **27.15.21(.2.7)**
pedagogue **26.7.6**
pedagogy **1.14.6, 1.26.6**
pedal **40.22.1, 40.22.4**
pedalo **19.29.12**
pedant **22.26.15(.10)**
pedantic **24.2.10(.14)**
pedantically **1.31.24(.9.5)**
pedantry **1.29.15(.15)**
pedate **22.4.10, 22.19.11**
peddle **40.22.4**
peddler **17.34.22**
pederast **22.29.6(.11)**
pederasty **1.10.26(.5)**
pedate **22.4.10, 22.19.11**
pedestal **40.21.18**
pedestrian **28.3.20(.11)**
pedestrianism **27.15.21(.2.9)**

pedestrianization **28.17.25(.3.12)**
pedestrianize **35.15.12(.3)**
pedicab **21.6**
pedicel **40.5.11, 40.31.12**
pedicellate **22.4.23(.7.2)**
pedicle **40.23.12(.8)**
pedicular **17.34.16(.21.2)**
pediculate **22.19.26(.13)**
pediculosis **34.2.17(.11.2)**
pediculous **34.18.29(.17.6)**
pedicure **12.22, 17.7.12(.5)**
pedicurist **22.29.2(.29.2)**
pediform **27.10.5(.2)**
pedigree **2.30.12**
pediment **22.26.15(.13.2)**
pedimental **40.21.17(.2)**
pedlar **17.34.22**
pedlary **1.29.11(.27)**
pedological **40.23.12(.17.2)**
pedologist **22.29.2(.26.3)**
pedology **1.26.10(.11.2)**
pedometer **17.12.16(.9.2)**
pedophile **40.13.9**
pedophiliad **23.7.2**
Pedro **19.27.16**
peduncle **40.23.15**
peduncular **17.34.16(.21.2)**
pedunculate **22.4.23(.7.3), 22.19.26(.13)**
pee **2**
Peebles **35.30.15**
peek **24.1**
peekaboo **16.6**
peekily **1.31.17(.11)**
peeky **1.12.1**
peel **40.1**
peeler **17.34.1**
peeling **29.1.31(.1)**
Peelite **22.16.25(.1)**
peen **28.1**
Peenemunde **17.13.20(.12)**
peep **20.1**
peep-bo **19.8, 19.9.12**
peeper **17.10.1**
peephole **40.18.13**
peepshow **19.22**
peepul **40.19.1**
peer **3**
peerage **39.2.22(.1)**
peeress **34.5.14, 34.18.27(.2)**
peer-group **20.12**
peerless **34.18.29(.3)**
peerlessly **1.31.33(.12.6)**
peerlessness **34.18.16(.31.6)**

peeve **31.1**
peevish **36.2.19**
peevishly **1.31.35(.7.3)**
peevishness
34.18.16(.33.6)
peewee **2.29**
peewit **22.2.23**
peg **26.4**
Pegasean **28.17.1(.9)**
Pegasus **34.18.20**
pegboard **23.12.2(.11)**
Pegg **26.4**
Peggotty **1.10.16(.11)**
Peggy **1.14.4**
peg-leg **26.4**
pegmatite **22.16.9**
pegtop **20.7.4**
Pegu **16.24.8**
Pei **4**
peignoir **10.22.9**
Peirce **34.3**
pejoration
28.17.25(.3.13)
pejorative **31.2.1(.9.4)**
pejoratively **1.31.30(.7.1)**
pekan **28.17.13(.4)**
peke **24.1**
Pekin **28.2.13**
Pekinese **35.1.12**
Peking **29.1.14**
pekingese **35.1.12**
pekoe **19.12.1**
pelage **39.2.23**
Pelagian **28.3.18,**
28.17.28(.3)
Pelagianism
27.15.21(.2.9)
pelagic **24.2.24(.2)**
Pelagius **34.3.13**
pelargonium **27.3.8(.10)**
Pelasgian **28.3.6, 28.3.18**
Pelasgic **24.2.13,**
24.2.24(.8)
Pelé **4.28.2**
pele **40.1**
pelerine **28.1.25(.3),**
28.2.29(.5)
Peleus **34.3.16, 34.18.28**
pelf **30.20.2**
pelham **27.15.28(.4)**
Pelias **34.7.2**
pelican **28.17.13(.13)**
Pelion **28.3.21(.1), 28.10.2**
pelisse **34.1.8**
pelite **22.16.25(.1)**
pellagra **17.32.22**
pellagrous **34.18.27(.17)**
pellet **22.2.25**
pelletize **35.15.7(.7)**
pellicle **40.23.12(.19)**
pellicular **17.34.16(.21.2)**

pellitory **1.29.11(.8.10)**
pell-mell **40.5.7**
pellucid **23.18.20**
pellucidity **1.10.16(.9)**
pellucidly **1.31.23(.14.7)**
pellucidness
34.18.16(.21.1)
Pelmanism **27.15.21(.2.9)**
Pelmanize **35.15.12(.5)**
pelmet **22.19.14**
Peloponnese **35.1.12**
Peloponnesian
28.17.26(.1), 28.17.32
Pelops **34.21.6**
pelorus **34.18.27(.8)**
pelota **17.12.9, 17.12.18**
pelt **22.32.2**
pelta **17.12.26(.3)**
peltae **2.12.16**
peltate **22.4.9(.10)**
peltry **1.29.15(.18)**
pelvic **24.2.17**
pelvis **34.2.15**
Pemba **17.11.17(.3)**
Pemberton **28.17.11(.15)**
Pembroke **24.16.15,**
24.18.13
pemmican **28.17.13(.13)**
pemphigoid **23.13.10**
pemphigous
34.18.14(.5)
pemphigus **34.18.14(.5)**
pen **28.5**
Peña **17.33.9**
penal **40.26.1**
penalization
28.17.25(.3.12)
penalize **35.15.21(.4.5)**
penally **1.31.17(.14.1)**
penalty **1.10.28**
penance **34.24.10(.15)**
pen-and-ink **24.19.1**
Penang **29.4.8**
penannular
17.34.16(.21.4)
Penarth **32.8**
penates **35.1.7(.2), 35.4.3**
pence **34.24.3**
penchant **11.14**
pencil **40.31.21**
penciller **17.34.16(.15)**
pend **23.24.5**
pendant **22.26.15(.10)**
pendency **1.22.23(.10.2)**
Pendennis **34.2.13**
pendent **22.26.15(.10)**
pendentive **31.2.1(.14)**
Penderecki **1.12.17(.8)**
Pendine **28.14.6**
Pendle **40.22.16**
Pendlebury **1.29.11(.7.2)**

Pendleton **28.17.11(.27)**
pendragon **28.17.15(.6)**
pendulate **22.4.23(.7.2)**
penduline **28.14.19(.11)**
pendulous **34.18.29(.17.5)**
pendulously
1.31.33(.12.6)
pendulum **27.15.28(.11)**
Penelope **1.8.11(.9)**
peneplain **28.4.19**
penetrability
1.10.16(.22.2)
penetrable **40.20.16(.27.6)**
penetralia **3.24.3**
penetrance **34.24.10(.16)**
penetrant **22.26.15(.23.4)**
penetrate **22.4.22(.8)**
penetratingly
1.31.28(.1.4)
penetration
28.17.25(.3.13)
penetrative **31.2.1(.9.4)**
penetratively
1.31.30(.7.1)
penetrator **17.12.4(.15)**
pen-feather **17.23.4**
Penfold **23.31.13(.7)**
penfriend **23.24.5(.14)**
Pengam **27.15.12**
Penge **39.17.3**
Pengelly **1.31.5**
penguin **28.2.28**
Penhaligon **28.17.15(.13)**
penicillate **22.19.26(.1)**
penicillia **3.24.2**
penicillin **28.2.31(.2)**
penicillium **27.3.18**
penile **40.13.8**
penillion **28.3.21(.15),**
28.3.22
peninsula **17.34.16(.21.4)**
peninsular **17.34.16(.21.4)**
penis **34.2.13**
Penistone **28.17.11(.25)**
penitence **34.24.10(.10)**
penitent **22.26.15(.9)**
penitential **40.33.12(.2)**
penitentially **1.31.17(.22)**
penitentiary **1.29.11(.20)**
penitently **1.31.22(.20.2)**
penknife **30.12**
penknives **35.28.6**
penlight **22.16.25(.17)**
Penmaenmawr **17.3.5**
penman **28.17.16(.25)**
penmanship **20.2.7(.19)**
Penn **28.5**
pennant **22.26.15(.14)**
penne **1.16.5**
penni **1.16.5**
penniä **10.1**

pennies **35.2.8**
penniless **34.18.29(.17.3)**
pennilessly **1.31.33(.12.6)**
pennilessness
34.18.16(.31.6)
pennill **40.2.10**
Pennine **28.14.9**
Pennington **28.17.11(.23)**
pennon **28.17.17(.4)**
Pennsylvania **3.9.3(.6)**
Pennsylvanian
28.3.8(.3)
penny **1.16.5**
penny-ante **1.10.23(.4)**
Pennycuick **24.2.25,**
24.14.5, 24.15.8
pennyfarthing **29.1.21**
Pennyfeather **17.23.4**
pennyroyal **40.16.5**
pennyweight **22.4.21**
pennywort **22.20.15**
pennyworth **32.14.12,**
32.14.15
penological
40.23.12(.17.2)
penologist **22.29.2(.26.4)**
penology **1.26.10(.11.4)**
penpusher **17.26.12**
Penrhos **34.20.16**
Penrhyn **28.2.29**
Pensacola **17.34.18(.5)**
pensée **4.18, 4.18.8**
Penshurst **22.29.16**
pensile **40.13.12**
pension **11.18,**
28.17.25(.16)
pensionability
1.10.16(.22.2)
pensionable
40.20.16(.16.3)
pensionary **1.29.11(.13.2)**
pensioner **17.18.16(.16)**
pensionless **34.18.29(.27)**
pensive **31.2.4(.13)**
pensively **1.31.30(.7.4)**
pensiveness
34.18.16(.28.2)
penstemon **28.17.16(.1)**
penstock **24.9.4**
pent **22.26.4**
pentachord **23.12.4**
pentacle **40.23.12(.7.3)**
pentad **23.7.7**
pentadactyl **40.21.16**
pentagon **28.17.15(.13)**
pentagonal **40.26.13(.7)**
pentagonally
1.31.17(.14.2)
pentagram **27.6.17(.5)**
pentagynous
34.18.16(.15.3)

p

pentahedra **17.32.20**
pentahedral **40.16.13(.17)**
pentahedron
28.17.31(.15)
pentamerous
34.18.27(.18)
pentameter **17.12.16(.9.1)**
pentamidine **28.1.10**
pentandrous
34.18.27(.15)
pentane **28.4.3**
pentangle **40.24.14(.2)**
pentaprism
27.15.21(.2.14)
Pentateuch **24.15.8**
pentateuchal **40.23.11**
pentathlete **22.1.18**
pentathlon **28.10.26,
28.17.33(.24)**
pentatonic **24.2.15(.6.1)**
pentavalent **22.26.15(.25)**
Pentax® **34.23.5(.3)**
Pentecost **22.29.9**
Pentecostal **40.21.18**
Pentecostalism
27.15.21(.2.15)
Pentecostalist
22.29.2(.31.2)
Pentel® **40.5.3**
Penthesilea **17.2.10**
penthouse **34.8.6(.11)**
pentimenti **1.10.23(.3)**
pentimento **19.10.17**
Pentire **17.6.3**
Pentland **23.24.16(.16.3)**
pentobarbital **40.21.12**
pentobarbitol **40.9.7**
pentobarbitone
28.19.4(.5)
pentode **23.20.5**
Pentonville **40.2.12**
pentose **34.20.4, 35.20.3**
Pentothal® **40.6.12**
pent-roof **30.13.4**
pentyl **40.13.3(.9)**
penuche **1.25.11**
penult **22.32.8**
penultimate **22.19.14**
penultimately
1.31.22(.15)
penumbra **17.32.18**
penumbrae **2.30.9**
penumbral **40.16.13(.15)**
penurious **34.3.15(.5)**
penuriously **1.31.33(.1.4)**
penuriousness
34.18.16(.31.1)
penury **1.29.11(.26)**
Penybont **22.26.9**
Penyghent **22.26.4(.7)**
Penza **17.25.18**

Penzance **34.24.4**
peon **28.10.1, 28.17.1**
peonage **39.2.15**
peony **1.16.15(.1)**
people **40.19.1**
pep **20.4**
Pepe **4.7**
peperino **19.15.1**
Pepin **28.2.9**
pepla **17.34.19**
peplum **27.15.28(.14)**
pepo **19.8**
Peppard **23.9.5**
pepper **17.10.4**
pepperbox **34.23.8(.2)**
peppercorn **28.11.5**
pepperiness
34.18.16(.2.9)
peppermint **22.26.1**
pepperminty **1.10.23(.1)**
pepperoni **1.16.17(.13)**
pepperpot **22.11.2**
pepperwort **22.20.15**
peppery **1.29.11(.6)**
peppily **1.31.17(.7)**
peppiness **34.18.16(.2.2)**
peppy **1.8.4**
Pepsi® **1.22.19**
Pepsi-Cola® **17.34.18(.5)**
pepsin **28.2.23(.12)**
Pepsodent® **22.26.4(.5),
22.26.15(.10)**
pep talk **24.10.2**
peptic **24.2.10(.12)**
peptide **23.15.4**
peptone **28.19.4(.6)**
peptonize **35.15.12(.5)**
Pepys **34.2.6, 34.21.1,
34.21.4**
per **18**
peradventure **17.28.22**
Perak **17.32.5, 24.6.21**
perambulate **22.4.23(.7.3)**
perambulation
28.17.25(.3.14)
perambulator
17.12.4(.16)
perambulatory
1.29.11(.8.10)
per annum **27.15.14(.5)**
percale **40.4.4, 40.8.6**
per capita **17.12.16(.3)**
per caput **22.17**
perceivable **40.20.16(.19)**
perceivably **1.31.21(.7.1)**
perceive **31.1.4**
perceived **23.26**
perceiver **17.21.1**
per cent **22.26.4(.11)**
percentage **39.2.10**
percentile **40.13.3(.9)**

percept **22.22.3**
perceptibility
1.10.16(.22.2)
perceptible
40.20.16(.11.4)
perceptibly **1.31.21(.4.3)**
perception **28.17.25(.14)**
perceptional
40.26.13(.14.6)
perceptive **31.2.1(.12)**
perceptively
1.31.30(.7.2)
perceptiveness
34.18.16(.28.1)
perceptivity **1.10.16(.15)**
perceptual **40.16.12**
perceptually **1.31.17(.24)**
perch **38.16**
perchance **34.24.6**
percher **17.28.16**
Percheron **28.10.24(.5)**
perchlorate **22.4.22(.4)**
perchloroethylene
28.1.27(.7)
percipience **34.24.2**
percipient **22.26.2(.1)**
percipiently
1.31.22(.20.1)
Percival **40.28.11**
percoid **23.13.9**
percolate **22.4.23(.7.1)**
percolation
28.17.25(.3.14)
percolator **17.12.4(.16)**
per contra **17.32.19(.10)**
percuss **34.14**
percussion **28.17.25(.9)**
percussionist
22.29.2(.18.2)
percussive **31.2.4(.6)**
percussively **1.31.30(.7.4)**
percutaneous **34.3.6(.3)**
percutaneously
1.31.33(.1.2)
Percy **1.22.17**
per diem **27.5.1**
Perdita **17.12.2**
perdition **28.17.25(.2.3)**
perdurability
1.10.16(.22.2)
perdurable
40.20.16(.27.2)
perdurably **1.31.21(.8)**
père **6**
peregrinate **22.4.14(.9.4)**
peregrination
28.17.25(.3.8)
peregrinator
17.12.4(.10)
peregrine **28.2.29(.11)**
pereira **17.32.2, 17.32.5**
Perelman **28.17.16(.35)**

peremptorily
1.31.17(.27.1)
peremptoriness
34.18.16(.2.9)
peremptory
1.29.11(.8.12)
perennial **40.3.7(.4)**
perenniality
1.10.16(.32.1)
perennially **1.31.3(.7)**
Peres **35.5.13**
perestroika **17.14.10,
17.14.15(.1)**
Pérez **35.5.13**
perfect **22.23.4(.5),
22.23.10**
perfecta **17.12.21(.2)**
perfecter **17.12.21(.2)**
perfectibility
1.10.16(.22.2)
perfectible **40.20.16(.11.5)**
perfection **28.17.25(.15.2)**
perfectionism
27.15.21(.2.9)
perfectionist
22.29.2(.18.2)
perfective **31.2.1(.13.2)**
perfectly **1.31.22(.19)**
perfectness
34.18.16(.20.4)
perfecto **19.10.16**
perfervid **23.2.15**
perfervidly **1.31.23(.14.7)**
perfervidness
34.18.16(.21.1)
perfidious **34.3.4**
perfidiously **1.31.33(.1.1)**
perfidiousness
34.18.16(.31.1)
perfidy **1.11.17**
perfin **28.2.19**
perfoliate **22.3.13**
perforate **22.4.22(.6),
22.19.24(.9)**
perforation
28.17.25(.3.13)
perforative **31.2.1(.9.4)**
perforator **17.12.4(.15)**
perforce **34.12.4**
perforin **28.2.29(.5)**
perform **27.10.5**
performability
1.10.16(.22.2)
performable
40.20.16(.15)
performance
34.24.10(.14)
performative **31.2.1(.9.2)**
performatory
1.29.11(.8.7)
performed **23.23.6**
performer **17.17.9**

perfume **27.14.7**
perfumer **17.17.13**
perfumery **1.29.11(.12)**
perfumier **3.8.6**
perfumy **1.15.12**
perfunctorily
1.31.17(.27.1)
perfunctoriness
34.18.16(.2.9)
perfunctory
1.29.11(.8.12)
perfuse **35.17.7**
perfusion **28.17.26(.4)**
perfusive **31.2.4(.8)**
Pergamene **28.1.13**
Pergamon **28.17.16(.16)**
Pergamum **27.15.13**
pergola **17.34.16(.10)**
perhaps **34.21.5**
peri **1.29.2**
perianth **32.21**
periapses **35.1.16(.12)**
periapsis **34.2.17(.12)**
periapt **22.22.4**
pericardia **3.5.5**
pericardiac **24.6.1**
pericardial **40.3.4**
pericarditis **34.18.11(.8)**
pericardium **27.3.4(.5)**
pericarp **20.6**
perichondria **3.22.16**
perichondrium
27.3.17(.7)
periclase **34.4.14, 35.4.18**
Periclean **28.17.1(.13)**
Pericles **35.1.23**
periclinal **40.26.11**
pericope **1.8.11(.5)**
pericrania **3.9.3(.8)**
pericranium **27.3.8(.3)**
peridia **3.5.2**
peridium **27.3.4(.2)**
peridot **22.11.5**
peridotite **22.16.9**
perigean **28.17.1(.11)**
perigee **2.27**
periglacial **40.3.10,
40.33.2**
perigynous
34.18.16(.15.3)
perihelion **28.3.21(.1)**
peril **40.16.13(.3)**
perilous **34.18.29(.17.5)**
perilously **1.31.33(.12.6)**
perilousness
34.18.16(.31.6)
perilune **28.16.14,
28.16.15**
perilymph **30.18**
perimeter **17.12.16(.9.1)**
perimetric **24.2.26(.14.2)**

perimysium **27.3.11**
perinatal **40.21.3**
perinea **17.1.7**
perineal **40.16.1**
perineum **27.15.1**
period **23.3**
periodate **22.4.10**
periodic **24.2.11(.7)**
periodical **40.23.12(.8)**
periodically **1.31.24(.9.7)**
periodicity **1.10.16(.16.1)**
periodization
28.17.25(.3.11)
periodize **35.15.8**
periodontal **40.21.17(.4)**
periodontics **34.23.2(.3)**
periodontist **22.29.2(.13)**
periodontology
1.26.10(.11.2)
periostea **3.4.13**
periosteal **40.3.3**
periosteum **27.3.3**
periostitis **34.18.11(.8)**
peripatetic **24.2.10(.3.1)**
peripatetically
1.31.24(.9.3)
peripateticism
27.15.21(.2.12)
peripeteia **3.4, 17.6.3**
peripheral **40.16.13(.12.2)**
peripherality
1.10.16(.32.13)
peripherally
1.31.17(.27.2)
periphery **1.29.11(.14)**
periphrases **35.1.16(.10)**
periphrasis **34.2.17(.10.4)**
periphrastic
24.2.10(.15.4)
periphrastically
1.31.24(.9.6)
peripteral **40.16.13(.12.1)**
perique **24.1.11**
periscope **20.15.4(.1)**
periscopic **24.2.8(.5)**
periscopically
1.31.24(.9.2)
perish **36.2.25**
perishability
1.10.16(.22.2)
perishable **40.20.16(.23)**
perishableness
34.18.16(.37.4)
perishably **1.31.21(.7.3)**
perisher **17.26.14**
perishingly **1.31.28(.1.13)**
perishless **34.18.29(.35)**
perisperm **27.16.1**
perissodactyl **40.21.16**
Perissodactyla
17.34.16(.7)

peristalith **32.2.9**
peristalsis **34.2.17(.16)**
peristaltic **24.2.10(.16)**
peristaltically
1.31.24(.9.6)
peristome **27.17.4**
peristyle **40.13.3(.10)**
peritonea **17.1.7**
peritoneal **40.16.1**
peritoneum **27.15.1**
peritonitis **34.18.11(.8)**
Perivale **40.4.9**
periwig **26.2.9**
periwinkle **40.23.15**
perjure **17.29.14**
perjurer **17.32.14(.20)**
perjury **1.29.11(.23)**
perk **24.17**
perkily **1.31.17(.11)**
Perkin **28.2.13(.7)**
perkiness **34.18.16(.2.4)**
Perkins **35.26.2**
Perks **34.23.16**
perky **1.12.14**
Perlis **34.2.22(.9)**
perlite **22.16.25(.10)**
perlocution **28.17.25(.11)**
perm **27.16**
permafrost **22.29.9**
Permalloy **13.17**
permanence
34.24.10(.15)
permanency
1.22.23(.10.3)
permanent **22.26.15(.14)**
permanentize **35.15.7(.8)**
permanently
1.31.22(.20.3)
permanganate
22.4.14(.9.1), 22.19.15(.9)
permeability
1.10.16(.22.1)
permeable **40.20.3**
permeance **34.24.2**
permeant **22.26.2(.4)**
permeate **22.4.2(.6)**
permeation **28.17.25(.3.1)**
permeator **17.12.4(.1)**
Permian **28.3.7**
per mil **40.2**
permissibility
1.10.16(.22.2)
permissible
40.20.16(.21.1)
permissibleness
34.18.16(.37.4)
permissibly **1.31.21(.7.2)**
permission **28.17.25(.2.4)**
permissive **31.2.4(.2)**
permissively
1.31.30(.7.4)

permissiveness
34.18.16(.28.2)
permit **22.2.11**
permittee **2.11**
permitter **17.12.2**
permittivity **1.10.16(.15)**
permutable
40.20.16(.11.2)
permutate **22.4.9(.5)**
permutation
28.17.25(.3.3)
permutational
40.26.13(.14.2)
permute **22.18.10**
Pernambuco **19.12.11**
pernicious **34.18.22(.2)**
perniciously
1.31.33(.12.4)
perniciousness
34.18.16(.31.4)
pernicketiness
34.18.16(.2.3)
pernickety **1.10.16(.10)**
pernoctate **22.4.9(.7)**
pernoctation
28.17.25(.3.3)
Pernod® **19.15.5, 19.15.13**
Perón **28.10.24**
peroneal **40.16.1**
Peronism **27.15.21(.2.9)**
Peronist **22.29.2(.18.3)**
perorate **22.4.22(.6)**
peroration **28.17.25(.3.13)**
Perot **19.27**
peroxidase **35.4.4**
peroxide **23.15.11(.11)**
perpend **23.24.5(.2)**
perpendicular
17.34.16(.21.2)
perpendicularity
1.10.16(.21.1)
perpendicularly
1.31.17(.29)
perpetrable
40.20.16(.27.6)
perpetrate **22.4.22(.8)**
perpetration
28.17.25(.3.13)
perpetrator **17.12.4(.15)**
perpetual **40.16.12**
perpetualism
27.15.21(.2.15)
perpetually **1.31.17(.24)**
perpetuance **34.24.10(.6)**
perpetuate **22.4.4**
perpetuation
28.17.25(.3.1)
perpetuator **17.12.4(.2)**
perpetuity **1.10.16(.5)**
perpetuum mobile
1.31.17(.8)
perplex **34.23.4(.12)**

perplexedly 1.31.23(.14.7)
perplexingly
1.31.28(.1.11)
perplexity 1.10.16(.16.3)
per pro. 19
perquisite 22.2.17
Perranporth 32.10
Perrault 19.27, 19.27.2
Perrier® 4.2.9
Perrin 8, 28.2.29(.2)
perron 11.17, 28.17.31(.3)
perruquier 4.2.3
perry 1.29.3
per se 4
perse 34.19
persecute 22.18.10
persecution 28.17.25(.11)
persecutor 17.12.15(.8)
persecutory 1.29.11(.8.4)
Perseids 35.23.2
Persephone 1.16.15(.12)
Persepolis 34.2.22(.8)
Perseus 34.3.10
perseverance
34.24.10(.16)
perseverate 22.4.22(.6)
perseveration
28.17.25(.3.13)
persevere 3.11
Pershing 29.1.25
Persia 17.26.15, 17.27.8
Persian 28.17.25(.12),
28.17.26(.5)
persiennes 28.5, 35.26.5
persiflage 37.4.11
Persil® 40.31.13
persimmon 28.17.16(.2)
persist 22.29.2(.22)
persistence 34.24.10(.10)
persistency 1.22.23(.10.2)
persistent 22.26.15(.9)
persistently 1.31.22(.20.2)
person 28.17.23(.15)
persona 17.18.18(.7)
personable
40.20.16(.16.3)
personableness
34.18.16(.37.4)
personably 1.31.21(.6)
personae 2.17.11, 14.13
personage 39.2.15
persona grata 17.12.8
personal 40.26.13(.12)
personality 1.10.16(.32.8)
personalization
28.17.25(.3.12)
personalize 35.15.21(.4.5)
personally 1.31.17(.14.2)
personalty 1.10.28
persona non grata
17.12.8

personate 22.4.14(.9.3)
personation
28.17.25(.3.1)
personator 17.12.4(.10)
personhood 23.16.5(.10)
personification
28.17.25(.3.5)
personifier 17.6.9(.4)
personify 14.14.4(.7)
personnel 40.5, 40.5.8
person-to-person
28.17.23(.15)
perspectival 40.28.11
perspective 31.2.1(.13.2)
perspectively
1.31.30(.7.2)
perspex 34.23.4(.1)
perspicacious
34.18.22(.3)
perspicaciously
1.31.33(.12.4)
perspicaciousness
34.18.16(.31.4)
perspicacity
1.10.16(.16.1)
perspicuity 1.10.16(.5)
perspicuous 34.18.6
perspicuously
1.31.33(.12.1)
perspicuousness
34.18.16(.31.2)
perspiration
28.17.25(.3.13)
perspiratory 1.29.11(.8.9)
perspire 17.6.1
persuadability
1.10.16(.22.2)
persuadable 40.20.16(.12)
persuade 23.4.14
persuaded 23.18.10(.2)
persuader 17.13.3
persuasible 40.20.16(.22)
persuasion 28.17.26(.3)
persuasive 31.2.4(.3)
persuasively 1.31.30(.7.4)
persuasiveness
34.18.16(.28.2)
pert 22.20
pertain 28.4.3
Perth 32.15
pertinacious 34.18.22(.3)
pertinaciously
1.31.33(.12.4)
pertinaciousness
34.18.16(.31.4)
pertinacity 1.10.16(.16.1)
pertinence 34.24.10(.15)
pertinency 1.22.23(.10.3)
pertinent 22.26.15(.14)
pertinently 1.31.22(.20.3)
pertly 1.31.22(.16)
pertness 34.18.16(.20.3)

perturb 21.15
perturbable 40.20.16(.10)
perturbation
28.17.25(.3.2)
perturbative 31.2.1(.9.1)
perturbed 23.21
perturbingly 1.31.28(.1.3)
pertussis 34.2.17(.7)
Pertwee 2.29
Peru 16.23
Perugia 3.19.7, 17.29.12
peruke 24.15.7
perusal 40.32.13
peruse 35.17.6
peruser 17.25.14
Perutz 34.22.13
Peruvian 28.3.10
perv 31.11
pervade 23.4.9
pervasion 28.17.26(.3)
pervasive 31.2.4(.3)
pervasively 1.31.30(.7.4)
pervasiveness
34.18.16(.28.2)
perverse 34.19.6
perversely 1.31.33(.12.6)
perverseness
34.18.16(.31.7)
perversion 28.17.25(.12),
28.17.26(.5)
perversity 1.10.16(.16.2)
perversive 31.2.4(.10)
pervert 22.20.9
pervertedly 1.31.23(.14.3)
perverter 17.12.17
pervious 34.3.8
perviously 1.31.33(.1.3)
perviousness
34.18.16(.31.1)
Pery 1.29.2, 1.29.3, 1.29.4
Pesach 24.8.12, 25.5
peseta 17.12.4(.12)
Peshitta 17.12.1(.11)
peskily 1.31.17(.11)
peskiness 34.18.16(.2.4)
pesky 1.12.17(.2)
peso 19.20.2
pessary 1.29.11(.18)
pessimism 27.15.21(.2.8)
pessimist 22.29.2(.17)
pessimistic 24.2.10(.15.2)
pessimistically
1.31.24(.9.6)
pest 22.29.5
Pestalozzi 1.22.21
pester 17.12.24(.4)
pesterer 17.32.14(.6)
pesthole 40.18.13
pesticidal 40.22.11
pesticide 23.15.11(.6)
pestiferous 34.18.27(.20)

pestiferously
1.31.33(.12.5)
pestilence 34.24.10(.24)
pestilent 22.26.15(.25)
pestilential 40.33.12(.3)
pestilentially
1.31.17(.22)
pestilently 1.31.22(.20.5)
pestle 40.21.18, 40.31.5
pesto 19.10.19
pestological
40.23.12(.17.2)
pestologist 22.29.2(.26.3)
pestology 1.26.10(.11.2)
PET 2.11, 22.5
pet 22.5
Peta 17.12.1
Pétain 8
petal 40.21.4
petaline 28.14.19(.11)
petal-like 24.13.7(.27)
petaloid 23.13.20
petalon 28.10.26,
28.17.33(.13)
pétanque 24.19.5
petard 23.9.7
petasus 34.18.20
petaurist 22.29.2(.29.2)
petcock 24.9.6
Pete 22.1
petechia 3.6.1
petechiae 2.3
petechial 40.3.5
peter 17.12.1
Peterborough
17.32.14(.5)
Peterhead 23.5.13
Peterkin 28.2.13(.6)
Peterlee 2.32
Peterloo 16.25
peterman 28.17.16(.16)
Peter Pan 28.7
Peters 35.18.8
Petersburg 26.14.1(.11)
Petersfield 23.31.1(.2)
petersham 27.15.22
Peterson 28.17.23(.14)
Petherick 24.2.26(.10)
pethidine 28.1.10
petiolar 17.34.14
petiolate 22.19.26(.2)
petiole 40.14.1
petit 1.10.4, 2.11
petit bourgeois 10.22.12
petite 22.1.3
petite bourgeoisie 2.23
petit four 12
petition 28.17.25(.2.2)
petitionable
40.20.16(.16.3)
petitionary 1.29.11(.13.2)

petitioner 17.18.16(.16)
petitio principii 14.2
petit-maître 17.32.19(.2)
petit mal 40.6
petits pois 10
petnapper 17.10.5
petnapping 29.1.10(.5)
Peto 19.10.1
Petra 17.32.19(.3)
Petrarch 24.8.15
Petrarchan 28.17.13(.6)
petrel 40.16.13(.16)
Petri dish 36.2
Petrie 1.29.15
petrifaction
　28.17.25(.15.3)
petrification
　28.17.25(.3.5)
petrify 14.14.4(.14)
petrochemical
　40.23.12(.10)
petrochemistry
　1.29.15(.17)
petrodollar 17.34.9
Petrofina 17.18.1(.6)
petrogenesis
　34.2.17(.10.3)
petroglyph 30.2.6
Petrograd 23.7.16
petrographer 17.20.12(.5)
petrographic 24.2.16(.3)
petrographical
　40.23.12(.12)
petrography 1.18.9(.3.2)
petrol 40.16.13(.16)
petrolatum 27.15.9(.2)
petroleum 27.3.18
petrolic 24.2.27(.9)
petrologic 24.2.24(.4)
petrological
　40.23.12(.17.2)
petrologist 22.29.2(.26.4)
petrology 1.26.10(.11.5)
petronel 40.26.13(.14.8)
Petronella 17.34.5(.8)
Petronius 34.3.6(.7)
petrous 34.18.27(.14)
petter 17.12.5
petticoat 22.21.5
Pettifer 17.20.12(.1)
pettifog 26.7.8
pettifogger 17.16.7
pettifoggery 1.29.11(.11)
Pettigrew 16.23.11
pettily 1.31.17(.9.1)
pettiness 34.18.16(.2.3)
pettish 36.2.11
pettishly 1.31.35(.7.1)
pettishness
　34.18.16(.33.3)
pettitoe 19.10.2

Pettitt 22.2.7
petty 1.10.4
petty bourgeoisie 2.23
Petula 17.34.15
petulance 34.24.10(.24)
petulant 22.26.15(.25)
petulantly 1.31.22(.20.5)
Petulengro 19.27.18
petunia 3.9.9
petuntse 17.24.19
Petworth 32.14.15
Peugeot® 19.23
Pevensey 1.23.20
Peveril 40.16.13(.12.2)
Pevsner 17.18.29
pew 16
pewage 39.2.6
pewee 2.29
pewless 34.18.29(.16)
Pewsey 1.23.12
pewter 17.12.15
pewterer 17.32.14(.6)
peyote 1.10.18
peyotism 27.15.21(.2.4)
Peyton 28.17.11(.3)
Pfennig 26.2.4
pH 38.3
Phaedo 19.11.1
Phaedra 17.32.20
Phaedrus 34.18.27(.15)
Phaethon 28.17.21
phaeton 28.17.11(.3)
phage 39.4
phagedaena 17.18.1(.4)
phagedaenic 24.2.15(.1)
phagocyte 22.16.19(.9)
phagocytic 24.2.10(.2.3)
phagocytize 35.15.7(.6)
phagocytose 35.20.3
phagocytosis
　34.2.17(.11.1)
Phaidon 28.17.12(.13)
Phalange 39.17.4
phalangeal 40.3.12
phalanger 17.29.16(.4)
phalanges 35.1.19, 35.1.21
phalangist 22.29.2(.25)
phalansterian 28.3.20(.2)
phalanstery
　1.29.11(.8.12)
phalanx 34.23.18
phalarope 20.15.8
phalli 2.32.6, 14.25.6
phallic 24.2.27(.6)
phallically 1.31.24(.9.12)
phallicism 27.15.21(.2.12)
phallism 27.15.21(.2.15)
phallocentric
　24.2.26(.14.4)
phallocentricity
　1.10.16(.16.1)

phallocentrism
　27.15.21(.2.14)
phallus 34.18.29(.7)
phanariot 22.3.12
phanerogam 27.6.7
phanerogamic
　24.2.14(.4)
phanerogamous
　34.18.15(.10)
Phanerozoic 24.2.7
phantasm 27.15.21(.3)
phantasmagoria 3.22.9
phantasmagoric
　24.2.26(.6)
phantasmagorical
　40.23.12(.18)
phantasmal 40.25.14
phantasmally
　1.31.17(.13)
phantasmic 24.2.14(.17)
phantasy 1.22.16(.4)
phantom 27.15.9(.14)
pharanges 35.1.19,
　35.1.21
pharaoh 19.27.3
Pharaonic 24.2.15(.6.1)
Pharisaic 24.2.3
Pharisaical 40.23.12(.2)
Pharisaically 1.31.24(.9.1)
Pharisaicalness
　34.18.16(.37.5)
Pharisaism 27.15.21(.2.1)
Pharisee 2.22.7
pharmaceutic 24.2.10(.9)
pharmaceutical
　40.23.12(.7.2)
pharmaceutically
　1.31.24(.9.4)
pharmacist 22.29.2(.22)
pharmacognosy
　1.22.16(.9)
pharmacological
　40.23.12(.17.2)
pharmacologically
　1.31.24(.9.11)
pharmacologist
　22.29.2(.26.3)
pharmacology
　1.26.10(.11.3)
pharmacopoeia 17.1.1
pharmacopoeial 40.16.1
pharmacy 1.22.16(.8)
pharos 34.10.16
Pharsala 17.34.4, 17.34.8
pharyngal 40.24.14(.1)
pharyngeal 40.3.12,
　40.16.1
pharyngitis 34.18.11(.8)
pharyngoscope
　20.15.4(.1)
pharyngotomy
　1.15.13(.1)

pharynx 34.23.18
phase 35.4
phasedown 28.8.2(.10)
phaseout 22.9.14
phasic 24.2.21
phasmid 23.2.12
Phasmida 17.13.15
phatic 24.2.10(.4.1)
PhD 2.13
pheasant 22.26.15(.18)
pheasantry 1.29.15(.15)
Pheidippides 35.1.8
Phelan 28.17.33(.1)
Phelps 34.21.14
phenacetin 28.2.11(.10)
phenobarbital 40.21.12
phenobarbitone
　28.19.4(.5)
phenocryst 22.29.2(.29.5)
phenol 40.9.12
phenolic 24.2.27(.9)
phenological
　40.23.12(.17.2)
phenologist 22.29.2(.26.4)
phenology 1.26.10(.11.4)
phenolphthalein 28.1.2,
　28.2.2
phenomena 17.18.16(.8)
phenomenal 40.26.13(.8)
phenomenalism
　27.15.21(.2.15)
phenomenalist
　22.29.2(.31.3)
phenomenalistic
　24.2.10(.15.3)
phenomenalize
　35.15.21(.4.5)
phenomenally
　1.31.17(.14.2)
phenomenological
　40.23.12(.17.2)
phenomenologically
　1.31.24(.9.11)
phenomenologist
　22.29.2(.26.4)
phenomenology
　1.26.10(.11.4)
phenomenon
　28.17.17(.10)
phenotype 20.10.2
phenotypic 24.2.8(.1)
phenotypical 40.23.12(.5)
phenotypically
　1.31.24(.9.2)
Phensic 24.2.20(.15),
　24.2.21
phenyl 40.2.10, 40.13.8,
　40.26.1, 40.26.4
phenylalanine 28.1.14,
　28.14.9
phenylketonuria 3.22.12
pheromonal 40.26.15

pheromone **28.19.9**
phew **16**
phi **14**
phial **40.16.6**
Phi Beta Kappa **17.10.5**
Phidias **34.7.2**
Phil **40.2**
Philadelphia **3.10.6**
Philadelphian **28.3.9**
philadelphus **34.18.17**
philander **17.13.20(.4)**
philanderer **17.32.14(.7)**
philanthrope **20.15.8**
philanthropic **24.2.8(.5)**
philanthropically **1.31.24(.9.2)**
philanthropism **27.15.21(.2.2)**
philanthropist **22.29.2(.11)**
philanthropize **35.15.5**
philanthropy **1.8.11(.8)**
philatelic **24.2.27(.4)**
philatelically **1.31.24(.9.12)**
philatelist **22.29.2(.31.2)**
philately **1.31.17(.9.1)**
Philbin **28.2.10**
Philby **1.9.24**
Philemon **28.17.16(.1)**
philharmonia **3.9.11**
philharmonic **24.2.15(.6.2)**
philhellene **28.1.27(.3)**
philhellenic **24.2.15(.1)**
philhellenism **27.15.21(.2.9)**
philhellenist **22.29.2(.18.3)**
Philip **20.2.13**
Philippa **17.10.14**
Philippi **14.6**
Philippian **28.3.1**
philippic **24.2.8(.1)**
philippina **17.18.1(.1)**
Philippine **28.1.7**
Philistine **28.14.5**
Philistinism **27.15.21(.2.9)**
Phillipines **35.26.1**
Phillips® **34.21.2**
Phillpott **22.11.2**
phillumenist **22.29.2(.18.1)**
phillumeny **1.16.15(.11)**
Philly **1.31.2**
Philoctetes **35.1.7(.1)**
philodendron **28.17.31(.15)**
philogynist **22.29.2(.18.3)**
philologer **17.29.13**

philologian **28.3.18**
philologic **24.2.24(.4)**
philological **40.23.12(.17.2)**
philologically **1.31.24(.9.11)**
philologist **22.29.2(.26.4)**
philologize **35.15.18**
philology **1.26.10(.11.5)**
philomel **40.5.7**
Philomela **17.34.1**
Philomena **17.18.1(.6)**
philoprogenitive **31.2.1(.9.2)**
philosophaster **17.12.24(.5)**
philosopher **17.20.12(.3)**
philosophic **24.2.16(.4)**
philosophical **40.23.12(.12)**
philosophically **1.31.24(.9.9)**
philosophize **35.15.13**
philosophizer **17.25.12(.7)**
philosophy **1.18.9(.1)**
Philostratus **34.18.11(.10)**
philtre **17.12.26(.1)**
phimosis **34.2.17(.11.2)**
phimotic **24.2.10(.6)**
Phineas **34.3.6(.2)**
Phipps **34.21.2**
phiz **35.2**
phizog **26.7.10**
phlebitic **24.2.10(.2.1)**
phlebitis **34.18.11(.8)**
phlebotomist **22.29.2(.17)**
phlebotomize **35.15.11**
phlebotomy **1.15.13(.1)**
phlegm **27.5**
phlegmatic **24.2.10(.4.2)**
phlegmatically **1.31.24(.9.4)**
phlegmy **1.15.4**
phloem **27.5.3**
phlogistic **24.2.10(.15.2)**
phlogiston **28.10.9, 28.17.11(.25)**
phlox **34.23.8**
Phnom Penh **28.5**
phobia **3.3.9**
phobic **24.2.9(.7)**
Phobos **34.10.7**
Phocaea **17.1.11**
Phocian **28.3.13, 28.3.15**
Phocis **34.2.17(.11.1)**
phoebe **1.9.1**
Phoebus **34.18.10**
Phoenicia **17.26.1, 17.26.2**
Phoenician **28.17.25(.1)**

phoenix **34.23.2(.6)**
pholas **34.18.29(.19)**
phon **28.10**
phonaesthesia **3.15.1**
phonate **22.4.14**
phonation **28.17.25(.3.8)**
phonatory **1.29.11(.8.7)**
phonautograph **30.7.5(.1)**
phone **28.19**
phonecard **23.9.9**
phone-in **28.2.18**
phoneme **27.1.6**
phonemic **24.2.14(.1)**
phonemicist **22.29.2(.22)**
phonemicization **28.17.25(.3.12)**
phonemicize **35.15.16(.4)**
phonendoscope **20.15.4(.1)**
phonetapping **29.1.10(.5)**
phonetic **24.2.10(.3.1)**
phonetically **1.31.24(.9.3)**
phonetician **28.17.25(.2.2)**
phoneticism **27.15.21(.2.12)**
phoneticist **22.29.2(.22)**
phoneticization **28.17.25(.3.12)**
phoneticize **35.15.16(.4)**
phonetist **22.29.2(.13)**
phoney **1.16.17**
phonic **24.2.15(.6.1)**
phonically **1.31.24(.9.8)**
phonily **1.31.17(.14.3)**
phoniness **34.18.16(.2.5)**
phono **17.18.18, 19.15.8, 19.15.14**
phonogram **27.6.17(.5)**
phonograph **30.7.5(.1)**
phonographer **17.20.12(.5)**
phonographic **24.2.16(.3)**
phonographical **40.23.12(.12)**
phonographically **1.31.24(.9.9)**
phonography **1.18.9(.3.2)**
phonolite **22.16.25(.9)**
phonological **40.23.12(.8)**
phonologically **1.31.24(.9.11)**
phonologist **22.29.2(.26.4)**
phonology **1.26.10(.11.4)**
phonometer **17.12.16(.9.2)**
phonon **28.10.14**
phonoscope **20.15.4(.1)**
phonotype **20.10.2**

phooey **1(.6)**
phoresy **1.22.16(.13)**
phoretic **24.2.10(.3.3)**
phormium **27.3.7**
phosgene **28.1.23**
phosphatase **34.4.4, 35.4.3**
phosphate **22.4.15**
phosphatic **24.2.10(.4.4)**
phosphene **28.1.15**
phosphide **23.15.9**
phosphine **28.1.15**
phosphinic **24.2.15(.2)**
phosphite **22.16.16**
phospholipid **23.2.6**
phosphor **17.20.18**
phosphorate **22.4.22(.6)**
phosphoresce **34.5.14**
phosphorescence **34.24.10(.18)**
phosphorescent **22.26.15(.17.2)**
phosphoric **24.2.26(.6)**
phosphorite **22.16.24(.9)**
phosphorous **34.18.27(.20)**
phosphorus **34.18.27(.20)**
phosphorylate **22.4.23(.7.2)**
phosphorylation **28.17.25(.3.14)**
phossy **1.22.9**
phot **22.21**
photic **24.2.10(.11)**
photism **27.15.21(.2.4)**
Photius **34.3.3**
photo **19.10.14**
photobiology **1.26.10(.11.1)**
photocall **40.10.7**
photocell **40.5.11**
photochemical **40.23.12(.10)**
photochemistry **1.29.15(.17)**
photochromic **24.2.14(.12)**
photocomposition **28.17.25(.2.5)**
photoconductive **31.2.1(.13.4)**
photoconductivity **1.10.16(.15)**
photoconductor **17.12.21(.6)**
photocopiable **40.20.3**
photocopier **3.2.5**
photocopy **1.8.7**
photodegradable **40.20.16(.12)**
photodiode **23.20.2**

photoduplicate
22.4.11(.6)
photoduplication
28.17.25(.3.5)
photodynamic
24.2.14(.4)
photoelectric
24.2.26(.14.3)
photoelectricity
1.10.16(.16.1)
photoelectron
28.10.24(.7)
photoemission
28.17.25(.2.4)
photoemitter **17.12.2**
photoengraving **29.1.20**
photo finish **36.2.16(.2)**
photofit **22.2.13**
photogenic **24.2.15(.1)**
photogenically
1.31.24(.9.8)
photogram **27.6.17(.5)**
photogrammetrist
22.29.2(.29.5)
photogrammetry
1.29.15(.8)
photograph **30.7.5(.1)**
photographable
40.20.16(.18)
photographer
17.20.12(.5)
photographic **24.2.16(.3)**
photographical
40.23.12(.12)
photographically
1.31.24(.9.9)
photography **1.18.9(.3.2)**
photogravure
17.7.12(.10)
photojournalism
27.15.21(.2.15)
photojournalist
22.29.2(.31.3)
photokinetic
24.2.10(.3.1)
photolithographic
24.2.16(.3)
photolithographically
1.31.24(.9.9)
photolithography
1.18.9(.3.2)
photolysis **34.2.17(.10.5)**
photolytic **24.2.10(.2.5)**
photolyze **35.15.21(.4.3)**
photomechanical
40.23.12(.11)
photomechanically
1.31.24(.9.8)
photometer
17.12.16(.9.2)
photometric
24.2.26(.14.2)
photometry **1.29.15(.8)**

photomicrograph
30.7.5(.1)
photomicrography
1.18.9(.3.2)
photomontage **37.4.3**
photon **28.10.9**
photonics **34.23.2(.6)**
photonovel **40.28.7**
photo-offset **22.5.13(.12)**
photoperiod **23.3**
photoperiodic **24.2.11(.7)**
photoperiodism
27.15.21(.2.5)
photophobia **3.3.9**
photophobic **24.2.9(.7)**
photopic **24.2.8(.5)**
photorealism
27.15.21(.2.15)
photoreception
28.17.25(.14)
photoreceptor **17.12.19**
photosensitive
31.2.1(.9.3)
photosensitivity
1.10.16(.15)
photosensitize
35.15.7(.7)
photoset **22.5.13(.4)**
photosetter **17.12.5(.8)**
photosetting **29.1.12(.4)**
photosphere **3.10.5**
photospheric **24.2.26(.4)**
photostat® **22.7.7**
photostatic **24.2.10(.4.1)**
photosynthesis
34.2.17(.10.4)
photosynthesize
35.15.16(.4)
photosynthetic
24.2.10(.3.2)
photosynthetically
1.31.24(.9.3)
phototransistor
17.12.24(.2)
phototropic **24.2.8(.5)**
phototropism
27.15.21(.2.2)
phototypesetter
17.12.5(.8)
phototypesetting
29.1.12(.4)
photovoltaic **24.2.3**
phrasal **40.32.3**
phrase **35.4**
phrasebook **24.14.3**
phraseogram **27.6.17(.5)**
phraseological
40.23.12(.17.2)
phraseology
1.26.10(.11.1)
phrasing **29.1.24**
phratry **1.29.15**

phreatic **24.2.10(.4.1)**
phrenetic **24.2.10(.3.1)**
phrenetically
1.31.24(.9.3)
phrenic **24.2.15(.4)**
phrenological
40.23.12(.17.2)
phrenologically
1.31.24(.9.11)
phrenologist
22.29.2(.26.4)
phrenology **1.26.10(.11.4)**
Phrygia **3.19.2**
Phrygian **28.3.18**
phthalate **22.4.23(.5)**
phthisic **24.2.20(.10)**
phthisical **40.23.12(.15)**
phthisis **34.2.17(.8)**
Phuket **22.5.5**
phut **22.15**
phut-phut **22.15.7**
phutt **22.15**
phycological
40.23.12(.17.2)
phycologist **22.29.2(.26.3)**
phycology **1.26.10(.11.3)**
phycomycete **22.1.9**
phyla **17.34.13**
phylactery **1.29.11(.8.12)**
phyletic **24.2.10(.3.3)**
phyletically **1.31.24(.9.3)**
Phyllida **17.13.15**
Phyllis **34.2.22(.2)**
phyllite **22.16.25(.2)**
phyllode **23.20.13**
phyllophagous
34.18.14(.5)
phyllopod **23.10.1**
phylloquinone **28.19.10**
Phyllosan **28.7.14**
phyllostome **27.17.4**
phyllotactic **24.2.10(.13)**
phyllotaxis **34.2.17(.14)**
phyllotaxy **1.22.22**
phylloxera **17.32.2,
17.32.14(.16)**
phylogenesis
34.2.17(.10.3)
phylogenetic
24.2.10(.3.1)
phylogenetically
1.31.24(.9.3)
phylogenic **24.2.15(.4)**
phylogeny **1.16.15(.17)**
phyloxera **17.32.14(.16)**
phylum **27.15.28(.9)**
physalis **34.2.22(.3)**
physic **24.2.21**
physical **40.23.12(.16)**
physicalism
27.15.21(.2.15)

physicalist **22.29.2(.31.2)**
physicalistic
24.2.10(.15.3)
physicality **1.10.16(.32.5)**
physically **1.31.24(.9.10)**
physicalness
34.18.16(.37.5)
physician **28.17.25(.2.5)**
physicist **22.29.2(.22)**
physicky **1.12.13**
physico-chemical
40.23.12(.10)
physio **15.1.8**
physiocracy **1.22.16(.13)**
physiocrat **22.7.20**
physiocratic **24.2.10(.4.5)**
physiognomic **24.2.14(.6)**
physiognomical
40.23.12(.10)
physiognomically
1.31.24(.9.8)
physiognomist
22.29.2(.17)
physiognomy **1.15.13(.5)**
physiographer
17.20.12(.5)
physiographic **24.2.16(.3)**
physiographical
40.23.12(.12)
physiographically
1.31.24(.9.9)
physiography **1.18.9(.3.2)**
physiological
40.23.12(.17.2)
physiologically
1.31.24(.9.11)
physiologist
22.29.2(.26.2)
physiology **1.26.10(.11.1)**
physiotherapist
22.29.2(.11)
physiotherapy **1.8.11(.8)**
physique **24.1.7**
physostigmine **28.1.13**
phytoalexin **28.2.23(.14)**
phytochemical
40.23.12(.10)
phytochemist
22.29.2(.17)
phytochemistry
1.29.15(.17)
phytochrome **27.17.13**
phytogenesis
34.2.17(.10.3)
phytogeny **1.16.15(.17)**
phytogeography
1.18.9(.3.2)
phytography
1.18.9(.3.2)
phytolith **32.2.9**
phytopathology
1.26.10(.11.5)

p

phytophagous **34.18.14(.5)**
phytoplankton **28.17.11(.20)**
phytotomy **1.15.13(.1)**
phytotoxic **24.2.20(.13)**
phytotoxin **28.2.23(.14)**
pi **14**
piacular **17.34.16(.21.2)**
Piaf **30.5.1**
piaffe **30.5**
Piaget **4.21**
pia mater **17.12.4**
pianism **27.15.21(.2.9)**
pianissimo **19.14.12**
pianist **22.29.2(.18.1)**
pianistic **24.2.10(.15.2)**
pianistically **1.31.24(.9.6)**
piano **19.15.6, 19.15.7**
piano-accordion **28.3.4(.7)**
pianoforte **1.10.10, 4.9.5**
pianola® **17.34.18(.8)**
piano nobile **4.28.7**
piassava **17.21.6**
piaster **17.12.24(.5)**
piastre **17.12.24(.5)**
Piat **22.19.1**
piazza **17.24.19**
pibroch **24.9.15, 25.6**
PIBS **35.21**
pic **24.2**
pica **17.14.12**
picador **12.6.6**
Picard **23.9.9**
Picardy **1.11.17**
picaresque **24.20.3**
picaroon **28.16.13**
Picasso **19.20.4, 19.20.5**
picayune **28.16.14**
Piccadilly **1.31.2**
piccalilli **1.31.2**
piccaninny **1.16.2**
piccolo **19.29.12**
pice **34.15**
pichiciago **19.13.3**
pick **24.2**
pickaback **24.6.6(.9)**
pickable **40.20.16(.13)**
pickaxe **34.23.5(.5)**
Pickelhaube **17.11.6**
picker **17.14.2**
pickerel **40.16.13(.12.1)**
Pickering **29.1.30(.8)**
picket **22.2.9(.1)**
picketer **17.12.16(.7)**
Pickett **22.2.9(.1)**
Pickford **23.18.16(.13)**
pickiness **34.18.16(.2.4)**
pickings **35.27**

pickle **40.23.2**
pickler **17.34.23**
Pickles **35.30.18**
picklock **24.9.16(.13)**
pick-me-up **20.9.1**
pickoff **30.8.6**
pickpocket **22.2.9(.5)**
pickpocketing **29.1.12(.14)**
Pickthorne **28.11.8**
pickup **20.9.7**
Pickwick **24.2.25**
Pickwickian **28.3.5**
picky **1.12.2**
pick-your-own **28.19**
picnic **24.2.15(.12)**
picnicker **17.14.15(.9)**
picnicky **1.12.13**
Pico **19.12.1**
picosecond **23.24.16(.5)**
picot **19.12.1**
picotee **2.11**
picquet **22.2.9(.1), 22.5.5**
picrate **22.4.22(.10)**
Pict **22.23.2**
Pictish **36.2.11**
pictogram **27.6.17(.5)**
pictograph **30.7.5(.1)**
pictographic **24.2.16(.3)**
pictography **1.18.9(.3.2)**
pictorial **40.3.14(.5)**
pictorially **1.31.3(.11)**
picture **17.28.20**
picturebook **24.14.3**
picturegoer **17.9.5**
picturesque **24.20.3**
picturesquely **1.31.24(.13)**
picturesqueness **34.18.16(.22)**
piddle **40.22.2**
piddler **17.34.22**
piddock **24.16.5**
pidgin **28.17.28(.2)**
pidginization **28.17.25(.3.11)**
pidginize **35.15.12(.5)**
pie **14**
piebald **23.31.6**
piece **34.1**
pièce de résistance **34.11**
piece-goods **35.23.11**
piecemeal **40.1.6**
piecer **17.24.1**
piece-rate **22.4.22(.14)**
piecework **24.17.6(.15)**
piecrust **22.29.12**
pied **23.15**
pied-à-terre **6.4**

piedmont **22.26.9**
Piedmontese **35.1.7**
Pied Piper **17.10.12**
pie-eyed **23.15**
pie in the sky **14**
pieman **28.17.16(.13)**
pier **3**
pierce **34.3**
piercer **17.24.3**
piercingly **1.31.28(.1.11)**
Piercy **1.22.3**
Pierian **28.3.20(.2)**
pierogi **1.14.13**
Pierre **3, 6**
Pierrot **19.27.1**
Piers **35.3**
Pierson **28.17.23(.3)**
pietà **10.6**
Pietermaritzburg **26.14.1(.10)**
Pietism **27.15.21(.2.4)**
pietist **22.29.2(.13)**
pietistic **24.2.10(.15.2)**
pietistical **40.23.12(.7.3)**
piety **1.10.16(.4)**
piezoelectric **24.2.26(.14.3)**
piezoelectrically **1.31.24(.9.12)**
piezoelectricity **1.10.16(.16.1)**
piezometer **17.12.16(.9.2)**
piffle **40.27.2**
piffler **17.34.26**
piffling **29.1.31(.23)**
pig **26.2**
pigeon **28.17.28(.2)**
pigeonhole **40.18.13**
pigeon pair **6**
pigeonry **1.29.20**
piggery **1.29.11(.11)**
piggin **28.2.15**
piggish **36.2.14**
piggishly **1.31.35(.7.1)**
piggishness **34.18.16(.33.4)**
Piggott **22.19.13**
piggy **1.14.2**
piggyback **24.6.6(.2)**
piggybank **24.19.3(.1)**
piggy in the middle **40.22.2**
piggywig **26.2.9**
pigheaded **23.18.10(.3)**
pig in the middle **40.22.2**
piglet **22.19.26(.20)**
piglike **24.13.7(.15)**
pigling **29.1.31(.20)**
pigmeat **22.1.5**

pigment **22.26.4(.8), 22.26.15(.13.3)**
pigmental **40.21.17(.2)**
pigmentary **1.29.11(.8.12)**
pigmentation **28.17.25(.3.3)**
pigmentosa **17.24.17**
pignut **22.15.6**
pig-out **22.9**
pigpen **28.5.2**
pigskin **28.2.13(.14)**
pigsticker **17.14.2**
pigsticking **29.1.14(.2)**
pigsty **14.8**
pigswill **40.2.19**
pigtail **40.4.2**
pigwash **36.9.5**
pigweed **23.1.10**
pi jaw **12**
pika **17.14.1, 17.14.12**
pike **24.13**
pikelet **22.19.26(.19)**
pikeman **28.17.16(.23)**
pikeperch **38.16**
piker **17.14.12**
pikestaff **30.7.2**
pilaf **30.5.9**
pilaster **17.12.24(.5)**
Pilate **22.19.26(.11)**
Pilatus **34.18.11(.6)**
pilau **9.17**
pilch **38.19**
pilchard **23.18.24**
pile **40.13**
pileate **22.3.13**
pileated **23.18.9(.3)**
piledriver **17.21.10**
piledriving **29.1.20**
pilei **14.2**
pileup **20.9.16**
pileus **34.3.16**
pilewort **22.20.15**
pilfer **17.20.19**
pilferage **39.2.22(.9)**
pilferer **17.32.14(.12)**
pilgrim **27.15.26(.13)**
pilgrimage **39.2.14**
pilgrimize **35.15.11**
piliferous **34.18.27(.20)**
piliform **27.10.5(.2)**
piling **29.1.31(.10)**
Pilkington **28.17.11(.23)**
pill **40.2**
pillage **39.2.23**
pillager **17.29.13**
pillar **17.34.2**
pillar box **34.23.8(.2)**
pillaret **22.5.19**
pillbox **34.23.8(.2)**
Pilling **29.1.31(.2)**

pillion 28.3.21(.2)
pilliwinks 34.23.18
pillock 24.16.16
pillory 1.29.11(.27)
pillow 19.29.2
pillowcase 34.4.6
pillowslip 20.2.13
pillowy 1(.7)
pillular 17.34.16(.21.4)
pillule 40.15.9(.11)
pillwort 22.20.15
pilose 34.20.17, 35.20.14
pilosity 1.10.16(.16.2)
pilot 22.19.26(.11)
pilotage 39.2.10
pilothouse 34.8.6(.11)
pilotless 34.18.29(.22)
pilous 34.18.29(.14)
Pilsen 28.17.23(.28),
    28.17.24(.17)
pilsner 17.18.28, 17.18.29
Piltdown 28.8.2(.5)
Pilton 28.17.11(.27)
pilule 40.15.9(.11)
pilulous 34.18.29(.17.6)
Pima 17.17.1
Piman 28.17.16(.1)
pimento 19.10.17
pi-meson 28.10.19
pimiento 19.10.17
Pimlico 19.12.12
Pimm 27.2
pimp 20.16.1
pimpernel 40.5.8
pimple 40.19.14
pimpliness
    34.18.16(.2.10)
pimply 1.31.20
PIN 28.2
pin 28.2
piña colada 17.13.7
pinafore 12.11.3
pinaster 17.12.24(.5)
piñata 17.12.8(.8)
pinball 40.10.4
PINC 24.19.1
pince-nez 4.14, 35.4.8
pincer 17.24.22(.1)
pincette 22.5.13
pinch 38.18.1
pinchbeck 24.4.3
Pincher 17.28.22
pinch-hit 22.2.22
pinch-hitter 17.12.2
pinchpenny 1.16.5
pinch-run 28.13.9
pinch-runner 17.18.12
Pincus 34.18.13(.13)
pincushion 28.17.25(.10)
Pindar 10.7

Pindaric 24.2.26(.5)
pin-down 28.8.2(.8)
Pindus 34.18.12
pine 28.14
pineal 40.3.7(.2), 40.16.1
pineapple 40.19.5
pinecone 28.19.6
pine marten 28.2.11(.6),
    28.17.11(.8)
Pinero 19.27.1, 19.27.3
pinery 1.29.11(.13.1)
pineta 17.12.1(.7)
pinetree 2.30.10
pinetum 27.15.9(.1)
pinewood 23.16.6(.14)
pinfeather 17.23.4
pinfold 23.31.13(.7)
ping 29.1
pinger 17.19.1
pingo 19.13.12
pingpong 29.6.1
pinguid 23.2.21
pinguin 28.2.28
pinhead 23.5.13(.14)
pinheaded 23.18.10(.3)
pinheadedness
    34.18.16(.21.1)
pinhole 40.18.13
pinion 28.17.32
pink 24.19.1
Pinkerton 28.17.11(.15)
pinkeye 14.10
Pink Floyd 23.13
pinkie 1.12.16
pinkish 36.2.13
pinkly 1.31.24(.12)
pinkness 34.18.16(.22)
pinko 19.12.15
Pinkster 17.12.24(.20)
pinna 17.18.2
pinnace 34.18.16(.2.1)
pinnacle 40.23.12(.11)
pinnae 2.17.2
pinnate 22.4.14(.2),
    22.19.15(.1)
pinnated 23.18.9(.3)
pinnately 1.31.22(.4)
pinnation
    28.17.25(.3.8)
Pinner 17.18.2
Pinney 1.16.2
pinnigrade 23.4.15
pinniped 23.5.1
pinnular 17.34.16(.21.4)
pinnule 40.15.9(.8)
pinny 1.16.2
Pinocchio 15.1.4
Pinochet 4.20
pinochle 40.23.7
pinol 40.9.12

pinole 1.31.19, 4.28.8,
    40.18.9
piñon 28.10.25, 28.17.32
Pinot Blanc 11
Pinot Noir 10
pinpoint 22.26.11
pinprick 24.2.26(.12)
pinsetter 17.12.5(.8)
pinspotter 17.12.9
pinstripe 20.10.5
pint 22.26.13
pinta 17.12.22(.1)
pintado 19.11.7
pintail 40.4.2
Pinter 17.12.22(.1)
pintle 40.21.17(.1)
pinto 19.10.17
pinup 20.9.9
pinwheel 40.1.14
pinworm 27.16.7
piny 1.16.13
Pinyin 28.2.30
piolet 4.28.7
pion 28.10.4
pionic 24.2.15(.6.1)
pious 34.18.5
piously 1.31.33(.12.1)
piousness 34.18.16(.31.2)
pip 20.2
pipa 10.4, 17.10.12
pipal 40.19.1
pipe 20.10
pipeclay 4.28.12
pipecleaner 17.18.1(.16)
pipefish 36.2.18(.13)
pipefitting 29.1.12(.2)
pipeful 40.14.6(.8)
pipeless 34.18.29(.20)
pipeline 28.14.19(.13)
pip emma 17.17.5
piper 17.10.12
piperade 23.9.20
piperidine 28.1.10,
    28.2.12
pipette 22.5.1
pipework 24.17.6(.6)
pipistrelle 40.5.18
pipit 22.2.5
pipkin 28.2.13(.8)
pipless 34.18.29(.20)
Pippa 17.10.2
pippin 28.2.9
pipsqueak 24.1.10
pipy 1.8.9
piquancy 1.22.23(.10.2)
piquant 22.26.15(.11)
piquantly 1.31.22(.20.2)
pique 24.1
piqué 4.11

piquet 4.11, 22.2.9(.1),
    22.5.5
piracy 1.22.16(.13)
Piraeus 34.18.1, 34.18.2
piragua 17.31.7
Pirandello 19.29.4
Piranesi 1.23.3
piranha 17.18.8(.11)
pirate 22.19.24(.8)
piratic 24.2.10(.4.5)
piratical 40.23.12(.7.1)
piratically 1.31.24(.9.4)
Pirie 1.29.1
piripiri 1.29.1
pirogue 26.15
pirouette 22.5
Pisa 17.25.1
pis aller 4.28.3
Pisan 28.17.24(.1)
Pisano 19.15.7
piscary 1.29.11(.10)
piscatorial 40.3.14(.5)
piscatorially 1.31.3(.11)
piscatory 1.29.11(.8.6)
Piscean 28.3.13
piscean 28.3.5, 28.3.13,
    28.17.1(.9)
Pisces 35.1.16(.8)
piscicultural
    40.16.13(.12.3)
pisciculture 17.28.26
pisciculturist
    22.29.2(.29.4)
piscina 17.18.1(.9)
piscine 28.1.11, 28.1.18,
    28.14.7, 28.14.13
piscivorous
    34.18.27(.21)
pisco 19.12.17
Pisgah 17.16.18
pish 36.2
Pisidia 3.5.2
Pisidian 28.3.4(.2)
pisiform 27.10.5(.2)
pismire 17.6.7
piss 34.2
Pissarro 19.27.5
pissoir 10.22.11
pisspot 22.11.2
piss-taker 17.14.3(.2)
piss-taking 29.1.14(.3)
piss-up 20.9.12
pistachio 15.1.9, 15.1.10
piste 22.29.1
pisteur 18.3
pistil 40.2.5, 40.21.18
pistillary 1.29.11(.27)
pistillate 22.4.23(.7.1),
    22.19.26(.13)
pistilliferous
    34.18.27(.20)

pistilline 28.1.27(.7), 28.2.31(.10)
pistol 40.21.18
pistole 40.18.5
pistoleer 3.24
piston 28.17.11(.25)
pistou 16.7.8
pit 22.2
pita 17.12.1
pit-a-pat 22.7.5
Pitcairn 28.6
pitch 38.2
pitchblack 24.6.23
pitchblende 23.24.5(.15)
pitcher 17.28.2
pitcherful 40.14.6(.7)
pitchfork 24.10.6
pitchman 28.17.16(.33)
pitchout 22.9.16
pitchpine 28.14.3
pitchpipe 20.10.1
pitchstone 28.19.4(.9)
pitchy 1.25.2
piteous 34.3.3
piteously 1.31.33(.1.1)
piteousness 34.18.16(.31.1)
pitfall 40.10.11
pith 32.2
pithead 23.5.13(.9)
Pithecanthropus 34.18.9(.8)
pithecoid 23.13.9
pithily 1.31.17(.18)
pithiness 34.18.16(.2.6)
pithless 34.18.29(.31)
pithoi 13.9
pithos 34.10.14
pithy 1.20.2
pitiable 40.20.3
pitiableness 34.18.16(.37.4)
pitiably 1.31.21(.1)
pitiful 40.27.2
pitifully 1.31.17(.16.1)
pitifulness 34.18.16(.37.2)
pitiless 34.18.29(.2)
pitilessly 1.31.33(.12.6)
pitilessness 34.18.16(.31.6)
Pitlochry 1.29.17
pitman 28.17.16(.21)
Pitney 16.19
piton 11.5, 28.10.9
pitpan 28.7.4
Pitsea 2.22.10
Pitt 22.2
pitta 17.12.2
pittance 34.24.10(.10)
Pittenweem 27.1.11

pitter-patter 17.12.6
Pitti 1.10.2
Pittman 28.17.16(.21)
pittosporum 27.15.26(.8)
Pitt-Rivers 35.18.15
Pitts 34.22.2
Pittsburgh 26.14.1(.10)
pituitary 1.29.11(.8.5)
pituri 1.29.11(.22)
pity 1.10.2
pityingly 1.31.28(.1.1)
pityriasis 34.2.17(.10.1)
più 16
Pius 34.18.5
pivot 22.19.17
pivotability 1.10.16(.22.2)
pivotable 40.20.16(.11.3)
pivotal 40.21.12
pix 34.23.2
pixel 40.31.18
pixie 1.22.22
pixilated 23.18.9(.3)
Pizarro 19.27.5
pizza 17.24.19
pizzazz 35.7
pizzeria 17.1.16
Pizzey 1.22.21, 1.23.2
pizzicato 19.10.7
pizzle 40.32.2
PJ's 35.4.13
placability 1.10.16(.22.1)
placable 40.20.16(.13)
placableness 34.18.16(.37.4)
placably 1.31.21(.5)
placard 23.9.9
placate 22.4.11
placatingly 1.31.28(.1.4)
placation 28.17.25(.3.5)
placatory 1.29.11(.8.2)
place 34.4
placebo 19.9.1
placeholder 17.13.23(.8)
placeless 34.18.29(.33)
placement 22.26.15(.13.5)
placenta 17.12.22(.3)
placental 40.21.17(.2)
placer 17.24.4
placet 22.5.13(.2), 22.19.18
placid 23.2.16
placidity 1.10.16(.9)
placidly 1.31.23(.14.7)
placidness 34.18.16(.21.1)
placing 29.1.23
placket 22.2.9(.3)
placoid 23.13.9
plafond 11.10, 23.24.9
plagal 40.24.3
plage 37.4
plagiarism 27.15.21(.2.14)

plagiarist 22.29.2(.29.1)
plagiaristic 24.2.10(.15.2)
plagiarize 35.15.20(.1)
plagiarizer 17.25.12(.14)
plagiocephalic 24.2.27(.6)
plagioclase 34.4.14, 35.4.18
plagioclastic 24.2.10(.15.4)
plagiostome 27.17.4
plague 26.3
plagueily 1.31.17(.12)
plagueiness 34.18.16(.2.4)
plaguesome 27.15.20(.16)
plaguily 1.31.17(.12)
plaguy 1.14.3
plaice 34.4
plaid 23.7
plaided 23.18.10(.4)
plain 28.4
plainchant 22.26.8
plainclothes 35.20.14, 35.29
plainly 1.31.27(.4)
plainness 34.18.16(.25)
plainsman 28.17.16(.30)
plainsong 29.6.9
plainspoken 28.17.13(.15)
plainswoman 28.17.16(.14)
plainswomen 28.2.17(.1)
plaint 22.26.3
plaintiff 30.2.1
plaintive 31.2.1(.14)
plaintively 1.31.30(.7.3)
plaintiveness 34.18.16(.28.1)
Plaistow 19.10.19
plait 22.7
plan 28.7
planar 17.18.3
planarian 28.3.20(.4)
planchet 22.19.20, 22.19.21
planchette 22.5.15
Planck 24.19.3
plane 28.4
planeload 23.20.13
planemaker 17.14.3(.3)
planemaking 29.1.14(.3)
planer 17.18.3
planet 22.2.12
planetaria 3.22.4
planetarium 27.3.17(.3)
planetary 1.29.11(.8.7)
planetesimal 40.25.10
planetoid 23.13.7
planetologist 22.29.2(.26.3)
planetology 1.26.10(.11.2)

plangency 1.22.23(.10.4)
plangent 22.26.15(.21)
plangently 1.31.22(.20.4)
planimeter 17.12.16(.9.1)
planimetric 24.2.26(.14.2)
planimetrical 40.23.12(.18)
planimetry 1.29.15(.8)
planish 36.2.16(.5)
planisher 17.26.14
planisphere 3.10.5
planispheric 24.2.26(.4)
plank 24.19.3
plankton 28.17.11(.20)
planktonic 24.2.15(.6.1)
planner 17.18.6
planoconcave 31.3.2
planoconvex 34.23.4(.8)
planographic 24.2.16(.3)
planography 1.18.9(.3.2)
planometer 17.12.16(.9.2)
plant 22.26.6, 22.26.8
plantable 40.20.16(.11.6)
Plantagenet 22.19.15(.9)
plantain 28.4.3, 28.17.11(.22)
plantar 10.6.7, 17.12.22(.4)
plantation 28.17.25(.3.3)
planter 17.12.22(.4)
plantigrade 23.4.15
Plantin 28.17.11(.22)
planting 29.1.12(.19)
plantlet 22.19.26(.17)
plantlike 24.13.7(.12)
plaque 24.6, 24.8
plaquette 22.5.5
plash 36.6
plashy 1.24.5
plasm 27.15.21(.3)
plasma 17.17.23
plasmacyte 22.16.19(.9)
plasmagel 40.5.15
plasmagene 28.1.23
plasmapheresis 34.2.17(.1)
plasmasol 40.9.14
plasmatic 24.2.10(.4.2)
plasmic 24.2.14(.17)
plasmid 23.2.12
plasmodesma 17.17.23
plasmodesmata 17.12.16(.9.3)
plasmodia 3.5.8
plasmodial 40.3.4
plasmodium 27.3.4(.8)
plasmolysis 34.2.17(.10.5)
plasmolyze 35.15.21(.4.5)
Plassey 1.22.6
plaster 17.12.24(.5)
plasterboard 23.12.2(.5)

plasterer **17.32.14(.6)**
plasterwork **24.17.6(.4)**
plastery **1.29.11(.8.12)**
plastic **24.2.10(.15.4)**
plastically **1.31.24(.9.6)**
Plasticine® **28.1.18(.6)**
plasticity **1.10.16(.16.1)**
plasticization **28.17.25(.3.11)**
plasticize **35.15.16(.4)**
plasticizer **17.25.12(.10)**
plasticky **1.12.13**
plastid **23.2.8**
plastral **40.16.13(.16)**
plastron **28.17.31(.14)**
plat **22.7**
Plataea **17.1.3**
platan **28.17.11(.6)**
plat du jour **17.7**
plate **22.4**
plateau **19.10, 19.10.6**
plateaux **35.20.3**
plateful **40.14.6(.10)**
platelayer **17.2.10**
plateless **34.18.29(.22)**
platelet **22.19.26(.17)**
platen **28.17.11(.6)**
plater **17.12.4**
plateresque **24.20.3**
platform **27.10.5(.4)**
Plath **32.6**
plating **29.1.12(.3)**
platinic **24.2.15(.2)**
platinization **28.17.25(.3.11)**
platinize **35.15.12(.5)**
platinoid **23.13.12**
platinotype **20.10.2**
platinum **27.15.14(.11)**
platitude **23.17.4(.1)**
platitudinarian **28.3.20(.4)**
platitudinize **35.15.12(.5)**
platitudinous **34.18.16(.15.2)**
Plato **19.10.3**
Platonic **24.2.15(.6.1)**
platonical **40.23.12(.11)**
Platonically **1.31.24(.9.8)**
Platonism **27.15.21(.2.9)**
Platonist **22.29.2(.18.1)**
platoon **28.16.3**
Platt **22.7**
Plattdeutsch **38.10**
platteland **23.24.6(.13)**
plattelander **17.13.20(.4)**
platter **17.12.6**
platy **1.10.3**
platyhelminth **32.21**
platypus **34.16, 34.18.9(.8)**

platyrrhine **28.14.18**
plaudit **22.2.8**
plausibility **1.10.16(.22.1)**
plausible **40.20.16(.22)**
plausibly **1.31.21(.7.2)**
Plautus **34.18.11(.7)**
play **4**
playa **17.6**
playability **1.10.16(.22.1)**
playable **40.20.16(.2)**
play-act **22.23.5(.1)**
playback **24.6.6(.3)**
playbill **40.2.4**
playbook **24.14.3**
playboy **13.3**
player **17.2**
player-piano **19.15.6**
Playfair **6.10**
playfellow **19.29.4**
playful **40.27.4**
playfully **1.31.17(.16.1)**
playfulness **34.18.16(.37.2)**
playgirl **40.17**
playgoer **17.9.5**
playground **23.24.7(.10)**
playgroup **20.12**
playhouse **34.8.6(.3)**
playlet **22.19.26(.3)**
playlist **22.29.2(.31.1)**
playmaker **17.14.3(.3)**
playmate **22.4.13(.1)**
playoff **30.8.1**
playpen **28.5.2**
playroom **27.14.6(.3)**
playschool **40.15.4**
playsuit **22.18.6**
Playtex® **34.23.4(.3)**
plaything **29.1.21**
playtime **27.12.1**
playwear **6.18.2**
playwright **22.16.24(.3)**
playwriting **29.1.12(.11)**
plaza **17.25.7**
plc **2.22**
plea **2**
pleach **38.1**
plead **23.1**
pleadable **40.20.16(.12)**
pleaded **23.18.10.1**
pleader **17.13.1**
pleading **29.1.13(.1)**
pleadingly **1.31.28(.1.5)**
pleasance **34.24.10(.19)**
pleasant **22.26.15(.18)**
pleasantly **1.31.22(.20.4)**
pleasantness **34.18.16(.20.4)**
pleasantry **1.29.15(.15)**
pleasaunce **34.24.10(.19)**

please **35.1**
pleasingly **1.31.28(.1.12)**
pleasurable **40.20.16(.27.5)**
pleasurableness **34.18.16(.37.4)**
pleasurably **1.31.21(.8)**
pleasure **17.27.3**
pleat **22.1**
pleb **21.4**
plebby **1.9.4**
plebe **21.1**
plebeian **28.17.1(.2)**
plebeianism **27.15.21(.2.9)**
plebiscitary **1.29.11(.8.8)**
plebiscite **22.2.16, 22.16.19(.9)**
plectra **17.32.19(.9)**
plectron **28.17.31(.14)**
plectrum **27.15.26(.10)**
pled **23.5**
pledge **39.5**
pledgeable **40.20.16(.25)**
pledgee **2.27**
pledger **17.29.4**
pledget **22.19.22**
pledgor **17.29.4**
pleiad **23.18.3**
Pleiades **35.1.8**
plein-air **6**
plein-airist **22.29.2(.29.1)**
pleiotropic **24.2.8(.5)**
pleiotropism **27.15.21(.2.2)**
pleiotropy **1.8.11(.8)**
Pleistocene **28.1.18(.6)**
plena **17.18.1**
plenarily **1.31.17(.27.2)**
plenary **1.29.11(.13.1)**
plenipotentiary **1.29.11(.20)**
plenitude **23.17.4(.1)**
plenteous **34.3.3**
plenteously **1.31.33(.1.1)**
plenteousness **34.18.16(.31.1)**
plentiful **40.27.14**
plentifully **1.31.17(.16.1)**
plentifulness **34.18.16(.37.2)**
plenty **1.10.23(.3)**
plenum **27.15.14(.1)**
pleochroic **24.2.7**
pleochroism **27.15.21(.2.1)**
pleomorphic **24.2.16(.5)**
pleomorphism **27.15.21(.2.10)**
pleonasm **27.15.21(.3)**
pleonastic **24.2.10(.15.4)**

pleonastically **1.31.24(.9.6)**
plesiosaur **12.14.2**
plesiosauri **14.24.4**
plesiosaurus **34.18.27(.8)**
plessor **17.24.5**
plethora **17.32.14(.14)**
plethoric **24.2.26(.6)**
plethorically **1.31.24(.9.12)**
pleura **17.32.10, 17.32.14(.3)**
pleural **40.16.13(.11)**
pleurisy **1.22.16(.13)**
pleuritic **24.2.10(.2.4)**
pleurodynia **3.9.2**
pleuron **28.10.24(.5)**
pleuropneumonia **3.9.1**
Pleven **28.17.20(.4)**
plew **16**
plexiform **27.10.5(.2)**
Plexiglass® **34.9.7**
plexor **17.24.20**
plexus **34.18.20**
pliability **1.10.16(.22.1)**
pliable **40.20.16(.5)**
pliableness **34.18.16(.37.4)**
pliably **1.31.21(.2)**
pliancy **1.22.23(.10.1)**
pliant **22.26.15(.4)**
pliantly **1.31.22(.20.1)**
pliantness **34.18.16(.20.4)**
plicate **22.4.11(.5), 22.19.12(.9)**
plicated **23.18.9(.3)**
plication **28.17.25(.3.5)**
plié **4.1**
pliers **35.18.4**
plight **22.16**
plimsole **40.18.10, 40.31.20**
plimsoll **40.31.20**
pling **29.1**
plink **24.19.1**
Plinlimmon **28.17.16(.2)**
plinth **32.21**
Pliny **1.16.2**
Pliocene **28.1.18(.6)**
plissé **4.18.1**
plod **23.10**
plodder **17.13.8**
ploddingly **1.31.28(.1.5)**
ploidy **1.11.12**
Plomer **17.17.13, 17.17.16**
Plomley **1.31.26(.9)**
plonk **24.19.5**
plonker **17.14.21(.4)**
plonko **19.12.15**
plop **20.7**

plosion 28.17.26(.6)
plosive 31.2.4(.11)
plot 22.11
Plotinus 34.18.16(.13)
plotless 34.18.29(.22)
plotlessness
   34.18.16(.31.6)
plotter 17.12.9
plough 9
ploughable 40.20.16(.3)
ploughboy 13.3
plougher 17.3
ploughland 23.24.6(.13)
ploughman 28.17.16(.8)
ploughshare 6.14
Plouviez 4.2.6
plover 17.21.9
plow 9
Plowden 28.17.12(.7)
plower 17.3
Plowright 22.16.24(.6)
ploy 13
pluck 24.12
plucker 17.14.11
pluckily 1.31.17(.11)
pluckiness 34.18.16(.2.4)
pluckless 34.18.29(.24)
plucky 1.12.9
plug 26.10
plugger 17.16.9
plughole 40.18.13
plugola 17.34.18(.6)
plug-ugly 1.31.25
plum 27.11
plumage 39.2.14
plumassier 3.14
plumb 27.11
plumbaginous
   34.18.16(.15.3)
plumbago 19.13.3
plumbate 22.4.8
plumbeous 34.3.2
plumber 17.17.10
plumbic 24.2.9(.8)
plumbiferous
   34.18.27(.20)
plumbism 27.15.21(.2.3)
plumbless 34.18.29(.26)
plumbline
   28.14.19(.18)
plumbous 34.18.10
plumbum 27.15.8
plume 27.14
plumeless 34.18.29(.26)
plumelike 24.13.7(.16)
plumery 1.29.11(.12)
Plummer 17.17.10
plummet 22.2.11
plummily 1.31.17(.13)
plumminess
   34.18.16(.2.5)

plummy 1.15.10
plumose 34.20.8
plump 20.16.5
plumpish 36.2.9
plumply 1.31.20
plumpness 34.18.16(.18)
Plumpton 28.17.11(.18)
Plumptre 2.30.10
plumpy 1.8.14
Plumstead 23.5.3,
   23.18.9(.20)
Plumtre 2.30.10
plumulaceous
   34.18.22(.3)
plumular 17.34.16(.21.4)
plumule 40.15.9(.7)
plumy 1.15.12
plunder 17.13.20(.10)
plunderer 17.32.14(.7)
plundering 29.1.30(.8)
plunderous 34.18.27(.15)
plunge 39.17.8
plunger 17.29.16(.7)
plunk 24.19.7
Plunket 22.2.9(.9)
pluperfect 22.23.2
plural 40.16.13(.11)
pluralism 27.15.21(.2.15)
pluralist 22.29.2(.31.4)
pluralistic 24.2.10(.15.3)
pluralistically
   1.31.24(.9.6)
plurality 1.10.16(.32.13)
pluralization
   28.17.25(.3.12)
pluralize 35.15.21(.4.7)
plurally 1.31.17(.27.1)
pluripotential
   40.33.12(.2)
pluripresence
   34.24.10(.19)
plurry 1.29.9
plus 34.14
plus ça change 37.5
plus-fours 35.12
plush 36.12
plushily 1.31.17(.22)
plushiness 34.18.16(.2.8)
plushly 1.31.35(.6)
plushness 34.18.16(.33.1)
plushy 1.24.9
Plutarch 24.8.4
plutarchy 1.12.6
Pluto 19.10.11
plutocracy 1.22.16(.13)
plutocrat 22.7.20
plutocratic 24.2.10(.4.5)
plutocratically
   1.31.24(.9.4)
plutolatry 1.29.15(.13)
pluton 28.10.9

Plutonian 28.3.8(.11)
Plutonic 24.2.15(.6.1)
Plutonism 27.15.21(.2.9)
plutonium 27.3.8(.10)
pluvial 40.3.8
pluviometer
   17.12.16(.9.2)
pluviometric
   24.2.26(.14.2)
pluviometrical
   40.23.12(.18)
pluviometrically
   1.31.24(.9.12)
pluvious 34.3.8
ply 14
Plymouth 32.14.11
Plynlimon 28.17.16(.2)
plywood 23.16.6(.5)
pneumatic 24.2.10(.4.2)
pneumatically
   1.31.24(.9.4)
pneumaticity
   1.10.16(.16.1)
pneumatocyst
   22.29.2(.22)
pneumatological
   40.23.12(.17.2)
pneumatology
   1.26.10(.11.2)
pneumatophore 12.11.3
pneumococcus
   34.18.13(.5)
pneumoconiosis
   34.2.17(.11.1)
pneumocystis 34.2.8
pneumogastric
   24.2.26(.14.5)
pneumonectomy
   1.15.13(.1)
pneumonia 3.9.11
pneumonic 24.2.15(.6.2)
pneumonitis 34.18.11(.8)
pneumothorax
   34.23.5(.14)
Pnyx 34.23.2
PO 19
po 19
poach 38.17
poacher 17.28.17
poblano 19.15.7
Pocahontas 34.18.11(.14)
pochard 23.18.24
pochette 22.5.15
pock 24.9
pocket 22.2.9(.5)
pocketable
   40.20.16(.11.3)
pocketbook 24.14.3
pocketful 40.14.6(.10)
pocketless 34.18.29(.22)
pockety 1.10.16(.10)
Pocklington 28.17.11(.23)

pockmark 24.8.8
pocky 1.12.7
poco 19.12.14
Pocock 24.9.6
pococurante 1.10.23(.4)
pococuranteism
   27.15.21(.2.1)
pococurantism
   27.15.21(.2.4)
Pocono 19.15.12
pod 23.10
podagra 17.32.22
podagral 40.16.13(.19)
podagric 24.2.26(.16)
podagrous 34.18.27(.17)
poddy 1.11.10
podestà 10.6.8
podgily 1.31.17(.25)
podginess 34.18.16(.2.8)
podgy 1.26.6
podia 3.5.8
podiatrist 22.29.2(.29.5)
podiatry 1.29.15(.1)
podium 27.3.4(.8)
podophyllin 28.2.31(.2)
podsol 40.9.14
podunk 24.19.7
podzol 40.9.15
podzolization
   28.17.25(.3.12)
podzolize 35.15.21(.4.6)
Poe 19
poem 27.15.6
poesy 1.23.13
poet 22.19.7
poetaster 17.12.24(.3)
poetess 34.5.2,
   34.18.11(.10)
poetic 24.2.10(.3.1)
poetical 40.23.12(.7.1)
poetically 1.31.24(.9.3)
poeticize 35.15.16(.4)
poetize 35.15.7(.7)
Poet Laureate 22.3.12
poetry 1.29.15(.2)
po-faced 22.29.4
pogey 1.14.13
pogo 19.13.11
pogrom 27.9, 27.15.26(.13)
Pogue 26.15
poi 13
poignance 34.24.10(.23)
poignancy 1.22.23(.10.4)
poignant 22.26.15(.24)
poignantly 1.31.22(.20.5)
poikilotherm 27.16.5
poikilothermal 40.25.11
poikilothermia 3.8.8
poikilothermic
   24.2.14(.11)
poikilothermy 1.15.14

poilu **16.25**
poinciana **17.18.8**
poind **23.24.2, 23.24.11**
Poindexter **17.12.24(.20)**
poinsettia **3.4.3**
point **22.26.11**
point-blank **24.19.3(.7)**
point duty **1.10.15**
pointe **22.8**
pointedly **1.31.23(.14.3)**
pointedness
   34.18.16(.21.1)
pointer **17.12.22(.9)**
pointillism
   27.15.21(.2.15)
pointillist **22.29.2(.30)**
pointillistic **24.2.10(.15.3)**
pointless **34.18.29(.22)**
pointlessly **1.31.33(.12.6)**
pointlessness
   34.18.16(.31.6)
Pointon **28.17.11(.22)**
pointsman **28.17.16(.29)**
point-to-point **22.26.11**
point-to-pointer
   17.12.22(.9)
pointy **1.10.23(.9)**
Poirot **19.27.5**
poise **35.13**
poison **28.17.24(.8)**
poisoner **17.18.16(.15)**
poisoning **29.1.17(.12)**
poisonous **34.18.16(.15.3)**
poisonously
   1.31.33(.12.3)
poisonousness
   34.18.16(.31.3)
Poisson distribution
   28.17.25(.11)
Poitier **4.2.2**
Poitiers **4.2.2**
Poitou **16.7**
poke **24.18**
poker **17.14.17**
pokerwork **24.17.6(.4)**
pokeweed **23.1.10**
pokily **1.31.17(.11)**
pokiness **34.18.16(.2.4)**
poky **1.12.15**
pol **40.9**
polacca **17.14.5**
Polack **24.6.23**
polacre **17.14.7**
Poland **23.24.16(.16.2)**
Polanski **1.12.17(.12)**
polar **17.34.18**
polarimeter **17.12.16(.9.1)**
polarimetric
   24.2.26(.14.2)
polarimetry **1.29.15(.8)**
Polaris **34.2.21**

polariscope **20.15.4(.1)**
polariscopic **24.2.8(.5)**
polarity **1.10.16(.21.1)**
polarizable **40.20.16(.22)**
polarization
   28.17.25(.3.11)
polarize **35.15.20(.2)**
polarizer **17.25.12(.14)**
polarly **1.31.17(.29)**
polarographic **24.2.16(.3)**
polarography **1.18.9(.3.2)**
Polaroid® **23.13.19**
polder **17.13.23(.5)**
pole **40.18**
pole-axe **34.23.5(.15)**
polecat **22.7.9**
Polegate **22.4.12(.13)**
polemic **24.2.14(.3)**
polemical **40.23.12(.10)**
polemically **1.31.24(.9.8)**
polemicist **22.29.2(.22)**
polemicize **35.15.16(.4)**
polenta **17.12.22(.3)**
Pole Star **10.6.8**
polevault **22.32.5, 22.32.6**
pole-vaulter **17.12.26(.5)**
poleward **23.18.26(.17)**
police **34.1, 34.1.8**
policeman **28.17.16(.29)**
policewoman
   28.17.16(.14)
policewomen **28.2.17(.1)**
policy **1.22.16(.14)**
policyholder **17.13.23(.8)**
polio **15.1.13**
poliomyelitis **34.18.11(.8)**
polis **34.2.22(.6)**
Polisario **15.1.12**
Polish **36.2.27**
polish **36.2.27**
polishable **40.20.16(.23)**
polisher **17.26.14**
Politburo **19.27.7, 19.27.11**
polite **22.16.25**
politely **1.31.22(.13)**
politeness **34.18.16(.20.2)**
politesse **34.5.2**
politic **24.2.10(.10)**
political **40.23.12(.7.1)**
politically **1.31.24(.9.3)**
politician **28.17.25(.2.2)**
politicization
   28.17.25(.3.12)
politicize **35.15.16(.4)**
politicking **29.1.14(.2)**
politicly **1.31.24(.2)**
politico **19.12.12**
polity **1.10.16(.33)**
polje **17.33.13**
Polk **24.18**

polka **17.14.25**
polka dot **22.11.5**
poll **40.9, 40.18**
pollack **24.16.16**
pollan **28.17.33(.7)**
pollard **23.9.22, 23.18.29**
pollee **2**
pollen **28.17.33(.7)**
pollenless **34.18.29(.27)**
pollex **34.23.4(.12)**
pollicitation
   28.17.25(.3.3)
pollie **1.31.10**
pollinate **22.4.14(.9.4)**
pollination **28.17.25(.3.8)**
pollinia **3.9.2**
pollinic **24.2.15(.2)**
polliniferous
   34.18.27(.20)
pollinium **27.3.8(.2)**
Pollitt **22.2.25**
polliwog **26.7.12**
pollock **24.16.16**
pollster **17.12.24(.25)**
pollutant **22.26.15(.9)**
pollute **22.18.11**
polluter **17.12.15(.8)**
pollution **28.17.25(.11)**
Pollux **34.23.15**
polly **1.31.10**
Pollyanna **17.18.6**
Pollyannaish **36.2.7**
Pollyannaism
   27.15.21(.2.1)
polo **19.29.14**
polocrosse **34.10.16**
polonaise **35.4.8**
polonium **27.3.8(.10)**
Polonius **34.3.6(.7)**
polony **1.16.17(.15)**
Polperro **19.27.2**
poltergeist **22.29.13**
poltroon **28.16.13**
poltroonery
   1.29.11(.13.1)
poly **1.31.10**
polyadelphous **34.18.17**
polyamide **23.15.7**
polyandrous
   34.18.27(.15)
polyandry **1.29.16**
polyantha **17.22.13**
polyanthus **34.18.19**
polyatomic **24.2.14(.6)**
polybag **26.5.1**
polybasic **24.2.20(.3)**
Polybius **34.3.2**
polycarbonate
   22.4.14(.9.1), 22.19.15(.9)
Polycarp **20.6**
Polycell® **40.5.11**

polychaetan **28.17.11(.1)**
polychaete **22.1.4**
polychaetous **34.18.11(.1)**
polychlorinated
   23.18.9(.3)
polychromatic
   24.2.10(.4.2)
polychromatism
   27.15.21(.2.4)
polychrome **27.17.13**
polychromic **24.2.14(.12)**
polychromous
   34.18.15(.12)
polychromy **1.15.15**
polyclinic **24.2.15(.2)**
Polyclitus **34.18.11(.8)**
polycotton **28.17.11(.9)**
Polycrates **35.1.7(.6)**
polycrystal **40.21.18**
polycrystalline
   28.14.19(.11)
polycyclic **24.2.27(.16)**
polycythaemia **3.8.1**
polydactyl **40.21.16**
polydaemonism
   27.15.21(.2.9)
polydipsia **3.14.12**
polyester **17.12.24(.4)**
polyethene **28.1.17**
polyethylene **28.1.27(.7)**
Polyfilla® **17.34.2(.8)**
polygamic **24.2.14(.4)**
polygamist **22.29.2(.17)**
polygamous **34.18.15(.10)**
polygamously
   1.31.33(.12.3)
polygamy **1.15.13(.4)**
polygene **28.1.23**
polygenesis **34.2.17(.10.3)**
polygenetic **24.2.10(.3.1)**
polygenic **24.2.15(.4)**
polygenism **27.15.21(.2.9)**
polygenist **22.29.2(.18.3)**
polygeny **1.16.15(.17)**
polyglot **22.11.17**
polyglottal **40.21.7**
polyglottic **24.2.10(.6)**
polyglottism
   27.15.21(.2.4)
polygon **28.10.12,
   28.17.15(.13)**
polygonal **40.26.13(.7)**
polygonum **27.15.14(.11)**
polygraph **30.7.5(.1)**
polygynous
   34.18.16(.15.3)
polygyny **1.16.15(.17)**
polyhedra **17.32.20**
polyhedral **40.16.13(.17)**
polyhedric **24.2.26(.15)**
polyhedron **28.17.31(.15)**

p

polyhistor 17.12.24(.2)
Polyhymnia 3.9.14
polymath 32.6.3
polymathic 24.2.18(.3)
polymathy 1.20.8
polymer 17.17.14(.12)
polymerase 35.4.16
polymeric 24.2.26(.4)
polymerism 27.15.21(.2.14)
polymerization 28.17.25(.3.12)
polymerize 35.15.20(.2)
polymerous 34.18.27(.18)
polymorph 30.9.2
polymorphic 24.2.16(.5)
polymorphism 27.15.21(.2.10)
polymorphous 34.18.17
Polynesia 3.15.1, 17.33.12
Polynesian 28.17.26(.1), 28.17.32
polyneuritic 24.2.10(.2.4)
polyneuritis 34.18.11(.8)
Polynices 35.1.16(.8)
polynomial 40.3.6
polynya 17.33.9
polyopia 3.2.7
polyp 20.13.7
polypary 1.29.11(.6)
polypeptide 23.15.4
polyphagous 34.18.14(.5)
polyphase 35.4.9
polyphasic 24.2.21
Polyphemus 34.18.15(.1)
polyphone 28.19.11
polyphonic 24.2.15(.6.3)
polyphonically 1.31.24(.9.8)
polyphonous 34.18.16(.15.3)
polyphony 1.16.15(.12)
polyphosphate 22.4.15
polyphyletic 24.2.10(.3.3)
polypi 14.6
polyploid 23.13.20
polyploidy 1.11.12
polypod 23.10.1
polypody 1.11.19
polypoid 23.13.5
polyposis 34.2.17(.11.1)
polypous 34.18.9(.2)
polypropene 28.1.7
polypropylene 28.1.27(.7)
polyptych 24.2.10(.12)
polypus 34.18.9(.8)
polyrhythm 27.15.19
polysaccharide 23.15.15
polysemic 24.2.14(.1)
polysemous 34.18.15(.1)

polysemy 1.15.1, 1.15.13(.8)
polystyrene 28.1.25(.2)
polysyllabic 24.2.9(.2)
polysyllabically 1.31.24(.9.2)
polysyllable 40.20.16(.29)
polysynthetic 24.2.10(.3.2)
polytechnic 24.2.15(.12)
polytetrafluoro-ethylene 28.1.27(.7)
polytheism 27.15.21(.2.1)
polytheist 22.29.2(.1)
polytheistic 24.2.10(.15.1)
polythene 28.1.17
polytonal 40.26.15
polytonality 1.10.16(.32.8)
polyunsaturate 22.4.22(.6)
polyunsaturates 34.22.15
polyurethane 28.4.11
polyvalence 34.24.10(.24)
polyvalent 22.26.15(.25)
polyvinyl 40.2.10, 40.26.11
polyzoan 28.17.8
Polzeath 32.1, 32.5
pom 27.9
pomace 34.2.12
pomade 23.9.11
Pomagne® 28.4.7
pomander 17.13.20(.4)
pomatum 27.15.9(.2)
pombe 4.8
pome 27.17
pomegranate 22.19.15(.3)
pomelo 19.29.4, 19.29.12
Pomerania 3.9.3(.8)
Pomeranian 28.3.8(.3)
Pomeroy 13.15
pomfret 22.19.24(.9)
pomiculture 17.28.26
pomiferous 34.18.27(.20)
pommel 40.25.5, 40.25.7
pommy 1.15.8
pomological 40.23.12(.17.2)
pomologist 22.29.2(.26.4)
pomology 1.26.10(.11.4)
Pomona 17.18.18(.5)
pomp 20.16.4
Pompadour 12.6.6, 17.7.4
pompano 19.15.12
Pompeii 1(.2), 4.7
Pompey 1.8.14
Pompidou 16.8.4
pompom 27.9
pompon 28.10.7

pomposity 1.10.16(.16.2)
pompous 34.18.9(.11)
pompously 1.31.33(.12.2)
pompousness 34.18.16(.31.3)
'pon 28.10
ponce 34.24.7
ponceau 19.20.16
ponceaux 35.20.10
poncey 1.22.23(.6)
poncho 19.22, 19.24
poncy 1.22.23(.6)
pond 23.24.9
pondage 39.2.11
ponder 17.13.20(.7)
ponderability 1.10.16(.22.1)
ponderable 40.20.16(.27.3)
ponderation 28.17.25(.3.13)
pondering 29.1.30(.8)
ponderosa 17.24.17, 17.25.15
ponderosity 1.10.16(.16.2)
ponderous 34.18.27(.15)
ponderously 1.31.33(.12.5)
ponderousness 34.18.16(.31.5)
Pondicherry 1.29.3
pondweed 23.1.10
pone 28.19
pong 29.6
ponga 17.19.4
pongal 40.24.14(.3)
pongee 2.27
pongid 23.18.23, 23.18.25
pongo 19.13.12
pongy 1.17
poniard 23.9.21, 23.18.28
pons 35.26.10
pons asinorum 27.15.26(.5)
Ponsonby 1.9.19
pons Varolii 14.2
pont 22.26.9
Pontardawe 1(.3)
Pontardulais 34.18.29(.2)
Pontefract 22.23.5(.9)
Ponteland 23.24.16(.16.1)
pontes 35.1.7(.9)
pontes Varolii 14.2
Pontiac 24.6.1
Pontianak 24.6.11
pontifex 34.23.4(.7)
pontiff 30.2.1
pontific 24.2.16(.1)
pontifical 40.23.12(.12)
pontificalia 3.24.3

pontifically 1.31.24(.9.9)
pontificate 22.4.11(.6), 22.19.12(.10)
pontification 28.17.25(.3.5)
pontifices 35.1.16(.10)
Pontin 28.2.11(.13)
Pontine Marshes 35.18.19
Ponting 29.1.12(.19)
Pontius 34.3.3, 34.18.22(.12), 34.18.23
pontoon 28.16.3
Pontormo 19.14.9
Pontus 34.18.11(.14)
Pontypool 40.15.1
Pontypridd 33.1
pony 1.16.17
ponytail 40.4.2
poo 16
pooch 38.14
poodle 40.22.12
poof 30.13
poofter 17.12.23
poofy 1.18.8
pooh 16
pooh-bah 10.5
pooh-pooh 16.5
Pook 24.15
pooka 17.14.14
pool 40.15
Poole 40.15
Pooley 1.31.16
poolroom 27.14.6(.20)
poolside 23.15.11(.17)
poon 28.16
Poona 17.18.15
poop 20.12
pooper-scooper 17.10.13
poor 12, 17.7
poorboy 13.3
poorhouse 34.8.6(.7)
poorly 1.31.11, 1.31.17(.4)
poorness 34.18.16(.15.1)
Pooter 17.12.15
Pooterish 36.2.25
pootle 40.21.11
poove 31.10
pop 20.7
popcorn 28.11.5
pope 20.15
popedom 27.15.10(.11)
popeless 34.18.29(.20)
Popemobile 40.1.2
popery 1.29.11(.6)
Popeye 14.6
popeyed 23.15
popgun 28.13.5
Popham 27.15.7
popinjay 4.23

popish 36.2.9
popishly 1.31.35(.7.1)
popishness
34.18.16(.33.2)
poplar 17.34.19
poplin 28.2.31(.13)
popliteal 40.16.1
Popocatépetl 40.21.4
popover 17.21.14(.3)
poppa 17.10.8
poppadom 27.15.10(.8)
popper 17.10.8
poppet 22.2.5
poppied 23.2.6
popple 40.19.7
Poppleton 28.17.11(.27)
Popplewell 40.5.17(.17)
popply 1.31.20
poppy 1.8.7
poppycock 24.9.6
Popsicle® 40.23.12(.15)
popsy 1.22.19
populace 34.18.29(.17.6)
popular 17.34.46(.21.1)
popularism
27.15.21(.2.14)
popularity 1.10.16(.21.1)
popularization
28.17.25(.3.12)
popularize 35.15.20(.2)
popularizer 17.25.12(.14)
popularly 1.31.17(.29)
populate 22.4.23(.7.3)
population
28.17.25(.3.14)
populism 27.15.21(.2.15)
populist 22.29.2(.31.5)
populistic 24.2.10(.15.3)
populous 34.18.29(.17.6)
populously 1.31.33(.12.6)
populousness
34.18.16(.31.6)
porbeagle 40.24.1
porcelain 28.4.19,
28.17.33(.13)
porcellaneous 34.3.6(.3)
porcellanous
34.18.16(.15.3)
porch 38.9
Porchester 17.12.24(.14)
porchless 34.18.29(.36)
porcine 28.14.13
porcini 2.17.1
porcupine 28.14.3
porcupinish 36.2.16(.11)
porcupiny 1.16.13
pore 12
porgy 1.14.7
Pori 1.29.8
porifer 17.20.12(.5)
poriferan 28.17.31(.11)

porism 27.15.21(.2.14)
porismatic 24.2.10(.4.2)
pork 24.10
porker 17.14.9
porkling 29.1.31(.19)
porky 1.12.8
Porlock 24.9.16(.4)
porn 28.11
porno 19.15.9
pornographer
17.20.12(.5)
pornographic 24.2.16(.3)
pornographically
1.31.24(.9.9)
pornography 1.18.9(.3.2)
poroplastic 24.2.10(.15.4)
porosity 1.10.16(.16.2)
porous 34.18.27(.8)
porously 1.31.33(.12.5)
porousness
34.18.16(.31.5)
porphyria 3.22.1
porphyrin 28.2.29(.5)
porphyritic 24.2.10(.2.4)
porphyrogenite
22.16.14(.6)
porphyry 1.29.11(.14)
porpoise 34.18.9(.6)
porrect 22.23.4(.10)
porridge 39.2.22(.5)
porridgy 1.26.10(.9)
porringer 17.29.16(.8)
Porsche® 17.26.9, 36.11
Porsena 17.18.16(.14)
Porson 28.17.23(.9)
port 22.13
portability 1.10.16(.22.1)
portable 40.20.16(.11.2)
portableness
34.18.16(.37.4)
portably 1.31.21(.4.1)
portage 39.2.10
Portakabin® 28.2.10
portal 40.21.8
portamenti 2.12.14
portamento 19.10.17
portative 31.2.1(.9.1)
Port-au-Prince 34.24.1
portcullis 34.18.29(.13)
Porte 22.13
porte-cochère 6.14
portend 23.24.5(.4)
portent 22.26.4(.4),
22.26.15(.9)
portentous 34.18.11(.14)
portentously
1.31.33(.12.2)
portentousness
34.18.16(.31.3)
Porteous 34.3.3
porter 17.12.10

porterage 39.2.22(.9)
porterhouse 34.8.6(.7)
portfire 17.6.9(.7)
portfolio 15.1.13
Porth 32.10
Port Harcourt 22.13.4
Porthcawl 40.10.7
Port Hedland
23.24.16(.16.3)
Porthmadog 26.7.4
porthole 40.18.13
Portia 17.26.9
portico 19.12.12
portière 6
portion 28.17.25(.8)
portionless 34.18.29(.27)
Portishead 23.5.13(.15)
Portland 23.24.16(.16.3)
portliness 34.18.16(.2.10)
portly 1.31.22(.10)
Portmadoc 24.16.5
portmanteau 19.10.17
portmanteaux 35.20.3
Portmeirion 28.3.20(.3)
Portnoy 13.7
Porto 19.10.9
Porto Alegre 17.32.22
Portobello 19.29.4
Port-of-Spain 28.4.1
portolan 28.17.33(.13)
portolano 19.15.7
Porton 28.17.11(.10)
Porto Novo 19.17
portrait 22.4.22(.8),
22.19.24(.12)
portraitist 22.29.2(.13)
portraiture 17.28.15
portray 4.26.11
portrayable 40.20.16(.2)
portrayal 40.16.2
portrayer 17.2.9
Portreath 32.1
Portree 2.30.10
portreeve 31.1.8
Port Said 23.15
Portsmouth 32.14.11
Port Stanley 1.31.27(.6)
Port Sudan 28.9.3
Port Talbot 22.19.9
Portugal 40.24.11
Portuguese 35.1.10
pose 35.20
Poseidon 28.17.12(.13)
poser 17.25.15
poseur 18.12
poseuse 35.19
poseuses 35.19
posey 1.23.15
posh 36.9
poshly 1.31.35(.5)

poshness 34.18.16(.33.1)
posit 22.2.17
position 28.17.25(.2.5)
positional 40.26.13(.14.1)
positionally 1.31.17(.14.3)
positioner 17.18.16(.16)
positive 31.2.1(.9.3)
positively 1.31.30(.7.1)
positiveness
34.18.16(.28.1)
positivism 27.15.21(.2.11)
positivist 22.29.2(.20)
positivistic 24.2.10(.15.2)
positivistically
1.31.24(.9.6)
positivity 1.10.16(.15)
positron 28.10.24(.7)
positronic 24.2.15(.6.4)
positronium 27.3.8(.10)
posological
40.23.12(.17.2)
posology 1.26.10(.11.5)
poss. 34.10
posse 1.22.9
posse comitatus
34.18.11(.6)
possess 34.5.10
possession 28.17.25(.4)
possessionless
34.18.29(.27)
possessive 31.2.4(.4)
possessively 1.31.30(.7.4)
possessiveness
34.18.16(.28.2)
possessor 17.24.5
possessory 1.29.11(.18)
posset 22.2.16
possibility 1.10.16(.22.1)
possible 40.20.16(.21.2)
possibly 1.31.21(.7.2)
possum 27.15.20(.6)
post 22.29.17
postage 39.2.10
postal 40.21.18
postally 1.31.17(.9.3)
postbag 26.5.1
postbox 34.23.8(.2)
postbus 34.14
postcard 23.9.9
post-chaise 35.4.12
postcode 23.20.7
postdate 22.4.10
postdoc 24.9.5
postdoctoral
40.16.13(.12.1)
posted 23.18.9(.20)
poster 17.12.24(.15)
poste restante 22.26.9
posterior 3.22.2
posteriority 1.10.16(.21.2)
posteriorly 1.31.3(.11)

p

posterity 1.10.16(.21.1)
postern 28.17.11(.25)
postface 34.4.9
postfix 34.23.2(.7)
Postgate 22.4.12(.7)
postglacial 40.3.10, 40.33.2
postgrad 23.7.16
postgraduate 22.19.5
posthaste 22.29.4
post hoc 24.9
posthole 40.18.13
posthorn 28.11.10
posthumous 34.18.15(.10)
posthumously 1.31.33(.12.3)
postiche 36.1
postie 1.10.26(.13)
postil 40.2.5
postilion 28.3.21(.2)
postillion 28.3.21(.2)
posting 29.1.12(.21)
Postlethwaite 22.4.21
postliminy 1.16.15(.11)
postlude 23.17.5
postman 28.17.16(.21)
postman's knock 24.9
postmark 24.8.8
postmaster 17.12.24(.5)
post meridian 28.3.4(.2)
post meridiem 27.3.4(.2)
postmistress 34.18.27(.14)
postmodern 28.17.12(.9)
postmodernism 27.15.21(.2.9)
postmodernist 22.29.2(.18.1)
postmodernity 1.10.16(.13)
postmortem 27.15.9(.7)
post-op 20.7
postoperative 31.2.1(.9.4)
postpaid 23.4.1
post-partum 27.15.9(.5)
postponable 40.20.16(.16.3)
postpone 28.19.2
postponement 22.26.15(.13.4)
postponer 17.18.18(.1)
postposition 28.17.25(.2.5)
postpositional 40.26.13(.14.1)
postpositive 31.2.1(.9.3)
postpositively 1.31.30(.7.1)
postprandial 40.3.4
post room 27.14

postscript 22.22.1
postulant 22.26.15(.25)
postulate 22.4.23(.7.3), 22.19.26(.13)
postulation 28.17.25(.3.14)
postulator 17.12.4(.16)
postural 40.16.13(.12.3)
posture 17.28.24
posturer 17.32.14(.19)
posturing 29.1.30(.8)
postvocalic 24.2.27(.6)
postwar 12.20
postwoman 28.17.16(.14)
postwomen 28.2.17(.1)
posy 1.23.15
pot 22.11
potability 1.10.16(.22.1)
potable 40.20.16(.11.3)
potableness 34.18.16(.37.4)
potage 37.4.3
potager 17.29.13
potamic 24.2.14(.4)
potamology 1.26.10(.11.4)
potash 36.6.3
potassic 24.2.20(.5)
potassium 27.3.11
potation 28.17.25(.3.3)
potato 19.10.3
potatory 1.29.11(.8.6)
pot-au-feu 18.9
potbelly 1.31.5
potboiler 17.34.11
potbound 23.24.7(.2)
potch 38.8
poteen 28.1.9, 28.1.22
Potemkin 28.2.13(.11)
potence 34.24.10(.10)
potency 1.22.23(.10.2)
potent 22.26.15(.9)
potentate 22.4.9(.8)
potential 40.33.12(.2)
potentiality 1.10.16(.32.1)
potentially 1.31.17(.22)
potentiate 22.4.2(.11)
potentilla 17.34.2(.2)
potentiometer 17.12.16(.9.2)
potentiometric 24.2.26(.14.2)
potentiometry 1.29.15(.8)
potentization 28.17.25(.3.11)
potentize 35.15.7(.8)
potful 40.14.6(.10)
pothead 23.5.13(.9)
potheen 28.1.9
pother 17.23.8
potherb 21.15

pothole 40.18.13
potholer 17.34.18(.13)
pothook 24.14.9
pothouse 34.8.6(.11)
potiche 36.1
potion 28.17.25(.13)
Potiphar 10.12, 17.20.12(.1)
potlatch 38.5
potlatching 29.1.27
Potomac 24.6.10
potoroo 16.23
potpie 14.6
potpourri 2.30, 2.30.6
potrero 19.27.3
Potsdam 27.6.5
potsherd 23.19.6
potshot 22.11.12
potstone 28.19.4(.9)
pottage 39.2.10
potter 17.12.9
potterer 17.32.14(.6)
Potteries 35.2.17
pottery 1.29.11(.8.4)
pottiness 34.18.16(.2.3)
pottle 40.21.7
potto 19.10.8
Potts 34.22.8
potty 1.10.9
pouch 38.6
pouchy 1.25.7
pouf 30.13
pouffe 30.13
Poughkeepsie 1.22.19
poulard 23.9.22
Poulenc 24.19.3(.7)
Poulson 28.17.23(.28)
poult 22.32.9, 22.32.10, 22.32.12
poult-de-soie 10.22.11
Poulter 17.12.26(.7)
poulterer 17.32.14(.6)
poultice 34.18.11(.17)
Poultney 1.16.19
Poulton 28.17.11(.27)
poultry 1.29.15(.18)
poultryman 28.17.16(.2)
pounce 34.24.5
pouncer 17.24.22(.4)
pouncet-box 34.23.8(.2)
pound 23.24.7
poundage 39.2.11
poundal 40.22.16
pounder 17.13.20(.5)
Pountney 1.16.19
pour 12
pourable 40.20.16(.27.2)
pourboire 10.22.4
pourer 17.32.10
pourparler 4.28.4

pousada 17.13.7
poussette 22.5.13
Poussin 8, 28.7.14
pout 22.9
pouter 17.12.7
poutingly 1.31.28(.1.4)
pouty 1.10.7
poverty 1.10.16(.15)
Povey 1.19.12
pow 9
powan 28.17.8
powder 17.13.6
powderiness 34.18.16(.2.9)
powderpuff 30.11.1
powdery 1.29.11(.9)
Powell 40.16.3, 40.16.9
power 17.3
powerboat 22.21.2
powerful 40.27.14
powerfully 1.31.17(.16.1)
powerfulness 34.18.16(.37.2)
powerhouse 34.8.6(.7)
powerless 34.18.29(.17.1)
powerlessly 1.31.33(.12.6)
powerlessness 34.18.16(.31.6)
powerpack 24.6.5
powerpoint 22.26.11
Powers 35.18.2
Powhatan 28.7.6, 28.17.11(.6)
powwow 9.15
Powys 34.2.2
pox 34.23.8
poxy 1.22.22
Poznan 28.7.11
pozzolana 17.18.8(.13)
praam 27.6, 27.8
practicability 1.10.16(.22.2)
practicable 40.20.16(.13)
practicableness 34.18.16(.37.4)
practicably 1.31.21(.5)
practical 40.23.12(.7.3)
practicality 1.10.16(.32.5)
practically 1.31.24(.9.5)
practicalness 34.18.16(.37.5)
practice 34.2.8
practicum 27.15.11(.9)
practise 34.2.8
practiser 17.24.15
practitioner 17.18.16(.16)
prad 23.7
Prado 19.11.7
praecipe 1.8.11(.7)
praecox 34.23.8(.5)
praedial 40.3.4

praemunire **1.29.2(.6)**
praenomen **28.5.7(.12), 28.17.16(.18)**
praepostor **17.12.24(.7)**
praesidia **3.5.2**
Praesidium **27.3.4(.2)**
praetor **12.5.1, 17.12.1**
praetoria **3.22.9**
praetorian **28.3.20(.7)**
praetorium **27.3.17(.4)**
praetorship **20.2.7(.6)**
pragmatic **24.2.10(.4.2)**
pragmatical **40.23.12(.7.1)**
pragmaticality **1.10.16(.32.5)**
pragmatically **1.31.24(.9.4)**
pragmatism **27.15.21(.2.4)**
pragmatist **22.29.2(.13)**
pragmatistic **24.2.10(.15.2)**
pragmatize **35.15.7(.7)**
Prague **26.6**
Praha **10.21**
prahu **16.21**
Praia **17.6**
prairie **1.29.4**
praise **35.4**
praiseful **40.27.26**
praiser **17.25.3**
praiseworthily **1.31.17(.19)**
praiseworthiness **34.18.16(.2.6)**
praiseworthy **1.21**
Prakrit **22.2.24**
praline **28.1.27(.2)**
pralltriller **17.34.2(.15)**
pram **27.6**
prana **17.18.8**
pranayama **17.17.7**
prance **34.24.6**
prancer **17.24.22(.3)**
prandial **40.3.4**
Prandtl **40.21.17(.3)**
prang **29.4**
prank **24.19.3**
prankful **40.27.20**
prankish **36.2.13**
pranksome **27.15.20(.15)**
prankster **17.12.24(.20)**
prase **35.4**
praseodymium **27.3.7**
prat **22.7**
prate **22.4**
prater **17.12.4**
pratfall **40.10.11**
pratie **1.10.3**
pratincole **40.18.7**

pratique **24.1.3**
Pratt **22.7**
prattle **40.21.5**
prattler **17.34.21**
prau **16.3**
Pravda **17.13.21**
prawn **28.11**
praxes **35.1.16(.14)**
praxis **34.2.17(.14)**
Praxiteles **35.1.23**
pray **4**
prayer **6, 17.2**
prayerbook **24.14.3**
prayerful **40.27.6**
prayerfully **1.31.17(.16.1)**
prayerfulness **34.18.16(.37.2)**
prayerless **34.18.29(.6)**
preach **38.1**
preachable **40.20.16(.24)**
preacher **17.28.1**
preachify **14.14.4(.12)**
preachiness **34.18.16(.2.8)**
preaching **29.1.27**
preachment **22.26.15(.13.6)**
preachy **1.25.1**
pre-adamite **22.16.13**
pre-adolescence **34.24.10(.18)**
pre-adolescent **22.26.15(.17.2)**
preamble **40.20.19**
preambular **17.34.16(.21.1)**
preamp **20.16.3**
preamplified **23.15.9**
preamplifier **17.6.9(.4)**
preamplify **14.14.4(.16)**
prearrange **39.17.2**
prearrangement **22.26.15(.13.6)**
preatomic **24.2.14(.6)**
prebend **23.24.16(.2)**
prebendal **40.22.16**
prebendary **1.29.11(.9)**
prebendaryship **20.2.7(.2)**
pre-book **24.14.3**
pre-bookable **40.20.16(.13)**
Precambrian **28.3.20(.10)**
precancerous **34.18.27(.23)**
precancerously **1.31.33(.12.5)**
precarious **34.3.15(.3)**
precariously **1.31.33(.1.4)**
precariousness **34.18.16(.31.1)**

precast **22.29.6(.5), 22.29.8(.3)**
precative **31.2.1(.9.1)**
precatory **1.29.11(.8.6)**
precaution **28.17.25(.8)**
precautionary **1.29.11(.13.2)**
precede **23.1.7**
precedence **34.24.10(.11)**
precedency **1.22.23(.10.2)**
precedent **22.26.15(.10)**
precedented **23.18.9(.19)**
precedently **1.31.22(.20.2)**
precent **22.26.4(.11)**
precentor **17.12.22(.3)**
precentorship **20.2.7(.9)**
precentrices **35.1.16(.10)**
precentrix **34.23.2(.12)**
precept **22.22.3**
preceptive **31.2.1(.12)**
preceptor **17.12.19**
preceptorial **40.3.14(.5)**
preceptorship **20.2.7(.9)**
preceptress **34.18.27(.14)**
precession **28.17.25(.4)**
precessional **40.26.13(.14.3)**
precinct **22.23.13**
preciosity **1.10.16(.16.2)**
precious **34.18.22(.4)**
preciously **1.31.33(.12.4)**
preciousness **34.18.16(.31.4)**
precipice **34.2.6**
precipitability **1.10.16(.22.3)**
precipitable **40.20.16(.11.3)**
precipitance **34.24.10(.10)**
precipitancy **1.22.23(.10.2)**
precipitant **22.26.15(.9)**
precipitantly **1.31.22(.20.2)**
precipitate **22.4.9(.5), 22.19.10**
precipitately **1.31.22(.15)**
precipitateness **34.18.16(.20.3)**
precipitation **28.17.25(.3.3)**
precipitator **17.12.4(.5)**
precipitin **28.2.11(.10)**
precipitous **34.18.11(.10)**
precipitously **1.31.33(.12.2)**
precipitousness **34.18.16(.31.3)**
precis **2.22.3**
precise **34.15.8**

precisely **1.31.33(.9)**
preciseness **34.18.16(.31.2)**
precisian **28.17.26(.2)**
precisianism **27.15.21(.2.9)**
precision **28.17.26(.2)**
precisionism **27.15.21(.2.9)**
precisionist **22.29.2(.18.3)**
preclassical **40.23.12(.15)**
preclinical **40.23.12(.11)**
preclude **23.17.5**
preclusion **28.17.26(.4)**
preclusive **31.2.4(.8)**
precocial **40.33.11**
precocious **34.18.22(.9)**
precociously **1.31.33(.12.4)**
precociousness **34.18.16(.31.4)**
precocity **1.10.16(.16.2)**
precognition **28.17.25(.2.4)**
precognitive **31.2.1(.9.2)**
pre-coital **40.21.12**
pre-coitally **1.31.17(.9.2)**
pre-Columbian **28.3.2**
precompensation **28.17.25(.3.10)**
preconceive **31.1.4**
preconception **28.17.25(.14)**
preconcert **22.20.10**
precondition **28.17.25(.2.3)**
preconization **28.17.25(.3.11)**
preconize **35.15.12(.5)**
preconscious **34.18.22(.12)**
preconsciousness **34.18.16(.31.4)**
precook **24.14.5**
pre-cool **40.15.4**
precordial **40.3.4**
precostal **40.21.18**
precursive **31.2.4(.10)**
precursor **17.24.16**
precursory **1.29.11(.18)**
pre-cut **22.15.4**
predacious **34.18.22(.3)**
predaciousness **34.18.16(.31.4)**
predacity **1.10.16(.16.1)**
pre-date **22.4.10**
predate **22.4.10**
predation **28.17.25(.3.4)**
predator **17.12.16(.6)**
predatorily **1.31.17(.27.1)**
predatoriness **34.18.16(.2.9)**

prep **20.4**
prepack **24.6.5**
prepackage **39.2.12**
preparation
28.17.25(.3.13)
preparative **31.2.1(.9.4)**
preparatively
1.31.30(.7.1)
preparatorily
1.31.17(.27.1)
preparatory **1.29.11(.8.9)**
prepare **6.2**
preparedness
34.18.16(.21.1)
preparer **17.32.5**
prepay **4.7**
pre-payable **40.20.16(.2)**
prepayment
22.26.15(.13.1)
prepense **34.24.3**
prepensely **1.31.33(.16)**
pre-plan **28.7.22**
preponderance
34.24.10(.16)
preponderant
22.26.15(.23.3)
preponderantly
1.31.22(.20.5)
preponderate **22.4.22(.6)**
prepose **35.20.1**
pre-position
28.17.25(.2.5)
preposition **28.17.25(.2.5)**
prepositional
40.26.13(.14.1)
prepositionally
1.31.17(.14.3)
prepositive **31.2.1(.9.3)**
prepossess **34.5.10**
prepossession
28.17.25(.4)
preposterous
34.18.27(.14)
preposterously
1.31.33(.12.5)
preposterousness
34.18.16(.31.5)
prepotence **34.24.10(.10)**
prepotency **1.22.23(.10.2)**
prepotent **22.26.15(.9)**
preppie **1.8.4**
preppy **1.8.4**
preprandial **40.3.4**
pre-preference
34.24.10(.16)
preprint **22.26.1**
preprocess **34.5.9**
pre-processor **17.24.5**
pre-production
28.17.25(.15.5)
preprofessional
40.26.13(.14.3)

pre-programme
27.15.26(.13)
pre-pubertal **40.21.12**
pre-puberty **1.10.16(.7)**
prepubescence
34.24.10(.18)
prepubescent
22.26.15(.17.2)
pre-publication
28.17.25(.3.5)
prepuce **34.17.13**
preputial **40.33.8**
prequel **40.35.3**
Pre-Raphaelism
27.15.21(.2.15)
Pre-Raphaelite
22.16.25(.3)
Pre-Raphaelitism
27.15.21(.2.4)
prerecord **23.12.4**
preregister **17.12.24(.14)**
preregistration
28.17.25(.3.13)
prerequisite **22.2.17**
pre-revolutionary
1.29.11(.13.2)
prerogative **31.2.1(.9.1)**
presage **39.2.19**
presager **17.29.13**
presbyopia **3.2.7**
presbyopic **24.2.8(.5)**
presbyter **17.12.16(.4)**
presbyteral
40.16.13(.12.1)
presbyterate **22.19.24(.9)**
presbyterial **40.3.14(.2)**
Presbyterian **28.3.20(.2)**
Presbyterianism
27.15.21(.2.9)
presbytership **20.2.7(.9)**
presbytery **1.29.11(.8.6)**
preschool **40.15.4**
pre-schooler **17.34.15**
prescience **34.24.2**
prescient **22.26.2(.7)**
presciently **1.31.22(.20.1)**
prescind **23.24.2**
Prescot **22.19.12(.14)**
Prescott **22.11.6,
22.19.12(.14)**
prescribe **21.12**
prescribed **23.21**
prescriber **17.11.11**
prescript **22.22.1**
prescription **28.17.25(.14)**
prescriptive **31.2.1(.12)**
prescriptively
1.31.30(.7.2)
prescriptiveness
34.18.16(.28.1)
prescriptivism
27.15.21(.2.11)

prescriptivist **22.29.2(.20)**
pre-season **28.17.24(.1)**
Preseli **1.31.5**
presence **34.24.10(.19)**
present **22.26.4(.12),
22.26.15(.18)**
presentability
1.10.16(.22.2)
presentable
40.20.16(.11.6)
presentableness
34.18.16(.37.4)
presentably **1.31.21(.4.3)**
presentation
28.17.25(.3.3)
presentational
40.26.13(.14.2)
presentationally
1.31.17(.14.3)
presentationism
27.15.21(.2.9)
presentationist
22.29.2(.18.2)
presentative **31.2.1(.9.1)**
present-day **4.10**
presentee **2.11**
presenter **17.12.22(.3)**
presentient **22.26.15(.19)**
presentiment
22.26.15(.13.2)
presently **1.31.22(.20.4)**
presentment
22.26.15(.13.3)
presentness
34.18.16(.20.4)
preservable **40.20.16(.19)**
preservation
28.17.25(.3.9)
preservationist
22.29.2(.18.2)
preservative **31.2.1(.9.3)**
preserve **31.11**
preserver **17.21.13**
preset **22.5.13**
preshrunk **24.19.7**
preside **23.15.12**
presidency **1.22.23(.10.2)**
president **22.26.15(.10)**
president-elect
22.23.4(.11)
presidential **40.33.12(.3)**
presidentially
1.31.17(.22)
presidentship **20.2.8**
presidiary **1.29.2(.3)**
presidio **15.1.3**
Presidium **27.3.4(.2)**
Presley **1.31.34**
presoak **24.18.9**
pre-Socratic **24.2.10(.4.5)**
press **34.5**
pressboard **23.12.2(.15)**

Pressburg **26.14.1(.10)**
pressgang **29.4.6**
pressing **29.1.23**
pressingly **1.31.28(.1.11)**
pressman **28.7.10(.20),
28.17.16(.29)**
pressmark **24.8.8**
pressmen **28.5.7(.24)**
pressroom **27.14.6(.17)**
pressrun **28.13.9**
press-up **20.9.12**
pressure **17.26.4**
pressurization
28.17.25(.3.11)
pressurize **35.15.20(.2)**
Prestatyn **28.2.11(.5)**
Prestcold **23.31.13(.4)**
Presteigne **28.1.9(.7)**
Prestel® **40.5.3**
Prester **17.12.24(.4)**
prestidigitation
28.17.25(.3.3)
prestidigitator
17.12.4(.5)
prestige **37.1, 39.1**
prestigeful **40.27.28,
40.27.30**
prestigious **34.18.24**
prestigiously
1.31.33(.12.4)
prestigiousness
34.18.16(.31.5)
prestissimo **19.14.12**
presto **19.10.19**
Preston **28.17.11(.25)**
Prestonpans **35.26.7**
prestressed **22.29.5(.12)**
Prestwich **38.2.9**
Prestwick **24.2.25**
presumable **40.20.16(.15)**
presumably **1.31.21(.6)**
presume **27.14.7**
presumedly **1.31.23(.14.6)**
presumingly **1.31.28(.1.7)**
presumingness
34.18.16(.26)
presumption
28.17.25(.14)
presumptive **31.2.1(.12)**
presumptively
1.31.30(.7.2)
presumptuous **34.18.6**
presumptuously
1.31.33(.12.1)
presumptuousness
34.18.16(.31.2)
presuppose **35.20.1**
presupposition
28.17.25(.2.5)
prêt-à-porter **4.9.5**
pretax **34.23.5(.3)**

p

preteen 28.1.9
pretence 34.24.3
pretend 23.24.5(.4)
pretender 17.13.20(.3)
pretense 34.24.3
pretension 28.17.25(.16)
pretentious 34.18.22(.12)
pretentiously 1.31.33(.12.4)
pretentiousness 34.18.16(.31.4)
preterhuman 28.17.16(.15)
preterite 22.19.24(.9)
preterition 28.17.25(.2.6)
pre-term 27.16.2
pretermission 28.17.25(.2.4)
pretermit 22.2.11
preternatural 40.16.13(.12.3)
preternaturalism 27.15.21(.2.15)
preternaturally 1.31.17(.27.2)
preternaturalness 34.18.16(.37.3)
pretest 22.29.5(.2)
pretext 22.29.20
pretone 28.19.4
pretonic 24.2.15(.6.1)
pretor 12.5.1
Pretoria 3.22.9
pretorian 28.3.20(.7)
pretreat 22.1.17
pretreatment 22.26.15(.13.3)
pretrial 40.16.6
prettification 28.17.25(.3.5)
prettifier 17.6.9(.4)
prettify 14.14.4(.4)
prettily 1.31.17(.9.1)
prettiness 34.18.16(.2.3)
pretty 1.10.2
prettyish 36.2.1
prettyism 27.15.21(.2.1)
pretty-pretty 1.10.2
pretzel 40.31.16
prevail 40.4.9
prevailingly 1.31.28(.1.18)
prevalence 34.24.10(.24)
prevalent 22.26.15(.25)
prevalently 1.31.22(.20.5)
prevaricate 22.4.11(.6)
prevarication 28.17.25(.3.5)
prevaricator 17.12.4(.7)
prevenient 22.26.2(.5)

preveniently 1.31.22(.20.1)
prevent 22.26.4(.10)
preventability 1.10.16(.22.2)
preventable 40.20.16(.11.6)
preventative 31.2.1(.9.1)
preventatively 1.31.30(.7.1)
preventer 17.12.22(.3)
prevention 28.17.25(.16)
preventive 31.2.1(.14)
preventively 1.31.30(.7.3)
preverbal 40.20.17
preverbally 1.31.17(.8)
preview 16.24.12
Previn 28.2.20
previous 34.3.8
previously 1.31.33(.1.3)
previousness 34.18.16(.31.1)
previse 35.15.14
prevision 28.17.26(.2)
previsional 40.26.13(.14.8)
prevocalic 24.2.27(.6)
pre-vocational 40.26.13(.14.2)
prevue 16.24.12
prewar 12.20
pre-wash 36.9.5
prex 34.23.4
prexy 1.22.22
prey 4
preyer 17.2
prezzie 1.23.4
Priam 27.6.2, 27.15.3
priapic 24.2.8(.3)
priapism 27.15.21(.2.2)
Priapus 34.18.9(.3)
price 34.15
priceless 34.18.29(.33)
pricelessly 1.31.33(.12.6)
pricelessness 34.18.16(.31.6)
pricer 17.24.13
pricey 1.22.13
priciness 34.18.16(.2.7)
prick 24.2
pricker 17.14.2
pricket 22.2.9(.1)
prickle 40.23.2
prickliness 34.18.16(.2.10)
prickly 1.31.17(.11), 1.31.24(.2)
pricy 1.22.13
pride 23.15
prideful 40.27.19
pridefully 1.31.17(.16.2)
prideless 34.18.29(.23)

prie-dieu 18.16
prie-dieux 18.16, 35.19
priest 22.29.1
priestcraft 22.27.4(.4)
priestess 34.5.2, 34.18.11(.16)
priesthole 40.18.13
priesthood 23.16.5(.6)
priest-in-charge 39.8
Priestland 23.24.16(.16.3)
priestless 34.18.29(.22)
Priestley 1.31.22(.22)
priestlike 24.13.7(.12)
priestliness 34.18.16(.2.10)
priestling 29.1.31(.17)
priestly 1.31.22(.22)
prig 26.2
priggery 1.29.11(.11)
priggish 36.2.14
priggishly 1.31.35(.7.1)
priggishness 34.18.16(.33.4)
priggism 27.15.21(.2.7)
prim 27.2
prima ballerina 17.18.1(.15)
primacy 1.22.16(.8)
prima donna 17.18.9
prima donna-ish 36.2.7
prima facie 2.3, 2.24
prima inter pares 35.1.22
primal 40.25.8
primally 1.31.17(.13)
primarily 1.31.17(.27.1)
primary 1.29.11(.12)
primate 22.4.13(.5), 22.19.14
primateship 20.2.7(.14)
primatial 40.33.2
primatologist 22.29.2(.26.3)
primatology 1.26.10(.11.2)
primavera 17.32.5
prime 27.12
primeness 34.18.16(.24)
primer 17.17.11
primeval 40.28.1
primevally 1.31.17(.17)
primigravida 17.13.15
primigravidae 2.13
primipara 17.32.14(.4)
primiparae 2.30.7, 2.30.8
primiparous 34.18.27(.12)
primitive 31.2.1(.9.2)
primitively 1.31.30(.7.1)
primitiveness 34.18.16(.28.1)

primitivism 27.15.21(.2.11)
primitivist 22.29.2(.20)
primly 1.31.26(.2)
primness 34.18.16(.24)
primo 19.14.1
primogenital 40.21.12
primogenitary 1.29.11(.8.7)
primogenitor 17.12.16(.10)
primogeniture 17.28.15
primordia 3.5.6
primordial 40.3.4
primordiality 1.10.16(.32.1)
primordially 1.31.3(.4)
primordium 27.3.4(.7)
primp 20.16.1
primrose 35.20.12
primula 17.34.16(.21.4)
primum mobile 1.31.17(.8)
primus 34.18.15(.8)
primus inter pares 35.1.22
prince 34.24.1
princedom 27.15.10(.17)
princelike 24.13.7(.22)
princeliness 34.18.16(.2.10)
princeling 29.1.31(.26)
princely 1.31.33(.16)
princeship 20.2.7(.22)
princess 34.5.9, 34.18.20
Princeton 28.17.11(.25)
Princetown 28.8.1
principal 40.19.11
principality 1.10.16(.32.2)
principally 1.31.17(.7), 1.31.20
principalship 20.2.7(.24)
principate 22.19.8
Príncipe 1.8.11(.7), 4.7
Principia 3.2.2
principle 40.19.11
Pringle 40.24.14(.1)
prink 24.19.1
Prinknash 39.2.15
print 22.26.1
printability 1.10.16(.22.1)
printable 40.20.16(.11.6)
printer 17.12.22(.1)
printery 1.29.11(.8.12)
printhead 23.5.13(.9)
printing 29.1.12(.19)
printless 34.18.29(.22)
printmaker 17.14.3(.3)
printmaking 29.1.14(.3)
printout 22.9.7
printwheel 40.1.14

printworks **34.23.16**
prion **28.10.1, 28.17.5**
prior **17.6**
priorate **22.19.24(.9)**
prioress **34.5.14,**
34.18.27(.11)
prioritization
28.17.25(.3.11)
prioritize **35.15.7(.7)**
priority **1.10.16(.21.2)**
priorship **20.2.7(.9)**
priory **1.29.11(.2)**
Priscian **28.3.15,**
28.17.25(.2.1)
Priscilla **17.34.2(.9)**
prise **35.15**
prism **27.15.21(.2.1)**
prismal **40.25.14**
prismatic **24.2.10(.4.2)**
prismatically
1.31.24(.9.4)
prismoid **23.13.11**
prismoidal **40.22.9**
prison **28.17.24(.2)**
prisoner **17.18.16(.15)**
prissily **1.31.17(.20)**
prissiness **34.18.16(.2.7)**
prissy **1.22.2**
Pristina **17.18.16(.4)**
pristine **28.1.9(.7)**
Pritchard **23.9.18, 23.18.24**
Pritchett **22.19.21**
prithee **2.21**
Pritt **22.2**
privacy **1.22.16(.11)**
private **22.19.17**
privateer **3.4**
privateering **29.1.30(.2)**
privateersman
28.17.16(.30)
privately **1.31.22(.15)**
privation **28.17.25(.3.9)**
privative **31.2.1(.9.3)**
privatively **1.31.30(.7.1)**
privatization
28.17.25(.3.11)
privatize **35.15.7(.7)**
privatizer **17.25.12(.2)**
privet **22.2.14**
privilege **39.2.23**
privileged **23.30**
privily **1.31.17(.17)**
privity **1.10.16(.15)**
privy **1.19.2**
prix **2, 35.1**
prix fixe **34.23.2**
Prix Goncourt **17.7.5**
prize **35.15**
prizefight **22.16.16**
prizefighter **17.12.13(.5)**
prizefighting **29.1.12(.11)**

prizeman **28.17.16(.30)**
prizewinner **17.18.2**
prizewinning **29.1.17(.2)**
PRO **19**
pro **19**
proa **17.9**
proaction **28.17.25(.15.3)**
proactive **31.2.1(.13.3)**
proactively **1.31.30(.7.2)**
proactivity **1.10.16(.15)**
pro-am **27.6**
probabilism
27.15.21(.2.15)
probabilist **22.29.2(.31.2)**
probabilistic
24.2.10(.15.3)
probability **1.10.16(.22.1)**
probable **40.20.16(.10)**
probably **1.31.21(.3)**
proband **23.24.6(.4),**
23.24.16(.2)
probang **29.4.2**
probate **22.4.8**
probation **28.17.25(.3.2)**
probational
40.26.13(.14.2)
probationary
1.29.11(.13.2)
probationer **17.18.16(.16)**
probationership
20.2.7(.9)
probative **31.2.1(.9.1)**
probe **21.16**
probeable **40.20.16(.10)**
prober **17.11.15**
probing **29.1.11**
probingly **1.31.28(.1.3)**
probit **22.2.6**
probity **1.10.16(.7)**
problem **27.15.28(.15)**
problematic **24.2.10(.4.2)**
problematical
40.23.12(.7.1)
problematically
1.31.24(.9.4)
problematization
28.17.25(.3.12)
problematize **35.15.7(.7)**
probosces **35.1.16(.6)**
proboscidean **28.3.4(.2)**
proboscidiferous
34.18.27(.20)
proboscidiform
27.10.5(.2)
proboscis **34.2.17(.6)**
Probyn **28.2.10**
procain **28.4.5**
procaine **28.4.5**
procaryote **22.17**
procaryotic **24.2.10(.6)**
Procea **3.14.11**

procedural **40.16.13(.12.3)**
procedurally
1.31.17(.27.2)
procedure **17.29.1**
proceed **23.1.7**
proceedings **35.27**
proceeds **35.23.1**
process **34.5.9**
processable
40.20.16(.21.1)
procession **28.17.25(.4)**
processional
40.26.13(.14.3)
processionary
1.29.11(.13.2)
processionist
22.29.2(.18.2)
processor **17.24.5**
procès-verbal **40.8.3**
procès-verbaux **19.9**
pro-choice **34.13**
prochronism
27.15.21(.2.9)
proclaim **27.4.9**
proclaimer **17.17.4**
proclamation
28.17.25(.3.7)
proclamatory
1.29.11(.8.7)
proclitic **24.2.10(.2.5)**
proclitically **1.31.24(.9.3)**
proclivity **1.10.16(.15)**
Procne **1.16.21**
proconsul **40.31.21**
proconsular
17.34.16(.21.4)
proconsulate
22.19.26(.13)
proconsulship **20.2.7(.24)**
Procopius **34.3.1**
procrastinate
22.4.14(.9.1)
procrastination
28.17.25(.3.8)
procrastinative
31.2.1(.9.2)
procrastinator
17.12.4(.10)
procrastinatory
1.29.11(.8.7)
procreant **22.26.2(.9)**
procreate **22.4.2(.14)**
procreation **28.17.25(.3.1)**
procreative **31.2.1(.2)**
procreator **17.12.4(.1)**
Procrustean **28.3.3**
Procrustes **35.1.7(.10)**
Procter **17.12.21(.5)**
proctological
40.23.12(.17.2)
proctologist
22.29.2(.26.3)

proctology **1.26.10(.11.2)**
proctor **17.12.21(.5)**
proctorial **40.3.14(.5)**
proctorship **20.2.7(.9)**
proctoscope **20.15.4(.1)**
procumbent **22.26.15(.8)**
procurable **40.20.16(.27.2)**
procural **40.16.13(.11)**
procurance **34.24.10(.16)**
procuration
28.17.25(.3.13)
procurator **17.12.4(.15)**
procurator fiscal
40.23.16
procuratorial **40.3.14(.5)**
procurators fiscal
40.23.16
procuratorship **20.2.7(.9)**
procuratory **1.29.11(.8.9)**
procure **12.22, 17.7.12(.5)**
procurement
22.26.15(.13.1)
procurer **17.32.14(.3)**
procuress **34.5.14(.3),**
34.18.27(.8)
Procyon **28.3.13**
prod **23.10**
prodder **17.13.8**
prodigal **40.24.11**
prodigality **1.10.16(.32.6)**
prodigalize **35.15.21(.4.4)**
prodigally **1.31.17(.12)**
prodigalness
34.18.16(.37.5)
prodigious **34.18.24**
prodigiously
1.31.33(.12.4)
prodigiousness
34.18.16(.31.5)
prodigy **1.26.10(.3)**
prodromal **40.25.12**
prodrome **27.17.13**
prodromic **24.2.14(.6)**
produce **34.17.13**
producer **17.24.14**
producibility
1.10.16(.22.2)
producible **40.20.16(.21.2)**
product **22.23.8**
production
28.17.25(.15.5)
productional
40.26.13(.14.6)
productive **31.2.1(.13.4)**
productively **1.31.30(.7.2)**
productiveness
34.18.16(.28.1)
productivity **1.10.16(.15)**
proem **27.5.3**
proemial **40.3.6**
Prof. **30.8**

profanation 28.17.25(.3.8)
profane 28.4.9
profanely 1.31.27(.4)
profaneness 34.18.16(.25)
profaner 17.18.3
profanity 1.10.16(.13)
profess 34.5.7
professedly 1.31.23(.14.7)
profession 28.17.25(.4)
professional
40.26.13(.14.3)
professionalism
27.15.21(.2.15)
professionalization
28.17.25(.3.12)
professionalize
35.15.21(.4.5)
professionally
1.31.17(.14.3)
professionless
34.18.29(.27)
professor 17.24.5
professorate 22.19.24(.9)
professorial 40.3.14(.5)
professorially 1.31.3(.11)
professoriate 22.3.12
professorship 20.2.7(.9)
proffer 17.20.7
proficiency 1.22.23(.10.4)
proficient 22.26.15(.19)
proficiently 1.31.22(.20.4)
profile 40.13.9
profiler 17.34.13
profilist 22.29.2(.31.1)
profit 22.2.13
profitability
1.10.16(.22.2)
profitable 40.20.16(.11.3)
profitableness
34.18.16(.37.4)
profitably 1.31.21(.4.2)
profiteer 3.4
profiterole 40.18.14
profitless 34.18.29(.22)
profligacy 1.22.16(.7)
profligately 22.19.13
profligately 1.31.22(.15)
profligateness
34.18.16(.20.3)
pro-forma 17.17.9
profound 23.24.7(.5)
profoundly 1.31.23(.17)
profoundness
34.18.16(.21.1)
Profumo 19.14.11
profundity 1.10.16(.9)
profuse 34.17.13
profusely 1.31.33(.11)
profuseness
34.18.16(.31.2)
profusion 28.17.26(.4)

prog 26.7
progenitive 31.2.1(.9.2)
progenitor 17.12.16(.10)
progenitorial 40.3.14(.5)
progenitorship 20.2.7(.9)
progenitress 34.5.14(.5),
34.18.27(.14)
progenitrices 35.1.16(.10)
progenitrix 34.23.2(.12)
progeniture 17.28.15
progeny 1.16.15(.17)
progesterone 28.19.17
progestogen 28.17.28(.9)
proglottid 23.2.8
proglottis 34.2.8
prognathic 24.2.18(.3)
prognathism
27.15.21(.2.12)
prognathous 34.18.19
prognoses 35.1.16(.11)
prognosis 34.2.17(.11.2)
prognostic 24.2.10(.15.4)
prognosticable
40.20.16(.13)
prognostically
1.31.24(.9.6)
prognosticate 22.4.11(.6)
prognostication
28.17.25(.3.5)
prognosticative
31.2.1(.9.1)
prognosticator
17.12.4(.7)
prognosticatory
1.29.11(.8.6)
program 27.6.17(.5)
programmability
1.10.16(.22.2)
programmable
40.20.16(.15)
programmatic
24.2.10(.4.2)
programmatically
1.31.24(.9.4)
programme 27.6.17(.5)
programmer 17.17.6
progress 34.5.14(.8)
progression 28.17.25(.4)
progressional
40.26.13(.14.3)
progressionist
22.29.2(.18.2)
progressive 31.2.4(.4)
progressively
1.31.30(.7.4)
progressiveness
34.18.16(.28.2)
progressivism
27.15.21(.2.11)
progressivist 22.29.2(.20)
pro hac vice 1.22.13
prohibit 22.2.6

prohibiter 17.12.16(.4)
prohibition 28.17.25(.2.1)
prohibitionary
1.29.11(.13.2)
prohibitionism
27.15.21(.2.9)
prohibitionist
22.29.2(.18.2)
prohibitive 31.2.1(.9.1)
prohibitively
1.31.30(.7.1)
prohibitiveness
34.18.16(.28.1)
prohibitor 17.12.16(.4)
prohibitory 1.29.11(.8.6)
project 22.23.4(.9)
projectile 40.13.3(.8)
projection 28.17.25(.15.2)
projectionist
22.29.2(.18.2)
projective 31.2.1(.13.2)
projectively 1.31.30(.7.2)
projector 17.12.21(.2)
prokaryote 22.11.1, 22.17
prokaryotic 24.2.10(.6)
Prokofiev 30.4
prolactin 28.2.11(.12)
prolapse 34.21.5
prolapsus 34.18.20
prolate 22.4.23
prolately 1.31.22(.4)
prolative 31.2.1(.3)
prole 40.18
proleg 26.4
prolegomena 17.18.16(.8)
prolegomenary
1.29.11(.13.2)
prolegomenon
28.17.17(.10)
prolegomenous
34.18.16(.15.3)
prolepses 35.1.16(.12)
prolepsis 34.2.17(.12)
proleptic 24.2.10(.12)
proletarian 28.3.20(.4)
proletarianism
27.15.21(.2.9)
proletarianization
28.17.25(.3.12)
proletarianize
35.15.12(.3)
proletariat 22.3.12
pro-life 30.12
proliferate 22.4.22(.6)
proliferation
28.17.25(.3.13)
proliferative 31.2.1(.9.4)
proliferator 17.12.4(.15)
proliferous 34.18.27(.20)
prolific 24.2.16(.1)
prolificacy 1.22.16(.6)

prolifically 1.31.24(.9.9)
prolificity 1.10.16(.16.1)
prolificness 34.18.16(.22)
proline 28.1.27(.8)
prolix 34.23.2(.13)
prolixity 1.10.16(.16.3)
prolixly 1.31.33(.15)
prolocutor 17.12.16(.19)
prolocutorship 20.2.7(.9)
PROLOG 26.7.14
prologize 35.15.10
prologue 26.7.14
prolong 29.6.15
prolongation
28.17.25(.3.6)
prolonger 17.19.3
prolusion 28.17.26(.4)
prolusory 1.29.11(.19)
prom 27.9
promenade 23.9.12
promenader 17.13.7
promethazine 28.1.19
Promethean 28.3.11
Prometheus 34.3.9
promethium 27.3.10
prominence 34.24.10(.15)
prominency
1.22.23(.10.3)
prominent 22.26.15(.14)
prominenti 1.10.23(.3),
2.12.14
prominently
1.31.22(.20.3)
promiscuity 1.10.16(.5)
promiscuous 34.18.6
promiscuously
1.31.33(.12.1)
promiscuousness
34.18.16(.31.2)
promise 34.2.12
promisee 2.22
promiser 17.24.15
promisingly
1.31.28(.1.11)
promisor 17.24.15
promissory 1.29.11(.18)
prommer 17.17.8
promo 19.14.14
promontory
1.29.11(.8.12)
promotability
1.10.16(.22.2)
promotable
40.20.16(.11.3)
promote 22.21.7
promoter 17.12.18
promotion 28.17.25(.13)
promotional
40.26.13(.14.5)
promotive 31.2.1(.11)
prompt 22.25

p

prospect **22.23.4(.1)**
prospective **31.2.1(.13.2)**
prospectively **1.31.30(.7.2)**
prospectiveness **34.18.16(.28.1)**
prospectless **34.18.29(.22)**
prospector **17.12.21(.2)**
prospectus **34.18.11(.13)**
prosper **17.10.18**
prosperity **1.10.16(.21.1)**
Prospero **19.27.11, 19.27.13**
prosperous **34.18.27(.12)**
prosperously **1.31.33(.12.5)**
prosperousness **34.18.16(.31.5)**
Prosser **17.24.9**
Prost **22.29.9**
prostaglandin **28.2.12**
prostate **22.4.9(.9)**
prostatectomy **1.15.13(.1)**
prostatic **24.2.10(.4.1)**
prosthesis **34.2.17(.1)**
prosthetic **24.2.10(.3.2)**
prosthetically **1.31.24(.9.3)**
prostitute **22.18.10**
prostitution **28.17.25(.11)**
prostitutional **40.26.13(.14.5)**
prostitutor **17.12.15(.5)**
prostrate **22.4.22(.8)**
prostration **28.17.25(.3.13)**
prostyle **40.13.3(.10)**
prosy **1.23.15**
protactinium **27.3.8(.2)**
protagonist **22.29.2(.18.1)**
Protagoras **34.7.18, 34.18.27(.17)**
protamine **28.1.13**
protandrous **34.18.27(.15)**
protanope **20.15.5**
protanopia **3.2.7**
protases **35.1.16(.10)**
protasis **34.2.17(.10.2)**
protatic **24.2.10(.4.1)**
protea **3.4.11**
protean **28.3.3, 28.17.1(.3)**
protease **34.4.1, 35.4.1**
protect **22.23.4(.2)**
protectant **22.26.15(.9)**
protection **28.17.25(.15.2)**
protectionism **27.15.21(.2.9)**
protectionist **22.29.2(.18.2)**
protective **31.2.1(.13.2)**

protectively **1.31.30(.7.2)**
protectiveness **34.18.16(.28.1)**
protector **17.12.21(.2)**
protectoral **40.16.13(.12.1)**
protectorate **22.19.24(.9)**
protectorship **20.2.7(.9)**
protectress **34.5.14(.5), 34.18.27(.14)**
protégé **4.21**
proteiform **27.10.5(.2)**
protein **28.1.9(.4)**
proteinaceous **34.18.22(.3)**
proteinic **24.2.15(.1)**
proteinous **34.18.16(.1)**
pro tem **27.5**
pro tempore **4.26.8, 4.26.9**
proteolyses **35.1.16(.10)**
proteolysis **34.2.17(.10.5)**
proteolytic **24.2.10(.2.5)**
Proterozoic **24.2.7**
protest **22.29.5(.2)**
Protestant **22.26.15(.9)**
Protestantism **27.15.21(.2.4)**
Protestantize **35.15.7(.8)**
protestation **28.17.25(.3.3)**
protester **17.12.24(.4)**
protestingly **1.31.28(.1.4)**
protestor **17.12.24(.4)**
Proteus **34.3.3**
prothalamia **3.8.3**
prothalamion **28.3.7**
prothalamium **27.3.7**
prothalli **2.32.6, 14.25.6**
prothallia **3.24.5**
prothallium **27.3.18**
prothallus **34.18.29(.7)**
Prothero **19.27.11**
Protheroe **19.27.11**
protheses **35.1.16(.10)**
prothesis **34.2.17(.10.4)**
prothetic **24.2.10(.3.2)**
prothetically **1.31.24(.9.3)**
prothonotary **1.29.11(.8.7)**
protist **22.29.2(.13)**
protistology **1.26.10(.11.2)**
protium **27.3.3**
protocol **40.9.9**
protogynous **34.18.16(.15.3)**
protomartyr **17.12.8(.7)**
proton **28.10.9**
protonate **22.4.14(.9.1)**
protonic **24.2.15(.6.1)**

protonotary **1.29.11(.8.7)**
protopectin **28.2.11(.12)**
protophyte **22.16.16**
protoplasm **27.15.21(.3)**
protoplasmal **40.25.14**
protoplasmatic **24.2.10(.4.2)**
protoplasmic **24.2.14(.17)**
protoplast **22.29.6(.12)**
protoplastic **24.2.10(.15.4)**
prototheria **3.22.2**
prototherian **28.3.20(.2)**
prototypal **40.19.9**
prototype **20.10.2**
prototypic **24.2.8(.1)**
prototypical **40.23.12(.5)**
prototypically **1.31.24(.9.2)**
protozoa **17.9.9**
protozoal **40.16.9**
protozoan **28.17.8**
protozoic **24.2.7**
protozoology **1.26.10(.11.1)**
protozoon **28.10.6, 28.17.8**
protract **22.23.5(.9)**
protracted **23.18.9(.17)**
protractedly **1.31.23(.14.3)**
protractedness **34.18.16(.21.1)**
protractile **40.13.3(.8)**
protraction **28.17.25(.15.3)**
protractor **17.12.21(.3)**
protrude **23.17.3**
protrudent **22.26.15(.10)**
protrusible **40.20.16(.21.2)**
protrusile **40.13.12**
protrusion **28.17.26(.4)**
protrusive **31.2.4(.8)**
protrusively **1.31.30(.7.4)**
protrusiveness **34.18.16(.28.2)**
protuberance **34.24.10(.16)**
protuberant **22.26.15(.23.3)**
protuberantly **1.31.22(.20.5)**
proud **23.8**
Proudhon **28.10.10**
proudly **1.31.23(.6)**
proudness **34.18.16(.21.1)**
Proust **22.29.14**
Prout **22.9**
provability **1.10.16(.22.1)**
provable **40.20.16(.19)**

provableness **34.18.16(.37.4)**
provably **1.31.21(.7.1)**
prove **31.10**
proven **28.17.20(.9)**
provenance **34.24.10(.15)**
Provençal **40.8.11**
Provence **34.11, 34.24.6**
provender **17.13.20(.13)**
provenience **34.24.2**
pro-verb **21.15**
proverb **21.15**
proverbial **40.3.2**
proverbiality **1.10.16(.32.1)**
proverbially **1.31.3(.2)**
Proverbs **35.21**
provide **23.15.10**
providence **34.24.10(.11)**
provident **22.26.15(.10)**
providential **40.33.12(.3)**
providentially **1.31.17(.22)**
providently **1.31.22(.20.2)**
provider **17.13.12**
province **34.24.1**
provincial **40.33.12(.1)**
provincialism **27.15.21(.2.15)**
provincialist **22.29.2(.31.4)**
provinciality **1.10.16(.32.1)**
provincialize **35.15.21(.4.6)**
provincially **1.31.17(.22)**
provision **28.17.26(.2)**
provisional **40.26.13(.14.8)**
provisionality **1.10.16(.32.8)**
provisionally **1.31.17(.14.3)**
provisionalness **34.18.16(.37.1)**
provisioner **17.18.16(.17)**
provisionless **34.18.29(.27)**
provisionment **22.26.15(.13.4)**
proviso **19.21**
provisor **17.25.12(.8)**
provisorily **1.31.17(.27.2)**
provisory **1.29.11(.19)**
Provo **19.17**
provocateur **18.3**
provocation **28.17.25(.3.5)**
provocative **31.2.1(.9.1)**
provocatively **1.31.30(.7.1)**

provocativeness
34.18.16(.28.1)
provokable **40.20.16(.13)**
provoke **24.18.8**
provoker **17.14.17**
provokingly **1.31.28(.1.6)**
provost **22.29.9,**
22.29.15(.15)
provost-marshall
40.33.5
provostship **20.2.8**
prow **9**
prowess **34.5, 34.18.3**
prowl **40.7**
prowler **17.34.7**
Prowse **34.8, 35.8**
prox. **34.23.8**
proxemic **24.2.14(.1)**
Proxima Centauri
14.24.4
proximal **40.25.10**
proximally **1.31.17(.13)**
proximate **22.19.14**
proximately **1.31.22(.15)**
proxime accessit **22.2.16**
proximity **1.10.16(.12)**
proximo **19.14.12**
proxy **1.22.22**
Prozac® **24.6.15**
Pru **16**
prude **23.17**
prudence **34.24.10(.11)**
prudent **22.26.15(.10)**
prudential **40.33.12(.3)**
prudentialism
27.15.21(.2.15)
prudentialist
22.29.2(.31.4)
prudentially **1.31.17(.22)**
prudently **1.31.22(.20.2)**
prudery **1.29.11(.9)**
Prudhoe Bay **4**
prudish **36.2.12**
prudishly **1.31.35(.7.1)**
prudishness
34.18.16(.33.3)
Prue **16**
Prufrock **24.9.15**
pruinose **34.20.9**
Pruitt **22.2.4**
prune **28.16**
prunella **17.34.5(.8)**
pruner **17.18.15**
prurience **34.24.2**
pruriency **1.22.23(.2)**
prurient **22.26.2(.9)**
pruriently **1.31.22(.20.1)**
pruriginous
34.18.16(.15.3)
prurigo **19.13.7**
pruritic **24.2.10(.2.4)**

pruritis **34.18.11(.8)**
prusik **24.2.20(.9)**
Prussia **17.26.10**
Prussian **28.17.25(.9)**
prussic **24.2.20(.9)**
pry **14**
Pryce **34.15**
Pryde **23.15**
pryingly **1.31.28(.1.1)**
Prynne **28.2**
prytany **1.16.15(.7)**
Przewalski **1.12.17(.15)**
psalm **27.8**
psalmbook **24.14.3**
psalmic **24.2.14(.5)**
psalmist **22.29.2(.17)**
psalmodic **24.2.11(.7)**
psalmodist **22.29.2(.14)**
psalmodize **35.15.8**
psalmody **1.11.17**
psalter **17.12.26(.5)**
psalteria **3.22.2**
psalterium **27.3.17(.2)**
psaltery **1.29.11(.8.12)**
psephological
40.23.12(.17.2)
psephologically
1.31.24(.9.11)
psephologist
22.29.2(.26.4)
psephology
1.26.10(.11.5)
pseud **23.17**
pseudepigrapha
17.20.12(.5)
pseudepigraphal
40.27.14
pseudepigraphic
24.2.16(.3)
pseudepigraphical
40.23.12(.12)
pseudo **19.11.10**
pseudocarp **20.6**
pseudograph **30.7.5(.1)**
pseudomorph **30.9.2**
pseudomorphic
24.2.16(.5)
pseudomorphism
27.15.21(.2.10)
pseudomorphous
34.18.17
pseudonym **27.2.6**
pseudonymity
1.10.16(.12)
pseudonymous
34.18.15(.10)
pseudonymously
1.31.33(.12.3)
pseudopod **23.10.1**
pseudopodia **3.5.8**
pseudopodium
27.3.4(.8)

pseudo-science
34.24.10(.5)
pseudo-scientific
24.2.16(.1)
pshaw **12**
p.s.i. **14**
psi **14**
psilanthropic **24.2.8(.5)**
psilanthropism
27.15.21(.2.2)
psilanthropist
22.29.2(.11)
psilocybin **28.2.10**
psilosis **34.2.17(.11.2)**
Psion® **28.10.4**
psionic **24.2.15(.6.1)**
psionically **1.31.24(.9.8)**
psittacine **28.14.13**
psittacosis
34.2.17(.11.1)
psoae **14.5**
psoai **2.8**
psoas **34.7.4, 34.18.8**
psoriasis **34.2.17(.10.1)**
psoriatic **24.2.10(.4.1)**
psych **24.13**
psyche **1.12.10**
psychedelia **3.24.1**
psychedelic **24.2.27(.4)**
psychedelically
1.31.24(.9.12)
psychiatric **24.2.26(.14.3)**
psychiatrical
40.23.12(.18)
psychiatrically
1.31.24(.9.12)
psychiatrist **22.29.2(.29.5)**
psychiatry **1.29.15(.1)**
psychic **24.2.12**
psychical **40.23.12(.9)**
psychically **1.31.24(.9.7)**
psychicism
27.15.21(.2.12)
psychicist **22.29.2(.22)**
psycho **19.12.9**
psychoactive
31.2.1(.13.3)
psychoanalysis
34.2.17(.10.5)
psychoanalyst
22.29.2(.31.3)
psychoanalytic
24.2.10(.2.5)
psychoanalytical
40.23.12(.7.1)
psychoanalytically
1.31.24(.9.3)
psychoanalyse
35.15.21(.4.5)
psychobabble **40.20.6**
psychobiological
40.23.12(.17.2)

psychobiologist
22.29.2(.26.2)
psychobiology
1.26.10(.11.1)
psychodrama **17.17.7**
psychodynamic
24.2.14(.4)
psychodynamically
1.31.24(.9.8)
psychogenesis
34.2.17(.10.3)
psychogenic **24.2.15(.4)**
psychograph **30.7.5(.1)**
psychokinesis **34.2.17(.1)**
psychokinetic
24.2.10(.3.1)
psycholinguist
22.29.2(.28)
psycholinguistic
24.2.10(.15.2)
psychological
40.23.12(.17.2)
psychologically
1.31.24(.9.11)
psychologist
22.29.2(.26.3)
psychologize **35.15.18**
psychology **1.26.10(.11.3)**
psychometric
24.2.26(.14.2)
psychometrically
1.31.24(.9.12)
psychometrist
22.29.2(.29.5)
psychometry **1.29.15(.8)**
psychomotor **17.12.18**
psychoneuroses
35.1.16(.11)
psychoneurosis
34.2.17(.11.2)
psychoneurotic
24.2.10(.6)
psychopath **32.6.2**
psychopathic
24.2.18(.3)
psychopathically
1.31.24(.9.10)
psychopathological
40.23.12(.17.2)
psychopathology
1.26.10(.11.5)
psychopathy **1.20.8**
psychopharmacology
1.26.10(.11.3)
psychophysical
40.23.12(.16)
psychophysics
34.23.2(.11)
psychophysiological
40.23.12(.17.2)
psychophysiology
1.26.10(.11.1)
psychoses **35.1.16(.11)**

p

psychosexual **40.14.8, 40.16.10**

psychosexually **1.31.17(.22)**

psychosis **34.2.17(.11.1)**

psychosocial **40.33.11**

psychosocially **1.31.17(.22)**

psychosomatic **24.2.10(.4.2)**

psychosomatically **1.31.24(.9.4)**

psychosurgery **1.29.11(.23)**

psychosurgical **40.23.12(.17.3)**

psychotherapeutic **24.2.10(.9)**

psychotherapist **22.29.2(.11)**

psychotherapy **1.8.11(.8)**

psychotic **24.2.10(.6)**

psychotically **1.31.24(.9.4)**

psychotropic **24.2.8(.5)**

psychrometer **17.12.16(.9.2)**

psylla **17.34.2**

psyllid **23.2.23**

psyllium **27.3.18**

ptarmigan **28.17.15(.13)**

pteranodon **28.10.10, 28.17.12(.16)**

pteridological **40.23.12(.17.2)**

pteridologist **22.29.2(.26.3)**

pteridology **1.26.10(.11.2)**

pteridophyte **22.16.16**

pterodactyl **40.21.16**

pteropod **23.10.1**

pterosaur **12.14.8**

pterygoid process **34.5.9**

ptisan **28.7.15**

Ptolemaic **24.2.3**

Ptolemy **1.15.13(.12)**

ptomaine **28.4.7**

ptosed **23.28.4**

ptosis **34.2.17(.11.1)**

ptotic **24.2.10(.11)**

ptyalin **28.2.31(.10)**

pub **21.11**

pubcrawl **40.10.18**

pubertal **40.21.12**

puberty **1.10.16(.7)**

pubes **35.1.6**

pubescence **34.24.10(.18)**

pubescent **22.26.15(.17.2)**

pubic **24.2.9(.4)**

pubis **34.2.7**

public **24.2.27(.14)**

publically **1.31.24(.9.12)**

publican **28.17.13(.13)**

publication **28.17.25(.3.5)**

publicism **27.15.21(.2.12)**

publicist **22.29.2(.22)**

publicistic **24.2.10(.15.2)**

publicity **1.10.16(.16.1)**

publicize **35.15.16(.4)**

publicly **1.31.24(.9.12)**

publish **36.2.27**

publishable **40.20.16(.23)**

publisher **17.26.14**

Publius **34.3.16**

Puccini **1.16.1(.12)**

puccoon **28.16.5**

puce **34.17**

puck **24.12**

pucker **17.14.11**

puckery **1.29.11(.10)**

Puckett **22.2.9(.6)**

puckish **36.2.13**

puckishly **1.31.35(.7.1)**

puckishness **34.18.16(.33.4)**

pucklike **24.13.7(.14)**

pud **23.16**

pudding **29.1.13(.10)**

puddingy **1.17**

puddle **40.22.10**

puddler **17.34.22**

puddly **1.31.17(.10), 1.31.23(.10)**

puddock **24.16.5**

pudency **1.22.23(.10.2)**

pudenda **17.13.20(.3)**

pudendal **40.22.16**

pudendum **27.15.10(.14)**

pudeur **18.4**

pudge **39.11**

pudgily **1.31.17(.25)**

pudginess **34.18.16(.2.8)**

pudgy **1.26.8**

pudic **24.2.11(.11)**

Pudsey **1.23.18**

pudu **16.8.3**

Puebla **17.34.20**

pueblo **19.29.16**

puerile **40.13.16**

puerilely **1.31.38**

puerility **1.10.16(.31)**

puerperal **40.16.13(.12.1)**

Puerto Rican **28.17.13(.1)**

Puerto Rico **19.12.1**

puff **30.11**

puffball **40.10.4**

puffer **17.20.9**

puffery **1.29.11(.14)**

puffily **1.31.17(.16.1)**

puffin **28.2.19**

puffiness **34.18.16(.2.6)**

puff-puff **30.11.1**

puffy **1.18.7**

pug **26.10**

Puget Sound **23.24.7**

puggaree **1.29.11(.11)**

puggish **36.2.14**

puggy **1.14.8**

Pugh **16**

Pughe **16**

pugilism **27.15.21(.2.15)**

pugilist **22.29.2(.31.4)**

pugilistic **24.2.10(.15.3)**

Pugin **28.2.27**

pugnacious **34.18.22(.3)**

pugnaciously **1.31.33(.12.4)**

pugnaciousness **34.18.16(.31.4)**

pugnacity **1.10.16(.16.1)**

Pugwash **36.9.5**

puisne **1.16.14**

puissance **34.11, 34.24.10(.18)**

puissant **22.26.15(.17.1)**

puja **17.29.12**

puke **24.15**

pukeko **19.12.4**

pukey **1.12.12**

pukka **17.14.11**

puku **16.9**

pul **40.15**

pula **17.34.14**

pulao **9.17**

Pulaski **1.12.17(.3)**

Pulborough **17.32.14(.5)**

pulchritude **23.17.4(.1)**

pulchritudinous **34.18.16(.15.2)**

pule **40.15**

puli **1.31.16**

Pulitzer **17.24.19**

pull **40.14**

pullback **24.6.6(.23)**

pull-chain **28.4.15**

pulldown **28.8.2(.13)**

Pullen **28.17.33(.11)**

puller **17.34.14**

pullet **22.19.26(.12)**

pulley **1.31.15**

Pullman **28.17.16(.35)**

pullout **22.9.19**

pullover **17.21.14(.15)**

pullthrough **16.23.13**

pullulant **22.26.15(.25)**

pullulate **22.4.23(.7.3)**

pullulation **28.17.25(.3.14)**

pull-up **20.9.16**

pulmonaria **3.22.4**

pulmonary **1.29.11(.13.2)**

pulmonate **22.19.15(.9)**

pulmonic **24.2.15(.6.2)**

pulmonically **1.31.24(.9.8)**

pulp **20.18**

pulper **17.10.19**

pulpiness **34.18.16(.2.2)**

pulpit **22.2.5**

pulpiteer **3.4**

pulpless **34.18.29(.20)**

pulpous **34.18.9(.13)**

pulpwood **23.16.6(.8)**

pulpy **1.8.16**

pulque **1.12.19, 4.11**

pulsar **10.15**

pulsate **22.4.18**

pulsatile **40.13.3(.4)**

pulsatilla **17.34.2(.2)**

pulsation **28.17.25(.3.10)**

pulsative **31.2.1(.9.3)**

pulsator **17.12.4(.12)**

pulsatory **1.29.11(.8.2)**

pulse **34.27**

pulseless **34.18.29(.33)**

pulsimeter **17.12.16(.9.1)**

Pulsometer **17.12.16(.9.2)**

pultrude **23.17.3**

pulverizable **40.20.16(.22)**

pulverization **28.17.25(.3.11)**

pulverizator **17.12.4(.13)**

pulverize **35.15.20(.2)**

pulverizer **17.25.12(.14)**

pulverulent **22.26.15(.25)**

pulvinate **22.4.14(.9.3)**

puma **17.17.13**

pumice **34.2.12**

pumiceous **34.18.22(.2)**

pummel **40.25.7**

pump **20.16.5**

pumpernickel **40.23.2**

Pumphrey **1.29.21**

pumpkin **28.2.13(.8)**

pumpkinseed **23.1.7**

pun **28.13**

puna **17.18.15**

punch **38.18.7**

Punch and Judy **1.11.16**

punchbag **26.5.1**

punchball **40.10.4**

punchbowl **40.18.4**

punchcard **23.9.9**

punchdrunk **24.19.7**

puncheon **28.17.27**

puncher **17.28.22**

punchily **1.31.17(.24)**

Punchinello **19.29.4**

punchiness **34.18.16(.2.8)**

punchline **28.14.19(.23)**

punchup 20.9.13, 20.9.14
punchy 1.24.15
puncta 17.12.21(.8)
punctate 22.4.9(.7)
punctation 28.17.25(.3.3)
punctilio 15.1.13
punctilious 34.3.16
punctiliously 1.31.33(.1.5)
punctiliousness 34.18.16(.31.1)
punctual 40.16.12
punctuality 1.10.16(.32.1)
punctually 1.31.17(.24)
punctuate 22.4.4
punctuation 28.17.25(.3.1)
punctum 27.15.9(.13)
puncture 17.28.20, 17.28.23
pundit 22.2.8
punditry 1.29.15(.5)
pungency 1.22.23(.10.4)
pungent 22.26.15(.21)
pungently 1.31.22(.20.4)
Punic 24.2.15(.7)
punily 1.31.17(.14.1)
puniness 34.18.16(.2.5)
punish 36.2.16(.10)
punishable 40.20.16(.23)
punisher 17.26.14
punishingly 1.31.28(.1.13)
punishment 22.26.15(.13.6)
punitive 31.2.1(.9.2)
punitively 1.31.30(.7.1)
punitiveness 34.18.16(.28.1)
punitory 1.29.11(.8.7)
Punjab 21.7
Punjabi 1.9.6
punk 24.19.7
punkah 17.14.21(.5)
punkah-wallah 17.34.9
punkish 36.2.13
punky 1.12.16
punner 17.18.12
punnet 22.2.12
punningly 1.31.28(.1.7)
punster 17.12.24(.23)
punt 22.26.12, 22.26.14
Punta Arenas 34.18.16(.4)
punter 17.12.22(.10)
puny 1.16.14
pup 20.9
pupa 17.10.13
pupae 2.9
pupal 40.19.10
pupate 22.4.7
pupation 28.17.25(.3.2)

pupil 40.19.10
pupilarity 1.10.16(.21.1)
pupillage 39.2.23
pupillar 17.34.16(.5)
pupillarity 1.10.16(.21.1)
pupillary 1.29.11(.27)
pupiparous 34.18.27(.12)
puppet 22.2.5
puppeteer 3.4
puppeteering 29.1.30(.2)
puppetry 1.29.15(.3)
puppy 1.8.8
puppyhood 23.16.5(.1)
puppyish 36.2.1
Purana 17.18.8(.11)
Puranic 24.2.15(.5)
Purbeck 24.4.3
purblind 23.24.13
purblindness 34.18.16(.21.1)
Purcell 40.5.11, 40.31.13
purchasable 40.20.16(.21.2)
purchase 34.18.23
purchaseable 40.20.16(.21.2)
purchaser 17.24.15
purdah 10.7, 17.13.16
Purdie 1.11.18
Purdon 28.17.12(.17)
Purdue 16.24.6
Purdy 1.11.18
pure 12, 17.7
pureblood 23.14
pureblooded 23.18.10(.10)
purebred 23.5.15
purée 4.26.7, 4.26.8
purely 1.31.11, 1.31.17(.4)
pureness 34.18.16(.15.1)
purfle 40.27.15
Purfleet 22.1.18
purgation 28.17.25(.3.6)
purgative 31.2.1(.9.1)
purgatorial 40.3.14(.5)
purgatory 1.29.11(.8.6)
purge 39.15
purger 17.29.14
purification 28.17.25(.3.5)
purificator 17.12.4(.7)
purificatory 1.29.11(.8.2)
purifier 17.6.9(.4)
purify 14.14.4(.14)
Purim 27.1.12, 27.2.14
purine 28.1.25(.1)
purism 27.15.21(.2.14)
purist 22.29.2(.29.2)
puristic 24.2.10(.15.2)
puritan 28.17.11(.15)
puritanic 24.2.15(.5)

puritanical 40.23.12(.11)
puritanically 1.31.24(.9.8)
puritanism 27.15.21(.2.9)
purity 1.10.16(.21.2)
purl 40.17
purler 17.34.17
Purley 1.31.18
purlieu 16.24.17
purlieux 35.17.7
purlin 28.2.31(.11)
purloin 28.12
purloiner 17.18.11
Purnell 40.5.8
purple 40.19.12
purpleness 34.18.16(.37.4)
purplish 36.2.27
purply 1.31.17(.7), 1.31.20
purport 22.13.1, 22.19.8
purportedly 1.31.23(.14.3)
purpose 34.18.9(.9)
purposeful 40.27.25
purposefully 1.31.17(.16.2)
purposefulness 34.18.16(.37.2)
purposeless 34.18.29(.33)
purposelessly 1.31.33(.12.6)
purposelessness 34.18.16(.31.6)
purposely 1.31.33(.12.2)
purposive 31.2.4(.9)
purposively 1.31.30(.7.4)
purpura 17.32.14(.21)
purpure 17.7.12(.2)
purpuric 24.2.26(.8)
purpurin 28.2.29(.5)
purr 18
purse 34.19
purseful 40.14.6(.19)
purser 17.24.16
pursership 20.2.7(.9)
purse-seine 28.4.12
purse-seiner 17.18.3
purse-strings 35.27
pursiness 34.18.16(.2.7)
purslane 28.4.19, 28.17.33(.26)
pursuable 40.20.16(.7)
pursuance 34.24.10(.7)
pursuant 22.26.15(.6)
pursuantly 1.31.22(.20.1)
pursue 16.24.14
pursuer 17.8
pursuivant 22.26.15(.16)
pursy 1.22.17
purulence 34.24.10(.24)
purulency 1.22.23(.10.4)
purulent 22.26.15(.25)

purulently 1.31.22(.20.5)
Purves 34.2.15
purvey 4.16
purveyance 34.24.10(.2)
purveyor 17.2.6
purview 16.24.12
Purvis 34.2.15
pus 34.14
Pusan 28.7.14
Pusey 1.23.12
push 36.13
pushbike 24.13.2
pushbroom 27.14.6(.7)
pushbutton 28.17.11(.11)
pushcart 22.10.5
push-chain 28.4.15
pushchair 6.16
pushdown 28.8.2(.11)
pusher 17.26.12
pushful 40.27.27
pushfully 1.31.17(.16.2)
pushfulnes 34.18.16(.37.2)
pushily 1.31.17(.22)
pushiness 34.18.16(.2.8)
pushingly 1.31.28(.1.13)
Pushkin 28.2.13(.15)
pushover 17.21.14(.10)
pushpin 28.2.9
push-pull 40.14.2
pushrod 23.10.12
pushstart 22.10.3
Pushtu 16.7.9
pushy 1.24.10
pusillanimity 1.10.16(.12)
pusillanimous 34.18.15(.10)
pusillanimously 1.31.33(.12.3)
pusillanimousness 34.18.16(.31.3)
puss 34.16
pussy 1.22.14
pussycat 22.7.9
pussyfoot 22.17
pussyfooter 17.12.14
pustulant 22.26.15(.25)
pustular 17.34.16(.18)
pustulate 22.4.23(.7.3)
pustulation 28.17.25(.3.14)
pustule 40.15.9(.3)
pustulous 34.18.29(.17.5)
put 22.17
putative 31.2.1(.9.1)
putatively 1.31.30(.7.1)
putdown 28.8.2(.5)
putlock 24.9.16(.11)
putlog 26.7.14
Putney 1.16.19

put-put 22.15.1
putrefacient 22.26.15(.19)
putrefaction
28.17.25(.15.3)
putrefactive 31.2.1(.13.3)
putrefy 14.14.4(.14)
putrescence 34.24.10(.18)
putrescent 22.26.15(.17.2)
putrescible
40.20.16(.21.1)
putrid 23.2.22
putridity 1.10.16(.9)
putridly 1.31.23(.14.7)
putridness 34.18.16(.21.1)
putsch 38.13
putt 22.15
puttee 2.11
Puttenham 27.15.14(.11)
putter 17.12.12, 17.12.14
putterer 17.32.14(.6)
putti 2.12.9
putting-green 28.1.25(.9)
Puttnam 27.15.14(.14)
putto 19.10.10
putt-putt 22.15.1
putty 1.10.12
putz 34.22.11, 34.22.13
puy 2
puzzle 40.32.11
puzzlement
22.26.15(.13.7)
puzzler 17.34.28
puzzling 29.1.31(.27)
puzzlingly 1.31.28(.1.18)
Pwllheli 1.31.5
pya 10
pyaemia 3.8.1
pyaemic 24.2.14(.1)
pycnic 24.2.15(.12)
Pye 14
pye-dog 26.7.4
pyelitis 34.18.11(.8)
pyelogram 27.6.17(.5)
pyelonephritis
34.18.11(.8)
Pygmalion 28.3.21(.3)
pygmean 28.17.1(.6)
pygmy 1.15.17
pyjama 17.17.7
pyknic 24.2.15(.12)
Pyle 40.13
pylon 28.10.26,
28.17.33(.10)
pylori 14.24.4
pyloric 24.2.26(.6)
pylorus 34.18.27(.8)
Pylos 34.10.17
Pym 27.2
pyoid 23.13.3
Pyongyang 29.4.16
pyorrhoea 17.1.16

pyosis 34.2.17(.11.1)
pyracantha 17.22.13
Pyrah 17.32.13
pyralid 23.2.23
pyramid 23.2.12
pyramidal 40.22.13
pyramidally 1.31.17(.10)
pyramidic 24.2.11(.2)
pyramidically
1.31.24(.9.7)
Pyramus 34.18.15(.10)
pyre 17.6
Pyrenean 28.17.1(.7)
Pyrenees 35.1.12
pyrethrin 28.2.29(.12)
pyrethroid 23.13.19
pyrethrum 27.15.26(.15)
pyretic 24.2.10(.3.3)
Pyrex® 34.23.4(.11)
pyrexia 3.14.15
pyrexial 40.3.10
pyrexic 24.2.20(.13)
pyrexical 40.23.12(.15)
pyrheliometer
17.12.16(.9.2)
pyridine 28.1.10
pyridoxal 40.31.18
pyridoxine 28.1.18(.7),
28.2.23(.14)
pyrimidine 28.1.10
pyrite 22.16.24(.8)
pyrites 35.1.7(.5)
pyritic 24.2.10(.2.4)
pyritiferous 34.18.27(.20)
pyritize 35.15.7(.6)
pyritous 34.18.11(.8)
pyro 19.27.9
pyroclast 22.29.6(.12),
22.29.8(.8)
pyroclastic 24.2.10(.15.4)
pyroelectric
24.2.26(.14.3)
pyroelectricity
1.10.16(.16.1)
pyrogallol 40.9.21
pyrogenic 24.2.15(.4)
pyrogenous
34.18.16(.15.3)
pyrography 1.18.9(.3.2)
pyrolatry 1.29.15(.13)
pyroligneous 34.3.6(.8)
pyrolysis 34.2.17(.10.5)
pyrolytic 24.2.10(.2.5)
pyrolyze 35.15.21(.4.7)
pyromancy 1.22.23(.4)
pyromania 3.9.3(.5)
pyromaniac 24.6.1
pyrometer 17.12.16(.9.2)
pyrometric 24.2.26(.14.2)
pyrometrically
1.31.24(.9.12)

pyrometry 1.29.15(.8)
pyrope 20.15.8
pyrophoric 24.2.26(.6)
pyrosis 34.2.17(.11.2)
pyrotechnic 24.2.15(.12)
pyrotechnical
40.23.12(.11)
pyrotechnically
1.31.24(.9.8)
pyrotechnist
22.29.2(.18.3)
pyrotechny 1.16.21
pyroxene 28.1.18(.7)
pyroxylin 28.2.31(.10)
Pyrrha 17.32.1
Pyrrhic 24.2.26(.1)
Pyrrhonian 28.3.8(.11)
Pyrrhonic 24.2.15(.6.4)
Pyrrhonism 27.15.21(.2.9)
Pyrrhonist 22.29.2(.18.3)
Pyrrhus 34.18.27(.1)
pyruvate 22.4.16
Pythagoras 34.18.27(.17)
Pythagorean 28.17.1(.12)
Pythia 3.12
Pythian 28.3.11
Pythias 34.3.9
python 28.17.21
Pythonesque 24.20.3
pythonic 24.2.15(.6.3)
pyuria 3.22.12
pyx 34.23.2
pyxides 35.1.8
pyxidia 3.5.2
pyxidium 27.3.4(.2)
pyxis 34.2.17(.14)
q 16
Qantas® 34.18.11(.14)
Qatar 10.6, 10.6.2
Qatari 1.29.6
Qattara 17.32.7
Q-boat 22.21.2
Q.C. 2.22
QED 2.13
Qinghai 14.22
Q-ship 20.2.7(.8)
q.t. 2.11
qua 4, 10
Quaalude® 23.17.5
quack 24.6
quackery 1.29.11(.10)
quackish 36.2.13
quad 23.10
quadragenarian
28.3.20(.4)
Quadragesima
17.17.14(.8)
quadragesimal 40.25.10
quadrangle 40.24.14(.2)
quadrangular
17.34.16(.21.3)

quadrant 22.26.15(.23.4)
quadrantal 40.21.17(.3)
quadraphonic
24.2.15(.6.3)
quadraphonically
1.31.24(.9.8)
quadraphony 1.16.9,
1.16.15(.12)
quadrat 22.7.20,
22.19.24(.13)
quadrate 22.4.22(.9),
22.19.24(.13)
quadratic 24.2.10(.4.5)
quadrature 17.28.15
quadrennia 3.9.4
quadrennial 40.3.7(.4)
quadrennially 1.31.3(.7)
quadrennium 27.3.8(.4)
quadric 24.2.26(.15)
quadriceps 34.21.4
quadrifid 23.2.14
quadriga 17.16.1, 17.16.10
quadrilateral
40.16.13(.12.1)
quadrilingual 40.35.4
quadrille 40.2.20
quadrillion 28.3.21(.2)
quadrinomial 40.3.6
quadripartite 22.16.9
quadriplegia 3.19.1,
17.29.1
quadriplegic 24.2.24(.1)
quadrireme 27.1.12
quadrisyllabic 24.2.9(.2)
quadrisyllable
40.20.16(.29)
quadrivalent
22.26.15(.25)
quadrivia 3.11.2
quadrivium 27.3.9
quadroon 28.16.13
quadrophonic
24.2.15(.6.3)
quadrophonically
1.31.24(.9.8)
quadrophony
1.16.15(.12)
quadrumanous
34.18.16(.15.3)
quadruped 23.5.1
quadrupedal 40.22.1,
40.22.4, 40.22.13
quadruple 40.19.10
quadruplet 22.19.26(.15)
quadruplicate
22.4.11(.6), 22.19.12(.10)
quadruplication
28.17.25(.3.5)
quadruplicity
1.10.16(.16.1)
quadruply 1.31.20
quadrupole 40.18.3

p
q

quick-witted 23.18.9(.2)
quick-wittedness
34.18.16(.21.1)
quid 23.2
quiddity 1.10.16(.9)
quidnunc 24.19.7
quid pro quo 19
quiescence 34.24.10(.18)
quiescency 1.22.23(.10.4)
quiescent 22.26.15(.17.2)
quiet 22.19.4
quieten 28.17.11(.15)
quietism 27.15.21(.2.4)
quietist 22.29.2(.13)
quietistic 24.2.10(.15.2)
quietly 1.31.22(.15)
quietness 34.18.16(.20.3)
quietude 23.17.4(.1)
quietus 34.18.11(.1)
quiff 30.2
Quigley 1.31.25
quill 40.2
quill-coverts 34.22.15
Quiller-Couch 38.14
quilling 29.1.31(.2)
Quilp 20.18
quilt 22.32.1
quilter 17.12.26(.1)
quim 27.2
quin 28.2
quinacrine 28.1.25(.8),
28.2.29(.10)
quinary 1.29.11(.13.1)
quinate 22.4.14(.6)
quince 34.24.1
quincentenary
1.29.11(.13.1)
quincentennial
40.3.7(.4)
quincuncial
40.33.12(.5)
quincuncially
1.31.17(.22)
quincunx 34.23.18
quinella 17.34.5(.8)
quingentenary
1.29.11(.13.1)
quinine 28.1.14
Quink® 24.19.1
Quinlan 28.17.33(.23)
Quinn 28.2
quinol 40.9.12
quinoline 28.1.27(.7),
28.2.31(.10)
quinone 28.19.10
quinquagenarian
28.3.20(.4)
quinquagenary
1.29.11(.13.2)
Quinquagesima
17.17.14(.8)

quinquelateral
40.16.13(.12.1)
quinquennia 3.9.4
quinquennial 40.3.7(.4)
quinquennially
1.31.3(.7)
quinquennium 27.3.8(.4)
quinquereme 27.1.12
quinquevalent
22.26.15(.25)
quinsied 23.2.17
quinsy 1.23.20
quint 22.26.1
quinta 17.12.22(.1)
quintain 28.17.11(.22)
quintal 40.21.17(.1)
quintan 28.17.11(.22)
quinte 22.8
quintessence
34.24.10(.18)
quintessential
40.33.12(.3)
quintessentially
1.31.17(.22)
quintet 22.5.3
quintile 40.13.3(.9),
40.21.17(.1)
Quintilian 28.3.21(.2)
quintillion 28.3.21(.2)
quintillionth 32.21
Quintin 28.2.11(.13)
Quinton 28.17.11(.22)
quintuple 40.19.10
quintuplet 22.19.26(.15)
quintuplicate
22.4.11(.2)
quintuplication
28.17.25(.3.5)
quintuply 1.31.20
Quintus 34.18.11(.14)
quip 20.2
quipster 17.12.24(.16)
quipu 16.5
quire 17.6
Quirinus 34.18.16(.13)
quirk 24.17
Quirke 24.17
quirkily 1.31.17(.11)
quirkiness 34.18.16(.2.4)
quirkish 36.2.13
quirky 1.12.14
quirt 22.20
quisling 29.1.31(.27)
quislingite 22.16.15
quit 22.2
quitch 38.2
quitclaim 27.4.9
quite 22.16
Quito 19.10.1
quitrent 22.26.4(.14)
quittance 34.24.10(.10)

quitter 17.12.2
quiver 17.21.2
quiverful 40.14.6(.7)
quivering 29.1.30(.8)
quiveringly 1.31.28(.1.17)
quivery 1.29.11(.15)
qui vive 31.1
Quixote 1.10.18, 22.19.18,
22.21.11
quixotic 24.2.10(.6)
quixotically 1.31.24(.9.4)
quixotism 27.15.21(.2.4)
quixotize 35.15.7(.7)
quiz 35.2
quizmaster 17.12.24(.5)
quizshow 19.22
quizzer 17.25.2
quizzical 40.23.12(.16)
quizzicality
1.10.16(.32.5)
quizzically 1.31.24(.9.10)
quizzicalness
34.18.16(.37.5)
Qum 27.13
Qumran 28.9.13
quod 23.10
quodlibet 22.5.2
quodlibetarian
28.3.20(.4)
quodlibetical
40.23.12(.7.1)
quodlibetically
1.31.24(.9.3)
quoin 28.12
quoit 22.14
quokka 17.14.8
quondam 27.6.5,
27.15.10(.14)
Quonset® 22.19.18
quorate 22.4.22(.4)
Quorn® 28.11
quorum 27.15.26(.5)
Quosh 36.9
quota 17.12.18
quotability 1.10.16(.22.1)
quotable 40.20.16(.11.3)
quotation 28.17.25(.3.3)
quotative 31.2.1(.9.1)
quote 22.21
quoth 32.16
quotha 17.22.11
quotidian 28.3.4(.2)
quotient 22.26.15(.19)
Quranic 24.2.15(.5)
q.v. 2.19
Qwaqwa 17.31.6
Qwerty 1.10.17
r 10
Raasey 4.18.7
Rabat 22.7.6, 22.10.2
Rabaul 40.7

rabbet 22.2.6
rabbi 14.7
Rabbie 1.9.5
rabbin 28.2.10
rabbinate 22.4.14(.9.1),
22.19.15(.9)
rabbinic 24.2.15(.2)
rabbinical 40.23.12(.11)
rabbinically 1.31.24(.9.8)
rabbinism 27.15.21(.2.9)
rabbinist 22.29.2(.18.1)
rabbit 22.2.6
rabbity 1.10.16(.7)
rabble 40.20.6
rabble-rouser 17.25.6
Rabelais 4.28.7
Rabelaisian 28.3.14,
28.17.26(.3)
rabi 2.10
rabid 23.2.7
rabidity 1.10.16(.9)
rabidly 1.31.23(.14.2)
rabidness 34.18.16(.21.1)
rabies 35.1.6, 35.2.2
Rabin 28.1.8
Rabindranath 32.8
Rabinowitz 34.22.2
raccoon 28.16.5
race 34.4
racecard 23.9.9
racecourse 34.12.2
racegoer 17.9.5
racegoing 29.1.9
racehorse 34.12.7
racemate 22.4.13(.14)
raceme 27.1.8
racemic 24.2.14(.1)
racemize 35.15.11
racemose 34.20.8
racer 17.24.4
racetrack 24.6.21
raceway 4.25.22
Rachael 40.16.12
Rachel 40.16.12
rachel 40.5.13
rachidial 40.3.4
rachis 34.2.10
rachitic 24.2.10(.2.1)
rachitis 34.18.11(.8)
Rachmaninov 30.8.7
Rachmanism
27.15.21(.2.9)
racial 40.33.2
racialism 27.15.21(.2.15)
racialist 22.29.2(.31.4)
racially 1.31.17(.22)
racily 1.31.17(.20)
Racine 28.1.18
raciness 34.18.16(.2.7)
racism 27.15.21(.2.12)

racist 22.29.2(.22)
rack 24.6
rack-and-pinion 28.17.32
racket 22.2.9(.3)
racketball 40.10.4
racketeer 3.4
rackety 1.10.16(.10)
Rackham 27.15.11(.5)
raclette 22.5.21
racon 28.10.11
raconteur 18.3
raconteuse 35.19
racoon 28.16.5
racquet 22.2.9(.3)
racy 1.22.4
rad 23.7
RADA 17.13.7
radar 10.7
Radcliffe 30.2.6
raddle 40.22.5
Radetsky 1.12.17(.8)
Radford 23.18.16(.12)
radial 40.3.4
radially 1.31.3(.4)
radian 28.3.4(.3)
radiance 34.24.2
radiancy 1.22.23(.2)
radiant 22.26.2(.3)
radiantly 1.31.22(.20.1)
radiate 22.4.2(.4)
radiately 1.31.22(.4)
radiation 28.17.25(.3.1)
radiational 40.26.13(.14.2)
radiationally
    1.31.17(.14.3)
radiative 31.2.1(.2)
radiator 17.12.4(.1)
radical 40.23.12(.8)
radicalism 27.15.21(.2.15)
radicalization
    28.17.25(.3.12)
radicalize 35.15.21(.4.4)
radically 1.31.24(.9.7)
radicalness
    34.18.16(.37.5)
radicchio 15.1.4
Radice 1.25.1
radices 35.1.16(.10)
radicle 40.23.12(.8)
radicular 17.34.16(.21.2)
radii 14.2
radio 15.1.3
radioactive 31.2.1(.13.3)
radioactively
    1.31.30(.7.2)
radioactivity 1.10.16(.15)
radio-assay 4.18, 4.18.6
radiobiological
    40.23.12(.17.2)
radiobiologically
    1.31.24(.9.11)

radiobiologist
    22.29.2(.26.2)
radiobiology
    1.26.10(.11.1)
radiocarbon 28.17.10
radiochemical
    40.23.12(.10)
radiochemist 22.29.2(.17)
radiochemistry
    1.29.15(.17)
radiogenic 24.2.15(.4)
radiogenically
    1.31.24(.9.8)
radio-goniometer
    17.12.16(.9.2)
radiogram 27.6.17(.5)
radiograph 30.7.5(.1)
radiographer 17.20.12(.5)
radiographic 24.2.16(.3)
radiographically
    1.31.24(.9.9)
radiography 1.18.9(.3.2)
radioimmunology
    1.26.10(.11.4)
radioisotope 20.15.3
radioisotopic 24.2.8(.5)
radioisotopically
    1.31.24(.9.2)
radiolaria 3.22.4
radiolarian 28.3.20(.4)
radiolocation
    28.17.25(.3.5)
radiologic 24.2.24(.4)
radiological
    40.23.12(.17.2)
radiologist 22.29.2(.26.2)
radiology 1.26.10(.11.1)
radiometer 17.12.16(.9.2)
radiometric 24.2.26(.14.2)
radiometry 1.29.15(.8)
radionics 34.23.2(.6)
radionuclide 23.15.16
radio-opaque 24.3.2
radiopacity 1.10.16(.16.1)
radiopaging 29.1.28
radiopaque 24.3.2
radiophonic 24.2.15(.6.3)
radioscopic 24.2.8(.5)
radioscopy 1.8.11(.5)
radiosonde 23.24.9
radiotelegraphy
    1.18.9(.3.1)
radiotelephone 28.19.11
radio-telephonic
    24.2.15(.6.3)
radiotelex 34.23.4(.12)
radiotherapeutic
    24.2.10(.9)
radiotherapist
    22.29.2(.11)
radiotherapy 1.8.11(.8)
radish 36.2.12

radium 27.3.4(.3)
radius 34.3.4
radix 34.23.2(.4)
Radlett 22.19.26(.18)
Radley 1.31.23(.5)
Radner 17.18.22
Radnor 17.18.22
Radnorshire 17.26.14
radome 27.17.5
radon 28.10.10
Radox® 34.23.8(.4)
radula 17.34.16(.19)
radulae 2.32.9(.8)
radular 17.34.16(.19)
Rae 4
Raeburn 28.18.3
Rael-Brook 24.14.10
RAF 30.4, 30.5
Rafe 30.3
Rafferty 1.10.16(.14)
Raffi 1.18.4
raffia 3.10.2
raffinate 22.4.14(.9.3)
raffinose 34.20.9, 35.20.8
raffish 36.2.18(.4)
raffishly 1.31.35(.7.3)
raffishness 34.18.16(.33.6)
raffle 40.27.7
Raffles 35.30.21
rafflesia 3.15.1, 3.17
Rafsanjani 1.16.8
raft 22.27.4
rafter 17.12.23
raftsman 28.17.16(.29)
rag 26.5
raga 17.16.6
ragamuffin 28.2.19
rag-and-bone 28.19.3
ragbag 26.5.1
rag doll 40.9
Ragdoll 40.9.8
rage 39.4
ragee 2.15
ragged 23.18.12
raggedly 1.31.23(.14.5)
raggedness
    34.18.16(.21.1)
raggedy 1.11.17
raggee 2.15
raggle 40.24.4
raggle-taggle 40.24.4
raglan 28.17.33(.21)
ragman 28.7.10(.14),
    28.17.16(.24)
ragmen 28.5.7(.18)
Ragnarök 24.9.15, 24.17.7
ragout 16.10
ragstone 28.19.4(.9)
rags-to-riches 35.18.20
ragtag 26.5.2

ragtime 27.12.1
ragtop 20.7.4
raguly 1.31.17(.28)
ragweed 23.1.10
ragworm 27.16.7
ragwort 22.20.15
rah 10
Rahman 28.17.16(.9)
rah-rah 10.23.2
rai 14
raid 23.4
raider 17.13.3
Raikes 34.23.3
rail 40.4
railage 39.2.23
railcar 10.8.18
railcard 23.9.9
railer 17.34.4
rail fence 34.24.3
railhead 23.5.13(.19)
railing 29.1.31(.4)
raillery 1.29.11(.27)
railless 34.18.29(.38)
railman 28.17.16(.35)
railroad 23.20.12
railway 4.25.26
railwayman 28.17.16(.4)
raiment 22.26.15(.13.1)
rain 28.4
Raina 17.18.1, 17.18.3
rainbird 23.19.1
rainbow 19.9.15
raincoat 22.21.5
raindrop 20.7.12
Raine 28.4
rainfall 40.10.11
Rainford 23.18.16(.16)
rainforest 22.29.2(.29.2)
raingauge 39.4.4
Rainhill 40.2.18
Rainier 3.9, 3.9.3, 4.2.4
rainily 1.31.17(.14.1)
raininess 34.18.16(.2.5)
rainless 34.18.29(.27)
rainmaker 17.14.3(.3)
rainmaking 29.1.14(.3)
rainproof 30.13.4
rainstorm 27.10.2
rainswept 22.22.3
rainwater 17.12.10(.7)
rainwear 6.18.11
rainy 1.16.4
Raisa 17.24.1
raisable 40.20.16(.22)
raise 35.4
raisin 28.17.24(.3)
raisiny 1.16.15(.15)
Raison 28.17.24(.3)
raison d'être 17.32.19(.3)
raisons d'être 28.10.19

r

Raistrick 24.2.26(.14.5)
raj 37.4, 39.8
raja 17.29.7
rajah 17.29.7
rajaship 20.2.7(.9)
Rajasthan 28.9.2
Rajasthani 1.16.8
Rajneesh 36.1
Rajput 22.17
Rajputana 17.18.8(.2)
Rajshahi 1.27
rake 24.3
raker 17.14.3
raki 1.12.5, 1.12.6, 2.14
rakish 36.2.13
rakishly 1.31.35(.7.1)
rakishness 34.18.16(.33.4)
raku 16.9
rale 40.6, 40.8
Ralegh 1.31.7, 1.31.9,
 1.31.11
Raleigh 1.31.7, 1.31.9,
 1.31.11
rallentando 19.11.14
rallier 3.24.5
ralline 28.14.19(.6)
rally 1.31.7
rallycross 34.10.16
Ralph 30.3, 30.20.3
ram 27.6
Rama 17.17.7
Ramadan 28.7.7, 28.9.3
Ramadhan 28.9.3
Ramakrishna 17.18.30
ramal 40.25.2
Ramayana 17.18.16(.21)
Rambert 6.3
ramble 40.20.19
rambler 17.34.20
rambling 29.1.31(.16)
ramblingly 1.31.28(.1.18)
Rambo 19.9.14
rambunctious
 34.18.22(.11)
rambunctiously
 1.31.33(.12.4)
rambunctiousness
 34.18.16(.31.4)
rambutan 28.17.11(.14)
Rameau 19.14.6, 19.14.7
ramee 1.15.6
ramekin 28.2.13(.6)
ramen 28.5.7(.6)
Rameses 35.1.16(.10)
rami 2.16, 14.12
ramie 1.15.6
ramification
 28.17.25(.3.5)
ramify 14.14.4(.6)
Ramillies 35.1.23
ramin 28.1.13

Ramírez 35.5.13
ramjet 22.5.17
rammer 17.17.6
rammy 1.15.6
Ramón 28.10.13
Ramona 17.18.18(.5)
Ramos 34.10.12
ramose 34.20.8
ramp 20.16.3
rampage 39.4.1
rampageous 34.18.24
rampageously
 1.31.33(.12.4)
rampageousness
 34.18.16(.31.5)
rampager 17.29.3
rampancy 1.22.23(.10.2)
rampant 22.26.15(.7)
rampantly 1.31.22(.20.2)
rampart 22.10.1
rampion 28.3.1
Rampton 28.17.11(.18)
Rampur 17.7.1
ram-raid 23.4.15
ramrod 23.10.12
Ramsaran 28.17.31(.11)
Ramsay 1.23.19
Ramsbotham 27.15.9(.6),
 27.15.18
Ramsbottom 27.15.9(.6)
Ramsden 28.17.12(.26)
Ramsey 1.23.19
Ramsgate 22.4.12(.11)
ramshackle 40.23.5
ramson 28.17.23(.23),
 28.17.24(.15)
ramus 34.18.15(.3)
ran 28.7
rance 34.24.4
ranch 38.18.4
rancher 17.28.22
ranchero 19.27.3
Ranchi 1.24.15
rancho 19.22, 19.24
rancid 23.2.16
rancidity 1.10.16(.9)
rancidness 34.18.16(.21.1)
rancor 17.14.21(.3)
rancorous 34.18.27(.16)
rancorously 1.31.33(.12.5)
rancour 17.14.21(.3)
rand 22.26.6, 22.26.8,
 22.26.9, 23.24.6
Randall 40.22.16
randan 28.7.7
R & B 2
R & D 2
Randers 35.18.9
randily 1.31.17(.10)
randiness 34.18.16(.2.3)

Randolph 30.20.4
random 27.15.10(.14)
randomization
 28.17.25(.3.11)
randomize 35.15.11
randomly 1.31.26(.11)
randomness 34.18.16(.24)
Randstad 22.7.7
randy 1.11.20(.4)
ranee 2.17
Ranelagh 17.34.16(.12)
rang 29.4
rangatira 17.32.2
range 39.17.2
rangé 4.21
rangefinder 17.13.20(.11)
rangeland 23.24.6(.13)
ranger 17.29.16(.2)
rangership 20.2.7(.9)
ranginess 34.18.16(.2.8)
Rangoon 28.16.6
rangy 1.26.13
rani 2.17, 2.17.5
Ranjitsinhji 1.26.13
rank 24.19.3
rank-and-file 40.13.9
ranker 17.14.21(.3)
Rankin 28.2.13(.13)
ranking 29.1.14(.14)
rankle 40.23.15
rankly 1.31.24(.12)
rankness 34.18.16(.22)
Rannoch 24.16.7, 25.10
ransack 24.6.14
ransacker 17.14.5
ransom 27.15.20(.18)
Ransome 27.15.20(.18)
ransomed 23.23.9
ransomer 17.17.14(.8)
rant 22.26.6
ranter 17.12.22(.4)
ranting 29.1.12(.19)
rantingly 1.31.28(.1.4)
rantipole 40.18.3
Ranulf 30.20.5
ranunculaceous
 34.18.22(.3)
ranunculi 2.32.9(.8),
 14.25.9
ranunculus
 34.18.29(.17.6)
Raoul 40.15
rap 20.5
rapacious 34.18.22(.3)
rapaciously 1.31.33(.12.4)
rapaciousness
 34.18.16(.31.4)
rapacity 1.10.16(.16.1)
rape 20.3
raper 17.10.3

rapeseed 23.1.7
Raphael 40.4.8, 40.16.2
raphide 23.15.9
rapid 23.2.6
rapid-fire 17.6.9
rapidity 1.10.16(.9)
rapidly 1.31.23(.14.2)
rapidness 34.18.16(.21.1)
rapier 3.2.3
rapine 28.2.9, 28.14.3
rapist 22.29.2(.11)
Rappahannock 24.16.7
rapparee 2.30
rappee 2.9
rappel 40.5.1
rapper 17.10.5
rapport 12.3
rapporteur 18.3
rapprochement 11.8
rapscallion 28.3.21(.5)
rapt 22.22.4
raptly 1.31.22(.18)
raptness 34.18.16(.20.4)
raptor 17.12.19
raptorial 40.3.14(.5)
rapture 17.28.18
rapturous 34.18.27(.26)
rapturously 1.31.33(.12.5)
rapturousness
 34.18.16(.31.5)
Rapunzel 40.32.17
Raquel 40.5.5
rara avis 34.2.15
rare 6
rarebit 22.2.6
raree-show 19.22
rarefaction
 28.17.25(.15.3)
rarefactive 31.2.1(.13.3)
rarefication
 28.17.25(.3.5)
rarefy 14.14.4(.14)
rarely 1.31.6
rareness 34.18.16(.6)
raring 29.1.30(.4)
rarity 1.10.16(.21.1)
Rarotonga 17.16.17(.3)
Rarotongan 28.17.15(.16)
rascal 40.23.16
rascaldom 27.15.10(.20)
rascalism 27.15.21(.2.15)
rascality 1.10.16(.32.5)
rascally 1.31.17(.11)
raschel 40.33.4
rash 36.6
rasher 17.26.6
Rashid 23.1.8
rashly 1.31.35(.3)
rashness 34.18.16(.33.1)
Rasmussen 28.17.23(.14)

rasp **20.17**
raspatory **1.29.11(.8.6)**
raspberry **1.29.11(.7.2)**
rasper **17.10.18**
raspingly **1.31.28(.1.2)**
Rasputin **28.2.11(.9)**
raspy **1.8.15**
Rasta **17.12.24(.5)**
Rastafari **1.29.6**
Rastafarian **28.3.20(.4)**
Rastafarianism
   27.15.21(.2.9)
raster **17.12.24(.5)**
rasterization
   28.17.25(.3.11)
rasterize **35.15.20(.2)**
rasterizer **17.25.12(.14)**
Rastrick **24.2.26(.14.5)**
Rastus **34.18.11(.16)**
rat **22.7**
rata **17.12.8**
ratability **1.10.16(.22.1)**
ratable **40.20.16(.11.1)**
ratably **1.31.21(.4.1)**
ratafia **3.10, 17.1.8**
rataplan **28.7.22**
rat-arsed **22.29.8(.2)**
rat-a-tat **22.7.7**
rat-a-tat-tat **22.7.7**
ratatouille **2.29**
ratbag **26.5.1**
ratcatcher **17.28.6**
ratch **38.5**
ratchet **22.2.20**
Ratcliffe **30.2.6**
rate **22.4**
rateability **1.10.16(.22.1)**
rateable **40.20.16(.11.1)**
rateably **1.31.21(.4.1)**
ratecap **20.5.1**
ratel **40.21.3, 40.21.6**
ratepayer **17.2.1**
ratfink **24.19.1(.3)**
Rathbone **28.19.3**
rathe **33.3**
rather **17.23.7**
rathe-ripe **20.10.5**
Rathlin **28.2.31(.22)**
rathole **40.18.13**
rathskeller **17.34.5(.5)**
ratifiable **40.20.16(.5)**
ratification **28.17.25(.3.5)**
ratifier **17.6.9(.4)**
ratify **14.14.4(.4)**
rating **29.1.12(.3)**
ratio **15.1.9**
ratiocinate **22.4.14(.9.3)**
ratiocination
   28.17.25(.3.8)
ratiocinative **31.2.1(.9.2)**

ratiocinator **17.12.4(.10)**
ration **28.17.25(.5)**
rational **40.26.13(.14.4)**
rationale **40.6.9, 40.8.9**
rationalism
   27.15.21(.2.15)
rationalist **22.29.2(.31.3)**
rationalistic
   24.2.10(.15.3)
rationalistically
   1.31.24(.9.6)
rationality **1.10.16(.32.8)**
rationalization
   28.17.25(.3.12)
rationalize **35.15.21(.4.5)**
rationalizer **17.25.12(.15)**
rationally **1.31.17(.14.3)**
ratite **22.16.9**
ratline **28.2.31(.15)**
Ratner **17.18.21**
ratoon **28.16.3**
ratrace **34.4.13**
ratsbane **28.4.2**
Ratskeller **17.34.5(.5)**
rat's-tail **40.4.2**
rattan **28.7.6**
rat-tat **22.7.7**
Rattenbury **1.29.11(.7.2)**
ratter **17.12.6**
Rattigan **28.17.15(.13)**
rattily **1.31.17(.9.1)**
rattiness **34.18.16(.2.3)**
rattle **40.21.5**
rattlebox **34.23.8(.2)**
rattler **17.34.21**
rattlesnake **24.3.8**
rattletrap **20.5.6**
rattling **29.1.31(.17)**
rattly **1.31.17(.9.1),
   1.31.22(.6)**
Rattray **1.29.15, 4.26.11**
ratty **1.10.6**
raucous **34.18.13(.6)**
raucously **1.31.33(.12.2)**
raucousness
   34.18.16(.31.3)
raunch **38.18.6**
raunchily **1.31.17(.24)**
raunchiness
   34.18.16(.2.8)
raunchy **1.24.15**
ravage **39.2.17**
ravager **17.29.13**
rave **31.3**
Ravel **40.5.10**
ravel **40.28.5**
ravelin **28.2.31(.10)**
raven **28.17.20(.3)**
Ravenglass **34.9.7**
Ravenna **17.18.4**
ravenous **34.18.16(.15.3)**

ravenously **1.31.33(.12.3)**
ravenousness
   34.18.16(.31.3)
raver **17.21.3**
rave-up **20.9.11**
ravin **28.2.20**
ravine **28.1.16, 28.2.20**
raving **29.1.20**
ravingly **1.31.28(.1.9)**
ravioli **1.31.19**
ravish **36.2.19**
ravisher **17.26.14**
ravishing **29.1.25**
ravishingly
   1.31.28(.1.13)
ravishment
   22.26.15(.13.6)
raw **12**
Rawalpindi **1.11.20(.1)**
Rawdon **28.17.12(.10)**
rawhide **23.15.13**
Rawle **40.10**
Rawlings **35.27**
Rawlins **35.26.2**
Rawlinson
   28.17.23(.24)
Rawlplug® **26.10**
Rawls **35.30.9**
rawly **1.31.11**
rawness **34.18.16(.10)**
Rawson **28.17.23(.9)**
Rawtenstall **40.10.5**
ray **4**
rayah **17.6**
Rayburn **28.18.3**
Rayleen **28.1.27(.2)**
Rayleigh **1.31.4**
rayless **34.18.29(.4)**
raylet **22.19.26(.3)**
Raymond **23.24.16(.7)**
Rayner **17.18.3**
Raynes **35.26.4**
rayon **28.10.3, 28.17.2**
raze **35.4**
razoo **16.16**
razor **17.25.3**
razorback **24.6.6(.9)**
razorbill **40.2.4**
razorblade **23.4.16**
razorshell **40.5.13**
razz **35.7**
razzia **3.15.4**
razzle **40.32.5**
razzle-dazzle **40.32.5**
razzmatazz **35.7**
re **2, 4**
Rea **2, 4, 17.1**
reabsorb **21.9**
reabsorption
   28.17.25(.14)
reaccept **22.22.3**

reacceptance
   34.24.10(.10)
reaccustom **27.15.9(.15)**
reach **38.1**
reachable **40.20.16(.24)**
reacher **17.28.1**
reacquaint **22.26.3**
reacquaintance
   34.24.10(.10)
reacquire **17.6.13**
reacquisition
   28.17.25(.2.5)
react **22.23.5**
reactance **34.24.10(.10)**
reactant **22.26.15(.9)**
reaction **28.17.25(.15.3)**
reactionary **1.29.11(.13.2)**
reactionist **22.29.2(.18.2)**
reactivate **22.4.16**
reactivation
   28.17.25(.3.9)
reactive **31.2.1(.13.3)**
reactively **1.31.30(.7.2)**
reactivity **1.10.16(.15)**
reactor **17.12.21(.3)**
Read **23.1**
read **23.1, 23.5**
readability **1.10.16(.22.1)**
readable **40.20.16(.12)** *
readableness
   34.18.16(.37.4)
readably **1.31.21(.4.4)**
readapt **22.22.4**
readaptation
   28.17.25(.3.3)
readdress **34.5.14(.6)**
Reade **23.1**
reader **17.13.1**
readership **20.2.7(.9)**
readily **1.31.17(.10)**
read-in **28.2.12**
readiness **34.18.16(.2.3)**
Reading **29.1.13(.4)**
reading **29.1.13(.1)**
readjust **22.29.12**
readjustment
   22.26.15(.13.3)
Readman **28.17.16(.22)**
readmission
   28.17.25(.2.4)
readmit **22.2.11**
readmittance
   34.24.10(.10)
readopt **22.22.5**
readoption **28.17.25(.14)**
readout **22.9.8**
readthrough **16.23.13**
read-write **22.16.24**
ready **1.11.5**
ready-to-serve **31.11**
ready-to-wear **6.18**

r

reaffirm **27.16.4**
reaffirmation **28.17.25(.3.7)**
reafforest **22.29.15(.17)**
reafforestation **28.17.25(.3.3)**
Reagan **28.17.15(.3)**
reagency **1.22.23(.10.4)**
reagent **22.26.15(.21)**
real **40.3, 40.8**
realgar **10.9, 17.16.19**
realign **28.14.19**
realignment **22.26.15(.13.4)**
realisability **1.10.16(.22.2)**
realism **27.15.21(.2.15)**
realist **22.29.2(.31.1)**
realistic **24.2.10(.15.3)**
realistically **1.31.24(.9.6)**
reality **1.10.16(.32.1)**
realizability **1.10.16(.22.2)**
realizable **40.20.16(.22)**
realization **28.17.25(.3.11)**
realize **35.15.21(.2)**
realizer **17.25.12(.15)**
reallocate **22.4.11(.6)**
reallocation **28.17.25(.3.5)**
reallot **22.11.17**
reallotment **22.26.15(.13.3)**
really **1.31.1, 1.31.3**
realm **27.18**
realness **34.18.16(.37.1)**
Realpolitik **24.1.3**
realtor **12.5.10, 17.12.26(.2)**
realty **1.10.28**
ream **27.1**
reamer **17.17.1**
reanalyses **35.1.16(.10)**
reanalysis **34.2.17(.10.5)**
reanalyse **35.15.21(.4.5)**
reanimate **22.4.13(.6)**
reanimation **28.17.25(.3.7)**
reap **20.1**
reaper **17.10.1**
reappear **3.1**
reappearance **34.24.10(.16)**
reapplication **28.17.25(.3.5)**
reapply **14.25.11**
reappoint **22.26.11**
reappointment **22.26.15(.13.3)**
reapportion **28.17.25(.8)**
reapportionment **22.26.15(.13.4)**
reappraisal **40.32.3**
reappraise **35.4.16**
rear **3**

Reardon **28.17.12(.3)**
rearer **17.32.2**
rearm **27.8**
rearmament **22.26.15(.13.2)**
rearmost **22.29.17(.4)**
rearrange **39.17.2**
rearrangement **22.26.15(.13.6)**
rearrest **22.29.5(.12)**
rearview **16.24.12**
rearward **23.18.26(.3)**
rear-wheel drive **31.9**
reascend **23.24.5(.11)**
reascension **28.17.25(.16)**
reason **28.17.24(.1)**
reasonable **40.20.16(.16.3)**
reasonableness **34.18.16(.37.4)**
reasonably **1.31.21(.6)**
reasoner **17.18.16(.15)**
reasoning **29.1.17(.12)**
reasonless **34.18.29(.27)**
reassemble **40.20.19**
reassembly **1.31.21(.12)**
reassert **22.20.10**
reassertion **28.17.25(.12)**
reassess **34.5.9**
reassessment **22.26.15(.13.5)**
reassign **28.14.13**
reassignment **22.26.15(.13.4)**
reassume **27.14.7**
reassumption **28.17.25(.14)**
reassurance **34.24.10(.16)**
reassure **12.16, 17.7.10**
reassuring **29.1.30(.8)**
reassuringly **1.31.28(.1.17)**
reattach **38.5**
reattachment **22.26.15(.13.6)**
reattain **28.4.3**
reattainment **22.26.15(.13.4)**
reattempt **22.25**
reave **31.1**
reawaken **28.17.13(.3)**
Reay **4**
reb **21.4**
rebadge **39.6**
rebalance **34.24.10(.24)**
rebar **10.5.1**
rebarbative **31.2.1(.9.1)**
rebase **34.4.3**
rebatable **40.20.16(.11.1)**
rebate **22.2.6, 22.4.8**
rebater **17.12.4(.4)**
rebbe **17.11.4**

rebbetzin **28.2.23(.13)**
rebec **24.4.3**
Rebecca **17.14.4**
rebeck **24.4.3**
rebel **40.5.2, 40.20.5**
rebellion **28.3.21(.2)**
rebellious **34.18.28**
rebelliously **1.31.33(.12.6)**
rebelliousness **34.18.16(.31.5)**
rebid **23.2.7**
rebind **23.24.13**
rebirth **32.15.1**
rebirther **17.22.10**
rebirthing **29.1.21**
reboot **22.18.3**
rebore **12.4**
reborn **28.11.2**
rebound **23.24.7(.2)**
rebounder **17.13.20(.5)**
rebozo **19.21**
rebroadcast **22.29.6(.5), 22.29.8(.3)**
rebuff **30.11.2**
rebuild **23.31.2**
rebuilder **17.13.23(.2)**
rebuilding **29.1.13(.16)**
rebuilt **22.32.1**
rebuke **24.15.8**
rebuker **17.14.14**
rebukingly **1.31.28(.1.6)**
reburial **40.3.14(.3)**
rebury **1.29.3**
rebus **34.18.10**
rebut **22.15.2**
rebutment **22.26.15(.13.3)**
rebuttable **40.20.16(.11.2)**
rebuttal **40.21.9**
rebutter **17.12.12**
rec **24.4**
recalcitrance **34.24.10(.16)**
recalcitrant **22.26.15(.23.4)**
recalcitrantly **1.31.22(.20.5)**
recalculate **22.4.23(.7.3)**
recalculation **28.17.25(.3.14)**
recalesce **34.5.16**
recalescence **34.24.10(.18)**
recall **40.10.7**
recallable **40.20.16(.29)**
recant **22.26.6**
recantation **28.17.25(.3.3)**
recanter **17.12.22(.4)**
recap **20.5.1**
recapitalization **28.17.25(.3.12)**
recapitalize **35.15.21(.4.3)**

recapitulate **22.4.23(.7.3)**
recapitulation **28.17.25(.3.14)**
recapitulative **31.2.1(.9.4)**
recapitulatory **1.29.11(.8.10)**
recapture **17.28.18**
recast **22.29.6(.5), 22.29.8(.3)**
recce **1.12.4**
re-cede **23.1.7**
recede **23.1.7**
receipt **22.1.9**
receivable **40.20.16(.19)**
receive **31.1.4**
receiver **17.21.1**
receivership **20.2.7(.9)**
recency **1.22.23(.10.4)**
recension **28.17.25(.16)**
recent **22.26.15(.17.1)**
recentness **34.18.16(.20.4)**
recep **20.4**
receptacle **40.23.12(.7.3)**
reception **28.17.25(.14)**
receptionist **22.29.2(.18.2)**
receptive **31.2.1(.12)**
receptively **1.31.30(.7.2)**
receptiveness **34.18.16(.28.1)**
receptivity **1.10.16(.15)**
receptor **17.12.19**
recess **34.5.9**
recession **28.17.25(.4)**
recessional **40.26.13(.14.3)**
recessionary **1.29.11(.13.2)**
recessive **31.2.4(.4)**
recessively **1.31.30(.7.4)**
recessiveness **34.18.16(.28.2)**
Rechabite **22.16.8**
recharge **39.8**
rechargeable **40.20.16(.25)**
recharger **17.29.7**
réchauffé **4.15**
recheck **24.4.11**
recherché **4.20**
rechristen **28.17.23(.2)**
recidivism **27.15.21(.2.11)**
recidivist **22.29.2(.20)**
recidivistic **24.2.10(.15.2)**
Recife **4.15**
recipe **1.8.11(.7)**
recipiency **1.22.23(.2)**
recipient **22.26.2(.1)**
reciprocal **40.23.12(.18)**
reciprocality **1.10.16(.32.5)**

reciprocally 1.31.24(.9.12)
reciprocalness 34.18.16(.37.5)
reciprocate 22.4.11(.6)
reciprocation 28.17.25(.3.5)
reciprocator 17.12.4(.7)
reciprocity 1.10.16(.16.2)
recirculate 22.4.23(.7.3)
recirculation 28.17.25(.3.14)
recision 28.17.26(.2)
recital 40.21.10
recitalist 22.29.2(.31.2)
recitation 28.17.25(.3.3)
recitative 31.1.1
recite 22.16.19
reciter 17.12.13(.7)
reck 24.4
reckless 34.18.29(.24)
recklessly 1.31.33(.12.6)
recklessness 34.18.16(.31.6)
reckon 28.17.13(.4)
reckoner 17.18.16(.6)
reckoning 29.1.17(.12)
reclaim 27.4.9
reclaimable 40.20.16(.15)
reclaimer 17.17.4
reclamation 28.17.25(.3.7)
reclassification 28.17.25(.3.5)
reclassify 14.14.4(.9)
reclinable 40.20.16(.16.2)
reclinate 22.4.14(.9.4)
recline 28.14.19(.16)
recliner 17.18.13(.14)
reclosable 40.20.16(.22)
reclothe 33.10
recluse 34.17.14
reclusion 28.17.26(.4)
reclusive 31.2.4(.8)
reclusiveness 34.18.16(.28.2)
recode 23.20.7
recognisability 1.10.16(.22.3)
recognisably 1.31.21(.7.2)
recognition 28.17.25(.2.4)
recognitory 1.29.11(.8.7)
recognizability 1.10.16(.22.3)
recognizable 40.20.16(.22)
recognizably 1.31.21(.7.2)
recognizance 34.24.10(.19)
recognizant 22.26.15(.18)
recognize 35.15.12(.7)
recognizer 17.25.12(.6)

recoil 40.11.4
recoilless 34.18.29(.12)
recoin 28.12
recollect 22.23.4(.11)
recollection 28.17.25(.15.2)
recollective 31.2.1(.13.2)
recolonization 28.17.25(.3.12)
recolonize 35.15.12(.5)
recolour 17.34.12
recombinant 22.26.15(.14)
recombination 28.17.25(.3.8)
recombine 28.14.4
recommence 34.24.3
recommencement 22.26.15(.13.5)
recommend 23.24.5(.7)
recommendable 40.20.16(.12)
recommendation 28.17.25(.3.4)
recommendatory 1.29.11(.8.6)
recommender 17.13.20(.3)
recommission 28.17.25(.2.4)
recommit 22.2.11
recommitment 22.26.15(.13.3)
recommittal 40.21.2
recompense 34.24.3
recompose 35.20.1
reconcilability 1.10.16(.22.2)
reconcilable 40.20.16(.29)
reconcilably 1.31.21(.9)
reconcile 40.13.12
reconciled 23.31.9
reconcilement 22.26.15(.13.7)
reconciler 17.34.13
reconciliation 28.17.25(.3.1)
reconciliatory 1.29.11(.8.1)
recondite 22.16.10
reconditely 1.31.22(.13)
reconditeness 34.18.16(.20.2)
recondition 28.17.25(.2.3)
reconditioner 17.18.16(.16)
reconduct 22.23.8
reconfiguration 28.17.25(.3.13)
reconfigure 17.16.2
reconfirm 27.16.4

reconfirmation 28.17.25(.3.7)
reconnaissance 34.24.10(.18)
reconnect 22.23.4(.4)
reconnection 28.17.25(.15.2)
reconnoitre 17.12.11
reconquer 17.14.21(.4)
reconquest 22.29.5(.11)
reconsecrate 22.4.22(.10)
reconsecration 28.17.25(.3.13)
reconsider 17.13.2
reconsideration 28.17.25(.3.13)
reconsign 28.14.13
reconsignment 22.26.15(.13.4)
reconsolidate 22.4.10
reconsolidation 28.17.25(.3.4)
reconstitute 22.18.10
reconstitution 28.17.25(.11)
reconstruct 22.23.8
reconstructable 40.20.16(.11.5)
reconstruction 28.17.25(.15.5)
reconstructive 31.2.1(.13.4)
reconstructor 17.12.21(.6)
reconvene 28.1.16
reconversion 28.17.25(.12)
reconvert 22.20.9
record 23.12.4
recordable 40.20.16(.12)
recorder 17.13.9
recordership 20.2.7(.9)
recording 29.1.13(.8)
recordist 22.29.2(.14)
record-player 17.2.10
recount 22.26.7
recoup 20.12
recoupable 40.20.16(.9)
recoupment 22.26.15(.13.3)
recourse 34.12.2
recover 17.21.9
recoverability 1.10.16(.22.2)
recoverable 40.20.16(.27.5)
recoverer 17.32.14(.13)
recovery 1.29.11(.15)
recreancy 1.22.23(.2)
recreant 22.26.2(.9)
recreantly 1.31.22(.20.1)
recreate 22.4, 22.4.2(.14)

recreation 28.17.25(.3.1)
recreational 40.26.13(.14.2)
recreationally 1.31.17(.14.3)
recreative 31.2.1(.2)
recriminate 22.4.14(.9.2)
recrimination 28.17.25(.3.8)
recriminative 31.2.1(.9.2)
recriminatory 1.29.11(.8.7)
recross 34.10.16
recrudesce 34.5.3
recrudescence 34.24.10(.18)
recrudescent 22.26.15(.17.2)
recruit 22.18.9
recruitable 40.20.16(.11.2)
recruital 40.21.11
recruiter 17.12.15(.7)
recruitment 22.26.15(.13.3)
recrystallize 35.15.21(.4.3)
recta 17.12.21(.2)
rectal 40.21.16
rectally 1.31.17(.9.3)
rectangle 40.24.14(.2)
rectangular 17.34.16(.21.3)
rectangularity 1.10.16(.21.1)
rectangularly 1.31.17(.29)
recti 14.8
rectifiable 40.20.16(.5)
rectification 28.17.25(.3.5)
rectifier 17.6.9(.4)
rectify 14.14.4(.4)
rectilineal 40.3.7(.2)
rectilinear 3.9.2
rectilinearity 1.10.16(.21.1)
rectilinearly 1.31.3(.7)
rectitude 23.17.4(.1)
recto 19.10.16
rector 17.12.21(.2)
rectoral 40.16.13(.12.1)
rectorate 22.19.24(.9)
rectorial 40.3.14(.5)
rectorship 20.2.7(.9)
rectory 1.29.11(.8.12)
rectrices 35.1.16(.10)
rectrix 34.23.2(.12)
rectum 27.15.9(.13)
rectus 34.18.11(.13)
recumbence 34.24.10(.9)

recumbency
　1.22.23(.10.2)
recumbent 22.26.15(.8)
recuperable
　40.20.16(.27.3)
recuperate 22.4.22(.6)
recuperation
　28.17.25(.3.13)
recuperative 31.2.1(.9.4)
recuperator 17.12.4(.15)
recur 18.5
recurrence 34.24.10(.16)
recurrent 22.26.15(.23.2)
recurrently 1.31.22(.20.5)
recursion 28.17.25(.12),
　28.17.26(.5)
recursive 31.2.4(.10)
recursively 1.31.30(.7.4)
recurvate 22.4.16
recurvature 17.28.15
recurve 31.11
recusance 34.24.10(.19)
recusancy 1.22.23(.10.4)
recusant 22.26.15(.18)
recyclable 40.20.16(.29)
recycle 40.23.10
recycler 17.34.23
red 23.5
redact 22.23.5(.5)
redaction 28.17.25(.15.3)
redactional
　40.26.13(.14.6)
redactor 17.12.21(.3)
redan 28.7.7
redback 24.6.6(.13)
red bark 24.8
red-blooded 23.18.10(.10)
red-bloodedness
　34.18.16(.21.1)
redbreast 22.29.5(.12)
redbrick 24.2.26(.13)
Redbridge 39.2.22(.10)
redbud 23.14
redcap 20.5.1
Redcar 10.8.12, 17.14.19
redcoat 22.21.5
redcurrant 22.26.15(.23.2)
redd 23.5
Reddaway 4.25.9
redden 28.17.12(.5)
reddish 36.2.12
reddishness
　34.18.16(.33.3)
Redditch 38.2.4
reddle 40.22.4
red-dog 26.7.4
reddy 1.11.5
rede 23.1
redecorate 22.4.22(.6)
redecoration
　28.17.25(.3.13)

rededicate 22.4.11(.6)
rededication
　28.17.25(.3.5)
redeem 27.1.3
redeemable 40.20.16(.15)
redeemer 17.17.1
redefine 28.14.10
redefinition
　28.17.25(.2.4)
redemption 28.17.25(.14)
redemptive 31.2.1(.12)
Redemptorist
　22.29.2(.29.3)
redeploy 13.17
redeployment
　22.26.15(.13.1)
redescend 23.24.5(.11)
Redesdale 40.4.3
redesignate 22.4.14(.13)
redesignation
　28.17.25(.3.8)
redetermination
　28.17.25(.3.8)
redetermine
　28.17.16(.17)
redevelop 20.13.7
redeveloper 17.10.14
redevelopment
　22.26.15(.13.3)
red-eye 14.9
red-faced 22.29.4
Redfern 28.18.7
redfish 36.2.18(.16)
Redford 23.18.16(.12)
Redgrave 31.3.7
redhanded 23.18.10(.14)
redhead 23.5.13(.10)
Redhill 40.2.18
redial 40.13.4, 40.16.6
redid 23.2.9
rediffuse 35.17.7
rediffusion 28.17.26(.4)
redingote 22.21.6
redintegrate 22.4.22(.11)
redintegration
　28.17.25(.3.13)
redintegrative 31.2.1(.3)
redirect 22.23.4(.10)
redirection
　28.17.25(.15.2)
rediscover 17.21.9
rediscoverer 17.32.14(.13)
rediscovery 1.29.11(.15)
redissolution
　28.17.25(.11)
redissolve 31.13
redistribute 22.18.10
redistribution
　28.17.25(.11)
redistributive 31.2.1(.8)
redivide 23.15.10

redivision 28.17.26(.2)
redivivus 34.18.18
redleg 26.4
redline 28.14.19(.15)
redly 1.31.23(.4)
Redmond 23.24.16(.7)
redneck 24.4.7
redness 34.18.16(.21.1)
redo 16.8
redoes 35.14
redolence 34.24.10(.24)
redolent 22.26.15(.25)
redolently 1.31.22(.20.5)
redone 28.13.4
redouble 40.20.12
redoubt 22.9.8
redoubtable
　40.20.16(.11.1)
redoubtably 1.31.21(.4.1)
redound 23.24.7(.4)
redox 34.23.8(.4)
redpoll 40.9.5, 40.18.3
redraft 22.27.4(.4)
redraw 12.21
redrawn 28.11.12
redress 34.5.14(.6)
redressable
　40.20.16(.21.1)
redressal 40.31.5
redresser 17.24.5
redressment
　22.26.15(.13.5)
redrew 16.23.9
Redruth 32.13
redshank 24.19.3(.5)
redshirt 22.20.12
redskin 28.2.13(.14)
redstart 22.10.3
reduce 34.17.13
reducer 17.24.14
reducibility 1.10.16(.22.2)
reducible 40.20.16(.21.2)
reductio ad absurdum
　27.15.10(.9)
reduction 28.17.25(.15.5)
reductionism
　27.15.21(.2.9)
reductionist
　22.29.2(.18.2)
reductionistic
　24.2.10(.15.2)
reductive 31.2.1(.13.4)
redundance 34.24.10(.11)
redundancy
　1.22.23(.10.2)
redundant 22.26.15(.10)
redundantly
　1.31.22(.20.2)
reduplicate 22.4.11(.6)
reduplication
　28.17.25(.3.5)

reduplicative 31.2.1(.9.1)
redux 34.23.11
Redvers 35.18.15
redwing 29.1.29
redwood 23.16.6(.10)
redye 14.9
reebok 24.9.3
re-echo 19.12.4
reed 23.1
reed-bed 23.5.2
reedbuck 24.12.1
reeded 23.18.10(.1)
reedification
　28.17.25(.3.5)
reedify 14.14.4(.5)
reedily 1.31.17(.10)
reediness 34.18.16(.2.3)
reeding 29.1.13(.1)
re-edit 22.2.8
reedling 29.1.31(.18)
re-educate 22.4.11(.6)
re-education
　28.17.25(.3.5)
reedy 1.11.1
reef 30.1
reefer 17.20.1
reefpoint 22.26.11
reek 24.1
reeky 1.12.1
reel 40.1
re-elect 22.23.4(.11)
re-election 28.17.25(.15.2)
reeler 17.34.1
re-eligible 40.20.16(.25)
re-embark 24.8.3
re-emerge 39.15
re-emergence
　34.24.10(.21)
re-emergent 22.26.15(.21)
re-emphases 35.1.16(.10)
re-emphasis
　34.2.17(.10.4)
re-emphasize
　35.15.16(.4)
re-employ 13.17
re-employment
　22.26.15(.13.1)
re-enact 22.23.5(.6)
re-enactment
　22.26.15(.13.3)
re-enforce 34.12.4
re-enforcement
　22.26.15(.13.5)
re-engagement
　22.26.15(.13.6)
re-engineer 3.9
re-enlist 22.29.2(.31.1)
re-enlistment
　22.26.15(.13.3)
re-enter 17.12.22(.3)
re-entrance 34.24.10(.16)

r

r

rental

relevantly 1.31.22(.20.4)
relevé 4.16
reliability 1.10.16(.22.1)
reliable 40.20.16(.5)
reliableness
  34.18.16(.37.4)
reliably 1.31.21(.2)
reliance 34.24.10(.5)
reliant 22.26.15(.4)
relic 24.2.27(.4)
relict 22.23.2
relief 30.1.9
relievable 40.20.16(.19)
relieve 31.1.9
reliever 17.21.1
relievo 19.17
relight 22.16.25
religion 28.17.28(.2)
religioner 17.18.16(.19)
religionism
  27.15.21(.2.9)
religionist 22.29.2(.18.3)
religionless 34.18.29(.27)
religiose 34.20
religiosity 1.10.16(.16.2)
religious 34.18.24
religiously 1.31.33(.12.4)
religiousness
  34.18.16(.31.5)
reline 28.14.19
relinquish 36.2.24
relinquishment
  22.26.15(.13.6)
reliquary 1.29.11(.24)
reliquiae 2.3
relish 36.2.27
relishable 40.20.16(.23)
relit 22.2.25
relive 31.2.5
reload 23.20.13
relocate 22.4.11
relocation 28.17.25(.3.5)
relucent 22.26.15(.17.3)
reluctance 34.24.10(.10)
reluctant 22.26.15(.9)
reluctantly 1.31.22(.20.2)
rely 14.25
REM 27.5
rem 27.5
remade 23.4.7
remain 28.4.7
remainder 17.13.20(.2)
remake 24.3.7
reman 28.7.10
remand 23.24.6(.8),
  23.24.8
remanence 34.24.10(.15)
remanent 22.26.15(.14)
remark 24.8.8
remarkable
  40.20.16(.13)

remarkableness
  34.18.16(.37.4)
remarkably 1.31.21(.5)
remarriage 39.2.22(.4)
remarry 1.29.5
remaster 17.12.24(.5)
rematch 38.5
Rembrandt 22.26.6
REME 1.15.1
remeasure 17.27.3
remeasurement
  22.26.15(.13.2)
remediable 40.20.3
remedial 40.3.4
remedially 1.31.3(.4)
remediless 34.18.29(.2)
remedy 1.11.17
remember 17.11.17(.3)
rememberable
  40.20.16(.27.3)
rememberer 17.32.14(.5)
remembrance
  34.24.10(.16)
remembrancer
  17.24.22(.7)
remex 34.23.4(.5)
remind 23.24.13
reminder 17.13.20(.11)
remindful 40.27.19,
  40.27.22
Remington® 28.17.11(.23)
reminisce 34.2.13
reminiscence
  34.24.10(.18)
reminiscent
  22.26.15(.17.1)
reminiscential
  40.33.12(.3)
reminiscer 17.24.2
remint 22.26.1
remise 35.15.11
remiss 34.2.12
remissible 40.20.16(.21.1)
remission 28.17.25(.2.4)
remissive 31.2.4(.2)
remissly 1.31.17(.20)
remit 22.2.11
remittable
  40.20.16(.11.1)
remittal 40.21.2
remittance 34.24.10(.10)
remittee 2.11
remittent 22.26.15(.9)
remitter 17.12.2
remix 34.23.2(.5)
remixer 17.24.20
remnant 22.26.15(.14)
remodel 40.22.7
remodification
  28.17.25(.3.5)
remodify 14.14.4(.5)

remonetization
  28.17.25(.3.12)
remonetize 35.15.7(.7)
remonstrance
  34.24.10(.16)
remonstrant
  22.26.15(.23.4)
remonstrantly
  1.31.22(.20.5)
remonstrate 22.4.22(.8)
remonstration
  28.17.25(.3.13)
remonstrative
  31.2.1(.9.4)
remonstrator
  17.12.4(.15)
remontant 22.26.15(.9)
remora 17.32.10(.6),
  17.32.14(.10)
remorse 34.12.3
remorseful 40.27.25
remorsefully
  1.31.17(.16.2)
remorsefulness
  34.18.16(.37.2)
remorseless 34.18.29(.33)
remorselessly
  1.31.33(.12.6)
remorselessness
  34.18.16(.31.6)
remortgage 39.2.13
remote 22.21.7
remotely 1.31.22(.17)
remoteness
  34.18.16(.20.3)
remould 23.31.13(.6)
remount 22.26.7
removability
  1.10.16(.22.2)
removable 40.20.16(.19)
removal 40.28.10
remove 31.10
remover 17.21.11
Remploy® 13.17
remunerate 22.4.22(.6)
remuneration
  28.17.25(.3.13)
remunerative 31.2.1(.9.4)
remuneratory
  1.29.11(.8.9)
Remus 34.18.15(.1)
Renaissance 34.24.6,
  34.24.10(.18)
renal 40.26.1
rename 27.4.5
renascence 34.24.10(.18)
renascent 22.26.15(.17.1)
Renata 17.12.8(.8)
renationalization
  28.17.25(.3.12)
renationalize
  35.15.21(.4.5)

Renault® 19.15.4
rencontre 17.12.22(.7)
rencounter 17.12.22(.5)
rend 23.24.5
Rendell 40.22.16
render 17.13.20(.3)
renderer 17.32.14(.7)
rendering 29.1.30(.8)
render-set 22.5.13(.4)
rendezvous 16.14
rendition 28.17.25(.2.3)
rendzina 17.18.1(.10)
René 4.14
Renée 1.16.1, 4.14
renegade 23.4.6
renegado 19.11.7
renege 26.1, 26.3
reneger 17.16.1, 17.16.3
renegotiable 40.20.3,
  40.20.16(.23)
renegotiate 22.4.2(.9)
renegotiation
  28.17.25(.3.1)
renew 16.24.10
renewability
  1.10.16(.22.1)
renewable 40.20.16(.7)
renewal 40.16.8
renewer 17.8
Renfrew 16.23.12
reniform 27.10.5(.2)
renitence 34.24.10(.10)
renitency 1.22.23(.10.2)
renitent 22.26.15(.9)
renminbi 1.9.19
Rennes 28.5
rennet 22.19.15(.2)
Rennie 1.16.5
rennin 28.2.18
Reno 19.15.1
Renoir 10.22.9
renominate 22.4.14(.9.2)
renomination
  28.17.25(.3.8)
renounce 34.24.5
renounceable
  40.20.16(.21.3)
renouncement
  22.26.15(.13.5)
renouncer 17.24.22(.4)
renovate 22.4.16
renovation 28.17.25(.3.9)
renovative 31.2.1(.3)
renovator 17.12.4(.11)
renown 28.8.4
Renshaw 12.16.12
rent 22.26.4
rentability 1.10.16(.22.1)
rentable 40.20.16(.11.6)
rent-a-car 10.8.8
rental 40.21.17(.2)

reproduction
28.17.25(.15.5)
reproductive
31.2.1(.13.4)
reproductively
1.31.30(.7.2)
reproductiveness
34.18.16(.28.1)
reprogram 27.6.17(.5)
reprogrammable
40.20.16(.15)
reprographer
17.20.12(.5)
reprographic 24.2.16(.3)
reprographically
1.31.24(.9.9)
reprography 1.18.9(.3.2)
reproof 30.13.4
reprovable 40.20.16(.19)
reproval 40.28.10
reprove 31.10
reprover 17.21.11
reproving 29.1.20
reprovingly 1.31.28(.1.9)
reptant 22.26.15(.9)
reptile 40.13.3(.7)
reptilian 28.3.21(.2)
Repton 28.17.11(.18)
republic 24.2.27(.14)
republican 28.17.13(.13)
republicanism
27.15.21(.2.9)
republication
28.17.25(.3.5)
repudiable 40.20.3
repudiate 22.4.2(.4)
repudiation 28.17.25(.3.1)
repudiator 17.12.4(.1)
repugnance 34.24.10(.15)
repugnant 22.26.15(.14)
repugnantly
1.31.22(.20.3)
repulse 34.27
repulsion 28.17.25(.17)
repulsive 31.2.4(.14)
repulsively 1.31.30(.7.4)
repulsiveness
34.18.16(.28.2)
repurchase 34.18.23
repurification
28.17.25(.3.5)
repurify 14.14.4(.14)
reputability 1.10.16(.22.2)
reputable 40.20.16(.11.3)
reputably 1.31.21(.4.3)
reputation 28.17.25(.3.3)
repute 22.18.10
reputed 23.18.9(.12)
reputedly 1.31.23(.14.3)
request 22.29.5(.11)
requester 17.12.24(.4)

requicken 28.17.13(.2)
requiem 27.3.16, 27.5.2
requiescat 22.7.9
require 17.6.13
requirement
22.26.15(.13.1)
requirer 17.32.14(.2)
requisite 22.2.17
requisitely 1.31.22(.15)
requisiteness
34.18.16(.20.3)
requisition 28.17.25(.2.5)
requisitioner
17.18.16(.16)
requisitionist
22.29.2(.18.2)
requital 40.21.10
requite 22.16.23
reran 28.7.20
rerate 22.4.22
re-read 23.1.11, 23.5.15
re-readable 40.20.16(.12)
re-record 23.12.4
reredos 34.10.9
re-release 34.1.8
re-roof 30.13.4
re-route 22.18.9
rerun 28.13.9
res 35.1, 35.4
resale 40.4.10
resaleable 40.20.16(.29)
resat 22.7.15
reschedule 40.15.9(.4)
rescind 23.24.2
rescindable 40.20.16(.12)
rescindment
22.26.15(.13.3)
rescission 28.17.26(.2)
rescript 22.22.1
rescuable 40.20.16(.6)
rescue 16.24.7
rescuer 17.8
reseal 40.1.10
resealable 40.20.16(.29)
research 38.16
researchable
40.20.16(.24)
researcher 17.28.16
reseat 22.1.9
resect 22.23.4(.7)
resection 28.17.25(.15.2)
resectional
40.26.13(.14.6)
resectionist 22.29.2(.18.2)
reseda 17.13.1, 17.13.15
reseed 23.1.7
reselect 22.23.4(.11)
reselection
28.17.25(.15.2)
resell 40.5.11
reseller 17.34.5(.11)

resemblance
34.24.10(.24)
resemblant 22.26.15(.25)
resemble 40.20.19
resembler 17.34.20
resent 22.26.4(.12)
resentful 40.27.18
resentfully 1.31.17(.16.2)
resentfulness
34.18.16(.37.2)
resentment
22.26.15(.13.3)
reserpine 28.1.7, 28.2.9
reservable 40.20.16(.19)
reservation 28.17.25(.3.9)
re-serve 31.11
reserve 31.11
reservedly 1.31.23(.14.7)
reservedness
34.18.16(.21.1)
reserver 17.21.13
reservist 22.29.2(.20)
reservoir 10.22.10
reset 22.5.13
resettability
1.10.16(.22.2)
resettable 40.20.16(.11.1)
resettle 40.21.4
resettlement
22.26.15(.13.7)
reshape 20.3
reship 20.2.7
reshuffle 40.27.11
reside 23.15.12
residence 34.24.10(.11)
residency 1.22.23(.10.2)
resident 22.26.15(.10)
residential 40.33.12(.3)
residentially 1.31.17(.22)
residentiary 1.29.11(.20)
residentship 20.2.8
residua 17.7.12(.4)
residual 40.34
residually 1.31.17(.25)
residuary 1.29.11(.3)
residue 16.24.6
residuum 27.15.4
resign 28.14.13, 28.14.14
resignal 40.26.19
resignation 28.17.25(.3.8)
resigned 23.24.13
resignedly 1.31.23(.14.6)
resignedness
34.18.16(.21.1)
resigner 17.18.13(.9)
resile 40.13.13
resilience 34.24.2
resiliency 1.22.23(.2)
resilient 22.26.2(.10)
resiliently 1.31.22(.20.1)
re-silver 17.21.19

resin 28.2.24
resinate 22.4.14(.9.3)
resiniferous
34.18.27(.20)
resinification
28.17.25(.3.5)
resiniform 27.10.5(.2)
resinify 14.14.4(.7)
resinoid 23.13.12
resinous 34.18.16(.15.3)
resist 22.29.2(.23)
resistance 34.24.10(.10)
resistant 22.26.15(.9)
resistibility 1.10.16(.22.2)
resistible 40.20.16(.11.7)
resistibly 1.31.21(.4.3)
resistive 31.2.1(.15)
resistivity 1.10.16(.15)
resistless 34.18.29(.22)
resistlessly 1.31.33(.12.6)
resistor 17.12.24(.2)
resit 22.2.16
resite 22.16.19
resize 35.15.16
resold 23.31.13(.8)
resole 40.18.10
resoluble 40.20.16(.28)
resolute 22.18.11
resolutely 1.31.22(.14)
resoluteness
34.18.16(.20.2)
resolution 28.17.25(.11)
resolutive 31.2.1(.8)
resolvability
1.10.16(.22.2)
resolvable 40.20.16(.19)
resolve 31.13
resolvedly 1.31.23(.14.7)
resolvedness
34.18.16(.21.1)
Resolven 28.17.20(.14)
resolvent 22.26.15(.16)
resolver 17.21.19
resonance 34.24.10(.15)
resonant 22.26.15(.14)
resonantly 1.31.22(.20.3)
resonate 22.4.14(.9.3)
resonator 17.12.4(.10)
resorb 21.9
resorbence 34.24.10(.9)
resorbent 22.26.15(.8)
resorcin 28.2.23(.6)
resorcinol 40.9.12
resorption 28.17.25(.14)
resorptive 31.2.1(.12)
resort 22.13.10, 22.13.11
resorter 17.12.10(.6)
resound 23.24.7(.7)
resoundingly
1.31.28(.1.5)
resource 34.12.6

r

r

revoker **17.14.17**
revolt **22.32.12**
revolting **29.1.12(.22)**
revoltingly **1.31.28(.1.4)**
revolute **22.18.11**
revolution **28.17.25(.11)**
revolutionary
1.29.11(.13.2)
revolutionism
27.15.21(.2.9)
revolutionist
22.29.2(.18.2)
revolutionize
35.15.12(.5)
revolvable **40.20.16(.19)**
revolve **31.13**
revolver **17.21.19**
revue **16.24.12**
revulsion **28.17.25(.17)**
revulsive **31.2.4(.14)**
reward **23.12.8**
rewardingly **1.31.28(.1.5)**
rewardless **34.18.29(.23)**
rewarewa **17.31.1**
rewash **36.9.5**
reweigh **4.25**
rewind **23.24.13**
rewinder **17.13.20(.11)**
rewirable **40.20.16(.27.2)**
rewire **17.6.13**
reword **23.19.8**
rework **24.17.6**
reworking **29.1.14(.12)**
rewound **23.24.7(.9)**
rewrap **20.5.6**
rewrite **22.16.24**
rewritten **28.17.11(.2)**
rewrote **22.21.14**
Rex **34.23.4**
Rexine® **28.1.18(.7)**
Rey **4**
Reyes **35.4, 35.15**
Reykjavik **24.2.17**
reynard **23.9.12, 23.18.14**
Reynolds **35.23.15**
Rh **38.3**
rhabdomancy **1.22.23(.4)**
Rhadamanthine
28.14.12
Rhadamanthus **34.18.19**
Rhaetian **28.3.15,
28.17.25(.1)**
Rhaetic **24.2.10(.1)**
Rhaeto-Romance **34.24.4**
Rhaeto-Romanic
24.2.15(.5)
rhapsode **23.20.11**
rhapsodic **24.2.11(.7)**
rhapsodical **40.23.12(.8)**
rhapsodically
1.31.24(.9.7)

rhapsodist **22.29.2(.14)**
rhapsodize **35.15.8**
rhapsody **1.11.17**
rhatany **1.16.15(.7)**
Rhayader **17.13.15**
rhea **3, 17.1**
rhebok **24.9.3**
rheme **27.1**
Rhemish **36.2.15**
Rhenish **36.2.16(.4)**
rhenium **27.3.8(.1)**
rheological
40.23.12(.17.2)
rheologist **22.29.2(.26.2)**
rheology **1.26.10(.11.1)**
rheostat **22.7.7**
rheostatic **24.2.10(.4.1)**
rheotropic **24.2.8(.5)**
rheotropism
27.15.21(.2.2)
rhesus **34.18.20**
rhesus-negative
31.2.1(.9.1)
rhesus-positive
31.2.1(.9.3)
rhetor **17.12.1**
rhetoric **24.2.26(.10)**
rhetorical **40.23.12(.18)**
rhetorically **1.31.24(.9.12)**
rhetorician **28.17.25(.2.6)**
Rhett **22.5**
rheum **27.14**
rheumatic **24.2.10(.4.2)**
rheumatically
1.31.24(.9.4)
rheumaticky **1.12.13**
rheumatism
27.15.21(.2.4)
rheumatoid **23.13.7**
rheumatological
40.23.12(.17.2)
rheumatologist
22.29.2(.26.3)
rheumatology
1.26.10(.11.2)
rheumy **1.15.12**
Rhiannon **28.10.14,
28.17.17(.5)**
rhinal **40.26.11**
Rhine **28.14**
Rhineland **23.24.6(.13)**
rhinestone **28.19.4(.9)**
rhinitis **34.18.11(.8)**
rhino **19.15.10**
rhinoceros **34.18.27(.23)**
rhinocerotic **24.2.10(.6)**
rhinopharyngeal
40.3.12, 40.16.11, 40.34
rhinoplastic
24.2.10(.15.4)
rhinoplasty **1.10.26(.5)**

rhinoscope **20.15.4(.1)**
rhizocarp **20.6**
rhizoid **23.13.17**
rhizome **27.17.11**
rhizopod **23.10.1**
rho **19**
Rhoda **17.13.17**
rhodamine **28.1.13**
Rhode Island
23.24.16(.16.2)
Rhodes **35.23.14**
Rhodesia **17.26.1, 17.27.1**
Rhodesian **28.17.25(.1),
28.17.26(.1)**
Rhodian **28.3.4(.10)**
rhodium **27.3.4(.8)**
rhodochrosite
22.16.19(.10)
rhododendron
28.17.31(.15)
Rhodope **1.8.11(.4), 1.8.13**
Rhodophyta **17.12.13(.5)**
rhodopsin **28.2.23(.12)**
rhodora **17.32.10(.3)**
Rhodri **1.29.16**
rhomb **21.17, 27.9**
rhombi **14.7**
rhombic **24.2.9(.8)**
rhombohedra **17.32.20**
rhombohedral
40.16.13(.17)
rhombohedron
28.17.31(.15)
rhomboid **23.13.6**
rhomboidal **40.22.9**
rhomboidally
1.31.17(.10)
rhomboidei **14.2**
rhomboideus **34.3.4**
rhombus **34.18.10**
rhona **17.18.18**
Rhondda **17.13.20(.7),
17.23.15**
Rhône **28.19**
Rhoose **34.17**
Rhos **34.20**
Rhossili **1.31.2**
rhotic **24.2.10(.11)**
rhoticity **1.10.16(.16.1)**
rhubarb **21.7**
Rhuddlan **28.17.33(.25)**
Rhum **27.11**
rhumb **27.11**
rhumba **17.11.17(.6)**
rhumb-line **28.14.19(.18)**
Rhydderch **24.16.10,
25.10**
Rhydding **29.1.13(.2)**
Rhyl **40.2**
rhyme **27.12**
rhymeless **34.18.29(.26)**

rhymer **17.17.11**
rhymester **17.12.24(.22)**
rhymist **22.29.2(.17)**
Rhymney **1.16.23**
rhyolite **22.16.25(.9)**
Rhys **34.1**
rhythm **27.15.19**
rhythm-and-blues
35.17.8
rhythmic **24.2.14(.15)**
rhythmical **40.23.12(.10)**
rhythmically
1.31.24(.9.8)
rhythmicity
1.10.16(.16.1)
rhythmist **22.29.2(.17)**
rhythmless **34.18.29(.26)**
ria **17.1**
rial **40.8**
rialto **19.10.21**
rib **21.2**
ribald **23.31.6, 23.31.15**
ribaldry **1.29.16**
riband **23.24.16(.2)**
Ribbentrop **20.7.12**
ribber **17.11.2**
ribbing **29.1.11**
Ribble **40.20.2**
ribbon **28.17.10**
ribbonfish **36.2.18(.19)**
ribcage **39.4.3**
Ribena® **17.18.1(.2)**
ribless **34.18.29(.21)**
riboflavin **28.2.20**
riboflavine **28.1.16**
ribonucleic **24.2.3**
ribose **34.20.3, 35.20.2**
ribosomal **40.25.12**
ribosome **27.17.10**
ribwort **22.20.15**
Ricardo **19.11.7**
rice **34.15**
ricer **17.24.13**
ricercar **10.8, 10.8.8**
ricercare **1.29.6, 4.26.5**
rich **38.2**
Richard **23.18.24**
Richards **35.23.12**
Richardson **28.17.23(.20)**
Richelieu **18.16**
richen **28.17.27**
Richie **1.25.2**
richly **1.31.36**
Richmal **40.25.15**
Richmond **23.24.16(.7)**
richness **34.18.16(.35)**
Richter **17.12.21(.1)**
ricin **28.2.23(.1)**
rick **24.2**
Rickard **23.9.9**

Rickards **35.23.5**
Rickenbacker **17.14.5**
ricketily **1.31.17(.9.2)**
ricketiness **34.18.16(.2.3)**
rickets **34.22.2**
Rickett **22.2.9(.1)**
Ricketts **34.22.2**
rickettsia **3.14.13**
rickettsiae **2.3**
rickettsial **40.3.10**
rickety **1.10.16(.10)**
rickey **1.12.2**
Rickover **17.21.14(.6)**
rickrack **24.6.21**
Ricks **34.23.2**
rickshaw **12.16.9**
Ricky **1.12.2**
ricochet **4.20, 22.5.15**
Ricoh **19.12.1**
ricotta **17.12.9**
ricrac **24.6.21**
rictal **40.21.16**
rictus **34.18.11(.13)**
rid **23.2**
riddance **34.24.10(.11)**
Riddell **40.5.4, 40.22.2**
ridden **28.17.12(.2)**
Ridding **29.1.13(.2)**
riddle **40.22.2**
riddler **17.34.22**
riddlingly **1.31.28(.1.18)**
ride **23.15**
rideable **40.20.16(.12)**
Rideout **22.9.8**
rider **17.13.12**
riderless **34.18.29(.17.2)**
ridge **39.2**
ridgel **40.34**
ridgepole **40.18.3**
ridgeway **4.25.25**
Ridgway **4.25.25**
ridgy **1.26.1**
ridicule **40.15.9(.5)**
ridiculous **34.18.29(.17.6)**
ridiculously **1.31.33(.12.6)**
ridiculousness
 34.18.16(.31.6)
riding **29.1.13(.9)**
Ridley **1.31.23(.1)**
Riemann **28.17.16(.1)**
Riesling **29.1.31(.26)**
Rievaulx **19.17, 35.18.15**
Rif **30.2**
rifampicin **28.2.23(.9)**
rifampin **28.2.9**
rife **30.12**
rifeness **34.18.16(.27)**
riff **30.2**
riffle **40.27.2**
riffraff **30.5.8**

Rifkind **23.24.2**
rifle **40.27.12**
rifleman **28.17.16(.35)**
riflescope **20.15.4(.1)**
rifling **29.1.31(.23)**
rift **22.27.1**
riftless **34.18.29(.22)**
rifty **1.10.24**
rig **26.2**
Riga **17.16.1**
rigadoon **28.16.4**
rigatoni **1.16.17(.3)**
Rigby **1.9.17**
Rigel **40.24.9, 40.34**
Rigg **26.2**
rigger **17.16.2**
rigging **29.1.15**
Riggs **35.24**
right **22.16**
rightable **40.20.16(.11.2)**
rightabout **22.9.6**
rightangle **40.24.14(.2)**
right-back **24.6.6(.12)**
righten **28.17.11(.12)**
righteous **34.18.23**
righteously **1.31.33(.12.4)**
righteousness
 34.18.16(.31.5)
righter **17.12.13**
rightful **40.27.18**
rightfully **1.31.17(.16.2)**
rightfulness
 34.18.16(.37.2)
righthand **23.24.6(.11)**
right-handed
 23.18.10(.14)
right-handedly
 1.31.23(.14.4)
right-handedness
 34.18.16(.21.1)
right-hander **17.13.20(.4)**
right-ho **19, 19.26**
rightish **36.2.11**
rightism **17.15.21(.2.4)**
rightist **22.29.2(.13)**
rightless **34.18.29(.22)**
rightlessness
 34.18.16(.31.6)
rightly **1.31.22(.13)**
rightmost **22.29.17(.4)**
rightness **34.18.16(.20.2)**
righto **19**
rightward **23.18.26(.9)**
rigid **23.2.20**
rigidify **14.14.4(.5)**
rigidity **1.10.16(.9)**
rigidly **1.31.23(.14.7)**
rigidness **34.18.16(.21.1)**
rigmarole **40.18.14**
rigor **12.8, 17.16.2**
rigorism **27.15.21(.2.14)**

rigor mortis **34.2.8**
rigorous **34.18.27(.17)**
rigorously **1.31.33(.12.5)**
rigorousness
 34.18.16(.31.5)
rigour **17.16.2**
Rigsby **1.9.22**
Rigveda **17.13.3**
Rijeka **17.14.4**
Rijksmuseum **27.15.1**
Rikki **1.12.2**
Rikki-Tiki-Tavi **1.19.3,
 1.19.6**
rile **40.13**
Riley **1.31.14**
rilievo **19.17**
Rilke **17.14.25**
rill **40.2**
rille **40.2**
rillettes **22.5.20**
rim **27.2**
Rimbaud **19.9.14**
rime **27.12**
rimester **17.12.24(.22)**
rimfire **17.6.9(.8)**
Rimini **1.16.15(.11)**
rimless **34.18.29(.26)**
Rimmer **17.17.2**
Rimmon **28.17.16(.2)**
rimose **34.20.8**
rimous **34.18.15(.8)**
rimrock **24.9.15**
Rimsky-Korsakov **30.8.6**
rimu **16.11**
rimy **1.15.11**
rind **23.24.13**
rinderpest **22.29.5(.1)**
rindless **34.18.29(.23)**
ring **29.1**
ringbark **24.8.3**
ringbinder **17.13.20(.11)**
ringbolt **22.32.12**
ring-dove **31.8**
ringent **22.26.15(.21)**
ringer **17.19.1**
ring-fence **34.24.3**
ringhals **34.27**
ringingly **1.31.28(.1.7)**
ringleader **17.13.1**
ringless **34.18.29(.28)**
ringlet **22.19.26(.23)**
ringletted **23.18.9(.13)**
ringlety **1.10.16(.37)**
ringmaster **17.12.24(.5)**
ringpull **40.14.2**
ringside **23.15.11(.13)**
ringsider **17.13.12**
ringster **17.12.24(.24)**
ringtail **40.4.2**
Ringwood **23.16.6(.15)**

ringworm **27.16.7**
rink **24.19.1**
rinkhals **34.27**
rinky-dink **24.19.1(.1)**
rinse **34.24.1**
rinser **17.24.22(.1)**
Rintoul **40.15.3**
Rio **19.1**
Rio de Janeiro **19.27.1**
Río de la Plata **17.12.8**
Río de Oro **19.27.7**
Río Grande **1.11.20(.4),
 23.24.6**
Rioja **17.14.8, 17.14.17,
 17.15**
Río Muni **1.16.14**
Riordan **28.17.12(.3)**
Ríos **34.20.1**
riot **22.19.4**
rioter **17.12.16(.1)**
riotless **34.18.29(.22)**
riotous **34.18.11(.10)**
riotously **1.31.33(.12.2)**
riotousness
 34.18.16(.31.3)
RIP **2.9**
rip **20.2**
riparian **28.3.20(.4)**
ripcord **23.12.4**
ripe **20.10**
ripely **1.31.20**
ripen **28.17.9**
ripeness **34.18.16(.18)**
ripieno **19.15.3**
Ripley **1.31.20**
rip-off **30.8.3**
Ripon **28.17.9**
riposte **22.29.9**
ripper **17.10.2**
ripple **40.19.2**
ripplet **22.19.26(.15)**
ripply **1.31.17(.7), 1.31.20**
Rippon **28.17.9**
riprap **20.5.6**
riproaring **29.1.30(.7)**
riproaringly
 1.31.28(.1.17)
ripsaw **12.14.10**
ripsnorter **17.12.10(.4)**
ripsnorting **29.1.12(.9)**
ripsnortingly
 1.31.28(.1.4)
ripstop **20.7.4**
riptide **23.15.4**
Ripuarian **28.3.20(.4)**
Rip van Winkle
 40.23.15
Risborough **17.32.14(.5)**
RISC **24.20.1**
Risca **17.14.23**
rise **35.15**

risen 28.17.24(.2)
riser 17.25.12
rishi 1.24.2
risibility 1.10.16(.22.1)
risible 40.20.16(.22)
risibly 1.31.21(.7.2)
rising 29.1.24
risk 24.20.1
riskily 1.31.17(.11)
riskiness 34.18.16(.2.4)
risky 1.12.17(.1)
Risorgimento 19.10.17
risotto 19.10.8
risqué 4.11
rissole 40.18.10
rit. 22.2
Rita 17.12.1
Ritalin® 28.2.31(.10)
ritardando 19.11.14
Ritchie 1.25.2
rite 22.16
riteless 34.18.29(.22)
ritenuti 2.12.10
ritenuto 19.10.11
ritornelli 2.32.5
ritornello 19.29.4
Ritson 28.17.23(.19)
Ritter 17.12.2
ritual 40.16.12
ritualism 27.15.21(.2.15)
ritualistic 24.2.10(.15.3)
ritualistically 1.31.24(.2),
    24.2.10(.15.3)
ritualization
    28.17.25(.3.12)
ritualize 35.15.21(.4.8)
ritually 1.31.17(.24)
Ritz 34.22.2
ritzily 1.31.17(.20)
ritziness 34.18.16(.2.7)
ritzy 1.22.21
rival 40.28.9
rivalry 1.29.24
rive 31.9
Rivelin 28.2.31(.10)
riven 28.17.20(.2)
river 17.21.2, 17.21.10
Rivera 17.32.5
riverain 28.4.18
riverbank 24.19.3(.1)
riverbed 23.5.2
riverboat 22.21.2
riverfront 22.26.12
Riverina 17.18.1(.15)
riverine 28.14.18
riverless 34.18.29(.17.4)
Rivers 35.18.15
riverside 23.15.11(.6)
rivet 22.2.14
riveter 17.12.16(.12)

Riviera 17.32.5
rivière 6
rivulet 22.5.21,
    22.19.26(.13)
Rix 34.23.2
Riyadh 23.7.1, 23.9.21
riyal 40.6, 40.6.1
Rizla® 17.34.28
roach 38.17
road 23.20
roadability 1.10.16(.22.1)
roadbed 23.5.2
roadblock 24.9.16(.10)
roadhog 26.7.11
roadholding 29.1.13(.16)
roadhouse 34.8.6(.12)
roadie 1.11.19
roadless 34.18.29(.23)
roadliner 17.18.13(.14)
roadman 28.7.10(.12),
    28.17.16(.22)
roadmen 28.5.7(.16)
roadroller 17.34.18(.14)
roadrunner 17.18.12
roadshow 19.22
roadside 23.15.11(.10)
roadstead 23.5.3
roadster 17.12.24(.19)
roadtest 22.29.5(.2)
roadway 4.25.13
roadwork 24.17.6(.9)
roadworthiness
    34.18.16(.2.6)
roadworthy 1.21
Roald 23.31.11
roam 27.17
roamer 17.17.16
roan 28.19
Roanoke 24.18.6
roar 12
roarer 17.32.10
roaring 29.1.30(.7)
roaringly 1.31.28(.1.17)
roast 22.29.17
roasted 23.18.9(.20)
roaster 17.12.24(.15)
roasting 29.1.12(.21)
Roath 32.16
rob 21.8
Robb 21.8
Robben Island
    23.24.16(.16.2)
robber 17.11.8
robbery 1.29.11(.7.1)
Robbie 1.9.7
Robbins 35.26.2
robe 21.16
Robens 35.26.13(.6)
Roberson 28.17.23(.14)
Robert 22.19.9

Roberta 17.12.17
Roberts 34.22.15
Robertson 28.17.23(.19)
Robeson 28.17.23(.18)
Robespierre 3.2.10, 6.1
Robey 1.9.13
robin 28.2.10
Robina 17.18.1(.2)
Robin Goodfellow
    19.29.4
Robin Hood 23.16
robinia 3.9.2
Robins 35.26.2
Robinson 28.17.23(.24)
Robinson Crusoe 19.20.9
roborant 22.26.15(.23.3)
robot 22.11.3
robotic 24.2.10(.6)
robotically 1.31.24(.9.4)
robotization
    28.17.25(.3.11)
robotize 35.15.7(.7)
Rob Roy 13
Robsart 22.10.9
Robson 28.17.23(.18)
robust 22.29.12
robustious 34.3.3,
    34.18.23
robustly 1.31.22(.22)
robustness 34.18.16(.20.4)
Roby 1.9.13
roc 24.9
rocaille 14.10
rocambole 40.18.4
Rocco 19.12.7
Rochdale 40.4.3
Roche 36.9, 36.16, 38.17
Rochelle 40.5.13
roche moutonnée 4.14
Rochester 17.12.24(.14)
rochet 22.19.21
Rochford 23.18.16(.21)
rock 24.9
rockabilly 1.31.2
Rockall 40.10.7
rock and roller 17.34.18
rock-bed 23.5.2
rock-bottom 27.15.9(.6)
rockbound 23.24.7(.2)
rockburst 22.29.16
rock-cake 24.3.6
rock-candy 1.11.20(.4)
Rockefeller 17.34.5(.9)
rocker 17.14.8
rockery 1.29.11(.10)
rocket 22.2.9(.5)
rocketeer 3.4
rocketry 1.29.15(.6)
rocketship 20.2.8
rockfall 40.10.11

rockfish 36.2.18(.17)
Rockhampton
    28.17.11(.18)
rockhopper 17.10.8
Rockies 35.2.5
rockily 1.31.17(.11)
rockiness 34.18.16(.2.4)
rockless 34.18.29(.24)
rocklet 22.19.26(.19)
rocklike 24.13.7(.14)
rockling 29.1.31(.19)
Rockne 1.16.21
rock 'n roll 40.18
rock 'n roller 17.34.18
Rockwell 40.5.17(.9)
rock-wool 40.14.7
rocky 1.12.7
Rocky Mountains
    35.26.13(.7)
rococo 19.12.14
rod 23.10
Roddenberry
    1.29.11(.7.2)
Roddick 24.2.11(.7)
Roddy 1.11.10
rode 23.20
rodent 22.26.15(.10)
rodential 40.33.12(.3)
rodenticide 23.15.11(.6)
rodeo 15.1.3, 19.2
Roderick 24.2.26(.10)
Rodger 17.29.8
rodham 27.15.10(.6)
Rodin 8, 28.7.7
rodless 34.18.29(.23)
rodlet 22.19.26(.18)
rodlike 24.13.7(.13)
Rodney 1.16.20
rodomontade 23.4.3,
    23.9.7
Rodrigues 35.5.7
roe 19
roebuck 24.12.1
Roedean 28.1.10
roe-deer 3.5.8
Roehampton
    28.17.11(.18)
Roffey 1.18.5
rogation 28.17.25(.3.6)
rogational 40.26.13(.14.2)
Rogationtide 23.15.4
roger 17.29.8
Rogers 35.18.21
Roget 4.21
rogue 26.15
roguery 1.29.11(.11)
roguish 36.2.14
roguishly 1.31.35(.7.1)
roguishness
    34.18.16(.33.4)
Rohan 28.17.8

roil **40.11**
roister **17.12.24(.9)**
roisterer **17.32.14(.6)**
roistering **29.1.30(.8)**
roisterous **34.18.27(.14)**
Rojas **34.7.17**
Rokeby **1.9.16**
Roker **17.14.17**
Roland **23.24.16(.16.2)**
rôle **40.18**
role-play **4.28.9**
Rolex® **34.23.4(.12)**
Rolf **30.20.4**
roll **40.18**
rollable **40.20.16(.29)**
rollaway **4.25.9**
rollback **24.6.6(.23)**
rollbar **10.5.14**
rollcall **40.10.7**
Rollei **14.25.10**
roller **17.34.18**
rollerball **40.10.4**
rollerblade **23.4.16**
rollerblader **17.13.3**
rollick **24.2.27(.9)**
rollickingly **1.31.28(.1.6)**
Rollins **35.26.2**
rollmop **20.7.6**
Rollo **19.29.8**
roll-on **28.10.26**
roll-on roll-off **30.8**
Rolls **35.30.13**
Rolls-Royce® **34.13**
rolltop **20.7.4**
Rolo® **19.29.14**
roly-poly **1.31.19**
ROM **27.9**
Rom **27.9, 27.17**
Roma **17.17.16**
Romaic **24.2.3**
romaine **28.4.7**
romaji **1.26.10(.4)**
Roman **28.17.16(.18)**
roman-à-clef **4.28.12**
Roman Catholic
24.2.27(.13)
Roman Catholicism
27.15.21(.2.12)
Romance **34.24.4**
romance **34.24.4**
romancer **17.24.22(.3)**
Romanesque **24.20.3**
roman-fleuve **31.11**
Romania **3.9.3(.5)**
Romanian **28.3.8(.3)**
Romanic **24.2.15(.5)**
Romanish **36.2.16(.13)**
Romanism
27.15.21(.2.9)
Romanist **22.29.2(.18.1)**

romanization
28.17.25(.3.11)
romanize **35.15.12(.5)**
Romano **19.15.7, 19.15.12**
Romanov **30.8.7, 31.7**
Romansh **38.18.4**
romantic **24.2.10(.14)**
romantical **40.23.12(.7.3)**
romantically **1.31.24(.9.5)**
romanticism
27.15.21(.2.12)
romanticist **22.29.2(.22)**
romanticization
28.17.25(.3.12)
romanticize **35.15.16(.4)**
Romany **1.16.15(.11)**
Romberg **26.14.1(.8)**
Rome **27.17**
Romeo **15.1.5**
romer **17.17.16**
Romero **19.27.3**
Romish **36.2.15**
Rommel **40.25.5**
Romney **1.16.23**
romneya **3.9.14**
romp **20.16.4**
romper **17.10.17**
rompingly **1.31.28(.1.2)**
rompy **1.8.14**
Romsey **1.23.19**
Romulus **34.18.29(.17.6)**
Ron **28.10**
rona **17.18.18**
Ronald **23.31.21**
Ronaldsay **4.18.11**
Ronaldsway **4.25.23**
Ronan **28.17.17(.12)**
Roncesvalles **40.6.11,
40.8.10**
rondavel **40.28.6**
ronde **23.24.9**
rondeau **19.11.14**
rondeaux **35.20.4**
rondel **40.22.16**
rondo **19.11.14**
Rondônia **3.9.11**
rone **28.19**
roneo **15.1.6**
ronggeng **29.3**
ronin **28.2.18**
Ronnie **1.16.9**
Ronsard **10.15**
Ronson® **28.17.23(.24)**
röntgen **28.17.15(.15),
28.17.32**
röntgenography
1.18.9(.3.2)
röntgenology
1.26.10(.11.4)
roo **16**
rood **23.17**

roodscreen **28.1.25(.8)**
roof **30.13**
roofage **39.2.16**
roofer **17.20.11**
roofing **29.1.19, 29.1.20**
roofless **34.18.29(.29)**
roofline **28.14.19(.20)**
roofscape **20.3**
rooftop **20.7.4**
rooftree **2.30.10**
rooibos **34.10.7**
rooinek **24.4.7**
rook **24.14**
Rooke **24.14**
rookery **1.29.11(.10)**
rookie **1.12.11**
rooklet **22.19.26(.19)**
rookling **29.1.31(.19)**
room **27.13, 27.14**
Roome **27.14**
roomer **17.17.12, 17.17.13**
roomette **22.5.8**
roomful **40.14.6(.14)**
roomily **1.31.17(.13)**
roominess **34.18.16(.2.5)**
roommate **22.4.13(.12)**
roomy **1.15.12**
Rooney **1.16.14**
Roosevelt **22.32.2**
roost **22.29.14**
rooster **17.12.24(.13)**
root **22.18**
rootage **39.2.10**
rootbeer **3.3.10**
rootedness **34.18.16(.21.1)**
rooter **17.12.15**
Rootes **34.22.14**
rootle **40.21.11**
rootless **34.18.29(.22)**
rootlessness
34.18.16(.31.6)
rootlet **22.19.26(.17)**
rootlike **24.13.7(.12)**
root-mean-square **6.18.9**
rootstock **24.9.4**
rootsy **1.22.21**
rooty **1.10.15**
rooves **35.28.7**
rope **20.15**
ropeable **40.20.16(.9)**
ropedancer **17.24.22(.3)**
ropemanship **20.2.7(.19)**
Roper **17.10.16**
ropewalk **24.10.9**
ropeway **4.25.10**
ropey **1.8.13**
ropily **1.31.17(.7)**
ropiness **34.18.16(.2.2)**
roping **29.1.10(.11)**
ropy **1.8.13**

roque **24.18**
Roquefort® **12.11.7**
roquelaure **12.23.2,
12.23.7**
roquet **1.12.15, 4.11**
Roraima **17.17.11**
Rorke **24.10**
ro-ro **19.27.12**
rorqual **40.35.3**
Rorschach test **22.29.5**
rort **22.13**
rorty **1.10.10**
Rory **1.29.8**
Ros **35.10**
Rosa **17.25.15**
rosace **34.4.11**
rosaceous **34.18.22(.3)**
Rosaleen **28.1.27(.7)**
Rosalie **1.31.17(.21)**
Rosalind **23.24.2**
rosaline **28.1.27(.7)**
Rosalyn **28.2.31(.10)**
Rosamund **23.24.12**
rosaniline **28.1.27(.7),
28.2.31(.10), 28.14.19(.11)**
Rosanna **17.18.6**
Rosanne **28.7.15**
rosaria **3.22.4**
rosarian **28.3.20(.4)**
Rosario **15.1.12**
rosarium **27.3.17(.3)**
rosary **1.29.11(.19)**
Roscian **28.3.13, 28.3.15,
28.17.25(.7)**
Roscius **34.3.10, 34.3.12**
roscoe **19.12.17**
Roscommon
28.17.16(.10)
rose **35.20**
rosé **4.19**
Roseanne **28.7.15**
roseate **22.3.9, 22.4.2(.10)**
rosebay **4.8**
Rosebery **1.29.11(.7.2)**
rosebowl **40.18.4**
rosebud **23.14**
rosebush **36.13**
rose-chafer **17.20.3**
rosehip **20.2.9**
roseless **34.18.29(.34)**
roselike **24.13.7(.23)**
rosella **17.34.5(.12)**
rosemaling **29.1.31(.8)**
rosemary **1.29.11(.12)**
Rosen **28.17.24(.14)**
Rosenberg **26.14.1(.9)**
Rosencrantz **34.22.18,
34.24.4**
Rosenthal **40.8.4,
40.10.12**
Rosenwald **23.31.6**

roseola 17.34.16(.1), 17.34.18
roseolar 17.34.16(.1), 17.34.18
roseolous 34.18.29(.17.1)
Rosetta Stone 28.19
rosette 22.5.14
Rosewall 40.10.17
rosewater 17.12.10(.7)
rosewood 23.16.6(.18)
Rosh Hashana 17.18.8(.9)
Rosicrucian 28.17.25(.11)
Rosicrucianism 27.15.21(.2.9)
Rosie 1.23.15
rosily 1.31.17(.21)
rosin 28.2.24
rosiness 34.18.16(.2.7)
rosiny 1.16.15(.15)
Roskilde 23.31.2
Roslea 4.28
rosolio 15.1.13
RoSPA 17.10.18
Ross 34.10
Rossellini 1.16.1(.16)
Rossendale 40.4.3
Rosser 17.24.9
Rossetti 1.10.4
Rossi 1.22.9
Rossini 1.16.1(.10)
Rossiter 17.12.16(.14)
Rosslare 6.21
Rosslyn 28.2.31(.23)
Ross-on-Wye 14.23
roster 17.12.24(.7)
Rostock 24.9.4
rostra 17.32.19(.11)
rostral 40.16.13(.16)
rostrally 1.31.17(.27.3)
rostrate 22.4.22(.8), 22.19.24(.12)
rostrated 23.18.9(.3)
Rostrevor 17.21.4
rostriferous 34.18.27(.20)
rostriform 27.10.5(.2)
Rostropovich 38.2.7
rostrum 27.15.26(.10)
Roswell 40.5.17(.16)
rosy 1.23.15
Rosyth 32.12
rot 22.11
rota 17.12.18
Rotarian 28.3.20(.4)
rotary 1.29.11(.8.11)
rotatable 40.20.16(.11.1)
rotate 22.4.9
rotation 28.17.25(.3.3)
rotational 40.26.13(.14.2)
rotationally 1.31.17(.14.3)
rotative 31.2.1(.3)

rotatively 1.31.30(.7.1)
rotator 17.12.4(.5)
rotatory 1.29.11(.8.2)
rotavate 22.4.16
Rotavator® 17.12.4(.11)
rotavirus 34.18.27(.10)
rote 22.21
rotenone 28.19.10
rotgut 22.15.5
Roth 32.9, 32.16
Rothamsted 23.5.3
Rother 17.23.8
Rotherham 27.15.26(.8)
Rotherhithe 33.7
Rothermere 3.8.7
Rothesay 1.22.25, 4.18.13
Rothko 19.12.16
Rothman 28.17.16(.28)
Rothschild 23.31.9
Rothwell 40.5.17(.14)
roti 1.10.18
rotifer 17.20.12(.1)
Rotifera 17.32.14(.12)
rotisserie 1.29.11(.18)
rotogravure 17.7.12(.10)
rotor 17.12.18
rotorscope 20.15.4(.1)
Rotorua 17.8
rot-proof 30.13.4
rotten 28.17.11(.9)
rottenly 1.31.27(.14)
rottenness 34.18.16(.25)
rotter 17.12.9
Rotterdam 27.6.5
Rottingdean 28.1.10
Rottweiler 17.34.13
rotund 23.24.12
rotunda 17.13.20(.10)
rotundity 1.10.16(.9)
rotundly 1.31.23(.17)
rotundness 34.18.16(.21.1)
Rouault 19
rouble 40.20.15
roucou 16.9
roué 4.5
Rouen 11.4
rouge 37.7
rouge-et-noir 10.22.9
rough 30.11
roughage 39.2.16
rough-and-ready 1.11.5
rough-and-tumble 40.20.19
roughcast 22.29.6(.5), 22.29.8(.3)
roughen 28.17.19
roughhouse 34.8.6(.18)
roughish 36.2.18(.8)
roughly 1.31.29

roughneck 24.4.7
roughness 34.18.16(.27)
roughrider 17.13.12
roughshod 23.10.10
Rough Tor 12
roughy 1.18.7
rouille 1(.6)
roulade 23.9.22
rouleau 19.29, 19.29.11
rouleaux 35.20.14
roulement 11.8
roulette 22.5.21
round 23.24.7
roundabout 22.9.6
round-arm 27.8.4
roundel 40.22.16
roundelay 4.28.7
rounder 17.13.20(.5)
Roundhay 4.24
Roundhead 23.5.13(.10)
roundhouse 34.8.6(.12)
roundish 36.2.12
roundly 1.31.23(.17)
roundness 34.18.16(.21.1)
round robin 28.2.10
round-shouldered 23.18.10(.15)
roundsman 28.17.16(.30)
roundup 20.9.6
roundworm 27.16.7
Rountree 2.30.10
roup 20.12
roupy 1.8.10
Rourke 24.10
rousable 40.20.16(.22)
rouse 35.8
rouseabout 22.9.6
rouser 17.25.6
rousingly 1.31.28(.1.12)
Rousse 34.17
Rousseau 19.20.9
Roussillon 11.18
roust 22.29.7
roustabout 22.9.6
rout 22.9
route 22.18
router 17.12.15
Routh 32.7
routine 28.1.9
routinely 1.31.27(.1)
routinism 27.15.21(.2.9)
routinist 22.29.2(.18.1)
routinization 28.17.25(.3.11)
routinize 35.15.12(.1)
Routledge 39.2.23
roux 16, 35.17
rove 31.12
rover 17.21.14
row 9, 19

Rowallan 28.17.33(.5)
rowan 28.17.3, 28.17.8
rowboat 22.21.2
Rowbotham 27.15.9(.6)
Rowbottom 27.15.9(.6)
rowdily 1.31.2
rowdiness 34.18.16(.2.3)
rowdy 1.11.8
rowdyism 27.15.21(.2.1)
Rowe 19
rowel 40.16.3
rowen 28.17.3
Rowena 17.18.1
Rowenta® 17.12.22(.3)
rower 17.9
rowhouse 34.8.6(.8)
Rowland 23.24.16(.16.2)
Rowlands 35.23.15
Rowlandson 28.17.23(.20)
Rowley 1.31.19
rowlock 24.9.16(.8), 24.16.16
Rowntree 2.30.10
Rowse 34.8
Rowton 28.17.11(.7)
Roxana 17.18.8(.8)
Roxanna 17.18.6
Roxanne 28.7.14
Roxburgh 17.32.14(.5)
Roxy 1.22.22
Roy 13
royal 40.16.5
royalism 27.15.21(.2.15)
royalist 22.29.2(.31.1)
royalistic 24.2.10(.15.3)
royally 1.31.17(.2)
royalty 1.10.28
Royce 34.13
Royle 40.11
Royston 28.17.11(.25)
rozzer 17.25.8
Ruabon 28.17.10
Ruaridh 1.29.8, 1.29.11(.3)
rub 21.11
rub-a-dub 21.11
rub-a-dub-dub 21.11
Rubáiyát 22.7.3
rubato 19.10.7
rubber 17.11.10
rubberiness 34.18.16(.2.9)
rubberize 35.15.20(.2)
rubberneck 24.4.7
rubbery 1.29.11(.7.1)
rubbing 29.1.11
rubbish 36.2.10
rubbishy 1.24.12
rubbity 1.10.16(.7)
rubble 40.20.12
rubblework 24.17.6(.19)
rubbly 1.31.17(.8)

Rubbra 17.32.18
rubdown 28.8.2(.4)
rube 21.13
rubefacient 22.26.15(.19)
rubefaction 28.17.25(.15.3)
rubefy 14.14.4(.3)
rubella 17.34.5(.2)
rubellite 22.16.25(.9)
Ruben 28.17.10
rubenesque 24.20.3
Rubens 35.26.13(.6)
rubeola 17.34.16(.1), 17.34.18
Rubery 1.29.11(.7.1)
Rubicon 28.10.11, 28.17.13(.2)
rubicund 23.24.12, 23.24.16(.5)
rubicundity 1.10.16(.9)
rubidium 27.3.4(.2)
rubify 14.14.1
rubiginous 34.18.16(.15.3)
Rubik 24.2.9(.4)
Rubin 28.2.10
Rubinstein 28.14.5
rubric 24.2.26(.13)
rubrical 40.23.12(.18)
rubricate 22.4.11(.6)
rubrication 28.17.25(.3.5)
rubricator 17.12.4(.7)
rubrician 28.17.25(.2.6)
rubricism 27.15.21(.2.12)
rubricist 22.29.2(.22)
ruby 1.9.10
ruche 36.14
ruck 24.12
ruckle 40.23.9
rucksack 24.6.14
ruckus 34.18.13(.7)
rucola 17.34.16(.9)
ruction 28.17.25(.15.5)
rudaceous 34.18.22(.3)
rudbeckia 3.6.4
rudd 23.14
rudder 17.13.11
rudderless 34.18.29(.17.2)
Ruddigore 12.8
ruddily 1.31.17(.10)
ruddiness 34.18.16(.2.3)
ruddle 40.22.10
ruddock 24.16.5
ruddy 1.11.13
rude 23.17
rudely 1.31.23(.13)
rudeness 34.18.16(.21.1)
ruderal 40.16.13(.12.1)
rudery 1.29.11(.9)
Rudge 39.11
Rudi 1.11.16

rudiment 22.26.15(.13.2)
rudimental 40.21.17(.2)
rudimentarily 1.31.17(.27.1)
rudimentariness 34.18.16(.2.9)
rudimentary 1.29.11(.8.12)
rudish 36.2.12
Rudolph 30.20.4
Rudy 1.11.16
Rudyard 23.9.21, 23.18.25, 23.18.28
rue 16
rueful 40.27.13
ruefully 1.31.17(.16.1)
ruefulness 34.18.16(.37.2)
rufescence 34.24.10(.18)
rufescent 22.26.15(.17.2)
ruff 30.11
ruffian 28.3.9
ruffianism 27.15.21(.2.9)
ruffianly 1.31.27(.3)
ruffle 40.27.11
ruffled 23.31.22
rufflike 24.13.7(.19)
Rufford 23.18.16(.7)
rufous 34.18.17
Rufus 34.18.17
rug 26.10
Rugbeian 28.17.1(.2)
rugby 1.9.17
Rugeley 1.31.37
Rügen 28.17.28(.8)
rugged 23.18.12
ruggedly 1.31.23(.14.5)
ruggedness 34.18.16(.21.1)
rugger 17.16.9
rugola 17.34.16(.10)
rugosa 17.25.15
rugose 34.20.7, 35.20.6
rugosely 1.31.33(.13), 1.31.34
rugosity 1.10.16(.16.2)
Ruhr 17.7
ruin 28.2.7
ruination 28.17.25(.3.8)
ruinous 34.18.16(.15.1)
ruinously 1.31.33(.12.3)
ruinousness 34.18.16(.31.3)
Ruislip 20.2.13
Ruiz 35.2.1
rule 40.15
rulebook 24.14.3
ruleless 34.18.29(.16)
ruler 17.34.15
rulership 20.2.7(.9)
ruling 29.1.31(.11)
rum 27.11

Rumansh 38.18.4
rumba 17.11.17(.6)
rum baba 17.11.7
Rumbelow 19.29.12
rumble 40.20.19
rumbler 17.34.20
rumbling 29.1.31(.16)
Rumbold 23.31.13(.2)
rumbustious 34.3.3, 34.18.23
rumbustiously 1.31.33(.1.1)
rumbustiousness 34.18.16(.31.1)
Rumelia 3.24.1
rumen 28.5.7(.9), 28.17.16(.15)
Rumi 1.15.12
rumina 17.18.16(.8)
ruminant 22.26.15(.14)
ruminate 22.4.14(.9.2)
rumination 28.17.25(.3.8)
ruminative 31.2.1(.9.2)
ruminatively 1.31.30(.7.1)
ruminator 17.12.4(.10)
rumly 1.31.26(.9)
rummage 39.2.14
rummager 17.29.13
rummer 17.17.10
rummily 1.31.17(.13)
rumminess 34.18.16(.2.5)
rummy 1.15.10
rumness 34.18.16(.24)
rumour 17.17.13
rump 20.16.5
Rumpelstiltskin 28.2.13(.14)
rumple 40.19.14
rumpless 34.18.29(.20)
rumply 1.31.17(.7)
Rumpole 40.18.3
rumpus 34.18.9(.11)
rumpy 1.8.14
rumpy-pumpy 1.8.14
rumrunner 17.18.12
run 28.13
runabout 22.9.6
runagate 22.4.12(.5)
runaround 23.24.7(.10)
runaway 4.25.9
runback 24.6.6(.17)
runcible 40.20.16(.21.3)
Runcie 1.22.23(.8)
Runciman 28.17.16(.2)
runcinate 22.19.15(.9)
Runcorn 28.11.5
rundale 40.4.3
Rundle 40.22.16
run-down 28.8.2
rundown 28.8.2(.8)

rune 28.16
rung 29.8
rungless 34.18.29(.28)
runic 24.2.15(.7)
run-in 28.2.18
runlet 22.19.26(.22)
runnable 40.20.16(.16.2)
runnel 40.26.10
runner 17.18.12
runniness 34.18.16(.2.5)
runningboard 23.12.2(.13)
runny 1.16.12
Runnymede 23.1.4
runt 22.26.12
runthrough 16.23.13
runty 1.10.23(.10)
run-up 20.9.9
runway 4.25.17
Runyon 28.17.32
rupee 2.9
Rupert 22.19.8
rupiah 17.1.1
rupturable 40.20.16(.27.5)
rupture 17.28.18
rural 40.16.13(.11)
ruralism 27.15.21(.2.15)
ruralist 22.29.2(.31.4)
rurality 1.10.16(.32.13)
ruralization 28.17.25(.3.12)
ruralize 35.15.21(.4.7)
rurally 1.31.17(.27.1)
ruridecanal 40.26.3, 40.26.13(.6)
Rurik 24.2.26(.8)
Ruritania 3.9.3(.2)
Ruritanian 28.3.8(.3)
rusa 17.24.14
ruse 35.17
rush 36.12
Rushdie 1.11.22
rushee 2.24
rusher 17.26.10
rush-hour 17.3.9
rushingly 1.31.28(.1.13)
rushlight 22.16.25(.20)
rushlike 24.13.7(.24)
Rushmore 12.9.13
Rusholme 27.17.12
Rushton 28.17.11(.26)
Rushworth 32.14.15
rushy 1.24.9
rusk 24.20.7
Ruskin 28.2.13(.14)
Russ 34.14
russe 34.17
Russell 40.31.10
russet 22.2.16
russety 1.10.16(.16.2)

Russia **17.26.10**
Russian **28.17.25(.9)**
Russianization **28.17.25(.3.11)**
Russianize **35.15.12(.5)**
Russianness **34.18.16(.25)**
Russification **28.17.25(.3.5)**
Russify **14.14.4(.9)**
Russki **1.12.17(.7)**
Russo **19.20.8**
Russophile **40.13.9**
Russophobe **21.16.1**
Russophobia **3.3.9**
rust **22.29.12**
rust-belt **22.32.2**
rustbucket **22.2.9(.6)**
rustic **24.2.10(.15.4)**
rustically **1.31.24(.9.6)**
rusticate **22.4.11(.6)**
rustication **28.17.25(.3.5)**
rusticity **1.10.16(.16.1)**
rustily **1.31.2**
rustiness **34.18.16(.2.3)**
rustle **40.31.10**
rustler **17.34.27**
rustless **34.18.29(.22)**
rustling **29.1.31(.26)**
rustproof **30.13.4**
rustre **17.12.24(.10)**
rusty **1.10.26(.8)**
rut **22.15**
rutabaga **17.16.3**
Rutgers **35.18.11**
ruth **32.13**
Ruthenia **3.9.1**
ruthenium **27.3.8(.1)**
Rutherford **23.18.16(.9)**
rutherfordium **27.3.4(.7)**
ruthful **40.27.24**
ruthfully **1.31.17(.16.2)**
ruthfulness **34.18.16(.37.2)**
ruthless **34.18.29(.31)**
ruthlessly **1.31.33(.12.6)**
ruthlessness **34.18.16(.31.6)**
Ruthven **28.17.20(.2)**
rutile **40.13.3(.3)**
rutin **28.2.11(.9)**
Rutland **23.24.16(.16.3)**
Rutledge **39.2.23**
ruttish **36.2.11**
rutty **1.10.12**
Ruwenzori **1.29.8**
R-value **16.24.17**
Rwanda **17.13.20(.4)**
Rwandan **28.17.12(.23)**
Rwandese **35.1.8**
Ryan **28.17.5**

Rycroft **22.27.5**
Rydal **40.22.11**
Ryde **23.15**
Ryder **17.13.12**
rye **14**
ryegrass **34.9.6**
Ryland **23.24.16(.16.2)**
Rylands **35.23.15**
Ryle **40.13**
Ryles **35.30.10**
Ryman **28.17.16(.13)**
ryokan **28.7.8,**
28.17.13(.15)
ryot **22.19.4**
Ryton **28.17.11(.12)**
ryu **16**
Ryvita® **17.12.1(.9)**
s **34.5**
Saab® **21.7**
Saadi **1.11.9**
Saar **10**
Saarbrücken **28.17.13(.11)**
Saarinen **28.17.17(.10)**
Saarland **23.24.6(.13)**
Saba **17.11.7**
sabadilla **17.34.2(.3)**
Sabaean **28.17.1(.2)**
Sabah **17.11.7**
Sabaism **27.15.21(.2.1)**
Sabaoth **32.9**
Sabatier **4.2.2**
sabayon **11.18**
sabbatarian **28.3.20(.4)**
sabbatarianism **27.15.21(.2.9)**
sabbath **32.14.7**
sabbatic **24.2.10(.4.1)**
sabbatical **40.23.12(.7.1)**
sabbatically **1.31.24(.9.4)**
sabbatization **28.17.25(.3.11)**
sabbatize **35.15.7(.7)**
Sabellian **28.3.21(.4)**
Sabian **28.3.2**
sabicu **16.9**
Sabin **28.2.10**
Sabina **17.18.1(.2)**
Sabine **28.1.8, 28.2.10,**
28.14.4
sabir **3.3**
sable **40.20.4**
sably **1.31.21(.1)**
sabot **19.9.3**
sabotage **37.4.3, 39.8**
saboteur **18.3**
sabra **17.32.18**
sabre **17.11.3**
sabretache **36.6.3**
sabretooth **32.13**

sabreur **18.15**
Sabrina **17.18.1(.15)**
sac **24.6**
saccade **23.9.9**
saccadic **24.2.11(.5)**
saccate **22.4.11(.3)**
saccharide **23.15.15**
saccharimeter **17.12.16(.9.1)**
saccharimetry **1.29.15(.8)**
saccharin **28.2.29(.5)**
saccharine **28.1.25(.3),**
28.2.29(.5)
saccharogenic **24.2.15(.4)**
saccharometer **17.12.16(.9.2)**
saccharometry **1.29.15(.8)**
saccharose **34.20.16,**
35.20.12
sacciform **27.10.5(.2)**
saccular **17.34.16(.21.2)**
sacculate **22.4.23(.7.3)**
sacculation **28.17.25(.3.14)**
saccule **40.15.9(.5)**
sacerdotage **39.2.10**
sacerdotal **40.21.14**
sacerdotalism **27.15.21(.2.15)**
sacerdotalist **22.29.2(.31.2)**
sacerdotally **1.31.17(.9.2)**
Sacha **17.26.6**
sachem **27.15.23**
Sachertorte **17.12.10(.2)**
Sachertorten **28.17.11(.10)**
sachet **4.20**
Sachs **34.23.5**
Sachsen **28.17.23(.21)**
sack **24.6**
sackable **40.20.16(.13)**
sackbut **22.15.2**
sackcloth **32.9**
sacker **17.14.5**
sackful **40.14.6(.12)**
sacking **29.1.14(.4)**
sackless **34.18.29(.24)**
sacklike **24.13.7(.14)**
Sackville **40.2.12**
sacra **17.32.21**
sacral **40.16.13(.18)**
sacrament **22.26.15(.13.2)**
sacramental **40.21.17(.2)**
sacramentalism **27.15.21(.2.15)**
sacramentalist **22.29.2(.31.2)**
sacramentality **1.10.16(.32.3)**

sacramentally **1.31.17(.9.3)**
sacramentarian **28.3.20(.4)**
Sacramento **19.10.17**
sacraria **3.22.4**
sacrarium **27.3.17(.3)**
sacred **23.18.27**
sacredly **1.31.23(.14.7)**
sacredness **34.18.16(.21.1)**
sacrementality **1.10.16(.32.3)**
sacrifice **34.15.6**
sacrificial **40.33.1**
sacrificially **1.31.17(.22)**
sacrilege **39.2.23**
sacrilegious **34.18.24**
sacrilegiously **1.31.33(.12.4)**
sacriligious **34.18.24**
sacriligiously **1.31.33(.12.4)**
sacring **29.1.30(.14)**
sacrist **22.29.2(.29.5)**
sacristan **28.17.11(.25)**
sacristy **1.10.26(.11)**
sacroiliac **24.6.1**
sacrosanct **22.23.13**
sacrosanctity **1.10.16(.8)**
sacrum **27.15.26(.12)**
sad **23.7**
Sadat **22.7.8**
sadden **28.17.12(.6)**
saddish **36.2.12**
saddle **40.22.5**
saddleback **24.6.6(.23)**
saddlebag **26.5.1**
saddle bow **19**
saddlecloth **32.9**
saddleless **34.18.29(.38)**
saddler **17.34.22**
saddlery **1.29.11(.27)**
Sadducean **28.17.1(.9)**
Sadducee **2.22.7**
Sadduceeism **27.15.21(.2.1)**
Sade **23.9**
sadhu **16.8.2**
Sadie **1.11.4**
sad-iron **28.17.5**
sadism **27.15.21(.2.5)**
sadist **22.29.2(.14)**
sadistic **24.2.10(.15.2)**
sadistically **1.31.24(.9.6)**
Sadler **17.34.22**
sadly **1.31.23(.5)**
sadness **34.18.16(.21.1)**
sadomasochism **27.15.21(.2.6)**
sadomasochist **22.29.2(.15)**

r
s

sadomasochistic 24.2.10(.15.2)
s.a.e. 2
saeter 17.12.4, 17.12.5
safari 1.29.6
safe 30.3
safebreaker 17.14.3(.8)
safe-conduct 22.23.8
safecracker 17.14.5
safeguard 23.9.10
safekeeping 29.1.10(.1)
safely 1.31.29
safeness 34.18.16(.27)
safety 1.10.24
safety-first 22.29.16
safetyman 28.7.10(.2)
safetymen 28.5.7(.2)
Safeway 4.25.19
safflower 17.3.11
saffron 28.17.31(.19)
saffrony 1.16.15(.18)
safranin 28.2.18
safranine 28.1.14
sag 26.5
saga 17.16.6
sagacious 34.18.22(.3)
sagaciously 1.31.33(.12.4)
sagaciousness 34.18.16(.31.4)
sagacity 1.10.16(.16.1)
sagamore 12.9.4
Sagan 28.7.9
Sagar 17.16.3
sage 39.4
sagebrush 36.12
sagely 1.31.37
sageness 34.18.16(.36)
Sager 17.16.3
sageship 20.2.7(.23)
saggar 17.16.5
saggy 1.14.5
Saginaw 12.10
sagitta 17.12.2, 17.12.16(.16)
sagittal 40.21.12
Sagittarian 28.3.20(.4)
Sagittarius 34.3.15(.3)
sagittate 22.4.9(.5)
sago 19.13.3
saguaro 19.27.5
sagy 1.26.2
Sahara 17.32.7
Saharan 28.17.31(.6)
Sahel 40.5.16
Sahelian 28.3.21(.1)
sahib 21.2, 21.7
Said 23.15
said 23.5
Saida 17.13.12
saiga 17.16.3, 17.16.10

Saigon 28.10.12
sail 40.4
sailable 40.20.16(.29)
sailbag 26.5.1
sailboard 23.12.2(.20)
sailboarder 17.13.9
sailboarding 29.1.13(.8)
sailboat 22.21.2
sailcloth 32.9
sailer 17.34.4
sailfish 36.2.18(.21)
sail-fluke 24.15.9
sailing 29.1.31(.4)
sailless 34.18.29(.38)
sailmaker 17.14.3(.3)
sailor 17.34.4
sailoring 29.1.30(.8)
sailorless 34.18.29(.17.6)
sailorly 1.31.17(.29)
sailplane 28.4.19
sainfoin 28.12
Sainsbury 1.29.11(.7.2)
saint 22.26.3
saintdom 27.15.10(.12)
sainted 23.18.9(.19)
Saint Elmo's fire 17.6
Saint-Étienne 28.5.19
sainthood 23.16.5(.6)
saintlike 24.13.7(.12)
saintliness 34.18.16(.2.10)
saintling 29.1.31(.17)
saintly 1.31.22(.20.1)
Saint-Malo 19.29.7
Saint-Moritz 34.22.2
saintpaulia 3.24.8
Saint-Saëns 11.12, 34.11, 35.11
saintship 20.2.8
Saint-Tropez 4.7
Saipan 28.7.4
Saisho 19.22
saith 32.5
saithe 32.4, 33.3
Sajama 17.17.7
Sakai 14.10
sake 24.3
saké 1.12.6, 4.11
saker 17.14.3
Sakhalin 28.1.27, 28.2.31
Sakharov 30.8.11, 31.7
saki 1.12.6
Sakta 17.12.21(.4)
Sakti 1.10.21
Saktism 27.15.21(.2.4)
sal 40.6
salaam 27.8.10
salacious 34.18.22(.3)
salaciously 1.31.33(.12.4)
salaciousness 34.18.16(.31.4)

salacity 1.10.16(.16.1)
salad 23.18.29
salade 23.9.22
Saladin 28.2.12
Salamanca 17.14.21(.3)
salamander 17.13.20(.4)
salamandrian 28.3.20(.12)
salamandrine 28.2.29(.9), 28.14.18
salamandroid 23.13.19
salami 1.15.7
Salamis 34.2.12
sal ammoniac 24.6.1
Salang 29.4.17
salangane 28.4.6
salariat 22.3.12
salary 1.29.11(.27)
salaryman 28.17.16(.2)
salat 22.10.13
Salazar 10.16
salbutamol 40.9.11
salchow 19.12.18
Salcombe 27.15.11(.17)
sale 40.4
saleability 1.10.16(.22.1)
saleable 40.20.16(.29)
Salem 27.15.28(.3)
salep 20.4, 20.13.7
saleratus 34.18.11(.3)
Salerno 19.15.13
saleroom 27.14.6(.20)
sales clerk 24.8.16
salesgirl 40.17
Salesian 28.3.14, 28.17.26(.1)
saleslady 1.11.4
salesman 28.17.16(.30)
salesmanship 20.2.7(.19)
salesperson 28.17.23(.15)
salesroom 27.14.6(.18)
saleswoman 28.17.16(.14)
saleswomen 28.2.17(.1)
Salford 23.18.16(.22)
Salian 28.3.21(.3)
Salic 24.2.27(.3)
salicet 22.5.13(.4)
salicin 28.2.23(.9)
salicine 28.1.18(.6), 28.2.23(.9)
salicional 40.26.13(.14.1)
salicylate 22.4.23(.7.2)
salicylic 24.2.27(.2)
salience 34.24.2
saliency 1.22.23(.2)
salient 22.26.2(.10)
salientian 28.17.25(.16)
saliently 1.31.22(.20.1)
Salieri 1.29.4
saliferous 34.18.27(.20)

salify 14.14.4(.16)
salina 17.18.13(.14)
Salinas 34.18.16(.1)
saline 28.14.19(.3)
Salinger 17.29.16(.8)
salinity 1.10.16(.13)
salinization 28.17.25(.3.11)
salinometer 17.12.16(.9.2)
Salisbury 1.29.11(.7.2)
Salish 36.2.27
saliva 17.21.10
salivary 1.29.11(.15)
salivate 22.4.16
salivation 28.17.25(.3.9)
Salkeld 23.31.4
sallee 1.31.7
sallenders 35.18.9
sallet 22.19.26(.5)
Sallis 34.2.22(.5)
sallow 19.29.5
sallowish 36.2.8
sallowness 34.18.16(.17)
sallowy 1(.7)
Sallust 22.29.15(.18)
sally 1.31.7
Sally Lunn 28.13
sally port 22.13.1
salmagundi 1.11.20(.7)
salmanazar 17.25.3
salmis 1.15.21
salmon 28.17.16(.7)
salmonella 17.34.5(.8)
salmonellosis 34.2.17(.11.2)
salmonid 23.2.13
salmonoid 23.13.12
salmony 1.16.15(.11)
Salome 1.15.15
salon 11.19, 28.10.26
Salonica 17.14.15(.9)
saloon 28.16.15
Salop 20.13.7
salopette 22.5.1
Salopian 28.3.1
salpiglossis 34.2.17(.6)
salpingectomy 1.15.13(.1)
salpingitis 34.18.11(.8)
salsa 17.24.24
salsify 1.18.9(.1)
salt 22.32.5, 22.32.6
Saltaire 6.4
salt-and-pepper 17.10.4
saltarelli 2.32.5
saltarello 19.29.4
Saltash 36.6.3
saltation 28.17.25(.3.3)
saltatorial 40.3.14(.5)

S

saltatory 1.29.11(.8.6)
saltbox 34.23.8(.2)
Saltburn 28.18.3
saltbush 36.13
saltcellar 17.34.5(.11)
salter 17.12.26(.5)
saltern 28.17.11(.27)
Salterton 28.17.11(.15)
Salthouse 34.8.6(.11)
saltigrade 23.4.15
saltimbocca 17.14.8
saltine 28.1.9
saltiness 34.18.16(.2.3)
salting 29.1.12(.22)
saltire 17.6.3
saltirewise 35.15.19
saltish 36.2.11
Salt Lake City 1.10.2
saltless 34.18.29(.22)
Saltley 1.31.22(.23)
saltlick 24.2.27(.15)
saltly 1.31.22(.23)
Saltmarsh 36.8
saltness 34.18.16(.20.4)
saltpan 28.7.4
saltpetre 17.12.1(.1)
saltshaker 17.14.3(.7)
saltus 34.18.11(.17)
saltwater 17.12.10(.7)
saltwort 22.20.15
salty 1.10.28
salubrious 34.3.15(.7)
salubriously 1.31.33(.1.4)
salubriousness 34.18.16(.31.1)
salubrity 1.10.16(.21.3)
saluki 1.12.12
salutary 1.29.11(.8.10)
salutation 28.17.25(.3.3)
salutational 40.26.13(.14.2)
salutatorian 28.3.20(.7)
salutatory 1.29.11(.8.6)
salute 22.18.11
saluter 17.12.15(.8)
salvable 40.20.16(.19)
Salvador 12.6, 12.6.6
Salvadoran 28.17.31(.8)
Salvadorean 28.3.20(.7)
salvage 39.2.17
salvageable 40.20.16(.25)
salvager 17.29.13
Salvarsan 28.7.14
salvation 28.17.25(.3.9)
Salvation Army 1.15.7
salvationism 27.15.21(.2.9)
salvationist 22.29.2(.18.2)
salve 31.13
salver 17.21.19

Salvesen 28.17.23(.14)
salvia 3.11.11
salvo 19.17
sal volatile 1.31.17(.9.1)
salvor 17.21.19
Salyut 22.18.10
Salzburg 26.14.1(.10)
Sam 27.6
samadhi 1.11.9
Samantha 17.22.13
Samar 17.17.7
samara 17.32.7
Samaria 3.22.4
Samaritan 28.17.11(.15)
Samaritanism 27.15.21(.2.9)
samarium 27.3.17(.3)
Samarkand 23.24.6(.7)
Samarra 17.32.7
Sama-Veda 17.13.3
samba 17.11.17(.4)
sambar 17.11.17(.4)
sambhar 17.11.17(.4)
sambo 19.9.14
sambur 17.11.17(.4)
same 27.4
same-day 4.10
samel 40.25.4
sameness 34.18.16(.24)
same-sex 34.23.4(.10)
samey 1.15.3
sameyness 34.18.16(.2.5)
samfu 16.13
Samhain 28.2.28, 28.17.3
Samian 28.3.7
samisen 28.5.10
samite 22.16.13
samizdat 22.7.8
Samlesbury 1.29.11(.7.2)
samlet 22.19.26(.21)
Sammy 1.15.6
Samnite 22.16.14(.11)
Samoa 17.9.6
Samoan 28.17.8
Sámos 34.10.12
samosa 17.24.14, 17.24.17
Samothrace 34.4.13
samovar 10.13
Samoyed 23.5
Samoyedic 24.2.11(.4)
samp 20.16.3
sampan 28.7.4
samphire 17.6.9(.8)
sample 40.19.14
sampler 17.34.19
sampling 29.1.31(.15)
Sampson 28.17.23(.17)
samsara 17.32.7
samsaric 24.2.26(.5)
samskara 17.32.7

Samson 28.17.23(.23)
Samsung 29.8, 29.9
Samuel 40.16.14
Samuels 35.30.12
samurai 14.24.6
san 28.7
Sana'a 10.11
San Andreas 34.18.2
San Antonio 15.1.6
sanataria 3.22.4
sanative 31.2.1(.9.2)
Sanatogen® 28.5.15, 28.17.28(.9)
sanatoria 3.22.9
sanatorium 27.3.17(.4)
sanatory 1.29.11(.8.7)
sanbenito 19.10.1
San Bernardino 19.15.1
Sánchez 35.5.11
Sancho 19.22, 19.24
San Clemente 1.10.23(.3)
sancta 17.12.21(.8)
sanctification 28.17.25(.3.5)
sanctifier 17.6.9(.4)
sanctify 14.14.4(.4)
sanctimonious 34.3.6(.7)
sanctimoniously 1.31.33(.1.2)
sanctimoniousness 34.18.16(.31.1)
sanctimony 1.16.15(.11), 1.16.17(.7)
sanction 28.17.25(.15.6)
sanctionable 40.20.16(.16.3)
sanctitude 23.17.4(.1)
sanctity 1.10.16(.8)
sanctuary 1.29.11(.3)
sanctum 27.15.9(.13)
sanctum sanctorum 27.15.26(.5)
Sanctus 34.18.11(.13)
Sand 11
sand 23.24.6
sandal 40.22.16
sandalwood 23.16.6(.22)
sandarac 24.6.21
Sandbach 38.5
sandbag 26.5.1
sandbagger 17.16.5
sandbank 24.19.3(.1)
sandbar 10.5.8
sand-bath 32.8
sandblast 22.29.6(.12), 22.29.8(.8)
sandblaster 17.12.24(.5)
sandbox 34.23.8(.2)
sandboy 13.3
Sandburg 26.14.1(.7)

sandcastle 40.31.6, 40.31.7
sander 17.13.20(.4)
sanderling 29.1.31(.12)
sanders 35.18.9
Sanderson 28.17.23(.14)
Sanderstead 23.5.3, 23.18.9(.20)
Sandes 35.23.15
sandfly 14.25.14
Sandford 23.18.16(.12)
Sandgate 22.4.12(.8)
sandglass 34.9.7
sandgrouse 34.8.7
sandhi 1.11.20(.4), 2.28
sandhog 26.7.11
Sandhurst 22.29.16
San Diego 19.13.3
sandiness 34.18.16(.2.3)
Sandinista 17.12.24(.2)
sandiver 17.21.12
sandlike 24.13.7(.13)
sandlot 22.11.17
sandman 28.7.10(.12)
Sandoval 40.6.11
Sandown 28.8.2(.8)
Sandoz 35.10
sandpaper 17.10.3
sandpiper 17.10.12
sandpit 22.2.5
Sandra 17.32.20
Sandringham 27.15.15
sandshoe 16.17
sandsoap 20.15.6
sandstock 24.9.4
sandstone 28.19.4(.9)
sandstorm 27.10.2
Sandwich 38.2.9, 39.2.21
sandwich 38.2.9, 39.2.21
sandwich-board 23.12.2(.18)
sandwich-man 28.7.10(.23)
sandwich-men 28.5.7(.27)
sandwort 22.20.15
sandy 1.11.20(.4)
sandyish 36.2.1
Sandys 35.23.15
sane 28.4
sanely 1.31.27(.4)
saneness 34.18.16(.25)
San Fernando 19.11.14
Sanford 23.18.16(.16)
sanforize 35.15.20(.2)
San Francisco 19.12.17
sang 29.4
sanga 17.16.17(.2)
sangar 17.16.17(.2)
sangaree 2.30

sang-de-boeuf **30.15**
Sanger **17.19.2**
sang-froid **10.22.13**
sangha **17.16.17(.2)**
Sango **19.13.12**
sangrail **40.4.14**
sangría **3.22.18, 17.1.16**
Sangster **17.12.24(.24)**
sanguification **28.17.25(.3.5)**
sanguinarily **1.31.17(.27.2)**
sanguinariness **34.18.16(.2.9)**
sanguinary **1.29.11(.13.2)**
sanguine **28.2.28**
sanguinely **1.31.27(.14)**
sanguineness **34.18.16(.25)**
sanguineous **34.3.6(.2)**
sanguinity **1.10.16(.13)**
Sanhedrim **27.2.14**
Sanhedrin **28.2.29(.9)**
sanicle **40.23.12(.11)**
sanidine **28.1.10**
sanies **35.1.1**
sanify **14.14.4(.7)**
sanious **34.3.6(.3)**
sanitaria **3.22.4**
sanitarian **28.3.20(.4)**
sanitarily **1.31.17(.27.1)**
sanitariness **34.18.16(.2.9)**
sanitarium **27.3.17(.3)**
sanitary **1.29.11(.8.7)**
sanitate **22.4.9(.5)**
sanitation **28.17.25(.3.3)**
sanitationist **22.29.2(.18.2)**
sanitization **28.17.25(.3.11)**
sanitize **35.15.7(.7)**
sanitizer **17.25.12(.2)**
sanitoria **3.22.9**
sanitorium **27.3.17(.4)**
sanity **1.10.16(.13)**
San Jacinto **19.10.17**
San José **4.19**
San Juan **28.9**
sank **24.19.3**
Sankey **1.12.16**
San Marino **19.15.1**
sannyasi **1.22.8**
sanpro **19.27.13**
San Quentin **28.2.11(.13)**
sans **35.26.7**
San Salvador **12.6.6**
sans-culotte **22.11.17**
sans-culottism **27.15.21(.2.4)**
Sanskrit **22.2.24**
Sanskritic **24.2.10(.2.4)**

Sanskritist **22.29.2(.13)**
Sansom **27.15.20(.18)**
Sanson **28.17.23(.24)**
Sansovino **19.15.1**
sans serif **30.14**
Santa **17.12.22(.4)**
Santa Ana **17.18.6**
Santa Catarina **17.18.1(.15)**
Santa Claus **35.12**
Santa Cruz **35.17**
Santa Fé **4**
Santander **6.5, 17.13.20(.4)**
Santayana **17.18.8(.12)**
Santiago **19.13.5**
Santiago de Compostela **17.34.5(.3)**
Santo Domingo **19.13.12**
santolina **17.18.1(.16)**
santonica **17.14.15(.9)**
santonin **28.2.18**
Santoríni **1.16.1(.15)**
Santos **34.10.8**
sanyasi **1.22.8**
Sanyo® **19.28**
São Paulo **19.29.6**
São Tomé **4.13**
sap **20.5**
sapajou **16.20**
sapan **28.7.4**
sapanwood **23.16.6(.14)**
sapele **1.31.1**
sapful **40.27.17**
saphenous **34.18.16(.1)**
sapid **23.2.6**
sapidity **1.10.16(.9)**
sapience **34.24.2**
sapiens **35.26.5**
sapient **22.26.2(.1)**
sapiential **40.33.12(.2)**
sapiently **1.31.22(.20.1)**
Sapir **3.1, 3.2.3**
sapless **34.18.29(.20)**
sapling **29.1.31(.15)**
sapodilla **17.34.2(.3)**
saponaceous **34.18.22(.3)**
saponifiable **40.20.16(.5)**
saponification **28.17.25(.3.5)**
saponify **14.14.4(.7)**
saponin **28.2.18**
sapor **12.3, 17.10.3**
sappanwood **23.16.6(.14)**
sapper **17.10.5**
Sapphic **24.2.16(.3)**
sapphire **17.6.9(.2)**
sapphirine **28.2.29(.5), 28.14.18**
Sapphism **27.15.21(.2.10)**

Sappho **19.16**
sappily **1.31.17(.7)**
sappiness **34.18.16(.2.2)**
Sapporo **19.27.7**
sappy **1.8.5**
saprogenic **24.2.15(.4)**
saprophagous **34.18.14(.5)**
saprophile **40.13.9**
saprophilous **34.18.29(.17.4)**
saprophyte **22.16.16**
saprophytic **24.2.10(.2.3)**
sapsucker **17.14.11**
sapwood **23.16.6(.8)**
Sara **17.32.5, 17.32.7**
saraband **23.24.6(.4)**
Saracen **28.17.23(.14)**
Saracenic **24.2.15(.4)**
Saragossa **17.24.9**
Sarah **17.32.5**
Sarajevo **19.17**
saran **28.7.20**
sarangi **1.14.14**
Saransk **24.20.13**
Saranwrap **20.5.6**
sarape **4.7**
Saratoga **17.16.15**
Sarawak **24.6.20**
sarcasm **27.15.21(.3)**
sarcastic **24.2.10(.15.4)**
sarcastically **1.31.24(.9.6)**
sarcelle **40.5.11**
sarcoma **17.17.16(.4)**
sarcomata **17.12.16(.9.3)**
sarcomatosis **34.2.17(.11.1)**
sarcomatous **34.18.11(.10)**
sarcophagi **14.11, 14.21**
sarcophagus **34.18.14(.5)**
sarcoplasm **27.15.21(.3)**
sarcoptic **24.2.10(.12)**
sarcous **34.18.13(.4)**
sard **23.9**
Sardanapalian **28.3.21(.3)**
Sardanapalus **34.18.29(.17.2)**
Sardegna **17.33.9**
sardelle **40.5.4**
sardine **28.1.10, 28.14.6**
Sardinia **3.9.2**
Sardinian **28.3.8(.2)**
Sardis **34.2.9**
sardius **34.3.4**
sardonic **24.2.15(.6.1)**
sardonically **1.31.24(.9.8)**
sardonicism **27.15.21(.2.12)**
sardonyx **34.23.2(.6)**
Sargant **22.26.15(.21)**

Sargasso **19.20.4**
sarge **39.8**
Sargodha **17.13.17**
Sargon **28.10.12**
sari **1.29.6**
sarin **28.1.25, 28.2.29(.3)**
sark **24.8**
sarkily **1.31.17(.11)**
sarkiness **34.18.16(.2.4)**
sarking **29.1.14(.5)**
sarky **1.12.6**
Sarmatia **3.16.3, 17.26.3**
Sarmatian **28.17.25(.3.7)**
sarmentose **34.20.4, 35.20.3**
sarmentous **34.18.11(.14)**
sarnie **1.16.8**
sarod **23.20.12**
sarong **29.6.14**
Saronic **24.2.15(.6.4)**
Saros **34.10.16**
Saroyan **28.17.4**
sarracenia **3.9.1**
Sarre **10**
sarrusophone **28.19.11**
sarsaparilla **17.34.2(.15)**
sarsen **28.17.23(.7)**
sarsenet **22.19.15(.9)**
Sarson **28.17.23(.7)**
Sarto **19.10.7**
sartorial **40.3.14(.5)**
sartorially **1.31.3(.11)**
sartorii **14.2**
sartorius **34.3.15(.5)**
Sartre **17.32.19(.4)**
Sartrean **28.3.20(.11)**
Sarum **27.15.26(.2)**
SAS **34.5, 34.7**
sash **36.6**
Sasha **17.26.6**
sashay **4.20**
sashimi **1.15.13(.10)**
sasin **28.2.23(.4)**
sasine **28.2.23(.2)**
Saskatchewan **28.17.6**
Saskatoon **28.16.3**
Saskia **3.6.9**
sasquatch **38.5, 38.8**
sass **34.7**
sassaby **1.9.11**
sassafras **34.7.18**
Sassanian **28.3.8(.3)**
Sassanid **23.2.13**
Sassenach **24.6.11, 25.4**
sassily **1.31.17(.20)**
sassiness **34.18.16(.2.7)**
Sassoon **28.16.10**
sassy **1.22.6**
sastrugi **1.14.10**
SAT® **2.11**

S

sat 22.7
Satan 28.17.11(.3)
satang 29.4.3
satanic 24.2.15(.5)
satanically 1.31.24(.9.8)
satanism 27.15.21(.2.9)
satanist 22.29.2(.18.1)
satanize 35.15.12(.5)
satanology 1.26.10(.11.1)
satay 4.9.2
satchel 40.16.12
satcom 27.9
sate 22.4
sateen 28.1.9
sateless 34.18.29(.22)
satellite 22.16.25(.9)
satellitic 24.2.10(.2.1)
satellitism 27.15.21(.2.4)
satem 27.15.9(.2)
satiable 40.20.16(.23)
satiate 22.3.10,
22.4.2(.11)
satiation 28.17.25(.3.1)
Satie 1.10.6
satiety 1.10.16(.4)
satin 28.2.11(.5)
satinette 22.5.9
satinflower 17.3.11
satinwood 23.16.6(.14)
satiny 1.16.15(.7)
satire 17.6.3
satiric 24.2.26(.1)
satirical 40.23.12(.18)
satirically 1.31.24(.9.12)
satirist 22.29.2(.29.3)
satirization
28.17.25(.3.11)
satirize 35.15.20(.2)
satisfaction
28.17.25(.15.3)
satisfactorily
1.31.17(.27.1)
satisfactoriness
34.18.16(.2.9)
satisfactory 1.29.11(.8.12)
satisfiability
1.10.16(.22.2)
satisfiable 40.20.16(.5)
satisfiedly 1.31.23(.11)
satisfy 14.14.6
satisfyingly 1.31.28(.1.1)
satnav 31.5
satori 1.29.8
satranji 1.26.13
satrap 20.5.6, 20.13.6
satrapy 1.8.11(.8)
satsuma 17.17.13
Satterfield 23.31.1(.2)
Satterthwaite 22.4.21
saturable 40.20.16(.27.5)
saturant 22.26.15(.23.3)

saturate 22.4.22(.6)
saturation 28.17.25(.3.13)
Saturday 1.11.17, 4.10.7
Saturn 28.17.11(.6)
saturnalia 3.24.3
saturnalian 28.3.21(.3)
Saturnian 28.3.8(.10)
saturnic 24.2.15(.9)
saturniid 23.2.2
saturnine 28.14.9
saturnism 27.15.21(.2.9)
satyagraha 10.21
satyr 17.12.6
satyriasis 34.2.17(.10.1)
satyric 24.2.26(.1)
satyrid 23.2.22
sauce 34.12
sauceboat 22.21.2
saucebox 34.23.8(.2)
sauceless 34.18.29(.33)
saucepan 28.17.9
saucepanful 40.14.6(.15)
saucepot 22.11.2
saucer 17.24.10
saucerful 40.14.6(.7)
saucerless 34.18.29(.17.5)
Sauchiehall 40.10.16
saucily 1.31.17(.20)
sauciness 34.18.16(.2.7)
saucy 1.22.11
Saud 23.8
Saudi 1.11.8
Saudi Arabia 3.3.3
Saudi Arabian 28.3.2
sauerbraten 28.17.11(.8)
sauerkraut 22.9.18
sauger 17.16.8
Saul 40.10
sault 16, 19
Saumur 17.7.12(.7)
sauna 17.18.7, 17.18.10
Saunders 35.18.9
Saundersfoot 22.17
saunter 17.12.22(.8)
saunterer 17.32.14(.6)
saurian 28.3.20(.7)
saurischian 28.3.5
sauropod 23.10.1
saury 1.29.8
sausage 39.2.19
Saussure 17.7.12(.11)
sauté 4.9.8
Sauternes 28.18.4
sauve qui peut 18
Sauveterrian 28.3.20(.4)
Sauvignon 11.18, 28.10.25
savable 40.20.16(.19)
savage 39.2.17
savagedom 27.15.10(.19)
savagely 1.31.37

savageness 34.18.16(.36)
savagery 1.29.11(.23)
savannah 17.18.6
savarin 28.2.29(.5)
savate 22.10.8
save 31.3
saved 23.26
saveloy 13.17
saver 17.21.3
Savernake 24.6.11
Savery 1.29.11(.15)
Savile 40.28.5
savin 28.2.20
savine 28.2.20
saving 29.1.20
saviour 17.33.10
Savlon® 28.10.26
savoir faire 6
savoir vivre 17.32.26
Savonarola 17.34.18(.14)
Savonlinna 17.18.2
savor 17.21.3
savorily 1.31.17(.27.2)
savory 1.29.11(.15)
savour 17.21.3
savourily 1.31.17(.27.2)
savouriness 34.18.16(.2.9)
savourless 34.18.29(.17.4)
savoury 1.29.11(.15)
savoy 13.8
Savoyard 23.9, 23.9.4
savvy 1.19.5
saw 12
sawbench 38.18.2
sawbill 40.2.4
sawbones 35.26.15
Sawbridgeworth
32.14.15
sawbuck 24.12.1
sawcut 22.15.4
sawdust 22.29.12
sawfish 36.2.18(.7)
sawfly 14.25.14
sawgrass 34.9.6
sawhorse 34.12.7
sawlike 24.13.7(.6)
sawmill 40.2.9
sawn 28.11
sawpit 22.2.5
sawtooth 32.13
sawtoothed 22.28
sawyer 17.5
sax 34.23.5
Saxa 17.24.20
saxatile 40.2.5, 40.13.3(.4)
saxboard 23.12.2(.15)
Saxby 1.9.21
saxe 34.23.5
Saxe-Coburg-Gotha
17.12.18

saxhorn 28.11.10
saxicoline 28.14.19(.11)
saxicolous 34.18.29(.17.2)
saxifrage 37.2, 39.4.9
saxist 22.29.2(.22)
Saxmundham
27.15.10(.14)
Saxo 19.20.15
Saxon 28.17.23(.21)
Saxondom 27.15.10(.14)
Saxone 28.19.13
Saxonism 27.15.21(.2.9)
Saxonist 22.29.2(.18.1)
Saxonize 35.15.12(.5)
saxony 1.16.15(.14)
saxophone 28.19.11
saxophonic 24.2.15(.6.3)
saxophonist
22.29.2(.18.1)
Saxton 28.17.11(.25)
say 4
sayable 40.20.16(.2)
Sayce 34.4
sayer 17.2
Sayers 35.18.1
saying 29.1.3
says 35.5
say-so 19.20.2
S-bend 23.24.5(.3)
scab 21.6
scabbard 23.18.8
scabbard-fish 36.2.18(.16)
scabbiness 34.18.16(.2.2)
scabby 1.9.5
scabies 35.1.6, 35.2.2
scabious 34.3.2
scablike 24.13.7(.11)
scabrous 34.18.27(.13)
scabrously 1.31.33(.12.5)
scad 23.7
Scafell 40.5.9
scaffold 23.31.13(.7),
23.31.22
scaffolding 29.1.13(.16)
scagliola 17.34.18(.15)
scalability 1.10.16(.22.1)
scalable 40.20.16(.29)
scalar 17.34.4
scalariform 27.10.5(.2)
scald 23.31.6
scalder 17.13.23(.6)
scale 40.4
scaleless 34.18.29(.38)
scalelike 24.13.7(.27)
scale-moss 34.10.12
scalene 28.1.27(.2)
scaleni 14.13
scalenus 34.18.16(.1)
scaler 17.34.4
Scalextric 24.2.26(.14.5)

Scaliger **17.29.13**
scaliness **34.18.16(.2.10)**
scallion **28.3.21(.5)**
scallop **20.13.7**
scalloper **17.10.14**
scallywag **26.5.7**
scaloppine **1.16.1(.1)**
scalp **20.18**
scalpel **40.19.16**
scalper **17.10.19**
scalpless **34.18.29(.20)**
scalpriform **27.10.5(.2)**
scaly **1.31.4**
scam **27.6**
Scammell **40.25.4**
scammony **1.16.15(.11)**
scamp **20.16.3**
scamper **17.10.17**
scampi **1.8.14**
scampish **36.2.9**
scan **28.7**
scandal **40.22.16**
scandalize **35.15.21(.4.3)**
scandalmonger
  17.16.17(.4)
scandalous **34.18.29(.17.2)**
scandalously
  1.31.33(.12.6)
scandalousness
  34.18.16(.31.6)
Scanderbeg **26.4**
Scandia **3.5.9**
Scandinavia **3.11.3**
Scandinavian **28.3.10**
scandium **27.3.4(.9)**
Scanlon **28.17.33(.23)**
scannable **40.20.16(.16.1)**
scanner **17.18.6**
scansion **28.17.25(.16)**
scansorial **40.3.14(.5)**
scant **22.26.6**
scanties **35.2.3**
scantily **1.31.17(.9.3)**
scantiness **34.18.16(.2.3)**
scantling **29.1.31(.17)**
scantly **1.31.22(.20.1)**
scantness **34.18.16(.20.4)**
scanty **1.10.23(.4)**
Scapa Flow **19**
scape **20.3**
scapegoat **22.21.6**
scapegoater **17.12.18**
scapegrace **34.4.13**
scaphoid **23.13.13**
scapula **17.34.16(.21.1)**
scapulae **2.32.9(.8)**
scapular **17.34.16(.21.1)**
scapulary **1.29.11(.27)**
scar **10**
scarab **21.14**

scarabaei **14.1**
scarabaeid **23.2.1**
scarabaeus **34.18.1**
scaramouch **36.14**
Scarborough **17.32.14(.5)**
scarce **34.6**
scarcely **1.31.33(.3)**
scarceness **34.18.16(.31.2)**
scarcity **1.10.16(.16.1)**
scare **6**
scarecrow **19.27.17**
scared **23.6**
scaredy-cat **22.7.9**
scaremonger **17.16.17(.4)**
scaremongering
  29.1.30(.8)
scarer **17.32.5**
scarf **30.7**
Scarfe **30.7**
Scargill **40.2.8**
scarification
  28.17.25(.3.5)
scarificator **17.12.4(.7)**
scarifier **17.6.9(.4)**
scarify **14.14.4(.14)**
scarily **1.31.17(.27.1)**
scariness **34.18.16(.2.9)**
scarious **34.3.15(.3)**
Scarisbrick **24.2.26(.13)**
scarlatina **17.18.1(.3)**
Scarlatti **1.10.6**
scarless **34.18.29(.9)**
scarlet **22.19.26(.7)**
Scarlett **22.19.26(.7)**
Scarman **28.17.16(.9)**
scaroid **23.13.19**
scarp **20.6**
scarper **17.10.7**
Scart **22.10**
scarus **34.18.27(.4)**
scarves **35.28.4**
scary **1.29.4**
Scase **34.4**
scat **22.7**
scathe **33.3**
scatheless **34.18.29(.32)**
scathing **29.1.22**
scathingly **1.31.28(.1.10)**
scatological
  40.23.12(.17.2)
scatologist **22.29.2(.26.3)**
scatology **1.26.10(.11.2)**
scatophagous
  34.18.14(.5)
scatter **17.12.6**
scatterbrain **28.4.18**
scatterer **17.32.14(.6)**
scattergram **27.6.17(.5)**
scattergun **28.13.5**
scatterplot **22.11.17**

scattershot **22.11.12**
scattily **1.31.17(.9.1)**
scattiness **34.18.16(.2.3)**
scatty **1.10.6**
scaup **20.8**
scauper **17.10.9**
scaur **12**
scavenge **39.17.9, 39.17.10**
scavenger **17.29.16(.8)**
scavengery **1.29.11(.21)**
scazon **28.17.24(.3)**
scean dhu **16**
scena **17.18.3**
scenario **15.1.12**
scenarist **22.29.2(.29.2)**
scend **23.24.5**
scene **28.1**
scenery **1.29.11(.13.1)**
sceneshifter **17.12.23**
scenester **17.12.24(.23)**
scenic **24.2.15(.1)**
scenically **1.31.24(.9.8)**
scent **22.26.4**
scentless **34.18.29(.22)**
sceptic **24.2.10(.12)**
sceptical **40.23.12(.7.3)**
sceptically **1.31.24(.9.5)**
scepticism
  27.15.21(.2.12)
sceptre **17.12.19**
Schadenfreude **17.13.10**
Schaefer **17.20.3**
Schaeffer **17.20.3**
schappe **17.10.5, 20.5**
schedule **40.15.9(.4), 40.34**
scheduler **17.34.15,
  17.34.16(.19)**
Scheele **17.34.4**
scheelite **22.16.25(.1)**
Scheherazade **17.13.7**
Schelde **17.13.23(.3),
  23.31.4**
Scheldt **22.32.2**
Schelling **29.1.31(.5)**
schema **17.17.1**
schemata **17.12.16(.9.1)**
schematic **24.2.10(.4.2)**
schematically
  1.31.24(.9.4)
schematism
  27.15.21(.2.4)
schematization
  28.17.25(.3.11)
schematize **35.15.7(.7)**
scheme **27.1**
schemer **17.17.1**
scheming **29.1.16**
schemingly **1.31.28(.1.7)**
Schenectady **1.11.17**
scherzando **19.11.14**
scherzo **19.20.14**

Schiaparelli **1.31.5**
Schick **24.2**
Schiedam **27.6.5**
Schiele **17.34.1**
Schiller **17.34.2**
Schilling **29.1.31(.2)**
schipperke **1.12.13**
schism **27.15.21(.2.1)**
schismatic **24.2.10(.4.2)**
schismatical
  40.23.12(.7.1)
schismatically
  1.31.24(.9.4)
schismatize **35.15.7(.7)**
schist **22.29.2**
schistose **34.20.4**
schistosome **27.17.10**
schistosomiases
  35.1.16(.10)
schistosomiasis
  34.2.17(.10.1)
schizanthus **34.18.19**
schizo **19.20.14**
schizocarp **20.6**
schizocarpic **24.2.8(.4)**
schizocarpous **34.18.9(.5)**
schizogenous
  34.18.16(.15.3)
schizogeny **1.16.15(.17)**
schizoid **23.13.16**
schizomycete **22.1.9**
schizont **22.26.9**
schizophrenia **3.9.1**
schizophrenic **24.2.15(.4)**
schizostylis **34.2.22(.7)**
schizothymia **3.8.5**
schizothymic **24.2.14(.8)**
schizotype **20.10.2**
Schlegel **40.24.3**
Schleicher **17.14.12, 17.15**
schlemiel **40.1.6**
schlepp **20.4**
Schlesinger **17.29.16(.8)**
Schleswig **26.2.5, 26.2.9**
Schliemann **28.17.16(.1)**
schlieren **28.17.31(.2)**
schlock **24.9**
schlocky **1.12.7**
schmaltz **34.22.20**
schmaltzy **1.22.26**
Schmidt **22.2**
Schmitt **22.2**
schmo **19**
schmoe **19**
schmooze **35.17**
schmuck **24.12**
schnapps **34.21.5**
schnauzer **17.24.19,
  17.25.6**
Schneider **17.13.12**
schnitzel **40.31.16**

schnook 24.14
schnorrer 17.32.8
schnozz 35.10
schnozzle 40.32.8
Schofield 23.31.1(.2)
scholar 17.34.9
scholarliness
34.18.16(.2.10)
scholarly 1.31.17(.29)
scholarship 20.2.7(.9)
scholastic 24.2.10(.15.4)
scholastically
1.31.24(.9.6)
scholasticism
27.15.21(.2.12)
Scholes 35.30.13
Scholfield 23.31.1(.2)
scholia 3.24.11
scholiast 22.29.6(.1)
scholiastic 24.2.10(.15.4)
scholium 27.3.18
Scholl 40.9, 40.18
Schönberg 26.14.1(.9)
school 40.15
schoolable 40.20.16(.29)
school-age 39.4, 39.4.10
schoolbook 24.14.3
schoolboy 13.3
schoolbus 34.14
schoolchild 23.31.9
schoolchildren
28.17.31(.15)
schooldays 35.4.4
schoolfellow 19.29.4
schoolgirl 40.17
schoolhouse 34.8.6(.24)
schoolie 1.31.16
schooling 29.1.31(.11)
schoolkid 23.2.10
schoolman 28.7.10(.24),
28.17.16(.35)
schoolmarm 27.8.6
schoolmarmish 36.2.15
schoolmaster
17.12.24(.5)
schoolmastering
29.1.30(.8)
schoolmasterly
1.31.17(.9.3)
schoolmate 22.4.13(.15)
schoolmen 28.5.7(.28)
schoolmistress
34.18.27(.14)
schoolmistressy
1.22.16(.13)
schoolroom 27.14.6(.20)
schoolteacher 17.28.1
schoolteaching 29.1.27
schooltime 27.12.1
schoolwork 24.17.6(.19)
schoolyard 23.9.21

schooner 17.18.15
Schopenhauer 17.3.10
schorl 40.10
schottische 36.1
Schreiber 17.11.11
Schrödinger 17.19.1
Schroeder 17.13.16,
17.13.17
Schubert 22.19.9
Schubertian 28.3.3
Schultz 34.22.20
Schumacher 17.14.5
Schumann 28.17.16(.15)
schuss 34.16, 34.17
Schütz 34.22.14
Schuyler 17.34.13
schwa 10
Schwann 28.7, 28.10
Schwartz 34.22.9
Schwarzkopf 30.8.6,
30.17
Schwarzwald 23.31.5
Schweitzer 17.24.19
Schweppes® 34.21.4
sciagram 27.6.17(.5)
sciagraph 30.7.5(.1)
sciagraphic 24.2.16(.3)
sciagraphy 1.18.9(.3.1)
sciamachy 1.12.13
sciatic 24.2.10(.4.1)
sciatica 17.14.15(.6)
sciatically 1.31.24(.9.4)
science 34.24.10(.5)
scienter 17.12.22(.3)
sciential 40.33.12(.2)
scientific 24.2.16(.1)
scientifically 1.31.24(.9.9)
scientism 27.15.21(.2.4)
scientist 22.29.2(.13)
scientistic 24.2.10(.15.2)
Scientologist
22.29.2(.26.3)
Scientology®
1.26.10(.11.2)
sci-fi 14.14.3
scilicet 22.5.5, 22.5.13(.4)
scilla 17.34.2
Scillies 35.2.19
Scillonian 28.3.8(.11)
Scilly 1.31.2
scimitar 17.12.16(.9.1)
scintigram 27.6.17(.5)
scintigraphy
1.18.9(.3.1)
scintilla 17.34.2(.2)
scintillant 22.26.15(.25)
scintillate 22.4.23(.7.1)
scintillatingly
1.31.28(.1.4)
scintillation
28.17.25(.3.14)

scintiscan 28.7.8
sciolism 27.15.21(.2.15)
sciolist 22.29.2(.31.1)
sciolistic 24.2.10(.15.3)
scion 28.17.5
Scipio 15.1.1
scire facias 34.7.2
scirrhi 14.24.1
scirrhoid 23.13.19
scirrhosity 1.10.16(.16.2)
scirrhous 34.18.27(.1)
scirrhus 34.18.27(.1)
scissel 40.31.2
scissile 40.2.14, 40.13.12,
40.31.2
scission 28.17.25(.2.1),
28.17.26(.2)
scissor 17.25.2
scissorwise 35.15.19
sciurine 28.2.29(.5),
28.14.18
sciuroid 23.13.19
sclera 17.32.2
scleral 40.16.13(.2)
sclerenchyma
17.17.14(.4)
sclerenchymata
17.12.16(.9.3)
sclerite 22.16.24(.2)
scleritis 34.18.11(.8)
scleroderma 17.17.15
scleroid 23.13.19
scleroma 17.17.16(.11)
scleromata 17.12.16(.9.3)
sclerometer
17.12.16(.9.2)
sclerophyll 40.2.11
sclerophyllous
34.18.29(.17.4)
scleroprotein 28.1.9(.4)
sclerosed 23.28.4
scleroses 35.1.16(.11)
sclerosis 34.2.17(.11.2)
sclerotherapy 1.8.11(.8)
sclerotic 24.2.10(.6)
sclerotin 28.2.11(.10)
sclerotitis 34.18.11(.8)
sclerotium 27.3.3
sclerotomy 1.15.13(.1)
sclerous 34.18.27(.2)
Scobie 1.9.13
Scoby 1.9.13
scoff 30.8
scoffer 17.20.7
scoffingly 1.31.28(.1.8)
scold 23.31.13
scolder 17.13.23(.8)
scolding 29.1.13(.16)
scolex 34.23.4(.12)
scolices 35.1.16(.10)
scoliosis 34.2.17(.11.1)

scoliotic 24.2.10(.6)
scollop 20.13.7
scolopendria 3.22.16
scolopendrium
27.3.17(.7)
scomber 17.11.17(.5)
scombrid 23.2.22
scombroid 23.13.19
sconce 34.24.7
Scone 28.16
scone 28.10, 28.19
scoop 20.12
scooper 17.10.13
scoopful 40.14.6(.8)
scoot 22.18
scooter 17.12.15
scooterist 22.29.2(.29.3)
scopa 17.10.16
scopae 2.9
scope 20.15
scopolamine 28.1.13,
28.2.17(.5)
scopula 17.34.16(.21.1)
scopulae 2.32.9(.8)
Scopus 34.18.9(.10)
scorbutic 24.2.10(.9)
scorbutically 1.31.24(.9.4)
scorch 38.9
scorcher 17.28.10
scorchingly 1.31.28(.1.15)
scordatura 17.32.14(.3)
score 12
scoreboard 23.12.2(.4)
scorebook 24.14.3
scorecard 23.9.9
scoreine 28.1.25(.1)
scorekeeper 17.10.1
scoreless 34.18.29(.11)
scorer 17.32.10
score sheet 22.1
scoria 3.22.9
scoriaceous 34.18.22(.3)
scoriae 2.3
scorification
28.17.25(.3.5)
scorifier 17.6.9(.4)
scorify 14.14.4(.14)
scoring 29.1.30(.7)
scorn 28.11
scorner 17.18.10
scornful 40.27.22
scornfully 1.31.17(.16.2)
scornfulness
34.18.16(.37.2)
scorp 20.8
scorper 17.10.9
Scorpian 28.3.1
Scorpio 15.1.1
scorpioid 23.13.2
scorpion 28.3.1
Scorpius 34.3.1

S

sculptress 34.18.27(.14)
sculptural 40.16.13(.12.3)
sculpturally 1.31.17(.27.2)
sculpture 17.28.18
sculpturesque 24.20.3
scum 27.11
scumbag 26.5.1
scummy 1.15.10
scuncheon 28.17.27
scunge 39.17.8
scungy 1.26.13
scunner 17.18.12
Scunthorpe 20.8
scup 20.9
scupper 17.10.11
scurf 30.15
scurfiness 34.18.16(.2.6)
scurfy 1.18.10
scurrility 1.10.16(.31)
scurrilous 34.18.29(.17.5)
scurrilously 1.31.33(.12.6)
scurrilousness
   34.18.16(.31.6)
scurry 1.29.9
scurvied 23.2.15
scurvily 1.31.17(.17)
scurviness 34.18.16(.2.6)
scurvy 1.19.11
'scuse 35.17
scut 22.15
scuta 17.12.15
scutage 39.2.10
scutal 40.21.11
Scutari 1.29.6,
   1.29.11(.8.4)
scutate 22.4.9(.4)
scutch 38.11
scutcheon 28.17.27
scutcher 17.28.11
scute 22.18
scutella 17.34.5(.3)
scutellate 22.4.23(.7.1),
   22.19.26(.13)
scutellation
   28.17.25(.3.14)
scutellum 27.15.28(.4)
scutiform 27.10.5(.2)
scutter 17.12.12
scuttle 40.21.9
scuttlebutt 22.15.2
scutum 27.15.9(.9)
scuzzy 1.23.11
Scylla and Charybdis
   34.2.9
scyphiform 27.10.5(.2)
scyphose 34.20.10
scyphozoan 28.17.8
scyphus 34.18.17
scythe 33.7
Scythia 3.13
Scythian 28.3.12

'sdeath 32.5
sea 2
seabag 26.5.1
seabed 23.5.2
seabird 23.19.1
seaboard 23.12.2(.1)
sea-boat 22.21.2
seaboot 22.18.3
seaborne 28.11.2
seacoast 22.29.17(.3)
seacock 24.9.6
seadog 26.7.4
seafarer 17.32.5
seafaring 29.1.30(.4)
sea floor 12
seafood 23.17.2
Seaford 23.18.16(.1)
Seaforth 32.10
seafront 22.26.12
Seaga 17.16.6
seagoing 29.1.9
seagull 40.12
seahorse 34.12.7
seakale 40.4.4
seal 40.1
sealable 40.20.16(.29)
sealant 22.26.15(.25)
Seale 40.1
sealed-beam 27.1.1
sealer 17.34.1
sealery 1.29.11(.27)
Sealey 1.31.1
Sealink 24.19.1(.8)
sealpoint 22.26.11
sealskin 28.2.13(.14)
sealstone 28.19.4(.9)
Sealyham 27.3.18
seam 27.1
seaman 28.17.16(.1)
seamanlike 24.13.7(.17)
seamanly 1.31.27(.14)
seamanship 20.2.7(.19)
seamark 24.8.8
seamer 17.17.1
seamew 16.24.9
seaminess 34.18.16(.2.5)
seamless 34.18.29(.26)
seamlessly 1.31.33(.12.6)
seamlessness
   34.18.16(.31.6)
seamstress 34.18.27(.14)
Seamus 34.18.15(.3)
seamy 1.15.1
Sean 28.11
Seanad 23.18.14
séance 34.11, 34.24.6
seaplane 28.4.19
seaport 22.13.1
seaquake 24.3.12
sear 3

search 38.16
searchable 40.20.16(.24)
searcher 17.28.16
searchingly 1.31.28(.1.15)
searchless 34.18.29(.36)
searchlight 22.16.25(.21)
searingly 1.31.28(.1.17)
Searle 40.17
Sears 35.3
Seascale 40.4.4
seascape 20.3
seashell 40.5.13
seashore 12.16.1
seasick 24.2.20(.1)
seasickness 34.18.16(.22)
seaside 23.15.11(.1)
season 28.17.24(.1)
seasonable 40.20.16(.16.3)
seasonableness
   34.18.16(.37.4)
seasonably 1.31.21(.6)
seasonal 40.26.13(.13)
seasonality 1.10.16(.32.8)
seasonally 1.31.17(.14.2)
seasoner 17.18.16(.15)
seasoning 29.1.17(.12)
seasonless 34.18.29(.27)
seat 22.1
seatbelt 22.32.2
seatless 34.18.29(.22)
seatmate 22.4.13(.9)
SEATO 19.10.1
Seaton 28.17.11(.1)
seatrein 28.4.18
Seattle 40.21.5
seawall 40.10.17
seaward 23.18.26(.1)
seawater 17.12.10(.7)
seaway 4.25.1
seaweed 23.1.10
seaworthiness
   34.18.16(.2.6)
seaworthy 1.21
Seb 21.4
sebaceous 34.18.22(.3)
Sebastian 28.3.3
Sebastopol 40.9.5,
   40.19.11
Sebat 22.7.6
sebesten 28.17.11(.25)
seborrhoea 17.1.16
seborrhoeic 24.2.1
Sebring 29.1.30(.12)
sebum 27.15.8
sec 24.4
secant 22.26.15(.11)
secateurs 35.19
secco 19.12.4
secede 23.1.7
seceder 17.13.1

secession 28.17.25(.4)
secessional
   40.26.13(.14.3)
secessionism
   27.15.21(.2.9)
secessionist 22.29.2(.18.2)
Secker 17.14.4
seclude 23.17.5
seclusion 28.17.26(.4)
seclusionist 22.29.2(.18.3)
seclusive 31.2.4(.8)
Secombe 27.15.11(.1)
second 23.24.9,
   23.24.16(.5)
secondarily 1.31.17(.27.1)
secondariness
   34.18.16(.2.9)
secondary 1.29.11(.9)
seconde 23.11
seconded 23.18.10(.14)
secondee 2.13
seconder 17.13.20(.13)
second hand 23.24.6
secondi 2.13
secondly 1.31.23(.17)
secondment
   22.26.15(.13.3)
secondo 19.11.14
secrecy 1.22.16(.13)
secret 22.19.24(.14)
secretaire 6.4
secretarial 40.3.14(.4)
secretariat 22.3.12, 22.7.2
secretary 1.29.3,
   1.29.11(.8.9)
secretary-general
   40.16.13(.12.2)
secretaryship 20.2.7(.2)
secrete 22.1.17
secretion 28.17.25(.1)
secretive 31.2.1(.9.4)
secretively 1.31.30(.7.1)
secretiveness
   34.18.16(.28.1)
secretly 1.31.22(.15)
secretor 17.12.1(.14)
secretory 1.29.11(.8.1)
sect 22.23.4
sectarian 28.3.20(.4)
sectarianism
   27.15.21(.2.9)
sectarianize 35.15.12(.3)
sectary 1.29.11(.8.12)
section 28.17.25(.15.2)
sectional 40.26.13(.14.6)
sectionalism
   27.15.21(.2.15)
sectionalist 22.29.2(.31.3)
sectionalize 35.15.21(.4.5)
sectionally 1.31.17(.14.3)
sector 17.12.21(.2)

sectoral 40.16.13(.12.1)
sectorial 40.3.14(.5)
secular 17.34.16(.21.2)
secularism 27.15.21(.2.14)
secularist 22.29.2(.29.4)
secularity 1.10.16(.21.1)
secularization 28.17.25(.3.12)
secularize 35.15.20(.2)
secularly 1.31.17(.29)
secund 23.24.12
Secunderabad 23.7.6, 23.9.6
secundly 1.31.23(.17)
securable 40.20.16(.27.2)
secure 12.22, 17.7.12(.5)
secured 23.12.10, 23.18.4
securely 1.31.11, 1.31.17(.4)
securement 22.26.15(.13.1)
Securicor® 12.7
securitization 28.17.25(.3.12)
securitize 35.15.7(.7)
security 1.10.16(.21.2)
sedan 28.7.7
sedate 22.4.10
sedately 1.31.22(.4)
sedateness 34.18.16(.20.1)
sedation 28.17.25(.3.4)
sedative 31.2.1(.9.1)
Sedburgh 17.32.14(.5), 26.14.1(.7)
Seddon 28.17.12(.5)
sedentarily 1.31.17(.27.1)
sedentariness 34.18.16(.2.9)
sedentary 1.29.11(.8.12), 1.29.15(.15)
Seder 17.13.3
sederunt 22.26.15(.23.1)
sedge 39.5
Sedgefield 23.31.1(.2)
Sedgemoor 12.9.15
Sedgewick 24.2.25
sedgy 1.26.3
sedile 1.31.14
sedilia 3.24.1, 3.24.2, 3.24.9
sediment 22.26.15(.13.2)
sedimentary 1.29.11(.8.12)
sedimentation 28.17.25(.3.3)
sedition 28.17.25(.2.3)
seditionary 1.29.11(.13.2)
seditionist 22.29.2(.18.2)
seditious 34.18.22(.2)
seditiously 1.31.33(.12.4)
seditiousness 34.18.16(.31.4)

seduce 34.17.13
seducer 17.24.14
seducible 40.20.16(.21.2)
seduction 28.17.25(.15.5)
seductive 31.2.1(.13.4)
seductively 1.31.30(.7.2)
seductiveness 34.18.16(.28.1)
seductress 34.18.27(.14)
sedulity 1.10.16(.35)
sedulous 34.18.29(.17.5)
sedulously 1.31.33(.12.6)
sedulousness 34.18.16(.31.6)
sedum 27.15.10(.1)
see 2
seeable 40.20.16(.1)
seed 23.1
seedbed 23.5.2
seedcake 24.3.6
seedcorn 28.11.5
seeder 17.13.1
seedily 1.31.17(.10)
seediness 34.18.16(.2.3)
seedless 34.18.29(.23)
seedling 29.1.31(.18)
seedsman 28.17.16(.30)
seedy 1.11.1
Seeger 17.16.1
seek 24.1
seeker 17.14.1
seel 40.1
Seeley 1.31.1
Seely 1.31.1
seem 27.1
seemingly 1.31.28(.1.7)
seemliness 34.18.16(.2.10)
seemly 1.31.26(.1)
seen 28.1
seep 20.1
seepage 39.2.8
seer 3, 17.1
seersucker 17.14.11
seesaw 12.14.1
seethe 33.1
seethingly 1.31.28(.1.10)
see-through 16.23.13
Seféris 34.2.21
Segal 40.24.1
segment 22.26.4(.8), 22.26.15(.13.3)
segmental 40.21.17(.2)
segmentalization 28.17.25(.3.12)
segmentalize 35.15.21(.4.3)
segmentally 1.31.17(.9.3)
segmentary 1.29.11(.8.12)
segmentation 28.17.25(.3.3)
sego 19.13.1

Segovia 3.11.8
Segrave 31.3.7
segregable 40.20.16(.14)
segregate 22.4.12(.5)
segregation 28.17.25(.3.6)
segregational 40.26.13(.14.2)
segregationist 22.29.2(.18.2)
segregative 31.2.1(.3)
segue 1.28, 4.25.15
seguidilla 17.33.1, 17.33.13
Sehnsucht 22.23.9, 22.24
sei 4
seicentist 22.29.2(.13)
seicento 19.10.17
seicentoist 22.29.2(.10)
seiche 36.4
seif 30.1, 30.3
Seifert 22.19.16
seigneur 17.33.9, 18.16
seigneurial 40.3.14(.6)
seigneury 1.29.11(.26)
seigniorage 39.2.22(.9)
seigniory 1.29.11(.26)
Seine 28.4
seine 28.4
seiner 17.18.3
seise 35.1
seisin 28.2.24
seismal 40.25.14
seismic 24.2.14(.17)
seismical 40.23.12(.10)
seismically 1.31.24(.9.8)
seismicity 1.10.16(.16.1)
seismogram 27.6.17(.5)
seismograph 30.7.5(.1)
seismographer 17.20.12(.5)
seismographic 24.2.16(.3)
seismographical 40.23.12(.12)
seismographically 1.31.24(.9.9)
seismography 1.18.9(.3.2)
seismological 40.23.12(.17.2)
seismologically 1.31.24(.9.11)
seismologist 22.29.2(.26.4)
seismology 1.26.10(.11.4)
seismometer 17.12.16(.9.2)
seismometric 24.2.26(.14.2)
seismometrical 40.23.12(.18)

seismometry 1.29.15(.8)
seismoscope 20.15.4(.1)
seismoscopic 24.2.8(.5)
seizable 40.20.16(.22)
seize 35.1
seizer 17.25.1
seizure 17.27.1
sejant 22.26.15(.21)
Sejanus 34.18.16(.4)
selachian 28.3.5
seladang 29.4.4
Selborne 28.11.2
Selby 1.9.24
seldom 27.15.10(.20)
select 22.23.4(.11)
selectable 40.20.16(.11.5)
selectee 2.11
selection 28.17.25(.15.2)
selectional 40.26.13(.14.6)
selectionally 1.31.17(.14.3)
selective 31.2.1(.13.2)
selectively 1.31.30(.7.2)
selectiveness 34.18.16(.28.1)
selectivity 1.10.16(.15)
selectman 28.7.10(.11), 28.17.16(.21)
selectmen 28.5.7(.15)
selectness 34.18.16(.20.4)
selector 17.12.21(.2)
Selena 17.18.1(.16)
selenate 22.4.14(.9.4)
Selene 1.16.1(.16)
selenic 24.2.15(.1)
selenide 23.15.8
selenious 34.3.6(.1)
selenite 22.16.14(.6)
selenitic 24.2.10(.2.2)
selenium 27.3.8(.1)
selenocentric 24.2.26(.14.4)
selenodont 22.26.9
selenographer 17.20.12(.5)
selenographic 24.2.16(.3)
selenography 1.18.9(.3.2)
selenologist 22.29.2(.26.4)
selenology 1.26.10(.11.4)
Seleucid 23.2.16
self 30.20.2
self-abandon 28.17.12(.23)
self-abandonment 22.26.15(.13.4)
self-abasement 22.26.15(.13.5)
self-abhorrence 34.24.10(.16)
self-abnegation 28.17.25(.3.6)

S

self-improvement **22.26.15(.13.5)**
self-induced **22.29.14**
self-inductance **34.24.10(.10)**
self-induction **28.17.25(.15.5)**
self-inductive **31.2.1(.13.4)**
self-indulgence **34.24.10(.21)**
self-indulgent **22.26.15(.21)**
self-indulgently **1.31.22(.20.4)**
self-inflicted **23.18.9(.17)**
self-insurance **34.24.10(.16)**
self-interest **22.29.5(.12), 22.29.15(.17)**
self-interested **23.18.9(.20)**
self-involvement **22.26.15(.13.5)**
selfish **36.2.18(.21)**
selfishly **1.31.35(.7.3)**
selfishness **34.18.16(.33.6)**
self-justification **28.17.25(.3.5)**
self-justifying **29.1.7**
self-knowledge **39.2.23**
selfless **34.18.29(.29)**
selflessly **1.31.33(.12.6)**
selflessness **34.18.16(.31.6)**
self-loader **17.13.17**
self-loading **29.1.13(.13)**
self-locking **29.1.14(.6)**
self-love **31.8**
self-made **23.4.7**
self-mastery **1.29.11(.8.12)**
selfmate **22.4.13**
self-mocking **29.1.14(.6)**
self-motion **28.17.25(.13)**
self-motivation **28.17.25(.3.9)**
self-moving **29.1.20**
self-murder **17.13.16**
self-murderer **17.32.14(.7)**
self-mutilation **28.17.25(.3.14)**
self-neglect **22.23.4(.11)**
selfness **34.18.16(.27)**
self-obsessed **22.29.5(.6)**
self-opinion **28.17.32**
self-parody **1.11.17**
self-perpetuating **29.1.12(.3)**
self-perpetuation **28.17.25(.3.1)**

self-pity **1.10.2**
self-pitying **29.1.2**
self-pityingly **1.31.28(.1.1)**
self-pollinated **23.18.9(.3)**
self-pollinating **29.1.12(.3)**
self-pollination **28.17.25(.3.8)**
self-pollinator **17.12.4(.10)**
self-portrait **22.4.22(.8), 22.19.24(.12)**
self-possessed **22.29.5(.7)**
self-possession **28.17.25(.4)**
self-praise **35.4.16**
self-preservation **28.17.25(.3.9)**
self-proclaimed **23.23.3**
self-propagating **29.1.12(.3)**
self-propelled **23.31.4**
self-propelling **29.1.31(.5)**
self-protection **28.17.25(.15.2)**
self-protective **31.2.1(.13.2)**
self-raising **29.1.24**
self-realization **28.17.25(.3.12)**
self-recording **29.1.13(.8)**
self-regard **23.9.10**
self-regarding **29.1.13(.6)**
self-registering **29.1.30(.8)**
self-regulating **29.1.12(.3)**
self-regulation **28.17.25(.3.14)**
self-regulatory **1.29.11(.8.10)**
self-reliance **34.24.10(.5)**
self-reliant **22.26.15(.4)**
self-reliantly **1.31.22(.20.1)**
self-renunciation **28.17.25(.3.1)**
self-reproach **38.17**
self-reproachful **40.27.29**
self-respect **22.23.4(.1)**
self-respecting **29.1.12(.18)**
self-restrained **23.24.4**
self-restraint **22.26.3**
self-revealing **29.1.31(.1)**
self-revelation **28.17.25(.3.14)**
Selfridge **39.2.22(.14)**
self-righteous **34.18.23**

self-righteously **1.31.33(.12.4)**
self-righteousness **34.18.16(.31.5)**
self-righting **29.1.12(.11)**
self-rising **29.1.24**
self-rule **40.15.8**
self-sacrifice **34.15.6**
self-sacrificing **29.1.23**
selfsame **27.4.7**
self-satisfaction **28.17.25(.15.3)**
self-satisfied **23.15.9**
self-satisfiedly **1.31.23(.11)**
self-sealing **29.1.31(.1)**
self-seed **23.1.7**
self-seeker **17.14.1**
self-seeking **29.1.14(.1)**
self-selecting **29.1.12(.18)**
self-selection **28.17.25(.15.2)**
self-service **34.2.15**
self-serving **29.1.20**
self-slaughter **17.12.10(.8)**
self-sown **28.19.13**
self-starter **17.12.8(.3)**
self-sterile **40.13.16**
self-styled **23.31.9**
self-sufficiency **1.22.23(.10.4)**
self-sufficient **22.26.15(.19)**
self-sufficiently **1.31.22(.20.4)**
self-sufficing **29.1.23**
self-suggestion **28.17.27**
self-support **22.13.1**
self-supporting **29.1.12(.9)**
self-surrender **17.13.20(.3)**
self-sustained **23.24.4**
self-sustaining **29.1.17(.3)**
self-tapping **29.1.10(.5)**
self-taught **22.13.3**
self-torture **17.28.10**
self-understanding **29.1.13(.14)**
self-will **40.2.19**
self-willed **23.31.2**
self-winding **29.1.13(.14)**
self-worth **32.15.2**
Seligman **28.17.16(.24)**
Selima **17.17.1**
Selina **17.18.1(.16)**
Seljuk **24.15.6**
Seljukian **28.3.5**
Selkirk **24.17.3**

sell **40.5**
sellable **40.20.16(.29)**
Sellafield **23.31.1(.2)**
Sellar **17.34.5**
Sellars **35.18.25**
sell-by date **22.4**
seller **17.34.5**
Sellick **24.2.27(.4)**
sellotape® **20.3**
sellout **22.9.19**
Selma **17.17.24**
Selous **16.25**
Selsey **1.22.26**
seltzer **17.24.19**
Selvas **34.18.18**
selvedge **39.2.17**
selves **35.28.10**
Selwyn **28.2.28**
Selznick **24.2.15(.18)**
SEM **27.5**
semanteme **27.1.2**
semantic **24.2.10(.14)**
semantically **1.31.24(.9.5)**
semantician **28.17.25(.2.2)**
semanticism **27.15.21(.2.12)**
semanticist **22.29.2(.22)**
semanticize **35.15.16(.4)**
semaphore **12.11.3**
semaphoric **24.2.26(.6)**
semaphorically **1.31.24(.9.12)**
Semarang **29.4.15**
semasiological **40.23.12(.17.2)**
semasiology **1.26.10(.11.1)**
sematic **24.2.10(.4.2)**
semblable **40.20.16(.29)**
semblance **34.24.10(.24)**
semé **1.15.4, 4.13**
semée **4.13**
semeiology **1.26.10(.11.1)**
semeiotics **34.23.2(.3)**
Semele **1.31.17(.13)**
sememe **27.1.5**
semen **28.17.16(.1)**
Semer Water **17.12.10**
semester **17.12.24(.4)**
semi **1.15.4**
semiaquatic **24.2.10(.4.4)**
semiautomatic **24.2.10(.4.2)**
semibreve **31.1.8**
semicircle **40.23.13**
semicircular **17.34.16(.21.2)**
semicolon **28.10.26, 28.17.33(.15)**

semiconducting **29.1.12(.18)**
semiconductor **17.12.21(.6)**
semi-conscious **34.18.22(.12)**
semicylinder **17.13.20(.13)**
semicylindrical **40.23.12(.18)**
semidemisemiquaver **17.21.3**
semidetached **22.31**
semidiameter **17.12.16(.9.1)**
semifinal **40.26.11**
semifinalist **22.29.2(.31.3)**
semigloss **34.10.17**
Semillon **11.18, 28.10.26**
seminal **40.26.13(.8)**
seminally **1.31.17(.14.2)**
seminar **10.11**
seminarian **28.3.20(.4)**
seminarist **22.29.2(.29.4)**
seminary **1.29.11(.13.2)**
seminiferous **34.18.27(.20)**
Seminole **40.18.9**
semiological **40.23.12(.17.2)**
semiologist **22.29.2(.26.2)**
semiology **1.26.10(.11.1), 39.14**
semiotic **24.2.10(.6)**
semiotical **40.23.12(.7.2)**
semiotically **1.31.24(.9.4)**
semiotician **28.17.25(.2.2)**
semiotics **34.23.2(.3)**
semipalmated **23.18.9(.3)**
semipermeable **40.20.3**
semiprecious **34.18.22(.4)**
semiprivate **22.19.17**
semi-professional **40.26.13(.14.3)**
semiquaver **17.21.3**
Semiramis **34.2.12**
semiretired **23.18.3**
semisoft **22.27.5**
semisweet **22.1.16**
Semite **22.16.13**
Semitic **24.2.10(.2.2)**
Semitism **27.15.21(.2.4)**
Semitist **22.29.2(.13)**
Semitization **28.17.25(.3.11)**
Semitize **35.15.7(.7)**
semitone **28.19.4(.2)**
semitrailer **17.34.4**
semitropical **40.23.12(.5)**
semivowel **40.16.3**
semmit **22.2.11**

semolina **17.18.1(.16)**
Semper **17.10.17**
sempervivum **27.15.17**
sempiternal **40.26.14**
sempiternally **1.31.17(.14.3)**
sempiternity **1.10.16(.13)**
Semple **40.19.14**
semplice **1.25.12, 4.22**
sempre **4.26.9**
sempstress **34.18.27(.14)**
Semtex® **34.23.4(.3)**
senarii **14.2**
senarius **34.3.15(.3)**
senary **1.29.11(.13.1)**
senate **22.19.15(.2)**
senator **17.12.16(.10)**
senatorial **40.3.14(.5)**
senatorially **1.31.3(.11)**
senatorship **20.2.7(.9)**
send **23.24.5**
sendable **40.20.16(.12)**
Sendai **14.9**
sendal **40.22.16**
sender **17.13.20(.3)**
sending-off **30.8**
Seneca **17.14.15(.9)**
senecio **15.1.7, 15.1.9**
Senegal **40.10.8**
Senegalese **35.1.23**
senesce **34.5.6**
senescence **34.24.10(.18)**
senescent **22.26.15(.17.2)**
seneschal **40.33.9**
Senghenydd **33.2**
Senhor **12.22**
Senhores **35.4.16**
senile **40.13.8**
senility **1.10.16(.25)**
senior **3.9.1**
seniority **1.10.16(.21.2)**
seniti **1.10.16(.13)**
Senlac **24.6.23**
senna **17.18.4**
Sennacherib **21.2**
sennet **22.2.12**
Sennett **22.2.12**
sennight **22.16.14(.2)**
sennit **22.2.12**
señor **12.22**
señora **17.32.10(.11)**
señores **35.4.16**
señorita **17.12.1(.14)**
sensa **17.24.22(.2)**
sensate **22.4.18**
sensation **28.17.25(.3.10)**
sensational **40.26.13(.14.2)**
sensationalism **27.15.21(.2.15)**

sensationalist **22.29.2(.31.3)**
sensationalistic **24.2.10(.15.3)**
sensationalize **35.15.21(.4.5)**
sensationally **1.31.17(.14.3)**
sense **34.24.3**
senseless **34.18.29(.33)**
senselessly **1.31.33(.12.6)**
senselessness **34.18.16(.31.6)**
sense-organ **28.17.15(.9)**
sensibility **1.10.16(.22.1)**
sensible **40.20.16(.21.3)**
sensibleness **34.18.16(.37.4)**
sensibly **1.31.21(.7.2)**
sensitive **31.2.1(.9.3)**
sensitively **1.31.30(.7.1)**
sensitiveness **34.18.16(.28.1)**
sensitivity **1.10.16(.15)**
sensitization **28.17.25(.3.11)**
sensitize **35.15.7(.7)**
sensitizer **17.25.12(.2)**
sensitometer **17.12.16(.9.2)**
Sensodyne® **28.14.6**
sensor **17.24.22(.2)**
sensoria **3.22.9**
sensorial **40.3.14(.5)**
sensorially **1.31.3(.11)**
sensorily **1.31.17(.27.2)**
sensorium **27.3.17(.4)**
sensory **1.29.11(.18)**
sensual **40.16.14**
sensualism **27.15.21(.2.15)**
sensualist **22.29.2(.31.4)**
sensuality **1.10.16(.32.1)**
sensualize **35.15.21(.4.6)**
sensually **1.31.17(.22)**
sensualness **34.18.16(.37.1)**
sensum **27.15.20(.18)**
sensuous **34.18.6**
sensuously **1.31.33(.12.1), 34.18.6**
sensuousness **34.18.16(.31.2)**
sensu stricto **19.10.16**
sent **22.26.4**
sente **1.10.23(.3)**
sentence **34.24.10(.10)**
sentential **40.33.12(.2)**
sententious **34.18.22(.12)**
sententiously **1.31.33(.12.4)**

sententiousness **34.18.16(.31.4)**
sentience **34.24.10(.20)**
sentiency **1.22.23(.2)**
sentient **22.26.15(.19)**
sentiently **1.31.22(.20.1)**
sentiment **22.26.15(.13.2)**
sentimental **40.21.17(.2)**
sentimentalism **27.15.21(.2.15)**
sentimentalist **22.29.2(.31.2)**
sentimentality **1.10.16(.32.3)**
sentimentalization **28.17.25(.3.12)**
sentimentalize **35.15.21(.4.3)**
sentimentally **1.31.17(.9.3)**
sentinel **40.26.13(.4)**
sentry **1.29.15(.15)**
Senussi **1.22.15**
Seoul **40.18**
sepal **40.19.1, 40.19.4**
separability **1.10.16(.22.1)**
separable **40.20.16(.27.3)**
separableness **34.18.16(.37.4)**
separably **1.31.21(.8)**
separate **22.4.22(.6), 22.19.24(.9)**
separately **1.31.22(.15)**
separateness **34.18.16(.20.3)**
separation **28.17.25(.3.13)**
separatism **27.15.21(.2.4)**
separatist **22.29.2(.13)**
separative **31.2.1(.9.4)**
separator **17.12.4(.15)**
separatory **1.29.11(.8.9)**
Sephardi **1.11.9**
Sephardic **24.2.11(.6)**
Sephardim **27.2.4**
sepia **3.2.1**
sepoy **13.2**
seppuku **16.9**
sepses **35.1.16(.12)**
sepsis **34.2.17(.12)**
sept **22.22.3**
septa **17.12.19**
septal **40.21.15**
septate **22.4.9(.6)**
septation **28.17.25(.3.3)**
septcentenary **1.29.11(.13.1)**
September **17.11.17(.3)**
septenarii **14.2**
septenarius **34.3.15(.3)**
septenary **1.29.11(.13.1)**
septenate **22.4.14(.1)**

septennia 3.9.4
septennial 40.3.7(.4)
septennium 27.3.8(.4)
septet 22.5.3
septfoil 40.11.7
septic 24.2.10(.12)
septicaemia 3.8.1
septicaemic 24.2.14(.1)
septically 1.31.24(.9.5)
septicity 1.10.16(.16.1)
septilateral 40.16.13(.12.1)
septillion 28.3.21(.2)
septimal 40.25.10
septime 27.1.2
Septimus 34.18.15(.10)
septivalent 22.26.15(.25)
septuagenarian 28.3.20(.4)
septuagenary 1.29.11(.13.1)
Septuagesima 17.17.14(.8)
Septuagint 22.26.1
septum 27.15.9(.12)
septuple 40.19.10
septuplet 22.19.26(.15)
sepulchral 40.16.13(.18)
sepulchrally 1.31.17(.27.3)
sepulchre 17.14.25
sepulture 12.17, 17.7.12(.3), 17.28.26
Sepulveda 17.13.15
sequacious 34.18.22(.3)
sequaciously 1.31.33(.12.4)
sequacity 1.10.16(.16.1)
sequel 40.35.3
sequela 17.34.1, 17.34.5(.14)
sequelae 2.32.1, 2.32.5
sequence 34.24.10(.22)
sequencer 17.24.22(.7)
sequent 22.26.15(.22)
sequential 40.33.12(.3)
sequentiality 1.10.16(.32.1)
sequentially 1.31.17(.22)
sequently 1.31.22(.20.5)
sequester 17.12.24(.4)
sequestra 17.32.19(.11)
sequestrable 40.20.16(.27.6)
sequestral 40.16.13(.16)
sequestrate 22.4.22(.8)
sequestration 28.17.25(.3.13)
sequestrator 17.12.4(.15)
sequestrotomy 1.15.13(.1)

sequestrum 27.15.26(.10)
sequin 28.2.28
sequitur 17.12.16(.17)
sequoia 17.5
sera 17.32.2
serac 24.6.21
seraglio 15.1.13
serai 14.24
serang 29.4.15
serape 1.8.6
seraph 30.14
seraphic 24.2.16(.3)
seraphical 40.23.12(.12)
seraphically 1.31.24(.9.9)
seraphim 27.2.7
Seraphina 17.18.1(.6)
Serapis 34.2.6
Serb 21.15
Serbia 3.3.8
Serbian 28.3.2
Serbo-Croat 22.7.4
Serbo-Croatian 28.17.25(.3.1)
Serbonian 28.3.8(.11)
SERC 2.22
sere 3
serein 8, 28.7.20
Seremban 28.7.5
Serena 17.18.1(.15)
serenade 23.4.8
serenader 17.13.3
serenata 17.12.8(.8)
serendipitous 34.18.11(.10)
serendipitously 1.31.33(.12.2)
serendipity 1.10.16(.6)
serene 28.1.25
serenely 1.31.27(.1)
sereneness 34.18.16(.25)
Serengeti 1.10.4
serenity 1.10.16(.13)
serf 30.15
serfage 39.2.16
serfdom 27.15.10(.16)
serfhood 23.16.5(.12)
serge 39.15
sergeancy 1.22.23(.10.4)
sergeant 22.26.15(.21)
sergeant-major 17.29.3
sergeantship 20.2.8
Sergei 4.12
Sergio 15.1.11
Sergius 34.3.13
serial 40.3.14(.2)
serialism 27.15.21(.2.15)
serialist 22.29.2(.31.1)
seriality 1.10.16(.32.1)
serialization 28.17.25(.3.12)

serialize 35.15.21(.2)
serially 1.31.3(.11)
seriate 22.3.12, 22.4.2(.14)
seriatim 27.2.3
seriation 28.17.25(.3.1)
Seric 24.2.26(.4)
sericeous 34.18.22(.2)
sericultural 40.16.13(.12.3)
sericulture 17.28.26
sericulturist 22.29.2(.29.4)
seriema 17.17.1
series 35.2.17
serif 30.14
serigraph 30.7.5(.1)
serigrapher 17.20.12(.5)
serigraphy 1.18.9(.3.1)
serin 28.2.29(.2)
serine 28.2.29(.1)
serinette 22.5.9
seringa 17.16.17(.1)
Seringapatam 27.6.4, 27.8.3
serio-comic 24.2.14(.6)
serio-comically 1.31.24(.9.8)
serious 34.3.15(.2)
seriously 1.31.33(.1.4)
seriousness 34.18.16(.31.1)
serjeant 22.26.15(.21)
serjeantship 20.2.8
Serkin 28.2.13(.7)
sermon 28.17.16(.17)
sermonette 22.5.9
sermonize 35.15.12(.5)
sermonizer 17.25.12(.6)
seroconvert 22.20.9
serological 40.23.12(.17.2)
serologist 22.29.2(.26.4)
serology 1.26.10(.11.5)
seronegative 31.2.1(.9.1)
seropositive 31.2.1(.9.3)
serosa 17.24.17
serosity 1.10.16(.16.2)
Serota 17.12.18
serotine 28.14.5
serotonin 28.2.18
serotype 20.10.2
serous 34.18.27(.2)
serow 19.27.2
Serpell 40.19.12
Serpens 35.26.5, 35.26.13(.5)
serpent 22.26.15(.7)
serpentiform 27.10.5(.2)
serpentine 28.14.5
serpiginous 34.18.16(.15.3)
SERPS 34.21.11

serpula 17.34.16(.21.1)
serpulae 2.32.9(.8)
serra 17.32.4
serradella 17.34.5(.4)
serradilla 17.34.2(.3)
serrae 2.30.2
serran 28.17.31(.3)
serranid 23.2.13
serrate 22.4.22
serration 28.17.25(.3.13)
serried 23.2.22
serrulate 22.4.23(.7.3), 22.19.26(.13)
serrulation 28.17.25(.3.14)
serum 27.15.26(.1)
serval 40.28.12
servant 22.26.15(.16)
serve 31.11
server 17.21.13
servery 1.29.11(.15)
Servian 28.3.10
service 34.2.15
serviceability 1.10.16(.22.2)
serviceable 40.20.16(.21.2)
serviceableness 34.18.16(.37.4)
serviceably 1.31.21(.7.2)
serviceberry 1.29.3
serviceman 28.17.16(.29)
servicewoman 28.17.16(.14)
servicewomen 28.2.17(.1)
serviette 22.5
servile 40.13.10
servilely 1.31.38
servility 1.10.16(.26)
serving 29.1.20
Servis 34.2.15
Servite 22.16.17
servitor 17.12.16(.12)
servitorship 20.2.7(.9)
servitude 23.17.4(.1)
servo 19.17
sesame 1.15.13(.8)
sesamoid 23.13.11
sesamum 27.15.13
Sesotho 19.10.14
sesquicentenary 1.29.11(.13.1)
sesquicentennial 40.3.7(.4)
sesquipedalian 28.3.21(.3)
sesquiplicate 22.4.11(.6), 22.19.12(.10)
sess 34.5
sessile 40.13.12

session 28.17.25(.4)
sessional 40.26.13(.14.3)
sesterce 34.19.3
sestertia 3.4.10, 17.26.15
sestertii 14.2
sestertium 27.3.3, 27.3.13, 27.15.22
sestertius 34.3.3, 34.3.12, 34.18.22(.8)
sestet 22.5.3
sestina 17.18.1(.3)
set 22.5
seta 17.12.1
setaceous 34.18.22(.3)
setae 2.12.1
set-aside 23.15.11(.6)
setback 24.6.6(.12)
Seth 32.5
SETI 1.10.4
setiferous 34.18.27(.20)
setigerous 34.18.27(.27)
seton 28.17.11(.1)
setose 34.20.4, 35.20.3
set-piece 34.1.1
setscrew 16.23.10
setsquare 6.18.9
Setswana 17.18.8(.10)
sett 22.5
settee 2.11
setter 17.12.5
setterwort 22.20.15
setting 29.1.12(.4)
settle 40.21.4
settleable 40.20.16(.29)
settlement 22.26.15(.13.7)
settler 17.34.21
settlor 17.34.21
set-to 16.7
setup 20.9.5
setwall 40.35.2
Seurat 10.23.4
seven 28.17.20(.4)
sevenfold 23.31.13(.7)
Sevenoaks 34.23.17
seventeen 28.1.9
seventeenth 32.21
seventh 32.21
seventhly 1.31.31
seventieth 32.14.1
seventy 1.10.23(.12)
seventyfold 23.31.13(.7)
Seven Up® 20.9
sever 17.21.4
severable 40.20.16(.27.5)
several 40.16.13(.12.2)
severally 1.31.17(.27.2)
severalty 1.10.28
severance 34.24.10(.16)
severe 3.11
severely 1.31.3

severity 1.10.16(.21.1)
Severn 28.17.20(.4)
Severus 34.18.27(.2)
severy 1.29.11(.15)
seviche 4.22
Seville 40.2.12, 40.28.4
Sèvres 17.32.26
sew 19
sewage 39.2.6
Seward 23.18.5, 23.18.26(.1)
Sewell 40.16.8
sewellel 40.16.15
sewer 17.8, 17.9
sewerage 39.2.22(.9)
sewin 28.2.7
sewn 28.19
sex 34.23.4
sexagenarian 28.3.20(.4)
sexagenary 1.29.11(.13.2)
Sexagesima 17.17.14(.8)
sexagesimal 40.25.10
sexagesimally 1.31.17(.13)
sexangular 17.34.16(.21.3)
sexcentenary 1.29.11(.13.1)
sexennial 40.3.7(.4)
sexer 17.24.20
sexfoil 40.11.7
sexily 1.31.17(.20)
sexiness 34.18.16(.2.7)
sexism 27.15.21(.2.12)
sexist 22.29.2(.22)
sexisyllabic 24.2.9(.2)
sexisyllable 40.20.16(.29)
sexivalent 22.26.15(.25)
sexless 34.18.29(.33)
sexlessly 1.31.33(.12.6)
sexlessness 34.18.16(.31.6)
sexological 40.23.12(.17.2)
sexologist 22.29.2(.26.4)
sexology 1.26.10(.11.5)
sexpartite 22.16.9
sexploitation 28.17.25(.3.3)
sexpot 22.11.2
sexstarved 23.26
sext 22.29.20
sextain 28.4.3
Sextans 35.26.13(.7)
sextant 22.26.15(.9)
sextet 22.5.3
sextile 40.13.3(.10)
sextillion 28.3.21(.2)
sextillionth 32.21
sexto 19.10.19
sextodecimo 19.14.12
sexton 28.17.11(.25)

sextuple 40.19.10
sextuplet 22.19.26(.15)
sextuply 1.31.20
sexual 40.14.8, 40.16.10
sexualist 22.29.2(.31.4)
sexuality 1.10.16(.32.1)
sexualize 35.15.21(.4.8)
sexually 1.31.17(.22)
sexvalent 22.26.15(.25)
sexy 1.22.22
Seychelles 35.30.4
Seychellois 10.22
Seychelloise 35.9
Seymour 12.9.1
sez 35.5
Sfax 34.23.5
sforzandi 2.13
sforzando 19.11.14
sforzato 19.10.6
sfumati 2.12.5
sfumato 19.10.7
sgraffiti 2.12.1
sgraffito 19.10.1
Sgurr 17.7
Shaba 17.11.7
shabbat 22.7.6
shabbily 1.31.17(.8)
shabbiness 34.18.16(.2.2)
shabbos 34.18.10
shabby 1.9.5
shabbyish 36.2.1
shabrack 24.6.21
shack 24.6
shackle 40.23.5
Shackleton 28.17.11(.27)
shad 23.7
Shadbolt 22.32.12
shadbush 36.13
shaddock 24.16.5
shade 23.4
shadeless 34.18.29(.23)
shadily 1.31.17(.10)
shadiness 34.18.16(.2.3)
shading 29.1.13(.3)
shadoof 30.13.2
shadow 19.11.6
shadowbox 34.23.8(.2)
shadower 17.9.3
shadowgraph 30.7.5(.1)
shadowiness 34.18.16(.2.1)
shadowless 34.18.29(.19)
shadowy 1(.7)
Shadrach 24.6.21
Shadwell 40.5.17(.8)
shady 1.11.4
SHAEF 30.3
Shaffer 17.20.5
shaft 22.27.4
Shaftesbury 1.29.11(.7.2)

Shafto 19.10.18
shag 26.5
shagbark 24.8.3
shagger 17.16.5
shaggily 1.31.17(.12)
shagginess 34.18.16(.2.4)
shaggy 1.14.5
shaggy-dog 26.7.4
shagreen 28.1.25(.9)
shah 10
shahdom 27.15.10(.5)
Shaka 17.14.7
shake 24.3
shakeable 40.20.16(.13)
shakedown 28.8.2(.6)
shaken 28.17.13(.3)
shaker 17.14.3
Shakeress 34.5, 34.5.14(.3), 34.18.27(.16)
Shakerism 27.15.21(.2.14)
Shakeshaft 22.27.4(.3)
Shakespeare 3.2.9
Shakespearean 28.3.20(.2)
Shakespeareana 17.18.8
shakeup 20.9.7
shakily 1.31.17(.11)
shakiness 34.18.16(.2.4)
shako 19.12.3, 19.12.5
shakuhachi 1.25.6, 1.25.8
shaky 1.12.3
Shaldon 28.17.12(.27)
shale 40.4
shaley 1.31.4
shaliness 34.18.16(.2.10)
shall 40.6
shalloon 28.16.15
shallop 20.13.7
shallot 22.11.17
shallow 19.29.5
shallowly 1.31.19
shallowness 34.18.16(.17)
Shalmaneser 17.25.1
shalom 27.9, 27.17.14
shalt 22.32.3
shalwar 10.13
shaly 1.31.4
sham 27.6
shaman 28.17.16(.4)
shamanic 24.2.15(.5)
shamanism 27.15.21(.2.9)
shamanist 22.29.2(.18.1)
shamanistic 24.2.10(.15.2)
shamateur 17.12.16(.9.1), 17.28.15, 18.3
shamateurish 36.2.25
shamateurishly 1.31.35(.7.4)
shamateurishness 34.18.16(.33.6)

shamateurism
27.15.21(.2.14)

shamble 40.20.19

shambolic 24.2.27(.9)

shambolically
1.31.24(.9.12)

shame 27.4

shamefaced 22.29.4

shamefacedly
1.31.22(.22), 1.31.23(.14.7)

shamefacedness
34.18.16(.20.4)

shameful 40.27.21

shamefully 1.31.17(.16.2)

shamefulness
34.18.16(.37.2)

shameless 34.18.29(.26)

shamelessly
1.31.33(.12.6)

shamelessness
34.18.16(.31.6)

shamingly 1.31.28(.1.7)

Shamir 3.8

shammer 17.17.6

shammy 1.15.6

shampoo 16.5

shamrock 24.9.15

Shamu 16.11

shamus 34.18.15(.3)

Shan 28.7, 28.9

Shandean 28.3.4(.11)

shandrydan 28.7.7

shandy 1.11.20(.4)

shandygaff 30.5.4

Shane 28.4

Shang 29.4

shanghai 14.22

Shangri-La 10.25

shank 24.19.3

Shankar 10.8.15

Shankill 40.2.7

Shanklin 28.2.31(.17)

Shankly 1.31.24(.12)

Shanks 34.23.18

Shannon 28.17.17(.5)

shanny 1.16.6

Shansi 2.22

shan't 22.26.8

shantung 29.8

shanty 1.10.23(.4)

shantyman 28.7.10(.2)

shantymen 28.5.7(.2)

shantytown 28.8.1

Shanxi 2.22

shap 20.5

shapable 40.20.16(.9)

SHAPE 20.3

shape 20.3

shapeable 40.20.16(.9)

shapechanger
17.29.16(.2)

shapechanging 29.1.26,
29.1.28

shapeless 34.18.29(.20)

shapelessly 1.31.33(.12.6)

shapelessness
34.18.16(.31.6)

shapeliness
34.18.16(.2.10)

shapely 1.31.20

shaper 17.10.3

shaping 29.1.10(.3)

Shapiro 19.27.1

shard 23.9

share 6

shareable 40.20.16(.27.1)

sharecrop 20.7.12

sharecropper 17.10.8

share-farmer 17.17.7

shareholder 17.13.23(.8)

shareholding 29.1.13(.16)

share-out 22.9.18

sharer 17.32.5

shareware 6.18.3

sharia 17.1.16

sharif 30.1.8

Sharjah 10.18, 10.20,
17.27.5, 17.29.7

shark 24.8

sharkskin 28.2.13(.14)

Sharman 28.17.16(.9)

Sharon 28.17.31(.4)

sharp 20.6

Sharpe 20.6

shar-pei 4.7

sharpen 28.17.9

sharpener 17.18.16(.3)

sharpening 29.1.17(.12)

sharper 17.10.7

Sharpeville 40.2.12

sharpie 1.8.6

sharpish 36.2.9

Sharples 35.30.14

sharply 1.31.20

sharpness 34.18.16(.18)

sharpshooter 17.12.15(.4)

sharpshooting
29.1.12(.13)

Sharwood 23.16.6(.3)

shashlik 24.2.27(.20)

Shasta 17.12.24(.5)

Shastra 17.32.19(.11)

shat 22.7

Shatner 17.18.21

Shatt al-Arab 21.14

shatter 17.12.6

shatterer 17.32.14(.6)

shatteringly
1.31.28(.1.17)

shatterproof 30.13.4

Shaughnessy 1.22.16(.9)

Shaun 28.11

shave 31.3

shaveling 29.1.31(.24)

shaven 28.17.20(.3)

shaver 17.21.3

shavetail 40.4.2

Shavian 28.3.10

shaving 29.1.20

Shavuoth 22.11, 34.18.7

shaw 12

Shawcross 34.10.16

shawl 40.10

shawm 27.10

Shawnee 2.17

shay 4

shchi 2

she 2

shea 2

sheading 29.1.13(.1)

sheaf 30.1

shear 3

shearbill 40.2.4

Sheard 23.3, 23.6, 23.19

shearer 17.32.2

shearing 29.1.30(.2)

shearling 29.1.31(.3)

Shearman 28.17.16(.3)

shearpin 28.2.9

sheartail 40.4.2

shearwater 17.12.10(.7)

sheatfish 36.2.18(.15)

sheath 32.1

sheathe 33.1

sheathing 29.1.22

sheathless 34.18.29(.31)

sheave 31.1

Sheba 17.11.1

shebang 29.4.2

shebeen 28.1.8

she-cat 22.7.9

she'd 23.1

shed 23.5

shedder 17.13.4

she-devil 40.28.4

shedhand 23.24.6(.11)

Sheehan 28.17.29

Sheehy 1(.1), 1.27

sheela-na-gig 26.2.3

sheen 28.1

Sheena 17.18.1

Sheene 28.1

sheeny 1.16.1

sheep 20.1

sheepdip 20.2.3

sheepdog 26.7.4

sheepfold 23.31.13(.7)

sheepish 36.2.9

sheepishly 1.31.35(.7.1)

sheepishness
34.18.16(.33.2)

sheeplike 24.13.7(.10)

sheepmeat 22.1.5

sheeprun 28.13.9

sheep's-bit 22.2.6

sheepshank 24.19.3(.5)

sheepskin 28.2.13(.14)

sheepwalk 24.10.9

sheer 3

sheerlegs 35.24

sheerly 1.31.3

sheerness 34.18.16(.3)

sheet 22.1

sheetfed 23.5.8

sheetfeeder 17.13.1

Sheetrock® 24.9.15

Sheffield 23.31.1(.2)

sheikh 24.1, 24.3

sheikhdom 27.15.10(.13)

sheila 17.34.1

shekel 40.23.4

Shekinah 17.18.13(.3)

Shelagh 17.34.1

Shelburne 28.17.10,
28.18.3

Sheldon 28.17.12(.27)

Sheldonian 28.3.8(.11)

sheldrake 24.3.13

shelduck 24.12.3

shelf 30.20.2

shelfful 40.14.6(.17)

shelf-life 30.12

she'll 40.1

shell 40.5

shellac 24.6.23

shellback 24.6.6(.23)

shell-bit 22.2.6

Shelley 1.31.5

shellfire 17.6.9(.13)

shellfish 36.2.18(.21)

shell-less 34.18.29(.38)

Shell-Mex 34.23.4(.5)

shellproof 30.13.4

shellshock 24.9.11

shelly 1.31.5

Shelta 17.12.26(.3)

shelter 17.12.26(.3)

sheltered 23.18.9(.21)

shelterer 17.32.14(.6)

shelterless 34.18.29(.17.2)

Shelton 28.17.11(.27)

shelty 1.10.28

shelve 31.13

shelver 17.21.19

shelves 35.28.10

Shem 27.5

Shema 10.10, 17.17.4

shemozzle 40.32.8

Shena 17.18.1

Shenandoah 17.9.3

shenanigan 28.17.15(.13)

Shenfield 23.31.1(.2)

S

Shensi **2.22**
Shenyang **29.4.16**
Shenzhen **28.5.13**
Sheol **40.9.1, 40.18.1**
Shepard **23.18.7**
shepherd **23.18.7**
shepherdess **34.5.3, 34.18.12**
Sheppard **23.18.7**
Sheppey **1.8.4**
Shepshed **23.5.12**
Shepton **28.17.11(.18)**
Shepton Mallet **22.2.25**
Sher **6, 18**
sherardize **35.15.8**
Sheraton **28.17.11(.15)**
sherbet **22.19.9**
Sherbourne **28.11.2, 28.17.10**
Sherbrooke **24.14.10**
sherd **23.19**
Shere **3**
sheria **17.1.16**
sheriff **30.14**
sheriffalty **1.10.28**
sheriffdom **27.15.10(.16)**
sheriffhood **23.16.5(.12)**
sheriffship **20.2.7(.21)**
Sheringham **27.15.15**
sherlock **24.9.16(.7)**
Sherman **28.17.16(.17)**
sherpa **17.10.15**
Sherrin **28.2.29(.2)**
Sherrington **28.17.11(.23)**
sherry **1.29.3**
Sherwood **23.16.6(.7)**
Sheryl **40.16.13(.3)**
she's **35.1**
Shetland **23.24.16(.16.3)**
Shetlander **17.13.20(.13)**
sheva **10.13**
Shevardnadze **17.25.16**
Shevat **22.7.14**
shewbread **23.5.15**
she-wolf **30.20.6**
she-wolves **35.28.10**
Shi'a **17.1**
Shiah **17.1**
shiatsu **16.15**
shibboleth **32.5, 32.14.17**
shicer **17.24.13**
shicker **17.14.2**
shicksa **17.24.20**
shied **23.15**
shield **23.31.1**
shieldbug **26.10**
shieldless **34.18.29(.23)**
Shields **35.23.15**
shieling **29.1.31(.1)**
shift **22.27.1**

shiftable **40.20.16(.11.7)**
shifter **17.12.23**
shiftily **1.31.17(.9.3)**
shiftiness **34.18.16(.2.3)**
shiftless **34.18.29(.22)**
shiftlessly **1.31.33(.12.6)**
shiftlessness **34.18.16(.31.6)**
shifty **1.10.24**
shigella **17.34.5(.6)**
shiglet **22.19.26(.20)**
shih-tzu **16.15**
Shiism **27.15.21(.2.1)**
Shiite **22.16.1**
shikar **10.8**
shikara **17.32.7**
shikari **1.29.6**
Shikoku **16.9**
shiksa **17.24.20**
shill **40.2**
shillelagh **1.31.4, 17.34.4**
shilling **29.1.31(.2)**
Shillong **29.6.15**
Shilluk **24.14.11**
shilly-shally **1.31.7**
shilly-shallyer **3.24.5**
Shiloh **19.29.9**
Shilton **28.17.11(.27)**
shim **27.2**
shimmer **17.17.2**
shimmeringly **1.31.28(.1.17)**
shimmery **1.29.11(.12)**
shimmy **1.15.2**
shin **28.2**
shinbone **28.19.3**
shindig **26.2.2**
shindy **1.11.20(.1)**
shine **28.14**
shiner **17.18.13**
shingle **40.24.14(.1)**
shingly **1.31.25**
shinily **1.31.17(.14.1)**
shininess **34.18.16(.2.5)**
shiningly **1.31.28(.1.7)**
shinny **1.16.2**
shinsplints **34.22.18**
Shinto **19.10.17**
Shintoism **27.15.21(.2.1)**
Shintoist **22.29.2(.10)**
shinty **1.10.23(.1)**
Shinwell **40.5.17(.12)**
shiny **1.16.13**
ship **20.2**
shipboard **23.12.2(.7)**
shipbroker **17.14.17**
shipbuilder **17.13.23(.2)**
shipbuilding **29.1.13(.16)**
shiplap **20.5.8**
shipless **34.18.29(.20)**

Shipley **1.31.20**
shipload **23.20.13**
Shipman **28.17.16(.19)**
shipmaster **17.12.24(.5)**
shipmate **22.4.13(.8)**
shipment **22.26.15(.13.3)**
shipowner **17.18.18(.1)**
shippable **40.20.16(.9)**
Shippam **27.15.7**
shipper **17.10.2**
ship-rigged **23.22**
shipshape **20.3**
Shipston **28.17.11(.25)**
Shipton **28.17.11(.18)**
ship-to-shore **12.16**
shipway **4.25.10**
shipworm **27.16.7**
shipwreck **24.4.12**
shipwright **22.16.24(.10)**
shipyard **23.9.21**
shiralee **2.32.9(.7)**
Shiraz **35.7**
-shire **3**
shire **17.6**
shire-horse **34.12.7**
shirk **24.17**
shirker **17.14.16**
Shirley **1.31.18**
shirr **18**
shirt **22.20**
shirtdress **34.5.14(.6)**
shirtfront **22.26.12**
shirtily **1.31.17(.9.2)**
shirtiness **34.18.16(.2.3)**
shirting **29.1.12(.15)**
shirtless **34.18.29(.22)**
shirtsleeve **31.1.9**
shirttail **40.4.2**
shirtwaist **22.29.4**
shirtwaister **17.12.24(.3)**
shirty **1.10.17**
shish kebab **21.6**
shit **22.2**
shitbag **26.5.1**
shit creek **24.1**
shite **22.16**
shithouse **34.8.6(.11)**
shitless **34.18.29(.22)**
shittim **27.2.3**
shitty **1.10.2**
shiv **31.2**
Shiva **17.21.1**
shivaree **2.30**
shiver **17.21.2**
shiverer **17.32.14(.13)**
shiveringly **1.31.28(.1.17)**
shivery **1.29.11(.15)**
shivoo **16.14**
shlemiel **40.3.6**
shlep **20.4**

Shloer® **18**
shmear **3**
shoal **40.18**
shoaly **1.31.19**
shoat **22.21**
shochet **22.5.5, 22.5.6**
shock **24.9**
shockability **1.10.16(.22.1)**
shockable **40.20.16(.13)**
shocker **17.14.8**
shocking **29.1.14(.6)**
shockingly **1.31.28(.1.6)**
shockingness **34.18.16(.26)**
shockproof **30.13.4**
shod **23.10**
shoddily **1.31.17(.10)**
shoddiness **34.18.16(.2.3)**
shoddy **1.11.10**
shoe **16**
shoebill **40.2.4**
shoeblack **24.6.23**
shoebox **34.23.8(.2)**
Shoeburyness **34.5.6**
shoehorn **28.11.10**
shoelace **34.4.14**
shoeleather **17.23.4**
shoeless **34.18.29(.16)**
shoemaker **17.14.3(.3)**
shoemaking **29.1.14(.3)**
shoeshine **28.14.15**
shoestring **29.1.30(.13)**
shoetree **2.30.10**
shofar **17.20.14**
shofroth **22.21.14**
shogun **28.13.5, 28.17.15(.14)**
shogunate **22.4.14(.9.1), 22.19.15(.9)**
Sholokhov **30.8.6**
Sholto **19.10.21**
Shona **17.18.9, 17.18.18**
shone **28.10**
shonky **1.12.16**
shoo **16**
shoofly **14.25.14**
shoo-in **28.2.7**
shook **24.14**
shoot **22.18**
shootable **40.20.16(.11.2)**
shoot'em up **20.9**
shooter **17.12.15**
shooting **29.1.12(.13)**
shoot-out **22.9.7**
shoot-up **20.9.5**
shop **20.7**
shopaholic **24.2.27(.9)**
shop-bought **22.13.2**
shopfitter **17.12.2**

shopfitting 29.1.12(.2)
shop-floor 12.23.9
shopfront 22.26.12
shopgirl 40.17
shopkeeper 17.10.1
shopkeeping 29.1.10(.1)
shopless 34.18.29(.20)
shoplift 22.27.1
shoplifter 17.12.23
shopman 28.17.16(.19)
shopper 17.10.8
shoppy 1.8.7
shopsoiled 23.31.7
shoptalk 24.10.2
shopwalker 17.14.9
shopworker 17.14.16
shopworn 28.11.11
shoran 28.7.20
shore 12
shore-based 22.29.4
shorebird 23.19.1
Shoreditch 38.2.4
shorefront 22.26.12
Shoreham 27.15.26(.5)
shoreless 34.18.29(.11)
shoreline 28.14.19(.8)
shoreward 23.18.26(.5)
shoreweed 23.1.10
shoring 29.1.30(.7)
shorn 28.11
short 22.13
shortage 39.2.10
short-arm 27.8, 27.8.3
shortbread 23.5.15
shortcake 24.3.6
short-change 39.17.2
short-circuit 22.2.9(.8)
shortcoming 29.1.16
shortcrust 22.29.12
shortcut 22.15.4
short-dated 23.18.9(.3)
shorten 28.17.11(.10)
Shorter 17.12.10
shortfall 40.10.11
shorthair 6.17
short-haired 23.6
shorthand 23.24.6(.11)
shorthanded
    23.18.10(.14)
shorthaul 40.10.16
short-head 23.5.13
shorthold 23.31.13(.9)
shorthorn 28.11.10
shortish 36.2.11
shortlist 22.29.2(.31.6)
shortly 1.31.22(.10)
shortness 34.18.16(.20.2)
short-order 17.13.9
shortsighted
    23.18.9(.10)

shortsightedly
    1.31.23(.14.3)
shortsightedness
    34.18.16(.21.1)
shortstay 4.9.10
shortstop 20.7.4
shortwave 31.3.6
shortweight 22.4.21
shorty 1.10.10
Shoshone 1.16.17(.11)
Shoshonean 28.3.8(.11)
Shostakovich 38.2.7
shot 22.11
shotgun 28.13.5
shotproof 30.13.4
shotten 28.17.11(.9)
should 23.16
shoulder 17.13.23(.8)
shouldn't 22.26.15(.10)
shout 22.9
shouter 17.12.7
shove 31.8
shove-ha'penny 1.16.18
shovel 40.28.8
shovelboard 23.12.2(.20)
shovelful 40.14.6(.22)
shovelhead 23.5.13(.19)
shoveller 17.34.16(.14)
show 19
show-and-tell 40.5
showband 23.24.6(.4)
showbiz 35.2.2
showboat 22.21.2
showcard 23.9.9
showcase 34.4.6
showdown 28.8.2(.2)
shower 17.3, 17.9
showerproof 30.13.4
showery 1.29.11(.1)
showgirl 40.17
showground 23.24.7(.10)
showily 1.31.17(.6)
showiness 34.18.16(.2.1)
showing 29.1.9
showjump 20.16.5
showjumper 17.10.17
showjumping
    29.1.10(.12)
showman 28.17.16(.18)
showmanship 20.2.7(.19)
shown 28.19
show-off 30.8.2
showpiece 34.1.1
showplace 34.4.14
showroom 27.14.6(.5)
showstopper 17.10.8
showstopping 29.1.10(.6)
showtime 27.12.1
showy 1(.7)
shoyu 16.24.2

shrank 24.19.3
shrapnel 40.26.16
shred 23.5
shredder 17.13.4
Shreveport 22.13.1
shrew 16
shrewd 23.17
shrewdly 1.31.23(.13)
shrewdness
    34.18.16(.21.1)
shrewish 36.2.6
shrewishly 1.31.35(.7.1)
shrewishness
    34.18.16(.33.1)
Shrewsbury 1.29.11(.7.2)
shriek 24.1
shrieker 17.14.1
shrieval 40.28.1
shrievalty 1.10.28
shrift 22.27.1
shrike 24.13
shrill 40.2
shrillness 34.18.16(.37.1)
shrilly 1.31.38
shrimp 20.16.1
shrimper 17.10.17
Shrimpton 28.17.11(.18)
shrine 28.14
Shriner 17.18.13
shrink 24.19.1
shrinkable 40.20.16(.13)
shrinkage 39.2.12
shrinker 17.14.21(.1)
shrinking 29.1.14(.14)
shrinkingly 1.31.28(.1.6)
shrinkpack 24.6.5
shrinkproof 30.13.4
shrive 31.9
shrivel 40.28.2
shriven 28.17.20(.2)
Shrivenham 27.15.14(.11)
Shropshire 17.26.17
shroud 23.8
shroudless 34.18.29(.23)
shrove 31.12
Shrovetide 23.15.4
shrub 21.11
shrubbery 1.29.11(.7.1)
shrubbiness
    34.18.16(.2.2)
shrubby 1.9.9
shrug 26.10
shrunk 24.19.7
shrunken 28.17.13(.17)
shtick 24.2
shtuck 24.14
shtum 27.13
shuck 24.12
Shuckburgh 17.32.14(.5)
shucker 17.14.11

shudder 17.13.11
shudderingly
    1.31.28(.1.17)
shuddery 1.29.11(.9)
shuffle 40.27.11
shuffleboard 23.12.2(.20)
Shufflebottom
    27.15.9(.6)
shuffler 17.34.26
Shufflewick 24.2.25
shuffling 29.1.31(.23)
shufti 1.10.24
shufty 1.10.24
shul 40.14, 40.15
Shula 17.34.15
shuln 28.20
Shumen 28.5.7(.9)
shun 28.13
shunt 22.26.12
shunter 17.12.22(.10)
shush 36.12, 36.13
Shuster 17.12.24(.13)
shut 22.15
shutdown 28.8.2(.5)
Shute 22.18
Shuter 17.12.15
shut-eye 14.8
shut-in 28.2.11(.7)
shut-off 30.8.4
shut-out 22.9.7
shutter 17.12.12
shutterbug 26.10
shutterless 34.18.29(.17.2)
shuttle 40.21.9
shuttlecock 24.9.6
Shuttleworth 32.14.15
Shuy 14
shwa 10
shy 14
shyer 17.6
Shylock 24.9.16(.5)
shyly 1.31.14
shyness 34.18.16(.13)
shyster 17.12.24(.11)
si 2
sial 40.16.6
sialagogue 26.7.6
Siam 27.6
siamang 29.4.7
Siamese 35.1.11
Siân 28.9
sib 21.2
Sibelius 34.3.16
Siberia 3.22.2
Siberian 28.3.20(.2)
sibilance 34.24.10(.24)
sibilancy 1.22.23(.10.4)
sibilant 22.26.15(.25)
sibilate 22.4.23(.7.1)
sibilation 28.17.25(.3.14)

Sibley **1.31.21(.1)**
sibling **29.1.31(.16)**
sibship **20.2.7(.13)**
sibyl **40.2.4, 40.20.2**
sibylline **28.14.19(.11)**
sic **24.2**
siccative **31.2.1(.9.1)**
sice **34.15**
Sichuan **28.9.12**
Sicilia **3.24.2**
Sicilian **28.3.21(.2)**
siciliana **17.18.8**
siciliano **19.15.7**
Sicily **1.31.17(.20)**
sick **24.2**
sickbay **4.8**
sickbed **23.5.2**
sicken **28.17.13(.2)**
sickener **17.18.16(.6)**
sickeningly **1.31.28(.1.7)**
Sickert **22.19.12(.2)**
sickie **1.12.2**
sickish **36.2.13**
sickle **40.23.2**
sickliness **34.18.16(.2.10)**
sicklist **22.29.2(.31.6)**
sickly **1.31.24(.2)**
sickness **34.18.16(.22)**
sicko **19.12.2**
sickroom **27.14.6(.10)**
Sid **23.2**
sidalcea **3.14.17**
Sidcup **20.9.7, 20.13.2**
Siddall **40.10.6**
Siddeley **1.31.17(.10)**
Siddons **35.26.13(.8)**
side **23.15**
sidearm **27.8.4**
sideband **23.24.6(.4)**
sidebar **10.5.8**
sideboard **23.12.2(.9)**
Sidebotham **27.8.3,
27.15.9(.6), 27.15.18**
Sidebottom **27.8.3,
27.15.9(.6)**
sideburn **28.18.3**
sidecar **10.8.12**
sidedish **36.2.12**
sidedness **34.18.16(.21.1)**
sidehill **40.2.18**
sidekick **24.2.12**
sidelamp **20.16.3**
sideless **34.18.29(.23)**
sidelight **22.16.25(.14)**
sideline **28.14.19(.15)**
sidelong **29.6.15**
sideman **28.7.10(.12)**
sidemen **28.5.7(.16)**
side-on **28.10**
sidepiece **34.1.1**

sidereal **40.3.14(.2)**
siderite **22.16.24(.9)**
siderostat **22.7.7**
sidesaddle **40.22.5**
sideshow **19.22**
sideslip **20.2.13**
sidesman **28.17.16(.30)**
sidesplitting **29.1.12(.2)**
sidestep **20.4**
sidestepper **17.10.4**
sidestroke **24.18.13**
sideswipe **20.10.4**
sidetrack **24.6.21**
sidewalk **24.10.9**
sideward **23.18.26(.10)**
sideways **35.4.15**
sidewinder **17.13.20(.11)**
sidewise **35.15.19**
Sidgewick **24.2.25**
siding **29.1.13(.9)**
sidle **40.22.11**
Sidmouth **32.14.11**
Sidney **1.16.20**
Sidon **28.17.12(.13)**
Sidra **17.32.20**
SIDS **35.23.2**
siege **39.1**
Siegel **40.24.1**
Siegfried **23.1.11**
Sieg Heil **40.13**
Siemens **35.26.13(.10)**
Siena **17.18.4**
Sienese **35.1.12**
sienna **17.18.4**
sierra **17.32.4**
Sierra Leone **1.16.17,
28.19**
Sierra Leonian
28.3.8(.11)
Sierra Madre **4.26.12**
Sierra Nevada **17.13.7**
siesta **17.12.24(.4)**
sieve **31.2**
sievelike **24.13.7(.20)**
sievert **22.19.17**
sifaka **17.14.5**
siffleur **18.17**
siffleuse **35.19**
sift **22.27.1**
Sifta **17.12.23**
sifter **17.12.23**
Sigal **40.24.1**
sigh **14**
sight **22.16**
sighter **17.12.13**
sighting **29.1.12(.11)**
sightless **34.18.29(.22)**
sightlessly **1.31.33(.12.6)**
sightlessness
34.18.16(.31.6)

sightline **28.14.19(.14)**
sightliness **34.18.16(.2.10)**
sightly **1.31.22(.13)**
sight-read **23.1.11, 23.5.15**
sight-reader **17.13.1**
sight-sang **29.4.9**
sightsaw **12.14.11**
sightscreen **28.1.25(.8)**
sightsee **2.22.10**
sightseeing **29.1.1**
sightseer **17.1.11**
sight-singing **29.1.18**
sigil **40.34**
sigillate **22.4.23(.7.2)**
Sigismund **23.24.16(.7)**
sigla **17.34.24**
siglum **27.15.28(.18)**
sigma **17.17.20**
sigmate **22.4.13(.11)**
sigmatic **24.2.10(.4.2)**
sigmoid **23.13.11**
sigmoidoscope
20.15.4(.1)
sigmoidoscopic
24.2.8(.5)
sigmoidoscopy **1.8.11(.5)**
Sigmund **23.24.16(.7)**
sign **28.14**
signable **40.20.16(.16.2)**
signal **40.26.19**
signalize **35.15.21(.4.5)**
signaller **17.34.16(.12)**
signalman **28.17.16(.35)**
signary **1.29.11(.13.3)**
signatory **1.29.11(.8.7)**
signature **17.28.15**
signboard **23.12.2(.12)**
signer **17.18.13**
signet **22.19.15(.11)**
significance
34.24.10(.12)
significancy
1.22.23(.10.2)
significant **22.26.15(.11)**
significantly
1.31.22(.20.2)
signification
28.17.25(.3.5)
significative **31.2.1(.9.1)**
signified **23.15.9**
signifier **17.6.9(.4)**
signify **14.14.4(.7)**
signing **29.1.17(.10)**
signor **12.22**
signora **17.32.10(.11)**
signorina **17.18.1(.15)**
signory **1.29.11(.26)**
signpost **22.29.17(.1)**
signwriter **17.12.13(.8)**
signwriting **29.1.12(.11)**
Sigurd **23.19.3**

Sihanouk **24.14.6**
Sihanoukville **40.2.12**
sika **17.14.1**
Sikh **24.1**
Sikhism **27.15.21(.2.6)**
Sikkim **27.2.5**
Sikkimese **35.1.11**
Sikorsky **1.12.17(.6)**
silage **39.2.23**
silane **28.4.19**
Silas **34.18.29(.14)**
Silchester **17.12.24(.4)**
Silcox **34.23.8(.5)**
sild **23.31.2**
silence **34.24.10(.24)**
silencer **17.24.22(.7)**
sileni **14.13**
silent **22.26.15(.25)**
silently **1.31.22(.20.5)**
silenus **34.18.16(.1)**
Silesia **3.15.1, 17.26.1**
Silesian **28.3.14,
28.17.25(.1), 28.17.26(.1)**
silex **34.23.4(.12)**
silhouette **22.5**
silica **17.14.15(.15)**
silicate **22.4.11(.6),
22.19.12(.10)**
siliceous **34.18.22(.2)**
silicic **24.2.20(.2)**
silicide **23.15.11(.6)**
siliciferous **34.18.27(.20)**
silicification
28.17.25(.3.5)
silicify **14.14.4(.9)**
silicon **28.17.13(.13)**
silicone **28.19.6**
Silicon Valley **1.31.7**
silicosis **34.2.17(.11.1)**
silicotic **24.2.10(.6)**
siliqua **17.31.6**
siliquae **2.29, 14.23**
silique **24.1.12**
siliquose **34.20.15**
siliquous **34.18.26**
silk **24.21**
silken **28.17.13(.19)**
silkily **1.31.17(.11)**
Silkin **28.2.13(.17)**
silkiness **34.18.16(.2.4)**
silklike **24.13.7(.14)**
silkscreen **28.1.25(.8)**
silkworm **27.16.7**
silky **1.12.19**
sill **40.2**
Sillars **35.18.25**
siller **17.34.2**
sillily **1.31.17(.29)**
sillimanite **22.16.14(.6)**
silliness **34.18.16(.2.10)**

Sillitoe **19.10.2**
Silloth **32.14.17**
Sills **35.30.2**
silly **1.31.2**
silo **19.29.9**
Siloam **27.15.6**
Silsoe **19.20.17**
silt **22.32.1**
siltation **28.17.25(.3.3)**
siltstone **28.19.4(.9)**
silty **1.10.28**
Silures **35.1.22**
Silurian **28.3.20(.7)**
Silva **17.21.19**
silvan **28.17.20(.14)**
Silvanus **34.18.16(.4)**
silver **17.21.19**
silver birch **38.16**
silverfish **36.2.18(.11)**
silveriness **34.18.16(.2.9)**
Silverman **28.17.16(.16)**
silvern **28.17.20(.14)**
silver-plate **22.4.23(.8)**
silverside **23.15.11(.6)**
silversmith **32.2.3**
silversmithing **29.1.21**
Silverstone **28.17.11(.25),**
28.19.4(.9)
silverware **6.18.4**
silverweed **23.1.10**
silvery **1.29.11(.15)**
Silvester **17.12.24(.4)**
silvicultural
40.16.13(.12.3)
silviculture **17.28.26**
silviculturist
22.29.2(.29.4)
Silvikrin® **28.2.29(.10)**
Sim **27.2**
sima **17.17.11**
simazine **28.1.19**
Simca® **17.14.20**
simcha **17.15, 17.28.21**
Simcox **34.23.8(.5)**
Simenon **11.9, 28.10.14**
Simeon **28.3.7**
Simes **35.25.8**
simian **28.3.7**
similar **17.34.16(.11)**
similarity **1.10.16(.21.1)**
similarly **1.31.17(.29)**
simile **1.31.17(.13)**
similitude **23.17.4(.1)**
Simla **17.34.25**
simmer **17.17.2**
Simmonds **35.23.15**
Simmons **35.26.13(.10)**
simnel **40.26.20**
simoleon **28.3.21(.11)**
Simon **28.17.16(.2)**

Simone **28.19.9**
simoniac **24.6.1**
simoniacal **40.23.12(.3)**
simoniacally **1.31.24(.9.1)**
Simonides **35.1.8**
simonize **35.15.12(.5)**
simon-pure **12.22,**
17.7.12(.2)
Simons **35.26.13(.10)**
simony **1.16.15(.11)**
simoom **27.14.5**
simoon **28.16.7**
simp **20.16.1**
simpatico **19.12.12**
simper **17.10.17**
simperingly
1.31.28(.1.17)
Simpkin **28.2.13(.8)**
Simpkins **35.26.2**
Simpkinson **28.17.23(.24)**
simple **40.19.14**
simple-hearted
23.18.9(.7)
simple-minded
23.18.10(.14)
simple-mindedly
1.31.23(.14.4)
simple-mindedness
34.18.16(.21.1)
simpleness
34.18.16(.37.4)
simpleton **28.17.11(.27)**
simplex **34.23.4(.12)**
simplicity **1.10.16(.16.1)**
simplification
28.17.25(.3.5)
simplify **14.14.4(.16)**
simplism **27.15.21(.2.15)**
simplistic **24.2.10(.15.3)**
simplistically
1.31.24(.9.6)
Simplon **28.10.26**
Simplot **22.11.17**
simply **1.31.20**
Simpson **28.17.23(.17)**
Sims **35.25.2**
Simson **28.17.23(.23)**
simulacra **17.32.21**
simulacrum **27.15.26(.12)**
simulate **22.4.23(.7.3)**
simulation **28.17.25(.3.14)**
simulative **31.2.1(.9.4)**
simulator **17.12.4(.16)**
simulcast **22.29.6(.5),**
22.29.8(.3)
simultaneity **1.10.16(.1)**
simultaneous **34.3.6(.3)**
simultaneously
1.31.33(.1.2)
simultaneousness
34.18.16(.31.1)

simurg **26.14.2**
sin **28.2**
Sinai **14.2, 14.13**
Sinaitic **24.2.10(.2.1)**
Sinanthropus **34.18.9(.8)**
sinapism **27.15.21(.2.2)**
Sinatra **17.32.19(.4)**
Sinbad **23.7.6**
sin-bin **28.2.10**
since **34.24.1**
sincere **3.14**
sincerely **1.31.3**
sincereness **34.18.16(.3)**
sincerity **1.10.16(.21.1)**
sincipital **40.21.12**
sinciput **22.15.1**
Sinclair **6.21**
Sind **23.24.2**
Sindebele **1.31.1, 1.31.4**
Sindh **23.24.2**
Sindhi **1.11.20(.1)**
sindonology
1.26.10(.11.4)
Sindy **1.11.20(.1)**
sine **28.14**
Sinéad **23.4.8**
sinecure **12.22, 17.7.12(.5)**
sinecurism
27.15.21(.2.14)
sinecurist **22.29.2(.29.2)**
sine die **2.6**
sine qua non **28.10**
sinew **16.24.10**
sinewless **34.18.29(.16)**
sinewy **1(.6)**
sinfonia **3.9.11, 17.1.7**
sinfonietta **17.12.5**
sinful **40.27.22**
sinfully **1.31.17(.16.2)**
sinfulness **34.18.16(.37.2)**
sing **29.1**
singable **40.20.16(.17)**
singalong **29.6.15**
Singapore **12.3**
Singaporean **28.3.20(.7)**
singe **39.17.1**
singer **17.19.1**
singer-songwriter
17.12.13(.8)
Singh **29.1**
singingly **1.31.28(.1.7)**
single **40.24.14(.1)**
single-lens reflex
34.23.4(.12)
single-minded
23.18.10(.14)
single-mindedly
1.31.23(.14.4)
single-mindedness
34.18.16(.21.1)
singleness **34.18.16(.37.5)**

singlestick **24.2.10(.15.4)**
singlet **22.19.26(.20)**
singleton **28.17.11(.27)**
singletree **2.30.10**
singly **1.31.25**
singsong **29.6.9**
singular **17.34.16(.21.3)**
singularity **1.10.16(.21.1)**
singularization
28.17.25(.3.12)
singularize **35.15.20(.2)**
singularly **1.31.17(.29)**
sinh **28.14, 38.3, 38.18.1**
Sinhala **17.34.8**
Sinhalese **35.1.23**
sinister **17.12.24(.14)**
sinisterly **1.31.17(.9.3)**
sinisterness
34.18.16(.15.2)
sinistral **40.16.13(.16)**
sinistrality **1.10.16(.32.13)**
sinistrally **1.31.17(.27.3)**
sinistrorse **34.12.8**
sinistrorsely **1.31.33(.7)**
Sinitic **24.2.10(.2.2)**
sink **24.19.1**
sinkable **40.20.16(.13)**
sinkage **39.2.12**
sinker **17.14.21(.1)**
sinkhole **40.18.13**
Sinkiang **29.4.16**
sinking **29.1.14(.14)**
sinless **34.18.29(.27)**
sinlessly **1.31.33(.12.6)**
sinlessness **34.18.16(.31.6)**
sinner **17.18.2**
sinnet **22.19.15(.1)**
Sinn Fein **28.4**
Sinn Feiner **17.18.3**
Sinnott **22.19.15(.1)**
Sino- **19.15.10**
Sino-Japanese **35.1.12**
sinological **40.23.12(.17.2)**
Sinologist **22.29.2(.26.4)**
Sinologue **26.7.14**
Sinology **1.26.10(.11.4)**
Sinomania **3.9.3(.5)**
Sinophile **40.13.9**
Sinophobe **21.16.1**
Sinophobia **3.3.9**
sinopia **3.2.7**
Sino-Soviet **22.3.7**
Sino-Tibetan
28.17.11(.4)
sinter **17.12.22(.1)**
Sintra **17.32.19(.10)**
sinuate **22.4.4**
sinuosity **1.10.16(.16.2)**
sinuous **34.18.6**
sinuously **1.31.33(.12.1)**

sinuousness **34.18.16(.31.2)**
sinus **34.18.16(.13)**
sinusitis **34.18.11(.8)**
sinusoid **23.13.16**
sinusoidal **40.22.9**
sinusoidally **1.31.17(.10)**
Siobhan **28.11.7**
Sion **28.17.5**
Sioned **23.18.14**
Siouan **28.17.7**
Sioux **16**
sip **20.2**
sipe **20.10**
siphon **28.17.19**
siphonage **39.2.15**
siphonal **40.26.13(.9)**
siphonic **24.2.15(.6.3)**
siphonophore **12.11.3, 12.11.4**
siphuncle **40.23.15**
sipper **17.10.2**
sippet **22.19.8**
sir **18**
sircar **10.8.9**
sirdar **10.7**
sire **17.6**
siren **28.17.31(.10)**
sirenian **28.3.8(.1)**
sirgang **29.4.6**
Sirhowy **1(.3)**
Sirius **34.3.15(.1)**
sirloin **28.12**
sirocco **19.12.7**
sirrah **17.32.1**
sirree **2.30**
Sirte **1.10.17**
sis **34.2**
sisal **40.31.11, 40.32.12**
siskin **28.2.13(.14)**
Sisley **1.31.34**
Sissie **1.22.2**
sissified **23.15.9**
sissiness **34.18.16(.2.7)**
Sissons **35.26.13(.13)**
sissoo **16.15**
sissy **1.22.2**
sissyish **36.2.1**
sister **17.12.24(.2)**
sisterhood **23.16.5(.3)**
sisterless **34.18.29(.17.2)**
sisterliness **34.18.16(.2.10)**
sisterly **1.31.17(.9.3)**
Sistine **28.1.9(.7)**
sistra **17.32.19(.11)**
sistroid **23.13.19**
sistrum **27.15.26(.10)**
Sisyphean **28.17.1(.8)**
Sisyphus **34.18.17**

sit **22.2**
Sita **17.12.1**
sitar **10.6**
sitarist **22.29.2(.29.2)**
sitatunga **17.16.17(.5)**
sitcom **27.9**
sitdown **28.8.2**
site **22.16**
sit-fast **22.29.6(.9)**
sit-in **28.2.11(.2)**
Sitka **17.14.18**
sitophobia **3.3.9**
sitrep **20.4**
sitringee **2.25, 2.27**
sits vac **24.6**
Sittang **29.4.3**
sitter **17.12.2**
sitter-in **28.2**
sitting **29.1.12(.2)**
Sittingbourne **28.11.2**
Sitting Bull **40.14**
situ **16.24.5**
situate **22.4.4, 22.19.5**
situation **28.17.25(.3.1)**
situational **40.26.13(.14.2)**
situationally **1.31.17(.14.3)**
situationism **27.15.21(.2.9)**
situationist **22.29.2(.18.2)**
sit-up **20.9.5**
sit-upon **28.10.7**
Sitwell **40.5.17(.7), 40.35.2**
sitz **34.22.2**
sitz-bath **32.8**
Sitzkrieg **26.1**
sitzmark **24.8.8**
Sivaism **27.15.21(.2.1)**
Sivaite **22.16.5**
Sivan **28.17.20(.1)**
Siwash **36.9.5**
six **34.23.2**
sixain **28.4.12**
sixer **17.24.20**
sixfold **23.31.13(.7)**
six-footer **17.12.14**
sixgun **28.13.5**
sixpenny **1.16.15(.5)**
six-shooter **17.12.15(.4)**
sixte **22.29.20**
sixteen **28.1.9**
sixteenmo **19.14.16**
sixteenth **32.21**
sixth **32.23**
sixth-former **17.17.9**
sixthly **1.31.31**
sixtieth **32.14.1**
Sixtine **28.1.9(.7), 28.14.5**
Sixtus **34.18.11(.16)**
sixty **1.10.26(.14)**
sixtyfold **23.31.13(.7)**

sixty-fourmo **19.14.9**
sizar **17.25.12**
sizarship **20.2.7(.9)**
size **35.15**
sizeable **40.20.16(.22)**
sizeably **1.31.21(.7.2)**
sizer **17.25.12**
Sizewell **40.5.17(.16)**
sizzle **40.32.2**
sizzler **17.34.28**
sjambok **24.9.3**
ska **10**
Skagerrak **24.6.21**
Skagway **4.25.15**
skald **23.31.5, 23.31.6**
skaldic **24.2.11(.18)**
Skanda **17.13.20(.4)**
Skara Brae **4**
skarn **28.9**
skat **22.7**
skate **22.4**
skateboard **23.12.2(.8)**
skateboarder **17.13.9**
skatepark **24.8.2**
skater **17.12.4**
skating-rink **24.19.1(.7)**
skean **28.1, 28.17.1**
skean dhu **16**
Skeat **22.1**
sked **23.5**
skedaddle **40.22.5**
skeet **22.1**
skeeter **17.12.1**
Skeffington **28.17.11(.23)**
skeg **26.4**
Skegness **34.5.6**
skein **28.4**
skeletal **40.21.1, 40.21.12**
skeletally **1.31.17(.9.1)**
skeleton **28.17.11(.15)**
skeletonize **35.15.12(.5)**
Skelmersdale **40.4.3**
Skelton **28.17.11(.27)**
skep **20.4**
skeptic **24.2.10(.12)**
skeptical **40.23.12(.7.3)**
skeptically **1.31.24(.9.5)**
skerrick **24.2.26(.4)**
skerry **1.29.3**
sketch **38.4**
sketchbook **24.14.3**
sketcher **17.28.5**
sketchily **1.31.17(.24)**
sketchiness **34.18.16(.2.8)**
Sketchley **1.31.36**
sketchpad **23.7.5**
sketchy **1.25.4**
skeuomorph **30.9.2**
skeuomorphic **24.2.16(.5)**

skew **16**
skewback **24.6.6(.8)**
skewbald **23.31.6**
Skewen **28.2.7**
skewer **17.8**
skewness **34.18.16(.14)**
skew-whiff **30.2.4**
ski **2**
skiable **40.20.16(.1)**
skiagram **27.6.17(.5)**
skiamachy **1.12.13**
skibob **21.8**
ski-bobber **17.11.8**
skiboot **22.18.3**
skid **23.2**
Skiddaw **12.6.1**
skidlid **23.2.23**
skidmark **24.8.8**
skidoo **16.8**
skidpan **28.7.4**
skidproof **30.13.4**
skid row **19**
skier **17.1**
skiff **30.2**
skiffle **40.27.2**
ski-jorer **17.32.10(.9)**
ski-joring **29.1.30(.7)**
ski-jump **20.16.5**
skilful **40.27.31**
skilfully **1.31.17(.16.2)**
skilfulness **34.18.16(.37.2)**
ski lift **22.27.1**
skill **40.2**
skillet **22.19.26(.1)**
skillfully **1.31.17(.16.2)**
skill-less **34.18.29(.38)**
skilly **1.31.2**
skim **27.2**
skimmer **17.17.2**
skimmia **3.8.2**
skimp **20.16.1**
skimpily **1.31.17(.7)**
skimpiness **34.18.16(.2.2)**
skimpy **1.8.14**
skin **28.2**
skincare **6.6**
skin-deep **20.1**
skin-dive **31.9**
skinflick **24.2.27(.18)**
skinflint **22.26.1**
skinful **40.14.6(.15)**
skinhead **23.5.13(.14)**
skink **24.19.1**
skinless **34.18.29(.27)**
skinlike **24.13.7(.17)**
skinner **17.18.2**
Skinnerian **28.3.20(.2)**
Skinnerism **27.15.21(.2.14)**
skinniness **34.18.16(.2.5)**

skinny **1.16.2**
skinny-dip **20.2.3**
skint **22.26.1**
skintight **22.16.9**
skip **20.2**
skipjack **24.6.18**
ski-plane **28.4.19**
skipper **17.10.2**
skippet **22.2.5**
skipping-rope **20.15.8**
Skipton **28.17.11(.18)**
skirl **40.17**
skirmish **36.2.15**
skirmisher **17.26.14**
skirr **18**
skirret **22.19.24(.1)**
skirt **22.20**
skirting **29.1.12(.15)**
skirtless **34.18.29(.22)**
skit **22.2**
skite **22.16**
skitter **17.12.2**
skittery **1.29.11(.8.1)**
skittish **36.2.11**
skittishly **1.31.35(.7.1)**
skittishness
  34.18.16(.33.3)
skittle **40.21.2**
skive **31.9**
skiver **17.21.10**
Skivvies **35.2.10**
skivvy **1.19.2**
skiwear **6.18.1**
Skoda® **17.13.17**
Skokholm **27.15.11(.11),**
  27.17.12
skol **40.9, 40.18**
skookum **27.15.11(.8)**
Skryabin **28.2.10**
skua **17.8**
Skues **35.17**
skulduggery **1.29.11(.11)**
skulk **24.21**
skulker **17.14.25**
skull **40.12**
skullcap **20.5.1**
skunk **24.19.7**
sky **14**
skycap **20.5.1**
skydive **31.9**
skydiver **17.21.10**
skydiving **29.1.20**
Skye **14**
skyer **17.6**
skyey **1(.5)**
sky-high **14.22**
skyhook **24.14.9**
skyjack **24.6.18**
skyjacker **17.14.5**
Skylab **21.6**

skylark **24.8.16**
skyless **34.18.29(.14)**
skylight **22.16.25(.8)**
skyline **28.14.19(.10)**
skyrocket **22.2.9(.5)**
skysail **40.4.10**
skyscape **20.3**
skyscraper **17.10.3**
skywalk **24.10.9**
skyward **23.18.26(.6)**
skywatch **38.8**
skyway **4.25.7**
skywriting **29.1.12(.11)**
slab **21.6**
slab-sided **23.18.10(.11)**
slack **24.6**
slacken **28.17.13(.5)**
slacker **17.14.5**
slackly **1.31.24(.5)**
slackness **34.18.16(.22)**
Slade **23.4**
slag **26.5**
slaggy **1.14.5**
slagheap **20.1**
slain **28.4**
slàinte **17.28.22,**
  17.29.16(.6)
Slaithwaite **22.2.2,**
  22.4.21
slake **24.3**
slalom **27.15.28(.6)**
slam **27.6**
slambang **29.4.2**
slammer **17.17.6**
slander **17.13.20(.4)**
slanderer **17.32.14(.7)**
slanderous **34.18.27(.15)**
slanderously
  1.31.33(.12.5)
slanderousness
  34.18.16(.31.5)
slang **29.4**
slangily **1.31.17(.15)**
slanginess **34.18.16(.2.5)**
slangy **1.17**
slant **22.26.6, 22.26.8**
slantways **35.4.15**
slantwise **35.15.19**
slap **20.5**
slap-bang **29.4.2**
slapdash **36.6.4**
slaphappy **1.8.5**
slapjack **24.6.18**
slapshot **22.11.12**
slapstick **24.2.10(.15.4)**
slap-up **20.9, 20.9.4**
slash **36.6**
slash-and-burn **28.18.3**
slasher **17.26.6**
slat **22.7**

slate **22.4**
slater **17.12.4**
slather **17.23.5**
slating **29.1.12(.3)**
slattern **28.17.11(.6),**
  28.18.4
slatternliness
  34.18.16(.2.10)
slatternly **1.31.27(.14)**
Slattery **1.29.11(.8.3)**
slaty **1.10.3**
slaughter **17.12.10**
slaughterer **17.32.14(.6)**
slaughterhouse
  34.8.6(.7)
slaughterous
  34.18.27(.14)
Slav **31.6**
slave **31.3**
slave-driver **17.21.10**
slaveholder **17.13.23(.8)**
slaver **17.21.3, 17.21.5**
slavery **1.29.11(.15)**
slavey **1.19.3**
Slavic **24.2.17**
slavish **36.2.19**
slavishly **1.31.35(.7.3)**
slavishness
  34.18.16(.33.6)
Slavism **27.15.21(.2.11)**
Slavonia **3.9.11**
Slavonian **28.3.8(.11)**
Slavonic **24.2.15(.6.3)**
Slavophile **40.13.9**
Slavophobe **21.16.1**
slaw **12**
slay **4**
slayer **17.2**
slaying **29.1.3**
Slazenger **17.29.16(.8)**
Sleaford **23.18.16(.1)**
sleaze **35.1**
sleazily **1.31.17(.21)**
sleaziness **34.18.16(.2.7)**
sleazoid **23.13.17**
sleazy **1.23.1**
sled **23.5**
sledge **39.5**
sledgehammer **17.17.6**
sleek **24.1**
sleekly **1.31.24(.1)**
sleekness **34.18.16(.22)**
sleeky **1.12.1**
sleep **20.1**
Sleepeezee **1.23.1**
sleeper **17.10.1**
sleepily **1.31.17(.7)**
sleepiness **34.18.16(.2.2)**
sleepless **34.18.29(.20)**
sleeplessly
  1.31.33(.12.6)

sleeplessness
  34.18.16(.31.6)
sleepwalk **24.10.9**
sleepwalker **17.14.9**
sleepwalking **29.1.14(.7)**
sleepwear **6.18.6**
sleepy **1.8.1**
sleepyhead **23.5.13(.1)**
sleet **22.1**
sleetiness **34.18.16(.2.3)**
sleety **1.10.1**
sleeve **31.1**
sleeveless **34.18.29(.30)**
sleeving **29.1.20**
sleigh **4**
sleight **22.16**
slender **17.13.20(.3)**
slenderize **35.15.20(.2)**
slenderly **1.31.17(.10)**
slenderness
  34.18.16(.15.2)
slept **22.22.3**
Slessor **17.24.5**
sleuth **32.13**
sleuthhound **23.24.7(.8)**
slew **16**
sley **4**
slice **34.15**
sliceable **40.20.16(.21.2)**
slicer **17.24.13**
slick **24.2**
slicker **17.14.2**
slickly **1.31.24(.2)**
slickness **34.18.16(.22)**
slid **23.2**
slidable **40.20.16(.12)**
slidably **1.31.21(.4.4)**
slide **23.15**
slider **17.13.12**
slideway **4.25.13**
slight **22.16**
slightingly **1.31.28(.1.4)**
slightish **36.2.11**
slightly **1.31.22(.13)**
slightness **34.18.16(.20.2)**
Sligo **19.13.7**
slim **27.2**
slime **27.12**
slimily **1.31.17(.13)**
sliminess **34.18.16(.2.5)**
slim-jim **27.2.12**
slimline **28.14.19(.18)**
slimly **1.31.26(.2)**
slimmer **17.17.2**
slimmish **36.2.15**
slimness **34.18.16(.24)**
slimy **1.15.11**
sling **29.1**
slingback **24.6.6(.18)**
slinger **17.19.1**

slingshot 22.11.12
slink 24.19.1
slinkily 1.31.17(.11)
slinkiness 34.18.16(.2.4)
slinkweed 23.1.10
slinky 1.12.16
slip 20.2
slipcase 34.4.6
slipcover 17.21.9
slipknot 22.11.9
slipover 17.21.14(.3)
slippage 39.2.8
slipper 17.10.2
slipperily 1.31.17(.27.1)
slipperiness 34.18.16(.2.9)
slipperwort 22.20.15
slippery 1.29.11(.6)
slippiness 34.18.16(.2.2)
slippy 1.8.2
slipshod 23.10.10
slipstitch 38.2.3
slipstream 27.1.12
slip-ware 6.18.6
slipway 4.25.10
slit 22.2
slither 17.23.2
slithery 1.29.11(.17)
slitter 17.12.2
slitty 1.10.2
sliver 17.21.2, 17.21.10
slivovitz 34.22.2
Sloane 28.19
Sloaney 1.16.17
slob 21.8
slobber 17.11.8
slobberiness
   34.18.16(.2.9)
slobbery 1.29.11(.7.1)
slobbish 36.2.10
Slocombe 27.15.11(.11)
Slocum 27.15.11(.11)
sloe 19
sloe-eyed 23.15
slog 26.7
slogan 28.17.15(.14)
slogger 17.16.7
sloid 23.13
Sloman 28.17.16(.18)
slo-mo 19.14.14
sloop 20.12
sloosh 36.14
sloot 22.18
slop 20.7
slope 20.15
slopewise 35.15.19
sloppily 1.31.17(.7)
sloppiness 34.18.16(.2.2)
sloppy 1.8.7
slosh 36.9
sloshy 1.24.7

slot 22.11
slotback 24.6.6(.12)
slot car 10
sloth 32.16
slothful 40.27.24
slothfully 1.31.17(.16.2)
slothfulness
   34.18.16(.37.2)
slouch 38.6
slouchy 1.25.7
Slough 9
slough 9, 30.11
sloughy 1.18.7
Slovak 24.6.12
Slovakia 3.6.5
sloven 28.17.20(.7)
Slovene 28.1.16
Slovenia 3.9.1
Slovenian 28.3.8(.1)
slovenliness
   34.18.16(.2.10)
slovenly 1.31.27(.14)
slovenry 1.29.20
slow 19
slowcoach 38.17
slowdown 28.8.2(.2)
slowish 36.2.8
slowly 1.31.19
slowness 34.18.16(.17)
slowpoke 24.18.1
slowworm 27.16.7
slub 21.11
sludge 39.11
sludgy 1.26.8
slue 16
sluff 30.11
slug 26.10
slugabed 23.5.2
slugfest 22.29.5(.4)
sluggard 23.18.12
sluggardliness
   34.18.16(.2.10)
sluggardly
   1.31.23(.14.5)
slugger 17.16.9
sluggish 36.2.14
sluggishly 1.31.35(.7.1)
sluggishness
   34.18.16(.33.4)
sluice 34.17
sluicegate 22.4.12(.10)
sluiceway 4.25.22
sluit 22.2.4
slum 27.11
slumber 17.11.17(.6)
slumberer 17.32.14(.5)
slumberous
   34.18.27(.13)
slumbrous 34.18.27(.13)
slumgullion 28.3.21(.2)
slumlord 23.12.11

slumminess
   34.18.16(.2.5)
slummock 24.16.6
slummy 1.15.10
slump 20.16.5
slung 29.8
slunk 24.19.7
slur 18
slurp 20.14
slurry 1.29.9
slush 36.12
slushiness 34.18.16(.2.8)
slushy 1.24.9
slut 22.15
sluttish 36.2.11
sluttishly 1.31.35(.7.1)
sluttishness
   34.18.16(.33.3)
sly 14
slyboots 34.22.14
slyly 1.31.14
slyness 34.18.16(.13)
slype 20.10
smack 24.6
smacker 17.14.5
smackeroo 16.23
Smail 40.4
Smails 35.30.3
Smale 40.4
small 40.10
smallage 39.2.23
Smalley 1.31.11
smallgoods 35.23.11
smallholder 17.13.23(.8)
smallholding 29.1.13(.16)
smallish 36.2.27
small-minded
   23.18.10(.14)
small-mindedly
   1.31.23(.14.4)
small-mindedness
   34.18.16(.21.1)
smallness 34.18.16(.37.1)
Smallpiece 34.1.1
smallpox 34.23.8(.1)
smalltalk 24.10.2
smallwares 35.6
Smallwood 23.16.6(.22)
smalt 22.32.5, 22.32.6
smarm 27.8
smarmily 1.31.17(.13)
smarminess
   34.18.16(.2.5)
smarmy 1.15.7
smart 22.10
smart-alecky 1.12.13
smart-arse 34.9.2
smart-ass 34.9.2
smarten 28.17.11(.8)
Smartie 1.10.8
smartingly 1.31.28(.1.4)

smartish 36.2.11
smartly 1.31.22(.8)
smartness 34.18.16(.20.2)
smartweed 23.1.10
smarty 1.10.8
smarty-boots 34.22.14
smarty-pants 34.22.18
smash 36.6
smash-and-grab 21.6
smasher 17.26.6
smashingly 1.31.28(.1.13)
smatter 17.12.6
smatterer 17.32.14(.6)
smattering 29.1.30(.8)
smear 3
smearer 17.32.2
smeariness 34.18.16(.2.9)
smeary 1.29.2
smectic 24.2.10(.13)
Smedley 1.31.23(.4)
smegma 17.17.20
smegmatic 24.2.10(.4.2)
smell 40.5
smellable 40.20.16(.29)
smeller 17.34.5
smelliness 34.18.16(.2.10)
smell-less 34.18.29(.38)
smelly 1.31.5
smelt 22.32.2
smelter 17.12.26(.3)
smeltery 1.29.11(.8.12)
Smersh 36.15
Smetana 17.18.16(.4)
Smethurst 22.29.16
Smethwick 24.2.19
smew 16
smidgen 28.17.28(.2)
Smike 24.13
smilax 34.23.5(.15)
smile 40.13
smileless 34.18.29(.38)
smiler 17.34.13
Smiles 35.30.10
smiley 1.31.14
smilingly 1.31.28(.1.18)
Smily 1.31.14
smirch 38.16
smirk 24.17
smirker 17.14.16
smirkily 1.31.17(.11)
smirkingly 1.31.28(.1.6)
smirky 1.12.14
smit 22.2
smite 22.16
smiter 17.12.13
smith 32.2
smithereens 35.26.1
Smithers 35.18.16
smithery 1.29.11(.16)
Smithfield 23.31.1(.2)

S

Smithson **28.17.23(.26)**
Smithsonian **28.3.8(.11)**
smithy **1.20.2, 1.21**
smitten **28.17.11(.2)**
smock **24.9**
smog **26.7**
smoggy **1.14.6**
smokable **40.20.16(.13)**
smoke **24.18**
smoke-free **2.30.13**
smoke-ho **19.26**
smokehouse **34.8.6(.13)**
smokeless **34.18.29(.24)**
smoker **17.14.17**
smokescreen **28.1.25(.8)**
smokestack **24.6.7**
smokily **1.31.17(.11)**
smokiness **34.18.16(.2.4)**
smoko **19.12.14**
smoky **1.12.15**
smolder **17.13.23(.8)**
smolderingly
    1.31.28(.1.17)
smoleable **40.20.16(.29)**
Smolensk **24.20.13**
Smollett **22.2.25**
smolt **22.32.12**
smooch **38.14**
smoocher **17.28.14**
smoochy **1.25.11**
smoodge **39.13**
smooth **33.8**
smoothable **40.20.16(.20)**
smooth-bore **12.4**
smoothe **33.8**
smoother **17.23.12**
smooth-faced **22.29.4**
smoothie **1.21**
smoothish **36.2.20**
smoothly **1.31.32**
smoothness **34.18.16(.30)**
smooth-talk **24.10.2**
smooth-tongued **23.25**
smorgasbord **23.12.2(.15)**
smorzando **19.11.14**
smote **22.21**
smother **17.23.10**
smothery **1.29.11(.17)**
smoulder **17.13.23(.8)**
smoulderingly
    1.31.28(.1.17)
smriti **1.10.2**
smudge **39.11**
smudgeless **34.18.29(.37)**
smudgepot **22.11.2**
smudgily **1.31.17(.25)**
smudginess **34.18.16(.2.8)**
smudgy **1.26.8**
smug **26.10**
smuggle **40.24.8**

smuggler **17.34.24**
smugly **1.31.25**
smugness **34.18.16(.23)**
smurf **30.15**
smut **22.15**
Smuts **34.22.11**
smuttily **1.31.17(.9.2)**
smuttiness **34.18.16(.2.3)**
smutty **1.10.12**
Smyrna **17.18.17**
Smyth **32.2**
Smythe **33.7**
snack **24.6**
Snaefell **40.5.9**
snaffle **40.27.7**
snafu **16.13**
snag **26.5**
Snagge **26.5**
snaggletooth **32.13**
snaggle-toothed **22.28**
snaggy **1.14.5**
snail **40.4**
Snaith **32.4**
snake **24.3**
snakebite **22.16.8**
snake-charmer **17.17.7**
snakelike **24.13.7(.14)**
snakeroot **22.18.9**
snakeskin **28.2.13(.14)**
snakily **1.31.17(.11)**
snakiness **34.18.16(.2.4)**
snaky **1.12.3**
snap **20.5**
snapdragon **28.17.15(.6)**
Snape **20.3**
snappable **40.20.16(.9)**
snapper **17.10.5**
snappily **1.31.17(.7)**
snappiness **34.18.16(.2.2)**
snappingly **1.31.28(.1.2)**
snappish **36.2.9**
snappishly **1.31.35(.7.1)**
snappishness
    34.18.16(.33.2)
snappy **1.8.5**
snapshot **22.11.12**
snare **6**
snarer **17.32.5**
snark **24.8**
snarl **40.8**
snarler **17.34.8**
snarlingly **1.31.28(.1.18)**
snarl-up **20.9.16**
snarly **1.31.9**
snatch **38.5**
snatcher **17.28.6**
snatchily **1.31.17(.24)**
snatchy **1.25.6**
snavel **40.28.5**
snazzily **1.31.17(.21)**

snazziness **34.18.16(.2.7)**
snazzy **1.23.5**
sneak **24.1**
sneaker **17.14.1**
sneakily **1.31.17(.11)**
sneakiness **34.18.16(.2.4)**
sneakingly **1.31.28(.1.6)**
sneak-thief **30.1.5**
sneak-thieves **35.28.1**
sneaky **1.12.1**
sneck **24.4**
Sneddon **28.17.12(.5)**
Sneek **24.1**
sneer **3**
sneerer **17.32.2**
sneeringly **1.31.28(.1.17)**
sneeze **35.1**
sneezer **17.25.1**
sneezeweed **23.1.10**
sneezewort **22.20.15**
sneezy **1.23.1**
Snelgrove **31.12**
Snell **40.5**
snib **21.2**
snick **24.2**
snicker **17.14.2**
snickeringly
    1.31.28(.1.17)
Snickers® **35.18.10**
snicket **22.2.9(.1)**
snide **23.15**
snidely **1.31.23(.11)**
snideness **34.18.16(.21.1)**
sniff **30.2**
sniffable **40.20.16(.18)**
sniffer **17.20.2**
sniffily **1.31.17(.16.1)**
sniffiness **34.18.16(.2.6)**
sniffingly **1.31.28(.1.8)**
sniffle **40.27.2**
sniffler **17.34.26**
sniffly **1.31.17(.16.1),
    1.31.29**
sniffy **1.18.2**
snifter **17.12.23**
snig **26.2**
snigger **17.16.2**
sniggerer **17.32.14(.9)**
sniggeringly
    1.31.28(.1.17)
sniggle **40.24.2**
snip **20.2**
snipe **20.10**
sniper **17.10.12**
snipper **17.10.2**
snippet **22.2.5**
snippety **1.10.16(.6)**
snippily **1.31.17(.7)**
snippiness **34.18.16(.2.2)**
snipping **29.1.10(.2)**

snippy **1.8.2**
snit **22.2**
snitch **38.2**
snitcher **17.28.2**
snivel **40.28.2**
sniveller **17.34.16(.14)**
snivellingly **1.31.28(.1.18)**
snob **21.8**
snobbery **1.29.11(.7.1)**
snobbish **36.2.10**
snobbishly **1.31.35(.7.1)**
snobbishness
    34.18.16(.33.2)
snobby **1.9.7**
SNOBOL **40.9.6**
Sno-Cat® **22.7.9**
Snodgrass **34.9.6**
snoek **24.15**
snog **26.7**
snood **23.17**
snook **24.15**
snooker **17.14.14**
snoop **20.12**
snooper **17.10.13**
snooperscope **20.15.4(.1)**
snoopy **1.8.10**
snoot **22.18**
snootily **1.31.17(.9.2)**
snootiness **34.18.16(.2.3)**
snooty **1.10.15**
snooze **35.17**
snoozer **17.25.14**
snoozy **1.23.12**
snore **12**
snorer **17.32.10**
snoringly **1.31.28(.1.17)**
snorkel **40.23.8**
snorkeller **17.34.16(.9)**
Snorri **1.29.7**
snort **22.13**
snorter **17.12.10**
snot **22.11**
snottily **1.31.17(.9.2)**
snottiness **34.18.16(.2.3)**
snotty **1.10.9**
snotty-nosed **23.28.4**
snout **22.9**
snoutlike **24.13.7(.12)**
snouty **1.10.7**
snow **19**
snowball **40.10.4**
snowbank **24.19.3(.1)**
snowbelt **22.32.2**
snowberry **1.29.3,
    1.29.11(.7.1)**
snowbird **23.19.1**
snowblind **23.24.13**
snowblower **17.9.13**
snowboard **23.12.2(.6)**
snowboarder **17.13.9**

snowboarding **29.1.13(.8)**
snowboot **22.18.3**
snowbound **23.24.7(.2)**
snow-broth **32.9**
snowcap **20.5.1**
snow-capped **22.22.4**
snowcat **22.7.9**
Snowcem® **27.5.8**
snowclad **23.7.17**
snowcone **28.19.6**
Snowden **28.17.12(.18)**
Snowdon **28.17.12(.18)**
Snowdonia **3.9.11**
snowdrift **22.27.1**
snowdrop **20.7.12**
snowfall **40.10.11**
snowfield **23.31.1(.2)**
snowflake **24.3.14**
snowily **1.31.17(.6)**
snowiness **34.18.16(.2.1)**
snowless **34.18.29(.19)**
snowlike **24.13.7(.9)**
snowline **28.14.19(.12)**
snowmaking **29.1.14(.3)**
snowman **28.7.10(.8)**
snowmen **28.5.7(.12)**
snowmobile **40.1.2**
snowplough **9.17**
snowscape **20.3**
snowshoe **16.17**
snowshoer **17.8**
snowstorm **27.10.2**
snowsuit **22.18.6**
Snow-white **22.16.23**
snowy **1(.7)**
snub **21.11**
snubber **17.11.10**
snubbingly **1.31.28(.1.3)**
snub-nosed **23.28.4**
snuck **24.12**
snuff **30.11**
snuffbox **34.23.8(.2)**
snuffer **17.20.9**
snuffle **40.27.11**
snuffler **17.34.26**
snuffly **1.31.17(.16.1),
1.31.29**
snuffy **1.18.7**
snug **26.10**
snuggery **1.29.11(.11)**
snuggle **40.24.8**
snuggly **1.31.17(.12),
1.31.25**
snugly **1.31.25**
snugness **34.18.16(.23)**
Snyder **17.13.12**
so **19**
soak **24.18**
soakage **39.2.12**
soakaway **4.25.9**

soaker **17.14.17**
soaking **29.1.14(.13)**
Soames **35.25.11**
so-and-so **19.20.16**
Soane **28.19**
soap **20.15**
soapbark **24.8.3**
soapberry **1.29.3**
soapbox **34.23.8(.2)**
soapily **1.31.17(.7)**
soapiness **34.18.16(.2.2)**
soapless **34.18.29(.20)**
soaplike **24.13.7(.10)**
soapstone **28.19.4(.9)**
soapsuds **35.23.9**
soapwort **22.20.15**
soapy **1.8.13**
soar **12**
soarer **17.32.10**
soaringly **1.31.28(.1.17)**
SOAS **34.7.4, 35.7**
Soay **4.6**
SOB **2.10**
sob **21.8**
sobber **17.11.8**
sobbingly **1.31.28(.1.3)**
Sobell **40.5.2**
sober **17.11.15**
soberingly **1.31.28(.1.17)**
soberly **1.31.17(.8)**
Sobers **35.18.7**
Sobranie® **1.16.8**
sobriety **1.10.16(.4)**
sobriquet **4.11**
soca **17.14.17**
socage **39.2.12**
so-called **23.31.6**
soccage **39.2.12**
soccer **17.14.8**
sociability **1.10.16(.22.1)**
sociable **40.20.16(.23)**
sociableness
34.18.16(.37.4)
sociably **1.31.21(.7.3)**
social **40.33.11**
socialism **27.15.21(.2.15)**
socialist **22.29.2(.31.4)**
socialistic **24.2.10(.15.3)**
socialistically
1.31.24(.9.6)
socialite **22.16.25(.9)**
sociality **1.10.16(.32.1)**
socialization
28.17.25(.3.12)
socialize **35.15.21(.4.6)**
socially **1.31.17(.22)**
social science
34.24.10(.5)
social service **34.2.15**
social studies **35.2.4**
societal **40.21.12**

societally **1.31.17(.9.2)**
society **1.10.16(.4)**
Socinian **28.3.8(.2)**
Socinus **34.18.16(.13)**
sociobiological
40.23.12(.17.2)
sociobiologically
1.31.24(.9.11)
sociobiologist
22.29.2(.26.2)
sociobiology
1.26.10(.11.1)
socio-cultural
40.16.13(.12.3)
socioculturally
1.31.17(.27.2)
socio-economic
24.2.14(.6)
socio-economically
1.31.24(.9.8)
sociolinguist **22.29.2(.28)**
sociolinguistic
24.2.10(.15.2)
sociolinguistically
1.31.24(.9.6)
sociological
40.23.12(.17.2)
sociologically
1.31.24(.9.11)
sociologist **22.29.2(.26.2)**
sociology **1.26.10(.11.1)**
sociometric **24.2.26(.14.2)**
sociometrically
1.31.24(.9.12)
sociometrist
22.29.2(.29.5)
sociometry **1.29.15(.8)**
sociopath **32.6.2**
sociopathic **24.2.18(.3)**
sociopathology
1.26.10(.11.5)
socio-political
40.23.12(.7.1)
sock **24.9**
socket **22.2.9(.5)**
sockeye **14.10**
sockless **34.18.29(.24)**
socko **19.12.7**
socle **40.23.7, 40.23.14**
Socotra **17.32.19(.8)**
Socrates **35.1.7(.6)**
Socratic **24.2.10(.4.5)**
Socratically **1.31.24(.9.4)**
sod **23.10**
soda **17.13.17**
sodalite **22.16.25(.9)**
sodality **1.10.16(.32.4)**
sodbuster **17.12.24(.10)**
sodden **28.17.12(.9)**
soddenly **1.31.27(.14)**
soddenness **34.18.16(.25)**
Soddy **1.11.10**

sodic **24.2.11(.13)**
sodium **27.3.4(.8)**
sodium bicarb **21.7**
sodium chloride
23.15.15
sodium hydroxide
23.15.11(.11)
sodium nitrate
22.4.22(.8)
Sodom **27.15.10(.6)**
sodomite **22.16.13**
sodomize **35.15.11**
sodomy **1.15.13(.2)**
Sodor **12.6.7**
soever **17.21.4**
sofa **17.20.14**
sofabed **23.5.2**
Sofar **10.12**
soffit **22.2.13**
Sofia **3.10.4, 17.1.8**
soft **22.27.5**
softa **17.12.23**
softback **24.6.6(.12)**
softball **40.10.4**
softbound **23.24.7(.2)**
softcore **12.7**
softcover **17.21.9**
soft-drink **24.19.1(.7)**
soften **28.17.19**
softener **17.18.16(.10)**
softie **1.10.24**
softish **36.2.11**
softly **1.31.22(.21)**
softly-softly
1.31.22(.21)
softness **34.18.16(.20.4)**
software **6.18.7**
softwood **23.16.6(.9)**
softy **1.10.24**
SOGAT **22.7.10**
soggily **1.31.17(.12)**
sogginess **34.18.16(.2.4)**
soggy **1.14.6**
soh **19**
Soho **19.26**
soi-disant **11.13**
soignée **4.27**
soil **40.11**
soiled **23.31.7**
soil-less **34.18.29(.38)**
soilpipe **20.10.1**
soily **1.31.12**
soirée **4.26.5**
sojourn **28.17.28(.7),
28.18.11**
sojourner **17.18.16(.19)**
soke **24.18**
sol **40.9**
sola **17.34.18**
solace **34.18.29(.10)**
solan **28.17.33(.15)**

S

solanaceous 34.18.22(.3)
solander 17.13.20(.4)
solar 17.34.18
solaria 3.22.4
solarism 27.15.21(.2.14)
solarist 22.29.2(.29.4)
solarium 27.3.17(.3)
solarization
 28.17.25(.3.11)
solarize 35.15.20(.2)
solar plexus 34.18.20
solar system 27.15.9(.15)
SOLAS 34.18.29(.19)
solatia 3.16.3, 17.26.3
solatium 27.3.13, 27.15.22
sold 23.31.13
soldanella 17.34.5(.8)
solder 17.13.23(.5)
solderable 40.20.16(.27.3)
solderer 17.32.14(.7)
soldier 17.29.16(.9)
soldierly 1.31.17(.25)
soldiership 20.2.7(.9)
soldiery 1.29.11(.23)
sole 40.18
solecism 27.15.21(.2.12)
solecist 22.29.2(.22)
solecistic 24.2.10(.15.2)
Soledad 23.7.8
solely 1.31.38
solemn 27.15.28(.7)
solemnity 1.10.16(.13)
solemnization
 28.17.25(.3.11)
solemnize 35.15.12(.8)
solemnly 1.31.26(.11)
solemnness 34.18.16(.24)
solenodon 28.17.12(.16)
solenoid 23.13.12
solenoidal 40.22.9
Solent 22.26.15(.25)
soleplate 22.4.23(.8)
sol-fa 10.12
solfatara 17.32.7
solfeggi 2.27
solfeggio 15.1.11
soli 1.31.19
solicit 22.2.16
solicitation 28.17.25(.3.3)
solicitor 17.12.16(.14)
Solicitor-General
 40.16.13(.12.2)
solicitous 34.18.11(.10)
solicitously 1.31.33(.12.2)
solicitousness
 34.18.16(.31.3)
solicitude 23.17.4(.1)
solid 23.2.23
solidago 19.13.3
solidarity 1.10.16(.21.1)

solidi 2.13, 14.9
solidifiable 40.20.16(.5)
solidification
 28.17.25(.3.5)
solidifier 17.6.9(.4)
solidify 14.14.4(.5)
solidity 1.10.16(.9)
solidly 1.31.23(.14.7)
solidness 34.18.16(.21.1)
solidungulate
 22.19.26(.13)
solidus 34.18.12
solifidian 28.3.4(.2)
solifluction
 28.17.25(.15.5)
Solihull 40.12
soliloquist 22.29.2(.28)
soliloquize 35.15.19
soliloquy 1.28
soliped 23.5.1
solipsism 27.15.21(.2.12)
solipsist 22.29.2(.22)
solipsistic 24.2.10(.15.2)
solipsistically
 1.31.24(.9.6)
solitaire 6.4
solitarily 1.31.17(.27.1)
solitariness 34.18.16(.2.9)
solitary 1.29.11(.8.10)
solitude 23.17.4(.1)
solleret 22.5.19
solmizate 22.4.19
solmization
 28.17.25(.3.11)
solo 19.29.14
soloist 22.29.2(.10)
Solomon 28.17.16(.16)
Solomonic 24.2.15(.6.2)
Solon 28.10.26,
 28.17.33(.15)
solstice 34.18.11(.16)
solstitial 40.33.1
Solti 1.10.28
solubility 1.10.16(.22.1)
solubilization
 28.17.25(.3.12)
solubilize 35.15.21(.4.2)
soluble 40.20.16(.28)
solus 34.18.29(.19)
solution 28.17.25(.11)
Solutrean 28.3.20(.11)
solvability 1.10.16(.22.1)
solvable 40.20.16(.19)
solvate 22.4.16
solvation 28.17.25(.3.9)
Solvay 4.16
solve 31.13
solvency 1.22.23(.10.4)
solvent 22.26.15(.16)
solver 17.21.19
Solway Firth 32.15

Solzhenitsyn 28.2.23(.13)
soma 17.17.16
Somali 1.31.9
Somalia 3.24.6
Somalian 28.3.21(.6)
Somaliland 23.24.6(.13)
somatic 24.2.10(.4.2)
somatically 1.31.24(.9.4)
somatogenic 24.2.15(.4)
somatology 1.26.10(.11.2)
somatotonic 24.2.15(.6.1)
somatotrophin 28.2.19
somatotropin 28.2.9
somatotype 20.10.2
somberly 1.31.17(.8)
sombre 17.11.17(.5)
sombrely 1.31.17(.8)
sombreness
 34.18.16(.15.2)
sombrero 19.27.3
sombrous 34.18.27(.13)
some 27.11
somebody 1.11.10, 1.11.17
someday 4.10.11
somehow 9.14
someone 28.13.8
someplace 34.4.14
Somerfield 23.31.1(.2)
Somers 35.18.12
somersault 22.32.5,
 22.32.6
Somerset 22.5.13(.4)
Somerville 40.2.12
something 29.1.21
sometime 27.12.1
someway 4.25.16
somewhat 22.11.14
somewhen 28.5.17
somewhere 6.18.10
somite 22.16.13
somitic 24.2.10(.2.2)
Somme 27.9
sommelier 3.24.4, 4.2.10,
 4.27
somnambulant
 22.26.15(.25)
somnambulantly
 1.31.22(.20.5)
somnambulism
 27.15.21(.2.15)
somnambulist
 22.29.2(.31.5)
somnambulistic
 24.2.10(.15.3)
somnambulistically
 1.31.24(.9.6)
somniferous
 34.18.27(.20)
somnolence 34.24.10(.24)
somnolency
 1.22.23(.10.4)

somnolent 22.26.15(.25)
somnolently
 1.31.22(.20.5)
Somoza 17.25.15
son 28.13
sonagram 27.6.17(.5)
sonancy 1.22.23(.10.3)
sonant 22.26.15(.14)
sonar 10.11
sonata 17.12.8
sonatina 17.18.1(.3)
sonde 23.24.9
Sondheim 27.12.6
sone 28.19
son et lumière 6.1
song 29.6
songbird 23.19.1
songbook 24.14.3
songfest 22.29.5(.4)
songful 40.27.23
songfully 1.31.17(.16.2)
songless 34.18.29(.28)
songsmith 32.2.3
songster 17.12.24(.24)
songstress 34.18.27(.14)
songthrush 36.12
songwriter 17.12.13(.8)
songwriting 29.1.12(.11)
Sonia 17.33.9
sonic 24.2.15(.6.1)
sonically 1.31.24(.9.8)
sonless 34.18.29(.27)
sonnet 22.19.15(.5)
sonneteer 3.4
Sonning 29.1.17(.7)
sonny 1.16.12
sonobuoy 13.3
son-of-a-bitch 38.2.2
son-of-a-gun 28.13.5
sonogram 27.6.17(.5)
sonograph 30.7.5(.1)
sonometer 17.12.16(.9.2)
Sonora 17.32.10(.7)
sonorant 22.26.15(.23.3)
sonority 1.10.16(.21.2)
sonorous 34.18.27(.19)
sonorously 1.31.33(.12.5)
sonorousness
 34.18.16(.31.5)
sonship 20.2.7(.19)
sonsie 1.22.23(.6)
sons-of-bitches 35.18.20
sons-of-guns 35.26.11
sonsy 1.22.23(.6)
Sontag 26.5.2
sool 40.15
sooler 17.34.15
soon 28.16
soonish 36.2.16(.12)
soot 22.17

S

sooterkin 28.2.13(.6)
sooth 32.13
soothe 33.8
soother 17.23.12
soothingly 1.31.28(.1.10)
soothsaid 23.5.10
soothsay 4.18.13
soothsayer 17.2.7
sootily 1.31.17(.9.2)
sootiness 34.18.16(.2.3)
sooty 1.10.14
sop 20.7
Soper 17.10.16
Sophia 17.1.8, 17.6.9
Sophie 1.18.11
sophism 27.15.21(.2.10)
sophist 22.29.2(.19)
sophister 17.12.24(.14)
sophistic 24.2.10(.15.2)
sophistical 40.23.12(.7.3)
sophistically 1.31.24(.9.6)
sophisticate 22.4.11(.6), 22.19.12(.10)
sophisticatedly 1.31.23(.14.3)
sophistication 28.17.25(.3.5)
sophistry 1.29.15(.17)
Sophoclean 28.17.1(.13)
Sophocles 35.1.23
sophomore 12.9.4
sophomoric 24.2.26(.6)
soporiferous 34.18.27(.20)
soporific 24.2.16(.1)
soporifically 1.31.24(.9.9)
soppily 1.31.17(.7)
soppiness 34.18.16(.2.2)
sopping 29.1.10(.6)
soppy 1.8.7
sopranino 19.15.1
sopranist 22.29.2(.18.1)
soprano 19.15.7
Sopwith 32.2.7
sora 17.32.10, 17.32.16
Soraya 17.6.14
sorb 21.9
sorbefacient 22.26.15(.19)
sorbet 4.8, 22.19.9
Sorbian 28.3.2
sorbic 24.2.9(.3)
sorbitol 40.9.7
sorbo 19.9.6
Sorbonne 28.10.8
sorbose 34.20.3, 35.20.2
sorcerer 17.32.14(.16)
sorceress 34.5.14(.3), 34.18.27(.23)
sorcerous 34.18.27(.23)
sorcery 1.29.11(.18)

sordid 23.2.9
sordidly 1.31.23(.14.4)
sordidness 34.18.16(.21.1)
sordini 2.17.1
sordor 17.13.9
sore 12
sorehead 23.5.13(.4)
sorel 40.16.13(.7)
sorely 1.31.11
soreness 34.18.16(.10)
Sorensen 28.17.23(.24)
sorghum 27.15.12
sori 14.24.4
sorites 35.1.7(.5)
soritical 40.23.12(.7.1)
Soroptimist 22.29.2(.17)
sororicidal 40.22.11
sororicide 23.15.11(.6)
sorority 1.10.16(.21.2)
soroses 35.1.16(.11)
sorosis 34.2.17(.11.2)
sorption 28.17.25(.14)
sorrel 40.16.13(.7)
Sorrell 40.16.13(.7)
Sorrento 19.10.17
sorrily 1.31.17(.27.1)
sorriness 34.18.16(.2.9)
sorrow 19.27.6
sorrower 17.9.11
sorrowful 40.27.14, 40.27.16
sorrowfully 1.31.17(.16.1)
sorrowfulness 34.18.16(.37.2)
sorry 1.29.7
sort 22.13
sorta 17.12.10
sortable 40.20.16(.11.2)
sortal 40.21.8
sorter 17.12.10
sortie 1.10.10
sortilege 39.2.23
sortition 28.17.25(.2.2)
sorus 34.18.27(.8)
SOS 34.5
so-so 19.20, 19.20.12
sostenuto 19.10.11
sot 22.11
soteriological 40.23.12(.17.2)
soteriology 1.26.10(.11.1)
Sotheby 1.9.11
Sothic 24.2.18(.4)
Sotho 16.7.3, 19.10.14
Soto 19.10.14
sottish 36.2.11
sottishly 1.31.35(.7.1)
sottishness 34.18.16(.33.3)
sotto voce 1.25.14

sou 16
soubrette 22.5.19
souchong 29.6.10, 29.6.11
souffle 40.27.13
soufflé 4.28.15
Soufrière 6
sough 9, 30.11
sought 22.13
sought-after 17.12.23
souk 24.15
soukous 34.17.6, 34.18.13(.9)
soul 40.18
Soulbury 1.29.11(.7.2)
soulful 40.27.31
soulfully 1.31.17(.16.2)
soulfulness 34.18.16(.37.2)
soulless 34.18.29(.38)
soullessly 1.31.33(.12.6)
soullessness 34.18.16(.31.6)
soulmate 22.4.13(.15)
soulster 17.12.24(.25)
sound 23.24.7
soundalike 24.13.7(.8)
soundbite 22.16.8
soundboard 23.12.2(.9)
soundbox 34.23.8(.2)
soundcheck 24.4.11
sounder 17.13.20(.5)
soundhole 40.18.13
sounding 29.1.13(.14)
soundless 34.18.29(.23)
soundlessly 1.31.33(.12.6)
soundlessness 34.18.16(.31.6)
soundly 1.31.23(.17)
soundness 34.18.16(.21.1)
soundproof 30.13.4
soundstage 39.4.2
soundtrack 24.6.21
Souness 34.18.16(.14)
soup 20.12
soupçon 11.12, 28.10.18
souped-up 20.9
soupily 1.31.17(.7)
soupiness 34.18.16(.2.2)
soupspoon 28.16.1
soupy 1.8.10
sour 17.3
source 34.12
sourcebook 24.14.3
sourdough 19.11.11
sour grapes 34.21.3
sourish 36.2.25
sourly 1.31.17(.1)
sourness 34.18.16(.15.1)
sourpuss 34.16
soursop 20.7.8

Sousa 17.25.14
sousaphone 28.19.11
sousaphonist 22.29.2(.18.3)
souse 34.8
souslik 24.2.27(.19)
Sousse 34.17
sous vide 23.1
soutache 36.6.3
soutane 28.9.2
souteneur 18.8
souter 17.12.15
souterrain 28.4.18
south 32.7
South African 28.17.13(.13)
Southall 40.10.12, 40.30
Southam 27.15.19
South American 28.17.13(.13)
Southampton 28.17.11(.18)
southbound 23.24.7(.2)
South China Sea 2
Southdown 28.8.2(.9)
southeast 22.29.1
southeaster 17.12.24(.1)
southeasterly 1.31.17(.9.3)
south-easterner 17.18.16(.4)
Southend 23.24.5
souther 17.22.4
southerliness 34.18.16(.2.10)
southerly 1.31.17(.19)
southern 28.17.22
Southerndown 28.8.2(.8)
southerner 17.18.16(.13)
southernmost 22.29.17(.4)
southernwood 23.16.6(.14)
Southey 1.21
southing 29.1.22
southland 23.24.6(.13)
southpaw 12.3
south-southeast 22.29.1
southward 23.18.26(.15)
southwardly 1.31.23(.14.7)
Southwark 24.16.10
Southwell 40.5.17(.14), 40.30
southwest 22.29.5(.11)
southwesterly 1.31.17(.9.3)
southwesterner 17.18.16(.4)
Southwold 23.31.13(.10)
Souttar 17.12.15

Soutter **17.12.15**
souvenir **3.9**
souvlaki **1.12.6**
souvlakia **3.6.6**
sou'wester **17.12.24(.4)**
sovereign **28.17.31(.20)**
sovereignly **1.31.27(.14)**
sovereignty **1.10.23(.12)**
soviet **22.3.7**
Sovietization **28.17.25(.3.11)**
Sovietize **35.15.7(.2)**
sovietologist **22.29.2(.26.3)**
Soviet Union **28.3.8(.9)**
sow **9, 19**
sowback **24.6.6(.5)**
sowbelly **1.31.5**
sowbread **23.5.15**
sower **17.9**
Sowerby **1.9.11**
Sowetan **28.17.11(.4)**
Soweto **19.10.4**
sowing **29.1.9**
sown **28.19**
sowthistle **40.31.2**
sox **34.23.8**
soy **13**
soya **17.5**
soybean **28.1.8**
Soyinka **17.14.21(.1)**
Soyuz **35.16**
sozzled **23.31.24**
spa **10**
space **34.4**
space-age **39.4.7**
spacecraft **22.27.4(.4)**
spaced-out **22.9**
spaceflight **22.16.25(.18)**
spacelab **21.6**
spaceman **28.7.10(.20), 28.17.16(.29)**
spacemen **28.5.7(.24)**
spacer **17.24.4**
spaceship **20.2.7(.22)**
spaceshot **22.11.12**
spacesuit **22.18.6**
spacewalk **24.10.9**
spaceward **23.18.26(.16)**
spacewoman **28.17.16(.14)**
spacewomen **28.2.17(.1)**
spacey **1.22.4**
spacing **29.1.23**
spacious **34.18.22(.3)**
spaciously **1.31.33(.12.4)**
spaciousness **34.18.16(.31.4)**
spade **23.4**
spadeful **40.14.6(.11)**

spadework **24.17.6(.9)**
spadiceous **34.18.22(.2)**
spadicose **34.20.6**
spadille **40.2.6**
spadix **34.23.2(.4)**
spado **19.11.6**
spae **4**
spaewife **30.12**
spaewives **35.28.6**
spaghetti **1.10.4**
spaghettini **1.16.1(.3)**
spahi **2.28**
Spain **28.4**
spake **24.3**
Spalding **29.1.13(.16)**
spall **40.10**
spallation **28.17.25(.3.14)**
spalpeen **28.1.7**
Spam® **27.6**
span **28.7**
spanakopita **17.12.16(.3)**
Spandau **9.4**
spandrel **40.16.13(.17)**
spang **29.4**
spangle **40.24.14(.2)**
Spanglish **36.2.27**
spangly **1.31.17(.12), 1.31.25**
Spaniard **23.18.28**
spaniel **40.16.14**
Spanier **4.27, 17.33.9**
Spanish **36.2.16(.5)**
Spanish-American **28.17.13(.13)**
Spanishness **34.18.16(.33.5)**
spank **24.19.3**
spanker **17.14.21(.3)**
spanking **29.1.14(.14)**
spanner **17.18.6**
Spansule® **40.15.9(.10)**
spar **10**
sparable **40.20.16(.27.1)**
sparaxes **35.1.16(.14)**
sparaxis **34.2.17(.14)**
spare **6**
sparely **1.31.6**
spareness **34.18.16(.6)**
spare part **22.10**
sparer **17.32.5**
sparerib **21.2**
spare-time **27.12.1**
sparge **39.8**
sparger **17.29.7**
sparid **23.2.22**
sparing **29.1.30(.4)**
sparingly **1.31.28(.1.17)**
sparingness **34.18.16(.26)**
spark **24.8**
Sparke **24.8**

sparkish **36.2.13**
sparkle **40.23.6**
sparkler **17.34.23**
sparkless **34.18.29(.24)**
sparklet **22.19.26(.19)**
sparklingly **1.31.28(.1.18)**
sparkly **1.31.24(.6)**
Sparks **34.23.7**
sparky **1.12.6**
sparling **29.1.31(.8)**
sparoid **23.13.19**
sparrow **19.27.4**
sparrowhawk **24.10.8**
sparry **1.29.6**
sparse **34.9**
sparsely **1.31.33(.5)**
sparseness **34.18.16(.31.2)**
sparsity **1.10.16(.16.2)**
Sparta **17.12.8**
Spartacist **22.29.2(.22)**
Spartacus **34.18.13(.10)**
spartan **28.17.11(.8)**
spasm **27.15.21(.3)**
spasmodic **24.2.11(.7)**
spasmodically **1.31.24(.9.7)**
spastic **24.2.10(.15.4)**
spastically **1.31.24(.9.6)**
spasticity **1.10.16(.16.1)**
spat **22.7**
spatchcock **24.9.6**
spate **22.4**
spathaceous **34.18.22(.3)**
spathe **33.3**
spathic **24.2.18(.3)**
spathose **34.20.12**
spatial **40.33.2**
spatiality **1.10.16(.32.1)**
spatialize **35.15.21(.4.6)**
spatially **1.31.17(.22)**
spatio-temporal **40.16.13(.12.1)**
spatio-temporally **1.31.17(.27.1)**
Spätlese **17.25.3**
Spätlesen **28.17.24(.3)**
spatter **17.12.6**
spatterdash **36.6.4**
spatula **17.34.16(.18)**
spatulae **2.32.9(.8)**
spatulate **22.19.26(.13)**
Spätzle **17.34.27, 40.31.16**
spavin **28.2.20, 28.17.20(.5)**
spawn **28.11**
spawner **17.18.10**
spawning **29.1.17(.8)**
spay **4**
Speaight **22.4**
speak **24.1**
speakable **40.20.16(.13)**

speakeasy **1.23.1**
speaker **17.14.1**
speakerphone **28.19.11**
speakership **20.2.7(.9)**
speaking clock **24.9**
spear **3**
spearfish **36.2.18(.2)**
speargun **28.13.5**
spearhead **23.5.13(.2)**
spearman **28.17.16(.3)**
spearmint **22.26.1**
Spears **35.3**
spearwort **22.20.15**
spec **24.4**
special **40.33.3**
specialism **27.15.21(.2.15)**
specialist **22.29.2(.31.4)**
specialistic **24.2.10(.15.3)**
speciality **1.10.16(.32.1)**
specialization **28.17.25(.3.12)**
specialize **35.15.21(.4.6)**
specially **1.31.17(.22), 1.31.35(.2)**
specialness **34.18.16(.37.5)**
specialty **1.10.28**
speciation **28.17.25(.3.1)**
specie **1.24.1, 2.24**
species **35.1.16(.1), 35.1.18, 35.2.11, 35.2.13**
speciesism **27.15.21(.2.12)**
speciesist **22.29.2(.23)**
specifiable **40.20.16(.5)**
specific **24.2.16(.1)**
specifically **1.31.24(.9.9)**
specification **28.17.25(.3.5)**
specificity **1.10.16(.16.1)**
specificness **34.18.16(.22)**
specifier **17.6.9(.4)**
specify **14.14.4(.9)**
specimen **28.17.16(.16)**
speciological **40.23.12(.17.2)**
speciology **1.26.10(.11.1)**
speciosity **1.10.16(.16.2)**
specious **34.18.22(.1)**
speciously **1.31.33(.12.4)**
speciousness **34.18.16(.31.4)**
speck **24.4**
speckle **40.23.4**
speckless **34.18.29(.24)**
specs **34.23.4**
spectacle **40.23.12(.7.3)**
spectacular **17.34.16(.21.2)**
spectacularly **1.31.17(.29)**
spectate **22.4.9**
spectator **17.12.4(.5)**

S

spectatorial 40.3.14(.5)
Spector 17.12.21(.2)
spectra 17.32.19(.9)
spectral 40.16.13(.16)
spectrally 1.31.17(.27.3)
spectre 17.12.21(.2)
spectrochemistry 1.29.15(.17)
spectrogram 27.6.17(.5)
spectrograph 30.7.5(.1)
spectrographic 24.2.16(.3)
spectrographically 1.31.24(.9.9)
spectrography 1.18.9(.3.2)
spectroheliograph 30.7.5(.1)
spectrohelioscope 20.15.4(.1)
spectrometer 17.12.16(.9.2)
spectrometric 24.2.26(.14.2)
spectrometry 1.29.15(.8)
spectrophotometer 17.12.16(.9.2)
spectrophotometric 24.2.26(.14.2)
spectrophotometry 1.29.15(.8)
spectroscope 20.15.4(.1)
spectroscopic 24.2.8(.5)
spectroscopical 40.23.12(.5)
spectroscopist 22.29.2(.11)
spectroscopy 1.8.11(.5)
spectrum 27.15.26(.10)
specula 17.34.16(.21.2)
specular 17.34.16(.21.2)
speculate 22.4.23(.7.3)
speculation 28.17.25(.3.14)
speculative 31.2.1(.9.4)
speculatively 1.31.30(.7.1)
speculativeness 34.18.16(.28.1)
speculator 17.12.4(.16)
speculum 27.15.28(.11)
sped 23.5
speech 38.1
speechful 40.27.29
speechification 28.17.25(.3.5)
speechifier 17.6.9(.1)
speechify 14.14.4(.12)
speechless 34.18.29(.36)
speechlessly 1.31.33(.12.6)

speechlessness 34.18.16(.31.6)
speed 23.1
speedball 40.10.4
speedboat 22.21.2
speeder 17.13.1
speedily 1.31.17(.10)
speediness 34.18.16(.2.3)
speedo 19.11.1
speedometer 17.12.16(.9.2)
speedster 17.12.24(.19)
speedway 4.25.13
speedwell 40.5.17(.8)
speedy 1.11.1
Speight 22.4
Speir 3
speiss 34.15
Speke 24.1
speleological 40.23.12(.17.2)
speleologist 22.29.2(.26.2)
speleology 1.26.10(.11.1)
spell 40.5
spellable 40.20.16(.29)
spellbind 23.24.13
spellbinder 17.13.20(.11)
spellbindingly 1.31.28(.1.5)
spellbound 23.24.7(.2)
speller 17.34.5
spellican 28.17.13(.13)
spelling 29.1.31(.5)
Spellman 28.17.16(.35)
spelt 22.32.2
spelter 17.12.26(.3)
spelunker 17.14.21(.5)
spelunking 29.1.14(.14)
Spen 28.5
Spenborough 17.32.14(.5)
spence 34.24.3
spencer 17.24.22(.2)
spend 23.24.5
spendable 40.20.16(.12)
spender 17.13.20(.3)
spendthrift 22.27.1
Spens 35.26.5
Spenser 17.24.22(.2)
Spenserian 28.3.20(.2)
spent 22.26.4
sperm 27.16
spermaceti 1.10.1, 1.10.4
spermacetic 24.2.10(.1)
spermary 1.29.11(.12)
spermatheca 17.14.1
spermathecae 2.14
spermatic 24.2.10(.4.2)
spermatid 23.2.8
spermatidal 40.22.11

spermatoblast 22.29.6(.12), 22.29.8(.8)
spermatocyte 22.16.19(.9)
spermatogenesis 34.2.17(.10.3)
spermatogenetic 24.2.10(.3.1)
spermatogonia 3.9.11
spermatogonium 27.3.8(.10)
spermatophore 12.11.3, 12.11.4
spermatophoric 24.2.26(.6)
spermatophyte 22.16.16
spermatozoa 17.9.9
spermatozoal 40.16.9
spermatozoan 28.17.8
spermatozoic 24.2.7
spermatozoid 23.2.5
spermatozoon 28.10.6, 28.17.8
spermicidal 40.22.11
spermicide 23.15.11(.6)
spermidine 28.1.10
spermine 28.1.13
spermoblast 22.29.6(.12), 22.29.8(.8)
spermocyte 22.16.19(.9)
spermogenesis 34.2.17(.10.3)
spermogonia 3.9.11
spermogonium 27.3.8(.10)
spermophore 12.11.3
spermophyte 22.16.16
spermozoa 17.9.9
spermozoid 23.13.17
spermozoon 28.10.6, 28.17.8
sperm whale 40.4
spessartine 28.1.9(.3)
spew 16
spewer 17.8
Spey 4
sphagnum 27.15.14(.15)
sphalerite 22.16.24(.9)
sphene 28.1
sphenoid 23.13.12
sphenoidal 40.22.9
spheral 40.16.13(.2)
sphere 3
spheric 24.2.26(.2)
spherical 40.23.12(.18)
spherically 1.31.24(.9.12)
sphericity 1.10.16(.16.1)
spheroid 23.13.19
spheroidal 40.22.9
spheroidicity 1.10.16(.16.1)

spherometer 17.12.16(.9.2)
spherular 17.34.16(.21.4)
spherule 40.15.8
spherulite 22.16.25(.9)
spherulitic 24.2.10(.2.5)
sphincter 17.12.21(.8)
sphincteral 40.16.13(.12.1)
sphincterial 40.3.14(.2)
sphincteric 24.2.26(.4)
sphingid 23.2.11, 23.2.19, 23.2.20
sphingomyelin 28.2.31(.10)
sphingosine 28.14.13
sphinx 34.23.18
sphragistics 34.23.2(.3)
sphygmogram 27.6.17(.5)
sphygmograph 30.7.5(.1)
sphygmographic 24.2.16(.3)
sphygmographically 1.31.24(.9.9)
sphygmography 1.18.9(.3.2)
sphygmological 40.23.12(.17.2)
sphygmology 1.26.10(.11.4)
sphygmomanometer 17.12.16(.9.2)
sphygmomanometric 24.2.26(.14.2)
spic 24.2
spica 17.14.12
spicate 22.4.11(.5), 22.19.12(.9)
spicated 23.18.9(.3)
spiccato 19.10.7
spice 34.15
spiceberry 1.29.3
spicebush 36.13
spicery 1.29.11(.18)
spicey 1.22.13
spicily 1.31.17(.20)
spiciness 34.18.16(.2.7)
spick 24.2
spick-and-span 28.7.4
spicknel 40.26.18
spicular 17.34.16(.21.2)
spiculate 22.19.26(.13)
spicule 40.15.9(.5)
spicy 1.22.13
spider 17.13.12
spiderish 36.2.25
spiderman 28.7.10(.6)
spidermen 28.5.7(.10)
spiderwort 22.20.15
spidery 1.29.11(.9)

S

spiegeleisen 28.17.24(.10)
Spiegl 40.24.1
spiel 40.1
Spielberg 26.14.1(.12)
spieler 17.34.1
spiffily 1.31.17(.16.1)
spiffiness 34.18.16(.2.6)
spiffing 29.1.19
spifflicate 22.4.11(.6)
spifflication 28.17.25(.3.5)
spiffy 1.18.2
spignel 40.26.19
spigot 22.19.13
spik 24.2
spike 24.13
spikelet 22.19.26(.19)
spikenard 23.9.12
spikily 1.31.17(.11)
spikiness 34.18.16(.2.4)
spiky 1.12.10
spile 40.13
spill 40.2
spillage 39.2.23
Spillane 28.4.19
spiller 17.34.2
spillikin 28.2.13(.6)
spillover 17.21.14(.15)
spillway 4.25.26
Spilsbury 1.29.11(.7.2)
spilt 22.32.1
spilth 32.24
spin 28.2
spina bifida 17.13.15
spinaceous 34.18.22(.3)
spinach 38.2.6, 39.2.15
spinachy 1.25.12, 1.26.10(.5)
spinal 40.26.11
spinally 1.31.17(.14.1)
spindle 40.22.16
spindleshanks 34.23.18
spindly 1.31.23(.17)
spindrift 22.27.1
spin-dry 14.24.8
spin-dryer 17.6.14
spine 28.14
spinel 40.5.8
spineless 34.18.29(.27)
spinelessly 1.31.33(.12.6)
spinelessness 34.18.16(.31.6)
spinet 22.2.12, 22.5.9
spinifex 34.23.4(.7)
spininess 34.18.16(.2.5)
Spink 24.19.1
Spinks 34.23.18
spinnaker 17.14.15(.9)
spinner 17.18.2
spinneret 22.5.19

spinney 1.16.2
spin-off 30.8.7
spinose 34.20.9
spinous 34.18.16(.13)
spin-out 22.9.11
Spinoza 17.25.15
Spinozism 27.15.21(.2.12)
Spinozist 22.29.2(.23)
Spinozistic 24.2.10(.15.2)
spinster 17.12.24(.23)
spinsterhood 23.16.5(.3)
spinsterish 36.2.25
spinsterishness 34.18.16(.33.6)
spinthariscope 20.15.4(.1)
spinule 40.15.9(.8)
spinulose 34.20.17
spinulous 34.18.29(.17.6)
spiny 1.16.13
Spion Kop 20.7
spiracle 40.23.12(.18)
spiracula 17.34.16(.21.2)
spiracular 17.34.16(.21.2)
spiraculum 27.15.28(.11)
spiraea 17.1.16
spiral 40.16.13(.10)
spirality 1.10.16(.32.13)
spirally 1.31.17(.27.1)
spirant 22.26.15(.23.2)
spire 17.6
spirilla 17.34.2(.15)
spirillum 27.15.28(.2)
spirit 22.2.24
spiritedly 1.31.23(.14.3)
spiritedness 34.18.16(.21.1)
spiritism 27.15.21(.2.4)
spiritist 22.29.2(.13)
spiritless 34.18.29(.22)
spiritlessly 1.31.33(.12.6)
spiritlessness 34.18.16(.31.6)
spiritous 34.18.11(.10)
spiritual 40.16.12
spiritualism 27.15.21(.2.15)
spiritualist 22.29.2(.31.5)
spiritualistic 24.2.10(.15.3)
spirituality 1.10.16(.32.1)
spiritualization 28.17.25(.3.12)
spiritualize 35.15.21(.4.8)
spiritually 1.31.17(.24)
spiritualness 34.18.16(.37.1)
spirituel 40.5
spirituelle 40.5
spirituous 34.18.6

spirituousness 34.18.16(.31.2)
spirketing 29.1.12(.14)
spirochaete 22.1.4
spirograph 30.7.5(.1)
spirographic 24.2.16(.3)
spirographically 1.31.24(.9.9)
spirogyra 17.32.13
spirometer 17.12.16(.9.2)
spirt 22.20
spiry 1.29.11(.2)
spit 22.2
Spitalfields 35.23.15
spit-and-polish 36.2.27
spitball 40.10.4
spitballer 17.34.10
spitchcock 24.9.6
spite 22.16
spiteful 40.27.18
spitefully 1.31.17(.16.2)
spitefulness 34.18.16(.37.2)
spitfire 17.6.9(.6)
Spithead 23.5.13
spitter 17.12.2
spittle 40.21.2
spittly 1.31.17(.9.1)
spittoon 28.16.3
spitty 1.10.2
spitz 34.22.2
spiv 31.2
spivish 36.2.19
spivvery 1.29.11(.15)
spivvish 36.2.19
spivvy 1.19.2
splake 24.3
splanchnic 24.2.15(.12)
splanchnology 1.26.10(.11.4)
splanchnotomy 1.15.13(.1)
splash 36.6
splashback 24.6.6(.21)
splashboard 23.12.2(.17)
splashdown 28.8.2(.11)
splashily 1.31.17(.22)
splashiness 34.18.16(.2.8)
splashy 1.24.5
splat 22.7
splatter 17.12.6
splay 4
splay-feet 22.1.6
splay-foot 22.17
splay-footed 23.18.9(.11)
spleen 28.1
spleenful 40.27.22
spleenwort 22.20.15
spleeny 1.16.1
splendent 22.26.15(.10)

splendid 23.2.9
splendidly 1.31.23(.14.4)
splendidness 34.18.16(.21.1)
splendiferous 34.18.27(.20)
splendiferously 1.31.33(.12.5)
splendiferousness 34.18.16(.31.5)
splendor 17.13.20(.3)
splendour 17.13.20(.3)
splenectomy 1.15.13(.1)
splenetic 24.2.10(.3.1)
splenetically 1.31.24(.9.3)
splenial 40.3.7(.1)
splenic 24.2.15(.1)
splenii 14.2
splenitis 34.18.11(.8)
splenius 34.3.6(.1)
splenoid 23.13.12
splenology 1.26.10(.11.4)
splenomegaly 1.31.17(.12)
splenotomy 1.15.13(.1)
splice 34.15
splicer 17.24.13
spliff 30.2
spline 28.14
splint 22.26.1
splint-bone 28.19.3
splint-coal 40.18.7
splinter 17.12.22(.1)
splintery 1.29.11(.8.12)
split 22.2
split-level 40.28.4
split-second 23.24.16(.5)
splitter 17.12.2
split-up 20.9.5
splodge 39.9
splodginess 34.18.16(.2.8)
splodgy 1.26.6
sploosh 36.14
splosh 36.9
splotch 38.8
splotchiness 34.18.16(.2.8)
splotchy 1.25.9
Splott 22.11
splurge 39.15
splutter 17.12.12
splutterer 17.32.14(.6)
splutteringly 1.31.28(.1.17)
spluttery 1.29.11(.8.4)
Spock 24.9
Spode® 23.20
spodosol 40.9.14
spodumene 28.1.13
Spofforth 32.14.13
spoil 40.11

spoilage 39.2.23
spoiled 23.31.7
spoiler 17.34.11
spoilsman 28.17.16(.30)
spoilsport 22.13.1
spoilt 22.32.7
Spokane 28.7.8
spoke 24.18
spoke-bone 28.19.3
spoken 28.17.13(.15)
spokeshave 31.3.4
spokesman 28.17.16(.29)
spokesperson
  28.17.23(.15)
spokeswoman
  28.17.16(.14)
spokeswomen
  28.2.17(.1)
spokewise 35.15.19
spoliation 28.17.25(.3.1)
spoliator 17.12.4(.1)
spoliatory 1.29.11(.8.1)
spondaic 24.2.3
spondee 2.13
Spondon 28.17.12(.23)
spondulicks 34.23.2(.13)
spondylitis 34.18.11(.8)
Spong 29.6
sponge 39.17.8
spongeable 40.20.16(.25)
spongelike 24.13.7(.26)
sponger 17.29.16(.7)
spongiform 27.10.5(.2)
spongily 1.31.17(.25)
sponginess 34.18.16(.2.8)
spongy 1.26.13
sponsion 28.17.25(.16)
sponson 28.17.23(.24)
sponsor 17.24.22(.5)
sponsorial 40.3.14(.5)
sponsorship 20.2.7(.9)
spontaneity 1.10.16(.1)
spontaneous 34.3.6(.3)
spontaneously
  1.31.33(.1.2)
spontaneousness
  34.18.16(.31.1)
spontoon 28.16.3
spoof 30.13
spoofer 17.20.11
spoofery 1.29.11(.14)
spook 24.15
spookily 1.31.17(.11)
spookiness
  34.18.16(.2.4)
spooky 1.12.12
spool 40.15
spoon 28.16
spoonbeak 24.1.2
spoonbill 40.2.4
spoon-bread 23.5.15

spooner 17.18.15
spoonerism
  27.15.21(.2.14)
spoonfed 23.5.8
spoonfeed 23.1.6
spoonful 40.14.6(.15)
spoonily 1.31.17(.14.1)
spooniness 34.18.16(.2.5)
spoonsful 40.14.6(.20)
spoony 1.16.14
spoor 12, 17.7
spoorer 17.32.10,
  17.32.14(.3)
Sporades 35.1.8
sporadic 24.2.11(.5)
sporadically 1.31.24(.9.7)
sporangia 3.19.9
sporangial 40.3.12
sporangium 27.3.14,
  27.3.15
spore 12
sporogenesis
  34.2.17(.10.3)
sporogenous
  34.18.16(.15.3)
sporophore 12.11.3
sporophyte 22.16.16
sporophytic 24.2.10(.2.3)
sporophytically
  1.31.24(.9.3)
sporozoite 22.16.6
sporran 28.17.31(.7)
sport 22.13
sporter 17.12.10
sportif 30.1.1
sportily 1.31.17(.9.2)
sportiness 34.18.16(.2.3)
sportingly 1.31.28(.1.4)
sportive 31.2.1(.5)
sportively 1.31.30(.7.1)
sportiveness
  34.18.16(.28.1)
sportscast 22.29.6(.5),
  22.29.8(.3)
sportscaster 17.12.24(.5)
sportshirt 22.20.13
sportsman 28.17.16(.29)
sportsmanlike
  24.13.7(.17)
sportsmanly 1.31.27(.14)
sportsmanship
  20.2.7(.19)
sportspeople 40.19.1
sportsperson
  28.17.23(.15)
sportswear 6.18.12
sportswoman
  28.17.16(.14)
sportswomen 28.2.17(.1)
sportswriter 17.12.13(.8)
sporty 1.10.10

sporular 17.34.16(.21.4)
sporule 40.15.8
spot 22.11
spot-check 24.4.11
spotlamp 20.16.3
spotless 34.18.29(.22)
spotlessly 1.31.33(.12.6)
spotlessness
  34.18.16(.31.6)
spotlight 22.16.25(.13)
spot-on 28.10
spottedness
  34.18.16(.21.1)
spotter 17.12.9
spottily 1.31.17(.9.2)
spottiness 34.18.16(.2.3)
Spottiswoode
  23.16.6(.17)
spotty 1.10.9
spotweld 23.31.4
spotwelder 17.13.23(.3)
spousal 40.32.6
spouse 34.8, 35.8
spout 22.9
spouter 17.12.7
spoutless 34.18.29(.22)
Sprachgefühl 40.15.6
sprag 26.5
Spragge 26.5
Sprague 26.3
sprain 28.4
spraing 29.2
spraint 22.26.3
sprang 29.4
sprat 22.7
Spratt 22.7
spratter 17.12.6
sprauncy 1.22.23(.7)
sprawl 40.10
sprawler 17.34.10
sprawlingly 1.31.28(.1.18)
spray 4
sprayable 40.20.16(.2)
spray-dry 14.24.8
sprayer 17.2
sprayey 1(.2)
spray-paint 22.26.3
spread 23.5
spreadable 40.20.16(.12)
spread-eagle 40.24.1
spreader 17.13.4
spreadsheet 22.1.11
spree 2
sprig 26.2
spriggy 1.14.2
sprightliness
  34.18.16(.2.10)
sprightly 1.31.22(.13)
sprigtail 40.4.2
spring 29.1

springboard 23.12.2(.13)
springbok 24.9.3
spring-clean 28.1.27(.10)
spring-cleaning
  29.1.17(.1)
springe 39.17.1
springer 17.19.1
Springfield 23.31.1(.2)
springform 27.10.5(.6)
springhouse 34.8.6(.17)
springily 1.31.17(.15)
springiness 34.18.16(.2.5)
springless 34.18.29(.28)
springlet 22.19.26(.23)
springlike 24.13.7(.18)
spring-loaded
  23.18.10(.13)
Springs 35.27
Springsteen 28.1.9(.7)
springtail 40.4.2
springtide 23.15.4
springtime 27.12.1
springwater 17.12.10(.7)
springy 1.17
sprinkle 40.23.15
sprinkler 17.34.23
sprinkling 29.1.31(.19)
sprint 22.26.1
sprinter 17.12.22(.1)
sprit 22.2
sprite 22.16
spritely 1.31.22(.13)
spritsail 40.4.10, 40.31.16
spritz 34.22.2
spritzer 17.24.19
sprocket 22.2.9(.5)
sprog 26.7
Sproughton 28.17.11(.10)
Sproule 40.15, 40.18
sprout 22.9
spruce 34.17
sprucely 1.31.33(.11)
spruceness
  34.18.16(.31.2)
sprucer 17.24.14
sprue 16
spruik 24.15
spruiker 17.14.14
spruit 22.4
sprung 29.8
spry 14
spryly 1.31.14
spryness 34.18.16(.13)
spud 23.14
spue 16
spumante 1.10.23(.4)
spume 27.14
spumoni 1.16.17(.7)
spumous 34.18.15(.9)
spumy 1.15.12

spun 28.13
spunk 24.19.7
spunkily 1.31.17(.11)
spunkiness 34.18.16(.2.4)
spunky 1.12.16
spur 18
spurge 39.15
Spurgeon 28.17.28(.10)
spurious 34.3.15(.5)
spuriously 1.31.33(.1.4)
spuriousness
    34.18.16(.31.1)
spurless 34.18.29(.18)
Spurling 29.1.31(.13)
spurn 28.18
spurner 17.18.17
spur-of-the-moment
    22.26.15(.13.2)
Spurrell 40.16.13(.9)
spurrey 1.29.9
spurrier 3.22.10, 3.22.13
spurry 1.29.12
spurt 22.20
spurwort 22.20.15
sputa 17.12.15
sputnik 24.2.15(.10)
sputter 17.12.12
sputterer 17.32.14(.6)
sputum 27.15.9(.9)
spy 14
spycatcher 17.28.6
spyglass 34.9.7
spyhole 40.18.13
spymaster 17.12.24(.5)
Sqezy 1.23.1
squab 21.8
squabble 40.20.9
squabbler 17.34.20
squabby 1.9.7
squab-chick 24.2.23
squacco 19.12.5
squad 23.10
squaddie 1.11.10
squadron 28.17.31(.15)
squail 40.4
squalid 23.2.23
squalidity 1.10.16(.9)
squalidly 1.31.23(.14.7)
squalidness
    34.18.16(.21.1)
squall 40.10
squally 1.31.11
squaloid 23.13.20
squalor 17.34.9
squama 17.17.4
squamae 2.16
squamate 22.19.14
Squamish 36.2.15
squamose 34.20.8
squamous 34.18.15(.3)

squamously
    1.31.33(.12.3)
squamousness
    34.18.16(.31.3)
squamule 40.15.9(.7)
squander 17.13.20(.7)
squanderer 17.32.14(.7)
square 6
square-bashing 29.1.25
square-built 22.32.1
square deal 40.1
square-eyed 23.15
squarely 1.31.6
squareness 34.18.16(.6)
squarer 17.32.5
square-rigged 23.22
square-rigger 17.16.2
square root 22.18
Squarial 40.3.14(.4)
squarish 36.2.25
squarrose 34.20.16
squash 36.9
squashily 1.31.17(.22)
squashiness 34.18.16(.2.8)
squashy 1.24.7
squat 22.11
squatly 1.31.22(.9)
squatness 34.18.16(.20.2)
squatter 17.12.9
squaw 12
squawk 24.10
squawker 17.14.9
squeak 24.1
squeaker 17.14.1
squeakily 1.31.17(.11)
squeakiness
    34.18.16(.2.4)
squeaky 1.12.1
squeal 40.1
squealer 17.34.1
squeamish 36.2.15
squeamishly 1.31.35(.7.2)
squeamishness
    34.18.16(.33.5)
squeegee 2.27
Squeers 35.3
squeezable 40.20.16(.22)
squeeze 35.1
squeezebox 34.23.8(.2)
squeezer 17.25.1
squelch 38.19
squelcher 17.28.26
squelchiness
    34.18.16(.2.8)
squelchy 1.25.16
squib 21.2
squid 23.2
squidginess 34.18.16(.2.8)
squidgy 1.26.1
squiffed 22.27.1

squiffy 1.18.2
squiggle 40.24.2
squiggly 1.31.17(.12),
    1.31.25
squill 40.2
squillion 28.3.21(.2)
squinancywort 22.20.15
squinch 38.18.1
squint 22.26.1
squinter 17.12.22(.1)
squinty 1.10.23(.1)
squirarchy 1.12.6
squire 17.6
squirearch 24.8.15
squirearchical
    40.23.12(.9)
squirearchy 1.12.6
squiredom 27.15.10(.8)
squireen 28.1.25
squirehood 23.16.5(.3)
squirelet 22.19.26(.13)
squireling 29.1.31(.10)
squirely 1.31.17(.3)
squireship 20.2.7(.9)
squirl 40.17
squirm 27.16
squirmer 17.17.15
squirmy 1.15.14
squirrel 40.16.13(.1)
squirrelly 1.31.17(.27.1)
squirt 22.20
squirter 17.12.17
squish 36.2
squishiness 34.18.16(.2.8)
squishy 1.24.2
squit 22.2
squitch 38.2
squitters 35.18.8
squiz 35.2
squoze 35.20
Sri Lanka 17.14.21(.3)
Sri Lankan 28.17.13(.17)
Srinagar 17.16.9
srubbiness 34.18.16(.2.2)
St. 22.1
stab 21.6
stabber 17.11.5
stabbing 29.1.11
stabile 40.13.2
stability 1.10.16(.22.1)
stabilization
    28.17.25(.3.12)
stabilize 35.15.21(.4.2)
stabilizer 17.25.12(.15)
stable 40.20.4
Stableford 23.18.16(.22)
stableful 40.14.6(.22)
stableman 28.7.10(.24)
stablemate 22.4.13(.15)
stablemen 28.5.7(.28)

stableness 34.18.16(.37.4)
stablish 36.2.27
stably 1.31.17(.8),
    1.31.21(.1)
staccato 19.10.7
stack 24.6
stackable 40.20.16(.13)
stacker 17.14.5
Stackhouse 34.8.6(.13)
stacte 2.12.13
Stacy 1.22.4
staddle 40.22.5
stadia 3.5.3
stadium 27.3.4(.3)
stadtholder 17.13.23(.8)
stadtholdership
    20.2.7(.9)
staff 30.7
Staffa 17.20.5
staffage 39.2.16
staffer 17.20.5, 17.20.6
Stafford 23.18.16(.5)
Staffordshire 17.26.18
staffroom 27.14.6(.15)
Staffs 34.25
stag 26.5
stage 39.4
stageability 1.10.16(.22.1)
stageable 40.20.16(.25)
stagecoach 38.17
stagecraft 22.27.4(.4)
stagehand 23.24.6(.11)
stage-manage 39.2.15
stager 17.29.3
stagestruck 24.12.8
stagey 1.26.2
stagflation 28.17.25(.3.14)
Stagg 26.5
stagger 17.16.5
staggerer 17.32.14(.9)
staggeringly 1.31.28(.1.17)
staghound 23.24.7(.8)
stagily 1.31.17(.25)
staginess 34.18.16(.2.8)
staging 29.1.28
stagnancy 1.22.23(.10.3)
stagnant 22.26.15(.14)
stagnantly 1.31.22(.20.3)
stagnate 22.4.14
stagnation 28.17.25(.3.8)
stagnicolous
    34.18.29(.17.2)
stagy 1.26.2
staid 23.4
staidly 1.31.23(.3)
staidness 34.18.16(.21.1)
stain 28.4
stainable 40.20.16(.16.1)
stained-glass 34.9.7
stainer 17.18.3

S

Staines 35.26.4
Stainforth 32.10, 32.14.13
stainless 34.18.29(.27)
stainlessly 1.31.33(.12.6)
stainlessness
  34.18.16(.31.6)
Stainton 28.17.11(.22)
stair 6
staircase 34.4.6
stairhead 23.5.13(.3)
stairlift 22.27.1
stairway 4.25.4
stairwell 40.5.17(.2)
staithe 33.3
stake 24.3
stakeboat 22.21.2
stakebuilding
  29.1.13(.16)
stakeholder 17.13.23(.8)
stakeout 22.9.9
staker 17.14.3
Stakhanovism
  27.15.21(.2.11)
Stakhanovist 22.29.2(.20)
Stakhanovite 22.16.17
stalactic 24.2.10(.13)
stalactiform 27.10.5(.2)
stalactite 22.16.9
stalactitic 24.2.10(.2.1)
Stalag 26.5.9
stalagmite 22.16.13
stalagmitic 24.2.10(.2.2)
St Albans 35.26.13(.6)
stale 40.4
stalely 1.31.38
stalemate 22.4.13(.15)
staleness 34.18.16(.37.1)
Stalin 28.2.31(.6)
Stalingrad 23.7.16
Stalinism 27.15.21(.2.9)
Stalinist 22.29.2(.18.3)
stalk 24.10
stalker 17.14.9
stalk-eyed 23.15
stalkless 34.18.29(.24)
stalklet 22.19.26(.19)
stalklike 24.13.7(.14)
stalky 1.12.8
stall 40.10
stallage 39.2.23
stallholder 17.13.23(.8)
stallion 28.3.21(.2)
Stallybrass 34.7.18,
  34.9.6
stalwart 22.19.23
stalwartly 1.31.22(.15)
stalwartness
  34.18.16(.20.3)
Stalybridge 39.2.22(.10)
Stamboul 40.15.2
stamen 28.5.7(.4)

stamina 17.18.16(.8)
staminal 40.26.13(.8)
staminate 22.19.15(.9)
staminiferous
  34.18.27(.20)
stammer 17.17.6
stammerer 17.32.14(.10)
stammeringly
  1.31.28(.1.17)
stamp 20.16.3
stampede 23.1.1
stampeder 17.13.1
stamper 17.10.17
Stanbury 1.29.11(.7.2)
stance 34.24.6
stanch 38.18.4
stanchion 28.17.25(.16)
stand 23.24.6
stand-alone 28.19.19
standard 23.18.10(.14)
Standardbred 23.5.15
standardizable
  40.20.16(.22)
standardization
  28.17.25(.3.11)
standardize 35.15.8
standardizer 17.25.12(.3)
standby 14.7
standee 2.13
stander 17.13.20(.4)
stand-in 28.2.12
standing 29.1.13(.14)
Standish 36.2.12
stand-off 30.8.5
standoffish 36.2.18(.6)
standoffishly
  1.31.35(.7.3)
standoffishness
  34.18.16(.33.6)
standout 22.9.8
standpipe 20.10.1
standpoint 22.26.11
St Andrews 35.17.6
standstill 40.2.5
stand-to 16.7
Stanford 23.18.16(.16)
Stanhope 20.13.3, 20.15.7
Stanislas 34.7.19, 34.9.7,
  34.18.29(.33)
Stanislaus 34.8.8, 34.12.9
Stanislavsky 1.12.17(.14)
stank 24.19.3
Stanley 1.31.27(.6)
Stanleyville 40.2.12
Stanmore 12.9.11
Stannard 23.18.14
stannary 1.29.11(.13.1)
stannate 22.4.14(.4)
stannic 24.2.15(.5)
stannite 22.16.14(.3)
stannous 34.18.16(.7)

Stansfield 23.31.1(.2)
Stansgate 22.4.12(.11)
Stansted 23.5.3,
  23.18.9(.20)
Stanton 28.17.11(.22)
Stanway 4.25.17
Stanwell 40.5.17(.12),
  40.35.5
Stanwick 24.2.15(.5),
  24.2.25
stanza 17.25.18
stanzaic 24.2.3
stapedes 35.1.8
stapelia 3.24.1
stapes 35.1.5
staphylococcal 40.23.7
staphylococcus
  34.18.13(.5)
staple 40.19.3
Stapleford 23.18.16(.22)
Staplehurst 22.29.16
stapler 17.34.19
Stapleton 28.17.11(.27)
star 10
Stara Zagora 17.32.10(.5)
starboard 23.12.2(.3),
  23.18.8
starburst 22.29.16
starch 38.7
starcher 17.28.8
starchily 1.31.17(.24)
starchiness
  34.18.16(.2.8)
starch-reduced 22.29.14
starchy 1.25.8
star-crossed 22.29.9
stardom 27.15.10(.5)
stardust 22.29.12
stare 6
starer 17.32.5
starfish 36.2.18(.5)
stargaze 35.4.6
stargazer 17.25.3
stargazing 29.1.24
stark 24.8
starkers 35.18.10
Starkey 1.12.6
Starkie 1.12.6
starkly 1.31.24(.6)
starkness 34.18.16(.22)
starless 34.18.29(.9)
starlet 22.19.26(.7)
starlight 22.16.25(.7)
starlike 24.13.7(.5)
starling 29.1.31(.8)
starlit 22.2.25
Starr 10
starrily 1.31.17(.27.1)
starriness 34.18.16(.2.9)
starry 1.29.6
starry-eyed 23.15

Stars and Bars 35.9
Stars and Stripes 34.21.8
starship 20.2.7(.5)
START 22.10
start 22.10
starter 17.12.8
startle 40.21.6
startler 17.34.21
startlingly 1.31.28(.1.18)
start-up 20.9.5
star turn 28.18
starvation 28.17.25(.3.9)
starve 31.6
starveling 29.1.31(.24)
starwort 22.20.15
stases 35.1.16(.2)
stash 36.6
Stasi 1.23.7
stasis 34.2.17(.2)
stat 22.7
statable 40.20.16(.11.1)
statal 40.21.3
state 22.4
statecraft 22.27.4(.4)
statedly 1.31.23(.14.3)
statehood 23.16.5(.6)
statehouse 34.8.6(.11)
stateless 34.18.29(.22)
statelessness
  34.18.16(.31.6)
statelet 22.19.26(.17)
stateliness 34.18.16(.2.10)
stately 1.31.22(.4)
statement 22.26.15(.13.3)
Staten Island
  23.24.16(.16.2)
state-of-the-art 22.10
stater 17.12.4
stateroom 27.14.6(.8)
stateside 23.15.11(.9)
statesman 28.17.16(.29)
statesmanlike
  24.13.7(.17)
statesmanly 1.31.27(.14)
statesmanship
  20.2.7(.19)
statesperson
  28.17.23(.15)
stateswoman
  28.17.16(.14)
stateswomen 28.2.17(.1)
statewide 23.15.14
Statham 27.15.18,
  27.15.19
static 24.2.10(.4.1)
statical 40.23.12(.7.1)
statically 1.31.24(.9.4)
statice 1.22.16(.4)
station 28.17.25(.3.1)
stationariness
  34.18.16(.2.9)

stationary **1.29.11(.13.2)**
stationer **17.18.16(.16)**
stationery **1.29.11(.13.2)**
station-keeping **29.1.10(.1)**
statism **27.15.21(.2.4)**
statist **22.29.2(.13)**
statistic **24.2.10(.15.2)**
statistical **40.23.12(.7.3)**
statistically **1.31.24(.9.6)**
statistician **28.17.25(.2.2)**
Statius **34.3.3, 34.3.12, 34.18.22(.3)**
stative **31.2.1(.3)**
stator **17.12.4**
statoscope **20.15.4(.1)**
stats **34.22.5**
statuary **1.29.11(.3)**
statue **16.24.5**
statuesque **24.20.3**
statuesquely **1.31.24(.13)**
statuesqueness **34.18.16(.22)**
statuette **22.5**
stature **17.28.6, 17.33.6**
status **34.18.11(.3)**
status quo **19**
statutable **40.20.16(.11.2)**
statutably **1.31.21(.4.1)**
statute **22.18.10**
statute-barred **23.9.6**
statutorily **1.31.17(.27.1)**
statutory **1.29.11(.8.10)**
staunch **38.18.6**
staunchly **1.31.36**
staunchness **34.18.16(.35)**
Staunton **28.17.11(.22)**
staurolite **22.16.25(.9)**
stauroscope **20.15.4(.1)**
stauroscopic **24.2.8(.5)**
stauroscopically **1.31.24(.9.2)**
Stavanger **17.19.2**
stave **31.3**
stavesacre **17.14.3(.6)**
stay **4**
stay-at-home **27.17.12**
stayer **17.2**
staysail **40.4.10, 40.31.4**
stead **23.5**
steadfast **22.29.6(.9), 22.29.15(.14)**
steadfastly **1.31.22(.22)**
steadfastness **34.18.16(.20.4)**
steadier **3.5.4**
steadily **1.31.17(.10)**
steadiness **34.18.16(.2.3)**
steading **29.1.13(.4)**
Steadman **28.17.16(.22)**
steady **1.11.5**

steak **24.3**
steakhouse **34.8.6(.13)**
steal **40.1**
stealer **17.34.1**
stealth **32.24**
stealthily **1.31.17(.18)**
stealthiness **34.18.16(.2.6)**
stealthy **1.20.12**
steam **27.1**
steamboat **22.21.2**
steamer **17.17.1**
steamfitter **17.12.2**
steamily **1.31.17(.13)**
steaminess **34.18.16(.2.5)**
steaming **29.1.16**
steamroller **17.34.18(.14)**
steamship **20.2.7(.18)**
steamshovel **40.28.8**
steamy **1.15.1**
stearate **22.4.22(.1)**
stearic **24.2.26(.5)**
stearin **28.2.29(.1)**
Stearn **28.18**
Stearne **28.18**
steatite **22.16.9**
steatitic **24.2.10(.2.1)**
steatopygia **3.19.2, 3.19.6**
steatopygous **34.18.14(.4)**
steatorrhoea **17.1.16**
steatosis **34.2.17(.11.1)**
Stechford **23.18.16(.21)**
stedfastly **1.31.22(.22)**
steed **23.1**
steel **40.1**
Steele **40.1**
steelhead **23.5.13(.19)**
steeliness **34.18.16(.2.10)**
steelwork **24.17.6(.19)**
steelworker **17.14.16**
steelworks **34.23.16**
steely **1.31.1**
steelyard **23.9.21, 23.18.28**
Steen **28.1**
steenbok **24.9.3**
steenkirk **24.17.3**
steep **20.1**
steepen **28.17.9**
steepish **36.2.9**
steeple **40.19.1**
steeplechase **34.4.12**
steeplechaser **17.24.4**
steeplechasing **29.1.23**
steeplejack **24.6.18**
steeply **1.31.20**
steepness **34.18.16(.18)**
steer **3**
steerable **40.20.16(.27.1)**
steerage **39.2.22(.1)**
steerageway **4.25.25**
steerer **17.32.2**

steersman **28.17.16(.30)**
steeve **31.1**
stegosaur **12.14.8**
stegosaurus **34.18.27(.8)**
Steichen **28.17.13(.10)**
Steiermark **24.8.8**
Steiger **17.16.10**
stein **28.14**
Steinbeck **24.4.3**
Steinberg **26.14.1(.9)**
steinbock **24.9.3**
Steiner **17.18.13**
Steinway® **4.25.17**
stela **17.34.1**
stelae **2.32.1**
stelar **17.34.1**
stele **1.31.1, 40.1**
Stella **17.34.5**
stellar **17.34.5**
stellate **22.4.23(.4), 22.19.26(.4)**
stellated **23.18.9(.3)**
stelliform **27.10.5(.2)**
stellini **2.17.1**
stellular **17.34.16(.21.4)**
stem **27.5**
stemless **34.18.29(.26)**
stemlet **22.19.26(.21)**
stemlike **24.13.7(.16)**
stemma **17.17.5**
stemple **40.19.14**
stemware **6.18.10**
stench **38.18.2**
stencil **40.31.21**
Stendhal **40.8.5**
sten gun **28.13**
steno **19.15.4**
stenograph **30.7.5(.1)**
stenographer **17.20.12(.5)**
stenographic **24.2.16(.3)**
stenography **1.18.9(.3.2)**
stenoses **35.1.16(.11)**
stenosis **34.2.17(.11.2)**
stenotic **24.2.10(.6)**
stenotype **20.10.2**
stenotypist **22.29.2(.11)**
stent **22.26.4**
stentor **12.5.8, 17.12.22(.3)**
stentorian **28.3.20(.7)**
step **20.4**
stepbrother **17.23.10**
step-by-step **20.4**
stepchild **23.31.9**
stepchildren **28.17.31(.15)**
stepdad **23.7.8**
stepdaughter **17.12.10(.3)**
step-down **28.8.2(.3)**
stepfamily **1.31.17(.13)**

stepfather **17.23.7**
Stephanie **1.16.15(.12)**
stephanotis **34.2.8**
Stephen **28.17.20(.1)**
Stephens **35.26.13(.11)**
Stephenson **28.17.23(.24)**
stepladder **17.13.5**
steplike **24.13.7(.10)**
stepmother **17.23.10**
Stepney **1.16.18**
step-parent **22.26.15(.23.1)**
steppe **20.4**
stepping-stone **28.19.4(.9)**
stepsister **17.12.24(.2)**
stepson **28.13.7**
stepstool **40.15.3**
Steptoe **19.10.15**
stepwise **35.15.19**
Steradent **22.26.4(.5)**
steradian **28.3.4(.3)**
stercoraceous **34.18.22(.3)**
stercoral **40.16.13(.8)**
stere **3**
stereo **15.1.12**
stereobate **22.4.8**
stereochemistry **1.29.15(.17)**
stereograph **30.7.5(.1)**
stereography **1.18.9(.3.2)**
stereoisomer **17.17.14(.8)**
stereometry **1.29.15(.8)**
stereophonic **24.2.15(.6.3)**
stereophonically **1.31.24(.9.8)**
stereophony **1.16.15(.12)**
stereopsis **34.2.17(.12)**
stereoptic **24.2.10(.12)**
stereopticon **28.10.11**
stereoscope **20.15.4(.1)**
stereoscopic **24.2.8(.5)**
stereoscopically **1.31.24(.9.2)**
stereoscopy **1.8.11(.5)**
stereospecific **24.2.16(.1)**
stereospecifically **1.31.24(.9.9)**
stereospecificity **1.10.16(.16.1)**
stereotactic **24.2.10(.13)**
stereotaxic **24.2.20(.13)**
stereotaxis **34.2.17(.14)**
stereotaxy **1.22.22**
stereotype **20.10.2**
stereotypic **24.2.8(.1)**
stereotypical **40.23.12(.5)**
stereotypically **1.31.24(.9.2)**

S

stereotypy **1.8.9**
Stergene **28.1.23**
steric **24.2.26(.2)**
sterile **40.13.16**
sterilely **1.31.38**
sterility **1.10.16(.31)**
sterilizable **40.20.16(.22)**
sterilization **28.17.25(.3.12)**
sterilize **35.15.21(.4.7)**
sterilizer **17.25.12(.15)**
sterlet **22.19.26(.14)**
sterling **29.1.31(.13)**
sterlingness **34.18.16(.26)**
stern **28.18**
sterna **17.18.17**
sternal **40.26.14**
Sterne **28.18**
sternly **1.31.27(.15)**
sternmost **22.29.17(.4)**
sternness **34.18.16(.25)**
Sterno® **19.15.13**
sternpost **22.29.17(.1)**
sternum **27.15.14(.12)**
sternutation **28.17.25(.3.3)**
sternutator **17.12.4(.5)**
sternutatory **1.29.11(.8.2)**
sternward **23.18.26(.13)**
sternway **4.25.17**
stern-wheeler **17.34.1**
steroid **23.13.19**
steroidal **40.22.9**
stertor **17.12.17**
stertorous **34.18.27(.14)**
stertorously **1.31.33(.12.5)**
stertorousness **34.18.16(.31.5)**
stet **22.5**
stethoscope **20.15.4(.1)**
stethoscopic **24.2.8(.5)**
stethoscopical **40.23.12(.5)**
stethoscopically **1.31.24(.9.2)**
stethoscopist **22.29.2(.11)**
stethoscopy **1.8.11(.5)**
Stetson® **28.17.23(.19)**
Steuben **28.17.10**
Stevas **34.18.18**
Steve **31.1**
stevedore **12.6.6**
Steven **28.17.20(.1)**
Stevenage **39.2.15**
stevengraph **30.7.5(.1)**
Stevens **35.26.13(.11)**
Stevenson **28.17.23(.24)**
stew **16**
steward **23.18.5**
stewardess **34.2.9, 34.5.3**

stewardship **20.2.7(.15)**
Stewart **22.19.6**
stewpan **28.7.4**
stewpot **22.11.2**
Steyning **29.1.17(.4)**
St George **39.10**
St Gotthard **23.18.9(.8)**
St Helena **17.18.1(.16)**
St Helens **35.26.13(.20)**
St Helier **3.24.4**
sthenia **3.9.4**
sthenic **24.2.15(.4)**
stichomythia **3.12**
stick **24.2**
stickability **1.10.16(.22.1)**
stickball **40.10.4**
sticker **17.14.2**
stickily **1.31.17(.11)**
stickiness **34.18.16(.2.4)**
stick-in-the-mud **23.14**
stickjaw **12.18**
stickleback **24.6.6(.23)**
stickler **17.34.23**
stickless **34.18.29(.24)**
sticklike **24.13.7(.14)**
stickpin **28.2.9**
stickshift **22.27.1**
stick-to-it-ive **31.2.1(.9.1)**
stick-to-it-iveness **34.18.16(.28.1)**
stickum **27.15.11(.2)**
stick-up **20.9.7**
stickweed **23.1.10**
sticky **1.12.2**
stickybeak **24.1.2**
Stieglitz **35.22**
stifado **19.11.7**
stiff **30.2**
stiffen **28.17.19**
stiffener **17.18.16(.10)**
stiffening **29.1.17(.12)**
stiffish **36.2.18(.1)**
Stiffkey **1.12.12, 2.14**
stiffly **1.31.29**
stiffness **34.18.16(.27)**
stiffy **1.18.2**
stifle **40.27.12**
stifled **23.31.22**
stifler **17.34.26**
stiflingly **1.31.28(.1.18)**
stigma **17.17.20**
stigmata **17.12.8(.7), 17.12.16(.9.3)**
stigmatic **24.2.10(.4.2)**
stigmatically **1.31.24(.9.4)**
stigmatist **22.29.2(.13)**
stigmatization **28.17.25(.3.11)**
stigmatize **35.15.7(.7)**
stilb **21.18**

stilbene **28.1.8**
stilbestrol **40.16.13(.16)**
stilbite **22.16.8**
stilboestrol **40.9.19, 40.16.13(.16)**
stile **40.13**
stiletto **19.10.4**
Stilgoe **19.13.15**
stili **14.25.8**
Stilicho **19.12.2**
still **40.2**
stillage **39.2.23**
stillbirth **32.15.1**
stillborn **28.11.2**
stillicide **23.15.11(.6)**
still-life **30.12**
stillness **34.18.16(.37.1)**
stillroom **27.14.6(.20)**
Stillson **28.17.23(.28)**
stilly **1.31.2, 1.31.38**
stilt **22.32.1**
stilted **23.18.9(.21)**
stiltedly **1.31.23(.14.3)**
stiltedness **34.18.16(.21.1)**
stiltless **34.18.29(.22)**
Stilton® **28.17.11(.27)**
Stimson **28.17.23(.23)**
stimulant **22.26.15(.25)**
stimulate **22.4.23(.7.3)**
stimulating **29.1.12(.3)**
stimulatingly **1.31.28(.1.4)**
stimulation **28.17.25(.3.14)**
stimulative **31.2.1(.9.4)**
stimulator **17.12.4(.16)**
stimulatory **1.29.11(.8.10)**
stimuli **2.32.9(.8), 14.25.9**
stimulus **34.18.29(.17.6)**
sting **29.1**
stingaree **2.30, 2.30.7**
stinger **17.19.1**
stingily **1.31.17(.25)**
stinginess **34.18.16(.2.8)**
stingingly **1.31.28(.1.7)**
stingless **34.18.29(.28)**
stinglike **24.13.7(.18)**
stingray **4.26.16**
stingy **1.17, 1.26.13**
stink **24.19.1**
stinkard **23.18.11**
stinkbomb **27.9**
stinker **17.14.21(.1)**
stinkhorn **28.11.10**
stinkingly **1.31.28(.1.6)**
stinko **19.12.15**
stinkpot **22.11.2**
stinkweed **23.1.10**
stinkwood **23.16.6(.11)**
stinky **1.12.16**

stint **22.26.1**
stinter **17.12.22(.1)**
stintless **34.18.29(.22)**
stipe **20.10**
stipel **40.19.9**
stipellate **22.19.26(.4)**
stipend **23.24.5(.2)**
stipendiary **1.29.11(.26)**
stipes **35.1.5**
stipiform **27.10.5(.2)**
stipitate **22.19.10**
stipitiform **27.10.5(.2)**
stipple **40.19.2**
stippler **17.34.19**
stipular **17.34.16(.21.1)**
stipulate **22.4.23(.7.3)**
stipulation **28.17.25(.3.14)**
stipulator **17.12.4(.16)**
stipulatory **1.29.11(.8.2)**
stipule **40.15.9(.1)**
stir **18**
stir-crazy **1.23.3**
stir-fry **14.24.10**
stirk **24.17**
stirless **34.18.29(.18)**
Stirling **29.1.31(.13)**
stirpes **35.1.5**
stirpiculture **17.28.26**
stirps **34.21.11**
stirrer **17.32.15**
stirring **29.1.30(.9)**
stirringly **1.31.28(.1.17)**
stirrup **20.13.6**
stishovite **22.16.17**
stitch **38.2**
stitcher **17.28.2**
stitchery **1.29.11(.22)**
stitchless **34.18.29(.36)**
stitchwork **24.17.6(.17)**
stitchwort **22.20.15**
stiver **17.21.10**
Stivichall **40.10.15, 40.16.12**
St John **28.10**
St John's **35.26.10**
St Kilda **17.13.23(.2)**
St Kitts **34.22.2**
St Kitts-Nevis **34.2.15**
St Lawrence **34.24.10(.16)**
St Leger **17.29.4**
St Louis **1(.6), 34.2.4**
St Lucia **3.16.6, 17.26.13**
stoa **17.9**
stoat **22.21**
stob **21.8**
stochastic **24.2.10(.15.4)**
stochastically **1.31.24(.9.6)**
stock **24.9**
stockade **23.4.5**

S

strabismic 24.2.14(.17)
strabismus 34.18.15(.18)
Strabo 19.9.2
Strachan 28.11,
28.17.13(.5), 28.17.14
Strachey 1.25.3
Strad 23.7
Stradbroke 24.14.10
straddle 40.22.5
straddler 17.34.22
Stradivari 1.29.6
Stradivarius 34.3.15(.3)
Stradling 29.1.31(.18)
strafe 30.3, 30.7
Strafford 23.18.16(.5)
strafing 29.1.19
straggle 40.24.4
straggler 17.34.24
straggly 1.31.17(.12),
1.31.25
straight 22.4
straightaway 4.25, 4.25.9
straight edge 39.5
straight-eight 22.4
straighten 28.17.11(.3)
straightener 17.18.16(.4)
straightforward
23.18.26(.5)
straightforwardly
1.31.23(.14.7)
straightforwardness
34.18.16(.21.1)
straightish 36.2.11
straightlaced 22.29.4
straightly 1.31.22(.4)
straightness
34.18.16(.20.1)
straight-out 22.9
straight-up 20.9
straightway 4.25
strain 28.4
strainable 40.20.16(.16.1)
strainer 17.18.3
strait 22.4
straiten 28.17.11(.3)
straitjacket 22.2.9(.3)
straitlaced 22.29.4
straitly 1.31.22(.4)
straitness 34.18.16(.20.1)
strake 24.3
stramonium 27.3.8(.10)
strand 23.24.6
stranding 29.1.13(.14)
Strang 29.4
strange 39.17.2
strangely 1.31.37
strangeness 34.18.16(.34)
stranger 17.29.16(.2)
Strangeways 35.4.15
Strangford 23.18.16(.17)
strangle 40.24.14(.2)

stranglehold 23.31.13(.9)
strangler 17.34.24
strangling 29.1.31(.20)
strangulate 22.4.23(.7.3)
strangulation
28.17.25(.3.14)
strangurious 34.3.15(.5)
strangury 1.29.11(.26)
Stranraer 10.23
strap 20.5
strap-hang 29.4.13
straphanger 17.19.2
straphanging 29.1.18
strap-hung 29.8
strapless 34.18.29(.20)
strapline 28.14.19(.13)
strappado 19.11.4, 19.11.7
strapper 17.10.5
strappy 1.8.5
Strasberg 26.14.1(.10)
Strasbourg 26.14.1(.11)
strass 34.7
strata 17.12.8
stratagem 27.5.11,
27.15.24
stratal 40.21.3, 40.21.6
strategic 24.2.24(.1)
strategical 40.23.12(.17.1)
strategically
1.31.24(.9.11)
strategist 22.29.2(.26.1)
strategy 1.26.10(.2)
Stratford-upon-Avon
28.17.20(.3)
strath 32.6
Strathclyde 23.15.16
Strathleven 28.17.20(.1)
Strathmore 12.9
strathspey 4.7
strati 14.8
straticulate 22.19.26(.13)
stratification
28.17.25(.3.5)
stratificational
40.26.13(.14.2)
stratify 14.14.4(.4)
stratigraphic 24.2.16(.3)
stratigraphical
40.23.12(.12)
stratigraphy 1.18.9(.3.1)
stratocirrus 34.18.27(.1)
stratocracy 1.22.16(.13)
stratocumuli 14.25.9
stratocumulus
34.18.29(.17.6)
stratopause 35.12
stratosphere 3.10.5
stratospheric 24.2.26(.4)
stratum 27.15.9(.2)
stratus 34.18.11(.3)
Strauss 34.8

Stravinsky 1.12.17(.12)
straw 12
strawberry 1.29.11(.7.1)
strawboard 23.12.2(.4)
strawboss 34.10.7
strawman 28.7.10(.5)
strawmen 28.5.7(.7)
strawy 1(.4)
stray 4
strayer 17.2
streak 24.1
streaker 17.14.1
streakily 1.31.17(.11)
streakiness 34.18.16(.2.4)
streaky 1.12.1
stream 27.1
streambed 23.5.2
streamer 17.17.1
streamless 34.18.29(.26)
streamlet 22.19.26(.21)
streamline 28.14.19(.18)
streamlined 23.24.13
Streatfield 23.31.1(.2)
Streatham 27.15.9(.3)
Streatley 1.31.22(.1)
Streep 20.1
street 22.1
streetcar 10.8.11
street-cred 23.5.15
Streeter 17.12.1
streetlight 22.16.25(.13)
streetwalker 17.14.9
streetwalking 29.1.14(.7)
streetward 23.18.26(.9)
streetwise 35.15.19
Streisand 23.24.6(.10),
23.24.16(.10)
strelitzia 3.14.13
strength 32.19
strengthen 28.17.21
strengthener
17.18.16(.12)
strengthless 34.18.29(.31)
strenuous 34.18.6
strenuously 1.31.33(.12.1)
strenuousness
34.18.16(.31.2)
strep 20.4
streptocarpi 14.6
streptocarpus
34.18.9(.5)
streptococcal 40.23.7
streptococci 14.10
streptococcus
34.18.13(.5)
streptomycin 28.2.23(.7)
stress 34.5
stressful 40.27.25
stressfully 1.31.17(.16.2)
stressfulness
34.18.16(.37.2)

stressless 34.18.29(.33)
stretch 38.4
stretchability
1.10.16(.22.1)
stretchable 40.20.16(.24)
stretcher 17.28.5
stretchiness
34.18.16(.2.8)
stretchy 1.25.4
Stretford 23.18.16(.11)
stretto 19.10.4
Stretton 28.17.11(.4)
streusel 40.32.10, 40.32.13
Strevens 35.26.13(.11)
strew 16
strewer 17.8
strewth 32.13
stria 17.6
striae 2.6
striate 22.4.3
striated 23.18.9(.3)
striation 28.17.25(.3.1)
striature 17.28.15
strick 24.2
stricken 28.17.13(.2)
Strickland 23.24.16(.16.3)
strickle 40.23.2
strict 22.23.2
strictly 1.31.22(.19),
1.31.24(.2)
strictness 34.18.16(.20.4)
stricture 17.28.20
strictured 23.18.24
stridden 28.17.12(.2)
stride 23.15
stridence 34.24.10(.11)
stridency 1.22.23(.10.2)
strident 22.26.15(.10)
stridently 1.31.22(.20.2)
strider 17.13.12
stridor 17.13.12
stridulant 22.26.15(.25)
stridulate 22.4.23(.7.2)
stridulation
28.17.25(.3.14)
strife 30.12
strigil 40.34
strigose 34.20.7
strikable 40.20.16(.13)
strike 24.13
strikebound 23.24.7(.2)
strikebreaker 17.14.3(.8)
strikebreaking
29.1.14(.3)
strikeout 22.9.9
strikeover 17.21.14(.6)
striker 17.14.12
strike-slip fault 22.32.6
strikingly 1.31.28(.1.6)
strikingness
34.18.16(.26)

strimmer® **17.17.2**
Strindberg **26.14.1(.7)**
Strine **28.14**
string **29.1**
stringboard **23.12.2(.13)**
stringency **1.22.23(.10.4)**
stringendo **19.11.14**
stringent **22.26.15(.21)**
stringently **1.31.22(.20.4)**
stringer **17.19.1**
stringhalt **22.32.5, 22.32.6**
stringily **1.31.17(.15)**
stringiness **34.18.16(.2.5)**
stringless **34.18.29(.28)**
stringlike **24.13.7(.18)**
stringy **1.17**
stringy-bark **24.8.3**
strip **20.2**
stripe **20.10**
stripling **29.1.31(.15)**
stripper **17.10.2**
stripperama **17.17.7**
striptease **35.1.7**
stripteaser **17.25.1**
stripy **1.8.9**
strive **31.9**
striver **17.21.10**
strobe **21.16**
strobila **17.34.13**
strobilae **2.32.7, 14.25.8**
strobile **40.13.2**
strobili **14.25.9**
strobilus **34.18.29(.17.2)**
stroboscope **20.15.4(.1)**
stroboscopic **24.2.8(.5)**
stroboscopical **40.23.12(.5)**
stroboscopically **1.31.24(.9.2)**
strode **23.20**
Stroganoff **30.8.7**
stroke **24.18**
strokeplay **4.28.9**
stroll **40.18**
stroller **17.34.18**
stroma **17.17.16**
stromata **17.12.16(.9.3)**
stromatic **24.2.10(.4.2)**
stromatolite **22.16.25(.9)**
Stromboli **1.31.17(.8)**
Stromness **34.5.6**
strong **29.6**
strongbox **34.23.8(.2)**
stronghold **23.31.13(.9)**
strongish **36.2.17**
strongly **1.31.28(.3)**
strongman **28.7.10(.16)**
strongmen **28.5.7(.20)**
strongpoint **22.26.11**
strongroom **27.14.6(.14)**

strongyle **40.34**
strontia **3.4.12, 3.16.8, 17.26.21**
strontium **27.3.3, 27.3.13, 27.15.22**
Strood **23.17**
strop **20.7**
strophanthin **28.2.21**
strophe **1.18.5, 1.18.11**
strophic **24.2.16(.4)**
stroppily **1.31.17(.7)**
stroppiness **34.18.16(.2.2)**
stroppy **1.8.7**
Stroud **23.8**
strove **31.12**
strow **19**
strown **28.19**
struck **24.12**
structural **40.16.13(.12.3)**
structuralism **27.15.21(.2.15)**
structuralist **22.29.2(.31.4)**
structurally **1.31.17(.27.2)**
structure **17.28.20**
structureless **34.18.29(.17.5)**
strudel **40.22.12**
struggle **40.24.8**
struggler **17.34.24**
strum **27.11**
struma **17.17.13**
strumae **2.16**
Strumble **40.20.19**
strummer **17.17.10**
strumose **34.18.15(.9), 34.20.8**
strumous **34.18.15(.9)**
strumpet **22.2.5**
strung **29.8**
strut **22.15**
struth **32.13**
struthious **34.3.9**
Strutt **22.15**
strutter **17.12.12**
struttingly **1.31.28(.1.4)**
Struwwelpeter **17.12.1(.1)**
strychnic **24.2.15(.12)**
strychnine **28.1.14**
strychninism **27.15.21(.2.9)**
strychnism **27.15.21(.2.9)**
Stuart **22.19.6**
stub **21.11**
stubbily **1.31.17(.8)**
stubbiness **34.18.16(.2.2)**
stubble **40.20.12**
stubbly **1.31.17(.8)**
stubborn **28.17.10**
stubbornly **1.31.27(.14)**

stubbornness **34.18.16(.25)**
Stubbs **35.21**
stubby **1.9.9**
stucco **19.12.8**
stuccowork **24.17.6(.5)**
stuck **24.12**
stuck-up **20.9**
stud **23.14**
studbook **24.14.3**
studding-sail **40.4.10**
studding-sail/stunsail **40.31.21**
Studebaker **17.14.3(.1)**
student **22.26.15(.10)**
studentship **20.2.8**
studiedly **1.31.23(.14.4)**
studiedness **34.18.16(.21.1)**
studio **15.1.3**
studious **34.3.4**
studiously **1.31.33(.1.1), 34.3.4**
studiousness **34.18.16(.31.1)**
Studland **23.24.16(.16.3)**
Studley **1.31.23(.10)**
study **1.11.13**
stuff **30.11**
stuffer **17.20.9**
stuffily **1.31.17(.16.1)**
stuffiness **34.18.16(.2.6)**
stuffing **29.1.19**
stuffy **1.18.7**
Stuka **17.14.14**
stultification **28.17.25(.3.5)**
stultifier **17.6.9(.4)**
stultify **14.14.4(.4)**
stum **27.11**
stumble **40.20.19**
stumblebum **27.11.2**
stumbler **17.34.20**
stumblingly **1.31.28(.1.18)**
stumer **17.17.13**
stump **20.16.5**
stumper **17.10.17**
stumpily **1.31.17(.7)**
stumpiness **34.18.16(.2.2)**
stumpy **1.8.14**
stun **28.13**
stung **29.8**
stunk **24.19.7**
stunner **17.18.12**
stunningly **1.31.28(.1.7)**
stunt **22.26.12**
stuntedness **34.18.16(.21.1)**
stunter **17.12.22(.10)**
stuntman **28.7.10(.11)**

stuntmen **28.5.7(.15)**
stupa **17.10.13**
stupe **20.12**
stupefacient **22.26.15(.19)**
stupefaction **28.17.25(.15.3)**
stupefactive **31.2.1(.13.3)**
stupefier **17.6.9(.4)**
stupefy **14.14.4(.2)**
stupefyingly **1.31.28(.1.1)**
stupendous **34.18.12**
stupendously **1.31.33(.12.2)**
stupendousness **34.18.16(.31.3)**
stupid **23.2.6**
stupidity **1.10.16(.9)**
stupidly **1.31.23(.14.2)**
stupor **17.10.13**
stuporous **34.18.27(.12)**
sturdied **23.2.9**
sturdily **1.31.17(.10)**
sturdiness **34.18.16(.2.3)**
sturdy **1.11.18**
sturgeon **28.17.28(.10)**
Sturmabteilung **29.9**
Sturminster **17.12.24(.23)**
Sturm und Drang **29.4**
Sturt **22.20**
Sturtevant **22.26.15(.16)**
Stuttaford **23.18.16(.9)**
stutter **17.12.12**
stutterer **17.32.14(.6)**
stutteringly **1.31.28(.1.17)**
Stuttgart **22.10.6**
Stuyvesant **22.26.15(.17.3)**
St Vincent **22.26.15(.17.3)**
St Vitus **34.18.11(.8)**
sty **14**
stye **14**
Stygian **28.3.18**
style **40.13**
stylebook **24.14.3**
styleless **34.18.29(.38)**
stylelessness **34.18.16(.31.6)**
styler **17.34.13**
Styles **35.30.10**
stylet **22.19.26(.11)**
styli **14.25.8**
stylish **36.2.27**
stylishly **1.31.35(.7.4)**
stylishness **34.18.16(.33.6)**
stylist **22.29.2(.31.1)**
stylistic **24.2.10(.15.3)**
stylistically **1.31.24(.9.6)**
stylite **22.16.25(.8)**
Stylites **35.1.7(.5)**
stylization **28.17.25(.3.11)**
stylize **35.15.21(.3)**

stylo **19.29.9**
stylobate **22.4.8**
stylograph **30.7.5(.1)**
stylographic **24.2.16(.3)**
styloid **23.13.20**
stylus **34.18.29(.14)**
stymie **1.15.11**
styptic **24.2.10(.12)**
styrax **34.23.5(.14)**
styrene **28.1.25(.2)**
Styria **3.22.1**
Styrofoam® **27.17.9**
Styron **28.10.24(.4)**
Styx **34.23.2**
Su **16**
suability **1.10.16(.22.1)**
suable **40.20.16(.7)**
suasion **28.17.26(.3)**
suasive **31.2.4(.3)**
suave **31.6**
suavely **1.31.30(.4)**
suaveness **34.18.16(.28.1)**
suavity **1.10.16(.15)**
sub **21.11**
subabdominal
   40.26.13(.8)
subacid **23.2.16**
subacidity **1.10.16(.9)**
subacute **22.18.10**
subacutely **1.31.22(.14)**
subagency **1.22.23(.10.4)**
subagent **22.26.15(.21)**
subahdar **10.7**
subalpine **28.14.3**
subaltern **28.17.11(.27)**
subantarctic **24.2.10(.13)**
subaqua **17.31.6**
subaquatic **24.2.10(.4.4)**
subaqueous **34.3.14**
subarctic **24.2.10(.13)**
Subaru® **16.23.3, 16.23.6**
subastral **40.16.13(.16)**
subatomic **24.2.14(.6)**
subaudition
   28.17.25(.2.3)
subaxillary **1.29.11(.27)**
sub-branch **38.18.4**
sub-breed **23.1.11**
Subbuteo® **15.1.2**
subcategorization
   28.17.25(.3.12)
subcategorize
   35.15.20(.2)
subcategory
   1.29.11(.11)
subcaudal **40.22.8**
subclass **34.9.7**
subclassification
   28.17.25(.3.5)
sub-clause **35.12**
subclavian **28.3.10**

subclinical **40.23.12(.11)**
subcommissioner
   17.18.16(.16)
subcommittee **1.10.2**
subcompact **22.23.5(.2)**
subconical **40.23.12(.11)**
subconscious
   34.18.22(.12)
subconsciously
   1.31.33(.12.4)
subconsciousness
   34.18.16(.31.4)
subcontinent
   22.26.15(.14)
subcontinental
   40.21.17(.2)
subcontract **22.23.5(.9)**
subcontractor
   17.12.21(.3)
subcontrary **1.29.11(.25)**
subcordate **22.4.10**
subcortical **40.23.12(.7.2)**
subcostal **40.21.18**
subcranial **40.3.7(.3)**
subcritical **40.23.12(.7.1)**
subcultural
   40.16.13(.12.3)
subculture **17.28.26**
subcutaneous **34.3.6(.3)**
subcutaneously
   1.31.33(.1.2)
subcuticular
   17.34.16(.21.2)
subdeacon **28.17.13(.1)**
subdean **28.1.10**
subdeanery
   1.29.11(.13.1)
subdecanal **40.26.13(.6)**
subdeliria **3.22.1**
subdelirious **34.3.15(.2)**
subdelirium **27.3.17(.1)**
subdiaconate
   22.4.14(.9.1), 22.19.15(.9)
subdivide **23.15.10**
subdivision **28.17.26(.2)**
subdominant
   22.26.15(.14)
subduable **40.20.16(.7)**
subdual **40.16.8**
subduct **22.23.8**
subduction
   28.17.25(.15.5)
subdue **16.24.6**
subdued **23.17.4(.2)**
subdural **40.16.13(.11)**
subedit **22.2.8**
subeditor **17.12.16(.6)**
sub-editorial **40.3.14(.5)**
subeditorship **20.2.7(.9)**
suberect **22.23.4(.10)**
subereous **34.3.15(.2)**
suberic **24.2.26(.4)**

suberose **34.20.16**
subfloor **12.23.9**
subform **27.10.5(.3)**
sub-frame **27.4.8**
subfusc **24.20.7**
subgenera **17.32.14(.11)**
subgeneric **24.2.26(.4)**
subglacial **40.33.2**
subgroup **20.12**
subhead **23.5.13(.8)**
subheading **29.1.13(.4)**
subhuman **28.17.16(.15)**
subjacent **22.26.15(.17.1)**
subject **22.23.4(.9),
   22.23.10**
subjection **28.17.25(.15.2)**
subjective **31.2.1(.13.2)**
subjectively **1.31.30(.7.2)**
subjectiveness
   34.18.16(.28.1)
subjectivism
   27.15.21(.2.11)
subjectivist **22.29.2(.20)**
subjectivity **1.10.16(.15)**
subjectless **34.18.29(.22)**
subjoin **28.12**
subjoint **22.26.11**
sub judice **2.22.7**
subjugable **40.20.16(.14)**
subjugate **22.4.12(.5)**
subjugation **28.17.25(.3.6)**
subjugator **17.12.4(.8)**
subjunctive **31.2.1(.13.5)**
subjunctively
   1.31.30(.7.2)
sublapsarian **28.3.20(.4)**
sublease **34.1.8**
sub-lessee **2.22**
sub-lessor **17.24.5**
sublet **22.5.21**
sub-librarian **28.3.20(.4)**
sub-licensee **2.22**
sublieutenant
   22.26.15(.14)
sublimate **22.4.13(.6)**
sublimation
   28.17.25(.3.7)
sublime **27.12.8**
sublimely **1.31.26(.10)**
Sublime Porte **22.13**
subliminal **40.26.13(.8)**
subliminally
   1.31.17(.14.2)
sublimity **1.10.16(.12)**
sublingual **40.35.4**
sublittoral **40.16.13(.12.1)**
sublunary **1.29.11(.13.1)**
subluxation
   28.17.25(.3.10)
submachine gun **28.13**

subman **28.7.10(.10)**
submarginal
   40.26.13(.14.8)
submarine **28.1.25**
submariner **17.18.16(.20)**
submaster **17.12.24(.5)**
submaxillary **1.29.11(.27)**
submediant **22.26.2(.3)**
submen **28.5.7(.14)**
submental **40.21.17(.2)**
submerge **39.15**
submergence
   34.24.10(.21)
submergible
   40.20.16(.25)
submerse **34.19.4**
submersible
   40.20.16(.21.2)
submersion **28.17.25(.12),
   28.17.26(.5)**
submicroscopic
   24.2.8(.5)
subminiature **17.28.15**
submission **28.17.25(.2.4)**
submissive **31.2.4(.2)**
submissively **1.31.30(.7.4)**
submissiveness
   34.18.16(.28.2)
submit **22.2.11**
submittal **40.21.2**
submitter **17.12.2**
submultiple **40.19.11**
subnormal **40.25.6**
subnormality
   1.10.16(.32.7)
sub-nuclear **3.24.14**
subocular **17.34.16(.21.2)**
suborbital **40.21.12**
suborder **17.13.9**
subordinal **40.26.13(.5)**
subordinary
   1.29.11(.13.2)
subordinate **22.4.14(.9.1),
   22.19.15(.9)**
subordinately
   1.31.22(.15)
subordination
   28.17.25(.3.8)
subordinative **31.2.1(.9.2)**
suborn **28.11.2**
subornation
   28.17.25(.3.8)
suborner **17.18.10**
suboxide **23.15.11(.11)**
sub-paragraph **30.7.5(.1)**
subphyla **17.34.13**
subphylum **27.15.28(.9)**
subplot **22.11.17**
subpoena **17.18.1(.1)**
subprior **17.6.14**
subprocess **34.5.9**

S

Suez 35.2.1
suffer 17.20.9
sufferable 40.20.16(.27.5)
sufferance 34.24.10(.16)
sufferer 17.32.14(.12)
suffering 29.1.30(.8)
suffice 34.15.6
sufficiency 1.22.23(.10.4)
sufficient 22.26.15(.19)
sufficiently 1.31.22(.20.4)
suffix 22.29.20, 29.1.18, 29.1.23, 34.23.2(.7)
suffixation 28.17.25(.3.10)
suffocate 22.4.11(.6)
suffocating 29.1.12(.3)
suffocatingly 1.31.28(.1.4)
suffocation 28.17.25(.3.5)
Suffolk 24.16.8
suffragan 28.17.15(.13)
suffraganship 20.2.7(.19)
suffrage 39.2.22(.14)
suffragette 22.5.17
suffragism 27.15.21(.2.13)
suffragist 22.29.2(.26.1)
suffuse 35.17.7
suffusion 28.17.26(.4)
Sufi 1.18.8
Sufic 24.2.16(.6)
Sufism 27.15.21(.2.10)
sugar 17.16.11
sugarbeet 22.1.2
sugarbush 36.13
sugarcane 28.4.5
sugarcoated 23.18.9(.15)
sugarhouse 34.8.6(.7)
sugariness 34.18.16(.2.9)
sugarless 34.18.29(.17.2)
sugarloaf 30.16
sugarloaves 35.28.9
sugarplum 27.11.14
sugary 1.29.11(.11)
suggest 22.29.5(.9)
suggester 17.12.24(.4)
suggestibility 1.10.16(.22.2)
suggestible 40.20.16(.11.7)
suggestion 28.17.27
suggestive 31.2.1(.15)
suggestively 1.31.30(.7.4)
suggestiveness 34.18.16(.28.1)
Sui 4
suicidal 40.22.11
suicidally 1.31.17(.10)
suicide 23.15.11(.6)
sui generis 34.2.21
sui juris 34.2.21
suint 22.26.1

suit 22.18
suitability 1.10.16(.22.1)
suitable 40.20.16(.11.2)
suitableness 34.18.16(.37.4)
suitably 1.31.21(.4.1)
suitcase 34.4.6
suitcaseful 40.14.6(.19)
suite 22.1
suiting 29.1.12(.13)
suitor 17.12.15
Sukarno 19.15.7
Sukey 1.12.12
Sukhotai 14.8
Sukie 1.12.12
sukiyaki 1.12.5, 1.12.6
Sukkur 17.14.13
Sulawesi 1.22.4
sulcate 22.4.11(.8)
sulci 2.14, 2.22.14, 14.10, 14.18
sulcus 34.18.13(.15)
Suleiman 28.17.16(.4)
sulfa drug 26.10
sulfamate 22.4.13(.6)
sulfate 22.4.15
sulfone 28.19.11
sulfuration 28.17.25(.3.13)
sulfurator 17.12.4(.15)
sulfuric 24.2.26(.8)
sulfury 1.29.11(.14)
Sulgrave 31.3.7
sulk 24.21
sulker 17.14.25
sulkily 1.31.17(.11)
sulkiness 34.18.16(.2.4)
sulky 1.12.19
Sulla 17.34.12, 17.34.14
sullage 39.2.23
sullen 28.17.33(.9)
sullenly 1.31.27(.14)
sullenness 34.18.16(.25)
Sullivan 28.17.20(.10)
Sullom Voe 19
sully 1.31.13
sulpha 17.20.19
sulphadimidine 28.1.10
sulphamate 22.4.13(.2)
sulphanilamide 23.15.7
sulphate 22.4.15
sulphide 23.15.9
sulphite 22.16.16
sulphonamide 23.15.7
sulphonate 22.4.14(.9.3)
sulphonation 28.17.25(.3.8)
sulphone 28.19.11
sulphonic 24.2.15(.6.3)
sulphur 17.20.19

sulphurate 22.4.22(.6)
sulphuration 28.17.25(.3.13)
sulphurator 17.12.4(.15)
sulphureous 34.3.15(.5)
sulphuretted 23.18.9(.4)
sulphuric 24.2.26(.8)
sulphurization 28.17.25(.3.11)
sulphurize 35.15.20(.2)
sulphurous 34.18.27(.11)
sulphury 1.29.11(.14)
sultan 28.17.11(.27)
sultana 17.18.8(.2)
sultanate 22.4.14(.9.1), 22.19.15(.9)
sultrily 1.31.17(.27.3)
sultriness 34.18.16(.2.9)
sultry 1.29.15(.18)
sulu 16.25
sum 27.11
sumac 24.6.10
Sumatra 17.32.19(.4)
Sumatran 28.17.31(.14)
Sumburgh 17.32.14(.5)
Sumer 17.17.13
Sumerian 28.3.20(.2)
Sumitomo 19.14.14
summa 17.17.10, 17.17.12
summa cum laude 4.10.3
summarily 1.31.17(.27.2)
summariness 34.18.16(.2.9)
summarist 22.29.2(.29.4)
summarizable 40.20.16(.22)
summarization 28.17.25(.3.11)
summarize 35.15.20(.2)
summarizer 17.25.12(.14)
summary 1.29.11(.12)
summation 28.17.25(.3.7)
summational 40.26.13(.14.2)
summer 17.17.10
Summerfield 23.31.1(.2)
Summerhayes 35.4.14
Summerhill 40.2.18
summerhouse 34.8.6(.7)
summerless 34.18.29(.17.3)
summerly 1.31.17(.13)
Summers 35.18.12
summersault 22.32.5, 22.32.6
summertime 27.12.1
summer-weight 22.4.21
summery 1.29.11(.12)
summing-up 20.9
summit 22.2.11

summiteer 3.4
summitless 34.18.29(.22)
summitry 1.29.15(.8)
summon 28.17.16(.12)
summonable 40.20.16(.16.3)
summoned 23.24.16(.7)
summoner 17.18.16(.8)
summons 35.26.13(.10)
summum bonum 27.15.14(.13)
Sumner 17.18.25
sumo 19.14.11
sump 20.16.5
sumpter 17.12.19
sumptuary 1.29.11(.3)
sumptuosity 1.10.16(.16.2)
sumptuous 34.18.6
sumptuously 1.31.33(.12.1)
sumptuousness 34.18.16(.31.2)
Sumter 17.12.19
sun 28.13
sun-baked 22.23.3
sunbathe 33.3
sunbather 17.23.3
sunbeam 27.1.1
sunbed 23.5.2
Sunbelt 22.32.2
sunbird 23.19.1
sunblind 23.24.13
sunblock 24.9.16(.10)
sunbonnet 22.2.12
sunbow 19.9.15
sunburn 28.18.3
sunburnt 22.26.16
sunburst 22.29.16
Sunbury 1.29.11(.7.2)
Sun City 1.10.2
Sunda 17.13.20(.10)
sundae 1.11.20(.7), 4.10.12
Sundanese 35.1.12
Sunday 1.11.20(.7), 4.10.12
Sunday best 22.29.5
Sunday school 40.15
sundeck 24.4.5
sunder 17.13.20(.10)
Sunderland 23.24.16(.16.2)
sundew 16.24.6
sundial 40.16.6
sundown 28.8.2(.8)
sundowner 17.18.7
sundrenched 22.30, 22.31
sundress 34.5.14(.6)
sun-dried 23.15.15
sundriesman 28.17.16(.30)
sundry 1.29.16

sunfast **22.29.6(.9)**
sunfish **36.2.18(.19)**
sunflower **17.3.11**
sung **29.8**
sunglasses **35.18.17**
sun-god **23.10.6**
sunhat **22.7.18**
sunk **24.19.7**
sunken **28.17.13(.17)**
Sunkist **22.29.2(.15)**
sunlamp **20.16.3**
sunless **34.18.29(.27)**
sunlessness
   34.18.16(.31.6)
sunlight **22.16.25(.17)**
sunlike **24.13.7(.17)**
sunlit **22.2.25**
sunlounger **17.29.16(.5)**
sun-lover **17.21.9**
sunn **28.13**
Sunna **17.18.12, 17.18.14**
Sunni **1.16.12**
sunnily **1.31.17(.14.1)**
sunniness
   34.18.16(.2.5)
Sunningdale **40.4.3**
Sunnite **22.16.14(.4)**
sunny **1.16.12**
sunproof **30.13.4**
sunray **4.26.15**
sunrise **35.15.20(.5)**
sunroof **30.13.4**
sunroom **27.14.6(.13)**
sunscreen **28.1.25(.8)**
sunset **22.5.13(.11)**
sunshade **23.4.12**
sunshine **28.14.15**
sunshiny **1.16.13**
sunspot **22.11.2**
sunstar **10.6.8**
sunstone **28.19.4(.9)**
sunstroke **24.18.13**
sunstruck **24.12.8**
sunsuit **22.18.6**
suntan **28.7.6**
Suntory® **1.29.8**
suntrap **20.5.6**
sunup **20.9.9**
sunward **23.18.26(.13)**
Sun Yat-sen **28.5.10**
sup **20.9**
super **17.10.13**
superable **40.20.16(.27.3)**
superableness
   34.18.16(.37.4)
superabound
   23.24.7(.2)
superabundance
   34.24.10(.11)
superabundant
   22.26.15(.10)

superabundantly
   1.31.22(.20.2)
superadd **23.7**
superaddition
   28.17.25(.2.3)
superaltar **17.12.26(.5)**
superannuable
   40.20.16(.6)
superannuate **22.4.4**
superannuation
   28.17.25(.3.1)
superaqueous **34.3.14**
superb **21.15**
superbly **1.31.21(.10)**
superbness **34.18.16(.19)**
Super Bowl **40.18**
supercalender
   17.13.20(.13)
supercargo **19.13.5**
supercelestial **40.3.3**
supercharge **39.8**
supercharger **17.29.7**
superciliary **1.29.2(.12)**
supercilious **34.3.16**
superciliously
   1.31.33(.1.5)
superciliousness
   34.18.16(.31.1)
superclass **34.9.7**
supercolumniation
   28.17.25(.3.1)
supercomputer
   17.12.15(.8)
supercomputing
   29.1.12(.13)
superconducting
   29.1.12(.18)
superconductive
   31.2.1(.13.4)
superconductivity
   1.10.16(.15)
superconductor
   17.12.21(.6)
superconscious
   34.18.22(.12)
superconsciously
   1.31.33(.12.4)
superconsciousness
   34.18.16(.31.4)
supercontinent
   22.26.15(.14)
supercool **40.15.4**
supercritical
   40.23.12(.7.1)
superduper **17.10.13**
superego **19.13.1**
superelevation
   28.17.25(.3.9)
supereminence
   34.24.10(.15)
supereminent
   22.26.15(.14)

supereminently
   1.31.22(.20.3)
supererogation
   28.17.25(.3.6)
supererogatory
   1.29.11(.8.6)
superexcellence
   34.24.10(.24)
superexcellent
   22.26.15(.25)
superexcellently
   1.31.22(.20.5)
superfatted **23.18.9(.5)**
superfecta **17.12.21(.2)**
superfecundation
   28.17.25(.3.4)
superfetation
   28.17.25(.3.3)
superficial **40.33.1**
superficiality
   1.10.16(.32.1)
superficially **1.31.17(.22)**
superficialness
   34.18.16(.37.5)
superficies **35.1.1, 35.1.18**
superfine **28.14.10**
superfluid **23.2.4**
superfluidity **1.10.16(.9)**
superfluity **1.10.16(.5)**
superfluous **34.18.6**
superfluously
   1.31.33(.12.1)
superfluousness
   34.18.16(.31.2)
supergiant **22.26.15(.4)**
superglue **16.25**
supergrass **34.9.6**
supergun **28.13.5**
superheat **22.1.15**
superheater **17.12.1(.13)**
superhero **19.27.1**
superhet **22.5.18**
superheterodyne
   28.14.6
superhighway **4.25.7**
superhuman
   28.17.16(.15)
superhumanly
   1.31.27(.14)
superhumeral
   40.16.13(.12.2)
superimpose **35.20.1**
superimposition
   28.17.25(.2.5)
superincumbent
   22.26.15(.8)
superinduce **34.17.13**
superintend **23.24.5(.4)**
superintendence
   34.24.10(.11)
superintendency
   1.22.23(.10.2)

superintendent
   22.26.15(.10)
superior **3.22.2**
superioress **34.18.27(.2)**
superiority **1.10.16(.21.2)**
superiorly **1.31.3(.11)**
superjacent
   22.26.15(.17.1)
superlative **31.2.1(.9.4)**
superlatively
   1.31.30(.7.1)
superlativeness
   34.18.16(.28.1)
superluminal
   40.26.13(.8)
superlunary
   1.29.11(.13.1)
Superman **28.7.10(.6)**
supermarket **22.2.9(.4)**
supermen **28.5.7(.10)**
supermini **1.16.2**
supermodel **40.22.7**
supermundane **28.4.4**
supernacular
   17.34.16(.21.2)
supernaculum
   27.15.28(.11)
supernal **40.26.14**
supernally **1.31.17(.14.3)**
supernatant **22.26.15(.9)**
supernatural
   40.16.13(.12.3)
supernaturalism
   27.15.21(.2.15)
supernaturalist
   22.29.2(.31.4)
supernaturalize
   35.15.21(.4.7)
supernaturally
   1.31.17(.27.2)
supernaturalness
   34.18.16(.37.3)
supernormal **40.25.6**
supernova **17.21.14(.7)**
supernovae **2.19**
supernumerary
   1.29.11(.12)
superorder **17.13.9**
superordinal **40.26.13(.5)**
superordinate
   22.19.15(.9)
superphosphate **22.4.15**
superphysical
   40.23.12(.16)
superpose **35.20.1**
superposition
   28.17.25(.2.5)
superpower **17.3.1**
supersaturate **22.4.22(.6)**
supersaturation
   28.17.25(.3.13)
superscribe **21.12**

S

superscript 22.22.1
superscription 28.17.25(.14)
supersede 23.1.7
supersedence 34.24.10(.11)
supersedure 17.29.1
supersession 28.17.25(.4)
supersonic 24.2.15(.6.3)
supersonically 1.31.24(.9.8)
superstar 10.6.8
superstardom 27.15.10(.5)
superstate 22.4.9(.9)
superstition 28.17.25(.2.2)
superstitious 34.18.22(.2)
superstitiously 1.31.33(.12.4)
superstitiousness 34.18.16(.31.4)
superstore 12.5.9
superstrata 17.12.4(.15), 17.12.8(.10)
superstrate 22.4.22(.8)
superstratum 27.15.9(.2)
superstructural 40.16.13(.12.3)
superstructure 17.28.20
supersubtle 40.21.9
supertanker 17.14.21(.3)
supertax 34.23.5(.3)
supertemporal 40.16.13(.12.1)
superterrestrial 40.3.14(.9)
supertitle 40.21.10
supertonic 24.2.15(.6.1)
supervene 28.1.16
supervenient 22.26.2(.5)
supervention 28.17.25(.16)
supervise 35.15.14
supervision 28.17.26(.2)
supervisor 17.25.12(.8)
supervisory 1.29.11(.19)
superwoman 28.17.16(.14)
superwomen 28.2.17(.1)
supinate 22.4.14(.9.1)
supination 28.17.25(.3.8)
supinator 17.12.4(.10)
supine 28.14.3
supinely 1.31.27(.11)
supineness 34.18.16(.25)
supper 17.10.11
supperless 34.18.29(.17.2)
suppertime 27.12.1
supplant 22.26.6, 22.26.8
supplanter 17.12.22(.4)

supple 40.19.8
supplejack 24.6.18
supplely 1.31.38
supplement 22.26.4(.8), 22.26.15(.13.2)
supplemental 40.21.17(.2)
supplementally 1.31.17(.9.3)
supplementarily 1.31.17(.27.1)
supplementary 1.29.11(.8.12)
supplementation 28.17.25(.3.3)
suppleness 34.18.16(.37.4)
suppletion 28.17.25(.1)
suppletive 31.2.1(.1)
suppliant 22.26.2(.10)
suppliantly 1.31.22(.20.1)
supplicant 22.26.15(.11)
supplicate 22.4.11(.6)
supplication 28.17.25(.3.5)
supplicatory 1.29.11(.8.2)
supplier 17.6.15
supply 14.25.11
support 22.13.1
supportability 1.10.16(.22.2)
supportable 40.20.16(.11.2)
supportably 1.31.21(.4.1)
supporter 17.12.10(.1)
supportingly 1.31.28(.1.4)
supportive 31.2.1(.5)
supportively 1.31.30(.7.1)
supportiveness 34.18.16(.28.1)
supportless 34.18.29(.22)
supposable 40.20.16(.22)
suppose 35.20.1
supposedly 1.31.23(.14.7)
supposition 28.17.25(.2.5)
suppositional 40.26.13(.14.1)
suppositionally 1.31.17(.14.3)
supposititious 34.18.22(.2)
supposititiously 1.31.33(.12.4)
supposititiousness 34.18.16(.31.4)
suppositious 34.18.22(.2)
suppositiously 1.31.33(.12.4)
suppositiousness 34.18.16(.31.4)
suppository 1.29.11(.8.8)
suppress 34.5.14(.4)

suppressant 22.26.15(.17.2)
suppressible 40.20.16(.21.1)
suppression 28.17.25(.4)
suppressive 31.2.4(.4)
suppressor 17.24.5
suppurate 22.4.22(.6)
suppuration 28.17.25(.3.13)
suppurative 31.2.1(.9.4)
supra 17.32.17
supralapsarian 28.3.20(.4)
supramaxillary 1.29.11(.27)
supramundane 28.4.4
supranational 40.26.13(.14.4)
supranationalism 27.15.21(.2.15)
supranationality 1.10.16(.32.8)
supraorbital 40.21.12
suprarenal 40.26.1
suprasegmental 40.21.17(.2)
supremacism 27.15.21(.2.12)
supremacist 22.29.2(.22)
supremacy 1.22.16(.8)
suprematism 27.15.21(.2.4)
supreme 27.1.12
suprême 27.5.13
supremely 1.31.26(.1)
supremeness 34.18.16(.24)
supremo 19.14.1
sura 17.32.14(.3)
Surabaya 17.6.2
surah 17.32.14(.3)
surahi 1.27
sural 40.16.13(.11)
Surat 22.7.20
Surbiton 28.17.11(.2)
surcease 34.1.5
surcharge 39.8
surcingle 40.24.14(.1)
surcoat 22.21.5
surculose 34.20.17
surd 23.19
surdity 1.10.16(.9)
sure 12, 17.7
sure-enough 30.11.7
surefire 17.6.9(.3)
surefooted 23.18.9(.11)
surefootedly 1.31.23(.14.3)
surefootedness 34.18.16(.21.1)

surehanded 23.18.10(.14)
surehandedly 1.31.23(.14.4)
surehandedness 34.18.16(.21.1)
surely 1.31.11, 1.31.17(.4)
sureness 34.18.16(.15.1)
surety 1.10.16(.21.2)
suretyship 20.2.7(.2)
surf 30.15
surface 34.18.17
surfacer 17.24.15
surface-to-air 6
surface-to-surface 34.18.17
surfactant 22.26.15(.9)
surfbird 23.19.1
surfboard 23.12.2(.14)
surfboat 22.21.2
surfeit 22.19.16
surfer 17.20.13
surficial 40.33.1
surficially 1.31.17(.22)
surfy 1.18.10
surge 39.15
surgeon 28.17.28(.10)
surgery 1.29.11(.23)
surgical 40.23.12(.17.3)
surgically 1.31.24(.9.11)
suricate 22.4.11(.6)
Suriname 27.6.9
Surinamer 17.17.7
Surinamese 35.1.11
surlily 1.31.17(.29)
surliness 34.18.16(.2.10)
surly 1.31.18
surmise 35.15.11
surmount 22.26.7
surmountable 40.20.16(.11.6)
surmullet 22.19.26(.10)
surname 27.4.5
surpass 34.9.1
surpassable 40.20.16(.21.1)
surpassing 29.1.23
surpassingly 1.31.28(.1.11)
surplice 34.18.29(.20)
surplus 34.18.29(.20)
surplusage 39.2.19
surprise 35.15.20(.3)
surprisedly 1.31.23(.14.7)
surprising 29.1.24
surprisingly 1.31.28(.1.12)
surprisingness 34.18.16(.26)
surra 17.32.12, 17.32.14(.3)
surreal 40.3.14
surrealism 27.15.21(.2.15)

surrealist 22.29.2(.31.1)
surrealistic 24.2.10(.15.3)
surrealistically 1.31.24(.9.6)
surreality 1.10.16(.32.1)
surreally 1.31.3
surrebuttal 40.21.9
surrebutter 17.12.12
surrejoinder 17.13.20(.9)
surrender 17.13.20(.3)
surreptitious 34.18.22(.2)
surreptitiously 1.31.33(.12.4)
surreptitiousness 34.18.16(.31.4)
surrey 1.29.9
Surridge 39.2.22(.7)
surrogacy 1.22.16(.7)
surrogate 22.4.12(.5), 22.19.13
surrogateship 20.2.8
surround 23.24.7(.10)
surrounding 29.1.13(.14)
surtax 34.23.5(.3)
Surtees 35.1.7(.7)
surtitle 40.21.10
surtout 16.7.5
Surtsey 1.22.21
surveillance 34.24.10(.24)
survey 4.16
surveyor 17.2.6
surveyorship 20.2.7(.9)
survivability 1.10.16(.22.2)
survivable 40.20.16(.19)
survival 40.28.9
survivalism 27.15.21(.2.15)
survivalist 22.29.2(.31.4)
survive 31.9
survivor 17.21.10
survivorship 20.2.7(.9)
Surya 3.22.12
sus 34.14
Susa 17.24.14, 17.25.14
Susan 28.17.24(.11)
Susannah 17.18.6
susceptibility 1.10.16(.22.2)
susceptible 40.20.16(.11.4)
susceptibly 1.31.21(.4.3)
susceptive 31.2.1(.12)
sushi 1.24.11
Susie 1.23.12
suspect 22.23.4(.1)
suspend 23.24.5(.2)
suspender 17.13.20(.3)
suspense 34.24.3
suspenseful 40.27.25

suspensible 40.20.16(.21.3)
suspension 28.17.25(.16)
suspensive 31.2.4(.13)
suspensively 1.31.30(.7.4)
suspensiveness 34.18.16(.28.2)
suspensory 1.29.11(.18)
suspicion 28.17.25(.2.1)
suspicious 34.18.22(.2)
suspiciously 1.31.33(.12.4)
suspiciousness 34.18.16(.31.4)
suspiration 28.17.25(.3.13)
suspire 17.6.1
Susquehanna 17.18.6
suss 34.14
Sussex 34.23.2(.10)
sustain 28.4.3
sustainability 1.10.16(.22.2)
sustainable 40.20.16(.16.1)
sustainably 1.31.21(.6)
sustainedly 1.31.23(.14.6)
sustainer 17.18.3
sustainment 22.26.15(.13.4)
sustenance 34.24.10(.15)
sustentation 28.17.25(.3.3)
susurration 28.17.25(.3.13)
susurrus 34.18.27(.9)
Sutch 38.11
Sutcliffe 30.2.6
Sutherland 23.24.16(.16.2)
Sutlej 39.2.23
sutler 17.34.21
sutra 17.32.19(.6)
Sutro 19.27.15
suttee 2.11, 2.12.7
Sutter 17.12.12
Sutton 28.17.11(.11)
Sutton Coldfield 23.31.1(.2)
Sutton Hoo 16
sutural 40.16.13(.12.3)
suture 17.28.14
Suva 17.21.11
Suwannee 1.16.9
Suzanna 17.18.6
Suzanne 28.7.15
suzerain 28.4.18, 28.17.31(.11)
suzerainty 1.10.23(.2)
Suzette 22.5.14
Suzuki® 1.12.12

Suzy 1.23.12
Svalbard 23.9.6
svarabhakti 2.12.13
svelte 22.32.2
Svengali 1.31.9
Sverdlovsk 24.20.14
swab 21.8
swabbie 1.9.7
Swabia 3.3.3
Swabian 28.3.2
swaddie 1.11.10
swaddle 40.22.7
swaddy 1.11.10
Swadeshi 1.24.3
Swadlincote 22.21.5
Swaffer 17.20.7
Swaffham 27.15.16
swag 26.5
swage 39.4
Swaggart 22.19.13
swagger 17.16.5
swaggerer 17.32.14(.9)
swaggeringly 1.31.28(.1.17)
swaggie 1.14.5
swagman 28.7.10(.14)
swagmen 28.5.7(.18)
Swahili 1.31.1
swain 28.4
Swainson 28.17.23(.24)
swale 40.4
Swaledale 40.4.3
Swales 35.30.3
swallow 19.29.8
swallowable 40.20.16(.8)
swallow-dive 31.9
swallower 17.9.13
swallow-hole 40.18.13
swallowtail 40.4.2
swam 27.6
swami 1.15.7
swamp 20.16.4
swampiness 34.18.16(.2.2)
swampland 23.24.6(.13)
swampy 1.8.14
swan 28.10
Swanage 39.2.15
Swanee 1.16.9
swandive 31.9
swank 24.19.3
swankily 1.31.17(.11)
swankiness 34.18.16(.2.4)
swankpot 22.11.2
swanky 1.12.16
Swanley 1.31.27(.9)
swanlike 24.13.7(.17)
Swann 28.10
swan-neck 24.4.7
swannery 1.29.11(.13.1)

Swanscombe 27.15.11(.15)
swansdown 28.8.2(.10)
Swansea 1.23.20
Swanson 28.17.23(.24)
swansong 29.6.9
Swanton 28.17.11(.22)
swan-upping 29.1.10(.7)
swap 20.7
SWAPO 19.8
swapper 17.10.8
Swaraj 39.8
Swarajist 22.29.2(.26.1)
Swarbrick 24.2.26(.13)
sward 23.12
sware 6
swarf 30.9
Swarfega® 17.16.1
swarm 27.10
swart 22.13
swarthily 1.31.17(.19)
swarthiness 34.18.16(.2.6)
swarthy 1.21
swash 36.9
swashbuckler 17.34.23
swashbuckling 29.1.31(.19)
swastika 17.14.15(.6)
swat 22.11
swatch 38.8
swath 32.9, 32.10
swathe 33.3
swatter 17.12.9
sway 4
Swazi 1.23.7
Swaziland 23.24.6(.13)
swear 6
swearer 17.32.5
swearword 23.19.8
sweat 22.5
sweatband 23.24.6(.4)
sweatbox 34.23.8(.2)
sweater 17.12.5
sweatily 1.31.17(.9.1)
sweatiness 34.18.16(.2.3)
sweatpants 34.22.18
sweatshirt 22.20.13
sweatshop 20.7.10
sweatsuit 22.18.6
sweaty 1.10.4
Swede 23.1
Sweden 28.17.12(.1)
Swedenborg 26.9
Swedenborgian 28.3.6, 28.3.18
Swedish 36.2.12
Sweeney 1.16.1
sweep 20.1
sweepback 24.6.6(.11)
sweeper 17.10.1

sweeping 29.1.10(.1)
sweepingly 1.31.28(.1.2)
sweepingness 34.18.16(.26)
sweepstake 24.3.4
sweet 22.1
sweet-and-sour 17.3.8
sweetbread 23.5.15
sweetbriar 17.6.14
sweetcorn 28.11.5
sweeten 28.17.11(.1)
sweetened 23.24.16(.3)
sweetener 17.18.16(.4)
sweetening 29.1.17(.12)
Sweetex® 34.23.4(.3)
sweetheart 22.10.11
sweetie 1.10.1
sweetie-pie 14.6
sweeting 29.1.12(.1)
sweetish 36.2.11
sweetly 1.31.22(.1)
sweetmeal 40.1.6
sweetmeat 22.1.5
sweetness 34.18.16(.20.1)
sweetshop 20.7.10
sweetsop 20.7.8
sweet-talk 24.10.2
swell 40.5
swelling 29.1.31(.5)
swellish 36.2.27
swelter 17.12.26(.3)
swelteringly 1.31.28(.1.17)
swept 22.22.3
swerve 31.11
swerveless 34.18.29(.30)
swerver 17.21.13
swift 22.27.1
swiftie 1.10.24
swiftlet 22.19.26(.17)
swiftly 1.31.22(.21)
swiftness 34.18.16(.20.4)
swig 26.2
swigger 17.16.2
swill 40.2
swiller 17.34.2
swim 27.2
swimmable 40.20.16(.15)
swimmer 17.17.2
swimmeret 22.5.19
swimmingly 1.31.28(.1.7)
swimsuit 22.18.6
swimwear 6.18.10
Swinburne 28.18.3
swindle 40.22.16
swindler 17.34.22
Swindon 28.17.12(.23)
swine 28.14
swineherd 23.19.7
swinery 1.29.11(.13.1)

swing 29.1
swingbin 28.2.10
swingboat 22.21.2
swinge 39.17.1
swingeingly 1.31.28(.1.14)
swinger 17.19.1
swingingly 1.31.28(.1.7)
swingle 40.24.14(.1)
Swingler 17.34.24
swingletree 2.30.10
swingometer 17.12.16(.9.2)
swingy 1.17
swinish 36.2.16(.11)
swinishly 1.31.35(.7.2)
swinishness 34.18.16(.33.5)
Swinnerton 28.17.11(.15)
Swinton 28.17.11(.22)
swipe 20.10
swiper 17.10.12
swipple 40.19.2
swirl 40.17
swirly 1.31.18
swish 36.2
swishily 1.31.17(.22)
swishiness 34.18.16(.2.8)
swishy 1.24.2
Swiss 34.2
Swissair® 6.12
switch 38.2
switchable 40.20.16(.24)
switchback 24.6.6(.22)
switchblade 23.4.16
switchboard 23.12.2(.18)
switcher 17.28.2
switcheroo 16.23
switchgear 3.7
switchman 28.17.16(.33)
switch-over 17.21.14(.11)
switchyard 23.9.21
swither 17.23.2
Swithin 28.2.22, 28.17.22
Swithun 28.17.22
Switzerland 23.24.16(.16.2)
swive 31.9
swivel 40.28.2
swizz 35.2
swizzle 40.32.2
swob 21.8
swollen 28.17.33(.15)
swoon 28.16
swoop 20.12
swoosh 36.13, 36.14
swop 20.7
sword 23.12
swordbearer 17.32.5
swordbelt 22.32.2

swordbill 40.2.4
swordfish 36.2.18(.16)
swordlike 24.13.7(.13)
swordplay 4.28.9
swordsman 28.17.16(.30)
swordsmanship 20.2.7(.19)
swordstick 24.2.10(.15.4)
swordtail 40.4.2
swore 12
sworn 28.11
swot 22.11
swotter 17.12.9
swum 27.11
swung 29.8
swy 14
sybarite 22.16.24(.9)
sybaritic 24.2.10(.2.4)
sybaritical 40.23.12(.7.1)
sybaritically 1.31.24(.9.3)
sybaritism 27.15.21(.2.4)
sycamine 28.2.17(.5), 28.14.8
syce 34.15
sycomore 12.9.4
syconia 3.9.11
syconium 27.3.8(.10)
sycophancy 1.22.23(.10.4)
sycophant 22.26.6, 22.26.15(.15)
sycophantic 24.2.10(.14)
sycophantically 1.31.24(.9.5)
sycoses 35.1.16(.11)
sycosis 34.2.17(.11.1)
Sydney 1.16.20
Sydneysider 17.13.12
syenite 22.16.14(.6)
syenitic 24.2.10(.2.2)
Sykes 34.23.12
syllabary 1.29.11(.7.1)
syllabi 14.7
syllabic 24.2.9(.2)
syllabically 1.31.24(.9.2)
syllabication 28.17.25(.3.5)
syllabicity 1.10.16(.16.1)
syllabification 28.17.25(.3.5)
syllabify 14.14.4(.3)
syllabize 35.15.6
syllable 40.20.16(.29)
syllabub 21.11
syllabus 34.18.10
syllepses 35.1.16(.12)
syllepsis 34.2.17(.12)
sylleptic 24.2.10(.12)
sylleptically 1.31.24(.9.5)
syllogism 27.15.21(.2.13)
syllogistic 24.2.10(.15.2)

syllogistically 1.31.24(.9.6)
syllogize 35.15.18
sylph 30.20.1
Sylphides 23.1.6
sylphlike 24.13.7(.19)
sylva 17.21.19
sylvae 2.19
sylvan 28.17.20(.14)
sylvatic 24.2.10(.4.4)
Sylvester 17.12.24(.14)
Sylvia 3.11.11
Sylvie 1.19.14
sylvine 28.1.16
sylvite 22.16.17
symbiont 22.26.9
symbioses 35.1.16(.11)
symbiosis 34.2.17(.11.1)
symbiotic 24.2.10(.6)
symbiotically 1.31.24(.9.4)
symbol 40.20.19
symbolic 24.2.27(.9)
symbolical 40.23.12(.19)
symbolically 1.31.24(.9.12)
symbolism 27.15.21(.2.15)
symbolist 22.29.2(.31.2)
symbolistic 24.2.10(.15.3)
symbolization 28.17.25(.3.12)
symbolize 35.15.21(.4.2)
symbology 1.26.10(.11.2)
symbolology 1.26.10(.11.1)
Symington 28.17.11(.23)
symmetric 24.2.26(.14.2)
symmetrical 40.23.12(.18)
symmetrically 1.31.24(.9.12)
symmetricalness 34.18.16(.37.5)
symmetrize 35.15.20(.4)
symmetrophobia 3.3.9
symmetry 1.29.15(.8)
Symon 28.17.16(.13)
Symonds 35.23.15
Symonds Yat 22.7
Symons 35.26.13(.10)
sympathectomy 1.15.13(.1)
sympathetic 24.2.10(.3.2)
sympathetically 1.31.24(.9.3)
sympathize 35.15.15
sympathizer 17.25.12(.9)
sympathy 1.20.8
sympatric 24.2.26(.14.3)
sympetalous 34.18.29(.17.2)

symphonic 24.2.15(.6.3)
symphonically 1.31.24(.9.8)
symphonious 34.3.6(.7)
symphonist 22.29.2(.18.1)
symphony 1.16.15(.12)
symphyllous 34.18.29(.2)
symphyseal 40.3.11
symphyses 35.1.16(.10)
symphysis 34.2.17(.10.4)
symplasm 27.15.21(.3)
symplast 22.29.6(.12)
sympodia 3.5.8
sympodial 40.3.4
sympodially 1.31.3(.4)
sympodium 27.3.4(.8)
symposia 3.15.8
symposiac 24.6.1
symposial 40.3.11
symposiarch 24.8.1
symposiast 22.29.6(.1)
symposium 27.3.12
symptom 27.15.9(.12)
symptomatic 24.2.10(.4.2)
symptomatically 1.31.24(.9.4)
symptomatology 1.26.10(.11.2)
symptomless 34.18.29(.26)
synaereses 35.1.16(.10)
synaesthesia 3.15.1
synaesthetic 24.2.10(.3.2)
synagogal 40.24.6
synagogical 40.23.12(.17.2)
synagogue 26.7.6
synallagmatic 24.2.10(.4.2)
synantherous 34.18.27(.22)
synanthous 34.18.19
synapse 34.21.5
synapses 35.1.16(.12)
synapsis 34.2.17(.12)
synaptic 24.2.10(.12)
synaptically 1.31.24(.9.5)
synarchy 1.12.6
synarthroses 35.1.16(.11)
synarthrosis 34.2.17(.11.2)
sync 24.19.1
syncarp 20.6
syncarpous 34.18.9(.5)
synchondroses 35.1.16(.11)
synchondrosis 34.2.17(.11.2)
synchro 19.27.17

synchrocyclotron 28.10.24(.7)
synchroflash 36.6.10
synchromesh 36.5
synchronic 24.2.15(.6.4)
synchronically 1.31.24(.9.8)
synchronicity 1.10.16(.16.1)
synchronism 27.15.21(.2.9)
synchronistic 24.2.10(.15.2)
synchronistically 1.31.24(.9.6)
synchronization 28.17.25(.3.11)
synchronize 35.15.12(.5)
synchronizer 17.25.12(.6)
synchronous 34.18.16(.15.3)
synchronously 1.31.33(.12.3)
synchronousness 34.18.16(.31.3)
synchrony 1.16.15(.18)
synchrotron 28.10.24(.7)
synclinal 40.26.11
syncline 28.14.19(.16)
syncopal 40.19.11
syncopate 22.4.7
syncopation 28.17.25(.3.2)
syncopator 17.12.4(.3)
syncope 1.8.11(.5)
syncretic 24.2.10(.3.3)
syncretism 27.15.21(.2.4)
syncretist 22.29.2(.13)
syncretistic 24.2.10(.15.2)
syncretize 35.15.7(.7)
syncytia 3.4.2
syncytial 40.33.1
syncytium 27.3.3
syndactyl 40.2.5, 40.21.16
syndactylism 27.15.21(.2.15)
syndactylous 34.18.29(.17.2)
syndactyly 1.31.17(.9.3)
syndeses 35.1.16(.10)
syndesis 34.2.17(.10.2)
syndesmoses 35.1.16(.11)
syndesmosis 34.2.17(.11.2)
syndetic 24.2.10(.3.1)
syndic 24.2.11(.16)
syndical 40.23.12(.8)
syndicalism 27.15.21(.2.15)
syndicalist 22.29.2(.31.2)
syndicate 22.4.11(.6), 22.19.12(.10)

syndication 28.17.25(.3.5)
syndrome 27.17.13
syndromic 24.2.14(.6)
syne 28.14
synecdoche 1.12.13
synecdochic 24.2.12
synecological 40.23.12(.17.2)
synecologist 22.29.2(.26.3)
synecology 1.26.10(.11.3)
syneresis 34.2.17(.10.4)
synergetic 24.2.10(.3.2)
synergic 24.2.24(.6)
synergism 27.15.21(.2.13)
synergist 22.29.2(.26.1)
synergistic 24.2.10(.15.2)
synergistically 1.31.24(.9.6)
synergy 1.26.10(.5)
synesis 34.2.17(.10.3)
syngamous 34.18.15(.10)
syngamy 1.15.13(.4)
Synge 29.1
syngenesis 34.2.17(.10.3)
syngnathous 34.18.19
synizeses 35.1.16(.1)
synizesis 34.2.17(.1)
synod 23.10.7, 23.18.14
synodal 40.22.13
synodic 24.2.11(.7)
synodical 40.23.12(.8)
synodically 1.31.24(.9.7)
synoecious 34.18.22(.1)
synonym 27.2.6
synonymic 24.2.14(.2)
synonymity 1.10.16(.12)
synonymous 34.18.15(.10)
synonymously 1.31.33(.12.3)
synonymousness 34.18.16(.31.3)
synonymy 1.15.13(.5)
synopses 35.1.16(.12)
synopsis 34.2.17(.12)
synopsize 35.15.16(.5)
synoptic 24.2.10(.12)
synoptical 40.23.12(.7.3)
synoptically 1.31.24(.9.5)
synoptist 22.29.2(.13)
synostoses 35.1.16(.11)
synostosis 34.2.17(.11.1)
synovia 3.11.8
synovial 40.3.8
synovitis 34.18.11(.8)
syntactic 24.2.10(.13)
syntactical 40.23.12(.7.3)
syntactically 1.31.24(.9.5)
syntagm 27.6.4
syntagma 17.17.20

syntagmata 17.12.16(.9.3)
syntagmatic 24.2.10(.4.2)
syntagmatically 1.31.24(.9.4)
syntagmic 24.2.14(.14)
syntax 34.23.5(.3)
syntheses 35.1.16(.10)
synthesis 34.2.17(.10.4)
synthesist 22.29.2(.22)
synthesize 35.15.16(.4)
synthesizer 17.25.12(.10)
synthetic 24.2.10(.3.2)
synthetical 40.23.12(.7.1)
synthetically 1.31.24(.9.3)
synthetize 35.15.7(.7)
syntype 20.10.2
Syon 28.17.5
syphilis 34.2.22(.8)
syphilitic 24.2.10(.2.5)
syphilize 35.15.21(.4.6)
syphiloid 23.13.20
Syracuse 34.17.13, 35.17.7
syrette® 22.5.19
Syria 3.22.1
Syriac 24.6.1
Syrian 28.3.20(.1)
syringa 17.16.17(.1)
syringe 39.17.1
syringeal 40.3.12
syrinx 34.23.18
Syro-Phoenician 28.17.25(.1)
syrphid 23.2.14
syrup 20.13.6
syrupy 1.8.11(.8)
syssarcoses 35.1.16(.11)
syssarcosis 34.2.17(.11.1)
systaltic 24.2.10(.16)
system 27.15.9(.15)
systematic 24.2.10(.4.2)
systematically 1.31.24(.9.4)
systematism 27.15.21(.2.4)
systematist 22.29.2(.13)
systematization 28.17.25(.3.12)
systematize 35.15.7(.7)
systematizer 17.25.12(.2)
systemic 24.2.14(.1)
systemically 1.31.24(.9.8)
systemization 28.17.25(.3.11)
systemize 35.15.11
systemizer 17.25.12(.5)
systemless 34.18.29(.26)
systole 1.31.17(.9.3)
systolic 24.2.27(.9)
Syston 28.17.11(.25)
syzygy 1.26.10(.8)
Szeged 23.5.5

S

talkie **1.12.8**
tall **40.10**
tallage **39.2.23**
Tallahassee **1.22.6**
tallboy **13.3**
Talley **1.31.7**
Talleyrand **23.24.6(.12)**
Tallinn **28.1.27, 28.2.31(.5)**
Tallis **34.2.22(.5)**
tallish **36.2.27**
tallith **32.2.9, 34.2.22(.5)**
tallness **34.18.16(.37.1)**
tallow **19.29.5**
tallowish **36.2.8**
tallowy **1(.7)**
Tallulah **17.34.15**
tally **1.31.7**
tally-ho **19.26**
tallyman **28.7.10(.2), 28.17.16(.2)**
tallymen **28.5.7(.2)**
Talmud **23.14, 23.18.13**
Talmudic **24.2.11(.10)**
Talmudical **40.23.12(.8)**
Talmudist **22.29.2(.14)**
talon **28.17.33(.5)**
talus **34.18.29(.4)**
Talybont **22.26.9**
Tal-y-llyn **28.2.31, 28.2.32**
TAM **27.6**
tam **27.6**
tamale **1.31.9**
tamandua **17.7.4, 17.7.12(.4), 17.8**
tamanoir **10.22.9**
Tamar **10.10.1**
Tamara **17.32.7**
tamarack **24.6.21**
tamari **1.29.6**
tamarillo **19.29.2**
tamarin **28.2.29(.5)**
tamarind **23.24.2**
tamarisk **24.20.1**
tambala **17.34.8**
tamber **17.11.17(.4)**
Tambo **19.9.14**
tambour **12.4, 17.7.2**
tamboura **17.32.10(.1), 17.32.14(.3)**
tambourin **28.2.29(.5)**
tambourine **28.1.25**
tambourinist **22.29.2(.18.1)**
Tamburlaine **28.4.19**
tame **27.4**
tameability **1.10.16(.22.1)**
tameable **40.20.16(.15)**
tameableness **34.18.16(.37.4)**
tamely **1.31.26(.3)**

tameness **34.18.16(.24)**
tamer **17.17.4**
Tamerlane **28.4.19**
Tamil **40.2.9, 40.25.4**
Tamilian **28.3.21(.2)**
Tamil Nadu **16.8.2**
Tamla Motown **28.8.1**
Tammany **1.16.15(.11)**
Tammie **1.15.6**
tammy **1.15.6**
tam-o'-shanter **17.12.22(.4)**
tamp **20.16.3**
Tampa **17.10.17**
tampan **28.7.4**
tamper **17.10.17**
Tampere **17.32.14(.4)**
tamperer **17.32.14(.4)**
tampering **29.1.30(.8)**
tamper-proof **30.13.4**
Tampico **19.12.1**
tampion **28.3.1**
tampon **28.10.7, 28.17.9**
tamponade **23.4.8**
tamponage **39.2.15**
tam-tam **27.6.4**
Tamworth **32.14.15**
tan **28.7**
tanager **17.29.13**
Tanagra **17.32.22**
Tánaiste **17.12.25, 17.28.25**
Tananarive **31.1.8**
tanbark **24.8.3**
Tancred **23.2.22, 23.5.15**
tandem **27.15.10(.14)**
tandoor **12.6, 12.6.11, 17.7.4**
tandoori **1.29.8, 1.29.11(.3)**
Tandy **1.11.20(.4)**
tang **29.4**
tanga **17.16.17(.2)**
Tanganyika **17.14.1**
Tanganyikan **28.17.13(.1)**
tangelo **19.29.12**
tangency **1.22.23(.10.4)**
tangent **22.26.15(.21)**
tangential **40.16.12, 40.33.12(.3)**
tangentially **1.31.17(.22)**
tangerine **28.1.25**
tanghin **28.2.15**
tangibility **1.10.16(.22.1)**
tangible **40.20.16(.25)**
tangibleness **34.18.16(.37.4)**
tangibly **1.31.21(.7.3)**
Tangier **3.19**
Tangiers **35.3**
tanginess **34.18.16(.2.5)**

tangle **40.24.14(.2)**
Tanglewood **23.16.6(.22)**
tangly **1.31.28(.2)**
Tangmere **3.8.11**
tango **19.13.12**
tangram **27.6.17(.5)**
tangy **1.17**
tanh **28.7, 38.3, 38.18.3**
Tania **3.9.5, 3.9.6**
tanist **22.29.2(.18.1)**
tanistry **1.29.15(.17)**
tank **24.19.3**
tanka **17.14.21(.3)**
tankage **39.2.12**
tankard **23.18.11**
tanker **17.14.21(.3)**
tankful **40.14.6(.12)**
tankless **34.18.29(.24)**
tanksuit **22.18.6**
tanktop **20.7.4**
tannable **40.20.16(.16.1)**
tannage **39.2.15**
tannate **22.4.14(.4)**
tanner **17.18.6**
tannery **1.29.11(.13.1)**
Tannhäuser **17.25.10**
tannic **24.2.15(.5)**
tannin **28.2.18**
tannish **36.2.16(.5)**
tannoy® **13.7**
Tanqueray **1.29.11(.10), 4.26.8**
tanrec **24.4.12**
Tansey **1.23.20**
tansy **1.23.20**
tantalic **24.2.27(.6)**
tantalisingly **1.31.28(.1.12)**
tantalite **22.16.25(.9)**
tantalization **28.17.25(.3.12)**
tantalize **35.15.21(.4.3)**
tantalizer **17.25.12(.15)**
tantalizingly **1.31.28(.1.12)**
tantalous **34.18.29(.17.2)**
tantalum **27.15.28(.11)**
tantalus **34.18.29(.17.2)**
tantamount **22.26.7**
tantivy **1.19.2**
tant mieux **18**
tant pis **2**
tantra **17.32.19(.10)**
tantric **24.2.26(.14.3)**
tantrism **27.15.21(.2.14)**
tantrist **22.29.2(.29.5)**
tantrum **27.15.26(.10)**
Tanya **3.9.5, 3.9.6**
Tanzania **17.1.7**
Tanzanian **28.17.1(.7)**

Tao **9, 19.3**
Taoiseach **24.16.13, 25.10**
Taoism **27.15.21(.2.1)**
Taoist **22.29.2(.4)**
Taoistic **24.2.10(.15.1)**
Taormina **17.18.1(.6)**
Taos **34.8**
tap **20.5**
tapa **17.10.5, 17.10.7**
tap-dancer **17.24.22(.3)**
tape **20.3**
tapeable **40.20.16(.9)**
tapeless **34.18.29(.20)**
tapelike **24.13.7(.10)**
taper **17.10.3**
taperecord **23.12.4**
tapestry **1.29.15(.17)**
tapeta **17.12.1(.1)**
tapetum **27.15.9(.1)**
tapeworm **27.16.7**
tapioca **17.14.17**
tapir **3.2.3, 17.10.3**
tapiroid **23.13.19**
tapis **1.8.5, 2.9**
tapless **34.18.29(.20)**
Taplin **28.2.31(.13)**
Taplow **19.29.15**
tapotement **22.26.15(.13.3)**
Tapp **20.5**
tappable **40.20.16(.9)**
tapper **17.10.5**
tappet **22.2.5**
tapping **29.1.10(.5)**
taproom **27.14.7(.6)**
taproot **22.18.9**
Tapsell **40.31.15**
tapster **17.12.24(.16)**
tapu **16.5**
tap water **17.12.10**
taqueria **17.1.16**
tar **10**
Tara **17.32.7**
taradiddle **40.22.2**
tarakihi **1.27, 2.14**
taramasalata **17.12.8(.11)**
Taranaki **1.12.5, 1.12.6**
tarantass **34.7.7**
tarantella **17.34.5(.3)**
tarantism **27.15.21(.2.4)**
tarantula **17.34.16(.18)**
taraxacum **27.15.11(.9)**
Tarbert **17.29.9**
tarboosh **36.14**
tarbrush **36.12**
Tarbuck **24.12.1**
Tardenoisian **28.3.14**
tardigrade **23.4.15**
tardily **1.31.17(.10)**
tardiness **34.18.16(.2.3)**

t

Tardis **34.2.9**
tardive dyskinesia **3.15.1**
tardy **1.11.9**
tare **6**
target **22.2.10**
targetable **40.20.16(.11.3)**
Targum **27.14.4, 27.15.12**
Targumist **22.29.2(.17)**
Tarheel **40.1.13**
tariff **30.2.5**
Tariq **24.2.26(.5)**
Tarka **17.14.7**
tarlatan **28.17.11(.15)**
Tarleton **28.17.11(.27)**
Tarmac® **24.6.10**
tarmacadam **27.15.10(.4)**
tarn **28.9**
tarnation **28.17.25(.3.8)**
tarnish **36.2.16(.7)**
tarnishable **40.20.16(.23)**
taro **19.27.4**
tarot **19.27.4**
tarp **20.6**
tarpan **28.7.4**
tarpaulin **28.2.31(.8)**
Tarpeia **17.1.1**
Tarpeian **28.17.1(.1)**
tarpon **28.17.9**
Tarporley **1.31.17(.7)**
Tarquin **28.2.28**
tarragon **28.17.15(.13)**
Tarragona **17.18.9**
Tarrasa **17.24.8**
tarrier **3.22.5**
tarriness **34.18.16(.2.9)**
tarry **1.29.5, 1.29.6**
tarsal **40.31.7**
Tarshish **36.2.22**
tarsi **14.18**
tarsia **3.14.5**
tarsier **3.14.5**
Tarski **1.12.17(.4)**
tarsus **34.18.20**
tart **22.10**
tartan **28.17.11(.8)**
tartar **10.6.3, 17.12.8**
tartare **10.6**
tartaric **24.2.26(.5)**
tartarize **35.15.20(.2)**
tartar sauce **34.12**
Tartarus **34.18.27(.14)**
Tartary **1.29.11(.8.4)**
tartily **1.31.17(.9.2)**
tartiness **34.18.16(.2.3)**
tartlet **22.19.26(.17)**
tartly **1.31.22(.8)**
tartness **34.18.16(.20.2)**
tartrate **22.4.22(.8)**
tartrazine **28.1.19**

Tartuffe **30.13.1**
tarty **1.10.8**
Tarzan **28.17.24(.6)**
Tashkent **22.26.4(.6)**
task **24.20.4**
Tasker **17.14.23**
taskmaster **17.12.24(.5)**
taskmistress **34.18.27(.14)**
Tasman **28.17.16(.30)**
Tasmania **3.9.3(.5)**
Tasmanian **28.3.8(.3)**
tass **34.7**
tassa **17.24.6**
tassel **40.31.6**
tassie **1.22.6**
Tasso **19.20.4**
taste **22.29.4**
tasteable **40.20.16(.11.7)**
taste bud **23.14**
tasteful **40.27.18**
tastefully **1.31.17(.16.2)**
tastefulness **34.18.16(.37.2)**
tasteless **34.18.29(.22)**
tastelessly **1.31.33(.12.6)**
tastelessness **34.18.16(.31.6)**
taster **17.12.24(.3)**
tastily **1.31.17(.9.3)**
tastiness **34.18.16(.2.3)**
tasting **29.1.12(.21)**
tasty **1.10.26(.3)**
tat **22.7**
ta-ta **10.6**
tatami **1.15.7**
Tatar **17.12.8**
Tatarstan **28.9.2**
Tatchell **40.16.12**
Tate **22.4**
tater **17.12.4**
Tatham **27.15.9(.4), 27.15.18, 27.15.19**
Tati **1.10.6**
Tatiana **17.18.8**
tatler **17.34.21**
tatou **16.7.1**
Tatra **17.32.19(.4)**
Tatras **34.18.27(.14)**
tatter **17.12.6**
tatterdemalion **28.3.21(.3)**
tattersall **40.10.14, 40.31.12**
tattery **1.29.11(.8.3)**
tattie **1.10.6**
tattily **1.31.17(.9.1)**
tattiness **34.18.16(.2.3)**
tattle **40.21.5**
tattler **17.34.21**
tattletale **40.4.2**

Tatton **28.17.11(.6)**
tattoo **16.7**
tattooer **17.8**
tattooist **22.29.2(.8)**
tatty **1.10.6**
Tatum **27.15.9(.2)**
tau **9, 12**
taught **22.13**
taunt **22.26.10**
taunter **17.12.22(.8)**
tauntingly **1.31.28(.1.4)**
Taunton **28.17.11(.22)**
Taunus **34.18.16(.8)**
taupe **20.15**
Taupo **19.8**
taupy **1.8.13**
Tauranga **17.16.17(.2)**
Taurean **28.3.20(.7), 28.17.1(.12)**
taurine **28.1.25(.1), 28.14.18**
tauromachy **1.12.13**
Taurus **34.18.27(.8)**
taut **22.13**
tauten **28.17.11(.10)**
tautly **1.31.22(.10)**
tautness **34.18.16(.20.2)**
tautochrone **28.19.17**
tautog **26.7.3**
tautologic **24.2.24(.4)**
tautological **40.23.12(.17.2)**
tautologically **1.31.24(.9.11)**
tautologist **22.29.2(.26.3)**
tautologize **35.15.18**
tautologous **34.18.14(.5)**
tautology **1.26.10(.11.2)**
tautomer **17.17.14(.2)**
tautomeric **24.2.26(.4)**
tautomerism **27.15.21(.2.14)**
tautophony **1.16.15(.12)**
Tavaré **4.26.8**
tavern **28.17.20(.5)**
taverna **17.18.17**
Taverner **17.18.16(.11)**
Taverners **35.18.13**
Tavistock **24.9.4**
taw **12**
tawa **17.31.2**
tawdrily **1.31.17(.27.3)**
tawdriness **34.18.16(.2.9)**
tawdry **1.29.16**
Tawe **1(.3)**
tawer **17.4**
tawniness **34.18.16(.2.5)**
tawny **1.16.10**
taws **35.12**
tawse **35.12**

tax **34.23.5**
taxa **17.24.20**
taxability **1.10.16(.22.1)**
taxable **40.20.16(.21.3)**
taxation **28.17.25(.3.10)**
tax-deductible **40.20.16(.11.5)**
tax-efficient **22.26.15(.19)**
taxer **17.24.20**
taxes **35.1.16(.14)**
taxi **1.22.22**
taxicab **21.6**
taxidermal **40.25.11**
taxidermic **24.2.14(.11)**
taxidermist **22.29.2(.17)**
taxidermy **1.15.13(.2), 1.15.14**
taximeter **17.12.1(.6)**
taxingly **1.31.28(.1.11)**
taxis **34.2.17(.14)**
taxiway **4.25.2**
taxless **34.18.29(.33)**
taxman **28.7.10(.20)**
taxmen **28.5.7(.24)**
taxol® **40.9.14**
taxon **28.10.18**
taxonomic **24.2.14(.6)**
taxonomical **40.23.12(.10)**
taxonomically **1.31.24(.9.8)**
taxonomist **22.29.2(.17)**
taxonomy **1.15.13(.5)**
taxpayer **17.2.1**
taxpaying **29.1.3**
Tay **4**
tayberry **1.29.11(.7.1)**
Taylor **17.34.4**
tayra **17.32.13**
Tay-Sachs **34.23.5(.10)**
Tayside **23.15.11(.4)**
tazza **17.24.19**
Tbilisi **1.22.1**
Tchaikovsky **1.12.17(.13)**
TD **2.13**
te **2**
tea **2**
teabag **26.5.1**
teaball **40.10.4**
teabread **23.5.15**
teacake **24.3.6**
teach **38.1**
teachability **1.10.16(.22.1)**
teachable **40.20.16(.24)**
teachableness **34.18.16(.37.4)**
teacher **17.28.1**
teacherly **1.31.17(.24)**
teach-in **28.2.26**
teaching **29.1.27**

teacup **20.9.7**
teacupful **40.14.6(.8)**
teacupsful **40.14.6(.19)**
teagarden **28.17.12(.8)**
teahouse **34.8.6(.1)**
teak **24.1**
teakettle **40.21.4**
teal **40.1**
tealeaf **30.1.9**
tealeaves **35.28.1**
team **27.1**
teammate **22.4.13(.12)**
teamster **17.12.24(.22)**
team-teaching **29.1.27**
teamwork **24.17.6(.12)**
teapot **22.11.2**
teapoy **13.2**
tear **3, 6**
tearable **40.20.16(.27.1)**
tearaway **4.25.9**
teardrop **20.7.12**
tearer **17.32.5**
tearful **40.27.3**
tearfully **1.31.17(.16.1)**
tearfulness
  34.18.16(.37.2)
teargas **34.7.10**
tearjerker **17.14.16**
tear-jerking **29.1.14(.12)**
tearless **34.18.29(.3)**
tearlessly **1.31.33(.12.6)**
tearlessness
  34.18.16(.31.6)
tearlike **24.13.7(.2)**
tear-off **30.8.11**
tearoom **27.14.6(.1)**
tearstained **23.24.4**
teary **1.29.2**
Teasdale **40.4.3**
tease **35.1**
teasel **40.32.1**
teaseler **17.34.16(.16)**
teaser **17.25.1**
teaset **22.5.13(.1)**
teashop **20.7.9**
teasingly **1.31.28(.1.12)**
Teasmade® **23.4.7**
teaspoon **28.16.1**
teaspoonful **40.14.6(.15)**
teaspoonsful
  40.14.6(.20)
teat **22.1**
teatime **27.12.1**
Tebay **4.8**
Tebbitt **22.2.6**
tec **24.4**
tech **24.4**
techie **1.12.4**
techily **1.31.17(.24)**
techiness **34.18.16(.2.8)**

technetium **27.3.13,
  27.15.22**
technic **24.2.15(.12)**
technical **40.23.12(.11)**
technicality **1.10.16(.32.5)**
technically **1.31.24(.9.8)**
technicalness
  34.18.16(.37.5)
technician **28.17.25(.2.4)**
technicist **22.29.2(.22)**
technicolour **17.34.12**
technique **24.1.5**
techno **19.15.16**
technobabble **40.20.6**
technocracy **1.22.16(.13)**
technocrat **22.7.20**
technocratic **24.2.10(.4.5)**
technocratically
  1.31.24(.9.4)
technological
  40.23.12(.17.2)
technologically
  1.31.24(.9.11)
technologist
  22.29.2(.26.4)
technology **1.26.10(.11.4)**
technophile **40.13.9**
technophobe **21.16.1**
technophobia **3.3.9**
technophobic **24.2.9(.7)**
technospeak **24.1.1**
Teck **24.4**
tectonic **24.2.15(.6.1)**
tectonically **1.31.24(.9.8)**
tectorial **40.3.14(.5)**
tectrices **35.1.16(.10)**
tectrix **34.23.2(.12)**
Tecumseh **17.24.21**
Tecwyn **28.2.28**
ted **23.5**
tedder **17.13.4**
Teddington **28.17.11(.23)**
teddy **1.11.5**
Te Deum **27.15.1, 27.15.2**
tedious **34.3.4**
tediously **1.31.33(.1.1)**
tediousness
  34.18.16(.31.1)
tedium **27.3.4(.1)**
tee **2**
tee-hee **2.28**
teem **27.1**
teen **28.1**
teenage **39.4.5**
teenager **17.29.3**
teensy **1.23.20**
teensy-weensy **1.23.20**
teeny **1.16.1**
teenybopper **17.10.8**
teeny-weeny **1.16.1(.14)**
Tees **35.1**

Teesdale **40.4.3**
teeshirt **22.20.12**
tee-square **6.18.9**
Teesside **23.15.11(.1)**
teeter **17.12.1**
teeterboard **23.12.2(.5)**
teeter-tatter **17.12.6**
teeter-totter **17.12.9**
teeth **32.1**
teethe **33.1**
teething ring **29.1**
teetotal **40.21.14**
teetotalism
  27.15.21(.2.15)
teetotaller **17.34.16(.7)**
teetotally **1.31.17(.9.2)**
teetotum **27.15.9(.11)**
teff **30.4**
TEFL **40.27.5**
Teflon® **28.10.26**
teg **26.4**
Tegucigalpa **17.10.19**
tegular **17.34.16(.21.3)**
tegularly **1.31.17(.29)**
tegument **22.26.15(.13.2)**
tegumental **40.21.17(.2)**
tegumentary
  1.29.11(.8.12)
Tehran **28.7.20, 28.9.13**
Teign **28.1, 28.2**
Teignmouth **32.14.11**
Teilhard de Chardin **8**
Te Kanawa **17.31.3**
teknonymous
  34.18.15(.10)
teknonymy **1.15.13(.5)**
tektite **22.16.9**
telaesthesia **3.15.1**
telaesthetic **24.2.10(.3.2)**
telamon **28.10.13,
  28.17.16(.16)**
Tel Aviv **31.1.3**
tele **1.31.5**
tele-ad **23.7.2**
telebanking **29.1.14(.14)**
telecamera **17.32.14(.10)**
telecast **22.29.6(.5),
  22.29.8(.3)**
telecaster **17.12.24(.5)**
telecine **1.16.2**
Telecom® **27.9**
telecommunication
  28.17.25(.3.5)
telecommute **22.18.10**
telecommuter
  17.12.15(.8)
telecoms **35.25.6**
teleconference
  34.24.10(.16)
teleconferencing
  29.1.23

telecottage **39.2.10**
telecourse **34.12.2**
teledu **1.11.5, 16.8.4**
tele-evangelism
  27.15.21(.2.15)
tele-evangelist
  22.29.2(.31.4)
Telefax® **34.23.5(.8)**
telefilm **27.18**
telegenic **24.2.15(.4)**
telegonic **24.2.15(.6.1)**
telegony **1.16.15(.10)**
telegram **27.6.17(.5)**
telegraph **30.7.5(.1)**
telegrapher **17.20.12(.5)**
telegraphese **35.1.13**
telegraphic **24.2.16(.3)**
telegraphically
  1.31.24(.9.9)
telegraphist **22.29.2(.19)**
telegraphy **1.18.9(.3.1)**
telekinesis **34.2.17(.1)**
telekinetic **24.2.10(.3.1)**
Telemachus **34.18.13(.10)**
Telemann **28.7.10(.6)**
telemark **24.8.8**
telemarketer **17.12.16(.7)**
telemarketing
  29.1.12(.14)
telemessage **39.2.19**
telemeter **17.12.1(.6),
  17.12.16(.9.1)**
telemetric **24.2.26(.14.2)**
telemetry **1.29.15(.8)**
teleologic **24.2.24(.4)**
teleological
  40.23.12(.17.2)
teleologically
  1.31.24(.9.11)
teleologism
  27.15.21(.2.13)
teleologist **22.29.2(.26.2)**
teleology **1.26.10(.11.1)**
teleost **22.29.9**
telepath **32.6.2**
telepathic **24.2.18(.3)**
telepathically
  1.31.24(.9.10)
telepathist **22.29.2(.21)**
telepathize **35.15.15**
telepathy **1.20.8**
téléphérique **24.1.11**
telephone **28.19.11**
telephonic **24.2.15(.6.3)**
telephonically
  1.31.24(.9.8)
telephonist **22.29.2(.18.1)**
telephony **1.16.15(.12)**
telephoto **19.10.14**
telephotograph
  30.7.5(.1)

telephotographic 24.2.16(.3)
telephotographically 1.31.24(.9.9)
telephotography 1.18.9(.3.2)
teleplay 4.28.9
telepoint 22.26.11
teleport 22.13.1
teleportation 28.17.25(.3.3)
teleprinter 17.12.22(.1)
teleprompt 22.25
teleprompter 17.12.19
telerecord 23.12.4
telerecording 29.1.13(.8)
telergy 1.26.11
telesales 35.30.3
telescope 20.15.4(.1)
telescopic 24.2.8(.5)
telescopically 1.31.24(.9.2)
teleshopping 29.1.10(.6)
telesoftware 6.18.7
Teletex® 34.23.4(.3)
teletext 22.29.20
telethon 28.10.17
teletype 20.10.2
teletypewriter 17.12.13(.8)
televangelism 27.15.21(.2.15)
televangelist 22.29.2(.31.4)
teleview 16.24.12
televiewer 17.8
televisable 40.20.16(.22)
televise 35.15.14
television 28.17.26(.2)
televisor 17.25.12(.8)
televisual 40.14.8, 40.16.11
televisually 1.31.17(.28)
telework 24.17.6(.1)
teleworker 17.14.16
Telex 34.23.4(.12)
telfer 17.20.19
Telford 23.18.16(.22)
tell 40.5
tellable 40.20.16(.29)
teller 17.34.5
tellership 20.2.7(.9)
telling 29.1.31(.5)
tellingly 1.31.28(.1.18)
telling-off 30.8
telltale 40.4.2
tellurate 22.4.22(.6)
tellurian 28.3.20(.7)
telluric 24.2.26(.8)
telluride 23.15.15
tellurite 22.16.24(.9)

tellurium 27.3.17(.4)
tellurous 34.18.27(.11)
telly 1.31.5
telnet 22.5.9(.7)
teloi 13.17
telomere 3.8.7
telos 34.10.17
telpher 17.20.19
telpherage 39.2.22(.9)
telson 28.17.23(.28)
Telstar® 10.6.8
Telugu 16.10
temblor 12.23.4
temerarious 34.3.15(.3)
temerity 1.10.16(.21.1)
Temne 2.17.13
temp 20.16.2
temper 17.10.17
tempera 17.32.14(.4)
temperable 40.20.16(.27.3)
temperament 22.26.15(.13.2)
temperamental 40.21.17(.2)
temperamentally 1.31.17(.9.3)
temperance 34.24.10(.16)
temperate 22.19.24(.9)
temperately 1.31.22(.15)
temperateness 34.18.16(.20.3)
temperative 31.2.1(.9.4)
temperature 17.28.15
temperedly 1.31.23(.14.2)
temperer 17.32.14(.4)
Temperley 1.31.17(.7)
tempersome 27.15.20(.11)
Temperton 28.17.11(.15)
tempest 22.29.15(.8)
tempestuous 34.18.6
tempestuously 1.31.33(.12.1)
tempestuousness 34.18.16(.31.2)
tempi 2.9
Templar 17.34.19
template 22.4.23(.8), 22.19.26(.15)
temple 40.19.14
templet 22.19.26(.15)
Templeton 28.17.11(.27)
tempo 19.8
tempora 17.32.14(.4)
temporal 40.16.13(.12.1)
temporality 1.10.16(.32.13)
temporally 1.31.17(.27.1)
temporarily 1.31.17(.27.1)

temporariness 34.18.16(.2.9)
temporary 1.29.11(.6)
temporization 28.17.25(.3.11)
temporize 35.15.20(.2)
temporizer 17.25.12(.14)
tempt 22.25
temptability 1.10.16(.22.1)
temptable 40.20.16(.11.4)
temptation 28.17.25(.3.3)
tempted 23.18.9(.18)
tempter 17.12.19
tempting 29.1.12(.17)
temptingly 1.31.28(.1.4)
temptress 34.18.27(.14)
tempura 17.32.14(.3)
ten 28.5
tenability 1.10.16(.22.1)
tenable 40.20.16(.16.1)
tenableness 34.18.16(.37.4)
tenace 34.4.8, 34.18.16(.5)
tenacious 34.18.22(.3)
tenaciously 1.31.33(.12.4)
tenaciousness 34.18.16(.31.4)
tenacity 1.10.16(.16.1)
tenacula 17.34.16(.21.2)
tenaculum 27.15.28(.11)
tenancy 1.22.23(.10.3)
tenant 22.26.15(.14)
tenantable 40.20.16(.11.6)
tenantless 34.18.29(.22)
tenantry 1.29.15(.15)
Tenbury 1.29.11(.7.2)
Tenby 1.9.19
tench 38.18.2
tend 23.24.5
tendance 34.24.10(.11)
tendencious 34.18.22(.12)
tendenciously 1.31.33(.12.4)
tendenciousness 34.18.16(.31.4)
tendency 1.22.23(.10.2)
tendentious 34.18.22(.12)
tendentiously 1.31.33(.12.4)
tendentiousness 34.18.16(.31.4)
tender 17.13.20(.3)
tenderer 17.32.14(.7)
tender-eyed 23.15
tenderfoot 22.17
tenderhearted 23.18.9(.7)
tenderheartedly 1.31.23(.14.3)

tenderheartedness 34.18.16(.21.1)
tenderize 35.15.20(.2)
tenderizer 17.25.12(.14)
tenderloin 28.12
tenderly 1.31.17(.10)
tenderness 34.18.16(.15.2)
tendinitis 34.18.11(.8)
tendinous 34.18.16(.15.2)
tendon 28.17.12(.23)
tendresse 34.5.14(.6)
tendril 40.16.13(.17)
tenebrae 2.30.9, 4.26.10
tenebrous 34.18.27(.13)
Tenedos 34.10.9
tenement 22.26.15(.13.2)
tenemental 40.21.17(.2)
tenementary 1.29.11(.8.12)
Tenerife 30.1.8
tenesmus 34.18.15(.18)
tenet 22.19.15(.2)
tenfold 23.31.13(.7)
ten-gallon hat 22.7
Teng Hsiao-p'ing 29.1.10
Teniers 35.3
Tenko 19.12.15
Tennant 22.26.15(.14)
tenné 1.16.5
tenner 17.18.4
Tennessee 2.22
Tennesseean 28.17.1(.9)
Tenniel 40.3.7(.4)
tennis 34.2.13
tenno 19.15.4
Tennyson 28.17.23(.14)
Tennysonian 28.3.8(.11)
Tenochtitlán 28.9.15
tenon 28.17.17(.4)
tenoner 17.18.16(.9)
tenon-saw 12.14.15
tenor 17.18.4
tenorist 22.29.2(.29.4)
tenosynovitis 34.18.11(.8)
tenotomy 1.15.13(.1)
tenour 17.18.4
tenpenny 1.16.15(.5)
tenpin 28.2.9
tenpin bowling 29.1.31(.14)
tenrec 24.4.12
tense 34.24.3
tenseless 34.18.29(.33)
tensely 1.31.33(.16)
tenseness 34.18.16(.31.7)
tensile 40.13.12
tensility 1.10.16(.27)
tensimeter 17.12.16(.9.1)
tension 28.17.25(.16)

tensional 40.26.13(.14.7)
tensionally 1.31.17(.14.3)
tensioner 17.18.16(.16)
tensionless 34.18.29(.27)
tensity 1.10.16(.16.3)
tenson 28.17.23(.24)
tensor 17.24.22(.2)
tensorial 40.3.14(.5)
tent 22.26.4
tentacle 40.23.12(.7.3)
tentacular 17.34.16(.21.2)
tentaculate 22.19.26(.13)
tentage 39.2.10
tentative 31.2.1(.9.1)
tentatively 1.31.30(.7.1)
tentativeness
    34.18.16(.28.1)
tenter 17.12.22(.3)
Tenterden 28.17.12(.16)
tenterhook 24.14.9
tenth 32.21
tenthly 1.31.31
tenth-rate 22.4.22
tenuis 34.2.3
tenuity 1.10.16(.5)
tenuous 34.18.6
tenuously 1.31.33(.12.1)
tenuousness
    34.18.16(.31.2)
tenure 17.33.9
tenured 23.18.28
tenurial 40.3.14(.6)
tenurially 1.31.3(.11)
tenuto 19.10.11
Tenzing Norgay 4.12
tenzon 28.17.24(.16)
teocalli 1.31.7
tepee 2.9
tephra 17.32.25
tepid 23.2.6
tepidaria 3.22.4
tepidarium 27.3.17(.3)
tepidity 1.10.16(.9)
tepidly 1.31.23(.14.2)
tepidness 34.18.16(.21.1)
tequila 17.34.1
terabyte 22.16.8
teraflop 20.7.13
terai 14.24
terametre 17.12.1(.6)
teraph 30.14
teraphim 27.2.7
teratogen 28.17.28(.9)
teratogenic 24.2.15(.4)
teratogeny 1.16.15(.17)
teratological
    40.23.12(.17.2)
teratologist 22.29.2(.26.3)
teratology 1.26.10(.11.2)
teratoma 17.17.16(.2)

teratomata 17.12.16(.9.3)
terawatt 22.11.14
terbium 27.3.2
terce 34.19
tercel 40.31.13
tercentenary
    1.29.11(.13.1)
tercentennial 40.3.7(.4)
tercet 22.19.18
terebinth 32.21
terebinthine 28.14.12
terebra 17.32.18
terebrae 2.30.9, 4.26.10
terebrant 22.26.15(.23.4)
teredo 19.11.1
Terence 34.24.10(.16)
Teresa 17.24.1, 17.24.4,
    17.25.3
Terese 34.1.7, 35.1.22,
    35.4.16
Teresina 17.18.1(.9)
terete 22.1.17
tergal 40.24.12
tergiversate 22.4.18
tergiversation
    28.17.25(.3.10)
tergiversator 17.12.4(.12)
teriyaki 1.12.5, 1.12.6
term 27.16
termagant 22.26.15(.12)
terminable
    40.20.16(.16.3)
terminableness
    34.18.16(.37.4)
terminal 40.26.13(.8)
terminally 1.31.17(.14.2)
terminate 22.4.14(.9.2)
termination
    28.17.25(.3.8)
terminational
    40.26.13(.14.2)
terminator 17.12.4(.10)
termini 14.13
terminism 27.15.21(.2.9)
terminist 22.29.2(.18.1)
terminological
    40.23.12(.17.2)
terminologically
    1.31.24(.9.11)
terminologist
    22.29.2(.26.4)
terminology
    1.26.10(.11.4)
terminus 34.18.16(.15.3)
termitaria 3.22.4
termitarium 27.3.17(.3)
termitary 1.29.11(.8.7)
termite 22.16.13
termless 34.18.29(.26)
termly 1.31.26(.12)
termor 17.17.15

tern 28.18
ternary 1.29.11(.13.3)
ternate 22.4.14(.10),
    22.19.15(.10)
ternately 1.31.22(.4)
terne 28.18
terne-plate 22.4.23(.8)
terpene 28.1.7
Terpsichore 1.29.11(.10)
Terpsichorean
    28.3.20(.7), 28.17.1(.12)
terra 17.32.4
terra alba 17.11.20
terrace 34.18.27(.3)
terracotta 17.12.9
terra firma 17.17.15
terrain 28.4.18
terra incognita
    17.12.1(.7), 17.12.16(.10)
terramara 17.32.7
terramare 1.29.6
Terramycin® 28.2.23(.7)
terrane 28.4.18
terrapin 28.2.9
terraria 3.22.4
terrarium 27.3.17(.3)
terra sigillata 17.12.4(.16)
terrazzo 19.20.14
Terre Haute 22.21
Terrell 40.16.13(.3)
terreplein 28.4.19
terrestrial 40.3.14(.9)
terrestrially 1.31.3(.11)
terret 22.19.24(.3)
terre-verte 22.6
terrible 40.20.16(.27.1)
terribleness
    34.18.16(.37.4)
terribly 1.31.21(.8)
terricolous 34.18.29(.17.2)
terrier 3.22.3
terrific 24.2.16(.1)
terrifically 1.31.24(.9.9)
terrifier 17.6.9(.4)
terrify 14.14.4(.14)
terrifyingly 1.31.28(.1.1)
terrigenous
    34.18.16(.15.3)
terrine 28.1.25
territ 22.2.24
territorial 40.3.14(.5)
territorialism
    27.15.21(.2.15)
territoriality
    1.10.16(.32.1)
territorialization
    28.17.25(.3.12)
territorialize 35.15.21(.2)
territorially 1.31.3(.11)
territory 1.29.11(.8.9)
terror 17.32.4

terrorism 27.15.21(.2.14)
terrorist 22.29.2(.29.4)
terroristic 24.2.10(.15.2)
terroristically
    1.31.24(.9.6)
terrorization
    28.17.25(.3.11)
terrorize 35.15.20(.2)
terrorizer 17.25.12(.14)
terry 1.29.3
terse 34.19
tersely 1.31.33(.12.6)
terseness 34.18.16(.31.7)
tertian 28.17.25(.12)
tertiary 1.29.11(.20)
tertium quid 23.2
Tertius 34.3.12,
    34.18.22(.8)
Tertullian 28.3.21(.8)
tervalent 22.26.15(.25)
terylene® 28.1.27(.7)
terza rima 17.17.1
terzetti 1.10.4
terzetto 19.10.4
Tesco 19.12.17
TESL 40.31.5
tesla 17.34.27
TESOL 40.9.14
Tess 34.5
TESSA 17.24.5
tessellate 22.4.23(.7.2)
tessellation
    28.17.25(.3.14)
tessera 17.32.14(.16)
tesserae 2.30.7, 2.30.14
tesseral 40.16.13(.12.2)
tessitura 17.32.14(.3)
test 22.29.5
testa 17.12.24(.4)
testability 1.10.16(.22.1)
testable 40.20.16(.11.7)
testaceous 34.18.22(.3)
testacy 1.22.16(.4)
testae 2.12.15
testament 22.26.15(.13.2)
testamental 40.21.17(.2)
testamentarily
    1.31.17(.27.1)
testamentary
    1.29.11(.8.12)
testamur 17.17.4
testate 22.4.9(.9), 22.19.10
testation 28.17.25(.3.3)
testator 17.12.4(.5)
testatrices 35.1.16(.10)
testatrix 34.23.2(.12)
Test-Ban Treaty 1.10.1
testee 2.11
tester 17.12.24(.4)
testes 35.1.7(.10)
testicle 40.23.12(.7.3)

testicular 17.34.16(.21.2)
testiculate 22.19.26(.13)
testification 28.17.25(.3.5)
testifier 17.6.9(.4)
testify 14.14.4(.4)
testily 1.31.17(.9.3)
testimonial 40.3.7(.9)
testimony 1.16.15(.11)
testiness 34.18.16(.2.3)
testis 34.2.8
testosterone 28.19.17
testudinal 40.26.13(.5)
testudines 35.1.12(.3)
testudo 19.11.10
testy 1.10.26(.4)
tetanic 24.2.15(.5)
tetanically 1.31.24(.9.8)
tetanize 35.15.12(.5)
tetanoid 23.13.12
tetanus 34.18.16(.15.2)
tetany 1.16.15(.7)
Tetbury 1.29.11(.7.2)
tetchily 1.31.17(.24)
tetchiness 34.18.16(.2.8)
tetchy 1.25.4
tête-à-tête 22.4.9
tête-bêche 36.5
tether 17.23.4
Tethys 34.2.16
Tetley 1.31.22(.5)
Teton 28.10.9
tetra 17.32.19(.3)
tetrachloride 23.15.15
tetrachloroethylene 28.1.27(.7)
tetrachord 23.12.4
tetracyclic 24.2.27(.16)
tetracycline 28.1.27(.10), 28.2.31(.17)
tetrad 23.7.16
tetradactyl 40.2.5, 40.21.16
tetradactylous 34.18.29(.17.2)
tetraethyl 40.13.11, 40.29
tetragon 28.10.12, 28.17.15(.13)
tetragonal 40.26.13(.7)
tetragonally 1.31.17(.14.2)
tetragram 27.6.17(.5)
Tetragrammaton 28.10.9, 28.17.11(.15)
tetragynous 34.18.16(.15.3)
tetrahedra 17.32.20
tetrahedral 40.16.13(.17)
tetrahedron 28.17.31(.15)
tetralogy 1.26.10(.10)
tetramerous 34.18.27(.18)

tetrameter 17.12.16(.9.1)
tetramorph 30.9.2
tetrandrous 34.18.27(.15)
tetraplegia 3.19.1, 17.29.1
tetraplegic 24.2.24(.1)
tetraploid 23.13.20
tetrapod 23.10.1
tetrapodous 34.18.12
tetrapterous 34.18.27(.14)
tetrarch 24.8.15
tetrarchate 22.4.11(.4)
tetrarchical 40.23.12(.9)
tetrarchy 1.12.6
tetrastich 24.2.10(.15.4)
tetrastyle 40.13.3(.10)
tetrasyllabic 24.2.9(.2)
tetrasyllable 40.20.16(.29)
tetrathlon 28.10.26, 28.17.33(.24)
tetratomic 24.2.14(.6)
tetravalent 22.26.15(.25)
Tetrazzini 1.16.1(.11)
tetrode 23.20.12
tetrodotoxin 28.2.23(.14)
tetroxide 23.15.11(.11)
tetter 17.12.5
Teuton 28.17.11(.14)
Teutonic 24.2.15(.6.1)
Teutonicism 27.15.21(.2.12)
Tevet 22.5.11
Teviot 22.3.7
Tewkesbury 1.29.11(.7.2)
Tex 34.23.4
Texan 28.17.23(.21)
Texas 34.18.20
Texel 40.31.18
Tex-Mex 34.23.4(.5)
text 22.29.20
textbook 24.14.3
textbookish 36.2.13
textile 40.13.3(.10)
textless 34.18.29(.22)
textual 40.16.12
textualism 27.15.21(.2.15)
textualist 22.29.2(.31.5)
textuality 1.10.16(.32.1)
textually 1.31.17(.24)
textural 40.16.13(.12.3)
texturally 1.31.17(.27.2)
texture 17.28.24
textureless 34.18.29(.17.5)
texturize 35.15.20(.2)
TGIF 30.4
Thackeray 1.29.11(.10), 4.26.8, 4.26.13
Thaddeus 34.3.4
Thai 14

Thailand 23.24.6(.13), 23.24.16(.16.2)
Thailander 17.13.20(.4)
thalamic 24.2.14(.4)
thalamus 34.18.15(.10)
thalassaemia 3.8.1
thalassic 24.2.20(.5)
thalassotherapy 1.8.11(.8)
thaler 17.34.8
Thales 35.1.23
Thalia 3.24.3, 17.6.15
thalidomide 23.15.7
thalli 2.32.6, 14.25.6
thallic 24.2.27(.6)
thallium 27.3.18
thalloid 23.13.20
thallophyte 22.16.16
thallous 34.18.29(.7)
thallus 34.18.29(.7)
thalweg 26.4
Thame 27.4
Thammuz 35.16
than 28.7
thanage 39.2.15
thanatology 1.26.10(.11.2)
thane 28.4
thanedom 27.15.10(.14)
thaneship 20.2.7(.19)
Thanet 22.19.15(.3)
thank 24.19.3
thankful 40.27.20
thankfully 1.31.17(.16.2)
thankfulness 34.18.16(.37.2)
thankless 34.18.29(.24)
thanklessly 1.31.33(.12.6)
thanklessness 34.18.16(.31.6)
thank-offering 29.1.30(.8)
thanksgiving 29.1.20
thank you 16
thar 10
that 22.7
thatch 38.5
thatcher 17.28.6
Thatcherism 27.15.21(.2.14)
Thatcherite 22.16.24(.9)
thaumatology 1.26.10(.11.2)
thaumatrope 20.15.8
thaumaturge 39.15
thaumaturgic 24.2.24(.6)
thaumaturgical 40.23.12(.17.3)
thaumaturgist 22.29.2(.26.4)
thaumaturgy 1.26.11

thaw 12
thawless 34.18.29(.11)
THC 2.22
the 2
Thea 17.1
theandric 24.2.26(.15)
theanthropic 24.2.8(.5)
thearchy 1.12.6
theatre 17.12.3
theatregoer 17.9.5
theatregoing 29.1.9
theatre-in-the-round 23.24.7(.10)
theatric 24.2.26(.14.3)
theatrical 40.23.12(.18)
theatricalism 27.15.21(.2.15)
theatricality 1.10.16(.32.5)
theatricalization 28.17.25(.3.12)
theatricalize 35.15.21(.4.4)
theatrically 1.31.24(.9.12)
Theban 28.17.10
thebe 4.8
Thebes 35.21
theca 17.14.1
thecae 2.14, 2.22.1
thecate 22.4.11(.1), 22.19.12(.1)
thé dansant 11.12
thee 2
theft 22.27.2
thegn 28.4
theine 28.1.1, 28.2.1
their 6
theirs 35.6
theirselves 35.28.10
theism 27.15.21(.2.1)
theist 22.29.2(.1)
theistic 24.2.10(.15.1)
theistical 40.23.12(.7.3)
theistically 1.31.24(.9.6)
Thelma 17.17.24
Thelwall 40.10.17
Thelwell 40.5.17(.17)
them 27.5
thematic 24.2.10(.4.2)
thematically 1.31.24(.9.4)
theme 27.1
Themistocles 35.1.23
themself 30.20.2
themselves 35.28.10
then 28.5
thenar 10.11, 17.18.1
thence 34.24.3
thenceforth 32.10
thenceforward 23.18.26(.5)
Theo 19.1

theobald 23.31.6
theobromine 28.1.13, 28.2.17(.7)
theocentric 24.2.26(.14.4)
theocentrism 27.15.21(.2.14)
theocracy 1.22.16(.13)
theocrasy 1.22.4, 1.22.16(.13)
theocrat 22.7.20
theocratic 24.2.10(.4.5)
theocratically 1.31.24(.9.4)
Theocritus 34.18.11(.10)
theodicean 28.17.1(.9)
theodicy 1.22.16(.5)
theodolite 22.16.25(.9)
theodolitic 24.2.10(.2.1)
Theodora 17.32.10(.3)
Theodorákis 34.2.10
Theodore 12.6.6
Theodoric 24.2.26(.10)
Theodosius 34.3.10
theogonist 22.29.2(.18.1)
theogony 1.16.15(.10)
theologian 28.3.18, 28.17.28(.11)
theological 40.23.12(.17.2)
theologically 1.31.24(.9.11)
theologist 22.29.2(.26.2)
theologize 35.15.18
theology 1.26.10(.11.1)
theomachy 1.12.13
theomania 3.9.3(.5)
theophany 1.16.15(.12)
Theophilus 34.18.29(.17.4)
theophoric 24.2.26(.6)
Theophrastus 34.18.11(.16)
theophylline 28.1.27(.1), 28.2.31(.2)
theorbist 22.29.2(.12)
theorbo 19.9.6
theorem 27.15.26(.1)
theorematic 24.2.10(.4.2)
theoretic 24.2.10(.3.3)
theoretical 40.23.12(.7.1)
theoretically 1.31.24(.9.3)
theoretician 28.17.25(.2.2)
theorist 22.29.2(.29.1)
theorization 28.17.25(.3.11)
theorize 35.15.20(.1)
theorizer 17.25.12(.14)
theory 1.29.2
theosoph 30.8.8
theosopher 17.20.12(.3)

theosophic 24.2.16(.4)
theosophical 40.23.12(.12)
theosophically 1.31.24(.9.9)
theosophism 27.15.21(.2.10)
theosophist 22.29.2(.19)
theosophize 35.15.13
theosophy 1.18.9(.1)
Thera 17.32.2
therabouts 34.22.6
Theran 28.17.31(.2)
therapeutic 24.2.10(.9)
therapeutical 40.23.12(.7.2)
therapeutically 1.31.24(.9.4)
therapeutist 22.29.2(.13)
therapist 22.29.2(.11)
therapsid 23.2.16
therapy 1.8.11(.8)
Theravada 17.13.7
there 6
thereabout 22.9.6
thereafter 17.12.23
thereanent 22.26.4(.9)
thereat 22.7
thereby 14.7
therefor 12.11
therefore 12.11.2
therefrom 27.9
therein 28.2
thereinafter 17.12.23
thereinbefore 12.11
thereinto 16.7.7
theremin 28.2.17(.5)
thereof 31.7
thereon 28.10
thereout 22.9
Theresa 17.24.1, 17.25.1
therethrough 16.23.13
thereto 16.7
theretofore 12.11
thereunder 17.13.20(.10)
thereunto 16.7, 16.7.7
thereupon 28.10.7
therewith 33.2
therewithal 40.10, 40.10.13
theriac 24.6.1
therianthropic 24.2.8(.5)
theriomorphic 24.2.16(.5)
therm 27.16
thermae 2.16
thermal 40.25.11
thermalization 28.17.25(.3.12)
thermalize 35.15.21(.4.5)
thermally 1.31.17(.13)

thermic 24.2.14(.11)
thermically 1.31.24(.9.8)
thermidor 12.6.6
thermion 28.3.7, 28.10.2
thermionic 24.2.15(.6.1)
thermistor 17.12.24(.2)
thermit 22.2.11
thermite 22.16.13
thermochemical 40.23.12(.10)
thermochemistry 1.29.15(.17)
thermocline 28.14.19(.16)
thermocouple 40.19.8
thermodynamic 24.2.14(.4)
thermodynamical 40.23.12(.10)
thermodynamically 1.31.24(.9.8)
thermodynamicist 22.29.2(.22)
thermoelectric 24.2.26(.14.3)
thermoelectrically 1.31.24(.9.12)
thermoelectricity 1.10.16(.16.1)
thermogenesis 34.2.17(.10.3)
thermogram 27.6.17(.5)
thermograph 30.7.5(.1)
thermographic 24.2.16(.3)
thermography 1.18.9(.3.2)
thermohaline 28.1.27(.2), 28.14.19(.3)
thermokarst 22.29.8(.3)
thermolabile 40.13.2
thermoluminescence 34.24.10(.18)
thermoluminescent 22.26.15(.17.2)
thermolysis 34.2.17(.10.5)
thermolytic 24.2.10(.2.5)
thermometer 17.12.16(.9.2)
thermometric 24.2.26(.14.2)
thermometrical 40.23.12(.18)
thermometrically 1.31.24(.9.12)
thermometry 1.29.15(.8)
thermonuclear 3.24.14
thermophile 40.13.9
thermophilic 24.2.27(.2)
thermopile 40.13.1
thermoplastic 24.2.10(.15.4)
Thermopylae 2.32.9(.2)

Thermos® 34.18.15(.11)
thermoset 22.5.13(.4)
thermosetting 29.1.12(.4)
thermosphere 3.10.5
thermostable 40.20.4
thermostat 22.7.7
thermostatic 24.2.10(.4.1)
thermostatically 1.31.24(.9.4)
thermotactic 24.2.10(.13)
thermotaxic 24.2.20(.13)
thermotaxis 34.2.17(.14)
thermotropic 24.2.8(.5)
thermotropism 27.15.21(.2.2)
theropod 23.10.1
Theroux 16.23
thesauri 14.24.4
thesaurus 34.18.27(.8)
these 35.1
theses 35.1.16(.1)
Theseus 34.3.10
thesis 34.2.17(.1)
thesp 20.17
thespian 28.3.1
Thespis 34.2.6
Thessalian 28.3.21(.3)
Thessalonian 28.3.8(.11)
Thessalonica 17.14.2
Thessaloníki 1.12.1
Thessaly 1.31.17(.20)
theta 17.12.1
thetic 24.2.10(.3.1)
Thetis 34.2.8
theurgic 24.2.24(.6)
theurgical 40.23.12(.17.3)
theurgist 22.29.2(.26.1)
theurgy 1.26.11
thew 16
they 4
they'd 23.4
they'll 40.4
they're 6
they've 31.3
thiamine 28.1.13, 28.2.17(.5)
thiazide 23.15.12
thiazole 40.18.11
thick 24.2
thick and thin 28.2
thicken 28.17.13(.2)
thickener 17.18.16(.6)
thickening 29.1.17(.12)
thicket 22.2.9(.1)
thickhead 23.5.13(.11)
thickheaded 23.18.10(.3)
thickheadedness 34.18.16(.21.1)
thickie 1.12.2

thickish 36.2.13
thickly 1.31.24(.2)
thicknee 2.17.12
thickness 34.18.16(.22)
thicknesser 17.24.15
thicko 19.12.2
thickset 22.5.13
thick-skinned 23.24.2
thick-skulled 23.31.8
thick-witted 23.18.9(.2)
thief 30.1
thieve 31.1
thievery 1.29.11(.15)
thieves 35.28.1
thievish 36.2.19
thievishly 1.31.35(.7.3)
thievishness
 34.18.16(.33.6)
thigh 14
thighbone 28.19.3
thill 40.2
thiller 17.34.2
thimble 40.20.19
thimbleful 40.14.6(.22)
thimblerig 26.2.10
thimblerigger 17.16.2
thimerosal 40.6.13
thin 28.2
thine 28.14
thing 29.1
thingamabob 21.8
thingamajig 26.2.8
thingum 27.15.15
thingummy 1.15.13(.6)
thingy 1.17
think 24.19.1
thinkable 40.20.16(.13)
thinker 17.14.21(.1)
think-tank 24.19.3(.2)
thinly 1.31.27(.2)
thinner 17.18.2
thinning 29.1.17(.2)
thinnish 36.2.16(.2)
thin-skinned 23.24.2
thio 19.5
thiocyanate 22.4.14(.8)
thiol 40.9.3
thionate 22.4.14(.8)
thionyl 40.2.10
thiopentone 28.19.4(.8)
thiosulphate 22.4.15
thiourea 17.1.16
Thira 17.32.2
third 23.19
thirdhand 23.24.6(.11)
thirdly 1.31.23(.15)
Thirlmere 3.8.16
Thirsk 24.20.9
thirst 22.29.16
thirstily 1.31.17(.9.3)

thirstiness 34.18.16(.2.3)
thirstless 34.18.29(.22)
thirsty 1.10.26(.12)
thirteen 28.1.9
thirteenth 32.21
thirtieth 32.14.1
thirty 1.10.17
thirtyfold 23.31.13(.7)
thirty-two-mo 19.14.11
this 34.2, 34.18
Thisbe 1.9.22
thistle 40.31.2
thistledown 28.8.2(.13)
thistly 1.31.17(.20)
thither 17.23.2
thitherto 16.7
thitherward 23.18.26(.7)
thixotropic 24.2.8(.5)
thixotropy 1.8.11(.8)
tho' 19
thole 40.18
tholepin 28.2.9
tholi 14.25.10
tholoi 13.17
tholos 34.10.17
tholus 34.18.29(.19)
Thom 27.9
Thomas 34.18.15(.6)
Thomasina 17.18.1(.9)
Thomism 27.15.21(.2.8)
Thomist 22.29.2(.17)
Thomistic 24.2.10(.15.2)
Thomistical 40.23.12(.7.3)
Thompson 28.17.23(.17)
Thomson 28.17.23(.23)
thong 29.6
Thor 12
Thora 17.32.10
thoracal 40.23.12(.18)
thoraces 35.1.16(.2)
thoracic 24.2.20(.5)
thorax 34.23.5(.14)
Thorazine® 28.1.19
Thorburn 28.18.3
Thoreau 19.27, 19.27.7
thoria 3.22.9
thorite 22.16.24(.7)
thorium 27.3.17(.4)
thorn 28.11
Thornaby 1.9.11
thornback 24.6.6(.17)
thornbill 40.2.4
Thorndike 24.13.3
Thorne 28.11
Thorner 17.18.10
Thorneycroft 22.27.5
Thornhill 40.2.18
thornily 1.31.17(.14.1)
thorniness 34.18.16(.2.5)
thornless 34.18.29(.27)

Thornley 1.31.27(.10)
thornproof 30.13.4
thorntail 40.4.2
Thornton 28.17.11(.22)
thorny 1.16.10
Thorogood 23.16.3
thorough 17.32.12
thoroughbred 23.5.15
thoroughfare 6.10
thoroughgoing 29.1.9
thoroughly 1.31.17(.27.1)
thoroughness
 34.18.16(.15.3)
thorow-wax 34.23.5(.13)
Thorpe 20.8
those 35.20
Thoth 22.21, 32.9, 32.16
thou 9
though 19
thought 22.13
thoughtful 40.27.18
thoughtfully
 1.31.17(.16.2)
thoughtfulness
 34.18.16(.37.2)
thoughtless 34.18.29(.22)
thoughtlessly
 1.31.33(.12.6)
thoughtlessness
 34.18.16(.31.6)
thought-provoking
 29.1.14(.13)
thousand 23.24.16(.11)
thousandfold
 23.31.13(.7)
thousandth 32.18, 32.21
Thrace 34.4
Thracian 28.17.25(.3.1)
thraldom 27.15.10(.20)
thrall 40.10
thrang 29.4
thrash 36.6
thrasher 17.26.6
thrashing 29.1.25
thrasonical 40.23.12(.11)
thrasonically
 1.31.24(.9.8)
thrawn 28.11
thread 23.5
threadbare 6.3
threader 17.13.4
threadfin 28.2.19
threadfish 36.2.18(.16)
threadlike 24.13.7(.13)
Threadneedle 40.22.1
threadworm 27.16.7
thready 1.11.5
threat 22.5
threaten 28.17.11(.4)
threatened 23.24.16(.3)
threatener 17.18.16(.4)

threateningly
 1.31.28(.1.7)
three 2
three-bagger 17.16.5
three-card trick 24.2
three-cornered 23.18.14
three-D 2.13
three-decker 17.14.4
three-dimensional
 40.26.13(.14.7)
threefold 23.31.13(.7)
three-handed
 23.18.10(.14)
three-legged 23.18.12
threeness 34.18.16(.1)
threepence 34.24.10(.8)
threepenny 1.16.15(.5),
 1.16.18
three-ply 14.25.11
three-point 22.26.11
three-pointer 17.12.22(.9)
three-point landing
 29.1.13(.14)
three-point turn 28.18
three-quarter
 17.12.10(.7)
three R's 35.9
threescore 12.7
threesome 27.15.20(.1)
three-way 4.25
three-wheeler 17.34.1
Threlfall 40.10.11
Threlkeld 23.31.4
thremmatology
 1.26.10(.11.2)
threnode 23.20.9
threnodial 40.3.4
threnodic 24.2.11(.7)
threnodist 22.29.2(.14)
threnody 1.11.17
threonine 28.1.14
thresh 36.5
thresher 17.26.4
threshold 23.31.13(.9)
threw 16
thrice 34.15
thrift 22.27.1
thriftily 1.31.17(.9.3)
thriftiness 34.18.16(.2.3)
thriftless 34.18.29(.22)
thriftlessly 1.31.33(.12.6)
thriftlessness
 34.18.16(.31.6)
thrifty 1.10.24
thrill 40.2
thriller 17.34.2
thrillingly 1.31.28(.1.18)
thrips 34.21.2
thrive 31.9
thriven 28.17.20(.2)
thro' 16

throat 22.21
throatily 1.31.17(.9.2)
throatiness 34.18.16(.2.3)
throaty 1.10.18
throb 21.8
throe 19
Throgmorton
28.17.11(.10)
thrombi 14.7
thrombin 28.2.10
thrombocyte 22.16.19(.9)
thrombolysis
34.2.17(.10.5)
thrombose 34.20.3,
35.20.2
thromboses 35.1.16(.11)
thrombosis 34.2.17(.11.1)
thrombotic 24.2.10(.6)
thrombus 34.18.10
throne 28.19
throneless 34.18.29(.27)
throng 29.6
throstle 40.31.8
throttle 40.21.7
throttlehold 23.31.13(.9)
throttler 17.34.21
through 16
throughout 22.9
throughput 22.17
throughway 4.25.8
throve 31.12
throw 19
throwable 40.20.16(.8)
throwaway 4.25.9
throwback 24.6.6(.10)
thrower 17.9
throw-in 28.2.8
thrown 28.19
throw-off 30.8.2
throw-out 22.9.4
throwster 17.12.24(.15)
thru 16
thrum 27.11
thrummer 17.17.10
thrummy 1.15.10
thrush 36.12
thrust 22.29.12
thruster 17.12.24(.10)
thrutch 38.11
thruway 4.25.8
Thucydides 35.1.8
thud 23.14
thug 26.10
thuggee 2.15
thuggery 1.29.11(.11)
thuggish 36.2.14
thuggishly 1.31.35(.7.1)
thuggishness
34.18.16(.33.4)

thuggism 27.15.21(.2.7)
thuja 17.29.12, 17.33.3
Thule 1.31.16, 17.34.15,
40.15
thulium 27.3.18
thumb 27.11
thumbless 34.18.29(.26)
thumbnail 40.4.7
thumbprint 22.26.1
thumbscrew 16.23.10
thumbs-down 28.8.2
thumbstall 40.10.5
thumbs-up 20.9
thumbtack 24.6.7
thump 20.16.5
thumper 17.10.17
thunder 17.13.20(.10)
thunderball 40.10.4
Thunder Bay 4
thunderbird 23.19.1
thunderbolt 22.32.12
thunderbox 34.23.8(.2)
thunderbug 26.10
thunderclap 20.5.8
thundercloud 23.8
thunderer 17.32.14(.7)
thunderflash 36.6.10
thunderfly 14.25.14
thunderhead 23.5.13(.5)
thunderiness
34.18.16(.2.9)
thundering 29.1.30(.8)
thunderingly
1.31.28(.1.17)
thunderless
34.18.29(.17.2)
thunderous 34.18.27(.15)
thunderously
1.31.33(.12.5)
thunderousness
34.18.16(.31.5)
thundershower 17.3.9
thunderstorm 27.10.2
thunderstruck 24.12.8
thundery 1.29.11(.9)
thunk 24.19.7
Thurber 17.11.14
Thurgau 9.6
thurible 40.20.16(.27.2)
thurifer 17.20.12(.5)
thuriferous 34.18.27(.20)
thurification
28.17.25(.3.5)
Thuringia 3.19.9
Thuringian 28.3.16,
28.3.18
Thurrock 24.16.15
Thursday 1.11.21, 4.10.15
Thurso 19.20.11
Thurston 28.17.11(.25)
thus 34.14

thwack 24.6
Thwaite 22.4
thwart 22.13
thy 14
Thyestean 28.3.3
Thyestes 35.1.7(.10)
thylacine 28.1.18(.6),
28.2.23(.9), 28.14.13
thyme 27.12
thymi 14.12
thymine 28.1.13
thymol 40.9.11
thymus 34.18.15(.8)
thymy 1.15.11
thyratron 28.10.24(.7)
thyristor 17.12.24(.2)
thyroid 23.13.19
thyrotoxicosis
34.2.17(.11.1)
thyrotropin 28.2.9
thyroxine 28.1.18(.7)
thyrsi 14.18
thyrsus 34.18.20
Thysanoptera
17.32.14(.6)
thysanopteran
28.17.31(.11)
thysanopterous
34.18.27(.14)
Thysanura 17.32.14(.3)
thysanuran 28.17.31(.11)
thysanurous
34.18.27(.11)
thyself 30.20.2
Thyssen 28.17.23(.1)
ti 2
Tia Maria® 17.1.16
Tiananmen Square 6
tiara 17.32.7
Tibbett 22.2.6
Tibbitts 34.22.2
Tibbs 35.21
Tiber 17.11.11
Tiberias 34.3.15(.2), 34.7.2
Tiberius 34.3.15(.2)
Tibesti 1.10.26(.4)
Tibet 22.5.2
Tibetan 28.17.11(.4)
tibia 3.3.2
tibiae 2.3
tibial 40.3.2
tibiotarsi 14.18
tibiotarsus 34.18.20
Tibullus 34.18.29(.15)
tic 24.2
tice 34.15
Tichborne 28.11.2
Ticino 19.15.1
tick 24.2
tick-bird 23.19.1
ticker 17.14.2

tickertape 20.3
ticket 22.2.9(.1)
ticketless 34.18.29(.22)
ticket-of-leave man 28.7
ticket-of-leave men 28.5
tickety-boo 16.6
ticking 29.1.14(.2)
tickle 40.23.2
tickler 17.34.23
tickless 34.18.29(.24)
ticklish 36.2.27
ticklishly 1.31.35(.7.4)
ticklishness
34.18.16(.33.6)
tickly 1.31.17(.11),
1.31.24(.2)
tickover 17.21.14(.6)
tick-tock 24.9.4
ticky-tacky 1.12.5
Ticonderoga 17.16.15
tic-tac 24.6.7
tic-tac-toe 19.10
tidal 40.22.11
tidally 1.31.17(.10)
tidbit 22.2.6
tiddledywink 24.19.1(.6)
tiddler 17.34.22
Tiddles 35.30.17
tiddly 1.31.17(.10),
1.31.23(.1)
tiddlywink 24.19.1(.6)
tide 23.15
tideland 23.24.6(.13)
tideless 34.18.29(.23)
tideline 28.14.19(.15)
tidemark 24.8.8
Tidenham 27.15.14(.11)
Tideswell 40.5.17(.16)
tidewaiter 17.12.4(.14)
tidewater 17.12.10(.7)
tidewave 31.3.6
tideway 4.25.13
tidily 1.31.17(.10)
tidiness 34.18.16(.2.3)
tidings 35.27
Tidmarsh 36.8
tidy 1.11.14
tie 14
tieback 24.6.6(.7)
tiebreak 24.3.13
tie-breaker 17.14.3(.8)
tie-breaking 29.1.14(.3)
tie-dye 14.9
tieless 34.18.29(.14)
Tientsin 28.2.23
tiepin 28.2.9
Tiepolo 19.29.12
tier 3, 17.6
tierce 34.3
tiercel 40.31.3, 40.31.13

t

tiercet **22.19.18**
Tierney **1.16.3**
Tierra del Fuego **19.13.3**
tiff **30.2**
tiffany **1.16.15(.12)**
tiffin **28.2.19**
Tiflis **34.2.22(.12)**
tig **26.2**
tiger **17.16.10**
tigerish **36.2.25**
tigerishly **1.31.35(.7.4)**
tiger moth **32.9**
Tigers **35.18.11**
tiger's-eye **14.19**
tigerskin **28.2.13(.14)**
Tighe **14**
tight **22.16**
tighten **28.17.11(.12)**
tightener **17.18.16(.4)**
tight-fisted **23.18.9(.20)**
tight-fistedly **1.31.23(.14.3)**
tight-fistedness **34.18.16(.21.1)**
tightly **1.31.22(.13)**
tightness **34.18.16(.20.2)**
tightrope **20.15.8**
tightwad **23.10.11**
Tiglath-pileser **17.25.1**
tiglic **24.2.27(.17)**
tigon **28.10.12, 28.17.15(.11)**
Tigray **4.26.14**
Tigrayan **28.17.2**
tigress **34.5.14(.8), 34.18.27(.17)**
Tigrinya **17.33.9**
Tigris **34.18.27(.17)**
Tijuana **17.18.8(.10)**
tiki **1.12.1**
tikka **17.14.1, 17.14.2**
'til **40.2**
til **40.2**
tilapia **3.2.3, 3.2.4**
Tilburg **26.14.1(.12)**
tilbury **1.29.11(.7.2)**
Tilda **17.13.23(.2)**
tilde **1.11.23, 17.13.23(.2)**
Tilden **28.17.12(.27)**
tile **40.13**
Tilehurst **22.29.16**
tiler **17.34.13**
tiling **29.1.31(.10)**
till **40.2**
tillable **40.20.16(.29)**
tillage **39.2.23**
tiller **17.34.2**
Tilley **1.31.2**
Tilley lamp® **20.16.3**
Tillich **24.2.27(.2)**

Tilly **1.31.2**
Tilsit **22.2.16, 22.2.17**
tilt **22.32.1**
tilter **17.12.26(.1)**
tilth **32.24**
tilt-hammer **17.17.6**
tiltyard **23.9.21**
Tim **27.2**
Timaru **16.23.6**
timbal **40.20.19**
timbale **40.8.3, 40.20.19**
timber **17.11.17(.1)**
timberjack **24.6.22**
Timberlake **24.3.14**
timberland **23.24.6(.13)**
timberline **28.14.19(.11)**
timberwork **24.16.14**
timbre **17.11.17(.1)**
timbrel **40.16.13(.15)**
Timbuktu **16.7**
time **27.12**
time-expired **23.18.3**
timekeeper **17.10.1**
timekeeping **29.1.10(.1)**
timeless **34.18.29(.26)**
timelessly **1.31.33(.12.6)**
timelessness **34.18.16(.31.6)**
timeliness **34.18.16(.2.10)**
timely **1.31.26(.10)**
timeous **34.18.15(.8)**
timeously **1.31.33(.12.3)**
time-out **22.9**
timepiece **34.1.1**
timer **17.17.11**
Times **35.25.8**
timesaving **29.1.20**
timescale **40.4.4**
timeserver **17.21.13**
timeserving **29.1.20**
timeshare **6.14**
time-sharing **29.1.30(.4)**
timesheet **22.1.11**
timetable **40.20.4**
timework **24.17.6(.12)**
timeworker **17.14.16**
timeworn **28.11.11**
Timex® **34.23.4(.5)**
timid **23.2.12**
timidity **1.10.16(.9)**
timidly **1.31.23(.14.6)**
timidness **34.18.16(.21.1)**
timing **29.1.16**
Timisoara **17.32.7**
Timms **35.25.2**
Timmy **1.15.2**
timocracy **1.22.16(.13)**
timocratic **24.2.10(.4.5)**
Timon **28.10.13, 28.17.16(.13)**

Timor **12.9.1**
Timorese **35.1, 35.1.22**
timorous **34.18.27(.18)**
timorously **1.31.33(.12.5)**
timorousness **34.18.16(.31.5)**
Timotei® **4.9.7**
timothy **1.20.8**
timpani **1.16.15(.5)**
timpanist **22.29.2(.18.1)**
Timpson **28.17.23(.17)**
tin **28.2**
tinamou **16.11**
tinctorial **40.3.14(.5)**
tincture **17.28.20, 17.28.23**
tindal **40.22.16**
Tindale **40.4.3**
Tindall **40.10.6, 40.22.16**
Tindell **40.5.4**
tinder **17.13.20(.1)**
tinderbox **34.23.8(.2)**
tindery **1.29.11(.9)**
tine **28.14**
tinea **3.9.2**
tinfoil **40.11.7**
ting **29.1**
tinge **39.17.1**
tinged **23.29**
tingle **40.24.14(.1)**
tingly **1.31.17(.12), 1.31.28(.1)**
Tingwall **40.10.17**
tinhorn **28.11.10**
tinily **1.31.17(.14.1)**
tininess **34.18.16(.2.5)**
tinker **17.14.21(.1)**
tinkerer **17.32.14(.8)**
tinkering **29.1.30(.8)**
tinkle **40.23.15**
tinkling **29.1.31(.19)**
tinkly **1.31.17(.11), 1.31.24(.12)**
tinner **17.18.2**
tinnily **1.31.17(.14.1)**
tinniness **34.18.16(.2.5)**
tinnitus **34.18.11(.8)**
tinny **1.16.2**
Tin Pan Alley **1.31.7**
tinpot **22.11.2**
tinsel **40.31.21**
tinselly **1.31.17(.20)**
Tinseltown **28.8.1**
Tinsley **1.31.34**
tinsmith **32.2.3**
tinsnips **34.21.2**
tinstone **28.19.4(.9)**
tint **22.26.1**
tintack **24.6.7**
Tintagel **40.34**
tinter **17.12.22(.1)**

Tintern **28.17.11(.22)**
tintinnabula **17.34.16(.21.1)**
tintinnabular **17.34.16(.21.1)**
tintinnabulary **1.29.11(.27)**
tintinnabulation **28.17.25(.3.14)**
tintinnabulous **34.18.29(.17.6)**
tintinnabulum **27.15.28(.11)**
Tintoretto **19.10.4**
tintype **20.10.2**
tinware **6.18.11**
tiny **1.16.13**
Tío Pepe® **1.8.4**
tip **20.2**
tip-and-run **28.13.9**
tip-cart **22.10.5**
tipcat **22.7.9**
tipless **34.18.29(.20)**
tipper **17.10.2**
Tipperary **1.29.4**
tippet **22.2.5**
Tippett **22.2.5**
Tipp-Ex® **34.23.4(.1)**
tipple **40.19.2**
tippler **17.34.19**
tippy **1.8.2**
tipsily **1.31.17(.20)**
tipsiness **34.18.16(.2.7)**
tipstaff **30.7.2**
tipstaves **35.28.2**
tipster **17.12.24(.16)**
tipsy **1.22.19**
tipsy-cake **24.3.6**
tiptoe **19.10.15**
tiptop **20.7.4**
tirade **23.4.15**
tirailleur **18**
tiramisu **16.15**
Tirana **17.18.8(.11)**
tire **17.6**
tiredly **1.31.23(.14.1)**
tiredness **34.18.16(.21.1)**
Tiree **2.30**
tire gauge **39.4**
tireless **34.18.29(.17.1)**
tirelessly **1.31.33(.12.6)**
tirelessness **34.18.16(.31.6)**
Tiresias **34.3.10, 34.7.2**
tiresome **27.15.20(.11)**
tiresomely **1.31.26(.11)**
tiresomeness **34.18.16(.24)**
Tirpitz **34.22.2**
'tis **35.2**
tisane **28.7.15**

Tishri 2.30.15
Tisiphone 1.16.15(.12)
Tissot 19.20.1
tissue 16.17, 16.24.14
tit 22.2
titan 28.17.11(.12)
titanate 22.4.14(.9.1)
Titaness 34.5,
  34.18.16(.15.2)
Titania 3.9.3(.2), 3.9.6
titanic 24.2.15(.5)
titanically 1.31.24(.9.8)
titanium 27.3.8(.3)
titbit 22.2.6
titch 38.2
titchiness 34.18.16(.2.8)
titchy 1.25.2
titfer 17.20.15
tit-for-tat 22.7.7
tithable 40.20.16(.20)
tithe 33.7
tithing 29.1.22
Tithonus 34.18.16(.17)
titi 2.11, 2.12.1, 14.8
Titian 28.17.25(.2.1)
Titicaca 10.8.4, 17.14.7
titillate 22.4.23(.7.1)
titillatingly 1.31.28(.1.4)
titillation 28.17.25(.3.14)
titivate 22.4.16
titivation 28.17.25(.3.9)
titlark 24.8.16
title 40.21.10
titleholder 17.13.23(.8)
Titmarsh 36.8
titmice 34.15.5
titmouse 34.8.4
Titmus 34.18.15(.13)
Tito 19.10.1
Titograd 23.7.16
Titoism 27.15.21(.2.1)
Titoist 22.29.2(.10)
titrant 22.26.15(.23.4)
titratable 40.20.16(.11.1)
titrate 22.4.22(.8)
titration 28.17.25(.3.13)
titre 17.12.13
titter 17.12.2
titterer 17.32.14(.6)
titteringly 1.31.28(.1.17)
tittle 40.21.2
tittlebat 22.7.6
tittle-tattle 40.21.5
tittup 20.13.1
tittuppy 1.8.11(.3)
titty 1.10.2
titubation 28.17.25(.3.2)
titular 17.34.16(.18)
titularly 1.31.17(.29)
Titus 34.18.11(.8)

Tiverton 28.17.11(.15)
Tivoli 1.31.17(.17)
tiz 35.2
Tizard 23.9.16, 23.18.21
Tizer® 17.25.12
tizz 35.2
tizzy 1.23.2
T-joint 22.26.11
T-junction 28.17.25(.15.6)
TKO 19
Tlaxcala 17.34.8
Tlemcen 28.5.10
Tlingit 22.2.10
tmesis 34.2.17(.1)
TNT 2.11
to 16
toad 23.20
toadfish 36.2.18(.16)
toadflax 34.23.5(.15)
toad-in-the-hole 40.18.13
toadish 36.2.12
toadlet 22.19.26(.18)
toadlike 24.13.7(.13)
toadstone 28.19.4(.9)
toadstool 40.15.3
toady 1.11.19
toadyish 36.2.1
toadyism 27.15.21(.2.1)
to-and-fro 19.27.20
toast 22.29.17
toasted 23.18.9(.20)
toaster 17.12.24(.15)
toastie 1.10.26(.13)
toastmaster 17.12.24(.5)
toastmistress
  34.18.27(.14)
toast rack 24.6.21
toasty 1.10.26(.13)
tobacco 19.12.5
tobacconist 22.29.2(.18.1)
Tobagan 28.17.15(.3)
Tobago 19.13.3
Tobagonian 28.3.8(.11)
Tobermory 1.29.8
Tobias 34.18.5
Tobin 28.2.10
Tobit 22.2.6
Toblerone® 28.19.17
toboggan 28.17.15(.8)
tobogganer 17.18.16(.7)
tobogganist 22.29.2(.18.1)
Tobruk 24.14.10
toby 1.9.13
toccata 17.12.8(.5)
Toc H 38.3
Tocharian 28.3.20(.4)
tocher 17.14.8, 17.15
tocopherol 40.9.19
Tocqueville 40.2.12
tocsin 28.2.23(.14)

tod 23.10
today 4.10
Todd 23.10
toddle 40.22.7
toddler 17.34.22
toddlerhood 23.16.5(.3)
toddy 1.11.10
todger 17.29.8
Todhunter 17.12.22(.10)
Todmorden 28.17.12(.16)
to-do 16.8
tody 1.11.19
toe 19
toea 17.5
toecap 20.5.1
toehold 23.31.13(.9)
toeless 34.18.29(.19)
toenail 40.4.7
toey 1(.7)
toff 30.8
toffee 1.18.5
toffeeish 36.2.1
toffee-nosed 23.28.4
toft 22.27.5
tofu 16.13
tog 26.7
toga 17.16.15
together 17.23.4
togetherness
  34.18.16(.15.3)
toggery 1.29.11(.11)
toggle 40.24.6
Togo 19.13.11
Togolese 35.1.23
toil 40.11
toile 40.8
toiler 17.34.11
toilet 22.19.26(.9)
toiletry 1.29.15(.13)
toilette 22.5.21
toilsome 27.15.20(.22)
toilsomely 1.31.26(.11)
toilsomeness
  34.18.16(.24)
toilworn 28.11.11
toing and froing 29.1.9
toings and froings 35.27
Tojo 19.25
tokamak 24.6.10
tokay 4.11
toke 24.18
Tokelau 9.17
token 28.17.13(.15)
tokenism 27.15.21(.2.9)
tokenist 22.29.2(.18.1)
tokenistic 24.2.10(.15.2)
Toklas 34.18.29(.24)
Tok Pisin 28.2.23(.1)
Tokugawa 17.31.2
Tokyo 15.1.4

tola 17.34.18
tolbooth 32.13
tolbutamide 23.15.7
told 23.31.13
Toledo 19.11.1, 19.11.4
tolerability 1.10.16(.22.1)
tolerable 40.20.16(.27.5)
tolerableness
  34.18.16(.37.4)
tolerably 1.31.21(.8)
tolerance 34.24.10(.16)
tolerant 22.26.15(.23.3)
tolerantly 1.31.22(.20.5)
tolerate 22.4.22(.6)
toleration 28.17.25(.3.13)
tolerator 17.12.4(.15)
Tolima 17.17.1
Tolkien 28.1.11
toll 40.18
tollbooth 32.13, 33.8
tollbridge 39.2.22(.10)
Tolley 1.31.10
tollgate 22.4.12(.13)
tollhouse 34.8.6(.24)
tollroad 23.20.12
Tollund 23.24.16(.16.2)
tollway 4.25.26
Tolpuddle 40.22.10
Tolstoy 13.4
Toltec 24.4.4
Toltecan 28.17.13(.4)
tolu 16.25
toluene 28.1.4
toluic 24.2.6
toluol 40.9.4
tom 27.9
tomahawk 24.10.8
tomalley 1.31.7
tomatillo 19.28, 19.29.2
tomato 19.10.7
tomatoey 1(.7)
tomb 27.14
tombac 24.6.6(.16)
tombak 24.6.6(.16)
Tombaugh 12.4
tombola 17.34.18(.2)
tombolo 19.29.14
tomboy 13.3
tomboyish 36.2.3
tomboyishness
  34.18.16(.33.1)
tombstone 28.19.4(.9)
tomcat 22.7.9
tome 27.17
tomenta 17.12.22(.3)
tomentose 34.20.4
tomentous 34.18.11(.14)
tomentum 27.15.9(.14)
tomfool 40.15.6
tomfoolery 1.29.11(.27)

Tomintoul **40.15.3**
Tomlin **28.2.31(.19)**
Tomlinson **28.17.23(.24)**
tommy **1.15.8**
tommyrot **22.11.15**
tomogram **27.6.17(.5)**
tomograph **30.7.5(.1)**
tomographic **24.2.16(.3)**
tomography **1.18.9(.3.2)**
Tomor **17.17.16**
tomorrow **19.27.6**
tompion **28.3.1**
Tompkins **35.26.2**
Tompkinson **28.17.23(.24)**
tompot **22.11.2**
Toms **35.25.6**
Tomsk **24.20.12**
tomtit **22.2.7**
tomtom **27.9**
ton **11, 28.13**
tonal **40.26.15**
tonality **1.10.16(.32.8)**
tonally **1.31.17(.14.3)**
Tonbridge **39.2.22(.10)**
tondi **1.11.20(.5)**
tondo **19.11.14**
tone **28.19**
tonearm **27.8.7**
toneburst **22.29.16**
tone-deaf **30.4**
toneless **34.18.29(.27)**
tonelessly **1.31.33(.12.6)**
tonelessness **34.18.16(.31.6)**
toneme **27.1.6**
tonemic **24.2.14(.1)**
tonemically **1.31.24(.9.8)**
tonepad **23.7.5**
toner **17.18.18**
tone-row **19.27.19**
tonetic **24.2.10(.3.1)**
tonetically **1.31.24(.9.3)**
tong **29.6**
tonga **17.16.17(.3), 17.19.3**
Tongan **28.17.15(.16), 28.17.18**
Tonge **29.6, 29.8, 39.17.7**
tongkang **29.4.5**
tongue **29.8**
tongue-and-groove **31.10**
tongue-in-cheek **24.1.8**
tongue-lashing **29.1.25**
tongueless **34.18.29(.28)**
tongue-tie **14.8**
tonguing **29.1.18**
Toni **1.16.17**
tonic **24.2.15(.6.1)**
tonically **1.31.24(.9.8)**

tonicity **1.10.16(.16.1)**
tonic sol-fa **10.12**
tonify **14.14.4(.7)**
tonight **22.16.14**
tonish **36.2.16(.15)**
Tonkin **28.2.13**
Tonks **34.23.18**
ton-mile **40.13.7**
tonnage **39.2.15**
tonne **28.13**
tonneau **19.15.8**
tonneaux **35.20.8**
tonometer **17.12.16(.9.2)**
tonsil **40.31.21**
tonsillar **17.34.16(.15)**
tonsillectomy **1.15.13(.1)**
tonsillitis **34.18.11(.8)**
tonsorial **40.3.14(.5)**
tonsure **17.7.12(.11), 17.26.21, 17.33.11**
tontine **28.1.9, 28.14.5**
Tonto **19.10.17**
Tonton Macoute **22.18.4**
ton-up **20.9.9**
tonus **34.18.16(.17)**
tony **1.16.17**
Tonypandy **1.11.20(.4)**
Tonyrefail **40.13.10**
too **16**
toodle-oo **16**
toodle-pip **20.2.1**
Toogood **23.16.3**
took **24.14**
tool **40.15**
toolbox **34.23.8(.2)**
toolchest **22.29.5(.8)**
tooler **17.34.15**
toolkit **22.2.9(.11)**
toolmaker **17.14.3(.3)**
toolmaking **29.1.14(.3)**
toolroom **27.14.6(.20)**
toolshed **23.5.12**
Toombs **35.25.9**
toot **22.18**
Tootal **40.21.11**
tooter **17.12.15**
tooth **32.13**
toothache **24.3.9**
tooth-billed **23.31.2**
toothbrush **36.12**
toothcomb **27.17.6**
tooth-glass **34.9.7**
toothily **1.31.17(.18)**
toothiness **34.18.16(.2.6)**
toothless **34.18.29(.31)**
toothlike **24.13.7(.21)**
toothpaste **22.29.4**
toothpick **24.2.8(.10)**
toothsome **27.15.20(.20)**
toothsomely **1.31.26(.11)**

toothsomeness **34.18.16(.24)**
toothwort **22.20.15**
toothy **1.20.7**
Tooting **29.1.12(.13)**
tootle **40.21.11**
tootler **17.34.21**
too-too **16.7, 16.7.3**
tootsie **1.22.21**
Toowoomba **17.11.17(.7)**
top **20.7**
topaz **35.7**
topazolite **22.16.25(.9)**
topboot **22.18.3**
topcoat **22.21.5**
top-dress **34.5.14(.6)**
tope **20.15**
Topeka **17.14.1**
toper **17.10.16**
topgallant **22.26.15(.25)**
Topham **27.15.7**
top-hamper **17.10.17**
top-hatted **23.18.9(.5)**
top-heavily **1.31.17(.17)**
top-heaviness **34.18.16(.2.6)**
top-heavy **1.19.4**
Tophet **22.2.13**
tophi **14.14.5**
tophus **34.18.17**
topi **2.9**
topiarian **28.3.20(.4)**
topiarist **22.29.2(.29.1)**
topiary **1.29.2(.1)**
topic **24.2.8(.5)**
topical **40.23.12(.5)**
topicality **1.10.16(.32.5)**
topicalization **28.17.25(.2.13)**
topicalize **35.15.21(.4.4)**
topically **1.31.24(.9.2)**
topknot **22.11.9**
Toplady **1.11.4**
topless **34.18.29(.20)**
toplessness **34.18.16(.31.6)**
toplofty **1.10.24**
topman **28.7.10(.9)**
topmast **22.29.6(.7), 22.29.8(.5)**
topmen **28.5.7(.13)**
topmost **22.29.17(.4)**
topnotch **38.8**
top-notcher **17.28.9**
topo **19.8**
topographer **17.20.12(.5)**
topographic **24.2.16(.3)**
topographical **40.23.12(.12)**
topographically **1.31.24(.9.9)**

topography **1.18.9(.3.2)**
topoi **13.2**
topological **40.23.12(.17.2)**
topologically **1.31.24(.9.11)**
topologist **22.29.2(.26.3)**
topology **1.26.10(.11.2)**
Topolsky **1.12.17(.15)**
toponym **27.2.6**
toponymic **24.2.14(.2)**
toponymy **1.15.13(.5)**
topos **34.10.6**
topper **17.10.8**
topping **29.1.10(.6)**
topple **40.19.7**
topsail **40.4.10, 40.31.15**
topside **23.15.11(.7)**
topslice **34.15.10**
top-slicing **29.1.23**
topsoil **40.11.8**
topspin **28.2.9**
topstitch **38.2.3**
Topsy **1.22.19**
topsy-turvily **1.31.17(.17)**
topsy-turviness **34.18.16(.2.6)**
topsy-turvy **1.19.11**
top-up **20.9.4**
toque **24.18**
toquilla **17.1.5, 17.33.1**
tor **12**
Torah **10.23, 17.32.10, 17.32.16**
Torbay **4.8**
torc **24.10**
torch **38.9**
torch-bearer **17.32.5**
torchère **6.14**
torchlight **22.16.25(.21)**
torchlit **22.2.25**
torchon **28.10.20, 28.17.25(.8)**
Tordoff **30.8.5**
tore **12**
toreador **12.6.2**
torero **19.27.3**
toreutic **24.2.10(.9)**
Torfaen **28.14.11**
torgoch **24.9.7, 25.6**
tori **14.24.4**
toric **24.2.26(.7)**
torii **2.3**
Torino **19.15.1**
torment **22.26.4(.8), 22.26.15(.13.1)**
tormentedly **1.31.23(.14.3)**
tormentil **40.2.5**
tormentingly **1.31.28(.1.4)**

tormentor **17.12.22(.3)**
torn **28.11**
tornadic **24.2.11(.5)**
tornado **19.11.4**
Tornio **15.1.6**
toroid **23.13.19**
toroidal **40.22.9**
toroidally **1.31.17(.10)**
Toronto **19.10.17**
torose **34.20.16**
torpedo **19.11.1**
torpefy **14.14.4(.2)**
torpid **23.2.6**
torpidity **1.10.16(.9)**
torpidly **1.31.23(.14.2)**
torpidness **34.18.16(.21.1)**
torpor **17.10.9**
torporific **24.2.16(.1)**
torquate **22.4.21**
Torquay **2.14**
torque **24.10**
Torquemada **17.13.7**
torr **12**
Torrance **34.24.10(.16)**
torrefaction
  28.17.25(.15.3)
torrefy **14.14.4(.14)**
Torremolinos **34.10.13**
torrent **22.26.15(.23.2)**
torrential **40.33.12(.3)**
torrentially **1.31.17(.22)**
Torres **34.2.21, 35.2.17**
Torrez **34.2.21**
Torricelli **1.31.5**
torrid **23.2.22**
torridity **1.10.16(.9)**
torridly **1.31.23(.14.7)**
torridness **34.18.16(.21.1)**
torse **34.12**
torsel **40.31.9**
Tórshavn **28.17.20(.6)**
torsion **28.17.25(.8)**
torsional **40.26.13(.14.5)**
torsionally **1.31.17(.14.3)**
torsionless **34.18.29(.27)**
torsk **24.20.6**
torso **19.20.7**
tort **22.13**
torte **17.12.10, 22.13**
Tortelier **4.2.10**
tortellini **1.16.1**
tortelloni **1.16.17**
torten **28.17.11(.10)**
tortfeasor **17.25.1**
torticollis **34.2.22(.6)**
tortilla **17.33.1**
tortious **34.18.22(.5)**
tortiously **1.31.33(.12.4)**
tortoise **34.13, 34.18.11(.7),
  35.13**

tortoise-like **24.13.7(.22)**
tortoiseshell **40.5.13**
Tortola **17.34.18(.3)**
tortrices **35.1.16(.10)**
tortrix **34.23.2(.12)**
tortuosity **1.10.16(.16.2)**
tortuous **34.18.6**
tortuously **1.31.33(.12.1)**
tortuousness
  34.18.16(.31.2)
torturable **40.20.16(.27.5)**
torture **17.28.10**
torturer **17.32.14(.19)**
torturous **34.18.27(.26)**
torturously **1.31.33(.12.5)**
torula **17.34.15,
  17.34.16(.21.4)**
torulae **2.32.8, 2.32.9(.8)**
torus **34.18.27(.8)**
Torvill **40.2.12**
Tory **1.29.8**
Toryism **27.15.21(.2.1)**
Toscana **17.18.8(.3)**
Toscanini **1.16.1(.8)**
tosh **36.9**
Toshack **24.6.16**
Tosk **24.20.5**
toss **34.10**
tosser **17.24.9**
tosspot **22.11.2**
toss-up **20.9.12**
tostada **17.13.7**
tostado **19.11.7**
tot **22.11**
total **40.21.14**
totalitarian **28.3.20(.4)**
totalitarianism
  27.15.21(.2.9)
totality **1.10.16(.32.3)**
totalization
  28.17.25(.3.12)
totalizator **17.12.4(.13)**
totalize **35.15.21(.4.3)**
totalizer **17.25.12(.15)**
totally **1.31.17(.9.2)**
totaquine **28.1.24**
tote **22.21**
totem **27.15.9(.11)**
totemic **24.2.14(.3)**
totemism **27.15.21(.2.8)**
totemist **22.29.2(.17)**
totemistic **24.2.10(.15.2)**
toter **17.12.18**
t'other **17.23.10**
totipotent **22.26.15(.9)**
Totnes **34.18.16(.20.2)**
toto **19.10.14**
Tottenham **27.15.14(.11)**
totter **17.12.9**
totterer **17.32.14(.6)**

tottery **1.29.11(.8.4)**
totting-up **20.9**
totty **1.10.9**
toucan **28.7.8,
  28.17.13(.12)**
touch **38.11**
touchable **40.20.16(.24)**
touch-and-go **19.13**
touchback **24.6.6(.22)**
touchdown **28.8.2(.12)**
touché **4.20**
toucher **17.28.11**
touchily **1.31.17(.24)**
touchiness **34.18.16(.2.8)**
touchingly **1.31.28(.1.15)**
touchingness
  34.18.16(.26)
touch-in-goal **40.18.8**
touchline **28.14.19(.23)**
touch-me-not **22.11.9**
touchpad **23.7.5**
touchpaper **17.10.3**
touchstone **28.19.4(.9)**
touchwood **23.16.6(.20)**
touchy **1.25.10**
Tough **25.9, 30.11**
tough **30.11**
toughen **28.17.19**
toughener **17.18.16(.10)**
toughie **1.18.7**
toughish **36.2.18(.8)**
toughly **1.31.29**
tough-minded
  23.18.10(.14)
tough-mindedness
  34.18.16(.21.1)
toughness **34.18.16(.27)**
Toulon **11.19**
Toulouse **35.17.8**
Toulouse-Lautrec
  24.4.12
toupée **4.7**
tour **12, 17.7**
touraco **19.12.12**
tour de force **34.12**
tourer **17.32.14(.3)**
touring car **10**
tourism **27.15.21(.2.14)**
tourist **22.29.2(.29.2)**
touristic **24.2.10(.15.2)**
touristically **1.31.24(.9.6)**
touristy **1.10.26(.11)**
tourmaline **28.1.27(.7)**
Tournai **4.14**
tournament
  22.26.15(.13.2)
tournedos **19.11.11**
tourney **1.16.10,
  1.16.15(.4), 1.16.16**
tourniquet **4.11**
Tours **17.7, 35.18.5**

tousle **40.32.6**
tousle-haired **23.6**
tous-les-mois **10.22.8**
tout **22.9**
tout court **12**
tout de suite **22.1**
tout ensemble **40.20.19**
touter **17.12.7**
tovarish **36.2.25**
Tovey **1.19.7, 1.19.12**
tow **19**
towable **40.20.16(.8)**
towage **39.2.7**
toward **23.12.8**
towbar **10.5.6**
towboat **22.21.2**
Towcester **17.12.24(.15)**
towel **40.16.3**
towelling **29.1.31(.7)**
tower **17.3, 17.9**
Towers **35.18.2**
towery **1.29.11(.1)**
towhead **23.5.13(.6)**
tow-headed **23.18.10(.3)**
towhee **2.28**
towline **28.14.19(.12)**
town **28.8**
town crier **17.6**
Towne **28.8**
Townes **35.26.8**
town hall **40.10**
townhouse **34.8.6(.16)**
townie **1.16.7**
townish **36.2.16(.6)**
townless **34.18.29(.27)**
townlet **22.19.26(.22)**
Townley **1.31.27(.7)**
town-major **17.29.3**
townscape **20.3**
Townsend **23.24.5(.12)**
townsfolk **24.18.7**
township **20.2.7(.19)**
townsman **28.17.16(.30)**
townspeople **40.19.1**
Townsville **40.2.12**
townswoman
  28.17.16(.14)
townswomen **28.2.17(.1)**
Townswomen's Guild
  23.31.2
townward **23.18.26(.13)**
towny **1.16.7**
towpath **32.8**
towplane **28.4.19**
towrope **20.15.8**
Towy **1(.3)**
towy **1(.7)**
Towyn **28.2.4**
toxaemia **3.8.1**
toxaemic **24.2.14(.1)**

toxaphene **28.1.15**
toxic **24.2.20(.13)**
toxically **1.31.24(.9.10)**
toxicant **22.26.15(.11)**
toxicity **1.10.16(.16.1)**
toxicological **40.23.12(.17.2)**
toxicologist **22.29.2(.26.3)**
toxicology **1.26.10(.11.3)**
toxicomania **3.9.3(.5)**
toxigenic **24.2.15(.4)**
toxigenicity **1.10.16(.16.1)**
toxin **28.2.23(.14)**
toxocara **17.32.7**
toxocariasis **34.2.17(.10.1)**
toxophilite **22.16.25(.9)**
toxophily **1.31.17(.16.1)**
toxoplasmosis **34.2.17(.11.2)**
Toxteth **32.5, 32.14.8**
toy **13**
Toyah **17.5**
toyboy **13.3**
toylike **24.13.7(.7)**
toymaker **17.14.3(.3)**
Toynbee **1.9.19**
Toyota® **17.12.18**
toyshop **20.7.9**
toystore **12.5.9**
toytown **28.8.1**
Tozer **17.25.15**
T-piece **34.1.1**
trabeate **22.4.2(.2)**
trabeation **28.17.25(.3.1)**
trabecula **17.34.16(.21.2)**
trabeculae **2.32.9(.8)**
trabecular **17.34.16(.21.2)**
trabeculate **22.19.26(.13)**
tracasserie **1.29.11(.18)**
trace **34.4**
traceability **1.10.16(.22.1)**
traceable **40.20.16(.21.1)**
traceableness **34.18.16(.37.4)**
trace-horse **34.12.7**
traceless **34.18.29(.33)**
tracer **17.24.4**
traceried **23.2.22**
tracery **1.29.11(.18)**
trachea **3.6.3, 17.1.5**
tracheae **2.2, 2.3**
tracheal **40.3.5, 40.16.1**
tracheate **22.4.1, 22.4.2(.5)**
tracheostomy **1.15.13(.1)**
tracheotomy **1.15.13(.1)**
trachoma **17.17.16(.4)**
trachomatous **34.18.11(.10)**
trachyte **22.16.11**

trachytic **24.2.10(.2.1)**
tracing **29.1.23**
track **24.6**
trackage **39.2.12**
track-and-field **23.31.1(.2)**
trackbed **23.5.2**
tracker **17.14.5**
tracking **29.1.14(.4)**
tracklayer **17.2.10**
tracklaying **29.1.3**
tracklement **22.26.15(.13.7)**
trackless **34.18.29(.24)**
tracklessness **34.18.16(.31.6)**
trackman **28.7.10(.13), 28.17.16(.23)**
trackmen **28.5.7(.17)**
trackside **23.15.11(.11)**
tracksuit **22.18.6**
trackway **4.25.14**
tract **22.23.5**
tractability **1.10.16(.22.1)**
tractable **40.20.16(.11.5)**
tractableness **34.18.16(.37.4)**
tractably **1.31.21(.4.3)**
Tractarian **28.3.20(.4)**
tractarian **28.3.20(.4)**
Tractarianism **27.15.21(.2.9)**
tractate **22.4.9(.7)**
traction **28.17.25(.15.3)**
tractional **40.26.13(.14.6)**
tractive **31.2.1(.13.3)**
tractor **17.12.21(.3)**
tractorfeed **23.1.6**
Tracy **1.22.4**
trad **23.7**
tradable **40.20.16(.12)**
trade **23.4**
trademark **24.8.8**
trader **17.13.3**
tradescantia **3.4.12**
tradesman **28.17.16(.30)**
tradespeople **40.19.1**
trades union **28.3.8(.9)**
trades unionist **22.29.2(.18.1)**
trade union **28.3.8(.9)**
trade unionism **27.15.21(.2.9)**
trade unionist **22.29.2(.18.1)**
trade-weighted **23.18.9(.3)**
tradewind **23.24.2**
tradition **28.17.25(.2.3)**
traditional **40.26.13(.14.1)**

traditionalism **27.15.21(.2.15)**
traditionalist **22.29.2(.31.3)**
traditionalistic **24.2.10(.15.3)**
traditionally **1.31.17(.14.3)**
traditionary **1.29.11(.13.2)**
traditionist **22.29.2(.18.2)**
traditionless **34.18.29(.27)**
traditor **17.12.16(.6)**
traditores **35.1.22**
traduce **34.17.13**
traducement **22.26.15(.13.5)**
traducer **17.24.14**
traducian **28.3.13, 28.17.25(11)**
traducianism **27.15.21(.2.9)**
traducianist **22.29.2(.18.1)**
Trafalgar **10.9, 17.16.19**
traffic **24.2.16(.3)**
trafficator **17.12.4(.7)**
trafficker **17.14.15(.10)**
trafficless **34.18.29(.24)**
Trafford **23.18.16(.5)**
tragacanth **32.21**
tragedian **28.3.4(.1)**
tragedienne **28.5**
tragedy **1.11.17**
tragi **14.11, 14.21**
tragic **24.2.24(.2)**
tragical **40.23.12(.17.1)**
tragically **1.31.24(.9.11)**
tragicomedy **1.11.17**
tragicomic **24.2.14(.6)**
tragicomical **40.23.12(.10)**
tragicomically **1.31.24(.9.8)**
tragopan **28.7.4**
tragus **34.18.14(.2)**
Traherne **28.18.12**
trahison des clercs **6**
trail **40.4**
trailblazer **17.25.3**
trailblazing **29.1.24**
trailer **17.34.4**
train **28.4**
trainability **1.10.16(.22.1)**
trainable **40.20.16(.16.1)**
trainband **23.24.6(.4)**
trainee **2.17**
traineeship **20.2.7(.1)**
trainer **17.18.3**
trainless **34.18.29(.27)**

trainload **23.20.13**
trainman **28.7.10(.15)**
trainmen **28.5.7(.19)**
train-mile **40.13.7**
trainsick **24.2.20(.15)**
trainsickness **34.18.16(.22)**
traipse **34.21.3**
trait **4, 22.4**
traitor **17.12.4**
traitorous **34.18.27(.14)**
traitorously **1.31.33(.12.5)**
traitorousness **34.18.16(.31.5)**
traitress **34.18.27(.14)**
Trajan **28.17.28(.3)**
trajectory **1.29.11(.8.12)**
tra-la **10.25**
Tralee **2.32**
tram **27.6**
tramcar **10.8.14**
Traminer **17.18.1(.6)**
tramline **28.14.19(.18)**
trammel **40.25.4**
trammie **1.15.6**
tramontana **17.18.8(.2)**
tramontane **28.4.3**
tramp **20.16.3**
tramper **17.10.17**
trampish **36.2.9**
trample **40.19.14**
trampled **23.31.14**
trampler **17.34.19**
trampoline **28.1.27**
trampolinist **22.29.2(.18.1)**
tramway **4.25.16**
trance **34.24.6**
tranche **38.18.4**
Tranmere **3.8.10**
tranny **1.16.6**
tranquil **40.35.3**
tranquilization **28.17.25(.3.12)**
tranquilizer **17.25.12(.15)**
tranquillity **1.10.16(.30)**
tranquillization **28.17.25(.3.12)**
tranquillize **35.15.21(.4.6)**
tranquilly **1.31.17(.26)**
transact **22.23.5(.8)**
transaction **28.17.25(.15.3)**
transactional **40.26.13(.14.6)**
transactionally **1.31.17(.14.3)**
transactor **17.12.21(.3)**
transalpine **28.14.3**
transatlantic **24.2.10(.14)**
transaxle **40.31.18**

t

transporter 17.12.10(.1)
transposable 40.20.16(.22)
transposal 40.32.15
transpose 35.20.1
transposer 17.25.15
transposition 28.17.25(.2.5)
transpositional 40.26.13(.14.1)
transpositive 31.2.1(.9.3)
transputer 17.12.15(.8)
transsexual 40.14.8, 40.16.10
transsexualism 27.15.21(.2.15)
transship 20.2.7
transshipment 22.26.15(.13.3)
trans-Siberian 28.3.20(.2)
trans-sonic 24.2.15(.6.3)
transubstantiate 22.4.2(.9)
transubstantiation 28.17.25(.3.1)
transudation 28.17.25(.3.4)
transudatory 1.29.11(.8.6)
transude 23.17.4(.5)
transuranic 24.2.15(.5)
Transvaal 40.8.10
Transvaaler 17.34.8
transversal 40.31.13
transversality 1.10.16(.32.11)
transversally 1.31.17(.20)
transverse 34.19.6
transversely 1.31.33(.12.6)
transvest 22.29.5(.5)
transvestism 27.15.21(.2.4)
transvestist 22.29.2(.13)
transvestite 22.16.9
Transworld 23.31.12
Transylvania 3.9.3(.6)
Transylvanian 28.3.8(.3)
tranter 17.12.22(.4)
trap 20.5
trap-ball 40.10.4
trapdoor 12.6, 12.6.8
trapeze 35.1.5
trapezia 3.15.1
trapezium 27.3.12
trapezoid 23.13.17
trapezoidal 40.22.9
traplike 24.13.7(.10)
trappean 28.3.1
trapper 17.10.5
trappings 35.27

Trappist 22.29.2(.11)
Trappistine 28.1.9(.7)
trapshooter 17.12.15(.4)
trapshooting 29.1.12(.13)
trash 36.6
trashcan 28.7.8
trashery 1.29.11(.20)
trashily 1.31.17(.22)
trashiness 34.18.16(.2.8)
trashman 28.7.10(.22)
trashmen 28.5.7(.26)
trashy 1.24.5
Trás-os-Montes 35.4.3
trass 34.7
trattoria 17.1.16
trauma 17.17.9
traumata 17.12.16(.9.1)
traumatic 24.2.10(.4.2)
traumatically 1.31.24(.9.4)
traumatism 27.15.21(.2.4)
traumatization 28.17.25(.3.11)
traumatize 35.15.7(.7)
travail 40.4.9
travel 40.28.5
traveller 17.34.16(.14)
Travelodge® 39.9
travelogue 26.7.14
Travers 35.18.15
traversable 40.20.16(.21.2)
traversal 40.31.13
traverse 34.18.18, 34.19.6
traverser 17.24.15, 17.24.16
travertine 28.1.9(.3)
travesty 1.10.26(.11)
Traviata 17.12.8
Travis 34.2.15
travois 13.8, 35.13
trawl 40.10
trawler 17.34.10
trawlerman 28.17.16(.16)
Trawsfynydd 33.2
tray 4
trayful 40.14.6(.3)
treacherous 34.18.27(.26)
treacherously 1.31.33(.12.5)
treacherousness 34.18.16(.31.5)
treachery 1.29.11(.22)
treacle 40.23.1
treacliness 34.18.16(.2.10)
treacly 1.31.17(.11), 1.31.24(.1)
Treacy 1.22.1
tread 23.5
treader 17.13.4
treadle 40.22.4

treadmill 40.2.9
treadwheel 40.1.14
treason 28.17.24(.1)
treasonable 40.20.16(.16.3)
treasonableness 34.18.16(.37.4)
treasonably 1.31.21(.6)
treasonous 34.18.16(.15.3)
treasure 17.27.3
treasurehouse 34.8.6(.7)
treasurer 17.32.14(.18)
treasurership 20.2.7(.9)
treasury 1.29.11(.21)
treat 22.1
treatable 40.20.16(.11.1)
treated 23.18.9(.1)
treater 17.12.1
treatise 34.2.8, 35.2.3
treatment 22.26.15(.13.3)
treaty 1.10.1
Trebizond 23.24.9
treble 40.20.5
treble clef 30.4
Treblinka 17.14.21(.1)
trebly 1.31.21(.1)
Trebor 12.4
trebuchet 22.5.15
trecentist 22.29.2(.13)
trecento 19.10.17
Tredegar 17.16.1
tree 2
treecreeper 17.10.1
treehouse 34.8.6(.1)
treeless 34.18.29(.1)
treelessness 34.18.16(.31.6)
treeline 28.14.19(.1)
treen 28.1
treenail 40.4.7, 40.26.4
treetop 20.7.4
trefa 17.20.3
Trefgarne 28.9.5
trefoil 40.11.7
Trefusis 34.2.17(.9)
Tregaron 28.17.31(.5)
trehalose 34.20.17
trek 24.4
trekker 17.14.4
Trelawney 1.16.10
trellis 34.2.22(.4)
trellis-work 24.17.6(.15)
Tremain 28.4.7
trematode 23.20.5
tremble 40.20.19
trembler 17.34.20
trembling 29.1.31(.16)
tremblingly 1.31.28(.1.18)
trembly 1.31.21(.12)
tremendous 34.18.12

tremendously 1.31.33(.12.2)
tremendousness 34.18.16(.31.3)
Tremlett 22.19.26(.21)
tremolo 19.29.12
tremor 17.17.5
tremulant 22.26.15(.25)
tremulous 34.18.29(.17.6)
tremulously 1.31.33(.12.6)
tremulousness 34.18.16(.31.6)
trench 38.18.2
trenchancy 1.22.23(.10.4)
trenchant 22.26.15(.20)
trenchantly 1.31.22(.20.4)
Trenchard 23.9.17, 23.9.18, 23.18.22, 23.18.24
trencher 17.28.22
trencherman 28.17.16(.16)
trend 23.24.5
trendily 1.31.17(.10)
trendiness 34.18.16(.2.3)
trendsetter 17.12.5(.8)
trendsetting 29.1.12(.4)
trendy 1.11.20(.3)
Trent 22.26.4
trental 40.21.17(.2)
trente-et-quarante 22.12
Trentham 27.15.9(.14)
Trentino-Alto 19.10.21
Trento 19.10.17
Trenton 28.17.11(.22)
Treorchy 1.12.8
trepan 28.7.4
trepanation 28.17.25(.3.8)
trepang 29.4.1
trephination 28.17.25(.3.8)
trephine 28.1.15, 28.14.10
trepidation 28.17.25(.3.4)
treponemata 17.12.16(.9.1)
treponeme 27.1.6
treponima 17.17.1
Tresillian 28.3.21(.2)
trespass 34.18.9(.12)
trespasser 17.24.15
tress 34.5
tressure 17.7.12(.11), 17.26.4
tressy 1.22.5
trestle 40.31.5
tret 22.5
Tretchikoff 30.8.6
Trethowan 28.17.8
Tretyakov 31.7
trevally 1.31.7
Trevelyan 28.3.21(.4)

Trevethick 24.2.18(.2)
Trevino 19.15.1
Trevithick 24.2.18(.1)
Trevor 17.21.4
trews 35.17
trey 4
triable 40.20.16(.5)
triacetate 22.4.9(.5)
triacid 23.2.16
triad 23.7.3
triadelphous 34.18.17
triadic 24.2.11(.5)
triadically 1.31.24(.9.7)
triage 37.4.1, 39.2.1, 39.2.5
trial 40.16.6
trialist 22.29.2(.31.1)
trial run 28.13
triandrous 34.18.27(.15)
triangle 40.24.14(.2)
triangular 17.34.16(.21.3)
triangularity
  1.10.16(.21.1)
triangularly 1.31.17(.29)
triangulate 22.4.23(.7.3),
  22.19.26(.13)
triangulately 1.31.22(.15)
triangulation
  28.17.25(.3.14)
Trianon 28.10.14
triantelope 20.15.9
Trias 34.7.3
Triassic 24.2.20(.5)
triathlete 22.1.18
triathlon 28.10.26,
  28.17.33(.24)
triatomic 24.2.14(.6)
triaxial 40.3.10
tribade 23.18.8
tribadism 27.15.21(.2.5)
tribal 40.20.13
tribalism 27.15.21(.2.15)
tribalist 22.29.2(.31.2)
tribalistic 24.2.10(.15.3)
tribally 1.31.17(.8)
tribasic 24.2.20(.3)
tribe 21.12
tribesman 28.17.16(.30)
tribespeople 40.19.1
tribeswoman
  28.17.16(.14)
tribeswomen 28.2.17(.1)
triblet 22.19.26(.16)
triboelectricity
  1.10.16(.16.1)
tribologist 22.29.2(.26.3)
tribology 1.26.10(.11.2)
triboluminescence
  34.24.10(.18)
triboluminescent
  22.26.15(.17.2)
tribometer 17.12.16(.9.2)

tribrach 24.6.21
tribrachic 24.2.12
tribulation 28.17.25(.3.14)
tribunal 40.26.12
tribunate 22.4.14(.9.4),
  22.19.15(.9)
tribune 28.16.14
tribuneship 20.2.7(.19)
tribunicial 40.33.1
tribunician 28.17.25(.2.4)
tribunitial 40.33.1
tributarily 1.31.17(.27.1)
tributariness
  34.18.16(.2.9)
tributary 1.29.11(.8.10)
tribute 22.18.10
tricameral 40.16.13(.12.2)
tricar 10.8.5
trice 34.15
Tricel® 40.5.11
tricentenary
  1.29.11(.13.1)
triceps 34.21.4
triceratops 34.21.6
trichiasis 34.2.17(.2)
trichina 17.18.1(.5),
  17.18.13(.3)
trichinae 2.17.1, 2.17.8
Trichinopoly 1.31.17(.7)
trichinosis 34.2.17(.11.2)
trichinous 34.18.16(.15.2)
trichloride 23.15.15
trichloroethane 28.4.11
trichogenous
  34.18.16(.15.3)
trichological
  40.23.12(.17.2)
trichologist 22.29.2(.26.3)
trichology 1.26.10(.11.3)
trichome 27.17.6
trichomonad 23.7.12
trichomoniasis
  34.2.17(.10.1)
trichopathic 24.2.18(.3)
trichopathy 1.20.8
Trichoptera 17.32.14(.6)
trichopteran
  28.17.31(.11)
trichopterous
  34.18.27(.14)
trichord 23.12.4
trichotomic 24.2.14(.6)
trichotomize 35.15.11
trichotomous
  34.18.15(.10)
trichotomy 1.15.13(.1)
trichroic 24.2.7
trichroism 27.15.21(.2.1)
trichromatic 24.2.10(.4.2)
trichromatism
  27.15.21(.2.4)

Tricia 17.26.2
tri-city 1.10.2
Tricity® 1.10.16(.16.1)
trick 24.2
tricker 17.14.2
trickery 1.29.11(.10)
trickily 1.31.17(.11)
trickiness 34.18.16(.2.4)
trickish 36.2.13
trickle 40.23.2
trickler 17.34.23
trickless 34.18.29(.24)
trickly 1.31.17(.11),
  1.31.24(.2)
trick-or-treat 22.1.17
tricksily 1.31.17(.20)
tricksiness
  34.18.16(.2.7)
trickster 17.12.24(.20)
tricksy 1.22.22
tricky 1.12.2
triclinia 3.9.2
triclinic 24.2.15(.2)
triclinium 27.3.8(.2)
tricolor 17.34.16(.9)
tricolour 17.34.12,
  17.34.16(.9)
tricoloured 23.18.29
tricorne 28.11.5
tricot 19.12.1, 19.12.2
tricotyledonous
  34.18.16(.15.2)
tricrotic 24.2.10(.6)
tricuspid 23.2.6
tricycle 40.23.12(.15)
tricyclic 24.2.27(.16)
tricyclist 22.29.2(.31.6)
tridactyl 40.21.16
tridactylous
  34.18.29(.17.2)
trident 22.26.15(.10)
tridentate 22.4.9(.8)
Tridentine 28.14.5
tridigitate 22.4.9(.5)
tridimensional
  40.26.13(.14.7)
triduum 27.15.4
tridymite 22.16.13
tried 23.15
triene 28.1.3
triennia 3.9.4
triennial 40.3.7(.4)
triennially 1.31.3(.7)
triennium 27.3.8(.4)
Trier 3
trier 17.6
trierarchy 1.12.6
Trieste 22.29.5
trifacial 40.33.2
trifecta 17.12.21(.2)
triffid 23.2.14

trifid 23.2.14
trifle 40.27.12
trifler 17.34.26
triflingly 1.31.28(.1.18)
triflingness 34.18.16(.26)
trifocal 40.23.14
trifoliate 22.3.13
triforia 3.22.9
triforium 27.3.17(.4)
triform 27.10.5(.1)
trifurcate 22.4.11(.6)
trig 26.2
trigamist 22.29.2(.17)
trigamous 34.18.15(.10)
trigamy 1.15.13(.4)
trigeminal 40.26.13(.8)
trigemini 14.13
trigeminus
  34.18.16(.15.3)
trigger 17.16.2
triggerfish 36.2.18(.11)
triglyceride 23.15.15
triglyph 30.2.6
triglyphic 24.2.16(.1)
triglyphical 40.23.12(.12)
trigon 28.10.12,
  28.17.15(.11)
trigonal 40.26.13(.7)
trigonally 1.31.17(.14.2)
trigoneutic 24.2.10(.9)
trigonometric
  24.2.26(.14.2)
trigonometrical
  40.23.12(.18)
trigonometrically
  1.31.24(.9.12)
trigonometry 1.29.15(.8)
trigram 27.6.17(.5)
trigraph 30.7.5(.1)
trigynous 34.18.16(.15.3)
trihedra 17.32.20
trihedral 40.16.13(.17)
trihedron 28.17.31(.15)
trihydric 24.2.26(.15)
trijet 22.5.17
trike 24.13
trilabiate 22.3.2
trilaminar 17.18.16(.8)
trilateral 40.16.13(.12.1)
trilaterally 1.31.17(.27.1)
trilateralness
  34.18.16(.37.3)
trilby 1.9.24
trilemma 17.17.5
trilinear 3.9.2
trilingual 40.35.4
trilingualism
  27.15.21(.2.15)
triliteral 40.16.13(.12.1)
trilith 32.2.9
trilithic 24.2.18(.1)

trilithon 28.10.17
trill 40.2
Trilling 29.1.31(.2)
trillion 28.3.21(.2)
trillionth 32.21
trillium 27.3.18
trilobate 22.4.8
trilobite 22.16.8
trilocular 17.34.16(.21.2)
trilogy 1.26.10(.10)
trim 27.2
trimaran 28.7.20
Trimble 40.20.19
trimer 17.17.11
trimeric 24.2.26(.4)
trimerous 34.18.27(.18)
trimester 17.12.24(.4)
trimestral 40.16.13(.16)
trimeter 17.12.1(.6),
  17.12.16(.9.1)
trimetric 24.2.26(.14.2)
trimetrical 40.23.12(.18)
trimly 1.31.26(.2)
trimmer 17.17.2
trimming 29.1.16
trimness 34.18.16(.24)
trimorphic 24.2.16(.5)
trimorphism
  27.15.21(.2.10)
trimorphous 34.18.17
Trimurti 1.10.16(.5)
trinal 40.26.11
Trincomalee 2.32
trine 28.14
Tring 29.1
Trini 1.16.1
Trinian's 35.26.3
Trinidad 23.7.8
Trinidad and Tobago
  19.13.3
Trinidadian 28.3.4(.5)
Trinitarian 28.3.20(.4)
Trinitarianism
  27.15.21(.2.9)
trinitrotoluene 28.1.4
trinitrotoluol 40.9.4
trinity 1.10.16(.13)
trinket 22.2.9(.9)
trinketry 1.29.15(.6)
trinomial 40.3.6
trinomialism
  27.15.21(.2.15)
trio 19.1
triode 23.20.2
trioecious 34.18.22(.1)
triolet 22.5.21,
  22.19.26(.13)
trioxide 23.15.11(.11)
trip 20.2
tripartite 22.16.9
tripartitely 1.31.22(.13)

tripartition 28.17.25(.2.2)
tripe 20.10
tripetalous 34.18.29(.17.2)
triphibious 34.3.2
triphosphate 22.4.15
triphthong 29.6.8
triphthongal 40.24.14(.3)
triphyllous 34.18.29(.2)
tripinnate 22.4.14(.2),
  22.19.15(.1)
Tripitaka 17.14.7,
  17.14.15(.6)
triplane 28.4.19
triple 40.19.2
triple crown 28.8
triple-header 17.13.4
triplet 22.19.26(.15)
triplex 34.23.4(.12)
triplicate 22.4.11(.6),
  22.19.12(.10)
triplication 28.17.25(.3.5)
triplicity 1.10.16(.16.1)
triploid 23.13.20
triploidy 1.11.12
triply 1.31.20
tripmeter 17.12.1(.6)
tripod 23.10.1
tripodal 40.22.13
tripoli 1.31.17(.7)
Tripolis 34.2.22(.8)
Tripolitania 3.9.3(.2)
Tripolitanian 28.3.8(.3)
tripos 34.10.6
Tripp 20.2
tripper 17.10.2
trippingly 1.31.28(.1.2)
trippy 1.8.2
triptych 24.2.10(.12)
triptyque 24.1.3
Tripura 17.32.14(.4)
tripwire 17.6.13
triquetra 17.32.19(.1)
triquetrae 2.30.10
triquetral 40.16.13(.16)
triquetrous
  34.18.27(.14)
trireme 27.1.12
trisaccharide 23.15.15
Trisagion 28.3.6
trisect 22.23.4(.7)
trisection 28.17.25(.15.2)
trisector 17.12.21(.2)
Trish 36.2
Trisha 17.26.2
trishaw 12.16.5
triskelion 28.3.21(.4)
trismus 34.18.15(.18)
trisomy 1.15.13(.8)
Tristan 28.17.11(.25)
Tristan da Cunha
  17.18.15, 17.33.9

Tri-Star 10.6.8
triste 22.29.1
tristesse 34.5.2
tristichous 34.18.13(.10)
tristigmatic 24.2.10(.4.2)
Tristram 27.15.26(.10)
tristylous 34.18.29(.14)
trisulcate 22.4.11(.8)
trisyllabic 24.2.9(.2)
trisyllabically
  1.31.24(.9.2)
trisyllable 40.20.16(.29)
tritagonist 22.29.2(.18.1)
tritanope 20.15.5
tritanopia 3.2.7
trite 22.16
tritely 1.31.22(.13)
triteness 34.18.16(.20.2)
triternate 22.4.14(.10),
  22.19.15(.10)
tritheism 27.15.21(.2.1)
tritheist 22.29.2(.1)
tritiate 22.4.2(.3)
tritiation 28.17.25(.3.1)
triticale 1.31.4
tritium 27.3.3
triton 28.17.11(.12)
tritone 28.19.4(.3)
triturable 40.20.16(.27.5)
triturate 22.4.22(.6)
trituration 28.17.25(.3.13)
triturator 17.12.4(.15)
triumph 30.18
triumphal 40.27.21
triumphalism
  27.15.21(.2.15)
triumphalist
  22.29.2(.31.4)
triumphally
  1.31.17(.16.2)
triumphant 22.26.15(.15)
triumphantly
  1.31.22(.20.4)
triumvir 17.21.16
triumviral 40.16.13(.12.2)
triumvirate 22.19.24(.9)
triune 28.16.14
triunity 1.10.16(.13)
trivalency 1.22.23(.10.4)
trivalent 22.26.15(.25)
trivet 22.2.14
trivia 3.11.2
trivial 40.3.8
triviality 1.10.16(.32.1)
trivialization
  28.17.25(.3.12)
trivialize 35.15.21(.2)
trivially 1.31.3(.8)
trivialness 34.18.16(.37.1)
trivium 27.3.9
tri-weekly 1.31.24(.1)

Trixie 1.22.22
Troad 23.20
Troas 34.7.4
Trobriand 23.24.3,
  23.24.6(.1)
Trocadero 19.27.1, 19.27.3
trocar 10.8.10
trochaic 24.2.3
trochal 40.23.14
trochanter 17.12.22(.4)
troche 36.16
trochee 2.14
trochi 14.10
trochlea 3.24.14
trochleae 2.3
trochlear 3.24.14
trochoid 23.13.9
trochoidal 40.22.9
trochus 34.18.13(.5)
troctolite 22.16.25(.9)
trod 23.10
trodden 28.17.12(.9)
trog 26.7
troglodyte 22.16.10
troglodytes 35.1.7(.5)
troglodytic 24.2.10(.2.1)
troglodytical
  40.23.12(.7.1)
troglodytism
  27.15.21(.2.4)
trogon 28.10.12
troika 17.14.10
troilism 27.15.21(.2.15)
Troilus 34.18.29(.12)
Trojan 28.17.28(.11)
Trojan Horse 34.12
troll 40.9, 40.18
troller 17.34.9, 17.34.18
trolley 1.31.10
trolleybus 34.14
trollop 20.13.7
Trollope 20.13.7
trollopish 36.2.9
trollopy 1.8.11(.9)
Tromans 35.26.13(.10)
trombone 28.19.3
trombonist
  22.29.2(.18.3)
trommel 40.25.5
tromometer
  17.12.16(.9.2)
tromometric
  24.2.26(.14.2)
tromp 20.16.4
trompe 20.16.4
trompe l'oeil 13.17
trona 17.18.18
tronc 24.19.5
Trondheim 27.12.6
Troon 28.16
troop 20.12

trooper **17.10.13**
troopship **20.2.7(.12)**
tropaeola **17.34.16(.1)**
tropaeolum **27.15.28(.11)**
trope **20.15**
trophic **24.2.16(.4)**
trophied **23.2.14**
trophoblast **22.29.6(.12)**, **22.29.8(.8)**
trophoneuroses **35.1.16(.11)**
trophoneurosis **34.2.17(.11.2)**
trophy **1.18.11**
tropic **24.2.8(.5)**
tropical **40.23.12(.5)**
tropically **1.31.24(.9.2)**
tropics **34.23.2(.1)**
tropism **27.15.21(.2.2)**
tropological **40.23.12(.17.2)**
tropology **1.26.10(.11.2)**
tropopause **35.12**
troposphere **3.10.5**
tropospheric **24.2.26(.4)**
troppo **19.8**
Trossachs **34.23.15**
trot **22.11**
troth **32.9, 32.16**
Trotsky **1.12.17(.8)**
Trotskyism **27.15.21(.2.1)**
Trotskyist **22.29.2(.2)**
Trotskyite **22.16.2**
trotter **17.12.9**
trotting race **34.4**
trottoir **10.22.5**
trotyl **40.2.5, 40.13.3(.6)**
troubadour **12.6.6, 17.7.4**
trouble **40.20.12**
troubled **23.31.15**
troublemaker **17.14.3(.3)**
trouble-making **29.1.14(.3)**
troubler **17.34.20**
troubleshoot **22.18.7**
troubleshooter **17.12.15(.4)**
troubleshot **22.11.12**
troublesome **27.15.20(.22)**
troublesomely **1.31.26(.11)**
troublesomeness **34.18.16(.24)**
troublous **34.18.29(.21)**
trough **30.8**
trounce **34.24.5**
trouncer **17.24.22(.4)**
troupe **20.12**
trouper **17.10.13**
trouser **17.25.6**

trouserless **34.18.29(.17.5)**
trousseau **19.20.9**
trousseaux **35.20.10**
trout **22.9**
troutlet **22.19.26(.17)**
troutling **29.1.31(.17)**
trouty **1.10.7**
trove **31.12**
trover **17.21.14**
trow **9, 19**
Trowbridge **39.2.22(.10)**
trowel **40.16.3**
Trowell **40.16.3, 40.16.9**
troy **13**
truancy **1.22.23(.10.1)**
truant **22.26.15(.6)**
Trubetskoy **13.5**
Trubshaw **12.16.7**
truce **34.17**
truceless **34.18.29(.33)**
trucial **40.33.8**
Trucial States **34.22.3**
truck **24.12**
truckage **39.2.12**
trucker **17.14.11**
truckie **1.12.9**
truckle **40.23.9**
truckler **17.34.23**
truckload **23.20.13**
truculence **34.24.10(.24)**
truculency **1.22.23(.10.4)**
truculent **22.26.15(.25)**
truculently **1.31.22(.20.5)**
Trudeau **19.11.10**
trudge **39.11**
trudgen **28.17.28(.7)**
trudger **17.29.10**
Trudgill **40.2.8**
Trudi **1.11.16**
Trudy **1.11.16**
true **16**
true-blue **16.25**
trueish **36.2.6**
true-life **30.12**
true love **31.8**
Trueman **28.17.16(.15)**
trueness **34.18.16(.14)**
Truffaut **19.16**
truffle **40.27.11**
trug **26.10**
truism **27.15.21(.2.1)**
truistic **24.2.10(.15.1)**
Trujillo **19.28**
Truk **24.12**
trull **40.12**
truly **1.31.16**
Trumbull **40.20.19**
trumeau **19.14**
trumeaux **35.20.7**
trump **20.16.5**

trumped-up **20.9**
trumpery **1.29.11(.6)**
trumpet **22.2.5**
trumpeter **17.12.16(.3)**
trumpeting **29.1.12(.14)**
trumpetless **34.18.29(.22)**
truncal **40.23.15**
truncate **22.4.11**
truncately **1.31.22(.4)**
truncation **28.17.25(.3.5)**
truncheon **28.17.27**
trundle **40.22.16**
trunk **24.19.7**
trunkful **40.14.6(.12)**
trunking **29.1.14(.14)**
trunkless **34.18.29(.24)**
trunklike **24.13.7(.14)**
trunnel **40.26.10**
trunnion **28.17.32**
Truro **19.27.11**
Truscott **22.11.6, 22.19.12(.14)**
truss **34.14**
trusser **17.24.12**
trust **22.29.12**
trustable **40.20.16(.11.7)**
trustbuster **17.12.24(.10)**
trustbusting **29.1.12(.21)**
trustee **2.11, 2.12.15**
trusteeship **20.2.7(.1)**
truster **17.12.24(.10)**
trustful **40.27.18**
trustfully **1.31.17(.16.2)**
trustfulness **34.18.16(.37.2)**
trustie **1.10.26(.8)**
trustily **1.31.17(.9.3)**
trustiness **34.18.16(.2.3)**
trusting **29.1.12(.21)**
trustingly **1.31.28(.1.4)**
trustingness **34.18.16(.26)**
trustworthily **1.31.17(.19)**
trustworthiness **34.18.16(.2.6)**
trustworthy **1.21**
trusty **1.10.26(.8)**
truth **32.13**
truthful **40.27.24**
truthfully **1.31.17(.16.2)**
truthfulness **34.18.16(.37.2)**
truthless **34.18.29(.31)**
try **14**
Tryfan **28.17.20(.2)**
tryingly **1.31.28(.1.1)**
trypanosome **27.17.10**
trypanosomiasis **34.2.17(.10.1)**
trypsin **28.2.23(.12)**
trypsinogen **28.17.28(.9)**

tryptic **24.2.10(.12)**
tryptophan **28.7.12**
trysail **40.4.10, 40.31.11**
tryst **22.29.2**
tryster **17.12.24(.2)**
tsar **10**
tsardom **27.15.10(.5)**
tsarevich **38.2.7**
tsarevna **17.18.27**
tsarina **17.18.1(.15)**
tsarism **27.15.21(.2.14)**
tsarist **22.29.2(.29.2)**
tsessebi **1.9.3, 1.9.11**
tsetse **1.22.21**
Tsinan **28.7.11**
Tsinghai **14.22**
Tsitsikamma **17.17.6**
T-square **6.18.9**
tsunami **1.15.7**
Tsushima **17.17.1**
Tswana **17.18.8**
TT **2.11**
t-test **22.29.5(.2)**
Tuareg **26.4**
tuatara **17.32.7**
tub **21.11**
tuba **17.11.12**
tubal **40.20.15**
tubbable **40.20.16(.10)**
tubbiness **34.18.16(.2.2)**
tubbish **36.2.10**
tubby **1.9.9**
tubbyish **36.2.1**
tube **21.13**
tubectomy **1.15.13(.1)**
tubeless **34.18.29(.21)**
tubelike **24.13.7(.11)**
tuber **17.11.12**
tubercle **40.23.12(.6)**
tubercular **17.34.16(.21.2)**
tuberculate **22.19.26(.13)**
tuberculation **28.17.25(.3.14)**
tuberculin **28.2.31(.10)**
tuberculin-tested **23.18.9(.20)**
tuberculosis **34.2.17(.11.2)**
tuberculous **34.18.29(.17.6)**
tuberose **35.20.12**
tuberosity **1.10.16(.16.2)**
tuberous **34.18.27(.13)**
tube worm **27.16**
tubful **40.14.6(.9)**
tubicolous **34.18.29(.17.2)**
tubicorn **28.11.5**
tubifex **34.23.4(.7)**
tubiform **27.10.5(.2)**
tubilingual **40.35.4**

tubing 29.1.11

Tubman 28.17.16(.20)

tub-sized 23.28.2

tubular 17.34.16(.21.1)

tubule 40.15.9(.2)

tubulous 34.18.29(.17.6)

tuck 24.12

tuckahoe 19.26

tuckbox 34.23.8(.2)

tucker 17.14.11

tuckerbag 26.5.1

tucket 22.2.9(.6)

tuckpoint 22.26.11

tuckshop 20.7.9

Tucson 28.10.18

Tudor 17.13.14

Tudorbethan 28.17.21

Tudoresque 24.20.3

Tuesday 1.11.21, 4.10.15

tufa 17.20.11

tufaceous 34.18.22(.3)

tuff 30.11

tuffaceous 34.18.22(.3)

tuffet 22.2.13

Tuffnell 40.26.21

tuft 22.27.6

tuftiness 34.18.16(.2.3)

tufty 1.10.24

tug 26.10

tugboat 22.21.2

Tugendhat 22.10.11

tugger 17.16.9

tug-of-love 31.8

tug-of-war 12.20

tugrik 24.1.11

tui 1(.6)

Tuileries 1.29.11(.27), 35.2.17

tuition 28.17.25(.2.1)

tuitional 40.26.13(.14.1)

tuitionary 1.29.11(.13.2)

Tula 17.34.15

tularaemia 3.8.1

tularaemic 24.2.14(.1)

tulchan 28.17.13(.19), 28.17.14

tulip 20.2.13

tulipwood 23.16.6(.8)

Tull 40.12

Tullamore 12.9.4

tulle 40.15

Tulloch 24.16.16, 25.10

Tully 1.31.13

Tulsa 17.24.24

tum 27.11

tumble 40.20.19

tumbledown 28.8.2(.13)

tumble-dry 14.24.8

tumble-dryer 17.6.14

tumbler 17.34.20

tumblerful 40.14.6(.7)

tumbleweed 23.1.10

tumbril 40.16.13(.15)

tumefacient 22.26.15(.19)

tumefaction 28.17.25(.15.3)

tumefy 14.14.4(.6)

tumescence 34.24.10(.18)

tumescent 22.26.15(.17.2)

tumid 23.2.12

tumidity 1.10.16(.9)

tumidly 1.31.23(.14.6)

tumidness 34.18.16(.21.1)

tummy 1.15.10

tumorous 34.18.27(.18)

tumour 17.17.13

tump 20.16.5

tumtum 27.11.3

tumular 17.34.16(.21.4)

tumuli 14.25.9

tumult 22.32.8

tumultuary 1.29.11(.3)

tumultuous 34.18.6

tumultuously 1.31.33(.12.1)

tumultuousness 34.18.16(.31.2)

tumulus 34.18.29(.17.6)

tun 28.13

tuna 17.18.15

tunable 40.20.16(.16.2)

Tunbridge Wells 35.30.4

tundish 36.2.12

tundra 17.32.20

tune 28.16

tuneful 40.27.22

tunefully 1.31.17(.16.2)

tunefulness 34.18.16(.37.2)

tuneless 34.18.29(.27)

tunelessly 1.31.33(.12.6)

tunelessness 34.18.16(.31.6)

tuner 17.18.15

tung 29.8

tungstate 22.4.9(.9)

tungsten 28.17.11(.25)

tungstic 24.2.10(.15.4)

tungstite 22.16.9

Tungus 34.16, 35.17.2

Tungusic 24.2.20(.11), 24.2.21

tunic 24.2.15(.7)

tunica 17.14.15(.9)

tunicae 2.14

tunicate 22.4.11(.6)

tunicle 40.23.12(.11)

tuning 29.1.17(.11)

Tunis 34.2.13

Tunisia 3.15.2

Tunisian 28.3.14

tunnel 40.26.10

tunneller 17.34.16(.12)

tunnel vision 28.17.26(.2)

Tunney 1.16.12

tunny 1.16.12

Tuohy 1(.6)

tup 20.9

Tupamaro 19.27.4, 19.27.5

tupelo 19.29.12

Tupi 1.8.10

tuppence 34.24.10(.8)

tuppenny 1.16.15(.5), 1.16.18

tuppenny-ha'penny 1.16.15(.5), 1.16.18

Tupperware® 6.18.4

tuque 24.15

tu quoque 1.28

turaco 19.12.12

Turandot 22.11.5

Turanian 28.3.8(.3)

turban 28.17.10

turbary 1.29.11(.7.1)

turbellarian 28.3.20(.4)

turbid 23.2.7

turbidity 1.10.16(.9)

turbidly 1.31.23(.14.2)

turbidness 34.18.16(.21.1)

turbinal 40.26.13(.3)

turbinate 22.4.14(.9.1), 22.19.15(.9)

turbination 28.17.25(.3.8)

turbine 28.2.10, 28.14.4

turbit 22.2.6

turbo 19.9.10

turbocharge 39.8

turbocharger 17.29.7

turbocharging 29.1.28

turbo-diesel 40.32.1

turbofan 28.7.12

turbojet 22.5.17

turboprop 20.7.12

turboshaft 22.27.4(.3)

turbot 22.19.9

turbulence 34.24.10(.24)

turbulent 22.26.15(.25)

turbulently 1.31.22(.20.5)

Turco 19.12.13

Turcophile 40.13.9

Turcophobe 21.16.1

turd 23.19

turdoid 23.13.8

tureen 28.1.25

turf 30.15

turfman 28.17.16(.27)

turfy 1.18.10

Turgenev 30.4

turgescence 34.24.10(.18)

turgescent 22.26.15(.17.2)

turgid 23.2.20

turgidescence 34.24.10(.18)

turgidescent 22.26.15(.17.2)

turgidity 1.10.16(.9)

turgidly 1.31.23(.14.7)

turgidness 34.18.16(.21.1)

turgor 17.16.14

Turin 28.2.29

Turing 29.1.30(.8)

turion 28.3.20(.8)

Turk 24.17

Turkana 17.18.8(.3)

Turkestan 28.9.2

turkey 1.12.14

turkeycock 24.9.6

Turki 1.12.14

Turkic 24.2.12

Turkish 36.2.13

Turkmenistan 28.9.2

Turkoman 28.7.10(.6), 28.9.6, 28.17.16(.16)

Turku 16.9

turmeric 24.2.26(.10)

turmoil 40.11.6

turn 28.18

turnabout 22.9.6

turnaround 23.24.7(.10)

turnback 24.6.6(.17)

Turnberry 1.29.11(.7.2)

turnbuckle 40.23.9

Turnbull 40.14.3

turncoat 22.21.5

turncock 24.9.6

turndown 28.8.2(.8)

turner 17.18.17

turnery 1.29.11(.13.3)

turning 29.1.17(.13)

turnip 20.2.4

turnipy 1.8.11(.6)

turnkey 2.14

turnout 22.9.11

turnover 17.21.14(.7)

turnpike 24.13.1

turnround 23.24.7(.10)

turnsick 24.2.20(.15)

turnside 23.15.11(.12)

turnsole 40.18.10

turnspike 24.13.1

turnspit 22.2.5

turnstile 40.13.3(.10)

turnstone 28.19.4(.9)

turnup 20.9.9

turpentine 28.14.5

turpeth 32.14.6

Turpin 28.2.9

turpitude 23.17.4(.1)

turps 34.21.11

turquoise 35.9, 35.13

turret **22.19.24(.7)**
turtle **40.21.13**
turtledove **31.8**
turtleneck **24.4.7**
turtleshell **40.5.13**
Turton **28.17.11(.16)**
turves **35.28.8**
Turvey **1.19.11**
Tuscan **28.17.13(.18)**
Tuscany **1.16.15(.9)**
Tuscarora **17.32.10(.10)**
tush **36.12**
tusk **24.20.7**
tusker **17.14.23**
tusky **1.12.17(.7)**
tussah **17.24.12**
Tussaud's **35.23.7,
35.23.14**
tusser **17.24.12**
tussive **31.2.4(.6)**
tussle **40.31.10**
tussock **24.16.11**
tussocky **1.12.13**
tussore **12.14.6, 17.24.12**
tut **22.15**
Tutankhamun **28.16.7,
28.17.16(.9)**
tutee **2.11**
tutelage **39.2.23**
tutelar **17.34.16(.7)**
tutelary **1.29.11(.27)**
tutenag **26.5.4**
Tutin **28.2.11(.9)**
tutor **17.12.15**
tutorage **39.2.22(.9)**
tutoress **34.18.27(.14)**
tutorial **40.3.14(.5)**
tutorially **1.31.3(.11)**
tutorship **20.2.7(.9)**
Tutsi **1.22.21**
tutti **1.10.14, 1.10.15**
tutti-frutti **1.10.15**
Tuttle **40.21.9**
tut-tut **22.15.3**
tutty **1.10.12**
tutu **16.7.3**
Tuva **17.21.11**
Tuvalu **16.25**
Tuvaluan **28.17.6**
tu-whit tu-whoo **16.22**
tux **34.23.11**
tuxedo **19.11.1**
tuyère **6.20**
Twa **10**
twaddle **40.22.7**
twaddly **1.31.17(.10)**
twain **28.4**
twang **29.4**
twangle **40.24.14(.2)**
twangy **1.17**

Twankey **1.12.16**
'twas **35.10**
twat **22.7, 22.11**
twayblade **23.4.16**
tweak **24.1**
twee **2**
tweed **23.1**
Tweeddale **40.4.3**
tweedily **1.31.17(.10)**
tweediness
34.18.16(.2.3)
Tweedledee **2.13**
Tweedledum **27.11.4**
Tweedsmuir **12.22,
17.7.12(.7)**
tweedy **1.11.1**
tweely **1.31.1**
'tween **28.1**
'tween decks **34.23.4(.4)**
tweeness **34.18.16(.1)**
tweeny **1.16.1**
tweet **22.1**
tweeter **17.12.1**
tweezer **17.25.1**
twelfth **32.22**
Twelfth Day **4**
twelfthly **1.31.31**
Twelfth Night **22.16**
twelve **31.13**
twelvefold **23.31.13(.7)**
twelvemo **19.14.17**
twelvemonth **32.21**
twentieth **32.14.1**
twenty **1.10.23(.3)**
twenty-first **22.29.16**
twentyfold **23.31.13(.7)**
twenty-fourmo **19.14.9**
twentysomething
29.1.21
twenty-twenty
1.10.23(.3)
'twere **18**
twerp **20.14**
Twi **2**
twibill **40.2.4**
twice **34.15**
twicer **17.24.13**
Twickenham
27.15.14(.11)
twiddle **40.22.2**
twiddler **17.34.22**
twiddly **1.31.17(.10),
1.31.23(.1)**
twig **26.2**
twiggy **1.14.2**
twilight **22.16.25(.8)**
twilit **22.2.25**
'twill **40.2**
twill **40.2**
twin **28.2**
twine **28.14**

twiner **17.18.13**
twinge **39.17.1**
twi-night **22.16.14(.5)**
Twining **29.1.17(.10)**
twink **24.19.1**
twinkle **40.23.15**
twinkler **17.34.23**
twinkly **1.31.17(.11),
1.31.24(.12)**
twinning **29.1.17(.2)**
twin-screw **16.23.10**
twinset **22.5.13(.11)**
twin-size **35.15.16(.7)**
twintub **21.11**
twirl **40.17**
twirler **17.34.17**
twirly **1.31.18**
twist **22.29.2**
twistable **40.20.16(.11.7)**
twister **17.12.24(.2)**
twistily **1.31.17(.9.3)**
twistiness **34.18.16(.2.3)**
twisting **29.1.12(.21)**
twisty **1.10.26(.2)**
twit **22.2**
twitch **38.2**
twitcher **17.28.2**
twitchily **1.31.17(.24)**
twitchiness **34.18.16(.2.8)**
twitchy **1.25.2**
twite **22.16**
twitter **17.12.2**
twitterer **17.32.14(.6)**
twittery **1.29.11(.8.1)**
twittish **36.2.11**
'twixt **22.29.20**
twizzle **40.32.2**
two **16**
two-a-penny **1.16.5**
two-bit **22.2.6**
two-by-four **12.11**
two-dimensional
40.26.13(.14.7)
twofold **23.31.13(.7)**
Twohy **1(.6)**
Twomey **1.15.12**
twoness **34.18.16(.14)**
twopence **34.24.10(.8)**
twopenny **1.16.15(.5),
1.16.18**
twopenny-halfpenny
1.16.15(.5), 1.16.18
twopennyworth
**32.14.12, 32.14.15,
32.15.2**
two-piece **34.1.1**
two-seater **17.12.1(.10)**
twosome **27.15.20(.10)**
two-timer **17.17.11**
two-tone **28.19.4(.4)**
'twould **23.16**

two-up **20.9**
two-way **4.25**
two-wheeler **17.34.1**
twyer **17.6**
Twyford **23.18.16(.8)**
Tyburn **28.17.10, 28.18.3**
Tyche **1.12.10**
tychism **27.15.21(.2.6)**
tychist **22.29.2(.15)**
Tycho **19.12.9**
Tychonian **28.3.8(.11)**
Tychonic **24.2.15(.6.1)**
tycoon **28.16.5**
Tye **14**
tying **29.1.7**
tyke **24.13**
Tyldesley **1.31.34**
Tyler **17.34.13**
tylopod **23.10.1**
tylopodous **34.18.12**
tympan **28.17.9**
tympana **17.18.16(.3)**
tympanic **24.2.15(.5)**
tympanites **35.1.7(.5)**
tympanitic **24.2.10(.2.2)**
tympanitis **34.18.11(.8)**
tympanum **27.15.14(.11)**
Tynan **28.17.17(.8)**
Tyndale **40.22.16**
Tyne **28.14**
Tyne and Wear **3**
Tynemouth **32.7**
Tyneside **23.15.11(.12)**
Tynesider **17.13.12**
Tynwald **23.31.11**
typal **40.19.9**
type **20.10**
typebar **10.5.7**
typecast **22.29.6(.5),
22.29.8(.3)**
typeface **34.4.9**
typefounder **17.13.20(.5)**
typescript **22.22.1**
typeset **22.5.13(.6)**
typesetter **17.12.5(.8)**
typesetting **29.1.12(.4)**
typewriter **17.12.13(.8)**
typewriting **29.1.12(.11)**
typewritten **28.17.11(.2)**
typhlitic **24.2.10(.2.5)**
typhlitis **34.18.11(.8)**
typhoid **23.13.13**
typhoidal **40.22.9**
typhonic **24.2.15(.6.3)**
Typhoo® **16.13**
typhoon **28.16.9**
typhous **34.18.17**
typhus **34.18.17**
typical **40.23.12(.5)**
typicality **1.10.16(.32.5)**

typically **1.31.24(.9.2)**
typification **28.17.25(.3.5)**
typifier **17.6.9(.4)**
typify **14.14.4(.2)**
typist **22.29.2(.11)**
typo **19.8**
typographer **17.20.12(.5)**
typographic **24.2.16(.3)**
typographical **40.23.12(.12)**
typographically **1.31.24(.9.9)**
typography **1.18.9(.3.2)**
typological **40.23.12(.17.2)**
typologist **22.29.2(.26.3)**
typology **1.26.10(.11.2)**
typonym **27.2.6**
Tyr **3, 17.7**
tyramine **28.1.13**
tyrannical **40.23.12(.11)**
tyrannically **1.31.24(.9.8)**
tyrannicidal **40.22.11**
tyrannicide **23.15.11(.6)**
tyrannize **35.15.12(.5)**
tyrannosaur **12.14.8**
tyrannosauri **14.24.4**
tyrannosaurus **34.18.27(.8)**
Tyrannosaurus Rex **34.23.4**
tyrannous **34.18.16(.15.3)**
tyrannously **1.31.33(.12.3)**
tyranny **1.16.15(.18)**
tyrant **22.26.15(.23.2)**
tyre **17.6**
tyre guage **39.4**
tyremark **24.8.8**
Tyrer **17.32.13**
Tyrian **28.3.20(.1)**
tyro **19.27.9**
Tyrol **40.16.13(.1), 40.18.14**
Tyrolean **28.3.21(.11), 28.17.1(.13)**
Tyrone **28.19.17**
tyrosine **28.1.18(.6)**
tyrothricin **28.2.23(.7)**
Tyrrell **40.16.13(.1)**
Tyrrhene **28.1.25**
Tyrrhenian **28.3.8(.1)**
Tyson **28.17.23(.12)**
Tyzack **24.6.15**
tzatziki **1.12.1**
tzigane **28.9.5**
u **16**
U-2 **16.7**
UAW **16.24.17**
UB40 **1.10.10**
Ubaid **23.4.2, 23.15.3**
Ubange **1.14.14**

U-bend **23.24.5(.3)**
Übermensch **38.18.2**
Übermenschen **28.17.25(.16)**
ubiety **1.10.16(.4)**
ubiquitarian **28.3.20(.4)**
ubiquitarianism **27.15.21(.2.9)**
ubiquitous **34.18.11(.10)**
ubiquitously **1.31.33(.12.2)**
ubiquitousness **34.18.16(.31.3)**
ubiquity **1.10.16(.20)**
U-boat **22.21.2**
U-bolt **22.32.12**
UCATT **22.7.9**
UCCA **4, 17.14.11**
Uccello **19.29.4**
Uckfield **23.31.1(.2)**
UCLA **4**
udal **40.22.12**
Udall **40.10.6, 40.22.12**
udaller **17.34.16(.8)**
udalman **28.17.16(.35)**
udder **17.13.11**
UDI **14**
Udmurtia **17.26.14**
udometer **17.12.16(.9.2)**
UEFA **17.20.3**
U-ey **1(.6)**
Uffizi **1.22.21**
UFO **19, 19.16**
ufologist **22.29.2(.26.4)**
ufology **1.26.10(.11.5)**
Uganda **17.13.20(.4)**
Ugandan **28.17.12(.23)**
Ugaritic **24.2.10(.2.4)**
ugli **1.31.25**
uglification **28.17.25(.3.5)**
ugli fruit **22.18**
uglify **14.14.4(.16)**
uglily **1.31.17(.29)**
ugliness **34.18.16(.2.10)**
ugly **1.31.25**
Ugrian **28.3.20(.14)**
Ugric **24.2.26(.16)**
UHF **30.4**
uh-huh **17.30**
uhlan **28.9.15**
UHT **2.11**
Uighur **17.7.6**
Uist **22.29.2(.8)**
uitlander **17.13.20(.4)**
ujamaa **10.10**
Ujjain **28.4.16**
UK **4.11**
ukase **34.4.6, 35.4.5**
ukiyo-e **4.27**
Ukraine **28.4.18**

Ukrainian **28.3.8(.3)**
ukulele **1.31.4**
Ulan Bator **12.5**
Ulanova **17.21.12**
ulcer **17.24.24**
ulcerable **40.20.16(.27.5)**
ulcerate **22.4.22(.6)**
ulceration **28.17.25(.3.13)**
ulcerative **31.2.1(.9.4)**
ulcerous **34.18.27(.23)**
ulema **10.10, 10.10.4, 17.17.14(.12)**
Ulfilas **34.7.19**
uliginose **34.20.9**
uliginous **34.18.16(.15.3)**
ullage **39.2.23**
Ullapool **40.15.1**
Ullmann **28.17.16(.35)**
Ulm **27.18**
ulna **17.18.32**
ulnae **2.17.14**
ulnar **17.18.32**
ulotrichan **28.17.13(.13)**
ulotrichous **34.18.13(.10)**
Ulpian **28.3.1**
Ulster **17.12.24(.25)**
Ulsterman **28.17.16(.16)**
Ulsterwoman **28.17.16(.14)**
Ulsterwomen **28.2.17(.1)**
ult **22.32.8**
ulterior **3.22.2**
ulteriorly **1.31.3(.11)**
ultima **17.17.14(.2)**
ultimacy **1.22.16(.8)**
ultimata **17.12.4(.9)**
ultimate **22.19.14**
ultimately **1.31.22(.15)**
ultimateness **34.18.16(.20.3)**
ultimatum **27.15.9(.2)**
ultimo **19.14.12**
ultimogeniture **17.28.15**
ultra **17.32.19(.13)**
ultracentrifuge **39.13**
ultradian **28.3.4(.3)**
ultraism **27.15.21(.2.1)**
ultramarine **28.1.25**
ultramicroscope **20.15.4(.1)**
ultramicroscopic **24.2.8(.5)**
ultramontane **28.4.3**
ultramontanism **27.15.21(.2.9)**
ultramontanist **22.29.2(.18.1)**
ultramundane **28.4.4**
ultrasonic **24.2.15(.6.3)**
ultrasonically **1.31.24(.9.8)**

ultrasound **23.24.7(.6)**
ultrastructure **17.28.20**
Ultrasuede® **23.4.14**
ultraviolet **22.19.26(.13)**
ultra vires **35.1.22**
ululant **22.26.15(.25)**
ululate **22.4.23(.7.3)**
ululation **28.17.25(.3.14)**
Ulverston **28.17.11(.25)**
Ulysses **35.1.16(.10)**
um **27.11**
umbel **40.20.19**
umbellar **17.34.5(.2)**
umbellate **22.4.23(.7.1), 22.19.26(.13)**
umbellifer **17.20.12(.6)**
umbelliferae **2.30.7**
umbelliferous **34.18.27(.20)**
umbellule **40.15.9(.11)**
umber **17.11.17(.6)**
umbilical **40.23.10, 40.23.12(.19)**
umbilically **1.31.24(.9.12)**
umbilicate **22.4.11(.6), 22.19.12(.10)**
umbilicus **34.18.13(.10)**
umble **40.20.19**
umbo **19.9.14**
umbonal **40.26.15**
umbonate **22.4.14(.9.1), 22.19.15(.9)**
umbones **35.1.12(.4)**
umbra **17.32.18**
umbrage **39.2.22(.10)**
umbrageous **34.18.24**
umbral **40.16.13(.15)**
umbrella **17.34.5(.15)**
umbrella-like **24.13.7(.8)**
umbrette **22.5.19**
Umbria **3.22.14**
Umbrian **28.3.20(.10)**
Umbriel **40.3.14(.8)**
umbriferous **34.18.27(.20)**
umiak **24.6.1**
umlaut **22.9.19**
ump **20.16.5**
umph **30.18**
umpirage **39.2.22(.8)**
umpire **17.6.1**
umpireship **20.2.7(.9)**
umpteen **28.1.9**
umpteenth **32.21**
umpty **1.10.19**
UN **28.5**
Una **17.18.15**
unabashed **22.30**
unabashedly **1.31.23(.14.7)**
unabatedly **1.31.23(.14.3)**

unable **40.20.4**
unabridged **23.30**
unabsorbed **23.21**
unacademic **24.2.14(.3)**
unaccented **23.18.9(.19)**
unacceptable
  40.20.16(.11.4)
unacceptableness
  34.18.16(.37.4)
unacceptably
  1.31.21(.4.3)
unaccepted **23.18.9(.16)**
unacclaimed **23.23.3**
unaccompanied **23.2.13**
unaccomplished **22.30**
unaccountable
  40.20.16(.11.6)
unaccountably
  1.31.21(.4.3)
unaccounted **23.18.9(.19)**
unaccustomed **23.23.9**
unaccustomedly
  1.31.23(.16)
unachievable
  40.20.16(.19)
unacknowledged **23.30**
unacquainted
  23.18.9(.19)
unadaptable
  40.20.16(.11.4)
unadapted **23.18.9(.16)**
unaddressed **22.29.5(.12)**
unadjacent
  22.26.15(.17.1)
unadjusted **23.18.9(.20)**
unadopted **23.18.9(.16)**
unadulterated **23.18.9(.3)**
unadventurous
  34.18.27(.26)
unadventurously
  1.31.33(.12.5)
unadvisable **40.20.16(.22)**
unadvisedly
  1.31.23(.14.7)
unadvisedness
  34.18.16(.21.1)
unaesthetic **24.2.10(.3.2)**
unaffected **23.18.9(.17)**
unaffectedly
  1.31.23(.14.3)
unaffectedness
  34.18.16(.21.1)
unaffectionate
  22.19.15(.9)
unaffordable
  40.20.16(.12)
unafraid **23.4.15**
unaggressive **31.2.4(.4)**
unaided **23.18.10(.2)**
unalienable
  40.20.16(.16.1)
unalienably **1.31.21(.6)**

unaligned **23.24.13**
unalike **24.13.7**
unallied **23.15.16**
unallotted **23.18.9(.8)**
unallowable **40.20.16(.3)**
unalloyed **23.13.20**
unalterable
  40.20.16(.27.3)
unalterableness
  34.18.16(.37.4)
unalterably **1.31.21(.8)**
unaltered **23.18.9(.21)**
unaltering **29.1.30(.8)**
unambiguous **34.18.6**
unambiguously
  1.31.33(.12.1)
unambitious **34.18.22(.2)**
unambitiously
  1.31.33(.12.4)
unambitiousness
  34.18.16(.31.4)
unambivalent
  22.26.15(.25)
unambivalently
  1.31.22(.20.5)
unamenable
  40.20.16(.16.1)
un-American
  28.17.13(.13)
un-Americanism
  27.15.21(.2.9)
unamiable **40.20.3**
unamplified **23.15.9**
unamused **23.28.3**
unamusing **29.1.24**
unaneled **23.31.1(.1)**
unanimity **1.10.16(.12)**
unanimous **34.18.15(.10)**
unanimously
  1.31.33(.12.3)
unanimousness
  34.18.16(.31.3)
unannounced **22.29.21**
unanswerable
  40.20.16(.27.5)
unanswerableness
  34.18.16(.37.4)
unanswerably
  1.31.21(.8)
unanswered **23.18.20**
unapologetic
  24.2.10(.3.2)
unapologetically
  1.31.24(.9.3)
unapostolic **24.2.27(.9)**
unapparent
  22.26.15(.23.1)
unappealable
  40.20.16(.29)
unappealing **29.1.31(.1)**
unappealingly
  1.31.28(.1.18)

unappeasable
  40.20.16(.22)
unappetisingly
  1.31.28(.1.12)
unappetizing **29.1.24**
unappetizingly
  1.31.28(.1.12)
unapplied **23.15.16**
unappreciable **40.20.3,
  40.20.16(.23)**
unappreciative **31.2.1(.2)**
unapproachable
  40.20.16(.24)
unapproachableness
  34.18.16(.37.4)
unapproachably
  1.31.21(.7.4)
unapt **22.22.4**
unaptly **1.31.22(.18)**
unarguable **40.20.16(.6)**
unarguably **1.31.21(.2)**
unargued **23.17.4(.3)**
unarm **27.8**
unarmed **23.23.5**
unarresting **29.1.12(.21)**
unarrestingly
  1.31.28(.1.4)
unartistic **24.2.10(.15.2)**
unartistically
  1.31.24(.9.6)
unary **1.29.11(.13.1)**
unascertainable
  40.20.16(.16.1)
unascertainably
  1.31.21(.6)
unashamed **23.23.3**
unashamedly
  1.31.23(.14.6)
unashamedness
  34.18.16(.21.1)
unasked **22.23.14**
unasked-for **12.11.5**
unassailability
  1.10.16(.22.3)
unassailable **40.20.16(.29)**
unassailableness
  34.18.16(.37.4)
unassailably **1.31.21(.9)**
unassertive **31.2.1(.10)**
unassertively
  1.31.30(.7.1)
unassertiveness
  34.18.16(.28.1)
unassignable
  40.20.16(.16.2)
unassigned **23.24.13**
unassimilable
  40.20.16(.29)
unassisted **23.18.9(.20)**
unassuageable
  40.20.16(.25)
unassuaged **23.30**

unassuming **29.1.16**
unassumingly
  1.31.28(.1.7)
unassumingness
  34.18.16(.26)
unattached **22.31**
unattackable
  40.20.16(.13)
unattainable
  40.20.16(.16.1)
unattainableness
  34.18.16(.37.4)
unattainably **1.31.21(.6)**
unattained **23.24.4**
unattempted **23.18.9(.18)**
unattended **23.18.10(.14)**
unattested **23.18.9(.20)**
unattractive **31.2.1(.13.3)**
unattractively
  1.31.30(.7.2)
unattractiveness
  34.18.16(.28.1)
unattributable
  40.20.16(.11.3)
unattributably
  1.31.21(.4.3)
unau **12.10**
unaudited **23.18.9(.13)**
unauthentic **24.2.10(.14)**
unauthentically
  1.31.24(.9.5)
unavailable **40.20.16(.29)**
unavailableness
  34.18.16(.37.4)
unavailing **29.1.31(.4)**
unavailingly
  1.31.28(.1.18)
unavenged **23.29, 23.30**
unavoidable **40.20.16(.12)**
unavoidableness
  34.18.16(.37.4)
unavoidably **1.31.21(.4.4)**
unavowed **23.8**
unawakened **23.24.16(.5)**
unaware **6.18**
unawareness **34.18.16(.6)**
unawares **35.6**
unawed **23.12**
unbackable **40.20.16(.13)**
unbacked **22.23.5(.3)**
unbaked **22.23.3**
unbalance **34.24.10(.24)**
unban **28.7.5**
unbar **10.5**
unbearable
  40.20.16(.27.1)
unbearableness
  34.18.16(.37.4)
unbearably **1.31.21(.8)**
unbeatable
  40.20.16(.11.1)
unbeatably **1.31.21(.4.1)**

u

unbeaten 28.17.11(.1)
unbeautiful 40.27.14
unbeautifully 1.31.17(.16.1)
unbecoming 29.1.16
unbecomingly 1.31.28(.1.7)
unbecomingness 34.18.16(.26)
unbefitting 29.1.12(.2)
unbefittingly 1.31.28(.1.4)
unbefittingness 34.18.16(.26)
unbegotten 28.17.11(.9)
unbeknown 28.19.10
unbeknownst 22.29.21
unbelief 30.1.9
unbelievable 40.20.16(.19)
unbelievableness 34.18.16(.37.4)
unbelievably 1.31.21(.7.1)
unbeliever 17.21.1
unbelieving 29.1.20
unbelievingly 1.31.28(.1.9)
unbelievingness 34.18.16(.26)
unbeloved 23.18.17
unbelt 22.32.2
unbend 23.24.5(.3)
unbendingly 1.31.28(.1.5)
unbendingness 34.18.16(.26)
unbent 22.26.4(.3)
unbiased 22.29.15(.4)
unbiblical 40.23.12(.19)
unbiddable 40.20.16(.12)
unbidden 28.17.12(.2)
unbind 23.24.13
unbleached 22.31
unblemished 22.30
unblessed 22.29.5(.13)
unblest 22.29.5(.13)
unblinking 29.1.14(.14)
unblinkingly 1.31.28(.1.6)
unblock 24.9.16(.10)
unbloody 1.11.13
unblown 28.19.19
unblushing 29.1.25
unblushingly 1.31.28(.1.13)
unbolt 22.32.12
unbonnet 22.2.12
unbookish 36.2.13
unboot 22.18.3
unborn 28.11.2
unbothered 23.18.19

unbound 23.24.7(.2)
unbounded 23.18.10(.14)
unboundedly 1.31.23(.14.4)
unboundedness 34.18.16(.21.1)
unbowed 23.8
unbrace 34.4.13
unbranded 23.18.10(.14)
unbreachable 40.20.16(.24)
unbreakable 40.20.16(.13)
unbreakably 1.31.21(.5)
unbreathable 40.20.16(.20)
unbribable 40.20.16(.10)
unbridgeable 40.20.16(.25)
unbridle 40.22.11
un-British 36.2.11
unbroken 28.17.13(.15)
unbrokenly 1.31.27(.14)
unbrokenness 34.18.16(.25)
unbrotherly 1.31.17(.19)
unbrushed 22.30
unbuckle 40.23.9
unbuild 23.31.2
unbuilt 22.32.1
unbundle 40.22.16
unburden 28.17.12(.17)
unburied 23.2.22
unburnt 22.26.16
unbury 1.29.4
unbutton 28.17.11(.11)
uncage 39.4.3
uncalculating 29.1.12(.3)
uncalled-for 12.11.6
uncandid 23.18.10(.14)
uncannily 1.31.17(.14.1)
uncanniness 34.18.16(.2.5)
uncanny 1.16.6
uncanonical 40.23.12(.11)
uncanonically 1.31.24(.9.8)
uncap 20.5.1
uncared-for 12.11.6
uncaring 29.1.30(.4)
uncaringly 1.31.28(.1.17)
uncase 34.4.6
uncashed 22.30
uncatchable 40.20.16(.24)
uncategorizable 40.20.16(.22)
uncaught 22.13.4
unceasing 29.1.23
unceasingly 1.31.28(.1.11)
uncensured 23.18.22

unceremonious 34.3.6(.7)
unceremoniously 1.31.33(.1.2)
unceremoniousness 34.18.16(.31.1)
uncertain 28.17.11(.16)
uncertainly 1.31.27(.14)
uncertainty 1.10.23(.12)
uncertified 23.15.9
unchain 28.4.15
unchallengeable 40.20.16(.25)
unchallengeably 1.31.21(.7.3)
unchallenging 29.1.26, 29.1.28
unchangeable 40.20.16(.25)
unchangeableness 34.18.16(.37.4)
unchangeably 1.31.21(.7.3)
unchanged 23.29
unchanging 29.1.26, 29.1.28
unchangingly 1.31.28(.1.14)
unchangingness 34.18.16(.26)
uncharacteristic 24.2.10(.15.2)
uncharacteristically 1.31.24(.9.6)
uncharismatic 24.2.10(.4.2)
uncharitable 40.20.16(.11.3)
uncharitableness 34.18.16(.37.4)
uncharitably 1.31.21(.4.2)
uncharming 29.1.16
uncharted 23.18.9(.7)
unchaste 22.29.4
unchastely 1.31.22(.22)
unchastened 23.24.16(.10)
unchasteness 34.18.16(.20.4)
unchastity 1.10.16(.8)
unchecked 22.23.4(.8)
unchivalrous 34.18.27(.28)
unchivalrously 1.31.33(.12.5)
unchosen 28.17.24(.14)
unchristian 28.17.27
unchristianly 1.31.27(.14)
unchurch 38.16
unci 14.18
uncial 40.3.10, 40.33.12(.5)

unciform 27.10.5(.2)
uncinate 22.4.14(.9.3), 22.19.15(.9)
uncircumcised 23.28.2
uncircumcision 28.17.26(.2)
uncivil 40.28.2
uncivilly 1.31.17(.17)
unclad 23.7.17
unclaimed 23.23.3
unclasp 20.17
unclassifiable 40.20.16(.5)
unclassified 23.15.9
uncle 40.23.15
unclean 28.1.27(.10)
uncleanliness 34.18.16(.2.10)
uncleanly 1.31.27(.1)
uncleanness 34.18.16(.25)
uncleansed 23.28.5
unclear 3.24.14
unclearly 1.31.3(.12)
unclearness 34.18.16(.3)
unclench 38.18.2
Uncle Sam 27.6
Uncle Tom 27.9
unclimbable 40.20.16(.15)
unclinch 38.18.1
unclip 20.2.13
uncloak 24.18.15
unclog 26.7.14
unclose 35.20.14
unclothe 33.10
unclouded 23.18.10(.5)
unco 19.12.15
uncoded 23.18.10(.13)
uncoil 40.11.4
uncollected 23.18.9(.17)
uncoloured 23.18.29
uncome-at-able 40.20.16(.11.1)
uncomfortable 40.20.16(.11.3)
uncomfortableness 34.18.16(.37.4)
uncomfortably 1.31.21(.4.2)
uncomforted 23.18.9(.13)
uncommercial 40.33.10
uncommon 28.17.16(.10)
uncommonly 1.31.27(.14)
uncommonness 34.18.16(.25)
uncommunicable 40.20.16(.13)
uncommunicative 31.2.1(.9.1)

uncommunicatively
1.31.30(.7.1)
uncommunicativeness
34.18.16(.28.1)
uncompetitive
31.2.1(.9.1)
uncompetitiveness
34.18.16(.28.1)
uncomplaining
29.1.17(.3)
uncomplainingly
1.31.28(.1.7)
uncomplimentary
1.29.11(.8.12)
uncompounded
23.18.10(.14)
uncomprehended
23.18.10(.14)
uncomprehending
29.1.13(.14)
uncomprehendingly
1.31.28(.1.5)
uncomprehension
28.17.25(.16)
uncompromising
29.1.24
uncompromisingly
1.31.28(.1.12)
uncompromisingness
34.18.16(.26)
unconcern **28.18.9**
unconcernedly
1.31.23(.14.6)
unconditional
40.26.13(.14.1)
unconditionality
1.10.16(.32.8)
unconditionally
1.31.17(.14.3)
unconditioned
23.24.16(.12)
unconfident **22.26.15(.10)**
unconfined **23.24.13**
unconfirmed **23.23.10**
unconformable
40.20.16(.15)
unconformableness
34.18.16(.37.4)
unconformably
1.31.21(.6)
unconformity
1.10.16(.12)
uncongenial **40.3.7(.1)**
uncongenially **1.31.3(.7)**
uncongested
23.18.9(.20)
unconjecturable
40.20.16(.27.5)
unconnected **23.18.9(.17)**
unconnectedly
1.31.23(.14.3)
unconnectedness
34.18.16(.21.1)

unconquerable
40.20.16(.27.3)
unconquerableness
34.18.16(.37.4)
unconquerably
1.31.21(.8)
unconquered **23.18.11**
unconscionable
40.20.16(.16.3)
unconscionableness
34.18.16(.37.4)
unconscionably
1.31.21(.6)
unconscious
34.18.22(.12)
unconsciously
1.31.33(.12.4)
unconsciousness
34.18.16(.31.4)
unconsecrated
23.18.9(.3)
unconsenting
29.1.12(.19)
unconsolable
40.20.16(.29)
unconsolably **1.31.21(.9)**
unconstitutional
40.26.13(.14.5)
unconstitutionality
1.10.16(.32.8)
unconstitutionally
1.31.17(.14.3)
unconstrainedly
1.31.23(.14.6)
unconstraint **22.26.3**
unconstricted
23.18.9(.17)
unconstructive
31.2.1(.13.4)
unconsumed **23.23.8**
uncontactable
40.20.16(.11.5)
uncontainable
40.20.16(.16.1)
uncontentious
34.18.22(.12)
uncontentiously
1.31.33(.12.4)
uncontested **23.18.9(.20)**
uncontestedly
1.31.23(.14.3)
uncontrollable
40.20.16(.29)
uncontrollableness
34.18.16(.37.4)
uncontrollably
1.31.21(.9)
uncontrolled
23.31.13(.11)
uncontrolledly
1.31.23(.14.7)
uncontroversial
40.33.10

uncontroversially
1.31.17(.22)
uncontroverted
23.18.9(.14)
uncontrovertible
40.20.16(.11.3)
unconventional
40.26.13(.14.7)
unconventionalism
27.15.21(.2.15)
unconventionality
1.10.16(.32.8)
unconventionally
1.31.17(.14.3)
unconverted **23.18.9(.14)**
unconvertible
40.20.16(.11.3)
unconvinced **22.29.21**
unconvincing **29.1.23**
unconvincingly
1.31.28(.1.11)
uncooked **22.23.9**
uncool **40.15.4**
uncooperative
31.2.1(.9.4)
uncooperatively
1.31.30(.7.1)
uncooperativeness
34.18.16(.28.1)
uncopiable **40.20.3**
uncord **23.12.4**
uncordial **40.3.4**
uncork **24.10.4**
uncorrected **23.18.9(.17)**
uncorroborated
23.18.9(.3)
uncorrupted **23.18.9(.16)**
uncountability
1.10.16(.22.2)
uncountable
40.20.16(.11.6)
uncountably **1.31.21(.4.3)**
uncounted **23.18.9(.19)**
uncouple **40.19.8**
uncourtly **1.31.22(.10)**
uncouth **32.13**
uncouthly **1.31.31**
uncouthness
34.18.16(.29)
uncovenanted
23.18.9(.19)
uncover **17.21.9**
uncrackable
40.20.16(.13)
uncracked **22.23.5(.9)**
uncreased **22.29.1**
uncreate **22.4**
uncreative **31.2.1(.3)**
uncritical **40.23.12(.7.1)**
uncritically **1.31.24(.9.3)**
uncropped **22.22.5**
uncross **34.10.16**

uncrossable
40.20.16(.21.2)
uncrowded **23.18.10(.5)**
uncrown **28.8.5**
uncrushable
40.20.16(.23)
uncrushed **22.30**
UNCTAD **23.7.7**
unction **28.17.25(.15.6)**
unctuous **34.18.6**
unctuously **1.31.33(.12.1)**
unctuousness
34.18.16(.31.2)
uncultured **23.18.24**
uncurb **21.15**
uncurl **40.17**
uncurtailed **23.31.3**
uncus **34.18.13(.13)**
uncut **22.15.4**
undamped **22.25**
undaunted **23.18.9(.19)**
undauntedly
1.31.23(.14.3)
undauntedness
34.18.16(.21.1)
undead **23.5.4**
undealt **22.32.2**
undecagon **28.10.12,
28.17.15(.13)**
undeceive **31.1.4**
undecidable **40.20.16(.12)**
undecided **23.18.10(.11)**
undecidedly
1.31.23(.14.4)
undecidedness
34.18.16(.21.1)
undecipherable
40.20.16(.27.5)
undeciphered
23.18.16(.8)
undeclared **23.6**
undecodable
40.20.16(.12)
undefended
23.18.10(.14)
undefinable
40.20.16(.16.2)
undefinably **1.31.21(.6)**
undefined **23.24.13**
undelivered **23.18.17**
undemanding
29.1.13(.14)
undemandingness
34.18.16(.26)
undemocratic
24.2.10(.4.5)
undemocratically
1.31.24(.9.4)
undemonstrable
40.20.16(.27.6)
undemonstrative
31.2.1(.9.4)

u

undemonstratively **1.31.30(.7.1)**
undemonstrativeness **34.18.16(.28.1)**
undeniable **40.20.16(.5)**
undeniableness **34.18.16(.37.4)**
undeniably **1.31.21(.2)**
undenied **23.15.8**
undenominational **40.26.13(.14.2)**
undented **23.18.9(.19)**
undependable **40.20.16(.12)**
under **17.13.20(.10)**
underachieve **31.1.5**
underachievement **22.26.15(.13.5)**
underachiever **17.21.1**
underact **22.23.5**
under-age **39.4**
underarm **27.8.9**
underbelly **1.31.5**
underbid **23.2.7**
underbidder **17.13.2**
underblanket **22.2.9(.9)**
underbody **1.11.10**
underbred **23.5.15**
underbrush **36.12**
undercapacity **1.10.16(.16.1)**
undercarriage **39.2.22(.4)**
undercart **22.10.5**
undercharge **39.8**
underclass **34.9.7**
underclay **4.28.12**
undercliff **30.2.6**
underclothes **35.20.14, 35.29**
underclothing **29.1.22**
undercoat **22.21.5**
underconsumption **28.17.25(.14)**
underconsumptionist **22.29.2(.18.2)**
undercook **24.14.5**
undercover **17.21.9**
undercroft **22.27.5**
undercurrent **22.26.15(.23.2)**
undercut **22.15.4**
underdeveloped **22.22.8**
underdevelopment **22.26.15(.13.3)**
underdid **23.2.9**
underdo **16.8**
underdoes **35.14**
underdog **26.7.4**
underdone **28.13.4**
underdrainage **39.2.15**
underdrawers **35.12**

underdrawing **29.1.5**
underdress **34.5.14(.6)**
underemphases **35.1.16(.10)**
underemphasis **34.2.17(.10.4)**
underemphasize **35.15.16(.4)**
underemployed **23.13.20**
underemployment **22.26.15(.13.1)**
underequipped **22.22.1**
underestimate **22.4.13(.6), 22.19.14**
underestimation **28.17.25(.3.7)**
underexploited **23.18.9(.9)**
underexpose **35.20.1**
underexposure **17.27.9**
underfed **23.5.8**
underfelt **22.32.2**
underfinanced **22.29.21**
underfinancing **29.1.23**
under-fives **35.28.6**
underfloor **12.23.9**
underflooring **29.1.30(.7)**
underflow **19.29.21**
underfoot **22.17**
underframe **27.4.8**
underfunded **23.18.10(.14)**
underfunding **29.1.13(.14)**
underfur **18.9**
undergarment **22.26.15(.13.1)**
undergird **23.19.3**
underglaze **35.4.18**
undergo **19.13**
undergone **28.10.12**
undergrad **23.7.16**
undergraduate **22.19.5**
underground **23.24.7(.10)**
undergrowth **32.16**
underhand **23.24.6(.11)**
underhanded **23.18.10(.14)**
underhandedly **1.31.23(.14.4)**
underhandedness **34.18.16(.21.1)**
Underhill **40.2.18**
underhung **29.8**
underlain **28.4.19**
underlay **4.28, 4.28.7**
underlease **34.1.8**
underlet **22.5.21**
underlie **14.25**
underline **28.14.19**

underlinen **28.2.18**
underling **29.1.31(.12)**
underlip **20.2.13**
underlit **22.2.25**
under-manager **17.29.13**
undermanned **23.24.6(.8)**
undermanning **29.1.17(.5)**
undermentioned **23.24.16(.12)**
undermine **28.14.8**
underminer **17.18.13(.4)**
underminingly **1.31.28(.1.7)**
undermost **22.29.17(.4)**
underneath **32.1**
undernourished **22.30**
undernourishment **22.26.15(.13.6)**
under-occupancy **1.22.23(.10.2)**
underpaid **23.4.1**
underpainting **29.1.12(.19)**
underpants **34.22.18, 34.24.4**
underpart **22.10.1**
underpass **34.9.1**
underpay **4.7**
underpayment **22.26.15(.13.1)**
underperform **27.10.5**
underperformance **34.24.10(.14)**
underpin **28.2.9**
underpinning **29.1.17(.2)**
underplant **22.26.6, 22.26.8**
underplay **4.28.9**
underplot **22.11.17**
underpowered **23.18.2**
under-prepared **23.6**
underprice **34.15.9**
underpriced **22.29.13**
underprivileged **23.30**
underproduction **28.17.25(.15.5)**
underproof **30.13.4**
underprop **20.7.12**
under-provision **28.17.26(.2)**
underquote **22.21.13**
underrate **22.4.22**
under-rehearsed **22.29.16**
under-report **22.13.1**
under-represented **23.18.9(.19)**
under-resourced **22.29.10**
underripe **20.10.5**

underscore **12.7**
undersea **2.22**
underseal **40.1.10**
undersecretary **1.29.3, 1.29.11(.8.9)**
undersell **40.5.11**
underset **22.5.13**
undersexed **22.29.20**
undersheet **22.1.11**
undershirt **22.20.12**
undershoot **22.18.7**
undershorts **34.22.9**
undershot **22.11.12**
undershrub **21.11**
underside **23.15.11(.6)**
undersign **28.14.13**
undersigned **23.24.13**
undersize **35.15.16**
undersized **23.28.2**
underskirt **22.20.4**
underslung **29.8**
undersold **23.31.13(.8)**
undersow **19.20**
underspend **23.24.5(.2)**
underspent **22.26.4(.2)**
understaffed **22.27.4(.2)**
understaffing **29.1.19**
understairs **35.6**
understand **23.24.6(.5)**
understandability **1.10.16(.22.3)**
understandable **40.20.16(.12)**
understandably **1.31.21(.4.4)**
understander **17.13.20(.4)**
understanding **29.1.13(.14)**
understandingly **1.31.28(.1.5)**
understate **22.4.9(.9)**
understatement **22.26.15(.13.3)**
understater **17.12.4(.5)**
understeer **3.4.13**
understood **23.16.1**
understorey **1.29.8**
understrapper **17.10.5**
under-strength **32.19**
understudy **1.11.13**
undersubscribed **23.21**
undersurface **34.18.17**
undertake **24.3.4**
undertaker **17.14.3(.2)**
undertaking **29.1.14(.3)**
undertenancy **1.22.23(.10.3)**
undertenant **22.26.15(.14)**

under-the-counter 17.12.22(.5)
underthings 35.27
undertint 22.26.1
undertone 28.19.4(.5)
undertook 24.14.4
undertow 19.10.12
undertrained 23.24.4
undertrick 24.2.26(.14.3)
under-use 35.17.7
underused 23.28.3
under-utilization 28.17.25(.3.12)
under-utilize 35.15.21(.4.3)
undervaluation 28.17.25(.3.1)
undervalue 16.24.17
undervest 22.29.5(.5)
underwater 17.12.10(.7)
underwear 6.18.4
underweight 22.4.21
underwent 22.26.4(.13)
underwhelm 27.18
underwing 29.1.29
underwire 17.6.13
underwired 23.18.3
underwood 23.16.6(.6)
underwork 24.17.6(.4)
underworld 23.31.12
underwrite 22.16.24
underwriter 17.12.13(.8)
underwritten 28.17.11(.2)
undescended 23.18.10(.14)
undescribed 23.21
undeservedly 1.31.23(.14.7)
undeservedness 34.18.16(.21.1)
undeserving 29.1.20
undeservingly 1.31.28(.1.9)
undesignedly 1.31.23(.14.6)
undesirable 40.20.16(.27.2)
undesirableness 34.18.16(.37.4)
undesirably 1.31.21(.8)
undesired 23.18.3
undesirous 34.18.27(.11)
undetectable 40.20.16(.11.5)
undetectably 1.31.21(.4.3)
undetected 23.18.9(.17)
undetermined 23.24.16(.7)
undeterred 23.19.2
undeveloped 22.22.8

undeviating 29.1.12(.3)
undeviatingly 1.31.28(.1.4)
undiagnosed 23.28.4
undid 23.2.9
undies 35.2.4
undigested 23.18.9(.20)
undignified 23.15.9
undiminished 22.30
undimmed 23.23.2
undine 28.1.10
undiplomatic 24.2.10(.4.2)
undiplomatically 1.31.24(.9.4)
undirected 23.18.9(.17)
undiscerning 29.1.17(.13)
undischarged 23.30
undiscipline 28.17.33(.16)
undisclosed 23.28.4
undiscoverable 40.20.16(.27.5)
undiscoverably 1.31.21(.8)
undiscovered 23.18.17
undiscussed 22.29.12
undisguisedly 1.31.23(.14.7)
undismayed 23.4.7
undisposed 23.28.4
undisputed 23.18.9(.12)
undistinguishable 40.20.16(.23)
undistinguished 22.30
undivided 23.18.10(.11)
undo 16.8
undock 24.9.5
undocumented 23.18.9(.19)
undogmatic 24.2.10(.4.2)
undone 28.13.4
undoubtable 40.20.16(.11.1)
undoubtably 1.31.21(.4.1)
undoubted 23.18.9(.6)
undoubtedly 1.31.23(.14.3)
undoubting 29.1.12(.6)
undramatic 24.2.10(.4.2)
undraped 22.22.2
undreamed 23.23.1
undreamed-of 31.7
undreamt 22.25
undreamt-of 31.7
undress 34.5.14(.6)
undrinkable 40.20.16(.13)
undrivable 40.20.16(.19)
UNDRO 19.27.16
undue 16.24.6
undulant 22.26.15(.25)

undulate 22.4.23(.7.2)
undulately 1.31.22(.15)
undulation 28.17.25(.3.14)
undulatory 1.29.11(.8.2)
unduly 1.31.16
undutiful 40.27.14
undutifully 1.31.17(.16.1)
undutifulness 34.18.16(.37.1)
undy 1.11.20(.7)
undyed 23.15.5
undying 29.1.7
undyingly 1.31.28(.1.1)
undynamic 24.2.14(.4)
unearth 32.15
unearthliness 34.18.16(.2.10)
unearthly 1.31.31
unease 35.1
uneasily 1.31.17(.21)
uneasiness 34.18.16(.2.7)
uneasy 1.23.1
uneatable 40.20.16(.11.1)
uneatableness 34.18.16(.37.4)
uneaten 28.17.11(.1)
uneconomic 24.2.14(.6)
uneconomical 40.23.12(.10)
uneconomically 1.31.24(.9.8)
unedifying 29.1.7
unedifyingly 1.31.28(.1.1)
unedited 23.18.9(.13)
uneducable 40.20.16(.13)
uneducated 23.18.9(.3)
unelectable 40.20.16(.11.5)
unelected 23.18.9(.17)
unembarrassed 22.29.15(.17)
unembellished 22.30
unemotional 40.26.13(.14.5)
unemotionally 1.31.17(.14.3)
unemphatic 24.2.10(.4.4)
unemphatically 1.31.24(.9.4)
unemployability 1.10.16(.22.2)
unemployable 40.20.16(.4)
unemployed 23.13.20
unemployment 22.26.15(.13.1)
unemptied 23.2.8
unenclosed 23.28.4
unendearing 29.1.30(.2)
unending 29.1.13(.14)

unendingly 1.31.28(.1.5)
unendingness 34.18.16(.26)
unendowed 23.8
unendurable 40.20.16(.27.2)
unendurably 1.31.21(.8)
unenforceable 40.20.16(.21.2)
unenforced 22.29.10
unenjoyable 40.20.16(.4)
unenlightening 29.1.17(.12)
unenterprising 29.1.24
unenthusiastic 24.2.10(.15.4)
unenthusiastically 1.31.24(.9.6)
unenviable 40.20.3
unenviably 1.31.21(.1)
unenvied 23.2.15
unenvironmental 40.21.17(.2)
UNEP 20.4
unequable 40.20.16(.26)
unequal 40.35.3
unequally 1.31.17(.26)
unequalness 34.18.16(.37.3)
unequipped 22.22.1
unequitable 40.20.16(.11.3)
unequitably 1.31.21(.4.2)
unequivocal 40.23.12(.13)
unequivocally 1.31.24(.9.9)
unequivocalness 34.18.16(.37.5)
unerring 29.1.30(.9)
unerringly 1.31.28(.1.17)
unerringness 34.18.16(.26)
unescapable 40.20.16(.9)
UNESCO 19.12.17
unessential 40.33.12(.3)
unestablished 22.30
unethical 40.23.12(.14)
unethically 1.31.24(.9.10)
uneven 28.17.20(.1)
unevenly 1.31.27(.14)
unevenness 34.18.16(.25)
uneventful 40.27.18
uneventfully 1.31.17(.16.2)
uneventfulness 34.18.16(.37.2)
unexacting 29.1.12(.18)
unexamined 23.24.16(.7)
unexampled 23.31.14
unexceptionable 40.20.16(.16.3)

u

unexceptionableness **34.18.16(.37.4)**
unexceptionably **1.31.21(.6)**
unexceptional **40.26.13(.14.6)**
unexceptionally **1.31.17(.14.3)**
unexcitable **40.20.16(.11.2)**
unexciting **29.1.12(.11)**
unexclusive **31.2.4(.8)**
unexhausted **23.18.9(.20)**
unexpected **23.18.9(.17)**
unexpectedly **1.31.23(.14.3)**
unexpectedness **34.18.16(.21.1)**
unexpired **23.18.3**
unexplainable **40.20.16(.16.1)**
unexplainably **1.31.21(.6)**
unexplained **23.24.4**
unexploded **23.18.10(.13)**
unexploited **23.18.9(.9)**
unexplored **23.12.11**
unexportable **40.20.16(.11.2)**
unexposed **23.28.4**
unexpressed **22.29.5(.12)**
unexpressible **40.20.16(.21.1)**
unexpressibly **1.31.21(.7.2)**
unexpressive **31.2.4(.4)**
unfaceable **40.20.16(.21.1)**
unfaded **23.18.10(.2)**
unfading **29.1.13(.3)**
unfadingly **1.31.28(.1.5)**
unfailing **29.1.31(.4)**
unfailingly **1.31.28(.1.18)**
unfailingness **34.18.16(.26)**
unfair **6.10**
unfairly **1.31.6**
unfairness **34.18.16(.6)**
unfaithful **40.27.24**
unfaithfully **1.31.17(.16.2)**
unfaithfulness **34.18.16(.37.2)**
unfaltering **29.1.30(.8)**
unfalteringly **1.31.28(.1.17)**
unfamiliar **3.24.2**
unfamiliarity **1.10.16(.21.1)**
unfancied **23.2.16**
unfashionable **40.20.16(.16.3)**

unfashionableness **34.18.16(.37.4)**
unfashionably **1.31.21(.6)**
unfasten **28.17.23(.7)**
unfathered **23.18.19**
unfatherliness **34.18.16(.2.10)**
unfatherly **1.31.17(.19)**
unfathomable **40.20.16(.15)**
unfathomableness **34.18.16(.37.4)**
unfathomably **1.31.21(.6)**
unfathomed **23.23.9**
unfavorableness **34.18.16(.37.4)**
unfavorably **1.31.21(.8)**
unfavourable **40.20.16(.27.5)**
unfavourableness **34.18.16(.37.4)**
unfavourably **1.31.21(.8)**
unfavourite **22.19.24(.9)**
unfazed **23.28.1**
unfeasibility **1.10.16(.22.2)**
unfeasible **40.20.16(.22)**
unfeasibly **1.31.21(.7.2)**
unfed **23.5.8**
unfeeling **29.1.31(.1)**
unfeelingly **1.31.28(.1.18)**
unfeelingness **34.18.16(.26)**
unfeigned **23.24.4**
unfeignedly **1.31.23(.14.6)**
unfelt **22.32.2**
unfeminine **28.2.18**
unfemininity **1.10.16(.13)**
unfenced **22.29.21**
unfermented **23.18.9(.19)**
unfetter **17.12.5(.6)**
unfilial **40.3.15**
unfilially **1.31.3(.12)**
unfilled **23.31.2**
unfinancial **40.33.12(.4)**
unfinished **22.30**
unfit **22.2.13**
unfitly **1.31.22(.2)**
unfitness **34.18.16(.20.1)**
unfitting **29.1.12(.2)**
unfittingly **1.31.28(.1.4)**
unfix **34.23.2(.7)**
unflagging **29.1.15**
unflaggingly **1.31.28(.1.6)**
unflappability **1.10.16(.22.2)**
unflappable **40.20.16(.9)**
unflappably **1.31.21(.3)**

unflattering **29.1.30(.8)**
unflatteringly **1.31.28(.1.17)**
unflavoured **23.18.17**
unfledged **23.30**
unfleshed **22.30**
unflexed **22.29.20**
unflickering **29.1.30(.8)**
unflinching **29.1.25, 29.1.27**
unflinchingly **1.31.28(.1.13)**
unflurried **23.2.22**
unflustered **23.18.9(.20)**
unfold **23.31.13(.7)**
unfoldment **22.26.15(.13.3)**
unforced **22.29.10**
unforcedly **1.31.23(.14.7)**
unfordable **40.20.16(.12)**
unforecast **22.29.6(.5), 22.29.8(.3)**
unforeseeable **40.20.16(.1)**
unforeseen **28.1.18**
unforgettable **40.20.16(.11.1)**
unforgettably **1.31.21(.4.1)**
unforgivable **40.20.16(.19)**
unforgivably **1.31.21(.7.1)**
unforgiveably **1.31.21(.7.1)**
unforgiven **28.17.20(.2)**
unforgiving **29.1.20**
unforgivingly **1.31.28(.1.9)**
unforgivingness **34.18.16(.26)**
unforgotten **28.17.11(.9)**
unformed **23.23.6**
unforthcoming **29.1.16**
unfortified **23.15.9**
unfortunate **22.19.15(.9)**
unfortunately **1.31.22(.15)**
unfounded **23.18.10(.14)**
unfoundedly **1.31.23(.14.4)**
unfoundedness **34.18.16(.21.1)**
unframed **23.23.3**
unfree **2.30.13**
unfreedom **27.15.10(.1)**
unfreeze **35.1.22**
unfrequented **23.18.9(.19)**
unfriended **23.18.10(.14)**
unfriendliness **34.18.16(.2.10)**
unfriendly **1.31.23(.17)**

unfrightening **29.1.17(.12)**
unfrock **24.9.15**
unfroze **35.20.12**
unfrozen **28.17.24(.14)**
unfruitful **40.27.18**
unfruitfully **1.31.17(.16.2)**
unfruitfulness **34.18.16(.37.2)**
unfuddled **23.31.17**
unfulfillable **40.20.16(.29)**
unfulfilled **23.31.2**
unfulfilling **29.1.31(.2)**
unfunded **23.18.10(.14)**
unfunnily **1.31.17(.14.1)**
unfunniness **34.18.16(.2.5)**
unfunny **1.16.12**
unfurl **40.17**
unfurnished **22.30**
unfussily **1.31.17(.20)**
unfussy **1.22.12**
ungainliness **34.18.16(.2.10)**
ungainly **1.31.27(.4)**
ungallant **22.26.15(.25)**
ungallantly **1.31.22(.20.5)**
ungenerous **34.18.27(.19)**
ungenerously **1.31.33(.12.5)**
ungenerousness **34.18.16(.31.5)**
ungenial **40.3.7(.1)**
ungentle **40.21.17(.2)**
ungentlemanliness **34.18.16(.2.10)**
ungentlemanly **1.31.27(.14)**
ungentleness **34.18.16(.37.5)**
ungently **1.31.22(.20.1)**
un-get-at-able **40.20.16(.11.1)**
unglamorous **34.18.27(.18)**
unglued **23.17.5**
ungodliness **34.18.16(.2.10)**
ungodly **1.31.23(.8)**
ungovernability **1.10.16(.22.2)**
ungovernable **40.20.16(.16.3)**
ungovernably **1.31.21(.6)**
ungoverned **23.24.16(.9)**
ungraceful **40.27.25**
ungracefully **1.31.17(.16.2)**
ungracefulness **34.18.16(.37.2)**
ungracious **34.18.22(.3)**

ungraciously
1.31.33(**.12.4**)
ungraciousness
34.18.16(**.31.4**)
ungrammatical
40.23.12(**.7.1**)
ungrammaticality
1.10.16(**.32.5**)
ungrammatically
1.31.24(**.9.4**)
ungrammaticalness
34.18.16(**.37.5**)
ungraspable **40.20.16**(**.9**)
ungrateful **40.27.18**
ungratefully
1.31.17(**.16.2**)
ungratefulness
34.18.16(**.37.2**)
ungreen **28.1.25**(**.9**)
ungrounded **23.18.10**(**.14**)
ungrudging **29.1.28**
ungrudgingly
1.31.28(**.1.16**)
ungual **40.16.7, 40.35.4**
unguard **23.9.10**
unguardedly
1.31.23(**.14.4**)
unguardedness
34.18.16(**.21.1**)
unguent **22.26.15**(**.5**)
unguessable
40.20.16(**.21.1**)
unguiculate **22.19.26**(**.13**)
unguided **23.18.10**(**.11**)
unguis **34.2.20**
ungula **17.34.16**(**.21.3**)
ungulae **2.32.9**(**.8**)
ungulate **22.4.23**(**.7.3**),
22.19.26(**.13**)
ungum **27.11.6**
unhallowed **23.20.13**
unhand **23.24.6**(**.11**)
unhandily **1.31.17**(**.10**)
unhandiness
34.18.16(**.2.3**)
unhandsome
27.15.20(**.18**)
unhandy **1.11.20**(**.4**)
unhang **29.4.13**
unhappily **1.31.17**(**.7**)
unhappiness
34.18.16(**.2.2**)
unhappy **1.8.5**
unharbour **17.11.7**
unharmed **23.23.5**
unharmful **40.27.21**
unharmonious **34.3.6**(**.7**)
unharness **34.18.16**(**.9**)
unharvested **23.18.9**(**.20**)
unhasp **20.17**
unhatched **22.31**
UNHCR **10**

unhealed **23.31.1**(**.6**)
unhealthful **40.27.24**
unhealthfulness
34.18.16(**.37.2**)
unhealthily **1.31.17**(**.18**)
unhealthiness
34.18.16(**.2.6**)
unhealthy **1.20.12**
unheard **23.19.7**
unheard-of **31.7**
unhearing **29.1.30**(**.2**)
unheated **23.18.9**(**.1**)
unheeded **23.18.10**(**.1**)
unheedful **40.27.19**
unheeding **29.1.13**(**.1**)
unheedingly **1.31.28**(**.1.5**)
unhelpful **40.27.17**
unhelpfully **1.31.17**(**.16.2**)
unhelpfulness
34.18.16(**.37.2**)
unheralded **23.18.10**(**.15**)
unheroic **24.2.7**
unheroically **1.31.24**(**.9.1**)
unhesitating **29.1.12**(**.3**)
unhesitatingly
1.31.28(**.1.4**)
unhesitatingness
34.18.16(**.26**)
unhidden **28.17.12**(**.2**)
unhindered **23.18.10**(**.14**)
unhinge **39.17.1**
unhip **20.2.9**
unhistoric **24.2.26**(**.6**)
unhistorical **40.23.12**(**.18**)
unhistorically
1.31.24(**.9.12**)
unhitch **38.2.8**
unholiness
34.18.16(**.2.10**)
unholy **1.31.19**
unhook **24.14.9**
unhoped-for **12.11.5**
unhopeful **40.27.17**
unhorse **34.12.7**
unhouse **35.8**
unhuman **28.17.16**(**.15**)
unhung **29.8**
unhurried **23.2.22**
unhurriedly
1.31.23(**.14.7**)
unhurrying **29.1.2**
unhurt **22.20.14**
unhusk **24.20.7**
unhygienic **24.2.15**(**.1**)
unhygienically
1.31.24(**.9.8**)
uni **1.16.14**
Uniat **22.7.2**
Uniate **22.3.6, 22.4.2**(**.7**)
uniaxial **40.3.10**
uniaxially **1.31.3**(**.9**)

unicameral
40.16.13(**.12.2**)
UNICEF **30.4**
unicellular **17.34.16**(**.21.4**)
unicolour **17.34.12**
unicorn **28.11.5**
unicuspid **23.2.6**
unicycle **40.23.10**
unicyclist **22.29.2**(**.31.6**)
unidea'd **23.3**
unideal **40.3.4, 40.16.1**
unidentifiable
40.20.16(**.5**)
unidentified **23.15.9**
unidimensional
40.26.13(**.14.7**)
unidiomatic **24.2.10**(**.4.2**)
unidirectional
40.26.13(**.14.6**)
unidirectionality
1.10.16(**.32.8**)
unidirectionally
1.31.17(**.14.3**)
UNIDO **19.11.11**
unifiable **40.20.16**(**.5**)
unification **28.17.25**(**.3.5**)
unificatory **1.29.11**(**.8.2**)
unifier **17.6.9**(**.4**)
uniflow **19.29.21**
uniform **27.10.5**(**.2**)
uniformitarian
28.3.20(**.4**)
uniformitarianism
27.15.21(**.2.9**)
uniformity **1.10.16**(**.12**)
uniformly **1.31.26**(**.8**)
unify **14.14.4**(**.7**)
Unigate® **22.4.12**(**.5**)
unilateral **40.16.13**(**.12.1**)
unilateralism
27.15.21(**.2.15**)
unilateralist
22.29.2(**.31.4**)
unilaterally **1.31.17**(**.27.1**)
Unilever® **17.21.1**
unilingual **40.35.4**
unilingually **1.31.17**(**.26**)
uniliteral **40.16.13**(**.12.1**)
unilocular **17.34.16**(**.21.2**)
unimaginable
40.20.16(**.16.3**)
unimaginably **1.31.21**(**.6**)
unimaginative
31.2.1(**.9.2**)
unimaginatively
1.31.30(**.7.1**)
unimaginativeness
34.18.16(**.28.1**)
unimpaired **23.6**
unimparted **23.18.9**(**.7**)
unimpeachable
40.20.16(**.24**)

unimpeachably
1.31.21(**.7.4**)
unimpeded **23.18.10**(**.1**)
unimpededly
1.31.23(**.14.4**)
unimportance
34.24.10(**.10**)
unimportant **22.26.15**(**.9**)
unimposing **29.1.24**
unimposingly
1.31.28(**.1.12**)
unimpressed **22.29.5**(**.12**)
unimpressionable
40.20.16(**.16.3**)
unimpressive **31.2.4**(**.4**)
unimpressively
1.31.30(**.7.4**)
unimpressiveness
34.18.16(**.28.2**)
unimpugned **23.24.15**
unindexed **22.29.20**
uninfected **23.18.9**(**.17**)
uninflammable
40.20.16(**.15**)
uninflected **23.18.9**(**.17**)
uninfluenced **22.29.21**
uninfluential **40.33.12**(**.2**)
uninformative
31.2.1(**.9.2**)
uninformed **23.23.6**
uninhabitable
40.20.16(**.11.3**)
uninhabitableness
34.18.16(**.37.4**)
uninhabited **23.18.9**(**.13**)
uninhibited **23.18.9**(**.13**)
uninhibitedly
1.31.23(**.14.3**)
uninhibitedness
34.18.16(**.21.1**)
uninjured **23.18.23,
23.18.25**
uninspired **23.18.3**
uninspiring **29.1.30**(**.8**)
uninspiringly
1.31.28(**.1.17**)
uninsurable
40.20.16(**.27.2**)
unintellectual **40.16.12**
unintelligent
22.26.15(**.21**)
unintelligently
1.31.22(**.20.4**)
unintelligibility
1.10.16(**.22.3**)
unintelligible
40.20.16(**.25**)
unintelligibleness
34.18.16(**.37.4**)
unintelligibly
1.31.21(**.7.4**)
unintended **23.18.10**(**.14**)

u

unmask **24.20.4**
unmasker **17.14.23**
unmatchable **40.20.16(.24)**
unmatchably **1.31.21(.7.4)**
unmatched **22.31**
unmated **23.18.9(.3)**
unmeaning **29.1.17(.1)**
unmeaningly **1.31.28(.1.7)**
unmeaningness **34.18.16(.26)**
unmeant **22.26.4(.8)**
unmeasurable **40.20.16(.27.5)**
unmeasurably **1.31.21(.8)**
unmeasured **23.18.23**
unmelodious **34.3.4**
unmelodiously **1.31.33(.1.1)**
unmemorable **40.20.16(.27.4)**
unmemorably **1.31.21(.8)**
unmended **23.18.10(.14)**
unmentionability **1.10.16(.22.2)**
unmentionable **40.20.16(.16.3)**
unmentionableness **34.18.16(.37.4)**
unmentionably **1.31.21(.6)**
unmentioned **23.24.16(.12)**
unmerchantable **40.20.16(.11.6)**
unmerciful **40.27.14**
unmercifully **1.31.17(.16.1)**
unmercifulness **34.18.16(.37.2)**
unmerited **23.18.9(.13)**
unmet **22.5.8**
unmethodical **40.23.12(.8)**
unmethodically **1.31.24(.9.7)**
unmetrical **40.23.12(.18)**
unmilitary **1.29.11(.8.10)**
unmindful **40.27.19, 40.27.22**
unmindfully **1.31.17(.16.2)**
unmindfulness **34.18.16(.37.2)**
unmingled **23.31.19**
unmissable **40.20.16(.21.1)**
unmistakable **40.20.16(.13)**

unmistakableness **34.18.16(.37.4)**
unmistakably **1.31.21(.5)**
unmistakeably **1.31.21(.5)**
unmistaken **28.17.13(.3)**
unmitigatedly **1.31.23(.14.3)**
unmixed **22.29.20**
unmodified **23.15.9**
unmolested **23.18.9(.20)**
unmoor **12.9, 17.7.7**
unmoral **40.16.13(.7)**
unmorally **1.31.17(.27.1)**
unmotherly **1.31.17(.19)**
unmounted **23.18.9(.19)**
unmourned **23.24.10**
unmovable **40.20.16(.19)**
unmoved **23.26**
unmoving **29.1.20**
unmown **28.19.9**
unmuffle **40.27.11**
unmurmuring **29.1.30(.8)**
unmurmuringly **1.31.28(.1.17)**
unmusical **40.23.12(.16)**
unmusicality **1.10.16(.32.5)**
unmusically **1.31.24(.9.10)**
unmusicalness **34.18.16(.37.5)**
unmuzzle **40.32.11**
unnail **40.4.7**
unnameable **40.20.16(.15)**
unnamed **23.23.3**
unnational **40.26.13(.14.4)**
unnatural **40.16.13(.12.3)**
unnaturally **1.31.17(.27.2)**
unnaturalness **34.18.16(.37.3)**
unnavigable **40.20.16(.14)**
unnecessarily **1.31.17(.27.1)**
unnecessariness **34.18.16(.2.9)**
unnecessary **1.29.3, 1.29.11(.18)**
unneeded **23.18.10(.1)**
unneighborly **1.31.17(.8)**
unneighbourliness **34.18.16(.2.10)**
unneighbourly **1.31.17(.8)**
unnerve **31.11**
unnervingly **1.31.28(.1.9)**
unnoticeable **40.20.16(.21.2)**

unnoticeably **1.31.21(.7.2)**
unnoticed **22.29.2(.13)**
UNNRA **17.32.24**
unnumbered **23.18.8**
UNO **19.15.11**
uno **19.15.11**
unobjectionable **40.20.16(.16.3)**
unobjectionableness **34.18.16(.37.4)**
unobjectionably **1.31.21(.6)**
unobliging **29.1.28**
unobservable **40.20.16(.19)**
unobservant **22.26.15(.16)**
unobservantly **1.31.22(20.4)**
unobservedly **1.31.23(.14.7)**
unobstructed **23.18.9(.17)**
unobtainable **40.20.16(.16.1)**
unobtainably **1.31.21(.6)**
unobtrusive **31.2.4(.8)**
unobtrusively **1.31.30(.7.4)**
unobtrusiveness **34.18.16(.28.2)**
unoccupancy **1.22.23(.10.2)**
unoccupied **23.15.2**
unoffending **29.1.13(.14)**
unofficial **40.33.1**
unofficially **1.31.17(.22)**
unoiled **23.31.7**
unopposed **23.28.4**
unordinary **1.29.11(.13.2)**
unoriginal **40.26.13(.14.8)**
unoriginality **1.10.16(.32.8)**
unoriginally **1.31.17(.14.3)**
unornamental **40.21.17(.2)**
unornamented **23.18.9(.19)**
unorthodox **34.23.8(.4)**
unorthodoxly **1.31.33(.15)**
unorthodoxy **1.22.22**
unostentatious **34.18.22(.3)**
unostentatiously **1.31.33(.12.4)**
unostentatiousness **34.18.16(.31.4)**
unowned **23.24.18**
unpack **24.6.5**

unpacker **17.14.5**
unpadded **23.18.10(.4)**
unpaid **23.4.1**
unpainted **23.18.9(.19)**
unpaired **23.6**
unpalatability **1.10.16(.22.3)**
unpalatable **40.20.16(.11.3)**
unpalatableness **34.18.16(.37.4)**
unpalatably **1.31.21(.4.2)**
unparalleled **23.31.4**
unpardonableness **34.18.16(.37.4)**
unpardonably **1.31.21(.6)**
unparliamentary **1.29.11(.8.12)**
unpatriotic **24.2.10(.6)**
unpatriotically **1.31.24(.9.4)**
unpatronizing **29.1.24**
unpeaceful **40.27.25**
unpeg **26.4**
unpeople **40.19.1**
unperceptive **31.2.1(.12)**
unperceptively **1.31.30(.7.2)**
unperceptiveness **34.18.16(.28.1)**
unperfected **23.18.9(.17)**
unperfumed **23.23.8**
unperson **28.17.23(.15)**
unpersuadable **40.20.16(.12)**
unpersuasive **31.2.4(.3)**
unpersuasively **1.31.30(.7.4)**
unperturbedly **1.31.23(.14.2)**
unphilosophic **24.2.16(.4)**
unphilosophical **40.23.12(.12)**
unphilosophically **1.31.24(.9.9)**
unphysiological **40.23.12(.17.2)**
unphysiologically **1.31.24(.9.11)**
unpick **24.2.8**
unpicturesque **24.20.3**
unpierced **22.29.3**
unpin **28.2.9**
unpitied **23.2.8**
unpitying **29.1.2**
unpityingly **1.31.28(.1.1)**
unplaceable **40.20.16(.21.1)**
unplaced **22.29.4**
unplait **22.7.21**
unplanned **23.24.6(.13)**

unplastered 23.18.9(.20)
unplasticized 23.28.2
unplausible 40.20.16(.22)
unplayable 40.20.16(.2)
unplayably 1.31.21(.2)
unplayed 23.4.16
unpleasant 22.26.15(.18)
unpleasantly 1.31.22(.20.4)
unpleasantness 34.18.16(.20.4)
unpleasantry 1.29.15(.15)
unpleasing 29.1.24
unpleasingly 1.31.28(.1.12)
unpleasurable 40.20.16(.27.5)
unploughed 23.8
unplucked 22.23.8
unplug 26.10
unplumbable 40.20.16(.15)
unplumbed 23.23.7
unpoetic 24.2.10(.3.1)
unpoetical 40.23.12(.7.1)
unpoetically 1.31.24(.9.3)
unpoeticalness 34.18.16(.37.5)
unpointed 23.18.9(.19)
unpolished 22.30
unpolitic 24.2.10(.10)
unpolitical 40.23.12(.7.1)
unpolitically 1.31.24(.9.3)
unpolled 23.31.13(.1)
unpompous 34.18.9(.11)
unpopular 17.34.16(.21.1)
unpopularity 1.10.16(.21.1)
unpopularly 1.31.17(.29)
unposed 23.28.4
unpossessed 22.29.5(.7)
unpowered 23.18.2
unpractical 40.23.12(.7.3)
unpractically 1.31.24(.9.5)
unpractised 22.29.2(.13)
unprecedented 23.18.9(.19)
unprecedentedly 1.31.23(.14.3)
unpredictability 1.10.16(.22.3)
unpredictable 40.20.16(.11.5)
unpredictableness 34.18.16(.37.4)
unpredictably 1.31.21(.4.3)
unpredicted 23.18.9(.17)
unprejudiced 22.29.2(.14)

unpremeditatedly 1.31.23(.14.3)
unprepared 23.6
unpreparedly 1.31.23(.14.7)
unpreparedness 34.18.16(.21.1)
unprepossessing 29.1.23
unpresentable 40.20.16(.11.6)
unpressed 22.29.5(.12)
unpresuming 29.1.16
unpresumptuous 34.18.6
unpretending 29.1.13(.14)
unpretendingly 1.31.28(.1.5)
unpretendingness 34.18.16(.26)
unpretentious 34.18.22(.12)
unpretentiously 1.31.33(.12.4)
unpretentiousness 34.18.16(.31.4)
unpreventable 40.20.16(.11.6)
unpriced 22.29.13
unprincipled 23.31.14
unprincipledness 34.18.16(.21.1)
unprintable 40.20.16(.11.6)
unprintably 1.31.21(.4.3)
unprinted 23.18.9(.19)
unproblematic 24.2.10(.4.2)
unproblematically 1.31.24(.9.4)
unprocessed 22.29.5(.6)
unproclaimed 23.23.3
unproductive 31.2.1(.13.4)
unproductively 1.31.30(.7.2)
unproductiveness 34.18.16(.28.1)
unprofessional 40.26.13(.14.3)
unprofessionalism 27.15.21(.2.15)
unprofessionally 1.31.17(.14.3)
unprofitable 40.20.16(.11.3)
unprofitableness 34.18.16(.37.4)
unprofitably 1.31.21(.4.2)
unprogressive 31.2.4(.4)
unpromising 29.1.23
unpromisingly 1.31.28(.1.11)

unprompted 23.18.9(.16)
unpronounceable 40.20.16(.21.3)
unpronounceably 1.31.21(.7.2)
unpropertied 23.2.8
unprophetic 24.2.10(.3.2)
unpropitious 34.18.22(.2)
unpropitiously 1.31.33(.12.4)
unpropitiousness 34.18.16(.31.4)
unprosperous 34.18.27(.12)
unprosperously 1.31.33(.12.5)
unprotected 23.18.9(.17)
unprotectedness 34.18.16(.21.1)
unprotesting 29.1.12(.21)
unprotestingly 1.31.28(.1.4)
unprovability 1.10.16(.22.2)
unprovable 40.20.16(.19)
unprovableness 34.18.16(.37.4)
unproved 23.26
unproven 28.17.20(.9)
unprovocative 31.2.1(.9.1)
unprovoked 22.23.12
unpruned 23.24.15
unpublicized 23.28.2
unpublishable 40.20.16(.23)
unpublished 22.30
unpunctual 40.16.12
unpunctuality 1.10.16(.32.1)
unpunctually 1.31.17(.24)
unpunishable 40.20.16(.23)
unpunished 22.30
unpurified 23.15.9
unputdownable 40.20.16(.16.1)
unqualified 23.15.9
unquantifiable 40.20.16(.5)
unquantified 23.15.9
unquenchable 40.20.16(.23)
unquenchably 1.31.21(.7.3)
unquenched 22.30, 22.31
unquestionability 1.10.16(.22.3)
unquestionableness 34.18.16(.37.4)

unquestionably 1.31.21(.6)
unquestioned 23.24.16(.13)
unquestioning 29.1.17(.12)
unquestioningly 1.31.28(.1.7)
unquiet 22.19.4
unquietly 1.31.22(.15)
unquietness 34.18.16(.20.3)
unquotable 40.20.16(.11.3)
unquote 22.21.13
unrated 23.18.9(.3)
unratified 23.15.9
unravel 40.28.5
unreachable 40.20.16(.24)
unreachableness 34.18.16(.37.4)
unreachably 1.31.21(.7.4)
unreached 22.31
unreactive 31.2.1(.13.3)
unread 23.5.15
unreadability 1.10.16(.22.2)
unreadable 40.20.16(.12)
unreadably 1.31.21(.4.4)
unreadily 1.31.17(.10)
unreadiness 34.18.16(.2.3)
unready 1.11.5
unreal 40.3.14
unrealism 27.15.21(.2.15)
unrealistic 24.2.10(.15.3)
unrealistically 1.31.24(.9.6)
unreality 1.10.16(.32.1)
unreally 1.31.3
unreason 28.17.24(.1)
unreasonable 40.20.16(.16.3)
unreasonableness 34.18.16(.37.4)
unreasonably 1.31.21(.6)
unreasoning 29.1.17(.12)
unreasoningly 1.31.28(.1.7)
unrebelliousness 34.18.16(.31.1)
unreceptive 31.2.1(.12)
unreckoned 23.24.16(.5)
unreclaimed 23.23.3
unrecognisableness 34.18.16(.37.4)
unrecognisably 1.31.21(.7.2)
unrecognizable 40.20.16(.22)

unscarred 23.9.9
unscathed 23.27
unscented 23.18.9(.19)
unscheduled 23.31.10
unscholarliness
34.18.16(.2.10)
unscholarly 1.31.17(.29)
unschooled 23.31.10
unscientific 24.2.16(.1)
unscientifically
1.31.24(.9.9)
unscramble 40.20.19
unscrambler 17.34.20
unscratched 22.31
unscreened 23.24.1
unscrew 16.23.10
unscripted 23.18.9(.16)
unscriptural
40.16.13(.12.3)
unscripturally
1.31.17(.27.2)
unscrupulous
34.18.29(.17.6)
unscrupulously
1.31.33(.12.6)
unscrupulousness
34.18.16(.31.6)
unseal 40.1.10
unsealed 23.31.1(.4)
unsearchable
40.20.16(.24)
unsearchableness
34.18.16(.37.4)
unsearchably
1.31.21(.7.4)
unsearched 22.31
unseasonable
40.20.16(.16.3)
unseasonableness
34.18.16(.37.4)
unseasonably 1.31.21(.6)
unseasoned
23.24.16(.11)
unseat 22.1.9
unseaworthiness
34.18.16(.2.6)
unseaworthy 1.21
unsectarian 28.3.20(.4)
unseeable 40.20.16(.1)
unseeded 23.18.10(.1)
unseeing 29.1.1
unseeingly 1.31.28(.1.1)
unseemliness
34.18.16(.2.10)
unseemly 1.31.26(.1)
unseen 28.1.18
unselect 22.23.4(.11)
unselective 31.2.1(.13.2)
unselfconscious
34.18.22(.12)
unselfconsciously
1.31.33(.12.4)

unselfconsciousness
34.18.16(.31.4)
unselfish 36.2.18(.21)
unselfishly 1.31.35(.7.3)
unselfishness
34.18.16(.33.6)
unsellable 40.20.16(.29)
unsensational
40.26.13(.14.2)
unsensationally
1.31.17(.14.3)
unsensitive 31.2.1(.9.3)
unsensitively
1.31.30(.7.1)
unsent 22.26.4(.11)
unsentimental
40.21.17(.2)
unsentimentality
1.10.16(.32.3)
unsentimentally
1.31.17(.9.3)
unserious 34.3.15(.2)
unserviceability
1.10.16(.22.3)
unserviceable
40.20.16(.21.2)
unset 22.5.13
unsettle 40.21.4
unsettledness
34.18.16(.21.1)
unsettlement
22.26.15(.13.7)
unsevered 23.18.17
unsewn 28.19.13
unsex 34.23.4(.10)
unsexy 1.22.22
unshackle 40.23.5
unshaded 23.18.10(.2)
unshakability
1.10.16(.22.2)
unshakably 1.31.21(.5)
unshakeability
1.10.16(.22.2)
unshakeable
40.20.16(.13)
unshakeably 1.31.21(.5)
unshaken 28.17.13(.3)
unshakenly 1.31.27(.14)
unshapeliness
34.18.16(.2.10)
unshapely 1.31.20
unshared 23.6
unsharp 20.6
unsharpness
34.18.16(.18)
unshaved 23.26
unshaven 28.17.20(.3)
unsheathe 32.1, 33.1
unshed 23.5.12
unshell 40.5.13
unshielded
23.18.10(.15)

unshiftable
40.20.16(.11.7)
unship 20.2.7
unshockability
1.10.16(.22.2)
unshockable
40.20.16(.13)
unshockably 1.31.21(.5)
unshod 23.10.10
unshorn 28.11.9
unshrinkability
1.10.16(.22.2)
unshrinkable
40.20.16(.13)
unshrinking 29.1.14(.14)
unshrinkingly
1.31.28(.1.6)
unshriven 28.17.20(.2)
unshut 22.15.8
unsighted 23.18.9(.10)
unsightliness
34.18.16(.2.10)
unsightly 1.31.22(.13)
unsilenced 22.29.21
unsimplified 23.15.9
unsinkability
1.10.16(.22.2)
unsinkable 40.20.16(.13)
unsized 23.28.2
unskilfully 1.31.17(.16.2)
unskilled 23.31.2
unskimmed 23.23.2
unslakeable 40.20.16(.13)
unslaked 22.23.3
unsleeping 29.1.10(.1)
unsleepingly
1.31.28(.1.2)
unsliced 22.29.13
unsling 29.1.31(.26)
unslung 29.8
unsmiling 29.1.31(.10)
unsmilingly
1.31.28(.1.18)
unsmilingness
34.18.16(.26)
unsmoked 22.23.12
unsmoothed 23.27
unsnarl 40.8.9
unsoaked 22.23.12
unsociability
1.10.16(.22.2)
unsociable 40.20.16(.23)
unsociableness
34.18.16(.37.4)
unsociably 1.31.21(.7.3)
unsocial 40.33.11
unsocialist 22.29.2(.31.4)
unsocially 1.31.17(.22)
unsold 23.31.13(.8)
unsolder 17.13.23(.5)
unsoldierly 1.31.17(.25)

unsolicited 23.18.9(.13)
unsolicitedly
1.31.23(.14.3)
unsolvability
1.10.16(.22.2)
unsolvable 40.20.16(.19)
unsolvableness
34.18.16(.37.4)
unsolved 23.26
unsophisticatedly
1.31.23(.14.3)
unsophisticatedness
34.18.16(.21.1)
unsophistication
28.17.25(.3.5)
unsought 22.13.10
unsound 23.24.7(.6)
unsounded 23.18.10(.14)
unsoundly 1.31.23(.17)
unsoundness
34.18.16(.21.1)
unsoured 23.18.2
unsown 28.19.13
unsparing 29.1.30(.4)
unsparingly
1.31.28(.1.17)
unsparingness
34.18.16(.26)
unspeakable
40.20.16(.13)
unspeakableness
34.18.16(.37.4)
unspeakably 1.31.21(.5)
unspeaking 29.1.14(.1)
unspecial 40.33.3
unspecific 24.2.16(.1)
unspecified 23.15.9
unspectacular
17.34.16(.21.2)
unspectacularly
1.31.17(.29)
unspent 22.26.4(.2)
unspilled 23.31.2
unspilt 22.32.1
unspiritual 40.16.12
unspirituality
1.10.16(.32.1)
unspiritualness
34.18.16(.37.1)
unspoilt 22.32.7
unspoken 28.17.13(.15)
unsporting 29.1.12(.9)
unsportingly
1.31.28(.1.4)
unsportingness
34.18.16(.26)
unsprayed 23.4.15
unsprung 29.8
Unst 22.29.21
unstable 40.20.4
unstableness
34.18.16(.37.4)

unstably **1.31.21(.1)**
unstaffed **22.27.4(.2)**
unstained **23.24.4**
unstamped **22.25**
unstarched **22.31**
unstatable **40.20.16(.11.1)**
unstatutable **40.20.16(.11.2)**
unstatutably **1.31.21(.4.1)**
unsteadfast **22.29.6(.9)**
unsteadfastly **1.31.22(.22)**
unsteadfastness **34.18.16(.20.4)**
unsteadily **1.31.17(.10)**
unsteadiness **34.18.16(.2.3)**
unsteady **1.11.5**
unsterile **40.13.16**
unsterilely **1.31.38**
unstick **24.2.10(.15.1)**
unstinted **23.18.9(.19)**
unstintedly **1.31.23(.14.3)**
unstinting **29.1.12(.19)**
unstintingly **1.31.28(.1.4)**
unstirred **23.19.2**
unstitch **38.2.3**
unstocked **22.23.7**
unstockinged **23.25**
unstop **20.7.4**
unstoppability **1.10.16(.22.2)**
unstoppable **40.20.16(.9)**
unstoppably **1.31.21(.3)**
unstopper **17.10.8**
unstrap **20.5.6**
unstratified **23.15.9**
unstreamed **23.23.1**
unstressed **22.29.5(.12)**
unstretched **22.31**
unstring **29.1.30(.13)**
unstripped **22.22.1**
unstructured **23.18.24**
unstrung **29.8**
unstuck **24.12.2**
unstudied **23.18.10(.10)**
unstudiedly **1.31.23(.14.4)**
unstuffed **22.27.6**
unstuffy **1.18.7**
unsubstantial **40.33.12(.4)**
unsubstantiality **1.10.16(.32.1)**
unsubstantially **1.31.17(.22)**
unsubtle **40.21.9**
unsubtly **1.31.17(.9.2)**
unsuccess **34.5.9**
unsuccessful **40.27.25**
unsuccessfully **1.31.17(.16.2)**
unsugared **23.18.12**

unsuggestive **31.2.1(.15)**
unsuitability **1.10.16(.22.2)**
unsuitable **40.20.16(.11.2)**
unsuitably **1.31.21(.4.1)**
unsuited **23.18.9(.12)**
unsullied **23.2.23**
unsung **29.8**
unsupplied **23.15.16**
unsupportable **40.20.16(.11.2)**
unsupportably **1.31.21(.4.1)**
unsupportedly **1.31.23(.14.3)**
unsupportive **31.2.1(.5)**
unsuppressed **22.29.5(.12)**
unsure **12.16, 17.7.10**
unsurely **1.31.11, 1.31.17(.4)**
unsureness **34.18.16(.15.1)**
unsurmountable **40.20.16(.11.6)**
unsurpassably **1.31.21(.7.2)**
unsurpassed **22.29.6(.2), 22.29.8(.1)**
unsurprising **29.1.24**
unsurprisingly **1.31.28(.1.12)**
unsurveyed **23.4.9**
unsurvivable **40.20.16(.19)**
unsusceptible **40.20.16(.11.4)**
unsuspected **23.18.9(.17)**
unsuspectedly **1.31.23(.14.3)**
unsuspecting **29.1.12(.18)**
unsuspectingly **1.31.28(.1.4)**
unsuspectingness **34.18.16(.26)**
unsuspicious **34.18.22(.2)**
unsuspiciously **1.31.33(.12.4)**
unsuspiciousness **34.18.16(.31.4)**
unsustainable **40.20.16(.16.1)**
unsustainably **1.31.21(.6)**
unsustained **23.24.4**
unswallowed **23.20.13**
unswathe **33.3**
unswayed **23.4.14**
unswept **22.22.3**
unswerving **29.1.20**
unswervingly **1.31.28(.1.9)**

unsworn **28.11.11**
Unsworth **32.14.15**
unsymmetrical **40.23.12(.18)**
unsymmetrically **1.31.24(.9.12)**
unsympathetic **24.2.10(.3.2)**
unsympathetically **1.31.24(.9.3)**
unsystematic **24.2.10(.4.2)**
unsystematically **1.31.24(.9.4)**
untack **24.6.7**
untainted **23.18.9(.19)**
untaken **28.17.13(.3)**
untalented **23.18.9(.19)**
untameable **40.20.16(.15)**
untamed **23.23.3**
untangle **40.24.14(.2)**
untanned **23.24.6(.5)**
untapped **22.22.4**
untarnished **22.30**
untasted **23.18.9(.20)**
untaught **22.13.3**
untaxed **22.29.20**
unteach **38.1**
unteachable **40.20.16(.24)**
untearable **40.20.16(.27.1)**
untechnical **40.23.12(.11)**
untechnically **1.31.24(.9.8)**
untenability **1.10.16(.22.2)**
untenable **40.20.16(.16.1)**
untenableness **34.18.16(.37.4)**
untenably **1.31.21(.6)**
untenanted **23.18.9(.19)**
untended **23.18.10(.14)**
Untermensch **38.18.2**
Untermenschen **28.17.25(.16)**
untestable **40.20.16(.11.7)**
untested **23.18.9(.20)**
untether **17.23.4**
Unthank **24.19.3(.3)**
unthanked **22.23.13**
unthankful **40.27.20**
unthankfulness **34.18.16(.37.2)**
unthatched **22.31**
untheological **40.23.12(.17.2)**
untheoretical **40.23.12(.7.1)**
unthickened **23.24.16(.5)**
unthink **24.19.1(.4)**
unthinkability **1.10.16(.22.2)**

unthinkable **40.20.16(.13)**
unthinkableness **34.18.16(.37.4)**
unthinkably **1.31.21(.5)**
unthinking **29.1.14(.14)**
unthinkingly **1.31.28(.1.6)**
unthinkingness **34.18.16(.26)**
unthought **22.13.9**
unthoughtful **40.27.18**
unthoughtfully **1.31.17(.16.2)**
unthoughtfulness **34.18.16(.37.2)**
unthought-of **31.7**
unthought-out **22.9**
unthread **23.5.15**
unthreatening **29.1.17(.12)**
unthreshed **22.30**
unthriftiness **34.18.16(.2.3)**
unthrifty **1.10.24**
unthrone **28.19.17**
untidily **1.31.17(.10)**
untidiness **34.18.16(.2.3)**
untidy **1.11.14**
untie **14.8**
until **40.2.5**
untilled **23.31.2**
untimeliness **34.18.16(.2.10)**
untimely **1.31.26(.10)**
untipped **22.22.1**
untired **23.18.3**
untiring **29.1.30(.8)**
untiringly **1.31.28(.1.17)**
untitled **23.31.16**
unto **16.7.7**
untold **23.31.13(.3)**
untouchability **1.10.16(.22.2)**
untouchable **40.20.16(.24)**
untouchableness **34.18.16(.37.4)**
untouched **22.31**
untoward **23.12.8**
untowardly **1.31.23(.9)**
untowardness **34.18.16(.21.1)**
untraceable **40.20.16(.21.1)**
untraceably **1.31.21(.7.2)**
untraced **22.29.4**
untracked **22.23.5(.9)**
untraditional **40.26.13(.14.1)**
untrainable **40.20.16(.16.1)**
untrained **23.24.4**

untrammelled 23.31.20
untransferable
40.20.16(.27.5)
untranslatable
40.20.16(.11.1)
untranslatably
1.31.21(.4.1)
untransportable
40.20.16(.11.2)
untravelled 23.31.23
untreatable
40.20.16(.11.1)
untrendy 1.11.20(.3)
untried 23.15.15
untrimmed 23.23.2
untrodden 28.17.12(.9)
untrue 16.23.8
untruly 1.31.16
untruss 34.14
untrusting 29.1.12(.21)
untrustworthily
1.31.17(.19)
untrustworthiness
34.18.16(.2.6)
untrustworthy 1.21
untruth 32.13
untruthful 40.27.24
untruthfully
1.31.17(.16.2)
untruthfulness
34.18.16(.37.2)
untuck 24.12.2
untunable 40.20.16(.16.2)
untuned 23.24.15
untuneful 40.27.22
untunefully
1.31.17(.16.2)
untunefulness
34.18.16(.37.2)
unturned 23.24.17
untutored 23.18.9(.12)
untwine 28.14.17
untwist 22.29.2(.28)
untying 29.1.7
untypical 40.23.12(.5)
untypically 1.31.24(.9.2)
unusable 40.20.16(.22)
unused 22.29.14, 23.28.3
unusual 40.16.11
unusually 1.31.17(.23)
unusualness
34.18.16(.37.1)
unutterable
40.20.16(.27.3)
unutterableness
34.18.16(.37.4)
unutterably 1.31.21(.8)
unvanquished 22.30
unvaried 23.2.22
unvarnished 22.30
unvarying 29.1.2

unvaryingly 1.31.28(.1.1)
unveil 40.4.9
unvented 23.18.9(.19)
unverifiable 40.20.16(.5)
unverified 23.15.9
unversed 22.29.16
unviability 1.10.16(.22.1)
unviable 40.20.16(.5)
unvisited 23.18.9(.13)
unvoiced 22.29.11
unwaged 23.30
unwanted 23.18.9(.19)
unwarily 1.31.17(.27.1)
unwariness 34.18.16(.2.9)
unwarlike 24.13.7(.6)
unwarmed 23.23.6
unwarned 23.24.10
unwarrantable
40.20.16(.11.6)
unwarrantably
1.31.21(.4.3)
unwarranted 23.18.9(.19)
unwary 1.29.4
unwashed 22.30
unwatchable
40.20.16(.24)
unwatched 22.31
unwatchful 40.27.29
unwavering 29.1.30(.8)
unwaveringly
1.31.28(.1.17)
unwaxed 22.29.20
unweaned 23.24.1
unwearable
40.20.16(.27.1)
unwearied 23.2.22
unweariedly 1.31.23(.1)
unweariedness
34.18.16(.21.1)
unweary 1.29.2(.10)
unwearying 29.1.2
unwearyingly
1.31.28(.1.1)
unwed 23.5.14
unwedded 23.18.10(.3)
unweddedness
34.18.16(.21.1)
unweighed 23.4.14
unweight 22.4.21
unwelcome 27.15.11(.17)
unwelcomely
1.31.26(.11)
unwelcomeness
34.18.16(.24)
unwell 40.5.17
unwept 22.22.3
unwhipped 22.22.1
unwholesome
27.15.20(.22)
unwholesomely
1.31.26(.11)

unwholesomeness
34.18.16(.24)
unwieldily 1.31.17(.10)
unwieldiness
34.18.16(.2.3)
unwieldy 1.11.23
unwilled 23.31.2
unwilling 29.1.31(.2)
unwillingly 1.31.28(.1.18)
unwillingness
34.18.16(.26)
Unwin 28.2.28
unwind 23.24.13
unwinking 29.1.14(.14)
unwinkingly
1.31.28(.1.6)
unwiped 22.22.7
unwired 23.18.3
unwisdom 27.15.10(.18)
unwise 35.15.19
unwisely 1.31.34
unwish 36.2.24
unwitnessed
22.29.15(.13)
unwitting 29.1.12(.2)
unwittingly 1.31.28(.1.4)
unwittingness
34.18.16(.26)
unwomanliness
34.18.16(.2.10)
unwomanly 1.31.27(.14)
unwonted 23.18.9(.19)
unwontedly
1.31.23(.14.3)
unwontedness
34.18.16(.21.1)
unworkability
1.10.16(.22.2)
unworkableness
34.18.16(.37.4)
unworked 22.23.11
unworldliness
34.18.16(.2.10)
unworldly 1.31.23(.18)
unworn 28.11.11
unworried 23.2.22
unworthily 1.31.17(.19)
unworthiness
34.18.16(.2.6)
unworthy 1.21
unwound 23.24.7(.9)
unwoven 28.17.20(.11)
unwrap 20.5.6
unwritable
40.20.16(.11.2)
unwritten 28.17.11(.2)
unwrought 22.13.14
unwrung 29.8
unyielding 29.1.13(.16)
unyieldingly 1.31.28(.1.5)
unyieldingness
34.18.16(.26)

unyoke 24.18.14
unzip 20.2.6
up 20.9
up-anchor 17.14.21(.3)
up-and-coming 29.1.16
up-and-over 17.21.14
up and running
29.1.17(.9)
up-and-under
17.13.20(.10)
up-and-up 20.9
Upanishad 23.7.14
upas 34.18.9(.7)
upas tree 2
upbeat 22.1.2
upbraid 23.4.15
upbraiding 29.1.13(.3)
upbringing 29.1.18
upbuild 23.31.2
upbuilt 22.32.1
UPC 2.22
upcast 22.29.6(.5),
22.29.8(.3)
upchuck 24.12.7
upcoming 29.1.16
upcountry 1.29.15(.15)
upcurrent 22.26.15(.23.2)
update 22.4.10
updater 17.12.4(.6)
Updike 24.13.3
updraft 22.27.4(.4)
updraught 22.27.4(.4)
upend 23.24.5
upfield 23.31.1(.2)
upflow 19.29.21
upfold 23.31.13(.7)
up-front 22.26.12
upgrade 23.4.15
upgradeable 40.20.16(.12)
upgrader 17.13.3
upgrowth 32.16
uphaul 40.10.16
upheaval 40.28.1
upheave 31.1.6
upheld 23.31.4
uphill 40.2.18
uphold 23.31.13(.9)
upholder 17.13.23(.8)
upholster 17.12.24(.25)
upholsterer 17.32.14(.6)
upholstery 1.29.11(.8.12)
UPI 14
Upjohn 28.10.22
upkeep 20.1
upland 23.24.16(.16.3)
uplift 22.27.1
uplifter 17.12.23
uplighter 17.12.13(.9)
upload 23.20.13
uplying 29.1.7

u

usurp **20.14**
usurpation **28.17.25(.3.2)**
usurper **17.10.15**
usury **1.29.11(.21)**
Utah **10.6.4, 12.5.4**
Ute **22.18**
utensil **40.2.14, 40.31.21**
uteri **14.24.6**
uterine **28.14.18**
uteritis **34.18.11(.8)**
uterus **34.18.27(.14)**
utile **40.13.3(.3)**
utilitarian **28.3.20(.4)**
utilitarianism
  27.15.21(.2.9)
utility **1.10.16(.23)**
utilizable **40.20.16(.22)**
utilization **28.17.25(.3.12)**
utilize **35.15.21(.4.3)**
utilizer **17.25.12(.15)**
Utley **1.31.22(.12)**
utmost **22.29.17(.4)**
utopia **3.2.7**
Utopian **28.3.1**
utopianism **27.15.21(.2.9)**
Utrecht **22.23.4(.10), 22.24**
utricle **40.23.12(.18)**
utricular **17.34.16(.21.2)**
Utrillo **19.29.2**
Utsire **17.32.2**
Uttar Pradesh **36.5**
utter **17.12.12**
utterable **40.20.16(.27.3)**
utterance **34.24.10(.16)**
utterer **17.32.14(.6)**
utterly **1.31.17(.9.2)**
uttermost **22.29.17(.4)**
utterness **34.18.16(.15.2)**
Uttley **1.31.22(.12)**
Uttoxeter **17.12.16(.14)**
U-turn **28.18.4**
uvea **3.11.6**
uvula **17.34.16(.21.4)**
uvulae **2.32.9(.8)**
uvular **17.34.16(.21.4)**
UWIST **22.29.2(.28)**
Uxbridge **39.2.22(.10)**
uxorial **40.3.14(.5)**
uxoricidal **40.22.11**
uxoricide **23.15.11(.6)**
uxorious **34.3.15(.5)**
uxoriously **1.31.33(.1.4)**
uxoriousness
  34.18.16(.31.1)
Uzbek **24.4.3**
Uzbekistan **28.9.2**
Uzi® **1.23.12**
v **2**
V/STOL **40.9.7**
Vaal **40.8**

Vaasa **17.24.8**
vac **24.6**
vacancy **1.22.23(.10.2)**
vacant **22.26.15(.11)**
vacantly **1.31.22(.20.2)**
vacatable **40.20.16(.11.1)**
vacate **22.4.11**
vacation **28.17.25(.3.5)**
vacationer **17.18.16(.16)**
vacationist **22.29.2(.18.2)**
vaccinal **40.26.13(.12)**
vaccinate **22.4.14(.9.3)**
vaccination **28.17.25(.3.8)**
vaccinator **17.12.4(.10)**
vaccine **28.1.18(.7)**
vaccinia **3.9.2**
vacillate **22.4.23(.7.2)**
vacillation **28.17.25(.3.14)**
vacillator **17.12.4(.16)**
vacua **17.7.12(.5)**
vacuity **1.10.16(.5)**
vacuolar **17.34.16(.3)**
vacuolation
  28.17.25(.3.14)
vacuole **40.18.2**
vacuous **34.18.6**
vacuously **1.31.33(.12.1)**
vacuousness
  34.18.16(.31.2)
vacuum **27.14.7**
vade mecum **27.15.11(.3)**
Vaduz **35.17.1**
vag **26.5**
vagabond **23.24.9**
vagabondage **39.2.11**
vagal **40.24.3**
vagarious **34.3.15(.3)**
vagary **1.29.11(.11)**
vagi **14.11, 14.21**
vagina **17.18.13(.12)**
vaginal **40.26.11**
vaginally **1.31.17(.14.1)**
vaginismus **34.18.15(.18)**
vaginitis **34.18.11(.8)**
vagotomy **1.15.13(.1)**
vagrancy **1.22.23(.10.4)**
vagrant **22.26.15(.23.4)**
vagrantly **1.31.22(.20.5)**
vague **26.3**
vaguely **1.31.25**
vagueness **34.18.16(.23)**
vaguish **36.2.14**
vagus **34.18.14(.2)**
vail **40.4**
vain **28.4**
vainglorious **34.3.15(.5)**
vaingloriously
  1.31.33(.1.4)
vaingloriousness
  34.18.16(.31.1)

vainglory **1.29.8**
vainly **1.31.27(.4)**
vainness **34.18.16(.25)**
vair **6**
Vaishnava **17.21.12**
Vaisya **17.33.11**
Vaizey **1.23.3**
Val **40.6**
Valais **5**
valance **34.24.10(.24)**
valanced **22.29.21**
Valda **17.13.23(.4)**
Valdemar **10.10.4**
Valderma **17.17.15**
Valdez **35.1.8**
vale **40.4**
valediction
  28.17.25(.15.1)
valedictorian **28.3.20(.7)**
valedictory **1.29.11(.8.12)**
valence **34.24.10(.24)**
valencia **3.14.16**
Valencian **28.3.13**
Valenciennes **28.5**
valency **1.22.23(.10.4)**
valentine **28.14.5**
Valentinian **28.3.8(.2)**
Valentino **19.15.1**
valerate **22.4.22(.6)**
valerian **28.3.20(.2)**
valeric **24.2.26(.2)**
Valerie **1.29.11(.27)**
Valéry **1.29.11(.27)**
valet **4.28.3, 22.19.26(.5)**
valeta **17.12.1(.15)**
valetudinarian
  28.3.20(.4)
valetudinarianism
  27.15.21(.2.9)
valetudinary
  1.29.11(.13.2)
valgus **34.18.14(.9)**
Valhalla **17.34.6**
valiant **22.26.2(.10)**
valiantly **1.31.22(.20.1)**
valid **23.2.23**
validate **22.4.10**
validation **28.17.25(.3.4)**
validity **1.10.16(.9)**
validly **1.31.23(.14.7)**
validness **34.18.16(.21.1)**
valine **28.1.27(.2)**
valise **35.1.23**
valium **27.3.18**
Valkyrie **1.29.11(.10)**
Vallance **34.24.10(.24)**
Valle Crucis **34.2.17(.9)**
vallecula **17.34.16(.21.2)**
valleculae **2.32.9(.8)**
vallecular **17.34.16(.21.2)**

valleculate **22.4.23(.7.3)**
Valletta **17.12.5(.11)**
valley **1.31.7**
vallum **27.15.28(.5)**
Valois **10.22.14**
Valona **17.18.18(.11)**
valonia **3.9.11**
valorem **27.15.26(.5)**
valorization
  28.17.25(.3.11)
valorize **35.15.20(.2)**
valorous **34.18.27(.28)**
valorously **1.31.33(.12.5)**
valour **17.34.6**
Valparaiso **19.21**
valproic **24.2.7**
valse **34.27**
valuable **40.20.16(.6)**
valuably **1.31.21(.2)**
valuate **22.4.4**
valuation **28.17.25(.3.1)**
valuator **17.12.4(.2)**
value **16.24.17**
valueless **34.18.29(.16)**
valuelessness
  34.18.16(.31.6)
valuer **17.7.12(.14)**
valuta **17.12.15(.8)**
valvate **22.4.16**
valve **31.13**
valveless **34.18.29(.30)**
valvular **17.34.16(.21.4)**
valvule **40.15.9(.9)**
valvulitis **34.18.11(.8)**
vambrace **34.4.13**
vamoose **34.17.8**
vamp **20.16.3**
vampire **17.6.1**
vampiric **24.2.26(.1)**
vampirism **27.15.21(.2.14)**
vampish **36.2.9**
vamplate **22.4.23(.8)**
vampy **1.8.14**
van **28.7**
vanadate **22.4.10**
vanadic **24.2.11(.3)**
vanadium **27.3.4(.3)**
vanadous **34.18.12**
Van Allen **28.17.33(.5)**
Vanbrugh **17.32.18**
Van Buren **28.17.31(.11)**
Vance **34.24.4, 34.24.6**
Vancouver **17.21.11**
Vanda **17.13.20(.4)**
vandal **40.22.16**
Vandalic **24.2.27(.6)**
vandalism **27.15.21(.2.15)**
vandalistic **24.2.10(.15.3)**
vandalistically
  1.31.24(.9.6)

vandalize 35.15.21(.4.3)
Van de Graaff 30.7
Vandenberg 26.14.1(.9)
Vanden Plas 34.7
Vanderbilt 22.32.1
Van der Post 22.29.9
Van Der Rohe 17.9
van de Velde 17.13.23(.3)
Van Diemen's Land
  23.24.6
Van Dyck 24.13
vandyke 24.13.3
vane 28.4
vaneless 34.18.29(.27)
Vanessa 17.24.5
van Eyck 24.13
vang 29.4
van Gogh 30.8
vanguard 23.9.10
vanilla 17.34.2(.7)
vanillin 28.2.31(.2)
vanish 36.2.16(.5)
vanitory 1.29.11(.8.7),
  1.29.15(.9)
vanity 1.10.16(.13)
vanload 23.20.13
vanquish 36.2.24
vanquishable
  40.20.16(.23)
vanquisher 17.26.14
Vansittart 22.19.10
vantage 39.2.10
vantage point 22.26.11
Vanuatu 16.7.1
Vanya 17.33.9
vapid 23.2.6
vapidity 1.10.16(.9)
vapidly 1.31.23(.14.2)
vapidness 34.18.16(.21.1)
vapor 17.10.3
vaporer 17.32.14(.4)
vaporetti 2.12.4
vaporetto 19.10.4
vaporific 24.2.16(.1)
vaporiform 27.10.5(.2)
vaporimeter
  17.12.16(.9.1)
vaporish 36.2.25
vaporizable 40.20.16(.22)
vaporization
  28.17.25(.3.11)
vaporize 35.15.20(.2)
vaporizer 17.25.12(.14)
vaporous 34.18.27(.12)
vaporously 1.31.33(.12.5)
vaporousness
  34.18.16(.31.5)
vapory 1.29.11(.6)
vapour 17.10.3
vapour-check 24.4.11
vapourer 17.32.14(.4)

vapourish 36.2.25
vapoury 1.29.11(.6)
vaquero 19.27.3
varactor 17.12.21(.3)
Varah 17.32.7
Varangian 28.3.16, 28.3.18
Vardon 28.17.12(.8)
varec 24.4.12
Varèse 35.5.13
Vargas 34.7.10, 34.18.14(.3)
varia 3.22.4
variability 1.10.16(.22.1)
variable 40.20.3
variableness
  34.18.16(.37.4)
variably 1.31.21(.1)
variance 34.24.2
variant 22.26.2(.9)
variate 22.3.12, 22.4.2(.14)
variation 28.17.25(.3.1)
variational 40.26.13(.14.2)
variationally
  1.31.17(.14.3)
variationist 22.29.2(.18.2)
varicella 17.34.5(.11)
varices 35.1.16(.10)
varicocele 40.1.10
varicoloured 23.18.29
varicose 34.18.13(.10),
  34.20.6
varicosed 22.29.15(.11),
  22.29.17(.3), 23.28.4
varicosity 1.10.16(.16.2)
varied 23.2.22
variedly 1.31.23(.14.7)
variegate 22.4.12(.1)
variegation 28.17.25(.3.6)
varietal 40.21.12
varietally 1.31.17(.9.2)
varietist 22.29.2(.13)
variety 1.10.16(.4)
varifocal 40.23.14
variform 27.10.5(.2)
variola 17.34.16(.2)
variolar 17.34.16(.2)
variolate 22.4.23(.2)
variole 40.14.1
variolite 22.16.25(.3)
variolitic 24.2.10(.2.5)
varioloid 23.13.20
variolous 34.18.29(.3)
variometer
  17.12.16(.9.2)
variorum 27.15.26(.5)
various 34.3.15(.3)
variously 1.31.33(.1.4)
variousness
  34.18.16(.31.1)
varistor 17.12.24(.2)
varix 34.23.2(.12)
varlet 22.19.26(.7)

varletry 1.29.15(.13)
Varley 1.31.9
varmint 22.26.15(.13.1)
varna 17.18.8
Varney 1.16.8
varnish 36.2.16(.7)
varnisher 17.26.14
Varro 19.27.4
varsity 1.10.16(.16.2)
Varsovian 28.3.10
varsoviana 17.18.8
varsovienne 28.5
varus 34.18.27(.4)
varve 31.6
vary 1.29.4
varyingly 1.31.28(.1.1)
vas 34.7
vasa deferentia 3.16.8,
  17.26.21
vasal 40.31.4, 40.32.3
Vasari 1.29.6
Vasco da Gama 17.17.7
vascula 17.34.16(.21.2)
vascular 17.34.16(.21.2)
vascularity 1.10.16(.21.1)
vascularize 35.15.20(.2)
vascularly 1.31.17(.29)
vasculum 27.15.28(.11)
vas deferens 35.26.5
vase 35.9
vasectomize 35.15.11
vasectomy 1.15.13(.1)
vaseful 40.14.6(.20)
vaseline® 28.1, 28.1.27
vasiform 27.10.5(.2)
vasoactive 31.2.1(.13.3)
vasoconstriction
  28.17.25(.15.1)
vasoconstrictive
  31.2.1(.13.1)
vasoconstrictor
  17.12.21(.1)
vasodilating 29.1.12(.3)
vasodilation
  28.17.25(.3.14)
vasodilator 17.12.4(.16)
vasomotor 17.12.18
vasopressin 28.2.23(.3)
Vásquez 35.5.12
vassal 40.31.6
vassalage 39.2.23
vast 22.29.6, 22.29.8
vastation 28.17.25(.3.3)
vastitude 23.17.4(.1)
vastly 1.31.22(.22)
vastness 34.18.16(.20.4)
VAT 2.11, 22.7
vat 22.7
Vatersay 4.18.10
VAT-free 2.30.13

vatful 40.14.6(.10)
vatic 24.2.10(.4.1)
Vatican 28.17.13(.13)
Vatican City 1.10.2
Vaticanism 27.15.21(.2.9)
Vaticanist 22.29.2(.18.1)
vaticinal 40.26.13(.12)
vaticinate 22.4.14(.9.3)
vaticination
  28.17.25(.3.8)
vaticinator 17.12.4(.10)
vaticinatory 1.29.11(.8.7)
Vättern 28.18.4
vaudeville 40.2.12
vaudevillian 28.3.21(.2)
Vaudois 10.22.6
Vaughan 28.11
Vaughn 28.11
vault 22.32.5, 22.32.6
vaulter 17.12.26(.5)
vaunt 22.26.10
vaunter 17.12.22(.8)
vauntingly 1.31.28(.1.4)
Vaux 19, 34.23.8, 34.23.9
Vauxhall 40.10.14,
  40.10.16
vavasory 1.29.11(.18)
vavasour 12.14.8, 17.24.15
Vavasseur 18.11
veal 40.1
Veale 40.1
vealy 1.31.1
Veblen 28.17.33(.17)
vector 17.12.21(.2)
vectorial 40.3.14(.5)
vectorization
  28.17.25(.3.11)
vectorize 35.15.20(.2)
Veda 17.13.1, 17.13.3
Vedanta 17.12.22(.4)
Vedantic 24.2.10(.14)
Vedantist 22.29.2(.13)
Vedda 17.13.4
vedette 22.5.4
Vedic 24.2.11(.1)
vee 2
veep 20.1
veer 3
veg 39.5
Vega 17.16.1, 17.16.3
vegan 28.17.15(.1)
veganism 27.15.21(.2.9)
Vegeburger 17.16.14
Vegemite® 22.16.13
vegetable 40.20.16(.11.3)
vegetal 40.21.12
vegetarian 28.3.20(.4)
vegetarianism
  27.15.21(2.9)
vegetate 22.4.9(.5)

vegetation 28.17.25(.3.3)
vegetational
40.26.13(.14.2)
vegetative 31.2.1(.9.1)
vegetatively 1.31.30(.7.1)
vegetativeness
34.18.16(.28.1)
veggie 1.26.3
vegie 1.26.3
vehemence 34.24.10(.14)
vehement 22.26.15(.13.1)
vehemently
1.31.22(.20.3)
vehicle 40.23.12(.1)
vehicular 17.34.16(.21.2)
veil 40.4
veiling 29.1.31(.4)
veilless 34.18.29(.38)
vein 28.4
veinless 34.18.29(.27)
veinlet 22.19.26(.22)
veinlike 24.13.7(.17)
veinstone 28.19.4(.9)
veiny 1.16.4
vela 17.34.1
velamen 28.17.16(.4)
velamina 17.18.16(.8)
velar 17.34.1
velarization
28.17.25(.3.11)
velarize 35.15.20(.2)
Velázquez 35.5.12,
35.18.22
velcro 19.27.17
veld 22.32.2
veldskoen 28.16.5
veldt 22.32.2
veleta 17.12.1(.15)
velic 24.2.27(.1)
velitation 28.17.25(.3.3)
velleity 1.10.16(.1)
vellum 27.15.28(.4)
Velma 17.17.24
velocimeter 17.12.16(.9.1)
velocipede 23.1.1
velocipedist 22.29.2(.14)
velociraptor 17.12.19
velocity 1.10.16(.16.2)
velodrome 27.17.13
velour 12, 12.23, 17.7.13
velouté 4.9.6
velum 27.15.28(.1)
velutinous
34.18.16(.15.2)
velvet 22.2.14
velveted 23.18.9(.13)
velveteen 28.1.9
velvety 1.10.16(.15)
vena 17.18.1
Venables 35.30.15
vena cava 17.21.3

venae 2.17.1
venae cavae 2.19
venal 40.26.1
venality 1.10.16(.32.8)
venally 1.31.17(.14.1)
venation 28.17.25(.3.8)
venational 40.26.13(.14.2)
vend 23.24.5
Venda 17.13.20(.3)
vendace 34.4.5, 34.18.12
Vendée 4.10.4
vendee 2.13
vendetta 17.12.5(.2)
vendeuse 35.19
vendible 40.20.16(.12)
vendor 12.6.11,
17.13.20(.3)
vendue 16.24.6
veneer 3.9
venepuncture 17.28.20,
17.28.23
venerability
1.10.16(.22.1)
venerable 40.20.16(.27.4)
venerableness
34.18.16(.37.4)
venerably 1.31.21(.8)
venerate 22.4.22(.6)
veneration 28.17.25(.3.13)
venerator 17.12.4(.15)
venereal 40.3.14(.2)
venereally 1.31.3(.11)
venereological
40.23.12(.17.2)
venereologist
22.29.2(.26.2)
venereology
1.26.10(.11.1)
venery 1.29.11(.13.1)
venesection
28.17.25(.15.2)
Venetia 17.26.1
venetian 28.17.25(.1)
Veneto 19.10.1
Venezuela 17.34.4
Venezuelan 28.17.33(.3)
vengeance 34.24.10(.21)
vengeful 40.27.28,
40.27.30
vengefully 1.31.17(.16.2)
vengefulness
34.18.16(.37.2)
venial 40.3.7(.1)
veniality 1.10.16(.32.1)
venially 1.31.3(.7)
venialness 34.18.16(.37.1)
Venice 34.2.13
venipuncture 17.28.20,
17.28.23
venison 28.17.23(.14),
28.17.24(.12)

Venite 1.10.1, 1.10.13
Venner 17.18.4
venom 27.15.14(.4)
venomous 34.18.15(.10)
venomously
1.31.33(.12.3)
venomousness
34.18.16(.31.3)
venose 34.20.9
venosity 1.10.16(.16.2)
venous 34.18.16(.1)
venously 1.31.33(.12.3)
vent 22.26.4
ventage 39.2.10
Vent-Axia® 3.14.15
vent-hole 40.18.13
ventiduct 22.23.8
ventifact 22.23.5(.7)
ventil 40.2.5
ventilate 22.4.23(.7.1)
ventilation 28.17.25(.3.14)
ventilative 31.2.1(.3)
ventilator 17.12.4(.16)
ventless 34.18.29(.22)
Ventnor 17.18.21
Ventolin® 28.2.31(.10)
ventouse 34.17.4
ventral 40.16.13(.16)
ventrally 1.31.17(.27.3)
ventre à terre 6
ventricle 40.23.12(.18)
ventricose 34.20.6
ventricular
17.34.16(.21.2)
ventriloquial 40.3.13
ventriloquially
1.31.3(.10)
ventriloquism
27.15.21(.2.13)
ventriloquist 22.29.2(.28)
ventriloquistic
24.2.10(.15.2)
ventriloquize 35.15.19
ventriloquous 34.18.26
ventriloquy 1.28
venture 17.28.22
venturer 17.32.14(.17)
venturesome
27.15.20(.11)
venturesomely
1.31.26(.11)
venturesomeness
34.18.16(.24)
venturi 1.29.11(.3)
venturous 34.18.27(.25)
venturously
1.31.33(.12.5)
venturousness
34.18.16(.31.5)
venue 16.24.10
venule 40.15.9(.8)

Venus 34.18.16(.1)
Venusian 28.3.13, 28.3.14
Vera 17.32.2
veracious 34.18.22(.3)
veraciously 1.31.33(.12.4)
veraciousness
34.18.16(.31.4)
veracity 1.10.16(.16.1)
Veracruz 35.17.6
veranda 17.13.20(.4)
veratrine 28.1.25(.6),
28.2.29(.8)
verb 21.15
verbal 40.20.17
verbalism 27.15.21(.2.15)
verbalist 22.29.2(.31.2)
verbalistic 24.2.10(.15.3)
verbalizable 40.20.16(.22)
verbalization
28.17.25(.3.12)
verbalize 35.15.21(.4.2)
verbalizer 17.25.12(.15)
verbally 1.31.17(.8)
verbatim 27.2.3
verbena 17.18.1(.2)
verbiage 39.2.2
verbose 34.20.3
verbosely 1.31.33(.13)
verboseness
34.18.16(.31.7)
verbosity 1.10.16(.16.2)
verboten 28.17.11(.10)
verb. sap. 20.5
Vercingetorix
34.23.2(.12)
verd 23.19
verdancy 1.22.23(.10.2)
verdant 22.26.15(.10)
verd-antique 24.1.3
verdantly 1.31.22(.20.2)
verdelho 16.24.17, 19.28
verderer 17.32.14(.7)
Verdi 1.11.6
Verdian 28.3.4(.4)
verdict 22.23.2
verdigris 2.30.12, 34.1.7
verditer 17.12.16(.6)
Verdun 28.13.4
verdure 17.29.14, 17.33.7
verdurous 34.18.27(.11)
Vere 3
Vereeniging 29.1.15
verge 39.15
vergence 34.24.10(.21)
verger 17.29.14
vergership 20.2.7(.9)
Vergil 40.34
Vergilian 28.3.21(.2)
verglas 10.25.9
veridical 40.23.12(.8)

V

veridicality 1.10.16(.32.5)
veridically 1.31.24(.9.7)
veriest 22.29.15(.2)
verifiable 40.20.16(.5)
verifiably 1.31.21(.2)
verification 28.17.25(.3.5)
verifier 17.6.9(.4)
verify 14.14.4(.14)
verily 1.31.17(.27.1)
verisimilar 17.34.16(.11)
verisimilitude 23.17.4(.1)
verism 27.15.21(.2.14)
verismo 19.14.18
verist 22.29.2(.29.1)
veristic 24.2.10(.15.2)
veritable 40.20.16(.11.3)
veritably 1.31.21(.4.2)
verity 1.10.16(.21.1)
verjuice 34.17.10
verkrampte 17.12.19
Verlaine 28.4.19
verligte 17.12.21(.1)
Vermeer 3.8
vermeil 40.2.9, 40.4.6
vermian 28.3.7
vermicelli 1.31.5
vermicide 23.15.11(.6)
vermicular
    17.34.16(.21.2)
vermiculate 22.4.23(.7.3)
vermiculation
    28.17.25(.3.14)
vermiculite 22.16.25(.9)
vermiform 27.10.5(.2)
vermifuge 37.7, 39.13
vermilion 28.3.21(.2)
vermin 28.2.17(.6)
verminate 22.4.14(.9.2)
vermination
    28.17.25(.3.8)
verminous 34.18.16(.15.3)
verminously
    1.31.33(.12.3)
verminousness
    34.18.16(.31.3)
vermivorous
    34.18.27(.21)
Vermont 22.26.9
vermouth 32.13, 32.14.11
vernacular 17.34.16(.21.2)
vernacularism
    27.15.21(.2.14)
vernacularity
    1.10.16(.21.1)
vernacularize
    35.15.20(.2)
vernacularly 1.31.17(.29)
vernal 40.26.14
vernalization
    28.17.25(.3.12)
vernalize 35.15.21(.4.5)

vernally 1.31.17(.14.3)
vernation 28.17.25(.3.8)
Verne 28.18
Verner 17.18.5, 17.18.17
Verney 1.16.16
vernicle 40.23.12(.11)
vernier 3.9.10
vernissage 37.4.6
vernix 34.23.2(.6)
Vernon 28.17.17(.11)
Verny 1.16.16
Verona 17.18.18(.10)
veronal 40.26.13(.14.8)
Veronese 1.23.3
veronica 17.14.15(.9)
veronique 24.1.5
verruca 17.14.14
verrucae 2.14, 2.22.6
verrucose 34.20.6
verrucous 34.18.13(.9)
versa 17.24.16
Versailles 14.18
versant 22.26.15(.17.3)
versatile 40.13.3(.4)
versatilely 1.31.38
versatility 1.10.16(.23)
verse 34.19
verselet 22.19.26(.26)
verset 22.19.18
versicle 40.23.12(.15)
versicoloured 23.18.29
versicular 17.34.16(.21.2)
versification
    28.17.25(.3.5)
versifier 17.6.9(.4)
versify 14.14.4(.9)
versin 28.2.23(.10)
versine 28.14.13
version 28.17.25(.12)
versional 40.26.13(.14.5)
vers libre 17.32.18
verso 19.20.11
verst 22.29.16
versus 34.18.20
vert 22.20
vertebra 17.32.18
vertebrae 2.30.9, 4.26.10
vertebral 40.16.13(.15)
vertebrally 1.31.17(.27.3)
vertebrate 22.4.22(.7),
    22.19.24(.11)
vertebration
    28.17.25(.3.13)
vertex 34.23.4(.3)
vertical 40.23.12(.7.2)
verticality 1.10.16(.32.5)
verticalize 35.15.21(.4.4)
vertically 1.31.24(.9.4)
vertices 35.1.16(.10)

verticil 40.2.14
verticillate 22.19.26(.1)
vertiginous
    34.18.16(.15.3)
vertiginously
    1.31.33(.12.3)
vertigo 19.13.9
vertu 16.7
Verulamium 27.3.7
vervain 28.4.10
verve 31.11
vervet 22.19.17
Verwoerd 22.19.5
very 1.29.3
Very light 22.16
Vesalius 34.3.16
Vesey 1.23.1
vesica 17.14.12,
    17.14.15(.12)
vesical 40.23.10,
    40.23.12(.15)
vesicant 22.26.15(.11)
vesicate 22.4.11(.6)
vesication 28.17.25(.3.5)
vesicatory 1.29.11(.8.6)
vesicle 40.23.12(.15)
vesicular 17.34.16(.21.2)
vesicularly 1.31.17(.29)
vesiculate 22.4.23(.7.3),
    22.19.26(.13)
vesiculation
    28.17.25(.3.14)
Vespa® 17.10.18
Vespasian 28.3.14,
    28.17.26(.3)
vesper 17.10.18
vespertilionid 23.2.13
vespertine 28.14.5
vespiary 1.29.2(.1)
vespine 28.14.3
Vespucci 1.25.11
vessel 40.31.5
vest 22.29.5
vesta 17.12.24(.4)
vestal 40.21.18
vestee 2.12.15
vestiary 1.29.2(.2)
vestibular 17.34.16(.21.1)
vestibule 40.15.9(.2)
vestige 39.2.10
vestigial 40.3.12, 40.34
vestigially 1.31.17(.25)
vestiture 17.28.2
vestment 22.26.15(.13.3)
vestral 40.16.13(.16)
vestry 1.29.15(.17)
vestryman 28.17.16(.2)
vesture 17.28.24
Vesuvian 28.3.10
Vesuvius 34.3.8
vet 22.5

vetch 38.4
vetchling 29.1.31(.28)
vetchy 1.25.4
veteran 28.17.31(.11)
veterinarian 28.3.20(.4)
veterinary 1.29.11(.13.2)
vetiver 17.21.12
veto 19.10.1
vetoer 17.9.2
vex 34.23.4
vexation 28.17.25(.3.10)
vexatious 34.18.22(.3)
vexatiously 1.31.33(.12.4)
vexatiousness
    34.18.16(.31.4)
vexedly 1.31.23(.14.7)
vexer 17.24.20
vexilla 17.34.2(.9)
vexillological
    40.23.12(.17.2)
vexillologist
    22.29.2(.26.4)
vexillology 1.26.10(.11.5)
vexillum 27.15.28(.2)
vexingly 1.31.28(.1.11)
Vi 14
via 17.6
viability 1.10.16(.22.1)
viable 40.20.16(.5)
viably 1.31.21(.2)
Via Dolorosa 17.24.17
viaduct 22.23.8
Viagra 17.32.22
vial 40.16.6
vialful 40.14.6(.22)
via media 3.5.1
viand 23.24.16(.1)
viatica 17.14.15(.6)
viaticum 27.15.11(.9)
vibes 35.21
vibist 22.29.2(.12)
vibracula 17.34.16(.21.2)
vibracular 17.34.16(.21.2)
vibraculum 27.15.28(.11)
Vibram® 27.6.17(.4),
    27.15.26(.9)
vibrancy 1.22.23(.10.4)
vibrant 22.26.15(.23.4)
vibrantly 1.31.22(.20.5)
vibraphone 28.19.11
vibraphonist
    22.29.2(.18.3)
vibrate 22.4.22(.7)
vibratile 40.13.3(.4)
vibration 28.17.25(.3.13)
vibrational
    40.26.13(.14.2)
vibrative 31.2.1(.9.4)
vibrato 19.10.7
vibrator 17.12.4(.15)
vibratory 1.29.11(.8.2)

V

V

Vivienne 28.5
vivification 28.17.25(.3.5)
vivify 14.14.4(.8)
viviparity 1.10.16(.21.1)
viviparous 34.18.27(.12)
viviparously
1.31.33(.12.5)
viviparousness
34.18.16(.31.5)
vivisect 22.23.4(.7)
vivisection 28.17.25(.15.2)
vivisectional
40.26.13(.14.6)
vivisectionist
22.29.2(.18.2)
vivisector 17.12.21(.2)
vivo 19.17
vixen 28.17.23(.21)
vixenish 36.2.16(.13)
vixenly 1.31.27(.14)
Viyella® 17.34.5
viz 35.2
vizard 23.18.21
vizcacha 17.28.6
vizier 3.15, 3.15.2
vizierate 22.4.22(.1),
22.19.24(.2)
vizierial 40.3.14(.2)
viziership 20.2.7(.3)
Vlach 24.8
Vlad 23.7
Vladimir 3.8.7
Vladivostok 24.9.4
vlei 4, 14
Vlissingen 28.17.18
Vlorë 17.32.10
Vltava 17.21.12
V-neck 24.4.7
vocab 21.6
vocable 40.20.16(.13)
vocabulary 1.29.11(.27)
vocal 40.23.14
vocalese 35.1, 35.1.23
vocalic 24.2.27(.6)
vocalism 27.15.21(.2.15)
vocalist 22.29.2(.31.2)
vocality 1.10.16(.32.5)
vocalization
28.17.25(.3.12)
vocalize 35.15.21(.4.4)
vocalizer 17.25.12(.15)
vocally 1.31.17(.11)
vocation 28.17.25(.3.5)
vocational 40.26.13(.14.2)
vocationalism
27.15.21(.2.15)
vocationalize
35.15.21(.4.5)
vocationally
1.31.17(.14.3)
vocative 31.2.1(.9.1)

Voce 34.20
vociferance 34.24.10(.16)
vociferant 22.26.15(.23.3)
vociferate 22.4.22(.6)
vociferation
28.17.25(.3.13)
vociferator 17.12.4(.15)
vociferous 34.18.27(.20)
vociferously
1.31.33(.12.5)
vociferousness
34.18.16(.31.5)
vocoder 17.13.17
vocoid 23.13.9
Vodaphone® 28.19.11
vodka 17.14.19
vodun 28.16.4
voe 19
Vogel 40.24.13
vogue 26.15
voguish 36.2.14
voguishness
34.18.16(.33.4)
voice 34.13
voiceful 40.27.25
voiceless 34.18.29(.33)
voicelessly 1.31.33(.12.6)
voicelessness
34.18.16(.31.6)
voiceprint 22.26.1
voicer 17.24.11
voicing 29.1.23
void 23.13
voidable 40.20.16(.12)
voidance 34.24.10(.11)
voidness 34.18.16(.21.1)
voilà 7, 10.25
voile 40.8, 40.11
vol 40.9
volant 22.26.15(.25)
Volapük 24.14.2, 24.15.1
volar 17.34.18
volatile 40.13.3(.4)
volatileness
34.18.16(.37.1)
volatility 1.10.16(.23)
volatilizable
40.20.16(.22)
volatilization
28.17.25(.3.12)
volatilize 35.15.21(.4.3)
vol-au-vent 11.11
volcanic 24.2.15(.5)
volcanically 1.31.24(.9.8)
volcanicity 1.10.16(.16.1)
volcanism 27.15.21(.2.9)
volcano 19.15.3
volcanological
40.23.12(.17.2)
volcanologist
22.29.2(.26.4)

volcanology
1.26.10(.11.4)
vole 40.18
volet 4.28.5
Volga 17.16.19
Volgograd 23.7.16
volitant 22.26.15(.9)
volition 28.17.25(.2.6)
volitional 40.26.13(.14.1)
volitionally 1.31.17(.14.3)
volitive 31.2.1(.9.4)
Volk 24.21
Völkerwanderung 29.9
Völkerwanderungen
28.17.18
völkisch 36.2.13
Volkswagen®
28.17.15(.6)
volley 1.31.10
volleyball 40.10.4
volleyer 3.24.7
Vólos 34.10.17
volplane 28.4.19
Volpone 1.16.17(.1)
Volscian 28.3.5
Volski 1.12.17(.15), 2.14
volt 22.32.5, 22.32.12
Volta 17.12.26(.5)
volta 17.12.26(.5)
voltage 39.2.10
voltaic 24.2.3
Voltaire 6.4
voltameter 17.12.16(.9.1)
volte 22.32.5, 22.32.12
volte-face 34.7.13, 34.9.5
voltmeter 17.12.1(.6)
volubility 1.10.16(.22.1)
voluble 40.20.16(.28)
volubleness
34.18.16(.37.4)
volubly 1.31.21(.9)
volume 27.14.7
volumetric 24.2.26(.14.2)
volumetrical
40.23.12(.18)
volumetrically
1.31.24(.9.12)
voluminosity
1.10.16(.16.2)
voluminous
34.18.16(.15.3)
voluminously
1.31.33(.12.3)
voluminousness
34.18.16(.31.3)
voluntarily 1.31.17(.27.3)
voluntariness
34.18.16(.2.9)
voluntarism
27.15.21(.2.14)
voluntarist 22.29.2(.29.3)

voluntary 1.29.11(.8.12)
voluntary-aided
23.18.10(.2)
voluntaryism
27.15.21(.2.1)
voluntaryist 22.29.2(.2)
volunteer 3.4
volunteerism
27.15.21(.2.14)
voluptuary 1.29.11(.3)
voluptuous 34.18.6
voluptuously
1.31.33(.12.1)
voluptuousness
34.18.16(.31.2)
volute 22.18.11
voluted 23.18.9(.12)
volution 28.17.25(.11)
Volvo® 19.17
volvox 34.23.8(.8)
vomer 17.17.16
vomit 22.2.11
vomiter 17.12.16(.9.2)
vomitoria 3.22.9
vomitorium 27.3.17(.4)
vomitory 1.29.11(.8.7)
vomitus 34.18.11(.10)
von 28.10
Vonnegut 22.15.5
voodoo 16.8.3
voodooism 27.15.21(.2.1)
voodooist 22.29.2(.8)
Voortrekker 17.14.4
Vopo 19.8
voracious 34.18.22(.3)
voraciously 1.31.33(.12.4)
voraciousness
34.18.16(.31.4)
voracity 1.10.16(.16.1)
Vorarlberg 26.14.1(.12)
Vorster 17.12.24(.8)
vortex 34.23.4(.3)
vortex ring 29.1
vortical 40.23.12(.7.2)
vortically 1.31.24(.9.4)
vorticella 17.34.5(.11)
vortices 35.1.16(.10)
Vorticism 27.15.21(.2.12)
Vorticist 22.29.2(.22)
vorticity 1.10.16(.16.1)
vorticose 34.20.6
vorticular
17.34.16(.21.2)
Vortigern 28.17.15(.13),
28.17.28(.9), 28.18.6,
28.18.11
Vosburgh 17.32.14(.5)
Vosene 28.1.19
Vosges 37.9
Voss 34.10
Vostok 24.9.4

votable **40.20.16(.11.3)**
votaress **34.5.14(.3),**
  34.18.27(.14)
votarist **22.29.2(.29.3)**
votary **1.29.11(.8.11)**
vote **22.21**
voteless **34.18.29(.22)**
voter **17.12.18**
voting paper **17.10.3**
votive **31.2.1(.11)**
vouch **38.6**
voucher **17.28.7**
vouchsafe **30.3**
voussoir **10.22.11**
Vouvray **4.26.18**
vow **9**
vowel **40.7, 40.16.3**
vowelize **35.15.21(.4.1)**
vowelless **34.18.29(.38)**
vowelly **1.31.38**
vowel-point **22.26.11**
Vowles **35.30.6, 35.30.13**
vox angelica **17.14.15(.15)**
vox humana **17.18.8(.5)**
vox pop **20.7**
vox populi **2.32.9(.8)**
voyage **39.14**
voyageable **40.20.16(.25)**
voyager **17.29.13**
voyageur **18.14**
voyeur **18.16**
voyeurism **27.15.21(.2.14)**
voyeuristic **24.2.10(.15.2)**
voyeuristically
  1.31.24(.9.6)
vraic **24.3**
vroom **27.14**
V-sign **28.14.13**
VTOL **40.9.7**
vug **26.10**
vuggy **1.14.8**
vugular **17.34.16(.21.3)**
Vulcan **28.17.13(.19)**
Vulcanian **28.3.8(.3)**
vulcanic **24.2.15(.5)**
Vulcanist **22.29.2(.18.1)**
vulcanite **22.16.14(.6)**
vulcanizable
  40.20.16(.22)
vulcanization
  28.17.25(.3.11)
vulcanize **35.15.12(.5)**
vulcanizer **17.25.12(.6)**
vulcanological
  40.23.12(.17.2)
vulcanologist
  22.29.2(.26.4)
vulcanology
  1.26.10(.11.4)
vulgar **17.16.19**
vulgarian **28.3.20(.4)**

vulgarism **27.15.21(.2.14)**
vulgarity **1.10.2**
vulgarization
  28.17.25(.3.11)
vulgarize **35.15.20(.2)**
vulgarly **1.31.17(.12)**
vulgate **22.4.12(.13),**
  22.19.13
vulnerability
  1.10.16(.22.1)
vulnerable **40.20.16(.27.4)**
vulnerableness
  34.18.16(.37.4)
vulnerably **1.31.21(.8)**
vulnerary **1.29.11(.25)**
vulpine **28.14.3**
vulture **17.28.26**
vulturine **28.14.18**
vulturish **36.2.25**
vulturous **34.18.27(.26)**
vulva **17.21.19**
vulval **40.28.16**
vulvar **17.21.19**
vulvitis **34.18.11(.8)**
vying **29.1.7**
Vyrnwy **1.28**
Vyvyan **28.3.10**
w **16.24.17**
WAAF **30.5**
Waal **40.8**
Wabash **36.6.2**
WAC **24.6**
Wace **34.4**
wack **24.6**
wacke **17.14.5**
wackily **1.31.17(.11)**
wackiness **34.18.16(.2.4)**
wacko **19.12.5**
wacky **1.12.5**
Waco **19.12.3**
wad **23.10**
wadable **40.20.16(.12)**
Waddell **40.5.4**
wadding **29.1.13(.7)**
Waddington
  28.17.11(.23)
waddle **40.22.7**
waddler **17.34.22**
waddy **1.11.10**
wade **23.4**
Wadebridge
  39.2.22(.10)
Wade-Giles **35.30.10**
wader **17.13.3**
wadge **39.9**
Wadham **27.15.10(.6)**
wadi **1.11.10**
Wadi Halfa **17.20.19**
Wadsworth **32.14.15**
wady **1.11.10**
WAF **30.5**

wafer **17.20.3**
wafery **1.29.11(.14)**
Waffen SS **34.5**
waffle **40.27.8**
waffler **17.34.26**
waffly **1.31.17(.16.1),**
  1.31.29
waft **22.27.4, 22.27.5**
wag **26.5**
wage **39.4**
wager **17.29.3**
Wagga Wagga **17.16.7**
waggery **1.29.11(.11)**
waggish **36.2.14**
waggishly **1.31.35(.7.1)**
waggishness
  34.18.16(.33.4)
waggle **40.24.4**
waggly **1.31.17(.12),**
  1.31.25
waggonload **23.20.13**
Wagnall **40.26.19**
Wagner **17.18.24**
Wagnerian **28.3.20(.2)**
wagon **28.17.15(.6)**
wagoner **17.18.16(.7)**
wagonette **22.5.9**
wagonful **40.14.6(.15)**
wagon-lit **2.32**
wagonload **23.20.13**
wagtail **40.4.2**
Wahabi **1.9.6**
wahine **1.16.1(.13)**
wahoo **16.21**
Wahran **28.9.13**
wah-wah **10.22.1**
waif **30.3**
waifish **36.2.18(.3)**
waif-like **24.13.7(.19)**
Waikato **19.10.7**
Waikiki **2.14**
wail **40.4**
wailer **17.34.4**
wailful **40.27.31**
wailing **29.1.31(.4)**
wailingly **1.31.28(.1.18)**
wain **28.4**
Waine **28.4**
Wainfleet **22.1.18**
wainscot **22.11.6,**
  22.19.12(.14)
wainwright
  22.16.24(.15)
waist **22.29.4**
waistband **23.24.6(.4)**
waist-cloth **32.9**
waistcoat **22.21.5**
waisted **23.18.9(.20)**
waistless **34.18.29(.22)**
waistline **28.14.19(.14)**
wait **22.4**

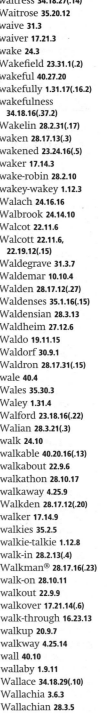

Waite **22.4**
waiter **17.12.4**
Waites **34.22.3**
waitress **34.18.27(.14)**
Waitrose **35.20.12**
waive **31.3**
waiver **17.21.3**
wake **24.3**
Wakefield **23.31.1(.2)**
wakeful **40.27.20**
wakefully **1.31.17(.16.2)**
wakefulness
  34.18.16(.37.2)
Wakelin **28.2.31(.17)**
waken **28.17.13(.3)**
wakened **23.24.16(.5)**
waker **17.14.3**
wake-robin **28.2.10**
wakey-wakey **1.12.3**
Walach **24.16.16**
Walbrook **24.14.10**
Walcot **22.11.6**
Walcott **22.11.6,**
  22.19.12(.15)
Waldegrave **31.3.7**
Waldemar **10.10.4**
Walden **28.17.12(.27)**
Waldenses **35.1.16(.15)**
Waldensian **28.3.13**
Waldheim **27.12.6**
Waldo **19.11.15**
Waldorf **30.9.1**
Waldron **28.17.31(.15)**
wale **40.4**
Wales **35.30.3**
Waley **1.31.4**
Walford **23.18.16(.22)**
Walian **28.3.21(.3)**
walk **24.10**
walkable **40.20.16(.13)**
walkabout **22.9.6**
walkathon **28.10.17**
walkaway **4.25.9**
Walkden **28.17.12(.20)**
walker **17.14.9**
walkies **35.2.5**
walkie-talkie **1.12.8**
walk-in **28.2.13(.4)**
Walkman® **28.17.16(.23)**
walk-on **28.10.11**
walkout **22.9.9**
walkover **17.21.14(.6)**
walk-through **16.23.13**
walkup **20.9.7**
walkway **4.25.14**
wall **40.10**
wallaby **1.9.11**
Wallace **34.18.29(.10)**
Wallachia **3.6.3**
Wallachian **28.3.5**

wallah **17.34.9**
wallaroo **16.23**
Wallasey **1.22.16(.14)**
wallchart **22.10.10**
wallcovering **29.1.30(.8)**
walled **23.31.6**
Wallenberg **26.14.1(.9)**
Waller **17.34.9**
wallet **22.19.26(.8)**
wall-eye **14.25.7**
wall-eyed **23.15**
wallflower **17.3.11**
wall-hung **29.8**
Wallingford **23.18.16(.17)**
Wallis **34.2.22(.6)**
wall-less **34.18.29(.38)**
Wallonia **3.9.11**
Walloon **28.16.15**
wallop **20.13.7**
walloper **17.10.14**
wallow **19.29.8**
wallower **17.9.13**
wallpaper **17.10.3**
wallplanner **17.18.6**
Walls **35.30.9**
wally **1.31.10**
Walmesley **1.31.34**
walnut **22.15.6**
Walpamur **17.7.12(.7)**
Walpole **40.18.3**
Walpurgis **34.2.11**
walrus **34.14, 34.18.27(.28)**
Walsall **40.10.14, 40.31.9, 40.31.22**
Walsh **36.17**
Walsham **27.15.22**
Walsingham **27.15.15**
Walter **17.12.26(.5)**
Walters **35.18.8**
Waltham **27.15.18**
Walthamstow **19.10.19**
Walton **28.17.11(.27)**
waltz **34.22.20, 34.27**
waltzer **17.24.19, 17.24.24**
Walvis Bay **4**
Walworth **32.14.15**
wampum **27.15.7**
WAN **28.7**
wan **28.10**
Wanamaker **17.14.3(.3)**
wand **23.24.9**
Wanda **17.13.20(.7)**
wander **17.13.20(.7)**
wanderer **17.32.14(.7)**
wandering **29.1.30(.8)**
wanderlust **22.29.12**
wanderoo **16.23**
wandoo **16.8**
Wandsworth **32.14.15**
wane **28.4**

waney **1.16.4**
wang **29.4**
Wanganui **1(.6)**
wangle **40.24.14(.2)**
wangler **17.34.24**
wank **24.19.3**
Wankel **40.23.15**
wanker **17.14.21(.3)**
Wankie **1.12.16**
wanky **1.12.16**
wanly **1.31.27(.9)**
wanna **17.18.9**
wannabe **2.10**
Wanstead **23.2.8, 23.5.3**
want **22.26.9**
Wantage **39.2.10**
wanter **17.12.22(.7)**
wanton **28.17.11(.22)**
wantonly **1.31.27(.14)**
wantonness **34.18.16(.25)**
wapentake **24.3.4**
wapiti **1.10.16(.6)**
Wapping **29.1.10(.6)**
war **12**
waratah **10.6**
warb **21.9**
Warbeck **24.4.3**
warble **40.20.10**
warbler **17.34.20**
Warboys **35.13**
Warburg **26.14.1(.1)**
Warburton **28.17.11(.15)**
warby **1.9.8**
ward **23.12**
Wardell **40.5.4**
warden **28.17.12(.10)**
wardenship **20.2.7(.19)**
warder **17.13.9**
Wardle **40.22.8**
Wardour **12.6.4, 17.13.9**
wardress **34.18.27(.15)**
wardrobe **21.16.2**
wardroom **27.14.6(.9)**
wardship **20.2.7(.15)**
ware **6**
Wareham **27.15.26(.2)**
warehouse **34.8.6(.4)**
warehouseman **28.17.16(.29)**
warfare **6.10**
warfarin **28.2.29(.5)**
Wargrave **31.3.7**
warhead **23.5.13(.4)**
Warhol **40.9.17, 40.18.13**
warhorse **34.12.7**
warily **1.31.17(.27.1)**
wariness **34.18.16(.2.9)**
Waring **29.1.30(.4)**
Warkworth **32.14.15**
Warley **1.31.11**

warlike **24.13.7(.6)**
warlock **24.9.16(.4)**
warlord **23.12.11**
warm **27.10**
warm-blooded **23.18.10(.10)**
warm-bloodedness **34.18.16(.21.1)**
warmed-over **17.21.14**
warmed-up **20.9**
warmer **17.17.9**
warm-hearted **23.18.9(.7)**
warm-heartedly **1.31.23(.14.3)**
warm-heartedness **34.18.16(.21.1)**
Warminster **17.12.24(.23)**
warmish **36.2.15**
warmly **1.31.26(.8)**
warmness **34.18.16(.24)**
warmonger **17.16.17(.4)**
warmth **32.20**
warm-up **20.9.8**
warn **28.11**
warner **17.18.10**
warning **29.1.17(.8)**
warningly **1.31.28(.1.7)**
Warnock **24.9.9**
warp **20.8**
warpage **39.2.8**
warpaint **22.26.3**
warpath **32.8**
warper **17.10.9**
warplane **28.4.19**
warrant **22.26.15(.23.2)**
warrantable **40.20.16(.11.6)**
warrantableness **34.18.16(.37.4)**
warrantably **1.31.21(.4.3)**
warrantee **2.11**
warranter **17.12.22(.12)**
warrantor **12.5, 12.5.8**
warranty **1.10.23(.12)**
warren **28.17.31(.7)**
Warrender **17.13.20(.13)**
warrener **17.18.16(.20)**
warrigal **40.24.11**
Warrington **28.17.11(.23)**
warrior **3.22.8**
Warsaw **12.14.5**
warship **20.2.7(.6)**
Warsop **20.7.8**
Warspite **22.16.7**
wart **22.13**
Wartburg **26.14.1(.6)**
warthog **26.7.11**
wartime **27.12.1**
Warton **28.17.11(.10)**
wartorn **28.11.3**

warty **1.10.10**
Warwick **24.2.25, 24.2.26(.6)**
Warwickshire **17.26.19**
warworn **28.11.11**
wary **1.29.4**
was **35.10**
Wasatch **38.5**
wash **36.9**
wash/wipe **20.10.4**
washability **1.10.16(.22.1)**
washable **40.20.16(.23)**
wash-and-wear **6.18**
washbag **26.5.1**
washbasin **28.17.23(.4)**
washboard **23.12.2(.17)**
Washbourne **28.11.2**
washbowl **40.18.4**
Washbrook **24.14.10**
Washburn **28.18.3**
washcloth **32.9**
washday **4.10.16**
washed out **22.9**
washed up **20.9**
washer **17.26.8**
washer/dryer **17.6.14**
washerman **28.17.16(.16)**
washerwoman **28.17.16(.14)**
washerwomen **28.2.17(.1)**
washery **1.29.11(.20)**
washeteria **3.22.2**
wash-hand basin **28.17.23(.4)**
washhouse **34.8.6(.22)**
Washington **28.17.11(.23)**
Washingtonian **28.3.8(.11)**
washing-up **20.9**
washland **23.24.6(.13)**
washout **22.9.15**
washroom **27.14.6(.19)**
washstand **23.24.6(.5)**
washtub **21.11**
wash-up **20.9.13**
washy **1.24.7**
wasn't **22.26.15(.18)**
Wasp **20.17**
wasp **20.17**
waspie **1.8.15**
waspish **36.2.9**
waspishly **1.31.35(.7.1)**
waspishness **34.18.16(.33.2)**
wasplike **24.13.7(.10)**
wassail **40.4.10, 40.31.8**
wassail-bowl **40.18.4**
wassail-cup **20.9.7**
wassailer **17.34.4, 17.34.16(.15)**

wast **22.29.9**
wastable **40.20.16(.11.7)**
wastage **39.2.10**
waste **22.29.4**
wastebasket **22.19.12(.14)**
wasteful **40.27.18**
wastefully **1.31.17(.16.2)**
wastefulness
  34.18.16(.37.2)
wasteland **23.24.6(.13)**
wasteless **34.18.29(.22)**
waster **17.12.24(.3)**
wastrel **40.16.13(.16)**
Wastwater **17.12.10(.7)**
Wat **22.11**
watch **38.8**
watchable **40.20.16(.24)**
watchband **23.24.6(.4)**
watchcase **34.4.6**
watchchain **28.4.15**
watchdog **26.7.4**
watcher **17.28.9**
Watchet **22.2.20**
watchfire **17.6.9(.12)**
watchful **40.27.29**
watchfully **1.31.17(.16.2)**
watchfulness
  34.18.16(.37.2)
watch-glass **34.9.7**
watchkeeper **17.10.1**
watchmaker **17.14.3(.3)**
watchmaking **29.1.14(.3)**
watchman **28.17.16(.33)**
watchnight **22.16.14(.12)**
watchspring **29.1.30(.11)**
watchstrap **20.5.6**
watchtower **17.3.3**
watchword **23.19.8**
Watendlath **32.14.17**
water **17.12.10**
waterbed **23.5.2**
waterbird **23.19.1**
waterborne **28.11.2**
waterbrash **36.6.9**
watercolour **17.34.12**
watercolourist
  22.29.2(.29.4)
watercourse **34.12.2**
watercraft **22.27.4(.4)**
watercress **34.5.14(.7)**
waterer **17.32.14(.6)**
waterfall **40.10.11**
Waterford **23.18.16(.9)**
waterfowl **40.7**
waterfront **22.26.12**
watergate **22.4.12(.5)**
waterhole **40.18.13**
Waterhouse **34.8.6(.7)**
wateriness **34.18.16(.2.9)**
watering **29.1.30(.8)**

waterless **34.18.29(.17.2)**
waterline **28.14.19(.11)**
waterlogged **23.22**
Waterloo **16.25**
waterman **28.17.16(.16)**
watermark **24.8.8**
watermelon **28.17.33(.4)**
watermill **40.2.9**
waterpower **17.3.1**
waterproof **30.13.4**
waterproofer **17.20.11**
waterproofness
  34.18.16(.27)
water-repellant
  22.26.15(.25)
water-repellency
  1.22.23(.10.4)
water-repellent
  22.26.15(.25)
water-resistance
  34.24.10(.10)
water-resistant
  22.26.15(.9)
Waters **35.18.8**
watershed **23.5.12**
waterside **23.15.11(.6)**
water-soluble
  40.20.16(.28)
Waterson **28.17.23(.14)**
watersport **22.13.1**
waterspout **22.9.5**
watertight **22.16.9**
waterway **4.25.9**
waterweed **23.1.10**
waterwheel **40.1.14**
waterwings **35.27**
waterworks **34.23.16**
watery **1.29.11(.8.4)**
Wates **34.22.3**
Watford **23.18.16(.11)**
Wath **32.9**
Watkin **28.2.13(.9)**
Watkins **35.26.2**
Watkinson **28.17.23(.24)**
Watling Street **22.1**
Watney **1.16.19**
Watson **28.17.23(.19)**
watsonia **3.9.11**
Watson-Watt **22.11.14**
Watt **22.11**
watt **22.11**
wattage **39.2.10**
Watteau **19.10.8**
watt-hour **17.3**
wattle **40.21.7**
wattlebird **23.19.1**
wattmeter **17.12.1(.6)**
Watts **34.22.8**
Watusi **1.22.15**
Watutsi **1.22.21**
Waugh **12**

waul **40.10**
wave **31.3**
waveband **23.24.6(.4)**
waveform **27.10.5(.7)**
wavefront **22.26.12**
waveguide **23.15.6**
wavelength **32.19**
waveless **34.18.29(.30)**
wavelet **22.19.26(.25)**
wavelike **24.13.7(.20)**
waver **17.21.3**
waverer **17.32.14(.13)**
waveringly **1.31.28(.1.17)**
wavery **1.29.11(.15)**
wavetop **20.7.4**
wavily **1.31.17(.17)**
waviness **34.18.16(.2.6)**
wavy **1.19.3**
wawl **40.10**
wax **34.23.5**
waxberry **1.29.11(.7.2)**
waxbill **40.2.4**
waxcloth **32.9**
waxen **28.17.23(.21)**
waxer **17.24.20**
waxily **1.31.17(.20)**
waxiness **34.18.16(.2.7)**
waxing **29.1.23**
wax-light **22.16.25(.19)**
wax-like **24.13.7(.22)**
waxplant **22.26.6, 22.26.8**
waxwing **29.1.29**
waxwork **24.17.6(.15)**
waxy **1.22.22**
way **4**
wayback **24.6.6(.3)**
waybill **40.2.4**
waybread **23.5.15**
wayfarer **17.32.5**
wayfaring **29.1.30(.4)**
Wayland **23.24.16(.16.1)**
waylay **4.28**
waylayer **17.2.10**
way leave **31.1.9**
waymark **24.8.8**
waymarker **17.14.7**
Wayne **28.4**
way-out **22.9**
waypoint **22.26.11**
wayside **23.15.11(.4)**
wayward **23.18.26(.4)**
waywardly **1.31.23(.14.7)**
waywardness
  34.18.16(.21.1)
way-worn **28.11.11**
wayzgoose **34.17.7**
wazzock **24.16.12**
WC **2.22**
we **2**
weak **24.1**

weaken **28.17.13(.1)**
weakened **23.24.16(.5)**
weakener **17.18.16(.6)**
weakfish **36.2.18(.17)**
weakish **36.2.13**
weak-kneed **23.1.5**
weakliness
  34.18.16(.2.10)
weakling **29.1.31(.19)**
weakly **1.31.24(.1)**
weakness **34.18.16(.22)**
weak-willed **23.31.2**
weal **40.1**
weald **23.31.1**
wealden **28.17.12(.27)**
Wealdstone **28.19.4(.9)**
wealth **32.24**
wealthily **1.31.17(.18)**
wealthiness **34.18.16(.2.6)**
wealthy **1.20.12**
wean **28.1**
weaner **17.18.1**
weanling **29.1.31(.21)**
weapon **28.17.9**
weaponless **34.18.29(.27)**
weaponry **1.29.20**
Wear **3**
wear **6**
wearability **1.10.16(.22.1)**
wearable **40.20.16(.27.1)**
wear-and-tear **6.4**
wearer **17.32.5**
weariless **34.18.29(.2)**
wearily **1.31.17(.27.1)**
weariness **34.18.16(.2.9)**
wearing **29.1.30(.4)**
wearingly **1.31.28(.1.17)**
wearisome **27.15.20(.2)**
wearisomely **1.31.26(.11)**
wearisomeness
  34.18.16(.24)
Wearmouth **32.7**
Wearside **23.15.11(.3)**
weary **1.29.2**
wearyingly **1.31.28(.1.1)**
weasel **40.32.1**
weaselly **1.31.17(.21)**
weather **17.23.4**
Weatherall
  40.16.13(.12.2)
weatherbeaten
  28.17.11(.1)
weatherboard
  23.12.2(.5)
weatherbound
  23.24.7(.2)
weathercock **24.9.6**
weather eye **14**
weathergirl **40.17**
weatherglass **34.9.7**
Weatherhead **23.5.13(.5)**

w

westernization **28.17.25(.3.11)**

westernize **35.15.12(.5)**

westernizer **17.25.12(.6)**

westernmost **22.29.17(.4)**

Westfield **23.31.1(.2)**

Westgate **22.4.12(.7)**

westing **29.1.12(.21)**

Westinghouse **34.8.6(.17)**

Westland **23.24.16(.16.3)**

Westmeath **32.1**

Westminster **17.12.24(.23)**

Westmorland **23.24.16(.16.2)**

Weston **28.17.11(.25)**

Weston-super-Mare **6.8**

Westphalia **3.24.3**

Westphalian **28.3.21(.3)**

westward **23.18.26(.9)**

westwardly **1.31.23(.14.7)**

Westwood **23.16.6(.9)**

wet **22.5**

wet-and-dry **14.24.8**

wetback **24.6.6(.12)**

wether **17.23.4**

Wetherall **40.10.18**

Wetherby **1.9.11**

wetland **23.24.6(.13), 23.24.16(.16.3)**

wetlook **24.14.11**

wetly **1.31.22(.5)**

wetness **34.18.16(.20.1)**

wet-nurse **34.19.5**

wetsuit **22.18.6**

wettable **40.20.16(.11.1)**

wetting **29.1.12(.4)**

wettish **36.2.11**

wetware **6.18.7**

wet-weather **17.23.4**

we've **31.1, 31.2**

Wexford **23.18.16(.18)**

wey **4**

Weybridge **39.2.22(.10)**

Weymouth **32.14.11**

whack **24.6**

whacker **17.14.5**

whacking **29.1.14(.4)**

whacko **19**

whale **40.4**

whaleback **24.6.6(.23)**

whaleboat **22.21.2**

whalebone **28.19.3**

whale-oil **40.11.10**

whaler **17.34.4**

whale-watching **29.1.27**

Whaley **1.31.4**

whaling-master **17.12.24(.5)**

Whalley **1.31.4, 1.31.10, 1.31.11**

Whalley Range **39.17.2**

wham **27.6**

whammy **1.15.6**

whang **29.4**

Whangarei **4.26**

whangee **2, 2.15**

whap **20.7**

whare **1.29.7**

wharf **30.9**

wharfage **39.2.16**

Wharfe **30.9**

Wharfedale **40.4.3**

wharfie **1.18.6**

wharfinger **17.29.16(.1)**

Wharton **28.17.11(.10)**

wharves **35.28.5**

what **22.11**

what-do-you-call-it **22.2.25**

whate'er **6**

whatever **17.21.4**

Whatmough **19.14.15, 30.11.6**

whatnot **22.11.9**

what's-her-name **27.4.5**

what's-his-name **27.4.5**

whatsit **22.2.16**

what's-its-name **27.4.5**

whatsoe'er **6**

whatsoever **17.21.4**

what-you-may-call-it **22.2.25**

whaup **20.8**

wheal **40.1**

wheat **22.1**

Wheatcroft **22.27.5**

wheatear **3.4.1**

wheaten **28.17.11(.1)**

wheatgerm **27.16.6**

wheatgrass **34.9.6**

Wheathampstead **23.2.8, 23.5.3**

Wheatley **1.31.22(.1)**

wheatmeal **40.1.6**

wheatsheaf **30.1.7**

wheatsheaves **35.28.1**

Wheatstone **28.19.4(.9)**

whee **2**

wheedle **40.22.1**

wheedler **17.34.22**

wheedlingly **1.31.28(.1.18)**

wheel **40.1**

wheelbarrow **19.27.4**

wheelbase **34.4.3**

wheelchair **6.16**

wheel-clamp **20.16.3**

wheeler **17.34.1**

wheeler-dealer **17.34.1**

wheeler-dealing **29.1.31(.1)**

wheelhouse **34.8.6(.24)**

wheelie **1.31.1**

wheeling **29.1.31(.1)**

wheelless **34.18.29(.38)**

wheelman **28.7.10(.24)**

wheelmen **28.5.7(.28)**

wheelslip **20.2.13**

wheelsman **28.17.16(.30)**

wheelspin **28.2.9**

wheelwright **22.16.24(.19)**

Wheen **28.1**

wheeze **35.1**

wheezer **17.25.1**

wheezily **1.31.17(.21)**

wheeziness **34.18.16(.2.7)**

wheezingly **1.31.28(.1.12)**

wheezy **1.23.1**

Whelan **28.17.33(.1)**

whelk **24.21**

whelp **20.18**

when **28.5**

whence **34.24.3**

whencesoever **17.21.4**

whene'er **6.9**

whenever **17.21.4**

whensoe'er **6**

whensoever **17.21.4**

where **6**

whereabouts **34.22.6**

whereafter **17.12.23**

whereas **35.7**

whereat **22.7**

whereby **14.7**

where'er **6**

wherefore **12.11.2**

wherefrom **27.9**

wherein **28.2, 28.2.29**

whereof **31.7**

whereon **28.10, 28.10.24**

wheresoe'er **6**

wheresoever **17.21.4**

whereto **16.7**

whereupon **28.10.7**

wherever **17.21.4**

wherewith **33.2**

wherewithal **40.10.13**

Whernside **23.15.11(.12)**

wherry **1.29.3**

wherryman **28.17.16(.2)**

whet **22.5**

whether **17.23.4**

whetstone **28.19.4(.9)**

whetter **17.12.5**

whew **16**

Whewell **40.16.8**

whey **4**

which **38.2**

whichever **17.21.4**

whichsoever **17.21.4**

whicker **17.14.2**

whiff **30.2**

whiffiness **34.18.16(.2.6)**

whiffle **40.27.2**

whiffler **17.34.26**

whiffletree **2.30.10**

whiffy **1.18.2**

Whig **26.2**

whiggery **1.29.11(.11)**

whiggish **36.2.14**

whiggishness **34.18.16(.33.4)**

whiggism **27.15.21(.2.7)**

while **40.13**

whilom **27.15.28(.9)**

whilst **22.29.23**

whim **27.2**

whimbrel **40.16.13(.15)**

whimper **17.10.17**

whimperer **17.32.14(.4)**

whimpering **29.1.30(.8)**

whimperingly **1.31.28(.1.17)**

whimsical **40.23.12(.16)**

whimsicality **1.10.16(.32.5)**

whimsically **1.31.24(.9.10)**

whimsicalness **34.18.16(.37.5)**

whimsy **1.23.19**

whim-wham **27.6.16**

whin **28.2**

whinchat **22.7.17**

whine **28.14**

whiner **17.18.13**

whinge **39.17.1**

whingeingly **1.31.28(.1.14)**

whinger **17.29.16(.1)**

whingey **1.26.13**

whingingly **1.31.28(.1.14)**

whingy **1.26.13**

whiningly **1.31.28(.1.7)**

whinny **1.16.2**

whinsill **40.2.14**

whinstone **28.19.4(.9)**

whiny **1.16.13**

whip **20.2**

whipcord **23.12.4**

whipcracking **29.1.14(.4)**

whip hand **23.24.6**

whiplash **36.6.10**

whipless **34.18.29(.20)**

whipper **17.10.2**

whipper-in **28.2**

whippersnapper **17.10.5**

whippet **22.2.5**

whippiness **34.18.16(.2.2)**

wield **23.31.1**
wielder **17.13.23(.1)**
wieldy **1.11.23**
wiener **17.18.1**
Wiener schnitzel **40.31.16**
wienie **1.16.1**
Wiesbaden **28.17.12(.8)**
Wiesel **40.31.1**
Wiesenthal **40.8.4**
wife **30.12**
wifehood **23.16.5(.12)**
wifeless **34.18.29(.29)**
wifelike **24.13.7(.19)**
wifeliness **34.18.16(.2.10)**
wifely **1.31.29**
wife-swapping **29.1.10(.6)**
wifish **36.2.18(.9)**
wig **26.2**
Wigan **28.17.15(.2)**
wigeon **28.17.28(.2)**
Wiggin **28.2.15**
wigging **29.1.15**
Wiggins **35.26.2**
wiggle **40.24.2**
wiggler **17.34.24**
Wigglesworth **32.14.15**
wiggly **1.31.17(.12), 1.31.25**
wight **22.16**
Wigley **1.31.25**
Wigmore **12.9.10**
Wigram **27.15.26(.13)**
Wigton **28.17.11(.21)**
Wigtownshire **17.26.21**
wigwag **26.5.7**
wigwam **27.6.16**
Wilberforce **34.12.4**
Wilbert **22.19.9**
Wilbraham **27.15.25, 27.15.26(.9)**
Wilbur **17.11.20**
Wilby **1.9.24**
wilco **19.12.18**
Wilcock **24.9.6**
Wilcocks **34.23.8(.5)**
Wilcox **34.23.8(.5)**
Wilcoxon **28.17.23(.21)**
wild **23.31.9**
Wildblood **23.14**
wild card **23.9**
wildcat **22.7.9**
Wilde **23.31.9**
wildebeest **22.29.1**
Wildenstein **28.14.5**
Wilder **17.13.23(.7)**
wilder **17.13.23(.2)**
wilderness **34.18.16(.15.2)**
wild-eyed **23.15**
wildfire **17.6.9(.13)**

wildfowl **40.7**
wildfowler **17.34.7**
wildfowling **29.1.31(.7)**
wild-goose chase **34.4**
wilding **29.1.13(.16)**
wildish **36.2.12**
wildlife **30.12**
wildly **1.31.23(.18)**
wildness **34.18.16(.21.1)**
wildwood **23.16.6(.10)**
wile **40.13**
Wiley **1.31.14**
Wilf **30.20.1**
Wilford **23.18.16(.22)**
Wilfrid **23.2.22**
wilful **40.27.31**
wilfully **1.31.17(.16.2)**
wilfulness **34.18.16(.37.2)**
wilga **17.16.19**
Wilhelmina **17.18.1(.6)**
Wilhelmshafen **28.17.19**
Wilhelmshaven **28.17.19, 28.17.20(.6)**
wilily **1.31.17(.29)**
wiliness **34.18.16(.2.10)**
Wilkerson **28.17.23(.14)**
Wilkes **34.23.19**
Wilkie **1.12.19**
Wilkins **35.26.2**
Wilkinson **28.17.23(.24)**
will **40.2**
Willa **17.34.2**
Willard **23.9.22**
Willemstadt **22.7.7**
Willenhall **40.10.16**
willer **17.34.2**
Willesden **28.17.12(.26)**
willet **22.19.26(.1)**
Willetts **34.22.15**
Willey **1.31.2**
willfully **1.31.17(.16.2)**
William **27.15.27**
Williams **35.25.10**
Williamsburg **26.14.1(.11)**
Williamson **28.17.23(.23)**
willie **1.31.2**
willing **29.1.31(.2)**
willingly **1.31.28(.1.18)**
willingness **34.18.16(.26)**
Willis **34.2.22(.2)**
will-less **34.18.29(.38)**
Willmott **22.11.8**
will-o'-the-wisp **20.17**
Willoughby **1.9.11**
willow **19.29.2**
willowherb **21.15**
willowy **1(.7)**
willpower **17.3.1**
Wills **35.30.2**

willy **1.31.2**
willy-nilly **1.31.2**
willy-willy **1.31.2**
Wilma **17.17.24**
Wilmcote **22.21.5**
Wilmer **17.17.24**
Wilmington **28.17.11(.23)**
Wilmslow **19.29.23**
Wilsher **17.26.25**
Wilson **28.17.23(.28)**
Wilsonian **28.3.8(.11)**
wilt **22.32.1**
Wilton **28.17.11(.27)**
Wilts **34.22.20**
Wiltshire **17.28.26**
wily **1.31.14**
wimble **40.20.19**
Wimbledon **28.17.12(.27)**
Wimborne **28.11.2**
Wimbush **36.13**
Wimoweh **4.25.9**
wimp **20.16.1**
wimpish **36.2.9**
wimpishly **1.31.35(.7.1)**
wimpishness **34.18.16(.33.2)**
wimple **40.19.14**
Wimpole **40.18.3**
wimpy **1.8.14**
win **28.2**
Winalot® **22.11.17**
Wincanton **28.17.11(.22)**
Wincarnis **34.2.13**
wince **34.24.1**
wincer **17.24.22(.1)**
wincey **1.22.23(.1)**
winceyette **22.5**
winch **38.18.1**
Winchelsea **2.22.14**
wincher **17.28.22**
Winchester **17.12.24(.14)**
winchester **17.12.24(.4)**
Winchmore **12.9.13, 12.9.14**
wincingly **1.31.28(.1.11)**
Winckelmann **28.7.10(.24)**
wind **23.24.2, 23.24.13**
windage **39.2.11**
Windaus **34.8.1**
windbag **26.5.1**
windblown **28.19.19**
windbound **23.24.7(.2)**
windbreak **24.3.13**
Windbreaker® **17.14.3(.8)**
windburn **28.18.3**
windcheater **17.12.1(.12)**
windchill **40.2.16**
windcone **28.19.6**
wind-down **28.8.2(.8)**

winder **17.13.20(.11)**
Windermere **3.8.7**
windfall **40.10.11**
windfarm **27.8.8**
windflower **17.3.11**
Windhoek **24.14.9**
windhover **17.21.7**
windily **1.31.17(.10)**
windiness **34.18.16(.2.3)**
windjammer **17.17.6**
windlass **34.18.29(.23)**
Windlesham **27.15.22**
windless **34.18.29(.23)**
windlestraw **12.21**
windmill **40.2.9**
Windolene® **28.1.27(.7)**
window **19.11.14**
windowless **34.18.29(.17.2)**
windowpane **28.4.1**
windowseat **22.1.9**
window-shop **20.7.9**
window-shopper **17.10.8**
windowsill **40.2.14**
windpipe **20.10.1**
windproof **30.13.4**
windrow **19.27.16, 19.27.19**
Windrush **36.12**
windsail **40.4.10, 40.31.17**
Windscale **40.4.4**
windscreen **28.1.25(.8)**
windshield **23.31.1(.5)**
windsock **24.9.10**
Windsor **17.25.18**
windstorm **27.10.2**
windsurf **30.15**
windsurfer **17.20.13**
windswept **22.22.3**
wind-up **20.9.6**
windward **23.18.26(.10)**
windy **1.11.20(.1)**
wine **28.14**
wineberry **1.29.11(.7.2)**
winebibber **17.11.2**
winebibbing **29.1.11**
wineglass **34.9.7**
wineglassful **40.14.6(.19)**
winegrower **17.9.11**
wineless **34.18.29(.27)**
winemaker **17.14.3(.3)**
winemaking **29.1.14(.3)**
winepress **34.5.14(.4)**
winery **1.29.11(.13.1)**
wineskin **28.2.13(.14)**
Winfield **23.31.1(.2)**
Winford **23.18.16(.16)**
Winfred **23.2.22**
Winfrith **32.2.8**
wing **29.1**

wolfcub **21.11**
Wolfe **30.20.6**
Wolfenden **28.17.12(.23)**
Wolfgang **29.4.6**
wolfhound **23.24.7(.8)**
wolfish **36.2.18(.21)**
wolfishly **1.31.35(.7.3)**
wolfishness
  34.18.16(.33.6)
Wolfit **22.2.13**
wolf-like **24.13.7(.19)**
wolf-man **28.7.10(.17)**
wolf-men **28.5.7(.21)**
wolfram **27.15.26(.14)**
wolframite **22.16.13**
wolfsbane **28.4.2**
wolfskin **28.2.13(.14)**
wolf's-milk **24.21**
Wolfson **28.17.23(.25)**
Wollaston **28.17.11(.25)**
Wollongong **29.6.6**
Wollstonecraft
  22.27.4(.4)
Wolof **30.8.12**
Wolseley **1.31.34**
Wolsey **1.23.22**
Wolsingham **27.15.15**
Wolstenholme **27.17.12**
Wolverhampton
  28.17.11(.18)
wolverine **28.1.25(.3)**
Wolverton **28.17.11(.15)**
wolves **35.28.10**
woman **28.17.16(.14)**
womanhood **23.16.5(.10)**
womanish **36.2.16(.13)**
womanishly
  1.31.35(.7.2)
womanishness
  34.18.16(.33.5)
womanize **35.15.12(.5)**
womanizer **17.25.12(.6)**
womankind **23.24.13**
womanless **34.18.29(.27)**
womanlike **24.13.7(.17)**
womanliness
  34.18.16(.2.10)
womanly **1.31.27(.14)**
womb **27.14**
wombat **22.7.6**
womb-like **24.13.7(.16)**
Wombwell **40.5.17(.11)**
women **28.2.17(.1)**
womenfolk **24.18.7**
womenkind **23.24.13**
women's lib **21.2**
women's libber **17.11.2**
womenswear **6.18.13**
won **28.10, 28.13**
wonder **17.13.20(.10)**
wonderer **17.32.14(.7)**

wonderful **40.27.14**
wonderfully
  1.31.17(.16.1)
wonderfulness
  34.18.16(.37.2)
wondering **29.1.30(.8)**
wonderingly
  1.31.28(.1.17)
wonderland **23.24.6(.13)**
wonderment
  22.26.15(.13.2)
wondrous **34.18.27(.15)**
wondrously **1.31.33(.12.5)**
Wong **29.6**
wonkily **1.31.17(.11)**
wonkiness **34.18.16(.2.4)**
wonky **1.12.16**
won't **22.26.17**
wont **22.26.9, 22.26.17**
wonton **28.10.9**
woo **16**
wooable **40.20.16(.7)**
wood **23.16**
Woodall **40.10.6**
Woodard **23.9.8**
woodbind **23.24.13**
woodbine **28.14.4**
woodblock **24.9.16(.10)**
Woodbridge **39.2.22(.10)**
woodcarver **17.21.6**
woodcarving **29.1.20**
woodchip **20.2.8**
woodchopper **17.10.8**
woodchuck **24.12.7**
woodcock **24.9.6**
woodcraft **22.27.4(.4)**
woodcut **22.15.4**
woodcutter **17.12.12**
woodcutting **29.1.12(.10)**
wooded **23.18.10(.12)**
wooden **28.17.12(.14)**
woodenhead **23.5.13(.14)**
woodenheaded
  23.18.10(.3)
wooden-headedness
  34.18.16(.21.1)
woodenly **1.31.27(.14)**
woodenness **34.18.16(.25)**
Woodford **23.18.16(.12)**
woodgrouse **34.8.7**
Woodhall **40.10.16**
Woodhead **23.5.13(.10)**
Woodhouse **34.8.6(.12)**
woodiness **34.18.16(.2.3)**
woodland **23.24.16(.16.3)**
woodlander **17.13.20(.13)**
woodlark **24.8.16**
Woodlesford
  23.18.16(.19)
woodless **34.18.29(.23)**
Woodley **1.31.23(.12)**

woodlice **34.15.10**
woodlot **22.11.17**
woodlouse **34.8.8**
woodman **28.17.16(.22)**
woodnote **22.21.8**
woodpecker **17.14.4**
woodpie **14.6**
woodpigeon **28.17.28(.2)**
woodpile **40.13.1**
Woodrow **19.27.16**
woodruff **30.11.10**
woodrush **36.12**
Woods **35.23.11**
woodscrew **16.23.10**
woodshed **23.5.12**
woodsman **28.17.16(.30)**
woodsmoke **24.18.5**
Woodstock **24.9.4**
woodsy **1.23.18**
woodturner **17.18.17**
woodturning **29.1.17(.13)**
Woodward **23.18.26(.10)**
woodwasp **20.17**
woodwind **23.24.2**
woodwork **24.17.6(.9)**
woodworker **17.14.16**
woodworking
  29.1.14(.12)
woodworm **27.16.7**
woody **1.11.15**
woodyard **23.9.21**
wooer **17.8**
woof **30.13**
woofer **17.20.11**
Woofferton **28.17.11(.15)**
Wookey **1.12.11**
wool **40.14**
Woolacombe **27.15.11(.9)**
Wooldridge **39.2.22(.12)**
woolen **28.17.33(.11)**
Wooler **17.34.14**
Woolf **30.20.6**
woolgathering
  29.1.30(.8)
Woollard **23.9.22**
woollen **28.17.33(.11)**
Woolley **1.31.15**
wool-like **24.13.7(.27)**
woolliness
  34.18.16(.2.10)
woolly **1.31.15**
woolly-bear **6.3**
woolly-headed
  23.18.10(.3)
woolpack **24.6.5**
woolsack **24.6.14**
woolsey **1.23.22**
woolshed **23.5.12**
Woolwich **38.2.11,
  39.2.23**
Woolworth **32.14.15**

woomera **17.32.14(.10)**
Woosnam **27.15.14(.17)**
Wooster **17.12.24(.13)**
Wootton **28.17.11(.13)**
woozily **1.31.17(.21)**
wooziness **34.18.16(.2.7)**
woozy **1.23.12**
wop **20.7**
Worcester **17.12.24(.12)**
Worcestershire **17.26.14**
word **23.19**
wordage **39.2.11**
wordbook **24.14.3**
wordfinder **17.13.20(.11)**
word for word **23.19**
wordily **1.31.17(.10)**
wordiness **34.18.16(.2.3)**
wording **29.1.13(.12)**
wordless **34.18.29(.23)**
wordlessly **1.31.33(.12.6)**
wordlessness
  34.18.16(.31.6)
word-perfect **22.23.2**
wordplay **4.28.9**
wordsearch **38.16**
wordsmith **32.2.3**
WordStar **10.6.8**
Wordsworth **32.14.15**
Wordsworthian **28.3.12**
wordy **1.11.18**
wore **12**
work **24.17**
workability **1.10.16(.22.1)**
workable **40.20.16(.13)**
workableness
  34.18.16(.37.4)
workably **1.31.21(.5)**
workaday **4.10.7**
workaholic **24.2.27(.9)**
workbasket **22.19.12(.14)**
workbench **38.18.2**
workboat **22.21.2**
workbook **24.14.3**
workbox **34.23.8(.2)**
workday **4.10.10**
worker **17.14.16**
workfare **6.10**
workforce **34.12.4**
workhorse **34.12.7**
workhouse **34.8.6(.13)**
working **29.1.14(.12)**
Workington **28.17.11(.23)**
workless **34.18.29(.24)**
workload **23.20.13**
workman **28.17.16(.23)**
workmanlike
  24.13.7(.17)
workmanship **20.2.7(.19)**
workmate **22.4.13(.10)**
workout **22.9.9**
workpeople **40.19.1**

w

w

zealotry 1.29.15(.13)
zealous 34.18.29(.5)
zealously 1.31.33(.12.6)
zealousness
34.18.16(.31.6)
Zebedee 2.13
zebra 17.32.18
zebrine 28.14.18
zebu 16.6, 16.24.4
Zebulon 28.17.33(.12)
Zech. 24.4
Zechariah 17.6.14
zed 23.5
Zedekiah 17.6.5
zedoary 1.29.11(.5)
zee 2
Zeebrugge 17.16.11
Zeeland 23.24.16(.16.1)
Zeffirelli 1.31.5
zein 28.2.1
Zeiss 34.15
Zeitgeist 22.29.13
zek 24.4
Zelda 17.13.23(.3)
Zelotes 35.1.7(.8)
zemstvo 19.17
Zen 28.5
Zena 17.18.1
zenana 17.18.8(.6)
Zend 23.24.5
Zener diode 23.20.2
Zenist 22.29.2(.18.1)
zenith 32.2.4
zenithal 40.29
Zeno 19.15.1
Zenobia 3.3.9
zeolite 22.16.25(.9)
zeolitic 24.2.10(.2.5)
Zephaniah 17.6.8
zephyr 17.20.4
Zephyrus 34.18.27(.20)
zeppelin 28.2.31(.10)
Zermatt 22.7.11
zero 19.27.1
zeroth 32.16
zest 22.29.5
zester 17.12.24(.4)
zestful 40.27.18
zestfully 1.31.17(.16.2)
zestfulness
34.18.16(.37.2)
zestiness 34.18.16(.2.3)
zesty 1.10.26(.4)
zeta 17.12.1
zetetic 24.2.10(.3.1)
Zetland 23.24.16(.16.3)
zeugma 17.17.20
zeugmatic 24.2.10(.4.2)
Zeus 34.17

Zeuxis 34.2.17(.14)
Zhang 29.4
Zhanjiang 29.4.12
Zhdanov 31.7
Zhengzhou 19.23
Zhenjiang 29.4.12
Zhivago 19.13.5
zho 19
Zhongshan 28.7.16
Zhou 19
Zhukov 30.8.6, 31.7
Zia 3
zibet 22.19.9
zibeth 32.14.7
Ziegfeld 23.31.4
Ziegler 17.34.24
ziff 30.2
ziggurat 22.7.20
zigzag 26.5.6
zilch 38.19
zillah 17.34.2
zillion 28.3.21(.2)
zillionth 32.21
Zimbabwe 1.28, 4.25.11
Zimbabwean 28.3.19,
28.17.2
zimmer 17.17.2
Zimmerman
28.17.16(.16)
zinc 24.19.1
zinco 19.12.15
zincograph 30.7.5(.1)
zincography 1.18.9(.3.2)
zincotype 20.10.2
zincy 1.12.16
Zinfandel 40.5.4
zing 29.1
zingari 2.30.7
zingaro 19.27.11
zinger 17.19.1
zingy 1.17
Zinjanthropus
34.18.9(.8)
zinnia 3.9.2
Zion 28.17.5
Zionism 27.15.21(.2.9)
Zionist 22.29.2(.18.1)
zip 20.2
zip-code 23.20.7
zip-fastener 17.18.16(.14)
zip-lock 24.9.16(.9)
zip-on 28.10.7
zipper 17.10.2
zippily 1.31.17(.7)
zippiness 34.18.16(.2.2)
zippy 1.8.2
zip-up 20.9.4
zircon 28.10.11
zirconia 3.9.11

zirconium 27.3.8(.10)
zit 22.2
zither 17.23.2
zitherist 22.29.2(.29.4)
zizz 35.2
zloty 1.10.9
zodiac 24.6.1
zodiacal 40.23.12(.3)
Zoë 1(.7)
zoetrope 20.15.8
Zoffany 1.16.15(.12)
Zog 26.7
zoic 24.2.7
zoisite 22.16.19(.5)
Zola 17.34.18
zollverein 28.14.18
Zomba 17.11.17(.5)
zombie 1.9.18
zonal 40.26.15
zonally 1.31.17(.14.3)
zonary 1.29.11(.13.3)
zonate 22.4.14(.11)
zonation 28.17.25(.3.8)
zonda 17.13.20(.7)
zone 28.19
zonk 24.19.5
Zonta 17.12.22(.7)
Zontian 28.3.3
zoo 16
zoogeographic
24.2.16(.3)
zoogeographical
40.23.12(.12)
zoogeographically
1.31.24(.9.9)
zoogeography
1.18.9(.3.2)
zoography 1.18.9(.3.2)
zooid 23.2.4, 23.13.4
zooidal 40.22.2, 40.22.9
zookeeper 17.10.1
zoolatry 1.29.15(.13)
zoological 40.23.12(.17.2)
zoologically 1.31.24(.9.11)
zoologist 22.29.2(.26.2)
zoology 1.26.10(.11.1)
zoom 27.14
zoomancy 1.22.23(.4)
zoometry 1.29.15(.8)
zoomorphic 24.2.16(.5)
zoomorphism
27.15.21(.2.10)
zoonoses 35.1.16(.11)
zoonosis 34.2.17(.11.2)
zoophyte 22.16.16
zoophytic 24.2.10(.2.3)
zooplankton
28.17.11(.20)
zoospore 12.3
zoosporic 24.2.26(.7)

zootomy 1.15.13(.1)
zoot suit 22.18
Zora 17.32.10
Zorah 17.32.10
zorbing 29.1.11
zori 1.29.7, 1.29.8
zoril 40.2.20
zorilla 17.34.2(.15)
Zoroaster 17.12.24(.5)
Zoroastrian 28.3.20(.11)
Zoroastrianism
27.15.21(.2.9)
zoster 17.12.24(.7)
Zouave 31.6
zouk 24.15
zounds 35.23.15
Zsa Zsa 10
Z score 12
Zubes 35.21
zucchetto 19.10.4
zucchini 1.16.1(.5)
Zuckerman 28.17.16(.16)
zugzwang 29.4.14, 29.5
Zuider Zee 2
Zuleika 17.14.1,
17.14.3(.9), 17.14.12
Zulu 16.25
Zululand 23.24.6(.13)
Zürich 24.2.26(.8)
zwieback 24.6.6(.1), 24.8.3
Zwingli 1.31.25
Zwinglian 28.3.21(.14)
zwitterion 28.17.5
Zwolle 17.34.9
Zworykin 28.2.13(.6)
zydeco 19.12.12
zygodactyl 40.2.5,
40.21.16
zygodactylous
34.18.29(.17.2)
zygoma 17.17.16(.5)
zygomata 17.12.16(.9.3)
zygomatic 24.2.10(.4.2)
zygomorphic 24.2.16(.5)
zygomorphous 34.18.17
zygosis 34.2.17(.11.1)
zygospore 12.3
zygote 22.21.6
zygotene 28.1.9(.3)
zygotic 24.2.10(.6)
zygotically 1.31.24(.9.4)
zymase 34.4.7, 35.4.7
zymological
40.23.12(.17.2)
zymologist 22.29.2(.26.4)
zymology 1.26.10(.11.4)
zymosis 34.2.17(.11.2)
zymotic 24.2.10(.6)
zymotically 1.31.24(.9.4)
zymurgy 1.26.11

Z